DICTIONARY
OF
FUNDAMENTAL
THEOLOGY

Edited by
René Latourelle
Rino Fisichella

DICTIONARY
OF
FUNDAMENTAL
THEOLOGY

*English-language edition
edited by
RENÉ LATOURELLE*

ST PAULS

ST PAULS
Middlegreen, Slough, SL3 6BT, United Kingdom
Moyglare Road, Maynooth, Co. Kildare, Ireland
7708 St. Paul Road, San Antonio Village, Makati 1203, Metro Manila, Philippines

Original edition: *Dizionario di Teologia Fondamentale*, René Latourelle and Rino Fisichella, Editors.
Italian edition edited by Rino Fisichella.
©Cittadella Editrice 1990

English language edition copyright © 1994 by The Crossroad Publishing Company

Published by ST PAULS by arrangement with The Crossroad Publishing Company, New York.

ISBN 085439 395 1

Printed in the United States of America

ST PAULS is an activity of priests and brothers of the Society of St Paul who proclaim the Gospel through the media of social communication.

LIST OF ARTICLES

The titles in bold print are the guiding threads of the *Dictionary of Fundamental Theology.*

ACKNOWLEDGMENTS

The English-language edition of this *Dictionary*
has been made possible
thanks to the generosity and contributions
of a significant number of Canadian bishops
and, in particular, of the following
English-speaking Provinces of the Society of Jesus:

California Province (USA)
Missouri Province (USA)
New England Province (USA)
New York Province (USA)
Australian Province
British Province
Canadian Jesuits
Irish Province

The Crossroad Publishing Company
wishes to express its gratitude
to René Latourelle
for his personal commitment to this edition
and for his individual contributions at every stage,
particularly in verifying the accuracy and quality
of all the translations into English.
Without his theological and linguistic expertise,
not to speak of fund-raising activities,
this dictionary would not have been possible.

Finally, our thanks to Alba House
for having authorized the use,
in condensed and modified form,
of selected chapters from René Latourelle's
Man and His Problems in the Light of Jesus Christ (1983).

INTRODUCTION
to the English-Language Edition

Purpose, Structure, and Originality of the Dictionary

I wish to emphasize from the outset that this work belongs in the category of dictionaries and not of treatises or manuals. The point is an important one, since a dictionary can be used in more flexible and varied ways, which in this case are enhanced by two indexes, a systematic and an analytic.

Why a dictionary of fundamental theology? To meet an urgent present need. There is no doubt that the four-volume *Dictionnaire apologétique de la foi catholique*, which A. d'Alès began a century ago, and the shorter work published in 1948 under the editorship of M. Brillant and M. Nédoncelle have rendered valuable service to generations of students. It must be recognized, however, that postwar changes in the social and religious spheres and consequently in outlooks, approaches, methods, and techniques have compelled revisions that have even led classical, traditional apologetics to change its name and be known henceforward as "fundamental theology."

There is, of course, continuity between the apologetics that held the field for centuries and present-day fundamental theology (after all, the basic questions remain, although they have become more numerous and more complex), but there is also a discontinuity so great as to outweigh the continuity. We are compelled to say that the discipline has a new status, a new identity, a new set of papers. We are in the presence now of a new discipline that has its proper object, its proper method, a new structure—or, in short, a specific character that identifies it and distinguishes it from the other theological disciplines. Among the changes that have brought about the shift from apologetics to fundamental theology I single out the following.

1. The entire intellectual and spiritual ambiance has changed. The human race finds itself in a situation in which *pluralism* has left its mark on the whole of contemporary society. The most divergent systems of thought coexist, with none of them managing to dominate the others. On the other hand, all the religions offer models that resemble one another (quest of salvation, mediators, rites, institutions); the conclusion people often draw from this is that all religions are of equal value and should henceforth restrict themselves to cultivating good neighbor relations with one another. Furthermore, the end of the cultural isolation of peoples is promoting the free exchange of ideas and helping to establish relations of equality among the varied viewpoints developed by reason and experience. In short, pluralism is a dominant characteristic of contemporary society. This is a fact with serious consequences for Christianity, which claims to be *the* revelation par excellence.

2. A second change directly affects religion. In the space of a few centuries the Christian West has passed from a state of religious wrangling to emancipation and finally to *indifference*. Nowadays a good many Christians think that Christianity is sure to disappear.

The crisis now being experienced by the peoples of the West, who are rebellious, embittered, or disillusioned, is the crisis of an entire civilization that was formed by Christianity but has become anemic and dreadfully ignorant and can no longer see that which Christianity is able to contribute to it, namely, the fullest interpretation of human existence. Our contemporaries are undergoing a *crisis of meaning:* they are confronted with their own mystery, in a broken world that is destroying itself. To fill the void, some have flung themselves headlong into the world of the sects, thousands of which have appeared since 1960. After belonging for a usually short period to a sect, these people become disillusioned and withdraw without any fuss; they then sink into indifference. Indifference, however, is a fluid thing, difficult to delimit and define.

3. A third change is the massive entry of *science* into contemporary thought. There is, for example, the renewal of the biblical and patristic sciences, the phenomenal advances of literary and historical criticism, the multifaceted progress of the linguistic sciences, the development of the human sciences (especially psychology and sociology), and the impact of the historical dimension on all problems. Located as it is on the boundary between the human sciences and the sacred sciences, fundamental theology, more than any other discipline, experiences repercussions from a world that no longer reaches it only through the mediation of philosophy, as was true in the past.

4. The most striking of all the changes, and one that directly affects fundamental theology, is a change of *attitude*. Fundamental theology is marked no longer by confrontation but by dialogue. This change of attitude reflects the new climate introduced into the church by the encyclical *Ecclesiam Suam* of Paul VI and the documents of Vatican II, the evident intention of which was to deliver the church from its silence and bring it once again into the contemporary world. To achieve this goal, Paul VI and the council chose the path of dialogue. The council itself was a great act of dialogue with the other Christian communities, the other religions, the various cultures, and the whole of the human race.

The profound changes I have been describing, together with the attitude of dialogue that henceforth characterizes fundamental theology, have resulted in the widening of its circle of addressees. The first of these addressees continues to be believers, who are never excused from reflecting on the foundations of Christianity and of their faith, this last being regarded as a reasonable, motivated choice and the source of the hope that is in them (1 Pt 3:15). But modern believers, immersed as they are in a world that is often lacking in any religious values, carry within them the doubts of the unbeliever. Consequently, when they enter into dialogue with unbelievers, it is with themselves as well that they are dialoguing. The addressees of fundamental theology are no longer the rationalists and the militant atheists, but rather former Christians who have become indifferent as well as the simply indifferent who no longer ask themselves about God or Christ. God and Christ do not come within the intellectual range of vision of those who are indifferent.

* * *

In what ways does this dictionary respond to the anxieties and desires of a world that has so radically changed? I shall briefly list some of the book's more obvious novelties:

For the first time, fundamental theology is defined in clear and decisive language, as a discipline that is one, distinct, and specific. It deals with the self-manifestation and self-giving of God in Jesus Christ and, at the same time, with the self-accreditation of this manifestation. This presence of God in the history, flesh, and language of Jesus is the subject and unifying center of fundamental theology. God-among-us-in-Jesus-Christ: this is the first mystery, the first event, the first reality that grounds faith and the whole of theological discourse. If fundamental theology uses an "integrational method" (combining the method of dogmatic theology with the methods of the human sciences of literary criticism, history, and philosophy), it does so because of the nature of revelation itself, since this, like the church or the resurrection, is at once a divine mystery and an event in history. The method is in the service of a reality that has two sides: the world of God and the world of human beings.

When Christ is placed "front stage" as the radiating center and point of convergence for fundamental theology (this is also the perspective adopted by the Gospels and Vatican II), it becomes possible to place in a hierarchical order all other problems, which are viewed as implications of the central core. The result is the following sequence: (1) Christian revelation, with its specific characteristics; (2) the credibility of revelation and the problem of its signs; (3) the response of faith and its specific discourse; (4) relations with the other Christian communities and the other religions; and (5) the relationship to history, philosophy, the sciences, culture, and language.

Despite the large number of articles it contains (223), the dictionary I am here introducing is far from being a labyrinth: it has its guiding threads, in the form of about thirty more important titles that clarify the structure of the whole. Some of these key articles stand out by reason of the large amount of space given to them. For example: Revelation, Credibility, approaches to Christology, Christological Titles, Interreligious Dialogue, Church, God, Gospels, Faith, Deposit of Faith, Fundamental Theology, History of Salvation, Inculturation, Kingdom, Philosophical and Theological Language, Messianism, Miracle, Mission, Ecumenism, Promise and Fulfillment, Prophecy, Religion (its various aspects, in ten articles), Resurrection, Testimony, Theology and Theologies, Tradition, Vatican II.

The dialogical approach is everywhere present, but especially in the articles on Ecumenism, the World Council of Churches, Anglicanism, Lutheranism, Calvinism, the Evangelical Churches, and Fundamentalism; on the great religions, such as Judaism, Islam, Buddhism, and Hinduism; on the forms taken by the religious crisis of the present age, such as Indifference, Christian Sects, New Age, Reincarnation, "pick and choose" religion, and so on.

A good many subjects which in the past did not appear at all or barely rose to the surface have become necessary parts of present-day fundamental theology. For example: Inculturation, Communication, Feminism, Philosophical Christology, Lay Apologetes, Structural Analysis, Language, Temporality, Beauty, Silence, Solitude, relation between Imagination and Theology and between Literature and Theology.

It was obviously impossible to pass over in silence the "greats" of classical apologetics and of contemporary fundamental theology. The criterion applied in choosing them is the impact that certain of them continue to have. For example: Irenaeus, Augustine, Origen, Pascal, Newman, Guardini, Barth, Blondel, Rosmini, Rahner, Teilhard de Chardin, de Lubac, von Balthasar.

If fundamental theology is to be "contextual," it must be "planetary" in character, and this aspect can be seen in the number of collaborators in this dictionary: almost a hundred, from twenty university centers and representing fifteen different countries (Australia, Austria, Belgium, Brazil, Canada. France, Great Britain, Germany, Holland, India, Italy, Malta, Spain, United States, and Yugoslavia). This international list of contributors and the cultural wealth it represents give the dictionary a novel character.

* * *

After the collapse of traditional apologetics, professors and students found themselves faced with a vacuum that had to be filled and a future that had to be built. Present-day fundamental theology takes up problems that cannot be passed over, but does so with new approaches to them, new methods of handling them, and new ways of presenting them; as a result, it shows itself to be a renewed and open, yet well identified and better structured, theological discipline. In our opinion, this dictionary will give a new impulse to a discipline that, more than others, needs air, space, and creative freedom.

The dictionary, which has been undertaken in a spirit of service and without any polemical aims, is addressed to students of universities, higher institutions of religious knowledge, those in the work of formation, and pastoral workers, as well as to bishops, diocesan priests, and lay persons: in short, to all men and women who are eager to reflect on the ultimate meaning of the human condition.

René Latourelle

INTRODUCTION
to the Original Edition

The creation of any dictionary is a difficult enterprise, but it is flirting with recklessness to attempt the project of a *Dictionary of Fundamental Theology.* Yesterday's apologetics has changed more than its name; it has changed its state and condition. By virtue of its peculiar condition as a "frontier discipline" vis-à-vis the sacred and human sciences, fundamental theology is constantly exposed to changes that we may quite legitimately regard as revolutionary.

The *Dictionnaire Apologétique de la Foi Catholique* (A. d'Alès), launched some hundred years ago now, rendered immense service in a period of relative theological stability. But the changes to which theology has been subjected for some decades now—in its methods; in its exegetical, historical, and literary analyses; in its response to the relationships prevailing among church, science, and today's world; and, especially, in its mentality—have obliged theologians to "rethink," from the ground up, the task of classic apologetics.

Substance and content abide, but approaches, presentations, and treatments have changed radically. Furthermore, many series of problems have become the object of a breadth of reflection that was scarcely recognizable in the apologetics of yesteryear. In a word, professors, scholars of the material, and students, find themselves confronted with a void to be filled and a future to be built. This is the background against which, in a spirit of ecclesial service, the present work has been conceived.

It may be useful to the reader to know the various propaedeutic steps in the composition of the *Dictionary.*

* * *

In the first phase of the editorial work, it was especially necessary to define the *Dictionary*'s broad lines. Then came a determination of the entries to be treated, in terms of a series of criteria that we may synthesize as follows.

1. The changes that have occurred in theology since the close of World War II, especially at the time of Vatican Council II and its aftermath.
2. The very notion of fundamental theology, which attends to the elements of a general consensus, of course, but also to divergencies arising in function of the variety of cultural traditions.
3. The *Dictionary*'s addressees, whose presence more directly conditions fundamental theology, inasmuch as the discourse and style of the latter take shape with readers in view who come from very diverse religious confessions and cultures.
4. The importance of building a team that would be genuinely international.
5. The specific dimension of each entry, in view of its peculiarity for our discipline.

6. The importance of an approach that would be at once diachronic and synchronic.
7. The deliberate decision to accord each separate entry an adequate, complete treatment. From this standpoint, an occasional repetition of data will represent a positive quality rather than a limitation, as it will foster a comprehensive view of the thematics under consideration and facilitate a better situating of the content of each entry.

* * *

The structure of the *Dictionary* has been conceptualized in such wise as to propose, to those who wish to avail themselves of it, a systematic study of all of the topics of fundamental theology: the basic principles as well as their implications.

This structure is articulated in the following manner:

I. *Christian Revelation and Its Singularity.* 1. Historical preparation. 2. Complement and plenitude in Jesus Christ. 3. Transmission: Scripture, tradition, inspiration, deposit of faith, magisterium. 4. Mission, evangelization, inculturation.

II. *Credibility of Revelation.* 1. Nature and object. 2. Dogmatic and apologetical perspectives: integration of the two approaches. 3. Study of signs. 4. Addressees.

III. *Faith: The human being's response to revelation.* 1. Nature. 2. Content. 3. Subject. 4. Expression. 5. Obstacles.

IV. *Implications of the Singularity of Christian Revelation.* 1. Problem of the knowledge of faith: theology. 2. Relationship with history. 3. Relationship with philosophies that reject the Incarnation: illuminism, Bultmannian theology. 4. Relationship with other churches: ecumenism. 5. Relationship with other religions. 6. Relation to culture, language, the sciences.

V. *Historical Outlook.* 1. *Triplex demonstratio: religiosa, Christiana, Catholica.* 2. Historico-thematic reconstruction. 3. Major authors.

Among the 220 terms studied, we have identified thirty-five as more important in the sense that they constitute the *Dictionary*'s broad structure. Thus, they are apportioned more space in their treatment, and they stand out from the others in the graphic design of the List of Articles (pp. v–x). They include Anthropology, Apologetics, Atheism, Church, Christology, Credibility, *Dei Verbum*, Deposit of Faith, Evangelization, Faith, Fundamental Theology, Gospel, God, Hermeneutics, History, Inculturation, Inspiration, Justice, Language, Magisterium, Martyrdom, Messianism, Method, Miracle, Paschal Mystery, Prophecy, Religion, Revelation, Signs of the Times, Semiology, *Sensus Fidei*, Testimony, Theologies, Theology, Tradition.

A goodly number of topics addressed in the *Dictionary* are of great currency. Indeed, frequently these terms do not appear in other dictionaries, or are only cursorily treated. For example: Apologists (Lay), Christology (Philosophical), Communication, Feminism, Imagination, Language, Literature, Realism, Sects (Christian), Silence, Solitude.

Naturally we could not pass over in silence the "greats" of classic apologetics and contemporary fundamental theology. But how were we to select them, and on what criteria? We have chosen authors who continue to have an incisive impact on the contemporary scene. Among our titles: Apologists (i.e., of the early centuries), Apologists (Lay) (i.e., of the eighteenth and nineteenth centuries), Augustine, Anselm, Barth, Blondel, Drey, Guardini, Irenaeus, Newman, Origen, Rahner, Rosmini, Teilhard de Chardin, Urs von Balthasar, Zubiri.

* * *

There are some one hundred collaborators on this work, and they write from more than twenty academic centers throughout the world. They constitute an authentically international team, Concretely, fifteen countries are thus represented: Australia, Austria, Belgium, Brazil, Canada, France, Germany, Great Britain, India, Italy, Malta, The Netherlands, Spain, the United States, Yugoslavia.

We have thought it useful to draw up two indexes: one, *systematic*, intended to afford the reader an overview of the organic structure of our approach to fundamental theology; the second, *analytical*, for the purpose of providing a cross-index not only of the various series of problems upon which our articles bear, but also of subjects whose treatment will be found scattered throughout various parts of the *Dictionary*.

* * *

In a time when fundamental theology comes forward as a discipline with a more crisply defined identity and with updated methodologies and research techniques at its disposition, we hope that the present *Dictionary* may correspond, in a spirit of renewed commitment, to that sense of responsibility for the Christian faith that challenges us, in the words of 1 Peter 3:15: "Should anyone ask you the reason for this hope of yours, be ever ready to reply."

In conclusion, we should like to express our profound thanks to the institutions that have made it possible for us to bring our project to realization: the Pontifical Gregorian University, the Pontifical Biblical Institute, and the Pro Civitate Christiana of Assisi.

17 September 1990
Rome
THE EDITORS

CONTRIBUTORS

1. Pontifical Gregorian University

ADNÈS, Pierre, Professor of Dogmatic Theology

AZEVEDO, Marcello de C., Guest Professor of Anthropology

BOSETTI, Elena, Director of New Testament Exegetical Studies

CABA, José, Professor of NT Exegesis

CARRIER, Hervé, Professor of Sociology

CHAPPIN, Marcel, Professor of Church History

CONROY, Charles, Professor of Old Testament Exegesis

CROUZEL, Henri, Guest Professor of Patristics

DE FINANCE, Joseph, Professor of General Ethics

DHAVAMONY, Mariasusai, Professor of Phenomenology of Religions and Theology of Religions

DUPUIS, Jacques, Professor of Dogmatic Theology

FISICHELLA, Rino, Professor of Fundamental Theology

FUČEK, Ivan, Professor of Moral Theology

FUELLENBACH, John, Director of Studies in Dogmatic Theology

FUSS, Michael, Director of Studies in Buddhism

GALOT, Jean, Professor of Dogmatic Theology

GILBERT, Paul, Professor of Metaphysics

GROTH, Bernd, Professor of Fundamental Theology

HAMEL, Édouard, Professor of Moral Theology

HENN, William, Professor of Dogmatic Theology

LADARIA, Luis F., Professor of Dogmatic Theology

LAFONT, Ghislain, Guest Professor of Methodology

LAMBIASI, Francesco, Guest Professor of Dogmatic Theology

LATOURELLE, René, Professor of Fundamental Theology

MCDERMOTT, John M., Professor of Dogmatic Theology

O'COLLINS, Gerald, Professor of Fundamental Theology

O'DONNELL, John, Professor of Dogmatic Theology

ORBE, Antonio, Professor of Patristics

PASTOR, Félix-Alejandro, Professor of Dogmatic Theology

PELLAND, Gilles, Professor of Dogmatic Theology

ROEST CROLLIUS, Arij A., Professor of Missionary Spirituality and of Islam

ROSATO, Philip J., Professor of Dogmatic Theology

SCARVAGLIERI, Giuseppe, Professor of Religious Sociology

SULLIVAN, Francis A., Professor of Dogmatic Theology

TILLIETTE, Xavier, Guest Professor of the History of Philosophy
VERCRUYSSE, Jos E., Professor of Ecclesiastical History and Ecumenical Theology
WICKS, Jared, Professor of Fundamental Theology and Ecumenics

2. Other University Centers

AMATO, Angelo, Professor of Dogmatic Theology, "Salesianum" Pontifical University
BEAUDE, Pierre-Marie, Professor of Catholic Theology, University of Metz
BERGERON, Richard, Center of Information on New Religions, Montreal
BLOESCH, Donald G., Professor of Systematic Theology, University of Dubuque
BUCKLEY, Michael J., National Council of Catholic Bishops, Washington, D.C.
CANÉVET, Mariette, Professor of Patristics, University of Strasbourg
CARNICELLA, M. Christina, Professor of Fundamental Theology, "Salesianum" Pontifical University
CARR, Anne E., Professor of Systematic Theology, Divinity School, University of Chicago
CHARRON, André, Professor of Fundamental Theology, University of Montreal
CIPRIANI, Nello, Professor of Patristics, "Augustinianum" Patristic Institute, Rome
COFFELE, Gianfranco, Professor of Fundamental Theology, "Salesianum" Pontifical University
CUCINOTTA, Filippo Santi, Professor of Fundamental Theology, Faculty of Theology of Sicily, Palermo
DE LA POTTERIE, Ignace, Professor of New Testament Exegesis, Pontifical Biblical Institute, Rome
DES PLACES, Édouard, Professor of History of Religion and of Greek Philosophy, Pontifical Biblical Institute, Rome
DULLES, Avery, Professor of Fundamental Theology, Fordham University, New York
FARRELL, Shannon-Elizabeth, Professor of Hebrew Prophetic and Wisdom Literature, Faculty of Theology, Laval University, Quebec
FARRUGIA, Mario, Professor of Theology, Theological Faculty, "San Luigi," Naples
GENEST. Olivette, Professor of Sacred Scripture, University of Montreal
GILBERT, Maurice, Professor of Old Testament Exegesis, Pontifical Biblical Institute, Rome
GODIN, André, Professor of Psychology of Religions, "Lumen Vitae" Center, Brussels
GRACIA, Diego, Professor of the History of Medicine, Complutensian University, Madrid
GRECH, Prosper, Professor of Hermeneutics, Pontifical Biblical University, Rome
JOSEPH, Howard, Rabbi and Professor, Department of Religion, Concordia University, Montreal
KAGEDAN, Ian J., Director of Government Relations of B'nai Brith Canada
KERN, Walter, Professor of Fundamental Theology, University of Innsbruck
KUSTERMANN, Abraham Peter, Director of the Academy, Diocese of Rottenburg-Stuttgart
LANGEVIN, Gilles, Professor of Dogmatic Theology, Laval University, Quebec
LANGEVIN, Paul-Émile, Professor of New Testament Exegesis, Laval University, Quebec
LANE, Gilles, Professor of Philosophy, University of Montreal
LEFEBVRE, Solange, Professor of Pastoral Theology, University of Montreal
LINDBECK, Georg, Professor of Ecumenical Theology, Divinity School, Yale University, New Haven
LÖSER, Werner, Professor of Dogmatic Theology, Hochschule "Sankt Georgen," Frankfurt
MAESSCHALCK, Marc, Professor of Philosophy, State University, Haiti
MANSINI, Guy F., Professor of Dogmatic Theology, St. Meinrad Archabbey, St. Meinrad, Ind.

MCMORROW, Kevin, Director of the "Atonement" Ecumenical Center, Rome
MURPHY, Anne, Professor of Historical Theology, Heythrop College, University of London
NAUD, Julien, Professor of Philosophy, University of Quebec, Trois-Rivières
NEUFELD, Karl H., Professor of Fundamental Theology, University of Innsbruck
PERKINS, PHEME, Professor of Theology, Boston College
PIÉ-NINOT, Salvador, Professor of Fundamental Theology, Theological Faculty of Catalunya, Barcelona
POTTMEYER, Hermann J., Professor of Fundamental Theology, University of Bochum
POZZO, Guido, Professor of Dogmatic Theology, "Caymari" Institute, Rome
PROVENCHER, Normand, Professor of Fundamental Theology, Saint Paul's University, Ottawa
ROCCHETTA, Carlo, Professor of Dogmatic Theology, Fiorentino Theological Institute, Florence
ROCHAIS, Gerard, Professor, Department of Religious Sciences, University of Quebec, Montreal
ROOT, Howard, Director of the Anglican Center, Rome
SABOURIN, Léopold, Author and Researcher in Sacred Scripture
SCHLITT, Dale M., Professor of Philosophy of Religion and Theology, Saint Paul's University, Ottawa
SECKLER, Max, Professor of Fundamental Theology, University of Tübingen
SKA, Jean-Louis, Professor of Old Testament Exegesis, Pontifical Biblical Institute, Rome
SPERA, Salvatore, Professor of Philosophy of Religion, "La Sapienza" University, Rome
STAGLIANÒ, Antonio, Professor of Fundamental Theology, Pius X Pontifical Seminary, Catanzaro
SULLIVAN, Francis, P., Professor of Fundamental Theology, Department of Theology, Boston College
VANHOYE, Albert, Professor of New Testament Exegesis, Pontifical Biblical Institute, Rome
VERWEYEN, Hansjürgen, Professor of Fundamental Theology, University of Fribourg im Breisgau
VISCA, Danila, Professor of History of Religions, "La Sapienza" University, Rome
WEGER, Karl Heinz, Professor of Philosophy, Berchmanskolleg, Munich

Translators

Robert Barr
David Kipp
Matthew O'Connell
Alan Neame
John Cummings
Stewart Foster
Staff of St. Paul's Publications

SYSTEMATIC INDEX

Italics are used in this Systematic Index for topics that are treated as parts of articles in the *Dictionary*; these themes are not the subjects of individual articles. The pages on which these topics are covered in the various articles of the *Dictionary* can be found in the Analytical Index at the end of this work.

I. Revelation

1.1. Nature and Object

Abba
Certitude
Christology
Church
Dialogue
God
Holy Spirit
Jesus of History
Kingdom/Reign of God
Love
Meaning
Mystery
Paschal Mystery
Salvation
Specificity of Revelation
Testimony
Trinity
Truth
Word of God

1.2. Preparation

Covenant
Election
Experience
History of Salvation
John the Baptist
Judaism
Law
Messianism
Patriarchs
Promise
Prophets
Sacred Scripture
Testaments: Promise

1.3. Fulfillment

Abba
Apparitions
Christology
Church: Jesus and the Church
Eschatology
Holy Spirit
Jesus of History
Messianism
Miracle
Paschal Mystery
Prophecy
Testaments: Old and New
Testimony
Uniqueness and Universality
Word of God

2. Credibility

2.1. Nature and Object

Christological Titles
Church
Faith
God
Gospel
History of Salvation
Jesus of History, Christ of Faith
Love
Meaning
Messianism
Mystery
Paschal Mystery
Revelation
Sacred Scripture
Salvation
Sign
Tradition
Truth
Word of God

2.2. Structuring

A. Dogmatic Reflection

Analogy
Canon of Scripture
Charism
Christocentrism
Deposit of Faith
Dogma
Faith
Gospel
History
Language
Magisterium
Method
Mystery
Revelation
Sensus Fidei

Testimony
Testaments: Old and New
Theology
Tradition
Truth

B. Apologetic Reflection

Analysis of the Faith
Gospel
Hermeneutics
Historical Jesus
Immanence
Knowledge of Jesus
Language
Literature
Meaning
Method
Philosophy (Christian)
Preamble of the Faith
Realism, Christian
Religion
Semiology
Testimony
Theology

2.3. Signs

Christ
Credibility
Evangelization
Inculturation
Justice
Kingdom/Reign of God
Loci Theologici
Love
Martyr
Miracle
Mission
Prophecy
Semiology

3. Faith

4. Epistemology

5. History

ABBREVIATIONS

Books of the Bible

Acts	Acts of the Apostles		2 Kgs	2 Kings
Am	Amos		Lam	Lamentations
Bar	Baruch		Lk	Luke
1 Chr	1 Chronicles		Lv	Leviticus
2 Chr	2 Chronicles		Mal	Malachi
Col	Colossians		1 Mc	1 Maccabees
1 Cor	1 Corinthians		2 Mc	2 Maccabees
2 Cor	2 Corinthians		Mi	Micah
Dn	Daniel		Mk	Mark
Dt	Deuteronomy		Mt	Matthew
Eccl	Ecclesiastes		Na	Nahum
Eph	Ephesians		Neh	Nehemiah
Est	Esther		Nm	Numbers
Ex	Exodus		Ob	Obadiah
Ez	Ezekiel		Phil	Philippians
Ezr	Ezra		Phlm	Philemon
Gal	Galatians		Prv	Proverbs
Gn	Genesis		Ps(s)	Psalms
Hb	Habakkuk		1 Pt	1 Peter
Heb	Hebrews		2 Pt	2 Peter
Hg	Haggai		Rom	Romans
Hos	Hosea		Ru	Ruth
Is	Isaiah		Rv	Revelation
Jas	James		Sir	Sirach
Jb	Job		1 Sm	1 Samuel
Jdt	Judith		2 Sm	2 Samuel
Jer	Jeremiah		Song(Sg)	Song of Songs
Jgs	Judges		Tb	Tobit
Jl	Joel		1 Thes	1 Thessalonians
Jn	John		2 Thes	2 Thessalonians
1 Jn	1 John		Ti	Titus
2 Jn	2 John		1 Tm	1 Timothy
3 Jn	3 John		2 Tm	2 Timothy
Jon	Jonah		Wis	Wisdom
Jos	Joshua		Zec	Zechariah
Jude	Jude		Zep	Zephaniah
1 Kgs	1 Kings			

Documents of Vatican II

AA	*Apostolicam Actuositatem*
AG	*Ad Gentes*
CD	*Christus Dominus*
DH	*Dignitatis Humanae*
DV	*Dei Verbum*
GE	*Gravissimum Educationis*
GS	*Gaudium et Spes*
IM	*Inter Mirifica*
LG	*Lumen Gentium*
NA	*Nostra Aetate*
OE	*Orientalium Ecclesiarum*
OT	*Optatam Totius*
PC	*Perfectae Caritatis*
PO	*Presbyterorum Ordinis*
SC	*Sacrosanctum Concilium*
UR	*Unitatis Redintegratio*

Acts of the Council

AS	*Acta Synodalia S. Concilii Oecumenici Vaticani II.* Typis Polyglottis Vaticanis, Civitas Vaticana. 26 vols. Rome, 1970–80.

Documents of the Magisterium

DS	Denzinger-Schönmetzer, eds. *Enchiridion symbolorum, definitionum et declarationum de rebus fidei et morum*

CL	*Christifideles Laici*
CT	*Catechesi Tradendae*
DM	*Dives in Misericordia*
EN	*Evangelii Nuntiandi*
ES	*Ecclesiam Suam*
PT	*Pacem in Terris*
RH	*Redemptor Hominis*
RM	*Redemptoris Mater*

Reference Works

BthW	*Bibeltheologisches Wörterbuch*, ed. J. Bauer. Graz, 1976.
Cath	*Catholicisme*, ed. G. Jacquemet. Paris, 1948–.
CChrCM	*Corpus Christianorum, Continuatio Mediaevalis.* Brepols, Turnholt, 1966.
CChrSL	*Corpus Christianorum, Series Latina.* Brepols, Turnholt, 1953.
CChrSG	*Corpus Christianorum, Series Graeca.* Brepols, Turnholt, 1977.
CG	Thomas Aquinas, *Summa Contra Gentiles.*
CCL	*Catholic Canon Law*
CSCO	*Corpus Scriptorum Christianorum Orientalium.* Rome, 1903.

CSEL	*Corpus Scriptorum Ecclesiasticorum Latinorum,* ed. Académie de Vienne. Vienna, 1906.
DAFC	*Dictionnaire apologétique de la foi catholique,* ed. d'Alès. Paris, 1931.
DBS	*Supplément au Dictionnaire de la Bible.* Paris, 1928.
DC	*Documentation catholique*
DECA	*Dictionnaire encyclopédique du christianisme ancien.* Paris, 1990.
DSp	*Dictionnaire de Spiritualité,* ed. M. Viller. Paris, 1937.
DTC	*Dictionnaire de théologie catholique,* ed. E. Vacant. Paris, 1937.
DTI	*Dizionario Teologico Interdisciplinare.* Turin, 1977–78.
EB	*Enchiridion Biblicum: Documenta Ecclesiastica Sacram Scripturam Spectantia.* Naples and Rome, 1961.
EC	*Enciclopedia Cattolica.* Vatican City, 1945–54.
EF	*Enciclopedia filosofica.* Novara, 1979.
EKL	*Evangelisches Kirchenlexicon,* ed. H. Brunotte and O. Weber. Göttingen, 1956–61.
EO	*Enchiridion Oecumenicum,* ed. S. J. Voicu and G. Ceretti. Bologna, 1986–88.
EP	Rouët de Journel, *Enchiridion patristicum.*
ER	*Encyclopedia of Religion,* ed. M. Eliade. New York and London, 1987.
ETF	*Enciclopedia di Teologia Fondamentale: Storia, Progetto, Autori, Categorie,* ed. G. Ruggieri. Turin, 1987.
EV	*Enchiridion Vaticanum.* Bologna, 1966.
GDR	*Grande Dizionario delle Religioni,* ed. P. Poupard. Assisi, 1988.
GLNT	*Grande lessico del Nuovo Testamento.* Italian trans. of *TWNT,* by F. Montagnini. Brescia, 1965–90.
GNO	*Gregorii Nysseni Opera,* ed. W. Jaeger and H. Langerbeck
HDG	*Handbuch der Dogmengeschichte.* Fribourg, 1956.
HFT	*Handbuch der Fundamentaltheologie,* ed. W. Kern, H. J. Pottmeyer, and M. Seckler. Fribourg, 1985–88.
HKG	*Handbuch der Kirchengeschichte,* ed. H. Jedin. Fribourg, 1962.
HWP	*Historisches Wörterbuch der Philosophie,* ed. R. Eisler. Bâle, 1971.
JBC	*The Jerome Biblical Commentary,* ed. R. E. Brown, J. A. Fitzmyer, and R. E. Murphy. Englewood Cliffs, N.J., 1968.
LTK	*Lexikon für Theologie und Kirche,* ed. J. Hofer and K. Rahner. Freiburg im Breisgau, 1956–65.
LW	*Luther's Works.* The American Edition. 55 vols. St. Louis and Philadelphia, 1955–86.
MystSal	*Mysterium Salutis,* ed. J. Feiner and M. Löhrer. Brescia, 1967–78.
NCE	*New Catholic Encyclopedia.* New York, 1967–74.
ND	N. Neuner and J. Dupuis, eds. *The Christian Faith in the Doctrinal Documents of the Catholic Church.* Rev. ed. Staten Island, N.Y., 1982.
NDL	*Nuovo Dizionario di Liturgia,* ed. D. Sartore and A. M. Triacca. Rome, 1984.
NDM	*Nuovo Dizionario di Mariologia,* ed. S. De Fiores and S. Meo. Rome, 1985.
NDS	*Nuovo Dizionario di Spiritualità,* ed. S. De Fiores and T. Goffi. Rome, 1985.
NDT	*Nuovo Dizionario di Teologia,* ed. G. Barbaglio and S. Dianich. Rome, 1977.

NDTB	*Nuovo Dizionario di Teologia Biblica*, ed. P. Rossano, G. Ravasi, and A. Girlanda. Rome, 1989.
NHTG	*Neues Handbuch theologischer Grundbegriffe*, ed. P. Eicher. Munich, 1984–.
PG	*Patrologiae Cursus Completus: Series Graeca*, ed. J. P. Migne. Paris, 1857–1945.
PhW	*Philosophisches Wörterbuch*, ed. W. Brugger. Fribourg, 1953.
PL	*Patrologiae Cursus Completus: Series Latina*, ed. J. P. Migne. Paris, 1844–1974.
PO	*Patrologia Orientalis*, ed. R. Graffin. Paris and Turnholt, 1907.
RGG 1–3	*Die Religion in Geschichte und Gegenwart: Handwörterbuch für Theologie und Religionswissenschaft*, ed. K. Galling. Tübingen, 1957–65.
SChr	*Sources chrétiennes*. Paris, 1941–.
SM	*Sacramentum Mundi*, ed. K. Rahner. Brescia, 1974–77.
ST	Thomas Aquinas, *Summa Theologiae*
TDNT	*Theological Wordbook of the New Testament*, ed. G. Kittel and G. Friedrichs. Grand Rapids, 1964–76.
TRE	*Theologische Realenzyklopädie*, ed. G. Krause and G. Müller. Berlin and New York, 1977.
TWAT	*Theologisches Wörterbuch zum Alten Testament*, ed. G. Botterweck and H. Ringgren. Stuttgart, 1973.
TWNT	*Theologisches Wörterbuch zum Neuen Testament*, ed. G. Kittel and G. Friedrich. Stuttgart, 1933–73.
WA	*Weimarer Ausgabe. M. Luther, Werke, Kritische Gesamtsausgabe.* Weimar, 1883–.
WKL	*Weltkirchenlexikon: Handbuch der Ökumene*, ed. F. H. Littell and H. H. Walz. Stuttgart, 1960.

Journals and Series

AAS	*Acta Apostolica Sedis*
ABG	*Archiv für Begriffsgeschichte*
AHC	*Annuarium Historiae Conciliorum*
ArchFil	*Archivio di Filosofia*
ARG	*Archiv für Reformationsgeschichte*
ArPh	*Archives de Philosophie*
ASSR	*Archives de Sciences Sociales des Religions*
ATh	*Année théologique*
Aug	*Augustinianum*
Bib	*Biblica*
BETL	Bibliotheca ephemeridum theologicarum lovaniensium
BJRL	*Bulletin of the John Rylands Library*
BTB	*Biblical Theology Bulletin*
BZ	*Biblische Zeitschrift*
CBQ	*Catholic Biblical Quarterly*
CivCatt	*La Civiltà Cattolica*
Comm	*Communio*
Conc	*Concilium*

EE	Estudios Eclesiásticos
EstBibl	Estudios Bíblicos
EsVie	Esprit et Vie
Et	Études
ETL	Ephemerides Theologicae Lovanienses
ETR	Études Théologiques et Religieuses
EvQ	Evangelical Quarterly
EvT	Evangelische Theologie
FrSA	Franciscan Studies Annual
FZPT	Freiburger Zeitschrift für Philosophie und Theologie
Greg	Gregorianum
HeyJ	Heythrop Journal
HTR	Harvard Theological Review
IBS	Irish Biblical Studies
IKZ	International kirchliche Zeitschrift
IPQ	International Philosophical Quarterly
Ir	Irénikon
ITQ	Irish Theological Quarterly
JAAR	Journal of the American Academy of Religion
JTS	Journal of Theological Studies
KuD	Kerygma und Dogma
Lat	Lateranum
LKD	Literatur des katholischen Deutschlands
MSR	Mélanges de Science Religieuse
MTZ	Münchener theologische Zeitschrift
NHS	Nag Hammadi Studies
NRT	Nouvelle Revue Théologique
NT	Novum Testamentum
NZST	Neue Zeitschrift für Systematische Theologie
PhJ	Philosophisches Jahrbuch der Görres-Gesellschaft
RAMy	Revue d'Ascétique et de Mystique
RB	Revue biblique
RBén	Revue Bénédictine
RCT	Revista Catalana de Teología
RdT	Rassegna di Teologia
REB	Revista Ecclesiástica Brasileira
RET	Revista Española de Teología
RFNS	Revista di Filosofia Neo-Scolastica
RHPhR	Revue d'Histoire et de Philosophie Religieuses
RSLR	Rivista di Storia e Letteratura Religiosa
RSPT	Revue des Sciences Philosophiques et Théologiques
RSR	Recherches de Science Religieuse
RThom	Revue Thomiste
RThPh	Revue de Théologie et de Philosophie
RTL	Revue Théologique de Louvain
RUnOtt	Revue de l'Université d'Ottawa
Sal	Salesianum
ScCatt	La Scuola Cattolica
ScE	Science et Esprit

SHR	Studies in the History of Religion
SNT	Schriften des Neuen Testaments
SNTU	Studien zum Neuen Testament und seiner Umwelt
StCatt	Studi Cattolici
StTh	Studia Theologica
StZ	Stimmen der Zeit
Teol	Teologia
Theol	Theology
TD	Theology Digest
TG	Theologie und Glaube
Thom	The Thomist
TP	Theologie und Philosophie
TPQ	Theologisch-praktische Quartalschirft
TQ	Theologische Quartalschrift
ThR	Theologische Rundschau
TS	Theological Studies
VD	Verbum Domini
ZAW	Zeitschrift für die alttestamentliche Wissenschaft
ZKT	Zeitschrift für die katholische Theologie
ZNW	Zeitschrift für die neutestamentliche Wissenschaft
ZThK	Zeitschrift für Theologie und Kirche

Other Abbreviations

LXX	Septuagint
NT	New Testament
OT	Old Testament
PT	Palestinian Targum

Other Early Jewish and Christian Writings

Ant.	Josephus, Antiquities of the Jews
Apoc. Mos.	Apocalypse of Moses
J.W.	Josephus, Jewish War
Pss. Sol.	Psalms of Solomon

Qumran Literature

CD	Damascus Document
1QH	Thanksgiving Hymns from Qumran Cave 1
1QM	War Scroll from Qumran Cave 1
1QpHab	Pesher on Habakkuk from Qumran Cave 1
1QS	Community Rule from Qumran Cave 1
1QSa	Rule of the Congregation from Qumran Cave 1
4QFlor	Florilegium from Qumran Cave 4

Practical Matters

1. Transliteration. Greek: Long o and e vowels in Greek are marked with a macron over the vowel (ō, ē). Accents are not indicated. Hebrew: Aleph = '; Ayin = '; Shin = š. Long vowels written defectively in Hebrew are indicated with a macron over the vowel. Long vowels with full writing are indicated by a circumflex over the vowel.

2. Cross-references. Cross-references to other articles in the *Dictionary* are indicated either by small capital letters within the text or by parenthetical references with arrows. For example: (→ THEOLOGY I).

A

ABBA, FATHER

The Gospels clearly present the figure of Jesus under the denomination "Son of God." They establish an explicit Christology, and they do so in programmatic fashion. Thus, the very first verse of the Gospel of Mark outlines the whole development of the work: "Jesus Christ, the Son of God" (Mk 1:1). John formulates the same thesis in his conclusion, explaining that it is to this end that he has composed his Gospel: "That you may come to believe that Jesus is the Messiah, the Son of God" (Jn 20:31). In order to arrive at this overt formulation, the evangelists take their point of departure in an implicit Christology, which they present to us in Jesus' behavior, in his words and preaching, in the execution of his work. A basic starting point for coming to this faith in Jesus as Son of God is Jesus' own use of the term *abba* ("father") to express his relationship with God. In order to grasp the dimension that this term acquires in Jesus' usage, we must contrast that usage with its precedents in the Judaic world that was the concrete matrix of Jesus' life.

1. To call the divinity "Father" belongs to a common legacy in the history of religions. The OT is no exception. There too, along with so many other designations, God is presented as 'āb ("father"). But Judaic piety has special characteristics. God is a father not in the sense of a forefather but as the Creator (Dt 32:6; Mal 2:10). The people of Israel have had the experience of a God as Father, and themselves as the firstborn of God, through a salvation history having its meaningful commencement in the flight and liberation from Egypt (Ex 4:22; Is 63:16; Jer 31:9). Here is the moment of the birth of the people created by God. Throughout the history of this people, God has shown it a father's love (Hos 11:1-4, 8). Thus, the fatherhood of God is Israel's special prerogative. However, Israel exercises great reserve in applying the name "Father" to God, perhaps owing to the danger of its being misunderstood in a mythological sense. God is designated "Father" only some fifteen times in the OT (Dt 32:6; 2 Sm 7:14; 1 Chr 17:13; 22:10; 28:6; Pss

68:6; 89:27; Is 63:16 [bis]; 64:7; Jer 3:4, 19; 31:9; Mal 1:6; 2:10). Among this people, these children of God, the king enjoys a special relationship of sonship with God, and God maintains with him a particular attitude of Father (2 Sm 7:14). In this adoption of predilection, God is said to engender the king on the day of his enthronement and to proclaim to him, "You are my son" (Ps 2:7): thus the king is invested with a messianic character and foreshadows an eschatological figure. Only in rare passages, and only in the more recent literature, does the OT treat of God as Father in a personal relationship with the individual (Sir 23:1, 4; Wis 14:3). In these texts of Hellenistic Judaism, sprung from a Greek matrix, God not only is denominated "Father" but is actually addressed as such: "Lord, Father, and master of my life" (Sir 23:1); "Lord, Father, and God of my life (Sir 23:4)—although the doubt remains open as to whether, in their point of departure, these expressions might represent not a personal invocation of God as Father but an appeal to God as "Lord of *my* father," in the spirit of the canticle of the children of Israel (Ex 15:2), or indeed of a text in Sirach itself (51:10). It is the book of Wisdom that offers us the first and only OT supplication of God as Father in the vocative case (Gr. *pater*), when, in speaking of the works of wisdom, the sacred writer addresses God as follows: "It is your providence, Father, that directs it" (Wis 14:3). Here we find an excellent preparation for the new route that Jesus will open.

2. As we move from the OT to the NT, we encounter a different panorama—although one still in keeping with the lines already initiated. First, the term "Father" is applied to God nearly 250 times. Second, a radical change occurs in the projection of the fatherhood of God—which now is no longer Israel's prerogative alone but belongs to all human beings. Third, and most radically, this fatherhood is now rooted in the exceptional and unique meaning assigned to the establishment of the relation between Jesus as Son and God as Father: this novelty of meaning is now extended to other human beings, in

an insistence that the latter, in imitation of Jesus, should not only refer to but actually address God as their "Father."

A. The *frequency* of the occurrence of the term "Father" in the NT may stem from Jesus' own use of it with reference to God. The Gospels place the expression "Father" on Jesus' lips with astonishing frequency in reference to God—no fewer than 170 times. Mark uses it 4 times, Luke some 15, Matthew 42, and John 109. We observe an increasing frequency as the Gospel tradition advances, so that the difference between Mark and John is enormous in this respect. Thus, we surmise that many of the texts in which Jesus is said to call God "Father" are the fruit of the evangelists' redaction.

B. The *designation of God as Father* originates, however, with Jesus himself. Jesus' own use of the term "Father" to designate God is present in the most ancient layers of the tradition, as it is found in Mark and in the common source of Matthew and Luke. We are referring to Jesus' denomination of God as "Father" not only absolutely—that is, without a modifier (Mk 13:32; Lk 11:13)—or with the addition of the second person plural possessive "your" (Mk 11:25; Mt 5:48 par. Lk 6:36; 6:32 par. Lk 12:30)—but also, and especially, with the possessive "my," as in common texts of Matthew (11:27) and Luke (10:22) and even, perhaps, in the Gospel of Mark (8:38). This expression—Jesus' calling God "my Father"—is almost without parallel in OT or rabbinic literature. The originality and novelty of this manner of referring to God further increase our confidence in tracing it back to Jesus himself.

C. Jesus' *invocation of God as Father* enjoys an even stronger warranty. All layers of the gospel tradition are consistent in presenting Jesus' personal invocation of God as a father. Mark records it (14:36 par. Mt 26:39 and Lk 22:42); Matthew does so in a text exclusively his (26:42); Luke has it twice (23:34, 46); and it occurs in John nine times (11:41; 12:27–28; 17:1, 5, 11, 21, 24, 25). In combination, these texts lead to the conclusion that Jesus begins every prayer with an invocation of God as a father, with the exception of one prayer on the cross (Mk 15:34 par. Mt 27:46)—in which Jesus quotes the words of the psalm: "My God, my God, why have you forsaken me?" But furthermore, we learn the concrete manner in which Jesus invoked God: not only does Mark hand it down to us by preserving, in the prayer of Gethsemane, the Aramaic word in its Greek transliteration (abba), followed by the corresponding Greek term, *ho patēr* (Mk 14:36); but the juxtaposition of the invocation in Aramaic and in Greek suggests that the invocative terms cited in Jesus' other prayers are only being substituted for the word he actually used in addressing God: 'abbā. The root of this invocation of Jesus is clear from Paul, who refers to the cry the faithful of his own community utter, when, under the impulse of the Spirit, they likewise call on God as *Abba* (Gal 4:6), as also does another community not founded by him (Rom 8:15).

D. The *strongest guarantee of Jesus' invocation* of God as a father is in the very term *abba*. We may rest assured that it was actually used by Jesus. Why? The word 'abbā originates in "baby talk"—the words children used to address their fathers—although, to be sure, it was used by adults as well in addressing their elders. True, from time to time in Hellenistic Judaism God was addressed as *pater* (see Wis 14:3). But it would have been simply unthinkable for anyone to use the term 'abbā in addressing God. It would have been regarded as disrespectful. This discontinuity with the usage of the era of the Gospel is our further surety for the historicity of its use by Jesus (→ GOSPELS).

E. The *relationship of filial intimacy* prevailing between Jesus and the Father is betrayed by Jesus' use of the term *abba*. The content of this relationship is enshrined in the hymn of jubilee pronounced by Jesus and calling upon God as a "father" (suggesting the Aramaic 'abbā). Addressing God as "Father" twice in that hymn, Jesus offers thanks to that Father for the latter's revelatory activity in behalf of the lowly (Mt 11:25-26 par. Lk 10:21). Next he declares the relationship that unites him, the Son, to God, his Father. Jesus asserts: "All things have been handed over to me by my Father" (Mt 11:27a; Lk 10:22a). In the context of Jesus' just-uttered prayer of thanksgiving, what has "been given" to the Son by the Father will be a full and total revelation. Whereas for the scribes and Pharisees the source of information has been the traditions of their forebears (see Mk 7:3, 9), Jesus' own source of knowledge is what he has received from God his Father. The knowledge between Jesus and the Father is reciprocal: "No one knows the Son except the Father, and no one knows the Father except the Son" (Mt 11:27bc par. Lk 10:22bc). In this mutual cognition, without excluding the noetic aspect, we may observe what biblical "knowledge" implies: the will is involved, as well, in a communion of life. The Father's preferential love for the Son — his "beloved Son" (Mt 3:17; Mk 1:11) — is presupposed, as well as a love on the part of the Son that leads him to an attitude of submission and obedience to the Father (Lk 2:49; Mt 26:39; Mk 14:6). As it is Jesus who knows the Father, it is he who can reveal that Father; the Father prefers to make divine revelation to the simple (Mt 11:25–26 and par.); the Son reveals the Father to whom he will (Mt 11:27d and par.). Commencing in the Synoptics, this Christology will reach its total, plenary development in the Christology of the Fourth Gospel: "It is God the only Son, who is close to the Father's heart, who has given to know him" (Jn 1:18). John, like the Synoptics, from a point of departure in Jesus' designation and invocation of God as Father, and from the submission and obedience he manifests, will arrive at a clear and explicit designation of Jesus as Son of God (Mk 1:1; Jn 20:31).

F. *Our own designation and invocation* of God as Father is at Jesus' behest (Mt 6:9; Lk 11:2): in virtue of the activity of the Spirit, we too address God as *Abba* (Rom 8:15; Gal 4:6). Of course, there will always remain the measureless difference established by Jesus himself, who does not include himself in the "our" of our invocation "Our Father," and who distinguishes "his" Father and "ours" in Jn 20:17: "I am ascending to my Father and your Father." And yet Jesus and we are both enveloped in one and the same love bestowed on us by the Father, as we learn from the petition that Jesus makes in behalf of his disciples: "That the love with which you have loved me may be in them" (Jn 17:26).

Bibl.: G. DALMAN, *Die Worte Jesu: Mit Berücksichtigung des nachkanonischen jüdischen Schrifttums und der aramäischen Sprache*, vol. 1 (Darmstadt, 1930², 1965) 150–59; G. KITTEL, "ἀββᾶ," *TDNT* 1:4–6; G. SCHRENK, "πατήρ," *TDNT* 5:945–1014; W. MARCHEL, *Abba, Père! La prière du Christ et des chrétiens: Étude exégétique sur les origines et la signification de l'invocation à la divinité comme Père, avant et dans le Nouveau Testament* (Rome, 1963); J. JEREMIAS, "Kennzeichen der ipsissima vox Jesu," in *Synoptische Studien* (Fs. A. Wikenhauser; Münster, 1958) 86–93; id., *Abba* (Philadelphia, 1978); id., *Neutestamentliche Theologie*, vol. 1: *Die Verkündigung Jesu* (Gütersloh, 1971) 45, 67–73 (*New Testament Theology*, vol. 1: *The Proclamation of Jesus* [London/New York, 1971]); J. CABA, *El Jesús de los evangelios* (Madrid, 1977) 281–84, 300–313; O. MICHEL, "Patêr," in H. BALZ et al., eds., *Exegetisches Wörterbuch zum NT*, vol. 3 (Stuttgart, 1982) 125–35; S. SABUGAL, *Abba! . . . La oración del Señor* (Madrid, 1985) 366–424.

José CABA

AGNOSTICISM

1. Explanation of the Term

The term "agnosticism" (from Gk. *agnostos*, "unknowable") usually refers to the (philosophical) position that everything transempirical, or transcendent, is unknowable. In line with this position, statements about the transcendent are regarded as scientifically unverifiable, and scientific status is consequently also denied to metaphysics (the science of the transempirical, immutable, and spiritual).

The concept was formulated by the English biologist and philosopher Thomas Henry Huxley (1825–1895) in contradistinction to "gnostic" cognitive certainty, and was introduced into philosophy in 1869. Huxley intended this concept to designate a position in which, presupposing that God is unknowable and that human knowledge is finite and limited, one refrains from making definite assertions of belief oneself and reacts skeptically to those made by others (see Huxley, 237–40).

In view of this, agnosticism is also critically distinct from atheism, which claims, of course, to have definite knowledge of God's nonexistence. Agnosticism, by contrast, relegates claims about the existence or nonexistence of God to the realm of cognitively unverifiable statements. Accordingly, contestation of God's existence is to be treated in the same way as affirmation of his existence.

Agnostic currents and attitudes of mind have been present from earliest times in Western thought, even if not always made the object of philosophical or theological reflection. In so-called negative theology, based on the understanding that, in relation to God, one can always know only what he is not, and not what he is, we find a religiously oriented agnosticism.

2. Modern Agnosticism

Critical philosophy (Hume, Kant) and neo-positivism (Vienna Circle, analytic philosophy) are regarded as the intellectual forerunners of modern agnosticism. There is a close intellectual kinship with modern skepticism.

According to Kant's (1724–1804) statements on transcendental dialectic in the *Kritik der reinen Vernunft* (*Critique of Pure Reason*), scientific statements are possible only regarding finite, spatiotemporal interrelationships. In his view, statements about the world as a whole lead to contradictions. Scientific knowledge, which ought to be reliable, is attainable only in the realm of finite appearances and interrelationships. Statements going beyond this are to be regarded as inadmissible crossings of the boundary and are thus to be rejected.

In the view of modern positivism, the logical inquiries undertaken by analytical philosophy demonstrate the contradictoriness of religious statements. How can God, e.g., be simultaneously infinite and a person?

Today agnosticism is indebted to thinkers like Bertrand Russell, Ernst Topitsch, and others for important stimuli. The Spanish legal philosopher Enrique Tierno Galván (1918–1986) attempted a general justification of agnosticism (see Bibliography). In his view, agnosticism is contrastingly opposed to both atheism and religious belief. Like Huxley, he rejects gnostic certainty of knowledge about the existence or nonexistence of God. His thought circles around the notion of "finitude." The agnostic is the person who consciously and sincerely confronts the finitude of being and endeavors to live positively. The life of a believer, by contrast, is split by a two-directional striving, by a this-worldly goal and an otherworldly one. Tierno Galván sees a fundamental contradiction between these two life goals; hence, he also speaks of the "theological tragedy" of the life of believers. He therefore wishes to restore to humanity the sense of the finitude—and thus the unity—of its existence that it has lost through religion. Agnosticism is

also a humanism: it aims at overcoming the loneliness and isolation of human beings and establishing community without thereby violating or annihilating the individual. Salvation represents no transcendental fact, but implies identifying oneself with the meaning of this world, which lies in finitude. In the end, however, just how this finitude can be lived in a world like ours remains open and without answer. The moral appeal to live one's finitude in a humane way is not really sufficient.

3. Theological Evaluation

Today the spirit of the times inclines more toward agnosticism than toward atheism, which means that contemporary theology perceives agnosticism ("indifference") as the real challenge (cf. Karl Rahner, H. R. Schlette).

In the past, the Catholic church has repeatedly condemned modern agnosticism.

Vatican I (1870), in the Dogmatic Constitution *Dei Filius* (DS 3000–3045), affirms the certain knowability of God with the aid of human reason (see DS 3004), and pronounces an anathema upon all who dispute this (see DS 3026)—something that agnosticism must also be counted as doing.

Pope Pius X, in his encyclical of 8 September 1907, *Pascendi dominici gregis* (cf. *AAS* 40 [1907] 596ff.; DS 3475–3500) and elsewhere, develops a detailed position on agnosticism. In the view of the pope, agnosticism forms the basis of the errors of modernism.

However, two theological convictions intrinsic to Christianity itself weigh against any overhasty condemnation of agnosticism: (1) the conviction that all human knowledge is "partial" (1 Cor 13:9), limited, and fallible, and (2) the traditional doctrine—based on the biblical way of speaking of the "hidden God" (Is 45:15)—of the "unknowability of God" (Jn 1:18a; Heb 11:27; Rom 1:20; Col 1:15; 1 Tm 1:17; and elsewhere), as was advanced theologically mainly by the Cappadocians (Basil; Gregory of Nyssa in his dispute with the Arian Eunomius). Involved here are not, of course, two completely different things; rather, the two problems are internally related. Human cognition and human knowledge are by nature referred to what is worldly because they are themselves components of worldly reality. Consequently, they are also subject to the contingency that is characteristic of everything worldly. Knowledge of God is no exception to this. Hence, by his very nature God cannot be an object of human cognition; he remains fundamentally unknowable.

That human cognition is in principle contingent, limited, and fallible is no modern insight that theology might have to owe, for instance, to modern *fallibilism* (Karl Popper, Hans Albert, et al.). Apart from the broad basic conviction of the partial nature of human cognition that is, as noted above, intrinsic to Christian philosophy and theology, Nicholas of Cusa (1401–1464) was preeminent, at the close of the Middle Ages, in discussing the *suppositional* nature (the "conjectural" nature) of human cognition ("Speaking of contingent realities, we run always the risk of erring" [*Docta ignorantia* bk. 2, chap. 11]).

The apparent contradiction between the traditionally taught unknowability of God and his knowability as maintained by the First Vatican Council results from a superficial reading of the text; for the added qualifying phrase *e creatis* (from the things that are made) is usually disregarded. The council maintains that there is a limited knowledge of God *"from the things that are made."* Not God himself is the object of the knowledge, but the world as God's creation. What is maintained, then, is the knowability of the world's creatureliness and its inherent referredness to something/someone that/who is radically different from it. Moreover, the creatureliness of the world initially implies no more than that the world cannot exist without what religious language calls "God." "God" appears as the one without whom nothing exists. This theological consideration is fully compatible with the biblical evidence, incorporates the fundamental insight of negative theology, and may well also provide a basis for dialogue with modern agnosticism.

Bibl.: L. STEPHEN, *An Agnostic's Apology* (1876); T. H. HUXLEY, "Agnosticism," in *Collected Essays*, vol. 5 (London, 1902); C. SEIDEL, "Agnostizismus," in *Historisches Wörterbuch der Philosophie*, vol. 1 (Basel/Stuttgart, 1971) 110–12; R. W. HEPBURN, "Agnosticism," in *The Encyclopedia of Philosophy*, vol. 1 (New York/London, 1972) 56–59; A. V. STRÖM, H. GÜNTHER, and B. GUSTAFSSON, "Agnostizismus I–III," in *Theologische Realenzyklopädie*, vol. 2 (Berlin/New York, 1978) 91–100; E. KANT, "Transcendental Dialectic," in *Critique of Pure Reason*; H. R. SCHLETTE, ed. *Der moderne Agnostizismus* (Düsseldorf, 1979); K. RAHNER, "Justifying Faith in an Agnostic World," in *Theological Investigations*, vol. 21 (1983; London/New York, 1988) 130–36; E. TIERNO GALVÁN, *¿Que es ser agnóstico?* (Madrid, 1986).

Bernd GROTH

ANALOGY

We may say without exaggeration that *analogy* is the essential form of discourse in Catholic fundamental theology. It denotes a way of using certain words so that, under certain specific conditions, they can effectively enunciate the reality of God, even if in a very approximate manner. In other words, analogy opens up a *via media* between two extremes. One is negative ("apophatic"), according to which none of the names attributed to God can properly signify him; the divine names then are metaphors, images, and indications, all with practical (i.e., liturgical) implications. They suggest, if people believe in God, a certain mode of human behavior, rather than the mode of God's being; or, one might say, they provide means with which God may be celebrated, but they never, in however limited a way, provide exhaustive knowledge of God. The other is the univocal extreme. With all the practical reservations needed to avoid the danger of anthropomorphism, one may allow that words can make a statement about God while making a statement about human beings, their essence and history. Behind these two positions, there are two ideas of God: the God beyond everything, who does not have to do with anything that is human, whether because it is human, or because it is culpable, so that there is no concept of God and no name for God. Conversely, God is so very much with us that we can neither conceive of him nor express him other than in this communication with human beings, at the level of human essence and human history.

Finally, we must remember that these two positions, precisely because they are extreme, do meet in a certain sense: if God can express himself only with us and by using our words (understood univocally) for the purpose, then our words do not allow access to that which he would be eventually in himself and apart from us. If we agreed to take this viewpoint into consideration, it would amount to sheer apophatism. Conversely, if we can say nothing proper about God, even though we must indeed speak of him (as the Bible itself does), we run the risk of actually hypostatizing the "indicative" words that we then use, thus lapsing surreptitiously into an uncritical form of univocity. From Plotinus to Heidegger, on the one hand, and from Oenomaus of Gadara to Hegel, on the other hand, there has been no lack of followers—including Christian thinkers—of the two ways.

Like everything that is "intermediate" or "moderate," the royal road of analogy is difficult to follow, and it is not easy to keep to it. Its philosophico-theological basis is the theme of creation: if God is the creator of human beings, then naturally they are led to search for knowledge of their Principle, and they are possessed of an intellect appropriate to that quest. Accordingly, certain human words that they use should be capable of enunciating the names of God; no disorder, however great, in human life can wholly eradicate this power of words, because it is impossible to quash God's creative work and absolutely corrupt the human intellect. On the other hand, if God is creator, he is not human and therefore cannot be named as human beings name themselves and the objects in their world; the names of God are the names of God as fundamental Principle.

To elaborate this important point somewhat: to say that the names of God are the names of God as Principle does not mean that they signify God only to the extent that he is *our* Principle, for it is not God in himself whom we wish to name but God in his relation to us, which is a functional and not a characteristic designation. Moreover, these names do not express God totally beyond his reality as Principle, for we have no means of access to him other than our acknowledgment of this essential creative quality. Then one would say that there is some kind of participation between the Principle and us: the Principle bestows on us some share, however small, in that which he is in himself; a discriminatory analysis of that which, in human being or in the world, does not necessarily bear the marks of finiteness, precedes all analogical attributions. Then a process that requires extremely refined management comes into play; it consists in retaining

the word and the concept while simultaneously depriving them of their finite aspects. Accordingly, we arrive at an attribution that signifies God properly but that, in accordance with analogy, is related to the proximity of Creator to creature and to the distance between Creator and creature.

Analogy comes fully into play in regard to the word "being," for then it concerns what is the most pregnant and at the same time the least specific category of the human vocabulary. To say that God is "he who is" does not mean merely "God is the cause (wholly unknown and unnamable) of our being," nor, conversely, "God is God as we are human beings." That is to say, God is, in the way in which he can be who produces in the creature not only this or that aspect but being pure and simple. Accordingly, this "mode of being" of God can indeed be enunciated, but such an utterance does not mean that our intellect has comprehended God, "for no similarity can be said to hold between Creator and creature which does not imply a greater dissimilarity between the two" (Fourth Lateran Council, DS 806).

The word "being," pronounced in accordance with analogy in awareness of this mysterious proximity/distance, thus offers a key for interpreting the other divine names, in that they relate to creation or to covenant, and in that they derive from revelation or from the exercise of human reason. All the riches of human intellect, feeling, and experience, when for example the name of the Father is in question, can be brought into play in order to know the divine fatherhood, in relation to Christ as in relation to us, but while respecting the ineffable transcendence of the level of being in accordance with which God is Father, and therefore Son and Spirit. The imagined notion of divinity, without which our religion would run the risk of impoverishment and desiccation, is channeled and in some way elevated, provided that there is a vital awareness of the unique being of that same divinity. Then, if we move from the undoubtedly proper names of God, relating to his invisible essence or to his history with humankind, as Father and Lord, to words that are more tinged with cosmic or human feeling, a sense of unique depth is bestowed on the resulting metaphors, confronted as they are with the mystery of being. Theology as a whole might be validly conceived as a concerted and organic evaluation of the divine names, the meaning and implications of which would be specified as far as is possible in each case. Then analogy becomes a privileged instrument of contemplation beyond all more or less idolatrous anthropomorphism and beyond any magnificent apophasis.

Bibl.: Var., *Analogie et dialectique* (Geneva, 1983); var., *Metafore dell'invisibile: Ricerche sull'analogia* (Brescia, 1984); var., *Origini e sviluppi dell'analogia: Da Parmenide a San Tommaso* (Vallombrosa, 1987).

Ghislain LAFONT

ANGLICANISM

1. Anglican Communion

The Anglican communion traces its roots to the Church of England, which separated from the Roman Catholic church in the sixteenth century. It may be seen as a communion of churches united to a common referent, the archbishop of Canterbury (England), who is the senior bishop and titular head, and, moreover, by a general acceptance of the doctrines and liturgical usages to be found in the *Book of Common Prayer*, a text first published in 1549 (which underwent radical modification in 1552, with further changes in 1559, 1604, and 1662).

From the time of the Reformation itself, the missionary, commercial, and colonial activities of the English ensured that their particular form of faith and its practices were introduced to the newly discovered lands and to the rich territories of the Americas. This in turn contributed to the creation and foundation of new churches, which gradually assumed a local identity different from that of the Church of England.

However, it is not until 1867, with the first Lambeth Conference, convened at the suggestion of the Church of Canada, that one may affirm the origins of an Anglican communion. From the outset, the Lambeth Conference emerged and described itself as one of the chief binding principles of the Anglican communion. It became the forum for the expression of different opinions among the churches on a variety of problems, from the directly theological and social to those of a political nature. However, because the Anglican communion does not have a centralized form of government, the decisions taken by the conference do not of themselves have any legal force in the individual churches but must be approved and adapted in accordance with the proper constitutions of each church. The Lambeth Conference normally meets every ten years under the presidency of the archbishop of Canterbury as *primus inter pares.*

Dialogue between the Anglican communion and other Christian churches is conducted on the basis of the so-called Lambeth Quadrilateral. This is formed from the four pillars that constitute the basis of the Anglican faith: (1) the acceptance of Sacred Scripture as the rule of faith; (2) the Apostles' Creed and the profession of faith of Nicea-Constantinople; (3) the sacraments of baptism and the Lord's Supper; and (4) the episcopate. These four principles were first issued by the General Convention of the Protestant Episcopal Church at Chicago in 1886 and thereafter amended and adopted on behalf of the entire Anglican communion at the Lambeth Conference of 1888.

The Anglican liturgy is generally to be located in the *Book of Common Prayer*, which bears testimony to the union of the *lex credendi* and the *lex orandi* and their expression in faith, theology, and the witness of the Christian life. The rediscovery of the fathers of the church, who so often constituted the very core of the return to ancient tradition, and, from the sixteenth century, a concern for writing in the vernacular are further developments of the Anglican tradition.

In this century the Anglican communion has been especially prominent in the ecumenical movement and ecumenical dialogue. The meeting between Pope John Paul II and Archbishop Runcie of Canterbury in 1982 was a milestone in Anglican relations with the Catholic church, when the prospects for reconciliation were addressed. This encounter was the natural outcome of preparations made at two previous meetings between Pope Paul VI and Archbishop Ramsey in 1966 and Archbishop Coggan in 1977.

Rino FISICHELLA

2. Fundamental Theology

"'Fundamental theology' is the word now used for what used to be called APOLOGETICS

Heinrich Fries, "Fundamental Theology," *SM* 2). This is a convenient, succinct definition that can serve also as a pointer to an Anglican approach to FUNDAMENTAL THEOLOGY. There would be no problem if *only* the word "apologetics" were at issue. Fundamental theology, however, is not a term much used by Anglican theologians. This fact is largely a difference in terminology. Since the term has been in Roman Catholic usage only since the earlier part of the nineteenth century, it is not part of that common Western inheritance which Anglicans and Catholics share. Apologetics was a shared term of that kind. There may, however, be a subtle difference of approach that is masked by the terminological variation.

Several terms have been used, often interchangeably: apologetics, natural theology, philosophy of religion, philosophical theology.

a. Apologetics. It has been said that the subject matter falls into three parts: (1) to show that it is more reasonable to have a religion than not; (2) to show that Christianity can give a more rational account of itself than any other religion; and (3) to show that it is more reasonable to profess orthodox Christianity than any other form ("Apologetics," *Oxford Dictionary of the Christian Church*). It has not usually been claimed that Christian apologetics can irrefutably show the truth of Christianity by the methods of science. It has been claimed that Christianity is congruent with reason in ways and to a degree that no other religion or system of belief can show itself to be. Christian apologetics has also been taken in a more wide-ranging sense to include the propagation and defense of particular Christian doctrines. There is also an element in twentieth-century thinking (e.g., Edwyn Hoskyns and D. M. Mackinnon) that is sympathetic to the dictum of K. BARTH that "apologetics" per se is the "great enemy" of authentic Christian theology. That is to say, an apologetic both aggressive and defensive can militate against proper Christian theological thinking and utterance. It is important to note a distinction increasingly made between apologetics and the theology and philosophy of the Christian religion. In the last twenty-five years or so some have wished to explore further "the philosophy of theology" as an inquiry related to the questions of fundamental theology but by

no means identical with them. D. M. Mackinnon is an outstanding example.

b. Natural Theology. According to the *Oxford Dictionary of the Christian Church,* natural theology is "the body of knowledge about God which may be obtained by human reason without the aid of Revelation and hence to be contrasted with 'Revealed Theology.'" The origins of this classification and distinction are clearly medieval and scholastic. The notion of both the possibility and the desirability of such a natural theology was prevalent in the late seventeenth and the eighteenth centuries in a context ironically remote from the medieval one. For a great many years, Anglican apologists were engaged in controversy with Deists: principally, Lord Herbert of Cherbury (*De Veritate* [1624]); J. Locke (*The Reasonableness of Christianity* [1695]); J. Toland (*Christianity Not Mysterious* [1696]); J. Clarke (*Demonstration of The Being and Attributes of God* [1704–6]). The influence of Deism (itself a term with varying emphases) in England was probably less than, say, in France — and therefore probably less for Anglicans than for Roman Catholics. The most impressive and original Anglican thinker of the time was Bishop Joseph Butler (1692–1752). His *Analogy of Religion* (1736) was of the greatest importance not only in the struggle with Deism but in the development of a distinctive Anglican approach and style in what many now call fundamental theology. Eventually, however, the content of natural theology came to be seen as more naturally part of philosophy rather than theology.

c. Philosophy of Religion. In more recent years the term "natural theology" has given way to "philosophy of religion." It is important to note, however, that this term is not to be understood in the sense of the German *Religionsphilosophie,* which has often had its own ideological connotation. Traditionally, the subject matter of the philosophy of religion, whether in England or in other countries with strong Anglican connections in universities and seminaries, has included apologetic issues. In the present century, however, it has been increasingly devoted to the critical study of religious concepts and language, analytic rather than apologetic, although the two have not always been separated. This emphasis is undoubtedly due to the powerful influence of linguistic analysis and logical empiricism in the Anglo-Saxon world. In Oxford and Cambridge, for example, from the 1930s until the 1970s and even later, the work of divergent philosophers from Russell to Wittgenstein was overpowering. In Oxford the Special Subject in the Final Honours School of Theology was called Philosophy of Religion, and its scope reflected these movements of thought.

d. Philosophical Theology. It is of interest that in Cambridge the term "philosophical theology" has in modern times been preferred to "philosophy of religion." It is possible that this usage reflects hesitancy about connotations suggesting *Religionsphilosophie.* It certainly reflects the importance of the work of F. R. Tennant (*Philosophical Theology,* 2 vols., 1928, 1930), who could well be esteemed as the greatest Anglican writer in this field since Bishop Joseph Butler. It is philosophical theology rather than philosophy of religion that is the formal title of the subject in the Theological Tripos Parts II and III at Cambridge. Oxford and Cambridge should not be considered normative for Anglican theology; historically, however, they have been the most prominent centers of Anglican theological thinking and learning. There are now other Anglican faculties of theology of distinction, but this does not change the historical fact that until quite recent times Oxford and Cambridge have virtually been Anglican preserves.

To understand the distinctive features of Anglican thinking about apologetics, philosophical theology, fundamental theology, or whatever it may be called, it is necessary to consider Anglican history. When European Christianity was one, until the separation of the sees of Rome and Canterbury, it would not be easy to discern any particular theological style that characterized, say, the ancient universities of England as opposed to those on the continent of Europe. Thereafter, however, two important differences show themselves. First, England never underwent the so-called Counter-Reformation. The importance of this fact is often underestimated. Second, the energies of Anglican theologians were very largely consumed by the establishing of an ecclesiastical identity in the series of controversies maintaining the Anglican *via media* between Rome and Geneva. Throughout the "classical" period of Anglicanism in the seventeenth century (the period of "The Caroline Divines") the theological and philosophical issues we are dealing with were of less concern. An important exception to this generalization might be Archbishop J. Bramhall (1594–1663). He was the outstanding contemporary adversary of T. Hobbes and therefore of philosophical materialism. (In his *Replication* of 1656 he also expressed the fervent hope that he might see the restoration of Christian unity.)

The eighteenth century saw a distinctive Anglican development. As already mentioned, there was the contest with the Deists (of several varieties) as well as with such philosophers as Hobbes. The case of David Hume was special. His first work, *Essays Moral and Political* (1741–42), had been warmly greeted by Bishop Joseph Butler. Although part of a particularly British kind of empiricism, that tradition was various; and it is too simple to speak of "Locke, Berkeley, and Hume" as though they were all more or less the same. Hume's skepticism, especially marked in his "Essay on Miracles," has never ceased to pose serious problems. One of the most interesting Anglican responses it evoked was that of A. E. Taylor, *David Hume and the Miraculous* (1927). In his own time Taylor was a writer whose influence was wide and especially noted, for example, by T. S. Eliot. D. M. Mackinnon had worked as Taylor's assistant in Edinburgh.

In more recent times William Temple, subsequently archbishop of Canterbury (see *Nature, Man and God* [1934]), and W. R. Matthews, subsequently dean of St. Paul's Cathedral (see *God in Christian Thought and Experience* [1930]) have continued the tradition of scholarly apologetics. In the last forty years or so there are many names to be mentioned. Perhaps the most original and brilliant Anglican theologian of this century was A. M. Farrer, whose *Finite and Infinite* (1943) has become a modern classic in philosophical theology. E. L. Mascall has been a prolific and penetrating writer in the Thomist tradition. C. C. J. Webb was a persuasive writer on both philosophical and theological themes. A layman, he was Nolloth Professor of the Philosophy of the Christian Religion at Oriel College, Oxford. His successor in that chair was L. W. Grensted, who made notable contributions in matters of the psychology of religion and of belief. His successor, in turn, was I. T. Ramsey (subsequently bishop of Durham), a brave thinker in Oxford at the time of the ascendency of linguistic philosophy in the 1950s. J. Macquarrie brought to Oxford keen attention to existentialist philosophy and has written a number of widely read books. Such thinkers have maintained something rather like an Anglican style in dealing with a certain range of questions.

Bibl.: F. R. TENNANT, *Philosophical Theology,* 2 vols. (Cambridge, 1928, 1930); A. M. FARRER, *Finite and Infinite* (Westminster, 1959); J. MACQUARRIE, *Principles of Christian Theology* (New York, 1977).

Howard E. ROOT

ANONYMOUS CHRISTIANS

This is Karl RAHNER's term for those who live in Christ's grace, even if (through no fault of their own) they do not know of Christ as savior, remain unbaptized, and do not belong to the Christian community (see *LG* 16; *GS* 22).

Rahner's theological anthropology emphasizes the unlimited horizon of the human spirit with its dynamic openness to God, whose universal salvific will (1 Tm 2:3–4) means that all men and women are offered the grace to be saved. Several things need to be clarified here.

First, all grace comes through Christ (Acts 4:12; 2 Cor 5:15; 1 Jn 5:11–12) and necessarily orients human beings toward Christ and his visible church. Second, although grace is universal, it is supernatural and gratuitous. It is freely and lovingly offered to all human beings, with a view to that final vision of God which goes beyond their "natural" powers and rights. Third, in this present order grace does not remain a mere "external" offer, but from the outset is a divine self-communication that really shapes our common human condition. Here Rahner speaks of the supernatural existential given along with our nature.

The universality of grace entails a free self-gift of God (the SUPERNATURAL existential), which intrinsically affects the inner structure of human existence (the supernatural *existential*) and calls us all to our ultimate goal.

Obviously not every human being has been or is in a position to respond to God's presence and call through explicit faith in Christ and his church. There are millions whose chance of knowing and relating to God has been mediated through Buddhism, Confucianism, Hinduism, Islam, traditional religions, and other systems of belief. Whenever and wherever such human beings open themselves in faith to God, Rahner recognized them as anonymous Christians— that is to say, as those who at least implicitly accept their supernatural vocation and, even without knowing this, are enabled through Christ's grace to open themselves to the mystery of God. Their faith relates such anonymous Christians to Christ and implicitly orients them toward his visible church.

In interreligious dialogue, Rahner's talk of "anonymous Christians" has not always been well accepted. It does not seem to concern itself sufficiently with the specific beliefs, practices, and experiences of non-Christian religions. It has prompted some followers of other faiths to speak of Christians as "anonymous Hindus" or "anonymous Muslims."

Nevertheless, Rahner offers a valid approach to a question that has concerned Christian thinkers since the time of such early fathers of the church as Irenaeus, Justin, and Clement of Alexandria. Given the divine will to save all through Christ, how can we understand and interpret the situation of those non-Christians who, at least implicitly, believe in God and accept their supernatural vocation? Some critics claim that Rahner takes away the motivation for missionary work. The truth, however, is that his thesis of "anonymous Christians" indicates how the gospel speaks to and calls to full expression a hidden reality of grace which is present, at least imperfectly, in every human life (see *AG* 19; *LG* 17).

Bibl.: K. RAHNER, "Anonymous Christians," in *Theological Investigations,* vol. 6 (1965; London, 1969), 390–98; id., "Anonymous Christianity and the Missionary Task of the Church," in *Theological Investigations,* vol. 12 (1970; London, 1975), 161–78; K.-H. WEGER, *Karl Rahner: An Introduction to His Theology* (New York, 1980) 112–41.

Gerald O'COLLINS

ANSELM OF CANTERBURY

After citing Karl Barth's thesis regarding Anselm's theology and the speculative context of his writing, I shall discuss a few methodological texts. First, however, a short biography.

1. Biography

Anselm (1033–1109) was born at Aosta. He left his native Piedmont around 1050 to look for an intellectual mentor in France. In 1058 he enrolled in the school of Lanfranc, prior of the very new (1040) abbey of Bec. He became a member of the community and its prior in 1062. Since his duties included teaching, he wrote an instructional text, the *Monologion* (1076), the themes of which he took up again in the *Proslogion* (1077–78). In 1078 he was elected abbot. From 1080 to 1085 he wrote a text of pure dialectics, the *De grammatico*, then three "studies on Holy Scripture": the *De veritate*, the *De libertate arbitrii*, and the *De casu diaboli*. Around 1092, in order to defend himself against Roscelin, he wrote his *Epistola de incarnatione Verbi*, with a longer recast version in 1094. In 1093 he became archbishop of Canterbury, in succession to Lanfranc, who had just died there. In 1098 he published his *Cur Deus homo*. There followed treatises in answer to specific theological questions: *De conceptu virginali* (1100), *De processione spiritu sancti* (1102; regarding the *filioque* clause and the Council of Bari), *Epistola de azimo et fermentato* and *Epistola de sacramentis Ecclesiae* (1106–7). These various texts were written during two periods of exile forced on him by the English monarch, for Anselm rejected the royal, and antipapal, view of investiture. In 1108 Anselm wrote his *De concordia praescientiae et praedestinationis et gratiae Dei cum libero arbitrio*. He died in 1109, leaving several prayers and an extremely lively and extensive correspondence.

2. The Issues

In order to preserve the gift of faith in all its purity, some theologians denied that it could be understood rationally, i.e., in accordance with the possibilities of the human mind. Peter Damian (1007–1072), a contemporary of

Anselm, accepted this notion, according to which theology makes no concession to mere human reflection. The contrary attitude is also traditional; Anselm shared it, but without implying that the gift of faith is in any way reduced to the limits of the human intellect.

The Interpretation of Karl Barth

According to BARTH, the Anselmian formula "id quo maius cogitari nequit" is "theological"; the negation that it includes (*nequit*) in fact expresses the interdiction of the decalogue: "You shall have no other gods" (Ex 20:3). This interdiction allows the Word of God to shine forth in all its purity. Human beings cannot talk of God if God does not freely bestow his Word on them; in fact, the human mind, made proportionate to the world, grasps God as a "thing" if it is not otherwise enlightened. For this reason, the *Proslogion* is structured as a prayer, in the sense of an address to God. "True knowledge is determined by God's prevenient and active grace. This truth of a general order and the fact that we should always pray to obtain this grace already suffices to indicate that the power of attaining to 'knowledge of faith' [*intellectus fidei*] does not coincide in the last resort with the spontaneity of human reason."

Hence "theology is a meditation on the faith of the church as it is expressed and compels our recognition in Holy Scripture, the creeds, the conciliar definitions, and the writings of the fathers" (H. Bouillard, 1:145). This doctrine of Barth's is traditional; nevertheless, for him theology "does not attempt to ground its object, but to understand it precisely in its incomprehensibility" (ibid.); for Anselm, in the *Monologion*, it is sufficient for reflection to understand by means of rational consideration that the divine mystery is incomprehensible (cf. 75.11 [the edition cited here is that of F. S. Schmitt; numbers refer to page, then line]).

Nevertheless, the inaccessibility of God does nullify the work of the mind; indeed, faith seeks to understand, *fides quaerens intellectum*. The work of the intellect originates not in a desire for knowledge but in a desire for faith. But the theological intellect does not reduce the content of faith to the level of the object of a "scientific" judgment; its way is interior to faith. For this purpose, however, the content of faith must already be intelligible, or at least possess a meaning. To say, for example, that God does not exist is meaningful if the word "God" has a meaning for the person who says it.

Meaning is thus given in advance, and the theologian searches for its truth—i.e., for the ground of its coherence. The truth envisaged by faith searching for knowledge is not ontological but logical; the intellect perfects the adherence of faith by showing that its propositions are logically true. Theology discloses the systematic unity of the dogma in which the simplicity of God resides. This perfecting of faith adds something new to "naked" faith, which means moving spontaneously from an accepted meaning to knowledge of the truth or, from reciprocal necessity, the articles of the creed. "Such are the known elements *a, b, c, d* . . . on the basis of which one demonstrates that the unknown *x* is 'rational' and 'necessary,'" Barth says of *Cur deus homo*. One does not show the intelligibility of an article of the creed by pretending that this article has no meaning and by looking subsequently for some reasonable validity in it; one proceeds in faith from one's acceptance of the meaningfulness of the creed to the point of understanding its logical truth, which is grounded a priori in its systematic totality.

Before verifying this thesis of Barth's in Anselm's texts, I shall look at the cultural situation in the eleventh century.

The Cultural Context

The word "philosophy" appears only twice in Anselm's works. For the *De grammatico,* "the philosophers who have examined the [paronym] problem admit that 'grammarian' is a quality" (146.1–2). According to the *Cur deus homo,* "since it is a fact that there is no human being who does not die, the philosophers include the notion of mortality in the definition of the human being" (109.17). The philosopher is a specialist in language.

In the Middle Ages, a philosopher was practical or existential. Peter Damian, to whom we owe the expression "philosophy the handmaid of theology," said that his treatise *Contempt for the World* was addressed to the "philosopher of Christ." But a dialectical philosophy developed alongside this monastic philosophy.

The theological effort of the twelfth century originated in the "theories of the grammarians" (Chenu, 92), Anselm's "philosophers." The scholarly education of the time was defined by the trivium (grammar, logic, and rhetoric). Grammar in fact included reading and writing, poetry, methodology and history; rhetoric was scarcely something distinct. The basic text was the grammar of Priscian and, to a lesser extent, that of Donatius. Anselm was also interested in the future question of the *suppositio*.

The problem of meaning was essential to Anselm's time, which the dispute about the Eucharist shows clearly. When Anselm arrived at the abbey of Bec in 1058, Bérenger and Lanfranc (then abbot of Bec) were disputing about the Eucharist. Bérenger speaks of the Eucharist in terms of a "sacred sign"; the Roman discourse is realist, almost carnalist: "verum corpus et sanguinem Domini Jesu Christi esse, et sensualiter, non solum sacramento; sed in veritate manibus sacerdotum tractari, frangi et fidelium dentibus atteri" (quoted by J. de Montclos 1971: 171–72), as Bérenger was forced to say in a profession of faith imposed in 1059. But scarcely had he uttered this credo, than Bérenger spoke out against the very concept that had been forced on him. His argument is dialectical. The Roman formula contrasts sacrament and truth, sign and reality. But if the "truth" is empirical reality, the proposition that has been imposed is incoherent; either the bread is bread and not flesh, or it is flesh and not bread. If, therefore, one says that the bread is "flesh," it is so as a sign. There is no ontological identity between that which is believed by virtue of a sign and that which is uttered literally. I should add that, for Bérenger, one can attain to the truth without recourse to human authorities—i.e., according to Augustine understood literally (cf. *De vera religione* 25.47), without recourse to the fathers.

But Anselm, a disciple of Lanfranc, wrote his *Monologion* in the style of Bérenger, "in no way persuaded to depart from the authority of Holy Scripture" (7.7–8). He sent a first version of his text to Lanfranc, then archbishop of Canterbury. Lanfranc probably asked his former disciple to adduce traditional grounds in his text, but Anselm did not think this change was necessary: "Often rereading my words, I have found nothing in them which does not accord with the writings of the Catholic fathers, especially the Blessed Augustine" (8.8–9) which means that the "necessary arguments" and the "necessity of reason" (7.10) are capable of re-creating the traditional affirmations.

This assurance of Anselm is even more in evidence when we compare the Prologue of the *Monologion* with its first paragraph, for these methodological texts have identical structures. The first paragraph served as a prologue to the text sent to Lanfranc; the present Prologue was added after Lanfranc's reactions (cf. Schmitt 1938: 203–4). The last sentence of the first paragraph states: "If what I say is not covered by a greater authority, I wish it to be received thus; although the reasons apparent to me are conclusive almost of necessity, I do not say that they are absolutely necessary for this reason, but that they may seem so on a wholly provisional basis" (14.1–4); the "provisional" disappears from the definitive version of the Prologue. Anselm affirms his conviction that reflection on God and the creation can indeed replace tradition.

Presumably this "rationalist" emphasis is there because Anselm takes the objector's presence into account. But when the literary form is meditative, he welcomes "objections, even if simplistic and rather irrational, which occur to me" (7.11–12). The objector follows rational processes alien to spiritual language, and Anselm acknowledges this procedure. Anselmian meditation is concerned with the content of faith. The *Monologion* is defined as an "example of meditation" (7.4–5 and 94.6–7) on "the divine essence and certain other points connected with this meditation" (7.3–4). As for the *Proslogion*, there he meditates on the "reason of faith" (94.7) and its contents: "God is truly, . . . he is the sovereign good . . . and all that we believe of the divine substance" (93.7–10). The expression "reason of faith" does not signify objective reasons, i.e., the principles of faith to be found assembled in the creed, for Anselm mentions them without taking them as a basis for reflection. The *Proslogion* in fact starts from the ignorance of the fool; the *Monologion* also starts from ignorance, though an assumed ignorance, on the part of the believer who wishes to purify his or her understanding of the mysteries (cf. 93.3–4). Thus reflection replaces the objective "reasons" of faith; accordingly, the argument on the basis of authority is excluded, and reason does not draw directly on revelation.

The meaning and truth of the articles of the creed are illumined by meditation, which assembles the principles of faith by "reasoning" (*ratiocinando*, 93.4). Since the role of the fathers gives way to that of reasoning, the a priori truth of faith is rediscovered by reflection. Apprehension of the rational meaning of the propositions of faith leads to an affirmation of their necessary, a priori "implicit" truth, but as constructed "for us" by intellectual inquiry. The overall structure of the argument is therefore that of the ontological argument, which proceeds from the idea to reality, from signification to the truth, thus following a path that, in principle, the objector can also follow.

3. The Methodological Texts

Monologion §1 (13.5–14.1): The Meaning of the Words of Faith

The *Monologion* defines its object as that which "we necessarily believe" (13.9); to what does this "necessarily" refer? Faith is what it is by reason of its "object" (objective faith) and the believer (subjectivity); that which is believed should have an intelligible meaning; *necessarily* indicates the immanent meaning of the articles of the creed, which is accessible to the intellect of the one who believes.

The investigation is entrusted to "reason alone" (13.11), which accompanies the one who "does not know" (13.10) of the existence of propositions of faith or their meaning. Indeed, one may be ignorant of what faith is saying "either because one has not heard speak of it, or because one does not believe it" (13.9: "aut non audiendo, aut non credendo"). That is why it seems inadequate to say that, from the moment reflection starts, one accepts that the propositions are known (*audiendo*) or that their meaning is received (*credendo*).

The *Monologion* starts from the universal human experience of desire (13.12–14.1). "All human beings ardently wish to enjoy that which they think alone is good" (13.13). Anselm goes on to show that this desire has but one direction, a meaning, and that this meaning is reasonable. The appropriateness of desire is shown by grounding its direction in reason. This demonstration that desire is rationally oriented results from reflective inquiry. The "eye of the spirit" discerns "the traces of that which causes to be good those things that it desires ardently, only if it judges them to be good" (13.14–15). The *Monologion* throws light on that in the name of which desire is rendered meaningful, i.e., is assigned its beginning and its end.

The reflection follows the categories of formal causality. It proceeds by representing the structure of creation in its explanation. The secularization of faith, or the understanding of this creation in terms of desire, necessitates a procedure "ratione ducente et illo prosequente" (13.15–16), this *illo* being "that by which all these things are good" (13.14–15). Accordingly, reason follows the testimony of inward experience as it tends toward the original good that endows it with movement and being. It thus perceives itself as dwelling in the goodness of creation, a privileged expression of desire, like the Word in the Spirit.

The Prologue of the Monologion *(7.2–12)*

Where the first paragraph of the *Monologion*, says *sola ratione*, we now read, at the same parallel point, "quatenus auctoritate scripturae penitus nihil in ea persuaderetur" (7.7–8). This alteration from one text to another shows Anselm's work replacing scriptural authority with reason. The steps in the argument are logical: "by means of plain arguments and straightforward discussion" (7.9–10). As for the conclusion, it is to be accepted "by force of the necessity of reason and the evident clarity of truth" (7.9–10). "Necessary" reason is not "objective reason," the latter being the articles of the creed. Its strength derives from the argument, which reaches a conclusion from its premises and what unites them, and not as a result of the a priori coherence of the creed. In this conclusion, however, the believer perceives the splendor of the creed. As for the "clarity of truth," it avoids scriptural meditation and replaces it with reflection on the universal structures of desire. Some commentators see an echo of Jn 14:6 in this truth, but in that case Anselm would have rationalized Scripture to an extreme degree.

The Proslogion *(93.2–94.7): The Truth of the Words of Faith*

In the *Proslogion*, faith seeks to understand (itself) "sub persona conantis erigere mentem suam ad contemplandum deum et quaerentis intelligere quod credit" (93.21–94.2). Accord-

ingly, the object of faith is given at the start of the reflection. Knowledge no longer advances by following the thread of the investigation, but in accordance with the rhythm of the "lifting up" of the spirit. Nevertheless the *Proslogion* allows room to the *insipiens*, the fool for whom the starting point of faith is not true, even though it may have a meaning. The unillumined mind therefore compels one to proceed beyond meaning in order to rediscover the truth of the propositions of faith. Chapter 2 introduces nonbelief into the study of the statements of faith; this same opposition to faith is to be found in Scripture (Ps 14:1); there is a certain darkness within faith. The faith of the *Proslogion*, as much at the start as at the end, does not intuit its "object"; it is also a nonfaith. Accordingly, by saying that the work's horizon is the truth of faith, one means that faith, incomplete at the start, is searching for something to supplement it, which is knowledge of its darkness and of that which illumines it in spite of everything, and not evidence of the "objective" reality of what is proclaimed in the creed.

By saying that it is not true that God exists (negation), the fool makes a rational affirmation (takes up a reasonable position). The *Proslogion* starts from this tension between a negative truth and a positive meaning. The *Proslogion*, unlike the *Monologion*, starts from the knowledge of the meaningfulness of the words of faith. The unillumined mind has heard tell of God, whom he or she pre-comprehends, in principle, in accordance with the *maius* that the *Monologion* established. In this tension between the negation of truth and the positive knowledge of its meaningfulness, we may discern the operation of the rational structure of creation, which reflection makes use of on the basis of self-experience. Indeed, when describing the object of his work, Anselm uses terms reminiscent of the *Monologion*'s references to creation:

Monologion §1	Proslogion
unam naturam,	Deus vere est . . .
summam omnium . . .	summum bonum . . .
solam sibi sufficientem	nullo alio indigens . . .
omnibus rebus . . . sunt . . .	omnia indigent ut sint
bene sunt.	et ut bene sint.

But the committed reflection of the *Monologion* is used in a new way in the *Proslogion*;

the latter demonstrates the truth of the propositions of faith that are meaningful for the former. The *Proslogion* contemplates at another level—that of the truth necessary for the spirit—the same dynamic force whose meaning the *Monologion* has demonstrated. Reflection on the life of the spirit provides the rhythm of the argument that seeks to make the thought appropriate to the fullness of its opening. The Augustinian trinitarian categories, by means of which the account of creation was articulated in the *Monologion*, are replaced by *unum argumentum* (93.6), adumbrating the stages of thought on the way toward that which exceeds thought and which it will never encompass, the "id quo maius cogitari nequit" of chapters 2–4, which becomes "quiddam maius quam cogitari possit" in chapter 15. The *Proslogion* apprehends the power of desire by integrating the negative aspect of the darkness of faith, whereas the *Monologion* interprets it in terms of the positive structures of humankind, made in the image of God.

The Cur Deus Homo (42.6–43.3)

The first book of the *Cur deus homo* wishes to prove, without recourse to the figure of Christ and by adducing necessary reasons, that it is impossible to be saved without him (cf. 42.12–13). The second book proceeds accordingly, "with a manifest reason and in truth" (42.14–15). For Barth, the term "reason" here means objective reason, the systematic coherence of the articles of the creed, on the basis of which one concludes that the Son of God must become incarnate. The axiomatic system at the beginning would include these propositions: (1) God exists, (2) he created human beings, (3) he created them to be good, (4) humanity is destined for eternal happiness, and (5) human beings are sinners. But in fact all these articles, except for the last-mentioned, were posed progressively in the preceding works, on the basis of a reflection on contingency and on the action of the spirit. However, in the *Commendatio* that introduces his text and in which he explains its intention, Anselm uses the word *ratio* several times (39.5; 40.2, 7, 14) to mean "principle of argument." Accordingly, the results of the preceding works are accepted as gifts of faith.

At the end of the inquiry, one is granted a deeper understanding of mystery, "inter fidem et speciem" (40.10). According to Barth, the understanding between faith and vision does not emerge from faith; indeed, knowledge of faith does not spring forth without receiving something to think about. Though its object is a work of grace, its own activity must dwell within the action of grace. Nevertheless, knowledge within the bounds of faith, at least if the latter is merely affirmative, cannot say that those without faith are prisoners of their negative viewpoint (50.16). Therefore it is necessary to deepen the relation between the operation of the mind and the act of faith. The process of understanding faith may be set out schematically:

faith (rehearsal of the articles of the creed)
 —the reasonableness of faith (apprehension of its a priori coherence)
 —understanding (reconstruction of this coherence by way of a negation)
species

The *species* is a direct and evident perception not of God, who is always "greater," but of the cogency of faith in him; the mind participates in this cogency (cf. 40.11–12). In fact, whereas contemplation of the *species* reveals the formal principle of the coherence of faith, and whereas faith tends toward the *intellectus* by approaching its intelligible principle, the work of the mind consists in simplifying and unifying the articles of faith under the guidance of that which unifies them a priori, the *species*. Here and now, therefore, theological reflection enacts the contemplation promised for the end of time.

The Letter De incarnatione Verbi: Meaning, Significance, and Truth

We now come to a final text of Anselm, in which the methodological approach seems quite different from that of the foregoing. Anselm prepared for the composition of the *Cur deus homo* in two successive editions of a letter in which he adumbrated his position against Roscelin (1050–1120), whose teaching on the Trinity accords with Bérenger's requirements. The letter was occasioned by an allusion that Roscelin made to Anselm. Roscelin is taken as saying that, even for Anselm, we may think that if the Son became incarnate, the entire Trinity is incarnate. The Trinity, indeed, being one, is but one substance, yet one person of the Trinity is also "substance"; consequently the incarnation of one substance necessitates the incarnation of all the "persons."

In the *Monologion*, in fact, essence, substance, and nature are identified with one another (cf. 16.27; 44.10; 45.14; 86.12). They connote an individual "thing"; person and substance are separated by a mere nuance: "Personhood may be predicated only of the individual rational nature, and substance, mainly of individuals who maintain themselves principally in a plurality" (86.7–8). Substance, conceived thus as the subject of an accidental plurality, does not suit God; "substance" is "person" writ large. In the *Lettera*, Anselm reverts to the Latin vocabulary; since substance, essence, and nature are always identical (cf. 23.3), the Father and the Son, i.e., different persons, are explicitly a single substance and not two substances (23.14, 15).

This new arrangement accords with a decision regarding the common words of faith. In *Epistola* 136, Anselm concurs with one of Roscelin's positions: "It is by reason that faith must be defended against the ungodly" (34–35). Although, however, it is possible to enter into discussion with the unbeliever, the infidel, or the ungodly, the same is not true of the heretic. The *Proslogion* welcomes the unbeliever, and the *Cur deus homo* the infidel; the heretic, however, does not accept that the words of faith can have any meaning. Hence, in *Epistola* 136, Anselm refuses to enter into discussion with the heretic. A heretic breaks the connection between faith and the human mind. Roscelin does not support the viewpoint imposed on him, because for him these words are meaningless. If the meaning of words is not made normative by a spiritual opening ultimately effected by rehearsing the act of faith, then either faith does not accord with the words said, or the words said do not accord with faith. In any case, faith can never seek the intellect; there is a gulf between them, and so Anselm finds the heretic's position untenable.

However, the heresiarch requires an answer. If he or she inquires into the mysteries dialectically, then the answer must come by way of the dialectic. But which dialectic? Roscelin is a practitioner of the dialectic *in voce*. On the other hand, to advance from meaning to truth

and to think the creed truly, one needs a logic of reference, of intentionality, a dialectic *in re*. Anselm tries to articulate these two types of dialectic, *in voce* and *in re*, precisely from the point of the *Proslogion*, where he expatiates on being "in intellectu et in re." The *maius* is anterior to and leads the intellect to that which exceeds it, proceeding thus from *in intellectu* to *in re*. The *De grammatico* and the *De veritate* now appear as essential works. Confronted with Roscelin, argument about the meaning of words is insufficient; in chapter 2 of his *Lettera*, Anselm recalls the priority of faith over its understanding. The faith of which he speaks here is ethical; it receives the meaning and a priori truth of its propositions by entering into the experience of God, and by purifying its heart in order to open it up to the Creator. Attached to the Creator, the spiritual person is able to judge all things, even the mysteries of God, because he or she lives by virtue of a new life (cf. 2 Cor 2:14–15). In this sense, "the person who does not believe does not experience; the person who has not experienced cannot know" (9.5–6). Ethical faith supports negation by opening itself up to a beyond that it welcomes and prepares to worship.

For the dialectic *in voce*, there is "nothing" to understand. Reflection is purely formal. The norm of meaningfulness curves back to the formal cohesion of the linguistic system, where meaningfulness is exhausted. The dialectic decides the extent of what can be known by virtue of the signifiers' capability of producing their significance of themselves, without normative reference to the actual present moment. Anselm speaks, at this point, of "heretics of the dialectic" (9.21–22).

Before engaging in dialectics, the soul must be disposed to God, if only confusedly, if only by way of negation. Without humble contemplation, without adherence to, or at least a possible opening up to, the meaning of God, the soul will never accede to the significance of the words of the creed, still less to their truth.

Bibl.: (1) Edition: S. ANSELMI CANTUARIENSIS ARCHI-EPISCOPI, *Opera omnia*, ed. F. S. SCHMITT (Edinburgh, 1946–61).

(2) Collective works: *Analecta Anselmiana*, 6 vols. (Frankfurt, 1969–); *Spicilegium Beccense*, vol. 1: *Congrès international du IXe centenaire de l'arrivée d'Anselme au Bec* (Paris, 1959); *Sola ratione: Anselm-*

Studien für Pater Dr. h.c. Franciscus Salesius Schmitt OSB zum 75. Geburtstag am 29. Dezember 1969 (Stuttgart/Bad Cannstatt, 1970); *Anselm Studies*, vol. 1 (London, 1983); *Spicilegium Beccense*, vol. 2: *Les mutations socioculturelles au tournant des XI-XIIe siècles: Actes du colloque international du CNRS. Études anselmiennes: IVe session, Le Bec, July 11–16, 1982* (Paris, 1984).

(3) Works cited in important recent works (a bibliography [until 1984] is found in the work below of S. Vanni Rovighi): K. BARTH, *Fides quaerens intellectum: Anselm's Proof of the Existence of God* (Richmond, 1960); H. BOUILLARD, *Karl Barth*, vol. 1: *Genèse et évolution de la théologie dialectique*, and vol. 3: *Parole de Dieu et existence humaine*, 2nd part (Paris, 1957); Y. CATTIN, *La preuve de Dieu: Introduction à la lecture du Proslogion d'Anselme de Canterbury* (Paris, 1986); M. D. CHENU, *La théologie au douzième siècle* (Paris, 1957); M. CORBIN, "L'événement de vérité," in *L'inouï de Dieu* (Paris, 1981), 59–107; H. DE LUBAC, "Seigneur, je cherche ton visage: Sur le chapitre XIV du Proslogion de saint Anselme," *ArPh* 39 (1976): 201–25, 407–25; J. DE MONTCLOS, *Lanfranc et Bérenger: La controverse eucharistique du XIe s.* (Louvain, 1971); G. R. EVANS, *Anselm and Talking about God* (Oxford, 1978); P. GILBERT, *Dire l'ineffable: Lecture du Monologion de saint Anselme* (Paris/Namur, 1984); J. GOLLNICK, *Flesh as Transformation Symbol in the Theology of Anselm of Canterbury* (Lewiston/Queenston, 1985); D. P. HENRY, *The Logic of Saint Anselm* (Oxford, 1967); J. JOLIVET, "Éléments pour une étude du rapport entre la grammaire et l'ontologie au Moyen Age," in J. P. BECKMANN et L. HONNENFELDER, eds., *Sprache und Erkenntnis in Mittelalter* (Berlin, 1981) 135–64; K. KIENZLER, *Glauben und Denken bei Anselm von Canterbury* (Freiburg, 1981); H. KOHLENBERGER, *Similitudo und ratio: Überlegungen zur Methode bei Anselm von Canterbury* (Bonn, 1972); F. S. SCHMITT, "Les corrections de saint Anselme à son Monologion," *RBén* 48 (1938): 194–205; R. W. SOUTHERN, *Saint Anselm and His Biographer: A Study of Monastic Life and Thought, 1059–ca.1130* (Cambridge, 1966); S. TONNINI, "La Scrittura nelle opere sistematiche di s. Anselmo: Concetto, posizione, significato," *Analecta Anselmiana* 2:57–116; S. VANNI ROVIGHI, *Introduzione a Anselmo d'Aosta* (Bari, 1987); H. Urs VON BALTHASAR, "La Concordantia Libertatis chez saint Anselme," in var., *L'homme devant Dieu*, vol. 2 (Paris, 1964) 29–45.

Paul GILBERT

ANTHROPOLOGY

I. BIBLICAL ANTHROPOLOGY: *1. The Dialogue between Biblical Sciences and Human Sciences. 2. Select Passages or the Entire Book. 3. The Biblical Uses of Images. 4. Anthropology and Anthropomorphism. 5. The Evolution of Biblical Anthropology. 6. An Anthropology of Transformation. 7. Anthropology and Theology. 8. Human Finiteness. 9. Biblical Anthropology as Solution.* (S.-E. FARRELL)

II. CHRISTIAN: *1. The Concept. 2. The Human Being Created in the Image of God. 3. The Human Being Called to Be a Child of God in Christ. 4. Unity of the Human Being in a Duality of Body and Soul. 5. The Human Being as a Personal Being Open to Transcendence.* (L. F. LADARIA)

I. BIBLICAL ANTHROPOLOGY

Histories and updates of research in biblical anthropology have already been presented by a number of authors. (See the works by Hahn, Osiek, and Rogerson in the bibliography.) Instead of describing yet again the development of this approach to biblical studies, the present article will examine a number of questions pertinent to the topic.

1. The Dialogue between Biblical Sciences and Human Sciences

If it is true that God took on flesh in Jesus Christ, then one can assume that human nature was respected in the process. There is therefore no need to fear subjection of the Christian faith to the scrutiny of anthropological sciences such as philology, sociology, or psychology. A similar viewpoint was put forward by Hans Urs von BALTHASAR in a 1958 lecture entitled "Dieu a parlé un langage d'homme." Gone are the times when many Catholic authors hesitated to do scientific research, fearing that it would endanger certain aspects of the Christian faith.

Nevertheless, dialogue between biblical and human sciences, however advanced it may be today, still leaves much to be desired. A great distance still separates the biblical vision of humanity from those views of humanity put forward by the human sciences. For example, a good number of publications in biblical anthropology seem to imply that a researcher has still to make a fundamental choice between subjecting the Bible to scientific hypotheses (as does N. K. Gottwald, in his use of a Marxist hypothesis) and submitting one's thoughts to the demands of Catholic dogma. (Many introductions to the Bible follow this second alternative.) Would it not be legitimate rather to try to reconcile the well-founded requirements of the biblical sciences with those of the human sciences?

2. Select Passages or the Entire Book?

Biblical research inspired by the anthropological approach raises another question that is rarely discussed in the histories of this type of research. It would seem as though the anthropological approach to the Bible restricts the researcher to the study of certain key passages, namely, those that directly pertain to human life. Whether creation myths, patriarchal sagas, or social laws, the number of texts that can be examined from the angle of anthropology seems limited. One is left with the impression that a considerable part of the Bible is of no interest to research of this kind.

However, if it is true that the Bible is the word of God transmitted by human persons, and if the evolution of this literature truly culminates in the Incarnate Word in whom divinity and humanity are perfectly united, it follows that the whole book—and not just a number of select passages—must develop a specific vision of humanity.

One way in which a biblical anthropologist is able to take the whole Bible into account is through the study of biblical vocabulary. Such an approach is taken by H. W. Wolff and, more recently, by S. Fernandez-Ardanaz. Again, a number of major exegetical approaches that have been applied to a wide variety of biblical texts do consider, among other things, anthropological aspects of the text. For example, historical criticism retraces the historical (and therefore human) development of a text, and structuralism seeks to highlight in the biblical text the universal structures of human thought.

3. The Biblical Use of Images

Wolff's study of biblical vocabulary demonstrates how the Hebrew Scriptures make known the inner, hidden life of the human being by speaking of outward, visible human life. Biblical use of the word "heart" is a good example of such a phenomenon: in biblical language, the word "heart" refers not only to an organ of the human body but also to such personal inner dynamics as feeling, desire, reason, and decision (*Gefühl, Wunsch, Vernunft, Willensentschluss*). Certain biblical uses of the word "heart"—a word that calls to mind something visible and concrete—evoke the more abstract characteristics of human life.

This relationship which the Scriptures establish between the physical organ of the human heart and certain inner qualities of the human being is not arbitrary. The heart is situated inside the human body, where one feels, desires, reasons, and decides. The heart is the center of one's physical energies, in somewhat the same way as decision is the source of behavioral energies. There are even moments when the physical organ and the inner person act together, such as in the state of excitement, measurable by an increased heartbeat. Therefore, in its "imaged" representation of the personal and subjective aspects of human life, Scripture objectifies this hidden area of the human person and renders it available for discussion.

But it is not the practice of "imaging" that is most significant to biblical anthropology; it is rather the *way* in which such imaging is done that is most important. In rendering certain invisible aspects of human life visible and concrete, Scripture employs a very special instrument, even that which is most familiar to each and every human being: in its efforts to express the invisible, Scripture uses that concrete, visible, and tangible reality which is the *human body*. And what could be more preeminently anthropological than the human body?

4. Anthropology and Anthropomorphism

Biblical practice of using corporeal terms to describe spiritual human realities prepares the mind to receive yet another use of anthropological images—that of anthropomorphism. An anthropomorphism is a reference to the divine made through the use of anthropological images. To say that God *speaks* is already an anthropomorphism. The God of the Scriptures speaks to Moses "mouth to mouth" (Nm 12:8). This same God is celebrated as a warrior whose "right arm" crushes the enemy (Ex 15:6).

If biblical traditions other than that of the Yahwist hesitate to use so visual a language in their descriptions of God, they nevertheless continue to apply to God terms borrowed from universal human experience. The Deuteronomist speaks of a "jealous" God (Dt 4:24). The Psalms praise the "goodness" and the "graciousness" of God (Ps 106:1). The prophets quote a God who says such things as "My heart recoils within me; my compassion grows warm and tender" (Hos 11:8).

Archaeological discoveries prove again and again that the Hebrews were not the only people of the ancient Near East to describe their God in anthropological terms. Indeed, there are very few biblical anthropomorphisms that do not find a parallel in the nonbiblical literature of the ancient Near East. However, when comparing biblical and nonbiblical religions, a few distinctions must be made. According to F. Michaeli, who in 1950 published a classical work on the subject, one must differentiate between a moral anthropomorphism and an anthropomorphism of the cruder form. That is, whereas certain religions ascribe to their gods forms of behavior that scarcely inspire respect, the Bible presents a God who has moral character and whose holiness is the source of moral obligations on the part of humanity.

Therefore, a close kinship exists between biblical anthropology and biblical anthropomorphism. Michaeli suggests as much when he poses the following questions: "Is the role of anthropomorphism uniquely to render *theological* knowledge, or does it not also have a *moral* knowledge to transmit to human beings? If God creates, speaks, and acts, is it not also this One who summons human beings to be, speak, and act?" (Michaeli, 161).

5. The Evolution of Biblical Anthropology

One must not conclude that anthropological studies bring to light the ultimate meaning of the biblical text. Nevertheless, it must be recognized that the human person remains important from one end of the Bible to the other. Furthermore, there is certainly a development in the understanding of humanity between the origins of the Hebrew people and the time of the early Christian community. In this regard, the first thing to note is the antiquity of the anthropological perspective.

The universality of biblical language predates that vision of human history put forward in the first chapters of Genesis. This language, which has the potential to speak to all members of the human race, existed long before the Isaian tradition of universal salvation.

Biblical language, of which anthropomorphism is only one component, developed as a result of various historical experiences of the Hebrew people. Its development was also the fruit of different encounters with ancient mythologies and philosophies. Hence it is appropriate to speak of an evolution of biblical language, an evolution that occurred not only by drawing on human physical, emotional, and moral experience but also, eventually, by exploiting human metaphysical experience—that which belonged to the Greek presentation of "being."

One can therefore retrace the development of biblical anthropology not only in the Hebrew books of the Bible but also in its Greek elements. Such development took place over a period of more than ten centuries of history and intercultural relations.

6. An Anthropology of Transformation

If ever there was one term that could describe the evolution of biblical anthropology, it would have to be the word "transformation." The anthropology developed in the Bible eventually transforms every aspect of human life. This tendency is evident already in the manner in which biblical thought makes use of nonbiblical literature and traditions. Whether one considers anthropomorphism, creation myths, or theories concerning the immortality of the soul, it is not sufficient to establish parallels between biblical and nonbiblical texts. Above all one must examine just how the Bible uses such borrowings. In most cases one can speak of a progressive adaptation of external sources that is discernible even in the case of that "primitive thought" which certain anthropologists seek to identify in the biblical texts.

What is the driving force behind such adaptation? In order to answer this question, one must recognize an element peculiar to biblical thought. In the history of a particular people—and, eventually, in all human life—biblical thought perceives the presence of God.

7. Anthropology and Theology

Therefore, biblical anthropology is necessarily linked to biblical theology. The Bible distinguishes itself from other forms of literature in that it puts *God*, not humanity, at the center of its anthropology. Such a vision is not natural to human beings. It demands a purification similar to that undergone by Job, who, after his encounter with God, made the following confession: "I know that you can do all things. . . . Therefore [I must admit that] I have uttered what I did not understand, things too wonderful for me, which I did not know. . . . I had heard of you by the hearing of the ear, but now my eye sees you; therefore I despise myself, and repent in dust and ashes" (Jb 42:2a, 3b, 5–6).

This text of Job, and other similar texts, can enlighten us concerning a most important and yet very difficult aspect of biblical anthropology—that of human sinfulness. It seems that only in his encounter with God does Job become conscious of his sinfulness, because, right up to chap. 42, Job protests his innocence! However, upon encountering God, Job becomes aware of the fact that human life is not situated at the center of space and time. Job's sin was not understanding this earlier.

According to Alonso-Diaz, the book of Job is responsible for a certain "de-anthropomorphisation" of the biblical concept of God. Whereas numerous biblical passages present God in anthropomorphic fashion, the God of Job is a God separated from humanity by an unfathomable abyss. The book of Job illustrates that difference of *nature* which exists between God and humanity. The God of the Bible lives for all eternity; the human life span attains seventy-odd years. Qoheleth puts it very eloquently: "No one has power over the wind to restrain the wind, or power over the day of death; there is no discharge from the battle" (Eccl 8:8).

8. Human Finiteness

And so is the human condition. Every culture, every religion, every race, and every individual must one day confront the finitude of human life. S. G. F. Brandon's book *Man and His Destiny in the Great Religions* (1962) presents the way in which each of the world religions has dealt with this anthropological reality.

In a study of the biblical texts, restored inasmuch as possible to their chronological order of composition, a solution to the problem of human finiteness slowly emerges. Ironically, the first spark of an answer is to be found in the book of Job. Despairing as he is, Job confesses his faith to God as follows: "I know that you can do all things, and that no purpose of yours can be thwarted" (Jb 42:2). This word of hope is located in a book that most exegetes date around the mid-fifth century B.C.E. Although the book of Job is put forward as the struggles of an individual, its presence in the Hebrew canon is the fruit of national sufferings—those of exilic and postexilic times.

Three centuries later, and as the result of religious persecution, appears the narrative of a woman who transmits to her sons the courage of martyrdom by speaking to them as follows: "I do not know how you became visible in my womb, nor was it I who graced you with spirit and life, nor I who arranged each of the elements. For that very reason the Creator of the cosmos, the One who molded the origin of the human being and of all inventions, with compassion that One will grant to you again both spirit and life because now you disdain yourselves for the sake of the Law" (2 Mc 7:22–23).

Such declarations of Job and of the woman of 2 Mc 7 are professions of faith pronounced by individuals who find themselves victims of situations that surpass them and for which they have no resources. Job and the woman of 2 Mc 7 are obliged—even despite themselves—to turn to God in an act of faith. Their declarations constitute the most serious of challenges to anthropologists who are interested in the Bible.

Indeed, is there a place in the human sciences for that which is "beyond reason"? Jung and his school would probably identify this "beyond reason" with the subconscious. Such a solution is accessible to the researcher who does not recognize the existence of "Other"; however, it restricts one to investigation of "humanity in itself" or, at best, the human being in relation to other human beings. It does not permit one to see the (limited) human being in relation to an Unlimited being.

9. Biblical Anthropology as Solution

Biblical anthropology is an anthropology of *transcendence*. It proposes a transformation of the human being that leads to the transcendence of the self. In the face of the human lot of seventy-odd years, it offers the possibility of life unlimited. This involves an unimaginable turn of events, able to transport the human being beyond the self and into life of the Other.

Unimaginable, but not impossible. The "supreme anthropomorphism" of the Gospels—which designates a mode of being, and not only a mode of verbal expression—is there to prove it: "And the Word became flesh and lived among us" (Jn 1:14).

The anthropological transformation proclaimed in biblical texts respects human nature. Thus the Word made flesh, divine and human, experienced even suffering and death. But this time human life did not stop at death. The God-man who died rises again. He says: "Look at my hands and my feet; see that it is I myself. Touch me and see; for a ghost does not have flesh and bones as you see that I have" (Lk 24:38–39).

During his appearances, the risen Jesus is identified by the wounds of the crucifixion. The very necessity to have recourse to these wounds in order to identify him proves that his physical body has now entered into a life that surpasses that of this world. Henceforth, one will speak of a transformation of the human being brought about by the gift of the "spirit of Jesus," or the "Holy Spirit." Far from violating individual freedom, such an anthropology enhances human liberty: "For the law of the Spirit of life in Christ Jesus has set you free from the law of sin and death" (Rm 8:2).

10. Conclusion

As the reader will notice, it remains difficult—if not impossible—to discover all the richness of biblical anthropology by resorting exclusively to theories elaborated by the human sciences. However, one must nevertheless consider the benefits that biblical studies draw from dialogue with the human sciences. This article has pointed out a good number of contributions that the human sciences have brought to the study of biblical anthropology.

Dialogue implies mutual exchange between two partners. Indeed, textbooks introducing the human science of anthropology often indicate the important role the Bible has played in the birth and development of this modern science. One might hope that biblical studies will continue to play such an essential role in the evolution of the human sciences. For example, biblical anthropology makes one wonder if there are cultural traditions other than that of the biblical text which propose so radical a transformation of the human being. Biblical anthropology leads one to ask the following question: In what measure are the human ideals proposed by other traditions able to be understood and lived out by all human persons? Finally, biblical anthropology reminds researchers that many cultural traditions are perhaps centered on realities other than that of the human being.

Bibl.: J. PEDERSEN, _Israel, Its Life and Culture_, 4 vols. (London, 1926); C. G. JUNG, _Psychology and Religion_ (New Haven, 1938); F. MICHAELI, _Dieu à l'image de l'homme_ (Neuchâtel, 1950); S. G. F. BRANDON, _Man and His Destiny in the Great Religions_ (Manchester, 1962); H. URS VON BALTHASAR, "God Has Spoken Human Language," in _Word and Revelation: Essays in Theology_, 1 (New York, 1964); H. F. HAHN, _The Old Testament in Modern Research_ (Philadelphia, 1966); J. ALONSO-DIAZ, "Proceso antropomorfizante y desantropomorfizante en la formación del concepto bíblico de Dios," _EstBibl_ 27 (1968): 333–46; M. JOUSSE, _L'anthropologie du geste_ (Paris, 1969); H. W. WOLFF, _Anthropologie des Alten Testaments_ (Munich, 1973); C. WESTERMANN, _Genesis (chs. 1–2)_ (Minneapolis, 1984); G. CUSSON, _Notes d'anthropologie biblique_ (Rome, 1977); N. K. GOTTWALD, _The Tribes of Yahweh_ (New York, 1979); G. DE GENNARO, _L'antropologia biblica_ (Naples, 1981); W. G. ROLLINS, _Jung and the Bible_ (Atlanta, 1983); J. W. ROGERSON, _Anthropology and the Old Testament_ (Sheffield, 1984); B. LANG, ed., _Anthropological Approaches to the Old Testament_ (London, 1985); S. FERNANDEZ-ARDANAZ, "Evolución en el pensamiento hebreo sobre el hombre: estudio diacronico de los principales conceptos antropologicos," _RCT_ 12/2 (1987): 263–311; J. BARR, "La foi biblique et la théologie naturelle," _ETR_ 64 (1989): 355–68; C. OSIEK, "The New Handmaid: The Bible and the Social Sciences," _TS_ 50 (1989): 260–78.

Shannon-Elizabeth FARRELL

II. CHRISTIAN ANTHROPOLOGY

1. The Concept

In the most authentically Christian conception of the term, the object of revelation is simply and solely God, who bestows a self-revelation through Christ, the Word Incarnate, to the end that human beings, in the Holy Spirit, by means of that same Christ, may have access to the Father (*DV* 2). The human being, in a first approach, is merely the addressee, and not the direct object, of the revelation and salvation proclaimed and realized by the Father. Still, the knowledge of God and salvation offered us in Christ make known to us the human being's definitive calling—God's design in our regard—with a profundity that otherwise would never have been accessible. In this sense, the human being, precisely as addressee of divine revelation, also becomes an object of the same. Only in the light of the salvation afforded us by Christ do we discover whither we are called and, consequently, who we are: "Christ, the final Adam, by the revelation of the mystery of the Father and His love, fully reveals man to man himself and makes his supreme calling clear" (*GS* 22). Christian revelation presupposes human beings, and therefore a particular notion the latter will have of themselves. On the other hand, the novelty of the incarnation of the Son will surely enrich and enlighten this vision. On the basis of revelation, therefore, Christianity can and must proclaim a particular idea of the human being, which in many respects will coincide with the one offered by philosophy and the human sciences and which ought to be enriched by their contributions, but which will also possess an inalienable originality. And so we speak of "Christian anthropology."

2. The Human Being Created in the Image of God

Indeed, while it is obvious that Sacred Scripture makes no attempt to provide us with a systematic anthropology, just as obviously it speaks of the human being on many of its pages, and this from the outset. In the Yahwist account of the creation and fall (Gn 2–3), we find the human being (*hā-'ādām*) at the center of God's creative work: "Adam" is formed by the hands of God and receives life from the divine breath itself (Gn 2:7). For the human being God plants the Garden of Eden and assigns *hā-'ādām* the task of assigning names to the animals (see Gn 2:9, 19–20). Last of all, he gives him a fitting helpmate—for it is not good that a human being should be alone (Gn 2:9, 20–24). Here we have the nucleus of a profound anthro-

pology: *hā-'ādām* is called to make use of and exercise dominion over creation; and he is an eminently social being, made to be in communion with others. But *hā-'ādām* will have life only if he maintains a relationship with God, who has created him and communicated to him the divine life itself; and only if he is faithful to God's commands (Gn 2:16). This means that a relationship with God is essential to the human being and that it constitutes the comprehensive dimension upon which all other relations are superimposed.

The Priestly account (Gn 1:1–2:4a) also indicates the human being's primacy over the rest of creation. Here for the first time we have the notion of the creation of the human being in the image and likeness of God (cf. Gn 1:26–27)—the human characteristic cited in first place by Vatican Council II (*GS* 12) in its explanation of the church's response to the anthropological question, regarding which such diverse and contradictory opinions have been held throughout history. It will be useful, then, to undertake a brief examination of the meaning of these expressions and of the manner in which they have been interpreted in the Bible and church tradition up to the present time.

The human being's dominion over creatures is also present in the Priestly document. Clearly, it derives from our creation in the image and likeness of God (see Gn 1:26–27). Once more, the social character of the human being is set in relief in these verses: the human being made to the image of God is male and female. But here again, the human being's relationship with God, even in the presence of the radical difference between Creator and creature, is determinative. The simple datum that God creates this being "to his image and likeness" is the primary characteristic of the divine deed, and this in turn determines the distinction between the human being and other creatures. The human being has been created to exist in a relation with God, to live in communion with God. We encounter these same elements in Gn 5:1–3, where, furthermore, a certain analogy is posited between the creation of the human being by God in the divine image and the generation of Seth according to the likeness and image of his father, Adam. The condition of image of God renders human life sacred (see Gn 9:6). Dominion over the rest of creatures and the divine call to share in God's immortal life are the salient points in the concept of the creation of human beings in the divine image and likeness in the other texts of the OT in which the image motif appears (see Sir 17:3, Wis 2:23; also Ps 8:5–9).

In the NT, the image of God is declared to be Christ (see 2 Cor 4:4; Col 1:15; also Heb 1:2; Phil 2:6). No neglect of the human being's condition as created in the image and likeness of God is implied. On the contrary, the human being is asserted to have been summoned to be transformed into the image of Jesus, by accepting, in faith, Christ's revelation and the salvation he offers (see 2 Cor 3:18): the Father has predestined us to be conformed to the image of his Son, that the latter may be the firstborn among many sisters and brothers (see Rom 8:29). And as we have borne the image of the first Adam, the one of earth, who became a living soul, so shall we bear the image of the Adam of heaven, Christ raised, in sharing in his spiritual body (1 Cor 15:45–49). Thus, the human being is destined to pass from the state of image of the first Adam to that of the second. This is in no wise marginal or supplementary to the human "essence." Rather this calling to a conformation with Christ and the donning of his image constitute the profoundest element of our being. Along with this christological reinterpretation of the theme of the image, we note a strong eschatological orientation of this motif in the NT (see also 1 Jn 3:2). However, it will not be rash to assert that, if the human being is oriented to Christ as the final target of his or her existence, then this ordination must somehow have been present from the outset. It is the general conviction of the NT that the orders of creation and salvation subsist in a profound relationship: all things have been made through Christ, and all things move toward him (see 1 Cor 8:6; Col 1:25–20; Eph 1:3–10; Jn 1:3, 10; Heb 1:3): Jesus is Alpha and Omega, the beginning or principle, and the end or goal, of all (see Rv 1:8; 21:6; 22:13).

The christological reinterpretation of the motif of the image continues to develop in patristic theology. The fathers emphasize that the "exemplarity" of the *Verbum*, the Word, functions in the very moment of creation, and not merely in the final consummation. Indeed, the Son alone is the image of God; the human being is not, strictly speaking, the image itself, but has only been made "according to the image." This is generally recognized by all schools of the ancient church. However, these currents of thought take varying approaches to a specification of the meaning and import of the image of God that is the Son. This fact will have immediate anthropological consequences. On the one hand, the Alexandrians (Clement, Origen, followed substantially by Augustine) hold the image of God to be the preexistent Word; then the human being is created according to this image. Thus, the vehicle of the image of God in the human being is the spiritual element, the soul. By contrast, other fathers and ecclesiastical writers (Irenaeus, Tertullian) hold that the image of God the Father is the incarnate Son, who thus makes known the invisible God. The human being has been created, from the first moment of his and her existence, according to the image of the Son who would one day take flesh and would rise glorious in his humanity. When God fashioned the first Adam of clay, the divine mind was already thinking upon the eternal Son who would become a human being and thus be the definitive Adam. According to this line of thought, we human beings have been created to the image of God in our whole substance, soul and body alike, with special insistence on the latter. No aspect of the human composite is excluded from this condition of image, inasmuch as the whole of it has been called to participate in the resurrection of Christ. Despite these notable differences, again we find the theology of the first centuries in agreement on the distinction between the divine image and the divine likeness: the former is had in our very creation; the latter refers to our eschatological perfection and final consummation. While the distinction does not have an altogether literal basis in Scripture, neither is it utterly foreign to the same (see 1 Jn 3:2). Indeed, it brings out very strongly a most important element of the NT: an emphasis on the character of human existence as a journey and on the constant need for progress in a oneness with, and following of, Jesus.

The distinction between image and likeness has not generally been maintained throughout later times. Indeed, even the christological sense of the creation of the human being in the divine image and likeness has become less explicit in theology and Christian consciousness. Thus, the contribution of Vatican Council II is all the more praiseworthy, when, in *Gaudium et Spes*, as we have already noted, the magisterium posits the human being's creation to the image and likeness of God as the wellspring and basis of the Christian response to the question of the mystery of the human being. According to no. 12 of this Pastoral Constitution, the condition of having been created according to the divine image and likeness means first and foremost that we have the capacity to know and love our Creator—that is, we are capable of entering into a personal relationship with God. To this it adds our position of dominion over the creatures of earth, of which we are to make use for God's glory, and the social condition of the human being, who is called to exist in an interpersonal communion. As we see, many of the intuitions we have discovered in our rapid survey of Holy Scripture, especially in the OT, are present here as well. But this passage (*GS* 12) must be read in conjunction with no. 22 (which we have likewise cited in our opening pages):

> The truth is that only in the mystery of the incarnate Word does the mystery of man take on light. For Adam, the first man, was a figure of Him who was to come [cf. Rom 5:14], namely, Christ the Lord. . . . It is not surprising, then, that in Him all the aforementioned truths find their root and attain their crown.
>
> He who is "the image of the invisible God" (Col 1:15), is Himself the perfect man. To the sons of Adam He restores the divine likeness which had been disfigured from the first sin onward.

The christological orientation of Christian anthropology has been heavily underscored, then, by the council (as also by the magisterium of John Paul II: see, e.g., *Redemptor Hominis*, nos. 8, 13, 28).

To be sure, the ecclesiastical magisterium has not gone into explicit detail in setting forth the relationship between Christology and anthropology. The contemporary theological understanding of these is not of a piece. It would go beyond the scope of this article to expound on the various positions and explanatory models, however succinctly. But theologians all agree that in accepting Christ's revelation the human being finds a response to his and her deepest questions. The following of Christ, then, is not something imposed only from without, and having no relationship with our being. Quite the contrary, only in Jesus does the essence of the human being reach its definitive determination, since from the first moment of creation God has stamped this orientation upon it. Therefore Vatican II (*GS* 41) can assert that one who follows Christ, the perfect human being, becomes more a human being herself. The unsuspected novelty of the incarnation of the Son of God, that fruit of the utterly gratuitous salvation plan of the Father, and of nothing else, and the orientation of the world and the human being to Christ in such wise that Christ constitutes the perfection to which that world and human being tend in this concrete order of creation, will be the two points (only seemingly contradictory) which Christian theology, and especially anthropology, will always need to maintain.

Christian faith tells us that the human being has not been faithful to this divine plan, and that, from the beginning, the reality of sin has hindered our relationship with God. But God has remained faithful and loving, and in Christ the twisted divine likeness has been restored (*GS* 22). Nor indeed has human nature, while profoundly affected by sin, been corrupted at its root.

3. The Human Being Called to Be a Child of God in Christ

Christian anthropology asserts that the human being's only perfection consists in a full conformation to Jesus, who is the perfect human being. This means participation in his divine filiation—in the unique, interable relationship prevailing between Christ, the only-begotten Son of God, and his Father. In the Gospels themselves, we read that Jesus, who always addresses God with the appellation "Father," teaches his disciples, without ever placing himself on the same level, to do the same (see Mk 11:25; Mt 5:48; 6:9, 32; Lk 6:36; 11:2; etc.). Paul will tell us that this is possible only through the gift of the Holy Spirit, who is sent to our hearts and who calls out within us, "Abba, Father" (Gal 4:6; cf. Rom 8:15). By virtue of this gift, we can lead a life authentically that of daughters and sons of God and brothers and sisters of one another. Thus, the only-begotten Son of God becomes the firstborn of many siblings (see Rom 8:29; Heb 2:11–12:17; perhaps Jn 20:17). Christian anthropology, then, contemplates a human being called to share in the very life of the triune God: in the same Spirit, we all have access to the Father through Christ (Eph 2:18). The very unity that prevails among the disciples of Christ—a oneness with one another to which all human beings are called—is a reflection of the unity of the divine persons (see Jn 17:21-23).

Our brief sketch of some of the points of Christian anthropology must not omit the category of "grace," which is essential to the Christian view of the human being. We have referred to the unsuspected, unanticipated novelty of the incarnation of Jesus. God freely bestows a self-communication in the divine Son and his Spirit. Likewise a gift of God, without merit on the part of human beings, is a personal incorporation into salvation (justification by faith). The Christian view of the human being must not forget: the fullness of humanity is always received as a free gift. It is not reducible to the gift of creation, any more than the incarnation of Jesus is deducible from that primordial event. Consequently, it is a new, inalienable element of the Christian view of the human being that the latter receives his plenitude as an unmerited gift, which in turn does not preclude the necessity of freely accepting it, and of cooperating with the God who grants it in the infinite divine goodness.

4. Unity of the Human Being in a Duality of Body and Soul

The biblical teaching of the human being's creation in the image and likeness of God shows forth the intimate relationship between the orders of creation and salvation. Christian faith throughout the centuries has been concerned not only to propound the meaning of salvation but also to insist on such a creaturely configuration of human beings, in their "nature," as will constitute them an apt receptacle for this free salvation of Christ as their intrinsic perfection. Without a doubt, an essential point of this concern has been the unity of the human being in the plurality of her dimensions. The NT itself, in the footsteps of the OT, while insisting on the original unity of the human being, is nonetheless cognizant of distinct aspects of the same. In their material dimension, human beings are "body," which makes them cosmic beings, inserted into this world, in solidarity with others, having a definite identity throughout the various stages of their existence (see 1 Cor 15:44-49). This corporeal condition of the human being is sometimes associated with the "carnal" condition, which in turn frequently acquires a negative connotation: it indicates our weakness (see Mk 14:38; Mt 26:41) or even, especially in Paul, our subjection to the dominion of sin (see Rom 6:19; 8:3-9; Gal 5:13, 16-17). Human beings are also "psyche"—life, soul: they have emotions and feelings (see Mk 3:4; 8:35; Mt 20:28; 26:38; Col 3:23). Finally, the human being also has a "capacity for the divine": he stands in a relationship with God. All of this is expressed in the term "spirit," which indicates both the life of God communicated to us and constituting our own life principle and our condition as moved by the Holy Spirit. It frequently stands in opposition to the "flesh" as weak or subject to sin (see Mk 14:38; Jn 3:6; Rom 8:2-4, 6, 10, 15-16; Gal 5:16-18, 22-25). While the NT enters upon no systematic reflection on the question, it shows us, beyond any doubt, taken overall, the human being as a being at once worldly and transcendent to this world, a being with a receptive capacity for a relation with God.

Throughout history, from the first Christian centuries on, this has been expressed in the notion of the human being as composed of soul and body. Christianity assimilated these notions from Greek anthropology, while transforming them in the process. Christological and soteriological schemas (incarnation, resurrection) led some of the fathers to center their anthropologies precisely on the body. Soon enough, it is true, owing to the predominance of Platonic schemas, the soul acquired a preeminence over the body—to the point that at times it was the soul, strictly speaking, that was regarded as the human being. But in Christian theology the body has never been regarded as evil in itself. It too has been created by God and is called to a final transformation in resurrection. Thomas Aquinas emphasized the unity of the human composite in his celebrated formula _Anima forma corporis_: the soul is the substantial form of the body. A primordial substantial unity prevails in the human being, embracing two aspects, soul and body, in such wise that neither of the two in separation from the other would be a human being or person. There is no soul without a body, then, nor human body without a soul (prescinding from the continued existence of the soul after death). The substantial unity of the soul and body was likewise underscored by the Council of Vienne, in the year 1312 (see DS 900, 902). The Fifth Lateran Council (1513) defined that the soul is not common to all human beings, but is individual and immortal (DS 1440). The body and soul of the human being are also spoken of in their unity in *GS* 14.

Modern anthropology prefers to say that, rather than *having* a soul and a body, the human being *is* at once soul and body. At the same time, it insists that both the soul and the body are "of the human being" (in the singular) — an apt way of enunciating the oneness that we are and experience. Our psychism and our corporeality are mutually conditioning. Being body, we find ourselves immersed in spatiotemporality, united with the rest of humankind, and subject to finitude and mortality. Being soul, we transcend the world and are called to immortality — an immortality that, from a Christian viewpoint, is meaningless if it is not both a life in communion with God and continuous with our present life, so that it will still be "I" who shall enjoy the plenitude of resurrection, when I shall at last be fully remolded to the shape of the risen Christ.

5. The Human Being as a Personal Being Open to Transcendence

The psychosomatic constitution of the human being, in virtue of which, while remaining a cosmic being, she nevertheless transcends this world, is intimately bound up with her "personal" being. The human being is not just one more object among so many others in the world. He is a unique, interable subject. Christian thought has developed the notion of "person" to express this character of the human being — the quality that renders us radically distinct from all the beings around us and confers on us a dignity and value in ourselves, rather than merely in function of our activities or the utility we may afford others. Vatican Council II points out that the human being is the only earthly creature that God has loved for itself (*GS* 24). It is not without significance that the anthropological development of the notion of person has been chronologically posterior to its application in trinitarian theology and in Christology. The meaning of the value and worth of the person, so widely recognized in our day (despite manifold contradictions, which must not be ignored), even beyond the Christian pale, receives from the Christian view of the human being the latter's ultimate foundation: we have an absolute value for one another because we have an absolute value for God, who loves us in Jesus, the Son of God, and who calls us to the divine communion. The condition of the human being as person and interable subject is indissolubly bound up with that of his freedom. This means not only that he is able to choose among various goods or concrete opportunities, although it necessarily includes this; but also, and especially, it means that he consists of a capacity to conform or mold himself, to form his very substance and personhood, in accordance with his own options. Thus it has been possible to say not merely that the human being *has* freedom, but that he *is* freedom. After all, in spite of the evident conditioning to which we find ourselves subject, we enjoy an authentic capacity for self-determination. In the exercise of our freedom, the human being primarily makes an option vis-à-vis herself. One must therefore speak not only of freedom *from* lets and hindrances, inward or outward, but of a freedom *for* a human project standing in need of implementation. Freedom has nothing in common with caprice. Hence, it attains its fullness only in an option for good. From a Christian viewpoint, this means permitting oneself to be freed by the Spirit: it means bursting the bonds of sin and selfishness, to live in the liberty of the sons and daughters of God, which is the freedom of Jesus, who delivers himself up even unto death, for love. It is important to observe that the human being is free even with regard to God and the divine word. In revelation God seeks to establish a dialogue with us, and calls us to a communion in the divine life itself. None of this would be possible on the hypothesis that God would force us to accept it. When we lay emphasis on human freedom, then, we are asserting that, even before God and in regard to God, we are and remain ever an authentic subject, a genuine "thou."

As a personal, free being, the human being finds himself necessarily open to the world and others. Facing these, he exercises his freedom, and in this very exercise is able to experience his own transcendence. We need the world around us for our very subsistence. This is a fundamental, universally recognized experience we have. But in this very relation of dependency vis-à-vis the world, we discover the meaning of our transcendence of that world: thanks to human beings and their ability to transform reality around them, something new is produced in that reality. Through human effort, nature realizes new possibilities—possibilities that it could have attained in no other way. Human toil, then, is a qualitatively new phenomenon on the face of the cosmos: thus, the human being can be characterized as a "creator." These possibilities in nature are in turn transformed into new possibilities for the human being herself—new possibilities for her freedom. Inserted into the world, in her very activity within that world she shows that she transcends it—that she is more than just a cog in a mechanism. Furthermore, we are perpetually unsatisfied with our attainments. A chasm ever yawns between what we have and what we yearn for. Hardly, then, will the world furnish human beings with the ultimate meaning of their lives.

Interpersonal communion is irreducibly distinct from all other relationships between human beings and the world around them. Only in another human being do we find the "fitting helpmate" of the ancient biblical wisdom. Only the human being is worthy of the human being. Solely in the exercise of his social dimensions—and, especially, in communion and interpersonal bestowal—can the human being be himself. The notion of person, even in its deep theological roots, to which we have alluded, entails this dimension. In the encounter with our neighbor *qua* person, we find ourselves in confrontation with an absolute value not created by ourselves. Nor is it this other, any more than society as a whole, who, taken simply, is the foundation of the absolute value with which we find ourselves face to face: after all, our own personal being, too, is an absolute value vis-à-vis other persons. The interpersonal relation, then, also opens out upon the mystery of human beings' transcendence of their surroundings.

Human limitation and indigence, as manifested especially in death—the sensation of truncation almost inevitably experienced at the thought of death—also places us before the question of the meaning of human existence, along with the problem of the difficulty of discovering that meaning if we attempt to confine ourselves to what we see. Christian hope, especially if it is manifested in the outward life of believers, offers a plausible response to these questions in the mind of the human being.

As we have seen, Christian revelation presents us with a view of the human being that focuses first and foremost on Jesus, the perfect human being, in whom we are the sons and daughters of God. Inasmuch as this filiation is our ultimate vocation, Christian theology may not ignore those aspects of our constitution and creaturely being that render us suitable receptacles of this divine call. In the concrete anthropology of our very makeup, we discover a trace of the plan of a God who would possess us. Thus, Christian revelation reveals the human being as a being available to God's own self-communication. Christian revelation shows us new perspectives. Of ourselves we should never have been able to imagine them. Christian revelation is pure grace, a gift of the divine benevolence. And yet it responds to our inmost yearnings and desires: we learn that we can indeed attain to the intimate communion with God made possible to us by Christ, who also opens to us the full communion with our sisters and brothers that we experience in the life of the church—that instrument of "intimate union with God, and of the unity of all mankind" (*LG* 1), a church gathered into one by the unity of the Father, the Son, and the Holy Spirit (*LG* 4).

Bibl.: H. CROUZEL, *Théologie de l'image de Dieu chez Origène* (Paris, 1954); A. ORBE, *Antropología de san Ireneo* (Madrid, 1969); L. SCHEFFCZYK, ed., *Der Mensch als Bild Gottes* (Darmstadt, 1969); M. FLICK and Z. ALSZEGHY, *Fondamenti di una antropologia teologica* (Florence, 1970); W. PANNENBERG, "Christological Foundation of Christian Anthropology," *Conc* 9.9 (1973): 425–34; id., *Anthropology in Theological Perspective* (1983; Philadelphia, 1985); K. RAHNER, *Foundations of Christian Faith: An Introduction to the Idea of Christianity* (New York, 1978); A. GANOCZY, *Der schöpferische Mensch und die Schöpfung Gottes* (Mainz, 1976); W. KASPER, "Christologie und Anthropologie," *TQ* 162 (1982): 202–21; L. F. LADARIA, *Antropología teológica* (Madrid/Rome, 1983); R. LATOURELLE, *Man and His Problems in the Light of Jesus Christ* (New York, 1983); G. GOZZELLINO, *Vocazione e destino dell'uomo in Cristo* (Turin,

1985); J. I. Gonzalez Faus, *Proyecto de hermano: Visión cristiana del hombre* (Santander, 1987); J. Alfaro, *De la cuestión del hombre a la cuestión de Dios* (Salamanca, 1988); J. L. Ruiz de la Peña, *Imagen de Dios: Antropología teológica fundamental* (Santander, 1988); G. Colzani, *Antropologia teologica: L'uomo, paradosso e mistero* (Bologna, 1988); H. Urs von Balthasar, *Theo-drama: Theological Dramatic Theory*, vol. 2: *Dramatis Personae* (San Francisco, 1990).

Luis F. Ladaria

APOCRYPHAL GOSPELS

The church believes that through the Gospels we are united with and know Jesus of Nazareth, in his life and in his message. This conviction is of an order that enables the church to take up a position in regard to apocrypha. We refer mainly to apocryphal *Gospels*, that is: (1) the Jewish-Christian Gospels known under four titles: the *Gospel of the Hebrews*, the *Gospel of the Nazarenes*, the *Gospel of the Ebionites*, the *Gospel of the Twelve Apostles*; (2) the *Gospel of Peter*; (3) the *Protogospel of James*; and (4) the *Infancy Gospel of Thomas*.

These Gospels contain certain positive characteristics purloined for the most part from the canonical Gospels. In their entirety they are painfully mediocre. Pandering to the popular taste for marvels and legends, the Apocrypha succumb to the temptation to "complete" the Gospels, whether to supply the lack of information which they deem insufficient on certain periods of Jesus' life (particularly that preceding his public ministry), or to embellish the resurrection narrative with details tending irrefutably to establish its reality in the face of incredulity. This attempt already represents the temptation to write a life of Jesus that would reconstruct the past completely, in order to answer the demands of popular curiosity or the requirements of some apologetical effort to explain the disagreement of our narratives, or to increase the realism of the main events in Jesus' life.

This aim of the Apocrypha represents a two-fold betrayal of the Gospels. On the one hand, it panders to popular curiosity by using the Gospel above all else as a source of information;

on the other hand, it tends to separate the event from its meaning and to give it a "plus value" by treating it as something in itself, something as it were "self-centered."

From the middle of the second century, our four Gospels were treated as a compact whole, as a *numerus clausus*: they are four in number, no more and no less. All the other texts that claim the title "Gospel" were rejected as apocryphal. The four canonical Gospels were considered to be the four forms of the one good news of salvation. This conviction is recorded in the expressions of Irenaeus, who speaks of the "fourfold Gospel"; of Tertullian, who speaks of "the gospel argument" (as of a single argument that may be invoked against heretics); and of Eusebius, who speaks of the "sacred quadriga" of the Gospels. These formulas, which see the Gospels as a whole with four aspects, express an uncontested acquisition with a long history.

Bibl.: L. Vaganay, "Apocryphes du N.T.," in *Catholicisme*, 1:699–703; E. Amann, "Apocryphes," in *DBS* 1, cols. 460–533.

René Latourelle

APOLOGETICS

I. History: *1. New Testament. 2. Patristic Age. 3. Middle Ages. 4. From the Sixteenth to the Eighteenth Century. 5. Nineteenth Century. 6. Twentieth Century.* (A. Dulles)

II. Nature and Task: *1. Negative Definition. 2. Nature of Apologetics. 3. Apologetic Methodology.* (R. Latourelle)

I. HISTORY

1. New Testament

The biblical books, including the NT, are pastoral writings directed to communities of faith. None of them, as it stands, is primarily apologetic. But indirectly the NT yields abundant information about how the early Christians, in dialogue with Jews and pagans, gave a reasoned "defense" (the original meaning of *apologia*) of the hope that was in them (see 1 Pt 3:15). The earliest Christian preaching, as reported in Acts, seeks to demonstrate to potential believers that Jesus, as the promised Messiah, died and rose again according to the Scriptures. The apostles, as there depicted, stress the evidential value of the appearances of the risen Lord and point to the gifts of prophecy and miracle working as proof that the risen Lord, in fulfillment of biblical prophecy, has sent his Spirit upon the Christian community (Acts 2:16–21; 1 Cor 14:25). In situations of persecution Stephen, Paul, and others explain for the benefit of their persecutors or captors the solid grounds of their faith and thus set examples for subsequent confessors and martyrs to follow.

Luke introduces his Gospel by expressing his intention to reassure Theophilus of the certainty of the teachings he has received (Lk 1:4). All four Gospels tell the story of Jesus in a way calculated to win belief in him as Messiah. His Davidic ancestry, his miraculous conception, and the very town of his birth, his flight into Egypt, his preaching and miracles, as well as the details of his passion and resurrection, are linked with prophetically interpreted texts from the OT. The authority with which Jesus spoke and the powerful deeds he performed are set forth as reasons for putting faith in him.

Among the NT letters the one directed to the Hebrews is notable for its elaborate argumentation that Christ surpassingly fulfilled everything for which Moses, Aaron, and other priests and prophets, and even the angels, had been revered. The letter is apologetic insofar as it aims to prevent Christian converts from relapsing into Judaism. A similar intention underlies the second letter of Peter, which contrasts the good news with "cleverly devised myths" (2 Pt 1:16).

The NT, therefore, contains many echoes of early Christian apologetics; it furnishes materials enabling Christians to justify their faith and defend it against adversaries; to some extent it is designed to reassure Christians that their faith is solidly grounded.

2. Patristic Age

In the second century, with the so-called apologists, apologetics became the dominant form of Christian literature. Some of this literature was directed to emperors and civil authorities to gain legal tolerance for Chris-

tians. Some was directed to Jews or pagans in the hope that they might abandon their errors; some, toward Christians to keep them from being swayed by objections and to move them to confess their faith boldly. The two apologies of Justin, the *Embassy for Christians* by Athenagoras, and the anonymous *Letter to Diognetus* all contend that Christians are not disloyal to the state and that they have done nothing deserving of death. In his *Dialogue with Trypho the Jew* Justin provides a model of frank debate about the fulfillment of biblical prophecy in Christianity. By the end of the century many of the standard forms of Christian apologetics had already been established.

In the third century, Tertullian carried on the apologetic task with rhetorical brilliance. In his *Apology* and *To Scapula* he pleaded eloquently for religious freedom and protested against the false and absurd charges made against Christians. He also wrote apologies *Against the Jews* and *To the Pagans*. In Alexandria, Clement composed a splendid exhortation to conversion, the *Protrepticus*, presenting Christianity as the true philosophy. ORIGEN, who took Clement's place as head of the catechetical school at Alexandria, produced in his *Contra Celsum* an erudite, closely argued, and full-fledged reply to the eclectic Platonist Celsus, who had stated the case against Christianity. With Clement and Origen apologetics achieved philosophical sophistication.

In the fourth century, Arnobius and Lactantius, carrying on the tradition set by Minucius Felix in the third century, composed literary apologies for the faith addressed to educated Romans who might be contemplating conversion. In the East, Eusebius of Caesarea, in his *Preparation for the Gospel*, responded in a learned and civil style to the neo-Platonist Porphyry. In his *Proof of the Gospel* Eusebius promoted a christological reading of the Hebrew Scriptures. He and Athanasius, although they differed in their attitudes toward the Arians, shared a common jubilation at the overthrow of paganism in the empire.

In the fifth century, the Antiochene Theodoret of Cyrrhus produced a respectable *summa* of the standard arguments against paganism, *The Cure of Pagan Maladies*, emphasizing the agreements between Platonic philosophy and biblical revelation. In the West apologetics reached a new level of brilliance in AUGUSTINE of Hippo (354–430). In his early dialogues Augustine refuted skepticism on purely philosophical grounds. He then wrote several brief works against the Manichaeans, including *Of True Religion* and *On the Usefulness of Belief*. Later he composed his monumental treatise *The City of God*, in which he responded to the charge that Christianity was reponsible for the fall of the Roman Empire. Besides exposing the weaknesses of pagan religion, as others had done, Augustine in this work laid the groundwork for a comprehensive theology of history. With his philosophical acumen, his literary power, and his exceptional grasp of the dynamism of the human spirit, Augustine ranks among the leading apologists of all time. His work was in some way continued by his disciples Orosius and Salvian, and in the sixth century by Popes Leo I and Gregory I.

3. Middle Ages

Beginning in the seventh century, apologetics took on the added task of answering the Muslims. John Damascene and his disciple Abu Qurrah wrote dialogues involving religious debates between Christians and Muslims. In the Latin West fictitious dialogues (in some cases based on actual debates) between Christians and Jews were composed by Isidore of Seville (seventh century), Peter Damian (eleventh century), Gilbert Crispin (eleventh century), Rupert of Deutz (twelfth century), and many others. Peter the Venerable (twelfth century) authored a polemical tract *Against the Inveterate Obstinacy of the Jews* and another *Against the Sect or Heresy of the Saracens*. In contrast to these rather vehement pieces Abelard wrote a remarkably open and unpolemical *Dialogue between a Philosopher, a Jew and a Christian*.

In the thirteenth century, THOMAS AQUINAS contributed importantly to the development of apologetics with his *Summa contra Gentiles*, otherwise called *On the Truth of the Catholic Faith against the Errors of the Unbelievers*, a work probably intended, at least in part, for the use of Christian missionaries in Spain. Thomas drew a sharp contrast between religious truths that are accessible to reason on the basis of ordinary experience, such as the existence of God and the immortality of the soul, and other truths, such as the Trinity and the incarnation,

that cannot be known without revelation. Faith in these indemonstrable truths, he contended, is rationally warranted by virtue of the testimony of authoritative teachers, whose credibility is authenticated by prophecies and miracles.

After the time of Aquinas, apologetic writing against the Saracens and Jews was carried on by the thirteenth-century Dominican Raymond Martini and, at the turn of the new century, by Raymond Lull and Ricoldus de Monte Croce. Lull composed several interesting dialogues between Christians, Jews, and Saracens. This tradition was continued in the fifteenth century by Georgios of Trapezon, Juan de Torquemada, and Denis the Carthusian, all of whom wrote against the Muslims. Cardinal Nicholas of Cusa, just after the fall of Constantinople, wrote a remarkably irenic dialogue *On Peace or Concord in Matters of Faith* (*De pace seu concordantia fidei*, 1454) in which the apologetic element is minimal.

From the beginning of the fourteenth century the Scotists and Okhamists maintained that it was possible to achieve a firm and fully warranted assent of faith (*fides acquisita*) on the basis of reason alone. Henry Totting of Oyta and Henry of Langenstein, following Scotus, carefully enumerated the extrinsic signs by which Christianity was in their view accredited.

During the Renaissance, Marsilio Ficino (1433–1499), the founder of the Platonic Academy at Florence, worked out an attractive synthesis between Platonic philosophy and Christian faith. In his *On the Christian Religion* he extolled Christianity as the most perfect religion and defended the immortality of the soul and the divinity of Christ. Ficino's contemporary Girolamo Savonarola, in his apologetic treatise *The Triumph of the Cross*, splendidly portrayed the beauty of Christ's passion and described the inner peace that comes from steadfast fidelity in the confession of Christ.

4. From the Sixteenth to the Eighteenth Century

The Protestant Reformers had varying attitudes toward apologetics. Luther often spoke as though reason were an incompetent guide in spiritual matters and could only engender doubts unless it submitted to the guidance of revelation. Revelation, he believed, should be accepted on the basis of faith alone. Yet Luther's close associate Philipp Melanchthon, at least in his later writings, made use of reason as a preparation for faith. Beginning with the 1536 edition of his *Loci communes,* he set forth the traditional arguments from the antiquity of biblical revelation, the excellence of Christian doctrine, the perpetuity of the church, and the attestation of miracles. John Calvin, in his *Institutes of the Christian Religion* (final edition, 1559), defends the revealed character of Holy Scripture on the basis of arguments similar to those used by Scotus and the fourteenth-century Nominalists.

Sixteenth-century Catholics, while engaging in polemical disputes with Protestants, continued to produce apologetic tracts such as *On the Truth of the Christian Faith* by the Spanish humanist Juan Luis Vivés (posthumous, 1543). This work, indebted to Augustine, Aquinas, and the subsequent tradition, emphasizes the need for religion and the grounds for accepting the Christian religion as a divinely given path to salvation. In a concluding section Vivés addresses the concerns of Jews and Muslims in dialogue form.

The Huguenot Philip du Plessis-Mornay in his *On the Truth of the Christian Religion* (1581) established the basic pattern for Calvinist apologetics. His work closely resembles, in its general structure, Catholic treatises such as that of Vivés. Hugo Grotius, an outstanding Dutch Calvinist apologist, produced a clear and systematically organized handbook, *The Truth of the Christian Religion* (1621, revised 1627). Moïse Amyraut, writing in France a few years after Grotius, particularly addressed the problem of religious indifference. Another Huguenot pastor, Jacques Abbadie, in his *Vindication of the Truth of the Christian Religion* (1684; Eng. trans. 1694), grappled with the new problems raised by Spinoza's biblical criticism and new paleontological theories of La Peyrère.

Seventeenth-century Catholics tended to accuse the Protestants of putting too much stock in reason and private judgment. Pierre Charron, responding to a polemical work of du Plessis-Mornay, established a three-stage approach, defending successively the validity of religion, that of Christianity in particular, and that of Catholicism as the authentic form of Christianity (*Les trois vérités . . . ,* 1596). He sought to unmask the excessive self-confidence of atheists, non-Christians, and Protestants, all of whom he accuses of claiming to know more than they really do about God and religion. Blaise PASCAL (1623–1662) in his *Pensées* ridiculed the metaphysical proofs for the existence of God and preferred to follow what he called the reasons of the heart. He spoke of faith as a wager in which we take a calculated risk that the message is true. It is reasonable, he asserted, to obey our inclination to believe if our hearts should be so inclined.

Some Catholic apologists of the seventeenth century, influenced by the climate of rationalism, were very bold in their apologetics. The Spanish Jesuit Miguel de Elizalde (1616–1678) and his disciple Thyrsus Gonzáles attempted a quasi-mathematical demonstration of the "fact of revelation." The influential court preacher Jacques Bénigne Bossuet (1627–1704), though he was no rationalist, seemed singularly free from doubts. In his *Discourse on Universal History* (1681) he illustrated at some length how the true church, always attacked but never conquered, is "a perpetual miracle and testifies brilliantly to the immutability of the divine counsels."

As an antidote to skepticism the English diplomat Edward Herbert of Cherbury (1583–1648) devised the system known as Deism, in which reason is deemed competent to establish all the truths of religion and in which all that is claimed as revealed must be validated by its conformity with reason. John Locke in *The Reasonableness of Christianity as Delivered in the Scriptures* (1695) maintained that Christianity could qualify as revealed because it was attested by miracles and prophecies and contained nothing contrary to reason. Two of his disciples, John Toland and Matthew Tindal, going beyond their master, denied that revealed religion could be anything but a republication of the religion of nature.

A host of Anglican apologists came to the defense of revealed religion. Samuel Clarke (1675–1729), strongly upholding the rights of natural theology, maintained that the NT is in full accord with reason. Joseph Butler, more empirical in his mentality, preferred to avoid arguments from metaphysics and from authority. In his *The Analogy of Religion, Natural and Revealed* (1736), he held that the missions of Christ and the Holy Spirit, surpassing the truths of natural religion, are essential to Christianity and are fully credible. The arguments for Christianity, he admitted, are only probable when taken singly, but "probable proofs, by being added, not only increase the evidence, but multiply it." In nearly all the practical decisions of life, he contended, we are guided by presuppositions and probabilities. Why not, then, in religion?

Toward the end of the eighteenth century, William Paley summed up in clear and systematic form the main arguments of the evidential school. His celebrated *A View of the Evidences of Christianity* (1794) amasses the standard arguments against the philosophical skeptics, who question the knowability of God, against the Deists, who deny revelation, and against the historical skeptics, who do not credit the claims of biblical revelation. Paley is chiefly remembered today for his argument from design, in which he, like others before him, compared God to a watchmaker.

On the European continent unbelief became increasingly virulent with Pierre Bayle (1647–1706). In a discourse prefixed to his *Theodicy* (1710) Gottfried Wilhelm Leibniz (1646–1716) argued against Bayle that faith is concordant with reason and that the fact of evil is no objection to the existence of God, who has created the best of all possible worlds. In a more scholastic vein the Jesuit Vitus Pichler, in his *Theologia polemica* (1713), maintained that one can prove by reason the possibility and necessity of revelation. Other German apologists, both Protestant and Catholic, took part in the debate set off by the Deist Hermann Samuel Reimarus (1694–1768), who attacked the historicity of the Gospels.

In France the Oratorian Alexandre Houtteville attempted to demonstrate, in his *The Christian Religion Proved by Facts* (1722), that the miracle stories of the Gospels are trustworthy according to the general norms of historical evidence. The Abbé Nicolas Bergier, who wrote several responses to Rousseau and other Deists, defended the historicity of the NT miracle stories along the same lines as Houtteville. Voltaire had many Catholic critics including Claude Nonnotte and Antoine Guénée.

The Sorbonne professor Luke Joseph Hooke combined the somewhat rationalist approach of Clarke and Pichler with the more historical approach of Houtteville. His *Religionis natu-ralis et revelatae principia* (1752–1754) used a step-by-step approach, defending first the truths of natural theology, then the possibility and necessity of revelation, and finally the fact of revelation. This general approach, developed in many standard works of the period (e.g., those of Benedikt Stattler, Ignaz Neubauer, and Engelbert Klüpfel), was most elaborately set forth by the Italian Dominican Pietro Maria Gazzaniga in his nine-volume *Praelectiones theologicae* (1788–1793). To show the necessity of revelation Gazzaniga emphasized the weakness of human reason, which he nevertheless deemed competent to establish criteria for discerning authentic revelation. For Gazzaniga the supreme miracle is the resurrection of Christ.

5. Nineteenth Century

At the close of the eighteenth century there was a reaction against the arid rationalism of the Enlightenment. In Germany Friedrich Schleiermacher (1768–1834) introduced a new style of apologetics which strove not to defend the dogmas of traditional orthodoxy but to give scope for the religious instinct that gives rise to faith. In his lectures *On Religion* (1799) Schleiermacher attacked the passion for calculation and deduction that tended to enfeeble the sense and taste for the infinite. In his dogmatic synthesis, *The Christian Faith* (1821–1822), he vindicated Christianity as the highest form of monotheism and monotheism as the highest form of religion. God's redeeming power in Christ, he held, is self-validating to those who experience it.

In French Catholicism the romantic revival is typified by the apologetics of François René de Chateaubriand (1768–1848) among many others. Chateaubriand's *The Genius of Christianity, or the Beauties of the Christian Religion* (Paris, 1802) took the literary world by storm. In the early nineteenth century, French traditionalists such as Joseph de Maistre and Louis de Bonald advocated the Catholic church as the channel by which divine tradition was best transmitted. The papacy, they believed, was essential to guard against religious anarchy, as was monarchy to prevent civil disintegration. Félicité de Lamennais wrote a four-volume *Essay on Indifference in Matters of Religion* (1817–1823), in which he contended that the true religion is that which rests on the greatest religious authority, namely, that of an infallible pope. The Abbé Louis Bautain, who had links with traditionalism, held that the only effective route to faith passes through a stage of hypothetically accepting, on the word of human witnesses, the truth of revelation. Only within such an attitude of acceptance can one gain the light to discern, in faith, the truth of the Christian message (*La philosophie du christianisme,* 1835).

Toward the middle of the nineteenth century, Spain produced two distinguished Catholic apologists. Jaime Balmés argued that submission to religious authority is the necessary condition of liberty and social progress. Juan Donoso Cortés maintained that by deifying the principle of authority the Catholic church has condemned the forces of pride and rebellion.

The Catholic restoration in Germany found an able champion in Bruno Liebermann (1759–1844), whose five-volume *Institutiones theologicae* (1819–1827) continued the anti-deistic apologetics of his scholastic teachers. More original was the approach of Georg Hermes (1775–1831). Influenced by Kant, he argued that practical reason can establish that the acceptance of Christian faith is essential for the observance of the self-evident moral imperative to respect the dignity of every human person. After Hermes' death, some of his works were placed on the index because they did not conform to the Roman doctrine of faith. Johann Sebastian DREY (1777–1853), the founder of the Catholic Tübingen School, wrote a three-volume *Apologetics as a Scientific Demonstration of the Divinity of Christianity* (1847). Influenced by Schleiermacher and Schelling, Drey emphasized the historical and social character of revelation.

The Roman school, under the leadership of Giovanni Perrone, S.J. (1794–1876), perpetuated the general style of apologetics found in Liebermann. In his *Praelectiones dogmaticae* Perrone, omitting the standard treatise on the importance of religion in general, focused on revealed religion in particular. He moved logically from the possibility of revelation, through its necessity, to the criteria and finally the actuality of revelation. In other works he answered rationalistic critics of the Gospels, such as H. E. G. Paulus, D. F. Strauss, and E. Renan.

In England the leading Catholic apologist was the convert John Henry NEWMAN (1801–1890). Building on the work of Joseph Butler, he probed deeply into the antecedent probabilities that underlie one's personal journey to faith. Christianity, he concluded in his *Grammar of Assent,* is the only religion in the world that can fulfill the "aspirations, needs, and foreshadowings of natural faith and devotion." In the final chapter of this work and in his *Apologia pro vita sua,* Newman set forth an impressive historical argument for the truth of Christianity based on a vast convergence of probabilities.

In the United States two remarkable converts from Protestantism, Orestes Brownson (1803–1876) and Isaac Hecker (1819–1888), revitalized apologetics. Brownson explained how he was led to the church by the writings of French utopian socialists. Hecker, more self-consciously American, praised Catholic Christianity as the religion that best harmonized with the national respect for reason, freedom, human dignity, equality, and progress. Shortly afterward Cardinal James Gibbons wrote his immensely popular *The Faith of Our Fathers* (1876), which combined an able response to common Protestant objections with an enthusiastic endorsement of the separation of church and state. The writings of Archbishop John Ireland (1838–1918) exuded optimistic progressivism and confidence in America's destiny.

Reacting against the type of apologetics taught in seminary manuals, the Belgian Victor Dechamps (1810–1883), who later became a cardinal, propounded a "method of providence" that relied on the correlation of two facts—the inner fact of a felt need for divine enlightenment and the exterior fact of the church as a "subsistent miracle." The correspondence between these two facts, he maintained, makes it possible to recognize Catholic Christianity as a providential means of grace and salvation.

Vatican Council I in its Dogmatic Constitution on Catholic faith (1870) taught that assent to the Christian revelation was rationally warranted on the ground of extrinsic arguments. The council appeared to support two different styles of apologetics—the one biblical and historical, along the lines of Perrone, and the other experiential and ecclesial, along the lines of Dechamps. In the latter part of the nineteenth century, theologians such as Franz Hettinger (1813–1890) continued the seminary-type apologetics, with a strong accent on extrinsic signs of credibility and on authority. In France Paul de Broglie (1834–1895) argued for the transcendence of Christianity in relation to the other religions. In Germany Albert Maria Weiss, O.P. (1844–1925), defended Catholicism as the religion of social progress.

Protestant apologetics after Schleiermacher developed in several strands. Pietists such as August Tholuck (1799–1877) built on the joyful experience of regeneration through Christ and on the self-evidence of the new life given by the Holy Spirit. Georg F. W. HEGEL (1770–1831) and his orthodox followers attempted to show the conformity between Christian dogma and the historical dialectic of world evolution. In Denmark, Søren Kierkegaard (1813–1855) attacked Hegelianism as a distortion of Christianity. Denying that Christianity could be made rationally plausible, he argued that the paradox of the incarnation, calling for a blind leap of faith, fulfills the supreme passion of reason to submit to an object totally transcending itself. Neo-Kantians such as Albrecht Ritschl (1822–1899), Wilhelm Herrmann (1846–1922), and Julius Kaftan (1848–1926) sought to show the practical benefits of Christian faith. Adolf von Harnack (1851–1930) appealed to a critical study of the Gospels to show that the original preaching of Jesus centered on the "higher righteousness" of love, a doctrine that commends itself by its simplicity and sublimity.

In England, Samuel Taylor Coleridge (1772–1834) and his friend Frederick Denison Maurice (1805–1872), rejecting the method of Paley and the evidentialists, called for a more personal and affective type of apologetics. As biblical criticism and biological evolutionism became more broadly accepted, English-speaking Protestant apologists were divided into two main schools. Conservatives, such as Benjamin B. Warfield (1851–1921) at Princeton Theological Seminary, rejected the new tendencies, whereas liberals, such as the Anglican bishop Charles Gore (1853–1932), held that the church should welcome the advances of science.

6. Twentieth Century

At the close of the nineteenth century, the Catholic layman Maurice BLONDEL (1861–1949) attempted to reconstruct metaphysics from a study of the dynamism of the human will (*Action*, 1893). He contended that this dyna-

mism cannot be satisfied except by a supernatural gift of communion with God. Apologetics, therefore, must show that Christianity satisfies the desire for the supernatural that is inherent in nature as it concretely exists. In various articles Blondel proposed a "method of immanence" that in some ways drew upon Dechamps' analysis of the "interior fact." The encyclical *Pascendi* (1907), directed against Catholic modernism, seemed to condemn the method of immanence, making it difficult for Blondel and his disciples to continue to urge their ideas.

The theory of apologetics was debated in scholastic circles by French theologians such as the Dominicans Ambroise GARDEIL (1859–1931) and Réginald Garrigou-Lagrange and the Jesuits J. V. Bainvel and H. Pinard de la Boullaye. Léonce de Grandmaison, S.J., composed a three-volume work *Jesus Christ: His Person, His Message, and His Credentials* (1928), which served for several decades as a standard reply to radical biblical criticism. In Germany Karl Adam wrote apologetic works on behalf of Catholic Christianity that combined modern phenomenology with a vivid sense of communal solidarity. Adam deliberately developed his apologetics from a position within the commitment of faith.

The 1930s and 1940s witnessed a spate of apologetically oriented convert stories, of which Thomas Merton's *The Seven Storey Mountain* (1948) is perhaps the best known. The French Thomist philosophers Jacques Maritain and Etienne Gilson popularized the concept of a Christian philosophy operating in a context of faith. The Jesuit paleontologist Pierre TEILHARD DE CHARDIN (1881–1955), espousing an evolutionary worldview, sought to achieve a synthesis between science and faith. Faith, in his view, promotes human progress. Maritain and Gilson, among others, denounced Teilhardism as a new gnosticism.

In more recent twentieth-century Calvinist theology one may find a conservative trend, in continuity with Benjamin Warfield and the Princeton school, that is highly suspicious of modern biblical criticism. Carl F. H. Henry, Gordon H. Clark, Bernard Ramm, and others of this school strongly insist on the rational preambles to faith. In neo-orthodox circles Karl BARTH (1886–1968) and Rudolf BULTMANN (1884–1976) repudiated apologetics as a capitulation of faith to human reason, but Emil

Brunner (1889–1966) vindicated apologetics on the ground that it could expose the falsity of reason's understanding of itself. Paul TILLICH (1886–1965), in response to Barth, insisted that apologetics is an omnipresent feature of systematic theology, which must exhibit the Christian message as a satisfying answer to human existential questions.

Anglicanism produced a group of talented lay apologists, such as C. S. Lewis (1898–1963), who placed their literary talents at the service of Christian faith. Other Anglicans such as Alan Richardson developed a historical approach to the Bible that was sensitive to modern critical findings and to the complexities of historical method.

In the period following World War II there was a move, especially in Protestant circles, toward a theology of secularization. Dietrich Bonhoeffer (1906–1945) in some posthumous writings, Friedrich Gogarten (1887–1967), and others contended that biblical monotheism, by desacralizing the world, promoted the process of secularization, and was thus in harmony with modern civilization. Other German-speaking Protestants, such as Gerhard Ebeling and the so-called post-Bultmannians, renewed, in slightly different form, the liberal Protestant effort to find in the Jesus of history the norm of Christian faith. Wolfhart Pannenberg and his circle have insisted, as did some Hegelians of the nineteenth century, that the truth of Christianity must agree with the demands of universal human reason. Yet there are Protestant and Catholic fideists who look upon faith as a purely private decision depending on inner feelings that are attributed to the Holy Spirit. Thus the status of apologetics is closely linked with the way in which the relations between faith and reason are understood in a given system.

In Catholic theology after 1940 there was a resurgence of the Blondelian inner apologetic in the work of Henri Bouillard and that of Karl RAHNER (1904–1984). Rahner's appeal to the "supernatural existential" and his hypothesis of "anonymous Christianity" have certain affinities with Blondel's method of immanence, though Rahner does not share Blondel's voluntarism. Hans Urs von BALTHASAR (1905–1988) opposed Rahner's transcendental theology as excessively anthropocentric. In dialogue with Barth he sought to construct an "aesthetic theology" that would preserve the objectivity and transcendence of the revealed datum. Edward Schillebeeckx (1914–) and Johann Baptist Metz (1918–) have developed Catholic counterparts of the Protestant theology of secularization.

Although apologetics has been practiced since the origins of Christianity, and even earlier in Judaism, it continues to have in some circles a dubious reputation. Its bad name is due not simply to the excesses of fideism but, in great part, to the limitations of the kind of apologetics that was dominant from the fourteenth century until the middle of the twentieth. Although outstanding thinkers such as Pascal, Kierkegaard, Newman, and Blondel have resisted apologetic rationalism, many apologists have overestimated the capacity of pure reason to demonstrate the fact of Christian revelation. In contemporary theology apologetics is increasingly seen as an articulation of the intelligibility that is inherent in faith itself, and thus as inseparable from good theology. The intelligibility in question is not that of pure deductive reason but that of actual men and women, tempted to sin, but impelled by grace and attracted toward the God who is dimly known in the yearning he implants in the human heart.

Bibl.: K. WERNER, *Geschichte der apologetischen und polemischen Literatur der christlichen Theologie*, 5 vols. (Schaffhausen, 1861–67); O. ZÖCKLER, *Geschichte des Apologie des Christentums* (Gütersloh, 1907); R. AIGRAIN, "Histoire de l'apologétique," in M. BRILLANT and M. NÉDONCELLE, eds., *Apologétique* (1st ed., Paris, 1937) 950–1029; A. DULLES, *A History of Apologetics* (London/Philadelphia/New York, 1971); G. HEINZ, *Divinam christianae religionis originem probare* (Mainz, 1984); G. RUGGIERI, ed., *Enciclopedia di Teologia fondamentale*, vol. 1 (Genoa, 1987).

Avery DULLES

II. NATURE AND TASK

Classical, traditional apologetics, which prevailed for three centuries, corresponds to only a part of present-day fundamental theology, which takes up but also extends the concerns of classical apologetics. Indeed, apologetics represents that aspect of fundamental theology which examines revelation as a *fact* but also the gamut of signs that allow us to conclude that this fact exists.

Classical apologetics did not examine revelation as a mystery; that was thought to be the task of dogmatic theology. From the latter it obtained its basic concepts (revelation, tradition, mystery, miracle, and so on) and concerned itself with the event, or fact. This apologetical approach is still entirely valid, but it is now integrated into a broader vision: revelation in its entirety as mystery, event, and theological category.

In this article I shall look at apologetics as its leading practitioners conceived and practiced it until 1950, when it became the fundamental theology that received the sanction of *Sapientia christiana* on 29 April 1979.

1. Negative Definition

Before explaining the concerns and nature of apologetics, it will be helpful to say what it is not:

a. Apologetics *is not a form of conversion.* Many of the ambiguities which trouble apologetics are attributable to the more or less explicit conviction that the task of apologetics is to "convert" people. But, since thousands of readers have finished works of apologetics without being converted, it is difficult to justify this particular claim for the science.

We have to make a distinction between apologetics as an *art*, and apologetics as a *science*. There is a practical *pastoral* theology of conversion which is the concern of missionaries and centers devoted to problems of conversion. It consists in presenting Christian doctrine as a whole and extending an invitation to faith to an individual or group. This pastoral approach takes extremely varied forms, which are in fact as different as individuals themselves. This pastoral theology of conversion is needed in the church. To a certain extent, it can even take a scientific form, but it is not what we call apologetic theology. The latter is a science proper, with its own subject matter, purpose, and methodology. The apologetic method follows a reasoning process and leads to a certainty of the same order. As such it does not approximate to faith. Whereas apologetics is a science, faith is a religious and beneficial act, a personal and total adherence to God and to his word. Whereas the apologetic judgment is speculative and scientific, the assent of faith is existential and the combined product of

freedom and grace. On the way of conversion, the manifestation of Christianity as a *value*, as revealed in an encounter with true sanctity, may well prove more attractive than the fullness and wisdom of the most rigorous apologetics.

b. Although its origins would suggest the opposite (conflict between Jews and Gnostics), apologetics *is not a system of defense against opponents.* For centuries apologetics devoted its greatest strength to the organization of crusades. Happily it has lost the polemical and assertive tone which so discredited it. Above all, apologetics is a *positive science* that would deserve to exist even if there were no opponent. What is more, students nowadays, who live in an ecumenical atmosphere, no longer welcome that kind of cut-and-thrust apologetics. A truly significant sign of the change of attitude is that today Orthodox, Protestant, or Islamic students can attend courses in apologetics in Catholic universities without the least embarrassment.

c. Apologetics is not, as some commentators, such as Dieckmann, have opined, a mere *philosophical-historical* treatise. Apologetics draws on history and philosophy, but that does not mean that it is void of theology. Apologetics is an authentic theology. It exists within faith, and for the believer it always represents the questing intellect applied to the data of revelation. The fact that this form of reflection, because of its goal, draws on the data of history, philology, and philosophy in no way detracts from its *essential purpose*, which is to understand the data of revelation, which it examines as historical fact, and dogmatic theology as mystery. An erroneous conception of what theology does has taken to an extreme the distinction between apologetics and dogma, neither of which alone has fullness and vitality, for the reality they examine is both event and mystery.

d. Apologetics is not *philosophy of religion.* The essential aim of the philosophy of religion is a philosopher's and not a believer's aim. It does not examine mysteries as objects of faith (dogmatics) or as worthy of faith (apologetics), but religion as a human activity and as a conscious activity. It studies the phenomena that religion gives rise to, the categories that it brings into play. For philosophy of religion revelation is never any more than a negative criterion. Apologetics, on the other hand, always operates under the direction of the church and under the pressure of faith in search of knowledge. As Yves Congar says, the philosophy of religion studies the religious act, the Christian faith, but *from below*. "The level at which it operates and its methodology prevent it from making an ultimate judgement about the existential conditions of faith or of its object in their entirety. That is the work of theology" (Y. Congar, *La foi et la théologie* [Brussels and Paris, 1962], 190).

2. Nature of Apologetics

After this review of what apologetics is not, I shall say what I think it is:

a. All theologians recognize that apologetics is an *authentic theology*. It functions through knowledge of the data of revelation in terms proper to the constitution of theology. Its concern is to understand this deposit of revelation precisely inasmuch as it is *revealed* and, consequently, is *worthy of faith*. To put it another way, it seeks to show the human appropriateness of the option of faith which constitutes the principle of all Christian theology. If faith is a free and reasonable act, reason must be able to demonstrate that it does not engage in it unreasonably. This prime consideration in theology is analogous to the function of ontology and criticism in philosophy.

2. The primary aim of apologetics is formulated in various ways that are substantially the same. If we look at apologetics from the viewpoint of *revelation*, we may say that it is the science of the credibility of revelation. It seeks to establish in a *methodical* way (in accordance with the demands of science) that the Christian religion is worthy of faith, since its origin is divine. It does so in terms of a *speculatively* valid discourse (which answers not only the requirements of practical life but those of the critical spirit) that is also *universally* effective (because of the objective value of the arguments, and not only because of the authority of whoever is speaking or the weakness of whoever is listening). In other words, it is a scientific exposition of signs that bear witness to the fact of revelation and, consequently, testify to the credibility of the Christian religion. If we

consider apologetics from the viewpoint of *faith*, we may say that it is concerned to "demonstrate, in terms of a discourse of value to the unbeliever, what the believer considers to be the rational bases of the decision of faith" (H. Bouillard).

c. Apologetics should be concerned not only with the *object* under examination (the testimony of Christ, signs of his mission, the ecclesial project), but with the *human subject* to whom revelation and the signs of revelation are addressed. By *human subject*, we mean human beings with their aspirations, inclinations, and profound needs, as described by PASCAL and BLONDEL, for instance. If apologetics neglected the human subject, it would soon succumb to an extremely dry form of extrinsicism. If it ignored divine facts and claimed to be wholly enclosed in the subject, it would dissolve into a language of no effective range. Objective and subjective apologetics are not two different modes of onslaught for the purpose of conversion, or two chronologically successive methods, but two aspects of an integral apologetics. In this perspective, consideration of subjectivity is not merely parallel to the demonstration but coextensive with the demonstration as a whole, and intervenes in the structure of each of the arguments. It is especially significant in two privileged aspects: At the start, in order to show that human beings, if they are attentive to the data of their inward universe, cannot refuse to be receptive at least to the hypothesis of a completion bestowed on them by God, as a gift, and in order to examine the conditions for reception of a possible divine word that would be the sign for them of this gift and this completion. Consideration of the subject also forms part of the treatment of the signs of revelation in order to show that the actual interpretation of signs cannot take place without a certain number of arrangements without which the signs would remain enigmatic, and not only deviant but exasperating. Authentic apologetics therefore maintains a course midway between a pure apologetics of the object and a pastoral apologetics directly concerned with conversion.

d. Apologetic reflection on the *fact* of revelation is an *ecclesial* function. It is the function by means of which the church becomes aware, on its own account and on the account of those who consult it, of the human integrity of the commitment of faith. If the church were to stop reflecting on the intervention of God in history and on the signs of that intervention, ultimately it would expose itself to the danger of fideism; committed to the venture of faith, it would no longer know why or how it was thus committed. This reflection primarily has to do with its children, whose faith it wishes to affirm, just as Luke writes to Theophilus to reassure him about the soundness of received teachings (Lk 1:1–4). In our times especially, the church should help the Christian to locate himself or herself in regard to atheism, non-Christian religions, and the cults that are mushrooming everywhere. This consideration also applies to the *missionary* function of the church, since as a matter of course the church should be in a position to introduce those who are drawing close to faith not only to the doctrine of Christ but also to the signs that accredit him as the Messiah and as the Son of the Father. It must be able to address the unbeliever and talk to him or her in a useful way. This is an increasingly urgent task, as the ignorance of Christians themselves is often abysmal.

e. The apologetic demonstration culminates in a high degree of certainty, of the same order as the forms of certainty that are vouchsafed in the human sciences, but with the difference that this certainty remains a *moral* certainty. The apologetic demonstration, indeed, relies on *signs*—that is, unusual and contingent realities—that it approaches only by way of *human testimony*, through documents that are always difficult to criticize. This *mediative* nature of a demonstration which takes place in terms of signs and a historical testimony, is complemented by that of a conclusion reached through *convergence*—the convergence of indications of divine intervention in human history. There is a form of certainty that is appropriate to the respective fields of mathematics, metaphysics, psychology, and sensible perception. When it is a question of signs and historical testimony, we are operating on the plane of history, psychology, and tangible actuality. We reach forms of moral certainty.

f. Apologetic science as a *whole belongs collectively* to the church as a social body. Just as no doctor on his own can master medical science in its entirety, so no Christian and no

theologian can exhaust the meaning of each and all the signs of Christian revelation. Apologetic science, indeed, presumes among other things a profound knowledge of Scripture, tradition, the history of Israel, the history of religions, linguistic sciences, and so on. As for the human sciences, possession of apologetic science is an *ecclesial* fact. The faithful, to various degrees, in accordance with the intelligence, culture, and grace of each one, participate in the science of the church. This sharing in science in collective certainty is important, especially when it is a matter of richly meaningful signs (for instance, the signs afforded by the fulfillment of the messianic promises), which are also very complex and consequently difficult to interpret. Many Christians, at any rate, are capable of attaining to a knowledge of Christianity's titles to credibility which amounts to a consistent and effective form of discourse, even for the unbeliever.

3. Apologetic Methodology

Apologetic reflection is concerned with the prime and fundamental facts of Christianity—that is, with the facts of revelation and Jesus' ecclesial project. In the course of its demonstration, therefore, it cannot appeal to the inspired nature of Scripture or to the divine character of the church, as these precisely are the characteristics at issue. Apologetic reflection avoids introducing any affirmation of faith into the texture of its argument and tries to maintain a form of discourse that is meaningful and effective even to the unbeliever. It considers the texts of Scripture as historical documents whose value has to be established on the basis of historical criticism and criteria it acknowledges. Accordingly, the arguments that apologetic reflection adopts from philosophy have to be acceptable to critical reason because of their intrinsic value and not because of the authority of the church. Its historical or philosophical discourse has to bear its own rational justification. For the theologian it is not a question of suspending faith but rather one of adapting the procedure to his or her aim, which is to establish critically the fact of God's intervention in history in Jesus Christ, by showing that there are historically effective signs of this incursion. Because this is the critical reflection of a believing theologian, it is produced under the pressure of a faith that seeks to understand this amazing novelty.

Bibl.: This list of publications is deliberately brief and is strictly limited to that part of theology which was formerly called apologetics until 1950. Following this date, fundamental theology—which has a broader scope—assumes the same task. Articles that specifically mention fundamental theology "in the state of renewal" will be listed after the articles entitled fundamental theology.

J. H. CREHAN, "Apologetics," *A Catholic Dictionary of Theology*, 1:113–22; A. LAIS, "Apologetik," in *LTK* 1:723–31; X.-M. LE BACHELET, "Apologétique," *DAFC* 1:189–251; L. MAISONNEUVE, "Apologétique," *DTC*, vol. 1, 2 (1923): 1511–80; J.-B. METZ, "Apologetik," in *SM* 1:266–76; H. DE LUBAC, "Apologétique et théologie," *NRT* 57 (1930): 361–78; H. STRAUBINGER, "Die Apologetik als theologische Disziplin," *TQ* 121 (1940): 14–25; D. J. SAUNDERS, "A Definition of Scientific Apologetics," *TS* 5 (1944): 159–83; A. DE BOVIS, *Bulletin d'Apologétique* 43 (1955): 599–624; A. GARDEIL, "Crédibilité," in *DTC*, vol. 3, 2, 2201–2310; N. DUNAS, "Les problèmes et le statut de l'apologétique," *RSPT* 43 (1959): 643–80; H. BOUILLARD, "Le sens de l'apologétique," *Bulletin du Comité des études*, no. 35 (Paris, 1961): 311–27; P. J. CAHILL, "Apologetics," in *NCE*, 669–74; A. DULLES, *Apologetics and the Biblical Christ* (Woodstock, 1964); M. GÖSSMANN, *Was ist Theologie* (Munich, 1966): 25–52; R. LATOURELLE, "Apologétique et Fondamentale: Problèmes de nature et de méthode," *Sal* 28 (1965): 256–73.

René LATOURELLE

APOLOGIA

1. General Semantics

The term *apologia* (here the most common transliteration in modern European languages) is already attested to in presocratic Greece. As with other terms connected to the stem *apolog-*, this indicates a fundamental link with speech (*legō*) and with the cause (*apo*) by means of which the word is expressed. In general the term means speaking in the presence of another with the intention of justifying one's own or someone else's conduct, or else in defense of philosophical and religious convictions. In fact, there are two contexts in which the term frequently occurs: philosophical (e.g., Plato, *Pol.* 286a) and forensic. In the latter context *apologia* is a technical term ("accusation," "defense").

Nevertheless, one also finds a more developed sense of the term, indicating simply an explanatory response.

2. Occurrence in Scripture

Scripture offers three derivations from the stem *apolog-*: *apologeomai* (3 times in the OT and 10 in the NT), *apologia* (once in the OT and 8 times in the NT) and *apologēma* (a single occurrence, Jer 20:12). The figures indicate a notable increase in the NT from five to eighteen occurrences.

On the other hand, and not surprisingly, one may observe that the term *apologia* does not appear in the most noteworthy biblical and theological dictionaries of our century (BL, BThW, GLNT, TBLNT). Perhaps this omission points to the problems associated with an apologetic theology too preoccupied with defending the faith from the attacks of adversaries (→ APOLOGETICS). At all events a degree of caution is made all the more necessary in seeking the biblical meaning of the term under examination.

To understand what the Scriptures mean by the terms *apologeomai* and *apologia* it is first necessary to examine the contexts in which they are used. Sometimes the forensic sense of the term is intended, while at other times the context is that of dispute, or yet again of persecution.

In the OT the word first appears in Jer 12:1, where it is used to translate the Hebrew word *rîb*, a classical term for contention, whether juridical or not. But the prophet employs it here to describe his relationship with God, his coming "to dispute" (*'ārîb/apologēsomai*) with him, his questioning of the way God acts. It translates the Hebrew *rîb* and also the Greek substantive *apologēma* found in Jer 20:12. The prophet, persecuted by his enemies, is upheld by having entrusted his defense to the Lord. The forensic usage of the term is thus clearly transferred to the religious sphere, where it concedes complete trust in divine justice. The word has a political meaning instead in 2 Mc 13:26, where it refers to Lysias's defense of himself against the citizens of Ptolemais.

It is significant that the only occurrence of *apologia* in the OT is in a sapiential context (Wis 6:10). It refers to a warning given to earthly rulers to acquire wisdom and to conduct themselves becomingly (Wis 6:1–11). Indeed, a severe judgment awaits the haughty. But the one who allows himself to be schooled by wisdom and who will have regard for "holy things" will find in them his own defense. An apologetic role is thus ascribed to wisdom, in the sense that she acknowledges her ability to defend her devotees.

In the NT the term appears almost exclusively in Paul and Luke (the only exception is 1 Pt 3:15), wherein one may speak of Hellenistic influence. The term is used in two basic spheres: situations of conflict (social or religious) and the missionary context. In the first case the language used expresses the confrontation/clash between the infant Christian religion and the pagan world, on the one hand, and the synagogue, on the other (see Lk 12:11; 21:14; 19:33; Acts 22:1; 24:10; 25:8; 26:1, 2, 24; 2 Tm 4:16). In the second case, the language refers to the missionary movement and shows the influence of Judeo-Hellenistic propaganda (1 Cor 9:3; 2 Cor 7:11; 12:19; Phil 1:7, 16).

3. 1 Peter 3:15

Of particular interest to fundamental theology is the meaning of *apologia* in 1 Pt 3:15. The document is addressed to Christians living in scattered groups in the Roman provinces of Asia Minor. The whole letter—and particularly the extract to which this passage belongs (3:13–17)—allows one to surmise a tense atmosphere, if not of persecution then certainly one of hostility and violence. To such a context the author brings a very positive line of argument. He has confidence in the logic of reciprocity that governs civil life. Generally speaking, the good is recognized and appreciated. The author thus maintains that the climate of opposition can be resolved if Christians, for their part, are resolved to work for the good: "Who will harm you if you are eager to do what is good?" (1 Pt 3:13). The question, which is clearly rhetorical, suggests a consoling reply (no one!). But this does not exclude the fact that things may turn out differently. In effect, Peter knows from experience—as a witness to the sufferings of Christ (1 Pt 5:1)—that good can sometimes be repaid by rejection and hostility.

The possibility of unjust suffering, already glimpsed in the exhortation to the servants (see 2:19–20), is a reality faced by every Christian and refers to the beatitude: "if you do suffer for

doing what is right, you are blessed (*makarioi*)" (1 Pt 3:14; cf. Mt 5:10). However, the author does not view suffering as an ordinary occurrence, and his intention is to reaffirm the idea that the power of good triumphs; Christians must be the proof of this. This conviction reappears at the end of the passage: it is always better to suffer—if God so wills—in order to have done good (*agathopoieō*) rather than evil (1 Pt 3:17), as God's exaltation of Christ attests (3:18–22; cf. 2:21–25).

The sense in which the term *apologia* is used is captured within the context of just such an argument. Believers are urged not to allow themselves to be paralyzed by the fear instilled by their enemies, and not to succumb to their criticisms and opposition, but rather to respond to the confrontation by being positive and discreet. With a bold expression, the author invites them to "reverence" Christ in their hearts, acknowledging him as *Kyrios*, the eschatological Lord. This close relationship with Christ will allow them to be open to others (*hetoimoi*) at all times (*aei*), to offer "explanation" (*apologia*) to those who seek the reason for their hope (3:15). And all this not by means of arrogance, but with meekness, respect, and "a clear conscience" (3:16a).

For Peter, the purpose of such an apologia is to disown calumny by pointing to deeds. Whoever speaks ill of Christians must be able to have their minds changed by observing the upright behavior of those who follow Christ (3:16b; cf. 2:12).

What therefore is the meaning of *apologia* in this context? It would appear to exclude a form of public and legal defense as practiced in the courts. Indeed, while the expression *aitein tina logon peri tinos* (to ask someone the reason for something) and the word *apologia* can have a legal sense, this does not seem to be the case in this passage. The author, having already spoken of obedience to the civil authority (see 2:13–17), does not make any mention at this stage of a specific category. The demand for an explanation can come to anybody (*panti*), and thus one must allow that an informal questioning is here intended, something that is part and parcel of everyday life. It is in daily living, laid open to sustained and critical scrutiny, that Christians must always be ready to engage in such an apologia.

In such a context the sense of apologia as "reasoned defense of the faith" likewise seems inadequate. The object upon which the question focuses is not, in the first place, faith but hope (elpis), a major theme in the writings of Peter (1:3, 21; 3:15). With this end in sight, more than adherence to a doctrine, the author seeks to explain the new direction on which life is founded, the regeneration secured through the resurrection of Jesus Christ from the dead (1:3).

The same questioning is stimulated by everyday experience since Christians, on account of the hope dwelling within them (en hymin: in each one and in the community), now live in a markedly different way. The forms of behavior once engaged in give rise to that all-embracing questioning rooted in the new direction of life, in the hope toward which Christians are deeply oriented.

Now, however, questioning about the meaning of life in general is met not with a "defense" or "self-justification," but with seeking to explain the profound reasons that have changed the course of one's life.

On the other hand, it is not even a question of offering reassurance that Christians are obedient to the constituted order, submissive to the authority and the laws of the social system. This hypothesis has been advanced by D. Balch on the basis of the apologetic discourses of Philo (Hypoth. 7.14) and Flavius Josephus (Contra Apionem 2.147, 178, 181). But the perspective of 1 Peter differs from that of Philo and Flavius Josephus. The term apologia is used in a broad sense; it surpasses the purely defensive level and encompasses the missionary dimension. The ability to allow oneself to question, and above all to "stare one's opponents in the eye" with dignity and gentleness, carries the value of a positive and a missionary apologetic.

In conclusion, the Petrine usage of apologia carries the reader beyond the confines of words spoken amid persecution to the sphere of daily life, where there is room to be challenged by that hope in which believers are still rooted today.

Bibl.: L. GOPPELT, Der 1 Petrusbrief (Göttingen, 1978); R. FABRIS, "L'Apologia nel Nuovo Testamento," ETF 1:3–14; M. SECKLER, "Fundamentaltheologie: Aufgaben und Aufbau, Begriff und Namen," HFT 4:455–67; D. BALCH, Let Wives be Submissive: The Domestic Code in I Peter (Chico, 1981), 90–93.

Elena BOSETTI

APOLOGISTS

"Apologists" is the name given to the second- and third-century writers who tried to answer the main criticisms of the Christian faith in their cultural environment. The oldest Greek document we know of is a fragment of the Apology that Quadratus addressed to Emperor Adrian (117–138). We know too that an Athenian philosopher offered another Apology to Adrian or to Antony the Pious (138–161). Here too we possess only a short fragment.

The most important author is Justin, who was born in Palestine but eventually settled in Rome, where he ran a school and died a martyr's death between 163 and 167. We have his Dialogue with Trypho and two Apologies (initially they probably formed parts of a single piece, ca. 153). Tatian (Discourse to the Greeks), Athenagoras (Supplication for the Christians) and Theophilus of Antioch (To Autolycus) also deserve mention. In the Latin world Tertullian has a major place in this respect as in so many others (To the Nations, the Apologetics, The Testimony of the Soul, To Scapula, etc.). Moreover, we should not ignore Minucius Felix, Cyprian, Arnobius, and Lactantius (the two last-mentioned, however, belong to the end of the third and to the beginning of the fourth century). The standard reference works should be consulted for the life and works of each of these authors. Here I shall confine myself to two major points that are of interest to fundamental theology.

1. Pagan Polemics: Christianity and Philosophy in the Second Century

At first, Christians had to withstand the attacks of popular credulity as well as scurrilous rumors. We find echoes of this reaction in such writers as Lucian of Samosata (The Life of Peregrinos), but also in Tacitus, Suetonius, and the Younger Pliny. For these writers, Christians are superstitious, stupid, and inimical toward humanity. In this context, the Epistle to Diognetus seems almost provocative. Who are the Christians? the author asks. "They love all men and everyone persecutes them. . . . They are killed and thereby gain life. They are poor and enrich many people. They lack everything and enjoy an abundance of all things. They are calumniated and in this calumniation they find their glory.... What the soul is in the body Christians are in the world.... The soul is enclosed in the body, and yet sustains the body. Christians are held in the prison of the world, yet they sustain the world" (*Epistle to Diognetus* 5.11–6.7; *S.Chr.* 33.65–67; cf. H. I. Marrou's analysis of this text in *S.Chr.* 33:119–76, and the valuable remarks of R. Joly, in spite of all his harsh criticism, in *Christianisme et philosophie: Études sur Justin et les Apologistes grecs du II*e *siècle*, Christianity and philosophy. Studies of Justin and the Greek apologists of the second century [Brussels, 1973], 210–20).

The Christians were also a target of systematic polemics, such as those of Celsus and later Porphyry. In its judgment of Christianity, this second type of attack readily drew on the traditional values of Hellenism (cf. Borret's very useful analyses in *S.Chr.* 227). Some apologists, such as Tatian and Tertullian, rejected pagan culture as a whole: "What could Athens and Jerusalem, the Academy and the Church, have in common?" (Tertullian, *De Praescr.* 7). But this was not the general tendency, of which Justin is a good example. For him, everything good in paganism belonged equally to Christians, because all truth accords with the Word in some way. In fact, what the pagans possessed only in part, or in a "seminal" form, we have received in full through revelation (cf. *Apol.* 2.10.1–8; 2.13.2–6). Therefore, in Christ Christians possess the truth of all philosophy in an eminent form, for philosophy is never anything other than sharing in the Logos.

These formulas inspired by the Stoic Porch recalled a topic of platonizing tradition, his sympathy with which Justin did not conceal (*Dial.* 2). They gave rise to various interpretations. They have been seen as indicating the increasingly emphatic hellenization of Christian thought in the second century, of which gnosis was the most extreme form, but which eventually produced Origen as one of its major representatives (cf. the "classic" theses of Harnack, Miura-Stange, E. de Faye, H. Koch, H. Jonas, etc.). H. Crouzel has shown convincingly that this presentation was tantamount to caricature in respect of ORIGEN (*Origène et la philosophie* [Origen and philosophy] [Paris, 1962]). It also poses the much broader question

of the Platonism of the fathers." In fact, the complex relations between Christianity and Hellenism lend themselves all the more readily to simplification, the less prepared we are to look critically at philological scholarship, and if we too promptly identify and assess elements that it looks on as borrowings or sources. The work, inter alia, of J. H. Waszink, H. Dörrie, E. P. Meijering, A. M. Ritter, C. de Vogel, and G. Madec (to mention only the most recent examples) has elicited some highly nuanced aspects of this subject that we can no longer afford to neglect.

Quite apart from what divided them, even radically, pagans and Christians necessarily participated in a cultural koine, in which Platonic tradition (more than Platonism in the strict sense) in fact occupied the main place. Theology encountered numerous themes that it found close to or "consonant with its own"—e.g., the immortality of the soul. It drew on them all the more readily because of its conviction that Christianity represented the integral truth, inasmuch, of course, as the Word was the ultimate and sole principle of all knowledge, and the best that the Greeks had to offer was purloined from the wisdom of the Scriptures! The Christian assimilation of Platonism remained a more restricted phenomenon than has been admitted. In many cases, it amounted for the most part to the adoption of metaphors or formulas that were very appropriate for apologetic use. As G. Madec writes, "We must look for a justification of the philosophical theory and practice of Christian thinkers in the implicit coherence of their teachings" (Madec 1976:402). They tried to "formulate in terms that were often Greek the irreducible distinction between the uncreated God and his creature (whereas the pagan distinction was that between the intelligible and the tangible), together with the insoluble paradox of a God who was simultaneously *absconditus* and *revelatus*, transcendent and immanent (whereas Platonic transcendence and Stoic immanence were mutually exclusive).... But that is not all.... Though the fathers developed the content of each of these two terms in a sometimes very extreme way, they always believed that keeping them together accorded with the nature of the mystery and was based on knowledge of the faith" (Rondeau, 55–56).

2. Jewish Polemics

In their defense of the Christian faith, the apologists had not only to confront problems emanating from the pagan world but to deal with those raised by the Jews. The central question was that of the hermeneutics of Scripture, or more exactly of its prophetic implications.

Israel already looked ahead to a telos. It lived in expectation. Each of the stages of its history precisely corresponded to an assumption of the promise that resided in the figures of the past. For the Torah it is essential to look beyond the laws to what gives them their ineffable value. Accordingly, reality does not merely follow on the figures, in all the "sedimentary" forms that they may have assumed in accordance with the rhythm of the successive "present moments" of the faith of Israel; it will eventually fulfill them. "We look on Abraham in the flesh in his yearning for a rich land! But then we forget that what he maintained was, on the one hand, the Word (=the Promise), firmly, and on the other hand, the lack of land, patiently. The material inadequacy of the image has faded for the reader who often retains the land quite emphatically and the Word less emphatically. What Abraham longed for was a land that was the whole truth of this Word" (Paul Beauchamp, *Le récit, la lettre, et le corps* [Narrative, letter, and body] [Paris, 1982], 49; cf. two other studies by the same author: "L'interprétation figurative et ses présupposés" [Figurative interpretation and its presuppositions], *RSR* 63 (1975): 299–312; *L'un et l'autre Testament* [One and the other Testament] [Paris, 1976]).

This is the theology that every page of the NT, in its turn, presents, though in a transfigured form. The kerygma is not restricted to proclaiming the facts, for it ascribes a meaning to them: "God fulfilled what he had foretold through all the prophets" (Acts 3:18). In a famous study, C. H. Dodd admirably delineated the method of the apostles. It consisted in taking certain passages from the Scriptures (especially the Prophets) and situating them in a broader context, so that this corpus formed by the OT quotations and their application to gospel events is common to the NT as a whole, and in particular provided a starting point for Paul's theological construction, and for those of the Epistle to the Hebrews and the Fourth Gospel. Dodd sees this as constituting the infrastructure of all Christian theology and as already comprising its main regulative themes. What was in question was something quite other than establishing a wholly material correspondence between prediction and event. The NT authors interpret and apply the OT prophecies on the basis of a certain understanding of history that is substantially the same as that of the prophets themselves (see Dodd). History proceeds in accordance with the "economy" of God's designs, the main lines of which were already revealed in the OT, but the full understanding of which can be shown only "in the fullness of time." Hence Christ is not only the exegete of the Scriptures; properly speaking, he is their exegesis (Jn 5:39; Lk 24:27).

Therefore the apologists' contribution does not consist in a systematic explanation of the OT in terms of the NT, and vice versa. In this respect, the *Dialogue with Trypho* also gives us a good idea of the kind of polemics that set Jews against Christians in the second century. To a considerable extent it represented the exegesis of the rabbinic schools and some of the arguments derived from it: the sacred and immutable nature of the Law above all, but also the human nature of the Messiah, however great and glorious he must necessarily be. Obviously, the conclusion of *Trypho* could have seemed decisive: "If you forsake God in order to place your hope in human beings, what salvation will you have then?" (no. 8).

Justin, as I said, did not dismiss pagan culture as a whole. He was also careful not to contrast the OT God with the God of the NT, as Marcion was to do. He also avoided as negative an attitude to the place of Judaism as that taken up in the *Epistle of Barnabas*. Others after him were to speak in the same spirit of "the symphony of the two Testaments" (cf. Irenaeus and Origen). Of course much remained to be done, after the apologists, in refining analytical methods and improving the definition of the transcendent novelty of Christianity. Origen in particular represented a major phase of exegesis with his account of the relations between history and the Spirit, within the framework of the manifold meanings of Scripture (see especially H. DE LUBAC, *Histoire et Esprit* [History and spirit] [Paris, 1950]). But he was also to influence theology decisively with his impressive demonstration of the relations between the one Word and the one Mystery (cf. H. Urs von BALTHASAR, *Parole et Mystère chez Origène* [Word and mystery in Origen] [Paris, 1957]). There was still a long way to go in the middle of the second century, but the road ahead was already marked out.

Bibl.: For texts, see C. OTTO, *Corpus Apologetarum*, 9 vols. (Iena, 1847); J. GEFFCKEN, *Zwei griechische Apologeten* (Berlin, 1907); E. J. GOODSPEED, *Die ältesten Apologeten* (Göttingen, 1914); G. KRÜGER, *Die Apologeten* (Freiburg, 1968).
Principle Studies (excluding patrological sources and dictionaries): C. ANDRESEN, "Justin und der mittlere Platonismus," *ZNW* 44 (1952–53): 157–95; J. H. WASZINK, "Der Platonismus und die altchristliche Gedankenwelt," *Entretiens sur l'antiquité classique* 3 (1955): 137–74; J. DANIÉLOU, *Message évangélique et culture hellénistique* (Tournai, 1961); id., "Bemerkungen zu Justins Lehre vom Logos spermatikos," in *Mullus* (Fs. Theodor Klauser; Münster, 1964), 380–90; C. H. DODD, *According to Scripture* (Philadelphia, 1963); P. PRIGENT, *Justin et l'Ancien Testament* (Paris, 1964); J. C. M. VAN WINDEN, "Le Christianisme et la philosophie: Le commencement du dialogue entre la foi et la raison," in *Kyriakon* (Fs. Johannes Quasten; Münster, 1970) 1:205–13; M.-J. RONDEAU, "Transcendance grecque et transcendance chrétienne," *Les quatre fleuves* 1 (1974): 41–56; G. MADEC, "La christianisation de l'hellénisme: Thème de l'histoire de la philosophie patristique," in *Humanisme et foi chrétienne: Mélanges scientifiques du Centenaire de l'Institut catholique de Paris* (Paris, 1976), 399–406; "Platonisme des Pères," *Cath*, cols. 491–507; D. BOURGEOIS, *La sagesse des anciens dans le mystère du Verbe: Évangile et philosophie chez saint Justin, philosophe et martyr* (Paris, 1981); H. DÖRRIE, "Die andere Theologie," *TP* 56 (1981): 1–46.

Gilles PELLAND

APOLOGISTS, LAY

The crucial assumption of apologetics on the part of the laity, based on their own critical reflection, offers two instances of great interest as much in terms of the subject (the lay theologian) and object (apologetics) as for the lived experience that forms part of the tradition of the church.

1. Overview

a. The question of the presence of lay apologists may be approached from two different perspectives. If by lay person one means a *non-cleric*, then from the time of Aristides this group is numerous, rich, and varied. But if we are referring to the emergence of a new consciousness of identity, at first cultural and then ecclesial, which becomes embedded in humanism and which in the modern era finds its complex and painful development, then such a group declines until, at certain times, it almost disappears. Retaining a greater variety of critical components and methodological questions, our approach will adopt this second perspective. Yet one must be conscious that any inquiry into those among the laity charged with reflection on the Christian faith may be conducted only by overcoming a number of recent epistemological models of *doing theology* in order to understand the vision of a sustained reflection on Christian experience on the part of all believers who give serious reflection to their own faith.

b. The impossibility of producing interpretative theories that tend toward a historical-ecclesial structuring of apologetical development — marked as it is by profound cultural and theological discontinuity — lead to a methodological preference for a return to a phenomenological synthesis relating to the figures who retain most significance in order to bring together the essential structures of the lay dimension of modern apologetics. The field of analysis extends geographically to Europe, confessionally to that part which is termed Catholic, and historically to the eighteenth and nineteenth centuries. This was a period in which the Catholic and theocratic continent found itself confronted by a new philosophical and scientific spirit that modified its cultural foundations and shifted the center of gravity of civilization toward the Protestant north. For the first time Christianity in general and Catholicism in particular began to embrace these elements, among others, in a new historical and sociocultural context characterized by the collapse of faith and the temptation to establish an atheist republic. The Catholic reaction will see as its protagonists a group of figures, almost entirely lay, charged with combatting *philosophical negativity* and giving a foundation to religiosity. Their chief limit, however, will be rooted in the assumption of the same misunderstanding present in the concept of enlightened *reason* centered only on the rational dimension of the human being rather than in the affirmation of the sufficiency of the common meaning which constitutes the norm of truth. Even on the social level, the perspective will appear heavily reduced in defending a hierarchically organized society, based on privilege, even if religiously united by the Catholic faith considered as the sole foundation of the state and of political and civil rights in every situation subordinated to it.

2. The Figures

a. While this form of apologetics flourished in northern Europe, in Italy there appeared a number of deluded figures immersed in sterile polemics against Protestantism, Jansenism, and Febronianism, thus justifying Lamennais' severe judgment: "If I were allowed to judge the Romans by the books that reach us from their country, I would be somewhat induced to believe that they are a little backward in social terms. One would say, on reading them, that nothing has changed in the world since the Middle Ages" (letter of 2 January 1821). Among the lay apologists we must remember Monaldo Leopardi (1776–1847), who defends a Catholic society organized in a heavily hierarchical fashion as a bastion against the damage that would have been inflicted by other sociopolitical structures deemed to be inadequate.

b. In Prussia we find Johann Joseph von Görres (1776–1848) and Franz Xavier Benedict von Baader (1765–1841). Görres's thinking, on account of its encyclopedic nature, starts with an analysis of the philosophical intricacies of history, arriving at the rediscovery of a religious foundation to individuality as a defense against every kind of Jacobinism, be it revolutionary or reactionary. His philosophical method and his apologetical thought are characterized by his having sought in Catholicism that foundation which he had found in the principles of revolution and which successive political restoration had negated, most especially with regard to his patriotic hopes and ambitions. His chief religious interests were taken up with the study of things *primitive* and *mythical* as well as with a reassessment of the Middle Ages and the church. The same conceptual and intellectual coherence was to be found in his intense political activity in the Catholic party, of which he was both a leading member and an indefatigable organizer.

The project of establishing an academy for the religious sciences at St. Petersburg puts von Baader in an extremely interesting light. The academy, with the support of other Russian lay figures, would have had as its principal aim the promotion and diffusion of the true meaning of religion—and in a manner different from that of either the Jesuits or the encyclopedic approach. For von Baader religion must have been akin to a philosophy through which the Catholic faith became a participation in knowledge of God— namely, a *con-scientia* in which awareness of things coincided with the recognition of their belonging to a higher form of knowledge. In fact, it is in the act of believing that the human person arrives not only at the right use of reason but, above all, at the fullness of his/her development. Moving from the philosophical to the sociopolitical level, and from the individual to the collective, one deduces how the same society must be founded on the recognition that communion in God is at the root of communion between individuals. As in the case of other lay apostles, so too the rigorous coherence of von Baader's thought and his life made him the object of deep respect and a springboard for a profound intellectual influence, especially for the Russian philosophers V. S. Soloviev and N. Berdiaev, for whom he always remained an eminent figure in the history of Christian thought.

c. Turning our attention to Spain, we find Juan Donoso Cortés (1809–1853), who placed at the very foundation of his thought a reflection on evil, the cause of the destruction of humanity, only broken by the sacrifice of the cross. His thinking takes as its point of departure the insufficient knowledge of human intelligence, which, although possessing the capacity to select and distinguish evil from good, does not have the power successfully to withstand it. As a result, one has the condemnation by the philosophy which would give humanity a false confidence in its ability to understand truth derived from its own judgments. On the contrary, only Christianity will be able completely to transform humanity. It is interesting to note how Donoso Cortés never wished to be called an *apologist* on account of his sensitivity and charity, which naturally distanced him from the often overtly offensive attitude of various *enemies*.

d. It will be France that will provide the richest and most significant body of lay thinkers, who, without a doubt, have left an indelible mark on modern apologetics and who, in good times and bad, have contributed to the birth of contemporary apologetics. They were thinkers who would never have been able to have imagined a political system other than that of a monarchy or one that was not supported by the vast canvas of history, namely, by that past which they projected into the future and of which they were tireless prophets for its restoration in their own times. To restore unity, truth, goodness, and beauty: this was at the heart of their vocation and of their intention to reunite the history of humanity with that of God in the wake of the rupture caused by the Enlightenment and the Revolution, and to do so in a visible church bearing the highest standards of political, ethical, and aesthetic perfection.

Joseph de Maistre (1753–1821) begins with the reality of the church. God has established but a single church and charges humanity to defend it against those who, in the course of history, seek to undermine its unity, competence, and stability. Protestantism will thus be regarded as the very principle of evil, which brings every form of disorder and rebellion: from confessional diversity to the French Revolution itself. He saw the bond between the heretic and the revolutionary as akin to that between church and state. Doctrinal disorder would emerge, followed by sociopolitical ferment, or vice versa; for this reason the Inquisition must strike the heretic and the revolutionary with equal force. His strong certainty of possessing the *truth* was not, however, a source of personal complacency or of public recognition, not even on the part of his foremost and natural beneficiaries: pope and king feared the headstrong obstinacy that was potentially a cause of exaggerated diplomatic reactions and incidents. His most famous work, *Il Papa* (1819), was written during his diplomatic appointment at St. Petersburg and was intended to placate the czar with regard to the proselytiz-

ing work of the Jesuits; it articulates its message in four books, beginning with a statement of principle which is then developed at greater length by a series of demonstrations derived from the very meaning of history: the priority of the *Word* over *Scripture*. In fact, while the Word is an uncontaminated light, Scripture is a corrigible text, susceptible of infinite and dangerous correction, addition, and interpretation. The Word is the image of God; Scripture is the text and the human expression of a truth open to conditioning by earthly and practical reason.

François-René de Chateaubriand (1768–1848) understood that religion was necessary to heal the wounds of the Revolution. In his most celebrated work, *The Genius of Christianity* (1802), he expounds the beauties of the religion to which he himself had made a dramatic return: a Christianity sublime through the antiquity of its memories, ineffable on account of its mysteries, adorable through its sacraments, interesting on account of its history, heavenly in its moral teaching, fascinating on account of its ceremonies, rich and inspiring through the deep traces it had left in the human heart. On the one hand, the book has come to be considered a document crucial to the rediscovery of Christianity in terms of its beauty and social values, capable of stimulating other works and studies of culture—and in the most varied and diverse fields, not only the theological—yet on the other hand there is no shortage of critics who have regarded it as something of a literary-historical treatise, at times even disjointed, an easy target for irony. In some of its descriptions it has been judged pompous and theatrical, but, above all, it has been criticized for being simplistic in its metaphysics. From a specifically apologetic point of view, it certainly bore more of a subjective-affective tendency, rather than being a strict example of intense apologetics. The essential characteristics of its apologetic methodology appear to be the predominance of the heart over reason with the glorification of all the affective faculties and the exaltation of the modern world over that of antiquity—of Christianity, that is, over paganism. He confessed to having embraced Christianity not because he had been stopped in his tracks by great intellectual enlightenment, but as a consequence of a calling, a vocation that had sprung from the heart: he had wept and thus had believed. He disclosed his apologetic sentiments with the affirmation that apologetics conducted against heretics must have been no more than a novelty of their times, having exhausted their mandate and being seen as useless for the present day. He no longer sought to defend a particular dogma, so much as the fact that the very foundations of faith had been rejected. By now it was necessary to pass from effect to cause, proving how Christianity came from God himself on account of its sublimity and not that it was sublime because it came from God. For this reason he needed to present religion under a wholly human light and to respond to the new errors of the great scientific and rationalistic (the Encyclopaedia) Babel, proving that among all the religions it was Christianity that was the most poetic and human, the most favorable to freedom, art, and letters, that the world had ever known and to which all were indebted.

Unlike de Maistre, who placed the criterion of truth and the guarantee of salvation in authority and tradition, Louis Gabriel Ambroise de Bonald (1754–1840) turned to that tradition of which political power is the expression and God the foundation. In so doing he tends to follow the same intuition on a more historical note (from this point of view he may be likened to Lamennais). His traditionalist attitude coincided with the joint defense of the Catholic religion and the institution of the monarchy. Vindicating God as the origin of society and religion, he begins from the idea of ancient humans without the faculty of speech. Thereby he introduces his own theory of language as divinely revealed and inspired. Thus it will be tradition that will guarantee science and the principles of human knowledge and reason itself. Tradition alone constitutes some discernible criterion between truth and error. The serious limitations of such a philosophical-theological concept lie in having deprived the individual reason of its cognitional function, reducing it to a simple instrument of interpretation of universal reason and thus of the authority of the community, removing from faith its primary and fundamental condition of rationality. As an inevitable corollary one will encounter theological confusion between the natural and the supernatural, thereby serving to reintroduce the yet-to-be resolved problems of Jansenism.

3. Hermeneutics

It is an undeniable fact that what exists is not so much a "lay apologetics" as figures from among the laity who have engaged in apologetics, albeit with all the depth and originality of their intellect and experience. And if it is true that the quality of their output, except for certain purposeful insights, is somewhat submerged into the very evaluation that marks the vast and complex period under discussion, others are nevertheless original contributions to such literature. In fact, if on the one hand it is to some extent aggressive, and perhaps more than that, yet on the other hand it is capable of taking on board horizons and approaches almost totally unknown to the clerical world—the philosophy of history, politics, and aesthetics—and of taking the first steps in linguistics and in the realm of myth. Such works are all attempts at a style of apologetics that is as much a prophetic anticipation of interdisciplinary approaches, from the viewpoint of methodology as, and above all, a global anthropology specifically related to current systematic methods. Yet perhaps what gives a distinctive character to such works is the coherence between thought and existence. The authors are lay people who knew how to express their own personal testimony, in a way in which clerics were often incapable—a witness founded on a faith at which they had generally arrived as a result of genuine conversion. For this reason, as we come to appreciate the whole apologetic endeavor from the viewpoint and the contribution of the laity, we may reinterpret it in the light of a fresh critical parameter, which, from being methodological, becomes anthropological: not only the apologia of conversion but the converts themselves, writing in such diverse ways from a fundamental intuitive expertise: *unum, bonum, verum et pulchrum quaerunt intellectum* ("unity, goodness, truth, and beauty seek to understand").

Bibl.: L. G. A. DE BONALD, *Théorie du pouvoir politique et religieux dans la société civile, démontrée par le raisonnement et l'histoire* (Konstanz, 1796); id., *Essai analytique sur les lois naturelles de l'ordre social* (Paris, 1860); J. DE MAISTRE, *Les soirées de Saint-Pétersbourg* (Paris, 1806); id., *Du pape* (Lyons, 1819); F. X. B. VON BAADER, *Beiträge zur dynamischen Philosophie* (Berlin, 1809); M. LEOPARDI, *Le illusioni della pubblica carità* (Lugano, 1838); J. DONOSO

CORTÉS, *Ensayo sobre el catolicismo, el liberalismo y el socialismo* (Barcelona, 1851).

Filippo SANTI CUCINOTTA

APOSTLE

In accordance with the Semitic substratum, the term "apostle" means a delegate, an ambassador, one who carries out a mission as a plenipotentiary on behalf of someone with authority, who in a certain sense becomes present through the delegate. The apostle represents the person who has commissioned him: "Very truly, I tell you, servants are not greater than their masters; nor are messengers greater than the one who sent them" (Jn 13:16). The term may not have an absolutely univocal meaning, but it occurs in all the NT writings, with the exception of 2 Thessalonians, James, and the Epistles of John. Used alone or in compound form, the term is characteristic of the apostolic age (from 50 to 80).

1. *Apostolos*, in the letters of Paul, is a privileged term. The testimony of 1 Thessalonians in this respect is significant, not only because of the antiquity of the document (51), but because the term is still free from any trace of polemics. Paul presents himself as an apostle of Christ (1 Thes 2:7), commissioned to proclaim the gospel (2:9; 4:4). Through him, God himself addresses the Corinthians: "So we are ambassadors for Christ, since God is making his appeal through us" (2 Cor 5:20). The apostle is an ambassador of Christ, commissioned by him. Paul has received his mission as an apostle from the risen Christ, not from human beings (Gal 1:1). This mission is primarily one of evangelization. The traditional trilogy "apostles, teachers, and prophets," which we find in Corinthians and Ephesians (Eph 4:11–12), also has to do with the missionary character, and it would seem that Paul obtained it from Antioch.

2. In Luke, the concept of apostle is closely related to that of *witness*. The apostles are men chosen by Jesus during his public life. Before the ascension they were given a definitive mission and thus became witnesses to his teaching, works, passion, and resurrection. In Luke

the delegation of power and the function of witness are one and the same, as seems to be the case in the account of the choice of Matthias. For Luke, the apostles are not only the ambassadors of Christ but, above all, men who take on the functions reserved for the Twelve, and mainly the task of acting as qualified witnesses to the life and resurrection of Jesus.

At this point we may ask whether Jesus, during his public life, gave his disciples the title of apostles (Lk 6:13). The question is subject to debate. It is not, to be sure, a matter of doubt that Jesus summoned a certain number of men to follow him and become his disciples. Nor is there any doubt that, during his public life, Jesus chose a certain number of his disciples "to be with him," with the mission of proclaiming the kingdom, of driving out demons, and of curing the sick. The founding of a group of twelve men forms part of the oldest tradition (Mk 3:14; Lk 9:1). Nevertheless, we cannot say as much of the term "apostle" and the expression "the twelve apostles." Present-day criticism thinks that *apostolos* came from Antioch and was applied to wandering missionaries. It is applied to Peter and to Paul in this sense. The expression "the twelve apostles" would seem to have resulted from a combination of the two expressions "the Twelve" and "the apostles," as used in the primitive church.

The essential point here is to know the meaning that the primitive church assigned to this term, and the attitude to Jesus that it reveals. In fact, the apostle, in the language and mentality of the primitive church, whether he is considered an ambassador and representative of Christ (Paul's conception) or a witness to the life of Jesus (Luke's conception), has a relation of loyalty to the one who commissions him to represent him, to whom he bears witness.

Bibl.: K. H. RENGSTORF, "ἀπόστολος," *TDNT* 1:407–47; A. MÉDEBIELLE, "Apôtre," *DBS* 1:533–388; X. LÉON-DUFOUR, "Apostle," *Vocabulary of Biblical Theology* (New York, 1967), 71–76; M. L. HELD, "Apostle," *NCE* 1:678–80; A. LEMAIRE, *Les ministères aux origines de l'Église* (Paris, 1971), 179–80; A. DESCAMPS, "Aux origines du ministère: La pensée de Jésus," *RTL* 2 (1971): 19–24; R. LATOURELLE, *Finding Jesus through the Gospels* (New York, 1979), 189–91; J. GUILLET, *Entre Jésus et l'Église* (Paris, 1985).

René LATOURELLE

APPARITIONS

The theme of apparitions is often encountered in fundamental theology, where it involves the use, though without any great precision, of a number of terms. The biblical narratives, however, describe various realities and belong to literary genres with characteristics that are quite reliable enough to allow of classification. It is possible to distinguish the following:

1. The *theophanies* are found mainly in the OT and are characterized as manifestations of God to an individual when communicating with his people through a mediator. Thus, on Sinai, Moses receives the words of the Lord in order to transmit them to the people (Dt 19). In prophetic literature theophanies are associated with inaugural visions in which the prophet receives the mission of approaching Israel in God's name (Is 1; Jer 1; Ez 1). The location is often the mountain, the cloud, the storm, or fire. Theophanies are rare in the NT, for Jesus himself is the Presence of God among us (Jn 1:18; Heb 1:1–13). Nevertheless this theophany comes into its own at certain times: e.g., at baptism (Mk 1:9–11; Mt 3:13–17; Lk 3:21–22) and on the occasion of the transfiguration (Lk 9:28–36; Mt 17:1–8; Mk 9:2–8). In the last-mentioned narrative we find the themes of the mountain and of God's presence in the cloud. Peter, James, and John are the privileged witnesses of the glory of Jesus, which they are to proclaim after his passion, death, and resurrection.

2. In the *christophanies*, or apparitions of Jesus after his resurrection, we find the following constants: the self-presentation of Jesus in order to overcome the resistance of the people he is talking to, a task that the Resurrected hands on with authority and that has a foundational value for the future (Lk 24:18–19; Mk 16:15–16; Mt 28:18–20), with God's assistance in accomplishing the mission that is entrusted. The Christ glorified and made manifest is identical with the Crucified of the day before, but with a mode of existence that is wholly unprecedented; now he is in contact with the earthly world, but no longer belongs to it.

3. The *epiphanies* refer to the earthly and prepaschal Jesus with his body of the here and now. The epiphany is a manifestation of a divine attribute of the person of Jesus, especially his power. Two typical instances of such epiphanies are Jesus' walking on the water and his calming the storm. The epiphany raises the question of the authority and the identity of Jesus. In the words of the disciples, "Who is this man?"

René LATOURELLE

ATHEISM

I. ORIGINS

1. A Point of Departure

The modern emergence of atheism in the Western world presents fundamental theology with almost insuperable ambiguities. The meaning of "atheism" is inescapably dialectical, its understanding parasitic upon the "theism" of which it is the denial. This semantic dependence is compounded when one recognizes that "atheism" has been applied to many different forms of hidden convictions or of systematic thought. "Atheism" has functioned as an invective hurled at one's adversaries or as a personal signature identifying a position taken and argued in public discourse.

Analyses and histories of atheism have often concentrated on the acknowledged or hidden implications of thought, distinguishing between atheism, agnosticism, and anti-theism, indifference and postulation, practical and theoretic atheisms. They tend to gather under each category a particular range of figures insofar as a line of argument was read to necessitate such a denial, even irrespective of protestation to the contrary. This reading of another's thought through the imposition of one's own concepts and structures can result in the most unsatisfactory indices. Socrates and the early Christians, Epicurus and Hobbes, Descartes and Spinoza, LaPlace, Hegel and Heidegger have all fallen prey to this manner of doing the history of thought.

It is but a short step from such disciplined study to the invective and suspicious terror that one finds at the beginnings of modernity. Walter, Earl of Essex (d. 1577), saw only religious ruin throughout England: "There is nothing but infidelity, infidelity, infidelity, atheism, atheism, atheism, no religion, no religion," while Thomas Nashe warned some twenty years later that there was "no Sect now in England so scattered [about] as Atheisme." Still a few decades later, Père Mersenne would find fifty thousand in Paris alone (M. J. Buckley 1987:10, 58). The attribution of atheism to one's adversaries, either as disciplined criticism or as accusation, seems at best a highly doubtful procedure.

A more promising point of departure, though not without its own ambiguities, would be to attend not to what was said about major thinkers, but what they advocated and what they said about themselves. This would be to take seriously the sense they gave to the terms they used, the arguments they mounted, and the conclusions they drew. Here the lists narrow considerably, but the story becomes more paradoxical.

Modern atheism was called into being not simply by social and economic forces, the logical consequences of political freedoms and the autonomy of modernity, much less by the development of science. These were certainly present, operative at times as critical factors in the emergence of the unprecedented phenomenon that is modern atheism. Ideas do not emerge and continue in existence without an organic or social matrix that gives them context and support. The presence and the influence of such a matrix have been recorded repeatedly in the histories of modernity in the West. The limitations of a single article do not allow for the summary of those histories here.

But atheism is also an idea, an argument, a persuasion that possesses its own intellectual integrity. As such, it makes a unique claim on fundamental theology's attention. What can theology learn from the argument over the centuries that originated and supported the denial of what is most fundamental to religion? The ideational origins of modern atheism are grasped most clearly when atheism is seen to be generated out of the very forces that were marshaled to counter it, when not only the meaning of its terms but its existence and form are seen to be dialectical.

Atheism as signature emerged in the Western world during the course of the Enlightenment; it arose in the circle surrounding Baron Paul

d'Holbach and Denis Diderot in the middle of the eighteenth century. That they were preceded by such hidden but remarkable figures as l'abbé Jean Meslier does not remove their pride of place among the initiators and defenders of admittedly atheistic public discourse. They introduced the denial of the reality of "god" into the intellectual tradition of the West with such strength that its presence was permanently secured.

Their numbers were initially small. In a celebrated conversation, David Hume told Baron Paul d'Holbach that he did not believe that any real atheists existed. D'Holbach suggested that the circle in which they spoke would number fifteen! (M. J. Buckley 1987:256). Atheism would increasingly assert its claim in the intellectual and social movements that were to form much of the century that followed. But the massive shadow that Nietzsche and Newman would later see descending on the belief of Europe took its origin and feature during those last years of the French Enlightenment. It was Hegel himself who wrote: "We should not make the charge of atheism lightly, for it is a very common occurrence that any individual whose ideas about God differ from those of other people is charged with a lack of religion, or even atheism. But here it really is the case that this philosophy has developed into atheism, and has defined matter, nature, etc. as that which is to be taken as the ultimate, the active, and the efficient" (*Lectures on History of Philosophy* 3:387).

But neither Denis Diderot nor Paul d'Holbach originated what they brought to birth. They were only the end of its beginning. Herein lies a critical lesson for fundamental theology. For just as the meaning of "atheism" is dialectically parasitic upon "theism," so are its origins.

Diderot and d'Holbach did not number John Toland (*Christianity Not Mysterious* and the *Letters to Serena*) nor Anthony Collins among their predecessors. Nor did they build upon Thomas Hobbes and Baruch Spinoza, though these latter were taken by Clarke and Bayle as instigators of a growing atheism. Diderot and d'Holbach counted as their heritage the major defenders of Christian belief. D'Holbach takes the structure of an entire chapter from Samuel Clarke and shows that it can be satisfied with dynamic matter. The physics of Isaac Newton occupy a central place for both Diderot and d'Holbach that no other scientific achievement would attain, but these French admirers were determined to save his physics by replacing the *dominatio* of Newton's God with a dynamic all-encompassing matter. For the question of God at the height of the Enlightenment had become one of philosophy and physics.

2. Philosophic Question and Religious Epoché

As indicated above, in the sixteenth and seventeenth century, atheists—like witches—had been seen everywhere. In 1572, for example, no less a figure than Lord Burleigh was informed that all of England was "divided into three parties, the Papists, the Atheists, and the Protestants. All three are alike favored: the first and second because, being many, we dare not displease them; the third, because having religion we fear to displease God in them" (M. J. Buckley 1987:9). Tracts and sermons came out against them from Checke, Rastell, Hutchinson, and Latimer. Among the most systematic and most symptomatic of this great company of books was that of a Flemish theologian, Leonard Lessius, *De providentia numinis et animi immortalitate* (1613), translated into English in 1631 as *Rawleigh: His Ghost.*

There are three notable factors in Lessius's broadside "against the Atheists and Polititians [*sic*] of our times." Lessius could name his politicians. There were Machiavelli and those who had taken the *Prince* for their guide in life. But who were the atheists? Lessius could name no contemporaries. He had to recall the indices drawn up in classical antiquity by Cicero, Sextus Empiricus, and Claudius Aelianus. From these lists, Lessius selected those he thought the most incontestable: Diagoras of Melos and Protagoras; Theodore of Cyrene and Bion of Borysthenes; and Lucian. To this group, Lessius joined the atomists, who denied any effective divine providence: Democritus, Epicurus, and Lucretius. What contemporaries there were—again like witches—"are not much knowne to the world; since the feare of the lawes doth impose silence to these kind of men, and only secretly among their familiars do they vomit out their Atheisme" (Lessius, cited in M. J. Buckley 1987:46).

The second factor is the treatment given to atheism. The typical atheists are ancient philosophers: atomists, sophists, and skeptics. Hence the question of atheism will be treated as if it were a philosophical, rather than a religious or theological, question. Lessius writes as if he were doing a seventeenth-century retrieval of Cicero's *De natura deorum* and as if sixteen hundred years of Christianity were irrelevant. Even miracles and prophetic tradition are taken up not as religious signs but within the classic Stoic categories; they are made another instance of nature's design bearing witness to the existence of God through such a spectacular intervention.

An additional reason, perhaps, fostered this shifting of the question to the purely philosophic. The warring churches were seen by some to furnish the soil of atheism. Francis Bacon had written: "The causes of atheism are, divisions in religions, if they be many" (*The Essays*, "On Atheism"). And many there were, and bloody besides. Philosophy opened a field that was common to all—even allowing *De providentia numinis* to be translated into Chinese for concerns about atheistic positions in the Middle Kingdom.

There was a further influence, that of a particular reading of Aquinas's *Summa theologiae.* Lessius had introduced into Louvain the practice of commenting on the *Summa* in place of Peter Lombard's *Sentences.* The question of the existence of God, with which the *Summa* begins, was read as resolving its issue by argumentation that is essentially philosophic in evidence and in method, though placed in a theological setting. Lessius was neither the first nor the last Thomist to maintain that this is how such a question must be handled. Étienne Gilson, for example, coming upon this section of the *Summa* as late as 1959 wrote: "It is natural that his [Aquinas's] first question should be about the existence of God. On this problem, however, a theologian cannot do much more than apply to the philosophers for philosophical information. The existence of God is a philosophical problem" (*Elements of Christian Philosophy* 43, 209). Lessius had contended very much the same centuries before. But he went further. He removed the whole issue from its theological location, marshaled a squadron of philosophical arguments, and sectioned off as not pertinent anything essentially involved in the religious or personal interchange between God and human beings. The crucial step here was not the introduction of philosophy or natural philosophy or natural theology; the crucial step was the religious *epoché*, the bracketing of all essentially religious phenomena or "information" as without cogency outside of confessional faith. The experiences and usages of religion had nothing to say about its foundational assertion.

The third factor that one should notice is the union between science and religion. The conventual wisdom speaks of the early and irresolvable conflicts between science and religion. As a matter of fact, almost the opposite was the case. With the exception of the tragedy of Galileo and its aftermath, science—called "natural philosophy" through the time of Newton—was not only not opposed to religion; it often believed that it could furnish the foundations for religious beliefs better than religion.

The great Minim theologian and polymath, Marin Mersenne, would follow a similar pattern. In his massive commentary in 1623 on Genesis, some nineteen hundred columns in the original folio, and in his more direct volume of the succeeding year, *L'Impiété des Déistes, Athées, et Libertins de ce temps*, Mersenne launched his own attacks on the putative atheism of his time. Almost anyone who was dangerous to his own thought is caught up in this category, but three names stand out before the rest: Pierre Charron, Geronimo Cardano, and Giordano Bruno—a skeptical fideist who wanted to become a Carthusian, a neo-Averroist bringing the school of Padua to Paris, and a thoroughgoing rationalist—each of whom would have repudiated the appellation with horror. To silence these and the countless other atheists with whom Mersenne invested Paris, he builds arguments that conjoin the devices of Epicurean physics with a Platonic ontology. Whatever space Lessius had left for miracles and prophecies was eliminated. Anything specifically religious—whether in experience or witness or tradition or practice—is bracketed off in the interest of providing it with foundations.

This religious *epoche* became much of the apologetic strategy of Europe. The existence of God became primarily a philosophic question. The greatest metaphysicians or natural philosophers of that period not only accepted this charge; they leapt to it.

3. Cartesian and Newtonian Settlement

To the theologians of the faculty of theology at Paris, Descartes dedicated his greatest work, his *Meditations on First Philosophy*. But in that very dedication he distinguished his task from theirs: "I have always considered that the two questions respecting God and the soul were the chief of those that ought to be demonstrated by philosophical rather than by theological arguments."

To Richard Bentley, Newton wrote about the *Principia*: "When I wrote my treatise about our Systeme [of the world], I had an eye upon such Principles as might work with considering men for the beliefe of a Deity; and nothing can rejoice me more than to find it usefull for that purpose" (*Origins*, 102). To the end of the second and third editions of the *Principia* and to the Queries at the end of his *Opticks*, Newton mounted a lengthy defense of the divine existence, "for thus much concerning God, to discourse of whom from the appearance of things does certainly belong to natural philosophy" (*Principia* III, "General Scholium"). But Newton goes further than this: "The main business of natural Philosophy is to argue from Phaenomena without feigning Hypotheses, and to deduce Causes from Effects, till we come to the very first Cause, which is certainly not mechanical" (*Opticks*, Query #28). This will, in turn, furnish the foundations for what the thirty-first Query in the *Opticks* called moral philosophy and what Newton's unpublished manuscript, "Short Scheme of the True Religion" would equate with fundamental religion: "our duty towards God and our duty towards man, or piety and righteousness, which I will here call Godliness and Humanity."

Two important factors came together in these movements against a putative atheism, one from Descartes and the other from Newton. Descartes had distinguished various kinds of philosophy: God would be treated in first philosophy, while mechanics would be explained by only mechanical principles, matter, and the laws of the motion initially given it by God. Newton, in sharp contrast, eliminated metaphysics and made mechanics a universal science. The Universal Mechanics provided the foundations not only for geometry but also for theology because it demanded a principle that was ultimately not mechanical. Theologians had not only prepared the way for these revolutions in the status of the affirmations of the reality of God; they welcomed them, and each in his way followed suit. Descartes generated his Malebranche and Newton his Samuel Clarke. Both erected entire systems of foundational thinking in theology on the conceptual structures provided by their masters; in this area, each was probably the most influential thinker in his respective country.

Newtonianism eventually came to predominate even on the Continent in the eighteenth century, physicotheologies flourished, and the existence of God was given its foundations most securely by *la physique expérimentale*.

4. The Enlightenment: Synthesis and Correctives

One can trace the overthrow of this settlement through its disintegration in the works of Denis Diderot. In his early *Pensées philosophiques* (1746), Diderot constructed an apologetic that transposed into an aphoristic idiom the argument from design of Newton. In his later *Lettre sur les aveugles* (1749), the problem of evil, embodied in Dr. Saunderson's blindness, was allowed to destroy the cogency of the argument from design, and Diderot introduced a theory of dynamic matter that could explain both good and evil. God was at best a *deus otiosus*. From the agnosticism of the *Lettre* came the frank atheism of the *Entretien entre d'Alembert et Diderot, Le rêve de d'Alembert*, and *Suite de l'entretien* (1769). One year later, *Système de la nature* of the prolific Baron Paul d'Holbach appeared pseudonymously, giving Diderot system and support and bringing to completion d'Holbach's own previous works, *Christianisme dévoilé* and *Contagion sacrée*. The writings of both espoused an atheism that would gather adherents and force. The nineteenth century took up their argument, transposing the area of evidence from the design in nature to the implications of human nature as foundational for any affirmation or denial of the divine reality.

What happened in the Enlightenment and what lies at the origins of the first argued and articulated atheism in modern times were basically quite simple. Diderot and d'Holbach put two ideas together. From Newton, they accepted the universality of mechanics—that

the mechanical method and it alone could deal with all reality. What they rejected from Newton was his claim, as it had been Aristotle's before him and would be Whitehead's afterwards, that the study of natural phenomena necessarily leads to a source that is above nature. From Descartes, they accepted the autonomy of mechanics—that all physical or natural reality must be explained in terms of mechanical principles, that is, in terms of matter and the laws of motion. What they rejected from Descartes was any prior first philosophy that could demonstrate the existence of God. In many ways, Diderot and d'Holbach built these beginnings of modern atheism by synthesizing lines of thought from the two greatest minds of the seventeenth century, philosophers celebrated by the theologians as guardians of the foundations of religion. The synthesis was a universal mechanics with only mechanical principles.

This synthesis was effected by making one pivotal change. Both Descartes and Newton had made matter inert, intrinsically without motion or movement. Descartes identified matter with the extension that made geometry possible. Newton identified matter with mass and found matter to differ only conceptually from the inertial resistance to change. Now Diderot and d'Holbach revolutionized natural philosophy and eliminated what had been taken as the foundation of religion—by making matter no longer inert but dynamic. They made motion part of matter's very existence, an intrinsic attribute of matter. Then one did not need God to confer the initial motion to matter, and whatever design matter realized would be the necessary effect of motion and of matter. Matter with its intrinsic motion becomes the creative, dynamic evolving source of all physical reality. It is no great wonder that Diderot was Karl Marx's favorite prose author.

Many other factors were also operative in the origins of atheism as in any great social and ideological revolution, and they have been charted in analyses of social, cultural, and economic movements. But what has been neglected in these genetic histories has been the evolution of the argument that gave these developments understanding and justifications. The origins of atheism most immediately came out of a shift in physics. But physics did not say that there was no God—any more than did

LaPlace in his celebrated conversation with Napoleon in 1802. LaPlace simply maintained that the chain of natural causes would explain the construction and preservation of the sidereal heavens. The physics of dynamic matter only asserted that it did not need a God to arrange and balance the system. Only those who had made physics, natural philosophy, foundational for asserting the divine existence were left with a groundless assertion.

So the question is: Who made the warrant for the existence of God depend on philosophy or natural philosophy in the first place? Who bracketed religion in order to argue to the central religious affirmation: that God is? It was the theologians centuries before who had accepted the religious *epoché* as an essential strategy, making the issue, the evidence, and the argument essentially philosophic to the exclusion of the profoundly religious nature of the question, the uniquely religious aspects of human life that must function as warrant, and the procedures by which one might understand religious questions and evidence and assess their implications. The more one insisted that the existence of God was essentially and solely a philosophic question, the more one was implicitly accepting the inner cognitive emptiness of religion to sustain with any cogency its own foundational affirmation. The more one came to insist on natural philosophy, the more the inevitable growth in the autonomy of natural philosophy became not simply a positive event in physics but a negative indication in religious thought. The origins of atheism in modernity, then, are profoundly dialectical: atheism was generated in part by the very efforts to combat it.

Further, as Alan Kors has recently demonstrated, even those philosophies which mounted a metaphysical argument rather than one from the growing natural philosophy made an analogous contribution. What the Cartesians built up, the Aristotelians tore down. What the Aristotelians appealed to as evidence for the divine existence, the Cartesians found insufficient, uncertain, and nondemonstrative. When an articulated atheism finally did break out, a few decades before the celebrated and public Diderot and d'Holbach, it issued from l'abbé Jean Meslier, a remarkable French Curé who left posthumous volumes to his startled parish proving that all religion was a hoax. And

where did his arguments come and those of the small group of atheists who were to surround or follow in the train of d'Holbach? From the polemics of the believers. There is no need to posit a secret history of free thought that finally broke into the open. Not only the dynamism that lies at the origins of atheism, but even its argumentation, comes out of the polemics and the apologetics of the orthodox.

5. A Lesson for Fundamental Theology

Does such a reading of the history of an idea imply that the speculation of metaphysics or the implications of natural philosophy are antireligious when they come to treat or suggest the reality of God—that such thought is secretly atheistic? By no means. That has not been true of the great tradition of wisdom from Plato and Aristotle through Pierce and Whitehead. Sartre remarked with disappointment that all of the great philosophers until his time had been believers in one form or another, that a truly great atheistic philosophy was something that philosophy lacked and to which he would bend his efforts (Simone de Beauvoir, *Adieux*, Panthéon, p. 436). Philosophy does not betray the genius of religion; religion can only betray itself.

This event in the development of an idea indicates that the religious *epoché* is ultimately self-destructive, that foundational thought cannot exclude the data and the experience of the religious in order to substantiate the existence of God. Religion, and the reflection upon it, must possess the principles and experiences within itself to disclose the divine existence. If there is nothing of cogency in the phenomenology of religious experience or nothing made known in the witness of personal histories of holiness, prayer, profound reverence, and religious commitments; nothing in that sense of claim by the absolute already present in the demands of truth or fidelity or goodness or beauty; nothing in the intuitive sense of the "givenness" of God or in an awareness of an infinite horizon opening up before inquiry or longing, in an awakening jolted into a more perceptive consciousness by such limit-experiences as death and joy, loneliness and radical desire; if there is nothing of cogency in the long history and wisdom of religious institutions and practices and in all of those dimensions of life that are legitimately called "religious"; above all, for anyone who takes the religious question seriously, if there is nothing in the claim of the life and meaning of Jesus of Nazareth—then it is ultimately counterproductive to look outside of the religious to another discipline or science or art to establish religion's foundational claim or to demonstrate, in Gilbert Murray's words, that there is a "friend behind the phenomena."

The term "God" has acquired too much depth or density through the multiform experiences of religious involvements to be established or satisfied simply and foundationally by inference. Few will long believe in a personal God with whom there is no personal communication. The value of metaphysical inference or even theological argument is not to establish the existence of God of whom we have no experience, but to indicate that what is already at the depth of human experience is the mysterious presence of God whom one already experiences in longing, joy, inquiry, and all reaches of the human spirit toward the ultimate. And concomitant with such inferential disclosure of what is already present must be the concrete personal embodiments of this sacred absolute in the lives of saints and prophets, in the dark striving of human beings toward a truth that is given absolute recognition, and in communities in which inexcusable sins are forgiven and the sacred has become sacramental.

In Rahnerian vocabulary, the lesson to be learned from this moment in the origins of atheism is that Catholic theology must explore together both the transcendental and the categorical disclosure of God. Among the elements that Baron von Hügel saw of the essence of sound religion, foundational thought must include all three basic factors: the rational and the speculative; the affective and the mystical and the actional; the institutional and the traditional. There is a necessary and an organic unity among them. Eliminate any one of these, and foundational theology will write a history not unlike that which emerged at the dawn of Western modernity. For to bracket the religious in all of its fullness and to attempt something else or to abstract a single factor as foundational or as a substitute, as Catholic theologians did at that time, are to move into a process of internal contradiction of which the ultimate resolution must be atheism.

Bibl.: A. B. DRACHMANN, *Atheism in Pagan Antiquity,* trans. Ingebord Anderson (London, 1922); R. P. PALMER, *Catholics and Unbelievers in Eighteenth Century France* (Princeton, 1939); P. HAZARD, *La pensée européenne au XVIIIe siècle de Montesquieu à Lessing* (Paris, 1946); A. VARTANIAN, *Diderot and Descartes: A Study of Scientific Naturalism in the Enlightenment* (Princeton, 1953); James COLLINS, *God in Modern Philosophy* (Chicago, 1959); L. FEBVRE, *Le problème de l'incroyance au XVIe siècle: La religion de Rabelais* (Paris, 1962); G. T. BUCKLEY, *Atheism in the English Renaissance* (New York, 1965); P. GAY, *The Enlightenment: An Interpretation,* vol. 1: *The Rise of Modern Paganism* (New York, 1966); H. BLUMENBERG, *Die Legitimität* (Frankfurt, 1966); id., *The Legitimacy of the Modern Age* (Cambridge, Mass., 1983); C. FABRO, *God in Exile,* trans. Arthur Gibson (Westminster, Md., 1968); A. C. KORS, *D'Holbach's Coterie: An Enlightenment in Paris* (Princeton, 1976); id., "The First Being of Whom We Have No Proof: The Preamble of Atheism in Early-Modern France," in A. C. KORS and P. J. KORSHIN, eds., *Anticipations of the Enlightenment in England, France and Germany* (Philadelphia, 1986); M. J. BUCKLEY, *At the Origins of Modern Atheism* (New Haven, 1987); id., "The Newtonian Settlement and the Rise of Atheism," in R. J. RUSSELL, W. R. STOEGER, and G. V. COYNE, eds., *Physics, Philosophy and Theology* (Vatican Observatory, 1988); A. C. KORS, *Atheism in France, 1650–1729,* vol. 1: *The Orthodox Source of Disbelief* (Princeton, 1990).

Michael J. BUCKLEY

II. ATHEISM, MODERN

1. Explanation of the Concept

As the opposite of *theism* (from the Greek *theos* = God; *atheos* = without God, without knowledge of God; cf. Eph 2:12), this refers to the (philosophical) position or school of thought that denies the existence of a God or gods, and also of transcendent entities in general.

Agnosticism differs from atheism in denying the possibility of certain knowledge about the existence of God (→ AGNOSTICISM).

2. Modern Atheism

Modern atheism arises in the context of the secularization process in Western industrial societies. It emerges originally from the *principle of methodological atheism,* which was intended to provide the basis for a natural law that is independent of all religious quarrels, is universally valid, and is thus binding even on God (Hugo Grotius: *Etsi Deus non daretur,* "as though there were no God"). Atheism as a *theory* represents the conscious *legitimation* of the secularization of society and all its spheres.

It is usual to distinguish between theoretical, practical, and hypothetical atheism. For purposes of rough initial analysis, this may also be sufficient; however, the branchings of modern atheism can be better differentiated according to their function. Correspondingly, one can speak (1) of atheism as a new, secular approach to reality, (2) of atheism as a secular hermeneutics of religion, (3) of atheism as a new, secularized form of life corresponding to the modern age, and finally (4) of transformations of atheism.

Modern atheism presents itself initially as a new—that is, secularized—approach to reality that contrasts with all religious forms. This aspect comes to the fore primarily in the works of d'Holbach and Comte. For d'Holbach, atheism is the rediscovery of nature and of an ethics appropriate to human nature. For the early Comte, atheism (in the form of Comtean positivism) is simply the most mature stage of human development.

As a secular hermeneutics of religion, modern atheism enters its perhaps most interesting phase of development. Here the philosophical work of Ludwig Feuerbach (1804–1872) has exerted a lasting influence. For Feuerbach, the contents of religious faith are projections of human wishes and needs. God appears to him to be the essence of humanity (the infinitude of its own consciousness) as contraposed to itself through projection into an imaginary beyond. Although Feuerbach did not wish to be seen as a materialist (in the sense of eighteenth-century materialism), he has nevertheless made a lasting contribution, through his effective critique of religion, to the development and strengthening of materialism. His influence on succeeding generations of critics of religion can hardly be overestimated. Karl Marx allied himself with the Feuerbachian philosophy of religion but gave it a social twist: religion is an expression of, and simultaneously a protest against, the misery that results from humanity's being forced to live in an "inverted world." Thus Feuerbach's projection theory receives a social explanation. Friedrich Engels, a friend

and colleague of Karl Marx, formulated the Marxist definition of religion. According to it, "all religion is nothing other than the fanciful reflection, in the minds of human beings, of those external forces that dominate their everyday existence, a reflection in which the worldly forces assume the form of other-worldly ones" (*MEW* 20: 294). In his later works, Engels attempted to apply his understanding of religion to the problem of the origin of Christianity. In three writings (*Bruno Bauer und das Urchristentum* [1882]; *Das Buch der Offenbarung* [1883]; and *Zur Geschichte des Urchristentums* [1895]), he occupies himself with problems concerning the dating of NT texts and with questions about the rise of early Christianity. Here he shows himself to be a disciple of Bruno Bauer, a radical representative of the "mythological school." In a different way, Sigmund Freud, the founder of psychoanalysis, continued the momentum of Feuerbachian ideas. He returned again and again to questions about the nature of religion, but without arriving at any consistent theory. His extant work contains merely several tentative approaches. Freud discerns in religion a univeral compulsive neurosis; he thinks that he can recognize prehistoric patricide as the source of religion; and finally, he regards religious consciousness as a nurturing of infantile consciousness, i.e., the refusal to become an adult.

As a new, secular form of life that corresponds to the conditions and demands of the modern age, atheism asserts itself everywhere. Special attention may be given here to Lenin and the system of atheistic education in countries under real socialism. For his understanding of religion, Lenin is indebted to Engels. His own significance lies in his formulation of the relationship between the revolutionary struggle and the struggle against religion. The struggle against religion must be subordinated to the general revolutionary struggle; it has no independent value. In the struggle against religion, the feelings of the faithful must not be hurt. The establishment of a system of education in atheism has its origins in Lenin. Education in atheism implies, moreover, the acquisition of a scientific-materialistic worldview.

At present, explicit atheism tends to be absorbed into other forms of basic intellectual outlook. Given this, it is both meaningful and justifiable to speak of *transformations* of atheism. Examples of such transformations are scientism, (atheistic) humanism, nihilism, rationalism, and, above all, agnosticism.

3. The Theological Dialogue with Atheism

Since the rise of modern atheism, theology too has engaged in critical discussion of it. Within this debate, a new approach was represented by the later theological writings of Dietrich Bonhoeffer, particularly his letters from prison, in which he calls for acceptance of the worldliness of the world and its adulthood. Only then can it be possible to proclaim the gospel under the conditions of modern times. Christians ought to live in the world, *etsi Deus non daretur.* Beyond that, he suggests a "nonreligious" interpretation of biblical concepts but does not set out in detail or explain how this might be effected.

Following in Bonhoeffer's wake, widely divergent attempts to come to terms with modern atheism can be identified. The most radical attempt is probably represented by so-called God-is-dead theology, which, however, cancels itself out as theology. The advocates of theology of "secularization" endeavor to take the worldliness of the world seriously at the theological level and to accept whatever consequences ensue.

Entire theological treatises can be understood, in their very essence, as critical confrontations with modern atheism without their needing to contain discussion of any particular atheistic author. In a certain respect, comprehensive formulations as differing as Rudolf BULTMANN's demythologization thesis and Karl BARTH's radical "word-of-God" theology can be viewed as independent attempts at critical confrontation with atheism. On the Catholic side, this contrast recurs, to a degree, in the relation between the anthropologically focused theology of Karl RAHNER and the aesthetic theology of Hans Urs von BALTHASAR.

The central problem between modern atheism and traditional Christian belief is the question about the *reality of GOD.* All varieties of modern atheism are at one in regarding "God" as an illusion held by religious people. In order to counter this charge of illusoriness, theology must reflect anew on the ontological presuppositions behind the question of God. Here it is not a matter of using the world as a basis for inferences about God; rather, the point is that without the assumption of a God the world itself cannot be described in a noncontradictory way (which is necessary for being able to act in it). For in the very description of fundamental aspects of the world (as, e.g., change or evolution), a problem of contradiction arises in the sense that the aspect in question cannot be described noncontradictorily. Thus, e.g., change must be described as a coincidence of identity and nonidentity. In order to distinguish this apparent contradiction from a real one, certain more probing reflections are needed about the principle of noncontradiction and, above all, its ontological (rather than just logical) validity. Only when one considers that the problematic state of affairs surrounding contradictoriness is, as a whole, entirely referred to something else from which, at the same time, it totally differs can the problem be solved, and the fact thus shown that the world is "creaturely," i.e., entirely referred to something else from which it totally differs. In religious language, this other is called "God." The world, because it has been created, is not conceivable apart from this other, while this other, God, is precisely that apart from which nothing can exist.

The objection that modern cosmology renders traditional talk of God impossible (cf. Hans Albert, *Traktat über kritische Vernunft,* Tübingen, 1968, chap. 5, "Glaube und Wissen") has its justification in the fact that one cannot speak of God in a cosmologically neutral way. But the claim that the notion of God is exclusively tied to the sociomorphic view of the cosmos characteristic of antiquity or the Middle Ages can be refuted by the considerations developed above.

4. Modern Atheism and the Theodicy Problem

Theological discussion with atheism cannot ignore the theodicy problem, generally regarded as the hard argument of modern atheism. In the framework of the points presented so far, however, a new approach is possible to this problem as well.

The classical question about how the existence of an all-powerful and all-benevolent God can be reconciled with the evil in the world allows no satisfactory resolution. It leaves only this alternative: evil exists either because God is indeed all-powerful but not all-benevolent, or because he is indeed all-benevolent but not all-powerful. Attempts to distinguish between physical and moral evil can clarify some things, but they no more amount to a solution than does the explanation of evil as *"privatio boni."* Further relevant considerations have been put forward by Peter Knauer (1986) and Peter Henrici (1988).

According to Knauer, the theodicy problem proceeds on a false presupposition, as if there were some concept covering both God and the world that would then enable one to move from God to conclusions about the world. God (as Creator) is understood as the one without whom nothing exists. A concept of God attained in this way cannot then be played off later against the reality of the world. The problem is more a practical one: How can we live in the world without deifying it in times of happiness and despairing of it in times of misfortune? The word "God" provides no answer to this. In the experience of the world, what holds true is simply that God "makes his sun rise on the evil and on the good, and sends rain on the righteous and on the unrighteous" (Mt 5:45). This experience of the world becomes good news solely through Christian revelation, which is the manifestation of God's love for humanity. In the Christian faith, humans live out of the experience of communion with a (merciful) God who is universally powerful and therefore overcomes suffering and death.

According to Henrici, the theodicy problem results from an intermixing of two complex lines of inquiry that have differing origins: (1) the Greek question about rational order in the world, and (2) the Christian question about the omnipotent Creator. From the mixing of the Greek concept of the cosmos with the Christian understanding of God arises the "nonsensical" theodicy problem (i.e., the question of a "justification of God" in view of the evil in the world). The reasonableness of the world is then called into question by God's omnipotence, while God's omnipotence, for its part, is measured by the reasonableness of the world. Based on assumptions like these, however, all inquiries are doomed to fail. There is no intellectual solution. Meanwhile, the human question about the possible meaning of suffering remains unclarified. The problem presents itself at the level of concrete reality, where suffering is a fact that cannot be argued away. At the level of reason, suffering remains something irrational, which cannot be integrated into a rational system. Thus, even in principle, there is no solution to the theodicy problem—humans must come to terms with evil (suffering) while remaining unable to escape this reality by making rationalizations. The problem of God's omnipotence receives its practical solution through God's self-revelation in history: (1) in the book of Job, suffering is explained as a trial permitted by God and is thus seen as meaningful; (2) the exilic biblical texts (Jeremiah and Deutero-Isaiah) point to the redemptive character of suffering: suffering is overcome through the bearing of it; and (3) the NT shows that God himself, in Jesus Christ, has borne suffering. The NT's answer is not if God suffers then suffering must have a meaning, but rather the fact that God suffers gives all suffering a meaning. This implies neither justification of God in view of suffering nor simple justification of suffering through God, but rather justification on the basis of suffering that God himself voluntarily took upon himself (as a historical fact). "Thus no genuine theodicy can disregard either the Incarnation or the Passion" (Henrici).

In the biblical sense, then, suffering can become the locus of encountering God to the extent that humans endeavor to come to terms with it, rather than suppressing it through rationalizations or fretful argumentation.

Bibl.: F. BILLICSICH, *Das Problem des Übels in der Philosophie des Abendlandes,* 3 vols. (Vienna, 1955–59); W. DANTINE, *Die Gerechtmachung des Gottlosen* (Munich, 1959); R. CAPORALE and A. GRUMELLI, *Religione e ateismo nelle società secolarizzate* (Bologna, 1972); H. M. BARTH, *Atheismus: Geschichte und Begriff* (Munich, 1973); J. FIGL, *Atheismus als theologisches Problem* (Mainz, 1977); id., *L'ateismo contemporaneo,* 4 vols., Pont. Univ. Salesiana (Turin, 1970); A. GRUMELLI, ed., *Ateismo, secolarizzazione e dialogo* (Rome, 1974); K. H. WEGER, ed., *Religionskritik: Beiträge zur atheistischen Religions-kritik der Gegenwart* (Munich, 1976); M. NEUSCH, *Aux sources de l'athéisme contemporain* (Paris, 1977); J. L. MACKIE, *The Miracle of Theism: Arguments for and against the Existence of God* (London, 1982); H. ZIRKER, *Religionskritik* (Düsseldorf, 1982); B. GROTH, *Sowjetischer Atheismus und Theologie im Gespräch* (Frankfurt, 1986); P. KNAUER, *Unseren Glauben verstehen* (Würzburg, 1986); M. J. BUCKLEY, *At the Origins of Modern Atheism* (New Haven, 1987); var., *Ateismo e Bibbia: Atti del XIII convegno Biblico Italiano Francescano* (Verona, 23–

28 sept. 1985) (Assisi, 1988); P. Henrici, "Von der Ungereimtheit, Gott zu rechtfertigen," *Archivio di Filosofia* 66 (1988) nos. 1–3, 675–81.

Bernd Groth

AUGUSTINE

The theme of revelation, although never treated by Augustine in an integrated or systematic fashion, was always at the forefront of his attention, from the beginnings of his conversion to the end of his life, present under a variety of forms and amid different concerns. Without making sharp chronological divisions, we may say that an apologetic interest is clearly predominant. Augustine, himself newly converted to Christianity, when faced with Manichaean rationalism and the pagan critics of the Christian religion's claim to a God-given character, had an overwhelming urge to defend the reasonableness of faith and the credibility of Christian revelation. His attention later focused on the more strictly theological and anthropological aspects of revelation (how to safeguard the simplicity and immutability of God, the trinitarian dimension, the nature and economy of revelation). Finally his interest in the hermeneutical and exegetical aspects of the sources of revelation, already nurtured in his polemical writings against the Manichaeans, grew and developed alongside the maturing of his theological speculation and at the behest of his zealous opposition to Donatism and Pelagianism. This will be the pattern, therefore, that will be followed in this exposition of Augustine's thinking on the subject of revelation.

1. Apologetic Dimension

Augustine's conversion, as we know, coincides with the overcoming of skeptic rationalism and Manichaean objections to the Catholic faith. He threw himself into the arms of the Manichees on account of their denunciation of the *terribilis auctoritas* ("the fearful power of the faith") of faith, which the church required prior to every demonstration of the truth, while the Manichees themselves promoted an approach to God and truth conducted "with pure and simple reason" (*Ut. cred.* 1.2). Only after nine

years did he come to see that Manichaeism "made rash promises of scientific knowledge, and then put forward a whole system of preposterous inventions which they expected their followers to believe on trust because they could not be proved" (*Conf.* 6.5, 7). Augustine's experience of Manichaeism compelled him to seek rational justification for the act of faith in general and for the submission of the mind to Christian authority (Christ, Scripture, church) in particular.

The echoes of this twofold preoccupation with paganism and Manichaeism are as evident in the writings of the period following immediately upon Augustine's conversion as they are in those of his maturity.

a. *Reasonableness of faith.* In order to make inroads into Manichaean criticisms of Catholic faith it was enough for Augustine to point to the innumerable facts in which he believed yet which he had not seen and in the development of which he had played no part. Examples thereof would be historical events, news about cities and places one had never seen, the many things that were absolutely essential to life but which one accepted on the testimony of friends, doctors, and a whole variety of people. One would not be certain even of the identity of one's parents were it not for the fact that one trusted what others said (*Conf.* 6.5, 7).

Similar considerations are developed in the first two chapters of *De fide rerum quae non videntur* and further still in the first chapter of *De utilitate credendi*, where by way of conclusion it is affirmed that in real life it is not even possible to imagine someone who does not believe in something (*Conf.* 11.25). Moreover, "if we decided not to believe in anything that we could not comprehend on the basis of evidence, then human society would retain nothing that is firm or unshakeable" (12.26). The strength of this type of argument lies in the recognition of the cognitive value of faith. It certainly does not offer a purely rational understanding, but neither can it be equated with simple belief or, worse still, credulity. If to understand (*intelligere*) is "to possess something with certainty through the reason," and if opinion is a rash conviction of knowing that which one does not know, faith is the knowledge of truth that is still not fully understood but which is guaranteed by the authority of testimony (*Ut. cred.*

11.25). Above all for Augustine, faith is always a degree of knowledge (*Disc.* 126.1.1). Together with reason it is a source of knowledge and, moreover, the actual mark of human perception and the starting point for that trust in authoritative testimony which leads to rational knowledge (*Ord.* 2.9.26). Authority demands faith, but faith prepares the way for reason, and reason leads to intellectual knowledge (*De vera rel.* 24.45). To believe, therefore, is not in itself an act contrary to reason; it may be thus if the content of faith is completely absurd or if one believes too easily, without due consideration given to the authority for a belief. Augustine concludes that such considerations simply demonstrate that faith "in realities that we do not yet understand" cannot be ascribed to the realm of rash conjecture. There is an important difference between thinking that one knows something and believing, on the basis of testimony deemed reliable by faith, in that of which one has still to attain knowledge (*Ut. cred.* 11.25). Yet how far is what is said to be true for faith at the human level also the case for faith in divine truths? Augustine offers a twofold response. With regard to the existence of God and his providence, one cannot attain certain knowledge as one can in the case of sensible objects or for interior acts grasped by the mind (*Ep.* 147.3); but one does not believe in God simply on the basis of someone else's testimony. Faith in God springs from the heart of one who knows how to listen to the cry that comes forth from all created things: "We are not your God. Seek what is above us" (*Conf.* 10.6.9; *De vera rel.* 29.52; 42.79). To those who already believe in God the reply to the question about the rationality of faith in divine truths is more complex. If in matters of everyday life (commerce, marriage, the education of children) no one doubts that it is better to avoid errors than to commit them, then this same principle must "be considered even more valid in religious matters; the things of man are in fact much easier to comprehend than those of God, and error in the case of the latter would be much more serious and dangerous" (*Ut. cred.* 12.27). The problems that one encounters in coming to knowledge of divine truths do not depend only on the absolute transcendence of God, but also on one's own sinful condition (*Mor. Eccl. Cat.* 1.7.11–12): "since men are too weak to discover the truth by reason alone, they have need of a God-given authority" (*Conf.* 6.5.8); "since we are seeking the true religion, only God can provide the remedy for such an immense obstacle" (*Ut. cred.* 13.29). Naturally, there is no form of necessity within God.

There has already been mention of a *populari quadam clementia* ("a certain particular clemency toward the people") in the *Contra Academicos* (3.19.42). In the *De vera religione* (24.45) he speaks quite explicitly of an "ineffable beneficence of divine Providence. . . . Because we had sunk amidst the things of the world and since love of such things took us far away from eternal realities, a specific earthly medicine calls us to salvation not by means of rational knowledge, but through faith."

The object of this revelation is "those truths that it is not salutary to disregard and which are not of the type that we can know by ourselves" (*Civ. Dei* 11.3); "they are truths that concern the doctrine of salvation and which we cannot yet understand by means of reason, but which can be known one day" (*Ep.* 120.1.3). Thus there is neither incompatibility nor exclusiveness between faith and reason, rather complementarity and mutual assistance. A similar optimism rests in the conviction that "God cannot despise that faculty (reason) in virtue of which he has created us as superior to the other animals." Therefore it is unthinkable "that faith prevents us from finding or searching for rational explanation of what we believe, since we would not be able to believe were it not for the fact that we had rational souls" (ibid.). Rational understanding of faith is always something to be hoped for; whosoever fails to desire this, remaining content with an uncomplicated faith, has not even begun to understand the benefit of faith (*Ep.* 120.2.8). In addition to this purificative function, as outlined above, faith also has a cognitive role: "the certainty of faith is somehow the beginning of knowledge" (*De Trin.* 9.1.1); it sows "the seeds of truth" (*Ut. cred.* 14.31).

b. *The credibility of the auctoritas cristiana* ("Christian authority"). If it is reasonable that faith precede reason in the temporal order at least, it is likewise true that reason must take precedence over faith when considering the motives for belief, whereby one has to give credence to particular persons or books (*De vera rel.* 24.45). Only after painstaking consideration of the reliability of a testimony is it permissible to give the assent of faith (*Ep.* 147.16.39).

In this inquiry Augustine usually has in mind the *saluberrima auctoritas* ("salutary authority"), constituted by God for the salvation of all humanity (*Ut. cred.* 16.34), which comprises Christ, Sacred Scripture, and the church. Throughout his polemical discourses against paganism one can readily detect a more pronounced apologetic preoccupation with the authority of Christ, while in his attacks on the Manichees the prevalent concern is for the authority of the church.

From the time of Aristotle, pagan culture had considered oracles a valid form of proof in exhibitions of rhetoric (Aristotle *Rhetoric* 1.15.35 1376a). Among the different forms of evidence for the divine, Cicero added various types of divination to that of oracles (*Topic* 20.77), in this regard following the Stoics, who had had recourse to divinatory predictions in order to establish divine providence (Cicero *De natura deorum* 2.65.166–67). For the Neoplatonists, such as Porphyry, the oracles became sources of that same philosophy, while theurgic practices were the means of purification for the masses. From the first sections of the *De civitate Dei*, precisely to counteract such a culture, Augustine set himself the task of unmasking the falsity of divine testimonies claimed by the pagans, and instead exalted the divine *auctoritas* of Christ. He is the self-same divine intellect who has taken human flesh in order to summon humanity back to God (*C. Acad.* 3.19.42). The authentic divine authority is that which not only transcends in the realm of sensible signs every human faculty (for such is also possible to demons), but which has assumed that same humanity and by its deeds manifests its own power, by its teaching its nature, and by its humility its mercy (*Ord.* 2.9.27). In *De utilitate credendi* the divine authority of Christ is seen as being confirmed by miracles and by the multitudes who followed him: "By means of the miracles he acquires authority, with authority he merits faith, with faith he gathers a multitude, with the crowds he obtains the tradition of antiquity, and with antiquity he strengthens religion" (*Ut. cred.* 15.33). Special attention is given to miracles in order to distinguish the true from the false. Augustine does not deny that even in pagan religions there must be all sorts of strange events (*mira*) and happenings and predic-

tions of the future, which outstrip every natural human capacity; but he insists that these are the work not of God but of demons who wish to win over human beings and play tricks on them in order to enslave them (*Ord.* 2.9.27; *Civ. Dei* 10.16.1–2).

The miracles performed by Christ are proof of his divine authority, because as well as admiration, they also elicited gratitude and love: "some were clearly of benefit to the bodies of the sick; others were signs given directly to the mind; all of them bore witness to the majesty of God." The miracles were thus occasions for increasing the numbers of believers and for strengthening the bond between them, so that Christ's authority would be effective in renewing religious custom and practice (*Ut. cred.* 16.34).

A further development of Augustine's apologetics is to be found in *De fide rerum quae non videntur*. Faith in Christ is justified by a number of signs (*indicia*) that point to his divinity: "They are committing a grave error who think that we believe in Christ without a single justification" (*De fide rerum* 4). One such proof is the prodigious nature of the birth and development of the church in the world. Surely, Augustine argues, the fact that all humanity invokes one God and that idolatry has come to an end, "is such a great marvel by which we are led to the belief that the light of God has suddenly shone upon the human race." Above all, this is so when one considers that such has come about through the work of a crucified man and poor, unlettered disciples. The moral renewal of the world is also quite extraordinary, and likewise the conversion of men and women of every sort who are willing to suffer persecution and to give their lives for the truth. Moreover, one may point to the growth of the church throughout the world notwithstanding the many contradictions that afflict it from both within and without (*De fide rerum* 7.10).

A further sign of the divinity of Christ is given through the fulfillment of the prophecies of the OT. With great anticipation the ancient prophets of Israel had announced not only his coming but also his birth of a virgin, and the passion, resurrection, and ascension (*De fide rerum* 4.7). The prophets of old had also linked the spread of the church throughout the world to the message of Christ's coming: this has now been realized (*De fide rerum* 3.5–6).

Connected to the divine authority of Christ

is the authority of the Scriptures. They occupy the highest summit of authority to the point that they must be read with absolute certainty as to their truth and inerrancy (*Ep.* 82.2.5).

The justification for this divine authority of the Scriptures rests in the fact that they contain the word of Christ himself, who has spoken first through the prophets, then in person, and finally by means of the apostles. The authors of the sacred books are worthy witnesses to the faith because they have perceived the truths revealed through the inspiration of the Holy Spirit (*Civ. Dei* 11.3–4.1). There are many proofs of this authority. Resorting to the categories of the science of rhetoric, Augustine lists among the extrinsic proofs the diffusion and consensus with which the Sacred Scriptures have been accepted throughout the world for many centuries: were the Christian Scriptures not worthy of such faith, then this would destroy the credibility of every other form of history (*Mor. Eccl. Cat.* 1.60–61). When compared with the Christian Scriptures, those of the Manichees are devoid of authority because they are of recent composition, obscure and accepted by few people; moreover, they are without any credibility (*Ut. cred.* 14.31). The authority of the Christian Scriptures is recognized throughout the world, and among all peoples, because they contain so many prophecies regarding the future which have now been perfectly fulfilled and among which is that concerning the faith of the nations in times to come (*Civ. Dei* 12.9.2). Lastly, God would not have conceded such great authority to the Scriptures unless he had willed that through them all should believe in him and search for him (*Conf.* 6.5.7–8).

The authority of the church is also fully recognized as being the authority of Christ from the very moment that "his teaching issued from Christ himself and through the apostles reached us and from us will pass to future generations" (*Ut. cred.* 8.20). The church has attained the highest degree of authority "from the apostolic see through the episcopal succession to the confession of faith of the whole human race" (*Ut. cred.* 17.35). The church's testimony of faith is now indispensable for believing in Christ: "I cannot consider how I might have believed in anything if not in the firm opinion and good repute to be found among the peoples, who everywhere have embraced the mysteries of the Catholic

church. . . . I repeat, I have believed on the testimony that draws its strength from diffusion, consensus and antiquity" (*Ut. cred.* 14.31; *C. ep. fund.* 4–5). Here too one may see that the categories used and the vocabulary employed are typical of the science of rhetoric (*opinio, fama, celebritas, consensus, vetustas*) and also that the emerging concept of apostolic tradition lies at the root of Augustine's method of argument.

As we have already stressed, in *De fide rerum quae non videntur* and *De civitate Dei* great emphasis is attached to the apologetic value of the OT prophecies together with the message of Christ himself, the prophets had also heralded the church and its growth among the pagan nations (*De fide rerum* 3.5–6). Furthermore, such evidence is not weakened by the suggestion that the prophecies must be the work of Christian authors: the Christians themselves saw from the writings of the Jewish people, who were the enemies of Christians, that even the incredulity of the Jews, itself foreseen and proclaimed, constituted an extrinsic proof of the *auctoritas cristiana* (*De fide rerum* 6.9). To conclude this section we may say that the authority of the church, besides protecting the authentic teaching of Christ, guarantees the true interpretation of Sacred Scripture (*Ut. cred.* 6.13) and determines the scriptural canon (*C. ep. fund.* 5).

2. Theological Dimension

a. *Subject and content of revelation.* At the heart of Augustine's reflection on divine revelation is the principle set out in the letter to Nebridius: "The Trinity of Catholic faith is made known and believed in as indivisible . . . so that whatsoever comes from it must be accomplished by the Father together with the Son and the Holy Spirit. And there is nothing that is done by the Father that is not also done by the Son and the Spirit" (*Ep.* 11.2). Consequently, "when God speaks and teaches, it is the Trinity that speaks and teaches" (*Io. Ev.* 77.2). Just as the incarnation is the work of the whole Trinity, although it is only the Son to whom human nature is united (*De Trin.* 2.10.18), yet the fullness of revelation is ascribed to the Trinity, even though it can be attributed properly and under different aspects to the specific divine persons. In keeping with this principle, Augustine consigns revelation now simply to

God, now to the Father, now to the Son, or on other occasions to the Holy Spirit. Schooled in the gospel, he knows that "God has said nothing that he has not said in the Son" (_Io. Ev._ 21.4) and that "all that the Father says to mankind he says through the Word" (ibid. 22.14); it is "through his Word and by his Wisdom that God reveals the past and the future to the angels" (_De Trin._ 4.17.22). On the other hand, when God speaks it is the Holy Spirit who is speaking (_Io. Ep._ 2.9), and when the psalmist speaks of Christ it is still the Holy Spirit who is speaking (ibid. 10.8). The inspiration and illumination of the prophets are ascribed to the action of the Holy Spirit (_Quaest. ad Simpl._ 2.2). It is the Spirit of prophecy itself which has enlightened and given assistance to the authors of the sacred books (_Io. Ev._ 1.6–7).

Yet as R. Latourelle rightly observes, the central point about which Augustine's thinking on divine revelation crystallizes is "Christ, Way and Mediator" (Latourelle, 138). He, in fact, is the "wisdom begotten of the Father" (_De fide et symb._ 3.3). It is always Christ who speaks in the OT, as in the Gospels, because he is the Word of God (_C. Adim._ 13.3). It was he who inspired the prophets, and he himself was a prophet (_Io. Ev._ 24.7); "he is the true heavenly teacher as much for men as for the angels" (ibid. 12.6); he is the master of the heart who teaches all who call upon him (ibid. 20.3). As the Word of God "Christ directs and guides every spiritual and material creature in the way most suited to times and places" (_Ep._ 102.11). Precisely because Christ is the Word of God, "his every action is for us a word; his miracles contain their own language for those for whom they are worked (_Io. Ev._ 24.2); "all his works are a sign, charged with a message" (ibid. 49.2).

With regard to the content of divine revelation, this cannot be other than the same Word of God himself. Christ, being the Father's Word, has come not to speak his own words to us but the Word of the Father (_Io. Ev._ 14.7). To be more precise: "God reveals his Son by means of that same Son, and he reveals himself through the Son" (ibid. 23.4). Moreover, it is the Trinity which has been revealed (ibid. 97.1). God is absolutely ineffable (_Doct. Ch._ 1.6.6) and incomprehensible to human beings (_Ep._ 147.8.21). Nevertheless, "the power of God is such that he cannot remain completely hidden to the rational creature who uses his reason. With few exceptions, where human nature is excessively depraved, the whole human race recognizes God as the Creator of the world. But his identity as the Father of Christ, through whom the sins of the world are taken away, has been revealed by that same Christ to those whom the Father has given him (_Io. Ev._ 106.4). God has sent his Word, who is his only Son, so that men and women might be purified by the Son's sacrifice and, enriched by that love which is diffused by the Holy Spirit, might attain eternal life (_Civ. Dei_ 7.31). This ineffable plan of God, opening up a universal route of salvation, was completely impenetrable to the human mind, had it not been revealed by God himself in ancient times to a few people, above all to the Jews, and then by the Mediator himself present in human flesh (_Civ. Dei_ 10.32.2).

b. _The economy of revelation._ A fundamental aspect of Augustine's teaching is that God has never hesitated to reveal himself to men and women in a way that can save them. And this has been so "from the very beginnings of the human race," "not only among the people of Israel, but also among other peoples prior to the Incarnation." On the contrary, the ways of revelation vary, "being now in a more obscure form, now more obvious, according as divine Providence thinks fit in different ages" (_Ep._ 102.15). To the pagans who, with Porphyry, objected: "Why so late and what was the lot of those before Christ?" Augustine replies: "because they realized that the times do not run of their own accord but in keeping with a sequence determined by divine Providence, such that what may be suitable or opportune for each age is something that surpasses human intelligence" (ibid. 13). Augustine distinguishes five epochs within this economy of salvation, "containing the prophecy directed towards all the peoples," from Adam to John the Baptist; the sixth epoch is the age of Christ, wherein the prophecies come to fulfillment (_Io. Ev._ 9.6; _De Trin._ 4.4.7). In this way the whole of human history falls into two great periods, that coming before Christ, the age of prophecy or sign, and the time of Christ, the age of reality and the fullness of revelation. "From the ancient times, from the very origin of the human race, the prophets always spoke about Christ: he was always present, though secretly" (_Io. Ev._ 9.4). Precisely because of this presence men and women of every age could believe in him, coming to know him in some way and able to lead a holy and righteous life, conforming to his precepts and in that way attaining salvation. "Just as we believe in him not only as living with the Father, but also as having taken flesh, so those of old believed in him as being with the Father and as taking flesh in the age to come" (*Ep.* 120.12). His coming in the flesh was prefigured with appropriate signs (*sacramenta*) (*Ep.* 11), by means of which the people of old were able to attain salvation, even though what would be revealed by Christ remained hidden to them: "In the OT there is a veil, which will be removed when each one passes into Christ" (*Ep.* 140.10.26). Contrary to the total rejection of the OT by the Manichees, Augustine always commits himself to giving emphasis to the unity and harmony between the OT and the NT, defending their sacred character and divine authority.

However, in his polemical writings against Pelagianism, and in order to highlight the uniqueness of the grace of Christ at a time when this was being greatly undervalued, Augustine tends to underline the difference between the OT and the NT. The old covenant is marked by what is carnal: the promises are those of an earthly kingdom; the new covenant, on the other hand, is marked by what is spiritual: the kingdom that is promised is a heavenly kingdom (*De vera rel.* 27.50). The difference between the two types of promises corresponds to the method chosen by God to instruct humanity, whereby "wishing to show that even earthly happiness is his gift, he saw fit to command the old covenant in former times, a covenant adapted to the men and women of that age, and from which this present life necessarily begins. . . ."

These earthly goods which were promised and given by God foretold, in an allegorical way, the blessings of the new covenant; and the handful of people who had received the gift of prophecy were able to understand this. When God finally sent his own Son into the world, then "the grace that was hidden under the veil of the Old Testament was revealed in the New, namely, the power to become children of God, given to those who believe in Christ" (*Ep.* 140.2.5–3.9).

c. *The nature and method of revelation.* Despite the paucity of explicit references, it appears undeniable that in the case of Augustine one must speak of private revelation, directed to individuals, and public revelation, directed to all people (*De vera rel.* 25.46; *Civ. Dei* 17.3.2). Yet the most frequently made distinctions are those which safeguard the simplicity and immutability of God, or those made in relation to humans and their cognitive faculties. In contrast to the materialist interpretations of the OT theophanies, Augustine distinguishes an immediate action of God (*per seipsum* or *per suam substantiam*) and a mediated action (*per creaturam*) (*De Trin.* 3.11.22; *Gen. litt.* 10.25.43). From the viewpoint of human beings, considered under their twin dimensions of what is interior and exterior, revelation will be both interior (its effects in the human soul) and exterior (the objective, historical means by which God reveals himself) (W. Wieland, 27). A further distinction is founded on the concept of the cognitive faculty held by the Stoics and Porphyry: *sensus, spiritus, intellectus,* to which there is a corresponding threefold cognitive vision: *bodily, spiritual, and intellectual* (*Ep.* 120.11). One may thus speak of revelation *per speciem corporalem,* by means of the bodily senses; revelation *per speciem spiritualem,* through the *spiritus,* "the part or faculty of the soul where images are formed" (*Gen. litt.* 12.9.20); and revelation *per illuminationem,* directly in the mind (*Gen. litt.* 8.27.49). The first two forms of revelation are effected by God by means of the angels working in visions, dreams, and ecstasy, but they could also be produced by demons when we are awake or during sleep (*De Trin.* 4.11.14). In order to receive true and authentic revelation, the illumination of the mind must be involved, for it is the mind that judges and interprets the other forms of seeing (*C. Adim.* 28.2). This concept of revelation leads to speculation about prophetic inspiration. Even authentic prophecy, the charism of which Paul speaks (1 Cor 13:2) and which was a gift enjoyed by the ancient prophets such as Isaiah, Jeremiah, and others, came to pass *per informationem spiritus,* namely, by means of the imaginative faculty and through the work of the angels, together with the *intelligentia* of the images of perception (*Quaest. ad Simpl.* 2.1). At this point a difficulty arises. In Wieland's words: "According to Augustine, what is the relationship of revelation to inspiration? Does he explain the first by using the model of prophetic inspiration or by means of the concept of a general charismatic enlightenment? In terms of biblical inspiration, must we distinguish the prophetic books from historical writings? What is Augustine's response to the difficult question of collaboration between God and man in the development of the biblical texts?" (Wieland, 119).

The author just cited is in no doubt as to the answer: this same concept of prophetic inspiration is valid for the biblical authors, and since this always comes about by means of the imaginative faculty through the work of the angels, it is through this same way that the sacred writers received divine revelation (Wieland, 123–24, 133–34). Among the evidence used to support this conclusion is a text in which Augustine, on the basis of the Acts of the Apostles (7:53), affirms that the law was given by God through the angels (*Civ. Dei* 10.15) and that this would hold true not only in the case of the Mosaic Law, but for the whole of Sacred Scripture (*Civ. Dei* 10.7). An alternative conclusion was reached by R. A. Markus, beginning from the concept of prophecy found in *Civ. Dei* 17.38: "An evangelist or an author of one of the historical books of the OT could be considered a prophet in a broad sense, not in the sense that he had received from God a special revelation with visions, but in the sense that his mind had been enlightened by a special gift for interpreting an episode in the national history of the Jews or in the life of Jesus" (R. A. Markus, "Saint Augustine on history, prophecy and inspiration," *Augustinus* 12 [1967]: 278). It seems to me that the same conception is confirmed by other texts. In *De Trinitate*, when discussing knowledge of future events, alongside the angelic revelation received by the prophets Augustine speaks of another type of revelation "not by means of the angels but given directly (*per seipsos*) from other human beings, in that their minds were raised up by the Holy Spirit so as to apprehend the causes of future events, as being already present in the supreme principle of things" (*De Trin.* 1.17.22). Elsewhere Augustine makes a distinction between revelation *per fidem rei creditae* and revelation *per visionem rei cospectae*, such as that received by Paul when he was transported to the heavenly realm or that received by Moses (*Ep.* 147.12.30). It is with this revelation *per fidem* that the psalmist, transcending all creatures *acie mentis forti et valida et praefidenti* and even

acie fidei, comes to see what was seen by the evangelist when, inspired by God, he said: "In the beginning was the Word" (*En. ps.* 61.18). In the same way the author of Genesis could say that in the beginning God created the heavens and the earth (*Civ. Dei* 11.4). Such affirmations about the work of the evangelists appear to confirm this interpretation. The Gospel is the word of God, dispensed by means of human beings (*Cons. Ev.* 2.12.28): they write as they are given inspiration, yet without making any unnecessary additions (ibid. 1.35.54). They write mindful of that which they have heard or seen, yet not all in the same way nor with the same words. The following truth is always respected: "they can change the order of the words or even substitute one word for another of the same meaning; they can forget something or, despite their efforts, may fail perfectly to recall that which they have heard" (ibid. 2.12.28–29).

It is not easy to understand such utterances in the sense of being an inspiration given by angels. Even if, as one must recognize, the things said about the *evangelists* seem to contradict what Augustine says about the verbal inspiration of the Seventy (*Civ. Dei* 18.42). Finally, revelation for Augustine is always an illumination of the mind given by God either in direct fashion or by the mediation of the angels, who act upon the *spiritus*, so that human beings might know the things of God. One should add that this interior revelation is always accompanied by the inspirations of love, whereby revelation is also attraction (*Io. Ev.* 26.5).

d. *Sources of revelation and the scriptural canon.* From what has been said about the authority of the church it is clear that for Augustine it is precisely the church that is the guardian of Christ's teaching (*Ut. cred.* 14.31). Certainly the evangelists had written down what Christ revealed and said to them (*Cons. Ev.* 1.35.54). It is also true that the apostles saw the same Lord and proclaimed to us what they had heard from his mouth (*Io. Ev.* 1.3).

However, "there are many other things, kept safe by the whole church, that are not to be found written down, for we believe that they were ordained by the apostles" (*De. bapt.* 5.23.31). Elsewhere we find mention of unwritten prescriptions, guarded and conserved by the whole church through tradition, because they are deemed to have been established and recommended on the authority of the apostles or by plenary councils (*Ep.* 54.1.1). The authority of the church provides the rule for the interpretation of Scripture (*Doct. Ch.* 3.2.2) and for the determination of the biblical canon. At a time still troubled by doubts and uncertainties, in both East and West, Augustine bequeathed the list of canonical books, that same list which was to be accepted at the Council of Trent (*Doct. Ch.* 2.8.13), with an indication of the criteria he followed. In general, the scriptural writings considered canonical are those recognized by the greater part of the Catholic churches, among which are numbered those churches merited with having an apostolic see or having received letters from the apostles.

More precisely, the biblical writings accepted by all the churches are to be preferred to those accepted only by some; among those not accepted by all preference is to be given to those accepted by the majority and by the higher authority; when one book has the numerical criterion in its favor and another that of authority, they must be considered as being of equal authority (*Doct. Ch.* 2.8.12).

With regard to the apocryphal books, these can also contain some truths, bearing the stamp of antiquity or even being attributed to authoritative writers considered as prophets by the canonical Scriptures, such as Enoch; yet they are still excluded from both the Hèbrew and Christian canons. Augustine observes that, in all probability, such must have been the difficulty of having watertight proof of their authenticity (*Civ. Dei* 18.38).

3. Hermeneutical Dimension

The problem of the interpretation of Scripture was always at the center of Augustine's attention. If at first he embraced with enthusiasm the spiritual interpretation of Ambrose, it was because it helped to overcome Manichaean objections to the OT, attempting at once to confront the problem in a more critical fashion, seeking directions from the best Catholic exegetes. We have a checklist of the initial results of these researches in *De genesi ad litteram liber imperfectus*, where there is an account of the four ways of explaining the Scriptures (2.5).

De Lubac denies that Augustine is the originator of the theory of the four senses of Scripture, which would be affirmed in the Middle Ages; he had spoken of the four interpretative modes for different texts, not for the same text (H. de Lubac, *L'Exégèse mediévale: Les quatre sens de l'Ecriture*, I,1 [Paris, 1959] 180–82).

Yet however things stand in this regard, Augustine's energies in arriving at a more satisfactory theory of hermeneutics culminated in *De Doctrina Christiana*, once described as "the manifesto of Augustine's theological hermeneutics" (Ripanti, 13). This particular work of Augustine addresses the problem of the *Tractatio Scripturarum* on the twofold matter of *inventio* and *elocutio*, on the basis of a specific linguistic theory, in which a fundamental distinction is drawn between *signum* and *res*. *Signum* is that which comes to be used to indicate something else; *res* is that which has value in itself and is not used to indicate something else (*Doct. Ch.* 1.2.2). In the light of such a distinction, the Sacred Scriptures are "*signa divinitus data*," signs given by God to reveal to mankind the *res* necessary for salvation (2.22.3), namely: God one and three, the incarnation of Christ, the church, the resurrection of the body, the love of God and neighbor. Scripture does not seek to teach anything but this Catholic faith (ibid., 3.10.15). The interpreter must therefore hold fast to the *regula fidei* in interpretation (3.2.2), without stepping beyond the limits of faith (*Gen. litt. l. imp.* 1.1.1).

The hermeneutic circle is the clear result: "the truths of faith and morals, which are sought in the text, are explained by means of the creed of the church as the authoritative interpretation, through which one comes to understand the contents of Scripture only if one already believes it" (Ripanti, 82). This prior theological understanding opens the horizons within which meaning is sought, yet the work of interpretation is not rendered void.

In order to establish true and specific exegetical principles, Augustine refers again to the theory of language. After the distinction between *signum* and *res*, he proposes another distinction, of no little importance, between the *signa propria* and the *signa translata*. The *signa propria* are "those which have come to be used to denote the things for which they have been instituted"; the *signa translata* are "the same things which, indicated by the proper words, serve to denote something else" (*Doct.*

Ch. 3.15.23). Upon this twin definition rests the distinction between literal sense and figurative or allegorical sense. Because Sacred Scripture has been given by God through human beings, if from one point of view this human mediation corresponds to profound anthropological and theological needs, as is well brought out in the prologue (4–9), then from another angle it stretches like a veil over the revealed message. This hiddenness, effected by the human word, is well expressed in the image of the cloud: "The sacred writings of the prophets and apostles . . . are rightly called clouds, because the words that resound and pass through the air are also charged with the obscurity of allegories, as if they must have been overtaken by darkness, becoming, so to speak, clouds" (*Doct. Ch.* 2.4.5). The consequences of this obscurity are not always, nor wholly, negative: in fact, divine providence always governs this darkness, in order to subdue pride and rekindle interest in that quest which, were it too easy, could be rendered wearisome (ibid. 2.7). The danger of erroneous interpretations, linked to the darkness of allegory, is still considerable and justifies every effort to establish clear exegetical principles. For Augustine the legitimacy of allegorical interpretation is beyond discussion, having been practiced by the apostle himself. Instead, another question presents itself: "with regard to the narration of facts must everything be understood in a figurative sense or must one also affirm and uphold the historical truth (*fides*) of facts?" (*Gen. litt l. imp.* 1.1.1). The reply is given in book 3 of *De Doctrina Christiana*: "all, or nearly all, the facts recounted in the OT can also be understood in the figurative, and not only the actual sense (literal)" (3.22.32; *Civ. Dei* 17.3.2). Thus the most pressing task facing the interpreter is that of deciding if the expression that one seeks to understand has a literal or a figurative sense (*Civ. Dei* 3.24.34). First, in order to achieve this, one must avoid taking in a literal sense that which is given in a figurative sense, lest one succumb to prosaic interpretations: "it would be a miserable form of slavery to substitute the signs for the reality signified" (3.5.9).

Second, it is not necessary to take in a figurative sense that which is given in a literal sense, because under the pretext of allegorical interpretations, every sort of moral behavior and heretical opinion may be justified (3.10.14–

15). Therefore they follow other principles of no less importance: all that which in the word of God, understood in the literal sense, cannot be related to custom or usage nor to the truth of faith, must be understood in a figurative sense (3.10.14); in allegorical speech, therefore, it is necessary to give careful consideration to that which one reads for as long as one fails to reach the realm of love. If love is already present in the literal sense, there is no need to think in terms of figurative speech (3.15.23).

At this point one is faced with the problem of the plurality of senses of the same figurative locution. Certainly the sought-after sense always remains that understood by the sacred author:

> Whoever searches the Word of God must strive to reach the *voluntas* (intention) of the writer by means of which the Holy Spirit has given us that Scripture. Only in cases where from the same words of Scripture one arrives not at one but at two or more senses, and on condition that one can show from other biblical passages that those senses accord perfectly with the truth, may one allow a plurality of senses, even if one is ignorant of the sense understood by the sacred author. (3.27.38)

Augustine does not wish to give the slightest license to what is arbitrary: the plurality of allegorical senses is allowed only on very precise and strictly limited conditions. He advances the theory of an interpretation based on reason but warns: "this is a dangerous method; one walks with much greater security by means of the same divine Scriptures" (3.28.39). The possibility of finding more meanings in allegory is considered a providential fact, foreseen and willed by the Holy Spirit for the good of the reader or the listener (*Conf.* 12.18.27).

A particular critical examination is reserved (for the rules of Ticonius: they can be very useful for the understanding of Scripture, but as Ticonius's own exegeses show, they are not enough to resolve all the obscurities (*Doct. Ch.* 3.30.42).

This insistence on the hermeneutical principles must not lead us to think that Augustine had neglected the more properly philological dimension. He dedicated the whole of book 2 and part of book 3 of *De Doctrina Christiana* to an understanding of the *signa propria* and the *signa translata ignota*. The interpretation of

Scripture required a profound knowledge of the conceptual and linguistic world of the Bible (2.9.14), and a mastery of languages, primarily Hebrew and Greek, so as to be able to verify the accuracy of the Latin versions of Scripture (2.11.16; 15.22). The interpreter must make a *collatio* of the various codices and versions (2.12.17–15.22), an *emendatio* of the text (3.2.2–3.7) and must have knowledge of all the sciences, from natural sciences to those of history and philosophy (2.16.24–40.60). It is this vast body of knowledge that Augustine would have sought to possess.

Bibl.: R. LATOURELLE, *Theology of Revelation* (New York, 1966); G. PELLAND, *Cinq études d'Augustin sur le début de la Genèse* (Tournai/Montreal, 1972); R. P. HARDY, *Actualité de la Révélation divine: Une étude des "tractatus in Johannis Evangelium" de S. Augustin* (Paris, 1974); W. WIELAND, *Offenbarung bei Augustinus* (Mainz, 1978); G. RIPANTI, *Agostino teorico dell'interpretazione* (Brescia, 1980).

Nello CIPRIANI

B

BALTHASAR, Hans Urs von

With the realization of the threefold themes of theological aesthetics, drama, and logic, von Balthasar has forged the missing link in theological tradition capable of reading the event of revelation in the light of these three transcendental modes.

Von Balthasar (8 December 1905–26 June 1988) did not write as a specialist in fundamental theology. In his great theological works we encounter, above all, different themes that are the special object of fundamental theology and which, as they are taken up and addressed more explicitly, the author himself has wished to consider as arguments within fundamental theology.

The construction of a "scheme" of fundamental theology on the part of von Balthasar could be outlined in the following way:

1. Epistemological Principles

The first characteristic that emerges from von Balthasar's work with respect to fundamental theology is the clarity of theological definition. Leaving to one side the content and methodology of the manuals (→ THEOLOGY II), which dealt chiefly with *demonstrationes* conducted with great philosophical-scholastic rigor and which used the *praeambula fidei* as their strong point, fundamental theology is met with here in its particular and specific reflection on faith, which already determines the content and the method of theological procedure.

One finds the following simple statement at the end of *Herrlichkeit* (*The Glory of the Lord*): "fundamental theology and dogmatic theology are inseparable." Already this bears a methodological consequence for itself and creates an epistemological presupposition of great importance. In fact, the typical form of reflection proper to fundamental theology is already set out under the common denominator of "theology," which in von Balthasar leaves no doubt as to its constitution in terms of reflection carried out in the light of faith. Thus the researches of fundamental theology are not considered either as an introduction or as foreword to dogmatics,

still less as a simple "function" for the whole theological endeavor. Making fundamental theology equivalent to the accomplishment of that reflection and that search, which are already part and parcel of the dynamic of *fides quaerens intellectum* ("faith in search of understanding"), von Balthasar writes: "the apologetic is already charged with the dogmatic when it accepts the attempt to show the plausibility of the image of divine revelation to those who do not yet believe" (1982–91: 1:111).

We are not, therefore, speaking of an ancillary role for philosophy in relation to theology, nor of a dependence of the latter on various philosophical systems. On the contrary, the epistemological foundation of theology will be that knowledge which comes from faith, and, strengthened and underpinned by this, theology will be able to recover philosophical knowledge.

To this initial observation can be added a second feature that allows us to evaluate the originality of von Balthasar's apologetical "scheme." Before all else, it is a prior understanding of a recovery of the unity of transcendentals as a primary transposition, in the theological sphere, of a reading of revelation.

It will be noted and underlined that one is in the midst of a global scheme that cannot be reduced to the sole reading of aesthetics. Revelation, for von Balthasar, comes to be given theological explanation in the dynamic reciprocal relationship of the three transcendental modes with the respective readings of "aesthetics," "drama," and "logic." Each reading or understanding that would confine itself, even in the realm of fundamental theology, to the purely aesthetic would in some way be compromised and, in any case, reductionist. The aesthetic dimension continues to take the primary position, the point of departure and the original intuition, that develops thereafter into a "drama" and a "logic," because in this way alone does the Gestalt (form) come to be perceived in its fullness.

The use of *pulchrum* ("beauty") as the starting point for understanding revelation brings into operation some principles that may be summarized thus:

a. At the epistemological level, *pulchrum* recalls as its corresponding form of knowledge, *perception* (*Wahrnehmung*). That which "appears" (*Erscheinung*) is at the same time that which constitutes truth in itself. The self-manifestation of being as *pulchrum* is what allows us to see the realization of the identity of phenomena and reality in itself. In other words, what "appears" is the same reality in itself, as it thus presents itself to the historical subject. Thus there is no distinction between being and that which is constituted by the appearance of *pulchrum*. What appears "phenomenologically" is what "ontologically" is.

Above all, there is an "indissolubility" between the form of appearance and what is in itself. This allows the conclusion that the truth of the form is not reducible to the various interpretations of the perceiving subject; on the contrary, it bears it within itself, without limits, in its own self-manifestation. *Sic et simpliciter* is reference made to the transparency of being.

b. Consequently, the form of knowledge produced by the perception of *pulchrum* establishes a relationship between subject and object. Faithful to a Thomist ontology in its most original interpretation, von Balthasar sees the realization of a particular modality which is the reception that works itself out in the subject.

It is not the subject that instigates being; on the contrary, he finds himself at all times and constantly in a condition of pure passivity before it. In no sense can the subject judge the beauty of the Gestalt. In every case, in fact, it presents itself as complete otherness and as that which escapes every possible tendency to rationalization or to an exhaustive definition.

c. No possibility, therefore, of an objectivization of the Gestalt by the subject suffers from the loss of real and coherent knowledge of the reality itself. This remains as a "whole," which comes to be received as such, without being able to be broken into fragments, in that as a "whole" it contains within itself the conditions of possibility for existence and credibility.

It is only at this point that we find the introduction of "ecstasy" (*Entrückung*), the aesthetic contemplation of the Gestalt. What comes to be created is, in fact, a "reference back" not to an external reality but to the very ground of being that is given by the Gestalt and which expresses itself therein:

the appearance, as a revelation of depth, is indissolubly and at the same time the real

presence of the depth, the whole, and remains real beyond itself, to that depth. . . . We perceive the Gestalt, but when we really perceive it, in terms of the depth which reveals itself therein, then we see it as the splendour and glory of being. Gazing upon this depth we are "enchanted" and "enraptured" by it. (1982–91: 1:111)

The key concept that needs to be extracted from this aesthetic understanding, besides those of *Erscheinung* and *Wahrnehmung*, is that of *Gestalt*, which acts as a foundation and informs all further understanding in terms of fundamental theology.

Gestalt gives expression to the absolute, revealing it outside of itself yet remaining in itself and returning to the depth that it expresses.

[Gestalt] means a totality of parts and elements which rests in itself and yet, by means of its stability, needs not only an environment (*Umwelt*), but being in its fullness; and in this necessity there is, as Nicholas of Cusa says, "a contracted representation" of the absolute, in that even this, in its own sphere, transcends and dominates the parts in which it is articulated (1982–91: 4:34)

With this category one is faced with a relationship that determines the theological understanding of revelation. In fact, Gestalt is complete immanence, yet like a guarantee for the expressiveness of transcendence, and a transcendence that opens into ontological difference, thus allowing the individuation of uniqueness and the uniqueness of Gestalt itself. *Erscheinung, Wahrnehmung,* and *Gestalt* are condensed into the *Erblickungslehre* that constitutes and presents fundamental theology as a discipline which focuses on perception: "the doctrine of perception or fundamental theology. Aesthetics (in the Kantian sense) in terms of the doctrine of perception of the Gestalt of God who reveals himself" (1982–91: 1:110).

2. Particular Themes

Perception binds the subject to entering into synthesis with that which comes to be perceived in order that it may possess the highest form of knowledge. To the capacity of being able to grasp the truth (*Wahrnehmung*), there must thus correspond the "simplicity of vision."

Because the *theological* character of this understanding unfolds in all its originality and detail, it is necessary to give their proper name to both *pulchrum* and Gestalt. Whatever *pulchrum* calls to mind on the part of the philosopher, it is surpassed theologically and biblically by images of *kābôd/doxa*, i.e., the self-manifestation of the glory of God, of theological beauty. Gestalt is Jesus of Nazareth in the unfolding of his thirty-three years on earth, the ultimate and definitive expression of the Father's love. He is both the revealer and the revelation of the mystery of the Trinity; what is decisive is that in his Gestalt-splendor there is no separation and distinction of what he is as man and what he is as God. In him, once and for all (*ephapax*), is the historical realization of that unrepeatable one which allows the radiance of God's glory to shine in the nature of a man, and this only and because of an essential and trinitarian equality to God.

Nevertheless, the dialectic described above acquires its full value and meaning when the reference of the Gestalt to its origin witnesses to and allows perception of the divine nature: full and complete reference to the other, perfect identity through total otherness. Pure gratuity as the form of utter unselfishness; in a word, the uniqueness and single-mindedness of Jesus Christ determined by his relation as Son within the life of the Trinity.

But even this perspective conditions subsequent theological reflection. Jesus Christ, as the center of the Gestalt of revelation, is not measured by anything or anyone other than himself. He has been given and must be accepted thus, without any conditions and without any presuppositions from the subjective point of view. To accept this objective evidence implies, therefore, the acceptance of that evidence that emanates from and is imposed by the phenomenon itself.

Of greatest importance to the theological vision of von Balthasar in this regard are the absolute freedom and gratuity of God, because in everything the transcendence and trinitarian meaning of his love are safeguarded as absolute and total gift by dint of the greatest freedom. In no case can the prior understanding of the subject determine, condition, or add something to the objective evidence. This reveals and asserts itself in the historical Gestalt of Jesus of Nazareth, who already "by the total fact of his presence and self-manifestation—by words and works, signs and miracles, but above all by his death and glorious resurrection from the dead, and finally by sending the Spirit of truth . . . [has] revealed that God was with us, to deliver us from the darkness of sin and death, and to raise us up to eternal life" (*DV* 4).

Consequently, it is the fact that God chooses to become human that allows a perfect "accord" (*Stimmung*) between his self-expression as God and the universal forms of his human communication. The language of Jesus of Nazareth can, in fact, be posited as "normative" of every language that reveals and communicates the divine, because God himself chooses to express himself through the structures of interpersonal communication.

Everything, in the creature and in creation, functions in terms of this communication of the life of the Trinity made visible in the historical presence of the Son; and at this point one may affirm that as in Jesus there is nothing of the human that is not of the language and expression of the divine, likewise there is not even anything of the divine in him that fails to communicate and reveal through the language of his humanity. Therefore, in his freedom of communication God chooses the Son, Jesus of Nazareth, as his personal alphabet and language; but the significance of this is to place the historicity of this language as the archetype and very foundation for every cultural or linguistic form that seeks to give expression to God.

The uniqueness of Christ, as well as making him his own interpretative key is also what makes him the universal and normative prototype for all human beings and for all ages (→ UNIVERSALE CONCRETUM). The only criterion of interpretation that is given to theology is thus Jesus of Nazareth, solely and exclusively, in terms of the testimony of his mission which constitutes the whole of his existence: the revelation of the trinitarian life of God.

Beginning with Jesus Christ, remaining in him and returning to him: only thus is it possible to see displayed the Gestalt in its mission of revelation. Although it may seem something of a paradox and create a suspicion that this centrality constitutes a kind of immobility, it is precisely this that epitomizes the dynamic of trinitarian love, the true, center of von Balthasar's theology.

In Jesus of Nazareth God's revelation is fulfilled *sub contrario*; this means that once the Gestalt has been perceived, it still remains even more hidden, and thus the human paradox reaches the peak of the twofold experience: that God will always remain greater than anything we can conceive of and that the believer is brought face to face with this when rationally he understands that it cannot be understood. The way forward for theological reflection will be that traced by ANSELM, to whom von Balthasar himself has recourse: viz., the way of consolation and adoration.

At this point we must examine another essential theme in fundamental theology: the credibility of the Gestalt of revelation.

Jesus of Nazareth, who has no other standard or form of measurement except himself in terms of the light and depth of revelation, is also the unique sign of the credibility of his person and his message. To be a sign, for him, amounts to having no point of reference other than himself with regard to the mystery of his existence. The uniqueness of his being prevents the search for alternative forms of the same rank or degree in terms of being able to explain his identity. And while this would appear to be an obstacle to created freedom, yet it reveals itself as the true measure of a total freedom that "does no violence" but manifests itself in that ultimate form expressive of a love that "persuades," i.e., by bearing witness to that which is beyond itself, overcoming all possible objections, drawing the subject into the same unique dynamic of love.

Love becomes the hermeneutic for the whole trilogy because, in the final analysis, it is the last word spoken by the triune God in the mystery of his revelation. However, it is a love that is definitively revealed in the paschal mystery, where the unrepeatable and unique one gives himself up to death, becoming the concrete expression of the love of a God whose very nature consists in complete and utter self-giving (see von Balthasar 1982–92: vol. 4).

Beginning with the incarnation, passing through the whole development of Jesus' earthly life, and arriving finally at the mystery of Holy Saturday, the believer is confronted with the revelation of a love that is pure reciprocity in its complete and total self-giving. Only in Jesus of Nazareth can it be affirmed

that the "theory and praxis of God's love" is made visible. It is the paschal mystery as the mystery of obedience unto death, death on the cross—or rather obedience until the silence of the sepulcher of Holy Saturday so as to be raised up in the glory of the Father. It is this obedience that gives visible and concrete shape to the Gestalt revealed as a renunciation of self and complete openness to the will of the Other, the Father. This love, which on the one hand reveals the transcendence of love in every human situation, to the point of not being able to be revealed at all unless by the Son, on the other hand "evidently" establishes itself as normative for every form of love that truly seeks to be like it, i.e., definitive and eternal love. The death of the innocent one, as the last word that God wishes to speak in human language in terms of knowledge of his being-essence, remains in human history as the final challenge to deciding and choosing to follow that same path.

To the perception of the Gestalt of revelation in its objective sense, there must be a corresponding *subjective evidence*, which expresses itself in the faith of the believer. Such complete and utter giving requires a response in terms of an all-inclusive form of action or behavior through which man finds himself, by the strength of grace, in relationship with divine revelation. And yet, even here, where the human response would be to claim itself as the mediator of the form and the measure of relationship, von Balthasar presents the Gestalt of Jesus as the archetype and norm of every response of faith: "it is by beginning with the testimony of the Trinity that human faith must be demonstrated and justified" (1982–91: 1:127, 280).

It is within the objective evidence, which allows the subject to perceive with the primary response of "wonder" and "marvel," that one already finds the power that urges humanity to recognize it as beautiful, and therefore as good and true, and by that same sense to be able to be loved and followed. It is the *fides Christi* which is offered to everyone as the example of the most faithful response to the Father. But each one feels enveloped in, and illuminated by, this faith through its proclamation and fulfillment in an intrapersonal-trinitarian, and thus "transpersonal," relationship (1982–91: 1:176). In a word, the simplicity of the act of faith is the same simplicity of love, because it is the fruit of the "seduction" worked by the appearance of the Gestalt. Not a human love, however, but the love of Christ, which alone is able to maintain in perfect harmony that which is inconceivable in human terms: the love of a being with the love of being.

Faith, which is the complete and total response to God who reveals himself (cf. _DV_ 5), is thus the simplest act that one can perform because it consists in allowing oneself to love in order to recognize and respond to love in that attitude or gesture recognized, in the mystical-spiritual tradition, as total _Gelassenheit_ (trusting repose in God, or total abandonment).

3. Summary

Von Balthasar's work, by its very composition, never permits a single conclusion or a simple judgment of its merits. It would always remain with the doubt about the contingency of our knowledge and the limits of any attempt at systematization. Yet it seems that this "scheme" of fundamental theology is marked by three features that open onto an inevitably new horizon of research for this discipline.

_a._ What emerges is, first, a clear stance against every form of _subjectivism_ when dealing with revelation. Neither the "cosmological reduction," which typified ancient times, nor the "anthropological" determining the modern era, have known how to avoid this difficulty. In the first case, on account of starting with the contingent and elevating it to become the expression of the universal; and in the second case because, having given center stage to humanity, equal weight has been given to every form of knowledge.

Von Balthasar's fundamental theology, as with all his theology, is characterized instead by the _objectivity_ of the Gestalt that is the person of Jesus of Nazareth. None of the different theological formulations has the ability to explain this mystery, but only a theology that will present itself as a simple "hermeneutic" of that which is the self-expression and self-explanation that come forth from the Christ-Gestalt.

It is the "all" of the Christ-Gestalt that forms the interpretative criterion of revelation. It is an "all" or "whole" that finds the grounds for

credibility only within itself, because in its own foundation, and only there, does being reveal itself in its freedom, transcendence, and love.

_b._ A second feature is the trinitarian character of revelation. The whole of the Trinity is encountered in the Christ-Gestalt. The evidence by which this is perceived is the typical evidence of the mystery that is dialectically revealed and hidden, until reaching its culmination in the death on the cross, where the trinitarian love of God gives expression to its ultimate and extreme form of freedom precisely when this freedom appears to be at its weakest. Christology, therefore, opens onto _Theo_-logy as the highest form and content of all Christian knowledge.

The theme of ANALOGY, which cuts through the whole of von Balthasar's work, constitutes the only possible means by which one may speak about God in a language that deprives neither the mystery of its nature nor the believer of the possibility of giving explanation to reality. Analogy remains for von Balthasar the most appropriate theological criterion and method by which we will ensure that we will not distance ourselves from, nor compromise, this same theological enterprise.

_c._ Von Balthasar's fundamental theology is one of the most expressive forms of theological learning available to the modern world, when the problem of existence is posed in an authentic fashion. The originality of this approach consists precisely in the balance given to its various constituent parts.

God does not come to be sacrificed for the pleasure of the development of humanity and its world; and humanity and its world do not come to be raised up and exalted on account of wishing to bestow upon them a purely immanent, and thus wholly illusory, salvation. There corresponds to the freedom of God the full consciousness of the creature which knows that it is not able to confer complete autonomy. It is with regard to such characteristics that each one has revealed to him the true sense of self, and in this way the path lies open for the most significant of human acts: the liberty of decision of wanting to accept a freedom greater than can be imagined.

To make the Christian message credible and acceptable to the world: this is the task that APOLOGETICS sees as its own on the strength of the Petrine injunction "Always be ready to make your defense to anyone who demands from you an accounting for the hope that is in you" (1 Pt 3:15). It is this hope that urges us to believe that the mystery of the incarnation is a reality today and that the love of God has meaning for the present condition of humanity. Von Balthasar has infused this hope into his writings, giving believers the courage to move forward untiringly on the journey of intelligent faith, and toward the "Other" of our faith, giving the power to be able to identify the light that comes forth from the person of Jesus of Nazareth, true God and true Man.

To von Balthasar may be accorded the merit of having outlined a model of fundamental theology which, though rooted in the context of contemporary theology, is rich in its resources. In fact, only a theology of "BEAUTY" will be of the caliber to make inroads into human history because it will contain within itself what is necessary for transformation and openness to what is new.

Bibl.: H. Urs VON BALTHASAR, *Word and Revelation: Essays in Theology 1* (New York, 1964); id., *Word and Revelation: Essays in Theology 2* (New York, 1965); id., *The Glory of the Lord: A Theological Aesthetics*, vol. 1: *Seeing the Form*; vol. 2: *The Realm of Metaphysics*; vol. 3: *Studies in Theological Style*; vol. 4: *The Realm of Metaphysics in Antiquity*; vol. 5: *The Realm of Metaphysics in the Modern Age*; vol. 6: *Theology: The Old Covenant*; vol. 7: *Theology: The New Covenant* (San Francisco, 1982–1991); id., *Theo-drama: Theological Dramatic Theory*, vol. 1: *Prolegomena*; vol. 2: *Dramatis Personae*; vol. 3: The Dramatis Personae: The Person in Christ; vol. 4: *The Action*; vol. 5: *The Last Act* (San Francisco, 1982–92); id., *Theologik*, vol. 1: *Wahrheit der Welt* (Einsiedeln, 1985); vol. 2: *Wahrheit Gottes* (Einsiedeln, 1985); vol. 3: *Der Geist der Wahrheit* (Einsiedeln, 1986); R. FISICHELLA, *Hans Urs von Balthasar: Amore e credibilità cristiana* (Rome, 1981); id., "Fundamentaltheologisches bei Hans Urs von Balthasar," in K. LEHMANN and W. KASPER, eds., *Hans Urs von Balthasar: Gestalt und Werk* (Cologne, 1989), 298–311; id., "Rileggendo H. U. von Balthasar," *Greg* 71 (1990): 511–46; B. KÖRNER, "Fundamentaltheologie bei Hans Urs von Balthasar," *ZKT* 109 (1987): 129–52; E. BRITO, "La beauté de Dieu," *RTL* 20 (1989): 141–61.

Rino FISICHELLA

BARTH, Karl

Karl Barth (1886–1968), the renowned Swiss theologian of the Reformed church, is generally acclaimed as a forceful and prolific advocate of the christocentric understanding of revelation and of faith. Yet a proper understanding of the works that Barth produced at the height of his academic career necessitates an acquaintance with the stages of his intellectual development. Only gradually was Barth able to assert that (1) God cannot be known at all except through the unique and free act of self-disclosure, in Israel and in Jesus Christ, as attested to in the Bible; (2) this christocentric viewpoint was seriously distorted by Catholic scholasticism, (3) was authentically rediscovered during the Protestant Reformation, and (4) was once again misconstrued by liberal Protestantism. At first Barth was an ardent proponent of the anthropologically centered theology that he had learned from his German professors Adolf von Harnack and Wilhelm Herrmann. Then he became a fiery defender both of the Christian existentialism of Søren Kierkegaard and of the eschatological socialism of Christoph Blumhardt. Finally he emerged as a tireless spokesman of the scripturally based dogmatic and ethical tenets of Martin Luther and John Calvin. These phases of Barth's evolution as a theologian provide a horizon against which to comprehend his fully evolved teaching on revelation and faith.

As a young pastor, Barth's preaching mirrored the insights of Friedrich Schleiermacher, the founder of liberal Protestantism, who regarded Jesus Christ as the historical verification and the unmatched symbol of the universal religious aspirations of humanity. Similarly, Barth's pastoral activity, based on the gospel and on socialist principles, sought to better the living conditions of working-class parishioners, who fondly called him "comrade pastor"; his opposition to the unjust behavior of Christian manufacturers rested on the Christian socialist conviction that the gospel is best grasped as an especially persuasive expression of the self-evident claim that God stands on the side of economic justice and human development. Thus, during this early period Barth held that Christian revelation is an authentic formulation, articulated by Jesus of Nazareth, of the innate knowledge of God's liberating and loving relationship to human beings, and thus is not absolutely different from the various similar teachings of other religious traditions. Like all forms of belief in the transcendent being, Christian faith is the sentiment of absolute dependence on the providence of God, although it adheres to the religious views and moral values of Jesus Christ, the Christian church is the body of believers whose corporate spirit comprehends and offers to others the profound piety and the liberating ethics of its founder.

When Barth's liberal German professors supported the militarist stance of their nation at the outbreak of World War I, he became disillusioned both with his excessively rationalistic theological training and with his allegiance to the predominantly political principles of Christian socialism. He then undertook an intensive study of the Pauline writings, so as to discern anew the uniqueness of Christian revelation, faith, and ethics. Subsequently, he published two consecutive editions of *The Epistle to the Romans*, which publicly announced his total rejection of the anthropological foundations of liberal Protestantism and of Christian socialism. In the edition of 1919, Barth's interpretation of Paul constituted an evangelical and existential reaction to the rationalism of his professors, and thus presented Christian revelation as the incomprehensible offer, on the part of God through Jesus Christ, of meaning and redemption to human persons, who in turn can accept this offer only by putting aside the principles of reason and relying on the wisdom of the Holy Spirit. In 1922, however, Barth repudiated Christian existentialism with its untenable stress on the human search for God and adopted instead the pristine Protestant position that God searches for humanity and is waiting for it at one point alone, the person of Jesus Christ. Therefore, humanity can know and love God solely at the precise locus where the divine tangent touches the human circle, the incarnation of the eternal Word.

Both the consternation and the interest aroused by Barth's first major publications caused him to be invited to teach systematic theology in Germany. In the course of preparing his lectures, Barth once again modified his view of revelation and of faith by no longer regarding the incarnation as a cryptic event that conceals more than it reveals about God. Instead, the incarnate Word is the unmerited self-disclosure of God in human form and in human words, so that believers in the crucified and risen Jesus can possess as sheer gift the revealed truth about God and can in the power of the Holy Spirit gratuitously practice the revealed love for God and for neighbor. Barth further maintained that revelation in its objective form can be encountered only in the written and oral modes by which the church confesses the divinity of the person and the definitiveness of the achievement of Jesus Christ, and similarly that revelation in its subjective form can be realized solely in the evangelical community of the church which is filled and guided by the power of the Holy Spirit. Barth was led to these distinctions while composing *Fides Quaerens Intellectum*, an analysis of the thought of ANSELM of Canterbury. The incarnate Word of God, Jesus Christ, is the ontic expression of divine revelation and thus comprises the one communication of God's self-knowledge which puts human reason in crisis. The poured-out love of God, the Holy Spirit, is the noetic expression of divine revelation, and therefore is the unique personal appropriation of God's self-effacement which places human morality into confusion.

With the rise of National Socialism in Germany, Barth's controversial return to Protestant orthodoxy was tested and strengthened in diverse ways. He considered Nazism to be blatant idolatry and collective suicide, and thus accused its Christian supporters of placing divine self-revelation on the same level as a wicked political system. Barth began to designate as "natural theology" not only the compromise made by the German Christians with the Third Reich but also any other culturally motivated tendency to attenuate the religious truth and the ethical demands of Scripture. Thus, in the acerbic pamphlet simply entitled *No!*, Barth castigated his fellow Protestant Emil Brunner for defending the inherent ability of human persons to have some preconception of divine truth and love that facilitates the act by which the Holy Spirit brings them to faith in Jesus Christ. This error was for Barth the root of the distortion of divine revelation systematically perpetrated by medieval Catholicism and still being championed by means of the concept *analogia entis* ("analogy of being") on the part of contemporary spokesmen such as Erich Przywara. Barth judged it imperative that genuine followers of Luther and Calvin deny the existence of an analogy of being between humanity and God. If there is a similarity between these two entirely different realities, it is found solely in the historical manifestation of the Word and is reflected thereafter only in believers filled by the Holy Spirit, so that an *analogia fidei* ("analogy of faith") continually comes to exist between the Word and the hearers of the Word.

Although Barth's Christocentrism was disputed because it summarily affirmed that all other pretensions to know and love God apart from Judaism and Christianity are false, because disobedient to the divine command to hear and accept the incarnate Word, this position did in fact motivate his courageous defense of the Jews during the Third Reich. When some of his Protestant colleagues attempted to mitigate the literal meaning of the phrase "salvation is from the Jews" (Jn 4:22), Barth responded that, since Jesus himself was a Jew and died for Gentiles and Jews, no Christian who held or practiced anti-Semitism could be regarded as his follower. Relying on the Pauline teaching that the salvation of the believers in Jesus is entwined with that of the Jews, Barth on the one hand reinforced his global rejection of the validity of all nonbiblical religions, and on the other became one of the few Christian theologians who resisted the mentality that caused the Holocaust as it was occurring. To Barth's mind, Friedrich Gogarten and other adherents to the German Christian movement were rendering the Word of God inaudible by echoing the voice of a stranger, that of National Socialism. Thus, during World War II, Barth repeatedly wove into the text of his ongoing major work, *Church Dogmatics*, the conviction that genuine reflection on Christian faith is a responsible ecclesial act and not a free philosophical inquiry. The true Christian theologian is bound humbly to explicate the three diverse but interrelated historical forms of divine revelation: the incarnate Word, the written Word, and the preached Word.

Until the end of his life, Barth reiterated this seemingly christomonistic stance, which his Catholic, Orthodox, and Protestant critics deemed poorly nuanced and excessively intolerant. Yet he insisted that revelation and faith cannot be said to exist in graduated degrees beyond Judaism and Christianity, lest the sovereign decision of God to disclose himself in

Jesus Christ and to assure for himself the response of humanity through the activity of the Holy Spirit in the church be negated. Thus, in later works such as *Evangelical Theology: An Introduction*, Barth warned Protestants that, should they replace the reflection on the Word of God with the description of the experience of the human person in general or of the Christian in particular, they would be unfaithful to the fundamental objection of the Reformers to the selfsame defect of Catholicism. In *Ad Limina Apostolorum*, the account of his journey to Rome and audience with Paul VI in 1968, Barth greatly lauded the prevalence of biblical theology in the documents of Vatican II, but in the list of questions he had posed to his Catholic counterparts he showed himself to be uncertain as to whether, with its emphasis on the mediatory role of the Virgin Mary, the infallibility of the pope and the bishops, and the sacramental rituals of the church, Catholicism was still replacing the reflection on the sovereign Word of God with the articulation of the ecclesial experience of believers.

Karl Barth's understanding of Christian revelation, faith, and theology has been most influential in fostering ecumenical dialogue between Catholics and Protestants in the twentieth century, since it has sharply etched both the agreements and the differences existing between them. Barth has urged Protestants to imitate the seriousness with which Catholic theology is allocating to Scripture and tradition the very center of its current attempt at renewal; and Barth has challenged Catholics to affirm ever more clearly the priority of the Word of God above every other secondary mediation which Catholics gratuitously employ in and for the life of the church. However, it has been demonstrated that Barth's avowed Christocentrism is contradicted by his own painstaking efforts constantly to balance it with pneumatocentric considerations. As Barth once observed, Christian revelation and faith are elliptical in nature: the theocentric focus is Jesus Christ and the anthropocentric focus is the believer, both of whom are held in a dynamic harmony by the action of the Spirit of Jesus Christ in the church. If Catholics such as Karl Rahner appreciated the attempts of some Protestants to ponder the hidden prompting of the Holy Spirit in human persons before the act of faith in Jesus Christ is made, and if Protestants such as Jürgen Moltmann praise some Catholics for their efforts to revive pneumatology as the prevailing theme of ecclesiology, then both the foci of Barth's theology of revelation and faith are still promoting the authenticity of the churches and the interchange between them which he foremost desired.

Bibl.: P. MONSMA, *Karl Barth's Idea of Revelation* (Sommerville, 1937); H. Urs VON BALTHASAR, *Karl Barth: Darstellung und Deutung seiner Theologie* (Cologne, 1951; see the abridged translation: *The Theology of Karl Barth* [New York, 1971]); H. BOUILLARD, *Karl Barth*, 3 vols. (Paris, 1957); H. M. RUMSCHEIDT, *Revelation and Theology: An Analysis of the Barth-Harnack Correspondence of 1923* (Cambridge, 1972); P. ROSATO, *The Spirit as Lord: The Pneumatology of Karl Barth* (Edinburgh, 1981); A. DULLES, *Models of Revelation* (Garden City, 1983).

Philip J. ROSATO

BEAUTY

Beauty is the point of departure in the contemplation of being. It is the last word that the intellect is able to utter before making way, as reason demands, for knowledge of the incomprehensible.

Everyone knows what beauty is because, quite simply, it reveals itself inasmuch as the presence of goodness and truth of being yields an all-embracing intuition.

People today have lost their relationship with beauty. We are incapable of grasping it rationally and turning it into a quantifiable "number"; instead we have opted to reduce it to the level of banality. Never, perhaps, as in our time of heightened aesthetic sense, has contact with works of art been so reduced. Astonishment and wonder accompanied by the feeling of joy, as experienced in the presence of *pulchrum*, have made way for indifference and noise. Beauty seems to have been shut out of our lives. Museums, to paraphrase Neitzsche, have become the tomb of *pulchrum*. Aesthetic experience and creation may not have been neglected or even denied, but they have unquestionably been reduced to being the privilege of the few.

And yet, when we lose contact with beauty, we also lose the sense of goodness and truth. The individual becomes ever more incapable of relating to essential universal values, and existence tends to assume less-human forms.

The history of theology can also trace a parabolic movement in relating to *pulchrum*.

In Scripture, as word of revelation, beauty extends from God to everything he has created. Beauty and goodness are synonymous because they enable us to see both Yahweh's creativity and the fact that he made himself known to us as the true God. Yahweh delivered us from slavery and death (Ex 3:8; 18:9) and demonstrated the beauty and goodness of his love; the Yahweh who introduced us to the "beautiful" country that flows with milk and honey (Dt 8:7–10) is the same Yahweh who is faithful to his promise.

But this God was also the same God who, after creating heaven and earth and everything there, described what he had made as "beautiful": "And God saw it was something beautiful and good" (Gn 1:3). The Hebrew *ṭôb* is imprecise, translated variously as *kalos* and *agathos*; later *kābôd* is used to convey very specifically the sense and content of God's beauty.

Kābôd is the glory of the radiant power of God revealing himself to humanity. This is what enables us to perceive the splendor of his beauty. It is a beauty that cannot be described or seen directly (Ex 33:18–23); it is there to be contemplated in its reflected manifestation (Ex 34:30–35). This same glory is the beauty which believers today see reflected on the face of the crucified Christ, "the most handsome of men" (Ps 45:2).

Throughout the patristic and medieval periods, theologians saw neither the demand nor the need to produce a specifically aesthetic theory. The relationship with the beauty of all creation, and of men and women within it, was so closely linked to the way of understanding reality in those times that theologians were intuitively inclined to see in beauty a manifestation of the irruption of the divine.

It was Irenaeus, with his felicitous insight *gloria Dei vivens homo* ("the glory of God is the living man"), that opened the way to a theology that made it possible to perceive beauty without having to articulate it. After him, Augustine, Pseudo-Dionysius, Anselm, Francis of Assisi, Thomas, Bonaventure, and many more continued to describe in their different-styles God's revelation in Jesus Christ, in the light of biblical glory and of beauty.

This theology was so rich and stimulating that it had a strong influence on poetry and art and found its fullest expression in Dante and the Gothic cathedrals of the Middle Ages.

Since Thomas Aquinas, and almost without interruption up to the present day, theology has sought to go down other avenues, which appeared to lead to more verifiable certainties; it has distanced itself from the original relationship with *pulchrum* and has occasionally become *Sententia* or *Commentarium* instead.

It was only the work of nonprofessional theologians that made it possible for the links with the original sources to survive: Petrarch, Nicholas of Cusa, Erasmus, John of the Cross, Teresa of Avila, Pascal, Johann Georg Hamann, Dostoievsky, Tolstoy, Gerard Manley Hopkins, and Charles Péguy are only some of those whose aesthetic work has sustained theology over the centuries.

In recent times, the only theologian to open up the treasures of aesthetics within the theological, patristic, and medieval traditions and to produce comparable literary output has been Hans Urs VON BALTHASAR.

Rino FISICHELLA

BLONDEL, Maurice

By descent or derivation Blondel's ties are with Pascal. The germ of the theory in his work *Action* (*L'Action*) is already present in Pascal's "wager." In any hypothesis, we have to make a wager, as though we had already "embarked" on something. Whether we like it or not, we have to face the question of meaning. Blondel sees life as a praxis. Human beings act and cannot not act. But why? What latent aspect of this action bears it along in spite of the human subject? An analysis of the internal logic of action inescapably poses the problem of a necessary fulfillment, which human beings are incapable of ordaining for themselves. Our actions are marked by an incompleteness that is not only a fact but a necessity; i.e., they manifest a natural and ineluctable unrealizability. Blondel's dialectic reveals a "gaping chasm" in us, which can be filled only by that which is

Other than us. To give our lives a meaning, we must remain open to the possibility of a divine Gift, which, for the believer, is clearly Christian revelation.

I concentrate on *L'Action* in this article because this work above all remains Blondel's masterpiece and directly poses the problem of fundamental theology: namely, the problem of the meaning of life, of human action and its relation to human aspirations and the promises of Christianity. In this respect, *L'Action* has not aged.

1. The Dialectic of *L'Action*

In the first few lines of his work Blondel poses the problem of action in terms reminiscent of Pascal: "Yes or no, does human life have a meaning, and does humanity have a destiny? I act, but without even knowing what action is, without having wished to live, without really knowing who I am or even if I am" (p. vii; page numbers throughout refer to *L'Action* [Paris, 1893], reprinted with the same pagination). Furthermore, I understand that my actions bear a responsibility that may incur life or death. I cannot even take refuge in nothingness. If there is anything to understand, I want to understand it. I want to know if this mystery that I am to myself has any consistency. "I shall probably find what is hidden in my actions in those ultimate depths where, without myself, in spite of myself, I undergo being and cling to it" (p. vii).

To understand the meaning of the human condition, we have to confront the problem of human action; i.e., we have to examine the dialectic of real life, to see what is inevitable and necessary in the unfolding of human life seen as a whole. "I am located, so to speak, within human action in order to recognize its demands, to estimate its entire, irresistible expression" (p. 20). If the approach is to be rigorous, I must presuppose nothing and avoid nothing. Human beings have invented a vast number of attitudes to avoid the demands of action. We should examine them all to see if they contain their own justification or condemnation. "At the roots of the most daring negations or the most insane extravagances of volition, we have to see if there is not an initial movement that nevertheless persists, and that we delight in and want, even though we may deny or abuse it. It is in each individual that the principle must be found for the judgment to be passed on each (p. xx). The problem of action is not "one particular question, any *one* question like any other that happens to pose itself to us. It is *the* question, without which there is no other" (pp. xxi–xxii).

In all those attitudes to which human beings resort to avoid the demands of action, Blondel wishes to show that there is always a certain "disproportion" (p. xxiii), a "discordance" (p. xxiv), between what we think we want and what we in fact deeply desire, between the object wanted and the "spontaneous" movement of wanting, between the *will-willing* ("la volonté *voulante*") and the *will-willed* ("la volonté *voulue*"). By "will-willing," we must understand the spiritual dynamism that gives life to a human being as a whole, including one's intellect. The will-willing is the "dynamized" being. After passing in review the entire range of human procedures and noting this disproportion throughout, this recurrent discordance between what is actually willed and the spontaneous human dynamism, we are in a position to assess the extent of this dynamism. It then becomes clear that human beings cannot fulfill themselves unless they open themselves up to an action other than their own. Hence, it would seem that in its depths, at its roots, human volition, which is always "fidgeting with impatience," always unsatisfied, is the expectation of and desire for a something more. Christianity would seem to be the appropriate answer to this demand and to this need. This is the approach taken in *L'Action*. Blondel's methodology depends essentially on the dialectic between will-*willed* and will-*willing*, of the reflective and spontaneous movements of volition. It is a reflective and thematic representation of action as it is lived.

L'Action is divided into five parts. The first three, which might well be entitled "Humanity in the World," conclude that the natural order is inadequate. The fourth part, "The Necessary Being of Action," deduces the necessity of yielding to divine action. The fifth part, entitled "The Fulfillment of Action," shows the necessity of taking seriously the idea of revelation and of the supernatural order, as defined by Christianity. These last two parts are of particular interest in the present context.

First Part: Is There a Problem Regarding Action?

To remain faithful to his method, which consists in supposing nothing and in avoiding nothing, Blondel begins by asking if this question is meaningful, if there are grounds for asking it. He first examines the attitudes of the dilettante and the aesthete. The dilettante eradicates the problem by allowing several contradictory lives to coexist within himself or herself at the same time; this is "trying-out in action" (p. 8). The dilettante tries to sample the relative pleasure of everything, but without ever making a basic commitment. But in fact this attitude reveals a contradiction, for to try to enjoy everything, without willing anything, without ever committing oneself, is to will oneself.

The analysis of the dilettantist attitude reveals two things: First, the very effort made to commit oneself to nothing at all contains a subtle and positive resolution to will only *oneself* as object (pp. 19–20). Second, if the dilettante tries to persevere in willing nothing, to be logical he or she must come to nothing, i.e., must disappear. But in reality, says Blondel, "the dilettante spits on life only to have a surfeit of it and of himself. He likes himself so much that he will sacrifice everything to his egotism; he likes himself little enough to melt away, to sacrifice himself and lose himself in everything else" (p. 20).

Second Part: Is There a Negative Solution to the Problem of Action?

Confronted with the inevitable problem of human destiny, one might propose the solution of taking nothingness as the conclusion of human experience, the end of knowledge, and the goal of human aspirations. The advocates of this solution prefer a radical solution to the games of the dilettante. Moreover, all those who have experienced life in its different forms (wealth, ambition, success) know that in the end there is only disgust and nothingness. We should expect nothing of life because it can offer us nothing. Knowledge leads to the same result: knowledge is pointless, since it reveals the vanity of being human. It only extends the area of mystery.

Blondel answers this negative solution to the problem of action by saying that we cannot conceive of or will absolute nothingness. We conceive of it only by affirming something else. We posit nothingness only because we need a more solid reality than the one we reject. In reality, the will to nothingness is derived from an absolute love of being, which is betrayed by the inadequacy of the phenomenon, of appearance (pp. 38–39). In reality, what we want is that there should be something, and that this something should be truly adequate. We want there to be something *consistent:* "these words— there is something—express the naïve movement of life that is enamored of itself and of everything that sustains it without knowing what it is. In my actions, in the world, in me, outside me, I know not where or what, there is something" (pp. 40–41). "Most people live by this conviction; it is the broad and long road along which the bulk of humanity proceeds" (p. 41). "This agreed fact must give rise by a hidden initiative, to the whole scientific, moral, and social order. . . . By following the thrust of the will to the end, we shall know whether human action can be defined and contained in this natural realm" (p. 41). The question is whether the declared will (the surface will, the will-willed) to limit humanity to the field of natural activity is in accordance with the deepest human will (the willing-will), whence all spiritual activity emerges. This brings Blondel to the third part of his work.

Third Part: The Phenomenon of Action

This well-developed section (pp. 33–223) corresponds to what one might call the first stage of the genesis of the supernatural, according to Blondel. There is something analogous in Pascal, in his analysis of the human condition, and in Teilhard de Chardin, in his analysis of the human phenomenon. Blondel reviews one by one the various spheres of human activity, while considering doctrines or attitudes that would limit human destiny to one or another sector of human activity: e.g., scientific activity, inspired by positivism; personal and individual activity; social activity, which gives rise to the family, one's country, and human society as a whole; moral activity, with its unsatisfied quest for an absolute; the tendency to make idols (science, nation) and to give them an absolute value that they do not possess but that we try to secure in order to use it.

After examining all the spheres of human activity, Blondel concludes that none of them, individually or as a whole, is sufficient to exhaust the profundity of human wanting. There is but one conclusion: "It is impossible not to recognize the inadequacy of the entire natural order and not to experience a further need; it is impossible to find within oneself anything that might satisfy this religious need. *It is necessary and it is impracticable:* such, quite badly put, are the conclusions from the determinism of human action" (p. 319). Blondel once again uses an indeterminate language. He simply concludes that the necessary condition for the fulfillment of human action is inaccessible to human action. "By his voluntary action, man goes beyond phenomena. He can be adequate to his own demands. In himself he has more than he can use of himself. He cannot succeed by his own efforts in putting into his willed action all that which is contained in the principle of his voluntary action" (p. 321). The human will has indeed become inextricably mired in an insoluble problem.

Fourth Part: The Necessary Being of Action

This section corresponds to the second stage of the genesis of the idea of the supernatural in Blondel's work. At the beginning, Blondel recapitulates everything that he developed in the first part and once again poses the problem of action, but on the basis of the self-inquiring human being.

The now-verified fact that human beings try unsuccessfully to discover that which is adequate to them in the natural order constitutes a crisis for them. This crisis not only appears at the heart of their particular projects but is immanent in the human condition itself. Indeed, we wish to be sufficient unto ourselves, and we cannot be. Moreover, in that which is wanted, human beings everywhere encounter self-conceit and suffering. Into what they do there creep weaknesses and faults, whose consequences they cannot repair. Finally, death puts the finishing touch to all human setbacks (pp. 324–32).

However, Blondel emphasizes, this apparent miscarriage of willed action (p. 325) reveals the indestructibility of the dynamism of willing action, for I should not be aware of this miscarriage if I did not contain a will that rises above all the contradictions of life. The presence in us of what is not willed (errors, failures) reveals the will-*willing* in all its purity. Such is the human condition. "Divided between what I do without willing it and what I will without doing it, I am always as if excluded from myself. How is the human subject to prove adequate to the subject itself? In order to will myself to be myself fully, I must will more than I have as yet been able to find. . . . Between me and myself there is an abyss that I cannot bridge" (pp. 337–38). When I think of the way that must be taken under the constraint of an inflexible determinism, I am forced to conclude that I cannot stop or go back or advance alone (p. 339). "In my action there is something that I have as yet been unable to understand or equal, something that prevents it from falling back into nothingness, and that is something only by virtue of being something other than what I have willed up to now." Blondel continues, "This conflict explains the ineluctable presence of a new affirmation in the consciousness; the reality of this necessary presence makes possible in us our very consciousness of this conflict itself. There is a *uniquely necessary*" (p. 339). And nothing else whatsoever is necessary.

But the dialectic continues. No longer having any finite object to pursue, nevertheless the will now cannot not will. After it has inventoried all that can be willed, there is still a gap, an inadequation between willing and the willed. As a result, voluntary action, which has gone from failure to failure, sees itself compelled to turn back on itself and is led back to the center of the subject, where the movement of the will originates, with a "supplementary inventory" in view.

Here Blondel introduces the proofs of the existence of God, which he presents in a new way and not one by one, but by making the classic so-called cosmological, teleological, and ontological arguments converge. It is not a matter of three different proofs, like the five proofs of Thomas, but rather of three different forms of the same approach. It is a question of a single way that changes name three times. Moreover, Blondel emphasizes, it is not a matter of "any sterile satisfaction of the mind," "of any purely logical argument" (pp. 340–41). It is a question rather of recognizing a gradually

emergent "presence" in ourselves (p. 340). The mind advances toward an *encounter*.

Only at the end of this dialectical argument does Blondel introduce the name of God. "At the term, quickly reached, of what is finite, we find ourselves in the presence of that which phenomenon and nothingness both harbor and manifest, before that of which we can never speak as if of a stranger or of someone who is absent: God" (p. 350).

Blondel's originality lies in his conceiving that the proof asks us to go much further. We cannot remain in the presence of this personal Absolute, God, without being simultaneously required to take up a position, to opt for the life or death of action.

The conflict that we have observed in human beings—i.e., that I cannot provide myself with the necessary being, and yet I cannot surrender the necessity to will—can be resolved only by means of an inevitable alternative (p. 353). "Yes or no, is man willing to live, until he dies thereby, so to speak, by agreeing to be replaced by God? Or will he try to be self-sufficient without God, to profit from his necessary presence without willing it, to take from him the power to avoid him, and to want infinitely without wanting the infinite? To will and not to be able, to be able and not to will, is the very option with which freedom is faced. . . . If the thought that there is something to make of life is available to all people, that is sufficient for even the most crass among them also to be summoned to resolve the greatest question of all, the one necessary thing" (pp. 354–55).

Blondel then examines the terms of the alternative in order to explain the inevitable consequences of each of the two possible options. First he analyzes the attitude of refusal, or the negative option. If human beings try to find in themselves what is needed, then they lose the very principle of life and are condemned. By locating the whole of their life where there is nothing to fulfill it, human beings are self-condemned to death everlasting. If a person chooses the second option, how is it possible *freely* to set God at the heart of human action? How are we to open ourselves up to the action of God? How are we to prepare, if there is one, for a more lucid revelation of human destiny? (p. 375).

Blondel answers this question with three points that define the approach of a sincere individual behaving consistently. Like Pascal, he finds these inward attitudes very important. First, a person should do all that he or she believes to be good, and everything that he or she thinks is in accordance with his or her conscience. Second, if detachment is part of the principle of good action, it is not astonishing that the moral life should be accompanied by sacrifice and renunciation. The yardstick for the human heart is the degree of acceptance of suffering. Third, to act with self-denial and to accept suffering are not enough. "After behaving entirely as if one expected nothing from God, one must still expect everything from God, as if one had never taken oneself into account at all" (p. 385).

The conclusion of the fourth part may be formulated thus: what Blondel sees as arising from the determinism of human action is the indeterminate idea of an Absolute that all human beings, even without knowledge of Christianity, want obscurely but that cannot be obtained *as a Thing*. In other words, it is the idea of the uniquely necessary thing that can be reached only by giving oneself up to it; it is the idea of divine action to which one has to surrender oneself, whatever the form under which it is presented.

Fifth Part: The Fulfillment of Action

This section corresponds to the third stage of the genesis of Blondel's notion of the supernatural. The supernatural as considered henceforth by Blondel is that which lies beyond what dogmas present us with. Blondel asks whether historical Christianity, with its dogmas and practices, is not the sought-for determination and identification of humanity's relation to the Absolute.

Blondel answers those who would avoid the Christian supernatural without examining it by saying that this is an attitude contrary to the true philosophical spirit. In fact, the approach of reflection on human action has led us to "awareness of an irresolvable disproportion between the élan of the will and the human term of action" (p. 390). We have seen that human beings cannot fulfill themselves unless they open themselves up to an action other than their own (p. 401). Therefore it would be unreasonable to ignore the Christian concept of the *revealed* supernatural. Aware both of its

powerlessness and of its demands, reason has to ask if Christian revelation does not accord with the original profound aspirations of the human will.

It is not a matter of rationally reconstructing the Christian revelation, for then Christianity would not be revelation. In its essential content, indeed, revelation is the intimate life of the God-in-Trinity, communicated to human beings through grace (p. 407). But if it is impossible to discover Christian dogmas and mysteries other than by revelation, it is legitimate to consider these dogmas not primarily as revealed but as revelatory, i.e., to confront them with the profound aspirations of the will and to find there, should it be there, the image of our real needs and the expected answer. It is legitimate to accept them as hypotheses, as geometricians do, by supposing the problem to be resolved and by verifying the supposed answer by means of analysis (pp. 391 and 401).

Christian revelation must thus be seen as a hypothesis that would allow us to see clearly into the demands of the will. If the attempt succeeds, that would not mean that the historical reality of Christian revelation would have been affirmed, nor even that its intrinsic possibility would have been established (p. 406), as its content as well as its existence do not yield to reason alone. But it would mean that we would have seen how "something analogous to what dogmas propose" seems necessary in order to explain the discordance between the will-willing and the will-willed. Moreover, we would have established the practical obligation to accept the supernatural as Christian teaching indicates, if ever Christian revelation happened to present itself as a historically and effectively given reality.

Blondel wishes to show that the expectation of the human will is oriented to something analogous to the Christian supernatural order. Hence the supernatural remains both *inaccessible* (gratuitous, like the divine initiative) but nevertheless *necessary* (necessary in the same sense as a practical necessity: it has to be accepted, if in fact it is given).

The "hypothetical" religion should possess dogmas and require a certain form of practice. Only an integrally lived Christian experience can demonstrate whether Christianity is that religion and whether it allows the will to will fully and action to be fulfilled. But at the end of his work, Blondel wishes to offer a personal testimony, while stressing yet again that it goes beyond philosophy. "It is up to philosophy to show that the alternative must be posed: Is it or is it not the case? It is also up to philosophy to study the consequences of one or the other solution and to assess the vast gulf; it cannot go further or say in its own right whether this is or is not the case. But it is allowed to add a single statement that exceeds the realm of human knowledge and the competence of philosophy: the only statement capable, when confronted by Christianity, of expressing that part—the better part—of the certainty that cannot be communicated because it arises only from the intimacy of wholly personal action—and this statement is itself an action and must be uttered: *It is*" (p. 492).

2. Stages in the Genesis of the Supernatural

I shall now offer a synthesis of the three stages of genesis of the notion of the supernatural in *L'Action*, while emphasizing the connection between them.

First Blondel establishes the insufficiency of human action. He shows that the *indispensable* condition for the fulfillment of human action is *inaccessible* to that action. This dialectic of the indispensable–inaccessible, or of the necessary-impossible, ordains and provides the rhythm of all subsequent procedure. It is always a matter of showing that the exigency of the will exceeds its power. This gives rise to the idea of the supernatural, in two modes. In the first mode, the necessity is absolute, but the supernatural remains indeterminate. In a second mode, the necessity is that of a hypothesis, but this hypothesis is the Christian supernatural order. What appears in the first mode is the absolute necessity of opening up to the action of God, whatever it may be. The second mode is characterized by the necessity of accepting the positive revelation, if this revelation appears to be real.

The decisive stage is not the last, but that in which the idea of God (in the fourth part) arises from the conflict within the will, confronts consciousness with an alternative, and makes it opt for or against yielding to a still-indeterminate divine action. This is so true that, in the manuscript submitted to the Sorbonne for permission to print his thesis, Blondel had written: "Fourth part: decisive part." At the end of the work, he writes: "*The only point* is to be found entirely in this necessary conflict arising at the heart of the human will and forcing it to choose in practice between the terms of an inevitable alternative, of an alternative such that man either tries to remain his own master and to stay wholly in control of himself, or to submit to the divine order more or less obscurely revealed to his consciousness" (p. 487). Blondel, to be sure, does not restrict his examination to this indeterminate supernatural. He looks beyond, but he knows that, as a philosopher, this is the only approach he can take to Christian revelation.

The phenomenology of *L'Action* is a *logic* of action. The strength of Blondel's dialectic is that it does not construct an ideal that would be the end of human action; it merely expresses the inevitable content of human activity. The boundless aspect of the will is not the starting point of his inquiry but his point of arrival. Blondel does not assess the various stages from action to fullness, which is assumed to be known by the will; on the contrary, it is the inexorable development of human action that gradually reveals the *fullness of the spiritual dynamism* that has secretly impelled the will from the beginning. On each occasion, an inadequacy of the will-willing to the will-willed, and a discordance between them, has been revealed.

The movement of thought that takes a person from an analysis of the volitional dynamism to that inward conflict that forces him or her to a decisive option by which he or she closes in on the self, or opens up to God and to the obscurely anticipated divine order, offers us a reflection that is still of value today. In fact, today as yesterday, we shall have done nothing if we do not succeed in showing that human beings must at the very least be open to an eventual Word of God addressed to humanity in history.

What Rahner tried to do on the basis of the dynamism of human knowledge (*Hörer des Wortes*), Blondel attempted on the basis of the dynamic being of the essential human person.

Blondel's philosophy is no mere apology for Christianity, or mere philosophy of religion. It is indeed a "philosophical apologetics." But because it is philosophical, this apologetics can be apprehended by all people of good will. It saves believers from fideism. It also shows sincere men and women that the leap into the supernatural is no less reasonable and no less necessary than the truths of everyday life.

Bibl.: H. DUMÉRY, *La philosophie de L'Action: Essai sur l'intellectualisme blondélien* (Paris, 1948); J. PAILLARD, *Maurice Blondel ou le dépassement chrétien* (Paris, 1950); H. BOUILLARD, *Blondel and Christianity* (Washington, 1969–70); A. CARTIER, *Existence et vérité: philosophie blondélienne de l'Action et problématique existentielle* (Paris, 1955); J. LACROIX, *Maurice Blondel: An Introduction to the Man and His Philosophy* (New York, 1968); R. LATOURELLE, *Man and His Problems in the Light of Christ* (New York, 1983), 195–214; F. LEFÈVRE, *L'itinéraire philosophique de Maurice Blondel* (Paris, 1966); R. SAINT-JEAN, *Genèse de l'Action 1882–1893* (Bruges/Brussels/Paris, 1965); id., *L'apologétique philosophique: Blondel, 1893–1913* (Paris, 1966).

René LATOURELLE

BUDDHISM

1. Buddhism is the most ancient of the major world religions. Rooted in the disturbing experience of the illuminations of Siddhartha Gautama in the sixth century B.C.E., in Northern India, its missionary dynamism, following its expansion throughout the whole of Asia, is today penetrating the West as well. From the second century B.C.E., after a period of scholasticism, two distinct currents developed: the *Theravāda* (School of the Ancients), also known disparagingly as *Hīnayāna* (The Little Way), which spread chiefly in southern Asia with its center in Sri Lanka; second, the *Mahāyāna* (Greater Way), inculturated in various forms in Tibet, China, Korea, and Japan. Whereas the first current has come to be seen as the original and orthodox form, directed toward the asceticism of the monastic life, the Mahāyāna gives somewhat greater emphasis for the laity to the principles of altruism in the light of a universal redemption.

Maintaining an apophatic silence about God, the way of salvation in Buddhism points to profound mystical experience and guides one away from knowledge of worldly vanity toward a transcendent serenity. Far from a purely speculative interest, Buddhism proclaims its doctrinal teachings "as a raft useful for crossing the river, but not to be clung to." By "seeing straight" (*Sn* 231) the world of phenomena, Buddhism offers a hermeneutic key rather than a dogmatic system and complements cultures and religions by means of intuitive wisdom. It dispenses redemption not through grace but in a passive way, the fruits of the essential work of a spiritual reawakening. The fundamental mystery is illumination in terms of an opening of the self, which is imprisoned in the painful cycle of birth and death, to an existence rooted in nirvana. Having first journeyed along just such a path of liberation, the Buddha becomes the model and spiritual friend (*kalyanamitra*) of humanity.

Everything that has been taught by the Buddha—from the night of illumination until the night of extinction—comes to be considered sacred word. The canonical sources fall into three groups (*Tripitaka*), gathered by the monastic community after the death of the Buddha, according to the quality of the texts: the *Vinaya-pitaka* contains the monastic rules; the *Sūtra-pitaka* contains the doctrinal discourses; and the *Abhidharma-pitaka* contains the scholastic texts of preliminary philosophical reflection. Of the various canonical collections, the only one to have been conserved as an integral unit is the *Tripitaka* of the Theravādin from Sri Lanka (codified ca. 80 B.C.E.), written in the ancient Pali language of Northern India. Notwithstanding the Buddha's custom of using the common language, many other texts are composed in Sanskrit. The problem of studying a body of ancient writings can be approached by applying the historical-critical method. With the beginnings of the Mahāyāna the canon was augmented by other works clearly dating from the early part of the first century B.C.E., yet containing later revelations of the Buddha's secret teachings. Among these are the texts of the *Prajñāpāramitā* (Supreme Wisdom), the *Avatamsaka Sūtra*, and the *Sūtra of Loto*, which develop new doctrines and which themselves form a separate canon (*vaipulya*). The major collections are found in Chinese and Tibetan and comprise 2,184 works in the last and most authoritative edition of the *Taishō Tripitaka*, published in Japan in fifty-five volumes (1924–29). The Tibetan canon, codified by Bu-ston (1290–1364), distinguishes between "the word of Buddha" (*bKa'gyur;* 1,055 texts) and scholastic works (*bsTan'gyur*; 3,962 texts).

From the simple formula "I take refuge in the Buddha, I take refuge in the Dharma, I take refuge in the Sangha," which from ancient times has constituted the clearest expression of the symbol of faith, spring the chief principles (*triratna*, three jewels) of salvation: the person of the "guide of men and of the gods" (Buddha); the body of doctrine (*Dharma*); and the community (*Sangha*), divided into monks and laity.

2. The biography of the Buddha consists in a story of salvation, together with elements of legend and historical facts. According to mythology, Sākyamuni is numbered among an enormous host of deliverers, of which one is revealed for every age of the world (*kalpa*, cycle of generation, existence, and destruction of the cosmos). Preceded by numerous other Buddhas and followed by his successor Maitreya in the next cosmic cycle, Sākyamuni prepared himself as a bodhisattva (one destined to be a Buddha) in many previous existences by the accumulation of great merits in order to save humanity in the present age, and had predestined all the circumstances of his historical life. With such complete sovereignty he becomes human in order to fulfill his steadfast decision to guide humanity from the slavery of death and rebirth.

Sakyamuni Gautama (the sage of the tribe of Sākya, of the Gautama family) was born ca. 566 B.C.E. at Lumbini, near Kapilavastu in present-day Nepal, of the family of Prince Suddhodana and of Māyā. He received the name Siddhārta. According to a prophecy, he would have been destined to become an emperor in the world or an important religious figure. He grew up within the peaceful atmosphere of the court, and at the age of 16 married Yasodharā, by whom he had a son, Rahula (the bond). Unable to find satisfaction in the carefree life of luxury, Sākyamuni was troubled by questions of an existential nature, such as age, illness, and death, and pondered upon immortality after the painful cycle of the birth and decomposition of the world (*samsāra*). At the age of 29 (537 B.C.E.) he abandoned the hidden life of the palace for that of an itinerant ascetic (*sramana*) and, as did so many of his contemporaries, spent six years visiting various masters of yoga. At last he came to understand that superhuman powers did not lead to spiritual progress, and he decided to

follow the *via media*, avoiding the extremes of laxity and exaggerated asceticism. Meditating alone under a tree at Bodh-Gaya, he received illumination and became the Buddha (the Awakened). This honorary title indicates his nirvana, i.e., the extinction of all subjugated aspects within absolute spiritual tranquillity. In the course of this sacred night (531 B.C.E.) Sākyamuni arrived at the knowledge of his past existences, at the certainty of the eternal cycle of birth and death of beings, and at the elimination of ignorance and desire. Finally he mastered understanding of the basic law of the conditional origin of all the phenomena of life (*pratitya-samutpada*). According to a chain of twelve causes, he analyzed the interdependence of the psychophysical elements in the cycle of formation and decomposition of every object, realizing in himself the rupture of just such a chain, i.e., the freedom of nirvana. The ineffable joy of this experience motivated him, out of compassion for human ignorance, to be a preacher. Beginning in the Park of the Deer at Benares in front of five ascetics who were his one-time companions, with the "Sutra on putting the Law into practice" (*Dharmacakra-pravartanasūtra*), the Buddha spent forty-five years traveling around Northern India, preaching and receiving disciples into his order (*Sangha*), in the same way as so many other masters. He died at Kusinagara at the age of 80 (486 B.C.E.), attaining by means of the dissolution of the psychophysical elements (*skandha*) the fullness of nirvana "like a flame extinguished without trace." Having completed his salvific mediation by indicating the "middle way," he referred his disciples to the supreme authority of the *dharma* as the guide for the future.

3. At the very heart of the doctrine (*dharma*) is a meticulous analysis of the state of the world, which is enunciated, in the first discourse of the Master at Benares, in the Four Noble Truths: (i) In the world everything is *duhkha*; (ii) *duhkha* is caused by desire (*trishnā*); (iii) this cause can be eliminated in nirvana; (iv) the remedy is found in the Eightfold Path. The meaning of *duhkha* is revealed only with "suffering" in its various psychophysical forms; in reality this is most often expressed in man's existential sphere by the sense of "passivity" (cf. Latin *pati*). *Duhkha*

comes to be tested out as privation of the unconditional activity of man and expresses the contingency thereof. The contrary term would be *sukha*, or absolute happiness, which is never realized in the human state except by illumination. Every being is composed of five aggregates (*skandha*): corporeality, sensation, perception, volition, knowledge; these are the ephemeral phenomena, in a state of continuous change (*samsāra*), impermanence (*anitya*), and lacking a nucleus of individuality (*anattā*, "non-being"). In contrast to Brahmanism, Buddha bases his teaching on just such a theory of nonsubstantiality, comparing the conventional concept of the human personality with the etiquette imposed in a purely functional way on the different parts that together form a cart. At the moment of death what remains is not a personal soul, which would be capable of transmigration, but only a series of aggregates that are continually fashioned afresh into new constellations. "The word is empty (*sunya*) of a self and of all that pertains to a self" (S IV.54).

The origin of these phenomena, however, must be linked to desire, to the thirst for life caused by the action of the passions. The chain of existence follows the eternal law of conditioned production (*pratitya-samutpāda*), according to which a number of factors give rise to a phenomenon, often illustrated by the analogy of the simultaneity of fire and smoke. From passion, composed of ignorance, desire, and self-centeredness, there flows in a cyclical fashion the action (*karman*) that leads to the production of aggregates or components that will constitute future generations. Because human beings inherit the fruits of their actions without ever being the masters of their activities, the whole of the Buddha's interest is directed toward a higher ethical conduct and, finally, at being able to finish the cycle of *samsāra*, to the elimination of all action. Inasmuch as *duhkha* constitutes the existential horizon of reality, its abolition (*nirvana* = extinction of every production) induces a state of ineffable tranquillity beyond the categories of this world. At the epistemological level the negative interpretation of nirvana is limited, while other texts (*It* 37) leave a positive concept of the character of uncaused Ultimate Reality. Rather than being a particular place, nirvana is a spiritual state that emerges once desire and suffering cease, leading to the overcoming of

what is illusory and contingent. The fourth Noble Truth presents the Eightfold Spiritual Path for the suppression of *duhkha* in the practice of moral rectitude, concentration, and wisdom. While morality reflects education in social behavior, meditative concentration induces peace of mind and places the human being in a position to act with benevolence, compassion, kindly joy, and fairness toward all other beings. Wisdom is the profound intuitive understanding of the essence of phenomena, i.e., the consciousness of their nonsubstantiality and of the law of conditioned production. This last attainment calls to mind the freedom-giving illumination mentioned above.

By concentric circles formed from monks, nuns, and laity, the *Sangha* unites the community by means of an attitude of reciprocal giving of material and spiritual goods. Because Buddhism is not organized in a hierarchical fashion, its doctrinal and social tradition has come to be guaranteed by the *Sangha*. From its very foundation, the monastic life has conserved a democratic structure, regular public confession, and the annual retreat. With the help of five precepts the laity are brought to free themselves spiritually from the world and to store up the merits of salvation. Their own particular ethic and form of worship fostered the emergence of the Mahāyāna.

4. The innovation of Mahāyāna is more a reelaboration of ideas contained in the Theravāda than a separate development. The popular need for an object of worship culminated in a progressive deification of the Buddha, and even to new sūtras. Sākyamuni is considered the historical manifestation of the transcendent Buddhas, such as Amitābha (Amida), which, being luminous and merciful, guide humanity with divine energy toward paradise. The doctrine of the "three bodies" (*Trikāya*) explains the absolute transcendence of the Ultimate Reality as an ungenerated and impersonal Buddha-like quality (*Dharmakāya*), perceptible only to a Buddha, and from which radiates the "body of reward" (*Sambhogakāya*), shown to the bodhisattva by means of the mystical vision. The final aspect of the unique Buddha is the historical Sākyamuni, who appeared in the "body of transformation" (*Nirmanakāya*) in order to save all beings. The ideal of the redemptive dynamic comes about in the figures

of the holy bodhisattva such as Mañjusrī and Avalokitesvara (the Lord with the kindly look; Japanese *Kwannon*), whose ascension into nirvana is deferred so that they may better exercise their "great compassion" (*mahākarunā*). In Japan, from the twelfth century, veneration and imitation of such altruistic figures found expression in the "Buddhism of faith" (*Jōdo Shin-shū*).

Like the moon, the image of which is reflected in the vast ocean as in a drop of water, the *Dharmakāya* is present in embryonic form in the "womb of Buddha-likeness" (*Tathāgata-garbha*) of individuals as also in the beginning of the cosmos. Its nature is *sūnyatā* (emptiness): everything exists only inasmuch as it is in communication with everything else. The existential interdependence of each phenomenon presupposes the emptiness of inherent existence and follows from the "law of conditioned production." The absolute identity of emptiness and form, intuited in meditation, changes human consciousness in a radical way and thrusts it into universal solidarity in the realization of compassion (*karunā*). Ontic non-substantiality and ethical altruism are complemented in the dynamic unity of the Ultimate Void, the highest symbol of which is the bodhisattva in his pro-existence.

5. The Second Vatican Council opened new perspectives for dialogue by the recognition of the presence of redemptive values in Buddhism (*NA*). This evaluation of the different currents within Buddhism is the culmination of a long history of encounters, beginning in the era of Clement of Alexandria (*Strom.* 1.15) and sporadically intensified during the age of the Nestorians (cf. the pillar of Xi'an Fu of 781), the missionary endeavors of the Franciscans in China (thirteenth–fourteenth centuries), and by Francis Xavier. While these first meetings revealed a rich literary witness in the parallelisms of the apocryphal Gospels and in the curious fact of the legend of the Buddha, christianized in Saints Barlaam and Josaphat (*PG* 96:857; in the Roman martyrology, 27 November), the encounters themselves point to the commitment to peace and justice in the world (WCRP: World Conference of Religions for Peace, founded in 1970, with the resolute participation of Buddhists and Christians), to mystical experience and the practice of medi-

tation, and to the exchanges of monastic life. Doctrinal dialogue values the existential depth of the journey of salvation in Buddhism. Buddha and Christ have been models because both are founders of revolutionary movements within the context of their respective religious traditions. Whereas Christ preaches salvation as the gift of the Father in the universal kingdom of God, the Buddha appears to refer humanity to the achievement of freedom through its own powers. Yet given the doctrine of non-being (*anattā*), even in Buddhism salvation is effected by the radical renunciation of self.

Meditation and the practice of compassion act as companions to humanity, together with the highest strengths of personal elevation, on the path to the threshold of the spontaneous gift of liberation. The extreme *kenōsis* of abandonment, both in Christianity (Lk 1:38) and in the holiness of Buddhism (*arhant; bodhisattva*), represents a fundamental point of contact. The peak of mystical experience, born of silence in Buddhism, and elsewhere taught in Christian theology, emerges as a point of challenge for dialogue. Today the focus of attention moves to the analogy between Mary and the Buddha, taking into account their shared human nature as opposed to the uniqueness of Christ's divine and human natures. Similarity and diversity between the two religions find expression in these two figures, inasmuch as both, in their great humility, conceive the Word. Whereas the Logos becomes definitively incarnate in Mary, in the sacred word of Buddha it remains *Dharma*. The divine veneration of the Buddha refers to his redemptive mediation and never to his nature, in contrast to that of Christ. Every dialogue, however, must begin from the fundamental qualification of the Sacred Scriptures and cannot ignore the mystical and mystagogical dimension.

Bibl.: Sources: *Canone Buddhista*, 2 vols. (Turin, 1967–68); E. CONZE, ed., *Buddhist Scriptures* (Baltimore, 1956); E. FROLA, trans., *L'orma della disciplina (Dhummapada)* (Turin, 1979); A. PASSI, trans., *Asvaghosa, Le Gesta del Buddha* (Milan, 1987).

Studies: H. OLDENBERG, *Buddha: Life, Doctrine, Community* (London, 1882); B. L. SUZUKI, *Mahayana Buddhism* (London, 1948); H. DE LUBAC, *Aspects of Buddhism* (1951; New York, 1954); id., *La rencontre du bouddhisme et de l'Occident* (Paris, 1952); E. LAMOTTE, *Histoire du Bouddhisme indien* (Louvain,

1958); H. Dumoulin, *Buddhism in the Modern World* (New York, 1976); H. Schumann, *Buddhismus: Stifter, Schule und Systeme* (Freiburg, 1976); Nyanaponika Thera, *Il cuore della meditazione buddhista* (Rome, 1978); A. Pezzali, *Storia del Buddhismo* (Bologne, 1983); H. C. Puech, ed., *Storia del Buddhismo* (Bari, 1984); W. Rahula, *L'insegnamento del Buddha* (Rome, 1984); E. Conze, *Breve storia del Buddhismo* (Milan, 1985); M. Zago, *La spiritualità buddhista* (Rome, 1986).

Dialogue: W. L. King, *Buddhism and Christianity* (London, 1963); H. Waldenfels, *Absolutes Nichts* (Freiburg, 1976); C. Geffré and M. Dhavamony, eds., *Buddhism and Christianity* (New York, 1979); M. Zago, *Buddhismo e Cristianesimo in dialogo* (Rome, 1985); M. Fuss, *Buddhavacana und Dei Verbum* (Leiden, 1989); P. Magnin, "Le vrai défi du bouddhisme à l'Occident chrétien," *Études* (mai 1992) 683–93.

Michael Fuss

BULTMANN, Rudolf

The article on methods of Gospel analysis offers an account of Bultmann's positive and undeniable contribution at a literary level. The work of form criticism (*Formgeschichte*), with Bultmann as one of its main protagonists, has been a major force behind exegesis. Form criticism, indeed, has furnished exegesis with a most precise analytical instrument for improved knowledge of the Gospels and their existential location (*Sitz im Leben*), or the environment in which they originated. But this methodological advance is matched by a doctrinal inadequacy too serious to overlook.

Rudolf Bultmann (1884–1976) was principally responsible for this lack. He was Professor of New Testament studies at Marburg (from 1921) and published works of exegesis, history of religion, and dogmatic theology. His interpretation of the NT, especially of the Gospels, of Jesus, and of his identity, message, mission, resurrection, and salvation has given rise to distortions. It is of interest to fundamental theology because of the influence it has exerted, and above all in order to show how philosophical and theological options can impair the quality of research even when its original intention was quite admirable.

In Bultmann we cannot separate historiography, hermeneutics, and theology. He confronts the Gospels as the heir of Strauss, Kähler, and Wrede, whose positions he radicalized. His hermeneutics and his "demythologization" of the NT owe much to Heidegger's existential analysis. Bultmann's theology depends on the Lutheran and Kierkegaardian paradox of faith conceived as a renunciation of all security and as an irrational "leap" within the enfolding acceptance of the God of salvation.

1. The Utopian Enterprise of History concerning Jesus

For Bultmann, Christianity began with *Christ as preached*, i.e., with the kerygma of the primitive church. This kerygma certainly assumes the historical existence of Jesus but shows no interest in that life as a chronicle. It is, however, interested in the *thatness* (the *Dass*) of Jesus' existence as the location of God's effective reply to human beings' question about the meaning of their existence. That Jesus was born, that he lived, that he was crucified, that he died—Christian faith needs no more than that: "facticity" is the sole necessary historical substrate of the event of faith and salvation. The *Was* (what)—i.e., the moral personality of Jesus—and the *Wie* (how)—i.e., his teaching, his message, and his action—are of no theological interest. "What happened in Jesus' heart [says Bultmann] I do not know and do not wish to know" (*Glauben und Verstehen* [Faith and Understanding] [Tübingen, 1933], 1:101, 251).

Bultmann, to be sure, does not deny the existence of a material and chronological continuity between Jesus of Nazareth and the Christ of the kerygma, but he proclaims a veritable break, an essential theological discontinuity, between Jesus and the Christ of faith. The following facts seem to indicate such a break: (a) instead of Jesus, the kerygma proposes the mythic figure of the Son of God; (b) whereas Jesus proclaims the imminence of the kingdom, the primitive church preaches Christ who died for our sins and rose again: the preacher is now the preached; (c) whereas Jesus speaks of unconditional obedience to the Father, the kerygma now speaks of obedience to the church.

For Bultmann, Jesus still belongs to Judaism. What, then, is the connection between Jesus and the church? Bultmann opines that the kerygma did not arise from the life of Jesus and that it does not depend on that life. The Synoptics do not try to legitimate the kerygma by means of history, but on the contrary to legitimate history by means of the kerygma: it is the latter which illumines everything and makes everything meaningful. Christian faith begins with the kerygma, which replaces the Jesus of history. It begins when he who preached is proclaimed as the eschatological action of God. Surely Paul constructed his theology without reference to the actual history of Jesus. In the failure of the prophet of Nazareth the kerygma sees God's reply to the human question. In the crucified, God utters a condemnation of human inadequacy and proclaims his will of forgiveness and authentic life for all those who accept that they must die to themselves. We may summarize this commentary by saying that Bultmann's approach to Jesus has two aspects: first, a radical critique which states that historiographical research regarding Jesus is an impossible, even illegitimate, enterprise; then, a demonstrably positive and creative aspect which seeks to replace historiography with a theology and a hermeneutics of the kerygma.

Bultmann thinks it is utopian to wish to write a life of Jesus—not only because Jesus wrote nothing but above all because the Gospels are primarily confessions of faith. Moreover, the image of Jesus that they put forward was considerably "mythized" by the primitive community. Bultmann expressed his skepticism in 1926, in his *Jesus* (London, 1934). That Jesus existed is beyond all doubt: he exercised his ministry as a rabbi and died under Pontius Pilate. But the Gospels mix historical and mythic elements so inextricably that it is impossible to detect a kernel of historical truth and a faithful succession of events. The Synoptics present Christ as the Son of God through the image of a Greek divinity. We can know almost nothing of the life and personality of Jesus because the Christian sources we know are very fragmentary, are permeated by legend, and show no interest in that point. Yet, even though we know very little about Jesus' life and personality, we know enough about his preaching to yield a consistent image of it. But here too the nature of the sources requires us to be exceptionally prudent. Before all else the sources offer us the preaching of the community, the greater part of which is attributed to

Jesus. Of course that does not mean that Jesus actually uttered all the words put in his mouth. In many cases we can even prove that they derive only from the community, or that it reworked them. The possibility of knowing what Jesus actually preached is therefore greater but "with a fairly relative coefficient of certainty" (*Jesus* [London, 1934]). In short, the Gospels arose from faith and have meaning for faith. They are a kerygma and not a chronicle.

2. A Theology of Kerygma and Faith

For Bultmann, faith has no justification apart from faith itself. What matters is the meaning of Jesus' existence, announced by the kerygma—that, as a result of their total reference to God through faith, human beings are saved. What lies behind or in front of the kerygma does not matter very much. Thus Bultmann proclaims his personal conviction that Jesus was not conscious of being the Messiah. But he also adds that, as far as his project is concerned, the question is not important, since recognition of Jesus as the one in whom the Word of God is realized decisively is a pure act of faith independent of the answer offered to the historical question of knowing whether Jesus thought he was the Messiah. Only the historian can answer this question, to the extent that an answer is possible; and faith, which is a personal decision, cannot depend on the historian's work. Faith, as a commitment of the whole person, has to free itself from the precarious nature of historical research.

In Bultmann, the historian and the theologian seem to coexist and to remain indifferent to one another. On the one hand, indeed, Bultmann in his *Jesus* and in his *History of the Synoptic Tradition*, studies the preaching of Jesus and tries to reconstitute it. On the other hand, the theologian seems to ignore his historical research. How are we to explain this kind of methodological dualism? Historical criticism surely has no purpose other than to demonstrate the impossibility of grounding the kerygma historically and thus of liberating faith from all human support.

Bultmann's indifference to the history of Jesus is attributable, so it seems, more to his theology of faith than to his historical skepticism. In fact, the historical interest in the prepaschal Jesus is not to be condemned in itself. This is clear from the fact that this was indeed a motive for Bultmann himself. But this interest must remain strictly within its due, that is, the *historical* order. As soon as a theological interest is added—i.e., a desire to legitimate kerygma and faith by means of historical maneuvers—the inquiry immediately becomes suspect. This kind of concern to legitimate faith annihilates faith. Any historical research behind the kergyma, any inquiry into the Jesus of the past, when inspired by an apologetic interest, must be sterile and must be disowned by believers, for it tempts us to rely on it. Authentic faith has nothing to do with historical knowledge, whether certain or probable. The kergyma bears its own credibility within itself. We need only be addressed for the possibility of faith to be assured. Therefore it is principally in the name of kergyma and faith that Bultmann denies the interest of the historical Jesus. Salvation does not come from objectifying and scientific knowledge, as if it were possible to appropriate God, but from *faith alone*. Bultmann's theology is therefore to be defined as a theology of kergyma and faith. The entire revelation event is concentrated in the kerygma and in the decision of faith in God, who calls upon and challenges us.

3. Necessary "Demythologization"

The kerygma comes first. But we must also add: on condition that, in its turn, it is subjected to a rigorous process of interpretation, for although the NT and its language could affect the people of the first century, they cannot elicit the decision of faith in contemporary men and women. Accordingly we have to *demythologize* the NT, i.e., to translate the message of Christ into a philosophical system intelligible to contemporary men and women. *Demythologization* poses the problem of the language of the NT with reference to the kerygma expressed through these data, whereas the problem of the historical Jesus is the problem of historical data concerning Jesus in relation to the Christ professed in faith as an eschatological event of salvation.

Myth, in the Bultmannian sense, speaks of the supernatural, divine, and transcendent world in terms of our spatial and temporal world. It describes the action of God in terms of historical, cosmological, and psychological causality. Bultmann says that he understands

myth in the sense in which it is used in the history of religion, where myth is any representation in which the noncosmic appears as cosmic, the divine appears human, and God himself appears as a far-off spatial being. Clearly this concept of myth is not to be confused with the modern sense of pure ideology.

It is clear that Bultmann sees the NT as a mythic universe, peopled with divine or demonic individuals, traversed by mysterious forces, and divided into spatial and temporal sectors. It describes Christ as a preexistent being, as the Son of God, incarnate in the womb of the Virgin Mary. When the NT speaks of the miracles of Jesus, of the transfiguration, of the resurrection, of Pentecost, it has recourse to mythical language. This way of speaking, Bultmann explains, betrays the influence of Hellenism, Gnosticism, and the Jewish apocalyptic tradition. Like the rationalists, we have to eradicate this way of talking. Above all, we have to reinterpret the evangelical narratives in terms adapted to modern human beings, particularly in the existentialist mode, on the model of Heidegger's philosophy. In this respect, those elements of the kerygma are important which have to do with our existence and our interpersonal relationship with God. Jesus above all has a value *indicative* of salvation, which we apprehend through faith. He is a great prophet but he is not the savior. He is rather the location chosen by God to proclaim salvation to us. Accordingly, the resurrection narrative does not refer us to the historical event of an actual corporeal resurrection but proclaims the meaning of the historical event of the cross. The cross of Jesus must be deciphered as a historical (*historisch*) and significant (*geschichtlich*) event, since it is only there that human beings feel the weight of their sin and the salvific judgment of God. The resurrection, on the other hand, is pure myth. The cross signifies judgment, the condemnation of the world, whereas the resurrection signifies the possibility of an authentic life bestowed on human beings as a result of obedience to faith. Accordingly, the resurrection forms part of the kerygma—not, like the cross, as a historical event that truly happened but as an announcement of our eschatological salvation. Bultmann says:

> Talking of Christ's resurrection amounts to nothing else than an expression of the meaning

of the cross. We must look on the death of Jesus Christ on the cross as a mere human death. It is God's judgment on the world. The cross and the resurrection make one whole, for together they are a single cosmic event, through which the world has been judged, and which has given us the possibility of authentic life. Jesus' resurrection cannot be a miracle which evokes faith, on the basis of which those who seek may quite securely believe in Christ. (R. Bultmann, "Nouveau Testament et mythologie" [New Testament and mythology], in Bultmann, _L'interprétation du N. T._ [The interpretation of the NT], ed. O. Laffoucrière [Paris, 1955], 177–78)

The salvific act does not occur through the freedom of Jesus. God uses the sad adventure of Jesus of Nazareth and his death on the cross to provide the effective symbol of salvation. Jesus' intention does not come into it. Salvation occurs only by means of a vertical event that tends toward our lives. This announcement was made first in the preaching of Jesus, but took its final form in the apostolic kerygma. This kerygma retains its power by virtue of the absolute event that was proclaimed for us once and for all in the historical event of Jesus of Nazareth. It was announced first in the preaching of Jesus but took its definitive form only in the apostolic kerygma. This kerygma remains up-to-date because of the preaching of the church. The kerygma tells us of the mystery of God which in the cross opens our eyes to our sinful condition, but simultaneously reveals his forgiving grace and henceforth offers us the chance to live from him and in him. Hence, Jesus is God's instrument, to some extent despite himself. Apart from the meaning bestowed on it by the kerygma, Jesus' earthly life and existence are of no interest.

In short, Bultmann's creed amounts to the following articles; Jesus is only a man; he is the last on the list of OT prophets. There is such a hiatus between kerygma and history that we know practically nothing of the life and personality of Jesus. The primitive church gave him the titles of Son of God and Savior, for "marketing" reasons—i.e., in order to allow him to compete with the Greek gods. When the NT speaks of miracles and of the resurrection of Jesus, it uses a mythic language, under the influence of Hellenism, Gnosticism, and Jewish apocalyptic, but the modern mind cannot accept the notion of a miracle or the resurrection of the dead. Finally, Jesus is in no way savior of humanity, redeemer of men and women, in the sense adumbrated by the present-day Catholic church, but merely the historical locus chosen by God in order to tell human beings about their salvation by faith.

Bibl.: R. BULTMANN, _Primitive Christianity in Its Contemporary Setting_ (1950; New York, 1956); id., _Theology of the New Testament_ (New York, 1951–55); id., _Das Verhältnis der urchristlichen Christusbotschaft zum historischen Jesus_ (Heidelberg, 1960); id., _History of the Synoptic Tradition_ (Oxford/New York, 1963); id., _Jesus Christ and Mythology_ (New York, 1956); id., _Faith and Understanding_ (New York, 1969).

Studies: L. MALEVEZ, _Le message chrétien et le mythe_ (Brussels/Bruges/Paris, 1954); R. MARLÉ, _Bultmann et l'interprétation du Nouveau Testament_ (Paris, 1956); A. MALET, _Mythos et Logos: La pensée de Rudolf Bultmann_ (Geneva, 1962); R. PALMER, _Hermeneutics_ (Evanston, 1969); R. RANDELLINI, "L'Ermeneutica esistenziale di R. Bultmann," _Atti della XXI Settimana biblica dell'Associazione biblica italiana_ (Brescia, 1972), 35–69; R. LATOURELLE, _Finding Jesus through the Gospels_ (New York, 1979); P. GRECH, "Ermeneutica," _Nuovo Dizionario di Teologia biblica_ (Milan, 1988), 464–89. → HERMENEUTICS.

René LATOURELLE

C

CALVINISM

Calvinism may be described as a network of systematic theological reflections upon the word of God (Sacred Scripture) as this is interpreted and proposed by John Calvin. Although all of Calvin's theological works should be studied to grasp the thoroughness and nuances of his thought, the classical source of his theology is his *Institutes of Christian Religion*, a work constantly revised by Calvin between its first edition in 1536 and its final edition in 1551.

John Calvin was born at Noyon in France on 10 July 1509. His father, Gerard Cauvin, was a notary and served as legal advisor to the Cathedral Chapter of Noyon. Little is known of his mother, Jeanne Le Franc, who died when John was about three years of age. Calvin's father was desirous that his son receive a university education, and so at the age of fourteen John was enrolled in the University of Paris in the Collège de la Marche. Here he was befriended by Mathurin Cordier, a priest noted for his interest in Latin and humanistic pursuits. The young Calvin soon transferred to the Collège de Montaigu in order to begin his theological studies. He studied under a certain John Major, who was known to be an advocate of nominalistic teachings. At this time he was influenced by the reformist thought of his cousin Pierre-Robert Olivetan. At the same Collège, Calvin began to study the works of Augustine and other early church fathers.

In 1528 Calvin received the master of arts degree and was directed by his father to begin the study of law at the University of Orleans. While at Orleans he became acquainted with the Lutheran professor Melchior Wolmar, with whom Calvin established a lifelong friendship. After his father's death in 1531, Calvin returned to Paris, where he continued his studies in Greek, Latin, and Hebrew. In late 1533 or early 1534 he underwent what he himself called a sudden conversion, which brought about his departure from the Catholic church. Unfortunately for posterity Calvin has left no detailed description of the internal and external factors that led him to embrace the fundamental principles of evangelical theology. But very probably his familiarity with Luther's teachings, the cruel treatment (imprisonment and death) of contemporaries who sought to reform the Catholic church, the superstitious practices that abounded in the church, and the worldly life of pope and bishops all moved him to look elsewhere for a purer expression of the Gospel.

Doctrines of Calvinism

Doctrine of God. In book 1, chapter 13 of his *Institutes* Calvin proposes the traditional doctrine of God as triune, explaining in orthodox fashion the distinction of the divine persons within the Trinity. The God of the Bible is eternal, merciful and just, omnipotent, etc., but the divine attribute especially stressed by Calvin is God's will. The latter is absolutely sovereign and is the foundation for all that exists: "For his will is, and rightly ought to be, the cause of all things that are. . . . When, therefore, one asks why God has so done, we must reply: because he has willed it" (*Inst.* 3.23.2).

While the created world and Sacred Scripture manifest that God is Creator, Scripture alone provides certitude that God is Redeemer (see *Inst.* 1.10.1; 2.9.1). While God is indeed transcendent and sovereign (a hidden God), he is likewise the one who reveals himself to the elect as merciful and who embraces the latter with the righteousness and saving benefits of Christ (*Inst.* 1.17.2; 3.24.5).

Christology. Calvin teaches that Jesus Christ is true God and true man who became incarnate for the sole purpose of our redemption. Calvin especially stresses Christ's role as mediator. In so doing he teaches that Christ as mediator must be fully divine and fully human: "In short, since neither as God alone could he feel death, nor as man alone could he overcome it, he coupled human nature with divine that to atone for sin he might submit the weakness of the one to death; and that, wrestling with death by the power of the other nature, he might win victory for us" (*Inst.* 2.12.3). The reconciliation between God and humanity is accomplished in and through Christ's death and resurrection:

> We have in his death the complete fulfillment of salvation, for through it we are reconciled to

God, his righteous judgment is satisfied, the curse is removed, and the penalty paid in full. Nevertheless, we are said to "have been born anew to a living hope" not through his death but "through his resurrection" (I Peter 1:3). For as he, in rising again, came forth victor over death, so the victory of our faith over death lies in his resurrection alone. (*Inst.* 2.16.13)

Pneumatology. Calvin employs many NT passages that attest to the divinity of the Holy Spirit. He likewise defends the Spirit's divinity on the basis of his role in creation: "For it is the Spirit who, everywhere diffused, sustains all things, causes them to grow, and quickens them in heaven and in earth. Because he is circumscribed by no limits, he is excepted from the category of creatures; but in transfusing into all things his energy, and breathing into them essence, life, and movement, he is indeed plainly divine" (*Inst.* 1.13.14).

In addition to the Holy Spirit's activity in creation and providence, the Spirit likewise guarantees the inspiration of God's word, makes that word fruitful in the heart of the believer, and applies to the believer the benefits of Christ's salvific work.

Sacred Scripture. According to Calvin both the Old and New Testaments are inspired by the Holy Spirit and have as their focal point the person of Christ: "The Scriptures should be read with a view to finding Christ in them" (*Commentary on St. John* 5.38, 39). As God's word, then, the Scriptures communicate to the believer both Jesus himself and his gift of salvation. The latter is appropriated through the gift of faith, which is conferred by the Holy Spirit, a gift that opens the believer's heart to Scripture's saving truth: "For as God alone is a fit witness of himself in his Word, so also the Word will not find acceptance in men's hearts before it is sealed by the inward testimony of the Spirit" (*Inst.* 1.7.4). For Calvin, God's word, the faith of the believer, and the action of the Holy Spirit must be held together in an indissoluble unity.

Church and sacraments. For Calvin the true universal church consists of all the redeemed of all times and places, and this church is invisible. Its members are the elect of God, and these latter are known only to God himself.

This one church also has a visible aspect and "designates the whole multitude of men spread over the earth who profess to worship one God and Christ" (*Inst.* 4.1.7). Within this community exist both saints and sinners. In agreement with Luther, Calvin affirms that this church of God can be recognized or is present (1) where the word of God is purely preached and heard and (2) where the sacraments are administered according to Christ's institution (*Inst.* 4.1.9).

The sacraments referred to by Calvin are baptism and Eucharist, instituted by Christ according to the testimony of the NT. They are instruments of the Holy Spirit and serve to make more concrete and visible the very word of God: "Therefore, let it be regarded as a settled principle that the sacraments have the same office as the Word of God: to offer and set forth Christ to us, and in him the treasures of heavenly grace. But they avail and profit nothing unless received in faith" (*Inst.* 4.14.17). Thus through baptism persons of faith are assured that their sins are remitted in the sense that sinfulness will not be imputed to them; and they are confirmed in faith that they exist as ones reborn into Christ (*Inst.* 4.15.6). In the Lord's Supper Christ is communicated to the believer in the signs of bread and wine, which while remaining the same effect in the worthy recipient "redemption, righteousness, sanctification, and eternal life, and all the other benefits Christ gives to us" (*Inst.* 4.17.11).

Doctrine of the human person. Prior to receiving the gift of faith, the human person belongs to the *massa damnata* and under the weight of original sin stands condemned and convicted before God (see *Inst.* 2.1.8). Original sin corrupts every part of the human person and brings forth further fruits of sin, which Calvin calls, following Paul, "works of the flesh" (Gal 5:19). In this condition the human person is incapable of initiating any activity that might lead to restoration of friendship with God. While unregenerate human remains at an infinite distance from God, Calvin does allow that one can, by the use of one's reason, order "earthly things" and thus contribute to good government, the advance of science, and the progress of the liberal arts (see *Inst.* 2.2.13).

Faith in Christ. The human person is delivered from the sinful condition through the gift of faith. Faith alone justifies and has as its object the embracing of Christ "clad in his own promises" (*Inst.* 2.9.3). In similar fashion Calvin explains: "We say that faith justifies, not because it merits righteousness for us by its own worth, but because it is an instrument whereby we obtain free the righteousness of Christ" (*Inst.* 3.18.8). This justifying faith does not render one sinless, but it does establish a new relationship between God and the believer. In this new relationship God as Judge does not impute human sinfulness to the person but rather imputes or reckons to that person the righteousness of Christ.

Concomitant with justification is sanctification, which Calvin attests to quite clearly in the following way:

> Why, then, are we justified by faith? Because by faith we grasp Christ's righteousness, by which alone we are reconciled to God. Yet you could not grasp this without at the same time grasping sanctification also. For he "is given unto us for righteousness, wisdom, sanctification, and redemption" (I Cor. 1:30). Therefore Christ justifies no one whom he does not at the same time sanctify. (*Inst.* 3.16.1)

This sanctification is to find expression in both the life of the believer and in that of society at large, so that all of human life might be an on-going hymn to God's glory.

Predestination. Since God's will is the cause of all things, it is likewise the cause of salvation and reprobation. "We call predestination God's eternal decree, by which he compacted with himself what he willed to become of each man. For all are not created in equal condition; rather, eternal life is foreordained for some, eternal damnation for others" (*Inst.* 3.21.5). By his doctrine of double predestination Calvin maintains both God's sovereignty and the human's total inability to achieve his or her own salvation. The latter rests solely in God's decree (will) and is the result of neither good works nor of the so-called merits gained via good works. Ultimately predestination is veiled in mystery. With faith, affirms Calvin, we must see God's decree of reprobation as just and as manifesting his glory (see *Inst.* 3.21.7).

John Calvin's doctrinal positions as outlined above were destined to undergo variation and modification when confronted with subsequent intellectual, cultural, and historical factors. A number of the Genevan scholar's teachings would be modified by such movements as Protestant orthodoxy, pietism, the rationalism of the Enlightenment, the rise of liberal Protestant theology, and so on. In recent decades the influence of Karl Barth and ecumenical dialogues have succeeded in reviving interest in Calvin's theological positions concerning the sovereignty and glory of God and the centrality of God's Word for the ordering of theology and Christian life.

Bibl.: J. Calvin, *Institutes of the Christian Religion*, ed. J. T. McNeill, 2 vols. (Philadelphia, 1960); J. K. S. Reid, ed., *Calvin: Theological Treatises* (Philadelphia, 1954); J. T. McNeill, *The History and Character of Calvinism* (New York, 1973); T. H. L. Parker, *John Calvin: A Biography* (London, 1975); B. A. Gerrish, *The Old Protestantism and the New: Essays on the Reformation Heritage* (Chicago, 1982); W. J. Bouwsma, *John Calvin: A Sixteenth Century Portrait* (New York, 1988).

Kevin McMorrow, S.A.

CANON OF SCRIPTURE

Paul wrote in large letters in Gal 6:14–16 about the rule (Gr. *kanon*) of those living under God's peace and mercy: the cross, freedom from the legal requirement of circumcision, and being a new creation in Christ. Thus a "canon" comprises what is normative and of criteriological relevance for Christian discourse and behavior. In the eventual development of Christian vocabulary in patristic times, the term "canon" came to stand for the official list of the books of Scripture that give authoritative testimony to God's revelation.

1. Conceptual Clarification

In its root sense the Greek term *kanon* refers to a stiff rod or ruler used by a carpenter or stonemason to ascertain whether he has assembled certain building materials in a level or straight manner. In the transferred sense, a canon is a standard or norm by which one judges correct thinking or teaching. In art and literature, scholars of the Hellenistic age drew up lists of those ancient works of exemplary form and linguistic style to which canonical status as models was ascribed.

In early Christian usage, the core of the transmitted apostolic teaching was the "canon of truth" (→ RULE OF FAITH) which provided a normative context for theological speculation (Clement of Alexandria, Origen) and served as a critical test by which to show that Marcionite and gnostic teachings were deviant and to be excluded (Tertullian, Irenaeus). After 300 C.E. the doctrinal and disciplinary provisions of episcopal synods were the "canons" which regulate church teaching and life.

The application of the term "canon" to the church's Scriptures is, in fact, a linguistic usage in which one term conveys two overlapping meanings. Athanasius wrote in 351 that *The Shepherd* of Hermas "is not in the canon" (*PG* 25:448). The same writer's Festal Letter of 367 catalogues the books of both the Old and New Testaments which are included in the now completed and closed canon (*ta kanonizomena*), in opposition to the apocryphal books not so included (*CSCO* 151:34–37). Thus, the canon is the complete list or index of the sacred books constituting the Bible of the church.

However, a different shade of meaning appears when Christians make reference to "the canonical Scriptures." Thomas Aquinas says that sacred doctrine uses the canonical Scriptures as its proper and genuine source of data and probative evidence. The reason is that "our faith is based on the revelation made to the Apostles and Prophets, who composed the canonical Scriptures" (*ST* I, 1, 8). Thus, the books of the canon are uniquely authoritative. Augustine venerated the books now termed "canonical" to the extent of firmly believing that none of the authors ever swerved in the least from the truth (*Ep.* 82.3; *CSEL* 34/2:354). In book 2 of *De doctrina christiana* (428), Augustine listed the canonical Scriptures of the churches and then added that these works provided quite sufficient guidance and nourishment for the whole Christian life of faith, hope, and charity ("In things openly declared by the Scriptures, we find everything concerning faith and morals, viz., hope and charity" [*CSEL* 80:42]).

The Christian canon of Scripture is, first, the complete enumeration of those books which the church officially receives as part of its foundation as a community of faith. But as canonical, these books then serve as the prophetic and apostolic norm or standard of what is proper and legitimate in the transmission of revealed truth and in shaping Christian lives.

Canonicity, however, is not simply identical with INSPIRATION. Faith acknowledges the canonical books as inspired, but of itself the canon does not exclude the possibility that other writings, not now recognized as canonical, could have been composed with the Spirit's charismatic assistance and guidance. Furthermore, inclusion in the canon is not a determination of literary *authenticity*, that is, of actual composition by the one named as author of the work. The canonicity of a biblical work is quite compatible with the work's being *pseudonymous* in origin. For example, the epistles to Timothy and Titus, as works included in the NT canon are thereby guaranteed to convey normative apostolic traditions of doctrine and church order. But canonical status does not preclude the possibility that these works were written not by the apostle Paul but by another author, who reformulated Pauline tradition for the situation of churches a quarter century after the death of Paul.

2. The Christian Old Testament Canon

In Judaism down to ca. 100 C.E., there was a solid core of authoritative books, divided into Torah, prophecy, and "other writings" (Sir, Prologue). The first two parts were closed collections at the time of Jesus, whereas the number of books in the third part of the Jewish Scriptures appears to have been considered differently by different groups (Sadducees, Pharisees, Essenes, Samaritans, diaspora Jews). But after the traumatic events of 70 C.E., with the destruction of the Temple, the Pharisees' conception of inspiration and canon prevailed in reconstituted Judaism. The prophetic charism of inspiration was held to have ceased in the fifth century B.C.E., and absolute authority for synagogue worship and teaching was ascribed to a closed canon of twenty-two books. These included the preeminent five books of Moses, twelve books of prophecy (both prophetic history from Joshua through Job and Ezra-Nehemiah as well as the prophetic books of Isaiah, Jeremiah-Lamentations, Ezekiel, Daniel, and the one book of the twelve minor prophets), and just five other writings (Esther, Psalms, Proverbs, Qoheleth, and the Song of Songs).

The complex history of the Christian reception of Israel's Scriptures has been studied from a variety of perspectives by A. C. Sundberg, H. von Campenhausen, R. A. Greer, R. Beckwith, and numerous others. In our exposition, we pass over Jesus' own view of the Scriptures of Israel and the apostolic church's extremely fruitful rereading of them in the light of the Christ-event and its own universal mission.

The definite closing of the Jewish canon had no immediate impact on the Christians of the second and third centuries. However, a development of major significance was the wide-ranging reaction in the church against Marcion's contestation of any relevance for Christians of the Scriptures of Israel. Justin Martyr, Irenaeus, Origen, and others mounted a major didactic campaign in defense of the OT as indispensable for Christians because of its wealth of instruction on the economy of salvation devised and carried out in history by the one God who is both Lord of Israel and the Father of Jesus Christ.

Eventually the issue of the material extension of the Christian OT emerged, specifically in the discussion concerning the status of certain books not included in the Jewish canon: Tobit, Judith, 1–2 Maccabees, Wisdom, Sirach, Baruch, and parts of Daniel (3:25–90, chaps. 13–14). These works are now called *deuterocanonical* in Catholic parlance, but are listed among the *apocrypha*, or noncanonical books, by most Protestants.

Some church writers in the East held that the Christian OT should be restricted to only those books used by their Jewish contemporaries. Origen knew that some Christian churches made catechetical use of Tobit, and Athanasius saw the deuterocanonical books as instructive in godly living; but for these fathers, and for Cyril of Jerusalem, the Christian canon did not include these works. Jerome, after moving to Palestine, became a convinced defender of the restricted canon of books originally composed in Hebrew, and he translated Tobit for the Latin Vulgate only under episcopal mandate. In the West, however, Augustine was an incisive defender of the larger canon, appealing to the use of the deuterocanonical books in the liturgy of numerous churches and arguing in detail for

their beneficial contribution to both doctrine and piety. Canons of Scripture issued by the councils of Hippo (393 C.E.) and Carthage (397) gave official sanction to the extended canon, which Pope Innocent I confirmed in 405 (DS 213).

The authority of Augustine, combined with that of the church of Rome, assured the inclusion of the deuterocanonical books in the Christian OT of late antiquity and the Middle Ages. But the Protestant Reformation challenged this situation of peaceful possession. In Luther's Leipzig Disputation of 1519 against Johann Eck, the Wittenberg reformer raised doubts about the theological use of 1–2 Maccabees to justify prayer, offerings, and indulgences for the souls in purgatory. The authority of Jerome figured prominently in a broader Protestant case against the seven deuterocanonical books, an argument given more systematic form by Luther's colleague Andreas Karlstadt in *De canonicis scripturis libellus* (1521). In their vernacular Bibles, both Luther and Zwingli had the contested books printed in an appendix, but the Calvinist editions expelled these works completely from the Bible.

Catholic controversialist writers, such as Johann Cochlaeus and Johann Dietenberger, argued on behalf of the canonicity of the disputed books, on the basis of the number and authority of their ancient defenders and the tradition of their use in the church. When the Council of Trent began its work in December 1545, early discussions showed that most of the bishops wanted to simply receive and solemnly promulgate the canon that had been presented by the Council of Florence a century before in its reunion negotiations with the Jacobite or Coptic Christians of Ethiopia (DS 1334–35). Jerome Seripando, the Augustinian Superior General, argued for admitting some differentiation within the OT, e.g., between books canonical for grounding matters of faith and others belonging to a *canon morum*, but an overwhelming majority objected to even discussing the content of the canon. Thus, at Trent's fourth session (8 April 1546), the council promulgated its *Decretum de libris sacris et traditionibus recipiendis*, which includes a formal espousal of the deuterocanonical books as part of the inspired and normative books of the OT (DS 1502).

3. The New Testament Canon

The canon of Christian apostolic writings was formulated over time through a gradual sifting and separation of certain books out of a larger body of early Christian literature. Numerous processes of this selection of normative works remain historically obscure, as do many of the norms and motives brought to bear on decisions concerning particular books. Although the process was well advanced by 200 C.E., another century and a half passed before the NT canon had the exact shape we know today.

The Christian communities of apostolic foundation had from the beginning a set of canonical writings taken over from Judaism, even if the outer boundaries of this collection were not a matter of early consensus. Furthermore, these communities had the authoritative words and deeds of Jesus, which were being passed on orally as a tradition superior to Israel's Scriptures and normative for their interpretation. Even before the traditions deriving from Jesus were set down in writing, some of the earliest communities also had valued letters of apostolic pastoral instruction which served both to recall the original preached gospel and to spell out its implications for worship and everyday life.

Second Peter, written ca. 100 C.E., gives witness to the existence in one area of the church of a *corpus Paulinum*, which stands on the same level as "the other Scriptures" (3:15–16). But even though the literature of 100–150 C.E. is rife with echoes of writings eventually included in the NT canon, most writers of the period seem to draw more on the ongoing oral transmission of Jesus' words and of apostolic instruction. In mid-century Tatian used the four Gospels as a quarry from which he took materials for his written harmony, the *Diatessaron*, which itself was widely used for two centuries in the churches of Syria. Tatian shows that the four Gospels were highly esteemed about 150 C.E., but also that their compositional shape did not yet have canonical status in the churches.

Two factors stimulated the formulation of a NT canon in the later second century. Marcion's radically Pauline notion of gracious salvation in Christ led to his establishing a small canon of authentic Christian instruction, consisting of ten letters of Paul and a version of Luke's Gospel purified of all references to the God of Moses. Second-century Gnosticism, however, moved in a direction opposed to Marcion. Its teachers, who often claimed to have instructions transmitted from secret meetings with the risen Jesus, were prolific in producing new gospels and letters of alleged dominical and apostolic origin. A group of representatives of the great churches, among whom Irenaeus of Lyons stands out, subjected both Marcionite and gnostic teachings to withering criticism and thus established the conditions in which a Christian canon could be articulated. This would include a fuller range of apostolic works than Marcion admitted, while sifting out and stamping as spurious the works of gnostic provenance.

Striking documentation of Christian canon formation in the late second century is given by the Muratorian Fragment (for the Latin text, see *EB*, 1–3; French translation available in A. Paul, *L'Inspiration et le Canon des Ecritures*, Cahiers évangile 49 [Paris, 1984], 42–43). Generally considered to reflect convictions held in Rome around 200 C.E., the Fragment sustains the normative character of just four Gospels, Acts of the Apostles, and thirteen Pauline and three other apostolic letters. John's Apocalypse is canonical, but beside it stands an apocalypse of Peter, deemed by some to be inappropriate for reading in church. Strangely, Solomon's book of Wisdom is accepted as Christian, while there is no mention of Hebrews, 1–2 Peter, James, and 3 John. The Fragment expresses strong convictions about excluding from Christian usage two letters infected with Marcion's ideas and certain unnamed works of the gnostic masters. The author recommends private reading of *The Pastor* of Hermas, while denying it a place in liturgical readings. Thus, by the year 200 C.E., a strong sense of having a canonical apostolic patrimony was present in at least one church, where definite criteria were being applied in order to show the canonicity of works received as fundamental for the life of the whole church.

From centers such as the one that produced the Muratorian "canon" there then radiated into numerous other churches a new clarity about the set of apostolic books that were foundational in an exclusive manner for Christianity. However, one century later, Eusebius relates that certain discrepancies still exist between the official lists of NT books used in the different churches. Some deny the canonicity of James, 2 Peter, Jude, and 2–3 John, and John's Apocalypse is also a subject of debate (*Ecclesiastical History* 3.25; *GCS* 9/1:250–53). Obscurity shrouds the way in which the canonicity of the Catholic letters and the Apocalypse came to be widely established. The earliest extant NT canon that conformed to all later usage is in Athanasius's Festal Letter of 367, which sought to impose a certain uniformity on the lectionaries of the Egyptian churches and to rule out use of gnostic gospels and apocalypses. The Western canons of Hippo (393), Carthage (397), and Pope Innocent (405) agreed with Athanasius in listing twenty-seven books, which together and exclusively make up the NT of the Christian churches.

4. Theological Significance of the Canon

The canon of Scripture serves to identify and delimit for believers a set of works received and read as "word of God," i.e., as conveying in written form a reliable precipitate of the experiences of chosen mediators of God's self-communication in history and personal enlightenment. Scripture evolves from what Moses wrote on Sinai (Ex 34:28), what Yahweh's prophets were sent to proclaim (Am 7:15; Is 6:8f.), and what the disciples of Jesus heard, saw, remembered, and recounted concerning the Word of life (1 Jn 1:1–3). Theological reflection on a closed and normative canon occurs in two general areas: (1) the relationship between canon and church, and (2) the hermeneutical relevance of the canon.

1. Sociologically, canon formation is a step toward standardizing doctrine and stabilizing community norms. The canon draws a precise borderline around a body of literature uniquely expressing the identity that a given community has by derivation from its foundation. This restrictive effect, however, is only one side of canon formation. For the canon also serves to identify those works which one fully expects to be truthful and instructive, with power to instill a vitality and life-style conformed to the community's authentic vision of itself (see 2 Tm 3:16f.). The canonical Scriptures, therefore, are an indispensable means by which "the Church, in her doctrine, life, and worship, perpetuates and transmits to every generation all that she herself is, all that she believes" (*DV* 8.1).

A somewhat sophistic Enlightenment argument claims to expose a vicious circle in the church that, on the one hand, asserts its derivation from the prophets and apostles, as they are known through their writings, and, on the other hand, arrogates to itself the legitimation of the Scriptures by its promulgation of their canon. This, however, is to misconstrue the nature of the Christian canon. Early on, Christians of the apostolic age simply found themselves in possession of Israel's Scriptures, which upon rereading proved to say much about Jesus (see Lk 24:44). In the second century, the four-Gospel collection quickly imposed itself, in spite of the overlap and discrepancies between the different Gospels. In the same period, the collected letters of Paul the apostle were simply assumed to be authoritative without question or discussion, as was such a central letter of apostolic instruction as 1 John. At the center, the church did not confer canonical status on its scriptures.

The further steps leading to the final canon then involved interventions by numerous churchmen, that is, by pastors who selected liturgical readings, by theologians who criticized works lacking genuineness, and by bishops who individually or in synod promulgated canons. But these actions do not *constitute* the authority of the books so "canonized."

A theological understanding of the canon can best be shown by noting its affinity to the DEPOSIT resulting from the many-sided apostolic ministry of preaching, instruction, and organization—with ample use of Moses, prophets, and Psalms—in the earliest churches. The late letters of the NT witness to the perception that the results of this ministry form an identifiable whole which is now complete. The canon of the NT recognizes that the same is true of those written works which faithfully express "the faith that was once for all entrusted to the saints" (Jude 3). Churchmen articulated with increasing precision the outer limits of this apostolic transmission, as they marked the historical point at which the privileged and truly founding communication of the apostles with the churches came to an end. The Christian OT canon emerged from an analogous process of recognition of those works which fitted harmoniously into the life, teaching, and worship deriving from Jesus the Christ and his apostles.

It is commonplace to list three factors as the criteria that figured centrally in the church's formation of the Christian biblical canon. These are the orthodox RULE OF FAITH, apostolicity, and continuous usage in worship. There is more than just a modicum of evidence for such an account, but the evidence is scattered and incomplete.

Irenaeus and the Muratorian Fragment argue from the tradition—i.e., the transmitted faith of the church—in their rejection of Marcionite and gnostic literature from further Christian consideration. The works they attack undermine faith in "God the Father almighty, Creator of heaven and earth," and they waffle on the enfleshed presence of God's Son in a fully human life and death. But, on the other hand, the central NT writings themselves had contributed much to solidifying these tenets of the ecclesial "canon of truth." It would be misleading to think that the RULE OF FAITH was applied to the canonical books from the outside. Tradition and Scripture, from the beginning, were coinherent with each other.

Apostolic provenance was decisive for the eventual inclusion in the canon of the "Catholic epistles" we know today. But then we are often constrained by exegetical evidence to see these letters as containing apostolic tradition rather than direct apostolic utterance. The criterion of apostolicity seems, in fact, to enshrine the church's acknowledgment of the unique and limited time-span in which its foundation was completed by the teaching ministry of the apostles and their close associates.

Usage in the liturgy did give Augustine persuasive arguments on behalf of the deuterocanonical books of the OT. But it is also true that certain books presently not in the canon had limited careers of liturgical usage, e.g., *1 Clement*, the *Diatessaron*, and *The Pastor*, which the Muratorian Fragment and Athanasius take pains to rule out. Liturgical use is a necessary precondition for inclusion, but of itself it did not suffice to settle disputed cases. In each critical advance toward the full canon, problems were resolved by a unique configuration of considerations and norms which came together in ways we can recover only partially and approximately.

What stands out is that church people of the early patristic age knew where their faith and life had come from. Consequently they took great pains to keep in contact with the foundational events, teachings, and personages of Christianity through the documents that had been transmitted. These documents remain canonical for the church in every age, because they serve to make the church "apostolic," as the creed professes that it is and will remain. Today, because of this canonicity, "it follows that all the preaching of the Church, as indeed the entire Christian religion, should be nourished and ruled by sacred Scripture" (*DV* 21).

2. The canon gives Christians a precise listing of the books they should always be reading and interpreting in order to deepen their own authenticity and to apply God's word to the changing circumstances of their lives. But questions arise concerning the proper contribution of the canon to the ongoing project of biblical interpretation, whether this be homiletic, scholarly, or doctrinal.

(a) The Christian canon has a peculiar shape, in linking together the books of God's prior covenant with Israel and the books directly relating to Jesus. This canonical configuration seems profoundly normative for all Christian thinking, as expressed in the suggestive title of the book by D. L. Baker, *Two Testaments, One Bible*, and as set forth in recent writings by L. Sabourin, P. Grelot, P.-M. Beaude, and H. Simian Yofre.

The cross and resurrection of the Christ of Israel, together with the universal mission embraced by his followers, combine to place the earlier revelatory experiences of Israel in a new context of fulfillment and amplification. But the new framework of understanding and the new inclusiveness do not sever Christian faith and life from their roots in Israel. Integral thinking by Christians, and specifically any biblical theology worthy of the name, must draw on the precious patrimony received from Israel. Christian preaching and teaching have a peculiar dynamic of movement from promise to fulfillment and have repeatedly been fructified by the recovery of forgotten themes of the prior covenant, such as God's benign intent toward all creation (Gn 9:8–17) and the identity of the church as preformed in the elect people ever moving in God-given freedom through the vicissitudes of life in this world (*LG* 9).

The two-part Christian canon is profoundly relevant for interpretation, while any species of recrudescent Marcionism is life-threatening for Christian theology and preaching.

(*b*) A recent wave of writing in North America, especially by B. Childs and J. A. Sanders, is urging that certain principles of "canonical criticism" become normative in biblical interpretation.

The canonical critics assert first that interpretation must focus on the final "canonical shape" of the Bible and of each biblical book. Historical-critical exegesis has too often featured hypothetical reconstructions of earlier strata of tradition and of precanonical editorial influences on the genesis of the biblical text. Exegetes often delight in isolating additions, reformulations, and rearrangements that change or even misunderstand the original stock of narrative or teaching. The danger here is that a precanonical unit is taken as normative, while later additions, which now form part of the canonical text, are devalued as secondary accretions. Canonical criticism insists that exegesis seek above all to grasp and explain the final form of the biblical texts. Interpretation should seek to recover what was communicated to the community of faith by the final redactor of the texts as we have them now.

If earlier strata are identified in the final text, canonical criticism urges that they be seen and explained, not just historically but precisely as canonical discourse. This is to see particular traditions in relation to the situations which they address in a normative manner. The traditions that survived to be included in the final text had already proved themselves in their canonicity, i.e., their experienced religious normativity for those who articulated and received them. Interpretation should bring out just how passages gave guidance and inspiration in the situation of their formulation.

On the level of our two testaments in their respective entirety, canonically oriented interpretation concerns itself with the innerbiblical relatedness of often quite diverse works included in the canon. One thinks of the contrary tendencies of works like Isaiah and Qoheleth, or of

Galatians and 1 Timothy. The canonical collections have united these works in the same Bible, in an apparent openness both to a diversity that manifests the richness of revelation and to a dynamic of mutual correction in opposition to the dominance of any single line of teaching.

Numerous practitioners of other modes of exegesis have reviewed negatively the works in which the canonical critics set forth their program. Still, their work is not without theological relevance, both because of their emphasis on the final text, which is surely the inspired text, and on the values for religious practice that all parts of Scripture manifested on their way to inclusion in the canon. The contemporary mind will remain, quite rightly, committed to explanation in terms of genetic development, but with the Bible it is right to urge constant attention to the religious actuality of the texts that proved normative, or canonical, in particular settings.

(*c*) Moving in a direction contrary to that of the canonical critics, a group of continental European theologians urge the importance of establishing a "canon within the canon," both as religiously beneficial and doctrinally necessary.

In this proposal, expounded by writers such as W. Marxsen, E. Käsemann, and I. Lønning, there is some influence of Lutheran hermeneutics, but the main motivation arises from the modern perception of striking diversities between the doctrinal and ecclesiological outlooks of different NT authors. This pluralism, in which these authors find some incompatible opposites, constrains the interpreter to find a standard of normative teaching by which to distinguish between what is authoritative in the NT and what is not such, because of its discrepancy from the truly canonical center of our collection of first-century Christian writings. Paul's eschatology is in disaccord with that of Luke-Acts, and Jesus' words on the required accomplishment of every "jot and tittle" of the Law (Mt 5:18) clash with Paul's programmatic declaration that Christ is "the end of the Law" (Rom 10:4). Close reading of the NT yields the imperative that one find a doctrinal core and thereby marginalize the portions of the collection that do not fit with the truly canonical center.

Strong opposition to a canon within the canon has been voiced—and not just by Catholics, who see the NT church developing toward the form it takes in "early Catholic" documents such as Luke-Acts and the Pastoral Epistles. Also, Protestant authors such as K. Stendahl, E. Best, and B. Metzger insist on the rich fruitfulness found in the very diversity of NT teaching. The canonical collection is pluralistic in content, but as a consequence the churches are provided with an abundance of texts and doctrines that prove relevant to the needs and challenges of vastly diverse cultures.

Opponents of a canon within the canon see the tensions present in the NT as due to the different situations in which Jesus and his apostles brought the message of salvation to bear on the lives of believers in quite different first-century situations. The selection of a normative center is not necessarily arbitrary and subjective, but by tending to focus on a particularly "up-to-date" message it runs the risk of soon becoming "out-of-date." The canon protects believers from extremes in the quest of relevance, while setting the limits of what is acceptable. The canon is ecumenically indispensable, since it keeps communities from lightly questioning the Christian legitimacy of other communities. In the end, the NT canon is the first instance of the ideal of unity in reconciled diversity.

Still, a personal and confessional set of priorities within the canonical collection seems inevitable. Jesus himself summed up the whole of the Torah in just two commandments, and Paul declared that the promise to Abraham in Gn 12:3 stands above the Law given on Sinai (Gal 3:7-22). One can admit that individuals and communities will have something like a *hierarchia librorum* ("hierarchy of books"), similar to the *hierarchia veritatum* ("hierarchy of truths") of *UR* 11. But the key to thinking and living in full accord with the Scriptures is to remain ever ready to hear the word of God, even when it sounds forth with its uncanny impact from places in Scripture which one might for a time take to be the outer ranges of the canonical collection.

Bibl.: P. G. DUNKER, "The Canon of the Old Testament at the Council of Trent," *CBQ* 15 (1953): 277–99; A. C. SUNDBERG, *The Old Testament of the Early Church* (Cambridge, Mass., 1964); W. MARXSEN, *Das Neue Testament als Buch der Kirche* (Gütersloh, 1966; E. KÄSEMANN, *Das Neue Testament als Kanon* (Göttingen, 1970); H. VON CAMPENHAUSEN, *La formation de la Bible chrétienne* (Paris, 1971); I. LØNNING, *Kanon im Kanon* (Oslo/Munich, 1972); D. L. BAKER, *Two Testaments, One Bible* (Leicester, 1976); E. BEST, "Scripture, Tradition, and the Canon of the New Testament," *BJRL* 61 (1979): 258–89; T. CITRINI, "Il problema del canone biblico: un capitolo di teologia fondamentale," *La Scuola cattolica* 10 (1979): 549–90; B. CHILDS, *Introduction to the Old Testament as Scripture* (Philadelphia/London, 1979); id., *The New Testament as Canon: An Introduction* (Philadelphia/London, 1985); L. SABOURIN, *The Bible and Christ: The Unity of the Two Testaments* (New York, 1980); P.-M. BEAUDE, *L'accomplissement des Écritures* (Paris, 1980); P. GRELOT, "Relations between the Old and New Testament in Jesus Christ," in R. LATOURELLE and G. O'COLLINS, eds., *Problems and Perspectives of Fundamental Theology* (New York, 1982), 186–205; K. STENDAHL, "One Canon is Enough," in *Meanings: The Bible as Document and Guide* (Philadelphia, 1982), 55–68; J.-D. KAESTLI and O. WERMELINGER, eds., *Le canon de l'Ancien Testament, sa formation et son histoire* (Geneva, 1984); J. A. SANDERS, *Canon and Community: A Guide to Canonical Criticism* (Philadelphia, 1984); R. BECKWITH, *The Old Testament Canon of the New Testament Church* (London, 1985); H. GAMBLE, *The New Testament Canon: Its Making and Meaning* (Philadelphia, 1985); R. A. GREER, "The Christian Transformation of the Hebrew Scriptures," in J. L. KUGEL, ed., *Early Biblical Interpretation* (Philadelphia, 1986); H. SIMIAN YOFRE, "Old and New Testament: Participation and Analogy," in R. LATOURELLE, ed., *Vatican II: Assessment and Perspectives Twenty-five Years After* (New York, 1989), 1:267–98; B. METZGER, *The Canon of the New Testament: Its Origin, Development and Significance* (Oxford, 1987).

Jared WICKS

CERTITUDE

An examination of our experiences of knowledge and certainty may yield the following distinctions.

Certainty is a *conviction* regarding the "truth" of this or that knowledge—that is, the fact that the content of our perceptions, images, or forms of understanding of things accords with those things themselves. Observably, in modern times the main concern of knowledge is not so much to attain to those things themselves, as to reach the point that our *certainties* should not manifest any kind of error or illusion. We acknowledge the fact that certain more or less troublesome doubts can accompany our convictions, but we recognize at the same time that certainty means an absence of grave or overwhelming doubt.

Certainty, therefore, is to be contrasted with mere *opinion*—that is, a matter of perceiving, conceiving, or understanding things whose truth is only probable or plausible. We recognize that "certainty" about such matters might well be subject to error or illusion. In other words, opinion can always be accompanied by doubts. At best it is a conscious form of conjecture, to be contrasted with conscious certainty.

For many contemporary thinkers, knowledge must be accompanied by conscious certainty, and even by a certainty based on wholly irrefutable reasons ("objective" certainty), if it is to be properly considered authentic knowledge. If the certainty is compelling or very strong—and therefore free from all factual doubt—but is in no way based on conscious and compelling reasons (a wholly "subjective" certainty), we would have not knowledge but mere "irrational" *belief*. Such an opinion lacks the recognition that its conviction could be illusory and therefore that it might indeed not be *knowledge*.

While requiring that "authentic" knowledge be accompanied by a certainty based on reasons, several contemporary scholars, in the absence of wholly compelling reasons, are content with reasons that are at least "sufficient"— that is, capable of "justifying" the fact that a conviction one has experienced is free from errors or illusions. Should not we ask, however, whether the certainty concerning the very sufficiency of the reasons finally perceived to be "sufficiently" convincing might not be, in its turn, the certainty of a mere unjustified "irrational" belief and, in accordance with the requirement in question, might contain no authentic knowledge?

It might be suggested that this demand for a certainty arising from compelling, or truly sufficient, reasons is in fact unrealizable and that it requires the imposition of too strict limitations on the possibilities of knowledge. For it is possible to distinguish immediate and direct knowledge (by way of "intuition" or "feeling") from knowledge by "representation" (a cognitive, mediated apprehension of the thing itself). But such a requirement would imply that there was knowledge by means of representation only

if one *knew* that the actual representation in fact accorded, or at least was equivalent to, the things or facts that it represented. But that is impossible. The most there could be would be *belief* in this accordance, or in a "sufficient" degree of accordance.

It should also be noted that in any field, people generally end up *believing* (perhaps unconsciously but with certainty) in the "cognitive equivalence" of numerous sensible or conceptual representations. This is true even of a scientist or a thinker who may be very attentive to certainties established on the basis of the strongest reasons. Belief may be supported by a very conscious wish, especially in the case of a belief that one would personally prefer to another, for particular reasons. Even in the sciences, there are a great many more instances of knowledge by means of representation, and therefore of beliefs, than there are examples of direct knowledge without belief—that is, of forms of knowledge imposed by evident intuitions or by wholly compelling "feelings."

The certainty of all forms of knowledge by means of representation and belief would be wholly illusory, in fact, if this kind of knowledge were never, at the same time, *direct* knowledge of unperceived realities. But that is often the case. When, indeed, one tries to picture something, the fact is that one has no actual apprehension of what, precisely, that reality is, nor of its precise constituents. One nevertheless knows that there is something there to conceive of, or to conceive of somewhat more effectively. One already has some knowledge of the fact that a certain reality exists, which one would like to grasp more effectively and know better. But if one is also aware that the constitution and actual conditions of that reality will never be *directly* known, and therefore that one will never be able to reach (duly grounded) certainty such that our representations of it accord with it so closely as to rule out any possibility of illusion, then one must revise one's conception of the role of our "representations." In many cases, of course, we do not expect our representations to operate as a description of what we might know of the internal constitution of that reality.

Furthermore, though not descriptive of things actually perceived, our representations—our images and our concepts—often help us to acquire a more conscious and more vital direct knowledge of realities that we have already observed, and to establish or to maintain closer relations between the knower and certain types of reality that are known in this way. Moreover, certainty about truly knowing (and acceding to) the reality itself is thereby both more effectively based and enhanced. If belief still enters in, it is not because there is no (direct) knowledge of the reality itself but because there is awareness that the actual nature of reality thus known is in some way lacking in clear and total apprehension. When, moreover, awareness of these imperfections evokes unease and doubt regarding the actual nature or the very existence of the reality in view, it often happens that a sudden exertion of belief is sufficient to reestablish certainty and thus to prompt a recovery and improvement of cognitive apprehension.

A first example will serve to illustrate the foregoing. Theoretical physicists—who seek only to *know* the world better—agree that the theory of subatomic particles is not (and cannot be) a representation that accords with unperceived reality. But this representation nevertheless enables them to maintain and to reaffirm their *cognitive* apprehension in a field of reality which they do not see directly, although certain of its sensible manifestations they have learned to recognize. Although researchers sometimes admit that they can only *believe* in the existence of this area of reality that they cannot see, that does not imply that they do not *know* that it exists (and know nothing of its reality itself). Rather it would imply that they know perfectly well that their representations are not descriptions that more or less approximate to the real thing in question, whose particular individual constitution and actual conditions of existence (or activity) they do not apprehend. In other words, this "belief" does not amount to a denial of the fact that there is *cognitive* apprehension of the reality itself.

A second example is drawn from more general experience. It sometimes happens that one person (M) may know that another person (N) is behaving toward M, at that moment, in a way that would be termed "kindly," and that, in spite of all arguments for determinism, M is not confronted with a mere robot. Because M does not *see* this attitude itself or anything in N that is directing it toward him, M might say that he only *believes* in the actual existence of this attitude, or in the fact that M is dealing here

with something other than a mere robot. Certain more or less pictured, more or less consistent, "representations" accompany the certainty that M has that he is not deceiving himself; but M could see that, even if they were not descriptions of realities that he attains by means of his knowledge, they nevertheless constitute indispensable aids to—though sometimes harmful distractions from—better *cognitive* apprehension of this actual reality.

We may note finally that in certain areas—that of human relations, for instance, or of religious faith—knowledge accompanied by "representations" and beliefs happens to impose personal and free choices. What happens, in fact, is that one inevitably must choose between two beliefs—that of trying to maintain (or improve) cognitive apprehension of an imperfectly known reality, or that of favoring instead an interruption of that same apprehension. When this concerns the very person of another, or the existence of God, we understand that the choice has a more particular meaning. It may mean, indeed, that one wishes to take (or not to take) a *personal* interest in another. It may mean that, of one's own free choice, one wants to believe—in the hope of knowing or more effectively apprehending the other. Alternatively, one may choose to cease believing thus, in order to break off all personal contact with a reality of *this* kind.

The problem of certainty, and of the various forms of knowledge and belief it accompanies, can arise just as readily in the realm of (ordinary or scientific) secular belief as in that of religious faith. In both cases, there are realities that are apprehended and known, but imperfectly. As Paul observed (1 Cor 13:12), we know these realities but only see them "in a mirror, dimly."

Gilles LANE

CHARISM

Because the term "charism" is part of the vocabulary of the NT, it is necessary to begin our study by examining the texts that contain this term in order to expound the theological question of charisms.

1. *Charisma* is a Greek substantive derived from the verb *charizesthai*, which means "to show oneself agreeably," "to do a favor." The suffix *-ma* indicates the effect of the action (e.g., *ktisma*, "creature"=the effect of *ktizein*, "to create"). The meaning of *charisma* is thus "generous gift." The term is not met in classical Greek and occurs only a few times in Greek papyri; it is found in two variants of Sirach (7:33 Sinaiticus; 38:30 Vaticanus) and in two passages in Philo, with the sense of "gift." However, it is found with greater frequency in the NT: sixteen times in the letters of Paul (Rom, 6 times; 1 Cor, 7 times; once each in 2 Cor, 1 Tm, and 2 Tm) and once in 1 Pt 4:10.

2. An initial problem with regard to a possible technical meaning of *charisma* in these texts is that one notices a certain specialization. The term is always found in a theological context; it never designates a gift given by one person to another, but always a divine gift. More often *charisma* is linked to the grace (*charis*) of God: Rom 5:15–16; 12:6; 1 Cor 1:4–7; 1 Pt 4:10. In this context, however, *charisma* retains its general meaning in a number of texts and cannot be translated as "charism"—which has a technical meaning—but must be rendered as "generous gift." This is the case in Rom 5:15–16, where redemption is described, and in Rom 6:23, where it is applied to eternal life, "the generous gift of God." In 2 Cor 1:11 *charisma* refers to an occasional favor of God, liberation from danger of death, graces received by the prayers of the community. Thus the meaning does not correspond to what we mean by "charism."

In other texts, however, the word is applied to a more specific reality, viz., to certain gifts of grace, which are not part of the fundamental graces essential for all but come to be distributed according to the omnipotence of God. "We have *gifts* (*charismata*) that differ according to the grace given to us" (Rom 12:6). "Each has a particular *gift* (*charisma*) from God, one having one kind and another a different kind" (1 Cor 7:7). Peter speaks in terms of a "*manifold* grace of God" (1 Pt 4:10).

Some texts offer a list of such "gifts" without ever pretending that it is complete. In the list given in 1 Cor 12:8–10, Paul places at its head a number of rather modest gifts ("a word of wisdom," "a word of knowledge"), proceeds to more impressive ones ("gifts of healing," "powerful works"), and finishes with the sensational gifts of prophecy" and "every sort of tongue," which disturb the assembled community (cf. 14:26). The distribution of all these gifts is attributed to "one and the same Spirit" (12:11). A little farther on (12:28) Paul no longer refers to the Spirit but attributes everything to God and presents a different list, which begins with a hierarchy of positions (God has given primacy of place in the church to apostles; in the second place are prophets; in third place are teachers) and continues with different gifts ("then miracles, then gifts of healing, help, guidance, different tongues"). In yet another list (Rom 12:6–8) Paul omits all reference to speaking in tongues, to healings, and to other miracles; he gives first place to prophecy and goes on to name only everyday activities of value to the life of the church: service or ministry, teaching, exhortation, works of charity, oversight, and mercy. In a more schematic way, Peter mentions but two major categories, that of service and that of the word (1 Pt 4:10). Two texts in the Pastoral Epistles speak of *charisma* in relation to pastoral ministry and specify that it is a question of a gift received through imposition of hands (1 Tm 4:14; 2 Tm 1:6).

The textual differences that have been noted demonstrate the fact that the term *charisma* did not have, even in the NT, the technical meaning that came to be given to "charism" in later theology. On the contrary, G. W. H. Lampe's *Patristic Greek Lexicon* reveals that not even in the Greek patristic texts did the term have a specialized meaning; in fact, its applications show greatest variety: the Holy Spirit is called *charisma*, likewise baptism, the Eucharist, the priesthood, forgiveness of sins, chastity, and, naturally, prophecy, miracles, and so on.

3. Nevertheless, it is still possible to look for the origin of the theological concept of "charism" in a number of NT texts. To tell the truth, in Latin theology the concept has been elaborated from certain texts, because the word *charisma* does not occur in the Latin Bible, except in one rather insignificant passage (1 Cor 12:31: "Aemulamini charismata meliora"). In the other passages the Vulgate does not render *charisma* in a uniform way, but by three different terms: *gratia* ("grace," eleven times),

donum ("gift," three times), and *donatio* ("donation," twice). For this reason Latin theology in the Middle Ages did not use the term "charism" but, inspired above all by 1 Cor 12:4–11, it spoke of particular "graces." A distinction came to be drawn between the *gratia gratum faciens* ("grace making gracious"), which, sanctifying the soul, rendered it favorable to God, and the *gratiae gratis datae* ("freely giving graces"), supernatural gifts that did not of themselves have this interior effect (*ST* I, II, 3, 1). Thomas Aquinas saw in 1 Cor 12:8–10 a complete and systematic list of these *gratis datae* graces (*ST* I, II, 3, 4). He gives full consideration to them in II, IIae 171–78, where he distinguishes the gifts that relate to knowledge (prophecy, faith, wisdom, discernment of spirits, knowledge) and those that relate to speech (the gift of tongues and *gratia sermonis*) and to action (the gift of miracles).

In order to define the scope of the *gratis date* graces, Thomas reiterates the assurance given in 1 Cor 12:7: "To each is given the manifestation of the Spirit *for usefulness*," but completing it with the sense of usefulness *for others: ad utilitatem, scil. aliorum.* Grace *gratis data* is a grace "through which a man helps the other to turn to God" (I, II, 3, 1, "Reply"; art. 4, "Reply"). This opinion has become the traditional one, and the translators introduced it into the text of 1 Cor 12:7, where they speak of "common" usefulness. But Paul did not write "common," and the way in which he then expresses himself with regard to tongues shows that the usefulness of certain gifts can be brought to perfection not by being shared but only in terms of being personal: "Those who speak in a tongue build up themselves. . . . [I]f I come to you speaking in tongues, how will I benefit you?" (1 Cor 14:4–6). Paul shows great regard for the gift of tongues (14:5, 8), but does not consider it to be of common usefulness; for this reason he does not permit its manifestation in the Christian assembly, except in cases where there is an interpreter who can reveal the meaning (14:27–28). To be faithful to Pauline teaching, it is thus necessary to abandon the restrictive definition which limits the range of charisms or graces *gratis date* to utility in an altruistic sense. In fact, useful charisms are frequently to be seen in, e.g., personal prayer or personal growth in the virtues.

Having said this, it is necessary to recognize that the majority of the gifts listed by Paul are useful in terms of the community, and that Peter invites each of the faithful to place the gifts of grace he or she has received at the service of others (1 Pt 4:10). On the other hand, it is possible that a grace *gratis data* is in no way useful to the one who has received it, but only to other people. However, this does not correspond to God's intentions; it happens on account of the sin of the individual. In Matthew's Gospel some very severe words are directed by Jesus to certain leading "charismatics," who had worked many wonders and who had even cast out demons in his name yet had not been receptive to God in a personal sense; these people will be rejected by the Lord, those "evildoers" (Mt 7:21–23). Paul takes an analogous view when he points out that without charity, the most striking gifts do not have the least usefulness for those who exercise them (1 Cor 13:1–3). Charismatic activity by itself does not offer the least guarantee of an authentic relationship with Christ and with God.

4. In more recent times the term *charisma* has entered the theological vocabulary of the Latin church. The Second Vatican Council adopted it fourteen times in its official texts. On the other hand, the question of charismatic gifts has acquired a new relevance with the appearance of pentecostal and charismatic movements. The pentecostal movement, characterized above all by the phenomenon of tongues (*glossolalia*), began in a Methodist church in Kansas on 1 January 1901 and then spread to the rest of the United States and to Europe (Scandinavia, Great Britain, and Germany). Its excesses provoked strong opposition (see *Die Berliner Erklärung* of 1909) but that did not stop it. The movement entered the Catholic church after the council, beginning in 1967; the first Catholic charismatic manifestations took place in the United States in Pittsburgh, Pennsylvania. The movement spread very quickly. In 1975 an international congress met in Rome, with ten thousand participants drawn from more than sixty countries.

5. During the council a very lively debate had contrasted two concepts of charism: charism as an extraordinary, miraculous gift granted by God in an exceptional fashion; and charism as

a gift of grace even in an ordinary sense and granted by God for the upbuilding of the ecclesial community. Cardinal Ruffini defended the first concept, which was considered "traditional," while Cardinal Suenens supported the second (see *Acta Synodalia Vaticani II* [Vatican City, 1972], II–III, 175–78). In the end, the position taken by Suenens prevailed, and a text on charisms was adopted by the council in the paragraph that deals with the "prophetic" office of the People of God (*LG* 12). Charisms are defined as "special graces" that the Holy Spirit "dispenses among Christians of every rank" and "with which they are fitted and made ready to assume various works and offices, for the renewal and greater upbuilding of the Church." The council specifies that the charisms can be quite spectacular, or else simpler and more diffused ("Quae charismata, sive clarissima, sive etiam simpliciora et latius diffusa"). With this definition the council refused to restrict the concept of charism to extraordinary and miraculous gifts but also applied it to more modest and less rare gifts, such as those listed in Rom 12:6–8. In his speech, Cardinal Suenens had spoken of people "endowed by the Holy Spirit with different charisms in the field of catechesis, evangelization, various forms of apostolic action, social works and charitable activities." It would be possible to add further examples.

6. Inspired by the theological distinction between *gratia gratum faciens* and *gratiae gratis datae*, the council presents charisms as functional gifts that render the faithful of every rank "fitted and made ready to assume various works and offices" for the good of the church (*LG* 12). These utterances highlight the relationship between charisms and ministries, which remains a controversial point. At the end of the nineteenth century A. Harnack proposed the distinction between two types of ministry in the primitive church, viz., the charismatic and the administrative (*Die Lehre der zwölf Aposteln* [Leipzig, 1884], 96ff.; *Das Wesen des Christentums* [Leipzig, 1900], 129). He gave preference to the charismatic ministries. Others of a more radical stance asserted that the church, in the beginning, was solely charismatic and had then lost its authentic nature, becoming a juridical institution. The discussion continues. In his article "Amt und Gemeinde,"

E. Käsemann argues that Paul "has contrasted his doctrine of the charisms with the idea of institutionally-guaranteed office" (in *Exegetische Versuche und Besinnungen* [Göttingen, 1960], 1:126). Inspired by this article, H. Küng describes the community at Corinth as a clear example of "charismatic organization," the expression of the "Pauline constitution of the Church." By this example he seeks to base his thesis on the "charismatic structure of the Church" (1965: 43–59; French ed.; *L'Église* [Paris, 1968], 248–64, 556–58).

In actual fact, this thesis is inconsistent. It demonstrates Paul's attitude when he addresses the charismatics at Corinth. In fact, the apostle does not permit free development of individual charisms but imposes strict and detailed rules on those same charismatics (1 Cor 14:27–29). Far from expressing a contrast between inspiration and institution, Paul declares in the same breath that God has established a hierarchy of positions and a multiplicity of gifts in the church (1 Cor 12:28). For this reason the article on *charisma* in the *GLNT* quite rightly concludes that "the celebrated distinction between the charismatics and the authority of the church does not hold up" (9:396), and in *DBS*, E. Cothenet remarks that "to oppose charism and hierarchy means to depart from Pauline categories" (8:1302).

It is certainly possible to distinguish institutional and charismatic aspects within the church, but it is not possible to separate completely these different aspects, still less to pretend that they are incompatible. The church is the body of Christ and, as such, the temple of the Holy Spirit. The institutional dimension of the body "is joined and knit together by every ligament with which it is equipped" (Eph 4:16; cf. 2:20–21) and is the concrete condition of authentic communion "in the Spirit" (Eph 2:22). The church thus has a charismatic-institutional structure, formed by means of the sacraments, in which institution and grace are closely united by virtue of the mystery of the incarnation.

The charisms of the lay faithful are rooted in baptism and confirmation, even if they are not necessary effects of these sacraments, but depend on the free initiative of the Spirit received through them. The pastoral charisms have as their source presbyteral or episcopal ordination, as attested to in two passages from the Pastoral Epistles (1 Tm 4:14; 2 Tm 1:6).

When the council declares that "the Spirit instructs and directs the Church with different hierarchical and charismatic gifts" (*LG* 4), it purposely avoids the error of an interpretation that separates the two categories; in fact, the hierarchical gifts are usually accompanied by various charismatic gifts which make the pastors "fitted and ready to assume" their ecclesial responsibilities in a personal, spiritual fashion. The lay faithful receive other charisms, which make them fit and ready to render other forms of service in the church and in the world.

Naturally, the council guards against saying that a definite gift gives the right to a corresponding ministry. To adopt such a thesis, based on the notion of "charismatic structure," would be to generate total confusion in the church, leaving the field open to all those who are ambitious and enlightened, to the detriment of the true faithful. Yet as Paul says, "God is a God not of disorder but of peace" (1 Cor 14:33). Put this way, the practice of the church, encouraged by the council, is to welcome the different charisms "with gratitude and consolation," and to take great care when admitting candidates for ordination and the conferring of ministries.

7. The teaching and the practice of Paul show that the fact of having received some particular gift does not dispense one from the duty of submission to the pastors of the church. The authentic recipient of a charism is not obstinately fixed in the subjective conviction of his or her own inspiration but remains open to other manifestations of God's will. In particular, recipients of charisms accept gracefully the expression of the Lord's will that comes to them by means of the authority of the church (see 1 Cor 14:37). With regard to "extraordinary" charisms, the council states: "Those who have charge over the Church should judge the genuineness and proper use of these gifts, through their office not indeed to extinguish the Spirit, but to test all things and hold fast to what is good (cf. 1 Thes 5:12 and 19–21)" (*LG* 12).

A relatively frequent application of this norm concerns the charism of visionaries who claim to be favored with special revelations (→ REVELATIONS, PRIVATE). Another application relates to the charism of founders of new institutes of consecrated life.

A particular feature of this second kind of charism, obviously not attested in the NT, is its influence among numerous people over long periods of time. In fact, the spiritual and apostolic orientation received from the founder communicates itself to the members of the institute. With regard to the renewal of religious life, the council has established as normative "the continual return . . . to the original inspiration of the institutes" and the fidelity of each religious family to the "spirit of the founders" (*PC* 2). To these different spiritualities, the council applies the Pauline expressions that contain the term *charisma* and act as a foundation for the theology of the charisms (Rom 12:5–8 and 1 Cor 12:4, cited in *PC* 8). The concept of charism thus moves from an individual sense (see 1 Cor 12:7–10: "to one . . . to another . . . etc.") to a communitarian sense and acquires the possibility of an indefinite duration, attached to an institution. Faithful to the teaching of the council, the new Code of Canon Law, promulgated in 1983, in a like manner applies to institutes of consecrated life the phrase in Rom 12:6 on the diversity of charisms and requires from the members of every single institute fidelity to the spirit of the founder (CCL cc. 577–78). In this way a fundamental agreement is reached between juridical norms and charismatic inspirations, corresponding to the charismatic-institutional structure of the church.

Nevertheless, a fundamental agreement does not mean the absence of concrete, and sometimes very acute, problems. It is inevitable that in the church there are often signs of tension between the institutional aspects, which are more or less fixed, and the charismatic impulses, which are to a greater or lesser degree authentic. Yet it is a question of a tension necessary to the life of the church. The solution to problems requires careful discernment and genuine effort at mutual acceptance in receptivity to the revelation of Christ and the dynamism of the Spirit.

Bibl.: E. KÄSEMANN, "Ministry and Community in the New Testament," in *Essays on New Testament Themes* (Naperville, Ill., 1963), 63–94; H. KÜNG, "The Charismatic Structure of the Church," *Conc* 4 (1965): 41–61; id., *The Church* (New York, 1967); M.-A. CHEVALLIER, *Esprit de Dieu, paroles d'hommes: Le rôle de l'Esprit dans les ministères de la parole selon l'apôtre Paul* (Neuchâtel/Paris, 1966); G. HASENHÜTTL,

Charism (Freiburg, 1969); U. BROCKHAUS, *Charisma und Amt: Die paulinische Charismenlehre auf dem Hintergrund frühchristlichen Gemeindefunktionen* (Wuppertal, 1972); H. CONZELMANN, "χάρισμα," *TDNT* 9:402–6; D. GRASSO, *Il carisma della profezia* (Rome, 1978); id., *I carismi nella Chiesa* (Brescia, 1982); S. LYONNET, "Agapé et charismes selon 1 Cor 12,31," in L. DE LORENZI, ed., *Paul de Tarse* (Rome, 1979), 509–27; J. SANCHEZ BOSCH, "Le Corps du Christ et les charismes dans l'épître aux Romains," in L. DE LORENZI, ed., *Dimensions de la vie chrétienne (Rm 12–13)* (Rome, 1979), 51–72; id., "La primera lista de carismas (1 Cor 12,8-10)," in *El misterio de la Palabra* (Fs. L Alonso Schökel; Madrid, 1983), 327–50; V. SCIPPA, *La glossolalia nel Nuovo Testamento* (Naples, 1982); F. A. SULLIVAN, *Charisms and Charismatic Renewal* (Ann Arbor, Mich., 1982); var., *Carisma e Istituzione: Lo Spirito interroga i religiosi* (Rome, 1983); L. DE LORENZI, ed., *Charisma und Agape (1 Ko 12–14)* (Rome, 1983); O. KNOCH, "Charisma und Amt: Ordnungs-elemente der Kirche Christi," *SNTU* 8 (1983): 124–61; N. BAUMERT, "Charisma und Amt bei Paulus," in A. VANHOYE, ed., *L'apôtre Paul* (Louvain, 1986), 203–28; id., "Zur Semantik von charisma bei den frühen Vätern," *TP* 63 (1988): 60–78; id., "The Biblical Question of 'Charisms' after Vatican II," in R. LATOURELLE, ed., *Vatican II: Assessment and Perspectives Twenty-five Years After*, 3 vols. (New York, 1989), 1:439–68; W. E. MILLS, ed., *Speaking in Tongues: A Guide to Research on Glossolalia* (Grand Rapids, 1986).

Albert VANHOYE

CHRISTOLOGY

I. FUNDAMENTAL CHRISTOLOGY

At the base and heart of any theology is the profession of faith: "Jesus is Lord" (Rom 10:9; Phil 2:11). The reflection of the Christian community has used this Christocentrism as an epistemological principle of learning and belief, and it has been transmitted without interruption to the critical conscience of contemporary believers.

Christology is the reflection, explanation, and communication of faith, and must be considered the pivot of all theological research. It has been thus since the beginning, when, through homological, nominal, and verbal formulas, the Christian community expressed in both the kerygma and the liturgy the mystery of Jesus of Nazareth in his relationship with his Father and the ancient promises ("You are the Messiah, the Son of the living God," Mt 16:16), the unequivocal explanation of the significant events of his life ("While we were still sinners Christ died for us," Rom 5:8; "God raised him from the dead," Rom 10:9).

The theology of the fathers was influenced by the various challenges that were encountered by faith, and these ranged from philosophy to a more directly political impact; it finally reached the great christological syntheses which in turn found their highest and most prescriptive expression in the dogmatic formulations of various councils.

Furthermore, the great masters of the Middle Ages had already allowed a glimpse of the relationships developing between Christology and the mystery of the Christian life: the sins committed by humanity (→ ANSELM), the sacraments (Abelard) and the plan of salvation (→ THOMAS AQUINAS). Subsequent theology was to lay itself open to other interpretations dictated by the "schools" of Molina and Suarez before finally condensing into manualistic theology (→ THEOLOGY II: EPISTEMOLOGY), and the latter managed to keep the product of christological reflection almost unchanged until Vatican II.

The council invited theology to find the basis and spirit of its research in the Scriptures (*DV* 24) and identified a further interpretative principle to be adopted: the centrality of the Gospels in that "they are the principal witness of the life and teaching" of the Lord (*DV* 18).

In fact, it was Vatican II, and particularly *DEI VERBUM*, that was the point of departure for a renewal of Christology. The presenting of revelation within Jesus of Nazareth's historical authenticity made it possible to rediscover proofs that the metaphysical emphasis on textbook learning had caused us to forget.

In other words, the re-proposing of the *person* of Jesus of Nazareth in the *historical* development of his existence enables theology not only to place Christology once again in the center of its research (after decades of church-centrism) but also to rediscover the biblical, patristic, and genuinely Thomist proofs that have characterized the life of faith for at least twelve centuries. Thus, the re-proposed centrality of Christology has made it possible to exploit to the full those themes which enable faith to present itself as having global significance for today. With so many perspectives to choose from, that of Jesus' historical authenticity together with his uniqueness and universal importance and redeeming powers is the most relevant.

There is another reversal that has become all the more evident as modern christological texts are compared with christological textbooks in use before Vatican II: that is the theological problem of a Christology that, because of its varied methodological instruments and the complexity of its themes, can claim that a systematic reading requires an interdisciplinarity.

Without doubt, one of the more positive results of Vatican II's theology is the awareness of the need for a systematic and interdisciplinary approach to the study of Christology. A systematic study is well capable of organizing all the critical knowledge around the person of Jesus of Nazareth, starting from the a priori position of faith concerning the fullness of the mystery that is realized within it.

Jesus of Nazareth constitutes that indissoluble center which, on the one hand, is the unmistakable Word of God addressed to humanity. On the other hand, Jesus is a sign that there can be no separation between his historical reality and his embodiment of salvation, the ultimate end of human existence (→ CREDIBILITY).

While systematic learning facilitates the organization of information for maintaining thematic unity, interdisciplinarity makes it possible, through diverse methods and approaches, for the same content to be researched and analyzed under more specific perspectives.

All disciplines must refer prescriptively to the Scriptures (in our case, the Gospels) so that research can be organized for a better comprehension of the revealed fact. Moreover, each discipline will find its own methods and aims, which will enable it to invest a given text with the truth that it already contains. In these circumstances, there are two elements: that of the text, which has to be prescriptive so that it can be expressed truthfully, and that of the theologian-exegete, who, by bringing the information up to date, develops his or her own creative role in respect of the text.

Biblical theology will have a perspective that is more closely linked to the demands of its exegetic and interpretative aims. Through an analysis of the various strata of *Traditionsgeschichte*, it will try to establish the basic level of the written text so that it will lead to Jesus of Nazareth. In this way, it will seek to produce results which will show what the Scriptures really mean but which, given the universal synchrony and diachrony of the languages, can also be seen as an exegesis according to the *sensus plenior* (*DV* 12). *Sensus plenior* alone can give the exegesis the power to recognize the specific character of the scriptural text.

Dogmatic theology, on the other hand, will broaden its horizon of research by concentrating specifically on the content and role of tradition. The figure of Jesus of Nazareth, reached through exegesis, will be studied within the prescriptive interpretation that the church's faith has developed over the centuries. The seven "christological" councils, with the statement of Chalcedon in the center, will make it possible to see the unity of the Christian faith intact before any of the schisms; in the context of interpreting dogma these councils will be essential for presenting christological faith to the contemporary reader.

Moral theology, which starts out from the

person of Christ, who, since the time of his historical existence, has been calling everyone to follow him, will also find that Christology is the basis of morality. It will take the form of a vocational call, which, together with the gift of grace and freedom of choice, makes one's personal existence to be fully realized.

The person of Christ will therefore be studied in the light of salvation as the archetype offered to each one of us and as the image to strive toward as a logical fulfillment of oneself within the context of daily life.

One further ingredient needs to be included in this interdisciplinary study, and that is fundamental theological research. This will be identified schematically in the following survey of five aims:

1. Historical Authenticity

The history of fundamental theology makes it possible to understand what losing sight of the historical dimension really means. The christological influence that can be measured in the textbooks clearly highlights the shortcomings that have developed over the last few decades. Christology, which is limited almost completely to the tract *De Legato divino*, underlined *de testimonio Jesu circa seipsum* ("the testimony of Jesus concerning himself" by means of a methodology in which the proofs for historical authenticity had been supplied from without and were therefore running the risk of outside influence. What emerged from the apologetic analysis was a historical-positivist reading.

The program for recovering historical authenticity is in three parts:

a. Access to sources. There is a two-pronged criticism of NT sources. The first is that of BULTMANN, who saw the Gospels as documents of faith and came to the conclusion that there could not possibly be consistent historical evidence; the second is that of Kierkegaard, who appealed to the radicalness of faith, which gives rise to obedience and therefore has no need of history. With these two criticisms overcome, fundamental theology can today demonstrate that the only viable approach is the one that keeps fidelity to history and interpretation of faith close together.

By passing exegetically through the various stages of *Traditionsgeschichte* and integrating information that comes from sources outside the Bible, fundamental theology manages to present results that incontrovertibly help to form the basic, historical figure of Jesus, which that faith has resolutely respected and preserved ever since. It is in this context that phrases, including *gestis verbisque* ("deeds and words") (*DV* 2), which make up the historical figure of Jesus, are analyzed. The most important features of this reconstruction are the annunciation of the KINGDOM OF GOD, the use of parables, the radicalness of the call, the miracles, and the prophetic statements.

b. Historical authenticity is a reminder also of Jesus' awareness of his person and his vision of the world: this is something that is frequently undervalued because of a tendency to overvalue the interpretation of the faith. Just as we all look at ourselves in order to understand ourselves and determine our future, so Jesus of Nazareth thought about and planned his historical existence. It is this self-awareness that has to emerge from evangelical sources because it was the earliest testimony of Jesus' "personality" and perspectives (*De Jesu autoconscientia quam scilicet ipse de se ipso et de sua missione habuit* [The Awareness Jesus Had of Himself and of His Mission], International Theological Commission, 1986). Here we can see that Jesus considered his existence to be a *mission*, a task received from someone else, which he felt he had to fulfill—and wanted to fulfill—in order to be truly himself (Jn 5:19; 10:25; 12:49; 14:31). His entire historical existence was an awareness of being constantly "sent back" to God, whom he addresses familiarly as "Abba" (Mk 14:36). He devoted his life to the Father, calling it perpetual obedience which would last till death.

As Jesus faced death, his self-understanding was complete: sources show beyond all possible doubt how lucidly he *knew* about his violent death and *wanted* to die in a way that had true finality. When he finally encountered the reality of death, Jesus was lucid and clear and quite consistent with his prediction; he also presented a faith in the Father who he was sure would call him from the dead within three days, thereby giving him the reward for his obedience (Jn 2:19; Acts 2:14–32).

These details are all about the historical authenticity of Jesus of Nazareth. A Christology that eschewed them would inevitably be nothing more than gnosis or Docetism, because it would lack that prescriptive interpretation that every historical person can and must have of himself as a person.

c. Jesus' self-awareness and the strength of his word have transmitted themselves to the faith of those people, today's generation included, who "ate and drank" with God (Acts 10:41) and who left everything and followed him (Mt 19:27). Indeed, something that characterizes historical authenticity is its relevance to the present day. The event of Jesus of Nazareth and his disciples' faith in him have given birth to a tradition that makes it possible to ascertain the unity between that fundamental past and the faith of today. The fact that so little has ever been committed to paper (Jn 20:30; 21:25) is what persuades today's believers to live God's important words and gestures again in their own lives. This tradition, which is still alive, makes it possible to see our understanding of the event and its significance for the present grow by the day (*DV* 8).

This relevance to the quest for meaning (→ MEANING II) is what each one of us encounters and what enables us to think of ourselves as contemporaries of Jesus himself.

2. The Centrality of Easter as the Culmination of Revelation

It is of paramount importance to emphasize the unity of Easter: the passion, the death, the resurrection, and the glorification constitute the only act through which God's trinitarian love comes into contact with human beings.

Here fundamental theology will have the task of presenting those elements which make it possible to see whether Easter is historically based or whether it is the driving force behind the theme of the credibility of the revelation itself. More specifically, as it has already been revealed, there is a need to collate all the information that enhances an understanding of Jesus prior to his death and his faith in his Father's answer.

Just the same, research will need to be restricted to two fronts:

a. On the one hand, it will be necessary to show that Jesus' death was the high point

around which all christological information revolves. From the point of view of apologetics, the death of Jesus will have to be presented as the event that in human terms expresses the totality and the insuperability of the revelation of God's trinitarian love. Mark's Gospel gives us a significant and relevant picture of this: "Now when the centurion, who stood facing him, saw that *in this way* he breathed his last, he said, 'Truly this man was God's Son!'" (Mk 15:39). The centurion represents the nonbeliever, the "other one" (→ FUNDAMENTAL THEOLOGY II: ADDRESSEE), who, when faced with the death of an innocent person—and this death in particular—summoned up an understanding of God that was capable of kindling in him his first profession of faith.

b. On the other hand, fundamental theology will be able to express the radical nature of death because it believes in the resurrection. It is from this point, in fact, that death retrospectively acquires its full meaning by revealing that the essence of trinitarian love does not stop at death, but *in* death becomes life. In addition to producing traditional information which makes it possible to support the resurrection with this baggage of historical "certainties," this approach must above all insist on the depth of meaning which emerges from opening up to faith in the promise of the Father.

In conclusion, the resurrection must take on the character of *uniqueness*, which itself recalls a corresponding statement of faith, and of eschatology, which already allows us a glimpse of the new creation tending toward final fulfillment. In this part of the research, the image to inspire us is that of John, the loving apostle who, on arriving at Christ's tomb, did not go in; he only went in when Peter arrived, and then "he saw and believed" (Jn 20:8).

3. Jesus of Nazareth and the Church

One of the fundamental studies in Christology will be devoted to the explanation of facts relating to the relationship between Jesus and the church (→ CHURCH II: JESUS AND THE CHURCH). It would be quite inappropriate here to force the texts and reach conclusions that have acquired a full meaning only within the dynamic of the Christian faith. Nonetheless, fundamental theology is aware that the church is an important element as well as a consequence of revelation; it will seek out the connection that fuses the origins of the church, its life, and its mission in the historical word of Jesus of Nazareth—or, more exactly, in the plan of Jesus, who saw in his own person the definitive establishment of the kingdom of God.

Fundamental theology is far removed from the juridical-canonical mentality which placed the conception of the church's "foundation" in classical apologetics; it sees the foundation of the church by Jesus as a universal act in his role as Messiah.

4. Universal Value of the Person of Jesus

From these factors we have discussed, there emerges yet another task for fundamental theology: the identification of Jesus' *universal* character. In this context, theology draws our attention to the themes that flow from the Christian faith's claim to have both within it and within the uniqueness of one person the definitive word that has been handed down to history and all people from time immemorial.

The christological impact is conveyed by fundamental theology on two planes: first on the perspective of the universality of salvation, and second on the relationship with other RELIGIONS. As for the former, there is the element of salvation that is part of the history of humanity and therefore imposes an assessment of the relation between the HISTORY OF SALVATION and the history of the world; as for the latter, we come up against the *specificity* of Christian revelation and its originality in relation to other religions that claim to lead to salvation.

5. Christology and Epistemology

With regard to theological epistemology, there is one final task that falls to fundamental theology: the *justification of the meaning* of the claims of Christology and the reasons for moving from *Christo*-logy to *Theo*-logy.

Giving the reasons for the meaning of Christology is the same as fixing the premises that justify theological work, but it also means considering the sensibleness of the claim, particularly the extent to which the content is expressed in a prescriptive and universal way. So as not to fall into the twin trap of an excess of metaphysics or historicism in answering this question, it is necessary for the meaning of faith to have an emphasis within the context in which it is placed.

From the perspective of apologetics, fundamental theology must be able to establish the foundations that will encourage an understanding of Christology in today's cultural climate, whether it is one that believes in God or not. In the same way, it will have to sustain and determine the proclamation of the good news in such a way that the original meaning and the cultural meaning can communicate with each other.

The second task is to bring about the ascendancy of theology over Christology. The principle of Christocentrism is essential for the foundation and development of theology, but the ultimate aim of a critical understanding of faith must remain the fullness of the revealed mystery, and this consists of the mystery of God's trinitarian love.

It is precisely by abiding strictly by the truths discovered within fundamental Christology that Christology can be consistent in submitting the reasons for its superiority. In Jesus of Nazareth himself, there is evidence of his "deferring" to his Father's will and therefore to the fullness of revelation (Jn 14:31).

Christology is surpassed by theology so that it can ultimately have a full meaning both as a historical reality and as the revelation of the mystery: "it is to your advantage that I go away, for if I do not go away, the Advocate will not come to you" (Jn 16:7).

To understand what Christology is, it is necessary to look at *Theo*-logy because the mystery will remain the mystery of the three hypostases, of which it will be possible to articulate only one, through the incarnation, in the terrestrial reality. This is how we come to the Pauline interpretation according to which the Son gives himself totally to the Father: "then the Son himself will also be subjected to the one who put all things in subjection under him, so that God may be all in all" (1 Cor 15:28).

How, then, is the contribution of fundamental theology specified in the interdisciplinary approach? In our opinion it consists in providing insights that are neither simply exegetical nor exclusively dogmatic. In fact, fundamental theology presents data that are both historical and exegetical, and are reflected as elements around all of Jesus' actions and sayings as the revealer of the Father. It is this identity between revealer and revelation that fundamental theology brings out as a unique detail of the realism of the incarnation. And so, if in terms of apologetics, fundamental theology presents the person of Jesus in his historical reality, and therefore in his self-awareness, it also makes use of this self-awareness in dogmatic terms to express the fullness of revelation and its uniqueness and universality.

To summarize, what fundamental theology helps us to rediscover, in accordance with its nature and method, is the unity of history and faith: in apologetics, fundamental theology is rooted in history, but in dogma it is true to the faith.

Bibl.: K. RAHNER, "Current Problems in Christology," in *Theological Investigations*, vol. 1 (1954; London, 1961); R. LATOURELLE, *Theology of Revelation* (New York, 1966); id., *Finding Jesus through the Gospels* (New York, 1979); var., *Il problema cristologico oggi* (Assisi, 1973); K. LEHMANN, "Über das Verhältnis der Exegese als historischkritischer Wissenschaft zum dogmatischen Verstehen," in *Jesus und der Menschensohn* (Freiburg, 1975), 421–34; R. LATOURELLE and G. O'COLLINS, *Problems and Perspectives of Fundamental Theology*, Part 3: *Christological Approaches* (New York, 1982); M. BORDONI, *Gesù di Nazareth Signore e Cristo*, Vol. 1: *Introduzione alla cristologia* (Rome, 1985); K. H. OHLIG, *Fundamentalchristologie: Im Spannungsfeld von Christentum und Kultur* (Munich, 1986), in *HFT* 4, chaps. 6–11, pp. 122–265; A. AMATO, *Gesù Il Signore* (Bologna, 1988); H. J. VERWEYEN, *Christologische Brennpunkte* (Essen, 1989).

Rino FISICHELLA

II. PHILOSOPHICAL CHRISTOLOGY

The term "philosophical Christology," modeled on philosophical theology, has been in use for some decades as a comprehensive term for the approach characterized by the phrase "the Christ of the philosophers." It meets with the same approval but also the same reservations as Christian philosophy, without which, anyway, it is inconceivable. Nevertheless, whereas Christian philosophy is compelled mainly to justify its philosophical status, philosophical Christology, which reverses the syntagma, has to demonstrate its christological bona fides. For many people Christ as the philosophers see

him must be a vain image, or a "ghost," as Baader puts it. The implicit or explicit disagreement between Christianity and philosophies increases with the introduction of Christ in person. On this point the demarcation line is not drawn between believers and unbelievers, for, as in the case of Christian philosophy, supporters and opponents are to be found on both sides. If by philosophical Christology we mean an independent form of speculative doctrine with Christ as its author, as M. Blondel and M. Nédoncelle among others would have it; or if, conversely, he is to be treated as a metaphysical object, as a metaphysically unique person, that is wholly inappropriate. Philosophy does not enjoy that kind of direct contact with the person and life of Jesus; it is not a substitute for faith and prayer. That is not the nature of the discipline. The terminology would be entirely misapplied if we were to interpret philosophical Christology, doctrinally or existentially, as an annexation of Christ by philosophy.

Yet there ought to be a philosophical approach to Jesus Christ. Philosophy and philosophers are not excluded or dispensed from answering the question on which life, whole and entire, depends: What do you think of Christ? Reinhold Schneider puts this movingly in a work that appeared just after the last war and still bore the harsh traces of that catastrophe. No one escapes the question of Caesarea: Who do you say that I am? Yet, contrary to the general opinion, the philosophers have not been slow to answer. No major philosopher of the modern era has avoided the question of Christ or has evaded the presence of Christ. There is much more reason for astonishment that historians and critics, except during the last few decades, should have paid the question so little attention or thought it inappropriate to consider it. In the glaring case of Kant, for example, and even in that of Hegel, their treatment remains superficial, as if some mere prefatory question were at issue. From this viewpoint, Henri Gouhier's fine little book, *Bergson et le Christ des Évangiles* (*Bergson and the Christ of the Gospels*) (Paris, 1961), is exceptional. But, in examining the place Christ occupies in the thought of philosophers (on the basis of a few select examples: Bergson, Spinoza, and Rousseau), Gouhier did not think that it was possible to go beyond the empirical philosophical Christologies. The philosopher always produces his or her own image of Christ, and philosophical Christology is tantamount to a portrait gallery.

Nevertheless, it is possible to do more than offer a series of monographs, useful as they may be, and a comparative study. The very diversity of the more or less developed Christologies inherent in the systems raises the problem of unity, which derives from the model, as well as the problem of tradition. Moreover, the unity underlying philosophy in general, and each philosophical discipline in particular, accords with the nature of things and with the essential relation of philosophy to its history. Similarly, the versions of philosophical Christology offered by the modern era are interconnected by the mere existence of philosophical affinities. Hence we meet with a more or less major emphasis on the Jesus of history or on the Christ of faith, depending on whether the philosophies in question are more critical or more systematic. A critical or historical starting point, as in Kant, Fichte, and Bergson, stresses Jesus the moral preceptor, the revealer, the mystic—though dogmatic accretions are not ignored, even if they demand the presence of the solid basis of historical appearance. On the contrary, the major speculative philosophies of religion tend to minimize historical contingency (though not to discard it), and above all to integrate the development of dogma. Ultimately we would have on the one hand a Christ without Christology, and on the other hand a Christology without Christ. For the recurrent problem of any Christology that claims the epithet "philosophical" is not palpably different from that of theology, holding a balance between Docetism and Arianism. This is also the dichotomy that some commentators have tried to decree between the Jesus of history and the Christ of faith. But since, for the philosopher (and in fact, anyway), the Jesus of history is the Christ of faith, the contrast is rather one between the Christ of history and the Christ of the idea or of speculation, and hence we have the twofold starting point to which I have just referred.

But it is a matter of tackling—by one means or another—Lessing's "vast and terrible gulf" (which faith leaps over) between the contingent testimony of history and the universal truth of speculative reason. The philosophers do not treat the "Jesus problem" properly speaking, but they too have their preferences for an ascending or a descending Christology. Spinoza starts with Jesus the "supreme philosopher," whose mind was in direct communication with God. Fichte seizes on the religious genius, the brilliant precursor of *The Science of Knowledge*. Bergson settles for the supermystic and the orator of the Sermon on the Mount. But Malebranche listens to the inward word, universal reason. The young Schelling naïvely opines that the only significant aspect is the "symbolic" individual and not that rather ordinary, transparent man, the Essene preacher (he changes his opinion later). Hegel constructs a majestic staurology (with, that is, negativity as the universal lever), in which the ineluctable *hic et nunc* of Jesus of Nazareth becomes a historical index and moment. In either direction, the difficulty is a matter of the connection or transition, unless the chasm is left yawning, as happens, for example, with Feuerbach and Strauss. Kant leaves open the question of the divine origin of the model, but he does not exclude the possibility that the master of the Gospel, as a phenomenal appearance, should accord perfectly with the noumenal archetype. To say anything more than that would mean going well beyond the permissible bounds. Fichte presents a Jesus overrun and possessed by the idea that he is unique, for whom metaphysics is historical; that will not do for the orthodox, but it is more than *The Science of Knowledge* will allow. Conversely, the older Schelling attributes a wholly dogmatic history to his Christ of so many metamorphoses. Hegel will not dissociate the most elevated speculation and the spirit of the community from the unique tangible appearance (this is where the "shoe pinches" in all speculative Christology).

Contrary to what might be supposed, most philosophies that make room for Christ and Christology in their reflective edifices are worthy attempts to do justice to the incarnation and exinanition. The competence of the *Idea Christi*, which empowers systems of an idealist bent, does not prevent a confrontation with history and contingency, and many examples of this tendency are available, from Hegel and Schelling to their numerous imitators. But it is true that Christ, when invited into these "conceptual constructs," suffers the effects. He is not only asked to reside there but to play a part. The resulting philosophical Christology can be invoked only as a kind of supplement to help out an understanding of Christ; this Christology operates mainly for philosophical ends. Its goal is obvious in the vast work of Hegel, where Christ is "recrucified." It is more subtly apparent in Schelling's positivism, where Christ assumes the Herculean labors of the median power, only to fall temporarily into mysterious abeyance during the period of the church and the work of eradicating evil, which— paradoxically enough—is allocated to Satan. But less openly christological philosophies also certify that Christ is—to borrow a phrase from Novalis—the "key to the world." That is the case with Spinoza, who ascribes to Christ and his Spirit that perfect and unsurpassable knowledge which he does not wholly enjoy himself. And so it is also with Fichte, for whom Christ, bursting with Johannine life, inimitably fulfills *The Science of Knowledge*, encompassing as it does the life and light of humanity. Even Bergson, who is usually so discreet, ascribes to the Christ of the Gospels an unprecedented ability to modify the life force (*élan vital*) and, finally, initiate a new ethical and spiritual creation.

While praising the intention, we can hardly avoid accusing philosophical Christologies as a whole of *polychristism*, the charge which Möhler reserved for heretics. Nevertheless, if we consider all these Christologies, in accordance with their intentions, as approximations and approaches, we shall find that they follow consistent and homogeneous procedures, and accord with what, for discussion purposes, may be called a threefold typology. The first type is the opening up of philosophy to Christology, "evangelical preparation," the philosophy that "leads to Christ," the *intellectus quaerens fidem* ("intellect in search of faith"). This type of Christian philosophy by anticipation and vocation is to be found, for example, in Jules Lequier, the later Maine de Biran, a number of phenomenologists, Max Scheler, the Bergson of *The Two Sources*, and the Blondel of the second period ("Open Philosophy" is the title of his tribute to Bergson). Conversely, in the same line as the *fides quaerens intellectum* ("faith in search of understanding"), and therefore to be ranked with the foregoing tendency, we have the kind of Christology committed to doing philosophy, underpinning it as it were. It sees its task as one of marking out the always difficult and dangerous road from theology to philosophy. Philosophically oriented Christology is inseparable from christologically oriented philosophy

and gives rise to a truly philosophical Christology which overtakes philosophy in order to reinforce and regenerate it, at the risk of secularization. We find it within philosophy in the form of schemata, images, and symbols that do not necessarily result from a reductive maneuver. The supreme example of this tendency is the Hegelian system, which is incomprehensible without the *analogia Christi*, but does not retain sufficient distance and mystery. Blondel's panchristism, mainly apparent in the fourth and fifth sections of *Action*, literally unearths a Christology with a philosophical theme. Similarly, the second phase of Gabriel Marcel's thought is deeply and variously indebted to Christianity and Christology, the echoes of which, though in a different order, recur in sometimes rather odd philosophemes. Of course these philosophical Christologies, even as mere outlines, draw their power from the fullness of Christ—i.e., from the full range of his characteristics, categories, and *epinoiai* ("afterthoughts"), for all the elements of Christ are compossible. The inadequacy of an approach like Marcel Légaut's is its—admittedly passionate— attachment to the aspect of the spiritual master alone. Should this kind of Christology actually encounter Christ's ontological reality of Christ, it is wholly powerless and ineffectual.

A third type of philosophical Christology derives from the second; it is scarcely evident at this time but is implicit in christological thought. This type is really more a phenomenology of Christ which, guided by sympathetic intuition, scrutinizes as efficiently as possible the *eidos* of his experiences and categories, and especially those which are philosophically pertinent: subjectivity, time, intersubjectivity, corporeality, suffering, death, sin, evil, and destiny. This christological phenomenology would have as much to contribute to anthropology (in Maine de Biran's sense) as to knowledge of Christ. Admittedly, it does not yet exist, but we may discern faint, though very suggestive, traces of it in studies by Jean Mouroux on awareness of time, and especially by Maurice Nédoncelle on intersubjectivity; and of course we must not forget Blondel in his letters. Alongside these pioneers, there are exegetes and theologians who have made several valuable contributions in this respect: Guardini, von Balthasar, Guillet, Guitton—but we already have Karl Adam, Léonce de Grandmaison, and the incomparable Newman. Oscar Cullmann's book with a promising title, *Christ and Time*, takes a quite different direction and is not an example to follow. Nevertheless, he provides a starting point for the conception of Christian time that is necessarily associated with the actual temporality of Christ. When Kierkegaard says that Jesus' words to Judas, "What you have to do, do quickly," are the most poignant words in the Gospel, he is indicating with all the urgency of anguished desire a special qualitative relationship to time.

In a famous passage, Augustine drew a line of demarcation between the Logos so familiar to pagan philosophy and the incarnate Word, which was not to be found in Plato and his successors. As was foreseeable, the powerful advance of Christian philosophy has repudiated Augustine's observation, which was relevant at the time. Even the emancipation of philosophy did not prevent the repercussions of christological faith on independent reason. The daring proposition advanced in regard to Teilhard de Chardin does not seem out of place: "The God of the philosophers just as much as the God of the theologians is the God of Abraham, Isaac and Jacob." This somewhat sibylline statement may nevertheless be interpreted as meaning that henceforth Christ occupies the position of the God of the philosophers, and that christological philosophy now takes the place of philosophical theology. But unsympathetic colleagues, whether philosophers or theologians, have still to be made aware of this.

I shall say only a few words about transcendental Christology. It is the prerogative and the achievement of Karl Rahner. The Innsbruck theologian did not claim to set it in the place of categorical or positive theology, of which it is an indispensable presupposition. In the tradition of Kant and Maréchal, he conceived of it as an examination of a priori conditions, or of the hypothetical a priori of a given possible experience (or reality). Rahnerian transcendental Christology refers to the possibility of incarnation or of the Man-God, and in fact refers to two interconnected questions: What are the conditions by which—subjectively—we can recognize the man who is God, the God made man? What are the conditions which allow someone to be said to be God; how is it possible for a human being to be God; how can a human being be capable of being God? In both

cases (and here he differs from Kant), Rahner prefers the currently fashionable ascending approach. The second question is resolved by recourse to the power of obedience—i.e., to a radicalized filial form of obedience. Here Rahner comes close to Schleiermacher. The first, complex question refers to Christ's historical humanity, and Christology is in quest of the reality of the absolute savior which its schemata of foreknowing (absolute availability and perfect surrender) allow it to predict. Even if this natural desire would be more appropriately fulfilled at the end of history, and therefore in eschatology, it responds to the language of faith by which Jesus of Nazareth is designated. Transcendental Christology cannot replace faith, the evidence of which testifies to the fact that Jesus fulfills the conditions. Hence Rahner indirectly justifies Kant, who thought it was impossible to equate the Master of the Gospel with the transcendent Archetype. Rahner is able to do so as a theologian demanding more elbow room than is conventionally proper to a theologian.

Rahner's powerful approach, which I have merely outlined, shows Christology and anthropology interacting to the benefit of Christology. There is nothing to prevent a similarly forceful use of the interaction of anthropology and Christology to the benefit of anthropology.

Bibl.: R. Schneider, *Die Heimkehr des deutschen Geistes: Über das Bild Christi in der deutschen Philosophie des 19. Jahrhunderts* (Baden-Baden, 1946); J. Mouroux, *The Mystery of Time: A Theological Inquiry* (New York, 1964); H. Boussé and J. J. Latour, eds., *Problèmes actuels de christologie* (Paris, 1965); M. Légaut, *Introduction à l'intelligence du passé et de l'avenir du christianisme* (Paris, 1970); A. Matheron, *Le Christ et le salut des ignorants chez Spinoza* (Paris, 1971); T. Pröpper, *Der Jesus der Philosophen und der Jesus des Glaubens: Ein theologisches Gespräch* (Mainz, 1975); K. Rahner, *Foundations of Christian Faith* (New York, 1978); E. Brito, *La christologie de Hegel (Verbum Crucis)* (Paris, 1983); X. Tilliette, *La christologie idéaliste* (Paris, 1986); id., *Filosofi davanti a Cristo* (Brescia, 1989); id., "Spinoza devant le Christ," Greg 58/2 (1977); id., *Le Christ de la philosophie (Cogitatio Fidei)* (Paris, 1990); id., "Is a Philosophical Christology Possible?" in R. Latourelle and G. O'Collins, eds., *Problems and Perspectives of Fundamental Theology* (New York, 1982), 135–50; id., *Pour une philosophie chrétienne* (Namur/Paris, 1983).

Xavier Tilliette

III. CHRISTOLOGICAL TITLES

Addressing the topic of Christological titles in a theological sense involves two elements. The first is taking account of the irreducibility of Jesus of Nazareth in terms of the innumerable classifications that the human mind, together with faith, has succeeded in expressing in the course of the centuries. In fact, the person of Jesus emerges with ever greater clarity, continually going beyond the different qualifications and revealing the grandeur of the mystery vis-à-vis the limits of the person, which one may understand always and only as a *novum* offered to us.

The second element is realizing that it is possible to foster both the perception of the historicity of Jesus of Nazareth, in his self-revelation as the One sent by the Father, and the understanding of the faith of the primitive Christian community. In a word, it is a question of being placed in front of that true synthesis between the historical fact and the experience of faith; it is this that allows fundamental theology its own particular approach to Christology (→ CHRISTOLOGY I: FUNDAMENTAL). This synthesis in no way lessens or contradicts the historical component nor that of faith; on the contrary, it values both. In fact, it shows that the experience of faith is always linked to a historical event, yet this is never a *factum brutum*; it is always related to a subject and to a culture that shapes it, giving it meaning in terms of the present and providing the basis for understanding the future, and thereby "history" as well.

1. A Glance at History

From the perspective of fundamental theology, the study of the christological titles has quickly followed a pattern of development that can be traced in three stages.

a. The treatment of the christological titles is not something new. From the very first period of Christian literature one may find significant examples: Dionysius wrote the thirteen books of the *De divinis nominibus* (*PG* 3:586–990); Orienzus wrote a poem entitled *De epithetis Salvatoris nostri* in ca. 450 (*PL* 61:1000–1005), in which a description and commentary are given of fifty-four titles.

An early document in the form of a monograph may be traced to the hand of Louis de Leon (1528–1591), who published his *De los nombres de Cristo* in 1583. The surprising thing about this work is that it came to be written with the intention of leaving some margin with regard to the serious danger for the people following the prohibition on publishing the Sacred Scriptures in the vernacular.

So as not to leave people in ignorance of Christian truth, with the effect of alienating them from the practice of their faith (pp. 4–5), Leon gathered ten principal titles with the aim of providing a means of catechizing simple believers: "Many names are given to Christ in the Scriptures; however, there are ten principal ones, within which it is possible to recognise a synthesis of all the others" (p. 12). The development of the book is thus: three young Augustinian monks, Sabino, Marcellus, and Julian, take refuge from the heat of Salamanca, and find refuge in the country. A discussion ensues on the names attributed to Jesus: Shoot, Face of God, Way, Shepherd, Mountain, King and Prince, Bridegroom, Beloved, Jesus, and Lamb. From the brief statement of the name there develops a demonstration that tries to illustrate its significance and thus imprint on the mind of the reader the truth of the underlying faith.

One is brought face to face with the christological titles as a substitute for reading Scripture in such a way that "knowing Christ, one comes to the truth and proper knowledge about human beings" (p. 8).

b. A second stage is represented by the theology of the manuals (→ THEOLOGY II: EPISTEMOLOGY) the true and proper origin of the problem of the titles in theology.

The context within which the study placed itself was that of the polemical struggle with illuminism and, more directly, rationalism. The *De legato divino*, which found its complement in the dogmatic treatise *De verbo incarnato*, constituted the apologetic impact on Christology.

The purpose of this methodology was to show how unfounded was the thesis that maintained the contradiction and contraposition between historical research into the life of Jesus and his image in dogma. In effect, what was presented was far from capable of consideration as a defense of the historicity of Jesus of

Nazareth. What the titles managed to achieve, besides an obvious functional purpose external to the subject in question, which in this way came to be distanced to an ever greater degree from its historical context, was the presentation of a Christ who had all the characteristics of being *exceptional*, both with regard to his humanity and in his historicity.

The image thus forged was well removed from the perspective found in the Gospels and from the historical reality that it sought to defend.

Being involved in the issues addressed in the earlier treatises (one has only to think of the first apologetic treatise, that of Joseph Hooke, *Religionis naturalis et revelatae principia* 1754 Liber II, pars I, art 1, which cited as proof of divinity only the messianic character of Jesus and his authority in preaching and working miracles), the manuals had reduced the contents of Christology to the demonstration of single titles.

The material used for consideration in this regard, and foreign to any exegetical methodology, was guided by the power of dogma. In this way, however, the apologetics of the manuals revealed its attempt to present Christology. In fact, Jesus of Nazareth was no longer considered in himself, neither as the source nor as described by the witness of the Gospels, but rather was the product of dogmatic formulation. Paradoxically, the gap between the historical Jesus and the Christ of faith, which the manuals sought to overcome, ended up by being widened.

c. Fundamental theology in the period following the Second Vatican Council, when it eventually comes to consider the titles, cannot ignore the fresh impetus given by the council to the theology of revelation and to Christology.

The recovery of the priority of Scripture for an exact theological understanding of the facts, the horizon of salvation history into which it is possible to insert the different components of the Bible and the structural systematization of the organization of known facts are the essential hermeneutical keys for considering the christological titles from the perspective of fundamental theology.

2. Systematic Presentation

One presentation or suggestion with regard to the use of the christological titles, a perspective outlined below, endeavors to make its treatment of the subject a ready foundation for a twofold aim:

a. Within a global reading of revelation, the titles may be considered a vehicle by which it is possible to reach that knowledge of Jesus which expresses the mystery of his existence and the purpose of his mission of salvation.

b. More specifically, in the order of hermeneutical methodology, the titles can allow that verification which shows the language of faith to be rooted in the historical language of Jesus of Nazareth. Thus, theology is given the possibility of a formulation that guarantees the scientific nature and proper sense of its own expression, against every form of reductionism that would lead to some type of linguistic analysis.

L. Sabourin, in an appendix to his work *Les noms et les titres de Jésus*, lists 187 titles, already found by the end of the seventh century, which, with different meanings, are present within the NT.

From our interest in the matter, we think it possible to distinguish three levels that would be able to constitute almost the most significant context for the arrangement and understanding of the titles: (1) Titles that express the popular knowledge of Jesus' contemporaries. The particular point of reference is the world of the OT. These titles—namely, "prophet" and "Son of David"—fell into disuse within the postresurrection community because clearly they no longer expressed the fullness of the mystery that had been revealed. (2) Titles applied to Jesus himself which, in this way, made explicit reference to his own understanding of himself (e.g., "Son of Man"). The community could not but have kept these expressions because they handed on the most authentic teaching of the master himself. (3) Titles which, in the light of the Easter mystery, the Christian community has made explicit or applied to Jesus in twofold way: either (a) bringing into present use the OT images that refer to him (e.g., "wisdom") or celebrating the liturgy (e.g., "Lord") or (b) recording the very teaching of Jesus himself, his actions and his conduct, in which he revealed that he was the "Messiah" and the "Son of God."

A rapid survey of these examples would point

us toward the theological perspective that has been expounded.

Jesus the Prophet. The Jewish world at the time of Jesus was characterized to a very strong degree by two factors: the definitive position of Scripture and constant reference to Moses and the law. The sense of prophecy, as it had been experienced in the period of Deuteronomy, had diminished; the will of Yahweh had now come to be known through reference to the Torah and the prophets, read and interpreted by the doctors. Although it was thought that the prophetic spirit had ended with Haggai, Zechariah, and Malachi, the people nevertheless knew the ways in which the experience of the prophets had been kept alive—above all, by the apocalyptic genre, which sustained the expectation of the Messiah, and then by the prophetic charism, which was seen to be present in the high priest by virtue of his office (see Jn 11:5). Finally, one must not forget the Qumran community, which by its written documents and its way of life was guided by the authority of the Master of Justice and by the constant expectation of the coming of the Aaronic Messiah.

The advent of the Baptist and his preaching had certainly maintained the climate of expectation that ran through the whole of Israel's history, subsequently attaching a prophetic connotation to this figure, thereby reawakening the sentiments mentioned already, feelings and expectations that had grown dim in the hearts of the people.

It is within this context that the preaching and the works of Jesus of Nazareth must first of all be placed. A number of facts found in the NT texts demonstrate, without a shadow of doubt, that beginning with the first disciples and then all the people, the person of Jesus was welcomed and interpreted by the same standards as that of the prophets of old. The appearance of Jesus in the public domain reawakened among those who encountered him that same image already presented by the Baptist, namely, that which led to a recovery of the image of the prophet.

It is easy to verify the general opinion, that of individuals and of groups, which refers to Jesus by the title "Prophet": Philip communicates the same to Nathaniel (Jn 1:45); Simon the Pharisee has the thought in his mind, although he doubts (Lk 7:39); the man born blind attests it

before the judges who question him (Jn 9:17); the Samaritan professes it publicly (Jn 4:19); the soldiers use it as a form of mockery (Mt 26:68), but for the crowd it is a reason for joy and praise (Mt 21:11; Lk 7:16).

These reactions have a historical foundation which allows one to conclude that one of the first facts expressed by preresurrection Christology was that which interpreted Jesus of Nazareth as a prophet who placed himself within the long line of Israel's prophetic figures (Mt 21:45; Jn 1:21; 7:40; Lk 24:19).

How can the application of this title to Jesus be explained? We do not think it can be traced to Jesus himself. The Gospels give only two texts (Mt 13:57; Lk 13:33) in which direct reference is made in Jesus' own words about himself as the prophet. Nevertheless, the context is that of the suffering and violent death which by then had appeared on the horizon of Jesus' own life. Thus, what we have is more of a *figure of explanation* employed to express the rejection by the people and the fate of a violent death, which was the common destiny of the prophets, as opposed to an identification with the prophets themselves.

Moreover, there is a conformity between this and the custom of Jesus to avoid giving clear expression of his personal identity and his ministry by means of titles. As we shall see with the expression "Son of Man," Jesus always seems to use formulas and images that, on the one hand, clarify the mystery of his existence and, on the other hand, serve to protect and conceal that same mystery.

To explain the reaction of Jesus' contemporaries, and likewise the consequent acquisition by preresurrection Christology of the title "Prophet," it is necessary to turn to another possible solution, which will reveal an attitude within the behavior and words of Jesus such that the people were intuitively reminded of the prophets.

Above all, it was the custom of Jesus to interpret the Scriptures so as to explain and to further understanding of the present situation. Luke, more than the other evangelists, underlines this aspect, placing it almost as an archetype of the whole of the master's public preaching (Lk 4:16–30). Therefore, Jesus prophesies; that is to say, he expresses himself in images and in the style reminiscent of the prophets. One thinks of the anathemas and warnings of misfortune

(Lk 13:34; Mt 23:34; Mk 13:1–2), or the judgments of salvation (Lk 12:32; 10:23) with the different beatitudes (Mt 5:3–12). Looked at in this way, one cannot deprive the historical Jesus of the heritage of the text from Mi 13:1–2, which has come to be considered, to all effects, as a prophecy, both for its style and also for its content. In fact this text is central to and constitutes an essential explanation for understanding both the accusations that were made against Jesus during his trial (Mk 14:58) and the mockery by those standing at the cross (15:29).

Furthermore, Jesus acted in such a way as to make clear reference to the many deeds performed by the prophets as explicit signs of revelation; in this sense one may think of the symbolic value of a number of miracles (Jn 6:1–66; 9:41; 11:1–44), but more directly of the cleansing of the Temple (Mt 21:12–16), with the consequent expulsion of the traders; of the warning in relation to the fig tree and the incredulity of the people (Mt 21:18–22); or of the writing in the earth before extending pardon and salvation to the woman taken in adultery (Jn 8:1–11).

Another expression of prophetic behavior can be seen in the different *visions* that Jesus had. Their contents were given expression both in relation to the human heart, wherein nothing could be hidden from him (Mt 12:25; Lk 9:47), and in the necessity of being open to the coming of the kingdom of salvation, with the consequent collapse of the kingdom of Satan (Lk 18:18).

Finally, one must consider the various predictions of the passion and the consequent promise of glorification from the perspective of prophecy (Mk 8:31; 9:31; 10:33). Yet with the various degrees of historicity adopted by the three stages of redaction, one is faced with an incontestable fact: Jesus had full knowledge of the destiny of the violent death, typical of the prophets, that lay before him, and he had the will to mark this event with a personal significance, which brought fulfillment and the deepest possible meaning to his mission.

The NT sources nevertheless allow us to verify a common fact, even if with different theological emphases: that of considering Jesus a prophet on the strength of his behavior. If, however, referring to this historical fact, one may speak of a *prophetic Christology*, it is also necessary to add that this is seen as a primitive form which allows evaluation of the immediate reaction of the crowd to Jesus. In fact, a dynamic within the text allows us to see that the NT sources are not content to refer to this dimension alone. The person of Jesus evokes reflections and attitudes that oblige us to see in him "one who is greater" (Mt 12:41; 12:42; 12:16). Thus it is possible to attribute to Jesus the title of prophet only in an *analogical* sense; the authority with which he expressed himself and the knowledge that was revealed of his relationship with God served to give emphasis to the dissimilarity more than the similarity with the reality contained within the title (→ PROPHECY).

Son of David. Another title, directly linked to the idea of messiahship, is "Son of David." Its absence from OT texts could be something of a surprise, and yet it is certain that the whole tradition never ceases thinking about the Messiah who must come, along the lines of the prophecy of Nathan (2 Sam 7:13–16). It is only the extrabiblical literature, which predates that of Christianity, which gives but one example from the *Psalms of Solomon* (17:21–25); however, the rabbinic texts reveal a usage of the formula "the Son of David who comes," which had by then become traditional.

The usage found in the Synoptic tradition in all probability reflects a pre-Christian mentality which saw in the title the connection with the *regal* identity of the Messiah and the establishment of his kingdom. In this way we have a political-kingly understanding of messiahship. This enables us to understand the reserve that can be detected in Jesus' attitude toward the title. The most explicit logion in which this appears is Mt 22:41–46.

The context of the dispute reveals that one is faced with the wish for a change of perspective in understanding the subject. Bringing up the matter of the "haggadic antinomy" (see J. Jeremias 1971: 295), Jesus accepts the truth that the title expresses, but corrects its interpretation, in order for it to be in greater conformity with the whole of his preaching, which prefers the figure of the suffering servant to that of the glorious Messiah.

The same point is found to be true in another passage, Mk 10:46–52. With regard to the historicity of this event, various factors can be brought together in order to reach a positive judgment. Here the blind man, Bartimaeus, calling upon Jesus as "Son of David" (v. 47), expresses a popular form of messianic hope that, together with that of the prophet, was among those most familiar to the people (A. Descamps, "Le messianisme royal," in *Attente du Messie*, 61).

In the light of the Easter mystery, this title, which is also found in the profession of faith in Rom 1:3–4, begins to give way to the more expressive and complete title Son of God.

Son of Man. This designation, even before being a christological title, is an expression that the primitive community had honored and esteemed because it related immediately not only to the master's own language but above all to that image which he had established in order to give expression to the mystery of his mission and his person.

The Son of Man became a christological title only after it had been understood that one had to go beyond the image contained in Dn 7 and its link with that of the 'ebed Yhwh of Deutero-Isaiah. Only when the community realized the impossibility of equivocation between the OT vision of the glorious eschatological judgment and its incarnation in the prophet-servant who suffers and gives his life as a ransom for the people, only then was it in a position to extend the usage of that expression and to transform it, in time, into a true christological title.

"Son of Man" is an expression firmly rooted in the Gospels. With the exception of three instances (which, moreover, refer back to OT citations [Rv 1:13; 14:15; Heb 2:6]), it is to be found in the other NT sources only in Acts 7:55; for the rest, one finds eighty-two occasions in which it is used exclusively by Jesus. This fact cannot be explained away; on the contrary, it calls for explanation.

The Greek translation *ho huios tou anthrō-pou* is an Aramaism; the second article is in fact unusual in Greek and would all the more express the usual determinative translation "Son *of* man."

This linguistic expression, which the Hebrew renders as *ben 'ādām* and Aramaic as *bar 'ĕnaš*, is used a great deal in the OT writings. In the book of Ezekiel there are at least fifty-three times when the vocative *ben-'ādām* is used to express the call of the prophet. The originating meaning is determined by the position of the prefix *ben/bar*. In fact, it can indicate descent if

joined to a proper name, or provenance if it precedes a geographical name. In this instance *ben-'ādām/bar 'ĕnaš* simply indicates a "man," one who belongs to the human race.

From the apocalyptic literature on, however, the expression is conditioned by the image found in Dn 7:13–14. Here the sacred author introduces the *symbolic* figure of "one like/as a son of man," expressing his fundamental understanding of a forthcoming intervention by Yahweh that would establish his messianic rule on earth after having destroyed the various kingdoms that were enemies of Israel (see Dn 2:31–45).

Biblical criticism has indulged its own whims in the course of decades of research into trying to identify this figure. In effect, the text, with all the complexity with which it expresses itself, allows one to glimpse the fact that the "son of man" may be understood either as one person (the king) or in collective terms (the people or the "holy ones"). The most recurrent interpretation at the present time makes use of the theory of *corporate personality*, because it succeeds above all others in harmonizing the apparent contradictions in the text. Thus, beginning with an individual sense, it is possible to recognize a collectivity within that same individual meaning, and vice versa. Beyond the particular interpretation, however, and within the messianic context of the OT, the image of the son of man helps to enrich the expectation of a Messiah by adding the connotations of glory (v. 14), of power (v. 15), and of eschatological judgment (v. 27), which until then the popular consciousness had lacked.

The uncertainty with regard to determining the setting and the identity of the son of man which so characterized studies of the OT literature, appears to have diminished in terms of the testimony of the Gospels.

NT studies that deal with the identity of the Son of Man can be placed into at least three categories: (1) those that hold that Jesus made use of the title but applied it not to himself but to another figure; (2) those that suggest that the primitive community invented the title to justify the proclamation of the glorification of the suffering servant; and (3) those that say Jesus created this expression himself in order to express his identity.

A careful examination of the texts reveals that the third position presents itself as being the most respectable on the basis of the evidence of the Gospels and as that best suited to drawing together the various factors that converge toward a solution.

The material to be found in the Gospels relating to the Son of Man can be subdivided into three groups: (1) logia referring to Jesus' earthly activity (e.g., Mk 2:10); (2) logia bearing the theme of the passion-death-resurrection (e.g., Mk 8:31); (3) logia that speak of the glory-parousia (Mk 13:26). Indeed, these few texts, while revealing their dependence on the figure in Dn 7, at the same time exhibit substantial differences from it. The first and most impressionistic, which produces complete discontinuity with the OT text, is that which sees the characteristics of suffering, passion, and death as constitutive of the Son of Man in the Gospels.

In fact, this characteristic comes from another OT image, the 'ēbed Yhwh ("servant of Yahweh") of Deutero-Isaiah (→ MESSIANISM). Although the title "servant" does not come to be applied directly to Jesus, his redemptive mission certainly refers to this figure for the purposes of explanation.

We have already seen that Jesus was welcomed and accepted by his contemporaries above all as a prophet. Moreover, several texts show that the preferred image of the prophetic vocation was that expressed by Deutero-Isaiah. Narratives such as that of the baptism (Mk 1:11, which cites Is 47:1), that of the predictions of the passion (Mk 10:33, which cites Is 50:6), and that of the Last Supper (Mk 14:27, which cites Is 53:12) make *implicit* reference to this figure; there are other texts as well that make *explicit* reference to the suffering servant (e.g., Mk 8:17 and Is 53:4; Lk 22:37 and Is 53:12).

For the Jewish world at the time of Jesus, the figure of the prophet is often linked with the image described in the four canticles to be found in the so-called Book of Consolation (first song=Is 42:1-4; second song=Is 49:1-6; third song=Is 50:4-9a; fourth song=Is 52:13-54:12). In these texts, parting from the description of the prophet's mission, there is evidence of his obedient response to Yahweh; they also describe the sufferings and laments that he must undergo on behalf of the people—a *vicarious* suffering therefore, which is asked of him because it is the realization of God's plan of salvation. Only after all these injuries and sufferings and

his consequent death will the prophet be able to sing of his victory and receive in glory the inheritance of the peoples.

These songs certainly came to Jesus' mind, particularly when it was clearly shown to him that his destiny was to suffer a violent death similar to that of the prophets. In fact, Jesus was fully aware of the fact that his behavior had caused scandal (Lk 4:28; 5:27–32) and violent reaction on the part of the leaders of the people (Mt 26:4; Mk 12:12). His solidarity with sinners and his messianic claims had already caused him a brush with death (Lk 4:29), and he was almost stoned (Jn 8:59; 10:31–33; 11:8). A clear realism in the face of these events, especially after the death of the Baptist and the disorder that he had caused in the Temple, had urged Jesus to seek his destiny and to give it a deeper, final significance.

Within this particular horizon, therefore, the figure of Deutero-Isaiah became the most familiar, whereby, more than all else that had gone before, Jesus understood his particular mission received from the Father, together with his death for the salvation of the people. Consequently, the mission of the servant found itself joined to the glorious image of the Son of Man in Daniel. Without a doubt this set up a striking contraposition of images which confused the popular mind yet certainly gave an indication of the originality of the person of Jesus. This was the case because this synthesis canceled every previous scheme and established its irreducibility in terms of all other messianic understandings of the day.

This originality, which is typical of the Gospels (the extrabiblical sources of the book of *Enoch* and of 4 Ezra are of the Jewish-Christian era and are thus later), is traced to Jesus himself. A full critique, which starts from the textual and passes to the form-historical, leads to the conclusion that, in some cases (e.g., Mk 3:28 with Mt 12:31), bar-'ĕnaš is transformed from the generic sense of "man" into that of the messianic title vis-à-vis Daniel. Moreover, one can verify the fact that thirty-seven out of fifty-one texts are given in duplicate form; one source gives the personal pronoun, while the other gives "Son of Man." One must conclude that the oldest and most original form is that which uses the pronoun; thus the evangelist, in using the title "Son of Man," has interpreted it in the light of the messianic title. However, there are thirteen instances which prove irreducible to other sources and which have reached the Gospels in their original, archaic, and primitive form (Mk 13:26; 14:62; Mt 24:27; 24:37b; 10:23; 25:31; Lk 17:22, 24, 26, 30; 18:8; 21:36; Jn 1:51). This antiquity must be taken into consideration when making an overall evaluation of the texts. If one adds a further stage of analysis to the facts that have already emerged, having a bearing on the necessary criterion of explanation, then one may achieve a further layer of historicity. In fact one must be in a position to respond to a number of questions which arise from the perspective of redaction: How to justify the abundant usage of the title (eighty-two times) always and only on the lips of Jesus? Why does the community hand it on but fail to make use of it even at the most important moments in his life? Why the apparent contradiction between the description of future glory and that of present suffering? Why the absence of a distinction between resurrection and parousia? Why does not John, who uses the title in his Gospel, employ the same term in his letters? To these questions one would need to add further elements which preclude one from thinking that the community created the title. One thinks of the pivotal text of Lk 12:8–9; here Jesus makes some sort of distinction between himself and the future Son of Man. Why would the community have maintained this distinction if it had created the title itself? Furthermore, why are there no logia in which resurrection and parousia are spoken of simultaneously, an identification such as would be natural for the postresurrection community? And why would the community have desisted from using the title almost immediately if it had not long before invented it? Finally, why would the community have referred the title of the glory of Daniel's vision to Jesus if the state of suffering then had to take place.

All these questions lead to the conclusion that "Son of Man" certainly became a title, but only because the primitive community, with that expression, memorized the most usual way in which the master expressed himself. True to his own style, Jesus of Nazareth did not wish to give a clear and exhaustive self-definition. "Son of Man" met this requirement above all by means of its ambiguous character. It was able to indicate the eschatological characteristics of the Messiah and at the same time recall the more generic meaning of "human." If one then adds that Jesus stamps the mark of his suffering on the figure of Daniel, the mark of his passion and death, then one understands more easily the reason for popular doubt in the face of this saying: "Who is this Son of Man?" (Jn 12:34).

Fully attuned to the dialectic of revelation, the saying serves to reveal and to conceal the mystery of Jesus. The primitive Christian community had wanted the use of "Son of Man" to be rooted in the unique language of the master; in fact, it was no longer used, either in liturgy or catechesis, nor even in the communities outside Jerusalem. The title "Son of Man" must have retained that sacred character because it formed part of the most authentic recollections of Jesus.

Son of God. The messianic consciousness of Jesus reached its peak at the moment in which he established such a unique relationship with Yahweh, one that had no precedent in the history of Israel, the relationship of sonship.

The title "Son of God" that is found in some OT formulas is overshadowed, in terms of its significance and originality, when the NT applies it to Jesus of Nazareth. The reality that comes to be expressed is a sharing of the very nature, something the monotheistic thinking of the Bible not only had never been able to articulate, but had expressly refused even to consider.

Israel had certainly been influenced by Egypt with regard to the idea of a filial relationship between the people and Yahweh. Exodus and Deuteronomy frequently take this route either to contrast Israel's sonship to that of the Egyptian traditions (Ex 4:22), or to set it above the other peoples (Dt 7:6–10; 32:10). The wisdom tradition will apply the title also to those individuals who devote themselves to maintaining the integrity of the faith of the fathers (Sir 4:10); but at different moments the king, the angels, or those who hold a particular office are also called "son of God" (Ps 29; Wis 2:12).

Beginning with David, a unique case in Israel's history, the formula of Ps 2:7 came to be applied to the king: "You are my son; today I have begotten you." Nevertheless, the characteristic of election and adoption that is taken up in this proclamation is evident enough. The prophets recaptured the correct understanding of sonship: it will be constituted by the correction that the father shows when confronted with the errors and betrayals of his sons with regard to the law, but in each case a correction that takes place and unfolds in the light of mercy and forgiveness.

The NT reveals how the title progressively became the patrimony of the faith of the church. "Son of God" is interchangeable with the absolute expression "the Son" or with that of the invocation "Father." Quite clearly there is a theology particular to each evangelist, yet the perspective is the same for all of them: Jesus Christ is the Son of the Father in a unique and absolute way.

This faith will not be able to lean on explicit sayings of Jesus; in fact he never used the title "Son of God" in reference to himself. Yet the faith of the church, in applying it to him, has done nothing more than make explicit what Jesus himself had said. In the first place one can examine the overall behavior of Jesus, which leads one to see in him the claim to a particular relationship with God: the authority with which he taught, the certainty with which he addressed the problems of those who questioned him, the finality of his judgment on the law, the radical commitment asked of those who follow him—all are facts that are justified only if one accepts Jesus' claim.

More directly, the *invocation* that he addressed to God, calling him "Abba," i.e., "Dad," in the order of natural generation, establishes complete discontinuity with the previous Jewish mentality.

Teaching the disciples to do the same when they pray to God, Jesus nevertheless distances himself even from them. Certainly, the Father is unique, but the relationship that comes to be expressed between "my" Father (Mt 11:20) and "our" Father (Mt 5:48) is substantially different: they are sons because he is *the* Son.

The primitive community, presenting Jesus as the Son of God, also recorded the purpose of his teaching: when, e.g., he narrated the parable of the wicked husbandmen (Mk 12:1–12 par.), he led them to recognize him in the figure that the Father sent "last of all," his "beloved son" who must be respected but who instead was killed and cast out of the vineyard.

Thus, with this title, there is first and foremost complete *coherence* with and *conformity* to both the behavior of Jesus and the whole of his teaching. The faith of the church, from the very moment it experienced the glory of Christ's resurrection, understood that the previous titles—Prophet, Servant, Son of David, Son of Man—no longer succeeded in containing the mystery of his person. Thus the title "Son of God" almost naturally gained precedence, because, over and above all considerations of functionality, it revealed the very essence of Jesus and gave explanation to his historical existence.

3. Conclusion

An excessive emphasis on the christological titles is certainly very dangerous, in that description of the person of Jesus is fragmented, with an onus on the functional. Nevertheless, the various titles have meaning only if they are derived from the person of Christ and if they refer back to him. This is the demand of a unifying principle that impresses itself upon theological study, and it is this that gives emphasis to the overall nature of the mystery of the person more than the partiality of those aspects which refer to his mission.

Fundamental theology starts from the centrality of Jesus of Nazareth as the revealer and the revelation of the Father, and from here the richness of the different titles springs forth. The specific task of fundamental theology is not analysis of the titles as such; rather it focuses on the referent of revelation who manifests himself by these titles. This choice of perspective means that a study from the discipline of fundamental theology gives emphasis only to a few titles, either because they are more directly involved in the particular scope of this same discipline or because they are of the kind best suited to showing the profound unity between Jesus of Nazareth and the Christ of the primitive community.

These christological titles provide the first theology of Jesus of Nazareth. One is confronted by the self-understanding of the mystery of God incarnate, which must be given preference with regard to all other analyses. It is certainly the case that the resurrection, breaking into the lives of the disciples, had created within them a new awareness of past events; but nothing had taken away that original love and respect that had led them to leave everything in order to follow the master. Therefore, Easter had not done away with Golgotha.

The Christian community was enabled to proclaim in faith that Jesus is the Son of God by means of unwavering fidelity in receiving and conserving his word as the word of him who fulfilled the Scriptures and the one who had always been awaited. In the first place, therefore, he had been received by the disciples as a prophet, then believed in as the Son of Man, even though he contradicted their expectations; he was finally proclaimed as the Christ and the Son of God because he himself had drawn them to do so, and because by then they were certain of but one thing: whatever formula or expression had been used, it would have been inaccurate and inadequate for giving a description of the uniqueness of his person.

To the disciples and to the whole community it thus remained only to communicate faithfully what their eyes had seen, their hands touched, and their ears heard (1 Jn 1:1–4): the face of God imprinted on the unrecognizable face of the innocent one who was crucified, who had given himself up to death in order to express the authenticity of the Father's love.

Bibl.: L. DE LEON, *De los nombres de Cristo* (Valencia, 1680); O. CULLMANN, *Christ and Time* (1946; Philadelphia, 1964); id., *The Christology of the New Testament* (Philadelphia, 1959); V. TAYLOR, *The Names of Jesus* (London, 1954); id., *The Gospel According to Saint Mark* (London, 1957); R. BULTMANN, *Theology of the New Testament* (New York, 1955); E. SJÖBERG, *Der verborgene Menschensohn in den Evangelien* (Lund, 1955); F. GILS, *Jésus Prophète d'après les évangiles synoptiques* (Louvain, 1957); W. ZIMMERLI and J. JEREMIAS, "υἱός," *TDNT* 5:636–717; C. COLPE, "παῖς," *EDNT* 8:400–477; var., *Attente du Messie* (Louvain, 1958); J. COPPENS and L. DEQUEKER, *Le Fils de l'homme et les Saints du Très-Haut en Daniel*, vol. 7: *Apocryphes et le Nouveau Testament* (Louvain, 1961); F. HAHN, *Christologische Hoheitstitel* (Göttingen, 1963); E. JÜNGEL, *Paulus und Jesus* (Tübingen, 1964); E. DHANIS, "De Filio hominis in vetere testamento et in judaismo," *Greg* 45 (1964): 5–59; E. SCHÜRER, *History of the Jewish People in the Time of Jesus* (New York, 1961); L. SABOURIN, *The Names and Titles of Jesus*, Themes of Biblical Theology (New York, 1967); C. DUQUOC, *Christologie: Essai dogmatique*, vol. 1: *L'homme Jésus* (Paris, 1968); vol. 2: *Le Messie* (Paris, 1972); H. CONZELMANN, *An Outline of the Theology of the New Testament* (New York, 1969); E. SCHWEIZER, *Cristologia neotestamentaria* (Bologna, 1969); R. N. LONGENECKER, *The Christology of Early Jewish Christianity* (London, 1970); H. McARTHUR, *In Search of the Historical Jesus* (London, 1970); J. JEREMIAS, *New Testament Theology* (London, 1971); id., *Abba* (1966; Philadelphia, 1978); id., "Die älteste Schichte der Menschensohn-Logien," *ZNW* 58 (1967): 158–72; W. MARCHEL, *Abba! La prière du Christ et du Chrétien* (Rome, 1971); R. KEARNS, *Vorfragen zur Christologie*, vol 3: *Religionsgeschichtliche und Traditionsgeschichtliche Studien zur Vorgeschichte einen christologische Hoheitstitels* (Tübingen, 1972); M. SERENTHÀ, *Gesù Cristo, ieri oggi e sempre* (Turin, 1972); var., *La venue du Messie* (Paris, 1972); N. FÜGLISTER, "Les bases vétérotestamentaires de la christologie du Nouveau Testament," in *MystSal* 9 (Paris, 1972); var., *Il problema cristologico oggi* (Assisi, 1973); F. SCHNIDER, *Jesus, der Prophet* (Göttingen, 1973); G. VERMES, *Jesus the Jew* (London, 1973); W. KASPER, *Jesus the Christ* (London, 1976); R. PESCH and R. SCHNACKENBURG, *Jesus und der Menschensohn* (Freiburg, 1975); M. HENGEL, *Der Sohn Gottes* (Tübingen, 1975); A. GRILLMEIER, *Christ in Christian Tradition* (Atlanta, 1975); L. SCHEFFCZYK, *Grundfragen der Christologie heute* (Freiburg, 1975); F. LAMBIASI, *L'autenticità storica dei vangeli* (Bologna, 1976); H. SCHÜRMANN, *Jesus ureigener Tod: Exegetische Besinnung und Aufblick* (Freiburg, 1976); J. CABA, *El Jesús de los Evangelios*, BAC 392, Historia salutis (Madrid, 1977); C. F. D. MOULE, *The Origin of Christology* (London, 1977); K. RAHNER, *Foundations of Christian Faith* (New York, 1978); P. GRELOT, *L'espérance juive à l'heure de Jésus* (Paris, 1978); id., *Les poèmes du Serviteur: De la lecture critique à l'herméneutique* (Paris, 1981); R. LATOURELLE, *Finding Jesus through the Gospels* (New York, 1979); D. HILL, *New Testament Prophecy* (Atlanta, 1979); var., *Jésus et Jésus Christ* (Paris, 1979); X. LÉON-DUFOUR, *Face à la mort: Jésus et Paul* (Paris, 1979); J. COPPENS, "Où en est le problème de Jésus Fils de l'homme?" *ETL* 56 (1980): 282–302; id., *Loghia: Les paroles de Jésus*, ed. J. Delobel (Louvain, 1982); id., *Le fils de l'homme vétéro-intratestamentaire* (Louvain, 1983); E. SCHILLEBEECKX, *Expérience humaine et foi en Jésus Christ* (Paris, 1981); M. E. BORING, *Sayings of the Risen Jesus* (Cambridge, 1982); M. BORDONI, *Gesù di Nazaret*, vol. 2 (Perugia, 1982); E. COTHENET, "Prophétisme dans le Nouveau Testament," *DBS* 8:1222–1337; D. E. AUNE, *Prophecy and Early Christianity* (Grand Rapids, 1983); B. LINDARS, *Jesus Son of Man* (London, 1983); S. KIM, *The Son of Man as Son of God* (Tübingen, 1983); R. FABRIS, *Gesù di Nazaret: Storia e interpretazione* (Assisi, 1983); B. FORTE, *Jésus de Nazareth: Histoire de Dieu et Dieu de l'histoire* (Paris, 1984); var., *Prophets, Worship and Theodicy* (Leiden, 1984); var., *Gesù e la sua morte* (Brescia, 1984); H. FRIES, *Fundamentaltheologie* (Cologne, 1985); R. FISICHELLA, *La Rivelazione: Evento e credibilità* (Bologne, 1985); H. J. VERWEYEN, *Christologische Brennpunkte* (Essen, 1985); W. KERN, H. J. POTTMEYER and M. SECKLER, in *HFT* 2: *Traktat Offen-*

barung (Freiburg, 1985); K. H. OHLIG, *Fundamental-christologie* (Munich, 1986); J. GALOT, *"Christ, qui es-tu?"* (Louvain, 1986); C. I. GONZALES, *El es nuestra salvación: Cristología y Soteriología* (Bogotá, 1987); A. AMATO, *Gesù il Signore* (Bologna, 1988); G. CLAUDEL, *La confession de Pierre* (Paris, 1988); H. Urs VON BALTHASAR, *The Glory of the Lord*, vol. 7: *Theology: The New Covenant* (San Francisco, 1989); J. DUPONT, *Jésus aux origines de la christologie* (Louvain, 1989); S. PIÉ-NINOT, *Tratado de Teología Fundamental* (Salamanca, 1989); C. A. EVANS, *Life of Jesus Research: An Annotated Bibliography* (Leiden, 1989); H. WALDENFELS, *Manuel de théologie fondamentale* (Paris, 1990).

Rino FISICHELLA

IV. VARIOUS APPROACHES

In this article I shall describe various approaches to Christology and assess the value of each type. I shall also try to elicit some methodological principles.

1. Biblical Christology, Patristic Christology, Speculative Christology

Biblical Christology is not identical with exegesis. The latter attempts an interpretation of each scriptural text in particular, whereas biblical Christology to a certain extent already comprises a doctrinal systematization of the results of exegetical research. This systematic treatment operates at various levels. It may apply only to a group of texts with a particular theme, such as a Christology of the cross in Paul; or examine the doctrine of an individual author—e.g., the Christology of Matthew, Mark, Luke, or John; or proffer a more global view of Christology in the NT as a whole. Exegetes rightly stress the importance of respecting the ideas and orientations of each individual author and the inappropriateness of mixed interpretations. We cannot, e.g., interpret John by invoking Paul, or Luke in terms of Matthew. Nevertheless, various testimonies are connected in different ways, and comparisons can be made and parallels established that sometimes do indeed imply the dependence of this one on that other. Moreover, while maintaining distinctions between authors and detecting any evident pluralism, a synthesis of biblical data is called for that will define Christ

as revealed throughout Scripture. It is not sufficient to characterize the Christ of Mark, or of each evangelist. Finally, the Christ of the Gospel does have a certain countenance, and we have to determine the essential traits of this image.

Patristic Christology examines the contribution of the fathers of the church, which is itself grounded in the interpretation of the biblical revelation. Christology in the patristic mode is concerned mainly to establish the doctrine peculiar to each of the fathers, but also studies the pertinent course of historical development and the salient currents of thought.

Accordingly, it is concerned with the two schools that divided theologians in the fourth and fifth centuries: the school of Alexandria, which emphasized the unity of Christ and his divinity; and the school of Antioch, which stressed the duality and integrality of his human nature. Patristic Christology is especially concerned to bring out the meaning of the definitions of faith which emerged from christological controversies: the definitions of the Councils of Nicea (325), Constantinople (381), Ephesus (431), Chalcedon (451), the second Council of Constantinople (553) (whose declarations are definitive only inasmuch as they exclude Nestorianism), and the third Council of Constantinople (681).

Speculative Christology reflects on the revealed deposit of faith in order to produce a systematic account of doctrine and organize it rationally. It confronts problems that the redemptive incarnation poses for human understanding and, with the help of philosophical concepts, tries to determine the ontological constitution of Christ. It inquires into the psychology of Jesus and takes into consideration the development of his human consciousness and his exercise of human freedom. It tries to outline the characteristic traits of the human saintliness of Jesus; to understand how the development of grace and virtue was verified in him; and to show how it is possible to reconcile perfect holiness and the experience of temptations, as well as impeccability and freedom. Speculative Christology tries to define the meaning of the savior's mission and to explain the nature of the paschal mystery, the value of sacrifice, and the meaning of the glorious triumph that followed Jesus' passion and death.

There is no alternative in the development of

biblical Christology, patristic Christology, and speculative Christology. Speculative Christology, indeed, has to rely on revelation as contained in Scripture and as expressed in the tradition of the church. It should be noted, too, that christological speculation draws not only on the Bible and patristics but on the whole development of doctrine over the centuries. It accepts the contributions of scholastic theology, especially those of the great thirteenth-century thinkers, and more particularly those of THOMAS AQUINAS. It works in continuity with the whole modern theological movement and, of course, with the teaching adumbrated by the councils. Although Vatican II decided not to treat Christology expressly, it nevertheless offered views and indications in this area, above all in *Lumen Gentium* and *GAUDIUM ET SPES*.

2. Ontological Christology, Functional Christology

Ontological Christology seeks to determine the nature of the being of Christ. In plain terms, it affirms that Jesus Christ is true God and true man, and more precisely that he is the Son of God who by the incarnation became a human being like us in everything except sin. Although he is perfectly God and perfectly man, Christ is one, an individual subject. In this doctrinal reflection on that essential datum of revelation, Christology has recourse to the profession of faith of the Council of Chalcedon, which affirmed the union of the two natures in one person, a single hypostasis (DS 302). By using the term "hypostasis," the council wished to stress the ontological nature of the one person. Christology tries to establish precisely what constitutes the reality of the person and its distinction from nature.

Functional Christology is concerned to define and explain the function of Jesus. It concentrates on the work that Christ accomplished and on what humanity has received and continues to receive from him. The very name of Jesus, "Savior God" (see Mt 1:21), indicates the God in him who bestows salvation on humankind.

We note in our own time a particular interest in the development of functional Christology. It is a mode of reaction against the form taken by the treatise on the incarnation when restricted to an examination of problems raised by the unity of the person in the duality of natures. A certain number of theologians have rightly observed that the incarnation cannot be separated from its redemptive purpose, and that Christ is essentially the savior. Consequently, ontological Christology cannot develop independently of functional Christology. All forms of Christology must try to understand the mission of the Word made flesh.

There is, nevertheless, a less acceptable position—that of theologians who understand functional Christology in an exclusive sense. They are not interested in the ontology of Christ and think that the only valid object of Christology is to be found in what Christ did for us. This position sometimes relies on the conviction that the function of Christ is easier to determine than his ontology, and less subject to controversy.

In this regard, we must remember that functional Christology necessarily requires an ontological determination. The mission that Jesus carried out has a value and an effect that depend on what he is. If he were only a man, his actions would be much more limited. If he is God he can communicate his divine life to human beings.

According to the Gospel narrative, Jesus himself posed the ontological problem in the question he addressed to the Twelve: "Who do you say that I am?" (Mt 16:15 par.). Rather than ask what he came to do or what work he undertook to carry out, he asks them to tell him, in a dynamic expression of faith, who he is.

Since 1968, there has been a development, first in Latin America and then in other countries, of a special form of functional Christology: the Christology of liberation. The tendency here is to demonstrate Christ's answer to acute and grave problems of social and political injustice. It discovers principles in the Gospel that should guide society toward a form of government in which the rights of all people and justice are more sincerely respected, and in which there is a more equitable division of earthly goods. The perspective marked out by this Christology also decides its limits, for we cannot reduce the liberation that Christ bestowed on humanity to the level of a social and political regime and nothing else. The problem of evil in the world is much greater than that, and the salvation of Christ frees human beings from all kinds of sin. It endows them with a spiritual life that transforms and illumines hearts with a love whose fruits should be to the advantage of social life, but should also inspire all other aspects of human existence, with an essential orientation to the hereafter.

3. Christology from Below, Christology from Above

The terms "from below" and "from above" have been used to distinguish two different starting points for Christology. In German Protestant theology, the Christologies of Bultmann and Barth, otherwise very different from one another, are considered to be Christologies from above, for they are grounded on the word of God. W. Pannenberg's, however, is a Christology from below, since it proceeds from the historical Jesus to demonstrate his divine Sonhood.

The two terms may be associated with different interpretations. Thus, Rahner's transcendent Christology claims to be a Christology from below, although it does not take the historical aspect of Jesus as its starting point; it is based on a given anthropological foundation common to all men and women. I shall not go into the various nuances and perspectives of these terms but restrict myself to an examination of two essential methodological problems which they highlight.

The first problem has to do with the kind of knowledge applied by Christology. Does Christology proceed from the kerygma, from affirmations of faith, and from the message as preached, or is it derived from knowledge of the historical Jesus? The second problem is much more closely concerned with the primary object of study: Do we have to start with the divinity of Christ in order to arrive at his humanity, or must we argue from his humanity to his divinity? The two problems are connected. When Christology starts with the kerygma, it tends above all to consider the divinity of Christ. When, however, it starts with the historical Jesus, it is more inclined to look first at his humanity before moving on to affirm his divinity. Nevertheless, each of these questions deserves separate treatment.

a. Historical Christology, Kerygmatic Christology

Is the starting point the Christ of faith or the historical Jesus? Some theologians have expressed this difference by making a distinction between "Jesusology" and "Christology." Jesus is the man who lived historically in Palestine, and Christ is the one whom we proclaim in our faith.

In fact, the answer to the problem is not a matter of choosing one to the exclusion of the other. On the one hand, we have to admit the objective precedence of the historical Jesus; in this sense Christology is from below. On the other hand, there is a subjective precedence of the knowledge of faith, so that from this viewpoint Christology is from above.

The object of Christology is the Jesus of history. Christianity began with a historical event. It arose neither from a mere idea nor from a dogma or message, but from the life, death, and resurrection of Jesus of Nazareth. Accordingly, all Christology is "Jesusology." Christ can only be the historical Jesus.

Therefore the Jesus of history has to be studied in his earthly life, as reported in the Gospels. We cannot simply take the risen Christ as the starting point for Christology, as if revelation had occurred only in the resurrection and could only have awakened faith from that moment. In reality, Jesus revealed his identity as the Son of God in his public life, and well before the resurrection he asked his disciples for a profession of faith. The resurrection brought a new light to bear on things, but essentially one that confirmed the preceding words and gestures of Jesus. Christ became manifest as the Son of God and Savior in the historical conditions of his earthly life and not only in his glorified state. Objectively speaking, therefore, Christology developed on the basis of the Jesus of history. Subjectively speaking, however, the Christ of faith is its starting point.

When a human subject undertakes christological studies, his or her intellectual effort is usually founded on a knowledge and conviction of faith. Faith requires this effort, the better to understand what and why it believes. It draws on all the resources and means of exegetical and historical scholarship to discover the person of Jesus as it was apparent in history.

Hence anyone seeking to discern the historical Jesus should not make his or her faith abstract. While respecting the demands of scientific research, he or she must be guided by faith oriented to truth. It is a question not only of the researcher's individual faith but of the faith of the church, which has been handed down in a long tradition and is always in progress.

b. Ascending Christology, Descending Christology

Should Christology start with the humanity of Jesus and move upward, or begin with his divinity and proceed downward? Here, too, it is not a question of choosing one direction to the exclusion of the other, but of understanding how the two have their necessary place in christological studies.

Christology has its starting point in the human countenance of Jesus as described in the Gospels. His divinity is revealed in his humanity. We cannot conceive of two levels of revelation in Jesus, one divine and the other human. All that is divine in him is manifested through the human aspect. The Gospel accounts never offer us purely divine apart from human actions. Therefore we have to try to know the human words and gestures of Jesus in order to discover the person of the Son of God in him. But that does not imply a method that consists in studying solely what is human in a first stage, and then proceeding, in a second stage, to consider the revelation of the divine aspect. In fact, the entire humanity of Jesus bears the revelation of his divine person, and we cannot separate the two aspects.

An ascending Christology has to be completed by a descending Christology. If Jesus revealed himself as the person of the Son, we are not dispensed from inquiring into the origin of his presence on earth and from retracing the movement by which he who is God became human. That is what John undertakes in the prologue to his Gospel, by affirming that the Word which existed from eternity has been made flesh. More particularly, a descending Christology shows how the act of incarnation is primarily the decisive demonstration of the love of the Father, who has given his Son to humanity through the Spirit.

It should be stressed that the incarnation consists essentially in a descending movement. It is the Word that is made human and not a man that is made Word. The divine initiative takes precedence. Therefore we cannot consider Christ as the product of a human evolutionary process.

On the other hand, the mission of Christ exhibits an ascending movement, which also has to be acknowledged and studied. The visible image and sign of this movement are the final ascent to Jerusalem, which is systematically developed in the narrative of Luke's Gospel. By his passion and death Jesus arrives at his glorious triumph, which, through the bestowal of the Holy Spirit, culminates in the ascension and his elevation to heaven, where he sits at the right hand of the Father.

4. Dogmatic Christology, Existential Christology

Christology has sometimes been conceived of mainly as dogmatic, i.e., as grounded in the dogmas defined by the councils of the first centuries, above all those of Nicea and Chalcedon. This conception ran the risk of offering merely an abstract exposition, which was both too systematically conceptual and too detached from the actual framework of the work of salvation. As a reaction, some theologians wanted to promote a more existential and less essentialist Christology—one that would appeal to experience not only of the origins but of the present-day life of the church.

Christology, to be sure, derives from a unique initial experience, when Christ revealed his own mystery to his disciples. In itself the entry of the Son of God into the world constitutes an exceptional experience of a divine individual who lived a human life. This experience cannot be reduced to the conditions of the common experience of humankind; it has to be apprehended in accordance with its transcendent nature. There was the experience of the disciples who lived with Christ, received his revelation, and handed it on to subsequent generations. Throughout its history, the church has continued to experience Christ's presence, which is a faith experience illumined by the gospel revelation.

This kind of experiential Christology is not at all contrary to dogmatic Christology, if the latter is understood properly. The dogmas proclaimed by the councils are actually the fruit of the church's experience—the experience of a faith in the process of development, and one that seeks a better definition of the Christ to whom it professes adherence. The declarations of Nicea and Chalcedon are professions of faith resulting from an increasingly profound reflection on the meaning of revelation. We must remember, too, that the experience of the Christian faith can remain authentic only by self-recognition in the church's professions of faith and by reliance on them.

Dogmatic Christology acquires its proper vitality if we replace it in the existential perspective of the work of revelation and salvation. Existential Christology finds support and due expression in dogmatic affirmations.

5. Kenotic Christology, Christology of the Resurrection

Kenotic Christology appeared as a tendency in the nineteenth century. Its starting point is the kenosis affirmed by Paul in the christological hymn of Philippians (2:7). Christ Jesus, who subsisted in the form of God, has now emptied himself. This self-emptying, which characterizes the act of incarnation, has given rise to various interpretations. Some of them have conceived of kenosis in a radical sense, as a renunciation of divine properties, or have even extended it to the eternal life of the Trinity. This radical trend found a new expression in death-of-God theology, which developed mainly in the 1960s and 1970s, and proposed the idea of an absorption of Jesus' divinity by his humanity, so that the incarnation would signify a real death of God.

Though this extreme interpretation is inadmissible, kenosis does express the condition of Christ's earthly life. The incarnation does indeed comprise a renunciation of any manifestation of divine glory. Jesus himself said that he had come to serve (Mk 10:45), and the humility of his behavior implies an intimate self-emptying. Any Christology should include kenosis, with its culmination in sacrifice.

A converse direction is represented by the Christologies of resurrection. The most noteworthy recent example is Pannenberg's Christology. He sees the resurrection as the decisive eschatological event, in which God reveals himself personally. Pannenberg believes that this viewpoint enables him to arrive at a historical demonstration of Christ's divinity. His ideas are less readily acceptable when he treats Jesus' earthly life as a mere "prolepsis," or preamble.

The whole value of the resurrection has to be brought out, but at the same time we have to recognize the value of kenosis, both for the revelation of Christ's godhead and for his work of salvation.

6. Pneumatological, Eschatological, and Cosmic Christology

Some Christologies have stressed major aspects of the revelation of the person and work of Christ that have not previously received the attention they deserve.

Pneumatological Christology

Theologians have recently looked more closely than before at the relations between Christ and the Holy Spirit. In the past it was mainly the sending of the Paraclete by the Son that attracted most interest. But the operation of the Holy Spirit in the development of the church, on the basis of Pentecost, lies in the extension of his role in the earthly life of Jesus, as is shown in Luke's Gospel. Christology therefore tries to decide in what sense we may say that Christ was infused with the life of the Spirit.

Eschatological Christology

Christ came to fulfill the eschatological pronouncements of the old covenant. Therefore the eschatological aspect is essential for an understanding of the mystery of the redemptive incarnation. Christology is asked to determine what aspect of the promised eschatology was fulfilled in the "now" or the "hour" of Christ, and what was left to develop later, either in the earthly life of the church or in the hereafter. The value and consequences of the event which is the resurrection of Jesus need closer examination in this perspective.

Cosmic Christology

The mystery of the incarnation implies the transformation of the destiny not only of humanity but of the universe as a whole. The cosmic aspect of Christology was brought out above all by Teilhard de Chardin. He tried to incorporate the significance of the presence of Christ in the world in a scientific worldview. He combined an eschatological viewpoint with the cosmic perspective and proposed at the end of the universal process of evolution an omega point which is identical with Christ.

These ideas drew the attention of theologians to the cosmic fullness of the coming of Christ, which is suggested or underlined by certain NT texts.

Bibl.: C. F. Mooney, *Teilhard de Chardin and the Mystery of Christ* (London, 1966); J. P. Jossua, *Le salut: Incarnation ou mystère pascal chez les Pères de l'Église de saint Irénée à saint Léon le Grand* (Paris, 1968); W. Beinert, *Christus und der Kosmos: Perspektiven zu einer Theologie der Schöpfung* (Freiburg/Basel/Vienna, 1974); L. Bouyer, *The Eternal Son: A Theology of the Word of God and Christology* (1974; Huntington, Ind., 1978); A. Schilson and W. Kasper, *Christologie im Präsens: Kritische Sichtung neuer Entwürfe* (Freiburg/Basel/Vienna, 1974); J. D. G. Dunn, *Jesus and the Spirit: A Study of the Religious and Charismatic Experience of Jesus and the First Christians as Reflected in the New Testament* (London, 1975); G. Aulen, *Jesus in Contemporary Historical Research* (Philadelphia, 1976); var., *Jesus Ort der Erfahrung Gottes* (Freiburg/Basel/Vienna, 1976); M. Breidert, *Die kenotische Christologie des 19 Jahrhunderts* (Gütersloh, 1977); J. Caba, *El Jesús de los Evangelios*, BAC 392, Historia salutis (Madrid, 1977); P. J. Rosato, "Spirit Christology," *TS* 38 (1977): 423–49; R. F. Aldwinckle, *More than Man: A Study in Christology* (Grand Rapids, 1978); K. Rahner, *Foundations of Christian Faith* (New York, 1978); Y. Congar, "Pour une christologie pneumatologique," *RSPT* 63 (1979): 435–42; A. Grillmeier, *Jesus der Christus im Glauben der Kirche*, 2 vols. (Freiburg/Basel/Vienna, 1979, 1986; Eng. trans., vol. 1, *Christ in Christian Tradition* [London, 1975]); id., *Mit ihm und in ihm: Christologische Forschungen und Perspektiven* (Freiburg/Basel/Vienna, 1975); W. Kasper, *Jesus the Christ* (New York, 1976); R. Latourelle, *Finding Jesus through the Gospels* (New York, 1979); id., *Theology of Revelation* (New York, 1966); J. Galot, *Christ, foi et contestation* (Chambray, 1981); id., *Christ, qui es-tu?* (Louvain, 1986); id., *Christ de notre foi* (Louvain, 1986); G. Marchesi, *La cristologia di Hans Urs von Balthasar* (Rome, 1977); E. L. Mascall, *Theology and the Gospel of Christ: An Essay in Reorientation* (London, 1977); B. Mondin, *Le cristologie moderne* (3rd ed.; Alba, 1979); K. Rahner and W. Thüsing, *A New Christology* (New York, 1980); E. Schillebeeckx, *Expérience humaine et foi en Jésus-Christ* (Paris, 1981); M. Bordoni, *Gesù di Nazaret, Signore e Cristo: Saggio di cristologia sistematica*, vol. 1: *Problemi di metodo* (Rome, 1982); R. Latourelle and G. O'Collins, eds., *Problems and Perspectives of Fundamental Theology* (New York, 1982); B. Sesboüé, *Jésus-Christ dans la tradition de l'Église: Pour une actualisation de la christologie de Chalcédoine* (Paris, 1982); R. Latourelle, ed., *Vatican II: Assessment and Perspectives Twenty-five Years After* (New York, 1982), vol. 1, especially "The Word of God" (pp. 123–382) and "Christ: Revealer, Founder of the Church and Source of Ecclesial Life" (pp. 385–406); C. E. Gunton, *Yesterday and Today: A Study of Continuities in Christology* (London, 1983); G. O'Collins, *Interpreting Jesus* (London/Ramsey, 1983); Pontifical Biblical Commission, *Bible et Christologie* (Paris, 1984); B. Forte, *Jésus de Nazareth: Histoire de Dieu et Dieu de l'histoire* (Paris, 1984); G. Segalla, *La cristologia del Nuovo Testamento: Un saggio* (Brescia, 1985); J. A. Sayes, *Cristología fundamental* (Madrid, 1985); M. Serentha, *Gesù Cristo ieri oggi e sempre* (2nd ed.; Turin, 1986).

Jean Galot

V. Christology in Perspective

1. The Christological Focus of the 1980s

A task that continues to face fundamental Christology is the determination of its epistemological constitution and a more exact definition of its sphere of inquiry with regard to dogmatic or systematic Christology. However, given that there is some agreement on their undeniable overlap, it is with reference to their intrinsic connection and complementarity that we offer some reflections that can, in substance, be welcomed and shared by both christological perspectives.

At the heart of every discourse on Jesus Christ is the convincing proclamation of the apostle Peter: "For there is no other name under heaven given among mortals by which we must be saved" (Acts 4:12). This means that the proclamation of the Gospel in history continues to be summed up by the assertion: *Christ is still today the one and universal savior of all mankind.* One sees that the first encyclical of John Paul II's pontificate was devoted precisely to Christ *"Redemptor Hominis"* and "centrum universi et historiae" (*RH* 1). The task of all Christology is to offer the reason for this hope (see 1 Pt 3:15), i.e., for the meaning and value of every element and implication of this solemn proclamation and claim.

In the wake of the *ecclesiological* emphasis of the council and the *anthropological* focus of the postconciliar period, the 1980s witnessed an undeniable concern with *Christology*. This shift of emphasis (*déplacement*) toward Christ did not come about, however, by the simple repetition of the past, but through new forms of speaking, new questions and perspectives, which came to be articulated and which were often provocative in a positive sense. In the course of a providential, though sufficiently stormy, debate there have been a number of authoritative replies setting out the Catholic faith with regard to semidogmatic or completely profane ventures in Christology. We are referring to the publication of the scholarly contributions by the International Theological Commission (ITC) and the Pontifical Biblical Commission (PBC).

Between 1980 and 1986, the ITC published three documents of a christological nature. The first, *Quaestiones selectae de christologia* (official Latin text in *Greg* 61 [1980]: 609–32), analyzes the historical approach to the figure of Christ, not only as being possible and legitimate but as an essential demand of Christian faith. The unity between the historical Jesus and the glorified Christ is then reaffirmed, and likewise the continuity of the biblical data with subsequent dogmatic and ecclesial data. The second document, *Theologia, Christologia, Anthropologia* (official Latin text in *Greg* 64 [1983]: 5–24), reasserts the existing, intrinsic connections between, on the one hand, Christology and, on the other, trinitarian revelation and anthropology. The third document, *De Iesu autoconscientia quam scilicet ipse de se ipso et de sua missione habuit* (official Latin text published by Libreria Editrice Vaticana in 1986), confirmed, among other things, Jesus' knowledge of himself as Son and Messiah. The document, given the extreme range of opinions, did not address the question of how Jesus reached his knowledge-consciousness (for a suggestion as to how to understand the problem, see Amato 1988:381–97).

The PBC's study document, *De Sacra Scriptura et Christologia* (for the official Latin and French text, see Commission Biblique Pontificale, *Bible et Christologie* [Paris, 1984]), is both full and well argued. The first part contains a summary of contemporary approaches to the figure of Christ (classical, speculative, historical, religious, anthropological, existential, social, and new forms of systematic theological approaches), assessing their value and limitations. In the second part, consideration is given to the universal testimony of Sacred Scripture which is yet again summarized in the proclamation of Jesus Christ as Lord and universal mediator of salvation.

From the complex stock of christological endeavor in the 1980s there emerges the task of giving great attention to the *analogia fidei* (analogy of faith) (see *DV* 12). An adequate understanding of the Christ-event cannot be separated from the mystery of the Trinity (above all, with regard to its pneumatological dimension), nor can it be divorced from its intrinsic relationship to the mystery of humanity (recreated in Christ in the image of God), in its moral, spiritual, and, above all, liturgical life, as the highest concentration of the indissoluble unity of the truth and lived experience of Christology.

Hermeneutically speaking as well, one is faced with the urgent task of rebuilding a more harmonious relationship between biblical exegesis and dogmatic theology where they touch on crucial questions of Christology, as, for example, the correct interpretation and theological motivation of the incarnation, the messianic consciousness of Jesus, the salvific purpose of his death, the historical-metahistorical foundation and meaning of the resurrection, the reality of Jesus' divinity, his salvific presence in the church and the sacraments, and of the absolute finality of salvation in Jesus.

On the other hand, one cannot ignore the need to pay greater attention to the dialogue with the human sciences. And this is the case not only with those disciplines traditionally in contact with theology, such as philosophy, literature, and history but also with regard to new sciences—some of which first developed in an antireligious setting—such as psychology, sociology, educational sciences, and the sciences of social communication. The dialogue cannot be left to some of the branches of practical theology alone, such as catechetics and pastoral theology, but must also extend to fundamental and systematic Christology. Overcoming the phase of mutual suspicion or of a partial and expedient use of the other sciences, Christology will have to enter a period of dialogue and collaboration underpinning a definite choice of criteria.

We outline in greater depth some of the patterns in Christology, of which a number have already been partially affirmed, while others are gradually being sketched on the theological horizon of the 1990s.

2. Reevaluation of the Historical Jesus and Pre-Easter Christology

A fairly widespread tendency in Christology is the rediscovery and reevaluation of the theological importance both of history itself, understood in the wider sense of free and authentically human events that also embrace the dialogue of salvation between God and humanity, and the history of Jesus, understood as the foundation and ultimate motivation of his unique and unrepeatable saving event (see, e.g., Kasper 1976; Forte 1981). The story of Jesus is not an "optional extra" of which theology can make what it likes, as maintained, e.g., by R. Bultmann. It is precisely in the concrete history of Christ and in the universality of his earthly life that the absolute nature of his existential call, in terms of salvation, is both rooted and justified (see Acts 2:22–24). History reaches its maximum soteriological receptivity and fruition in Christ, from the point when his existence (=actions, words, behavior, miracles, paschal mystery) is simultaneously definitive salvation for us.

From this point of view, liberation theology's emphasis on the historical Jesus is completely justified, provided that it fully respects the personal continuity with the Christ of post-Easter faith and ecclesial dogma. In this way there emerges the real possibility of an *implicit* or *pre-paschal Christology* as the indispensable basis for understanding the Easter Christ and an explicitly post-Easter Christology. The pre-Easter Jesus has an intrinsic christological and soteriological significance, and together with the Easter mystery constitutes a fully salvific event. It is by beginning with his extraordinary pre-Easter *exousia* (authority) that one can legitimately make the transition to his equally extraordinary *ousia* (divine reality). We are speaking about implicit Christology, not in the sense that in the historical Jesus there was any lack of decisive signs of christological identity, but in the sense that these signs were not sufficiently understood by the disciples. The existence of Jesus, as the expression of his intimate self-knowledge, is completely oriented in a christological sense or direction. He always presents himself as the one who bears the absolute authority of God in the spiritual realm. For this reason one can also speak of an *implicit* or *open Christology*, in the sense that pre-paschal

Christology—and such is the incipient faith of the disciples—remains open to its completion in the resurrection, which is the decisive event of illumination and authentic understanding with regard to the entire Christ-event.

This historical rooting of the Christ-event means that every hypothesis intent on a mythological understanding of the incarnation is untenable. On the contrary, the light of the resurrection presents the final disclosure of the salvific originality of the historical figure of Christ, in absolute discontinuity with the interpretation and appropriation that make of him, e.g., the contemporary Jewish *Leben-Jesu-Forschung*, where Jesus is considered simply the "great brother" or enlightened master and official interpreter of the law of Israel (see, e.g., S. Ben-Chorin, *Fratello Gesù: Un punto di vista ebraico sul Nazareno* [Brescia, 1985]; H. Falk, *Jesus the Pharisee: A New Look at the Jewishness of Jesus* [New York, 1985]).

3. Christology "Of the Others" or "From Outside"

Within modern culture one sees the emergence of an extraordinary *Christology "of the others" or "from outside."* We are dealing with the understanding of Jesus Christ, in its most positive, yet also reductionist, sense as engaged in outside Christianity—by atheists, non-Christians, and agnostics—or outside traditionally approved theological circles, e.g., by the psychological sciences, literature, and art. Above all, one detects a *humanistic* model of Christ, who is held up as the universal man, the most decisive of all ordinary human beings, the source of genuine humanity, the model of a liberated existence, the insuperable support of precious moral ideals, without which even the richest, best-organized, and most technically perfect society remains uncivilized. According to this humanistic view, Jesus is acknowledged as having attributed an absolute value to each person and as having replaced the tyranny and arrogance of power with the action of giving and sharing (see Jaspers 1957; Kolakowski 1975: 32–39; Machovec 1974: 40ff.; Lombardo Radice 1976: 24ff.; Belo 1974). Even the psychological approach sees in him not only "the exemplary man," and thus a completely balanced human personality, lacking animosity, hypocrisy, cruelty, and rigidity, but also an unequalled "psychotherapist," whose great psychological maturity becomes for others the instrument of creative and humanizing transformation (see H. Wolff, *Jesus Der Mann: Die Gestalt Jesu in Tiefenpsychologie* [Stuttgart, 1975]; id., *Jesus als Psychotherapeut: Jesu Menschenbehandlung als Modell moderner Psychotherapie* [Stuttgart, 1978]).

This humanistic interpretation opens up uncharted areas for reevaluation of the human richness of the figure of Jesus as the just man who, reaffirming the dignity of each person independently of his or her economic, intellectual, moral, psychic, or physical status, offers himself as a model of humanity fully relevant today. Moreover, the freshness of language has a salutary, life-giving, and innovative function in comparison with the dry and often repetitive style of conventional theological vocabulary. On not a few occasions, these humanistic interpretations, while coming from a view of the world that is one-dimensional and materialistic, and which on principle denies the transcendent, paradoxically give expression to the urgent need to escape from the gravitational pull of wicked and inhuman systems. What seems at first to be a history of the "disinterpretation" of Jesus accepted only as human, could also be considered an extreme attempt to anchor Christ as the authentic support of the task of being human.

In addition to the humanistic model, we can also detect a *religious model* of Jesus, such as appears in the Jewish, Hindu, and Islamic interpretations of Jesus. He comes to be viewed as a teacher of true religious living (*guru*), a martyr to self-sacrifice and to universal brotherhood, the full incarnation of God for the enlightenment and salvation of the world (*avatāra*), a prophet of the Most High, guide to true human morality, a martyr to justice. The human and religious significance of the "Jesus-for-others" is a refreshing antidote to quite a few Christians confused in their faith and dubious of the relevance in human terms of being a Christian today (see de Rosa 1989; Küng 1993; Vernette 1987).

4. Plurality of Christological Perspectives and Understandings

This assimilation and appropriation of Jesus by others challenges Christians to reconsider the timeless question of Christology: "But who do you say that I am ?" (Mt 16:15), with the consequent need to be motivated afresh by Simon Peter's reply: "You are the Christ, the Son of the living God" (Mt 16:16). For Christians, Jesus is not someone or something relative, and thus one among many models of humanity and religiosity; in terms of salvation he is absolute. He is the universal reconciler (Col 1:20; Eph 1:10), the liberator from the slavery of sin (Rom 6:17–18), the creator anew of humanity and nature (Rom 5:1; Ti 3:5–6), the Son of God incarnate (Jn 1:14), profoundly human while being the Son of God (Heb 2:17ff.; 4:15; 5:7ff.), the sole mediator between God and humanity (1 Tm 2:5). The Christian understanding surpasses and fulfills the non-Christian interpretations.

While the central core of christological proclamation has remained intact, from the very beginning Christians have employed different models for interpreting the Christ-event. If the perspective of orthodox Christology is, by tradition, that of *glory*, that of Lutheranism is of *the theology of the cross*. Contemporary Catholic Christology is characterized at its roots by the emphasis on the *humanity* of Jesus, by an *existential-praxical call*, and by *dialogue with modern culture*. This has given rise to a plurality of models and approaches. One has, e.g., Christology from below or from above, and Christologies that are variously cosmic, historical, transcendental, or aesthetic, as well as those from the perspective of liberation theology, inculturation, and popular religiosity (→ CHRISTOLOGY IV: VARIOUS APPROACHES). The theological legitimacy of these models is given by their ability and willingness to mediate the universality of the Christ-event, avoiding the pitfalls of fragmentation, reductionism, and mutual incommunicability. On account of their notable capacity for evolution and future development, we will pause to examine only some of these approaches.

5. Christology and Inculturation

For the Second Vatican Council, the history of Christian evangelization has been and continues to be a constant process of "cultural adaptation," "dialogue with cultures," and "vital exchange with different cultures" (see *GS* 44, 58): "Verbi revelati 'accomodata praedicatio' lex omnis evangelizationis" (*GS* 44). From the 1977

Synod of Bishops on, the term INCULTURATION refers to an essential demand of engaging in theology today (see ITC, "Fides et inculturatio," *Greg* 70 [1989]: 625–46). A list of theological criteria with regard to inculturation has already been drawn up. This is essentially the incarnation of the mystery of Christ in a specific culture and its expression anew in the language, cultural symbols, experience, indeed in the "flesh" of the different peoples being evangelized (*Christological criterion*). This "re-creation" of culture, purified of what is potentially unworthy, is effected by the whole ecclesial community (*ecclesiological criterion*) and serves to liberate and enlighten the person who is evangelized (*anthropological criterion*).

The acute sensitivity to the originality and identity proper to the different cultural zones of the church offers the fullest of panoramas with regard to inculturated or contextual Christologies. In addition to Latin American Christology, one sees the emergence of both Asian and African understandings of the person of Christ. There are, e.g., interesting possibilities for Christology in the Philippines, India, Japan, Korea, and New Guinea. In Africa too an inculturated Christology is being developed, such as viewing Christ as chief, ancestor, elder brother, healer, master of the rites of initiation. They are African names and concepts that would lead to a better understanding of the person of Jesus Christ and his saving mystery. Among the most fitting titles, it seems that that of "elder brother" has emerged as being particularly appropriate. African authors are conscious, however, that the mystery of Jesus Christ cannot be totally assimilated and expressed by indigenous categories without loss of originality. In Christ there has to remain an irreducible and untranslatable "otherness."

6. Liberation Christology

We are dealing with a specific contemporary example of an *inculturated* interpretation of Jesus Christ arising from the liberation theology of Latin America (→ THEOLOGIES). We may illustrate this by referring to the Christologies outlined by L. Boff and J. Sobrino. Boff begins from two interpretative factors with regard to the Christ-event: the historical circumstances and the poverty of Latin America. This means "on the social level: collective oppression,

exclusion, and marginalization; on the human level: injustice and the denial of human dignity; on the religious level: social sin, which is something 'contrary to the plan of the Creator and the honor which must be given to Him' (Puebla 28)" (see L. and C. Boff, *Come fare teologia della liberazione* [Assisi, 1986], 12).

The theology of liberation is rooted in the encounter between the poor Christ and the poor of this world: "The Crucified One is present in the crucified of this world, lamenting and uttering his cry of invocation" (ibid., 12). Jesus Christ "is God in the midst of our distress, the eternal Son who has assumed the form of a real Jew," who "makes his own the hopes of the oppressed and proclaims that now (today) they are fulfilled. The Messiah is thus he who brings about the liberation of the needy today" (ibid., 83). Christ comes to be seen as the liberator, and as the one who promotes a praxis of liberation in the church: "The Christology that proclaims Jesus Christ as liberator seeks to commit itself to the economic, social, and political liberation of groups suffering oppression and domination. It endeavors to consolidate the theological dimension of the historical liberation of the vast masses of our continent. . . . In this way it offers to articulate the contents of Christology and to create a style that highlights the liberative dimensions in the historical course of Jesus' life" (L. Boff, "Jesus Cristo Libertador: Uma visão cristológica a partir da periferia," *REB* 37 [1977]: 502).

J. Sobrino also places an eminently practical purpose on his Christology: "Hermeneutics seeks not only to resolve the problem of the truth of affirmations that come to be made about Christ, but also to find the way to make them understandable and effective, that is, to make existing tradition concerning Christ something that continues to be living and real" (see *Christología desde América Latina: Esbozo a partir del seguimiento del Jesús histórico* [Mexico City, 1977], 299). To do this he adopts two criteria of fidelity: that of the hermeneutics of praxis, which implies fidelity to the actual situation, and that of the historical Jesus, which entails being faithful to the practice of the biblical Christ.

Both Boff and Sobrino, having given emphasis not so much to the understanding and truth about Christ as to his transforming and liberating effect on the reality of oppression, select and accentuate those elements that are to be found in special relationship with the paradigm of liberation (kingdom of God, resurrection as utopia), and with the proper practical attitude to attain it (the social activity of Jesus, the duty to follow it). It is a decision that elicits from the saving work of Christ those occasions capable of shaping and transforming the present: "We believe that the historical Jesus is the hermeneutic principle at the noetic level as at the level of praxis with regard to approaching the totality of Christ, in whom is the actual fulfillment of the unity of Christology and soteriology" (ibid., 8; for further details see J. Sobrino, *Jesús en América Latina: Su significado para la fe y la cristología* [Santander, 1982]).

Let us say straight away that the term *liberation* is highly attractive to the modern world; it has a strongly emotive impact, and it evokes the image of human life that is both free and fulfilled (see the Instruction *Libertatis nuntius*, n. 1). The *preferential option for the poor* is the choice or decision that underpins the theology and Christology of liberation. It is a question of an evangelical obligation that arises from the actual praxis of Jesus Christ and which the church in Latin America made its own at the Conference of Latin American Bishops in Puebla in 1979. Puebla accepted the theme of liberation as being required by, and indispensable to, the doctrine and mission of the church (nn. 355, 562, 1254, 1270, 1283, 1302), dedicating much space to evangelization, liberation, and human promotion (nn. 470–506) and to the preferential option for the poor (nn. 1134–65). The "liberative" and "active" application of the christological message—on account of the strong emphasis given by the theology of liberation—is today much more widely known throughout the church, having become a *precious and liberating resource.* The same instructions from the Congregation for the Doctrine of the Faith issued in 1984 and 1986 (see *AAS* 76 [1984]: 876–909; 79 [1987]: 554–99) have not failed to legitimize the freedom-giving expressions and applications of the theology of liberation (see the Instruction *Libertatis nuntius* [1986] I–IV), while guarding against a rigid and uncritical assumption of Marxism as the principle determinative of theological research (ibid., nn. VII–VIII). The option for the poor is sustained by a marvelous *concrete witness*,

even to the point of martyrdom, by our brothers and sisters in Latin America, which allows the poor and dispossessed to claim both dignity and freedom. Through such an interpretation of the liberating effect of the Christ-event, some often neglected elements of the Gospel are recovered, such as the political and social implications of the christological message on the Latin American situation. Jesus comes to be regarded as a force for challenge and liberation, capable of removing the mechanisms of injustice and oppression, and of promoting the task of building a new, fraternal, just, and truly evangelical world in present-day Latin America. Finally, the Christology of liberation "represents the first marginal theology developed from the problems arising therein, yet having universal aims" (L. and C. Boff, *Come fare teologia della liberazione*, 134). It carries within itself the features of modernity and universality because it concerns itself with the poor, with men and women howsoever humiliated and discriminated against (economically, socially, politically, racially, sexually, culturally, religiously), by redeeming and freeing them through preaching the Gospel of Jesus Christ. The Christology of liberation presents Jesus Christ as the true source of *humanization* for the modern world.

Despite these undoubted merits, we can mention some criticisms offered and accepted by the Boffs (ibid., 99–100). They allow that the theology of liberation devalues somewhat the mystical dimension of Christianity; they also admit an exaggerated emphasis on the political sphere, to the detriment of other, more deeply human and evangelical aspects; likewise a certain subordination of the discourse of faith to the discourse of society and an inappropriate emphasis on issues of class, without taking account of what is specifically religious and Christian; an exaggerated absoluteness given to the theology of liberation, with a consequent carelessness with regard to the validity of other theological viewpoints; too great a concentration on the socioeconomic figure of the poor in the Gospel, thus minimizing the importance of other aspects of social oppression, such as racial and sexual oppression; too great an emphasis on the fragmentation, as opposed to the continuity, of the church's pastoral action; insufficient attention to the doctrinal and social teachings of the pontifical and local magisterium, and too little attention given to understanding the different expressions of the church; the use of a method—that of Marxist analysis—"that no longer holds the monopoly on historical change" (ibid., 133). To these criticisms one may add that the almost exclusive insistence on the social-structural working of the Gospel and on orthopraxis runs the risk of elevating the principle of the practical efficacy alone of the Christ-event into an absolute criterion of truth. If this were true, much would be lost of the meaning of the central mystery of Christian redemption and salvation, represented by the passion, death, and resurrection of Jesus. With further reference to content, the Christology of liberation underlines those aspects of the story of the earthly Jesus which can be interpreted as a concrete model of liberation: his solidarity with the poor, his lack of conformity to oppressive structures, his attitude of challenging the powerful. The emphasis on the historical Jesus alone risks neglecting the biblical-ecclesial Christ, who is approached with a certain degree of distrust and as without concrete incidence in the praxis of liberation. In this way an overwhelming gap is created between the Jesus of history and the Christ of ecclesial faith, dogma, liturgy, and sacraments, who is the real agent in the history of the praxis of full human liberation. The risk is that a "profane" reading of Jesus emerges. His figure and person, cut loose from his true trinitarian and pneumatological context, are reduced almost exclusively to the empirical-factual level, regarded only as a privileged, if not unique, bearer of christological meaning. In this way there is a tendency to minimize the witness of the Gospels to Jesus' obedience to the Father, to his messianic knowledge of being the liberator from sin and death, to his redemptive sacrifice, and his death on the cross. "These temptations," we may conclude with the Boffs, "will be the more easily avoided as theologians of liberation come to be imbued with the meaning of Christ (see 1 Cor 2:16), bound to the ecclesial community and nourished in a life-giving way by the strong mystical infusion of religion and popular faith" (ibid., 100).

7. Christology and Popular Religiosity

Popular religiosity, also known as "popular devotion," "popular piety," "religiosity of the people," is a universal and complex reality in the church. Describing the popular religiosity of Latin America, Puebla affirms:

> by the religion of the people, popular religiosity or piety, we mean the complex of deep beliefs sealed by God, of fundamental attitudes that are derived from these convictions and the expressions by which they are manifested. It is a question of the cultural or existential form adopted by religion in a particular people. The religion of the Latin American people, in its most characteristic cultural form, is an expression of the Catholic faith. It is a popular Catholicism. (Puebla 444)

Popular religiosity is rich in positive elements. It contains a mixture of values that respond with Christian wisdom to the great questions of existence. It has the sense of the sacred, displays a thirst for God, expresses a most moving fervor and purity of intention that only the poor and the simple can have (EN 48; CT 54); it is open to the Word of God, having faith in the providence and in the constant, loving presence of God the Father, and it has a great sense of prayer (EN 48; Puebla 454, 913); it is a popular Catholic wisdom that has a capacity for making a vital synthesis which unites the divine and human in a creative way, and likewise Christ and Mary, spirit and body, communion and institution, person and community, faith and country, intellect and emotion (Puebla 448, 913); it celebrates Christ in the mystery of his incarnation (Christmas, the infant Jesus), in his crucifixion, in the Eucharist, and in devotion to the Sacred Heart (Puebla 454, 912); it progresses in knowledge of the mystery of Christ and his message, of his incarnation, redemptive cross, his resurrection, the working of the Spirit in every Christian (CT 54); it gives expression to love of Mary, who is venerated as the Immaculate Mother of God and of humanity (Puebla 454); when it is a question of witnessing to the faith, it is capable of heroic sacrifice and generosity (EN 48; Puebla 913); it has a strong sense of sin and the need for expiation (Puebla 454); it expresses the faith in a full-bodied way (song, images, action, color, dance), situating it in time (feasts) and places (sanctuaries and churches), and lives it deeply in the sacraments and sacramentals of personal and social life (Puebla 454); it fosters interior attitudes rarely seen to the same degree elsewhere: patience, an awareness of the cross in daily life, openness to others, devotion (EN 48), practice of the evangelical virtues (CT 54), detachment from material things, solidarity (Puebla 454, 913); it has filial respect for the pastors of the church and a lively affection for the Holy Father (Puebla 454). Through its profound human and Christian wisdom, popular religiosity can constitute an authentic "Christian humanism that asserts the radical dignity of each person as a child of God, establishes a basic fraternity, teaches a true encounter with nature, an understanding of work, and provides the motives for a certain good humor and wit, even though it finds itself living a very hard life" (Puebla 448).

Yet one cannot underestimate the dangers of popular religiosity, above all when it is ignored and overlooked by the work of evangelization and catechesis. The limitations of an ancestral pattern are superstition, magic, fatalism, idolatry of powers, fetishism, and ritualism (EN 48; Puebla 456). Catechesis is stunted by the following: a static archaism, misinformation and ignorance, syncretistic reinterpretations, reduction of faith to a simple contract in one's relationship with God; likewise, an exaggerated value given to the cult of the saints to the detriment of knowledge of Jesus Christ and his saving mystery (EN 48; Puebla 456, 914). The threats to popular religiosity are secularism spread by the means of social communication; consumerism; sects; oriental and agnostic religions; ideological, economic, social, and political manipulation; messianic movements of a secular, political nature; urban poverty and uprooting on account of cultural change (Puebla 456). There is thus an urgent need for purification, of continual rectification (CT 54), but above all, theological consideration of popular religiosity in order to make it a model for the proclamation of the Gospel throughout the world.

We must point out that Puebla also refers to what we may call "the Christ of popular religiosity." Whatever the level of real understanding, or debasement, of Jesus by popular religiosity, he remains forever a Christ who is seen, heard, welcomed, and loved by the people. However disfigured or impoverished from the point of view of reason—perhaps to the gain of the Blessed Virgin or some of the saints (Puebla 914)—it is he who enlightens and sustains the people's entire existence, support-

ing and guaranteeing their highest values and authentic aspirations. This is proved by participation in the mass and other sacraments, and above all by receiving the Eucharist; by the celebration of important liturgical feasts of the Lord; by the use of christological devotions, such as that of the Sacred Heart; by Christ's protective presence in their houses in the form of images, altars, and statues (Puebla 912). Students of folklore and popular religiosity have identified a number of images of Christ typical of popular piety in Latin America. There is a particularly strong devotion to *the dead Christ* (with whom the people identify; the famous crucifix in the church of St. Francis at Bahía in Brazil, which is a synthesis of the "popular Christology" of Latin America), to the infant Jesus (which arouses feelings of tenderness), to *Christ the heavenly king* (which stimulates courage and strength amid the difficulties of life and persecution of the faith), and to Christ the King of Peace (proclaimed by those who first evangelized the continent). These images are more than simply of Spanish origin.

Faced with the reality of this popular Christology, Puebla stipulated a renewed evangelization, without any reduction or preconceived selectivity with regard to the figure of the biblical-ecclesial Christ, who is "true God and true man" (171): "Christ, our hope, is in our midst as the One sent by the Father, enlivening the church with his Spirit and offering mankind today his own word and his very life, in order to bring them to the fullness of his liberation" (166). "It is our duty to announce clearly, without leaving room for doubt or equivocation, the mystery of the incarnation: both the divinity of Christ as the church professes it, and also the reality and power of his human and historical dimension" (175); "We cannot deform, reduce or ideologize the person of Christ, either as a political figure, a leader, a revolutionary, or a simple prophet, or by restricting to the merely private sphere he who is the lord of history" (178; cf. 179). It is thus at the very basis of the dogmatic integrity of the mystery of Christ that the church in Latin America situates the proclamation of complete (including the socioeconomic) liberation of oppressed peoples: "In solidarity with the sufferings and hopes of our people, we feel the urgency of giving them what is specifically ours: the mystery of Jesus of Nazareth, the Son of God. We feel that this is the "strength of God" (Rom 1:16), capable of transforming our personal and social situation and bringing us toward freedom and brotherhood, toward the full revelation of the kingdom of God" (181).

8. Christology and Non-Christian Religions

Plurality of Models

A decisive challenge for contemporary Christology is that posed by the meaning and universality in terms of salvation of the Christ-event, not only with regard to non-Christian religions and the sects but also for Christianity itself in relation to those authors who have developed a theology of non-Christian religions which assigns them an efficacy in salvific terms. Thus the "myth of God incarnate" (see J. Hick, ed., *The Myth of God Incarnate* [London, 1977]) was followed ten years later by the "myth of Christian uniqueness" (see J. Hick and P. Knitter, eds., *The Myth of Christian Uniqueness: Towards a Pluralistic Theology of Religions* [Maryknoll, N.Y., 1987]), with the single-minded development of a line of argument set upon questioning, relativizing, and even denying the two-thousand-year-old knowledge of the Christian faith with regard to the incarnation of the Son of God and the unique and absolute nature of the salvation of the whole human race in the one mediator, Jesus Christ.

The point at issue in this challenge to Christology stems from the council's reevaluation of the salvific value of non-Christian religions, by the weakening of the missionary spirit within Christianity, and by the modern resurgence of other religions, which after centuries of lethargy and cultural subordination, have rediscovered the source and guarantee of basic human values, national identity and independence, universal peace and harmony. Joint INTERRELIGIOUS DIALOGUE, emigration, the end of colonialism, proselytism, the mysterious preoccupation with Eastern exoticism, and the offer of an alternative style of life and culture to the postmaterial existence of the Western world—each of these factors appears to add a new dimension to the so-called arrogance of Christianity with regard to salvation. Thus it is that quite a few Christian theologians openly question the assertion of Christ as the unique and universal savior, developing at the same time a new frame of soteriological reference in relation to the other offers of salvation available in our planetary culture.

In the most schematic sense one may point to five models that seem to have emerged with regard to the soteriological significance of Christ today. The *exclusive* model, on the one hand, rejects non-Christian religions as idolatrous and erroneous and, on the other hand, reasserts the unconditional absoluteness of Christianity (see, e.g., K. Barth). This model proposes an ecclesiocentric universe and a Christ who is *exclusive* mediator of salvation.

A second model, termed *inclusive*, has a dialectical attitude of acceptance and criticism: it accepts the partial validity of non-Christian religions in the order of salvation (see *LG* 16; *GS* 22); but it contests their claim to absolute salvation. The possible presence therein of faith, grace, and salvation is brought by Christ, who is the constitutive source of all salvation available both within and outside Christianity. This model envisages a christocentric universe and a Christ who is the *constitutive* mediator of salvation. This is the view of the council, shared by authors such as A. Dulles, K. Rahner, and P. Rossano (see Dulles 1983; Rahner 1966, 1978; Rossano 1981).

The *normative* model rejects the view of the uniqueness of salvation in Christ and asserts instead that all religions have an intrinsic salvific value independent of the founder of Christianity. They would all be relatively true, even if "made normative" by Christ. Rather than being the constitutive mediator of salvation, Christ is the *normative* mediator, who by the exemplary nature and fullness of the same Christ-event corrects and fulfills the other media of salvation, which remain intrinsically salvific. "And since one can say that God has said and done more than has been said and done in Christ, Christians engage in dialogue with other religions not only to teach, but to learn, possibly, much that they had never known before" (P. Knitter, "La teologia cattolica delle religioni a un crocevia," *Conc* [1986]: 137). According to P. Knitter, this understanding "has become . . . a commonly held view among Catholic theologians today. In different ways it is representative of H. Küng, H. R. Schlette, M. Hellwig, W. Bülmann, A. Camps, P. Schoonenberg" (ibid., 138; cf. Bülmann, 1983; Camps 1983; Hellwig 1983: 127–55; Küng 1966, 1993; Schlette 1963; Schoonenberg 1966: 89–109). In this vision of Christ as the normative savior, the perspective is neither ecclesiocentric nor strictly christocentric, but theocentric.

The fourth model, the *pluralistic* model, takes as its explicit starting point the myth of Babel, more than the mystery of Pentecost. It advocates a multiplicity and an absolute pluralism of mediators and salvific media, all of equal validity. Christ would be one of many mediators, since it would be impossible to offer objective historical evidence for the uniqueness of his saving event: "More concretely and uncomfortably, one may say that Buddhism and Hinduism are just as important for the history of salvation as Christianity, or that the other agents of revelation, the other saviours, are just as important as Jesus of Nazareth" (Knitter, "La teologia cattolica," 138ff.; the same author has developed his position in the book *No Other Name? A Critical Survey of Christian Attitudes toward the World Religions* [Maryknoll, 1985]). The authors who follow this line think that the single founders and single religions of the world are absolute means of salvation for their followers, with a decisive importance for other religions, which can find in them both completion and inspiration (see, e.g., Maurier 1976; Panikkar 1981; Pieris 1983, 1982; Puthiadam 1980; Thompson 1985). The uniqueness of Christianity is considered a myth to be overcome in view of a pluralistic theology of religions (this is the thesis defended in the volume edited by Hick and Knitter, *The Myth of Christian Uniqueness*; see also L. Swidler, ed., *Toward a Universal Theology of Religion* [Maryknoll, 1987]). For them Jesus Christ is a *relative* savior in a generically sacred universe.

There is, finally, a fifth model, that of *liberation* or of *religions without reference to Christ*. This is the latest stance of Knitter, outlined in 1986 and then developed with greater precision the following year (see Knitter, "La teologia cattolica," 133–44; id., "Toward a Liberation Theology of Religions," in Hick and Knitter, eds., *Myth of Christian Uniqueness*, 178–200). He begins from the presupposition that theologians of liberation and theologians of religions must work together because they have the same end in view. Rather than an INTER-RELIGIOUS DIALOGUE rooted in God, it is incumbent upon human beings to secure liberation by means of orthopraxis. It is humanity, not God, which is the theological locus for dialogue.

There is a need to move away from an ecclesiocentric, christocentric, or theocentric position to a "kingdom-centeredness" or "soteriocentric" position (see Knitter, "Toward a Liberation Theology," 187). In Knitter's view, the problem does not concern the way in which each religion is related to the church, to Christ, or to God, but how it is committed to promoting human welfare and to bringing liberation to the poor and the marginalized. The criteria of distinction between religions are not, therefore, doctrinal but practical: they depend on their soteriological effectiveness in terms of humanization. Christians do not need to understand Jesus Christ to be the sole universal savior in order to be committed to promoting salvation. On the contrary, it is ORTHOPRAXY that constitutes the ultimate criterion of religious value. In this sense Jesus would be simply a *complementary* savior (ibid., 194) from an anthropocentric perspective.

Some Possible Solutions

The conciliar model, that of Christ as the constitutive mediator of salvation, is founded substantially on the assertion of God's universal salvific will and on the unique mediation of Christ "[God] desires everyone to be saved and to come to the knowledge of the truth. For there is one God; there is also one mediator between God and humankind, Christ Jesus, himself human, who gave himself a ransom for all" (1 Tm 2:4–6). Yet in the positive evaluation of non-Christian religions, even though they are a gift of God to humanity, the ultimate distinguishing feature between Christianity and non-Christian religions is still the Christ-event, his self-revelation in history, his privileged presence in the church, and his identity as the sacrament of salvation in human history. There is no conflict between Christianity and non-Christian religions, but a transcendence accepted by faith, a faith motivated by history. History, not in a positivistic sense, is fitted to display particular signs of a possible incarnation and presence of the absolute savior. If in fact history entertains more than one manifestation of a high priest, it can also offer the Christophany. If history is able to sustain the myth of Babel, it can also entertain the mystery of Pentecost, the event whereby all the peoples are saved in Christ.

The absolute nature in salvific terms of the

Christ-event has a bearing on the claims of the historical Christ and on the historical-theological understanding of that event as it has been transmitted by the NT, whose historical trustworthiness is not without reason considered inferior to its testimony of faith. The decisive factors of such a claim may be reduced to seven points: the proclamation of the kingdom and its advent-identification with that same person of Christ, in whom are fulfilled all the promises of creation and the covenant; the preresurrection knowledge of Jesus that he is Son and Messiah; the paschal mystery of his death and resurrection; the revelation of God as love and as trinitarian communion; the experience of divine sonship in each human person; the experience of the saving encounter of humanity in Christ through the church; the historical-metahistorical universality of Christian salvation. From these factors emerges the absolute discontinuity of Jesus with regard to the other mediators of salvation, and at the same time the complete fulfillment in him and in the church of all the desires for salvation of humanity and the cosmos.

9. The Need for a "Lived" Christology

The practical application of the theology of liberation and the urgency of the preferential option for the poor highlight the necessity to forge a strong link between the truth-bearing criteria of the Christ-event and the criteria essential to a "lived" Christology. An adequate christological position will not have to assure an "orthodox" christological stance alone. It would not have to limit itself to proclaiming the truth of the Christ-event, summarized thus: (a) by narrating its history (biblical dimension); (b) by recognizing his presence as the Living One today (ecclesial dimension); (c) as the unique and universal mediator; (d) of a salvation that is intrinsically important to humanity and the world. It would also have to outline and give thematic expression to a "lived" Christology in complete correspondence with the truth proclaimed. Indeed, the truth-bearing criteria are also essential criteria. Thereby the narration of the story of Jesus comes to be experienced as a personal encounter with him (personal criterion); the recognition of his presence as the Living One today becomes the experience of meeting him in the ecclesial setting, where the church celebrates the Eucharist and the other *mirabilia Dei* (communitarian criterion); faith in Jesus as the absolute and definitive savior becomes the experience of an integral personal and communitarian salvation (salvific criterion); and, finally, the affirmation of the saving importance of Christ translates itself into an authentically Christian culture (practical-cultural criterion). One would then have the summit of the practical and cultural importance of Christology. It is not that life in Christ is exhausted and neutralized in its historical fulfillment, but rather that Christian culture continually moves human history to transcend its own limits and imperfections until it is completely fulfilled in him.

This universal christocentric perspective does not mean an entirely christomonist position, but rather it sees Christ as the one who reveals, and acts as the catalyst for, all personal and communitarian existence, the lord of history and of the cosmos, the origin, the providential sustainer, the orientation, the purpose and end of every creature. This is the mystery of the Father that led the apostle Paul to cry out with joy:

> May you be made strong with all the strength that comes from his glorious power, and may you be prepared to endure everything with patience, while joyfully giving thanks to the Father, who has enabled you to share in the inheritance of the saints in the light. He has rescued us from the power of darkness and transferred us into the kingdom of his beloved Son, in whom we have redemption, the forgiveness of sins.
>
> He is the image of the invisible God, the firstborn of all creation; for in him all things in heaven and on earth were created, things visible and invisible, whether thrones or dominions or rulers or powers—all things have been created through him and for him. He himself is before all things, and in him all things hold together. He is the head of the body, the church; he is the beginning, the firstborn from the dead, so that he might come to have first place in everything. For in him all the fullness of God was pleased to dwell, and through him God was pleased to reconcile to himself all things, whether on earth or in heaven, by making peace through the blood of his cross. (Col 1:11–20)

Completely enraptured by the reality of this mystery, the apostle exclaims, "For to me, living is Christ" (Phil 1:21); "it is no longer I who live, but it is Christ who lives in me" (Gal 2:20). The goal of all Christology is life in Christ.

General Bibliography: (1) For an overview: A. AMATO, *Gesù il Signore: Saggio di Cristologia* (Bologna, 1988), 381–97. (2) See especially: W. KASPER, *Jesus the Christ* (New York, 1976; German original, Mainz, 1974); B. FORTE, *Jésus de Nazareth: Histoire de Dieu et Dieu de l'histoire* (Paris, 1984). (3) K. JASPERS, *Die grossen Philosophen* (Munich, 1957), 280–307; M. MACHOVEC, *Gesù per gli atei* (Assisi, 1974); F. BELO, *Lecture matérialiste de l'Évangile de Marc* (Paris, 1974); L. KOLAKOWSKI, *Senso e non-senso della tradizione cristiana* (Assisi, 1975), 32–39; L. LOMBARDO RADICE, "Figlio dell'uomo," in I. FETSCHER and M. MACHOVEC, *Marxisti di fronte a Cristo* (Brescia, 1976), 24–25. (4) J. VERNETTE, *Jésus dans la nouvelle religiosité* (Paris, 1987); G. DE ROSA, *Cristianesimo, religioni e sette non cristiane a confronto* (Rome, 1989); H. KÜNG, ed., *Christianity and World Religions* (New York, 1993). (5) See K. RAHNER, "History of the Word and Salvation-History," in *Theological Investigations*, vol. 5 (1962; London/New York, 1966), 97–114; id., *Foundations of Christian Faith* (New York, 1978); P. ROSSANO, "Christ's Lordship and Religious Pluralism," in G. ANDERSON and T. STRANSKY, eds., *Christ's Lordship and Religious Pluralism* (Maryknoll, N.Y., 1981), 96–110; A. DULLES, *Models of Revelation* (New York, 1983). (6) H. R. SCHLETTE, *Die Religionen als Thema der Theologie* (New York, 1963); P. SCHOONENBERG, "The Church and Non-Christian Religions," in D. FLANAGAN, ed., *The Evolving Church* (Staten Island, N.Y., 1966), 89–109; H. KÜNG, *On Being a Christian* (New York, 1966); W. BÜLMANN, *God's Chosen Peoples* (Maryknoll, N.Y., 1983); A. CAMPS, *Partners in Dialogue* (Maryknoll, N.Y., 1983); M. HELLWIG, *Jesus the Compassion of God* (Wilmington, Del., 1983). (7) See H. MAURIER, "The Christian Theology of Non-Christian Religions," *Lumen Vitae* 21 (1976): 59–74; I. PUTHIADAM, "Fede e vita cristiana in un mondo di pluralismo religioso," *Conc* 17 (1980): 895–915; R. PANIKKAR, *The Unknown Christ of Hinduism* (Maryknoll, N.Y., 1981); A. PIERIS, "The Place of Non-Christian Religions and Cultures in the Evolution of Third World Theology," in V. FABELLA and S. TORRES, eds., *Irruption of the Third World: Challenge to Theology* (Maryknoll, N.Y., 1983), 113–39; id., "Parlare del Figlio di Dio in culture non cristiane," *Conc* 19 (1982): 429–39; W. M. THOMPSON, *The Jesus Debate* (New York, 1985.

Special Bibliography: For Christology and inculturation, see the general bibliography in A. AMATO, "Inculturazione, Contestualizzazione, Teologia in contesto," *Sal* 45 (1983): 442–46. For Christology in the context of the Philippines, see E. MENGUITO, "Christology in the Philippines" (bibliography) *DIWA* 6 (1981): 93–100; N. T. YATCO, *Jesus Christ for Today's Filippino* (Quezon City, 1983); B. BELTRAN, *The Theology of the Inarticulate: An Inquiry into the Filippino Understanding of Jesus Christ* (Manila, 1987). For Christology in India, see PANIKKAR 1981 (above); M. M. TOMAS, *The Acknowledged Christ of the Indian Renaissance* (London, 1969); K. CRAGG, "Christology and India," in id., *The Christ and the Faiths* (London, 1986), 173–241; M. VEKATHANAM, *Christology in the Indian Anthropological Context* (Frankfurt/Bern/New York, 1986). For Christology in Japan, see H. S. TAKAYANAGI, "Christology and Postwar Theologians in Japan," in *Postwar Trends in Japan: Studies in Commemoration of Rev. Aloysius Milles, S.J.* (Tokyo, 1975), 119–67; id., "La cristologia nell' attuale teologia giapponese," in K. KITAMORI, *Teologia del dolore di Dio* (Brescia, 1975), 9–27; Y. KUMAZAWA, "Confessing Christ in the Context of Japanese Culture," *The North East Asia Journal of Theology* 12 (1979): 1–14; R. J. SORLEY, "A Christology for Japan," *The Japan Christian Quarterly* 50 (1984): 31–40. For Christology in China, Korea, New Guinea, and the cultures of the Southern Pacific, see, e.g., J. SANGBAE RI, *Confucius et Jésus-Christ* (Paris, 1979); C. WRIGHT and L. FUGUI, eds., *Christ and South Pacific Cultures* (Suva Fiji, 1985); R. COVELL, *Confucius, the Buddha, and Christ: A History of the Gospel in Chinese* (Maryknoll, N.Y., 1986). For African Christology, see F. KABASELE, J. DORÉ, and R. LUNEAU, eds., *Cristologia africana* (Cinisello Balsamo, 1987). See also A. NGINDU MUSHETE, "The Figure of Jesus in African Theology," *Conc* 196 (1988): 73–79. For liberation Christology, see C. BUSSMANN, *Befreiung durch Jesus? Die Christologie der lateinamerikanischen Befreiungstheologie* (Munich, 1980); M. COOK, "Christology from the Other Side of History: Christology in Latin America," *TS* 44 (1983) 258–87; EQUIPO SELADOC, *Panorama de la teología latino-americana*, vol. 6: *Cristologia en América Latina* (Salamanca, 1984); J. MEJIA, "Cristologia en algunos autores latinoamericanos," *Medellín* 10 (1984): 176–86; J. VAN NIEUWENHOVE, "Jésus-Christ dans la réflexion chrétienne en Amérique Latine: Analyse d'une problématique," in id., *Jésus et la libération en Amérique Latine* (Paris, 1986), 19–52; S. CAJIAO, "La cristologia en América Latina," *Theologia Xaveriana* 36 (1986): 363–404. For Christology and popular religion, see J. DANTSCHER, "Jesus in der Frömmigkeitsgeschichte der Kirche: Der fromme Jesus," in F. J. SCHIERSE, ed., *Jesus von Nazareth* (Mainz, 1972), 174–86; S. GALILEA and R. VIDALES, *Christología y Religiosidad Popular* (Medellín, 1977); D. D. FERNANDEZ, "Cristología y cultura de masas en minimilagros," *Christus, Mexico* 46 (1981): n. 542, 9–21. For Christology and non-Christian religions, besides the bibliography mentioned in the article, see the following general studies: R. F. ALDWINCKLE, *Jesus A Savior or The Savior? Religious Pluralism in Christian Perspective* (Macon, Ga., 1982); H. BÜRKLE, "L'unicità dell'evento di Cristo di fronte alla mentalità asiatica," *Comm* 101 (1988): 59–79; E. HILLMANN, *Christ and Other Faiths* (Maryknoll, N.Y., 1988); id., "Jesus Unsurpassable Uniqueness: A Theological Note," *Horizons* 16 (1989): 101–30; P. MOJZES, ed., "Universality and Uniqueness in the Context of Religious Pluralism," *Ecumenical Studies* 26 (1989): n. 1, 1–216); L. NEWBIGIN, "Religious Pluralism and the Uniqueness of Jesus Christ," *International Bulletin of Missionary Research* 13 (1989): 30–54; M. BARNES, *Religions in Conversation: Christian Identity and Religious Pluralism* (London, 1989).

Angelo AMATO

CHURCH

I. FUNDAMENTAL ECCLESIOLOGY

1. Origin of the Tractate *De Ecclesia*

The problem of the scientific demonstration of the truth of the Catholic church, and thus of establishing that Roman Catholic Christianity is in complete continuity with the intentions and work of Jesus Christ, the founder of the church, is a question that, in principle, was posed with the appearance of the first schisms. But the chapter of classic apologetical ecclesiology designated *Demonstratio Catholica* is a modern creation. Neither the heresies of antiquity nor the medieval separation of Christians of East and West had provoked a religious crisis of the magnitude of that of the sixteenth century, with its various opposing communions claiming to be the true heirs of Christ: Catholicism, Anglicanism, and Protestantisms of different kinds. Despite certain anticipations (the earliest being that of Giacomo of Viterbo, 1301–1302), the treatise *De Vera Ecclesia* appeared only in the sixteenth century, to be consolidated, developed, and transformed without interruption over a number of cen-

turies, up until its great revival in VATICAN COUNCIL I (1870).

This ecclesiology subsists in three traditional forms, typfied in three respective "ways." The *via historica* attempts to demonstrate, by way of an examination of ancient documents, that the Roman Catholic church is the Christian church of all times, appearing in history as a single, visible, ongoing, and hierarchically organized society. In practice, this "way" is reduced to the so-called *via primatus*, which is a simplification of the *via historica* in that it restricts itself to an effort to show the truth of the Roman church on the basis that its head, the bishop of Rome, is the legitimate successor of Peter, prescinding from all the other aspects of historical continuity.

The second way is the *via notarum*, which unfolds in terms of the following syllogism. Jesus Christ endowed his church with four distinctive notes or marks: unity, holiness, catholicity, and apostolicity. But the Roman Catholic church alone possesses these four marks. Therefore, it is the true church of Christ, to the exclusion of the remaining Christian confessions, such as Lutheranism, Calvinism, Anglicanism, and Orthodoxy, which do not possess them.

Finally, the third "way" is the *via empirica*, adopted by Vatican Council I thanks to its champion, Cardinal Dechamps. That council follows a simpler method: abandoning all confrontation between the current Roman Catholic church and antiquity, in order to escape the difficulties encountered in an interpretation of the historical documents, as well as to obviate the need for a concrete verification of the notes (→ CHURCH V. NOTES), it emphasizes instead the value of the church in itself as a moral miracle functioning as a divine sign confirming its transcendence.

The treatise on the church, then, after its early anticipations in the fourteenth century with Giacomo of Viterbo, and in the fifteenth with Juan de Ragusa and Juan de Torquemada, by the sixteenth century was commonly presented in two steps: the tractate *De Vera Religione*, followed by the *De Ecclesia*. The latter adopted a forthright persuasive and apologetic perspective—appearing as it did at the moment of the first struggles with Lutheranism and Calvinism—and by the year 1550 had been diffused throughout the length and breadth of Europe, if with widely differentiated nuances.

On the basis of this initial formulation, the treatise on the church, especially in terms of its most common "way," the *via notarum*, underwent a number of changes, in function of the particular sensibilities of a given moment. Thus, in the sixteenth and seventeenth centuries, the "notes" in question tended to appeal to Scripture and the fathers as their source. On the other hand, in the eighteenth and nineteenth centuries the emphasis was usually on the four intrinsic notes of ecclesiastical society. At the close of the nineteenth and in the first half of the twentieth centuries—i.e., between Vatican I and Vatican II—these four notes were presented by and large in a romantic spirit, with the emphasis on the worldwide expansion of Catholicism, and the cohesion and fecundity of the church.

Of these three ways, the *via notarum* has been the one most utilized in ecclesiological treatises and, while distinct from the other two, has not always been distinguished from them very clearly. Its spirit calls for premises in the *via historica*: the notes must be historically verified. And its matter is intimately bound up with the *via empirica*: when all is said and done, the notes are perceived as constituting a miracle of the moral order.

In this process, the ecclesiological legacy of Vatican Council II is relevant, with its twin contribution, a reference to the *via primatus*, centered on papal infallibility (DS 3053–74), and the essence of the *via empirica*, the orientation to the church as a sign, and therefore motive of credibility (DS 3012–14). The conciliar text, while citing the *via notarum* in passing—"*Ecclesiam 'notis' instruxit*" (DS 3012)—goes no further.

2. Perspectives of Vatican II in Fundamental Ecclesiology

The church as sacrament of communion—a specific category of Vatican II—is rich in material for an orientation of fundamental theology. The expression reflects a decentralization of the church vis-à-vis itself, as it centers the church altogether on Christ. The concept has a twofold value: *internally*, it posits the church, the primordial sacrament, as the root of the sacraments; and *externally*, it visualizes the

mission and "significative" mediation of the church for the world, with both values united in "one interlocked reality" (*LG* 8). This proposition now constitutes a restatement of the classic syllogisms of the three "ways" of apologetic demonstration of the true church. It manifests the "difficulty" of grasping its external-internal "globality" by way of its sacramental character—i.e., by way of being not a "demonstrative sign" but an indicative, "monstrative" one and, at most, a sign revelatory of mystery, hence perceptible only to the eyes of faith.

In turn, Vatican II makes an explicit reference to the notes of the church: "This is the unique Church of Christ which in the Creed we avow as one, holy, catholic, and apostolic." And the text goes on to specify at once that "this Church, constituted and organized in the world as a society, subsists in (*subsistit in*) the Catholic Church" (*LG* 8). As we readily observe, both the language and the very intention of the text reject all exclusivity and oneness of the true church as these would be conceived in a closed fashion, while leaving room for positivity and acknowledgment of the Catholic church as the true church. The verb *subsistit* (replacing the *est* of the original draft) underscores not exclusivity (which *est* could easily have implied) but a character of openness and positivity. Thus, the *subsistit* has the intention and discharges the function of avoiding an uncontrolled identification of the church of Christ with the Roman Catholic church, maintaining an openness to the ecclesial reality present in the other Christian confessions.

Furthermore, the category "sacrament" used by Vatican II recalls the expression of Vatican I: "Ecclesia, signum levatum in nationes" (DS 3013). Indeed this formula is explicitly cited in *SC* 2; *LG* 50; *AG* 36; and *UR* 2, and always focuses on the sign of unity in charity. The church, then, is a sign of the coming of salvation among human beings, inasmuch as it reflects in our world the oneness and the love of trinitarian life. Vatican II, through a process of personalization that extends to the entire economy of salvation and its transmission, speaks of individual and community witness, where Vatican I speaks of miraculous attributes of the church. Thus fundamental ecclesiology receives a new orientation across the board.

Conclusion: Witness is an ecclesial sign of credibility and a paradigm for fundamental ecclesiology. The category of "witness" has gradually come into theological language, especially since Vatican II, where it is omnipresent (133 times). In the Bishops' Synods on Evangelization (1974) and the Laity (1987), the theme was vigorously emphasized, just as in the corresponding Apostolic Exhortations, *Evangelii Nuntiandi* and *Christifideles Laici*. In this perspective, witness becomes an ecclesial sign of credibility and a paradigm for fundamental ecclesiology.

Indeed, the category of witness, besides typifying the Christian and ecclesial life par excellence, is adopted by current reflexive philosophy (J. Nabert, Emmanuel Levinas, Paul Ricoeur) in its triple empirical, juridical, and ethical dimension, to become the hermeneutic locus that "reveals" the confluence of two elements occurring in witness: its vector of historical observation and verification, and its vector of the expression of self-witness. Rightly, then, may one speak of an authentic "metaphysics of witness," a body of cognition having the capacity to demonstrate the reasonable possibility of testimony to an absolute that is also fully historical.

In its own turn, theological reflection recalls that, if witness is to be an ecclesial sign of credibility, it must always refer to the apostolic church (along the vector of historical objectivity) as transmitter of the "DEPOSIT OF FAITH" (*DV* 10; *GS* 62; *UR* 6). It is in this framework and in terms of this perspective that we may speak of *Ecclesia mater congregans* ("the church as the gathering mother"): the vehicle of that *founding witness* that is the apostolic church functioning as the presence of the risen Lord to the end of the ages (see Mt 28:26–30). At the same time, this founding testimony will set the stage for the realization of its correlative: the *Ecclesia fraternitas congregata* ("the church as the gathered community"), a formulation of the subjective vector, that of the church as witness to itself, consisting in the *living testimony* offered by Christians through their lives and their history (see 1 Cor 1:2; Rom 1:7; Eph 5:27; 1 Thes 4:7; 2 Thes 2:13–14; etc.). Functioning as mediation between the two is the *witness of the Spirit* who animates the church as *Spiritus in Ecclesia* (see *LG* 4).

Thus emerges the decisive function of witness as a route of ecclesial credibility and a synthesis of the best of the three classic "ways" of access to the truth of the church. This approach is not reducible to a focus either on a merely outward, extrinsic credibility—the risk run by a classic ecclesiological apologetics—or on a merely inward, subjective credibility, the fideist danger, the upshot of an attempt to compensate for the first approach. Rather, it centers its attention on an understanding of credibility as a simultaneously (by reason of its integrating character) external and internal invitation to faith. Thus, in this *credibility of ecclesial witness* all three dimensions intersect: (1) the outward dimension, the fruit of a historical connection with the *founding apostolic witness* of the church; (2) the interiorized dimension, arising from the ecclesial experience of *living witness*; and (3) the inward and interiorizing dimension, due to the *witness of the Spirit*, who animates and sanctifies the church.

Bibl.: Y. CONGAR, *L'ecclésiologie de S. Augustin à l'époque moderne* (Paris, 1970); R. LATOURELLE, *Le témoignage chrétien* (Montreal, 1971); id., *Christ and the Church: Signs of Salvation* (New York, 1972); id., "Évangélisation et témoignage" in M. DHAVAMONY, ed., *Évangelisation* (Rome, 1975), 77–110; A. ANTÓN, *El Misterio de la Iglesia*, 2 vols. (Madrid, 1986, 1987); S. PIÉ-NINOT, "Hacia une eclesiología fundamental basada en el testimonio," *RCT* 9 (1984): 401–61; id., *La Chiesa come tema teologico fondamentale*; in R. Fisichella, ed., *Gesù rivelatore* (Casale Monferrato, 1988), 140–63; id., "Ecclesiologia fundamental: Status questionis," *RET* 49 (1989): 361–403.

Salvador PIÉ-NINOT

II. JESUS AND THE CHURCH

1. Historical Sketch

A consideration of Jesus and the church, especially the origins of the church, is basic for the Christian faith. The NT writings themselves present these origins, in a variety of germinal strokes, in terms of a believing description of the church's own self-comprehension. The preeminent locus of the development in question is the Pentecost event and the ensuing activity on the part of the APOSTLES, especially Peter, as the pioneer of the first Christian community, and Paul, the missionary of the Gentiles, who thus become the great bearers of this development and formation of the church. The requirements for membership in the first Christian community were conversion to faith in Christ, baptism, the pentecostal gift of the spirit, celebration of the Eucharist, and an operative, communitarian love (see Acts 2:38, 42–47). In the Gospels themselves, throughout the Jesus narrative, we frequently encounter elements of the formation of a church conceived as a continuation of Jesus' preaching and mission, especially through the apostles. Still more relevantly, theological and organizational elements of the infant church appear in the Pauline literature and the other NT writings.

Only with the fathers of the church, however, as with Ignatius, Irenaeus, Origen, John Chrysostom, and especially Ambrose and Augustine, does the question of the formation of the church come under theological consideration as an actual founding or institution of that church. This is the focus that, by and large, will be maintained until the Enlightenment and the dispute over modernism in the early years of the twentieth century. Indeed, beginning with the great fathers, the formation of the church is seen in the mysterious image of the birth of the church from the side of the crucified One, as Eve sprang from the side of Adam (Ambrose *In Psalmum 36*, no. 37 [*PL* 14:986], *Epistola 76*, nos. 3–4 [*PL* 16:1260]; Augustine *In Johannem Tractatus*, book 9, chap. 2, no. 10; book 15, chap. 4, no. 8; book 120, chap. 19, no. 2 [*PL* 35:1463, 1513, 1953, etc.]. The symbolism is an important one and survives into the Middle Ages. In particular, it is cited by the Ecumenical Council of Vienne in 1312 (DS 901).

In the subsequent period, characterized by ecclesiastical power struggles, a new element enters theological reflection on the founding of the church: the election and mission of the apostles, especially of Peter, as the first members of the ecclesiastical hierarchy. Under the influence of juridical thinking, the concept of *jus divinum* ("divine right") is introduced as warranty for the historical and "foundational" fidelity of the church and its institutions. With the dispute over Scripture as the *norma non normata* ("norm not normed"), the criterion of the *jus divinum* becomes the touchstone of LUTHERANISM, which has adopted the formula *sola Scriptura* ("Scripture only"). The Council of TRENT will give special attention to these two concepts, situating them in their proper places.

Thereafter, the Counter-Reformation will place great emphasis on the ministry of Peter and on the papacy as a guarantee of continuity between Jesus and the church.

It was not until the Enlightenment, then, and the controversy over modernism properly so-called, that the critical question of the "singular foundation of the church by Jesus of Nazareth" was posed. Vatican I (1870) itself declared that Christ "determined to build the holy church" ("sanctam aedificare ecclesiam decrevit," DS 3050). But it was the documents of the magisterium issued in connection with MODERNISM that dealt with the problem more directly: concretely, the decree *Lamentabili* (DS 3452) and the encyclical *Pascendi Gregis* (DS 3942), both published in 1907 and both recapitulated in the Oath against Modernism of 1910, which reads: "The church was instituted immediately and directly by the actual, historical Christ himself while he lived among us" (DS 3540).

On the basis of these texts issuing from the magisterium, manuals of fundamental theology and ecclesiology introduced an important new treatise into their respective subjects, intending it as an apologetic prolegomenon to all theology. The expressions "instituting," "founding," and "building" now achieved common currency where the relationship between Jesus of Nazareth and the church was concerned. The specific "founding" acts of Jesus were explicitly listed: the calling and sending of the Twelve, the institution of the primacy of Peter and its succession, the transmittal to the apostles of the threefold power of Christ (the "power of teaching, sanctifying, and ruling"), and the institution of the Eucharist as the new covenant (J. B. Franzelin, H. Dieckmann, A. Tanquerey, J. Salaverri, T. Zapelena, M. Schmaus, F. A. Sullivan, and others).

Only with Vatican II does this theme achieve a more complete and integrated focus. Indeed, *LG* 2–5 sketches an entire processual view of the institution of the church. Only in no. 5 are the words "foundation" and "Founder" finally used. In the aftermath of the council, an important document issued from the International Theological Commission on 7 October 1985, on the occasion of the twentieth anniversary of the conclusion of Vatican II. It deals with "select topics in ecclesiology," beginning precisely with that of the "foundation of the church by Jesus Christ" (*EV* 9:1673–80) and represents both a response to certain perhaps rather skeptical or critical positions (Hans Küng, Leonardo Boff, etc.) and an adjusted, updated Catholic synthesis on this question.

Let us now review the more relevant theological points of this historical panorama, since, in the articulation of a state of the question proper to fundamental theology and ecclesiology concerning Jesus' originating and founding relationship with the church, we shall do well to keep account of a number of theological questions implied in this theme.

2. Two Classic Binomials of the Relationship between Jesus and the Church

Actually, the specific question provoked by the Enlightenment and by the modernist controversy over the foundation of the church, despite its novelty, and consequently its parallelism with the appearance of fundamental theology as a discipline, has its roots in two broader theological questions, to which we have already referred and which have been debated all through the history of theology. We mean the relationship between, respectively, Scripture and the church, and *jus divinum* and *jus ecclesiasticum*—the classic binomials of our topic, "Jesus and the Church." It will be in order, then, to indicate the salient elements of these binomials, as we shall thereby have the basic points we need for a correct theological state of our question.

Scripture and Church

Since the first origins of the life of the church, Scripture has been regarded as a normative instrument of all activity, communitarian and private alike. This is the meaning of the celebrated formula *norma normans—norma non normata* ("norm norming–norm not normed") employed to designate Sacred Scripture as the literary objectification of the faith of the apostolic church, which in turn is the norm and foundation of the church of all times. As supreme criterion of all Christian behavior, Scripture acquired a function of exceptional importance for the definition and preservation of the deposit of faith, by reason of the basic significance attributed to the deposit of faith as a fundamental, characteristic component of the authentic church of Christ. Now, in the fathers

and in medieval theology alike, Scripture and tradition were regarded as subsisting in intimate connection. Only with the Protestant crisis did that connection come to be questioned, and Luther responded with his famous axiom *Sola Scriptura*.

The matter came in for debate at the Council of Trent and was taken up anew in Vatican II. As for the Tridentine decree (DS 1501) and its interpretation, there is now considerable consensus among Catholic scholars that, where the object of faith is concerned, Sacred Scripture is materially sufficient, and that tradition, in this case, exercises the mere function of *traditio interpretativa* ("interpretative tradition"). As for the mores and customs of the church, however, Scripture is insufficient and must be completed materially (in its content) by tradition, which in this case is *traditio constitutiva* ("constitutive tradition") (J. R. Geiselmann, Georges Tavard, Yves M.-J. Congar, Joseph Ratzinger, J. Beumer, J. M. Rovira Belloso, etc.).

This interpretation of the text of Trent—not common before Geiselmann's pioneering study on the question—helped Vatican II formulate an approach calculated to transcend various dualisms of Scripture and tradition. Thus, *DV* avoids the extremes by stressing the integration of the two, speaking not of two fonts, but sacred tradition and sacred Scripture as "flowing from one and the same divine wellspring" (*ex eadem scaturigine promanantes, DV 9*). From this single font or source, Scripture arises as the sole word of God, to be transmitted by church tradition. The function of the latter, basically, is a decisively criteriological one, explicitly indicated by the council under three aspects: tradition (1) identifies the canon of sacred books (ibid.), (2) specifies the certitude entertained by the church with respect to all revealed truths (ibid.—the point that occasioned the most debate at the council), and (3) creates an in-depth application of Scripture to the problems of today (ibid., 8, 12, 21, 24–25). The meaning attributed to polemical formulations like the theory of the "two fonts" among Catholics, or that of "Scripture alone" among Protestants, is thereby rendered an anachronism (see the commentaries on the council by U. Betti, P. Lengsfeld, B.-D. Dupuy, A. Franzini, and others).

Jus Divinum and Jus Ecclesiasticum

The question of a *jus divinum* ("divine right") was first broached by the Council of Trent and became a bone of contention with Lutheranism, especially in directly sacramental questions: Were the sacraments actually "instituted" by Jesus? Rather than propounding an ecclesiological viewpoint and a definition of the theological framework of the ministries of the church, Trent determines the power of the priesthood in terms of a theology of the sacraments. In this context, the concept of a *jus divinum* arises as a relevant argument for the revealed nature of a corresponding question—one that will arise again at Vatican I—of the primacy. Vatican II, adopting the declarations of both of these earlier councils, frames them in a specifically ecclesiological and ecumenical perspective. Let us examine the most important points of this question—which is generally relegated to treatises on law (perhaps owing simply to the form of its expression, *jus*), but which is of basic theological and ecclesiological importance.

In general terms, we may say that the expression *jus divinum* usually designates a reality of positive divine institution for which a scriptural reference can be cited. Augustine himself defined it as equivalent to that which is attested in Scripture: "Divinum ius in Scripturis habemus" (*In Johannem Tractatus*, book 6, chap. 25; *PL* 35:1436). Indeed, there is a *jus divinum* because there is Scripture (*PL* 33:665, n. a). Thomas Aquinas took his position along these same lines—"Jus divinum est quod pertinet ad legem novam" (*ST* I–II, q. 107, a. 4; and elsewhere)—and specified that this law does not suppress the *jus humanum* ("human right") or the *jus ecclesiasticum* ("church right") since the "jus divinum quod est ex gratia non tollit jus humanum quod est ex naturali ratione" (II–II, q. 10, a. 10).

The Lutheran reform, and Luther himself, frequently employed the notion *jus divinum*, meaning that which is legitimated by Scripture. Thus, Luther wrote: "Sacra Scriptura, quae est proprie jus divinum" (*WA* 2279:23–24). In fact, the equivalency between *jus divinum* and Scripture is altogether clear in the Esmacalda article—redacted by Luther—which reads: "Quod Papa non sit jure divino seu secundum verbum Dei, . . ." as well as in Melanchthon's commentary, which introduced the concept of

jus humanum to explain the superiority of the pope over the bishops. This expression of the *jus humanum* is very similar to the perspective indicated by the *votum* of Franciscan Juan Antonio Delphino at the Council of Trent, which situates it in the "third degree" of *jus divinum*: the first degree designates everything found explicitly in Scripture; the second refers to anything implicit or concomitant in Scripture; the third degree consists of the statutes of the church and the councils and may be qualified as *jus humanum*.

Significantly, the expression *jus divinum* is absent from direct references to the episcopate in the councils of Trent (DS 1776) and Vatican II (*LG* 28). At the same time, the entire context, and the formulas used to replace the expression *jus divinum*—especially *divina ordinatio* or *institutio*—indicate a broader comprehension. On the other hand, the explicit expression is used in Vatican I apropos of the perpetuity of the succession of Peter, which is qualified as *de jure divino* (DS 3058). Here the formula occurs at the conclusion of the second chapter, where no explicit Gospel text is invoked—although Mt 16:18 and Mt 28:20 are paraphrased, along with a lengthy citation of Philip, the papal legate at the Council of Ephesus, and texts of Leo the Great, Irenaeus, and Ambrose. The meaning of Scripture in the interpretation of the church, then, is plain: "This utterly clear doctrine of the Scriptures, in the substance and manner that the Catholic church has always understood it" (DS 3054), is a legitimate route to the acknowledgment that an institution is *de jure divino*. Indeed, it seems obvious that neither the "divine institution/ordination" of Trent or Vatican II, nor the *jus divinum* of Vatican I, may be identified with an exclusive, explicit foundation on the part of the Lord, since various structures can be instituted by the apostolic church under the direction of the Holy Spirit, as the Scriptures attest, or by the divine providence that has guided the post-apostolic church.

Along these same lines of a broad understanding of the *jus divinum*, we find various Catholic theologians holding that a series of ecclesiastical structures (e.g., a monarchical-episcopal constitution and an ongoing Petrine ministry) can be understood as proceeding from Jesus and being *juris divini*, even without being reducible to an actual utterance of Jesus that would be unequivocally apprehensible by ourselves on the historical level. The premise here is only that it would be understandable that such decisions (such acts of the church that create a constitution) might be found among the authentic possibilities offered by Jesus and by faith in him. These acts, as well, may be irreversibly obligatory, and in this sense be *juris divini* for later generations, under the presuppositions just mentioned (Karl Rahner, Y. Congar, C. T. Peter, Avery Dulles, A. Antón, M. Miller, etc.).

In terms of this state of the question, then, the emphasis falls on the human, historical determination of this *jus divinum:* divine law will be found in an enunciation or historical realization frequently referred to as *jus ecclesiasticum.* This is the position of the "Lutheran–Roman Catholic Report" in the Malta document of 1972:

> The *jus divinum* is never totally distinct from the *jus humanum*. We possess the *jus divinum* only in the mediation of forms that always bear the seal of history. These forms of mediation must not be regarded as a pure product of the sociological process of development, but may be perceived as the fruit of the Spirit, by reason of the pneumatic nature of the Church. (No. 31)

Further on, the document continues:

> The Church, in its institutions, abides in a constant bond with the Gospel, which has an ineluctable priority over it. Attending to this bond, the Catholic tradition speaks of a *jus divinum*. However, for the institutions of the Church, the Gospel can be a criterion only in living relationship with the particular social reality of a given era. Just as the Gospel can be legitimately explained in dogmas and professions of faith, so also is there a historical realization of law in the Church. [No. 33]

By way of complementing this text, it may be useful to refer as well to the declaration "Authority in the Church II" (Windsor, 1981) from the mixed Anglican and Roman Catholic Commission, which identifies the application of the concept of "divine right" to the "Petrine service" as one of the "four problems of importance in this matter that we have seen as requiring further study" (no. 1). Let us extract the most relevant points of this reflection.

> Although there is no universally accepted interpretation of the expression, *jus divinum*, there is every indication that . . . it expresses God's

plan for his Church. There is no need to understand *jus divinum* as implying in this context that . . . [the Church] was directly founded by Jesus during his earthly life. (No. 11)

And further on:

> In view of the interpretation of the phrase concerning divine right or law in Vatican Council I, it is reasonable to wonder, as we have done above, whether any difference actually obtains between the assertion of a primacy by divine right ("jure divino") and the acknowledgement of its emergence by virtue of divine providence ("divina providentia"). (No. 13)

To conclude this point, let us observe the importance of distinguishing between the "fact" of institution on the part of the Lord and the use of an argument from Scripture. This distinction—not always employed by the authors of treatises on the subject—may be useful when it comes to avoiding the frequent ambiguity of the expression *jus divinum*, especially where no account is taken of the theological tradition and confessional context in which it is used.

3. Recent Theological History

The first to adopt an approach to the life of Jesus in the line of historical criticism, Lutheran H. S. Reimarus (1694–1768), asserts that Jesus' objective, which was shared by the apostles, was not to establish a church or separate religious community but to reestablish the Davidic kingdom in the land of Palestine. After Jesus' failure and execution, his disciples' disappointment occasioned the propagation of the notion of a church. This view has been frequently repeated, and justly rejected, in our own time and, quite in conformity with its original context, accompanies an eschatological interpretation of Jesus' preaching. Indeed, the controversy at the dawn of our century over modernism and the discovery of the eschatological meaning of the reign of God, constitute the background of the contemporary discussion of the relationship between Jesus and the church. Following, in brief, are the most significant stages of the discussion.

The First Consensus of Liberal Historical Research: 1932

Initially Adolf von Harnack, modernists A. Sabatier, G. Tyrrell, Alfred Loisy, and, later, R.

Bultmann and his followers. These authors deny any kind of organized church in Jesus' thought and preaching. In 1932, O. Linton synthesized the "consensus" reached in this stage of the development of our theme as follows: The global church arose as a later confederation of local communities. Indeed, the church in its Catholic mold as a sacramental community took shape under the influence of Hellenism and the Roman Empire, after it was seen that the parousia would be delayed. Here let us recall Loisy's celebrated dictum "Jesus proclaimed the Kingdom, and there came the church," which was originally used not in a negative sense but, in the polemic with Harnack, was merely intended to emphasize that there came a moment when, without the church, it would henceforth be impossible to continue to preach the reign of God. Later this assertion was transformed into a paradigmatic slogan of modernism, reflecting a negative appraisal of the church (cf. F. M. Braun, Oscar Cullmann, H. Conzelmann, H. Fries, Leonardo Boff, etc.; on the other hand, the original, non-negative sense has been rehabilitated in the monographs of E. Poulat and G. Heinz).

The New Consensus of New Testament Eschatological Research: 1942

F. Kattenbusch, K. L. Schmidt, A. Nygren, T. W. Manson, V. Taylor, F. J. Leenhardt, W. A. Visser't Hooft, L. Goppelt, E. Stauffer, and others; and more recently, Joachim Jeremias. This step, characterized by Catholic F. M. Braun in 1942 as that of a "new consensus," defines the church as the people of God of the "end-time," gathered into one by the Messiah Son of Man, constituted on the basis of the death and resurrection of Jesus, and confirmed by the eschatological bestowal of the Spirit at Pentecost. On this view, even before the first Easter, the circle of the Twelve proclaimed the establishment of the eschatological people of God, which Jesus expected would be composed not only of Jews but of Gentiles as well.

E. Käsemann's Synthesis: EARLY CATHOLICISM (Frühkatholizismus)

Here, a proposition already present in Rudolf Bultmann is propagated and popularized by E. Käsemann, beginning in 1963. It underscores the contrast prevailing between Pauline ecclesiology, oriented solely to charisms, and the later one attested especially in the deutero-Pauline letters and the Lukan work, focused on the authority of ordained ministers, and identifies it as an ecclesiology of a Catholic type, not attributable to the will of the historical Jesus. These propositions comport a revision of the traditional concept of CANON, inasmuch as they impose what Käsemann—in a radical attempt to apply the Lutheran axiom "Urgemus Christum contra Scripturam" ("We stand for Christ against Scripture"), which touches the epicenter of the relationship between Jesus and the church—characterizes as a "canon within a canon." The position of Early Catholicism has had great influence on various Protestant exegetes (F. Hahn, L. Goppelt, S. Schulz, U. Luz, etc.—and initially H. Schlier, who, precisely in his positive evaluation of this evolution, passed from Protestantism to Catholicism) and is relevant in the more polemical ecclesiological studies of Hans Küng.

The New State of the Question and the Positions of Catholic Theologians

On the basis of the previous, basically Protestant, steps, we next find, in Catholic theology, the beginnings of a "new state of the question," which adopts the most valid elements of the methods of historical criticism. Thus, two great Catholic exegetes, R. Schnackenburg and A. Vögtle, as early as the eve of Vatican II, declared that, strictly speaking, one may speak of the church only after the glorification and Pentecost. In turn, however, and with equal emphasis, they stressed the continuity of the post-paschal manifestation of the church with Jesus and with his works and words: hence they also speak of the *kirchenstiefenden Akte Jesu* ("acts of Jesus founding the church"). This position, intuited by R. GUARDINI as early as 1937, has been generally disseminated by recognized exegetical commentator J. Schmid in his contributions to the *Ratisbon New Testament Commentary* and has undergone a more recent formulation at the hands of fundamentalist H. Fries, in his notion of the *kirchenrelevante Akte* of Jesus of Nazareth.

There are more critical voices in Catholic theology, such as those of Hans Küng (1967) and Leonardo Boff (1980). Both of these authors, in the spirit of the "new state of the question," tend to accentuate certain more radical conclusions:

they do not speak of properly "ecclesial" acts on Jesus' part, although both agree that Jesus' preaching and actions laid the "foundations" for the appearance of the post-paschal church (see the critical observations on Küng in the Declaration of the Congregation for the Doctrine of the Faith of 15 December 1979=EV 6:1942–51, and the letter of John Paul II of 15 May 1980= EV 7:374–99; and on Boff, in the Notification of the Congregation for the Doctrine of the Faith of 11 March 1985=EV 9:1421–32).

The New Exegetical-Theological Synthesis:
The Implicit Ecclesiology of Jesus of Nazareth

In terms of the previous steps and their difficulties, and in the spirit of an "implicit Christology" attributed to Jesus of Nazareth, what we may term a "new exegetical-theological synthesis" has been suggested and has been called an "implicit ecclesiology." The formula has been consecrated by the 1986 document of the International Theological Commission on the consciousness of Jesus (no. 3). This focus adopts the results of various Catholic studies in recent years (A. Descamps, H. Schlier, followed by A. Antón, who speak of a *Präformation der Kirche* in Matthew; W. Trilling, H. Frankemölle, M. M. Garijo-Guembe). In terms of an "implicit ecclesiology," God, in furthering the reign inaugurated by Jesus, remains faithful precisely to its historical beginnings, entrusting the reign to a post-paschal church that thereby is linked to the same historical beginnings (Trilling). Special mention should be made of G. Lohfink, who criticizes certain presentations of this position but defends the identification of the eschatological people of God with the church: Jesus was not precisely the founder of a new institution, but the savior of Israel, the one who gathers together the true Israel of the end-time—the church. Let us also observe here the suggestive reflections of Francis Schüssler · Fiorenza, who does not restrict the concept of "founding" to the explicit intention of the subject, but situates it in an a posteriori interpretation of history on the basis of the hermeneutics of reception. Within this framework, especially important are the sociological studies on the first group of followers of Jesus, especially those of G. Theissen and R. Aguirre, who regard nascent Christianity as an intra-Judaic move-- ment of renewal that gradually consummated its breach with "official" Pharisaic Judaism.

4. Theological Perspectives

Vatican II was the first council to set forth a broad theological state of the question of the originating, founding relationship of Jesus to the church. Following is a detailed analysis of the substance of the apposite texts in *LG* 2–5. According to this Dogmatic Constitution on the church, the church is bound up with the three divine Persons as "a people made one with the unity of the Father [*LG* 2], the Son [*LG* 3], and the Holy Spirit [*LG* 4]" (*LG* 4, citing a text of Cyprian; cf. Augustine, John Damascene, Fulgentius, Cyril, etc.), and furthermore maintains a relationship with the reign of God (*LG* 5). Further on, in *LG* 18, apropos of the institution of the hierarchy, the document refers to the text of Vatican I that is cited above ("built the holy church," DS 3050), adopting its texts and argumentation to the effect that the apostles were called and sent forth as a group (*LG* 18–29).

LG 2 speaks of the salvific plan of God the Father, who convokes the holy church prefigured from the foundation of the world, prepared in the history of Israel, constituted in the end-time, manifested by the outpouring of the Spirit, and to be consummated at the end of the ages. In this context, *LG* 2 cites the famous patristic *ecclesia ab Abel* (Gregory the Great, Irenaeus, Origen, Augustine, Leo the Great, John Damascene; cf. Thomas's synthesis: "patres antiqui pertinebant ad idem corpus Ecclesiae" ("the ancient fathers were belonging to the same body of the church"), *ST* III, q. 8, a. 3, ad 3).

LG 3 tells of the mission and work of the Son, who "inaugurated the kingdom of heaven on earth and revealed to us the mystery of the Father. By His obedience He brought about redemption." It is here that a relationship with the church is introduced, by way of a striking formula: "The church, or, in other words, the kingdom of Christ now present in mystery, grows visibly in the world through the power of God," while, in turn, "this inauguration and this growth are both symbolized by the blood and water which flowed from the open side of the crucified Jesus"—that image invoked by the great fathers (Ambrose, Augustine), adopted by the Council of Vienne in 1312 (DS 901) and proclaimed once more in Vatican II's conciliar Constitution on the Liturgy (*SC* 5).

LG 4 speaks of the Spirit, who sanctifies the

church, along the lines of *LG* 2, centering its whole import on the dynamics of the phrase "thus all believers would have access to the Father through Christ in the one Spirit"—a compendium of the whole economy of salvation—and giving us to understand how "the Spirit dwells in the church" (*Spiritus in Ecclesia*). This observation, in turn, recalls the distinction drawn by Thomas Aquinas between truths *de medio* and *de fine*, in his commentary on the Apostles' Creed, where he observes that the truth of the church is one of the former, so that, rather than "believing *in* the church," it is better to say that we "believe *in* the Holy Spirit, who sanctifies the church" (*ST* II-II, q. 1, a. 9). Finally, the conciliar text points to the eschatological nature of this presence of the Spirit and the church, who "both say to the Lord Jesus, 'Come!'" and concludes with the synthetic text cited above of Cyprian on the "Ecclesia de Trinitate."

In *LG* 5, the conciliar text focuses on the relationship between the church and the reign of God. Here is the only occurrence of the use of the words "foundation" and "Founder." The text states, "The mystery of the holy church is manifest in her very *foundation*," and lists the following founding acts: Christ's inauguration of the church in his proclamation of the promised reign; the manifestation of that reign in his words, works, and presence; his miracles attesting to its actual arrival on earth; and especially the manifestation of the reign "in the very person of Christ." Then the text goes on to say that Jesus "poured out upon his disciples the Spirit promised by the Father (cf. Acts 2:33). The church, consequently, "equipped with the gifts of her Founder, . . . receives the mission to proclaim and to establish among all peoples the kingdom of Christ and of God. She becomes on earth the initial budding forth (*germen et initium*) of that kingdom."

As we see, then, Vatican II stands in the line of current reflection on the data of the NT, in terms of which the most accurate conceptualization is that of a foundation of the church throughout all of Jesus' activity, on earth as well as in his exaltation. In the movement of convocation at the hands of the earthly Jesus, in the circle of his disciples, in his meals, especially his last supper before his death, and so on, we behold pre-paschal *vestigia ecclesiae* ("sketches of the church") (cf. Walter Kasper),

either explicit, perhaps, or, more probably, implicit. All of the elements and perspectives of the pre-paschal Jesus are utilized as building materials in the new, post-paschal situation.

In the framework of an understanding of these pre-paschal *vestigia ecclesia*, an advance is made, and further precisions are offered, by the more recent document of the International Theological Commission of 7 October 1985 on certain questions of ecclesiology. This text provides us with a detailed list of the development and stages of the process of the foundation of the church, synthesized as ten:

1. The promises of the OT with regard to the people of God, which are presupposed in Jesus' preaching, and which retain all of their salvific force.
2. Jesus' broad summons of all human beings to conversion and faith.
3. The calling and institution of the Twelve as a sign of the future reestablishment of all Israel.
4. The imposition of a name on Simon Peter, and his preeminent place in the circle of the disciples and their mission.
5. Israel's rejection of Jesus, and the breach between the Jewish people and Jesus' disciples.
6. The fact that, in instituting the Supper and in confronting his passion and death, Jesus persists in preaching the universal reign of God, which consists in the gift of life to all human beings.
7. The restoration, in the Lord's resurrection, of the broken bond between Jesus and his disciples, and the post-paschal introduction of the ecclesial life properly so-called (*proprie ecclesialem*).
8. The sending of the Holy Spirit, who makes the church a true "creature of God" (see the narrative of Pentecost in the writings of Luke).
9. The mission to the pagans, and the constitution of the church of the pagans.
10. The definitive breach between the "true Israel" and Judaism.

In turn, the text concludes, altogether unambiguously:

No stage, taken separately, is totally meaningful. All of them together, however, clearly demonstrate that the foundation of the Church is to be understood as a historical process, as the becoming of the Church within the history of revelation. The Father "planned to assemble in the holy Church all those who would believe in Christ. Already from the beginning of the world the foreshadowing of the Church took place. She was prepared for in a remarkable way throughout the history of the people of Israel and by means of the Old Covenant. Established in the _present era of time_, the Church was made manifest by the outpouring of the Spirit. At the end of time she will achieve her glorious fulfillment" (_LG_ 2). In this same process is constituted the basic ongoing, definitive structure of the Church. [=_EV_ 9:1677–79]

By way of a complement of the above, we have a later document from the same International Theological Commission on the consciousness of Jesus, dated 31 May 1986. In its third proposition on that question, it states:

> In order to carry out his salvific mission, Jesus willed to gather together human beings in view of the Reign, and to join them around himself. In order to realize this purpose, Jesus performed concrete acts whose sole possible interpretation, taking them conjointly, is the preparation of the church, which was definitively constituted by the events of Easter and Pentecost. Thus, it must be asserted that Jesus willed to found the church ("Jesum voluisse Ecclesiam fundare").

In its commentary on this proposition, we read of the category, "implicit ecclesiology" with respect to Jesus' intent. "It is not a matter of asserting that this intention of Jesus implies an express will to found and establish all institutional aspects of the church as these have developed over the course of the centuries." But further on, we have the following specifications:

> Christ had an awareness of his salvific mission. This comported with the foundation of his "Church"—that is, the convocation of all human beings in the "family of God." The history of Christianity is ultimately based on the intention and will of Jesus to found his Church. (No. 3.2=_Greg_ 67 [1986]: 413–28, 422–24)

5. Conclusion

Synthesizing the relationship between Jesus and the church, we can make use of a tripartite theological view of the origins of the sacra-mental church in the image of the essential structure of the sacraments. That structure is established by way of three determinations: (1) "institution by Christ," (2) "outward sign," and (3) "inward effect of grace."

This tripartite theological view arises from the conciliar texts themselves, especially _LG_ 2–5. Instead of focusing solely on the question, posed by modernism, of the historical "foundation" of the church by Jesus of Nazareth, these texts contribute a comprehensive theological statement of the question of a foundational, originating, and founding relation of Jesus to the church. Thus, let us keep in mind that the three determinations contributed by sacramentology must be applied conjointly if we are to have a correct solution, in terms of fundamental theology, of the problem of the relationship between Jesus and the church. Viz.:

Institution by Christ: Jesus Christ as Founder of the Church

As we have already observed, this first determination is profoundly interconnected with questions bearing on the person, and personal consciousness, of Jesus. Thus, in terms of the development and the stages of the life and ministry of Jesus of Nazareth, we are struck by the genesis, throughout that life, of an "implicit, processual ecclesiology." This formula expresses the notion that (1) the reign of God inaugurated by Jesus and entrusted to the post-paschal church is in authentic continuity with these first beginnings of the church during Jesus' earthly life; and (2) this fact, in turn, authentically links the post-paschal church to its origin in Jesus' earthly life. In these terms, then, we have the concrete manner in which Jesus Christ is properly denominated the "founder" of the church (cf. _LG_ 5 and the ITC documents of 1985, 1986).

Outward Sign: Jesus Christ as Origin of the Church

The second determination is clarified by the origin of the church as a historical formation. Jesus' salvific action unfolds in our world only through human beings and their history. In this historical transmission, a relevant mission belongs to the apostles and their successors, who have the ministry of preserving in its integrity the "deposit of faith" (_DV_ 10). Thus, the "Church, in her teaching, life, and worship, perpetuates and hands on to all generations all that she herself is, all that she believes" (*DV* 8). For this reason, the church can be described as a "universale sacramentum salutis" ("universal sacrament of salvation") (*LG* 1, 9, 48, 59; *GS* 42, 45), formed of a divine and a human element (by analogy with the mystery of the incarnate Word), "at the same time holy and always in need of being purified" (*LG* 8). Along these lines we must emphasize that the church is "mystery" and at the same time "historical subject," with the consequent "plenitude and relativity" that this fact comports in its "historical existence." That existence must be analyzed with the help, as well, of historical and sociological methodology: the church must be seen as the "people of God 'in via,' in a situation never complete here on earth" (ITC 1985, no. 3), and yet a people conscious of being "the Reign of God already present in mystery" (*LG* 3), and in some sort a "sacrament of the Reign" (cf. the specifications above concerning this formula of the ITC 1985, no. 10.3).

Inward Effect of Grace:
Jesus Christ in the Function
of Foundation of the Church

The third determination is realized in the founding of the church upon the saving mysteries of Christ, prepared from the beginning (see "Ecclesia ab Abel," *LG* 2), and articulated in his incarnation, paschal mystery, and sending of the Spirit. The incarnation of the Word transforms that word into the father of the new humanity (see Rom 8:3, 29) and makes possible the recapitulation of universal history in Christ (Eph 1:10), by mediation of the church, the creature of the Word (see *DV* 1).

The second foundational event is the paschal mystery of Christ, that maximal expression of Christ's service to all human beings (see Mk 10:45; 14:24): "For to this end Christ died and lived again, so that he might be Lord of both the dead and the living" (Rom 14:9). In this event Christ creates a new sacramental economy (see *SC* 61): hence the image of the birth of the church from his side (see *LG* 3; *SC* 5).

The third event of the life of Christ is the sending of the Spirit (Acts 2), who is the authentic foundational protagonist of all history and of the life of the church, of which

the Spirit is the "soul" (see *LG* 7), and which fully manifests its proper being as the *Ecclesia de Trinitate* (see *LG* 4).

Thus we have a more precise determination of the (1) foundational, (2) originating, and (3) founding relationship of Jesus Christ vis-à-vis the church, understood from a point of departure in its sacramental structure, the true fulcrum of the ecclesiology of Vatican II. In this fashion, the mystery of the "one interlocked reality" (*LG* 8) of the historical-and-transcendent church is totally referred to and illuminated by Christ, that sole "Lumen Gentium" of whom the church, founded by, originated by, and founded upon him, is "a kind of sacrament or sign of intimate union with God, and of the unity of all mankind" (*LG* 1).

Bibl.: H. SCHLIER, "Ekklesiologie des NT," *MystSal* 4/1 (1972): 101–221; G. HEINZ, *Das Problem der Kirchenentstehung* (Mainz, 1974); A. ANTÓN, *La Iglesia de Cristo* (Madrid, 1977); G. THEISSEN, *Soziologie der Jesusbewegung* (Munich, 1977); J. AUER, *Die Kirche* (Ratisbonne, 1983); B. FORTE, *La chiesa icona della Trinità* (Brescia, 1984); H. FRANKEMÖLLE and H. HÄRING, "Kirche/Ekklesiologie," *NHTG* 2 (1984): 294–323; F. S. FIORENZA, *Foundational Theology: Jesus and the Church* (New York, 1985); H. FRIES, *Fundamentaltheologie* (Graz/Vienna/Cologne, 1985); G. LOHFINK, "Jesus und die Kirche," *HFT* 3 (1986): 49–96; A. DESCAMPS, *Jésus et l'Église* (Louvain, 1987); R. AGUIRRE, *Del movimiento de Jesus a la Iglesia cristiana* (Bilbao, 1987); M. M. GARIJO-GUEMBE, *Gemeinschaft der Heiligen* (Düsseldorf, 1988).

Salvador PIÉ-NINOT

III. MOTIVE OF CREDIBILITY

1. From Vatican I to Vatican II

We may say in a general sense that the church is a sign of salvation, for it represents and communicates the invisible grace of salvation. It is the efficacious sign of a spiritual reality—of human union with God and, as a result of that union, the union of people with one another.

When this mystery of salvation shines forth brightly among people, even for nonbelievers it becomes a perceptible sign of the event of salvation in the world. Then we speak of the church as a motive of credibility. When, indeed, the People of God are assembled in unity, faithful to their calling to sanctity, and, when they live to the full their life of union with God and with other people, by their very presence they bear witness to the fact that the salvation proclaimed and preached by the church has been truly bestowed on humanity in order to transform and sanctify it. In other words, when the life of unity and love lived by the members of Christ accords with the gospel, that life becomes a sign that not only alludes to but *expresses* the reality signified. Then it visibly shows that the church is indeed the location of salvation in Jesus Christ, and that the Spirit of Christ truly dwells among human beings. Then the church becomes the visible and historical sign of the Spirit of Christ, the invisible principle of the unity of the church.

The idea that the presence of the church in the world, throughout the centuries, with all the benefits that it represents, constitutes a sign of its divine origin, was not discovered by the first Vatican Council, for the argument is traditional in the church. Its roots are to be found in Acts, where the life of the primitive community is described (Acts 2:44–45). It would seem to be prefigured in the OT, in the presence of the People of God, a sign raised up to the nations. From the first centuries, the fathers—especially Irenaeus, Tertullian, Origen, and Augustine—cited in Christianity's favor its miraculous expansion, the constancy of its martyrs, and the splendor of its saints. Savonarola developed the argument afterward, in the fifteenth century; Bossuet and Pascal in the seventeenth; Fénelon in the eighteenth; Balmes, Lacordaire, Bautain, and Dechamps in the nineteenth; and, directly after Vatican I, J. Kleutgen and J. B. Franzelin. Vatican I set the stamp of its authority on the validity of this sign and provided its major if not definitive formulation. "The Church," said the council, "because of its astonishing prolongation, its eminent sanctity, and the inexhaustible abundance of all its benefits, its catholic unity, and its unvanquished solidity, is *of itself* a great and everlasting motive of credibility and an irrefutable testimony to its divine mission" (DS 3013–14).

Accordingly, the approach suggested by the council is different from the *historical* procedure that established the foundation of the church by Christ and the continuity of that church with the present Catholic church. In other words, this is not the method known as the Notes of the Church, which consists in discerning in the present-day church the essential and exclusive marks that Christ bestowed on the institution that he founded. It is a matter rather of an *empirical* procedure that takes as its starting point the church as an observable and extraordinary spatiotemporal phenomenon. The Notes method examines the essence of the church of Christ. The approach proposed by Vatican I is directly concerned with the image of the church, or the characteristics of its appearance as presented to the observer, even an unbeliever, and makes no appeal to Christ's historical foundation of the church.

The council lists five of these apparent traits that are characteristic of the phenomenon of the church: its *astonishing* prolongation, its *eminent* sanctity, its *inexhaustible* benefits, its *catholic* unity, and its *unvanquished* solidity. The five qualifications attached to the substantives stress the unique nature of these manifestations. The church appears in the world as an extraordinary, exceptional, and miraculous phenomenon. These characteristics are to be considered not in isolation but together, and qualitatively. As with Christ, it is a matter of *many-sided* convergence.

The Vatican I formulation does not claim to be definitive or to be immune from criticism. In this regard, we may ask whether the image proffered does indeed represent a proper awareness of the actual complexity of the sign of the church. This sign is in fact more ambiguous and infinitely more difficult to present than the sign of Christ. The unity of the church is real, but it is a disrupted unity, one that has to be mended. It is a unity that has to be protected and always requires to be perfected. Its stability is continually threatened, and its catholicity is subject to constant tensions. Its sanctity arises in sinful ground. To be sure, the Vatican I formulation must be understood in the sociological context of the nineteenth century, in which the church was conceived as a perfect, autonomous, and transcendent society removed from the vicissitudes of human societies. Admittedly, it scarcely betrays the fact that the sign of the church resembles a *tissue of paradoxes* that make the church an enigma to be deciphered. The church of Vatican I seems an abstract, ideal church with absolute attributes, rather than a fragile and sinful pilgrim community of the faithful. The adjectives applied to the church's characteristics (astonishing, eminent, inexhaustible, unvanquished) evoke intensity rather than paradox. Moreover, in a twentieth-century context the Vatican I formulation seems highly subject to the charge of unreality.

That is why Vatican II, aware of the different context, altered the perspective and the formulation, while retaining the reality of the sign. Indeed, Vatican II often refers to the Vatican I text but never quotes it in full. It is noteworthy, too, that in the passages in question, the sign of the church is reduced in practice to the sign of unity in charity. The church is the sign of the bestowal of salvation among human beings in that it reflects in our own world the loving unity of trinitarian life. Moreover, Vatican II, by a process of personalization that extends to the entire economy of revelation and its transmission, speaks of personal and communitarian *witness*, whereas Vatican I speaks of the miraculous attributes of the church. The individuals themselves, by their holy lives; the Christian communities, by their life of unity and charity; and the whole People of God, by their life in conformity with the gospel, demonstrate to human beings that the church is the locus of salvation.

2. In Search of an Approach

The sign of the church undoubtedly received a stable valuation from the last two councils, although the viewpoints and formulations differed, with Vatican I offering a more abstract formulation, and Vatican II a more personally and discreetly phrased version.

Moreover, we must admit that it is rather difficult to present the sign of the church to people in our own era. Because of publicity that makes the least local event a worldwide occurrence, we now know more about the weaknesses of churchmen and the institutions of the church. Magazines, papers, radio, and television describe the everyday tribulations that the church is subject to. We are also more aware of the church's historical errors.

In studying the church as a motive of credibility, I avoid two approaches that seem inadequate, for different reasons. I eschew the *comparative* approach (at least as a direct approach), which consists in comparing the church with other religious communities (separated Christian communities or great his-

torical religions, such as Buddhism, Hinduism, or Islam) and in stating that, compared with those communities, the church is incalculably superior, above all at the level of unity, universality, duration, and sanctity. Of course this approach does suppose that we acknowledge some elements of sanctity and of the church outside the Catholic community. In this way of thinking, however, the church represents an excellence, a fullness of sanctity and salvation, that would not seem to be apparent to the same degree in the other communities of salvation. I find this approach complicated, scarcely satisfactory, and subject to very serious risks. In particular, it can hardly escape charges of ignorance, imprecision, self-congratulation, and even injustice, and an accusation that the true facts are still minimized in order to reveal Catholic superiority. I think that the main value of this approach is confirmative.

I also avoid the *transcendent* approach, at least as formulated by Vatican I, which sees the church as a transcendent phenomenon analogous in the moral order to a physical miracle, and as one that testifies directly to the divine origin of the church and its mission. If one tells anyone nowadays about the *astonishing* prolongation, the *eminent* sanctity, the *inexhaustible* abundance, the *catholic* unity, and the *unvanquished* solidity of the church, one will pointlessly evoke the uncontrollable antipathy of one's audience.

Instead I propose to approach the question in terms of *internal comprehensibility* and a *search for meaning*. This method starts with the paradoxes and tensions that constitute the actual reality of the church and not with its absolute and glorious attributes. This approach tries to understand those paradoxes and tensions in themselves and in their mutual relations, and in terms of the explanation that the church offers of itself. The appropriateness of the suggested explanation to the observable facts (nature and extent) leads us to think that the witness of the church is truthful—that it is truly, among human beings, a sign of salvation in Jesus Christ. The comprehensibility of the phenomenon resides in the *mystery* that is attested. I shall not deny the miraculous attributes of the church: the transcendence of the church seems instead to be the key to an understanding of the full range and complexity of the phenomenon.

Therefore it is possible to distinguish at least three major paradoxes in the church: the paradox of *unity*, the paradox of *perpetuity*, and the paradox of *sanctity*. These are not simple paradoxes. Each of them represents a number of *tensions*, some of which are strong enough to split any society that has to undergo them and simultaneously face the test of time. This set of paradoxes and tensions makes the church an enigmatic sign for which we need a cipher or key.

The simultaneous existence of characteristics that are seemingly incompatible in the light of human experience and history, and yet harmonized within it, enables the church in some way to evoke the major paradoxes of the presence of Christ in the world: the simplicity and authority, humility and unprecedented claim of the one who says that he is the Son of the Father, the eschatological judge, sinless and yet with a greater understanding than anyone else of the meaning of sin and its universality. The church, like Christ, is an enigma to be deciphered.

3. Paradoxes and Tensions of Unity

The first of the great paradoxes of the church is that of *unity*. On a superficial inspection, the unity of the church is reducible to the unity of baptism, the creed, and authority. In reality, this unity comprises many sizable tensions. There were times in the church when theology stressed Catholic unity, but without any very accurate notion of its complexity. Our age is more aware of the diversity and complexity that go to make up this unity.

Unity of Complexity and Challenge

One of the first discernible facts about the church is that its unity is no superficial unity of an ordinary kind but a unity in complexity. The Catholic faith is not merely a vague, sentimental, and not very demanding religious attitude, nor is it merely adherence to a certain number of external observances. Rather, it is a faith in mysteries that can overwhelm human reason: the Trinity, the incarnation, the divinization of humanity, the resurrection of the body, and so on. This unity in complexity is also a unity of *challenge*, which asks human beings to submit not only their external actions but even their most secret thoughts and inti-

mate desires to the word of Christ. It is a demand for a choice that can extend as far as the possibility of a martyr's death.

In spite of this unity of complexity and challenge, in the course of the centuries the church has welcomed and incorporated vast numbers of human beings. This membership of the church, which is usually accompanied by a profound integration of personalities, establishes a "communion" between all the members of the church, no matter how unknown or isolated in space and time. According to the testimony of the faithful themselves, the principle of this cohesiveness and communion of the church is the union of all its members in Christ and in his Spirit.

Loyalty and Realization

As a word addressed to a specific milieu, at a precise moment in time, revelation nevertheless has to encounter people of all times, in this particular and always unique historical situation. It has to answer their questions and anxieties in order to lead them to God. The church has to remain attentive to the Word of God and to the voices of all times.

The church may succumb to stagnation, lack of movement, and transient forms of fashion and time. There is certainly an inevitable tension between a peaceably possessed deposit and its necessary adaptation to the present and to the imminent future. The church has to live in a precarious situation, for a church that lives in hope is one that constantly discerns the future in the present and discovers today the loyalty of tomorrow.

Accordingly, the church in its preaching shows its determination not to sacrifice any part of the message that it has received, and not to alter it. At the same time it recognizes its obligation to understand the gospel in a constantly fresh way so that it can elicit from the gospel novel answers to novel questions. It must, says *Ecclesiam Suam*, "introduce the Christian message into current thought, expression, culture, customs, tendencies and humanity, so that it remains vital and effective today over the face of the earth."

The church is loyal to the past but not its slave; it shows an equal and unyielding will to remain loyal to the unique message of the faith, and simultaneously to the realization of that message, in order to answer the questions of each age. Such loyalty is one of the most significant aspects of the paradox of the unity of the church.

Unity of Faith and Theological Pluralism

The problem of making the word contemporary is intimately linked to that of interpreting the faith and of grasping the multitude of expressions of that understanding of faith. To what extent is the Catholic faith itself capable of making room for a certain theological pluralism?

Pluralism is a matter of fact and has always existed. Even at the level of revelation, we find, if not pluralism, at least plurality and a complementarity of perspectives in the presentation of one and the same mystery. Accordingly, we have Synoptic, Johannine, and Pauline approaches to the mystery of Christ. When no longer revelation but theological reflection is at issue, "pluralism" is even more evident. In patristic times problems regarding the inculturation of the gospel led to very different linguistic and philosophical presentations of it. In the Middle Ages, schools formed, proliferated, and even opposed one another (e.g., Thomists, Scotists, and Suarezians).

Theological pluralism is the result of several factors: first, *different mentalities and cultural environments*. Hence the East developed an ecclesiology of communion, whereas the West worked out an institutional ecclesiology. A second factor is *basic philosophical options*: Platonism, Aristotelianism, personalism, existentialism. Third is *intuitions and preoccupations*, giving rise subsequently to various systematic expressions, such as Dominicans, Jesuits, Carmelites, Franciscans, and Benedictines. Fourth, because of the *languages and approaches* appropriate nowadays to various disciplines (exegesis, history, semiotics, and so on), theology always seems more complex and various. Finally, more than in the past, theology seeks to be *in context*, located in a given cultural field and more attentive to the hierarchy of truths.

In the past, orthodox and heterodox could confront and contradict one another but at the same time could clearly identify themselves and the reasons for their disagreement. That is no longer the case today. We are faced with theologies that claim to be Christian but that constitute a different universe. How are we to relate Bultmann to Catholic theology, or merely to Christian faith? We can recognize a Christian vocabulary, yet it is no longer suffused with Christianity but with a radical rationalism.

Theological pluralism is inevitable. It can even be beneficial. Vatican II recognized its legitimacy and fruitfulness (*UR* 17; *GS* 62; *LG* 23; *AG* 22). Nevertheless, it is undeniable that theological pluralism is accompanied by a continual tension that can reach a critical point. A many-sided and multidirectional pluralism produces the risk of dissipating the fundamental viewpoint of faith, which is the person of Christ, the Son of God among us. Here unity threatens to split. Accordingly, we may legitimately ask how a society that has undergone such tensions for so many centuries persists without dislocation and even without vanishing altogether.

Violated Unity and Will to Ecumenism

It is no mere hypothesis but a fact of history that the tensions within unity can reach a crisis point and compromise the equilibrium of the church.

The unity of the church persisted for a thousand years and more. Then it experienced two especially serious historical breaks: the schism with the East in 1054, and Luther's Protestant Reformation in the sixteenth century. The responsibilities for these breaks were shared, which the Decree on Ecumenism openly recognizes: "Large communities became separated from full communion with the Catholic Church—developments for which, at times, men of both sides were to blame" (*UR* 3).

Although the church succeeded in preserving its internal unity, it nevertheless was affected by those great historical divisions. Though the storm did not destroy the church, it weakened and impoverished it, like a tree that loses a number of key branches. It sometimes affected its equilibrium. The separated communities, however, are not lifeless branches. They continue to live by the Spirit of Christ and his gospel. They have often valued even more than we have the treasures that they have preserved: the meaning of Scripture and the Word of God, the meaning of God's transcendence and the gratuitous nature of salvation among Protestants; the meaning of mystery and liturgical prayer in the Eastern churches.

The church does not passively accept this wound to its unity. The foundation of a Secretariat for Christian Unity in 1960 and the Decree on Ecumenism of Vatican II indicate the church's firm and sincere will to reestablish dialogue and communion with the separated churches. Paul VI's gestures of friendship toward Patriarch Athenagoras and Archbishop Ramsey are actual expressions of this attitude as adumbrated in the texts. In the Decree on Ecumenism the Catholic church assumes its share of the responsibility for the great divisions of history; it recognizes the riches of salvation and life of the various communities; it avoids the wounding terms "schismatics" and "heretics"; it speaks of ecclesial communities or churches; and it invites all the faithful to a conversion of hearts and to offer the testimony of a holy life.

Therefore the church is aware that its unity has been gravely affected, partly by its own fault, and that this is a scandalous division. It is not a question of a triumphant and definitive unity but of an actual internal unity, and one that is nevertheless active and desirous not only to incorporate new members but to rediscover those who have left it. It is a shattered unity that has to be repaired and perfected. If the church did not exhibit this ecumenical thrust, its unity would lack awareness both of the seriousness of the divisions that occurred and of any consciousness of Christ's precept ". . . that they may all be one" (Jn 17:21). Any such lack of a will to ecumenism would be a condemnation of the church. But the fact that the church is aware of its wounds, and also anxious to rediscover the fullness of its unity, is a sign of a salutary tension within it.

Unity and Catholicity

These two substantives seem contradictory. Unity in fact means elimination of elements that tend to differentiation. Unity, above all, if it wishes to be firm and consistent (like the unity of the Jewish people, whom God compelled to reject everything alien), easily becomes authoritarian, intransigent, and centralizing and sacrifices the elements of legitimate diversity; or, to protect itself, it transforms itself into a closed sect. Catholicity, on the contrary, means welcome and communion; it willingly accepts divergences and, if need be, sacrifices internal unity. Catholicity is prepared to simplify things, provided that there is a common denominator, even if it is inferior, which allows the greatest possible number to come together.

The paradox is that the church seeks unity and catholicity at one and the same time. It is not only called together and assembled in itself (internal unity) but also, as the history of the missions shows, summons together all the people of the earth. It seeks to construct, beyond the earthly geography, a new geography that would reunite all the people of the earth, without distinction of language, color, race, or institution. It constructs the body of Christ and assembles the children of the Father, "For in the one Spirit we were all baptized into one body" (1 Cor 12:13). The church asserts itself not against human beings but in a union of love with all people.

What is noteworthy in this universality is not so much the outward phenomenon (the space covered and the number of members) as its quality. It is a question of an expansion accompanied by a profound transformation of minds and hearts, on the basis of a free choice obtained not by force of arms but by the beguiling power of love: God's love in Jesus Christ.

The Universal Church and Local Churches

Unity and catholicity give rise to many and many-sided tensions even within the church. There is first of all tension between _local churches_. The NT already shows the coexistence in the church of unity in plurality. There are structured and relatively autonomous local churches: the churches of Jerusalem, Corinth, Antioch, and so on; there are also _regional churches_: Asia, Palestine, Greece. Moreover, certain churches have their own Gospel: Mark for the Romans, Matthew for the Judeo-Christians, Luke for the Greeks, and John for Asia Minor. There is also a plurality of languages, customs, and mentalities. Unity does not mean uniformity. There are even tensions between Jerusalem and the diaspora, between Judeo-Christians and Christians of the Gentile dispensation. In spite of this regionalism, the churches maintain the communion of faith and the sacraments, the communion of bishops, and the communion of fellowship. There are local churches, and yet there is a communion of churches.

There is a similar tension between the *local* churches and the *universal* church, which arises from the communion of all the churches. Over the centuries these two lines of force have come together and synthesized but have also known rivalry and opposition. Because the church as a society is organized and structured with its central administrations and all its organs, with its law and lawyers, there has been a tendency to think of local churches as branches of the one great universal church, the latter consisting of all the faithful united under the authority of the pope. In the church the West has privileged the aspect of unity and universality, but without always attending sufficiently to the diversity of local churches. For the East, on the contrary, the basic unit is the local church, which fully realizes the essence of the church, brought together by the word, the Eucharist, the Holy Spirit, and also by the bishop, who is at the basis of this unity. Collegiality resides in the dialogue of local churches. The successor of Peter presides over this synergy.

There is an unavoidable tension between an ecclesiology of the universal church and an ecclesiology of local churches, between the primacy of the pope and the collegiality of the bishops. It is true that the church contains all the organs needed to ensure both unity and diversity. Hence the function of the primate is to maintain unity, whereas collegiality guarantees the universality in pluriformity of the local churches and safeguards unity by means of the communion of bishops with one another and with the pope.

Nevertheless a certain dialectical tension between unity and diversity remains unavoidable and impossible wholly to absorb. Too great a concern for unity can lead to autocratism and leveling down. Too much diversity may bring about a disintegration of unity and sheer anarchy. There must be unity without uniformity, pluriformity without division. This swinging of the pendulum between the universal church and the local churches, between primacy and collegiality, is characteristic of the very reality of the church. The most foresighted prescription of canon law will never succeed in preventing inevitable conflicts. The paradox is rather that the church can survive so many tensions of this kind.

Internal Unity and Missionary Unity

Unity is characteristic of the church as a gift of Christ to his spouse. This unity, however, has to be accommodated to earthly dimensions and to encompass all the centuries. This dynamic missionary unity of the church is not mere proselytism, a desire for numerical grandeur, but a natural demand. The church would not be itself—that is, a "universal sacrament of salvation" (*LG* 9, 13, 48; *AG* 1)—if it were apparent only on a single continent or in a single nation, for then it would not display its true nature. If the church were not one, it would not be the new People of God that Christ came to gather together; furthermore, if it were not a missionary church, it would no longer be the sacrament of salvation for all human beings.

History shows in fact that missionary activity is one of the major characteristics of the church, although along with strong periods in that history are others so weak as to be almost dead.

The first century, with the great thrust begun by the apostles, especially by Paul, was the springtime of the church and of the missions. The third century and the start of the fourth marked the evangelization of Africa. From the seventh century there was a certain slowing down because of the obstacle represented by Islam, and also because of ignorance of the New World. At the end of the sixteenth century, with the great discoveries and the Tridentine Counter-Reformation, there was a burst of missionary activity: in India, China, Japan, the Philippines, and the two Americas. The eighteenth century was a dead period because of the persecutions and the suppression of the Jesuits. In the nineteenth century, missionary activity underwent a revival with the foundation of more than twenty missionary communities. In the twentieth century there has been a certain setback because of the vocations crisis and also because of the scarcely enlightened attitude of certain theologians who, on the pretext of asserting the value of universal salvific grace, have decided to marginalize the need for a church "in missionary mode." The Vatican II decree on the missionary activity of the church, and much deeper thinking about missions, inculturation, and the various forms and stages of the process of evangelization have enlivened the dynamic unity of the church.

Unity Pursued Yet Always Evanescent

The unity of the church must always be sought anew because it is always under threat: within, because of the scandal caused by Catholics themselves; and outside, because of persecution. The task of bringing all human beings together in the unity of charity seems always to be subject to setbacks. The activity of Christians seems constantly to come up against moments of failure and never prevails entirely. The quest for unity is *urgent and unrelenting.* Indeed the church never gives up, never despairs, and never surrenders to skepticism, in spite of the constant new beginnings forced on it by war, persecution, sloth, or human disloyalty. The church never gives up. It places itself halfway between utopia and despair. It tends to "recapitulate" all the nations and to resume its task in each century. A hundred times and more it has had reason to despair and to surrender. We need think only of the church's efforts to establish itself in China and its experiences of rejection there. Contradiction, rebuffs, rejection, ridicule, and persecution — in spite of them all, the church begins again and, following the same paths of love, with patient obstinacy sets about its work of building up the body of Christ.

A Self-Questioning Paradox

Many serious paradoxes and enigmas exist within the church: a unity in complexity and challenge, established on the basis of freedom and love; a unity that is both loyalty to the message of Christ and a constant effort to listen to the world and its requests; a unity of belief among a plurality of viewpoints, formulations, and systematizations; a broken unity that is nevertheless followed by repentance, reformation, and attempts to reestablish communion with the separated churches; a unity in catholicity, in spite of all particular features; a unity of the universal church in the pluriformity of local churches; an internal unity that is simultaneously a missionary unity; and a unity that is precarious but also continuously threatened yet never discouraged, and that has persisted for two thousand years. All these tensions form

part of the phenomenon of the church. They are all observable and visible for any witness to see. Any one of them might well provoke a collapse of the church, and yet the church carries on. They said of Christ: "Who is this man?" We may say of the church: "What is this church?"

4. The Paradox and Tensions of Temporality

In its encounter with time and history, the church is constantly threatened by two dangers, and we may well ask which is the more serious: too deep an entry into time and history, or a lack of presence. On the one hand, indeed, the church should enter into the life of human beings; it should confront them at the level of their problems and take hold of them in their existential and working environment, in the structures that bring them together. But even though this entry into life represents strength for the church, it is also a threat. The more the church is present in the history of a certain age, and the more it adopts the rhythm, structures, ways of thought, and action of that time, the more too it risks losing its identity and foundering with them. On the other hand, if the church, to escape the risks of temporality, cuts itself off from the world in order to live in a ghetto, it runs the risk of no longer understanding the people to whom it addresses its message, and of speaking to them in an incomprehensible tongue and thereby losing them. The risk of a church absorbed by temporality and controlled by it, or the risk of a church cut off from the world and ultimately reduced to silence: history bears witness to the fact that this dual threat has always menaced the church. I shall take a brief look at some of these moments in the history of the church when the tension between an excessive degree of inclusion and a lack of any inclusion at all reached a critical point.

The Threat of Judaism

The first danger that the church had to confront in its bid to become a universal religion came from the very nation in which it had its roots. From the start it had to overcome a dual danger: the defection of the Judeo-Christians who, under the pressure of Jewish nationalism, took the risk of a return to Judaism; and the pressure of the pagan-Christians who ran the risk of forsaking the new faith rather than remain within the bounds of former Judaism. If the primitive church had listened to the Judaizers, it would have remained a minor Jewish sect and would have become a historical curiosity, like the Essenes. By separating from the synagogue and strict Judaism, the church overcame its first major threat.

The Power of the Roman Empire

After escaping the danger of too great an inclusion in its original environment, the church had to confront persecutions, above all by the paganism of the Roman Empire. For almost three centuries, with alternating periods of relative calm, the church lived in an atmosphere of mockery, suspicion, and hatred. This constant threat explains the voluntary near self-effacement of the church in the official life of the period. Opinion and the law forced it to live on the periphery of society. However, even though Christian life could not openly advertise its existence in public life, it was no less vitally active. It won over people one by one. It penetrated society at all levels. It transformed its spirit. A day was to come when the empire would acknowledge itself as Christian.

Historically, this change of situation coincided with the Edict of Milan in 313, which put an end to the persecutions and officially recognized the church. Henceforth the church was free and could enter into the life of the empire. It grew with the empire, accepted its protection, and supported it. It shared the universal belief in the perpetuity of Roman civilization and the empire. This was a compromising situation. By associating itself with the centralizing, totalitarian policy of the empire, the church ran the risk of Christian statism. It risked becoming the first victim of the emperor's protection. It ran the risk of golden chains — but chains nonetheless. The church adopted the structures of civil society. The civil seat of government and that of the church were intimately related and enjoyed the same prestige. Hence, when the seat of the empire moved from Rome to Constantinople, the ecclesiastical see of Constantinople became a rival to the pontifical see of Rome. This connection between the ecclesiastical see and the civil seat of government led ultimately to the schism of the East. We should note too that

Christianity in its turn, when it became all-powerful as a result of the patronage of Constantine and his successors, turned intolerant and became a persecuting power. It persecuted pagans, treated schism and heresy as equivalent to crime, and made them offenses punishable by the state. Scarcely liberated from oppression, the church underwent an even more telling test: that of the protection of the state, and in its turn became the oppressor.

Feudal Subjection of the Church

Identified with the empire, the church seemed destined to perish with it. But at the very moment when the empire went under, by some mysterious device the church undertook to evangelize the conquerors and opened up the way of salvation to the new peoples. In less than three centuries, the people known as barbarians were converted to Christianity. In this respect the baptism of Clovis had a symbolic value. The church in the West dissociated itself from the empire just when it was going under. Once again the church entered into the life of nations, but not without encountering another danger, perhaps the most serious in its history. The church introduced the barbarians to the gospel of Christ. In return, monasteries, local churches, and sanctuaries benefited from the generosity of the great. Kings shared their authority with prelates, who became temporal princes.

All these riches and honors, far from adding to the real strength of the church, became a supreme snare and delusion. After enriching the church, the feudal order tried to absorb and subject it. By conferring the dignity of temporal princes on them, the monarch exercised increasing authority over the nomination of bishops and priests, whom he chose from among his most loyal friends. In addition, for a century (from 962) the German kings appointed the sovereign pontiffs. The church was annexed to the state. The church became a victim of the machinery of feudalism. The feudal church slid toward the abyss. Having lost the power to choose its own ministers and hierarchy, from the pope to an ordinary priest, it was no longer in control of its own destiny. Benefice had become more important than office and gave rise to simony and immorality. Lords more than bishops, the latter had no pastoral concern and allowed the people to rot in ignorance. Sacramental practice scarcely existed. The times were ripe for heresy. Indeed, in the eleventh century, the Albigensian heresy erupted, accompanied by a plethora of sects and superstitions. The situation of the church probably never seemed so desperate. The church's entry into the social and political structures of the time became absorption by those structures, a loss of its freedom, and the ruination of its spiritual thrust.

The Grandeur and Ambiguity
of Medieval Christianity

The situation was desperate. Nevertheless the church took hold of itself and revived. The movement started from Cluny, a tenth-century Benedictine abbey and, thanks to its priests, many of whom were real saints, spread gradually to the monasteries of France, Italy, Spain, Britain, and Portugal. Founded in 910, by the year 1100 Cluny had more than ten thousand monks divided among 1,450 houses, which had taken root over the entire West. Gradually the movement spread until it covered the whole of Christianity, supported and propagated by saints such as Romuald, John Gualbert, Peter Damian, and Bernard, and by popes such as Leo IX, Gregory VII, and Urban II. Gregory VII was the main propagator of this reform. With an iron energy and blazing zeal, he suddenly realized that to save the church he had to *liberate* it. After fifty years of struggle, the church won the freedom of canonical elections, from that of the pope to those of lesser dignitaries.

Henceforth free from the control of temporal lords, the authority of the pope grew from day to day. The church tended to organize itself as a strongly centralized monarchy, with its curia and nuncios. As the head of Christianity surrounded by imperial splendor, the pope proffered sovereign decisions in matters of faith and discipline. He could judge the emperor, depose him, excommunicate him, and free his subjects from all bonds of loyalty to him. The pope was not only sovereign of the pontifical state but lord of a number of states. The Crusades were holy wars declared by the pope and conducted by him. They made him the first man of his time, head of Christianity and of all the West.

Thus, in over almost three centuries, from 1050 to 1350, the church seems to have succeeded in raising the divine dwelling-place of Christianity on earth. They built cathedrals, they left for the conquest of the Holy Sepulchre, they fought against Islam, and they set off for the conquest of the New World. There is something astonishing about the growth of the monastic orders, such as Cistercians, Premonstratensians, Franciscans, and Dominicans. It was the age of the great theological syntheses of Bonaventure and Thomas, the age of Dante and Roger Bacon. But there was no more room for the unbeliever in this society than for the Christian in the pagan system. The heretic was treated as a traitor. After having been dominated by the state, the church itself became dominant. The heritage of the Middle Ages was a heavy one. It plunged the church into profound ambiguity. As human and secular activities developed under the aegis of the church, the latter became an accomplice in everything done in its name. It took the church centuries to get rid of the ambiguities that arose from this situation, in respect of war, science, politics, philosophy, and theology. The Crusades, the Inquisition, Copernicus, Galileo, Descartes, Pascal, and Leibniz are so many facts and names that express the nature of this ambiguous situation that was sometimes so painful and tragic.

Modern Nations and Neo-Caesarism

From the fourteenth century the power of the state, partly eclipsed by the universal dominative power of the medieval papacy, recovered at the national level a form of autonomy followed by an authority that soon became absolute, then aggressive and hostile. In addition, in all fields, the thrust of the church relaxed. The Crusades were in the past. The zeal of the builders of cathedrals diminished. Theology became repetitive and lost its creativity. A taste for luxury began to infect the clergy and even the religious orders. Above all, the unity of Christianity began to dissolve. The grandiose image of an intellectually and religiously united society, using Latin in its liturgy and schools, was in full decline. Paris was no longer the only major university center. Oxford, Prague, Salamanca, and Coimbra were rivals. Intellectual life ceased to be a clerical monopoly. National languages rivaled Latin and assumed an ever greater place in education and in literary production.

The era of *nationalisms* opened up, and the church had to take account of it. It was in the setting of the nations that the church had to do its work and to find its place. This was a new form of inclusion, with new dangers. Especially in France and Spain, within the centralizing and authoritarian monarchist system, where the king was a deputy-god, the church was a cog in the machinery of the state. From 1516, the bishops were appointed by the king, provided with benefits, and became lords, dukes, equals, and counselors of the monarch. Once again the church, after gaining entry to the life of nations, was domesticated by them. The nations became guardians of the clergy and almost separated them from Rome. Now the swing of the pendulum favored the state.

Renaissance, Humanism, and Cultural Entry

Much more than a mere return to the study of ancient arts and letters, the Renaissance was a revolution that affected Western society at all levels: social, moral, aesthetic, and philosophical. It was characteristic of an entire epoch (from the fourteenth to the sixteenth century) and was represented by a new intellectual dynamism, contrary to that of the medieval age and society. The Renaissance was not yet a total human emancipation in regard to God and the Christian message but a fierce affirmation of humanity and its own values.

Humanism was the literary and cultural component of this revolution. It wished to educate and shape people (grammarians, orators, poets, teachers, and philosophers) by means of Latin and Greek classical literature. Humanists were characterized by the cultivation of letters, a love of wisdom, confidence in humanity, and an interest in uniting culture and piety. They rejected neither sin nor grace but emphasized all that was beautiful and good in humanity. Taken as a whole, the humanist movement was not pagan, and it cannot be made directly responsible for the immorality of the Renaissance, which existed long before and proliferated in quarters that were quite alien to humanist culture. Nevertheless, we must recognize that the humanists put themselves in a state of lasting ambiguity by accommodating a coexistence of the Christian ideal and pagan ideals.

The church for its part had good reasons for associating with the cultural movement of the time and for keeping its contacts with the elite. Unfortunately, it was unable to resist the disintegrative elements propagated by that same culture. Together with the art and cult of antiquity, it absorbed the spirit of antiquity and was won over to a way of life in which the dominant values were those of money, luxury, ostentation, and pleasure. The disastrous effects of this change were evident in the popes themselves. For over thirty years, with Sixtus IV, Innocent VIII, and Alexander VI, the example of the pontifical court comprised the greatest scandals and provocative display. The church touched the lower depths of immorality and crime. It was an age in which poison and daggers were extraordinarily commonplace. During this period Savonarola at Florence proclaimed reformation and the punishments of God on an adulterous church. The pilgrims who passed through Rome returned to their own countries shocked by the venality and the spirit of luxury, covetousness, and debauchery of churchmen and even the popes. The scandal of pontifical Rome was vastly to the discredit of the entire church.

The Reformation came, but very late, after initiatives that escaped the control of the church and led to the drama of Luther and to the loss of half of Europe. The church had entered into the culture and life-style of the Renaissance but to the point of being swallowed up by them.

The Nineteenth Century and a Lack of Inclusion

After a period of excessive inclusion in the culture and political life of the nations, in the nineteenth century and at the beginning of the twentieth the church experienced a new but more subtle danger: that of keeping apart from the world. For a century and a half, indeed, it was as if the church was a stranger in the world, and consequently slow in understanding it. It developed an odd and distressing inferiority complex toward modern philosophy and science. It was faced with a civilization that it found disconcerting and eventually disturbing. It resisted new ideas. It relied on the bourgeoisie, which represented the new form of power, but it simultaneously lost the working classes.

Throughout the nineteenth century, however, irreligion spread increasingly and bit deeper. It became sectarian, aggressive, and determined to destroy not only Christ and the church but God himself. The entire humanism of the nineteenth century was atheistic. The Christian conception of humanity was felt to be a shackle. The result of a development that started with the Renaissance, this attitude developed in the eighteenth century and was formulated in the nineteenth century in the philosophy and writings of Hegel, Feuerbach, Marx, Comte, Taine, and Littré.

Faced with this rising sea of rationalism, all the church could oppose to it was a form of apologetics that had more fine intentions than real strength. Polemical and poorly equipped at a scientific level, it hastily tried to stop up the most urgent breaches in the fortress. To answer the historical criticism of the age, it needed a vital exegesis, philosophy, and theology. But the Catholic scholarship of the nineteenth century was weak and decadent. The church was behind the times and incapable of making a synthesis of old and new. It could do no more than oppose an unreceptive attitude to the theses of rationalism.

The secular notions of the nineteenth century (liberty, equality, democracy, a separation of politics from religion, historical and literary criticism) undoubtedly contained not only some dubious components but valuable elements that the church could assimilate. Faced with these attacks, however, the church rejected them in toto. For almost a century it continued to multiply its condemnations.

There are certainly explanations for the church's attitude. But the fact remains that the church of the nineteenth century, when confronted by the world in progress, went on the defensive. It gradually isolated itself. After having been far too committed to the social, political, and cultural structures of the past, it ran the risk of no longer committing itself sufficiently, of no longer trying to understand the world that it had to lead to the gospel, and of ceasing all dialogue with it. It concentrated its life on its own affairs and on itself, but it was increasingly *absent* from the world and increasingly isolated and consequently had no real impact on the world. This lack of inclusion in the world was no less serious a risk for the church than the excessive commitment of the past.

The Twentieth Century: In Search of New Forms of Commitment

After a long period of protest against the modern world, then of isolation, the twentieth-century church, above all after Vatican II, underwent a veritable conversion in its attitude to the world. It experienced a multiple transformation of its various aspects. However defiant it seemed, the church became accessible and welcoming. Remember in this respect the gestures of John XXIII and of Paul VI (at the United Nations). It changed from a policy of prestige to a policy of discretion, and even of self-oblivion. Previously, it had affected to give without receiving, to know everything without having anything to learn. Now it recognizes that it has much to receive and learn from the world. It acknowledges the world as the free partner in an open dialogue. It recognizes other cultures and other mentalities and trusts them. The long-interrupted dialogue with the philosophies of the present time has been resumed. The church also engages in dialogue with the separated Christian communities, with the great world religions, and even with modern atheistic humanism.

More aware of its true nature and of its relation to the world, the twentieth-century church is searching for new forms of commitment. This is a difficult quest, since the world to which it has to commit itself is itself searching for a language, for new social and political structures, and for a new image of the cosmos. The church has to make its commitment in this world in which the indefinite and unforeseeable is the only definite element. In addition, the church lives in a cultural, civic, political, scientific, economic, and artistic context that is no longer the work of Christianity alone. Christians live in a state of diaspora in a secularized world. Accordingly, the life of faith is no longer a matter of inheritance and of environment but of personal decision and constant conquest. In this new world, the church has to be a church of living, active members who bear the gospel within themselves and the spirit of the gospel within their familial, professional, and social occupations. This mode of activity is characteristic of the kind of influence known as witness, or life commitment, which takes effect by means of an infusion of meaning and personal influence. This activity has to penetrate and vitalize all social milieus and levels.

This commitment to a secularized world also has its dangers, which are palpable—for example: a reduction of Christianity to a form of humanism, under the pretext of openness to the world; a tendency to make humanity the yardstick and criterion for God's initiatives; a danger, for the sake of bringing people together, of reducing Christ to intersubjectivity; a danger of reducing religion to ethics; a danger of setting hierarchy to one side in favor of the basis; a danger of a generalized relativism and of a practical indifference. The commitment of the church to the world that is in the process of formation is still too indefinite to allow one to speak with exactitude of the depth of these dangers or of their transient nature.

A Challenging Paradox

Hence, distinct from the world but committed to the world and to human history, the church cannot escape the risks of temporality. The problem of having to maintain equilibrium between excessive commitment to history and a lack of commitment to it is certainly one of the most pressing problems that the church has to resolve. No satisfactory solution has been found to it, which is probably because none exists.

That said, how are we to explain the lasting nature of the church, in spite of all these risks of temporality that surround it like so many factors of decay and death? Even if every aspect of history were to have a consistent and plausible explanation in the context of the age, how are we to explain the fact that circumstances always favor the church and allow it to survive? If we appeal to chance, how are we to explain the fact that chance always comes out in its favor? Looked at in each stage, the church seems something improbable, faltering, vulnerable, outpaced, a heap of ruins and new shoots, suffering now from enfeeblement and now showing signs of recovery. The church remains an *enigma*. It should have been dead long ago. Yet it persists. More effectively than the Jewish religion, which has never been able to free itself from circumstances of race, institutions, and rites, the church constantly commits itself and surrenders its commitment. It is not afraid to commit itself to a novel and difficult world, which confronts it with the threat of assimilation and the risk of decay.

Sharing in and engulfed by the structures of the political life of the Roman Empire, feudalism, medieval Christianity, and the modern nations, like them, the church should have collapsed and died. But in the last few centuries, increasingly liberated from the temporal power but also increasingly absent from the world, the church, like some ancient if aristocratic survivor of an era long gone, should really have withered away in an isolation worse than death. But the astonishing thing, the paradox, is that it persists and always finds the strength to renew and rejuvenate itself. Its vitality has not been exhausted over the twenty centuries of its existence. In human history as we know it, that kind of persistence within the temporal order constitutes a *true enigma*. Of course faith tells us that the church will never perish, because the principle of its persistence is not humanity but God and his Spirit. Nevertheless the historical expression of this activity is amazing. Anyone aware of all the fragility and decay in human history must be astonished that an institution that has been so very present in and so committed to human history, and subject to such tensions for twenty centuries, should have kept its identity and its dynamic thrust. The phenomenon does indeed seem tantamount to a mystery.

5. The Sinfulness–Sanctity Paradox of the Church

The third and greatest paradox of the church is that of the coexistence within it of sin and holiness. This is also the point that evokes most questions, even among believers, since for many people this is a stumbling block, a scandal, or sheer nonsense. However, the texts of the magisterium are similarly assured in affirming the holiness and the sinfulness of the church.

"Holy" is the first attribute to be attached to the word "church." In the baptismal creed of Jerusalem (ca. 348), the believer affirms his or her faith in the holy church (DS 41). In 374, the creed of Epiphanius also says that the church is holy (DS 42). The Nicene-Constantinopolitan creed of 381 declares in its turn: "We believe in the holy Church" (DS 150). Much more recently, Vatican II repeats the assertion that the church is holy (*LG* 2, 5, 8, 10, 12, 48). With the same assurance, however, the magisterium maintains that the church is a pilgrim church of sinners, which is vulnerable, beset with temptations, and constantly in need of repentance and reformation (*LG* 8, 9, 15, 65; *GS* 43).

The letters of Paul already bear witness to the existence in the primitive communities of instances when faith and charity were lacking, and to envy, lies, covetousness, and indecency. It is inescapable; unless we think of the church as an idealized hypostasis separated from the believers themselves, we have to admit that the sins of the members of the church are the sins of the People of God, and we must acknowledge that the sins of Christians affect the church itself, tarnishing and soiling the mysterious and holy body of Christ.

Therefore the church is both a community of sinners and a communion of saints. In spite of its sinfulness, the church is called holy; though holy, it is marked by sin. In the very expressive words of the fathers of the church, the church is a *casta meretrix*, a "chaste prostitute." That is the paradox. Accordingly the question arises, How can a church affected by sin still be an *expressive sign* of the salvation that it announces? Surely it is rather an antisign, a countertestimony? Some points from Scripture and theological reflection may help us to adjust our sights to the reality of this problem and to say something more precise about the relation between sin and holiness in the church.

Illuminating Scripture

Sanctity, in the biblical sense, is somewhat double-sided. First, God alone is holy, and all holiness comes from God. The People of God are holy, the church is holy, because it is chosen, called by God, and consecrated to God and to Christ in baptism. Second, this holiness of initiative and grace on the part of God summons up a responsive holiness on the part of humanity, that is, an ethical holiness. These points already help to clarify the paradox of the holiness and sinfulness of the church. They set us in a personalistic context of grace and love on the part of God, and of free and loving response on the part of human beings.

The images that Scripture uses to describe the mystery of the church shed even more light on the sin-sanctity paradox of the church. Thus Vatican II adopted the image of the *People of God* as a fundamental image in its presentation of the church. The image stresses the initiative of God. Israel exists only by virtue of the gracious and decisive divine initiative. It is born of nothing, and it consists of those on whom God has bestowed his grace. Choice, salvation, covenant, and law are pure gifts. The image also stresses the fact that the church is a pilgrim people—a caravan, as it were—on its way toward the eschatological kingdom. The church is in transit. Because it is on the way, the People of God are subject to the vicissitudes of time. They are weak and sinful; they are in constant need of reformation and forgiveness. Since the exodus the People of God have murmured and have been unfaithful. But this image also emphasizes the fact that the church is on its way toward an ending that will be its peace and joy.

The image of the *Bride and Bridegroom* also stresses the initiative of God. He was the first to love and choose his spouse. He has remained faithful to her in spite of her infidelities. The image also emphasizes the interpersonal nature of the relations between God and his church. It underlines the nature of freedom in the love and reciprocity of the gift. The love of God's initiative requires the answer of the church's love, for what would a love be without answer and reciprocity? Finally, the image emphasizes the lasting gifts of the Bridegroom to the Bride: the gospel, sacraments, and above all the Spirit. In the OT the Spirit was an episodic gift; in the NT he is a permanent gift. For this reason the church will never entirely traduce the Bridegroom.

Though it is many-layered, the image of the People of God does not exhaust the entire richness of the mystery of the church. We may say that this image constitutes the generic element that expresses the continuity of the two covenants. But the status of the church under the new covenant is expressed also in the image of the *body of Christ*. Since the union of the divine nature with the human nature in the incarnation, and since the resurrection of Christ, the church has been the body of Christ. Because Christ loves the church, his spouse, as his own body, the church is indissolubly united to him. The Bridegroom and the Bride will never separate. Some members may voluntarily remove themselves from the vital sanctifying influence of Christ and the Spirit, just as an illness can affect this or that member of the human body, but nothing can separate Bridegroom from Bride. Nothing can spoil or contaminate the source of life that incessantly vitalizes the body of Christ, for that source is God himself.

In each image we may note an aspect of initiative, calling, vocation, and active sanctification that comes from God. We also note an element of free response to this initiative and summons. Union and communion with the holy God demand a way of life that accords with so high a vocation.

Theological Reflection

In recent theological research (e.g., of C. Journet, A. de Bovis, Y. Congar, K. Rahner, G. Martelet, and H. Küng), we find, together with divergent viewpoints, a certain number of points of clear agreement. First, rather than think of the church as an unreal hypostasis, we should speak of the church as the People of God and thus as an assembly of saints and as an assembly of sinners. Second, the decisive note of the church is not in fact sin but holiness, and it is so by virtue of the choice of vocation and the action of God, who, through Christ and his Spirit, maintains the church and incessantly gives it life. Third, the church is subjectively holy, as a totality, because of the indefectible loyalty by which it has deserved Christ, who has united himself with it forever as his spouse and body. Fourth, the church shares in the general mystery of the sacramentality of the Christian economy; in spite of its sufferings, it always remains, at heart, the instrument of salvation for the world. Fifth, in its members, ethical sanctity depends on their more or less generous response. Finally, the wholly pure and entirely holy church will come about only eschatologically.

A Challenging Paradox

It is undeniable that the church is a visible community whose testimony assumes not only a personal but a communitarian form. The quality of the members of this community affects the quality of the community itself and the quality of the image that it offers to the world. This community lives by the gospel and simultaneously affirms the ascendancy over it of the gospel, recognized as a supreme value. The result is an *image* that is faithful to Christ

and to his Spirit. Sin, in contrast, establishes sinful interpersonal relationships between the members of a community. A community whose members are divided, egotistical, full of hate, cruel, immoral, and liars and thieves is rightly called sinful. It presents a sinful body and countenance to the world. It constitutes an antisign of salvation, for it contradicts the gospel that it proclaims.

We cannot ignore or reduce the importance of this aspect of the church. The image that the church presents to the world makes it an expressive and infectious sign or a negative sign of the salvation that it preaches. On the level of fundamental theology, it is therefore legitimate to speak of a sinful church, while recalling that it is a matter of the *image of the church* that results from the witness of the community.

What, then, are the *facts*, apparent even to people outside, that are so astonishing and evoke the question, If there is salvation in the world, surely it is in this community, which claims to be established by Christ to save human beings? In other words, what are the visible manifestations of holiness in the church that, in spite of the sinfulness of its members, can attract the attention of even the nonbeliever? Here are some of them: (1) the church does not cease to preach the gospel of salvation and the means of salvation; (2) the church never ceases to work to raise the moral level of the individual and of humanity; (3) the church welcomes sinners; (4) the church constantly proposes the ideal of evangelical perfection; (5) the church produces saints constantly and in all ages—Peter and Paul, Ignatius of Antioch, Basil, Gregory, Athanasius, Augustine, Ambrose, Bernard, Benedict, Clare, Francis, Dominic, Thomas Aquinas, Bonaventure, Ignatius Loyola, Francis Xavier, Vincent de Paul, Jean-Marie Vianney, John Bosco, John of the Cross, Francis of Sales, Teresa of Ávila, Teresa of Lisieux, John Brébeuf, Isaac Jogues, Maximilian Kolbe, and so on—all of whom belong to the universal church; (6) the periodical reformation of the church.

The church includes, together with its heroic saints, a considerable number of sinners. Moreover, in its whole body, as in its members, it is constantly in need of reformation. This is a necessity that Vatican II insists on. The church constantly needs reform, and it is aware of this. Periodically, in order to remain faithful to the gospel, which requires continual conversion, the church enacts its own rejuvenation in successive reforms. For examples, we may list the Cluniac reform of the eleventh century as extended and prolonged until the thirteenth century; the Tridentine Counter-Reformation of the sixteenth century extended by Ignatius, Charles Borromeo, Francis of Sales, and Vincent de Paul; the present reform of Vatican II: an authentic revolution at the level of texts and attitudes, the repercussions of which are still unpredictable.

In short, even in the midst of its trials and tribulations, the church remains a *paradox*. It makes itself the judge and reformer of its own weaknesses. In the very depths it finds the strength to take stock of itself. The paradox is that people, who are so weak and wretched, find the strength to look ahead and upward. The paradox is that the church, in spite of its infirmities, constantly and regularly produces saints great and loyal enough to be put forward for universal imitation.

6. In Search of Meaning: From Phenomenon to Mystery

In its totality and with all its paradoxical characteristics, the phenomenon of the church appears as an *enigma* to be deciphered. It does not reveal its secret straightaway but acts as a mental and spiritual stimulus calling for a quest for comprehensibility and a search for meaning. It is related to another paradox that it also appeals to: the paradox of Christ.

The church, as we have seen, offers the observer—even the unbeliever—a range of paradoxical characteristics, which in themselves comprise a variety of tensions and such explosive potential that any one of them alone would be enough to bring about the collapse of the church. It is a question not of theoretical threats or the abstract demons of some learned discourse but of historical realities that have failed to capsize the church. The phenomenon of the church, as a whole, is a question that demands a sufficient and appropriate explanation. It demands that we look elsewhere to find the principle to explain the major antinomies of the church: unity-Catholicity, endurance-temporality, sinfulness-holiness. What is the key to the enigma?

The church for its part proposes as an explanation of its own mystery that its entire being and action proceed from a special intervention of God in Jesus Christ. It testifies that of itself it is nothing, but that its entire power of expansion and cohesion, of sanctification and salvation, come to it from God in Jesus Christ, the epiphany of the Father. The real meaning of the phenomenon of the church is the active presence in it of Christ and of his Spirit, the source of unity and charity.

We cannot reject this kind of explanation without examining it, as it seems to be the only satisfactory key to the facts as we observe them. If we accept it, then everything is explained and becomes coherent and intelligible. Otherwise, we would certainly fail if we went in search of "natural" explanations. Then the church with all its paradoxes and all its tensions and twenty centuries of history would remain an undecipherable enigma. Faced with the nature and importance of the observable facts, it is prudent to acknowledge the truthfulness of the church's testimony regarding itself: among human beings it is the community of salvation in Jesus Christ required by God.

The conclusion is all the more reasonable when we realize that there is a marvelous accordance between the observable facts and the message of Christ, to which the church bears witness. The church indeed proclaims that Christ is the Son of God come among human beings to inaugurate the kingdom of God on earth: that is, to transform the hearts of human beings into the hearts of loving children and to bring all human beings together in the one People of God, so that they become one body, the body of Christ, empowered by the Spirit of love that unites the Father and the Son. But the church appears on earth as the visible and at least inchoative presence of this proclaimed transformation. In the *saint* especially, we see the appearance of a new type of humanity—that of a son or daughter of God living and acting under the influence of the Spirit. Moreover, a new type of society becomes apparent in the church, giving evidence, with indications of its human and earthly condition, of more radiant characteristics, which are like the first draft of a humanity ultimately gathered in unity and charity, in the image of the communion of the Trinity. This accord between the gospel of Christ and the paradoxical characteristics of the church leads us to conclude that the church is truly, among human beings, as it says, the sign of the coming of God, the location of the presence of salvation in Jesus Christ. The *paradox* conceals a *mystery.*

I must stress the fact that this approach is one of internal comprehensibility. It does not start from the absolute and glorious attributes of the church but from the paradoxes that it comprises. It tries to understand those paradoxes in themselves and in association with the explanation that the church offers of itself and of its relation to Christ. The consistency of the suggested explanation and its appropriateness to the observable phenomena lead us to conclude that the testimony of the church is a truthful one; among human beings it is indeed "the universal sacrament of salvation" in Jesus Christ. The phenomenon finds its explanation in the mystery that is testified to. This approach does not lead to any evidence, but rather it conveys a moral certainty that may ground a prudent decision. In order to open up to the presence concealed in the flesh of the phenomenon and in the fragility of the institutional church, it is necessary to lose oneself and to allow oneself to be borne along by the Spirit, who whispers within us in the most secret recesses of our being.

Definitively, the church is a sign to the extent that it tends to approach the Reality that it represents — namely, Christ in his universal charity. The more it reflects Christ faithfully, like an unblemished mirror, the more the holiness of the Bride tends to echo that of the Bridegroom, and the more too it signifies and attracts. Just as Christ was the epiphany of God for the Jews of his time, the church should be the epiphany of Christ for the people of the present time. It is from this viewpoint that Vatican II almost desperately emphasized the need for the testimony of a holy life. The church, in each of its members and in the communities that go to make it up, must be the living witness of Christ throughout the centuries. The more the communion of people among themselves, and of people with God, is visible and radiant, the more attractive the sign will prove.

Bibl.: General Works, Documents of Vatican II, especially: *LG, GS, AG, AL; Handbuch der Kirchengeschichte;* A. FLICHE and V. MARTIN, *Histoire de l'Église* (Paris, 1934–55); L. PASTOR, *The History of the Popes: From the Close of the Middle Ages* (1988; St. Louis, 1898).

Monographs: K. ADAM, *The Spirit of Catholicism* (New York, 1930); J. GUITTON, *The Church and the Gospel* (Chicago, 1961); H. Urs VON BALTHASAR, *Sponsa Verbi* (Einsiedeln, 1960); M. GRAND-MAISON, *L'Église par elle-même motif de crédibilité* (Rome, 1961); Y. CONGAR, *Sainte Église* (Paris, 1961); E. SCHILLEBEECKX, *Christ the Sacrament of the Encounter with God* (New York, 1963); G. MARTELET, *Sainteté et vie religieuse* (Toulouse, 1964); H. HOLSTEIN, "L'Église, Signe parmi les Nations," *Études* (Oct. 1962); J. HAMER, *L'Église est une communion* (Paris, 1962); R. SCHUTZ, *The Power of the Provisional* (1965; London, 1969); R. LATOURELLE, "La testimonianza della vita, segno di salvezza," in *Laici sulle vie del concilio* (Assisi, 1966), 377–95; K. RAHNER, *Belief Today* (New York, 1967); H. MÜHLEN, *Una Mystica Persona* (2nd ed.; Paderborn, 1967); H. DE LUBAC, *Paradoxe et Mystère de l'Église* (Paris, 1967); A. MANARANCHE, *Je crois en Jésus-Christ aujourd'hui* (Paris, 1968); H. KÜNG, *The Church* (New York, 1968); R. LATOURELLE, *Christ and the Church: Signs of Salvation* (New York, 1972); R. FISICHELLA, *H. U. Von Balthasar: Amore e credibilità cristiana* (Rome, 1981); N. COTUGNO, "La testimonianza del Popolo di Dio, segno di Rivelazione alla luce del Concilio Vaticano II," in R. FISICHELLA, ed., *Gesù Rivelatore* (Casale Monferrato, 1988), 227–40.

René LATOURELLE

IV. VIA EMPIRICA

The *via empirica,* or empirical way, is referred to as an "ascending way" and employs a "regressive" or "analytical" method. It figures in fundamental ecclesiology (→ CHURCH I) by virtue of its point of departure in a consideration of the Catholic church as it exists and lives *today* for a demonstration of the credibility of that church. Thus, while the other two ways (the *historical* and that of the *notes*) both move from Christ to the church, the *via empirica* proceeds in the opposite direction, "ascending" from the church to Jesus Christ.

We find a suggestion of this approach as long ago as Augustine: "The power of God is no longer manifested to us in the life of Christ, which we see no more; now it is shown in the living church, which is present to our eyes. We see the Body, and believe in the Head" (*PL* 38:659-60). Thomas Aquinas, again, holds that conversion to Christianity constitutes a "maximal miracle, manifest deed, and secure index of divine inspiration" (*CG* I, 1, 6).

In the fifteenth century, Savonarola, O.P., inaugurated the "apologetic method," arguing to the truth of the church from a starting point in its life. In the seventeenth century the principal authors using this kind of approach were J.-B. Bossuet and Blaise Pascal; and in the nineteenth, J. Balmes, H. Lacordaire, and especially Cardinal Dechamps, who regarded this "way" as the nucleus of his method (consisting in an argumentation "from providence") and who exerted a decisive influence on Vatican I.

That council was crucial for the fortunes of the *via empirica*. It declared the Catholic church to be, "through itself" (*per se ipsa*), a basis for its own credibility: the church as a "sign raised among the nations" (*signum levatum in nationes*; cf. Is 11:12), although the demonstration involved is indicative rather than demonstrative (DS 3013–14). With the first volume (1925) of H. Dieckmann's *De Ecclesia*, this "way" began to be designated the "empirical." Henceforward it operated on the premise of the church as a "moral miracle" typifying the extraordinary nature of the church and thus inferring its transcendence and divinity.

Since Vatican II, certain traits of the church as "sign" in the spirit of Vatican I have given way to a new focus on the "sacramentality" of the church, in which the ecclesial body is approached as a single *complexa realitas* (*LG* 8), an entity at once visible and spiritual. More specifically, a verification of the church as "sign" is concentrated more and more in the category of witness. At work here is the entire process of personalization: while Vatican I understood the "sign" of the church in terms of the *miraculous* attributes of the same, Vatican II appeals to personal and community *witness*. This witness becomes an ecclesial sign of credibility and a paradigm for fundamental ecclesiology. Currently, four emphases appear in the newer approach:

1. The *hagiophanic way* presents the church as a testimony of hagiophany. The miracle in question is no longer approached as an effect of the power of God, but now is seen as a sign of the divine presence, and of a call inviting human beings to conversion. The church is more an ostensive hagiophany, then, than a probative one (Y. Congar, G. C. Berkouwer).

2. The *way of the sociological institution* begins with the observation that the institution is the only way to salvage "concrete freedom" (G. W. F. Hegel), and with the empirical-sociological value of the institution (Peter Berger, T. Luckmann, Jürgen Habermas). Thus, the ecclesial institution presents itself as an identifying, integrating, and liberating sign of the power of the Spirit (M. Kehl, L. Dullaart) and of its prophetic visibility (P. A. Liégé).

3. The *way of self-explanation* is the "way" of internal intelligibility or search for meaning (Karl Rahner). Its point of departure is no longer the church's glorious attributes, but its paradoxes: the explanation for its paradoxical witness lies in "mystery attested" (Henri de Lubac, Avery Dulles). The church as a moral miracle is not the premise of the argumentation, but precisely its point of arrival. Like the others, this examination purports to generate not an "evidence" but a moral certitude constituting an adequate basis for a prudent decision (René Latourelle).

4. The *way of signification* points to the authentic *notae Ecclesiae* as *notae Christianorum* (Hans Küng), along the basic lines of the church as sacrament and sign (Otto Semmelroth, Leonardo Boff, Walter Kasper). The "significativity" of this witness is manifested in doctrinal consistency (Gregory Baum, Joseph Ratzinger), catholicity (W. Beinert, John Meyendorff, A. Dulles), the visualization of love (G. Thils, Hans Urs von Balthasar, R. Fisichella), the perception of communion (Jérôme Hamer, Henri de Lubac, S. Dianich, J. M. R. Tillard, M. M. Garijo-Guembe), the eucharistic dimension (J. Zizioulas, B. Forte, Jürgen Moltmann), the commitment to liberation (liberation theologians), openness and ecumenical dialogue (Congar, H. Fries, Rahner, H. Döring), and, finally, the church as sign of the reign of God (Wolfhart Pannenberg, F. A. Sullivan). Special mention is in order for the bishops' synods on justice in the world (1971), evangelization (1974), the aftermath of the council (1985), the laity (1987), and the priesthood (1990), as well as the Apostolic Exhortations *Evangelii Nuntiandi* (Paul VI) and *Christifideles Laici* (John Paul II).

A good synthesis of the postconciliar understanding of the *via empirica* is to be found in the conclusion of document issuing from the 1985 synod:

> An evangelization of unbelievers presupposes the self-evangelization of the baptized, indeed of deacons, priests, and bishops. Evangelization occurs through witnesses; but the witness gives testimony not only in words but in life. Let us not forget that the Greek word for witness is "martyrdom." (II: B-2 = *EV* 9:1795)

Bibl.: G. GIANFROCCA, *La via empirica del concilio Vaticano I a noi* (Rome, 1963); R. LATOURELLE, *Christ and the Church: Signs of Salvation* (New York, 1972); L. BOFF, *Die Kirche als Sakrament im Horizont der Welterfahrung* (Paderborn, 1972); B. HIDBER, *Glaubenatur-Übernatur: Studien der "Methode der Vorsehung," von Kardinal Dechamps* (Frankfurt, 1978); S. PIÉ-NINOT, *Tratado de Teología Fundamental* (Salamanca, 1989), 340–54, 363–66.

Salvador PIÉ-NINOT

V: NOTES OF THE CHURCH

Practically all Christians are united in professing their faith in the "one, holy, catholic, and apostolic church." This fourfold description of the church is part of the baptismal creed that was adopted as its profession of faith by the First Council of Constantinople, was confirmed by the Council of Chalcedon, and subsequently became the liturgical creed of the churches of both East and West. These four attributes are, like the church itself, professed in the creed as objects of the act of faith, sharing the nature of the church as mysteries. Hence, like the church, they are complex realities, being in some respects experientially verifiable and in other respects knowable only by faith. Ecclesiologists consider these properties of the church in all their aspects, seeking a fuller understanding of what we believe about the church. Catholic apologists, especially since the seventeenth century, have focused their attention on those aspects of the four creedal attributes which can lead a person who is sincerely seeking the true church of Christ to identify it as the Catholic church alone. For this purpose, apologists have selected those aspects of the four properties of the church which can function as the "notes" or distinguishing "marks" of the one true church. Such "notes" would have to be (1) more easily identifiable than the church itself; (2) proper to the true church; (3) inseparable from it; and (4) recognizable by every sincere inquirer, even the unlearned.

The apologetic argument known as the *via notarum* involved two basic steps: (1) the demonstration that by the will of Christ its divine founder, the church must be visibly and recognizably one, holy, catholic, and apostolic, with a specific kind of unity, holiness, catholicity, and apostolicity that is proper to the true church alone; and (2) the demonstration that precisely *such* unity, holiness, catholicity, and apostolicity characterize the Roman Catholic church and no other.

In the course of the eighteenth and nineteenth centuries, the *via notarum* became a standard feature of Catholic apologetics, undergoing various developments and adaptations as the problems inherent in it became better known and measures were taken to meet them. One such problem lay in the fact that it was clearly impossible to claim that there was simply no unity, holiness, catholicity, or apostolicity at all to be found in the non-Catholic churches. This was particularly evident in regard to the separated churches of the East, whose sacraments certainly could produce holiness in those who received them devoutly, and whose episcopal orders were apostolic in origin. Such problems as these made it necessary to further specify the notions of unity, holiness, catholicity, and apostolicity which are proper to the true church, in such a way as to be able to conclude that they are found uniquely in the Roman Catholic church. In other words, the Catholic use of the *via notarum* depended on a distinctively Catholic understanding of the four creedal properties of the church. Naturally, other Christians could claim these same properties for their churches, by understanding them in a way that corresponded to their realization in those churches.

The weakness of this procedure lay in the fact that inevitably the description of the unity, holiness, etc. that the church must have tended to be determined by the kind of unity, etc. that one's own church actually possessed. Whether consciously or not, one began with the presumption that one's own church had the right kind of unity, holiness, etc., and then returned to the NT and the documents of the early church in order to prove that this was the kind of unity, holiness, etc., that Christ wanted his church to have. Thus the *via notarum* involved all the problems of a strictly confessional use of the sources. It meant returning to the sources in order to prove a pre-established thesis, rather than an inquiry that would allow the sources themselves determine what kind of properties a church must have in order to be true to its NT origins.

One solution to this problem was proposed by V. A. Dechamps, the archbishop of Malines, and was adopted by the First Vatican Council. This obviated the need of returning to the sources by insisting that the unity, holiness, and universality that are unique to the Catholic church constitute a moral miracle and, therefore, of themselves provide sufficient proof that this is the true church of Christ (DS 3013). Of course this solution does not lack its own difficulty, as it involves the necessity of showing not only that the Catholic church alone enjoys these properties but also that the church's possession of them is an undeniable proof of its divine origin.

Despite the endorsement of this *via empirica* by Vatican I, Catholic apologists continued to propose the *via notarum*, either including the Roman primacy within this, in their treatment of unity and apostolicity, or proposing two distinct approaches, the *via notarum* and the via *primatus*.

However, developments during the twentieth century have led, if not to the total abandonment of the *via notarum*, at least to a quite different approach to the question of identifying the "true church of Christ." In the first place, the far-reaching advances made in biblical, patristic, and historical studies have led to increasing dissatisfaction with the use of the sources that was characteristic of the apologetic method. As more light came to be shed on the early church, it became increasingly evident that Catholic apologists had only too easily been finding in those sources what they wanted to find rather than what was objectively there. The weakness of the "proof-text" use of the sources became more and more apparent.

The development that has most radically affected Catholic apologetics in this century is the opening of the Catholic church to the ecumenical movement that was endorsed by Vatican II. This has led to a profound revision of some of the basic premises of the old apologetic argument. One of these premises was stated in its most emphatic form in the *Schema de Ecclesia* that was drawn up by the Preparatory Theological Commission for Vatican II, which declared not only that the Roman Catholic church is the one true church, but that there is no other that has a right to call itself a church at all (*AS* I/4, 15). However, this preparatory schema met such severe criticism during the first period of the council that it was withdrawn without being put to a vote. The new schema discussed by the council in 1963, while it continued to identify the church of Christ with the Roman Catholic church, recognized the presence, outside of it, of "elements of sanctification" which by nature belong to the church. Subsequently, the council approved an emendation by which the statement that the church of Christ *is* the Catholic church, was changed to say: *subsists in* the Catholic church. The reason given for the change was "so that the expression might better agree with the affirmation about the ecclesial elements which are found elsewhere" (*AS* III/1, 177).

Practically all commentators have seen in this change of wording a significant opening toward the recognition by the Catholic church of ecclesial reality in the non-Catholic world. This was confirmed in *LG* 15, where the council recognized the role of non-Catholic churches and ecclesiastical communities in providing baptism and other sacraments for their members. This was further developed in the Decree on Ecumenism, which declared that these non-Catholic churches and communities were used by the Holy Spirit as means of grace and salvation (*UR* 3).

What are the consequences for Catholic apologetics of this momentous change of attitude regarding the ecclesial status of the churches and ecclesial communities separated from Rome? It is no longer a question of having to prove that the Roman Catholic church is the "one true church" to the exclusion of the right of any other to be called a church. Vatican II, recognizing the ecclesial status of those other churches and communities, clearly acknowledged that the one church of Christ is present and salvifically operative in them also. In other words, the task of Catholic apologetics is no longer to prove that the church of Christ, in an exclusive sense, *is* the Roman Catholic church, but rather to justify the claim that the church of Christ *subsists in* the Catholic church. What this task involves depends on how the term *subsists in* is to be understood.

An important indication of the mind of the council on this question is given by the statement in the Decree on Ecumenism: "We believe that the unity with which Christ from the beginning endowed his church is something it cannot lose; it subsists in the Catholic church, and we hope it will continue to increase until the end of time" (*UR* 4). On the other hand, the same Decree had stated that the separated churches and communions "are not blessed with that unity which the Holy Scriptures and the revered tradition of the church proclaim" (*UR* 3). It would seem fully consistent with what the council has said about the unity Christ gave to his church "subsisting" in the Catholic church, to conclude that the other three creedal properties of the church can be said to "subsist" in the Catholic church as well.

From this it follows that the use of the *via notarum* in Catholic apologetics, since Vatican II, would be to show that the church of Christ subsists in the Catholic church precisely because it is there that the four creedal properties of the church of Christ continue to subsist.

The question then is: How would a Catholic *via notarum* done in the light of Vatican II differ from the preconciliar apologetic? There would be several important differences. The first stems from the fact that the term *subsists in*" does not have the exclusive sense of the word "is," which it replaced in the conciliar text. To say that the church of Christ subsists in the Catholic church does not mean that it is not found elsewhere; indeed the council recognized that it is present and operative in other churches and communities also in virtue of the ecclesial means of grace they provide for their members. Likewise, to say that the unity, holiness, catholicity, and apostolicity which Christ gave to his church subsist in the Catholic church does not imply that they are found exclusively there. One key to the council's opening to ecumenism lies in the recognition that such things as ecclesial communion admit degrees of fullness in their actualization, so that to claim a certain fullness of ecclesiality, unity, etc., for the Catholic church does not mean a

denial of their presence elsewhere. What the Catholic apologist now has to justify is the claim of his church to have a certain fullness of what it means to be a church, and a fullness of the church's essential properties, such that it can rightly be said that the church of Christ subsists there in a way that it is not found in other churches.

Two further differences must also be noted. The first is that, in the light of Vatican II, a claim to such "fullness" is not the same thing as a claim to realize the nature of the church or its properties in their absolute perfection. The council declared, for instance, that while the church is "indefectibly holy" (*LG* 39), still, on this earth, "it is marked with a holiness that, while genuine, is also imperfect" (*LG* 48). Similarly, it acknowledged that the divided state of the church prevents it from realizing the fullness of catholicity that is proper to it (*UR* 4). The church's unity is something that "must increase to the end of time" (*UR* 4). Post-Vatican II Catholic apologists have no reason to indulge in the triumphalism that marked some preconciliar apologetics.

Finally, as has been noted above, one of the problems of the earlier use of the *via notarum* was that it depended on a distinctively Catholic understanding of the four "notes" of the church. Since Vatican II important ecumenical studies have been devoted to the elucidation of the four creedal properties of the church. Hence there is reason to hope that in the future a Catholic apologist will be able to base the *via notarum* on an understanding of these properties that would represent at least a convergence, if not a full consensus, that had been achieved through ecumenical study and dialogue.

Bibl.: G. THILS, *Les Notes de l'Église dans l'apologétique catholique depuis la Réforme* (Gembloux, 1947); J. L. WITTE, "One, Holy, Catholic and Apostolic," in H. VORGRIMLER, ed., *One, Holy, Catholic and Apostolic* (London, 1968), 3–43; Y. CONGAR, *L'Église: Une, Sainte, Catholique et Apostolique* (Paris, 1970); H. J. POTTMEYER, "Die Frage nach der wahren Kirche," in W. KERN, H. J. POTTMEYER, M. SECKLER, eds., *Handbuch der fundamentaltheologie*, vol. 3: *Traktat Kirche* (Freiburg, 1986), 212–41; F. A. SULLIVAN, *The Church We Believe In: One, Holy, Catholic and Apostolic* (Mahwah/Dublin, 1989).

Francis A. SULLIVAN

VI: THE CHURCH AS INTERPRETER OF SCRIPTURE

As the assembly of believers, the church lives from God's Word. In prayer, liturgy, and study, Christians seek daily guidance and sustenance from the privileged expression of the Word in Scripture (DV 21–26). Consequently, interpretation of Scripture is of vital importance, and the Second Vatican Council took pains to set forth the principles of "integral EXEGESIS" of the Bible. The main hermeneutical statement of the council, Dei Verbum 12, encourages the historical-critical retrieval of the original or literal sense of texts but then goes on to insist on a broader theological interpretation of the Bible's meaning in the perspective of faith. Dei Verbum 12 then concludes by stating that interpretation of Scripture "is ultimately subject to the judgment of the church, which exercises a divinely conferred commission and ministry of preserving and interpreting the Word of God."

This role of the church in biblical interpretation, especially through authentic teaching by the ecclesial magisterium, can be misunderstood. A simplistic approach, for example, might contrast Protestant principles of "free examination" and private interpretation with the obligation of Catholics to accept the church's authoritative instruction on the meaning of the Bible. In actual fact, however, most Protestants read Scripture under the guidance of the catechesis and preaching which transmit to them the theological tradition of their particular denomination.

Catholic faith includes an explicit commitment to the church's tradition, especially as that is formulated in solemn teaching. But DOGMA is essentially protective of God's revelation in Christ as this has been originally mediated by the apostles and evangelists and further explained in the church. Tradition, however, is more than dogma; it is also the process by which the comprehensive DEPOSIT OF FAITH becomes present in every age (DV 8.1). Thus, tradition is also the community milieu formed by liturgy and spirituality, and Catholics believe that this ambience has a native congeniality with Scripture and is in fact the context in which the written text is fruitfully read, understood, and lived out as inspired testimony to God's own Word addressed to faith (DV 9).

Ultimately, the connection Catholics make between biblical interpretation and the church's teaching authority rests on the conviction that Christ provided an institutional means to ensure the integral transmission, protection, and explanation of what has been revealed for our salvation (DV 10; → MAGISTERIUM). This conviction, however, has a history that shows both continuity through the ages and considerable variety in ways of articulating and realizing a judicial role for the church in the interpretation of Scripture.

The fathers of the second and third centuries were sure that the churches, especially those of apostolic foundation, had in their "RULE OF FAITH" a body of teaching expressing the global meaning of Scripture in summary form. Origen could say that the truth of the word of God, a reality deeper than the letter of the text, is known to the church now converted to the Lord. For the Holy Spirit has conveyed the inspired sense (spiritualem sensum) to the church (In Leviticus 1.1; 5.5). Consequently, the ancient councils repeatedly evaluated doctrines, including those advanced with the backing of biblical texts, in terms of their conformity with the transmitted faith and its confession in the churches (→ CREED). Adoptionist Christology was rejected because its exponents, while citing the Gospels, did not understand them in accord with sound doctrine, i.e., in the way the Catholic fathers had confessed their faith and explained the texts. The Scriptures, to be sure, were the source of teaching and daily nourishment, but the creed coalesced with the doctrine of the fathers to constitute the norm by which interpretations of Scripture were assessed.

A new situation was created around 1500, due both to the increasing diffusion of printed Bibles for personal reading and to sporadic outbursts of apocalyptic fervor and expectation. A decree of the Fifth Lateran Council (session XI, 19 December 1516) censured those who twist the meaning of Scripture in sermons woven out of rash and idiosyncratic interpretations. Individualism in biblical preaching was ruled out, and preachers were mandated to announce and explain the truth of the Gospel in accord with the teaching of the approved doctores.

When the Council of TRENT took up its work of responding to the Reformation, its first solemn action was the formal reception of the traditional creed as the principle and foundation, prior to Scripture and apostolic traditions, for teaching and reform (session III, 4 February 1546). Trent's declaration on biblical interpretation (session IV; DS 1507) is part of a reform decree against abuses in preaching and clerical education, but it has long-term doctrinal implications. Trent asserts that the sense of Scripture handed on by the church—e.g., in its conciliar tradition—is the negative norm of interpretation. The Bible should not be construed in a manner contrary to either the central doctrinal heritage or the consensus of the fathers. Trent modified a draft formulation that had said that the church is the *only* legitimate interpreter of the Bible, but it went on to affirm that the church is indeed empowered to assess and judge that which biblical interpreters put forth as the Bible's teaching in reference to faith and concrete forms of worship and Christian life.

The First Vatican Council's Dogmatic Constitution *Dei Filius* reaffirmed Trent, but with a change from Trent's negative formulation, which ruled out interpretations contrary to the church's *sensus*, to a positive assertion that the ecclesial sense is true to Scripture in matters of faith and the Christian life (DS 3007). Vatican I's main concern in *Dei Filius* was to set forth both the differences and the relationships between natural reason and supernatural revelation and faith. Especially through the interventions of Bishop Meignan of Châlons, the council was aware of the danger of an overly restrictive approach to Scripture that would handicap Catholic scholars in their defense of revelation and the Bible against radical attacks. Thus, although Vatican I was stronger than Trent in its statement of the normative character of the doctrinal tradition, it did not claim that church teaching exhausts the meaning of Scripture. Vatican I did not shut the door to the eventual Catholic espousal of that work of reason which is the application of critical methods in the retrieval of the original communicative intention of particular biblical authors.

The further development of Catholic doctrine on the inspiration and interpretation of Scripture between the two Vatican Councils, with the repression of scholarship after the condemnation of modernism, has been told elsewhere (Beumer; Grelot; Brown and Collins). The papal encyclicals of 1893, 1920, and 1943, along with the decrees of the Pontifical Biblical Commission (especially 1905–15) are now of historical interest as background to *Dei Verbum*. We cited above Vatican II's concise restatement in *DV* 12 of the traditional claim of the church's role as a judicial instance in interpretation. What the same text says about the exegetical retrieval of the original sense and about theological interpretation in the light of faith indicates that the magisterium *is indeed* a final instance in interpretation. Further, the traditional claim, with which *DV* 12 concludes, is immediately preceded by an appreciative statement on the work of biblical scholars in contributing to the maturation of the church's judgment when it fulfills its mission of preserving and interpreting God's word.

The final word has surely not been said about the role of the church in interpreting Scripture, but two points can be stated in conclusion. (1) In doctrinal interventions by the magisterium, one must distinguish between the use of biblical texts to illustrate the doctrine taught and an authentic declaration on a biblical passage. The former practice does not intend to give an interpretation of the passages cited or referred to. But other magisterial statements do refer to the original sense of specific biblical passages. Cases of the latter would be Trent's chapter on the words of eucharistic institution (DS 1637) and on the grounding in Jas 5:14 of the sacrament of the anointing of the sick (DS 1695, 1716). These instances do illustrate the magisterium's judicial role in settling disputes over interpretations of Scripture. However, such declarations do not seem to identify formally the content of later dogma with the literal sense of the original passage. What is at stake is instead the homogeneity of the original meaning and what has developed in the church. The two senses are linked by a trajectory of organic and legitimate development, as seems clear in Vatican I's declarations on the Petrine texts and papal primacy (DS 3053–55).

Vatican II grounds the foregoing explanation, when it underscores the distance between the biblical authors, with their ancient Middle Eastern culture and modes of thought, and what came afterward as the fruit of doctrinal development. Retrieving the literal sense of texts demands the application of attentive study and critical methods (*DV* 12.2). This seems to rule out a retrojection of the meaning of later dogma into the communicative intent of the biblical authors.

(2) *DV* 12.3 insists on a reading "in the Spirit," which links particular biblical texts with the whole scope of revelation and with their interpretive actualization in ecclesial tradition. The history down to Trent indicates that the primary expression of this interpretive tradition is the objective complex of creed, dogma, and liturgy. For example, the major cycles of liturgical observance, focused on Christmas and Easter, give pointed expression to what faith takes as central in the Bible. The ascending movement of eucharistic prayer shows faith coming to authentic expression by giving all honor and glory to the Father, through the Son, in the Spirit. The church's *sensus Scripturae* has an identifiable content, and this should not be obscured by construing it solely in terms of the formal authority to intervene with an authentic judgment.

Bibl: J. BEUMER, *Die katholische Inspirationslehre zwischen Vaticanum I und II* (Stuttgart, 1965); H. KÜMMERINGER, "Es ist Sache der Kirche, judicare de vero sensu et interpretatione scripturarum sanctarum: Zum Verständnis dieses Satzes auf dem Tridentinum und Vaticanum I," *TQ* 149 (1969): 282–96; H. J. POTTMEYER, "Die historisch-kritische Methode und die Erklärung zur Schriftauslegung in der dogmatischen Konstitution *Dei Filius* des 1. Vaticanums," *AHC* 2 (1970): 87–111; M. MIDALI, *Rivelazione, chiesa, scrittura e tradizione alla IV sessione del concilio di Trento* (Rome, 1973); R. E. BROWN, *Biblical Exegesis and Church Doctrine* (New York/Mahwah, 1985); W. BRANDMÜLLER, "Die Lehre der Konzilien über die rechte Schriftinterpretation bis zum 1. Vaticanum," *AHC* 19 (1987): 13–61; P. GRELOT, *Evangiles et Histoire* (Paris, 1986), 22–70; R. E. BROWN and S. SCHNEIDERS, "Hermeneutics," and R. E. BROWN and T. A. COLLINS, "Church Pronouncements," in R. E. BROWN et al., eds., *The New Jerome Biblical Commentary* (Englewood Cliffs, N.J., 1990), 1163–74.

Jared WICKS

VII. EVANGELICAL CHURCHES

Evangelicalism as a religious movement has its genesis in both the Protestant Reformation of the sixteenth century and the evangelical awakenings of the seventeenth to nineteenth centuries. It therefore embraces the various church bodies that emerged out of these momentous spiritual upheavals.

The churches that came directly out of the Protestant Reformation constitute four distinctive strands: Lutheran, Reformed, Anglican, and Anabaptist. The Lutheran Reformation produced these important confessions of faith: the Augsburg Confession, the Smalcald Articles, Luther's Small Catechism, and the Formula of Concord. From the Reformed movement we have the Geneva Catechism, the Heidelberg Catechism, the First and Second Helvetic Confessions, the Belgic Confession, the Scots Confession, the Canons of Dort, and the Westminster Confession. The Anglican church adopted the Thirty-Nine Articles, which reflect to some degree the theology of the Calvinist Reformation.

Evangelical Protestantism can be fully understood only against the background of the movements of spiritual purification after the Reformation: Pietism, Puritanism, and the Evangelicalism associated with Wesley and Whitefield. These movements sought to complete the Reformation by calling for a reform in life as well as in doctrine. An iconoclastic bent was evident among the Puritans, who pressed for simplicity in worship. It was out of this spirit of revival that Protestantism experienced a remarkable upsurge of interest and activity in foreign missions.

While their purpose was to reform the churches from within, the movements of renewal unwittingly contributed to the rise of new denominations. Church bodies that trace their origins to separatistic Puritanism include Baptists, Congregationalists, and Plymouth Brethren. Pietism gave birth to the Moravian church, the Church of the Brethren, the Evangelical United Brethren (now part of the Methodist church), the Churches of God of North America, the Evangelical Covenant Church, and the Evangelical Free Church (these latter two bodies originating in Sweden). Out of the Wesley-Whitefield revivals in eighteenth-century Britain came the Methodist churches and later the Holiness movement, which urged the return to Wesleyan roots. Churches that show the impact of Holiness theology include the Christian and Missionary Alliance, the Salvation Army, the Church of the Nazarene, the Free Methodist church, the Wesleyan church, the Pilgrim Holiness church, the United Missionary church, the Church of God

(Anderson, Indiana), and the Evangelical Congregational church. Churches that stem from the Restoration movement in the nineteenth century, which upheld the NT model of the church, include the Disciples of Christ and the Churches of Christ.

The most significant movement of spiritual renewal in recent years is Pentecostalism, which has its genesis in revivals in the later nineteenth and earth twentieth centuries. Originating mainly within the Holiness family of churches, Pentecostalism is distinguished by its emphasis on the charismatic gifts—especially prophecy, healing, and speaking in tongues. It also shares with most evangelical bodies a sense of the urgency of evangelism.

Churches that belong to this latest stream of religious consciousness include the Assemblies of God, the Church of God (Cleveland, Tennessee), the Church of God in Christ, the Open Bible Standard church, and the International Church of the Foursquare Gospel, all based in the United States; the Pentecostal Assemblies and the Evangelical churches of Pentecost in Canada; the Apostolic church and the Elim church in Britain; the Fellowship of Christian Assemblies and the Mülheim Association of Christian Fellowships in Germany; the Christian Pentecostal church in Yugoslavia; the Apostolic church in Nigeria; the Apostolic Faith Mission and Full Gospel Church of God in South Africa; the Evangelical Pentecostal church, the Congregation of Christ, and the Assemblies of God in Brazil; the Methodist Pentecostal church in Chile; and the Pentecostal church, the Full Gospel Bethel church, and the Church of Jesus Christ in Indonesia. Because of their extraordinary expansion in Third World countries, Pentecostals now constitute the largest single family of churches within Protestantism.

With so many different churches involved, evangelical theology shows remarkable diversity, but there are nevertheless points of commonality that reflect the impact of the mainstream Protestant Reformation. Themes that are given special prominence in evangelical theology are the sovereignty of God, the authority and primacy of Holy Scripture, the radical pervasiveness of sin, the substitutionary atonement, salvation by grace (*sola gratia*), justification by faith (*sola fide*), the experience of conversion, the call to personal holiness, the priesthood of all believers, the urgency of mission, and the approaching end of the world.

Besides the classical marks of the church—oneness, holiness, catholicity, and apostolicity—evangelicals in the Reformation tradition cherish these two practical marks of the church: the preaching of the Word and the right administration of the sacraments. Under the impact of Pietism and Puritanism, many evangelicals also uphold church discipline, involvement in mission, and the fellowship of love (the *koinonia*) as authentic signs of the church in its fullness.

Theologians who have made a significant contribution to evangelical life and thought include Martin Luther, John Calvin, Ulrich Zwingli, Philip Melanchthon, Martin Chemnitz, John Wesley, Jonathan Edwards, Abraham Kuyper, Charles Hodge, and in the twentieth century P. T. Forsyth, Karl Barth, Emil Brunner, Anders Nygren, G. C. Berkouwer, Dietrich Bonhoeffer, and C. S. Lewis. Indubitably the three most influential thinkers have been Calvin, Luther, and Wesley. Calvin's *Institutes of the Christian Religion* has had a wide distribution not only in Reformed and Presbyterian circles but also among Congregationalists, low church Anglicans, Baptists, Plymouth Brethren, Evangelical Free churches, and independent Bible churches. Wesley's theological emphases have been crucial not only to Methodism but also to the Holiness and Pentecostal branches of Christendom.

On occasion, evangelical theologians have drawn upon the theological heritage of the Roman Catholic church, though with discrimination. Among Catholic thinkers who have been held in high esteem by evangelicals are Athanasius, Irenaeus, Augustine, Bernard of Clairvaux, and Pascal. Thomas Aquinas, too, has been commended for his emphasis on the priority of grace and his firm commitment to scriptural authority, though his natural theology has been criticized by evangelicals of a neo-orthodox bent. The Rhineland mystics, including John Tauler and the anonymous author of the *Theologica Germanica*, have been shown to have had a palpable influence on the thought and spirituality of Martin Luther.

Modern Protestantism is presently divided into two camps—the liberal and the evangelical. Protestant liberalism has its source in the Enlightenment of the eighteenth century, when higher criticism began to undercut biblical authority. Theological luminaries in the liberal tradition include Friedrich Schleiermacher, Albrecht Ritschl, Wilhelm Herrmann, Adolf von Harnack, Ernst Troeltsch, Horace Bushnell, Paul Tillich, Rudolf Bultmann, Henry Nelson Wieman, Jürgen Moltmann, and Wolfhart Pannenberg. Reinhold Niebuhr and his brother H. Richard Niebuhr (both Americans) were forceful critics of liberal theology within this tradition, but their thought also had a noticeable biblical thrust, which accounts for the fact that they have come to be appreciated by many evangelicals.

Among the distinctive emphases in liberal theology are the priority of religious experience over biblical revelation; a naturalistic or idealistic worldview over supernaturalism; a keen sense of the historical relativity of doctrine; a situational or contextual ethic over a revealed ethic; a belief in progress; and the reconception of revelation as rational insight or an intimation of transcendence rather than a definitive divine disclosure of meaning in the particular history recorded in the Bible.

The divisions in Protestantism today are not so much between denominations as between theological positions that cross denominational lines. The polarity between liberal or modernist theology on the one hand and evangelical theology on the other is deepening rather than dissipating. As the conflict intensifies, evangelicals are increasingly seeking contact with Roman Catholic and Eastern Orthodox charismatics and conservatives in order to establish a common front against secularism and modernism.

Much of the present-day strength of the evangelical movement lies in evangelistic parachurch organizations that make a special effort to work with young people on high school or university campuses. Among these are InterVarsity Christian Fellowship, Young Life, the Navigators, Youth for Christ, Scripture Union, and Campus Crusade for Christ.

Within the evangelical movement, some have advocated a catholic evangelicalism in which commitment to the gospel is united with a respect for church tradition and authority. This ecumenical thrust is discernible in a number of theologians in the modern era: Wilhelm Löhe, Philip Schaff, John Nevin, P. T. Forsyth, Nathan Söderblom, Gustaf Aulén, Friedrich Heiler, Thomas F. Torrance, and Karl Barth. Contempo-

rary theologians in America who espouse a catholic evangelical stance include Jaroslav Pelikan, Robert Webber, Richard Neuhaus, Carl Braaten, Richard Lovelace, and Donald Bloesch. Some of these scholars see the need for a restoration of religious community life on an evangelical foundation as well as for new statements on the sacraments, the church, the saints, and the role of Mary as the mother of all Christians.

Bibl.: P. SCHAFF, ed., *The Creeds of Christendom*, vol. 3: *Evangelical Protestant Creeds* (4th ed.; New York, 1919); J. PELIKAN, *The Christian Tradition*, vol. 4: *Reformation of Church and Dogma (1300–1700)* (Chicago, 1984); A. C. PIEPKORN, *Profiles in Belief: The Religious Bodies of the United States and Canada*, vol. 3: *Holiness and Pentecostal;* vol. 4: *Evangelical, Fundamentalist, and Other Christian Bodies* (San Francisco, 1979); W. J. HOLLENWEGER, *Enthusiastisches Christentum: Die Pfingstbewegung in Geschichte und Gegenwart* (Zurich, 1969); F. S. MEAD, *Handbook of Denominations in the United States* (6th ed.; Nashville, 1975); D. G. BLOESCH, *The Future of Evangelical Christianity: A Call for Unity Amid Diversity* (New York, 1983); M. ELLINGSEN, *The Evangelical Movement* (Minneapolis, 1988); B. RAMM, *The Evangelical Heritage* (Waco, Tex., 1973).

Donald G. BLOESCH

VIII. ORIENTAL CHURCHES

1. Historical Overview

The "oriental churches" are so called because they originate in the Orient (more precisely in the Eastern part of the Roman Empire) from the time of the schisms resulting from the contested dogmatic formulas of the Council of Ephesus in 431 and the Council of Chalcedon in 451 (see *UR* 13). Thus, we are dealing with ecclesial communities that became separated because they accepted neither the Cyrillian direction of Ephesus nor the new christological formula of Chalcedon. Toward the end of the fifth century, the Syrian Oriental church of Persia rejected Cyril's doctrine of the *mia physis tou theou logou sesarkomeni* (one incarnate nature of the Word of God), giving rise to the so-called Nestorian Christians, who carried on great missionary activity, above all in India. The Chalcedonian formula of "the one person or hypostasis of Jesus Christ in two natures" was rejected by Alexandria (and by its dependent Ethiopian church), by half of the patriarchate of Antioch, and by the Armenian church. These are the "non-Chalcedonian" churches, incorrectly known as "monophysite," because they adhere to the wording of Cyril of Alexandria's formula, which after the linguistic refinement that took place at Chalcedon (i.e., the distinction between "nature" and "person") emerged as being highly ambiguous. However, it seems unfair to ascribe this partial lack of success to the conciliar formula. There were other factors, not always theological, which led to schisms, opposition, and rejections. A careful reexamination of the so-called non-Chalcedonian Christology does not, in fact, succeed in determining substantial divergences of content from the formula of 451. The Christology of "Syrian monophysitism," e.g., rather than being theologically improper, may be considered only as "extraneous to Chalcedon," "pre-Chalcedonian," and "anti-Nestorian."

2. Dialogue

Notwithstanding their undeniable theological, liturgical, and juridical differences, together with their different experiences, these churches accept the dogmas of the Trinity and the incarnation, the mystery of the church, the liturgical and sacramental life, and monasticism. For this reason, even in the confrontations between these oriental churches, an atmosphere of dialogue has prevailed since Vatican II. A number of representatives of these communities were present at the council. Meetings between the pope and some of the oriental patriarchs have taken place either in Rome or abroad during the journeys of Paul VI and John Paul II. We may cite a number of concrete examples of the "bilateral" dialogue between the Catholic church and some of these Oriental churches. In 1973, Paul VI and Shenuda III, Coptic patriarch of Alexandria, met in Rome and issued a joint declaration, the christological part of which is absolutely correct but avoids the Chalcedonian wording "one person in two natures." Among other things, this affirms:

> In keeping with our apostolic traditions transmitted to our churches and conserved therein, and in conformity with the first three ecumenical councils, we confess a common faith in the One and Triune God and in the divinity of the Only Begotten Son of God, the Second Person of the Most Holy Trinity, the Word of God, the splendor of His glory and the revealed image of His substance, who for us became incarnate, taking to Himself a real body with a rational soul, and who shares our humanity with us, but who is without sin. We confess that Our Lord and God and Savior and King, Jesus Christ, is perfect God with regard to His divinity, and perfect man with regard to His Humanity. (EV 4:2500)

The dialogue between the Catholic church and the Coptic church continued through a joint commission, at the first plenary session of which (Cairo, 26–30 March 1974) an agreed statement on Christology was issued. In this statement precise definition was given of the respective christological formulas. In this way one sees the maintenance, even after Chalcedon, of Cyril of Alexandria's formula of the "one incarnate nature of the Word of God": "When the Orthodox [in this case, the Copts] profess that the divinity and the humanity of Our Lord are united in one nature, they take the word 'nature' not as a pure and simple nature, but rather as a composite nature in which the divinity and humanity are united inseparably and without confusion" (EO 1:2225). The same joint commission recommended further study of the christological councils, the sacraments in relation to the church and the economy of salvation, the recognition of saints, and other practical questions regarding cooperation between the two churches (EO 1:2230–42). The report of the second plenary session (Cairo, 27–31 October 1975), after having reaffirmed the actual tensions concerning effective unity of faith, in sacramental life and in harmonious mutual relations, took up a number of ecclesiological differences between the Coptic church (the local church as a constitutive reality of the universality of the church; the ecumenical council as the supreme instance of the universal church) and the Catholic church (the local church, the community of the faithful united around the bishop; the particular church, a union of a series of local churches; the universal church, constituted by the local churches and in the local churches; universal ministry of unity, at the service of the communion between the local churches, exercised by the bishop of Rome). The report lists a collection of themes to be given further reflection, among which are the structure of the church's unity before 451, the specific role of Peter and his successors, the Marian dogmas, and the sacraments (*EO* 1:2243–60). The meetings of this joint commission continue with a certain regularity (the most recent, the sixth, was scheduled for December 1989). In 1984 there was a common declaration between Pope John Paul II and the patriarch of Antioch, Mar Zakka I Iwas. These official exchanges are also accompanied by local talks and by unofficial meetings between theologians. In the United States, for example, there have been some joint declarations by the Oriental Orthodox-Roman Catholic Council on the aims, method, and themes of interecclesial dialogue (1982: *EO* 2:3080–97), and on the Eucharist (1983: *EO* 2:3098–99). From 18 to 25 September 1988 the fifth unofficial colloquium between Oriental and Catholic theologians took place in Vienna. Among other things, this gathering reaffirmed the possibility of a certain pluralism in christological formulas; the acceptance of a common platform of faith established by the first three ecumenical councils, and further study on the reception of the other councils and papal primacy.

Bibl.: W. DE VRIES, *Der christliche Osten in Geschichte und Gegenwart* (Würzburg, 1951); T. UQBIT, *Current Christological Positions of Ethiopian Orthodox Theologians* (Rome, 1973); R. KOTTJE, ed., *Storia ecumenica della chiesa*, 2 vols. (Brescia, 1980, 1981); P. GREGORIOS, W. H. LAZARETH, and N. A. NISSIOTIS, *Does Chalcedon Divide or Unite? Towards Convergence in Orthodox Christology* (Geneva, 1981).

Angelo AMATO

IX. ORTHODOX CHURCHES

1. Historical Overview

One may fix 1054 as the date of the first great schism between the churches of the East and West, officially marking the division of the *Orthodox* church (literally, "the church which maintains the correct faith") and the *Roman Catholic* church (literally, "the universal church," which has the pope, the bishop of Rome, as its supreme leader). *Orthodoxy*

embraces those oriental churches that recognize the first seven ecumenical councils (from Nicea I to Nicea II), which also have in common the Byzantine Rite and their own canon law, and which are not in communion with Rome. While maintaining their intrinsic independence, the Orthodox churches consider the patriarch of Constantinople as their spiritual focus and their leader; it is he who supervises preparations for the great panorthodox synod soon to be celebrated. The Orthodox churches are divided into nine *patriarchates* which have emerged through the centuries—from the most ancient to the most recent, such as that of Romania, erected as recently as 1925—and into more *autocephalous* ("autonomous") churches. Until 1989 the Orthodox church's largest presence in the free world was in Greece, with more than eight million members. With the liberalization and opening up of the Soviet Union under Gorbachev, and with the collapse of Communist regimes in the Soviet satellite states at the end of 1989, the other Orthodox churches—above all the Moscow patriarchate, erected in 1589—appeared to have been restored to freedom of worship, together with their faithful (numbering more than 120 million people).

Beginning from the time of the schism of 1054—which in the West came to be known as "the Eastern schism" but in the East as "the schism of the Western church"—the history of relations between Rome and Constantinople has been marked by a number of traumatic events, often not recognized as such in the West. In addition to the schism, the Orthodox have experienced several painful episodes, including the crusades (with the conquests of Jerusalem in 1099 and Constantinople in 1204), the attempts at union at the Councils of Lyons (1274) and Florence (1439), the fall of Constantinople to the Turks (1453) and the subsequent distress of the period under Turkish rule. This latter episode, which ended with the liberation of Athens in 1821 and of Salonika in 1912, made it impossible in practice for Orthodoxy, above all in Greece, to enjoy freedom of expression in theological and cultural matters. The atmosphere of suspicion and defensiveness in relations with the Catholic church, and from the end of the sixteenth century with Protestantism as well, was thus strengthened.

To all this, one must add the differences between East and West that had already emerged within the first millennium: diversity of liturgical rites; differences in hierarchical structure, with the formation of patriarchates; the concept of the church and interecclesial communion. After the schism other differences were affirmed: the contrast between scholastic theology and that of the tradition of Palamas; the almost absolute emphasis on ancient patristic and conciliar tradition (the "paradosis"); the rejection of papal infallibility and of papal primacy of universal jurisdiction; opposition to the more recent Marian dogmas (the Immaculate Conception and the assumption); the meaning given to the epiclesis in the liturgy of the Eucharist; perplexity with regard to the formula of sacramental absolution used in the West. Another reason for contrast and misunderstanding between the Orthodox church and the Catholic church is that those churches which for centuries had been in union with Rome were condemned to legal extinction by the Communist regimes of Eastern Europe (for example, the Ukranian church in 1946 and that of Romania in 1948) and were forcibly absorbed by the Orthodox churches. With the recent collapse of these regimes, the Catholics are reasserting their rights to their sacred buildings and confiscated goods, but, above all, to the freedom of worship and membership of the Catholic church.

Despite these differences and disagreements, the two churches share a vast amount in common, founded on the essential appeal to Scripture and the fathers, on the acceptance of the fundamental dogmas of the faith (the Trinity and the incarnation), on the liturgical and spiritual life, the acknowledgment of the seven sacraments, the experience of monasticism, devotion to Our Lady, the life of the apostolate, the missions, and holiness. The fact that these basic elements are viewed and interpreted in their proper and original way in the East and in the West, by means of a discipline, a juridical tradition and a theology, each of which is legitimately different one from another (see *UR* 15–17), must be seen as a ground for complementarity and harmony, and not of opposition and contrast.

2. The Dialogue of Charity

The age-old official silence between the Catholic and Orthodox churches, which was also caused by the dictates of political survival (differences with the Turkish authorities, the closure of the theological school of Chalkis, the closing down of some of the patriarchate's publications, the reduction of the Orthodox community of Istanbul to its lowest-ever number), was broken by Patriarch Athenagoras of Constantinople in October 1958. In two printed communiqués (7 and 10 October) he showed his profound sadness at the illness of Pope Pius XII and shared "in the great sorrow of the venerable Church of Rome" on the death of the pope. The same patriarch rejoiced at the election of John XXIII and responded positively to the pope's appeal for unity. For his part, on 5 June 1960, John XXIII instituted the Secretariate for Christian Unity (renamed "the Pontifical Council for the Promotion of the Unity of Christians" in 1989). Thus began the dialogue of charity, forged by concrete gestures of respect, esteem, and openness. We may list some of these deeds: the meeting in Jerusalem between Athenagoras and Paul VI (5–6 January 1964); the conciliar decree *Unitatis Redintegratio* on ecumenism (21 November 1964); the lifting of excommunications, decreed in 1054, by Rome and Constantinople (7 December 1965); the courageous visit of Paul VI to Constantinople (25–26 July 1967) and the consigning of the bull *Anno ineunte* (25 July 1967) to the patriarch, in which there was developed an original "theology of the sister churches," with the promise of fraternal dialogue between theologians; Patriarch Athenagoras's visit to Rome (26–28 October 1967); the publication in 1971 of the *Libro della carità* (=*Tomos agapis*) with testimonies to this network of cordial relations between Rome and Constantinople (revised in 1987 and translated into English as *Towards the Healing of Schism*); the extraordinary gesture of reconciliation and forgiveness by Paul VI, who, in the ceremony to commemorate the tenth anniversary of the lifting of the excommunications (1975), went down on his knees and kissed the feet of Metropolitan Melitus, the representative of Patriarch Dimitrios I of Constantinople, who had succeeded Athenagoras in 1972; the sending of delegations, from 1978 on, for the patronal feasts of the two churches, i.e., 29 June (the feast of the apostles Peter and Paul) and 30 November (the feast of the apostle Andrew); the visit of Pope John Paul II to Constantinople (30 November 1979) and his great concern for the problem of the unity of the church; the anniversary celebrations of a number of councils (Constantinople I, 381; Ephesus, 431; Nicea II, 787) and of the eleventh centenary of the death of St. Methodius (6 April 1985), which led to many contacts between Catholics and Orthodox in academic conventions and gatherings for prayer; the participation of Orthodox observers at the Extraordinary Synod of Bishops on the twentieth anniversary of the closure of Vatican II (1985); the visit of Patriarch Dimitrios I to Rome (3 to 7 December 1987); the celebration of the millennium of the conversion and baptism of Russia (6 to 16 June 1988), with the participation of a Catholic delegation invited by Patriarch Pimen of Moscow.

3. The Dialogue of Truth

The dialogue of charity, which continues to bear fruit with all the Orthodox churches, is also accompanied by common theological research, which seeks to understand and outline the problems that time and prejudice had aggravated beyond measure. At Fanar, on 30 November 1979, Dimitrios I and Pope John Paul II signed a joint declaration by which they signaled the beginning of the dialogue of truth between the two sister churches. A joint Catholic-Orthodox commission was also established and given the task of bringing this dialogue into being. This dialogue, which is still in progress, represents the most solid guarantee of a real opening toward unity between the churches. The first stage of the foundations were laid at Patmos and Rodi from 29 May to 4 June 1980. The method of procedure was established: a number of themes for study were selected and subcommissions were formed to prepare the terms of study for the plenary meetings. At the second plenary meeting at Munich, from 30 June to 6 July 1982, the joint commission gave unanimous approval to the text on "The Mystery of the Church and the Eucharist in the Light of the Mystery of the Holy Trinity." The document, which could not be traced back to one particular school of theology, presented a true and

proper language of unity, above all with the emphasis on eucharistic ecclesiology. The third plenary meeting was held on Crete (30 May to 8 June 1984), and its theme was "faith and communion in the sacraments: the sacraments of initiation and their relation to the unity of the church. It did not give its approval to any joint text. From 29 May to 7 June 1986 the fourth meeting, held at Bari, considered the following theme: "The sacrament of order in the sacramental structure of the church. In particular, the importance of the apostolic succession for the sanctification and unity of the People of God." Yet again there was no approval given to a final text; moreover, a number of representatives withdrew. However, one year later (16 June 1987), and again at Bari, unanimous approval was given to the joint international commission's second document, "Faith, sacraments and the unity of the church." In the final part of this document, in the section dealing with the sacraments of initiation, the theological and liturgical unity of baptism, confirmation, and the Eucharist was affirmed. The different forms of celebration of these sacraments was also revealed: baptism by immersion in the East, by infusion in the West; the simultaneous conferring of the three sacraments in the East (even in the case of babies), (first) communion given to children before confirmation in the West. The joint commission held its fifth plenary meeting at Valamo in Finland (19 to 27 June 1988), with its theme "the sacrament of order in the sacramental structure of the church." The final document was given unanimous approval, and having underlined the relation between Christ and the Holy Spirit, the commission took up the question of the function of the priesthood in the economy of salvation, expounding upon the ministry of the bishop, the priest, and the deacon, and finally giving emphasis to the apostolic succession as the continuous presence in history of the same and unique ministry of Christ and the apostles. The document also pointed out that, in the course of the centuries, the church in the East and the West had known different forms of the realization of communion between bishops, giving rise to special orders of preeminence between the churches, wherefrom arose the five principal sees of Rome, Constantinople, Alexandria, Antioch, and Jerusalem. The document concluded by underlining the function of ecumenical councils as the expression of the communion between the local churches, within which it urged consideration of the problem of the primacy of the bishop of Rome, "which constitutes a serious difference between us and which will be discussed further" (n. 55). The theme of the sixth meeting, held in Munich in 1990, was "the ecclesiological and canonical consequences of the sacramental structure of the church: Councils and authority in the church."

4. The Problems of Dialogue

The speed with which this process of reconciliation has taken place could not but have provoked lack of understanding and, at times, rejection, above all in communities that had grown accustomed to a certain degree of immobility. It must be remembered that while the Catholic church has witnessed substantial optimism with regard to the movement forward undertaken by Vatican II, the other Christian churches—if one excepts the patriarchate of Constantinople—have not shared the same pace. Therefore, one must recognize that in the last thirty years the two sister churches have recovered centuries of spiritual estrangement. It is a given fact that today they meet, understand, and speak to one another with sincerity and in truth. Yet for all these signs of brotherly freedom, theological dialogue is not easy. On the contrary, it presents very real difficulties and demands. There have already been interruptions, a lessening of momentum and great tensions. Despite the importance and novelty of the process—there were centuries during which there were no theological texts officially approved by both churches—the impact in the ecclesiastical world has not been very visible. There was no little disappointment, therefore, at the unsuccessful attempt to issue a final document in the plenary sessions at Crete and Bari in 1984 and 1986 respectively.

Among the difficulties experienced in the course of theological discussions, e.g., one may refer to those which arose on Crete and which have fortunately been overcome. If one acknowledges that the two churches, Orthodox and Catholic, while professing the same faith, would be able to have different baptismal symbols, then it is also agreed that the Oriental church has adopted the Nicene-Constantinople creed in its ritual of baptism, while the West has taken the ancient "apostolic" text. On the part of the Orthodox, however, there remained a question that was not given explicit formulation: the Latin church, in adding the "Filioque" clause to the Nicene-Constantinople creed (at the beginning of the eleventh century), acted unilaterally. Would it not now be opportune to remove this adjunct to the creed? Moreover, while in the East the three sacraments of Christian initiation are united in the sequence of baptism-confirmation-Eucharist, in the West these are conferred separately: for pastoral reasons, baptism is followed by (first) communion and then confirmation. Yet one may at once reply that, notwithstanding Orthodox objections to the custom of giving communion to the baptized before confirmation, it can be shown historically that the Catholic liturgical practice is very ancient (being traced back directly to the formation of the great sacramentaries) and wholly justifiable. Furthermore, what was also "unspoken" on the part of the Orthodox was that Greek custom permitted every priest (and not just bishops) to administer confirmation (the sacred "myron") immediately after baptism. On the part of the Catholics, however, the conciliar Decree on the Oriental Catholics (1964) had already given official recognition to the legitimacy of such power in the case of priests (OE 13–14). These and other difficulties have now been amicably resolved, with recognition given to the presence of different liturgical and pastoral usages and customs in the East and the West, and by accepting the fact that the same faith, founded on Scripture and the fathers, can have different formulations and practices.

The same spirit of understanding and acceptance has been brought to bear on the other points of theological contention between the two churches; e.g., the problem of Eastern Rite Catholics in communion with Rome, the models of the unity of the church in terms of future full communion, and the interpretation of the pope's primacy and infallibility. In the case of the relations between the Orthodox and Eastern Rite Catholics in the Ukraine, we may cite the example of the meeting held in Moscow from 12 to 17 January 1990 between the representatives of the Moscow patriarchate, the see which forcibly absorbed the Ukrainian Catholics in 1946, and a delegation from the Holy

See led by Cardinal Willebrands, president emeritus of the Pontifical Council for the Promotion of the Unity of Christians, and by Mgr. Edward Cassidy, president of the same council. The meeting agreed on the following recommendations as a first step toward regulating the whole issue: normalization must guarantee the Catholics of the Eastern Rite the right to religious activity recognized by the constitution and legislation of the Soviet Union and consequently must provide them with property for the purposes of religious worship.

The problems that beset the dialogue of truth cannot be resolved except in terms of the dialogue of charity, with both churches acting with complete freedom, as in the case of the meeting in Jerusalem between those two great prophets of ecumenism, Athenagoras and Paul VI. Let us recall the Byzantine icon painted by a monk of Mount Athos and given by Athenagoras to Paul VI to commemorate this historic meeting which took place on 5 January 1964. It depicts the fraternal embrace between St. Peter and St. Andrew. Under the gaze of Christ Pantocrator, who extends his arms of blessing in order to draw all to himself (Jn 12:32), there is the inscription: "The holy brother apostles." To the left of Peter there is the symbol of the upturned cross, upon which Peter "the leader" was martyred. To the right is the St. Andrew cross, with the inscription "Andrew the first to be called" (*protoklitos*; see Jn 1:31). The theological intention of the icon is obvious: the sister churches embrace one another in their bishops. The gaze of the two apostles toward the faithful is an invitation to do likewise.

Bibl.: Y. CONGAR, *Diversity and Communion* (1955; Mystic, Conn., 1985); W. DE VRIES, *Orthodoxie und Katholizismus* (Freiburg, 1965); A. AMATO, "Der Ökumenische Dialog zwischen Katholiken und Orthodoxen: Situation und entstandene Probleme," *Forum Katholische Theologie* 2 (1986): 184–200; J.-E. DESSEAUX, *Lessico ecumenico* (Brescia, 1986); E. J. STORMON, ed., *Towards the Healing of Schism: The Sees of Rome and Constantinople. Public Statements and Correspondance Between the Holy See and the Ecumenical Patriarchate, 1958–1984* (Mahwah, 1987). Particularly useful are the public bulletins of the Information Service of the Council for the Promotion of Christian Unity, as well as the documents published by *Irénikon*.

Angelo AMATO

COMMUNICATION

1. Science in Relation to Fundamental Theology

To speak of communication means immediately to focus one's attention on humanity, in that it is universally recognized that communication is a reality intrinsic to, and determinative of, human nature. Human beings can no more do without communicating than they can do without relating. For the realization of their own humanity, in order to grow in every way, human beings need in some sense to objectify their thoughts and decisions, to share and to verify in relation to others the validity of their own intuitions. Were it not possible to communicate, it would not be possible for progress itself to take place, and people would remain trapped in themselves and in their own inertia. It is certainly possible to define communication as a type of instinct connected to that of socialization, an instinct that brings human beings to discover life in community as an existential dimension. But at the same time we must say that communication involves a psychological demand that brings them to reveal their feelings in such a way as to provoke a response to the expression of their profound need to be loved, and that leads them to seek help from their fellows when they are aware of being in difficulty. Moreover, it is thanks to communication that it is possible to acquire the experience of things secondhand, and for that reason to relate the past to the shaping of the future.

Communication has always been present in history, therefore, from the very moment that human beings appeared—present, that is, as the very condition that makes it possible for humankind to realize its own history and thus to develop and improve its lot. Yet until about 1500 C.E., despite the variety of means and forms of communication, this was extremely limited in terms of its possibilities because of the slowness of spreading news. A decisive change came with the invention of printing, which made the transmission of messages far more precise and much quicker and which greatly added to the possibility of diffusing material. But above all, in recent years, the pace of development in the means of communication has become so overwhelming, and distances have contracted so much, that humankind is faced with a problem. Today's world is saturated by the knowledge of communication, and the ever-increasing developments in the field of communications are no longer simply a function of technological and scientific progress. They are dictated instead by the ever-increasing demands of an evolution that has its origins in the social, cultural, psychological, and spiritual spheres, in that it embraces not only the specific dimensions of word or image but the whole spectrum of human behavior and the relational realities by which it is shaped.

It is for precisely this reason that THEOLOGY cannot ignore the phenomenon of communication. In fact, theology, in its classic definition, means "the study of God"—not of God considered in himself and apart from the destiny of the world and humankind, but in strict relation to living beings and their existence in the world. Theology thus is concerned with people as social beings who are journeying toward levels of progress and development that are images that reveal the coming of the kingdom, wherein faith and love are not vague dimensions but concrete, visible realities. In this sense theology cannot but be concerned with disciplines such as sociology, the political and economic sciences, and HISTORY itself. Thus, inasmuch as it is interested in men and women as spiritual beings endowed with their own interior life, which grows and finds fulfillment through prayer and living the gospel, theological research is supported by sciences such as psychology, anthropology, and philosophy.

Theology is a science that focuses on humankind and for that reason it has to place itself at the level of human beings, structuring itself to them, and must reflect on the problems that most disturb them, offering them valid suggestions and alternatives, and above all developing its way of thinking in categories that modern men and women are familiar with. If the opposite happens, then the theological endeavor would be empty. But theology is not merely of interest in an intellectual sense, giving its students exercise in their powers of reflection; it is at the same time in tension with practice and intimately linked to the whole scheme of salvation, whereby it points to the urgency of spreading the gospel. In this sense theology presumes and implies an adequate treatment of communication and thereby makes reference to

"the science of communication." Moreover, this emerged in a clearer and more definite fashion after the great period of reflection on the problems of modern humanity which developed in the context of the Second Vatican Council.

Nowadays, theologians cannot ignore the connection with just such a science, since they are all the more aware of the fact that within Christianity, religion of the word of God, there is a basic structure of communication. If, in fact, we define communication along the general lines of the process by means of which information is sent from a source with a certain (more or less conscious) intention to a receiver who accepts it, we will have reached a sufficiently precise initial point of contact between the two disciplines. In fact, both in the science of communication and in theology we may speak of senders (God, the apostles, the faithful, etc.) who produce codified messages, by means of which they transmit information that seeks to convince, to change something in the person who receives it. In both disciplines also there are receivers who, once they have performed the operation of decodifying and understanding the messages, give their own *feedback*. In both disciplines an attitude is formed that defines and qualifies the relation between sender and receiver in the creation of links, even at a minimal level. Moreover, it is an undeniable fact that theology, insofar as it is a science, commits itself to a process of communication in transmitting the possibility of the experience of God to other human beings in a way that opens them to the dimension of community, in ordering the contents of faith such that the message of salvation can be made known, and in offering the results of its own reflection.

If theology in general cannot ignore this relationship with the science of communication, this is all the more so in the case of FUNDAMENTAL THEOLOGY, in that it identifies itself as a boundary discipline and thus open to those aspects of culture that while not having a specific theological structure, nevertheless exert a marked influence in the theological sphere. Furthermore, its object of study is REVELATION, not only as God's word to humankind and thus knowledge of the communication of the divine will, but also as the human need to transmit, and to share with others, individual being in dialogue with the divine, and the effects that this experience produces in one's life. Revelation is not an end in itself but requires transmission to all men and women in every age; if it seeks to be an effective "communication," it cannot ignore the needs of people as beings who communicate, especially today when such needs are somewhat numerous and complex. And again we find ourselves in a context of communication as soon as we speak of a response of FAITH and TESTIMONY. Faith in fact is the unspoken and personal commitment to the choices made by one's conscience, yet faith also requires nourishment from an external dimension that expresses openness, witness, and sharing with one's neighbor.

When viewed in this way, it is thus important to analyze, for example, both religious language in general and the language of Christianity in particular, in the light of developments in the science of communications. Likewise it is important to examine the various ways in which it is possible to transmit the message of the gospel through the mass media; the intellectual, linguistic, and visual categories employed by the media; the effect that these have on our way of thinking and speaking; and the changes that their widespread use brings to modern culture, both in shaping attitudes and in expression. In fact one must realize that the gospel has its origins in a setting that is very different from ours in terms of culture, and thus one must attempt, as far as it is possible, to give a constant reassessment of its relationship to current reality and the translation of the content of the gospel into those forms of language and artistic expression more consonant to the understanding of humankind in the twentieth century. At the same time one needs to weigh the possibility of using the mass media to spread the Christian message and of new ways of using traditional means of communication in such a way that the message is made fully capable of reception in our own day. Moreover, one must take account of the fact that new techniques of communication are ever giving rise to new symbols and create new ways of employing images and sounds, while at the same time giving life to new forms of political and economic structures, and thereby to new forms of manipulation, power, and the exploitation of human beings. These are methods against which Christians, following the teaching of the gospel, are called to struggle and to resist.

Fundamental theology cannot remain passive when confronted by such ferment, and it must address the problem of how, and in what way, divine truth is to be expressed today, and by which of the means for transmitting revelation of which the church is heir and custodian. Fundamental theology has the specific duty to address the problem of communication and likewise that of the effect on human beings of changes in this field. It must also ask itself to what degree different information systems can have an impact upon human beliefs, or how the analogy of trinitarian communication may be offered to men and women today as the ideal model of communication, to which they can relate all communication. Christ, as the "perfect communicator," is the model for all in the process by which relations with one's neighbor are established.

In this sense we may say that today it is necessary for fundamental theology to open itself to dialogue and collaboration with the science of communication. There have already been many steps taken in this direction, but we are only at the first stages of a path that seems rather long and difficult, even if at the same time it is rich in possibilities and challenges for theological research.

2. Communication as the Relationship of Revelation between God and Humankind

Revelation is communication between God, who reaches out from his own mystery, and humankind, which is saved and transformed in the dialogue of love. It involves a complex and highly structured process of communication, in defining which the Second Vatican Council used the term "economy."

From a technical point of view, communication between God and humankind seems impossible in that it is a question of two completely distinct levels, between which there is an infinite distance. Nevertheless, God has already overcome this difficulty. Not only does he reach out to humankind, but he does so by using all the possible ways offered by human strategies of communication. Already from the time of the OT it clearly emerges how revelation is conveyed through specific structures of communication that issue not from the will of human beings but from divine initiative. In fact, it is God who makes himself present in history in an infinite number of ways and means, and who at the same time offers himself as an object of thought, language, and experience. The Jews incisively expressed this series of communications from God as self-revelation, and they were perfectly aware that it was not a question of communication taking place at impersonal or abstract levels but that of a God who "spoke" with human beings, bringing them to a knowledge of his ways, explaining his ways of acting, making promises, uttering warnings, proclaiming happiness or punishment.

We are talking about a God who used a unique code of communication that was capable of assuming the multiformity necessary to express an infinite number of resonances. We are speaking, in fact, of "the word of God," but in an analogical sense. It differs from all human words. It reveals itself as a word containing many meanings, which directs itself toward the physical senses of human beings, but also toward their internal senses. It is word that also manifests itself under the form of the physical elements: thunder, lightning, wind, and fire. His word reveals, but at the same time obscures. It cannot be completely reduced to simple meanings of verbal communication in that it is the word that is "generative," not only of meanings but also of things and events, and that at the same time is an image, vision, feeling, encounter, and action that burst forth in history and shape its course irrevocably, thereby defining the will of the sender and the disposition that the receiver must adopt in order to be attuned to it. This is what appears in a clear way from the very moment in which words and actions are based on the manifestation of this complex system of signs that determines the dynamic of evolution with regard to God's plan of salvation, and in particular of those signs that mark the basic stages and then cast light upon daily life, giving it a new meaning.

Because this communication can be effectively established, the code by which it takes place must be interpreted correctly and must encourage humankind to develop in understanding this code. This task is not trivial, for the divine message is unique in kind, and the code by which it is expressed does not have parameters comparable to anything else.

Moreover, the true scope of communication is not only that of the transmission of information but of urging human beings to total com-

mitment to God's will, by which, having been drawn into the process of communication, they become capable not only of understanding the designs by which the divine plan operates but also of moving beyond the process of transmission. They become in turn transmitters in the dialogue with God, in a faithful relationship to him that transcends everyday human life: thereby they become effective protagonists of their own history and likewise that of the world.

In the OT, God was the one who communicated in the unfathomable depths of his own mystery, but in the NT he becomes the God who, now incarnate, meets humankind "face to face," thereby overcoming the inequality of the different natures by communicating in such a way as not to leave any room for uncertainty; now, in fact, sender and receiver are in the same spatio-temporal dimension. Thus we can say that Christ is the perfect communicator, in that in him we find both the focus and the realization of the possibility of the ideal communication that inspires every form of human communication—namely, the gift of self to the other, not only in the expression of one's own ideas and feelings but in the total giving of oneself in a mutual exchange and indwelling of love that leaves no room for misunderstanding. In this process, Christ is not only the one who conveys God's message, as in the case of the prophets; he is that very message itself, which is made visible in a concrete way in his taking human flesh and assuming the countenance of humankind. For this reason we can say that we are faced with a unique and irrepeatable communication, in that the elements that go to make up the process of communication, instead of being lost in the diversity of functions and thereby increasing the risk of disturbing the same process—as happens in the case of communication between human beings—converge and are condensed into a single person, wherein the threefold rhythm of the Trinity is perfectly exhibited.

Ontologically speaking, the human word presents itself as a dynamic entity. It is a dynamism that unfolds itself at different levels: first, with regard to the consciousness of the individual being and giving it a definite function and direction; second, with regard to the power of production, since this is a human product, but at the same time it displays a tendency to produce something else in its own turn; and third, with regard to the power of transformation, because it seeks to modify aspects of the reality to which it addresses itself, if not the whole of that reality. Christ, who is the image and word of the invisible God, is himself the very concentration of the power of the image and the word, which he reinforces through his own affirmation of God and humanity, which he engraves upon the human situation, changing its very structures and transforming it from a fallen humanity to one that is saved. Just as the human word is not limited simply to bringing men and women into relation one to another but also to strengthening and deepening those relationships in terms of covenant and union, so too the word of God unites in itself the whole of humanity and restores it to the Father in the bond of sonship.

The means by which this communication takes place are the same as those used by human beings in their everyday communication. Jesus uses an intimate union of words and actions, but employs them in a different way from others, using them with authority, effectiveness, and power—as vehicles of truth. This truth, however, though being conditioned by history, cannot but be referred back time and again to the eternal Truth from which it originates and of which it is the substance. In this way one can say that, through this variety of means, some highly polyvalent signs are transmitted, so that they can become keys of access to the transcendent. These signs create the possibility of translating the divine language into human categories, particularly into the form of words and actions.

Christ, in and by his earthly life, has done nothing other than speak of the Father's love for humanity. He has not, however, presented some philosophical doctrine or some speculation on a particular theme; in him, however, his very message is forever realized in a practical way, the concrete and visible revelation of mercy and compassion toward humankind. This happens not by miracles alone but in the conscious acceptance of suffering and death, in his wish to remain in the midst of humanity even after his ascension through the institution of the Eucharist, in not deserting his disciples but sending them the Holy Spirit, the Comforter, and

above all by founding the church (→ CHURCH II), through which it will be possible to spread his gospel in all the world.

It is a case of words and actions that find their internal cohesion in that same person of Christ, who is himself the Word and the Word who acts; yet at the same time they never lose their specific character, nor do they become confused one with another. Words and actions maintain their proper shape and identity in Christ until the moment of death on the cross, wherein this tension of relationality reaches its summit and arrives at the point of no return— that is, the overcoming of every possibility to the point that all words and actions are concentrated in the supreme sacrifice. The inexhaustible love of Christ-God, which did not have absolute need of suffering or death, becomes the point at which every mode of relating is rendered void, and every relationship taken up into the fullness of giving, into the death of the immortal God.

It is also a question of a process that reaches another peak in the resurrection. Christ, by entering history, asserts his divinity and his identity as Son of the Father and likewise makes it possible for communication between two different levels to take place at the human level; so too, by his resurrection, he ratifies the truth of these assertions and recapitulates this historical experience of the divine in taking the whole of humanity to himself, transposing the possibility of communication from the human level to that of the divine. Christ's becoming a man thereby becomes the vehicle through which one has the full expression and manifestation of his being God, in that his true, glorious destiny is conferred upon bodily nature, and the whole of humanity is drawn together in a process of solidarity. With the "resurrection event," Christ gives definitive ratification to his identity as the code, and at the same time the interpretative key to that code, which allows us to penetrate the divine message, thus excluding any possibility for equivocation: God has spoken with humankind, and to human beings fall the task and duty of reply.

Christ reveals the truth about humankind and places each man and woman, inasmuch as they receive him, face to face with their own reality. Christ says, "I am the truth," but with this assertion he establishes himself as the criterion of truth. But those who are faced with the truth but who seek it within themselves will discover themselves in their own selfishness and misery. The response to this can be either complete rejection of the truth or acceptance of one's limitations as the starting point for interior change. To accept the truth means to place oneself within a context of liberation. However, while Christ is the "perfect communicator," communication with human beings is not yet perfect. There exists what in technical terms is called "noise" or "clamor" (a disturbance in communication). The disturbance comes from human beings, and it is the fear of risk-taking. It is selfishness, the inability to submit everything for discussion, the search for pleasure or money or success, the need always to have signs in order to believe and then not wanting to believe even these.

Perfect communication between God and human beings will be realized only in an eschatological context. The economy of revelation in history would not make sense if God had not decided to communicate with humankind in the fullness of time. In fact this sense of perfection pertains to God's nature, whereby it is impossible to think of a partial or fragmentary process. Once he has begun this communication with human beings, God brings it to fulfillment. The word of God will make itself present in just such a context, and there will be the definitive recognition of the vision in toto. This does not mean full knowledge of God but an encounter with, and recognition of, the mystery as such, and at the same time in terms of a continual source of newness and originality. And it will be this possibility of fresh discovery in the dialogue with God that will be the basis for the possibility of perfect communication. If in fact the contents of communication had been exhausted, then this would no longer have any meaning. It would be pure and mechanical repetition of something already assimilated. It would mean an end to every possibility of productivity and progress in reciprocal relationships. On the contrary, eschatological communication will be the source of inexhaustible progress toward the never-ending discovery of God, of his immensity and of his love.

In this context, communication with God will fully coincide with the vision of God, and all distance between God and human beings will disappear in the universality of the act, in keeping with an unceasing form of dialogue that will be conducted in ever-greater depth within the divine glory and in the ever-clearer knowledge of the mystery of God, the world, and humankind. The relationship between God and humanity will be shaped in the same way in which the persons of the Trinity are in dialogue one with another: a dialogue that generates the power and communion of love in which human beings are called to share. That potential for relating, the pressing need that guides every man and woman to seek the other in communication, will be full and complete in an eschatological context and will find its own fulfillment in relationship to God, the world, and other human beings.

The intellectual capacity of human beings, perfectly synchronized with the sphere of emotions and feelings, will be capable of direct access to the truth in the vision of, and eternal renewal of commitment to, faith in God. This moment will be not only that of reaching perfect communication with God but also that in which perfect communication between all human beings is realized. Each person will be able to have the very essence of the other person before him or her and will be successful in "reading" that other person, thereby recognizing the reflection of the mystery of God, which gives life to the other, understanding that it is a question of the same movement of seeking completion and wholeness that has animated that one's earthly life, but now without anything being able to get in the way of true encounter. In this eschatological communication, therefore, each man and woman will be completely fulfilled; one will not be able to will anything, desire anything, or have need of anything, unless it be to nourish this communication of infinite and unbounded love.

Bibl.: E. BARAGLI, _Comunicazione, comunione e Chiesa_ (Rome, 1967); id., _Inter Mirifica_ (Rome, 1969); J. L. L. ARANGUREN, _La comunicatión humana_ (Madrid, 1967); F. CACUCCI, _Teologia dell'immagine_ (Rome, 1971); A. M. THIBAULT-LAULAN, _Le langage de l'image_ (Paris, 1971); M. FLICK and Z. ALSZEGHY, "L'evangelizzazione come communicazione," in M. DHAVAMONY, ed., _Evangelization_ (Rome, 1975); W. BARTHOLOMÄUS, "Communication in the Church: Aspects of a Theological Theme," _Conc_ 111 (1978): 95–110; G. GAIRD, _The Language and Imagery of the Bible_ (London, 1980); A. DULLES, "The Symbolic

Structure of Revelation," *TS* 41 (1980): 51–73; E. ROBINSON, "Loneliness and Communication," *Theol* 83 (1980): 196–203; J. O. MILLIS, *Mac Bride and the Kingdom* (Rome, 1981); N. COPRAY, *Kommunikation und Offenbarung: Philosophische und Theologische Auseinandersetzungen auf dem Weg zu einer Fundamentaltheorie der menschlichen Kommunikation* (Düsseldorf, 1983).

M. CRISTINA CARNICELLA

CONVERSION

In theological usage, conversion usually means a spiritual movement toward God as he communicates himself in Christ and the Holy Spirit.

1. Biblical Data

The NT concept is rooted not primarily in the Greek philosophical notion of conversion, which is predominantly intellectual, but rather in the OT concept of *šûb* (to turn toward, turn away from, return). The prophets look on Israel as having turned its back on Yahweh and as needing conversion to Yahweh to escape collective punishment (Hos 7:10–12; Am 4:6, 11). According to Is 6:10, as interpreted in the LXX and in the NT, the Israelites would be healed if they were able to see, hear, and be converted; their blindness and deafness are punishments for sin. Jeremiah and Ezekiel emphasize the interior and personal dimensions of conversion as an acceptance of God's covenant impressed upon the heart (Jer 31:33; 32:37–41; Ez 11:19; 18:19–32).

John the Baptist and Jesus make individual conversion (*metanoia*) a basic theme of their proclamation. John calls for repentance and good works in view of God's imminent judgment (Mt 3:1–2; Mk 1:1–8; Lk 3:1–20). Jesus adds to John's message the good news that God is already establishing his reign through love and forgiveness. Conversion is for Jesus a condition for faith, discipleship, and salvation.

The terms *epistrophē* and *metanoia* are frequent in Lk and Acts, which connect conversion with forgiveness (Lk 10:47; 24:47; Acts 3:19), faith (Acts 2:38; 10:43), baptism (Acts 2:38; 10:47), inner peace and joy (Lk 7:50; 15:32; 17:6), the gift of the Holy Spirit (Acts 2:38; 10:45; 11:15–18), life (Acts 11:18), and salvation (Lk 8:12; 19:9). Paul and Barnabas exhort the pagans to turn from idols to the living God (Acts 14:15). The conversion of Paul, three times described in Acts, involves both personal enlightenment and a vocation to the apostolate (Acts 9:1–19; 22:3–16; 26:9–18).

Paul occasionally uses terms such as *metanoia* (Rom 2:4; 2 Cor 7:9–10; cf. 12:21) and *epistrophē* (1 Thes 1:9; cf. 2 Cor 3:16), but he more often conveys the idea of conversion by metaphors such as dying and rising again, and attaining newness of life (Rom 6:4; 1 Cor 6:11). He speaks of progressive transformation into new degrees of glory (2 Cor 3:18). For John, as for Paul, coming to faith includes the idea of conversion; it is a passage from death to life, from darkness to light. In the Apocalypse conversion is seen as a condition for forgiveness (Rv 2:16, 22; 3:3). It is a matter of opening one's heart to Jesus, who knocks and desires to enter (3:19). The centrality of conversion in the primitive catechesis is indicated in Heb 6:1, in a context that emphasizes the necessity of perseverance (Heb 6:4–6).

2. Church History

The rapid expansion of Christianity during the first centuries occurred principally through conversions. The success of Christianity in attracting converts was due to its sacramentalism, which rivaled the appeal of the mystery religions; its respectability as a philosophy excelling the Greek schools; the communal bonds of love and fellowship; and the moral integrity of its adherents. The conversion stories of Justin, Clement of Alexandria, and Augustine show how the philosophical, religious, and moral motivations interpenetrated.

Modern conceptions of conversion are heavily marked by the writings of American revivalists (J. Edwards), British Methodists (J. Wesley), Catholic saints (Ignatius of Loyola) and spiritual leaders who came into the church as adults (J. H. Newman, T. Merton, D. Day).

3. Official Church Teaching and Liturgy

Several councils in the West have decisively shaped Catholic teaching on conversion. The Council of Orange II (529), endorsing some of Augustine's anti-Pelagian positions, taught the absolute necessity of grace and of the illumination of the Holy Spirit to bring about assent to the preaching of the gospel and even the desire for faith and baptism (DS 373–77).

The Council of Trent in its Decree on Justification (1547) asserted both the freedom of conversion and the primacy of God's grace (with quotations from Zech 1:3 and Lam 5:21; cf. DS 1525). In its description of the acts by which people dispose themselves for justification, Trent mentioned faith, fear of God's justice, hope in God's mercy, incipient love, detestation of sin, and repentance leading to a desire for baptism and a determination to obey God's commandments (DS 1526). Trent also indicated that conversion continues throughout life, as one progresses in faith, hope, and charity through the performance of good works (DS 1535).

Vatican Council I (1869–70) asserted that, while the church "as a standard lifted up among the nations" invites to herself all who do not yet believe, the Lord stirs up and aids with his grace those who are seeking the light of truth, leading them toward Catholic faith (DS 3014). Christian and Catholic faith, while it is always a gift of God, is a reasonable and not a blind assent (DS 3009–3110).

For Vatican Council II (1962–65) conversion begins with being "snatched away from sin and led into the mystery of the love of God, who calls people to enter into a personal relationship with Him in Christ" (AG 13). Conversion must be morally and physically free; unworthy tactics of proselytization are to be avoided. The converts' motives should be scrutinized and, if necessary, purified (AG 13; cf. DH 11). The council used the term "conversion" when speaking of missionary activity directed to non-Christians, but for Christians coming to the Catholic church it spoke rather of "the work of preparing and reconciling those individuals who wish for full Catholic communion" (UR 4).

In order to facilitate the full conversion of persons entering the church, Vatican II decreed that the catechumenate for adults should be restored (SC 64–66; AG 14). The new postconciliar Rite of Christian Initiation of Adults, with its several successive stages, is designed to ensure a sincere renunciation of evil and a committed participation in the death and resurrection of Christ, as well as an effective socialization into the church as a community of faith and worship.

4. Theology

In classical theology (Augustine, Thomas Aquinas) conversion is the process by which an individual turns to God and becomes more closely united to him. This process is a free response to God's self-gift in Christ and the Holy Spirit. Conversion normally occurs in a gradual way, but sometimes manifests itself in intense peak experiences and in a radical shift of one's mental and emotional horizons.

In terms of the objectives envisaged, one may distinguish between types of conversion such as the following: theistic (to God as transcendent reality), Christian (to Jesus Christ as the supreme manifestation of God), ecclesial (to the church as a community of faith), and personal (to a way of life in which one's commitment is lived out). These types sometimes overlap or even coincide, e.g., when one finds God and Christ in the acceptance of a new mode of life within the church.

For Bernard Lonergan religious conversion is a dynamic state of otherworldly falling in love in response to the love of God poured into our hearts by the Holy Spirit (cf. Rom 5:5). Religious conversion brings about new degrees of cognitional, moral, and affective self-transcendence. Some theologians of the Lonergan school, making use of developmental psychology, have distinguished stages of conversion corresponding to degrees of personal appropriation of faith and degrees of deliverance from self-centeredness.

In contemporary usage the term "conversion" applies especially to sudden and unexpected advances often involving a passage from alienation to reconciliation. Movements toward God that are slight, gradual, and continuous are designated by other terms. The adoption of explicit Christian faith may properly be called conversion, since it enables one to relate to God in a radically new way, thanking and trusting him because of what he has done for us in Christ. The process of conversion, therefore, should not be separated from the transmission of the gospel.

5. Fundamental Theology

From one point of view, fundamental theology may be understood as a systematic reflection on the structures of conversion and, more specifically, on conversion to the Christian faith. The genesis of faith cannot be adequately grasped unless account is taken of the workings of grace as known through revelation. Fundamental theology should also spell out the rational discernment by which the gospel is distinguished from systems that are incoherent, superstitious, or fraudulent. The claims of Christianity stand or fall with its perceived ability to shed light on questions of ultimate meaning and to give richness, purpose, and direction to human life. The words, deeds, and transformed lives of committed believers are crucial factors in rendering the gospel credible. The theology of conversion should take account of the organic connection between the decision to believe and the inclination to join a specific community of faith.

Bibl.: B. LONERGAN, *Method in Theology* (New York, 1972); W. E. CONN, ed., *Conversion: Perspectives on Personal and Social Transformation* (New York, 1978); A. DULLES, "Fundamental Theology and the Dynamics of Conversion," *Thom* 45 (1981): 175–93; R. DUGGAN, ed., *Conversion and the Catechumenate* (New York, 1984); W. CONN, *Christian Conversion: A Developmental Interpretation of Autonomy and Surrender* (New York, 1986).

Avery DULLES

CREDIBILITY

1. *As a Premise* 2. *Pattern of Development (Augustine, Thomas, Vatican I, Analysis Fidei, Vatican II)* 3. *Ambroise Gardeil (1859–1931)* 4. *Pierre Rousselot (1878–1915)* 5. *Systematic Outline (explicatio terminorum; Christological and Soteriological focus)*

1. As a Premise

"These are written so that you may come to believe that Jesus is the Messiah, the Son of God, and that through believing you may have life in his name" (Jn 20:31). This text, which marks the conclusion of the Gospel of John, likewise marks the beginning of our own story as believers. The evangelist, thinking of those who would believe in the Master without having seen him (see 1 Pt 1:8), presents Jesus of Nazareth in the inseparable unity of his self-expression by means of signs and words as the supreme and unsurpassable meaning of human existence.

To those who already believe, he thereby declares his profession of faith in the Lord; he is the fulfillment of the ancient promises and the very revelation of God because he is his Son. Henceforth the faith of each person, set firm on this foundation, may grow and fortify itself with greater knowledge and awareness, and thus attain to life.

However, the evangelist is also conscious of those who have yet to believe; he presents Jesus of Nazareth and his message of salvation as the favorable time for completing the passage from "darkness" into the light of life (Jn 1:9; 3:17–19). This text can just as easily be chosen as the most meaningful background for reflecting on the theme of the credibility (that is, worthiness of belief) of Christian revelation, which we examine here.

Two principles that seem to emerge from this passage help to direct us toward a renewed theological understanding of the theme of credibility. The main principle is the *focus or concentration upon Christology.* Jesus of Nazareth, the one who reveals the Father, is the true and explicit center of the Christian faith. That which has been written is nothing other than the interpretation, in the light of Easter faith, of a historical event that transformed the lives of John and the disciples. To believe that Jesus is the fulfillment of the promises of old is to profess one's faith in his divine sonship, without, however, being able to overlook his words and actions in history.

The historicity of Jesus is the foundation of John's theological reflection; as a leitmotiv, this is to be found throughout his Gospel. In fact, the Jesus one encounters is essentially a man with full knowledge of having received a mission that he firmly wishes to follow until the very end. He is the one who reveals a definitive message and, surprisingly, claims that he himself has the ability to instill awareness of the mystery of the trinitarian life of God. He is the "one who is sent" and the "bridegroom"; after him there is none else who can be awaited. The "way" that leads to the Father is identified with his own person, and thus no one will be able to come to God without him (Jn 14:4–11). An initial consequence that arises from this, with regard to our treatment of the theme of credibility, will be the necessary reference to the Christocentric nature of faith.

A second principle that emerges from the text is the *ultimate purpose* to which the profession of faith is directed: "life in his name." Johannine Christology, and with it the whole of the theology of the NT, remains incomprehensible without its soteriological referent. The act of believing and professing faith "in his name"— that is, in the whole person—is not an end in itself; thus, one does believe in order to believe, but through believing one may attain to salvation.

To recognize the Father's love in the life of the Son, and particularly in his death on the cross (Jn 3:16; 12:31), is for believers the same as breaking the chains of slavery and to free the world from sin. Jesus is the "Savior of the world" (Jn 4:42), and his death becomes life for the world (Jn 3:17).

Yet what is all the more striking about John is the *universal* value that comes to be attached to salvation. In contrast to Paul, John does not hold back in considering the salvation first of the Jews and then of the pagans (Rom 1:16); instead, for him, the whole of humanity, without exception, is placed before the Son of Man. In him the judgment of salvation is definitively accomplished (Jn 3:17; 19:30), and nothing or no one can ever undo it. Consequently, the theme of credibility must retrieve the soteriological perspective as an essential ingredient in that it is the final purpose of the act of believing.

2. Pattern of Historical Development of the Problem

To give a historical summary of the stages of development of the theme of credibility would be equivalent to engaging in a study of some two thousand years of the history of Christianity and theology. In effect, in a scheme such as this, it is easy to include all the texts that have been written on the subject of faith from the APOLO-GETICS of the fathers, through the whole of the medieval period, until our own times. The injunction of 1 Pt 3:15 (→ APOLOGIA), to which constant reference is made, is the common thread that binds together the most disparate ideas and theories. The responsibility to offer reasons for faith has been addressed (→ FUNDAMENTAL THEOLOGY II) to men and women, in a fully contemporary way, in the different historical epochs, providing and creating categories of thought expressed in communication.

In the course of the centuries solutions are attributed to some of the most significant names and others less well known. Yet all have made a determinative contribution to understanding the act of faith.

Among the first contributions is that of the *Augustinian tradition*, which, with a strongly expressed text that takes up the Johannine terminology almost to the letter, returns the act of faith to a threefold basis: *credere Deo, credere Deum, credere in Deum*. With the first, Augustine underlines the acceptance of the very fact that it is God who reveals himself; with the second, he accepts the contents of revelation; with the third (taking up the Latin construction *in*+acc.), he outlines an interpersonal movement that is a dynamic enduring until the full attainment of the eschaton. The anonymous author of the *Sermo de Symbolo*, attributed to Augustine, expresses himself in this way: "Believing *what he says* is indeed one thing; believing *him* is another; believing *in him* is yet another. To believe *what he says* is to believe that the things he says are true; to believe *him* is to believe that he is God; to believe *in him* is to love him" (PL 40:1190–91; cf. 35:1631, 1778; 38:788; 40:235; 36:988; 37:1704).

A further example is supplied by *Thomas Aquinas*. The *Summa Theologiae* dedicates the first sixteen questions of part 2.2 to the theme of faith, where Thomas expounds the contents of faith (q. 1), the act of faith (q. 2), and faith as virtue (q. 4). For Thomas the primary dimension of the act is sought in the personal reality ("actus specificatur ab objecto"); since it is God who reveals himself and in whom we believe, the act of faith will have to be essentially a personal act. As such, it shows a tendency toward a relationship of communion ("actus autem credendi non terminatur ad enuntiabile, sed ad rem," ST 2.2, q. 1, a. 2 ad 2). Faith is thus none other than a reflection on humankind; created by God, believers are in an incessant and ever new path by which they return to the Creator through exercise of the theological virtues.

Thereafter, the Council of TRENT, charged with evaluating the position of Luther, who emphasized the element of trust in faith and relegated its objective data to secondary importance, expressly asserted the necessity of the objective contents of revelation as being of the first importance for justification: "Disponuntur autem ad ipsam iustitiam, dum excitati divina gratia et adiuti, fidem 'ex auditu' concipientes, libere moventur in Deum, credentes, vera esse, quae divinitus revelata et promissa sunt" (DS 1526).

The names of *Suarez* and *De Lugo* are among the most significant for understanding the theology of faith from this point onward.

Above all, it is VATICAN I, which by synthesizing the complete treasury of the patristic and medieval tradition, and citing the text of Trent, reaches a definitive canonization of faith as humankind's free response to God's revelation, as a consequence of the intervention of grace that enlightens the intellect and disposes it to accept the contents of revelation. The third chapter of *De Fide* expresses it thus: "Ecclesia catholica profitetur, virtutem esse supernaturalem, qua, Dei aspirante et adiuvante gratia, ab eo revelata vera esse credimus, non propter intrinsecam rerum veritatem naturali rationis lumine perspectam, sed propter auctoritatem ipsius Dei revelantis qui nec falli nec fallere potest" (DS 3008).

Condemning the two extremes of RATIONALISM and FIDEISM-pietism (DS 3009–10; 3031–36), the council introduces the theme of the signs of revelation as the form that allows the act of faith to correspond to the demands of reason. Miracles and prophecies are considered "signa certissima et omnium intelligentiae accomodota" (DS 3009). In the works of Cardinal Dechamps in particular, the church is described as *signum levatum in nationes*, thus capable of representing for everyone the most consonant form of credibility both of itself and of the message it bears (DS 3013–14) (→ CHURCH III).

Far from wishing to force the act of faith or to demonstrate the *fact* of revelation, these signs are presented by the council as elements that can guarantee the *credibility* of that which comes to be expounded; therefore they are given as contents that, while they come to be known by reason according to its own laws, yet are equally fitted to be believed and accepted through an act of the will.

The theology that echoed this foundation, especially after the publication of Leo XIII's *Aeterni Patris* in 1879, sought to develop, using the neoscholastic method, an apologetics of the act of faith that included essentially the *motivum fidei* and the *motivum credibilitatis*. A theology that had underlined the objective contents of revelation was replaced by a

theology that took greater account of the conditions that were necessary for the subject to be in a position to adhere to faith. Theological reflection thus began to take into consideration two elements characteristic of the act: the suprarational moment and the contribution of the human reason.

Consequently, the authors of the manuals sought to produce a theological scheme pertaining to the act of faith that can be outlined by means of a few key words:

a. Praeambula fidei. Here it is a question of the religious and moral truths that can be known by the light of human reason. With the praeambula the decision to believe comes from the sphere of the arbitrary because it justifies itself as a free act in the presence of the demands of reason.

b. Motivum fidei. This is the reason or motive by which one believes. In essence, it is given by the authority of God in his self-revelation in a true and infallible form (DS 3008).

c. Motivum credibilitatis. This constitutes the moment of analysis of the motives by which it is possible to believe. Peculiar to this moment are the "signs" of revelation—in particular, the church, miracles, and prophecies; they are arguments that attest to the divine origin of revelation, arguments directed at reason. While analysis of the signs allows one to attain to the certainty of the revealed fact, it consequently allows one to conclude that the contents of revelation are worthy of belief.

d. Motivum credenditatis. This is the reason in terms of which one *must* believe and thus give assent to revelation. While God makes the way of salvation evident, it is up to the subject to see the connection between the act of faith and the salvation that is given to the subject.

Beyond the different terminologies, even the authors of the manuals tried in this way to respond to the ever-present problem: how to join together the presence of grace and human freedom?

Under the name *analysis fidei* one may gather all the attempts that have tried to describe the theological doctrine concerning the understanding of the act of faith as a typically human act, but yet one involving grace given to the subject in order to complete an act that of itself requires divine intervention so as to raise it to knowledge of the transcendent mystery of God.

In other words, it is the classic problem: how can the authority of God, which makes itself the guarantee of the truth of the contents of faith (DS 3008), be the ultimate motive or reason by which the human reason arrives at the certainty of the truth of the original act as one that is typically human? In a word, how are divine revelation and human knowledge related to each other?

As one can well appreciate, there was, and is, no easy solution to the problem, which requires that we keep the two elements firmly balanced. If one were to accentuate unduly the role of the divine presence, the act of faith would almost of necessity receive the assent of the believer because the evidence would be such that one could not but give one's consent; yet this act would no longer be fully human because it would not be free, in that it would be bound by the evidence of revelation. The result would be to fall into fideism.

In contrast, if one were to stress the intellectual dimension of the believer, which by means of its own speculation was to reach the clarity necessary for a decision, then the act would certainly be free but would lack certainty because it no longer referred to the divine authority in certifying belief. This second path would result in rationalism.

Thus the act of faith appears destined to remain within a dialectic that is inexorably stretched between understanding the facts and the concealed role of a much greater mystery, where grace plays a determining role.

On the one hand, therefore, we have the mark of the *supernatural*; this means that the act of faith absolutely requires the presence of grace, which allows the subject to trust in the God who makes himself known; on the other hand, the *natural* is necessarily present, for the *will* of the believer must be completely free in its movement toward God so as to guarantee that the salvation offered is truly chosen and not given in a compulsory way. Finally, the human *intellect* must make sure of being in the presence of a certain and secure act so that it reaches the conclusion of a logical procedure.

The history of the problem has witnessed

solutions that have revolved around three poles that make up the act of faith (grace, intellect, and will), at times giving emphasis to one at the expense of the others. Nevertheless, it is in terms of the whole of this history of the effects that one will be able to find a solution in the future, a solution that bears a greater conformity to modern sensibilities.

In this respect history is the witness to a great battlefield; not by chance has this topic become the *crux theologorum*. The theologian must possess the ability and the knowledge to move with circumspection between the Scylla and Charybdis of fideism and rationalism, being careful not to fall into an unwarranted Pelagianism or an exasperated supernaturalism.

It is easy to locate the point reached by the theology of faith between the two most recent councils in a vivid passage from Mouroux:

> A theology of faith can be built upon two different points of view. The first is analytic and abstract: it treats of the genesis of the structure of faith, usually making a particular study of elements such as: subjective factors (intelligence, will, grace), or objective data (credibility, natural object, formal reason). This is the customary viewpoint of theology. The second is synthetic and concrete: it looks at faith above all as a *concrete whole* and attempts to explain its existential nature. It is the customary viewpoint of Scripture and the fathers. On this level it seems to us that faith explains itself as an *organic whole of personal relations*. We consider it useful for theology to bring this point of view into evidence. (J. Mouroux, *Je crois en toi* [Paris, 1949], 8)

As far as this topic is concerned, Vatican II, from its singularly pastoral perspective, signaled a recovery of the *biblical* understanding, which brought about a renewed concept of *pistis* as an act that is at once faith, knowledge, and action. Moreover, the whole question is also directed toward adopting solutions that find their philosophical points of reference in the personalism inspired by E. Mounier, G. Marcel, and J. Mouroux but that had already been anticipated in the studies of J. H. NEWMAN and M. BLONDEL, and especially, even if with rightful exception and distinction, in the theological perspective of P. Rousselot.

Something that emerges from the theology of Vatican II is the return to the contents of faith. Wishing to forget the emphasis on what was extrinsic to be found in the manuals, the council restored the event of revelation to the center of theological reflection. The focal point is thus once again modified: revelation, with its objective contents, is returned to the horizon of salvation history as a primary datum; consequently, faith comes to be regarded as the "obedience by which man entrusts his whole self freely to God" (*DV* 5), and thus as a referent dependent upon the event of revelation.

A number of authors merit special mention as characterizing the present theology regarding the understanding of the credibility of the act of faith. From the Catholic tradition, J. Alfaro, E. Biser, W. Kasper, J. Ratzinger, and M. Seckler have gained a reputation for reintroducing to theological reflection the more biblical and patristic concept of faith. In this way they have tried to understand the act of belief in the light of new philosophical referents and have held in greater esteem the value of the believer's freedom in his or her act of responding with faith to God's revelation.

Without wishing to detract from the objective value of these studies, nevertheless there are two authors in particular who have emerged as the points of reference for contemporary Catholic research in this field: RAHNER and VON BALTHASAR. To the first we are indebted for the emphasis upon the transcendental structure of the subject and the introduction of the existential dimension into the question of the act of faith; to the second author we must be grateful for underlining the objective evidence of revelation and the "otherness" vis-à-vis the believing subject.

The magisterial work of R. Aubert, *Le problème de l'acte de foi*, has responded in a complete and overall way to the needs of a historical reconstruction of this problem. This work, which was finished in 1945, thus predating the renewal effected by Vatican II, may also be considered to be fully relevant today. In fact, while in the immediate aftermath of the council the theology of faith knew how to update its subject matter, yet thereafter it has experienced a period of stagnation. While the biblical perspective has by now become common patrimony, the dimension that bears a more subjective character, thus pertaining to the one who responds to the call of revelation, has yet to produce significant results such as will allow one to see that the schematic approach of the manuals has been overcome.

In terms of the present article, with its direct reference to apologetics, it remains to offer a more detailed, if somewhat schematic, presentation of the two endeavors that shaped the theological scene until Vatican II—A. GARDEIL and P. Rousselot.

3. Ambroise Gardeil (1859–1931)

Gardeil was the author of *La crédibilité et l'apologétique*, the first edition of which appeared in 1908 as a collection of articles previously published in the *Revue Thomiste*; a second edition, to which reference is made in this article, was published in 1912, the original work having been revised in the light of criticism by a number of authors, including M. Bainvel and Sertillanges. Gardeil has had a notable influence on the academic treatment of the topic of credibility. The classic manuals of Garigou-Lagrange, Tromp, Calcagno, Parente, and Nicolau show this in a very clear fashion. His interpretation signals what is perhaps the most successful attempt to produce a study of credibility that considers both the strong pressures for renewal enjoined by the publication of Blondel's *L'Action* and the retention of the classical subject matter of traditional forms of teaching. In whatever way one wishes to judge it, this work represented, at that particular time, the most successful attempt at renewal and adaptation of the scholastic doctrine vis-à-vis the topic under consideration.

To understand the logic of our author's way of proceeding about his subject, one must also appreciate his understanding of apologetics. For Gardeil, apologetics, is the science of the credibility of dogma. A primary form of apologetics is the "scientific," the special object of which is the *rational* demonstration of credibility (p. 230). A demonstration is possible if it upholds and respects the rules of scientific knowledge, laws that produce an absolute intellectual submission. This concept is pursued throughout the work of Gardeil, and it is this that characterizes the premises and demonstrations with regard to the credibility of the act of faith.

Given the definition of credibility as "the believability of an assertion" (p. 1), Gardeil begins his demonstration by making a psychological analysis of the act of faith, with the purpose of indicating the precise role that this plays within credibility.

Taking as his starting point the analysis of the human act as described by Aquinas (cf. *ST* 1.2, qq. 8–21), he establishes a parallel between this and the psychological process of the act of faith, demonstrating that while the act of faith is a human act, in its development it has to follow the psychological phases of ordinary human acts. The parallel thus established, which could at first sight seem deceptive, in fact exhibits truly authentic features. Above all, in concrete actions, there is an *intentio finis* by means of which each one thinks of projecting oneself, of giving oneself a purpose that endures. Similarly, in the act of faith this corresponds to the *intentio fidei*, by means of which the human being is fitted to believe in the God who reveals himself.

However, this correspondence does not suffice for our author; in fact it is necessary that the intelligence intervene to establish, on the strength of facts or signs, that one is truly in the presence of divine revelation and its utterances. The problem of a *judgment of credibility* thus depends on demonstrating the veracity and divine origin of the message that is said to have come from God. For something to be worthy of belief, therefore, it must be proved *rationally* because "neither the object of faith, nor the terms of the assertion furnish the evidence of this factual element" (p. 35). Therefore, one cannot stop at the "reasons of the heart," which at the very most can "desire" that the object be true. Apologetics must reach a judgment of credibility that "demonstrates that it is true" (p. 36).

Consequently, the journey from a sentiment of faith to an effective attestation of divine faith is brought about by making an analysis of the reasons for credibility, which, as in the traditional method, are brought back to miracles and prophecies.

This "rational" credibility is classified by Gardeil as "simple credibility" because it is known precisely through rational analysis of the reasons for credibility. But this can attain only to possible credibility and must be distinguished from "necessitating credibility," which constitutes the form of utterance for a judgment of capacity for belief. That is, the object of faith is not only possible but "exactable"; the conclusion that is drawn is that "one must

believe." Finally, there is "imperative credibility," which carries the moral obligation to believe once the judgment of capacity for belief has been reached; at this level there is but the imperative, "Believe!" (cf. "Credibilité," in *DTC* 3.2: 2206–10).

As with all works that refer to the scholastic tradition, so too is Gardeil's method of demonstration clear, precise, and logical. Nevertheless, even if it began as an honest attempt at renewal (one only has to think of "certitude probable" or "suppléances subjectives"), it was still tied to a metaphysical scheme that impeded one from seeing the involvement of the "real person" in the act of faith.

The structure put forward by Gardeil still places itself at the level of antithesis between intellect and will; this explains why the latter, in the psychology of faith, appears as an act that assists the impotence of the intellect in its inability to make any further progress. Thus the will balances the *sacrificium intellectus* set in place by fallible reason in the presence of the mystery of God.

Such a project, notwithstanding all its valuable elements, was doomed to failure. During this same period a start was made on a fresh and more realistic presentation, one that corresponded to the needs of the age and that recognized an intrinsic unity in the subject; this approach was found in P. Rousselot, its most authoritative representative.

4. Pierre Rousselot (1878–1915)

An attentive reader of Newman, an admirer of Blondel, and endowed with an extensive training in theology and philosophy, Rousselot was perhaps the person best suited to create a new impact on the study of the act of faith. His particular concern seemed to start from paying direct attention to simple, uncomplicated faith and, at the same time, to take into consideration the specifics of Christian faith. It is for this reason that, from the very first pages of his work, he parts company with Gardeil and outlines his own essential solution, namely, the way in which the act of faith operates within the individual believer: "The act of faith is not apologetic but purely theological" (1910: 241).

Symptomatic of this approach is the way in which he puts the problem: "How does one find in the simple peasant who studies the catechism scientific faith, the demonstration of rationality, or at the very least, complete certainty of credibility founded on absolutely valid reasons? How does one find it in the colored person who believes the word of the missionary? It is not quite enough to give a psychological explanation that illustrates the mechanism of the act of faith or of the disposition to believe. Such an explanation would be just as applicable to the faith of a Muslim as to that of the Christian. If the Catholic child has reason to believe its mother and its parish priest, is the Protestant child at fault in believing his pastor and his mother?" (1910: 245–46).

The crucial point for Rousselot is not to forget that within the individual there exists a "synthetic activity of the intellect" that attains to what is real by overcoming all merely conceptual expressions. Taking his terminology of "the eyes of faith" from Augustine ("Habet namque fides oculos suos" is placed at the foot of the page in the introduction to the first part of the work), but above all having the support of Aquinas with regard to the form of knowledge, and Blondel for the concept of the subject's dynamic openness to the fullness of being, Rousselot recaptures the biblical idea of faith and thinks that there is something "to see" by means of faith; rather, faith constitutes none other than the capacity to see that which God wishes to reveal, which cannot be seen without faith.

More directly, God does not reveal himself by means of an internal experience on the part of individuals but through a historical testimony that has been transmitted up to our own day. In order to explain this testimony and guarantee its legitimacy, God has given outward signs that bear objective validity, addressed to everyone without discrimination. Therefore, as far as our author is concerned, there are "external" facts, but these require the "eyes of faith" in order to be understood as signs from God. In fact, the human spirit, as such, does not have the ability to see these signs; for that reason it needs to receive the "capacity to see"—both to see the signs and to understand them as the data of revelation.

Grace is thus nothing other than the possibility given to us that the eyes might see their object correctly and in true proportion. Consequently, it is not that new objects of knowledge present themselves with regard to the credibility of the act but that the ability is given to understand them in such a way that signs, external reasons, and the *lumen gratiae* concur to yield the certainty of the act that is accomplished.

From the point of view of apologetics, it follows that the judgment of credibility and the act of faith constitute one and the same act, through which attestation is given to both the affirmation of the truth of believing and the perception of the reasons by which what is believed is found to be worthy of such belief: "The perception of credibility and the confession of the truth are the same act" (1910: 254). Thus it is the case that grace allows perception of credibility, but this, in its turn, gives them a reason and a meaning. Rousselot's thesis then develops by considering love as an act that stirs the faculty of knowledge and renders the act of believing a free act. By means of a synthetic expression it can thus be affirmed that "the act of faith is reasonable because the perceived sign carries the testimony of the natural order to the new truth. The act is free because the human being has the power to refuse the love of the supernatural good" (1910: 457).

As may be seen, one is presented with a very impressive prospect in that it recovers the essential unity of the subject beyond every form of dualism; moreover, it restores a form of unity between knowledge and faith because it reclaims the rationality proper to the very act of believing. The influence of this perspective on the theology of Vatican II is well attested.

5. Systematic Outline

These two examples are governed by two different philosophical and theological sensibilities. In their own, different ways they have marked a particular epoch; in fact, the first has been at the very roots of a tradition of manuals that have shaped generations of students preparing for the priesthood. The second has determined the renewal that came about in the church in the aftermath of the movement that led to the Second Vatican Council.

We think it more in keeping with our own times, which are marked by certain conflicting movements (*GS* 4–10) but also by a deep and sincere search for MEANING, which seems to be just as evident in bringing about the failure of the ideologies and forms of humanism that have characterized the postwar period, that the theme of credibility be exposed to the light of a new category: "significativity" (namely, that which is worthy of meaning).

Explicatio terminorum

A number of premises are necessary for understanding what follows.

a. When speaking about credibility, it must be observed that one is faced with a terminology that requires a degree of precision. The history of the topic, as we have seen, shows that different contents can be ascribed to credibility. In the past the credibility of *Christianity* has been spoken of, showing that, as a religion, it is superior to all others by virtue of its revelatory character and its sense of fulfillment; mention has also been made of the credibility of *the act of faith*, which in particular has witnessed to the possibility of people giving correct expression to their humanity yet entrusting themselves to the transcendent; and of the credibility of the *church*, which has been founded more directly on the demonstration of its "notae" and on the mystery of its historical development (→ CHURCH III). In the present article the chief objective is the description of the credibility of the *revelation* that comes to be seen in the light of "significativity."

Above all, to speak about the credibility of revelation means that we wish to bring into greater focus the central and determinative event of fundamental theology: revelation as given definitive expression in Jesus of Nazareth. In fact this allows us to give a more overall interpretation of the theme of credibility; it likewise offers the most fitting scenario whereby one speaks of faith not on its own, as if it were an isolated element, but as a response to the event of revelation (*DV* 5). With revelation as the object of credibility, we think it better to favor the interpretation of a priority of God's intervention in human history. In fact, revelation is given to theology as a free and gracious act of God, who out of love alone, comes forth from the depths of his own mystery to communicate himself, and thus bring salvation, to the human race.

Credibility thus presents itself as an act that does not originate in mere human subjectivity; rather, it arises from the objectivity of the event of revelation. For this reason credibility is not equivalent to the conclusion of a process of knowledge conducted according to the methodology of logic or psychology. Rather, it is the source, the beginning, of a challenge that comes to the subject so as to complete an anthropologically determined act—that of the self freely entrusting itself to another.

From this perspective credibility means, above all, that a unique and profound coherence is given to the subject of knowledge, a coherence between that which is and that which allows itself to be seen and understood; this seems worthy of consideration as something that cannot be overlooked, lest its own capacity for knowing remain incomplete. This fact impresses itself on humankind in that, *historically* speaking, it exists as a piece of evidence of which everyone is aware.

b. We may speak of "significativity" as a process that tends toward relating the event of revelation to the individual subject. Revelation is certainly something that is given from without, but the logic of its being and its very nature are such that they enter into communication with human beings in every time and place because they understand themselves to be called to a communion of life with God through belonging to Christ, who, in historical terms, is professed in the church. As a consequence of this, revelation presents itself as the place in which perennial questions of the subject, but also those that are more limited in cultural and historical terms, find a possibility of being answered.

However, there is also a tension on the part of a given era that challenges revelation into considering its historical situation, thereby to explain the present. In fact, only in this way is there created a permanent relationship that will be able to lead each person to consider the act of believing as a meaningful response to the question put.

From this perspective, credibility means to be in a position to see the realization, even in our own times, of that fullness of meaning that revelation represented for the first believers, who, on the strength of their faith in the Master, were able to leave everything in order to follow him (Mk 10:28). This means that credibility is equivalent to giving those reasons in terms of which the Christian life is not only understood in an intellectual sense as the response to the question of meaning but is at the same time the introduction to a praxis and witness of life that allows one to see the realization of the meaning that has been promised.

"Significativity," therefore, is the relationship between revelation and subjects in their act of understanding themselves as persons in view of the final purpose of the self.

This term "significativity" requires further explanation.

c. By "significativity," we mean a theological category that contains three elements: sense, meaning, and significance. By means of *sense*, one is inserted into the horizon of the epistemological foundations; by *meaning*, into the subject or contents; and by *significance* (i.e., that which is significant), one enters the typically anthropological horizon.

The category of "significativity" is brought about only by the unity of these three components and their reciprocal relationship. What suggests itself, therefore, is an interpretation of credibility that can be contained within a single act. In this single act the objectivity of the sense on which the contents are founded, and by which they are sustained, can also be related to the act of the subjects, who see that sense and those contents as the reality that is able to give a purpose to their life because it can supply an overall meaning to the whole of their existence.

We will now try to give a better account of the three elements of "significativity."

Sense. It is not easy to respond to the question, What is sense? Different disciplines refer to it as a particular object of study; there flows from it, therefore, a complexity of linguistic relationships that do not always admit of giving clear expression to the concept itself.

From the viewpoint of linguistic analysis, sense is linked to the laws of verification; in a wider philosophical interpretation, which brings one back to the theoretical principles of reflection, it would be much more the problem of the judgment of the question about sense. Finally, from the point of view of ethics, sense will be identified with the purpose and meaning of life.

From the viewpoint of theology, the meaning of revelation indicates (→ MEANING I), rather, the agreement or coherence that comes to be established within the form of revelation. The person of Jesus of Nazareth is the sense of revelation because in him, once and for all, the trinitarian mystery of God is revealed. There is complete coherence and consonance between this historical figure, in the totality of his existence, and that which seeks to be revealed. His *being* is expressed and manifested as a return to a much greater mystery, knowledge of which is given, however, only through him and by the words and actions that come from him.

Precisely this *reference* to another, without ever being able to ignore or separate itself from the person of Jesus, bestows sense—better still, is that by which sense is *constituted*. Indeed, it is only here that one has the final answer to the question about sense, and what it is exactly. It is the ultimate reply to the question because it refers back to the mystery of God, beyond or apart from which nothing can take place; it is the ultimate offering of sense, because it is in this figure that the definitive knowledge of the mystery is given, a mystery beyond which one cannot proceed. Thus it is that sense, as coherence between that which seeks to communicate itself and that which is reached, is here fully and definitively given. Jesus of Nazareth is the only way to a knowledge of God's revelation, but at the same time he is the Father's definitive offering who utters the call to salvation.

Consequently, what we have here is the concentration of the two most fundamental expectations: that of God, who sends the Son for the salvation of the human race, and that of men and women who, holding fast to Christ, at last attain to knowledge of God. Every intermediate grade of knowledge and salvific action can be considered preparatory or anticipatory, but never as completely definitive such as that given in history through revelation.

Meaning. In common parlance meaning is what is expressed, made visible, by that which is significant; yet for the purpose of definition, it can never be fully defined. Of its very nature, meaning eludes every possible categorization that one wishes to give. For human beings, it constitutes that which is perceived by intuition but that which is never fully expressed. Meaning, as such, has a universal value; each person can grasp it, even if it expresses itself by means of an indicator of significance that is arbitrary and that can vary according to linguistic expressions.

Once the relationship has been realized, the bearer of meaning will be able to modify or adjust itself. It will acquire shades of expressed meaning that were not at first revealed, but by dint of a "collective inertia" (De Saussure) the meaning can never lose its original sense.

In terms of the present discussion, meaning is expressed by the totality of the mystery of the incarnation. Hence we intend to express the global nature of the history of salvation, which sees in this event the culmination of the possibilities offered to humankind with regard to the final purpose and the very sense of human existence and history.

The incarnation of God constitutes the definitive way by means of which, in human history and beginning with human nature itself, meaning is given, a meaning that gives direction and final purpose. The history of the Jewish people is oriented toward "the one who is to come" (Mt 11:3: *ho erchomenos*); the history of believers is illumined by the one who has come. In history, once and for all (Heb 9:12), a union has been established between the divine and the human, a union that is not realized at the level of dialectic, but at that of unity in what cannot be mixed, of unity with respect to two natures, without which neither of the two fails in its freedom; a unity bestowed upon a single subject, not in the form of representation or deputation, but because it remains forever in history as the *unicum irrepetibile* (→ UNIVERSALE CONCRETUM).

As part of this mystery, which also involves Mary, because Christ is the child of her flesh and blood of her blood, the gift of the Holy Spirit is bestowed; this allows Mary and all believers to express their "yes"—their confidence and trust in God. Through the incarnation as a universal mystery, the church is introduced as the primary mediator of the everlasting meaning of revelation in human history.

And yet the meaning of revelation is never completely exhausted. It is definitively given but not exhaustively fulfilled. The gift of the Spirit enables the meaning of revelation, itself God's enduring call to salvation, to persist in different periods and cultures. It is not only a problem of interpretation of the revelation or understanding of this; in fact, in the course of the centuries meaning must find significant expressions, the fruit of a constant application of the SENSUS FIDEI, because it can emerge through this whole dynamic of truth that it has been bestowed in the originating historical event (*DV* 7–8; cf. *LG* 12).

The active witness of believers takes nothing from the original sense, but faith and the action of the Spirit focus the attention because a referent is established that is always in a position to act reciprocally in terms of its genuineness.

Significance. This is the specific point at which the subject perceives the relationship between sense and meaning in his or her personal life. Confronted by the evidence of sense, subjects still need to see it in relation to their personal context in order that the choice to accept it may be completely free. The universality of sense and meaning is not an impediment; on the contrary, it favors the personal relationship by means of which each person discovers that that reality is for him or her. Certainly, it is valid for everyone and must remain so, but people see it as directed to themselves *personally* and for precisely this reason perceive it as *significant*, in that within the final purpose of their existence this reality expresses the overall way in which they may be guaranteed to attain to their own end.

Consequently, significance qualifies personal freedom because it puts each one in the position of having to make a choice. Indeed, it is here that the universal reality comes to be seen as qualifying personal existence. It thus pertains to subjects to make the choice that shows full coherence between the universal meaning and the understanding of its validity in a personal context. Through that which is significant subjects express all their powers of criticism and purpose of decision because they complete the act that designates or qualifies them in anthropological terms, that of finite freedom that chooses to embrace a far greater freedom. This freedom is acknowledged and adhered to as the guarantor of having attained unto being itself. Only by freely choosing to make existence their ultimate goal can subjects guarantee their own freedom of choice in the various moments and actions in the future; but this finality demands that knowledge of the ultimate purpose outstrips the contradictions and limitations of our personal experience.

Theologically speaking, that which is significant is what qualifies and designates believers in their act of trusting in revelation as the supreme instance of their own destiny. Thus believers, in that they are sustained by the grace that allows them to understand the "unfathomable riches" of the mystery they encounter, see in the figure of Jesus of Nazareth the archetype of a completely free and fulfilled humanity, just as the church has handed it down in an unbroken and living tradition (*DV* 10).

Jesus of Nazareth is the prototype of every form of faith because he entrusts himself completely to the Father, to whom he makes constant reference in terms of the full identity of his own being. Jesus becomes the one who is significant for our personal lives because, on the one hand, he embodies universal meaning and, on the other hand, he reveals the possibility of an authentic personal existence that is at once free and finds its fullness in commitment to the other.

What is significant is given its ultimate value by choosing and living the *sequela Christi* (the following of Christ in accord with his style of life). The *sequela* does not, in fact, follow upon the act with which one sees the sense and meaning of revelation, but it is simultaneous to it. It is a unique act that believers accomplish in the moment at which they perceive revelation as the fullness of sense and *significance* for themselves; it is the act that envelops the intelligibility of the event into an indivisible whole, trusting it because it is worthy of belief and following it because life has at last reached its completion.

Having said this, one can find it confirmed in the following points, which seek to embody and expand upon what has been outlined and which, as we have already emphasized, hinge on a christological and soteriological focus.

Christological and Soteriological Focus

a. The person of Jesus of Nazareth — that is, the mystery of the incarnation of God — comes across as the universal form that establishes itself, on the strength of this characteristic, as the highest expression of sense and meaning in history.

The critical faculty of human beings has always sought the universal by which to express the ultimate norm, which, eschewing the individual or particular, will become valid for each person. The great philosophical systems that have endured to the present day are marked by this concern for individuation and identification. And yet critical knowledge lives with contradiction all the time, or intervention from outside, or with an unjustified elevation of the individual or particular above all else.

From this condemnation to what is contradictory one may salvage only the critical knowledge of the faith that confesses the ontological union of God with humankind in a single historical subject, who thereby becomes unique and unrepeatable.

This unity in uniqueness does not come about by a simple transposition or assumption of a single historical subject to a more exalted (even the ultimate) ontological status. It presents itself as the original decision of God, who, in his freedom, refuses to retain his divinity "jealousy for himself" but partakes in humanity (Phil 2:6–8; cf. Jb 42:2). Theologically speaking, therefore, this *unicum irrepetibile* can be bestowed only by means of *kenosis*, in such manner that it is always considered an action of God's freedom and grace and not a human initiative.

The God who takes flesh in human nature does not cease to be God; at the same time, however, he does not *exalt* himself proudly above human nature, because "he had to become like his brothers and sisters in every respect" (Heb 2:17), even in being tested, in suffering and in death (Heb 2:18; 4:15), which constitute the drama and the ultimate contradiction for a humanity that ever seeks to step beyond every form of limitation, conclusion, and barrier set upon personal will.

Instead, it is in this event that humanity is lifted up, because the whole of humankind comes to be saved by this union, in that it partakes of that singular humanity assumed by the Word (Heb 2:10).

This unrepeatable uniqueness, by which "one among us," as the fathers loved to say, yet remaining like unto us, reveals the mystery of God: it is this which becomes the universal norm for each and every one of us. This is determined by the fact that with Jesus of Nazareth one is no longer in the presence of something theoretical but of a concrete *historical* subject. His speech and behavior, while being human (*DV* 2), is not liable to be "confused" with ordinary human behavior. What Jesus communicates is his *being*—that is, his person—which is encountered as the expression of revelation, namely, a self-consciousness that is aware of being God and of revealing him in human form.

This behavior is charged with meaning because it is given by God, and it allows history to experience an internal thrust of direction in terms of specifying its final purpose and the possibility of attaining that end. Humankind and its history are thus no longer wandering toward an "infinite nothingness," incapable of finding a goal on the horizon. The uniqueness of the man Jesus of Nazareth guarantees that each person, and the whole of history, will find a conclusive result, because his historical being is assumed by the divine and henceforth joined with it. The returning and reference to the Father—in his plan of salvation, his time, and his "hour," as in all Jesus' decisions—are the "response" given to humankind at the point at which it seeks the sense and direction of its own personal existence.

This trust and confidence are salvation, because God alone can guarantee that the contradiction experienced by human beings is overcome and conquered from within, by means of a free act that allows entry into the kingdom, and thus to the highest form of communion.

b. A knowledge that is historical must respect the laws placed upon it; not even God goes against his own creation. The historical subject desires and needs a form of knowledge that will confirm that God truly expresses himself in Jesus of Nazareth; only this will lead to the overcoming of the last barrier that impedes recognition of the uniqueness and the evidence of the presence of God in Jesus.

Yet again one must take stock of the logic of this theological procedure, which seeks to respect the primary action of God. In fact, previous methods of theology had for too long expended energy in giving demonstration of external signs that, above all, were not successful in focusing upon the true center of gravity. Contemporary theology, in considering the signs of credibility, must instead be in a position to give pride of place to showing the centrality of the unique sign placed within history, from within which all other signs emerge and upon which they converge (cf. Jn 5:36–37). Thus there are the "signs of the Father," which must be the primary object of theological inquiry (Jn 14:10).

The sign given by the Father is none other than the Son nailed to the cross, dead, and risen. The primary sign of the credibility of Christian revelation is therefore the PASCHAL MYSTERY of the Crucified One.

In the death of Jesus, accomplished in human language, God has revealed himself, his nature, and his life. The God who communicates his very life expresses it as the love that "endures until the end." Such complete self-giving (Jn 3:16 *edōken*) characterizes the intratrinitarian dynamic of God's being.

The Father is like this in the very moment in which he gives himself *wholly* to the Son, and the Son himself is the Son in the very act in which he is *fully receptive* to the "all" of the Father. This very act of holding back nothing for oneself, but handing everything to the other and returning everything thereto characterizes the life of the Father and the Son; the Spirit is the third person who bears witness to the totality of the giving and receiving.

Everything is given to humankind in the incarnation of the Word, but the visible expression of this total giving is to be found only in the death on the cross, where God himself accepts death as the utmost sign, by which people may believe in the totality of his love.

The Son's death, which the Father accepts within himself, is not the extreme point of estrangement from his being. Instead, it is at the same time the beginning and the end of his self-giving. If love is "to give all," this becomes visible to humankind in the moment at which God gives himself completely—that is, loving "to the end" (Jn 13:1) and thus becoming through love that which could never be: death.

In the presence of this death of the innocent one, one can no longer produce the alibi of not believing, holding against God his inability to understand human suffering and sorrow even to the contradiction and drama of death, even the death of the innocent. Jesus of Nazareth, who is nailed to the cross and who cries out to the Father in his sorrow at having been given up by him into the hands of death (Mk 15:34), is the same God who shares all the sorrows of humankind and, what is more, sorrow on behalf of the suffering and death of the innocent.

Quite rightly Mark places the profession of faith made by the centurion, and thus by a nonbeliever, in the presence of Jesus' cry of abandonment and death: "When the centurion, who stood facing him, saw that in this way he breathed his last, he said, 'Truly this man was God's Son'" (Mk 15:39). The truth about God and the truth of God are engraved in the sign of the Crucified One, because here it emerges that the foolishness of the cross is the starting point of the divine logic, and thus the highest expression of true wisdom (1 Cor 1:23–28).

But the centrality of the Crucified One takes nothing away from the fullness of the mystery. If believers place the love made manifest in death as the sign of credibility, this is only because their profession of faith arises out of the news of the Easter proclamation. The resurrection is already present in the death on the cross, because that death is the act of trustful abandonment into the hands of a Father who does not allow the one who trusts in him to see the corruption of the tomb (Ps 16:10).

The completeness of the sign, which permits the very radicalization of Golgotha, is given by the dialectic of "the sign of the prophet Jonah" (Mt 12:39–41), by which it is only for three days that he must remain in the belly of the earth. It would not be possible for us to have any real interest in the Easter faith were it not for the complete identification between the one who has suffered and died and the one who is risen. In that death, one sees the love that, humanly speaking, expresses complete self-giving; in the resurrection this becomes evident. The resurrection does not become an alibi for escaping the drama of Golgotha; instead this is taken up into the fullness of its truth, yet overcome, without being destroyed, by a hope that only faith knows how to express.

_c._ The mystery of the cross and resurrection remains in the world, transmitted by the preaching of the church; it endures as the authentic and definitive sign of the trinitarian love of God, capable of being perceived as genuine love by those who seek to lead their lives in a prudent fashion.

There is a risk, at least nowadays, that the demand of love that has ever been placed upon the subject will be trivialized. In terms of "significativity," the theme of the credibility of revelation would have to be such that it showed a theological understanding of love capable of urging and challenging the subject in its search for meaning.

What is love? At the very moment in which critical understanding would find a definition capable of answering this question, then would love be forever destroyed and defeated in our world. It has a meaning and significance that remains a mystery. And yet it is necessary, theologically speaking, that one gives a _caritas quaerens intellectum_ ("charity in search of understanding") so that the act of faith can be authentically human.

In the presence of the radical newness of the revelation of Jesus of Nazareth, the first expression that emerges in terms of an understanding of love is that this can be given by means of revelation alone. In fact, the love that is thus encountered is not in the first place mediated by a human experience, which as such would participate in limitation and what is contradictory, but it is the unique and absolute love that issues from the very divine nature, the form of which, humanly speaking, is put into action. In theological terms this means that the credibility of love cannot be supplied by external elements but first and foremost is from within itself and by the forms that this progressively assumes in human language.

Nevertheless, the subject must be in a position to understand this form as the definitive expression of love that carries it beyond the contradictions that it _naturally_ experiences. This is possible because, when coming face to face with this particular form, the subject understands itself as being loved for what it is, with no other condition than that of a disinterested and gratuitous love. Indeed, the subject comes to perceive love not as a generic reality but as a personal dimension that realizes itself only in the degree to which two subjects relate one to the other to the point of giving themselves to one another completely. In fact, each time one of them loves, he or she becomes for the other a personal subject who can no longer understand itself apart from the personal relationship with the beloved. One desires to be loved by this person; and yet, in order to arrive at this moment, each must be in a position to let go of self in order to become the other, to make space for the other and to give oneself totally.

Without overlooking the other NT texts, it is Johannine theology that seems to give deepest expression in this regard and that is capable of shedding light upon these facts concerning a phenomenology of love in human terms.

As we have already seen, the ultimate form of love revealed by God is that which reaches to the point of assuming the death of the Son. In this context, Jn 3:16 seems to represent almost a synthesis: "God *so* [*houtōs*] loved the world that he gave [*edōken*] his only son, so that everyone who believes in him may not perish but may have eternal life." Love, therefore, is to give all, even if the other person, as the theology of Paul reminds us, is at fault and unworthy of love (Rom 5:6–8).

It is here that the Johannine concept of love takes shape, which finds its fulfillment in 11:50–13:35. The First Letter of John continues this reflection adding elements of extraordinary richness: "God is love" (1 Jn 4:8) becomes the highest expression of this theology. The recognition of such love, which consists in the fact that Jesus "laid down his life for us" (1 Jn 3:16), is not only life and salvation (1 Jn 1:1–4) but also constitutes the *newness* of Christianity; from the reciprocal love of brothers and sisters it will, in fact, be possible to keep alive this sign for all ages to come (1 Jn 2:3–11).

The assertion "God is love" thus indicates the recognition that *God loves.* He is a personal reality who expresses his nature in tripersonal relationality. God loves, and only God can love as God loves; nevertheless, this love, given once and for all in human history, remains the fullest possible sign of every love that seeks to be truly as much.

Every person can understand it and adhere to it, because each one understands his or her own personal reality vis-à-vis love as complete self-denial and detachment; only in this perspective may one be sure that it is genuine love.

The sign of love given by revelation takes nothing from the power of personal freedom. The Jesus who loves to the point of total self-giving is the one who, in this very act, also expresses his own awareness of being a completely free person: "I lay down my life *in order* to take it up again. No one takes it from me, but I lay it down of my own accord" (Jn 10:17–18). In the light of this, believers also see the full freedom of their own action, because it is the choice that is experienced as being fully conformed to their being and final destiny—that is, conceiving of itself only in terms of a love that is truly *eternal.*

d. In the presence of this sign, from which springs the significance of all other signs—the church, the miracles, prophecies, the preaching of the kingdom—each person is in the position to make a choice. Paraphrasing a scene from the Gospel of John, one would say that one wishes to believe not because someone has spoken about Jesus but because one has directly encountered his very person (Jn 4:42; Jb 42:5).

On the one hand, therefore, the offer of salvation is given universally, whereby, at this level, the figure of Christ presents itself as the archetype and center of history; on the other hand, and at the same time, the ultimate expression of judgment is made with regard to every form of religion and on the definitive meaning given to personal existence (cf. Jn 3:17–18; 5:27–30; 8:15–16; 12:47–48).

Credibility, seen as "significativity," now reaches its phase of completeness when the subject comes face to face with the evidence of revelation and sees it as being significant for itself. This process can be verifiable if the following elements are kept in mind.

First, there is a transcendent dimension to the subject that enables it to give an ultimate purpose to its own existence by means of comprehending objects that direct it toward an infinite space of knowledge. In a word, each person enjoys the capacity for perception of the meaning that comes about through a constant dynamic of human living.

The human being conceives of itself as a subject stretched between the finite of its historical condition and the infinite of its speculative reflection. It is precisely at the moment in which as a person—that is, as a subject that realizes itself by means of free choices—one makes a decision about the whole of one's existence, that one detects an ideal of life that is firmly *believed* to be the ultimate element capable of giving meaning to the whole of one's existence. This ideal remains as such, yet for the subject it acquires specific and historical value at the point of verification of its having been attained in dynamic fashion.

It is not attained—in fact, it is an ideal. Yet one *believes*—that is, trusts—that it alone will be capable of realizing itself through anticipation or expectation. This condition straightaway allows us to say that all people, in themselves, in that they are human, have their individual capacity both for the perception of meaning and for being able to attain to it.

Second, when subjects place themselves in

the presence of another subject, then the afore-mentioned process assumes particular dimensions. Subjects cannot "use" this purpose or end at their own pleasure; indeed, this is no longer a value or an object in their own hands. Rather, like them, the other is a person, a free subject.

At this point two almost conflicting freedoms enter the picture. These freedoms can be reconciled only to the extent to which one feels oneself loved to such a degree that one sees no violence at the very moment in which something of oneself is renounced so that one can accept the other person.

This act, which is reawakened in the subject by an originating experience that allows perception of a gratuitous and disinterested love, is foremost in permitting a real "focusing" upon the other person. In other words, the capacity for belief, in that it is possible for it to adhere to an ideal, is already situated within the onto-logical structure of subjects inasmuch as they perceive meaning and absorb it as their final object or purpose; yet because they can see what is significant in terms of revelation, it is necessary that revelation be the source of the primary action (→ Obediential Potency) that reawakens the subject's capacity for knowing how to gather all the evidence of that event.

This action, before being a merely intellectual act that grasps the truth of the fact, is a properly personal act of the unity of the subject, which at the same time intuitively _knows_ it is loved and sees in that form the supreme expression by which it is guaranteed the fullness of self.

Thus in order to know the "true God," it is necessary to have understanding (_dianoia_, which the Vulgate translates as _sensum_), which only the Son can communicate and which, historically speaking, he has communicated by the paschal mystery of his death. But "understanding" must of necessity be taken in the biblical sense. It is not primarily an intellectual activity; rather, it is complete adherence of the self to the mystery, and this embraces at one and the same time intellect, will, heart, and soul.

Third, and consequently, in the historical person of Jesus of Nazareth, humankind is given the supreme witness that, at the same time, reveals the mystery of God and stirs within human beings the power to see him as significant. In the last analysis, everyone desires life, although paradoxically, it can seem as if even the suicidal person is the one who dreams of a different, and perhaps better, life. Believing in "your word" (Jn 17:6) is equivalent to wishing to continue living. Johannine theology, more than any other, favors this soteriological perspective.

Those who believe cannot allow themselves to repeat the line in _Macbeth_: "Life is just a shadow." Life is neither a shadow nor something theoretical, because when each one of us comes face to face with life, we see that _res mea agitur_: the whole of myself comes into play. Thus, precisely in the presence of the event of revelation, life is made visible (see 1 Jn 1:1), and one discovers that one is not projected toward a theoretical eternal life beyond death; rather, one binds oneself to giving significance to this personal, historical existence.

Through his own historical existence (_DV_ 2), Jesus of Nazareth becomes "the light of life" (Jn 8:12) and "the light of all people" (Jn 1:14), because the very trinitarian life of God is in-serted into this process (1 Jn 5:11–12; Jn 1:3; 2:23; 3:16; 5:26; 6:57). Into the human situation, which would content itself with partial solutions, those of "water" (Jn 4:5–20) or "bread" (Jn 6:27), something is revealed that endures and remains right up until the present moment: "This is eternal life, that they may know you, the only true God, and Jesus Christ whom you have sent" (Jn 17:3). This is the offer that has been revealed to each person in order that one might understand oneself and one's existence. Life is salvation, and salvation is knowledge of God; but knowledge is to be called into communion with him and to share with one's brothers and sisters (1 Jn 3:11; 4:12; Jas 2:14–19).

Discernment of this promise of salvation cannot leave us neutral. Each person is called to make a choice: either to remain content with absurdity or to live the _sequela Christi_ as a son or daughter of the light.

Conclusion

"Truly your decrees are very such" (i.e., to be trusted) (Ps 93:5). In all probability it is by this psalm that we must seek entry to the terminology of credibility. It is to be worthy of faith—that is, capable of accomplishing what is, anthropologically speaking, the most important action, that of knowing how to trust and wishing to entrust oneself to another.

Credibility, in terms of "significativity," can serve to unite a number of the needs of current theology—above all, the personalist dimension in terms of which Vatican II has presented the theme of revelation. What one encounters is neither an object nor a theory but a person. Jesus of Nazareth is in a position to encounter the contemporary world because within himself, in that he is the Son of Man and Son of God, he can communicate the mystery of his being.

Through fidelity to the person of Christ, the church will be found worthy of trust, credible, notwithstanding its human and very apparent contradictions. The credibility is in terms of its lasting proclamation to the people of every land.

In Jesus of Nazareth each person can discover the meaning and ultimate significance that life can give, along with its own contradictions. This is possible because revelation here comes to be encountered in the light of love. It is not just any form of love that comes to be revealed but the love by which each one first attains to the most profound and personal mystery, and for this reason the love that alone is worthy of the name (1 Jn 4:10–19).

From this perspective even the most serious difficulties with regard to a theory and praxis of faith can be overcome because they are restored to the fundamental unity that is the personal act by which one meets God and decides to follow him forever. Within love there no longer exists either fear or timidity (1 Jn 4:18); people know themselves to be profoundly free, because they are taken up into a relationship that is far and beyond personal categories, immersed in the call to trinitarian life.

Consequently, it is love alone that remains as the last word that renders revelation worthy of belief, because only here do subjects rediscover, in a most obvious fashion, the equilibrium of the mystery of their own self. In fact, it is only through love that they recognize that they are loved, and only by loving are they able to *know* and *understand* what it is to love. Only by love can they be certain of their freedom in wanting to give and offer themselves, because here alone does every choice become clear in that, at the same time, it is seen and understood as a reality that appertains to them and yet one by which they are overcome.

Bibl.: P. ROUSSELOT, "Les yeux de la foi," *RSR* 1 (1910); A. GARDEIL, *La crédibilité et l'apologétique* (Paris, 1912); id., "Crédibilité," in *DTC* 3.2:2001–2310; S. HARENT, "Foi," *DTC*, 6/I: 55–514; R. AUBERT, *Le problème de l'acte de foi* (Louvain, 1945); id., "Questioni attuali intorno all'atto di fede," in var., *Problemi e orientamenti di Teologia Dogmatica* (Milan, 1957), 2:655–708; E. HOCEDEZ, *Histoire de la théologie au XIXe siècle* (3 vols.; Paris, 1947); J. MOUROUX, *I believe: The Personal Structure of Faith* (1949; New York, 1959); G. EBELING, *Was heisst glauben?* (Tübingen, 1959); R. GUARDINI, *Wunder und Zeichen* (Würzburg, 1959); J. ALFARO, "Fides in terminologia biblica," *Greg* 42 (1961): 463–505; id., *Fides Spes Caritas* (Rome, 1968); id., *Cristologia e antropologia* (Assisi, 1973); id., *Rivelazione cristiana, fede e teologia* (Brescia, 1986); J. PIEPER, *Belief and Faith* (New York, 1962); N. DUNAS, *Connaissance de la foi* (Paris, 1963); H. BOUILLARD, *The Logic of the Faith* (1964; New York, 1967); G. DE BROGLIE, *Les signes de crédibilité de la révélation chrétienne* (Paris, 1964); H. Urs VON BALTHASAR, *Glaubhaft ist nur Liebe* (Einsiedeln, 1966); id., *The Glory of the Lord: A Theological Aesthetics*, vol. 1: *Seeing the Form* (San Francisco, 1982); vol. 7: *Theology: The New Covenant* (San Francisco, 1991); id., *Theo-drama: Theological Dramatic Theory*, vol.2,1: *Dramatis Personae* (San Francisco, 1990); id., "Fides Christi," in *Sponsa Verbi: Saggi teologici* (1961; Brescia, 1972), 2:41–72; id., "Mysterium pascale," in *MystSal* (Brescia, 1971), 6:172–404; R. LATOURELLE, *Theology of Revelation* (New York, 1966); id., *Christ and the Church: Signs of Salvation* (New York, 1972); id., *Finding Jesus through the Gospels* (New York, 1979); id., *Man and His Problems in the Light of Jesus Christ* (New York, 1983); id., *The Miracles of Jesus and the Theology of Miracles* (New York, 1968); J. TRUTSCH, "La fede: Linee dello sviluppo del dogma e della teologia," in *MystSal* (Brescia, 1968), 2:405–504; K. RAHNER, *Hearers of the Word* (New York, 1969); id., *Foundations of Christian Faith* (New York, 1978); id., "The Human Question of Meaning in Face of the Absolute Mystery of God," in *Theological Investigations* (1978; New York, 1983), 18:89–104; id., "What Does it Mean Today to Believe in Jesus Christ?" in ibid., 143–56; J. RATZINGER, *Introduction to Christianity* (New York, 1969); id., *Principles of Catholic Theology* (1982; San Francisco, 1987); W. KERN and P. KNAUER, "Zur Frage der Glaubwürdigkeit der christlichen Offenbarung," *ZKT* 93 (1971): 418–42; E. SCHILLEBEECKX, *The Understanding of Faith* (London, 1974); E. BISER, *Glaubensverständnis* (Freiburg, 1975); id., *Glaubenswende* (Freiburg, 1987); J. B. METZ, *Faith in History and Society* (New York, 1979); W. KASPER, *An Introduction to the Christian Faith* (New York, 1980); G. RUGGIERI, *La compagnia della fede* (Milan, 1980); R. FISICHELLA, *Hans Urs von Balthasar: Amore e credibilità cristiana* (Rome, 1981); id., *La Rivelazione: evento e credibilità*

Bologna, 1981); id., ed., *Gesù Rivelatore* (Casale Monferrato, 1988); R. Sanchez-Chamoso, *I fondamenti della nostra fede* (Assisi, 1983); H. Fries, *Fundamentaltheologie* (Cologne, 1985); P. Neuer, "Der Glaube als subjektives Prinzip der theologischen Erkenntnis," in *HFT* (Freiburg, 1988), 4:51–67; E. Kunz, "Glaubwürdigkeitserkenntnis und Glaube," in *HFT* 4:414–49; U. Casale, *L'avventura della fede* (Turin, 1988); var., *La carità* (Bologna, 1988); S. Pié-Ninot, *Tratado de teologia fundamental* (Salamanca, 1989).

Rino Fisichella

CREED

Concise but comprehensive texts used for formally declaring one's adherence to the faith of the church are known from the first half of the fourth century. In his appeal to Pope Julius I in 340 C.E., Marcellus of Ancyra set forth his faith by citing the text known as the old Roman creed (*vetus Romanum*, DS 11). At the Council of Nicea, Eusebius of Caesarea tried to overcome suspicions about his orthodoxy by setting forth the confession of faith transmitted to him during his own catechetical instruction, which he claimed to have believed and taught, as presbyter and bishop, down to the present day (for Greek, see *Athanasius Werke*, ed. H. G. Opitz (Berlin, 1934), vol. 3/2, p. 29; for Latin, see *PL* 20:1538).

1. The Early Development

The fixed confessional formulas, known from the time of the Arian controversy, have deep roots in the times of Christian beginnings. An initial way of professing faith in Christ was to declare "Jesus is Lord" (1 Cor 12:3) or to "confess with your mouth that Jesus is Lord and believe in your heart that God raised him from the dead" (Rom 10:9; cf. Phil 2:10; Acts 2:36). In other churches of NT times, the central confession was that Jesus was uniquely "Son of God" (1 Jn 4:15; Mt 16:16).

Late in the first century, as reflected in Matthew's Gospel, the baptism of a new disciple was a solemn consecration "in the name of the Father, of the Son, and of the Holy Spirit" (28:19). A century later, in North Africa, as Tertullian mentions on occasion, the one being baptized first renounced Satan and then professed his or her adherence to the Christian faith in response to a set of three stereotyped questions about belief in God as Father, Son, and Holy Spirit.

About 215 C.E. Hippolytus described the baptismal rite of the church of Rome, relating the fixed text of the rite. In the water, before each immersion, the minister posed these questions:

> Do you believe in God the Father almighty? Do you believe in Christ Jesus, who was born by the Holy Spirit of the Virgin Mary, and was crucified under Pontius Pilate, and was dead and buried, and rose again the third day, alive from the dead, and ascended into heaven, and sat at the right hand of the Father, and will come to judge the living and the dead? Do you believe in the Holy Spirit, in the holy church, and the resurrection of the flesh? (*Traditio apostolica* 21; *SC* 11 [bis], 80–93; creed only in DS 10).

Thus, a very early profession of the church's faith was interrogative or dialogical in structure. Faith took the form of responding "I believe" to the questions about God and his economy of salvation asked by a church minister at the central moment of the liturgical act of baptism and incorporation into the community.

The fourth-century declarative formulas, such as the *vetus Romanum* and the Caesarean creed, had their principal *Sitz im Leben* in the catechumenate. While the question-and-answer format remained central in baptism itself, the handing over of the church's creed (*traditio symboli*) to the catechumens marked their passage into an advanced stage of preparation for baptism. They were told the formula used in the church they were entering, were required to learn it by heart, and heard instructions, usually by the bishop, on the meaning of each part of the text. The best-known example of such instruction is Cyril of Jerusalem's *Catechetical Lectures* (*PG* 33).

Shortly before being baptized, the candidates marked the end of their prebaptismal instruction at the rite of the *redditio symboli*. Augustine includes in his *Confessions* an account of how this was done in Rome around 355 C.E., when the distinguished scholar Marius Victorinus entered the church. "At Rome those who are about to enter into your grace usually make their profession in a set form of words which they learn by heart and recite from a raised platform in view of the faithful." The priests could offer the option of a private profession. "But

Victorinus preferred to declare his salvation in full sight of the assembled faithful. . . . When he mounted the platform to make his profession, all who knew him joyfully whispered his name to their neighbors. . . . He made his declaration of the true faith with splendid confidence, and all would gladly have seized him in their arms and clutched him to their hearts" (*Conf.* 8.2.5).

These declarative creeds expand somewhat the interrogative creeds of baptism itself, in accord with the RULE OF FAITH of the different local churches, in order to give compendious expression to the faith into which the candidates are being initiated. A whole series of fourth- to sixth-century Western creeds are known (DS 13–26) which differ somewhat from the *vetus Romanum* and out of which came the *textus receptus* of the "Apostles' Creed" of the Western church (DS 30). These texts were not meant to set forth the complete rule of faith, but rather to formulate the evangelical core of God's revelation of himself and his work of salvation in Christ.

But the Council of Nicea in 325 began a new movement, by promulgating a declarative creed for the whole church, which aimed at expressing a part of the common rule of faith in terms that exclude a specific error (→ DOGMA). This creed was less for use by individual believers as their personal profession than for setting forth a common norm of orthodoxy by which legitimate bishops might be known and other bishops might maintain the bond of ecclesial communion with them.

The Nicene Creed (DS 125) rules out certain tenets promoted by Arius of Alexandria, especially by specifying that the Son of God is generated of the Father's being or substance (*ousia*) and is "consubstantial (*homoousios*) with the Father." The intention here was not to impose a metaphysics on the church, but instead to counteract quite specific ways in which Arius had spoken of the divine monarchy and of the beginning of the Son as "firstborn of his ways" (Prv 8:21). Arius interpreted the NT from the viewpoint of texts like Jn 14:28, "The Father is greater than I." The Nicene definition declares above all that it is God himself who reveals himself in Jesus of Nazareth. The meaning of *ousia* and *homoousios* was not elaborated by the bishops in council. The intention of their action is especially clear from the addi-

tion to the creed they promulgated of a short list of Arian formulations that deny the Son's divinity, e.g., "There was a time when he was not," which are now prohibited under pain of excommunication (DS 126).

The Nicene Creed was exemplary of all future dogmatic declarations in being a regulative measure regarding the language of instruction in the church and a guideline to apply in interpreting Scripture. Privilege of place should be given, e.g., to a text like Jn 10:30, "The Father and I are one." The Nicene Creed excludes an erroneous rule of belief and principle of interpretation; it establishes a criterion of communion between bishops and churches, and it transmits the text that the churches eventually accepted and made the starting point of further dogmatic specifications of the faith they had received.

2. Theological Significance

After Nicea, the creed of the church clearly took on a new function, becoming a pointed expression of orthodoxy and a condition of *communio* between the churches. It would be impoverishing, however, to lose sight of the primordial role of the creed in expressing the believer's adherence to Christ as Son of God, risen, and Lord. The trinitarian structure of the oldest baptismal creeds makes clear that these texts fit into the action by which an individual consigns his or her life over to the saving purposes of the triune God. The creed is one element in the liturgical and ecclesial expression of conversion. The setting—i.e., initiation into the community of faith—makes it clear that the creed belongs to a rite of passage from sin and alienation into the "household of God" (Eph 2:19), as a person turns "from idols, to serve a living and true God, and to wait for his Son from heaven, whom he raised from the dead—Jesus, who rescues us from the wrath that is coming" (1 Thes 1:9–10).

The ancient practice of the *traditio/redditio symboli* has been given renewed prominence in the Catholic Rite of Christian Initiation of Adults. Such a placement of the creed brings out a second essential element of its meaning. For the creed is not the candidate's own invention, but instead a precious part of that which the church has and faithfully transmits as trustee (→ DEPOSIT OF FAITH). The creed derives ultimately from the preaching and teaching ministry of Christ's apostles and is professed under the lead of those who have acceded to responsibility for teaching, guarding, and expounding the transmitted word (*DV* 10). But the ultimate subject of the Christian declaration "I believe in God . . ." is the corporate person of the church itself. The "I" of the creed is the community of those who are joined in a common faith, a community of witnesses and believers who share life with each other and with God (see 1 Jn 1:1–3). The dialogue of the baptismal creed is, first, the offer of the church's faith to a new member and, second, the new member's willing appropriation of his or her participation in that faith. And in faith, where revelation reaches its intended term, one has new life and access to the Father, through the Son, in the Holy Spirit.

A final insight into the sense of the creed has been articulated by Thomas Aquinas. Concerning the multiplicity of distinct "articles" of creedal content, Thomas holds that all the diverse articles should be seen as implicitly contained in the primordial tenets that God exists and has a providential care for our salvation. The creed gives further articulation to the being of God, which we will know as our ultimate beatitude, and to his dispensation of historical means toward reaching that beatitude. The number of articles does increase, but this is by way of explicitation of what is present in the most fundamental conviction of faith (*ST* II–II, 1, 7). The ultimate object of faith is not the multitude of articles that we confess. We do need them because of our historical, ever-partial way of knowing, but that to which God is leading us by faith is the simplicity of himself as *prima Veritas* (*De veritate* 14.8 ad 5, ad 12).

From the viewpoint of faith itself, Thomas enunciates a principle to be applied both to each article of faith and to the creed as a whole: "Actus autem credentis non terminatur ad enuntiabilem sed ad rem" ("The believer's act does not reach its goal in the creedal enunciation itself, but beyond it in the reality thereby revealed") (*ST* II-II, 1, 2, ad 2). Faith is a movement of the graced human spirit which reaches its term not in the creedal article it professes but in the reality that is thereby revealed. An article of the creed formulates a truth of divine revelation, but the article does not constitute the ultimate object of the dynamic movement of faith. "The article of faith is but the perception of the divine truth transcending itself" (II–II, 1, 6). The acceptance and profession of a creedal article are thus but one moment in a movement that transcends the article itself. Faith brings the person into union with God, the *prima Veritas*, who even now, by revealing himself, shines the light of his presence into human hearts.

Bibl.: H. DE LUBAC, *La foi chrétienne: Essai sur la structure du Symbole des Apôtres* (Paris, 1969); J. N. D. KELLY, *Early Christian Creeds* (3rd ed.; London, 1976); F. E. VOKES et al., "Apostolisches Glaubensbekenntnis," *TRE* 3 (1978): 528–71; G. LANCZKOWSKI et al., "Glaubensbekenntnis(se)," *TRE* 13 (1984): 384–446; A. DE HALLEUX, "La réception du Symbole oecuménique de Nicée et Chalcédoine," *ETL* 61 (1985): 5–47; S. SABUGAL, *Credo: La fe de la iglesia* (Zamora, 1986); T. SCHNEIDER, *Was wir glauben: Eine Auslegung des apostolischen Glaubensbekenntnisses* (Düsseldorf, 1986); J. RATZINGER, *Principles of Catholic Theology* (San Francisco, 1987); M.-T. NADEAU, *Foi de l'Église: Évolution et sens d'une formule*, Théologie historique 78 (Paris, 1988).

Jared WICKS

D

DEATH

Gaudium et Spes says, with good reason: "It is in the face of death that the riddle of human existence becomes most acute" (*GS* 18).

1. A Seeming Absurdity

Many of our contemporaries call death the last and supreme absurdity of life. According to Jean-Paul Sartre, death is a breaking off, a rending, a boundary, a fall into emptiness. Death, like birth, is unexpected and absurd. We are born in a motiveless way and we die accidentally. Death deprives human beings of their freedom and puts an end to all possibilities of fulfillment. It makes us the prey of the living and puts us at the mercy of their judgments. For Albert Camus, at the center of life stands the human person with its absurd and meaningless existence that is full of suffering and bounded by death. It is clear that life tends to fulfillment, while death is a source of absurdity. Life has the first word, but death always has the last. The thousands and thousands of people who commit suicide each year draw that same conclusion: life is meaningless, absurd; better to put an end to it.

The living, be they believers or unbelievers, who are conscious of being condemned to death, are open to the temptation of thinking in the same way as these suicides. The press, television, plays, novels, and films constantly carry news and images of death: civil war, genocide, terrorism, brutal invasions, tragedies in the air and on the highways. Why so many lives diminished or snatched away at the very moment when they were about to become fruitful? Why so many fatal and undeserved illnesses? Why does the human race, despite its progress and technology, keep committing the same injustices, the same crimes? The threat of death, thus brutally present at every moment, begets a worldwide psychosis. At the very time when humanity is experiencing the intoxication of progress, it is sad and afraid. Is it really working for its own destruction? Is its destiny death or life? Faced with this nightmarish

stumbling block of death, many take refuge in forgetfulness; they seek diversion, they deaden their feelings, they take drugs—and die of them. And yet, even if we are reluctant to talk about death, we must do it, because life has whatever meaning we give to death. If death is for the sake of life, then we can have hope. But if life must inevitably end in a total shipwreck of body and possessions, then life itself has no meaning because it is a blind alley.

2. Death as Completion and Beginning

In the face of the meaninglessness and seeming absurdity of death, Christianity offers an utterly new fullness and even superabundance of MEANING. This capacity to give meaning, which comes to it from revelation, helps make Christianity credible.

As a matter of fact, the only answer to the mystery of death is another mystery: the mystery of temporal death for the sake of eternal life. Death is both a completion and a beginning. As seen by Christian faith, the human person is not a being-for-death but a being-for-life; this means that the Christian faith affirms death but at the same time looks beyond it. Life has a meaning because death has a meaning; it is a "passover," a passage leading into eternal life.

The most surprising aspect of the Christian revelation regarding death is that God has turned death into a mystery of Christ's love for the Father and, at the same time, a mystery of the Father's love for Christ and, through him, for all human beings. Human death has become a saving event for Christ and for the world. Christ does not deny death but gives it its deepest meaning. Christ has an experiential knowledge of our death with all its menacing darkness, with its power to shatter, its agony, its utter confusion and human helplessness. More than any other human being, Christ experienced a death marked by utter SOLITUDE, indescribable bodily sufferings, humiliations, and complete failure. He was spared nothing of the destruction death brings to a human existence.

But Christ also gave death its true reality and deepest meaning. Death, which is the concrete manifestation of humanity's sin and its alienation from God, becomes in Christ the supreme expression of submission to God. Both sin and love here reach their maximum effectiveness.

At the very moment when the sin of human beings finds its climactic expression by crucifying the Just One, the death of Christ becomes the Son's loving embrace as he surrenders himself to the Father. Love thus finds its climactic embodiment, for Jesus keeps covenant with the Father to the very end: "You are my God." By this complete surrender to and trust in the Father, Christ conquered death. It is this gift of self to the mystery of God who is Love, in acceptance of failure on the cross, that has given a meaning to human life as finally "fulfilled" in death. Without losing the element of darkness, death becomes something quite different, namely, a surrender of the whole person to God in order to share God's life.

3. Death as Sacrament and as Theological Act

Christ reveals to us a new dimension of saving grace. In the very moment when sin abounds, his death acquires the superabundant power that enables him to overcome it. Death, which had been the destruction of human existence and an expression of sin, becomes in Christ an act of surrender to the saving power and saving love of God, a loving dialogue with Love. Christ transforms death into a _sacrament_, i.e., an expression and efficacious sign of the absolute fulfillment of human existence in God.

For those who live their life as a mystery of dying and living with Christ, death becomes the point at which the appropriation of salvation, begun through faith and the sacraments, reaches its highest degree. It is less a boundary, therefore, than the completion of a process of maturation and fruit bearing. It means the loss of self but also encounter with God and life in God.

Death is in fact the _supreme theological act._ Through FAITH Christians ground their life on the word of God. The reality of the world to come invades the present world and inspires all their actions. But in death they stake everything for the sake of everything. Death is seemingly nothing but utter darkness, despair, and deadly coldness, but they believe, "on God's word," that this downfall leads to life and that they will live eternally. Faith can go no further; it has exhausted its possibilities. In death Christians hope against hope and surrender themselves to the God of the promise. Death thus met and accepted in total, trusting aban-

donment becomes truly an encounter with God in Christ. By hope Christians throw themselves on God and entrust their life to him for all eternity. Finally, charity too, which is love of God above all else, finds its supreme expression and completion in death. By our sins we have often resisted God's calls. Now we have an opportunity to say an unreserved yes. We have often been sorry that we were unable to give everything or able to give only with our lips. Now we are able in a sense to gather up our entire being and offer it to God as a living sacrifice: "Lord, into your hands I surrender my spirit." By permeating death, these three powers that ground Christian life—faith, hope, and charity—transform death. Death is not bankruptcy but a definitive victory of the life of God over death—life for good and for ever.

Death thus becomes a real assimilation to the death of Christ that was mystically effected in us through the sacraments and that now transforms our death. For through _baptism_ we are immersed in the death of Christ (Rom 6:3), crucified with him (by a death to sin), buried and raised up with him. Christian life is simply the gradual and continuous development or practical application, throughout a lifetime, of the twofold effect—death and life—that was produced by our baptism. In our real death we crown our life of configuration to Christ. We really die with him in order that we may rise with him. Sign and reality coincide here; we truly die and rise.

In the _Eucharist_ we unceasingly proclaim the death of Christ, which is our death and our life. But if we proclaim in the Eucharist the Christ who was "handed over for us," then we must share in this mystery by experiencing it in the reality of our own lives; this experience reaches its completion in our real death.

The _anointing of the sick_, finally, is the sacrament meant for the situation of death. It renders visible the fact that Christians, strengthened by the grace of Christ, are here meeting the final test of their lives and performing their final action—their death—in communion with the Lord. Thus the beginning, middle, and end of Christian life are consecrated by three sacraments in which we progressively make the death of Christ our own as the source of our salvation and resurrection.

The great truth underlying this Christian vision of death is the truth of our relationship with God, which is a vertical, direct, continuous, and ever-present relationship. When we respond at each moment to the call of God, we prepare ourselves to enter into the Lord's rest; the final moment differs only in that it recapitulates and ratifies all the preceding moments and brings us into eternal life in a definitive way. The essential thing in our life is the presence of God in each moment of a life wholly directed to him, like the flower that keeps following the sun all day long. God is not located at the end of our life, waiting for us there; his gaze is constantly upon us at every moment. In the final moment, however, this great presence will be unveiled and become everlasting light. A diaphanous veil makes the difference between these two presences: now, and at the hour of our death.

This vision of things can help us rise above the scandal of a death that crushes life in its prime and leaves some work unfinished. Whatever the character and duration of a human life, it is to be measured in the final analysis by the immensity of the love that dwells in it, the love of God himself. But who can measure the immensity of that love? The active indwelling of divine love in us means that at every moment we are at the end of our own history. That human beings are saved by grace means that the human history of each person, which is never finished, is constantly reaching its goal, namely, entrance into communion with God, into the love that bathes us in the Light that knows no darkness.

Now that Christ has died, there is no event in the universe that is more important than death. If we die with him, the commonplace act of dying is taken up into the mystery of God. The true meaning of life is that it is a preparation for dying, which means that it is a maturing into eternal life. To die is to be born forever; after our birth into temporal life, after our birth in baptism, which is a rebirth from water and the Spirit, there is a birth into eternal life. Christians are people who believe in the good news that death leads into a life in which there is no more death. We may be impatient with not seeing, but we know that a day will come which will never end. "My desire is to depart and be with Christ" (Phil 1:23).

The thoughts offered here have evidently been developed within the Christian faith. On the other hand, if, as I look at the seeming meaninglessnes of death, I see one appear who sheds light into this darkness, one who has a face, should I not turn to this gaze that plumbs my depths far more than I can myself? Is Christ not this fullness of meaning in a world that is in search of its lost meaning? Christ, like death itself, remains a mystery, but a mystery that sheds light, an ever-flowing source of meaning. All who open themselves to him will see a path of light open up before them.

Bibl. P. GRELOT and E. BORNE, "Mort," *DS*, 1747–69; R. TROISFONTAINES, *Je ne meurs pas* (Paris, 1960); K. RAHNER, *On the Theology of Death* (New York, 1961); V. JANKÉLÉVITCH, *La Mort* (Paris, 1966); M. BORDONI, *Dimensioni antropologiche della morte* (Rome, 1969); G. MARTELET, *Victoire sur la mort* (Paris, 1962); L.-V. THOMAS, *Anthropologie de la mort* (Paris, 1976); P. ARIÈS, *L'homme devant la mort* (Paris, 1977); R. LATOURELLE, *Man and His Problems in the Light of Jesus Christ* (New York, 1983), 337–56; G. COUTURIER, A. CHARRON, and G. DURAND, eds., *Essais sur la mort* (Montreal, 1985); H. BOURGEOIS, *La mort* (Paris/Ottawa, 1988).

René LATOURELLE

DEI VERBUM

I. HISTORY. *1. The Schema* De Fontibus Revelationis. *2. The Text of the "Mixed Commission." 3. Drafting of the New Text.* (R. FISICHELLA)

II. COMMENTARY. *1. Vatican II and Dei Verbum. 2. Change of Perspective. 3. The Economy of Revelation. 4. The Centrality of Jesus Christ. 5. Faith, Response to Revelation.* (R. LATOURELLE)

I. HISTORY

It is safe to say that the Dogmatic Constitution *Dei Verbum* (DV) is the most significant document to emerge from the Second Vatican Council—at least in the sense that it covers the whole gamut from the preparation for the council to its actual deliberations. All the important themes of the Christian faith are dealt with in it, but *Dei Verbum* also contains a step forward in dogmatic teaching and, what is more, a fresh presentation of it to the contemporary reader.

This article owes a double debt to the main contributor of *Dei Verbum*, Fr. Umberto Betti. First, he was responsible for the publication of a series of documents and texts to be studied by the council's preparatory and theological commissions; they not only throw light on the genesis and restructuring of the critical phases of the constitution but are also the main source referred to here, apart from the *Acta et Documenta* and *Acta Synodalia*. I am also grateful for a long, fruitful, and friendly meeting I had with Fr. Betti: his personal recollections and the wealth of detail on persons and events were yet another source of information I have been able to draw on in writing this article.

The long *Dei Verbum* odyssey began with the preconciliar consultation in 1959 and ended with its publication on 18 November 1965, twenty days before the council closed. The time taken to produce it was certainly not spent in vain: its content has such a great influence on the faith that it has become a crucial document for the church. Believing in it and making it work only make sense insofar as these gestures reflect the acceptance of the revealed Word of God.

The focus of debate on the doctrine of divine revelation may be described as the phase that attempted to bring it from its state of ferment, a characteristic of the period prior to the council, to a state of full maturity. The task was to meet the need to reconcile the fundamental truths, indispensable to the faith, with new factors and modes of expression that are more in tune with the new understanding of the historical nature of the church.

For reasons of space, we shall only outline the three main stages in the composition of *Dei Verbum*.

1. The Schema *De Fontibus Revelationis*

Having announced his intention on 25 January 1959 of calling a council, John XXIII appointed the following 17 May a prepreparatory commission headed by the cardinal secretary of state, Domenico Tardini. It was charged with "establishing appropriate contacts with the Catholic episcopate in different countries with a view to seeking advice and suggestions; collating the proposals made by the various departments of the Roman curia; and setting down guidelines for issues to be discussed at the council after listening to the opinions of the theological and canonical faculties of Catholic universities" (*Acta et Documenta Con-*

cilio Oecumenico Vaticano II apparando, series I, vol. I [Vatican City, 1960] 23). With that, there began a worldwide consultation the like of which had never been known before.

Among the major issues that were proposed for discussion at the council, particular emphasis was laid on the problem of the nature of revelation, ways of transmitting the revelation, and the relationship between the church's magisterium and God's word. The Preparatory Theological Commission was made up of seven members (Tromp, Piolanti, Garofalo, Ciappi, Gagnebet, Hurth and Balič) and two consultors (Staffa and Philippe), and was chaired by Cardinal Ottaviani. Fr. S. Tromp, professor of apologetics at the Gregorian University, was appointed secretary, and he ensured that the complex subject was discussed in an organized manner by providing a draft summary plan as a work proposal.

This document, entitled *Schema Compendiosum Constitutionis de Fontibus Revelationis*, was sent out to members of the Theological Commission but was not fundamentally amended. To give it further impetus, an internal subcommission chaired by Garofalo and charged with the job of drawing up a schema on the sources of revelation was set up.

The text of the schema was finished by 23 June the following year, and, after it was reviewed by the Theological Commission, it was sent to the Central Commission on 22 June 1962, and the *Schema Constitutionis Dogmaticae de Fontibus Revelationis* was finally approved by John XXIII on 13 July of the same year and sent out to members of the council prior to discussion within the council itself.

The schema on the sources of revelation was debated by the council on 14 November 1962. It is worth noting in passing that council members were already entering into the spirit of modernization which the pope had been insisting, ever since his opening address on 11 October, should be the council's best achievement. We should also bear in mind that the discussion on the renewal of the liturgy was already bearing its firstfruits. All of this explains why the setting in which our document was to be discussed was somewhat precarious.

There was yet another problem: the three other schemas that were rivals to the official document had been privately circulated. The first had been drawn up by the Secretariat for the Unity of Christians with decisive contributions from Stakemeier and Feiner; the second, *De Revelatione Dei et Hominis in Jesu Christo Facta,* had been prepared at great speed and was submitted by Karl Rahner with the support of the episcopal conferences of Austria, Belgium, France, Germany, and the Netherlands; the third was a paper produced by Yves Congar, entitled *De Traditione et Scriptura.*

Against such a background, it was hardly surprising that in his official presentation Cardinal Ottaviani argued strongly in favor of the schema prepared by the Theological Commission. The report was read, however, by Garofalo, who sought to present the document with the intention of salvaging as much as possible. The question, though, was what could still be saved? Speech followed speech in rapid succession, and the atmosphere was tense. Some participants who had been influenced by the rival texts found the schema absolutely unacceptable, while others, trying to preserve formal correctness, preferred to indicate shortcomings and spoke of the need for radical change.

The reasons that were pointing to a rejection of the schema were concentrated in the first chapter. Reference was made to the allegedly improper and equivocal use of the phrase "double source" with an insistence that almost amounted to obsession; however, it was pointed out that such a formulation had doctrinal consequences that saw the Scriptures and tradition as independent sources. In other words, the line taken by the commission was challenged because it amounted to a unilateral and completely unjustified theological choice.

The powerful attack on the schema had now become patent aggression. The critical voices that had been raised in St. Peter's effectively meant rejection. But at the moment of decision, the request to move to a vote was made in an unusually enigmatic formula. The proposal put to the fathers ran thus: "Should discussion on the Schema of the Dogmatic Constitution on the Sources of Revelation be halted?" Nobody understood from this question whether a halt to discussion on the schema meant it had been rejected or that it had not been rejected but that the debate was to be adjourned and deferred to a more opportune time.

The result of the vote, announced on 20 November, was as follows: *placet* ("approved"), 1,368; *non placet* ("not approved"), 822; invalid, 19; total votes, 2,209. Under the rule of a two-thirds quorum, 115 more votes were needed for a majority, but continued discussion of the issue was not in jeopardy. The minority could no longer approve a text that the majority had rejected.

Thanks to the wise advice of John XXIII, the council was spared any further troubles. On his authority, the document was remitted on condition that it be heavily amended.

2. The Text of the "Mixed Commission"

It was the pope's decision that the rewriting of the schema should be handed over to a special commission. This was made up of members of both the Doctrinal Commission and the Secretariat for the Unity of Christians, together with consultors and cardinals of the pope's choosing. In view of the type of commission it had now become, it was called a "mixed" commission; cardinals Ottaviani and Bea were appointed chairmen and Tromp and Willebrands secretaries.

To be able to proceed quickly, the commission was divided into five subcommissions each dealing with one of the schema's five chapters that had to be reworked. The commission reached an early agreement of principle on the following matters: (a) the basic structure of the new document particularly as the title had been changed to *De Divina Revelatione;* (b) the drafting of an "introduction" aiming to set out the doctrine on revelation; (c) the title of the first chapter, *De Duplici Fonte Revelationis,* being replaced by *De Verbo Dei Revelato.*

The first advance made by the new mixed commission was to avoid the question of the greater objective superiority of tradition over Scripture. In this respect, the commission was greatly assisted by the pope's approval of a formula put together by Cardinal Browne and Monsignor Parente. The real debate concentrated, therefore, on two items: the introduction and the first chapter. With regard to the introduction, it was noted that it had been produced in a hurry and that it was inconsistent with the rest of the document; as far as the first chapter was concerned, there was the thorny problem of the relationship between Scripture and tradition, but the commission looked more closely at the relationship between the church in general and the magisterium in particular.

The structure of the new schema was finally

sent to the coordinating commission; it was approved on 27 March 1963 and was forwarded to the council members for comment.

The text was more a point of departure than an arrival. A brief summary demonstrated immediately the fundamental flaws that had resulted from various compromises agreed on during the drafting stage. The new document ended up displeasing everybody and managed to engender a sense of anguish even among the best intentioned. It was providential that no room was found for it in the discussions of the second session (29 Nov.–4 Dec. 1963), thereby avoiding further disagreement. It was the widely held view of the council participants that the schema put forward by the mixed commission should be further amended but that the basic structure should be left intact. It very much sounded as if the document was going to be thrown out and not approved. However, there was one radical solution on the horizon, and that involved abandoning the constitution on revelation once and for all. This idea, which could have done the council serious damage, persuaded some fathers from the Italian and French episcopates to say that, if that happened, the central points should appear anyway in the document on the church. This did not, however, come about.

With this aim in mind, a subcommission was set up within the doctrinal commission on 7 March 1964 consisting of seven fathers (Charue, Florit, Barbado, Pelletier, van Dodewaard, Heuschen, and Butler) and nineteen experts (Betti, Castellino, Cerfaux, Colombo, Congar, Gagnebet, Garofalo, Grillmeier, Kerrigan, Moeller, Prignon, Rahner, Ramirez, Rigaux, Schauf, Semmelroth, Smulders, and Turrado); Ratzinger and van den Eynde were later added to the group of experts. Charue was appointed chairman and Betti secretary.

3. Drafting of the New Text

Much of the commission's heavy work load was borne by the experts: it was their job to reconcile the various and conflicting observations that came in from individual members and from episcopal conferences, and to combine them into a text that the whole council could accept.

The new document now had an introduction, which sought to give the schema a pastoral emphasis, and six chapters: (1) *De Ipsa Revelatione;* (2) *De Divinae Revelationis Transmissione;* (3) *De Sacrae Scripturae Divina Inspiratione et Interpretatione;* (4) *De Vetere Testamento;* (5) *De Novo Testamento;* (6) *De Sacra Scriptura et Vita Ecclesiae.* This appeared to be in keeping with the council's expectations.

Paul VI inaugurated the third session of the council on 14 September 1964. By now, the members of the council were used to a debate that was unique in many ways.

Discussion on this document lasted an entire week—from the ninety-first to the ninety-fifth assembly (30 Sept.–6 Oct.)—and the time was divided into two periods corresponding to the two parts of the document: first, the introduction and the first two chapters, and then the four remaining chapters. Rapporteur for the first part was E. Florit, archbishop of Florence, but minority views were also articulated by Franič, bishop of Split; the report for the second part was given by J. van Dodewaard, bishop of Haarlem.

The response of the members was positive in the main, and observations that were made in writing or in the assembly were examined closely by the experts on the subcommission. The outcome was that the document was considered to have been very well revised and not twisted out of shape: the overall content and structure had remained substantially the same as before.

This text *denuo emendatus* was once again sent back to the council to be voted on during the fourth session, but this time the members of the council could only vote in one of three ways: *placet, non placet,* and *placet iuxta modum* ("approved, not approved, and approved with amendments"), and by virtue of the third option, extra changes were made to the text without changing the basic position. The fact that the total *placet iuxta modum* vote was 1,498 for the entire document gives some idea of the difficulty the experts had in weaving last-minute observations into the final text.

When the amendments had at last been added and the overall balance deemed right, the schema could be confidently put to general assembly 155 on 29 October. This was now the last stage at which all the various amendments could be passed, and the council approved the schema almost unanimously. The voting was as follows: *placet,* 2,081; *non placet,* 27; invalid votes,

7; total votes, 2,115. The schema now had all the requirements necessary to be passed on to the full session of the council.

Promulgation was fixed for the session to be held on 18 November 1965, the eighth public session of the council, and the result was a landslide victory for the schema: *placet, 2,344; non placet, 6;* total votes, 2,350.

And so, with the signatures of the pope and of all the members present, the document on divine revelation, which had run into such complexities that it had to be drafted six times, now passed through the council's full procedure and became a Dogmatic Constitution. The chapter headings speak for the most important issues dealt with: (1) *De Ipsa Revelatione;* (2) *De Divinae Revelationis Transmissione;* (3) *De Sacrae Scripturae Divina Inspiratione et Interpretatione;* (4) *De Vetere Testamento;* (5) *De Novo Testamento;* (6) *De Sacra Scriptura in Vita Ecclesiae.*

Thus yet another document entered the corpus of Catholic teaching. The impact, which is not so much one of innovation as of renewal, will not be seen for some time to come. What is certain, however, is that this constitution is one of the many council proceedings which, as Paul VI said on 18 November, the day the document was finally voted on, would be the beginning of many new things happening in the life of the church.

Bibl.: *Acta et Documenta Concilio Oecumenico Vaticano II apparando* (Vatican City, 1960–71); U. BETTI, "Cronistoria della costituzione dogmatica sulla divina rivelazione," in var., *Commento alla costituzione dogmatica sulla divina rivelazione* (Milan, 1966), 33–67; id., "Storia della costituzione dogmatica Dei Verbum," in var., *La costituzione dogmatica sulla divina rivelazione* (Turin, 1967), 13–68; id., *La rivelazione divina nella Chiesa* (Rome, 1970); id., *La dottrina del Concilio Vaticano II sulla trasmissione della Rivelazione* (Rome, 1985); G. RUIZ, "Historia de la constitución Dei Verbum," in var., *Comentarios a la constitución Dei Verbum* (Barcelona, 1969), 3–35; *Acta Synodalia sacrosanti Concilii Oecumenici Vaticani II* (Vatican City, 1970–78); var., *La Révélation divine* (Paris, 1968).

Rino FISICHELLA

II. COMMENTARY

1. Vatican II and *Dei Verbum*

After the period of panic, deceleration, and stagnation resulting from the modernist crisis, the Constitution *Dei Verbum* seems like a breath of fresh sea air dispersing a heavy fog. The transition to a personalist, historical, and christocentric conception of revelation amounts to a kind of Copernican revolution, compared with the extrinsicist, atemporal, and notional approach that prevailed until the 1950s.

This transition has not been an easy one. On the contrary, *Dei Verbum*, one of the first constitutions submitted for discussion by the conciliar fathers, was one of the last to be voted on. Before this approval, it met with considerable resistance, went through a number of storms, and somehow managed to escape shipwreck. The definitive text, passed by the assembly on 27 October 1965, and almost unanimously approved, represents the sixth official draft. On the doctrinal level, *Dei Verbum* is the source document of the council's efforts, the hermeneutical key to all the other texts. On the ecumenical level, its importance can scarcely be exaggerated.

I do not intend to review here the history of the schemata that preceded the definitive vote but will consider only the points that have to do with revelation. This analysis is all the more important, since it was the first time that a council had systematically studied the nature and specific characteristics of this prime and fundamental Christian reality. A constant of all Christian life and theological discourse, it was nevertheless the last to be examined. In philosophy, the same is true of the concepts of existence, action, and knowledge. We live by these realities before subjecting them to critical reflection.

I shall use the first chapter of *Dei Verbum* as a general framework for my study of the text. I shall highlight the points that are original when compared with those in preceding documents.

2. Change of Perspective

a. In contradistinction to Vatican I, which spoke first of God's revelation through creation, then of the historical revelation, Vatican II reversed the perspective and began with the personal revelation of God and salvation in Jesus

Christ. This was a first general working plan, i.e., a consideration of the explanatory data before looking at what was unexplained. Having affirmed the fact of revelation, the council stated that it was essentially a divine initiative and a pure act of grace like all the rest of the work of salvation: "We announce to you the eternal life which was with the Father, and has appeared to us" (*DV* 1). "In his goodness and wisdom, God chose to reveal himself" (*DV* 2). "God sent his Son" to tell human beings "the innermost realities about God" (*DV* 4). Revelation is beyond all human demands and constraints. The fact that the God who is an invisible and a pure spirit has decided to reveal himself to human beings in this way, in an economy of flesh and language, is characteristic of his unpredictable love. As an epiphany of God in Jesus Christ (*DV* 4), revelation is a vertical light thrown on the mystery of God and on human destiny (*DV* 2). It is not human beings who are the parameter of God and dictate to him the ways in which he should act, but the word of God that asks for "the obedience of faith" (*DV* 5). It is important to remind people today that Christianity is not a more noble form of humanism but a *divine gift*. Revelation is a work of love and proceeds from "his goodness and wisdom" (*DV* 2). Here Vatican II recalls the terms used by Vatican I, but it stresses first the goodness of God, then the wisdom of God.

b. To define the *object* of revelation, the council makes generous use of biblical categories, especially those of Paul. Instead of speaking, like Vatican I, of the decrees of the divine will, it uses the Pauline term "mystery" (*sacramentum*). "God chose to reveal himself and to make known to us the hidden purpose [*sacramentum*] of his will" (Eph 1:9; *DV* 2). In article 6 the council says again: "Through divine revelation, God chose to show forth and communicate himself." Revelation is both a self-manifestation and a self-giving of God in person. By revealing himself, God gives himself. The evident intention of the council is to personalize revelation. Before he makes something known, namely, his salvific design, God himself manifests himself. God's design, in the sense of the mystery of Paul, is that "through Christ, the Word made flesh, man has access to the Father, in the Holy Spirit and comes to share in the divine nature" (*DV* 2). The

divine plan, expressed in terms proper to interpersonal relations, includes the three main mysteries of Christianity: Trinity, incarnation, and grace. Revelation is essentially a revelation of persons: the revelation of the mystery of the life of three divine persons, the revelation of the mystery of the person of Christ, and the revelation of our life as adoptive children of the Father. This revelation appears in its trinitarian dimension. The description of the object of revelation in its threefold personalist, trinitarian, and christocentric nature gives the text a richness and resonance that contrast with the formulation of Vatican I, which spoke of revelation without any explicit and direct mention of Christ, except by way of a reference to the Epistle to the Hebrews.

c. After affirming the existence and the object of revelation, the council outlines its nature: "Through this revelation, therefore, the invisible God (cf. Col 1:15; 1 Tm 1:17) out of the abundance of his love speaks to men as friends (cf. Ex 33:11; Jn 15:14–15) and lives among them (cf. Bar 3:38), so that he may invite and take them into fellowship with himself" (*DV* 2). To define revelation, therefore, the council retains the analogy of language, present throughout the OT and NT, in the patristic and medieval tradition, and in the documents of the magisterium. Language is the higher form of exchange between intelligent beings, used by one individual to address another in order to communicate with him or her. The terms used (*accessum habere, consortes fieri, alloqui, conversari, invitare, suscipere*) all point in the direction of a dialogue with encounter as its aim. These realities acquire an unsuspected dimension when the Word of God in person assumes human flesh and language in Christ, and the Word of God becomes human among human beings and converses with them. By the Word, transcendence becomes proximate to us. These analogies of language and encounter should not be treated lightly, like one more human attempt, among so many others, to translate the ineffable. Instead we are dealing with revealed analogies, based on the incarnation, used by the inspired texts, and therefore to be considered within the very core of the revelation that articulates them. Revelation initiates a long dramatic dialogue between God and human beings that is carried on over the centuries and reaches all human beings. Seeing is initiated through language; the movement is from hearing to believing, then to seeing.

d. God revealed himself, then, in order to invite human beings to a communion of divine life and with God to "share in the divine nature" (*DV* 2). That is the purpose of revelation. Revelation is the work of love and pursues a program of love ("ex abundantia caritatis . . . tamquam amicos . . . ut ad societatem secum"). God enters into communication with human beings and initiates them into the mystery of divine intimate life with a view to a sharing and communion in that life. The council increases the number of scriptural quotations and references so that we understand revelation as the manifestation of God's *agapē*.

3. The Economy of Revelation

As yet the analogy of language-and-meeting that is used to represent revelation says nothing about the actual "attitude" that God assumes to enter into personal contact with human beings. There are, indeed, many ways of communicating between people (gestures, actions, words, images, symbols, articulated or graphic signs, etc.). Therefore it is consonant with an understanding of revelation to attempt to describe its economy.

God addresses human beings, creatures of flesh and mind located in time, and communicates with them by means of history and the incarnation. This is the first time that a document of the extraordinary magisterium has described the actual expression of the economy of revelation in this way, by representing it in the active phase of its inception. Here, too, Vatican II goes beyond Vatican I, which describes revelation as a vertical action giving rise to a doctrine but scarcely touches on history. Vatican II, in describing the economy of revelation as occurring by the combined action of "deeds and words having an inner unity" (*DV* 2), keeps its distance from the two unilateral conceptions of revelation. The first, represented by W. Pannenberg (*Offenbarung als Geschichte* [Göttingen, 1961]), reduces revelation to an opaque tissue of events and all but sheds the *verba* that interpret them and enunciate their true meaning. The second was current in preconciliar Catholic theology, which showed an invincible tendency to confuse the word-revelation with revelation by way of articulated discourse, thus reducing revelation to a superior form of gnosis.

The council, by resorting to the pair *gesta-verba*, expresses the all-encompassing nature of revelation. Events and interpretation, works and words, form an organic and indissociable whole; it is an economy that reaches its fullness in Christ, the Word . . . made flesh . . . who dwells among us. It should also be noted that *gesta* has a more personalist resonance than *facta*. It also has its equivalent in the related phrase *opera et verba*, works and words, which always emanate from a personal center (*DV* 2 and 4). These gestures or indissociable works of God are, e.g., in the OT, the exodus, the covenant, the founding of the royal line, the exile and captivity, and the restoration. In the NT, they are the actions of the life of Christ, especially his preaching, miracles, examples, and passion. The words are the words of Moses and the prophets who interpret the divine gesture in history. They are also the words of Christ himself stating the meaning of his actions. Finally, they are the words of the apostles, witnesses, and authorized interpreters of the life of Christ.

The council then briefly explains how deeds and words are mutually dependent and assist one another. "The deeds wrought by God in the history of salvation manifest and confirm the teaching and realities [God's salvific plan and actions] signified by the words." Thus, deliverance from the Egyptian yoke manifests the intervention of the omnipotent and saving God but at the same time confirms the promise that Yahweh made to Moses to save his people. The cure of the paralytic manifests the liberating power of Christ and simultaneously confirms the words of the Son of Man, who claims to remit sins. The resurrection of Christ manifests his sovereign rule over life and death but simultaneously confirms the truth of his testimony and the reality of his mission as Son of the Father who has come to save human beings from sin and death. The words, in their turn, "proclaim the deeds, and clarify the mystery contained in them" (*DV* 2). The events and actions, admittedly, are already replete with meaning; thus the liberation of a people and a cure are already "significant."

But works and events always run the risk of

ambiguity, of partial or equivocal interpretation. These, however, are words intended to dissipate that ambiguity and to disclose the authentic meaning, the mysterious profundity, that God intends. The meaning of the event matures in the word. Without the words of Moses, who in the name of God interprets the migration of Israel as a liberation anticipating a covenant, would that event have been so very different from so many other even bigger migrations that took place over the centuries? Without Moses, the event would not be replete with the fullness of meaning that makes it the basis of the religion of Israel. In the NT, though Christ's merciful actions superbly express his love for humankind, his death remains open to various interpretations. It is the word of Christ, extended by that of the apostles, which discloses for us the unprecedented dimension of that death and presents for our faith the event itself together with its salvific implications. The events are replete with a religious meaning that the words are intended to proclaim and illumine.

This intimate union between works and words is clearly structural and not chronological in nature. Sometimes, there is a simultaneity of event and word; at other times, the event precedes or follows the word. We should note once again that the proportion of works and words can vary considerably. In the historical books, the events prevail, whereas in the wisdom books and in the Sermon on the Mount, the word is dominant. By stressing the works and words as constitutive elements of revelation, the council underlines their historical and sacramental nature. God intervenes in history and utters the meaning of his intervention. He acts and comments on his action. This general structure of revelation is affirmed by the council on five occasions (DV 2, 4, 14, 17) and suffices to distinguish it from any other form of knowledge—philosophical, mythic, metatemporal, or metaspatial.

This revelation allows the profound truth about God and humanity to shine forth in Christ for our contemplation. In Christ, indeed, we learn who God is: i.e., the Father who created us and loves us as his children; the Son and Word who invites us to become adoptive sons and daughters of our Father in Christ. This anthropological character of revelation is expressed much more clearly in the Constitu-

tion Gaudium et Spes: "The truth is that only in the mystery of the incarnate Word does the mystery of man take on light" (22). It is by Christ, "the Mediator and . . . fullness of revelation" (DV 2), that human beings manage to understand themselves and surpass themselves. Christ is the new man (GS 22), the perfect man, who alone is able to make human beings more human (GS 41).

After considering the internal structure of revelation, the council examines its historical development. Dei Verbum in fact distinguishes between two aspects of the dual manifestation of God. The first, by which God gave human beings "a permanent testimony" of his existence, is inscribed in the universe that he created (Rom 1:19–20). The council does not call this divine manifestation "revelation"—henceforth a technical term for the historical revelation—but a "self-testimony" of God: about divine existence, power and majesty, addressed to all people. If we insist on using the term "revelation" to designate this testimony about existence, it seems permissible to speak of a "cosmic" revelation, to distinguish it from the "historical" revelation.

Though the council does not go into any detail about the relation between these two divine manifestations, it nevertheless states that the very God who manifested himself to human beings by his creative Word is the same God who, "planning to make known the way of heavenly salvation, . . . manifested himself to our first parents" and therefore by means of a historical revelation in time (DV 3). By speaking of the cosmic revelation as of a testimony about God himself, and of the historical revelation as the way to heavenly salvation, the text allows the judgment that, in the mind of the conciliar fathers, the testimony to the existence of God, and his recognition by humanity, also constitutes a way of salvation, even though partial and incomplete, and awaiting a higher manifestation of God—one, that is, of a supernatural order.

To be sure, revelation in the strict sense begins with the historical revelation, the stages of which the council describes, referring only to the high points. After the fall of our first parents, God granted them the hope of a salvation to come: this light of salvation, cited by Genesis, is the proto-gospel. With the promise, whose salvific implications are universal, the history of salvation is begun, and God will not omit anyone from this "higher salvation." "To those who by patiently doing good seek for glory and honor and immortality, he will give eternal life" (Rom 2:6–7). This is an allusion to the inward testimony of the conscience, which God has inscribed in human hearts and which is the equivalent for pagans of the Mosaic law. This grace of salvation given to all human beings awaits the most explicit summons of the historical revelation. The text says in fact. "Suo autem tempore," i.e., at the time chosen by him, God summoned Abraham to establish a great people (Gn 12:2). After the patriarchal age God taught this people through Moses and the prophets (*DV* 3; *LG* 9). He revealed himself to them "through words and deeds" (*DV* 14). He taught them to recognize God as a Father who takes care of his children, as a very just Judge, and to expect the promised savior (*DV* 3). The essential revelation of the OT is both promise and instruction. Over the centuries, God formed his people in this way and traced out the paths of the gospel. Israel knew God not abstractly but by experiencing the way of God in history.

4. The Centrality of Jesus Christ

In article 4 the council returns to its affirmation of Christ as "Mediator and . . . fullness of revelation," but now in a *historical* perspective (Heb 1:1). After having persisted as fragments of a discourse, the word reaches wholeness and perfection. Christ is the summit of revelation because he is the Son sent by the Father, as his eternal Word, to dwell among us and to tell us about the innermost realities about God (*DV* 4). The revelatory function of Christ originates in his function as Son and Word of God within the Trinity. "Jesus Christ, therefore, the *Word* made flesh, sent as 'a man to men,' 'speaks the *words* of God' (Jn 3:34), and completes the work of salvation which his Father gave him to do" (*DV* 4). This association of the Word with the words that it utters by way of the flesh and language marvelously emphasizes the Son of God's entry into history and into the human dimension, making use with full entitlement of the human condition and its means of expression. The Word, who is a spirit, becomes one of us, a human being among human beings, sent to humanity to meet them at their own level, by means of human words that are simultaneously the Word of God. Since Christ is thus the Son

of the Father and the eternal Word, it follows that revelation must reach its fullness, its realization (*complendo*) and perfection (*perficit*), in him.

The constitution then applies what was said in article 2 to the general structure of revelation. Christ exercised his revelatory function "through his whole work of making himself present and manifesting himself: through his deeds, his signs and wonders, but especially through his death and glorious resurrection from the dead and final sending of the Spirit of truth" (*DV* 4). Christ is the epiphany of God. Revelation through Christ, the incarnate Word, sets to work all the resources of human expression, both *facere* and *docere*, in order to manifest the Son of God and, in him, the Father, to us. The incarnation of the Son, understood in a concrete sense, is revelation. The entire human existence of Christ (action, gestures, attitudes, behavior, words) is a perfect way of revealing the Son and, in him, the Father.

The originality of *Dei Verbum* is to present Christ simultaneously as the Revealer and as the Sign that allows him to be identified as such. The signs of revelation are not external to Christ. They are Christ himself in the radiance of his power, holiness, and wisdom. In this radiance we see his glory as the Son. We move directly from the reflection to the source. All this radiance of the being and action of Christ constitutes a "divine testimony." Christ "perfected revelation" and confirms it by revealing that "God is with us to free us from the darkness of sin and death, and to raise us up to life eternal" (*DV* 4).

The last sentence in the paragraph appears as a conclusion of everything that has been said about Christ. He is the eternal Word of God, the only Son of the Father, sent to human beings to reveal to them the intimate life of God, the Epiphany of the Father (*DV* 4), in whom "the full revelation of the supreme God is brought to completion" (*DV* 7). Therefore the economy he brings with him cannot be thought of as merely transient. It is "definitive" and "will never pass away"; i.e., it will never be replaced by another, more perfect one. "We now await no further public revelation before the glorious manifestation of our Lord Jesus Christ" (*DV* 4). Since God has uttered his only Word for us, what more can he say? What more can there be than his only Son? Here the NT is duly *novum et defini-*

tivum. Jesus Christ is the last word of revelation. In him everything is accomplished, both salvation and its manifestation.

Of course, this does not exclude "private revelations" with a particular purpose, addressed to particular individuals. Above all, it does not exclude an increasingly profound assimilation and a increasingly rich and adequate formulation of the mystery that has been revealed. This second process, whose implications are incommensurable, nevertheless differs from the process of revelation as given, which constitutes all others. In this respect, Christ is both an end and a beginning. What progress, for example, was made in the understanding of revelation, between Vatican I and Vatican II.

5. Faith, Response to Revelation

We believe in the God who reveals. This Revelation itself constantly affirms (Rom 1:5; 16:26; 2 Cor 10:5–6; Eph 1:13; 1 Cor 15:11; Mk 16:15–16), as do the documents of the magisterium (DS 2778, 3008, 3542). Revelation and faith are realities that meet and answer one another. The revelation described by Vatican II is the initiative of the living God and a manifestation of his personal love. God comes toward humanity and condescends to open up to human beings the secrets of his intimate life, looking for a reciprocal love. Human beings, for their part, turn to God through faith and open up to him in friendship. The council says explicitly that by faith "man entrusts his whole self freely to God, offering 'the full submission of intellect and will to God who reveals,' and freely assenting to the truth revealed by him" (*DV* 5). The council therefore avoids two incomplete notions of faith: the conception of a faith-as-homage, almost devoid of content, and the depersonalized conception of a faith-as-assent to a doctrine. Authentic Christian faith is both gift and assent.

The human response to revelation is not the result of a mere human action but is a gift of God. It is not enough to hear the teaching of the gospel, for the action of prevenient grace is needed, which moves us to belief (*ad credendum*) and enables us to believe (*in credendo*). God, through his grace, has to "co-naturalize" us to the mystery to which the gospel introduces us, for how could we, of ourselves, open ourselves to this unheard-of word of the Quite

Other? This action of grace is described subsequently in more biblical terms. It is a matter of the assistance of the Holy Spirit (DS 3009), who moves the hearts of human beings and converts them to God, enlightens their intellects, and shapes the capabilities of their desire (DS 3010, 377). On several occasions Scripture emphasizes this action of grace that opens the human spirit to the light from above (Mt 11:25; 16:17; Acts 16:14; 2 Cor 4:6) and draws human beings to Christ (Jn 6:44). This inward action is the "testimony of the Spirit" (1 Cor 5:6), who takes effect within so that people recognize and confess the truth of Christ. The more profound understanding of revelation is also ascribable to the Spirit and his gifts (*DV* 5). In the movement of human beings toward faith, it is the Spirit who opens the mind to the new world of the gospel. Within faith it is also the Spirit who develops the penetrative power of the intellect (the gift of intelligence) and schools the faithful to understand by the ways of love (gift of wisdom), by infusing them with an affective agreement that co-naturalizes them to the gospel.

Having begun with a statement of loyalty to Vatican I, the first chapter of *Dei Verbum* closes by recalling the teaching and terms of Vatican I. This process of literary inclusion adds scarcely anything to what has already been said but represents a compromise intended to satisfy proponents of the former viewpoint. From articles 2 and 4 we know that revelation is both manifestation and communication, and that its object is God himself and his plan of salvation. This final paragraph nevertheless adds two interesting points. First, it splits the *revelare* of Vatican I, which becomes *manifestare* and *communicare*, thus aligning Vatican I with Vatican II. It also emphasizes—with a gravity justified by the context of contemporary atheism—the fact that it is possible to know God by the exercise of human reason reflecting on the world, because the created world offers incontestable evidence of its creator. On the other hand, though mysteries in the true sense remain the privileged object of revelation, the council remarks that we must also attribute to revelation the fact that religious truths accessible to reason can easily be known by all people "with solid certitude, and with no trace of error" (*DV* 6).

Finally, I summarize the significant points of *Dei Verbum*: First, the council considers in an ordered way all the essential aspects of revelation: nature, object, purpose, economy, progress, instruction, the central position of Christ, the summit of the history of salvation and of revelation, God revealing and revealed, self-testifying and self-identifying, the decisive and definitive nature of the Christ-revelation, acceptance by faith, and a more profound understanding under the influence of the Spirit. Second, the exposition is calm and profoundly religious and expressed in biblical categories (there are thirty-two references to Scripture, notably to Paul and John). Indeed, all the basic texts are represented. Third, the personalist, trinitarian, christological perspective, and of course the anthropological dimension, are present throughout. Fourth, on the basis of *Dei Verbum* we can define revelation as the self-manifestation and self-giving of God, in and through a historical economy, culminating in Jesus Christ, the author, object, center, mediator, fullness, and sign of the revelation that he in person is. Christ is the crown of this vast cathedral with the two Testaments as its arches. It is by way of faith in Christ and his gospel that we enter into the life of the Father, Son, and Spirit. Henceforth revelation in its active and objective aspect is a technical term that we know cannot be used loosely and irrelevantly.

The Constitution *Dei Verbum* is an unusually rich and powerful text. We surely owe this splendid result to the many-sided provocations of rationalism. Nevertheless, all the evidence was already to hand in the data of Scripture and patristic tradition. Because of its distance from its sources, however, the theology of revelation gradually became impoverished and eventually ran dry.

Bibl. *AAS* 58 (1966): 817–36; C. REYMONDON and L. A. RICHARD, *Vatican II au travail* (Paris, 1965); G. BAUM, "Vatican's Constitution on Revelation: History and Interpretation," *TS* 28 (1967): 51–75; U. BETTI, E. FLORIT, A. GRILLMEIER, A. KERRIGAN, R. LATOURELLE, R. RANDELLINI, O. SEMMELROTH, *Commento alla Costituzione sulla Divina Rivelazione* (Milan, 1966); P. GRELOT, "La Constitution sur la Révélation," *Études* 324 (1966): 99–113, 233–46; R. LATOURELLE, "La Révélation et sa transmission selon la Constitution Dei verbum," *Greg* 47 (1966): 5–40; id., "Le Christ, Signe de la Révélation selon la Constitution Dei Verbum," *Greg* 47 (1966): 685–709; id., *Theology of Revelation* (Staten Island, N.Y., 1966), 453–88; id., "Vatican II et les signes de la Révélation," *Greg* 49

(1968): 225–52; I. DE LA POTTERIE, "La vérité de la Sainte Écriture et l'histoire du salut d'après la Constitution dogmatique Dei Verbum," *NRT* 98 (1966): 149–69; O. SEMMELROTH and M. ZERWICK, *Vatikanum II über das Wort Gottes* (Stuttgart, 1966); G. H. TAVARD, "Commentary on De Revelatione," *Journal of Ecumenical Studies* 3 (1966): 1–35; J.-P. TORRELL, "La Constitution Dei Verbum," *RThom* 74 (1966): 63–85; H. HOLSTEIN, "La Constitution sur la divine Révélation," *Bible et Vie chrétienne* 73 (1967): 43–59; J. RATZINGER, A. GRILLMEIER, B. RIGAUX, "Vatican II," *LTK*, 497–583; K. MCNAMARA, "Divine Revelation," *ITQ* 34 (1967): 3–19; R. SCHUTZ and M. THURIAN, *Das Wort Gottes auf dem Konzil* (Freiburg/Basel/Vienna, 1967); B. D. DUPUY, ed., *La Révélation divine*, 2 vols. (Paris, 1968); A. ANTÓN, "Revelación y Tradición: Gesta et Verba sus elementos constitutivos," *EE* 43 (1968): 225–58; L. ALONSO-SCHÖKEL, ed., *Comentarios a la constitución sobre la divina Revelación* (Madrid, 1969); H. WALDENFELS, *Offenbarung: Das Zweite Vatikanische Konzil auf dem Hintergrund der neueren Theologie* (Münster, 1969); H. DE LUBAC, R. LATOURELLE, M. PHILIPPON, *Essor et permanence de la Révélation* (Paris, 1970); L. PACOMIO, *Dei Verbum: Genesi della Costituzion sulla divina Rivelazione* (Rome, 1971); C. M. MARTINI, L. PACOMIO, eds., *I Libri di Dio* (Rome, 1975); R. LATOURELLE, "Il Vaticano II e il tema della Rivelazione," in J. FEINER and M. LÖHRER, eds., *MystSal* 1 (2nd ed.; Brescia, 1967); H. WALDENFELS, "Das Offenbarungsverständnis auf dem 2. Vatikanischen Konzil," *Handbuch der Dogmengeschichte*, vol. 1, fasc. 1b, 193ff.; G. LAFONT, "La Constitution Dei Verbum et ses antécédents préconciliaires," *NRT* 110 (1988): 58–73.

René LATOURELLE

LUBAC, Henri de

The French theologian Henri de Lubac became known worldwide through his contributions to the ongoing development of Catholicism and to his engagement with issues regarding modern atheism, the church, and exegesis. Above all, his studies on the problem of the *"surnaturel"* led to debates and criticisms, as well as to his suspension in 1950 from his teaching duties in fundamental theology at the Facultés Catholiques de Lyon. His participation as a council theologian in the Second Vatican Council, along with his ultimate appointment to the cardinalate, signified official recognition of his person and his work. From 1929, when, as successor to Albert Valensin, he took over the professorship in apologetics at Lyon, de Lubac's activity was devoted to fundamental theology. This was at a time when the church, through *Deus Scientiarum Dominus* was not only giving new external form to its institutions of theological training, but was preparing to support a new synoptic view arising from the internal connectedness of Christian truth. At any rate, from the very start of his teaching activities, and because he was concerned to be able to fulfill his task as a theologian, de Lubac engaged in fundamental reflection on the status of apologetics. Up to then, apologetics had often been regarded as a kind of philosophical and historical task in an area precursory to theology, a narrow perspective within which a whole series of difficulties was generated. H. de Lubac was of the opinion that these difficulties could, in principle, be dealt with if Catholic apologists affirmed their standpoint of faith and integrated it consciously and explicitly into their task. That, for him, was fundamental theology. He was able to show that the advantage supposedly accruing to traditional apologetics from sharing a common basis with its opponents was an illusion, which also explained the ineffectualness of the old apologetics among those at whom it was actually aimed. H. de Lubac nonetheless took the task of apologetics itself quite seriously; he was just of the view that it could not be performed in the traditional way and under the customary presuppositions. This insight proved fully exemplary regarding the nature of his subsequent contributions, insofar as his works show a constant striving to overcome false distinctions, to replace ineffectual programs with better ones, and to respect the given interconnections between things. An initial field of activity for such strivings presented itself when he was appointed to teach the study of religion. Encounter with the various world religions, and with the mission as understood in the thirties, gave him occasion— at a time when he was assimilating observations and impulses from P. Teilhard de Chardin and J. Monchanin—to inquire into the nature and claim of Catholicism in such a way that approaches and possible connections would come to light. Catholicism offers scope for all genuine values, so that conceiving of Christian faith merely as a religious alternative—with the implication that Christianity must absolutely replace whatever had previously constituted the life of a non-Christian and would be discardable simply through conversion—cannot correspond to the gospel itself. Buddhism, in particular, more and more won de Lubac's respect, a fact which he later underscored publicly through detailed studies. Above all, it was very important to assure Asians who were interested in the Christian faith that they would not have to renounce any of their traditional values in order to become Christians.

With this intention, de Lubac developed, in the context of discussion with P. Charles, a new conception of Christian mission and its theological foundation. It was based on a view about the origin of religion that seemed novel to some. In its perspective, Christianity appeared as a broadening and comprehensively enriching force, as a "Catholic" reality in the original sense of the word, which bridges over constrictions and oppositions. For de Lubac, this viewpoint bore directly on the distinction—so decisive precisely for religious life—between Christian existence in the personal, individual sense and in the social sense. In 1936, as one of the first to do so, he spoke of the social character of Christian dogma, thereby initiating the reflections that he summed up, in the series "Théologies d'occasion" (1984), as "political theology."

Conversion and becoming a Christian are thus understood as events in a community whose message cannot be sustained without that community. Accordingly, redemption through Jesus Christ applies to humanity and the world, rather than to the individual soul taken in exclusion. That this entailed giving a new accentuation to a series of traditional interpretations was not at once fully clear; but to readers of de Lubac's *Catholicisme* (Paris, 1938)—his first book summarizing his earlier essays and reducing them to a common denominator—the difference in outlook and treatment was immediately obvious. It resulted from a theological deepening of those topics which, since the time of the Reformation, had been treated in a very superficial, juridical way, and whose theological significance had, in the process, been gradually forgotten. This program of theological deepening, because it was discussed almost solely in social and legal terms, necessarily had a quite specific effect on the image of the church. In such a framework, however, the quality of Catholicity could be accommodated only in the sense of numerical and geographical expansion, i.e., in a sense reduced to positive actualities. With the historical study *Corpus mysticum: L'Eucharistie et l'Église au Moyen Âge* (Paris, 1939), de Lubac had contributed, in his fashion, to the elaboration of a theological image of the church, although for having done so he later had to endure harsh criticism. Nonetheless, in his focus on the ties between church and Eucharist, he went right to the theological center of the communion of the faithful. At the same time, he thereby exposed the root from which the life of the church is constantly nourished and derives its decisive inner structure. The author of these works was obviously not always fully aware, at the time, of their fundamental-theological significance; a series of external circumstances contributed to his choice of particular themes. Still, he always did this in such a way that something of consequence for fundamental theology was generated, whose importance not infrequently became estimable only later on. The political situation during the Second World War meant that, for de Lubac, other questions came immediately to the fore: on the French side, Marxist ideas exercised a certain influence, while on the German side, National Socialism likewise aimed at undermining faith and Christianity. The question of atheism posed itself in a new way at that time, because the wider masses, and no longer just the intellectuals, were affected by it. De Lubac's scholarly articles, which he subsequently brought out as *The Drama of Atheist Humanism*, served the purpose of resistance. At the same time, he took quite seriously the humanistic impulse and spiritually oriented approach that he believed he discerned in these atheists. It was thus no matter of rational refutation of abstract theoretical views. This explains the choice of authors to whom, in this connection, de Lubac turned his attention. Nietzsche, Comte, and Dostoyevsky are not the names that come first to mind when the question of modern atheism is raised. But they represent a movement which, along with its humanistic concern, chooses a spiritual approach, and to that extent constitutes a challenge that had been completely ignored by classical Christian apologetics.

For this reason, de Lubac was also aware that a positive process of guidance toward the reality of God was required in order to counter the creeping dissolution of faith in God. Exposing the nature of an atheistic humanism in all its tragedy was only one part of the task to be accomplished. He inquired into the *Causes de l'atténuation du sens du sacré* (1942) and, at the end of the war, brought out his essay "De la connaissance de Dieu," from which issued, in 1956, the book *Sur les chemins de Dieu*—a work to be read, and reflected on, as a positive counterpart to *The Drama of Atheist Humanism* (New York, 1949). Only then is it understandable why the question of God is not simply broached and dealt with in the customary manner here, but rather, in such a way as to become a means of spiritual and existential guidance for human beings, who are taken seriously as regards all their special relevant difficulties. Admittedly, this book, like most of de Lubac's larger publications, grew out of a collection of individual essays, yet in such a way that its internal unity and coherence strike the reader as unquestionable and required by the nature of the subject. Because the element of inner cohesiveness is so strong, discovery of the fact that these books were not conceived and composed as one unified project is likely to cause surprise. As well, however, the way that the themes are mutually interlinked is astonishing. H. Urs VON BALTHASAR rightly spoke of de Lubac's "organic life's work." Nevertheless, for present purposes, everything turns on correctly identifying the core of this organic unity so as to comprehend the meaning of the whole.

Some have claimed that the core of de Lubac's thought coincides with his famous efforts to grasp the *The Mystery of the Supernatural* (1946), which primarily occasioned the above-mentioned difficulties for him. Certainly these inquiries and reflections are concerned with determining the nature of the concrete relationship of God to humanity and humanity to God, a false view of which, according to de Lubac, is one of the main preconditions for the intellectual possibility of modern atheism. He is convinced that, until the advent of the modern age, all humans were, in one way or another, so religious in outlook that the existence of a world and humanity without God, or something godly, was unthinkable. Only after the idea of *natura pura* emerged in theology and led to an intellectual system for conceiving the relationship between God and humanity did the distant possibility arise of an existence assumed to contain its entire meaning in itself, rather than in a relationship pointing inherently beyond it. This new discovery explains de Lubac's decisive struggle against the system of *natura pura,* in the pursuit of which, to be sure, he was also able to bring sufficient inner-theological arguments to bear. For this reason, *Surnaturel* is logically linked to the works and publications on modern atheism and modern approaches to God. A main factor in the development, in the sixteenth century, of the system of *natura pura* was, according to de Lubac, the medieval separation of spirituality and theology, of existential relevance to life and theoretical formulation of religious reflection. This separation allowed theology to generate a conceptual system that was logically consistent in itself, a total body of rational exposition to be judged by linguistic, philosophical, and historical standards, for which relevance to life or to any reality beyond the rational sphere was not of decisive importance. De Lubac's critics have failed to grasp these interrelationships, and have usually tried to examine and evaluate his statements on the basis of positions quite dissimilar to his. From a historical standpoint, to be sure, scarcely any significant criticisms could be made of his studies; hence all the more effort was devoted to criticizing them from the standpoint of systematic positions that, in de Lubac's view, stemmed precisely from the idea of *natura pura.* He himself felt that these criticisms were not really applicable; but he also had to dispute, above all, that they were actually able—in accordance with their general intent—to establish with certainty the fact of the gratuitous nature of grace. The enormous energy expended on these reflections did not lead to the desired result; rather, it generated, at best, some auxiliary constructs from which—assuming that certain, but still decidedly questionable, hypotheses were made— even de Lubac did not withhold qualified validity.

Personally, he regarded the separation between theology and spirituality, which extends all the way back to the Middle Ages, as having particularly serious consequences, even assuming that it had not led to the system of *natura pura.* From his studies of the history of religion, and particularly his research on Buddhism, he recognized the importance of spiritual life for religious conviction. He therefore occupied himself extensively with questions about mysticism and spiritual experience, but also with the problem of its reliable documentation and interpretation. In this connection, he was less concerned with remarkable manifestations than with existential experiences of Christian faith that were accessible and familiar to all. For it is through these that the precise significance of religious statements and creeds becomes clear, which means that religious language must not simply be isolated and studied, or used, as if it were complete in itself. De Lubac was forced by circumstances to probe these insights more concretely in his *The Religion of Teilhard de Chardin* (1962) and *Teilhard de Chardin: The Man and His Meaning* (1964); for Teilhard's religious statements, measured against narrow criteria of what constitutes a valid form of statement, were strongly contested and repeatedly misunderstood. The study on *Claudel et Péguy* (1974) can also be classed with efforts of this kind, since it is similarly concerned with religious statements that, by the standards of rigid orthodoxy, appear problematic. The connection between mysticism and language—two aspects of present-day fundamental theology—probably came to be discussed by de Lubac largely as a result of external factors and accidental circumstances, yet this served to deepen the studies and reflections that had long preoccupied him.

Quite obviously, e.g., one must regard his four-volume work *Exégèse médiévale* (1959–64) as the most comprehensive study resulting from his scholarly research activity. If *Histoire et Esprit: L'intelligence de l'Écriture d'après Origène* (1950) is placed alongside this, then it quickly becomes evident that the study and interpretation of Holy Scripture is the central concern in de Lubac's creative work, traces of which can be uncovered, beyond the context of these volumes, throughout the whole of his life. The question is not posed and treated as a mere theological source among others, but as an attempt to bring out, against the background of the spiritual presuppositions current at specific times, the nature of Scripture as a testimony to revelation. What did the people of antiquity and the Middle Ages obtain for their faith from their reading and use of Scripture? Why was Scripture able to offer them such sustenance? What implications does this have for present-day approaches to God's word in Scripture? Significantly, the central chapter of

Catholicisme was already devoted to the topic of "The Interpretation of Scripture." This is the perspective from which de Lubac's total work must be interpreted. Here, consideration must naturally also be given to tradition, which does not, however, come to expression under that heading in de Lubac's thought, but rather—in a number of his contributions—as part of his treatment of the topic of "the church." This is of great importance for the understanding of his writings. Since further points about his approaches to a theological understanding of the church have already been made above, there is no need to add to this here. For de Lubac, these main concerns of his work as a theologian converged in his collaboration in the Second Vatican Council and its Dogmatic Constitutions *Lumen Gentium*, on the church, and *Dei Verbum*, on divine revelation. Above all, the Constitution on revelation, with its foreword and first chapter, was given detailed commentary by him in "La révélation divine" (1968) and highlighted in its significance. From the very first in this document, H. de Lubac lays stress on the personal character of God's word and on the christological focus of both the occurrence of revelation and its experience and transmission. His own endeavors to formulate a fundamental theology that is appropriate to present-day thinking and also capable, under existing conditions, of opening the way to faith and arousing understanding of its message he finds to be confirmed, yet challenged anew, by the council. For the task of providing a proper theological foundation for the truth of Christianity redefines itself in the light of the council's expanded perspectives, given that previous reductions and constrictions, previous fixations on concepts and images and rigid, almost mechanical ways of dealing with them were thereby broadened and deepened. Within this newly expanded sphere, however, one no longer pursues fundamental theology for itself alone, but becomes capable of genuine and living encounter with religious conceptions and spiritual currents whose values are fully recognized and can be made fruitful for Christianity and its task. The work has not been finished.

In his endeavors, H. de Lubac was closely linked to a number of thinkers. His work is inconceivable apart from dialogue with these associates. Only two may be mentioned here, who were undoubtedly for him the most signifi-

cant partners: Gaston Fessard (1897–1978), the philosopher, and Henri Bouillard (1908–1981), the fundamental theologian, each of whom, together with de Lubac, stimulated in a particular way the study of the philosophy of M. BLONDEL. In style of thinking and scholarly specialization, but also in temperament, they were all quite different. Nonetheless, they felt themselves impelled by similar aims in their intellectual work, so that their exchange of ideas was fruitful and enriching in more than just one respect. They were convinced that theological thought cannot get by without philosophy, a position that Bouillard emphatically defended in his great debate with K. BARTH. But they were also convinced that the way in which philosophical thought is to be utilized for theological reflection must be determined from the standpoint of Christianity. To them, the philosophy of M. Blondel seemed to offer presuppositions favorable to this, namely, in its openness and strict awareness of, and respect for, its own limitations. Blondel's immanence method promised, in today's world, not only a more convincing type of argumentation, but also the possibility of incorporating modern humanity and its self-consciousness into theological reflection. In this way, an opportunity suggested itself for fundamental ontology to overcome reservations and unjustified criticisms from the standpoint of its own truth, and also to create a basis upon which theological expositions and disciplines could build. This necessary service was underestimated in many ways, and taken too lightly, with the result that many proposals lacked anchoring in the ground of existing reality. H. de Lubac's critical warnings were usually directed against positions that seemed to him to have no solid foundation in the faith of the church. Precisely for that reason, he became increasingly mistrustful of large-scale theoretical projects and schemes. The detailed historical work from which, throughout his life, he had drawn his insights proved too wearisome for some, and was avoided or only eclectically and arbitrarily pursued. But precisely religious history is always also intellectual history, and not just a random collection of inconsequential facts or interchangeable details. If, at first glance, de Lubac is seen to be working as a historian, then he does not do so without a philosophical conception and constant intellectual reflection on his subject matter from the standpoint of mystery. In this way of proceeding, the classical methods of apologetics are fully preserved, but broadened and integrated into an ongoing process of interchange. Here, spirituality and thought are no longer disjoined and isolated; here, the intellectual realities of the modern world are taken seriously, but in such a way that Christians need not allow themselves to be intimidated, or have their viewpoint simply dictated, by them. This kind of fundamental theology is characterized by a search and by constant examination or discrimination, a process that cannot be captured in some simply convenient theoretical formula. Yet it has the advantage of being flexible enough to be capable of recognizing and meeting whatever challenges might chance to arise, and of repeatedly bringing, amidst the rapid flux of circumstances, God's word to appropriate expression.

Bibl.: K. H. NEUFELD and M. SALES, eds., *Bibliographie H. de Lubac 1925–1974* (Einsiedeln, 1974); id., "Bibliographie H. de Lubac, corrections et suppléments, 1942–1989," in H. DE LUBAC, *Théologie dans l'histoire*, vol. 2 (Paris, 1990), 408–20; H. DE LUBAC, *Mémoire sur l'occasion de mes écrits* (Namur, 1989).

Karl H. NEUFELD, S.J.

DEPOSIT OF FAITH

1. Introduction. 2. Biblical Notion. 3. Historical Perceptions. 4. Modern Catholic Teaching. 5. Ecumenical Perspectives. 6. Further Questions. (J. WICKS)

1. Introduction

A late letter of the apostolic age encouraged its readers to continue contending "for the faith delivered once for all to the saints" (Jude 3). The "deposit" is the inclusive term for this faith and way of life bequeathed by the apostles and their coworkers to the churches founded by their proclamation of the good news about Jesus Christ. The apostles left as their legacy a coherent pattern of faith, teaching, and modes of biblical interpretation, of worship and community structures of service, and of life in the world according to the word and example of the Lord Jesus. By holding to the apostolic patrimony, expressed in a special way in the NT writings, the people of God in every age sustain their faith, seek to live in holiness, and renew their perception of revealed truth (see *DV* 8). By its own virtuality, the apostolic legacy comes to be clothed in different forms in successive ages, as the church is guided by the Spirit to live according to the rule and inspiration given at the beginning. But the source and norm of the church's teaching and life remain the "deposit" left by those whom Jesus sent out as his emissaries to communicate his revelation and divine gifts.

2. Biblical Notion

In antiquity, the legal codes of both Greece and Rome stipulated the obligations of persons receiving objects or sums of money deposited by another, e.g., when the latter was leaving on a journey. The depositary was above all bound to faithful safekeeping, which excluded any personal use of the deposit. Restitution *in specie* to the owner had to be made on demand. Violation of these provisions could lead to indictment and the wrath of the gods. Administrators of religious sanctuaries were esteemed guardians of deposits, and such service redounded to the good name of the god of the sanctuary. The Twelve Tables, the earliest Roman code of laws, laid down that a negligent or otherwise unfaithful depositary must repay twice the value of the original deposit. Similar obligations of fidelity devolved upon the executor of a last will and testament, in whose care the inheritance was left, much like a deposit, but for faithful distribution to the designated beneficiaries.

The Scriptures of Israel stipulate simple laws of deposit as part of the Mosaic ordinances of the covenant of Sinai (Ex 22:6–12). When a deposit is damaged or lost, the depositary must swear on oath that he has not misappropriated what was given for his safekeeping. An unfaithful depositary must make double compensation when convicted of a breach of trust in the matter of a deposit. The ritual law of Israel set down the way in which an unfaithful depositary, upon repentance, had to make restitution to the depositor and offer an expiatory sacrifice in order to gain forgiveness of the Lord who is guarantor of the contract of deposit (Lv 5:26). The Temple itself received the deposits of the poor in sacred trust under the protection of the Lord of the same Temple (see 2 Mc 3:7–30).

Late in the first century C.E., Flavius Josephus referred to deposits in his account of the code Moses gave to regulate the Israelites' life on the land they were about to occupy. A depositary is bound by solemn obligation: "Let the recipient of a deposit esteem it worthy of custody as a sacred and divine object and let no one venture to defraud the one who entrusted it to him, . . . not even if he might thereby gain an untold amount of gold" (*Antiquities* 4.38 §285).

Against this background of the depositary's sacred obligation before God of conscientious safekeeping and faithful transmission, the Pastoral Epistles refer to the Pauline tradition as a deposit (*parathēkē*) to be maintained intact and guarded against falsification (1 Tm 6:20; 2 Tm 1:12, 14). Furthermore, Paul's onetime collaborator Timothy is himself to entrust what he has received to trustworthy persons who will then be able to transmit further what was once given over by the apostolic founder (2 Tm 2:2).

Modern scholarship views the Pastoral Epistles as insistent expressions of the normative validity of the Pauline tradition written by an unknown author in the last years of the first century C.E. The letters both reaffirm and reinterpret Paul's legacy for churches facing crises that their missionary-founder did not himself have to confront. The Pastorals update doctrine, ethics, and especially the ministerial duties of pastors, in order to ward off the subversive influence of false doctrines, myths, and alleged "knowledge" (*gnosis*), which threaten to destroy the line of continuity with Paul by which these communities have their identity as the household of God, the church of the living God" (1 Tm 3:15).

The Pastorals envisage the "deposit" as the result of Paul's many-sided founding ministry. They do not catalogue the content of Paul's deposit, but instead insist on its continuing adequacy and normativity for community life well after Paul's death. The pastors of the contemporary church are depositaries who must energetically protect the apostle's patrimony by their own fidelity in announcing his gospel (e.g., Ti 3:4–7), giving sound instruction (passim), teaching the inspired and efficacious Scriptures (1 Tm 4:3; 2 Tm 3:14–17), regulating community prayer (1 Tm 2:1–6), carefully select-

ing other ministers (1 Tm 3:1–13; 5:15–22; Ti 1:5–9; 2 Tm 2:2), and withstanding alien and subversive doctrines (1 Tm 1:3–4; 4:1–3; 6:3–5, 20–21; Ti 3:9–11; 2 Tm 2:14). The actual situation, with its potential for confusion, required authentic reformulation of certain doctrines, e.g., the meaning of the law (1 Tm 1:8–11), the universality of redemption in Christ (1:15; 2:3–7), and the value of marriage and all foods (4:1–5). Still of fundamental importance is the example of Paul's own life, both as a sinner forgiven by God's grace (1 Tm 1:12–16), and as one who suffered for the sake of the gospel (2 Tm 1:8–15; 2:3).

Thus the NT deposit is apostolic tradition in its ample and complex form, in communities for which it is the norm of faith and the source of life. Survival in the identity once given these communities now depends on fidelity to the deposit received. What Paul transmitted has in fact been realized in the life of these communities. Now, the Pastorals insist on renewed attention to keeping his deposit inviolate and transmitting it in its integrity. For such a work, human effort does not suffice and so the author expresses Paul's confidence in the divine protector of deposits (2 Tm 2:12) and in an enabling power given to the communities and their pastors: "Guard the deposit with the help of the Holy Spirit dwelling within us" (1:14; cf. 1:6–7).

Other late works of the NT share the concern that the churches remain rooted in the life-giving soil of the apostolic deposit and preserve it from contamination. In Acts, the last discourse of Paul's missionary work incisively commends his legacy to the college of elders of the church of Ephesus (20:17–35). As Paul looks to the end of his ministry (20:24), the Ephesian pastors are to look to what he had taught about repentance and faith in the Lord Jesus (20:20–21). From him they know of the entire dispensation of God and in the light of this they are to "keep watch . . . over all the flock of which the Holy Spirit has made you overseers (*episkopoi*)" (20:28). Pure Pauline doctrine is endangered by those who try to pervert the truth (20:29–30), and so renewed vigilance and careful discernment are imperative.

The Gospels of Luke and Matthew can be seen as authentic formulations of the apostolic legacy in the eighties of the first century in forms that give it definite profile in that time of turmoil. In a similar vein, what is probably the latest NT writing inveighs against false teachers (2 Pt 2), while commending rightly interpreted Scripture (1:19–21). More pointed in reference to a deposit is 2 Peter's insistence on renewed remembering of what has been transmitted as basic teaching, i.e., "the words spoken in the past by the holy prophets, and the commandment of the Lord and Savior spoken through your apostles" (3:2).

3. Historical Perceptions

Yves Congar's magnum opus on tradition surveys the shifting understandings of the apostolic deposit and its mode of presence in the church in later ages. Our presentation will be selective, relating the views of just three authors who spoke perceptively of the deposit of faith with regard to its inner constitution and its relevance for the church: Irenaeus of Lyons, Vincent of Lérins, and John Henry Newman.

Late in the second century, Irenaeus contested the legitimacy of a variety of fully developed Gnostic doctrines by appealing to the "rule of truth" received from the apostles of Christ and now accessible in the preaching and baptismal profession of faith of churches of apostolic foundation (→ RULE OF FAITH). The Gnostics, by contrast, propagate their confused myths of cosmic fallenness and redemptive knowledge in secret conventicles, whereas the single tradition coming from the apostles is preserved as a public possession in numerous churches, in which Christ's apostles had appointed fully instructed presbyters and bishops to continue their ministry of teaching. In Rome, e.g., in the church founded by Peter and Paul, one can learn of the economy of salvation in Christ and share "one and the same life-giving faith that has been preserved in the church from the apostles until now, handed down in truth" (*Adversus Haereses* 3.3.3).

Thus, at the very time the church began delimiting its official list of authentic apostolic writings (→ CANON OF SCRIPTURE), Irenaeus enunciated a correlative principle, namely, a normative pattern of faith in God the Creator, in the Son of God who in our flesh carried out the work of salvation, and in the Holy Spirit given to believers as "the earnest of incorruption, the confirming power of our faith, and the ladder of ascent to God" (3.24.1). Holding to this faith, in the church, a person can read all the Scriptures of both testaments with the firm assurance of knowing their meaning, i.e., the full range of the dispensation to which they give testimony. Outside the ambit of the apostolic and ecclesial rule of faith, the biblical texts give no solid nourishment, for they have been chopped up by the gnostic savants and their pieces forced to serve the alien purpose of illustrating their myths.

Irenaeus's "rule of truth" is present in the Scriptures, and finds right expression in the churches' catechesis and in their various patterns of professing the faith. But the rule is not simply identical with any one of these and not exhaustively stated by them. The rule gives rise to diverse expressions in different places, but "the power of the tradition (*dynamis tēs paradoseōs*) is one and the same" (1.10.2). It is not only the true meaning of apostolic teaching that these churches receive and transmit, for they also "acknowledge the same gift of the Spirit, strive to walk in the same commandments and preserve the same form of ecclesiastical constitution, and expect the same advent of the Lord and long for the same salvation of the whole person, i.e., both body and soul" (5.20.1; cf. 4.33.8).

Irenaeus thus thought in terms of a complete apostolic deposit, but, unlike the author of the Pastorals, he did not stress the duties of the episcopal depositaries. He emphasized instead the great gain accruing to believers from the legacy of the apostles, who "as in a rich depository left in the church most copiously all that pertains to the truth, so that all who wish may draw upon this source and drink the water of life" (3.4.1). The apostolic tradition of truth is in the church, where Christians believe in God's full dispensation. "The faith received from the church we do guard and protect, but it acts continually, by the Spirit of God, like a valuable deposit in a precious vessel, to rejuvenate both itself and the very vessel that contains it" (3.24.1). The apostolic deposit, in the Irenaean vision, is a comprehensive and invigorating spiritual possession, found in the milieu of the church, as a pattern of belief and way of life.

Vincent of Lérins, writing in southern Gaul in 434 C.E., is best known for formulating classical criteria for testing whether a doctrine pertains to revealed truth: "In the Catholic church, every care should be taken to hold fast to what has been believed everywhere, always, and by all" (quod ubique, quod semper, quod ab omnibus [Commonitorium 2]). Novel teachings are ruled out by their nonconformity with what has been handed on from the beginning as part of the traditional rule of faith. This rule is the "catholic and ecclesiastical sense of Scripture" (ibid.), which the decrees of general councils make known. However, Vincent makes no reference to the Council of Nicea and its dogmatic norm for understanding biblical texts on the relation of the Father and the Son. Vincent ascribes great importance to the unmasking of particular opinions as deviant by showing their divergence from a collation of the views of revered Catholic teachers whose consensus will prove the genuineness of the truth they transmit (Comm. 27–28).

Vincent does not rule out progressive development in the church, but this occurs within the strict ambit of past tradition. No tenet of Catholic dogma may be renounced, but what grows is understanding, knowledge, and wisdom in the selfsame teaching: "in eodem scilicet dogmate, eodem sensu eademque sententia" ("in the same dogma, the same meaning, the same formula," Comm. 23). However, if the deposit is taken as formulated teaching, one naturally wonders how to apply this notion of progress in the case of a new question arising in a time and culture greatly different from the apostolic age.

It is no surprise that Vincent of Lerins was much taken by the mandate given Timothy to guard the apostolic deposit. This word, for Vincent, applies in his day either to the universal church or to all its leaders, and it should instill a definite cast of mind. For the deposit "is what was entrusted to you, not what you have invented; what you have received, not what you have devised; not a matter of creativity, but of doctrine; not a private acquisition, but a public tradition; something delivered to you, not produced by you; a matter you did not create, but are to guard; not as the master, but as an adherent; not leading, but following. This deposit, he says, guard. Preserve the talent of the Catholic faith inviolate and wholly intact" (Comm. 22).

As an Anglican, John Henry Newman opposed the notion that Scripture was its own sufficient interpreter. Against the doctrinal fragmentation arising from the Protestant principle of private judgment, Newman appealed to the tradition and rule of faith derived from the apostles, by which the church grasps inerrantly the "one direct and definite sense" of revealed biblical teaching.

Writing on apostolic tradition in 1836, Newman cited 1 Timothy to show that the apostles delivered over to their successors a doctrinal deposit for further transmission. Newman cited Vincent of Lérins's explanation of depositum (see above), but added a characteristic description that points beyond an original set of dogmas. What the apostles transmitted cannot be circumscribed in documents. It was "too vast, too minute, too complicated, too implicit, too fertile, to be put in writing, at least in times of persecution; it was for the most part conveyed orally, and the safeguard against its corruption was the number and unanimity of its witnesses." The creed listed the main headings, but in the churches the substance of tradition "was manifold, various, and independent in its local manifestation" (Essays Critical and Historical [London, 1871], 1:126f.). For Newman, apostolic tradition resulted from living contact, not just indoctrination, and this resulted in the profuse body of truth that penetrates the church like its very atmosphere.

When Newman became a Roman Catholic, the amplitude and fecundity of the apostolic deposit had a central place in his reflections. His studies of the Arian crisis and of Chalcedon convinced him that revealed truth was meant to develop under the guidance of an inerrant teaching authority. As he explained in An Essay on the Development of Christian Doctrine (London, 1845), Christianity is a fact which impresses itself upon the believing mind in a way leading to a multitude of repercussions. It is dogmatic, devotional, social, and practical all at once, and no single expression serves to define it. Scripture introduces us to a vast territory that we cannot map out or describe in a single catalogue. In the time of the church, exploration of the many parts of revelation is a work of inquiry, contemplation, and the resolution of controversy. New dogmas have to be declared at times, but fundamentally they only manifest the church's newly attained awareness of what was implicit in the deposit given at the beginning.

What the apostles transmitted had its own unity and cohesion and so one perception leads in time to another. Great ideas, Newman notes, are not taken in all at once, but grow toward perfect comprehension in the course of time. Devout and enlightened minds give scope to the word of God with its expansive force, as it generates further knowledge of itself in its diverse parts and multiform relations to the different spheres of life. Scripture itself is rife with questions that the apostles did not answer in a peremptory manner. For they left many decisions to mature over time, e.g., the biblical canon, baptism for newborn infants, and forgiveness of sins committed after baptism. Answers to these issues came by gradual and homogeneous developments of the deposit. Newman saw that this dynamism for growth in explicitation of content should not be cut off by declaring any point in time to be the end of an alleged classical age. Much like the Eternal Word made flesh, so also God's revealing word has resolutely entered history.

Clearly, human minds can twist and deform revealed truth, e.g., by incautiously asserting just one doctrine to the detriment or exclusion of other truths of faith. And so Newman set forth his famous criteria or tests for sifting the doctrinal wheat from the chaff, i.e., discerning true developments from corruptions of the deposit. True doctrinal developments are preservative of the same type of doctrine found in more rudimentary formulations; they conform to certain enduring principles deeply embedded in the believing mind; they successfully assimilate other realities of value, e.g., philosophical systems; they stand in a logical relation to earlier positions, even if the development itself was a more spontaneous growth; they bring to realization earlier, fragmentary anticipations of what comes later; they act conservatively upon antecedent developments, illustrating and confirming the whole body of thought from which they arise; finally, true developments manifest chronic vigor and staying power, while corruptions quickly fade from the scene.

Newman's tests were mainly an apologetic tool for showing that later Catholic teachings stand in dynamic continuity with the original apostolic word. But they also raise the correlative question about the proper way to discover the apostolic deposit amid the great variety of what the church hands on in any given age. How is the believer to lay hold of the tradition amid the traditions? G. O'Collins (see bibliography) has proposed a way that overcomes the severe limitations of Vincent of Lérins's classicizing canon of antiquity, universality, and consensus, while not going to the other extreme of simply identifying apostolic tradition with the utterances of its living magisterial interpreter. Here the *sensus fidei*, the NT writings, and the risen Christ himself are given their due place, without denying the difficulties of rightly interpreting these realities of spirit, word, and life.

4. Modern Catholic Teaching

Between the two Vatican councils, the teaching church manifested an acute sense of being the appointed depositary of the apostolic legacy of revealed truth. What Christ and his apostles entrusted to the church for safekeeping and infallible declaration is the *Verbum Dei scriptum vel traditum*, the meaning of which one finds above all in the church's dogmatic pronouncements. Developments do occur, but the preferred way of describing doctrinal progress came from Vincent of Lérins, not John Henry Newman (see Vvatican I, *Dei Filius*; DS 3011, 3018, 3020).

The modernist crisis then elicited a powerful current of official response that shaped the normal theology of Catholic seminary instruction down to 1960 (→ Modernism). Here the deposit was seen as the summa of truths contained in Scripture and apostolic tradition. This objective doctrinal corpus was closed with the death of the last apostle and from this the church derives its teaching, commissioned as it is to preserve and render explicit the meaning of the apostolic legacy. Personal and interior factors in the spiritual lives of believers are only incidental to supernatural revelation itself, as is any notion of a historical evolution of the authentic meaning of doctrines (DS 3420–22, 3541).

In the encyclical *Humani Generis* (1950), Pope Pius XII accentuated the normative role of the hierarchical magisterium in formulating the content of the deposit for acceptance by believers and theologians. The latter must immerse themselves in the apostolic sources, but their study and teaching are strictly ancillary: "It is for them to show how the teachings of the living magisterium are found, whether explicitly or implicitly, in Sacred Scripture and the divine tradition" (DS 3886). Thus the deposit is a territory over which the hierarchical teaching authority has certain exclusive rights. "For together with these sacred sources, God gave his church the living magisterium, which is to clarify and elaborate those matters contained in the deposit of faith only obscurely or implicitly. The task of authentically interpreting the deposit was entrusted by our divine redeemer, neither to individual Christians nor to the theologians, but solely to the magisterium of the church" (DS 3886).

From 1959 to 1962 hostility to modernism and a defensive concern over independent work with the sources dominated the official preparation of materials for the Second Vatican Council. But decisive interventions by Pope John XXIII, especially his opening discourse *Gaudet Mater Ecclesia* (11 October 1962), gave Vatican II a fresh spirit and creative direction. Pope John emphatically declared the magisterium's responsibility for transmitting a doctrine of great potential benefit for people in all sectors of their lives. The church is the depositary of a message of great potential for nourishing faith in God and giving guidance and inspiration to life in this world. Clearly, the council will teach in continuity with the doctrinal corpus elaborated by previous councils. But a more efficacious communication is imperative, because the teaching itself has beneficent power in its affirmation of personal dignity and contribution to humanizing life in this world. The times call for a fresh attempt to communicate the precious deposit of saving truth, not for anxious preoccupation with condemning errors. Thus Vatican II began with an authoritative invitation to restate the church's fundamental doctrine, the deposit of faith, in a manner more likely to enhance the lives of believers and of all people of goodwill.

Vatican II's Dogmatic Constitution on the Church spoke of the deposit of faith, first, in connection with the special charism of infallibility, with the latter being essentially protective of the deposit against error and misrepresentation in solemn expressions of church teaching (*LG* 25,3). As official teachers, the bishops and the pope must, however, study attentively the prophetic and apostolic testimonies to the deposit given once for all, because their teaching does not fall from heaven as new revelation, but aims instead to clarify and to actualize the definitive revelation already given (*LG* 25.5).

The Decree on Ecumenism affirms that ongoing ecclesial reform may on occasion call for updating the manner in which doctrine is enunciated. The deposit of faith remains definitive and perennial, but its articulation by the church can stand in need of adaptation based on a better understanding of the inexhaustible early sources or the requirements of more effective communication (*UR* 6). In 1973 the Congregation for the Doctrine of the Faith commented on the issue of doctrinal reformulation. Such magisterial updating may be needed, first, because of the transcendent grandeur of the mysteries of salvation themselves, which are not fully communicated in any single expression of truth. Second, because language is a historical reality, even the most penetrating formulations can with the passage of time wane in their communicative efficacy. They thus can stand in need of complement or revision, in order to bring out more clearly that beneficent fecundity of the message of Christ transmitted by his apostles (*Mysterium Ecclesiae* 5; *EV* 4:1674–76).

Vatican II's Pastoral Constitution on the Church in the Modern World addresses itself in one chapter to human cultural development (*GS* 53–62). Clearly certain difficulties have impeded a fully creative influence of Christian and ecclesial teaching upon modern culture. Here the constitution underscores the need for theology to contribute to overcoming these obstacles by fostering better communication between the church and people of the modern world. As Pope John pointed out, the deposit and truths of faith are one thing in their meaning and substance, but the way they are formulated can develop and be made more enriching for the diverse sectors of human life (*GS* 62.2).

Vatican II's principal statements on the deposit of faith occur in chapter 2 of the Dogmatic Constitution on Divine Revelation (*DV* 7–10). Since these dense paragraphs have been treated in the commentaries on *Dei Verbum* we limit ourselves to drawing out just three points of teaching that speak in a fresh way of the apostolic deposit and its mode of presence in the church.

First, the apostolic patrimony delivered to the church is more than a doctrinal *corpus* deriving from revelation. Jesus did teach and his apostles then carried out a ministry of instruction in the churches they founded. But the apostles were personally formed as well by witnessing the works of Jesus and by their sharing of life (*conversatio*) with him. Then, in the communities of those who accepted the gospel, the apostles transmitted divine gifts by what they said, by how they lived, and by the structures (ministries, forms of worship) they instituted (*DV* 7). Their many-sided influence created an ethos that is formative of both belief and behavior: "What was handed on by the apostles comprises everything that serves to help the people of God live holy lives and grow in faith." After the apostolic age, what is handed on is a comprehensive form of shared faith and life: "The church, in her doctrine, life, and worship, perpetuates and transmits to every generation all that she herself is, all that she believes" (*DV* 8). Tradition, thus, creates a milieu of life in communion, with a multiplicity of concretizations ordered to personal formation in wisdom and holiness.

Second, although God's founding revelation is completed in Jesus and with his apostles (*DV* 4), what was given once for all is intrinsically ordered to development and progress. The apostles themselves were gradually led by the Holy Spirit to that full understanding of salvation in Christ expressed in the NT writings (*DV* 7). In the era of the church, the meaning of the apostolic deposit emerges gradually and comes progressively to expression. Over time, numerous factors influence a fully historical process of development, not the least of which is the ongoing influence of the Holy Spirit. "There is a growth in the understanding of the realities and words which have been handed down. This happens through the contemplation and study made by believers, who treasure these things in their hearts (cf. Luke 2:19, 51); the intimate understanding of spiritual things they experience, and through the preaching of those who have received through episcopal succession the sure gift of truth" (*DV* 8).

Vatican II, however, did not fall victim to smug optimism about progress in the church, for the same council stated as well the need of recurrent interventions to reform church discipline and doctrine (*UR* 6). Clearly, however, Newman has made a decisive contribution and historical modes of thought have been accepted regarding the presence of the apostolic deposit in the

church. Silently, the static classicism of Vincent of Lerins has been set aside.

Third, the importance ascribed to reflection on lived experience, taken together with the supernatural *sensus fidei* of the whole people of God (*LG* 12), manifests a notable change from the teaching of Pius XII in *Humani Generis*. The deposit, the council declares, is delivered over to the whole church as the basis and inspiration of its life in the image of the ideal apostolic community of Acts 2:42: "Sacred tradition and Sacred Scripture form one sacred deposit of the word of God, which is committed to the Church. Holding fast to this deposit the entire holy people, united with their shepherds, remain always steadfast in the teaching of the apostles, in the common life, in the breaking of the bread, and in prayer" (*DV* 10.1).

The hierarchical magisterium has a key contribution to make, namely, that of authentically interpreting the deposited word, a word, however, to which the magisterium itself is subordinate, as listener, protector, and official expositor. All official teaching proposed in the church for belief derives from the one deposit of faith given by the apostles (*DV* 10.2). Thus the magisterium is not an isolated and sovereign office, nor does it create church teaching *ex nihilo*. The deposit itself impinges on believers in a variety of ways, and is accessible through a variety of its expressions. But the dangers of imprecision arising from the very abundance of what is handed on can, when necessary, be averted by clarifying magisterial interventions. Thus the magisterium serves the ongoing contribution of the deposit to faith and life, as it critically sifts ecclesiastical and theological expressions and adapts church teaching to new situations.

A perceptive reference to the deposit was made by Pope Paul VI in his concluding discourse of Vatican II (7 December 1965). The council was now offering to the world a refurbished image of the church and, at the same time, a newly clarified, determined, and ordered presentation of the legacy received from Christ as a deposit. "This the people have over the course of centuries meditated upon; this they have assimilated, as it were, into their own flesh and blood; this they have in a way expressed by the way of life. . . . It is a living deposit, by reason of the force of divine truth and grace which constitute it, and therefore one must judge it well able to vivify whoever devoutly receives it and takes from it nourishment for life" (Conc. Vat. II, *Constitutiones, Decreta, Declarationes* [1966], 1062).

In modern Catholic teaching, the apostolic deposit is complex but life-giving, a reality of natural growth through new expressions, a family treasure that surely must be guarded in the community, but more importantly it is an abundant source to be made accessible to all who have need of its light and guidance.

5. Ecumenical Perspectives

The Eastern Orthodox doctrine of revelation is centered on the incarnation of the Son of God, his glorious resurrection, and the ongoing transformation of present life by the Holy Spirit. The church is the presence of eschatological salvation already projected into time and realized in sacramental celebration. Especially in the eucharistic synaxis, the renewed world, centered on Christ and his saints, manifests itself to the eyes of faith. Revelation and the sacraments thus bring about the deification of humankind and the world in the Holy Spirit.

Historical revelation in Christ was entrusted as a saving deposit by the apostles to the church, both in writing and as a tradition that conveyed the true sense of the Scriptures. The early councils expressed in dogmatic form the central mystery of Christ, while the Eastern fathers, down to Maximus the Confessor, expounded the same revelation synthetically and brought out the truth of human divinization by the Spirit of the risen Christ. Today tradition is actualized in the church, and in a sense is the church as the form of Christ's presence revealed to faith (Staniloe). Tradition is saving revelation complete in itself, but in time it opens up a space for our gradual appropriation in faith and for theological penetration into its essential meaning.

Western Catholic thought shares the Orthodox conviction that revelation is transmitted through Scripture read in the church in the light of tradition. But Catholicism sees the church deeply immersed in human history, where it continues to look ahead with longing for the not-yet-realized eschatological fullness of divine truth.

The apostolic gospel of Christ is for Catholics the one source of all saving truth and guidance for life (*DV* 7, restating the Council of Trent), but even in the apostolic age the gospel resulted in a wealth of instruction and different forms of belief and life in the world. This gospel and apostolic teaching must be further expressed and applied to believers' lives amid a great variety of cultures. Thus, for Catholics, dogmatic development continues to offer new expressions of the original deposit well after the close of the patristic age. Here there is room for ongoing interpretation of the deposit, both by way of spiritual experience and learned reflection, and by timely interventions of the episcopal and papal magisterium.

Protestant thought understands revelation from its center, namely, the gospel of God's prevenient mercy and his gratuitous gift of salvation *propter Christum*. This gospel created the church, and continues to do so, as the assembly of those who by faith lay hold of the evangelical message. In the midst of the earliest churches the gospel was formulated once for all in the NT Scriptures. After the apostolic age the ecclesial ministry of word and sacrament continues to communicate the gospel and so serves the calling forth of saving faith in Christ. Revelation can even be said to continue in the church, but when it occurs it does not have the normative value proper to the Bible. The biblical books retain an unsurpassable authority as the measure of truth and, more importantly, as the source of the *viva vox* of the gospel in every age.

The churches, to be sure, continue to formulate and interpret the gospel in creeds, doctrines, catechisms, and theologies. The gospel may well resound in a genuine manner in these postapostolic forms, but they are of themselves vulnerable, i.e., liable to error. In fact all ecclesial speech and action must be critically tested for its conformity to the original biblical norm of the gospel and its real contribution to fostering faith in God's gracious gifts in Christ.

The Scriptures, for Protestants, *are* the apostolic deposit, and they have their luminous center in the gospel of unmerited salvation. This gives them a self-interpreting capacity, which renders superfluous any hermeneutic of tradition or magisterium. In the influential view of Oscar Cullmann, the church of the second century C.E. recognized the danger of losing the gospel and responded by subordinating its whole life, i.e., all ecclesiastical tradition, to the clear rule of apostolic tradition expressed in the books of the NT canon. From that time on, faith may not venture with assurance outside this strictly drawn ambit of the apostolic deposit.

Catholic teaching also esteems the gospel of Christ as a message of saving efficacy and agrees that the NT has unique value as expressing apostolic preaching and faith. But Catholics are convinced that the ample gifts conveyed by the apostles form a complex unity in which the gospel is but one part. The apostolic legacy resulted in communities, i.e., in centers of corporate life illumined by teaching, inspired by living example, structured institutionally, and worshiping according to transmitted forms. The gospel is central, but is from the beginning fruitful in creating shared life and witness.

After the apostolic age the deposit developed through expressions that bring out its inherent meaning. To guard the deposit is not to retain it unchanged but to make it apply fruitfully to belief and life in every age. Transmission of revelation involves adaptation to new needs and leads to fresh perceptions of the original gift. Various factors interact to bring about such development: contemplation and reflection on experience, learned study of the biblical witness, preaching, and the magisterial activity of the bishops and the pope. On occasion, definitions formulate key points of revelation itself for acceptance by faith as part of the substance of the deposit of faith.

Catholic belief is optimistic about the potential for true growth in the church. Thus it insists on the corporate context of believers' encounters with the apostolic legacy. A whole gamut of witnesses impinge on the Christian in the community that professes its faith, celebrates the memorial of Christ, and seeks to serve all humankind. Only in such a network of interaction, according to the Catholic vision, does the integral meaning of the original apostolic deposit come to light.

As of 1990, one can judge that the Orthodox–Catholic dialogue provides grounds for envisaging future reconciliation and restoration of communion. The differences over revelation and the deposit seem open to eventual unity in reconciled diversity based on a future mutual recognition of each other's ecclesial reality. The dialogue must still promote greater readiness to see the Christian substance that the two communities clothe in diverse but not contradictory forms of preaching, sacraments, and ministry.

Protestant–Catholic ecumenism is fragmented in numerous bilateral dialogues, and most of these have not yet taken up the cluster of issues raised by consideration of the apostolic deposit and its development in church teaching and life. Important advances have been made, e.g., in the Lutheran–Catholic dialogues on sacraments, ministry, and justification. What were once considered significant obstacles to unity have proven to be practically nonexistent. But much still needs to be treated in the area of ecclesiology, where a central point is the churches' respective "doctrine about doctrine," where serious divergences appear to persist. Most Protestants are loathe to see the gospel's saving power compromised by entanglement with magisterial pronouncements or obfuscated by appeals to the _sensus fidelium_. Catholics, for their part, feel that the full range of apostolic provisions can be compromised by certain reductive appeals to the original gospel. Also, they refuse to leave the interpretation of the meaning of God's revelation solely in the hands of biblical exegetes. The full apostolic patrimony is a spiritual treasure too precious to give over to the undisciplined plurality of those who try to reconstruct it from the biblical books with the tools of historical and literary criticism. The dialogue needs to continue.

6. Further Questions

The illuminating teaching on the apostolic deposit by major figures such as Irenaeus and Cardinal Newman contributed to the fresh accents with which Vatican II spoke of the deposit of faith. A reduction of the apostolic legacy to a set of doctrines that anticipate later dogma has been overcome by the more comprehensive account of how the apostles contributed and continue to contribute to the formation of Christians in community. The apostolic patrimony is no longer seen as the possession solely of the hierarchy, but as a life-giving presence impinging on the lives of believers to build them up in the wisdom of faith and help them walk in holiness. Still, however, certain topics regarding this deposit of faith and life stand in need of further theological clarification. We take up three of these here.

(1) While the church as a whole lives from the deposit in its teaching, worship, and life, there

is also a contemporary presence of portions of the apostolic deposit in the written books of the NT. The apostolic letters and Gospels have a privileged place in Christian life, especially in personal prayer and the liturgy.

But the original expressions of apostolic faith and instruction are also accessible to analytic study of their meaning by the methods of historical and literary criticism. The use of these methods have been authoritatively recommended (Pius XII, *Divino Afflante Spiritu*; *DV* 12). Such learned analysis can result in the recovery of the particular didactic intention of Jesus or of an apostolic author, e.g., in a learned commentary on a Gospel or epistle. Such study of the "sacred page" is one way of retrieving portions of the apostolic deposit.

But how do the results of critical exegesis fit together with the graced experience of believers who live from the riches of the deposit? How does historical and literary interpretation of the teaching of the apostolic authors relate to the doctrinal tradition of the church resulting from the interventions of those who interpret the deposit in virtue of their pastoral office and the sure charism of truth"? Vatican II was cognizant of this duality of interpretive methods and recommended both of them (*DV* 12). But the council's teaching at this point is more a juxtaposition than an account of how to fit together the different methods as a coherent unity. Further theological clarification seems needed on the interrelation of the diverse ways in which we today perceive the content of the apostolic legacy.

(2) The deposit of faith, however it may become present, is also a deposit of life-giving inspiration and guidance for Christian practice. Apostolic teaching gives witness both to God's self-communication in grace and to a range of ways of responding to his word and gifts. The apostolic legacy has consequently often been seen as communicating an articulated moral teaching. In the NT we encounter numerous expressions of both ethical principles and particular directives for life as a follower of Jesus. The church has not hesitated to specify numerous Christian duties in its catechesis and official teaching.

Questions, however, arise first over the normative character of particular apostolic directives in their binding force for Christian consciences today, e.g., Paul's teaching on marriage in 1 Cor 7. Does everything contained in the apostolic legacy have continuing relevance as a norm for shaping Christian behavior in later ages? Second, further clarification seems needed concerning the ecclesial magisterium in its role as guardian and expositor of the deposit. With what kind of competency does the magisterium formulate moral norms for believers? Are portions of the natural law included in the apostolic deposit? How far is the magisterium empowered to go, both in enunciating moral principles implicit only in apostolic teaching and in applying such teaching to particular cases arising in the changed circumstances of later history?

(3) Finally, there is the connection between the apostolic deposit in its mediation of communion with God and in its potential to enhance human life in the world. The social and mundane relevance of the message of Jesus must never overshadow the gifts of divine life poured out by the Holy Spirit. The apostles gave testimony to what they had seen and heard with Jesus, precisely so believers could enter community with them and share the joy of communion with Christ and his Father (see 1 Jn 1:1–3). The apostles, and the Christian teachers who come after them, dedicate themselves primarily to expressing the transcendent meaning of this gift.

But there is a further radiation of the light of this religious message over the whole of human life — in families, in political society, in the professions. Pope John XXIII, at the opening of Vatican II, underscored the potential blessings of the deposit for humanizing and enhancing life in this world. The council's Pastoral Constitution explicitly affirmed this connection and represents a broad-ranging attempt to radiate the light of Christ over a multitude of human problems. The deposit, precisely in its account of the gift and way of divine salvation, also enhances human dignity, supports social bonds, and gives human work a new depth of meaning (*GS* 40.3).

Thus, at every level, Christian teaching must aim to maintain balance, as it seeks to offer an inclusive articulation of the liberating and elevating truth brought into the world by Jesus and formulated by his apostles as their precious deposit given to the church.

Bibl.: C. SPICQ, *Les Épîtres pastorales* (2nd ed.; Paris, 1947), Excursus XV, "Le bon dépôt," 327–35; Y. CONGAR, *Tradition and Traditions*, 2 vols. (1960–63; New York, 1966); G. BIEMER, *Überlieferung und Offenbarung: Die Lehre der Tradition nach John Henry Newman* (Freiburg, 1961); N. BROX, *Offenbarung, Gnosis und gnostischer Mythos bei Irenäus von Lyon* (Salzburg/Munich, 1966); J. RATZINGER, "Kommentar zum 2. Kap. von Dei Verbum, Das zweite Vatikanische Konzil," *LTK*, vol. 2. Ergänzungsband, 515–28, Eng. trans. in H. VORGRIMLER, ed., *Commentary on the Documents of Vatican II* (London/New York, 1969), 3:181–98; O. CULLMANN, "La Tradizione, problema esegetico, storico, teologico," in *Studi di teologia biblica* (Rome, 1969), 203–56; J. SCHUMACHER, *Der apostolische Abschluss der Offenbarung Gottes* (Freiburg, 1979); G. O'COLLINS, "Criteria for Interpreting the Traditions," in R. LATOURELLE and G. O'COLLINS, eds., *Problems and Perspectives of Fundamental Theology* (New York, 1982), 327–39; U. BETTI, *La Dottrina del Concilio Vaticano II sulla trasmissione della rivelazione* (Rome, 1985); D. STANILOE, *Il Genio dell'Ortodossia* (Milan, 1985); R. FABRIS, *Le Lettere pastorali* (Brescia, 1986); J. WICKS, "Il deposito della fede: un concetto cattolico fondamentale," in R. FISICHELLA, ed., *Gesù Rivelatore* (Casale Monferrato, 1988), 100–119; M. WOLGER, *Die Pastoralbriefe als Paulustradition* (Göttingen, 1988).

Jared WICKS

DOGMA

Ordinarily, "dogma" refers to a dogmatic statement, a proposition expressing some part of the content of divine revelation, publicly proposed as such by the church and to be assented to in faith. Such proposal is by way either of the ordinary and universal or by way of the extraordinary and infallible magisterium of the church. Thus the articles of the creeds, as well as the canons of ecumenical councils, are to be recognized as expressing dogmas.

1. Dogmatic Statements as an Aspect of Revelation in Christ

a. The Eschatological Word of and about Christ

The propositional statement of the content of revelation and the role of such statement in the tradition of revelation are to be understood as one aspect of the comprehensive form of revelation, which is the history of God's saving words and deeds first to and then through Israel, the summation and culmination of which is the Incarnate Word in his life, death, resurrection, and bestowal of the Holy Spirit. Contemporary theology, as also the Second Vatican Council (*DV* 2), is in fact far from conceiving revelation only or in the first place as a collection of propositions. However, since the deeds of the history of salvation and revelation are no brute facts but the personal acts of a personal God, they contain a meaning and an intelligibility in themselves, which is ordinarily partially expressed in an accompanying prophetic word, and capable of elaboration in inspired sapiential reflection: Thus, even in Israel, there comes to be at least this one normative expression of the covenantal faith of God's people: "Hear, O Israel: The LORD is our God, the LORD alone" (Dt 6:4–9; 11:13–21; Nm 15:37–41).

The deeds of God and the prophetic interpretation of and sapiential reflection upon them within the OT are, however, unfinished, and constitute but an incomplete statement of the promise of God. Only with Christ is God's word completely spoken and the fullness of his promise perfectly delineated (*DV* 2; 4). Now the preeminent activity of Christ's life is that of proclaiming in word and deed that the kingdom of God is at hand: in word, "the time is fulfilled and the kingdom of God has come near" (Mk 1:15), and again, "let us go on to the neighboring towns, so that I may proclaim the message there also; for that is what I came out to do" (Mk 1:38); in deed, such as in the gathering of disciples to an unconditional following of him, in table-fellowship with sinners, in the forgiveness of sins, in healings and exorcisms. Moreover, this life and teaching constitute a claim on Jesus' part that the presence of his person, as declared in his word and manifested in his deeds, is a sufficient witness to and demonstration of the credibility of the truth of the message of the kingdom. For his word is authoritative: "You have heard that it was said. . . . But I say to you . . ." (Mt 5:21–22; see Mk 1:22). And similarly, his deed objectively calls for a response of faith: "But if it is by the Spirit of God that I cast out demons, then the kingdom of God has come to you" (Mt 12:28; see Jn 5:36; 9:32–33; 10:38; 14:11). This witness and demonstration thus identify Jesus as the one without whom the good news of the kingdom, and so the kingdom itself, is inaccessible, in that his cause and that of the gospel are one (Mk 8:35; 10:29), and so identify him positively, if perhaps only implicitly, as the Christ, and as the mediator who is what he mediates, God as God's Son. This witness and demonstration, both to the truth of his message and to the identity of his person, is perfected and confirmed only in the resurrection, the unmistakable sign that God's salvific ending of time is already anticipated and present within time, and indeed, in Jesus.

The resurrection *is* a "word": it means that the word of the crucified is true, that God's eschatological word spoken within time in Jesus' words has been guaranteed by God's eschatological act within history, and that the crucified is who he claimed to be, the eschatological savior who saves by his death (Mk 14:24–25). Also, the resurrection is to be declared in word (Mk 16:6–7). "He is risen" has therefore claim to be the initial and comprehensive statement of revelation (see Acts 2:24), a statement that is not merely a human response to God's deed ("confession" narrowly understood), but God's very word itself, creative of its human expression, since it is a word commissioned by Jesus himself (Mt 28:10, 18–19; Luke 24:46–48), and this is formal to the grounding of the Catholic understanding of dogma: the proclamation of the resurrection, as also dogma, is a "teaching" with a content, the result of a "decision," God's free *placet* that redeems humanity, as well as a teaching guaranteed by God, and so *his* teaching known as such.

Thus, originally, the possibility of dogmatic statements resides in (1) the teaching *of* Jesus himself, i.e., the eschatological word of God spoken in the human words of Jesus, (2) the at least implicit claim about the person and significance of Jesus made by Jesus, which claim is made explicit already in the NT by statements *about* Jesus, and (3) the confirmation of this teaching and claim in the event of the resurrection, which is itself a word and a word to be spoken. Thus, to be a follower of Christ includes (1) holding as true what Jesus taught to be held as true, the gospel he spoke, for he retains his title of "Teacher," and (2) holding as true about Jesus what the NT church held as true about him, the gospel that "concerns" him (Rm 1:3), the "confession of the Son" (1 Jn 2:23) and the "testimony" of the apostle that the Father has sent his Son as the savior of the world (1 Jn 4:14), which is the "good deposit" of teaching to be guarded (2 Tm 1:14), and (3) holding these truths as truths revealed by God.

b. The Eschatological Word Maintained across Time

Dogmatic statements are, however, ordinarily thought of as something distinct from and in addition to the statements of Scripture. The necessity of such further statement follows from the fact that an eschatological word has been spoken within time, the properly human time of merely the partial domination of temporal succession, i.e., the time of forgetfulness and loss as well as of progress, and in any event the time of such difference as threatens the identity of memory, the sameness of meaning of a once-spoken word. If the Eternal Word is to remain the eschatological word spoken within time, and thus indefectibly in the faith of the hearers, then it must contrive some way to remain what it is in and through the temporal words of men and women. This means that, just as human words themselves, so also the human act of interpretation must be taken up by the Word of God. For human meanings spoken in human words do not remain what they are, in their identity and sameness, except through interpretation, which keeps the meaning of a human word present in a time outside of its original time of utterance. The product of the interpretation of the once expressed eschatological word of Christ is "dogma."

Thus, just as Jesus himself interpreted the prior words of the OT revelation (as in the saying on divorce, Mt 19:4–6; as in the teaching on the resurrection, Mt 22:31–32; → 3a below), so also does the church, his body, not divorced from her head, interpret the word of Christ contained in Scripture. Or one can say: the eschatological word of the gospel, continually in the church's memory (Jn 14:26), continues to interpret and judge the various questions and words that men and women bring to the reception of the gospel. There is no difference between these formulations in a Catholic understanding that recognizes the priority and gratuity of grace, indeed, but as well recognizes the fact that grace is truly given to human beings and truly transforms them.

That the power to interpret authoritatively God's Word made flesh, and so uttered in human words, is exercised in and through the company of those united in the Spirit with Christ is already implicit in the reception of the canon of the NT, where such reception means that the theologies of the NT, the authors of which are also the evangelists and the apostles, are normative. If the interpretations of which the NT is composed were necessary after the time of the Lord, one may expect a like necessity for subsequent normative formulations, a making present of the NT itself in more and further human words, so that the word of the NT, and so the Word of God, can remain in time.

2. Emergence of the Notion of Dogma

a. The Modern Notion of Dogma

It is common to find in the First Vatican Council's *Pastor Aeternus* an expression of the modern, technical notion of dogma: "All those things are to be believed with divine and Catholic faith which are contained in the word of God, written or handed down, and which, either by solemn judgment or by her ordinary and universal magisterium, are proposed for belief by the church as having been divinely revealed" (DS 3011). What is formal to the notion, beyond the fact that dogma is a teaching contained in revelation, is that such teaching is proposed by the teaching authority of the church to be believed as such. So understood, "dogma" includes more than the medieval *articulus fidei*, which refers more narrowly to the propositions of the creed, but less than "doctrine," or "dogma" in its medieval theological usage, which does not include the note of being proposed by the extraordinary or ordinary infallible magisterium.

This technical notion of dogma first emerges with Melchior Cano, *De locis theologicis* (1563), who does not so much define the word as use it to mean some teaching that is both (1) apostolic, passed on by way either of Scripture or tradition, and (2) defined by pope or council or held to by all the faithful. Philip Neri Chrismann, *Regula fidei catholicae et collectio dogmatum credendorum* (1792), is usually credited with expressing the modern definition of dogma: "Dogma of faith is nothing else than doctrine and divinely revealed truth, which the church, by means of a solemn declaration, proposes as to be adhered to by divine faith, in such a way that a contrary position is condemned by the church as a heretical doctrine." In the context of its formulation, therefore, it is a notion that faces two ways: first, polemically, against Protestantism; second, constructively, as an answer to what the principles of theological science are and how they may be determined.

There is both gain and loss in the formulation of this technical notion, as with any objectification: it is useful, for both theological and controversial (and ecumenical) purposes, to have seized this object accurately and precisely; it is dangerous, in that such definition invites both a narrowly juridical consideration of dogma in isolation from the broader realities of revelation and faith, and as well a certain narrowing down of the very object of faith itself.

b. Dogma in the New Testament

Just as the formulation of any single dogma within, say, Christology or trinitarian theology leads to the question of its relation to Scripture and tradition, and the sense in which the dogma may be seen to be contained therein, so the formulation of the notion of dogma itself leads to the question of its relation to Scripture and tradition, and the sense in which it may be seen to be already living therein.

In common Greek, *dogma* (from *dokein*, "to think," "suppose") is an opinion, and more specially: (1) the opinion or teaching of a philosophical school; or (2) the resolution or decree of an assembly or ruler. It is this last sense that is prominent in the NT. Acts 17:7 speaks of the "decrees of the emperor" (see Lk 2:1). Again, we read of "legal *dogmata*" of the Mosaic dispensation, done away with in Christ (Col 1:14; Eph 2:15; see Col 2:20). Last, note is taken of the *dogmata*, the "decisions," of the apostles and elders made in Jerusalem concerning dietary and sexual purity (Acts 16:4; see 15:22, 25, 28). While the precise content of these *dogmata* is disciplinary and ethical, one may note that the context is more than ethical, for in not deciding to impose circumcision on the Gentiles, a matter is touched on that is of the essence of the gospel. It is in second- and third-century Christian literature that dogma becomes something doctrinal as well as disciplinary, congruently with the conception of Christianity as the "true philosophy."

The chief NT warrants for the notion of dogma as doctrine, beyond what has been said in (1) above, are to be found: (1) in the usage of *pistis* and *pisteuein*, for NT faith is not only confidence in the Lord and obedience to God, but as well a holding of certain things as true (e.g., Rm 10:8–9; Jn 6:69); (2) in the creedal or "precreedal" formula, especially hymnic, contained in the NT, Paul's appeal to which (e.g., Phil 2:5–11; 1 Cor 15:1–3) indicates that the idea of a relatively fixed expression of the faith is by no means foreign to the NT; (3) in that use of *homologia* and *homologein* where the object confessed, acknowledged, assented to is the kerygma about Christ, e.g., "Jesus is Lord" (Rm 10:9; see also 1 Tm 6:12; Heb 4:14; 1 Jn 4:15); and (4) in the emphasis in the Pastorals on the *didaskalia*, the "sound doctrine" (Ti 1:9; 2:1) that Timothy and Titus are urged to be faithful to, the "good treasure" they are to guard (2 Tm 1:14), which is the "truth" (2 Tm 2:25; 3:7), and is one and the same as "the standard of sound teaching" they have received (2 Tm 1:13).

c. Nicea

In the NT and early Christianity, therefore, "dogma" subsists already as a lived reality, but with no great emphasis on a standardization of verbal formula; with Cano and Chrismann, there is a reflex possession of the reality of dogma, an expression of which possession one can find in *Pastor Aeternus*. But between the lived reality, which includes the possibility of express standardization of formula, and the reflex possession there is the making actual of dogma precisely as a propositionally expressed teaching proposed by church authority to be assented to with divine faith. This making actual is prepared for by the emergence of catechetical and baptismal creeds, as well as by the raising to consciousness of the *regula fidei* in the controversy with Gnosticism. But it occurs fully for the first time at Nicea. "But those who say 'there was a time when he was not,' . . . or 'that he was made from what does not exist or from another hypostasis or ousia,' . . . these the Catholic church anathematizes' (DS 126). Thus, what one must say in order to belong to the community of salvation is that the Logos is eternal, uncreated, and *homoousios* with the Father. The emphasis is on what is said, because what we say sententially and propositionally, making a judgment, is a claim to the possession in knowledge of what is. Independently of what we think or what the Arians say about it, what is the case about the Logos is as it is. Moreover, this can be known; the knowledge is expressed in a true judgment, a true proposition that corresponds to what is; and this possession of reality by a mind illumined by faith is a part of what it means to be saved.

3. Development of Dogma

a. Sacred Scripture, Tradition, Magisterium

Presupposing the common understanding of Scripture, tradition, the magisterium, and the relations among them, their relation to dogmatic statements is capable of the following brief statement. If Scripture is understood as the materially sufficient inspired witness of the apostolic community to the Incarnate Word of God, Christ, and so as *norma non normata* of faith, and if tradition, the principle of which is the same Spirit who inspired the Scriptures, and whose comprehensive subject is the church, is the formally necessary context in which correctly to read and interpret Scripture, since it includes the experience of the very realities of which Scripture speaks (*DV* 8), then a dogmatic statement will be related to Scripture and previous expressions of tradition as a normative interpretation thereof, and the role of the magisterium in the production of that interpretation will be that simply of an infallible recognition, according to the gift of the Holy Spirit given it, that such an interpretation is indeed correct (*DV* 10).

The production of a dogmatic statement can, therefore, rightly be considered in the first place simply as a kind of exegesis, and indeed, "spiritual exegesis," i.e., a reading of Scripture, and in its service, in the Spirit of Christ, who removes the veil from the face of Moses, that "hardness of heart" that prevents the OT from being understood as speaking of Christ (2 Cor 3:12–18). The warrant for such exegesis, moreover, is the example of Christ as understood according to Luke-Acts. In Lk 4:16–21, the meaning of Is 61:1–2 is declared by Christ to be Christ himself: he provides by his teaching and is in his reality the normative context of the interpretation of Scripture. In Lk 24:27, the meaning of Scripture ("Moses and all the prophets") is once more declared by Christ to be Christ. And this example, moreover, is followed by others, for in Acts 8:27–35, Philip declares the meaning of Is 53:7–8 to the Ethiopian eunuch, and the meaning is Christ.

b. Theories of Development

Four theories of dogmatic development are commonly distinguished. For those who continue to admit the notion of "development" at all, the last is much the more common position.

(1) Development as restatement or clearer statement of what is already conceptually possessed and known (Bossuet). With the passing of the idea of tradition as a collection of orally transmitted teachings not contained in Scripture, and with keener attention given to the history not only of outward verbal expression but of expressed conceptuality in Christian tradition, this idea of development has been abandoned.

(2) Development as the logical work of drawing conclusions from revealed premises (e.g., F. Marin-Sola). On this view, it should be possible strictly logically to demonstrate the continuity of dogma with Scripture. The difficulty of this demonstration has led to the abandonment of this view.

(3) Development as the material transformation of the didactic expression of faith according to the scientific and philosophical conceptuality of the age (Schleiermacher, modernism). This view is ordinarily criticized on the ground that the continuity of Christianity is more than a continuity of experience and piety and includes a continuity of teaching.

(4) Development as properly theological contemplation of revealed reality by a necessarily historically conditioned reason illumined by faith (Newman, Moehler, Blondel). Recognition of the historical conditionedness of reason accounts for the leaps in development that cannot be logically bridged as a passage from already possessed premises to previously unarticulated conclusion. Delimitation of the object of contemplation as revealed *reality* (the

Christ), while not denying the role of propositions in the transmission of revelation, explains how there can be more in the developments than was previously already propositionally expressed. Finally, the specification of the contemplation as "theological" and of reason as "illumined by faith" makes of the actual process of development an act of faith, and so one not wholly reducible to naturally human capacities, and makes of the subsequent recognition of authentic developments likewise an act of faith.

c. The Interpretation of Dogma

In general, dogmatic statements are to be interpreted according to the same canons as Scripture: historical critical objectivity is brought to bear within the horizon of faith and tradition. Since they are themselves interpretations of Scripture and tradition, they find their own interpretation according to the norm of what they interpret. In what they bind the believer to confess, they are by their nature to be interpreted strictly. The "irreformability" of dogmatic statements (DS 3074) does not mean that they do not call for interpretation and even reformulation; it means that, in the sense in which they were understood at the time and in the context of their definition, they are to be assented to as true.

4. The Denial of Dogma

In the NT, heresy and schism are not clearly distinguished as denial of some part of revelation on the one hand, and breaking of communion but without departing from the rule of faith, on the other. The "schisms" in Corinth (1 Cor 1:10) seem rather to be "parties," partially distinguished at any rate merely by adherence to some party leader (1 Cor 1:12). But in Acts, the basis of "schism" among the citizens of Iconium (14:4) and within the Sanhedrin (23:7) is clearly some intellectual disagreement. *Hairesis* (from *haireomai*, "to choose," "select"), which in pre-Christian Greek means a sect, especially a philosophical school, is used in Acts in a similar fashion: "the sect of the Sadducees" (5:17; see also 15:5; 24:5; 26:5). It seems rather to be a description of a group from outside the group (see 24:14), and tending to a hostile description. Paul's use of it is hard to distinguish from schism (cf. 1 Cor 1:10 and

11:18). It is only in 2 Pt 2:1 that "heresy" is clearly understood to be based on a denial of doctrine, indeed, doctrine about Christ. That such differences entail already in the NT the breaking of communion is clear from 1 Jn 1:18ff. The indefectibility of the church's faith belongs to the church as a communion, not to the individual as such.

With the Nicene production of dogma, there is possible a correlatively exact notion of heresy as the denial of a dogmatic statement. This is in continuity with the more plastic notion of a heretic as one who does not interpret Scripture according to the rule of faith (Ignatius), itself in continuity with the sense of heresy in 2 Pt 2:1. The clarity of dogma past Nicea, however, changes the nature of doctrinal controversy: while it took Irenaeus four books to demonstrate the fact that the Gnostics did not interpret Scripture according to the rule of faith, Arians and semi-Arians are rendered easily identifiable against the measure of the *homoousios*.

Modern problems with the notion of heresy are not to be distinguished from modern problems with the notion of dogma, and turn on the question of whether some knowledge of the truth, propositionally expressed, belongs essentially to the presently possessed goods of salvation, and so, is formal to membership in the community of the saved.

5. Modern Problems and Perspectives on Dogma

a. Anthropological Presuppositions

Modern problems with the notion of dogma begin with difficulties over the anthropological presuppositions of dogma. These presuppositions, as the possibility of dogma itself, are known theologically only from the actuality of revelation. Just as, before revelation, we cannot know that God's word can be spoken in human words, so also, before revelation, we cannot know we can hear him. The anthropological conditions of dogma can be stated variously. But classically and with St. Thomas, one can say that the fundamental presupposition is that there is a natural human desire for the vision of God. Such a natural desire, supernaturally known as it is, is of course strictly dependent on that character of the human mind as *quodammodo omnia* ("in a certain way all

things"), and such that the analogical stretch of our language extends beyond the realm of materially conditioned being: the human mind is really capable of understanding something of God, or more properly, of what God is not, and human words can speak of divine things. These natural conditions of dogma can be seen to be strictly implied in Jesus' preaching of the kingdom: if human beings can hear an eschatological word, then their time is not that of animal immersion in a mere succession of perceptions, but that of a perception of succession: to that extent they dominate the time they are nonetheless subject to, are capable of making history, and so possess an openness to a word about an end of history not of their own making, but of God's. Such an openness implies that humanity's mind extends in desire beyond all regions of being, even the whole of the material and temporal cosmos, and so has being as such for its adequate object.

The anthropological possibility of dogma is commonly denied in two ways. First, if a critical philosophy holds that the adequate object of the mind is not being as such, the mind is confined to the knowledge of phenomena, and analogous predication of God collapses into equivocity: all religious discourse is at best metaphorical, and so there can be no proper word spoken to us by God, received and expressed in our words. Second, if a postcritical idealism holds that being is not only the adequate, but the proper object of the mind, there is no intelligibility that surpasses the mind, analogous predication of God collapses into univocity, and there is no need to accept any truth on the authority of the revealing God.

b. Modern Questions

The very idea of dogma induces a crisis of faith, however, not simply in virtue of the various denials of post-Christian philosophy, but also according as one takes seriously the following questions.

(1) The first is that of the Reformation. Does not the church's claim to propound dogma contradict the freedom of the Christian conscience, as well as the freedom of the gospel, of the word of God, to address that conscience? Does it not do so by inserting a human authority between the Christian and the one mediator

between God and humanity, Jesus Christ? And does it not reduce the faith that alone saves and whose sole term is God to a series of intellectual "works," assents to humanly formulated propositions, humanly understood?

Modern attention to the Reformation question is usually bound up with the liberal Protestant reading of the history of doctrine for which dogma is the expression of the Greek intellectualizing corruption of the Christian piety of the NT. Further, it is given exegetical urgency by proponents of a consistent eschatology for whom dogma is the solution of early Catholicism to the problem of the delay of the parousia. In general, the Protestant inclination is to understand church dogma more narrowly as "confession," understood as a human response to the word of revelation, but falling short of a participation in the authority of revelation itself.

(2) The second question is the question of the Enlightenment. Does not the very idea of dogma contradict human freedom? A *fides imperata*, such as the notion of dogma supposes, is a *fides servilis*; free faith, which alone is moral, requires assent to nothing beyond the principles of morality tied to the idea of God as postulated by practical reason (Kant). Again, dogma contradicts the spirit of free inquiry (Heidegger) and is opposed to the openness of scientific method (J. Dewey, B. Russell). The Enlightenment indictment of dogma can be summarized as follows: a "dogma" is an opinion that is not and cannot be known to be true illegitimately imposed on others by some human authority. The imposition of dogma is "heteronomy"; it denies the autonomous character of human inquiry and action. As doing so in the interest of some social class, dogma becomes "ideology" in the Marxist sense.

(3) How restore Christian unity given the divisiveness of dogma, which is not overcome by the simple recognition of a hierarchy of truths (Second Vatican Council, *UR* 11)?

c. Modern Proposals

All the difficulties broached by these questions seem to arise only on a cognitivist-realist view of dogma: dogmatic statements tell us something about God, Christ, the ways of God with man; furthermore, dogmatic statements are true in the sense of corresponding; e.g., the statement "there are three persons in God" is true because there are three persons in God. All difficulties can be seen to be met, therefore, by abandoning this notion, either by denying the nature of dogmas as informative utterances, or by abandoning the correspondence view of truth. The following represent the chief lines of reformulation.

(1) The experiential-expressivist notion of dogma. Proponents of this view think with Schleiermacher to respond to the Enlightenment critique both of knowledge and of revealed religion. Dogmas are misunderstood if we take them as giving us information about some reality transcendent to our ordinary experience. Rather are dogmas expressions and evocations of a unique kind of experience, the experience of "absolute dependence," our "God-consciousness." For instance, "Jesus is *homoousios tǭ patri*" is an expression of the God-consciousness— broadly, of the religious experience or ultimate concern—of the one making the assertion. Making the assertion evokes the God-consciousness of the one making it; it keeps him or her in the experience. It is, as it were, a metaphor that points to the experience, which is itself properly ineffable, outside of the realm of the kind of intelligibility that our language and our concepts are capable properly of expressing.

The statement is true with respect to the experience of the one making it insofar as it does really express and evoke his or her God-consciousness; it is true with respect to Jesus insofar as he really did have an unsurpassable God-consciousness.

The statement is reformable as long as the reformulation is similarly expressive of the God-experience of the one making the statement, as long as the reformulation makes a like commitment to the uniqueness of Jesus. It is to be expected that the reformulation of the statement will keep pace with the scientific and philosophic idiom of the age. The continuity of dogmatic development is one of experience, not of conceptual content.

Congruently with the above, church doctrines can have but a temporally and culturally relative normativity. They bind neither the freedom of the gospel nor freedom of conscience. And they therefore erect no great obstacle to Christian unity.

(2) Pragmatism, modernism. The meaning of any statement just is the expectation of experience that it implies, and the action it enjoins. Thus "Jesus is _homoousios tǭ patri_" means that we should act toward Jesus as we do toward God, and it means that we may expect him to act toward us as does God; e.g., if God is the agent of our salvation, we may expect Jesus to be likewise. The meanings of two statements are distinct only according as they imply different experiences, enjoin different actions. Thus, if "Jesus is the revelation of God" implies the same experiences, enjoins the same actions as the Nicene doctrine, then it is equivalent to it in meaning, for meaning is the intention not of reality but of our relation to it.

The truth of the statement is a function of its coherence with our experience and practice, as well as all other statements we are committed to, for a truth can be true and can be known to be true only as part of a whole. The free progress of science and philosophy may therefore require a reformulation of dogma.

Pragmatic holism and coherentism, combined with both a historicist (often Heideggerian) view of the relation of being to language and a futurist eschatology, produce that view of dogmatic statements according to which they are merely provisionally serviceable pointers toward the eschatological truth yet to be revealed. Their truth consists not of a present correspondence to reality but in their keeping us in the way of an orientation toward a truth we cannot now possess in language, but of which our language can express only the hope.

(3) Antifoundationalism, constructivism. A third and twofold possibility for reformulating the sense of dogma arises from the contemporary construal of discourse as a disparate collection of culturally and historically constituted vocabularies or frameworks, none of which is privileged in respect to another, none of which can be known to relate us to the real any better than another. Like pragmatism, this view also is a function of Hegelian holism and coherentism but asserts a plurality of incommensurable discourses or vocabularies, each of them historically and culturally constituted for some extracognitive end, e.g., the unity of some community, the maintenance of some ethical practice. Two lines can be taken. Either dogmas are seen to be statements made within frameworks,

capable of truth only within and presupposing them; or dogmas are the meta-statements that constitute the frameworks. In the first, it is the relation of the framework to reality that is problematic: if the framework is not true of reality, then no truth within the framework really puts us in possession of the real either. This is a return to pragmatism.

The second line can be developed as follows. The foundation of a discourse is a matter of delimiting what is important to talk about by way of inventing the categories in which to talk about it. Dogmatic statements are instances of such delimitation. Like rules, they are themselves neither true nor false; rather, they establish a discourse within which statements capable of truth and falsity can be made. "Jesus is _homoousios tǭ patri_" is a shorthand for several rules: always speak of God as one; always speak of Jesus and the Father as really distinct; always speak of Jesus so as to maximize his importance. One stays within the meaning of the dogma as a norm according as one follows the rules. If "Jesus is the supreme revelation of God" can be shown to fall within the space for the formation of statements outlined by the rules, then it falls within Nicene orthodoxy. The dogma itself is true, not in the sense of corresponding, but according as the categories (divine unity, real distinction, maximal importance of Jesus) are adequate for the purpose of Christian discourse as a whole, which is to help us to get into the right relation to ultimate reality. Different rules of categorial adequacy pose no serious obstacle to Christian unity.

Proposals like the above have contributed greatly to an apprehension of the relation of dogma to experience and action (praxis), history and culture, and to appreciating it as a special mode of discourse in relation to the religiously prior discourse of prayer and praise. But they are criticized on the ground: (1) that no council or church authority understood itself to be evoking experience or giving rules of conduct or stating conditions of categorial adequacy, where any of those things are distinct from stating how things are, when they enunciated a dogma; and (2) that none of the proposals, on the example, really exclude Arianism or even adoptionism. Evidently, the questions they respond to call for a demonstration that, if the cognitivist-realist understanding of dogma is correct, dogma is not only not opposed to the freedom of the gospel and the freedom of the Christian, but positively serves them in maintaining the presence of the word of the gospel in time, and that the heteronomy of dogma, as of revelation itself, is the instrument of a human freedom greater than which one can conceive of or attain to on his or her own.

Bibl.: J. H. NEWMAN, *An Essay on the Development of Christian Doctrine* (1878); M. BLONDEL, "Histoire et Dogme," in *Les Premiers écrits de Maurice Blondel* (Paris, 1956); K. RAHNER, "What is Heresy", in *Theological Investigations*, vol. 5 (1962; London, 1966); id., "What is a Dogmatic Statement?" in *Theological Investigations*, vol. 5 (London, 1966), 42–66; W. KASPER, *Dogme et Évangile* (Tournai, 1967); J. WALGRAVE, *Unfolding Revelation: The Nature of Doctrinal Development* (London/Philadelphia, 1972); B. LONERGAN, "The Origins of Christian Realism," in *A Second Collection* (Philadelphia, 1974); id., *The Way to Nicea* (Philadelphia, 1976); P. SCHRODT, *The Problem of the Beginning of Dogma in Recent Theology* (Frankfurt/Bern/Las Vegas, 1978).

Guy F. MANSINI

DREY, Johann Sebastian von (1777-1853)

1. Biographical Sketch

J. S. Drey was born, in impoverished circumstances, on 17 October 1777, in Killingen (now Ellwangen-Röhlingen). After a conventional higher education (1787–97) and merely second-rate theological training (theological college, St. Salvator [ex-Jesuit] in Augsburg, 1797–99; seminary, 1799–1801), he was ordained a priest in 1801. In 1806, having utilized the period of his curacy for purposeful independent study, he became professor of mathematics and physics at the lyceum in Rottweil. In 1812, when the short-lived Friedrich University was founded in Ellwangen, he was offered, with no special preparation, the professorship in dogmatics and history of dogma (including contribution to the theological encyclopedia). By 1814 he had begun—in creative divergence from the set curriculum—presenting lectures in apologetics. The transfer of the Ellwangen Institute to the University of Tübingen in 1817, where it became the Faculty of Catholic Theology (alongside the existing Faculty of Protestant Theology), suited his aims. While retaining his areas of specialization, he established, on a permanent basis, the discipline and teaching of apologetics in Tübingen. Within a short time, Drey came to be regarded as the faculty's outstanding theologian. In addition to his innovations in Catholic theology (*Revision des gegenwärtigen Zustandes der Theologie*, 1812), he was staunchly active (less notably after 1830) on behalf of ecclesiastical reform at all levels (roughly in the spirit of I. H. v. Wessenberg [1774–1860]). From 1822 to 1827, he was four times designated first bishop of Rottenburg by the Wurtembergian crown; just as often, for reasons of church politics, his confirmation was refused by Rome. This course of things, disappointing to Drey, made it easier for him to retreat into a scholarly life which, although externally inconspicuous and uneventful, was internally dynamic and left its stamp on the basic form of theology at Tübingen (a theology of scholarly rigor, concern for the present, and closeness to the church under the motto of "thinking for oneself"). Besides *Kurze Einleitung* (1819) and his main work, *Apologetik I–III* (1838–47), the body of his publications are contained in the *Theologische Quartalschrift*, which he cofounded in 1819. He never published a comprehensive dogmatic work, but manuscripts of his lectures on dogmatics and the history of dogma have been preserved. Two separate ennoblements (1823, 1846) serve as the highest recognition of his work. Granted emeritus status in 1846, Drey died on 19 February 1853 in Tübingen. No comprehensive bibliography has yet been published.

2. Influence and Present State of Research

J. S. Drey's theological significance is evident from the fact that today, by consensus, he is accorded the role of "founder" or "father of modern fundamental theology." His own insistence on the denotatively enduring disciplinary term "apologetics" (despite all his conceptual reliance on "fundament[al]" metaphors) is primarily a result, on the one hand, of a resistance to older and coextensive Catholic terms and categories like "universal" or "general dogmatics" (*dogmatica generalis*), "introduction to dogmatics" (*introductio* or prolegomena), and so on, and of a positive interest in having similarity of nomenclature with parallel endeavors in Protestant theology on the other (especially by F. Schleiermacher [1768–1834]); hence it implies no rehabilitative affirmation of the apologetic tradition.

Noteworthy, however, is that the earliest attribution of the role of founder to J. S. Drey (which occurred in Protestant theology well before it did in Catholic), and even more the nonuniform way in which this gained recognition, were not exclusively linked to any *one* of his relevant writings. The reasons are related initially, before publication of his *Apologetik* (1838ff.), to his *Kurze Einleitung* (1819) — although the conceptions of apologetics/fundamental theology in the two works partially differ — and only later to both writings together. Corresponding to this is the positive fact that, in Drey, the concept of "apologetics" embraces not only a certain published work (*Apologetik*), but a *didactic*, a *literary*, and a *theological* program, all of which, in frequently intertwining ways, underwent multileveled development from their inception to their final form. Each of these three strands exerted its specific effect. Drey's apologetics/fundamental theology is therefore not simply identical with his *Apologetik*. That work already reflects the impact of conceptual criticisms (and even tabooings) of his intellectual project, although without abandonment of the core of his creative new approach.

The process of broad and continuous influence of the apologetics/fundamental theology of J. S. Drey (who himself founded no "school") was interrupted when he acquired emeritus status, or after his main work was concluded. For reasons of theological principle, his successor, J. E. Kuhn (1806–1887), opposed granting disciplinary independence to apologetics as a field of study clearly distinguishable, within theory of the sciences, from dogmatics. In effect, but for quite different reasons, the dominating paradigm of academic apologetics in the second half of the nineteenth century led in this same direction. Insofar as Catholic fundamental theology associates more than an honorary title with the idea of Drey's "foundership" or "fatherhood," this appears to reflect a key orientational move in the multileveled process of present-day formulation of its theory.

With regard to their sources, the stages of development of Drey's project between 1814 and 1819 (Ellwangen lectures and the *Kurze Einleitung*) and 1847 (vols. 2 and 3 of the *Apologetik*) are still open for research. To that extent, and insofar as it meets with any interest, the methodological proposition of substantiating the concrete-analytical and systematic representation of his apologetics through parallel historicogenetic inquiries is, in principle, realizable. For decades, however, this customary methodological approach has been largely ignored in the research on Drey, which first really began in 1930, with the work of J. R. Geiselmann. Geiselmann's own research, which has left a long-lasting mark on the hermeneutics of interpretation of Drey, is partly itself an embarrassing case in point. Thus some of the aforementioned tabooings have been able to remain effective even after the commendable "rediscovery" of J. S. Drey. Symptomatic of this is the fact that, for a long time, Drey's apologetics/fundamental theology (especially in the form of his *Apologetik*) drew attention solely because of some of its individual themes, but has never, even up to recent times, been delineated in its genesis, distinctive integral structure, and systematic approach.

3. Early Conceptualization

J. S. Drey's development of independent ideas becomes graspable with his turn away from the categories of (still dogmatically current) "prolegomena" (viz., E. Klüpfel [1733–1811]) or "introductio" (viz., P. B. Zimmer [1752–1820]). As early as 1812 to 1813, he already understood his introductory lecture in dogmatics as a "philosophical exposition of Christianity," as an exposition of the "idea of Christianity in general": of the *kingdom of God*. This notion clearly points beyond the foundation of dogmatics alone to the "philosophical foundation of Christian theology" as a whole. The change in the lecture's title (1814: "apologetics") makes obvious the connection between this notion and F. Schleiermacher's concept of "philosophical theology." Drey's ideational and conceptual synergy with Schleiermacher manifests itself comprehensively in his initial encyclopedic conception (without concrete elaboration) of apologetics in 1819 (*Kurze Einleitung* §§221–47): it is (1) *in content*, an examination of the "essence of Christianity" (as religion and as church) that demonstrates (a) through internally applied argument its inner, intellectual and intelligible truth (concept of the kingdom of God), and (b) through external, historical method its divine origin (revelation); (2) *in method*, a "philosophical construction" of the essence of Christianity that, although historically informed, operates in the realm of essential reason and employs its principles; (3) *in structure*, the constructive component of the "foundation" of "scientific theology" (and in that respect related more closely to systematic theology than to theology in its entire scope), although not in the sense of constructive formalism, but as substantial, "scientific knowledge" of Christianity with the power "to vindicate belief in Christianity before all reason"; and (4) *in function*, the systematic basic discipline of theology that (for Drey differently than for Schleiermacher) transforms the historical facts of Christianity ("matter") into the ideas of reason ("knowledge"), or integrates them into the internally coherent and interdependent *system* of human knowledge.

In making a priori rational construction of the leading basic concept (kingdom of God) the starting point of apologetics, Drey is linked, on the Catholic side, especially to M. Dobmayer (1735–1805). Drey's *interpretatio apologetica* of Dobmayer's work (paralleling a certain distancing from Schleiermacher, 1821 and on) marks a phase of new reflections (until about 1834) on the attainment of independent status, within theory of the sciences, for apologetics and on its basic principle. In this process, his final working out of the actual theological themes is not always clearly reflected in their didactic translation to lecture form. But in the course of it, (a) apologetics acquires its sharp profile (chiefly in contrast to dogmatics) as the discipline in which faith is *grounded*, in an epistemological and objective sense, and (b) the previous leading principle of apologetics, the kingdom of God, is replaced by the fundamental transcendental concept of *revelation*, which then functions to systematize Drey's apologetics fully.

4. Nature of Thought and Approach

In contrast to the antagonism between naturalism/rationalism and transnaturalism/transrationalism (including mysticism) that polarized the theology of the times, Drey's intellectual program takes the form of *positive rationalism in the church*. He begins with actually given Christianity, as expressed "positively" in the origin and historical tradition of the church all the way up to its contemporary manifestation in her. As "a positive and historical religion, Christianity is initially recognizable only historically" (*Apologetik* I,3), i.e., in the church as the objective, unbroken, pure, and consistent continuation of the (biblically certified) original actuality. Therefore, the church ("the true basis of all theological knowledge," *Kurze Einleitung* §54) is the transsubjective guaranteeing authority in the world of theological objects. Clarification of the *truth* of the claims to validity implicit in this cannot, however, rest content with substantiation of the sources (exegesis, church history) or demonstration that actual religious consciousness either is identical with the individual testimonies of tradition or can be interpreted as in agreement with tradition (dogmatics). It requires essential theological rationality, i.e., conversion of the (in theory and practice) positively pregiven facts, in a critically normative way and by demonstration of their inner intelligibility, into universally discussible rational form (apologetics). Whatever is, by virtue of its *origin*, part of the content of revelation must also be capable of being expressed, by virtue of its *structure*, as an evident idea of reason. The relation between revelation and reason is an absolute one: "everything *from* God—*through* reason—and *for* reason" (ibid., §291). In the full scientific sense, apologetics is to be understood as that *theological* (not pretheological) discipline which transforms "initially just believed truth into understood truth," comprehends the "content of revelation" as a "nexus of teachings" "that carry their truth and necessity in themselves," and allows the "mystery" to pass over "into the idea and the truths of revelation into truths of reason" (ibid., §305f.). The essential characteristic of Drey's approach is its basic reliance on the principle of intrinsicality in apologetics.

5. Hermeneutic Circle

A critical and normative method of correlation is possible, however, only as a testing of revelation against itself, i.e., under the presupposition of revelation and as an originally self-induced process. Among the *overt* hermeneutic presuppositions of Drey's apologetics is that something a posteriori is intellectually treated, in the interest of its internal authentication, as an a priori, namely, historically positive revelation. The interrelation between the transcendentality and the phenomenality of revelation, or between the ideal-transcendental concept of revelation and the historical unfolding of revelation, which is constantly presupposed in it, as a reflective system, acquires its total verification only through concrete history. Since the basic categories of Drey's apologetics have been conceived as *historical*, it implies the inner comprehension of the whole of (revelatory) history. To that extent, part of its background is formed by his philosophy and theology of history, in which the epistemological model of "ideal-realism"—given its (idealistic) stamp by F. W. J. Schelling (1775–1854) and thoroughly affirmed by Drey—exerts a continuing influence.

6. Personal and Participative Understanding of Revelation

The basic categories of Drey's apologetics have also been conceived as *personal*. For him, revelation is grasped not in terms of didactic categories, but essentially as the "self-revelation of God" (*Apologetik* I,1, 119–21, 124f.) in the sense of the participative communications-theoretical model (M. Seckler) of God's self-communication for the sake of human redemption. In the person of Christ, this reaches its unsurpassable apex in both form and content (ibid., 199–204). The incarnation is therefore the central point of apologetics, containing in itself the starting point and the goal (ibid., 26): as basic teaching (ibid., 124), basic truth (ibid., 3, 15), basic fact (ibid., VII), and basic actuality (ibid., 3). The discrete purposes of revelation (intellectual: instruction; ethical: moral awakening; social: founding of the church) converge, within historical time, in the *one*: redemption (ibid., 177). Christian revelation is the "revelation of salvation" (ibid., 245).

7. Apologetics as Fundamental Theology

In the framework of the theory of the sciences current at the time, apologetics secures the possibility and existence of theology as a science through discursive demonstration of its material (revelation) and its formal (scien-

tificality) principles (twofold formal object). Along with that, it elaborates the foundation for the whole of theology (in all its methodological and material multidimensionality) in four main respects: (a) *materially:* with its demonstration of Christianity as a religion of revelation and its related establishment of the material of theology and the suitability of theology to function as theology of revelation; (b) *epistemologically:* in its inwardly (in the mode of understanding) and outwardly (in the mode of explaining) directed eliciting of the "basic idea" of Christianity (incarnation); (c) *methodologically:* through its elaboration of the initial and the ultimate groundings of the theological system of argumentation and its correlated ordering of that system's rational components; and (d) *pedagogically:* in the sense of providing an introduction to the subject matter of theology. As accords with its basic approach (→ 4 above), apologetics, the fundamental discipline, relates all particular theological results back to their common ground, namely, to revelation as manifested, in present-day form, in the church. With regard to this grounding function of the church vis-à-vis theology, it is fairly clear that the influence of M. Dobmayer's theological epistemology lives on in Drey's work.

8. Basic Methodological Structure and Inherent Tenor

The traditionally established *loci theologici* reappear in Drey's apologetics, but have been functionally altered as a result of the adaptation of the basic methodological structure to the purposes implicit in the content.

The *ratio philosophica* (*Apologetik* I: *Philosophy of Revelation*), as theoretical philosophy of revelation (more fully, as philosophy, theory, and critique of revelation) grounds the critical and regulative norms (ontological and epistemological principles of revelation) required for comprehending the fundamental concept. Revelation appears there as the "transcendental ground of everything empirically Christian" (*Apologetik* I,15): as the unity of the varied phenomena in view of the idea.

The *ratio philosophico-historica* (*Apologetik* II: *Religion in its Historical Development up to its Fulfillment through Revelation in Christ*), as applied (to Judaism and pre-Christianity paganism) philosophy of revelation, or philosophicocritical history of religion, traces the categorical manifestations of revelation (revelations) under the criterion of its idea. Implicit in this is postulation of a coherent system for the whole of (revelatory) history "that discloses itself precisely in the sequence of these manifestations" (ibid., 132). This is the successively unfolding "plan of education that God has in view for humanity" (ibid., 245).

Finally, the *ratio historica* finds its application in cases where the facticity of a transcendentally disclosed idea cannot be apodictically proven although it can be confirmed, through the understanding of historical reason, to be a realized fact on the basis of a congruence between historical actuality and idea, e.g., the case of positive-historical proof of the incarnation. It has, within the system of apologetic argumentation, not a positivistically isolated logic of validation, but rather, a normatively controlled one.

In the first two volumes of the *Apologetik*, this basic methodological structure is placed above the classical subdivision of the treatises. Moreover, for internal reasons (interdependence of the concepts of religion and revelation), the treatises on religion and revelation (*demonstratio religiosa* and *demonstratio christiana*) have been combined in them.

The treatise on the church (*Apologetik* III: *Christian Revelation in the Catholic Church*) repeats the basic structure outlined above in an independent new context (idea of the church;

establishment of the church; *via notarum;* etc.), but is, on the whole, more closely tied to apologetic tradition. Here, Drey's elaboration of the concept of "living tradition" (the church as both product and bearer of revelation) remained pioneering.

Bibl.: Sources. J. S. VON DREY, *Kurze Einleitung in das Studium der Theologie mit Rücksicht auf den wissenschaftlichen Standpunkt und das katholische System* (Tübingen, 1819; mod. edition, Darmstadt, 1971); id., *Die Apologetik als wissenschaftliche Nachweisung der Göttlichkeit des Christentums in seiner Erscheinung*, 3 vols. (Mainz, 1838–47; mod. edition, Frankfurt, 1967).

Studies. M. SECKLER, "Ein Tübinger Entwurf: Johann Sebastian Drey und die Theologie," in M. SECKLER, *Im Spannungsfeld von Wissenschaft und Kirche: Theologie als schöpferische Auslegung der Wirklichkeit* (Freiburg, 1980), 178–98; F. J. NIEMANN, *Jesus als Glaubensgrund in der Fundamentaltheologie der Neuzeit: Zur Genealogie eines Traktats*, Innsbrucker Theologische Studien 12 (Innsbruck, 1983), 301–48; R. LACHNER, *Das ekklesiologische Denken Johann Sebastian Dreys: Ein Beitrag zur Theologiegeschichte des 19. Jahrhunderts*, Europäische Hochschulschriften XXIII/280 (Frankfurt/Bern/New York, 1986); E. TIEFENSEE, *Die religiöse anlage und ihre Entwicklung: Der religionsphilosophische Ansatz Johann Sebastian Dreys*, Erfurter Theologische Studien 56 (Leipzig, 1988); A. P. KUSTERMANN, *Die Apologetik Johann Sebastian Dreys: Kritische, historische und systematische Untersuchungen zu forschungsgeschichte, Programment-wicklung, Status und Gehalt*, Contubernium 36 (Tübingen, 1988), with research bulletins and bibliography.

Abraham Peter KUSTERMANN

E

EARLY CATHOLICISM

In 1958 German theologian W. Marxsen published (at Neukirchen) a little book entitled *Der Frühkatholizismus im Neuen Testament*. In the following year F. Mussner, a Catholic theologian, offered some thoughts on the subject in the *Trierer Theologische Zeitschrift*, pp. 237–45. But, although it was not the earliest work on the subject, it was S. Schulz's book, *Die Mitte der Schrift: Der Frühkatholizismus im Neuen Testament als Herausforderung an den Protestantismus* (1976), that elicited the most reactions and thus called attention to a subject hitherto relegated to obscure appendixes. Until about 1950 Protestant scholars tended to locate early Catholicism in the post–NT period, but R. Bultmann, in his *Theology of the New Testament* (New York, 1953), recognized that "the tendencies that were operative in the earliest church" already "appear in that tradition [i.e., Acts, Pauline letters, and the Synoptics]" (1:33). Not long afterwards, E. Käsemann, a disciple of Bultmann, began to raise seriously the question of whether it is possible to find in the NT itself different levels of evangelical authenticity, or a "canon within the canon."

Schulz's important work takes up this question. The subject is indeed a fascinating one, for if it be true that developments proper to the early church go back to the NT, then it is no longer possible for the "evangelical" confessions simply to appeal to the NT as the basis of their conviction that they represent authentic Christianity, or to continue claiming that the "Catholicization" of the faith represents a decline (*Abfall*) by comparison with the primitive kerygma. Schulz takes the presence of early Catholic elements in the NT as a challenge to Protestantism. In his book he describes at length these "Catholic" infiltrations into the NT and, in order to defend against the danger they represent, he proposes a reassertion of the Reformation principle: the "center of the scriptures," the "canon within the canon," is the Pauline teaching on justification by faith.

I shall now list in chronological order the studies that have appeared on this subject and that have the term "early Catholicism" in their title. A. Ehrhard pioneered with his *Urkirche und Frühkatholizismus* (1st ed., Bonn, 1935; 3rd ed., 1951). Subsequently came W. Marxsen, *Der Frühkatholizismus im Neuen Testament* (Neukirchen, 1958); H. Küng, "Der Frühkatholizismus im Neuen Testament als kontroverstheologisches Problem," *TQ* 142 (1962): 385–424; idem, "'Early Catholicism' in the New Testament as a Problem in Controversial Theology," in *The Council in Action: Theological Reflections on the Second Vatican Council* (New York, 1963), 159–95; E. Käsemann, "Paulus und der Frühkatholizismus," *ZTK* 60 (1963): 75–89, reprinted in his *Exegetische Versuche und Besinnungen* 2 (Göttingen, 1964), 239–52 (also translated into English and French); K. Beyschlag, *Klemens Romanus und der Frühkatholizismus* (Tübingen, 1966); J. M. Elliott, "A Catholic Gospel: Reflections on 'Early Catholicism' in the New Testament," *CBQ* 31 (1969): 213–23; E. Lohse, "Die frühkatholische Kirche," in R. Kottje and B. Moeller, eds., *Ökumenische Kirchengeschichte* I. *Alte Kirche und Ostkirche* (Mainz/Munich, 1970), 61–69; I. de la Potterie, "Le problème oecuménique du Canon et le protocatholicisme," *Axes* 4 (1972), no. 4, pp. 7–19; U. Luz, "Erwägungen zur Entstehung des 'Frühkatholizismus,' eine Skizze," *ZNW* 65 (1974): 88–111; I. H. Marshall, "Early Catholicism' in the New Testament," in R. N. Longenecker and M. C. Tenney, eds., *New Dimensions in New Testament Study* (Grand Rapids, 1974), 217–31; H. J. Schmitz, *Frühkatholizismus bei Adolf von Harnack, Rudolf Sohm und Ernst Käsemann* (Düsseldorf, 1977); F. Hahn, "Das Problem des Frühkatholizismus," *EvT* 38 (1978): 340–57; G. Kretschmar, "Frühkatholizismus: Die Beurteilung theologischer Entwicklungen im späten ersten und im zweiten Jahrhundert nach Christus," in J. Brantschen and P. Selvatico, eds., *Unterwegs zur Einheit: Festschrift für Heinrich Stirnimann* (Freiburg, Switz., 1980), 573–87; C. Bartsch, *"Frühkatholizismus" als Kategorie historischkritischer Theologie: Eine methodologische und theologiegeschichtliche Untersuchung* (Berlin, 1980); V. Fusco, "Sul concetto di Protocattolicesimo," *RivB* 30 (1982): 401–34; J. Rogge and G. Schille, eds., *Frühkatholizismus im ökumenisch-theologischen Arbeitskreise in der DDR* (Berlin, 1983); C. Clifton Black II, "The Johannine Epistles and the Question of

Early Catholicism," *NT* 28 (1986): 131–58. To these studies should be added: K. Giles, "Is Luke an Exponent of 'Early Protestantism'? Church Order in the Lukan Writings," *EvQ* 54 (1982): 193–205; 55 (1983): 3–20.

S. Schulz lists (*Mitte*, 80f.) the most characteristic traits of "early Catholicism" as identified by scholars writing prior to his own work: the gradual abandonment and final disappearance of the expectation of an imminent coming or apocalyptic expectation of the irruption of God's reign; the failure to understand the true Pauline message of the justification of the wicked, which is now replaced by a focusing of attention on the just; the new value given to the Law, contrary to Paul's teaching (but what "law" is in question here?); a new understanding of faith, which becomes increasingly a virtue or a hope, instead of being that by which salvation is appropriated (Paul); the vicarious satisfaction offered by Christ no longer occupies a central place in theology; the subordination of the Spirit to the ecclesiastical institution; the teaching of the ecclesiastical magisterium becomes increasingly important; the attacks by Gnosticism lead to a clearer definition of heresy as contrasted with orthodoxy; the repression of the "enthusiast" movement finds partial expression in a new attention paid to the historical aspect of Jesus and the church (Gospels and Acts of the Apostles); Christ is seen more and more as the inaugurator of a new law and a morality that presupposes the idea of merit; the great importance assigned to miracles; the idea of salvation through the sacraments bulks larger; elements of a natural theology find growing acceptance; the dangerous reconciliation of the church with the state; a tendency to attach the label "apostolic" to everything, whence the abundance of anonymous or pseudonymous literature during the early Catholic period.

Schulz divides his study of "early Catholic theology" into three parts. The first is entitled "The Catholicization of the Person, History, and Theology of Paul" (86–130). I am interested here especially in his references to various passages in the writings of Paul.

1. The figure of the church as "body of Christ" makes its appearance as early as the letter to the Colossians (1:24; 2:19), as does the church's role in the development of the Christian faith, a role that the tradition must preserve (2:6f.) at

any price, just as it must the gospel itself (1:23). Present hope, focused on individual salvation (1:5, 27), gains the upper hand over expectation of the end. Contrary to what is taught in Romans 6:4–5, the baptized are already risen (Col 2:12f.; 3:1) and freed from the ascendancy of the cosmic powers. The *Haustafeln*, or codes of domestic morality (3:18–4:1), are found in a good number of writings regarded as "early Catholic." Schulz finds in Colossians, especially in 2:8–23, allusions to gnostic heresy that are not consistent with what is to be found in 1 Corinthians. His view is that it was a disciple with "early Catholic" tendencies who wrote Colossians around the year 80 in order to bring the authority of Paul to bear in the struggle against Gnosticism. A number of studies of the *Haustafeln* have appeared recently. There is a list in L. Sabourin, *Early Catholicism and Ministries* (Burlington, Ont., 1989) n. 17.

2. In the letter to the Ephesians, the vocabulary again includes a number of words that do not seem to go back to Paul but are found in postapostolic writings. More than Colossians, on which it depends, the letter to the Ephesians belongs among early Catholic writings by reason of its content and especially of the way it speaks of the church as the "fullness" of Christ (1:23), who is her head and the savior of her who is his body (5:23). The next verses (5:24–27) suppose that the church is the spouse of Christ, a theme that becomes explicit in many subsequent early Catholic writings such as the *Didache* (11.11) and the Epistle of Ignatius of Antioch to Polycarp (5.1). Thus in Ephesians the church becomes a necessary mediator of salvation: a view that again shows the early Catholic perspective. Furthermore, there is a tendency to identify the church with the kingdom of God on earth. Ephesians contains no reflections on the salvation of the Jewish people, such as are found in, e.g., Rom 9–11. Slavery to sin seems to be something in the past (2:1–3) or else the lot of pagans (4:17–19), whereas Paul speaks of it as a personal experience (Rom 7:13–25). Schulz concludes that Ephesians must be a document from the end of the first century and therefore post-Pauline, early Catholic in inspiration, and addressed to the communities of Asia Minor in order to instruct them on the nature of the "one, holy, catholic" church.

3. As many critics recognize, it is difficult to attribute the second letter to the Thessalonians to the author of the first, so different is the second in style but also in content, especially in what has to do with eschatology. Christians need no longer look forward to the proximate coming of the Lord, and signs will make that coming known in advance (2 Thes 2:1–12). In addition, the moralization of salvation replaces the Pauline message of justification by faith: faithful Christians have rewards in store, and sinners punishment (1:6–12). The ready acceptance of the authority to command that is attributed to the apostle (2:15; 3:4–15) seems also to show the early Catholic origin of the document.

4. Recent exegesis readily assigns the Pastoral letters (1–2 Tm, Ti) to a writer later than Paul, although it is not possible to be more specific. Schulz, for his part, thinks that these letters represent instructions to *Amtsträger*, holders of authority in the church, who are represented by Timothy and Titus. The letters bear clear witness to the antignostic struggle and the early Catholic exegesis of Paul that was being practiced in Asia Minor at the beginning of the second century. Some of the recognizable early Catholic traits in these letters are the reference to *eusebeia* ("godliness," "piety"), which occurs only here, in Acts, and in 2 Peter, as well as the reference to the *Haustafeln* and the lists of vices. As in 2 Peter, so here there is a tendency to rationalize the Christian life and turn it into a morality.

5. There is agreement that the third Gospel and the book of Acts come from one and the same author. According to ancient Catholic tradition both are the work of Luke, a doctor and friend of Paul (Col 4:14). But, relying on the Protestant scholarship that has been in fashion for a century now, Schulz thinks that this Luke is not the author of Luke-Acts. He maintains that it is not possible to see a companion of Paul as author of a book (Acts) that gives an "early Catholic" picture of the person, apostolate, and theology of the apostle (109). Moreover, in the prologue of the Gospel the author himself shows that he is a Christian of the second generation (Lk 1:1–4). He must have composed his work in the first third of the second century, for it attests to a period in which Paul has already become an almost legendary figure who is fitted into the framework of the early Catholic interpretation of "salvation history."

6. According to Schulz (123–30), even the authentic letters of Paul have undergone revisions at the hands of their early Catholic editor. This is true especially of 1 Thessalonians, 1–2 Corinthians, and Romans. I shall limit myself to a few examples. The call for watchfulness in 1 Thessalonians 5:1–11 reflects the content of passages in "Luke" (see Lk 21:25–27; Acts 3:20f.) and recalls other passages with an early Catholic content (e.g., 2 Pt 3:10–13). 1 Corinthians 14:33b–36 seems to be part of an antignostic polemic against the emancipation of women; it is in disagreement with the role that Paul grants women in liturgical assemblies (1 Cor 11:5) but is consistent with texts in the Pastoral Epistles (see 1 Tm 2:11f.). The reviser of these letters (it is claimed) was drawing Paul into the fold of the early Catholic tradition. In 2 Cor 6:14–7:1 not only does the reviser use words that are not Pauline, but we also find there an idea of "justice" that is no longer that of the apostle. The contrast drawn between the "just" and the "wicked" in this passage appears again in Eph 1:1; 1 Tm 4:10, and elsewhere in writings that show an early Catholic tendency. Rom 7:25b seems to be an early Catholic gloss that has been added to Paul's text: "So then, with my mind I am a slave to the law of God, but with my flesh I am a slave to the law of sin." This is an example of that increased attention to the "just," which I mentioned earlier among the characteristic traits of early Catholic theology. It is also probable that the great doxology in Rom 16:25–27 was added to Paul's text by a different hand. The preaching of the gospel is also often described in the deutero-Pauline writings as the revelation of a mystery, and 2 Peter 3:16 likewise speaks of "prophetic writings" in the sense of canonical texts.

The second part of Schulz's study of early Catholic theology is entitled: "The Catholicization of Legalist and Apocalyptic Jewish Christianity." He explains (131) that Mark, Q, and the material proper to Matthew and Luke come from "life of Jesus" traditions that represent the conservative, legalist, and apocalyptic Jewish Christianity of Syria-Palestine. However, the original source of these writings is often obscured by an early Catholic editing that has transformed them in a significant way. In comparison with the parable of the murderous vine growers in which the son plays a part (Mt 21:37-39), the parable of the wedding feast (22:1-14) represents teaching on ecclesiology rather than on Christology: this again is a characteristic of early Catholic theology. According to Schulz, Matthew's conclusion, "For many are called, but few are chosen," suggests precisely that the early Catholic church seeks to be an "assembly of the just," whereas in v. 10 the wicked as well as the good are assembled in the wedding hall.

Without being as clear as in Matthew, evidence of early Catholic editing appears even in the earliest Gospel, that of Mark. Here too we find specifically a history of salvation plan, a lessening of expectation of an imminent end, the proclamation of punishment for Israel, and the dramatic end of the former economy (Mk 15:38). On the other hand, we do not find here the doctrine of merit as maintained by Matthew who adds to Mark 8:38 a sentence having to do with merit: "For the Son of Man is to come with his angels in the glory of his Father, and then he will repay everyone for what has been done" (Mt 16:27; the second half of the sentence draws on Ps 62:13: "For you repay to all according to their work"). Mark's silence on merit can be explained in part by the fact that he reflects the teaching of the synagogue in a pagan land, whereas the Q source for the sayings of Jesus is linked rather with Palestinian Judaism.

There is very little sign of Paul's influence in the Gospel of Mark. For example, Paul prefers to speak of sin in the singular number, as a power that enslaves; Mark prefers to speak of the forgiveness of sins, in the plural (1:4f.; 2:5, 9; 3:28; 11:25), and his Gospel also contains a catalogue of sins (7:10-23), similar to those in the Pastorals (1 Tm 1:9f.; 6:4f.; 2 Tm 3:2-5; Ti 2:2-5; 3:3). It is true that these lists of sins may spring from early Catholicism, which tends to turn the Christian life into a morality, but they are also found in Wis 14:15f., Rom 1:29f., Gal 5:19f., and Eph 4:17-32. On this subject, see G. Segalla, "I cataloghi dei peccati in S. Paolo," *Studia Patavina* 15 (1968): 205-28; N. J. McEleney, "The Vice Lists of the Pastoral Epistles," *CBQ* 36 (1974): 202-19; E. Schweizer, "Gottesgerechtigkeit und Lasterkataloge bei Paulus (inkl. Kol und Eph)," in J. Friedrich et al., eds., *Rechtfertigung: Festschrift für Ernst Käsemann zum 70. Geburtstag* (Tübingen/ Göttingen, 1976), 415-42.

The miraculous undoubtedly receives special attention in early Catholic writings, but this is due, in part, to the intention of showing that Jesus was not an ordinary person but could readily be compared to the kind of person to whom the title *theios anēr* ("divine man") was given. See T. Tagawa, *Miracles et Évangile: La pensée personnelle de l'évangeliste Marc* (Paris, 1966). The title of Mark's Gospel (1:1), the considerable room given to miracle stories, and the centurion's confession (15:39) show that Mark aimed to stress the divine character of Jesus. It is doubtless not a mere coincidence that the same tendency appears in the sermons of Peter (Acts 2:22; 3:16; 4:9-12), since Mark would be reflecting Peter's teaching. According to Schulz, the profusion of miracle stories in Mark's Gospel shows early Catholic influence (219). Readers might believe that the miraculous was a deeply rooted element in the religious literature of the people, but in fact it was mainly toward the end of the second century that miracle stories began to proliferate. This literary genre reached its high point in *The Life of Apollonius* by Philostratus; see L. Sabourin, *The Divine Miracles Discussed and Defended* (Rome, 1977), 41-46, and G. Petzke, *Die Traditionen uber Apollonius von Tyana und das Neue Testament* (Leiden, 1970). The question of the Gospel miracles continues to hold the attention of scholars. See the annotated bibliography in my *Divine Miracles*, 237-71. In a recent study R. Latourelle stresses the need of seeing the miracles of Jesus for what they are, namely, signs that make known the coming of the kingdom; see *The Miracles of Jesus and the Theology of Miracles* (New York, 1988), 9-40. In *Divine Miracles* I raised the question of "faith and healing" (115-17). On three different occasions Jesus says to the person who has been healed: "Your faith has saved you!" (Mk 5:34; 10:5; Lk 17:19). See D. Merli, *Fiducia e fede nei miracoli evangelici* (Genoa, 1973), and my review in *BTB* 3 (1973): 231f.

Schulz also finds early Catholic influence in the Gospel of John, a document that represents for him "the Catholicization of gnostic enthusiasm" (227-56). Making his own a rather widespread but often refuted thesis, he distinguishes between the Gospel as we now have it and a *Grundschrift*, which was in fact a gnosticizing document impregnated with dualism. Schulz thinks he sees this origin reflected in the contrasts that John or the Johannine Christ draws between light and darkness, truth and falsehood, life and death, freedom and slavery, things above and things below. Furthermore, as Bultmann had already argued, it is as Revealer that the Christ of John saves the world, for his incarnation and presence are a challenge to every human being. In particular (Schulz says), the added twenty-first chapter is the work of an early Catholic editor, whose hand also appears in various verses of the prologue as we have it (Jn 1:1–18). The "sacramentalization" of various passages (3:5; 6:53–55; 19:34) is to be explained in the same way. The allegory of the vine (15:1–8) goes with the theme of the meritorious life of the just (see 5:29), another early Catholic trait. Some passages of the first Letter and the Revelation of John can be read in the same light.

Distinctive marks of early Catholic theology also appear in the letter to the Hebrews. Hebrews is the only NT document that describes Christ as a priest and in particular calls him the celebrant of the true sanctuary and true tent (see 8:2 and 9:11f., together with my explanation of these passages in *NTS* 18 [1971]: 87–90 and in greater detail in *Priesthood* [Leiden, 1973], 178–212). "Faith" in Heb 11 is not the christological faith of Paul but rather the hope of reaching the goal (11:14–16), and in this respect, too, the letter is close to early Catholic thinking. The same holds for the reference to forgivable and unforgivable sins, which indicates the possibility of recourse to the sacrament of penance.

Like other authors who display an early Catholic tendency, Jude in his letter is particularly opposed to false teachers, who are described in stereotyped terms that make their identification difficult. The real author of the letter cannot have been Jude (Judas), the brother of James (see Lk 6:16; Acts 1:13), since he is writing, at the earliest, at the end of the first century, while on the other hand the letter predates 2 Peter, which makes use of it. Among the "early Catholic" traits in Jude mention may be made also of his idea of "faith," his appeal to tradition, and his reminder of the reward awaiting the just.

As might be expected, the influence of early Catholic theology is also to be seen in the writings of the apostolic fathers: in chronological order, *1 Clement*, the *Didache*, Ignatius of Antioch, Barnabas, the *Shepherd* of Hermas, *2 Clement*, and the Epistle of Polycarp (Schulz, 257–381). The letter of Clement to the Corinthians, which dates from 93 to 96, is contemporary with several NT writings. The thing that most clearly marks it as an "early Catholic" document is its Judeo-Hellenistic conception of the eternal order of creation, similar to that found in the natural theology of the Stoics (Schulz, 310). In keeping with this line of thought, God is frequently named (ninety times) and given the titles Creator, Master, and Lord. There is not enough space in the present article for me to list all the "early Catholic" traits in the writings of the apostolic fathers.

I have drawn upon S. Schulz's book, *Die Mitte der Schrift*, for this presentation of "early Catholicism"; my use of his book does not, however, mean that I accept his thesis, which two theologians have criticized rather severely. The reader will find in my book *Early Catholicism and Ministries* an extended review of P.-G. Müller, "Destruktion des Kanons—Verlust der Mitte. Ein kritisches Gespräch mit Siegfried Schulz," *TRev* 73 (1977): 177–86. In Müller's judgment (178) Schulz's book displays a "fanatical aversion" to Catholicism. Schulz has no doubt at all that Catholicism is an *Abfall* (a defection) from the *Evangelium*, and he does his utmost to prove this in his book. He refers occasionally to Catholic authors such as Schlier, Schelkle, and Mussner, but only to discredit them (see 179), while finding support for his views in Küng. The bulk of his work (86–381) is devoted to showing that Paul's gospel constitutes the center (*Mitte*), the very heart of the Scriptures, whereas most of the NT has been "Catholicized": see the repeated use of the word *Katholisierung* in the titles of the chapters. Guided by a cumbersome and controlling a priori, Schulz finds almost everywhere in the NT traces of an early Catholic degeneration, an early Catholic disfiguration of the pure *Christusevangelium*. As one reads Schulz's book, one is led to ask whether "the gospel of justification" is not a pipe dream, an idea that cannot be found in its pure state in the NT. Can Jesus himself be said to have been free of "pre-Catholic" tendencies, since he makes fraternal charity the criterion of authentic religion, somewhat like James, who rejects a justification solely by faith? In *TP* 52 (1977): 98–102, J. Beutler has a review of Schulz's work that brings out its good points and its defects.

Léopold SABOURIN

ECCLESIAM SUAM (Encyclical)

John XXIII and Paul VI wished to take the church into the history of the twentieth century and to make it a resourceful church in dialogue with the world. In this respect, among all those changes in attitude that express the *metanoia*, or conversion, effected by the council itself (especially those of service, opening up to the world, dialogue, inwardness, search for meaning, and care for the spirit rather than the letter), the dialogic attitude brought about the most profound revolution in the life of the church.

It came, indeed, after a period during which the church had protested against the modern world, followed by a period of isolation and silence—indeed of dumbness. At Vatican II, the church underwent conversion; it was no longer defiant and hostile but became accessible and receptive. Beforehand it had claimed to know everything, without having to learn anything. Henceforth it recognizes the world as its partner in open dialogue. It acknowledges other cultures and mentalities and trusts them. The long-interrupted dialogue with the sciences and philosophies of the modern era was reestablished. The church also engaged in dialogue with the separated Christian communities, with the great world religions, and even with atheistic humanism. It looked for forms of cooperation, or at least of understanding, with the Communist states.

The year 1964 represents a point of maturity in this ecclesiastical realization of the urgent need to adopt an attitude of dialogue. Four major documents appeared in the space of four months, all essentially concerned with the word of God and dialogue. First was Schema III

on revelation, which contains an entirely new paragraph, of more than fifteen lines, on revelation understood as dialogue between God and human beings, through the mediation of Jesus Christ. This text was published in July 1964 and remained unchanged until the promulgation of *DV* in 1965. Second was the encyclical *Ecclesiam Suam*, which describes the attitude of the church to the world in terms of dialogue. It appeared on 6 August 1964. Finally the Constitution on the Church and the Decree on Ecumenism were promulgated on 21 November 1964.

This convergence of major texts, so close in time, and all intimately concerned with dialogue, cannot have been the work of chance. Ecclesiastical awareness had matured, and the dialogic attitude had become part of the church's life. The interest of *Ecclesiam Suam* is grounded in the encyclical's concern to express the theological bases of this rediscovered attitude by appealing directly to the heart of revelation. "The church [says *ES*] should enter into dialogue with the world in which it lives. It must turn to talk, message and discussion" (*AAS* 56 [1964]: 639). But the prototype of this dialogue of the church with the world was the dialogue of God with human beings, which we know as revelation. "Revelation, which [is] the supernatural relation that God himself has taken the initiative of establishing with human beings, may be represented as a dialogue in which the word of God is expressed by the incarnation, and then by the gospel. The paternal and holy colloquy between God and human beings interrupted because of original sin has been marvelously resumed in the course of history. Salvation history is a precise account of this long and varied dialogue, which starts with God and undertakes a varied and extraordinary conversation with human beings. It is in this conversation of Christ with people (Bar 3:38) that God allows an understanding of something regarding himself—namely, the mystery of his life, which is one in its essence and trinitarian in its persons. Here he has finally stated how he wishes to be known—he is love—and how he wishes to be honored and served. Our supreme commandment is love. Dialogue is pursued in a full and trusting way. The child is invited to it, and mystical theology is exhausted in it. We must always ensure the presence of that ineffable and real relation of dialogue offered and established with us by God the Father, through the mediation of Christ in the Holy Spirit, if we are to understand what relation we, the church, should seek to establish and to promote with human beings" (*AAS* 56 [1964]: 641–42).

This is the first time that an encyclical has described so emphatically the dialogic cast of revelation and has proposed it as a prototype of the dialogue between the church and the world. By adopting the terms of Schema III on revelation—"dialogue" (*ES = colloquium*; *DV = et homines alloquitur*) and "conversation" (*ES = sermoninatio*; *DV = et alloquitur*, taken from the same text in Bar 3:38)—it lays an unprecedented emphasis on the dynamic and interpersonal nature of revelation. The living God, through an initiative of love, leaves his mystery and enters into communication with human beings. God engages in dialogue and speaks with human beings in order to establish a communion of thought and life. The main object of this dialogue, which is the confidence of love, is the very mystery of the divine life. The dialogue of revelation, *ES* stresses, enlightens us about the church's dialogue with humanity. At the basis of all dialogue there is profound respect for the other person and an availability and readiness to listen, which already represent a beginning of love itself. Dialogue, says *ES*, implies a "desire for courtesy, respect, sympathy and kindness, on the part of the person who undertakes it" (*AAS* 56 [1964]: 644). Perfect dialogue occurs when a speaker listens so effectively to another person speaking that the speaker inspires confidence in the person who has to reply, and likewise when the listener shows such a degree of attention and sympathy that he or she makes the speaker inclined to stop talking in order to listen to the listener. The great temptation of dialogue is to indulge in monologue in order to dominate the other person, or to reject dialogue in order to eliminate the other person. True dialogue always implies the possibility of a death or a holocaust, even on the part of the church; that is why it cannot be sustained without charity. *ES* summarizes the foregoing by listing the four qualities of dialogue as charity, equanimity, trust, and prudence, following the example of Christ himself (*AAS* 56 [1964]: 645).

There is analogy but not identity between the dialogue of God with human beings and the dialogues of human beings with one another.

Once we have stressed this essential difference, it remains true that the dialogue of salvation can act as an inspiration in the relations between the church and the world, and between each Christian and his or her human brothers and sisters. *Ecclesiam Suam* describes both types of dialogue.

The encyclical lists the characteristics of the dialogue of revelation. First, it is a dialogue "spontaneously inaugurated by the divine initiative: it is God who loved us first" (*AAS* 56 [1964]: 642). Second, it is a dialogue inaugurated by "charity, by divine loving-kindness" (ibid., 642). Third, it is a dialogue "which is not assessed according to the merits of those to whom it was addressed, or the results it may or may not have obtained" (ibid., 642). Fourth, although it is ineffably serious, because of the salvation which it expresses, it nevertheless infinitely respects human freedom. "The dialogue of salvation does not physically compel anyone to accept it. It is a redoubtable request for love that, though it represents a considerable responsibility for those to whom it is addressed, nevertheless leaves them free to match that address or to repudiate it" (ibid., 642). Fifth, the dialogue of salvation "is addressed to all human beings, without discrimination" (ibid., 643). Finally, this kind of dialogue has been a work of patience and wise instruction. It has experienced successive developments and humble beginnings before reaching complete success" (ibid., 643), which show respect for the delays in human maturity.

In a second section the encyclical describes the church's duties in regard to revelation. On the one hand, it must deepen its awareness of "the deposit of truth which it has inherited and guards" (*AAS* 56 [1964]: 644). Yet, "neither guardianship nor defense exhausts the Church's duty regarding the riches in its possession" (ibid., 639). It must also propagate the inheritance that it has received. It must also exhibit, in its teaching, "a concern to come to terms, as far as that is possible, with the experience and understanding of the contemporary world" (ibid., 650). It has to adapt to "the life of people at a certain time, in a certain place, in a certain culture, and in a certain social situation" (ibid., 646). This theme is developed at length in *GS*, especially in regard to culture (*GS* 58).

Loyalty and adaptation are the two poles of the church's action in regard to the gospel and in its dialogue with humanity. It should set the gospel before people of our own time—the gospel that has been given once and for all and that is nevertheless always present and always relevant. The church has to reconcile these two attitudes. It should avoid anxious, chilly, and sterile conservatism but also a too liberal form of adaptation that would be no more than "irenicism and syncretism" (*AAS* 56 [1964]: 647). The search for this balance between a concern for loyalty and a concern for adaptation gives rise to authentic dialogue. It is a delicate balance, but it is part of the very condition of a revelation introduced into history in order to address human beings of all times and places.

Bibl.: J. LACROIX, "La Filosofia del Dialogo," *StCatt* 8 (Nov.–Dec. 1964): 57–64; VATICAN II, Constitution *Dei Verbum* (1965), chap. 1; R. LATOURELLE, "La Révélation comme dialogue dans Ecclesiam suam," *Greg* 46 (1965): 834–39; id., *Theology of Revelation* (Staten Island, N.Y., 1966), 407–24; id., *Christ and the Church: Signs of Salvation* (New York, 1971), 198–207.

René LATOURELLE

ECUMENISM

1. Terminology

The word *ecumenism* and especially the adjective *ecumenical* are used actually in two different senses. In expressions as "ecumenical patriarch" or "ecumenical council" it has an ancient meaning linked to its classic Greek use, in which *oikoumenē* indicated the inhabited world, more specifically the world of Greek or Roman culture, the Byzantine empire and later the Christian world, linked as it was with the not yet divided Roman Empire. So it also referred to the official, orthodox doctrine, common to the Eastern and Western church. It is only in the period 1920 to 1930 that "ecumenism/ecumenical" began to be used currently as an expression to indicate the movement toward Christian unity. The word is sometimes used in a still larger meaning, indicating any effort toward unity among religions or within the world. We use it here in its more restricted, contemporary meaning to indicate the endeavors toward unity among the separated Christian churches.

2. Definition

In the decree on ecumenism, *Unitatis Redintegratio*, the Second Vatican Council has described the ecumenical movement as follows:

> Everywhere large numbers have felt the impulse of this grace [i.e., of remorse over division and longing for unity], and among our separated brethren also there increases from day to day a movement, fostered by the grace of the Holy Spirit, for the restoration of unity among all Christians. Taking part in this movement, which is called ecumenical, are those who invoke the Triune God and confess Jesus as Lord and Savior. They join in not merely as individuals but also as members of the corporate groups in which they have heard the gospel, and which each regards as his church and, indeed, God's. And yet, almost everyone, though in different ways, longs that there may be one visible church of God, a church truly universal and sent forth to the whole world that the world may be converted to the Gospel and so be saved, to the glory of God. (*UR* 1)

The decree indicates thus some essential features of the ecumenical movement, namely, its reference to the work of the Holy Spirit, its communal and ecclesial character, and its missionary orientation. The Holy Spirit works beyond the boundaries of any church and brings them to unity for the salvation of the world. Because of its pneumatologic and ecclesiologic roots the ecumenical dimension is part of any theological reflection.

3. Historical Survey

Even though the history of disunity weighs heavily in the history of the Christian churches, this unfortunate state of affairs has never been accepted with a good conscience. Always there have been efforts to reconcile and to restore unity. Let us recall only the vain efforts of the councils of Lyon (1274) and Florence (1439) with regard to the Oriental churches and the influence of Desiderius Erasmus upon the religious colloquies in Germany and France at the time of the Protestant Reformation. It is only in the twentieth century that the scandal of the division among Christians has been fully recognized. Many historical reasons have contributed to the development of this conscience: e.g., the international philanthropic movements of the nineteenth century, the interconfessional youth and student movements, and the expansion of the missionary idea within the Protestant world. As a matter of fact, it is the World Missionary Conference at Edinburgh (1910) that is generally considered the starting point of the modern ecumenical movement. It was in the aftermath of this conference that the International Missionary Council was founded in 1921, in order particularly to "foster world-wide fellowship among Christians and to further united planning and action in presenting the Gospel to all men" (Rouse and Neill 1945: 1:368). The Faith and Order Movement was created to tackle the theological problems that were consciously left out at Edinburgh but continued to burden all further contact. The movement organized two important world conferences, first in 1927 in Lausanne, and the second in Edinburgh in 1937. A third mainstream that led to the first Universal Christian Conference on Life and Work [*Conférence mondiale du Christianisme pratique*] in Stockholm in 1925 and a second one in Oxford in 1937, originated in the concerns of the Lutheran bishop of Uppsala, Nathan Söderblom (1866–1931), for peace during the First World War (1914–18). This movement was built upon the conviction that unity was best served with a common concern and collaboration for peace and justice. Along with this major current other groups worked for a rapprochement among Christians. The Christian Student Movement should be remembered as the spiritual nursery for many an ecumenical leader. It was Faith and Order and Life and Work that formally decided in 1937 to merge into the World Council of Churches. The International Missionary Council decided at that moment not to join formally but worked in close contact with the World Council. The three strands, namely, doctrine, service, and mission, that gave raise to the WCC remained at work in the further evolution of the council: they continue to develop within the one structure of the WCC their own programs, e.g., by convoking their own world conferences.

It is fair to say that when the Roman Catholic church showed interest in the ecumenical movement in the early sixties with the setting up of the Secretariat for Promoting Christian Unity with Cardinal Augustin Bea (1881–1968) as its first president, the sending of official observers to the New Delhi general assembly of the WCC (1961), and by inviting non-Catholic observers to the Second Vatican Council, it joined a movement that was already fully constituted. For many years the Catholic church had stood aloof from the ecumenical movement. Pius XI's encyclical *Mortalium Animos* (6 January 1928) was an official refusal to collaborate. This attitude remained fundamentally unaltered until 1960, even though the instruction of the Holy Office of 20 December 1949, *De Motione Ecumenica*, showed already some openness. Entrance into the movement had been prepared by the private interest of several Catholic ecumenists such as Y. M. Congar (b. 1904), P. Couturier (1881–1953), M. Pribilla (1884–1956), and L. Beauduin (1873–1960), the founder of the Benedictine priory of Amay (now relocated at Chèvetogne). The Catholic Conference for Ecumenical Questions, of which Johannes Willebrands was the secretary, should also be remembered. The overture of the Catholic church was momentous for the whole ecumenical movement. Through a conciliar act Vatican II gave its backing to the ecumenical endeavor and made it enter as never before among the official priorities of the Catholic church, as well as of other churches.

The entrance of the Catholic church changed the ecumenical panorama. If previously the ecumenical movement could largely be identified with the achievements of the WCC, the council now became an important part of a much larger movement. In this panorama the *bilateral dialogues between the confessions and the churches* acquired a great importance. Although the network of the dialogues is larger than the ones the Catholic church is involved in, it is true also that the latter has a certain preference for them. Let us mention some of the more fruitful dialogues on a world level: the Orthodox-Roman Catholic International Dialogue, the Anglican-Roman Catholic International Theological Commission (ARCIC), the Lutheran-Roman Catholic Joint Commission, the Reformed-Roman Catholic International Dialogue. There are also dialogues with the ancient Eastern churches, with the Baptists, the Disciples of Christ, the Pentecostals, and the Methodists. Some important dialogues on a local level, such as the Lutheran-Roman Catholic Dialogue in the United States and the work of the French Groupe des Dombes, have had an important impact on ecumenical consensus building. Getting acquainted with the results of these dialogues, available in many reports and statements and assembled now in various collections, will expand the ecumenical horizon of theology and further the reception of their findings.

The ecumenical venture is not limited to official contacts and doctrinal dialogues. It is more than merely one concern among others. It has become a demanding way of being related to one another in various ways and on various levels of church life, from official bodies to the most informal ways of living together at the grass-roots. These new relations express themselves in common prayer, Bible reading and worship, in common witness and service toward the various needs of the world, especially for peace and justice. Christians, as a matter of fact, should do together all that they are not obliged to do separately. The ecumenical movement is a provisional way of living together as Christians, born from the acute suffering for the scandal of disunity and the recognition of a common faith. The concern for unity and the unequal reception of the ecumenical advance will unavoidably create tension and fermentation in the churches and in the Christian commonwealth. The experience of communion, however imperfect it may still be, can never be adequately covered by rules and directives, which are necessarily codifications of yesterday's reality. The patience and prudence the ecumenical venture is calling for conflict with the urgency of the goal, namely, the lifting up of the separation and the restoration of the broken communion.

4. Theological Problems

I do not intend to give a complete panorama of the theological problems raised in the ecumenical dialogues. According to the orientation of this encyclopedia, we mention some that seem more relevant for fundamental theology.

a. Method of Ecumenical Theology

The relations between the confessions have been characterized for centuries through *controversy*, each one defending its own position by opposing it in an apologetic and polemical way to another church or community. Often such a way of arguing led to exalting one's own views by belittling, caricaturing, and globally condemning the divergent viewpoints as heretical, not to say, devilish. Thus controversy has built up impressive libraries and amounts of prejudice. Since the start of the ecumenical movement ways have been looked for to improve mutual understanding. One of the first ones was the *comparative method*, "a neutral and simple method of self-explanation and comparison without raising the question of who is right and wrong" (Pathil 1981: 398). Although comparison still remains unavoidable, the ecumenical experience has led us to look at diversity in the light of a hermeneutic of unity. A breakthrough has been the so-called *christological method* presented in the final report of the Third World Conference of Faith and Order in Lund (1952): "Once again," the report says, "it has been proved true that as we seek to draw closer to Christ we come closer to one another" (Vischer 1963:85). Though not ignoring the differences, one tries to look beyond them by recognizing a more fundamental unity in Christ and by studying the common sources in Scripture and in the common tradition of teaching, worship, and prayer. But again and again one was confronted with the great diversity and plurality of traditions and theologies, related to particular historical, sociocultural, political, and psychological life situations. This variety of contexts is taken into account in the *contextual method* that tries to relate them to one another in an effort to express the unity in diversity of the church (Pathil 1981:346).

A major tool to achieve the goals of these methods is *dialogue*, a catchword in the modern ecumenical movement. For the Decree on Ecumenism meetings and dialogues "where each can treat with the other on an equal footing *(par cum pari)*" are most valuable for the discussion of theological problems (*UR* 9). In a working paper of the Secretariat for Promoting Christian Unity with reflections and suggestions concerning ecumenical dialogue (1970) is the following:

> In general terms, dialogue exists between individuals and groups from the moment when each party begins both to listen and reply, to seek to understand and to be understood, to pose questions and to be questioned in turn, to be freely forthcoming and receptive to the other party, concerning a given situation, research project, or course of action, with the aim of

progressing in unison toward a greater community of life, outlook, and accomplishment. (*SPCU/Information Service* [1970], no. 12, p. 5, II/1)

The Vatican Council accepted dialogue on the grounds of well-tested ecumenical methodology. The theological foundation can be found in the "communion" ecclesiology. Though not yet in full communion, churches do consider themselves because of their ecumenical commitment already as *church-in-relation,* as *church-in-dialogue.* The churches hesitate, however, to reflect on the ecclesiological implications and significance of the wider context in which they are *church in relation with other churches and communities.* The roots lie anthropologically in the dignity and the social nature of the human person. Ecclesiologically they are rooted in the fact that God's Spirit is working beyond the borders of any community: "Christians are in a position to communicate to each other the riches that the Holy Spirit develops within them. This community of spiritual goods is the first basis upon which ecumenical dialogue rests" (*SPCU/Information Service* [1970], no. 12, p. 6, III/1). Dialogue among the Christian churches has taken an extension and depth that could not have been foreseen by the Second Vatican Council. Expressing one's own convictions of faith on one hand, and careful and patient listening to the convictions of the dialogue partners on the other will always remain a painstaking requirement of living together as churches, be it in imperfect or full communion. There is no communion without permanent willingness to listen, to understand, and to be changed in the process (see "Ecumenical Findings," *ER* 41 [1989]: 126). Stressing the dialogical dimension has sometimes been felt to be in tension with the missionary task of the church.

b. Credibility

Among the most fundamental problems in ecumenical reflections is without doubt the *credibility* of the Christian message preached by the church. At the origin of the ecumenical movement stands the problem of the mission. Jesus' prayer that "they may all be one . . . so that the world may believe that you have sent me" (Jn 17:21) pervades the whole ecumenical movement. It shows that unity of the church is not an end in itself but has a missionary goal and must finally witness to the all-transcending reign of God. This outlook implies that the ecumenical movement must reflect upon the salvific function of the Christian faith and the church in front of the other religions and faiths, and thus of the proper meaning of the absoluteness of the Christian message. More and more also is the ecumenical movement aware of the theological urgency of its responsibility for the world and for humankind, for justice, peace, and the integrity of creation. In the face of the many threats that endanger humankind and the world, the ecumenical movement has become more sensitive to its responsibility for a creation whose survival is entrusted to all human persons.

c. Models of Church Unity

All the churches confess the unity of the church with the words of the Creed of Constantinople. In its most intimate being the church is one and cannot exist as divided. Where division arises it should be mended by forgiveness and reconciliation. Many central texts of the Bible teach us this duty: "Forgive us our debts as we also have forgiven our debtors" (Mt 6:12); "So when you are offering your gift at the altar, if you remember that your brother or sister has something against you, leave your gift there before the altar and go; first be reconciled with your brother or sister" (Mt 5:23–24). In the letter to the Ephesians Paul puts before our eyes Christ, our Peace, who reconciled the two— Gentiles and Jews—in a single body to God through the cross, on which he killed the enmity. He broke down the dividing wall (Eph 2:11–22). In different situations these summons become seeds of reconciliation in one believing community.

The contemporary ecumenical movement has attempted to chart paths toward future restored unity. These models have to consider the essentials of Christian faith and church order, as well as the pluriformity of Christian confessions, rites, and traditions that have arisen in the Christian commonwealth for different cultural, historical, and psychosociological reasons. One of the major challenges of the search for unity is how to reconcile necessary unity with permissible and legitimate diversity.

These models are conditioned by the proper ecclesiological convictions and views of the different dialogue partners.

Orthodoxy stresses the necessity of a return to the common faith of the ancient and undivided church of the first seven ecumenical councils. That pure, unchanged, and common heritage of the forefathers of all separated Christians has been kept full and intact by the Orthodox church alone. Unity is seen as a harmonious symphony of autocephalous national churches, which have kept or recovered the orthodox faith and the total episcopal structure of the church (see *Declaration of the Orthodox Delegates...*, in Vischer 1963: 141–43; also Patelos 1978: 94–96).

In agreement with the seventh article of the Confession of Augsburg (1530) the Protestant tradition, Lutherans as well as Reformed, teach that "it is sufficient for the true unity of the Christian church that the gospel be preached in conformity with a pure understanding of it and that the sacraments be administered in accordance with the divine word." Uniformity of ceremonies, humanly instituted, is not of necessity. What looks like a rather formal principle is in fact filled by the Reformers with a concrete theological content regarding justification by faith alone and the divine institution of the sacraments. The unity of the church requires an agreement about the essentials of the faith and gives great freedom for the shaping of the institutional forms of the community. The great institutional variety of existing historic churches cannot destroy the essential unity of the church, when an agreement on faith and sacrament is existing. The search for visible unity remains a fragile working of human beings, looking for forms that make the historical churches answer somewhat better to the unity we confess in the creed.

Anglicanism has expressed its view in the so-called Lambeth Quadrilateral. It contains the four fundamental requirements for achieving unity: the acceptance of (1) the Holy Scriptures, (2) the Nicene and the Apostles' Creed, (3) the divinely instituted sacraments of baptism and Holy Communion, and (4) the episcopate as providing the means for a ministry "acknowledged by every part of the church as possessing not only the inward call of the Spirit, but also the commission of Christ and the authority of the whole body" (Lambeth Conference, 1920,

An Appeal to All Christian People 5). Anglicanism thinks of a visible, corporate, comprehensive, and organic unity in which the sources of the original heritage of faith and the fundamental church order are fully kept, notwithstanding a great diversity of cultural expressions. The Anglican communion thinks of itself as a provisional model of such a universal communion.

Within the Christian commonwealth the Roman Catholic church takes a peculiar place. As no other church it has the awareness of being a universal, worldwide, and also in its appearance a truly catholic church. Though it largely appears on the world scene as a culturally *Latin* church, it never lost the conscience of being in fact a communion of local churches with various rites and traditions. Before the Second Vatican Council the Catholic church considered the restoration of unity, as expressed in the encyclical *Mortalium Animos* (1928) of Pope Pius XI, as a *return* to the one true church of Christ, "to the Apostolic See, set up in the City which Peter and Paul . . . consecrated by their blood." Vatican II put the idea of *communion* in the center of its ecclesiology stating in the Decree on Ecumenism: "For men who believe in Christ and have been properly baptized are brought to a certain, though imperfect, communion with the Catholic Church. Nevertheless, all those justified by faith through baptism are incorporated into Christ. They therefore have a right to be honored by the title of Christian, and are properly regarded as brothers in the Lord by the sons of the Catholic Church" (*UR* 3). Full communion is restored when Christians, "possessing the Spirit of Christ, accept her entire system and all the means of salvation given to her, and through union with her visible structure are joined to Christ, who rules her through the Supreme Pontiff and the bishops" (*LG* 14). It is clear from this statement and from the history of the ecumenical dialogue that the role of a personal ministry of unity in the universal church as present in the bishop of Rome is a key issue. Through the entrance of the Catholic church in the ecumenical dialogue this issue has become an unavoidable topic.

Next to these mainstream views are Christian communities that have a quite low understanding of future unity, stressing particularly the ecclesiological significance of the local congregation and considering all broader institutions, as may be useful, but altogether accidental instruments for collaboration and exchange, without real ecclesiological significance.

From dialogue, actual living together, and common experience in the ecumenical movement some models of future unity arose. Church unions were even achieved on a national level. More experience was thus gathered. Leading in further reflection has been the brief description given by the general assembly of the WCC in New Delhi, 1961:

> We believe that the unity which is both God's will and his gift to his church is being made visible as all in each place who are baptized into Jesus Christ and confess him as Lord and Savior are brought by the Holy Spirit into one fully committed fellowship, holding the one apostolic faith, preaching the one gospel, breaking the one bread, joining in common prayer, and having a corporate life reaching out in witness and service to all and who at the same time, are united with the whole Christian fellowship in all places and all ages in such wise that ministry and members are accepted by all, and that all can act and speak together as occasion requires for the tasks to which God calls his people. (Vischer 1963:146–47)

The Nairobi assembly (1975) described unity as *conciliar fellowship*. Referring also to New Delhi, it stated:

> The one church is to be envisioned as a conciliar fellowship of local churches which are themselves truly united. In the conciliar fellowships, each local church possesses, in communion with the other, the fullness of catholicity, witnesses to the same apostolic faith, and therefore recognizes the others as belonging to the same church or Christ and guided by the same Spirit. As the New Delhi assembly pointed out, they are bound together because they have received the same baptism and share in the same Eucharist; they recognize each other's members and ministries.

The statement stresses especially the exchange between the churches and invites them accordingly to be one in their common commitment to confess the gospel of Christ by proclamation and service to the world and aims at maintaining sustained and sustaining relationships with the sister churches, expressing it in conciliar gatherings whenever required for the fulfillment of their common calling (*Breaking Bar-*

riers. Nairobi 1975, ed. David M. Paton [London, 1976], 60). This model is connected with the conciliar and synodal tradition existing in nearly all churches. It does not only indicate the goal, but it tells also something about the journey, which must be lived already in a "conciliar" way of increasing trust and exchange between the churches.

Some, however, thought that this description did not take sufficiently into account the existing confessional diversity and blurred the particularity of the various traditions. This led to the development of the model of *unity in reconciled diversity*. The Lutheran World Federation described it as

> a way to unity which does not automatically entail the surrender of confessional traditions and confessional identities. This way to unity is a way of living encounter, spiritual experience together, theological dialogue and reciprocal correction, a way on which the distinctiveness of each partner is not lost sight of but rings out, is transformed and renewed, and in this way becomes visible and palpable to the other partners as a legitimate form of Christian existence and of the one Christian faith. There is no glossing over the differences. Nor are the differences simply preserved and maintained unaltered. On the contrary, they lose their divisive character and are reconciled to each other. (*In Christ—A New Community* [Geneva, 1977], 174; *Models of Unity* 15)

Other descriptions and terms have been offered, such as "church of churches" or "communion of communions." In the dialogue with the Orthodox churches one speaks of "communion of sister-churches." In the dialogue with the Anglican communion, *koinonia* became a catchword. All models, however, must take into account the two poles, *unity* and *diversity*.

A crucial question then arises: What diversity is tolerated by the unity? "How wide a latitude is permissible before diversity in interpretation effectively destroys real commonality in consensus?" ("Ecumenical Findings," *ER* 41 [1989]: 132). What are the criteria for defining legitimate diversity? A vision that leaves no room for the differences between the confessions and the variety of types and spiritual worlds in the Christian commonwealth is unfit. Historically, various types of Christian life-style and thinking became embodied in social and ecclesiastical forms. These types form different spiritual worlds, bodies of ideas, values and customs, nurturing a Christian's life in view of his or her spiritual destiny.

The restoration of full church fellowship will be the outcome of a long and patient process of coming together. As wounds heal over their full length, so is the restoration of unity the result of a comprehensive and prolonged learning process, of which the way and the end are intimately interlocked. It is only by furthering communion on the way that full communion will ever be achieved at the end. Static concepts will never do justice to the living reality of reconciliation that is at the heart of any quest for unity. Evolution goes along various stages, while creating already real unity. Growing relations between the churches must lead to an intrinsic desire for further steps. The authorities of the churches should examine courageously the progress achieved and take official action. Such a gradual growth toward church fellowship has been described in the document of the Roman Catholic/Lutheran Joint Commission, *Facing Unity* (1985): "Reconciliation is not possible without dialogue and constant communication. It is a process of discerning the spirits and of searching for steps along a pathway known only to God. Reconciliation is thus a dynamic process, even where church unity exists or has been re-established" (48).

d. Quest for Church Fellowship

The quest for church fellowship raises several specific questions, often of a hermeneutic nature. They are conditioned by sometimes divergent theological, anthropological, and ecclesiological presuppositions that have often been built up in a polemical and controversial way against one another. Though these differences should not be unduly exaggerated, they cannot be overlooked. They must be integrated in the unity schemes. Rather than be exclusive, they could well be warnings to each other and draw attention to the one-sidedness of every attempt to speak about the One who is Ineffable and self-manifests in the Lord Jesus Christ. Faith and unity rest finally on the One who is *beyond* all our endeavors.

(1) A first area of discussion treats the existence or not of a *fundamental difference*, which could question radically the relevance of

the ecumenical agreements on specific issues already reached in the bilateral dialogues. It calls into question the assertion that a fundamental *consensus* is still extant and that the churches still agree on the most essential elements of the Christian faith, notwithstanding some more superficial differences. The issue has been raised in the context of the dialogue between Catholics and Protestants. But could not analogous questions be raised in the relations between the Occidental and Oriental churches? In the West the problem was raised since the early nineteenth century in many a book of controversial systematic theology. The ecumenical dialogue, however, made a burning issue of it. There is no question that many superficial differences reveal deeper and even more fundamental differences. We think they must be looked for in the area of "sacramental mediation," namely, of the so-called synergism between God and human beings in the order of salvation. They manifest differences in the description of the relation between God and the human being. The tension created by the essential and unbridgeable difference between God and the human person, between creator and creature, have been differently stressed in the Catholic and Protestant tradition. This difference has important implications for theological anthropology and ecclesiology. It is therefore no surprise that the latest ecumenical dialogues want to deal with problems such as justification and the nature of the church. But do these diversities have to be exclusive? Can they not be complementary and draw the attention to some forgotten truths? Do they not show healthily the limits of our efforts to express systematically the unfathomable mysteries of God's dealing with humankind?

(2) The reference to the HIERARCHY OF TRUTHS in *Unitatis Redintegratio* (11) remains important for the ecumenical dialogue. The decree states: "When comparing doctrines with one another, they should remember that in Catholic doctrine there exists an order or 'hierarchy' of truths, since they vary in their relation to the foundation of the Christian faith." The council did not want to adopt the distinction between "essential" and "not essential" truths. Though all articles of faith are equally true and binding, they do not all have the same closeness to the

core of the faith about God and salvation through Christ. Faith is a structured whole in which certain articles are more closely linked to the "foundation" than others. Considering this perspective in faith can be of help for a missionary catechesis and for discerning what is required and what is secondary in view of unity.

(3) The *relation between the Holy Scripture and the tradition* is a key issue particularly in the dialogue with the Protestant churches. The report on "Scripture, Tradition and traditions" studied at the World Conference of Faith and Order in Montreal (1963) marked a break-through. The question cannot anymore be envisaged merely in the terms of the Council of Trent. The relation between Scripture and tradition was no longer viewed as the external juxtaposition of two sources, but rather in a comprehensive fashion within a single *paradosis* or *Tradition* (with a capital T). "By the *Tradition* is meant the Gospel itself, transmitted from generation to generation in and by the church, Christ himself present in the life of the church. By *tradition* is meant the traditionary process. The term *traditions* is used in two senses, to indicate both the diversity of forms of expression and also what we call confessional traditions" (*The Fourth World Conference on Faith and Order*, ed. P. C. Rodger and L. Vischer [New York, 1964], 50, no. 39). Holy Scripture itself and the various traditions have developed under the guidance of the Holy Spirit within the englobing, living Tradition. This new perspective does not lift all the traditional differences and accentuations of the various components of the process, but it puts them within a larger and more dynamic process. *Baptism, Eucharist and Ministry* (BEM) gave new impulse to the reflection on the meaning of tradition when speaking of "the faith of the Church through the ages." How must this expression be understood in an ecumenical context? The discussion on tradition raises immediately the question of the role of the various authorities. Holy Scripture and the authoritative documents of the church are "authorities" in a quite different way than the living "magisterium" in the church, which has the task to interpret and to decide about the faith of the church, in faithful obedience to the divine foundation of the church in the Christ-

event and to the founding witness. The Scriptures remain thus always irreducible challenges to all its later interpreters. The questions linked with authority, the bearers and the extension of the teaching office in the church, are among the most difficult ones of the ecumenical dialogue.

(4) The *apostolicity of the church*, including the *apostolic succession* of the ministry, particularly of the episcopate, is intrinsically linked to the understanding of tradition. The latter question has now been taken up in a more comprehensive view of apostolicity, as can been seen, e.g., in the study document prepared by the joint theological commission on "catholicity and apostolicity" (1968) (*One in Christ* 6 [1970] 452–82). The more recent document *Baptism, Eucharist and Ministry* (1982) states:

> Apostolic tradition in the church means continuity in the permanent characteristics of the Church of the apostles: witness to the apostolic faith, proclamation and fresh interpretation of the Gospel, celebration of baptism and the eucharist, *the transmission of ministerial responsibilities*, communion in prayer, love, joy and suffering, service to the sick and the needy, unity among the local churches and sharing the gifts which the Lord has given to each. (*Ministry* 34)

The orderly succession of the ordained ministry and the succession of bishops are, the document agrees, an expression of the continuity of the apostolic faith. It must be clarified still what the proper function and effectivity of the ministerial succession is within the englobing apostolicity of the church. In what sense can it be said that the episcopal succession is a "guarantee" and an "effective sign" of the continuity of the church through the ages?

(5) Even though the ecumenical movement is essentially a movement of reconciliation of what is separated, it has to deal unavoidably also with diversity and pluralism in the Christian commonwealth. These many forms of diversity are the result of quite complex developments, due to cultural and historic processes, to separation and excommunication in the church, as well as to the building up of confessional ideologies and life-styles with an intricate set of psychosocial idiosyncrasies, prejudices, and memories, which burden the

reciprocal relations between the churches. They make themselves felt in the discussion of apparently merely theological problems. One should be aware of these components when expressing convictions we consider intimately connected with faith. A hermeneutics of unity thus becomes an exercise in relating one's own convictions to the faith of other Christians, believing that the Holy Spirit is speaking in many unexpected ways. It is true indeed, as stated in *Baptism, Eucharist and Ministry*, that "openness to each other holds the possibility that the Spirit may well speak to one church through the insights of another" (*Ministry* 54).

e. Conclusion

Ecumenical consensus building cannot be reduced to theological research and dialogue. But without serious theological reflection and exchange it will build on sand. Such an exchange has to be carried on with great humility and readiness to listen earnestly to the questions of other traditions: "We must be prepared to admit that the word of God may come to us through our partners in dialogue" ("Ecumenical Findings," *ER* 41 [1989]: 126). Furthermore, no teaching of a church can be simply identified with its viewpoints of centuries ago, when churches separated from one another. Time has healed wounds. But sometimes too areas of divergence have shifted. Real progress has been made in the interconfessional dialogue. The ecumenical movement should accordingly cultivate its memory and build on the convergences and even the agreements already reached.

However, all ecumenical work must be carried by convictions. The disunity of Christians is and remains a scandal, yet more so that it has been recognized as such. The gospel contains an urgent and lasting appeal to do everything possible, again and again—"seventy times seven" (Mt 18:22)—to break down walls and to forgive and to convert one another in order that the witness should be unanimous, so "that the world may believe" (Jn 17:21). They call for conversion of the heart, looking up together—burdened with the weight of our disunity and its consequences in history—to the crucified Lord (Jn 19:37). This conversion to God and to one another is at the heart of all ecumenical commitment.

Bibl.: R. ROUSE and S. C. NEILL, eds., *A History of the Ecumenical Movement*, vol. 1: *1571–1948* (London, 1945); vol. 2 (H. E. FEY, ed.): *The Ecumenical Advance, 1948–1968* (London, 1970, 1986); L. VISCHER, ed., *A Documentary History of the Faith and Order Movement* (St. Louis, 1963); C. G. PATELOS, ed., *The Orthodox Church in the Ecumenical Movement: Documents and Statements 1902–1975* (Geneva, 1978); K. PATHIL, *Models in Ecumenical Dialogue* (Bangalore, 1981); W. RUSCH, *Ecumenism: A Movement toward Church Unity* (Philadelphia, 1985); id., *Towards the Healing of Schism: The Sees of Rome and Constantinople*, Ecumenical Documents 3, ed. E. J. STORNON (New York/Mahwah, 1987); T. F. STRANSKY and J. B. SHEERIN, eds., *Doing the Truth in Charity*, Ecumenical Documents 1 (New York, 1982); J. F. PUGLISI and S. J. VOICU, *A Bibliography of Interchurch and Interconfessional Theological Dialogues* (Rome, 1984); H. MEYER and L. VISCHER, eds., *Growth in Agreement: Reports and Agreed Statements of Ecumenical Conversations on a World Level* (New York, 1984); *Les dialogues oecuméniques hier et aujourd'hui*, Chambésy, Les Études théologiques de Chambésy 5 (Geneva, 1985)]; J. W. WITMER and J. R. WRIGHT, eds., *Called to Full Unity: Documents on Anglican–Roman Catholic Relations 1966–1983* (Washington, 1986); H. KRÜGER et al., *Ökumene-Lexikon* (Frankfurt, 1987); M. KINNAMON, *Truth and Community: Diversity and Its Limits in the Ecumenical Movement* (Grand Rapids/Geneva, 1988).

Jos E. VERCRUYSSE

ELECTION/COVENANT/LAW

We have included these three topics in a single entry, because they are so closely interconnected. Each covenant, indeed, is preceded by a divine election, or choice, and, after Sinai, the law is indissolubly joined to the covenant and is then subjected, as is the covenant, to a gradual process of interiorization.

1. The Covenant with Abraham

The covenant with Abraham is preceded by a summons of *election* by God. Yahweh says to Abraham: "Go from your country and your kindred and your father's house. . . . I will make of you a great nation" (Gn 12:1–2). This summons separated him from his people, his land, and the domination of a culture that looked back to Babel and its consequences (Gn 12). Yahweh chose Abraham to form a nation that would inherit the ancient blessings and promises bestowed by God on the occasion of the first creation (Gn 3:15) and the second, that is, the covenant with Noah (Gn 9:17). By divine choice Abraham will become the root of a blessed generation that one day will welcome his true descendant, Christ (Gal 3:16).

This covenant with Abraham is not a bilateral pact by means of which two parties make an agreement with each other, but a promise, a unilateral oath in which Yahweh solemnly promises an inheritance to Abraham and his descendants. This oath may indeed be called a covenant, for it effectively creates a new relationship between Yahweh and Abraham. Nevertheless, this "agreement" is very odd, for the initiative comes exclusively from Yahweh, whereas Abraham is content to accept this promise and to pay homage, in total surrender, to the word Yahweh has uttered (Gn 15:6).

The Abrahamite covenant, as a supremely free and gratuitous act on the part of Yahweh, could not be made subject to conditions or compromised by human beings: it was indefectible and eternal. Yahweh will always be the God of Abraham and of his descendants, and the promises made will be infallibly fulfilled when the time comes for them.

But these promises were not addressed to all his descendants. Including an election on the part of Yahweh, they will be transmitted through certain descendants, to the exclusion of others, and this is the result of God's own design, and not because of the fault of human beings (S. Lyonnet). Election affirms the freedom of God, who expresses himself in the differentiation of the elect and is already manifest in the strange phenomenon of pairs of brothers: there must be at least two sons for an election to take place. Isaac will be chosen and not Ishmael. In accordance with the law of the nation, it is Ishmael, the "firstborn," who should receive the first promise of Abraham's inheritance. But here it is a question of the appropriateness of the free grace of God. The entire story of Isaac has only one aim: to express the fact that he is born solely by the power of God. He is the son of promise, born of Sarah, the "free woman" (Gal 4:22), whereas Ishmael, the son of a slave, will have no direct connection with the

summons to Abraham. The true posterity of Abraham is Isaac, because of God's free initiative.

Freedom of election is affirmed also in the case of Esau and Jacob, the twins whose fates cross in a characteristic way. Genesis presents Esau as the elder (Gn 25:35). Yet Yahweh will choose Jacob and make him the heir of the divine promises. Because of this choice, and as a sign, Yahweh changed Jacob's name to Israel. After having renewed with Isaac (Gn 26:3–5) the covenant concluded with Abraham (Gn 17:19), Yahweh extends it to the person of Jacob and to the twelve sons, ancestors of the twelve tribes of Israel, which constitute the basic structure of the people of God. "Your name is Jacob . . . but Israel shall be your name . . . a nation and a company of nations shall come from you, and kings shall spring from you . . ." (Gn 35:9–11). Jacob-Israel is the chosen one of God and, as such, he will become the father and founder of the elect people, on whom God will bestow his favors rather than on his equals or his rivals. Israel will be formed from the descendants of Abraham, through Isaac and Jacob, and not by Esau, ancestor of the Edomites, hereditary enemies of Israel, who certainly do not form part of the elect people (S. Lyonnet). Thus, once again, the freedom of Yahweh's elective action is affirmed.

It will be part of the work of the NT to reveal that the fatherly love of God has never, in spite of outward appearances, forgotten the other brother. The two-brothers theme reappears in two of Jesus' parables: the prodigal son (Lk 15:11–32) and the two sons (Mt 21:28–32).

Women will also have their part to play in this mystery of divine election. In the Bible, sterility is a curse and fruitfulness a blessing. But Sarah is sterile, whereas Hagar is fruitful. But things are reversed. The fertile Hagar has to fight the threat of rejection and is finally sent away (Gn 21:14), whereas Sarah becomes the blessed one and gives birth to Isaac, the son of promise. The same reversal will occur with other pairs of sterile and fertile women: Rachel and Leah (Gn 29:30), and Hannah and Peninnah (1 Sm 1 and 2). In her canticle, which anticipates Mary's Magnificat, Hannah, the mother of Samuel, celebrates this reversal of values: "The barren has borne seven, but she who has many children is forlorn" (1 Sm 2:5). Mary, the fruitful virgin, will be the superior version of these

these sterile women who bear children with God's aid.

2. The Sinai Covenant

"The Lord called to him from the mountain, saying, 'Thus you shall say to the house of Jacob . . . : You have seen what I did to the Egyptians, and how I bore you on eagles' wings and brought you to myself. Now, therefore, if you will obey my voice and keep my covenant, you shall be my treasured possession out of all the peoples'" (Ex 19:3–5). In this "overture," which amounts to a résumé of the entire Mosaic covenant, we have, simultaneously, the exodus, election, the promise of the alliance and the law.

The *exodus* is carried out by Yahweh himself, who has "heard their groaning, and God remembered his covenant with Abraham, with Isaac, and with Jacob . . . [and came] down to deliver them out of the hand of the Egyptians . . ." (Ex 2:24; 3:8). The exodus is the continuation of a unique history of liberation that began with Abraham. Yahweh's aim is to establish a covenant that will make Israel a free people, giving them their dignity, their law, and their mission in history.

Election. The relationship of Israel with Yahweh depends solely on the free will of Yahweh, who chose Israel. There is no example in the history of religion of an alliance between an individual deity and a single nation. The case of Israel is unique: "For what other great nation has a god so near to it as the LORD our God is whenever we call on him?" (Dt 4:7). "It was not because you were more numerous than any other people that the LORD set his heart on you and chose you—for you were the fewest of all peoples. It was because the LORD loved you and kept the oath that he swore to your ancestors, that the LORD has brought you out with a mighty hand, and redeemed you from the house of slavery" (Dt 7:7–8). Israel is chosen among the nations, blessed and showered with blessings by Yahweh. Everything is ready for a new relationship between Yahweh and Israel.

The offer of the covenant. ". . . if you obey my voice and keep my covenant" (Ex 19:5).

The mere fact that Yahweh requires a free response from the people underlines the unique nature of the Mosaic covenant. The relations between the deity and human beings are wholly changed: there is no more rivalry but the possibility of free cooperation. In the surrounding religions, on the other hand, human beings have no choice, no freedom to refuse or accept. Yahweh certainly presents himself as the powerful Lord but not as a dictator: "God is not a tyrant. He wants those who serve him to do so freely, so that they freely accept his plan of salvation and do good not out of fear but by their own free choice" (Origen). Yahweh's yes to his people should be answered by the yes of the people who commit themselves to do his will freely. The Mosaic covenant is a free exchange of promises and commitments. God has chosen a people that has freely agreed to advance along the ways he has pointed out. It is a step in the history of Israel, and neither the first nor the last. It is a new testimony of the loyalty of Yahweh to his promises of salvation, and it acquires all its meaning from the covenant with Abraham, of which it is a continuation. It is preceded by the promise made to Abraham and to Isaac, of which it is the firstfruits. Israel will always remain under the blessing of the Abrahamite covenant, which will remain valid even when Israel takes the road of exile because of its disloyalty: "then will I remember my covenant with Jacob; I will remember also my covenant with Isaac and also my covenant with Abraham" (Lv 26:42).

The law. The Sinaitic covenant had a twofold result: it gave birth to the people of Yahweh; it also gave them a law the aim of which was to ensure that Israel's actions accorded with the demands of its sublime vocation. On Sinai, the covenant with Abraham assumed its complete form, in order to introduce and establish the law that henceforth would remain inseparable from the covenant. This law, like the covenant itself, is God's gift to his people: "what other great nation has statutes and ordinances as just as this entire law that I am setting before you today?" (Dt 4:8).

The law is connected with the exodus, election, and blessing of Yahweh on his people. It is derived from the exodus and expresses and continues it. It is the means by which the people advance along their way of exodus-liberation, which they have already begun but have not yet completed. The law did not exist at the beginning of the history of the elect people. Israel was chosen, saved, and liberated without the law. It was already a free people when it received the law. The law could not be given in Egypt but only directly after the liberation: slaves have no law! Yahweh the liberator appeals to the freedom of the people so that they will remain liberated and become increasingly free. Established on the memory of the liberation from Egypt, the law is a consecration of freedom. It does not save or give life, although it is related to salvation and life. It is the gift of God to Israel, inseparable from the grace of the covenant and therefore from the divine assistance that is needed in order to observe it. It is the way to remain in a salvation that has already been given and freely accepted. It is never a means to "win" the relationship with Yahweh, but the means to live that relationship. The Mosaic covenant was given as a pure grace from God, but included religious and moral demands that must be observed if Israel wishes to remain in the covenant. Just as, with the election of the people and the covenant, Yahweh had shown his designs for salvation in Israel, with the law he indicates the way to stay a people pure and simple—no human community can live without law—and to remain the people of God with a special vocation. There is continuity between the way of liberation and that of the law. By living according to the law, Israel advances with its God and becomes an actor responsible for its own destiny and increasingly free inwardly. But a divine gift like the law should be shared among all. The one who has been freed from slavery cannot treat his or her brother or sister as a thing, by disposing of life, a spouse, reputation, or goods (Ex 20:13, 17). The law of God should never be separated from its giver, Yahweh (otherwise it would no longer "speak" and would become a dumb thing), or from other beneficiaries of the covenant with whom it may be shared, that is to say, observed.

3. The Covenant with David (2 Sm 7:1–29)

The unexpected choice of David underlines yet again the freedom of God's designs. Entrusted because he is the youngest son with the care of his people's sheep, David, the youngest, was nevertheless the one among all the sons of Jesse chosen to be the successor to King Saul, who had been rejected by Yahweh (1 Sm 16:10–12).

The kingship of the Davidic dynasty is described in terms of the Abrahamite tradition. In David the promises given to the patriarchs are fulfilled and renewed. Whereas the Mosaic covenant was conditional, the covenant with David explicitly excludes any notion of a break. It will be eternal and, in this respect, connects with the covenant with Abraham. The triumph of Yahweh the King, which began with the exodus (the idea of the kingdom was present even on Sinai; see Ex 19:6), will end with the triumph of the Messiah King, "son of David." Israel's hope relies on continuity between the past, present, and future. God's loyalty to his word in the past (Abraham) guarantees his promises for the present and the future (David and the Messiah), and this is what Mary eventually proclaims in the Magnificat (Lk 1:54–55).

The covenant with David assumes great significance at the time of the exile, when, from the depths of its wretchedness, Israel asks itself if, after having broken the Mosaic covenant so often, it is still the people of Yahweh and worthy of his promises. The prophets, especially Jeremiah, Ezekiel, and Isaiah, then reveal new aspects of the divine covenant. They remind the people that it is a wholly gratuitous arrangement that relies not on the merits of the people but solely on the mercy of Yahweh. The covenant is not so much a pact as a gratuitous act of Yahweh, who remains loyal to his people. His oath endures forever. Israel's disloyalty does not automatically break the covenant, for Yahweh is free to show patience and to forgive.

An appeal is then made to a covenant formulated not in terms of blessings and curses, and dependent not on its observation by the people but on an alliance that is wholly a matter of God's promise and valid in spite of human failings. The unconditional promise made to David is recalled, which does not destroy the Sinaitic covenant but confirms it by centering it on the king. Henceforth God will be present to his people through the line of David.

From David on, God's covenant with the people passes through the king. The throne of Israel will be the throne of David. God will save his people through an intermediary, the king, successor of David's successor. Accordingly, Israel's hope becomes dynastic.

4. Jeremiah and Ezekiel Announce a New Covenant

Jeremiah. The long history of the disloyalty of Israel, punished in the time of Jeremiah by an unprecedented disaster, clearly proclaimed the ineffectiveness of the law and of the covenant that was its basis. The people were in exile in Babylon. All human hope of a repetition was in vain. Everything seemed finished. Then it all began again. Yahweh revealed to Jeremiah his intention to reunite Israel with him by means of an eternal covenant. Thus Yahweh will remain loyal to the promises made to Abraham. Apart from the divine judgment, Jeremiah predicts a divine miracle. He announces a new type of covenant that will go beyond external mediation and effect a more profound form of union with Yahweh. "But this is the covenant that I will make with the house of Israel after those days. . . . I will put my law within them, and I will write it on their hearts" (Jer 31:33).

Jeremiah describes the curative and liberating action of Yahweh, which goes directly to the "heart" of the problem in order to cure the wrongdoing of the human heart, where evil things are born (Mk 7:21). Under the new covenant, the law of God will change its location. It will no longer be written on tablets of stone but in the hearts of human beings. It will change its function: it will no longer be a condition of the promise but the object of the promise. It will be more effective. Until now Israel *had* to observe the law, but now it will be *able* to observe it, for it will receive the full capability to do so.

Ezekiel. Noting that the "inclination of the human heart is evil from youth" (Gn 8:21), Ezekiel announces a change of heart. The novelty is not that of the covenant, as in Jeremiah, but that of the heart and of the spirit. Ezekiel admirably describes the internal action that God is going to bring about in the human heart, the profound inward transformation of the human partner: removal of the heart of stone, transplantation of a new heart, and the continuous action of the Holy Spirit, who alone is capable of canceling the works of the flesh and allowing the fruits of the Spirit to ripen (Gal 5:19–22): "A new heart I will give you, and a new spirit I will put within you, and I will remove from your body the heart of stone and give you a heart of flesh. I will put my spirit within you . . ." (Ez 36:26–27).

Ezekiel describes the new covenant in terms of the most personalistic and spiritual categories of *heart* and *spirit*, thus showing that the inward law of which Jeremiah spoke was not only a standard but a principle of action, being none other than the Holy Spirit, who will effect a profound transformation of the human heart. Jeremiah's concept of the "inward law" is connected, in Ezekiel, with a theology of the Holy Spirit. In Jeremiah, God gives a law by inscribing it in the heart. In Ezekiel, this gift is given a name: the Holy Spirit, God's gift par excellence. There is a movement from the law written in the heart to the "law of the Spirit" (Rom 8:2); which lives and acts in the heart.

It is in Jesus' human heart, at the end of the passion, that the prophecies of Jeremiah and Ezekiel are first realized. God's law is written perfectly in his heart. He has the new heart promised by Ezekiel, and God has put his Spirit in him. Thanks to his sacrifice, these very prophecies are effected in us: it is in Jesus' heart that we in our turn possess the "new heart" (A. Vanhoye).

5. Salvation History in Diabolo Form

If we were to make a diagram of the history of Israel we might picture it as a *diabolo*, or hourglass shape (Henry Cooper suggested this image). Throughout the times of the old covenant there is a process of contraction resulting from a succession of choices and rejections.

Abraham is chosen from among much more polished Mesopotamians. Among the sons of Abraham, Ishmael is rejected whereas Isaac is chosen. Of the two sons of Isaac, Esau is rejected whereas Jacob is chosen. Although the "least numerous of all the nations," Israel is chosen to be the consecrated people of Yahweh. David, the youngest, is preferred to other sons of Jesse. The process of contraction gathers pace at the time of the Babylonian exile: only a small remnant will return. This notion of an elite remnant is associated with the very structures of the faith of Israel: election, covenant, judgment, and salvation. The strict preaching of the prophets, which speaks of rupture and disloyalty, is tempered by references to a holy remnant that will be saved. Even in the worst moments of the history of Israel there was always a tiny loyal remnant in which the word of God found a fully human response, an elite remnant for which Yahweh reserved his favors and in which the entire future of the people was preserved. Beyond the discontinuity there is always a certain small continuity. Because of his love, Yahweh rebuilds his people on the basis of this remnant, which is "humble and contrite in spirit" (Is 66:2). *Pars pro toto:* The part will fulfill the whole. This little remnant represents the entire community in Yahweh's eyes. It is the loyal part that persists because of a divine choice that takes place within the people themselves. God acts in their favor to obtain forgiveness and salvation for all Israel. It is the root that communicates holiness to the whole, the kernel of a new Israel that will live ultimately in holiness and obedience. At the end this little remnant will be reduced to a few holy families, Elizabeth and Zachary, Simeon and Hannah, and Joachim and Anna, who will eventually give birth to Mary. With the "little daughter of Israel" the first cone of the diabolo reaches its point: finally the Lord God will be able to visit his people. From this central point, the process is reversed and the second cone will grow larger and larger. We move from the unique and exceptional blessing conferred on Mary, full of grace, to a universal blessing which concerns us all: through the beloved Son of the Father and of Mary, we are all destined in love to be his children . . . "according to the good pleasure of his will, to the praise of his glorious grace that he freely bestowed on us in the Beloved" (Eph 1:5–6).

Mary is at the point of intersection of the two cones, at the meeting point of the two covenants, the old and the new. In her the past and the future come together. The chain of prophecies and promises of the old covenant led toward the annunciation to Mary. Israel, the bearer of promises, is fulfilled in Mary, the true daughter of her people. Without her *fiat*, the change of direction could not have taken place. Her yes marks the end of the old covenant and the beginning of the new. All the light of the old covenant, from Eve to the book of Wisdom, shines in her, for the "sun of righteousness" (Mal 4:2) has entered her womb, where the new covenant begins, the kingdom of the true David, whose reign will have no end (Lk 1:33).

Mary is the true Israel in whom the old and new covenants are inseparably joined. There is a continuity of faith from Abraham to Mary. She is the people of God that bears fruit because of God merciful power. Theodore of Ancyra greets Mary as the new volume of the new covenant, *novus tomus scriptionis novae.*

There is no break between the covenants, as there is only one economy of salvation, with the Father as its author, the Son as savior, and the Holy Spirit as promise and gift. The God of Jesus Christ is also the God of the old covenant. The entire history of the old covenant has a typological value: it signifies the hope of the one who relies on God's promises (Abraham, Moses, David), and it is fulfilled in Christ. Looking forward to the coming of Christ, each moment in this history is extended forward, in accordance with a dynamics of continuity and increase.

The entire old covenant is a "parable." The faith of Abraham is already the substance of Christian faith, though concealed. The Apocalypse locates the twelve tribes of Israel (21:12) and the twelve thrones of the new covenant (21:14) together in a row before the throne of God. Christ is the culmination of the old covenant. He is the sum of all promises: "For in him every one of God's promises is a 'Yes'" (2 Cor 1:19).

This concentration on a single descendant, Christ, was the condition of a true universality, so that the "blessing of Abraham might come to the Gentiles" (Gal 3:14). From Christ on there is a reversal of perspective. The sociological inclusion in Israel is no longer necessary for salvation: it is enough to keep to Christ, the authentic descendant of Abraham. Christ is simultaneously our covenant (Is 42:6), our law (Gal 6:2), and the elect of the Father (Is 42:1). Henceforth, in him and by him we are all chosen (Eph 1); the new covenant is concluded in favor of everyone (Mt 26:28); and the Holy Spirit is offered to all people in the shape of the law "of the Spirit of life in Christ Jesus" (Rom 8:2).

Bibl.: G. E. MENDENHALL, *Law and Covenant in Israel and the Ancient Near East* (Pittsburgh, 1955); W. MORAN, "De Foederis mosaici Traditione," *VD* 40 (1962): 3–17; É. HAMEL, *Les Dix Paroles: Perspectives bibliques* (Paris, 1969); id., "Alleanza e Legge," *RdT* 16 (1975): 513–32; J. GIBLET and P. GRELOT, "Covenant," in *Vocabulary of Biblical Theology*, ed. X. Léon-Dufour (New York, 1967), 75–79; P. GRELOT, "Law," ibid., 263–69; J. GIBLET, "Election," ibid., 115–19; L. MON-LOUBOU and F. M. DU BUIT, "Alliance," *Dictionnaire* *biblique universel* (Paris, 1985), 22–25; id., "Élection," ibid., 198–99; id., "Loi," ibid., 428–31.

Édouard HAMEL

ESCHATOLOGY

Two inseparable aspects must be kept in mind in any discussion of eschatology from the Christian viewpoint. First, the full revelation of God has already occurred in Jesus. The apparition of God in the world in the Jesus-event is the event of events, and stamps history with its definitive orientation. In the coming of Christ, the "Last" has burst forth upon the world: indeed, it is he who *is* the "Last." On the other hand—still in terms of this first aspect—one must not neglect the concrete content of Christian hope, which is not only the supreme "Last," but also the "last things": what we human beings hope for, whether at the close of history (collective or final eschatology), or at the term of our individual mortal lives (personal or "intermediate" eschatology). This second aspect, as well, bears directly on Christ. Christian hope can have no other ultimate object than God, who is manifested to us in Christ. Thus Christian eschatology speaks to us not of an intramundane future—a future whose events, at least in principle, could be transcended by some later event—but of the absolute future that is very God. Jesus as the eschatological event opens us to the meaning of the ultimacies of the world and the human being. What has occurred in Jesus, although as yet in a veiled manner—that which, since his resurrection, is reality in him who is the head—awaits full manifestation in his entire body.

The fundamental characteristics of Christian eschatology are determined by that eschatology's christological orientation. First of all, we cannot lay claim to an ability to "describe" the future world. Jesus manifests to us a Father whom no one has seen (see Jn 1:18). God's revelation in its fullness not only immensely outstrips all that our eye has seen or ear heard; it immensely outstrips all that our mind can imagine (see 1 Cor 2:9). The very attempt to describe what we hope for would therefore be precisely destructive of Christian hope: it would mean reducing to our worldly param- eters that which by definition goes beyond them.

Second, Christian eschatology is a message of salvation. It proclaims to us the full realization of the salvation occurring in Jesus. If the entire Christ-event is salvation, then its definitive manifestation will scarcely be anything else. True, Christian faith affirms, in all seriousness, the possibility of the human being's condem- nation—the possibility that we may reject the grace offered to everyone (since only in this way will faith be compatible with our authentic freedom and therefore with the authentically human character of adherence to God and the divine invitation to loving communion). But it is equally clear that this negative possibility cannot constitute the core of the Christian message. Christian eschatology is an aspect of the salvation proclamation: it is "gospel" in the purest sense of the word. This is how it was understood by the first Christians, whose burn- ing desire was for the full manifestation of Jesus in glory.

Finally, Christian eschatology knows it must assert both the already present reality of the "Last," and the future of the "last things." On the one hand, Jesus has already come, died, and risen; but on the other, we do not yet fully share his glory. The sovereignty of Christ over all things has been real since the moment of his resurrection; but it has not as yet been fully manifested. Jesus has already conquered sin and death, but we still experience their weight. We live under the paradox of present and future, of continuity and breach between this world and the new heavens and new earth. The absolute future is genuinely anticipated in Jesus (other- wise we could make no statements about it whatsoever)—it is already relevant for us—and at the same time it continues to be the radical novelty that outstrips even our desires. This tension, while naturally admitting of various accentuations of one or the other aspect, is present in the great majority of the writings of the NT. I believe that, as a hermeneutic rule, it will be valid in principle simply to assert both extremes at once, without setting them in opposition. The reality of salvation in Jesus must not be minimized: baptism signifies a sharing in his death and resurrection. On the other hand, full participation in his glory sup- poses participation in his death, as well—and not only by way of a sacramental anticipation.

All that we and the world around us are must be subjected to the judgment of the cross of Christ.

The concrete content of Christian eschatology (which we cannot present in detail here) also bears the seal of Jesus: it shows us that this content is simply the unfolding of the eschatological event that has taken place in the world with Jesus' presence here. The Nicene-Constantinopolitan creed proclaims a faith that Christ will come in glory to judge the living and the dead, and it adds that his reign will have no end. Jesus' glorious manifestation was the object of the hope of the first Christians. In his resurrection, Jesus has been enthroned as Lord: now this dominion must come to its full manifestation. The Lord's coming or parousia, therefore, is the consequence of his resurrection: that future coming is the full realization of the salvation whose foundation is in the victory Jesus has already won. Paul has expressed the theological content of this event in 1 Cor 15:23–28: Christ constitutes the firstfruits of the resurrection, upon which will follow, in his coming, the resurrection of all human beings. (We shall return to the latter aspect below.) Christ's parousia will be the "end," and will entail the destruction of all the powers hostile to God and human beings, including death, doubtless contemplated here in its intimate relationship with sin (1 Cor 15:54–56). In that final moment, all things will at last be subjected to Christ: his dominion over the world will become reality. Then Jesus will hand over his REIGN to the Father, by whose initiative all salvation history, concluded in this moment, has been accomplished. Jesus' reference to the Father, which was constantly present in all of the times and events of his life, finds its expression here as well. With his full dominion over all creation, God will be "all in all things."

The full manifestation of God's dominion means the full salvation of the human being. The passage to which we have just referred as well as others (cf., e.g., Phil 3:21; 1 Thes 4:14–18) indicates the connection between the parousia and resurrection. The latter, as the human being's fullness, becomes the correlative of Jesus' apparition in his glory. Christ's dominion over all things means our own full salvation. Resurrection, therefore, is equivalent to our fullness in all our dimensions, personal, cosmic, and social. Conformation to the raised Christ is the human being's sole definitive calling. Christ is the firstfruits, in terms of which the resurrection of all who belong to him becomes reality (see 1 Cor 15:20–23). He is also the firstborn from the dead (Col 1:18), and consequently "just as we have borne the image of the man of dust, we will also bear the image of the man of heaven" (1 Cor 15:49). Resurrection on the last day also means the fullness of the body of Christ: the heavenly church. We must not forget, in any discussion of eschatology, the social dimension of the Christian life, which is set in such high relief in other areas of theology as well. Chapter 7 of the Second Vatican Council's Dogmatic Constitution Lumen Gentium is sufficiently clear in this respect.

Perfect conformation to the raised Christ and participation in his life constitute precisely "eternal life," or "heaven." The human being's salvation can actually be nothing else but God, inasmuch as, from the first moment of creation, we have been made for God. Only in God can the human heart find rest (see Augustine, Confessions 1.1). The tradition of the church, then, with the clear authority of Scripture (1 Cor 13:12; 1 Jn 3:2) has spoken of the intuitive, "face-to-face" vision of God as the fundamental content of the reward of the just. This vision of God is not to be understood in a merely intellectual sense. It is to be a full communion of love with the triune God, in total accomplishment of our divine filiation. The condition of the saved human being, for many other passages in the NT, is "being with Christ" (see Lk 23:43; 1 Thes 1:17; Phil 1:23; Jn 17:24; etc.). In being grafted onto the Lord's glorious body, we shall attain to fullness of life.

Jesus as definitive presence of salvation, and in this sense as eschatological event, has opened to us a hope of the last things; and these, as well, are definitively concentrated in him by whom, in the Spirit, we have access to the Father. Indeed, it would be meaningless for the One who was to come to have referred us to someone or something distinct from himself.

Bibl.: K. RAHNER, "The Hermeneutics of Eschatological Assertions," in *Theological Investigations* (1960; London, 1966), 4:323–46; J. RATZINGER, *Eschatologie: Tod und ewiges Leben* (Regensburg, 1977); C. POZO, *Teología del más allá* (Madrid, 1981); H. U. VON BALTHASAR, *Theo-dramatik*, vol. 4: *Das Endspiel* (Einsiedeln, 1983); M. KEHL, *Eschatologie* (Würzburg,

1986); J. L. Ruiz de la Peña, *La otra dimensión: Escatología cristiana* (3rd ed.; Santander, 1986); M. Bordoni and N. Ciola, *Gesù nostra speranza: Saggio di escatologia* (Bologna, 1988).

Luis F. Ladaria

EVANGELIZATION

I. Evangelization and Mission: *1. Mission and Missions. 2. The Purpose of Mission: From Implantation of the Church to Evangelization. 3. What Is Evangelization? In Search of a Broader Concept. 4. Mission of Jesus and Mission of the Church. 5. Theological Conclusions.* (J. Dupuis)

II. Evangelization of the Culture: *1. Culture as Field of Evangelization. 2. A Long Experience of the Evangelization of Culture. 3. A Renewed Approach to Evangelization. 4. The Challenge of Mass Culture. 5. Modernity as Culture.* (H. Carrier)

III. A New Evangelization: *1. To Whom Is the New Evangelization Directed? 2. How Re-evangelize Cultures? 3. An Anthropology Open to the Spirit. 4. Toward the Redemption of Cultures* (H. Carrier).

I. Evangelization and Mission

1. Mission and Missions

From the beginning of his ministry Jesus "called to him those whom he wanted . . . and he appointed twelve . . . to be with him, and to be sent out to proclaim the message" (Mk 3:13; see Mt 10:1–42); after the resurrection he entrusted to them the mission of his church (Mt 28:16–20; Mk 16:14–19; Lk 24:36–49; Jn 20:19–29; Acts 1:6–11). Mission is thus a biblical term and at the foundation of the church. It has never ceased to be part of the vocabulary of theology. And yet in a modern, although already centuries-long, tradition people have spoken more of missions (in the plural) than of mission. This practice goes back especially to the great missionary movements of the modern period, beginning in the sixteenth century. Attention was focused on the "missions" (mission countries) of traditionally Christian countries (Christendom); the latter sent out missionaries to evangelize the "non-Christian" peoples. The missionary task was entrusted (*ius commissionis*) to the large religious congregations and to missionary institutes. The Congregation for the Propagation of the Faith was established in 1622 to organize and direct this work. (After Vatican II this Roman congregation was renamed the "Congregation for the Evangelization of Peoples.")

Not long ago, the term "mission" (in the singular) made a strong comeback in the vocabulary of the church. There has been a renewed awareness that the church is essentially missionary in all circumstances and in all the countries of the world, whether or not these countries are traditionally Christian. The recent "dechristianization" of the Christian world has, paradoxically, helped foster this new awareness. Thus in 1943 Henri Godin could publish a book that had a remarkable influence at the time, *La France, pays de mission?* (Lyons: Ed. de l'Abeille). His primary subject was the dechristianization of the working class, which now had to be reevangelized at great cost. Inspired by the secularization of the Western world, Christians once again became conscious that mission is a universal task of the church. People today speak of the church's mission of evangelization as its essential task; they speak specifically (but perhaps inaccurately, since evangelization is a never-finished process) of a "new evangelization" of the "post-Christian" Western world. The church is everywhere and always in a state of mission.

Recent ecclesiology has developed along this line—a development that is, in fact, a rediscovery of the early tradition. The essential place that mission holds in the mystery of the church has been emphasized anew. This development reflects a movement from a static ecclesiology (the ecclesiology of the "perfect society") to a dynamic concept of the church as an essentially missionary communion journeying through history. The church is mission, or it does not exist. The Apostolic Exhortation *Evangelii nuntiandi* of Paul VI, which followed upon the 1974 Synod of Bishops, which took the evangelization of the modern world as its subject, echoes this renewed consciousness. Speaking of evangelization, the pope writes: "Evangelizing is . . . the grace and vocation proper to the church, her deepest identity. She exists in order to evangelize" (*EN* 14).

The Second Vatican Council had already taken this renewed consciousness into account. Not that it stopped speaking of "missions" (plural) in the usual sense, but it located these in the broader context of the church's "mission," within which they are to be understood. The decree devoted to them is characteristically entitled "Decree on the Church's Missionary Activity" (AG). This document first develops the broad context—namely, the church's universal mission (AG 1–5)—and then situates within this the "missions," that is, the mission of the church as exercised and carried out progressively in territories in which it has not yet reached its full stature (AG 6ff.). The priority given to mission over missions thus shows that the vocation of the church is fundamentally the same everywhere, even if its level of development varies from place to place.

2. The Purpose of Mission: From Implantation of the Church to Evangelization

A relatively recent "missiology" endeavored to define the purpose of the missions. The formula it uses is "the implantation of churches." The church must become solidly established in countries in which it has only recently taken root. Solid establishment means, in addition to the development of the Christian community, the development of an "indigenous" clergy and hierarchy. Once the church is solidly and fully established in a place, the mission will have achieved its purpose. This view of the matter is not without merit. In fact, compared with ideas previously current it represents a certain progress; no longer is there talk simply of saving souls who otherwise would have no access to eternal salvation. The aim, rather, is to establish the church throughout the world as the universal means intended by God for the salvation of humankind.

This thesis, however, falls short in more than one way. It still represents what in the final analysis is a negative vision of the salvation of "non-Christians." It asserts the universal salvific will of God and the possibility of individual salvation for all human beings, but it assigns the "non-Christian" religions no positive role in this mystery of salvation. Furthermore, there is an undue focus on the church itself, as though it were an end in itself. The need, in fact, is to

decenter the church away from itself by centering it in Jesus Christ and in God's reign in the world; then one would think of the church as a sign leading human beings, on the one hand, to their Lord and, on the other, to the establishment of his reign in history. Finally, and in consequence, the accepted thesis defines the mission in a one-sided way as the proclamation of the gospel, catechesis, and the administration of the sacraments; it is dominated by an exaggerated preoccupation with the numerical growth of the Christian community. Also to be noted is that most of the time the "implantation" of the church, which was the central perspective adopted in this approach, is in fact a "transplantation": an established model of ecclesial life, developed in the West, is transplanted to the "mission" country, with little concern for adaptation or INCULTURATION. What should be done is to follow the gospel parable of the sower (Lk 8:4–15) and sow the word of God in the soil of the various peoples so that it might germinate there and develop while transforming that soil (see AG 22). The true image of mission is the seed sowing of which the gospel speaks, not the transplantation of alien models of ecclesial life.

This explains why, even before Vatican II, a new theology of mission was developed that reflected the evolution, mentioned above, from missions to mission. The mission of the church is everywhere the same, even if it admits of degrees and varied forms. The purpose is to evangelize, that is, to communicate the good news, the gospel of Jesus Christ; or, again, it is to make the mystery of Jesus Christ visibly present and active, through word and action. It is easy to see that such an approach made it possible to move beyond the one-sided ecclesiocentrism of the preceding approach by recentering the church itself in Christ and the gospel, in God's reign that began in Christ and is growing throughout history. This new approach is also more biblical, since it focuses directly on the gospel image of the sowing of the good news. In addition, it makes it possible to move beyond the narrowly Western outlook, according to which the old continent, and later North America, established "foreign missions" throughout the world. This narrow view has been replaced today by the theology of the local churches that are established in every place, though these are not all equally ancient, and by the theology of mission as a reciprocal activity between sister churches. This new theology of mission applies universally to all the churches, even while not denying their differences.

Vatican II did not choose between the two theories. It was concerned rather to achieve unanimity among its members, and it therefore juxtaposed the two, perhaps without realizing that they represented divergent perceptions and perspectives. Thus in the Decree on the Missionary Activity of the Church we read the following about "missions": "'Missions' is the term usually given to those particular undertakings by which the heralds of the gospel are sent out by the Church and go forth into the whole world to carry out the task of preaching the gospel and planting the Church among peoples or groups who do not yet believe in Christ" (*AG* 6). And, more clearly: "The special purpose of this missionary activity is evangelization and the planting of the Church among those peoples and groups where she has not yet taken root" (ibid.).

It would be wrong to oppose one approach to the other as though they were contradictory. At the same time, however, postconciliar ecclesiology and missiology have increasingly chosen a more biblical and more fundamental conception of evangelization. The postconciliar church has increasingly expanded the concept of evangelization to the point that it contains everything dealing with the church's mission. In fact, we have reached the point of identifying the two terms or of speaking, redundantly, of the church's evangelizing mission. The passage, cited above, from Paul VI's Apostolic Exhortation *Evangelii nuntiandi* was moving in this direction: "Evangelizing . . . is the vocation proper to the Church. . . . She exists in order to evangelize" (*EN* 14).

If the purpose of mission is evangelization, the question still needs to be asked: What is evangelization? What ecclesial activities does the church's mission of evangelization include by its very nature? Does evangelization mean simply preaching or proclaiming the gospel and urging others to be converted to Jesus Christ and to become his disciples in his church? Or does evangelization have a more inclusive meaning that can be restricted only at the price of cramping the church's mission?

3. What Is Evangelization?
In Search of a Broader Concept

Once the universal mission of the church had been defined in terms of evangelization, the word itself took on an increasingly inclusive meaning in postconciliar ecclesiology. I shall not attempt to follow the course of this development through the many congresses and theological meetings on evangelization that were held in the postconciliar years, but I must at least outline the development as seen in some official documents of the ecclesial magisterium. In general, the development manifests itself as a passage from a narrow idea of evangelization, in which it is identified with the preaching or proclamation of the gospel, to a broader idea of it, in which such activities as human development and the struggle for justice, or even interreligious dialogue, have a fully legitimate place in the mission of evangelization.

The 1974 Synod of Bishops, which took the evangelization of the modern world as its theme, marks an important stage in this development. The results of the synod were included, with the very personal stamp of the pope himself, in the Apostolic Exhortation that Paul VI published in 1975. After showing that evangelization is "the vocation proper to the church" (sec. 14), the pope develops a broader idea of evangelization, remarking, "Any partial and fragmentary definition that attempts to render the reality of evangelization in all its richness, complexity and dynamism does so only at the risk of impoverishing it and even of distorting it. It is impossible to grasp the concept of evangelization unless one tries to keep in view all its essential elements" (sec. 17). Regarding the subject or agent of evangelization, the pope says that it is the entire person: words, actions, testimony (sec. 21–22). As for the object, this includes all that is human: "For the church, evangelizing means bringing the Good News into all the strata of humanity, and through its influence transforming humanity from within and making it new" (sec. 18). The church must therefore "evangelize man's culture and cultures" (sec. 20).

What activities of the church, then, are included in evangelization? Paul VI observes that certain aspects of the church's evangelizing activity "are so important that there will be a tendency simply to identify them with evangelization. Thus it has been possible to define evangelization in terms of proclaiming Christ to those who do not know Him, of preaching, of catechesis, of conferring Baptism and the other sacraments" (sec. 17)—a view that the pope seems to some extent to make his own (see sec. 14). Paul VI, however, is not claiming that this understanding of evangelization excludes others but is trying to bring out the privileged and necessary place that the proclamation of the gospel has in the mission of evangelization: "There is no true evangelization if the name, the teaching, the life, the promises, the kingdom and the mystery of Jesus of Nazareth, the Son of God, are not proclaimed" (sec. 22). This proclamation in turn "only reaches full development when it is listened to, accepted and assimilated, and when it arouses a genuine adherence in the one who has thus received it" (sec. 23).

What, then, is the place of other ecclesial activities in the mission of evangelization? Paul VI elaborates on the advancement, development, and liberation of the human person. He notes that there are "profound links" of an anthropological, theological, and evangelical kind between these activities and evangelization (sec. 31). Mission cannot, of course, be reduced "to the dimensions of a simply temporal project," and the pope does not fail to assert "the specifically religious finality of evangelization" (sec. 32). This being understood, the church does, however, have "the duty to proclaim the liberation of millions of human beings . . . the duty of assisting the birth of this liberation, of giving witness to it, of ensuring that it is complete. This is not foreign to evangelization" (sec. 30). Generous though this statement is, it appears timid when set beside what the Synod of Bishops had said in 1971 in a document entitled "Justice in the World": "Action on behalf of justice and participation in the transformation of the world fully appear to us as a constitutive dimension of the preaching of the Gospel, or, in other words, of the Church's mission for the redemption of the human race and its liberation from every oppressive situation" (sec. 6).

At the synod on evangelization, some bishops, especially from Asia, had urged that a broader concept of the church's evangelizing mission should also include interreligious dialogue as an integral part. But the Apostolic Exhortation *Evangelii nuntiandi* does not echo this view. Speaking of the "non-Christian" religions, the pope says that "they have, as it were, their arms stretched out towards heaven" but are not able to establish "with God an authentic and living relationship," such as Christianity alone "effectively establishes." Even though the other religious traditions contain "natural religious expressions most worthy of esteem," only "the religion of Jesus, which she [the church] proclaims through evangelization, objectively places man in relation with the plan of God, with His living presence and with His action" (sec. 53). It follows that "non-Christians" have a place only as recipients of the proclamation of the good news by the church, which "keeps alive her missionary spirit." Nor is anything said about interreligious dialogue between Christians and other believers as having a role to play in the mission of evangelization (ibid.).

Pope John Paul II in his teaching has on more than one occasion called attention to the close connection between evangelization and the furthering of justice. Even in his first encyclical, *Redemptor hominis* (1979), this concern for humanity is seen as "an essential, unbreakably united element of her [the church's] mission" (sec. 15). This thought will be often repeated later on in equivalent terms. The same encyclical tackles the theme of the other religions with great openness. The pope sees in "the firm belief of the followers of the non-Christian religions" an "effect of the Spirit of truth operating outside the visible confines of the Mystical Body." He supports every activity "for coming closer together" with them "through dialogue, contacts, prayer in common, investigation of the treasures of human spirituality, in which . . . the members of these religions also are not lacking" (sec. 6). Making his own the views of some fathers of the church, the pope sees in the various religions "as it were so many reflections of the one truth, 'seeds of the Word,' attesting that, though the routes taken may be different, there is but a single goal to which is directed the deepest aspiration of the human spirit as expressed in its quest for God and also . . . in its quest for the full dimension of its humanity" (sec. 11). "The missionary attitude always begins with a deep feeling for 'what is in man' (Jn 2:25). . . . It is a question of respecting everything that has been brought about in him by the Spirit, which 'blows where it wills' (Jn

3:38)" (sec. 12). The pope thus calls for acknowledgment of the active presence of the Spirit of God in the faithful of other religions, and he gives a theological basis for the importance of interreligious dialogue in the mission of the church. The same teaching will be repeated in subsequent documents; what still needed to be done was to formulate it expressly in terms of evangelization.

This step seems to have been taken in a document published in 1984 by the Secretariat for Non-Christians: "Attitude of the Catholic Church to Believers of Other Religions: Reflections and Guidelines for Dialogue and Mission." The document explains that the mission of the church "is one, but it is carried out in different ways depending on the conditions in which the mission is undertaken" (sec. 11). It goes on to bring together "the modalities and various aspects" of the mission (sec. 12). It does so in a passage that, without aiming to be exhaustive, lists five "principal elements" of "the one but complex and organized reality" that is the church's mission of evangelization. These elements are (1) presence and witness; (2) involvement in service to humanity, that is, action for social development and human liberation; (3) liturgical life, prayer, and contemplation; (4) interreligious dialogue; and (5) preaching or proclamation and catechesis (sec. 13). "All these elements have their place in the mission" (ibid.).

"All these elements have their place in the mission," but the list is not complete. Some remarks are in place. The proclamation of the gospel through preaching and catechesis comes at the end ("finally, there is . . ."), and rightly so, since mission or evangelization should be seen as a dynamic reality or a process. This process culminates in the proclamation of Jesus Christ by preaching (→ KERYGMA) and catechesis. But "liturgical life, prayer and contemplation" could have been placed after the proclamation of Jesus Christ with which they are directly connected (as in Acts 2:42, to which the document refers) and of which they are the natural completion. The order would then have been: presence, service, dialogue, proclamation, sacramentalization, with the last two being the ecclesial activities that, in a narrower but traditional vision of things, are the sum total of evangelization. In the wider perspective adopted in this document, the "one reality" of evangelization is presented as both "complex and organized"; it indeed is a process. This means that while all the elements in the process are forms of evangelization, they do not all have the same value or the same place in the mission of the church. Interreligious dialogue, for example, precedes proclamation. It may or may not be followed by this last, but the process of evangelization occurs only when proclamation follows dialogue, since proclamation and sacramentalization are the climax of the church's mission of evangelization.

4. Mission of Jesus and Mission of the Church

Does the NT provide a foundation for this broadened idea of evangelization as conceived by the church in its present stage of self-awareness? At first sight, it would seem not to provide such a foundation. If we look at the missionary mandate of the apostles after the resurrection of Jesus, as it is described in the Gospels and Acts, one would be led to think of evangelization as identical with the preaching or proclamation of the good news. But the different versions of the mandate have their own nuances. Matthew speaks of making discples among all the nations and of baptizing and teaching (28:19–20); Mark, of proclaiming the good news to the whole creation (16:15); Luke, of proclaiming and giving witness (24:47–48), while Acts adds that this witnessing must reach "the ends of the earth" (1:8). John, finally, speaks of being sent on a mission that continues the sending of Jesus by the Father (20:21). Witness, teaching, proclamation, baptism — these are different components that nonetheless are all parts of what I have called the narrower concept of evangelization.

Note, however, that for Mark the good news (to euangelion) of God that Jesus proclaims refers, in its noun form, to the entire event, words and actions included (1:14), the same event that the church will be obliged to proclaim after Jesus (16:15). In Luke, who prefers the verb form, "evangelize" (euangelizein) seems to have the narrower sense of "to proclaim" the good news (4:18; 7:22; 16:16), to preach the gospel; in other passages the same idea is expressed by the verbs kēryssein or katangellein, with "gospel" (euangelion) as their object. But from the linguistic viewpoint the verb *euangelizein* can signify every action, and not just proclamation, that bears upon the good news.

Behind the terminology, however, it is to the mission of Jesus himself, which is continued by the church, that we must look in order to discover the scope of the mission of evangelization. We will find that it is not reducible to proclamation, essential though this is, but extends beyond it in the direction sketched out above.

The mission of Jesus, which is continued in the mission of the church, and the good news that his mission makes real and applies are the event of Jesus himself in all its extent. He carries out his mission of evangelization not only by his words but also by his actions and deeds. Ultimately, it is he himself, in his person, who is the Good News of God that is at work in the world. The gospel in action, of which Mark speaks in a programmatic summary of Jesus' missionary activity (1:14–15), is his entire human life, ending in his death and resurrection. This author gives the whole account of this life the title "the good news of Jesus Christ" (1:1). This gospel of Jesus includes his actions as well as his words: his actions first, then his words, since God reveals himself in actions, which the words of the prophets then explain (this is already the case in the OT). Thus it is the entire human life of Jesus that is the foundation of the church's mission of evangelization.

The words of Jesus are the gospel in action. It will be enough here to mention the "discourse on the good news," which Matthew (5–7) and Luke (6:20–49) each report. The subject of this discourse is not first and foremost a new law that must be observed if one is to be saved; still less is it an unattainable ideal that would make faith alone the disposition required for salvation. The Sermon on the Mount is "gospel" rather than moral code (J. Jeremias). It describes the new kind of life that follows on acceptance of the reign that God is beginning in the world through his messenger; it proclaims the coming of a new age rather than new moral demands. That is why it begins with the "Beatitudes," which in their seemingly older Lukan form (6:20–23) proclaim the joy flowing from acceptance of God's reign: Happy are you! In the other parts of the sermon, too, the emphasis is on the assertion that the reign has come, on the beginning of the good news rather than on the moral demands it makes.

Similar remarks apply to the parables (Mt 13). These are not moral exhortations illustrated by examples but "defenses of the good news" (J. Jeremias). The parables express certainty about the realization of God's reign, the power of which is already active and which nothing can hold back; they also describe its manner of growth. The element of the unexpected that the parables display points to the newness of this reign, shows its mysteriousness, and urges the listener to accept it. Thus all the discourses of the Gospel, the parables included, bring out the centrality and present reality of the reign of God in the words of Jesus.

The same is true of Jesus' gestures and actions. His actions are prophetic actions, the true meaning of which needs to be grasped. This is especially the case with the healing miracles and the exorcisms. The answer of Jesus to the emissaries of John the Baptist (Mt 11:4–6) makes clear the significance of his miracles: they show that the good news is already being proclaimed through his actions. The miracles are thus the gospel in action. They are not to be understood, as they too often have been, simply as proofs of Jesus' credibility as a messenger; they are, in themselves, an integral part of the establishment of the reign of God.

The same holds for the exorcisms. Like the healing miracles, they display the already real victory of God's reign over the powers of evil. They liberate human beings from subjugation to evil spirits, from the state of alienation to which they had been reduced. As symbolic actions of Jesus the liberator, they contain the good news that in him the forces of evil have already been overcome, that God is beginning to rule not only in souls but also in the bodies of human beings and in their physical environment, that the world is reconciled with God and with itself. They are the reign of God in practice, as is very clear from the answer that Jesus gives in his debate with the Pharisees on the expulsion of demons (Mt 12:26–28).

It is not only to the words and actions of Jesus but to his entire life that we must look if we are to understand his mission of evangelization. His whole manner breathes freedom, just as it shows his apartness. His attitudes, choices, and ways of looking at things distinguish him and set him apart. He takes stands in opposing the legalism of the scribes, the self-justification of the Pharisees, the ritualism of the priests and Levites. He is not afraid to oppose those exercising authority unjustly, even if they are the religious leaders of his own people. He rejects every form of social discrimination and prefers to associate with the poor, the oppressed, and the marginalized. He proclaims that it is to them first of all that the good news is addressed. He is indeed not a political revolutionary, but his life and death do have a political dimension inasmuch as his attitudes are a challenge and a threat to the authorities both religious and political. It is this threat that brings him to the suffering of the cross.

This human and political dimension of the activity of Jesus does not detract from its transcendental dimension, from his unique relationship with the God whom he calls ABBA. He attributes to his own teaching a unique authority that comes to him from God; he claims divine prerogatives for himself; he asserts that in his person the reign of God is being established in the world. The horizontal and vertical dimensions of his person and activity cannot be separated or disconnected. What begins in him is both divine and human, transcendent but also social and political. Human beings are in need of an integral liberation, both from sin and from the unjust structures to which sin leads. The social gospel is part of the reign of God.

This last point is an important one if we want to draw conclusions about the evangelizing mission of the church from the evangelizing mission of Jesus. It is clear from the latter that the furthering of justice and human liberation are part of the church's mission and therefore that this mission cannot be reduced to the proclamation of salvation in Jesus Christ, or to evangelization in the narrow sense.

Still to be asked is whether the mission of Jesus also justifies including interreligious dialogue in the mission of evangelization. The answer would at first glance seem to be no. Did not Jesus declare explicitly that he "was sent only to the lost sheep of the house of Israel" (Mt 15:24)? During his ministry, moreover, when he was sending the twelve apostles on their first mission, did he not expressly command them to "go nowhere among the Gentiles" and to "enter no town of the Samaritans"? They were to

go, rather, "to the lost sheep of the house of Israel" (Mt 10:5–6).

The gospel story, however, depicts a Jesus who shows openness to men and women who are not Israelites. He admires the centurion's attitude of faith and even says that he has not found this kind of faith in Israel (Mt 8:5–13); he performs healing miracles for "foreigners" (Mk 7:24–30; Mt 15:21–22). He converses with a Samaritan woman and tells her that an hour is coming "when the true worshipers will worship the Father in spirit and truth" (Jn 4:23). In the eyes of Jesus, the reign of God that is being established in the world through him is already present and is at work beyond the borders of the chosen people. In fact, he explicitly announces the entrance of Gentiles into the reign of God (Mt 8:10–11; 11:20–24; 25:31–32)—a reign that is both historical and eschatological. It can be said without forcing the evidence that Jesus displays an attitude that justifies us in regarding the church's readiness to dialogue with the other religious traditions as an integral part of its mission of evangelization.

5. Theological Conclusions

Evangelization is therefore to be understood in the broad sense of the term and in the comprehensive perspective according to which it is not reducible to the proclamation or preaching of the gospel, irreplaceable though this is. The following theological conclusions may therefore be proposed.

A Broader and More Comprehensive Concept of Evangelization Is Needed

This broader and more comprehensive concept signifies not only that the entire person of those who evangelize is involved (their words and works, the testimony of their lives) and that evangelization looks to everything that is human and therefore tends to the transformation of culture and cultures by gospel values; it also means that evangelization includes all the varied kinds of ecclesial activities by which the gospel is spread. It must therefore include activities, such as the furthering of justice and interreligious dialogue, which are not part of the proclamation of Jesus Christ or of the ensuing administration of the sacraments. These other activities must be rightfully regarded as authentic forms of evangelization. This requires us to overcome the ingrained habit of reducing evangelization to explicit proclamation and to the administration of the sacraments within the ecclesial community, while regarding as secondary the furthering of justice and the task of human liberation, and while forgetting completely about interreligious dialogue.

The Furthering of Justice and Interreligious Dialogue Are Intrinsic Elements of Evangelization

The 1971 Synod of Bishops declared forcefully that the furthering of justice and participation in the transformation of the world are a "constitutive dimension" of the church's evangelizing mission. The same ought therefore to be said of interreligious dialogue. We are dealing here not so much with distinct parts of the mission but with different elements or dimensions or, better still, with distinct forms, modalities, or expressions of a mission that is "a single but complex and organized reality." The concrete forms that the mission of evangelization takes in practice will depend largely on the concrete circumstances of time and place and on the human (social, economic, political, and religious) context in which it is being carried out. Given the present context— namely, the very rich variety of religious traditions, which continue even today to be the source of inspiration and values for millions of believers, interreligious dialogue will quite naturally be a privileged form of evangelization. There may even be circumstances making it, at least for a time, the only possible form that mission can take.

Evangelization Is Coextensive with the Mission of the Church

Once evangelization is understood as identical with the church's mission, even while it finds expression in a variety of forms, then some distinctions long regarded as traditional are manifestly outdated—for example, the distinctions between preevangelization and evangelization and between direct and indirect evangelization, since these distinctions are based on an identification of evangelization with the explicit proclamation of Jesus Christ. The drawback in such distinctions is that everything included in the ideas of preevangelization or indirect evangelization seems to

belong to the order of means, which looks, more or less closely, and leads, more or less directly, to the explicit proclamation of Jesus Christ in evangelization as such. But this is not the case. The furthering of justice and interreligious dialogue—among others—are not simply means capable of leading to evangelization; they are in themselves authentic forms of evangelization.

Evangelization Leads to the Proclamation of Jesus Christ

What I have been saying in no way detracts from the fact that the proclamation of Jesus Christ is the summit of the church's mission of evangelizaion. The mission process leads to proclamation and sacramentalization. As for interreligious dialogue, the opportune moment at which it will in fact lead to proclamation must be left in each case to God and his providence. Morover, circumstances may be such that proclamation is possible at the very beginning of the evangelization process.

Bibl.: VATICAN II, *Ad Gentes;* PAUL VI, *Evangelii Nuntiandi* (1975); SECRETARIATE FOR NON-CHRISTIANS, "The Urgency of Dialogue with Non-Christians," in *Origins,* vol. 14 (1984), 641–50; E. HILLMANN, *The Church as Mission* (London, 1966); J. SCHÜTTE, ed., *L'activité missionnaire de l'Église,* Unam Sanctam 67 (Paris, 1967); R. LAURENTIN, *L'évangélisation après le quatrième synode* (Paris, 1975); M. DAGRAS, *Théologie de l'évangélisation* (Tournai, 1978); id., "Evangelization in the World Today," *Conc* 114 (1979); *La missione negli anni 2000,* Sedos 1981 (Bologna, 1983); M. DHAVAMONY, ed., *Prospettive di missiologia, oggi,* Documenta Missionalia 16 (Rome, 1982); D. SENIOR and C. STUHLMUELLER, *The Biblical Foundations for Mission* (New York, 1983); id., *Missiologia oggi* (Rome, 1985); S. DIANICH, *Chiesa in missione: Per una ecclesiologia dinamica* (Milan, 1985); H. TEISSIER, *La mission de l'Église* (Paris, 1985); L. LEGRAND, *Le Dieu qui vient: La mission dans la Bible* (Paris, 1988).

Jacques DUPUIS

II. EVANGELIZATION OF CULTURE

The expression "to evangelize cultures" is a relatively new one in the church. In the traditional view, evangelization is addressed strictly to individual persons, each being urged to respond to the proclamation of the good news of Christ. Properly speaking, only persons can be converted, receive baptism, make an act of faith, and join the church. But, while acknowledging that the primary addressees of evangelization are indeed persons, the church speaks today of *evangelizing cultures*, that is, mentalities, collective attitudes, and life-styles. How is this extended sense of "evangelization" to be understood? There have been two main reasons for this evolution of meaning. On the one hand, the concept of culture itself is expanded and applies not only to persons but also to human communities. These two uses—the individual and the collective—of the term "culture" can be seen in two sets of expressions: "intellectual culture" or "a cultured person," and "French culture" or "the youth culture." On the other hand, inspired by Vatican II, the church has been engaging in a new dialogue with the modern world and its cultures, which are seen as playing a vital role in the religious future of humanity.

1. Culture as Field of Evangelization

We may begin with the idea of culture. The word has traditionally been applied to persons, their intellectual development, their artistic creations, and their scientific productions. Thus we speak of persons as cultured—that is, learned, educated, having developed their gifts and talents. This usage is still valid, but alongside this kind of culture, which is called "classic" or "humanistic," an "anthropological" concept of culture has emerged among our contemporaries. Using the word in this way, we speak of a cultural identity, popular culture, cultural changes, cultural development, and dialogue among cultures. In this usage, culture means the characteristic traits of a human group, its typical ways of thinking, behaving, and humanizing a given milieu. Each human community is recognized by its particular culture.

Cultures in this collective and historical sense of the word are today seen as a proper subject of evangelization. It is no longer enough to reach individuals one by one; it is also necessary to reach the collectivity in all that makes up its culture, in order to evangelize this. As Paul VI forcefully put it:

For the Church it is a question not only of preaching the gospel in ever wider geographic areas or to ever greater numbers of people, but also of affecting and as it were upsetting, through the power of the Gospel, mankind's criteria of judgment, determining values, points of interest, lines of thought, sources of inspiration and models of life, which are in contrast with the Word of God and the plan of salvation. (*Evangelii nuntiandi* 19)

The gospel, then, must be addressed to both the individual and the collective consciousness and must seek to regenerate not only the culture of individuals but the culture of human groups, that is, the mentalities typical of a given milieu.

If we are to look beyond formulas to the meaning of "evangelizing cultures," we must start with what may be called a sociotheological fact, namely, that the gospel by its nature creates a culture. John Paul II referred to this fact in his address to UNESCO (2 June 1980), when he stressed "the fundamental link between the gospel, that is, the message of Christ and the Church, and human beings in their very humanity. This link lays the very foundation of culture." The entire history of Christianity gives evidence of the civilizing power of the gospel.

2. A Long Experience of the Evangelization of Culture

From the outset, the church acted on cultures by enlightening, purifying, and elevating the human mind through the preaching of the gospel. The great Christian thinkers, such as Origen and Augustine, expressed the message of Christ in categories intelligible to their contemporaries. Later on, theologians of genius, such as Thomas Aquinas, enriched rational and religious thought by developing bold syntheses of classical philosophy and the teaching of Christ. This chiefly intellectual aspect of the evangelization of culture is still relevant and a vital challenge to the church in each Christian generation. History bears witness to a real evangelization of the worlds of the imagination and symbol through creations, inspired by the Christian faith, in the areas of painting, architecture, music, and poetry. Think, for example, of the astounding multiplicity of images of Christ and the Virgin Mary that have permanently enriched the history of art. Think of Fra Angelico, who created marvelous works that are the fruits of prayer and evangelization. Recall the treasures of Gregorian music. Thus it is possible to show a clear connection between the progress of evangelization and the birth of an authentically Christian humanism.

The spread of the gospel throughout the Roman Empire introduced a new training of minds and consciences. Beginning with modest schools whose focus was on the study of Scripture as the food of the interior life and the source of preaching, the church brought into being the earliest faculties of theology and of the sciences known at the time. Thus were born the universities that made so deep a mark on all of Europe and on the countries that Europe influenced. The culture of the time was characterized by a humanism that was at once theological, literary, and scientific and that formed the intellectual elite engaged in the building of Europe and its civilization. It was this culture of mind and heart that produced the great explorers and evangelizers of genius, such as Matteo Ricci in China, Roberto de Nobili in India, and Bartolomé Las Casas in Latin America.

By a slow process of osmosis the whole of civilization was impregnated with the values of the gospel and all aspects of society were influenced by the Christian spirit. Leo XIII reminded us in a striking way of this result of evangelization: "There was a time when the philosophy of the gospel governed states. During that period the sovereign power and influence of the Christian spirit had penetrated the laws, institutions, and customs of peoples and the organizations of the state" (*Immortale Dei*, 1 November 1885, no. 9).

These brief historical observations give some idea of what it means for cultures to be transformed by the power of the gospel. They suggest the way in which the gospel acts at the level of persons, customs, and institutions. This action of the church on the culture of individuals and human communities has gone on since the beginning of Christianity, that is to say, long before our contemporaries began to speak of *evangelizing cultures*. We must therefore ask how the surprising success of this relatively new expression is to be explained, and what novelty it implies in the pastoral approach of the present-day church.

3. A Renewed Approach to Evangelization

The novelty is due to several factors. First of all, there is the fact that all cultures today are being subjected to deep and rapid changes. All our contemporaries are asking what is to become of the cultural values that used to give stability to customs, attitudes, institutions, and traditional modes of behavior. All human groups, now that they have been thrown headlong into the modern age, are asking what their own cultural identity is and are feeling the need to take their own future into their hands and to make choices in which the spiritual and moral stakes are clear to all. All this has made our contemporaries very sensitive to cultural changes and to the meaning and direction of these. The insights of anthropologists and sociologists in the area of cultural analysis and action are today widely shared by the majority of people. As a result, governments have committed themselves to bold cultural policies, creating ministries of culture and various agencies for cultural development.

The church, especially at Vatican II, welcomed this modern view of cultures as human realities that need to be understood, discerned, and evangelized. It was for this reason that John Paul II established the Pontifical Council for Culture—namely, to make the entire church aware of the concrete tasks involved in the evangelization of cultures and cultural development. Culture has become, for the church no less than others, a dynamic category that is indispensable for social analysis and for defining Christian involvement in the modern world. In this historico-anthropological perspective, in which the future of societies henceforth requires *analysis of cultures* with a view to *action on cultures*, the full importance of the evangelization of cultures becomes clear.

The evangelization of cultures, which the church carried out in the past through slow action and patient osmosis in dealing with minds and manners, must today be the object of a much more conscious and methodical effort.

Split between Faith and Culture

The massive and dramatic phenomenon of secularization requires a revised approach to the evangelization of minds and mentalities. In the modern world, religion and culture no longer go hand in hand as in past societies. Desacralized and dechristianized cultures have become a new area for evangelization. It is this awareness that motivates and justifies the evangelization of culture. Paul VI emphasized the dramatic urgency of such an evangelization: "The split between the Gospel and culture is without a doubt the drama of our time, just as it was of other times. Therefore every effort must be made to ensure a full evangelization of culture, or more correctly of cultures" (EN 20).

This requires, first of all, that evangelizers have an intellectual grasp of the culture as an area that is to be christianized. They need to be trained in the observation, discernment, and discovery of areas of the culture into which the gospel can be brought. This means that the work of evangelization must explicitly aim both at the conversion of individual consciences and at the conversion of the collective conscience. Paul VI described these two aspects of evangelization, the personal and the collective, as follows: "The Church evangelizes when she seeks to convert, solely through the divine power of the message she proclaims, both the personal and collective consciences of people, the activities in which they engage, and the lives and concrete milieu which are theirs" (EN 18).

Evangelizing the Ethos

Understanding the culture as a field for evangelization means distinguishing, in a given cultural setting, between that which contradicts the gospel and that which needs to be purified, regenerated, and elevated. Since a culture is made up precisely of ideals of behavior and typical ways of thinking, judging, and feeling, it is upon collective activity that the light and power of the gospel must be brought to bear. It is the ethos of a milieu, that is, the commonly accepted codes of conduct of a human group, that must be dealt with. This ethos may often clash with ethics, because it puts forward as "normal" behaviors that end up destroying the human person and its dignity; we need only think of such practices as abortion, euthanasia, racism, or of permissiveness and individualism turned into life-styles.

The evangelization of cultures will often oblige Christians to prove themselves countercultural people; they will need to criticize and condemn things that their culture accepts as obvious but that tend to darken consciences and dull the moral sense. The pressure of collective fashions, judgments, and interests has a profound influence on living cultures and conditions common behaviors. To evangelize means to judge these types of behavior according to the norms found in the teaching of Jesus Christ, who came to save human beings in their personal, social, and cultural dimensions.

But the condemnation of evil, of individual and collective sin, requires on the positive side the proclamation of the evangelical ideal, which taps into the most secret aspirations of every human being and every culture. The gospel must exert an influence on the key areas of collective activity, such as the family, work, education, and leisure, and on social, economic, and political environments. The need is not simply to remind people of the principles of a code of social morality but to convert mentalities and, by the power of the gospel, to change drastically the set of values that are at work, for good or for evil, in a living culture. The effects of redemption must transform the ways of thinking and the behaviors regarded as ideal in a particular culture. Each culture needs to be challenged in its fashions, customs, and traditions. A cultural milieu must discover, in very concrete ways, that there is a "Christian way" of working, living as family, educating children, running a school, serving the common good, engaging in politics, and defending human rights. This kind of action on mentalities is not easy; it is carried on, in the first place, by individuals and families. It endeavors to introduce greater awareness into collective opinions and judgments and so prepare the way for a real conversion of behavior.

Conversion of Consciences and Cultures

It is undoubtedly indispensable to offer to a culture a social ethic, but the teaching of morality is only a first step in evangelization. There is no evangelization without conversion, without a change in consciences. Faith must reach the point of transforming the living culture of a group. True enough, the conversion of cultures is only analogous to individual conversion, but the point needs to be made that the collective conscience likewise needs purification and _metanoia_. Societies possess "sinful structures" or "social sins," which have resulted from many personal sins, from shared responsibilities or complicities that are more or less acknowledged, from collective omissions, forms of greed, and prejudices. The conversion of the collective conscience will require a joint effort and the collaboration of a large number of people who are ready to acknowledge the fact that sin is spread throughout society and that the culture is in need of redemption. The evangelization of cultures is accomplished, then, by individuals who accept the saving message of Christ for their individual life and their social setting. There is thus a kind of reciprocal influence between individual conversions and collective conversions. Faith must make its mark at the same time on both consciences and cultures. It is this synthesis that the evangelization of culture must bring about according to John Paul II: "A synthesis of faith and culture is required not only by the culture but by faith as well. A faith that does not embody itself in a culture is a faith that has not been fully accepted, thought through, and lived faithfully" (Letter establishing the Pontifical Council for Culture, 20 May 1982).

4. The Challenge of Mass Culture

In order to understand the full scope, and the difficulty, of acting on cultures, it is worth looking closely at mass culture and at the impact that the media have on modern mentalities. The mass media of our time are an especially effective means of acting on the culture. They have become powerful agents for the production and transmission of a mass culture that conditions minds and consciences. Any methodical effort to evangelize cultures will have to devote special attention to the media, and Christians must learn to be discerning and to criticize in an effective way the culture produced by these modern media. Above all, Christian values must find expression in the production and widespread use of the mass media. At stake here are issues important for the future both of the culture and of evangelization. It is precisely the impingement of the media on modern life that has caused a radical upheaval in values and mentalities, to the point where families, schools, and churches feel threatened in their traditional ways of educating new generations.

If I stress the importance of the mass media

in modern society, it is not because I regard it as the sole cause of cultural change, but primarily because the media make clear all that is at stake in any action on present-day cultures. The media certainly produce culture, but first and foremost they reveal the modern conscience and its typical values, tastes, and aspiration. It is at this level that the new field for evangelization is located. It is this aspect of civilization that challenges Christians.

5. Modernity as Culture

The new and very complex question being asked of the churches is whether the phenomenal creations of modern civilization are to bring spiritual benefit or ruin to consciences. Modernity itself must be understood as a culture to be evangelized. Contemporary culture is characterized by the influence that urbanization and industrialization are continually exercising on ways of thinking and acting. Modern culture undeniably brings with it human advances and expectations, which evangelizers must be able to make their own with a view to the development of a culture that is open to Christian hope. At the same time, the negative aspects of modern culture must be subjected to criticism because they are an obstacle to the human and spiritual progress of individuals and societies. The modern conscience is now being forced to confront moral problems that are planetary in scope: for example, the establishment of peace, solidarity in the development of all peoples, and the protection of the natural world. The answers to these questions are beyond the powers of the individual, but no one can be indifferent to these communal responsibilities. These problems and the demands they make are henceforth part of the culture that is emerging around the world.

Efforts at evangelization must henceforth deal with this vast dimension of new cultures. The breadth of the challenge suggests that the task cannot be successfully completed without a more concerted and methodical effort of all those in charge of evangelization. No diocese, no parish, and no religious institute or movement can successfully take on, by itself, the mission of evangelizing today's cultures. A joint effort at all levels will henceforth be indispensable. It is here that the novelty, and the promise, of the evangelization of cultures is to be found. This approach is today the object of special study and investigation that focuses on the connected problem of the inculturation of the gospel. The two problems shed light on each other; the evangelization of culture and the INCULTURATION OF THE GOSPEL must be seen in their mutual and complementary relationships.

To sum up: What is needed is a new awareness on the part of those in charge of evangelization. They must grasp the cultural dimension of pastoral activity and must foster a concerted approach, in every Christian community, aimed at making the faith penetrate and renew the living cultures. This is one of the most urgent challenges of evangelization, as John Paul II has said: "You must help the church give answer to these questions that are so fundamental for present-day cultures: How is the message of the church to be made accessible to new cultures, to contemporary modes of understanding and feeling? How can the church of Christ make itself understood to the modern mind, which is so proud of its accomplishments and at the same time so uneasy about the future of the human family? *Who is Jesus Christ* for the men and women of our day?" (To the Pontifical Council for Culture, 16 January 1984).

Bibl.: H. CARRIER, *The Gospel and Cultures: From Leo XIII to John-Paul II* (Vatican City/Paris, 1987); L. J. LUZBETAK, *The Church and Cultures: New Perspectives in Missiological Anthropology* (Maryknoll, N.Y., 1988); H. CARRIER, *Lexique de la culture* (Louvain, 1992), 161–70.

Hervé CARRIER

III. A NEW EVANGELIZATION

The term "new evangelization" has come into current use in the church and has been made familiar especially by the teaching of John Paul II. Variants are also used: second evangelization, reevangelization, or new stage of evangelization. The concept reflects the new conditions in which evangelization is carried on in the contemporary world. In simple fact, the task of evangelizing consciences and cultures offers a new challenge in our day, since in many instances the milieus to be christianized received

the message of Christ in an earlier age, but the good news has been suppressed, as it were, by indifference or practical agnosticism. In addition, the secularization of society has to a notable degree favored this climate in which faith is suppressed or dormant. As a result, the church sees itself obliged to undertake a *new evangelization.* What is the difference between first evangelization and a new evangelization?

First evangelization is that which makes known the *newness* found in Christ the Redeemer, who comes "to the poor" in order to liberate, convert, and baptize them and to implant the church. The process of evangelization takes place in consciences and in the structures that sustain faith, including family, parish, school, Christian organizations, and communities in which a way of life is shared. At this point there is already a true evangelization of the culture, that is, a christianization of mentalities, hearts, minds, institutions, and human creations. In this way the traditional cultures were christianized by a slow osmosis. The conversion of consciences had a profound transformative effect on institutions. We are all familiar with the prototypical agents of first evangelization: Paul, Irenaeus, Patrick, Cyril and Methodius, and Francis Xavier.

Many evangelizers in the past accomplished a wonderful work of inculturation, long before the term came into use. John Paul II reminded us that "Sts. Cyril and Methodius anticipated certain advances in the area of the INCULTURATION OF THE GOSPEL message [which the church fully adopted at Vatican Council II], by accepting without reservation the language, customs, and spirit of each nation" (Address at Compostella, 9 November 1982). It must be observed that the first evangelization is still going on in the world and that it often proves very difficult, such as in India, Japan, Islamic and Buddhist cultures, and in many sectors of society that resist religious values.

The *new evangelization* takes place under very different conditions. A second or new evangelization is directed to populations that were christianized in the past but are now living in a secularized world that denies religion any value and simply tolerates a private religion or sometimes directly attacks even this or hinders it indirectly by policies and practices that marginalize believers and their communities. This new situation is one that has never before occurred on such a scale in the history of the church. It calls for a collective effort of thought in order to determine the *subjects* or *addressees* of a new evangelization; this is an indispensable condition for *reevangelizing the cultures.*

1. To Whom Is the New Evangelization Directed?

We must try to understand the mentality of those who are the addressees of a new evangelization.

A New Kind of "Rich" Person

These individuals do not think of themselves as psychologically the "poor of the gospel" but rather as "rich" people, satisfied people whose focus is on their possessions, autonomy, comfort, and self-fulfillment. It is necessary to enter into this collective psychology in a sympathetic way in order to make it see its limitations in the face of the Absolute that is God. It will thus be possible to bring to light the "spiritual poverty" that often lies hidden behind attitudes of seeming self-satisfaction or indifference.

A Rootless Faith

In many people their initial faith has never developed because it lacks roots and has not been entered into in depth. The first evangelization was often inadequate and superficial and has gradually lost its savor and died away for lack of interiorization and solidly rooted motivations. Faith has not been strengthened by personal experience of Christ and by a loving and joyous sharing of this faith, nor has it been intensified by the support of a close-knit and vital Christian community.

A Faith Rejected and Repressed

Many nominal Christians who live a life of practical indifference have rejected a religion that in their psychic development has remained in an infantile stage and seems to them morally oppressive, for popular culture often confuses religion with moralism. Religion as they experience it evokes fear and stirs unconscious anxieties. In the name of freedom they then reject religion and the church as causes of alienation. It is necessary to ask what defects in the first evangelization might have led to this kind of mental perception of Christianity.

A Dormant Faith

It may be wrong to say that faith is entirely dead in these individuals, but it is certainly dormant, inactive, forgotten, buried by other interests and concerns—money, prosperity, comfort, and pleasure—which have become, in effect, idols. When Christendom still existed, the pressure of traditional religion could be enough to make Christians receive the sacraments regularly. This kind of social pressure does not necessarily negate the value of popular or traditional religion, which has produced great Christian men and women. It is a fact, however, that today's new culture leaves individuals spiritually isolated as they face themselves and their own responsibilties, which are often perceived only in a confused way. Disenchantment and spiritual uncertainty make individuals frail, anxious, and likely to be gullible. Isolation leaves the person ready for a word of welcome. The sects understand this—better than we do at times. We need to pay careful attention to this psychological and spiritual approach.

Psyches without Moral Structure

An even more disturbing phenomenon is a kind of radical "demoralization" that causes the loss of any moral or spiritual structure. Belief becomes almost impossible when individuals distrust every ideology, every belief, every great cause that forces them to go out of themselves. The tendency is augmented when individuals withdraw into an illusory moral self-sufficiency. Modern society tends to turn this individualistic outlook into a system. Evangelizers will appreciate the formidable obstacle to be surmounted in the effort to touch the consciences of such persons. But despite all the difficulties, we must convince ourselves that at bottom every human heart feels the need for hope.

A Latent Hope

Modern men and women have their characteristic anxieties and hopes. Have Christians really grasped the deeper spirit of the council, which was so attentive to the mentality of our contemporaries? We must try to divine the anxiety hidden behind so many seemingly serene attitudes and behaviors. Never, perhaps, has there been such a thirst for meaning and such a passionate search for reasons for living as today. The bringing to light of this latent need of hope is a first important step in evangelization. We must look beyond the anxieties and see the positive aspirations that are often being expressed in the midst of confusion. These aspirations for justice, dignity, shared responsibility, and brotherhood and sisterhood show a need of becoming more human and a thirst for the absolute. Evangelizers will know how to read in these anxieties and aspirations a first openness to the message of Christ. Such sociopastoral interests are to be found in all the conciliar documents and represent a very concrete concern for evangelization. Vatican II needs to be reread in this light. A latent hope and a spiritual hunger are hidden in the depths of hearts. We must winkle out the traces of this hope and this hunger in present-day culture in order that we may bring to them the answer of faith. This is a new stage in evangelization.

2. How Reevangelize Cultures?

The Culture Is No Longer an Ally

When a second evangelization becomes necessary, the issue is precisely a *new culture*. There is no longer a "supporting culture," as in the past. The church is today faced with a culture that is opposed to it (producing persecution and oppression) or else with a culture that is indifferent to it or quietly ridding itself of it, a culture that relativizes all beliefs.

A pluralistic culture, though it has the drawback of putting all beliefs on the same footing, may offer evangelizers a new opportunity and the possibility of showing their unique point of view to advantage amid the chorus of opinions. Often they can even profit from the modern media to proclaim the novelty of their message. From now on a special education will be required for living and acting in a pluralist culture.

Recognizing the Obstacles
to a New Evangelization

These obstacles can vary greatly from one country or region to another. In many countries of what used to be Christendom the church has been, as it were, disfigured by slow erosion, by a process of evacuation or rejection of the faith on the part of a progressively secularized culture. The result has been a culture of indifference, which is one of the most formidable obstacles to reevangelization, since religion no longer seems to interest, touch, or raise questions for an ever-growing mass of individuals who spiritually exist "elsewhere" and live in an "areligious" world.

It is to be noted that the climate of unbelief is quite different from country to country. In many countries, reevangelization is directed to people whose memory is marked by persecutions, religious wars, revolutions, and aggressively atheistic policies. Others have experienced foreign colonization and exploitation, or, again, the loss of the working class in the last century. It is extremely important to have a correct understanding of the collective psychology of each people being evangelized, since this psychology is the result of historical experience.

Piercing the Wall of Indifference

In the Western countries, secularization has created a climate of RELIGIOUS INDIFFERENCE — of unbelief, spiritual obtuseness, and disinterest in religion. The tragedy is that the gospel is neither completely unknown nor completely new. The religious pscyhology that confronts us is ambiguous. Faith is both present and absent from the minds of people. The evangelical salt has lost its savor, the very *words* have lost their edge. The words "gospel," "church," and "Christian faith" are no longer new but have become hackneyed and trite. Any identity between culture and Christianity has become superficial; think, for example, of what has happened to our Christmas and Easter celebrations and how they have been commercialized and secularized. The good news is simply an element in a set of customs, comparable to the other traditions, folklore, and cultural traits of the society. Christians must recover the value of their treasures in the eyes of public opinion, the media, and ordinary behavior. They must react against a *culturalization of Christianity*, which is thereby reduced to words, secularized happenings, and desacralized customs.

Christians Must Not Allow Themselves
to be Marginalized

Christians may not resign themselves to becoming marginalized people, people rejected by the prevailing culture. They must become aware that our central values have been progressively emptied of content. Consider, for example, the words that have become taboo in our cultural environment: virtue, interior life, renunciation, conversion, charity, silence, adoration, contemplation, cross, resurrection, life in the Spirit, imitation of Christ. Do these words, so typically associated with the spiritual life, still have any meaning in the language of our contemporaries? If the latter no longer understand the words that express our hope, how can we draw them to Jesus Christ? The young, in particular, are strongly affected by the spirit of the times, which radically devalues religion. The young are the witnesses and victims of the religious crisis, but they are also and above all the revealers of contemporary aspirations. It is with their collaboration that we shall be able truly to create a new culture of hope.

3. An Anthropology Open to the Spirit

One of the most striking "new" aspects of a new evangelization is that it aims explicitly at the conversion not only of individuals but of cultures as well. But the evangelization of cultures calls for a new anthropological approach to pastoral practice. The human sciences can render valuable service in achieving indispensable discernments and analyses. The chief advantage of modern anthropology is that it "defines" human beings in terms of *culture* and thus comes to grips with them in the psychosocial context in which their associations, their creations, their hopes and fears are all located. John Paul II has several times emphasized this approach to evangelization: "The human person becomes in an ever new manner the way of the church" (Encyclical on the Holy Spirit, no. 58 [1986]). The understanding of the human person as a being endowed with reason and freedom is greatly enriched by the cultural vision of human reality that modern anthropology provides. John Paul II put it this way: "Recent advances in cultural and philosophical anthropology show that a no less accurate definition of human reality may be obtained by referring to culture. Culture is proper to human beings and distinguishes them from other beings no less clearly than do reason, freedom, and language" (Address at the University of Coimbra, 15 April 1982).

When evangelizers seek out historical human beings in the setting of living cultures, they are able to bring to light the tragedy of so many people who are enduring a kind of spiritual agony; this is, in my opinion, the cruel state of a great many persons. If we look deeper, we will perhaps see that this spiritual anxiety often prepares the way for the discovery of salvation in Jesus Christ. Paul Tillich gave the following description of this experience of human transitoriness that can predispose a person for faith: "Only those who have experienced the shock of transitoriness, the anxiety in which they are aware of their finitude, the threat of nonbeing, can understand what the notion of God means. Only those who have experienced the tragic ambiguities of our historical existence and have totally questioned the meaning of existence can understand what the symbol of the Kingdom of God means" (*Systematic Theology* [Chicago, 1951], 1:61–62). Not only the ability to read the signs of the times but also the profound need of hope that a secularized culture creates, will open a new way for evangelization.

4. Toward the Redemption of Cultures

Finally, evangelization confronts cultures with the mystery of Christ dead and risen. A radical break is unavoidable, since, as Paul says, this mystery is "a stumbling block to Jews and foolishness to Gentiles." A constant conversion is required. The dynamism at work in evangelization reaches its goal only in the encounter with Jesus Christ. He is the sole mediator through whom the reign of God comes about. The evangelization both of cultures and of individuals derives its effectiveness solely from the power of the Spirit, prayer, the witness of faith, and participation in the mystery of the cross and redemption. Any attempt to change cultures by purely psychosocial or sociopolitical means is useless. Evangelization, especially in the dark night of faith—and the spiritual night of cultures—supposes a conversion to the mystery of the cross. Willingness to endure this purification and hope in the mysterious but sure ways of the Spirit are indispensable dispositions for tackling the work of evangelization. It is not pleasant to live amid the anxieties of a new world that is obscurely taking shape around us.

When all is said and done, to reevangelize is

to proclaim unceasingly the radical salvation in Jesus Christ that purifies and elevates all of human reality by bringing it through death to resurrection. In this sense, every evangelization is new, because it proclaims the abiding need of conversion. The cultures are filled with a burning desire for hope and liberation. Evangelization thus becomes the supreme way of elevating cultures and consciences that yearn for deliverance from all the forms of selfishness that hinder the reign of God. Evangelization requires this proclamation of definitive salvation in Jesus Christ, and this is true both for individuals and for cultures, as John Paul II has reminded us: "Since salvation is total and integral, it embraces the individual and all human beings, thereby affecting historical and social reality, the culture and communal structures in which they live." Salvation is not a matter solely of earthly pursuits nor of the purely human capacities of the person. "In the final analysis, human beings are not their own saviors; salvation is beyond the power of the human and the earthly; it is a gift from on high. There is no self-redemption, for God alone saves human beings in Christ" (Address at the Pontifical Urban University, 8 October 1988).

The new evangelization is directed to all human beings and all cultures. John Paul II has proclaimed the need of it for all continents. This evangelization, he has said, will be "new in its fervor, new in its methods, new in its expression" (Address to CELAM, 9 March 1983).

Bibl.: Hervé CARRIER, *Évangélisation et développement des cultures* (Rome, 1990); id., *The Gospel and Cultures: From Leo XIII to John-Paul II* (Vatican City/Paris, 1987); id., *Lexique de la culture* (Louvain, 1992), 247–55

Hervé CARRIER

INTEGRAL EXEGESIS

Exegesis is the interpretation of, commentary on, or explanation of the biblical text. This article will deal only with the principles or rules of Catholic exegesis and not with the entirety of exegesis. By "biblical text" is meant Sacred Scripture or the Bible as understood by Catholics, i.e., the OT, including the "deutero-

canonical" books, and the NT. In speaking of "integral" exegesis, the intention is to show, if possible, the entire process involved in exegesis. The fundamental principles of this integral exegesis have been heavily emphasized in the Constitution *Dei Verbum* of Vatican II. The conciliar document will be supplemented from some addresses of Paul VI and John Paul II.

1. Scientific Dimension

> Since God speaks in sacred Scripture through men in human fashion, the interpreter of sacred Scripture, in order to see clearly what God wanted to communicate to us, should carefully investigate what meaning the sacred writers really intended, and what God wanted to manifest by means of their words. (*DV* 12.1)

The ultimate goal of exegesis is theological: "to see clearly what God wanted to communicate to us." Exegesis supposes faith in the divine inspiration of the Scriptures (*DV* 11.1) and also faith in the purpose God had when his Spirit inspired the sacred writers: "The books of Scripture must be acknowledged as teaching firmly, faithfully, and without error that TRUTH which God wanted put into the sacred writings for the sake of our salvation" (*DV* 11.2). At bottom, therefore, exegesis is not a purely profane or secular science but an integral part of theology, and the exegetes who practice it are and ought to be theologians by the same title as dogmatic theologians or moral theologians. For the subject matter of their study, namely, the word of God, is eminently theological and even theologal. The implications of these claims will become clear further on (section 2).

It is nonetheless true that in order to carry out his purpose God "chose human beings and while employed by Him they made use of their own powers and abilities" (*DV* 11.1); that he "has spoken through human beings in a human manner" (*DV* 12.1). Consequently, "interpreters . . . should carefully investigate what meaning the sacred writers really intended, and what God wanted to manifest by means of their words" (*DV* 12.1).

To this end, many sciences need to be used, and many methods as well. Recourse to secular knowledge can cause no uneasiness, provided scientific tools and methodologies are used properly and without any accompanying arbitrary presuppositions. Dealing with this question in 1974 (*DC* 71 [1974]: 326) Paul VI referred to a passage Father Lagrange had written in 1918; John Paul II returned to the subject in 1989:

> More than once, some methods of interpretation have admittedly seemed to be dangerous to the faith, because unbelieving interpreters have used them in order to subject the statements of scripture to destructive criticism. In such cases, a clear distinction must be made between, on the one hand, the method as such, which will contribute to the enrichment of knowledge provided it meets real needs of the human mind, and, on the other, questionable presuppositions (rationalistic, idealistic, or materialistic) that can influence and invalidate the interpretation. Obviously, exegetes working in the light of faith cannot accept such presuppositions, but they can profit from the method. (*DC* 86 [1989]: 472)

a. The first task is to establish the text by comparing the manuscript witnesses that have come down to us. In most cases, exegetes will be able to rely with confidence on the excellent works published in recent decades, both for the Hebrew text of the OT and the Greek text of the NT and the Septuagint. At the same time, as scholars who have themselves been trained in textual criticism, they must check the critical apparatus in the classic editions of these books. They must explain to their students how these apparatuses are to be used. They must also take into account the increasingly recognized fact that some books of the Bible have come down to us in varied forms; this is true especially of Sirach, Esther, Tobit, and even Acts, while the church has never required one specific form in its canon. Textual criticism can at times establish different stages in the transmission of a text.

Once the text or texts have been established, they must be translated. This is a much more complex labor than the general public often realizes. The reason is that the texts of the Bible received their present form nineteen centuries ago in the case of the most recent and about thirty centuries ago in the case of the oldest, and this in a particular culture within an Eastern, Semitic, and then Hellenistic world, and in languages that have either disappeared (Aramaic) or have greatly changed (Hebrew and Greek). The evolution of modern languages gives an idea of the complexity of the problem:

thus, the Italian of Dante can hardly be understood by the average person in present-day Italy. Here exegetes will have to draw on the services of orientalists, who are specialists in the languages and cultures of the ancient Near East. Dictionaries of the biblical languages—Hebrew, Aramaic, and Greek—give information about the kinship between words in the several languages used in a particular setting.

In order to get an idea of the variety of possible solutions to problems of translation, one might compare the translation of the same passage in different Bibles in current use. Students will be impoverished or even exposed to risk if they use but a single translation of the Bible. They must learn to read the critical notes in various Bibles and to compare them. But here a new difficulty arises. It is true that Thomas Aquinas knew none of the biblical languages, but in the twentieth century the words of Thérèse of Lisieux are still valid: "If I had been a priest, I would have studied Hebrew and Greek in depth so that I might know the thought of God as he deigned to express it in our human language." Any self-respecting program of theology will include a course in Biblical Hebrew and another in NT Greek. The value that any servant of the church must attach to the word of God should be a sufficient stimulus to a serious study of the biblical languages, especially today when international meetings oblige so many people to speak several languages. Following Pius XII (*Divino afflante Spiritu* 11.1), Vatican II has encouraged this direct access to the original texts of the Bible (*Optatam totius* 13).

b. Once the text has been established, its variants recognized, and the exact sense of the words ascertained (sometimes with several possible meanings in some passages), there comes the difficult stage of trying to determine "the intention of the sacred writers" (*DV* 12.2). If the council dwells on the study of "literary genres" in particular, it does so in order to endorse what Pius XII said in 1943 in *Divino afflante Spiritu* and implicitly to extend the study of these genres to the NT, as had been urged by the Pontifical Biblical Commission in its Instruction *Sancta Mater Ecclesia* of 1964. But *DV* 12 also accepts the validity of the following general principle: "In order to understand correctly what a sacred writer wanted to say in his writing, it is necessary to pay careful attention both to the customary and characteristic ways of perceiving, speaking, and storytelling that were current in the sacred writer's time and to the conventions commonly followed in human relationships in that period." Pius XII had already given official recognition to this procedure.

This need can already be felt in the analysis of the vocabulary of the sacred writers, as I said above; it is felt also when the effort is made to analyze particular passages or even larger wholes. Thus an understanding of the covenant in the oldest part of the OT has been sought in some basic patterns seen in the "vassal treaties" that were used in international treaties at that period (→ ELECTION). The wisdom of the ancient peoples of the Near East is the setting in which biblical wisdom developed, and the latter often developed through dialogue with pagan wisdom rather than in isolation. The pagan myths of the Semites enable us to see the originality of the biblical writers. Numerous other examples could be cited. This kind of work requires exegetes to possess knowledge they often do not have, but they can turn for it to the studies of orientalists. Paul VI openly acknowledged the need for such collaboration in 1974: "Just as it is difficult to understand the work of Christ apart from the biblical tradition which he made his own, so too, since truth must be our first concern, we must acknowledge the difficulty of reading the Old Testament today if we take a cavalier attitude toward the culture in which it was rooted" (_Orientalia_ 45 [1976]: 6).

The text requires of us a care not to confuse analogy with similarity, likeness with identity, and, above all, similarity with dependence; otherwise we shall miss the real message of the biblical writer.

In any case, the determination of a literary genre supposes a comparison between a number of biblical and extrabiblical texts, so that we can see resemblances in subject matter, themes, vocabulary, and even structure. With regard to this last point, our methods have become quite refined. In order to avoid imposing on a text a structure that is in fact the product of our own ideas and our own culture (a danger not always avoided in the past), we must set out to read the biblical text in its original language and to find in it all the linguistic and verbal elements that

show its internal organization. Repetitions of the same words, variations in grammatical forms, and so on, make it possible to detect inclusions, distinct divisions within a discourse, and so on; as a result, we discover the literary structures of extremely varied texts. But, in order not to fall into the habit of seeing, e.g., concentric structures everywhere, we must be sure to take into consideration all the textual evidence. This kind of reading ensures a better basis for comparing a text with others and determining its literary genre. The book of Wisdom would be a good example.

If we may suppose that the text itself is well written, the method makes it possible to detect glosses and additions that have been introduced into the text. Such findings will not infrequently be confirmed by the ancient translations of the Bible.

There are cases, however, in the Pentateuch, e.g., or in the prophets, when we discover, from disturbances in the flow of the text as well as from an analysis of its literary structure, that it contains, along with the original text, the rereadings in which successive communities have left traces of their own readings and interpretations. What comes to light in such cases is the entire history of the life and transmission of a text in the community.

The important thing in regard to glosses, additions, and rereadings is not to become a prisoner of the cult of the _Urtext,_ or primitive text, and thus end up denying any value to later supplementary material. Our focus must ultimately be on the biblical text in its final state, as it has come down to us, since this is the text retained by the church. Otherwise we might well find ourselves in conflict with the scriptural canon as understood by the church. The book of Sirach provides a good example.

In the final analysis, any study of the literary genre and literary structure of a text implies the conviction that there are such things as literary wholes and that they must be treated as such. When the text contains a narrative—which will normally be in prose—a different method has been in use for the last two or three decades, especially in France. The method is known as structural or semiotic analysis (→ EXEGESIS AND STRUCTURAL ANALYSIS). It draws on the work of Russian theoreticians who were endeavoring to understand how stories function, and it has produced a real grammar of narrative. Despite a vocabulary that is too often sybilline, and despite an excessive emphasis on the formal aspects of the text with the concomitant risk of paying too little attention to the message, this method is useful and frequently complementary to the others.

Concern for wholes, which has the great advantage of preventing fragmentation of a text, leads also to looking at a book or even a series of books as a totality. Attention is then focused no longer on occasional disturbances in the text that, as I said, reveal additions and rereadings, but on everything that unifies the material into a whole. This approach has led, for example, to insight into the originality of each evangelist; it has also made it possible to speak of the Deuteronomistic History, which runs from Deuteronomy through 2 Kings.

This is perhaps the place to mention the method recently developed in North America and known as "close reading"; this consists in reading the text very attentively, step by step, and making sure at every point that one has grasped all the nuances of the author's meaning; attention is paid also to all that is implicit and even to what is not said, which often reveals much about the author's thinking. This method is good for bringing out the deeper unity of a text—e.g., a narrative—and it calls into question theories that have been overly ready to see various redactional levels in the document. At times this method may even be able to show how such redactional levels have finally been harmoniously integrated in the textual unit that has come down to us.

c. Thus far I have dealt with literary criticism; since the object being studied is a text, we ought not be surprised by these developments in its study. However, a considerable number of the biblical books (at least the Pentateuch and the historical books in the OT; the Gospels and Acts in the NT) are concerned with events, and it is important to determine the historical status of these. Literary criticism provides light for historical criticism but does not do away with the need of it. When speaking of literary genres, Vatican II makes the timely point that "historical" texts can be historical in different ways (*DV* 12.2), and it "unhesitatingly" maintains "the historicity" of the four Gospels (*DV* 19). Historical criticism seems to be receiving little attention today, and a perhaps excessive

skepticism has settled in, at least as regards the historicity of events prior to the capture of Jerusalem by Nebuchadnezzar in 585 B.C.E. As for the Gospels and Acts, Catholic exegetes seem to have reached a consensus that respects their historicity.

There is nonetheless a fundamental need of the historical criticism that seeks to ascertain the historicity of the events recorded in the texts. For, just as, according to St. Thomas, faith has for its object not propositions but the reality that these express, so too exegesis does not deal exclusively with texts but also with the reality of which the texts speak. And this reality is our salvation, which God has brought about in human history and definitively so in the person of Jesus Christ. But it is also clear that historical criticism can be carried out only on the basis of a literary criticism of the texts, and not exclusively in the light of testimonies external to the texts. Archaeology, which has been making such important discoveries for the last centuries, renders valuable help here, as do all the sciences to which archaeology has given rise: epigraphy, numismatics, and so on.

2. Theological Dimension

All this scientific study with its various branches, textual, philological, literary, and historical, has for its purpose to "investigate what meaning the sacred writers really intended" (*DV* 12.2). But this is only one side of the exegete's task. The other is properly theological and keeps exegesis from being a purely secular work. We do not read Isaiah or Paul as we read Homer or Virgil.

"Holy Scripture must be read and interpreted according to the same Spirit by whom it was written" (*DV* 12.3). The reason for this statement is that what we are reading and interpreting is Sacred Scripture, and Sacred Scripture is unique in that it has for its authors both God and human beings chosen and inspired by him (however we may explain this joint action, a question that Vatican II did not intend to settle). The result of this joint action is that "everything asserted by the inspired authors or sacred writers . . . must be held to be asserted by the Holy Spirit" (*DV* 11.2).

As exegetes set out to understand this unique object that is the Scriptures, they also begin to listen to the Spirit who caused the Scriptures to be written. Since the object here is unique, it can be said that in all their scientific and critical investigation of what the sacred writer meant to say, exegetes are already submitting themselves, as the sacred writer did before them, to the action of the Spirit, inasmuch as the affirmations of the sacred writer are also those of the Spirit. This disposition has traditionally been demanded of exegetes in the church; the call for it goes back at least to Origen and Jerome and was repeated at Vatican II by the Eastern church. It is noteworthy that *DV* 12.3 is here repeating a recommendation made by the Pontifical Biblical Institute, which has done so much to win respect in the church for a biblical science that is thoroughly critical.

a. From the exegetical point of view, "interpreting in the light of Spirit" means at least what Paul VI pointed out with his usual sagacity, in 1970: if the word of God is "living and effective" so as to lead to salvation, then "those who scrutinize the scripture are in turn scrutinized by it; they must therefore approach it with the attitude of humble openness that alone prepares them to understand the message fully." The pope also stressed "the necessity of cultivating a certain connaturality of their interests and problems with the thought of the text so that they may be able to open themselves to it and hear what it says. . . . It is important above all to see the need of a real fidelity to the text. . . . Christ is the primary exegesis of the Father; his own word that manifests the Father, and every further word about God and Christ are based on this primal revelation of the Father." In 1974 the pope added: "Without the light of divine grace, for which we must always humbly ask, we cannot maintain the real existential openness to the mystery of the God of love, without which our exegesis, however learned, necessarily remains darkened."

b. Vatican II limits itself to specifying some basic characteristics of the goal of exegesis. Since the Scriptures must be read and interpreted in the light of the Spirit who caused them to be written, attention must be paid equally to their content and to the unity of the entire corpus (see *DV* 12.3). The church seems never before to have so clearly stated this principle of biblical hermeneutics. The reason for this requirement is given: It is the Holy Spirit who caused the Scriptures to be written. The human authors are indeed numerous and scattered through time, but the Spirit who inspired them all gives unity to the Scriptures in their entirety. Moreover, this totality that is unified by the Spirit has for its purpose to set down the truth needed for our salvation, and this truth is given its full embodiment in the person of Jesus Christ, the sole mediator. The Scriptures are a unity—a point repeated in *DV* 16—and the unity is to be seen most especially in their content. Anyone familiar with the Scriptures perceives this unity of content; we may be especially alert to the special message of one or other biblical writer, but we must not fail to recognize its harmony with the whole of which it is but a part. Note that the council is speaking of the content or message and no longer of the literary form in which this is expressed.

c. The council goes still further in this concern for wholes that is characteristic of contemporary exegetical study. Attention to the content and unity of the Scriptures as a whole must take into account the living tradition of the entire church and the analogy of faith (*DV* 12.3). The conciliar text is carefully phrased here: it says that in order to grasp the content and unity of the Scriptures we must take into account the living tradition of the entire church and the analogy of faith. In trying to determine the intention of the council it will be helpful to look at the history of this part of the document.

In choosing this formulation, the conciliar Theological Commission intended to do justice to some amendments proposed by the bishops: the latter were asking that the document speak of tradition (rather than the traditions of the fathers of the church), of the SENSUS FIDEI of the people of God, and of the MAGISTERIUM.

The connection of the Scriptures with the church is seen with increasing clarity nowadays. The church received the OT via Jesus and the first Christian community, whose only Scriptures it was. It was within the church's own bosom, however, and in order to express the mystery which she received and carried within her, that the NT was written. It was the church, too, that defined her canon of Scriptures. The best exegete is one who reads the Scriptures in vital harmony with the church; in 1918 Father Lagrange had already given a careful justification of these requirements.

The Bible is, after all, not the personal property of exegetes; the latter are only servants of the people of God, to whom the Bible speaks generation after generation and through whom, in turn, it speaks to the entire human race that is called to salvation. As a gift of God that is entrusted to the church, for the church's sake and by its mediation, the Scriptures suppose the whole of the faith if they are to be understood from within and in accordance with the intention of the sacred writers and of God, who wills the salvation of all. They require communion with the church of the present age as well as communion with those who for two millennia have lived and are still living by the Scriptures. The Scriptures are constantly building the church and cannot become a piece of private property, access to which is limited to a few privileged individuals who appeal to "science" in order to arrogate to themselves the right to throw doubt on the most deeply rooted beliefs of the people of God. Moreover, by the will of Christ this people, the church, possesses within itself a regulatory institution, the magisterium, which is assisted by the same Spirit who spoke through the prophets and apostles and who ever since Pentecost has been the power at work in the life of the church. It is for the magisterium to declare the authenticity of any and every exegesis.

d. The living tradition of the entire church also finds expression in the both the Eastern and Western fathers of the church and in the great exegetes who have gone before us. We are seeing increasingly today a return to the exegesis of the early church, and our knowledge of that exegesis is becoming more extensive due to better editions and better contemporary research. This is true not only of patristic exegesis but also of the exegesis of the medieval Latin theologians, not to mention the still too little known biblical renewal of the sixteenth and seventeenth centuries as revealed to us in, e.g., the books of H. DE LUBAC. It is true that our knowledge of the ancient Near East is superior to that of those earlier exegetes and that our methods are more rigorous. But, though they had fewer scientific tools and met less-stringent scientific requirements, they were ahead of us in their more open insertion of their work into the life of the church; their exegesis was truly theo-

logical and pastoral. We must recover and enrich these tendencies in our own exegesis.

The living tradition of the entire church also includes the *sensus fidei* of the people of God. This means that if exegetes are correctly to interpret the word of God, they must remain in touch with the people of God and share in everything that gives vitality to their faith. Exegesis cannot be a form of library work or research carried on in the privacy of one's study. The more that exegetes enter into dialogue with the people of God, the more they will see how the Scriptures are a real food and the more they will avoid the temptation to indulge in mind games that lack both significance and content. A pastoral practice inspired by the Bible can be for exegetes the place where they test the value of their understanding of the Bible. They will feel led, in their words and in their writing, to greater authenticity and truth and will derive a powerful encouragment to pursue their studies, for they will have come to see the real good they can do. They will understand how the Scriptures are truly the word of God for all of us today, and not simply something to be displayed in a museum of antiquities. They will attain to the same insight if, following a long Christian tradition that has been revived in our time, they devote themselves to *lectio divina*, the reading in which one listens to what the Lord is saying to us here and now through the Bible. This experience will be even more intense if they base their retreat on the Scriptures. It is perhaps here more than anywhere else that they will understand what it means to read the Scriptures with the aid of the same Spirit who caused them to be written.

The SENSUS FIDEI of the people of God finds expression chiefly in the liturgy. *Lex orandi lex credendi* (Rule of prayer, rule of faith). Along with the tradition, especially the Latin tradition, *DV* 21 reminds us that the church is fed at "the one table of the word of God and the body of Christ." The need is to have an intense experience of the liturgy of the word as we have it today, but also to undertake the study of the ancient liturgies (see *DV* 23). The use that all these make of the Scriptures often shows the direction to be followed in a Christian interpretation. Is it a fact of no importance that many liturgies, though not that of Paul VI, read Job in the context of the paschal mystery?

The *sensus fidei* includes, finally, the great

enterprises to which the church sees itself called in our time: ecumenism, dialogue with Judaism, openness to cultures. These are areas from which exegetes may not absent themselves. Since God wills the salvation of all; since Jesus Christ is the sole mediator of this salvation, and the Scriptures for their part advance it (see Heb 4:12) within the unity of the human race; and since the Scriptures are the good news proclaimed to all, exegetes must faithfully participate in every kind of study that makes it possible better to understand and communicate the message of the Scriptures. The Letter to the Romans, e.g., is of fundamental importance in the dialogue with the churches and communities of the Reformation, but also in determining the way in which Christians see Judaism. If we go beyond past generations to a more accurate and respectful knowledge of non-Catholic Christian traditions and of the Jewish tradition, our understanding of the Scriptures will often prove deeper. In particular, exegetes can no longer ignore the testimonies (the Targums, e.g.) of ancient Judaism that were contemporary with early Christianity. The dialogue with the non-Christian religions and with the cultures in which these religions have developed is no less important, especially in certain parts of the world, and the active presence of exegetes in this dialogue is a necessity. The Bible itself did not overlook this kind of dialogue, any more than did the Christian generations that preceded us, and it is extremely important that in those milieus the Bible should not give the impression of being an unassimilable foreign body, supposedly a Western one, which it certainly is not.

In all these dialogues certain basic requirements must be met. First: respect for the biblical text as it stands and an integral fidelity to the DEPOSIT OF FAITH and to communion with the entire church (which will mean an effort among exegetes working in different settings to share the riches they have discovered and the questions they face). Second, and more specifically: acceptance of the evident fact that every exegetical method is the product of a culture and that twentieth-century Western exegesis does not escape this law; other cultures raise other questions and produce a different hermeneutic. This is already true of patristic and medieval Christian exegesis; can we be surprised to find the same to be true when we turn to Jewish exegesis or try to adapt to Brazil or India or Zaire our manner of truly accepting the Bible and its message?

e. Finally, *DV* 12.3 says that attention to the content and unity of the entire Scriptures must also take into account the analogy of faith. The term comes from Rom 12:6, where it seems to refer to the harmony that exists between all the affirmations of the Christian faith. This implies that there is coherence between the teaching of the Scriptures and the teaching of the church. It must be kept in mind that the Scriptures are "the rule of faith." Using an expression of Leo XIII (who in turn got it from the Jesuits; see Lera 1984), *DV* 24 says that the Scriptures should be "the very soul of theology," that is, that theology is to derive its very life, as it were, from the Scriptures. Such a statement means that exegetes are first of all theologians. They are expected to bring out the theological significance of the biblical texts and, by taking the analogy of faith into account, show the harmony between this meaning and the teaching that the dogmatic theologians and moral theologians (to mention but two of the exegetes' colleagues) are saying in the name of the church. Over and above the scriptural arguments these colleagues offer (which must amount to more than simple citations from the Bible), it can be said that they are engaged in a common, interdisciplinary study of the great questions which the human race is asking itself today and on which theology must shed light. Dismissing the biblical witness or passing over it in silence with the excuse that it is anachronistic are ways of acting that are not in conformity with the Catholic faith. In 1973 Paul VI called for the help of the exegetes in answering the moral problems with which the Christian conscience is faced today. In like manner, the affirmations of Christology and other areas of dogmatics must be continually reread in the light of the Scriptures.

For a century now, the church has been continually refining the rules of its biblical hermeneutics; it is even the only community of believers to have done so. Open though it is to all the demands of science, it nonetheless firmly maintains that the primordial focus of the Scriptures is on the salvation of all human beings; that is why the church's hermeneutics is theological. Finally, since God in Christ proclaims and brings about our salvation in the course of our history, the church urges us not to separate ourselves from those who preceded us as guardians and transmitters of the word of God and as witnesses to its MEANING.

Bibl.: M.-L. LAGRANGE, *The Meaning of Christianity according to Luther and His Followers* (1918; New York, 1920); id., *La méthode historique: La critique biblique et l'Église* (Paris, 1966); H. DE LUBAC, *The Sources of Revelation* (1966; New York, 1968); L. ALONSO-SCHÖKEL, *Il dinamismo della tradizione* (Brescia, 1970); É. HAMEL, "L'Écriture, âme de la théologie," *Greg* 52 (1971): 511–35; P. DREYFUS, "Exégèse en Sorbonne, exégèse en Église," *RB* 82 (1975): 321–59; id., "L'actualisation de l'Écriture," *RB* 86 (1979): 5–58, 161–93, 321–84; P. GRELOT, "L'exégèse biblique au carrefour," *NRT* 98 (1976): 416–34, 481–511; B. MAGGIONI, "Esegesi," *DTI* (Turin, 1977), 2:101–10; id., "Esegesi biblica," *NDT Bib.* (Cinisello Balsamo, 1988), 497–507; C. BUZZETTI, "Esegesi ed ermeneutica," *DTI* (Turin, 1977), 2:110–26; M. GILBERT, "Paul VI: In memoriam," *Bib* 59 (1978): 453–62; J. M. LERA, "Sacrae paginae studium sit veluti anima Sacrae Theologiae (Notas sobre el origen y procedencia de esta frase)," in A. VARGAS MACHUCA and G. RUIZ, eds., *Palabra y vida: Homenaje a J. Alonso Díaz* (Madrid, 1984), 409–22; R. LATOURELLE, ed., *Vatican II: Assessment and Perspectives Twenty-five Years After (1962–1987)*, 3 vols. (New York, 1989), 1:139–388.

Maurice GILBERT

EXEGESIS AND STRUCTURAL ANALYSIS

Since the 1970s, the new methodology of structural and/or semiotic exegesis has extended the scope of biblical studies. A quick inspection of the relevant specialist dictionaries, introductions to the Bible, preliminary guides to the theological sciences, scholarly journals, and more popular reviews will reveal the extent to which this addition to Bible studies has been recognized. All these recent publications (in the French-speaking world, at least) include articles, chapters, and special issues on the subject. They serve to emphasize the integration into exegesis of the extraordinary development of the linguistic and textual sciences. They also use a specialized vocabulary that requires some clarification before examining this development of the exegetical method itself.

By tacit agreement, the *analysis of structure* is a practice distinct from *structural analysis* itself. The former is based mainly on the literary phenomenon of parallelism and refers to a number of operative procedures involved in the observation of certain recurrent textual elements and the ways in which they are associated and juxtaposed, and in studying sentences and their grammatical and stylistic links. In the analysis of structure, a synchronic reading—i.e., one not concerned with the diachronic editorial genesis of its subject matter—seeks to elucidate the literary composition and to demonstrate the contribution it makes to the explicit meaning of the work by virtue of the coherence it bestows on the text (see the works of Albert Vanhoye, Pierre Aufret, and Marc Girard). Rhetorical criticism also functions at this level of superficial stylistic structures. (See its definition and situation in relation to classical rhetoric in the practice of James Muilenburg and his followers in the U.S.A.)

The second of the two approaches is the structural approach proper. It confronts the text as a structure and as a system of structures, at all levels, superficial and deep. It maintains that there is a primacy of structure over discrete semantic elements, inasmuch as the latter derive their particular meaning from their inclusion in an overall network. Structural analysis wishes to extricate the organization of the underlying discourse from the ultimate literary and regulative organization of the text. As structural analysis has gradually established itself as an authentic methodology, in the particular field of development of interest to us here it has come to be known as *semiotic analysis*. (Compare Dumézil's structural analyses of Indo-European traditions and Vernant's and Détienne's analyses of Greek myths.) As it has developed, it has passed through formalist, structuralist, post-structuralist, deconstructionist, reconstructionist, and postmodernist periods. This terminology neither helps direct understanding nor, unfortunately, does it stand for the same things in continental Europe as in America.

Use of the terms "semiology," "semiotics," and "semanalysis" also involves a certain degree of confusion and disagreement among authors and readers. Broadly speaking, *semiology*, which derives from F. de Saussure, denotes the study of systems of linguistic and nonlinguistic signs and for many commentators connotes an inclusive vision of an ideological cast. *Semiotics*, which we owe to Hjelmslev, is often defined as the application of semiology to a particular system of signs (the semiotics of space, music, rites, literature, and so on), or to the analysis of linguistic communications. The term seems to allude to a specific scientific project in its own right. It is used in the Anglo-American tradition and in post-Hjelmslevian circles in France. A. J. Greimas and his school interpret it in the strict sense of the theory of signification coupled with a critical and operative formal language. Since exegesis has mainly drawn on the school of Greimas, this article will hold to the term semiotics and examine the following points: (1) structural semiotics; (2) biblical exegesis and structural semiotics; (3) structural semiotic exegesis in the area of biblical studies.

1. Structural Semiotics

History

Since other articles in the *DFT* are concerned with the millennial antecedents of semiology, I shall choose as a starting point its rediscovery in France, under the aegis of structuralist epistemology around 1960. What was to become present-day semiotics arose from a confluence of efforts originating in various disciplines. The actual origin of semiotic methodology is to be found in Dumézil's (1945) and C. Lévi-Strauss's (1964–71) treatment of myths. Anthropology and phenomenology, together with the interest shown in folktales by the formalist mythographer Propp, provided the conceptual framework and the basic hypotheses. In linguistics, on the other hand, the theories of Saussure (1857–1913), extended by Hjelmslev (1859, 1966, 1968), Bröndal (1943), R. Jakobson (1963, 1973), Benveniste (1966, 1974), and by a profusion of schools (Prague, Frankfurt, Warsaw, Constance, etc.), enabled these foundations to be transformed into a coherent project. In the 1960s–1970s some leading exponents (R. Barthes, U. Eco, A. J. Greimas, Mounin) emerged and finally realized in practice the possibility of analysis of discourse and of entry into interphrastic and transphrastic fields. In addition, we should not overlook those (Genette, Kristeva, Todorov) working on the boundaries of now

classic positions: of course this is not an exhaustive list, for other important figures could be included.

The same period saw a renewed and widespread interest in the United States in the linguistic theories of the American philosophers Charles Sanders Peirce (1839–1914) and Charles Morris (1901–), and an independent development in anthropology which had surpassed the European equivalent. This ferment produced an American structuralism that was able to profit from the presence of major European theorists, such as Roman Jakobson and Claude Lévi-Strauss, who had taken refuge in America during World War II. The two parallel lines of development, irreducible to each other and not linked by essentially identical features, eventually emerged as what are now known as the "two semiotics": that deriving from Peirce and that deriving from Saussure and Hjelmslev. This article will concentrate on the latter, mainly apparent in France in the progress of structuralism and around A. J. Greimas.

Characteristics

When we speak of the "school of Greimas" or the "French school of semiotics" or the "school of Paris," we refer to a group of researchers working under the impetus of the theory of Greimas, who until recently occupied the chair of structural semantics at the École des Hautes-Études en Sciences Sociales (Advanced School of Social Sciences) in Paris. Its working name is the "Semio-linguistic Research Group," and since 1979 it has published the journal *Actes sémiotiques*, which comprises two series of reviews, the Bulletins and the Documents, with a considerable international circulation. Its members are united in their adherence to the Greimas model, but tend to diverge from one another both in their semiotic epistemology and in the application of the general theory. Convergences and divergences give rise to sturdy growth among young practitioners of the method. They have achieved major breakthroughs in ethnosemiotics, sociosemiotics, psychosemiotics, visual semiotics, musical semiotics, and the semiotics of space, as well as the semiotics of literary, poetic, religious, scientific, and didactic discourse. This confrontation with such varied fields has contributed to a refinement of the conceptual apparatus of the method.

The elaboration of the "standard theory" began in 1966 and may be considered to have reached maturity in the 1970s. It is to be found in the publications of Greimas in 1966, 1970, 1979, and 1983. A. Courtès 1976 and J. Hénault 1979 offer an amenable overview. The *Dictionary* produced by Greimas and Courtès (1979, 1986) provides a generous exposition of the main lines of the theory of the Greimas school, and the second volume indexes the articles, which are signed by some forty contributors, under the classifications "new entry," "complementary entry," "discussion," and "proposition." The whole presentation is thus far from closed and dogmatic, but rather emerges as an invitation to continue exploration and discussion.

Since the "standard theory," after its introduction into the field of exegesis, has led to a new and practical view of the biblical text, it is appropriate to look somewhat more closely at a number of its basic possibilities, those in fact which are used by semioticist exegetes. Greimas derives from the Saussurian tradition, but nevertheless departs from central Saussurian theory in considering language not as a system of signs but as a system of signification. For Greimas and his school semiotics is not a general theory of signs but rather a general theory of systems of signification. This distinction allows of a considerable shift of the semiotic subject matter from a system of signs to meaning conceived of as a network of relations subtending the system of signs. Hjelmslev had already supplemented Saussure's static notion of signification with the dynamic concept of relations of functions seen as giving rise to meaning, thus empowering the semiotician with the adumbration of a theory regarding the genesis of meaning. On the basis of this "inchoative view," Greimas has developed a coherent metatheory supported by his own transpositive notion of meaning. Consequently semiotics for Greimas becomes that discipline which works out techniques of transposition, the transposition of meaning being conceived of as that condition that allows the possibility of meaning itself (see Parret 1989).

The transposition carried out by semiotic activity according to Greimas is description, which is itself a form of semiotic production and one that is never complete but open, and therefore reconstructive, as it eventuates in the formation of an object. It is contrasted with translation and explanation as it is also interpretative.

The Greimas method is also to be distinguished from those semiotics which derive from communication sciences. The latter, in one or other respect, or as a whole, relate to the well-known schema of Roman Jakobson (1963): sender, message, receiver; to be successfully received the message has to be clarified by a common context, code, and contact. Code and communication are of course the key terms of the semiology of Umberto Eco, who also tends to postulate an eclectic theory with various semiological currents. For Greimas, communication does not control signification and the genesis of meaning but, on the contrary, the statement that is produced is communicable primarily because it is significant (see J. Delorme 1982). That is, the intentional statement of the text, its intentionality, proceeds from its capability as statement controlled by the immanent structures of signification. It is this capability of enunciation which conditions the reading capability of the reader and not the other way around.

In this regard there is more than one dispute between schools on the primacy of either that which is stated or the actual stating of that which is stated, and on the position and the value of the referent in the sign and the systems of signification. It should be noted, on the one hand, that those arguing "for" the statement made have developed and applied techniques for identifying the circumstances of the statement in the text which were never previously available in the history of literary criticism. On the other hand, whereas the 1960s were characterized by interest in the statement made, the 1970s have seen the appearance, though still within the Greimasian tendency, of a semiotics concerned with the making of the statement, with enunciation, which takes into account the pragmatics or operativity of the text. This particular semiotics has been added to a sum total of wholly original developments: narrative grammar and the concept of narrativity; modal, deontic, volitive, and epistemic semiotics; the theory of action, passions, and the quest for values and aesthesis. There has also been the progressive achievement of the status of tested methodology, continually giving rise to its own self-criticism, and the production of an extremely rich and versatile array of analytical tools in the most varied fields.

Prospects

On the boundaries of the basic model, a sustained research effort constantly seeks to extend the horizon of the Greimas method. Efforts are being made to consolidate a fundamental semantics with the aid of validations carried out in conjunction with psychoanalysis, mathematics, and a transcendental philosophy of a Husserlian and Kantian cast. Above all the parentheses in which, as it were, the subject was enclosed during the structuralist beginnings of the semiotic project are now being reopened. The theorization of nature, and of the status and function of subjectivity, invokes the aid of the thymic category: that of intersubjectivity, the category of tensivity. Since the subject constitutes the intersection of the spatio-temporal positions it occupies, an attempt is made to reformulate time and space, no longer in terms of narrative or discursive grammar but in terms of fundamental semantics (see Parret 1989).

Discursive grammar also benefits from an attempt at strict specification in regard to the enunciative concept of meaning, an understanding of rhetoric as a manifestation of underlying rationality and of the theory of argument and informal logic. Finally, there is a clear realization of the need to formulate the rules of correspondence between the various subsystems of this discursive grammar.

2. Biblical Exegesis and Structural Semiotics

History

No body of literature except the Bible can claim to be surrounded with such a plethora of specialists, to have elicited such a vast number of commentaries, paraphrases, and studies, and to have had so many libraries devoted to it. When some pioneers ventured on a form of exegesis still scarcely deserving to be called structural, let alone semiotic, did biblical studies really need such a novel addition?

At the end of the 1960s, the historical approach reigned supreme in scientific exegesis. It was firmly buttressed by a vast amount of spectacular scholarship, produced by the best humanist culture—philology and the satellite historical disciplines of archaeology, numismatics, epigraphy, paleography, and so on. Since the beginning of the century it had profitably

and successfully passed through a radical critical phase. In 1906 Albert Schweitzer surveyed the schools that, since Reimarus (1694–1768), had expressed their activity in the form of the "Life of Jesus." His words on the subject are indeed well known; they are often quoted but are still as vital as ever:

> The study of the Life of Jesus has had a curious history. It set out in quest of the historical Jesus, believing that when it had found Him it could bring Him straight into our time as a Teacher and Saviour. It loosed the bands by which He had been riveted for centuries to the stony rocks of ecclesiastical doctrine, and rejoiced to see life and movement coming into the figure once more, and the historical Jesus advancing, as it seemed, to meet it. But He does not stay; He passes by our time and returns to His own. (*The Quest of the Historical Jesus* [London, 1910], 397)

Preceded by the *religionsgeschichtliche Schule*, intersected by the two-source hypothesis, interrupted by the two world wars, the schools of *Formgeschichte, Redaktionsgeschichte, Überlieferungsgeschichte, and Traditionsgeschichte* succeeded one another. From one to the other, however, the historical approach that characterized these methods tended to a literary emphasis and furnished no instruments appropriate to its own project, apart from techniques that lacked both the effective associations and critical verification of theories developed within the literary and linguistic sciences.

History may throw light on a text, but it does not resolve its meaning. It is understandable that some French exegetes, profoundly affected by the upheaval in French literary criticism and by the extraordinary development of the linguistic sciences, should have been impelled to enter into dialogue with colleagues who, like them, were concerned with reading and interpretation. They presented the semioticians with an exceptional corpus and common questions and were able to recenter their multiple resources in a general literary theory and problematics. They also wanted to take a new approach—within the theological disciplines—to the question of meaning and the hermeneutical perspective (Delorme 1982; *Sémiotique, L'Ecole de Paris*). They brought about a shift in exegesis toward the synchronic approach, a transition that all the human sciences, one after the other, were making.

Mixed teams of exegetes and semioticians were formed in 1967. The meeting with Greimas took place the following year at his Versailles seminar and Roland Barthes participated in the Chantilly biblical congress in 1959. The first major publications came from the side of the semioticians with *Sémiotique de la Passion: Topiques et figures* (Semiotics of the Passion: Topics and figures) (Paris, 1971) by Louis Marin, and *Le récit évangélique* (The Gospel Narrative) (Paris, 1974) by Claude Chabrol, Louis Marin, and others. During this period exegetes were gradually learning about all the theoretical and practical aspects of semiotics at the Hautes Études seminar in Paris and at Umberto Eco's center at Urbino. Research groups were founded, among them ASTRUC, *A*(nalyse) *struc*(turale) (structural analysis) (also the name of Louis XV's doctor, who originated source criticism of the Pentateuch) in Paris, and the Entrevernes group in Lyons in 1971, which eventually—in 1976—became CADIR (Centre pour l'analyse du discours religieux [Center for the analysis of religious discourse]). Numerous training sessions multiplied in France and in neighboring countries, which were extended by the foundation of Bible study groups offering a very high-level popularization of semiotics. The journal *Sémiotique et Bible*, which appeared from 1976, bears abundant witness to that. CADIR also emigrated as far as Madagascar and Korea; as it spread, it inspired several disciples in Denmark, the SEMANET group in the Netherlands and ASTER (Ateliers de sémiotique du texte religieux [Workshops for the semiotics of religious texts]) in Quebec, Ontario. Daniel Patte made the connection with the United States, where he inspires research in religious semiotics at Vanderbilt University, Nashville, and publishes the bulletin *Structuralist Research Information*. The abundance of works on the Bible is indicated by the journals *Linguistica biblica* (German), *Semeia* (American), *Sémiotique et Bible, Cahiers bibliques, Foi et Vie* (French), and *Theolinguistics* (Belgian).

Characteristics

The Greimas school

Since the great majority of works of semiotic exegesis are of the Greimasian persuasion, they owe allegiance to a theology of systems of signification rather than a theology of systems of signs. They are interested in the specificity of texts, of *this* text which is under analysis, and probe below sentences to discover the organization of the underlying discourse. They proceed from external to internal conditions of signification all the way to those of language. For the most part these semiotician-exegetes are not linguists, and this probably protects them from any temptation to explain the text by reference to the structures of language, or makes them less vulnerable.

Following on Greimas, these works also favor the enunciation as against its communicational environment, the exploration of its signifying power as against that of its transmission. The consequences of this position for the treatment of the biblical text are vast and radically distinguish semiotic exegesis from classic historical criticism. On a methodological presupposition, the former places in parentheses the external sources of the written text, its author, its historical coordinates, the communities and societies in which it was produced, and its original reception, all of which it terms transcending the text or transcendence of the text. It does not deny their existence or their interest, but takes them into account only to the extent that their traces are to be found inscribed in the matter of the text; these traces in their turn are extraordinarily numerous and yield considerable information when subjected to refined analytical techniques. Semiotic exegesis also omits any examination of the internal history of the text in the sense of its literary genesis, but operates at the final level of editing, or redaction as the official critical editions of the Bible restore it for us, at the point where the rehandled sources merge in another form of coherence.

It is the option for immanence as against transcendence (not to be confused with the transcendence of a superior divinity), of a synchronic as against a diachronic reading, which confronts the to-and-fro and before-and-after of the text with the aid of methods borrowed from history. The semiotician, on the contrary, considers texts as homogeneous discourses to be subjected to instruments appropriate to their nature as discourse, namely, to linguistic instruments. This is not to be confused, reductively or simplistically, with a choice of the closed as against the open, of restriction as against openness to an interdisciplinary approach. Instead, the semiotician's approach allows the delineation of an exact epistemic course. In practice, the semiotician constructs an object in accordance with tested criteria. Here it is not an a priori idea that governs the closure of the text, but the initial hypothesis of identification of fields of coherence, which must always remain subject to verification by analysis, and thereafter by the possibly effective demarcation of the object under examination. Given adequately developed samples, the systems of representations of humanity and of the world revealed by an analysis of the discursive component will soon disclose links with representations of communities, discursive societies and entire cultural areas connected by their written texts. Provided that there is no admixture of methodologies, these open boundaries will easily submit to the historical approach, and vice versa, for in constructing the historical referent the historian of the Middle East in antiquity possesses an adequate basis in the biblical texts before it is hypostatized as so-called historical reality.

Of course the question of textual meaning was certainly also an inspiration for the noteworthy diachronic work of past centuries. But the signification of a written text consists in the synchrony of all its linguistic and literary components. Semiotics in the Greimas tradition uses the appropriate tool to explore and elicit this signification in its own conditions of production, and no longer does so by fixing it under the analyst's microscope in the form of isolated snippets, slices, and samples of the system that bears and animates them. Observation of literary composition and of a concatenation of topics as practiced in the classic French method of textual analysis known as *explication de texte* has been an inadequate means of disclosing a book's unity since the textual sciences discovered the existence of networks of relations both syntactical and semantic, and of the different levels, each with its own structures, of a deep structural matrix by which they are articulated and integrated.

It is the task of biblical semiotics to describe this totality of meaningful structures. Biblical semiotics is concerned with the organization of contents, of contents modalized by virtue of their inclusion in a hierarchy of structures which are themselves articulated in an overall system. In this process biblical semiotics seeks out meaning and meanings step by step, and reproduces their conditions of production in its description-*cum*-transposition.

Achievements

The small group of exegetes turned semioticians proved themselves initially on mininarratives taken from the Gospels, then moved on to intermediary units and, passing from micro- to macro-organization, were able to consolidate a number of conclusions on the narrative organization of the Gospels themselves (Panier 1979). While developing the method in regard to the figurative aspect, they also tackled the cognitive dimension and elicited a complex interplay in respect of knowledge, believing, and the operation of veridiction, including the reader and an apparent homologation, but subject to the refractive effect of a pluri-isotopic discourse, leading to a virtual recategorization of semantic values both cultural and linguistic. Starting from units that historical criticism and liturgical convention had accustomed them to see as independent and connected secondarily by editorial or hermeneutical efforts, they discovered that "signification inheres in relations underlying discursive forms of expression and social communication" (Delorme 1982; *Sémiotique: L'École de Paris*). For exegetes with a classical formation, this was a powerful challenge to former criteria for identification of literary forms, and even the whole complex of problems regarding literary genres and forms in the Bible. Accordingly, a considerable number of studies have worked from the smallest to the largest wholes, but the converse movement is not yet in evidence—that is, from the whole Gospel seen whole and entire toward its smallest units. No one, moreover, has yet examined the question of the corpus of the Gospels as a text with several variants.

Almost all, if not all, the books of the biblical corpus have been subjected to semiotic treatments on varying scales. We are already able to draw certain conclusions regarding the characteristics of various forms of prophetic and apocalyptic discourse, and of epistolary and psalmic literatures; the poetic passages are still the poor relations. In the area of extrabiblical religious discourse, some soundings have been taken in regard to theological, mystical, and liturgical discourse. In general, semiotic exegesis, which is a young—indeed very young—science, has produced an astonishingly large number of studies covering the maximum possible area, but too few studies of a really vast corpus. This is also true of other semiotic and semiological fields, where the really extended efforts are almost exclusively concerned with theoretical development.

Nevertheless, there is now a list of solid achievements that will soon mature into valuable syntheses as the initial period, which has taken up so much energy, recedes into the past. Among others, I would draw attention to integrative models developed on the basis of textual analysis, and models of miracle narratives, parabolic language, and the literature of biblical commentary. Attention given to the passion narrative since the first joint ventures between exegesis and semiotics has produced an impressive number of results that have only to be formalized. Finally, we are now sufficiently well acquainted with the semantic functioning of the Gospels to conclude that, in the typology of discourses, they are distinct from mythic discourse and from that of tales and legends, and are to be classified among innovative discourses the particular characteristic of which is to articulate incompatible categories "not in order to eradicate their antinomy but in order to organize the transition and permit the establishment of a new axiological deixis" (Greimas in *Signes et paraboles*, 1977).

Prospects

A summary account of achievements to date reveals certain perspectives already in view that are more or less desirable according to one's particular viewpoint. Among work in progress, initial soundings disclose a number of complexes of problems. I would cite those concerned with paratextuality and intertextuality and with quotation—of which the Bible throughout its length provides so many explicit and implicit indications, in the form of integrated *midrashim*, from one testament to the other, and from one Gospel to the other, in the mutual integration of discursive forms and in their connections with underlying relations that allow them their authentic signification. In the same line, we find questions regarding proper biblical commentary right up to the functioning of

modern commentary. Beyond the text, so to speak, there are those that indicate an opening up to the phenomenon of reading and the existence of the reader, and to *Scriptura* in the literal Latin sense of writings that are still to be written and still to be spoken. Before the text, as it were, there are questions which derive from special features of biblical enunciation. The constitution of these features in a canon forming as a whole a corpus with an identity dependent on an external instance, and thus yielding a meaningful world, places it in an atemporal situation (in the sense of making it contemporaneous for all generations) with its own values to be revealed not according to the languages used, but in terms of the contexts that modalize and recategorize them, and endow them with authority and normativity. There are also questions that take as their object the community of readers and users and its interpretative presuppositions; the establishment of an enunciative system for the delineated signifying system; and the evaluation of gaps between this system and the literary structures of the corpus, and between the interpretation of the system and that of an external reading. Finally, there are allusions to a revival *ab origine* of questions of the (literal, spiritual, historical, full) meanings of Scripture inherited from the fathers, and of the theory of literary genres that inspired critical exegesis when there was agreement on the subject, but which now has to be recalibrated, as well as adverse comments on the "gospel as genre."

In short, the "already here, not-yet" situation of semiotic exegesis shows powerful promise of resulting in tested partial syntheses and their theorization. There should now be nothing to delay semiotic exegesis on its way to analysis of much more extensive corpus. In Europe and in Canada the 1970s served mainly to familiarize adepts with Greimas' propositions and to demonstrate their value. The 1980s indicated a return of the precedence of the text over methodology understood as an instrument in its service.

In the United States, where the avant-garde is taken up with "reader-oriented critique" or "poststructural reader response," exegetes well versed in semiotic-structural analysis in the style of Peirce, Greimas, or Lévi-Strauss are variously distributed on the methodological map of their discipline. Some of them persist in a philologic-historical practice out of kilter with the group of colleagues to which they owe their formation and which constitutes their academic network and support. They call their particular orientation formalism-structuralism, or formalist criticism. Some of those who have gone over to American poststructuralism, and therefore to a deconstructionist view of the object under study, claim that this is not tantamount to rejecting the utility of a positivist, empirical, and logical type of analysis. Others abandon the heuristic approach and adopt a hermeneutical viewpoint without the "objective" positivist preliminaries postulated by the study of ancient writings.

Hesitation at different transitional thresholds is an understandable reaction to the uneasy destabilizing effects of beginning all over again. In two continents, however, practitioners have come through the pioneering phase of enfranchisement to the point where they now have solid and reliable foundations to build on.

3. Structural Semiotic Exegesis in the Field of Biblical Studies

The entry of semiotics into exegesis came at the point of an isotopic break. *Traditionsgeschichte, Formgeschichte,* and *Redaktionsgeschichte* proceeded in logical sequence within the same paradigm. The semiotic method has a wholly alien epistemological horizon; it contributes to the field of biblical studies a different attitude to the text and an apparatus that has nothing in common with that of historical criticism. Sometimes the break has been too easy, and there has been a readiness to set aside the results of a monumental scholarly effort, the result of hard struggles on the territory of uncriticized religious ideologies. Fortunately, after the initial clashes, people have begun to profit from the positive effects rather than spend time counting the cost and staunching wounds.

The favorable effects appear primarily in the form of beneficial adjustments to methodology. It is possible to restate within the domain of exegesis the fundamental problems of the conception of history, of meaning, and of text and language; exegesis can no longer remain isolated from discussion regarding these questions outside the area of specialist biblical studies. How, for example, could methods grounded in the historical approach ensure the recognition in the historical sciences of the literary value of historical discourse, and also of scientific discourse in general, and of its connotative rather than denotative value? Of course scholars did not wait until the current of structuralism was flowing powerfully to interest themselves in language in exegesis and theology, as all those treatises on the divine names produced over the centuries bear witness. Semiotics proffers an invaluable instrument in the direct line of this tradition.

Another benefit is the renewal of reflection on the meaning and meanings of the Bible, on the meaning and meanings of the discourses produced on its basis, and on an improved knowledge of their functioning which we are now, and since a recent point in the history of literary criticism, capable of characterizing and describing scientifically. As a formal method, semiotics offers those who articulate these forms of discourse the benefit of distance in relation to their pronouncements, and the benefit of the space needed to evaluate their relation to the texts on which they are grounded. This is true of all discourses with a starting-point in the Bible: commentaries, paraphrases, patristic literature, theology, catechesis, homily, liturgies of the written or oral word, readings emanating from the magisterium, communities and individuals, and doctrinal and pastoral directions. It falls to exegesis as its proper mission to construct the discourse of a text as given to us at the point of its manifestation in the critical editions; as, indeed, it reaches us through the organization of its semantic contents. It is an exacting discipline that calls for the framework of a proven and sufficiently developed apparatus. Rigorous as it is, it ought to be capable of providing for textual surprises and of fine-tuning its methodology in accordance with the texts as they enact the production of meaning.

Exegesis has passed beyond the stage in which it was believed that we possessed the one valid method: that is, the historical-critical method. Nevertheless, certain reflexes and certain teachings reveal a persistent temptation to retreat before the proliferation of collective works examining the same pericope in accordance with several approaches or grids. An erroneous notion of complementarity soon restores the divergent readings to the classic schema or else to the application of a hierarchical approach that involves subordination. Semiotic exegesis, however, like other approaches that enjoy the status of method, is scarcely inclined to fill a gap in the phases of application of the historical-critical method, and to adopt the conceptual framework of that method. It cannot offer a solution to a problem of a historical nature or shed light on the event behind the narrative, any more than history or the historical referent can give an account of the textual discourse, of its means of signifying and of the meanings produced. Complementarity acts differently, for it offers a real and reciprocal stimulus. Diachrony and synchrony, history and systemics themselves exist in a systemic condition. Much more light can be shed on their symbiosis if they are not confused methodologically.

Adjustments, renewal, and even a reason for starting again are the valid consequences of confrontation with a variety of inputs. In spite of the flood of exegetical publications, the constantly increasing number of students, and the growing interest in the process of exegesis at all levels, biblical studies have entered a period of latency. Answers are still given, often brilliantly, to questions that are now of a certain age. Where are the new questions coming from, the questions that point ahead? Perhaps from the imminent entry of semiotic exegesis into the discussion on fundamental biblical subjects? There is every reason to hope that that is the case. Above all we may expect new departures within each of the methods reactivated by their interrelations.

Apart from its usefulness in particular instances, and its original value where theories of literature take over from history, semiotic exegesis for its part opens up privileged access to greater knowledge of the Bible as text. It conveys the best advantages of the spectacular advance in the sciences of language and of the literary object in the twentieth century. We can never have too many conceptual devices appropriate to research into meaning, which are all irreplaceable in their due location and supremely profitable when their particular identity and benefits are duly recognized and respected. Above all, the semiotic project in its roots and throughout the whole course of its development is a school of reading, and that, in the end, is what everything amounts to before the Scriptures.

Bibl.: A. J. GREIMAS, _Sémantique structurale_ (Paris, 1966); id., _Du sens_, 2 vols. (Paris, 1970, 1983); A. J.

GREIMAS and J. COURTÈS, _Sémiotique: Dictionnaire raisonné de la théorie du langage_, 2 vols. (Paris, 1979, 1986); J. COURTÈS, _Introduction à la sémiotique narrative et discursive_ (Paris, 1976); L. PANIER, _Récits et commentaires: Tentation de Jésus au désert: Approches sémiotiques du discours interprétatif_ (Lyons, 1976); D. PATTE, _What Is Structural Exegesis?_ (Philadelphia, 1976); GROUPE D'ENTREVERNES, _Signes et paraboles_ (Paris, 1977); Y. ALMEIDA, _L'opérativité sémantique des récits-paraboles_ (Louvain/Paris, 1978); GROUPE D'ENTREVERNES, _Analyse sémiotique des textes: Introduction, Théorie, Pratique_ (Lyons, 1979); A. HÉNAULT, _Les enjeux de la sémiotique_ (Paris, 1979); L. PANIER, "Sémiotique du discours religieux et sémiotique générale," _Actes sémiotiques: Bulletin_ 8 (1979): 5–17; J. CALLOUD and F. GENUYT, _La première épître de Pierre_ (Paris, 1982); J.-C. COQUET et al., _Sémiotique: L'École de Paris_ (Paris, 1982); J. DELORME, "Incidence des sciences du langage sur l'exégèse et la théologie," in B. LAURET and F. REFOULÉ, eds., _Initiation à la pratique de la théologie_, vol. 1 (Paris, 1982), 299–311; J. DELORME, ed., _Parole: Figure, Parabole_ (Lyons, 1987); H. PARRET, "La sémiotique: tendances actuelles et perspectives," in A. JACOB, ed., _Encyclopédie philosophique universelle_, vol. 1 (Paris, 1989), 1361–68.

Olivette GENEST

EXPERIENCE

Before sketching the valuable role that the concept of experience can play in contemporary fundamental theology, it could be useful to say something about the historical background of this concept. It is only fairly recently that the language of experience has been readily accepted by Catholic theologians.

1. Historical Background

Up to the time of the Second Vatican Council most Catholic theologians—and, in particular, fundamental theologians—avoided using the notion of experience. The father of liberal Protestantism, F. Schleiermacher (1768–1834), interpreted religion as based on intuition and feeling; detaching it from dogma, he argued that its highest experience lay in the sense of union with the infinite. Eventually defining religion as the feeling of absolute dependence, he saw Christianity as merely the finest expression which this feeling has assumed. At the end of the nineteenth century and the beginning of the twentieth, other factors reinforced Catholic suspicions about the terminology of experience. Some modernists, for example, overemphasized the place of individual religious experience and reduced the value of common statements of faith in Christian life. A similar antidogmatic strain appeared in the 1902 Gifford Lectures of William James (1842–1910), *The Varieties of Religious Experience.* Although they did not always articulate their fears this way, many Catholic theologians and bishops avoided talk of experience as being somehow incompatible with church doctrines and institutions and prone to encourage an emotional, irrational style of Christianity.

However, both among Catholics and other Christians more positive views on experience were being expressed and gradually came to affect Catholic fundamental theology. In a classic defense of his faith, *Apologia pro Vita Sua* (1864), and other writings, J. H. Newman (1801–1890) did not believe his deeply cherished "dogmatic principle" to be threatened by his constant appeals to experience, both collective and personal. The existentialism of Søren Kierkegaard (1813–1855), despite its strain of fideism and excessive individualism, eventually won a hearing in Catholic circles. In their differing ways, other philosophers like Wilhelm Dilthey (1833–1911), Edmund Husserl (1859–1938). A. N. Whitehead (1861–1947), Maurice Blondel (1861–1949), Max Scheler (1874–1928), Karl Jaspers (1883–1969), Gabriel Marcel (1889–1973), Martin Heidegger (1889–1976), Maurice Merleau-Ponty (1908–1961), and H.-G. Gadamer (b. 1900) also helped to raise the agenda of experience for Catholic fundamental theology. So too did the debate about understanding and interpretation encouraged by the existential hermeneutics of Rudolf Bultmann (1884–1976).

Often harder to pinpoint but, nonetheless, very real, other influences were affecting apologetics or fundamental theology as the discipline was coming to be called. The work of Rudolf Otto (1869–1937) on the role of the numinous (*mysterium tremendum et fascinans*) in religious consciousness, increasing dialogue with other religions, a growing openness to the psychology of religion, the impact of sociology and, in general, the pervasive influence of the experimental sciences encouraged Catholic reflection on the human experience of God. At times, interfaith dialogue with other Christian communities and theologies raised the question of religious experience. So too did the biblical and liturgical movements within Catholicism. One could hardly talk about the divine pedagogy operative in the OT, the apostolic testimony to Christ (1 Jn 1:1–3), or the liturgy as a theological source without moving into the area of experience.

Although such scholars as Jean Mouroux (1901–1973), Henri Bouillard (1908–1981), Yves Congar (b. 1904), and especially Karl Rahner (1904–1984) had developed approaches to the theme of experience, in its sixteen documents the Second Vatican Council used this language rather sparingly: the noun *experientia* thirty-two times and the verb *experior* seventeen times. Naturally the most frequent usage (the noun eleven times and the verb eleven times) came in the Pastoral Constitution on the Church in the Modern World (*Gaudium et Spes*), which was not only the council's longest document but also the one dealing extensively with the experiences and questions of men and women in today's world. The Constitution on Divine Revelation (*Dei Verbum*) spoke of Israel "experiencing" the ways of God (*DV* 14) and of various causes of development in the postapostolic traditions, one of them being "the intimate sense of spiritual realities" that believers "experience" (*DV* 8). This latter statement did not pass unchallenged by a few bishops who heard echoes of modernist privileging of an inner consciousness falsely divorced from the church and her public teachings. However, the language of experience turned up naturally in a document which dealt with the divine self-communication (*DV* 6) in the history of salvation (*DV* 3, 4, 14, 15, 17) that invited human beings to commit their entire selves freely to God (*DV* 5). Nowadays lingering fears that somehow experience and authority are opposed or even mutually exclusive seem to have pratically disappeared. In his teaching Pope John Paul II has frequently adopted the language of experience. His second encyclical, *Dives in Misericordia* (1980), uses the noun thirteen times and the verb six times in referring to our religious experience, in both its communal and individual aspects.

2. The Notion and Reality

Regarding fundamental theology it is relatively easy to illustrate the pervasive role of experience. If the addressees of fundamental theology are human beings not in the abstract but in their concrete historicity, where and how do we experience the mystery of God? How do we know that we are experiencing God, and interpreting correctly that experience? What are the things in our human experience that lend credibility to the Judeo-Christian message we receive?

That message derives first from the experiences of God enjoyed by the people of God, prophets and others in the unfolding history of the OT. Then fundamental theology studies the foundational revelation mediated through Jesus' own unique experience of God, the disciples' experience of Jesus and the experience of the apostolic church as its mission developed in the power of the Holy Spirit.

The postapostolic tradition can be seen as the collective memory of those privileged experiences which constituted the foundational revelation that reached its definitive and unsurpassable climax with Jesus Christ and the coming of the Holy Spirit. In all its written and unwritten forms, tradition means handing on, from one generation to another, the church's collective and specifically Christian experience of God in Jesus Christ.

Granted that the theme of experience constantly touches the central issues of the revelation of God in Jesus Christ, its credibility and its transmission, fundamental theology needs to analyze carefully what human and religious experience entails. Otherwise this complex notion and reality will not prove very productive in developing the discipline.

At least seven major points call for reflection in any analysis of human experience: (1) While normally taken to be a process, experience is also the condition which results. (2) Experience puts the subject in direct contact with the object. (3) Such immediacy does *not* mean that experiences are presuppositionless. Social, historical, and religious factors of all kinds condition and make possible our experiences. (4) In some experiences the subject is more active (e.g., in scientifically controlled experiments) in others more passive (e.g., in moments of powerful grace). The active and passive elements are inseparably there in all experiences. (5) The evidence and authority of experience are clear and direct. Nevertheless, new experiences can modify and correct what has already been learned. (6) Experiences are always interpreted experiences. The work of interpretation

begins right in the very event of experience. (7) Personal experience and tradition (which can be seen as the product of the community's or society's experiences) mutually affect each other. Tradition helps us to interpret our experiences, which in turn help us to understand and modify tradition.

Only some human experiences are consciously religious: that is to say, situations that let us sense the revealing and saving self-communication of God and which invite us to make or renew a faith commitment.

Spatial language has often been used in describing these experiences as "boundary situations," "limit experiences," "peak experiences," and "depth experiences." It is also possible to identify such deeply felt experiences in terms of deliverance from death to life, from absurdity to meaning, and from hatred or isolation to love and community. Such an interpretation recognizes a trinitarian face in all religious experiences, inasmuch as they move us toward the fullness of life (the Father), the ultimate meaning and truth (the Logos), and the plenitude of love (the Holy Spirit).

The historical, categorical experiences at the conscious level are to be distinguished from the transcendental, a priori dynamism that creates the possibility for any particular religious experience. Transcendental Thomism, in particular, as developed by Karl Rahner, has shown how in every specific experience we concurrently experience ourselves and our openness to absolute, unlimited being. In this sense all human experiences have an ultimate, religious dimension, which is the primordial form of God's revealing and saving self-communication.

To conclude: "experience" has not become the only way for developing a fundamental theology. Clear and careful analysis, however, can let it serve as a productive approach to this discipline. Besides clarifying the concept itself, fundamental theologians need also to establish criteria for interpreting and evaluating religious experiences.

Bibl.: J. Mouroux, *Christian Experience* (1952; New York, 1954); H. Bouillard, *The Logic of the Faith* (1964; New York, 1967); var., "Revelation and Experience," *Conc* 113 (1979); G. O'Collins, *Fundamental Theology* (London, 1981); C. Geffré, "La rivelazione e l'experienza storica degli uomini," in R. Fisichella, ed., *Gesù Rivelatore* (Casale Monferrato, 1988), 164–77.

Gerald O'Collins

F

FAITH

1. Faith according to Sacred Scripture. 2. The Transcendence of Faith. 3. The Theological Character, or Divine Origin, of Faith. 4. The Comprehensiveness of the Act of Faith. 5. The Unity of Faith. (G. Langevin)

1. Faith according to Sacred Scripture

In the view of the Bible, faith is the integral response of the human being to God who reveals himself as Savior. Faith accepts the messages, promises, and commandments of God; it is both a trusting submission to God who speaks and an assent of the mind to a message of salvation. The OT emphasizes the aspect of trust; the NT brings out more fully the assent to the message. The basic vocabulary of faith suggests the reliability of the one in whom believers trust, as well as the security and confidence of those who rely on God.

The Old Testament

In the OT, to believe means in effect to rely on God (Gn 15:6; Ex 14:31; Nm 14:11), to surrender to the saving message of a God who directs history and enters into covenant first with the patriarchs and then with "his people," Israel. Thus Abraham trusted unreservedly in the promise of God, being fully convinced that it would be fulfilled: Abraham "believed the LORD, and the LORD reckoned it to him as righteousness" (Gn 15:6). Israel was born as a people from faith in the power, overlordship, and concern of Yahweh, the God of the covenant (Ex 19–24). This experience of Israel, in which God manifested himself as sole savior (Is 43:10–13), was later translated into the doctrine of monotheism. The call for faith in this doctrine would be put in increasingly clear and more developed formulas (Dt 6:20–24; 26:5–9; Jos 24:2–13; Neh 9:5–25).

The New Testament

In the NT, in which salvation history and the incarnate Word of God are joined in Jesus Christ, the object of faith is more explicitly defined. Faith, which is the first requirement set by Jesus, is the sufficient condition for salvation according to the Synoptics; in Acts, no more than this is required for the purification of hearts and the reception of salvation; in John faith is a process involving the entire human person — knowledge and commitment — as he or she advances toward the person of Jesus Christ.

The interpersonal aspect of this faith makes it akin to the faith of the OT. It is both trust and surrender to God who is present in the words and actions of Jesus (Synoptics); it is an obedience that assimilates the person to the crucified and risen Jesus and bestows the Spirit of the children of God (Paul); it is an acceptance of the testimony of the Father and the Son (John).

To a greater degree than in the first testament, however, faith is an assent to a message. The message is presented under various of its aspects: in the Synoptics it is the announcement of the kingdom of God and proclamation of the Father's merciful love; in the letters of Paul and in Acts it is the good news of the death and resurrection of Jesus, Lord and only savior of all humankind; in John it is the very person of Jesus, the Word made flesh, full of grace and truth, in whom we contemplate the glory of the Father.

Although faith is an action of the human being, its original source is in God. It is sustained by the saving power of God, which is at work in the preaching and activity of Jesus (Synoptics). For Paul and the author of Acts, faith proceeds from the eschatological action of God in the raising of Jesus and in the preaching that makes him known. In the Gospel of John, faith is born of the attraction exerted by the Father, who invites human beings to share in the life of the Trinity.

2. The Transcendence of Faith

Because faith is properly a personal activity, the conditions that make its appearance possible must be found in us. If it were otherwise, we would have to say that, no matter what role we were to assign to God in the origination of faith, faith would be an alien phenomenon or would not concern us. It is possible, then, to use the term "preambles of faith" in a more radical sense than it used to have. In the person as subject and in its structures, not simply in the objects presented for the person's consideration, we must see conditions required for the possibility of faith.

The process of faith is not, in Christian thought, an abdication or capitulation of the spirit but a sovereign exercise in which human beings make the thinking of God their own. Acceptance of the word of God does not mean a renunciation of the personal search for truth; rather, it means access to the divine level of truth. Thus we would fail completely to account for the action of the believer if we thought of it as a simple weakness of spirit or as a falling back on another created or finite intelligence.

The Infinity of the Spirit, or Openness to God

These preliminary considerations suppose that the spirit bears the mark of infinity and that it is therefore an openness to God. What would the reception of the word of God mean to a person who was not already linked to God in some way? In fact, because persons have an openness to being, they are already geared to the infinite. Their concern in all they do from the moment when the spirit is awakened is with being: What is this or that which exists? The question, so characteristic of human activity, shows that children already have an affinity with being, that they already know what being is, without any one having, or being able, to show them; we know being by instinct. There would be no reason to ask these questions, however, and we would not in fact ask them, if what was presented for our consideration was fully being or being by identity. Our questions show that the objects of our experiences have their being from one who does not have it from another created being.

The spirit has an irrepressible desire to be one with the essence of this Absolute that both draws and sustains our thinking. The desire we have to reach the inner reality of every being is no less strong when it comes to that which the spirit knows to be the source and summit of being. At present we know God only by analogy, and we are driven by a passion to see him in his transcendent uniqueness. Several centuries ago a theologian wrote: "This desire appears to be something negative or something whose nature it is to leave us in suspense; we see that this desire cannot stop short at, or be

satisfied by, anything in this world. We set out, in the midst of this ignorance, for a beyond [*ita nesciens, aliquid altius quaerit*] that God will help us to know and reach when he gives us the light of faith and the help of grace" (Joannes Tinctoris, *Lectura in Primam Sancti Thomae,* q. 12, a. 1, fol. 20r–v). Thus, the mystery of God is both that which we cannot bestow on ourselves and that to which we aspire with all our strength.

The Word as Privileged Medium of Divine Revelation

While the boundlessness of the created spirit provides the basic conditions needed for the emergence of faith, the word provides the medium best suited for expressing the secrets of God. Creation does, of course, tell us something about God (it shows him to be the ultimate source and supreme exemplar of all that is), but the elements that make up creation fix our gaze initially on themselves: they tell us, first of all, about themselves, and only in a second movement does the spirit use creation as a starting point from which to rise to God. The word, in contrast, is unique in that it exists only in relation to something other than itself; its very nature is to point to the person who expresses himself or herself in it and to that which the person signifies by means of it. Words are spoken only to turn attention from themselves; they are a transparency that nothing can freeze or limit and that, participating as they do in the infiniteness of the spirit, can set their sights on what is attained only by analogy. In divine revelation, says Vatican II, "the words proclaim the deeds [of God] and clarify the mystery contained in them" (*DV* 2).

The Moral Dispositions of Trust and Surrender

In the moral order, faith implies a deliberate acceptance of the creaturely condition; it supposes trust and surrender: an unconditional trust in a wisdom and love that infinitely surpass any idea we can form of them; we can rely without fear on one who is absolute truth and goodness. Faith also supposes a surrender to the creative power of God, or a rejection of self-sufficiency. Acknowledgment of their limitations disposes persons not to let themselves be imprisoned by them; it may not directly make it possible to transcend these limits, but it does make possible the recognition that submission to the one who is without limit is not alienating.

> The gospel of John teaches us that the recognition of the Father's seal upon Christ, of his word in the words of Christ, of God's glory in the signs which Christ gives, requires certain spiritual dispositions. Thus faith reveals not so much the power of intelligences as the quality of the gaze. . . . In the eyes of faith humankind seems divided into two spiritual races: the children of darkness and the children of light. The former, being strangers to the truth, do not see the signs performed in their presence (6:26; 12:37); the word does not enter into them (8:37); the light blinds them (9:39). For the others, who 'do the truth' (3:21), everything is light, sign, work, witness, and seal of the Father. (D. Mollat, _Études johanniques_ [Paris, 1979], 84–85)

3. The Theological Character, or Divine Origin, of Faith

If faith is to be truly ours, it must be rooted in us or be produced by our powers. At the same time, however, it has its origin in God himself. This is a claim that the Judeo-Christian tradition has made with increasing assurance and clarity. The prophets who proclaim the blessings of the messianic covenant speak of the new heart and the new spirit—his Spirit—which God will bestow on human beings in order that they may know him. According to the NT, as we have seen, faith involves the divine saving power that is at work in the words and actions of Jesus; assent to the resurrection of the Lord Jesus, which is the heart of the Christian faith, comes from the same power that caused the resurrection; finally, faith is a response to an interior, freely offered call from God.

The Creative and Restructuring Initiative of God

If the acceptance of the word of God is not to be reductive, it must suppose a participation in the understanding from which this word derives its specific luminosity and density. A new creation, located within the first, is needed; otherwise we would end up reducing God's word to the level of human talk about God. It is clear what such an elevation of the human spirit involves. It supposes in us an adaptation to the horizon or object of the divine understanding. The proper object of this divine understanding is God himself in his interiority or mystery—therefore not an idea of God but the reality of God. Consequently, nothing less than the beginning of the vision of God is required if we are to rely on God as on the means by which we have the knowledge of faith.

When looked at from the viewpoint of believers, faith thus implies the creative and restructuring initiative of God, for it is on God as on a basic or absolute foundation that the spirit relies. Correlatively, when God makes himself known in ways that transcend analogy, he cannot rely on anything other than himself in support of his testimony. If absolute truth is to demand recognition of itself as such from a created spirit, it cannot depend on any truth other than itself.

The Function and Scope of the Reasons for Believing

The fact that the absolute is here bearing witness to itself obliges us to reflect on the function and scope of the reasons for believing, or signs, that accompany divine revelation. On the one hand, the Scriptures tell us that all prophets must prove the authenticity of their mission by means of "signs," i.e., wonders performed in the name of God (Is 7:11; see Jn 3:2; 6:29–30; 7:3–31; 9:16–33). Reason, for its part, requires that if persons are to give their assent, they must have reasons for believing. What respect for human dignity and responsibility would be shown by an unmotivated faith? Augustine's view was that no one has a right to believe who does not have reasons for believing.

On the other hand, no matter how strong and numerous my reasons for believing may be, it is not on them that I formally rely when I make my act of faith in God. In the final analysis, reasons alone would confront me simply with my own mind and not with God. Indispensable though these reasons are, they are insufficient and even belong, properly speaking, to another, lower order. It has been well said that reasons for believing do not dispense us from believing.

What, then, is the function of these signs or reasons for believing? Must we not admit that in fact they leave us destitute when we are faced with the decision of faith? Juan Alfaro writes:

"The signs, and his rational knowledge of them, give man control not of the intrinsic credibility of the divine word but of his *own knowledge* of the duty to believe and of his *own free decision* to believe. . . ." The possibility of rational knowledge of the signs of revelation is merely a condition of the uprightness of the free decision which man takes to believe God.

> The signs that God has spoken are not presented to man simply as objective data but as proof of a divine intervention in the world that gives human life a new meaning: in these signs God draws near to man and summons him. Before this summons human liberty, and therefore also divine grace, comes into play. . . . The inward light of grace transforms our rational knowledge of the signs into a realization that '*God is calling me to believe in him*': the 'practical judgment of credibility' involves an element that is personal, unutterable, incommunicable, the resonance in our consciousness of the divine call. Inwardly drawing man to itself, Personal Truth gives him a knowledge *per connaturalitatem* in which he virtually experiences an invitation to rise above creatures and trust in the transcendent credibility of God's word. ("Faith IV. Preambles of Faith," *SM* 3:325)

4. The Comprehensiveness of the Act of Faith

Faith, which has often been wrongly identified as a purely intellectual process, has a global character or comprehensiveness that it is important to emphasize. Vatican II says: "The 'obedience of faith' (Rom 16:26; cf. 1:5; 2 Cor 10:5–6) must be given to God who reveals, an obedience by which man entrusts his whole self freely to God, offering 'the full submission of intellect and will to God who reveals,' thus freely assenting to the truth revealed by him" (*DV* 5). Thus, before speaking of assent to the message, the council refers to surrender of the person to God who speaks. Faith belongs, first of all, to the interpersonal order of the covenant.

The Understanding: Witness to the Divine Origin and Radical Character of Faith

This self-surrender affects the understanding, the heart, behavior, and action; it affects us in all the dimensions of our being. The present age, which has rediscovered affective values, has trouble seeing the role of the understanding in faith. How can assent to a message or doctrine be salvific? Is God a schoolmaster who expects us to repeat back to him what he has taught us, if we are to be in his good graces? Does God ask of us anything besides the trust and surrender that come from the heart?

Assent to divine revelation expresses, first of all, the absolute otherness of the wisdom and love that save us. The actions that save us do not come from our creaturely resources; they do not belong to us in the way that the just-mentioned surrender and trust belong to us. The words and actions of revelation come out of the mystery of God, i.e., from that which is most radically Other. But we have access to otherness only through our understanding, which is a power enabling us to perceive the nonself, or other, precisely as other.

Does not this movement of the understanding also express the radical character of the mutual gift that God and creature make to each other? The first trinitarian procession, that of the Word, has its counterpart in the first movement of our spiritual being. Then, too, this role of the understanding bears witness to the respect that God has for the conscious beings he has made. As we shall see, the message simply sets before the clear consciousness the gift that God makes of himself, and the reality he causes to exist in us.

Love and Freedom: The Attraction of Communion in the Divine Life

Love and freedom also come into play when we believe in the God who speaks to us. It is even the attraction of the good set before us by revelation that triggers the activity of faith: "I believe because I want to believe." The ultimate existential good set before me is not part of my creaturely condition but transcends that for which nature equips me, namely, a knowledge and love of God that depend on analogy, an asymptotic process—"bliss in process but not beatitude," as Maritain put it (*Neuf leçons sur les notions premières de la philosophie morale* [Paris, 1951], 99). It is with full freedom that I allow myself to be won over by the new calling that God sets before me—a participation, made possible by the incarnation, in the condition of the very Son of God. The decisions that believers make concern not only the means that will put them on the road to a goal already assigned to them but also the ultimate end itself.

Faith, then, is not free only because it requires dispositions of trust and obedience in regard to God who speaks, or because the message of faith cannot be controlled by the reasoning mind that is always looking for evidence. Faith is free basically because I agree to be drawn by a good that transcends anything I can conceive or will by myself, namely, access to the world of the trinitarian relations. Grace comes to meet us in this decision in which we accept a new meaning for our being in its totality. As Augustine wrote in his refutation of Pelagius, "It is not by the external proclamation of law and doctrine, but by a powerful action which is interior and hidden, wonderful and indescribable, that God becomes the author in human hearts not only of genuine revelations but also of decisions of the will that are in conformity with the good" (*De gratia Dei et de peccato originali* 24, 25 [CSEL 42:145]).

Behavior: The Sequela Christi

This assent of the heart and spirit finds its completion in behavior that befits the children of God, in the *sequela Christi*; faith includes a total commitment. The word that believers receive is the word of God. This word, being Truth, is act; it is a word that brings into being that which it says, and therefore a word that wills to transform any life that opens itself to it. Faith without the works that embody it is empty; it is "dead," according to James (2:14–26; see 1:22–25). Paul holds the same view, for while he rejects the idea that the works of "the law" have an innate power to merit salvation, he nonetheless maintains that authentic faith is necessarily accompanied by works that the Spirit produces in us (Rom 8:4; Eph 2:8–10).

While loss of friendship with God through sin does not necessarily imply the disappearance of faith in the sinner, it does not follow from this that faith can exist apart from any desire to love God. Faith necessarily implies a desire for salvation and reconciliation, and also for complete and definitive union with God. "Christian life . . . is not the result of faith but its authentic working out in man; in his actions, man gives his full assent to the fact that the mystery of Christ is real" (Alfaro, 1967:58).

Gestures and Rites: The Sacramental Life

Faith also finds means of expressing and celebrating itself in gestures wherein God condescends to encounter us in our bodily and communal reality. Ever since the early Christian centuries Baptism has been regarded as the sacrament of faith. "In Christ Jesus you are all children of God through faith. As many of you as were baptized into Christ have clothed yourselves with Christ" (Gal 3:26–27). "When you were buried with him [Christ] in baptism, you were also raised with him through faith in the power of God, who raised him from the dead" (Col 2:12). Then, too, the Gospel of John shows how faith and the Eucharist are interconnected in a wonderful counterpoint (chap. 6). While faith is required for reception of the Eucharist, the Bread of Life is seen in turn as the summation and supreme test of faith.

5. The Unity of Faith

While faith draws on all our resources, it possesses in its very structures a unity that reflects the simplicity of God and his action. This unity is to be seen at three levels. Formally considered, faith is inseparably an acceptance of the reality of God and an assent to his revelation of himself. Second, the content of this revelation is homogeneous both with the action of God and with the action of the created spirit; it is an expression of the very process whereby God gives himself and whereby human beings accept him. Finally, these two viewpoints, of form and content, are combined in the association of the believer with the religious experience of Christ Jesus, who is the Mediator and fullness of revelation.

Acceptance of the Reality of God and Assent to the Revealed Message

A vital acceptance of the mystery of the tripersonal inner life of God and of our communion in this mystery implies something different from the ordinary factors involved in our affirmations. Much more is involved than the exercise of our innate powers of intuition, observation, and deduction. Nor does the kind of credence we give to our fellow human beings explain adequately what happens in the act of faith.

An acceptance of God's word that does not distort it implies, as I said earlier, that the divine truth, which is the means or basis of our knowledge, is incorporated into the process by which we affirm and that the spirit of the believer is attuned to the mystery of God as to an object that is henceforth connatural. No longer, then, is it a concept, however lofty a one we may invent, that attracts the human dynamism, but the unique and strictly nonrepresentable reality of God.

Juan Alfaro writes:

> He [God] communicates and manifests himself through grace, with no other mediation than his ineffable attraction toward himself, and man knows God a-conceptually in living the experience of his call. This knowledge is not a vision of God or an immediate experience of him, but the living of a tendency toward the transcendent one in himself and, in this tendency, an a-conceptual grasp of man's final end—the absolute as grace. (1967:60)

Homogeneity of the Process and Content of Faith

Also startlingly clear is the unity between the propositional content and the process of faith. Far from being a collection of statements without any internal connection to the activity that supports them, the object of faith is co-extensive with the twofold movement whereby God and the human person give themselves each to the other. For what is at issue in faith if not the pure acceptance from God *of a message that is involved with our history and fully revelatory of God*, a message that we make our own with full realization and freedom? Thus there are three steps: acceptance, hearing, and appropriation, which place us in the presence of a God who is Source or Father, Word or incarnate Son, and Spirit or Love, and who gives himself to our spirit in order to ensure our gift of ourselves in return. Our activity is thus correlative to the internal fruitfulness of the God who is Father, Son, and Spirit, of the incarnation of the Word in our human race, and of the communion of life that God wills should exist between himself and humanity. It is precisely of this that the formulas of the Christian creed speak.

Because of this correspondence between process and content, faith shows a *mystagogi-cal* aspect of which the fathers of the church were very much aware; faith gives access to the mystery that is the source and object of divine revelation. "In his goodness and wisdom, God chose to reveal himself and to make known the hidden purpose of his will (cf. Eph 1:9) by which through Christ, the Word made flesh, man has access to the Father in the Holy Spirit and comes to share in the divine nature" (*DV* 2).

Christ Jesus, Mediator and Fullness of Revelation

Finally, faith receives its vital unity from the person of Jesus Christ. For in Christ, who is God's unqualified gift to the human family, faith has its foundation, its object, and its end. First of all, faith rests on Christ as sole mediator of revelation in its fullness. "All things have been handed over to me by my Father; and no one knows the Son except the Father, and no one knows the Father except the Son and anyone to whom the Son chooses to reveal him" (Mt 11:27). "The man Jesus cannot become conscious of himself without having an unmediated consciousness of the person of the Word as subsistent relation to the Father, that is, without having an unmediated vision of the Father" (J. Alfaro, "Les fonctions salvifiques du Christ comme prophète, roi et prêtre," *MystSal* [Paris, 1975]: 297).

Christ is not only mediator of faith but its plenary object. Paul writes: "When I came to you, brothers and sisters, I did not come proclaiming the mystery of God to you in lofty words or wisdom. For I decided to know nothing among you except Jesus Christ, and him crucified" (1 Cor 2:1–2). It is the totality of the mystery that is revealed to us in Jesus, the Son of God: Trinity, redemptive incarnation, and adoptive sonship or daughterhood through the gift of the Spirit of Jesus.

It is Christ, finally, who sets faith in motion inasmuch as he is the good or end that faith seeks. "There is salvation in no one else," says Peter to the Sanhedrin (Acts 4:12). "God sent his Son . . . so that we might receive adoption as children. And because you are children, God has sent the Spirit of his Son into our hearts, crying, 'Abba! Father!'" (Gal 4:4–6). For God reconciles us to himself by uniting us to his beloved Son, and the happiness that draws believers is a sharing in the condition of the risen Christ.

Bibl.: J. ALFARO, "The Dual Aspect of Faith: Entrusting Oneself to God and Acceptance of the Christian Message," *Conc* 21 (1967): 53–56; id., "Foi et existence," *NRT* 90 (1968): 561–80; id., "Faith," in *Sacramentum Mundi: Encyclopedia of Theology,* 6 vols. (Montreal/New York/London), vol. 2 (1968) 313–22; H. BOUILLARD, *The Logic of the Faith* (1964; New York, 1967); J.-M. FAUX, *La foi du Nouveau Testament* (Brussels, 1977); K. RAHNER, *Foundations of Christian Faith* (New York, 1978); id., "Observations on the Situation of Faith Today," in R. Latourelle and G. O'Collins, eds., *Problems and Perspectives of Fundamental Theology* (New York, 1982), 274–91; H. URS VON BALTHASAR, *The Glory of the Lord: A Theological Aesthetics,* vol. 1: *Seeing the Form* (San Francisco, 1982); B. WELTE, *Was Ist Glauben!* (Freiburg, 1982).

Gilles LANGEVIN

FEMINISM

Feminism refers to the movements for the emancipation of women which, in the nineteenth century and again in the twentieth, emerged in North America and Europe and then throughout the world. It is part of the historical consciousness that afforded the insight that political, social, and cultural structures are the product of human creativity and not merely natural or God-given. The feminist movements occurred in both society and the churches as women worked for equality of participation in the political processes of their nations and in the institutions of society and culture: education, family and church life, and the professions. As the movements developed, the initial demand for equality deepened into calls for reform of the structures of social and political life and of the systems of thought that legitimated them. In both the nineteenth- and twentieth-century movements, women saw that the Christian churches, and their traditional views of women, were among the causes of their subordination and inferiority in social, political, and ecclesial life.

Thus, as part of the academic work of the women's movement, feminist theology and women's studies in religion brought to light *both* the massive exclusion *and* the active involvement and creativity of women in Christianity. On the one hand, feminist thinkers have shown the threefold ideology about women in Western religious traditions, including Christianity: women as property, objects, or tools; women as polluting, dangerously sexual, or carnal; women romantically idealized as morally and spiritually superior to men but childlike and in need of protection in the private realm (Ruether 1975). On the other hand, women scholars have shown that, despite the ideologies which severely limited their autonomy and participation, women exercised significant leadership in virtually all the Christian traditions and historical periods (Ruether and McLaughlin). Women have held an important place in a tradition and a theology that has systematically denigrated and subordinated them. Some scholars hold that Christianity is intrinsically patriarchal and urge women to leave its oppressive environment (Daly).

Yet many feminist women remain in the churches and find the Christian symbols of God, Christ, the Spirit, grace, and the redemptive community to be life-giving, even as they quarrel with the fathers of the theological and ecclesiastical tradition and urge that the experience of women be taken into account in the history, theology, and practice of Christian life (Carr). These Christian feminist women and the scholars who have developed the many forms of Christian feminist theology hold that the pattern of thought developed in the textbooks and histories which record only the theories and deeds of men is inadequate. That pattern fails to acknowledge either the oppressive character of biblical religion or the active leadership of women in its historical and theological development. Christian feminist theology today can be described in its moments of protest and critique, historical revisioning, and theological construction.

1. Protest and Critique

Christian feminist thought shows the systematic distortion of women within the history of Christianity. Its critique of ideology exposes the idolatry of the tradition as it envisions God as a male in heaven and so makes the male superior to women on earth. Christian feminist thought argues that theology has legitimated patterns of domination in relations between God and humankind, Christ and the church, men and women, adults and children, clergy and laity, rich nations and poor, whites and people of color, humankind and the earth. "God as dominator," extended into human relationships, from the perspectives of women and other oppressed groups, is a distortion of the Christian message, a distortion often found in the historical expressions of Christian theology.

In this extension of feminist reflection to the other dominations of historical Christianity and contemporary life, Christian feminist thought strives to be internally self-critical and to avoid reversal of dominative patterns. There are other issues to which it relates itself, e.g., as it examines the interstructuring of racism, classism, elitism, and clericalism. At the same time, feminism focuses on the personal and public issue of women who are not just one group among many struggling for liberation today but who are evenly distributed across _all_ subordinated groups and across all races and classes. Women are a unique case. Neither a caste nor a minority, women are more than half the human race. Many feminist thinkers argue that the domination of women is the original oppression that is analogous to the other oppressions of history. Thus, contemporary feminism protests against sexism as the distortion of male/female relationship that results in the rape, torture, pain and exploitation of women and fails to reverence the lives and contexts of real women. Feminist theology has exposed the texts and traditions of Christianity that denigrate women as the source of sin and evil, as inferior or incomplete human beings, and as incapable of leadership in the Christian community.

2. Historical Revision

While sexism, as exemplar of dominative power, is the impetus for feminism's protest and critique, it is also true that women have been not simply victims but agents in their religious lives, have participated vigorously in every Christian period, have touched the highest reaches of religious transcendence, and have produced their own spiritual and theological points of view. As some secular historians have noted, the recovery of women's lost, forgotten or suppressed history has provided the most recent redefinition of history itself. To look at the historical terrain through the eyes of women, from the perspective of women's domination or freedom, changes usual views and reorients

historical periods. The goal of integration of women's history into "history" itself—men's history—stems from awareness that the historical record is pervaded by patriarchal values and androcentric concerns (war and politics, not childrearing), and that only the elaboration of women's history will lead to a truly universal history.

The implications of women's history for Christian history, a history of ministry and theology that would incorporate the activity and theological vision of women, in popular religion, spirituality, mysticism, preaching, teaching, and the organization and reform of religious groups, are significant. Historians of ancient Near Eastern religions, the Hebrew Bible, NT, and early Christianity have put forward views that challenge the androcentric record. They suggest that gender is relatively unimportant in polytheistic cultures, whereas it is central in the monotheistic religions of the Bible (Ochshorn); that "countervoices" in the Hebrew Bible judge its dominant patriarchal themes, show the equality of female and male in creation and in erotic and mundane relationships, reveal the saturation of Scripture with female imagery (Trible). They show that the ancient goddess was positively appropriated by Jewish and Christian monotheism (Ruether 1983); that the Jesus movement began as a reform within Judaism which embodied an inclusive vision of the kingdom, goddess language and mythology, and equal discipleship of men and women (Schüssler Fiorenza). Scholars show that women exercised leadership as prophets and disciples in the earliest Christian communities, as scholars and founders in patristic and medieval times, as socially activist organizers in Counter-Reformation circles, and as religious and social reformers in nineteenth-century Europe and America (Ruether and McLaughlin). Studies of medieval mystics have brought new attention to theological symbols of "Jesus as mother" and the "motherhood of God" (Walker Bynum), while traditions of androgynous and spirit Christology inclusive of women have been discovered throughout Christian history (Ruether 1983). These patterns of female leadership and positive female imagery and symbolism represent an important undercurrent to the androcentric mainstream of ecclesiastical and theological history.

3. Theological Construction

Beyond protest, criticism, and the revision of history, feminist theology has begun to speak of God and the meaning of human relationship to God in Christ from the perspective of women's experience. One example from many illustrates this constructive work. The radical feminist critique—Is God male?—raises the question. In spite of theological denials, it appears to be so from the persistent use of masculine pronouns for God and the reaction of many Christians against reference to God as "she." Yet it is apparent that "she" is not only as appropriate as "he," but is perhaps necessary to reorient Christian imagination from the idolatrous tendencies of exclusive masculine God-language and the dominant uses and effects of the father image in the church. There have been suggestions for the use of "father and mother" or reference to God as "parent," or for the balancing use of feminine language for the Spirit. On the other hand, some feminist scholars have urged the move away from parental images as suggestive of childish rather than adult religious dependence. While parental images express compassion, acceptance, guidance, and discipline, they do not express the mutuality, maturity, cooperation, responsibility, and reciprocity demanded by personal and political experience today.

Feminist theologians call for the use of many metaphors and models for God and for divine–human relationships, since none alone is adequate. One suggestion is the metaphor of God as "friend" (McFague 1982; 1987). There is biblical basis in Jesus' saying about laying down one's life for one's friends (Jn 15:13) and his reference to the Son of Man as friend of tax collectors and sinners (Mt 11:19); Jesus *is* the parable of God's friendship with people. That friendship is shown in his parables of the Lost Sheep, the Prodigal Son, the Good Samaritan, and the "enacted parable" of his table fellowship with sinners. The Gospels describe Jesus as critical of familial ties and his presence as transforming the lives of his friends. Friendship to the stranger, both as individual and as nation or culture, is a model "for the future on our increasingly small and beleaguered planet where, if people do not become friends, they will not survive" (McFague 1982).

The metaphor of God as friend corresponds to the feminist ideal of "communal personhood," a relationship among persons and groups that is noncompetitive and mutual. It responds to feminist concerns for expressions of divine–human relation that overcome images of religious self-denial that have shaped women's experience and engendered internalized patterns of low self-esteem, passivity, and irresponsibility and to the search for concepts of mutuality, self-creation in community, and the creation of ever-wider communities with other persons and with the world (Plaskow). The theme of God's friendship is intensified in the life and death of Jesus, who reveals a God who suffers for people and invites them into a fellowship of suffering for others (J. Moltmann). It unites theology with feminist spirituality in its emphasis on women's friendship and noncompetitive, nonhierarchical mutuality and interdependence.

Feminism and feminist theology and spirituality are now vigorous movements across the world and in the churches, both Protestant and Roman Catholic, embodying the struggle of women everywhere for their own liberation and for the liberation of the social, political, and ecclesial structures that are the context of their lives.

Bibl.: M. DALY, *Beyond God the Father: Toward a Philosophy of Women's Liberation* (Boston, 1973); R. R. RUETHER, *New Woman, New Earth: Sexist Ideologies and Human Liberation* (New York, 1975); id., *Sexism and God-Talk: Toward a Feminist Theology* (Boston, 1983); id. and E. McLAUGHLIN, eds., *Women of Spirit: Female Leadership in the Jewish and Christian Traditions* (New York, 1979); P. TRIBLE, *God and the Rhetoric of Sexuality* (Philadelphia, 1978); J. GRANT, "Black Theology and the Black Woman," in G. Wilmore and J. Cone, eds., *Black Theology: A Documentary History 1966–1979* (New York, 1979), 418–33; M. KATOPPO, *Compassionate and Free: An Asian Woman's Theology* (Maryknoll, 1980); J. PLASKOW, *Sex, Sin and Grace: Women's Experience and the Theologies of Reinhold Niebuhr and Paul Tillich* (Washington, DC, 1980); J. OCHSHORN, *The Female Experience and the Nature of the Divine* (Bloomington, 1981); C. W. BYNUM, *Jesus as Mother: Studies in the Spirituality of the High Middle Ages* (Berkeley, 1982); S. McFAGUE, *Metaphorical Theology: Models of God in Religious Language* (Philadelphia, 1982); id., *Models of God: Theology for an Ecological, Nuclear Age* (Philadelphia, 1987); E. MOLTMANN-WENDEL and J. MOLTMANN, *Humanity in God* (New York, 1982); C. MORAGA and G. ANZALDÍA, eds., *This Bridge Called*

My Back: Writings by Radical Women of Color (New York, 1982, 1983); E. SCHÜSSLER FIORENZA, *In Memory of Her: A Feminist Theological Reconstruction of Christian Origins* (London/New York, 1983); J. GRANT, "A Black Response to Feminist Theology," in J. Kalven and M. L. Buckly, eds., *Womanspirit Bonding* (New York, 1984), 117–24; A. E. CARR, *Transforming Grace: Christian Tradition and Women's Experience* (San Francisco, 1988); V. FABELLA and M. A. ODUYOYE, eds., *With Passion and Compassion: Third World Women Doing Theology* (Maryknoll, 1988).

Anne E. CARR

FIDEISM AND TRADITIONALISM

The problem of the balance to be maintained between faith and reason was at the forefront in France throughout the nineteenth century as a result of the upheavals caused by the Enlightenment and by Kant's Critiques. The MAGISTERIUM subsequently intervened several times in order to correct ambiguous views.

Traditionalists and fideists excessively downgrade the competence of reason in religion, while rationalists and semirationalists exalt the power of reason beyond measure. Fideism and rationalism are to be understood in terms of a choice: Everything is within the reach of reason, or everything comes from revelation.

1. Fideism and Traditionalism among Catholics in the Nineteenth Century

While faith is free, i.e., it is not the outcome of a series of compelling arguments, it is nonetheless an *obsequium rationabile*, i.e., a reasonable decision. We do not have strict evidence that Christ is God, but his statements, life, works, message, and resurrection are motives for believing the revelation that he is in his person. Catholic theology avoids two incomplete concepts of faith: faith that is a trustful act of homage with practically no content, and faith that is an assent to a doctrine, but a depersonalized doctrine. The assent of faith involves both knowledge and love.

In the history of Catholic theology the term "fideism" refers to a movement of thought that developed in France at the beginning of the nineteenth century in reaction to the rationalism of the eighteenth century. Its chief representatives were P. Gerbert (1798–1864), L.-E. Bautain (1796–1867), A. Gratry (1805–1872), a disciple of Bautain, and A. Bonnetty, to whom may be added L. de Bonald and F. de Lamennais, though these last two are usually called traditionalists. All these men were bent on humbling reason, which the encyclopedists had exalted; they did so by emphasizing its weakness, errors, contradictions, and uncertainties. They did not regard the motives of credibility as sufficient to ground a solid decision. But what did that matter, since faith stands on its own and is its own foundation? In Bautain's view, faith is possible only for those who have a sense of the divine, which is in turn the work of grace. Grace alone makes it possible to recognize the truth of revelation through an interior experience, and not through the external signs, or motives of credibility, that accompany revelation. Bautain later retracted his views and acknowledged the value of the motives or signs that are intended to show revelation to be "believable."

The magisterium has repeatedly denounced the deviations of the fideists, especially Gregory XVI (DS 2751–56); Pius IX in 1846, in the encyclical *QUI PLURIBUS* (DS 2775–80); above all, Vatican I (DS 3008–9); Leo XIII in 1879, in the encyclical *Aterni Patris* (DS 3135–38); and Pius XII in 1950, in the encyclical *Humani Generis* (DS 3875). These documents stress the value of the proofs of the existence of God (→ GOD II) and of the motives of CREDIBILITY, without, however, denying the interior aid of the Spirit. Fideism is correct in its rejection of RATIONALISM, AGNOSTICISM, and liberalism, but it goes to the opposite extreme when it bases faith on faith itself. While the magisterium warns against the exaggerated depreciation of reason by the fideists and traditionalists, its primary concern is to oppose the claims of the rationalists and to remind us of the preponderant role of grace in the economy of salvation.

2. Fideism in a Protestant Context

Fideism has an entirely different meaning in the vocabulary of Protestantism, where it means salvation by faith alone. Thus Luther rejects philosophy as being an exaltation of reason and nature. He conceives of faith as a pure, trustful self-abandonment to God who saves and justifies. Through faith, human beings cast themselves upon God, independently of any assent to a set of doctrines. Therefore, alongside knowledge of the revealed DOGMAs that they accept, Protestants urge a second kind of faith—an unreserved trust in the divine promises in general and, above all, the unqualified conviction that they are justified by the merits of Christ. This trust-faith is regarded as the only authentically Christian faith; it is through this faith, independently of any good works, that human beings are saved. In this understanding of faith the interior testimony of the Holy Spirit obviously plays a major role. K. BARTH carried this early Protestant conception of faith to its extreme, arguing that human beings are filled with pride and sin; the only thing they can do is accept God's action in them.

3. Unconscious and Practical Fideism in Contemporary Catholicism

I refer here to the attitude of numerous Catholics who attach no importance, or at least an insufficient importance, to problems regarding the credibility of revelation. Paradoxically, this attitude is found in the postconciliar period. Since Vatican II and the *Normae quaedam* that were to guide the reform of ecclesiastical studies failed to say anything about fundamental theology, many seminaries and faculties of theology yielded to temptation and sacrificed a discipline that the magisterium itself seemed not to value. In some places fundamental theology was simply abolished. In others it was broken up and reduced to fragments that were inserted in one or other fashion into the other disciplines—e.g., the historicity of the Gospels into exegesis; revelation, tradition, and inspiration into the introduction to theology. The question of the signs of credibility was simply evaded or else partially dealt with in connection with exegesis (e.g., the theme of the miracles of Jesus, which have been denied rather than really discussed). In still other places, finally, under the influence of *DEI VERBUM*, fundamental theology was reduced to a study of revelation and its transmission, thereby losing half of its territory and especially the whole subject of credibility. In short, by fragmenting fundamental theology

and assigning its problems to other disciplines as though they were the remnants of a mortgaged inheritance, these various educational institutions stripped fundamental theology of its specific task (to confirm the brothers and sisters in their faith) and helped cause the shipwreck of thousands of the faithful, who were now left helpless before disturbing questions that were too difficult for them to handle without the help of specialists.

But reality is stronger than theories. Fundamental theology deals with problems that are too serious and too real to be ignored, including the historical origins of Christianity; the reality and identity of Jesus; the historical reality of his message, his works, especially his miracles, and his resurrection; his will to found a church on Peter and the apostles, and the nature of this planned church. It is possible for a time to play the ostrich and take refuge in a disguised fideism, but the problems remain and are always at the gates of the city (i.e., the church). We may refuse to look at them, but we cannot do away with them. The spirit in which we approach the problems must certainly change, especially in the present climate created by ecumenism, but the function exercised by fundamental theology is a permanent one. In addition, the questions with which it deals constitute a whole that has its own proper unity and makes fundamental theology a distinct province of theology.

Bibl.: S. HARENT, "Fidéisme," *DTC* 6,1:174–236; G. ROTUREAU and Y. CONGAR, "Fidéisme," in *Cath* 4:1260–61; R. AUBERT, *Le problème de l'acte de foi* (Louvain, 1945), 102–130; H. BOUILLARD, *Karl Barth*, 3 vols. (Paris, 1957), esp. vol. 2; P. POUPARD, *L'abbé Louis Bautain: Un essai de philosophie chrétienne au XIXe siècle* (Paris/Tournai/New York/Rome, 1961); R. LATOURELLE, "Dismemberment or Renewal of Fundamental Theology," *Conc* 46 (1969): 29–42; id., "Absence and Presence of Fundamental Theology at Vatican II," in R. Latourelle, ed., *Vatican II: Assessment and Perspectives Twenty-five Years After* (New York, 1989), 378–415.

René LATOURELLE

FUNDAMENTALISM

In the English-speaking world, the fundamentalist current in Protestant Christianity reaffirms the absolute inerrancy of the Bible and its sovereign authority for faith and life. As a twentieth-century movement, fundamentalism is a critical reaction against the erosion of traditional certainties through modernism in theology and the historical-critical investigation of Scripture.

A widely distributed series of twelve short tracts, *The Fundamentals: A Testimony to the Truth* (1910–15) set forth the basic tenets on which traditional faith should admit no doubt or accommodation: the full inspiration of Scripture as God's word; the divinity of Jesus Christ; his virginal conception, miracles, atoning death, physical resurrection, and future return; the reality of sin and of salvation by faith; the power of prayer and duty of evangelism. Between 1920 and 1940, disruptive disputes between fundamentalists and modernists divided major denominations such as the Baptists, Methodists, and Presbyterians, but in its resurgent form in the 1970s and 1980s fundamentalist religiosity has been most typically found in independent congregations and among the followers of television evangelists such as Jerry Falwell and Pat Robertson.

Fundamentalist communities and believers are intensely devoted to the biblical word, see Christianity as centered on conversion to accepting Jesus Christ as personal Lord and savior, and strive to follow a strict moral code in personal and family living. Earlier fundamentalism repudiated the "social gospel," but more recent fundamentalists are prominent in backing conservative political causes, such as restrictive legislation on abortion and homosexuality. The missionary outreach of fundamentalist communities is typically through sponsorship of preachers sent to Latin America. Fundamentalist interpretation of biblical prophecy often fosters the eager expectation of Jesus' return to take believers out of the decadent and doomed world, where the Antichrist will then reign until his eventual defeat and the opening of the thousand-year reign of the saints of God.

Fundamentalist faith in the prophetic and apostolic word does not admit interest in the historical conditioning and ecclesial contexts of the mediators of revelation. God's definitive word is immediately at hand in inspired and inerrant biblical texts. Fundamentalist hermeneutics, however, does not depend on a theory of verbal dictation by the Holy Spirit, but rather on the complete consistency and self-manifesting authority of the Bible as a whole and in all its parts. Fundamentalist preaching typically asserts the facticity of the biblical narratives, shows how one passage is supported by probative texts in numerous other biblical books, and regularly sets forth the divine plan of offering salvation in Christ to those who admit their sin and helplessness, decide to accept Jesus, and open their lives unreservedly to his power and guidance for fulfilling God's moral will.

Many analysts see fundamentalist Christians as seeking a secure shelter against the moral chaos of modern Western society and some observers note its analogies with integrist movements in contemporary Islam and even Roman Catholicism. Fundamentalism is alien to, and often hostile toward church traditions that affirm the role of reason and critical study (e.g., *DV* 12; *GS* 62). Still it serves as a strong reminder that Scripture constitutes a comprehensive world of thought with untold potential for enriching daily life with fresh motivation and guidance.

Bibl.: E. R. SANDEEN, *The Roots of Fundamentalism: British and American Millenarianism 1800–1930* (Chicago, 1970); J. BARR, *Fundamentalism* (London, 1977); N. T. AMMERMAN, *Bible Believers: Fundamentalists in the Modern World* (New Brunswick, NJ, 1987); T. F. O'MEARA, *Fundamentalism: A Catholic Perspective* (Mahwah, NJ, 1990).

Jared WICKS

FUNDAMENTAL THEOLOGIAN

1. From Confrontation to Dialogue

Present-day fundamental theology was born in large measure of a reaction against the apologetics of recent centuries, which was always on a war footing and engaged in clashes, always looking for adversaries to fight. Not only the rationalists but even Protestants, though they are baptized Christians, were cast in the role of enemies. Because of its polemics, carried on in an intransigent spirit that was as cutting as a lancet, apologetics had destroyed people's trust in it. For three decades it experienced the emptiness of the catacombs. But this also proved to be a fruitful period, for it provided the opportunity for apologetics to be "converted" and to reflect on the changes taking place in our time and on the tasks it was expected to carry out.

The most obvious sign of this "conversion" is the change of name: the old "apologetics" has been discreetly rebaptized and is to be known henceforth as FUNDAMENTAL THEOLOGY. But the change of name is more than the attaching of a new label to an old product. A change has also taken place that affects its status and its outlook. Those doing fundamental theology realized that the age of the crusades had passed and that twentieth-century Christians, who are open to the world and the sciences and have an ecumenical mentality, want above all to be heard. For they are tormented by problems of an unparalleled seriousness; they want to be taken seriously and to be informed in a dispassionate way of what Christianity has to say to them about these problems. Instead, therefore, of making statements couched in terms of opposition and refutation, fundamental theology now takes positions, offers explanations, and sets forth propositions. It has shifted from indictment to calm exposition, from confrontation to dialogue, and has thus adopted the attitude of the recent council that set out to listen and to dialogue.

Fundamental theology, as a contemporary discipline, has emerged from a critical period of "adolescence." It is now more modest, more serene, more aware of the complexity of the problems it faces, and better equipped; as a result, it is more concerned with the search for meaning and intelligibility than with sledge-hammer arguments. This attitude of dialogue extends to the sciences, the religions, the churches, and the cultures. Christ is still fundamental theology's point of departure and reference point, but not a bridgehead thrown forward for a new attack.

2. The Partner in Dialogue

Professors of fundamental theology address people who, thanks to the media, are much better "informed" than their counterparts of old; people who are also more critical, immersed as they are in a world in which all the ideologies rub shoulders and the strangest sects proliferate, in a culture increasingly alienated from the Christian vision of the human person and the world. These teachers run up against vast areas of indifference begotten by a secularized world of progress and technology, and therefore against a complete lack of interest in religious questions, as well as an abysmal ignorance of the Christian message.

When these people come or are met from time to time, it is not enough to tell them: "The church says," or "The gospel says," or, more ingenuously still, "I say." Believers and unbelievers alike demand answers that are precise and well argued. If professors of fundamental theology are to answer today's questions, they must acquire a formation that is as good as or better than that of the biologist, the physicists, the lawyer. If they reject this challenge to an austere, demanding, and lengthy preparation, they will be unable to lead the questioners to the faith and unable even to strengthen their own believing brothers and sisters in their faith (1 Pt 3:15). For nowadays believers carry within them the doubts of the unbeliever. "The same things that feed the thinking and attitude of unbelievers also keep uncertainty and doubt alive in many Christians" (H. Bouillard). When we dialogue with unbelievers we are dialoguing with ourselves; in such a setting, reflection on the rational bases of the decision to believe is not an intellectual game but a vital necessity. If such reflection does not take place, the present crisis of faith will only grow more serious until it becomes a vast underground schism or a sea of indifference.

3. Theological Status of Fundamental Theology

The Anselmian principle, *fides quaerens intellectum*, which provided a three-word definition of theology nine centuries ago, has hardly been outdated. But each term of the definition has been so expanded and has taken on such a fullness of meaning that the balance within the whole has been altered.

a. Fundamental theologians, like all theologians, find their ground in one and the same faith. Believers who try to understand themselves as believers cannot behave as if they did not believe; such an attitude would be utterly contradictory. In like manner, fundamental theology cannot regard it as accidental that the theologian is a believing Christian; rather this is essential to its very existence. This starting point is all the more important to the extent that the thinking of fundamental theologians has for its focus the central affirmation of the Christian faith, namely, that God manifests and gives himself in Jesus Christ. If these theologians have as their mission the complete and rounded study of revelation, which is the primordial reality of Christianity, then it is required of them, more than of anyone else, that they be "witnesses" to this faith which has already illumined and inspired their lives. In their persons understanding of the mystery must be inseparable from an experiential cleaving to the mystery. If they seek to understand, the reason is that their faith itself "urges" them to "seek" in order that they may more perfectly understand that which gives meaning to their lives.

It is true, of course, that the study of revelation takes fundamental theology into an area that pertains directly not to dogmatic theology but to apologetics; nonetheless it is the very nature of the reality being studied that makes this procedure necessary, since that reality is at once mystery and historical event. For fundamental theology investigates not only revelation as object of faith but also revelation as irruption of God into the history, flesh, and language of Jesus. It inquires into the presence of God-among-us-in-Jesus-Christ and into the historical signs of this presence. It inquires not only into what we believe but also into why we believe. It asks whether the claim that "God is among us in Jesus Christ" is "believable"; it asks whether the decision to believe is reasonable, sensible.

While fundamental theology, by reason of its subject matter, calls on the human sciences (literary and historical criticism, philosophy), it remains nonetheless the activity of believers. At no point does it set faith aside. It is bound to state its presuppositions, but it is also bound never to abandon them, under pain of ceasing to be itself.

b. The second word in the Anselmian definition, "seeking" (quaerens), is perhaps the one that has been broadened the most. For, overnight as it were, seekers have found themselves in possession of skills that have renewed and even revolutionized theology, and this especially in areas that most nearly affect fundamental theology: biblical and patristic sciences, linguistic sciences, and anthropology (philosophy, history, sociology, psychology). The real novelty, however, is that the human sciences have been freed of their connection with philosophy and have claimed their own full autonomy. As a result, the dialogue of fundamental theology with the sciences is now carried on directly with these, without the mediation of philosophy. The "seekers," i.e., fundamental theologians, have thereby seen the field of their study immensely broadened.

Among the disciplines that have had a more direct impact on the task of fundamental theology, priority belongs to history, the linguistic sciences, and, in general, the sciences of the human person. First of all, HISTORY. Awareness of the historical dimension has radically altered theology. This dimension plays such an essential role in contemporary thinking that any attempt to operate outside this horizon ensures not being understood by our contemporaries. The impact made by history is all the greater since revelation itself can be understood only in a historical setting. Next come the linguistic sciences: philosophies of languages, types of language (conceptual, symbolic, gestural; → LANGUAGE), problems of interpretation or HERMENEUTICS; problems of inculturation or transculturation. I may mention finally the triumphant rise of the *sciences of the human person* (sociology, psychology, psychoanalysis). Fundamental theology, being a discipline on the boundary, necessarily engages in dialogue with all these sciences that have shaped the thinking of our contemporaries. This dialogical receptivity represents an advance over the old apologetics, but it also entails dangers, especially that of losing sight of what is specifically Christian and diluting the message in order to turn it into a product acceptable to all. In short, the danger is of ending up with a Christianity that is faded and colorless, flattened out and without a physiognomy of its own. On the other hand, fundamental theology cannot retreat. It must maintain its attitude of dialogue, but with an even sharper awareness of its identity and mission.

4. Needed Preparation

Given all these conditions, is it still conceivable that there should be an adequate preparation for the teaching of fundamental theology? Must we require of all professors that they have a complete knowledge of ancient and modern philosophies, exegesis, the problems of language, the world's religious traditions, the methods of literary and historical criticism, and the rapidly developing human sciences? Would that not be a utopian challenge and one that would discourage even the best goodwill?

A distinction must be made between, on the one hand, fundamental theology as an activity of the church and an area of theological science, and, on the other, the teaching of fundamental theology by a particular professor and in a particular school. Just as no physician can in his or her single person possess all of medical science, so no theologian and no school can take on the teaching of all the subjects belonging to fundamental theology. That ability belongs to the church as a social body. Having said this, I think it possible to distinguish various levels and stages of preparation for the teaching of fundamental theology.

(a) A basic literary and philosophical formation (such as is normally given in a lycée, college, or German gymnasium) that prepares students for university studies. At this level, students acquire a knowledge of the great works of literature and the main currents of philosophy.

(b) A basic theological formation, with an emphasis on anthropology, Christology, and ecclesiology.

(c) A specialized formation in fundamental theology, crowned by a doctorate and a published dissertation. To this level belongs the thorough knowledge of that which constitutes the hard, irreducible nucleus of fundamental theology, namely, the problem of REVELATION and its CREDIBILITY. This nucleus includes the study of the origins of Christianity in their historical context; the coming on the scene of the person Jesus; the knowledge we can have of him that will give us access to his teaching, his works, his attitudes, his consciousness of being the Son, and his statements about his identity and his intention of founding a Church; the reality of his MIRACLES and resurrection

(→ PASCHAL MYSTERY II; the fidelity of the church to the interpretation Jesus gives of himself.

(d) This specialization in fundamental theology should be accompanied by specialization in a discipline that will enable future professors to familiarize themselves with the methods of literary and historical analysis. Concretely, this means a doctorate, or at least a licentiate, in exegesis or history.

(e) Many other problems have to do rather with the dialogue between fundamental theology and its outside partners: the churches, religions, cultures, and sciences. It is here that interdisciplinary aid comes to the rescue of the principal specialization. In a university of any size, the dialogue among colleagues and faculties will normally enable professors of fundamental theology to discover rather quickly what is not within their immediate competence.

Even with this distinction between levels of preparation and the contribution to be expected of each, the preparation of professors of fundamental theology will always be one of the most rigorous and demanding among the theological disciplines. It is meant above all for candidates whose inborn, many-sided curiosity equips them most easily to meet the demands of a discipline located at the crossroads where all the questions regarding the human person, Christ, and the church meet.

Bibl.: H. BOUILLARD, *The Logic of the Faith* (New York, 1967); SACRED CONGREGATION FOR CATHOLIC EDUCATION, "The Theological Formation of Future Priests," in *Origins* (1976): 173–90; R. LATOURELLE, *Theology: Science of Salvation* (Staten Island, NY, 1969); id., *Finding Jesus through the Gospels* (New York, 1979); id., "A New Image of Fundamental Theology," in R. Latourelle and G. O'Collins, eds., *Problems and Perspectives of Fundamental Theology* (New York, 1982), 37–58; R. LATOURELLE, "Absence and Presence of Fundamental Theology at Vatican II," in R. Latourelle, ed., *Vatican II: Assessment and Perspectives Twenty-five Years After* (New York, 1989), 3:378–415; M. CHAPPIN, "Dalla difesa al Dialogo: L'insegnamento della teologia fondamentale alla PUG, 1930–1988," in R. Fisichella, ed., *Gesù Rivelatore* (Casale Monferrato, 1988), 33–45.

René LATOURELLE

FUNDAMENTAL THEOLOGY

I. History and Specific Character. *1. From Apologetics to Fundamental Theology. 2. Reaction against Classical Apologetics. 3. Phase of Expansion. 4. Phase of Focusing. 5. A Distinct and Specific Theological Discipline. 6. A Structured Discipline. 7. Pedagogical Organization.* (René Latourelle)

II. Whom Is It For? *1. Positive Elements. 2. Problems.* (Rino Fisichella)

I. History and Specific Character

1. From Apologetics to Fundamental Theology

Present-day fundamental theology was born of classical APOLOGETICS and of reflection on the fact that this apologetics had either to disappear or to undergo reform so that it might respond to a new mentality, updated techniques, and new demands. Apologetics had indeed been accustomed to changes, to unforeseen shifts of direction. But in the postwar period the change that took place was so radical, so spectacular, that apologetes thought it good to change the name, and apologetics became *fundamental theology.*

This change of name is only the superficial sign of a much deeper change that affected the very character of the science. Fidelity to reality required a new passport, as it were, for apologetics, since the changes that took place affected not only its name but its content, its method, and its identity. On the other hand, since the problems faced by present-day fundamental theology remain substantially the same (→ REVELATION; → CREDIBILITY), it would be wrong to regard this fundamental theology as a completely new enterprise.

The formation of the new image of apologetics, henceforth known as fundamental theology, dates from the postwar years. It covers a period of three decades that are linked to a threefold movement of theological reflection: a phase of reaction against classical apologetics; a phase of expansion, during which the name "fundamental theology" was definitively adopted; and a phase of reflection on the identity of this theology and the hierarchization of its tasks. Taking Vatican II as a point of reference, one may schematize and speak of a preconciliar, a conciliar, and a postconciliar phase.

I shall speak of three phases rather than three chronological stages, because in fact we are dealing with three waves which overlap as much as they succeed each other. When the second arose, the movement of the first could still be felt; and while the second was unfurling, the third had already begun.

2. Reaction against Classical Apologetics

What is known as "traditional" or "classical" apologetics with its three stages—proof of religion (*demonstratio religiosa*), proof of Christianity (*demonstratio Christiana*), and proof of Catholicism (*demonstratio Catholica*)—was the result not of critical reflection on its object, purpose, and method, but of historical necessity, namely, the struggle against the Protestants of the sixteenth century, the libertines and practical atheists of the seventeenth, and the Deists and encyclopedists of the eighteenth. It was necessary to meet the atheists and libertines with a rigorous theodicy and to show the necessity of religion. Against the Deists, who were content with a natural religion and rejected any idea of a historical revelation, Christianity had to be shown to be the true religion by means of convincing proofs that Jesus Christ speaks in the name of God. Against the Protestants, finally, it was necessary to show that among the various Christian confessions the Catholic church is the only true CHURCH. In dealing with faith, Protestantism emphasized subjective elements, especially the action of the Spirit, who causes us to cleave to the word of God and gives us certitude regarding its origin. Catholic apologetics, on the other hand, stressed the objective criteria. As seen by Vatican I, these criteria are primarily MIRACLES and PROPHECIES. Behind this three-stage process lay the conviction that faith is the necessary end-result of the proof of Christianity, while entrance into the Catholic church will follow from the proof of Catholicism. This tripartite scheme was already in place in the sixteenth century. The term "apologetics" became current around 1830. Only at the beginning of the present century, however, did works appear that not only aimed at a rational and systematic justification of the decision to believe but at the same time endeavored to define the epistemological status of apologetics as a science distinct from both philosophy and dogmatics. I shall mention, as a point of reference, the classical works of A. GARDEIL, R. Garrigou-Lagrange, and S. Tromp.

The postwar setting is quite different from the one that saw the rise of classical apologetics. A vast renewal has stirred theology, especially in areas that most strongly affect apologetics. I am thinking in particular of the renewal of biblical and patristic studies, which have shown revelation and faith to be a much richer, more concrete, more personal, and more adaptable reality; the renewal of exegetical methods and techniques; the many-sided progress achieved in the linguistic sciences; the contribution of philosophies of the human being; and, finally, the ecumenical renewal, which has turned an aggressive and polemical attitude toward Protestants into an attitude of openness and dialogue. There is no doubt that the entire intellectual atmosphere has changed. This new cultural and religious context soon revealed the weakness and limitations of the old apologetics. Here are some of the criticisms brought against it:

a. Classical apologetics seeks to show the credibility of revelation, but it does so without having engaged in any serious study of the reality that it intends to handle in a critical way. And yet it is not unimportant to stress the fact that the revelation in question here is not a revelation of a philosophical kind, the model for which can be projected in advance, but a very special reality that comes to us via history and the incarnation. Revelation alone can tell us what revelation is. The first need in apologetics, therefore, is to look closely at this intervention of God in Jesus Christ and study all its riches and all its dimensions. In like manner, the only valid treatment of signs is one that sees them as unified in the person of Christ. This very special revelation is the basic datum on which theologians must reflect in order to grasp its historical coherence and its *meaning*.

b. Meaning is the subject of the second criticism of classical apologetics. After establishing by external arguments that Jesus is the messenger of God and that he founded a church, apologetes concluded that our faith in its entirety must be received from this church. They failed to see (at least in practice) that the Christian message is supremely intelligible and that its fullness of meaning is already a motive of credibility. Revelation is "believable," not only because of external signs but also because it reveals human beings to themselves; it is even the only key to an understanding of the mystery of the human person. It is not possible, therefore, to isolate the historical fact of revelation from the meaning of this revelation. Apologetics did not venture into this question, doubtless in order not to seem to be encroaching upon an area reserved to dogmatics.

c. Many practitioners of traditional apologetics dealt only with the messiahship of Jesus. It was enough, they thought, to show that Jesus presented himself as a divine messenger speaking in the name of God. The other testimonies of Jesus to his own person belonged in dogmatics. Once again, such a position is unacceptable. First of all, because it necessitates continual and unjustified reductions in the picture of Jesus as he is presented and confessed in the Gospels, namely, as the Christ, the Son of Man and the Son of the Father. Second, because it forces a simple messenger to put forth the radical demands proper to a supreme judge of the human race. Finally, because it makes unintelligible the miracle that is utterly unparalleled in the history of salvation: the resurrection into glory (→ PASCHAL MYSTERY II). This dichotomy between divine messenger and Son of the Father is artificial; it is contrary to the testimony of Jesus to himself and even more to the kerygma regarding him.

d. A fourth criticism has to do with the limited attention or, more accurately, the lack of attention in classical apologetics to the conditions for the acceptance of revelation and its signs by the human beings to which they are addressed. Out of a desire for scientific objectivity apologetics neglected one whole aspect of credibility. If apologetics is to deal not with an abstract credibility but with the human credibility of revelation, it cannot be satisfied to study revelation "in itself" or the signs of this revelation "in themselves"; it must pay equal attention to the conditions that determine the subject's effective reception of the revelation and its signs. This attention to the subjectivity of the recipient was brought out by BLONDEL and is now an established part of apologetics.

e. Until well into the twentieth century apologetics continued to cross swords with its

Protestant, deistic, and rationalistic adversaries. In the present ecumenical climate this is no longer a "defensible" attitude. The first step is not to refute but to create the conditions needed for drawing closer and listening to each other. As a result of its focus on self-defense the old apologetics closed in on itself and closed itself off from the others. Happily, it has lost this polemical tone. Its approach is now one not of confrontation but of presenting positions and propositions. Moreover, today's adversary is to be found in the heart of the believer no less than of the unbelievers. The people of the twentieth century are looking less for refutations than for serious reflection on their problems, together with a serious presentation of the claims of Christianity. This is a task that apologetics would have to take on even if there were no adversaries.

The difficulties just listed represent less an indictment from without than the self-criticism of those whose mission it was to teach apologetics in the years after the war. As they sought to determine the status of their discipline in a completely different cultural and intellectual setting, these teachers had to undertake a number of adjustments that served as so many liberating choices.

3. Phase of Expansion

The second phase in the history of postwar fundamental theology began in about the sixties and reached its climax in the promulgation of *Dei Verbum*. After having exorcized the ghost of the old apologetics and dissociated itself from the name by which it had been identified, the "new style" apologetics experienced the joy of a second spring. Books and articles on REVELATION multiplied. The characteristic mark of this period was an expansion of the discipline that was to be seen at all levels: extension of its tasks, enrichment of its special themes, dialogue with new partners. All this found a concrete expression in the definitive adoption of the name "fundamental theology," which signified its new image and new identity.

It can be said that the enrichment and deepening of fundamental theology came chiefly through its two privileged themes: revelation and its credibility.

Ever since 1940 there has been a ceaseless outpouring of works on the subject of revela-tion. The stimulus for this has come in part from Protestant work, which has been especially abundant in this area, but also from factors operating in Catholic circles: the biblical and patristic renewals and the development of the theologies of faith, preaching, and missions, all of which have acted as catalysts. It can be said that this renewal of the theology of revelation, begun by the works of H. Niebecker (1940), R. GUARDINI (1940), K. RAHNER (1941), and L. M. Dewailly (1945), and patiently continued for two decades in ever more numerous monographs, found its culmination and, to some extent, its canonization in the constitution DEI VERBUM of 18 November 1965.

For in *Dei Verbum* revelation is described not only in its objective aspect as doctrine and message but also as an action of God, namely, his self-manifestation and self-giving in Jesus Christ. Christ is the epiphanic Word of God: he *is* revelation. A further merit of the Constitution is that it presents Christian revelation not as an isolated phenomenon, but as an "economy," i.e., a vast and mysterious plan which God implements across the centuries in ways arranged by him. The Constitution thus emphasizes the historical, interpersonal, dialogical, christological, and ecclesiological dimensions of revelation. By thus expanding the idea of revelation in fidelity to what we are told about it in revelation itself, the Constitution accomplished a work of liberation. It also rendered a valuable service to fundamental theology by pulling together in a single vision themes formerly scattered or else artificially grouped in, e.g., a *De Inspiratione*, regarded as belonging to *De Sacra Scriptura*, and a *De Traditione*, regarded as belonging sometimes to *De Ecclesia*, sometimes to *De Locis Theologicis*.

The theme of credibility has been the subject of a no less spectacular expansion. Without denying a certain legitimacy to the traditional treatment of credibility in terms of the historical signs of revelation (miracles, prophecies, message, resurrection), fundamental theologians of the conciliar period could not but point out the limitations of this treatment: an insufficient understanding of the methods and tools of modern exegesis; a simplistic use of certain arguments (e.g., the fulfillment of messianic promises); a purely apologetic approach to signs; an inflated value set on certain signs (miracles, prophecies) to the detriment of the greater signs, which are Christ himself and his church; a separation of the signs from the person who makes use of them and from the message that gives them their full meaning; insufficient consideration of the testimony given by one's life or the harmony between gospel and life; inadequate attention or none at all to the conditions for the acceptance of the signs by human beings and, correlatively, a tendency to overvalue their power to persuade persons.

But, above and beyond these grievances, fundamental theologians of the conciliar period became aware that if the theme of credibility was to be correctly treated, it had to have wider horizons. Three major directions can be seen in this process of expansion.

A first has to do with problems of *history and hermeneutics*. For the theologians quickly realized that the knowledge of Jesus given to us by the GOSPELS, which are the place where revelation is most heavily concentrated, is not something to be taken for granted. While it is true that God has revealed himself through the words and deeds of Jesus and through his entire presence in the world, it is supremely important to know whether, how, and to what extent we can get at this epiphany of God, at least in its historical reality. It follows that the problem of access to Jesus through the Gospels is a fundamental one in thinking about Christian credibility.

The second direction, which has to do with *anthropology*, is in response to the objection leveled at the old apologetics, that it left a gap between the fact and content of revelation, that it inquired into the event without any concern for the *meaning* that the event has for human beings. A hermeneutic focused solely on the origin of Christianity in Jesus would be barren, since Jesus was not simply an irruption of God into human history, but an irruption that reveals human beings to themselves, decoding and transfiguring them. It is not enough, therefore, to show that we have access to Jesus of Nazareth through the Gospels; it is necessary also to show that the Christian message concerns human beings and the fundamental questions they ask. This human questioning is clear and insistent: human beings are waiting to be shown that Christ is the only key to the human riddle. This anthropological aspect of credibility, which Blondel had already empha-

sized in his *L'Action*, has been extensively developed by R. GUARDINI, K. RAHNER, H. Bouillard, H. URS VON BALTHASAR, M. Zundel, G. Marcel, J. Mouroux, M. Légaut, and J. Ladrière, each of them from quite different philosophical perspectives.

The third direction has to do with the *signs* of revelation. The issue here is the identification of Jesus as God-among-us. Since Jesus is the human, bodily form in which God encounters human beings and manifests himself to them, the saving presence of God can, strictly speaking, be authenticated only through the mediation of the man Jesus. He is the riddle, the mystery, that needs to be unlocked. Therefore, fundamental theology, like the old apologetics, takes up the study of the signs of revelation, but it does so with a more alert critical sense, with improved exegetical and historical tools, with a keener awareness of the complexity of the problems it is taking up, and, consequently, with a less categorical approach to its claims. The study of signs is likewise affected by the hermeneutical problem (→ HERMENEUTICS) in its interpretation of the texts that tell of the signs. Its most distinctive characteristic, however, is its concern to connect the signs with the person who gives them. The signs are, in fact, Jesus Christ himself, the complete living person, in the manifold aspects of his epiphany in this world.

Finally, the range of *addressees* has also been expanded. Fundamental theology aims at being a theology in dialogue, not only with believers but with all forms of religion and unbelief. The partner in dialogue is thus believers themselves, not only because each of them shares the doubts of unbelievers, but also because present-day believers, living as they do in a world of unbelief and indifference, are necessarily influenced by it. When we dialogue with unbelievers, we dialogue with ourselves. In such a setting, reflection on the intellectual basis for the decision of faith is not a game for intellectuals but a vital necessity.

4. Phase of Focusing

In the aftermath of the council, i.e., during the period when ecclesiastical studies were being reformed, fundamental theology found itself threatened by two equally deadly dangers. On the one side, the danger was that its traditional themes would be broken up and scattered; on the other the danger was that it would undergo an excessive enlargement that would turn it into a kind of "sacral pantology" with a consequent loss of its specific character.

Neither in the decree *Optatam Totius* of Vatican II nor in the later *Normae Quaedam* was any mention made of fundamental theology. Historians can only record this complete lack of judgment at a time when the most critical problems of theology were concentrated in the area of fundamental theology. Lacking the support of the council, seminaries and faculties yielded to the temptation of sacrificing a discipline which the council itself did not seem to recognize. In many places, fundamental theology was dismembered and reduced to fragments that were inserted as best they could into other disciplines: the historicity of the Gospels into exegesis; revelation, tradition, and inspiration into the introduction to theology. The theme of the signs of credibility was simply avoided or else parts of it were dealt with when exegesis required (e.g., the miracles of Jesus). Elsewhere, fundamental theology no longer existed at all. When fundamental theology was thus fragmented and its problems were passed on to other disciplines like the remnants of a mortgaged inheritance, it was deprived of its specific task; in addition, the result was that theology failed in part of its mission (to confirm the brothers and sisters in their faith) and contributed to the shipwreck of thousands of the faithful, who found themselves defenseless in the face of disturbing questions that were too difficult for them to tackle without the help of experts.

On the other hand, the postconciliar period was also characterized by an ever-increasing enlargement of the scope of fundamental theology. But this expansion, which was made necessary by the renewal in biblical and historical studies, by the new ecumenical openness, and by the development of the human sciences, proved deadly. Fundamental theology developed a spirit of annexation that risked turning it into an encyclopedia of the sciences. Because it wanted to include and embrace everything, fundamental theology was coming to lose its center of unity and its specific character. As a result of working on the periphery it was reaching the point of forgetting the heart of its concerns, namely, revelation and its credibility.

In the face of these two threats, fundamental theologians everywhere felt a need to *focus*, to *establish the identity* of the discipline and to *hierarchize* the themes that are its subject matter. In any case, it is characteristic of recent articles on the problems of fundamental theology that they speak increasingly of a "search for identity," of a "center of unity," a "focal point," a "structure" or "basic structure." Also characteristic of this felt need of unity and structure is the fact that the articles to which I am referring sometimes offer outlines for a renewed treatise on revelation or a fundamental theology. The present article is the logical place to defend the view that fundamental theology is a distinct and structured discipline.

5. A Distinct and Specific Theological Discipline

Fundamental theology is a distinct discipline not only because it is the first to be mentioned in the Constitution *Sapientia Christiana* (29 April 1979)—as it had been in *Deus Scientiarum Dominus*—among the principal and required disciplines, but also because it has its own subject matter, its own method, and its own structure.

a. It is, therefore, not a form of theodicy nor a simple introduction to theology nor a mere function of theology. As a *specific* discipline, it has its own proper material and formal object, namely, the *self*-manifestation and *self*-giving of God in Jesus Christ, and the *intrinsic* credibility of this manifestation that he is by his presence in the world. The subject matter and center of unity of fundamental theology are the unprecedented intervention of God in history in the flesh and language of Jesus Christ: this is the fundamental mystery, the fundamental event, the fundamental reality that is the basis for all theological discourse. Dogmatic theology breaks this reality down into particular mysteries and studies these one by one; fundamental theology considers this mystery as a *whole* and as an inviolable *unity*. It is true, of course, that dogmatic theology also speaks of revelation and takes it as its starting point, but it does not make revelation the first and exclusive object of study, nor, in dealing with this reality, does it have the same perspective, the same method, and the same concerns that fundamental theology has.

If I combine *self*-manifestation and *intrinsic* credibility, it is in order to emphasize the point that the sign, given in Jesus Christ, is inseparable from the person. By becoming incarnate, God manifests himself as both revealer and revealed, and at the same time bears witness to himself as such. Jesus Christ is simultaneously mediator, fullness of revelation, and sign of revelation. *Dei Verbum* succinctly states that Christ completes and perfects revelation and attests that he is God among us (*DV* 4). Fundamental theology takes Christian revelation, understood as a *self*-manifestation that has an *intrinsic* credibility, as the essential object of its study. It does not separate Christ from the particular signs which identify him, for he is at once the sign of God and the radiating center of all the signs that proceed from his person. He is the epiphany of God and is identified as such by his entire presence and his entire self-manifestation. The sign and the signified, the believable and the believed are inseparable.

b. The specificity of the subject matter of fundamental theology necessarily entails a *specific method*, which I describe as *dynamic integration*. I do so, not arbitrarily nor out of a desire to be conspicuous, but simply because the reality being studied demands this approach.

The word *integration* suggests a concern to establish and maintain the unity of elements or aspects that are distinct but are and must be organically combined, under penalty of destroying the coherence and very existence of the reality which calls for the identification of the elements that are its integral parts.

Revelation, however, is inseparably both mystery and irruption of this mystery into human history, with all the characteristics belonging to historical existence. It follows directly that the methodical discussion of this mystery-event must be adjusted so as to respect its *uniqueness*.

Since revelation is the primordial mystery that conveys all the others, fundamental theology must take a dogmatic approach to this mystery, just as is done with the particular mysteries. It proceeds, therefore, from faith to understanding of the faith, in reliance of Scripture as an inspired source and on the church as a divine institution. On the other hand, since revelation is also God's irruption into history in Jesus Christ at a particular point in time and place, fundamental theology subjects this revelation-event to the questions and methods of the human sciences, especially literary and historical criticism. At this point, it is looking at the texts of Scripture as historical documents, the value of which must be established in accordance with the criteria of historical science. In like manner, the arguments it derives from philosophy must appeal for critical acceptance on the basis of their intrinsic value and not of the authority of the church.

This integration of methods is an aspect of the kenosis of the Incarnate Word. It is as impossible to reject the integration of the two methods as it is to separate revelation as mystery from revelation as event, the church as mystery from the church as institution, the resurrection as mystery from the resurrection as event. For a long time, apologetics reduced revelation to a historical event, while leaving the mystery aspect to the care of dogmatic theology. But one may not thus separate what is inseparable in reality. H. de Lubac and H. Urs von Balthasar commented long ago that only barren prejudgments and a truncated image of reality could have refused to integrate the methods of dogmatic theology and apologetics (in the old sense of this word). The dogmatic treatment normally precedes the apologetic treatment, not in order to disparage the latter method to the profit of the former, but quite simply because revelation is first of all a mystery and because it is important to give a correct description of the reality to which, as historically manifested in Jesus, theology then directs a critical eye. The method of *integration* is the only one that does justice to a reality which is at once mystery and historical event and therefore requires two different approaches, each of which serves the other. Method is at the service of reality: if the method must be adapted, it is because the reality requires it. But, like every form of theology, fundamental theology is always faith in search of understanding of a reality which, in this case, is both mystery and event.

Not without reason have I used the term *dynamic* integration, since the two elements in the pair revelation-as-mystery and revelation-as-event dynamize or energize each other. The fullness of the mystery that in the person of Jesus enters history and brings it to a high point never to be reached again causes historians to ask questions. They look at the message, works, and behavior of the man Jesus and attempt to penetrate to the deeper *meaning* of this life. At the term of their inquiry, in which they use the methods of their discipline, they find a *meaningful existence*, but one in which the "meaningfulness" is utterly unique, so much so that it launches the historians upon a movement back to the mystery, where they may satisfy their curiosity and come to know "ever more" about the real identity of this human being and his purpose in life. At the end of this second study, historians are increasingly fascinated by the mystery and direct new questions to it. The result is a constant back and forth, at ever deeper levels, between the mystery set forth and its historical emergence. But it is always the *whole reality* of revelation that feeds this dynamism. Consequently, I say that this kind of *dynamic integration* specifies fundamental theology in the area of *method*.

6. A Structured Discipline

A study of the various treatises on fundamental theology yields an impression of chaos rather than of structured unity. The following are the results of observations based on some thirty such works.

Everywhere we see a *solid core*, namely, the study of God's revelation in Jesus Christ and of its credibility by means of signs. But once this universally accepted sequence of subjects is posited, the divergences begin. German thinkers remain faithful to the tripartite division found in classical apologetics (proof of religion, proof of Christianity, proof of Catholicism). (See, e.g., *HFT; MystSal;* Kolping; Fries; Waldenfels.) The Latin approach, evidently influenced by Vatican II, is biblical, christocentric, concerned with the history of salvation, sensitive to questions of hermeneutics and meaning. The Anglo-Saxon approach reflects German influence, but with an emphasis on experience and on language (sign, symbol).

As the Gospels have their wandering or nomadic sayings (e.g., "The last shall be first, and the first shall be last") that are put into varying contexts, so too works of fundamental theology have their "wandering" or nomadic themes. Thus some works speak of religion and the religions at the beginning (Waldenfels; *HFT*), while others hold back this theme until the end. The themes of theology and fundamental theology may be discussed by way of introduction or by way of conclusion. Ecumenism is looked on in some works as a dimension found throughout fundamental theology, while in others it is the subject of a special chapter. The theme of faith may be connected with that of theology or with that of revelation. The church usually comes at the end but is treated with varying fullness, sometimes so fully as to include (in the *HFT*) the entire question of the knowledge of faith as well as the forms this knowledge takes (Scripture, tradition, magisterium, theology).

Amid this *mare magnum* there is lacking, in my opinion, a principle of discernment that makes it possible to situate the problems and put them in some hierarchical order so as to arrive at a reasoned structure. Vatican II can provide a model in this respect. The council does not begin with declarations or decrees on religion and the religions, on ecumenism, or on culture and the sciences. The source-document, which provides the hermeneutical key to all the others, is *Dei Verbum*, and in this source-document the "first close-up" has for its focus the revelation of God in Jesus Christ, the Incarnate Word, and the mediator, fullness, and sign of the revelation that he is in his very person. The first chapter of the document describes this reality and its specific traits: sacramental structure (*gesta et verba*); development, economy, pedagogy; incarnational principle; light of God shed on the mystery of the human person; tension between past and present and between present and eschatology. The primal reality that explains all the others is the revelation of God in its specific character as a self-manifestation that carries its own credibility with it. Other questions are seen as *implications* of this very *specific* revelation.

If we follow this principle of discernment, the *nomadic* themes find a way of locating themselves, and the structure of fundamental theology takes shape and emerges more clearly.

The basic sequence is: revelation conceived as the *self*-manifestation and *self*-giving of God in Jesus Christ, the Incarnate Word and the mediator, fullness, and sign of revelation, a revelation that has an *intrinsic* credibility. The implications of this basic principle can be hier-archically organized as follows:

a. This specific revelation begets a faith and a knowledge (theology) that are no less specific.

b. Being an event as well as a mystery, revelation is connected with history. Therefore questions arise on the historical origins of Christianity, the historical existence and iden-tity of Jesus, the values of the Gospels as an access to Jesus, the reality present in his message and his works, and his intention of founding a church.

c. The incarnational principle of Christian revelation compels fundamental theology to study currents of thought that exclude the incarnation: the Age of Enlightenment; Bult-mann's existential theology.

d. The continuity between the ecclesial plan of Jesus and the present plurality of Christian communities gives rise to the problem of ECUMENISM.

e. The claims of Judaism, Islam, and Hin-duism to be likewise "revealed" religions raises the problem of the relation between the specific character of Christian revelation and the other RELIGIONS.

f. Connected as it is with a culture, a language, and a people, Christian revelation faces unavoidable problems of HERMENEUTICS and INCULTURATION.

Fundamental theology is thus structured by (1) *a basic principle,* namely, Christian revelation with its specific traits; (2) *the series of "impli-cations" deriving from the basic principle:* (a) a specific kind of knowledge; (b) relationship to history; (c) relationship to nonincarnational philosophies; (d) relationship to other Christian communities; (e) relationship to religions which also claim to be "revealed"; (f) relation-ship to language and culture.

7. Pedagogical Organization

If we follow what I have just been saying about present-day fundamental theology and the dimensions of it that I have described, each theological center ought to have a teaching staff that is familiar with the most recent dis-coveries of exegesis and history and completely au courant with modern philosophies, ecu-menical problems, other religions, and the linguistic sciences. These phenomenal pro-fessors ought then to have students who are no less exceptional.

Let me distinguish immediately between fun-damental theology as an ecclesial function and a distinct area of theological science and, on the other hand, the pedagogical problem of fitting it into a faculty or seminary. As a specialized science whose full range I have described, fundamental theology is a matter for the entire church; it is something to be accomplished collegially.

This having been said, there are questions that require treatment at the very outset of the theological curriculum; these are the questions that deal with the hard core of fundamental theology, namely, revelation and its credibility, as well as some of its implications, such as theology as a science and the connections of revelation with history. Other questions having to do with the various philosophies, the various religions, hermeneutics, and inculturation can be reserved for the second and third cycles, or else treated in an abridged form in the first cycle and then taken up again more fully in monographic form in the later cycles. The old curriculum, governed as it was by *Deus Scien-tiarum Dominus,* which jammed theological studies into four years, made it difficult to handle such a vast material and made it simply impossible to arrange the problems in a hier-archical sequence. What used to be impossible can be accomplished today due to the new Con-stitution *Sapientia Christiana.* Now that fundamental theology has been renewed, more clearly identified, better unified, and better structured, there is room for the free expansion of a discipline that, more than others, needs air, space, and creative freedom. The important thing is that it be fully conscious of its identity as a distinct discipline, and of its subject matter, method, and structure.

Bibl.: H. BOUILLARD, "Human Experience as the Start-ing Point of Fundamental Theology," *Conc* 6 (1965): 79–92; R. LATOURELLE, "Apologétique et Fondamen-tale," *Sal* 27 (1965): 255–74; A. LOCATELLI, "L'insegna-mento della teologia fondamentale nel rinnovamento degli studi ecclesiastici," *ScCatt* 96 (1967): 95–123; A. KOLPING, *Fundamentaltheologie,* 3 vols. (Freiburg, 1968, 1974, 1981); R. LATOURELLE, *Theology: Science of Salvation* (Staten Island, N.Y., 1969), 101–6; F.

ARDUSSO, "Teologia fondamentale," *DTI* 1:182–202; R. LATOURELLE, "Dismemberment or Renewal of Fundamental Theology," *Conc* 46 (1969): 29–42; J. ALFARO, H. BOUILLARD, H. CARRIER, G. DEJAIFVE, R. LATOURELLE, and G. MARTELET, "La théologie fondamentale à la recherche de son identité," *Greg* 50 (1969): 756–76; H. FRIES, "From Apologetics to Fundamental Theology," *Conc* 46 (1969): 57–68; J. SCHMITZ, "Fundamentaltheologie im 20 Jahrhundert," in H. Vorgrimler and R. V. Gucht, eds., *Bilan de la théologie du XXe siècle* (Tournai/Paris, 1970), 233–72; H. BOUILLARD, "La tâche actuelle de la théologie fondamentale," *Le Point théologique* 2 (1972): 7–43; W. JOEST, "Fundamentaltheologie," in *Theologisches Grundlagen und Methoden-Problem* (Stuttgart, 1974); H. BOUILLARD, "De l'apologétique à la Fondamentale," in *Les quatre fleuves* (Paris, 1974), 57–70; R. LATOURELLE, *Finding Jesus through the Gospels* (New York, 1979); J.-P. TORRELL, "Questions de théologie fondamentale," *RThom* 79 (1979): 273–86; S. PIÉ-NINOT, "La teología fondamental hoy," *RCT* (1980): 479–502; C. COLOMBO, "Dall'apologetica alla teologia fondamentale," *Teol* 3 (1981): 232–42; G. O'COLLINS, *Fundamental Theology* (London, 1981); R. LATOURELLE, "L'istanza storica in teologia fondamentale," in var., *Instanze della Teologia fondamentale* (Bologna, 1982), 55–94; id., "A New Image of Fundamental Theology," in R. Latourelle and G. O'Collins, eds., *Problems and Perspectives of Fundamental Theology* (New York, 1982), 37–58; D. TRACY, "Necessity and Insufficiency of Fundamental Theology" in R. Latourelle and G. O'Collins, eds., *Problems and Perspectives of Fundamental Theology* (New York, 1982), 47–66; R. LATOURELLE, "Das II Vaticanum: Eine Herausforderung an die Fundamentaltheologie," in E. Klinger and K. Wittstadt, eds., *Glaube im Prozess: Christsein nach den II Vaticanum: Für Karl Rahner* (Freiburg, 1984), 597–614; W. WALDENFELS, *Manuel de théologie fondamentale* (Paris, 1985), 94–105; R. LATOURELLE, "Absence and Presence of Fundamental Theology at Vatican II," in R. Latourelle, ed., *Vatican II: Assessment and Perspectives Twenty-five Years After* (New York, 1989), 3:378–415; M. SECKLER, *HFT* 4: 450–514; R. FISICHELLA, "Il contributo di René Latourelle alla teologia fondamentale," in R. Fisichella, ed., *Gesù Rivelatore* (Casale Monferrato, 1988), 11–22; G. O'COLLINS, "Problemi e Prospettive di Teologia fondamentale," in *Gesù Rivelatore*, 46–59; M. CHAPPIN, "Dalla difesa al Dialogo: L'insegnamento della teologia fondamentale alla PUG, 1930–1988," in *Gesù Rivelatore*, 33–45; S. PIÉ-NINOT, *Tratado di Teologia fundamental* (Salamanca, 1989), 17–54; R. FISICHELLA, *La Révélation et sa crédibilité* (Montreal/Paris, 1989), 25–51; R. LATOURELLE, "Spécificité de la théologie fondamentale," in J.-P. Jossua and N.-J. Sed, eds., *Interpréter: Hommage amical à Claude Geffré* (Paris, 1992), 104–22.

René LATOURELLE

II. WHOM IS IT FOR?

If theology were not addressed to someone, it would be no more than the theologian's theoretical solipsistic speculation and there would be no point to it. Who the addressee is to be cannot be a matter of pure choice; it is to some extent conditioned by the very rise of theological activity and by the differing social and cultural conditions in which this activity takes place.

Fundamental theology too is addressed to someone. As a theological discipline based on the "Why" (Dt 6:20) of faith, its role is always and responsibly to give an answer to the event of faith in revelation. This above all in harmony with 1 Pt 3:15, where the apostle invites us never to give up responding to the stimuli that occur, and above all always to be ready to furnish our reasons to other people who question us about the hope that is in us (→ APOLOGIA).

One is sometimes tempted to fix the identity of the addressee on the basis of sociocultural analysis, due to which the discipline came into existence. This sort of investigation is certainly basic; but fundamental theology cannot disregard — not even for an instant — the fact that it is primarily a theological discipline and that, this being so, the first analysis to be undertaken is already within the knowledge of faith.

In this connection we discover that although revelation is addressed to everyone, faith on the other hand creates a kind of distinction. For within faith, the theologian discovers there are those who believe, and those who do not yet believe but need to be given reasons for believing.

Paul's experience as he wanders the streets of Athens and his speech to the Areopagus (Acts 17:16–23) are normal conditions for fundamental theology today. We too as believers walking the city streets run across the altar dedicated to "the Unknown God." There are real people, capable of believing thought, and faith has a duty to approach them and reveal to them that their lives are as yet incomplete all the while they have not encountered Christ,

Within the reasons of faith therefore and our responsibility for it, we are called to approach "others" so as to give a definitive answer to their question about MEANING.

Thus regaining the very context of revelation, which invites everyone to believe and to adhere to Christ, we can in general terms already identify the addressees of fundamental theology: our own contemporaries.

Such a statement needs some clarifying distinctions.

In the history of fundamental theology it is easy to pick out different addressees determined by theological writers at various periods. Thus, it is well known that the earliest APOLOGISTS addressed their words to the pagans, to convince them of the goodness of faith in Jesus of Nazareth and of the truth of the sacred texts.

Thomas Aquinas was to write the *Contra Gentiles* with the Muslims largely in mind; for them he was to express the reasons of the faith or "the truths of Catholic doctrine," as the subtitle of the work makes clear: *Contra Gentiles seu de veritate catholicae fidei.*

In the age of humanism, Raymond of Sabunde (d. 1436) was to turn for preference to believers who had become a little skeptical; he was to work in the dimension of a humanity in which all are brothers and sisters ("Ista scientia docet omnem hominem cognoscere realitates, infallibiliter, sine difficultate et labore" ["This science teaches everyone how to know things infallibly, without difficulty and toil"]), with the aim of showing that the truth of revelation is necessary for human beings as such, so that they can know themselves as well as the mystery of God: "omnem veritatem necessariam homini cognoscere tam de homine, quam de Deo, et omnia quae sunt necessaria homini ad salutem et ad suam perfectionem, et ut perveniat ad vitam aeternam" ["All the truths man must know about man and about God, and all the things that are necessary for his salvation, and to obtain eternal life"] (*Theologia naturalis seu Liber creaturarum*, 27–30): theology seems to be much the same as anthropology.

Pierre Charron (1541–1601), as first inspirer of the threefold *demonstratio* later to take its final form in Hooker's *Ecclesiastical Polity*, was to write the volume *Les trois verités contre les athées, idolâtres, juifs, mahométans, hérétiques et schismatiques*; a collection of enemies to mask the real addressee of his book: Protestants in general and here more particularly the foe Duplessy-Mornay.

Deists, men of the Enlightenment, and rationalists in general were to be the addressees of fundamental theologies from the seventeenth to the nineteenth centuries. Pierre

Daniel Huet was to write a *Demonstratio evangelica*; Vitus Pichler, who was the first to introduce the expression "fundamental theology," was to write a *Theologia polemica* and René de Chateaubriand produced *Le Génie du Christianisme*.

The main theme of this period is the defense of supernatural religion against rationalism and every form of reductionism, and hence the defense of the value of Scripture as sacred and inspired against every form of historicism or positivism.

Lastly, the "atheist" will be the addressee of the treatises produced in the nineteenth century, before we come to MANUALIST THEOLOGY, which, having demolished the need for speculation on first principles, has "metaphysical man," divorced from any social context and hence lacking any specific point of view, as the partner in its discourse.

As may be seen from this quick survey of half a dozen authors and books selected from among the most significant, three characteristics seem to emerge as relevant to our theme:

(a) The first thing to strike us is the constant preoccupation with "enemies." Responsibility for the faith, which had motivated 1 Pt 3:15 and the early apologists, gradually degenerates into various kinds of polemics until finally it does not *present* the riches of the faith to anyone at all and only addresses enemies and heretics against whom Catholic doctrine has to be *defended.*

(b) A second characteristic is the preponderant activity of "pointing out errors." Whereas in the early centuries the effort was all to find common ground between believers and nonbelievers as a solid basis for discussion, instead we now encounter a forceful claim to exclusive possession of the truth, by virtue of which apologetics becomes a *critique* and judgment on any other way of understanding revelation.

Indeed there were objective errors and heretical forms, but *methodologically speaking* a different situation had been created; there was no further searching for a common ground, no more attempted maieutics. What counted was defending one's own truth in polemical opposition to anyone who might have different notions.

(c) A final element observable, which seems

paradoxical enough, is the gradual disappearance of the addressee altogether. For a living addressee is substituted merely the study of doctrine or, at best, the principles that regulate the demonstrational process. The addressee becomes the mere instrumental cause from which to set out, but the central and basic objective is the pointing out of errors to be found in someone else's teaching. No longer therefore a physical partner with his own historical, political, cultural, and religious coordinates, but doctrine, theses, or ideologies.

PASCAL, in the project that can be inferred from his *Pensées*, had strongly insisted on the primacy of the physical subject; so too NEWMAN in his *Grammar of Assent*; but it was essentially to be BLONDEL who, with *L'Action*, was to effect a synthesis between the two requirements by producing a metaphysics, yes, but with direct reference to the historicity of the subject.

Today's fundamental theology cannot ignore past history nor insulate itself from the changes taking place today. With the former, it is compromised *volens nolens*; the latter it has to tackle by virtue of *responsibility* for the faith, which is its raison d'être.

In considering the people whom we should be addressing, two groups of factors spring to mind, some positive, others more problematic.

1. Positive Elements

A first positive factor to be considered is certainly that of a renewed ecumenical sense, allowing a more open approach to our fellow Christians. Looking for "enemies" therefore would not only be anachronistic but deeply wrong-headed for a discipline that has rediscovered the basic reasons for its existence in the faith.

The historical consciousness (HISTORY I) characterizing our century makes us give serious consideration to the historicity of our theological approach and the typical conditions in which addressee and theologian are likely to meet. This recovered sense of history too is a positive element, allowing fundamental theology—assumptions about "metaphysical man" now having been overcome—to encounter people today deeply rooted in their own history and culture and fiercely proud of being so rooted.

This allows us to recover an initial common base. First of all, it is easier to present the person of Jesus of Nazareth as someone deeply a part of the history of his people, believed to be the fulfillment of salvation history and right up to today proclaimed as hermeneutical principle for an overall understanding of universal history. Furthermore, a heroic role in the transformation of this history is offered to the addressee: a life lived, in authentic liberating witness, mindful of the constant presence of evil and sin that have to be overcome, and of the seeds of salvation and hope that have already been sown and are now ripening.

In this context, particular importance is assumed by the theme of proclaiming the gospel in differing cultures and a kind of contextuality of theology (THEOLOGIES VII), giving evidence of the richness derived from integration and of the yield of the various cultural models.

2. Problems

So much for the positive factors; other facts and considerations arise that cause not a few problems for fundamental theology.

A first point to note is, now that there is no unity of philosophic reference, the selection of today's addressee is affected by differing philosophical and ideological coordinates. A pluralism of this sort creates in its turn a pluriformity of terms and ways of saying things that do not make it very clear who the partner in the dialogue may be.

With this kind of problem the temptation may arise to take the easiest path of a renewed neoabstractism in singling out the person to be addressed, with more unfortunate results than those of the manual period.

We must therefore be quite clear in our minds that an apologetical presentation of the Christian event having a single addressee in view will never be possible again. Also, the prospect of the "other" as hypothetical partner would be too simple an exemplification, and must be avoided. The forms of ATHEISM seem so varied today (from the methodological to the philosophical, psychological, or linguistic and pragmatic) that they cannot be reduced to a single factor.

On the other hand, a big problem is created by the permanence up till now of a deep crisis affecting rationalism. An unjustified importance is given to emotionalism and to a one-sided interpretation of "pastorality," inasmuch as there is no longer any vision of the constituent value of a critical consciousness for the content of the faith. It seems that "togetherness" or "praying together" is now the recipe for solving every problem. But for the theologian, whose obligation it is to maintain responsibility for _understanding_ the faith, these attitudes create more anxieties and problems than the difficulties they might solve.

A true union and a serene conversion, for these to be fully human and genuinely Christian, occur by way of the intellect: _fides si non intelligitur nulla est._ The wish to fulfill oneself in "praxis" and the insistence that this be the _locus theologicus_ on which to judge the truth of the faith is no less one-sided than a faith that might try to adjudge itself orthodox solely from its intellectual content.

The unity of personal activity, the typical means given to the church for it to remain in the truth and the reasons that theology supplies in the historicity of its reflection are all expressions to be considered on their respective merits, as regards the value they assume in the quest for the fullness of truth; in no case can they be disregarded.

For whom then is fundamental theology intended today?

Certainly the _believer_, for he or she is always the first person to whom theological thought is directed; then the "other" from our faith, because the latter is especially envisaged by fundamental theology within theological science.

Things as they are today, however, though they may allow us to see two types of addressee by virtue of the faith, do not on any account allow us to see the believer as "someone different" from his or her contemporaries. Inevitably, the words of the _Epistle to Diognetus_ spring to mind: "Christians are not different from the rest of men in nationality, speech or customs; they do not live in states of their own, nor do they use a special language, nor adopt a peculiar way of life. . . . Whether fortune has given them a home in a Greek or foreign city, they follow local custom in the matter of dress, food and way of life; yet the character of the culture they reveal is marvellous and, it must be admitted, unusual" (chap. 5).

Today, as yesterday, the faith creates something specific, yet the reality of characteristics that are properly human remains unchanged for all.

Our contemporaries, at their most positive, strike one as people full of _hope_. Hope seems to be the characteristic best qualifying the end of our century. Having come through two world wars and seen massacre and what hatred can do, with the _Shoah_ as climactic expression of human folly, our contemporaries are still living under the threat of nuclear destruction. Yet they entertain a growing hope that the nations will be able to coexist without trying to dominate one another and that justice will at last be able to embrace peace (Is 9:5–6). Consequently, they carefully mark every step the Great Powers take with a view to banishing war throughout the world.

A basic hope, then, takes concrete form in different objectives: an expanding economy raises hopes of affluent living conditions; all the new discoveries in medicine encourage people to think they will live longer; technological progress—particularly in the field of communications—makes everyone aware of being a "citizen of the world"; the news broadcast simultaneously throughout both hemispheres increases the feeling of world solidarity.

But to this growing hope, there corresponds a strong sense of mistrust and malaise, particularly as regards political organs and institutions. Never as today has such indifference and skepticism greeted the declarations of politicians or the political programs of party leaders. These, growing ever remoter from the sense of and quest for the common good, have become equally remote from the common man and woman and their deeply held need for a better kind of life. Owing to the way the laws of an élitist economy operate, social inequalities grow greater, making the very few rich ever richer and the very many poor ever poorer.

Frustrated by economic trickery and nihilistic ideologies, the essential values of respect for others, for life in its totality and nature in its entirety, have collapsed, to be replaced by a sense of helplessness and loneliness. Never before today, perhaps, has the sense of personal frustration been so acute, caused and dramatized as it is by the fact that we are each fully aware of it but each feel unable and too alone to do anything about it.

If we then look to the area of religion, here too we may observe the great frustration of our contemporaries. A renewed "sense of the sacred" seems to be replacing Nietzsche's prophecy of the death of God from our world. But in many respects, this phantom recovery of the sacred does no more than confirm the death of God, our cities being littered with empty churches like graveyards of the Christian God.

On the Christian side, there is more and more talk about a "crisis of participation"; the great capital cities of the West, on Sunday, have empty churches to show; catechesis as the systematic approach to a study of the faith is only followed by a tiny percentage; when the moral norm is referred to, we seem to be assisting at an undisclosed schism in which believers, appealing exclusively to their own conscience, apparently no longer accept the teaching of the magisterium. And while the young show a strong religious impulse, this is not exempt from intellectual crisis, since often they are exploited by charismatic personalities whose appeal is to the emotions rather than to the brain.

On the non-Christian side, we seem to be witnessing a neopaganism. Perverse rites are on the increase, RELIGIOUS SECTS proliferate at great speed; anyone can see for themselves how many people resort to crystal gazing and fortune-telling in order to feel secure and happy; new seers weave their spells, pulling the wool over their clients' eyes by means of the cards or the indestructible crystal ball, while the daily papers are often only read for their horoscopes.

All this is the sign of a void, of a depth that has not been filled by values that can truly satisfy since they involve personal responsibility. In a word, in the religious sphere, *indifference* seems to be supreme.

Another thing about our contemporaries is that they are always in more and more of a hurry and have no time to listen or reflect; they love slogans that produce an instant effect, without making any attempt to analyze their content; they cannot read anymore, because they are permanently crouched over the television set; they are no longer able to contemplate the beautiful, for they are confined in the chaos of the metropolis, which is destroying, by various forms of pollution, whatever past genius and faith have bequeathed as their legacy; they are constantly subjected to the clandestine attraction of crime and violence; lastly, when dramatically confronted with the problem of DEATH, they repudiate it, either by refusing to think about it or by deceiving themselves with new sophisms. But will these contemporaries of ours still be able to hear the prophetic voices of those who proclaim God?

Yes, certainly, since—all that sounds negative in the foregoing portrait notwithstanding—these contemporaries of ours are still able to take a serious attitude to the MEANING of life and are capable of grasping the significance of LOVE.

In every part of the world you will find people capable of the loving gesture. Examples would take us too far and would not convey the depth of the experienced reality. In each of these signs, however, it is possible to recognize and understand a language of love. Not a pure feeling, however; rather as a qualifying dimension of the person, allowing the performance of actions which are, humanly speaking, significant, since free and directed to an end.

Before it, fundamental theology has a listener, whether believer or not, who has a strong need for meaning (→ CREDIBILITY). The need is all the more urgent today because people are more aware of it and because everything around them seems to be dragging them away toward the absurd.

To them, in a new idiom, we have to bring the trinitarian love of God that reaches its highest point in the Easter mystery of Jesus of Nazareth.

To this revealed love—true love since fully free and able to reach total self-giving—our contemporaries cannot be insensible. They realize the message is for them, they *know* they will have to take the risk of believing and following, since this is the last opportunity open to them for truly grasping the mystery of their own existence and for feeling truly free.

Bibl.: G. RUGGIERI, *La compagnia della fede* (Turin, 1980); id., ed., *Enciclopedia di Teologia Fondamentale,* vol. 1 (Genoa, 1987); R. LATOURELLE, *Man and His Problems in the Light of Jesus Christ* (New York, 1983); F. J. NIEMANN, *Jesus als Glaubensgrund in der Fundamentaltheologie der Neuzeit: Zur Genealogie eines Traktats,* Innsbrucker Theologische Studien 12 (Innsbruck, 1983); G. HEINZ, *Divinam christianae religionis originem probare* (Mainz, 1984); G. FERRAROTTI, *Una teologia per laici* (Bari, 1984); M. SECKLER, "Fundamentaltheologie: Aufgaben und Aufbau, Begriff und Namen," *HFT* 4:451–513.

Rino FISICHELLA

G

GARDEIL, AMBROISE (1859-1931)

Entering the Dominican order in 1878, Gardeil received a solid formation in neoscholastic philosophy and theology, which introduced him to St. Thomas Aquinas, his lifelong master. Starting in 1883 with the tract *De locis theologicis*, he went on to teach apologetics and various courses in dogmatic and moral theology. Before abandoning the classroom after 1911 for writing, preaching, and spiritual direction, he had exercised a great, personal influence on his students and helped form the program of studies for Le Saulchoir. Although he did not write a detailed apologetics, Gardeil's understanding of theological method, particularly the relation between faith and reason, established the parameters for that science.

Fundamental to Gardeil's early understanding of theology was his philosophical "conceptual realism." Following Cajetan and John of St. Thomas, he held that the human intellect attained the real in and through the universal concept. Being, ultimately conceptualizable, provided the bedrock for all objective thought. Since the concept was received in the passive intellect whereby the mind was assimilated to reality and truth resulted, the distinction of spiritual faculties, intellect and will, in terms of their formal objects, the true and the good, allowed him to understand the will as the active faculty, responding to the perceived good and carrying human beings to external reality. However much voluntary efforts might subjectively facilitate intellection by removing impediments and focusing attention, the will did not directly influence the intellect, which grasped the objective real. This grasp of the real permitted a natural knowledge of God, the moral law, and the soul's immortality. Humanity's struggle to lead the moral life in the face of sin prompted it to look about in history for a salvation that transcended its natural powers. There the Christian message met it and demanded belief.

The utter primacy and objectivity of intellection meant that the truths of revelation were proposed in conceptual statements. As supernatural, purely gratuitous from God's point of view, revealed propositions exceeded every effort of the natural intellect to intuit their truth by its own light. How then might one accept the faith necessary for salvation? Analyzing the psychological process concluding in the act of faith, Gardeil replied that the will is moved ultimately by human being's final end, the infinite good of God, and should choose the means appropriate for attaining that end. The gospel's promise of redemption certainly attracts the will, but how might humanity, without offending against its moral obligation to truth, affirm the propositions of faith whose interior truth its natural intellect cannot perceive?

At this juncture Gardeil appealed to veridical testimony as a way of providing truths extrinsically in history. If God chose to reveal supernatural truths to humanity, it stood under a moral obligation to believe whatever its Creator said. But humanity needed evidence, or motives of credibility, to ascertain the fact of revelation. The task of apologetics, therefore, consisted in a rational presentation of arguments so as to justify prudentially the absolute intellectual assent of faith. By examining the external, historical signs given by God, especially miracles and fulfilled prophecies, to confirm his legates' testimony, as well as the veracity and competence of the witnesses to them, apologetics might prove their trustworthiness. Since Jesus entrusted his message to disciples, apologetics also identified them with the concrete church, one, holy, catholic, and apostolic, which had remained faithful to Christ's message and mission through the centuries.

Apologetics led to an absolutely sure judgment of credibility, a "scientific faith," about the fact of revelation. Even if not everyone need come to such certitude—faith as a divine gift could employ a merely probable argument to attain its certitude—the church required at the basis of her faith eyewitnesses, who then instructed others. The apostles and others had seen Christ's miracles and heard his words. Once the fact of revelation was established, one duty to obey the revealing God resulted in a judgment of credentity, absolute in the order of natural morality, but conditional since subordinated to the possibility of an act of divine faith. For that grace was needed. Under grace an absolutely obligatory, or necessitating, supernatural judgment of credentity moved one to adhere to revealed truths, whose very obscurity left room for freedom's response. Thence resulted the election, accomplished first by the will when the truths of faith were seen as good to believe; then the will enjoined the command "believe" upon the speculative intellect and applied it to its normal act, the judgment of adhesion to the terms asserted, thus culminating the act of faith. Thereafter the habit of faith and the gifts of the Holy Spirit might develop and cause a more profound understanding of revealed truths from within.

That understanding of reason and faith based faith squarely upon the authority of veridical witnesses, Christ and the church. Speculative theology had to accept its basic principles on authority before it could organize and illuminate those dogmas by relating them to their last end and finding appropriate analogies among revealed and natural truths. So positive theology had first to search and weigh the sources, Scripture and tradition, to discover what the church believed. Such was the continuity, under the guidance of the Spirit, between Christ and the present, infallible church that a "regressive method" might be employed. Starting from the present teaching of the magisterium, theologians should examine the previous tradition to find support for the church's current beliefs. This method applied not only to positive theology but also to apologetics insofar as the continuity of present teachings with Christ's was presupposed and proved on that supposition.

The development of dogma posed a great problem to Gardeil's position. For insofar as revelation was given in words that express concepts and concepts abstract from conditions of time and space to grasp eternally valid laws of reality and historical judgments regard matters of fact that cannot be otherwise, revealed truths were not subject to revision. At most there was a movement from implicit to explicit, as various ecclesial creeds further explicated conceptually what their predecessors affirmed. Expressions and images may change, but what is signified, the underlying form, or concept, remains invariable. The lack of explicit, historical testimony to various dogmas later defined

was explained on the presumption that extant documents represent but partial traces of the church's full oral tradition.

Alongside the strict conceptualist approach to apologetics and theology, other elements left room for development and flexibility. Already in the first edition of *La crédibilité et l'apologétique* (1908) Gardeil admitted that in exceptional cases without exterior signs God could attract people to faith—an objective process insofar as the First Truth interiorly instructs human beings—and devoted many pages to the subjective substitutes (*suppléances*) of credibility. Yet he did not consider an immanent apologetics (Blondel et al.), however useful subjectively, capable of being reconciled with an objective, scientific apologetics. Four years later the second edition adopted a concrete, dynamic viewpoint to replace the previous abstract, "ontological" analysis of faith's act. Here Gardeil discovered in the initial act of moral, reflective consciousness the divine call to affirm and choose one's final end, which de facto was supernatural. This "intention of faith" placed grace's role at the beginning of faith's genesis, where it functioned implicitly until it developed into explicit faith upon encountering ecclesial preaching. Though maintaining the validity and necessity of abstract analysis and rational credibility, Gardeil emphasized the supernatural continuity of faith's process. Thus only one, supernatural judgment of credentity was required and the judgment of credibility was scarcely distinguishable by abstraction from the judgment of credentity.

The polarity between abstract and concrete analyses permitted Gardeil to affirm a rigorous rational credibility and scientific faith while acknowledging the relative certitude, or verisimilitude, attainable from historical signs, which served in the majority of cases as the rational basis of faith's absolute assent under grace. Apologetics accordingly was both considered a "rational closed circle" and subordinated to theology. Similarly, without abandoning the validity of concepts, the intention of faith involved a supernatural, non-conceptual knowledge and love of God previous to explicit faith and charity. The more unified relations between natural and supernatural orders as well as among intellect, will, and grace prepared for Gardeil's later studies of mysticism. After arguing that the soul had to possess a habitual, obscure knowledge of itself lest it remain incapable of identifying itself as the knowing subject in a subsequent act of reflection, he concluded that the self-conscious soul could recognize God's supernatural presence in its own depths through an immediate, experiential, connatural knowledge and love. This openness to nonconceptual knowledge and supernatural experience without abandoning conceptual analysis or objective apologetics marks the pivotal role played by Gardeil in the evolution of Cajetanian Thomism. Whereas his student Garrigou-Lagrange followed his earlier works with their strong conceptualism, other students like Chenu preferred to develop his later writings. In Gardeil one may find a figure of transition from the objectivist, concept-based apologetics to the modern, more subjectively oriented apologetics of explicitation. He actually tried to balance the imperative demands of objective truth with the needs of individual subjects and to defend the validity of concepts without absolutizing them. Such polar tensions stand at the heart of Thomism and a successful apologetic.

Bibl.: A. GARDEIL, *Les dons du Saint-Esprit dans les saints dominicains* (Paris, 1903); id., *La crédibilité et l'apologétique* (Paris, 1908); id., *Le donné révélé et la théologie* (Paris, 1910); id., *La structure de l'âme et l'expérience mystique* (Paris, 1927); id., "La réforme de la théologie catholique," *RThom* 11 (1903): 5–19, 197–215, 428–57, 633–49; id., *RThom* 12 (1904): 407–43; R. AUBERT, *Le problème de l'acte de foi* (Louvain, 1950), 393–450; H.-D. GARDEIL, *L'oeuvre théologique du père Ambroise Gardeil* (LeSaulchoir, 1956); id., "Ambroise Gardeil," in *DSp* 6 (1967): 122ff.; see also *Bulletin thomiste* 4 (1931): 69–92 (bibliography); *RSPT* 40 (1956): 629–69.

Alessandro DONI and John M. McDERMOTT

GAUDIUM ET SPES

The sensitivity shown by thinkers of our time (R. GUARDINI, F. M. Sciacca, M. BLONDEL, TEILHARD DE CHARDIN, K. RAHNER, G. Marcel, H. URS VON BALTHASAR, M. Légaut, M. Zundel, A. Solzhenitsyn) to the problems of the human person and its condition is as old as Christianity itself, for Christianity is essentially a religion concerned with the salvation of human beings in Jesus Christ. Never before, however, has this sensitivity found such clear and explicit expression as in church documents during the last two decades, and especially in Vatican II's *Gaudium et Spes*, "Pastoral Constitution on the Church in the Modern World" (7 December 1965).

Gaudium et Spes is a novel document. It is the longest document in the entire history of church councils. Second, it is the first document of the extraordinary magisterium to speak of the directly temporal aspects of Christian life. Never before has a council spoken so directly about human beings coming to grips with the problems of their earthly lives. Third, the document proceeds in a way that is likewise novel. Instead of taking the data of faith as its starting point, it takes as its basis a description of the human person in the modern world. Thus it proceeds first empirically and then theologically. In the five successive drafts that mark the stages of the document's history, the only element of real continuity was this concern to remain in contact with the world, to speak to its problems, and to offer it the services of the church and, more concretely, the light of the gospel. Finally, the world addressed by the Constitution is the whole person: individual and society, matter and spirit, located in an indeterminate duration. The human person is both individual and social being, but the person addressed here is the "modern" person in "today's" world, the person searching for the MEANING of the human condition. The perspective is identical with that of fundamental theology in its renewed form.

The Constitution begins with a description of the present state of the human collectivity (secs. 4–10). The plain fact is that humanity has taken giant steps toward real progress, and in the process its picture of the world has been turned upside down (sec. 3). The first to experience the repercussions of this accelerated change are human beings themselves. The Constitution lists, in the form of antitheses, the principal changes and their negative side (sec. 4): (1) phenomenal growth in wealth and economic well-being, but at the same time hunger and extreme need on the part of a large part of the human race; (2) a keen sense of freedom, but at the same time the existence of many forms of social and psychic enslavement (including domination, oppression, and tyranny of public opinion); (3) awareness of the interdependence of all or universal solidarity, but at the same time social, racial, and ideological rifts and the threat of total war; (4) the spread of ideas throughout the world by the media, but at the same time the same words (e.g., "freedom," "work," and "progress") hide different meanings depending on the ideologies that manipulate them; and (5) an elaborate organization in the temporal sphere, but a waning spiritual development.

What effect does such rapid and radical change have on human beings? They are torn between hope and anxiety. They have difficulty seeing through ambiguities and discerning permanent values. Why devote so much effort to things of this world? Of what good is technology? Why make progress? To what end the ascent of the mass of humanity toward culture if all the effort is not leading toward a state in which the human person and human values are saved? The development of the world is a challenge that must be met.

The church must first of all become aware of the extent of this development and of its impact on the human collectivity. It must be more human in order to be more Christian. The human person is the point at which human beings, politics, and religions meet. This is why *Gaudium et Spes* takes as its starting point the human condition today; this is the basic datum undergirding the document. If the church seeks to understand "the world in which we live, its expectations, its longings," it does so in order that, "in language intelligible to each generation, she can respond to the perennial questions which men ask about this present life and the life to come and about the relationship of the one to the other" (sec. 4).

The phenomenological description, then, is not an end in itself but is for the sake of better service of human beings. If the church studies the signs of the times, it does so because it is more concerned for human beings than they are for themselves and because it exists only for their salvation. The phenomenology is in the service of an anthropology, and the anthropology is inspired by a vision of humanity in Jesus Christ, a vision of the new human being.

The conclusion drawn from this analysis of the social, psychological, political, economic, moral, and religious changes that the human race has experienced and is experiencing is

stated at the end of section 9 and in section 10, which serve as a transition to the remainder of the document. "The imbalances under which the modern world labors are linked with that more basic imbalance rooted in the heart of man" (sec. 10). "In the face of the modern development of the world, an ever-increasing number of people are raising the most basic questions or recognizing them with a new sharpness: what is man? What is this sense of sorrow, of evil, of death, which continues to exist despite so much progress? What is the purpose of these victories, purchased at so high a cost? What can man offer to society, what can he expect from it? What follows this earthly life?" (sec. 10). "In the light of Christ, . . . the Council wishes to speak to all men in order to illuminate the mystery of man and to cooperate in finding the solution to the outstanding problems of our time" (sec. 10).

In the first chapter of its first part ("The Church and Man's Calling"), *Gaudium et Spes* sets out to prove that Christian revelation indeed sheds light on the mystery of the person. It starts with the basic question: "But what is man? . . . He ofter exalts himself as the absolute measure of all things or debses himself to the point of despair. The result is doubt and anxiety. The Church understands problems. Endowed with light from God, she can offer solutions to them so that man's true situation can be portrayed and his defects explained, while at the same time his dignity and destiny are justly acknowledged" (sec. 12). Thus does *Gaudium et Spes* express, in language that calls to mind the *Pensées* of PASCAL, the paradox of wretchedness and greatness that is at the very heart of the human person.

Next, sections 12–18 describe the main lines of Christian anthropology. The document says first that human beings were originally created in the image of God (sec. 12), but that they then sinned (sec. 13). It moves on to the basic structure of the human person, the structure that embodies the image of God, which is the foundation of human greatness. It discusses unity and interiority (sec. 14), intelligence (sec. 15), moral conscience (sec. 16), and freedom (sec. 17). Section 18 reflects on an especially tragic problem—the problem of death: "It is in the face of death that the riddle of human existence becomes most acute." Death is the dread that stands on the horizon of the modern consciousness. For reasons that are historical (e.g., death camps, unending war, atomic threat, death on the roads and in the air), cultural (death is a subject pervasive in the novel, the theater, television, and the press), and philosophical (note the definition of the human person as a being-destined-for-death), and also for one other reason found in every age—namely, the animal, human, and spiritual fear of death—human beings, compounded as they are of greatness and wretchedness, struggle with death as with an insoluble and intolerable riddle. "[Man] rightly follows the intuition of his heart when he abhors and repudiates the absolute ruin and total disappearance of his own person. Man rebels against death because he bears in himself an eternal seed which cannot be reduced to sheer matter" (sec. 18). Consequently, in the midst of a life leading to inevitable disintegration, human beings feel that they are destined simultaneously to die and not to die.

An answer to this abyss can come only from another abyss: that of the Christian mystery. God did not make human beings for death but for resurrection, which simultaneously affirms death and says that death is overcome. Death is a passage opening into an "everlasting communion" with God. Christ first passed through death in order to deliver us from it. A Christian death is an act in which a human life reaches full maturity and acquires its definitive meaning. Death is the possibility of a "communion in Christ" with all those who died with him and in him. At the point, therefore, at which human beings have no more answers, faith in him who is resurrection and life teaches us that they are transported beyond death to everlasting life (sec. 18).

After speaking of those who reject this close and lifegiving relationship of human beings with God (→ ATHEISM), *Gaudium et Spes* has a lengthy section (22) on Christ, the *new human being*, as the real answer to the mystery of the human person. The important words in this section are the ones with which it begins: "The truth is that only in the mystery of the incarnate Word does the mystery of man take on light." Christ is seen as the key to the human riddle, the one who unveils its meaning, because he is the new human being, the new Adam of the new creation and new state of the human race.

In the paragraphs that follow Christ is presented as: (1) the image in which the human person is created and re-created, the one who restores to humanity the likeness to God that has been distorted by sin; (2) "an innocent lamb" who "merited life for us by the free shedding of His own blood," so that each person can say: "[He] loved me and gave himself up for me"; (3) the salvation of Christians, persons interiorly renewed and made like Christ by the gift of the Spirit; and (4) the salvation of all human beings of good will who are thus made sharers in the paschal mystery (sec. 22).

This first chapter of Part 1 of *Gaudium et Spes* ends thus: "Such is the mystery of man, and it is a great one, as seen by believers in the light of Christian revelation. Through Christ and in Christ, the riddles of sorrow and DEATH grow meaningful. Apart from His gospel, they overwhelm us." Christ, the Son, has given us life "so that, as sons in the Son, we can cry out in the Spirit: Abba, Father" (sec. 22). In the final analysis, it is the mystery of Christ that reveals human beings to themselves. The truth about human beings is that they are children of God and called to enter into the trinitarian life. Revelation, far from being something alien to human beings, is so closely linked to the mystery that they are to themselves that without it they cannot penetrate to their own identity. It follows, too, that if revelation comes to human beings as a historical reality, they must ponder this history and, above all, must reflect on themselves in order to find out whether God is calling them.

René LATOURELLE

GNOSIS

In the religious syncretism of the Greco-Roman world the Greek term for knowledge, *gnosis* (see Aristotle *Anal. post.* 2.99b–100b) came to be used of esoteric revelation that brought salvation to those who received it (see Irenaeus *Adv. haer.* 1.6.2). Grounded in revelation and available only to the elect few who are awakened to the inner divine nature that separates them from the material and perceptible cosmos, gnosis claims a truth that is not found by human reason or in the exoteric religious traditions of humanity (cf. *Tri. Trac.*,

Corpus Gnosticum [Corp. Gnos.], 12 vols. [Cairo] I 5 108, 12-114, 30; Orig. World, Corp. Gnos., II 5 97, 24–98, 10). 1 Tm 6:20 refers to the doctrine of heretical teachers as a false gnosis. The word "gnosis" was also used by some writers to refer to Christian doctrine (see Irenaeus Adv. haer. 4.33.8).

The Epistle of Barnabas uses "gnosis" of insight into God's activity in salvation history through exegesis of the OT as well as for understanding of God's commandments (Barn. 1:5; 2:3; 6:9; 9:8; 13:7). Such understanding is a gift of the Spirit (1:2f.; 9:9). By perfecting the gnosis of his readers, the author supplements their faith and assists their progress toward salvation. While not all persons have gnosis, the insights of those who do are addressed to the whole Christian community. The more technical usage, which treats gnosis as wisdom for elite, mature, or specially enlightened Christians, emerges in the second century. The claim to possess gnosis, revealed by a heavenly redeemer through Jesus, characterized various sects of heretical Christians. Some appear to have called themselves "Gnostics." Others, referred to by the name of founding teachers like Valentinus, Basilides, Marcus, Simon, or by peculiar traits of their teaching, shared with the self-proclaimed "Gnostics" a mythological cosmology, traditions of exegesis, similar images of the heavenly redeemer and fallen humanity, as well as ascetic and ritual forms of rejecting the material world (cf. Irenaeus Adv. haer. 1.xi.1–5 xxv.6; Hippolytus Ref. 5.6.4). In the catalogue of sectarian divisions that formed part of Celsus's attack on Christianity those who claim to be Gnostics are distinguished from those who claim that the Christian God is not the God of the Jews and from Valentinians, though all three groups agree that the Christian God is a heavenly entity far removed from the Jewish God, who is a malevolent and ignorant creator (see Origen c. Cels. 5.61).

Origen's response treats each group separately. Unlike his refutation of exegetical passages from the commentary of the Valentinian, Heracleon, in his own commentary on John, Origen does not require detailed knowledge of Christian theology in this context. First, he insists that the existence of sects within Christianity no more tells against its truth than does the existence of different schools of philosophy. Against those who claim that the Christian

God is not the God of the Jews, Origen notes that others can prove from Scripture that there is only one God for Jews and Gentiles. Paul, e.g., continued to worship the God of his ancestors after becoming a Christian. Origen's approach to the Valentinians focuses on the "classes" of human being, here "natural" and "spiritual," found in their writings. The twofold division may have been derived from Celsus, since the more common Valentinian anthropology holds that humanity is divided into material, psychic, and spiritual persons. Spiritual ones are the true Gnostics. The psychics are often described as mainstream Christians. They require conversion, repentance, the material sacraments and reach a lesser level of heavenly salvation. The material persons never attain any gnosis or spiritual insight. Some writings suggest that these divisions are "inborn" in individuals. Origen insists that those who belong to the church will never accept a determinism based on how persons are born. Finally, Origen equates the Gnostics with Epicureans. The latter do not deserve the title "philosopher" because they reject providence. Gnostics cannot be called Christians because they introduce new teachings which cannot be harmonized with the traditional doctrines received from Jesus.

Though gnosis is frequently identified with its use in the heretical sects, both Clement of Alexandria and Origen use "gnosis" to refer to knowledge about Christian teaching that is only possible for some Christians. They argue that from a pedagogical perspective some teachings ought to be concealed from those whose simple faith renders them unable to comprehend the meaning of such teaching. Clement's definition of the true Gnostic Christian fits the tradition found in Barnabas; a person who knows certain truths, who is spiritually mature and who brings others to gnosis (Strom. 2.10.46). Because gnosis is grounded in revelation by the Truth, itself, gnosis is more certain than anything that human reason using the tools of Greek philosophy might have discovered (Strom. 6.9.78). Clement adopts a tradition with roots both in Jewish apocalyptic writing and Platonic philosophy that the goal of gnosis is the soul's ascent through heavenly spheres to rest in a vision of the divine. The soul that achieves such a vision is itself akin to the divine (Strom. 7.10.57).

Clement speaks of gnosis as instruction from

the Lord to the apostles that had been handed down in oral form (*Strom.* 6.7.61). Distinctions between true and false gnosis are grounded in the doctrines of the church (*Strom.* 6.97.5; 125.2; 141.3). False gnosis treats the creator God of the OT as inferior to the God of Christians, rejects creation as the work of an evil demiurge and attacks such legitimate expressions of the passions as fear of God and marriage (*Strom.* 3.9.1; 103.1; 4.147.1; 163.1). True Christians will also reject the claim that gnosis only comes to certain humans who are naturally able to receive it.

Clement insists that gnosis, the perfecting of faith, belongs to a freely chosen path of progress from a good to a better state. It depends upon the free choice of individuals, study, ascetic discipline, and the grace of God (*Strom.* 1.6.3; 4.92.2).

While Clement understands received traditions and doctrines as ways of evaluating claims about what belongs to Christian gnosis, Origen links gnosis to the interpretation of Scripture. Scripture has a typological sense in which events in the OT prefigure realities of the new covenant. They also have a spiritual or moral meaning by which Christians are instructed in a life of virtue. However, their hidden, gnostic meaning cannot be universally shared. It concerns the soul's destiny, ascent to the spiritual world, and origin, descent from that world (*Hom. Num.* 27.2–4). Gnosis can only be found in the tradition of those teachers who know how to interpret Scripture. Faced with heretical commentaries on Scripture, which claimed to reflect its hidden, esoteric meaning, Origen attacks their interpretations as violating the logic of what Scripture reveals elsewhere (e.g., *Comm. in Jo.* 2.2).

For both Clement and Origen, pursuit of gnosis is the mark of a spiritually mature Christian. Gnosis enables the soul to grasp its true likeness to God, but it is not a necessary condition for salvation. The gnostic heretics, on the other hand, treat gnosis as the spiritual awakening from ignorance and delusion. Only then is one aware of one's divine origin and destiny (e.g., *Gos. Truth, Corp. Gnos.* I 3 22,3–20). *Gospel Phil.* (*Corp. Gnos.* II 3 76, 17–77,31) grounds the claim that knowledge of the gnostic truth about the self is necessary for salvation in an interpretation of Jn 3:1–12, Jn 8:34, and 1 Cor 8:1 as well as allusions to Paul's

treatment of baptism in Rom 6. Gnosis provides the Gnostic with an understanding of the true significance of traditional Christian rites like Baptism, Eucharist, and anointing.

Without gnosis sacramental rites have no effect. Some Gnostics opposed the orthodox understanding of sacraments as channels of salvation (cf. *Adv. haer.* 1.21.4; *Testim. Tr., Corp. Gnos.* IX 3 69,7–32). Since gnostic mythologies trace the origins of the material world to a loss of "light" from the divine world and its subsequent entrapment in matter through the actions of the evil or ignorant lower God, neither Judaism or orthodox Christianity, which worship that God, nor philosophy, which lacks divine revelation, can attain truth. Only the descent of a redeemer from the heavenly world can bring gnosis to those trapped in the ignorance of this cosmos. Hymnic fragments of a Jewish-Christian gnostic sect celebrate Jesus as the one who brings knowledge into this world and yet remains unstained by the filth of the world (cf. *1 Apoc. Jas., Corp. Gnos.* V 3 28,7–20; *2 Apoc. Jas., Corp. Gnos.* V 4 47,8–20). The revealer's teachings were transmitted to the apostles in secret. Consequently, such teaching is not found explicitly stated in the gospel traditions derived from the circles of the Twelve (cf. *Ap. Jas., Corp. Gnos.* I 2 1,1–2,39; *1 Apoc. Jas.* 42.20–24). Whereas the canonical texts present the risen Lord reestablishing the community of disciples and commissioning them to proclaim the gospel, gnostic writings frequently claim that Jesus revealed gnosis during the period between the resurrection and ascension (cf. *Ap. Jn., Ap. Jas., Soph. Jes. Chr., Pist. Soph.*). True understanding of the sayings of the earthly Jesus requires this later revelation.

Gnostic myths about the origins of the heavenly realms, with their numerous divine beings and the earthly antitype of the heavens ruled by a blind demiurge who claims to be the one true God, trace all things back to the unfolding of the one, unknown divine Father or Father-Mother. But the myth serves to establish a rigid, cosmic dualism. Only the spark of light trapped in gnostic souls can be awakened and ascend to union with its heavenly counterpart. Everything characteristic of the material, sensible world will be stripped away and ultimately destroyed when all that belongs to the divine has returned to its true home (see *Orig. World, Corp. Gnos.* II 5 124,33–127,17). The savior who brings this revelation is usually identified as the counterpart of the female figure of divine Wisdom whose activity led to the emergence of the lower worlds out of the divine (cf. *Soph. Jes. Chr., Corp. Gnos.* III *4* 112,4–114,25). The divine Wisdom figure plays a revelatory role in the cosmological myth. She chides the arrogant ruler-god for boasting in his superiority and reveals the heavenly archetype of humanity. Out of passionate desire for the beauty of the heavenly Adam, the ruler-god and his angels create the psychic and material bodies of human beings, which are subject to ignorance and death (see *Orig. World, Corp. Gnos.* II *5* 103,1–116,8). Frequently, the true Eve, "mother of the living," is said to have awakened Adam with gnosis about the superiority of humans to the lower gods in the events which the Genesis stories connect with the tree of knowledge.

This mythological cosmology was clearly developed in Jewish circles where speculation about Adam's creation and the stories of the fallen angels played a major role. In many texts, the heavenly Seth is the source of revelation for gnostic souls, which contain his seed (see *Gos. Eg.*). The myth of cosmological origins, the fallen soul and its redemption by a heavenly Wisdom/Immortal Adam/Seth figure seems to be quite independent of its appropriation by Christian Gnostics. Equating the Christ with one of the heavenly beings of the myth enabled the Gnostics to claim that this mythic story constitutes the saving gnosis that Christ taught.

An emphasis upon the dualism of this mythic story renders the "historical Jesus" as well as claims about the redemptive significance of Jesus' death on the cross irrelevant. For the Gnostic, "Jesus" is only the necessary material, psychic vehicle through which the divine redeemer can enter the world in order to make contact with the lost gnostic souls. Christian Gnostics explained the cross in docetic terms. The ignorant, demonic rulers of the cosmos thought they had crucified the savior. All they had really done was hang a discarded body on the cross. The Immortal Savior was never subject to death. Orthodox Christians who claim to find salvation in the cross, not gnosis, have been deluded into placing their hope in a dead human being rather than the living savior (see *Apoc. Pet., Corp. Gnos.* VII *3* 81,15–84,6). Similarly, orthodox belief in the resurrection as the future, bodily transformation of persons into

the image of Christ was attacked as a misplaced hope grounded in attachment to the material world. The true significance of resurrection must be found in the soul's awakening to its inner divine nature (see *De Res., Corp. Gnos.* I *4* 45,14–48,2).

Another line of development, evident in Plotinus's opposition to Gnostics (*Enn.* 2.9), combined the myth of the soul's return to the divine with Platonic speculation about the ascent of the soul to a divinizing vision of God. The neoplatonic triad, life-mind-existence, is used to describe the deity in writings from this school (cf. *Allogenes, Steles Seth, Marsanes, Zostr*). To the orthodox Platonist, gnostic dualism and mythological speculation are as offensive as they are to the orthodox Christian. Gnostic dualism severs the connection between the material world and heavenly archetypes. Beauty and order as images of the divine in this world no longer enable the soul to ascend to rational contemplation of the divine. Mythological speculation underlies the ritual baptisms linked to purification and ascent of the soul found in such gnostic writings as well as their speculation about angelic names and multiplication of heavenly beings.

Platonic speculation is more hospitable to the tripartite anthropology of many gnostic writings than orthodox Christianity. Christian writers frequently protest that the division of human beings into spiritual, psychic, and material persons makes salvation dependent upon one's nature rather than upon free will responding to God's grace (see *Exc. Theod.* 45.1; *Adv. haer.* 1.4.1; *Tri. Trac., Corp. Gnos.* I *5* 62,2–5). Other gnostic writings, less influenced by philosophic anthropology, describe Gnostics as those who belong to a different "race," that of Seth or the Immortal Man. Though gnostic writers can describe awakening to gnosis as a response to the divine "call" and in that sense an experience of divine grace or election (see *Exeg. Soul, Corp. Gnos.* II 6 in which the tale of the soul's repentant return to God is told), most of their speculative mythology does presume that only a few persons possess natures capable of gnosis. Various schools differ on their treatment of the "psychics," whom Valentinians identify with orthodox Christians. Some hold that they attain a form of salvation in a lower region of the heavens. However, the most striking element in gnostic anthropology is its exaltation of the human being over the creator God and his angels (cf. *Gos. Phil., Corp. Gnos.* II 3 71,35–72,4). Identification with one's inner divine nature not only renders the Gnostic superior to the religious and cultural authorities who decide how most of humanity lives, it even makes the Gnostic superior to the divine creator of this world.

This motif of alienation from the cosmos, its gods and authorities, is fundamental to the symbolic and mythical language of Gnosticism. Gnostics describe themselves as members of a "kingless" race, strangers to the demiurge and his powers (see *Apoc. Ad., Corp. Gnos.* V 5 65,18–19; 69,17–18; 76,5–6). Biblical stories of the flood, Sodom and Gomorrah, and the destruction of the earth by fire were frequently read as attempts by the Demiurge to destroy the gnostic race, which was preserved by angelic powers (see *Apoc. Ad., Corp. Gnos.* V 5 75,9–28; 76,8–15; *Gos. Eg., Corp. Gnos.* III 2 63,4–8). Whenever revelation appeared in the world, its rulers were agitated and attempted to destroy those who had been enlightened. Gnostics understood the opposition they faced from church authorities as yet another manifestation of this pattern (see *Treat. Seth, Corp. Gnos.* VII 2 58,14–60,12).

Though the church fathers report that some gnostic groups demonstrated their freedom from the restraints of the world in libertine ritual practices (see Irenaeus *Adv. haer.* 1.23.3; Epiphanius *Pan.* 26), the surviving gnostic writings show a decidedly ascetic strain. The passions, especially those connected with sexuality, are devices used by demonic powers to enslave the soul and prevent its reintegration into the heavenly world. The widespread inclusion of women in gnostic sects seems to have been predicated on the claim that through ritual and ascetic practice, they could "become male" (e.g., *Gos. Thom.* 114). The fallen soul is always pictured as "female" seeking to be reunited with her heavenly "male" counterpart. The central rite of Valentinians, the bridal chamber, apparently enacted this reunification (see *Gos. Phil., Corp. Gnos.* II 3 86,4–18).

Asceticism, ritual practices, and the development of patterns of scriptural interpretation in the context of a unique form of mythological speculation are all evident in the earliest forms of gnostic tradition, which have clearly developed in a milieu of Jewish apocalyptic sec-

tarianism. Gnostic teachers in the second century assimilated the traditional materials to middle-Platonic speculation about the unknown God, the emanation of the world and divine providence, as well as to emerging Christianity. The latter provided a social and religious context for the expanded development of gnostic sects. Where orthodox writers insisted that true gnosis required exegesis that deepened faith and was consistent with doctrinal traditions of the church, Gnostics rejected any interpretation that had not been formulated to symbolically express the revealed story of the soul's heavenly origins, fall into the world, and restoration through gnosis. For the Gnostic, salvation history has been rewritten on the mythic plane. Narratives of Israel's history or the earthly life and teachings of Jesus have no revelatory power in themselves. The divine Christ of gnostic speculation is a mythic being untouched by his descent into the human world.

Rejecting the gnosis of mythological speculation and individual enlightenment led orthodox Christians to insist upon the special revealed status of the narratives in the Gospels and Acts. Instead of the gnostic salvation history of mythic inversion and opposition to the God of Judaism, the orthodox insisted that the heavenly Father revealed by Jesus was the same God who had created this world and been revealed In the OT. Asceticism and the quest for a religious experience of the soul's union with God belong to the religious practice of orthodox Christianity. But they are not permitted to set the conditions for salvation in such a way that the atoning death of Christ or the sacraments lose their power to communicate salvation to the believer. Faith and grace rather than gnosis are the basic terms in which Christians describe salvation. Augustine's experience of the last great expression of gnosis in patristic times, Manichaeism, played an important role in shaping his understanding of evil and grace in human experience.

Bibl.: Texts: Editions of individual texts from Nag Hammadi along with translations, notes, and commentary are appearing in the series *Nag Hammadi Studies* (Leiden: Brill) and *Bibliothèque copte de Nag Hammadi* (Quebec: Les Presses de l'Université Laval). For an English translation of all the texts from the Nag Hammadi collection, see J. M. ROBINSON, ed., *The Nag Hammadi Library in English* (San Francisco, 1988). Collections that contain extensive material from patristic accounts of Gnosticism along with selections from surviving gnostic texts: W. FOERSTER, *Gnosis*, vol. 1: *Patristic Evidence*, trans. R. McL. Wilson (Oxford, 1972); vol. 2: *Coptic and Mandaic Sources* (Oxford, 1974); B. LAYTON, *The Gnostic Scriptures* (Garden City, 1987). Secondary sources, treatments of Gnosticism within the context of the theological development of Christian thought: J. DANIÉLOU, *A History of Early Christian Doctrine*, vol. 2: *Gospel Message and Hellenistic Culture* (London, 1973); J. PELIKAN, *The Christian Tradition*, vol. 1: *The Emergence of the Catholic Tradition (100–600)* (Chicago, 1971); M. J. EDWARDS, "Gnostics and Valentinians in the Church Fathers," *JTS* n.s. 40 (1989): 26–47. Treatments of Gnosticism as a religious phenomenon: H. JONAS, *The Gnostic Religion* (Boston, 1962); K. RUDOLPH, *Gnôsis* (San Francisco, 1983); G. STROUMSA, *Another Seed: Studies in Gnostic Mythology*, NHS 24 (Leiden, 1984). Collections of essays by leading scholars: B. ALAND, ed., *Gnôsis: Festschrift für Hans Jonas* (Göttingen, 1978); B. LAYTON, ed., *The Rediscovery of Gnosticism*, vol. 1: *The School of Valentinus*, SHR 12 (Leiden, 1980); vol. 2: *Sethian Gnosticism*, SHR 12,7 (Leiden, 1981; C. W. HEDRICK and R. HODGSON, eds., *Nag Hammadi, Gnosticism and Early Christianity* (Peabody, MA, 1986).

Pheme PERKINS

GOD

I. THE GOD OF REVELATION. *1. The Question of God. 2. Current Debate. 3. The Logic of Christian Theism. 4. The God of Revelation. 5. The Faith of the Catholic Church.* (F.-A. PASTOR)

II. GOD, PROOFS OF EXISTENCE OF. *1. Prefatory Considerations. 2. Basic Types of Proof of God's Existence.* (HANSJÜRGEN VERWEYEN)

I. THE GOD OF REVELATION

1. The Question of God

Christian Theology

A theological language for the affirmation of God arises out of the encounter between Greek philosophical culture and the religious message of Christianity. The first Christian apologists themselves manifest an attempt at a systematic reception of the philosophical concept of God.

Christianity proclaimed that the unknown, mysterious God, the creator of the world, was the very God of Abraham and the Father of Jesus, the one God living and true, revealed in the covenant, who is Lord of universal history, transcendent object of the religious sentiment of all peoples, and ultimate principle of all reality (Acts 17:23ff., Rom 1:18ff.). With the help of Greek philosophy, especially Platonism and Stoicism, the first Christian intellectuals arrived at a description of the soul as a singular, spiritual, and immortal reality. They emphasized the ecstatic nature of the religious experience and indicated the determining attributes of the divine reality, which was one and ultimate, spiritual and transcendent, eternal and provident, thus contradicting the materialistic pantheism of the Stoics and the indifferentism of Epicurean deism (Justin, Ignatius of Antioch, Clement of Rome). The confrontation of Christian monotheism with gnostic dualism (Valentinus, Marcion, Celsus) led to the orthodox formulation of the language of the first article of faith, in terms of the absolute singularity and unicity of the divine monarchy, with an unequivocal identification of the God of creation of the old covenant with the saving God and Father of Jesus of the new covenant (Irenaeus, Tertullian, Origen).

In the Christian theology of Alexandria and Cappadocia, God emerges as the absolute and infinite, transcendent and superessential reality from which the reality of created multiplicity proceeds. Through both the natural order and the salvific order, the divine light illumines all things. The presence of God fills the universe and history. The human being, as a creature, can achieve oneness with the Creator, not only by the "cataphatic way" of an affirmation of the divine names, but, especially, by the "apophatic way" of negative theology and by the "mystical way" of ecstatic union (Clement of Alexandria, Gregory of Nyssa, Denis). Latin theology underscores not only the ontological transcendence of the divine reality, but, especially, the incomprehensibility of the salvific design of the will of a God who is utterly free and almighty. With absolute love, with an inscrutable salvific will, God draws the universe precisely toward God, revealing an infinite mercy and predestining grace, in the election and the covenant, in the splendor of creation, and in the mystery of the *historia salutis*. The religious human being seeks and finds infinite truth, not only by contemplating the *vestigia Dei* in sensible creation, but, principally, by the "interior way," by which divine truth reveals itself in an illuminating, immediate, and unconditional manner, as truth loved, absolute, and certain (Ambrose, Victorinus, Augustine). The ancient church, in its professions of faith, affirmed the one, living God not only as absolute reality, but as personal reality as well, in the divine identity as Creator of the universe and Lord of history, almighty benefactor and holy Father (DS 125, 150). In rejecting the concept of a comprehensible, finite God (DS 410), the believing community affirmed God as essentially incomprehensible and mysterious, infinite and ineffable, foundation and abyss, unbegotten Father, unoriginated origin and *principium sine principio* of all reality, created and uncreated, visible and invisible.

With its acceptance of Aristotelianism, scholastic theology was able to develop—as an alternative to the contemplative way of the *descent* of the infinite to the finite, typical of Augustinian Platonism (Anselm, Bernard, Bonaventure)—a *deductive* way of the finite to the infinite, the creature to the Creator, through the ANALOGY of being (Thomas Aquinas). On the premise of an anthropology of human openness to transcendence, in the dynamism of the true and the good, and supposing the ontology of causality, the scholastics managed a logical legitimation of the affirmation of God, in terms both of an absolute, and a personal, divine reality. I.e., in the attributes of God's subsistent being and in the perfections of the eternal, spiritual divine life, God is supremely real and all-perfect in being, everlasting and omnipresent in living, omniscient and omnipotent in acting. God's wisdom and goodness act in concert—in the order of nature as creation and providence, and in the order of salvation as grace and predestination. The scholastic perspective fuses the conception of Christian Platonism (of a God who is the origin and goal of the universe, as the supreme God) with the causal ontology of Aristotle, which posits God as both first cause—as the being necessary for the universe of creatures—and ultimate final cause of the dynamism of that universe, in the sense of its purpose, as it will find its perfection and consummation only in a participation in the divine beatitude. Not only theology, but the medieval church magisterium as well, in its dogmatic declarations, maintains the horizon of mystery, asserting God to be one and unique, true and holy, eternal and immutable, "incomprehensible, omnipotent, and ineffable"; and yet language about God will be possible, by way of creaturely participation: after all, between creature and Creator both "likeness and unlikeness" obtain, although the unlikeness is "always greater" (DS 806; cf. 800). Accordingly, theology and the church will always speak of a *Deus semper major.*

Reason and Faith

With the dawn of the modern age, the apophatic and mystical way of Christian Platonism, like the speculative and dialectical way of Christian Aristotelianism, must confront the new methodic perspective of autonomous reason, which seeks, in mathematics and in the science of the universe, the possibility of a new rational theology (Descartes, Leibniz, Newton). The new rational religion encounters revealed faith as its critical instance in the theoretical sphere; and at the same time, in the practical sphere, as its ethical instance: rational religion now engages in a polemic with the intolerance, fanaticism, and superstition of the religions as they are found in history (Diderot, Voltaire, Hume). As a replacement for these religions, and for the positivity of Christian revelation, theological rationalism defends the universality of the religion of reason, positing God as artificer of the universe and guarantor of the mathematical laws that govern it. Theological rationalism also defends the primacy of moral reason over religious faith, which latter now becomes a mere corollary of ethicity (Shaftesbury, Rousseau). With rationalism, theology seems to dissolve either into a kind of pantheistic philosophy of an all-perfect nature (Spinoza, Lessing), or into a religion of reason as a popular quest for moral uprightness (Kant). In opposition to rationalism, Christian fideism (Luther, Pascal, Jacobi) stresses the difficulty of a sure affirmation of the infinite from a point of departure in the opacity of finitude. God is revealed as evident not to the light of reason, but only to the light of faith. Salvation history is a theophany of the mysterious God of Abraham, not of the rational God of the philosophers. Revelation alone, furthermore, knows the mystery of the human being—that finitude with a nostalgia for the infinite, that alienation in need of correction and grace. Theological rationalism itself was conscious of the impossibility of affirming the God of faith in the essential divine sublimity by way of a purely rational faith. Theological fideism is fully aware of the originality of the God of faith, in immanence and transcendence, personhood and unconditionality.

In rationalism and fideism alike, theological assertions stand on human subjectivity: as critical intelligence, as ethical will, or as believing sentiment. But for the autonomous reason of modernity, both religious anthropomorphism and biblical personalism are always problematic. The difficulty of thinking the Absolute as infinite and simultaneously as personal becomes acute in philosophical idealism (Fichte, Hegel). Seeking to bridge the gap between subjectivity and objectivity, between idea and reality, between the "I" and the world, idealism will posit an orientation of the finite subject to the infinite object, which subsequently will be recognized as absolute subject (Schelling). In the question of the relation between finite and infinite, idealism succumbs to the seduction of the principle of identity. On the premise of its conviction of the inobjectifiability of the infinite and the nonconceptuality of the unconditional, theological idealism seems doomed to a total apophaticism. The sole *via* of mediation now consists in the development of a subjective sentiment of radical dependency vis-à-vis the divine reality, with the acknowledgment of God as the unconditional foundation from which such dependency derives (Schleiermacher). The risk of idealistic theology, with its fascination for the principle of identity, consists in abandoning the notion of difference—thus, of the difference between conditional reality and unconditional ground— and dissolving into a kind of pantheistic monism.

By way of an alternative to romantic idealism, a current of thought now arises that is existential in its nature. Here, human beings are evaluated in their concrete being: body and spirit, feeling and reason, instinctuality and normativity, alienation and anguish, sociality and historicity (Feuerbach, Marx). This tendency, when it comes into competition with religion and faith, readily shifts to a kind of nihilism or postulatory atheism, as well as to a naturalism and existential pessimism (Schopenhauer, Nietzsche). However, the existential viewpoint remains valuable as a tool for plumbing the universe of faith, in terms of an awareness of the qualitatively infinite difference between the concrete human being—that being of finitude and alienation, desperation and sin—and the Absolute, as a personal God of holiness (Kierkegaard). In order to overcome rationalism and fideism, pantheism and atheism, ecclesial Christianity will have to propose a new methodology—one of a dialectic between reason, contemplative and critical, and faith in the God of religion and revelation. Vatican Council I had this problematic to deal with. Integrating the twin instances of reason and faith, the magisterium of the church will see itself obliged to reassert "Christian theism," in opposition both to the doubts of agnosticism and religious skepticism, and the denial of God, as both absolute and personal reality, in the various forms of atheism and pantheism (DS 3001–5). Between God and the world, as between Creator and creature, a qualitatively infinite difference obtains; but between the mysterious God of creation and the God revealed as Lord of history and salvation a profound identity prevails, as the first article of faith has asserted down all the centuries.

2. Current Debate

Apophaticism and cataphaticism, rationalism and fideism, idealism and existentialism continue their confrontation today. They manifest themselves in opposite, contrasting currents of thought: in theologies, respectively, of transcendence and immanence.

Theologies of Transcendence

In the Protestant arena, "liberal theology," with its reduction of Christianity to an ethical theism and its proclivity to a pantheistic rationalism, will be answered with a "dialectical theology," which recovers the transcendent moment of the religious experience, the personalism of biblical revelation, and eschatological Christocentrism in faith and theology. Knowledge of God is possible only in Christ: in his divine word, which reaches us through Scripture and the preaching of the church. The God of Abraham and Jesus engages in a self-revelation as the God who loves us freely. The encounter with the God of faith cannot occur by the dialectical *via* of the analogy of being, but only by the paradoxical way of the analogy of faith, in the encounter with the divine grace that justifies the sinner (Karl Barth). The encounter with the divine word of salvation, in the *kerygma*, entails the simultaneous discovery of one's own existence: one accepts the challenge to live that existence in authenticity and faith. The cross reveals the meaning of personal authenticity. The program of a "theology of the word" must be integrated with the use of an existential hermeneutics and a demythologizing reading (Rudolf Bultmann).

While dialectical theology underscored the discontinuity between the "hidden God" of religion, a concept that can lead to impiety, and the "revealed God," who justifies by faith and in grace, the "correlation method" places the accent on the profound identity between the God of the experience of transcendence, in the dimension of the unconditional, and the God of the irruption of the sacred, in the experience of Christian revelation. True, eschatological revelation occurs in Christ; but its religious relevance is verified only in the existential echo of the great Christian religious symbols, via an encounter between personal experience and that same revelation. Human reality finds itself threatened on all sides—ontically by death, ethically by moral evil, and spiritually by the absurd. The human condition is one of essential finitude, existential alienation, and vital ambiguity. God is revealed in a meaningful way only in the methodic confrontation between this human condition and Christian symbols, as irruption of the unconditional, ultimate meaning of all reality (Paul Tillich). Between the finite and the infinite, between the human being and God, both a maximum tension and a profound correlation prevail: for the human being, God is both foundation and abyss. Although theology is basically concerned with the God of revelation and faith, it will only be able to approach the thematics of belief satisfactorily from the perspective of the unconditional and sacred, which invades the world of relativity and profanity as ground of being and ultimate meaning of reality. Only from a point of departure in the "hidden God" can one affirm the "revealed God": only in terms of the God of

religion will there be any understanding of the God of faith.

In Catholic theology, survival of the modernist crisis, with its emphasis on religious immanentism, required the recovery, along with the logical and mediate moment, of the mystical, immediate moment in religious experience (Maurice Blondel, A. Gardeil. The so-called *nouvelle théologie* strove for a movement of renewal oriented in various directions: toward a recovery of the mystical moment in religious experience; attention to the living God of biblical revelation; contact with the apophatic spirituality of the patristic tradition; an emphasis on a *historia salutis* rendered present in the liturgical action; endorsement of the religious yearnings of the great Eastern religions; and cultural confrontation with the religious problem in the universe of secularity and atheistic humanism (Henri de Lubac, Jean Daniélou, Hans Urs von Balthasar). A sensitivity to the God of transcendence and mysticism did not prevent the development of a theology of culture and history, work and earthly realities, and politics and the temporal, with the accent on a theonomous outlook for the believer immersed in the world of secularity and profanity (M.-D. Chenu, G. Thils, Jacques Maritain). In the quest for the living God—in biblical revelation and Christian mysticism, in liturgical doxology and theological tradition (E. Przywara, R. GUARDINI, Hugo Rahner, Josef Jungmann)—the "transcendental method" contributes a theoretical elaboration consisting in a believing reflection in the perspective of the anthropological shift of the modern age. It associates a transcendental gnoseology and existential ontology to the perennial Christian meditation on mystery. An analysis transcendental in character, brought to bear on the inevitable a priori conditions in the actual knowing subject, reveals the human being both as "spirit in the world" (in our structure of conscious freedom and spatiotemporal ubication), and as "hearer of the word" (open to a possible divine revelation and plunged in an ambience of divine mystery). Thus human beings stand before God as "holy mystery," discovering themselves in their creaturely and historical structure, their spiritual component and their openness to transcendence, as beings anguished in their finitude, immersed in a world that resists grace, and invited by that same victorious grace as objects and addressees of the divine self-communication. In denominating this victorious grace, which envelops the world and human history, an authentic "supernatural existential," the theologian asserts a positive ontological determination of the historical human being as object of the universal salvific will of God (Karl RAHNER). Open to mystery, addressee of a possible divine self-communication that transcends and repairs evil in history and recovers the supernatural dimension of the divine design, the human being, in the *historia salutis* of revelation and grace, receives the free self-communication of the mercy of the Father, who is revealed as absolute truth in the Son, the absolute mediator, and as sanctifying goodness in the divine Spirit.

Theologies of Immanence

In Protestant theology, with its accent on the dimension of immanence in the religious experience, the "theology of secularization" seeks a worldly language about God, with a view to explaining the Christian message to the secular human being. Salvation will be announced as liberation, and Christ will be proclaimed as Lord of the world and paradigm of behavior in solidarity. A supposedly religious image of a God conceived as a mere *deus ex machina*, to be invoked in extreme situations of human existence, goes by the board. The theologians of secularization propose the acceptance of God from a point of departure in the reality and autonomy of the world, but this acceptance will be lived against a background of faith. The believer lives amidst the provocation of secularization, in a world that seems to function perfectly *etsi deus non daretur* ("even though there were no God"). The God of faith is revealed in the theology of the cross, manifested as the God who "abandons us." In Jesus' humiliation, revelation proclaims not a God of power, who solves human problems magically, but a God of weakness, affirmed in the paradox of faith (Dietrich Bonhoeffer, F. Gogarten). Numerous believers, unable to live their faith serenely in the conventional manner, undergo a crisis of human authenticity and religious sincerity. As an alternative to conventional Christianity, the theologians of secularization attempt to transcend any anthropomorphic understanding of the religious experience and theological language, accepting the program of demythologization and the critique of superstition. They likewise seek to discover that dimension of depth and ultimacy in which the human being opens up to the infinite. In a view of our neighbor as our brother or sister and the vicar of Jesus, the Christian praxis of mutual responsibility and solidarity is restored to its pristine priority (John A. T. Robinson, Harvey Cox, Dorothée Sölle). For the death of God theologians, the eclipse of the sacred in secular culture can be developed theologically only by way of a replacement of the categories of Christian Platonism, as well as of the dialectic of contingency proclaimed in theological Aristotelianism, by way of an empirical confrontation with the religious phenomenon, indeed with the reality of irreligiousness. The crisis of conventional theism will be countered with a christocentric focus in theological reflection, together with an emphasis on the praxic dimension in acceptance of the commitment of siblingship and the social and historical dimension. The God of transcendency is eclipsed; but thereby the God of immanence, manifested in Christ and history, is revealed (G. Vahanian, Paul Van Buren, Thomas J. J. Altizer, William Hamilton, H. Braun). The dimension of history and the future is also revalidated in the "theology of hope" (Jürgen Moltmann), with its accent on the tension of the "not yet" and its dialectic of the *novum* as tension between possibility and event. The category of the future is fundamental for human existence, individual and social. We all live in the dimension of hope, and our community lives in the perspective of "utopia." Revelation must be conceptualized not as an epiphany of the eternal present, but as a historical manifestation of the God who comes—in other words, the God of hope and the future.

Catholic theology, as well, has felt the need to face the challenge of secularization and senses the urgency of seeking a new theological paradigm in response to the phenomenon of secularity (Edward Schillebeeckx, Piet Schoonenberg, Hans Küng, Leslie Dewart). Thus it, too, blazes new trails. A "theology of modernity" attempts to integrate the demands of secular culture's critical rationality with the believing tradition of the Christian community, proposing an experience of God to be lived in the very depths of an "awareness of being," appealing to an in-depth trust as the basis of a believing affirmation, transcending any schema of rivalry between created freedom and omnipotent freedom, and, in the ethical enterprise, seeking a new paradigm of the transcendent in terms of the future. The process of mundanization, or affirmation of the secular in its autonomy, is now seen as a legitimate form of liberation from an oppressive heteronomy. In its worldly opacity and historical ambiguity, the world manifests before all else the *vestigia hominis*. Only in its character as creaturely reality, and in a transcendental perspective, can the world detect the *vestigia Dei*. The affirmation of the secular and worldly is seen as a corollary of the Christian experience: the world regarded as creation and as covenant, as divine work and as addressee of salvation history (Johannes B. Metz).

In the concrete historical context of Latin America, and in the presence of a search for a new emancipation of the popular classes and subordinate races and cultures there, the theology of liberation discovers the political relevance of the God of biblical revelation, a God who delivers the oppressed, and a God of prophetic religion. Here is a God of holiness and justice, who condemns social injustice and sins against one's sisters and brothers as tantamount to idolatry (Gustavo Gutiérrez, Hugo Assmann, Juan Luis Segundo). Through salvation history, God engages in a self-manifestation as Lord of hope and the future — as a God of the liberation of the oppressed and lowly. In a theological consideration of the meaning of revelation, the poor become a privileged epistemological locus, and the exodus paradigm illuminates a believing reflection upon the historical present (Leonardo Boff, Clodovis Boff, Enrique Dussel). A reading of the comprehensive meaning of the Christian message, on a tortured continent afflicted with truly subhuman poverty, the gospel and the divine reign, as moment of liberation and hope for the doomed and oppressed of history, become a kind of "canon within a canon," producing a denunciation of the contrast between conflictive social reality and the Christian ideal of siblingship.

3. The Logic of Christian Theism

The Possibility of a Theological Theory

In addressing the problem of the affirmation of God, principally considered in the light of the first article of Christian faith, we may not ignore the question of the best *method* for analyzing religious language. The theologian must attempt to discover the meaning and signification of Christian language concerning God, its logical articulation, and its theoretical and practical consequences. Accordingly, certain methodological presuppositions need explication:

(a) *Language concerning God.* The theological language of Christian theism may be regarded as a linguistic expression of the affirmation of God in the perspective of the first article of faith. Faith in God as almighty creator and merciful parent constitutes the basic assertion for the believing profession not only of the Catholic community but of all of the Christian confessions, and indeed, in various senses, of all of the great monotheistic religions. In its denunciation of a mythical, anthropomorphic, naïve, or superstitious understanding of a language of faith, secularization has provoked a crisis of conventional religious language. The best response to this provocation will be found in an understanding of the precise significate of the language of faith.

(b) *Theoretical method.* Important concepts of logic and theory of science, of philosophy of language and theory of communication, have a useful application in the construction of a general theory of language concerning God. Transcending a purely empiricist, naïvely positivistic language, theoretical method must set forth the preliminary hypotheses and general axiomatics, the linguistic rules, and the theological theorems best calculated to express religious meaning: the theoretical signification and practical relevance of Christian language concerning God.

(c) *A theological theory.* In its character precisely as theory, a theological theory will have to proceed methodically, from a point of departure in preliminary hypotheses, which will subsequently be subjected to a process of verification and corroboration. The general hypotheses of an understanding of the language of faith will be submitted to verification in terms of the criterion of normative Christian experience, objectified in biblical revelation. Subsequently, such hypotheses may be corroborated in confrontation with the solutions and dogmatic formulas of the orthodox language of church tradition. The intelligence of the problem must precede, partially, a theological solution of the same, in a fruitful equilibrium or balance of tension between an understanding in quest of faith (*intellectus quaerens fidem*) and the thrust of faith to gain an understanding of its own logic (*fides quaerens intellectum*).

(d) *Kerygma and logos.* Theological discourse may not dispense with the use of the logical reason that seeks an intelligence of faith. But neither may it neglect the witness of biblical revelation or orthodox tradition. The tension between apologetical, or dialogical theology and kerygmatic theology, that of obedience to faith, must not be resolved in a reductive, exclusive alternative. In order to discharge its specific diaconia, theology must take care not to renounce its dialogue with the cultural and social situation in which it finds itself; but neither may it refuse to hear the gospel of faith, or the tradition of that faith as maintained by the church community.

Preliminary Hypotheses concerning Theism

With regard to the question of the possibility of a religious affirmation and a profession of faith, along with the question of the possibility of a subsequent theoretical elaboration of that affirmation and profession in a theological system, four alternative hypotheses, by and large, are proposed.

(a) *First hypothesis.* "No affirmation of God is possible, either in the immanence of history or the transcendence of the spirit." The reality of God is undiscoverable, by reason of God's nonexistence or unknowableness, both *qua* absolute reality and as personal reality. This is the response of atheism and antitheism, agnosticism, and, in some measure, pantheism.

(b) *Second hypothesis.* "An affirmation of God is possible only in terms of transcendence of the world." This is the response of religion's mystical experience, as well as that of contemplative theology. It underscores the transcendent character of religious experience, which consists principally in an encounter with the holiness of God and with the presence of mystery.

(c) *Third hypothesis.* "An affirmation of God is possible only in terms of an ethical commitment to historical immanence." This is the response of religion's prophetical, experience of religion, and of theologies of praxis. The tendency here is to place an exclusive emphasis on the ethical dimension of religious experience—the encounter, individual and social, with the divine justice, which abominates evil both in the individual and in society.

(d) *Fourth hypothesis.* "Christianity's religious experience presupposes a dialectical synthesis of the transcendence and immanence of the reality of God in the life of the believer." The dilemma that proposes vertical faith or horizontal siblingship as the religious option's only alternatives contributes to the reduction and impoverishment of the complexity and wealth of the Christian religious experience. That experience is characterized by a tension between mystical contemplation and ethical exigency, a tension that will find its synthesis and transcendence in the experience of the mercy of God, in the mysterious light of the cross and grace.

General Axiomatics

The denomination "axiom" will be reserved to certain postulates of a basic, general nature, referring to the logic of the believing affirmation, and the structure of the significate in the religious affirmation. Among these axioms, the following will be proposed.

(a) *Fundamental axiom.* "The revealed God is the hidden God." This axiom posits an equation of the terms of the fundamental antinomy of Christian theological language—the tension between divine revelation and the mystery of God. In other words, the God who is self-revealed as merciful and faithful in the *historia salutis* is the same veiled, hidden God, creator of the universe, ultimate referent of contingent reality, that dwells in the inaccessible light of mystery. The fundamental axiom formulates the equivalency of the *deus revelatus* and the *deus absconditus*.

(b) *Gnoseological axiom.* "The known God is the incomprehensible God." This axiom posits an equation, on the theoretical level of truth, between the terms of the noetic antinomy proper to the affirmation of God: i.e., the tension between the knowability of God and the divine incomprehensibility inasmuch as God is affirmed as incomprehensible mystery. The second axiom, then, posits a logical equivalency between the *deus cognoscibilis* and the *deus incomprehensibilis*. This means that the infinite God is affirmed by human beings in transcendence of the limits of their own finitude, thus verifying the concept of a *finitum capax infiniti*.

(c) *Ontological axiom.* "The immanent God is the transcendent God." In rhetorical language, this axiom expresses the tension between "nearness" and "distance" in the religious experience. The God of covenant and election, of predestination and grace, is identical with the meta-temporal, meta-spatial God of creation, who transcends the world. Far from denying the divine transcendence, the divine immanence in reality and history precisely demands it. The third axiom enunciates the logic of equivalency between immanence and transcendence in Christian language concerning God.

(d) *Axiom of identity.* "God is God, and the Lord alone is God." The sixth axiom enunciates, on the theoretical level of truth, God's absolute singularity in the divine identity. An understanding of the divine reality under the principle of identity can occur only in the form of a logical tautology; but, as has been observed, we are dealing with a "signifying tautology." *Solus Deus est Deus* proclaims the exclusive monotheism of prophetical religion, asserting the divine monarchy over religion and history.

(e) *Axiom of reality.* "God must necessarily be thought of as reality." The fifth axiom formulates, on the theoretical level of reality, God's absolute, unconditional necessity. In the ontology of the *summum esse* (Supreme Being) is a perfect coincidence of idea and being, potency and act, existence and essence. The logical translation of the fifth axiom requires the use of the "existential quan-

tifier," inasmuch as we are always speaking of *ipsum esse per se subsistens* ("the pure Act of Existence").

(f) *Ethical axiom.* "The God of trust is the God of fear, and vice versa." The divine reality is revealed not only as absolute and necessary, transcendent and unconditional, but also as personal and spiritual, intelligent and free. The sixth axiom expresses the twofold aspect of *fascinans* and *tremendum* in the experience of numinous mystery, that encounter with the God of "fear and trembling" and with the God of "faithfulness" and "hope." The present axiom enunciates, on the practical and pragmatic level, the maximal tension provoked in the believer by the spiritual polarity of *amor Dei* and *timor Dei*.

(g) *Axiom of relation.* "Theological language is based on the religious relation between the human being and God." The seventh axiom underscores the relational character of the religious experience underlying language concerning God. It would be nonsense to speak, in the language of faith, of the object of religion while ignoring the religious subject—all the more so in that God transcends the subject-object schema, being ontologically the absolute subject while at the same time being recognized as personal reality. In replacing syllogistic logic with bivalent logic, the present axiom sets the stage for a more adequate understanding of, e.g., biblical language concerning the justice and mercy of God.

(h) *Conclusive axiom.* "The holy, eternal God is revealed as Lord of the covenant and Father of faithfulness and goodness." The eighth axiom asserts an identification between the God encountered in sacral theophany, in sacramental experience, or in mystical ecstasy, and the God of biblical revelation, who announces the divine justice and fidelity, proclaiming the victory of grace over evil and over sin. The conclusive axiom is invested with great ecumenical significance: the God sought in the great world religions or in personal spirituality is the same God as is revealed in the biblical religion and eschatological epiphany that are at the origin of Christianity.

Linguistic Rules

Certain rules will be proposed—general indications, formal in their nature—with reference to religious language, especially in Christian theology.

(a) *Fundamental rule.* "Language concerning God may not ignore the fact that its referent is always the ineffable God." This rule asserts the basic paradox of religious language: theology claims to speak of a God who simply cannot be circumscribed in a discourse. Theological language can only exist by way of a compromise between assertion and mystery. The ineffability of God is the linguistic version of the divine mystery and incomprehensibility, of the divine transcendency and utterly elusive freedom, of the holiness of God's justice and the eternity of God's faithfulness and goodness.

(b) *Rule of linguistic usage.* "Christian language concerning God is irreducible to any single kind of linguistic usage." E.g., the language of doxology as used in worship will be preponderantly expressive of Christian hope; the use of analogy in theology will tend to be informative; the language of a profession of faith or dogmatic declaration will prefer a normative linguistic usage.

(c) *Rule of the significate.* "The hermeneutics of language concerning God must take cognizance of the multiple semeiotic relevance of that language." A study of theological language will have to concern itself not only with the material significate or logical syntax of the discourse in question but with its theoretical significate and practical signification, as well.

(d) *Rule of functions.* "An interpretation of the meaning of religious language will find it useful to consider the various linguistic functions attendant upon any process of communication." Language concerning God presupposes a believing community, and serves as a means to communicate a message, within a complex process of acceptance and reception of faith. In religious communication—a dialectic of revelation and faith, proclamation and conversion, reception and transmission—the fundamental linguistic functions of any communicative process are present: emission and reception, message and referent, code and contact.

(e) *Rule of analogy.* "The existence of doxological language and orthodox language legitimizes the use of analogy in discourse upon God." Language concerning God proclaims to the believer the supreme reality, as revealed and mysterious, assertable and ineffable, singular in its identity and absolute in its freedom, the object of infinite love and unconditional fear. Language concerning God will be positive or cataphatic in an assertion of the perfections of God through the divine names. It will be negative or apophatic as well, in denying of God the imperfections of finitude or contradiction, and in refusing to set limits to its function of correcting the meaning of the believing proposition. The language of analogy, which shares this dialectic of affirmation, negation, and correction of meaning, should be regarded not as a *via media* between equivocation and univocity but as a moderated form of equivocation, and therefore as a moderated form of apophaticism.

(f) *Rule of paradox.* "Language concerning God expresses the paradoxical character of the believing assertion." Any analogy includes a paradoxical element. In the analogy of being, the tension between creature and creator, finite and infinite, conditional and unconditional will have to find a language in which the unconditional is expressed through conditional forms, and therefore in an objectively paradoxical way. In the analogy of faith, only a paradoxical language can express the tension between revelation of grace and justification of the sinner, as both are altogether unmerited and therefore logically unexpected. In the analogy of the symbol or image, Christianity itself appears as a paradoxical religion, in its theology of election and cross. The reign of God elects the lowly to confound the wise, and the cross, logically, is foolishness and scandal. Christian language concerning God is limited to showing the paradoxical character of Christianity itself.

Theological Theorems

Unlike the rules, which refer to the *formal* aspect of Christian religious language, the theorems refer to the *content* of Christian language concerning God, in the perspective of the first article of faith:

(a) *Fundamental theorem.* "God is revealed to all human beings, while remaining incomprehensible, strictly ineffable, mystery." The first theorem refers both to the real possibility of an affirmation of God, and to the limits of such an affirmation. This theorem, whose referent is the "revealed God," proposes, under the form of a complex enunciate, three questions of fundamental theological gnoseology: the question of the real possibility of an affirmation of God by human reason, as an affirmation necessarily possible *in se* and universally possible *quoad nos;* the question of the divine incomprehensibility; and the question of the ineffability of God, and, accordingly, of the limitation of any possible theological language. From the first theorem, a fundamental practical corollary derives: all theological language presupposes a religious experience of a *numinous* character—a personal encounter with the incomprehensible, ineffable God of faith.

(b) *Theorem of the divine holiness.* "God is revealed as infinitely holy, necessary and all-perfect, absolutely singular and unique." The second theorem refers to the divine reality as being. Again under the form of a complex enunciate, this theorem responds to three questions that bear on the divine being: its infinite holiness, its unconditional necessity and omniperfection, and its absolute singularity and uniqueness. From the second theorem derives a practical corollary with reference to the *sacramental* moment of the believing act, inasmuch as religious experience also signifies an existential encounter with the holiness of God.

(c) *Theorem of the divine presence.* "God is revealed as an eternal, omnipresent, and immense living being; the divine presence is manifested as spiritual and personal." The third theorem refers to the "revealed God" as a living being. Under the form of a complex enunciate, this theorem responds to three questions referring to the divine life as eternal presence: its eternity, its omnipresence, and its spiritual or personal character. From this third theorem as well, a practical corollary can be deduced: in existential confrontation with the presence of God, the believer is in the *mystical* moment of the religious experience.

(d) *Theorem of the divine justice.* "God is revealed as all-knowing and almighty also in the divine justice and reprobation of evil." The fourth theorem faces three decisive questions referring to the "revealed God" not only as absolute, supreme reality but also as spiritual, personal—i.e., intelligent and free—reality: the question of the infinite intelligence and omniscience of God; the question of the divine will as absolutely free and omnipotent; and finally, the question of the justice of a God who is omniscient and omnipotent precisely in rendering a judgment upon evil. Again, from the fourth theorem a practically corollary is deduced: the believer lives the *ethical* moment of the religious experience in personal confrontation with God's justice.

(e) *Theorem of the divine fidelity.* "God is revealed as good Creator, in the mysterious, holy divine providence; as faithful Lord, in the universal divine covenant of salvation; as merciful parent, full of fidelity and goodness." The fifth theorem refers to the reality of God as active in the orders of creation and salvation, and alludes to three fundamental questions: the creative and providential activity of God; God's universal divine salvific will and predestination to good; and God's salvific behavior in salvation history. From the present theorem, the following corollary is deduced: in existential confrontation with the merciful fidelity of God, who without any merit on their part grants sinners the grace of justification, the converted believer can undergo the *paradoxical* moment of the Christian religious experience.

(f) *Religious corollary.* The foregoing theorems have implicitly confirmed the complex structure of the Christian religious act as a confrontation of the believer with the mystery of God, in God's ineffable holiness and presence, justice and merciful fidelity. In Christianity, the religious act, as a dialectic of revelation and faith, is an act of great complexity, and is irreducible to any single principle. To the irruption of the unconditional element of the sacred, as revelation or as theophany, corresponds a mystical worship of the divine presence, as the expression of the fascinating moment of the religious experience; but likewise manifested is the unconditional exigency of the divine justice, in the tension of infinite fear and moral norm. While the mystical experience can be regarded under the principle of *identity* as tension of the finite toward the infinite, the ethical experience can only be regarded under the principle of *difference* as an expression of the tension between the divine holiness and the sinner's alienation. The tension between mystique and ethics, or the dialectic of identity and difference, is resolved, in paradoxical fashion, in the theology of grace.

4. The God of Revelation

Faith in God

Let us examine, first of all, the basic stages traversed by the explicitation of faith in God in biblical religion:

(a) *Archaic henotheism.* Primitive biblical piety acknowledges a mysterious, universal, and benevolent God ('*El*), sovereign of nature and the world (Gn 33:20), and the God revealed to Abraham, Isaac, and Jacob, the God of the Fathers who protects his worshipers (Gn 30:43). The polarity implied here is clearly resolved in an identification, in historical times, between the hidden God of the world and the Lord of the Patriarchs revealed in history. Subsequently, the theology of the exodus and covenant, proper to Mosaic Yahwism, proclaims a monolatry of historical liberation and ethical loyalty. The religious faith of Yahwism is at the origin of a historical experience of liberation from slavery (Ex 3:7). This intimate linkage between religious transcendence and salvific immanence, typical of biblical theism, implies a personal conception of the sacred, as well as a theology of hope and the future (Ex 6:7). The theology of the covenant precludes a false opposition between cultic religion and ethical religion (Ex 20:3ff.). The religion of the covenant clearly expresses the religious note of the ethical question, and stresses the personal moment of the

encounter with God, in an existential dialectic of trust and fear (Ex 20:18ff.).

(b) *The prophetic theology.* The prophets transmit the divine oracle and ethical norm of the religion of the covenant. The prophets express an ethical conscience and sense of difference through a proclamation of the coming of divine justice upon human wickedness (Am 5:18ff.; Is 5:16). The prospect of divine punishment never assumes demonic overtones, but is always conditioned by the will of the holiness of God to destroy evil and injustice (Am 8:4ff.). The dialectic of the prophets counterpoises an ideal moment in the religious relation, seen as covenant in history (Hos 12:10; Jer 2:7), with a real moment of moral contradiction, seen as apostasy (Hos 4:2; Jer 3:1ff.). The prophetic polemics do not conclude with this negative moment, but invite the hearer to a conversion—i.e., to a return to the dimension of the unconditional, which is made possible by the paradox of God's faithfulness (Am 5:15; Is 12:2; Jer 31:31). With the prophets, religious language affirms a transcendent and personal theism: i.e., an explicit theoretical monotheism (Is 43:10–11). Against any polytheistic temptation, the prophet uses the weapon of irony (Is 44:8–9). The Lord revealed to Israel is identified with the one, universal God, the transcendent Creator and incomparable Lord of the future, the just God who is the savior of all nations (Is 45:12–13, 21–22).

(c) *Sapiential and apocalyptic theology.* For the sages of Israel, the principle of wisdom coincides with the fear of God, identified with a practical knowledge of the divine will (Prv 1:7; 2:5). Sapiential reflection does not neglect the contemplative dimension of the religious experience in the form of an admiration for God's glory as revealed in the works of creation (Sir 42:15ff.) and salvation history (Sir 44:1ff.). But the sapiential theology also meditates God's silence, and faces the question of evil and the suffering of the just (Jb 42:3, 6). The sage even wonders about the problem of the possibility of establishing, from a point of departure in the beauty and power of the world as created effect, the omnipotence and intelligence of the divine artificer as creative principle (Wis 13:1–9). In turn, an apocalyptic propheticism maintains an interest in the relationship between God and history (Dn 10:21; 11:40; 12:1). The Most High guides the course of history and pronounces eschatological judgment on individuals and nations, nor is there any escaping that guidance or that judgment (Dn 10:13–14).

The apocalyptic theology of history is a corollary of monotheism: an immutable divine decree predetermines history, which is one as God is one (Dn 7:22; 8:13–14).

(d) *The message of Jesus.* The God of the imminent reign announced by Jesus is the very God of the Fathers and Lord of the covenant (Mk 12:26, 29). Jesus' religious message proclaims God as "Father" (Mt 6:6, 9), manifesting a singular awareness of his filial relation, a consciousness that was the fruit of an unlimited trust in the almighty goodness of God (Mk 14:36). The Gospel also proclaims God as sole, exclusive "Lord" of a divine reign (Mt 6:24). The disciple must seek exclusively the accomplishment of the divine will, pursuing the design of providence (Mt 6:10, 32). According to the Synoptic tradition, a world conditioned by finitude and alienation, and under the dominion of wickedness and evil, will behold the coming of the divine monarchy as salvific power (Mk 1:15), now become present in the humble ministry of Jesus, who is the teacher of the new law and prophet of the divine good pleasure, wonderworker of life and exorcist of evil (Mk 1:21ff.), the just one unjustly persecuted, and the servant of reconciliation with God (Mk 1:11). Jesus teaches the mysteries of the divine plan and the perfection of the divine observance (Mt 11:27; 5:17). The new praxis of discipleship will need to imitate the divine perfection, especially God's mercy, which will be translated into a generous benevolence of being a sibling, even toward one's enemies (Mt 5:48; Lk 6:36).

(e) *Theology of primitive Christianity.* The community of the first disciples founds its hope on a theology of resurrection. Trusting in the God of resurrection and life, Jesus' almighty Father (Acts 2:22–24), the entire community feels graced with the new justice of faith, and hopes in its own resurrection (Rom 3:24–25; 1 Cor 15:20). The believing community professes an eschato-logical panentheism: through the messianic dominion of the Son, the divine power will subject all adverse forces to the sovereignty of the Father (1 Cor 15:28). For Pauline theology, the unknown God can be recognized through creation and moral conscience (Rom 1:19–20; 2:14–15). However, human beings, inexcusably, do not acknowledge or worship their creator. The word of the cross takes on a revelatory meaning: God the Father is revealed as just, and as justifying those, Jews or Gentiles, who live in impiety (Rom 3:25). The gospel is the proclamation of God's parental love, which is revealed in Jesus' cross, that scandal and folly in the logic of the wise of this world (1 Cor 1:23). For Johannine theology, in turn, true knowledge of God is mediated by the revelatory activity of Jesus, eternal Word of the Father (Jn 10:14–15; cf. 1:14), and by the enlightening activity of the Spirit, that instructor of the community and accuser of the world (Jn 14:16–17; 16:7–8). Divine knowledge is not the fruit of pure reflection but requires a praxis of charity (1 Jn 4:16). To know God is to keep God's commandments, especially the new commandment of love (1 Jn 2:5). This should be the believer's basic response to the love of God revealed in the gift of Jesus (Jn 3:16; 17:25–26).

Biblical Theism

Let us analyze the affirmation of God in biblical revelation as a tension between mystery and theophany, history and transcendence, exclusivity and universality, unconditionality and personhood.

(a) *Epiphany of mystery.* In biblical religion, the dialectic of revelation and mystery determines the "fascinating" and "tremendous" character of the religious experience (Is 45:15). The theophanic experience is resolved in a veiled epiphany of mystery (2 Cor 5:7). To this fundamental religious tension corresponds the basic polarity of the language of biblical theism, as the dialectic of a God revealed and hidden: the God revealed in primitive henotheism (Ex 6:2–3), in monolatric worship (Dt 6:4), in prophetic monotheism (Is 6:3), or in sapiential meditation (Wis 13:5) is manifested through the world as creation and through history as salvation (Acts 17:24, 31). But the "Unknown God" (Acts 17:23) remains invisible and inaccessible (Rom 1:20; Jn 1:18; 1 Tm 6:16). Accordingly, language concerning God only expresses a basically ineffable religious situation.

(b) *History and transcendence.* Biblical theism is characterized by its conviction of a communion with the transcendent God, realized in the immanence of history. The institution of the covenant constitutes the paradigm of this kind of religious relationship (Ex 19:4–6). This fundamental category dominates the whole history of Israel's faith and is the theological condition of all of its traditions: creation and election (Gn 2:16–17; 9:9; 17:4), revelation and liberation (Ex 3:12–14), reign and grace (Is 52:7–9; 54:7–8). The eschatological community of the new covenant lives an intense, definitive experience of communion with God (1 Jn 1:3); in this communion, the dialectical tension between history and transcendence is radicalized. The one God becomes present in Jesus (Col 1:13–15). The holiness and glory of the Father are revealed in the Son (Jn 1:18). The divine grace gives us life in the power of the Spirit (Rom 8:26–27; Jn 14:17). Jesus is the mediator of the definitive revelation (Heb 1:2), and mediator as well of the new covenant of salvation (Heb 9:15).

(c) *Unicity of God.* In biblical theism, the believer's basic question with regard to God was that of the divine unicity. The God of the covenant and of Israel's religious piety was identified with the Creator of the universe and the eternal King (Pss 121:2; 47:3; 146:10). Unlike the polytheism of the surrounding nations (Jos 24:2), or its own primitive henolatry (Gn 15:1), the faith of Israel was lived as an exclusive monolatry (Dt 12:2) and explicit monotheism (Is 46:9–10). Israel's salvific monotheism is at once national and universal, communitarian and personal. The religious background of biblical theism enables us to grasp the originality of the Christian message. The God of the imminent reign, proclaimed by Jesus, is the very God of the Fathers and the covenant (Mt 22:32, 37). The message of Jesus proclaims God as compassionate Father and exclusive Lord (Mt 6:6, 24). The divine reign announced by Jesus in his parables is precisely God, in the divine holiness and power, justice and goodness (Mt 18:23ff.; Lk 15:11ff.).

(d) *God as reality.* By way of the fundamental identity of the mysterious God who is creator of the world with the Lord of the covenant revealed in history (Ps 95:3–7), the believer becomes aware of the divine reality. As Lord of history and creator of the world, God may be contemplated through creation. Idolatry, therefore, is judged inexcusable (Pss 10:4; 14:1; cf. 19:2; 33:6). The revelation of God's reality can be experienced in various ways: as assertion of the possibility of a religious question concerning ultimate reality, as ground of all created reality (Rom 1:20; Wis 13:4), as religious experience of the consciousness of moral duty and unconditional ethical imperative (Ps 51:4; Rom 2:14), as revelation of an unconditional salvific power of liberation and redemption in history (Ex 3:12), as experience of the divine, which in the paradox of the cross and grace is revealed and hidden (1 Cor 1:23; Phil 2:8).

(e) *A salvific monotheism.* In biblical religion, the affirmation of God takes the form of an exclusive theism, transcendent and personal, universal and salvific (Is 45:14, 18, 22). God is revealed as one and unique (Ex 20:3; Dt 6:4), holy and eternal (Is 6:3; Jer 10:10). The divine reality is absolutely singular and all-perfect, transcendent and omnipresent (Is 40:22; Jer 23:24). God is inaccessible mystery of holiness (Ex 33:19; Ez 10:18ff.), Most High in the divine majesty and glory (Ez 11:22–23; Is 59:19), transcending space and time, nature and history (Pss 90:2; 139:7ff.). As the eternal living One, God dominates the earth and fills the heavens with the divine salvific omnipresence (Jb 11:7–10; Prv 15:3). The living and true God is always revealed not only as absolute, unconditional reality, but as personal reality as well: God is the Holy One of Israel and Lord of the covenant (1 Sm 6:20; Ex 20:1ff.), redeemer from servitude and liberator from slavery (Ex 6:5–6), artisan of the universe and potter of the world (Gn 1:1ff.; Wis 13:5). As creator and as partner in the covenant, God is present in personal, salvific power, and one may call upon that power in the prayer of supplication (Wis 9:1ff.). Unlike the blind, deaf, mute, impotent idols, God is ever faithful and true, firm in resolution, unchangeable in oneness, almighty and all-knowing, in creation and providence, in election and grace (Pss 136:5; 135:6). The living, omniscient, omnipotent God is also the just and faithful, compassionate and merciful Lord. God is revealed as just—faithful to the divine covenant of salvation (Is 45:8; 51:7). God is just since God saves, revealing the divine justice in a defense mounted in behalf of the poor and persecuted (Pss 10:17–18; 18:3–4). God is Lord of hope, and does justice to the humiliated (Is 33:5; 51:6–7). God is zealous for good, and the divine anger will tolerate no evil (Ex 20:5; Dt 4:24). Against the religious background of the covenant, the divine comportment is characterized by a loyalty of love and benevolence (Ex 34:6; Dt 7:9): God is constant in mercy and compassion (Pss 25:10–11; 89:3).

In the eschatological community of the new covenant, Jesus renews the monolatric imperative (Mk 12:29–30). He also teaches veneration for the divine name, that expression of unapproachable holiness (Mt 6:9; cf. 5:33ff.). Especially, Jesus inculcates trust in a divine providence that does not abandon its creatures (Mt 6:25ff.). The Father is Lord of heaven and earth (Lk 10:21). The living God and Father of Jesus (Mt 16:16) is identical with the Creator, who is almighty and omniscient in salvific providence (Mt 6:26; 10:29). With the eschatological revelation, the divine plan has been definitively unveiled: God has created the world in order to save it in Christ (Eph 3:8–11; Col 1:26–27). The Father of Jesus adopts and sanctifies us in the Spirit (Gal 4:4–7). In the community of the disciples, Jesus declares the divine design to be absolutely free and filled with love, oriented to God's triumph in the divine mercy and forgiveness (Mt 18:14, 35). On the cross, Jesus reveals the Father's definitive love (Jn 3:16–17). The NT endorses biblical monotheism not only as a transcendent, personal theism, but as a theism of fidelity and bounty as well, and thus definitively affirms the compassionate monarchy of the Father (1 Jn 4:9–19).

5. The Faith of the Catholic Church

Identity and Difference

All of the creeds of the early church posit faith in one God, the Father and Creator, as the first article proposed to the believer's acceptance. This is the case with the most ancient formulas (DS 1–6) and the so-called Apostles' Creed (DS 10; 40ff.; 60), as well as with the conciliar creeds of Nicea (DS 125) and Constantinople (DS 150). The declaration of the synod condemning Origen is relevant as well, in its reprobation of any negation of the divine infinitude and incomprehensibility, and its corresponding insistence on a primordial apophaticism in language concerning God (DS 410). Likewise important are assertions of a divine monarchy coexisting with a hypostatic triplicity (DS 112–15), and an interpersonal equality in the one, undivided divine essence (DS 71–76). Initially, the language of ecclesial orthodoxy professes its faith in one God the Father almighty, creator of the visible and invisible reality of the universe (DS 13–19, 25–30)—thus identifying the God of creation and providence of the old covenant, in opposition to any gnostic dualism, with the merciful Father of the new. The unbegotten and eternal, infinite and incomprehensible, almighty God of creation is identified ever more clearly with the holy Father of the eternal divine Son, with the active inspirer of the Spirit who is the Paraclete, and with the omniscient judge of history (DS 139, 441, 451–2, 490, 525, 617). The king of ages, immortal and invisible (DS 16, 21–22, 29), is the unoriginated origin and unprincipled principle of both the intradivine life and the history of salvation (DS 71, 284, 470, 485, 525–26).

In the Latin West, the magisterium of the church constantly proposes the teaching of the first article of faith, defending it against any heretical interpretation. The councils of Carisiaco (DS 623) and Valentino (DS 626–27, 633) reject various errors concerning God's foreknowledge and predestination that would entail the theological necessity of evil. The Council of Seno rejected as heretical certain propositions of Peter Abelard to the effect that the divine behavior was in some way necessitated, both with regard to good (God could not have created a better world than the one actually created) or with regard to evil (not even God could have prevented evil, DS 726–27). The

Council of Rhiems (DS 745) criticized the theological language of Gilbert of Poitiers, which posited a real distinction between the divine essence, as substantial reality, and the divine Trinity, as tripersonal reality.

The Albigenses and Cathari renewed the dualistic heresy, distinguishing between a God of creation, the principle of evil, and a God of salvation, the principle of good, thus irreparably dividing the old and new covenants. Against this position, Lateran IV reasserted the unicity of the divine monarchy, professing "one sole true God, eternal, immense, and immutable, incomprehensible, omnipotent, and ineffable" (DS 800). This council also rejected the pantheistic doctrine of Amalrico of Bena, which identified God with the universal all (DS 808). The council's analogical theory is obviously intended for the purpose of demonstrating the simultaneous viability of a theology of identity and a theology of difference: between creator and creature, a dialectic of likeness and unlikeness obtains, in which the unlikeness is always greater. Thus Lateran IV takes a position under the umbrella of a moderately apophatic position (DS 806).

Lyons II once more reasserted the doctrine of God's unity and unicity, in opposition to any theological dualism or any cosmic pessimism (DS 851). Likewise the Council of Florence reasserted the doctrine of the oneness of the divine monarchy (DS 1330–36). John XXII, in his constitution *In Agro Dominico* condemned various propositions of Meister Eckhart that appeared to assert the eternity of the world, the personal unicity of God, and the impossibility of speaking of the divine goodness (DS 951ff., 973–74, 978).

At the dawn of the modern era, the Council of Trent proclaimed its faith from a starting point in the Nicene-Constantinopolitan formula, thus manifesting its fidelity to the tradition of the church (DS 1862). By way of such creeds, together with theological definitions and dogmatic declarations, the ecclesial magisterium reemphasized the faith of the Catholic church, proclaiming the believing conviction of a profound *identity* between the mysterious God of creation and providence manifested in the OT, and the God revealed in the NT as Lord of salvific history and Father of goodness and mercy. At the same time, that magisterium posited an irreducible *difference* between God and the world, between Creator and creation. During the first Christian millennium, the threat to faith was a loss of awareness of the *identity* of God as both Creator and Father: the divine monarchy was in danger of being supplanted by a supreme diarchy, two distinct ultimate principles—one of good and one of evil, one of the creation of matter and the other of the salvation of the soul, one of darkness and one of light, one of the old covenant and the other of the new. During the second millennium, the threat of a rejection of the first article of faith proceeds instead from the loss of an awareness of the *difference* between creature and creator, finite and infinite, world and God, which occurs in pantheism and atheism alike.

Furthermore, modernity abandons the model of a profound integration between REASON AND FAITH, typical of Christian Platonism, as well as the model of a moderate subordination of reason to faith, typical of scholastic Aristotelianism. Thus it is left with models either of an exaggerated subordination of critical reason to the conventional manner of living a traditional faith (fideism); or at the opposite extreme, of a subordination of piety and faith to the control of critical reason, with the attendant risk of RATIONALISM. Both errors are rejected by the magisterium, which reasserts the theological utility of an integration of the demands of faith with rational method. During the pontificates of Gregory XVI and Pius IX, the fideistic errors of L. E. Bautain (DS 2751–56, 2765–68) and A. Bonnety (DS 2811–14) were rejected, as well as the rationalistic theses of A. Günther (DS 2828–29) and I. Froschammer (DS 2853–57). The magisterium also opposes the tendency to pantheism—absolute, essential, or evolutionary—and defends the divine liberty in creation and providence, as well as the infinite difference between the world and God (DS 2841–47, 2901–5).

Affirmation of God

In the context of the religious crisis of secular culture, the magisterium of VATICAN I is relevant. This council rejects, as errors against faith, atheism and pantheism, AGNOSTICISM and Deism, fideism and rationalism (DS 3021–24). It also reasserts the reality and identity of God, together with the essential difference between God and the world, and proclaims its endorsement of a fidelity to the religious language of biblical revelation and Catholic theological tradition (DS 3001–3). Particular importance must be ascribed to the teaching of Vatican I regarding the concrete possibility of an affirmation of God from a point of departure in created reality, by means of the "light of human reason"– as well as, by the "light of faith," from a point of departure in divine revelation (DS 3004–5; cf. 3026–27). In the face of the modern challenge of unbelief and atheism, in function of the first article of faith, the magisterium condemns nihilism and religious indifference, anathematizing theoretical ATHEISM as well as any rejection of Christian monotheism (DS 3021), and positing the legitimacy of an affirmation of God. This condemnation of atheism, and the proposal of a rationally legitimate theism, is not tantamount to the acceptance of a kind of theological rationalism. The magisterium always speaks of a God who is absolute and holy mystery—transcendent and personal, incomprehensible and ineffable— both in the divine reality itself and in its salvific self-communication. Again, an endorsement of a "natural knowledge of God" as a precondition of the act of faith, by contrast with the thesis of fideism, does not entail a rejection of the positive influence of the believing community with its tradition of faith and its cultural piety. Still less does it mean a denial of the relevance of the religious phenomenon, or of the utility of Christian revelation: indeed, in the practical order, these are precisely necessary if the truths that bear on human beings' religious attitude and moral behavior are to be knowable and acceptable "universally, with certitude, and without error" (DS 3032, 3041).

The pontifical magisterium, as well, has asserted the possibility of an affirmation of God. On the occasion of the modernist crisis (→ MODERNISM), Pius X pointed to the way of causality as a path to a demonstrability of the reality of God, thus rejecting a form of piety reduced to an immanentism of subjectivity and an individualism of inner awareness (DS 3538; cf. 3420, 3475–77). Later, taking a position in the debate over the *nouvelle théologie* in the church, Pius XII also proposed the traditional thesis of the concrete possibility of an affirmation of God through the light of reason, so that one arrives at an acceptance of the existence of God as unique and transcendent, absolute and personal, reality (DS 3875; cf. 3892). On the other hand, the assertion of a possible culpability in atheism does not imply exclusion from the activity of a mysterious divine salvific providence in behalf of those who, being inculpably ignorant of God, seek the divine reality in some implicit way (DS 3869–72).

For Vatican II, as well, the theoretical and practical question of the affirmation of God is of the highest importance. On the problem of atheism, there is a significant reference in the Pastoral Constitution on the Church in the Modern World, which cites the gravity of the phenomenon when it involves an explicit denial of the concrete possibility of an affirmation of God. Human beings' loss of an awareness of transcendence deprives them of any avenue to a resolution of the problem. Frequently, of course, rather than denying the "God of the gospel" (*GS* 19), what a so-called atheism actually rejects is a false, distorted caricature of the divine (*GS* 19). The situation of those who seem to have lost the religious concern itself, or who ascribe an unconditional value to the goods of earth, is more serious. At other times, the "atheistic" intent is not so much to deny God as to assert the human being, in a responsible autonomy, with a defense of a legitimate emancipation from any form of oppression, including the experience of religion as heteronomy. Not rarely, the quest for a historical liberation is undertaken against a background of the world alone, with all of one's activity being restricted to the social, economic, and political spheres (*GS* 20). On the other hand, religion must be careful not to afford a pretext for irresponsible alienation from the problems of interhuman justice. But neither may the struggle for human life waged in the immanence of history neglect the profound dimension of a religious concern or an existential openness to transcendence and the God of faith (GS 21).

While the council's teaching alludes to the possibility that atheism be morally culpable, it goes no further into the question. Neither, however, does it fail to recognize the fact that responsibility for the unbelief of atheists may be a shared one: believers themselves may exert a negative influence here, when their comportment is inconsistent with their religious experience (*GS* 19). The question of the possibility of an inculpable atheism, in the theoretical sphere of reflexive consciousness, were atheism to coincide with an ethically upright life, finds an echo in some of the council documents. After all, no one can be regarded as excluded from the reign of God if he or she is living a righteous life, even in the event of a failure to arrive at an explicit theoretical positing of the religious act, since moral rectitude cannot survive in the absence of divine grace, and the elements of truth and justice in such a life constitute an authentic "preparation for the gospel" (LG 16). The teaching of the council also asserts that God can draw to faith, in a mysterious manner, any who are inculpably ignorant of the gospel, in virtue of the divine universal salvific will (AG 7).

It has likewise been the merit of the council to have recognized the validity of religious knowledge, and the authenticity of an experience of the sacred, in the ongoing search for the divine that finds its most meaningful expression in the great world religions, whether in a religious experience of the mystical moment in worship of the divine mystery, or in the experience of a prophetic revelation in the Abrahamic faith. Thereby Vatican II acknowledges the theological value of a religious experience of God as provident creator and merciful parent. In the religious experience, believers wrestle with the ultimate existential questions: being and life, good and evil, suffering and happiness, desire for God and religious fear (NA 1). The council magisterium acknowledges the presence of numerous spiritual, moral, and cultural values in the devotees of the non-Christian religions, who find in these religions a way of purification and ethical refuge, together with the supreme enlightenment of the spirit and a pathway to liberation from human passions and worldly selfishness (NA 2). In the great monotheistic religions, such as ISLAM or JUDAISM, worship is offered to the one God living and true, provident creator of the universe, protector of Abraham and all believers, omnipotent and merciful Lord of a salvation covenant in history, which will culminate in the Christian event (NA 3–4). Particularly significant is the doctrine of Vatican II concerning divine revelation, which propounds the mystery of a God of revelation and faith who, moved by the divine wisdom and goodness, has willed to bestow a self-revelation

and manifest the divine plan of salvation. Thus the council affirms faith in an invisible, merciful God who speaks to human beings, inviting them to a mysterious participation in the divine life and infinite beatitude. The manifestation of the mystery and design of God occurs in the words and deeds of the history of revelation and salvation, which will find their crown in Christ, the mediator and plenitude of eschatological salvific revelation itself (DV 1). The God of creation, through created works, offers an ongoing self-witness. To those who persevere in the practice of good, the God of salvation offers everlasting life. Through the history of the election of and covenant with the people of the promise, the God of revelation has been manifested to humanity, as the one God living and true, benevolent creator of the world and just judge of universal history (DV 2–3). God's revelation has culminated in the manifestation of the eternal Son, the divine Word who became incarnate for our enlightenment and salvation, as well as in the mission of the divine Spirit, that witness of the presence of the grace that delivers us from evil and bestows on us life eternal in consummate communion with infinite love (DV 4). To the Father, revealed in the divine Son Jesus Christ, believers, moved by the light and grace of the Holy Spirit, ought to offer a total, free assent of their understanding and consent of their will (DV 5). A divine self-communication, together with a communication of the reality of a universal salvific will, reveals God's mysterious design. Thus divine revelation actually offers the believer a universal and readily attained, infallible and certain, religious knowledge concerning God as principle and end of the universe, as ground of being and of the meaning of contingent, concrete reality (DV 6).

The documents of Vatican II manifest a doctrinal continuity with the earlier magisterium, reasserting faith in the one God, revealed and mysterious, and preserving the unity and singularity of the monarchy of the living and tender Father almighty, the *principium sine principio* (AG 2) and unoriginated origin of the intradivine life and salvation history alike, utterly different and distinct from the created world, who restores the universe by a redemptive activity in the divine Son Jesus Christ, and definitively sanctifies it by the eschatological gift of the divine Spirit (LG 2–4).

Bibl.: (1) G. AULEN, *Das christliche Gottesbild in Vergangenheit und Gegenwart* (Gütersloh, 1930); R. JOLIVET, *The God of Reason* (New York, 1958); M. MIEGGE, ed., *Religione* (Florence, 1965); G. B. MONDIN, *Il problema del linguaggio teologico dalle origine ad oggi* (Brescia, 1971); W. WEISCHEDEL, *Der Gott der Philosophen I–II* (2nd ed.; Munich, 1979). (2) P. TILLICH, *Systematic Theology*, vol. 1 (Chicago, 1951); H. DE LUBAC, *Sur les chemins de Dieu* (Paris, 1956); J. DANIÉLOU, *God and the Ways of Knowing* (New York, 1957); F. FERRÉ, *Language, Logic and God* (London, 1961); J. C. MURRAY, *The Problem of God Yesterday and Today* (New Haven/London, 1962); I. T. RAMSEY, *Religious Language* (London, 1967); E. SCHILLEBEECKX, *God and Man* (New York, 1969); K. RAHNER, *Foundations of Christian Faith* (New York, 1978); F. A. PASTOR, *La Lógica de lo Inefable* (Rome, 1986). (4) B. BALSCHEIT, *Alter und Aufkommen des Monotheismus in der israelitischen Religion* (Berlin, 1938); K. RAHNER, "Theos in the New Testament," in *Theological Investigations*, vol. 2 (1955; London, 1963), 79–148; W. EICHRODT, *Das Gottesbild des Alten Testaments* (Stuttgart, 1956); J. JEREMIAS, *Abba* (1966; Philadelphia, 1978); J. COPPENS, ed., *La notion biblique de Dieu* (Gembloux/Leuven, 1975). (5) R. AUBERT, *Vatican I* (Paris, 1964); J. GOETZ, "Summi Numinis vel etiam Patris," in *L'Église et les missions* (Rome, 1966), 51–63; K. RAHNER, "On the Importance of the Non-Christian Religions for Salvation," in *Theological Investigations*, vol. 18 (1978; London, 1984), 288–95; B. NEUNHEUSER, "Cum altari adsistitur semper ad Patrem dirigatur oratio: Der Canon 21 des Konzils von Hippo 393: Seine Bedeutung und Nachwirkung," *Augustinianum* 25/1–2 (1985): 105–19; F.-A. PASTOR, "L'homme en quête de Dieu," in R. Latourelle, ed., *Vatican II: Assessment and Perspectives Twenty-five Years After*, 2 vols. (New York, 1989), 2:392–407.

Félix-Alejandro PASTOR

II. PROOFS FOR THE EXISTENCE OF GOD

1. Prefatory Considerations

a. If every human being is responsible before God, then human reason must, in its essential predisposition, have access to knowledge of God. Explicating this "natural knowledge of God" in a philosophically reflective way is the real goal of "proofs of God's existence." The notion of a "proof" of God's existence has its justification in the fact that this natural predisposition is not a matter of mere feeling, but precisely one of reason, and must therefore be discussable with rational stringency. Still, the term "proof" is, in principle, limited here by the fact that knowledge of God is realizable only in freedom and, in that sense, is not demonstrable. On the one hand, an act of human freedom is presupposed, that can also close itself to God. On the other, knowledge of God (like knowledge of a human person) is possible only on the basis of a freedom that opens itself to the knower, and actualization of a "natural predisposition" to knowledge of God thus depends on God's freely disclosing himself (see Anselm *Prosl.* 1).

Beyond these limitations that apply in principle, proofs of God's existence are subject, in various respects, to historically conditioned problems of understanding.

b. Attempts at proof of God's existence can be traced all the way back to the origins of both Western and Eastern philosophy. They were first elaborated with systematic rigor only in contexts where theology recognized philosophy as a discipline relatively independent, at least methodologically, from itself. In the Christian West, that was the case from the beginning of scholasticism (→ REASON/FAITH). During the Age of Enlightenment, proofs of God's existence often subserved an attempt to found—in (sometimes hostile) contrast to the actual, historically established religions—a universal rational religion, and thus they came under suspicion, from the theological side, of being misdirected undertakings. Moreover, as an integral part of a revival of scholastic philosophizing that was supported by Catholic doctrinal office, proofs of God's existence were increasingly perceived, in view of modern thought, as reactionary, and have ever since been regarded less than favorably in both theological and philosophical circles.

c. In addition to these difficulties, conditioned by the history of scientific knowledge, attempts at proof of God's existence also meet with opposition or misunderstanding because of their ultimate groundedness in the intuitively evident. In an age when humans knew themselves to be contained within a cosmos ordered by the divine Logos, proofs of God's existence that were developed on the basis of general experience of the world could expect wide acceptance. The modern subject, however, thrown back upon itself in the face of a universe more readily perceived as threatening, sought increasingly for routes to rational knowledge of God in which the cosmic order no longer functions as a premise. But even those pathways that begin from individual self-experience seem blocked to the extent that the subject has been alienated from itself. The question of the validity of proofs of God's existence is closely bound up with the particular possibilities that show themselves (or that seem excluded) regarding a "first philosophy," i.e., a thinking that experiences itself not just as fragmented or even manipulated, but that is able to articulate itself within the horizon of an all-embracing concept of meaning.

2. Basic Types of Proof of God's Existence

In the following brief survey, only the "classical" proofs of God's existence can be covered, i.e., arguments sufficiently persuasive to have provoked thought on a continuing basis. An initial classification can be made according to the nature of their starting point, which may lie either in experience of the world or in human self-discovery. This classification is also suggested by the train of thought in the first two chapters of the Epistle to the Romans (see Rom 1:19f.; 2:14f.).

Experience of the World as the Starting Point

In his classification of proofs of God's existence, Kant cites two types of argument that begin with our experience of the sensible world, namely, the "physico-theological" and the "cosmological" argument. The first proceeds on the basis of "determinate experience and resultant cognition of the particular nature of our sensible world," while the second rests merely on "indeterminate experience" (see *Kritik der reinen Vernunft* B, 618f.).

For both historical and systematic reasons, it is advisable to follow this classification.

a. The theological, or physico-theological, argument. Kant regarded the "physico-theological" argument as the "oldest, clearest, and most suited to common human reason" (see *Kritik der reinen Vernunft* B, 651). In fact, it can be traced back, in the West, to Socrates (see *HWP* 3:820), and is also widespread in Indian philosophy (see *TRE* 13:751). This kind of proof, which reasons from the meaningful orderedness

("teleological") of nature back to a divine intelligence governing it, occurs in more modest form in Thomas Aquinas (*ST,* 1, q.2, a.3, "fifth way"), where the assumption is only that, in the sensible world, certain beings not endowed with reason always, or at least frequently, behave in goal-pursuing ways. In the Enlightenment, by contrast, the world order as a whole— in analogy to a clockwork—was often taken as the starting point. For the agnostic Hume, and even in Kant's critique, in principle, of all proofs of God's existence that are generated by theoretical-contemplative reason, this argument still enjoyed high esteem; but its cogency vanishes in the context of an evolutionary view of the cosmos.

b. The cosmological argument. The cosmological proof—introduced to the Christian West primarily from Aristotle by way of Islamic and Jewish scholars—has been highly influential, especially through its formulations in Aquinas's first three "ways." Based on (what Kant calls) only "indeterminate" experience of the sensible world, it is, because of this abstractness, not so easy to follow as the teleological argument, yet also seems, by resting on experience of a more general kind, less easily disputable. The central idea is that contingent being requires, for satisfactory explanation of its existence, necessary being. The most logically convincing formulation of this probably occurs in the version that Thomas presents as the "first way" of the *Summa Theologiae*, the "proof from motion": anything that, from a state of being merely potential, arrives at actualization of that potentiality, requires for this an "energy transfer." If this increase results from something that only passes the energy on, rather than deriving it originally from itself, then even the assumption of an infinite series of such mere "handings on" does not answer the initial question about the origin of the added measure of actuality. An adequate answer can come only from assuming that there is a "prime mover" whose pure actuality is bound up with no mere potentiality. But even this kind of reasoned proof cannot have evidential force without presupposing that the nature of motion corresponds, in at least some degree, to how it appears to the senses. In the context of a view of nature in which changes are understood as nothing more than local displacements of energy within an overall quantity of energy that remains constant, the cogency of the proof can hardly still be made intelligible.

Beyond this suggestion of the difficulties that arise in the context of present-day paradigms for explaining nature, the philosophical problems that attach, in principle, to the teleological and cosmological forms of proof must be briefly noted.

c. Fundamental problems regarding proofs of God's existence that start out from experience of the world. If, after starting out from experience of the world, the path of argument is to lead back to God, then the world must be experienced as basically ordered and not devoid of meaning. The perception of even partial breakdowns of meaning for which no finite freedom can be held responsible (*malum physicum*) throws open the theodicy problem, which cannot be answered by means of theoretical reason. Reflection on nature can avoid this problem if it reduces its perspective to the level of the merely quantifiable and excludes the category of meaning (of the "cosmic" in its original sense). With that, however, as noted above, "cosmological" or "teleological" proofs of God's existence also drop from its field of vision. And yet, even after the demise of a metaphysics that proceeds on the assumption of a well-ordered cosmos, one may still be permitted to cite the phenomenon—as stunning on occasion as a bolt of lightning—of natural beauty, which can hardly be fully accommodated within quantifying reflection, and can at least keep alive the *question* about God.

A shortcoming, in principle, of proofs of God's existence that begin with experience of the world is the fact that they usually fail to take into account the perceiving subject itself. Thus, on the one hand, nothing is determined about how much of its experience can actually be traced back to a separate reality confronting it and how much has to be regarded as a projection of its own preunderstanding. On the other, the disclosed God remains, at least initially, within a horizon of being understood as that of objects. Is the rational power that transcends the experienced objects in the direction of their highest cause itself surpassed in this process of transcending? Or must it grasp itself as a last residuum confronting this whole world of objects, together with its highest cause, and ultimately, in fact, as the constitutive source of the "world as such"?

Self-discovery as the Starting Point

a. The ontological argument. Why the proof of God's existence that Kant describes as "ontological" is included among subject-oriented types of argument here needs further explanation. Not all formulations of this proof start out from subjectivity. In the case of an approach that is based, e.g., on the concept of a "supremely perfect" (Descartes) or "supremely real" (Kant) being, God is definitely conceived in an object-oriented way. Only the original form of the argument, as advanced by ANSELM OF CANTERBURY (*Prosl.* 2–4), can be characterized as "subject-oriented," insofar as the notion of "that than which nothing greater can be conceived" (*id quo nihil maius cogitari potest*) speaks of God by way of reflecting on the utmost capabilities of human reason itself. In grasping this notion, thought does not represent God to itself as the "greatest" being (in which case there would be constant temptation to go beyond any concretely imagined example of this "greatest"— more or less as applies in relation to the potentially infinite series of natural numbers in mathematics—yet once again by positing an "n + 1"). Rather, inasmuch as reason (like Dr. Faust in the pact with Mephistopheles) comes to savor fully its own sublimity of transcendence, which can be tied down to no objectively given thing, it catches sight of a wholly other kind of infinitude and transcendence, whose locus does not lie within the realm of thought's projective potentialites. *This* concept of God is not attained (by starting from experienced objects or their qualities) through projection (as for Feuerbach), but can be comprehended only as the ultimate ground of all human projective capacities (see the next section).

Criticism of the "ontological proof" is directed primarily at its move from a mere concept to a conclusion about real existence: something that exists is "greater" than something merely conceived; hence the notion "than which nothing greater" includes the existence of what is conceived; for otherwise it has not been conceived in its fullness. Kant (similarly to Anselm's contemporary, Gaunilo and, more recently, Frege,

Scholz, and Russell) objected that attribution of existence moves on a totally different plane from that of conceptual predication, and thus cannot be inferred through conceptual analysis. The limitation of this criticism lies in its universalization of a logic derived from *contingent* objects (see Hegel's dissatisfaction with Kant's example of the "hundred thalers"). Anselm claims persuasiveness for his conclusion solely in relation to his concept of *God*—and as regards at least the *conceptual* act of the "I think," Kant admits that the *factuality* of this "I" is simultaneously evident (see *Kritik der reinen Vernunft* B, 157). One will have to concede to Anselm that God's existence is, in the act of thinking the concept formulated by him, also *necessarily thought* (see *Prosl.* 3). Here, however, it is not clear why this conceptual necessity should be paralleled by a corresponding actuality. This shortcoming is overcome only with the transcendental-logical argument.

b. The transcendental-logical arguments. In the notion of a "transcendental-logical proof" of God's existence, several forms of argument are summarized that have otherwise been given quite varied names (e.g., "noetic," "noological," "ideological," "anthropological," or "transcendental" proofs). The original form of the argument is found in Augustine (see especially *De lib. arb.* 2.3–15).

Augustine takes as his starting point the certainty, as secured by the process of methodological doubt, of one's own conscious being (*si fallor, sum*). This self-conscious reason recognizes itself as superior to its sense-perceptions and the "internal sense" that coordinates them because it *judges over* all this. The question of whether there might be something that is higher still and, in contrast to human reason, immutable leads to the question of what judges over reason itself. In this—or in "something" placed "above and beyond this"—one would have to recognize God, *quo nullus est superior* ("than whom none is greater"). Such an immutable and universally valid actuality, to whose judgment reason is subject, Augustine sees as constituted by "number and wisdom." For him, "number" is the supreme standard of value in the realm of the aesthetic, just as "wisdom" provides the criterion in the realm of the search for happiness.

A more developed form of this type of argu-

ment was presented by Descartes (*Med.* 3). Also starting out from the basis of the intuitive evidence, unshakable by all doubt, of the "I think/I am," Descartes seeks a specific content for this thought that can be traced back to nothing other than God. Among all the contents of thought, the idea of God alone fulfills this condition. It cannot have entered reason in an a posteriori way, nor can it be attained through negation of the finite. Rather, the concept of the "finite" presupposes, transcendental-logically, the concept of the infinite, just as, too, universal doubt itself—the starting point for the "Meditations on First Philosophy"—has this idea of the unconditioned as the condition of its possibility.

The fascinating element in this type of argument consists in its indissoluble combining of the concept of God with certainty of existence, which is not present in the "ontological" proof: reason recognizes itself, even in its seemingly—in relation to truth—most eccentric kinds of act, as stamped in its innermost core by an unconditioned being.

However, even in this case, one can speak of a real proof of God's existence only with qualifications. For the theodicy problem, which cannot be avoided when starting out from experience of the world, is only apparently overcome by the bracketing of all empirical sources of uncertainty in methodological doubt. In reality, the "transcendental-logical" proof represents merely the most stringent formulation of the situation of the absurd (in A. Camus's sense): the inescapable determinedness of Sisyphus by the idea of something unconditioned that nevertheless appears unrealizable. Regardless of whether this idea must necessarily be traceable back to "God," it would still be "better for God if he did not exist," as long as Sisyphus is incapable of glimpsing any meaning in such a "curse of God." Nonetheless, the human self-discovery that is effected by the transcendental-logical argument keeps alive, more intensely than does experience of the world, the question about a possible meaning despite the situation of the absurd, and thus about "that than which nothing greater can be conceived."

c. The moral proof of God's existence. Kant regarded the physico-theological, cosmological, and ontological arguments as exhausting the list of proofs of God's existence that were achievable (although not with strict cogency) by theoretical reason. He did not entertain the possibility of a transcendental-logical proof, even though, given the question of whence something like the idea of God derives its nature as *regulative* for all rational practice (cf. *Kritik der reinen Vernunft* B, 380, 384–86), this might have suggested itself.

On the basis of ethico-practical reason, however, Kant developed an independent argument that he himself described as a "moral proof" (*Kritik der Urteilskraft* § 87). This argument occurs in various formulations, among which only the last one (in the *Kritik der Urteilskraft* [Critique of Judgment]) is convincing.

An initial precondition for recognizing the necessity of this "postulate of God's existence" is the intuitive self-evidence of an absolute "ought"—under whose obligatory force individual reason, through "pure practical reason" (and not, e.g., through God as a heteronomous lawgiver), knows itself to lie. This absolute "ought" requires, however, not only an appropriate mental disposition but also a realization in the sensible world. Complete structuring of the sensible world according to the moral law that is obligatory upon all human beings is the final goal of pure practical reason.

Now, the sensible world nevertheless obeys its own natural law, and thus the course of things appears to conform but rarely to the laws of practical reason. If, therefore, humanity's obligation to further the final goal is not to be meaningless—because this "ought" is not matched, in principle, by a potential for realization—then humans must postulate God, as the guarantor of the nevertheless ultimately possible harmony between the law of freedom and the law of nature, and as the ultimate source of both kinds of lawfulness. Structurally similar to Kant's moral proof are present-day attempts, starting out from the notion of universal solidarity, to conceive God as the ultimate horizon of that idea—for instance, in the communications-theoretical approach of H. Peukert's fundamental theology.

The foundation of the moral proof of God's existence is not some indubitable certainty, but rather, a fact of unconditionally committed freedom. What the argument seems, in this sense, to lose by way of "being a proof" it gains,

in turn, with respect to the observation made above (see "Prefatory Considerations"): that true knowledge of God is realizable only in freedom.

On the basis of the argument developed by Kant, a philosophical answer can be given to the theodicy problem. According to it, God enters the human field of vision to the very extent that humans become committed to one another in unconditional solidarity, and do not break off this commitment in view of the apparent senselessness of existence that yawns before them in the sufferings of innocent victims. This endured solidarity in the face of incomprehensible annihilation is like the signature on an uncovered check that only God can cash.

Bibl.: Detailed analysis and bibliographical references in: D. Schlüter, "Gottesbeweis," in *HWP* 3:818–30; J. Clayton, "Gottesbeweise" II–III, in *TRE* 13:724–84. (1) K. Kienzler, *Glauben und Denken bei Anselm von Canterbury* (Freiburg, 1981); H. Verweyen, *Nach Gott fragen: Anselms Gottesbegriff als Anleitung* (Essen, 1978); J. Rohls, *Theologie und Metaphysik: Der ontologische Gottesbeweis und seine Kritiker* (Gütersloh, 1987). (2) F. Alquié, *La découverte métaphysique de l'homme chez Descartes* (Paris, 1950); W. M. Neumann, *Die Stellung des Gottesbeweises in Augustins De libero arbitrio* (Hildesheim, 1986). M. Albrecht, *Kants Antinomie der praktischen Vernunft* (Hildesheim/New York, 1978); H. Huber, "Die Gottesidee bei Immanuel Kant," *TP* 55 (1980): 1–43, 230–49; A. Winter, "Der Gotteserweis aus praktischer Vernunft: Das Argument Kants und seine Tragfahigkeit vor dem Hintergrund der Vernunftkritik" in K. Kremer, ed., *Um Möglichkeit oder Unmöglichkeit natürlicher Gotteserkenntnis heute* (Leiden, 1985), 109–78; H. Verweyen, "Kants Gottespostulat und das Problem sinnlosen Leidens," *TP* 62 (1987): 580–87; H. Peukert, *Wissenschaftstheorie Handlungstheorie Fundamentale Theologie* (Frankfurt, 1987); H. Verweyen, *Gottes Letztes Wort* (Düsseldorf, 1991).

Hansjürgen Verweyen

GOSPEL

I. Gospel as Literary Genre. *1. From Oral Gospel to the Gospel of Mark. 2. Characteristics of the Literary Genre "Gospel."*

II. Methods of Analysis. *1. Form Criticism. 2. Redaction Criticism.*

I. GOSPEL AS LITERARY GENRE

The literary genre known as gospel is a creation of Christianity. The Gospels are unique, just as is the event with which they are concerned.

1. From Oral Gospel to the Gospel of Mark

"Gospel" is a very ancient word in the church. Paul uses it without feeling obliged to explain it (1 Thes 1:5; 2:4; Gal 2:5, 14; 1 Cor 4:15; Rom 10:16). The word is taken, it seems, from the OT, where it is connected with the messenger or herald who proclaims the kingship of Yahweh and who by his effective proclamation inaugurates the messianic age. In the key passage, Is 52:7, the "bringer of good news," the messenger of joy, announces that with Cyrus's liberation of the captives in Babylon, the age of salvation has begun. Psalm 96 echoes this good news: "Tell [the good news] of his salvation from day to day. . . . Say among the nations, 'The LORD is king'" (vv. 2, 10). The entrance of all the nations into the history of salvation already places us in the NT setting.

In the NT it is Jesus who comes on the scene as messenger of the messianic good news (Mt 11:5; Is 35:5–6; 61:1). The time of salvation becomes a reality in him, as do the signs accompanying it. The essential content of this good news is the imminent coming of the kingdom, whose requirements Jesus proclaims: "Repent, for the kingdom of heaven has come near" (Mt 4:17). In addition, the announced kingdom begins with him. Where Jesus is, hostile forces fall back, and the life-giving and saving power proclaimed by the prophets is at work. Healings and exorcisms show that the reign of Satan is collapsing and that the reign of God is at work (Lk 7:22; Mt 12:28).

All this makes understandable the shift in meaning that can be seen in the language of the NT. Jesus is presented not only as the messenger of the good news but also as the one of whom the message is speaking. He proclaims the kingdom, but in the final analysis the proclamation is concerned with Jesus himself, who is established as messianic king by his resurrection and exaltation to the Father's right hand; it is he who saves. This outlook is even clearer in the language of Christians, who look upon the death and resurrection of Christ as the heart of the gospel.

"Gospel," one of the most frequently used words in Paul, appears sixty times in his letters. To proclaim the gospel is equivalent for Paul to proclaiming Christ and especially his death and resurrection, which mark the advent of eschatological salvation. To Paul, then, can be attributed, if not the introduction of the word "gospel" into the NT, at least its widespread use to describe the church's active preaching of the message of salvation.

When Mark introduces the word into the Synoptic tradition, he does not contradict Paul's use of it but rather comments on it and broadens it. It is not possible today to speak of the literary genre called "gospel" without referring first of all to Mark, for it is he who created the genre, even if he does not yet use the word to mean the written gospel. He did, however, conceive of his written work in so close a connection with the event and proclamation of salvation that the title "gospel" is justified for his book.

In Mark's view the gospel is still more an event than a message. This event includes the entire existence of Christ, but in comparison with the culminating moments of his life, namely, the passion and resurrection, everything else is only a beginning. This explains the words that serve as a quasi-title for his work: "The beginning of the good news of Jesus Christ" (Mk 1:1). It is through the ministry of John the Baptist and through the baptism and preaching of Jesus that the salvation foretold by the prophets begins to be a reality. Mark, writing from his present moment in the church, wants to go back to the beginning (archē) of a story, that is, to the first manifestations of the decisive action of God in this world. In his conception of the gospel, then, Mark differs from Paul, who thinks primarily of the passion and resurrection of Christ; for Mark the entire existence of Jesus, from baptism to resurrection, is a gospel.

By thus linking his work so closely to the *entire* event that is the life of Christ and to the good news of salvation, Mark made it easier to pass from oral gospel to written gospel. He was, as it were, the catalyst that facilitated the passage. Mark's work became the prototype for the gospel genre. Matthew, Luke, and John later made Mark's literary format their own, even if they never described their own works as gospels. It was only in the course of the second century that the word "gospel" came to designate our present canonical writings. Justin speaks of the "memoirs of the apostles," which "are called gospels" (*Apologia* 1.63.3; *EP* 129). The Muratorian Canon describes the Gospel of Luke as "third book of the gospel" (*tertius evangelii liber*) and the Gospel of John as "fourth gospel" (*quartum evangelium*) (*EP* 268). The present titles of the four Gospels date from the third century. Even when "gospel" came to refer primarily to the written gospel, the church always remained aware that the word refers first of all to the content of the works, namely, the proclamation of salvation in Jesus Christ, and that in the final analysis there can be only one gospel; Irenaeus thus speaks of the "fourfold gospel" (*Adv. Haereses* 2.2.7–8; *EP* 215).

2. Characteristics of the Literary Genre "Gospel"

The Gospels cannot be put into any of the literary categories known to antiquity: large-scale history (as practiced by Polybius, Thucydides, or Livy), Greek biography, "memoirs" such as Xenophon wrote about Socrates, or literary portraits. Within the NT itself the Gospels are unique. The other writings make it clear that they do not lack information about the life of Christ, but their attention is focused essentially on the event of the cross and resurrection. The remainder of Christ's activity is hardly mentioned. The Gospels alone display an obvious interest in his earthly activity. The compilers of the Gospels, however, are not writers working in a studio, using archival documents and intent on writing a life of Jesus from birth to death. We do not find in the Gospels any lengthy treatment of the origin of Jesus or of his education, character, or personality. We find no precise chronology or topography, though these are fundamental co-ordinates in historical writing. Information on place and time remains vague and general, with phrases such as "then; at that time; afterward; in the house; on the lake; as they were journeying; on the mountain." The whole of the tradition about Jesus is structured with the aid of an elementary framework and stereotyped connectives. How, then, are we to characterize a genre that evidently locates itself within history but at the same time ignores history to an often disconcerting degree? We can only describe each of its traits and allow a picture to emerge from the description.

a. The Gospels are the proclamation of a news that is utterly unique and original (an *Ur-Kunde*) because its object is the most important event of human history, namely, the decisive intervention of God in Jesus Christ. The manifestation of Christ among human beings is a historically unique "beginning" (an *archē*) because in and through him the salvation promised and awaited for centuries has become a reality. The fullness of time is "now," "today." Consequently, the gospel cannot be a neutral proclamation but is a call to radical decision. All human beings are called to conversion. All who wish to read the Gospels in the proper way must allow themselves to hear this stupendous call that makes salvation known in Jesus. Peter's hearers on Pentecost felt the impact of this call and "welcomed his message" (Acts 2:41).

b. The Gospels *tie in with a tradition* already formed, which in turn was a *rereading*, in the Spirit, of the Jesus-event (seen in the light of Easter), of the OT, and of the newborn church's experience. This dependence on a tradition can be seen in the fact that the Gospels introduce into the narrative framework already-existing units or series of units. Thus, before being works composed as such, the Gospels are witnesses to a literature that they collect, organize, and approve. It is also to be noted that this living tradition had been taken and frozen, as it were, at different stages of its development before being at last introduced into the work of the final editor. The evangelists report a tradition that has undergone the influence of several theologies; the latter have not been completely eliminated from the final redaction. The evangelists in their turn *rewrite*, each from his own perspective, what they have received from earlier traditions and theologies, for they are aware that they must proclaim the good news of salvation to men and women in a particular setting and that they must respond to the problems of these readers.

c. The *framework* of the Gospels, which is the same in all four, owes its *structure* and *basic themes* to the primitive kerygma, which it is possible to reconstruct from the letters of Paul (1 Cor 15:3–5; 11:23–27; Rom 1:1–4) and the sermons in Acts (Acts 2:22–36; 3:12–26; 4:8–12; 5:29–32; 10:34–43; 13:16–41). The Gospels develop and expand this traditional outline, whose main elements are the following: the time for the fulfillment of the promises has come; Jesus is of the family of David; after the preaching of the Baptist, Jesus began his own ministry in Galilee, where he healed the sick and liberated all who had fallen into the power of Satan; he then went up to Jerusalem, where he suffered and was crucified; he was raised from the dead and appeared to many witnesses; he is now exalted; all human beings are called to repentance and conversion. Mark sticks to this framework, which had now become obligatory, while taking the passion and resurrection as the basis from which to work back.

d. The proclamation of salvation takes the form of a *historical narrative.* Since the Gospels are first of all a "proclamation" of salvation, we must not think of them as being lives of Jesus. The proclamation, however, does take the form of a historical account because the salvation proclaimed is an event connected with an earthly, historical life. A description of this life as it unfolds will at the same time be a proclamation of the saving event. Mark is the first thus to set forth the good news within a simplified framework of the life of Jesus. He does so not out of mere love for the past but out of respect for the real situation. For in fact it is not to just any Christ in glory that we cling by faith but to a Christ who was glorified because he accepted the self-emptying of his earthly life with its lowliness and suffering. In Mark, the historical movement of Jesus' life, which is focused on his death and resurrection, is presented in only an outline form, with a single journey to Jerusalem before the passion and a fourfold division that retains only the major turning points of the life. Mark not only adopts a narrative form for events that he describes in

the past or the historical present; he also makes a clear distinction between periods of time. It is for the *present* church that he describes the history of salvation in its beginnings (preaching of the Baptist, baptism and preaching of Jesus), its progress in Galilee and neighboring regions, and its tragic end (account of the passion, with events put in a more careful chronological order). Furthermore, the activity of Christ as Son of Man embraces future, present, and past. The Son of Man, who will be condemned before the Sanhedrin, is one who even now has the authority to forgive sins (Mk 2:10) and who will come some day on the clouds of heaven. Past, present, and future flow into each other but remain distinct.

In Luke, this historical perspective emerges even more clearly, because the history of Jesus is extended backward, in the infancy stories, and forward, in the history of the apostles. The history of salvation is marked by a historically verifiable continuity and by an unfolding in which Christ is the center. Jesus and the church both pass through stages. Luke thus becomes the first historian of Christianity as he endeavors to narrate and define the major periods of the history of salvation.

e. The Gospels are at once *narrative* and *confession*: narrative of Jesus and testimony of the community that believes in him. Furthermore, narrative and testimony are so thoroughly interwoven that the narrative becomes a confession and the testimony of faith takes the form of narrative or account of Jesus, just as in the OT "creeds," which take the form of a concise account of God's saving acts (Dt 6:20–24; 26:5–9; Jos 24:2–13). There is nothing like this in secular literature. The basic reason for this combination of narrative and testimony is that in the eyes of the narrator-witness (the evangelist), the risen Lord, living and always present, is identical with Jesus of Nazareth, who saved us by his life and death. To tell his story is to confess him, to affirm that "Jesus is Lord." It is because the Gospels are concerned with the historical person of Jesus, who is Christ and Lord, that they are at once history and kerygma.

f. Since the Gospels are the proclamation of salvation in Jesus Christ to groups of human beings who are geographically and culturally distinct, they have an element of *actualization* and *dialogue.* Each Gospel is geared to a particular community and a concrete situation: the Jerusalem community, the Antioch community, Greek communities, communities in Asia and Rome. The Gospels record the dialogue of the church with the human beings and problems of these communities. Thus the Gospel of Matthew, which was composed in Syria during the eighties, is responding to the questions of a Jewish-Christian community that is defining itself in relation to the synagogue, which at that time was in a process of complete reorganization after the disaster of the year 70. The evangelist answers these questions in reliance on a tradition that draws its authority from Jesus himself and especially from his message. Thus the dialogue of Jesus with the Jews of his time is carried on by the church with new interlocutors and new groups of people; the various Gospels are, as it were, four voices in this polyphonic dialogue. We cannot read the Gospels properly if we abstract from this element of actualization.

Since the Gospels deliberately adopt the narrative form proper to history in order to describe the earthly activity of Jesus of Nazareth, it follows that the literary genre "gospel" is subject to the conditions imposed by history and the questions that are to be asked of history. When the Gospels recognize historicity as a dimension of salvation in Jesus Christ, they submit themselves to the criteria of historical study.

Bibl.: G. FRIEDRICH, "'Εὐαγγελίζομαι, εὐαγγέλιον," *TDNT* 2:707–37; L. VAGANAY, "Évangile," *Cath* 4:767–69; L. F. HARTMAN, "Gospel," *NCE* 6:635–36; D. DEELS, "The Holy Gospels," *NCE* 6:636–40; J. A. EVAN DODEWAARD, "Jésus s'est-il servi lui-même du mot Évangile?" *Bib* 35 (1954): 160–73; B. BLAESER, "Évangile," in H. FRIES, ed., *Encyclopédie de la foi,* vol. 2 (Paris, 1965), 87–95; J. LAMBRECHT, "Qu'est-ce qu'un Évangile?" *Revue du Clergé africain* 22 (1967): 6–14; A. VÖGTLE, "Formazione e Struttura dei Vangeli," in var., *Discussione sulla Biblia* (Brescia, 1967), 82–123; F. MUSSNER, "Évangile et Centre de l'Évangile," in var., *Le message de Jésus et l'interprétation moderne* (Paris, 1969), 151–76; A. GABOURY, *La structure des Évangiles synoptiques: La structure-type à l'origine des Évangiles* (Leiden, 1970); N. PERRIN, "The Literary Gattung Gospel," *Expository Times* 82 (Oct. 1970): 4–7; R. SCHNACKENBURG, "Das Evangelium im Verständnis des ältesten Evangelisten," in K. HOFFMANN, ed., *Orientierung an Jesus* (Freiburg/Basel/

Vienna, 1973), 309–23; R. LATOURELLE, *Finding Jesus through the Gospels* (New York, 1979), 97–129.

René LATOURELLE

II. METHODS OF ANALYSIS: (FORM CRITICISM AND REDACTION CRITICISM)

When it comes to the written sources used by the evangelists, no explanation has as yet succeeded in definitively replacing the two-source theory. According to this theory Matthew and Luke depend on Mark for their narrative elements and on the *Quelle* (source) for the words of Jesus; this latter source has been reconstructed on the basis of the sayings (logia) common to Matthew and Luke. The theory obviously does not explain all the material in the Synoptic Gospels, but none of the theories offered in resolution of the problem has managed to win full adherence. P. Vielhauer claims, rightly or wrongly, that having produced the two-source theory, source criticism (*Quellenkritik*) has completed its work and must pass the baton to form criticism (*Formgeschichte*) or find itself in an impasse.

1. Form Criticism

The form criticism school and its leaders (K. L. Schmidt, M. Dibelius, R. Bultmann, G. Bertram, A. Albertz) represent the most important attempt by modern criticism to break the "steel bands" that kept it a prisoner of the written sources and to follow the stream of tradition back to its origin in the preached gospel.

For, before being written down, the gospel was preached, actualized, and applied to the various situations in which the church found itself. It had a full life there, and a whole tradition of interpretation developed around it. The merit of the form criticism school has been precisely to study this first stage in the history of the gospel tradition. The school came into being between 1919 and 1922 and dominated criticism until the more recent works on tradition or transmission history by H. Conzelmann (*The Theology of St. Luke* [1954; New York,

1960]) and W. Marxsen (*Mark the Evangelist* [1956; Nashville, Tenn., 1969]).

At first glance, form criticism seems to be a *literary* undertaking. It identifies, describes, and classifies the literary forms used in telling the gospel stories. It goes on, however, to bridge the gap between the literary forms and the social settings that produced them; it asks what particular situations in the ecclesial community could have produced, developed, and transmitted a particular story. It is concerned with the genesis, formation, and development of oral traditions before they were written down. It inquires into the laws that governed this development. In broader terms, it can be said that after having studied the horizontal dimension of the gospel (its breakdown into literary units), form criticism descends to the deepest and oldest levels of the tradition in order to travel the road leading back from evangelist to church and then from church to Jesus. In the last analysis, then, the aim of form criticism is by its nature *historical*. Its ambition is to reconstruct the entire history of the gospel tradition from oral gospel to written gospel. In the first phase, its method is literary, but its ultimate aim is historical. The principle underlying the work of the form criticism school is that the primitive community was responsibile for the entire process of gospel transmission.

To put it very briefly, form criticism seeks to write the prehistory of the Gospels. This ambition provides the title of R. Bultmann's work *Die Geschichte der synoptischen Tradition* (3rd ed.; Göttingen, 1957; Eng. trans., *The History of the Synoptic Tradition* [Oxford, 1963]) or Vincent Taylor's *Formation of the Gospel Tradition* (London, 1935). The form-critical undertaking has been accurately compared to that of geology, which studies the successive forms of the earth's crust; or to morphological linguistics, which retraces the forms a word has taken down through the centuries; or, again, to modern analytical procedures that make it possible to take a painting and ascertain the successive forms the artist gave to the work, starting with the initial sketches. In an analogous way, form criticism seeks to ascertain the earliest forms of the tradition as well as its successive states during the years preceding the writing of our Gospels.

If the enterprise has ended in a degree of historical skepticism, or, in the case of Bultmann, even in a radically negative judgment, regarding the possibility of reaching Jesus through the Gospels, this is due less to the method itself than to the principles that guided its representatives—i.e., the sociological principle of the creative community; the rationalist principle that rejected the hypothesis of a divine intervention in history in the form of incarnation, miracles, and resurrection; and the theological principle that if faith is to ensure a vertical relationship with God, it must detach itself from history. Sixty-five years' distance (1925 to 1990) has made it possible for us to pass an accurate judgment on the contribution made by form criticism and to retain those elements that can be taken over and that are located primarily at the literary level. Among these positive elements the following may be noted:

a. Paradoxically, form criticism highlights the full importance of the oral tradition. The gospel was preached before it became Scripture. For a period of twenty-five to thirty years the material of the Gospels was preached in the early church; it was used in missionary work, catechesis, worship, and polemics. It follows that the material was colored by the whole life of the church and that it bears the marks of actualization and theological interpretation by that community. This influence of the tradition at the heart of the Gospels—as conceived by form criticism in reaction against *Quellenkritik*—was something new in the world of Protestant thought.

b. At all times and in all literatures people have had a more or less confused sense of the diversity of literary genres. A speech for the defense, a drama, a lyric poem, a legal document, and a chapter of Titus Livy all call for different kinds of commentary. The novelty of form criticism is to apply the principle of literary genres not only to the Gospels as complete documents but also to the smaller units that make them up. The ambition of form criticism is to draw up a complete list of the genres and subgenres to be found in our Gospels. Within the narrative material, for example, this school of thought distinguishes paradigms (Dibelius) or apophthegms (Bultmann), summaries, miracle stories, legends, myths, and the passion story. Within the doctrinal material, it recognizes allegories, parables, statements that are sapiential, polemical (controversial), prophetic, or apocalyptic in nature, as well as disciplinary norms, rules for living, and sayings in which Jesus speaks of himself (*Ich-Worte*). These various types can be subdivided. The sapiential genre, for example, comprises exhortations, explanations, proverbs, and apologues.

In this spate of literary genres with its types and subtypes, the focus of attention in form criticism is less on the stylistic elements, which display literary virtuosity, than on the elements that reveal a *real life setting*. In other words, the school is interested less in the literary imprint of the author on the material (the redactional aspect of his work) than in the imprint of the social and religious setting on the author. The school's concern is less with the personal contribution of the author than with the socioreligious influence of the community, which forces the author to one literary form rather than another. We are faced, then, with a new kind of literary analysis. Form criticism sees that our Gospels obviously have a molecular form; i.e., they resemble a mosaic of passages, each of which in turn displays a characteristic literary form. The aspect of a Gospel that interests form criticism is less the existence or absence of sources than the observable literary structure, along with the socioreligious setting that could have given rise to this structure.

c. A further positive trait of form criticism is that by analyzing forms, critics endeavor to gain knowledge of the life of the primitive church, which form criticism pictures as a living organism. It is the conviction of the form critics that each style or each *typical* literary form reflects a real life setting, a socioreligious context, a particular *Sitz im Leben*. If indeed the milieu or setting imposes a certain literary form, it follows that knowledge of the forms will lead with certainty to knowledge of the corresponding setting. There is an interaction, a continual interplay, of text and setting.

The literary types brought to light by form criticism connect us with settings that can be briefly listed. (1) In dealing with those outside, i.e., pagans and diaspora Jews, the church adopted the style of *missionary preaching*, or kerygmatic style: a broad proclamation of salvation, focused on the event of the death and resurrection of Jesus. (2) When dealing with converts, it was appropriate, in addition to stressing the essentials of kerygmatic preaching as formulated in the first creeds, to exhort them to a fully moral life: this was *parenesis*. The *liturgy*, with the breaking of bread as its center, included the narrative of the death and resurrection of Christ, as well as hymns to Christ the Savior. In the setting of a group of converts, *catechesis* focused on the teachings of Jesus as well as on the more important mysteries of his life, while in a *polemical* setting, the stories of controversies brought out the answers Jesus gave to his adversaries.

At the level of method, then, by analyzing literary forms, form criticism leads to a knowledge of real life settings and of the functions or activities of the primitive church. This undertaking is completely justifiable, although it is also not without its risks, for by using the analysis of forms to gain historical knowledge, the school makes a difficult move from literary criticism to historical criticism.

The fact remains, however, that at the literary level form criticism has made the most significant contribution to modern exegesis. It has developed a finely tuned and penetrating analytic tool. Through internal criticism it has succeeded in throwing light on the multiform activity of the church as a living community, with its internal life and its difficulties in dealing with the world.

2. Redaction Criticism

Absorbed as they were in a detailed analysis of the primary units making up the Gospels, Dibelius and Bultmann said relatively little about the final redaction. Form criticism reduces to a minimum the role of the redactors, treating them as rather naïve compilers (*Sammler*) who have, more or less skillfully, collected various elements of the tradition. Happily, the pendulum movement that criticism has shown during the last two centuries of its history has now led critics to pay more attention to the evangelists as authors. For over forty years now they have been investigating the contribution of the evangelists. In fact, as a result of emphasizing the theological concerns and redactional activity of the evangelists, the critics have even come to suspect their fidelity to Jesus. First, form criticism made the primitive church hide Jesus from us; now the evangelists supposedly do the same. Form criticism stripped the evangelists of any initiative; redaction criticism, on the contrary, makes their initiative and freedom its entire focus. One thing is certain: redaction criticism takes over from form criticism in investigating the history of the gospel tradition. It marks the second stage in a process in which, from the historian's point of view, form criticism was simply the first stage.

After the Second World War three important works established redaction criticism as a method and as a stage in the history of exegesis: *Die Mitte der Zeit,* by H. Conzelmann (Tübingen, 1954; Eng. trans., *The Theology of St. Luke* [New York, 1960]), *Der Evangelist Markus,* by W. Marxsen (Göttingen, 1956; Eng. trans., *Mark the Evangelist* [Nashville, Tenn., 1969]), and *Das wahre Israel,* by W. Trilling (Munich, 1964).

Redaction criticism sets itself the task of studying the particular organization and character of each of the Gospels, including the author's theological approach, his structuring of the material he has chosen, and his stylistic impress on the material. The Instruction of the Biblical Commission of 1964 and then the Constitution *Dei Verbum* of Vatican II (no. 19) of 1965 describe the essential aspects of the evangelists' work: the gospel writers *choose* from among the materials provided by the tradition, they *synthesize* and they *adapt* their Gospels to the needs of the churches.

a. The materials for the Gospels are not invented but found, already existent, in written or oral form. From among these materials the evangelists make a choice, leaving aside some stories or sayings. That a selection has been made is clearly attested in both the first and the second conclusions of the Gospel of John (20:30; 21:25). It is no less clear in the Gospel of Mark, especially in the narrative section, which reports only two discourses: the parables (chap. 4) and the eschatological discourse (chap. 13). Luke omits some of Mark's stories, e.g., the second multiplication of loaves. The omission of certain materials is no less revealing than the retention of others.

b. The material retained by the evangelists is organized in a way that expresses their point of view. Typical in this respect is the use made by Matthew and Luke of their main sources, namely, Mark and the *Quelle.* Matthew organizes his Gospel into five groups of deeds and words, so as to symbolize the new Pentateuch that the new Moses gives to the new Israel. The Sermon on the Mount is a synthesis, partly redactional, of the logia uttered by Jesus in varying circumstances. Taken together, this discourse (chaps. 5–7) and the following cycle of miracles (chaps. 8–9) form a synthesis intended to show Jesus as the legislator and miracle worker of the messianic age. This large collection is included between two summaries (Mt 4:23; 9:35) that sum up the twofold activity of Jesus: work and word. Luke, for his part, respects the traditional four-part structure of the ministry of Jesus (preaching of the Baptist, Galilee, journey to Jerusalem, Jerusalem), but he introduces two sections into this framework; the longer of these (Lk 9:51–18:14), which is inserted into the journey to Jerusalem, signifies that Jerusalem is the center of Christ's sacrifice and victory but also, undoubtedly, that Christian life consists in following Jesus in suffering in order to enter with him into glory.

c. Finally, in their redactions the evangelists take into account the different conditions and situations of their readers. Matthew writes for Jewish Christians, while Luke addresses Gentiles. As a result, each Gospel takes a different direction.

In order to appreciate the real extent of the redactional activity of the evangelists, a detailed list of the various kinds of redactional activity is needed. Here are the main types: (1) *Stylistic adjustments:* e.g., use of the aorist tense instead of the historical present (in the story of the calming of the sea); subordination of clauses instead of their juxtaposition. (2) *Clarifications:* to help the reader, an evangelist will sometimes add to his source text a word that clarifies. (3) *Omissions:* e.g., in the story of the healing of the leper, Matthew and Luke omit Mark's words: "After sternly warning him he sent him away at once" (Mk 1:43); they probably thought this too harsh sounding for their readers. (4) *Adaptation of a metaphor:* in the parable of the house built on rock or on sand (Mt 7:24–27), Matthew has in mind a Palestinian kind of house, while Luke is evidently thinking of a Greek house (Lk 6:47–49). (5) *Transposition of pericopes:* Luke combines in a single story (Lk 3:1–20) two events in the life of the Baptist that are separated in the Gospel of Mark: his preaching (Mk 1:1–8) and his imprisonment (Mk 6:17–29). (6) *Transposition within a single pericope:* in the story of the threefold temptation of Jesus in the wilderness, the second temptation in Matthew becomes the third in Luke. (7) *Reduction of two stages in a story to a single stage:* in the story of the raising of Jairus's daughter, Matthew does not mention the delegation of servants but restricts himself to the announcement of the little girl's death (Mt 9:18; Mk 5:35). (8) *Addition of a "nomadic" logion:* thus the verse "The last will be first, and the first will be last" (Mt 20:16) is found again in Mt 19:30 in connection with the rich young man, in Mk 10:31 in connection with the reward promised to detachment, and in Lk 13:30 in connection with the narrow door that gives entrance to the kingdom of heaven. This "nomadic" saying serves as an interpretive key in different situations, for it admirably illustrates the change of perspective and mentality brought about by the gospel. (9) *Addition of a story from another tradition:* e.g., in his story of Jesus' trial before Pilate (Mt 27:15–26), Matthew adds a verse (27:19) on the dream of Pilate's wife; in all probability, this detail comes from a different source. (10) *Abbreviation of the source document:* Luke and Matthew often shorten Mark in the narrative sections. Matthew in particular keeps only the essentials of miracle stories, to such a degree that his text often acquires a linear and hieratic character. His concern is with catechesis, even when he is telling a story. (11) *Use of hook words (mots-crochets):* this device, frequently used in rabbinic literature, is also found in the gospel tradition; e.g., in Mt 6:5–13, the phrase "when you pray" is used in order to bring the Our Father into the Sermon on the Mount. (12) While Mark is often content simply to juxtapose pericopes, Luke and Matthew take pains to *interconnect* them. These connectives—e.g., "then," "at that time," "afterward"—often have a purely literary value. (13) *Summaries:* these serve as transitions but are also recapitulations that describe an aspect of the life of Jesus. Since they are compositions of the evangelist, they are very important for knowledge of his theology; thus Mt 4:23 and 9:35 present Jesus as the prophet and wonder-worker of the messianic age. (14) *Geographic information,* which sometimes has biographical value: Nazareth, Caesarea Philippi, Nain, Emmaus, Jericho. Often, too, it has a theological value; thus, for Luke, Jerusalem is both the geographic and the mystical center of the history of salvation. (15) *References to the OT:* the evangelists see Christ as fulfilling the OT. This sense of fulfillment, which is very keen in Matthew, who is writing for Jewish Christians, is shown explicitly in a formula that recurs like a leitmotiv: "to fulfill what had been said by the prophet" (Mt 1:22; 2:5, 15, 17; 3:3; 4:14–16; 8:17; 12:7, 17; 13:35; 21:4; 27:9). (16) *Theological interpretation of the tradition:* e.g., Mark gives a christological meaning to the miracle of the multiplication of the loaves, using the miracle to show Jesus as the Messiah, the Shepherd of his people, the one who teaches and feeds his followers (Mk 6:34). Again, when Luke says that we must carry our cross *daily* (Lk 9:23; Mk 8:34), he undoubtedly wants to make his readers understand that abnegation is something that pervades Christian life.

Form criticism had reduced the role of the evangelists to that of mere compilers. Redaction criticism "rehabilitates" them by showing that, on the contrary, they are guided by personal requirements of a literary and theological kind. Detailed study of the redactional phenomena in question has shown the special character of each evangelist as writer and as theologian. While redaction criticism has helped to "personalize" each author, this "profile of the author" is to be understood less as the information on a passport than as the sum total of redactional elements and motifs that are characteristic of a particular Gospel.

Like form criticism, redaction criticism has its dangers, and it has not always escaped them. The chief danger is of being interested only in the theological value of the Gospels and in practice paying no attention to their connection with Jesus. This defect is to be seen in Conzelmann and Marxsen. The reality is more complex. Investigation of the redactional procedures used by an evangelist shows that he experiences a real tension between his fidelity to tradition and his creative freedom. His freedom is relative. It is bound, first of all, by fixed earlier sources: the main sources identified by *Quellenkritik* and the shorter materials identified by form criticism. It depends also on the way in which tradition weighs upon his plan and on the reduced freedom he has when it comes to emancipating himself from this tradition and from the communities whose spokesman he is. Redaction criticism enables us to measure and, as it were, put our finger on the degree of freedom and fidelity that the evangelists exercise toward their sources. Their freedom to interpret is real, but it can also be tested and checked. It appears to be exercised soberly, for good reason, and always under the sign of fidelity.

It is possible for us henceforth to take literary criteria as a starting point, to retrace the course of the tradition back to its earliest stage, to distinguish between older and more recent strata, and to distinguish, on the one hand, between what is part of the redactional activity and theological interpretation of the evangelist and, on the other, what betrays an actualizing interpretation by the church. But reliance on literary criteria is inadequate. It must still be shown that the message conveyed in these primitive literary forms is truly from Jesus. Thus the study of form criticism and redaction criticism necessarily leads to a study of the *historical content* of the literary forms that have been identified. The baton must be passed from the literary critic to the historian. The need now is to establish *specific criteria of historicity* that are valid and critically tested and that make it possible to bring to light and isolate the gospel material that goes back to Jesus himself. The study of form criticism and redaction criticism requires completion by a criteriology of historicity.

Bibl.: K. SCHMIDT, *Der Rahmen der Geschichte Jesus* (Berlin, 1919); X. LÉON-DUFOUR, "Formgeschichte et Redaktionsgeschichte des Évangiles Synoptiques," *RSR* 46 (1958): 237–69; P. BENOIT, "Réflexions sur la Formgeschichtliche Methode," *RB* 53 (1946): 481–512; id., in *Exégèse et théologie*, vol. 1 (Paris, 1961), 25–61; R. BULTMANN, *The History of the Synoptic Tradition* (New York, 1963); K. KOCH, *Was ist Formgeschichte* (Neukirchen, 1964); H. ZIMMERMANN, *Neutestamentliche Methodenlehre* (Stuttgart, 1967); A. DESCAMPS, "Progrès et continuité dans la critique des Évangiles et des Actes," *RTL* 1 (1970): 5–44; N. PERRIN, *What Is Redaction Criticism* (London, 1970); M. DIBELIUS, *From Tradition to Gospel* (Cambridge, 1971); B. DE SOLAGES, *Critique des Évangiles et méthode historique* (Toulouse, 1973); R. LATOURELLE, *Finding Jesus through the Gospels* (New York, 1979), 147–58, 199–213; V. FUSCO, "Vangeli," in *Nuovo Dizionario di Teologia biblica* (1988), 1612–19.

René LATOURELLE

III. HISTORICITY

The basic problem of the CREDIBILITY of Christianity is one of HISTORY and HERMENEUTICS. Since Jesus was a real human being whose existence cannot be seriously doubted, it follows that his words and deeds, which were an object of experiential knowledge during his lifetime, became an object of historical knowledge after his death. The investigation of his words and deeds takes the same form, in principle, as it does for any other individual of the past. In fact, however, it was soon realized that in this case the historical approach brought with it a hermeneutical problem. If we conceive of the hermeneutical problem as the problem posed by the levels of reality made available to us in the reading of a document, then it can be said that the problem of access to the reality of Jesus through the mediation of the Gospels is the first and most serious hermeneutical problem posed by Christian revelation.

1. A Real Problem

We know Jesus, not directly through any writings of his, but indirectly through the movement that he launched in the first century of our era. Now the first Christian community, and the evangelists who were members of it, had a religious purpose in mind: they bore witness to the saving event that took place in Jesus Christ. There can be no doubt that the Gospels are neither chronicles nor biographies but documents reflecting faith. The only Jesus that we reach through them is a Jesus who is professed and confessed to be Christ and Lord. A historical-critical study that respects the faith intention that controls the Gospels is therefore the only possible point of departure for gaining knowledge of the historical Jesus.

If we consider the image given of Christ in the Gospels, we have the impression, especially in John but also in Matthew and Mark, of a Jesus considerably more hieratic than the earthly Jesus would have been. Christ is so divine that his earthly life resembles a kind of interlude between his descent into humanity and his return to the heavenly world. If this impression is valid, are we to conclude that the original image of Jesus is to some extent hidden from us or that Jesus has been so transfigured by the Christ of the confession of faith that the historical shape of his life and person disappear in the dazzling light of Easter? Is it still possible to gain access to the reality of his message when he was among us?

We know, in addition, that the Gospels as we presently have them were the result of a lengthy process of reflection that the church began after Pentecost. For several decades, the material in the Gospels was used in catechesis, worship, controversy, and missionary work (→ KERYGMA/CATECHESIS/PARENESIS). As a result, it bears the marks of the actualization and interpretation carried on by the primitive church. We know, finally, that while the evangelists made the earlier tradition their own, they did not simply reproduce it but rethought and rewrote it according to the theological and literary perspectives appropriate to each of them.

The question therefore arises: Is it still possible to find, under the many strata of early actualization, events that "really happened" and to hear the message of Jesus in its original freshness? Just think, for example, of the great difference between the language Jesus uses in the Synoptics and the language he uses in the Gospel of John. In exercising their freedom, the evangelists seem to deal carelessly with reality. Under these conditions is there still any hope of getting back, if not to the *ipsissima verba Jesu* (a dream abandoned long ago), at least to the essential content of his teaching, the nucleus that fed further reflection, and to the solid rock of his most important actions? Is it possible to establish criteria by which we can be sure of coming to know the itinerant rabbi who unsettled Palestine and drastically changed the history of the human race? In short, What is the relationship between HISTORY and KERYGMA, between text and event?

Fundamental theology cannot avoid reflecting on this relationship between faith and history, for if Jesus did not exist or if he was the kind of person who cannot justify the interpretation that faith has given of him, but only

a quite different or even totally different one, then the very first claim of Christianity collapses. The Christian FAITH implies a continuity between the reality of Jesus and the primitive church's interpretation of him, because it was in the earthly life of Jesus that God manifested himself, and that life sanctions the Christian interpretation of it as the only authentic and true interpretation. If the apostles were able to confess Jesus as Christ and Lord, then Jesus must have performed certain actions and shown behavior, attitudes, and language that justify the Christian interpretation of the man Jesus in his earthly state.

2. The Answers of the Critics

Critics give many answers to the problem of the possibility of reaching Jesus through the Gospels.

a. The uncritical and utterly confident answer that prevailed in exegesis down to the eighteenth century. For a long time, the problem of the historical authenticity of the Gospels was identified with the problem of the authenticity of their authors. Relying on the testimony of the tradition, exegetes attributed the Gospels either to apostles (Matthew and John) or to disciples of apostles (Mark and Luke). Since the gospel thus came, immediately or mediately, from eyewitnesses, it followed that everything reported in the Gospels brings us into the presence of Jesus himself. The texts are transparently clear, and historical authenticity is no longer a problem.

b. The answer of historical skepticism, begun by Reimarus, developed by Strauss, Kähler, and Wrede, and given radical form by BULTMANN. The last-named acknowledges a material or chronological succession between Jesus and the apostolic preaching, but he claims that there is a radical break between Jesus of Nazareth, of whom we know practically nothing, and the kerygma in the Gospels. This historical skepticism is accompanied by a dogmatic principle—i.e., faith is independent of the results reached by historical study. The encounter with the word of God through faith is an encounter of two subjectivities and takes place in a realm beyond objective data. Such a situation may dismay the historian but not the believer or the theologian.

c. The more moderate answer of Bultmann's disciples, especially Käsemann, Bornkamm, and the "New HERMENEUTIC," represented by Fuchs, Ebeling, and Robinson. All of these scholars regard their teacher's skepticism as exaggerated, and they seek to find an essential continuity between the Jesus of history and the Christ of the Gospels. In addition, the present generation of Protestant theologians, as represented by Pannenberg and Moltmann, comes down solidly in favor of the primacy of history. "Faith is concerned first of all with what Jesus was. Only in light of that can we see what he is for us today and how it is possible to preach him today" (W. Pannenberg, *Gründzüge der Christologie* [Gütersloh, 1964]; *Principle Features of Christology* [1964]).

d. Finally, the answer of contemporary Catholic exegetes, who are convinced that it is possible to get back to Jesus of Nazareth through the kerygma in the Gospels but who are also much more critical than in the past because they are more aware of the difficulties of this undertaking. Their new position can be formulated in the following way. In Catholic theology the Christ of Easter is the same concrete individual as Jesus of Nazareth. There can be no separation or opposition between the earthly Jesus and the Christ of the Gospels, but only unity and continuity. We are always dealing with the same Jesus, but a Jesus now identified as Messiah and Lord as a result of his resurrection. The present glorified Jesus is yesterday's crucified Jesus; his condition has changed, but the person is one and the same. The resurrection is the catalyst or, we might say, the source of light that makes it possible to understand and grasp the full identity of Jesus of Nazareth. To separate Jesus from the kerygma would be to succumb to Gnosticism; to speak only of the Jesus of history would be to forgo understanding of him, even in his earthly condition.

The Lord whom the church adores, the Son of God, is also the carpenter's son. The fortunes of this person were the historical fortunes of a man of his age. We are dealing here not with the everlasting event proper to myth but with a history that cannot be repeated; not with an idea or a cipher but with a story; not with a cultic drama but with a historical reality; not with metaphysics but with a coming in time.

To reject the idea of Jesus as mythical, however, does not mean that we must close our eyes to the process of reflection and growing consciousness on the part of the church. We know in fact that the *rereading* of the Jesus-event and of Jesus' earthly life in the light of the resurrection launched a process of interpretation that is at the heart of our Gospels. Between Jesus and our present text, then, there are several intervening stages and several mediations that have undoubtedly enriched our knowledge and understanding of Jesus, but that have at the same time increased the hermeneutical distance separating us from him. It is this distance and this organic process that exegetes apply themselves to uncovering and evaluating. Is it possible, through the Gospels' perception of the glorified Christ, to recover their perception of Jesus of Nazareth?

3. Outline of a Demonstration

If it is to take into account investigations of the Gospels that have been carried on for over a century, historical criticism has no choice but to come to grips with several areas and questions.

a. The contribution of external criticism, even if this contribution has been reduced and reappraised.

b. The question, Is it possible and even highly probable that the words and actions of Jesus were faithfully and actively transmitted from the group consisting of Jesus and his disciples before Easter to the newborn church after Easter?

c. The question, Can we establish that the primitive church was concerned to transmit faithfully the words and actions of Jesus? Can we see in the newborn church a determination to exercise an *unbroken* fidelity to Jesus?

d. Finally, the question, Is it possible to establish that this fidelity to Jesus was a reality, a fact? This raises the cardinal problem of the criteria of historical authenticity.

The need, then, is to show the possibility of faithful transmission, the concern and determination to ensure this faithful transmission, and the fact of faithful transmission. If these points can be proved, our trust in the Gospels has a historical basis.

4. The Contribution of External Criticism

External criticism looks at the Gospels "from the outside" and endeavors to answer questions about the author, date and place of composition, sources, and integrity of the document. In the case of the Gospels external criticism relies on writings other than the Gospels (letters of Paul, Acts of the Apostles) and especially on the testimony of the postapostolic churches (in the second and third centuries) that speaks explicitly of the Gospels.

External criticism long enjoyed an almost exclusive and unchallenged authority, whereas internal criticism was regarded with suspicion and accused of subjectivism. Today, perspectives have been reversed. Internal criteria now are the focus of interest in criteriology, while external criticism has fallen into almost total discredit. The truth is probably to be found somewhere in the middle. Contemporary scholarship has indeed shown that because of the very nature of the Gospels and the history of their formation, external criticism no longer has the importance once assigned to it, but this does not mean that scholars are excused from inquiring into it. Even if its contribution is minimal, it still has something to tell us about the authors of the Gospels, the authority of these writers in the church of the first centuries, and the attitude of the church toward the tendencies of the Apocrypha and the Gnostic writings to distort the gospel (→ GNOSIS).

The Concept of Author

Until the twentieth century the problem was expressed in very simple terms. People attributed each Gospel to the author named by a tradition that generally does not go back beyond the second century. The author thus named—an apostle or a disciple of an apostle—was a firsthand witness who in addition was granted the charism of inspiration. The exegetes of the early church thus assigned the Gospels a privileged position, believing that the Gospel gave direct access to the reality. In these circumstances readers could dispense with internal criticism.

It can be said in general that the tradition tended to "individualize" the authors and assign them a close relationship with some apostolic authority. The earliest documents we have (Papias, the Muratorian Canon, the anti-Marcionite prologues, and IRENAEUS of Lyons) regard Mark and Luke as authors in the proper sense of the term. Contemporary scholarship, by and large, accepts this testimony for the following reason: If the tradition dating from the second century had been simply inventing Mark and Luke as evangelists, we would expect them to have proposed in turn the names of two eyewitnesses, namely, two apostles, thus adding one gratuitous assertion to another, one invention to another. If the second-century church accepted the names of Mark and Luke as authors, it doubtless did so under the pressure of the facts.

It is clear, though, that the tradition tended to link Mark and Luke as closely as possible with the apostles in order to lend their Gospels the full prestige of apostolic authority. This is true of Papias, who makes Mark not only a companion of Paul (which we know from elsewhere) but also the interpreter or spokesman of Peter. In addition, Clement of Alexandria claims that Mark wrote his Gospel during the lifetime of Peter. But earlier witnesses—Irenaeus of Lyons, Papias, and the anti-Marcionite prologues—maintain the contrary. What we have in Clement is doubtless the beginning of a legend and an example of the tendency to tighten the links between the apostles and the evangelists. One thing is certain. By making Mark a companion of Paul and a spokesman for Peter, the tradition made him a privileged witness of the life of Jesus. As for Luke, the tradition was content to see in him a companion of Paul. The tradition was right in proposing Mark and Luke as authors, especially since internal criticism confirms its testimony, but it overestimated their position as witnesses. Mark is much more a faithful reporter of the primitive preaching than he is a spokesman for Peter.

The tradition attributes the First Gospel to Matthew and the fourth to John. We know that the First Gospel is a substantial revision of an Aramaic work attributed to Matthew and that it directly or indirectly incorporates elements from other sources, especially Mark. In addition, we know that if the Fourth Gospel has its source in the testimony of John, it also reflects the influence of a community with specific characteristics, in which the Johannine tradition has been preached for a long time and in which it has developed.

It is certain that the early church tended to personalize the authors of the Gospels and to place these works under the aegis of an apostle, thus bestowing maximum authority on them. This concept of author, which prevailed until the twentieth century, has important consequences. For if our Gospels had for their authors eyewitnesses or disciples of eyewitnesses, then they bring us into the presence of the original events and of Jesus himself. The distance between Jesus and the Gospels is eliminated, and internal criticism is superfluous.

The Concept of Author Subjected to Criticism

Unfortunately, this concept of author does not stand up to contemporary criticism. If the First and Fourth Gospels were directly attributable to Matthew and John, their "eyewitness" character would show through, visibly and undeniably, in the final redaction. The same is true of Mark and Luke. In fact, exegetes doubt that the latter two were even witnesses at one remove, i.e., that they collected the testimonies of eyewitnesses (e.g., Peter) and later put them in writing. Their documents do not show the marks of live reporting.

It is not to be concluded from this that modern criticism achieves only negative results. A certain amount of information from antiquity is confirmed, while other points are better understood when placed in a new light.

With regard to the First Gospel, critics acknowledge that its author, though unknown, is a Greek-speaking Jewish Christian who has a rather profound knowledge of the Jewish and rabbinic milieu and who has preserved and made substantial use of the Aramaic work attributed to Matthew. Critics also acknowledge that Luke is a physician and companion of Paul (Acts 13–28) and a Christian converted from paganism. They acknowledge that Mark was a companion of Paul and that his Gospel influenced the work of Luke and the canonical Matthew. Mark depends much more on the primitive tradition, which he faithfully reports and transmits, than he does on Peter. On the other hand, the influence of Paul on Mark is being increasingly recognized. Mark's Christology, in particular, could have been inspired by Paul and would thus serve as a key for interpreting the Christology of the Synoptics. The personality of John, as immediate author of the Fourth Gospel, has become vague, although, in recompense, we have a better knowledge of the history of the redaction of the Fourth Gospel, as well as of its author's abilities as writer and theologian.

A New Conception of Authorship

To sum up: internal criticism has shown us that the modern concept of authorship cannot be applied univocally to the authors of the Gospels. The redactors of the Gospels were linked to the events of Jesus' ministry by an oral and written tradition that stretched over several decades. We must therefore put aside the idea of a redaction of the Gospels that was based on direct testimonies received from individuals who had taken part in the events and immediately written down by our authors. Between Jesus and the documents as we have them there were several intermediaries, whose respective contributions must be assessed. As a result, the authorship of Matthew and John is to be defined by a set of characteristic tendencies and traits, the discovery of which internal criticism alone has made possible. The same must be said, after due allowances have been made, of Mark and Luke. Investigation of the oral and written sources used by the redactors has opened the way to source criticism (*Quellenkritik*) and form criticism (*Formgeschichte*). The redactors themselves, moreover, were not simply reporters of the tradition; they were also interpreters and theologians. Each of them has his own perspective and literary methods. Investigation of this redactional activity has given rise to redaction criticism (*Redaktionsgeschichte*).

What the evangelists have lost as individuals, as persons, they have thus recovered as servants of the tradition and as theologians. This new conception of authorship has been made necessary by a more careful study of the ancient testimonies and especially by a study of the very fabric of the Gospels. Internal criticism has found in our texts discrepancies and even incoherences that cannot be attributed to an eyewitness, even a secondhand eyewitness. To explain these phenomena, exegetes have been forced to shift their ground: they have had to move from external criticism to internal criticism, and from criticism of the author to the problem of the sources and their formation.

The Authority of the Gospels

External criticism provides us with a further important piece of information. Running through all the documents one conviction finds forceful expression, namely, the unchallenged authority that the Gospels enjoyed in the early church. The acceptance of this authority is manifested in various ways.

a. In the faithful preservation of the text of the Gospels. Thus the recently discovered Bodmer Papyri (published in 1956–58) show that the present text of the Gospel of John was already in circulation at the end of the second century.

b. In the fact that from the second century on, the text of the Gospel was read during liturgical services and that this reading was regarded as no less important than the reading of the Prophets. Justin writes: "On the day of the sun [Sunday] all who live in the city and countryside assemble, and the memoirs of the apostles or the writings of the prophets are read" (*Apologia* 1.67). In another passage Justin, who is speaking to pagans, tells them that these memoirs are called gospels (1.66).

c. In the fact that when the church engaged in debate with heretics, it appealed to the Gospels as to a decisive authority. This is the case with Irenaeus of Lyons when addressing the Ebionites, Marcionites, Docetists, and Valentinians. Moreover, Irenaeus notes that though each of these sects broke away from the church, it always retained one of the four Gospels, at least in order to justify its doctrinal position. Thus the Ebionites, who were fanatical Jews, kept Matthew; Marcion and the Marcionites, who were hostile to Judaism, rejected the OT but retained Luke; Cerinthus and his followers invoked the Gospel of Mark, while Valentinian and his disciples based their speculations on the Gospel of John. Thus, in their own way, heretics confirmed the authority of the Gospels.

d. Finally, all the witnesses are unanimous in recognizing that the Gospels possess their authority because through them we have access to the person of Christ. For this reason the local churches, though differing in language, mentality, and culture, acknowledged the four Gospels as norms of faith and life. It was also for this reason that the apocryphal gospels were rejected.

These witnesses obviously do not use technical language and are not familiar with our critical requirements. They even tend to exaggerate the connection of the Gospels with the apostles. One thing remains clear, nonetheless: the very firm, unanimous, and spontaneous conviction that through the Gospels we truly know Jesus and his message because the Gospels contain the preaching of the apostles about Jesus. It is difficult to deny the importance of this testimony, even if it is uncritical and naïve in its expression, because it comes from generations still close to the event. It is the task of internal criticism to determine the precise connection between the message of Jesus and the present text of our Gospels. But literary criticism can never invalidate the massive and irrepressible conviction of the first Christian generations that through the Gospels we truly come in contact with the life and message of Jesus of Nazareth.

5. The Primitive Community before and after Easter

Once external criticism has made its contribution, *internal* criticism takes over. The primitive church is the setting in which Jesus and the evangelists come in contact with each other; the evangelists in turn ensure continuity between the primitive church and us. If there is a discontinuity at the very beginning between Jesus the preacher and the Christ who is preached, between Jesus and the primitive church, who can guarantee that the kerygma is indeed the gospel of Jesus? The *first task of internal criticism*, then, is to verify the real relationship between the pre-Easter community, on the one side, and the post-Easter community, on the other. Is it possible, then, that there was a genuine continuity, not only in time, but also in "tradition," between these two groups?

In a demonstration that no one has been able to invalidate, H. Schürmann (*Die Vorösterlichen Anfänge der Logientradition* [Berlin, 1961]) distinguishes a twofold *Sitz im Leben* in the pre-Easter community: one external and formed by the situations and visible activities of this community, the other internal and formed by the interpersonal relationships that linked the members of this community in their profession of the same faith and the same values.

The Pre-Easter Community

Schürmann first examines the life setting consisting of the close association of Jesus and his disciples; in his study he uses the very tools of form criticism.

Even one who adopts a reductive outlook cannot deny that Jesus preached and had disciples. The tradition on this point is unyielding. On several occasions Jesus calls individuals whom he has recruited and set apart to be his companions. He requires these individuals to leave everything in order to attach themselves to him and share his work.

This group, consisting of Jesus and his followers, forms a separate community, distinct from the surrounding society, precisely because the disciples have undertaken to follow this teacher and because they believe in him. Their community is not a casual one that is kept going by fleeting encounters; it is marked by stability. The entire tradition shows us a Jesus who is never separated from his disciples. The disciples share Jesus' insecure way of life; they are always with him and as a result become witnesses of his life and teaching.

This stable presence of disciples around Jesus does not come about spontaneously or by chance; it requires a cause. The cause is not only the call from Jesus but also faith in the message he preaches as being God's final message before the end of time. The authority with which he speaks strikes his listeners, who comment that no one has spoken as this man speaks. The respect his activities win for him is unprecedented; the crowds have never seen anything like this. The testimonies to the impact produced by the appearance of Jesus on the scene are undeniably historical.

Such is the setting in which the preaching of Jesus is heard. Those whom he calls gather around him and live in close familiarity with him. They have been fascinated by his message and have been won over. How is it possible, then, that they should allow this message to vanish into thin air or be forgotten? Their familiarity with such a teacher justifies us rather in thinking that they preserved the treasure of his words with the utmost care and that they did everything they could to maintain it unchanged.

If we accept the fact of the faith (in the sense of a deep attachment) of the disciples in the message of Jesus, we have an important methodological principle, namely, that the message of Jesus, in the form in which he gave it, was regarded as worth preserving and passing on and that in fact it *could* be so preserved and passed on because of the close familiarity in which Jesus and his followers lived. Furthermore, the very fact that logia of Jesus have been passed down is already a sign of this esteem and concern. In particular, attachment to Jesus explains the preservation of logia that could hardly have been understood during the lifetime of Jesus because they are deliberately obscure and prophetic and wholly directed toward the future. I am thinking especially of the logia about Jesus' own tragic lot. Had these sayings been composed after Easter, they would not have the enigmatic character they now have.

The faith of the disciples in the message of Jesus explains not only the possibility of a transmission but also the specific shape of the transmission. A community of disciples is not the same when its center is a teacher as when the center is a wise man or a leader or a prophet or a messianic figure. The person who becomes the center drawing this community together also determines the kind of fidelity he elicits and the solidity of the tradition he begets. Now it is clear that to his disciples Jesus was more than a rabbi or a wise man and that the circle of his disciples cannot be simply compared to circles made up of disciples of teachers in Israel. The pre-Easter community resembles, rather, the communities of prophets and their disciples, and it is here that we must look for an analogy. For the message of Jesus is uttered as the decisive message, proclaiming the supreme hour that will see the coming of the kingdom. Furthermore, the personality of Jesus shows itself to be that of a prophet, or rather of the greatest of the prophets. Jesus acts as a gatherer of human beings, as a shepherd who leads his flock.

It is easy, then, to see how important the disciples would think it to preserve not only the literary form but also, and even more, the message of Jesus with all its original content. The element of urgency and uniqueness that marks this message is a guarantee of a fidelity far greater than that achieved by all the rabbinic techniques. We should not deny, however, that Jesus himself used mnemonic devices current in an age of oral transmission.

The influence of the internal *Sitz im Leben* does not render superfluous the study of the external setting. Understanding of the private life of the community leads to the meaning of its external activity, while the latter in turn brings to light factors that show a new coherence in the process of transmission. Two of these factors are the missionary activity of the disciples and the requirements of communal life in the pre-Easter community.

Schürmann stresses the point that Jesus preached and set forth his message with the intention of providing his disciples with an appropriate tool for missionary activity, which they were to carry on not only after Easter but even during his own lifetime as ambassadors and preachers of the kingdom. For while Jesus issued a special call to individuals whom he set apart to be sharers of his life, the call undoubtedly meant that they would also share in his religious mission. A good many of the logia that have come down to us reflect, it seems, this intention of providing the disciples with a tool for evangelization. In this respect, the *mission* of the apostles prior to Easter is an especially important factor in understanding the origin and process of transmission of the gospel tradition.

The point is that Jesus likely gave his words a particular stamp in order precisely to impress them on the memory of his disciples. The very fact that there was one or, probably, several missions of the disciples before Easter suggests that Jesus really had this concern. If, then, Jesus intended to give his disciples a mission, even before Easter, he had to prepare them, especially since they were uneducated and uninstructed persons, or, rather, persons belonging to an oral culture in which everything was memorized: the Psalms, the Law, the Prophets. In this setting, the only way in which Jesus could avoid having his message of salvation and its moral requirements be distorted and trivialized was to express them in a more or less stereotyped form.

Matthew, Mark, and Luke tell us that after a lengthy period of ministry with his disciples around him, Jesus sends these disciples on a mission (Mk 6:7). On this point, authors such as Dibelius and Bornkamm agree with Catholic exegetes in acknowledging that the disciples did share in the activity of Jesus even before Easter. Jesus' intention of sending his followers on a mission is attested in Mk 3:14–15; 6:7, as well as in the missionary discourse, the central part of which (Mt 10:5b–6; Lk 10:8–12) reflects very old material. The context, the vocabulary, and the turn of phrase in this discourse reflect a pre-Easter situation. The collaboration of the disciples in the activity of Jesus finds expression in the power given to them so that they might, on the one hand, preach and, on the other, expel demons and effect cures; these two powers and two activities are also linked in the ministry of Jesus. When the apostles return from their mission, they gather around Jesus and tell him everything they have done and taught (Mk 6:30). The essential themes of this first preaching by the disciples are the proclamation of the kingdom (Mk 1:15; Mt 10:7) and the exhortation to repentance (Mk 6:12).

The second factor that serves to explain the formation and transmission of a tradition is the undeniable fact that Jesus and the disciples live a *communal life*. The group made up of the first disciples does not, of course, have a well-defined rule, such as the Qumran sect had, but it does have requirements that are intended to link the members more closely together. The disciples must abandon possessions, family, and profession in order to attach themselves to an itinerant preacher and follow him everywhere. These radical demands of Jesus are to be explained by the fact that his call is addressed to human beings who must devote themselves completely to the kingdom. The requirement of a communal life, as well as the other radical demands, are reflected in the logia describing the calling of the disciples and the following of Jesus.

Schürmann's study has thus shown that the logia of Jesus originate before Easter and that the transmission of these also begins before Easter in the very circle of his disciples. The one who initiates the transmission is Jesus himself, as is attested in 1 Jn 1:1ff.; Lk 1:2; Acts 1:21-22. A genuine continuity, not only temporal and sociological, but also of *tradition* (i.e., of acceptance, activity, and message) between the pre-Easter community and the post-Easter community is possible and highly probable.

The Post-Easter Community

After Easter, Jesus is more clearly identified and understood. His authority, far from lessening, increases. Acceptance of his message reaches a deeper level. The preaching of the kingdom continues but becomes more specific. There is no break, but continuity amid deeper understanding between the pre-Easter community and the post-Easter community. The discontinuity between phases does not obliterate memories or interrupt the process of continuity in transmission and in fidelity to Jesus. Easter is not an atomic bomb that wipes out everything that has gone before; it is a flame that sheds light on everything. The apostles, who are witnesses of Jesus, are still present. The post-Easter community does not live in a vacuum, cut off from its founders and sunk in ignorance.

Quite the contrary, for the Acts of the Apostles describes a community gathered around the *witnesses of Jesus*, who are also the *leaders* of this community, namely, the apostles with Peter at their head. Peter takes the initiative in the election of Matthias (Acts 1:15–26). On Pentecost he is the first to speak (Acts 2:14). When Peter and John are arrested, it is Peter who addresses the Sanhedrin (Acts 4:8). The Twelve call the disciples together and choose seven deacons (Acts 6:5–6). The apostles send Peter and John into Samaria to confirm the baptized (Acts 8:14–17). It is the apostles who object to people who go about causing disturbance without having received an apostolic mandate (Acts 15:24). It is the apostles who promulgate and broadcast the decree of the council of Jerusalem (Acts 15:27–28). It is said of Peter that "he went about everywhere" (Acts 9:32); he preaches in Lydda, Joppa, and Caesarea. Of the body of Christians, in contrast, it is said that "they devoted themselves to the apostles' teaching" (Acts 2:42). And when the apostles must choose between two ministries, they choose the ministry of the word (Acts 6:4).

Furthermore, the post-Easter community is in no sense an anonymous society. On the contrary, it is *fully identified* by the names of many of its important members. In addition to the apostles, who are universally known, it includes relatives of Jesus (James); disciples, such as Matthias, Barnabas, Barsabbas, Silas, Mark, Cleophas, Nicodemus, Joseph of Arimathea, and Mnason; deacons (of whom Stephen in one); Paul; the mother of Jesus and her immediate entourage.

The post-Easter community is thus not an amorphous, unstructured society. It is to be compared not with mollusks but with vertebrates. In this community, those who have authority to rule it are the very ones who have been the close associates and table companions of Jesus, the witnesses to his life and ministry. Such is the setting in which the tradition about Jesus develops, a setting characterized by fidelity to Jesus.

6. A Persevering Determination to be Faithful to Jesus: Language and Attitudes

As the tradition diversified and became further removed in time from the event, did it persevere in fidelity to Jesus as it developed? This is the second challenge to historical criticism.

In order to take up this challenge, which has to do with the years preceding the redaction of the Gospels, I shall try to enter into the mentality at work in the primitive church.

What is needed here is a kind of psychoanalysis that will bring to light the spontaneous, almost visceral responses of the primitive community to Jesus and his word, and, consequently, the psychological and mental structure of this community. I think it possible to carry out this kind of investigation with the aid of semantics, i.e., with the help of *words* that occur with such frequency in the newborn church that they fill the entire horizon, as it were, of the Christian consciousness and express its deepest orientation. I appeal to texts that directly describe the primitive ecclesial setting—in particular, the letters of Paul and the Acts of the Apostles. In this literature references to Jesus are less direct than in the Gospels, but they are for that reason all the more significant. For we know that communities, like individuals, betray themselves by their language, their use of certain privileged words. To be truly revelatory, these words need not only to be used frequently but also to be used in important contexts. In the present case, what we need to find out is whether the mentality shown in the basic vocabulary of Paul's letters and the Acts of the Apostles is one of fidelity to Jesus or of creative fabrication.

If we can successfully use these privileged words to discover the fundamental outlook of the primitive church, we will have an important criterion for evaluating the kind of ecclesial setting in which the gospel tradition was formed and developed. We will have shown that there is continuity not only from Jesus to the church but also from the church to Jesus, because the attitude of the young church during the years in which the tradition is formed is one of radical fidelity.

Among the words that thus display the attitude of the primitive church to Jesus we can distinguish three groups that mark out three concentric circles around Jesus. The first group, which is general but very old, is connected with the idea of tradition: "receive" (*paralambanein*) and "hand on" (*paradidonai*). The second group refers to the immediate collaborators of Jesus: "witness" (*martys*), "apostle" (*apostolos*), and "service" (*diakonia*) of the word. The third has to do with the broader and more comprehensive activity of all who preach the gospel: "teach" (*didaskein*), "proclaim" (*kēryssein*), "evangelize" (*euangelizesthai*), and "gospel" (*euangelion*). In examining these words, our aim is not so much to produce an exhaustive semantic study as it is to see how these key words and this basic vocabulary of the primitive church give us access to the Christian consciousness and subconsciousness as these relate to Jesus.

Paradosis: Reception and Transmission in the Letters of Paul

The letters of Paul, which go back to the years 50–60, i.e., to a period before the redaction of the Gospels, bear witness to the great importance that this set of words had for the Christian consciousness. The noun "tradition" (*paradosis*) recurs in the NT and refers to the content that is passed on. The verb "hand on" (*paradidonai*) occurs 120 times, with several meanings. When referring to tradition, it signifies the action of handing on: to institutions (Mk 7:3, 4, 5, 9) received through oral tradition, or to a teaching (1 Cor 15:3) communicated by other persons.

Paul had first been a Pharisee and, as such, an inflexible observer of the tradition contained in the written or oral Torah (Gal 1:13–14). He abandoned this tradition and adopted that of Jesus. But when he refers to this new tradition, he continues to use the terminology he has received from Judaism: "receive" (*paralambanein*) and "hand on" (*paradidonai*). Whatever he has received he must hand on. Though he is the most independent of the apostles, he says in his letter to the Galatians that he has submitted his gospel to the church of Jerusalem in order to confirm its authenticity, "in order to make sure that I was not running, or had not run, in vain" (Gal 2:2).

Paul sets up a strict correspondence between *receiving* and *handing on*, especially in two important passages, one about the resurrection (1 Cor 15:3), the other about the Last Supper (1 Cor 11:23). The identity of what has been received with what is handed on underscores Paul's fidelity in carrying out his mission. The content of the tradition in these two passages is the essential mysteries of salvation and their deeper meaning, including the Last Supper, and the passion, death, and resurrection. The authority that the *paradosis* has is due to the fact that Paul faithfully hands on that which it is his mission to hand on: "We are ambassadors for Christ, since God is making his appeal through us" (2 Cor 5:20).

In many passages we find the same outlook, if not always the same words. Thus he urges the Thessalonians to fidelity: "Stand firm and hold fast to the traditions that you were taught by us, either by word of mouth or by our letter" (2 Thes 2:15; see also 3:6). He writes to the Philippians: "Keep on doing the things that you have learned and received [from me] and heard and seen in me" (Phil 4:9). He praises the fidelity of the Colossians: "As you therefore have received Christ Jesus the Lord, continue to live your lives in him, rooted and built up in him and established in the faith, just as you were taught" (Col 2:6–7). In contrast, he rebukes those who have abandoned the gospel that he has preached: "If anyone proclaims to you a gospel contrary to what you received, let that one be accursed!" (Gal 1:9). Abandonment of the tradition contained in the gospel of Paul is equivalent to abandonment of the gospel of Christ.

It is not by accident that Paul takes over the vocabulary of Jewish *paradosis*; he shows by this vocabulary that the action of *receiving* and *handing on* in Christianity resembles the kind of transmission practiced in Judaism. The second letter to Timothy contains another example of Jewish and rabbinic influence on the Pauline conception of *paradosis*. Any tradition that claims to be authentic must produce an uninterrupted list of those who have handed it on. The second letter to Timothy lists five of the links in the transmission: Christ (1:10); Paul, apostle and teacher (1:11); Timothy, disciple of Paul (1:6); the faithful and other human beings (2:2). By thus listing an uninterrupted series of witnesses to the tradition, Paul shows the fidelity and therefore the authority of this tradition.

If we bring together the data on *paradosis* in the letters of Paul, we see that the term sometimes refers to the summations of the Christian faith that are, as it were, the first creeds (1 Cor 15:3ff.). Paul has received these formulas as constituting the core of his gospel; he hands them on just as he has received them, thus showing that he is the servant of the message. In the Jewish and rabbinic conception of *paralambanein-paradidonai*, the words imply an attitude of fidelity to what has been received and handed on. The issue is one not of creating, innovating, or transforming but simply of handing on. The word reveals a mentality and an environment in which the concern to preserve the message received as though it were a trust, an inheritance, is predominant. The authenticity of the tradition is ensured by the chain of qualified "handers on," a chain that links Christ to the apostles, the apostles to their disciples, and these disciples to the faithful. It must be stressed that the Pauline tradition, like that of Jesus (Acts 1:1), consists of actions and examples as well as instructions (Phil 4:9). A community that thus lives under the sign of *paradosis*, lives under the sign of fidelity and not of risky innovation.

The Uppsala school, represented by H. Riesenfeld and B. Gerhardsson, has studied the methods of transmission used in Jewish and rabbinic circles. Two principles were at work in rabbinic pedagogy: memorization and the unchanged preservation of a text that has been memorized with the help of techniques that can all be seen in the Gospels, including use of resumes or summaries, rhythmic sequences, parallelisms, antitheses, key words, and inclusions. After the death of Jesus the apostles remained in Jerusalem for fifteen or twenty years, i.e., during the period when the gospel tradition was being formed. In the setting of this oral culture, controlled here by the presence and influence of the Twelve, the tradition about Jesus took definitive shape. The logia of Jesus were collected, with various kinds of groupings being used. Most of the time, a unit took shape around a single theme (parables of the kingdom, advice to missionaries, miracle stories) or was determined quite simply through application of the same memorization techniques used in an oral culture. The logia of Jesus were passed from mouth to mouth in accordance with a pedagogy that Jesus himself began. But the Christian tradition has a characteristic peculiar to it. It is dynamized by fidelity to Jesus but also by a concern for actualization and deeper understanding that is connected with the fact that the logia of Jesus must shed light on ever-new problems of human living. For the church has received the message of Jesus not as a lifeless treasure but as a living message that can shed light on new situations. The activity elicited by this dynamic is visible and can be controlled, especially in the case of the parables, in which the message is not only preserved but also actualized in dependence on new conditions in which the church finds itself. This twofold dynamic of fidelity and actualization is already at work in the attitude and mentality of the primitive church.

Witness, Apostle, Service of the Word

a. "To give witness" and "witness" (noun) are found chiefly in the vocabulary of Acts and in the theology of Luke. The title "witnesses" belongs first and foremost to the apostles. Like the prophets, the apostles were chosen by God (Acts 1:26; 10:41). They saw and heard Christ (Acts 4:20; 1 Jn 1:1–3); they lived in close association with him and therefore had a direct experience of his person, teaching, and deeds. They ate and drank with him both before and after his resurrection (Acts 10:41). Other persons could preach; the apostles alone could bear witness in the strict sense of this phrase. They received from Christ the mission of bearing witness (Acts 10:41). In the apostolic testimony described in Acts there is an indissoluble combination of the historical event and its religious significance. The same is true of the kerygma of Paul. In Paul's eyes, the *Jesus* who was persecuted, crucified, and then raised from the dead is the *Christ*. Thus, far from denying or minimizing the historical reality, the apostolic testimony reaffirms and confirms it in order to bring to light its interior dimension. It does not attribute a historical existence to an event that did not happen; rather, it brings to light the salvific significance of what did happen. The category of testimony involves not only a reference to Jesus but a conscious, deliberate reference to him. If Jesus did not in fact do the deeds he is said to have done, the apostolic testimony no longer has any force, and the gospel no longer exists.

b. Although the term "apostle" is not used in a completely univocal way, it occurs in all NT writings with the exception of 2 Thessalonians, the letter of James, and the letters of John. In Paul's letters, "apostle" is a privileged term. Paul is an ambassador of Christ, appointed by him to represent him as his delegate. In Luke the idea of apostle is closely connected with that of witness. The apostles are not only ambassadors of Christ but also, and above all, men who take over the functions reserved to the Twelve, especially as authoritative witnesses to the life and resurrection of Christ. The essential point is that, in the language and mentality of the primitive church, an apostle, whether thought of as an ambassador and representative of Christ (Paul's conception of apostolate) or as a witness to the life of Jesus (Luke's conception), is in a relationship of fidelity to the one who delegates him as representative and to whom he bears witness.

c. In Paul *diakonia* is not a technical term. It is first applied to all itinerant missionaries, including the apostles (Rom 16:1; 1 Cor 3:5; 2 Cor 3:6; Eph 3:7; Col 1:23, 25); then it refers to collaborators of the apostles and of Paul in particular, such as Crescens, Titus, Luke, and Mark, who travel with him in accordance with the requirements of evangelization (2 Tm). In the letter to the Colossians Paul describes himself as *diakonos* of the gospel and *diakonos* of the church, commissioned to establish the word of God (Col 1:25). Being a servant of the gospel, Paul is also *diakonos* of Christ (2 Cor 11:23); he is even the *doulos*, or "slave," of Christ (Ti 1:1; Rom 1:1), a designation that gives even more forcible expression to the way in which he belongs to Christ.

In the Acts of the Apostles, the highest form of Christian service — namely, the proclamation of the good news of salvation in Jesus Christ — is described as "service of the word" (Acts 6:4). This *diakonia tou logou* is the same as what Luke describes as the *didachē* of the apostles (Acts 2:42).

For the apostles this service of the word is identified, in the concrete, with the testimony they must give to Jesus (Acts 1:1). In the prologue of his gospel Luke says that the "eyewitnesses" became "servants of the word" (Lk 1:2). This word, or message, is acknowledged as being, for the same reason as the OT message, not only a message about God but also a message from God. The attitude of respect and service owed to the Torah becomes in the NT respect for the message of Jesus, the message about Jesus. The tradition stemming from Jesus is a tradition about Jesus. Paul thus calls himself both a *diakonos* of the gospel and a *diakonos* of Christ (2 Cor 11:23). Such an outlook is evidently the expression of a fidelity.

Teach, Preach, Evangelize

These words, which are part of the vocabulary of EVANGELIZATION, are not reserved to the apostles alone; they are also applied to the apostles' coworkers in the spread of the good news.

In Acts, the testimony of the apostles is spread by their preaching, or kerygma. While these two nouns have the same field of reference in the concrete activity of the apostles, the fact remains that bearing witness is a properly apostolic activity, whereas "announce," "proclaim," and "preach" emphasize the dynamic, promulgational character of this testimony and are applied to other preachers besides the apostles (Acts 15:35; 18:25): Paul, Barnabas, Silas, Philip, Timothy.

"Evangelize" is also used with the meaning "proclaim." Thus Peter and John "evangelize" numerous Samaritan villages (Acts 8:25). Paul and Barnabas "evangelize" the city of Derbe (Acts 14:21). "Evangelize" and "teach" often go together. Paul and Barnabas "taught and proclaimed the word of the Lord" at Antioch (Acts 15:35; see also 5:42; 18:25; 29:31).

What the apostles announce, preach, proclaim, and teach, and what their listeners are urged to hear and receive, is "the good news about Jesus" (Acts 8:35), the message "about the Lord Jesus Christ" (Acts 28:31). The word that is common to all these passages and unifies them is *Jesus*, who is identified as Christ and Savior.

In some passages Paul briefly summarizes his entire mission. "We do not proclaim ourselves; we proclaim Jesus Christ" (2 Cor 4:5). Similarly, new life comes from Christ, for "surely you have heard about him and were taught in him, as truth is in Jesus" (Eph 4:21). Correlatively, the faith that is a response to this preaching is "faith in Jesus" (Rom 3:26), a faith that confesses that "Jesus is Lord" (Rom 10:9; 1 Cor 12:3).

The object of Paul's preaching, as well as of the testimony of the apostles and all who evangelize and teach, is always *Jesus* of Nazareth, now fully identified by his resurrection as being the Christ, the Lord, and the Son of God.

Although the limitations of the present *Dictionary* prevent pushing this inquiry further, what has been said thus far justifies a conclusion. A community whose basic attitudes are focused on mission, testimony, tradition, and service is entirely different from a community that changes position in every wind, has no center or point of reference, and is ignorant of its past and careless about its future. A human group whose conscious intention is to hand on undiminished what it has received, to bear witness to what it has seen and heard, to act as the delegate and representative of the one who appointed it, and to give this service a privileged place over every other—such a group definitely lives under the sign of *fidelity*. The soul of the primitive church was fashioned and permeated, as it were, by these basic words. To eliminate them or minimize them would be like depriving a language of its basic vocabulary. To list them is to describe the primary reactions and essential attitudes of the primitive church; it is to define that church's language and mentality. The important thing here is that this basic vocabulary in its original usage has only one object and displays a single intention: *Jesus* and *fidelity to Jesus*. We are thus justified in claiming that in the primitive church there is not only a continuity of tradition between Jesus and the church (as H. Schürmann has shown) but also a concern and will to keep the church *constantly faithful* to Jesus. In order to complete my demonstration, I must go on now to verify the *factual reality* of this fidelity by having recourse to the criteria of historical authenticity.

7. Criteria of the Historical Authenticity of the Gospels

In establishing the historical authenticity of the content of the Gospels, it is not enough to show that an active and faithful transmission of the words and actions of Jesus was possible from the very beginning, or, in addition, that throughout the formation of the tradition until the point when it was put in writing there was a concern and determination to be faithful to Jesus. It is also necessary to establish that this fidelity was *really operative* and can be shown; in other words, it is necessary to establish that the writings correspond to the reality they depict. In this final demonstration the criteria of historical authenticity are applied; literary criticism now yields to historical criticism. For even if literary criticism can get back to the earliest forms of the tradition with the help of the techniques used in form criticism and redaction criticism, it cannot by itself determine the historicity of a story or a logion.

The application of the criteria of historicity to the Gospels is a recent undertaking that began with Käsemann in 1954. Since then there has been a constantly growing interest in problems of criteriology. The first attempts at a systematic presentation began in 1964, as an effort was made to define and group the criteria and even to produce a hierarchical organization of them. This phase of research has produced the works of H. K. McArthur, N. Perrin, I. de la Potterie, L. Cerfaux, M. Lehmann, J. Jeremias, R. S. Barbour, D. G. A. Calvert, J. Caba, N. J. McEleney, D. Lührmann, E. Schillebeeckx, R. Latourelle, F. Lambiasi, and F. Lentzen-Deis.

Pieces of Evidence, Criteria, and Proof

Before proceeding to a study of criteria in the strict sense, several distinctions need to be made:

a. The first distinction is between *pieces of evidence* and *criteria*. A piece of evidence can lead to a likelihood, a probability, but not to a sure judgment of historical authenticity. Thus the fact that the evangelists have preserved a certain number of utterly "neutral" details, i.e., details that do not reflect any visible theological intention (e.g., that Jesus was sleeping on a *cushion* during the storm: Mk 4:38), is a favorable bit of evidence but not a criterion in the strict sense. Similarly, the color and liveliness of some stories in Mark do not deserve the name of criterion. Such things may indeed show the tradition's fidelity to the real events, but they may also be the result of redactional activity. The same must be said of the "impression of truthfulness" that the Gospels produce. Most people are aware of the reserve and even mistrust that historians show in regard to this kind of argument.

b. It is also important not to confuse the *archaic character of forms* with the historical authenticity of their *content.* Form criticism can successfully reach back to the earliest forms of the tradition, but it still operates within the limits of literary criticism. Tradition history takes a sounder and more valid approach when it sets out to uncover those elements that are attributable to the evangelists. Thus when exegetes succeed in discovering, in a logion or story, those elements that originate with the evangelist or the primitive church, we can assume that we have serious evidence of historicity, since we have eliminated as completely as possible the mediations separating us from Jesus. Such a procedure takes us back, for practical purposes, to the life setting of Jesus himself (*Sitz im Leben Jesu*). Strictly speaking, however, all this is still literary criticism and not yet historical criticism. Still to be demonstrated is the historical reality underlying the logion or story. It is at this point that the criteria, properly so called, of historical authenticity come into play. Nonetheless, the results of literary criticism are so weighty and so compelling that they come close to serving as criteria of historicity. This shows that the boundary between piece of evidence and criterion, between literary criticism and historical criticism, is sometimes difficult to define and that the transition from the one to the other may be imperceptible.

c. Finally, we must avoid confusing *criterion* and *proof.* Criteria are *principles* that, when applied to the gospel material, make it possible to test the historical coherence of stories and to pass a judgment of authenticity or inauthenticity on their contents. The convergent application of criteria makes possible a *proof,* or demonstration, of historical authenticity.

Primary or Basic Criteria

By *basic* criteria is meant criteria that have value in and of themselves and therefore justify a sure judgment of historical authenticity. We do not mean that these criteria must be employed exclusively, but we do mean that they have an intrinsic value, so that they lead to certain and fruitful results. These criteria, which are used in general history and are acknowledged by the majority of exegetes, are the following: criterion of multiple attestation, criterion of discontinuity, criterion of continuity or conformity, criterion of necessary explanation or sufficient reason.

a. The criterion of multiple attestation. We may formulate this criterion as follows: "we may regard as authentic a gospel datum that is solidly attested in all (or most) of the gospel sources: Mark, who is a source for Matthew and Luke; the *Quelle,* a source for Luke and Matthew; the special sources used by Matthew, Luke, and possibly Mark; the other NT writings, especially Acts, the Gospel of John, the letters of Paul, Peter, and John, and the Letter to the Hebrews." The criterion becomes all the more weighty if the datum is found in different literary forms, and if these in turn are attested in multiple sources. Thus the theme of the compassion and mercy of Jesus for sinners appears in all the gospel sources and in the most varied literary forms: parables (Lk 15:11–32), controversies (Mt 21:28–32), miracle stories (Mk 2:1–2), and vocation stories (Mk 2:13–17).

This criterion is currently used in general history. Concordant testimony from different sources that are not under suspicion of having been deliberately harmonized deserves to be accepted by all. Historical criticism will say, in practice: *testis unus, testis nullus* (one witness is no better than no witness). Certitude depends on the convergence of independent sources.

The chief difficulty that historians find in applying this criterion to the Gospels is obviously the difficulty of showing the independence of the sources. To what extent is this independence certain, when we know that behind the written sources there is an *oral* tradition, in the course of which the material being studied may have been introduced into the several sources because of the part it played in the primitive church? This difficulty must not be ignored or minimized. For this reason the conditions for a valid application of this criterion need to be defined.

It is a fact that oral tradition and the primitive church are the combined source that gave birth to the gospel tradition in its various written formulations. But this statement must be nuanced and explained. It is to be noted, first of all, that *single source* is not to be confused with *single attestation*. A source can represent a potentially high number of witnesses; this is the case in 1 Cor 15:3–9, which bears witness to the resurrection and appearances of Jesus. The more important thing, in the case of the Gospels, is the *character of the ecclesial setting*. This is why the second critical step in our demonstration was devoted to the study precisely of this setting. The result of the study undertaken there was clarity on the fact that the basic attitude of the primitive church toward Jesus was one of *fidelity*. We know, moreover, that the churches of the second century were convinced that the Gospels really gave them access to Jesus, so much so that the Gospels were for them a norm of faith and life, including even the commitment of martyrdom. We know, too, the laws governing oral transmission in the Judaism of the time. We know, in addition, that diversity and regionalism in ecclesial communities (differences of language, mentality, and culture) were a factor ensuring an independence that counteracted the danger of uniformism. Finally, by way of redaction history we can check the degree of fidelity of the written tradition in relation to the oral tradition. The fidelity of the former enables us to deduce the fidelity of the latter.

Against this background of fidelity amid freedom and of unity amid diversity, we can trust the criterion of multiple attestation and regard it as a fundamental criterion, especially when the issue is one of discerning the essential traits of the person, preaching, and activity of Jesus: e.g., his position in regard to the law, the poor, and sinners; his resistance to royal and political messianism; his activity as wonderworker; and his preaching in parables.

When it comes to logia or particular details, this criterion must usually be supplemented by others. The reason is that gospel material may have been introduced before the sources took shape. Thus Mk 8:34 on the need for the disciples of Jesus to carry their crosses is better explained in the context of post-Easter preaching than in that of the preaching of Jesus. At the same time, however, the conformity of this logion with the whole of Jesus' message on the necessity of dying to oneself in order to enter the kingdom, as well as with the example of his own life and death, makes it possible to assert that it represents a faithful interpretation of Jesus. In other cases, the criterion of multiple attestation is sufficient by itself to ground a judgment of authenticity. Thus the fact that Jesus died for the salvation of humanity is attested in all the sources and influences all pericopes.

In short, we can conclude that the criterion of multiple attestation is valid, and is in fact acknowledged as such, when we use it to establish the essential traits of the person, preaching, and activity of Jesus. In consideration of particular pericopes, the criterion is valid when supported by other criteria or when there is no serious reason for doubting the authenticity of the attested material.

b. The criterion of discontinuity. Agreement on this criterion is practically unanimous. The criterion can be stated thus: "A datum of the Gospels (especially one involving the words and attitudes of Jesus) can be regarded as authentic if it is not reducible either to concepts current in Judaism or to concepts current in the primitive church."

Before consideration of particular stories, it can be said that the Gospels as a whole are an instance of *discontinuity*, in the sense that they are unique and original in relation to any and every other literature. The literary genre "gospel" is discontinuous both with older Jewish literature and with subsequent Christian literature. The Gospels are not biographies or apologias or doctrinal speculations but *testimonies* to the unparalleled event of the coming of God into history. Their content is the person of Christ, which cannot be classified in the categories either of secular history or the history of religions. Jesus presents himself to the historian as an utterly unique being. The pericopes show countless examples of this discontinuity, both in their form and in their content. Jeremias has devoted special attention to cases of discontinuity in *form*. Thus, in the very frequent use that Jesus makes of antithetical parallelism, he differs from the OT by putting the emphasis on the second part of the parallelism rather than on the first (Mt 7:3–5). Again, unlike the OT, which uses "Amen"

("Truly") to express agreement with words already spoken, Jesus uses "Amen" (in the Synoptics) or "Amen, amen" (in John, followed by "I tell you") to introduce his own words. This kind of utterance, analogously to that of the prophets, manifests the unique authority of this man who also says: "I Am."

Discontinuity in the area of attitudes and content is even more important. Thus the expression "Abba," which Jesus uses in addressing God, displays an intimate relationship that is unheard of in ancient Judaism. Jesus alone is able to address God as his Father, and he alone can authorize his followers to say after him: "Our Father." As regards the law, Jesus does not share the attitude of the Pharisees, whose focus is on the details of external observance; his attention is directed immediately to the spirit of the law. His attitude and example in relation to the Sabbath and to legal purifications represent a break with the rabbinic world. Again, his vision of the kingdom differs radically from that of the average Jew. His vision combines the grandeur of the Davidic kingdom with a humble preaching to the poor, and the final glorification of the Son of Man with the redemptive sufferings of the Servant of Yahweh.

Let us look now at some instances of discontinuity with concepts current in the primitive church:

• The baptism of Jesus places him among sinners. How could the primitive church, which proclaims him to be "Lord," have invented a scene that contrasts so violently with its faith? The same must be said of the triple temptation, the agony, and the death on the cross.

• The order given to the apostles not to preach to the Samaritans and Gentiles no longer corresponds to the situation of a church that is now open to all nations.

• All passages in the Gospels that emphasize the apostles' lack of understanding, their defects, and even their defection (betrayal by Judas, denial by Peter) stand in contrast to the post-Easter situation, in which the primitive church cultivated a great veneration for the apostles.

• The Gospels have retained enigmatic sayings of Jesus that the church, in a position now to understand them, might well have been tempted to eliminate (Mt 11:11–12; Mk 4:11; 9:31; 14:58; Lk 13:32).

• The retention in the Gospels of such expressions as "kingdom" and "Son of Man" reflects a situation now anachronistic by comparison with the more-developed theology of Paul.

The majority of critics regard this basic criterion as valid but also think it must be used in combination with others, especially the criterion of conformity. Too exclusive a use of the criterion of discontinuity would tend to excise as unauthentic anything consonant with Judaism or the primitive church. Such an approach would turn Christ into a timeless being, cutting him off from his environment and period. It would put him into a vacuum in which he was uninfluenced by Judaism and in turn exercised no influence on the church; or it would be to accept the presupposition that the church either distorted or invented anything having to do with Jesus. The fact is that Christ belonged to his age and that he had to make his own the milieu and history of his people, with their linguistic, social, and religious traditions. In addition, Acts shows us how attached the church remained to Judaism and how painful it was for it to free itself of Judaism in order not to founder with it.

The criterion of discontinuity is especially effective in discovering and identifying certain sayings of Jesus, certain events of his life, and certain essential themes of his preaching. But it would not be legitimate to use this criterion exclusively and to eliminate everything in harmony with the Jewish tradition or the tradition of the church.

c. The criterion of conformity. This criterion is not understood in the same way by all critics. Thus B. Rigaux (*RB* 68 [1958]: 518–20) prefers to emphasize the conformity of the gospel stories with the Palestinian and Jewish environment in the time of Jesus, as this is known to us from history, archaeology, and literature. And in fact the gospel description of the human setting (work, housing, occupations); the linguistic and cultural setting (patterns of thought, Aramaic substratum); the social, economic, political, and juridical setting; and, above all, the religious setting (with its rivalries between Pharisees and Sadducees, its religious focus on clean and unclean, law and Sabbath, demons and angels, poor and rich, kingdom of God and end of time)—this description is remarkably faithful to the complex picture of Palestine in the time of Jesus. This conformity with the unique moment in time when Jesus appeared in Israel constitutes, in Rigaux's judgment, an indisputable sign of authenticity. No one could have invented out of whole cloth so wide-ranging and complex a collection of data that are reflected in the smallest details of the Gospels as in a piece of finely knit material; the explanation of this fidelity is that it reflects the reality.

Bultmann and Perrin regard as authentic only materials that are in conformity with those shown to be valid by the criterion of discontinuity. In other words, once an authentic nucleus of sayings and deeds of Jesus (in particular, his death on the cross and his preaching of the kingdom) has been uncovered by means of the criterion of discontinuity, anything more that is in conformity with these elements and with the image that emerges from them belongs to the Jesus of history. Thus the application of this criterion shows the parables of the kingdom to be authentic.

Broadening and extending this criterion, de la Potterie accepts as authentic everything that is in conformity with the central teaching of Jesus on the imminent coming of the kingdom. The theme of the reign of God belongs to the oldest strata of the gospel tradition. In addition, it is attested by the criterion of discontinuity. It is everywhere present in the Synoptics and has an element of eschatological urgency that distinguishes it both from previous Judaism and from the early preaching of the church.

Conformity with the setting, as understood by Rigaux, seems a valid argument in establishing the overall historicity of the Gospels. For when such extensive narratives reflect a setting in so faithful a manner, it can be said that there is a well-grounded presumption of authenticity. This is all the more so since the gospel description of this setting comes from the source and does not show the least sign of a post factum reconstruction. It must be said, however, that this kind of conformity does not lead directly to the historical Jesus, but only to the *setting* in which he lived. It cannot suffice by itself.

It is for this reason that the following definition of the criterion of conformity is offered, a definition that incorporates the positions of Rigaux, Perrin, and de la Potterie: "A saying or action of Jesus can be regarded as authentic if it is not only in close conformity with the times

and setting of Jesus (the linguistic, geographic, social, political, and religious setting) but also and above all fully consistent with the essential teaching of Jesus, the heart of his message, namely, the coming and establishment of the messianic reign." Examples that are typical from this point of view are the parables, which are wholly focused on the kingdom and the conditions for its development; the beatitudes, which are originally a proclamation of the good news of the coming of the messianic kingdom; the Our Father, which is originally and essentially a prayer for the establishment of the kingdom; the miracles, which are closely connected with the theme of the kingdom of God and the theme of conversion; the triple temptation, which is conformed to the setting of Jesus' life and to his conception of the kingdom (note the persistent calls of the Jews for a miracle, and the constant refusal by Jesus; Jewish expectation of a political and temporal Messiah, and the preaching by Jesus of an interior kingdom; confrontation between the kingdom of God and the kingdom of Satan).

The two criteria of discontinuity and conformity are at once different and complementary. It is the conformity with the setting that makes it possible to locate Jesus in history and to conclude that he was truly a man of his age, while the criterion of discontinuity shows him to be unique and original. He stands out against his age but at the same time belongs to it. The criterion of discontinuity also makes it possible to ascertain the essential traits of his personality and teaching. Operating on this still limited but solid basis, the criterion of conformity then extends and broadens the areas of authenticity, in a series, as it were, of concentric circles. The theme of the kingdom, for example, reaches out to include the parables, the beatitudes, the miracles, the triple temptation, and the Our Father. Finally, it is by using both of these criteria that we establish what I shall call, further on, the *style of Jesus*. It is necessary, therefore, to avoid isolating each of these criteria in practice, as though each were an absolute. Each is valid in itself, but each is also meant to shed light on, and to support, the others.

d. The criterion of necessary explanation. We propose the following description: "If a sizable collection of facts or data requiring a coherent and sufficient explanation are given an explanation that clarifies and harmoniously combines all these elements (which would otherwise remain puzzling), then we may conclude that we are in the presence of an authentic datum (a deed, action, attitude, or statement of Jesus)" (see René Latourelle, *The Miracles of Jesus and the Theology of Miracles* [New York, 1988], 67). This criterion brings to bear a set of observations that derive their value from their convergence and that as a group require an intelligible explanation, namely, the reality of the fact that is the starting point. This criterion is regularly applied in history, law, and most of the human sciences.

In the case of the Gospels, critics are justified in regarding as authentic an explanation that solves a large number of problems without giving rise to greater problems or even without giving rise to any new problem.

Thus a great number of facts in the life of Jesus (e.g., his attitude to prescriptions of the law, to the Jewish authorities, to the Scriptures; the prerogatives he claims; the language he uses; his prestige and his attractiveness to the disciples and the people generally) are intelligible only if we accept that behind them is a unique and transcendent personality. Such an explanation is more consistent than recourse to a supposed ecclesial creation of a mythical Jesus.

In the case of the miracles we are confronted with at least seven important facts that even the most rigorous criticism cannot dispute and that call for an adequate explanation: the excitement aroused by Jesus, the faith of the apostles in his messiahship, the place of miracles in the Synoptic and Johannine traditions, the hatred felt by the high priests and Pharisees because of the miracles worked by Jesus, the constant connection between miracles and the message of Jesus about the definitive coming of the kingdom, the place of miracles in the primitive kerygma, and the close relationship between the claims of Jesus to be the Son of the Father and miracles as signs of his power. All these facts call for an explanation, a sufficient reason.

While the privileged area for the application of the criterion of necessary explanation is the major themes of the gospel, we must insist that it applies no less well to particular pericopes. In the case, for example, of the multiplication of the loaves it is necessary to explain (1) why, as a result of this event, Jesus was regarded as a great prophet and even as the prophet for whom the nation was waiting, and why the people wanted to make him their king; (2) why Jesus forced his disciples to reembark without delay, as if they were unwilling to abandon something to which they were overly attached; (3) why this episode, which they initially misunderstood, marked a decisive stage in the disciples' journey toward faith in the messiahship of Jesus; (4) why Mark so strongly emphasizes the christological significance of the event and its value as a revelation of the Messiah; and (5) why this story, and no other, unexpectedly acquired such an unlikely importance in the successive stages of the tradition, first in liturgical catechesis, then in the composition of the Synoptics and the Gospel of John, and finally in the patristic tradition and the iconography of the early centuries. All these facts taken together call for a satisfying explanation. If we accept that Jesus did in fact perform this messianic action, the multiplication of loaves, we find in this fact the foundation and sufficient reason for all the facts we have just listed.

*A Secondary or Derived Criterion:
The Style of Jesus*

By "style" is meant here less a literary style than the *living, personal* style of Jesus. A style is a way of thinking that shapes language; it is the energy and movement that find expression not only in language but in the person's attitudes and entire behavior; it is the inimitable impress that the person puts on everything he or she does and says. The elements that make up this style cannot, however, be established except by applying the basic criteria of multiple attestation, discontinuity, conformity, and necessary explanation. For this reason we speak of style as secondary and derived. Once recognized and defined, however, style becomes a criterion of authenticity in its own right.

The language of Jesus, as Schürmann points out, is characterized by an exceptionally majestic self-consciousness that is without parallel; by a note of solemnity, elevation, and sacredness; by a tone at once of authority, simplicity, kindness, and eschatological urgency. In his own person Jesus begins a new age.

In his behavior, says Trilling, we can see "an unchanging love for sinners, compassion for those who suffer or are in some way enslaved, a pitiless severity toward every form of self-sufficiency, a holy anger at lying and hypocrisy, and, above all, a radical reference of himself to God, his Lord and Father" (1968:59).

These characteristics are to be seen in both the action and the teaching of Jesus. His words are marked by simplicity, gentleness, and, at the same time, sovereign authority. Thus the Jesus who describes himself as the servant of all, the good shepherd, and the friend of the poor and the lowly is also the Jesus who says: "I have come . . ."; "But I tell you . . ."; "Truly, I tell you . . ."; "Whoever acts on my word . . ."; "Go . . ."; "Come . . ."; "Follow me"; "Arise and walk." His words are marked by a sense of eschatological urgency: "You have heard that it was said. . . . But I say to you . . ."; "Heaven and earth will pass away, but my words will not pass away."

His activities show the same traits of simplicity and authority, and, above all, of kindness and compassion for sinners and all who suffer. Thus the Lukan parable of the prodigal son describes the incomparable goodness of God toward sinners, but at the same time it justifies Jesus' own attitude in socializing with tax collectors and sinners and eating at their table. The same attitude is to be seen in the parable of the lost sheep. It is part of the "style" of Jesus. The style he shows in his miracles is the same as that which he shows in his teaching, one combining simplicity, restraint, and authority.

Mixed Criteria

A piece of literary evidence is sometimes combined with one or more historical criteria; the result is a mixed criterion. Here are two especially important criteria of this kind.

a. Internal intelligibility of a story. When a datum of the Gospel fits perfectly into its immediate or mediate context and, in addition, is completely consistent in its internal structure, we may judge that we are dealing with a datum that is authentic. But this fact of the internal intelligibility of a story or a series of pericopes cannot by itself be a criterion of historical authenticity, for we are still dealing with literary evidence. If the fact of internal intelli-

gibility is to have value at the historical level, it must be supported by one or more criteria of historicity: multiple attestation, discontinuity, or conformity. The combination constitutes a mixed criterion.

Thus the fact of Jesus' burial is attested in the Synoptics, John, 1 Corinthians, and Acts. In addition, we find in Mark's account a set of details that are fully consistent among themselves. Pilate is surprised that Jesus is already dead: that is why he summons and questions the centurion in charge. The request to bury Jesus comes from a member of the Sanhedrin, whose name is Joseph of Arimathea; this is a fact which anyone could check. The interested parties make haste to bury Jesus because it is the eve of the Sabbath. The frightened women are content to look on. The body of Jesus is laid in a tomb close to Calvary—but a tomb is something permanent, whose existence can be checked. All these many consistent details form a piece of literary evidence that, when joined to the criterion of multiple attestation, acquires the status of a mixed criterion.

b. Different interpretations, substantial agreement. Considered in itself, different interpretations of a teaching or a miracle are a phenomenon in the area of redactional activity. They bear witness both to the freedom of the writers and to their respect for their sources. They take us back to very old traditions and thereby reduce both the number of mediations separating us from Jesus and the possibilities of distortion, but they do not on that account constitute a criterion of historicity. Thus the fact that Luke emphasizes the social bearing of the beatitudes, while Matthew brings out their moral significance, allows J. Dupont to reconstruct with probability the original literary form. However, it is only by application of the criteria of discontinuity and conformity that the passage from literary criticism to historical criticism becomes possible; once again, we have a mixed criterion. But the substantial agreement amid diversity of interpretation does constitute a strong presumption of historical authenticity.

In telling of the multiplication of loaves, John emphasizes, more than Mark does, the sacramental symbolism of the miracle. Mark in turn lays greater stress than Luke does on the christological significance of the miracle and shows

Christ as the Good Shepherd who has compassion on these sheep without a shepherd (Mk 6:34). The Gospel of John contains many details found only here: the place and time of the miracle, the dialogue with the disciples, the people's identification of Jesus as messianic prophet, the attempt to take him and make him king, the discourse on the bread of life, and the disagreement among the disciples when faced with the demands of Jesus (Jn 6). The event is the same, but it has been interpreted and studied more deeply. This piece of literary evidence is supported by the criterion of multiple attestation, since the fact is attested by both the Synoptic and the Johannine traditions; by the criterion of conformity, since the miracle is worked as a sign of the messianic and eschatological kingdom; and, finally, by the criterion of necessary explanation, since if there were no real event, a number of points would lack any sufficient reason.

The cure of the epileptic boy is attested by the three Synoptic Gospels but interpreted in three different ways. Luke sees in the miracle an act of kindness for the grieving father (Lk 9:42); in keeping with the general perspective of his Gospel, Mark sees in it primarily a resounding victory of Jesus over Satan (Mk 9:14–27); Matthew, finally, emphasizes the necessity of faith in the mission of Jesus (Mt 17:19) — because the disciples lacked this faith they could not rescue the possessed boy. Thus there is agreement on the event but differences in interpreting it. These different interpretations are due to the multilayered significance of the event itself.

One conclusion is unavoidable: the proof or demonstration of the historical authenticity of the Gospels depends on a *convergent application* of criteria. Even if it turns out that one or another criterion does not apply in a particular case (e.g., multiple attestation), in most instances several convergent criteria do come into play; at the very least, a single, clearly valid criterion will be confirmed by one or more of the others. When we come to the major themes of the Gospels, all the criteria apply.

8. Knowledge of Jesus through the Gospels

We have studied the results of external criticism; the pre-Easter setting, its makeup and cohesiveness, its fidelity to Jesus amid daily intimacy in a world shaped by oral culture; the consciously willed fidelity to Jesus that the primitive church maintained and that found expression in a basic vocabulary that came into being under the sign of fidelity; and the application of the criteria of historicity. All these approaches and convergent arguments allow us to draw some conclusions regarding knowledge of Jesus. Even when we adopt a moderately critical position, halfway between confidence in principle and suspicion in principle, we reach surprising results. Historical criticism allows us to salvage almost the whole of the gospel material and to obtain a knowledge of Jesus that yields in turn a solidly based Christology and ecclesiology. This knowledge includes: (a) the linguistic, human, social, political, economic, cultural, juridical, and religious setting; (b) the main phases of the ministry of Jesus: the beginnings in Galilee and the intense joy of people and apostles at the miracles worked; the growing lack of understanding as the messiahship of Jesus reveals its true character; the ministry in Jerusalem; the political and religious trial, condemnation, passion, and death; (c) the major events in the life of Jesus: baptism, transfiguration, teaching on the definitive coming of the kingdom, call to repentance and conversion, parables of the kingdom, beatitudes, Our Father, miracles and exorcisms as signs of the kingdom, betrayal by Judas, agony, trial, crucifixion, burial, and resurrection; (d) the controversies with the scribes and Pharisees over prescriptions for the Sabbath, legal cleanness, divorce, and taxes; (e) the attitude of Jesus with its contrasting elements of simplicity and authority; utter freedom from sin and compassion for sinners, the poor, the sick, and the oppressed; the spirit of service, even to the point of surrendering his life; (f) the formulas expressing an obscure, sometimes enigmatic Christology: sign of Jonah, sign of the temple, Son of Man; (g) the logia that humble Jesus, as it were, and make him inferior to God; (h) the rejection of a political and temporal messianism, the preaching of a kingdom into which people enter through repentance, conversion, and faith; (i) the astonishing claims displayed in the antitheses of the Sermon on the Mount, in attitudes toward the prescriptions of the law, in the use of the word *Abba* to express his relationship with God, in his identification of himself with Daniel's Son of Man, and in the statements that will bring him to his death; (j) the calling and sending of the apostles with a view to the formation of a community; the apostles' great excitement, followed by their misunderstanding; their betrayal and abandonment of him. For each of the themes just listed we can invoke the agreement of the most important in a throng of exegetes. As study of the texts proceeds, the extent of the material accepted as authentic is continually growing and will eventually cover the entirety of the gospel.

After the demonstration whose steps we have retraced, it is no longer possible to say with Bultmann: "We know nothing or almost nothing about Jesus of Nazareth." Such a claim is no longer tenable but is merely a reflection of an outdated myth.

Furthermore, an entire attitude to the Gospels needs to be changed. For over a century, people fostered a systematic prejudgment of suspicion in regard to these texts; the burden of proof was always regarded as falling on the Gospels themselves. After the investigations conducted during recent decades, it is no longer possible to maintain this attitude of the "masters of suspicion," for it is opposed by arguments that history itself provides. Nowadays the opposite stance is required: the burden of proof falls not on those who acknowledge Jesus as the source of the words and actions recorded in the Gospels but on those who regard these words and actions as creations of the primitive church. The presupposition that the Gospels deserve trust is well founded, while the prejudgment that the Gospels are not trustworthy is not well founded. This reversal of outlook does not mean that critics have settled for an attitude of naïve and uncritical trust. The point is simply that the Gospels have regained their credibility in the eyes of historical criticism.

9. Faith and History

It should be clear that this effort to reach Jesus by the paths of historical study is not a return by the back door to the perspectives of the old *Leben-Jesu-Forschung*, or critical investigation of the life of Jesus. If readers think so, they have not understood what we have been about here. The point is not at all to make faith dependent on historical investigation. Nor is the aim to reduce Christ to the man Jesus and then offer him as the religious ideal for the human race. Nor is there any intention of abandoning the christological interpretations found in the kerygma and the councils, in order to retain only a Jesus who has been immunized against any and every further interpretation. The aim is rather to gain access to Jesus of Nazareth, now identified as Christ and Lord, by way precisely of what he really said and did during the time he spent among us here on earth.

A historical and critical study obviously does not compel faith, but it does offer important services to faith. It can furnish it with a concrete content. It can show that the retrieval of the authentic Jesus and his authentic message is a possible and feasible undertaking. It can show that the church's interpretation of Jesus is consistent with the historical life and message of Jesus. That is an important contribution, since one may not just say anything whatsoever about Jesus. For in the final analysis faith has to do with Jesus of Nazareth, in whom God revealed himself. Historical investigation can also show that the call to the decision of faith is part of the original message of Jesus. By enlightening us about this message, it can even dispose us for it and show us how credible it is. But historical study cannot impose the decision of faith or force us to acknowledge him who speaks to be the Son of the living God. Historical scholarship does not impose faith, but it does make it possible by giving access to the authentic gospel of the authentic Jesus. We are still left with the responsibility for allowing Christ to challenge us and for surrendering to the Spirit who speaks within and causes us to see the living message of Jesus as a living message addressed to us individually.

Historical study also renders a valuable service to believers. First of all, it shows them that the age-old confidence of the church in the Gospels as a source of knowledge of Jesus is based on solid arguments that are proof against the attacks of criticism. It also teaches them how to read the Gospels properly. It is important in reading the Gospels not only to ask them what they have to say to us today but also to ask them the meaning for us today of what Jesus—as read and understood by the church and the evangelists—did and said yesterday. Otherwise the gospel runs the risk of being a mere doctrine or even an ideology that is divorced from its author, a message without a messenger. In the case of the Gospels, this is the supreme danger, since the message in this case is concerned with the messenger himself.

Bibl.: V. TAYLOR, *The Formation of the Gospel Tradition* (London, 1935); L. CERFAUX, *La voix vivante de l'Évangile au début de l'Église* (Tournai, 1946); id., *Jésus aux origines de la Tradition* (Bruges/Brussels/Paris, 1968); F. MUSSNER, "Der historische Jesus und der Christus des Glaubens," *BZ* 1 (1957): 224–52; H. ZAHRNT, *Es begann mit Jesus von Nazareth* (Stuttgart/Berlin, 1960); J. M. ROBINSON, *A New Quest of the Historical Jesus* (Naperville, Ill., 1959); id., *The Problem of the Historical Jesus* (Philadelphia, 1964); B. GERHARDSSON, *Memory and Manuscript* (Lund, 1961); W. RISTOW and K. MATTHIAE, eds., *Der historische Jesus und der kerygmatische Christus* (Berlin, 1961); R. BULTMANN, *History of the Synoptic Tradition* (New York, 1963); J. JEREMIAS, *The Problem of the Historical Jesus* (Philadelphia, 1964); id., *The Central Message of the New Testament* (New York, 1965); J. LEAL, *Nuestra confianza en los Evangelios* (Madrid, 1965); I. DE LA POTTERIE, ed., *De Jésus aux Évangiles* (Paris, 1967); J. R. SCHEIFLER, *Así nacieron los Evangelios* (2nd ed.; Bilbao, 1967); X. LÉON-DUFOUR, *The Gospels and the Jesus of History* (New York, 1967); W. TRILLING, *Fragen zur Geschlichtlichkeit Jesu* (Düsseldorf, 1966); J.-J. WEBER, "Les Évangiles méritent-ils notre confiance?" in J.-J. WEBER and J. SCHMITT, eds., *Où en sont les études bibliques?* (Paris, 1968), 185–212; P. GRECH, "Jesus Christ in History and Dogma," in *A New Catholic Commentary on Holy Scripture* (London, 1969), 822–37; M. BOUTTIER, *Du Christ de l'histoire au Jésus des Évangiles* (Paris, 1969); I. BERTEN, "Christologie et recherche historique sur Jésus," *RSPT* 53 (1969): 233–44; id., "Le retour de la question historique de Jésus," *RSPT* 54 (1970): 128–65; H. RIESENFELD, *The Gospel Tradition* (Oxford, 1970); J. CABA, *De los Evangelios al Jesús histórico* (Madrid, 1970); S. ZEDDA, *I Vangeli e la critica oggi* (Treviso, 1970); id., *Il Gesù della storia* (Trévise, 1970); L. VAGANAY, "Apocryphes du N.T.," *Cath* 1:699–704; R. BROWN, "Apocrypha," *JBC* 543–46; A. DESCAMPS, "L'approche des Synoptiques comme documents historiques," *ETL* 46 (1970): 5–16; E. SCHILLEBEECKX, *L'approccio a Gesù di Nazaret* (Brescia, 1972); J. DELORME, *Des Évangiles à Jésus* (Paris, 1972); A. DESCAMPS, "Portée de la recherche historique sur Jésus," in J. DUPONT, ed., *Jésus aux origines de la christologie* (Gembloux, 1975), 23–45; F. LAMBIASI, *L'autenticità storica dei Vangeli: Studio di criteriologia* (Bologna, 1976); R. LATOURELLE, *Finding Jesus through the Gospels* (New York, 1979); J. GUILLET, *Entre Jésus et l'Église* (Paris, 1985).

René LATOURELLE

GREGORY OF NYSSA

The mystery of Christ is gradually made known to the peoples of the world as they become capable of accepting it and understanding it in light of their own cultures. This phenomenon of inculturation, to which our century is especially sensitive, first played a role in the Greco-Latin culture in which Christianity spread far and wide. From the viewpoint of inculturation, the fourth century is all the more revealing because, on the one hand, it was the age in which, from Theodosius on, Christians had a sense of truly belonging to the empire, of moving "with the stream of history," and of being able to open themselves without reservations to the culture of which they were becoming the jewel; on the other, it was the age in which the Arian crisis made very clear the discontinuities and incompatibilities between Christianity and this same Greco-Latin mentality.

Gregory of Nyssa is a good example of both aspects. After having intended, it seems, to enter the priesthood, he allowed himself to be seduced by the final brilliant outburst of pagan culture in the reign of Julian; he became a rhetorician and probably married. Like many fathers of the church, he accepted, to the very end of his life, the idea that secular culture is useful to Christians (see the *Life of Moses* 2.12; *SChr* 1 [3rd ed.; Paris, 1968], 112–13), provided it is not separated from "the nutritious milk of the Church." He says that his own teachers were Paul and Libanios the rhetorician (see *Letter* 12.4–6; GNO 8/2, 45, 15), but at the same time he praises his sister Macrina for ignoring secular culture and deriving her instruction from the Scriptures alone (see *Life of Macrina* 3; *SChr* 178 [Paris, 1971], 148–51). Beginning with the *Treatise on Virginity*, written in 371, a year before his election to the episcopate, he expresses his regret that he had not shared this idea of virginity, "to which one cannot return once one has set foot in the life of the world" (*Treatise on Virginity*, *SChr* 119 [Paris, 1966], 274–75). After having tasted "the predicaments of the world" and having devoted his energies to theological debate, Gregory seems to have become increasingly enamored of monastic spirituality, as can be seen from the addressees of his last two works: the *Life of Moses* is addressed to a monk, and the *Homilies on the*

Song of Songs to a devout woman of Constantinople.

It is, however, in his work, more than in his life (of which we know little), that Gregory shows himself the balanced representative of the Christianity of his age. His high level of culture and his elegant style, which bear the mark of the aestheticism of the Second Sophistic, reflect the successful cultural assimilation of the Christianity of the imperial age. At the same time, his strength as a metaphysician and his spiritual depth make him better able than others to highlight the points at which Christianity is at odds with that same culture. It is in this twofold light that I shall study his expression of Christian revelation.

1. Christ and Human Beings

The first point at which there is a break between Greek philosophy and the metaphysics of Gregory of Nyssa is to be found in the conception of the universe and of the ladder of being. For his adversary, Eunomius, whom Gregory accurately describes as a "technologist," that is, a manipulator of human arguments, God is entirely comprehensible to the human mind and can be strictly enclosed in a human concept—the concept of the Unbegotten. In answering, Gregory takes into account the transcendence of the divine nature. The real abyss that cannot be bridged is not the one between the intelligible world and sensible matter but the one between the uncreated and the created. Intelligible nature is divided into two parts: "The one is uncreated and creates all beings; it is eternally what it is and always remains like itself; in its complete self-sufficiency it is beyond any addition or subtraction. The other, which has been brought into existence by an act of creation, is always turned toward the first cause of beings, and it is its participation in the transcendent Good that keeps it in existence" (*In Cant.* 6; GNO 6, p. 174, 1–7).

Created nature is confined within its own limits; it is finite and separated by an immense and impassable gulf from the uncreated nature, which is infinite; this infinity makes the divinity incomprehensible to us, elusive and inexpressible. Only one being makes it possible to cross this abyss: Christ, who unites humanity and divinity in himself and therefore becomes the sole and necessary mediator. "He has concealed himself beside our bed, this Beloved of ours, who is beautiful and full of delights. And indeed, if he had not concealed himself by hiding the light of his divinity under the form of a slave, who could have endured his manifestation? No one can see the face of God and live. You came therefore, you who are full of delights, but you became such that we could receive you" (*In Cant.* 6; GNO 6, pp. 107, 11–108, 6). Breaking with the Greek tradition, which thought of salvation as coming through knowledge, Gregory speaks of a salvation through the faith that unites human beings to Christ and alone gives them access to God: "And thus for the rest of his life there was the law of faith, which, through the story of Abraham, teaches those desirous of approaching God that this is impossible for them unless faith serves as mediator and unites the seeking spirit to the incomprehensible nature. Abandoning the curiosity that seeks knowledge, the Apostle says: 'Abraham believed in God, and this was accounted to him as justice'" (*Against Eunomius* 2; GNO 1, p. 253, 23–30).

2. The Scriptures and the Problem of Human Language

While God is transcendent, he does make himself known in two ways: through his wonderful works in creation and through Christ, who is taught to us in the Scriptures and given to us in the sacraments. The wonderful works of God are like the perfume of his presence throughout creation. On the basis of the traces that we can apprehend, we construct ideas about God and, in accordance with these ideas, words that enable us to give expression to what we grasp of the divine reality in each instance, though not to the divine reality as it is in itself. "On the one hand, the very perfume of the divinity—I mean, that which the divinity is by its essence—is beyond any and every name and concept; on the other, the wonders that we see in the universe provide us with the material for names which we apply to God, calling him wise, powerful, good, holy, blessed, eternal, judge, savior" (*In Cant.* 1; GNO 6, p. 37, 12–17). We can only form conjectures about God; that is, we can only move toward him without ever encompassing him. By the very fact that our language is limited to the created world of which we are a part, it is powerless to contain the infinite reality of God; it does not tell us what God is, but only that by means of which our thought can move toward him. Gregory of Nyssa's critique of language is harsh and even radical.

What is the status, then, of the language of the Scriptures, in which Christ reveals himself? In his condescending love for humankind, God reveals himself through human words, words shaped by human beings and therefore deficient when kept within the boundaries natural to them as part of created language. On each occasion, therefore, an effort is needed to move beyond the overly narrow and overly human meaning that words have for us and to allow God to reveal himself each time a little more fully. We are always tempted to substitute our "base, earthbound" ideas for the transcendent God who is revealing himself. The Word knocks at the door of our understanding and allows his knowledge to trickle into us: "For it is impossible that those who find themselves within the invisible sanctuary should experience a rain or shower of knowledge. Rather they should rejoice if the truth bedews their minds with tenuous and confused thoughts, since the spiritual water trickles down drop by drop from the saints and inspired persons" (In Cant. 11; GNO 6, pp. 325, 21–326, 5). The conditions for God's revelation in the Scriptures are neatly set down here: it must be the Word who knocks at our door; but he does this preeminently in the Scriptures (comprising prophets, evangelists, and apostles, to whom Gregory refers a few lines further on). But if we are to understand the Word, we must be within the invisible sanctuary, that is, Christ, and must be led by the Spirit. Through the words of Scripture, which are human words, and thanks to a correct exegesis, we reach some conjectural knowledge about God and move toward him. Revelation guarantees that it is indeed God to whom we are moving and not an illusion, because we are united with him by faith. Pagans and Christians alike are in great danger of trying to enclose God in our base, earthbound conceptions and concepts, or in an idea of him that is too small because it is limited to what we are capable of grasping of him. Here, too, Christ is the mediator through whom we can reach the true God.

3. Christ and Sinful Humanity

Sin does not radically destroy any and every relation between human beings and God. For,

according to Gn 1:26, a verse of Scripture that controls the whole of Gregory's anthropology, human beings are created in the image of God, that is, turned to God, called to know God because only like can know like, and destined to become an image increasingly like God through transforming contemplation.

Sin is due to the application of an erroneous norm of judgment. Instead of judging things in God, according to the reason that God has given them as his images, human beings choose their own senses as their norm. They become "material" (we today would say "materialistic") and choose their good according to appearances and not according to truth. But that which flatters the senses is not really good; only that which turns us toward our supreme Good, which is God, is really good. This error in direction has two consequences. First, the image of God that was reflected in the human heart as in a mirror becomes tarnished, since the mirror, being turned now to something else, reflects a different reality. Furthermore, human beings have the fearsome power of transforming themselves into that on which they gaze: into toads if they fasten their gaze on toads; into beauties if they focus their gaze on beauty (see In Cant. 4; GNO 6, pp. 102, 4–104, 15). The bond between them and God becomes distorted, and their ability to return to God disappears, unless they are given a Savior.

The second consequence: having condemned themselves to lead a base and earthbound life to which God had not called them, human beings must adapt to this kind of life. God therefore gives them a constitution enabling them to live the kind of life they have freely chosen, and this constitution does not correspond to that required for the happy life that alone God willed for them. Gregory explains this by saying that when human beings left paradise, they found themselves clad in "tunics of skin"; pleasure, greed, and anger develop, but so does a whole series of traits connected with biological life, especially sexuality and death. These last two characteristics are strictly connected with our earthbound condition and will disappear in the next life, where there will no longer be male and female and where death will have been destroyed. We see here the transformation of an idea that was extremely important in Greek philosophy: the distinction between the self and what is not the self. Like the philosophers,

Gregory says that honors, power, money, beauty, and health are not the self. But the philosophers (Plato, the Stoics, and others) also say that the body is not the self. Gregory distinguishes between the heavenly tunic, which is our risen body, and the tunic of skin, which is simply an adaptation to a life that passes away. The proclamation of the resurrection thus takes over a secular theme and transforms it.

Drawn thus by sin and the attraction of matter, human beings find themselves subject to a twofold necessity. On the one hand, as creatures, they are beings who have emerged from nothingness, and their nature continues to be determined by this original passage. They are called upon at every moment to pass from nothingness to being, or at least from a certain degree of being to greater being. If they turn aside from being, their essentially changing character draws them back again toward nothingness. On the other hand, sin links human beings to matter, that is, to the cyclic movement of material time. Sin bears the mark of this cyclic time; for example, we are hungry, we eat, and hunger returns. The same is true of our passions. We are like someone who is trying to climb a dune, but the sand keeps slipping away at each step (see *Life of Moses* 2.244; *SChr* 1:274–75). Evil is not limitless, since it was invented by human beings, whose power is limited precisely because they are only creatures. Consequently, evil cannot continue endlessly to find new forms. Human beings, however, do fall endlessly into the same sins. And, given the ancient conception of cyclic time, there is no reason to expect an end to this continued falling. It is Christ's intervention in the incarnation that breaks the cycle of evil and introduces a linear movement of continual progress in goodness. United with him, human beings pass through the zone of evil and enter into that of the Good, as the *Sermon on Christmas* explains: "Understand, then, that the night of sin had become as dark as possible and through the invention of all possible vices had reached its greatest extent, but also that today [Christmas, the day of Christ's birth] the law of sin's growth was abrogated and that henceforth sin is being reduced, to the point where it will disappear and be annihilated" (*PG* 45).

Christ thus introduces a break into the cyclic movement of time; he also halts a major effect of sin on creation, namely, division. Because Christ is one with his Father and because the divine nature is one and indivisible, the incarnation introduces a principle of reunification into divided humanity. It is thus that Gregory explains, for example, the victory of Christ over death. Death is only the final moment in the victory of evil, since it brings about the separation of what God had intended should be united: soul and body. In Christ, death does its work by separating his soul from his body, but at the final point of separation death comes up against that which is indivisible and is permanently united to both soul and body, namely, the divinity of Christ. The indivisible oneness of this divinity is the basis for the reunification of soul and body in the resurrection. "Before union with the flesh, during this union, and after the passion the divinity remains ever the same. . . . But in the suffering of the human nature it brought the divine plan to completion for our sake. For in due time it separated soul from body, but it did not separate itself from either of these two components to which it had been united once and for all; then it again reunited what had been separated, so as to give the whole of human nature a new point of departure and of linkage with his resurrection from the dead, in order that everthing corruptible might put on incorruptibility and everything mortal immortality" (*Refutation of Eunomius' Confession of Faith*; GNO 2, p. 387, 14–23).

Death, therefore, is not a destruction of the body, as the pagan Greek world teaches, but a destruction of what is corrupting and corrupted in us because of the presence of evil: "It is then that the part of us which is no longer of any use because it has received the contrary element is dissolved. . . . Let us suppose that a clay vessel has, out of mischief, been filled with molten lead; once poured in, the lead hardens and cannot be poured out. The owner of the vessel asserts his rights and, being a potter, breaks the clay that now forms a shell around the lead; then he refashions it in its original form so that he can use it, now that it is emptied of the material that had gotten mixed in with it. The artist who shapes our vessel acts in the same way, once evil has been mingled with the sentient part. . . . After seeing the dissolution of the matter that had contained the evil, the creator will, by means of the resurrection, fashion anew the vessel that is now purified of the contrary element; by thus regenerating its elements he will restore it to its original beauty" (*Catechetical Discourse* 7).

Christ's reunification of what had become divided in us begins at baptism. That is why Gregory lays special emphasis on the necessity of harmonizing the interior self and the exterior self, purity of soul and the rectitude produced by the virtues. If Christ is truly the cornerstone in us, then the two walls forming the angle must arise at the same place: "The head of the universe becomes our head as well, fitting himself to the two walls of our life, those consisting of our body and our soul, which are erected by means of good outward behavior and purity of soul, since it is their nature to form a two-sided angle. Consequently, when one of the two walls is defective (when good outward behavior is not developed along with purity of soul, or when the spiritual virtue of the soul is not manifested in the visible aspect), Christ cannot be the head of a life in which half is missing" (*On Perfection*; GNO 8/1, p. 193, 8–17). When everything is made one again in us, the flesh will no longer war against the spirit, for our entire being will be permeated by a single desire that is directed in Christ to God (see *In Cant.* I).

4. The New Birth, Mary, the Church

By his incarnation Christ inaugurated a new world from which evil and sin are excluded. Christ is the Firstborn, not because he is first in the creation we have inherited from Adam, but because he is the source of a new kind of birth, the birth of baptismal regeneration that begins with the baptism of Christ himself, and of a new creation in which there is no death and which begins with his resurrection. The sign of this birth, which is of a different order than the transmission of transitory bodily life that is doomed to death, is the virginal birth: "If we look at the twofold rebirth that is effected by baptism and resurrection, he is the leader in both births; in the flesh, on the other hand, he has become the Firstborn by being the first and only one to establish in his person a virginal birth, which is unknown to the natural order and of which no one else provides an example down through so many human generations" (*Against Eunomius* III, 2; GNO 2, p. 69, 14, 19).

Gregory considers it very important to emphasize the fact that this birth in the flesh is not a mere material continuation of the human race but is an interruption in the passing on of death. Thus he stresses the significant absence, from this birth, of the transitory marks of sin: "He was conceived without marital union, brought into the world without stain to the mother, birthed without pain. . . . Just as a son has here been given to us without a father, so this child has been brought into the world without the normal birth process. . . . He does not owe his origin to pleasure nor his coming to birth pangs. This is neither unreasonable nor improbable. Since the woman who by her sin brought death upon her own nature was condemned to give birth amid suffering and pain, it was absolutely necessary in the case of the mother of life that her conceiving should have its origin in joy and that her giving birth should reach its term in joy" (*In Cant.* XIII; GNO 6, pp. 388, 8–389, 9).

This passage is the first trace we have of the claim that Mary remained a virgin *in partu*. The doctrinal logic is clear enough: the birth of Christ is the re-creation of a new world, namely, the future church, from which every trace of evil is necessarily excluded. Arianism used the title "firstborn" to turn Christ into one creature among other, even if the first among them; Gregory answers by saying that Christ is firstborn, not as a preeminent specimen of humanity, but as the source and beginning of a new creation. The characteristic signs of this creation are manifested in Mary at the birth of Christ. They are also continued in the church, "for the founding of the church is the creation of a world; in the church, to use the prophet's words, a new heaven is created . . . a new earth is established . . . a new human being is fashioned who is renewed by the birth from on high in the image of its creator" (ibid., pp. 384, 21–385, 6). Those who see the church see Christ in her: "Those who turn their gaze to this new world brought into being by the creation of the church see in this world Him who is and who becomes all in all" (ibid., p. 386, 4–7). This birth is also ours in baptism, which leads us "to the blessed, divine state that does away with all suffering" (*Catechetical Discourse* 36).

5. The Concrete Way of Salvation

"I maintain," says Gregory, "that human beings cannot rise from the dead unless they have been reborn through baptism" (ibid., 35). This does not mean, he explains, that the unbaptized do not rise, but that they do not rise to the same life as the baptized. What God's action in baptism effects is the birth of the baptized into a pure, divine life: "Those who have been purified will share in the state of purity; and true purity is God" (ibid.). The change brought about by baptism is twofold: on the one hand, it brings purification from all the evil that is mingled with human nature; on the other, it causes human beings to leave behind their condition as limited creatures and raises them, through union with God in Christ, beyond their natural limits to an endless life of communion with God: "From mortal, human beings become immortal, from perishable imperishable, from ephemeral eternal; in short, they become God" (*On the Beatitudes*). This gift of divine life and purification from all evil does not, of course, take place automatically through the administration of the sacrament. Also needed is the cooperation of the human will that receives the sacrament, the assent of faith, and the manifestation of the work of grace through the practice of the virtues: "If the life after initiation does not differ from the life that preceded it, then I will say straight out, however daring I may sound: the water in this case is nothing but water. The gift of the Spirit is nowhere manifested in the action performed, if the person is not satisfied to go on insulting the divine image within him, but, due to the shameful vice of anger or the passion of greed, the unseemly disorder of the mind, and the noxious vapors of pride, envy, and arrogance, he even persists in keeping his unjustly gotten gains, while the woman he has acquired by adultery continues to serve his pleasure" (*Catechetical Discourse* 40). We should keep in mind that in Gregory's view, wherever Christ is at work, the external person and the interior person must develop in parallel fashion until they become one.

In Gregory's thought, all the sacraments have the same double function of healing human beings of their sins and enabling them to transcend the limitations of their creaturely condition in order to achieve a participation in the infinity of the godhead. Consequently, what he says of baptism is repeated in connection with the Eucharist. The Eucharist is first of all a remedy, namely, "this glorious body which has proved itself stronger than death and has become a source of life for us" (ibid., 37). In accordance with the division of the world into a sensible part and an intelligible part, a division that Gregory always respects, the Eucharist is already a remedy for the corruptibility of our bodies and is given to us in the appropriate form of food and drink. But this food and drink do not maintain what is mortal and transitory in the body; rather they feed the new life of the re-created body. The Eucharist also nourishes spiritual progress by leading men and women from the stage of childhood to that of the perfect adult. It brings about their emergence from a lower world in the direction of an ever higher world. The entrance of Christ into a person prompts a going out of the self, or what Gregory calls an "ecstasy": "What he urges his friends by his words to do here [Cant 5:1], he accomplishes in reality in the gospel, if it be true that every drunkenness ordinarily produces a going out of the spirit from itself under the influence of the wine. Thus the drunkenness which the Canticle urges took place long ago and always takes place as a result of the divine food and drink, for along with the food and drink the soul is transported and goes out from the lower world to the higher world" (*In Cant.* X; GNO 6, pp. 308, 15–309, 2).

6. The Revelation of Christ through the Members of the Church

As a result of this going out of the self, Christians grow constantly in Christ. But all do not grow at the same rate; some still stammer, while others can say with Paul, "It is no longer I who live, but it is Christ who lives in me." Persons thus transformed can then pass on to others what they themselves have already made their own. Gregory calls this the "economy of the church," thanks to which the Holy Spirit extends his influence: "Those who were the first to be taught by grace and who became the eyewitnesses of the Word did not lock this treasure up within themselves but engendered the same grace by transmission to those who came after them" (*In Cant.* I; GNO 6, p. 40, 14–17). Thus prophets, evangelists, and apostles, each taking "all that he could contain of the dark, hidden, invisible treasures, became for us a swollen river of water" (*In Cant.* XI; GNO 6, p. 362, 6–9). But this transmission does not take place only down through time, for each member, according to his or her capacity for receiving Christ and being transformed into him, is "the sweet fragrance of Christ" for others. The Holy Spirit thus spreads throughout the entire body and ensures its unity, each member being both one who fills others and one who is filled, or, in the image of the Canticle, being both queen and concubine. The final unity of this body is guaranteed by the oneness of its desire for God, a desire inspired by the total presence of Christ: "It is in the nature of all to strain with desire of blessedness and excellence. If, then, the young girls proclaim the doves blessed, they certainly desire to become doves themselves. And the fact that the concubines and the queens extol the dove is proof that they are also full of zeal for what they praise, until the moment when all those whose desires are fixed on the same goal become one and no trace of evil is left in anyone. God will be all in all, while all are blended together, each with the others, in the unity given by their communion in the Good" (*In Cant.* XV; GNO 6, pp. 468, 18–469, 8).

Even the angels are called to contemplate and love the beauty of the Bridegroom in the body of Christ, which is the church; consequently, it is a single love that restores the unity of all creation, which sin had broken. This one desire and one love thus reunite all of creation in Christ, but Christ, being God and man, remains a mediator, while humanity never loses the stamp of creaturehood, that is, an always limited, even if constantly expanding, capacity for knowing God. This is why humanity will always have something more to discover and why its desire will be forever both fulfilled and straining to reach out into the ocean of the divine infinity.

Bibl.: F. DIEKEMP, *Die Gotteslehre des heiligen Gregor von Nyssa: Ein Beitrag zur Dogmengeschichte der patristischen Zeit*, vol. 1 (Münster, 1896); J. DANIÉLOU, *Platonisme et théologie mystique* (Paris, 1954); id., *L'Être et le temps chez Grégoire de Nysse* (Leiden, 1970); E. MÜHLENBERG, *Die Unendlichkeit Gottes bei Gregor von Nyssa* (Göttingen, 1966); M. CANÉVET, "Grégoire de Nysse," *DSp* 6:971–1011 (Paris, 1967); id., *Grégoire de Nysse et l'herméneutique biblique: Étude des rapports entre le langage et la connaissance de Dieu* (Paris, 1983); R. M. HÜBNER, *Die Einheit des Leibes Christi bei Gregor von Nyssa: Untersuchungen zum Ursprung der "physischen" Erlösungslehre* (Leiden, 1974); H. DÖRRIE, "Gregor von Nyssa," *RAC* fascicle 94 (1983): 863–95; H. URS VON BALTHASAR, *Présence et pensée: Essai sur la philosophie religieuse de Grégoire de Nysse* (Paris, 1988).

Mariette CANÉVET

ROMANO GUARDINI (1885–1968)

On 11 November 1934, Romano Guardini remarked that Scripture was the source of almost all his creativity, together with a deep experience of himself and an intensive encounter with the people and things of the world. He presented his thoughts as lectures or sermons, progressively building up a system that handled the following questions: What is God? What is humanity? What is the world? The foundation stone had to be Christ's incarnation. He planned his major work to be his anthropology, where all knowledge would be gathered around the one question: What is man?

1. A Hermeneutics of Existence

Together with Karl Neundörfer, the young Guardini tackled the philosophical problems raised by Kant and Hegel—i.e., human autonomy and the multiplicity of existence. They elaborated a hermeneutics of existence, *Der Gegensatz: Versuche zu einer Philosophie des Lebendig-Konkreten* (1925). As the title suggests, it starts from an appraisal of objectivity and then proposes an original epistemological model.

Avoiding Kantian apriorisms and any simplistic reduction of objectivity, Guardini tried to safeguard the basic dynamism of human existence, with its characteristics of transcendence, freedom of choice, and freedom of activity. He also steered clear of romantic interpretations of existence and of the radical antithesis between reason and understanding.

Life is an ongoing encounter between subjectivity and objectivity, between a person and his or her world (*Umwelt*). In expressing oneself, a person establishes a "without" and a "within," constituting an interplay of polarities (*Gegensätze*) that form one's *Gestalt*. People can move increasingly inward or can transcend themselves by moving toward the world of objects and toward others, thus increasing their own *Umwelt* and establishing new patterns of relationships. Every human being thus has an individual rhythm of qualitative and quantitative change.

In *Welt und Person* (1939), Guardini developed his vision of humanity as involving a dialogic encounter between subjects. When two subjects override their existential seclusion, open up their *Gestalt* through language and communication, and decide to respect the freedom of the other, they—each "I"—give themselves the chance to be themselves, to express themselves freely, and to shape their own destiny (see *Freiheit, Gnade, Schicksal* [1948]). People also can widen their own *Umwelt* and their horizons to comprehend the totality of existence. Thus they encounter God's first spoken word in creation and his providence that accompanies creation throughout history. It is God's creative word that starts history; the person should respond with a *Weltanschauung* consonant with God's own vision (*Blick*) of the totality of being.

Guardini's hermeneutics comprehends human existence within the framework of the human encounter with objectivity, with history, and with God. Reaching beyond Schleiermacher's and Dilthey's hermeneutics based on their vision of human understanding, Guardini tried to found the basic framework of interpretation within existence itself.

2. Humanity and Revelation

Die Offenbarung (1940) is Guardini's main contribution to fundamental theology. Eventually he revised his material and started publishing it under the title *Religion und Offenbarung*. The first volume, dealing with the religious dimension of human existence, appeared in 1958; the second, specifically about revelation, still lies unpublished in the Guardini Archives.

Human existence is incomplete without God's revelation, which reinterprets and fulfills God's creative word.

In line with his *Gegensatz* methodology, Guardini explores four directions along which people can experience the limit (*Grenze*) of their being. People feel themselves called to a nameless and formless beyond, whence they hope to attain the meaning of existence. Along

with the "without" and the "within," Guardini moved backward and forward in history— toward the beginning of humanity and toward its end and the goal of its being.

Guardini identified the human experience of finitude and contingency as the human religious experience. Even the fall forms part of this basic experience, in the light of what is expressed in different mythologies. The symbolic nature of language and of so many things in life points also to the human experience of the limit. Guardini borrows heavily from Rudolph Otto's theory of numinosity to express these ideas, though he distances himself from Otto on two counts. The different manifestations of the numinous are not the various expressions of one basic reality; according to Guardini, varied human experience of the limit brings together these expressions. Besides, though we may speak of the beyond as the other, we should never consider it to be the counterpart of being, since the beyond envelops it completely.

Whenever people speak of this limit, their comments explain both the limit itself as well as the person giving the definition. "I believe in a world spirit" or "I believe in God" specify both the meaning given to existence as well as the subject's personal relationship to that totality. Guardini developed this thought in his *Den Menschen erkennt nur wer von Gott weiss* (1965).

One's experience of the limit is a dynamic encounter; human life is therefore a continual searching, a finding and losing again so as to move forward to a deeper encounter. One's understanding of the limit takes the form of yearning for meaning, leads to the understanding of a certain content, then shatters what has become known in the quest for further truth. Notwithstanding the symbolic nature of being, though everything speaks of and points to God, everything remains undetermined, disguised, and even confusing in one's quest for meaning. Only God's own self-manifestation gives a clear answer to the human existential quest for truth.

Revelation is God's encounter with humankind in history. This dialogic encounter therefore becomes a historical event that cannot be undone. Assuming the nature of a word, God's self-manifestation is an instance of his *kenōsis* within history. God's word can pass unnoticed, has to be deciphered, can be misunderstood, and can even give rise to scandal. A person should consequently be prepared to recognize God's word among the various words and events of history.

God chooses to reveal himself in a word spoken to one specific people, so that revelation takes the form of God's action (*Handeln*) with that people. It is made up of words and events within determined historical and spatial settings. God's word is nevertheless still addressed to all and elicits from humankind a personal response in obedience and faith together with one's partnership in a universal mission. God's intervention in history does not add another religion to the Babylonian, Canaanite, Egyptian, etc.; on the contrary, God encounters the totality of human history and dialogues with the people of all races and all times.

The perfect realization of God's encounter with humanity is the incarnation. God personally enters human history, so that Jesus becomes the expression (*Ausdruck*) and the epiphany of the living God. In Jesus, God manifests his tripersonal "I" and his own mind (*Gesinnung*). The God-made-human thus constitutes God's ultimate word about himself and about humanity, now called to a full personal communion with God. Christ ushers in a new creation, a new humanity, which Guardini called Christian interiority.

Relationship with Christ is everything (*das alles*). Christ is the God who speaks, the God who reveals everything, the infinite meaning that unfolds itself, while at the same time truly a man. With Adolf Harnack's *Essence of Christianity* in mind, Guardini affirms that there is no abstract definition of this essence. There is no teaching, no fundamental system of moral values, no religious stance and lifestyle detached from the person of Christ: "The content of Christianity is Christ himself."

Guardini can therefore insist that only revelation can explain itself. Coming from God's being, revelation can never lose its relevance and its novelty. It calls us to go beyond its symbolic nature, which can even conceal God's self-manifestation and move deeper into God's own being.

3. The Continuation of the Incarnation

In spite of the individualism of his day, Guardini presented the church as the continua-tion of Christ's unique mediation in time and, according to Newman, the realization of God's kingdom on earth; the church is truly the one and all (*Vom Sinn der Kirche* [1922]). People can never address God out of their isolated existence, but only out of the encompassing and embracing totality of the church, out of its living tradition and out of its communitarian "I." This "I" is not a formless "we" but the encounter of all those who constitute the living and believing community (*Vom Leben des Glaubens* [1935]).

People respond to God in obedience and faith. They must decide whether to keep or give away their own self (see Mt 10:39) — in the last instance not so much before God as with reference to the human mediation, the church, which is where people must make their decision for or against revelation. Only in and through the church, not in Kantian autonomy, can people attain their full freedom as expressed in their act of faith.

In and through the church, Christ comes to dwell in people and, through his Spirit, to bring them to a new level of existence. A person's redeemed existence is based upon the fact that the "thou" that is God and that approaches humanity in Christ draws the "I" of a person in itself and itself enters the "I," thus bringing into being a new polar relationship. Through the action of the Spirit, Christian interiority beckons people forward to ever greater heights and depths, away from any mediocrity and false security.

Only God's grace permits humanity to be itself, to achieve its being truly God's own image. A person responds in faith and love. Faith means a continual openness to the novelty of God, based on one's acceptance of God's revelation and one's obedience to God's call. Polemicizing against Kantian autonomy, Guardini believed obedience to be the critical point of a person's faith. In it we surrender our being in God's hands and realize what has been promised to us. This surrendering of self nonetheless demands a responsible and intelligent faith, together with a life of love that can unite a person with God and with others. We are directed in all this by the promptings of our heart that, in line with Augustine and Pascal, direct our search for the ultimate truth, God himself.

Bibl.: Works of R. GUARDINI: *Auf dem Wege* (Mainz, 1923); *Romano Guardini in Gespräch mit Erich*

Gorner 1933–34 (n.d.); The World and the Person (1939; Chicago, 1954); The Lord (Chicago, 1954); Das Wesen des Christentums (Würzburg, 1949); Unterscheidung des Christlichen (Mainz, 1963); "Kirche und Dogma," in M. Galli and M. Plate, eds., Kraft und Ohnmacht (Frankfurt, 1963); Berichte über mein Leben (Düsseldorf, 1984)

Studies: H. ENGELMANN and F. FERRIER, Romano Guardini: Le Dieu vivant et l'Existence chrétienne (Paris, 1966); A. LOPEZ QUINTAS, Romano Guardini y la dialéctica de lo viviente: Estudio metodológico (Madrid, 1966); id., Romano Guardini: Der Mensch—Die Wirkung—Begegnung (Mainz, 1979); R. WUCHERER-HULDENFELD, Die Gegensatzphilosophie Romano Guardinis in ihren Grundlagen und Folgerungen (Vienna, 1968); A. BABOLIN, Romano Guardini: Filosofo dell'Alterità, 2 vols. (Bologna, 1968, 1969); H. URS VON BALTHASAR, Romano Guardini: Reform aus dem Ursprung (Munich, 1970); H. B. GERL, Romano Guardini (1885–1968): Leben und Werk (Mainz, 1985); H. KLEIBER, Glaube und religiöse Erfahrung bei Romano Guardini (Freiburg, 1985); A. SCHILSON, Perspektiven Theologischer Erneuerung: Studien zum Werk Romano Guardinis (Düsseldorf, 1986).

Mario FARRUGIA

H

HEGEL, Georg Wilhelm Friedrich (1770–1831)

1. Works on Religion

In early adulthood Hegel briefly studied theology before turning to philosophy. Throughout his philosophical career he maintained a deep and abiding interest in religion in general, in the various religions of the world in particular, and especially in Christianity.

Hegel's own writings and lectures bear witness to the earnest effort with which he approached the philosophy of religion. At the beginning of the twentieth century Hermann Nohl gathered Hegel's earlier philosophical reflections on religion and on Christianity into a volume entitled *Hegel's Theological Writings*. Hegel's *Phenomenology of Spirit*, published in 1807, marked the beginning of his more mature, or systematic, philosophical reflection. In this fascinating but complex volume Hegel treated religion as the penultimate step in the phenomenological movement from consciousness to self-consciousness on to what he called "absolute knowledge." Hegel published his three-part *Science of Logic* during the years 1812 to 1816. He described his proposed movement of logical or pure thought in religious terms when he referred to it as "the presentation of God as God is in God's eternal essence before the creation of nature and a finite spirit." Hegel published three editions, successively augmented, of the summary of his philosophical system, *The Encyclopedia of the Philosophical Sciences in Outline*. Here again, in these 1817, 1827, and 1830 editions, he placed religion as penultimate sphere in the movement or self-development of philosophical thought. In 1821, at least partially in response to Friedrich Schleiermacher's approach to religion in *The Christian Faith*, he began the first of his four series of Berlin lectures on the philosophy of religion. Hegel himself never published these 1821, 1824, 1827, and 1831 religion lectures, which were in effect varied elaborations of the *Encyclopedia* outline of the philosophy of religion. However, their hasty publication in a first edition shortly after his death, and then again in a much-revised edition several years later, gave rise to considerable controversy concerning just how seriously he took religion and especially Christianity. Now in the latter part of the twentieth century the publication, by Walter Jaeschke, Ricardo Ferrara, and Peter C. Hodgson, of a critical edition of his 1821 philosophy of religion manuscript and of various auditors' transcripts of the later philosophy of religion lectures makes these lectures truly available for the first time. Their publication rounds out a century of renewed and growing interest in his philosophy and especially in his thought on religion and on Christianity.

2. Philosophy of Religion

In Hegel's mature view, religion was the elevation of human consciousness or finite spirit to God or the Infinite. Hegel proposed that this elevation took place in and as a movement of reflexive, conceptual thought. In fact, he insisted that spirit as such, including finite spirit, was a movement of thought. He defined the divine and the human literally in terms of thought. Since religion was that which was most characteristic of the human being both as an individual and in community, it was also a movement of thought. Hegel had several reasons for proposing to develop both his overall system as the movement of spirit in general, and his constructive philosophical reading of religion in particular, in terms of a dynamic movement of unifying or encompassing thought. One important reason, which is of particular present interest, was his intention to philosophize in the public realm. He was convinced that reflexive thought was publicly available and critically examinable. Therefore he chose to work with reflexive thought rather than, for example, something like intuition or feeling.

Hegel not only described religion as the elevation of finite religious consciousness to God or the infinite; he also consistently maintained that this elevation presupposed a more inclusive movement of spirit. From 1824 on, but especially in 1827, he more clearly and more systematically organized his lectures to reflect the structure of this more inclusive movement. He insisted that the elevation of finite to infinite was really the continuation, so to speak, of a logically prior movement from an initial, unitary infinite to differentiation or finitude. With such an affirmation Hegel was able to develop his philosophy of religion as a dynamic, dialectical, and self-positing movement of spirit. Religion—or, more specifically, the philosophy of religion—was for Hegel the dialectical movement of spirit othering itself into finitude and, by means of a negation of this finitude, returning in an enriched way to itself. Put more concretely, and in terms made explicit in the lectures of 1827, the philosophy of religion was the development of God as absolute spirit. Hegel presented the philosophy of religion as a movement from the concept of God to the various particular or determinate religions other than Christianity. He concluded his philosophy of religion with the presentation of the consummate religion as the negation of the limitation and the particularity of these finite or determinate religions. He identified the consummate religion, in its historical realization, with Christianity, and especially with his own Lutheran Christian tradition.

Hegel worked out his philosophy of religion as a movement of thought in the form of this internally self-developing movement of spirit. Since he identified this movement with the development of God as divine subject, he interpreted religion as a movement of divine subjectivity. It was a movement from God as substance to God as internally differentiated, and therefore true, divine subject or person. It was, indeed, a movement of inclusive divine subjectivity, since God came to be seen as inclusive of finitude or the world. Thus religion was, for Hegel, a movement of reconciliation between human and divine, a reconciliation occurring in the form of a self-positing, inclusive divine subjectivity.

Throughout the Berlin lectures Hegel consistently developed his philosophy of religion in three parts. He called part 1 "The Concept of Religion." He used the logical term "universality" to describe this first moment in the philosophy of religion. This first moment was as yet a more formally structured one. It remained on the level of the implicit. It was, he said, the divine idea as yet "in itself." Though it took him some years to work out an adequate structure for this first part of the philosophy of religion, he always began its presentation by insisting that religion was a question neither of the human nor of the divine alone, but of the

two together. He always started the presentation of the concept of religion with the affirmation of an original unity, namely, with religion as the relationship between human and divine. He would then go on to posit, as arising immediately out of this initial unity, the distinction between God and finite religious consciousness. He spoke of this second step—i.e., the arising of distinction—in terms of otherness. He came to see it as a moment of what he called theoretical or distinguishing reason. This arising of distinction or difference, more properly speaking, constitutes the moment of religion, since it is here with this second step that one can properly speak of an elevation from finite to infinite. Hegel would, in a third step, affirm the negation of this distinction by means of the movement of what he called practical or integrating reason. Especially in the later lectures this last step came more clearly to be seen as the moment of community and cultus or worship. Practical or integrating reason was, for Hegel, the movement of thought in the form of will. He insisted that these three, more formally developed steps or moments in the concept of religion were instantiated, in various ways, in each of the finite religions of the world. They were fully realized in the consummate religion.

Hegel named part 2 of his philosophy of religion "Determinate Religion." He described it as the moment of particularity. It was the appearance of the concept of religion or the divine idea "for itself" or as explicitly realized in finite otherness. "Determinate Religion" consisted in a series of dialectically juxtaposed, and typologically elaborated, presentations of the various religions of the world other than Christianity. Hegel's successive, and in certain ways significantly varying, elaborations of this second part witness to the fact that he continued to study these religions very seriously. Throughout the years of his Berlin lectures he regularly incorporated considerable amounts of new material into his presentations of these religions. Some would say that, with regard to these religions, he was the best-informed European of his day.

From one lecture series to the next Hegel made significant changes in the internal organization and the order of presentation of some of the finite or determinate religions. Nevertheless, he always began this part 2 with what might today be called primal religions, notably those of Africa and North America. In these phenomenologically earlier religions God was present more in the form of substance. Though Hegel placed these religions at an earlier stage in the phenomenological progression of determinate religions, he would not simply reject or abandon their views of God. He insisted that, though God was as yet understood and worshiped in some form of internally undifferentiated substance, such conceptions of God were still to be valued as more immediate instantiations of God. God as substance was subject, spirit, and person—but still only implicitly so. Hegel continued his presentation of the various finite religions, which he ranged, generally speaking, according to their increasingly more explicitly developed and complex conceptions of God and of the relationship between human and divine. Hegel grouped the finite religions geographically, treating of the religions of China, India, the Middle East, Greece, and Rome. He also rather boldly proposed that his phenomenological ranking and geographic grouping reflected the overall historical development of the various religions.

Hegel's dialectical dynamic of the realization of spirit in and through a series of finite forms of religion is extremely complex, yet fascinating. He tried at one and the same time to present this second moment, "Determinate Religion," both as one in which the concept of God gained in complexity and as one in which there occurred, finally, a total alienation. He saw this total alienation realized in Roman religion, which he always placed last within the series of determinate religions. In its degradation and debauchery Roman religion marked the low point or the turning point in the phenomenology and in the history of religion. Here the previously more complexly developed notions of God seemed to collapse in a religion of ever-greater negativity. For Hegel, Christianity arose dialectically out of the negation of that negativity.

Hegel entitled part 3 of his philosophy of religion lectures "The Consummate Religion." Here, in a way generally consistent throughout the four lecture series, he gave to Christianity and its basic doctrines a constructive philosophical interpretation in line with his overall understanding of spirit as dialectical movement of self-positing thought. As he had done with

his presentations of the various determinate religions, so here he constructed a sort of typological presentation of Christianity. He called his philosophical reading of Christianity the consummate religion because it consummated, or fully realized, the structure of what he had earlier, in part 1, established as the more formal structure and movement of religion. The consummate religion was able to serve as this fulfillment of the structure of the concept of religion because it incorporated the reality that that concept had attained in and through the various finite religions. He presented this third moment, the consummate religion, as the moment of individuality. What was initially present to thought or religious consciousness "in itself" and what was then realized "for itself" in the otherness of the various finite religions came, in the consummate religion, to be integrated in a moment Hegel referred to as the appearance of the divine idea "in and for itself." Thus the consummate religion is the religion of spirit. It is the religion in which God is known explicitly as spirit and in which God exists as spirit for finite spirit. In the consummate religion God is a movement of inclusive divine subjectivity.

From 1824 on, Hegel more clearly develops his presentation of the consummate religion in three parts. The first element or sphere of the consummate religion is the one in which he returns to the originary unity of God and religious consciousness. But now this unity has become a more-developed and internally differentiated sphere. In the 1831 lectures Hegel speaks of it as the kingdom of the Father. In this sphere the concept of God, the divine idea, is present to thought in the form of Trinity, i.e., of what would today be called "immanent" Trinity. According to Hegel, in Christianity God is the doubled dialectical movement of divine self-othering and of return spoken of figuratively as Father, Son, and Holy Spirit. This is a movement of the momentary arising of differentiation as a dialectical moment of negation. The Son, or second moment, is not the immediacy of the first moment. Rather, this second moment is one of distinction or difference that immediately disappears. The Holy Spirit is this disappearance of difference, the overcoming of otherness. Hegel characterizes this overall movement of spirit—i.e., one of differentiation and of return—as a movement of life and of love.

In the first sphere of the consummate religion otherness is only apparent or implicit. It becomes real and explicit and phenomenologically available in and as the second sphere. The second sphere is that of God or the divine idea positing itself as a finite world of nature and finite spirit. This second sphere is, at least from the 1824 lectures on, the doubled sphere of differentiation and immediate reconciliation. In 1831 Hegel calls it the kingdom of the Son. In his various lecture presentations Hegel carries out a long and impressive analysis of the Christian notions of creation, original innocence, and original sin. He gives them a philosophical and existential reading as he works out a dialectical reading of the relationship between good and evil. He pursues his analysis of the alienation, which arises with the distinction between God and finite spirit, on to the point where he can say that alienation constitutes the very core of what it means to be human. The human person is trapped in a sort of self-enslavement. And yet, to be human is to be a thinking being and, consequently, to be spirit. The human person is not only internal self-alienation but, as thinking being, also and equally in principle the very overcoming of such alienation.

Hegel sets up the human person as finite spirit and, essentially, as thinking being. By so casting his understanding of what it means to be human, namely, in terms of internal alienation and the possibility of overcoming that alienation, he can establish what might be called the transcendental context in which revelation and incarnation can and do occur. He often speaks of divine self-revelation, and with the incarnation, he affirms a total divine self-revelation in the form of a single human being, the Christ. He in various ways insists that this divine self-revelation must occur in one individual if it is to be available to humankind as a whole. God reveals God's self in a form of self-othering to the uttermost depths of finitude, namely, to the death of Christ on the cross. The resurrection is the transition to a spiritual presence to and in the believing community.

The third sphere of the consummate religion is that of community or cultus. In the second sphere Hegel had, at least from 1824 on, presented the doubled moment of differentiation and of immediate reconciliation in one divine-human self as the fulfillment of the second moment of the concept of religion,

namely, that of theoretical knowledge. Now he presents the third sphere as the fulfillment of the movement of practical knowing. This is the moment of inclusive individuality. It is the moment in which immediate reconciliation is made available to, and realized in, the community of finite spirits. Here, by means of a philosophical reading of faith, doctrine, sacrament, and sacrifice, Hegel presents the progressive realization, in the members of the spiritual community, of the reconciliation between human and divine that had already been achieved in Christ. Hegel speaks freely of the Holy Spirit as divine presence within the members of the spiritual community. Throughout the various lectures he calls this sphere the kingdom of the Spirit. In this kingdom—namely, in and through finite spirit—God has become spirit for spirit. This consciousness of being at one with God—what Hegel calls the peace of God—is itself to be expressed in ethical living. Yet for Hegel the reconciliation between human and divine, a reconciliation really achieved here in this third sphere, remains burdened with religious representational form. That is, the overcoming of alienation occurs as yet in the form of an otherness still identified as God the Holy Spirit. For Hegel the reconciliation and peace achieved in the spiritual community, and in ethical living, find their final and appropriate expression in the renewed immediacy of pure philosophical thought. In such thought mediation is self-mediation without remainder of externally presented otherness.

Though Hegel insisted that it was for philosophy to make explicit the internal coherence of religious thought, he equally, and especially from the 1824 lectures on, argued that religion, as the penultimate form of absolute spirit, was the perduring vehicle of truth and the valid representation of reconciliation for the general population. He consistently presented religion, and especially the Christian religion, as a dynamic phenomenological realization of the movement of spirit. Religion was the sphere or level on which spirit manifested itself as a dialectical movement of differentiation and enriched return. Here in this sphere of religion Hegel reformulated the more general religious notion of God into a movement of inclusive divine subjectivity, a movement of absolute spirit. To put it somewhat more crudely, Hegel argued that God was absolute spirit because

God included the world. To put it more philosophically, the true infinite was the infinite inclusive of the finite, and not merely a pseudo-infinite set over against the finite. By working with this reformulation of the notion of God, Hegel was able to create a unique philosophy of religion in the form of a movement of self-positing inclusive divine subjectivity. He could then affirm that this movement was one of divine and human freedom. It was a movement of human freedom because the human person was freed both from external alienation and from self-enslaving internal alienation. It was a movement of divine freedom because it was a movement of divine self-determination. God was spirit, i.e., God was at home with God's self in the other.

3. Hegel and Fundamental Theology

There are at least three classic functions or tasks that Christian fundamental theology has at various times carried out: first, the apologetic task of laying out the Christian tradition's basic justification and inner coherence; second, the foundational task of establishing the basis on which Christian theology goes about its further analytic, systematic, and constructive tasks; and third, the task of shedding light on basic themes in Christianity from the perspective chosen in working out the previous apologetic and foundational tasks. It will be helpful to consider Hegel's philosophy of religion from the point of view of each of these functions or tasks in order both to come to a better understanding of his overall position and to reflect on the relationship between his philosophy of religion and Christian fundamental theology.

Indeed, it would not be unfair to Hegel to describe his philosophy itself as a fundamental philosophical theology. He himself wrote that philosophy begins and ends with God. (Of course, he had primarily his own reformulated concept of God in mind.) And his philosophical interpretation of religion shows striking parallels to fundamental theology. Within the context of his overall philosophical project, in his philosophy of religion Hegel proposes for himself certain apologetic, foundational, and elucidational tasks quite analogous to those characteristic of fundamental theology.

In fact, Hegel's entire systematic philosophical project was apologetic in the sense that he constantly strove to set out the basic justification and inner coherence of his philosophy of absolute spirit. He seemingly entered into critical dialogue with any and every religious or philosophical position he came across. Of particular present interest are the critical attitudes he took toward the Christian theologians of his day, toward Christian theology itself, and toward religion in general or concrete religions in particular.

He was strongly critical of Christian theologians, whom he accused of having abandoned their fundamental task of examining the inner rational content and coherence of the major Christian dogmas. Furthermore, he argued that they took refuge either in reflections on merely subjective feelings or in less serious forms of historical studies. He felt that philosophy had to take up the tasks that fundamental and systematic theology had left undone.

Hegel insisted that religion, including the Christian religion in its reflected form as Christian theology, does indeed make available the truth of reconciliation to humankind in general. But he always qualified this positive valuation of religion with a further qualification. He argued that it is philosophy's task ever to identify the inner logical and rational coherence of religious beliefs. He found that even Christian theological reflection often remained too closely tied to "childish," or insufficiently critiqued and therefore seemingly disparate, images. Still, even when he accords to philosophy this all-important task of discerning the inner logical structure of religious reconciliation, he continues to maintain that religion as such, and Christianity with its theological reflection in particular, has a perduring value and importance. In their own way religion and Christian theology make an ongoing contribution not simply replaceable by philosophical thought. From different perspectives Hegel gives a certain continuing dialectical priority at one moment to religion and at another to philosophy. Though from the perspective of his systematic and speculative presentation he placed religion in a penultimate position just before the final moment of spirit as philosophical thought, he did not simply subordinate religion to philosophy. Religion remained the necessary historical embodiment of the truth expressed in philosophy. However, even when these qualifications concerning the respective roles of religion and philosophy are kept in mind, it would seem that Hegel gives a mediating and interpretational function to philosophy vis-à-vis religion that many religious thinkers find unacceptable.

An interesting critical stance of Hegel's, which many religious thinkers find considerably more attractive, is his de facto criterion for the evaluation of any religion or religious worldview. For Hegel this criterion is the question of whether, and to what extent, a particular religious tradition gives expression to freedom. For him it was a question of whether, and to what extent, a religion adequately represents divine freedom and, consequently, frees both the individual human person and the community from slavery to dehumanizing and one-sidedly objectifying tendencies. The theme of freedom constitutes the leitmotiv running through Hegel's philosophy of religion. The way in which Hegel works with this theme needs considerable further study. It is a theme that has also come back time and again in post-Hegelian religious reflection. Often this theme of freedom as constitutive characteristic of true religion, and even some of its more specific twentieth-century formulations, can be traced directly back to Hegel.

Hegel's apologetic stance involved a constant concern for exposition in the public realm, for inner coherence, and for the internal purification of religion. He in fact carried out this more apologetic task by concentrating on what could be called the foundational task. That is, he worked out a basic understanding of spirit as movement of inclusive subjectivity. He proposed a dialectical movement of thought that, in its most fundamental movement, was a positing of the other and an overcoming of the estrangement involved in the arising of such otherness. He identified this doubled movement of spirit with a creative reinterpretation of the various classic proofs for the existence of God. He saw in the ontological proof an expression of what he called the movement from concept to reality, namely, the self-differentiation of God as absolute spirit. He intriguingly reformulated the more cosmological and teleological proofs for the existence of God as the dialectical return of spirit, namely, as the elevation of finite spirit to the infinite. His fundamental understanding of the dynamic of spirit as differentiation and dialectical return, religiously and

theologically expressed in terms of the various proofs for the existence of God, provided the paradigm on the basis of which he worked out his overall philosophical system. He carried out his further analytic, systematic, and constructive reflections on the basis of this understanding of spirit. It will be of particular interest to fundamental theology to recall that for Hegel this movement of spirit found appropriate religious expression in the Christian doctrine of the Trinity.

Hegel used his fundamental understanding of spirit to elucidate basic themes in the various religions he examined. His efforts bore particularly rich fruit in his constructive philosophical interpretations of Christianity. Long before the Second Vatican Council he had spoken forcefully of divine self-revelation. It could even be argued that he introduced the notion into modern philosophical and theological discussion. His dialectical reconceptualization of God, and of the relationship between God and the world, allowed him to propose a moment of negativity in God. This he identified as the second moment in the "immanent" Trinity. When Hegel referred to this moment in terms of negation, he was in fact introducing the structure of crucifixion and death into the divine itself. Strikingly, with the affirmation of differentiation in God, namely, of an identity inclusive of difference, he was confirming the infinite value and importance of the realm of history, which is by definition the realm of difference and change.

A more detailed list of Hegel's insights that have made their way into theology and into the various attempts to establish a contemporary Christian fundamental theology would prove quite long. Perhaps one way to allude to these would be simply to indicate that Hegel integrated many Christian religious doctrines and theological themes that were seemingly less internally related. He brought together, for example, the themes of Trinity, revelation, grace, the kingdom of God, salvation history as the history of God, alienation, sin, and reconciliation, Christology, church and spiritual community, presence of the Holy Spirit, and responsible ethical living all into one overall sequence. He was able to interrelate these religious themes because he presented them as aspects of the dialectical development of God as absolute spirit and inclusive divine subjectivity.

Hegel's impressive philosophy of religion continues to pose constant challenges to Christian fundamental theology. From an apologetic perspective it challenges fundamental theology to work creatively in the public realm and to be self-critical in whatever it does. From a foundational perspective, it challenges fundamental theology to reflect on the most basic religious questions, including that of the structure of the experience of God as dynamic spirit. Hegel will not allow the theologian to remain content with merely external forms of argumentation. Rather, he forces the theologian to go to the heart of the matter, namely, to the question of the articulation of the dynamic inner relationship between finite and infinite, human and divine. From an elucidational perspective, he provides a great many insights into, and concrete observations on, Christian themes. In a sense his philosophy is a theological goldmine. However, there are two theological approaches to his philosophy that, it would seem, should be avoided. One is that of simply picking up a theological insight here or there in merely eclectic fashion. The result would surely be an eclectic theology. Another is that of taking over Hegel's system without further critical reflection on its inner coherence. This second approach would result in too easily carrying over into theology weaknesses internal to Hegel's own philosophy.

It is really not possible for the Christian fundamental theologian to remain neutral before Hegel's philosophy of religion and the challenges it poses. Either Hegel has basically succeeded in giving expression to the inner logical structure of Christianity or he has not. In the former case, then the fundamental theologian would have to follow Hegel quite closely. If Hegel has not succeeded, then it falls upon the fundamental theologian to come up with a rigorously formulated and more satisfying alternative position. In the past many Christian theologians have profited from the impressive scope and richness of Hegel's insight. More of them, perhaps, have resisted his overall philosophical position, and this for various reasons, including hesitations as to whether Hegel has in fact preserved divine freedom with regard to creation, whether he has adequately expressed either the radical character of evil or the continuity of otherness, or, more fundamentally, whether he has been able to argue convincingly

his own philosophical position. But perhaps the most concrete challenge facing the Christian fundamental theologian, when confronted with Hegel's unique and most impressive philosophy of religion, is to be able to acknowledge his or her immense debt to Hegel without, then, letting that debt become a burden.

Bibl.: Bibliographies: Kurt STEINHAUER, *Hegel Bibliography/Bibliographie* (Munich, 1980); Falk WAGNER, "Bibliographie zu Hegels Religionsphilosophie," in Friedrich Wilhelm Graf and Falk Wagner, eds., *Die Flucht in den Begriff: Materialen zu Hegels Religionsphilosophie* (Stuttgart, 1982) 309–45. Hegel Texts: *Hegels theologische Jugendschriften*, ed. Hermann Noh (Tübingen, 1907; Eng. trans. *Early Theological Writings*, trans. T. M. Knox [Chicago, 1948]); *Vorlesungen, Ausgewählte Nachschriften und Manuskripte*, vols. 3–5: *Vorlesungen über die Philosophie der Religion*, ed. W. Jaeschke (Hamburg, 1983, 1984, 1985; Eng. trans. *Lectures on the Philosophy of Religion*, 3 vols., ed. P. C. Hodgson, trans. R. F. Brown, P. C. Hodgson, and J. M. Stewart with the assistance of J. P. Fitzer and H. S. Harris [Berkeley, 1984, 1985, 1987]); *Lecciones sobre filosofía de la religión*, 3 vols., ed. and trans. R. Ferrara (Madrid, 1984). Secondary literature: Philosophy of Religion: C. BRUAIRE, *Logique et religion chrétienne dans la philosophie de Hegel* (Paris, 1964); A. CHAPELLE, *Hegel et la religion*, 4 vols. (Paris, 1964–71); F. BIASUTTI, *Assolutezza e soggettività: L'idea di religione in Hegel* (Trient, 1979); P. C. HODGSON, "Hegel's Approach to Religion: The Dialectic of Speculation and Phenomenology," *Journal of Religion* 64 (1984): 158–72; W. JAESCHKE, *Die Religionsphilosophie Hegels* (Darmstadt, 1983); id., *Die Vernunft in der Religion* (Stuttgart, 1986); D. M. SCHLITT, *Hegel's Trinitarian Claim: A Critical Reflection* (Leiden, 1984); id., *Divine Subjectivity Understanding: Hegel's Philosophy of Religion* (Scranton, 1989). Hegel and theology: H. RONDET, "Hégélianisme et Christianisme: Réflexions théologiques," *RSR* 26 (1936): 257–96, 419–53; G. ROHRSMOSER, "Die theologische Bedeutung von Hegels Auseinandersetzung mit der Philosophie Kants und dem Prinzip der Subjektivität," *NZST* 1 (1962): 87–111; W. G. SHEPHERD, "Hegel as a Theologian," *HTR* 61 (1968): 583–602; G. FESSARD, "Dialogue théologique avec Hegel," in H.-G. Gadamer, ed., *Stuttgarter Hegel Kongress 1970* (Bonn, 1974), 231–48; id., *Hegel et la théologie contemporaine* (Neuchâtel, 1977); W. KERN, "Philosophische Pneumatologie: Zur Theologischen Aktualität Hegels," in W. Kasper, ed., *Gegenwart des Geistes* (Freiburg, 1979), 45–90; F. W. GRAF, "Der Untergang des Individuums: Ein Vorschlag zur historisch-systematischen Rekonstruktion der theologischen Hegel-Kritik," in F. W. Graf and F. Wagner, eds., *Die Flucht in den Begriff:*

Materialen zu Hegels Religionsphilosophie (Stuttgart, 1982), 274–307; W. PANNENBERG, "Die Bedeutung des Christentums in der Philosophie Hegels," in H.-G. Gadamer, ed., *Stuttgarter Hegel Kongress 1970* (Bonn, 1974), 175–202; R. AHLERS, "Hegel's Theological Atheism," *HeyJ* 25 (1984): 158–77; P. CODA, *Il negativo e trinità: Ipotesi su Hegel* (Rome, 1987).

Dale M. SCHLITT

HELLENISM AND CHRISTIANITY

Was Christianity hellenized, or Hellenism christianized?

What did happen, so it would seem, was a major example of interpenetration or reciprocal action. Two worlds that diverged from one another in so many ways came together during the first centuries after the birth of Christ. The fact that Christ's birth inaugurated a new era, on the basis of which our centuries are now counted ("anno domini"), does not mean that Greco-Roman civilization did not survive and even penetrate the ancient world more deeply as the Christian religion progressed. Greece, to be sure, then Macedonia, had ceded their hegemony in the fourth and second centuries B.C.E. But Athens had ceased to draw a foreign, mainly Roman élite, and Alexandria had remained a Greek city whole language, with the help of the Septuagint translation, became the language of the Bible. Even before Byzantium, this museum of pagan culture was to be a focus of Christian theology.

Not a few historians of Greek religion have stressed the increasingly close relations between Hellenism and Christianity. The names of M. P. Nilsson, A.-J. Festugière, and A. D. Nock are the first to come to mind; their main works were published before E. R. Dodds's "polyvalent masterpiece" *Pagan and Christian in an Age of Anxiety* (1965).

There were many similarities between adherents of the old religion and disciples of Christ. The "service" of earthly existence could be interpreted optimistically or pessimistically. The dream revelations that were so significant for Aelius Aristides may be compared to the visions recorded in the *Passion* (prison journal) of the martyr Perpetua. Lucian's *Peregrinos* helps us to understand Pontius. To combat Christianity the pagans had to rely on a certain religious attitude; pagans, however, could not compete in the area of charity. Dodds emphasizes not so much doctrinal debates as "differences in mentality and feelings."

Dodds's book concludes with the observation that the Christians were "members one of another," and that this, far from being a mere formula, was the major cause of, and possibly the sole and most forceful reason for, the progress of Christianity. In a footnote he quotes a sentence from a lecture by A.-J. Festugière: "If that had not been the case, the world would still be pagan." Festugière had previously summed up the main differences that set paganism against Christianity. Though religious anxiety was common to pagans and Christians (if in very different ways), and though the "Greeks" of the first century were scarcely unacquainted with the essential meaning of religion (to the extent that Paul found them "almost too religious"), they had radically opposed views of sin. The religious person in classical antiquity "did not know the meaning of sin" as Christians understood it "as a direct affront to God."

I have just referred to Paul's speech on the Areopagus. In ten verses (Acts 17:22–31) the apostle sums up the Christian message; an analysis of his speech will indicate the main lines of the "first-century religious mentality." Let us take v. 22 first. *Deisidaimōn*, used here in the comparative—"somewhat too (religious)"—would be more appropriately translated into Latin as *religiosiores* rather than the *superstitiosiores* of the best Vulgate manuscripts. This adjective usually implies "superstitious" in the religious sense and is an inadequate translation of the orator's intention, for he is anxious to win his audience's good will. Neither of the components of the Greek adjective ("fear," "demon") necessarily indicates a blameworthy opinion. Fear of God can be a good thing (the Bible even calls it "the beginning of wisdom"), and the Greek devils are distinct from the gods and inferior to them, but nonetheless messengers between heaven and earth right up to Plato.

V. 23 is the sole literary testimony to a Greco-Roman cult of an "unknown god." The altar that Paul could have seen at Phaleron (Pausanias 1.1–4) bore an inscription in the plural: "to the unknown gods," and in *In Titum* (1.12) Jerome criticizes the apostle's "unfair ploy." We must suppose that the pagans dedicated altars to "unknown gods" lest any omission should offend the forgotten god.

In vv. 24 and 25, there are several points of agreement between pagans and Christians. A God who made the world, who is Lord of heaven and earth, who does not live in man-made shrines, who does not need the service of human hands, as if he lacked something—this is how poets and philosophers in Greece and Rome represented the "supreme Being." Though a Platonist was not necessarily prepared to accept the suppression of the temples, a Stoic loyal to Zeno's teaching was quite ready to do so; "No temple is to be built, for no mason's or workman's effort is precious." Part of the patristic tradition extends the prohibition to statues. For the Plato of the _Timaeus_ and the _Laws,_ the world is the true temple, and the stars are the images of the gods with which he replaces the divinities of Olympus. In the speech on the Areopagus the rejection in v. 24 of "shrines made by human hands" is extended in v. 25 as a general principle: "nor is he served by human hands, as though he needed anything." Here "service," _therapeia,_ is worship, and the _colitur_ of the Vulgate is a good rendering of the Greek verb. In spite of the suggestion of novelty, the reason given is traditional and appears in the OT as much as in Greco-Roman philosophy; five centuries after Xenophanes (sixth century B.C.E.), Lucretius (2.650) had written of godhead: _nihil indigna nostri._ Acknowledgment of divine independence led to a rejection of sacrifice, which is already a favorite topic of Hellenistic theology.

The second part of v. 25 gives the reason for the divine "autarchy": the present _didous_ is against the "ongoing creation" by means of which God supports the world in the instantaneous action by which he created it; hence the aorist _epoiēsen_ at the beginning of v. 26. The triad of v. 28—life, movement, being—expresses the total dependence of human beings in relation to God, but here again the idea is characteristic of the Plato of the last dialogues, who closely associates movement and life in his definition of the soul, and more directly characteristic, perhaps, of the Stoic Porch. To support these associations, Paul himself quotes v. 5 of the _Phenomena_ of Aratus: "For we too are his offspring."

V. 29 excludes idols, thus returning to the prohibition of shrines in v. 24. Up to that point the Athenian audience could have accepted the entire speech. Possibly they found the reminder of their ignorance (v. 30a=23b) less pleasing. But the call to repent in 30b, and above all the proclamation of the last judgment and the resurrection of the dead, could only have caused them annoyance or elicited a scathing reply.

That was the major stumbling block: mention of the resurrection brought the speech to an end, as nothing was more contrary to Greek ideas. The Plato of the _Phaedo_ wished to prove the immortality of the soul, but not that of the body. People had not forgotten Aeschylus's denials: "Once the black blood of a human being stains the ground, no magician can summon it back to the veins from which it flows" (_Agamemnon_ 1019–21); "when the dust has drunk a man's blood, if he is dead, he will not rise again" (_Eumenides_ 647–48). At the end of the fourth century C.E., Synesius, a convert from paganism who became bishop of Ptolemais, found it extremely difficult to accept the dogma of the resurrection, and his most recent commentators still debate the extent to which he finally did so.

This short account cannot do justice to the opposed features of the two ethical systems. "Greek ways" were a major obstacle to baptismal renewal. But Paul castigates the "vices of the pagans" often enough for the differences to resound when reading him alone. It seems more pertinent to stress the resemblances, and in this respect the speech on the Areopagus appears entirely appropriate.

Bibl.: A.-J. FESTUGIÈRE, "Aspects de la religion populaire grecque," _RTP_ 1 (1961): 31; E. R. DODDS, _Pagan and Christian in an Age of Anxiety_ (Cambridge, 1965); É. DES PLACES, _Religion grecque_ (Paris, 1969), 327–61; G. MADEC, "Platonisme des Pères," in _Cath_ 50 (1986): 492.

Édouard DES PLACES

HERMENEUTICS

1. Introduction. 2. History of Biblical Hermeneutics. 3. Modern Hermeneutics. 4. The Theological Dimension of Modern Hermeneutics. 5. Consequences for Fundamental Theology. (P. GRECH)

1. Introduction

The word "hermeneutics" has a much broader meaning in the context of a dictionary of fundamental theology than it would have in the context of biblical theology. In the latter discipline the term can refer simply to the method of exegesis, i.e., arriving at the original intention of a biblical writer, or else extracting from the biblical text thoughts useful for Christian living. From the following explanation of hermeneutics it will be seen that it also includes the relationship between REASON and faith in the interpretation of the Bible, the relationship between history and theology, and that between a possible scriptural "myth" and the prior understanding of contemporary philosophy. In fact various present-day theologies that are derived from the contact between sacred texts and different philosophical and ideological schools are also included within the sphere of hermeneutics.

While all this comes to be understood by hermeneutics in a context of fundamental theology, after the Reformation the interpretative form of hermeneutics became a discipline in its own right. According to the opinions of different writers, it touches upon problems such as the art of understanding, the value and interpretation of the humanist tradition, knowledge as the hermeneutics of being, the historicity of truth, the role of the subject in interpretation, the different functions of language, and the relationship between philosophies and ideologies, thus seeing hermeneutics as responsible for the cognitive, ontological, historical, and linguistic problems that invade the entire field of fundamental theology. On these depend radical decisions concerning the unchanging nature of truth, the possibility of knowledge of the truth, the value of the church's dogmas, demythologization, and the possibility of understanding different cultures. In this dark jungle it is always difficult to give a basic rationale to understanding revelation,

even for the reason that hermeneutics itself, while seeking to clarify things, is trapped in a labyrinth from which, at the moment, one cannot see clearly a way out. This article will give a historical exposition of the problem and will end by pointing out the exegetical, philosophical, and theological problems that have a bearing upon fundamental theology.

2. History of Biblical Hermeneutics

Apart from the demythologized and allegorical interpretation of the Homeric tales made by the Greeks, the influences that shaped the Christian hermeneutical tradition are to be found in the OT. The Hebrew text of the Bible was established by rabbinic scholars in the first century of our era; until then the text was quite fluid, and the same scribes were able to annotate it with explanatory expressions or theologically important comments (→ CANON). But even before this, in the period of collection and redaction of traditional texts, we find a continuous reinterpretation that adapts legal provisions to the circumstances of the day and rereads prophecies in the light of the latest events in the history of salvation by the method of the haggadah. To this must be added the semantic interpretation of dreams and visions. The significance of this is that, for the Jews, the Torah and the prophets always speak to the generation that reads them. They recount their history in this way, not merely for purely historical interest, but as a living history with a message for their contemporaries. The authors' historical sense has value only insofar as it also speaks to the present.

The literature of the intertestamental period, for the most part apocalyptic in character, is also of a hermeneutical kind. It sought to interpret its own times in the light of the biblical tradition with which it was linked, and to do so by means of references, implicit citations, or midrashic elaboration. By the time of Jesus, therefore, there were specific schools of exegesis that ranged from the midrash of the Targums to the literalism of the rabbis of a Pharisaic tendency who wished to justify their tradition of oral interpretation by hermeneutics of a literary nature; and likewise from the exegesis of the Qumran sect to the allegorism of Philo and the Alexandrians.

First-century Jewish exegesis is reflected in

the NT. The literary technique adopted in rereading the OT is similar, but the content is completely different, although in line with the traditional pattern of reinterpretation found in the Bible, which rereads the texts with the understanding offered by the most recent events in the history of salvation. It is obvious that for Jesus the chief event is the advent of the KINGDOM OF GOD, while for the NT authors it is the coming of Christ, together with his death and resurrection, the fullness of God's work of salvation. Consequently, the Christ-event sheds light on the meaning of the biblical text, which thereby receives its full significance. The NT thus offers certain types of hermeneutics that later become models for patristic exegesis: literal explanation, midrashim, midrash of the Peshitta, allegory, and typology, especially in passages such as Rom 9–11, Gal 4, 1 Cor 10, and Hebrews.

However, the hermeneutics of the second century was thrown into crisis by the Pauline thesis that denied all salvific value attached to the Torah per se. This was the reason for the rejection of Paul by the Ebionite Jewish-Christians, who were rooted in the Law. On the other hand, it gave an opportunity to the gnostics and to Marcion to attribute the OT, in whole or in part, to the Demiurge, otherwise known as "the righteous God." Gnostic exegesis began from the presupposition of different systems, attributed to the apostles, who handed them down by a secret tradition. Individual phrases, from either the OT or the NT, were interpreted in the context of these systems, often taken out of context and manipulated to give a gnostic meaning.

The Great Church did not find the least difficulty in interpreting the OT. The *Letter of Barnabas* had already begun to offer an allegorical explanation, while Justin, in offering an apology of Christianity against the pagans and Jews, gave a christological reading to the prophets in a way that would convince a Christian believer but that would leave many doubts in the mind of a rabbi who did not accept Christian presuppositions. This dichotomy in explaining the OT has always divided Christian exegesis from that of Judaism, especially if it is taken for granted, as with Justin and all the ante-Nicene fathers after him, that the Logos not only had created the world but was also the author of the OT and had enlightened the Greek philosophers.

It was Irenaeus, who, through his dealings with the gnostics, established certain rules of Christian interpretation that exist to this day. In contrast to the gnostics, obscure passages in Scripture must be explained by those that are much clearer (*Adv. Haer.* 2.10), every phrase must be understood in its immediate context (*Adv. Haer.* 1.8.1; 1.9.4), but also within the context of the whole of the Bible, both OT and NT, which has but one God for its author. Yet this is not enough; the Bible must be read in the context of the *regula fidei* (1.10.1), which is handed down to us not in an esoteric fashion but publicly by the bishops of the various churches (4.26.1–4). These rules for finding the true meaning of Scripture were elaborated by Irenaeus in the context of the gnostic controversy.

But when the OT is explained to believers for their spiritual nourishment, what sort of explanation must be given to the history and laws of the Jews? The problem was resolved by Origen by means of allegorical exegesis, which had already been practiced by Philo and the Hellenists. This does not mean that Origen did not care about the historical and literal meaning; the *Hexapla*, which he produced at great cost, gives ample demonstration of this. But history, at the level of a straightforward account of events, is good for the *simpliciores*, the "body" in the church; those who are more accomplished, the "soul" of the community, look for a moral sense; while the spiritual ones have need of allegory, i.e., the theological meaning. One must pay attention to Origen's terminology, which he expounds in *De principiis* 4, because the "spiritual sense" is not always contrasted with the "literal meaning" but often with the "material meaning," which more often than not corresponds to our redactional meaning.

The Antiochenes—Diodorus of Tarsus, Theodore of Mopsuestia, and John Chrysostom—reacted against the use of allegory, even if they did make use of it in their preaching. But they insisted on the literal meaning, namely, the meaning given by the authors, by searching among the historical circumstances surrounding the composition of the book. However, by engaging in this form of exegesis, they soon discovered that some prophetic texts, usually interpreted as messianic, were not really speaking about the Messiah in a direct fashion. Thus they proposed the theory of the *theoria*, or vision. By this they supposed that a prophet spoke of an event in the near future that would become a type for another event by which it would be fulfilled at an indefinite future date: hence Diodorus in his preface to the Psalms, especially Ps 118, and Theodore on Gal 4:22–31. The commentaries of Chrysostom appear somewhat dry in comparison to the theological richness of an Origen. The link between the Antiochenes and Alexandrians was provided by the Cappadocian fathers, who, engaging in biblical theology, spoke of the *skopos* and *akolouthia* that embraced both the purpose of the author and the salvific accompaniment of God's work.

But it is AUGUSTINE, who in books 2 and 3 of *De doctrina Christiana*, codified the hermeneutical principles of textual, literary, and theological criticism that dominated the Middle Ages in the Latin West. The rhetorician from Hippo, distinguishing between *res* and *signa*, with the latter subdivided between *propria* and *impropria*, set out the rules for discerning metaphor from allegory, while underlining the literal sense that is the true meaning intended by the Holy Spirit, although the OT still had a spiritual sense if read through Christian eyes. The context is either immediate or expository, or it pertains to the *regula fidei* (→ RULE OF FAITH). He thus acknowledges a certain *sensus plenior* to which he gives expression, particularly in his commentary on the Psalms, by enlisting the help of the seven hermeneutical rules of Ticonius. The medieval period codified the exegesis of Augustine into the four classical senses: literal, allegorical, moral, and anagogical: "Litera gesta docet, quid credas allegoria, moralis quid agas, quo tendas anagogia."

If we wish to summarize the hermeneutical theory of tradition, which we have been examining until now, we can say that we have a biblical text that contains within itself more possibilities for explanation than the historical author intended. The author's own intention will always be the primary meaning, but the community that reads the text, whether in synagogue or in church, extracts other meanings from it, informed by the unfolding of history, in such a way that the text speaks continually to every succeeding generation. Text and community are thus inseparable, in that the community becomes the context in which the text is read, together with the actual moment in history. The way in which this continuous understanding is expressed or explained is influenced by the cultural atmosphere in which it is read, which sometimes requires a translation or, better still, transfer from one cultural language to another, or from a language of the past to one of the present. When considering an inspired tent, it is the Spirit working within the community that realizes the possibilities of the text in relation to the living out of the *regula fidei*.

3. Modern Hermeneutics

A veritable revolution in biblical hermeneutics took place under Luther. With his principles of "sola Scriptura" and "Scriptura sui ipsius interpres," the Reformation separated biblical interpretation from tradition, the church, and the magisterium, making of the Bible a book that one can interpret as an individual with the help of the Holy Spirit. The hermeneutical methods of the fathers no longer sufficed because Scripture, notwithstanding its quasi divinization by the Reformers, was reduced to the level of any of the books of antiquity. Thus the way in which it was read, apart from the piety and veneration of the reader, was the same as the reading of classical works in general. From that moment, therefore, hermeneutics, instead of being strictly a method of interpreting sacred Scripture, began to be a discipline in its own right, having as its object literary or artistic works. One of the founding fathers of this new discipline was Matthias Flacius Illiricus (1520–1575), a Lutheran theologian who emphasized the self-sufficient character of Scripture by proposing the "hermeneutic circle," by which to explain the whole by means of the parts and the parts by means of the whole.

During the period of the Enlightenment, however, rationalism also entered theology, particularly through the works of Spinoza. The supernatural was often reduced to the limits of the rational, and thus, with J. H. Ernesti, "sacred" hermeneutics became a branch of philosophy or literature. But the writer who posed the problem and offered solutions that are still very much alive was, without a doubt, F. D. E. Schleiermacher (1768–1834), who lived within the full current of German romanticism as well as the spirit of Protestantism and that of the Enlightenment. This author is generally known for his theory of original intuition which unites reader and writer, solving the problem of the temporal distance that separates one from the other. Nevertheless, this is but a secondary aspect of Schleiermacher's work. His philosophy of hermeneutics is much fuller.

First, hermeneutics is the art of understanding, not explaining, the object of rhetoric. It does not confine itself to written works of antiquity but examines every type of discourse, even that which is oral. The act of speaking (or writing) is a linguistic fact that must be considered either on the historical level of the development of language or on that of the development of the one who is speaking. The mode of expression is at the core of everything. Thus there is both a structural and a phenomenological aspect. Philological analysis serves to explain the linguistic aspect, while the psychological aspect is grasped by all the historical and literary means that contribute to the individual psychology of the author and give rise to the basic intuition. To understand an author, however, does not mean to objectify the person and to exhaust the conscious meaning of his or her assertions. Since speaking or writing is an "act" that almost leaves the "I" on one side, so the circle of understanding never closes itself because the inventiveness of the interpreter finds in the text truths not understood by the author; through the very act of comprehension these truths become a fresh historical happening and thus a way of interpretation in different circumstances. The subjectivity of the interpreter comes to be included in the hermeneutical circle. The transparency of the text is not an end but is a means for this new stage in comprehension that in turn becomes an object of understanding on its own account.

Before reaching Dilthey, who is the next milestone in the history of hermeneutics, it will be well to say a brief word about some other German authors of the nineteenth century. W. von Humboldt, for example, emphasizes the role of the subject in understanding, not only in the linguistic field (I can understand only if I feel what I think, put into words by another), but also in historical research, wherein the researcher is the one who must give logical unity to the fragments that issue from documents, a logical unity analogous to that of the point in time in which the historian is living.

For J. G. Droysen, what contributes to the awareness and historical knowledge is the fact that the objects of our research are the events of which we are the heirs in our daily lives. However, the documents not only have a factual content but also reveal the state of soul, the psychology, and the ethos of the one who composed it; they reveal, therefore, a completely different world. It is possible to understand them only because we share our human nature with this other world, a human nature that, as it will be said much later, acts as a prior intention or understanding.

A. Boeckh is in agreement with the historical notion of Droysen in that he refers to historical knowledge as knowledge of what is already known because everything is the fruit of the human spirit. To understand authors from the past does not only mean that we explain them, but that we gain a better understanding of what they are in themselves, in that many factors that influenced writers from other eras are now brought to light—factors unknown to the authors but not so to us. The task of interpretation has to be carried out with the whole work in view; the fruit of criticism is the work considered in relation to its background and context.

W. Dilthey (1833–1911), working with the framework of the "objective spirit" of Hegel, makes a distinction between _Naturwissenschaften_ (sciences of nature) and _Geisteswissenschaften_ (human sciences). These are regulated in autonomous fashion by their own laws. While Schleiermacher regarded understanding to be a linguistic fact, for Dilthey it is a vital category. The experience of life shared by all men and women—their feelings, their understanding of their own social and cultural world—are externalized by means of vital expressions (_Lebensäusserungen_), those of everyday life, or indeed the higher expressions of art, literature, institutions, and so forth. The object of hermeneutics is such manifestations in that they express humankind's knowledge and intentions with regard to its essential world. In the course of history such expressions crystallize themselves in exterior forms that have lost contact with the source of experience. Hermeneutics makes this its proper object of study, and its task is to reconvert these human manifestations into the essential experience of men and women today. The human reason is the continuum that holds them together. For Dilthey, therefore, understanding becomes an existential principle without ceasing to be a methodological concept of the human sciences; the distinction between understanding and interpretation, however, becomes ever more obscure.

In the last decade of his life Dilthey leaned toward the phenomenological method of Husserl. Heidegger used both Husserl and Dilthey to bring hermeneutics to its existential climax. The philosopher from Marburg wanted to study being as such, that which kept beings from falling back into nothingness. One cannot study beings directly without falling into the category of subject-object, but since the privileged place where being manifests itself is the Dasein, i.e., the human being, it is here that one can study it. As with Dilthey, the human being is not seen as a preconstituted and absolute essence but is itself its own possibility and acquires its own *existentia* by the choices it makes. It is a finite transcendence whose structures encompass the relations with the world around it (*in-der-Welt-sein*). Whether the Dasein personalizes itself as a being that falls into a less-than-authentic existence, or whether on the contrary it truly accepts that it is the place wherein being reveals itself and realizes all its possibilities for becoming authentic existence, that which is continually struggling to avoid failing back to the level of an object (*Verfallenheit*)—this is the heart of the matter. The anxiety always to be creating one's own future can become a true fear, especially when faced with death. Time—past, present, and future—is the dimension or horizon in which being develops. The study of the way in which human beings have understood and worked out their own potential in the past opens the horizon to present possibilities for projecting themselves into the future and "explaining" or realizing themselves as human beings.

Philosophy is thus essentially a form of hermeneutics, the ontology and interpretation of being. But human beings must not explain what is external to them because what is constitutive of the Dasein's being-in-the-world is a certain basic existential understanding that emanates from prior knowledge or intention. Human understanding is by nature linguistic; language orders understanding, and authentic assertions by thinkers or poets interpret existence. Their study, therefore, is the study of the history of the self-understanding of the Dasein and its own potentiality, if such assertions are to be something more than idle nonsense (*Gerede*). This linguistic dimension is developed in the "later" Heidegger. Truth is *a-lētheia*, the unveiling of Being to humankind, which through its powers of understanding and language becomes a spokesperson for the muted voice of Being. The practitioner of hermeneutics is thus not simply one who explains words because these serve only to reveal the language of a particular age, a language that is perhaps too limited to express the fullness of understanding and thus capable of translation into an everyday language better adapted to our understanding of ourselves.

This insistence on language by the later Heidegger leads to the study of H. G. Gadamer in *Truth and Method*. Hermeneutics is understanding, but this understanding comes about when the reader, living in the present and thus heir to certain prejudices that reach the reader through the continuum of cultural history, is confronted with the text. The horizon of the text and that of the reader are founded the one within the other such that the former understanding is modified and becomes a new understanding. But even this is not absolute; it is still a link in the chain of different historical understandings of the past. The continuity of tradition is the *Wirkungsgeschichte* (the history of the effect) of the texts at the beginnings of our culture and revealed in language, into which cultural values are inserted. Although the text is normative, its interpretation is a continuous process, and one cannot say that an interpretation is definitive because the act of comprehension renews itself from one generation to the next through each interpreter giving rise to a fresh truth; this truth itself becomes the object of interpretation. In Gadamer's view, tradition is the chain of explanations that gives concrete expression to understanding.

4. The Theological Dimension of Modern Hermeneutics

At this point we must leave the field of philosophy and move to that of theology, returning to the former in due course. It is well known that the hermeneutical debates considered so far, especially Heidegger in *Being and Time*, have had repercussions in the theology of R. BULTMANN. Modern fundamental theology can no longer fail to take account of the problems raised by Bultmann, which can be developed at three levels: the questioning of the historicity of the Gospels, the relevance of our knowledge of the historical Jesus to our faith in the Christ of kerygma, and the question of the demythologization of the NT message.

Beginning with the *Formgeschichte*, according to which the majority of Jesus' sayings and the gospel stories have been created by the primitive Christian community, Bultmann has removed the supports for the historicity of the Gospels themselves. His was not a new thesis; from the time of Reimarus at the end of the eighteenth century, just such a conviction was taking shape. The consequences of this kind of thesis for fundamental theology are harmful. But this fact did not deter Bultmann, who, being a good Protestant, did not accept that his faith in Christ was based on any form of reason whatsoever, even of a historical nature. Thus, even if the life of Jesus could have been known in detail from hour to hour, according to this principle this knowledge would have added nothing to his security in the faith because for Bultmann, faith is not a question of acceptance of revealed truth but one of faith in God's future that makes us abandon our self-will, which is the essence of "sin" (parallel to Heidegger's nonauthentic existence). Moreover, the traditional truths of Christianity can act as an initial understanding in order to arrive at such a faith, but they are not its proper object. They are formulated in a language that dates back two thousand years and that shows signs of the mystical vision of the Judeo-Hellenistic world. In order to be acceptable to humankind today, they need to be translated anew, or demythologized, into a more modern language. Bultmann finds this language in the existential philosophy of Heidegger, just as H. Jonas did in the case of Gnosticism. Thus incarnation, resurrection, redemption, grace, and the sacraments are given an anthropocentric interpretation as a function of the decision of faith that comes about by contact with the word of God and that is at the same time salvation, redemption, and judgment, a realized and "precise" eschatology.

Just as Bultmann relied upon the early

Heidegger of *Being and Time*, so those devoted to the so-called New Hermeneutics, particularly E. Fuchs and G. Ebeling, have continued the line of argument of the later Heidegger and that of Gadamer. These writers also develop the history of forms as their method, but they are less skeptical than Bultmann about establishing some definite facts about Jesus. The return to the historical Jesus is not only possible but is also necessary in that he is the initiator of our language of faith, a language that comes from contact with God, conceptualized in language, but that in every generation that studies it is freed and becomes an experience of faith, which in its own turn becomes a language to be interpreted. To reproduce within myself the faith of Jesus means to believe in Christ. Knowledge of the historical Jesus is thus indispensable to faith.

The separation of history and faith in Bultmann has been criticized from all sides: because it removes the *extra nos* of salvation (Käsemann), because it smacks of Gnosticism and Docetism (Jeremias), and because there remains no criterion for judging the various postresurrection Christologies (Robinson). Bultmann's critical skepticism is nowadays much reshaped by the studies of Schürmann on the *Sitz im Leben Jesu*, of Jeremias on the parables, of Gerhardsson on the Semitic mode of oral transmission, while K. Berger has recently revolutionized the *Formgeschichte* as a literary method.

Even demythologized hermeneutics did not fare too well. After an initial success, when theologians from different philosophical backgrounds produced different hermeneutical "theologies" (van Buren from positivism, Belo and Gutiérrez from Marxism, the "process theology" of Whitehead, etc.), it began to be seen that Bultmann's theology emptied Christianity of its revealed content together with its historical foundation, and thus the criticism of Gnosticism was not without justification. If instead of "myth" we speak of symbolic language, one could look at the writings of P. Ricoeur. Like Dilthey before him, he maintained that humankind must be studied through the cultural manifestations in its history. Ricoeur takes this line of argument but asserts that many of these cultural manifestations are codified in signs, symbols, or myths that have a retrospective function toward their own origin and a theological dimension that looks forward to the maturation of the human being. These symbols must be decoded through the methods of psychoanalysis and other sciences because they are able to speak in a language intelligible to human beings at a certain stage of maturity.

The language of the Bible is often symbolic. We have only to think of the stories in Gn 3–11. Myth must neither be reduced to the basic instincts of Freud nor be emptied of its intellectual contents as in the case of Bultmann; on the contrary, it must be integrated into theological reflection on the true meaning of revelation. Myth is concerned with the outer shell of faith, not its core.

In a series of documents beginning with *Providentissimus Deus* of 1893 right through the Second Vatican Council's *Dei Verbum*, the Catholic church has encouraged the study of sacred Scripture, which had been almost monopolized by Protestantism. These documents include references to hermeneutics as rules for arriving at the true *sensus auctoris*, that which is really intended by the Holy Spirit, who inspires the Bible. They give progressive admission to technical apparatus such as the study of literary genres, certain methodological aspects of *Formgeschichte*, and the practice of philology in the knowledge that one is dealing with a sacred book that requires interpretation in the context of tradition with the guidance of the magisterium. However, these declarations do not touch upon hermeneutics in the philosophical sense of the word, thus leaving a great many questions open. Exegesis, and fundamental theology in particular, cannot ignore such issues if an adequate reply is to be given to the questions raised today. We will address these questions below.

We must return here to the discussion of hermeneutics in the period after Gadamer. We can do so only by highlighting a number of problems that have a bearing upon our subject. It was only to be expected that Gadamer's thesis would not go unchallenged. E. Betti, E. D. Hirsch, and P. Szondi reacted against the subjectivism of Gadamer's interpretation, each critic approaching the problem from his own particular point of view. They insisted that the criteria used by Gadamer did not leave a single means for verifying the truth or falsity of an interpretation because the subject comes to replace the author to such a degree that there is a lack of Hegelian total vision and a descent into historical fragmentation. The true meaning of a passage, so they maintain, is that intended by the author, and it is a closed and complete meaning. What this objective meaning says to me (*Bedeutung* vs. *Bedeutsamkeit;* meaning vs. significance) is something completely different and depends on my own (subjective) standpoint in relation to the text, the meaning of which may be deepened by further study that leads to a better understanding of the author but that does not depart from the *mens auctoris*.

From the philosophical point of view, L. Pareyson gives substantial correction to the position taken by Gadamer. Pareyson gives an ontological foundation to interpretation, maintaining the unity of the truth and the plurality of its manifestations, in that the truth of being reveals itself continuously or sporadically in important cultural events. Pareyson thus gives us a personal ontology.

Finally, the literary criticism of Hirsch also gives rise to a school that, drawing together structural analysis and aspects of classical and modern rhetoric, seeks to discover what impact a text (especially scriptural texts) has had on its immediate readership. R. Jewett and other biblical scholars in the United States have applied this method of research.

One further criticism of Gadamer closes this historical review of hermeneutics. Habermas, who is in sympathy with the Frankfurt school, in his criticism of ideology argues that Gadamer's evaluation of tradition imprisons society in an unreal traditionalism that fails to give consideration both to actual conflicts and to those psychopathological conflicts indicated by psychoanalysis, thus blocking the way to full modernity and freedom. Gadamer replies that such a criticism does not have a good understanding of the concept of hermeneutical tradition expounded in *Truth and Method* in that it is precisely the critical tradition viewed from present horizons that constitutes modern knowledge.

5. Consequences for Fundamental Theology

Having outlined the history of hermeneutics, both as a method of biblical criticism and as a philosophical discipline, we must now summarize matters by trying to understand the consequences of this discussion for fundamental theology. From this review it is clear that the concept of hermeneutics is not quite the same for all the authors, and nowadays there is a tendency to extend the task of this particular discipline to that of interpretative coordination not only of the spiritual sciences but also of ideologies and the natural sciences. It has thus become almost synonymous with philosophy and likewise shares the uncertainties and conflicts of the present moment. The same is obviously true of theology, which has always sought close relations with philosophy (→ THEOLOGY V) and now finds itself fully immersed in the world of hermeneutics. We can enumerate briefly the problems that the controversy in this field raises for fundamental theology, indicating both the contributions and the limitations and dangers of the different positions.

The area most affected is obviously that of biblical exegesis. Hitherto both Catholic and Protestant traditions have thought that the true meaning of Scripture, that inspired by the Holy Spirit, is the literal sense, namely, that intended by the author. We have seen that, with the strengthening of the role of the subject who is interpreter, the *mens auctoris* is in danger of disappearing. On the other hand, we have noted how certain OT texts have come to be used theologically in the NT, not according to their literal meaning, but read anew from the viewpoint of the latest events in the history of salvation. Thus the fathers drew allegorical meanings from the text that are by no means the fruits of pure fantasy. From these we may conclude that the text as such, as entrusted to the church, contains greater possibilities of meaning than the meaning(s) foreseen by the human author, and that these meanings are realized by the historical process of God's saving activity in the church and in the world. History is thus a hermeneutical principle of the interpretation of revelation in which the Spirit has inspired the initial author to continue speaking by his own words, surpassing the original historical limitation. The link with the original meaning, however, cannot be broken without going against the *mens auctoris* or the obvious meaning of the text. Theories to the contrary, such as those of Gadamer and Betti, may thus be reconciled with exegesis if they allow the continuity of the Spirit as author and interpreter, and if

they understand the "subject" to be not the individual but the church.

Gadamer's insistence on language as the constant underpinning of cultural tradition, which makes it possible for the fusion of perspectives between the "prejudice" of the author and the text, is an aid to understanding the connection between tradition and Scripture. The language of Christianity arose from the very preaching of the apostles that also gave birth to the NT. The church developed this language in dependence upon, and independently of, the NT. The two are inseparable for a proper understanding of both the Bible and tradition. The language of tradition is that into which we are born and which provides the basic understanding by which we understand the NT as a book. When the Reformers wanted to separate Scripture from TRADITION and from the living voice of the church, they removed the Bible from the river by which it steered only to bring it to a halt on the dry bank.

Even the very concept of tradition would be able to be acquired from the hermeneutical speculations of Dilthey and Gadamer. Tradition is certainly not material repetition but organic growth. The various dogmas of the church are hermeneutical interpretations of apostolic revelation in the language of the age in which they have been formulated. The mistake would be to identify language and substance in such a way that in reformulating the dogma in the language of our own day, we were to modify the contents. It would then no longer be tradition but invention. Herein lie the limits set by Ebeling, which see in tradition the reformulation of Jesus' self-understanding before God (faith) but without containing the *traditum* that forms one half of the joint foundation or underpinning.

Among the reasons for many misunderstandings is the insistence of Dilthey, for example, on the historicity of humankind and of truth. Human beings would not possess a nature capable of unchanging definition, but such definition changes with their own self-understanding in history. Truth would not have an ontological foundation but changes with history. It is here that one sees the importance of the corrective provided by Pareyson, who wants to draw attention to the identity of being and truth in the process of historical interpretation. The unchanging character of dogmas presupposes the stability of a truth that remains thus, even if it is obvious that a dogma must be interpreted in relation to its historical origin and translated anew within the present-day perspective of the church.

Bultmann's separation of history and faith has had a harmful effect on Christian hermeneutics. Käsemann had already noted that Bultmann deprived the Christian of the *extra nos* of salvation, rendering it immanent and gnosticizing, but in the final analysis, if I fail to refer to history, then no other criterion remains by which I am obliged to believe that Jesus is the Christ, and not Abraham or Muhammad. In fact, Bultmann maintains that I do not believe in Jesus because he is the Christ, but that he is the Christ because my faith has yielded as much.

The demythologized hermeneutics of Bultmann is thus the consequence of this separation. Allotting the term "myth" to every intervention by the transcendent world in the interlocking series of earthly causes (with the sole exception of my act of faith, which Bultmann maintains to be supernatural), the theologian from Marburg wishes to spare modern men and women from a *sacrificium intellectus*." Yet, apart from the fact that Bultmann has already demanded a *sacrificium intellectus* when he denies faith a rational or historical foundation, a Christian language that does not correspond to a transcendent reality, but only to our immanence, restricts us to a *sacrificium spei* of breaking the circle of an existence enclosed by sin. An abstract work of salvation on the part of God has no meaning if we detach it from the history of salvation in its harsh reality.

There now comes into play the distinction mentioned above, namely, that between *Bedeutung* and *Bedeutsamkeit* (meaning and significance), i.e., the meaning of something in itself and its meaning for me. How can I hope that a doctrine will have a meaning for me if I deny the validity of the meaning in itself.

Here too we enter the vast field of the theory of knowledge into which flows the whole of modern hermeneutics. Identifying hermeneutics with understanding *sic et simpliciter*, we do not move outside our intentionality in a phenomenological sense in order to be able to define the object of our understanding.

Fundamental theology requires an episte-mology that presupposes not only an ontology but also a metaphysics in order to break free from intersubjectivity and to reach some form of objectivity as understood by philosophy. In the final analysis it is a question of knowing whether we can assert that God exists or does not exist outside of ourselves.

Today's climate of nihilism in philosophy and of the disintegration of values is certainly not a help to fundamental theology, and a part of contemporary hermeneutics finds itself immersed in this atmosphere. From this situation there arises the urgent need for believers to engage in hermeneutics, in both the philosophical and theological fields, who will light up the way for Christian hermeneutics in the midst of the babel of voices that surround them.

Bibl.: M. HEIDEGGER, *Unterwegs zur Sprache* (Pfüllingen, 1927); id., *Being and Time* (1950; New York, 1962); E. FUCHS, *Zur Frage nach dem historischen Jesus* (Tübingen, 1960); id., *Marburger Hermeneutik* (Tübingen, 1969); P. ALTHAUS, *Die Theologie Martin Luthers* (Gütersloh, 1963); R. M. GRANT, *A Short History of the Interpretation of the Bible* (New York, 1963); R. BULTMANN, *History of the Synoptic Tradition* (New York, 1963); id., *Jesus Christ and Mythology* (New York, 1958); H. DE LUBAC, *Exégèse médiévale*, 4 vols. (Paris, 1961–64); G. EBELING, *Wort Gottes und Tradition* (Göttingen, 1964); id., *Einführung in die theologische Sprachlehre* (Tübingen, 1971); "Hermeneutik" and "Tradition" in *RGG* 3rd ed., 3:242–62; 6:974–84; W. SCHMITHALS, *Die Theologie Rudolf Bultmann* (Tübingen, 1966); E. D. HIRSCH, *Validity in Interpretation* (New Haven, 1967); P. H. JORGENSEN, *Die Bedeutung des Subjekt-Objektverhältnisses für die Theologie* (Hamburg, 1967); R. E. PALMER, *Hermeneutics* (Evanston, 1969); L. PAREYSON, *Verità e interpretazione* (Milan, 1971); N. HENRICHS, *Bibliographie zur Hermeneutik* (Düsseldorf, 1972); R. HEIJNE, *Sprache des Glaubens: Theologie von E. Fuchs* (Tübingen, 1972); P. RICOEUR, *The Conflict of Interpretation: Essays in Hermeneutics* (Evanston, 1974); id., *Essays on Biblical Interpretation* (Philadelphia, 1979); H.-G. GADAMER, *Truth and Method* (New York, 1975); I. MANCINI, "Ermeneutica" *NDT* (Rome, 1977), 370–80; B. DE MARJERIE, *Introduction à l'histoire de l'exégèse*, 3 vols. (Paris, 1980); V. MANNUCCI, *Bibbia come parola di Dio* (Brescia, 1981); H. J. SIEBEN, *Exegesis Patrum: Saggio bibliografico dell'esegesi biblica dei Padri* (Rome, 1983); D. K. McKIM, *What Christians Believe about the Bible* (New York, 1985); M. SIMONETTI, *Lettera e/o allegoria* (Rome, 1985); P. GRECH, *Ermeneutica e teologia biblica* (Rome, 1986); id., "Ermeneutica" *NDTB* (Milan, 1988), 464–89; G. MURA, *Emilio Betti:*

L'Ermeneutica come metodo generale delle scienze dello spirito (Rome, 1987); G. VATTIMO et al., *Il pensiero ermeneutico* (Geneva, 1988); K. MUELLER-VOLLMER, ed., *The Hermeneutics Reader* (New York, 1989); M. FERRARIS, *Storia dell'ermeneutica* (Milan, 1989).

Prosper GRECH

THE HIERARCHY OF TRUTHS

A recent addition to the theological vocabulary, this phrase conveys a way of considering Catholic doctrine, which was encouraged by Vatican II's *Decree on Ecumenism* and applauded by many involved in the ecumenical movement. On 25 November 1963, Archbishop Andrea Pangrazio suggested to the council that attention to the *hierarchical order* of revealed truths would provide a better estimate of the actual unity and division between Christians in matters of doctrine. Pangrazio stated that, while all revealed truths must be believed, they do not all have the same importance when one considers revelation as a whole. Some truths pertain to everlasting realities, such as the mysteries of the Trinity or the incarnation or redemption, while others pertain to the means of salvation that will one day pass away, such as truths about the church. Most Christian divisions concern these latter truths about the pilgrim life of the church. Christians are already united in faith about many of the most significant truths of revelation.

The council did not take up Pangrazio's language distinguishing truths about the end of salvation from truths about its means. But on 11 November 1964, just ten days before the final vote on *Unitatis Redintegratio,* the bishops voted to include in that decree the following sentence: "When comparing doctrines, they [Catholic theologians] should remember that in Catholic teaching there exists an order or 'hierarchy' of truths, since they vary in their relationship to the foundation of the Christian faith" (*UR* 11). Appearing in the section of chapter 2 of *Unitatis Redintegratio* that addresses dialogue, the concept of the hierarchy of truths is intended to help Catholics engaged in dialogue not only explain their church's doc-

trine more correctly but also achieve, together with their dialogue partners, an even more adequate expression of the "unfathomable riches of Christ" (Eph 3:8). Christian truths, in the plural, are seen in relationship to each other. The pattern that can be discerned among these truths allows the church to grasp Christian truth more adequately and to grow in its comprehension of revelation.

The phrase "hierarchy of truths" has several antecedents in the twentieth century, particularly among some theologians writing in the late 1930s about the theological methodology of Thomas Aquinas. But the precise phrase rarely appears until after Vatican II. Then it gave rise to a large number of publications and not a few courses at various theological centers. Several ecumenical dialogues commented favorably about the hierarchy of truths, and it was the subject of a number of consultations sponsored by the Joint Working Group of the Vatican Council for the Promotion of Christian Unity and the World Council of Churches. The results of all of this attention may be summarized under the categories of the historical and the systematic.

1. Historical

Theologians have suggested many historical antecedents for the notion of the hierarchy of truths. The NT itself suggests that Christian truth is centered in the very person of Jesus (see Jn 14:6–"I am the way, and the truth, and the life"– as well as the overall Johannine emphasis on the importance of personal attachment in loving discipleship to Jesus). Various expressions of the kerygma of the good news (e.g., 1 Cor 15:3–5 or the speeches by Peter and Paul in Acts 2:14–36; 3:12–26; 4:8–12; 10:34–43; 13:16–41), references to the "foundation" of the faith (1 Cor 3:10–11; Heb 6:1), hymns about the mystery of Christ (Eph 1:3–10; Phil 2:5–11; Col 1:12–20), and trinitarian formulas all point to a focal point of Christian truth in which the whole Christian message is centered. This idea of order also touches the existential response of the disciple in passages that speak about the "greatest" commandment (Mt 22:34–40), the danger of making dogmas of mere human precepts (Mt 15:9), and the preeminence of love (1 Cor 13).

This sense of proportion continues throughout the course of Christian tradition. Early on, creeds were developed as a means of fulfilling the liturgical need for expressing the heart of Christian truth at the celebrations of baptism and Eucharist. The patristic theologians of the early church had a sense for the trinitarian core of the faith and tended to relate any particular theological theme to that core. Later, scholastic theologians were fond of showing that all Christian truths derived from articles of the creed. The Reformation recognized the centrality of the gospel message about salvation in Christ as the principle for correctly interpreting the Scriptures and the norm for reforming the life of the church. Among the churches of the Reformation, some of the earliest efforts to achieve Christian unity were based on such notions as "fundamental articles," "truths necessary for salvation," and the consensus of the first five centuries or of the first seven ecumenical councils—notions that in various ways presuppose that Christian truth has a somewhat adequately identifiable center. In nineteenth-century Catholic theology, M. J. Scheeben's effort to show that all Christian truths can be reduced to several central mysteries once again echoed this theme, as did Vatican I's teaching that human reason, guided by faith, could make valuable progress in understanding revelation by considering the interrelation of revealed truths among themselves and with the final end of humankind (DS 3016). Thus, while the expression "hierarchy of truths" appears only in the twentieth century and especially after the Second Vatican Council, what it intends to say deeply resonates with much in Christian tradition.

2. Systematic

The notion of the hierarchy of truths is of particular interest for fundamental theology because of its profound connection with Vatican II's understanding of revelation. Some have even said that Unitatis Redintegratio's teaching about the hierarchy of truths is inconceivable without Dei Verbum's teaching about revelation. There, revelation is presented as God's self-manifestation (DV 2, 4, 6). Revelation does not concern all possible truths, but rather has a definite focus, the prima veritas, which is ultimately utterly simple. Faith is a complete personal response to this revelation and, as

such, is ultimately a response to the utterly simple mystery of God himself (DV 5). The hierarchy of truths is thus expressive of the very nature of revelation. This touches on an issue of deep consequences for fundamental theology—i.e., What is the relationship between the one simple truth that is God and the many individual truths that the church has come to assert over the course of many centuries?

A second major issue relative to fundamental theology concerns the relationship between faith and revelation. If revelation is ordered, must not faith that responds by a loving and grateful acceptance of that revelation be in some way determined by that order? Here one touches on the relationship between the "objective" order inherent in the very content of revelation itself and the "subjective," or "existential," order that characterizes the faith of individuals and communities. So far, theologians have noted that believers seem to exhibit an "existential hierarchy of truths" insofar as the faith of individuals and of groups can express a particular focus. Some have suggested that the objective focus of revelation should serve as a guide and corrective for existential faith. Faith should not place at the center something that is relatively peripheral to God's self-manifestation.

The hierarchy of truths raises the question of the obligation to believe the whole of revealed truth. In Mortalium Animos (1927), Pius XI rejected attempts at Christian unity based upon a distinction between fundamental and nonfundamental articles of faith on the basis that all truths that are revealed by God must be believed. In terms of the authority supporting the truths of revelation, all such truths are equal. Thus, the notion of the hierarchy of truths must not be thought of in such a way as to compromise the authority of God who reveals; it must safeguard the "obedience of faith" (Rom 16:26). The affirmation of the hierarchy of truths should indeed be an expression of such obedience. In this regard, the hierarchy of truths implies that the obedience of faith obeys also the order inherent in revelation. Emphasis on the formal authority underlying revelation must not obscure the differences between revealed truths. This gives an additional meaning to the word "indifferentism." Indifferentism is not only a laissez-faire attitude toward religious doctrine. Another form of indifferentism treats as equal truths that, in terms of their respective connections "with the foundation of Christian faith," are not equal. In this sense, *Unitatis Redintegratio* may be said to complete the teaching of *Mortalium Animos* by putting it in a more comprehensive context.

Ecumenically, the hierarchy of truths can be helpful in two ways. First, as a tool for dialogue between divided Christians, the notion can both help the dialogue partners more accurately understand one another's doctrine as well as assist them in grasping, expressing, and confessing together the apostolic faith today. Second, the hierarchy of truths could help the churches to identify the unity in faith that is necessary for full communion. This second element would be possible only under the guidance of the teaching office of the church, which could discern what significance the hierarchy of truths has for identifying and promoting unity in faith. In this regard, the hierarchy of truths needs to be brought to bear on the discussion of theological pluralism. Can a legitimate pluralism encompass not only differences in expression but also differences in the number of doctrines believed, granting always the intention to believe all that God reveals and the explicit profession of the central truths of faith? A positive response to this question could be given only under the discerning guidance of the teaching authority of the church, which would also have to address the pastoral need of showing how such a response does not jeopardize the authority of the various exercises of official church teaching in the course of the centuries.

The hierarchy of truths is relevant to several other theological issues as well. It could provide a guideline for the task of handing on the Christian faith, whether in terms of evangelization and inculturation or in terms of catechesis. It promises to be a useful tool in the dialogue between Christianity and world religions and in the task of credibly addressing the Christian message to a secularized society. Furthermore, it can serve as a hermeneutical framework for the perennial task of studying and expressing anew the Christian tradition. Emphasizing as it does the ordered nature of revelation, the hierarchy of truths could prove very useful for a more profound understanding of doctrinal development. It remains a conciliar teaching that is full of promise.

Bibl.: H. Mühlen, "Die Lehre des Vatikanum II: Über die Hierarchia veritatum und ihre Bedeutung für den ökumenischen Dialog," *TG* 57 (1966): 303–35; U. Valeske, Hierarchia veritatum (Munich, 1968); O. Cullmann, "Einheit in der Vielfalt im Lichte der 'Hierarchie der Wahrheiten,'" in E. Klinger and K. Wittstadt, eds., *Glaube im Prozess: Christsein nach dem II Vatikanum: Für Karl Rahner* (Freiburg, 1984), 356–64; W. Henn, "The Hierarchy of Truths Twenty Years later," *TS* 48 (1987): 439–71; H. Witte, "Alnaargelang hunband met het fundament van het christelijk geloof verschillendis," in *Wording en verwerking van de uitspraak over de 'hierarchie' van waarheden van Vaticanum II* (University of Tilburg, 1986).

W. Henn

HINDUISM

1. Introduction

Hinduism is a highly complex and rich religion. No founder's initiative, no dogma, and no reform have imposed restrictions on its domain of essential beliefs and practices. It is the product of a history that can be traced back about 3,500 years. Every period of that long history has left an impact on it that endures in today's beliefs and practices. A Hindu can be a polytheist, a monotheist, a pantheist, or even an atheist, while still believing in some kind of ultimate principle. Hindus belong to one of the caste groups and socially observe the customs and laws as formulated in the Hindu sacred writings. Hinduism is both a way of life and a highly organized social and religious system.

2. The Ancient Religious Tradition

The Hindus divide their sacred writings into two distinct categories that they call Śruti (what is heard) and Smriti (what is remembered). The former comprises the Veda (knowledge) itself, which is considered to be the eternal Śabda (word) heard by the sages of immemorial antiquity. The Veda, as we now have it, is historically divided into three groups: the Samhitas (collections) of hymns and formulas (the four Vedas), the Brāhmanas (sacrificial texts), and the Āranyakas (forest treatises), which culminate in the Upanishads (esoteric treatises). The Hindus believe that the whole of the Veda is uncreated; it is the Word uttered by the Absolute in eternity and "heard" or "memorized" by sages of old. The second category (Smṛiti) which does not have the rank of being the eternal truth, comprises the Sūtras (philosophical aphorisms), Dharma-Śāstras (the law books), the Purāṇas (stories about the great gods), and the two national epics, the Mahābhārata and the Rāmāyana. The Bhagavad Gītā, though not part of the sacred canon of the Veda, is in practice at least as highly regarded by all Hindus. These sacred writings do not contain an account of God's dealings with humankind in history; rather, they are a gradual and human realization of the being of God and of humanity. It is the human search for the Real, the Light, and the Immortal, both in the person and in the world that surrounds us. "From the unreal, lead me to the Real; from darkness lead me to Light; from death lead me to Immortality" (*Br. Up.* 1.3.28).

3. Basic Hindu Beliefs

Although Hinduism is free from dogmatic assertions concerning the nature of God and of human beings, still there are certain beliefs in post-Vedic Hinduism that are in no way disputed and are accepted as self-evident. These are *dharma, karma, samsāra, Brahman,* and *moksha.*

The Hindus themselves call their religion *sanātana dharma* (eternal religion). *Dharma* is the form of things as they exist and the power that keeps them as they are. It is that which maintains in being the whole universe in the cosmic order and humankind in the moral order in accordance with the eternal law. This *dharma* is set down in the sacred texts, particularly in those that deal with Hindu customary laws (Dharma-Śāstras). The term is also applied to the religious assumptions in which these laws are based. *Brahman* is the eternal substrate of the universe from which the eternal *dharma* proceeds. It also founds the spiritual prerogative of the Brahman caste. In earlier texts, Brahman meant "the sacred"; hence, whatever was sacred, whether a formula or a chant or a sacrificial action, was called *brahman.* Since the sacred as manifested in the sacrificial ritual was considered to be the bond linking temporal humanity with the eternal, *brahman* came to signify the eternal as it is in itself beyond space and time and as it manifests

itself in the phenomenal world. Consequently the term *brahman* was also applied to the state of the liberated soul (*moksha*); to the source from which all phenomenal existence derives its being; to the link between the world of *samsāra* conditioned by space and time, cause and effect, and the *moksha* that transcends these; to the eternal being, which is the unchanging source of all change; and finally to the eternal *dharma,* the law that is based on the eternal and that governs the world of *samsāra.*

Karma is the universal law according to which every action is the effect of a cause and is in its turn the cause of an effect. The whole process is called *samsāra,* the cycle of birth and death, to which all phenomenal existence is subject. The world of experience is in bondage to the fetters of time and desire because desire to do and to live implicates the doer in the wheel of *samsāra.* Escape from this cycle of time and action is possible and is called release of liberation (*moksha*). Time is conceived as a revolving wheel returning ever again to the point from which it started and in which there can be neither purpose nor salvation.

The Vedic mythology contains thirty-three gods, divided into terrestrial gods (Agni, Prithivi, Sarasvati), atmospheric gods (Indra, Rudra, Maruts, etc.), and celestial gods (Dyaus, Varuna, Mitra, Surya, etc.) The Vedic mythology is concerned not only with nature myths or with functional deities or with the social structure of a tribal society but also with a combination and integration of all these three into an ordered whole. There is the cosmic order (*ṛta*) on which human order, ethics, and social life depend. Thus there is correspondence between the world of human beings (the performers of sacrifice) and the world of gods (the recipients of the sacrifice). The Vedic worshiper keeps perfect balance between these two orders by means of the right performance of sacrifice, which is really the meeting ground between human beings and gods.

4. Basic Hindu Ritual

Vedic sacrifice consists in paying homage to the gods in the form of a lengthy ceremony culminating in offerings made to the sacred Fire (Agni). Its purpose is to commune with the gods, whose help is sought for general well-being or some particular benefit. In later

Hinduism, the Vedic ritual gave place to inward worship in the form of mental adoration, and symbolic gestures became widespread. Prayer in the form of the *mantra* on the occasions of initiation, expiation, etc. and the practice of *japa* (mental recitation) became universally established. Adoration (*pūja*) is the form par excellence of Hindu religious practice. In a series of operations partly based on Vedic models, the image of a deity is anointed, dressed, and adorned; food and drink are offered to it; flowers are placed, and lamps are lighted. Annually the image is carried out of the temple precincts in processions in which the image is installed in a chariot, and at the end it is immersed in some sacred river.

Much in Vedic religion is purely sacrificial, hieratic, and ritualistic. Even here, however, a certain personal relationship between the worshiper and the god is undoubtedly manifested in many of the Rig Veda hymns. In them, one finds both a healthy fear of the gods' wrath and an inner piety to the main gods, in whose benevolence worshipers place their faith and whom they profusely praise and confidently invoke in all their needs. The prayer for forgiveness of guilt is characteristic of the Varuna hymns, which are the most exalted and ethical in the whole Veda.

5. Monistic and Theistic Trends

With regard to the Hindu and especially Vedic polytheism, it should be noted that the frequent practice of invoking individual gods as the highest or the supreme has made scholars call it henotheism, which is defined as the belief in individual gods alternately regarded as the highest, the god addressed being for the moment treated as the Supreme Deity. This practice has led to an identification of one god with another and even with all. "What is but one, the wise call by manifold names" (*Rig Veda* 1.164.46).

As the early Indians tried to account for the origin of the world and the development of multiplicity out of unity, they stood before the mystery of existence. In the Vedic hymns creation is regarded as the transition from a chaos to a diversified order through a preexistent creator god who may or may not be divine. The quest for the Absolute (Brahman) begins in the Upanishads. What is Brahman? What is the innermost Self (Ātman) of all things and of human beings? Some said that Brahman was food in the sense of matter in a constant state of transformation, for one cannot live unless one eats, and one cannot eat unless one takes other lives, whether animal or vegetable. The process of eating and being eaten constitutes the unity underlying the diversity of existence. Others said that Brahman was the breath of life, since one needs it more than food to live. Yet others said that it was mind in the human being, since it can know all. Still others said that it was ether or space, which, since it pervades everything, can well be considered to be the ground of all things of the external world. Or again, it might be better to say no more of it than "Not this, not this," since once one defines it, one limits it, and whatever it is, Brahman is certainly not limited or circumscribed. Or again, if living beings are real in spite of their being subject to change and mortality, then Brahman, the true Self of all things, must be the Real of the real. It is the inner controller, the inmost self, the unseen seer, the unheard hearer, the unthought thinker, the unununderstood understander, the warp and woof of all things, other than the world but controlling it from within. In brief, Brahman is both eternal Being and the source of all the phenomenal universe; besides, it is also the inmost self within the essence of humankind. Thus is reached the famous identification of the eternal essence of humanity (Ātman) with the changeless Absolute (Brahman) that indwells and controls the whole universe.

Although this tendency to pure nonduality or monism appears more prominently in the early Upanishads, a tendency to conceive of the Supreme Being in personal terms, distinct from the universe, is not absent even in the earlier ones and becomes more prominent in the later Upanishads. Perhaps the first formulation of the Hindu idea of God is found in the so-called *Śandilya-Vidyā*, in which Brahman is called "this whole world" which also transcends the world, for it is greater than the great, and indwells the human soul. The idea of God as origin, sustainer, and indweller of the universe and of the human self emerges as something distinct from them. In the *Katha Upanishad*, the figure of a personal God appears as the Lord of both the ideal world and the world of becoming. "More subtle than the subtle, yet greater than the great, the Self is hidden in the depth of creatures. The man without desire, [all] sorrow spent, beholds it, the Majesty of the Self, by the grace of the Creator" (2.20). In the *Śvetāsvatara Upanishad* a fairly clear and consistent theism is proposed. God (Rudra-Śiva) is the one who presides over all causes endowed with time and self. God and his power (*śakti*) form an indissoluble unity. As God, he is unmoved; as Śakti, he is the mover. Śakti is the creative power of God by whom all things were made. Souls as fragments of God must therefore be of the same substance as God and will be merged into him at the end of time. God is regarded as Lord and Creator of the universe, immanent as well as transcendent, who loves righteousness and hates evil, and who has positive qualities and a distinct personality.

6. Bhagavad Gītā

The *Bhagavad Gītā* is the crowning of Indian theism. Brahman is cosmologically Primal matter (*prakriti* or *māyā*); psychologically it is the realization of immortality. God is creator, sustainer, and destroyer of the universe. God is its beginning, middle, and end, transcendent as the highest Person as well as immanent, and dwells in the hearts of people as the essence of all things and their seed. Though some passages of the *Gītā* are pantheistic, yet some key passages do not imply pantheism and understand the divine immanence correctly. Of the constituents (*gunas*) of nature, Krisha says: "Know that these are from me; I am not in them, but they are in me" (7.10; 9.18). Similarly God sustains all creatures but does not subsist in them. "All creatures subsist in me, but I am not established in them. And yet creatures do not subsist in me. Behold my sovereign power. My own Self sustains creatures without subsisting in them; it causes them to exist" (9.4–5). The *Gītā* teaches the doctrine of *avatāra* (incarnation) of the supreme God Vishnu. "Though I am unborn and of changeless substance, though I am the Lord of creatures, yet do I by my creative power (*māyā*) resort to nature which is of me, and thus come into being" (4.6). The real message of the *Gītā* is that God is not an impersonal absolute but the lover of the human soul—indeed, love itself. Krishna says: "I am that love in created things which is not contrary to righteousness" (7.10; 9.18). He is father,

comrade, and beloved (11.44). The relationship between human beings and God is one of grace and love. "With strong desire I have desired thee; therefore shall I tell thee thy salvation. Think of me, worship me, sacrifice to me, pay me homage; so shalt thou come to me. I promise thee truly, for I love thee well. Give up all things of the law; turn to me only as thy refuge. I will deliver thee from all evil; have no care" (18.64–66). For the first time in the long history of Indian religious experience God seems to be speaking directly to people, a God of love, mercy, and terror (11.24, 30).

7. The Hindu Ways of Salvation

Common Hindu belief finds three main causes of human bondage—evil actions, desire, and ignorance. Rebirth is the necessary consequence of our actions, which proceed from and are qualified by our desires, which in turn stem from our egoism. People are playthings of desires and egoism owing to their ignorance of true reality and hence of the true self. For the problem of bad actions, the proximate remedy is to do good and avoid evil, which involves ethical and religious observance. Very few will hold that this by itself will lead to final liberation, but all require it at least in the preparatory stage. (2) For the problem of desire, the remedy is to control and subdue one's passions, aiming at disinterested activity through ascetic practice, and to purify and transcend all desires by a single-hearted love of God. Love of God will either imply or easily lead up to true knowledge by the connaturality of love and the grace of God. For the problem of ignorance, the true knowledge of reality and, in particular, the knowledge of the true self is to be acquired, thus destroying egoism at its root. The attainment of intuitive, saving knowledge is commonly held to require, with or without the help of grace, a sustained asceticism and a technique of mental concentration (yoga).

Hinduism seeks the way for the imperfect people to realize the ultimate Reality, whether God or the Absolute, and to realize their ultimate goal of life.

What for the Hindu constitutes liberation (*moksha*) is release not from sin but from the human condition, i.e., release from action (*karma*) of any kind, whether good or evil, liberation into a condition where time and space are abolished and all is seen as one. Liberation for the nondualist Upanishads means merging into Brahman, the supreme principle, as a river merges into the sea, by which a person is freed from the fetters of the phenomenal life and passes into a mode of being that is infinite, omnipresent (because space is transcended), and deathless (because time is transcended); this is precisely to become Brahman. The Saṁkhya-Yoga is content to define liberation as *kaivalyam*, or isolation of the individual soul in its eternal essence. But theistic *bhakti* sects see the pathway to God as loyalty and love between the soul and God, and liberation means with a personal God in love and total surrender.

As to the way of salvation, the Hindus traditionally speak of three paths (*mārgas*): ascetic and religious observance (*karma-mārga*), intuitive knowledge of the true Reality (*jñāna-mārga*), and the love of God and surrender to him (*bhakti-mārga*). The distinction between these three paths, though helpful to understand the Hindu spirituality, is never adequate, for they interpenetrate one another in actual practice.

Hindu Asceticism

The early Brahmanic asceticism consists mainly of sacrifices and ritual. The word "yoga" (to yoke, link) was used in the sacrificial context. The performer of sacrifice "yokes" the heavenly powers to the offering, or "yokes" by mental concentration his or her own thought to the spiritual formula and action. After a ritual bath the performer of sacrifice undergoes a rigorous fast, sitting in ascetic immobility in embryo posture, in the dark between sacred fires, and thus communes with the gods. Internal asceticism, sacred recitation, and meditation are helps for union with God.

The *Bhagavad Gītā* gives a deeper meaning to the Hindu asceticism. If one's goal is to pass beyond all action into a timeless peace, then why should one act at all? The *Gītā* answers that it is not action, strictly speaking, that binds but attachment to action and to its fruits. When action is performed with complete detachment, it ceases to bind one to the world. Right action, moreover, automatically leads to a state of detachment of the mind, and detachment in its turn leads to a higher stage of

spirituality in the way of liberation. The *Gītā* says in its last chapter: "By giving up self, force, pride, lust, anger, and acquisitiveness, with no thought of 'mine,' at peace, so is a man fitted to realize his eternal essence."

Hindu Way of Knowledge (jñāna)

By knowledge is understood not simply book learning or rational-empirical knowledge but the intuitive apprehension of the true self. The Hindu doctrines differ among themselves in proposing this knowledge because of difference of their views on the true nature of the self and of the quality of their asceticism. The ignorance that requires rebirth may be the nondiscrimination between the self and the nonself (Saṁkhya-yoga), the ignorance of the true self's identity with the All-One (nondualism), or the ignorance of the self's true relation to God and lack of knowledge of God (theism). The intuitive realization of the true self and its relation to the Absolute, or God, is to be reached either by mystical apperception or, much more often, in a concrete mystical experience at the summit of an ascetic-mystical ascent. The nondualist (*advaita*) mysticism consists in knowing the difference between the Absolute and illusory being. Besides the preparatory methods of renunciation and devotion, this type of Hindu mysticism proposes the method of transcendental knowledge of one's own inner self. "One has to know the Self in the self alone through the self." Knowledge based on Hindu Scriptures is merely the finger that points to the object and that disappears when it is itself looked upon. The real knowledge is that which is one's own vision, an awareness of identity with Brahman in the sense of mystical insight. This awareness cannot be produced or reasoned out for it is not a work. The way to this vision may be prepared by the words of the Veda, by the loving devotion (*bhakti*) to a personal God, and by meditation on the ultimate Truth; in the end it is the seeing of the identity between the Absolute and the self.

The Hindu Way of Love of God

By love of God (*bhakti*) is meant a specific religious attitude and sentiment, the essential features of which are faith in, love for, and trustful surrender to the Deity. It is an affective participation of the soul in the divine nature, a most intense love for God, a clinging of the heart that focuses on the Lord's greatness. The object of *bhakti* is the Blessed Lord, the Holy, the Adorable. It is both a preparation for liberation and its completion. As the supreme goal, it is union and communion with God in the bond of love, implying a deep sense of dependence on, and submission to, God. Rāmānuja says that the knowledge that most radically destroys selfishness is that which arises from the devout meditation on the Lord as transcendent and as the true self of the soul. This devout meditation is a continuity of steady remembrance, moving uninterrupted like a flow of oil. Because of its exceptional intensity, it acquires the character of an intuitive perception and is exceedingly dear to the soul on account of the supreme lovableness of its object. But this intuitive and loving sense of God does not arise from meditation alone. It is due to grace, a choice of God.

In the Upanishads God is said to choose and favor whom he loves; by his grace alone a person gains knowledge and is liberated. In a way, all is grace in *bhakti*. The means of *bhakti* are only aids; *bhakti* is the fruit of a divine election. Madhva and Vallabha teach a doctrine of predestination, according to which some are predestined to *bhakti* and liberation; others are predestined to remain endlessly in a cycle of rebirth. The Lord's grace is healing, illuminating, conforming to divine nature, and uniting with him. But all this takes place within a system of immanent creation. Though God undoubtedly gives his grace freely, this help is never strictly supernatural, for grace restores the soul to its natural divine life. It does not raise the soul to a higher, supernatural level of being, life, and action.

The followers of Rāmānuja were divided over the doctrine of grace into two schools, northern and southern, distinguished as the ape-way and the cat-way. When a mother ape falls into danger, her young immediately clings fast to her. When the mother makes a leap to safety, this act saves them both. It does so, however, in such a way that the young one cooperates a little, because it clings to the mother by its own act. It is therefore synergist. When danger threatens a cat with her young one, however, the mother cat takes the young kitten in her mouth. The young one does nothing for its salvation. It remains merely passive. All cooperation is excluded. We can put the difference between the two schools briefly thus: in the northern, the soul gains God for itself; in the southern, God gains the soul for himself.

The bhakti mysticism believes in and strives for real union with a personal God through love of him. This love of God includes knowledge of God. Through love the religious soul comes to know God, who and how great he is in his being and love. Knowing God in his essence, the God-lover forthwith enters into union with him. This highest state of participation in God's essence is realized by the grace of God.

Bibl.: A. BARTH, *The Religions of India* (London, 1882); H. VON GLASENAPP, *Der Hinduismus* (Munich, 1922); S. N. DASGUPTA, *Hindu Mysticism* (Chicago, 1927); B. DAS, *An Advanced Textbook of Hindu Religion* (Adyar, 1930); O. LACOMBE, *L'Absolu selon le Vedanta* (Paris, 1938); F. EDGERTON, *The Bhagavadgita* (Cambridge, MA, 1944); K. W. MORGAN, ed., *The Religion of the Hindus* (New York, 1953); P. D. DEVANANDAN, *Living Hinduism* (Bangalore, 1959); J. GONDA, *Die Religionen Indiens*, 2 vols. (Stuttgart, 1960); id., *Vishnuism and Saivism* (London, 1970); T. M. P. MAHADEVAN, *Outlines of Hinduism* (Madras, 1960); S. RADHAKRISHNAN, *The Hindu View of Life* (London, 1963); M. HIRIYANNA, *Outlines of Indian Philosophy* (London, 1964); JESUIT SCHOLARS, *Religious Hinduism* (Allahabad, 1964); K. KLOSTERMAIER, *A Survey of Hinduism* (1965; Albany, 1989); V. IONS, *Indian Mythology* (London, 1967); A. M. ESNOUL, *L'hindouisme* (Paris, 1971); M. BIARDEAU, *Clés pour la pensée hindoue* (Paris, 1972); M. DHAVAMONY, *Love of God According to Saiva Siddhanta* (Oxford, 1972); id., *Classical Hinduism* (Rome, 1982); W. D. O'FLAHERTY, *Hindu Myths* (Harmondsworth, 1975); J. E. CARPENTER, *Theism in Medieval India* (Delhi, 1977); L. RENOU, *L'hindouisme* (Paris, 1979).

Mariasusai DHAVAMONY

HISTORIE/GESCHICHTE

One can understand the difference between *Historie* and *Geschichte* by examining the anthropological basis of the distinction. According to existentialist philosophy (as represented, for example, by M. Heidegger), Dasein is ex-sistence; i.e., human being stands out from itself. Human being is the process of coming to be. This implies that human being is temporal, or *geschichtlich*. Dasein comes to itself as thrown into the world, thus with a certain facticity, and is a project, being-toward-the-future, hence that being with possibility as its authentic mode of Being. Dasein's present is constituted by the appropriation of its future within the limits of its real possibilities. *Geschichte*, therefore, refers to that history which is Dasein's own history. In this sense *Geschichte* is an existential or an ontological structure of Dasein's Being. Every Dasein is *geschichtlich*.

At the same time, Dasein's transcendental *Geschichtlichkeit* is expressed objectively or categorically in the world, thereby giving rise to the public events of our human history. These historical events are open to objective, empirical investigation and are scientifically verifiable. The objective study of these empirical events is *Historie*.

The difference between *Historie* and *Geschichte* lies in the fact that *Historie* can be perceived by the detached, objective knower. *Geschichte*, on the other hand, is knowable only through the participation of subjects who realize themselves through their temporal self-expressions.

John O'DONNELL

HISTORY

I. HISTORICAL CONSCIOUSNESS

"The acquisition of a historical consciousness is probably the most important of the revolutions we have undergone since the advent of the modern age." Better than any, these words of H. G. Gadamer (*Le problème de la conscience historique* [1963]) introduce us to the problems and indicate their scope for contemporary thought. Nothing perhaps so uniquely characterizes our century as our historical consciousness, offering as it does an ever-expanding scenario in which to set the conquests of human knowledge, as also the responsibility for future progress.

Since the father of historical consciousness, W. Dilthey, started the process by diverting

thought from a critique of pure reason to one of historical reason, historical consciousness has become more and more a feature of the sciences (not only history and historiography, but philosophy, theology, and all the *Geisteswissenschaften* too), to the point where it is now regarded as normative for a correct system of knowledge.

The concept of historical consciousness is subject to at least three complementary interpretations.

a. By historical consciousness we mean above all *the situating of ourselves within a state of becoming*, a state characterized by the dynamic of facts which become events within the particular viewpoint of the subject and which so become a "history."

It is interesting to compare this with the conception of history among the Greeks. For them, one could only *tell* what happened; with the passage of time, the facts were regarded as mutable. The transitoriness of human affairs provides the background for the great "stories" of antiquity, a concept all the more surprising when one considers how well the Greeks understood the stability and permanence of the heavenly bodies and the unchanging order of the universe.

The narration of facts is what permits their survival in time. In this way, they do not fall into oblivion and can be remembered in the future.

Augustine's understanding of the matter was very different, representing possibly the first major breakthrough in the history of thought. He saw time as a stimulating factor, imposing *attentio animi* ("attention of the mind"). The human spirit is constantly drawn in a threefold motion—*memoria* ("memory"), *contuitus* ("contemplation"), and *expectatio* ("expectation")—which allows the classification of time into past, present, and future. At this level, historical consciousness is thus an awareness of the passing of time, allowing human nature to perceive and grasp what time is.

We might therefore say that historical consciousness is our awareness of ourselves being temporal beings and hence makers of history. Time becomes the medium for our personal encounter with reality; our temporality, however, allows us to grasp the separateness of the "other" from ourselves.

In other words, we have self-awareness within the limitations of time, which we are yet able to transcend. According to this interpretation, we have historical consciousness because here we find a thoughtful relationship that we have with ourselves. We are aware of being introduced, "flung" into history (Heidegger's *Geworfenheit*), but at the same time of being individuals who "pro-ject" ourselves (*Entwurf*).

Without historical consciousness, therefore, we should not have full self-awareness and would remain unfulfilled on the two planes of our own existence: the givenness of our own being, and the freedom of our will-to-be. For in this we complete the original experience contextualized in our wonder at discovering our having been given an existence.

I do not belong to me; I arrive at a moment in time and history decided on by others and receive what others have prepared. For no one is alone in history. On the contrary, here we discover the paradox of our existence. Our personal aspirations, our demands and ideals in life, are shared by others. Almost at once we discover that what we want, other people want. Consciousness leads to the discovery of the other as "other" than myself, even though deeply united to me. While therefore we discover a shared aspiration and ideal, our particular points of view and individuality set us apart.

b. At a second level, historical consciousness is *the perception of meaning in history*. It is not so much the connection and interdependence of events as it is an immediate seeing and knowing of a constant tendency toward fulfillment.

This consciousness does not permit us to assume that one absolute can impose itself as the one possible fulfillment of history and exclusively possess the characteristics of history—i.e., temporality and contingency.

The meaning of history permits us to see an initial balance achieved between the fragmentariness of events and a whole that can embrace them all by giving them meaning. It is therefore a perception and grasp of a universality eluding the limitations of the individual and extending to the personal, the social, and the transcendent.

c. Finally, historical consciousness is *that which permits historical knowledge*. The philosophy of history and historiography both refer to it as the basis for establishing objectivity in historical knowledge.

Burdened with the present and unable to get free of it, historians approach the past in an effort to find out, reconstruct, and interpret what history is made up of. But historical consciousness, at this level, imposes awareness of a vaster horizon against which the study of historical fact must be set. For the past can never be objective, as though it were some extraneous body or a neutral factor. All of today's problems present themselves when we interpret it, and oblige us to speak as though of something happening now.

Past history, like any other story, is contemporary because it is that which makes the present what it is and is reflected in it. With that past, we are involved and, willingly or not, compromised. Past and present therefore tend toward a higher synthesis that is both a new understanding of events and the foundation of the future.

H. I. Marrou rightly spoke of the *sympathie théorique* that has to be exercised by the historian. To know the past but, more important, to know what is other than me, should always "move" us or, to use M. Weber's word, produce an *Einfühlung*, a taking part so as to penetrate ever deeper into the event.

A historical consciousness prompts us to accept a *Wirkungsgeschichte* (Gadamer, *Wahrheit und Methode*), obliging us to see ourselves within an ever vaster horizon in which acceptance of tradition is the condition of survival for the present.

Historical consciousness would therefore have us give serious thought to the fact that we are so totally immersed in history that we cannot make sense of ourselves except as *historical persons*. We should thus be in a position to see the present clearly and project it into the future by being aware of a past with which we are burdened and by sorting out what was true in it and inevitably remains so even for our own time, notwithstanding the limitations and contingencies in which that truth has been revealed.

Bibl. H.-I. MARROU, *De la connaissance historique* (Paris, 1954); W. DILTHEY, *Gesammelte Schriften*, vol. 11: *Vom Aufgang des geschichtlichen Bewusstseins* (Göttingen, 1960); R. ARON, *Dimensions de la con-*

science historique (Paris, 1961); H. G. GADAMER, *Truth and Method* (New York, 1975); id., *Le problème de la conscience historique* (Louvain, 1963); R. LATOURELLE, *Finding Jesus through the Gospels* (New York, 1979).

Rino FISICHELLA

II. PHILOSOPHY OF HISTORY

Today we are heirs to illusion and disappointment, witnesses, moreover, to a world in ferment and a human race continually torn between hopes and fears, apprehension, and the will to live. (Note the opening words of *Gaudium et Spes:* "The joys and the hopes, the griefs and the anxieties. . . .") The *mysterium iniquitatis* (2 Thes 2:7), that first fall that put us into a *status deviationis*, or radical evil (see Kant, *Die Religion innerhalb der Grenzen der blossen Vernunft* [1793]) or original sin, cause of a *natura lapsa*, has always used the sense of the wretchedness of life to feed the tendency to millenarianism and apocalyptic vision. Revelation has added a substantial *et reparata* in a history, the continuity of which is represented by God's faithfulness and the dynamic growth of which shatters any linearity and any circularity of mystery (and of sin) in the newness of grace.

1. Individual—Community—Environment

The individual and the community (and, rightly, today the environmental component, *Le milieu divin* [1926–1927], of which T. de Chardin used to write) are now the locus of a salvation that sees as superficial that (past!) actualism of an identification with the universal subject of history, in the conviction that past and present can be reconciled in the one spiritual act. In the ebb and flow of historical debate, however, we must also guard against a recurring apocalyptic, being acutely aware of life's ambiguities and the precariousness of salvation, which sees salvation as improbable. Without explicitly denying the possibility of salvation, in a paradoxical and absolutist manner, "Fiat iustitia et pereat mundus" rings forth once more. Pauline thought, adopted by Augustine and interpreted by Luther, has to some degree nourished a motif dear to that perennial Gnosticism reaching the same conclu-

sions of theological solipsism. In disillusionment over a kingdom that has not come (immediately) and not been realized (manifestly), the denial of life (*vanitas vanitatum*), sanctifies the world by annihilation. The cynics of old had anticipated what was to reappear in the *De Contemptu Mundi* of Innocent III, or in the *De Divina Omnipotentia* of Peter Damian, or in the *De Servo Arbitrio* of Luther, or in an obsessive kind of apocalyptic of the period. As well as a *dignitas hominis* (until pressed too far), with the "theologian painters" and the Flemish and Rhineland mystics, humanism also strongly stresses an *indignitas hominis*—mad, tormented by every kind of affliction, and making even religion the object of strife (Reformation or Counter-Reformation) and war. The *ars moriendi* has the task of illustrating effectively (i.e., so as to inspire terror) that, if "talis vita finis ita," avarice, gluttony, lust, power, and riches are a death anticipated under the guise of life. Life is a "Haywain" (Bosch), where everyone grabs without scruple; the only remedy is loving conversation far from the fray, or the *fuga mundi* of the pilgrim (Bosch, *The Wayfarer*). Meanwhile, amid the general indifference and obtuseness, the painter gazes, perplexed and worried, beyond appearances into the mystery of the world and history (P. Bruegel the elder, *Self-portrait*). An anomaly too, as regards the Italian humanistic spirit, is Machiavelli, with his political realism, nor must we overlook its offshoot *Ad maiorem Dei gloriam*, lasting into the Counter-Reformation baroque.

2. Time and History

If within the Enlightenment itself (and particularly with the severe Kant) the enthusiastic belief in progress was thrown into confusion (first Mendelssohn, then Hamann), on the socio-economic plane rationalist-idealist optimism was wrecked by class war, and on the spiritual-interior plane by Kierkegaard and existentialism. With the waning of the ideologies, and notwithstanding the sorry legacies of war, genocide, destruction, the imminent nuclear threat, and that of the deterioration of the environment, today perhaps we can once more begin to hope and rethink history in unambiguous terms.

All kinds of models have now been devised in the search for an end and meaning for an unfragmented, uncompartmentalized history that, however, does not work to the detriment of the individual. Models that are circular (*l'éternel retour*), linear (continuous progress), punctual (absolutization of the contingent), pendular (apocalyptic-antagonistic), and ending in the spiroid would seek to gather up all positive elements; personal decision, however, still perhaps does not find its rightful place.

Augustine had the historiographic experience of the Greeks and Romans to go on, as well as the complaints of the tragedians at the infinite calamities afflicting the human race and the thought of the philosophers. For Plato, there was no liberation by history but only from history: we need to escape from time (*kronos*) to reach the paradigm of time that is the eternal (*aiōn*). For Plotinus (*Enneads* 3), time is the life of the soul, its movement from one state to another. Note the Augustinian *distensio animae:* "It is incorrect to say that there are three times—past, present, and future. But there are three presents: a present of things past, a present of things present, and a present of things future" (*Confessions* 11.20.26). The *De Civitate Dei*, written under the impact of the sack of Rome in 410, is a decisive and violent critique of pagan polytheism, which instigates an unbridled hedonism in private life and unrestrained violence in public. The worship of the gods and the importation of new rites and mysteries have not saved Rome from worldly catastrophe; by the same token, from careful examination of poetic and popular mythology, by naturalistic interpretation and various philosophical theories, we rediscover monotheism— unless, that is, we are prepared to adopt a ridiculous pantheism and immanentism.

The Augustinian view is illuminated by revelation; his philosophy cannot but become a theology of history: "Two loves have thus given life to two cities: the earthly one, that is to say, love of self in contempt of God; and the heavenly one, love of God in contempt of self" (14.28). Providence guides the human race, just as it does the individual; but the race is divided into the wicked and God's people. "There are two cities, one of the wicked, the other of the just, which endure from the beginning of the human race even to the end of time, which are now intermingled in body but separated in will, and, which, moreover, are to be separated in body also on the day of judgement" (*De Cat.*

Rud. 19.31). From Augustine's vision of history arises his conception of the perpetuity of the Christian religion: "This same, which today we call the Christian religion, already existed among the ancients and was not absent from the very beginnings of the human race right up to the time when Christ appeared in the flesh. The true religion, which had first and always existed, at this point began to be known as the Christian religion" (*Ep.* 102.12.5). This stimulating theme of the connection and reciprocity of philosophy of history and philosophy of religion extends from Lessing and Schleiermacher to Herder, Schelling, and Hegel and on to Troeltsch. Thought on the absoluteness of Christianity seeks to reconcile uniqueness and universality, the polemical and the ecumenical, the visible and the invisible, history and philosophical ecclesiology (see M. M. Olivetti, *Filosofia della religione come problema storico. Romanticismo e idealismo romantico* [Padua, 1974]).

3. Political Augustinianism and Civil and Religious Tolerance

Political Augustinianism, which begins abruptly with the seven books of the *Historiarum adversus paganos* of Orosius (a theology of history drawing its inspiration not only from Augustine but also from Athanasius's *Life of Antony*), contains overtly theocratic statements "to take up arms externally in defense of Christ's Holy Church against the incursions of pagans and the devastations of infidels, and to fortify her internally in knowledge of the Catholic faith" (*Epistula Caroli* 10). The universal vision of history takes solid form in the *imperium christianum:* "May it please Almighty God that under one single most devout king all people may be governed by a single code of law; this would be of great profit to the concord of the city of God and of equity among peoples" (Agobard, *Liber adversus legem Gundobaldi*). Augustinianism tempered with servility characterizes the *Politique tirée des propres paroles de l'Ecriture sainte*, which J. B. Bossuet dedicated to his Sun King in 1709, justifying superstitions, crimes, and every kind of tyranny. That it should have been preceded in 1681 by a *Discours sur l'histoire universelle* tells us that not even a theodicy will protect a writer from dishonest arguments. The *Essais de Théodicée sur la bonté de Dieu, la liberté de l'homme et l'origine du mal* (1710) of Leibniz at least has theoretic rigor when, with a contribution from Thomas Aquinas, they take up biblical thought.

Spinoza's *Tractatus theologico-politicus* (1670) is not only a defense of religious, civil, and political freedom, but it defends the autonomy of the political and the religious powers (pointing out the damage that the union of these powers in the state has inflicted on religion and piety during the struggle between the papacy and Luther). In the author's refusal to dedicate it to the Sun King (for any price he cared to name), it receives the seal of a dignity unknown to courtiers. To the *Leviathan* (1651) of Hobbes, who bases political absolutism on his bitter observation of *homo homini lupus* and interprets history in terms of *bellum omnium contra omnes*, Spinoza replies with the evolution *iuxτα propria principia* of natural law, from the state of nature to the state of law, from the slave to the subject and to the citizen.

Mindful of the Senecan adage "Fate leads the willing, drags the unwilling," Spinoza warns that the only way to interpret history realistically is to avoid the abstractions of those who "conceive of people not as they are but as they could wish them to be." Such a conception of human nature and of history characterizes the antihumanism of Machiavelli, who seeks the "effectual truth of the thing" without thinking up "republics and principalities which have never been seen nor known to be" and not leaving "what is done for what ought to be done" (*The Prince* [1513]). The following interpretation becomes the basis for a political program: "In their determination not to be alarmed, men make a point of putting the wind up others; and the wrongs of which they have rid themselves, they in turn inflict on someone else, as though it were necessary to ill-treat others or to be ill-treated" (*The Discourses on the First Ten Books of Titus Livius* [1514] 1.46).

4. A New Science

The systematic project for a philosophy of history antithetical to Cartesian rationalism, a project ignored by the Enlightenment (Montesquieu, *Esprit des lois* [1748]) but reappraised by Herder, consists in G. B. Vico's *Principi di una scienza nuova d'intorno alla natura delle nazioni* (1725), with the axiom "verum ipsum

factum" being the central point of a philosophy of history conceived as a historical science. A critical art is intended to "distinguish the truth" so as to recognize the guiding hand of Providence through human intentions and actions: "The eternal ideal [is] history, over which the histories of all nations run in time" (§ 349). If the *Scienza Nuova* demonstrates the truth of the Bible, Providence is a *List der Vernunft ante litteram*: "This world has undoubtedly issued from a mind often different and at times quite contrary and always superior to those particular ends that human beings have proposed" (§ 310). Vico himself translates his philosophy of history into "the logical civil theology of Divine Providence" (§ 342).

A new model of human history, framed on "the enlightened person" without reference to Scripture, was proposed by Voltaire in his *Essai sur les moeurs et l'esprit des nations* (7 vols., 1754–58), a critical reassessment of Bossuet's *Discours* (a providentialist conception of universal history), to which he opposed the gradual assertion of reason over superstition and the arbitrary, of civilization over barbarism.

The Lisbon earthquake of 1755 was a historical watershed, not so much on account of the material damage it caused but because of the debates to which it gave rise by confounding philosophical optimism and a facile providentialism (of which Voltaire's *Candide ou l'optimisme* [1759] is an echo). Kant too repeatedly intervenes, to warn against pietistic or moralistic interpretations (*On the Causes of Earthquakes: on the Occasion of the Disaster That Struck the Western Regions of Europe toward the End of Last Year*, and *Natural History and Description of the Most Singular Events That Convulsed a Great Part of the World at the End of the Year 1755*). The rebellious and progressive, as well as the Enlightenment myth of the progress of an abstract reason, sustained a rude shock.

5. Philosophy of History and Philosophy of Religion

The concept of revelation as a moment of history in Lessing's *Die Erziehung des Menschengeschlechts* (1780), while projecting a rational Christianity onto the background of an eternal gospel, sends away the meaning of history beyond time indefinitely; it says, "A time will come . . . !" In history, however, there is no possibility of absolute truth (*Sulla prova dello spirito e della forza* [1777], a point made also in the rambling *Eine Duplik* [1778]). Through the hypothesis and paradox of Christianity, Kierkegaard in his *Philosophical Fragments* (1844) and *Concluding Unscientific Postscript* (1846) localized in the "moment" the meeting point between the eternal and time, between God and human beings, the place of the decision made in faith, which is the basis of salvation. So too Schleiermacher (*On Religion: Speeches to Its Cultured Despisers* [1799]), while keeping to the "general connection" of history, and to an eternal destiny that seems to crush "the isolated commitment of the individual," sees in the world-spirit a One, the All, the Infinite, permeating and gently leading us.

For J. G. Herder, human life on earth is the prelude to a later state of humanity; of humanity, of the human race, one may speak as the living tradition of language attests. The plan of Providence (an element not identified with the Enlightenment) is concretely realized in the relationship between the individual and the human race. Herder enthusiastically equates "philosophy of humanity" with "the true history of the same!" (*Provincial Letters* [1774]). A "priest or God" ought to write the kind of history that is the "divine order of the human race! God's economy on earth!" His preamble to identifying the philosophy of history with the philosophy of religion begins with the affirmation: "All religion is basically and essentially fact! history!" So too for Herder, reason and revelation go together; the Bible illuminates the history of the human race by giving overall meaning to the "fragmentary histories of pagan philosophers." Furthermore, "As little as the human race could have become without creation, so little could it have lasted without divine help, and have grasped what it knows without divine instruction" (*Notes on the N.T.* [1775]). The *Ideen zur Philosophie der Geschichte der Menschheit* (1784–91) opens with the need for "a philosophy and a science of that which concerns us most closely, that is to say, the history of the human race in its totality," so as to find in the times the same order as in the spaces. We feel joy "at the wisdom and goodness of the Creator," which are manifest in all his works. The individual is molded by the human race and religion: "All are permeated with the self-same Humanity. . . . The study of this Humanity is the task of genuine *human philosophy*. . . . Religion is the supreme Humanity of the human. . . . it is the intellect's task to ferret out the relationship between cause and effect. . . . the first and last philosophy has always been religion." In the complex of philosophical, historical, and religious thought is an aspiration to give meaning, including religious meaning, to history, where individuals taken together form the human race.

Meanwhile, not only Mendelssohn (*On the Question: What Does Enlightenment Mean?* [1784]) but above all Kant upset the Enlightenment notion of continual and irreversible progress. The latter too put forward his *Idee zu einer allgemeinen Geschichte im weltbürgerlicher Absicht* (1784) and, though in different terms from Mendelssohn (*Jerusalem* [1783]) and Herder (*Ideen . . .* [1784–91]), held to an "absolutely irrevocable progress toward the best," a progressive fulfillment of the law, with Nature-Providence as guarantee of equilibrium in the battles for the triumph of Reason (*Grundlegung zur Metaphysik der Sitten* [1785]). But this yearning could not be given a theoretical basis (*Über das Misslingen aller philosophischen Versuche in der Theodicee* [1791]). Kant's philosophical approach to the history-philosophy of religion was to be deeper in the essay *Sul male radicale della natura umana* (1792), which led into the work *Die Religion innerhalb der Grenzen der blossen Vernunft* (1793). The original disposition toward the good and the tendency toward evil are at the basis of the historic struggle between good and evil principles, and of the tracing in history of the way the good principle gradually establishes itself on earth.

Schelling's *Philosophie der Offenbarung*, linked with the *Philosophie der Mythologie* and drawn from the *Età del mondo*, is a romantic and speculative interpretation of the history of the world as being interwoven with the history of God; God "becomes" as the world and as human beings "become." In Hegel, individuals (and historic personages) are at the disposal of the *Volksgeist; Volksgeister* in their turn are a manifestation (*Selbstauslegung*) of the Absolute Spirit. The Absolute Spirit unfolds and realizes itself in history, so as to achieve the freedom of absolute knowledge, in which the individual will become free. "The thinking spirit of universal history, having at once canceled the limitations of the spirits of particular peoples and its own earthly character, achieves its own concrete universality and ascends to knowledge of the Absolute Spirit, as of the truth, eternally real, in which cognitive reason is free per se, and necessity, nature, and history are instruments for the revealing and honoring of the Spirit" (*Enzyklopädie der philosophischen Wissenschaften* [1817], § 552). Kierkegaard, in the name of the inalienable rights of the individual, which are founded in God, and Marx with his dialectical definition of freedom as struggle with nature and class struggle, were to challenge the Hegelian system and stand it on its head. Later figures, such as Heidegger and Bloch, have given due emphasis to the historical dimension of existence — the former with the authentic existence that is the projection of the subject, unfolding in the Dasein; the latter, with the "hope-principle," which sustains the dialectical existence of humanity in the world and in history.

After Nietzsche's *Unzeitgemässe Betrachtungen* (the second entitled "On the Usefulness and Harmfulness of History for Life"), which stigmatizes the disaccord between a certain kind of historical culture and life, W. Dilthey, with his *Critique of Historical Reason* (cf. *Gesammelte Schriften*, vols. 5, 7 [Stuttgart, 1858, 1864]), came to the conclusion that life must be grasped through life. As against a naturalistic view of history proposing a weary and resigned fatalism (O. Spengler, *Untergang des Westens* [1918–22]) or a positivism vaguely tempered by natural providence (A. Toynbee, *A Study of History* [1934] and *Civilisation on Trial* [1948]), we affirm our faith and our certainty: "Crux probat omnia. Stat crux dum volvitur orbis."

Bibl.: J. G. DROYSEN, *Historik* (Munich, 1937); J. DANIÉLOU, *Essai sur le mystère de l'histoire* (Paris, 1963); N. BERDIAEV, *Il senso della storia* (Milan, 1971); K. LÖWITH, *Significato e fine della storia: I presupposti teologici della filosofia della storia* (Milan, 1975); P. MICCOLI, ed., *Filosofia della storia* (Rome, 1985).

Salvatore SPERA

III. THEOLOGY OF HISTORY

When faith first encountered history, not merely as its vital space but essentially as a question of meaning, the theology of history was born. The history of theology shows on numerous occasions what different views have been held about time and history.

1. Traditional Thought

Justin, Irenaeus, Clement of Alexandria, and Tertullian constructed the first theology of history; this had as its basis an understanding of the old covenant made with the people of Israel as a preparation for the new and eternal covenant brought about in Christ. By the same token, against the attacks of Celsus, the theses about the centrality of Christ in history were to be formulated by Origen and Athanasius. In general then, the APOLOGISTS were to present Christianity as a truth that was set in history, not to humble history but to bring it to a complete synthesis.

The first proper theorist of a theology of history, however, is AUGUSTINE, whose thinking on the subject remains the best organized and complete of any, even today. History is interpreted by him as a constant progress, having its beginning in God's free and unconditional act in willing to create and enter into time, and finding its fulfillment in the person of Jesus Christ. Central to history is the salvific event of the death and resurrection of Jesus of Nazareth; henceforth history opens onto the eschatological promise. Meanwhile, Cain and Abel symbolize a human race made up of the ambitious and the obedient. The *De Civitate Dei*, expressing their eventual synthesis, shows history as the place of continual conflict between faith and sin.

The Middle Ages, though still bound to the ancient cosmological and metaphysical scheme of things, nonetheless presents certain elements that allow us to glimpse a rough draft of a theology of history. Bonaventure and Thomas, for example, reinterpret and revitalize the Augustinian thesis. Joachim of Flora's interpretation, however, with his historico-philosophical vision and his division of history into three ages corresponding to the successive self-revelations of the three divine persons, is the most stimulating and original of the period.

In the modern age, J. B. Bossuet's writings met with success. They represent the first systematic attempt at a theology of history, one that in turn provoked Voltaire into writing the first ever philosophy of history (→ HISTORY II). In his *Discours sur l'histoire universelle* of 1681, the Dauphin's tutor seeks to prove that "profane histories narrate only fables or, at best, confused facts, of which half remain buried in oblivion. Scripture, however, leads back with many a precise event and the right sequence of things to their real origin, that is, God the Creator of all things" (1707 ed., 135–36). The three parts of the work embody the bishop of Meaux's ideas. The first part classifies history into twelve ages, which extend from Adam to the foundation of the new empire by Charlemagne. The second shows God's activity toward his people. The third describes the changes that occur in history because of, and superintended by, Providence.

As can be easily seen, the apologetic principle concealed behind Bossuet's theory is that of a loving but nonetheless despotic control of history by God; he is eternal and unchanging, hence without any possibility of real involvement in everyday events. History and thought about it are proper to human beings, but whether they are interested in it or not, it is the business of princes and kings only (cf. pp. 1–2); God, however, is completely outside it.

From the 1950s onward, contemporary theology in both Catholic and Protestant circles has shown a new interest in this subject. The studies of Barth, Brunner, Cullmann, von Balthasar, Daniélou, Marrou, Pannenberg, Rahner, and Ratzinger reveal differing sensibilities and complementary methods of approach. In them, however, one must distinguish between (1) a historico-salvific concept as a component of an interpretation of revelation and (2) a theology of history *ex professo*, which they do not always treat as a subject for study.

2. Proposal for a Systematic Interpretation

The expression "theology of history" has a number of different meanings; here it is used to denote the study of the meaning of history that is based on theological premises and methods.

For Christianity, a theology of history is made possible by the understanding Jesus of Nazareth had of his own life on earth as the fullness and completion of earlier history. Mark reports the earliest features of Jesus' preaching in unequivocal terms: "The time is fulfilled, and the kingdom of God is at hand" (Mk 1:15). With this as starting point, theology sees the possibility of a critical understanding of history in the light of a principle given to it, i.e., the salvation brought about by Jesus Christ's historical existence.

The various models that are repeatedly suggested for describing the biblical conception of time (e.g., cyclic, linear, parabolic, point, spiral, pendular) do not always do justice to an overall interpretation, for insistence on one aspect does not do justice to other elements that are equally real and compelling. It is therefore preferable to view the biblical conception of time and history through a series of perspectives that, taken together, furnish a less one-sided picture of the truth.

We may hence think of history as being the space that has its beginning in the creative activity of God and that is open to receiving his revelations. In this space, human beings are called to make definite choices about Yahweh that allow their natural completion and purpose to be achieved, i.e., their final reunion with God.

God is at the origin of time, but simultaneously he enters it, thus making himself history. The various mediations of revelation take place in a historical context. History is the natural scenario in which the revelatory event occurs.

History thus becomes God's manifestation, the place where he appears, and also the place of our decision to try to follow him. When one of these two components is missing, we no longer have a historical event; time becomes mere "passing days."

Only God's interventions, which become memory in the consciousness of the people, constitute history; this is kept alive by celebration. The "Remember, O Israel" becomes a constant imperative, lest the passing of time cause the events of the past to fade into oblivion (Dt 4:9–10; 11:18–21). Biblical history may thus be regarded as the time that passes between the giving of a promise and its long-awaited fulfillment.

But the Christian religion is born from the centrality and newness of Christ, who, accompanying his disciples on the road to Emmaus,

explains to them that he himself is the fulfillment of all history: "Beginning with Moses and
all the prophets, he interpreted to them the
things about himself in all the Scriptures" (Lk
24:27).

Here we have a hermeneutical principle of
incalculable scope for a theology of history. For
the primitive community sees that the understanding of the ancient Scriptures, and hence of
all history, is possible only by reference to the
Master. He henceforth is the interpretative key
to all history. If the Law and the Prophets refer
to him, then if he does not accompany them
now, now that the sun is setting, their history
as individuals and as a community becomes
void of meaning. The centrality of the event of
Jesus Christ thus constitutes the pivot on
which to construct a theology of history.

From this principle, three further ways of
understanding can be derived:

a. In Jesus of Nazareth, God himself
intervenes in a direct form in history, which
means that a Christian understanding of time
and history cannot yield place to a merely
philosophical interpretation of temporality. An
interpretation that saw God relegated to outside all time, motionless in his eternity, would
not be true to the biblical dynamic, which
primarily conceives of eternity, not negatively
as absence of time, but more positively as lordship over time and in time.

The eternal God is the God who is always
present in the events of his people's history,
precisely because he is Yahweh (Ex 3:14), i.e.,
Lord of time. God thus manifests his freedom
when, entering history and submitting to its
dynamic, he still remains free to transcend it,
since the mystery of his life-in-Trinity consists
precisely in being *semper maior* with regard to
any human limitation.

The fact, therefore, that in Jesus of Nazareth
God himself intervenes in history limits
neither human history nor him, since he
remains eternal, and history is ever free to make
its own decision about God. The UNIVERSALE
CONCRETUM can be regarded, in this context, as
the attempt at interpretation that, better than
any other, harmonizes the two extremes of the
debate: the presence of the *all*, which remains
such, in the fragment, and the *fragmentariness*
that finds its center of synthesis in the
universal.

b. The second proposition follows from the
above. A theology of history cannot ignore the
fact that the essence of believers is our historicity (→ HISTORY IV). This being so, we all
realize ourselves as historical beings by actions
and choices that express our personal freedom.

With the coming of Christ, sentence has
already been passed on the world, but we all
ought to present ourselves before him with our
individual capacity for choice (Mk 16:16; Jn
5:24). Salvation, achieved in the event of Easter,
requires that each of us recognizes it as directed
to ourself, choosing hence to place ourselves in
the *sequela Christi* and thus, by that choice,
creating the beginnings of a personal history as
a free and radical decision about the aim of our
own existence.

For believers, history is where we can see the
gift of salvation brought about and where, as
those who have been called, we may opt for it.
In this context, a theology of history ought to
formulate expressions to help us understand
both the relation between salvation history and
universal history (→ HISTORY V), and the relation between the history of the Christian
revelation and the history of other religions, in
such a way as to demonstrate the uniqueness of
the Christian faith (→ INTERRELIGIOUS DIA-
LOGUE).

Since history is where we believers physically
live out our decision of the *sequela Christi*, we
ourselves create situations and conditions that
determine history's progress or lack of progress.
Revelation and creation of the SIGNS OF THE
TIMES become the special object of a theology
of history, which should give a critical account
of the way believers contribute to transforming
the world and society (*GS* 4, 11, 44).

c. If a beginning to history is given by God's
free intervention in it, its ultimate purpose is to
wait for the time that "God may be all in all"
(1 Cor 15:28). Christ's centrality in human
history does not eliminate its moving toward a
completion; on the contrary, it anticipates this
completion and is evidence of it. History, like
the human race, seeks for a MEANING that will
be such as to allow a qualitative leap toward the
overcoming of its own contradictions.

The unknowability and unpredictability of
the future fix history's limitations and signal its
end. The Easter-event, occurring in history and

lived by Jesus of Nazareth, gives all history the strength to overcome its own limitations.

By Christ's death and resurrection, history is thrust in a new direction toward the goal of its own fulfillment. The crucifixion of the Son of God gives meaning to the limitations imposed on all history, since death is accepted into the "life story" of the Trinity as movement toward the resurrection. History thus sees a promise fulfilled within itself, yet suffering no damage to its nature; all it has to do is embrace it and carry it into a wider perspective.

A theology of history therefore sees a constant advance of all history toward fulfillment. This has already come about in the individual and personal history of Jesus Christ and continues to come about in the life of faith of the church, through the perpetuation of this event in the sacraments.

Between the anticipation and the complete fulfillment there hence unfolds an ESCHATOLOGY attesting to the already realized and to the not yet definitively given. In this context, the history of the church becomes the *sign* of a potentiality for constant transformation toward the definitive. As critical awareness, the eschatological sense stimulates history and the church within it to a constant mindfulness of its own salvific past and of the values essential for its total fulfillment.

A theology of history differs substantially from a philosophy of history (→ HISTORY II). While the latter must remain tied to the existential structure of the subject, which requires that meaning transcend itself, the theology of history presents itself with its claim to meaning already completed, since it is charged with the Easter-event. Thus only a deep consciousness of salvation history can allow a theology of history to express the best of itself. For while consciousness of salvation history, on the one hand, being simple historical consciousness, recovers a sense of becoming for us, on the other, being salvific, it introduces the *novum* of revelation. Consciousness of salvation history makes it possible for the present to be genuinely prophetic, since, by bringing the past into the present and keeping the tradition of ecclesial faith *alive* (*DV* 10), it impresses on the history of today the original characteristics of an eternal humanity, while laying the foundations for a real future existence.

Bibl.: AUGUSTINE, *Confessions*; id., *The City of God*; J.-B. BOSSUET, *Discours sur l'Histoire universelle* (Paris, 1707); K. BARTH, "Der christliche Glaube und die Geschichte," in *Schweizerische Theologische Zeitschrift* 1–2 (1912); R. NIEBUHR, *Faith and History* (New York, 1949); K. LÖWITH, *Weltgeschichte und Heilsgeschehen* (Stuttgart, 1953); H. SCHLIER, *Die Zeit der Kirche* (Freiburg, 1955); E. BISER, *Erkenne dich in Mir* (Einsiedeln, 1955); K. RAHNER, "History of the World and Salvation-History," in *Theological Investigations*, vol. 5 (1962; London, 1966), 97–114; J. DANIÉLOU, *Essai sur le mystère de l'histoire* (Paris, 1963); id., *L'entrée de l'histoire du salut* (Paris, 1967); H. Urs VON BALTHASAR, *A Theology of History* (New York, 1963); id., *A Theological Anthropology* (New York, 1967); O. CULLMANN, *Christ and Time* (Philadelphia, 1964); H. I. MARROU, *Théologie de l'histoire* (Paris, 1968); W. PANNENBERG, *Revelation as History* (New York, 1968); id., *Basic Questions in Theology* (Philadelphia, 1971); E. CASTELLI, ed., *Rivelazione e storia* (Rome, 1971); J. ALFARO, *Cristologia e antropologia* (Assisi, 1973); id., *Christianisme: Chemin de la libération* (Paris, 1975); W. KASPER, "Linee fondamentali di una teologia della storia," in *Fede e storia* (Brescia, 1975), 62–96; J. RATZINGER, *Principles of Catholic Theology* (San Francisco, 1987).

Rino FISICHELLA

IV. HISTORICITY OF REVELATION

One could conveniently develop this theme in four stages: the historicity of humanity, the historicity of revelation, the historicity of God, and the historicity of theology. Let us begin with the first.

The fact that we begin with humanity is no accident. The most significant shift in philosophy from the Middle Ages to the modern period is the transition from a cosmological to an anthropological point of view. In modern philosophy, especially in the tradition of German idealism, the human being is understood not in terms of the cosmos but in terms of freedom. The world is interpreted in the light of the human subject and his or her freedom, not vice versa.

An analysis of human freedom reveals that the person is poised between the finite and the Infinite. In every human act of choice, subjects seek to realize themselves. In choosing finite objects in the world, they are really choosing themselves. At the same time, in choosing categorical objects, they become aware that no finite object can satisfy the dynamism of their transcendence. Finite freedom is thus necessarily a reference to an infinite horizon that grounds the human freedom that the person is and makes that freedom possible. Without this infinite horizon, the person would be determined to some finite object. Hence finite freedom and infinite freedom are correlative. A further reflection alerts us to the fact that one cannot conceive the relationship between finite freedom and infinite freedom in a static way. Human transcendence is dynamic. Every choice of a finite good opens up the possibility of other choices. But no choice can ever satisfy the dynamism of human transcendence. The goal of human freedom eludes every attempt to grasp and possess it. The dynamic character of human freedom reveals that freedom is temporal or historical. Freedom is precisely the sphere of possibility. Human freedom is an openness to the future.

In our own century it was Martin Heidegger, who, drawing upon the research of Dilthey, most significantly deepened the historical dimension of human existence. Heidegger stressed the temporal character of existence, pointing out that humans are the only beings who can be said to exist in the strict sense. That is, humankind stands out of itself (ex-sistere). People do not possess their being; rather, their being is something to be realized. Naturally the possibilities that people possess are not infinite. People find themselves with a givenness; they ex-ist in a situation. To highlight the finite character of human being, Heidegger appropriated the term "Dasein." In *Being and Time* Heidegger gave a phenomenological analysis of Dasein and described the unity of Dasein as care (*Sorge*). At the same time he showed that care has a temporal structure. Care consists of three dimensions: facticity (past), possibility (future), and fallenness (present). By fallenness Heidegger meant that there is a tendency for Dasein to be dragged into a preoccupation with beings in the world and to forget its own transcendence and openness to being (this openness is its authentic futurity).

The import of Heidegger's analysis of Dasein is that a person does not exist in history like an object in a box. Rather, Dasein's being itself is radically historical. Heidegger expressed this fact by calling historicity an *existential*, or a structure pertaining to a person's being. History is not something objective apart from humanity. Rather, the primary historical is humanity itself. As John Macquarrie expresses it, summing up Heidegger's position: "History is possible for man because his temporality is not just a being within time [*Innerzeitigkeit*] but rather a being constituted by past, present and future in such a way that at any given moment not only the present but the past and future as well are disclosed to him and are real to him" (John Macquarrie, *An Existentialist Theology*, Pelican Book, New York, p. 151).

Humanity's openness to the future immediately poses a theological question: What is the ultimate future to which humanity is open? In Heidegger's philosophy, this future can only be death, since Dasein's possibilities are strictly circumscribed by finitude. Yet if the future is not primarily the unfolding of what lies in the past but the drawing near of what is still outstanding (*Zu-kunft*), then it is possible to see God as the ultimate future that draws near to humanity and offers himself as the goal of human freedom, a goal that opens up the possibility of transcending death in resurrection. Here we can link this reflection with our earlier analysis of finite freedom's basic openness to infinite freedom. At the beginning of the Enlightenment, Kant had shown that human freedom can be intelligible only if it exists within a free universe. Human freedom presupposes a kingdom of freedom. Otherwise human freedom is doomed to frustration and cannot realize itself. This analysis led Kant to postulate God as absolute freedom. Following the contemporary German theologian Walter Kasper (*The God of Jesus Christ* [London, 1983], 98–99, 105–5), we could interpret Kant in the following way. An analysis of human freedom raises the question of God. But since freedom is always a matter of self-gift, the relation of human transcendence to absolute freedom can never be a matter of necessity. People stand before the Ground of their freedom in poverty and expectation. On the philosophical level their human freedom remains a question mark. If their freedom is to make sense, it must await a free self-disclosure of God. This self-disclosure of God in freedom is what Christians experience in God's revelation of himself in Jesus Christ.

In the event of revelation, we see the encounter of two freedoms, human and divine.

Just as human freedom expresses itself in history, so God manifesting himself does so in history. Thus history is the meeting place of God and humanity in freedom. With this affirmation we have arrived at the historicity of revelation. Contemporary theology speaks of the historicity of revelation in two senses. First, there is God's categorical revelation, namely, the objective events in the history of the world in which God manifests himself. Obviously for a Christian the historical event par excellence in which God reveals himself is Jesus Christ. This event, however, cannot be isolated but bears within itself the whole preparatory history of God's revelation to Israel. If Jesus Christ is God's revelation in person, then revelation itself is temporal and historical. As Barth expressed it in his ground-breaking theology of revelation, revelation demands historical predicates. God expresses himself in time. The eternal God becomes temporal.

The other significant way in which contemporary theology speaks of the historicity of revelation is in reference to humanity's being as such. Here theology speaks about transcendental revelation, i.e., the revelation that takes place in human subjectivity as such. The point of departure is God's desire to communicate himself to every man and woman and his desire that all be saved. Since God's desire is universal and since every person can be saved only through grace, it follows that grace is offered to every person. But if what we said above about humanity is true—namely, that a person's being as such is historical, and if God's offer of himself is universal—then we must conceive a universal history of God's self-communication. This implies that God is revealing himself to every person implicitly in the depths of his or her being (transcendental level). Hence not only on the categorical level but also on the transcendental level, God's revelation of himself is historical.

A critical theological question today is how these two aspects of revelation are related to one another. All would agree that the universal transcendental offer of God reaches its fulfillment in the categorical event of Jesus Christ. Nonetheless, despite this fundamental agreement, significant differences emerge as to how the relationship between transcendental and categorical revelation should be conceived. Here we can mention in passing two significant lines of interpretation in Catholic theology. Karl Rahner places a greater emphasis on transcendental revelation and sees the categorical revelation as giving expression on the objective level to God's offer of himself on the transcendental level. In Rahner's interpretation the categorical revelation interprets the transcendental one. Another line of interpretation is pursued by Kasper. He argues that humanity's transcendental freedom remains basically ambiguous without the aid of God's categorical revelation of himself in history. For Kasper, a person's openness to the future is openness to an infinite horizon that can be interpreted in a pantheistic, theistic, or atheistic sense. Only God's revelation of himself categorically in history resolves the dilemma of human freedom and historicity. For Kasper, it is history that interprets humanity's transcendentality, not vice versa.

The reflections that we have pursued to this point indicate the astounding thesis that God reveals himself in history and therefore that God becomes temporal for our sake. As I indicated above, revelation demands historical predicates. But from this assertion, we can go even further and speak not only of the historicity of revelation but of the historicity of God himself. Here contemporary theologians strive to avoid two extremes, both of which would falsify the Christian experience of God in Jesus. One extreme would be a Deism or weak form of theism according to which God cannot in any way be influenced by the world. For such a theism the world makes absolutely no difference to God. This theism easily leads to atheism, since a God to whom I can make no difference is surely a dead god and not the living God of the Bible. The other extreme is a becoming God such as that proposed by Hegelianism or process theology who stands in need of the world to realize himself. Beyond these two extremes, on the basis of God's identification of himself with time in the incarnation of his Son, Christian faith seeks to reflect on God's historicity. In short, since God has become temporal, he has the capacity to become temporal. This capacity we can define as God's historicity (*Geschichtlichkeit*).

A number of contemporary theologians such as Rahner and Balthasar, Jüngel and Moltmann, stress this point. God's being is not static. Rather, God's being must include something analogous to becoming. Ultimately this becoming, which is not the becoming of a finite creature, can be understood only in trinitarian terms. Jüngel speaks of God's being as a triple coming. God comes from himself (Father), God comes to himself (Son), and God comes as God (Holy Spirit). There is a movement in God, from the Father to the Son in the Holy Spirit. The Holy Spirit is the guarantee of the unity of trinitarian love and of its infinite fullness. The love of the Father for the Son and the Son's response to the Father is so rich that it contains the quality of being ever greater, ever new, ever young. Balthasar speaks in similar terms, using the category of event to explain the dynamic character of God's eternal Being. For Balthasar, God's being is the event of the Father's self-donation and the Son's obedient response, which contains an overflowing fruitfulness that is the Holy Spirit. For all these authors the event that God is, is so dynamic, fruitful, and altruistic that it opens out toward the world. God's being is a being of ecstatic movement. The Holy Spirit both completes the circle of love and is the infinite fruitfulness of love for the world and so can be described as the ecstasy of God. God's love is not retained for himself but is a free gift for the world. In such trinitarian terms, God's historicity is the ground for his history with the world, which reaches its climax in the Christ-event.

We have continually spoken of the Christ-event as the fulfillment of God's revelation. For all the authors of the New Testament, Jesus Christ represents God's eschatological deed. There can be no subsequent revelation, for God has expressed himself completely in his Son. For this reason the church has taught that revelation is closed with the death of the last apostle. Nonetheless it must be equally stressed that precisely because of humanity's historicity, the revelation-event can never be grasped once and for all in its totality but is always perceived perspectively according to the limitations of the cultural situation in which the gospel is preached. Thus, on the one hand, Jesus always remains the absolute truth about God and humanity (see *DV* 2); on the other hand, this truth is always grasped in a fragmentary way. Hence there is a genuine historicity of doctrine and of theology. Revelation never comes to us in a pure, unadulterated way but is always embodied in some historical form. The truth

that Jesus Christ is, is expressed in the conceptual patterns of a given culture with all their richness and with all their limitations. This implies that theology, which is faith seeking understanding and which forms an intrinsic part of faith itself, is a hermeneutical process in which one generation attempts to translate the faith of previous generations and cultures into the self-expression of its own age and mentality.

Such attempts at translation presuppose, on the one hand, that each generation seeks to retrieve the unique and unsurpassable origin of faith, namely, Jesus Christ. On the other hand, the historicity of humanity implies that no translation attempt will ever be final. There is no possibility of creating an absolute theological system, for as we have seen, all theological affirmations share in the time-bound character of human existence. What is required is rather what Gadamer calls a conversation with tradition (cf. A. Louth, *Discerning the Mystery* [Oxford, 1983], 39–44). Tradition is not something objective, outside of me. Rather, I "indwell" my tradition. There is a connaturality between the subject seeking understanding and the subject's tradition.

Such a conversation implies a hermeneutical circle in which I question the tradition and the tradition questions me. Unless I had some horizon of questioning, I could not ask anything of the tradition, I would not know what I was seeking. But by placing the questions within my horizon of understanding, I am able to understand anew. The act of understanding takes place. I am able to hear the meaning of the past event of salvation history in my present. In turn this act of understanding opens up my horizon of meaning and lets me pose new questions. Such is the hermeneutical circle of theology. By entering into a conversation with the past, theologians come into contact with the unsurpassable origin of their faith and render that origin actual for intelligible belief today. The historicity of humanity as well as the historicity of revelation implies that such translation attempts and such conversations with the past will never cease. Theology as a historical science will continually wrestle with the past and attempt to translate the once-for-all truth of Christ ever anew until he comes again in glory.

Bibl.: J. Jüngel, "God's Being is in Becoming," in *The Doctrine of the Trinity* (Edinburgh/London, 1976),

61–108; id., "The Crucified Jesus Christ as 'Vestige of the Trinity,'" in *God as the Mystery of the World* (Edinburgh, 1983), 343–68; K. RAHNER, "The Historicity of Theology," in *Theological Investigations*, vol. 9 (1967; London, 1972), 64–82; A. LOUTH, "The Legacy of the Enlightenment," in *Discerning the Mystery: An Essay on the Nature of Theology* (Oxford, 1983), 17–44.

John O'DONNELL

V. UNIVERSAL HISTORY AND THE HISTORY OF SALVATION

The contrast between these two types of history seems at first a representation of the classic philosophical opposition between universal and particular, form and matter. Yet, if approached in those terms, the very notion of universal history proves paradoxical. For history is the realm of particulars, whereas the philosophical universal refers either to a conceptual abstraction from all particulars or to the widest extension of being—God, who transcends history. Hence universal history must deal with all the particulars of time and space, discovering their meaning, while the history of salvation apparently claims that some moments of history enjoy a priority of significance that alone permits the interpretation of universal history; in view of that extra significance, salvation is made available to people in particular places and times. This "elitist" view of history does not sit well with radical democratic egalitarians nor with those determined to find rationally a universal meaning in history. This particularity has often caused scandal, yet it remains ineradicable from Christianity.

Unlike most "natural" religions, Christianity does not stem from myths supposedly occurring at some indeterminate time and place while supplying the foundation for the regularity of seasonal processes and feasts. Neither does it subsist on philosophical speculations in principle available to every individual, as in Hinduism, Theravada Buddhism, Stoicism, Scientology, etc. Instead, like Judaism and Islam, Christianity depends on the reception of a divine revelation accomplished at definite times and places in history. The fact of God's speaking in history implies a personal God concerned with humanity's well-being and behavior.

It also establishes the importance of memory and the necessity of tradition to keep his words present to believers. Finally, the same concern of God for historical action implies his omnipotent mastery over history, his power to lead it where he will, while allowing for human freedom. This theme remained especially dear to the major prophets and the whole apocalyptic tradition. Christians thus live in the continuing tension between past and future, in a present where their response to God's revelation is demanded.

In Christianity the particularity of historical religions found its unsurpassable acme in the incarnation. Here the dialogue between God and Israel was concluded and a new, everlasting testament was established. The book of Hebrews stresses that "once and for all" Christ sacrificed himself, won an eternal salvation, and sanctified believers (7:27; 9:12; 10:10). That historical conjunction of time and eternity, divine initiative and human response, constitutes the central moment of history, to which all subsequent Christianity is bound. How history, the realm of the finite and relative, can bear something unsurpassable and definitive while still continuing remains a fundamental question for Christian theology. Alongside this tension between definitive and relative, Christianity yokes together another fundamental pair of apparent opposites. Though the man Jesus Christ is sole mediator between God and humankind, God wishes all people to be saved and to come to the knowledge of the truth (1 Tm 2:3–6). If God's will is not reduced to a mere good intention, how can all people, so distant in time and space, have contact with the historically limited humanity of Christ? How can the historically definite become definitive?

1. Answers from Earlier History

Without doubt, early Christians emphasized the novelty and particularity of Christ. When Celsus protested against the view that a simple Galilean carpenter should render superfluous all the great cultural achievements of paganism, Origen did not hesitate to repeat with Peter that in Christ's name alone salvation was offered to mortals (Acts 4:12). Cyprian's phrase "outside the church no salvation" faithfully mirrors Christian tradition, since the church alone had the charisma of correctly teaching

Christ's message. Not that this doctrine was interpreted too narrowly. The patriarchs and prophets of the OT were understood to be men of faith (Heb 11) who had accepted God's revelation about the Christ, whose coming they foretold. The early apologist Justin borrowed from Greek philosophy the notion of *logoi spermatikoi*, or rational (logical) seeds pervading the universe that reflected the Logos, its creator, and allowed even pagans to perceive and follow the Logos's teaching. The Alexandrian tradition, in which Origen stood, likewise was generous in finding traces of revelation and faith outside the Jewish tradition.

The heavily Platonic influence among the fathers led them to conceive of revelation mainly in terms of truths that Christ revealed in time but that remain eternally valid. Augustine knew Christ as the interior Master who enlightened the soul from within; the necessity of the church he attributed to the obfuscation caused by original sin and to concupiscence, which demanded an external authority to guarantee the truth taught exteriorly by Christ in history. History became primarily the struggle between the city of God (those who, from Adam on, have loved God's truth) and the city of man (those who have preferred themselves and the devil to God). Even the discovery of God's positive infinity and negative theology did not displace among the fathers the Platonic emphasis on interior illumination and eternal truths. The Aristotelian revolution in the West placed Platonic forms again in matter as the dynamic, essential principles of change, but Aristotle's notion of science as of the universal led the scholastics to conceive theology primarily as the explication of essential truths transmitted by Scripture and the church's unbroken tradition.

The first major break with such an understanding of historical truth came through the Renaissance's love of antiquity. Not only did classical texts have to be critically edited and the ancient historians compared, but also the difference between the Christian present and the pagan past awoke a sense of historical epochs that need be understood merely in terms of falsehood overcome by Christian truth. The Reformation also contributed to historical awareness insofar as Luther and Calvin appealed to the primitive church's purity of life and teaching in rejecting the decadence of the intervening centuries. Thus the ecclesial continuity with Christ presupposed by medieval thinkers was radically questioned and had to be proven in the face of criticism.

The baroque age saw the marshaling of historical apologetics along the lines established by Bellarmine and Baronius, but its expanding geographic horizons simultaneously led to a reinterpretation of Christian particularity. Whereas Thomas Aquinas presupposed that the whole inhabited world had heard of Christ and that God would send an angel to announce the Christian message to whatever simple man or woman, dwelling in sylvan isolation, had never heard it, the age of discovery uncovered millions in both Indies who had remained in ignorance of Christ. Convinced that there was no salvation outside the church, zealous missionaries like Francis Xavier traversed oceans, jungles, and deserts at great personal risk and inconvenience to offer Christ's salvation to all people. The thought of so many pagans dying in sin and the acknowledgment by missionaries that many pagans lived lives of great natural virtue led to a rethinking of the ancient dogma "outside the church no salvation" affirmed solemnly by the Council of Florence (DS 1351). Bellarmine expanded the notion of baptism of desire to include many good pagans who did all in their power to follow God's will as far as it was known to them through nature and would doubtless have accepted the Christian faith once it was preached to them. Despite Jansenist narrowness in limiting the number of the saved, Jesuits and other theologians refused to deny any the mercy of God. In their argument they were supported by the Catholic insistence upon the basic goodness of nature and its reliability in providing knowledge of God, in the face of the Protestant doctrines of nature's total corruption and the need of faith in God's word alone.

The inconclusiveness of European religious wars; the missionary reports about highly moral, non-Christian cultures, especially in the Orient; and the startling success of Galilean science contributed mightily to the Enlightenment and its radical critique of tradition as a source of truth. Since the God of battles apparently favored no one religious tradition over another in interpreting Scripture, another source of truth had to be sought in order to resolve conflicts—namely, human reason, common to all combatants. In pagan civilizations the same human reason had developed great moral doctrines that had much in common with the supposed excellence of Christian teaching. Was not human reason then capable of grounding a "natural" theology and morality applicable to all times and places, just as the laws of science were universally valid? Priesthood and tradition were condemned for introducing into religion unwarranted superfluities that could not stand before the bar of reason. Not only were divergences in doctrine among the various Christian confessions explained away or mocked, but also tradition itself was severely attacked, as contradictions and absurdities were highlighted. In the battle of the books enlightened observation, scientific discovery, and current genius were to prevail against memory, repetition, and traditional models of excellence. Eternally valid truths grounded in human nature obviated the strict need to search the past for fragments of wisdom. G. E. Lessing highlighted the most telling Enlightenment critique of Christianity in maintaining that "contingent historical truths can never become the proof of necessary truths of reason" ("Über den Beweis des Geistes und der Kraft," in _Lessings Werke_, vol. 5, ed. F. Bornmüller [Leipzig], 494).

The gap between the necessity and universality of truth and the contingency of historical events and personalities led to various attempts in German Protestant thought to subsume the latter under the former. Kant saw in Jesus' teaching a pure, rational morality and religion and interpreted Jesus as its ideal exemplification. Hegel considered Jesus, the union of God and humanity, as the historical revelation and anticipation of the inevitable goal of historical process. Schleiermacher interpreted Jesus as the supreme realization of God-consciousness, the religious sentiment of absolute dependence upon God. Liberal Protestantism, heir to the Enlightenment's historical criticism, tried to reconstruct the historical life of Jesus, purified from the "supernatural" veneer applied by the evangelists and tradition. Jesus was presented as the ideal religious-moral teacher who corresponded to the highest ideals of human nature and spoke a pure message to the present age.

So varied and contradictory were the portraits of Jesus offered by the "critical research" of erudite German scholars that by the end of the nineteenth century the search for the historical Jesus had rendered itself suspect. World War I ended liberal Protestant theories of a universal human nature, basically sound and advancing to ever-greater realization of the kingdom of God. Besides, A. Schweitzer had alleged that Jesus had actually expected an imminent, apocalyptic end of the world (Mt 10:23; Mk 9:1). Not inner-worldly development but radical supernaturalism characterized Jesus' message; despite Jesus' error, Schweitzer thought that liberal (i.e., nondogmatic) Protestantism could survive, since in disproving Jesus' eschatology, history had opened the way to accept the pure morality of the Sermon on the Mount without dogmatic encumbrances.

But skepticism about historical reconstruction had grown to such an extent that M. Kähler, W. Wrede, and R. Bultmann denied our ability to know the historical Jesus. Since historical "facts" do not exist apart from their perceivers, and since the perceivers necessarily bring their own interpretative categories to reality, no pure objectivity of fact can be hoped for; hence the resurrection of Jesus could not be grounded on historical evidence but depended on the faith of the witnesses. Christianity has to live from the kerygma, the event of the proclamation of the word that called people to an existential decision for God and his love in the face of the world's meaninglessness. The various schemata of thought employed by NT authors to transmit the event of Christ were considered myths, since no human words could adequately grasp the ineffable, infinite mystery of God in his saving presence. Hence NT interpretations that appeared outmoded had to be demythologized and reinterpreted in view of Jesus' existential summons to authentic existence. E. Käsemann stressed the irreducible pluralism of NT theologies that only the Spirit could unify. Though Käsemann called for a renewal of the search for the historical Jesus, the effect of his criticism and Bultmann's was to deny to past history any perduring validity. History had become the mere occasion of salvation, not its bearer.

Many were the reactions among Protestants against Bultmann's radical existential interpretation of the gospel's message. C E. Dodd claimed to find in Jesus and major NT authors a realized eschatology whereby the kingdom of God was already present through Jesus' preaching. Ongoing history, however, forced the church to abandon this view in favor of a kingdom of God that transcended history while guaranteeing the moral order of the universe. Particular events thus tended to lose their salvific significance. K. Barth rejected all attempts to reconstruct the historical Jesus and the formation of the NT as sinful, human attempts to dominate the omnipotent Word of God. Instead, people were called to accept God's word in its entirety as judging them and to believe in Jesus Christ, God and human, as the content of Scripture. While taking the literal content of Scripture seriously, Barth has basically reduced all intelligible history to the one event of Jesus Christ, as known in Scripture. O. Cullmann developed the notion of salvation history insofar as Jesus Christ was understood as the culmination of the OT preparation and the criterion for all subsequent history; the time between Christ and the end was understood as the difference between D-Day, the decisive victory, and V-E Day, the final manifestation of that victory.

E. Jüngel developed a radical critique of human philosophy whose very lack of success in trying to absolutize itself pointed people to history, where God spoke and gave himself to humankind in the event of Jesus Christ. That God united himself to the man Jesus made history meaningful, allowing for the nondivine in the most intimate union with God. Ultimately history was understood as entering through Jesus' life, death, and resurrection into the trinitarian life of God's love. For God not only established the distinction between life and death, being and nonbeing, but also entered that struggle in favor of life. In God the past remains ever present, for God remains the subject of his own history, but we are referred to it by the narration of Christ's story. The Christocentrism of all these views, however, deprives all subsequent history, even church history, of its significance. Whether with Barth we must overleap in faith all intervening time to be joined to Christ or with Jüngel God has taken all history into himself with Jesus, history has no meaning of itself apart from Christ. Without a significance of its own, universal history cannot be intelligibly distinguished from salvation history. Outside of Christ all is darkness.

To avoid a christocentric devaluation of subsequent history, some Protestants have looked to the end of history as normative and decisive. J. Moltmann saw the kingdom of God as the eschatological ideal to be realized by Christian praxis in history. This praxis was grounded in God's promises, which became definitive at Jesus' resurrection, the basis of all Christian hope. Unfortunately he never clarified how the resurrection could be considered definitive, especially when it was understood merely as the perception of the crucified Jesus in the glory of God's coming by passive witnesses who drew conclusions from it about their call and mission. Thus, despite his wish to maintain the definitiveness of Jesus and even to interpret his death as a death in God, Moltmann tended to relativize Jesus before the end of the world.

W. Pannenberg held that the ambiguity of all history will be overcome only at the end of time, when God's full plan will be realized. Indeed, a being's reality is given only with its goal. To avoid relativizing Jesus, however, Pannenberg saw the end of history as proleptically actualized in Christ's resurrection, which had been proleptically active through all of Jesus' earthly life. Hence, although Jesus can be said to have become divine at the resurrection, the resurrection rendered his previous life divine. Clearly Pannenberg wished to respect the full humanity of Jesus' life in all its contingency while making it definitive (divine) and, despite its definitiveness, to preserve the significance of subsequent history that the end of time would bring to completion. Unfortunately by neglecting to explain how something can be both relative (historical) and definitive, he seemed to wish to have his cake while eating it too. The strange dialectic of being both and neither demands a metaphysics that the doctrine of human nature's corruption seems to deny Protestant thought.

Catholic theology long remained untroubled by Protestant dilemmas about history. In the first place, it was profoundly skeptical about any alleged science that claimed to find in the Gospels, the only substantial witnesses to Jesus' life, an understanding of Jesus at odds with the clear testimony of the evangelists. Moreover, to presuppose, however hypothetically, that the church's faith is discontinuous with the reality of the historical Jesus would entail a surrender to Protestants, an intellectual suicide that a Catholic theologian could never condone. Finally, the clear distinction between nature and (supernatural) grace fundamental to Catholic theology avoided many problems of excessive Christocentrism.

The natural-supernatural distinction was historically grounded in the new initiative of God for a special revelation that culminated in the incarnation, life, death, and resurrection of Jesus Christ as the divine redemption of humankind from sin. What people of themselves were incapable of accomplishing in history was freely bestowed by God, namely, salvation as the full sharing in his divine life through Christ. The distinction preserved God's freedom in initiating salvation as a second gift of grace beyond creation. It also guaranteed humanity's freedom in response to God's supernatural initiative, for, as long as people could discover a sense in reality and attain a knowledge of God with their natural intellect, their will would have reasons for a free choice. Thus, when revelation occurred, people would have some preunderstanding of its meaning and would be capable of freely accepting it. Indeed it was precisely to deny the cooperation of human freedom in response to revelation that Protestants had denied any possibility of a natural knowledge of God, i.e., knowledge apart from revelation.

The scholastics had subtly shifted the basis of the natural-supernatural distinction from historical novelty to whatever surpassed the natural powers of human intellect and will. The scholastic epistemology presupposed that a person attained knowledge of reality (being) through concepts abstracted from sensible experience. Conceptual knowledge of God, however analogous, constituted natural knowledge. The beatific vision, the direct intuition of God, surpassed all abstractions; therefore it and whatever led to it — faith and the corresponding gifts to intellect and will — might be considered properly supernatural. Moreover, revelation, as adapted to human intelligence, was understood as formulated in conceptual propositions. As supernatural, these propositions surpassed the capacity of the natural human intellect to affirm their truth. A person's will had to be attracted by the promises of forgiveness of sins and eternal life, but lest its acceptance of these propositions be irrational, hence neither free nor human, the external motives of credibility in Jesus' working of miracles and fulfillment of prophecies sufficed to guarantee the veracity of his testimony. Since Jesus entrusted his revelation to his disciples, the church, with authority to proclaim and interpret his message, the role of authority for a faith preached from without was essential. From such an interpretative schema a clear distinction between universal and salvific history resulted. Historical events, known by a person's natural intellect, belonged to the former; whatever pertained to the knowledge of faith and supernatural charity constituted salvation history.

The primacy of concepts, produced in the passive intellect under the unvarying illumination of the agent intellect, guaranteed the objectivity of universal, abstract knowledge. Historical "facts" might be recognized through the passivity of sense knowledge and interpreted, as far as necessary, by the objective abstractions resulting from the sensible evidence. Thus faith could rest upon the facts of Jesus' life, especially the resurrection, which was a divine miracle par excellence and fulfilled prophecies. These scholastics had finessed Lessing's dilemma. Not only are the truths of revelation not "necessary" to human beings, since they are freely revealed by God, but also sure knowledge of facts grounds Jesus' and the church's authority in proclaiming supernatural truths.

Considerable difficulties accompanied this position. If the facts supporting Christ's authority were historically, naturally verifiable, how might faith remain both supernatural and free? Inversely, if they were historically unverifiable, how might the assent of faith be certain? Moreover, the universality or effectiveness of God's salvific will seemed imperiled. If the act of faith affirms explicit teaching accepted on authority, how can the implicit, natural desire to obey God on the part of a good pagan, who never heard the church's authoritative preaching, be rendered supernatural? A final difficulty concerned the type of supernatural truths involved. They involved either facts or conceptual propositions. "Facts" are what they are in time and place once and for all. Concepts, which abstract from the material individuality of time and space, provide a timeless, essential "absolute." As more and more evidence about the formation of the church's dogmatic creeds came to light through historical research, it became increasingly difficult to explain dogmatic evolution as the later rendering precise of a treasury of propositional truths closed with the death of the last apostle.

2. Tentative Modern Solutions

Transcendental Thomism, represented by such thinkers as P. Rousselot, K. Rahner, and B. Lonergan, at first seemed to offer a solution to these problems. Since the judgment affirms truth and attains reality, the concept, which is at best only part of a judgment, does not adequately grasp reality. As the conversion to the phantasm, the judgment refers the phantasm to a transcendent horizon of intelligibility. Since the judgment involves a synthetic and referential activity of the intellect, the intellect is conceived primarily as a dynamic faculty, and objectivity is known only over subjectivity. Because the intellectual dynamism is oriented to the true as its good, the traditional distinction of intellect and will in terms of their formal objects, the true and the good, is sublated in the fundamental movement of knowing and loving. The ultimate grounding of the spiritual desire revealed in the dynamism can be nothing finite, for any perception of limitation involves its transcendence. Hence neither a concept nor a Marxist social utopia can satisfy the basic human desire. Yet this dynamism must be capable of fulfillment, otherwise the original judgment—implying the intelligibility, goodness, and consistency of reality—would have been impossible. God alone can fulfill the conditions of possibility for the judgment's actuality. Since God, who alone can terminate a person's spiritual dynamism, would be known in a manner surpassing concepts, one can speak, with Aquinas, of a "natural desire" for the beatific vision. Given the universal salvific will, God would offer grace to all.

Faith involves no longer the assent to propositions on the basis of an external authority but the knowing-loving response to God's self-revelation that as grace effects its own acceptance in the soul. This is not pure interiority, for the fundamental structure of thought and love revealed in the conversion to the phantasm involves a reference to the historical concrete. There is no transcendence to the Infinite unless over the finite. Because there exists no opposition between the Infinite and the finite, the Infinite can employ the finite as a symbol of his self-revelation in time. So people must hold themselves open to God's possible self-revelation in history. In fact, this revelation has occurred and reached its culmination in Jesus Christ, who is the perfect expression of God and simultaneously the perfect human response to God. Since the highest in a genus is the cause of all others in the genus, in the order of grace Christ can be said to cause the faith of all others, even "anonymous Christians" who never heard of him explicitly. Within the Christian tradition the development of dogma is allowed a great flexibility, since the ineffable God, who makes himself present in the grace to which faith responds, can never be exhausted by any finite, intellectual formula. Hence in various ages the church can employ various conceptual categories in approximating the original, not fully thematized object of faith given in Christ.

Against that background Rahner drew a distinction between secular and salvific history. The latter occurs within the former while giving the former its meaning, just as the supernatural presupposes nature while leading it to its completion. For secular history can deliver no verdict about its own final meaning and can be identified only as that history without salvation. Any more precise definition is impossible, since human freedoms, which respond to grace, cannot be fully objectified. Indeed, since grace is offered to all people, the distinction between secular and salvific history is formal, not material. In contradistinction to this universal salvific history, materially identical with secular history, a particular salvific history is recognized in which God's self-communication in grace came to its necessary thematic expression under special divine guidance in a sufficiently continuous and "official" tradition leading to Jesus Christ, who henceforth provides the definitive criterion against which all previous revelations are measured.

The very flexibility that enabled transcendental Thomism to respond to the difficulties of a conceptual scholasticism led in turn to difficulties. How can the ineffable mystery of God experienced in grace come to adequate thematic expression? Rahner ever allowed that Jesus had erred concerning the imminent arrival of God's kingdom but explained this error as an inadequate thematic expression of God's proximity experienced in his human consciousness. If such inadequate expressions are possible for

Jesus, how can the church claim a greater surety in its dogmas? If every dogmatic expression is fundamentally inadequate to God's infinite mystery, what permanent value do dogmatic formulas maintain? What makes one formula preferable to another if the formulas are revisable with the changing philosophical terminology of diverse epochs or within the pluralism of one epoch? Though Rahner insisted on the necessity of an infallible magisterium to guarantee the continuing presence of God's definitive revelation in Christ, on what basis does the magisterium prefer one formula to another and authoritatively demand the adherence of the faithful to it? Given that God communicates himself to everyone and, axiomatic for Rahner, being is self-consciousness, everyone enjoys an immediacy to God surpassing the imperfections of dogma; one sees how for some unwary followers of Rahner the danger of a fall into liberal Protestantism threatens.

With the vagueness of his natural-supernatural distinction and his emphasis on the unity of God's salvific plan culminating in Christ, Rahner might seem to be driven into an excessive Christocentrism. Yet other passages of his writings maintain that the event of Christ and his resurrection are not mere facts but have to be interpreted against the wider horizon of expectation and intelligibility provided by the human desire for the infinite horizon of being. This oscillation illustrates the underlying difficulty of explaining how an absolute may be found in the relativity of history, the Infinite in the finite. This is the modern hermeneutical problem of finding meaning when all finite statements can be relativized from another viewpoint, when being conceals itself even while revealing itself. Though a particular tradition may provide a linguistic set of meanings that help the members of that tradition to operate relatively effectively within it and even probe beyond, when traditions meet and come into conflict, what allows one tradition to be preferred to the other besides habit, comfort, or power? The relativization of truth claims and of the values connected with them that was undertaken by Nietzsche, Heidegger, and Sartre has flowered into the current relativism and deconstructionism dominating much of modern thought. Even modern science, after quantum mechanics and relativity, has become very aware of the revisable, partial nature of its hypotheses.

Actually the hermeneutical problem is but another variant of the basic epistemological-metaphysical dilemma, namely, how the finite might know the Infinite, how the finite can exist "alongside" the Infinite. If there is a fundamental opposition between finite and Infinite, not only is the incarnation impossible, but also God cannot be known in and through any finite sign, whether the world or Scripture. Indeed, the difficulty goes deeper, for God is not the only infinity that one encounters. What the ancients and scholastics dubbed "prime matter," the principle of individuality, also represents an infinity. For no abstraction or series of abstractions can exhaust the individuality of any being. If the individual, however, constitutes reality, conceptual abstractions do not reach reality and their validity is radically placed in question. Without a stable coordinate system of concepts, the individual "facts" of history lose their meaning; since a fact can never be perceived apart from an interpretation and no interpretation can claim objectivity for itself, a world of partial viewpoints threatens to dissolve into incommunicability, unintelligibility, and moral chaos—in short, total subjective relativism of thought and action. Indeed, if the progressive, or divisible, infinity of matter is to be at all intelligible, only the pure infinity of God can comprehend it. But how does the finite know the infinite or the Infinite?

Just as total skepticism contradicts itself, so total relativism implies an absolute. For to affirm that all is relative establishes that statement as a truth beyond question. Just as all communication implies an objectivity common to subjectivities, all thought implies that the mind can know an objective truth beyond itself. Actually all knowing implies both objectivity and subjectivity, absolute and relative, known and knower. Every basic judgment joins a finite and an infinite element, and every concept involves a finite form abstracted from and in relation to the infinity of matter (e.g., "man" is an abstract form, but man implies corporeality). So not only cannot the Infinite and the finite be juxtaposed, much less set in exclusive opposition as two finite realities might be, but also all thought implies their conjunction. Potency and act, form and matter, being and nonbeing, knowledge and ignorance—all seem to be joined in human persons, paradoxical beings who must rely on their finite reason while recognizing that they cannot absolutize it. Constantly referred beyond themselves in space and time, people nonetheless seem incapable of ever exhausting the reality encompassing them. Where, then, does a person find meaning?

Certainly finite human reason cannot fully explain or justify itelf. One's sense of meaning is derived primarily not from discussions with a philosopher but from the love experienced at the hands of one's parents. An analysis of the human sense of moral obligation reveals it to be *absolute*, in that one should remain faithful even unto death, thus relativizing the attraction of all the world, past, present, and future; *suprarational*, in that any rational argument to persuade someone to give his or her life can be distinguished by playing the individual off against the universal, or vice versa; *personal*, in that one dies not for an abstraction or for something subhuman but for a being capable of knowing and loving; *free and liberating*, in that one is neither physically nor psychologically forced to respond but overcomes all finite attractions in responding positively to one's duty. This characterization of the moral experience reveals that it is ultimately love.

But is it not impossible for finite humankind to perceive anything absolute? The response is clear. Since human reason cannot absolutize itself, its critique of love as nonrational cannot destroy love. In fact, the structures of love and reason are identical, involving the conjunction of finite and Infinite. Reason, left to itself, implicates itself in contradictions, but if it is seen as reflecting the structure of love and love is reality, then reason is justified. The one who loves, remaining faithful, or true, to the demands of love, can recognize the correspondence of reason and reality, which is truth. Thus is attained a natural knowledge of God, i.e., apart from historical revelation in Christ. God's omnipotence, which summons people to surrender their life and the whole world's attractions, is seen as the condition of human freedom. For, if people cannot attain an absolute, any relative reason offered for their choices could be put in question and their choices would be deprived of an intelligent foundation, hence rendered arbitrary, not free. Furthermore, if God calls a person to the total, free sacrifice of himself or herself, one may trust that the God who has just effected the

highest self-awareness in that person will not destroy what he created. He remains faithful to the creative love that he is and grants immortality.

The structure of reality so far uncovered is sacramental. In and through a finite reality the infinite God makes himself present in a call for the total response of love, and upon one's response depends one's eternal destiny. God would be present in true friendship, and marriage emerges as the highest natural sacrament. But sin destroyed the primordial unity among people and between God and each person. The present world order with all its selfishness and suffering does not clearly reflect love. Since no one is an island but each is constituted by relations to others, the external disunity of humankind is repeated in the individual's internal, fractured unity. No one, examining one's own heart, can assure another that love is a reality or claim a total allegiance for oneself. If there was to be any further communication between God and people or any restoration of the unity of humankind, the initiative must come from God. Since the world no longer served as an unambiguous sign of God's love, God became a human being and gave his life as the clearest sign of love. In death the divine person totally made his own the human nature as a sign of love, and it was not abandoned to death but rose.

So the previous proof for Love's omnipotence, which now has conquered sin and death, as well as for life after death has itself been proven by the fact of Easter. Humanity's natural faith in love, without which reason is destroyed, has, despite the evidence of sin, been thereby strengthened; thus supernatural faith is more certain than any natural faith and reason in this world. The resurrection becomes paradoxically the surest fact of history because only in view of it can reason's validity be upheld. If reason is doubted, no fact is sure. For every fact depends upon an interpretation, and the interpretation is valid only insofar as its wider philosophical presuppositions can be justified. Easter, the concrete witness vindicating love, becomes the touchstone of true love and all meaning.

The divine love of Christ manifested clearly at Easter causes a responding love in human hearts or else results in their hardening. Those responding with love to Christ become one with him in personal love and so constitute the body of Christ. This church, Christ's bride, continues through time, preserving in word and sacrament the life of love that animates her, offering people the crucial, concrete point for conversion and growth in love. Lest God's final revelation, his personal entrance into time, be frustrated in its salvific intent, the church has been guaranteed continued existence until the final judgment. All of its dogmas may be shown to reflect the same sacramental structure realized in the incarnation, preached by Christ and the apostles, defended by Augustine, and coming to its most adequate expression at Chalcedon as interpreted by Maximus Confessor. Just as God's infinite reality and omnipotence leave room for creation and human freedom, so the kingdom of God, already historically present in Jesus' demand for total conversion, allows room for the kingdom's final coming; similarly the Son of Man is both present and to come in judgment.

Paul's "already" must be balanced by "not yet," his indicative by the imperative following from it, the fullness of time in Christ by the superabundance of grace overflowing into present and future. Whether the emphasis is placed on the "not yet," as by Luke and Matthew, or on the "already," as in John's realized eschatology, the tension between present fullness and future completion in the sacramental structure of divine omnipotence and human freedom is maintained consistently throughout the NT. Christ has accomplished human salvation once and for all, but individuals must still respond, and the end of time will reveal God's judgment upon human freedom. So Christ is the norm of reality, but subsequent time is not superfluous; it is the battlefield of his grace to human beings, where his victory achieves itself ever more fully.

3. Love and Mission

Within this context universal history would be the world without the supernatural grace of Christ. Since, however, God wishes all people to be saved in and through Christ, the one mediator, this universal history is factually salvation history. How salvation is effected in those who never heard of Christ remains a mystery of grace and freedom, but since all time is present to God, the effects of Christ's offer of love can be made retroactively or proleptically present in every relation of human love; for the basic intellectual structure of finite-Infinite would remain present in human beings even if it were not fulfilled sacramentally in love, and it is up to God to intervene when and where he wills. Whether this call to love through other human beings outside the area of verbal revelation is continuous or intermittent, we cannot judge. Alongside this universal salvific history stands the particular history of salvation leading to Jesus Christ. As in him the explicit, divine–human sign of love constitutes human salvation as well as announces it, so the particularity of the sign gives a privileged place to those blessed by encountering it. Not only do they possess a greater intellectual surety about life's meaning, but also this surety permits them to act more decisively. The joy of being loved infinitely by God naturally overflows into mission as they wish to share the blessings of love with others. Non-Christians are called to conversion, to a salvation outside themselves, from darkness or, at best, twilight into the full glory of grace.

Although no one can ever pronounce an infallible judgment about the perdition of another and one can hope for the salvation of all non-Catholics whom one meets, nonetheless, knowing how difficult it is to live Christ's sacrificial love even with all the helps of the church, recognizing the power of evil that resulted in the Christ's crucifixion and made clear the absolute need of conversion, and having received Christ's explicit command to make disciples of all nations, believers correctly admit that the gospel's emphasis rests upon the necessity of mission. The tension between God's universal salvific will and the particularity of the one mediator did not lead Paul to apostolic indolence and a false optimism about the salvation of the heathens. Instead that tension animated his preaching (1 Tm 2:7). Were Christian truth merely particularist, there would be no need to preach to others; were it merely universal, it would already be available to all and not need preaching. But preaching is needed to make the particular of salvation available to all people, for whom it was intended. Its particularity is due to sin and the subsequent need of conversion; its universality is due to the divine love that knows no bounds. In fulfilling his mission, Paul was but continuing the work of his Lord, the concrete universal, who demanded conversion and belief in the gospel because the time had been fulfilled and the kingdom of God had come close (Mk 1:15).

Bibl.: A. GARDEIL, *La crédibilité et l'apologétique* (Paris, 1907); id., *Le Donné révélé et la théologie* (Paris, 1909); P. ROUSSELOT, "Les yeux de la foi," *RSR* 1 (1910); K. BARTH, *Epistle to the Romans* (1919; Oxford, 1935); id., *Church Dogmatics*, vol. 1/1 (Edinburgh, 1936); R. BULTMANN, *Der Begriff der Offenbarung im Neuen Testament* (Tübingen, 1929); id., *Jesus Christ and Mythology* (New York, 1958); id., *Kerygma and Mythology* (New York, 1961); A. SCHWEITZER, *Das Messianitäts- und Leidensgeheimnis* (Tübingen, 1950); E. KÄSEMANN, "Begründet der neutestamentliche Kanon die Einheit der Kirche?," in *EvT* 2 (1951–52), 13–21; id., "Unity and Multiplicity in the New Testament Doctrine of the Church," in *New Testament Questions of Today* (1964; Philadelphia, 1969), 252–59; Y. CONGAR, "Ecclesia ab Abel," in M. Reding, H. Helfers, and E. Hofmann, eds., *Abhandlungen über Theologie und Kirche* (Düsseldorf, 1952), 79–108; CONGAR, "Vaste Monde, ma paroisse," in *Témoignage chrétien* (1959): 100–177; C. H. DODD, *The Parables of the Kingdom* (London, 1953); id., *The Apostolic Preaching and Its Developments* (London, 1936); H. DE LUBAC, *Paradoxe et mystère de l'Église* (Paris, 1967); W. PANNENBERG, *Jesus: God and Man* (Philadelphia, 1968); id., *Theology and the Kingdom of God* (Philadelphia, 1969); K. RAHNER, *Hearers of the Word* (New York, 1969); id., "History of the World and Salvation History," in *Theological Investigations*, vol. 5 (1962; London, 1966), 97–115; id., "Anonymous Christians," in *Theological Investigations*, vol. 6 (1965; London, 1969), 390–98; id., *Foundations of Christian Faith* (New York, 1978); H. Urs VON BALTHASAR, *Cordula ou l'épreuve décisive* (Paris, 1969); J. RATZINGER, *Le nouveau peuple de Dieu* (Paris, 1971); O. CULLMANN, *Christ and Time* (Philadelphia, 1964); id., *Le salut dans l'histoire* (Neuchâtel, 1966); J. MOLTMANN, *The Experiment Hope* (Philadelphia, 1975); id., *The Crucified God* (New York, 1974); J. M. McDERMOTT, "A New Approach to God's Existence," *Thom* 44 (1980): 219–50; id., "Proof for Existence of God," in J. Komonchak et al., eds., *New Dictionary of Theology* (Wilmington, 1987), 804–8; E. JÜNGEL, *God as the Mystery of the World* (Grand Rapids, 1983); id., "Jesus and the Kingdom of God in the Synoptics, Paul and John," in *Église et Théologie* 19 (1988): 69–91; G. ANGELINI, "Storia-Storicità," *DTI*, 3:337–64.

John M. MCDERMOTT

HOLY SPIRIT

What place should the Holy Spirit occupy in fundamental theology? If one consults the *Dictionnaire apologétique de la foi catholique* (ed. D'Alès [Paris, 1909–31]), one may be surprised to find there is no separate article on the Holy Spirit. This cannot be put down to general oversight, since a glance through the analytical index of the dictionary (which itself is a significant example of classic apologetics) shows not a few references to the Holy Spirit, e.g., in the articles on papal infallibility and grace. Of all the ample work of the Spirit, such as is attested by revelation and the liturgy, preconciliar theology generally confined itself to stressing two aspects: the Holy Spirit presented as the guarantor and faithful conserver maintaining unchanged the institution founded by Christ (traditionalism) and, with regard to the faithful, considered as the *dulcis hospes animae*, the theme of the divine indwelling being usually given a devotional turn and an inflection of intimacy.

Development was to come with VATICAN II, but not without travail; in the first draft of *De Ecclesia* three grave defects were still to be detected in the text: triumphalism, clericalism, and legalism—in a word, real sins against the Holy Spirit. In identifying the church with Christ and with the kingdom of God, triumphalism overlooks the fact that, whereas at the redemption the Word acted through a human nature free from sin, now, in the era of the church, he works with his Spirit through people marked by and subject to sin. Then, clericalism puts the person appointed to an office in the foreground as protagonist of salvation, and not Christ glorious and present in the Spirit. Lastly, legalism so stresses the ecclesiastical institution as to throw the interior working of the Spirit into the shade, who alone can make an act done by the church a saving event.

The council in fact not only overcame these dangers but, because of the broad perspectives opened up by biblical, patristic, and liturgical renewal, made important and weighty contributions in pneumatology that, if made the most of at the right moment, will make a significant impression on the main junctures of fundamental theology.

Since the specific feature distinguishing this discipline is the establishing of the CREDIBILITY of the revelation of God wrought in Jesus Christ and made present by the Spirit by means of the church in the historical present, it seems appropriate to organize our material according to three main topics: Spirit and revelation, Spirit and church, Spirit and history.

1. Spirit and Revelation

The salvation-history approach favored by Vatican II has led to a reconsideration of revelation in terms of a trinitarian event, an event unfolding in history and reaching toward beatific fellowship. Earlier apologetics preferred to identify the subject of revelation as God, i.e., the unique divine nature, prescinding from his being a Trinity of persons (so-called pretrinitarian monotheism). Vatican I also used the same terms: "It has pleased his [God's] wisdom and goodness . . . to reveal himself" (DS 3004). Contrast this strongly theocentric passage with that similar but markedly triadocentric one in *Dei Verbum:* "In his goodness and wisdom, God chose to reveal himself and to make known to us the hidden purpose of his will (cf. Eph 1:9) by which through Christ, the Word made flesh, man has access to the Father in the Holy Spirit and comes to share in the divine nature" (*DV* 2).

All revelation, therefore, is a love story that comes "*a* Patre *per* Filium *in* Spiritu Sancto *ad* Patrem." The council's vision is clearly christocentric, but not christomonistic: the Father reveals himself to the human race and draws it to himself by means of "the two hands" (see Irenaeus, *Adv. Haer.* 5.6.1), i.e., by the joint action of the Word and the Spirit. Christ lays out the objective reality of salvation and revelation, and the Spirit inspires and interiorizes it. The latter does not emit new words but renews Christ's words. According to John, he is the other (*allos*) Paraclete with respect to Christ, but he is not another Paraclete, i.e., different (*heteros*) from Christ (Jn 14:16). As Spirit of truth, he is to teach and to remind of everything Jesus has said (Jn 14:26), but "he will not speak on his own authority"; he will guide us into all the truth by drawing continually on Jesus' revelation (Jn 16:13–14).

In line with patristic and especially Augusinian-Thomist thought, the council seeks to summarize the revelatory work of the Spirit by means of the two categories of *universalization* and *interiorization:* "What was once [*semel*] preached by the Lord, or what was once wrought in him for the saving of the human race, must be proclaimed and spread abroad to the ends of the earth (Acts 1:8), beginning from Jerusalem (cf. Lk 24:47). Thus, what he once accomlished for the salvation of all [*pro omnibus*] may in the course of time come to achieve its effect in all [*in universis*]" (*AG* 3). If hence the Son becomes incarnate in history, the Spirit it is who opens history to eschatology by making Christ the eschatological being, the Last Adam. Thus, by operation of the Spirit, the unique event of Christ acquires an abiding presentness; his saving power crosses every latitude and extends to every hour of history. But the fulfillment wrought by the Spirit with regard to Christ must be rightly understood. It is not something added from outside, for nothing is lacking to the work of Christ, and in him all has been performed to perfection (cf. Jn 19:30); the Spirit makes universal the redemption by completing it *from within*, i.e., by interiorizing it. "To accomplish this goal [the universal spreading of salvation to the ends of the earth and the end of time], Christ sent the Holy Spirit from the Father. The Spirit was to carry out his saving work inwardly [*intus*]" (*AG* 4).

Thus the two loving arms of the Father—Christ and the Spirit—operate in a way that is united but not confounded, the one by expressing, the other by impressing; the one as word, the other as breath accompanying and introducing it into the hearts of believers: "For no one can accept the gospel preaching without the illumination and inspiration of the Holy Spirit, who gives delight to all who consent to and believe in the truth" (DS 377; 3010; *DV* 5).

A more carefully pneumatic reinterpretation of the revelatory event, such as was performed by Vatican II, allows the overcoming of various risks, of which preconciliar apologetics had fallen foul.

a. First of all was the risk of *intellectualism.* To define revelation, classic apologetics had favored the category of the word; revelation is *locutio Dei attestantis.* This, then, is the omnipresent analogy in the OT, as in the NT (Heb 1:1), but to protect the concept of revelation from the negations of rationalism and the contamination of liberal Protestantism, the described in terms of teaching, by analogy with the relationship between master and pupil. The result of this was an insistence on the conceptual aspect of revelation, which tended to make it the manifestation of a system of ideas rather than the communication of a person, Christ, the Truth in person. In a conception of this sort, words took precedence over deeds, the latter appearing merely as guaranteeing the revelation and not as the medium for it.

By conceiving of revelation not only in the context of the *Logos* but also in that of the *Pneuma*, the council recovers the historical dimension of the Trinity's self-communication, by showing how this occurs *in* history and *by means of* history: "This plan of revelation is realized by deeds and words having an inner unity: the deeds wrought by God in the history of salvation manifest and confirm the teaching and realities signified by the words, while the words proclaim the deeds and clarify the mystery contained in them" (*DV* 2). Without omitting the doctrinal character of revelation, *Dei Verbum* emphasizes how the word-history of the self-revealing God is born of love and tends to love: "Through this revelation, therefore, the invisible God out of the abundance of his love speaks to men as friends and lives among them so that he may invite and take them into fellowship with himself" (*DV* 2). The covenant includes teaching, but so as to arrive at fellowship.

b. This defect of intellectualism was reflected especially in the conception of Holy Scripture. To the aggressive onslaught of rationalism, which denied the divine inspiration of the Bible, claiming to point out various errors of logic in it, apologetics reacted by defending its inerrancy, but always on the plane of logical, i.e., propositional, truth (*propositionalism*). Starting from the conception of language, seen as a series of propositions, both rationalist polemics and apologetic counteroffensive identified the word with the proposition. The result of this was to fragment the Bible into thousands of different propositions, each one of which would contain an objective religious truth. As is clear, only the cognitive aspect of Scripture was taken into account, and recourse was had to this as to a *locus argumentorum*. In the theological manual, the Bible was quoted as proof of this or that thesis, but none of these took

account of the saving value of the word. For example, of that classic text in 2 Tm 3:16, only the aspect of inspiration was ever quoted (which served as basis for the doctrine of inerrancy), while the other aspect of the salvific efficacy of Scripture—"useful for teaching, for reproof, for correction, and for training in righteousness" though receiving more emphasis in the text—was passed over in silence. In point of fact, in Scripture it is easier to meet with statements about the salvific dynamism of the word than it is about its truth. Charged with the energy of the Spirit, the inspired word is seen as a word that works (*energeitai*, 1 Thes 2:13); not only does it teach, but it effectively produces salvation by making the potent voice of the Spirit ring out (*DV* 21; see Rom 1:16; Jas 1:21; 1 Cor 1:18; 2 Tm 2:9, etc.).

c. Traditional apologetics confined itself to dealing with Christ's messianic role, presenting him as "divine emissary" come to speak on God's behalf, while consigning other testimonies of Jesus about himself as Son of the Father to dogmatics. A presentation of this sort, making an artificial dichotomy between divine emissary and Son of the Father risks presenting us with a curtailed Jesus (*Jesuanism*), who only in part corresponds to the Christ of the Gospels.

However, a sound fundamental Christology (→ CHRISTOLOGY I) cannot but develop in the light of a "pneumatic" understanding of the Christ-event, for "Christ" means "consecrated with the Holy Spirit." We see "Christ's entire life unfolded in the presence of the Spirit" (Basil, *De Spir. S.* 16), from his birth ("incarnatus est de Spiritu Sancto," DS 150), to his baptism ("after the baptism that John announced . . . God anointed [*echrisen*] Jesus of Nazareth with the Holy Spirit and with power," Acts 10:37–38), up to his passover ("declared to be Son of God with power according to the Spirit of holiness by resurrection from the dead," Rom 1:4).

A truly fundamental Christology therefore is not confined to considering a part of Christ (his function as divine emissary) and claiming on this to found the subsequent dogmatic construction. By refusing any knowledge of Christ according to the Spirit, this kind of Christology would sooner or later end in slipping into a more or less disguised "Jesusology," i.e., a knowledge of Jesus Christ "according to the flesh," rightly refuted by revelation (see 2 Cor 5:16).

d. An adequate understanding of the fact and work of the Revealer cannot therefore depend on logic and dialectic alone, those favorite weapons of classic apologetics. In setting out the foundations of the Christian religion so as to be valid for believers and nonbelievers alike, one certainly cannot renounce the data of human experience and reason; nonetheless, the fundamental theologian should not be required to suspend his or her faith or put basic certainties in doubt. A "threshold apologetics" of this sort would inevitably fall into the arid tracts of a *rationalism* that claims to advance toward faith by eliminating any kind of presupposition by means of Cartesian doubt, so as to begin from supposedly neutral ground. A real fundamental theology, in contrast, rejects the artificial pretense to methodological neutrality, in the certainty that genuine scientific objectivity is not to be attained in theology by deluding oneself into thinking one can set out without any presuppositions—the claim would in fact be the most colossal of prejudgments!— but by honestly recognizing those religious presuppositions and subjecting them to critical thought.

Apologetics can never lower itself to the level of human wisdom, nor can it rest "with plausible words of wisdom, but with a demonstration of the Spirit" because "those who are unspiritual do not receive the gifts of God's Spirit" (1 Cor 2:4, 14). So too fundamental theology is *fides quaerens intellectum* and therefore will never be constructed in opposition to dogmatics. Since revelation—as christological-pneumatic event—is both mystery of faith and historical event, its course will necessarily be both apologetic and dogmatic.

2. Spirit and Church

Since the Holy Spirit comes forth as love, he comes forth as the first gift" (*ST* 1, q. 38, a. 2). First in the all-exceeding opening of God to us, the Spirit is also the first to arouse the adoring acceptance and obedient faith of human beings in the gift that comes from on high. This loving encounter between God and us comes about "by the operation of the Holy Spirit," hypostatically in Jesus, to be fulfilled mystically in us: "The Word and Son of the Father united to the flesh has become flesh, completely human, so that human beings united to the Spirit, might

become one sole Spirit. He is God, bearer of the flesh [*sarkophoros*], and we human beings are bearers of the Spirit" [*pneumatophoroi*] (Athanasius, *De Inc. Ver.* 8). The obedient return to the Father, inaugurated by Jesus, takes "body" in the church, in whom all her children, reborn by water and the Spirit, relive the Son's prayer: "Abba! Father!" (Rom 8:15).

From the very beginnings of its self-awareness, the Christian community has always conceived of itself as God's people, Christ's body, and so too as temple of the Spirit (1 Cor 3:16; 6:19; 2 Cor 6:16), and it has explicitly linked its existence to faith in the third person of the Trinity. The Constantinopolitan Creed demonstrates this, where the article "I believe in the Holy Spirit" is immediately followed by the one on "one, holy, catholic, and apostolic church" (DS 150).

Indeed, from the first steps of its journey through history, the Christian community has had to contend with a twofold temptation: on the one hand, that of dreaming about a totally spiritual church with no further need of signs and visible structures (Spirit without church), and on the other, that of taking shape as a society entirely centered on the hierarchical institution (church without Spirit). Classic apologetics, having developed in a climate of anti-Protestant and antirationalist polemics, was naturally exposed to the risk of heavily accentuating the juridical-social component in the church-reality, and of alarmingly reducing ecclesiology to the single, hierarchical dimension. The glaring neglect of the Spirit became acute during the Enlightenment, which infected certain second-rate theological manuals. They presented the church like a machine set going in the first instance by Jesus and then entrusted once and for all to the hands of the hierarchy. The theological renewal of the school of Tübingen, and particularly the work of J. A. Möhler (d. 1838), reacted against the sterility of rationalism by stressing the primacy of the Spirit over the institutional element and conceived of the church as the continued incarnation of Christ. Vatican I did not have a chance to gather up these very promising stimuli and was obliged to restrict the intended constitution on the church to the single question of the Roman pontiff. The Constitution *Pastor Aeternus* of 18 July 1870 defined the primacy and infallibility of the pope, while the Holy Spirit received mention only as guaranteeing help to the Petrine magisterium (DS 3060).

The recovery of the spiritual and charismatic element, occurring thanks to the encyclical *Mystici Corporis* of Pius XII (1943) — although still closely integrated in the context of a juridical ecclesiology — led to the balanced and dynamic synthesis of *Lumen Gentium*: "The society furnished with hierarchical agencies and the Mystical Body of Christ are not to be considered as two realities, nor are the visible assembly and the spiritual community, nor the earthly church and the church enriched with heavenly things. Rather they form one interlocked reality which is comprised of a divine and a human element" (*LG* 8). As is clear, the council rightly tries to avoid two most dangerous ecclesiological errors: *naturalism*, which sees the church as a simple, human institution furnished with disciplinary rules and external rites; and the opposite one of *mysticism*, which stresses the church's supernatural and interior component to such a degree as to regard it as a hidden and completely invisible entity. *Mystici Corporis* (AAS 35 [1943]: 220–24) and, some time before that, *Satis Cognitum* of Leo XIII (AAS 28 [1896]: 710) had linked these two errors with the two most serious christological heresies: Nestorianism, which took only Christ's visible nature into account, and Monophysitism, which took account only of his divine, invisible nature. Actually, no true opposition can exist between the invisible mission of the Holy Spirit, which has as effect the formation and animation of the mystical body, and the juridical office that the pastors have received from Christ, on the basis of which the church is a hierarchical community. "By an excellent analogy, [the church] is compared to the mystery of the incarnate Word. Just as the assumed nature inseparably united to the divine Word serves him as a living instrument of salvation, so, in a similar way, does the communal structure of the church serve Christ's Spirit, who vivifies it by way of building up the body (cf. Eph 4:16)" (*LG* 8).

Vatican II has maintained the essentially christological point of reference. By integrating this into an ample pneumatological perspective, however, it has thrown certain aspects of the church into relief, to which Latin theology, and especially certain treatises *De Ecclesia*, had not always devoted due attention.

a. The CHURCH cannot be regarded as merely a second edition of the life of Jesus but must be seen as the *event* of his Spirit. In other words, the relationship between Jesus and the church cannot be reduced to that between a founder and the foundation (a succession relationship of first Jesus, then the church); rather, it is a sacramental relationship of first Jesus, preparing the church, then Jesus in the Spirit living within the church. Without the gift of the Spirit, there would be no ecclesial "we" (see Acts 15:28). There is thus no church without Spirit: "Where the church is, there is the Spirit of God; and wherever the Spirit of God is, there is the church, and every kind of grace" (Irenaeus, *Adv. Haer.* 3.24.1).

Consequently, the memory of Jesus, or *anamnesis*, can never block the church into turning back but will set it in motion toward the *epiclesis*, projecting it forward. This is why the church is ever the same yet ever new; it is identical to itself, not with the identity of a stone but with that of a living being. The saving event is a grace never to be repeated in time and space, as such, but is forever the sign of the free and unpredictable visit of the Spirit. True, the Spirit is not inconsistent. Even when his coming obeys the constant laws (which he himself has laid down) of salvation history, even when he delivers himself freely through signs established in advance by himself, such as the sacraments or the apostolic succession, the Spirit is ever new; in sacramental celebrations, as in the great sacrament the church, the unrepeatable event of Christ is reproduced not only in new ways, bound up with ever varying human situations, but also with increased potentialities, because of the Spirit's inexhaustible fertility.

b. As fruit of the twofold mission of the second and third persons of the Trinity, the church is the *sacrament* of Christ and the *place* of the Spirit. According to patristic teaching, the church is the *organum* of the Spirit, as, by analogy, the human nature of the Logos is the organ into which flows the *dynamis*, the *energeia* of the second divine person. For the Spirit, "existing as one and the same being in the head and in the members, vivifies, unifies, and moves the whole body. This he does in such a way that his work could be compared by the holy Fathers with the function which the soul fulfills in the human body, whose principle of life the soul is" (*LG* 7).

As may be seen, this context is the "somatic" model of ecclesiology, much loved by Augustine and Thomas Aquinas. The council, however, toned down the traditional formula of the earlier magisterium, according to which Christ is the head of the mystical body and the Holy Spirit is its soul (DS 3328; 3808). *LG* takes a position on the functional plane, for on the ontological level, the soul forms a single being with the body, but the Spirit does not form a single being with the church. The union of the Spirit with the church is also different from the union of the Word with human nature in Jesus ("the hypostatic" union); all the doings of the Man-God had the divine Word as their subject and were therefore covered by an absolute guarantee of his Person. The union of the Spirit with the church, however, is in fact a covenantal union, which does not nullify the personalities of the human subjects with their acts of loyalty and betrayal. The church is indeed the sacrament of the Spirit, i.e., an indicative and effective sign of his presence, but only as sacrament; it is not itself the reality in question.

This perspective of the church as sacrament allows us to set out correctly the problem of how to discern the true church. Traditional apologetics, structured on the basis of an institutional, not a sacramental, paradigm, undertook to prove that only the church of Rome was Christ's true church, while all the others were "synagogues of Satan" (see Rev 2:9) and could not be called churches. Given, however, that only the Trinity is the absolute church of the Three, no earthly and historical agency can claim to identify itself, without qualification, as the church of Christ. To quote the council's words: "This Church . . . subsists in [N.B. *not* is] the Catholic Church, which is governed by the successor of Peter and by the bishops in union with that successor, although many elements of sanctification and of truth can be found outside of her visible structure. These elements, however, as gifts properly belonging to the Church of Christ, possess an inner dynamism toward Catholic unity" (*LG* 8). An analogous answer, even if more complicated and articulated, will have to be given to the question about the relationship between the Christian religion and others (see *AG* 3; 11; *NA* 2; *LG* 16).

c. Quickened by the "*koinōnia* of the Holy Spirit" (2 Cor 13:13), the church is much more than a society defined by juridical relationships. It is a mystery of *fellowship*, of which the Trinity is the source, form, and goal. In this ecclesial fellowship, the personal chain uniting Christians to one another and to God is the Holy Spirit, "who, on behalf of the whole Church and each and every one of those who believe, is the principle of their coming together and remaining together in the teaching of the apostles and in fellowship, in the breaking of bread and in prayers (cf. Acts 2:42)" (*LG* 13; cf. *UR* 2).

"Baptized into one body by one Spirit" (1 Cor 12:13), believers are sustained and quickened in their fellowship by the word, the Eucharist (the source and apex of every sacrament), the ministries, and the charisms, of which charity is the greatest.

As concerns fundamental theology, two gifts of the Spirit demand particular attention: holy tradition and ordained ministry.

The Spirit, "qui locutus est per prophetas," and who presided with his inspiration at the forming of Scripture, also presides over its conservation and interpretation by the dynamism of tradition. "To keep the gospel forever whole and alive within the church, the apostles left bishops as their successors, handing over their own teaching role to them" (*DV* 7). This tradition, which "develops in the church *with the help of the Holy Spirit"* (*DV* 8, emphasis added), makes the Christian community the vital environment in which the word of God is kept alive and active. For even outside the church the volumes of the Scriptures may be had, materially speaking, but not the living gospel, not the true understanding of the Scriptures. Inside the church is where the living Spirit is, and the church itself is the living gospel. The unique deposit of sacred tradition and sacred Scripture has been entrusted to the whole church, so that the whole church may live by these, but "the task of authentically interpreting the word of God, whether written or handed on, has been entrusted exclusively to the living teaching office of the church, whose authority is exercised in the name of Jesus Christ" (*DV* 10).

As concerns the word of God, the Spirit operates the "co-spiration" of all the faithful in endless growth toward the fullness of divine truth. From the Holy Spirit, every one of the baptized receives the *sensus fidei*, i.e., the gift of discerning what the true faith is, and the *gratia verbi*, the gift of accurately proclaiming it (*LG* 12; 35). In so doing, the Spirit does not open the way to arbitrary anarchy but makes himself the active principle of fellowship by giving to all to consent to the Truth. In this way the church, guided by the magisterium, stimulated by the study and thought of believers, sustained by the witness they bear in their lives, conforms to the word of God; SENSUS FIDEI becomes *consensus fidelium*.

3. Spirit and History

Committed to providing an answer for those who want an explanation of Christians' hope (see 1 Pt 3:15), fundamental theology cannot limit itself to checking off the traces of God's intervention in the story of Jesus of Nazareth but, aware of its responsibilities to the world, must deal with the questions of people demanding to see signs of the presence of the Spirit of Christ in the world of today. This is the theme of discerning the Spirit.

If we turn to the Bible, we see how, from the creation to the final consummation, the Spirit is as though magnetized by that which is corporeal and historical. He gives life to the cosmos, he dwells in a people and even "rests" in a physical human body, that of Christ; at Pentecost, he is poured out "on all flesh" (Acts 2:17), and at the end will be the agent of the "redemption of our bodies" (Rom 8:23). He is indeed God's power to make history; under his breath everything is transfigured. The tortured body of the Crucified becomes the glorious body of the Risen One, the human word "conveys" the word of God, bread becomes the body of Christ, and the church the anticipation of the kingdom, while the world becomes the vision restored of our home in heaven.

But if the Spirit "directs the unfolding of time" (*GS* 26), we must ask ourselves what the criteria are for deciphering his presence in history. "The People of God believes that it is *led by the Spirit of the Lord*, who fills the earth. Motivated by this faith, it labors to decipher authentic signs of God's presence and purpose in the happenings, needs, and desires in which this People has a part along with other men of our age" (*GS* 11, emphasis addded).

In partial analogy with the criteria for the historical authenticity of the Gospels, the following range of criteria may be outlined for discerning the authenticity of the Spirit's activity in history.

a. A first criterion may be defined as *continuity*. Faithful to the new everlasting covenant, the Spirit is present wherever people are led to Christ, for the Spirit does not bring a new revelation but will recall what Jesus has already said (Jn 14:26; 16:14); he will not therefore bring one beyond or above Christ. What the Spirit has said and brought about in Jesus remains normative forever; any novelty that does not tally with that past comes not from the Spirit but from the anti-Spirit. But it must be said that this return to an already-completed history is not a flight backward but a thrust forward, a going toward the Father. A sign of the Spirit is that which sends the church forward toward God's future: every true reform, every authentic scrap of human progress, must be consistent with the eschatological perfection of the heavenly Jerusalem. For the church, this means putting the *memoria Jesu* to good use so as continually to be open to the free and powerful breathing of the Spirit. Only thus can it manage to be faithful to the Christ of yesterday, of today, of eternity; only thus can memory not lapse into nostalgia, but open into eschatology.

b. A second criterion may be called that of *discontinuity*. A sign of the presence of the Spirit is that which is not referable to the flesh and to the world: "For what the flesh desires is opposed to the Spirit, and what the Spirit desires is opposed to the flesh" (Gal 5:17). The two most certain anticarnal and hence spiritual signs will be freedom and love. "Where the Spirit of the Lord is, there is *freedom*" (2 Cor 3:17); "To each is given the manifestation of the Spirit for the common good . . . and the greatest of these [gifts] is *love*" (1 Cor 12:7; 13:13). The sign of the Spirit is given above all in the freedom that makes itself love, in the love that blossoms in freedom; this freedom-love holds sway only in anti-Babel, the *Ecclesia ab Abel*, which the Spirit is endlessly preparing at every turn of history.

c. A third criterion may be called the criterion of *paradox*. The Spirit is present where those higher syntheses take place in which one aspect is not only balanced by but supported by its opposite; it is in these paradoxical syntheses that the proper nature of the Spirit is reflected. As, in the Trinity, he is unity in distinction, so in salvation history his activity is forever diversifying and unifying by a process in which unity and distinction neither annul nor dissolve one another but are involved the one in the other. The Spirit unites but does not standardize, fuses but does not confound, distinguishes but does not separate.

The other great antinomy that in salvation history always bears the stamp of the Spirit is that of cross and glory, of death and life. He who guided Jesus to total obedience to the Father on the cross and raised him up from death, making him alive and life-giving, guides the church too and the human race to lose itself in order to find itself, because he is himself the almighty weakness, the power of infinite love that makes itself poor and defenseless so as to arouse the response of finite love and enter into fellowship with it. The Spirit breathes there where life is given for love, where consolation is experienced in tribulation, forthrightness in persecution, forgiveness in hatred and desertion. This new life is the "guarantee of the Spirit" (see 2 Cor 5:5), the earnest of the church in heaven, where all will be "one in the other, one in the perfect Dove" (Gregory of Nyssa, *Homil. 15 in Cant.*).

Bibl.: Var., "πνεῦμα," *TDNT* 6:332–451; H. Mühlen, *Una Mystica Persona* (Paderborn, 1964); P. Evdokimov, *L'Esprit Saint dans la tradition orthodoxe* (Paris, 1969); W. Kasper, "Spirito, Cristo, Chiesa," in var., *L'esperienza dello Spirito* (Brescia, 1974); L. Bouyer, *Le consolateur* (Paris, 1980); J. D. Zizioulas, "Cristologia, pneumatologia e istituzioni ecclesiali: un punto di vista ortodosso," in G. Alberigo, ed., *L'ecclesiologia del Vaticano II: dinamismi e prospettive* (Bologna, 1981), 111–27; M. Bordoni, "Cristologia e pneumatologia: L'evento pasquale come atto del Cristo e dello Spirito," *Lat* 47 (1981): 432–92; var., *Credo in Spiritum Sanctum*, 2 vols. (Vatican City, 1983); A. Milano, "Spirito Santo," *NDT*, 1533–58; S. Bulgakov, *Il Paraclito* (2nd ed.; Bologna, 1987); F. Lambiasi, *Lo Spirito Santo, mistero e presenza: Per una sintesi di pneumatologia* (Bologna, 1987).

Francesco Lambiasi

HUMANISM

I. History

Definitions and division into periods are fundamental aspects of setting out in time and space any historical and cultural phenomena. They are all the more problematic in the case of humanism because of the difficulty of applying clear terminology and unambiguous meanings to this complex phenomenon, much of which defies definition and yet recurs to a greater or lesser extent throughout the history of culture and humanity. Culture refers to humanity, and humanistic culture seeks to make it unequivocal that it refers to culture in a particular way. This culture exalts the worldly, human values of independence, freedom, *dignitas hominis*, and *virtus*, all of which are to be found one way or another in our lives, our quests, and our reflection. We will be able to give as examples of this, of the revival of ancient, classical values going beyond the historical-philological movement to an acceptance of an anthropological-philosophical position, and of sensibility and a poetic language besides metaphysical and philosophical terms.

1. "Human" Values and the "Natural" Person

Dignitas (Pico della Mirandola, *Oratio de Hominis Dignitate* [1463–94]) goes hand in hand with pleasure (Lorenzo Valla, *De Voluptate* [1431]: "Voluptas est bonum undecumque quaesitum, in animi et corporis oblectatione positum") and glory; freedom (from Valla's *De Libero arbitrio* down to Erasmus's work of 1524 of the same title and engaged in polemic with Luther's *De Servo Arbitrio*) goes with fate and fortune (Coluccio Salutati, *De Fato et Fortuna* [1396]), before exploding in free examination and the religious Reformation. *Virtus* is not necessarily dependent on a moral teleology or on a reward in heaven. It is clear that our classical legacy, naturally mediated by Christianity, has been filtered by the disputes of scholasticism and will be taken up again at some time in the future. The *studia humanitatis* have not so much rejected theology as repudiated its comprehensiveness. Philosophy acquired a greater philological awareness before science and technology (in the persons of Francis Bacon, Leonardo da Vinci, Galileo, and many others) sought to make their own unique contribution to the establishment of the *regnum hominis.*

Anthropocentrism characterizes everything that human beings think and do. It is characterized by the Renaissance and humanism, even in the Middle Ages. Machiavelli departed from the humanistic spirit and even broke with the classical tradition; the relationship between theology and philosophy was transformed (→ THEOLOGY V). Philosophy was no longer relegated to the role of *ancilla theologiae* and even claimed to be an equal with dignity and liberty. The theoretical impossibility of conflict between these two methodologically different approaches to the single Truth demonstrates the limitations of human inquiry when that conflict is shown to be a valid one; it is one in which genuine religion and real philosophy are incapable of living side by side when subjected to inquiry or in human experience. With Pietro Pomponazzi's *De Immortalitate Animae* of 1516, reason separated from faith ("Anyone who wants to find the truth must be a heretic in philosophy"), and there was the formulation of a tragic "double truth" (Pomponazzi). Salutati may have succeeded in reading fate and fortune with Christian eyes, but the old, perennial question of free will, only shortly before treated by Lorenzo Valla and strenuously defended by Erasmus, is finally subjected to rigorous scrutiny by Luther and the thinkers of the Reformation. In the charged atmosphere of the time, the *indignitas hominis* (which harked back to Innocent III's *De Contemptu Mundi*, underlay Flemish mysticism, and was illustrated by the so-called "theological painters") had to deal with madness, anonymity, the distortion of nature (a metaphysical-religious prelude to present-day ecological problems), temptation, and the uncertainty of salvation.

The medieval conquest of the "inner person" is not disregarded, but it is replaced by the "natural person," and the conflict between flesh and spirit, body and mind (if not pushed to extremes by northern humanism and by the Reformation) is resolved in a heightened sensibility to all values. The human creatural condition is not denied, and the visible world becomes the place where blessedness begins; the medieval dialectical conception is no more exemplified by the "unhappy conscience" of the *Phenomenology of the Spirit* than the assertion

of aristocratic values is explained by the "reassessment of Christian values" of the *Antichrist.* The rebirth of old values accompanies the rebirth of the human being, but the awareness that "we are dwarfs carried on giants' shoulders" did not abandon reason so much as transform it into an ideological instrument. Continuity with the classical world was mediated by the Christian renascence as reflected not only in Joachim of Fiore and Francis of Assisi but also Dante and Petrarch. *De Vulgari Eloquentia* and *Convivio* convert the experience of poetry into an unveiling of reality, almost an *itinerarium in Deum.* The poet, argued Albertino Mussato (1261–1329), has the sacred function of revealing beings; poetry is a divine art, the philosophy and theology of the world. Poets were the first to speak to us of God. Even Boccaccio (1313–1375) believed that the profound meanings of mythology were in no way an attack on Christianity (*Genealogia Deorum*); indeed, poets were *pii homines* (*Vita di Dante*). Petrarch stands somewhere between Jerome's mistrust ("Ciceronian you are, but not Christian") and Erasmus's legitimate pride ("I have ensured that humanism—amongst the Italians, and the Romans in particular, it seemed to be little more than paganism— should take steps to celebrate Christ in a noble manner" [*Lettera a Maldonato*]). Petrarch, with his acute sense of the insufficiency of culture, settled for "Christus est Deus noster, Cicero autem princeps nostri eloquii" ("Christ is our God, Cicero the master of our language"); he dealt with this in *De sui ipsius et multorum ignorantia liber* (1367), although ignorance was more clearly expressed in Cusano's *De docta ignorantia* (1440) by reference to humanity's definitive state (*De visione Dei*).

There is a line of continuity running from Stoic *zōon logikon,* which has a background in Aristotle, the scholastic "animal rationale," and through Pascal's thoughtful "roseau pensant" to Kant's *Vernunft.* Humanism added grace and harmony to the unitary, medieval view of the world that has carried over in the modern period to Descartes' *cogito ergo sum* ("I think, therefore I am"), Berkeley's *esse est percipi* ("To be is to be perceived"), and Hegel's idea and absolute spirit. Moreover, humanism did so before magic (Giordano Bruno), and then science and technology upset the balance. Bloch's *Prinzip Hoffnung* (3 vols., 1954–59) with its eschatological, crypto-religious background to the dialectics of progress, Sartre's *L'existentialisme est un humanisme* (1946), and Heidegger's *Brief über den Humanismus* (1949) are only a few examples of humanism's survival. Furthermore, the enduring qualities of humanism inevitably give rise to problems, partly because times have changed but also because language has changed, too. Indeed, Sartre wrote, "I am condemned to be free, that is to say, the only limit to my freedom is freedom itself. Or, to put it in another way, we are not free to cease being free" (*L'être et le néant* [1943], 515). Heidegger's point of departure is very different, but it also seems to be more coherent, and it conveys very well the fundamental enduringness of humanism: "No question can be asked without the questioner being called into doubt and without the questioner himself becoming the question" (*What Is Metaphysics?*).

2. Toward a New World

Using Flavio Biondo's fundamental, although inevitably debatable, division into parts (*Evo Antico—Evo Medio—Evo Moderno*), we can say that the present period begins with the appearance of Petrarch as a major poetical figure in the first half of the fourteenth century. There is still debate, however, as to whether the period should go as far as the last thirty years of the fifteenth century or be allowed to include the death of Francis Bacon in 1626. All things considered, it does not really matter all that much. It is unquestionably more useful to recall the opposition in the Italian city-states of the mercantile aristocracy and the diminished importance of scholastic clerics and chivalry. One other critical event was the Council of Ferrara-Florence (1438–39); another was the fall of Constantinople (1453), which led to the spread of texts of Greek culture (including the Accademia Platonica of Florence and Ficino's *Theologiae Platonicae de immortalitate animarum libri XVIII* [1469–74]) and Plotinian mysticism. There was also interest in the cabala, and more generally in both Hebrew and Islamic culture and religion with irenic influences (see Cusano's *De pace fidei* [1453]), preceded by *De Gentili et Tribus Sapientibus* by Lull (1233?–1315?) and followed by the *Colloquium Heptaplomeres de Abditis Rerum Sublimium Arcanis* by Jean Bodin (1530–1596).

The Reformation accentuated and aggravated the problems of humanism—e.g., individualism and the criticism of philosophy and of scholastic theology. It also, in various ways, posed questions in areas such as natural theology, freedom of the individual, and the relationship between the individual and the community, and it did so to such an extent that it would be an understatement to talk of humanism in *crisis*. The notion that Rome better represented continuity with the past by saving Italy from the Reformation is open to quite different interpretations. What is important for us here is to emphasize the theme of madness as taken up in a satirical, anti-Lutheran manner (Thomas Murner, *Von dem grossen lutherischen Narren wie in doctor M. beschworen hat* [1523]).

Through Leonardo Bruni (1370–1444) as well as through philology (*De Studiis et Litteris*) and what we now call hermeneutics (*De Recta Interpretatione*), the *studia humanitatis* must "form the good man, than whom nothing more useful can be conceived of." Inevitably, with works such as Lorenzo Valla's *Adnotationes* and the Greek and Latin critical edition of the NT (1516) completed by Erasmus, and with the importance of philology, there was enthusiasm for a Christian humanism; this was set out in *Enchiridion militis christiani* (1503) and *Institutio principis christiani* (1516). The religious peace ("una religio in rituum varietate," *De pace fidei*) that was declared in the year that Constantinople fell to the Turks (1453) was itself an exhortation to tolerance—not the indifferentist tolerance of the Deists or the skeptical tolerance of the Enlightenment, but the convergence within Christianity of the only natural religion. Rational religion involved the existence of God and the immortality of the spiritual soul, itself open to revelation of the incarnation and the Trinity. In the unique *ordo catholicus universalis*, Cusano recognized the validity and legitimacy of the *conjecturae* that the human mind had developed over the centuries to represent divine reality. This was also the direction in which *Cribratio Alchorani*, published in 1461 and praised for its objectivity, was moving. Diversity and truth had to be reconciled in a harmonious way, and only Christianity was capable of comprehending all the faiths. The face of God was now visible as if through a veil, *in aenigmate*; everyone conceived of him in his or her own image and likeness until in the end he revealed himself (*De visione Dei*). To achieve the *concordantia catholica*, i.e., the unity of all peoples within the Christian doctrine, the church had to undergo internal reformation, a renewal. More and more voices were being raised even prior to the moment when the Reformation burst upon us. Savonarola rejected pagan culture ("Ecce Magi relinquunt gentilitatem et ad Christum veniunt et tu, relicto Christo, curris ad gentilitatem," *Discourse on the Epiphany*) and was against accepting any *docta religio* or *pia quaedam philosophia*, a polemical reference to Marsilio Ficino's *De christiana religione liber* (1474).

3. Humanism and Antihumanism

The argument was complicated with the introduction of cabalistic and mystery elements. In *Conclusiones philosophicae, cabalisticae et theologicae* (1486), Pico della Mirandola introduced the universal theosophical tradition, alongside the philosophical and religious tradition, into Christian truth; in his introduction to his translation of *Corpus hermeticum*, Marsilio Ficino wrote that he considered the mythical Mercurius Trismegistus to be "the original founder of philosophy," a true theologian. According to Giordano Bruno (1548–1600), the occult *philosophia* of Agrippa von Nettesheim became the apologia for a new religion consisting of art, philosophy, mathematics, and magic and retaining the ancient magic religion that had been obscured and corrupted by Judaism and Christianity. Its diseased nature ("Sometimes things that appear to us are not true: sometimes we dream them up in their presence," in Ficino, *Theologia platonica* 14.7) was splendidly captured in Dürer's copper engraving *Melancholia*.

Meanwhile, a school of thought developed in southern Europe that was opposed to humanism and had been inspired by the mystical, trinitarian, and christocentric experience of Jan van Ruysbroeck (1293–1381) and the Brothers of the Common Life. It was such mystical writing, and the even earlier *Vita Antonii* by Athanasius, that inspired the works of the theologian painters such as Bosch and Bruegel, the iconography of *Ars moriendi*, and the obsession with demonism in Jacob Sprenger's *Malleus maleficarum* (ca. 1484). The *indignitas*

hominis is rooted in the *insecuritas* of salvation, distrusts reason ("Aristotle ridden by the prostitute"), and takes refuge in anonymity ("Nemo"). The sadism of reason and the madness of the person seeking to cure madness ("Extracting the stone of madness") became a destructive irony, an ethical and religious appeal in Erasmus's *Moriae Encomium* (1509) or an evasion, which is certainly not ingenuous, in Thomas More's *Utopia* (1516).

An artist of the stature of Michelangelo who could live the yearnings of the Reformation without surrendering to the claims of the Counter-Reformation was needed to interpret the human condition with modern sensibility and perfection of form.

Bibl.: J. BURCKHARDT, *La civilisation de l'Italie au temps de la Renaissance* (1860); E. CASTELLI, ed., *L'Umanesimo e "la Follia"* (Rome, 1972); E. CASSIRER, *Individu et cosmos dans la philosophie de la Renaissance* (Paris, 1983); E. GARIN, ed., *Medioevo e Rinascimento* (Rome/Bari, 1987); id., *L'uomo del Rinascimento* (Rome/Bari, 1988).

Salvatore SPERA

II. CHRISTIAN HUMANISM

In contemporary usage the term "humanism" carries strongly secular if not atheistic overtones and can mean almost any kind of concern with human values. It is more usually associated with the modern German elaborations of philosophical humanism (Feuerbach, Marx, or Heidegger), with the existential humanism of Jean-Paul Sartre, or with contemporary secular humanisms. The root problem concerning the meaning of the word "humanism" seems to lie in the fact that the Latin word *humanus* has carried three distinct meanings: (1) human, or pertaining to human nature; (2) humane, meaning benevolent or compassionate; and (3) a learned person, as in the customary address to a scholar as *humanissime vir*. Modern humanisms tend to use the first two meanings and ignore the third, but an older tradition began with the third and believed that through a study of the humanities a scholar would come to understand the meaning of *humanitas*, what it means to be truly human.

1. Renaissance Christian Humanism

The word "humanism," first coined in 1808 by the German scholar F. J. Niethammar, was clearly derived from a similar word *humanista* (Ital. *umanista*) used at the time of the Renaissance for a professor, teacher, or student of the *studia humanitatis*. The *humanae litterae* emphasized five subjects in particular, all concerned with language or morals: grammar, rhetoric, poetry, history, and ethics. In each of these areas it was necessary to read and interpret the classical Greek and Latin authors. Most of the *umanisti* belonged to one of three professional groups: teachers at the universities or secondary schools; secretaries in the employment of princes, cities, or the church; or individuals who had the wealth and leisure to combine study with their other obligations. They were a significant and influential segment of the Italian and later the wider European Renaissance. Though many lived relatively obscure lives, a good number were distinguished scholars and public figures. These included Francesco Petrarch and Coluccio Salutati in the fourteenth century, Lorenzo Valla, Marsilio Ficino, and Giovanni Pico della Mirandola in the fifteenth, and across the Alps in the sixteenth century Desiderius Erasmus, Thomas More, Johannes Reuchlin, Juan Luis Vivés, Lefevre D'Etaples, Guillaume Budé, and many others.

Throughout the Christian tradition other scholars from Augustine to Karl Rahner have been recognized as Christian humanists. But the title belongs in a very precise and specific sense to the Christian *umanisti* of the Renaissance who caught the spirit of their times and sought to articulate their convictions about human and Christian life as these intersected with contemporary concerns. At its core Renaissance humanism was neither religious nor irreligious, but most, if not all, of the *umanisti* were believing Christians, many devoted to the renewal of Christendom. This article will explore their specific contribution to the religion and theology of their age. That contribution is to be found in their rhetorical style of writing, in their scholarly and critical treatment of religious texts, in their new vision of history, and in their ability to relate their anthropological and existential concerns to contemporary religious questions. Furthermore, as Kristeller shows, the way that scholars brought their humanist training to bear upon the Christian sources and theological subjects was an important factor in the great changes of Christianity in the early modern period. The attempts of these thinkers, who were often laymen in a secular profession, to read the signs of their own times is of particular interest for Christians of the post–Vatican II church.

2. The Rhetorical Tradition of Eloquence

The precise nature of Renaissance humanism is still a much-debated issue, since it embraced philosophical, political, ethical, educational, and aesthetic interests. However, Paul Oskar Kristeller's thesis that it was primarily a cultural and educational movement concerned with oral and written eloquence has gained wide acceptance. To view Renaissance humanism as a characteristic phase within the rhetorical tradition of Western culture provides a single unifying approach to a remarkably diverse and multifaceted movement. The central concern of the humanists was less the substance or content of ideas—though this remained important—but rather more how ideas were obtained, expressed, and communicated. They were concerned with the significance of language and with speech as *the* most characteristic of human endowments. Theirs was a "philosophy of discourse," and they had an acute sense of the importance of having learning occur in the context of human communication. This was to have a direct bearing on their understanding of God's self-revelation to humankind through the *Word* made flesh.

As a professional class, the humanists were in direct continuity with the medieval *dictatores*, who taught and practiced the art of composing documents, letters, and public speeches. But the humanists also believed that in order to speak and write well it was necessary to study and imitate the ancient classical authors. To this end they initiated a program of reviving classical Greek and Latin languages and literature through the recovery, editing, and careful study of as wide a range of material as possible. At the same time, they developed the skills of textual and historical criticism. Fruitful contacts with Byzantine scholars enabled the discovery of many Greek classical authors largely unknown in the medieval West. They introduced Greek into universities and schools and recovered almost the entire extant corpus of Greek literature, including Greek patristic theology. They also translated or retranslated most of this literature into Latin so that it would reach a wider readership. Thus the humanists were responsible for a very distinctive and influential movement that not only led to a revival of the humanities but in time meant that nearly every scholar received a basic humanistic training at school that was to be the foundation of future studies in all disciplines. The "new learning" was an influential component of education in both the Protestant Reformation and the Catholic reform movements. Both the Jesuit *ratio studiorum* and the English public school curriculum were indebted to it.

3. The Renaissance Philosophy of Man

Humanism was not simply a movement generating an academic enthusiasm for the retrieval of classical literature. It was related to a quest for intellectual and moral development through contact with some of the greatest minds and lives of the past. The humanists were much indebted to classical philosophy. Some were professional philosophers, like Ficino, Pico and Egidio of Viterbo (Platonists), and Pietro Pomponazzi, who represented the Paduan-Bolognese Aristotelian tradition. But the perception that the humanist movement was not basically a philosophical one is correct. Renaissance humanists were primarily interested in practical or moral philosophy, which included political philosophy. They sought the *ars bene beateque vivendi*, or the wisdom or philosophy that did not remain at the theoretical level but could be translated into the ordinary, everyday, urban world of human living.

What has loosely been called the Renaissance philosophy of humanity corresponds more exactly to an early form of religious anthropology. Christian humanists shaped their distinctive ideas on human nature and the human predicament, they were influenced by several currents of thought, of which two were central: the classical concepts of *humanitas* (Gk. *paideia*) and *virtus*, and the medieval tradition of discussion on the *conditio hominis*. *Humanitas* was that civilizing and "cultural" ethos acquired by growing up in a particular society. The Greeks and Romans saw it as a participation in a universal *vera humanitas* rather than as specifically their own; however, their superior *mores* enabled them to acquire *humanitas*, whereas those of the barbarians or the *vulgus* did not. *Humanitas* also came to mean the bondedness and sympathy that arise from a recognition of the similarity and universality of all human experience: "Homo sum, humani nihil a me alienum puto" ("I am a man, and nothing human leaves me insensible" [Terence]). It was embodied in the *vir humanus* who sought to communicate with others, to console, enhearten, enliven, and form friendships. Speech, after all, is the common possession of humankind. Time, place, and circumstances determine the appropriateness of its expression. Charles Trinkaus has shown that the humanist ideal of *vir humanus*—the sage—intersected with that of the Christian saint to provide a new ideal of lay piety and civic holiness. For Erasmus (d. 1536) it was to provide the christological model for the "Word made speech for us." God's divine wisdom had taken the form of human eloquence that accommodated itself to the human condition.

A further key to the humanist understanding of human nature was the classical concept of *virtus*, which was retrieved in its original meaning of "uttermost energy." The ancients believed that the human predicament was essentially a struggle between a person's will and Fortune's willfulness. The Romans worshiped the goddess Fortuna, who turned the wheel of a person's fate according to her capricious will. Whereas the Greeks submitted to *moira* (fate), the Romans admired the person who stood up and succeeded against destiny. *Fortuna* can be subdued and tamed by *virtus*. Human beings can shape their own destinies. The great source of this philosophy of self-reliant action was Plutarch's *Vitae parallelae*, forty-eight lives of great men of classical times. Translated from Greek into Latin by various humanists, these narratives enjoyed great popularity, and were first printed ca. 1470. The *Vitae* and also Petrarch's *De viris illustribus* (1337) corresponded exactly to the reading interests of the new social class, the bourgeoisie, whose knowledge of biography and history was thus considerably extended. History was seen as a resource from which many *exempla* (precedents) could be gathered. They shared Seneca's view: "Long is the way if one follows exhortations, but short and efficacious if one follows patterns."

This affirmative and optimistic view of the power of human beings to shape their own destinies was only gradually incorporated into a late medieval Christian view of God's providence, omnipotence, and grace. The symbol of *homo triumphans* in the later Renaissance was first voiced as a "remedy and alternative spiritual strategy for the moral sickness of a guilt-ridden overburdened conscience" (Trinkaus 1982:455). A long tradition of discussion and writing on the *conditio hominis*, seen under the complementary aspects of human dignity and human misery, was part of the Renaissance heritage. Human beings are subject to either exaggerated optimism or pessimism as they experience the ups and downs of life. They need to be counseled against despair or arrogance. However, there is much evidence that by the mid-trecento, the age of the black death, it was the image of human misery and helplessness that prevailed. Francesco Petrarch (ca. 1304–1374) realized that despair over one's misfortune often generated a sense of religious guilt. In his *De remediis utriusque fortunae* he offered advice for cultivating a kind of double awareness: in time of success be aware of human suffering, in time of despair be aware of the dignity of the human person. More significantly, he showed how human beings, under grace, could take responsibility for their own subjectivity, offering a sense of personal dignity that was compatible with piety and a theodicy for religious faith in the midst of the horrors of the age.

People of the Renaissance were to fully "make trial of their own powers" and did so as Christians by reviving the earlier patristic exegesis on the text of Genesis, "Let us make humankind in our image and likeness" (Gn 1:26). Augustine himself had seen a correspondence between the Trinity and the triple functions of the human soul. Father, Son, and Spirit were imaged by human memory, understanding, and will. Greater familiarity with patristic theology led the humanists to understand that divine creativity could be a model for human creativity. Human beings could shape their own destinies and create their own culture and civilization. They had the ability to confront and solve many of the problems they faced by

applying human reason and ingenuity. "Man was certainly not born to pine away in indolence but to stand up and do things," wrote Alberti in *De iciarchia*. This was not presumption or pride but part of God's creative intention for humankind.

Human dignity became a favorite theme of humanistic oratory and was significantly developed by Marsilio Ficino (1433–1499), Giovanni Pico della Mirandola (1463–1494), Pietro Pomponazzi (1464–1525), and the Spanish humanist Juan Luiz Vivés (1492–1540). Poggio Bracciolini (1380–1459), however, continued to focus on the theme of human misery, rejecting consolatory rhetoric and any merely human means of escaping from the miseries of life. He represents the darker and less optimistic side of Renaissance reflection on the human condition, one closest to that of the Reformation. But Giannozza Manetti (1396–1459) and Pico gave full expression to the ideal of the God-like person, who was energetic, creative, and constantly acting. In the second part of Pico's famous *Oratio*, usually misnamed *On the Dignity of Man* (1484), God addresses Adam: "We have made thee neither of heaven nor of earth, neither mortal nor immortal, so that with freedom of choice and with honor, as though the maker and molder of thyself, thou mayest fashion thyself in whatever shape thou shalt prefer." The theme of human creation in the image and likeness of God was to radically change ideas of both divinity and humanity in Renaissance religious thought. Human beings were not only the guardians of God's original creation but through their inventiveness and ingenuity were the creators of the "second nature" of civilized existence.

4. History under Providence: Stoicism or Augustinianism?

It would be a mistake, however, to suggest that humanists' ideas on human dignity and freedom anticipated the spirit of the Enlightenment, or "man's release from his self-incurred tutelage" (Kant). Jacob Burckhardt's thesis of Renaissance individualism has given way to a more nuanced view of humanist growth in self-awareness with the help of God's grace and within the Christian community. The Renaissance humanists struggled to understand and articulate the precise relationship between human freedom and human dependence upon God's grace, between history as shaped by human beings and God's providence, between the knowledge gained from human experience and that revealed by God. In their search for answers to these questions, Renaissance humanists drew upon two sets of opposing and antithetical ideas represented by the rhetorical traditions of Stoicism and Augustinianism. For Stoic writers such as Seneca and Cicero, God was the immanent, all-pervading energy by which the natural world was created. Human beings participated in this "world soul" through their reason, understood as the divine spark or seed within them. The highest good was to live according to the law of their own nature and reason, disregarding the misfortunes and pleasures of contemporary existence. The ideal of the wise and virtuous person, who lived by reason, avoiding the perturbation of mind that resulted from contact with the outer world, was at times very attractive to humanist scholars. Stoicism was classicist and resistant to change, since the latter usually meant a deviation from eternal, perennially valid, and so perennially retrievable principles. It also provided a bridge between classical antiquity and Christianity.

But Stoicism had no remedy to offer for the misery of the great majority of humankind. Augustine, in contrast, spoke directly to Everyman, as engaged in a political life in an urban setting (*The City of God*), and as involved in the inner struggles of his complex personality (*The Confessions*). Augustine operated within the actual dynamic of human experience. For him to *know* the good was not enough; the real problem was how to *do* the good, for the center of human life lay in the heart, not the intellect. Only the heart could be touched by grace. Augustine stressed the disjunction between nature and grace, the uniqueness of the Christian revelation of God in Jesus Christ. Even more significantly, he saw God's purposes worked out in the messy, unpredictable, disordered patterns of human history and human behavior. In contrast to Stoic self-sufficiency Augustine yearned for the grace of God. His emphasis on human subjectivity before God and the primacy of the will over the intellect profoundly influenced humanist thought. But some of its complexity, ambiguity, and inconsistency is often the consequence of attempting to harmonize elements from Stoic and Augus-

tinian traditions. Erasmus (1466–1536) tended toward Stoicism, while Valla (ca. 1406–1457) was markedly more Augustinian. This dialectic at the heart of Christian humanism would partly account for radical differences in the options of the humanists at the time of the Reformation.

The humanists' view of history under Providence came to differ considerably from that of preceding generations. The role assigned to human choice and responsibility in shaping and determining events led them to recognize that any given present state of affairs need not have been so, and could have been different. It was possible to trace a way back into the past and re-create it in the present. It was possible to project an ideal of what might be for the future and use it as a stimulus to create something better than the present, as in Thomas More's *Utopia*. This was a wholly new way to view past, present, and future, the early stirrings of what we would call change and evolution in history. From the time of Petrarch onward, humanists invented the concept of the Middle Ages or Dark Ages, lying between classical civilization and their own. The Christian-providential view of the past had equated the birth of Christ with the dispelling of darkness from the human condition. There were two periods—the age of preparation and the age of the gospel. The new humanist view of history equated darkness with the sack of Rome (A.D. 410) and the subsequent decline of culture and civilization. History was more usually divided into three periods: antiquity, the Middle Ages, and the present, which had potential for either progress or decline. As Christians, the humanists continually sought to relate rather than to distinguish between sacred history and secular history. Both were within and under God's providence. But they had a strong perception that God's revealed truth and God's grace were offered within a concrete historical context.

Despite a nostalgia for classical culture valid for all time, humanist classicism actually led them to a sense of cultural and linguistic conditionedness. Their sense of history made them acutely aware not only of the continuity but also of the radical discontinuity between past and present; the past had to be studied on its own terms. This was the beginning of the science of hermeneutics, the application of linguistic and historical criticism to the texts of the ancient world. Scholars such as Lorenzo Valla, Angelo Poliziano (1459–1494), and Guillaume Budé (1467–1540) studied the texts of Roman law as embodied in the Code of Justinian. They gradually came to see that far from being a homogeneous body of law, the code was a "loosely assembled and poorly translated series of enactments designed for a long defunct empire, with little or no bearing on the very different legal and political conditions of early modern Europe" (Skinner, 207). One of the most unsettling discoveries was Lorenzo Valla's proof that the so-called *Donation of Constantine* was a forgery from the eighth or ninth century. Papal claims to temporal authority in the West and spiritual primacy over the four imperial patriarchates had been based on the now discredited document.

Humanist scholars also applied their new skills to the study of biblical texts. The scholastic method had favored either a direct analytical assault on a text or the collation of texts around a specific theme or doctrinal point. The humanists read the NT not as a source for theological ideas but as a record of *early Christian experience transmitted in a literary and historical form*. They related each text directly to its historical context. For example, when John Colet, on his return from Italy to Oxford in 1497, lectured on Paul's Epistle to the Romans, he related it to the context of imperial Rome in the reign of Emperor Claudius and to the reasons why Paul exhorted *Roman* Christians to act circumspectly. Paul addressed a specific audience, using words that had a precise meaning at that time. As subsequent transcriptions or translations could obscure or misrepresent the original meaning, humanists sought to provide newer and more exact translations of the ancient Greek and Hebrew texts. Valla undertook a critical comparison between the Vulgate and the Greek NT. Erasmus, drawing on Valla's *Annotations on the New Testament* (1449) and his own collation of texts, issued his parallel Greek and Latin version of the NT in 1516. He strongly advocated the availability of the Scriptures in the vernacular. Manetti began the study of Hebrew under a young Jewish scholar, consulted medieval Hebrew biblical commentaries, and assembled a small library of Hebrew manuscripts. Johannes Reuchlin (1455–1522) taught himself Hebrew and Greek and in 1506 published his *Rudiments of Hebrew*, combined with a Hebrew-Latin dictionary. Trilingual colleges were established in many northern universities and in 1520 the first polyglot Bible, commissioned by Cardinal Ximénez de Cisneros, was printed at the new University of Alcalá.

5. Theologia Rhetorica

The Renaissance humanists were not usually professional theologians, yet in a variety of ways the *studia humanitatis* impinged upon the *studia divinitatis* and had a vital contribution to make to it. The humanists' renewal of biblical studies is well known, as is also the predictable scholastic hostility to their method and discoveries. But until comparatively recently their contribution to the theological and religious thought of the age has received less attention because it was concealed in an informal, unsystematic, and highly rhetorical body of humanistic writings. Aware of the human person as a living, feeling subject, they avoided the "clenched fist" of scholastic dialectical method and substituted the "open palm" of rhetorical discourse (Thomas More, *Letter to Dorp* [1515]). They used the treatise, the dialogue, the lay sermon, and the essay to communicate persuasively their preferred religious themes. Other literary genres included funeral orations, letters, admonitions, historiography, and biography. Such material provides much information about the religious and intellectual preferences of educated laypeople engaged in a life of creative service and Christian piety. Trinkaus and others have called this concealed humanistic theology a *theologia rhetorica*, partly because of the style of writing, but also because the humanists deliberately sought to combine the intellectual function of the theologian with the pastoral and affective function of the preacher. They were convinced that neither contemporary scholastic theology nor the current styles of preaching and spiritual guidance met their actual needs and aspirations.

The correlation between the rhetoric of classical oratory and Christian preaching was even more obvious to the humanists than it is to us. Effective orators or effective preachers must by definition be in touch with the feelings of their audience and be responsive to them. Humanists were well aware that a renewal of biblical studies would remain a barren exercise if not translated into an effective ministry of the word that would move people to lead lives of greater Christian depth. So they tried to determine what kinds of language, reasoning, *exempla*, or styles of delivery would best produce meaningful persuasion and corresponding action. They were aware that the ministry of the word extended beyond the pulpit to forms of catechesis, counseling, or the dialogue between confessor and penitent. Many asked whether current sacramental theory or practice *affectively* touched the core of a person's subjectivity before God—the areas of conscience, inwardness, choice, fear, and anxiety. They did not seek to replace but rather to deepen current sacramental understanding. But they attached more importance to the formation of conscience than to external formalities. Many humanists were to assume the role of lay counselors and were convinced that it was necessary to have a theological and pastoral synthesis adequate to the lived experience of Christians living a secular life in the world. It follows that in an unthematic way they were concerned about the credibility of the gospel in relation to contemporary life.

The rhetorical interest in how to influence and move people both as individuals and as groups was directly related to humanist understanding of the way in which the faith is transmitted. They did not underestimate faith as a gift of God nor the role of the Spirit but highlighted rather the human sensibilities of the one who receives this gift. As educators, they were convinced that the transmission of truth took place within a community setting and through a meeting of minds rather than in academic isolation. The act of faith involved the whole person, intellect and feelings as well as the external context in which the Christian life was led. They were much more aware than their predecessors of the knowledge gained from personal and shared experience as this impinged on their Christian faith. As they understood something of the extent to which human experience is historically and linguistically conditioned, they realized that this was also true of the transmission of the faith from apostolic times to the present. Hence there was a need to reach back *ad fontes* to the *vera theologia*, the sources of revelation contained in the Bible. *Theologia Rhetorica* was biblical, historical, anthropocentric, and experiential in

its scope and content. Erasmus's *Ratio verae theologiae* (1513) formulated the ideals of this theology programmatically with its sketch of a biblically based formation for the enterprise transforming contemporary society through a fresh communication of the gospel of Christ.

6. Christians in Relation to Pagans and Jews

It was difficult, if not impossible, to engage in so much discussion on the human condition without an awareness that it is shared by all peoples of differing cultures, faiths, and personal histories. Not only human experience but also religious experience seemed to be a universal phenomenon, and all religious traditions had something of the divine within them. In dealing with pre-Christian pagan religions, the humanists tried to eliminate elements that were clearly incompatible with Christian values—e.g., the obscenity, sensuality, and cruelty of many pagan rites. But there remained a core of genuine religious beliefs and practices that could be said to anticipate or even replicate those of the Christian era. The crux of the problem lay in the fact that God's gracious accommodation to the human condition as made visible in Jesus Christ meant that the Christian experience was a profoundly human one, yet also unique and separate. The themes of accommodation and separateness, continuity and discontinuity are frequently addressed in humanist writings. Many came to see Christianity as the complete revelation of what had been partially and imperfectly revealed in other traditions. Pre-Christian faiths, at their best, could serve as a preparation for the gospel. In God's providential plan, this was preeminently the role of Judaism. But the more usual view was that Judaism had been superseded by Christianity and only the willfully blind could ignore the evidence.

It was far easier to forge a retrospective reconciliation of pagan and Jewish faiths in the past than to deal with rival beliefs in the present. One can hardly overestimate contemporary Christian fear and hate of the invading Muslim "infidel," equated in popular imagination with "the scourge of God." Such a theodicy was not entirely absent from humanistic writers, nor were they free from anti-Semitism. The usually pacifist Erasmus observed that "if it is the part of a good Christian to hate the Jews, then we are all good Christians." Nevertheless humanists went further than most of their predecessors or contemporaries in arriving at an intellectual and religious accommodation of non-Christian faiths to that of Christianity.

Most humanist writers had a vision of the unitary nature of truth in the diversity of religious experience. Manetti's study of Hebrew with a Jewish scholar made him very sensitive to the thought world from which Christianity had emerged. He was one of the first to see Western Christian tradition as nurtured by both a Hellenism and a Hebraism. Yet Manetti's *Contra Iudeos et Gentes* (1454) was a defense of Christianity and a critique of paganism and Judaism as religions now historically superseded. However, he sought to persuade and convince Jews of their erroneous ways rather than to blame them directly for blindness. Marsilio Ficino wrote his *De religione christiana* in 1447, which influenced the later apologetical writings of Vivés, Duplessis-Mornay, Charron, and Grotius. It can be considered an early work of fundamental theology. Ficino was interested in religion as a universal characteristic of humankind, in how to distinguish good from bad religion, the true from the false. He considered that God's providence has permitted "a universal but partial revelation to all men, true and perfect revelation to a chosen few, all as part of a design for the opening of ultimate revelation and the possibility of salvation to all" (Trinkaus 1970:737). Pico, in the second part of his *Oration*, put forward a plan for a philosophical and theological peace. He sought a synthesis from among the variety of religious approaches to the truth. He listed those Christian authors who had most influenced him but added Arab scholars (Averroes, Avicenna, etc.), the Greeks, and the Jewish tradition through the cabala. His search for a mystical, esoteric universal revelation was more elitist than that of his contemporaries.

In 1492 Columbus discovered the natives of the New World and filled his diaries with references to the gentle, beautiful people of Hispaniola, who seemed eminently ready to receive the Christian faith. Thomas More's *Utopia* (1516) captured some of the contemporary interest in the idea of the noble savage. It is a fictitious narrative that presents a community of human beings untouched by either pagan classical civilization or the Christian religion. Yet through the use of their human intelligence and ingenuity they had arrived not only at a high degree of civilization but also at a highly developed belief in God, providence, morality, and the immortality of the soul. According to More, it was clear that evangelization was not identical with either civilization or education, but that they could develop reciprocally. The Utopians were ready to receive the gospel and in some respects were more admirable than many so-called Christians in Europe. Clearly More thought that a rational religion and philosophy could shape a just and equitable society, and that such could be a sure foundation for subsequent evangelization.

7. Erasmus against Fideism

Though recent scholarship is wary of attributing the word "Erasmian" to the rich diversity of sixteenth-century humanism, the characteristics of Christian humanist writers are summed up in a striking way in the work of Desiderius Erasmus, Prince of Humanists. An early work of Erasmus, the *Antibarbari* (1489, rev. 1494–1521), illustrates very clearly a humanist attack on contemporary forms of fideism and can serve as a summary and conclusion to this article. *Antibarbari* has more usually been seen as a veiled attack on Erasmus's scholastic critics in Louvain, but a recent and convincing analysis suggests that it was intended as the first part of a projected four-volume work rebutting the arguments of the main opponents of humanism (Bradshaw, 412). Early in the work Erasmus identifies three groups of such opponents: those who totally reject the classical heritage, those who partially reject it, and those who accept it too enthusiastically. Bradshaw convincingly identifies these groups as (1) those who reject secular learning and make undue claims for revelation and grace, such as *barbari* or contemporary fideists; (2) those who accept classical philosophy but reject rhetoric and literature, such as the scholastics; and (3) those who make undue claims for human reason and nature and undervalue Christian revelation and grace, such as enthusiastic humanist scholars who were in fact contemporary reductionists.

Erasmus deals with the third group—the enemy within his own camp—in *Ciceronianus*. He attacks his scholastic enemies in *Praise of Folly* (1511) and elsewhere. But the scholastics are his natural, if uneasy, allies in his fight against anti-intellectual elements in the church. *Antibarbari* is not a polemic against the scholastics but a direct assault on those who most undermined the humanist enterprise—the antirationalists whom later theologians would call fideists.

Two powerful and related movements in late medieval Christianity can be associated with a fideist position. First, the *theological position* of William of Ockham and his school, who shared in a tradition stretching back to Tertullian, which stressed the uniqueness and exclusiveness of revealed knowledge available through grace, while disparaging the knowledge acquired through human reason and experience. Second, there existed a *spiritual tradition* of evangelical simplicity and worldly renunciation that advocated a "holy ignorance," since God's Holy Spirit alone illuminated the hearts of the faithful. Erasmus saw many of the religious orders as bastions of antirationalist fideism, especially those who had undergone a fundamentalist kind of renewal. This outlook was also characteristic of the lay spirituality of the *devotio moderna* as expressed in the very influential *Imitation of Christ*: "Leave off that excessive desire of learning because there is found therein much distraction and deceit" (1.2). Thus the *Antibarbari* gives a Christian humanist answer to the age-old question of Tertullian, "What has Athens to do with Jerusalem?"

The rhetorical conventions of Renaissance polemic make it difficult for us to grasp readily the theological content of Erasmus's arguments. What would have most impressed his contemporaries is least helpful to us. Essentially he outlined an earlier version of his *Philosophia Christi* that he later developed more fully in the *Paraclesis* (1516). Erasmus's christological model was not the prophet but the Divine Master and teacher of wisdom, who came as the culmination of the long human search for truth and goodness. Plato's ideal philosopher found its perfect expression in Christ. Reason and nature, especially as represented in the classical tradition, were the divinely ordained agents of revelation and grace. To express the precise relationship between pre-Christian paganism and Christianity, Erasmus rejected Augustine's metaphor of "spoiling the Egyptians," or appropriating

what was valuable from the pagan heritage for the benefit of Christianity. He preferred Jerome's metaphor of the freeman marrying the captive slave in order to procure her freedom. Christianity lovingly appropriated the classical heritage so that it now had its place within the new setting.

Erasmus deployed a Platonic concept of existence as unity in diversity, an ordered relationship of all the parts to the whole. *Nature and grace* are not in conflict but in harmony, so that the human search for excellence is an integral part of the Christian search for sanctification. Similarly *reason and revelation* are not mutually exclusive, since both are directed to the truth. Christ as the incarnation of God's truth and goodness brings to perfection the natural processes. Furthermore, if virtue is the proper object of reason (Plato), the idea of holy ignorance is simply nonsense. Christ as the Word of God communicated with his disciples through human speech and accommodated himself to the human condition, so that it is a graced condition. Christ is permanently present to his church in the form of the scriptural word, and so linguistic and rhetorical skills are essential for the transmission of the Christian message. Finally Erasmus deployed the parable of the talents (Lk 19:11–27) in support of the use rather than the denial of human giftedness. God has actually commanded us to "make trial of our own powers."

Erasmus's most important defense of the freedom of the human will took place against Luther (1524–26). Of all the issues that he might have taken up, he chose this one because it seemed to him that Luther's theology was a version of fideism, albeit as a radically and brilliantly reformulated version of it. Luther, for his part, had already rejected Erasmus's *philosophia Christi* on the grounds that human power weighs more with Eramsus than divine. But Luther commended Erasmus for really grasping what was at stake. Luther believed that contemporary Catholic understanding of the role of human reason and will in the process of salvation was Pelagian and that it underestimated the unique power of God's grace. Luther saw the doctrine of "facienti quod in se est, Deus non denegat gratiam" ("God does not refuse grace to one who does his best") as being tantamount to saying that God's grace is not a free initiative but instead the reward for human effort. The debate between Eramus and Luther over the freedom or bondage of the human will was fraught with consequences for the future of Christendom. But it cannot be fully understood without reference to humanist reflections on divinity and humanity during the previous centuries.

8. Conclusion

The *theologia rhetorica* of the Renaissance humanists as it unfolded and developed in its variety and pluralism from the mid-fourteenth to the late sixteenth century was one of the most affirmative and creative articulations of lay theology within the whole Christian tradition. It had its obvious limitations. It can rightly be criticized as too elitist, deliberately distancing itself from the concerns and preferences of the *vulgus*, just as its classical counterpart had done. Today we would recognize that it was also sexist. Peter Burke has noted that of six hundred listed Italian Renaissance artists, writers, and humanists, only three were woman: Vittoria Colunna, Veronica Gambara, and Tullia d'Aragona. All three were poets and came near the end of the period. Contemporary ecological movements reject the anthropocentric orientation of both Renaissance and modern humanisms, which seem to place humankind in dominion over nature, of which we are all a part. But despite certain limitations, Renaissance Christian humanism remains a rich source for reflection on the human condition and human experience in its universal quest for religious and moral fulfillment, and for an understanding of God's revelation in Jesus Christ as the culmination of this search.

Bibl.: K. RAHNER, "Christian Humanism," in *Theological Investigations*, vol. 9 (1967; London, 1972), 187–204; C. TRINKAUS, *In Our Image and Likeness: Humanity and Divinity in Italian Renaissance Thought*, 2 vols. (Chicago/London, 1970); id., "The Religious Thought of the Italian Humanists and the Reformers," in C. Trinkaus and H. E. Oberman, eds., *The Pursuit of Holiness in Late Medieval and Renaissance Religion* (Leiden, 1974), 339–66; id., *The Scope of Renaissance Humanism* (Ann Arbor, 1983), 343–404; P. BURKE, *The Italian Renaissance: Culture and Society in Italy* (Oxford, 1972; rev. ed. 1986); W. BOUWSMA, "Two Faces of Humanism: Stoicism and Augustinianism in Renaissance Thought," in H. A. Oberman and T. A. Brady, eds., *Itinerarium Italicum* (Leiden, 1975), 3–60; Q. SKINNER, *The Foundations of Modern Political Thought*, vol. 1 (Cambridge, 1978); P. O. KRISTELLER, *Renaissance Thought and Its Sources* (New York, 1979); J. O'MALLEY, *Praise and Blame in Renaissance Rome: Rhetoric, Doctrine, and Reform in the Sacred Orators of the Papal Court* (Durham, N.C., 1979), cols. 1450–1521; id., "Introduction," *Collected Works of Erasmus*, vol. 66 (Toronto, 1988), ix–li; B. BRADSHAW, "The Christian Humanism of Erasmus," *JTS* 33 (1982): 411–47; V. R. GIUSTINIANI, "Homo, Humanus and the Meanings of Humanism," *Journal of the History of Ideas* 46 (1985): 167–95.

Anne MURPHY

III. ATHEISTIC HUMANISM

1. Explanation of the Term

The term "humanism" is one of the most overworked catchwords of our time, and what it signifies is therefore also highly ambiguous and imprecise. It must not, however, be confused with "philanthropy" (love of humanity), which is limited, in practice, to charitable benefaction; it does not necessarily regard humans as the highest value, nor does it necessarily have the "humanization" of humans as its goal. Both of these are, however, essential characteristics of humanism.

In the narrow sense, humanism refers to the *cultural ideal* of the (Italian) Renaissance in the fourteenth and fifteenth centuries, which was oriented toward the study of classical antiquity. But precisely the study of classical literature and the intellectual world of antiquity led to the formation of a new self-understanding. Humanity became conscious of itself as the creator of both itself and the world. At the center was the ideal of the *uomo universale*, the personality that is developed in every aspect, physically and intellectually (see P. O. Kristeller, *Humanismus und Renaissance*, vol. 1 [Munich, 1973]).

In the wider sense, the concept represents movements and intellectual outlooks that include a strong anthropocentric component. Thus the notion became linked to the rationalistic and humanitarian ideas that were developed in the period following the Enlightenment. Humanity becomes the "measure of all things," is declared the highest value for humanity itself, and is essentially characterized by his liberty. It is therefore hardly surprising if the radically anthropocentric orientation of humanism not infrequently takes on an antireligious cast, turning into explicit ATHEISM. Negation of God follows from the affirmation of the central position of humanity and its freedom. God's freedom and that of humanity are seen as mutually exclusive. God appears to stand in the way of the human striving for self-realization.

In his *Fröhliche Wissenschaft* (Joyful science), Nietzsche captured this outlook in a striking image. The religious person is compared to a lake whose water flows out into God and is therefore deprived of self-realization. Not until the lake has been blocked by a dam, so that its water no longer flows into God but actually rises higher, can a person achieve his or her self-realization, but now apart from God (fragment 285). The extent to which a particular image of God can "poison" an individual's life is illustrated quite vividly by the German psychoanalyst Tilmann Moser in his autobiographical work *Gottesvergiftung* (The Poisoning of God) (Frankfurt am Main, 1977). There, the author describes his liberation from the image of God he acquired in childhood, which he holds responsible for his feelings of guilt, his self-hatred, his self-destruction, and the futility of his life. The God of his childhood, from which he frees himself through psychoanalysis, had hindered him from finding himself as a human being and seeking others as human beings.

2. Systems, Thinkers, Discussions

Even though, from its very beginning, modern atheism exhibits a strong anthropocentric element, this does not find clear expression until the advent of the philosophy of Feuerbach. The interpretation of religion offered by Feuerbach becomes pivotal to the whole modern critique of religion. In 1844, when Marx wrote, "For Germany, the critique of religion has been essentially completed," he was writing with reference to Feuerbach, whose work *Das Wesen des Christentums* (The Essence of Christianity) had appeared only three years earlier, eliciting an enormous response from European intellectuals of the time. The history of Feuerbach's influence can be traced, via Marxism and existentialism, all the way to Bloch and Sartre. It

has also had a certain effect on present-day theological self-criticism (Martin Buber, Karl Barth, etc.).

Generally regarded as being the classical representatives of modern atheistic humanism are Feuerbach, Marx, Bloch, Sartre, and Fromm. Pertinent here, too, is the discussion that began in western and eastern Europe in the early sixties about a "humanistic Marxism."

Ludwig Feuerbach (1804–1872)

The basic insight underlying Feuerbach's critique of religion can be summarized in the proposition that God did not create humanity, but conversely, humanity created God in its own image. Thus, in his main work in criticism of religion, *Das Wesen des Christentums*, Feuerbach aims to uncover the true essence of (Christian) religion, which lies in anthropology (see his *Sämtliche Werke*, ed. W. Bolin and F. Jodl, vol. 6 [Stuttgart, 1960]). At the basis of the Feuerbachian critique of religion and theology is a genetico-secular interpretation of religion. Religion rests on the distinction between humans and animals. The essence of a human being is defined by the infinitude of his or her consciousness. Whereas an animal is equipped with instinct, a human being possesses consciousness. This consciousness is characterized by its ability to take something other than itself, and above all its own essence, as an object for itself. The infinite essence of humans expresses itself in the basic human faculties of reason, will, and love.

Religion is the attitude adopted by humans toward their own essence; its truth consists in the idea "the consciousness of the infinite." Its untruth results from the fact that theology separates the nature of humanity from human persons, places it outside of themselves, and indeed, with the help of the notion of God, turns it into an essence opposed to themselves. God is everything that human beings are not, and vice versa. God is the essence of humanity that has been relocated outside of humans; in him, humans contemplate their own essence as something alien to themselves. The true transcendence is not God but the species, which goes beyond the individual. The classic theistic attributes of God are transferred to it.

Feuerbach views both the concept of God and the content of religion as projections. He sees his critical task as one of tracing the other-worldly, supernatural, and superhuman essence of God back to the basic elements of human nature. Humanity is the center of religion, not God. The atheism thus asserted is only a seeming negativity. It negates God in order to affirm and liberate humanity; hence, it is true humanism.

Karl Marx (1818–1883)

Even though Marx soon distances himself from Feuerbach (see his eleven-part *Thesen über Feuerbach* [Theses on Feuerbach] of 1845), he nevertheless adopts Feuerbach's basic approach regarding both criticism of religion and humanism. In Marx's "Zur Kritik der hegelschen Rechtsphilosophie, Einleitung" (published in 1844 in the *Deutsch-Französische Jahrbücher*), he observes that, for Germany, criticism of religion has been essentially completed. This refers to the criticism of religion by the so-called Hegelian Leftists (David Friedrich Strauss and Bruno Bauer), but primarily to that by Feuerbach. Marx attributes to religion a twofold function: it is an expression of misery (in an "inverted world") and also an illusory consolation ("opium of the people") aimed at deceptively concealing that misery. Criticism of religion issues in the demand for an actual happiness. "Thus the criticism of religion is, in embryonic form, the criticism of that vale of tears whose halo is religion" (MEGA, Band 2 [I/2] [East Berlin, 1982], 171).

In style and choice of words, the Parisian manuscripts of 1844 reflect the humanistic pathos of Feuerbach. There, for the first time, Marx grapples theoretically with economic theories and problems, attempting to synthesize national economy and philosophy. The basic theme is the *humanization* of human beings, while the basic concept is *alienation* (a concept from Hegelian philosophy of human rights). Marx sees the basic contradiction as rooted in private property, which rests on alienated labor. According to him, workers are alienated from themselves because they have to realize themselves through the owners of capital; they have become commodities that themselves produce commodities. They are so alienated from themselves that they no longer even recognize themselves in their own products, which confront them as alien entities, as

alien power. Work becomes something forced upon them, something oppressive. Here, Marx is fighting not simply for the elimination of poverty and oppression, for the attainment of social well-being, but for humanity itself.

The goal is communism, under which no one is dependent upon another, no one can become the commodity of another, and the development of the individual becomes the condition making possible the development of everyone. Marx does not, however, develop communism as a humanistic ideal that is to be striven for; rather, for him it is more the internal stage in a goal-directed evolution whose theoretical explanation he attempts to evolve. "Communism is the positive abolition of private property as human self-alienation, and therefore is the authentic appropriation of the human essence by and for humans; it thus is the complete, conscious return, generated out of the total richness of the preceding evolution, of humans to themselves as social—i.e., human—beings. This communism, as complete naturalism, is equivalent to humanism, and as complete humanism, equivalent to naturalism; it is the actual resolution of human conflict with nature and with humans, the true resolution of the disharmony between existence and essence, between objectivization and self-activation, between freedom and necessity, between individual and species. It is the resolved riddle of history and recognizes itself as this resolution" (MEGA, 263).

The Paris manuscripts, long forgotten, were not published in their entirety until 1933, in Moscow. The conditions existing at that time in western Europe and the Soviet Union meant that discussion of these manuscripts did not begin until after World War II, in the late fifties. The humanistic pathos of the early Marx evoked an immense response. There was an attempt to play off a humanistically oriented early Marx against an economically and scientifically oriented later Marx (e.g., by Ernst Fischer and Erich Fromm). Louis Althusser, by contrast, sees the humanistic element as "ideological" and wishes to exclude it from the real core of Marx's theory in favor of a purely scientific theory amounting to theoretical antihumanism. It is certainly not easy to specify the place and status of the humanistic aspect in Marx's complete work. It is clear, however, that the cognitive-analytical elements are inextricably bound up with the practical ones that involve social liberation.

Ernst Bloch (1885–1977)

Bloch's philosophy is clearly and fundamentally stamped and inspired by Marx and Hegel, yet it cannot be unambiguously categorized. After many years of toil, and with an encyclopedic breadth of conception, Bloch completed a monumental work on the principle of hope as a philosophy designed to be practiced (*Das Prinzip Hoffnung*, Gesamtausgabe, vol. 5 [Frankfurt am Main, 1968]). No one else has reflected on hope in a comparable way. For Bloch, humans are by nature the essence of hope, directed toward the future; in this respect, they differ from animals. Because of this, they are inclined to look forward rather than backward. Humans do not, however, hope for a religious yet illusory beyond, but for happiness in an earthly world where alienation has been abolished and poverty and oppression overcome. Human striving and longing thus do not take an upward direction, but a forward one. One function of hope is the daydream.

Radically new and unusual is Bloch's view of Christianity and the Bible. In this, he also differs radically from Marx. Atheism and Christianity are not mutually exclusive, but mutually encompassing. Bloch's criticism of religion seeks to uncover the revolutionary elements in religion and to free it from distortion. He is mainly concerned not with negation but with clarification. Religion is profoundly bound up with hope: "Where there is hope, there is also religion" (*Atheismus im Christentum*, Gesamtausgabe, vol. 14 [Frankfurt am Main, 1968], 23).

Bloch understands religion (from "re-ligio") in the negative sense as a repressive, regressive system. The upward directedness is actually a tying back to the past (God as creator). Humans should, however, be freed of the past and have hope in the future. "Humans are not hermetically sealed"—i.e., they are not closed off in themselves but open toward the future. Human beings are transcendence without transcendence.

In *Atheismus im Christentum*, Bloch maintains: "Only an atheist can be a good Christian—equally, only a Christian can be a good atheist" (Gesamtausgabe, vol. 14, p. 24). Although it is a religion, Christianity is centrally oriented toward the future. It aims to lead out of the present state of things (note the subtitle to *Atheismus im Christentum: On the Religion of the Exodus and the Kingdom*). In Christianity, the position of the creator God in heaven is assumed by the Son of Man, Jesus. Jesus supplants the God of the established: "Behold, I make all things new" (Rv 21:5). Jesus is therefore an atheist. As opposed to the *fear of the Lord*, Jesus posits the *good tidings of the arrival of the new* (cf. Gesamtausgabe, vol. 14, 172ff.). For Bloch, it is beyond doubt that Jesus was a preacher of rebellion and struggle for the new.

Bloch, with his philosophy of hope, has heavily influenced present-day theology, both Protestant and Catholic. Jürgen Moltmann's *theology of hope* and Johann Baptist Metz's *political theology* are inconceivable without Bloch.

Jean-Paul Sartre (1905–1980)

Sartre is the main representative of French (atheistic) existentialism. By "existentialism" is meant a philosophy that makes human existence the central focus of its attention. Sartrean existentialism propounds its case with an emancipatory pathos. Humans are to be liberated from the constricting embrace of essence—hence, from that which is as it is. Humans achieve their existence only through a struggle against essence, in the course of which they attain self-realization. In Sartrean existentialism, as distinct from Marxism, humans are viewed less as members of a society than as individuals. Human beings (as individuals) must themselves each come to terms with their state of "being thrown into nothingness."

Sartre expressly describes his philosophy as *atheistic existentialism* (see *L'existentialisme est un humanisme* [Paris, 1946], 21). The central thesis of this existentialism is the claim that, if God does not exist, then existence precedes essence. This means that humans are given over to themselves; a person is initially a project that lives itself out subjectively. According to Sartre, the starting point for such an existentialism is Dostoevsky's observation that, if God did not exist, then everything would be permitted (ibid., 36). In fact, Sartre thinks, humans are wholly dependent upon themselves. Such a view excludes any element of determinism; rather, "a human being is freedom" (ibid., 37)—or, indeed, "condemned to freedom."

Sartre distinguishes two sorts of humanism. Humanism as a theory considers humans to be the final goal and highest value (see *L'existentialisme est un humanisme*, 90ff.). In contrast to this, existentialistic humanism posits something different: human beings are continually outside of themselves. What allows humans to exist is precisely the fact that they project themselves and lose themselves in something outside themselves. Insofar as humans pursue "transcendent goals," they are able to exist. There is no universe other than the human one, the universe of human subjectivity. Hence, transcendence is constitutive of humanity—not in a religious sense, however, but in the sense implying surpassing and subjectivity. This means, moreover, that humans are not closed up in themselves but are present in a human universe. There is no lawgiver other than humans themselves.

In this connection, Sartre thinks that existentialism is nothing other than an attempt to draw all the consequences of a coherent atheistic outlook (ibid., 94ff.). Consequently, he is also less concerned with atheism as a negation of God than with the recognition that, even if God existed, nothing would be changed. What is definitive is not the existence of God but the need for humans to find themselves and convince themselves that—apart from themselves—nothing can rescue them. In this sense, existentialism also amounts to optimism and a program for action.

Erich Fromm (1900–1980)

The central theme in Fromm's work is the humanity of human beings (see the "Einleitung des Herausgebers" in Gesamtausgabe, vol. 1: *Analytische Sozialphilosophie* [Munich, 1968]; vol. 9: *Sozialistischer Humanismus und humanistische Ethik* [Munich, 1989]). He attempts to synthesize Freudian psychoanalysis and Marx's critical social theory. Therefore he supplements psychoanalysis with social psychology and criticism of society. Fromm's humanism does not, however, rest merely on Freud and Marx, but on an attempt to integrate quite differing traditions and directions into his system, including Jewish Hasidism, the mysticism of Meister Eckhart, and Buddhism.

Hence, criticism of religion plays a significant role in Fromm's work (see Gesamtausgabe,

vol. 6: *Religion* [Munich, 1989]), given that he understands the question of the humanity of human beings as a religious question that traditional religion not only fails to treat correctly but positively distorts. Ultimately, then, he is concerned with outlining a new, true religion in which everything revolves exclusively around the humanity of human beings. With this, he moves far beyond Marx and Freud and actually comes closer to Feuerbach. In opposition to traditional, authoritarian religion, Fromm tries to conceive a radically humanistic religion in which the concept of God (essentially, the deification of humanity) is integrated into the concept of a true human being. The humanity of human beings becomes the content of the new religion and the new faith, which in turn implies the dissolution of any theological concept of God.

Fromm's work includes brilliant analyses of the factors that stand in the way of authentic human existence. In his final major work, *Haben oder Sein* (cf. Gesamtausgabe, vol. 2: *Analytische Charaktertheorie* [Munich, 1968]), the two basic attitudes specified in the title are taken as a basis for showing that the alienation of human existence is rooted in the orientation toward *having*. By contrast, it is in the *being* mode that human existence first comes to itself. The humanistic religion aimed at by Fromm wholly subserves two ends: personality development and the humanity of human beings. For him, as for Sartre, human beings are dependent on themselves alone. The process of human self-realization is seen as a kind of cyclic movement; only those humans who come out of themselves can arrive at themselves.

The Discussion about a Humanistic Marxism in the Socialist Countries

In the middle of the 1960s, discussion sprang up throughout the socialist countries of eastern Europe about the humanistic values of Marxism. At issue in that discussion were topics such as the meaning of life, the happiness of the individual, and the balanced development of the human personality. Naturally, the early writings of the young Marx, with their emphasis on emancipation and humanism, played a decisive role. The discussion was, however, probably stimulated and inspired more by really concrete problems that stemmed from the difficult everyday life in the socialistic countries. The attempts of Christians and Marxists to engage in dialogue also represented a significant contribution. Worth noting in this connection are the discussion meetings held by the German *Paulus Society* in 1965 at Salzburg (Austria), in 1966 at Herrenchiemsee (West Germany), and in 1967 at Marienbad (Czechoslovakia). With the violent termination of the so-called Prague Spring by invading troops from the Warsaw Pact states, this dialogue also came to an end.

Among the first of those in eastern Europe to have broached humanistic issues and attempted to provide answers from the Marxist viewpoint was the Polish philosopher Adam Schaff. His book *Marksizm a jednostka ludzka* (Marxism and the human individual) (Warsaw, 1965) also became known, in translation, in western Europe. Schaff attempts a reinterpretation of Marxism on the basis of Marx's early writings and reaches the conclusion that only a humanistic Marxism (in contrast to one whose orientation is exclusively economic and sociological) has any future. According to his thesis, "Marxism is a radical humanism" (ibid., 235). The starting point for Marxism is the human being as the highest good and the struggle to alter social relationships that degrade humans. In Schaff's view, the role of revolutionary praxis in humanistic Marxism is to promote the happiness of the individual.

Like Schaff, the Czech philosopher Milan Machovec poses these same questions and problems. In his book *Smysl lidského zivota* (The meaning of human life) (Prague, 1964), he depicts Marxism as humanism. For Machovec, the most important task today consists in interpreting Marxism as a living philosophy for present-day humanity.

In Soviet philosophy, similar attempts can be discerned since the start of the sixties. The questions about achieving humanization of human beings and balanced development of personality are central to the books of Eduard Struktov (e.g., *The Human Being in Communist Society* [Moscow, 1961]; *The Complete and Harmonic Development of the Personality* [Moscow, 1963]). The problems and difficulties standing in the way of such an undertaking in modern socialist society are treated most notably by Sergei Kovalev in his book *On Human Beings, Their Enslavement, and Liberation* (Moscow, 1970), in which he analyzes modern Soviet society against the backdrop of Marx's early writings. While questions about the sense of viewing meaningfulness or happiness in terms of an individual's life had long been rejected, one of the first to have taken up these issues is Petr Egides (see his *Meaning of Life* [Moscow, 1963] and *The Marxist Conception of the Meaning of Life* [Moscow, 1963]). Even if the answers turn out to be rather unconvincing, a start is nevertheless made that provides an impulse to further thought. Finally, Ivan Frolov, in a variety of publications (e.g., *Progress in Science and the Future of Humanity* [Moscow, 1975] and *The Prospects for Humanity* [Moscow, 1979]), addresses the threats posed to humane life by our scientific-technological world.

It is understandable that, at least prior to Gorbachev's assumption of power, all these inquiries presented their solutions and responses from a Marxist standpoint.

3. The Theological Debate

Atheistic humanism fundamentally opposes God and humanity (although not directly addressing the question of God's existence). Not surprisingly, modern Catholic and Protestant theology sees itself initially faced with the problem of overcoming this opposition.

Theology's critical response to atheistic humanism must begin with the movement's own basic experience, which is that of threatened, oppressed, and frustrated human existence. About the fact of this experience, all the representatives of atheistic humanism are in agreement. They diverge in determining the relevant causes of this condition and the means for recovering the human. They agree, however, that the causes are to be sought in social relationships, which, in turn, are rooted in human practice. Neither can be separated from the other. The thing, however, that decisively shapes human beings, and thus also their social practice, is anxiety about their own diversely threatened existence. Philosophers such as Kierkegaard, Heidegger, Sartre, and Russell have pointed out this factor, as have psychologists (see, e.g., H. J. Schultz, ed. *Angst* [Stuttgart, 1987]). This anxiety about one's own life undoubtedly plays a great role both in the humanization process and in the formation of human social structures. Every religion, including Christianity, aims to liberate people from anxiety about their own lives (see Oskar Pfister, *Das Christentum und die Angst* [Olten, 1975]).

Anxiety about one's own existence is a central experience of the human being as a limited creature threatened by death. This insight of modern existentialism and psychology coincides with the significance attributed to the topic in the Bible. This is pointed out by Bruna Costacurta in her thorough exegetical inquiry into the theme of anxiety in the Hebrew Bible (*La vita minacciata: Il tema della paura nella Bibbia Ebraica* [Rome, 1988]). In her view, "Anxiety appears in the Hebrew Bible as an emotion accompanying human beings throughout their existence and thus continually evidencing itself in an extraordinarily wide range of subjects and situations. . . . Anxiety shows itself to be a constant element in creaturely existence, which, as such, is transient and therefore structurally threatened" (ibid., 284ff.). The author goes on to indicate the particular significance of anxiety toward God, whose transcendence exposes the transient creatureliness of humans and in whose presence the individual feels as defenseless as when faced with a terrible danger.

With reference to Heb 2:14–15, a text dealing with the effects of human anxiety about death, Costacurta writes:

> A person becomes truly free by taking leave of anxiety about death and entering into a life that possesses the dimensions of the eternal. But this involves a transition requiring abandonment of anxiety about one's own existence and learning to accept death. In this way, . . . human beings, driven by anxiety about death, will no longer have to make themselves slaves to that which kills. (ibid., 279)

This passage from Hebrews refers to ways that faith in Christ deprives anxiety of its power.

Out of anxiety about their own lives, human beings tend to want to create, at any price, a sense of security for themselves. In attempting to realize this, they resort to personal or structural violence. "The means by which structural violence is usually sustained is that the powerful convert other human beings into instruments of their inhumanity by playing on the anxiety those others have about themselves. Dictatorships are chain-reactions of blackmail" (P. Knauer, *Der Glaube kommt vom Hören* [Bamberg, 1986], 20ff.). As opposed to this, the Christian message, which announces a communion with the living and death-conquering God of Jesus Christ, seeks to impart a certainty that is stronger than anxiety and that frees human beings for true humanity. In this consists the practical contribution of Christian faith to the humanization of human beings.

Bibl.: H. DE LUBAC, *The Drama of Atheist Humanism* (London, 1949); W. SCHUFFENHAUER (with introduction and selections), *Der Mensch schuf Gott nach seinem Bild* (Berlin, 1958); J. LACROIX, *Le sens de l'athéisme moderne* (Tournai, 1961); H. PFEIL, *Der atheistische Humanismus der Gegenwart* (Aschaffenburg, 1961); C. WACKENHEIM, *La faillite de la religion d'après Karl Marx* (Paris, 1963); W. POST, *Kritik der Religion bei Karl Marx* (Munich, 1969); J. KADENBACH, *Das Religionsverständnis von Karl Marx* (Munich/Paderborn/Vienna, 1970); M. XHAUFFLAIRE, *Feuerbach et la théologie de la sécularisation* (Paris, 1970); U. DUCHROW, "Die Frage nach dem neuen Menschen in theologischer und marxistischer Anthropologie," in *Marxismusstudien*, Series 6 (Tübingen, 1972); H. FLEISCHER, "Zum marxistischen Begriff der Humanität," in *Marxismusstudien*, Series 6 (Tübingen, 1972); G. HASENHÜTTL, *Gott ohne Gott: Ein Dialog mit Jean-Paul Sartre* (Graz/Vienna/Cologne, 1972); F. v. d. OUDENRIJN, *Kritische Theologie als Kritik der Theologie* (Mainz/Munich, 1972); E. SCHNEIDER, *Die Theologie und Feuerbachs Religionskritik* (Göttingen, 1972); L. CASINI, *Storia e umanesimo in Feuerbach* (Bologna, 1974); K. H. WEGER, ed., *Religionskritik von der Aufklärung bis zur Gegenwart* (Freiburg/Basel/Vienna, 1979); var., *Diagnosi dell'ateismo contemporaneo* (Rome/Brescia, 1980).

Bernd GROTH

I

IDEALISM, GERMAN

By means of the tradition of modern thought that led from Descartes and Spinoza to Kant, the idealists were heir to the autonomous position of philosophical rationality with respect to the problems of religious consciousness and theological discourse. By contrast with their predecessors, however, they go beyond the strictly demarcated domains of knowledge to encompass more broadly the various fields of discourse and grasp the particular relation that consciousness bears to itself. In this way theological discourse is integrated into areas of thought that have to do with the realization of freedom. As such, this discourse gives rise to a true "reformation of the understanding" for the examination and integration of the logic proper to theology and, in particular, its source in a revelation that is a mode of immediate contact chosen by the Absolute itself in history. The critique focuses on the theme of revelation, more in order to provide it a new epistemological justification than to disqualify it in the style of the rationalists. At issue in this new epistemological justification is respect for the autonomy of knowledge and thereby liberation from the model of ANALOGY, which had tended to supply the key to knowledge in general in the order of finite substances. We thus shall study the evolution of philosophical methods that cluster about the problem of revelation, with an eye to locating, for fundamental theology, the interest and even the fecundity of this "philosophical insistence" on its own ground.

1. Fichte

If Fichte never ceased urging people to go beyond the external forms of religion, he nevertheless evolved considerably in his speculative appreciation of Christianity, developing its ethical import, which he had already acknowledged in his sermons, in unexpected ways, through the transformation of his method. No doubt it had first seemed to him, following Kant, more urgent to complete the liberation of the mind from religious formalism, so as to guide it to its moral destination, the realization of rational autonomy, than to investigate directly the pertinence of religious discourse within the structure of a philosophy of action.

For the young Fichte, religion is acceptable only within the limits of a well-defined moral project, and the revelation by which it justifies itself is of interest only from this practical point of view, since its humbling at the hands of the laws of the transcendental field of consciousness leaves it no theoretical value. The only acceptable criterion is the action religion arouses within the structure of the free moral exercise of the will. If in this context we lose supersensible justification for our actions, we gain the certainty that only free moral effort can be a true help in concrete life, and that we must expect nothing but what in our wretchedness we can strive to realize. The idea of a supernatural supplement making up for our moral deficiencies is a serious illusion, leading directly to all the moral deviations religion can generate when it sets out to raise certain people's action above the law, on the grounds that such action answers to supernatural precepts. Religion properly understood does not set itself up against morals; it seeks only to improve people, to cultivate their heart in order to facilitate their *decision* in favor of moral progress. Religion has as its function the preparation in secret for the reign of morality; it is *faith* in one's possibility to surpass oneself, to improve oneself, to raise oneself toward the Good. At this level, the concept of revelation is the target of the strongest charge of ambiguity, since it always risks directing reflection toward the establishment of an order above morality whose interference in concrete experience will contravene the elementary laws of freedom. But when freedom regards itself as exempt from the moral order, it thereby loses the self-determination that in fact characterizes its relation of obedience to the duty it has settled on. The institution of a supernatural order strips free beings of responsibility, reducing them to actors in a drama that eludes them, whose "higher" interests are substituted for the temporal goals that are really in their reach. True religion, on the contrary, liberates people from the illusion of a preexisting "higher" order, a preestablished divine plan, converting them to produce concrete acts, to exercise their responsibility, to engage themselves with terrestrial structures. Religion must not lead us to flee the humbleness of our practices, but it should encourage us to accept our essential dependence on our own selves, on the fragility of our moral effort.

These radical positions on behalf of a religion enclosed within the human heart, as the source of moral effort and measured by the standard of the moral progress it sustains, provoked a violent reaction against Fichte's philosophy from intellectual religious spheres in 1798 and 1799 — the famous episode of the *Atheismusstreit*. Fichte never succeeded in dispelling the suspicions aroused in this period against his philosophy, and so the transformation of his philosophical method, and a fortiori the import of this transformation for his conception of religion, passed completely unnoticed in the eyes of his detractors. The break with Schelling in 1806 is a good example of the universal scorn directed at Fichte's entire enterprise after 1798. His new philosophy sought to think on the basis of eternal essence — that is, the absolute ideality that constitutes the field of consciousness, which is the source of the intensive and no longer extensive dynamism of knowledge. To think under the direction of eternal essence as a regulative notion no longer has meaning; one must think on the basis of it and regard oneself as a particle of that infinite Love, of that unmingled felicity, at the critical point of contact between the real and the ideal where knowledge and action are articulated. Concrete effort is a more or less successful replica of the ideality that guides it. It is nevertheless the ideal, the projective structures of reason, which guarantees that reflection always has a bearing on a problematically real, on an approximate reflection. Spirit determines itself and limits itself as a function of its ideal and absolute constitution, which is the originating act (*Urtat*) of freedom, eternal Love. All that matters definitively is this mysticism of action that considers the *manifestation* of Love under the most unexpected forms. Certainly "the philosophy of action grounded on duty in 1794–95 remains valid. The same could be said of the theory of creative morality. . . . Nor is action ever abandoned. Instead contemplation is added to it and moves it from a deeper level. This provides a sound justification for the formulas, at once religious and active, which Fichte uses in the *Addresses to the German Nation* to characterize life and existence."

Fichte always went beyond any representation of action that would completely assimilate it to the tension exacerbated by the finite morality that discovers as its inverse, by distortion or negation, the Absolute that justifies it, but from which it can hope for nothing on the grounds that mingling an interest with it in this way would pervert the rational affirmation from which the notion of divinity and absolute derives its force as a postulate of practical reason. Nevertheless, it is the manifestation of love that matters, and consciousness must be directed (*anweisen*) to take up its position and its task of reflection within concrete experience, both internal and external, ethical and political; it is here a question of *participating* in this metamorphosis of Love in me. This participation consists in reflecting the action of the Absolute within us, i.e., in the correlation of the idealization of the real (beginning with the limited) and the realization of the ideal (beginning with the limiting) that defines the activity of our freedom-in-the-world concerned with the creation of ways to affirm its virtualities. To participate in Love consists therefore in increasing our consciousness of being-free-in-the-world, in reuniting as intimately as possible action and thought of my freedom, to the point of identifying oneself progressively with the infinite Love of self that is full coincidence with oneself, full assumption of self, joy and felicity in being-oneself, "the self-possession of Me by itself."

This endeavor in which Fichte raises the religious ethics of his first philosophy to the level of a theological aesthetic leaves unanswered numerous questions about the historical fact of revelation. It is clear that Fichte retains from the Gospels in particular the Johannine speculations concerning the eternal Word, and the metaphysics of charity deducible from it that is also present in the preaching of the kingdom in Paul's letters and the Synoptic Gospels. Our time has meaning only as so ordained by the kingdom present within it, by the Eternal, by the absolute freedom incarnated in the person of Christ. Is the essence of Christianity in question here, the diversion of the kerygma toward a "speculative Gospel" like that of Lessing? We think that it is more fundamentally a "first theology" linked with an absolute philosophy of freedom — a foundation, in a way, that leaves open the possibility of religious or ethical construction, in the manner of Rahner's theological anthropology. In Fichte philosophical discourse does not claim to bridge the gap separating the relative self-contemplation of the Absolute in history from the astonishing kenosis of the Word, which is contemplated in the unique engagement with an ethical destiny. That would require something like a hermeneutical reversal, which for Fichte is not legitimated by philosophical rationality, which is essentially self-reflexive. Revelation in its historical concreteness remains the province of science, which takes it as its positive principle. Philosophy stands at the zero point of religious experience and, without contradicting it or standing in for it, or still less supplanting it, proposes to critical freedom the meaning to give to the value for human destiny of this confrontation with the Absolute that somehow really directs the course of this destiny toward the advent of a rational society (the *Vernunftreich*). Such a philosophical admonition, correctly understood, would keep theological reflection from going beyond its object and on a totally empirical basis reconstituting itself a metaphysics *après coup*, which in the name of a determinate experience would spiritualize or "theologize" the problem of the world and action. This "theologized metaphysics" would thus evacuate the aporia inherent in the finite understanding of the finite — an aporia that ceaselessly dynamicizes that understanding.

2. Hegel

An impassioned reader of Lessing's *Nathan the Wise*, Hegel does not hesitate, under the romanticist impulse, to assimilate the affirmation of the moral life to the pure and simple affirmation of life itself, across the caesuras of existence, that long disorder of being intersected by astonishing regenerations. Whether we consider morality, religiosity, politics, or popular culture, all these forms reveal the vital force that totalizes itself in each moment of history and gathers them into itself without losing their dissonances. In this work of absolute Life upon negativity, Christianity appears as a "positivity" that extracts consciousness from the hegemony of the negative, opposition, and dualism, to raise it to the spirit of the Whole that sustains all our negations. Contrary

to Hyppolite's suggestion, the positivity of Christianity does not lie in the "event of Jesus Christ," in this singularity thenceforth endowed with universality of meaning. The Christian revelation derives its positivity from its rupture with the order of representation. When it is thought in its positivity, outside the precepts and truths of the catechism, it appears that it opposes nothing to consciousness, that it imposes nothing foreign or arbitrary upon it, but that on the contrary it lies within the very heart of this consciousness, as the inner manifestation of its reference to the spirit of the Whole. It is the response of the divine within me to the "divine milieu," the communion or harmony of existence portentous with the ground of its being, the "in-existence" of difference, to use a term of G. Jarczyk. The true revelation of Christ to Peter in Mark's Gospel (Mk 8:29) could be glossed as follows: "The divine which is in you has recognized me as divine; you have understood my essence; it has resonated in your own." Revelation does not reside in acquaintance with an externality, since those who saw and touched Jesus rejected him or were content to believe in him without yet truly being born to the truth by becoming "worshipers in spirit," children of the light within them, without "being born again" by uniting with the life of the Whole like the branches on the vine.

According to the young Hegel, revelation therefore has significance only when understood as inner manifestation of communion with the life of the Whole. It becomes absurd, however, when used to legitimate the doctrinal exposition of metaphysical propositions and moral precepts. Now this new concept of revelation is imposed as a requirement of thought addressed to speculative reason; it is necessary to withdraw the thought of revelation from the order of the negative in order to point out something unthought within Christianity on this side of the moral, cultural, and political oppositions to which it has yielded. Christianity must be distinguished from its history; Christianity, in its spirit, must be conceived as the way to true reconciliation with the divine, to inner unity with universal Spirit.

This task is the duty of philosophy alone, even if the term "philosophy" cannot yet signify at this time everything it later will for Hegel. The *spirit of Christianity* again presents itself in the lineaments of a speculative hermeneutic ceaselessly in contact with the texts it is struggling to rethink. The task does not yet presuppose that self-possession in the rigor of the dialectical procedure that will characterize philosophy in its maturity. Eight or nine years later, *The Phenomenology of Spirit* will no longer be able to conceive the relation of religious consciousness to the phenomenon without the spirit on the way directly attempting to give the encountered content a determinate form in its efforts at coherence. Henceforth it is less a matter of destiny than of logic, and the Christian drama that Hegel will indefatigably seek to put on the stage now corresponds more to a logic of action—that is, to the tribulations of the Idea in the structures of conceived history. Hegel's method is forged in the Jena period, as he separates himself from and then derides the confusions nourishing the polemic of Schelling and Fichte. By stigmatizing spirit's transcendental act of self-reflection (I=I) and absolute substance's formal act of self-affirmation (A=A), Hegel rebuffs the false logics of identity that mask the relation of consciousness to itself in every process of reflection and proposes instead a dialectical logic in which difference redoubled is the only way of synthesis, which, in the image of the ancient method of the syllogism, always remains a procedure of negation-determination of its extremes by a middle term.

In order to achieve philosophical synthesis, the new method (the dialectic) emphasizes the negative thought of revelation as externalization of the Absolute, which is thus posited in the field of externality of the self-consciousness. The experience of the believing community only produces a false internalization of this externality, because it preserves in its spirituality, its living memory, and its doctrine the difference that opposed the individual Christ-person to his disciples and continues to encourage attitudes of belief instead of leading to the baptism of the spirit by which the faithful one is made the *alter Christus* who reinvents the good news. Religion and theology have in fact become the greatest obstacles to Christian truth. To dissolve this impasse it is necessary to hazard an approach predicated on another point of view and attempt to transport Christianity back to its fundamental essence. At this point the form of philosophical knowledge properly so called intervenes, the suppression of all dualism, the self-negation of the self in its other, the abolition of the subject in the concrete determination which it effects and thereby suppresses as pure factuality, dead to its own ideality. The truth of the concept lies in the very act that tears both Subject and Object from their unilaterality and conceives them in the double negation in which they penetrate one another without confusion, and comprehend the one in the other. In this way true philosophical Christianity emerges, which refused to conceive God without the world or the world without God, since in their double death there appears the only authentic reflection of the life of the Spirit, which is neither expiation on the cross nor justification at the end of time but the radical presence of the Eternal in the face of the false universal-singular of individuality and the false infinite that it generates in the impossible desire to reproduce it. The truth of the Spirit lies in the historical freedom it generates in the present, which itself produces the concrete forms of the universal which it desires infinitely . . . the community of freedom, mediation achieved and posited as the formal principle of the co-existence of individuals, and scope for struggle and respect.

Christianity teaches nothing else (but is there anything else to teach?) but to be the child of one's time— "without being better than one's time, to be one's time best!" in the context of its concrete political realizations. Understood philosophically, revelation remains the inner rebirth of consciousness in its historical career, the present response within me of Spirit which plays within the singularity of my history and my political community, the *Volkgeist* that determines my responsibility in the face of the Absolute of history, the universal freedom that must always be made concrete.

Thus Hegel sets himself radically against every reading of theological consciousness that would withdraw the "religious truth" it defends from its historical and even political implications. Religious truth is not a matter of indifference for the destiny of the ethical community. Quite to the contrary. Consciousness habitually formulates its projects in terms of this truth's categories, and it is through the caesura of Christian consciousness in the Reformation and the accompanying religious wars that modern consciousness is born. The desire of clarified consciousness to evacuate the religious problem has simply ended up showing that the modern ethical project could not be posed without the attempt to reconcile it with the demands of Christian consciousness, because theology retains a nonnegligible part of the keys to the political problem, since it claims to anticipate the end of humanity and reflects here on earth the conditions of a new collective being. In addition to Marx's declarations in his *Critique of Hegel's Philosophy of Right*, the writings of Metz, Moltmann, and Xhaufflaire among others issue this proclamation. More than an interest on the part of theology in politics, as understood by Clodovis Boff and much earlier by Thomas Aquinas, the political dimension of theology is at issue here. As a critical reflection on the origins and the meaning of the collective destiny of humanity, it attacks numerous limited representations of collective freedom and affirms its conception of salvation in relation to order, obedience, wealth, sexuality, power, and so forth by relativizing other positions elaborated on different foundations. It is impossible to minimize the function of this discourse in cultural space or to avoid analyzing the ways in which it mobilizes and also orders consciousness.

3. Schelling

The major periods of Schelling's "philosophy of becoming" are certainly among the most helpful, within German idealism and even beyond it, for clarifying the various aspects of rational discourse about revelation. Beyond the dispute over the active and passive senses of revelation that characterized the discussion of the Aufklärung and emerging idealism (1794–1800), Schelling investigates the wide and the narrow senses of the concept, aiming to redefine its extension from the point of view of his absolute philosophy, based on the intellectual intuition of God's self-knowledge in all things (1801–6). The traditional categories of the one and the many, at once the romantic *hen kai pan* and the philosophies of Spinoza and Leibniz, then dominated the philosophy of identity. But even as he critically reappropriated the parameters of this cosmic philosophy, still too static and purely formal, Schelling took part in a new discussion over the drama of freedom in revelation (1809–21), which raised in a clear way the question of a self-mediation,

itself mediated by its contrary (*sub contrario*), by the proof of necessary evil, and after 1810 by that of the willing abasement (the kenosis) of the original contraction, which inaugurated the process of the revelation/realization of divine freedom. In his final philosophical period (1821–53), this type of absolute self-mastery, by which God allows himself to be contained by what is more humble, points the way to rational access to the God who is *sui securus*, sovereign, Lord of being and its powers. During the period of the Hegelian dramatic, in which the rule of revelation is that of dereliction and contradiction overcome by that of liberation, the categories of power and action dominate over reflection, and revelation is questioned from the point of view of the value of the schemes that analogically express it: natural schemes or spiritual schemes, process or free action, essential necessity or sovereign and free decision or gift.

From 1800 to 1821, then, we move slowly from the idea that God is essentially his own self-revelation (the transcendental theogony of absolute reason) to the idea that God must reveal himself in order to realize his freedom (1809), to arrive at the idea that God reveals himself because that is his will, his free initiative, the extraordinary action of his goodness (after 1815). In the course of this philosophical itinerary Schelling moves beyond the rationalist approach to revelation, which seeks to define its validity a priori within the structures of the system that gives an account of the unified totality. Revelation is less the *Was* that preoccupies conceptualist approaches (the ones based on the notion of fitness to the divine essence) than a *Dass*, an unforeseeable occurrence, which destabilizes rational effort and disengages the mechanisms of apriority. The divine initiative is not explained. It can be understood, should anyone so desire, only by following it through its consequences for the freedom to which it addresses itself in the already-given order in which it occurs. The initiative can arouse only a *ratifying* thought, an effort at refiguration, itself based at first on "attentive listening," a reading of the occurrence, a configuration. What is needed is an astonishment, a radical abandonment of oneself, a death, to follow the affirmation of God in history and to seek to understand its significance for the human freedom that sees a new world opening up. The ecstasy of the *Schwärmerei* resolves none of the problem, because it claims to speak another language, regenerated and purified, which simply no longer concerns the world to which it addresses itself. Mystics say what they experience, but without knowing how their testimony redefines the already-present idea of the historical relation to the Absolute. The problem for historical consciousness is to determine the value, for its structures of humanity, of the opening of a spiritual destiny against all expectations, within the very heart of its resignation, though it was already accepting the false departure of the mysteries, the mythical opium of a death with nothing beyond except the hell of this world, the exterior of the exterior, the entrance into the magic of the varieties of existence.

In his study of the mythic past of revelation, Schelling shows that it has overcome (*überwinden*) the enclosing of consciousness within a world falsely external to the divine, which conceives of union with God in purely external terms. Union with God is the history of an astonishing fidelity present deep within all free actions, which finally comes to envelop them, by breaking into their externality. Christ is the hero of this reconciliation. The heart of his personality is the mind, the *Gesinnung*, which unites him intimately to the Father from the immemorial time of the fall, throughout his cosmic and anonymous preexistence—this apparent externality, freely willed for the salvation of humankind. This *Gesinnung* shatters the reign of pagan divinities and Judaism's external image of the Father, to reveal in the obedient man Jesus the inner grace that frees from death and leads to the right hand of the Father. It is only in love for the Father, obedient unto death, that the repressed figure of the god of life bursts forth, he who desires the victory of love in the time of sin.

Revelation henceforth must be conceived in terms of the structures of free action as *Überwindung*, linking kenosis and glorification, destruction and rebirth. In each action an externalization recedes and an internalization is made manifest; in Christ mystical glory recedes into annihilation, and true glory—that of obedience to the gift of the Father, to the call of love, to the creative initiation—shines through and is confirmed as new life and new creation.

In order to elaborate this new concept of revelation as a response to the horizon of modern thought, a revelation that is intensive, active, and "spiritual," and thus possesses an intrinsically sociocultural significance, Schelling had to set himself against several types of theology. From 1803 on, he attacked the exegetic empiricism and dogmatic moralism that forbade all reflection on the speculative significance of Christianity, that is, on its absolute intuition of the universe as history and on its concept of revelation as coextensive with the historical drama of humanity, culminating in the trinitarian fulfillment of time. In his middle philosophical period he argued against the presuppositions of a certain mystical theology that he found incapable of "desubstantializing" its discourse about revelation and therefore always in quest of a necessitarian explanation that would assimilate God to the end of the ecstatic process of spiritual regeneration. In fact, mystical theology suffers from the same disorder as the rationalist theology that is yoked to the perfecting of its proofs of God's existence. Life does not lead one back to the origin, or existential affirmation to the a priori idea of the Absolute, any more than ideas lead to life, or the thesis of absolutely necessary existence leads to the reality of the personal God. Mystical experience and rational demonstrations are each incapable of generating a science of revelation, because they always presuppose the priority of the explanatory process to the explanation of himself that God gives in the very act of self-revelation.

Schelling's formulations at this point are very close to those of Karl Barth. But he means to derive other consequences from them. For Schelling, it is philosophically important to grasp, in the human experience of freedom, the scope of the Christian fact of revelation. His concern is not so much to say in what way revelation concerns us, but rather to say that precisely because it does befall us and concern us, it implies a mode of existing in reference to Scripture and to the collective memory that determines particular structures of action in society and a meaningful attitude in the face of death, of the other, and of social existence. As Bruaire said, if God is Someone, all of my philosophy of existence is concerned with and summoned to a critical reappropriation of itself in order to determine the existential value of this relation to the Absolute, without which all that remains is an option or an act of faith. The task is to grasp the way in which being-Christian in relation to revelation also has implications for being-human in relation to the structures of social existence. In this way we are already part way to a postmodern natural theology that leaves itself open to challenge so that it in its turn may challenge the objective modalities of freedom in its struggle to christianize its practices. This natural theology presupposes an "epistemological break" with the ancient practice of the *praeambula fidei*; the task is not that of rationally positing the existence of God, but that of investigating the existential scope of God's free initiative in history, thanks to a rationality stripped of its principled apriority and dispossessed of its will to produce, so that, by following a hypothetico-deductive method, it may be transformed into attestation, ratification, "a posteriori progression," "a priori empiricism," or again "theo-logic of history."

4. Rendering Theological Reason "Dialectical"

Considered from these different points of view, idealism tends to focus theological attention upon the "material synthesis" of history, in which there is variously invented the figure of love's ceaselessly renewed fidelity to itself (the Fichtean aesthetic), there is variously made concrete the internality of the gift animating the Whole (the Hegelian dramatic), and there is again manifested the astonishing initiative of absolute freedom, which envelops time (the Schellingian theo-logic). Reflection on Christianity cannot take up a position on the definitions of natures without relation to a lived history; it cannot make reference to sacramental logics without a real relation to social relations historically conceived. There is no "automatic thought" of salvation whose conditions and effects might be mastered. Theology must be *made dialectical* in its relation to the historical structures of existence or it cannot be! A theological representation of history gives way to a historical reading of theology, whose epistemological framework is a dialectic of the ways of knowing (as so many ways of being-in-the-world) that completely escapes the "great genre of analogy." Theology must be *thought* with reference to lived history (salvation economy), *centered* on the event that institutes it in its

questioning and continues to address it (Christology), and finally it must *circulate* between its original contingency (the gift) and its (hermeneutic) reappropriation in time, employing categories that engage it with a culture always in motion. Along this circular path between source and present reality it traverses the text of the Scriptures, which must always, even as a privileged witness to the source, be revivified by contact with the present. The concretization of theological discourse that is envisaged by German idealism already betokens theology as a historical, exegetic, and hermeneutic science. Furthermore, this effort at clarification of theological consciousness, *grappling with its history through the interpretation of Christ "for us,"* has significance only if it rejoins the political project of modernity and helps fix religion's role in theory and practice in struggles for power, including power over consciousnesses and their moral and social imaginary. Concrete "dialecticized" theology, which posits Christ in history for interpretive consciousness, is also political because it acknowledges the impact of this religious aspect of consciousness on power structures. Rather than guiding such structures (by assisting or supervising), the church must then be one of the transcendental instances of culture that critically ensure the career of freedom within its power structures.

In this way idealism has stimulated theological discourse to render its method and contents "dialectical," in order to promote a notion of Christianity based on history and not the other way round, a theology in direct conversation with the historicity of its intelligible structures. The theology it awaits, while remaining speculative, must also be historical, christocentric, and political. To be sure, it can be seen that "idealism" is an improper term to signify the systematic apprehension of the theme of the actualization of historical consciousness, of which theology and (much more widely) religion form a domain susceptible of being examined and summoned to being rethought.

The project of a hermeneutical theology responds in a fundamental way to this challenge, since it seeks to articulate the historical labor of comprehension and the Christ-event in its singularity and its resistance to every effort at pure theorizing. The entire problem is, in our historical actuality, to come into possession of the novelty that the covenant offered to human beings in Jesus Christ never ceases to be. The task of fundamental theology is then in each period to create the conditions for the invention of this tradition/inheritance, by signifying the historical scope of the Christ-event within the self-ordering of concrete modalities of action. The word is spoken only on condition that it is "speakable" for a consciousness taken up with the present confrontation of theories and practices. It is necessary to fix the totality of performative categories that make the word audible, that is, to raise the circle of interpretive consciousness (or comprehension) to the circle of historical configurations (or spoken events), so that they may continually interact and remodel themselves as a function of that interaction. Such a theology must be ready to risk an "ecological doctrine of creation," for example, or to conceive the provisional (transitory) character of all our representations of the kingdom (as abuses or excesses) in connection with the eschaton of secular projects. The worth of a theology is measured by the risk it assumes in adapting its *episteme* to new categories, proper to the self-comprehension in time of the person to whom its word is addressed.

5. Theology as Symbolic Writing

In pursuing the conversation of critical consciousness with religion, idealism has displaced the poles of interest and at the same time the stakes of the conversation. It first showed on methodological grounds that consciousness cannot posit itself as purely external to the critique. On the contrary, it must think itself according to the logic it imposes on itself in its relation to that critique. Its language is therefore always double, so that it may conceive itself in the movement of its objectivization. Beyond this "genealogy" of theological and religious consciousness, attested by the deconstruction and reconstruction of its language, the religious phenomenon as a set of practices and theories is also rethought as a cultural dimension, this time as *writing*, which elaborates a true grammar of meaning for historical events. Philosophical consciousness first follows the logic of its image, the logic of its religious metamorphoses, in which it appears now as sinner, now as saved; now as disgraced, now as elect. But beyond the logic of the image there remains the economy of the sign or symbol, the excess that religion and its theoretic discourse have inscribed within the cultural *epos*. While imagining itself within the religious and theological horizon, consciousness discovers the religious economy of the sign, which breaks the circle of reflection and diverts the speculative effort. The theologico-religious existential of human thought and action challenges the economy of reflection, the logic of the image, which still imprisons Kant's analyses when he transfers the schematism of moral consciousness to the christological representation of morality in general. Reflecting itself in its theological reflection, consciousness is, so to speak, displaced in the direction of the self-reflection carried out on itself by the Absent of theology, the transcendent Origin, the divine opening that itself makes possible discourse about God.

At this point critical discourse undergoes a crisis because it cannot recapitulate itself in its own tension and thereby justify the absent that has itself voiced its entreaty. This is the crucial point of the "speculative Christology" of the idealists, and it is also the point where Schelling seeks to make a decisive step beyond Hegel: reason cannot prevail over a principle it received only in the negative, by developing it and assimilating it in its effort at intercoherence. If theology is elaborated strictly on a regimen of concepts, it will be, at its level and without betraying itself for all that, the image of reason's permanent effort to affirm itself in its history. But precisely at this moment it loses its own economy, its will to attest or signify or symbolize Absence. Theological doubling is not simply the doubling of hermeneutic consciousness. Theology is more than a language; it is a writing whose text in part eludes the one who produces it because that one always produces it from another text, from an absence, from a sign. There is no center in the play of theological writing; the hermeneutic circle is broken. There is instead an incomplete covenant, always compromised, within which the work of writing is pursued and constitutes itself as tradition, with no fusing of horizons, but with a sort of report by Absence on other horizons of the period. The attestation is effaced so that the old text may appear, with its disparities and deficiencies—the foreignness that defies interpretation. Theological writing is thus characterized by a self-surpassing in the direction of history. It constitutes itself a tradition by creating anew, for each period, its own interpretive site, the horizon of its problematic.

6. Returning to the Theological Task: Revelation and Social Destiny

Beginning by examining Christian consciousness with an eye to modernizing it, the idealists concluded by conceiving their modernity in terms of a new locus for Christian consciousness to examine. They did not seek so much to Christianize their thought as to think a modern Christianity. The nuance is present above all in the specific character of the philosophical task: it consists in grasping the possibility and the value of the historicity of religion, both from the existential and from the doctrinal point of view, but it does not include taking up the ensuing crisis in dogma. It awakens theological responsibility before the crisis of its *language* in order to provoke a new effort at *writing*, a reformation of the religious grammar of meaning for this time. Theology writes with the material of history to signal what is absent from it. Idealism finally calls in question the manner in which religious speech constitutes itself tradition by the play of its writing and thereby comes to assume or reject the questions of its time in the field proper to it. Theological writing is a crucible of meanings in which God humanized and humanity divinized skirt one another to determine a surplus of meaning, a "dialectical utopia," an alternative called the reign of reason (Fichte) or the rational state (Hegel) or the Johannine society of love (Schelling). Theology is the privileged writing of "social palingenesis" because it is constantly articulated upon the absence that mobilizes its thinking. Theological production thus maintains an organic relationship with the career of collective praxes. This is less a matter of a subject comprehending his or her God (the economy of the image) as of a history played out in the unlimited personalization of social relations, well articulated in theology as early as the combinatory language of Leibniz.

Idealism leads theology to the central question of the kingdom as the collective and "societal" dimension of revelation, in the very logic of its irreducibility.

Let us say of a word that it is a matter of articulating a *singular* option [the Christian faith] in response to *general* questions [social, economic, political, cultural]. . . . The tradition that can help us treat the theological question as it is henceforth asked must henceforth be sought first in modern "philosophy": where Spinoza, Hegel, Heidegger, and still others construct in terms of politics or history or linguistics . . . the discourse relative to questions of existence; where literature, in the genre of novel or poem, explicates by a work internal to language the problem raised by the disappearance of signifying institutions other than language itself; where work organizes practices articulated among "discourses" of gestures rich with rationalities, as efficacious as they are silent.

Bibl.: Concerning the period studied: A. RITSCHL, *Der Pietismus im Würtemberg* (Bonn, 1886); J. R. GEISELMANN, *Geist des Christentums und des Katholizismus* (Mainz, 1940); K. BARTH, *Protestant Thought: From Rousseau to Ritsch* (New York, 1959); R. KRONER, *Von Kant bis Hegel* (Tübingen, 1961); E. KLINGER, *Offenbarung im Horizont der Heilsgeschichte* (Zurich/Einsiedeln/Cologne, 1969); G. A. MCCOOL, *Catholic Theology in the Nineteenth Century* (New York, 1977); W. SCHULZ, *Le Dieu de la métaphysique moderne* (Paris, 1978); A. SCHURR, *Philosophie als System bei Fichte, Schelling und Hegel* (Stuttgart/Bad Cannstatt, 1974); K. SCHWAIGER, ed., *Kirche und Theologie im 19. Jahrhundert* (Göttingen, 1975); G. STIEHLER, *Der Idealismus von Kant bis Hegel* (Berlin, 1970); J. TAMINIAUX, *La nostalgie de la grâce et l'aube de l'idéalisme allemand* (The Hague, 1967); X. TILLIETTE, *Le Christ des philosophes*, vol. 1 (Paris, 1974); id., *La christologie idéaliste* (Paris, 1986); E. CASSIRER, *Les systèmes post-kantiens* (Lille, 1983); M. KESSLER, *Kritik aller Offenbarung* (Mainz, 1986); V. A. MCCARTHY, *Quest for a Philosophical Jesus* (Macon, Ga., 1986).

Concerning Fichte: X. LÉON, *La philosophie de Fichte* (Paris, 1902); id., *Fichte et son temps* (Paris, 1922–27); E. LASK, "Fichtes Idealismus und die Geschichte," in *Gesammelte Werke*, vol. 1 (Tübingen, 1923); M. GUEROULT, *L'évolution et la structure de la Doctrine de la Science* (Paris, 1930); M. MARÉCHAL, *Le point de départ de la métaphysique*, Cahier IV (Brussels/Paris, 1947); L. PAREYSON, *Fichte* (Turin, 1950); E. CORETH, "Le développement de la théologie de Fichte," in *Archives de Philosophie* 25 (1962): 484–540; D. JULIA, *La question de l'homme et le fondement de la philosophie* (Paris, 1964); R. LAUTH, *Zur Idee der Transzendentalphilosophie* (Munich/Salzburg, 1965); B. BOURGEOIS, *L'idéalisme de Fichte* (Paris, 1968); H. RADEMACHER, *Fichtes Begriff des Absoluten* (Frankfurt, 1970); I. SCHUSSLER, *Die Auseinandersetzung von Idealismus und Realismus in Fichtes Wissenschaftslehre* (Frankfurt, 1972); P.-P. DRUET, *Fichte* (Namur, 1977); A. PHILONENKO, *La liberté humaine dans la philosophie de Fichte* (2nd ed.; Paris, 1980); id., *L'oeuvre de Fichte* (Paris, 1984); L. FERRY, *Philosophie politique*, vol. 1 (Paris, 1984).

Concerning Hegel: R. HAYM, *Hegel und seine Zeit* (Leipzig, 1927); J. WAHL, *Le malheur de la conscience dans la philosophie de Hegel* (Paris, 1929); A. KOJÈVE, *Introduction et la lecture de Hegel* (Paris, 1947); A. CHAPELLE, *Hegel et la religion*, 4 vols. (Paris, 1963–71); C. BRUAIRE, *Logique et religion chrétienne dans la philosophie de Hegel* (Paris, 1964); P.-J. LABARRIÈRE, *Structures et mouvement dialectique dans la Phénoménologie de l'Esprit de Hegel* (Paris, 1968); G. A. KELLY, *Idealism, Politics and History: Sources of Hegelian Thought* (Cambridge, 1969); E. OESER, *Begriff und Systematik der Abstraktion* (Vienna/Munich, 1969); A. LÉONARD, *La foi chez Hegel* (Tournai/Paris, 1970); M. J. PETRY, *Hegel's Philosophy of Nature* (London, 1970); M. RÉGNIER, "Hegel," in *Histoire de la philosophie 2*, "La Pléiade" (Paris, 1973); T. LITT, *Hegel* (Paris, 1973); F. GUIBAL, *Dieu selon Hegel* (Paris, 1975); E. BRITO, *Hegel et la tâche actuelle de la christologie* (Namur/Paris, 1979); id., *La christologie de Hegel* (Paris, 1983); G. JARCZYK, *Système et liberté dans la logique de Hegel* (Paris, 1980); K. MARX, *Critique de la philosophie politique de Hegel*, in *Oeuvres*, vol. 3: *Philosophie*, "La Pléiade" (Paris, 1982); G. GÉRARD, *Critique et dialectique* (Brussels, 1982); J. HYPPOLITE, *Introduction à la philosophie de l'histoire de Hegel* (Paris, 1983); W. JAESCHKE, *Die Religionsphilosophie Hegels* (Darmstadt, 1983); O. POGGELER, *Études hégéliennes* (Paris, 1985); M. FUJIMA, *Philosophie und Religion beim jungen Hegel* (Bonn, 1985); G. JARCZYK and P.-J. LABARRIÈRE, *Hegeliana* (Paris, 1986); R. LAUTH, *Hegel critique de la Doctrine de la Science de Fichte* (Paris, 1987).

Concerning Schelling: H. FUHRMANS, *Schellings Philosophie der Weltalter* (Düsseldorf, 1954); J. HABERMAS, *Das Absolute und die Geschichte* (diss., Bonn, 1954); W. SCHULZ, *Die Vollendung des deutschen Idealismus* (Stuttgart, 1955); G. SEMERARI, *Interpretazione di Schelling* (Naples, 1958); H. ZELTNER, *Schelling* (Stuttgart, 1954); K. JASPERS, *Schelling* (Munich, 1965); W. KASPER, *Das Absolute in der Geschichte* (Mainz, 1965); A. BAUSOLA, *Metafisica e Rivelazione* (Milan, 1965); H. HOLZ, *Spekulation und Faktizität* (Bonn, 1970); X. TILLIETTE, *Schelling: Une philosophie en devenir* (Paris, 1970); id., *L'absolu et la philosophie* (Paris, 1987); J.-F. MARQUET, *Liberté et existence* (Paris, 1973); R. LAUTH, *Die Entstehung von Schellings Identitätsphilosophie* (Freiburg/Munich, 1975); M. VETO, *Le fondement selon Schelling* (Paris, 1977); M. THEUNISSEN, "Die Dialektik der Offenbarung," *Philosophisches Jahrbuch* 83 (1976): 1–29; T. F. O'MEARA, *Romantic Idealism and Roman Catholicism: Schelling and the Theologians* (London, 1982); E. BRITO, *La création selon Schelling* (Louvain, 1987); M. MAESSCHALCK, *Philosophie et révélation dans l'itinéraire de Schelling* (Louvain/Paris, 1989).

Other reference works: H. BOUILLARD, *Karl Barth*, 3 vols. (Paris, 1957); R. BULTMANN, *Geschichte und Eschatologie* (Tübingen, 1958); E. SCHILLEBEECKX, *Révélation et théologie* (Brussels/Paris, 1965); M. FOUCAULT, *Les mots et les choses* (Paris, 1966); E. WEIL, *Logique de la philosophie* (Paris, 1967); J.-B. METZ, *Theology of the World* (London/New York, 1969); R. LATOURELLE, *Theology: Science of Salvation* (Staten Island, NY, 1969); H. KÜNG, *Incarnation de Dieu* (Paris, 1972); B. J. LONERGAN, *Method in Theology* (New York, 1972); E. BLOCH, *Atheism in Christianity* (New York, 1972); M. CORBIN, *Le chemin de la théologie chez Thomas d'Aquin* (Paris, 1974); G. MOREL, *Problèmes de la religion* (Paris, 1968); M. DE CERTEAU, *L'écriture de l'histoire* (Paris, 1975); id., *La faiblesse de croire* (Paris, 1987); H. PEUKERT, *Wissenschaftstheorie—Handlungstheorie— Fundamentale Theologie* (Düsseldorf, 1976); K. RAHNER, *Foundations of Christian Faith* (New York, 1978); M. SERRES, *Le système de Leibniz et ses modèles mathématiques* (Paris, 1968); C. BOFF, *Teologia de lo politico* (Salamanca, 1980); P. VEYSSET, *Situation de la politique dans la pensée de saint Thomas d'Aquin* (Paris, 1981); G. THILS, *Pour une théologie de structure planétaire* (Louvain-la-Neuve, 1983); H. DELHOUGNE, *Karl Barth et la rationalité* (Lille/Paris, 1983); C. GEFFRÉ, *Le christianisme au risque de l'interprétation* (Paris, 1983); J. LADRIRE, *L'articulation du sens*, 2 vols. (Paris, 1984); J. GREISCH, *L'age herméneutique de la raison* (Paris, 1985); J. MOLTMANN, *God in Creation* (San Francisco, 1985); id., *The Future of Hope: Theology as Eschatology* (New York, 1970); id., *Trinity and the Kingdom* (New York, 1981); X. XHAUFFLAIRE, *Feuerbach et la théologie de la sécularisation* (Paris, 1970); id., *La "théologie politique"* (Paris, 1972).

Marc MAESSCHALCK

IDEOLOGY

There is always the latent risk of absolutizing one aspect of reality and of making it into all-truth; it is equally true that ideologies are born and die with the multiple forms of the "will-to-power" and with external defeats and internal disappointments. If this is true for the individual's experience, how much the more persistent is that risk for *religion*, claiming as it does to offer humanity total salvation, by an all-embracing vision of the real, the truth that transcends the phenomenon and history. For this reason it may be useful to consult the *philosophy of religion* (→ RELIGION VI); one can easily see how all the above-mentioned categories are interwoven, how they are related to one another and are mutually involved in their fate. But it is also clear to see that, at a theoretical level, the concept of TRUTH is fundamental for determining ideological thought: a system of thought not claiming to be all-truth can, by its very structure, be easily removed from the category of ideology.

At the beginning of the decade which will (we hope) bring us to the third millennium of the Christian era, our eyes behold the decline and fall of many an ideology (while others persist or arise, let us be under no illusion), notably Marxism—a singular landing stage for the philosophy of religion, to be sure. Ideology, characterized by a strong, abrogative, deconstructive charge, ends up destroying itself; just as the most radical demythicization, whether containing much or little truth, must eventually recoil on itself. Ideology is not interchangeable with *myth* (as De Gaulle would have it in his *Mémoires*) but contains it and, so, demythicization goes hand in hand with demystification.

It is a cultural fact: modes of thinking and acting, systems of values, symbolic codes, give a group structural unity. In Marxist ideology, there is (was?) a *structure:* capital in bourgeois society, capital and labor relations, the classes and all the legal, political, artistic, philosophic, and religious *superstructures.* With denouncing one ideology (*Die deutsche Ideologie*) goes the task of striving to put an end to it and, inevitably, the affirming of another one (*Das Kapital*), until this one's sun sets too. Ideology, as R. Aron so truly used to say, is the idea of one's opponent and consequently forms groups by imitation, aggregation, identification (inevitably, especially by the weakest). Whence the difficulty of a *science* of ideology, especially if to the dialectical *copulae* prejudice/reason, critical principle/authority and tradition, is inevitably added the interest that also sustains the analysis of science and technology (see J. Habermas, *Erkenntnis und Interesse* [Frankfurt, 1968]; idem, *Technik und Wissenschaft als 'Ideologie'* [Frankfurt, 1968]). Thought is constantly threatened by ideological deviation that offers justification for that which cannot be justified: the interests command and orient knowledge. Even though thought, at the time, is in itself negation, resistance to everything attempting to impose itself from outside (T. W. Adorno, *Negative Dialektik* [Frankfurt, 1966]), as Goethe's Mephistopheles had so well put it: "*Ich bin der Geist der stets verneint.*"

After the romantic nostalgia for the past and the Enlightenment-inspired struggle against prejudice, giving rise to other myths (e.g., "natural religion," "progress," or the absolutization of "reason"), a more precise attention to language (e.g., U. Eco, *Semiotica delle ideologie*) has alerted us to the fact that this message hides, instead of communicating, the conditions it was supposed to express. Mystification lies in the fact that it prevents us from seeing the various semantic systems in the totality of their mutual relationship. In fact, ideology overloads language; no meaning is possible except the "one meaning" that becomes the measure of all things, and woe betide anyone who expresses doubts about it. Here too HERMENEUTICS has a word to say (H. G. Gadamer, *Verità e metodo* [Milan, 1972]) in its attempt to study the effects of history on consciousness, to relate authority and reason, to distinguish between prejudice and authority and tradition.

The approach by way of the mental sciences (Gadamer) or the sciences of sociological criticism (Habermas) has the merit of regaining the historical dimension (Marx, "Ideology Has No History," in *Die Deutsche Ideologie* [1846]) and, to the systematic distortion of communication, opposes as a possible regulating idea a "communication without limitation or restraint" (Ricoeur). For when not only the relations but also the ambiguities of the ideology/utopia relationship have been elucidated, and a nonscientific system of judgment in which affirmations of fact were not sufficiently distinct from value judgments has been denounced, and the impetus of protest and the thrust of the great political-social units have become exhausted, the result will still not be noncommitment or transformism or ideological void. If the "threshold of tolerance" is a function of ideology, this is not to say that a weak ideology will be more tolerant than a strong one. And if the ideology means subjugation of the reason and of truth, the reduction of thought, as against a philosophy that reveals the truth, this good ideology is a more subtle travesty of the truth.

From Destutt de Tracy's "invention" of the term (*Mémoire sur la faculté de penser* [1796–98]; *Projet d'Eléments d'idéologie*, vols. I–IV [1801–45]) to the present-day debate now running out of steam, ideology has been given the most varied definitions and has been loaded with every kind of contradictory quality. Small wonder, when you consider that the most "natural" term (*nature*, to be precise), not even to mention the myth of "natural religion" or the ambiguities of the *anima naturaliter christiana* (ending with the anonymous Christians), has attracted the harshest critics. Nothing more ambiguous than *physis*, than *nature*, wrote J. Chr. Sturmius (*Philosophia eleatica* [1689]), and R. Boyle (*De ipsa natura sive libera in receptam naturae notionem disquisitio* [1686]) had as early as then suggested abolishing a term that would not have satisfed Leibniz either and was to be considered "vague and indeterminate" by Hume.

To the *idola* (*tribus, specus, fori, theatri*), prejudices of the dogmatism of traditional Aristotelean thought, Francis Bacon (*Novum Organon* [1620]) counterposes the true ideas that arise from experience (*signacula Creatoris super creaturam*). But David Hume's *Natural History of Religion* (1757) and the *Dialogues concerning Natural Religion* (1799), while indirectly hypothesizing a pure, philosophic religion, charge natural belief with credulity, superstition, fanaticism, and immorality.

The psychologistic criticism of Bacon and the deist/rationalistic empiricism of later English philosophers becomes sensistic materialism in Destutt de Tracy and the *idéologues*: Condillac, *Traité des sensations* (1754); D'Alembert, *Discours préliminaire de l'Encyclopédie* (1751); the many writings occasioned by Holbach's *Le Système de la nature* (1766–76); C. A. Helvetius (1715–1771), De La Mettrie, *L'homme Machine* (1748). Ideas are facts of consciousness, and ideology, of course, is the science of ideas. Sociology of ideologies, while avoiding any detailed metaphysical discourse on causes, substance, inquires into the origins of ideas and the law according to which they take shape. Napoleon's accusation of "shadowy metaphysics," not unprompted by political animus, was reinforced by that of "futile metaphysics" on the part of Chateaubriand (*Le Génie du Christianisme* [1802]), due to the "separation of the history of the human spirit from the history of things divine."

In the *Phänomenologie des Geistes*, Hegel defines culture as "the spirit that has gone *outside* the self" and religion as "unhappy conscience, appearance of movement, without substance, without awareness even." Further on, religion is "the purely useful" inasmuch as related to absolute essence. In conclusion: "In the world of culture itself, self-awareness does not succeed in intuiting its negation . . . either it is the heaven of faith or the useful instrument of the Enlightenment." In the context of an exposition, though brief, yet general, of the relationship between Kierkegaard and Hegel and idealistic/romantic philosophy in connection with the philosophy of religion, a few quotations from the Danish philosopher may illustrate his opposition to an ideologized Christianity (even though, inevitably, it is charged with a different ideological veneer). Betraying Christianity is to make every concept fade away: faith, revelation . . . just as Schleiermacher did, and to put one's own thought (*Philosophie der Offenbarung*) at the service of politics, as Schelling did at the court of Prussia. "Everything is politics, these days. The religious view differs *toto coelo* . . ." (*Il singolo*, SV XIII, 589). Truth is made to depend on the consensus of the majority, of the masses, and the paradox of Christianity has become state church: "By nothing am I so perplexed as by all this, which just reeks of this wretched mixture of politics and Christianity." The divinized political principle of socialization is the negation of the principle of religious individuality before God, of personal responsibility. "One may well reflect on what it would mean to live in a Christian state, in a Christian nation, where everything is Christian and where all are Christians" (*Il momento*, SV XIV, 128).

Engels, the theorist of the Marxist critique of religion, completes the critique of reaction's final effort against free philosophy in *Schelling and Revelation* (1842), denouncing, not unjustifiably, the ideological aspect of Schelling's "positive philosophy" and his *Philosophy of Revelation* with its claim to construct a "Christian philosophy" for a "Christian state." Engels's conclusion passes sentence on similar projects and admits of no appeal: "From such a doctrine one may once again clearly see how feeble the feet are, supporting modern Christianity."

Marx has a different theoretical premise: Feuerbach, whose extreme subjectivity of feeling resolves theology into anthropology, and for whom religion is "the sum of the relations of man with himself, but as though this himself were a being different from him" (*Das Wesen des Christentums* [1841]). The "groaning of the oppressed" and the "opium of the people" (K. Marx, Introduction to *Per la critica alla filosofia del diritto di Hegel* [1843]) find their context in the denunciation of all superstructures born of and battening on the false awareness of reality which divorces theory from practice, diverts people's attention from the historical, material, and social conditions of thought, and serves the interests of the ruling class (*Die Deutsche Ideologie* [1846]). As against the mystery-mongering of religion and Christianity, communism is defined as "*real* moment—and necessary for the next historical development—of human emancipation and restoration" (*Economico-philosophical MSS* [1844]). However lucid the Marxian analysis of an ideological reality has been, so much more evident (and ultimately admitted unreservedly) the ideological nature of the Marxist adventure has been, with results we all know.

The second of Nietzsche's *Unzeitgemässe Betrachtungen*, "On the utility and harm of history for life" (1873–76), offers a sort of antidote, even though Superman's will-to-power foretells the destruction of values hitherto held to be supreme (*Die fröhliche Wissenschaft* [1882–87]: "God is dead"), There is not much point (since tragedy cannot be explained) in trying to see how much direct or indirect responsibility Nietzsche's ideology bore for the racist ideologies of destruction, war, and death.

Freud, Marx, and Nietzsche have been described as "masters of mistrust," but even mistrust has become an ideology; one more, since there have always been ideologies with diverse and conflicting signs, in perpetual motion between "myth" and "logos." In the *extensive* sense (set of ideas, convictions, and doctrines appropriate to a period, a society, a class) and the *reductive* (one-dimensional reasoning in the service of the ruling class or as aid to seizing power); *theoretic/pluralistic* (cultural system of a human group at a historic period) and *pragmatic/exclusivist* ("persuasive belief" directed to action, to changing the world); *descriptive* (system of all-embracing interpretation of the real) and *valuative* (with, in addition, the identification of one's own interest with the general interest).

In *Ideologia e Utopia* (1929), K. Mannheim distinguished between an ideological consciousness, which tries to avoid the present in its efforts to understand it in terms of the past (*negative ideology*), and a utopian consciousness, which transcends the present and is directed toward the future (*valuative/dynamic ideology*). As can be seen, beyond the more or less deliberate frauds and travesties perpetrated by human interest-groups (ideology), utopia, with its critical and revolutionary stance, sets its gaze on the future. On this basis, P. Ricoeur (*Tradizione o alternativa* [1980]) has set out the basic function of ideology: to mold, to consolidate, to order the course of action. A function of conservation, also positive, of integration, with regard to the utopian function of "social subversion." Both being partial and dangerous, they react to one another in a very positive and fanatical way.

The radical absoluteness of revelation, discoursing as it does on the Absolute, while excluding identification with any particular interpretation ("the word of God won't allow itself to be captured"), cannot prescind from the historic human categories in which perforce it has been accepted and understood. Of course one may know (not prove the existence of) God, the beginning and end of all things, by considering the creation by the natural light of human reason: but to revelation alone pertains *Ab omnibus, expedite, firma certitudine et nullo admixto errore* (DS 3004–3005). The rebuke of stupidity (Wis 3) and perversity (Rom 1) does not let us forget that "my kingdom is not of this world" (Jn 18:36) and that what is due to Caesar is still distinct from what is due to God (see Mk 12:17). For Innocent III (*Unam Sanctam* [1302]), the *potestas temporalis* had to submit to the *potestas spiritualis*, which was exempt from all criticism. It is preoccupation with survival and institutional expansion that transforms Christianity into ideology and utters condemnations (from Erasmus to Galileo) which betray a fear of the unknown in their violent imposition of orthodoxy or their forging of securities (*Donatio Constantini*), doomed inevitably to fall apart. The ideological legitimization of the claims of the power of the pope in the struggle against the emperor, in Bossuet becomes continuity between the mysterious divine sovereignty of God, who makes use of human beings for his purposes (*Discours sur l'Histoire universelle* [1681]), and the justification of an absolutist power supposedly derived immediately from God (*Politique tirée des propres paroles de l'Ecriture sainte* [1709]). The gospel message, presented in the "patois de Canaan," demands free study, in contrast to ideological conformism; in fact, obedience to the gospel is, for the Christian, the only possible way of rebelling against the many ideologies. Perhaps Paul was alluding to this when he warned: "See to it that no one deceives you with his philosophy" (Col 2:8), and Anselm was on the right lines with his *fides quaerens intellectum.* The lack of critical attention to the active movements of history was perhaps one of the reasons why the Counter-Reformation became one of the greatest ideologies in the whole of Christian history, and is the critical thrust motivating Thomas More's *Utopia* (1516) and Erasmus's *Encomium Moriae* (1509). Its very affinity with ideology (a system of all-embracing interpretation of reality) and the inevitability of revelation's being received through conditioning *schemas* demand that theology be aware how precariously placed it is, and of the constant risk of becoming ideology. Also, due reservations made, we should take note of the polemic between C. Schmitt (*Politische Theologie* [1922]) and E. Peterson (*Il monoteismo come problema politico* [1935]). Only because of the dogma of the Trinity was the Christian religion freed from its bonds with the Roman Empire; God is no longer "the archetype of the mighty ones of this world, but the Father of the Christ who was crucified and rose again for our sakes" (J. Moltmann, *Trinità e regno di Dio* [Brescia, 1983], 212).

A "Catholic culture" longed for by nineteenth-century-type integralists and ultramontanists, but with modern trimmings, is like a plaster cast constraining the church from making free and open movements. Such an approach could not escape the pitiless analysis of the ruling culture Marx made in *Die deutsche Ideologie* and would moreover place us outside the perspectives of the *Epistle to Diognetus:* "As the soul is to the body, so Christians are to the world." And, contrariwise, Tertullian's virulent opposition to pagan culture ended up alienating him from the church as well. The task of evangelizing contemporary culture, and awareness of the tragic breach between gospel and culture characterizing our age (*EN* 20), cannot in any case mean mourning the disintegration of a monolith of Constantinian, Counter-Reformist, premodern design. Better a faith less protected, yet more free, feebler yet purer, less compromised with power, but so much the more evangelical. The "household of the faith" supplies the strength for denouncing whatever may attempt to detract from the absoluteness of God and the primacy of the human person; in a word, sin and the structures of sin. Just as we need to recognize the stimulating role of utopia without getting carried away by stupid enthusiasms, so we also need to free ourselves from iconoclastic frenzies and blind subjection to ideology. Through hermeneutics, in fact, the faith can be connected with culture and ideology: with due precaution, lest religion be ideologized, the ideologies should be able to be tackled freely on their own ground, at an equal distance from religious integralism and religious heteronomicity, care always being taken to grasp "a certain affinity of an earthly project with the profound logic of salvation" (I. Mancini, *Fede e Cultura* [Turin, 1979], 44).

Bibl.: E. Castelli, *De mitizzazione e Ideologia* (Rome, 1973); I. Mancini, *Teologia, ideologia, utopia* (Brescia, 1974); S. Dicaro, "Ideologia," in *DTI* 2:264–69; H. R. Schlette, "Ideologia" in *Concetti fondamentali di Filosofia* (Brescia, 1982), 2:988–99; G. Ruggieri, "Resistenza e dogma: Il rifiuto di qualsiasi teologia politica in Erik Peterson," in *Il monoteismo come problema politico* (Brescia, 1983), 5–26.

Salvatore Spera

IMAGINATION

Imagination supplies the basic materials for fundamental theology to think about. Revelation, in any religious system, occurs within imaginative constructs—myth, symbol, narrative, sacramental presentation, etc. So imagination shows itself as an irreplaceable power of knowing in its own right. What it knows cannot be gotten at directly. As a result, imagination, in religion, must invent means of knowing who or what is in relationship with whom. An example would be Ps 104 of the Hebrew Bible. To catch the sense that God creates, the psalmist creates a language that even imitates what God did at the origin of the world. The crucial problems for fundamental theology about such knowledge are (1) the openness of imaginative material to any understanding, anywhere; (2) the reality of the knowledge; and (3) the varieties of religious vision, e.g., about creation.

1. Imaginative constructs, in or outside religious traditions, endeavor to be self-explaining, though often much of their meaning can depend on a surrounding tradition. The parable of the Good Samaritan does depend on a tradition that understands social distinction, though, once that is explained, the basic internal point about kinship based on charity stands forth on its own and serves as a paradigm for many other situations far beyond the parable's time and place. The same may be said for the icon, whose beauty resides within it, though its theme derives from outside it. Where meaning is not immediately clear in an imaginative construct, fundamental theology interprets, but in its own way, through patterns of thought. It can happen that the interpretation then substitutes for the imaginative material. We then get a Platonic Christianity or an Aristotelean Christianity or, as more recently, an existentialist or a process Christianity. The purpose of interpretation in these instances has been to make up for the supposed lack of universality in the imaginative material. But another approach takes the imaginative material and makes it universal by calling it unique and unrelated to any other religious expression anywhere. Interpretation becomes the activity of applying untouchable revelation to historical circumstances. Liturgical approaches, however, tend to make imaginative materials do their own work from generation to generation, much as a work of art expresses itself from generation to generation.

The basic posture of fundamental theology has to be to find the way a specific tradition of religious imagination explains the whole, and yet does not exclude as meaningless other specific traditions of religious imagination that try, in their own ways, to explain the whole. An example would be Mircea Eliade's use of the experience of Romanian icon as the basis for understanding the imaginative constructs other religions use to grasp themselves and the

sacred. One always returns to the specific imaginative construct after having seen it in its relationship to constructs using similar materials. This is a historical study as much as it is a reflective one. The imaginative material retains primacy of place; it is seen as irreplaceable.

2. Imaginative constructs, in or outside of religion, endeavor to make sense of the real world. So they must be left inside their own natures as imaginative constructs. This is what reflective interpretation has discovered. A literalized reading of Ps 104 would miss the reality of the psalm and one of its deeper messages, i.e., that the sense of divine creativity is caught out in the experience of human creativity, and that the many creation stories found in the many religious traditions enhance rather than diminish the human reading of the world as created. The world intimates its origin. That is a delicate message. The effect of that message is as delicate. One imitates in life and liturgy the act of creation revealed in the psalm. That imitation must remain within imaginative terms. The psalm has some violence toward the end, where God is asked to destroy what is wicked. That is a contradiction to the meaning of the psalm that a literalist would not notice, i.e., one for whom the psalm is about the power of God, creation or no creation. But one for whom creation, even in God, is never an act of destruction would notice the contradiction. What is implied here is the judgment that imaginative constructions make about the meaning of life and the judgment that life must enter into about whether the imaginative constructions are true or not. If this does not happen, then imaginative religious material is pure imposition within varying traditions who cannot then talk to one another. The colloquy between Is 52–53 and the crucified Jesus of the Gospels would have to disappear as something internal to the two, and as something that made sense of life wherever life is found.

3. Imaginative constructs, in or outside religion, endeavor to relate to one another. The figure of Christ, for example, easily draws in other images, if one is to judge by the history of Christian art—the image of rabbi, of Orpheus, of the philosopher, of the ruler, of the monk, etc. The process can also be reversed, if one is to judge by some modern art in which a human being is depicted as being freed, and that person bears the marks of crucifixion, though he or she is not Christ. Images retain their own integrity even when absorbed by other images, e.g., the Suffering Servant motif from Isaiah as used to clarify the meaning of Jesus crucified. When images influence one another, there is an increment of meaning. It is true that a process of propaganda can violate images and force them to submit to something not themselves. But on the aesthetic level, images can recover themselves and reveal that they are being forced, such as with gnostic and apocalyptic imagery. The mark of integrity in an image or imaginative construct is its power to relate in a way that is co-creative; the image does not lose itself or efface the other. Psalm 104, except for the last few lines, intensifies Gn 1–2 and the prologue to John's Gospel. To have all three expressions of God creating is an enrichment, not a confusion. It is the doctrine of creation from nothing that tends to impoverish consciousness of relationship because such creation is inimitable.

Imaginative constructs, in or outside religion, do teach that they are constructs and that they cannot be idolatrized. They show that they are words, paint, sound, or motion. They also show that they are irreplaceable. The language that expresses Jesus' resurrection looks in its beauty like the language of a long poetic tradition, but it is used of a specific event in a specific time and place. It is only language, however beautiful, but it is historically irreplaceable. This is true of surviving art works as well, all stating their own fragility and irreplaceability.

Thinking about imaginative material in religious traditions can result in patterns of thought that then seek to validate themselves on their own terms. That is a distinctive human work, truth for truth's sake. But then the relationship to the imaginative material must be clarified. The hardest task is to think an image and have the image remain primary, not the thought.

At this point the role of creativity in a tradition becomes paramount, for the artist thinks within imagery if he or she accepts responsibility for the tradition. The state of fundamental theology depends on the state of aesthetic consciousness in a specific tradition. The more

imagination is recognized as synthetic in a truth-finding way—however unusual its products may be—the more reflective mind is called upon to be synthetic, and the more it will risk. For example, the book of Jonah forces a rethinking, then and now, of violence in the psalm tradition and requires a thinking today that must entertain the truth of varying religious systems. The same may be said for the parable of the Good Samaritan.

What would a modern book of Jonah be, or a modern parable of the Good Samaritan? They would be imaginative works that handle the problem of the Holocaust victim—or victim of any other genocide—vis-à-vis his or her victimizer, or that handle the problem of those struck down by disease or natural disaster vis-à-vis those left unharmed. If imaginative works of the size of the modern problem are created, then thinking on the same scale can begin. According to a phrase from the "Lamentatio" section of Penderecki's oratorio *Dies Irae*, taken from the poet Louis Aragon, "Even Christ did not follow such a path of doom." One must imagine that Christ truly followed all the paths of doom before one can think it. For that to be a truthful imagining, one must have an enormous empathy for everyone who followed any path of doom. From them may come the way of understanding Jesus. Penderecki's *Dies Irae* concludes with Paul's phrase: "Death has been swallowed up in victory" (1 Cor 15:54).

Bibl.: G. DURAND, *Les structures anthropologiques de l'imaginaire* (Paris, 1960); M. ELIADE, *A History of Religious Ideas*, 3 vols. (Paris, 1987); H. G. GADAMER, *Truth and Method* (London, 1975); M. GRIAULE, *Conversations with Ogotemmeli* (Oxford, 1965); R. HART, *Unfinished Man and the Imagination* (New York, 1968); J.-P. MANIGNE, *Pour une poétique de la foi* (Paris, 1969); H. MARCUSE, *The Aesthetic Dimension* (Boston, 1977).

Francis Patrick SULLIVAN

IMMANENCE METHOD

The concept of the "immanence method" was introduced by Maurice BLONDEL in order to designate the approach to philosophy of religion that he inaugurated in *L'Action* (1893).

1. Origin of the Concept

Blondel's doctoral dissertation of 1893 can be seen as the first—and so far most thorough—attempt to come to terms, in a rigorously scholarly way, with one of the most fundamental problems confronting the philosophy of religion in modern times, namely, how can a divine revelation that was effected as a concrete historical fact have an absolute claim on a humanity inherently characterized by autonomy? Here, it is not enough to show that reason is marked by a general openness to the transcendent or that a relationship of mere convenience or correspondence exists between the content of revelation and the fundamental structure of humanity. If the claim that Jesus Christ came "once and for all" is justified, then recognition of the absolute necessity of assenting to Christian revelation must occur in the innermost core of reason as soon as that revelation presents itself to humanity within history, and this necessity must, then, always have constituted the final goal of human existence.

From the very start, the driving force behind Blondel's attempt was the endeavor to resolve—on its highest plane and in debate with contemporary philosophy—a problem in philosophy of religion that had impressed itself upon his consciousness as a result of painful experience of the social and scholarly ghettoization of the postrevolutionary church in France. The initial reactions to the publication of _L'Action_ confirmed Blondel in this endeavor (I 539). For one thing, well-meaning reviewers from the Catholic side, who either stressed the kinship of Blondel's work with the thought of Pascal or Maine de Biran (II 4, but also II 14) or classed it with contemporary attempts to transfer philosophical apologetics to the terrain of psychology (II 22), gave him occasion to define more precisely his thoroughly dissimilar method. For another thing, Blondel was strengthened in his intention to make even more plainly obvious the fact that the character of his work satisfied the standards of modern philosophy. A factor here, for example, was the laudatory comparison with the philosophy of Fichte and Hegel accorded him by A. Lasson (II 17). Of first importance, however, was the accusation by L. Brunschvicg that Blondel had unwittingly transformed philosophy into an apology for positive religion (II 15) and disregarded the

concept of immanence that was among the fundamental preconditions of modern philosophizing (II 1). Probably the most significant document for understanding the reflections on method that Blondel then undertook in the _Lettre_ of 1896 is his penetrating critical response to the attempt by his friend V. Delbos to grasp the whole of philosophy, from Spinoza through Kant, Fichte, and Schelling to Hegel, as a progressive development of Spinozism (_évolution du Spinozisme;_ see I 26).

For Spinoza, and especially in the great idealistic systems that followed, an insight considered as fundamental was the assumption of _immanence,_ i.e., the idea that the truth of things does not show itself when they are grasped randomly and in isolation, but only after their particular place within the system of absolute spirit has been determined. Blondel does not dispute the necessity for demonstrating the dialectical interconnectedness of the phenomena within the immanence of the spirit. However, he rejects any purely speculative resolution of this task, as this would inevitably entail viewing all reality as a monistic or pantheistic unity subject to whatever constructions thought might impose upon it. If, by contrast, one grasps all the phenomena in the particular place (certainly to be determined systematically) that each occupies within its original context of living action—and not first within some system defined by speculation, which comes after the fact and can thus never definitively capture action—then the immanent dialectic of the spirit becomes itself manifest as an open-ended movement able to arrive at its own fulfillment only by opting in favor of a supernaturally guaranteed gift.

From the intensity of Blondel's critical examination of the most significant directions in modern philosophy, one can understand (1) the sharpness with which he (in part 1 of the _Lettre_) rejects the previous undertakings in apologetics that do not withstand thorough criticism; (2) the conceptual framework, oriented on the demands of modern criticism, in which (in part 2) he presents his "immanence method"; and finally, (3) the confidence with which (in part 3) he anticipates a future reconciliation between Catholicism and secular science, if only the path of modern critical reason is thought through logically to its end. But no less understandable, too, is how irksome this "Discours de la méthode" must have appeared in the eyes of those for whom any affiliation with the spirit of modernism was, in itself, already suspect.

2. Theological Controversies about the Immanence Method

Blondel's *Lettre* helped various philosophers who were thinking in terms of modern categories to make an appropriate evaluation of the character of his work as philosophy of religion (e.g., Brunschvicg, II 24; R. Eucken, II 36). L. Laberthonnière had already allied himself with Blondel in 1894 and became so decisive a champion of the immanence method that it was hard, up to 1913, to distinguish the approaches of the two friends from one another (cf. I 540; II 44; 80). The first strong attacks by neo-scholastic theologians (M. B. Schwalm, II 26; H. Gayraud, II 28; C. Pesch, II 54) foreshadowed the sorts of misunderstanding to which the categories employed by Blondel, interpreted from a Thomist perspective, would soon be exposed as a fundamental dispute arose between traditional theology and modern thinking.

To be sure, when the "crisis of modernism" broke out, criticism was initially centered (see esp. II 1050) on the two "little red books" by A. Loisy, from whose position of "historicism" Blondel dissociated himself in 1904 (I 80; cf. I 536; II 989). Since, however, Blondel simultaneously branded the traditional (fundamental-) theological approach as "extrinsicism," mistrust of his immanence method was strengthened. In a series of articles in 1905-7 (I 97; 98; 108), Blondel undertook a comparison between the immanence method and the apologetic method (unknown to him until 1904) of Cardinal Dechamps ("consacrée par le concile du Vatican"), emphasizing—as opposed to the apologetics of extrinsicism—their common assessment of the "fait intérieur," the necessary subordination of human reason to revelation. Here, in relation to Blondel himself (and not just to his committed theological defenders like L. Laberthonnière, J. Wehrlé, and Auguste Valensin), it is noticeable how much some of the distinctions pertaining to philosophy of religion that were elaborated by him in 1896 recede into the background as he attempts to defend the immanence method within the horizon of scholastic thought.

The controversies reached a peak when, after the appearance of the encyclical *Pascendi* (1907), the question was raised about the extent to which the immanence method ought to be numbered among those teachings classified as dangerous or even among those that were condemned (I 118; 531; 566; II 119-91). Contributions from this time showing a high level of scholarly distinction include, on the one side, the two-part article written by Albert and Auguste Valensin in the *DAFC* of 1912 (II 175; 176) and, on the other side, J. de Tonquédec's "Summa of Anti-Blondelism" (II 177), which was published in 1913 under the title "Immanence."

The article in the *DAFC* was cleverly divided into a treatise written by Albert Valensin entitled "Doctrine of Immanence" and a second entitled "Immanence Method" by Auguste Valensin, with critical response by Albert Valensin. This arrangement made it possible to engage initially in critical discussion of the doctrine of immanence condemned in *Pascendi* without, however, endangering the immanence method. The former is traced back to Spinoza. Its influence was then felt in philosophy of religion and theology, especially through Schleiermacher, Lutheran pietism, and, in France, primarily Sabatier. From there, finally, an "immanentistic apologetics" sprang up. In the representation and critique of this apologetics, the main censures made in the encyclical were linked to ideas and works that obviously could not be associated with the immanence method.

The representation of the immanence method by Auguste Valensin was expressly characterized by Blondel as a genuine expression of the essential lines of his thought (I 168). The oft-cited fact that the concept of immanence was introduced as a guiding principle of modern thought in Blondel's *Lettre* (p. 34) is immediately supplemented, by Auguste Valensin, with the point that the concept is, to no less extent, a guiding idea that was definitive for tradition (especially Thomas Aquinas). After some precisely formulated ideas on the necessity of an immanent referredness of reason to positive revelation ("Even when imposed by God, a law can permeate the conscience only through an element within already present in the conscience itself" [*DAFC*[1] II 582]), a lengthy attempt is made to resolve the problem thus implied of the relationship between nature and grace. Similar to

Blondel's earlier interpretation of the "fait intérieur" of Cardinal Dechamps, the decisive statements appear to anticipate the introduction of the "supernatural existential" by K. RAHNER. In conclusion, after reference to earlier approaches to an immanence method (especially by AUGUSTINE, PASCAL, Bossuet, Fénélon, Malebranche, and Dechamps), the basic argument of *L'Action* is concisely outlined.

Already in 1912, J. de Tonquédec had published parts (I 168) of his devastating critique, fully published in 1913, of Blondel's philosophy from a Thomist perspective. Against this background, it is understandable that the two-part article by the Valensin brothers barely escaped being placed on the Index (II 176). The outbreak of World War I, of course, had the effect of silencing the vehement debates about the immanence method. Nevertheless, the editor of the *DAFC* found himself forced, in the new edition of 1926, to replace the critical evaluation of the immanence method authored by Albert Valensin with excerpts from de Tonquédec's book, and even on the occasion of Blondel's death (1949) — and in view of the many modifications that Blondel's thought had undergone in the meantime — de Tonquédec withdrew nothing of his fundamental critique, although now, on the eve of the encyclical *Humani Generis*, this was aimed more at his fellow brothers in Lyon (II 751).

3. Status of the Immanence Method in Fundamental Theology

Blondel himself never spoke of an "immanence apologetics," emphasizing instead that the immanence method was to be conceived as part of, and serviceable to, an "integral apologetics" (I 155). Understood in this sense, the immanence method is an indispensable component of present-day fundamental theology. Through P. Rousselot and J. Maréchal, Blondel's approach influenced the "theological anthropology," or "transcendental theology," of Karl Rahner, thereby leaving an enduring mark on recent theology.

Under grace, we may view the gift of divine revelation — not in a didactic-theoretical way, as a repository of doctrines that are to be regarded as true, doctrines that essentially transcend human understanding and, like the contents of a letter closed by the seal of a king, are certified to reason as requiring belief only through the external signs of divine authority (see *ST* 3, q. 43, a. 1; DS 3008) — but as God's personal address to, and loving intimacy with, humanity (cf. *DV*, chap. 1). In that case, the question then necessarily arises of human nature having an inherent reference to revelation, of a structural framework of reason within which God's word discloses itself as meaningful and as bringing salvation.

As much as present-day fundamental theology goes beyond the original approach of the immanence method in many respects — e.g., as a result of the development of HERMENEUTICS and linguistic philosophy — it has, in another respect, also lagged behind it. There is no work in philosophy of religion comparable to Blondel's early work, which brings out the internal dynamics of the relation of human reason to revelation through a critically sound and detailed analysis of the total interconnectedness of the phenomena of the spirit. Further, Blondel's warning about attempts to explain the reference to revelation by means of a demonstration of mere correlations, with the free, supernatural gift appearing as an integral part of the immanent context of the human (cf. *Lettre*, part 1), is not always sufficiently regarded.

What remains of the sharp theological critique that the immanence method was subjected to from the very first? Can it be understood solely as a final act of resistance by an apologetics already moribund at the core? In posing this question, one should not forget that a thinker so little suspected of "extrinsicism" as H. U. von Balthasar expressed reservations not only about the transcendental approach of J. Maréchal and K. Rahner but also — albeit with greater caution — about B. and P. Rousselot. The legitimacy of the fundamental concern behind the immanence method — namely, to uncover within the inner nature of human reason the conditions of the possibility of being compellingly claimed by God's historically proclaimed word — was never seen by von Balthasar as a matter for debate. However, he set himself decisively against any notion of a dynamically anticipatory subjectivity that, in the performance of the act of faith, would be responsible for the actual synthesis of the diverse, contingent signs of revelation in such a way that the decisive quality of intuitive evidence can no longer be regarded as deriving from the historical configuration of revelation itself. This stress on the priority of the question of the reality and objectivity of the historical fact was also a central concern in the Thomist-oriented critique of the immanence method.

Just as for K. Rahner the question of the "categorial" and objective aspect of revelation recedes in favor of the emphasis on "transcendental revelation" (as an impressing of reason by the "supernatural existential"), so Blondel, too, exhibits a deficient interest in taking fundamental-theological account of the "fait extérieur" in relation to the "fait intérieur" (to use the categories of Dechamps). This one-sidedness is probably not solely attributable to the methodological self-restriction of this philosopher of religion but rests ultimately on the fact that there is no place in the perspective of L'Action for direct intuitive insight into an unconditioned truth from the side of historically occurring fact (see II 1302, pp. 41–44, 54–55, 74–75).

Already regarding Blondel's early deliberations on miracles ("It is beyond doubt that, if we get down to the bedrock, there is nothing more in miracle than in the most trifling facts" [*Lettre*, 14]), one could rightly ask by which means, according to Blondel, a positive-historical revelation might show itself to be ultimately valid. It then appears especially remarkable that Blondel—despite his own pioneering understanding of tradition in *Histoire et dogme* (I 80)—obviously fails to grasp the crucial point of Dechamps's "via empirica" (the presence of the historical "once-and-for-all" in the "now" of the church, with no objectivizing recourse to the "historical Jesus") when he writes, concerning this method, "It isn't of any value, unless one resorts implicitly to the rational preambles and the historical foundations of Catholic faith. One does not adhere to the divinity of the church without tacitly admitting its supernatural origin, and granting that its divine foundation has been already proved and can still be proved. The method of the learned is shrouded and implied by that of the simple-minded themselves" (I 108, p. 575). Precisely the comparison of the immanence method with the position of Dechamps shows that (as with K. Rahner) Blondel's main concern is to demonstrate the possibility of a salvation-mediating option for the subject, even outside of any encounter with positive-historical

revelation—on the basis of the "anonymous presence" of the "immanent supernatural" (see ibid., p. 585).

This closeness of Blondel's immanence method to K. Rahner's transcendental approach—and also the similar criticisms raised against both—is one evidence that the essential sorts of questions posed by the immanence method are not consignable to the past but still belong at the center of fundamental-theological discussion (→ FAITH; REASON/FAITH).

Bibl.: M. BLONDEL, *Action 1893: Essay on a Critique of Life and a Science of Practice* (1893; New York, 1984); id., "Lettre sur les exigences de la pensée contemporaine en matière d'apologétique" (1896) in *Les premiers écrits de M. Blondel* (Paris, 1956); R. VIRGOULAY and C. TROISFONTAINES, *Bibliographie analytique et critique*, vol. 1: *Oeuvres de M. Blondel (1880–1973)* (Louvain-la-Neuve, 1975); vol. 2: *Études sur M. Blondel (1893–1975)* (Louvain-la-Neuve, 1976); P. HENRICI, "Maurice Blondel und die 'philosophie der Aktion,'" in E. Coreth, ed., *Christliche Philosophie im katholischen Denken des 19. und 20. Jahrhunderts*, vol. 1: *Neue Ansätze im 19. Jahrhundert* (Graz, 1987), 543–84; C. TROISFONTAINES, "L'étude philosophique du christianisme suivant M. Blondel," in B. Willaert, ed., Philosophie de la religion, Godsdienstfilosofie: Miscellanea Albert Dondeyne (Louvain-la-Neuve, 1987), 93–106; H. J. VERWEYEN, *Methodik der Religionsphilosophie: L'Action* (1893) in *Spiegel der "Lettre"* (1896), TP 64 (1989): 210–21.

Hansjürgen VERWEYEN

INCULTURATION

I. THE PROBLEM. *1. Semantics of Inculturation. 2. Foundations of Inculturation in Terms of Biblical Theology. 3. New Awareness of the Necessity of Inculturation. 4. Indispensable Elements of an Inculturated Evangelization. 5. Elementary Data of a Model of Inculturation.* (M. C. AZEVEDO)

II. INCULTURATION OF THE GOSPEL. *1. The Lessons of History. 2. New Aspects of Inculturation. 3. Norms of Inculturation. 4. Extension of Inculturation.* (H. CARRIER)

I. THE PROBLEM

1. Semantics of Inculturation

Since the Second Council of the Vatican, and especially since the Synod on Evangelization

(1974) and the subsequent publication by Paul VI of *Evangelii Nuntiandi* (8 December 1975), theological reflection and ecclesial praxis have demonstrated a deepening sensitivity to the relation between faith and culture, which has come to be denoted *inculturation*. Inculturation is not a theological, missiological, or pastoral fad; it is an essential quality of revelation, evangelization, and theological reflection.

Revelation takes place within the context of a people, within the evolutionary framework of the sociocultural formation of that people (Heb 1:1–2). *Evangelization*, too, must take account of the extremely diversified sociocultural reality of its audience. Finally, *theological reflection* has always developed within, and in terms of, an identifiable sociocultural universe, so that the universe in question becomes important for an understanding, interpretation, and evaluation of any product of the theological process.

Inculturation is a theological term connoting elements of cultural anthropology. It is to be distinguished from the purely anthropological notions of *acculturation* (the process of transformations occurring in a person or a human group upon contact with a different culture), *enculturation* (a concept analogous to *socialization*: the process of initiation of a person or group into one's own culture or society), and *transculturation* (a term denoting either the presence of determinate cultural elements throughout various cultures or the ethnocentric, unidirectional transfer of cultural elements from one culture to another, generally subordinate, culture). Inculturation is likewise to be distinguished from *adaptation* in the sense of the phenomenological adjustment of both the evangelizer (ways of being and acting) and the message (translation and expression) to the culture addressed.

Inculturation denotes the active process emerging from within the culture that receives revelation through evangelization and that understands and translates it according to its own way of being, acting, and communicating. The process of inculturated evangelization not only sows the seed of the gospel in that culture. The germ of faith now comes to develop in terms of, and according to the peculiar character of, this particular culture receiving it.

Inculturation, then, is a process of evangelization by which the Christian life and message are assimilated by a culture in such a way that not only are this life and message expressed through the elements proper to this culture, but they come to constitute a principle of inspiration as well, and eventually a norm and power of unification that transforms, re-creates, and revitalizes that culture. Inculturation therefore always implies and connotes a relationship obtaining between faith and culture(s), which are realities that reach and embrace the totality of the human life and person, on the individual and communitarian plane alike.

By Christian *faith* we understand, here, neither a rational assent to a body of ideas or of doctrine nor the sociologically identifiable religious organization of an ensemble of beliefs or symbolic system of rituals and disciplines. Christian faith is taken here as the full existential response of acceptance made by a human person or group to the living gift of God in Jesus Christ. By *culture*, we understand here not only the human group taken in itself (an ethnological datum), with its describable phenomenology (an ethnographic datum), nor only the ensemble of human actions upon nature or congeries of creations of the human mind and spirit in all of their various possible expressions (art, science, and technologies). Culture is taken here as the ensemble of meanings and significations, values and models, underlying or incorporated into the activity and communication of a human group or concrete society and regarded by it as proper and distinctive expressions of its human reality.

Inculturation, therefore, is not an act but a process; i.e., it presupposes and involves history and time. It is an active process, requiring mutual acceptance and dialogue, critical awareness and discernment, transformation and growth, renovation and innovation. Inculturation supposes an interaction between a living faith and a living culture, and thus it is not cultural archaeology. The process of an inculturated evangelization does not lead to the absolutizing of some ideal culture, as if a culture could be an abstraction, or to the restoration of a historical culture having claims to validity only in the reality of its past. Inculturation supposes an interaction between faith and culture as the latter exists in actual life, in its dynamic process, which integrates tradition and change, fidelity to origins and new creations.

Nor is inculturation reducible to a theological archaeology. Although the message of the Bible and the gospel must remain faithful to itself and to the God revealed in and by Jesus Christ, it nevertheless is proclaimed to specific persons and groups. Its expressions, emphases, formulations, and ways of understanding conform to human rhythms. These must be proportioned to the specific life contexts in which the process of evangelization unfolds.

As we see in the pedagogy of Yahweh in the OT, of Jesus and Paul in the NT, and of the church under the action of the Spirit throughout history, the evangelization process incorporates the dimensions of education and communication in an organic unity. Both of these dimensions presuppose and involve attention to the interlocutor—to their addressees' own universe, historical context, level of absorption, and capacity for assimilation. Methodologically, then, there can be no single, uniform "way to evangelize." Evangelizer and evangelized are each the subject, the agent, of the process, and each must be attentive to the framework of his or her respective cultural history and the particular activity of the Holy Spirit in that history.

Finally, the process of inculturation does not prioritize the evangelization of a _culture_ over that of a _society_, to the exclusion, or relegation to a subordinate place, of the latter. Culture and society are distinct concepts and realities, but every culture has social expressions. Every society rests on cultural presuppositions that it proposes and sponsors, transmits and implements. There are different degrees of coincidence between the cultural humus of a human group and the concrete framework of its social mediations and institutions. There may even be a breach, and discrepancy, between these two realities. In an inculturated evangelization, then, a relation among faith, culture, and society is implied. Inculturated evangelization is therefore not present in the mere transfer or modification of languages and methods, rites and symbols, organization and norms, outward manners of action and expression. It must go further and reach the foundations, the roots, of culture and cultures (_EN_ 20); i.e., it must reach the meanings and criteria of a given culture, its worldview, and the tacit or patent, but genuinely determinative, inspiration of the sociocultural praxis of this human group, as translated in the

dynamic development and historical transformations of its sociocultural ethos. Thus, an inculturated evangelization touches the deepest level of human reality, on both the individual plane as well as the social. It is performed, then, at the level of the concrete person, and from a point of departure in that person, while taking into account the complex network of relationships among persons and between persons and God (ibid.) in a dynamics of individual and community conversion. It is also performed in terms of the whole gamut of ethical expressions of faith, which entail a demand for the transformation and perfecting of societal structures.

2. Foundations of Inculturation in Terms of Biblical Theology

The raw fact of inculturation is as ancient as salvation history itself. God's relationship with humanity, and with the people of Israel in particular, is attested by the divine self-revelation, which is a free gift, but which is tailored to well-defined sociocultural contexts. Inculturation presupposes the universality of the salvific plan of God and the potential for a response to God on the part of all human beings, in terms of the sociocultural diversity in which they live. Here the historical reality of the people of Israel is paradigmatic. Manifold cultures enter into the sociocultural development of this people, to be translated into the nomadic or sedentary reality of its tribes. God makes use of this cultural plurality—involving the cultures of Mesopotamia, Egypt, Canaan, Persia, post-exilic Judaism, Hellenism, late Judaism, and the Greco-Roman world—in order to convey to humanity various facets of the divine mystery. God even makes a nonsimultaneous, successive use of these cultures, without that succession implying any rejection, negation, or replacement of the stage coming before. The self-revelation of God is a process at once continuous and discontinuous, iterative and integrative, among the various cultural elements at hand. It is a process that will elevate Israel into an important—indeed unique—reference point in cultural history for the process of inculturation (_DV_ 15–16).

This manifestation of God occurs from a point of departure in the very reality of the life of the people, as well as in the reality of the evolution of its understanding of itself and its

God. God's self-communication to the people arrives by way of persons, situations, and events—all by the route of contingent, relative expressions (*DV* 13). On the one hand, no culture, not even Israel, can be absolutized as the one fixed form of expressing God's revelation, although Israel remains an indispensable, decisive point of reference—precisely because it was among this people that the very inculturation of God occurred in Jesus Christ. On the other hand, no culture can be deprived of its potential condition as a vehicle of revelation of some sort, just as no culture can be singled out as an exclusive mediation of that revelation. This proposition is founded on faith and attested by the actual reality of salvation history. It therefore transcends the value-equality of cultures postulated in cultural anthropology.

Inculturation is thus a problem of a theological order, although it makes use of the anthropological datum and analysis of the multiplicity of cultures, as a diversified expression of a profound human oneness. The Word who is God, without ceasing to be God, becomes fully human in Jesus Christ (Jn 1:1–14; Phil 2:5–8). Thus, the incarnation constitutes the primordial and most radical of inculturations. The incarnation occurs in a definite cultural space and time and thus establishes both the theological relevance of the people of Israel and the fundamental inspiration of any process of inculturation. By the incarnation, the divine nature takes on human nature; God becomes a human being, in a relationship between natures. In the attendant inculturation, the divine nature is translated into *this human being,* into this people, this culture, and this human group in which the particular human individual that is Jesus finds himself in this time and this space. By the incarnation, the Word that has become a human being in Jesus is a human being in the way that any other human being is a human being. Through this inculturation, the Word becomes a human being in the same way as certain other human beings, in the diversified reality of their culture and society, are human beings—namely, the Jews of Jesus' time. Historically, in Jesus, the Word became at one and the same time both a human being as any other (on the level of nature) and a human being *not* as any other (on the level of culture) because he was a Jew.

The inculturation occurring today in the evangelization process is a replica, as it were, of the inculturation in which Jesus realized himself existentially. Based theologically and christologically on the mystery of the incarnation, inculturation projects itself upon evangelization as an expression of mission. For his part, Jesus, while so deeply rooted in his own culture, maintains a critical freedom in its regard. He adopts and endorses that which is evangelically valid within it; he corrects or reorientates, in a dynamic of conversion and transformation, that which is deviant or distorted within it, thereby implementing the salvific plan of God. This discernment to be exercised upon culture—both the culture of the evangelizer and that of the evangelized—is indispensable to inculturation and inherent in it. Indeed, *qua* human reality, each culture is but one among many and shares in the limits that stamp the human being, on the ontological and psychological levels, as they do on the moral and theological. No culture, then, may be absolutized as the adequate, unique vehicle of revelation. In every culture there is room for, and there must be a demand for, conversion, transformation, and growth.

The process of implanting of the church, in its first beginnings and throughout the first centuries of its history, likewise reveals a great openness to the various cultures it encountered, and a constant adjustment to them. Semitic in its origin, the church nevertheless implanted communities in the diaspora, doing so within a broad process of cultural mediation: first, through the written fixing, by the evangelists, of the content of the new covenant, in a Greek narrative expression; second, through the doctrinal and conciliar fixing of the Christian mystery in its Greek rational and cultural expression. In the Greco-Roman symbiosis of the empire, the holy fathers, together with Eastern and Western monasticism, gradually laid the foundations, in terms of Latin and Hellenistic culture, of the theology, spirituality, and pastoral activity of practically the entire first millennium of our Christian era. Thus occurred the great, and perhaps the only, full process of inculturation of the Christian faith. This faith was actually assimilated and re-expressed on the basis of the elements and particular character of the culture being evangelized. The slow Christian incorporation of the Nordic peoples (barbarians) and the Slavs, while it was attentive to their cultures and receptive to them in many aspects, itself was largely conditioned by this Christian mold of Greco-Roman cultural extraction.

In the first centuries of the second millennium, the church played a crucial role in the construction of the great pluricultural synthesis of the European West, which had its catalyst in medieval Christianity and which then became the Catholic Christian culture. Thereupon this culture constituted the reference point for evangelization throughout practically three-fourths of the second millennium. It was regarded as the preferred expression, and often enough the only valid vehicle, of revelation. Its reaction to the Protestant Reformation, and the missionary movement springing from the Counter-Reformation, which coincides with the discovery, colonization, and evangelization of new continents, at the same time was an effort to construct a universal Christian unity upon the cultural uniformity of the West and the diffusion of the message of the gospel in exclusive terms of this single culture, at the price of the eclipse, repression, or suppression of the cultural dimension of other peoples. Thus we can say that the theological and christological phenomenon of biblical inculturation was supplanted by the christological and ecclesiological phenomenon of the inculturation of the first centuries of the Christian era.

The final vector in the first millennium, and to a great extent in the second, was the appearance in the West, from thence to be imposed in various other parts of the world as well, of the phenomenon of European Christian cultural hegemony as a phenomenon of political history. The crystallization and propagation of this cultural model as the preferred, even unique, vehicle of evangelization resulted in the wane and demise of inculturation. Replacing it was a hegemonic acculturation and transculturation of a Western tenor and hue, with a consequent dissociation between faith and culture — between Christian faith in its Western cultural attire and the multiplicity of cultures entering the consciousness of world history. For the non-European peoples, to embrace the faith increasingly came to mean letting go of their own culture and internalizing the Western cultural framework within which this faith was proposed. As Paul VI said, the dissociation between faith and culture(s) is the trauma of our time, as it has been the trauma of other eras.

3. New Awareness of the Necessity of Inculturation

Three factors especially favored the resurgence of an ecclesial awareness of the need for inculturation: (1) the diversified experience of a church now become actually worldwide, (2) a recognition of the ecclesiological status of the local churches and the consequences of this new appreciation, and (3) the rehabilitation or reemergence of cultures long repressed or oppressed by the constitution of the national states or by the process of colonization.

Consciousness of Being a Worldwide Church

Unlike the Councils of Trent and Vatican I, Vatican II was celebrated by a significant number of bishops from all parts of the world. That world, since World War II, had become conscious both of its planetary unity and of its profound diversity. Although the theology of Vatican II was formulated preponderantly in European terms, the council's decisions, and their gradual implementation, were a powerful reflection of the broad and varied presence of the church. This would later become clear with the World Synods of bishops, among which three are of special importance for our topic: the synods on justice (1971), evangelization (1974), and catechesis (1977). All three revealed this worldwide geographic and cultural dimension characterizing the church of this second half of the twentieth century.

In this context, even before Vatican II, and especially during and after it, two basic theological positions were consolidated, with immense consequences for the recent historical journey of the church and therefore of Christian faith in the world. The first position, centered in _Lumen Gentium_, spills over into various other conciliar documents. That position presents a church-in-relation, a church ready for dialogue and open to the diversity of the quest for God by human beings and to the multiple concretization of this effort (_Ad Gentes_). Here, then, is a church sensitive to the ecumenical dimension of the Christian traditions and denominations (_Orientalium Ecclesiarum_ and _Unitatis Redintegratio_) and to the relationship with the non-Christian religions (_Nostra Aetate_), entailing a new perspective on both the missionary enterprise of the church and the very character and quality of its presence in the world (*Dignitatis Humanae, Apostolicam Actuositatem,* and *Gravissimum Educationis*) and intercommunication with that world (*Inter Mirifica*).

The second position, centered in *Gaudium et Spes,* explicitates and reinforces especially the relationship between church and world. It does so above all through the analytical and hermeneutical key that is culture (*GS* 53–63). Culture is taken in a perspective that, while transcending the humanistic philosophical focus that had prevailed in the nineteenth century, which is still typical of a great deal of theological reflection, integrates and underscores the current contribution of the social sciences. Thereby light is shed on the multiplicity and diversity of cultures. We are encouraging a deeper appreciation of the importance of faith as it relates to culture and cultures.

In the singular, "culture" is seen both as the presence and activity of the human being vis-à-vis nature, and as a creation of the human mind. A fundamental emphasis is laid on the relationship between faith and modern culture, in an optimistic view that contrasts with the age-old breach between the church and the world and their divergent development in the last five centuries. In the plural, the word "cultures" sets in relief mainly the diversity both of ethnic groups and social formations, on the one hand, and, on the other, of the meanings, values, and worldviews copresent in a complex, plural world. Thus, the consciousness of being an actually worldwide church, in the living experience of a pluricultural reality, has sent the church down the road to a new sensitivity to the need for inculturation.

Recognition of the Status of the Local Churches

This second factor also flows from a fundamental position taken in *Lumen Gentium,* namely, the importance of episcopal collegiality, and therefore of the identity and relative autonomy of the local churches (*Christus Dominus, Presbyterorum Ordinis*). One of the main consequences of this position has been the modification or disappearance of the estrangement of pastors from their faithful, along with a keener perception of the situations and problems, needs and aspirations, of the latter. This ecclesial attitude was clearly present among the first Christians and lasted through a large part of the first millennium.

The principal consequences of the ecclesiological focus adopted by Vatican II have been (1) a contextualized reading of the council itself—e.g., in the episcopal assemblies of Medellín (1968) and Puebla (1979), which, while bearing directly only on Latin America, had broad repercussions on the entire church; (2) the celebration of the World Synods, which brought out the variety of pastoral concerns emerging from the historical and sociocultural diversity of the various regions of the world; (3) the growing individuation of the national, regional, or continental bishops' conferences, with their particularized treatment of kindred problems—e.g., the dissimilar approach to the nuclear question by the North American, German, and French episcopates, corresponding to the variety of the situations and responsibilities of their respective countries; (4) the multiplication of diversified theological projects, in consonance with a sensitivity to the varied realities of Latin America, Africa, and different areas of Asia such as India and the Philippines; and (5) a theological and pastoral focus on transcultural realities such as the youth culture, women's culture, black culture, and so on, generating specific readings of the Bible and sacred tradition in function of the demands proper to each of these various living realities.

To all of this we must add the direct cultural experience of Paul VI, and especially John Paul II, through their pastoral journeys. As we know, the preparation and execution of these journeys have contributed a great deal—far more than could have been accomplished by any exchange of correspondence with the bureaucracies of the Vatican City State or the Holy See—to a knowledge, analysis, and interpretation of the immense variety of ecclesial cultures that are part and parcel of the daily life of the Christian faithful in various parts of the world. The later real or potential repercussions of these journeys on an interaction between the pope and the respective episcopates is of genuine importance. This mass of data, together with the development of new ecclesial perceptions flowing from an enhanced appreciation of collegiality and of the local churches, has rendered the inculturation perspective imperative, for it is still far from engaging its whole potential for the service of the people of God.

Rehabilitation or Reemergence of Cultures

In itself, the rehabilitation or reemergence of the cultures is extrinsic to the life of the church, although it is a factor of great influence on that life. In the first place, studies in cultural and social anthropology conducted over the course of the past hundred years have given the world a more concrete and detailed knowledge of the diversity of ethnic groups and their historical and cultural presuppositions. Even before Vatican II, the slow assimilation of these new data by the church had been endowing its missionary sensitivity with a new orientation. The reformulation of the missiological vocabulary, through a semantic evolution involving words like transplantation, adaptation, accommodation, incarnation, insertion, indigenization, contextualization, and inculturation, reveals an entire new understanding of the relationship between evangelizer and evangelized. It is a function of a new ecclesiological perspective arising from the new anthropological appreciation of the value of the various cultural identities. In the second place, the demise of the empires and of the process of political colonization on various continents has resulted in the independence of young nations, especially in Africa, Asia, and Oceania. While cultural boundaries have not always been respected in the designing of political units, this process has represented a reassumption of cultural identities that had been repressed by colonization. Almost without exception, the phenomenon has had repercussions on the relationships obtaining between the church and these new situations in which its faithful find themselves. The principal consequences have been the implantation of a native clergy and episcopate; the development of an active, participating laity; and a wholesale revision of the church's educational, pastoral, and promotional processes in these countries.

Third, the consciousness-raising that has occurred among cultural minorities repressed by the formation of the national states in the Western world has aroused the participation of the church, as well as a new sensitivity on the part of that church to realities that had lain dormant for centuries, as we see in the case of the Basques and Catalans in Spain, or in Quebec in Canada—situations analogous to that of Central Europe—and more recently, with the Hispanics in the United States.

Fourth, the very viability of the new intercultural relationship, whether through communication and information or through the accelerating development of the tourist industry, while it has unified or compressed the world, has also contributed to an awareness of the irreducible cultural diversity of the populations of this same world. Even the hegemonic propagation of modern Western culture, which in one of its stages called forth the hypothesis of the imminent materialization of a homogeneous universal culture, has been revealing precisely the contrary: a growing willingness to safeguard specific cultural and subcultural diversity and autonomy. The recent phenomenon of the gradual de-Westernization of the Far East, together with its development and its increasing participation in Western economies, is a significant datum of this transformation. That datum was preceded by the defeat of the colonial empires and the consequent independence of various countries or creation of new ones, mainly in Africa, Asia, and Oceania. In Africa, this movement was marked by the recovery of a cultural awareness. The patient preservation of a rich oral culture has contributed to a new appreciation for cultural legacy and identity. As for Asia, the remarkable wealth of various written traditions, intimately bound up with religions thousands of years old, has permitted the conservation of well-defined cultural profiles subsisting, for that matter, in population majorities coexisting with Christian minorities. In each of these cultural areas, this diversification poses specific anthropological and theological problems for inculturation, as we see from experience, research, and an ever more abundant bibliography on the subject.

Finally, we note the creation and functioning of pluricultural international forums like the United Nations and its subsidiaries UNESCO, FAO, UNICEF, and so on, alongside other organizations and movements like international congresses and conventions of a thematic or corporative nature. All of this has revealed the experience and awareness of the cultural diversity of our world, and the concrete impossibility of hegemonic units built on uniformity or based on a lack of awareness or appreciation of the concrete, historical sociocultural diversity so evident in today's world. This reemergence of the cultures, and the new respect these cultures are accorded, is another access route for the church to a consciousness of the urgency of inculturation, and to the constructive redevelopment of a relationship between faith and culture.

4. Indispensable Elements of an Inculturated Evangelization

The conceptualization of culture that we have proposed—as an ensemble of meanings and significations, of values and models, underlying and/or incorporated into the activity and communication of a specific human group—is anthropologically well founded and theologically operational. Indeed, it can be applied to macrocultures (national or ethnic cultures) as well as to microcultures (small groups, urban ghettos, and so on), or, finally, to any kind of subculture (organizations and institutions, individuated transcultural conjuncts such as those of youth, the poor, women, campesinos, and so on). In this last sense, a university, a religious order, a political party, or a labor union is and, in a way, has a culture. That is, each is distinguished by a specific series of meanings and significations, values and models, a perception and a worldview, through which it asserts its identity, in itself and in relation to other human groups.

Inculturation, then, as a process of evangelization that strikes an organic link between faith and culture, is not limited to the evangelization of groups and communities to which the gospel has not been previously proclaimed (in "mission territories" or "on the foreign missions," in the preconciliar vocabulary). Inculturation must qualify any and every process of evangelization, whether in relation to human groups of Christian tradition or origin in their cultural formation (e.g., the majority of Western countries, stamped today by the modern or contemporary culture) in relation to groups without the determining influence of a Christian past on its cultural formation (as in the majority of the regions of Asia, Africa, and Oceania), or, lastly, in relation to subcultures within each of these groups (as organizations, institutions, specific regions, transcultural groups). The reason for this thesis is precisely the fact that, by inculturation, a living faith and a living culture, both marked by the dynamism of transformation and growth, are set in a concrete relationship.

An authentic process of evangelization, then, will always be attentive to a threefold dimension. First, there is no such thing as an evangelical nucleus or core in the abstract, that could be isolated and transmitted from one culture to another culture. What actually exists is the gospel message already concretely inculturated into some culture—in this case, into the culture that evangelizes by proposing the message to another culture, the one being evangelized. Accordingly, proposing or transmitting the message (evangelizing), just as receiving and assuming it (being evangelized), is an interaction between cultures. The faith that motivates the proposing of the message and the faith that results from the acceptance of the message is the same faith (i.e., the full existential response of acceptance given by a human person or group to the living gift of God in Jesus Christ), but it will be a culturally qualified faith, and therefore differentiated in its perception and expression.

Second, in this relationship between cultures that is the evangelization process, both the evangelizer and the evangelized are active subjects or agents. Evangelization, therefore, is not simply a unilateral transmission or translation of the gospel message, in the terms of the evangelizing culture. It is not a mere extrinsic or superficial adaptation, on the merely phenomenological level of the expression. Nor is it the passive reception of this message as conveyed and transported by the evangelizer. Evangelization is a process of dialogic interaction between the two cultures, that of the evangelizer and that of the evangelized, in a dialogue conducted in function of the message. An inculturated evangelization is therefore a critical process of discernment vis-à-vis both the culture of the evangelizer and the culture of the evangelized. The evangelizer is not asked to renounce his or her own culture, but only to be aware of the identity that characterizes it in its particular way of perceiving and living the gospel message, and not to impose this way as an obligatory vehicle of the message. The evangelizer is further asked to assist the person being evangelized to reach an active understanding, assimilation, and expression of the message from a point of departure in the latter's own cultural identity, that of the person being evangelized, in the terms of and according to the particular character of his or her own culture.

Third, because an inculturated evangelization is a process of relation between cultures in function of the gospel message, it is important to keep in mind that, in the concrete reality of history, a relation between cultures is not, generally speaking, symmetrical or egalitarian, but is asymmetrical. Cultures interrelate not as equals but as dominant and subordinate cultures. This is the case on the political and economic plane, the social and military, and, surely at least before now, on the ecclesial (as witness the evangelization of the past five centuries especially).

In any manner of relationship between cultures—whether of acculturation, transculturation, or inculturation—we must always suspect the concrete possibility of the domination of the one by the other. These intercultural relationships will not of themselves, therefore, be naturally tranquil, easy ones. On the contrary, they will be relations marked by tension, conflict, and perplexity. Hence the need for discernment, which aims at purification and deliverance from the elements of imposition and pressure, of power and violence. The process of inculturated evangelization, as the expression of an intercultural relationship focused on faith, is a dialectical process of the liberation of both cultures—that of the evangelizer and that of the evangelized—with a view to affording room for the action of the Spirit upon the subjects of evangelization in their proposal of the message and their arousal of its acceptance by faith. After all, faith, which is the end result of evangelization, is not an achievement of human effort, or the product of a method, but a free gift of God's self-manifestation and communication. The authentic process of an inculturated evangelization, then, is also a process of the liberation of culture. In turn, an evangelization process for the deliverance and transformation of society will be authentic only if it is also an inculturated process. Thus, there is no contradiction, but rather an integral complementarity, between the theological thematics of _inculturation_ and _liberation_. The one calls for the other.

5. Elementary Data of a Model of Inculturation

The gospel cannot be identified with cultures, but neither is it independent of them. It was revealed in the context of a culture (Israel);

it has been lived in concrete cultural contexts (tradition); and finally, the persons to whom it has been proclaimed are integrated into specific cultures. However, the gospel is not to be confused with a particular culture. It is always transmitted from a starting point in an apostolic dialogue that is necessarily associated with a dialogue between concrete cultures. The _models of evangelization_ proposed in missiological theological studies are numerous. From the outlook of an inculturated evangelization, it seems impossible to prescind from the following elements. The following four stages are analytically distinct. However, they may develop in integral, even simultaneous fashion.

First stage: The culture is identified anthropologically. A knowledge of the principal traits of the culture to be evangelized is fundamental. The evangelizer must come to know the mediations, channels, and vehicles that express and incorporate the meanings, values, and criteria characterizing the worldview, activity, and communication of this particular culture. The main source of this knowledge will be the members of the culture itself, but this source can be supplemented by other sources and documents, especially with respect to these persons' spontaneous, unconscious experience.

This anthropological knowledge is followed by a quest for a theological knowledge of the culture in question. How has God acted and been present in the life and history of this culture before the arrival and initiative of the evangelizer? Where does one find the traces of God, the latent or patent marks of the divine love, in the history of this people or this human group? The criteria for such a theological reading will be the human being and Jesus Christ. Any doubts concerning the validity of the criteria dictated by the constitution or character of the human being (and it is only natural that such perplexities should arise in pluralistic contexts) will have their possible solution in a reference to the human being Jesus Christ. Anything meeting these criteria in a given culture may be preserved "as is"—retained in the expression it already has in the code of the culture. But how, from this point onward, can one travel the path of evangelization precisely in the company of the members of the culture? How can one respect their identity and their rhythms with a view to their gradual, growing acceptance of the gospel message?

Second stage: As we have observed, limitation is inherent in all human reality, personal or cultural. We shall always find, in any culture, concrete deviations vis-à-vis the basic teleology of the good of the human being, to which, in principle, culture ought to be oriented. These perversions or warps of culture are the existential mark, in a particular concrete culture, of sin, frailty, and inconsistency. Just as the process of inculturation has previously identified the profound harmonies between a given culture and the gospel, it must now critically sort out and discern their mutual incompatibilities. There may be *absolute* incompatibilities of a moral, structural, or functional order in this particular culture—e.g., violence, injustice, oppression, or discrimination—which the culture may regard as legitimate, and, likely enough, even institutionalize. There may be cultural practices that are incompatible with human dignity or the teaching of Jesus Christ. There will surely be *relative* incompatibilities between the gospel and certain concrete modalities of any culture—aspects in which conversion or outright breach are not indicated, as in the previous case, but calling for a reorientation or better explicitation of the means by which a culture may rediscover or reassume its proper teleology (as with Jesus' position regarding the Sabbath). The message of the gospel can also open a culture to the prospect of growth in the direction of its original orientation (as with Jesus' antitheses in the Sermon on the Mount between the demands of the old law and the new).

These first two stages of a basic model of inculturated evangelization concern a culture as it is found in its concrete, present human reality. They stipulate a search for the existing harmonies, or the needed or possible corrections and complementarities, with regard to the acceptance and assimilation or interiorization of the gospel, in fidelity both to that gospel and to the cultural identity at hand. In this fashion, a dialogic and dialectical relationship, to which we have already referred, is established between faith and culture. The homologization (first stage) or reorientation (second stage) of the culture in the light of the human being and of Jesus Christ is itself an implicit form of proclamation—which, however, continues to stand against the immanent background of the culture itself.

Third stage: Next comes the explicit announcement, to the subjects of the culture in question, of what for them is a gift, a novelty vis-à-vis their culture. This gift will transcend the immanent scope of the culture in its original state—what a culture can attain by itself in the maximal development of its human potential. This gift is made by God to all human cultures in and by Jesus Christ. It is a gift that the cultures must not wrench or disfigure. On the contrary, they should be led by it to the optimization of their immanent scope, in a full realization of their human, individual, and social possibilities, as well as to a transcendence of this plane, in a full openness of the culture to God. It is in this third stage that the explicit proclamation of the gospel and the announcement of its project and identity, in the light of the totality of the mystery of Jesus Christ, occurs.

Fourth stage: The announcement of which we have just spoken is made on the foundation of a community that has accepted the gift of the gospel and seeks to live it and share it with others. This community of faith is the church. The bearer of the good news—of the gift that is manifested to the culture in the third stage—is the church. But the church is itself part of that gift, part of what is proclaimed. The acceptance and experience of Christian faith always occurs in community. Thus, a gradual evangelization of the concrete human community constituted by a given culture will lead that community, as a specific cultural group, also to be part of the gospel community of those who believe and who share their faith, in hope and love.

The evangelizing process that unfolds according to this elementary model naturally implies a consistent, credible witness (*martyrion*) on the part of those who already live the message and carry it to the culture in question. No less does it imply a dialogic interaction with the members of the community (*koinōnia*). It involves the enablement that consists of a service to the human and Christian growth of the members of the culture (*diakonia*). It issues in the announcement properly so-called of the gospel message, as God's free gift in and by Jesus Christ (*mystērion*), to be experienced in the community of ecclesial faith (*ekklēsia*).

The result of this process, in time, is an increasing inculturation of the faith. It is the creation of a new community in the sense of an ecclesial culture, in integral fidelity to the basic inspirations of this particular culture and of the faith, of the human being and of Jesus Christ. This outcome is characterized by the mediations and expressions of its activity and communication. These will have a particular identity, inasmuch as they owe their origin to specific cultural roots. But they will also create the mutual encounter of a profound oneness among communities, since all of these church-and-cultural communities take their inspiration in the same faith, which becomes the source and sustenance of an intercommunion and intercultural relationship. Thus is realized the church's unity of faith. Church unity does not rest on the *uniformity* of some one cultural paradigm or any potential that might be attributed to that paradigm for being a preferential or exclusive mediator of a faith de facto imposed, however unduly, on the various cultures. Rather, it is a *unity* built on the conscious diversity of cultures—all impregnated, however, with the same gospel and reshaped by it in the light of the gratuitous novelty of gift.

Bibl.: PAUL VI, "Apostolic Exhortation on Evangelization," *Origins* (Jan. 8, 1976): 459–68; A. A. ROEST CROLLIUS, "What Is So New about Inculturation? A Concept and Its Implications," *Greg* 59 (1978): 721–38; JOHN-PAUL II, "Exhortation apostolique Catechesi tradendae," in *Insegnamenti di Giovanni Paolo II*, II/2, 1979 (Vatican City, 1979); P. BEAUCHAMP, *Le récit, la lettre et le corps* (Paris, 1982); M. AZEVEDO, *Inculturation and the Challenges of Modernity*, Working Papers on Living Faith and Cultures, I, Pont. Univ. Gregoriana e Pont. Ist. Biblico Editrice (Rome, 1982); JOHN-PAUL II, "Lettera autografa di fondazione del Pontificio Consiglio per la Cultura" (20 May 1982), *AAS* 74 (1982): 683–88; id., "Discorso ai membri del Pontificio Consiglio per la Cultura" (18 janvier 1983), in *Insegnamenti di Giovanni Paolo II*, cit. VI/1, 1983; K. MULLER, "Accommodation and Inculturation in the Papal Documents," *VERBUM/ SVD* 24/4 (1983): 347–60; C. KRAFT, *Christianity in Culture* (New York, 1984); T. NKERAMIHIGO, "On Inculturation of Christianity," in A. A. ROEST CROLLIUS, ed., *What Is So New about Inculturation 2*, Working Papers on Living Faith and Cultures, Pont. Univ. Gregoriana e Pont. Ist. Biblico Editrice (Rome, 1984), 21–29; JOHN-PAUL II, enc. "Slavorum Apostoli per l'XI centenario dell'opera evangelizatrice dei santi Cirillo e Metodio" (June 2, 1985), in *Insegnamenti di Giovanni Paolo II*, cit. VII/2, 1985; H. CARRIER, "Understanding Culture: The Ultimate Challenge of

the World Church," in J. Grémillion, ed., *The Church and Culture since Vatican II* (Notre Dame, 1985); R. SCHREITER, *Constructing Local Theologies* (New York, 1985); M. AZEVEDO, *Comunidades Eclesiais de Base e Inculturação da Fé* (S. Paulo, 1986), 255–377; H. CARRIER, *The Gospel and Cultures: From Leo XIII to John-Paul II* (Vatican City/Paris, 1987); A. SHORTER, *Toward a Theology of Inculturation* (New York, 1988); L. LUZBETAK, *The Church and Cultures: New Perspectives in Missiological Anthropology* (Maryknoll, N.Y., 1988); P. SUESS, "Companheiro-Peregrino na Terra dos Pobres, Hóspede-Irmão na Casa dos Outros: Deafios para uma missiologia a partir da América Latina," *REB* 48/191 (1988): 645–71; N. STANDAERT, "L'histoire d'un néologisme: Le terme Inculturation dans les documents romains," *NRT* 110 (1988): 555–70; INTERNATIONAL THEOLOGICAL COMMISSION, "Faith and Inculturation," *Origins* 18 (May 4, 1988): 800–808; P. SUESS, "Inculturação, Desafios, Caminhos, Metas," *REB* 49/193 (1989): 81–127; G. LANGEVIN and R. PIRRO, eds., *Le Christ et les cultures dans le monde et l'histoire* (Montreal, 1991).

Marcello de C. AZEVEDO

II. INCULTURATION OF THE GOSPEL

"Inculturation" is a concept used to describe the cultural changes brought about by the entrance of the gospel into a human environment. Inculturation is related to "acculturation," a term used by anthropologists since the end of the last century to describe the cultural changes produced when two human groups come to live in direct contact with each other. The meeting of cultures usually causes numerous changes in, for example, language, customs, beliefs, and behavior. Catholics began very quickly to use the concept of acculturation as a tool for studying relations between Christianity and the cultures. Nowadays, the term "inculturation" is preferred and is more common. It has the advantage of making it clear that the encounter of the gospel with a culture is not reducible solely to the relations between two cultures (acculturation). It refers specifically to the interaction between the *message of Christ* and a given culture. The word has been used among Catholics since the 1930s, but only beginning in 1970 have the official documents of the church made use of it. In 1988 the International Theological Commission published a document entitled *Faith and Inculturation*, which was prepared in collaboration with the Pontifical Council for Culture; the document (sec. 11) gives the following definition:

> The process known as *inculturation* can be defined as the effort by the Church to bring the message of Christ into a particular sociocultural setting, while calling upon the latter to grow in accordance with all its own values, provided these are reconcilable with the gospel. The term inculturation includes the idea of the growth and mutual enrichment of persons and groups as a result of the meeting of the gospel with a social milieu. "Inculturation is the incarnation of the gospel in native cultures and, at the same time, the introduction of these cultures into the life of the Church." (Encyclical *Slavorum Apostoli*, 2 June 1985, no. 21)

There is reason for emphasizing both the novel and the traditional aspects of inculturation. I shall consider later the reasons for viewing inculturation as a renewed approach to evangelization, but it must also be noted that contemporary thought on the subject profits by a long and rich experience in the church.

1. The Lessons of History

Strictly speaking, the process known as inculturation—that is, the copenetration of the church and cultures—is as old as Christianity itself. The first evangelizers learned the languages, customs, and traditions of the peoples to whom they were announcing the message of Christ. The first Christian thinkers had to face the problem raised for them by the meeting of the gospel and the cultures of their age. As early as the second century we find in the *Letter to Diognetus* quite relevant reflections on the life-style of Christians, who are "citizens of heaven" but at the same time share the ways of their fellow human beings on earth:

> Christians do not differ from other people in country, language, or customs. They do not live apart in their own cities, or speak an unusual dialect of their own, or live an eccentric way of life. . . . They spend their lives on earth, but they are citizens of heaven. They obey the established laws, and their way of life is more perfect than the laws require. (*Letter to Diognetus*, ed. Funk, *Patres Apostolici* [1901], 396–400)

At the time when colonialism was growing and missionary work was keeping pace with it, the church issued some rules for a real inculturation, long before the term came into use.

For example, the Congregation for the Propagation of the Faith published the following directive in 1659:

> Do not be zealous, or advance any arguments, to persuade these people to change their rituals, customs, and habits, unless these are evidently inconsistent with religion and morality. What could be more absurd than to transplant France, Spain, Italy, or any other European country among the Chinese? Bring them not our countries but the faith, a faith that does not reject or offend against the rituals and customs of any people (provided these rituals and customs are not odious) but on the contrary means to safeguard and protect them. (*Le Siège apostolique et les missions* [Paris: Union missionaire du clergé, 1959])

The modern period brought a considerable development of missionary activity that was characterized by an increasingly careful preparation of the priests and the religious men and women who were being sent to Africa, Asia, and the Americas. A number of new missionary institutes were established in the nineteenth century to bring the gospel to vast regions that the church had not yet entered and sought to implant itself. These institutes gradually became more and more expert in defining the missionary task and the methods for adaptation to the various peoples.

After the First World War and down to the Second Vatican Council, the popes published a number of documents on the missions, in particular *Maximum illud* (1919), *Rerum Ecclesiae* (1926), and *Evangelii Praecones* (1951). These contain clear guidelines for the work of securing a better adaptation of the gospel to the character and traditions of each people. The first need is to master the language of the country. Quite special importance is given to the establishment of a native clergy. Native priests are to be trained to understand the ways, customs, and soul of their people. They must be accepted and respected by the local elites and be able some day to exercise the responsibilities of government over these new churches. Religious men and women are also encouraged to accept and form candidates drawn from the native populations. All evangelizers should profit from the modern sciences—linguistics, ethnography, history, geography, medicine—in order better to know and serve their peoples.

These guidelines offer valuable help in the

work of inculturation and show a maturing theology of the missions. The first norm is to respect the character and genius of the peoples being evangelized, by cultivating their best talents, purifying these, and elevating them through Christian faith. In his first encyclical, *Summi Pontificatus* (1939), Pius XII urged every church "to gain a deeper understanding of the civilization and institutions of the various people and to promote their best qualities and gifts. . . . Everything in the customs of a people that is not inseparably bound up with superstition or error should be studied with a benevolent attitude and, if possible, be preserved intact." Many of these directives, as we shall see, were taken over by Vatican II, especially in its Decree *Ad Gentes*.

2. New Aspects of Inculturation

Several events that left their mark on the world after the Second World War were to give a new urgency to inculturation. As the movement of decolonization and liberation advanced, the young churches were called upon to redefine themselves in relation to the countries that had brought the gospel to them. Pastors and theologians of the churches of Africa and Asia, and many Westerners along with them, undertook a revision of the methods of evangelization that missionaries were using. The church had certainly been implanted, but had the native cultures been converted at any deep level? In many instances, a latent paganism had hardly been affected at all. In addition, the religious potentialities present in many customs or cultural traits had not been understood and taken over by the missionaries. Other criticisms, sometimes excessive, were leveled at European evangelizers: too often the latter had transplanted their own languages, institutions, and thought patterns from one country to another. Was it not necessary, therefore, to strip Christianity of its Western garb, inculturate the faith in local cultures, and undertake an Africanization (or Indianization or, in general, an indigenization) of the native churches? The debate extended to every aspect of the church's life, including language, theology, morality, liturgy, and the possible acceptance by the church of elements of the traditional religions, such as sacred texts and forms of prayer.

The extent and seriousness of the questions being debated underscored the urgent need for more thorough studies of the conditions, norms, and methods of inculturation. It became clear that the whole question had to be reexamined in light of theological principles and a better knowledge of anthropology.

3. Norms of Inculturation

The norms to be followed are based on the nature of inculturation, this being conceived as a methodical approach to the evangelization of cultures. The fundamental presupposition that must inspire every effort at evangelization is this: the end sought is the EVANGELIZATION OF CULTURES. The inculturation of the gospel and the evangelization of the culture are two complementary aspects of the one mission of evangelization. Thus viewed, inculturation must proceed according to the norms that govern the relations between faith and cultures. Both of the spheres—theological and anthropological—that come into play in the process of inculturation must be respected.

At the outset, there is the given fact of the incarnation of Jesus Christ and its repercussions on the historical cultures. The spread of the gospel now summons all cultures to a new destiny. The *cultural implications of the incarnation* need to be emphasized. Jesus became a human individual in a particular culture. "Christ [bound] Himself, in virtue of His incarnation, to the definite social and cultural conditions of those human beings among whom He dwelt" (*AG* 10). Furthermore, the incarnation affects every human being and all human realities. Christ thus reaches out to all human beings in their complementary cultures. In a sense, the incarnation of the Son of God was also a cultural incarnation. The incarnation of Christ by its nature calls for the inculturation of the faith in all human environments.

The second principle governing inculturation is that there must be an *anthropological discernment* applied to the cultures to be evangelized. This is required by the complex character of evangelization in human milieus that are rapidly changing and are often passing through a crisis of cultural and religious identity. A methodical study and reflection are indispensable in our age. We must learn to analyze cultures in order to perceive the obstacles they contain but also their potentialities for the reception of the gospel. Inculturation will promote the preservation and growth of all that is sound in the customs, traditions, arts, and thought of peoples. The life of the church and even the liturgy will be enriched by the cultural heritage of the nations to be evangelized. As Vatican II tells us, the church does not impose a rigid uniformity:

> Rather she respects and fosters the spiritual adornments and gifts of the various races and peoples. Anything in their way of life that is not indissolubly bound up with superstition and error she studies with sympathy and, if possible, preserves intact. Sometimes in fact she admits such things into the liturgy itself, as long as they harmonize with its true and authentic spirit. (*SC* 37)

The needed discernment cannot be improvised but requires a concerted effort and presupposes that the local churches subject the data of the faith and the cultural elements of each region to "a new examination" in order to determine what can and cannot be made a part of Christian life. Although it does not use the word "inculturation," the decree of Vatican II on the missions clearly explains the rules that must guide its practice (*AG* 22).

In summary, authentic inculturation depends on respect for the conditions, both theological and ethnological, that govern the missionary task. There is need of a full understanding of the realities of faith and of the cultural realities that are involved in evangelization. This sociotheological discernment is absolutely necessary in order to reconcile the several elements that enter into a relation of dynamic tension during the process of evangelization. Inculturation must preserve, first of all, the distinction between faith and culture and, second, both the unity and the pluralism that the church needs. These requirements are fundamental in the practice of inculturation.

Distinguishing Faith and Culture

First of all, faith must be seen to be radically distinct from any and every culture. Faith in Christ is not the *product* of any culture; it is not identifiable with any of them but is unqualifiedly distinct from them because it comes from God. In the view of the cultures, faith is a "stumbling block" and "foolishness," to use Paul's words (1 Cor 1:22–23). But this distinction between faith and culture is not a *dissocia-*

tion of the two. It is intended that faith permeate every human culture in order to save it and to elevate it according to the ideal of the gospel. Furthermore, faith is not truly lived out unless it becomes culture, that is, unless it transforms mentalities and behaviors. There is a dialectic that must be respected between the transcendence of the revealed word and its goal of rendering all cultures fruitful. If we reject one or the other of these requirements, we expose inculturation to the risk of becoming a syncretism that confuses faith and human traditions or a false and superficial accommodation of the gospel to particular cultures.

Preserving Unity and Pluralism

Inculturation must also seek to preserve both the unity of the church and pluralism in the ways in which this unity finds expression. Evangelization works to build a church that has an essential unity and identity. It is true that in the past the message proclaimed was translated into categories of thought borrowed from particular cultures, but these cultural dependencies do not detract from the permanent value of the basic conceptualizations of the faith and the church's organic structures. Evangelizers now transmit a teaching that has been enriched by generations of believers, thinkers, and saints, whose contribution is now an integral part of the Christian heritage. In evangelization, it is this essential and foundational identity that must be passed on to the human cultures in terms accessible to all of them.

But *unity* is not to be confused with *uniformity*. Those engaged in inculturation must therefore know how to reconcile unity and diversity in the church. In this area, the lengthy experience of the Eastern churches provides a model that Paul VI regards as exemplary: "It is precisely in the Eastern churches that the validity of the pluralist pattern has been anticipated and completely proved, so that modern scholars looking to test relations between the proclamation of the gospel and human civilizations, between faith and culture, find already present in the history of these venerable churches conceptual developments and concrete forms ordered to the preservation of both unity and diversity." The pope thus makes it clear that the church "welcomes this kind of pluralism as a manifestation of unity" (Address to the Greek College in Rome, 1 May 1977).

The principle that guides every effort at the inculturation of theology, preaching, and discipline is the growth of the *communio ecclesiae*, the communion of the universal church. But this unity is not the unity of a uniform and undifferentiated system; it is rather the unity of a body that grows in an organic way. The universal church is a communion of local churches. It is also, by extension, a community of nations, languages, traditions, and cultures. Each age or each civilization contributes its gifts and patrimony to the life of the church. Through inculturation the cultures receive the treasures of the church and in exchange offer to the entire church the riches of their best traditions and the fruits of their wisdom. It is this complex and delicate exchange that inculturation must promote for the growth both of the church and of each culture.

4. Extension of Inculturation

Recent thinking has led to the extension of the practice of inculturation not only to traditional mission territories but also to modern societies, whose cultures have been dechristianized and are characterized by an increasing secularization. Modern culture is an obstacle to evangelization and calls for a methodical effort at inculturation. This is the challenging *second evangelization* that is called for in settings in which a faith that is dormant, suppressed, or rejected makes it difficult to proclaim the gospel in all its freshness. The document *Faith and Inculturation*, which the International Theological Commission published in 1988, devotes its final part to the culture of modernity. We read there:

> The inculturation of the gospel in modern societies will require a methodical effort at concerted study and action. This effort will demand of those in charge of evangelization (1) an attitude of receptivity and critical discernment; (2) the ability to perceive the spiritual expectations and human aspirations of new cultures; (3) a talent for cultural analysis aimed as an effective encounter with the modern world.

Inculturation has now taken on new dimensions. It no longer has to do solely with individuals, countries, nations, and institutions that await the gospel. Inculturation of the gospel also means coming to grips with psychosocial phenomena, mentalities, ways of thinking, and life-styles, in order to let the saving power of the Christian message make its way into them. In short: it is necessary to move beyond a *geographic* conception of evangelization to a more *cultural* one. The two perspectives do not completely exclude one another, but they do show the direction that the development of the mission of evangelization must take.

There are undoubtedly geographical regions still to be evangelized, but the main need now is to evangelize cultures themselves. The light of the gospel must permeate mentalities and life settings that are presently characterized by indifference and agnosticism. These last two outlooks tend to spread everywhere in the train of modernity. With discernment and confidence the church means to proclaim Christ to the cultures of the day; this will require *a lengthy and courageous process of inculturation*, as John Paul II has said:

> The church must become all things to all as it sympathetically reaches out to the cultures of the day. There are still groups and mentalities, as well as entire countries and regions, that need to be evangelized. This requires a lengthy and courageous process of evangelization, in order that the gospel may penetrate the soul of living cultures, as it responds to their highest expectations and enables them to grow in Christian faith, hope, and charity.

The term "mission," says the pope,

> applies henceforth to ancient civilizations on which Christianity has left its mark but which are now threatened by indifference, agnosticism, or even hostility to religion. In addition, new areas of culture are making their appearance, with their varied aims, methods, and languages. Intercultural dialogue is thus an obligation for Christians in all countries. (Address to the Pontifical Council for Culture, 18 January 1983)

Bibl.: Hervé Carrier, *The Gospel and Cultures: From Leo XIII to John-Paul II* (Vatican City/Paris, 1987); Louis J. Luzbetak, *The Church and Cultures: New Perspectives in Missiological Anthropology* (Maryknoll, N.Y., 1988); International Theological Commission, "Faith and Inculturation," *Origins* 18 (4 May 1989): 800–809; G. Langevin and G. Pirro, eds., *Le Christ et les cultures dans le monde et l'histoire* (Montreal, 1991); H. Carrier, *Inculturation de l'Évangile* (Louvain, 1992), 195–204.

Hervé Carrier

INSPIRATION

1. A Brief Look at History. 2. The Innovation of Vatican II. (R. FISICHELLA)

Scripture is a privileged expression of God's witness through the means of human communication.

The inspiration of Scripture is closely linked to the content of revelation, in addition to being an important matter in its own right. God's free choice to communicate with humanity found its full and culminating expression in Jesus of Nazareth. God's way of expressing himself through the work of the sacred writers, however, was a critical and fundamental part of his work.

It is remarkable that the dynamic of revelation was born at such an early stage. Yet what is adopted as an instrument of expression is good in itself, and appropriate for expressing God, albeit in a kenotic form; in fact, human language is never up to the task of expressing the fullness of divine reality.

The theme of the inspiration of the Scriptures appertains to the area of interdisciplinary research in a special way; fundamental theology defines the importance of inspiration in relation to revelation. We shall see that the truth that is contained in the sacred text is indeed the truth as an act of revelation by God. We shall also discover how this single truth, placed once and for all in history by dint of human learning and expression, can even today be true for someone opening oneself to revelation and also how it can be a source of self-knowledge and of the mystery of God.

The study that fundamental theology has made of inspiration is the conclusive assessment of the act of revelation; it is revelation's claim to have been welcomed and historically understood down through the centuries by means of a truth given to history and using the instruments of a particular period of history. In other words, it is the study of the fact of the inspiration of the Scriptures, and it must ensure that the implications that it contains are not lost from sight, namely, the possibility of a historic expression of the truth and the possibility that it can reach men and women throughout history ($\rightarrow$ TRUTH).

1. A Brief Look at History

The history of inspiration has been interesting for a variety of reasons.

a. The OT lacks the specific vocabulary needed and has opted for synonyms and more fluid expressions, describing the reality of inspiration in highly explicit terms. It is understood as an action of the spirit of Yahweh, who takes hold of humanity and encourages men and women to perform words and gestures in order to communicate his will to them.

Simple gestures such as the anointing with oil (1 Sm 16:13) express a more profound reality: Yahweh possessing his "chosen one" so that, when "consecrated," he or she can become a sign of revelation. By virtue of their mission, the prophets express the reality of inspiration more directly. It was said explicitly of Hosea that he was inspired. Micah was similarly self-aware (Mi 3:8), and Nehemiah went so far as to say that the prophets were the mouth of the Spirit (Neh 9:30).

The major prophets have left evidence in their writings of the importance they attached to acting, proclaiming, and writing in the name of Yahweh (Is 6; Jer 1; Ez 2). The words used by the prophets hardly seem to be any different from those of God himself: phrases like "oracle of Yahweh," "the word of the Lord," and "thus says the Lord" are evidence from the OT that God was communicating with his people through the prophets' use of human symbolism and language.

b. The NT is the only place where the word "inspiration" (Gr. *theopneustos*) has been used to give a technical explanation of the particular act with which God inspired the Scriptures. It appears in 2 Tm 3:16: "All scripture is inspired [*theopneustos*] by God and is useful for teaching, for reproof, for correction, and for training in righteousness." It is, however, to the focus provided by Jesus of Nazareth that we must turn in order to understand fully the teaching of the NT on inspiration.

In the days of the early church, there was a certainty that all the Scriptures were directed at Christ and found complete meaning only in him. The prophets spoke of him and predicted the reasons for his existence (Lk 24:27); when the apostles had shared the event of the revelation, they too were moved by the Spirit of the risen Lord to announce to the world that the ancient promise had been fulfilled.

Theirs was an experience of giving something freely that put them in direct contact with the experience of the old prophets. It is appropriate here to reflect on two of Peter's programmatic texts: the first one announcing the central character of Christ (1 Pt 1:10–12); the second announcing the direct influence of the Holy Spirit on the writers (2 Pt 1:20–21).

In the early church, the presence of the minister-prophet (→ PROPHECY) made the action of inspiration visible in two ways. During liturgical ceremonies, some men and women would pray for the community under the influence of the Holy Spirit and would refer directly to the word of the Master (Acts 15:22–32; 1 Cor 12:7–8). Moreover, some of the prophets together with the apostles were more directly involved in the growth of the community; their particular task was to transmit the word of Jesus by illuminating and rereading the events and needs of the community (Eph 2:20; 3:5; 4:11; 1 Cor 12:28). Their authority was accepted by the community because they were acknowledged to be men moved by the Spirit and directly inspired at the moment that they established the relationship between the announcement of the word of the Lord and the life of the community (2 Pt 3:2).

From the very beginning, the Gospels and the letters of the apostles have thus constituted the privileged testimony of the power of the Spirit, who ensured that the word of the Lord remained in the community's midst (Eph 4:11; 2 Pt 3:15–16).

c. During the patristic period, which was marked by a profound faith that naturally accepted Scripture as the word of God, inspiration did not present any particular problem. A text by the Venerable Bede commenting on Luke's prologue demonstrates clearly how the fathers felt in this regard: "If what the evangelist wrote seemed good to him, it is not to be interpreted that his writing seemed good only to him; for what he considered good was by the inspiration of the Holy Spirit" (PL 92:307).

The APOLOGISTS Justin, Origen, and Cyril of Alexandria tended to present the truth of the Scriptures as a response to the attacks of the pagans. Augustine and Jerome, in contrast, were the first to introduce the necessary distinctions and, more positively, gave the motivations for offering the redeeming truth of the sacred texts as a reply.

d. It was with the scholastics, and Thomas Aquinas in particular, that the theme of inspiration began to receive serious theological study. Thomas interpreted prophecy as the charism that made it possible to see revelation and inspiration as closely linked (ST 2 of 2, qq. 171–74).

Revelation is the knowledge of divine truths and accordingly demands the supernatural elevation of the spirit, or inspiration. Prophetic inspiration, in constrast, should be thought of as complementary to revelation: through it and the work of the Spirit, the prophet is raised to a higher level of knowledge and can therefore communicate and transmit divine revelation.

e. The subsequent history of the church is characterized by the involvement of the magisterium and theologians at different levels. After the Council of Trent, which amended the formulation *Spiritu Sancto inspirante* by the Council of Florence (DS 1334) with its own *Spiritu Sancto dictante* (DS 1501), theologians sought bolder interpretations. For some, led by Bañez, the influence of the Holy Spirit on the sacred writer was heading for the *singula verba*; for others following the ideas of Lessio, it was necessary to distinguish between revelation and inspiration and a book could be written without the help of the Holy Spirit. If the Holy Spirit subsequently stated that there was nothing false in the book, however, it would then become a sacred and inspired book.

In 1879 J. B. Franzelin published a book entitled *Tractatus de divina Traditione et Scriptura* that had a profound influence on the declarations of VATICAN I. Franzelin's position is that God is the author of the sacred books by virtue of supernatural influence over the sacred writers. The author is the one who personally conceives and produces the writings with his own mind; the role of God consists of influencing the writer's intellect and will and ensuring that he conceives in his own mind, and willingly writes, only what God wishes to communicate.

Inspiration is, therefore, not conceived as knowledge of truth (which the author may already know about independently) but as what influenced the writing. God, however, is conceived as the principal cause and true author of the text, while the sacred writer is viewed as the instrumental cause that acts under his influence and is thereby a formal part of the text, although he remains free to use language that is appropriate to the period.

Vatican II was an opportunity to present a broad synthesis regarding inspiration. There was a rejection of certain minimalist texts that sought to reduce inspiration to the level of subsequent acknowledgment by the church or of help to make sure no mistakes were made; instead, the following fundamental principle was affirmed: "Sacred texts . . . have God as their author, and as such are entrusted to the church" (DS 3006).

Leo XIII's *Providentissimus Deus* (DS 3291–93) and Pius XII's *Divino Afflante Spiritu* (DS 3826–30) were to be subsequent interventions of the magisterium to put the matter in focus. A more attentive exegesis and a new methodology also made it easier to understand literary genres and the personality of the sacred writer.

It was Vatican II, however, that gave a real impulse to find new solutions. The third chapter of *Dei Verbum* only seems to refer to the traditional doctrine on inspiration; in fact, only the three sections that form the chapter present real progress in the teaching on inspiration.

The council received a number of suggestions that had been arrived at through studies carried out over the previous decade. On both the biblical and dogmatic fronts, they had cleared the field of various reductionist positions that contained references to the problem and had identified new and promising potential solutions. On the biblical side McKenzie, McCarthy, Coppens, Lohfink, and Alonso-Schökel had opened up reflections that were more directly connected with the question of the sacred writer and the truth. Coming from a more theological standpoint, Rahner, Grelot, and Benoit put forward useful theories for a reinterpretation concerning ecclesiastical mediation, the function of the author, and the linguistic value of written mediations.

2. The Innovation of Vatican II

The innovation of Vatican II can be summarized in three headings.

a. The Identity of the Author. The sacred author was no longer seen in the role of a simple, passive interpreter or instrument in the hands of God as he has been identified by earlier theology. The *Spiritu Sancto dictante* of the Council of Trent was replaced by a more positive and biblical language that says the writer is chosen, one of God's elect, a person who writes his text as a real author.

This is followed by a highly positive definition of the author: a person who studies, reflects, researches, and communicates through his writings the redeeming experience of what he has been part of. Every sacred writer is considered totally free in the context of God's plan; the writer has responsibility for a mission to build the church. This mission is accomplished through the special nature of his writing, and it is the writer who has to do the work and has the burden of originality through which his personality is expressed.

At all events, God is undoubtedly the author (*Urheber*) because it is he who enacts the history of salvation by his various acts of revelation. Moreover, it is he who is at the very origin of the sacred text, whether it is a single book or several; he and his actions are what the sacred writer tries to express, although within the logic of revelation itself.

b. Precomprehension of "Truth." A second innovation concerns the understanding of "truth." Although texts circulating before the council had focused on inerrancy, and on the absence of any error in the Scriptures on account of their being revealed through inspiration, the council introduced a more biblical use of truth, which was above all a faithful and merciful communication of God as he tries to save the world.

However, the truth of the Scriptures is the full and universal truth of God's redeeming plan for humanity. *Dei Verbum* 11 marked a clear theological advance: "The books of the Scriptures teach the truth that God for our salvation wanted to be placed in the Sacred Scriptures, and does so faithfully, with certainty and without mistake."

c. Inspiration and Revelation. A third innovation was the renewed union of inspiration and revelation. It cannot be denied that the two had drifted further and further apart between the two councils. Vatican II put inspiration back where it belongs, within the more all-embracing reality that represents the event of revelation.

The guidelines pointing the new way for the theological study of the revelation will also apply for inspiration. Above all, it is a question of the *centrality of Christ*. Jesus of Nazareth, insofar as he is the Word of God, is also the truth of humanity. He is the true inspired book for communicating and giving salvation.

There is also the *freely given charism*. The sacred writer lives the experience of being the chosen and elected one of the Spirit; he is the author in every way, but aware at the same time of being in an intimate relationship with God in whom he trusts and from whom he freely accepts the mission to communicate his will through his writings.

Finally, we come to the *historical authenticity* of the event. Inspiration does not destroy the author's characteristics; on the contrary, it elevates them. Nonetheless, things proceed in the other direction with God, who humbles himself so as to be able to communicate. The event of inspiration takes place within history, and that is why the truth that is given in its entirety in the sacred text is only arrived at eschatologically. This is a case of a gradual maturing of the church as it reinterprets the text and rediscovers an ever more profound meaning, thereby creating a living tradition by analogy with faith (*DV* 12).

Inspiration therefore presents itself as a characteristic of the written form of the word of God. Only to the extent that it remains closely linked to revelation does it acquire its more meaningful and significant sense. The profound significance of the value and reality of inspiration is evocatively captured by these words of Ugo da San Vittore: "The whole of Scripture is one book, and that one book is Christ."

Bibl.: A. Bea, "Inspiration," *LTK* 5:703–5; G. Courtade, "Inspiration," *DBS* 4:544; P. Benoit, *Exégèse et Théologie*, 2 vols. (Paris, 1961); P. Grelot, *La vérité de l'Écriture: La Bible Parole de Dieu* (Paris, 1965); K. Rahner, *Inspiration in the Bible* (New York, 1966); J. Beumer, *Die katholische Inspirationslehre zwischen Vatikan I und Vatikan II* (Stuttgart, 1967); I. de la Potterie, *La "verità" della Bibbia nel dibattito attuale* (Brescia, 1968); V. Mannucci, *Bibbia come parola di Dio* (Brescia, 1981); R. Fisichella, *La Révélation: La révélation et sa crédibilité* (Montreal/Paris, 1989); M. A. Tabet and T. McGovern, "El principio hermenéutico de la inspiración del hagiógrafo en la constitución dogmática DV," in J. M. Casciaro, ed., *Biblia y Hermenéutica* (Pamplona, 1986), 697–713.

Rino Fisichella

INTERRELIGIOUS DIALOGUE

1. Dialogue in the Magisterium of the Church

Even though "interreligious dialogue" is a recent term in the church's vocabulary, it is not in fact all that new. Quite apart from the era of such missionary pioneers as Nobili in India or Ricci in China, dialogue was already evident during the pre–Vatican II period in countries where the church came into daily contact with members of other religious traditions. There was such a thing as dialogue, then, though of course it occurred sporadically and was often on the verge of descending into sterile debate. We must also acknowledge the unprecedented impetus that the council gave to dialogue between religions by making it one of the key themes in the renewal and opening up of the church that it promoted. In so doing, the council was following the infectious enthusiasm of Paul VI.

On 6 August 1964, between the second and third sessions of Vatican II, Paul VI published his programmatic encyclical *Ecclesiam Suam*, when the Vatican II documents that were to examine interreligious dialogue (*NA, AG,* and *GS*) were still in the drafting stage. The pope set up the Secretariat for Non-Christians less than a month before the encyclical appeared (17 May 1964). *Ecclesiam Suam* marked the entry of dialogue in general into the new perspective inherent in the church's program of renewal and the opening up to the world that the council desired. The term "dialogue" itself appeared here for the first time in an official church document.

In the pope's own words, the encyclical is concerned with the "problem of dialogue [*colloquium*]" between the church and the modern world (AAS 56 [1964]: 613). "The Church should enter into dialogue with the world in which it lives and works. It has something to say, a message to deliver, a communication to offer" (639). Dialogue, as the pope sees it, is to be conceived as "a method of accomplishing the apostolic mission, a means of spiritual communication" (644). Making a distinction between the various forms that the "dialogue of salvation" may take, he stresses the "prime importance retained by the proclamation of the word of God . . . for the Catholic apostolate. . . . Preaching is the primary form of apostolate" (648). The church, says the pope, should be prepared to "enter into dialogue with all people of good will, within and outside its own sphere" (649). The encyclical continues with an outline of a number of concentric circles "around the central point where God has placed us [the Church]" (650). In saying this, he hopes to show how the dialogue of salvation, implicit in the church's mission, reaches various classes of people in different ways. The pope makes a distinction between four concentric circles, beginning with the most remote (all humanity and the universe), then proceeding through a second (the faithful of other religions) and a third (other Christians), and ending with the innermost circle (dialogue within the church itself).

The second circle "consists essentially of those who worship the one supreme God, he whom we also worship," including not only the Jews and Muslims, but also the "faithful of the great Afro-Asian religions" (654–55). "By reason of a duty of loyalty," the pope emphasizes, "we should manifest our conviction that the true religion is unique and that it is the Christian religion, while preserving the hope of seeing it recognized as such by all those who seek and worship God" (655). Nevertheless, "we do not wish to withhold respectful recognition of the spiritual and moral values of various religious denominations, and we are ready to enter into dialogue and to take the initiative in doing so—which means dialogue regarding the ideals that we share in the realm of promotion and defense of religious freedom, human fellowship, culture, social welfare, and the civil order" (655).

This part of the encyclical ends with this real, though restrained, opening up. The theological evaluation offered of other religions, like the area open to religious dialogue, is still restricted. The role and place of this dialogue in the church's mission are not otherwise developed or specified.

Nevertheless a breakthrough had been made, which Vatican II was able to extend. This council was the first in the church's conciliar history

to speak positively of other religions of humankind. On the one hand, the conciliar documents exhibit a will to recognize "whatever truth and grace are to be found among the nations" (*AG* 9), not only in the objective elements of the religious traditions themselves, whether it is a matter of their "religious practices and cultures" (*LG* 17), of "those multiple endeavors [*incepta*], including religious ones, by which men search for God" (*AG* 3), or of other "riches which God in his generosity has dispensed to the nations" (*AG* 11). These elements are seen as "a ray of that Truth [*illius Veritatis*] which enlightens all men" (*NA* 2).

On the other hand, the council showed increasing awareness of the universal influence of the Holy Spirit well beyond the frontiers of Christianity, affecting indeed the whole universe. The Spirit of God—who is also the Spirit of Christ—fills the universe (*GS* 11). *Ad Gentes* and *Gaudium et Spes*—both products of the last session of the council—refer explicitly to this universal presence of the Spirit in space and time: "Doubtless, the Holy Spirit was already at work in the world before Christ was glorified" (*AG* 4); he is also there in the present-day world, in the aspirations of all men and women for a better quality of life (*GS* 38), a social order more worthy of humanity (*GS* 26.4), and universal fellowship (*GS* 39). His enduring influence keeps alive in humanity the question of human religious destiny (*GS* 41), offering men and women the light and strength to confront it (*GS* 10). Men and women have been bought by Christ and have become new creatures in the Holy Spirit (*GS* 37). In fact, the Spirit now summons all humankind to Christ, not only in the preaching of the gospel, but even by "the seed of the Word" (*AG* 15). He, "in a manner known only to God offers to every man the possibility of being associated with this paschal mystery" (*GS* 22). Thus revitalized and brought together in the Spirit of the risen Christ, humanity advances toward the consummation of human history (*GS* 45)—with a living hope that is the gift of the Spirit (*GS* 93).

That is the profound basis of interreligious dialogue in the conciliar documents. The documents ask members of the church to initiate this dialogue. We already find an exhortation of this kind in *Nostra Aetate*. The church exhorts its children:

prudently and lovingly, through dialogue and collaboration [*per colloquia et collaborationem*] with the followers of other religions, and in witness of Christian faith and life, acknowledge, preserve, and promote the spiritual and moral goods found among these men, as well as the values in their society and culture. (*NA* 2)

We find similar appeals in *AG* and *GS*. Following the very example of Jesus himself, his disciples,

profoundly penetrated by the Spirit of Christ, should know the people among whom they live, and should establish contact with them. Thus they themselves can learn by sincere and patient dialogue [*dialogo*] what treasures a bountiful God has distributed among the nations of the earth. But at the same time let them try to illumine these treasures with the light of the gospel, to set them free, and to bring them under the dominion of God their Savior. (*AG* 11)

The Magna Carta of dialogue according to Vatican II is to be found in *GS* 92, where the council recalls, but in the reverse order, the four concentric circles already described in the encyclical *Ecclesiam Suam*. In regard to the believers of other religious traditions, the text wants "frank conversation to compel us all to receive the inspirations of the Spirit faithfully and to measure us to them energetically." These generous words, however, never before uttered by an ecumenical council, do not indicate the place of interreligious dialogue in the church's mission. It was left to the postconciliar period gradually to clarify this aspect, up to the point of treating interreligious dialogue as an integral part and authentic expression of the church's evangelizing mission (→ EVANGELIZATION I).

2. The Aim of Dialogue

Interreligious dialogue is a fully entitled part of the overall mission of the church and cannot be reduced to an extrinsic element or merely treated as a useful means for proclamation of the gospel, however much it may help in making an initial approach to "non-Christians." Accordingly, it is not merely complementary to proclamation as a means to an end but is already an end in itself because it is good in itself. In order to perceive this—and to see in what ways dialogue nevertheless remains open

to the proclamation of the gospel—its meaning and intentions require some discussion.

Interreligious dialogue is a form of the "dialogue of salvation" that Paul VI spoke of (see above). Its reason is the universal and active presence of the mystery of Christ through his Spirit in all people, Christians and others. Accordingly, dialogue does not stop at mutual understanding between and friendly relations with other believers, nor even at collaboration in social projects. It goes beyond all this and proceeds to the level of the mind and spirit, where Christians and members of other religions can exchange a mutual witness to faith. In dialogue, says a document published by the Secretariat for Non-Christians (1984), "Christians meet believers of other religious traditions in order to advance together toward the truth and to collaborate in works of common interest" ("Attitude of the Catholic Church to the Believers of Other Religions—Reflections and Guidelines on Dialogue and Mission," 13). In dialogue, Christians and others are summoned to undergo a more profound conversion to God and a deeper commitment of faith. On the Christian side the aim of dialogue is not the conversion of others to Christianity and the numerical growth of the Christian community but, rather, mutual enrichment and communion in the Spirit with those who do not share our faith.

Proclamation, or the announcement of the gospel, is also intended to communicate to others the explicit knowledge of Jesus Christ and of what God has accomplished in him for the salvation of all humanity, and therefore wishes to invite them to become his disciples by entering into the Christian community. In this way, therefore, in the kerygmatic proclamation of the gospel, the church exercises a prophetic function. It proclaims Jesus Christ as the source of the mystery of salvation, in which the partners in dialogue already communicate, and invites to recognize it those who until now shared in this mystery without being able to identify its origin or to name its author.

Accordingly, dialogue and proclamation represent different approaches in the evangelizing mission of the church. They have distinct aims. Whereas interreligious dialogue cannot be thought of only as a means of proclaiming the gospel, it nevertheless remains open to that possibility. In fact, the church's evangelizing mission is a dynamic process that, in itself—even if that is not always realized in fact—culminates and comes to fruition in the proclamation and announcement of Jesus Christ.

3. The Demands of Dialogue

Beyond the psychological readiness to be open and to listen, which is indispensable to all dialogue, interreligious dialogue possesses certain internal requirements without which it is neither true nor authentic. Insofar as that is possible, each partner must enter into the religious experience of the other party, in order to understand it from within. This effort to understand and sympathize has been termed "intrareligious dialogue" (R. Panikkar). It is an indispensable condition of true dialogue.

This does not mean that we must or can, even temporarily, put our own faith "to one side." On the contrary, the honesty and sincerity of dialogue require the various partners to commit themselves to it in the integrity of their faith. Any methodological doubt, and any mental reservations, are out of question here, as is any compromise in the terms of real faith or any reduction of its content. Authentic faith does not allow of syncretism or eclecticism. Without wishing to dissimulate possible contradictions between respective religious faiths, it should patiently apprehend them in the actual circumstances of their existence. Dissimulation would be tantamount to cheating and would run counter to the purpose of dialogue.

Moreover, to enter, as far as that is possible, into another person's religious experience while firmly adhering to our own faith does not mean participating in two different religious faiths, while making each of them our own and combining them within our own personal lives. Apart from possible confrontations within each individual between contradictory aspects of these two shared faiths, each religious faith constitutes an indivisible whole and postulates total commitment. It seems impossible a priori for such abolute commitment to be shared and, as it were, divided between two faiths.

All necessary guarantees having been given, it is nevertheless certain that, to be true, interreligious dialogue demands from each partner the positive effort that is needed to enter into the religious experience and overall vision of the other. This kind of encounter, within one and the same person, of two ways of being, seeing, and thinking, represents the arduous but necessary preparation for a sincere meeting and true exchange between individuals.

4. Forms of Dialogue

Interreligious dialogue must not be conceived narrowly, as if it consisted solely in the mutual exchange of religious experiences at the level of mind and spirit. The above-mentioned document of the Secretariat for Non-Christians divides dialogue into four types. It is a matter of the dialogue of life, which is open to everyone (nos. 29–30), of mutual commitment to works of human justice and liberation (nos. 31–32), intellectual dialogue among experts (nos. 33–34), and sharing of religious experiences in the mutual quest for the Absolute (no. 35).

The actual content and order of these "principal models" of dialogue (no. 28) require some examination. I must stress first the primary role of the dialogue of life, accessible to everyone, which the document rightly puts to the fore. "It comprises attention to, and respect and welcome for the other person, to whom one allows the space necessary for his or her identity, his or her own form of expression, and his or her values" (no. 29). This form of dialogue is something that "every disciple of Christ, by virtue of his or her human and Christian vocation, is called to live in his or her everyday life" (no. 30).

The document also speaks in this regard, in second place, of the common commitment to justice and human liberation, according it precedence over theological discourse. It is also appropriate to emphasize the fact that this mode of dialogue should take the form of common action rather than that of shared discussion: "At another level we have the dialogue of action and cooperation, regarding aims of a humanitarian, socioeconomic and political nature, which promote the liberation and development of humanity" (no. 31). This dimension of dialogue assumes great significance in the present context of a culturally and religiously pluralist society, characterized both by universal problems of human rights and justice and by those of human promotion and liberation. The members of different religious traditions can and should commit themselves jointly, on the basis of their respective religious convictions, to the promotion and establishment of a more human world. The dialogue of life should give rise to the dialogue of action. Together they form the common human substrate without which theological discussion among specialists and the exchange of religious experience would have no basis.

We may also inquire into the merits of the order of the final two forms of dialogue as set out in the secretariat's document. The order should probably be reversed. Surely religious experience comes before theological discourse. Should not exchange at the experiential level in its turn serve as a basis for mutual discussion? Theological talk about the respective world-views and religious doctrines of the partners in dialogue is, to be sure, possible in principle, even if it is not based on a mutual exchange at the level of religious experience. Actual experience shows, however, that mutual understanding at the level of theological discourse remains difficult—if not impossible—unless it is preceded by a profound spiritual communion, which can be established only by a mutual exchange of religious experience. If that is absent, discourse runs the risk of turning into abstract debate, or even of degenerating into confrontation. It is at the level of spiritual exchange that dialogue is both most demanding and most promising. It is on the basis of this kind of spiritual exchange in depth that theological dialogue can best proceed if it is to bear the fruit of mutual understanding. True, exchange and communion usually give rise to talk.

5. The Starting Point of Dialogue

Where is theological dialogue to begin? What will be on the agenda? Of course it is impossible to decide a program in advance, for the Spirit blows where he chooses. We still can ask, however, where we can find common ground on which Christians and others can begin to conduct theological discourse?

It has been suggested that the meeting point should be the "Christ mystery," which is universally present and active, even though it affects Christians and others in different ways (R. Panikkar). The starting point for theological dialogue is not to be found in any doctrine, however, for doctrines, even though they may partly coincide in terms of their deep purpose, do not differ any less profoundly. The "Christ mystery," however, is common to everyone.

It must be noted, however, that the universal and active presence of the mystery of Jesus Christ comprises the theological basis that makes interreligious encounter and dialogue possible, more than it represents the actual starting point of that dialogue in its theological manifestation. Clearly the mystery of Jesus Christ, as understood by Christian faith, cannot function as a starting point on which there is assured advance agreement. We have to look elsewhere.

One possible starting point is the experience of the divine mystery in the Spirit. Spiritual exchange and communion in the Spirit indeed constitute a necessary condition for fruitful theological dialogue. They can also serve as its direct object.

Another starting point, one that is certainly less ambitious but no less valid and more accessible, is to be found in the basic questions that any religious person, in any tradition, asks in the depths of his or her heart: Where do we come from, and where are we going? What is the meaning of human existence? What is the meaning of suffering and death? What is the origin of this impulse in us—experienced and shared by the partners in dialogue—that compels us to emerge from our own selves in friendship, fellowship, and communion with others, and to advance beyond ourselves in order to answer a divine Absolute that always precedes us? The Second Vatican Council found that these utterly fundamental questions were asked nowadays by an increasing number of human beings and felt by them with renewed urgency (*GS* 10). The declaration *Nostra Aetate* lists these "profound mysteries of the human condition which, today even as in olden times, deeply stir the human heart" in answer to which "men look to the various religions" (1).

The Constitution *Gaudium et Spes* also formulates a series of analogous questions in regard to people of our own time (*GS* 10). It is not accidental, moreover, that the same conciliar document draws attention, on the one hand, to questions that everyone asks nowdays and, on the other hand, to the universal presence of the Spirit in them, in such a way that it is apparent in the hopes and aspirations, projects and initiatives of contemporary humanity. After all, the same Spirit inspires projects and provokes questions.

The question about humanity leads to the question about God. As such, it serves as a trustworthy starting point for theological dialogue. Thereafter, the agenda for this dialogue should be left to the Spirit, who inspires the partners in it. Its main agent is the Spirit, who is the source of all spiritual communion, which necessarily grounds all common theological discourse.

6. The Challenges and Fruits of Dialogue

Because the Spirit is at work in both partners in interreligious dialogue, there cannot be a one-way dialogue. Christians must not only give but receive. The fact that they may have received the fullness of revelation in Jesus Christ does not excuse them from listening. Christians do not have a monopoly on truth; rather, they should allow themselves to be possessed by truth. In fact, the other partner in the dialogue, even without having heard of the revelation that God has offered of himself in Jesus Christ, may be more deeply affected by "this Truth," which he or she is still seeking, and by the Spirit of Christ who shines his rays into him or her (cf. *NA* 2). We may certainly say that, through dialogue, Christians and others "advance together toward truth" (Secretariat, no. 13).

Consequently, a Christian has something to gain from dialogue and will in fact derive a dual advantage from it. On the one hand, there will be an enrichment of the Christian's own faith; through the experience and the witness of the other person, the Christian will be able to discern more profoundly certain dimensions of the divine mystery that he or she might not see so clearly and that perhaps do not stand out so clearly in the Christian tradition. On the other hand, he or she will receive a purification of faith. The shock of encounter will often force the Christian to question something, whether it is a matter of revising certain gratuitous assumptions or of destroying deep-rooted prejudices or even of revising too narrow notions or viewpoints. The benefits of dialogue also constitute a challenge for the Christian.

Hence the fruits and challenges of dialogue go together. Apart from certain benefits, we may say that encounter and exchange are valuable in themselves. Whereas they originally presume an opening to the other person and to God, they may lead to an opening to God of each person through the other.

Dialogue does not act as a mere means to an ulterior goal. Neither on one side nor on the other does it serve to advance the "conversion" of one partner to the other's religious tradition. It tends instead to a more profound conversion of the one and the other to God. For the same God speaks in the heart of each of the partners, and the same Spirit is at work in both of them. In the midst of reciprocal witness, the very same God issues the challenge of one partner to the other. For one another and reciprocally they thus become, we may say, a sign pointing to God. In the last analysis, the proper end of interreligious dialogue is the common conversion of Christians and members of other religious traditions to the same God—the God of Jesus Christ—who calls them together by summoning and challenging them through others. This reciprocal challenge, a sign of God's summons, is mutual evangelization.

Bibl.: Vatican II, *Nostra Aetate, Gaudium et Spes*; Secretariat For Non-Christians, "The Urgency of Dialogue with Non-Christians," *Origins* 14 (1984): 641–50; H. LE SAUX, *La rencontre du christianisme et de l'hindouisme* (Paris, 1965); R. PANIKKAR, *Interreligious Dialogue* (New York, 1978); K. CRAGG, *The Christ and the Faiths* (London, 1986); H. KÜNG, *Christianity and the World Religions* (Garden City, N.Y., 1986); M. ZAGO, *Il dialogo interreligioso a 20 anni dal concilio* (Rome, 1986).

Jacques DUPUIS

IRENAEUS AND REVELATION

The question of Irenaeus and revelation arises in connection with Irenaeus's use of Mt 11:27 (Lk 10:22) in his polemic against the Valentinians and Marcionites. The pages of greatest interest are in *Adversus Haereses*, book 4, chap. 6. From this passage we summarize here (1) the Valentinian position and exegesis and (2) the Irenaean positions and exegesis.

1. Valentinian Position and Exegesis

Irenaeus cites the logion in question, adduces its obvious meaning, and then presents his adversaries' exegesis:

> But those who would regard themselves as better qualified than the Apostles proceed as follows: "No one knows the Son but the Father, and no one knows the Father but the Son—and anyone to whom the Son wishes to reveal him" (Mt 11:27). And they interpret this as if the true God had been known by no one before Our Lord's coming, and say that the God who was announced by the prophets is not the Father of Christ. (*Adv. Haer.* 4.6.1.9ff.; 1.20.3.39ff.)

The saint attacks not the logion's variant readings but the meaning ascribed to it by his adversaries. While for Irenaeus (following Justin) the evangelical oracle expresses a universal economy, without limits of space and time, the sectaries urge the chronological aspect of both verbs: *egnō* ("know") and *apokalypsai* ("reveal"). Thus, the "no one" could seem to refer only to all who lived before the proclamation of the Father in Jesus' preaching.

The literal meaning of the logion, in and of itself, does not seem to justify the heretical position. Marcion, who in sound logic sought support in Lk 10:22, interpreted it in the sense of the present, just as did Irenaeus and Tertullian. Besides, Marcion is typically unconcerned with verbal formulas. Nevertheless, he agreed, to a large extent, with the heterodox gnosis.

Whether the verb was read in the present or in the aorist could prejudice its interpretation. Among the Valentinians, the technical meaning of both verbs came into play. For the non-Gnostic, to "know" (*ginōskein, epi-*) had an obvious meaning. On the contrary, among the Valentinians, with their connections with the Gnosis, it took on a very particular one. The same must be said for "reveal" (*apokalyptein*) through its technical meaning, in connection with "knowing."

The logion (Mt 11:27) attributes to the Father a *gnōsis* of the Son, without any allusion to his revelation. In place of the latter, it attributes to the Son a *gnōsis* of the Father and his revelation (to human beings). There is no reason why the mutual *gnōsis* of Father and Son should be differentiated. In all probability it indicates intuitive, perfect knowledge in both cases. One must determine whether the *revelation* ascribed

to the Son is correlative to the *gnōsis* to the extent that it would attain to the heights of the knowledge he seeks to communicate; and consequently, whether to the revelation of the Word there corresponds in human beings a perfect *gnōsis*. But among the Valentinians, only the "pneumatic" possess a perfect *gnōsis* of God. Only the spiritual, then, with their natural (*physei*) aptitude for the *gnōsis*—not the "psychical," and still less the "hylic"—will have a capacity for the Savior's strict, full revelation.

In these terms, the logion has a twofold meaning. Both verbs ("to know" and "to reveal"), in the strictest sense, apply solely to the Savior's message to the "pneumatic." With the latter, the divine knowledge, by correlation with Jesus' revelation, reaches the same level as that of the knowledge of the Father by the Son, or of the Son by the Father. Thus, the same family intimacy (*oikeiotēs*) that unites Jesus with God joins the spiritual with Jesus.

Irenaeus attends to the verbs in the Gospel, but he does not denounce the Valentinian technical interpretation. He is usually thinking of the Word incarnate, and not of the simple logos. No angelic soteriology enters his horizon. His interest lies in the salvation of human beings, by way of the Son who become a human being.

It is surprising that Irenaeus never understands the two verbs in the strong sense given them by the Valentinians. As his position is poles apart from that of the heretics, we may even wonder whether, according to him, the human being is even capable of a *perfect* gnosis. The Valentinians believed that, in this very world, on the basis of their illumination, they possessed a complete and perfect knowledge and understanding of the mysteries of God—or at any rate, an understanding on a par with the *gnōsis* of the Son. Not content with an arbitrary denial of such knowledge here below, Irenaeus seems to envision, in the future understanding of the saints as well, an indefinitely perfectible knowledge. Even in the next life, God will always have mysteries to communicate, so that the human being will always have them to receive. Their *gnōsis*—compatible, then, with faith and hope—will never be absolutely perfect, nor commensurable with that of God.

Although the church is the legatee of the apostolic tradition, it is incapable of solving all questions posed by the Scriptures. Even in the age to come, in the presence of God, there will be things to learn. God is ever the Teacher, the human being ever the disciple.

> Of the things subjected to examination in the Scriptures—all of the Scriptures being spiritual—some we solve by the grace of God, while others we leave to God: and this not only in the present age, but in the age to come, as well, in such wise that God will ever teach, and the human being ever learn the things that come from God. (*Adv. Haer.* 2.28.3.59ff.)

Paul confirms this (1 Cor 13:9–13):

> So also spoke the Apostle. With the destruction of all else beside, there abide these: faith, hope, charity. For faith in our Master abides unshaken. He warrants us that he is the one true God; and he desires us to love him ever as the one Father, and to hope to receive, hereafter, something more, and to learn of God, for he is good and possesses endless riches, the endless reign and doctrine to be learnt without measure. (*Adv. Haer.* 2.28.3.65ff.)

In the next life, with the destruction of the imperfect, the perfect remains: faith, hope, and charity (see 1 Cor 13:13). Faith remains, for our faith in our Teacher, the one true God, will only be consolidated. Love remains, for we shall always have God as our only Father. Hope remains, for we shall always have something to receive and learn from God. Being so good, God possesses inexhaustible wealth, a reign without end, a discipleship (or magisterium) without measure or end.

For the Valentinians, the *gnōsis* already received in this world dislodges faith and hope. For Irenaeus, not even the gnosis of the next world, bestowed on the human being as *salus carnis* ("salvation of the flesh"), will dislodge faith. We shall contemplate the Creator face to face; contemplation will nourish our faith in that Creator, as the one true God and source of endless truths. The sight of the Creator will feed our hope, uncovering to us endless riches, attainable only throughout eternity.

For Irenaeus, *gnōsis* and *pistis* (knowledge and faith) will go hand in hand with each other, like *elpis* and *agapē* (hope and love), in testimonial of the infinite distance between God the Teacher and us the disciples.

The Valentinians, puffed up with foolish pride, vaunt a knowledge of the mysteries of God here in this world. The Son has asserted that it is the Father's alone to know the day and hour of the judgment. These disciples that are above their Master, the so-called spiritual, understand the manner of the procession of the Word, the time and manner of the creation of matter, the reason why some angels transgressed and others did not (see *Adv. Haer.* 2.28.6–7)! They seem to want us to believe that the *gnōsis* they have received from the Savior makes them equal to Christ the Teacher—indeed, even to God.

According to Irenaeus, gnosis without charity is vain. Charity alone confers and seals perfection (*Adv. Haer.* 4.12.2.36ff.). Gnosis itself, at the highest degree of intuition, is ordered to charity. "Charity is of greater value than gnosis" (4.33.8.146ff.). Instead of erecting the latter as "pinnacle and crown of the rule" of Christians, with autonomy over faith, hope, and charity, as the sectaries would have it, one ought humbly to take up *pistis* and submit to charity, that Queen of Christians, both in this age and in the age to come.

Under Irenaeus's pen, the logion exalts the humble, loving knowledge of faith. The real *gnōsis* is not the perfect, definitive knowledge of certain privileged ones. Rather, the *gnōsis* of faith is available to all and holds its treasures in store for the day when the Son, the Father's Gnosis in person, will be revealed directly. A recognition of the Son and the Father, in free-willed awe at the witness of the Savior, is the *gnōsis* that is authentic knowledge of God, as well as being faith—the knowledge conditioned by the current economy of salvation.

2. Irenaean Positions and Exegesis

God has sent his only begotten Logos into the world for human salvation. The Son's revelation, human by reason of being addressed to human beings, is human as well by reason of the means selected—the incarnation, that supreme "apocalypse" of God to us (see *Adv. Haer.* 4.6.3.40ff.). God is ineffable and thus incapable of being revealed to anyone but the Son. Three things are required for the Logos to be able to reveal God to us: (1) that it know the unknowable Father personally, at every stage; (2) that it make the unknowable, unrevealable God revealable in itself—in the person of the Son; (3) that, furthermore, it make God *humanly* revealable to human beings.

The first requirement presents no difficulty. As for the second, in virtue of the ineffable divine generation of the Logos, the Infinite is circumscribed in the person of the Son, who is the image and substantial measure of the Father. The third requirement suggests that, although being the fruit of the divine generation, the Logos is also humanly engenderable, for the salvation of human beings.

There are two (substantial) revelations of the Son, then: creation and a manifestation of salvation. The creation only is a preliminary to the salutary manifestation.

The sectaries agreed with Irenaeus that a natural divine filiation was the sole radical title to a knowledge of the Father. Without God, no one arrives at God; one reaches neither the Father without the Son, nor the Son without the Father. For the sectaries, however, without divine nature and lineage, no one is called by the Son to the possession of the Father. For the church, meanwhile, a divine calling (and free response of faith) suffices in order to arrive at God by means of the Son. The Valentinians posit the divine consubstantiality of the individual as a requirement for reception of the Son's revelation. Irenaeus demands only that the individual be free to respond meritoriously to the message of the Logos.

> And for this has the Father revealed the Son, that through him he be manifested to all: that those who believe in him he may justly receive into incorruption and everlasting refreshment (now, to believe in him is to do his will), while those who do not believe, and therefore flee his light, he may justly shut up in the darkness that they have chosen for themselves. (*Adv. Haer.* 4.6.5.77ff.)

Here is the origin of the divine economy. The Father has willed to give himself to human beings to be known. Unable to do so personally, he must use the mediation of the Son. Nor was it feasible to reveal the Son to human beings—with sufficient efficacy to raise them to salvation (of the flesh)—unless the Son were first to become a child (a human being with the human being). And so the Father sent him to the womb of the Virgin, in order to give him—enfleshed and born of her—to the world to be known, making him available to view in human flesh.

Of itself alone, the revelation of the incarnate Son would have remained insufficient. Revelation must have the response of faith. Faith must accept Jesus' witness as authentic, recognizing in him the only begotten Word of the Father.

Irenaeus does not pause to list the signs of Jesus' divine sonship: the proofs of his sending by the Father. But he insists that these, which are sufficient to oblige one to believe in his person and testimony, offer to all the option through faith of ascending to incorruptibility and repose with the Father, or without faith of withdrawing finally from him.

One might justly fail to follow the Logos, had God not placed him within reach of all. Will someone who denies the indispensable means for the knowledge of his will be able justly to demand its accomplishment? God has offered the necessary means to all, namely, by sending the divine Son, and then by excluding no one from a knowledge of that Son, who is made visible to all through the logophanies and the incarnation (see *Adv. Haer.* 4.6.5.83ff.).

The Jews refused faith in the Son and thus are to blame for their perishing. They had the means to believe; they saw what all saw and heard what all heard. Has everyone contemplated the Word who became a human being and heard the message of revelation he has borne from the Father, as Jesus' Jewish contemporaries did? Surely not. Although not rendering him equally visible to all, God has made him attainable in sufficient measure to lead all to faith.

This brings us to a consideration of the various forms of the revelation of the Word. Irenaeus writes:

> The Word *reveals*: God the Creator by way of creation itself; and the Lord, Demiurge of the world, by way of the world; and the Artificer who has molded [the human being] by way of that which has been molded; and the Father who has begotten the Son by way of the Son. And these things are asserted by all alike, but not all believe them alike. So also the Word proclaimed himself and the Father by means of the Law and the Prophets: and the whole people heard [him] alike, but not all believed [in him] in the same way. (*Adv. Haer.* 4.6.6.88ff.)

Here are several universal manners of revelation. In all of them, the Logos indeed reveals the Father, but not in the same way or in conformity with a single aspect. They are manifold (and salutary) revelations of the one Word of God.

One of these revelations is *creation*. As God

the Father has created amorphous matter, the Logos reveals God, through this first creation. To this first revelation the human being responds, appropriately, by faith alone — receiving the language of the Word salvifically, through creation, in order to ascend to the Father.

A second revelation on the part of the Logos is the *world* — matter that has now been actually fashioned (the second creation). By means of this fashioning, this world, the human being arrives at the "Fashioner of the world," i.e., the Lord who is Logos. Unlike the revelation *per conditionem* (by way of the first creation) — in which one ascends from the substance of matter (or formless matter) to God the Father as its Author — in the revelation *per mundum* (by way of the second, or demiurgic, creation), one arrives at the Logos Demiurge.

The third form of revelation is the *plasma* — that which is "molded," or the human body. The mystery of the plasma, the creature molded and modeled to the image and likeness of God, is not something that can be discovered at a glance. A special revelation of the Logos is required for an understanding of the divine dimension of the human body, and for an ascent from it to the Father, who commits the Son and the Holy Spirit to its ongoing formation.

The fourth and last form of revelation is *the Word made flesh* (i.e., the revelation *per Filium*). The novelty of this form of revelation lies not in the natural divine sonship of the Logos but in the (personal) sonship of the human *plasma* in Christ. The Son of Man is the Son of God. Through creation, that of the world and the human body, faith must pierce to the person of the Son, who lives in the bosom of the Father, and must discover in the life of Jesus the ineffable mystery of the supreme God. No one discovers by the senses alone the revelation of God in Jesus. The revelation of the Logos is required. The same Logos that manifests the sacrament of creation, the deed of the Father, that of the world, the deed of the Word, and that of the human *plasma* (the joint task of the Father with his two divine Hands) also reveals the mystery of the form of a slave adopted by the Son, that the Logos may be manifested to human beings and proclaim the Father.

Being common and equally sensible to all, the four forms of revelation ought to have led all without distinction to a saving knowledge of God. But as these forms are founded on faith, and thus are humanly realizable by free acknowledgment alone, they force themselves on no one. Some persons accept revelation, and others do not.

Revelation *per ipsam conditionem* did not find equal acceptance among human beings, despite having been extended to all. The same is the case with the forms of revelation *per mundum, per plasma,* and *per Filium.* The story of Jesus demonstrates the fact that only believers have accepted the revelation of the incarnate Logos. "While all assert this alike, not all believe alike" (*Adv. Haer.* 4.6.6.91ff.). All — heretics and ecclesiastics alike — employ similar terms, as if all had ascended alike "by way of creation" to the Author of the universe, "by way of the world" to its Demiurge, and "by way of the human body" to its Artificer. But such is not the case. The heretics, by the three ways of revelation, reach the demiurge-soul, without ever encountering the Logos of God or discovering its mediation. They lack the humble, loving disposition needed for recognizing the word of truth. While they say the same thing outwardly, they do not believe in the same way, since, when all is said and done, they do not believe.

Good and wicked, believers and unbelievers, all testified to Jesus' wonders and teachings. The very demons recognized in him the Son of God. Of one accord in seeing, hearing, and even proclaiming in words the Son of God, and thereby the Father, not all believed in the Logos, or in the Father rendered visible in him. They did not recognize the Son and the Father as would be expected (i.e., unto salvation); they did not accept, with salvation in view, the revelation of both, through the Word.

No one directly called Jesus "God," although many called him "of God," in the genitive. Irenaeus adduces two examples, placing them on the lips of the devil, or the demons: "Holy One of God, Son of God." The denomination "God," applied in the genitive to Jesus, was the best proof that the very demons confessed both: God (the Father) and the Son:

> And on this account all called him Christ to his face, and denominated him God. But even the demons, seeing the Son, said: "We know who you are — the Holy One of God!" And the tempter, the devil, seeing him, said: "If you are the Son of God. . . ." Thus, all saw him and spoke of

the Son and the Father, but not all believed.
(*Adv. Haer.* 4.6.6.100ff.)

To paraphrase: Therefore all, even the demons, on the basis of his presence in the flesh, not only confessed him *orally* (*loquebantur*) as the Christ, but, in calling him Son *of God,* named him conjointly with his Father.

The diabolic witness is singularly relevant in view of certain errors. As the declaration of a witness with nothing to gain, it confirms the truth proclaimed by Christ. It condemns the fanaticism of those who refuse to profess what the very demons have openly asserted when confronted with the evidence of the facts (see *Adv. Haer.* 4.6.7.107ff.).

Against the Jews, the witness of the demons highlights the facility with which, on the basis of the incarnation of the Logos, they could have come to a saving knowledge of the Father and the Son.

The same accusation is valid against the Valentinians. They had invented a gratuitous distinction of persons between the unbegotten Son of God and the Christ who had a human soul. The facts spoke otherwise. It was not that one (the Christ with a human soul) spoke, while another (the only begotten) knew the Father in order that he be revealed to the spiritual. One and the same, true God and true human being, knew and revealed; the only begotten become a human being and come to reveal the Father.

Let us summarize. The logion Mt 11:27, Lk 10:22 refers to a *saving revelation.* The Son reveals the Father to those who hear him *in faith.* The saving revelation of the Logos does not require that the objective means of cognition be linked to God by the same order of causality. Creation, the world, and the human being come from God in ways very different from the way in which the Son comes from God. The revelation of the Logos is not intended to supply the causal order in the physical, as if the objective means were physically inadequate to manifest God; it is intended solely to supply, for supernatural effects, what physical cognition does not give. It leaves the objective truth untampered with, but it makes it the object of the knowledge of faith.

This is how we should understand the disposition Irenaeus requires of the Gentiles themselves. The Word cannot *reveal* the saving news of God if it collides with a spirit dominated by idolatry and concupiscence. The testimony of Epicurus as to the existence of God does not enter into the Irenaean horizon. Epicurus's dissolute life-style rendered him incapable of a saving knowledge.

Irenaeus never spoke of a "natural" and a "supernatural" knowledge. Such a vocabulary is foreign to the second century. Nor did he imply any such distinction. To ascribe to Irenaeus an express or implied distinction between a natural (that of reason alone) and a supernatural knowledge of God (that of faith), as if he had here anticipated, *quoad rem,* that later theological distinction, would be to anticipate history. Actually it would have represented the Valentinian distinction of the two orders ("psychical" and "pneumatic"), or that of the pagan theologians between a knowledge of mere existence (that of God) and a knowledge of essence, in terms of their two "ways"—physical (or cosmic) and divine (i.e., spiritual, *secundum cognitionem*). The antithesis between the nonsaving knowledge had by pagans, unbelieving Jews, and evil spirits, on the one hand, and that of faith positively bestowed by the Word, on the other, likewise recalls our modern distinction between the natural and the supernatural.

The saint has his favorite formulas. One of these contrasts knowledge *secundum magnitudinem* and knowledge *secundum dilectionem* (see *Adv. Haer.* 4.20.1.1ff.; 4.20.4.72ff.). While the divine Majesty is invisible and unattainable, infinite Love makes it attainable by the human being.

> In terms of magnitude, there is no way to know God: the Father cannot be measured. However, in terms of Love—which leads us to God by way of his Logos—in docility to him, we ever [both before and after Christ] learn that this great God exists, and that it is he who himself has established and selected and adorned, and who contains, all things. (*Adv. Haer.* 4.20.1.1ff.)

God does not change. The infinite abyss between the divine Unknown and the human intellect abides intact. But thanks to the measureless divine Love or Benignity, God invites all, even the unworthy, to the wedding banquet (see *Adv. Haer.* 4.36.5–6).

Benignity and Love do not, of themselves alone, explain the human being's knowledge of God. They only indicate the initial title of the economy of salvation, which is oriented toward a *gnōsis* of God.

The means or forms this cognition takes, like the entire dispensation of salvation, originates in the gratuitous love of God for the human being. But these forms are not to be confused with that love. The human being will never know God by way of love as a cognitive means. We know God by way of the Word, the Son of God, the visible expression of the Invisible.

The complexity of the aspects of *revelation*, which Irenaeus indicates without departing from an exegesis of Mt 11:27 (Lk 10:22), corresponds *a contrario* to the doctrine of his great adversaries, especially the Valentinians.

According to the latter, the gnoseology of the psychical Demiurge is one thing, while that of God the Spirit is another. The gospel logion, we hear, refers only to the revelation (or knowledge) of God the Spirit. The mediation of the Verbum does not affect knowledge of the Creator. By one route, one reaches the soul-god, and by another, God the Spirit.

Against the Valentinians, Irenaeus stresses the identity of the Demiurge and God the Spirit, the single economy of the Old and New Testaments, and the mediation of the Verbum for the human being's attainment of saving knowledge.

As the God of both Testaments is one, as the only begotten Logos of the Creator and Father is one, as the *plasma* summoned to salvation in virtue of a gnosis of God is one, as the economy presiding over human history before and after Christ is one—so also there is no reason to multiply routes of salvation: *gnōsis* for the "spiritual" and *pistis* for the "psychical." Nor may we distinguish, in terms of various human lineages (or generations), two manners of revelation: *apart from* the Logos in the OT and *by way of* the Logos in the NT.

The economy of salvation, common to both Testaments, is rooted in the love and benignity of the Creator, from whom proceed the four principal forms of revelation on the part of the Logos: creation, the world, the *plasma* that is the human body, and the Son (the Word Incarnate). The mediation of the Logos is necessary for an understanding of the first three forms of revelation as well as it is for the last.

Bibl.: J. LEBRETON, "La connaissance de Dieu chez saint Irénée," *RSR* 16 (1926): 385–406; L. ESCOULA, "Saint Irénée et la connaissance naturelle de Dieu," *RSR* 20 (Strasburg, 1940): 252–70; A. HOUSSIAU, "L'exégèse de Matthieu XI, 27b selon saint Irénée," *ETL* 26 (1953): 328–54; id., *La Christologie de saint Irénée* (Louvain, 1955), 72–73; R. LUCKHART, "Matthew 11, 27 in the 'Contra Haereses' of Saint Irenaeus" *Revue de l'Université d'Ottawa* 23 (1953): 65–79; J. OCHAGAVIA, *Visibile Patris Filius* (Rome, 1964), 62–69; A. Orbe, "San Ireneo y el conocimiento natural de Dios," *Greg* 47 (1966): 441–71; id., "La revelación del Hijo por el Padre según san Ireneo (Adv. Haer. IV, 6)," *Greg* 51 (1970): 5–83; P. BACQ, *De l'Ancienne et la Nouvelle Alliance selon S. Irénée* (Paris, 1978).

Antonio ORBE

ISLAM

In this article, revelation will be set forth according to the Islamic point of view. We begin by placing it in the Islamic conception of the history of revelation. Next, we describe the revelatory process in prophetic experience. After briefly mentioning the transmission of the Qur'anic text, we list some of the hermeneutical principles that operate in the various types of Qur'anic exegesis and conclude with a glance at a few aspects of Catholic theological thought about the Qur'an. Figures in parentheses below refer to chapters (*sūra*, pl. *sūrāt*) and verses of the Qur'an.

1. The History of Revelation

According to Islamic doctrine, revelation began with the history of the human race, The Qur'an says: God "taught Adam all the names" (2:31). It is a matter here of a teaching that comes from him who "knows the mystery of the heavens and the earth" (2:33), Furthermore, the concept of the "religion of the origin" (*dīn al-fiṭra*) is developed on the basis of the Qur'an. It concerns that religion, that is, with which God created human beings (from the beginnings) (cf. 30:30), Such was the religion when "human beings formed a single community [*umma*]" (2:213). But they split up into sects and became hostile to one another "after knowledge had come to them" (42:14). God then sent them the prophets to bring them the good news (cf. 2:213); there is no human community [*umma*] in existence to which a messenger from God has not been sent (cf. 10:47; 35:24). Of these messengers, the Qur'an mentions some, but not all, by name (cf. 4:164). Noah, Abraham, Moses, and Jesus receive special mention as predecessors of Muhammad. Their message was always: "Maintain the faith, and do not split into sects" (cf. 42:13).

The Qur'an states that human beings have often not accepted the words of those sent and have treated them as impostors. Almost the whole of *sura* 26 relates the facts of such missions. The mission of Muhammad and the revelation of the Qur'an are seen as the conclusion of the history of revelation. Muhammad is called "the Seal of the Prophets" (33:40), and in the codex (*mushaf*) of Ubbay his community is called "the ultimate *umma*" (61:6). In believing in the message proclaimed by Muhammad, Muslims thus profess their belief in all previous revelations: "We believe in God and in that which has been revealed to us, and in that which was revealed to Abraham, and Ishmael and Isaac and Jacob and the [twelve] tribes, and in that which was given to Moses and Jesus, and in that which was given to the Prophets from their Lord; we do not make any distinction between any of them, and to Him do we submit" (2:136).

In the Islamic view, the history of revelation flows into the Qur'anic revelation, which brings it to an end. Whereas, as regards the previous revelations, there is no talk of a development of revelation and the emphasis falls rather on the messages' being identical, Islamic scholars have made a careful study of the chronology of the words and texts contained in the Qur'an. This type of preoccupation, however, is not directed to establishing evidence of progressive revelation in the Qur'an, but rather to showing the intrinsic consistency and basic identity of everything contained in the text. An important exegetical principle is that of *al-nāsiḫ wa-l-mansūḫ*, based on the text: "Whatever verse We abrogate or cause to be forgotten, We bring one better than it or one like it. Do you not know that God is possessor of power over all things?" (2:106; cf. 16:101; 22:52). Evidently, for the application of such a principle, an exact knowledge of the chronology of the Qur'anic revelation is indispensable.

The ultimate basis for the sameness of the prophetic messages is their single, common source, which exegetes identify with the Qur'anic expression "the Mother of the Book"

(13:39; 43:4; cf. 58:78), which is the "heavenly prototype" of the scriptural revelations. The Qur'an is presented as the unique exact "copy" of the heavenly Scripture and therefore as norm for the authority of every other sacred SCRIPTURE, the transmission of which is held to be imperfect and defective.

2. Revelation in Prophetic Experience

In the language of the Qur'an, there are two key terms for indicating the process of revelation: *tanzīl* (lit. "sending down") and *wahy* ("inspiration"). In prophetic experience, the divine word to be transmitted to human beings is perceived as coming from a higher, external source; at the same time, the perception of such a word is an interior process, in the Prophet's heart. In describing the experience of revelation, the rich vocabulary of the Qur'an makes it clear that the divine word comes as a *call* and an *order* from God, with whom lies the absolute initiative for the revelatory act. The function of the word is to *teach* human beings what they do not know, to *make clear* what is obscure to them, to *remind* them of what they have forgotten, to *warn* them that judgment is imminent, and, above all, to *proclaim the good news* of God's mercy and to *summon* everyone to the faith, to worship the one God and obey his law.

The word directed to the Prophet establishes the latter in a special relationship with God and confers on him the function of apostle (*rasūl*). The "word of mission" is expressed in the Qur'an with formations on the root *klm*. This is particularly evident in the accounts of the call and mission of Moses (4:164–65; 7:143–44). The word (*kalima*) that comes from God in the revelatory process is the *order of the mission* and the *promise* of divine assistance and victory over enemies. When the Qur'an speaks of Jesus as "a word [*kalima*] of God" (3:45, 49; cf. 4:171), the most satisfactory way of interpreting the expression is along the lines of his being the organ and intermediary of revelation.

In the Qur'an, the word of God is made Scripture. Even the verse regarded as having been the first communicated to Muhammad refers to the recitation of a sacred text: "Recite in the name of your Lord who creates!" (96:1). Yet in the early *sūrāt* there is never any mention of a Scripture presented by the Prophet of Islam. Rather, his preaching is affirmed as conforming with that which is contained in preceding Scriptures (26:196; 87:18f.; etc.). Gradually there appear expressions representing Muhammad as the man on whom God "has sent down" the Scripture (2:231; 4:113; etc.). The Qur'an is called "a Scripture in the Arabic language, verifying [previous scriptures]" (46:12).

3. The Transmission of the Qur'anic Text

As regards the most intricate question of the history of the present-day Qur'anic text, the following points seem to be accepted by most Islamic and non-Islamic scholars: (1) Muhammad did not himself commit his message to writing; (2) the Qur'an was originally recorded and preserved in the hearts of the faithful; (3) when Muhammad died (632 C.E.), there existed collections of *sūrāt* or parts of *sūrāt*; (4) a first edition of the text was made under the Caliph 'Uthmān around the year 650 C.E.; (5) a vocalized edition of the text was produced during the caliphate of 'Abd al-Malik (685–705), although collections of seven, ten, or fourteen "readings" of the Qur'an, each regarded as canonical, continued to enjoy a certain authority; (6) with the first printed editions the need became felt to have greater conformity among the different readings still in circulation; and (7) in 1923 an edition of the Qur'an according to the "reading" of Hafs was published in Cairo. This text (revised in 1952) is now regarded as the standard text more or less throughout the Islamic world.

4. Hermeneutical Principles in Qur'anic Exegesis

The various types of classic Qur'anic exegesis are guided by a variety of hermeneutical principles.

Textual exegesis aims to establish the unique, authentic reading of the text and is based on the principle that the Qur'an constitutes a unitary text, the internal consistency of which must also be evident at the level of expression. Elements of the method used in this type of exegesis are lexicographical explanation, grammatical analysis, and the composition of a critical apparatus of variant readings.

Narrative exegesis aims to make relevant the Qur'anic message for the faithful. It places the Qur'anic text in a narrative setting to bring out its meanings. Sometimes it even proceeds by a method of interpolation, in which elements gathered from the Bible and the Talmud are to be found.

Legalistic exegesis seeks to clarify the content and the obligatory character of the moral and legal prescriptions contained in the Qur'an. For this exegesis, a knowledge of Qur'anic chronology is of the greatest importance, with a view to the right application of the aforementioned principle of *al-nāsiḫ wa-l-mansūḫ*. In establishing the chronological order of the text, the narrative method has an important role, concentrating as it does on the *asbāb al-nuzūl* ("the causes of the revelation")—that is, the circumstances or events that occasioned a given revelation and can therefore help to explain what it means. The traditions (*ḥadīth*) of the Prophet's life are the main source for these "causes." In this connection, "the science of the *ḥadīth*" has grown up as an auxiliary exegetical science, the function of which is to determine the degree of authenticity of the various *ḥadīth*.

Dogmatic exegesis aims to establish a probative relationship between doctrinal positions of apologetic theology and the Qur'anic text. Of methodological importance here is the explanation in a metaphoric sense of certain texts, with the help of principles of rhetoric, poetry, and Arabic linguistics. Another procedure consists in reasoning according to the principles of logic.

Mystical exegesis is the recourse to religious experience as hermeneutical principle for reaching the deep, "real" meaning hidden in the revealed text under the outward appearances of verbal expression.

In the vast field of *contemporary exegesis*, different currents with diverse preoccupations can be singled out:

Traditionalist exegesis reacts against the secular, materialistic, and rationalistic spirit of modern culture in demonstrating the validity for all time of Qur'anic truths and ordinances.

Ethical exegesis aims to make the Qur'an contemporary for the younger generation and lays stress on the moral values contained in it. In some cases, exegetes of this current invert the principle of *al-nāsiḫ wa-l-mansūḫ*, seeing the revelatory basis of religion in the most ancient verses, whereas the subsequent revelations would apply only to the specific historical circumstances that prompted them.

Scientific exegesis proceeds according to the principle that Scripture "makes all things plain" (6:155). It applies harmonistic methods in an effort to discover references to all the achievements of modern science in the Qur'anic text.

Philological exegesis attempts by applying principles of modern philology and linguistics to the Qur'an to establish the exact meaning of the words and expressions in the sacred text.

5. Positions of Catholic Theology

From the beginnings of Islam, Christian theological thought has been concerned with the Qur'anic revelation and the mission of Muhammad. After centuries of alternating periods of polemic, prejudice, and mutual disregard, the Second Vatican Council has given a clear signal to encourage objective and positive reflection about the Qur'anic revelation. Among modern theologians, differing approaches are to be discerned. One approach attempts to establish a link between the Qur'anic message and the faith of Abraham, to whom Islam refers. Such reference to the monotheistic faith of Abraham would give Islam and its holy book a special status in the "universal history of revelation." Another tendency seeks to identify the elements common to the Qur'anic and Christian revelations. The Qur'an is thus regarded as a reminder of biblical revelation and a reflection of certain revealed truths therein contained. A third approach attempts to explain the way in which the prophetic charisma operated in Muhammad's mission and in the formation and reception of the Qur'anic text.

Bibl.: A. A. ROEST CROLLIUS, *The Word in the Experience of Revelation in Qur'an and Hindu Scriptures* (Rome, 1974); J. WANSBROUGH, *Quranic Studies* (Oxford, 1977); R. CASPAR, *Traité de théologie musulmane*, vol. 1 (Rome, 1987).

Arij A. ROEST CROLLIUS

J

JESUS OF HISTORY AND CHRIST OF FAITH

To understand this distinction we must locate it in the historical context in which it first appeared. It goes back to Martin Kähler and his little book *Der sogenannte historische Jesus und der geschichtliche, biblische Christus,* published in 1892 (Eng. trans. *The So-Called Historical Jesus and the Historic Biblical Christ,* trans. C. Braaten [Philadelphia: Fortress, 1964]). Kähler used the distinction to show that the only real Jesus is the Christ of preaching and faith, and not the Jesus of a past time. He thus introduced a distinction that was to become popular between the Jesus of history and the Christ of the kerygma. Our interest is in the Christ of apostolic preaching and not in the Jesus of history, of whom, in any case, we know very little, at least with scientific certainty. Kähler did not deny that the Gospels have some minimal historical basis, but he did think that the investigation of the liberal school into the life of Jesus was pointless and fruitless.

For clarity's sake we should bear in mind that for Kähler the "historical (*historische*) Jesus" is the man of Nazareth, as a biography of Jesus might depict him, while the "historic (geschichtliche) Christ" already implies faith in the savior whom the church proclaims.

There is obviously no question of denying the earthly existence of Jesus or the preaching of Christ by the primitive church; it must be remembered, however, that these are one and the same person, who is henceforth "identified" as Christ and savior on the basis of his statements and works. In combining the two names into one, "Jesus Christ," the church emphasizes the point that it is speaking of a single person. The gap between the Jesus of history and the Christ of faith is artificial and the result of a false problem.

Contemporary scholarship has no intention of returning to the perspectives of the *Leben-Jesu-Forschung*; its focus is rather on access to Jesus of Nazareth, identified now as Christ and Lord, on the basis precisely of what he really said and did during his time on earth. Kähler's distinction, which was taken over by Bultmann, rests on a conception of faith that does away with the very event that is faith's foundation; it represents a return to *gnosis*.

Bibl.: R. BULTMANN, "Das Verhältnis der urchristlichen Christuskerygmas zum historischen Jesus," in H. Ristow and K. Matthiae, eds., *Der historische Jesus und der kerygmatische Christus* (Berlin, 1961), 233–35; M. KÄHLER, *The So-Called Historical Jesus and The Historic Biblical Christ* (1892; Philadelphia, 1964, 1988); F. MUSSNER, "Der historische Jesus und der Christus des Glaubens," *BZ* 1 (1957): 224–52; R. MARLÉ, "Le Christ de la foi et le Jésus de l'histoire," *Études* 302 (1959): 65–76; R. LATOURELLE, *Finding Jesus through the Gospels* (New York, 1979), 31–41.

René LATOURELLE

JUDAISM

I. THE SPIRIT OF JUDAISM

No matter the geographical location, Jews have felt more or less as if they were living in the Holy Land—some more than less, such as Judah Halevi, the Spanish poet whose great love poems for Zion have been a constant source of inspiration for Jews.

1. The Patriarchal or Ancestral Covenant: *Běrît 'Ābôt*

The beginning of this intimate linkage with the land is much earlier than medieval times. Jews have always understood themselves as being part of a covenant between their people and God which derives from Abraham, Isaac, and Jacob. From the beginning this relationship included the Land of Israel as an indispensable constituent of the covenantal reality. Their God, who called Abraham from his native land, was *'Elôhê hā-'āreṣ*, the God of the Land. When Abraham arrived in the land, the covenant was established:

> I will establish my covenant between me and you, and your offspring after you throughout their generations, for an everlasting covenant, to be God to you and to your offspring after you. And I will give to you, and to your offspring after you, the land where you are now an alien, all the

land of Canaan, for a perpetual holding; and I will be their God. (Gn 17:7–8)

The designation and sanctification of the people are inseparable from the sanctity of the land. The promise to Abraham was confirmed to the descendant patriarchs, Isaac and Jacob. Later, when Moses was sent to Egypt to deliver the people from bondage, it was in the name of the patriarchal covenant that he labored. There was only one destination possible after the exodus: the Land of Israel. As the people enter the land, their leader Joshua is charged: "Be strong and courageous, for you shall put this people in possession of the land that I swore to their ancestors to give them" (Jos 1:6).

After taking possession of the land, the Israelite farmer was to come with his tithe to the sanctuary. As part of the tithe confession, he was to offer the following prayer:

> Look down from your holy habitation, from heaven, and bless your people Israel and the ground that you have given us, as you swore to our ancestors—a land flowing with milk and honey. (Dt 26:15)

The references are too numerous to recite. What they all indicate is an inseparable bond between the people and the land, between Holy People and Holy Land. The destinies of this people and this land are linked, bound together by God's promise. Whether they are in the land or in exile, the covenant remains part of their identity and consciousness.

2. The Sinai Covenant: _Bĕrît Sinai_

There is a second covenant of importance for our purposes. This alliance is already hinted at in the Abraham cycle of stories. However, it does not emerge into full consciousness until Mount Sinai. We read the following in Genesis in the prelude to the destruction of Sodom:

> Shall I hide from Abraham what I am about to do, seeing that Abraham shall become a great and mighty nation, and all the nations of the earth shall be blessed in him? No, for I have chosen him, that he may charge his children and his household after him to keep the way of the LORD by doing righteousness and justice; so that the LORD may bring about for Abraham what he has promised him. (Gn 18:17–19)

Later, at Mount Sinai, this intimation of keeping the way of the Lord becomes the Torah, the

pattern of 613 commandments that are to guide the life of Abraham's descendants, the newly liberated people of Israel. Jewish thinkers have usually understood that these two covenants continue to function, the second not superseding the first. Thus, the people of Israel has a double covenantal sanctity: the ancestral covenant with its promise of the land and the Sinai covenant with its commandments. From the perspective of the first, Israel abroad, out of its land, is incomplete. It is not fulfilling its duty to settle the land and dwell in it as God's people; its sanctity is diminished. However, the Sinai covenant is not dependent on land. The Torah is portable, and its sanctity accompanies the people in all its dwelling places. Many of the commandments cannot be fulfilled outside of the land, for they are related to the settlement and cultivation of the land and celebration in the Jerusalem Temple. Nevertheless, the Sinai-Torah sanctity prevails everywhere.

3. The Content of the Covenants

My teacher, Rabbi Joseph B. Soloveitchik, discussed these two covenants in a now famous address to the Religious Zionists of America, the Mizrachi, in the 1960s. He noted that the content of the Sinai covenant is clear to us. "It expresses itself in statutes and judgments, in undertaking to observe 613 commandments." This gives the Jewish people its distinct character and purpose—its _yiud_. He then asked:

> But what is the content of the patriarchal covenant? Apart from circumcision, God did not give _miṣwôt_ to the patriarchs. . . . It seems to me that the content of the patriarchal covenant manifests itself in the sense of seclusion of the Jew; in his existential isolation; in the fact that he must struggle against secular philosophies and political forces which the cultured non-Jew ignores; in the fact that the security of society generally does not ipso-facto provide security for the Jew. In other words, the Judaism of the patriarchal covenant is expressed in our identification with Abraham the Hebrew—"All the world on one side and he on the other." (This latter quotation is a midrashic comment on the word "Hebrew," _'ibrî_. The root _'br_ can mean "on the other side.")

> The patriarchal covenant is realized within Jewish consciousness because others point at him and say: "He is a Jew!" In a word, the patriarchal covenant finds expression in the sense of

oneness with Klal Yisrael (the entire collective of Israel), in one's participation in the lot of all Jews, and in the consciousness of the fact that being Jewish is singular and unique. One who lacks this mentality and does not sense himself as bound to the strange, paradoxical Jewish fate, lacks the sanctity of the patriarchal covenant. One may observe the Torah and the commandments and be fully within the covenant of Sinai, yet at the same time profaning the patriarchal sanctity.

In other words, this covenant is one of fate, destiny—*gôrāl*.

Thus, we can say that from the ancestral or patriarchal covenant Jews derive their strong sense of family belonging: we are the children of the fathers and mothers of Israel. As members of the same family we care for each other, rejoice in each other's successes, and cry when any segment of the family faces tragedy. The Sinai covenant is one of learning—specifically, to do that which was commanded to us. The central figure in this mode is Moses, who is known in Jewish tradition as "our Teacher."

4. Messianic-Redemptive Implications

Each of the covenants has its own redemptive dynamic. For the *běrît 'ābôt* the drama of redemption is focused on the land. Away from the land, Israel is incomplete, in exile, the covenant remaining unfulfilled. The return to the land, therefore, has messianic significance. The covenant is actualized: once again the God of the land is their God. Possession of and sovereignty over the land are the sign of return to redemptive favor, possibly the beginning of a messianic era. The Sinai covenantal consciousness is concerned for the actualization of its program of Torah commandments as the guiding force of every phase of the life of the people. It is focused on the question of Jews having the power to create the circumstances in which to implement the covenantal terms. Return to the land may be a sign of forgiveness for whatever sins caused the people to go into exile and is for the purpose of a new opportunity to improve on past performance. It is hoped that the more perfected Torah-inspired society will result.

To understand the religious significance of Israel for Jews, both covenants must be appreciated. They work in tandem and produce different emphases. They exist in religious and secularized forms. Thus, in the development of Zionism, we find religious Jews as well as secular Zionists concerned for the survival of the Jewish people. They feared that the Emancipation and its aftermath would lead either to total assimilation or anti-Semitic annihilation. Their anticipations were unfortunately realized and confirmed in the Holocaust as well as in the general assimilation that pervades diaspora communities. We also find religious Jews who are motivated by the Sinai concerns, the opportunity to fulfill more of the covenantal responsibilities in the land than outside of it, including the command to settle the land and make it thrive. Secular Zionists also have a version of the Sinai consciousness: they wish to build a society rooted in Jewish values of justice.

The Zionist enterprise is thus motivated by both forms of covenantal consciousness. The Emancipation led to the loss of sovereignty over Jewish communal life, a heavy price to pay for integration into the modern state. Now Jews would be integrated into their locale of residence as full citizens. This attachment, it was feared, would be an insuperable challenge to identification with the Jewish nation. The *běrît 'ābôt* was in danger. Soon the *běrît Sînai* would be threatened as well, as the process of indigenization proceeded. Attempts to retain a strong sense of communal life were met with the development of modern political and racial anti-Semitism. Jewish sovereignty in the ancient Jewish homeland was a necessity for the survival of both covenantal impulses. A strong nation-state would be the guarantor of the physical survival and spiritual renewal of the Jewish people everywhere.

5. The State of Israel

The fulfillment of the Zionist aspiration and the ancient dream of our people came about in the creation of the State of Israel in 1948 by a resolution of the United Nations General Assembly. Since that time the state has progressively developed into a significant element of the religious, spiritual, and moral life of Jews everywhere. This has been especially true since June 1967, when Jerusalem came under Israeli control during the Six-Day War.

The war had been preceded by weeks of terror which overcame Jews as they heard the threats and saw the preparations to push all Israeli Jews into the sea. The swift, dramatic, decisive, and wholly unanticipated escape from disaster and the return to Jerusalem became a turning point for most Jews. They now identified with Israel as their reborn spiritual patrimony, and as a wholly fresh and new venture for modern Jewish life. They came to appreciate that the rebirth of Israel represents a commitment to survival by the Jewish nation, the determination to rebuild itself after the onslaught of the Holocaust. After two thousand years of relative powerlessness to defend themselves, Jews would now have the power to protect themselves and, more significant, to chart their destiny as a modern people with ancient roots.

Learning to use this power to create a new state has been a source of constant challenges. These include assimilating vast numbers of refugees from Europe and Arab lands, building a modern and just society, and attempting to create a spiritual center for world Jewry while defending the nation and trying to find a peaceful way of living with neighbors. Jews are proud of the state's accomplishments but are acutely aware of the many problems that Israel faces. Indeed, Jews throughout the world try to act as responsible partners in the development of Israeli life. They are highly sensitive to issues that relate to the security, stability, and morale of Israel's citizens. Many Jewish communal activities in the diaspora relate to Israel—lectures by prominent Israeli scholars or leaders, fundraising for educational and humanitarian purposes, encouragement of economic investment. Visits to Israel are frequent, and many youths pursue some part of their education there. These activities give individual Jews and Jewish communities a meaningful sense of participation with Israeli Jews in the building of the nation. All of this has led to a vital sense of Jewish communal and national identity—the fulfillment of the patriarchal covenant—which includes efforts to maintain well-serviced diaspora communities with much attention to aid for Jews in distressed circumstances such as Russia, Syria, and Ethiopia.

Thus, the rebirth of the State of Israel in its ancestral covenanted land has signaled a renewed commitment to Jewish peoplehood, which has always been the essence of the patriarchal covenant consciousness. In that perspective, the survival of the people through history is itself a sacred phenomenon, inspiring many Jews today—committed Jews as well as those somewhat alienated from tradition—to strengthen their Jewish attachments and even deepen their understanding of the religious, spiritual, and moral teachings that constitute their heritage and are derived from the Sinai covenant.

6. Power: Blessings and Dilemmas

Power is necessary for Jews to survive as a unique people. Power is also necessary for the implementation of the vision of Sinai. That challenge demands that Judaism deal with the real world and the issues of modern life. Those without power may sit on the sidelines and moralize. It is infinitely more difficult to eradicate poverty, create jobs, and fight terrorism and wars with dignity. Choices must be made and mistakes often result. Often even the best choices have some unfortunate and unforeseen consequences.

The power of the state means an opportunity to make Judaism come alive, to put God's commandments into practice as the guide for a modern society. Can the sacred enter the world and transform it, or must the sacred be cloistered in synagogue or study hall away from the tensions of real life? Can Jews create a society that is faithful to the values of kindness and justice? Or are these relevant only to dreams and not reality? Because Jews consider the struggle with power and its implications as so critical an issue today, we must dwell on this and amplify the dialectics. In our time, we have come to realize that harsh words and implied attitudes might result in a particularly nasty form of articulation. Jews are often worried that we might not remember the lessons of power. Throughout our history we have had sufficient power to negotiate our existence, maintaining ourselves as a distinct physical and spiritual entity. From time to time the balance was tipped against us. We lacked the power to protect ourselves and we suffered for it. The most extreme instance of the latter occurred in our own time. During the Holocaust we suffered extreme powerlessness. We could do almost nothing to save the six million Jews that were destroyed and the numerous communities that experienced dislocation. This fateful event is still fresh in our minds and evokes nightmares in many of those who survived. However, our generation has also experienced a miracle. The birth and development of the State of Israel, despite its many problems, are no less than a modern miracle. We hope and pray that it is rē'šît šĕmîḥat gĕ'ullātēnû, the first flowering of the promised grand redemption. Israel is considered to be today among the top world powers in terms of military capacity. In our entire history we have probably not been as absolutely or relatively strong as we are today. In living memory, we have gone from extreme powerlessness to extreme powerfulness. But that power is not only an asset; it is a challenge. A nation can become drunk with its power, as was ancient pharaoh's Egypt. Are we to ignore the lesson of the prophet Zechariah: "Not by might, nor by power, but by my spirit, says the LORD of Hosts" (Zec 4:6). We read these verses on Hanukkah recalling the victory and might of the Maccabees. They are a constant challenge to those with power.

What is this spirit of God to which Zechariah refers? Most definitely, it is part of the Sinai consciousness. Prior to Zechariah it had already been beautifully described by Isaiah in regard to the messianic leader: "The spirit of the LORD shall rest on him, the spirit of wisdom and understanding, the spirit of counsel and might, the spirit of knowledge and fear of the LORD" (Is 11:2). A sense for truth, justice, and kindness will characterize his actions. Notice what will result. "The wolf shall live with the lamb, the leopard shall lie down with the kid, the calf and the lion and the fatling together, and a little child shall lead them. The cow and the bear shall graze, their young shall lie down together; and the lion shall eat straw like the ox" (Is 11:6–7). The spirit of God is manifest when the powerful do not abuse the weak but learn to live with them in the same world. In addition, it is up to the rich and powerful to initiate this process. They must take responsibility, using their affluence—the strength and wealth entrusted to them by God—to assist others. That is our vision of the future.

The arrogance of power consists of an insistence that one's way be forced upon others totally and completely. In effect, the needs of others are to be ignored, their dignity and rights treated as nothing. The temptation of power is to dream that one can achieve all that one wishes, forcing the issue if necessary by might. Rather than modest success one thinks that one can have it all. Humble persons know that

in the imperfect world that we live in the inadequate will usually have to be adequate. The arrogance of wanting it all can lead to having nothing. In the language of Pirqe 'Abot, Tafasta merubah, lo tafasta, "if you try to take or grab too much, you end up taking nothing." It is a truth that applies in so many areas of life.

Words uttered within the community as mere words may eventually prompt and justify murderous deeds that were far from the original intention of those who spoke them. I am, of course, again referring to our twentieth-century experience of the Holocaust, which has taught us that harsh beliefs and attitudes ultimately affect our behavior toward others. Deeds catch up with words, and eventually the process of dehumanization can lead to destruction. After centuries of dehumanizing Jews, the deeds caught up with the words and we faced our notorious tragedy. In today's escalated pace of life, the process is quicker. Locking innocent Arabs in a shack and burning them to death is an example of that phenomenon. Those with power and authority must be even more careful with their words, for even their words have power. Hakhamim, heezeharu bedibreykhem ("Sages, be careful with your words") we are counseled in Pirqe 'Abot. Wise counsel, indeed.

7. Covenants in Conflict

The two types of covenantal consciousness can be in conflict. For the Sinai mode of thinking, the implementation of Torah norms of peace, justice, and compassion must be balanced with the other commands of land settlement and cultivation as well as the duty to create a secure existence for Jews. Decision makers must conclude how to balance the competing norms and weigh each component of the situation. Not all the elements may be totally or absolutely satisfied in the attempt to reach a balanced solution. However, the ancestral covenantal consciousness has only one item on the agenda: the possession of the land—sovereignty and power with which to protect Jewish survival according to its covenantal vision. Other considerations are irrelevant.

The current reality in Israel often reflects the conflict of these modes. Traditionally, Jews have operated with a dominant Sinai consciousness, trying to apply the commandments to the daily reality. The mood of post-Emancipation and post-Holocaust Jewry seems to be more worried about sheer survival. There has been a decided shift toward ancestral covenantal consciousness even among the bearers of the Sinai learning tradition. Jewish life and thinking should reflect both of these ancient foundational covenants that shaped our people over the centuries. It remains to be seen how Jews will choose to meet their responsibilities.

Howard JOSEPH

II. JEWISH LIFE

1. Hebrew Scriptures/Christian Understanding

The most basic of Jewish Scriptures is called by the Jewish people the Tanakh—and in English, the Hebrew Bible. This is what Christians call the "Old Testament," but that appellation imposes a Christian interpretation on the role and purpose of these Scriptures. It suggests that, in contrast to the "Old" Testament, the "New" is better and is to be preferred as the completion of the "Old," which is seen as incomplete.

Jews do not see the Hebrew Scriptures, and particularly the first five books (the Pentateuch, or Books of Moses) as complete in and of themselves either. They see a written text but also an oral interpretation which completes the Hebrew Bible. This interpretation, which completes the text and makes its message applicable to daily life, begins at the same time as the written message. The oral interpretations are as valid as the written material, and the text and interpretation must be understood together. In effect, the oral and written traditions are one. Christians are aware of the written text, but they are largely ignorant about the oral tradition.

The complex of text and interpretation may be divided into two broad areas: legal material and moral directives. All this together is called *Torah*. The term "Torah" itself is most commonly understood in three ways: (a) the first Five Books of Moses, Genesis through Deuteronomy (the Pentateuch); (b) the whole of the Hebrew Bible, with non-Pentateuchal Scripture providing an understanding of the Pentateuch; and (c) the whole of the Hebrew Bible plus its practice-oriented interpretation. A religious Jew

would opt for the latter description. Jews who live a life based on the text alone are considered to be heretics. The Pharisees, in spite of the often biased and negative publicity of the NT, championed the idea of an ongoing, living relationship between text and interpretation and between the written tradition and God, its author, and the individual. They made it possible for all people, rich and poor, laborer and prince or priest, to become fully part of the tradition. In that spirit, Jewish tradition has always sought to make possible for every person a relationship with God, in every age and under any circumstances, whether at home or among Gentiles, in times of tolerance or persecution.

The Hebrew Bible

The Hebrew Bible has three major divisions: the Books of Moses, or Pentateuch; the Prophets; and the Writings. The Books of Moses are Genesis, Exodus, Leviticus, Numbers, and Deuteronomy. The division called the "Prophets" is divided into two main units, Former and Latter Prophets. The Former Prophets include the books of Joshua, Judges, 1 and 2 Samuel, and 1 and 2 Kings. These books advance the covenantal story of the ancient Jewish community, begun in the Pentateuch. The Latter Prophets include the various books of prophecy of the Hebrew Bible. These are presented not in terms of chronological sequence, but more in terms of length, following the style of textual collection in the ancient world. These books are: Isaiah, Jeremiah, and Ezekiel; and the Book of the Twelve Prophets—Hosea, Joel, Amos, Obadiah, Jonah, Micah, Nahum, Habakkuk, Zephaniah, Haggai, Zechariah, and Malachi.

The division called "Writings" consists of a collection of materials of various sorts. The Psalms are prayer poems, written in the style of ancient Near Eastern religious poetry. They address all aspects of human concern. The Proverbs deal with the human condition; the book of Job is a lengthy reflection on the question of divine justice in our world. Following these three longer works are five "scrolls": the Song of Songs is a love poem, variously understood as describing passionate human love or God's love for Israel; Ruth is a tale of human friendship, set in the time of the judges; Lamentations is a lament on the fall of the kingdom of Jerusalem to the Babylonians in 586 B.C.E.;

Ecclesiastes is another reflection on the human condition; and Esther is a court tale describing the perilous circumstances in which the Jewish community found itself in foreign lands after the Babylonian defeat of the kingdom. Next comes the book of Daniel, a prophetic-type narrative also set in the period after 586 B.C.E.; then the books of Ezra, Nehemiah, and 1–2 Chronicles, works that detail the story of the Jewish people through the Babylonian exile and into the period of the restoration of the community in its ancestral homeland under the Persians, to about the year 400 B.C.E.

Story and Covenant

As we saw above, the story of the Jewish people in ancient times is contained in the Pentateuch and Former Prophets, then extended in Ezra, Nehemiah, and Chronicles. The story is one of promise and fulfillment. It begins with creation and continues on to reflect on human society as a whole and on God's special relationship with the descendants of Abraham, Isaac, and Jacob—the people Israel. The whole story is based on the notion of covenant, a contractual agreement between God and humanity. Covenant makes security available to believers, but at the same time it imposes responsibility. Key elements in any such relationship are consistency and fidelity. A hallmark of any long-standing contractual agreement freely entered into is patient love. God displays such constancy and love in this relationship with the chosen people, whom God has singled out to be a model of holiness and godly behavior. God accepts human nature and, after every straying from the covenantal agreement, is ever ready to accommodate to the creatures and people God has created and loves.

Prophets are raised up by God to remind the people of their covenantal obligations. Their calls for goodness, justice, and righteousness are ordained by God, who will not punish without warning. Even in their chastisement, there is an open offer of security and restoration for the penitent, and even in the most severe condemnation, there is hope.

Even after the Babylonian exile, which the prophets see as the result of numerous covenantal breaches in the moral and ethical realms and in the ritual realms as well, God restores the people in their homeland, and the ancient Temple in Jerusalem is ultimately rebuilt. The prophet Ezekiel describes God going into exile along with the people.

As one notices from the above, the order of the books of the Hebrew Scriptures differs from that of Christian Scriptures in that the Hebrew Bible concludes with the Writings, and Christian versions of the same Scriptures place the Latter Prophets after the Writings and just before the Gospels. The Scriptures of the Hebrew Bible are ordered so that they teach lifestyle in the context of story (Genesis–2 Kings), then focus on the operation of the covenantal relationship (Latter Prophets). The Hebrew Bible closes with Writings, texts of various sorts, not necessarily tied into specific aspects of the story or issues in prophecy, yet embodying aspects of the believer's relationship with and experience of God. It would seem that the intent of the Christian order is to underline the direct relationship of "promise" in the Prophets to "fulfillment" in the Gospels.

Individual and Community
in the Covenantal Relationship

In our society, we prize the individual, and individual rights are carefully balanced against the rights of society. At least in theory, individuals stand or fall in accord with their own actions. Whereas our laws and moral injunctions address the individual, and only then the community as a whole, the Hebrew Bible addresses the nation first, and only secondarily the individuals who compose it. Moses speaks to the people. In each generation and period in the story of ancient Israel, few individuals are identified; and whether they are singled out for good or bad, the entire people shares in their fate. Until the Babylonian exile, covenant operates within a system of community (or corporate) responsibility. When a prophet condemns a king for wrongdoing, the condemnation affects the people as a whole. All the people share in the fate of the kingdom, irrespective of their particular action or inaction on any issue.

The "individual" begins to emerge from the people at the time of the Babylonian exile, when, no doubt, many a good person could not accept a sorry fate, brought on by the actions of a sinful king or misleading leaders. The individual only fully emerges in the Hellenistic period, some three hundred years later. By this time, the Pharisees are advancing the cause of Torah by making it accessible to every person.

The Purpose of the Story and the Laws

Torah is a blueprint for life. Its purpose is to direct people's actions so that they may lead godly lives. This direction is accomplished through story and through legislation or commandments. As we have said, Torah is designed to be available to all, and its evolution and growth are in human hands. Its goal is to create a godly world.

Repentance and the Messiah

One great difference between the Jewish and Christian views of humanity is that Judaism is totally lacking any notion of the fall or of an original sin that is passed on from one generation to the next. Christianity sees the effects of Adam and Eve's sin passed down through the generations. It is a flaw in humanity, a distortion of the divine image in which human beings were created. Thus, the notion of Messiah differs for Christians and Jews. For Jews, no other can undo the sins of the individual; the restoration of a proper relationship with God is in the individual's hands alone. Temple cult and, later, prayer facilitate the restoration or reconciliation, but no intermediary may intervene between God and humanity, no intermediary (priest) is necessary for forgiveness. God listens to the penitent person and examines that person's actions for signs of sincerity or insincerity. There is always forgiveness for the truly penitent. The true test is in the individual's subsequent behavior. From this understanding, one may appreciate why for Judaism, the Torah is "complete." The early church evolved a different sense of the problem of ultimate forgiveness of the individual by rebirth into a new life of righteousness through Jesus; thus, for Christians, the "New Testament" is seen as the fulfillment of the "Old," a new covenant for life, displacing (although not denying) the older covenant. The NT begins with the birth of the Messiah and his revelation after the baptism of John (Mt 3:13–17), with John identified as Elijah (Lk 1:17). This is fulfillment of the promise in the prophecy of Malachi (Mal 4:5), which for Christians ends the OT.

Jews of today, even as in ancient times, vary in their interpretation of the messianic idea.

Some Jews today see the Messiah as a Davidic king, fully human and beloved of God, who would act as a protector to all Jews, enabling them to lead a godly life. There is in Judaism a conscious attempt to play down the person of the Messiah. In the past, when Jewish communities have recognized figures as the Messiah, this has brought tragedy, bloodshed, and disappointed hope. Virulent anti-Semitism has often followed a messianic claim. Jewish ideas concerning the Messiah tend to be this-worldly and concrete; thus, Jews ask, "If Jesus is the Messiah, how is it that nothing has changed?" To some Jews, the Messiah may not be a person as much as a state of being, a time of worldwide peace and freedom, as in the prophet Isaiah's vision of the lion and the lamb.

As with Christians, so with Jews: some are fundamentalists, and claim a very clear vision of the person and role of the Messiah. On the whole, while the messianic idea is present in Judaism today, it is godly actions that are emphasized. Perhaps Christians have a similar attitude toward the second coming. The time is not known; such is only for speculation. It does, however, offer hope. The key point is that, until the second coming, Christians have a mission and are also challenged to live out the Sermon on the Mount. Further, Christians have found that groups expecting an imminent return have caused great damage. Many have found a direct relationship between a too lively and concrete Christian messianism and anti-Semitism. In this regard, some of the wisest Jewish leaders have counseled great caution.

Disputation and Dialogue

The differing senses of how one might achieve the goal of godliness led Jews and Christians to different interpretations of Hebrew Scriptures as a whole, and of specific passage in particular. In ancient and medieval times, disputations occurred between Jews and Christians regarding interpretations of Scripture, Christians having claimed Hebrew Scriptures as their own and viewing them as fully connected to the NT Scriptures. Indeed, from the outset, Christianity sought to underline its deep connections with Judaism, even in its tracing of Jesus' Jewish lineage. By demonstrating Christian references in the OT, Christianity not only advanced the appropriation of the Hebrew Scriptures but gave Christianity the antiquity that any newly evolving religious tradition would seek to support its claims to legitimacy. For their part, Jewish people continued to live by Torah and, by their actions, validated their claim to its completeness. Some engaged in disputations regarding scriptural interpretation, not so much to deny Christianity its basis as to emphasize its absolute separation from Judaism on various key questions of belief. In addition, they sought to defeat the notion, often voiced by Christians, that the Jewish exile and powerlessness were proof of abandonment by God. As one might expect, the advent of the Messiah, or lack thereof, was the major focus of the debate.

It has taken almost two thousand years of thinking, and numerous accusations and oppressions—even attempted annihilation of the Jews and Judaism—for us to come as a group from disputation to dialogue. Through dialogue, we seek a better appreciation of each other's interpretations of Scripture, and we aspire to respect Jewish scriptural interpretation in its own right. We have come to understand that Christians and Christian Scriptures have been "grafted in" to the Jewish scriptural tradition. The World Council of Churches speaks of an "asymmetry" regarding these Scriptures: While Christians need the OT, the OT does not need the NT. Not only this, but the Jewish people, whose Scripture is the OT, which we have referred to as the Hebrew Bible, have developed a fruitful ethical and religious life without the NT. It is a special challenge for Christians, and for Jews as well, to understand what each appreciates in its own scriptural tradition and to see that although what constitutes Scripture for each group does differ, each is complete in its own right; and although method may differ, a goal of goodness and godliness for a troubled world is held in common.

In dialogue, as Jew and Christian listen to each other's interpretation of Scripture, both parties can be enriched and can begin to understand the other. Such a dialogue means change in the participants, and hopefully each begins to see the other not as an enemy who needs to be conquered but as a friend who brings new insight from the God who is revealed in Scripture.

2. Jesus and the Early Christian Community

Jesus of Nazareth: Who Was He?

Have you ever thought about who this Jesus of Nazareth really was? We all seem to assume we know the answer to this question, and that it is simple. Of course, he is one we read about in the NT and whose image in one form or another meets us every time we attend church or remember the pictures that we saw in Sunday school. It is all rather vague, perhaps confused, and maybe not too many of us are interested in finding out who he really was. We think we know and do not have to inquire any further.

What follows is an attempt to challenge us to think again and to read at least some parts of the NT anew on the assumption that there is still more to be seen and learned about him. As it is part of a study series on what has come to be known as the "Holocaust," and since many of the tensions and difficulties between Christians and Jews now and in the past have their origin to some extent in the NT, special emphasis will be placed on the relationship of Jesus with the Jews, of whom, of course, he was one himself. One of our tasks today is to rediscover Jesus' Jewishness—which, by the way, was vigorously and violently denied by Nazi ideology.

It is just not good enough to leave it at the statement in the creed that Jesus was made man. He was not made human in general, or a neutral or colorless man without any racial features—if there can be such a being. He became a concrete human being as a Jew and in no other way. He was born a Jew, brought up to go to synagogue and Temple piously and as a matter of course. It was as a Jew he lived and as a Jew he died. You might meditate anew on the meaning of the verses indicated and what they say in our context (Jn 1:46; Lk 2:42, 51; Lk 4:16; Jn 2:13; Mk 15:34; Ps 22:1). He was known as the son of a carpenter (Lk 4:22; Mk 6:2–3; Jn 6:42), had four brothers and at least two sisters (Mk 6:2–3), was esteemed as a learned man and therefore addressed as a teacher (Jn 1:38; 3:2; Mk 10:17; Mt 19:16; Lk 18:18) and was invited to and attended dinners in the homes of leading citizens (Lk 7:36). Often he worked as an exorcist and a healer (Mk 1:32–34; Jn 5:2–8), more often still as a teacher in the prophetic tradition (Mk 1:14–15; Mt 5:1–2; Lk 4:43–44) like one of the Pharisees. Nothing very extraordinary seems to have happened around him, though from time to time Jesus ran into opposition and criticism (Lk 4:28; 5:21). Often these were no more than disputes about exegetical points in which theologians in general and the Pharisees in particular liked to indulge (Mk 7:1–23). What is certain, however, is that Jesus' somewhat unconventional concern for the lost and outcast often caused protest and created conflict (Lk 15; Mt 18:12–14).

The situation changed radically for the worse once Jesus had come to Jerusalem on what was to be his last pilgrimage there (Mk 11:1ff.; Mt 21:1ff.; Lk 19:28ff.; Jn 2:12 ff.). His popularity all over the country won him a noisy welcome. Trouble began the moment he entered the Temple precincts and started to throw out the bankers and the dealers that custom had long established there (Mk 11:15–18; Jn 2:13–16). Once he started making critical remarks about the Temple itself (Mk 13:1–2; Lk 21:5–6; Jn 2:18–22), the hierarchy in charge of the Temple, its services and administration began to question his authority (Mk 11:27–33; Mt 21:23; Lk 20:1–2; Jn 2:18). The sequence of events leading to the crucifixion is recorded by the writers of all four Gospels. It appears clear that the hierarchy did a great deal of preparatory work but was not in the end a party to it. In fact they could not be, as capital punishment by crucifixion was not provided for in their law. Crucifixion was a traditional Roman form of executing rebels who had endangered the security of the state. It is difficult to be certain of the extent to which the Jewish leadership was involved, but some points can be made:

The Crucifixion: Who Was Responsible?

(1) It is not likely that the whole of the sanhedrin (as Mk suggests) would assembly in the official residence of the high priest (Mk 14:53) rather than in the judgment hall or official courtroom. Matthew, Luke, and John speak of a smaller meeting, perhaps something like an executive committee.

(2) It is noteworthy that the Pharisees, with whom from time to time Jesus had clashed in arguments (but remember also the Pharisee's attempt to save the life of Jesus, Lk 13:31), do not appear in the passion and crucifixion story at all. They were not responsible for the Temple and its ceremonies and the method and content of their teaching or their status in society were not at all endangered by the rabbi from Nazareth. In many ways Jesus' teaching seemed to parallel theirs and quite often he might have appeared to be one of them.

(3) The majority of the people appeared to have been on the side of Jesus. He had to be got rid of quickly lest all believe in him (Jn 11:48:); the people hung on his words (Lk 19:48); and a riot in favor of Jesus was anticipated (Mk 14:2). The crowd that is described as present outside the governor's palace (Mk 15:11; Mt 27:20; Lk 23:13; Jn 18:38) was in all likelihood no more than rabble hired by the executive to assist in their cause.

(4) The verse that has so often been used in history as evidence of Jewish guilt in Christ's death and to justify their punishment (Mt 27:25) should be seen in this context also. The Jewish nation was not present, although the language used by Matthew seems to refer to it, whereas in preceding verses (15, 20, 24) he had clearly indicated the presence of just the assembled and organized mob. It is most unfortunate that our translations fail miserably to make clear the vital difference! It should also be pointed out that washing hands as a sign of innocence is Jewish (Dt 21:1–9) rather than Roman and that Pilate is unlikely to have done it. A certain theological bent rather than historical facts lies behind both of these verses, and what unbelievable miseries have they become responsible for!

To sum up briefly: In no way can it be said that all "the Jews" of the NT generation were responsible for the crucifixion and death of Jesus of Nazareth. Nor is there, of course, the slightest justification for holding Jews of all times responsible.

John's Gospel

A more hostile attitude toward the Jews seems to be taken in the Gospel according to John. In several places in the Gospel the adversaries of Jesus are simply named "the Jews." We should be aware of the fact that this Gospel was most likely written at a relatively late date, when the breach between the Christian community and the synagogue had taken place, to which reference is made in Jn 9:22. It was in the interest of the Christian community to stress the differences between itself and the "mother church," the synagogue. Outward events helped to accentuate the division, e.g., the destruction of the Temple by the army of Titus in the year 70, widely seen by Christians as an outward and visible sign that God had shifted his favor away from the Jews. To lay the blame for the crucifixion at the feet of the Jewish community was a consequence of this "displacement" theology.

Considering that by no means all of the people were actively engaged in the events leading up to the crucifixion, we need not see John's language as trying to correct the reports of the first three Gospels. Perhaps, instead of "the Jews" in the inclusive sense, we might try to read "the other Jews" or "the adversaries of Jesus" or "the Jewish leaders." Sometimes the term means simply people from the province of Judea. We should also not overlook the stress that is laid on this problem in the "Book of Alternative Services" and its suggestion that the term "the Jews" in John's Gospel applies to particular individuals and not to the whole Jewish people. Insofar as we ourselves turn against Christ, the note goes on to say, we are responsible for his death (Good Friday liturgy, second rubric on p. 309).

In the talk Jesus has with the Samaritan woman (Jn 4:22) he makes the statement that "salvation is from the Jews." The discussion between him, a Jew (Jn 4:9), and the Samaritan is about the place of worship, Mount Gerizim or Jerusalem, and Jesus makes the point that worship must take place in spirit and in truth regardless of location (Jn 4:24). Jesus indicates that the Jewish place of worship is better or, rather, more appropriate. Jews know that salvation is from within their midst; the permanent prerogative of Israel, out of whom the Messiah comes, is thus indicated by Jesus. Israel's post-Jesus permanency is proclaimed—and that in a supposedly anti-Judaic Gospel!

Israel's Place in the History of Salvation

The debate about the spiritual or religious fate of "the Jews" must have started early in the Christian community, in fact soon after the crucifixion and well before any of the Gospels had been written. "The Jews," as represented by their leaders, were taken as responsible for the crucifixion of Jesus of Nazareth, who had been widely taken and acclaimed as the Messiah (Mk 8:29; 11:9–10) and acknowledged by the Father through his being raised from the dead. The question now arose: What about the future of the Jews, of Israel? Are they lost and condemned forever? Was killing Jesus committing deicide? Were they not the chosen people (Hos 11:1) that had hoped for and wanted the Messiah? Now they have forfeited their place in God's scheme of things by not recognizing that Jesus was the Messiah, and the vacated position is occupied by those who do believe in Jesus. One must not forget that in the beginning at least this was an inter-Jewish debate between those Jews who accepted Jesus as Messiah and those who had not. It was not yet a Gentile–Jewish or Christian–Jewish dispute in the way we might understand it today.

Paul and the Jews

Paul takes up the discussion. In no way have the Jews lost their position in God's salvation history! I who was a Pharisee (Acts 23:6), highly educated in Jewish law and religion (Acts 22:3), who am now a disciple and messenger of Jesus of Nazareth (Acts 9:15), would like to remind you of a few facts, he writes in his letter to the Roman congregation. To the Jews (I am one of them, don't forget!) "belong adoption, the glory, the covenants, . . . and the promises" (Rom 9:4f.). The Father who has chosen them simply because he loved them (Dt 7:7–8) does so still, "for the gifts and the calling of God are irrevocable" (Rom 11:29). Temporarily—and we should remember that the first generation of Christians expected the imminent return of Christ Jesus and the ending of all history—some Jews do not believe in the Messiah Jesus, but they all will (Rom 11:25f.). Others do believe, like Paul (Rom 11:1), all the disciples, the women in the passion story, and many more. It is important to remember this point, that the original breach was not between Gentile and Jew, or between Christian and Jew, but between Jew and Jew, Christian Jew and Jewish Jew.

Since the beginning of the second century those Jews who accepted Jesus as Messiah have been called apostates by the Jewish community, the synagogue. In their own eyes, however, the followers of Jesus were the true Jews, whereas, for the time being, the hearts of the others were seen as hardened (Rom 11:25) because of their refusal to recognize the messianic event of Jesus' death and resurrection. Christian Jews were in their own understanding citizens with dual nationality, members of the Jewish people as well as of the congregation of Jesus Christ. While Paul, as one of them, is deeply concerned about the present and future of Israel, his main interest concerns pagans and Gentiles (Gal 2:7–9). Gentile Christians do not have to observe the Torah (Acts 15:10, 19; 10:34–35, 44ff.): their only pro-Jewish obligation is to remember the poor in the Jerusalem congregation (Gal 2:10). Jewish Christians, on the other hand, continued to worship in the Temple (Acts 2:46) and were still bound to the Torah, the Law. Both groups, of course, had to live moral lives and were not permitted to eat ritually unclean food (Acts 15:20).

Christ and the Torah thus are not seen as canceling each other out. Jesus is not the Law's historical end, as Paul's words seem to suggest (Rom 10:4). Jesus himself had reinterpreted but not abrogated the Law (Mt 5:17–20, 21, 48), and now his disciples and followers should go on joyfully being guided by it in their master's spirit (Rom 12:1). God's holy, just, and good will continues to guide and direct the Lord's disciples into worship and service (Rom 13:8ff.). The coming of Jesus is not the end of the Jews (and the Torah) in God's plan. It is, rather, the opening of doors to let the multitude of Gentiles in. The drama goes on and the players are the same; only their numbers increase.

3. The Widening of the Breach

*The Rupture between the Church
and the Jewish Community*

It would be unfair and also incorrect to maintain that the roots of the Holocaust lie exclusively in the NT or with people and movements within the Christian church. It cannot be denied, however, that parts of the NT appear to be strongly anti-Jewish, that some church fathers and persons like Martin Luther were full of anti-Jewish bias, their language virtually anti-Semitic, and that the actions of many church councils were reprehensible. In enumerating the causes of the Holocaust mention must also be made of other than strictly religious ones. Political decisions and actions have been directed against Jews; speeches made against them, meetings organized, pamphlets and books written, denouncing their alleged cultural, political, and economic danger to Christian or Western civilization.

Sometimes measures were undertaken by the church on order of the civil authorities. At others times the church provided inspiration, if not active encouragement, to a book or other publication, a trend of thinking, or even violent actions. In many cases it might not be easy to determine the original cause of an event or a series of them, but some cross-fertilization may well be assumed. In view of the purpose for which this paper is written, major emphasis will be laid on developments within the church and Christian theology that contributed to the Holocaust, though it must be stressed that there have been other influences as well.

The destruction of the Temple in Jerusalem by the Roman army under Titus in 70 C.E. had several consequences. It brought the Jewish puppet government of the Sadducean regime to an end. For almost two thousand years, until the State of Israel was founded, Jews as a people were without a state or political responsibility for a territory. In Christian eyes, God's presence had departed from this people and divine favor had shifted from them. The old covenant was felt to be over, and a letter attributed to Barnabas was written, not long after the year 70, to the church as the true Israel. The fact that from now on the headquarters of the two communities were at different places did not help to cement friendly neighborliness. The Christians moved to Pella, east of the Jordan, and the Jews to Yavne-Jamnia, then to Babylon, which had been the second Jewish center since 556 B.C.E. Up until then Jewish Christians continued to worship in the synagogue. At this time they were declared a heretical sect, and, to make it impossible for Christians to worship there any longer, a curse on them was inserted into the twelfth of the daily blessings (*birkat-ha-minim*). The period was also used by the Jews to complete their organizational structure by firmly establishing the synagogue system worked out by the Pharisees, finalizing the canon of Jewish Scripture, and the calendar and by making the rabbi a *de facto* leader of the community who had to play a multiple role as teacher, exegete, judge, and arbitrator.

While the break took place on the level of leadership in both communities, there are numerous instances reported of good relations among ordinary people. However, the breach became complete and even more official after 135 C.E., when a period of general unrest ended with the revolt and death of Bar Kokhba. In conflict with the emperor Hadrian, who intended to rebuild the city and Temple of Jerusalem along Greco-Roman lines, Bar Kokhba had declared himself the Messiah and had received wide support. Obviously, there could not be two Messiahs, and Christians and Jews could not but be hostile to each other.

The hostility increased. The Jewish patriarch of Palestine sent letters and instructions to all Jews outside of Palestine, not only to request money as a substitute for the old Temple tax but also to condemn and curse those who did not keep the law and had accepted Jesus as Messiah. Jesus' teaching and his resurrection were formally condemned. On the other hand, Christians could not entirely do without Jewish protection. Judaism was still recognized as a *religio licita*, an officially recognized and permitted religion in the Roman Empire and so far Christians had simply lived as members of one of the sects of that religion. Being officially condemned by and excluded from the synagogue meant that Christians now had to justify their own existence.

They began to reinterpret the Hebrew Scriptures, declaring them to be their Old Testament. The Jews were thus disinherited from their sacred books. All that was promise and encouragement in the Hebrew Bible was said to have passed to the Christians. The law and the promises led to Jesus as the Messiah. The Jews by rejecting him had lost their share in the law and the promise. The history of Israel came to be interpreted as a history of decline and defection, its downward movement finally ending with the killing of God. Jewish suffering was said to be a punishment for their faithlessness.

This may have been the official theology of Christian–Jewish relations, but the practice was often quite different. We know of personal and professional friendships between Christian and Jewish theologians, of patient discussion between them of Christians taking lessons in Hebrew (how could they hope to refute or

reinterpret Jewish Scriptures if they did not know the language properly!), of daily contact between ordinary people (both living in a pagan environment!), of Passover and Easter being celebrated together (forbidden only in the fourth century), of many Christians influenced by the teaching and practices of the synagogue and converting (forbidden in the fourth century). Nor was Jewish life as different then from the life of Christians as it later became in the ghetto.

In spite of many such friendly relations the political consequences of the religious breach were unavoidable; from now on Christianity had to make its own peace with Rome. It could not and did not want to be seen any longer as a subdivision of Judaism.

The Constantinian Settlement

The next stage in the alienation between the Christian and Jewish communities was reached in the fourth century as a consequence of the so-called Constantinian settlement. It proved decisive for future developments and attitudes, whether it is seen as the taking over of Christianity by the emperor and its incorporation into the state or simply as the official recognition of Christianity as the most important religion. The consequences for other religious communities were grim, especially for Judaism, the source and in many ways the close relative of Christianity. The good fortune of the Christians was soon turned into the misfortune of the Jews. The attitude of the emperor was matched by the imperialism of the church, the legislation of one shaping the life of the other. Church laws and state laws became indistinguishable. The Christian hierarchy did everything in its power to extend its position and decrease that of the Jewish community. By this time the majority of Christians were Gentile converts from various religions. When required to assume Christianity, more often than not they became nominal adherents and their ethical standards remained lax.

As seen by most fourth-century writers and preachers, the Jew was not a contemporary human being at all but rather a theological abstraction or a caricature, based on his failings recorded in the OT. If contemporary Jews look and behave as a normal human being, it was felt, they must have disguised themselves to deceive their neighbors! Jews were seldom charged with ordinary human crimes, only with religious ones, with sin. Ideology replaced reality; generalizations became the order of the day. The special place of Israel in God's plan of salvation was never seen or inquired about by the church fathers. All curses in the OT were applied to one group, the Jews; all blessings to the Christians, their heirs and successors. This reading of Jewish history guided official and popular Christian thinking for centuries to come, much of it into the present.

Sermons in those days fulfilled both ecclesiastical and political purposes. They were to guide and instruct the faithful but were also a means of publicizing recent or forthcoming laws and ordinances. They were also instruments for forming policies that either church or state intended to introduce. Thus Ambrose, bishop of Milan, spoke against synagogues as "temples of impiety," the homes of devils and idolaters. They were worse than the circuses of the heathen, and to enter them was an act of blasphemy. If you attended the Jewish Passover with neighbors or friends you were insulting Christ. It was obvious that God hated the Jews, and you were expected to do likewise.

The most violent anti-Jewish preacher was John Chrysostom, bishop of Constantinople. In his *Eight Orations against the Jews* he preached against synagogues, the Passover, the absence of a lawful Jewish ministry, the Jewish failure to understand the Scriptures properly, Jewish festivals, and Christians who had any sympathy for Jews or fellowship with them. Councils of the church forbade marriages between Jews and Christians, in fact all sexual relations. The exchanging of gifts was prohibited, as was accepting hospitality offered by Jews. Jews were forbidden to own slaves and thus could no longer own and work land or work in industry. New synagogues could not be built, and missionary activities of any kind were forbidden. Jews were excluded from the military and could not act as advocates in court or become civil servants. Would it have been necessary to forbid all this, had it not been part and parcel of ordinary social life and relationships?

In spite of the multitude of restrictive measures against them, by the eighth century Jews had spread across the Mediterranean world: to Spain, then into Frankish and Teutonic territory, and the valleys of the Rhine and the Moselle. In the West they could still engage in agriculture and commerce, and in the Iberian Peninsula they often served as intermediaries between Christians and Muslims, as they were trusted by both sides. The two communities, Christian and Jewish, lived relatively peacefully side by side, the Jewish one at times even under close supervision if not the protection of the bishop. There were, of course, local difficulties from time to time, like the expulsion of the Jews from Mainz by Emperor Henry II in 1012, but on the whole life was peaceful and the future looked bright.

The Crusades

Things changed with Pope Urban II's call for the First Crusade on 26 November 1095, opening up a period of persecution such as Jews had never before experienced. The largely undisciplined hordes of crusaders, whipped into a religious frenzy by agitators, began to argue: Why should we trek to the Holy Land to free Jerusalem from Christ's Muslim enemies while we have his Jewish enemies here in our midst? Let's get rid of them first. And they tried, with bloody consequences, especially along the Rhine Valley and in France. Apostasy or death was the option offered to the Jews, who, it should be said again, were often protected by the local bishop or even the king.

Since the Jews were no longer needed as traders or middlemen and their farms were destroyed, they were forced into becoming moneylenders, pawnbrokers, and usurers. They were accused of plotting against Christians, poisoning wells, and the ritual murder of children. Ordered to wear special badges (Council of Narbonne, 1227) and special dress (Government of Castille, 1412), they were forced to live in special districts, and by the time of the Reformation ghettos were the rule. These were enclosed districts or streets, closed at night. Books belonging to Jews were publicly burned in Paris in 1242 and 1248. Pope Innocent III in the thirteenth century officially declared the Jews guilty of the crucifixion, and for their perpetual guilt they were condemned like Cain to be wanderers and fugitives forever. The Inquisition, established in 1233 against Christian heretics, was used in Spain in the fifteenth century to weed out Jews who had become nominal Christians but still practiced their religion in secret.

In 1290 the Jews were expelled from England to France, a century later from France to Spain, only to be thrown out again after another hundred years. On the other hand, a voluntary migration took place toward the East, to Lithuania and Poland, which came to have the largest number of Jews in Europe.

The Influence of Luther

The next low point in the shameful and embarrassing history of Christian–Jewish relations occurred in the days of Martin Luther (1483–1546). After 1517 Luther had become immensely popular. He was perceived not only as a reformer of the church but also as a national hero in Germany. Many of the common people and their leaders, including many regional princes and electors, had begun to follow him. While they all saw themselves as loyal but protesting sons and daughters of the church, they gladly accepted the reforms in worship that the monk and professor from Wittenberg introduced. The mass and other services were held in German; the Bible could be read in that tongue; and hymns were either translated into it or written in that language by Luther and others.

Luther had taken lessons in Hebrew from a famous humanist scholar who was also a member of the Dominican Order (originally set up to combat enemies of the church, heretics and Jews included), Johannes Reuchlin. Reuchlin had recently come to the rescue of Jews in Frankfurt and Cologne, where copies of the Talmud had been publicly burned by Pfefferkorn, a violently anti-Jewish convert from Judaism, also a Dominican. Luther was very willing to follow Reuchlin's advice to study Jewish books rather than to burn them. His lectures on the book of Genesis are proof of this. At that time, he saw in the Jews something like early protesters against the Christian church and was willing to assist them however he could. In return, he seems to have expected a mass conversion toward the new Protestant movement. In a pamphlet "Jesus was born a Jew" he declared that Jesus belonged more to the Jews than German Gentiles and that therefore Jews should be treated kindly and with Christian love rather than with the "law of the Pope." He wrote of the shameful way in which Jews had been treated by Christians throughout history "as if they were dogs not human beings."

However, in the course of time Luther was forced to recognize that his expectation of the conversion of the Jews was not to be fulfilled. They appeared to be as little interested in his interpretation of the gospel as they had been in that preached by the church during the previous fifteen hundred years. He was bitterly disappointed, and three years before his death in 1546 he wrote a pamphlet entitled *Of the Jews and Their Lies*, the tone of which was so vile that it has hardly been surpassed since, not even by the anti-Semitic Nazi press. In fact, much that can be found there was taken straight over from Luther. One should be aware that a great deal of the anti-Semitism that was found in so many Lutheran churches had its origin in this pamphlet of the reformer. It should be pointed out, however, that the Lutheran churches have since repudiated anti-Semitism.

Consequences of the Enlightenment

The Enlightenment, or the Age of Reason as it has also been called, began as a trend of thinking after the English revolution of 1688. The rationalism of Descartes, Newton's discovery of a fundamental universal order, and the empiricism of Francis Bacon were influences leading to it. Its aim may be said to have been the application of rational and scientific thought to social, political, economic, and religious issues. An end was to be made of medieval (including of course Reformation) attitudes of religious intolerance and obscurantism, but also of the restrictions on trade and commercial enterprises. Freedom, reason, and humanitarianism became the slogans by which one should live. The rights of man—today we might say human rights—were proclaimed not only by philosophers and essayists in England, France, and Germany but also by the "enlightened despots," as they wanted to be known, in Russia and Prussia, in Austria and even in Spain.

It was the Jews, as the most despised segment of society, who were to benefit most by the Enlightenment. It must not be forgotten, however, that human rights are not necessarily the same as civil rights, and it took years for Jews to gain their full rights as citizens. France in 1791 was the first country to grant these rights, followed by Holland in 1796 and Prussia in 1812. Oddly enough, England officially followed very much later, but by then the social integration of the Jews had been in effect for a long time.

It might well have appeared to the Jews that their troubles were almost over and that the persecution they had been suffering for hundreds of years was about to come to an end. Alas, this was not to be the case. Objections to their civil liberation continued from the circles that had to fear most for their property and their privileges—landowners, the middle classes who were in the process of becoming more affluent because of the industrial revolution, and the army.

The victories of Napoleon and their consequences also influenced the thinking of the educated classes and that of the general population. This enemy from outside, who was defeated with the help of other nations in a relatively short period of time, left a lasting impression on those responsible for the mental development and education of their fellow citizens: professors at the German universities, writers, and journalists. They looked for and found, they thought, a lesson of lasting value. The Napoleonic wars proved that states came and went, their boundaries could be changed and bypassed. Something more permanent was needed to provide a firm foundation for life, both personal and political. The idea of the nation, or "Volk," natural in the sense of being God-given, not created by humans and thus changeable, was born. Johann Gottfried Herder's outline of the Philosophy of Man became fundamental for subsequent thinkers like Hegel and Fichte, Schleiermacher, E. M. Arndt and H. von Goerres. They were followed a generation or so later by Marx, Eugen Duhring, Richard Wagner, H. von Treeitschke, Adolf Stoecker, Paul de Lagarde.

Before all else, there was the nation. It was pure and holy and had to be preserved in its purity at all costs. Foreigners could not be members of it, but were accommodated and looked down upon. The Jews, spread out among the nations, were seen as bent on destroying the unity of the nation and were therefore unwelcome. Their influence must be held in check if it could not be destroyed. Anti-Semitic propaganda in the daily press was barely surpassed by the papers in the time of the Nazis. Popular riots in cities like Hamburg and Frankfurt and in towns and villages of Badenia and Bavaria forced the authorities to call out the army to suppress them. While the lives of individual Jews might have been reasonably safe, their existence as an identifiable group was rather less so. Jews continued to be depicted as enemies of Christ, and anti-Jewish sermons and church pronouncements were common. A good deal of the anti-Jewish Nazi ideology was born in the thinking of nineteenth-century educated Germany.

In all of Christian history, the conflict between Christians and Jews had been a religious one, a struggle between two different religious faiths. In the middle of the nineteenth century, the perspective changed. Anti-Judaism, as it had been so far, changed into anti-Semitism (a term originally belonging to the science of languages) and the struggle was transferred into the field of race. Judaism as a religion became unimportant; Judaism as a race became the enemy. Race was seen as something fixed and immutable, something that never would change and never could be changed. Because of race the Jew was seen as evil and unchangeable; baptism would make no difference. Joseph Arthur Comte de Gobineau's essay "The Inequality of the Human Races," which appeared in 1855, provided the scientific foundation for subsequent racial theories. These were followed in Germany by the writings of the anti-religious philosopher Eugen Duhring and by Richard Wagner's English son-in-law Houston Stewart Chamberlain. His "Foundations of the Nineteenth Century," originally written in German (1899), became a textbook for Nazi ideologues with its glorification of Teutonic achievements and violently anti-Semitic views.

Two other events, important for their influence on future developments, must be mentioned. The Dreyfuss affair took place in France in 1894, when a Jewish army captain was accused and then convicted of high treason for selling military secrets to Germany. He was sentenced and banned for life to Devil's Island. Emile Zola's book *J'accuse*, along with the voices of many French people, including that of the president of France, helped to call him back to Paris after four years when he was rehabilitated. However, the damage had been done; anti-Semitism divided the French population and helped to increase the number of socialists. It also fostered the growth of the Zionist movement among the Jews of western Europe.

Mention has also to be made of the "Protocols of the Elders of Zion," first published in France with financial help from the Russian imperial secret police. They purported to be the minutes of secret meetings of an international Jewish high command whose intention was to conquer and rule the world. The pamphlet first appeared in Russia and was widely used after 1917 by the monarchists against the October Revolution, in which of course Jews were involved. It has since been translated into all eastern and western European languages as well as into Arabic. Hitler knew it well and made use of it in his book *Mein Kampf*. So did Goebbels and Alfred Rosenberg (*The Myth of the Twentieth Century*). The *Protocols* would hardly have been such a success in Russia and in Poland, had there not been wave after wave of Jewish persecutions and pograms (especially in the 1880s), though these were never of the magnitude of the Holocaust.

The ideological framework for the events of the Holocaust period had been firmly laid throughout European history, not least in the nineteenth century. Only a spark was needed to set the structure ablaze. World War I and its aftermath provided it.

It should not be forgotten that, following the Enlightenment, countless Jewish individuals and families abandoned all things Jewish and joined the majority in Germany, England, and other Western countries. Their influence on cultural, economic, and political developments was great, and they occupied chairs at universities, became writers and publicists, doctors and lawyers. They felt themselves to be Germans, British, and so on. Consequently, when war broke out in 1914, many of them fought for their country alongside their fellow citizens.

4. The Holocaust Years: 1933–1945

Prelude to Extermination

If there are days in human history out of which nothing but evil could come, 30 January 1933 must surely be counted among them. This was the day on which Adolf Hitler, the leader of the National Socialist German Workers Party was made chancellor of Germany, quite legally and democratically though not without behind-the-scenes dealing and trading off between the parties of the political right. To clarify that situation elections were held on 5 March which gave the party an overwhelming victory.

Unfortunately, many middle-class people were ill-prepared for the events of 30 January and for what was to follow. It had been beneath their dignity to make themselves acquainted with that loud and boisterous former Austrian corporal, a house painter, street fighter, and beer-cellar orator. He had even written a book, published in 1923, *Mein Kampf* (My Struggle), but why should one take it seriously? It was full of exaggeration and hyperbolic language about things that could never happen in Germany, such as "a citizen can only be one who is a member of the nation; a member of the nation can only be one who is of German blood regardless of religious confession; no Jew therefore can be a member of the nation." Why should one bother about such things? There were not that many Jews around in the first place, and had not paragraph 24 of the party program of 1923 declared that "the party stood for positive Christianity without binding itself in the matter of creed to any particular confession"? That was good enough as a guarantee of civilized Christian behavior, even if the next sentence in the program had stated that "the party combats the Jewish spirit of materialism within and without." One should not forget either that, as a result of Germany's defeat in the First World War, economic, political, and social conditions throughout the 1920s cried out for a strong leader who could bring order out of the existing chaos and lead people and country into a future of peace and security. Another reason for wanting a political savior was the "Bolshevist peril," the fear that Russian communism would spread into Germany and the West while conditions were so unstable.

Things developed rapidly and according to Nazi ideology. On 1 April 1933, a boycott of Jewish-owned stores all over the country was declared; those who wanted to enter them were forcibly prevented from doing so by Nazi brownshirts stationed outside, or their names were noted. A few days later, on 7 April, the first anti-Jewish law was passed; it was a "Law for the Restitution of the Professional Civil Service" excluding all Jews (except those who had served in the First World War). The practice of Jewish lawyers was severely restricted, as was that of physicians; entry into schools and universities was denied to children and young people of Jewish and half-Jewish extraction (two Jewish grandparents) including those who were Christians by reason of having been baptized. All this was perfectly legal, with laws and bylaws passed in the usual parliamentary manner.

Local incidents of an anti-Semitic nature were plentiful; the Nazi press had articles and comments directed at Jews every day; and district leader Streicher's *Der Stuermer* (The Stormtrooper) could not possibly have sunk any lower in its vile and deliberately dirty anti-Jewish articles and caricatures. In 1933 about five hundred thousand Jews lived in Germany. During subsequent years many of them who had the opportunity left the country, sometimes only for a neighboring state where, after the outbreak of war, the Nazis caught up with them. Of those staying on, a good number believed that their situation could not possibly get worse.

The next milestone in anti-Jewish measures was reached in September 1935. During the annual rally of the party at Nuremberg, the strongest anti-Jewish laws up to that time were proclaimed. From then on only members of the nation—i.e., so-called Aryans—were citizens with full rights and privileges; Jews could only be citizens of the state with duties to fulfill but without any rights. Marriages between Jews and Aryans were no longer allowed; those between Aryans and half-Jews needed special permission, which in the following months and years was not given (unless one was able and willing to make a very substantial financial contribution to the party treasury). Applicants were told that their children would be mongrels and that therefore marriage could not be permitted. Sexual relations between Jews and Aryans were punishable, and no Aryan woman below the age of 45 was allowed to do domestic work in a Jewish household.

Shortly after, the right to take part in parliamentary elections was taken away from all Jewish citizens, but during the Olympic Games in the summer of 1936 anti-Jewish signs, placards, and other indications of official anti-Semitism were carefully removed to make a good impression on visiting foreigners and to tell them that what they had read in the press at home was not true or was at least grossly exaggerated. In November 1937 the privilege of obtaining passports to travel abroad, except in special cases like emigration, was taken away. In July of the following year the right to certain jobs was cancelled, and the order was issued that from next January 1st all Jews had to carry special identity cards. From July 1938 Jewish physicians could practice only as "medical attendants," and in August of that year all Jews were required to add either Israel or Sarah to their first names if they were not already recognizably Jewish. Beginning that October Jewish passports had to be stamped with a large "J."

In October 1938 the large-scale deportation of Jews began. Fifteen thousand Jews who had been declared stateless were sent to Poland, which was quite unwilling to receive them. They had to spend months in the region between the two countries in a no-man's-land, hungry and suffering appalling physical and sanitary conditions. Among them were the parents of a young Jew living at that time in Paris. In his despair he tried to assassinate a councillor at the German Embassy who died two days after the attempt. On the urging of Goebbels, the Nazi propaganda minister, several days of anti-Jewish rioting followed, culminating in the "Crystal Night" (8 November 1938) during which streets, public places, and backyards were littered with glass from the windows of synagogues, stores, and private Jewish homes.

As "reparation" for the assassination in Paris a levy of one billion marks was demanded from the entire Jewish community, and the Jews were ordered to repair all damage of the Crystal Night at their own expense. As a further consequence, Jews could no longer own businesses and were forbidden to attend concerts, plays, or other cultural events. Shortly afterward all Jewish business establishments were closed down and taken over by Nazis. Some districts were closed to Jews during certain hours of the day, and local authorities were permitted to bar Jews from the streets on Nazi festivals and holidays. Universities were closed to them by the end of 1938. Real estate, securities, and jewelry had to be handed over to the authorities. By the spring of 1939 the number of Jews in Germany had shrunk to 215,000.

The War Years

At the beginning of war in September, a curfew was instituted and Jews had to hand over their radios. At once atrocities began against the Jews in Poland, committed by the invading German army and by special detachments of the Nazi security forces. Jews from Austria began to be deported to Poland, where all Jews were forced to wear a yellow Star of David.

With the invasion of Russia in June 1941 the last phase in dealing with the "Jewish question" began. A decree in that same month required all Jews to designate themselves as "unbelievers": Jews in Germany henceforth also had to wear the Star of David and they could no longer leave their places of residence without the permission of the police. Jews were no longer to have any social contact with Germans, nor were they allowed to use public telephones. In October, large-scale deportations of Jews to concentration camps began. By January 1942 their numbers in Germany had decreased to 130,000.

A conference was held on 20 January 1942 in Wannsee, a few kilometers outside Berlin, to come up with plans for the "Final Solution" of the Jewish Question both in Germany and all over occupied Europe. All the secretly planned measures Hitler and his assistants had ever schemed were put into practice. Only after the war did the full extent of this organized genocide become known to most Germans and the world at large. More than six million Jews, gypsies, Poles, and other "undesirables" in Germany and occupied Europe, who stood in the way of the pure nordic race the Nazis and others before them had been dreaming of, were brutally and inhumanly murdered. The conference itself was attended by high officials of various German ministries, the party, and special security services and was dominated by R. Heydrich, who had been appointed by Reichs-Marschall Goering as the man to execute all plans. Emigration and concentration camps had not proved sufficient, so a new solution had to be found: evacuation of all Jews from all over Europe to camps in Eastern Europe. A few months earlier, in the autumn of 1941, the experimental gassing of inmates at camps near Posen and in Auschwitz had taken place. Now an all-out effort was called for. The labor required to build the extermination camps could be provided by those Jews who were physically strong. They could work until they collapsed and died of exhaustion or were shot. All those transported to the East were told that they would have to work for the war effort. The ultimate reason for their journey would be kept secret from them and from the German population. Europe was systematically combed for Jews.

All told, six extermination camps were built. These were different from ordinary concentration camps, which, in the beginning of the Nazi period at least, were advertised as "protection camps" in which the prisoners were to be protected for their own good from the fury of the population. They were also termed "reeducation camps."

Many of the measures taken by Hitler against the Jews had been used before in history: ghettos, special dress, the yellow star, curfew, travel restrictions, supervision by police and neighbors. What was new was the mass scale and the systematic and scientific application of modern technologies, techniques of control and bureaucratic refinement. The pursuit of the war was less important than the destruction of the Jews in Germany and all over occupied Europe. Trains were diverted; new railway lines were built and staffed; thousands of freight cars were commandeered into which Jewish men, women, and children were crowded. Units of the armed forces and the Nazi security guards were ordered to Poland and other districts where there were extermination camps. Engineers, chemists, and physicists were directed away from the war effort to work in those camps to invent and then to supervise the diabolical means of destruction of millions of people. Ideology had to win at all costs! Something like a religious fanaticism dictated politics. In order to create the desired heaven on earth that was to last at least a thousand years, the chaotic hell out of which it would come had to be created first: the murder of six million Jews.

We probably cannot truly imagine the reactions of those who first entered the camps in the spring of 1945. It must have appeared unbelievable, inhuman, godless. Why did nobody do anything about it and help to save at least some of the victims from this mass brutality? Governments in Moscow, in London, in Paris, and in Washington were well aware of it, but for political, military, and strategic reasons were unable or unwilling to do anything.

And the people in Germany? The full extent of the genocide might have been unknown to most, but people knew at least vaguely what was going on, as the persecution of Jews and "non-Aryans" had grown stronger, more open, and "legal." People had relatives coming home from the eastern front, soldiers and S.S. personel directly involved in the atrocities. They must have talked to their wives, their doctors, perhaps even their pastors. But they were probably told to keep quiet about it or they would pay for it with their lives or be sent to a camp for reeducation. In the general atmosphere of terror and lack of freedom, many kept silent.

Of course there were many others, but statistics are lacking. There were people who protected Jewish friends or neighbors, or simply any Jews, by hiding them or smuggling them across borders into neutral Switzerland or Sweden. There were people who spoke up: the names of the cardinal archbishops of Munich and Münster, Faulhaber and von Galen, should not be forgotten, nor that of Bernhard Lichtenberg, the courageous Roman Catholic dean of Berlin who frequently protested in his parish magazine and who died while being taken to concentration camp. Nor that of Pastor Dietrich Bonhoeffer, who early in the days of the regime wrote against the persecution of the Jews, who helped not a few to get out of the country, and who in despair over the Nazi treatment of the Jews became involved with the underground movement in the armed forces, for which he was hanged a week before the war officially ended. The church's attitude toward the Jewish question, he wrote, will determine whether or not it is still Christian. The expulsion of the Jews from the West would necessarily bring with it the expulsion of Christ, for Christ was a Jew; "and the people of Israel will remain in eternity the people of God; the only people that will not pass away, for God has become its Lord, God has taken residence in it and built his house."

There were two other men, both Lutheran pastors, whose names frequently were mentioned as helping Jews and non-Aryan Christians either to hide in Germany or to emigrate, H. Grueber in Berlin and Maas in Heidelberg. Nor should one forget people like Fr. Maximilian Kolbe, the Roman Catholic priest who elected to be killed in the camp at Auschwitz in the hope that thereby the life of another inmate could be spared. All this may not appear to be, in fact may not have been, much more than crying in the wilderness but even a bit of crying may be better than no crying at all.

All the names mentioned so far were those of people, many of them in prominent positions, who spoke or acted not as representatives of their organizations but in an individual capacity. The churches, both Protestant and Roman Catholic, preferred to stay silent. They were not interested in the fate of Jews as such. The old story of the Jews having lost their position before God had not yet been forgotten; the substitution theory still held good. There were relatively few baptized Jews among their members, even fewer among the clergy. There was the tendency not to interfere in what was seen as the state's domain, and there was the all too human tendency to keep silent when speech might have proved costly. The command of Prv 31:8–9 that played such a role in the circles around Bonhoeffer was not heeded: "Speak out for those who cannot speak, . . . the poor and the needy." Considering that most of the people who worked in the extermination camps had probably been baptized or at least claimed to believe in what Hitler called "positive Christianity," and considering the silence of both the churches and the population in general, it is surely no exaggeration on the part of Franklin H. Littell to speak and write of "wholesale apostasy" and of the "apostasy of the millions who collaborated."

Unfortunately those millions were not confined to Germany and the countries occupied by or allied with Germany. Indirect collaboration went further by those who simply did nothing or refused to do more. Mass murder of Jews was paralleled by the mass apostasy of Christians outside Germany who refused to raise their voices on behalf of the persecuted and force their governments to open their frontiers and let them in. The United States was unwilling to change its quota system in favor of persecuted Jews. Great Britain at the beginning of the war sheltered a mere seventy thousand "refugees from Nazi oppression." It would not be right in this connection to forget one man in England who never grew tired of mentioning the plight of the Jews and who spent a great deal of time and energy helping those who had been able to emigrate from Germany to Great Britain, George K. A. Bell, bishop of Chichester. Australia admitted only a few thousand; South Africa allowed twenty-six thousand into its territory; Argentina and Brazil each admitted something like sixty-four thousand. Canada, on the advice of the director of the Immigration Branch, Frederick Charles Blair, acted on the principle that "none is too many" with the exception of several hundred who came by accident as they had been mistaken as prisoners of war and shipped to Canada as such. Mention should, however, be made of a "Resolution re: Persecution of the Jews" passed by the General Synod of the Church of England in Canada (as it then still was), meeting in Montreal, 12–21 September 1934. The only country willing to receive Jews in large numbers was Palestine, and it was prevented from doing so by the mandatory power, Great Britain. In a White Paper in 1939 the number of people to be admitted per year was fixed at fifteen thousand, and in fear of Arab reaction that figure was not to be changed under any circumstances.

There are many questions raised by the Holocaust still being asked today by those touched by that cruel tragedy or by those who are interested in the history of our century. How was it possible for the Nazis to divert so much of their effort from the war to pursue, against all strategic considerations, the attempt to rid the world of the Jews? Why did the Allies not interfere, and even keep completely silent? Why only in Germany and by Germans, when anti-Semitism had been much stronger in the past in France and Russia? Why was there no active resistance to anti-Semitic laws and the deportation of the Jews from Germany and countries occupied by Germany?

Jewish Reflections

There is, of course, also the question of how the Jewish community reacted. A very brief and incomplete answer shall be attempted here. After the first stunned silence, various reactions came out into the open. On the extreme Hasidic European right—what was left of it—a few voices were heard in terms of the Deuteronomic law (Dt 30:15ff.) of sin and punishment. While one cannot help being impressed by such a biblically orthodox fundamentalist view even when facing such an unbelievable evil as the Holocaust, one should not forget that the majority of European thinkers were closer in

their appraisal to the view in North America. In the United States, Richard Rubinstein, in his book *After Auschwitz*, maintained in effect that God was dead; only on such an assumption could Auschwitz be grasped. Emil Fackenheim answers No! To assume that God is dead is tantamount to giving Hitler a posthumous victory by destroying the Jewish soul after the body had been gassed in the camps. He saw it as the 614th of the Jewish laws not to grant this. Elie Wiesel was silent for a long time. As a survivor he could not and did not want to speak, especially as God himself had so obviously remained silent. Why? Does and did God not care? Is God indifferent to the suffering of God's people? Is God mad? Can anyone argue and dispute with such a God? In general there is agreement that to be able to understand Auschwitz would be worse than not to understand it at all. It would mean the end of one's religious worldview. Near the end of Wiesel's *The Gates of the Forest* the rabbi says: "How can you not believe in God after what has happened?" Jews after Auschwitz feel, of course, justified in maintaining that the Messiah has not yet come, and after the misery and evil of Auschwitz they are bound to ask more urgently than before, When will he come? Christians, on the other hand, who maintain that he has come, are also faced with the question, Why is there still so much evil in the world?

This questioning about the Messiah is something that unites Christians and Jews as much as it separates them. It is something that has to be on the agenda of any current or future dialogue between the two faith communities.

5. Judaism: A Celebration of Life

Judaism is a celebration of life, and life is especially a celebration of a community of people. Notwithstanding the extreme hardships faced by Jews throughout the last three thousand years, and notwithstanding the catastrophe of the Holocaust, itself an event of great pain and destructive of one out of every three of the world's Jewish community of the time, the tradition has maintained a positive approach to life and a positive view of the individual human and has sustained an investment in the thiswordly experience of the ordinary person at any given moment of existence.

Concepts

A number of concepts interact in the experience of a Jewish person and shape the life experience. A key concept in the tradition is God. As Creator, God is singular and unique. God is timeless and not bound to any place. God's ancient biblical name Yₕwₕ, or *"Ehyeh Asher Ehyeh,"* i.e., "I am what I am," or, "I shall be what I shall be," suggests timeless existence; the biblical name *Elohim* suggests strength to be applied in a constructive sense; and the appellation *Adonai* indicates the lordship that derives from God's being Creator. In the Judaism of the Greco-Roman period, other appellations became current: *haššēm,* "the Name," suggests the special creative power of God, who brings into being, who imparts specific identity, to animate and inanimate objects through speech (e.g., Let there be light . . .), while *hammāqôm,* "the Place," suggests omnipresence. God is the place to be.

The epitome of God's creation is the human. Judaism sees the reference to humanity's being created in God's image more as a challenge than as a simple statement of fact. Ancient Near Eastern people worshiped idols—forms. The theory underlying the use of the form was that it would be placed in the midst of the human community, in a special house (temple) designed for its comfort. If the form were a perfect fit, the god would indwell it, in-form it, and thereby dwell in the midst of the human community, which would benefit from the god's presence.

Judaism sees the individual human, created in God's image, as the form to be in-formed—by God. We are all challenged to act in a godly manner. Judaism places a great emphasis on the worth of the ordinary individual. We lead our lives as partners with God in the ongoing creation of our world.

In the incident of the Garden of Eden, Judaism sees no "fall from grace," rather a move toward fulfillment of God's purpose in creating us. The knowledge gained from the tree of knowledge is knowledge arising from an act of human free will and in itself is liberating. It is variously understood as sexual knowledge, the key to procreation; or the knowledge of the certainty of death, which ought to be a major stimulus for productive activity at every moment; or the general knowledge that permits us, testing, inquisitive, creative creatures, to apply the fruits of our testing and inquiry to the improvement of the human environment, i.e., the world in which God places us.

For all its delight, the garden of Genesis 3 is far too limiting a place for human expression. This world—our world—is our garden. We enjoy its fruit on account of our investment in its production. The woman of Genesis 3 is "cursed" with pain in childbirth. The pain is indeed great, but the joy is great as well, as is the appreciation of the great potential each new human life holds. The birth experience itself—the forceful expulsion of the new human from the womb—shocks the new human into a consciousness of life. This consciousness will develop and grow and will make possible great deeds. The expulsion from Eden may be understood in like manner. It is the stimulus necessary to set humanity on God's intended course.

The relationship between the human and God, between one person and one's fellow, and the complex of personal experience and "feelings" of the individual in response to one's total environment is described most essentially by the covenantal idea, which is the essence of Torah. The notion of covenant—an arrangement, agreement, or treaty to describe the complex relationships mentioned above is one modeled after covenants that existed in the political world of the ancient Near East. In its revolutionary appropriation of this idea from the political realm to the realm of human–divine relations, Judaism freed the world from the ultimately limiting experience of the ancient world, with its many capricious gods with conflicting interests, each demanding human allegiance. In Torah, God's will is revealed, and God's expectations of humanity are stated. We are freed from the inefficiencies of divination. The great scholar Abraham Joshua Heschel describes our God as a "God in search of man." God's first question to the human is (Gn 3) "Where are you?" God is asking "Where are you in your relationship with me, given the actions you have taken?" Human action is significant in God's eyes, and responsibility is a key aspect of human existence. God loves humanity, created in God's own image, and through the biblical story God demonstrates readiness to accommodate to the human creature.

The covenants of promise with Noah (that the world would never again suffer global destruction) and with David (that the Davidic line would always be the source of the ultimate human leadership) afford a measure of security and confidence for the human community. The covenant at Sinai, in which God's design for a productive and forward-moving human community is described, is the basis for the ultimate human challenge to make our world a godly place, in which all humanity and all the natural world might experience the greatest pleasure and joy. The ritual and ethical expectations of covenant are complementary, and all serve the purpose of a celebration of life.

Torah is revealed to the Jewish people; it is the blueprint for model community. Torah is not at all static, but it evolves in harmony with the evolving human experience. It is intended for everyday use, for every person. Deuteronomy says "It is not in heaven" — it is not distant or unreachable. It is a realistic plan, and it poses realistic challenges. In particular, it appreciates that the greatest human achievements will occur when humans work together, in community, to make our world a more wonderful place. The productive expression of any contemporary community is the cumulative expression of decision making of the historical community — all the Jewish people who have come before. There is a deep sense in Judaism of attachment simultaneously of one Jew to all other contemporary Jews and all Jews who have ever lived. All Jews identify with the joys and the pain of Jewish existence through the ages.

Although Judaism is not predominantly occupied with consideration of space or place, God being the key space (māqôm, as we noted above), the Land of Israel is a most special place, for it is there that the model community described by Torah finds its first expression. Through its inhabitation by the model community, the Land is to be a model land. Its varied topography and its central location in the ancient world suggest it to be the real-world response or reflection of the garden of Genesis 3. The land is the garden in which, through our knowledge, guided by covenant and articulated in communal action, we are able to achieve greatness to be shared and enjoyed by all humanity. The end, in 1948, of the long separation of the majority of Jews from their special land, is seen by many Jews as the beginning of a process that will lead to the most productive expression of all the ideals embodied in this complex of concepts we have discussed. In contemporary Jewish expression, Israel's Independence Day (1948; in the Hebrew calendar, the fifth day of the month of Iyyar) and the anniversary of the liberation and reunification of Jerusalem (1967; in the Hebrew calendar, the twenty-eighth day of Iyyar) are marked in the ritual and social life of the Jewish community as having very special significance. It is a new and special challenge for Jews, particularly for those who live outside the State of Israel, to see the State of Israel as home and, at the same time, enjoy, appreciate, and contribute to the experience of another home (Canada, or anywhere else Jews may live), often more familiar and, in many ways, more comfortable.

The Articulation of Concepts of Life

The vast, complex of human interactions — with one another, within the self, and with the cosmos — are directed by Torah and, specifically, by commandments or directives (miṣwōt) based in the ancient Jewish Scriptures and elaborated on in each generation and in each place where Jews live. The elaboration is part and parcel of the tradition itself. It responds to the new challenges of time and place and benefit from the cumulative experience of the worldwide Jewish community, and also the worldwide community of all peoples, Jews having lived among many peoples and having benefitted from their insights as well.

The complex of miṣwōt is, in its totality, Jewish religious expression. For a Jew, living a Jewish life is living a life of service to God. In a sense, every act is liturgical, every action one of prayer or praise. At the same time, various miṣwōt, particularly in the area of ritual, are specific as to time — the hour of the day for daily prayers, or the season of the year for seasonal festivals — or place — the synagogue for communal prayer or study, although any place where a group of ten gathers is suitable, or the home for the many home-based rituals.

Jewish tradition identifies three types of commandments, or miṣwōt, covering the range of human experience. Not all Jews, as they interact with others or with the natural environment, are conscious of the specific miṣwōt involved. While the tradition appreciates the relevance of consciousness of the special place in the complex of existence that each interaction fills, what is ultimately important is the action, not the consciousness of its fit in the system.

The three types of *miṣwōt* are identified as: (1) *bēn 'ādām lammāqôm*, i.e., between a human and God; (2) *bēn 'ādām laḥăbērô*, i.e., between a human and other humans; and (3) *bēn 'ādām lĕ'aṣmô*, i.e., between a human and the self—within oneself.

A Jew experiences Jewish history as a balancing of joy and pain, of acceptance and rejection by others. The Holocaust looms large as the catastrophically horrifying and ultimately disappointing example of such rejection. It is horrifying in its pain and in its destruction of a way of life. It is disappointing in that it subverted and, for many Jews, continues to subvert unwavering faith in the essential goodness of others. There is no easy recovery from such physical and emotional scars as the Holocaust inflicted. In many ways, there is no recovery at all. The great challenge is to not let those scars be incapacitating. For Judaism, the challenges and exciting potentials of existence are the essentials of life, and the path to such positive challenges—attachment to the tradition—is a social obligation to pass on. Deuteronomy calls out: "Therefore, choose life." We choose life! And our involvement in life, as individuals and in community, is cause for celebration.

6. Toward a Future Different from the Past

Let us begin with a passage from Andre Schwarz-Bart's novel *The Last of the Just*, set in Nazi-occupied Paris. The two characters concerned here are young Jews:

> He [Jesus] was really a good Jew, you know—a merciful man, and gentle. The Christians say they love him, but I think they hate him without knowing it. So they take the cross by the other end and make a sword of it and strike us with it. You understand, Golda . . . they take the cross and they turn it around, they turn it around, my God! . . . Poor Jesus, if he came back to earth and saw that the pagans had made a sword out of him and used it against his sisters and brothers, he'd be sad. He'd grieve forever. And maybe he does see it!

Thus does the novelist poignantly summarize what has unfortunately been a common pattern in the Christian world's attitudes and behavior toward Jews and Judaism for nearly twenty centuries. What of the future of the Christian–Jewish relationship? In light of the truly dreadful past, is there any realistic hope for a future radically different from that past? If there is, on what basis must such a future be built, and is there both the knowledge and the will to do so, particularly by those of us who are committed to the Christian faith? If we are prepared to do so, have we the requisite courage and honesty to pursue what we believe to be demanded of us by both God and humanity?

These questions are prompted by both the past history of the Christian–Jewish relationship and the presently available knowledge which, if taken seriously by us Christians, must lead to a radical rethinking of our own self-understanding as followers of the faithful Jew Jesus, whom we acknowledge as our savior and Lord. Among the many interrelated factors that have led prominent Christian thinkers, as well as ordinary layfolk, to engage in such a task, few can have been as significant as the horror known to us by the term "Holocaust," as well as the unique phenomenon known to us as the birth of the modern State of Israel. To these two events we should add the discovery of the Qumran documents and the interrelated growth in biblical scholarship, with its increasingly sophisticated methodologies, in both the Roman Catholic and non-Roman Catholic branches of Christianity.

We must, at the outset, keep two points firmly in mind. First, anti-Semitism as a historical phenomenon predates the advent of Christianity on the world scene. Second, Christian anti-Semitism has proved far more perduring and pernicious than anything known to us from "pagan" (especially Greco-Roman) history. The latter is hardly surprising, when one considers the potential of a theologically based prejudice. For what could be worse than to invest a human propensity to fear (and hence to hate) "the other" with a supposedly divine sanction? The examples furnished by so-called religious wars, such as the Crusades, the Thirty Years' War, and more recent conflicts in such places as Northern Ireland, India, and the Middle East are well known. Hence, the mix of human competitiveness and theological rationalization evident in the church's relationship to the Jews proved disastrous for the latter in terms of the historical consequences.

Theological Rationalizations

If we are to ensure that such tragic attitudes and behavior never recur, then we Christians must in the first instance be aware and rid ourselves of certain distorted theological rationalizations inherent in our tradition. Only then will we be in a position to construct a positive model of future relations with our Jewish brothers and sisters. Let us, then, summarize the more significant theological rationalizations from our Christian past and, in doing so, follow the tabulation of "Anti-Jewish Impressions Generated by Early Christian Writings," as prepared by Michael Cooke:

(1) There is the charge—perhaps the most historically pernicious of all—that the Jewish people, both of Jesus' time and ever afterwards, were collectively guilty of his death; and, as Jesus is, on orthodox Christian belief, the incarnation of God, the charge became one not of mere homicide but of "deicide." Besides being the most potent anti-Semitic indictment, this charge is, from a strictly historical perspective, ludicrous and baseless. Most Jews of Jesus' time in Palestine, as well as the vast majority of Jews dispersed throughout the Greco-Roman world, knew nothing of Jesus. The assertion of collective guilt is untenable in the light of the developed ethics of both the Hebrew Scriptures and the NT itself.

(2) It has also been alleged that the historic misfortunes of the Jewish people, particularly their dispersion throughout the world, were the fitting penalty for the act of "deicide." This charge is likewise, in historical perspective, groundless. The Jewish diaspora long predates the advent of Christianity and occurred in a major way approximately five hundred years prior to the birth of Jesus. As the majority of Jews were already resident outside of Palestine during Jesus' ministry, it is difficult to see how this can honestly be enlisted in aid of a bankrupt theological theory.

(3) Another weapon in the Christian polemical arsenal has been the charge of "displacement" or "supersession," according to which God's covenant with the people of Israel had been abrogated in view of the Jews' rejection of Jesus as Messiah (=the Greek term, "Christ"),

and a "new covenant" has been instituted with Christians, who now displace or supersede the Jews as the People of God. It is this type of thinking that produced the term "Old Testament" as an inherently pejorative description of the Hebrew Scriptures.

In addition to these three charges, we may note two further ones that tended to reinforce the former and increase their acceptance among the Christian faithful:

(4) It became common Christian practice, evidenced as early as the NT itself—to indulge in a particularly malicious and blinkered interpretative methodology whereby, particularly in the case of the prophetic literature in the Bible, negative criticisms made out of love and concern for religious fidelity by the prophets of their fellow Jews were seized upon by Christians—most of whom were ultimately Gentile in origin—as polemical weapons with which to beat the Jews. In contrast to this procedure, the positive passages of the prophetic literature dealing with promises of hope and redemption were applied by Christians not to the Jews, to whom the prophets had addressed these words, but to the church, which had now replaced the "Old Israel" and become the "New Israel." As has been well said by the Roman Catholic scholar Rosemary Radford Ruether:

> In the Christian exegesis of the Old Testament, Jewish history becomes split down the middle. The dialectic of judgment and promise is rendered schizophrenic, applied not to one elect people, but to two peoples: the reprobate people, the Jews, and the future elect people of the promise, the Church. . . . The rejection and murder of the Messiah is the logical climax of the evil history of the Jewish people. It is the Church which is the true heir of the promise to Abraham. (*Faith and Fratricide* [1974])

We may also note that this same method of a selective hermeneutic may be seen in the later church's use of Jesus' reported criticisms of some of his religious contemporaries. These criticisms, again motivated by a genuine concern for and love of his own people, were later converted into a polemical device, whereby purely internal (Jewish) self-criticism became externalized and used as a means of "de-Judaizing" Jesus himself.

(5) It has also been alleged that the Judaism of Jesus' day had become corrupt and lifeless, with no power of self-regeneration, and that its most notable feature was a barren and cruel "legalism" devoid of spiritual content or motivation. This charge became crystallized in the notoriously and almost uniformly negative depiction of the religious party known to us as the Pharisees. This charge has, like the preceding ones, happily fallen victim alike to historically demonstrable facts, theological sanity, and sheer common sense. It is now known that the Judaism of Jesus' day was in fact a rich and lively mixture of diverse schools of thought, as shown by (a) the varied canonical and extracanonical literature dating from ca. 200 B.C.E. to Jesus' time; (b) the Qumran documents discovered in the late 1940s and popularly known as the Dead Sea Scrolls; and (c) the vastly improved picture we now possess of the Pharisees themselves. The "rehabilitation" of the latter over the past few decades has been remarkable, as has been the effect of the Qumran discoveries in revolutionizing our knowledge of the history of both pre-Christian Judaism and early Christianity itself.

It must be emphasized yet again that the anti-Judaic polemic just outlined is to be found not only in a specific body of patristic literature but also, to a significant degree, in the primordial foundation of the NT itself. This latter fact, while acknowledged by many competent and respected Christian theologians of our own day, is nevertheless unknown to, or evaded by, large numbers of Christians who have yet to come to terms with its implications for the church and the world. Indeed, even certain NT passages that, when historically understood, may be less pejorative toward the Jews than might appear at first are often read without sound exegesis and hence are misunderstood and misapplied. And certain passages of potentially great value in restoring a proper Christian respect for Jews and Judaism have, until relatively recently, received inadequate attention from Christian biblical scholars, to say nothing of the average layperson.

Correcting the Errors of the Past

What, then, has been done thus far to correct the errors of the past, and what remains to be done? If forced to select one event of particular import for any hope of a future Christian–Jewish relationship radically different from the past, many would unhesitatingly cite the Second Vatican Council's Declaration *Nostra Aetate*, "Relationship of the Church to Non-Christian Religions," section 4. This section deals specifically with the church's relationship to the Jews and Judaism and was officially promulgated on 28 October 1965. Behind this relatively brief passage lies, of course, a very long and at points controversial history, but the fact that it was promulgated at all is owed in large part to singularly persistent and irenic efforts of the French Jewish scholar Jules Isaac, whose researches on the past history of Christianity's "teaching of contempt" vis-à-vis the Jews and Judaism had a significant impact on the resolve of Pope John XXIII to see this declaration passed by the council. Perhaps its most important sentences deal with two of the most pernicious charges summarized above, namely, the charge of "deicide" and the "displacement theory."

Nostra Aetate states:

> According to the Apostle [Paul], the Jews still remain most dear to God because of their fathers, for He does not repent of the gifts He makes nor of the calls He issues (cf. Rom 11:28–29).

These words, if taken at their full import, remove any grounds for a "displacement" or "supersessionist" theory of Judaism in relation to Christianity. They in fact imply a very significant rethinking by Christians of the place and role of Jews and Judaism in the redemption of the world in the context of an ongoing, valid covenant between God and the people of Israel.

Equally significant is the following explicit disavowal of the "deicide" charge:

> What happened in His [Jesus'] passion cannot be blamed upon all the Jews then living, without distinction, nor upon the Jews of today. . . . The Jews should not be presented as repudiated or cursed by God, as if such views followed from the Holy Scriptures.

It is also noteworthy that this section of *Nostra Aetate* recognizes the great importance of correct preaching and biblical exegesis as a sound basis for religious instruction. It is precisely such careful, scholarly exegesis that can provide the means once and for all to demolish the related myth of a punitive diaspora, as well as of a historical interpretation of the Hebrew Scriptures, treated as a mere "preparation" for the Christian gospel. And such scholarly inquiries can also put paid to the myth of a supposedly degenerate state of Judaism at the time of Jesus. Likewise of moment is the fact that subsequently issued guidelines from both the Vatican and the Roman Catholic bishops of the U.S.A. regarding the implementation of *Nostra Aetate* have made even more explicit and precise the implementation of this pivotal document for liturgy, preaching, and catechesis.

Owing to the Roman Catholic church's size and historic place within Christendom, any such steps toward the improvement of the past, tragic relationship between Christians and Jews must be of deep significance for all Christians. In this connection, one should also be aware of the fact that many of the major Protestant and Anglican churches have made similarly explicit statements on the theological roots of historic Christian anti-Semitism (including its theological formulation as anti-Judaism).

The role of the preacher is also crucial, who can perhaps be of most service not by continually "harping" on the dangers of anti-Semitism but rather by being sufficiently sensitized and knowledgeable as to express clearly, where appropriate, the positive values of the Jewish inheritance upon which Christians must draw. Catechesis likewise must be based on materials, at whatever level, devoid of the anti-Judaic elements of the past and reflective of our current understanding of the value and validity of the Jewish matrix whence we, as Christians, have come. In the latter connection the development and continued vitality of postbiblical Judaism need to be stressed, both as a dissuasion against any lingering remnants of the "displacement" and "degeneration" myths and as a rich source of spiritual insight and hope in our ongoing pilgrimage as spiritual descendants of Abraham, our common father in faith.

Such reassessments of our liturgy, preaching, and catechesis imply the continuing need — and the need at the scholarly level — for a developed, positive theology of Judaism and a rethinking of Christology, such that the church and the people of Israel may be seen as standing not over against one another but beside each other as each seeks to be faithful to its covenant with the one God whom we both acknowledge and seek to serve.

Mending the World

This latter point reminds us that there remain many areas in which, as committed Christians and Jews, we can combine our efforts honestly and without compromise in the pursuit of the noble goal of *tikkûn 'ôlām* (mending the world). It is here that our common ethical values can be expressed as we seek in solidarity to grapple with the serious problems of social justice so apparent in our world.

While Christians and Jews differ from one another concerning the identity and advent of the Messiah, we surely must each nevertheless confess that our world, in its present state, is yet far removed from that total redemption which is our common hope for humanity. It is that hope and courageous vision which must sustain us together in the years ahead.

There remains yet one final area that must be appreciated by us Christians if we truly wish to understand and respect our Jewish brothers and sisters, i.e., the tremendous significance of the modern State of Israel for the Jewish people as a whole. Since Israel's rebirth in 1948, the Christian world's assessment of the import of this event has been highly ambivalent. No doubt the reasons for such ambivalence are complex, but in the light of the past it seems not at all farfetched to suggest that part of that ambivalence is owing, even at the unconscious level, to the persistence of ideas of "deicide" and a "punitive diaspora" among many Christians. A serious rethinking of these untenable theological assumptions, together with a much greater realization of the role of peoplehood among Jews, will go a long way toward enabling Christians to deal more fairly and positively with the fact of modern Israel. As Christians, we may not agree with particular policies of a particular Israeli government. Such diversity of views will be found in the Jewish community as well. As Christians we shall naturally be concerned to see adequate provision being made for the various Christian (and other minority) groups within Israel. In any event we must not indulge in "the type of criticism that would use the failure of Israel to live up to the standards as an excuse to deny its right to exist." What we must affirm is our unequivocal acceptance of Israel's right to live in peace and justice with its neighbors; the lack of such acceptance would make effective dialogue and amity between Christians and Jews impossible.

Our dialogue must be based on mutual acceptance and respect as equals. Such respect will entail the willingness to allow each community to define itself in its own terms, free of the prejudicial stereotypes of the past. Dialogue will never be used as a covert attempt at proselytism but will rather be the basis for developing and sustaining that trust which is so necessary for the carrying out of the joint task of *tikkûn 'ôlām*. Such dialogue must therefore become a reality at the local, congregational level if there are to be any lasting changes of attitude and behavior in our inextricably tied relationship. Let us, as Christians, ensure the authenticity of that ending as we enter upon the future in company with our Jewish brothers and sisters!

Bibl.: Jewish Life: Jews and Judaism: M. M. KAPLAN, *Judaism as a Civilization* (Philadelphia, 1957); M. I. DIMONT, *Jews, God and History* (New York, 1962); T. H. GASTER, *Festivals of the Jewish Year* (Gloucester, Mass., 1962); A. J. HESCHEL, *Between God and Man: An Interpretation of Judaism* (New York, 1965); A. EBAN, *My People, the Story of the Jews* (New York, 1968); A. HERTZBERG, ed., *The Zionist Idea* (New York, 1970); H. KAUFMAN, *Jews and Judaism since Jesus* (New York, 1978); J. W. PARKES, *A History of the Jewish People* (London, 1964); id., *Whose Land? A History of the Peoples of Palestine* (New York, 1970); C. ROTH and G. WIGODER, eds., *Encyclopedia Judaica* (New York, 1972).

Jewish–Christian Relations: G. BAUM, *Is the New Testament Anti-Semitic?* (Mahwah, N.J., 1965); R. DE CORNEILLE, *Christians and Jews: The Tragic Past and the Hopeful Future* (New York, 1966); R. R. RUETHER, *Faith and Fratricide* (New York, 1974); K. STENDAHL, *Paul among Jews and Gentiles* (New York, 1976); E. FISCHER, *Faith Without Prejudice* (Mahwah, N.J., 1977); J. W. PARKES, *The Conflict of the Church and the Synagogue* (New York, 1977); H. CRONER and L. KLENICKI, *Issues of the Jewish-Christian Dialogue* (Mahwah, N.J., 1979); A. T. DAVIES, *Anti-Semitism and the Foundations of Christianity* (Mahwah, N.J., 1979); M. HAY, *The Roots of Christian Anti-Semitism* (New York, 1981); J. ISAAC, *L'enseignement du mépris* (Paris, 1961); id., *L'antisémitisme a-t-il des racines chrétiennes?* (Paris, 1960); J. PAWLIKOWSKI, *Christ in the Light of the Christian-Jewish Dialogue* (Mahwah, N.J., 1982); C. WILLIAMSON, *Has God Rejected his People?* (Nashville, 1982); A. J. RUDIN, *Israel for Christians* (Philadelphia, 1982); J. KOENIG, *Jews and Christians in Dialogue* (Philadelphia, 1983); P. M. VAN BUREN, *A Christian Theology of the People Israel* (New York, 1983); L. KLENICKI and G. WIGODER, *A Dictionary of the Jewish-Christians in Dialogue* (Mahwah, N.J., 1984); E. H. FLANNERY, *The Anguish of the Jews* (Mahwah, N.J., 1985); S. E. ROSENBERG, *The Christian Problem: A Jewish View* (New York, 1986).

The Holocaust—Historical viewpoint: A. FRANK, *The Diary of a Young Girl* (New York, 1965); L. S. DAWIDOWICZ, *The War against the Jews: 1933–1945* (New York, 1975); P. HALLIE, *Innocent Blood Be Shed: The Story of Le Chambon* (New York, 1980); I. ABELLA and H. TROPER, *None Is Too Many* (New York, 1982); G. CLARE, *Last Waltz in Vienna* (New York, 1982).

Ian J. KAGEDAN

JUSTICE

1. Introduction

The semantics of the concept of justice (*ṣedāqâ, dikaiosynē, iustitia, Gerechtigkeit*, justice, fairness, *pravednost*) is polyvalent: it has biblical, theological, philosophical, juridical, social, political, ethical, religious, and secular meanings. Hence it is an analogous concept, neither unambiguous nor ambiguous. It expresses a type of personal or social behavior, either in the microstructure or in the macrostructure. The Greek philosophers, with Aristotle, insisted on the *theory* of justice, which gradually became a rational system of principles, almost exclusively of "commutative" justice, in accordance with the criterion "*suum cuique*" ("to each his own"), with a strong accent on the *suum* ("one's own") and on the *alienum* ("not one's own"). The OT prophets, in contrast, insisted on the *praxis* of justice, dwelling on the will of Yahweh, in accordance with the criterion "take care for your neighbor." Hence, whereas the justice of the Greeks has a philosophical, juridical, social, political, ethical, and secular meaning, the justice of the prophets of the chosen people has a biblical, theological, social, moral, and religious significance.

Diversity of meaning notwithstanding, there is a basic continuity between the notions of the Greeks and of the Jews. As *pars in toto* thus, the Greek concept *cuique suum* is in fact contained in the biblical notion of justice. But the concept of justice is to be found as a sacred heritage in every culture and religion. Archaeologists in 1901–1902 discovered the codex of Hammurabi (about 1717–1665 B.C.E.), written in cuneiform characters on an obelisk; it contains 282 articles: Hammurabi is appointed by the gods to administer justice in the country, to "give justice" to the people, to protect widows and orphans, and to see to it that the strong do not oppress the weak. The concept of justice is not seldom ideologized in accordance with social, economic, and political systems and cultural traditions. In Western culture, it in fact comprises a three-dimensional *synthesis:* Judeo-Christian, Greco-Roman, Germano-Slav. The result of this is, today in the West, the concept of "justice" has different nuances from country to country, from one cultural circle to another. But not only in the West: this pluralism of the notion of justice is to be found worldwide. Throughout history, indeed, the concepts of "justice" and "just" behavior have been enriched but also obscured by philosophical, juridical, political, and ideological elements derived from differing theories and ideologies. So one may say today justice represents one of the most complex and hence most difficult of concepts to explain *ad captum*. At the same time, it is one of the most compromised of concepts, in that every regime and every system invents its own justice, in accordance with which it proceeds in theory (though using the same terms), but also in practice and in legislating.

Our intention is to describe the true notion of "justice"; we shall therefore have to investigate the roots, analyze and synthesize the prudence and wisdom of the Judeo-Christian socioreligious experience on the one hand, and the Greco-Roman philosophical-juridical theory on the other. The biblical concept of justice is religious, personal, and spiritual. It concerns the chosen people and the individual member, not from outside but from within the nation.

Indeed it comes to be identified with the concept of *perfection, holiness;* for the perfect, holy person is "just."

In the theocratic society of Israel, Yahweh is the just (perfect, holy) king on whom the covenant depends; Israel should be just (perfect, holy); it should imitate Yahweh-the-Just-king. The justice of Yahweh the Just is the *call* to the chosen people. The works of Yahweh the Just King, especially as regards the poor, the oppressed in general, the *'ānāwîm*, are the moral imperative for the chosen people to imitate. Consequently the justice of the chosen people is the concrete *rediscovery* of this call. Thus, the prophets insist on religio-moral practice rather than on theory, comparing Israel the Just with Yahweh the Just.

It may be said that a similar relationship between humanity and the absolute is to be found in all the great ethical religions of the East and in some African religions too (W. Schmidt, *The Culture Historical Method and Ethnology* [New York, 1939]). The adherents to these religions do and ought to do justice: something that in a certain sense is close to the justice of the Bible. The concept of justice in Greco-Roman philosophy has a profane, philosophical, juridical, political, secular character. It concerns the individual and living as a community within the *polis* and fixes the limits of the laws that regulate the life of the *polis*. For the sophists, just laws have a purely conventional value; for Socrates, Plato, and Aristotle, however, just laws are an expression of the rationality of human nature; whereas Greek philosophy develops the theory, Stoicism, particularly the Roman brand with Seneca, also stresses the practice, the *ascesis*. For the purpose of fundamental theology, the most suitable starting point is the biblical concept (divine/human justice), which throws light on the *basis* of all justice; only after this, shall we tackle other concepts of justice, before finishing up with the present-day debate on the concept of social justice.

2. In the Old Testament

The *origin* and the *model* of the concept of justice in Israel are *profane*. Israel in the nomadic period shared the same concept as the other peoples of the ancient Middle East: the king's activity in administering justice with special regard to the poor and oppressed was to protect them (Hammurabi). The king must be just, for protecting the needy is one of the king's main tasks. It is the privilege of the needy to be defended and protected by their king. Those who, humanly speaking, have no hope, throw themselves on the goodwill of their king.

With revelation, the profane concept of justice became a religious ones The just king is the God of Israel. In translating the Bible, the Septuagint uses the word _dikaios_ (just) to render _ṣaddîq_, which occurs 180 times and 43 times in its derivatives. The noun _dikaiosynē_, however, appears 220 times for _ṣĕdāqâ_ or _ṣedeq_ (justice). OT justice is _relational_, primarily in a _communal_ context (Yahweh/Israel), all members of the community being included. But the communal character of OT justice does not mean social in the sense of the Greek _polis_ or of some modern notion, but basically in the sense of personal relationship. It is based on the covenant and not on the relationship between absolute laws and the concrete activities of the people and the individual. Rather than legal, the relationship is always personal, between the two contracting parties to the covenant: the "I" of Yahweh and the "you" of Israel. So it is a question of sincerity and genuineness of attitude within the two-sided, personal-type relationship (Yahweh/Israel as individual).

As all Israel's morality is of a personal character, rather than of a legal or legalistic one (as was once thought), so too this attitude is inward, two-sided, shared, and reflects (follows, imitates) the justice of Yahweh the Just (Is 45:21; 51:5f.; 56:1; 62:1; Ps 24:5).

Hence Yahweh reveals himself as the just king of Israel; as the just God (Gn 18:15; Dt 32:4; Zep 3:3; Ps 111:7); the _deliverer_ (with Abraham: Gn 12:1–4; in the exodus: Ex 1–15) who demonstrates his _power_; the Mighty One of Jacob (Gn 49:24; Is 1:24; 49:26; 60:16) who demonstrates his watchfulness (over the patriarchs: Gn 20:6f.; 28:15; over Joseph "so that many people should be kept alive": Gn 45:8; 50:20; in the wilderness: Ex 16:15-18). Yahweh gives the _Decalogue_ (ten freedoms: Ex 20; Dt 5:6–21; Ex 24:3–15); he founds and makes justice possible in Israel. His love, his redemptive and saving activity by which he delivers an oppressed, enslaved people shines on every page of the Bible: "a righteous God and a savior; there is no one besides me" (Is 45:21). "My salvation

will be forever, and my deliverance will never be ended. Listen to me, you who know righteousness, you people who have my teaching in your hearts. . . . my deliverance will be forever, and my salvation to all generations" (Is 51:6–8). Yahweh is the _lord_ of the land and of the _soil_ given to Israel; the chosen people are only God's tenants and will always be "a stranger and a guest" (Lv 25:23; Ps 119:19). For this reason, Israel should praise Yahweh, be grateful to him and acknowledge dependence on him. Just as the agricultural festivals (Ex 23:14f.) correspond to the rhythms of nature: feast of Unleavened Bread, of firstfruits, of harvest (Ex 23:16) and ingathering of the harvest, so too the use of what is produced is specially regulated: the poor people and aliens must be allowed to glean (Dt 14:29; 24:19–21); so as not to exhaust the soil, no crops are to be harvested every seventh year (Ex 23:11). "This land-law, at once religious and social, indicates the authority of God to whom the soil belongs by right. Observance of it was to distinguish Israel from the heathen country-folk surrounding them" (G. Becquet). But the great temptation for Israel was presented by the Canaanites with their farming life and Baal, Lord of the countryside: the temptation to adopt their usages in field and vineyard and to adopt their religious, idolatrous, materialistic, prostitutional customs at the same time.

God reveals himself as a God who _condemns_ any kind of injustice done to his people: he who does justice to the oppressed, to all who suffer injustice (Is 41:10f.; 54:17; Ps 129:4f.). He is the head of the _armies_ of Israel (Ex 12:41), a warrior giving _victory_ to his people (Ex 15:12f.; 1 Sm 17:45), making them strong (Dt 8:17f.); his _presence_ reassures (2 Sm 6:2; Ps 132:8), but Yahweh is ever the _strength_ of his people (Ps 144:1f.; 28:7f.; 68:34f.). Yahweh continually acts _for the benefit_ of his people; he is _faithful_ to his promises (the "Rock" of Israel: Dt 32:4). Because of this, his justice is displayed in the _magnalia Dei_ ("the mighty acts of God") and God's kingship is always conceived of in the dynamic and relational sense. Once Israel has given itself a king, this kingship is subordinated to Yahweh's kingship; it is an organ of the theocracy founded on the covenant granted and decided on by Yahweh, entered into with Saul (1 Sm 10:24), with David (1 Sm 16:12), and the entire Davidic dynasty (2 Sm 7:12–16). The kingdom is, above all, the radiation of divine sovereignty at work; this sovereignty in its turn manifests itself in a particular relationship with the poor, the oppressed, the wretched, the little, the weak ("Yahweh's poor," Ps 74:19; 149:4f.; they are the object of his love, Is 49:13; 66:2; they are the firstfruits of a "people humble and lowly," Zep 3:12f.). In all these aspects the just king is protector and guarantor of justice. He is not so much an arbiter between two parties (Yahweh/people) as the protector of the weak against the strong.

Hence the *vertical* link (Yahweh/Israel) and the *horizontal* one (members of the chosen people among themselves). It could be said, with some modern authors, that by virtue of the covenant a link of kinship (Yahweh/Israel) is set up, especially in relation to the very poor. The brotherhood of all is based on descent "from one" (Gn 1–2; Acts 17:26), on the covenant ("You shall not hate in your heart anyone of your kin . . . you shall love your neighbor," Dt 19:17f.). In the patriarchal tradition, there are example models of this brotherly relationship: Abraham and Lot remote from discord (Gn 13:8); Jacob is reconciled to Esau (Gn 33:4); Joseph in a moving manner forgives his brothers (Gn 45:1–8). By way of contrast, the prophets deplore Israel's having forsaken brotherly love (Hos 4:2); "no one spared another" (Is 9:19f.); injustice is universal; there is no more trust (Mi 7:3–6); no one can put "trust in a brother, for every brother is a supplanter" (Jer 9:4; cf. 11:18; Job 6:12), though "a brother helped by a brother is a fortress" (Prv 18:19 LXX). But violation of the rights of the *poor* is an even greater wound inflicted on the brotherly community that holds Israel together; it is a personal affront to Yahweh, Creator of covenantal solidarity; it is a corruption of that justice (Am 5:7; Is 10:1f.; Jer 22:13–17) of which Yahweh is the guarantor. Therefore, he who tramples on his brother, especially his poor brother, falls under the judgment of the Lord, who as just king is the avenger of the poor and as ally-kinsman is the defender of the people founded and willed by him to be a community of brothers.

So Israel as community, and each of its members, is called to share in God's justice (Ps 24:5) and especially to follow Yahweh in caring for the poor and little brothers since they are in a special way loved and protected by Yahweh. Since they are the most threatened because the most needy, most wretched, and weakest, Yahweh the Just protects them all the more, defends them, avenges them, helps them and hears their cry for help. For the rural proletariat on occasion finds itself in incredible misery (Job 24:2–12). In contrast to the enslavement of the little ones, the prophet Jeremiah proclaims the freeing of the slaves, "that all should set free their Hebrew slaves, male and female, so that no one should hold another Judean in slavery" (Jer 34:9). Yahweh the Just is the avenger of injustice inflicted on the little brothers: "You have not obeyed me by granting a release to your neighbors and friends; I am going to grant a release to you, says the LORD—a release to the sword, to pestilence, and to famine. I will make you a horror to all the kingdoms of the earth" (Jer 34:17). The prophets often remind the people of Yahweh's call to be just: "Maintain justice and do what is right, for soon my salvation will come, and my deliverance be revealed" (Is 56:1). "For Zion's sake I will not keep silent, and for Jerusalem's sake I will not rest, until her vindication shines out like the dawn, and her salvation like a burning torch. The nations shall see your vindication, and all the kings your glory" (Is 62:1).

Here we see a deep sense of the religious concept of OT justice, since Yahweh desires the welfare and happiness of everyone in the community of the chosen people, Yahweh's justice to Israel is the *foundation* of Israel's justice and makes it possible, The people as a whole and the individual member of the Israelite community can only be just to other people when participating in Yahweh's justice and cooperating with it. To be just in Israel, hence, is the response made to Yahweh under the guise of faithfulness to the covenant (→ ELECTION/COVENANT/LAW): Yahweh is faithful to and full of love for Israel, always and in any circumstances; Israel must reciprocate Yahweh's faithfulness and love; so, faithfulness for faithfulness, love for love. Only thus will Israel be just in Yahweh's eyes and in those of "all the kingdoms of the earth" (Jer 34:17).

This said, the social dimension of justice in Israel, among the brothers within that community, means observing the social commandments given by Yahweh, so that harmony, brotherly love, solidarity, and well-being may reign within the community. "Ah, you who make iniquitous decrees, who write oppressive statutes, to turn aside the needy from justice and to rob the poor of my people of their right" (Is 10:1–2). But Isaiah has praise for the justice of the just: "Those who walk righteously . . . , who despise the gain of oppression, who wave away a bribe instead of accepting it, who stop their ears from hearing of bloodshed and shut their eyes from looking on evil, they will live on the heights" (Is 33:15–16).

> If a man is righteous and does what is lawful and right—if he does not eat upon the mountains or lift up his eyes to the idols of the house of Israel . . . , does not oppress anyone, but restores to the debtor his pledge, commits no robbery, gives his bread to the hungry and covers the naked with a garment . . . , follows in my statutes, and is careful to observe my ordinances . . . such a one is righteous; he shall surely live, says the LORD GOD" (Ez 18:5–9).

Before the Babylonian captivity, there is still little said about the personal justice of the individual; more importance is attached to remaining in the justice that Yahweh displays to the whole people (Ps 15; 24:3f.; 143:1). In this period, "human justice" is nearly always understood as a relationship between persons (Gn 38:26; 1 Sm 24:15; Am 5:7; 6:12). The just individual belongs to the people to whom Yahweh has granted the privilege of sharing in his divine justice (Ps 7:9; 17:1–15; 18:22–24; 26:1–6). With rabbinical Judaism, a deterioration sets in. Justice, be it social or personal, is nothing other than harmony with the law. The Qumran community speaks of justice also in the sense of "justification" and is convinced that "with God is my [your, our] justification" since "he cancels my sins with his acts of justice" (1QS 11:2, 3, 4, 12). On the other hand, Qumran particularly stresses the doctrine of justice with its mysterious Teacher of Justice or Teacher of Righteousness (→ MESSIANISM II).

In conclusion, let us bring out four points that synthesize this brief consideration of the OT concept of ṣĕdāqâ:

(a) *Poverty* in the OT is a social fact bound up with economic, political, and social conditions and giving rise to religious reflection. In nomadic times the entire people was poor. In the Book of the Covenant, there appears to be little social distinction. With the monarchy, a more differentiated economic state of affairs

sets in: a class of poor people comes into existence. Yet, condemning the scandal of poverty, the prophets fix on poverty as an ideal: a discovery of the spiritual values of poverty and of the peril of riches.

(b) Yahweh's justice is revealed in an event of salvation history, that is to say, the *covenant.* God becomes humanity's partner to create a community faithful to his Word and at peace with itself. Yahweh presents himself as kinsman of his people who accept the covenant. It is a matter of a "consanguinity" stronger than an ethnic one. Yahweh is united to Israel by bonds of kinship, which get all the tighter where the poorest are concerned. The beneficiaries of the covenant are thus bound to one another by bonds of kinship: they are "brothers," brothers on the religious and moral plane. With this, the concept of ṣĕdāqâ acquires an ever stronger acceptation as mutual support, love, charity, and goodness, especially if the chosen people stays faithful to the covenant. This new family fellowship of love, charity, and goodness ought not to exclude anyone, and so it demonstrates its genuineness in its care for the poor.

(c) The Bible's justice is in conformity with Yahweh's nature, which is always on the side of the poor, the oppressed, the needy, and which human beings should imitate and share with a pure heart (*lēb ṭahôr*); this goes for the whole chosen people and each of its individual members. If we say that justice is in conformity with Yahweh's nature, this introduces the theological thought that God's nature is love. So the ultimate basis of OT justice is Yahweh's love for his people. Israel is a participant in Yahweh's love, whence the obligation on each individual to imitate this shared love of God. All individuals have their own personal dignity, which, theologically speaking, is to be sought in union with God, that is to say, in love, in participating in God's love for everyone.

(d) With this, we have touched the analogy of the faith, expressed in the following *equation:* Yahweh faithful = Israel faithful; Yahweh just = Israel just; Yahweh love = Israel love. In ethical terms we could say that the internal *moral indicative* to be just (supportive, charitable) is the very nature of the human person, created in the image and likeness of God (Gn 1:26–27):

each individual is "in the image"; hence all are equals, neighbors, brothers, and sisters. The *moral imperative* consists not in external rules but in the person's being, which is obliged to imitate and reflect in its dignity its original or prototype, i.e., God's creator-love, in the perfect image of Christ (*GS* 22). In OT justice, the being of the individual counts for more than the individual's actions; or, rather, the importance of the actions is seen in the person. So the dimension of OT justice is personal, religio-theological in relation to Yahweh and religious-social in relation to the neighbor. Whatever the human justice or injustice, it is a welding or a breaking of this interpersonal loyalty and solidarity; but, above all, it is at the same time a discharglng or a transgressing of the loyalty and faithfulness due to Yahweh the just king and kinsman and absolute Lord.

3. In the New Testament

The better to grasp the dimension of revealed justice (a dimension that is external and internal, personal and social) and having seen the origin and development of that concept in the OT, we must now highlight certain aspects of *higher justice* in the NT. Here we are dealing with a qualitative leap. Let us take three outstanding points.

The *Nazareth episode* in Luke (4:18–19) is of fundamental importance to our subject, since it constitutes the core of Jesus' messianic program. It calls four parallel texts to mind: Is 61:1–2; 58:6–10; Lk 7:22–23; Mt 25:31–46. Jesus' homily on this occasion, at the inauguration of his ministry, has pride of place. The reading delivered by Jesus in the synagogue and his exposition of the passage from the prophet Isaiah are central, inasmuch as Jesus presents himself through the prophet Isaiah. The Spirit resting on him will carry him to evangelize the poor, to proclaim release to prisoners, to redeem the oppressed, to proclaim the Lord's year of grace, the year of jubilee when debts will be canceled and slaves set free. This stress on social outcasts with their respective needs—the poor, the prisoners, the blind, the oppressed (Lk 4:18–19), the lame, the lepers, the deaf, the dumb (Lk 7:22–23)—indicates the totality and universality of his mission. Isaiah continues: "the day of vengeance of our God, to comfort all who mourn" (Is 61:2), a passage that Jesus does

not read out, so as not to increase his listeners' irritation. However, the passage from Isaiah that he does read out (61:1–2) is as follows: "The Spirit of the LORD GOD is upon me, because the LORD has anointed me; he has sent me to bring good news to the oppressed, to bind up the brokenhearted, to proclaim liberty to the captives, and release to the prisoners, to proclaim the year of the LORD's favor." A parallel text in Isaiah is to be found at 58:6–10, recycled in the parable of the last judgment (Mt 25:31–46), where Jesus enumerates the works of justice/charity: "I was hungry, thirsty, a stranger, naked, sick, in prison; you gave me food and drink; you welcomed me, clothed me, visited me, came to look for me. . . . Truly I tell you, just as you did it to one of the least of these who are members of my family, you did it to me."

In the Nazareth synagogue episode, a physical and a spiritual aspect are both in evidence. In Isaiah, the restoration of "sight to the blind" is not limited to physical fact, but rather points to spiritual blindness and a new enlightening of the heart. With Jesus too, visible acts signify spiritual acts. The response to the Baptist's messengers follows the same line (Lk 7:22–23): The blind recover their sight; the lame walk; the lepers are cleansed; the deaf hear; the dead come back to life; the good news is preached to the poor. It is symptomatic that, of a whole series of miracles wrought by Jesus, the last sign should be the most specific and decisive, since it characterizes his messianic mission as foretold by Isaiah (61:1–2): "The good news is preached to the poor."

In its historical setting, Jesus' homily was charged with a strong eschatological and con-solatory tension: Christ offers eschatological salvation to those who are spiritually poor in the sense of the first beatitude (Mt 5:3: "Blessed are the poor in spirit"), to those, i.e., who possess nothing, who are totally destitute before God. Those are totally poor before God who receive all from God with humble and grateful hearts. For these have absolute faith in him. Here we see a *wider* conception of "the poor," which stresses the inner aspect of *detachment* from the things of this world and of total availability for the kingdom. There are three ways of looking at "the poor": poor in comparison with the rich, poor in relation to God, God in relation to the poor. But how does God compensate the poor?

He fills them, making himself the treasure of whoever is poor; he fills them by giving and communicating himself, not necessarily by enriching them with money. The gospel reveals this self-communication on God's part in Christ and in the Spirit. God reveals himself to the poor in all his power. The latter stand before him in their need, as those who call on him, entreat him, wait for him. (Martini 1978)

Of course, Luke 4:18 is deliberately ambiguous, general, enigmatic, and so it must remain. Both interpretations—the eschatological and the consolatory—have their weight, since without the eschatological there would be no consolation and vice versa. That said, one might object that there are rich people who cannot be put in the category of "the poor." But the answer has already been given: we are all spiritually poor before God in one way or another. Jesus' message is not about class; the outcasts, the ignorant, the sick, the devil-possessed, lepers, women, infants, children, pagans, Samaritans, tax collectors, and sinners are to be understood not primarily in the material sense but in the spiritual sense, not in the exclusive but in the preferential. Thus the concept ṣĕdāqâ, dikaiosynē, justice, in Jesus' program attains its supreme meaning, its zenith.

Let us now take the *central event*, the parable recorded in Mt 25:31–46. Once salvation history has come to an end, the most dramatic eschatological event is the last judgment, with the tremendous reality of higher justice. Although the parable is not entirely clear, it is about judgment—indeed, the last judgment. And the judgment is concerned with justice. Jesus Christ, in the form of the just king, is the judge; he is the main figure, central to the parable. This just king has a real relation of *kinship* with the poor, the least, the oppressed, the forsaken, for he calls them "members of my family" (Mt 25:40, 45). What then is the criterion of judgment? The criterion is the person of the king-judge; all the good and evil done to the poor, the least, and so on, is done to him: "Truly, I tell you, just as you did it to one of the least of these who are members of my family, you did it to me" (v. 40). The beatitudes are thrown into high relief once and for all: "Blessed are the poor"; "blessed are those who mourn"; "blessed are those who hunger and thirst for righteousness"; "blessed are those who are persecuted for righteousness' sake" (Mt 5:1–10).

This triumph of justice had already been perfectly described and in almost the same words, centuries before by the prophet Isaiah (58:6–10). So the revelation of justice is consistent from the beginning of history to the end, always in the ascendant, ever more human and humanized, ever more spiritual and spiritualized. The justice of the "king" and the justice of the "just" who follow the king become enriched with solidarity, charity, and mercy, but these virtues do not lose their own character.

But there are also wrong interpretations (Martini 1978). The first is *atheistic*, in that in the whole Matthean parable it sees no higher reason or reason of faith, no trace of religious feeling, as a result of which it fosters an atheistic view. Yet the champions of this absurd opinion do not see that the words "you have done it to me" and "you have not done it to me" (Mt 25:40, 45) are actions illuminated by faith in Christ and by the welcoming of his theandric person. This, however, has nothing to do with mere philanthropy. Then again, they do not grasp that this kind of charity is theological, that it does not exclude the appeal to believe in the gospel but actually assumes it. Now, it is of course true that the text does not explain how (theological) charity would be possible for those who have not accepted the gospel. Perhaps, indeed, Jesus did see in brotherly generosity a way that might lead to acceptance of the mystery of his person.

The second of the false interpretations is *superficial*, inasmuch as it affirms that all that is being spoken about in the parable is works, while the human heart does not come into it. A spiritual attitude is not required of anyone who helps the needy; neither intention nor conscience is of importance in the person giving the help; the only thing that matters is having given or not given it. But in many a text, Jesus stresses the person's intention, conscience, will, heart: "Beware of practicing your piety before others in order to be seen by them; for then you have no reward from your Father in heaven" (Mt 6:1).

The third opinion is *one-sided*, in that it affirms that the works listed form a complete and exclusive catalogue of all the works coming under the heading of justice, as though it were a definitive list of the corporal works of mercy.

> It would however be a mistake to drain from this text a kind of *exclusive catalogue* of the things

one must do to be saved. . . . The passage is very daring but, as is the case with many a biblical text, is to be taken in its symbolic sense, by looking into the depths of the message and not exaggerating one aspect or another. (Martini 1978)

There is more: if this Matthean parable is read in the context of the whole Gospel, one sees that all sorts of other works are recommended, such as mercy, forgiveness, silent prayer, and so on. Modern exegetes emphasize, among other things, three dimensions of Matthew's parables as being of main importance.

(1) The christological dimension is clear in this final Christophany: Jesus (Son of Man, king, Lord) is the center and arrival point both of the Father's salvific intention and of human action (just/unjust). Now the truth becomes clearer than ever that the person of Christ is the norm of moral conduct, "the measure of all things." "When all things are subjected to him, then the Son himself will also be subjected to the one who put all things in subjection under him, so that God may be all in all" (1 Cor 15:28).

(2) The *universal* extension of the judgment to all peoples and nations. The kinship relationship between the king and the least in the world, because they are the king's "brothers" (the hungry, the pilgrims, the sick, the prisoners, the poor, the least), calls for justice in personal works (love, charity, solidarity, tolerance). It is not enough just to have juridical-social justice, which is the *minimum moralitatis* and can be understood in the minimalistic and merely legalistic sense. On the contrary, with the Matthean parable we are in full, revealed gratuitousness: not the little ones in place of the king, not a full identification or univocity, but the two together in hierarchy: Christ wills to be helped in the poor, because what is done to the poor is done to him.

(3) The *lordship of Christ* is brought about in serving the little ones: "The Son of Man came not to be served but to serve, and to give his life" (Mk 10:45); "I have set you an example . . . servants are not greater than their masters" (Jn 13:15f.); "I am among you as one who serves" (Lk 22:27). By which we see how the accent falls on the seriousness of the *everyday,* of the ordinary, of the obvious, since by following the just king

on the threefold path of a threefold need in simple service of our fellow beings, we promote their rights. *Nourishment* (food and water) pertains to the first basic right, i.e., to the human right to a personal life. Inclusion in a *community* (stranger without homeland, without clothes, without the warmth of a community) pertains to the second basic right, i.e., the right to a community, to society (family, country, community of believers, social protection). The need for *freedom* (sickness, prison) pertains to the third fundamental human right, i.e., freedom of conscience, freedom of religion, external and individual freedom far from any coercion or limitation.

So, to conclude, the decisive *criterion* is the theandric person of Christ ("you have done it to me"). This criterion makes it that all the works done to the "brothers" fall within the extended, i.e., biblical, theological, religious, precisely Christian concept of justice. The object is the works of charity, mercy, and solidarity, which unquestionably express a more elevated philanthropy, a nobler humanity, a higher justice, than that perhaps required by some sort of positive law or justice set out in a code and expressed in the formula *cuique suum.* So, in the Matthean parable of the last judgment, many lofty, sublime, and spiritual values are involved, which transform the already perfect justice of the OT into a new, grand, salvific, specifically Christian justice.

There have been numerous writers on higher justice in Paul: J. Blank, G. Bornkamm, F. F. Bruce, R. Bultmann, C. H. Dodd, G. Friedrich, H. Hübner, S. Johnson, E. Käsemann, S. Lyonnet, H. Räisänen, S. Schlier, W. Schrage, H. Schürmann, U. Wilckens, and more recently Brice L. Martin, *Christ and the Law in Paul* (1989) and Frank Thielman, *From Plight to Solution: A Jewish Framework for Understanding Paul's View of the Law in Galatians and Romans* (1989).

The concept of justice in Paul is consistent with the biblical line already explained. But it becomes progressively interiorized toward inner growth, in the justification of the forgiven sinner in Christ. Let us note the following considerations: The debtor, in Roman culture, had to pay his debts or else go to prison, the existence of the *aequitas romana* notwithstanding, i.e., that legal even-handedness that made the Romans the envy of the world. Paul emphasizes the concept of justification: for the person forgiven in Christ, every debt is canceled. The justified person becomes just, holy. Whereas Roman justice emanates from the laws, Pauline justification comes about within the person, in the grace of Christ, without laws, and also has positive effects on society. For the Stoics, the Godhead is only a model of self-liberation; for Paul, God in Christ is the one who liberates and saves human beings from their own injustice, from *sklērokardia*. The liberated distance themselves from worldly possessions; this makes them available to use these for the benefit of the needy. Thus Paul relativizes the law and material possessions, gives a deeper social perspective, and rejects the Stoic ideal of self-sufficiency.

This indeed leads on to the real Pauline concept of justice. Following the biblical line, Paul is concerned about the poor (e.g., those belonging to the mother church in Jerusalem) but in a widened concept of poverty. He is concerned about the poor and outcast in the social sense, but still more so in the *spiritual* sense: about spiritual slaves. Paul defends the rights of the least, by proclaiming the authority of the universal kingdom of the risen Christ. On this basis, all, even the most wretched, have the same rights and the same duties: in marriage (the husband as well as the wife), in the family (the head of the family as well as the children and the slaves) (Eph 5:22–23; 6:1–9), in society, no discrimination between rich and poor, Greeks and Jews, masters and slaves (Col 3:18; Gal 3:26–28). This was an unheard-of social revolution, for until then slaves had been the chattel of their masters; the woman had been the weaker partner in the family; and children were exposed to the despotic will of their fathers. Now, "in the LORD," the slave has the same rights and duties as the master (Col 3:18–19).

With this, Paul did not overturn the contemporary social order politically, but he did relativize it. His own expression *"en Christō Iēsou tō Kyriō hēmōn,* in Christ Jesus our Lord" (Rom 6:23 and passim) changes everything from *within,* since, "set free from sin and become slaves of God" (Rom 6:22), Christians are able to transform society. The slave, unjust social position notwithstanding, is already set free in Christ. For this reason, many slaves accepted Christianity. They could not be converted to

Judaism unless they had already been set free by their masters, since slaves were unable to observe the Mosaic Law. Paul has to deal with slavery in Corinth, in Rome too, but what matters about people is not the outward, social, economic, political condition as such, but God's *call* (1 Cor 7:17f.). The slave can thus discharge his duty as a Christian by serving his master as he would Christ (cf. Eph 6:5–8): the Christian master for his part will treat his slave as his "brother in Christ" (Eph 6:9). This emerges from the short letter to Philemon:

> Onesimus . . . my very heart . . . that you might have him back forever, no longer as a slave but more than a slave, a beloved brother—especially to me but how much more to you, both in the flesh and in the Lord. So if you consider me your partner, welcome him as you would welcome me." (Phlm 14–21)

Those who have been baptized into Christ have been freed from sin, from death, from the law (Rom 6–8; Gal 5:1), since they have become slaves of God and justice (1 Cor 7:22f.; Rom 6:16–22). From being slaves they have become "children in the Son" (Gal 4:4–7, 21–31). Free in regard to all, they, however, become servants and slaves to all, after the example of their Lord (1 Cor 9:19; cf. Mt 20:26–27; Jn 13:14f.).

Hence this higher Pauline justice identified with the justification offered by God (Rom 3:5), which penetrates to the heart of the slave to sin (Rom 3:26) is different from human, social, political, economic justice. Yet the social fruits of this divine justice, which is neither partial nor based on class, are the only ones truly able to transform society in every age.

4. The Philosophical-Juridical Concept

There are two views about the philosophical-juridical concept of justice: the traditional one and the modern one.

(a) The *traditional or classical* view, beginning with Greek culture (*dikaiosynē* = justice; *dikaios* = just; *dikaiōsis* = justification), is derived from the substantive *dikē* = directive, indication, order. *Dikē* is the daughter of Zeus and shares in his governance of the world. This expresses the excellence of justice in Greek culture. The *dikē* is necessary so that people may develop a personal and communal life in an ordered manner. In the juridical and administrative sense, it can mean three things: the egalitarian order that ought to be established in a normal society; the complex of laws guaranteeing that same order; and the organ or regime that, without discrimination or favoritism, applies these laws equally to all. The opposite of juridical and administrative order is *biē*, violence, or power destructive of order. In its personal and person-to-person application, here are some definitions from antiquity. For Plato, justice is an act, i.e., "to give someone what is his due" (*Repub.* 1.6.331). For Aristotle, it is a disposition of mind: "the virtue by which the 'just' act from choice" (*Nic. Eth.* V.1129). So too for Ulpian it is a disposition: "a constant and perpetual wish to give every man what is his" (*Dig.* 1.1.10). For Thomas Aquinas, it is "the virtue by which each, with constant and perpetual will, gives each what is rightly his" (*ST* 2.2, q. 58a, a. 1).

To these and similar classic definitions (with the exception of Aquinas's doctrine) comprehensively considered, one may generally say that they show a too *objectivistic*, too "*thingified*," quantified, or mathematical justice—"to give every man what is his"—as though it were only a question of exterior possessions which have nothing to do with the subject-agent, nor with his conscience, nor with the subjective intention, as though neither the person of the agent nor the person to whom his due must be given respectively are in fact to be taken into consideration. This type of justice, which is limited to the material or quantified is unable to grasp the *personal* dimension of the law; it is a minimal, external justice, which may even become inhuman, and hence an "unjust justice."

(b) Every ethical quality is of the subject-agent and not of the thing due. This means that the formally just according to a law or an agreement may be unjust in terms of human dignity. A salary, a satisfying of the obligations of commutative justice, a bureaucratic and formal distribution: all these and other forms of objective, external justice may be "just" *ad rigorem litterae* but not *ad dignitatem personae*, since the subject-agent remains uninvolved.

But the new principle requires, first of all, that we recognize the fundamental right of the person with all that this implies, as we shall see further on; as a consequence, whereas before the *quantitative* (minimal) due was favored,

today the *qualitative* due is ("just" not in legal but in human terms). Here, however, one might object that beyond the strict duty and legal measure, there is only charity, and charity is not justice. Therefore the personal dimension of the subject-agent does not come into it and has nothing to do with justice as such. Quite right: it does have nothing to do with justice understood in the traditional, classic, objectivistic, and quantified sense, but it does have to do with the justice that is primarily the guarantee of the person's well-being, of the right that springs not from positive law but from the nature of the person, which affects the person and not merely his or her possessions.

The *history of the concept* of justice shows that, although having sprung from two sources (the biblical/theological first and the philosophical/juridical second), after the fathers of the church the biblical/theological dimension was virtually forgotten by the scholastics, whereas the Greco-Roman concept of justice "to each his own" became, practically speaking, the only one in a conservative, static, unchanging social order. In the treatise *De Gratia*, OT law is ignored and divine justice and human justification are considered in the Pauline sense, without any influence on Christian morality, catechesis, or training. Even today we still have authors who think of justice exclusively in the categories of Aristotelian justice. The historical fact is that the writers of the manuals did not know on what scriptural basis to organize the treatise *De Iustitia*. Commutative justice takes first and virtually exclusive place as the paradigmatic model. For evidence of this, see Chiavacci 1986: 13–23; commutative justice in G. Genicot's manual (*Institutiones Theologiae moralis*, I [1931]) takes up 201 pages; in H. Noldin's manual (*Summa Theologiae moralis*, I–II, 28th ed. [1941]) it takes up 233 pages; in D. M. Prummer's manual (*Manuale theologiae moralis*, II [1940]) it takes up some 200 pages; in T. A. Iorio's manual (*Theologia moralis*, II [1946]) it takes up 255 pages out of 580 in the section on the laws of God and the church. Thus, too much law and little theological content, virtually without any personal, ecclesial or social dimension.

Let us make the point once again: the Aristotelian concept of *cuique suum* held the field alone. The consequence was that all scholastic treatises were without deep biblical or theological dimensions. They neither took account of the links between justice and love/charity, nor between justice and the dignity of the human person, nor between justice and the rights of the needy (the poor, the little ones, widows).

> The treatise was called _De Iustitia et Iure_ and was bound up with civil law and thus of little use for uncovering social injustices. The correction of the great inequalities was entrusted to charity/beneficence, a virtue _par excellence_ of the rich, who were praised for their generosity to the poor. (Hamel, "The Foundations of Human Rights in Biblical Theology, Following the Orientations of _Gaudium et Spes_," in R. Latourelle, ed., _Vatican II: Assessment and Perspectives, Twenty-five Years After (1962–1987)_, 3 vols. [Mahwah, N.J., 1989], 2:460–77)

Hamel adds that for a long time the virtue of justice could find no place in treatises of spirituality. But there is more. Up to today, the concept of justice has not been dealt with in any scholastic textbooks—not, e.g., in the _Nuovo Dizionario di spiritualità_ (3rd ed., 1982), nor in the _Nuovo Dizionario de teologia_ (2nd ed., 1979), nor in the _Dizionario di catechetica_ (1986), nor in the _Dizionario di pastorale giovanile_ (1989), and so on.

Many urgent new factors outside the church (respect for native cultures, the common fate of all owing to exhaustion of energy resources, bioethical and environmental problems, the political and economic collapse of real socialism, and so on) and factors influencing a new way of thinking in the community of those who believe in Christ (the birth and rapid expansion of the "fourth" world, the renewed social teachings of the church, today's virtue of justice, and so on) generate a new need for _integration_ between the teachings of the Christian biblical-theological tradition, the classical philosophical-juridical tradition, and the modern notion that lays more and more stress on humanity in its socio-anthropological integrity. Thus we move toward a new _synthesis_ of the concept of justice, toward a renewed and modernized biblical-theological and philosophical-juridical concept, which is more human, more Christian, more comprehensive and acceptable, more credible and more effective for our times.

There are those who will object that with a broader concept of justice, i.e., personalized and theologized, we may have made two mistakes.

The first is that justice is very close to love/charity, and so the concepts of justice and charity are going to become more or less identical, such that the Lord's two great commandments could be rephrased: "justice toward God and one's neighbor." Would this not be a confusion of doctrine? The second objection is that, understood thus, justice comes very close to Christian faith, such that faith and justice would be more or less identified with each other. But a concept of this sort is too Christian and neither realistic nor attractive; it is therefore alien to the secularized folk of today. Yes, of course, there is a drawing together of the concepts of justice, charity, and faith, but let us examine the question point by point.

5. Some Characteristics of the New, Broadened Concept

The concept of "his" (_suum jus_) is that of the _right_ that lies at the origin (base, root) of justice. If we analyze the Platonic/Aristotelian/Thomist formulation, we find that the individual "his" predominates, and not the communal or social. For ethics too being rather individual—not to say "individualistic"—has through the centuries been too much focused on _commutative_ justice, as we have already said. But the _suum_ has at least two precise meanings: _objective_, in the case when that which is due belongs to a person (this due can be a thing, an action, a service); or _subjective_, in the case when a person might have a certain power of demanding or of disposing of a thing or an action. To these meanings of the concept "his," we can add two other aspects concerning human rights: the _legislative_ aspect, or _ratio juris_, which is the rational regulation of the rights and relationships of the person, based on natural or positive law; and the _scientific_ aspect, which denotes the science of law inasmuch as it deals in a scientific and systematic way with the topic of "his."

Justice is also a _virtue_. The habit of attributing to each "his own" rights is a virtue; not to give what is each rightly "his own" is a sin. Yet to be just, we need the constant, positive attitude (_habitus_)—i.e., the _virtue_—and not merely some isolated or sporadic act. But justice is a very special virtue.

For Plato, it is a human virtue exercised on two levels: _social_ inasmuch as, by giving to each his own, it ensures the maintenance of the social classes (rulers, warriors, artisans) in their proper order; *personal* inasmuch as order is safeguarded in the relationship between the three "souls" (covetous, irascible, rational) which, according to him, make up the human being.

For Aristotle, who has improved on the thought of his teacher, the virtue of justice takes three main forms, which will be a more or less absolute paradigm throughout history.

The first form, which we have already discussed, expresses the burden incumbent on citizens in their reciprocal relations *suum cuique*, called *commutative justice*, being particular, "linear" (between I–You–We), interpersonal, "arithmetical." It orders the just relationship between individuals or groups, according to the principle of a balancing of their rights and duties.

The second form expresses the onus incumbent on citizens toward the state or the common good and consists in the principle of keeping its laws. Laws order the members of society to the common good, where society is the subject of the rights, toward which individuals have their respective duties, while the common good is the object to be safeguarded and developed. This is called *legal justice*, being contributive, general, "from the bottom up."

The third form emphasizes the rights and duties of the citizens of the state or society and orders the relationship between society and its members. It does this by guaranteeing the common good. The subject of duty is society, which gives to each his own. This is called *distributive justice*, being proportional, "geometrical," from the top down.

For Aquinas, "justice is the habit whereby a person with a lasting and constant will renders to each his due" (*ST* 2.2, q. 58, a. 1). In theology it has its place with the four cardinal virtues: prudence, *justice*, fortitude, and temperance. We may observe that, for Aristotle, justice (*dikaiosynē*) is one of the "cardinal" virtues, with prudence (*phronēsis*), wisdom (*sophia*), temperance (*sōphrosynē*) and fortitude (*andreia*) (*Nic. Eth.* 1.3). Hence it is a moral virtue and actually takes first place, since the other virtues deal with the good of the individual *in se*, whereas justice looks to the common good, which transcends that of the individual. Justice-value and virtue establish equality between the

parties, reciprocity between right and duty, parity between persons and equalization of aims.

Hence the virtue of justice is *different* from the others, since the *aequalitas* or fundamental equality between the persons does not depend of itself on the will of the agent as in other virtues. Here *medium rei*, or "just measure," looks to the just *object* and not to the agent's intention, which is the force, but also the limit, of the virtue of justice. Whence the danger that rigid equality may become unjust, as Cicero puts it in his much quoted axiom: *summum ius, summa injuria*("rigid equality: supreme injustice," *De Officiis* 1.10.33).

And indeed justice should not be used rigidly, either when expressing the *suum* or when representing the *virtus*: it can and should remit the debt in *brotherly love* in the tradition of OT and NT justice, following the paradigm and teaching of the Lord Jesus (Lk 10:29–36, the Good Samaritan; Mt 20:1–16: the laborers in the vineyard; Mt 18:23–35: the unmerciful servant). In justice, therefore, for it to be truly human, there needs to be integration in the person and redemption effected by solidarity, human love, and Christian charity.

In this sense, the Second Vatican Council, throughout the second part of *Gaudium et Spes* (46–90) develops the church's social teaching within a theological-moral focus. In §29, it describes "the basic equality of all," since "all possess a rational soul and are created in God's likeness," "having the same nature and origin, having been redeemed by Christ, and enjoy the same divine calling and destiny." So the same basic human rights, based on the same dignity of the human person, of themselves deserve the same justice. All this reawakens deep, basic anthropological and theological arguments, and not merely socioeconomic ones although it includes them.

But who is the *subject* of the law? Only people, with their variety of institutions and societies? Could an *animal* be it? As regards this problem, there are three possible positions today. The first one, the *classic* one, says that the law pertains exclusively to the human being: only the human person can be the subject of the law. This is for two reasons: because only the person (be it physical person or moral person) is aware, free, and responsible; only the person has value *de fine* and not as object or as instrument. Consequently, no subhuman being is an aware, free, responsible person, nor has final value (the end is not in itself but in the higher personal being). Therefore, it can only have value as a means and be an object at law. Hence, to talk about rights in an analogous sense is incorrect. But this does not mean that people do not have *duties*, sometimes serious ones (and today there can be no doubt about this, as there used to be in the past) toward animals—for those domestic ones which ought to be looked after, fed, and cared for healthwise, and so on, since the dignity of the human person and of the subject at law is projected onto them. By the same token, no one may torture them or put them to inhumane uses, "If however he does such things, it is not specifically a sin of injustice against animals or against God that he commits, but one against himself in misusing his own property and per se, in itself, this sin does not exceed the venial" (B. H. Merkelbach, *Summa theologiae moralis*, II, n. 374). This last statement, "*veniale non excedit*," is generally regarded today as behind the times, and present-day debate does not exclude the possibility of really grave sin with regard to animals, especially when people torture them merely for sadistic pleasure, indulging intemperate passions and brutal instincts.

The second position, the *modern* one, poses the question in new terms with persistence and sensitivity. In recent years, what with vivisection and every type of biomedical experiment involving every kind of cruel manipulation of animals, which have now become the "live material" to be studied and put to use for the advance of modern science, the problem has taken on a new form and a new seriousness. Since the coordinates too are new, in which the problem arises, we may single out three aspects. The protagonist of animal rights is *secular-lay ethics*. But of these rights, can ethics say whether these are "natural" or "positive," i.e., founded in the animal's nature, or conferred by positive human law? Of course, ethics cannot speak of the animal's natural rights, since secular-lay ethics does not even grant us human beings constant values and rights rooted in nature (e.g., natural laws, inherent moral conscience, etc.) but only concedes our historical nature. Logically, therefore, in its teaching it ought only and exclusively to grant the animal "positive rights." On this point, however, it

seems to be inconsistent, since for it the animal not only has the "nature of object and value as means" but is not in essence different from a human being except in degree: something that Christian anthropology cannot allow. Next, it states that the animal, as a living being, even if it cannot reason or speak, can *suffer*, on which Christian anthropology of course agrees. So a new principle can be laid down: the animal's capacity to suffer. Now, faced with anybody's suffering, we have a duty to do all we can to relieve it. And some law codes have actually embodied this: the Austrian, that of the Italian League for Animal Rights, that of the International League for Animal Rights, published in Brussels at UNESCO (which at a political and juridical level does not, however, have the force of a convention or resolution). We should also mention some authors, such as P. Singer, J. Bentham, T. Regan. Certainly the principle of suffering has something to be said for it from the ethical point of view, as we shall say further on.

There is a *middle* position espoused by our schizophrenic culture, inasmuch as on the one hand it bases animal rights on the capacity to suffer, whether on the basis of the fact that suffering hurts, or on the basis of the rank, the ontological dignity of the being capable of suffering. Logically, defenders of animal rights ought also to defend the human embryo (which they do not), and the defenders of the human embryo should defend animals too, on the basis of the common principle of the dignity of life as such.

Here we hit on the incongruity of a legal system and a mentality which on the one hand rightly protect animals from human ill-treatment but, on the other, leaves unpunished the slaughter of millions of human beings in the womb, even in the ninth month of pregnancy (Canada, 1990). We are, however, in agreement that suffering and life itself are based on the *ontological* nature of living beings. But this is precisely the obstacle that secular-lay ethics cannot overcome, without at the same time renouncing the ethical-positivist principle.

The modern *Christian/Catholic* position is more nuanced. Whereas the manualistic approach stressed the anthropocentrism of human lordship over the creation (Gn 1–2), theological ANTHROPOLOGY in the ultimate analysis links the respect due to life to theocentrism, based on God—Love. The theologies of creation and of love reveal the sign on which the moral imperative is based. It is based not so much on the justice due to animals, nor on the principle of suffering, as, following in the footprints of traditional theology, on the *dignity of the human person*, for our duty is to encourage the progress of the other species of living creatures and not to wipe them out.

All said, we have *two* valid principles that ought to regulate human behavior toward animals. On the one side, we have the respect due to God, since God protects all his creation and he who attacks the creation, in a certain (analogical) sense attacks God himself. On the other, there must be the respect due to human dignity, which is the classic principle: *peccat erga se ipsum qui male utitur de re sua* ("He sins against himself who misuses his possessions") for we sin against our own human *dignity*, which is damaged by any kind of cruelty to animals, since by being cruel we demean ourselves, make ourselves contemptible, show ourselves as less than human.

6. The Worldwide Debate on Human Rights and Freedoms

By a logical progression, we must at this point broach this modern topic, which is closely bound up with the debate on the concept of justice. From what has already been said, it is obvious that justice presupposes and is based on *rights* (be they natural or positive), which express the *"suum"* of a moral subject. It is also obvious that the *natural* right of the human person, whether from the logical or temporal point of view, is anterior to any society, organization, and state, since it is anterior to any legislation and positive law, hence to any positive right. This being so, human rights are already in existence before any state and any positive legislation; hence, they are "pre-statal" and "supra-statal," just as the person is before any state and above any state. E. Ginters says that "human rights are conceived of here as pre-positive, pre-fixed and pre-existent to any statal legislation whatsoever. In other words, human beings are conceived of as beings who possess a *vocation* or an orientation not subject to discussion, before ever it gets fixed by any sort of human community or even by themselves" (*Valori, norme e fade cristiana*, 97).

Human rights are innate and unalienable, as are the person itself and its dignity, in which they are based (*GS* 25.1; 26.3). "To have a right means having a title to ask, demand or claim something from others, who have the corresponding duty not to frustrate us in what the requirement or object of the right is (negative aspect) and to satisfy the requests that we have just title to make (positive aspect)" (Ginters, *Valori*, 77). The contemporary, worldwide, or planetary debate on human rights and freedoms, in accordance with the principle *cuique suum*, proceeds in three sectors: in the church (Catholic and Protestant) and other religions, in the domain of international law, and in real socialism (when still existing). So we have *three* aspects of this new theological-moral and social-political topic, and this keeps increasing the scope of any treatment of justice. We are living the SIGNS OF THE TIMES, which express themselves in a fundamental ethical factor of today's world, affecting everybody, not only Christians. World society is increasingly becoming a single community, in which all separatism is anachronistic, all violation of rights and freedoms offend human dignity and society too. Alas, the rights of the individual and the community are always vulnerable. So here the universal coprinciples come into play: *pacta sunt servanda* ("agreements are to be kept"); damages unjustly caused must be repaired; promises made must be kept, and so on—i.e., the basic rights of every person, group, or nation must be recognized.

A glance at *history* tells us that the ecumenical agreement on rights in the church is something recent. It begins with the Protestants at *Oekumenischer Rat* in Amsterdam (1948), Uppsala (1968), St. Polten (1975). Many of their theologians took part, e.g., J. Moltmann, T. Rendtorff, H. E. Tödt, M. Honecker, W. Huber, and others; they worked out various explanations and plausible arguments. The Catholic church's position is a cautious one on teaching about rights. The reasons are well known: the charter of the *Declaration of the Rights of Man and the Citizen*, approved by the French National Assembly (26 August 1789), with the "immortal principles of 1789" (*liberté, égalité, fraternité*) of the French Revolution. The popes of the Catholic church (from Pius VI to Pius XII) stayed on the alert. What created the difficulties were articles 10 and 11 of the

Declaration itself. In the ordering of the state, the *Declaration* put the "confessions" and the "ideologies" on the same level as values. Add to this the Enlightenment in general and its grand master I. Kant in particular (1724–1804). There was also a special factor: in the Catholic church the topic of rights and freedoms goes together or primarily with the question of religious freedom, only set out in a new light by Vatican II with the declaration *Dignitatis Humanae* (7 December 1965), in which "the right of the individual and of the community to social and civil liberty in the matter of religion" is explained. There was silence from Pius VI until Pius XI, who in his encyclical *Mit brennender Sorge* (1937) against Nazism, affirmed the inalienable rights of the human person. On the occasion of the fifteenth anniversary of the United Nations Charter on rights and freedoms (1948), Pope John XXIII published the encyclical *Pacem in Terris* (1963) and gave the first systematic treatment of basic human rights on the church's part: the right to live and to a reasonable standard of living (*PT* 11), to respect for private property, to the search for truth, to the objectivity of information (*PT* 12), to honor God (*PT* 14), to choose one's own state of life (*PT* 15), to work (*PT* 18), to hold meetings and associations (*PT* 23), to emigrate and immigrate (*PT* 25), to hold a position in public life (*PT* 26). Then followed the famous pastoral constitution on the church in the modern world, *GAUDIUM ET SPES* (7 December 1965) of the Second Vatican Council, which is very rich in this field. One quotation will suffice:

> By virtue of the gospel committed to her, the Church proclaims the rights of man. She acknowledges and greatly esteems the dynamic movements of today by which these rights are everywhere fostered. Yet these movements must be penetrated by the spirit of the gospel and protected against any kind of false autonomy. For we are tempted to think that our personal rights are fully ensured only when we are exempt from every requirement of divine law. But this way lies not the maintenance of the dignity of the human person, but its annihilation. (*GS* 41.3)

So we can single out the characteristics of the magisterium's teaching: from questions on labor, race, class, women, ecology, underdevelopment, and so on, to the problem of world government, human rights, injustice, inequality, and so on. In this connection we need to study the pontifical documents on the church's teaching: from Leo XIII: *Rerum Novarum* (1891), Pius XI: *Quadragesimo Anno* (1931), Pius XII: *Summi Pontificatus* (1939), John XXIII: *Mater et Magistra* (1961), the aforementioned *Pacem in Terris* (1963), to Paul VI: *Populorum Progressio* (1967) and *Octogesima Adveniens* (1971), John Paul II: *Laborem Exercens* (1981)—eighty years after the encyclical *Rerum Novarum*—up to *Sollicitudo Rei Socialis* (1987). We should also add the courageous document issued by the Synod of Bishops, *Justice in the World* (1971), the less well known but no less important one from the Pontifical Commission *Iustitia et Pax* called *Self-reliance: Compter sur soi* (1978); that of the International Theological Commission (ITC) *The Dignity and Rights of the Human Person* (1983), and that most recent one of all from the Congregation for Catholic Education, *Guidelines for the Study and Teaching of the Church's Social Doctrine in the Formation of Priests* (1989), for an eventual teaching program. The *Code of Canon Law* (1983), which John Paul II calls "the last act of the Second Vatican Council" speaks of the "duties and rights of all the Christian faithful" (canons 2-8-223). In the meantime, many Catholic theologians and sociologists have gone deeper into the topic of human rights (A. Auer, F. Böckle, K. Demmer, J. Schasching, E. Hamel, O. von Nell-Breunig, and others).

The history of the teaching on human rights can be summarized into *five* phases: (*a*) Classic teaching did not deal with human rights and freedoms. (*b*) The concept was used pretty cautiously both by the Catholic magisterium and by theologians until the 1960s. (*c*) The subject came to prominence with the debate on the *specificum christianum* (the specifically Christian component) in morality (1970 on). (*d*) This teaching only enters Catholic political ethics after "signals" given by the magisterium. (*e*) Today, Catholic theology cannot ignore it any more. Thus, on this topic, the pontificate of Pius XII was still cautious; the pontificates of John XXIII and Paul VI were open, Vatican II even more so (specifically in *DH* and *GS*). But the subject comes into its own with the pontificate of John Paul II. It is important to point out the teaching's internal dimension: i.e., in the pontifical documents and the treatises and articles on the subject, the concepts of justice, charity, solidarity, and sharing go more and more together, as concepts very closely related. Without love/charity, there is neither peace nor real justice worthy of the human person, nor acknowledgment of one's neighbor, nor communication, nor information, nor truthfulness. Love/charity allows people to see things more humanly, more biblically, more Christianly in the personal and personalized dimension. All these aspects, however, are not intended to replace the virtue of justice.

As for the _hierarchy of human rights_, some are _essential_ or major: these are the _basic_ or primary ones, such as life; dignity; equality; and freedom of thought, of conscience, and of religion. There are also the _non-basic_ or secondary ones, e.g., certain civil rights: political, economic, social, cultural, personal. Other rights are _contingent_ or accidental, as resulting from or conditional on the basic rights or bound up with them; they are less "inviolable." Finally, there exist the so-called _postulated_ or minor rights. The "immediate" _basis_ of rights—i.e., "the dignity of the human person"— is arrived at by an "ascending" path (K. Rahner) or by a "descending" one (H. Urs von Balthasar). One may debate to what degree the dignity of the human person is already a foundational argument for human rights, or rather an appellative postulate. When, however, the teaching on human rights is analyzed point by point in relation to the dignity of the human person, by application of the most appropriate theological/philosophical hermeneutics, this seems to be more of a pseudo-problem than a real one, since the base on which the rights are founded is the reality of the _nature_ of the person, understood in its philosophical/theological and natural/supernatural totality.

Human rights may be considered _in terms of "worlds"_ (as the ITC does in the document mentioned above (B I, 2, 3, 4). The _First World_ has two characteristics: rights and freedoms are proclaimed, but this takes place in a moral vacuum in which dignity and freedom get distorted: consumerism, individualism, naturalism, false autonomy, lax behavior, unbridled liberty, social class differences, stronger nations "end up making other nations subservient to their interests" (_EV_ 9:1053).

The _Second World_ of so-called real socialism, while crumbling to pieces in the social-economic-political sense, is determined to salvage Marxist-Leninist ideology with its historical-ideological profile focused on the total withering away of the state and the law and, as a final phase, "the perfect communist society" (→ MARXISM). Everything is based on the positivist doctrine of law: the state, guided by the Communist Party, by means of constitution and positive legislation, assures the citizens their social, political, economic, and personal rights, who before were entirely lacking in any "natural right" (K. Marx). "Human rights" do not exist and have no meaning, no such expression is to be found in socialist legislation. On the other hand, "real socialist" regimes do use the same language as the free world (freedom, equality, law, conscience, and so on) but mean something quite different. That is, the content is different; everything has to be understood uniquely within the system. Everyone, therefore, has to think in the same way, while "dissidents" and those who "think differently" get severely punished.

In the _Third World_, with the differing conditions of young nations who believe in their own culture, independence, politics, and technological and economic progress, the social aspects of human rights take first place. "They maintain that the rights of a full international justice are often not fully accorded them" (_EV_ 9:1056), both on account of their little political clout and of their poverty. On the international plane, economic and commercial conditions are often subjected to unfair stipulations: minimal help from the rich nations ("hardness of heart") the values of native cultures still insufficiently appreciated.

The second major factor in the debate on human rights and in the human rights movement is the various _international declarations_ of the United Nations and the Helsinki Final Act of the Conference on Security and Cooperation in Europe (CSCE), with their respective organizations. The United Nations, with its _Statute of the United Nations_ (1945) at San Francisco, "reaffirms its belief in fundamental human rights, in the dignity and value of the human person, in equality of rights for men and women and for large and small nations" (§2). The aims of the United Nations are set out in chapter 1, art. 1, among which is that of "promoting and encouraging respect for human rights and the basic freedoms of all, without distinction of race, sex, language or religion"

(n. 3). Following the fundamental document of the United Nations—"a milestone on the long and difficult journey of the human race" (John Paul II), the *Universal Declaration of Human Rights* was approved by the General Assembly on 10 December 1948. The Catholic contribution had been made by J. Maritain, basing himself on the teachings of Thomas Aquinas, TEILHARD DE CHARDIN and others. In the Preamble (§1), the basis on which the entire *Declaration* is constructed is clearly and unambiguously set out. This basis is the human person, considered not as a being "empty in himself," virtually stripped of all existential value pertaining to the person (K. Marx), but as a being whose dignity is actually rooted in personal and ontological reality. This dignity of the human person is, according to the *Declaration*, the basis of, or the source from which all human rights flow, those "of man as concrete individual, and of man in his universal dimension" (John Paul II). We are not talking here of some sort of dignity added on from outside or accidentally, but "inherent in all members of the human family" as such (§1). This being so, "their rights" are "equal and unalienable" (§1). The "recognition of this dignity inherent in all members of the human family, and of their equal unalienable rights constitutes the basis of freedom, justice and peace in the world" (§1). By contrast, "refusal to recognize, and contempt for, human rights have led to acts of barbarity which offend the conscience of humanity" (§2). This excellent document, proclaimed as a common ideal to be striven for by all peoples and nations, has undoubtedly exerted an immense influence for good throughout the world—but, not being embodied in a treaty, has remained legally ineffective.

The United Nations has also undertaken the further task of codifying these principles into treaties, to be presented for approval and ratification by member states, so as then to be incorporated into national constitutions and codes of law. So today basic human rights are guaranteed by two pacts or treaties. Both the pacts, in the introduction to the text, state that "in due time they will become legally binding on those states that have ratified them." We are talking here of the *Declaration on Economic, Social and Cultural Rights*, adopted by the General Assembly on 16 December 1966, which came into force on 3 January 1976, after

the 35th instrument of ratification had been deposited by Jamaica; and the *Declaration on Civil and Political Rights*, adopted by the General Assembly on 16 December 1966, which came into force on 23 March 1976, after the 35th instrument of ratification had been deposited by Czechoslovakia. Among those states that have ratified them are all those of the former Eastern bloc: Bulgaria, Czechoslovakia, Poland, East Germany, Romania, Hungary, Ukraine, Russia (all Warsaw Pact members) and Yugoslavia. The United Nations has also passed various *Conventions* and *Declarations*.

The Conference on Security and Co-operation in Europe (CSCE) affirmed the same thing in the Final Act, promulgated in Helsinki on 1 August 1975 and confirmed by the thirty-five participating states. In the *Declaration on the principles regulating relations between the participating states*, the most important of the ten principles solemnly laid down is Principle VII: "Respect for human rights and basic freedoms, including freedom of thought, conscience, religion or belief." In this most important international document too the emphasis falls on the source of all human rights. It explicitly states that this source is "the dignity inherent in the human person" (§2) and that the most important task for the participating states is to promote and encourage "the effective exercise of the freedoms and civil, political, economic, social, cultural and other rights which are all derived from the dignity inherent in the human person and are essential for its free and full development" (§§1, 2). The CSCE from then on has used its plenary sessions to keep these principles constantly alive (Belgrade, Madrid, Ottawa, Vienna).

This rapid survey of the international charters leads to the obvious conclusion that the source of human rights is the human person—or, more exactly, "the dignity of the human person," which is more valuable than anything else in the world. Since the source from which human rights flow is human dignity—of every person—it follows that all human beings enjoy equality of basic rights and freedoms, without any distinction among them, inasmuch as all are endowed with the same dignity, even when they happen to be in error. This dignity furthermore does not come from outside but is inherent in humanity and therefore inalienable.

"Inherent" means that it is so closely connected with the human person as to be identified with it. This being so, this dignity is the human person's heritage from birth.

Humans are born *free, equal* in dignity and freedom, endowed with reason and conscience. This being so, human rights have *universal* importance, not by the will of some state or other, nor because world organizations proclaim them, but because they exist in humans independently of the state or of any other authority whatsoever. Consequently, it is natural for humans to act in a spirit of *solidarity* and *kinship* toward one another, precisely because they are equals in dignity and in rights. That then this inherent and inalienable dignity should be accepted by human beings and many states as constituting the *basis* for *freedoms* expressed in innumerable private and public ways is a recognition already operating at the international level too. Persons live their human dignity when no one interferes with their acting as free beings, not subject to anyone, even less to a community, to a system, to a state or to any other communal form that makes them slaves of society rather than responsible protagonists.

We may, however, say that the question of the *source*, or rather of the *base*, on which human rights stand (human dignity), as the international declarations so accurately put it, is not merely of legal/philosophical character (in the Hegelian sense or that of some other *bourgeois* philosophy) but represents the departure point for every legal/practical demand affecting the concrete behavior required of the citizen by the state. Were the government of a state to treat a person as though the latter had no rights or as though the *content* of the person's basic rights were not derived from personal dignity, the result would be that the inviolability or sanctity of this content would have no real meaning. According to these international documents, one cannot proceed downward from the state or collective to the individual as their subject; the only legitimate process is the one that starts from *adhesion* to the personal rights of every person — through protective measures — and debouches into the community or into the state. Further, whatever measure is taken by the state comes originally from the individual as citizen and is based on every person's *intangible*

right as person, *inviolable* in the dignity that person was born with.

7. Social Justice before the Encyclical *Sollicitudo Rei Socialis*

We return to the concept of justice, but now as *social justice,* and ask ourselves whether this concept, which is typically and exclusively philosophical and juridical, economic, social and political in nature, can also be *theological.* Yes, it certainly does have a theological dimension, inasmuch as the theological yardstick measures its ethical-religious importance. So, when we talk about social justice we are *in theologia.* This nexus with ethical-religious importance goes to show that social justice is closely bound up with person-to-person relations, with people's behavior toward one another, no longer limited merely to a society or a state. It is a virtue in the sense already explained, belonging among the cardinal virtues. Social justice is preeminently a part of the social teaching of the church. It thus pertains to the field of theology (*Sollicitudo* 41). This new theological perspective, for moral theology too, can be gathered from the new document issued by the Congregation for Catholic Education, *Guidelines for the Study and Teaching of the Church's Social Doctrine in the Formation of Priests* (1989) 30–46, 47–53.

Let us now consider social justice in the social teaching of the church in its *historical* aspect, that is to say, before *Sollicitudo Rei Socialis,* and after. Generally speaking, we may say that the concept of social justice has not yet been stabilized, owing to new social, economic, and political factors. We can see two phases in the development of the concept nonetheless.

The *first phase* covers the period lasting from the beginning of the church's social teaching up to the Second World War. The concept of social justice in the documents of the magisterium is identified with *distributive* and *legal* justice inasmuch as it regulates the relations between the rulers and the ruled within a nation, a state, a society. There is as yet no clear awareness that social justice *transcends* the dimensions of a self-contained society and has supranational, supra-statal, international, intercontinental, worldwide, planetary, and interplanetary dimensions. On the other hand, the concept of solidarity, although not identical with it, comes closer and closer to the concept of social justice.

This development has only become clear since the Second World War, in recent years, and is primarily bound up with the great advances made in at least two fields: in the *mass media* (press, radio, television), by means of which the entire human race has become aware that injustices (imbalance, discrimination) affect not only individuals but also nations and continents; in a *new mentality* that regards our globe as a shared "village," a single home for the whole human race. Today we are all more or less one community, equally protected, equally threatened. The great credit for this must go to the United Nations and CSCE, as we have seen; to the sensitization of the church to the problem of social justice with its ever-stronger emphasis on its social teaching. This, transcending national and continental boundaries, has made it possible not only for Christians but also for all people of goodwill to see and acknowledge the Catholic church's leading role in this field. What is important, however, for our subject is that in contemporary pontifical documents we find justice, charity, solidarity, and sharing linked together more and more, though without any blending of the concepts or weakening of the concept of justice as such. It is taken for granted that without love/charity there is neither peace, nor true justice worthy of the human person, nor respect for one's neighbor. Love/charity allows us to see things as they are, but it is not a substitute for the virtue of justice. The documents are more and more insistent on the duty of the baptized to operate on the basis of the virtue of justice, so as to achieve it always and everywhere, with new qualitative stress—i.e., more and more in the personalized and personalistic, biblical and theological sense.

There is still debate over the *nature* of social justice. There are three main opinions: (1) It is a new form of legal justice, inasmuch as it regulates the social, economic, and political relations between the ruled and the rulers, nowadays not only on the national plane but on the international plane as well. The objection to this is that it regulates not only those sorts relations but intercontinental, planetary, and interplanetary ones also. Evidently it goes well beyond classic legal justice. (2) It is a new form of legal and distributive justice at once. The

previous answer goes for this view also. (3) It is a new fourth form of proportionate justice at the world level. The reasoning runs as follows: (*a*) Here we have a *new moral principle*, which transcends the principles of the three classic "justices" by requiring an equitable distribution of wealth between the social, national, international, and worldwide groups. (*b*) There is also a *new moral criterion* for this *equity:* the right/duty to a decent human life in the worldwide and planetary sense; the right/duty to a sharing in economic, social, political, and cultural development; the right/duty to contribute to the *common good* of nations, continents, the world. Today particularly, account is taken of profits, salaries, conflicts between rich and poor, solidarity, tolerance, charity, subsidiarity, interdependence, sharing, social injustice, violence, terrorism, environmental and ecological problems, as well as problems about energy, disarmament, rejection of total war, and not least the idea of creating a new economically and politically united world (*Sollicitudo* 11–26, 27–34, 35–40).

On the negative side, social justice condemns all social-economic-political *systems*, with their ideologies, that in one way or another manipulate and oppress individuals, groups, and nations. Systems that have been condemned include *liberalism* and *communism* by Pope Pius XI in *Quadragesimo Anno* (1931; n. 101) and *Divini Redemptoris* (1937; n. 8); Marxist ideology by Pope John Paul II in *Laborem Exercens* (1981; n. 11); the *two blocs*, i.e., liberal capitalism and Marxist collectivism by Pope John Paul II in *Sollicitudo Rei Socialis* (1987; n. 22).

What is required hence is a world based on *solidarity*, on *kinship*, a virtue that has its source in real human love and supernatural charity. On this at once human and Christian basis, the three greatest present-day social and theological-moral problems await solution at the world level: (1) *The future of work.* In the world situation the ever-increasing number of unemployed, which in the Western industrialized states alone amounts to some forty million, contributes to the most serious existential-moral problem of growing poverty in an affluent world. (2) *The dignity of human life and survival.* This issue has specific reference to the environment and the ecological situation, and to nuclear energy and nuclear and chemical weapons. (3) *common responsibility* for the Third and Fourth Worlds (see Schasching 1989:3:1455–1456). So these and similar problems today can only be solved with social justice, which debouches into solidarity, kinship, love and charity, where Christians are called to give a more telling, concrete example by the way they live.

8. Social Justice in the Encyclical *Sollicitudo Rei Socialis*

It has been objected that the *material* of this encyclical is too economic-social—in fact, for the first time ever almost exclusively so in a papal encyclical. How can this be a subject for theology? True, this is the first novelty about *Sollicitudo*, but everything is presented actually in a theological light. The second novelty is the extending of social justice to the entire planet, with the demands of interdependence. The third new thing about it is the identifying of development with peace; in fact, there is a combining of justice-development-peace. With this, the genuine development of social justice has taken on an indisputable urgency in *Sollicitudo*, under sociological, biblical, theological, and ecclesial aspects.

The *sociological aspect* of the present-day world is very disappointing, pessimistically unstable. There are many "short-comings and obscurities" (25) in its development: economic and social disparities (north/south), the birth of the Fourth World, a growing contempt for human rights throughout the world, a dramatic crisis over housing, unemployment and underemployment, a huge international debt, a paradoxical contrast between overdevelopment and underdevelopment (28), temptations to and yieldings to despair, to pessimism, to passivity, to cowardice. There is hence a prevalent economic, cultural, and political underdevelopment, but there is also a human and spiritual underdevelopment (15). The encyclical examines the *causes* that make the situation worse in developing countries. Among others, it mentions the following: the perversity of certain economic, financial, and social mechanisms (16); the "logic of blocs" with four opposing elements: political, ideological, economic, military (20). Consequently, all humanity is aware of still living under a perpetual threat of open and total war. For today the merest handful of people run the whole world. The richer, technologically and economically more advanced North outweighs the South twice over (21). There is a temptation for the leader nations to withdraw into isolation, which the common good of humanity cannot permit (23). We may list further different *deviations of development*, such as arms production and the arms race, the product of the "logic of blocs" (23–24); the presence of millions of refugees because of discrimination, persecution, and so on, who have been deprived of home, employment, family, homeland, and will to live (24); the phenomenon of terrorism and hostage-taking (24); the systematic campaign to reduce the birthrate (25); drugs, the typical form of escapism of our day, which represents an insidious distortion of the concept of personal and social development (26). But there are also *reasons for hope*, such as the growing awareness of the dignity of the person of every individual; the growing conviction of a radical interdependence; a common concern for peace, which is something new in the world; ecological and environmental concern, which is gradually sensitizing politicians and people in general; and the growing awareness in the Third World of a certain self-sufficiency in food and of guaranteeing sources of employment.

The *biblical/theological aspect* clearly tells us two things: that undirected and limitless progress in the Enlightenment sense—a mere accumulation of goods and services—leading to consumerism and crass materialism, is not true development. True development concerns the *integral* and total *person* with all essential relationships. The human person is the parameter of development, not merely in the lay and profane sense but in the interior sense that it is innate in the specific nature of the human person, which is a corporeal and spiritual creature, a finite creature but, inasmuch as the image of God, kin to the infinite God. All creation ought to be subordinated to the divine image of humanity and its vocation to love/charity, which Love, the Creator, has given it (29). Humanity's vocation is not merely an earthly one; it has immortal dimensions. This vocation is also to orderly development, as Genesis says (1:26–30; 2:15). So humans must not allow themselves to be distracted by earthly things to the point of forgetting about their eschatological destination. In this sense, even according to Christian tradition before Vatican II. The human person has three moral duties: of all to all, promotion of human rights and freedoms, respect for the creation (34).

The *theological/moral aspect* involves two points: the structures of sin and the way of conversion (36). These *sinful structures*, in very different forms and differently nuanced, have causes of an economic, political, and moral nature, particularly in two aggravated forms: the exclusive desire for profit and the thirst for power. These can contaminate everything. CONVERSION, although it may be very arduous, demands social justice in the sense already explained—i.e., justice personalized in solidarity, charity, fellowship. Here once again we find justice being transformed into solidarity, and this into love/charity, the root of which is God—Love, God—trinitarian fellowship. Here we touch the identity of the reality justice/ solidarity/love/charity/fellowship/faith. The Christian hence lives a commitment to justice as faith-event, as one "created according to the likeness of God in true righteousnes and holiness" (see Eph 4:24). Justice lived by the Christian today is the credible sign of faith and of the sincerity of his evangelization, far from any double-talk or Pharisaism. Thus, the fact becomes clear that Christian morality and spirituality are not two different things but the same thing: to do justice and to be just, without measure or limitation, according to the measure of love/charity, which is measureless. We do not deny that these disciplines may, from the scientific point of view, be differently structured, but the life is one, has no plus and minus, only plus.

Therefore everyone is a brother or sister (Mt 25:40, 45) who not only has rights and basic equality as the image of God, in the likeness of the perfect image of the incarnate Word (GS 22), but has also been ransomed by Christ's blood and is under the activity of the Holy Spirit. One therefore must be loved, even if one is an *enemy* (Mt 5:44; Lk 6:27–35), with the same love with which the Lord loves that person. Only by loving like this can one become just, not with one's own justice but with the justice bestowed by God.

Under the *pastoral/catechetic* aspect, after what has been said so far, it becomes clear that the church's social teaching is not a third way between liberal capitalism and Marxist collectivism but is part of the church's spiritual mission. The church has no other task than the salvation and sanctification of human beings, be it in the personal or communal dimension. This means that the church's mission is to the integral person with all its relationships and in its earthly and eschatological vocation. With this, it is also clear that the encyclical *Sollicitudo Rei Socialis* is absolutely up-to-date in its interpretation of social justice, indicating and developing eminently theological lines of sight for the one part and pastoral/catechetic ones for the other.

9. Conclusion

Having followed the course of development of the concept of justice from the profane notion of the times of Middle Eastern culture and nomadism to the religious concept of OT revelation and the higher religious concept of NT revelation, passing by way of the philosophical/ juridical concept of the Greeks and Romans and on to the scholastics' concept and that of the manuals, and examining the Enlightenment's concept of justice and that of Vatican II, we have traced a *sinusoid*: from the profane to the religious, to the spiritual, to the philosophical/juridical, to the juridical strongly stressed, to the religious, social, personalistic again.

Since Vatican II, two phases may be discerned: the first covers the first ten years from 1965 to 1975, during which the concepts justice, charity, and faith (the turning point of Vatican II notwithstanding) were not as yet treated much together. Justice was usually presented as social-economic-political, even after the synod document of 1971. The second phase covers the past fifteen years, that is, from 1975 to today. A new turning point in depth occurred with Paul VI's apostolic exhortation *Evangelii Nuntiandi* (8 December 1975), particularly nn. 17–41, where *justice* is personalized once more and enriched with biblical/theological aspects from now on in a continuing process of drawing closer—indeed of assimilation, between *faith* and *justice*.

> Evangelization would not be complete if it did not take account of the unceasing interplay of the Gospel and of man's concrete life both personal and social. This is why evangelization involves an explicit message, adapted to the different situations constantly being realized,

about the rights and duties of every human being, about family life, about international life, peace, justice and development—a message especially energetic today about liberation. (*EN 29*)

Bibl.: S. SCHMIDT, "S. Pauli 'iustitia Dei' notione iustitiae, quae in V.T. et apud S. Paulum habetur, dilucidata," *VD* 37 (1959): 97–105; J. M. CASABÒ SUQUÉ, "La justicia en el Antiguo Testamento," *Strom* 25 (1969): 3–20; E. CHIAVACCI, *Principi di morale sociale: Morale sociale générale* (Bologna, 1971); id., *Teologia morale*, vol. 3/1: *Teologia morale e vita economica* (Assisi, 1986); J. DUPONT, *Les béatitudes*, 3 vols. (Bruges, 1958–73), 3:65–90; J. ALFARO, *Teologia della giustizia* (Rome, 1973); L. DI PINTO, *Volontà di Dio e legge antica nell'Epistola agli Ebrei: Contributo ai fondamenti biblici della teologia morale* (Naples, 1976); É. HAMEL, "I fondamenti dell'etica cristiana in ordine alla giustizia sociale: fede e giustizia sociale," *Comm* 38 (1978): 74–85; id., "Iustitia et jura hominum in Sacra Scriptura," Investigatio biblico-teologica," *Periodica* 69 (1980): 201–17; id., "Fondement théologique des droits de l'homme," *Seminarium* 23 (1983): 309–18; id., "The Foundations of Human Rights in Biblical Theology, Following the Orientations of *Gaudium et Spes*," in R. Latourelle, ed., *Vatican II: Assessment and Perspectives Twenty-five Years After (1962–1987)*, 3 vols. (New York, 1989), 2:460–78; C. M. MARTINI, *Evangelizare pauperibus* (Brescia, 1978); K. DEMMER, "Christliches Ethos und Menschenrechte," *Greg* 60 (1979): 453–79; I. FUČEK, "Il fondamento dei diritti umani nei documenti internazionali," *CivCatt* 4 (1982): 548–57; id., *Giustizia alla luce della fede e dell'esperienza* (Rome, 1989); S. MOSSO, *Il problema della giustizia e il messagio cristiano* (Casale Monferrato, 1982); V. ROSSI AGBANOU, *Les discours eschatologiques de Matthieu 24–25: Tradition et rédaction* (Paris, 1983); var., "Human Dignity and Human Rights," *Greg* 65 (1984); L. LORENZETTI, "Etica sociale cristiana," in T. Goffi and G. Piana, eds., *Corso di morale*, vol. 4: *Koinonia: Etica della vita sociale* (Brescia, 1985), 9–82; var., "Instrumenta communicationis socialis in formatione sacerdotali," *Seminarium* 37 (1986); F. REJON MORENO, *Teologia moral desde los pobres: Planteamientos morales de la teologia latinoamericana* (Madrid, 1986); G. OERSTREICH, *Geschichte der Menschenrechte und Grundfreiheiten in Umriss* (2nd ed.; Berlin, 1987); J. PUNT, *Die Idee der Menschenrechte: Ihre geschichtliche Entwicklung und ihre Rezeption durch die moderne katholische Sozialverkündigung* (Paderborn/Munich/Vienna/Zurich, 1987); P. PAVAN, *L'Enciclica "Pacem in Terris": A venticinque anni dalla publicazione* (Rome, 1988); J. BRYAN HEHIR, "John Paul II: Continuity and Change in the Social Teaching of the Church," in C. E. Curran and R. A. McCormick, eds., *Official Catholic Social Teaching*, Readings in Moral Theology 5 (New York/Mahwah, N.J., 1986), 247–63; D. HOLLENBACH, "Global Human Rights: An Interpretation of the Contemporary Catholic Understanding," in ibid., 366–83; var., *Solidarietà, nuovo nome della pace: Studi sull' Enciclica "Sollicitudo Rei Socialis" di Giovanni Paolo II offerti da don Giuseppe Gemellaro*, ed. M. Toso (Turin, 1988); Pont. Univ. Lateranense, *Le ragioni della speranza: Studi sull'enciclica Sollicitudo rei socialis* (Vatican City, 1988); E. BIFFI, "Cinque Letture dello sviluppo dei Popoli: Guida introduttiva all'Enciclica 'Sollicitudo rei socialis,'" in ibid., 137–73; J. KRAŠOVEC, *La justice (SDQ) de Dieu dans la Bible hébraïque et l'interprétation juive et chrétienne* (Freiburg/Göttingen, 1988) (abundant bibl.); J. N. SCHASCHING, "From the Class War to the Culture of Solidarity: A Fundamental Theme of the Church's Social Teaching," in R. Latourelle, ed., *Vatican II: Assessment and Perspectives Twenty-five Years After (1962–1987)*, 3 vols. (New York, 1989), 3:466–78; var., "De dottrina sociali Ecclesiae in formazione sacerdotali," *Seminarium* 41 (1989); M. MATTÉ, "Diritti e valori nella fattoria," *Il Regno-Attualità* 4 (1989): 97–99.

Ivan FUČEK

JUSTICE IN THE VISION OF THE MAGNIFICAT

This article studies the theme of justice in light of the interpretive key provided by the Magnificat (Lk 1:47-55). The Magnificat is a lyrical expression of a personal event: Mary is speaking of herself and her destiny as a historical individual. She contemplates her own history and that of humanity in the light of God the savior, the Almighty who does wonders with our creaturely "feebleness." Mary is the true Israel, in whom the old and new covenants are inseparably united. She is the people of God that bears fruit thanks to the merciful power of God.

1. Mary Looks at the World through the Eyes of God

> He has shown strength with his arm;
> he has scattered the proud in the thoughts of their hearts.
> He has brought down the powerful from their thrones,

and lifted up the lowly;
he has filled the hungry with good things,
and sent the rich away empty.

(vv. 51–53)

This second part, so forceful, almost harsh, so rich in antitheses, makes the Magnificat at once the most refined and the strongest song in the NT. J. Moltmann notes that in the Bible the most robust hymns are always sung by women: Miriam (Ex 15:21), Judith (Jdt 16), Deborah (Jgs 5), and Hannah (1 Sm 2).

As Mary looks at the world, she sees it with the eyes of God, strong and merciful eyes, and tells us how God intervenes in the history of human beings. After recalling the mighty works that God has accomplished for Israel, she points out a kind of constant in the divine action: the Father's love for the lowly, the poor, the oppressed. In choosing Mary for his plan of salvation God illustrates the "wonderful rule" according to which weakness becomes the preferred instrument of his power (1 Cor 1:27).

Mary, on whom God has looked with favor, is the privileged locus of all the reversals he brings about in the world; she is at the heart of the revolution caused by divine love and the divine work of liberation. She embodies the power of God that is manifested in weakness, and she exemplifies the law of the inversion of the values of the world in favor of those of the gospel. This is why she is the hope of the poor and the oppressed.

Mary is the "strong woman" who gives us a glimpse of the historical and social ways in which God carries out his plan of salvation, disappointing the expectations of the rich and the powerful and effecting his salvation by means of the poor and the humble. The Magnificat is a serene and objective challenge to the values that the human beings of every age glorify—power, knowledge, and possessions—in favor of the poor and lowly, who are raised up and exalted and of whom Mary is the perfect example.

The Magnificat echoes the canticle of Hannah, mother of Samuel (1 Sm 2:1-10), which has as its main theme the reversal of values as a sign of God at work. Hannah's song shows us a God who reverses the situation of all those who take themselves for gods and who constantly oppress their neighbor. It already contains the gospel in which Jesus embodies the care his Father takes of the hungry, the lowly, and the

oppressed. In showing us a God who chooses and loves the poor, Jesus offers the grace of a liberating redemption that will transform human history. The liberation of which the Magnificat sings is a liberation effected by God: it goes beyond the social level, even if it does have consequences there. It takes place without hatred and is based on love. God offers his mercy even to the unjust who repent and turn to him (Zacchaeus the publican, and others); once liberated, these individuals are advanced to the status of the lowly and the poor and become more like Christ.

If God in his mercy "scatters" the proud, it is in order that they may cease to be inhuman; if he brings down the mighty, it is in order that they may turn their power into service; if he sends the rich away, it is in order that they may share with the poor.

If God lifts up the lowly and fills the hungry, it is not in order that they may become proud, rich, and oppressors in their turn, nor that they may avenge themselves on those who made them suffer.

2. Mary's Prophetic Vision

The central section of the Magnificat is made up of verbs in the past definite tense, which signifies an action already accomplished. "He has scattered the proud in the thoughts of their hearts. He has brought down the powerful from their thrones, and lifted up the lowly. He has filled the hungry with good things, and sent the rich away empty."

Exegetes have stressed the prophetic power with which Mary sings of these actions as completed and regards as fully accomplished events that are beginning almost imperceptibly with her and will reach completion only at the end of time. In her prophetic faith she sees in advance, as it were, the definitive fulfillment of the promises of salvation once given to the patriarchs and now offered to the entire human race. Mary announces the final liberation, even though for the moment she sees only its very modest beginnings. After the annunciation and the nativity, nothing seems to have changed: the powerful are still in their places; the oppressed are still oppressed; yet salvation is being given in silence and obscurity to the humble and the poor who are able to see—Mary, Elizabeth, and the shepherds. Mary nonetheless already glimpses the final outcome. She sings of liberation as something past and regards it as accomplished in the eyes of God, who transcends time and guarantees the future. She sings of the great works of God, prophetically proclaiming even now their full future accomplishment. All that humanity hopes for will come to pass: Mary is sure of this and tells us of it. This is why the Magnificat contains not only a salutary threat and therefore an offer of salvation to the mighty and the rich, but also a message of hope for the poor and the oppressed.

3. The Magnificat, Song of Social Liberation?

In his encyclical *Mother of the Redeemer* (*Redemptoris Mater*) John Paul II invites us to reread and make present application of this hymn, which is both the gentlest and the most forceful in the NT. The gentlest because Mary's poetic inspiration leads her to sing of the God who is faithful and merciful; the most forceful because it denounces the false greatnesses of this world, the knowledge turned proud, the violent power that oppresses, the riches that close the heart. In short, the hymn reveals God's preferential love for the poor and the humble.

From this profession of faith in which Mary's personal experience and her interior ecstasy show through, the church learns that it cannot separate the truth that God saves, from the manifestation of his preferential love for the poor and the humble. In this way the church avoids the danger of focusing in a unilateral way on praise of Mary that would set aside her dynamic attitude of Mary in the "secular" sphere of justice. It is significant that Luke puts on Mary's lips the first song of liberation in the NT.

Our age needs a theology of freedom and liberation that will faithfully echo Mary's Magnificat as preserved in the memory of the church.

> Mary is totally dependent upon God and completely directed toward him and, at the side of her Son, she is the most perfect image of freedom and of the liberation of humanity and of the universe. It is to her as mother and model that the church must look in order to understand in its completeness the meaning of her own mission. (John Paul II, *Redemptoris Mater*, no. 37)

Why must the church thus look to Mary? Because the church in its fullness was present in her whose yes allowed the church to be born.

The church must preach the Magnificat in its totality as it came from the mouth of Mary, without either watering it down or forcing its meaning: with its salutary threats to the proud, the powerful, and the wealthy, and with its hopes for the lowly, the poor, and the oppressed.

The liberation of which Mary sings is a liberation that God effects, but this fact does not give us permission to lapse into smug resignation in the face of human misery. The God who "fills the hungry with good things" asks us to imitate him. Because he fills, we too must fill in our own way and as we find it possible. "He has filled the hungry with good things" cannot be separated from "I was hungry and you gave me food" (Mt 25:35).

Luke, who has given us Mary's Magnificat, emphasizes in the Acts of the Apostles the enduring concern for the poor in the primitive church.

The Magnificat must be sung not to the tune of the *Internationale* or the *Marseillaise*, but to the tune of Mary, e.g., without any spirit of vengeance or hatred. The prophets sternly reminded the rich of their responsibilities to God and the poor, and they made themselves the spokesmen of the poor, not in order to rouse the poor to vengeance or hatred but simply to represent them before the powerful and the rich, whom they reminded of the demands of justice and love.

Like the prophets before him, Jesus does not limit the grace of salvation to a single social category; he is mindful of all and wills the salvation of all. His message to the rich—his invitation to them to share their wealth, the serious threats of what will happen if they do not share—will be salutary for them if when touched by grace they decide at last to share with the impoverished. Thus understood, Jesus' threats to the rich are indirectly good news for the poor!

The evangelical option for the poor is preferential, not exclusive: it does not imply a systematic rejection of others, since the message to the rich has for its purpose to bring them to share and so reduce the great inequalities that exist in the world.

Furthermore, very few people can say that they are completely oppressed and nothing but oppressed. In every oppressed person there is almost always a sleeping oppressor. There is no real liberation without liberation from hatred. Without the liberation of the heart, which God alone can effect, other liberations are transitory. Only those who are liberated can in turn bring about a true and integral liberation.

The preferential option for the poor has reconciliation for its aim, and not division or elimination. As Paul VI reminded us, it must not be one group *against* others, nor one *without* others, but one *with* others.

Furthermore, the book of the Acts of the Apostles, in which the law of the Spirit that is written in hearts (Jer 31:31) is seen triumphing, describes social reversals that are peaceful, not violent. In the new covenant it is now the Holy Spirit who is the father of the poor, as we sing in the hymn *Veni Sancte Spiritus* (see Jb 29:15). By his action in the depth of hearts where he urges Christians to a spontaneous sharing, the Spirit already brings about a peaceful, non-violent reversal of situations. Under the action of the Spirit, the first Christians themselves righted social imbalances, leading oppressors to understand that they must no longer oppress and the rich that they must share. Under the action of the Spirit at work in hearts, the reversal of situations became part of the general process of interiorization and was often effected quietly and without violence. The magi of whom the Gospel of Matthew speaks (2:1–12) are a perfect example of such a reversal. When touched by grace, they open their hearts and their hands. Their knowledge has led them to adore the child king; their power is placed at his service, and their possessions become a freely given homage to the king of kings.

All the spiritual dispositions that had characterized the poor of the old covenant and were to be canonized in the beatitudes, converge in Mary and make up the spiritual portrait that she sketches of herself in the Magnificat: joy, service of God, reverential fear, awareness of her own weakness, sense of justice, solidarity with her people, openness and readiness to serve the divine plan.

The Magnificat shows us a Mary who is "not a passively submissive woman or one whose religion alienates her, but one who sings of a God who is savior and liberator, who lifts up the humble and the oppressed, and if need arises, pulls down the mighty from their thrones." It provides us in her with "a perfect model of the disciple of the Lord: one who builds the earthly and temporal city, but who is also a pilgrim hastening toward the heavenly and lasting city; a promotor of justice, who liberates the oppressed, and of charity, who helps the needy, but, above all, an active witness to the love that builds up Christ in hearts" (Paul VI, *Marialis Cultus*, no. 37).

These two articles on justice are meant to complement each other, even though the tone and method are different. The first is concerned with the historical development of the biblical, philosophical, theological, and juridical concept of justice, while the second, which comes under the heading of narrative theology, highlights the model of justice that is set forth in the Magnificat. In fact, the Magnificat is the only place in the entire history of salvation and of humanity, where God's positions on justice in every age are described and synthesized. Thus the biblical concept of justice, which includes all other perspectives, is the hyphen, as it were, linking the old self without Christ and the new self in Christ.

Bibl.: É. HAMEL, "La donna e la promozione della giustizia nel Magnificat," *RdT* 18 (1977): 417–34; R. SCHNACKENBURG, "Il Magnificat, la sua spiritualità e la sua teologia," in *La vita cristiana* (Milan, 1977), 215–34; É. HAMEL, "Le Magnificat, la femme et la promotion de la justice," *Cahiers marials* 113 (1978): 157–75; id., "Le Magnificat et le renversement des situations," *Greg* 60 (1979): 55–84; J. DUPONT, "Le Magnificat comme discours sur Dieu," *NRT* 102 (1980): 321–43; H. MUÑOZ, "Il Magnificat," *Parola, Spirito e Vita*, no. 6 (1982): 100–105; E. PERETTO, "Magnificat," *NDM*, 853–65; C. M. MARTINI, "La prophétie du Magnificat," in *Sur les Chemins du Seigneur* (Paris, 1987), 198–204; H. Urs VON BALTHASAR, *Marie pour aujourd'hui* (Paris, 1988), 63–68.

Édouard HAMEL

K

KERYGMA, CATECHESIS, PARENESIS

These three terms designate the forms and stages in a single process of evangelization that has been followed since the beginning of the church's existence. It will be helpful, therefore, to group them in order better to define and distinguish them.

1. The Greek word *kērygma* is a noun derived from the verb *kēryssein* and signifies broadly the preaching of the good news of the salvation wrought by Christ. It represents the first impact of the gospel, and the sound of it has echoed down the centuries. Kerygma is essentially a matter of proclaiming the event of salvation and of leading human beings to conversion and faith.

Because this event is unparalleled and has endless repercussions, its proclamation resembles the cry of a herald announcing an unprecedented victory. Kerygma represents a bursting through and has an expansive power. Thus on Pentecost Peter raises his voice and tells the crowd of the good news of salvation through Christ; his intention is to make the news public and official (Acts 2:14). This intention is manifested in many ways. Peter and Paul address crowds (Acts 3:12; 13:16; 15–22). Their message spreads throughout Jewish and Gentile circles. They multiply their appeals for attention and their instructions: listen (Acts 2:14, 22), repent (Acts 2:38), save yourselves (Acts 2:40). Everything the apostles do shows their burning desire to bring the word of God everywhere and to all. Under the influence of the Spirit they are gripped by a kind of fervor that compels them to proclaim, to evangelize. How could they remain silent? The fullness of time has come "now," "today." Nothing more important can ever happen in the future. All human beings are called to salvation. No one can remain neutral before this fact.

The unifying element in all the short formulations of the kerygma is the person of Jesus, identified now as Christ and Lord (Acts 8:5; 19:13; 1 Cor 1:23). If we move beyond these summary formulas to such examples of preaching as the addresses in Acts (chaps. 2, 3, 5, 10, 13), we see the kerygma enriched by inclusion of the following points: the time of fulfillment has come; this final period is characterized by ministry; the passion, death, resurrection, and glorification of Jesus. Salvation is wrought through faith in Christ and through baptism, which effects the forgiveness of sins and bestows the Spirit. The kerygma establishes an indissoluble bond between the Jesus-event and its salvific significance.

The kerygma does not belong to the past; it is not something outdated. Today as in the past, the impact of the good news is to disturb and shake people throughout the entire world. This proclamation of the good news by the church (*LG* 26) makes the event of salvation permanently present. The kerygma must be heard today in order that Jesus may be acknowledged and identified as Christ, Lord, universal Savior, and Center of history, who invites every human being to conversion and faith, which is the assent of the whole person in which he or she surrenders to Christ, who gave himself without reserve — in other words, a transforming, operative faith (*DV* 5).

2. The initial impression made by the good news is normally followed by *catechesis*, which brings out the content of the kerygma in explicit detail. Catechesis offers more-developed instructions for new converts, explanations of a more didactic kind in which the Scriptures are explained in light of the Christian event. Thus the first Christians "devoted themselves to the apostles' teaching" (Acts 2:42). The apostles were "standing in the temple and teaching the people" (Acts 5:25, 28). They also appointed seven deacons in order that they themselves might devote themselves exclusively "to prayer and to serving the word" (Acts 6:4). Paul remained in Corinth for a year and a half, "teaching the word of God among them [i.e., among 'my people']" (Acts 18:11).

The kerygma continues, however, to be the point of departure and of constant reference for catechesis. Thus the explanation of the sacraments and the principles governing the moral life have meaning only in light of the paschal event.

Beginning in the second and third centuries, catechesis usually meant teaching by which adults were prepared for baptism. Subsequently, when the church was given its freedom, catechesis increasingly acquired a specific form of its own. We may think, e.g., of the catechetical instructions of Cyril of Jerusalem and Theodore of Mopsuestia, Ambrose's explanations of the sacraments of initiation (baptism, confirmation, Eucharist), Gregory of Nyssa's lengthy *Oratio catechetica,* and Augustine's *De catechizandis rudibus.* There was thus a movement toward forms of teaching that anticipated our modern or contemporary catechisms, such as those of Luther, Peter Canisius, the Council of Trent, various episcopal conferences, and Vatican II. The purpose of these is not only to prepare persons for baptism but to deepen the faith of believers.

3. *Parenesis* differs from catechesis only by the direction it takes (it deals with moral conduct) and its tone (exhortation). Thus, several letters of Paul begin with an explanation of doctrine and end with parenesis (Rom 12–15; Gal 5–6; Eph 4–6).

In the OT, Israel received the Decalogue in order that it might live in a way befitting its covenant with the thrice-holy God. Similarly in the NT, since Christians are called by God to become his children, they must live in accordance with this vocation. Their call to follow Christ has as a necessary corollary a life like that of Christ. Call is accompanied by commandments. "If you are led by the Spirit, you are not subject to the law" (Gal 5:18) but are "under grace" (Rom 6:14). To live in Christ means to adopt Christ's manner of life, his views, and his tastes. The exhortations, the calls for vigilance and the practice of the virtues, and the particular precepts contained in parenesis all make the general commandment of love more specific and apply it to the detail of everyday life. Openness to Love does not obviate the need of setting out a number of channel markers, lest Christians get lost in the fog and risk shipwreck. Parenesis is therefore not mere moralism but rather realism about life in Christ, which, though it transcends norms in its thrust and its objective, does not therefore lack norms.

Bibl.: Concerning kerygma: K. H. RENGSTORF, *Apostolat und Predigtamt* (2nd ed.; Stuttgart, 1954); G. FRIEDRICH, "Κήρυγμα," *TDNT* 3:714–18; D. GRASSO, *L'Annuncio della salvezza* (Naples, 1965); R.

LATOURELLE, *Theology of Revelation* (Staten Island, N.Y., 1966), 46–81; id., *Finding Jesus through the Gospels* (New York, 1979), 193–98; F. X. MURPHY, "Catéchèse," *NCE* 3:208; id., "Kerygma," *NCE* 8:167–68; K. RAHNER, *La salvezza nella Chiesa* (Rome/Brescia, 1969); P. SABINI, "Kerygma," *Dizionario di Pastorale* (Assisi, 1980), 297–300.

Concerning catechesis: G. BARDY, "Catéchèse," *Cath* 2:646 and bibliography.

René LATOURELLE

KINGDOM OF GOD

The most historical datum about Jesus' life is the symbol that dominated his whole preaching, the reality that gave meaning to all his activities—the kingdom of God. The Synoptic Gospels summarize Jesus' teaching and preaching with the lapidary sentence: "The time is fulfilled, and the kingdom of God has come near; repent, and believe in the good news" (Mk 1:14–15; Mt 4:17; Lk 4:43). The phrase occurs 122 times in the Gospel and 90 times on the lips of Jesus.

Jesus preached the kingdom of God, not himself (K. Rahner), yet in his own teaching Jesus figures as the representative (Lk 17:20–21), the revealer (Mk 4:11–12; Mt 11:25–26), the champion (Mk 3:27), the initiator (Mt 11:12), the instrument (Mt 12:28), the mediator (Mk 2:18–19), and the bearer (Mt 11:5) of the kingdom of God (Beasley-Murray 1986: 296). The kingdom is not only the central theme of Jesus' preaching, the reference point of most of his parables, and the subject of a large number of his sayings; it is also the content of his symbolic actions, which form such a large a part of his ministry, e.g., his table fellowship with tax collectors and sinners, his healings, and exorcisms. In his communion with outcasts Jesus lived out the kingdom, demonstrating in action God's unconditional love for undeserving sinners (Soares-Prabhu 1981:584).

The death and resurrection of Jesus put his message into a new context, with the result that in Paul and John the kingdom of God is no longer directly at the center of the Christian preaching. "Jesus, the preacher of the Kingdom of God, became after Easter Christ preached" (R. Bultmann, *Glauben und Verstehen,* I [Tübingen, 1933], 101,251). This is not an early falsification of the message. There are two central topics in the NT: the kingdom of God and Jesus the Christ.

It is not easy to define precisely what the term "kingdom of God" means. In the course of the history of theology the interpretation of this phrase has often changed according to the situation and the spirit of the age. The word "reign" or "kingdom" is an archaic phrase that does not evoke a resonance in our present experience of reality. The expression needs to be retranslated in order to render its meaning. The question concerning the kingdom message of Jesus is therefore: How can we bridge the hermeneutical gulf between what the kingdom of God meant in the teaching of Jesus and what it can mean for us today? (Perrin 1976:32–56).

In the biblical and theological discussion on the kingdom in modern times we can distinguish three foci: the kingdom as concept, the kingdom as symbol and a new way of focusing, and the kingdom as related to liberation. Each approach raises different questions, which should be seen as complementary.

Kingdom as Concept

The first approach may be described as "author-centered." What did the authors of the Bible mean with this concept? To treat the phrase "kingdom of God" as a concept assumes that behind it we find one clear and constant idea. For example, the kingdom of God is the final, eschatological and decisive intervention of God in the history of Israel in order to fulfill the promises made to the prophets. The concern is to find out what the phrase meant in the teaching of Jesus, although Jesus himself never defined the kingdom in precise terms.

Kingdom as Symbol

The second may be referred to as a "text-centered" approach. It aims to explore what the text itself means and says today. Viewing the kingdom as a symbol opens the phrase to evoke a whole series of ideas, since a symbol by its definition provides a set of meanings that cannot be exhausted or adequately expressed by one referent only (Perrin 1976:33). As a symbol, kingdom evoked in Israel the remembrance of God's activity, be it as Creator of the cosmos, Creator of Israel in history, or ultimately the expectation of his final intervention at the end

of history. It is God acting in history on behalf of his people and ultimately on behalf of creation as a whole that is the underlying referent to which all of Jesus' teaching and preaching refers. The expression stands for a rich and multifaceted religious experience. It expresses a personal relationship and is even linked to geographical areas.

Kingdom as Liberation

The third approach that has emerged in recent times may be called a "reader-centered" approach. Liberation theologians appeal to the kingdom of God in order to help them articulate and deal with the fundamental question of liberation theology: the relationship between the kingdom of God and the praxis of liberation in history. "We are dealing here with the classic question of the relation between faith and human existence, between faith and social reality, between faith and political action, or in other words, between the kingdom of God and the building up of this world" (Gutiérrez 1973:45). What is at stake is the world-transforming dimension of the kingdom. Here the question is: What does the phrase "kingdom of God" have to say to the situation in which we find ourselves now, a situation marked by utter oppression and exploitation. This approach, while not denying the others, brings out very strongly the dynamic aspect of the kingdom. The message of Jesus aims at transforming all reality rather than offering us new information and ideas about it. It intends to recover the historical dimension of God's message and to move that message away from all abstract universalism so that the biblical message may be more responsive to the world of oppression and to the structures of an unjust social order (Fuellenbach 1989:37–48).

Thus, the first approach tries to get "behind the text"; the second stays "with the text"; and the third stands "in front of the text." The discussion in terms of the first focus, the kingdom as concept, was carried out largely in Europe (Germany and Britain); the second, the kingdom as symbol, in North America; and the third focus, kingdom and liberation, emerged from Latin America.

1. The Kingdom of God in the Old Testament

The phrase "kingdom of God" does not occur in the OT, but it is said nine times that God rules in a kingdom. Most exegetes insist that the abstract term *malkût* is associated with Yahweh, Israel's God, only very late in the OT and denotes the act of God. The emphasis is on kingly rule and domination rather than on a territory or a place. It is therefore regarded as a religious idea. In recent times this thesis has been challenged, as the notion of kingdom has been approached not only from a historical-critical viewpoint but also from a social-political one (Lohfink 1987:33–86) The faith of the OT rests on two certainties: first, that God has come in the past and that he has intervened in favor of his people; second, the firm hope that God will come anew in the future in order to accomplish his purpose for the world he has made. As Martin Buber put it: "The realization of the all embracing rulership of God is the Proton and Eschaton of Israel" (Beasley-Murray 1986:17).

The following can be regarded as the basic elements of the notion of the kingdom of God in the OT. (1) God is king over all creation and over Israel in particular, on the basis of the covenant. (2) This kingship over Israel is experienced in a particular way in the liturgical celebration, i.e., in the cult. (3) There is hope of a final and decisive coming of Yahweh on behalf of his people in the future in order to fulfill his promises made to the fathers and the prophets (Schnackenburg 1963:11–74).

What is unique was Israel's experience of Yahweh as Lord of history who acts on behalf of his people; who cares, protects, forgives, heals, and makes a covenant with them. All this becomes part of what it means to say that God is king of Israel and of all the nations. The actual care and presence of God among his people are then expressed in symbols such as father, mother, pastor, bridegroom, and so on. The functions of Yahweh as king who reigns among his people become components of this experience: he creates a people; he organizes its structure; he feeds them and protects them; he directs, corrects, and redeems them; and he imparts justice to them. All this forms the background of the "religious experience" expressed in the symbol kingdom of God (Cabellio 1985:16–18).

2. The Kingdom Message in the New Testament

Jesus never defined the kingdom of God in discursive language. He presented his message of the kingdom in parables, which are to be regarded as "Jesus' choice of the most appropriate vehicle for understanding the Kingdom of God" (Scott 1981:11). They are the preaching itself and should not be looked upon as merely serving the purpose of a lesson that is quite independent of them. Here participation precedes information. The parables have to remain the reference point for understanding the message of the kingdom (Crossan 1973:51–52). The basic content of the kingdom message can be summarized in the following characteristics:

It is "Already" Present and "Yet" to Come

Jesus' own mentality, his teaching and preaching were formed most profoundly by the great prophets of the OT, particularly by Deutero-Isaiah. According to Luke (4:16–21) and Matthew (11:1–6), he understood his mission in the setting of the jubilee tradition announcing the "great year of favor" as the ultimate visitation of God on behalf of his people (Lohfink 1986:223). Jesus proclaimed this final visitation of God not as future, nor as an object of anxious expectation (Lk 3:15), but as having arrived with him. The kingdom has become a present reality; it is "at hand" (Mk 1:14), "in our reach" (Lk 17:21); it demonstrates its effective presence as a liberating force through exorcisms (Mt 12:28), healing, and forgiving of sins.

Although the historical presence of the kingdom in and through the ministry of Jesus is strongly affirmed, the fulfillment of what is now dimly experienced in an anticipatory way is still to come. This creates the tension of the "already" and the "not yet." The emphasis either on the "not yet" or the "already" determines the way the kingdom message of Jesus is seen as affecting this world. If the emphasis is put on the "not yet," the "trials of the kingdom" in the present world stand out and the hope for its final coming becomes the determining factor for action. While no one denies the presence of the kingdom, the emphasis in traditional theology is put on the "not yet," to the detriment of the "already." In the words of Lohfink: "In order to be fair to Jesus' message and practice, one must, more than anything else, hammer out the presence of the *basileia* that Jesus himself maintained" (Lohfink 1989:103).

Although Jesus stood in the tradition of the great prophets, his message is deeply influenced by the apocalyptic expectations of the time. Yet he did not share the pessimism of the apocalyptic writers concerning this world, but he portrays a realistic view of the power of evil. His message of the kingdom of God can be understood only in contrast to the kingdom of evil that is at work in this world. Jesus understood his mission as undoing and overthrowing of the evil powers and bringing a liberation that aims at the end of all evil and the transformation of the whole of creation (Kelber 1974:15–18).

The Kingdom Is a Gracious Gift from God and a Task for Human Beings

Since the kingdom of God is God himself offering his unconditional love to his creatures and giving to each a share in his own life, the kingdom is to be understood as a gracious gift to which we have absolutely no claim. We can accept it only as a love gift from God in gratitude and thanksgiving. This is the main teaching of the growth parables (Mk 4 and Mt 13). One can pray "thy kingdom come" (Mt 6:10), may cry out to God day and night (Lk 18:7), may hold oneself in readiness like the wise virgins (Mt 25:1–13); it is God who "gives" it (Lk 12:31).

However, the gracious character of the kingdom does not make human beings mere passive objects. The parables of the talents (Mt 25:14–30) and the treasure in the field (Mt 13:44) show that human beings are actants of the kingdom as well. Here the kingdom is a pure gift, but also it comes only with incredible risks. The coming of the kingdom of God is totally and completely God's work, but at the same time it is also totally and completely the work of human beings (Lohfink 1989:104–5).

The Religious and Political Dimensions of the Kingdom

The religious character of the kingdom is so evident in Scripture that it does not need special attention. The kingdom transcends this world and aims at the new heaven and the new earth. This aspect, however, is often stressed to the extent that the kingdom has no place in this world anymore. Consequently, the message of Jesus becomes totally a private affair, and the social shape of the kingdom is completely neglected and disregarded. Attempts are made today to rescue Jesus from the prison of individualism and to bring him back into social life again (Hollenbach 1989:11–22). By placing Jesus in the sociocultural situation of his time and seeing his mission primarily in the setting of restoring Israel and announcing the "great year of favor" to his people, the political implication of Jesus' message becomes obvious as a demand for a radical restructuring of all present social structures on the basis of the covenant.

How political was Jesus? Jesus relativized all authority to the Father and to the kingdom. He undertook action that had political significance, the most radical of which was the denial of absolute authority to any power of his time. In that way Jesus presents us with a "normative politics": i.e., all legitimate authority must be put under the inbreaking kingdom, which demands the restructuring and reordering of all human relationships.

To insist that Jesus' message on the kingdom was purely religious and had nothing to say about sociopolitical structures cannot be maintained on the basis of Scripture but only on the basis of a rather dualistic view of the world which denies any relevance of the gospel for inner-earthly realities (Steidl-Meier 1984:15–16).

The Salvational and Universal Character of the Kingdom

John the Baptist announced the immediate coming of the kingdom and rejected any Jewish particularism and ethical passivism. Jewish ancestry was no guarantee of salvation. By adopting baptism as a rite used for Jewish proselytes he declares in fact that Jews stood on the same level with the Gentiles in view of the coming messianic visitation. In contrast to Jesus, who shared most of John's view of the coming kingdom, John announced first the great judgment that would precede the coming of the eschatological kingdom. No one could enter the coming kingdom before having passed through this judgment. For Jesus the absolutely certain event that is happening at this very moment in his words and actions is that God is offering his final salvation to all now in this precise hour. This offer is absolutely unconditional and has only one aim: the salvation of all, but specially the sinners and outcasts who hoped least for it. Its coming does not depend on us, nor can we prevent it. The motive for action in the face of the inbreaking kingdom now is not the coming judgment as in John's preaching but this unconditional offer of salvation. The function of the coming judgment, which Jesus did not deny, is not so much a threat of condemnation but rather a warning not to remain deaf and closed to the present offer of salvation (Merklein 1978:146–49).

For Jesus, the kingdom is a message of peace and joy. Now is no time to mourn and fast (Mk 2:18ff.). Satan's reign is collapsing (Lk 10:18). Now is a time of salvation; the separation of good from bad will be done at the end (Mt 13:24–30). The offer of salvation now is for all: Jews and Gentiles, righteous and sinners. Although Jesus restricted his mission to the "house of Israel," he foresaw the coming of the Gentiles (Mt 8:11) in the image of the great pilgrimage of the nations as outlined in Is 2:2–3.

The Challenge of the Kingdom: Conversion

To the indicative proclamation that the kingdom of God was a reality at hand, Jesus adds an imperative—a call to conversion as a response to God's coming in person. This response to the kingdom "at hand" is expressed with the words: "convert and believe." Since the kingdom is a dynamic power that constantly breaks into this world, the call for repentance is a permanent one directed to everyone, not only to sinners but also to the righteous who have committed no great sins.

To convert means to turn toward, to respond to a call. One is asked to let this message into one's life, to let oneself be overwhelmed by this great news. Such a turning around toward the kingdom will include a turning away from. But the motive for conversion is the inbreaking kingdom of God as having already arrived and not any demand to make oneself ready for its future coming. Conversion is a joyful occasion, not a terrible event of judgment and condemnation. The lost child has come home (Lk 15:25); the dead one has become alive again. "This son of mine was dead and is alive again; he was lost and is found" (Lk 15:24, 32). Conversion, therefore, is preceded by God's action, to which we are called to respond. Only his love makes it possible at all. Conversion is a person's reaction to God's prior action (Fuellenbach 1989:58–59).

It is important that the constantly inbreaking kingdom of God be regarded as being always good news and never judgment or condemnation. Jesus did not abandon judgment (the word appears fifty times in his preaching) but postponed it. Only the one who does not heed the message of the kingdom now will have to face judgment at the time when the fullness of the kingdom will come. Therefore, wherever the kingdom is preached, judgment should not be anticipated. The gospel has always to remain good news and to be preached accordingly.

Commitment to the Person of Jesus

The symbol kingdom of God ultimately points to and reveals in a very concrete way God's unconditional love for his creatures. This incomprehensible love (Eph 3:18–19) became visible and tangible in the person of Jesus of Nazareth. Therefore, the kingdom is not just a "grand design," a utopian dream come true, God's ultimate plan with creation. It is ultimately a person: Jesus Christ. What the kingdom really is we can only sense and imagine in a personal encounter with him "who loved me and who gave his life for me" (Gal 2:20). Conversion means to turn to someone. It means to welcome, to accept Jesus as the center of our whole life. For him and his gospel we subordinate everything else (Mk 10:28), even life itself (Mk 10:32). Prior to the question of what the kingdom is, comes the question, Who is Jesus for me? (Cabellio 1985:22). Conversion in the last analysis is a personal commitment to Jesus, an open declaration for him. The person of Jesus becomes the decisive factor for salvation, for acceptance or rejection in the kingdom of God. This personal attachment is a new and unparalleled element in the claims of Jesus.

To sum up, then, the key message of Jesus contains an indicative, which epitomizes all Christian theology, and an imperative, which sums up all Christian ethics. Its indicative is the proclamation of the kingdom, i.e., the revelation of God's unconditional love for everyone. Its imperative is a call to turn toward this inbreaking kingdom and to let its power into my life.

A Definition of the Kingdom

Jesus never defined the kingdom of God. He described the kingdom with parables and similes (Mt 13; Mk 4), with images such as life, glory, joy, and light. Paul in Rom 14:17 presents a description that comes closest to a definition: "For the kingdom of God is not food and drink but righteousness and peace and joy in the Holy Spirit." Albert Schweitzer regarded this text as "a creed for all times." Some scholars have argued from here that the symbol kingdom of God is not only the center of the Synoptics but also of the whole NT. Justice, peace, and joy are key concepts expressing relationships—to God, to ourselves, to our fellow human beings, and to nature. Wherever Christians relate in justice, peace, and joy in the Holy Spirit, there the kingdom becomes present. The kingdom defined in a short formula is nothing other than justice, peace, and joy in the Holy Spirit (Wenz 1975:20–24).

3. The Person of Jesus and the Kingdom of God

How is the kingdom of God related to the person of Jesus?

The Origin of Jesus' Kingdom Experience

Jesus' proclamation of the kingdom is ultimately rooted in his "*Abba* experience." The message of the kingdom was "sent" to him in his prayer and is therefore intimately tied to and determined by his personal experience of God as *Abba*. Jesus experienced God as the one who was coming as unconditional love, who was taking the initiative and was entering human history in a way and to a degree not known by the earlier prophets. This experience of God determined his whole life and formed the real core of his kingdom message (H. Schürmann, *Gottes Reich* [Freiburg im Breisgau, 1983] 21–64).

At some stage of his life, Jesus realized that Yahweh wanted to lead Israel and ultimately all human beings into that intimacy with Yahweh which Jesus himself experienced in his own relationship with God, whom he called Father. This is most explicitly expressed in the Lord's Prayer. Here Jesus authorized his disciples to follow him in addressing God as *Abba*. By doing so he lets them participate in his own communion with God. Only those who can say this "*Abba*" with a childlike disposition will be able to enter the kingdom of God (Jeremias). In Jesus, the Father wanted to make the covenant come true and be finally established. This is what Jesus thought of as being the kingdom of

God that was to come through him into the world: God's unconditional love, which does not know limits when it comes to fulfill the age-old promise of salvation for every person and the whole of creation. Since Jesus himself is God's ultimate offer to us, it can be said that he is God's kingdom present in the world. Jesus is the kingdom in person, the *autobasileia*, or, as Origen put it, "Jesus is the Kingdom of God realized in a self."

Jesus' Death and the Kingdom

What is the connection between the kingdom that Jesus preached and his death on the cross? Was Jesus' death necessary that the kingdom in its fullness might come? How did Jesus understand his death? How did he interpret his failure?

A. Schweitzer argued that Jesus would not have proclaimed the arrival of the eschatological kingdom of God without knowledge of the trials and suffering that were evoked by this apocalyptic phrase. If Jesus proclaimed the kingdom of God as imminent, then the thought of suffering had to come to him quite naturally. It was not possible to separate from the eschatological kingdom the thought of eschatological trial, of the coming Messiah, and of suffering in the age that would immediately precede the arrival of the kingdom. Suffering had to be proclaimed as necessary for the final coming of the kingdom of God. Jesus, who understood himself clearly in relation to the coming kingdom, realized that he had to undergo suffering and death as a necessary prerequisite to the coming of the kingdom. W. Kasper, making Schweitzer's view his own, concludes: "Jesus certainly saw the trials of suffering and persecution as part of the lowly and hidden character of the Kingdom of God, and as such they passed into the main stream of his preaching. There is, therefore, a more or less straight line from Jesus' eschatological message of the *basileia*, the kingdom, to the mystery of his passion" (Kasper 1976:116).

The Last Supper and the Kingdom of God

The eschatological perspective of Jesus' death is evident in the story of the Last Supper (Mk 14:17–25; 1 Cor 11:23–25). The gatherings at table, which provoked such scandal because Jesus excluded no one from them, even open sinners, and which thus expressed the heart of his message, were types of the feast to come in the time of salvation (Mk 2:18–20). The Last Supper, like all gatherings at table, was an anticipation or "antidonation" of the consummation of the kingdom. It is an "already" of the "not yet," a foreshadowing of the consummation of the kingdom, the advent of the perfect reign of God, the fulfillment of the great banquet — all that can only become a full reality after Jesus' death. The final gathering presupposes this giving of himself for the many.

The eschatological reference in Luke 22:16 has the following meaning: Jesus will no longer sit at table with the disciples on earth but will do so again during a new meal in the coming kingdom of God. For this to happen, his awaited death is a necessary condition. The disciples can partake of the final eschatological banquet only if Jesus first lays down his life for them (Lk 22:20). (Jeremias 1971:299). To share in the kingdom of God is possible only after Jesus has fulfilled the precondition for it; after he has drunk the cup and has been baptized with a baptism (see Mk 10:35–40) (Schnackenburg 1963:193). The true nature of the task that Jesus had to fulfill in order to bring the kingdom in its fullness is expressed in the words regarding the bread and wine. He must surrender his life so that men and women may share the feast of the kingdom with him.

> His resolution to complete the mission that God had given him in relation to the kingdom and his confidence that he would soon be participating in its joy sound the keynote of his last meal with his disciples. The Last Supper is framed in affirmation of the death of Jesus in prospect of the kingdom of God. (Beasley-Murray 1986:263)

The Death of Jesus: God's Ultimate Revelation

At one point in his life Jesus must have realized that the only way left to fulfill his mission was to demonstrate the immensity of God's love for us to the very end (Jn 13:1). The cross and his death appear as the only way that remained to prove God's redeeming love in a sin-permeated history of humankind. In what precisely do these "eschatological tribulations and sufferings" consist that he had to undertake in order to make the final coming of the kingdom possible? The solution offered is the following: The life of Jesus portrays a tension

that exists between his intimate life with the Father and his "living our life to the very end," his faithfulness to his mission, which is most adequately expressed with the two words "identification" and "representation." Jesus felt that the more he identified himself with us, the more he would experience our sinfulness, our forlornness, our insecurity as those who had rejected God's gift of love. He came to realize that in order to carry his mission through to the end he would have to experience the full reality of what it means for a creature to be cut off from God. For Jesus it would mean to experience in himself being cut off from the Father, who meant everything to him, from whom he drew life, and whose will he had come to do. The thought that this moment was coming horrified him.

The Father would take him as humankind in its God-forsaken, abandoned state. Jesus would have to experience this being completely identified with us in our sinfulness and being treated as our representative before God. The cry on the cross is to be seen as the moment when Jesus identified himself most with our God-forsakenness (Mk 15:34). In this moment it seemed as if the love of the Father, from which he drew life, had stopped flowing. The eschatological tribulations are precisely this experience of our true state without God: forsaken, condemned without any hope on our part. On the cross Jesus experienced God as the one who withdrew (Mk 15:34) and let him experience all our forlornness, the real trial of the inbreaking kingdom, which was to overcome sin, condemnation, and death (Fuellenbach 1989:85–95).

In experiencing the effect of sin as condemnation, God took upon himself in Jesus Christ what would have been the destiny of humankind. "He descended into hell!" These are the eschatological tribulations that had to be endured in order that the kingdom could finally come in its full glory.

4. The Hope Spirit and the Kingdom

The Holy Spirit is described in Scripture as the "agent of life" or as the "giver of life." Through the Spirit the old creation came to exist and remained in existence. The same Spirit is believed to bring about the new heaven and the new earth at the end of time. The eschatological time is foreseen as the golden age of the Spirit. Jesus' mission in the Gospel of John is described as "releasing the Spirit of the end-time" who will accomplish the transformation of the old into the new. As the ultimate revelation of God's unconditional love for his creatures, Jesus' death releases this love and transforms it into the power of the Holy Spirit. The first deed of this crucified love set free in the Spirit is the resurrection of the dead body of Jesus into the new creation. According to Paul, the Holy Spirit is the power by which the Father raised Jesus from the dead. By the same Spirit the kingdom, realized in a new way through the death and resurrection of Jesus, now becomes a world-transforming, life-giving force. It is, therefore, the Holy Spirit who continues the work of Christ down through the ages and is leading humanity and creation as a whole to its final completion in the fullness of the kingdom (Fuellenbach 1989:97–107).

5. The Church and the Kingdom

The Spirit of the risen Lord, the Spirit of the new creation, brings forth the new eschatological community, the church. The church is, therefore, an anticipation in space and time of the world to come. It is "in the world but not of the world." The church's essence and mission have to be understood in the light of the kingdom present in the church but directed to the transformation and salvation of the whole of creation.

Vatican II describes the church as the mystery of Christ. In it is realized the "eternal plan of the Father, manifested in Jesus Christ, to bring humankind to its eternal glory." The church is seen in relation to the "bringing about of the secret hidden for ages in God" (Col 1:16; Eph 3:3–9; 1 Cor 2:6–10), which is none other than the kingdom of God. The kingdom aims at the transformation of the whole of creation into its eternal glory, and the church must be seen and understood in the context of this divine intentionality. The church's mission is to reveal through the ages the hidden plan of God and to lead all humankind toward its final destiny. The church must see itself entirely in the service of this divine plan meant for the salvation of all creation (Pannenberg 1985:72–75).

The Church Is Not the Kingdom of God on Earth

Contrary to what many dogmatic textbooks before the council said, the church is not the kingdom of God now. Vatican II expressed this in *Lumen Gentium* (art. 5) and again in *Gaudium et Spes* (art. 45). "It replaces what was perhaps the most serious pre-Vatican II ecclesiological misunderstanding, namely, that the Church is identical with the Kingdom of God here on earth. If it is, then it is beyond all need for institutional reform, and its mission is to bring everyone inside lest salvation elude them" (McBrien 1981:686). The kingdom makes itself felt outside the church as well. The mission of the church is to serve the kingdom and not to take its place.

The Kingdom Is Present in the Church

It is the kingdom present now that creates the Church and keeps it constantly in existence. The church is therefore the result of the coming of God's kingdom into the world. The dynamic power of the Spirit who makes God's final saving intentionality effectively present is the true source of the community called church. Although the kingdom cannot be identified with the church, this does not mean that the kingdom is not present in the church. The kingdom makes itself present in a particular way. We can say that the church is an initial, proleptic, or anticipated realization of the plan of God for humankind. In the words of Vatican II: "She becomes on earth the initial budding forth of that Kingdom" (*LG* 5). Second, the church is a means or sacrament through which this plan of God with the world realizes itself in history (*LG* 9; 48). "The Kingdom creates the Church, works through the Church, and is proclaimed in the world by the Church. There can be no Kingdom without the Church—those who have acknowledged God's rule—and there can be no Church without the Kingdom; but they remain two distinguishable concepts: the Rule of God and the fellowship of men" (Ladd 1974:277).

The Mission of the Church

Jesus bound the reign of God, which previously belonged to the people of Israel, to the community of his disciples. With this election of a new community, the purpose of the OT people was transferred to this new people. They are now to become a visible sign of God's intention with the world and the active carrier of his salvation. They are called out of the nations in order to take up a mission for the nations. What matters is that the kingdom will remain bound to a visible community which must put itself in the service of God's ultimate plan of salvation for all (Lohfink 1985:17–29).

From this perspective the church is necessary in order for the kingdom to remain in the world. "It is the community which has begun to taste (even only in foretaste) the reality of the kingdom, which alone can provide the hermeneutic of the message. . . . Without the hermeneutic of such a living community, the message of the Kingdom can only become an ideology and a program, it will not be a gospel" (Newbigin 1980:19). The church's mission in the light of the kingdom is described in a threefold way: (1) To proclaim in word and sacrament that the kingdom of God has come in the person Jesus of Nazareth (2) To offer its own life as a test case, that the kingdom is present and operative in the world today. This can be seen in the church's own life, where justice, peace, freedom, and respect for human rights are concretely manifested. The church offers itself as a "contrast society" to society at large (Lohfink 1985:157–180). (3) To challenge society as a whole to transform itself along the basic principles of the inbreaking kingdom: justice, peace, kinship, and human rights. This is a constitutive element of proclaiming the gospel since the ultimate goal of the kingdom is the transformation of the whole of creation, and the church must understand its mission in the service of the imminent kingdom (McBrien 1981:717).

Bibl.: R. Schnackenburg, *God's Rule and Kingdom* (New York, 1963); J. Jeremias, *New Testament Theology* (London, 1971); J. D. Crossan, *The Parables: The Challenge of the Historical Jesus* (San Francisco, 1973); G. Gutiérrez, *A Theology of Liberation* (New York, 1973); W. Kelber, *The Kingdom in Mark: A New Place and a New Time* (Philadelphia, 1974); G. E. Ladd, *The Presence of the Future* (Grand Rapids, 1974); H. Wenz, *Theologie des Reiches Gottes* (Hamburg, 1975); H. Merklein, *Die Gottesherrschaft als Handlungsprinzip* (Würzburg, 1978); N. Perrin, *Jesus and the Language of the Kingdom* (Philadelphia, 1976); W. Kasper, *Jesus the Christ* (London/New York, 1976); J. Sobrino, "Jesús el Reino de Dios significado y objectivos ultimos de su vida y misión," *Christus* 45 (1980): 17–25; L. Newbigin, *Sign of the Kingdom* (Grand Rapids, 1980); R. Nordsieck, *Reich Gottes: Hoffnung der Welt* (Neukirchen, 1980); B. Scott, *Jesus, Symbol-Maker for the Kingdom* (Philadephia, 1981); G. M. Soares-Prabhu, "The Kingdom of God: Jesus' Vision of a New Society," in D. S. Amalopavadass, ed., *The Indian Church in the Struggle for a New Society* (Bangalore, 1981), 579–629; R. McBrien, *Catholicism* (London, 1981); L. Boff, *Jésus-Christ Libérateur* (Paris, 1983); P. Steidl-Meier, *Social Justice Ministry* (New York, 1984); G. Lohfink, *Jesus and Community* (London, 1985); id., "The Exegetical Predicament concerning Jesus' Kingdom of God Proclamation," *TD* 36:2 (1989): 103–11; id., "The Kingdom of God and the Economy in the Bible," *Comm* 13 (1986): 216–31; id. "Der Begriff des Gottesreichs vom Alten Testament her gesehen," in *Unterwegs zur Kirche Alttestamentliche Konzeptionen* (Freiburg, 1987), 33–86; R. Cabellio, "El Reino de Dios," *Christus* 50 (1985): 16–22; P. Hollenbach, "Liberating Jesus for Social Involvement," *BTB* 15 (1985): 151–57; id., "The Historical Jesus Question in North America Today," *BTB* 19 (1989): 12–19; W. Pannenberg, *Theology of the Kingdom* (Philadelphia, 1985); G. R. Beasley-Murray, *Jesus and the Kingdom of God* (Grand Rapids, 1986); J. Fuellenbach, *The Kingdom of God: The Heart of Jesus' Message for Us Today* (Manila, 1989); id., *Hermeneutics, Marxism and Liberation Theology* (Manila, 1989).

John Fuellenbach

L

LANGUAGE

I. Philosophical. *1. Presuppositions. 2. Survey.* (G. Lafont)

II. Theological. *1. The Basis of Theological Language. 2. The Distinctiveness of Theological Language.* (R. Fisichella)

I. Philosophical Language

The question of language plainly lies at the heart of fundamental theology, since the word "theology" itself includes the *logos*. Our task is thus to state the correct modalities of language insofar as it concerns God, to establish critically the validity and limits of these modalities, to contemplate the possibilities for truth and meaning they offer. Ideally this should all be elaborated only on the basis of a confirmed general theory of language that articulates language's forms of manifestation (phenomenology), mechanisms (linguistics), and scope and value (criticism and interpretation).

But the truth is that no such unitary theory exists. To the contrary, the field of the sciences of language is both vast and unordered, and we cannot yet foresee a time when a principle will be unearthed capable of ordering and articulating this diversity. The difficulty perhaps arises out of our cultural situation. As disciples of Socrates, we have sought "real truth" and have been swept up through a process of purification and internality to the place we supposed this truth to be; but we have also been suspicious of the incarnate human instruments that instead of pursuing this pure pathway, swerved from it toward the private interests of power and riches. Classical epistemology devoted little attention to language in its own right, as though it had an intrinsic role to play in disclosing truth; it was scarcely more than an instrument, to be kept under strict control.

At present an effort is certainly being made, sometimes indeed with excessive fervor, to break with Socrates; there is a willingness to consider that we operate from the outset *within language*. Language is not—or not simply, and in any event not at first—the expression of a thought and the clothing of a truth; it is more like an ontological dimension of human existence, one of its elements, if not its characteristic element. It is an already given structure that one converts to one's own use in existing, or at least exists only in so converting. It must therefore be studied in its own right, including its functioning, its mechanisms, its stages of development, and their communication with one another. However legitimate this new perspective may be, it is not without its paradoxes. Thus it is not easy to reconcile this "ontological" reflection on language with its role as vehicle of significance. If language has a truly primitive status, how can it have reference, to what, for whom? Again, what is to be made of the fact that we have only language to use in the study of language? Do we have here an a priori exception to the new discipline?

The same paradox may be seen in another way. Language appears at once as necessary and central to human existence and as outstripped on every side. It is as though, in spite of everything, we were pining for a "true discourse," to use Celse's expression, even as we recognized its impossibility. The meaning of discourse is limited by what lies beyond it: silence, as *fons et origo*, or conversely as pinnacle overarching everything; communication, as acknowledgment taking place between unique persons, which neither being nor becoming nor speech can reduce to pure logic; practice, which is justified more as obedience, fidelity, and competence than as conceptual coherence. Are the contents of language possible only under such conditions?

Finally, taking language on all its levels as a whole, its disorders stand out: conscious or concealed lying, sophisticated manipulation, and, perhaps most seriously, discourse's claim to appropriate reality, all the more perilous perhaps when discourse is or takes itself to be more true. Truth, real or supposed, may then become an instrument of power and even persecution.

It must then be understood that at a juncture so rich and difficult, the present article can do no more than take up some presuppositions that seem essential to any authentic perception of language and propose a possible route surveying the various operations of language, following an order that is satisfying though not unique.

1. Presuppositions

Here we limit ourselves to locating language with respect to *desire*, doubtless a more global perspective than one that immediately considers language's relation to truth; we next set out the *references* that are present whenever there is speech. The two problematics of desire and reference allow us to point out an essential property of language: *metaphor*. We then briefly mention *writing*, which is practically inseparable from language, but whose place is difficult to discern. Finally, we say a word about *symbol* and its relation to *image*.

Among all the spaces of meaning, it is language that puts words in play. We propose here as a working hypothesis that the word organizes the inexhaustible resources of sound and voice in the service of what might be called the three primordial desires of humanity: the desires to communicate, to know, and to do. These three forms of desire define three domains of language: a symbolic domain, in which words are instigators of relation more than of knowledge and in which truth lies in the reciprocity of invocation; a rational domain, which establishes science and in which truth derives from the logical coherence of discourse; and a practical domain, which allows performance and in which truth is found in success. These three domains need not be separate to be distinct; it is clear that the truth of one cannot be fully established without the truth of the others. On the other hand, there can be and is in fact transfer of languages, in which one of these domains is used "metaphorically" for the expression of another.

However matters may stand with critical problems, of which we shall venture a word further on, this triple language of desire immediately develops a reference that is itself triple. In other words, it continually presupposes a triple alterity: the world of things and people proportioned to the person speaking, transcendence, and time. This means that in each of the domains just considered, language is acquainted with dimensions that can be called (in a sense different from the one singled out above) metaphoric; it is capable of transferring the meanings formed at the level homogeneous with it to levels that are not. It is here that the problem of theological language properly arises. Which languages express (and produce) communion with God, the reality of God, in himself and in relation to us—a specific practice (if there is one) of an individual who is related to God and knows him? As for time, it introduces into the idea and the practice of language the word "tradition" and its reality. On the human plane alone, a language, and therefore a culture, is from the very start transmitted on a small scale by a human being, in the course of living out desire. Now this gift is appropriated and used in an original manner by its beneficiary; the instrument once bestowed does not emerge exempt from new uses. Thus no language is given once for all; univocal usage, itself personalized and therefore inflected, develops on the horizon of prospect (future) and interpretation (past) and obtains from this situation part of its power to signify. Moreover, if there is a relation that God bears to time, theological language also admits of an ineradicable element of interpretation.

Within a problematic of language that is developed even a little, some consideration must be given to *writing*. The orality of the word, indeed, cannot be maintained without the plasticity of writing. Midway between a simplistic vision of writing as a simple and intrinsically passive recording of speech and a sophisticated theory that would make of writing the original, undefined, and barely sensed pattern on which speech may in time come to be erected, we shall take writing here to have a double function—of construction and of memory. It involves construction, insofar as writing accords space to the desire to signify; words are in a way set down, displayed, "manipulated" in the strict sense of the word, until their spatial order at once engenders a complex meaning and corresponds to it. From this point of view, writing is essential to the development of the prospective function of speech, both at the level of real projects and at the level of fiction; at this point the idea of literature is articulated. Once composed by the act of writing itself, however, the words remain at one's disposal and constitute, as it were, material always freshly available for speech, interpretation, and action. In constant reciprocity, writing provokes speech, even as speech comments on (and therefore in a certain sense re-creates) writing. Finally, since writing belongs to the plastic domain, it constitutes the bridge between the word and the other fields of spatial meaning, which could be collectively labeled the vocable of art.

What we have proposed thus far makes it possible to distinguish among the various senses that may be given to the word "symbol" in the field of language. From the perspective of the desire to communicate, it is an element for *recognition*; in this way proper names can appear to be symbolic words par excellence. At the same time, any word, taken from any category of knowledge whatever and applied metaphorically, may play this role of instrument for recognition. This, then, is the second meaning of the word "symbol": an imaged designation, something that is always possible from the moment an interpretation decodes a metaphor by disclosing its power of invocation or evocation. Finally, outside of the formal process of recognition and therefore apart from the desires for *knowing* and *doing*, there is a symbol each time a word in one linguistic category is employed to say what could be said more exactly if less pregnantly in another. But here we need to make a distinction. In certain cases symbolic language can be, with gains and losses, retranscribed in a proper language, as prose succeeds poetry, but in other cases no proper language is immediately at our disposal. In this way symbolic language is essential (though not exclusive) to the language of transcendence and to the language of time, at least when the latter has reference to the future, which by definition is absent from our knowledge as well as from our recognition.

2. Survey

The shape of a survey depends in large measure on its origin. Since language gathers together the totality of the symbolism of voice and sound, we begin here with their first manifestations: *voice/cry/song*, only to observe immediately that these are arrayed against a reality that is perhaps more primordial: *listening/silence*. The voice, it is said, "breaks" the silence. Silence is double; there is a surrounding silence, and then the voice is a taking possession of this silent world and a self-affirmation present to it. But there is a more essential silence. The voice breaks a personal silence, in response to the silent expectation and listening of others; words do not burst forth if there is no one to hear. Conversely, silence may be a request for language. *Silence/listening* is then doubly prior to speech: there is the priority of a world, and the priority of others listening in reciprocity.

But on the horizon there stands the priority of God; here an entire line of thought becomes available for locating all of theology within a listening to the double word of creation (of the world) and of (interpersonal) covenant, to which as *logos*, theology responds. In this way we may discover the specific character of the original silence in Christian theology. This is not a matter of an *Abgrund*, infinite and terrifying in its impersonality, which would condemn all speech, but of the depth of a God who in his very transcendence creates and speaks. The primordial silence of God liberates speech and calls forth the response, first of all in God himself, and then in every human being and every community on earth.

The primacy of the pair *listening/silence*, further verified by the human body itself, in which the ear is always in a state of audition while the tongue is subject to the will, is clarified by another pair: *invocation/evocation*. There is no speech that is not addressed. The primal cry of the infant is already a call, and normal people do not speak when they are alone (even if one of the many linguistic disorders is abstraction from the hearer, speech that asks and admits of no reply). What is said ("evocation") is registered within the very act of speaking, which is always a "saying-to" ("invocation"); language is essentially interlocution. In linguistic terms, we might speak at this point of the primacy of the *proper name* (of the one being addressed) and of the *first-person personal pronoun* (for the one engaging in speech). The proper name contains and suggests the imaginary, symbolic, affective values that mediate the desire to be heard by the other, while the pronoun is said effectively only when personalized by unique characteristics of voice and tone. In both cases, the proper name and the pronoun have reference to the mystery of communication, of terms that communicate; they *designate* before *representing* (even if an element of representation is always, by right as well as in fact, inseparable from designation). If we continue this line of thought, we come to see, even on the human plane, but still more in language marked out as divine, the primacy of the hymnal, the liturgical, within which alone it is possible for every other form of language to gain meaning and truth. The doxology is without doubt the proper space of speech.

The next step in this phenomenological consideration of language is ethical in nature. Reciprocal invocation is most often charged with *question/answer* content: one who invokes the other by name enters the other's field of existence to invite that one to give, to collaborate; speech becomes prohibition (of continuing alone), proposal (to do something with)—in a word, *law*. Law is the form of language that results from the desire to communicate and the desire to do; it seeks to create a covenant and tends to introduce a story. If it is grounded on an accepted reciprocity of desires, it is also *grace*. In this way language is the locus of the effective appearance of liberties in their capacity as proposal and compliance, as commandment and obedience—in a word, as covenant. It is perhaps also at this level of law that language unveils its relation to death. Ethical speech cannot gain self-sufficiency without renunciation, or progress toward community without transcending isolated narcissism.

A sign of the ethical dimension's primacy in theological language can also be recognized if we recall that the first word God addresses to the man in the Garden of Eden is one of gift and prohibition: the proposal of a covenant, which occurs even before the man has begun to name the living beings around him and to reflect on God who has created him and addresses him. Thus the whole of the truth of theological discourse cannot be severed from fidelity to the covenant.

If language manifests itself first of all as ethical, it brings *narrative* along with it, for no word can be uttered but on the foundation of the memory of decisions made and registered, for good or ill, in the body, the world, and the history of a human being. At this point, then, the element of time comes into play in language, in the form of memory, as return of the past and anticipation of the future in speech. In this sense narrative is an act of language by means of which both narrator and auditors together ground their hope and action on the evocation of a meaningful past. It must be emphasized here that the element of anticipation, as well as that of account given, is part of the language of the story. That which is not yet,

and cannot therefore properly be mentioned, partially determines the interpretation of that which has been and the discrimination of that which is. It must also be observed that it is at this narrative level that language makes most clearly apparent the evil that inhabits it; narrative is always in some way confession of injustice committed and request, even if implicit, for pardon. The anticipated future is not only the symbolized completion that bestows its meaning on speech uttered today; it is also the eschatological purification of history and of all speech that accompanies it.

Considered in this perspective, theological language is redeemer and founder—redeemer in the sense that it heals the wounds of a memory forgetful of its true past; founder insofar as it reveals the true coordinates of the covenant, not only past and present, but still to come; in this sense it supplies a hermeneutical key for proper interpretation of the present. To say that theology is essentially narrative does not mean that it is limited to "telling stories" but that all of its language rests in the last analysis on a founding narrative, that of the paschal mystery of Jesus Christ, as remembrance, covenant, pardon, and mission—none of which, to be sure, can occur without evoking many "stories."

If silence as original space has a certain primacy over the speech of meeting or the speech of and for knowing, and if the process of speech begins from the primacy of what can be called reciprocal address (invocation, law, narrative), investigation can nevertheless not end with these points. On the foundation of silence and within communication, indeed, *knowledge* is displayed. Ancient epistemology tended to make of language the pure vocal transposition of thought; today, in contrast, it is difficult to discern a thought in language at all; the primacy of saying often rules out any serious analysis of what is said. Nevertheless this analysis is part of the theory of language, as can be shown in each of the steps we have considered. Reciprocal invocation is in reality not possible without the aid of an image, both of the one to whom one addresses oneself and of oneself, the one who is speaking. That this image is linked to the very act of interlocution is certain; that it runs the risk of constituting a veil, rather than conducing to the reciprocal appearance of the speakers, is also quite certain. But the provisos and the perils do not cancel the necessity for and the reality of an image; the category of seeing is less distant than it seems from that of saying. And at the heart of the image the idea is displayed.

In the second place, what ethical communication would there be if the names we use—the grammar that gathers them, and the logic that organizes them—were stripped of all objectivity? Lacking it, could an apparent dialogue be anything but the mute juxtaposition of expressions closed upon themselves? The normativeness of law is not external to the process of prohibition fundamental to narrative recital; in fact it discriminates its criteria. Again, it must be granted that a certain objective figure of the event is always at work within historical knowledge; a narrative assumes the values true and false insofar as its figuring is or is not faithful to a certain number of givens, which concern the future as well as the past.

Furthermore, we must examine the means that the *desire to know* is given for attaining its object—science with its various levels, not only in its practical uses, but also in its proper function, the gaining of knowledge. Here, too, names, grammar, and logic import into language the conceptual at all its levels and strive toward the manifestation of being. There is no basis for excluding the categories of theory, of the speculative, of contemplation from the analysis of language, since they are part of its resources.

In sum, the ancient analysis privileged the *contents* of language and made their truth the highest of values, perhaps neglecting the presence of metaphor and the constant possibility of interpretation. If today, probably with good reason, we exalt what was neglected then, it falls to us anew to define within this altered perspective the presence and the necessary meaning of the contents of language.

Here we find the immense theological question of the divine names, not only when they are proper names, terms of human prayer, when they accompany the confession of the covenant and the narrative of its vicissitudes, but also when they strive to express God, both in himself and in his creative activity. The truth of theology presupposes that these names are interpreted correctly and placed in proper relation to one another. The theory of this interpreting and relating is precisely the object of inquiry into theological language; the truth

aimed at here is a little like the asymptote of our human desires, when it comes to expressing God.

To conclude these fragmentary reflections on language, we recall that at the root of all language stands the hypothesis that "speech states the truth to the other." If the question of truth is contained in the question of language, what can we suggest about it here? We may say that truth is located at the confluence of the desires we have postulated at the source of language, which we take up here in a different order. The desire to *know*, to be acquainted, to comprehend; the noetic, centripetal desire for a relative appropriation of reality, according to the axiom that "the soul is called to become all things"; the extraversion of a limited self toward the amplitude of a cosmos in a vision either diachronic or synchronic. The desire to *become*, to develop in a definite direction, therefore to remember, conspire, and hope, to interpret and project; language that implicitly speaks of immortality. The desire to *communicate*, not to appropriate for oneself, but to enter into an ethical play of invocation and reply, of gift, of reception and exchange. The totality of truth would result from the articulation of the truth proper to each of these desires, which is in effect to say that it is a limit and that once attained, it is obliterated, to give way to a resumption and a deepening.

These reflections also orient us toward a theory of theological language that unites more than it excludes. We must not play off doxology against analogy, interpretation against science, invocation against representation, ethics against ontology, etc. Conversely, we cannot be satisfied, without running some risk of arrogance, with an articulation of concepts that expresses precisely the properties of some essence, as though there were no one speaking or the person speaking were not in the throes of some unknown but real salvation. The difficult task of fundamental theology when it comes to language is to distinguish in order to unite, so as to promote speech that is directed, and engaged, as faithful to reality as to memory and hope, and in the end active in contributing to the advent of truth.

Bibl. I. U. DALFERTH, *Religiöse Rede von Gott* (Munich, 1981); A. LOUTH, *Discerning the Mystery* (Oxford, 1983); J. LADRIÈRE, *L'articulation du sens,*

2 vols. (Paris, 1970, 1984); G. LAFONT, *Dieu, le temps et l'être* (Paris, 1986).

G. LAFONT

II. THEOLOGICAL LANGUAGE

There is no question of evading the problem of theological language: it needs to be studied with great precision even when the solution appears to be very remote and when the undertaking seems, in many ways, likely to be impeded by subsidiary problems.

The case for the importance of theological language does not need to be made; it is a reality facing us from the moment we acknowledge that it is characteristic both of the human condition to have to communicate and of revelation to become part of the universal heritage (Mt 28:19).

When a theologian prepares to explain the peculiarity of theological language, two issues need to be discusses: (1) the basis of theological language, and (2) the distinctiveness of theological language.

1. The Basis of Theological Language

The possibilities of theological language are determined by God's revelation, and the consequences of this are direct. In fact, it makes possible the identification of certain basic hermeneutic principles for a theory of theological language. Let us be more precise: (a) If theology can "say" God, it is because God has said it of himself. God's first and free self-revelation is at the root of all theological language. (b) This means that the form in which God has communicated with humanity has been established within a human language once and for all. The identification of this form involves acknowledging it as the norm for all subsequent languages that want to "say" the mystery of God.

One of the first consequences is evident. The economy of revelation presents a gradual increase in the individuation of the form in which God's self-communication is expressed. At a basic, intuitive, and universal level, the *creation* is seen as God's language. What words cannot yet express is manifested and revealed by nature: "The heavens are telling the glory of God; and the firmament proclaims his handiwork. Day to day pours forth speech, and night to night declares knowledge" (Ps 19:1–2).

In creation, everything becomes the word of God that speaks to guide men and women toward an understanding of the mystery (Rom 1:20–21). Moreover, in a creative act God also gives people the gift of language so that they may recognize him and praise him. A document found at Qumran is of considerable significance in this respect: "You created the spirit of language and knew its words; you established the fruits of the lips before they existed. You placed the words in order and directed the flow of the spirit of the lips, causing the words to come out in order according to their mysteries and the spirits to flow according to their ends; to make your glory known and to describe your wonders in all the works of your truth and justice; so that your name may be exalted by the mouths of all who know you (1QH 1:27–31).

From the creation to the events that made up the history of the people of the old covenant, God's word became ever more precise and assumed the form of a more personal communication. It was left to the prophets particularly to establish a language that in an indivisible unity of word and gesture expressed God's wish to save humanity.

However, everything in the creation and history was within range of the only real word the Father uttered, that of his Logos, who had always heard his words and therefore could be his true interpreter (Jn 1:18). He is God, just as the Father is; and in human terms his language is the same language that God uses when talking to humankind: "Long ago God spoke to our ancestors in many and various ways by the prophets, but in these last days he has spoken to us by a Son, whom he appointed heir of all things, through whom he also created the worlds" (Heb 1:1–2). *Dei Verbum* 4 makes a similar point in terms that seem to be a commentary on the Letter to the Hebrews:

> To see Jesus is to see His Father (Jn 14:9). For this reason Jesus perfected revelation by fulfilling it through His whole work of making Himself present and manifesting Himself: through His words and deeds, His signs and wonders, but especially through His death and glorious resurrection from the dead and final sending of the Spirit of truth.

The self-awareness of Jesus of Nazareth speaking the words of the Father (Jn 5:19; 8:26) suggests that his language is the only one that is consistent with God's by virtue of his being the Son of God: for in him "the whole fullness of deity dwells bodily" (Col 2:9). From the moment fundamental theology lays down theological premises for a theory of language, it cannot exclude this fact a priori, or else it loses the sense of any analysis. It will be observed that, even in awareness of a mediation of such an event determined by NT theologies, theology does not forgo finding this typical and specific form of Jesus' language *through* these theologies precisely because they are *mediations.*

This original language was made up of the unity of Jesus' words and gestures together with the language that mediates it, and is the first and prescriptive source of any subsequent theological language. The reason is that, whether as the word of Jesus or through the inspiration of the Holy Spirit, the revelation of God is the basis of all theological learning.

2. The Distinctiveness of Theological Language

Theological language has simultaneously a basic similarity with and a specific difference from other languages that express the divine mystery.

Theological language is not the language of *revelation* and *faith.* It is a basic language which, in the unity and uniqueness of the event of the incarnation, expresses the language of God in just one word: Jesus of Nazareth. The language of revelation is a paradoxical language because it makes the essence of trinitarian love present in Christ's death and resurrection. As we have already stated, theological language is based on this language, and in the plurality of concepts and linguistic expressions it struggles to make the singularity of the event intelligible. Theological language is not *liturgical* language. This is a special language of initiates and is by its nature doxological and mystagogical. Theological language "says," while liturgical language "celebrates." The former seeks to understand; the latter to contemplate. Theological language is not *religious* language. Religious language occupies an area that is contiguous to cultural anthropology, sociology, psychology, and the phenomenology of religion (→ RELIGION II). By its very nature, it must leave aside identifying the divinity so as to remain in the more general field of the *sacred* and of the attitudes of human beings to their perception of it. Theological language is not *catechetic* language. Catechetic language is used in the systematic training of the believer in such a way that, by referring to concrete situations in life, it can make the choice of the *sequela Christi* more significant.

Finally, theological language is not *pastoral* language. Pastoral language studies cultural situations and therefore seeks to translate the unique Christian message by means of various ways of preaching the gospel (*GS* 44–62).

We may conclude that theological language is above the many languages referred to because it is their source, a first mediation of the language of the revelation dealing with the mystery's *intelligibility.* A liturgy that was solely mystagogical and did not make intelligible the mystery that is being celebrated would rapidly slip into magic ritual. Catechesis or pastoral work that eschewed a theological basis in its teaching would have little evangelical impact if the teachers were trying to bring together the immutability of the revealed fact and the current relevance of the historic moment.

However, the movement is not simply in one direction from theology to the various manifestations of the life of faith. We must try to move in the other direction so that theological language can draw on different representations and expressions to revitalize its ways of communicating ideas.

Within the language of the faith, theological language may be described as a basic language that has a role in the dynamic of faith which aims at making the object intelligible. It follows that it is a language that expresses faith within revelation and at the same time it critically reflects on what it says.

The following are observations on the specificity of theological language:

a. One of the most important characteristics is interaction. By definition, an interactive language is one that engages the subject as soon as it is set in motion. In this case, the linguistic sign is not simply a verbal expression but contains a check on the behavior of the subject who is engaging or committing himself or herself with that language. There is a self-involvement that makes speech and action inseparable.

The interaction of theological language is an essential premise that derives from the faith of the believer as a fundamental act of theological learning. Nonetheless, every theological language is implicitly or explicitly determined by the formula "I believe that. . . ."

Interaction suggests above all that people have taken up a position vis-à-vis the content of language, a position of "believing" as a basic element of personal engagement and of the language itself. It follows that the believer does not question the goodness and truth of the content of his or her language; this comes from a knowledge of faith and from a universal application of faith, and with that it is accepted as a fact of God's revelation. Insofar as theological language is interactive, it analyzes its own content critically but with an attitude that is determined by faith.

b. Like any other language, theological language is determined by the historical context. This has a very natural origin in that it is a human language, and from *nature* it derives expressions that might characterize the creativity of the subject. However, as language exists for the purpose of communication, it becomes part of a *social* and cultural function that encourages personal freedom to assume responsibility. For that reason, we function best within a linguistic system that facilitates the communication of facts.

This dimension applies also to theological language. We think of theological language as dynamically constructed on a triad of foundation, development, and going beyond (or transcending).

Foundation. As we have already said, theological language is based on the word of God. Scripture and tradition constitute the prescriptive and fundamental moment of faith. This language must therefore make the life of Jesus of Nazareth its prime task.

Let us take an example: each of us speaks and expresses ideas in his or her mother tongue. This mother tongue is learned from birth; it is learned naturally. It is born; it grows and evolves in the characteristic relationship between the subject, who can express ideas, and the context in which those ideas can be expressed. The believer, who receives the life of faith at baptism, is also given the chance to learn his or her mother tongue as an innate reality that comes with the choice of living the faith. This language which expresses faith is the same as what it expresses: Jesus Christ. His words, which already express the reality of his incarnation kenotically, are consistent with the words of God.

The following will be expressed in him: the *fullness of love*, because it is a language that is born of the nature of God (1 Jn 4:16); the *totality of the truth*, because it is the source of full freedom before the Father (Jn 10:18; 8:16); the *evident credibility*, because it is consistent and significant in itself (Jn 8:13–14; 10:25–38).

Development. It is from these sources, which are completely free because they are the fruit of revelation, that there emerges a language that then seeks to reflect on the content. To pick up the earlier illustration, we might say that this is the moment when the believer acquires languages other than his or her mother tongue. Once a language has been learned, however, it cannot be substituted for the mother tongue, which, by definition, will always be better developed and expressive than a language that has been acquired. In fact, this is the only time when the subject naturally expresses himself or herself.

Development of theological language consists in finding concepts and formulations that make the intelligibility of the fact explicit and comprehensible to the outside. This principle is not unrelated to the very source of theological language. Scripture and tradition are the first opportunities of acquiring means of expression that are appropriate to the intelligibility and communication of the content of faith.

Literary genres, principles of philosophical learning, and various narrative formulations all point the way to keeping the development of theological language up-to-date. When the content of faith is in different contexts and cultures, it needs conceptual and linguistic developments that are consistent and consonant with the degree of intelligibility reached (→ INCULTURATION). The application of hermeneutic norms, the reference to principles of philosophical learning, and attention to important objective situations in which believers might find themselves will be needed in order to construct the essential material for the theologian, who has the responsibility of bringing out the most profound meaning of revelation.

Going Beyond. By its very nature, faith is directed toward the final encounter with the Lord, and therefore every reality we encounter is qualified by this absolute and unique occurrence.

Not even the theological language that interprets faith can avoid this fact. Each result that is achieved is the springboard for an even bigger discovery. The inexhaustibility of the revealed mystery is naturally reflected in the fragmentary nature of the formulations that go to explain it. There is no theological language, however, that can advance the claim of exhaustibility. The constant dialectic of an ever-increasing knowledge of the mystery encourages believers to discover fresh linguistic expressions that can make faith credible within every changing historical situation.

The ability that theological language has to "go beyond" is neither relativism nor an abandoning of the language so far attained. It is a true ability to "go beyond" which can grasp the value of an earlier tradition but at the same time be always looking at its basis. It is nonetheless a critical awareness, one that has to animate theological language, and therefore an awareness of a form of research with a particular interest in the scientific method.

There are attempts at different levels to solve the problem of theological language: these include prescriptiveness, symbolism, and tautology. The range of solution is an indication of the immensity of our language when it encounters the divine.

The situation for people living in biblical times was easier than it is for us now: they were born in the shadow of an instruction forbidding the naming of Yahweh; only God could utter his name and speak of himself (Ex 3:14). People today, on the other hand, see the word used freely and easily, and in consequence feel the need to call God by name and stretch reason to the limits in order to be able to fool themselves that they have explained the mystery.

A theological language that wishes to be faithful to what is said knows the *paradoxical* nature of itself from the outset. On the one hand, it cannot speak of God without using the forms that he has given, and it therefore calls itself *theological*. On the other hand, it must remain linked to human nature or else no longer be a "language."

This paradoxical character opens the way to a double characteristic, which will probably have to be kept constant. The first characteristic is the law of ANALOGY, which, as never before, explains the inadequacy of our speech compared with what has to be expressed. Without taking analogy on board, theological language could be rich in expressive formulations to delight the philosopher or scholar, but will sadly no longer express the content of revelation.

The second characteristic is that of *universality.* Theological language has to be catholic and recognizable by every believer in every part of the world. The universality of theological language is no impediment, however, to the originality and distinctiveness with which different churches will wish to formulate the content of their faith. On the contrary, it is precisely what makes diversification of the statements possible: they will thus have a common base, a mother tongue in which to recognize one another.

Nonetheless, theological language will not be afraid to count SILENCE as one of its ingredients, because it is aware that silence is both the source and the end of any theological language when confronted with the revelation of the trinitarian mystery of God: *Verbo crescente, verba deficiunt* ("Insofar as the Word appears, human words fail").

Bibl.: I. T. RAMSEY, *Religious Language* (London, 1957); H. URS VON BALTHASAR, *Word and Revelation* (New York, 1964); id., *Das Ganze im Fragment* (Einsiedeln, 1967; cf. *A Theological Anthropology* [New York, 1967]); E. CASTELLI, ed., *L'analisi del linguaggio teologico: Dire Dio* (Rome, 1969); J. LADRIÈRE, *L'articulation du sens,* 2 vols. (Paris, 1970, 1984); D. ANTISERI, *Filosofia analitico e semantica del linguaggio religioso* (Brescia, 1970); E. BISER, *Theologische Sprachtheorie und Hermeneutik* (Munich, 1970); G. B. MONDIN, *Il problema del linguaggio teologico dalle origini ad oggi* (Brescia, 1971); C. MOLARI, *La fede e il suo linguaggio* (Assisi, 1972); F. FERRÉ, *Le langage religieux at-t-il un sens? Logique moderne de la foi* (Paris, 1970); S. FAUSTI, *Ermeneutica teologica* (Bologna, 1973); I. MANCINI, *Teologia, Ideologia, Utopia* (Brescia, 1974); E. SCHILLEBEECKX, *The Understanding of Faith* (London, 1974); J. MACQUARRIE, *Thinking about God* (New York, 1975); G. LAFONT, *Dieu, le temps et l'être* (Paris, 1986).

Rino FISICHELLA

LITERATURE AND THEOLOGY

At its deepest level and in its most specific thrust, literature has for its purpose a fuller understanding of the mystery of the human person. It originates in the most irreducible core of the person, that mysterious level at which the person is first of all SILENCE and SOLITUDE, before opening itself to others through the medium of LANGUAGE. Literature is life, conscious of itself, that reaches its full self-expression through use not only of all the conceptual resources of language but also of the power of suggestion that language exercises through image, rhythm, and harmony.

From this point of view, poetry, drama, and the novel are privileged forms of interpersonal communication. Scripture, too, in its endeavor to express the ineffable Absolute, makes spontaneous use of images, symbols, poems, and lyric songs. The same is true of the great mystics (John of the Cross, Teresa of Avila, Francis of Assisi), who have no means except poetry to express the inexpressible. For in mystical experience as in poetic experience, expression originates in preconceptual or supraconceptual sources.

Taken in a broader sense, literature is the irreducible activity whose goal, like that of any artistic activity, is creation, but that in this case uses a specific material, language, and has specific purposes. Literature, understood in this broad sense, uses a great variety of literary genres: poetry, legend, epic, drama, chronicle, history, tale, novel, criticism, journalism, etc.

Human knowledge would be greatly impoverished without literature, for literature is a mirror reflecting the human person down the ages. This knowledge is of concern to theology, because while Christianity offers its own vision of the human person and the world, it needs to know those to whom the gospel is addressed, the expectations it is to fulfill, the problems to which it is to give an answer. It needs, consequently, to know how the gospel is perceived and received, and why it is accepted or, on the contrary, rejected and attacked. Vatican II, in its constitution *Gaudium et Spes*, recognizes the importance of literature:

> Literature and the arts are also, in their own way, of great importance to the life of the Church. For they strive to probe the unique nature of man, his problems and his experiences as he struggles to know and perfect both himself and the world. They are preoccupied with revealing man's place in history and in the world, with illustrating his miseries and joys, his needs and strengths, and with foreshadowing a better life for him. Thus they are able to elevate human life as it is expressed in manifold forms, depending on time and place. (*GS* 62)

As a matter of fact, all the currents of thought that have made their mark on the human mind have had their repercussion in literature. If we want to know human beings, we cannot do without literature. It stands at the crossroads of all human experience and all human problems: individual and social life, silence, solitude, otherness, work and progress, evil and freedom, sin and DEATH, etc. All forms of commitment, as well as all the gropings in darkness, all anxieties and doubts, find expression in literature. What would our knowledge of the human person be without Homer, Sophocles, Aeschylus, Dante, Shakespeare, Pascal, Montaigne, Molière, Racine, Tolstoy, Dostoyevski, Cervantes, Hemingway, Péguy, Claudel, Camus, Bernanos, and others?

Despite all this, until recently, theology allowed literature only a quite limited and even shamefaced place, with an insult added at times: "But, of course, that's only literature!"—a judgment that evidently discredited theology even more than it did literature. The result was that for a long time anthropology was deprived of an immensely rich resource. The fact that so many literary works were placed on the Index hardly promoted a dialogue between literature and theology. Those times are happily now past, and Vatican II openly acknowledged all that the church owes to literature. Present-day theologians not only turn to literature as an indispensable source; many of them are both literary persons and theologians. Think, for example, of Urs VON BALTHASAR, H. DE LUBAC, and J. Daniélou.

It seems possible to distinguish two ways in which theology and literature enrich each other.

Sometimes, while retaining its "literary" character (on which writers themselves insist), literature can at the same time convey the Christian message, which has become the life of the author's life. Thus such men as Chesterton, Bloy, Mauriac, Papini, Claudel, Bernanos, and Péguy, despite their not being professional theologians, lead us to a much better understanding of the faith than that which we may derive from many professional theologians. Some striking examples: the theme of the communion of saints, and the sense of sin and forgiving love, in Bernanos; or the theme of the abiding power of the priesthood to sanctify, despite the person's unworthiness, in Graham Greene's *Power and the Glory*.

But there are also instances of literature that, without being explicitly Catholic or even Christian, attains to such a knowledge of human beings and their problems that it becomes a fruitful and stimulating challenge to theology. Because literature has at its disposal all the rich resources of language, it describes the problems of human beings with an analytic penetration and a power to express and evoke that a strictly theological language cannot attain. How, for example, is it possible to surpass the dramatic intensity of the poem about the Grand Inquisitor in Dostoyevski, or the power of hatred, excelled only by the still-greater power of love, in Bernanos's *Diary of a Country Priest?* Theological reflection will never substitute for the poetic and prophetic power of these pages.

Literature, then, is not in competition with theology or even with the studies of the human being that are conducted in sociology, psychology, and psychiatry. Literature develops at a different level. Its aim is not erudition or information; instead, the medium of language with its magically evocative and creative power makes literature capable of a *qualitative* penetration of the mystery of the human person, an understanding that differs from the knowledge collected by the human sciences. The analyses of Jung and Freud will never succeed in equaling the human universe revealed by Shakespeare, Dostoyevsky, Tolstoy, and Pascal. It is true, of course, that these great works of literature raise more questions, expectations, and problems than they give answers, but this is precisely their special contribution to anthropology.

As we know, the real answer to the problems of the human person comes from "revelation." In a passage that is Pascalian in inspiration and even in language, *Gaudium et Spes* has this to say:

But what is man? About himself he has expressed, and continues to express, many divergent and even contradictory opinions. In these he often exalts himself as the absolute measure of all things or debases himself to the point of despair. The result is doubt and anxiety. The Church understands these problems. Endowed with light from God, she can offer solutions to them so that man's true situation can be portrayed and his defects explained, while at the same time his dignity and destiny are justly acknowledged. (12)

Then comes the key passage: "The truth is that only in the mystery of the incarnate Word does the mystery of man take on light" (22).

But we must immediately add: The illumination that Christ brings is measured by the thickness of the darkness that it dissipates. But it is literature that describes the dimensions of this darkness, i.e., the doubts, anxieties, questions, problems, and aspirations of human beings. What a different effect, then, one and the same light has when focused on a bush and when focused on the depths of an abyss! Literature brings to light the abysses within the human person, while revelation and then theology take over to show how Christ enters these depths and illumines them. In short, an anthropology that is developed without lengthy prior contemplation of the subject it is studying—namely, the human person—is in danger of being trivial. Literature can help it avoid this danger by showing it the dimensions of the human mystery that the mystery of Christ comes to illumine.

Bibl.: P.-H. SIMON, *La littérature du péché et de la grâce* (Paris, 1957); P. DUPLOYÉ, *La religion de Péguy* (Paris, 1965); C. MÖLLER, "La théologie devant l'évolution de la littérature au XXe siècle," in R. V. Gucht and H. Vorgrimmler, eds., *Bilan de la théologie du XXe siècle*, vol. 1 (Paris, 1970); L. GUISSARD, "Littérature," *Cath* 7 (1974): 842–61; H. CARRIER, *The Gospel and Cultures: From Leo XIII to John-Paul II* (Vatican City/Paris, 1987).

René LATOURELLE

LOCI THEOLOGICI

In modern theology, the loci are a cluster of standard organizing principles governing theological work. With roots in Aristotle, the Western rhetorical tradition spoke of the "commonplaces" as ordered sets of knowledge, such as historical exempla, useful citations, figures of speech, which the trained speaker or writer has acquired and has ready to hand. Rudolph Agricola's *De inventione dialectica* (1479) set forth thirty such loci, which are perspectives on reality from which one can discover material for use in constructing an argument. But the subsequent theological appropriation of the loci-method took place in two quite different ways.

A major early work of Protestant pedagogy was P. Melanchthon's *Loci communes rerum theologicarum* (1521; revised as the *Loci praecipui theologici* in 1559). Here the loci are the main themes found at the center of Scripture, such as our human fallen condition, sin, the gospel, justification, faith, and so on, in which one should garner data and instruction through study of all the canonical books. The loci constitute an ordered list of topics or headings that define the scope of theological formation. Mastery of the loci equips one for expounding Scripture's own manifold witness to God's beneficence to sinful humankind through Christ.

But another approach to the loci shaped the premier methodological treatise of modern Catholic theology, Melchior Cano's *De locis theologicis* (Salamanca, 1563; reprinted thirty times down to 1890). Cano, a Dominican student of Francesco de Vitoria and imperial theologian at the Council of Trent in 1551–1552, set forth the loci as the documentary fields in which the theologian discovers evidence in support of doctrines to be articulated or in rebuttal of doctrines rejected as heterodox. Cano's influential work of method is essentially an account of the sources from which a Catholic theologian draws his material. Certain rules govern work with each locus, showing how to derive specific testimonies to God's revealed truth in the manner appropriate to the locus. Making explicit the contrast between his notion and the loci of Melanchthon, Cano borrowed from Cicero's *De oratore* to call the loci the "domiciles" of all those elements with which one carries on theological argumentation. Cano places Holy Scripture first among the loci and explains its truth and canonical authority. Unfortunately, Cano's

death in 1560 prevented him from composing book 13 of his *De locis*, which was to be a treatise on biblical hermeneutics. The second focus is the complex of those apostolic traditions coming from Christ or the Holy Spirit's instruction of the apostles, which have proved to belong to the perennial doctrinal patrimony. These two fundamental sources, in which God's revealing word gives immediate attestation of itself, are in turn interpreted, protected, and developed by what the believer and theologian encounter in five diverse expressions of God's truth in the life of the church: the faith of the universal body of believers, synods and councils, the Roman church and its pastor, the fathers, and the scholastic theologians. When investigated properly—according to rules based on the nature of each—these seven areas give rise to specific kinds of testimony to God's revelation. Each locus can provide a proper and authoritative witness to the content of Christian doctrine.

Cano, as a disciple of Thomas Aquinas, did not construe theological work in a narrowly supernaturalistic manner, but instead went on to list three further fields from which one should draw materials of doctrinal relevance. These loci are the "annexes" of the main dwelling places of theological evidence, but they have nonetheless their specific contribution to make. Cano thus listed as the final three loci natural reason, the views of philosophers, and the lessons of human history.

Fundamental theology has traditionally included an exposition of the doctrinal sources and of theological method. Such a "doctrine of principles" is the natural complement of this discipline's account of revelation, credibility, faith, and the transmission of the gospel in the church for the world. A contemporary doctrine of the loci or sources will want to introduce themes not found in Cano, such as the witness of the liturgy and the experience of regional or local churches. But Cano's presentation retains its relevance.

(1) His account stands as a salutary warning against constricting the scope of theological research, whether by seeking the actuality of special experiences or by a quest for preemptive certitude, such as might be had from a literal reading of Scripture or from the ecclesial magisterium. Cano's breadth indicates the proper amplitude and complexity of a Catholic

theologian's *auditus fidei*. No single locus may exercise monopolistic control.

(2) What Cano's loci yield are testimonies having "authority." But this is not an authority due primarily to the will-act by which this or that mediating structure of the church was historically instituted. The testimonies of the loci impress themselves by reason of the Word of God, which comes to articulation in each of them.

(3) Finally, the system of numerous loci constitutes a profound indication that the gospel impinges on the believer "in many and various ways" (Heb 1:1). The witnesses to revealed truth speak with voices of different pitch and timbre, which a Christian teacher seeks to fuse into a symphonic whole. Other combinations and configurations are obviously possible. But good teaching attracts and charms precisely by reason of the harmonious interaction of its diverse components.

Bibl.: A. LANG, *Die loci theologici des Melchior Cano und die Methode des dogmatischen Beweises* (Munich, 1925); A. GARDEIL, "Lieux théologiques," *DTC* 9:712–47; E. MARCOTTE, *La nature de la théologie d'après Melchior Cano* (Ottawa, 1949); A. SCOLA, "Chiesa e metodo teologico in Melchior Cano," *RSLR* 9 (1973): 203–34; M. ANDRES, *La teologia española en el siglo XVI*, 2 vols. (Madrid, 1976, 1977), 2:311–29, 386–424; M. SECKLER, "Die ekklesiologische Bedeutung des Systems der 'loci theologici,'" in W. Baier et al., eds., *Weisheit Gottes— Weisheit der Welt* (Festschrift J. Ratzinger), 2 vols. (St. Ottilien, 1987), 1:37–65, reprinted in M. SECKLER, *Die schiefen Wande des Lehrhauses* (Freiburg, 1988), 79–104; J. TAPIA, *Iglesia y teología en Melchior Cano* (Rome, 1989).

Jared WICKS

LOVE

The specific task of fundamental theology is to understand and interpret the credibility of God's self-revelation that has definitively come through Jesus Christ This divine self-communication in human history reached its climax with the paschal mystery and the sending of the Holy Spirit.

Beyond question, fundamental theologians must also address other questions. Never-

theless, two central issues that give their discipline its basic character are revelation and resurrection, both understood not only dogmatically but also apologetically. In a particular way the nature and credibility of God's self-revelation and Christ's rising from the dead are illuminated by the theme of love.

1. Revelation

In and through the created universe God is manifested. The act of creation can be rightly seen as the primordial sign pointing to the divine benevolence. Love means an approval that wills and works for the good of others. The God revealed in the act of creation is a God who approves of human beings and their world and with effective divine power says, "I will that you exist."

While acknowledging the revelation of God mediated through the works and signs of nature (e.g., Gn 9:12–17; Jb 38–39; Ps 19:1–6; Wis 13:1–9), the OT gives precedence to the divine self-manifestation in human history. God has intervened in a special way to choose a people, bring them out of captivity, and so guide their story as to reveal ever more clearly the divine love toward them. An ancient creed that confesses the Lord's mighty acts revealed in the exodus experience and the conquest of Canaan (Dt 26:5–10) does not explicitly speak of the divine love but clearly presents a God whose faithful concern has repeatedly blessed the people.

Hosea's own life dramatizes God's redeeming and compassionate love toward Israel. The prophet witnesses to an intensely personal love of the Lord, a husband who will not abandon his harlot-people (Hos 1:2–3:5). Second Isaiah pictures God as crying out "like a woman in labor" (Is 42:14) or like a woman who has given birth to and carried Israel (Is 45:3–4; 49:15). The prophets and others feel constrained to describe God as mother, father, or spouse (e.g., Dt 32:6). They can do no less, since they have experienced God as loving, saving, and tenderly devoted to them.

Vatican II draws on both OT and NT to portray revelation as God "out of the abundance of His love" speaking to us as friends and drawing us into the divine fellowship (*DV* 2). This self-communication of God (*DV* 6) is no self-indulgent activity, but aims at our salvation through a sacramental structure of words and events (DV 2). The words light up and convey the revealing and saving value of events, which might otherwise remain merely anonymous and meaningless episodes.

The climax of the divine self-communication came with Jesus Christ and the events of his life, death, and resurrection. In *Redemptor Hominis*, John Paul II's encyclical of 1979, which, like his second encyclical of 1980 (*Dives in Misericordia*) has much to teach about revelation, the pope writes of God's "revelation of love" being also "described as mercy." He adds: "In human history this revelation of love and mercy has taken a form and a name: that of Jesus Christ" (*Redemptor Hominis* 9). The heart of the divine self-communication in Christ has been classically formulated by saying "God is love" (1 Jn 4:8, 16).

It is not that the revelation of God's love was absent from the OT. We have seen above how the prophets, among others, witnessed to the intensely personal love of God toward Israel. Such evidence gives the lie to the old dictum that God revealed his justice in the OT and his love in the NT.

What Christ brings, however, is first of all the visible, tangible, and audible presence of "Emmanuel, God with us" (Mt 1:23). Second, God is now disclosed as tripersonal. The Father is known as the ultimate source of divine life and love. The Son is the perceptible presence of this love. The Holy Spirit is experienced as the Gift of love (Rom 5:5) who moves us toward our eschatological fulfillment.

The Synoptic Gospels speak of "love" sparingly when presenting the ministry of Jesus. Luke, for instance, does not introduce the language of love in that most powerful expression of God's merciful love toward the lost and sinful, the parable of the prodigal son. What the Synoptics portray is a largely implicit but extremely real self-revelation of love in words and deeds. Jesus obeyed his Father, served others, suffered for them, healed them, gave himself away with unlimited generosity and, finally, died on a cross between two of the unrighteous, to whom he offered divine compassion and mercy. Jesus was love personified. His crucifixion, however, left the question open: Is such obedient love ultimately self-destructive and doomed to empty failure (Phil 2:8)?

2. Resurrection

The resurrection of the crucified Jesus revealed "the love of the Father which is more powerful than death" (*Dives in Misericordia* 8). The dialogue of love between Jesus and his Father, interrupted (at least in terms of Jesus' humanity) by the silence of death, is now resumed in a full and final way. To use the frequent NT image, Jesus is assumed into heaven and sits at the right hand of the Father (e.g., Acts 2:33; Rom 8:34; Col 3:1).

The paschal mystery can be explored and interpreted in various keys; e.g., as the climax of human redemption, as the foundation of Christian faith, and as the basis of all our hopes. No single approach can ever expect to do justice to the mystery. Nevertheless, the effective and definitive revelation of God's love is perhaps the most appropriate key for interpreting the resurrection of the crucified Jesus.

In John's Gospel it is no accident that from chap. 11 on, as the paschal mystery draws near, the language of love becomes more prominent. The Last Supper and the farewell discourses of Jesus begin (Jn 13:1) and end (17:26) with that language. In fact, the final prayer of Jesus, which interprets the point and purpose of his imminent death and resurrection, concludes with a petition to the Father on behalf to the disciples, "that the love with which you have loved me may be in them, and I in them" (Jn 17:26).

By rising from the dead, Jesus finally founds his community of love—the church, which is to be described in bridal imagery (Eph 5:21–33; Rv 21:2, 9). During his earthly existence Jesus has been the visible sign and living symbol of his Father—a theme classically expressed by Jesus' words to Philip, "Whoever has seen me has seen the Father" (Jn 14:9). With his death and resurrection Jesus himself is no longer directly and immediately seen. His community comes fully into being as the visible, living sign of his desire to save and bring home to the Father all men and women of all times and places. Despite their sinful failures, Christians remain strengthened by the Holy Spirit to be the special sign for the whole world of the risen Lord's presence and power.

To conclude: The loving self-manifestation of God climaxed with the resurrection of the crucified Jesus. The resurrection, one can also say, revealed the church, God's new community of love that lives in expectation of the final appearing of our savior (Ti 2:13), when his divine glory will be fully revealed (1 Pt 4:13).

Bibl.: H. Urs VON BALTHASAR, *Glaubhaft ist nur Liebe* (Einsiedeln, 1966; French: *L'amour seul est digne de foi* [Paris, 1966]); R. FISICHELLA, *H. U. von Balthasar: Amore et credibilità cristiana* (Rome, 1981); R. LATOURELLE, *Le témoignage chrétien* (Montreal/Paris, 1971).

Gerald O'COLLINS

LUTHERANISM

I. A LUTHERAN PERSPECTIVE

Fundamental theology has been little discussed and less practiced in the Reformation tradition. Unlike natural theology, it has not even been much attacked. This article is therefore an attempt to explain why it has been ignored. It starts with a description of the original Reformation position, briefly mentions developments during the intervening centuries, and concludes with comments about the present situation, including the possibility that fundamental theology as a distinct genre may have some future among the heirs of the Reformation.

This essay, though written by a Lutheran, is not confessionally distinctive. On the issues that here concern us, in contrast to certain others, there is little difference between the Reformed (Calvinist) and Lutheran traditions. It seems best, therefore, to speak simply of Reformation (or, as a synonym, following German usage, "evangelical") theology.

a. It is not the concern of fundamental theology but rather its existence as a distinct discipline that is alien to the Reformation tradition. This estrangement becomes understandable when one reflects on the implications of the *sola scriptura* in conjunction with the *sola fide.* Despite these watchwords, the Reformers were not anti-intellectual or fideistic. They marshaled all the cognitive resources of their day, including those of pagan provenance, for the task of understanding Scripture and the

faith for which it calls. No theologians in history have more vigorously pursued the enterprise of *fides quaerens intellectum* ("faith seeking understanding"). It was, however, a particular kind of *intellectum* they sought; the understanding of what may be called the internal *logos* or logic of faith. Like many pre-Reformation thinkers, not least Anselm in *Cur Deus Homo,* they focused on the inner connections of scriptural teachings. To this they added, more than had been done before, methodologically self-conscious concern for kerygmatic import, for applications *pro nobis.* These tasks we now generally divide between dogmatic or systematic and practical theologies, but they were for them a single enterprise, and they did their work in both areas as biblical theologians with constant reference to the language and conceptual grammar of Scripture.

Yet in their pursuit of *fides quaerens intellectum internum,* they did not exclude that other, "external" dimension of faith's self-understanding which is the special province of fundamental theology, the relation of faith's affirmations to that which is knowable apart from faith. Intent as they were on proclaiming the biblical message, they reflected at times on what seems reasonable or unreasonable to unbelievers outside the church and to the unbelief in the heart of every Christian. If one does not do this, one cannot make the crucial distinctions between true and false offenses to the intellect, and will substitute other scandals for the scandal of the cross. There are after all, to put it at an elementary level, such things as logical confusions, which can inhibit faith and which need to be cleared up by logic. (Luther, e.g., expatiates at length on the usefulness of Ockhamist logic in dealing with Zwinglian difficulties regarding the real presence.)

One thing must be eschewed, however. There must be no suggestion that the reasoning, knowledge, or experience available apart from faith sustains or enhances its authority or the authority of the Scripture to which it clings. The Bible, to use the classic phrases, is self-interpreting and the *norma normans non normata* ("normative norm not normed"). Its authority is that of God himself, and this cannot be increased by any amount of human reasoning. To try to do so is as misguided as the attempt to reinforce the certitude of the Pythagorean theorem by measuring more and more right triangles (Aquinas makes a similar logical point, e.g., in *ST* 1, q.1, a.8). Thus, while reason is needed both internally to explicate the faith and externally to clarify confusions and stop the mouths of mockers, it provides not the slightest foundation or legitimation for accepting the scriptural message. In relation to reason, that message is self-founded. It cannot be anything else if it is heard as truly God's word.

What has just been said about the foundational irrelevance of reason in general applies to all the other supports that could be proposed for the authority of Scripture: tradition, church, theories of inspirations or revelation, or faith itself. These are not excluded but rather included as content or consequence by the *sola scriptura*. Faith, to start with, does not validate Scripture but rather is validated by it. Similarly, though the Bible speaks of inspiration and revelation and theologians are at liberty to construct theories about such matters, scriptural authority does not depend on their success or failure (Aquinas follows a similar route in his discussion of, e.g., inspiration in *ST* 2.2, 171–73). Further, listening to the Word is a communal or ecclesial activity, not an individualistic one, for we need the help of other hearers, past as well as present, in order to distinguish God's voice from our own imaginings. Yet that voice is its own authority, not dependent on the church.

Nor, finally, is tradition excluded, though dependence on it is. This point needs amplification because of the Reformers' supposed anti-traditionalism. Their referent for the word was narrower than ours, and usually pejorative. First, when the word "tradition" is used in the sense in which contemporary historians generally employ the term, one can say that for them it is tradition that makes Scripture into Scripture just as analogously traditional conventions of reading make Euclid's *Elements* into geometry or Homer's *Iliad* into an epic poem rather than, as for philologists, mere sources of information about ancient Greek. The Bible is a heterogeneous collection of ancient writings unless it is read and used, as the Reformers insisted it should be, as the word of the triune God incarnate *pro nobis* in Jesus Christ, the one who alone is to be trusted for salvation. When thus functioning as hermeneutical principles, these doctrines are not extra-scriptural

developments but central parts of biblical content. Second, there is yet another sense in which traditions are contained in Scripture. These came to be called "necessary consequences." Luther placed infant baptism in this category because *inter alia*, he saw it as the paradigmatic instantiation of the *sola gratia*. Third, there are enduringly desirable extra-biblical traditions such as, for Luther, private confession and absolution, and also those that are contingently approvable, such as medieval mass vestments and ceremonials (on which Calvin was not so permissive). When, therefore, the Reformers rejected tradition, they were referring only to a fourth category: developments opposed to Scripture interpreted *sola gratia, sola fide, sola Christo*. In sum, the Bible is the self-founded touchstone for judging all traditions, reasonings, experiencings, and church authorities. It is normative primacy, not material exclusiveness, that is the import of the *sola scriptura*.

b. Yet this reformatory outlook, though not excluding the concerns of fundamental theology, makes it difficult for these to be organized into a distinct discipline. Appeals to the reasoning and evidence that believers share with nonbelievers occur as ad hoc responses to specific problems within the context of reflection on the logic internal to Scripture or, more particularly, on its kerygmatic applications. While there is no objection in principle to systematizing and generalizing the strategies these responses involve, there is also no need to do so. That need arises only if one thinks it possible and desirable to base the authority of Scripture on deeper certitudes.

This is not the place to trace the origins of the demand for epistemological foundations which has dominated Western philosophy from Descartes and Locke on and which, when unfulfilled—as has happened increasingly in the last hundred years—has no recourse except relativism or nihilism. Suffice it to say that it was in this context that apologetic and fundamental theologies were transformed from the incidental exercises they had historically been into systematic foundational disciplines, programmatically distinct from each other and from dogmatic or systematic theology.

Protestants, except for fideists, have on the

whole been more radically foundationalist than Roman Catholics, and this helps account for their neglect of the intermediate path represented by fundamental theology. The orthodox among them sought to base scriptural authority in inspiration and developed proto-fundamentalist theories of verbal inerrancy. Rationalists capitulated to purportedly universal Enlightenment criteria of reasonableness and tended toward unitarianism and deism. Simple pietists and their more sophisticated liberal descendants appealed, on analogy with faith alone, to experience alone as the foundation of scriptural authority (thus inverting the Reformation relationship). The long-regnant ideal of objectivity decreed an apologetic starting point, i.e., one outside the circle of faith. Those who, like Roman Catholic fundamental theologians, admitted to beginning with faith or were suspected of doing so were regularly accused of intellectual dishonesty. The search for foundations, so it was supposed, could not be successful if it was biased by personal prejudices.

c. The situation has changed in the twentieth century. Virtually all religious thought now resembles fundamental theology, inasmuch as the pretentions of objectivity have been abandoned and the inevitability of moving within some kind of circle of faith has been recognized. Further, those Protestants who are closest to the old liberals share with fundamental theologians the concern to exhibit the reasonableness of the faith by general rather than faith-specific criteria. Yet the differences are also great. The desire to make religion intelligible and attractive to the cultured among its despisers often dominates the entire theological program, and this results in a conflation of apologetics and dogmatics. The logic of believing which is internal to Christian faith tends to be distorted or replaced by one of the logics of coming to believe (e.g., through some type of rationality, or conversion, or existential authenticity) which are often common to a variety of religions. Thus recent Protestant liberals, of whom Paul Tillich is the greatest, have affinities to Roman Catholic fundamental theology, but do not have a place for it as a distinct discipline clearly separated from dogmatics.

At the other end of the spectrum is Karl Barth, for whom the authority of Scripture is as wholly self-founding as for the Reformers, but who went beyond them in his attacks on any efforts, no matter how nonfoundational, to show that the faith is reasonable by externally available standards. He made no distinction between apologetics and fundamental theology on the one hand, or foundational and nonfoundational positions on the other. Largely under Barth's influence, this undiscriminating rejection of all forms of fundamental theology was virtually universal until the 1960s among those confessionally committed to the Reformation traditions.

The beginnings of a new attitude are evident in the writings of some German Lutheran theologians in the last twenty-five years. In contrast to more liberal Protestants, but in agreement with Roman Catholics, they maintain the distinctions between apologetic, fundamental, and dogmatic theology. They are not, however, as clearly nonfoundational in reference to the authority of Scripture as were Barth and the Reformers.

A further development is now taking place in North America under the influence of widening Anglo-American philosophical claims that the modern search for epistemological foundations is itself thoroughly irrational and a major source of contemporary relativism and nihilism. Under the influence of this antifoundationalism, some theologians—chiefly Protestant but including Roman Catholics—argue that Barth, the Reformers, and pre-Reformation thinkers, not least Anselm and Aquinas, were reasonable in their refusal to give reasons that purport to enhance or warrant the authority of the Scripture or tradition to which they adhered. Indeed, the attempt to advance such reasons is self-contradictory and fails to meet the criteria of what is rational in such matters. Thus, an evangelical fundamental theology fully consistent with Reformation concerns may be coming into existence; and, what is more, it may be an ecumenical one.

Bibl.: G. EBELING, "Erwägungen zu einer evangelischen Fundamental-theologie," *ZTK* 67 (1970): 479–524; id., *The Study of Theology* (London, 1979), 153–65; W. JOEST, *Fundamentaltheologie* (Stuttgart, 1974); W. PANNENBERG, *Theology and the Philosophy of Science* (London, 1976); G. LINDBECK, *The Nature of Doctrine* (Philadelphia, 1984); F. S. FIORENZA, *Foundational Theology: Jesus and the Church* (New York,

1984); R. THIEMANN, *Revelation and Theology* (Notre Dame, Ind., 1985).

George LINDBECK

II. LAW AND GOSPEL

Martin Luther asserted on occasion that the correct distinction between law and gospel was the *summa* of Christian doctrine. In *The Freedom of a Christian* (1520) he explained that all Scripture is divided into two kinds of content: commandments of law and promises of grace and salvation in Christ. Biblical words first demand an obedience that, it turns out, a person cannot give or achieve by natural and innate power; but other words to us are gracious offers of unmerited righteousness and freedom in Christ (*WA* 7:23–24; *LW* 31:348f.). For sound theology, biblical interpretation, and preaching, it is essential to preserve both law and gospel, each in their distinctive character while never separating them.

Luther's notion of law/gospel does not refer to the division of OT and NT, for important evangelical promises are recorded in the Scriptures of Israel, e.g., Gn 3:15; 22:18; and the prophecies of the savior (*WA Deutsche Bibel* 6:4–7 *LW* 35:359f.). In the NT, while Jesus is the very content of the gospel and his apostles are its heralds, both also take pains to show the radical depth and extent of what God's law demands of us, as in the Great Commandment of love of God and neighbor.

God's revealed law, with the sanctions it threatens, does serve public order by reining in human destructiveness and thus protecting God's good creation against the forces of chaos. But the truly theological work of law, in either testament, is to place the human person in crisis, by imposing a demand that in fact asks more than what fallen human nature, with its *cor incurvatum in se*, can do. God wants willing service and threatens with death and loss those who fail to render this. Salvation, however, comes uniquely through the blessing of forgiveness and new life given because of Christ, all of which the gospel sets forth. The gospel announces that God's law has been observed perfectly by Jesus Christ and invites sinners to partake of this, as a pure gift, by faith. Under the gospel the believer does begin, by God's gifts of grace, to observe the law to an extent, but this is a work of grateful response, not the fulfillment of a requirement set down as the condition for attaining salvation.

Luther, as a biblical translator, found the distinction between law and gospel a great help in getting to the meaning of difficult biblical passages (*WA Tischreden* 1:128; *LW* 54:24f.). The distinction also underlies Luther's general hermeneutical principle that Scripture itself provides the rightful guidelines for its own interpretation (*"sacra Scriptura sui ipsius interpres," WA* 7:97). He worked this out in numerous detailed biblical commentaries by treating texts either as illustrating and urging the demands of an ultimately unfulfillable law or as announcing the pure grace of the gospel. This is the key to grasping all of God's dealings with his human creatures. Scripture means to show us our sinfulness and thereby to prepare us for the good news of God's gratuitous mercy, which can be rightly heard only by one sensing his or her dire straits.

Luther saw misrepresentation of Scripture and bad theology on two sides. A doctrine of merited salvation, with the mentality of expecting God to reward one's good works on the basis of *quid pro quo*, had to be opposed by urging the pure grace of what God has done on our behalf in Christ. On the other side, an "antinomian" view emerged in the teaching proposed by Luther's disciple Johann Agricola, that the law had no place at all in Christian life. Luther proved relentless in attacking Agricola's obfuscation of the genuine nature of faith as a form of resolution of a dire crisis and his transfer to Christ and the gospel of some of the law's functions.

Ultimately, the distinction of law and gospel is not about biblical texts or the discourse of theology. More basically it raises the question of the essence of Christianity (Söhngen, 1957) by witnessing to the nature of God's action in his creation and our relation to the God who overtakes us. God works in a fundamentally twofold manner, revealing himself thus in two distinct but interrelated ways. As sovereign Lord, he expresses his will and command, but as Father of mercies he speaks effective promises of forgiveness and mercy. Thus, "the proper subject of theology is man guilty of sin and condemned, and God the justifier and savior of sinful man" (*WA* 40/2: 318; *LW* 12:311). Christian existence, conformed to proper theology, focuses both on confessing one's own sin and helplessness and on ever again laying hold of God's word of saving grace because of Christ.

Bibl.: G. Söhngen, *Gesetz und Evangelium: Ihre analoge Einheit* (Freiburg/Munich, 1957); G. Ebeling, *Luther: Introduction à une réflexion théologique* (Geneva, 1983), chaps. 7–8; A. Peters, *Gesetz und Evangelium* (Gütersloh, 1981); J. Rogge, "Innerlutherische Streitigkeiten um Gesetz und Evangelium, Rechtfertigung und Heiligung," in H. Junghans, ed., *Leben und Werk Martin Luthers von 1526 bis 1546* (Berlin/Göttingen, 1983), 187–204.

Jared Wicks

MAGISTERIUM

The word *magisterium* in classical Latin meant the role and authority of one who was a "master" in any one of the various applications of the term: one could be "master" of a ship, of servants, of an art or trade, as well as a schoolmaster. However, by the Middle Ages, *magisterium* had come to mean the role and authority of the teacher. The traditional symbol of teaching authority was the chair; thus, Thomas Aquinas could speak of two kinds of *magisterium:* that of the pastoral chair of the bishop and that of the professorial chair of the university theologian.

In modern Catholic usage, the term "magisterium" has come to be associated almost exclusively with the teaching role and authority of the hierarchy. An even more recent development is that the term "the magisterium" is often used to refer not to the teaching office as such but to the body of men who have this office in the Catholic church: namely, the pope and bishops. In the documents of the Second Vatican Council one finds the term used in both of these senses. The council also several times described the magisterium of the pope and bishops as "authentic" and declared that "the task of authentically interpreting the word of God, whether written or handed on, has been entrusted exclusively to the living *magisterium*" (*DV* 10). It is important to understand that the term "authentic" as used here does not mean "genuine" or "true," but rather "authoritative," and, specifically, "endowed with pastoral or hierarchical authority." The council did not intend to deny that theologians and exegetes can interpret the word of God with such authority as their learning confers on them. What it asserts is that only the pastors of the church have inherited the mandate Christ gave to the apostles to teach in his name with such authority that he who hears them hears Christ, and he who rejects them rejects Christ and him who sent him (see Lk 10:16).

Catholic belief that the bishops have inherited the teaching mandate that Christ gave to his apostles, is expressed in the following statements of Vatican II: "By divine institution bishops have succeeded to the place of the apostles as shepherds of the Church" (*LG* 20). "The order of bishops is the successor to the college of the apostles in teaching authority and pastoral rule" (*LG* 22). "As successors of the apostles, bishops receive from Him [Christ] the mission to teach all nations and to preach the gospel to every creature" (*LG* 24).

These assertions obviously need to be substantiated by evidence from the NT and the documents of the early church. Space in this article permits only a brief indication of how this could be done. The following points would have to be developed: (1) the apostles received from Christ the mandate to teach in his name; (2) they shared this mandate with others whom they enlisted in the pastoral ministry; (3) the principle of succession in this mandate is already operative during the period of the writing of the NT; (4) the second- and third-century church recognized its bishops as the rightful successors of the apostles in teaching authority.

Since Christ himself left nothing in writing, Christian faith depends entirely on the witness of his disciples, and especially on the witness of the twelve men whom Christ had personally chosen "to be with him and to be sent out to proclaim the message" (Mk 3:14). To be a Christian means to be one who "believes in Christ through their word" (see Jn 17:20), for, apart from the testimony of the apostles, we would know nothing of what Christ said or did. The Gospels tell us that these men were sent out by the risen Christ with a mandate to "proclaim the good news to the whole creation" (Mk 16:15); to "make disciples of all nations . . . teaching them to obey everything that I have commanded you" (Mt 28:19–20). In fulfilling this mandate, the apostles would be authorized to speak in the name of Christ, with the consequence that "whoever welcomes you welcomes me, and whoever welcomes me welcomes the one who sent me" (Mt 10:40).

The clearest example of how an apostle shared his teaching mandate with his coworkers is found in the Pastoral Letters, where Timothy and Titus are repeatedly reminded of their mission as teachers. Timothy is told: "These are the things you must insist on and teach" (1 Tm 4:11). "Until I arrive, give attention to the public reading of scripture, to exhorting, to teaching" (1 Tm 4:13). "Pay close attention to yourself and to your teaching" (1 Tm 4:16). "Be persistent . . . with the utmost patience in teaching" (2 Tm 4:2). And Titus likewise: "But as for you, teach what is consistent with sound doctrine" (Ti 2:1).

The principle of succession in the mandate to teach is also evident in the Pastorals, e.g., in 2 Tm 4:1–8, where it is clear that Timothy is to carry on this ministry after Paul's death. It is also evident in the instructions given to Timothy to choose for the role of _episkopos_ men who are "apt teachers" (1 Tm 3:2). He is told: "What you have heard from me through many witnesses entrust to faithful people who will be able to teach others as well" (2 Tm 2:2). Titus likewise is instructed that among the qualifications of one to be chosen as elder is taht "he must have a firm grasp of the word that is trustworthy in accordance with the teaching, so that he may be able both to preach with sound doctrine and to refute those who contradict" (Ti 1:9). Similar ideas are found in Acts, where the address of Paul to the elders of the church of Ephesus looks to the time after Paul's death, when "savage wolves will come in among you." Then it will be the role of those whom "the Holy Spirit has made _episkopoi_" to be alert to safeguard the faith of the flock from corruption by those "speaking perverse things" (Acts 20:28–31). Here again we find the principle of succession in the apostolic teaching mandate already operative in the NT period.

It is true that in the NT we do not find the situation in which the teaching mandate is held by one bishop in each local church. The development from the earlier collegial form of local church leadership to the historical episcopate took place during the second century, with varying rapidity in different regions. Much in that period remains obscure; what we do know, however, is that by the end of the second century each church was led by a single bishop, assisted by presbyters and deacons, and that the bishops were recognized as the legitimate successors to the apostles. The Christian church accepted the bishops as the authorized

witnesses to apostolic tradition, with authority to formulate the creed with which the community was called upon to profess its faith. In other words, the whole church recognized the teaching of the bishops as normative for its faith.

Now it is surely a basic article of Christian faith that the Holy Spirit maintains the church in the true faith. This is a consequence of Christ's definitive victory and of his promise that the Spirit of truth would lead his church into all truth (cf. Jn 16:13). The church that is divinely maintained in the true faith could hardly have been mistaken when it determined the norms of its faith. If, then, our confidence that the Holy Spirit must have guided the second- and third-century church in its discernment of the writings that were going to be normative for its faith justifies our acceptance of the NT as inspired Scripture, we have equal reason for confidence that the Holy Spirit must have guided the same second- and third-century church in the universal recognition of its bishops as the authoritative teachers whose decisions about matters of doctrine would be normative for its faith.

2. Magisterium and the Word of God

The relationship between the _magisterium_ and the word of God as found in Scripture and tradition, is spelled out in the following passage of _DV_ 10:

> The task of authentically interpreting the word of God, whether written or handed on, has been entrusted exclusively to the living magisterium of the Church, whose authority is exercised in the name of Jesus Christ. This magisterium is not above the word of God, but serves it, teaching only what has been handed on, listening to it devoutly, guarding it scrupulously, and explaining it faithfully, by divine commission and with the help of the Holy Spirit; it draws from this one deposit of faith everything which it presents for belief as divinely revealed.

Practically every phrase here deserves some comment. The authority of the magisterium is an authority not over the word of God but over human interpretations of it. It is an authority within the community of faith, serving the unity of the church in the profession of the true faith. The term "what has been handed on" refers to the whole "sacred deposit of the word of God which is committed to the church." It is extremely significant that the council says that it is to the church (and not just to the magisterium) that the whole deposit of the word of God has been entrusted. Likewise, "the church, in her teaching, life, and worship, perpetuates and hands on to all generations all that she herself is, all that she believes" (DV 8). This is a salutary correction of the notion found in earlier treatises on this subject, according to which the deposit of faith was entrusted uniquely to the successors of the apostles, and is handed on primarily, if not exclusively, in the official teaching of the magisterium.

The phrase "listening to it devoutly" tells us that before the bishops can be preachers of the word they must first be hearers; and since "the sacred deposit of the word of God has been entrusted to the Church," they must listen to this word as it is handed on in the faith, life, and worship of the church. This will involve "consulting the faithful," as Newman put it, and also listening to the exegetes and theologians who spend their lives studying the word of God. The phrase "guarding it scrupulously" suggests the special concern of the magisterium: its primary function is not to penetrate into the depths of the mysteries of faith (the task of theology) but rather to safeguard the priceless treasure of the word of God and to defend the purity of the faith of the Christian community. They perform this task "with the help of the Holy Spirit." While the Holy Spirit dwells in all the faithful and arouses and sustains the supernatural sense of faith which characterizes the people as a whole (LG 12), Catholics believe that the sacrament of episcopal ordination, which confers the function of pastoral magisterium, is a divine pledge of a special assistance given to bishops in the fulfillment of their teaching office. While this assistance provides an absolute guarantee of the truth of their teaching only in certain rare cases, it gives us reason for confidence in the reliability of their teaching even when it is not infallible.

3. Various Forms of the Exercise of Magisterium

The first distinction to be made is between the ordinary and the extraordinary exercise of teaching authority. The extraordinary exercise is the pronouncing of a "solemn judgment" (see Vatican I, DS 3011), either by an ecumenical council or by a pope speaking *ex cathedra*, by which a doctrine is defined. To define a doctrine is to commit the church to holding and teaching this point of doctrine irrevocably, calling for an absolute assent to it on the part of all the faithful. Canon law prescribes that no doctrine is to be understood as having been defined unless this is manifestly the case (can. 749,3). Any other exercise of magisterium is ordinary. In this technical sense, the documents of Vatican II are examples of ordinary magisterium, since this council, even though it was an extraordinary historical event, chose not to define any doctrine. It must be noted that the distinction between extraordinary and ordinary magisterium is not identical to the distinction between infallible and non-infallible, since, under certain conditions that will be explained, the concordant *ordinary* teaching of the whole episcopal college also enjoys infallibility. In what follows we shall first describe the various instances of the ordinary, non-infallible exercise of the teaching function.

Each bishop who is the pastor of a diocese has responsibility and authority regarding the teaching of Christian doctrine in his diocese. He exercises this responsibility by his own teaching, whether orally or in pastoral letters, and by his promotion of sound teaching in the catechetical and educational institutions of his diocese.

Since Vatican II, bishops have been exercising their teaching function together in episcopal conferences. An episcopal conference is the permanent body composed of all the bishops of a country or territory, in which they exercise their pastoral office jointly. Vatican II strongly recommended this form of regular collaboration among all the bishops of each nation (CD 37), and Paul VI made the establishment of such conferences obligatory (AAS 58 [1966]: 774). Since teaching on matters of faith and morals is obviously part of the pastoral office of bishops, a great many episcopal conferences have issued pastoral letters or made other declarations of a doctrinal nature in the past few decades. The 1983 Code of Canon Law sanctioned this exercise of episcopal magisterium, stating: "Whether they teach individually, or in episcopal conferences, or gathered in particular councils, bishops in communion with the head and members of the college, while not infallible in their teaching, are the authentic instructors and teachers of the faith for Christ's faithful entrusted to their care" (can. 753).

The "particular councils" to which this canon refers can be either a "plenary council," in which all the bishops of an episcopal conference take part, or a "provincial council" of the bishops of one ecclesiastical province (consisting of an archdiocese and the neighboring dioceses associated with it). The regular meetings of an episcopal conference are not plenary councils, but the conference can decide, with the approval of the Holy See, to hold a plenary council, to which canon law attributes wider powers than it does to the regular meetings of the conference.

In recent years there has been a difference of opinion among theologians and canonists about the teaching authority of episcopal conferences. Some hold that it is only each individual bishop, and not the conference as a body, that has a "mandate to teach." Others insist that doctrinal statements that have been voted on and approved by the assembly of an episcopal conference come to the faithful of that region with the teaching authority of the episcopal conference as such, and not merely with that of the local bishops. Whatever the juridical case may be, it should be recognized that the real effectiveness of doctrinal statements to win the assent of the faithful depends not so much on their strictly juridical authority as on their moral authority, which can be measured by the reception which those subject to that authority are disposed to give to it. On that score, one can hardly doubt that Catholics will attribute more authority to a statement issued after full deliberation by the whole episcopal conference than to one issued only by their local bishop. The moral authority of some doctrinal statements made by episcopal conferences has been enhanced by the fact that the document itself makes the clear distinction between principles on which all Catholics are expected to be in agreement and concrete proposals that the bishops present as the fruit of their deliberations but about which they agree that there may be legitimate differences of opinion.

As has been mentioned, the documents issued by Vatican II are also examples of the ordinary exercise of magisterium, since the council chose not to define any doctrine. However, although "ordinary," this is still an exercise of the supreme teaching authority of the whole episcopal college together with its head, the pope. Hence, as the council declared, all the faithful are obliged to accept its doctrine, "according to the mind of the sacred Synod itself, which becomes known either from the subject matter or from the language employed, according to the norms of theological interpretation" (*AS* III/3, 10). These last phrases point to the varying degrees of binding force that are proper to different kinds of statements that one finds in the sixteen documents of Vatican II; it would be a mistake to give equal weight to all of them. One has to reckon with varying degrees of authority within the general category of ordinary magisterium.

What Vatican II said about the authority of its own teaching, it also said about the ordinary, nondefinitive exercise of magisterium by the Roman pontiff. *LG* 25 declares:

> Religious submission of will and of mind must be shown in a special way to the authentic teaching authority of the Roman Pontiff, in such a way that his supreme magisterium is acknowledged with reverence, the judgments made by him are sincerely adhered to, according to his manifest mind and will. His mind and will in the matter may be known chiefly either from the character of the documents, from his frequent repetition of the same doctrine, or from his manner of speakng.

The Roman pontiff exercises his ordinary teaching authority in papal encyclicals, apostolic exhortations, and other documents that are addressed to the whole church. He can also do this by his explicit and formal approval of doctrinal statements that are promulgated by the Congregation for the Doctrine of the Faith.

The term "religious submission" in the above citation from *LG* 25 is used by both the Abbott and the Flannery versions of the documents of Vatican II to translate the Latin *obsequium religiosum;* however, others prefer to render *obsequium* by the word "respect." In view of this lack of agreement as to the proper translation of the Latin term, it would seem wise to give neither too strong a meaning to "submission" nor too weak a meaning to "respect." Or one might use "submission" when speaking of the response due to the supreme teaching authority of the pope and the whole episcopal college, and "respect" of the response to the teaching authority of an individual bishop, at least when it is not evident that he is proposing what is already the common teaching of the whole episcopate.

How then is "religious submission of will and of mind" to be understood? The term "religious" refers to the motive that Catholics have for such an attitude: namely, their recognition that the pope and college of bishops have authority from Christ to teach matters of faith and morals in his name. It is "of will and of mind" in the sense that, acknowledging the teaching authority of their lawful pastors, the Catholic faithful are called upon to be willing to accept their teaching and to make it their own. This readiness of will brings its influence to bear on the judgment, to move it to assent to the teaching, even beyond the extent to which the person might naturally find the reasons given for it convincing. If people have already formed an opinion on the matter at variance with the official doctrine, they are called upon to make a serious and sustained effort to reject any tendency to obstinacy in that opinion and to convince themselves of the truth of the official teaching, so as to be able to adhere to it with a sincere interior assent of the mind. However, the standard manuals of Catholic theology take account of the fact that an attitude of religious submission to nondefinitive teaching authority does not always and in every single instance result in actual interior assent to what has been taught in this way. These approved manuals recognize that interior non-assent to this kind of teaching can be subjectively and even objectively justified when, despite sincere efforts to give one's sincere assent, reasons opposing the particular point of doctrine remain so convincing to one's mind that one is really unable to give an honest interior assent to it. Reference to this common teaching of Catholic theologians was made by the Theological Commission at Vatican II, in reply to an emendation proposed by three bishops, who had "invoked the case in which a learned person, in the face of a doctrine that had not been infallibly proposed, could not, for well-founded reasons, give his interior assent." The reply of the commission was: "On this case, the approved theological treatises should be consulted" (AS III/8, 88).

4. The Infallible Exercise of Ordinary Magisterium

While neither an individual bishop nor the pope himself speaks infallibly in the ordinary exercise of teaching authority, Vatican II lays down conditions under which the ordinary magisterium of the whole episcopal college enjoys the gift of infallibility. The conditions are these: that, while maintaining the bond of unity among themselves and with Peter's successor, and while teaching authoritatively on a matter of faith or morals, they concur in a single viewpoint as the one which must be definitively held (LG 25). The case that is envisioned is one where a particular point of doctrine has never been solemnly defined, but it is nevertheless evident that the pope and Catholic bishops all over the world have been in agreement in teaching this doctrine as something which Catholics are bound to hold in a definitive way. As an example one could mention the doctrine of the assumption of Our Lady, during the century prior to its definition as a dogma of faith by Pope Pius XII in 1950. There are also articles of the Apostles' Creed that have never been the specific object of a solemn definition but are undoubtedly proposed by the ordinary universal magisterium as doctrines of Catholic faith. Such, for instance, would be our belief in the "communion of saints."

5. The Extraordinary, Infallible Exercise of Magisterium

Here we are speaking of the "solemn judgments" by which an ecumenical council or a pope defines a doctrine. Some examples of such acts in modern times have been the definition of the immaculate conception by Pope Pius IX in 1864, the definition of papal infallibility by Vatican I in 1870, and the definition of the assumption of Our Lady by Pope Pius XII in 1950. Catholic belief in the infallibility of such solemn acts of the magisterium is based on two premises: that all the faithful are obliged to give their absolute assent of faith to dogmas that are proclaimed as such by the magisterium, and that in doing so they will not be led into error in their faith. From this it follows that such dogmas cannot be erroneous. And since no merely human teacher is immune from making errors, one rightly speaks of a "charism of infallibility," that is, a gift of grace, a work of the Holy Spirit, who alone can guarantee that such definitive teaching will necessarily be true. Solemn definitions are "irreformable," not in the sense that their formulation is so perfect or unchangeable that it could never be improved but in the sense that their authentic meaning will always be true.

When Vatican I declared that solemn definitions pronounced by the pope were "irreformable of themselves and not by virtue of the consent of the church" (DS 3074), its intention was to exclude the doctrine of Gallicanism, which had claimed that papal definitions would not be irreformable unless they were confirmed by the episcopate (DS 2284). In rejecting the Gallican position, Vatican I did not, and could not, rule out a real dependence of papal definitions on the faith of the church. For the pope can define as a dogma of faith only what is contained in the deposit of revelation, which has been entrusted to the church (*DV* 10), and is handed on "in her teaching, life, and worship" (*DV* 8). Since the pope has no independent source of revelation, he cannot define a dogma of faith without having in some real way consulted the faith of the church. However, one cannot on that account lay down the prior consensus of all the bishops or the faithful as a condition absolutely to be fulfilled prior to a papal definition, because this would eliminate the possibility of a decisive act of the papal magisterium that might be needed to overcome a threat to the church's unity in the faith and bring about a consensus, or restore one that had been lost.

6. The Subject Matter of Teaching Authority

Both Vatican I and Vatican II have described the object of authoritative and eventually infallible teaching as "matters of faith and morals." This means that bishops and popes cannot claim to speak authoritatively, much less infallibly, unless the matter about which they speak pertains to Christian belief or to the practice of the Christian way of life. It is important to note that there are two ways in which something can pertain to this object: either directly, as formally contained in the revealed word of God, or indirectly, as something in itself not revealed, but so connected with revealed truth that the magisterium could not

defend or expound some revealed truth unless it could make absolutely definitive statements about this other matter as well. Matters of faith and morals that are formally revealed constitute what is called the "deposit of faith"; this is the primary object of teaching authority. Other things that are not in themselves formally revealed but about which the magisterium needs to be able to speak definitively in order to defend or explain some revealed truth constitute the secondary object of magisterium. Only that which is in the primary object can be defined as a "dogma of faith"; matters in the secondary object can be defined as true but not as to be believed with "divine faith," i.e., faith directed to God as revealer. While the infallibility of the magisterium in defining matters in the primary object is a dogma of faith, the infallibility of the magisterium with regard to the secondary object is not a dogma of Catholic faith but a doctrine commonly held by Catholic theologians and confirmed by the ordinary magisterium (see *AAS* 65 [1973]: 401).

A question that is much discussed today is whether all the norms of the natural moral law fall within the object of infallible magisterium. It is generally agreed that some of the basic principles and norms of such law are also divinely revealed, and as pertaining to the primary object, could be infallibly taught. It does not seem, however, that any such norm has ever been solemnly defined. There is no dispute about the fact that questions of the natural moral law fall within the competence of the ordinary, non-infallible exercise of the magisterium. The question about which there are different opinions among Catholic theologians is whether the magisterium can make definitive and infallible statements about every question pertaining to the natural moral law, even regarding the complex modern problems whose solution is not found in revelation but must be sought by the application of human intelligence to the search for moral truth, with other people of good will, "in the light of the gospel" but also in the light of "human experience" (*GS* 46).

The first point to be kept in mind regarding this dispute is that, if such moral norms are not formally contained in the revealed word of God, they can only belong to the secondary object of infallible teaching. In that case, they could be determined by the magisterium with infallibility only if it could be shown that if the magisterium could not make a definitive judgment about such a matter, it would be unable to defend or explain some formally revealed truth. The second point is that, if the magisterium has made an infallible judgment on a question, that judgment must be held as absolutely final and irreversibly true. Many reputable Catholic theologians question whether it is appropriate to speak of absolutely final and irreversible judgments about this kind of problem. They argue that it is difficult to exclude the possibility that future experience might put a concrete moral problem into a new frame of reference which would call for a revision of a norm that, when formulated, could not have taken such new experience into account. Finally, it must be recalled that the infallibility of the magisterium regarding nonrevealed matter is not a dogma of faith. If the magisterium were ever to define such a question, Catholics would not be called upon by that definition to make an act of faith, in the strict and proper sense of the term, either in the truth of the defined proposition, or in the infallibility of the church in defining it.

Bibl.: P. CHIRICO, *Infallibility: The Crossroads of Doctrine* (Kansas City, Kan., 1977); K. RAHNER, "On the Church's Teaching Office," in *Foundations of Christian Faith* (New York, 1978), 378–88; J. ALFARO, "Theology and the Magisterium, in R. Latourelle and G. O'Collins, eds., *Problems and Perspectives of Fundamental Theology* (New York, 1982), 340–56; H. J. POTTMEYER, "Das Lehramt der Hirten und seine Ausübung," *TPQ* 128 (1980): 336–48; var., "Les théologiens et l'Église," *Les Quatre Fleuves* 12 (1980): 7–133; C. E. CURRAN and R. McCORMICK, eds., *The Magisterium and Morality*, Readings in Moral Theology 3 (New York, 1982); F. A. SULLIVAN, *Magisterium, Teaching Authority in the Catholic Church* (Mahwah, N.J./Dublin, 1983); J. BOYLE, "Church Teaching Authority in the 1983 Code," *The Jurist* 45 (1985): 136–70; M. LÖHRER, "Das besondere Lehramt der Kirche," in *MystSal*, 1:555–87; J. MOINGT, ed., "Le Magistère, institutions et fonctionnements," *RSR* 71 (1983): 1–336; L. ÖRSY, *The Church, Learning and Teaching* (Wilmington, 1985); A. DULLES, "Lehramt und Unfehlbarkeit" in *HFT* 4: *Traktat Theologische Erkenntnislehre* (Freiburg, 1988), 153–78.

Francis A. SULLIVAN

MARTYR

The martyrs are no strangers to us. We know who they are, we can distinguish between the personality and historical importance of each; yet all too often their images seem to conjure up a world no longer ours. They seem remote, relegated to the distant past, at best only recalled to memory in the liturgy. Described as having heroic qualities which arouse an allergic reaction in us moderns, the martyrs, in Western society particularly, seem to have become museum pieces.

And yet the martyrs are our contemporaries. Were they not, the church would long since have stopped presenting the kerygma as a saving proclamation comprehensible today to people and relevant to their lives. For, in the martyr, everyone can see human consistency at its most transparent, where a perfect identity is achieved between faith and life, between verbal profession and daily activity.

The church needs the martyrs, to highlight fully the reality of a love that freely accepts death while also becoming forgiveness of the persecutor. The martyrs, however, belong to the church not only because it in its two thousand years of history has always been characterized by the presence of martyrs, but rather because the church itself is by nature a martyr. Before being *ecclesia martyrum*, the church is *ecclesia martyr*. Indelibly once and for all impressed in the church's ontological constitution is the *forma Christi*, expressed in the Son's *kenōsis* culminating in his passion and death on the cross.

That which pertains to Christ is also true of his church; for the church too, therefore, the kenotic form must be produced as expression of the church's obediential following, which culminates in suffering and dying for love's sake. The church thus is born, lives, and is built on the foundation of the martyred Christ; the church's mission in the world must be to direct the eyes of all to "him who was pierced" (Jn 19:37; Rev 1:7), so that the revelatory word of the Father may be made explicitly clear.

Pauline theology supports this view, where it describes the apostle's activity in these words: "My little children, for whom I am again in the pain of childbirth until Christ is *formed* in you" (Gal 4:19). Christ's form, which the apostle is imprinting, cannot be other than that of the suffering servant who gives his life for the salvation of all (→ CHRISTOLOGY III). These "feelings" which characterize the historical figure of Jesus of Nazareth must also be for those who choose to follow him, so as to complete "what is lacking in Christ's afflictions" (Col 1:24).

In such terms we can fully understand the importance of the martyrs in the history and life of the Christian community. By their witness, the church certifies that only by such a road can the gospel proclamation be fully credible. And we can also explain why from the earliest years the church has seen in martyrdom a special place for verifying the truth and effectiveness of its proclamation; for in these events, bearing witness to the gospel was no longer confined merely to verbal form but involved life itself. Because of this, the church realized that the martyrs had no need of the church's prayers; on the contrary, the church prayed to them to obtain their intercession. So there was no praying for the martyrs, but praying to the martyrs for the church. The day of martyrdom was recorded and committed to memory as a time to which the faithful returned and kept holiday, to recover strength and encouragement for maintaining their evangelistic work.

The Christian community has therefore always maintained the ecclesial value of martyrdom; it has a highly communal quality, since lived for the church and by the whole church as an efficacious sign of love.

1. Historical Survey of the Facts

It is not the task of this article to analyze the various problems the term has given rise to in the course of its semantic evolution: a theology of martyrdom ought, however, to cover two essential facts at least: first, the origins of the semantic value we accord it today; second, the origins of a "theology" of martyrdom.

These two phases do not in fact coincide. From the OT to the NT, to the first decades of the primitive church, we observe a continual

evolution of the term *martys*. Semantic evolution hides the conceptual progress affecting the phenomenon; we shall thus see a gradual transition from a general concept of "witness" of a fact, to that more precise one of "bearing witness" to a truth or to other convictions, to the point of bearing witness by the shedding of one's own blood.

The concept of martyr in the modern acceptation of the word begins to be stabilized, it would seem, about 155 C.E. with the *Martyrium Polycarpi*: "Polycarp suffered martyrdom at Smyrna with eleven others from Philadelphia. Not only was he a celebrated teacher but also an outstanding martyr, whose martyrdom all desire to imitate because it was in accord with the gospel of Christ" (19.1). Being a martyr here and henceforth is identified with giving one's life for the truth of the gospel. A passage of Origen is very much to the point here:

> Everyone who testifies to the truth, whether he presents his testimony in words or deeds or in whatever way, would correctly be called a "witness." But it is already currently the custom of the brotherhood, since they have been amazed at the disposition of those who have struggled to death for truth or courage, to give the name "witnesses" (*martyres*) in a special sense only to those who have borne witness to the mystery of godliness by the pouring out of their own blood." (*In Iohannem* 2.210)

The reason why this transition in meaning should gradually have taken place is the subject of differing theories; what remains to be noted is the distinction that came to be drawn between *confessores* and *martyres*. All are witnesses to the Lord, but, even though they suffer persecution, the title of martyr is conferred only on those who give their lives; the others are generally regarded as *confessores*.

The salient features in Scripture that contribute to a first sketch of the figure of the martyr can be summarized as follows:

Old Testament

For identifying the martyr in the OT, two elements immediately leap to the eye:

a. The figure of the prophet. A series of texts gives us to suppose that the state of prophet has as natural background and within its coordinates of interpretation contains the possibility of a violent death. The prophet can be called "martyr" although still remote from martyr theology as it will later be interpreted. Examples of prophets' being killed are common enough: Jer 26:8–11 describes the listeners' reactions to the prophet's sermon in the Temple: "You shall die! . . . This man deserves the sentence of death because he has prophesied against this city." A few verses farther on, it is related of the prophet Uriah (Jer 26:20–23) that he actually was killed for having prophesied. In 2 Chr 24:17–22, there is reference to the killing of Zechariah, who was stoned to death in the courtyard of the Temple. In Elijah's outburst to the Lord in 1 Kgs 19:10–12, we learn that "the Israelites have forsaken your covenant, thrown down your altars, and killed your prophets with the sword. I alone am left, and they are seeking my life, to take it away." In Neh 9:26, we find the clearest example of the admission of this practice. Ezra, who has been reading the Torah, then accuses the people of having sinned: "They were disobedient and rebelled against you and cast your law behind their backs and killed your prophets, who had warned them in order to turn them back to you." The figure too of the 'ebed YHWH of Deutero-Isaiah may be taken as a symbolic picture of the prophet's fate.

The prophet hence is the witness of the word revealed to him by the Lord; he must obey it faithfully to the end. His death will be avenged by Yahweh alone: "I may avenge . . . the blood of my servants the prophets, and the blood of all the servants of the Lord" (2 Kgs 9:7).

b. Historical Events in Israel. In the way the Jews interpreted their history and, more particularly, the bloody events interspersed in it, we may detect an early "theology of martyrdom." More precisely, it is in the Maccabean period, in the decade when Israel came under the rule of Antiochus IV Epiphanes (175–163 B.C.E.) of Syria, that we can pinpoint the rise of this way of thinking. The attempt to relate suffering and death for the sake of the ancestral faith to a common matrix constitutes the seminal idea of a theology of martyrdom, which, strangely enough, has its roots in a "theology" of history (→ HISTORY III; cf. Dn 11–12; 2 Mc 6–7).

In these texts it is easy to see that the death of the innocent is regarded as a deep, effective witness, able to keep faith firm and to raise

hopes that the Lord will intervene. Very significant in this connection is the story in 2 Mc 6:12–30, which tells of the persecution of the Jews and the killing of Eleazar. Several telling facts emerge from this pericope: first, that the season of testing and persecution is interpreted as being a season of grace (v. 12); for the Lord admonishes his people by this experience and strengthens them in their faith (vv. 14–16); the witness of the righteous man who accepts death so as to stay faithful to the ancient law tends furthermore to confirm younger men in the faith of the fathers (vv. 24–28); death is thus accepted as a sign of love (v. 30); to conclude, the righteous man persecuted is described as having full freedom in the face of death and the persecutor, and is not afraid to choose death (v. 30).

For the OT, therefore, witnesses who accept death for the sake of the faith are innocent and without fault; their sufferings and death are regarded as purifying for the people and a sign of the greatest testimony that the people can receive. The content of the prayer of Judas Maccabeus does indeed correspond to this:

> They called on the Lord to have regard for the people oppressed on all sides, to take pity on the Temple profaned by the godless, to have mercy on the city now being destroyed and levelled to the ground, to hear *the blood of the victims that cried aloud to him,* and not to forget the criminal slaughter of innocent babies. (2 Mc 8:2–4)

New Testament

The NT is characterized by the centrality of Jesus of Nazareth, The mystery of his saving death is pivotal to the interpretation of Christian martyrdom. His life, and particularly his passion and death (→ PASCHAL MYSTERY), become the center and hermeneutic key to illuminate those same sufferings of his disciples and the life of the primitive community, which, in these moments, gives concrete proof of its loyalty to the Master: "As they left the council, they rejoiced that they were considered worthy to suffer dishonor for love of the name" (Acts 5:41; cf. 7:58–60; Phil 1:13; 2 Tm 2:3).

Two elements will be considered with a view to an overall interpretation of the NT evidence:

a. The fact that *Jesus meant to give meaning to his death.* Among the sure facts that can be recovered as pertaining to the historical Jesus are certainly his awareness of a violent death in store and the saving significance that he attached to it.

With complete lucidity Jesus of Nazareth knew that his behavior and words would inevitably bring him to a violent death. The fact that his contemporaries and his own disciples had understood him to be a PROPHET (Mk 8:28), the death of the Baptist (Mt 14:1–12), his feeling of kinship with public sinners (Mk 2:15–16), the challenge over the Mosaic Law (Mt 5:17–48), the accusation of blasphemy (Mk 2:6; 14:64), the suspicion of practicing magic or sorcery (Mt 9:34), the expulsion of the traders from the Temple and his harsh words against the priests (Mk 11:15–18, 28–33), and above all his claim to be in a special sense the Son of God (Jn 5:18): any one of these facts by itself allowed violent death to be glimpsed as a possibility. Nor should it be forgotten that, as the Gospels report, Jesus was several times on the point of being stoned (Jn 8:59; 10:31–33; Lk 4:29).

Jesus did not remain indifferent at the prospect this kind of death; rather, he drew from it the resolution to direct his whole life toward a death that would be acceptable for the salvation of all (Jn 3:14–15).

b. The fate of his disciples. A second element to be taken into account is the constant insistence in the texts concerned with following the Lord (see 8:34; 13:9) on the deep unity linking the lot of the disciples to that of the Master. For NT theology one certain fact is that following Christ means joining in his mission and hence in sharing his sufferings and death (Mt 16:24; 20:22–23).

The NT of course does not identify the idea of martyrdom with acceptance of death; those who bear faithful witness and attest the truth of the gospel are also called martyrs in the NT. The clearest example of this is provided by Stephen, who is not called martyr because he dies but simply because he has borne witness to Christ by his evangelistic work. The fate of the Master is, however, clearly expected for the disciple who elects to follow him.

The conclusion emerging, therefore, from the NT texts is that the martyr is essentially the eyewitness to the Lord's life, passion, death, and resurrection. Consequently, the disciples are all called martyr-witnesses, since they attest the truth of the gospel in their various states of life, even at the risk of persecution and suffering (1 Pt 4:12–19). Pauline theology was to be particularly sensitive to the unifying of the apostolate and mission of spreading the gospel with the acceptance of suffering (see Rom 6:4–15; Gal 5:16–25; 2 Cor 5:14–15; 6:8–11; 11:20–31; 13:4–7; 1 Tm 6:12).

Only a long process, as has already been mentioned, would lead to identifying the martyr with someone who becomes a witness to the faith to the point of giving up his or her life. The writings of Clement (96 C.E.), Ignatius (115 C.E.), and the Shepherd of Hermas (140 C.E.), while already familiar with the experience of martyrdom, do not as yet use the word in this sense.

From the *Martyrium Polycarpi* on we observe an interesting theological development with regard to martyrdom. The new meaning of martyr now gets applied to Christ, and hence an authentic theology of martyrdom comes into being, where the martyrs by following Christ's example are understood to be witnesses to perfect charity.

2. Martyrdom in Fundamental Theology

As object of theological scholarship, martyrdom belongs to various disciplines that analyze its different aspects with a view to complementarity in an overall interpretation.

Dogmatic theology, for instance, will concentrate on the component of bearing witness to the truth of the gospel; *spirituality*, however, will study martyrdom's forms and characteristics so that it may be presented today too as the model of Christian life; church *history* will seek to reconstruct the causes that gave rise to martyrdom situations and assess the accuracy of the annals despite their legendary trimmings; finally, *canon law* will assess the forms and matters in which the martyr's witness was given, to establish their soundness with a view to canonization.

Fundamental theology studies martyrdom in the apologetic dimension to show that it is the *language* expressive of revelation and a credible *sign* of God's trinitarian love. The witness of the martyrs shows that revelation still has its stimulating power today as regards the modern world, whether to permit the choice of faith or to live that faith consistently and meaningfully.

Martyrdom as Language

Whether we like it or not, the term "martyr" calls a definite reality to mind for speaker or for listener. Like any term used in human speech, this one too is subject to linguistic analysis, which seeks to reach a judgment about it and hence about whether it is true or not in everyday experience. As human language, it reveals the most personal dimension of the subject, who by this means is aware of himself as creative subject.

One particular form of human language is what takes place through the language of TESTI-MONY. A hermeneutics of this allows us to assemble facts permitting us a more organic and meaningful view of martyrdom.

Testimony is intuitively linked to the "juridical" sector of human experience; for it is conceived of as an act by which the object of personal knowledge is communicated. This dimension, however, is only the first form of our knowledge; for testimony, on deeper analysis, reveals characteristics that go directly to the subject's most personal nature.

Any testimony entails at least two elements: first, the *act* of communicating; then, the *content* expressed. This form of communication inevitably necessitates the presence of a recipient to receive the testimony. So we can say that testimony is a person-to-person relationship that comes into being between two subjects by virtue of a content that is communicated. The quality of the relationship formed belongs to the deepest sphere of interpersonal relationship inasmuch as, on the basis of the content expressed, the two subjects take the risk of trusting one another and of jeopardizing personal credibility. The witness, in proportion to the honesty with which he expresses the content of his experience, reveals his own truthfulness or lack of it; the person receiving the testimony, for his part, having assessed the degree of reliability of what has just been communicated to him, ventures to put his trust in the other party. Both subjects, however, evince a willingness to share a part of their life and so to come out of themselves with a view to communicating.

Seen in this way, testimony cannot be reduced to a simple telling of facts; instead it becomes a concrete commitment deliberately to communicate and express, by one's own death if need be, the truth of what one is saying, using one's own life as guarantee of the truth. With testimony, the subject disposes of himself with that primary freedom allowing him to prove that he is truthful and consistent; in a word, testimony represents one of the constituent features of human language, since it is backed up by action in a way the mere spoken word can never be.

Martyrdom has always been seen as the supreme form of testimony that the believer could give for the truth of faith in the Lord. The *Acta Martyrum* make it absolutely clear that martyrdom was understood to be that definitive testimony which, begun before the magistrate, ended with acceptance of death.

Martyrdom as Sign

The examples reported in the *Acta Martyrum* show clearly that the martyr's testimony was interpreted as a sign of God's presence in the community. In the martyr's death, the Trinity itself revealed the ultimate expression of its nature: love that goes to complete self-giving. The church has always understood the importance of this testimony, interpreting it as the abiding sign of God's unchanging and constant love which had its climactic expression in the death of Jesus.

The sign (→ SEMIOLOGY I), with its qualities of mediation and communication, has the characteristic of creating consensus about its meaning and of arousing those who see (or hear) it to make a decision. The essential features of the sign are fully expressed in martyrdom too. For unanimous consensus about the martyr's strength of mind and consistency is easily achieved; the content of the martyr's action makes it possible for anyone who so wishes to pass on to the meaning expressed in that death: the very love of God.

The stimulating force coming from martyrdom and prompting others to reflect on the meaning of existence and on the essential significance of giving up one's life is so obvious as to need no demonstration. Here the decision to reach a consistent and final choice finds its vital space. The history of the martyrs clearly shows that each one's death, while on the one hand leaving people astounded, on the other so shook the individual conscience as to lay it open to conversion and faith: *sanguis mar-*

tyrum semen christianorum ("The martyr's blood is a seed for Christians").

3. The Significance of Martyrdom

In martyrdom, fundamental theological thinking today still finds one of the most appropriate expressions for genuinely advancing the CREDIBILITY of the Christian revelation.

The apologetic perspective of preconciliar days normally confined itself to studying martyrdom in the context of an attempt to recover the heroic virtues the martyrs displayed for the sake of Christian truth. In superseding this interpretation, it is possible to see martyrdom more in relation to the perennial human questions and hence more as a sign to illuminate someone setting out on the quest for the meaning of existence.

Three issues seem constantly to affect the human person: the truth of one's personal life, freedom in face of death, and the option for eternity.

As regards the first of these—the truth of one's own life—one may observe that, from the church's very earliest days, martyrdom has been interpreted as being one of the most consistent deeds a human being could perform. The believer who had accepted the faith saw the deepest consistency between profession of faith and daily life acted out in the martyr's death. Analysis of the accounts of the martyrs' trials reveals that the martyrs conceived of the way of martyrdom as being the road they had to follow if they were finally to achieve their true identity as Christians and fulfill their destiny.

The truth of the faith, which ultimately for the martyrs became a matter of "giving up their lives for their friends" (see Jn 15:13), is a concrete experience of truth about themselves; for the martyrs understood that giving up their lives to the tyrant for Christ's sake was what constituted and formed the truth of their existence. Truth about their lives and the truth of the gospel flowed together into a synthesis such that it was no longer thinkable for them to imagine themselves as being outside the truth accepted in faith. They therefore became witnesses to the truth of the gospel by discovering the truth about their own lives which, in any perspective but this one, would no longer make sense.

And martyrdom is, in this context, an expression of honesty and consistency which leads to the putting of universal truth before one's personal preferences in life. For the martyrs show not only that one can know all the truth about one's own life but that, going even further, one can give up one's own life to convince other people of the truth that guides one's own convictions and choices.

As regards the second issue, personal freedom in the face of death, it may be said that, in martyrdom, this becomes so paradoxical as to seem a contradiction in terms: How can people think they are free at precisely that moment when their lives depend on the will of someone else?

Besides K. Rahner's enlightening treatment of the topic (1961: 75–108), the following points are worth noting:

a. DEATH is an event finishing the life of each of us and molding each one's personal history. It is a significant element for discerning the truth about us and about what we have achieved. In a word, death touches the entire individual and is a universal fact; nothing and no one is exempt from it.

And yet death is not a mere biological fact against which we see the parabola of our life; it is something more, because at that very moment we discover we are not made for death, but made for life. The refusal to see oneself disappear with one's physical dissolution shows us how essential it must be for the person knowingly to face this event, notwithstanding the fact that one wishes to put it out of mind.

b. Death is a mystery infinitely surpassing our understanding and by turns arousing the most disparate reactions: fear, flight, doubt, contradiction, curiosity, mistrust, serenity, desperation, cynicism, resignation, fight. . . .

In death, we each make our winning move, since we are forced into that chess game (cf. Bergman's remarkable film *The Seventh Seal*) which cannot be postponed and which in the end we look forward to as necessary and inevitable.

This is why we can say that the martyrs too, and especially the martyrs, reveal their full freedom in the face of death, particularly when there seems no room for freedom. For they, faced with death, give supreme meaning to their lives by accepting death for the sake of the life that comes to them from faith. The martyrs thus, although condemned to die, choose to die;

for them, dying is the same as freely choosing to entrust themselves completely to the Father's love. Martyrs know that, in this sense, accepting death is the same as freeing themselves from a life which, outside this context, would be meaningless. Here, what John's theology teaches becomes very clear: "I lay down my life in order to take it up again. No one takes it from me, but I lay it down of my own accord. I have power to lay it down, and I have power to take it up again" (Jn 10:17–18).

And now for the last question: What comes after death? The martyr succeeds in investing this with new meaning too.

Running like a *leitmotiv* through the martyrs' trials, we find the expression "being reunited with the Lord." In death, thus, one recovers that intimate and personal ability to make up one's own mind. Although it may seem paradoxical, the most authentic decision the subject can make, hence also the freest, is that of entrusting oneself to the mystery one perceives. Human nature is a mystery, yet within ourselves we grasp the presence of a greater mystery enfolding us but not destroying us. Outside this context we should become insoluble riddles; within it, on the other hand, we find the key for self-understanding.

Martyrs, being signs of love, are also signs of those who lovingly accept the mystery of the other. At this point there is no more questioning, only the certainty of being loved and so accepted. The martyr's strength lies in the knowledge that, since Christ has overcome death, so those who trust in him will reign forever. The palm in the martyr's hand becomes the abiding sign of the victory that transcends the defeat of death.

The elements we have described allow martyrdom to be seen as a contributing sign in the quest for the meaning and credibility of revelation. The martyr's death becomes the sign of what it means to die like a Christian: the putting on of Christ's very death in life, the supreme act of freedom admitting to the Father's love.

To sum up, the martyrs are those who give death a human face; paradoxically, they express the beauty of death. For going forth to meet it, they see it certainly as a dramatic moment in their existence even if not as a tragic one, and yet one worthy to be lived because it is an expression of their ability to love to the very end.

4. Toward an Extension of the Martyr's Identity

A swift survey of the history of the concept of martyr shows that at different periods different aspects have been stressed. Thus, Augustine was to say that "*martyres non facit poena, sed causa*" ("It is not the suffering that makes martyrs, but the cause for which they suffer") (*Enarrationes in Ps 34*); which Thomas Aquinas echoes by saying that "*causa sufficiens ad martyrium non solum est confessio fidei, sed quaecumque alia virtus non politica sed infusa, quae finem habeat Christum,*" ("What is required for martyrdom is not only confession of faith, but any other not political but infused virtue having Christ as purpose") and again: "*Patitur etiam propter Christum non solum qui patitur propter fidem Christi, sed etiam qui patitur pro quocumque iustitiae opere pro amore Christi*" ("Not only does he suffer on account of Christ, but also whoever suffers for some deed of justice for the love of Christ") (*Epistula ad Romanos* 8:7). Pascal's position is telling: "The example of the death of the martyrs touches us, for they are our members. We have a common tie with them, their resolution can form ours, not only by example but because it has perhaps made ours possible" (*Pensées*, 481). And Kierkegaard's is very much to the point: "If Christ were to return to earth, he would not perhaps be put to death, but be laughed at. This is martyrdom in the age of intelligence: to be put to death, in the period of passion and feeling," and in another passage he goes on to say: "No life has greater effect than that of the martyr, for the martyr only begins to act after death. So the human race either clings on to him or stays imprisoned in itself" (*Journal*). Manualistic theology, in defining martyrdom, was to make a point of stressing *odium fidei*: "martyrdom is defined theologically thus: voluntary acceptance of the death sentence inflicted out of hatred for the faith or the divine law, firmly and patiently borne and allowing immediate entry into bliss" (Tromp 1950:348).

The council too made a point of giving its own view of martyrdom, which is clearly articulated on the following characteristics: first the *christological premises*, then insertion into the *ecclesial scenario*, next stress on the *exceptional quality* of the martyr-believer, and finally the *parenesis*, so that all the baptized may be ready to profess the faith even to the point of giving up their lives. "Since Jesus, the Son of God, manifested his charity by laying down his life for us, no one has greater love than he who lays down his life for Christ and his brothers" (*christological premise*). From the earliest times, then, some Christians have been called upon—and some will always be called upon—to give this testimony to all humans, but especially to persecutors (*ecclesial scenario*). By martyrdom a disciple is transformed (*assimilatur*) into an image of his Master, who freely accepted death on behalf of the world's salvation; the martyr perfects that image even to the shedding of blood. The church therefore considers martyrdom an exceptional gift and the highest proof of love (*exceptional quality of martyrdom*). Though few are presented with such an opportunity, nevertheless all must be prepared to confess Christ before men, and to follow him along the way of the cross through the persecutions which the church will never fail to suffer (*parenesis*)" (*LG* 42; cf. also *LG* 50; *GS* 20; *AG* 24; *DH* 11, 14).

As can be seen from the above passage, Vatican II places martyrdom in a clear, christocentric perspective; the saving death of Jesus of Nazareth constitutes the normative principle for discerning Christian martyrdom. This centrality, however, is described by the expression "to lay down one's life for one's brothers," which recalls Christ's words in Jn 15:13 and reminds us that what moves the martyrs to lay down their lives is Christ's archetypal and normative love. Even recall to the ecclesial dimension no more than underlines the continuity of the loving testimony given by the martyrs to confirm the brothers in the faith. Even where the conciliar text refers to the special quality of Christian martyrdom by saying that it is "an exceptional gift," hence a grace and charism granted to those who love most, and "the highest proof of love," hence definitive testimony of love, the one and the other are seen as given within the church and for the church. Thus, the church may grow "into him who is the head, into Christ, from whom the whole body, joined and knit together by every joint with which it is supplied, when each part is working properly, makes bodily growth and upbuilds itself in love" (Eph 4:15–16; cf. 1 Cor 12–14).

Hence one may think that, with this description, Vatican II has opened the way to a new and more comprehensive interpretation of the martyr's testimony, in view of the new forms of martyrdom which we see today to bring about social change. It is therefore lawful to think that with the council martyrdom has been identified with giving up one's life for love.

The text of *LG* 42 quoted above speaks neither of profession of faith nor of *odium fidei*; no doubt it presupposes this, but it chooses rather to speak of martyrdom as a sign of the love that opens up to become a total giving of self.

If love is stressed rather than faith, we can see how much easier it is to bring out the normative quality of Christ's love, which is the basis of the martyr's testimony; for this kind of love still remains credible to our contemporaries, who can understand being stimulated by someone at the deepest level of their being.

If then the emphasis is put on the love that forms the basis for the martyr's testimony, we can also see how much easier it becomes to identify the martyr with someone who not only professes the faith but bears witness to it in any form of JUSTICE, this being the minimal form of Christian love.

Love therefore allows us to identify the martyrs by their personal testimony and direct involvement in the development and progress of humanity; for they bear witness that the basic elements for a decent human life are the dignity of the person and its elementary rights, universally recognized today though not respected. If we take this particular view, it becomes clear that the martyrs are no longer isolated to a few sporadic cases but are easy to find in all those places where, for love of the gospel, people live consistent lives to such a point as to give them up, side by side with the poor, the outcast, and the coerced, in defense of their downtrodden rights.

A widening of the concept of martyr does not, however, mean indiscriminate or inflationary use of it. Not all those who die for human rights or for their deepest aspirations could be regarded as martyrs, which goes to show there is further need for defining martyrdom so as to take in those new forms of persecution by which the truth of the faith and the credibility of love are compromised.

A good example of the modern usage for martyrdom is provided by the case of Maximilian Kolbe. When Paul VI beatified him on 17 October 1971, the pope numbered him among the *confessores*. At the canonization on 10 October

1982, however, John Paul II numbered him among the *martyres*. Here is the history of how this came about:

On 5 June 1982, Polish and German bishops representing their respective episcopal conferences, address a letter to the pope, published in the *Osservatore Romano* only on 7 October, in which an explicit request is made for Blessed Maximilian Kolbe to be canonized as "a martyr of the Catholic faith." The reasons accompanying the request move on a plane of canonical justification and conform to the pattern of an old conception of martyrdom: mainly the fact that Nazi ideology conflicted with Christian ethics and that Fr. Kolbe's imprisonment was due to Nazi hatred of the faith; furthermore, that the Beatus, while imprisoned in the concentration camp at Auschwitz had harbored no hatred toward his persecutors, who for their part tormented him relentlessly; and, finally, that he had offered to take the place of the father of a family (who had been condemned to death) with the simple words: "I am a Catholic priest."

The same day, on its second page, the *Osservatore Romano* carried an article—its being unsigned making it all the more authoritative—in which an extension of the concept of martyrdom was augured in these words:

> It will be up to theologians to justify on the theoretical plane an option perhaps not thoroughly approved of in the schools. I wish theology should as soon as possible give us an exact profile of the "modern marty," since I am persuaded it represents a source of energy for the Christian faithful to be able informedly and consistently to contemplate the modern "reality of martyrdom."

More expressive and extraordinarily modern, however, is the homily pronounced by John Paul II during the mass of canonization. The expression "martyr of the faith" never occurs in the pope's words; instead, the entire homily is designed to show the testimony of love given by Fr. Kolbe. The pope evokes the category of *sign* as the linguistic and theological expression best suited to manifest that testimony given for love.

The homily begins with reflections on Jn 15:13, the same text as was used in *LG* 42. The word "love" is used more than eleven times, and some synonymous expression at least five times; six times Kolbe is said to be a "sign" of love, which makes it easy enough to understand why the pope then went on to say:

> Is not this death, spontaneously faced for love of his fellow man, a particular fulfillment of Christ's words? Does it not make Maximilian particularly like Christ, the model of all martyrs, who gives his life on the cross for the brethren? Does not such a death possess a particular, penetrating eloquence for our own day? Does it not constitute a particularly genuine testimony of the church in the modern world? And so, by virtue of my apostolic authority I have decreed that Maximilian Kolbe, who after being beatified was venerated as a confessor, from now on is to be venerated as a martyr too.

It will be noted that an extension of the concept is therefore possible and has already come about in the case cited. But this still requires critical consideration on the part of theology.

We now propose a definition of martyr designed to combine the various requirements already expressed and to fit within the context of fundamental theology: The martyr, sign of greatest love, is a witness who, in following Christ, is prepared to give up his or her life to attest the truth of the gospel, acknowledged as such by the voice of the people of God and confirmed by the church as a faithful witness to Christ.

Some elements of this definition need a little expanding:

a. Sign of greatest love. By this expression we seek to reinstate the centrality of love as the ultimate sign to stimulate someone into making the decision of faith. Love, furthermore, summons to the dimension of gratuitousness and giving; inasmuch as martyrs, more than anyone else, are configured to Christ, they understand themselves to be recipients of a grace that is only explicable and comprehensible in love.

b. Following Christ. By this we mean the individual's freedom in opting for the faith and for the consequences this may have. The *sequela Christi* is not an act of mere profession, it is concrete practice of life and at the same time ecclesial testimony, since it incorporates the individual into the one mission of the church.

c. To give up one's life. By this we indicate the constituent feature of martyrdom, i.e., death. But this is to be understood not in a negative way — death as privation of life — but in a positive sense: the martyr does not die but hands over his or her life in full freedom, and this is gain. Martyrdom is an act by which one goes on living.

d. *The truth of the gospel.* We are talking about salvation. The ultimate and definitive element of the gospel proclamation is life eternal, i.e., salvation brought in the person of Jesus of Nazareth. Salvation makes the person a free subject, fully realizable in nature and, precisely because of this, capable of dialogue with God. This means that the truth of the gospel is also the saving proclamation of the dignity and sanctity of human life. Any action therefore that promotes human dignity has in itself a saving character, and any activity tending to suppress or obstruct this kind of proclamation is to be regarded as an obstruction and persecution of the faith.

e. *Acknowledged by the people of God.* In this way we try concretely to reassert the importance of the local community, in harmony with the practice of the church in the early centuries. The community always shares in the martyrdom of one of its members; and precisely because of this, it alone is in a position to grasp the importance of that testimony and to judge the sign it constitutes as being an authentic expression of Christian love. It is the local community that can recognize when the martyr's life is given for the truth of the gospel and not for other ends; for in it the martyr has been born, has grown up and grown strong, either in religious experience or in actual preparation for martyrdom. For the martyrs of the early centuries, life was impossible outside the community, and in many cases we have the testimony of a community that went to the lengths of bribing jailers so as to be able to stay near its martyr.

f. *The church confirms.* We certainly do not want to diminish the importance of canonization, which is bound up with the infallible action of the pope; rather, we aim to bring out the universal character of the holiness of the martyr, who is put forward for the veneration of, and as an example to, all Christians.

5. Conclusion

Martyrdom is no intellectual speculation; it is a concrete event of life. Indeed, it is the climactic point of a fully human existence, since it expresses the full freedom of the individual when faced with death.

On Holy Saturday 1979, the martyr-bishop O. Romero said in his homily: "God be thanked, we have pages of martyrdom not only from past history but from the present day too. Priests, religious, catechists, simple country-folk, have been put to death, stripped, beaten up, tortured, persecuted for being faithful children of this one God and Lord." So . . . no believer who has given serious thought to his or her faith can think of not being summoned to martyrdom. It is so much of the very essence of the Christian vocation that it constitutes a serious possibility in everyone's life.

Here we feel ourselves called upon to give the ultimate response to love's request, because we understand and are certain that someone has freely given up his life for us as a testimony of his love.

Martyrdom therefore figures as that reality today which the church can still proudly offer to the world as the greatest sign of love that a human being can achieve. Each individual is summoned to take a position before this sign. To wonder therefore if even today there are martyrs and who they may be is to wonder whether today the church is still able to present God's unchanging and constant trinitarian love.

If the martyrs are the sign of the greatest love of all, they are also a sign that today too, in the world, there is rejection of God, and people resistant to the prophetic proclamation and to the Christian community's strength of witness. Yes, there are new persecutors, more skillful than ever since linked to ever more obscure forms of power, and these do not allow believers to bear witness to faith and love as in the church's early days. They are not condemned to death; no legal sentence is handed down by the court. . . . An increasingly underhanded, serious, and dishonest approach is rife among the persecutors of our day: derision, vulgarization, indifference, or calumny — death later.

The courage of the martyrs thus requires the courage — always, unceasingly — to devise new forms and styles of life proclaiming the victorious force of the person of Christ still living today in the midst of his people, who in their turn proclaim him, as those first believers did, as Lord and faithful witness.

Bibl.: P. ALLARD, "Martyre," *DAFC*, 331–492; E. HOCEDEZ, "Le concept de martyre," *NRT* 55 (1928): 81–99, 199–208; R. HEDDE, "Martyre," *DTC*, 220–54; O. MICHEL, *Prophet und Märtyrer* (Gütersloh, 1932); H. DELAYHE, *Les origines du culte des Martyrs* (Brussels, 1939); S. TROMP, *De Revelatione Christiana* (Rome, 1950); E. ESKING, *Das Martyrium als theologisch-exegetisches Problem* (Stuttgart, 1951); M. LODS, *Confesseurs et Martyrs* (Neuchâtel, 1958); N. BROX, *Zeuge und Märtyrer* (Munich, 1961); M. PELLEGRINO, "Le sens ecclésial du martyre," *RSR* 35 (1961): 151–75; K. RAHNER, *On the Theology of Death* (New York, 1961); L. BOROS, *The Mystery of Death* (New York, 1962); H. VON CAMPENHAUSEN, *Die Idee des Martyriums in der alter Kirche* (Göttingen, 1964); A. KUBIS, *La théologie du martyre au XXe siècle* (Rome, 1968); H. Urs VON BALTHASAR, *Cordula, ou l'épreuve décisive* (Paris, 1969); id., *Nouveaux points de repère* (Paris, 1980); H. STRATHAM, "μαρτυς," *TDNT* 4:474–508; R. LATOURELLE, *Christ and the Church: Signs of Salvation* (New York, 1972); I. GORDON, "De conceptu theologico-canonico martyrii," in var., *Ius populi Dei* (Rome, 1972), 1:485–521; P. RICOEUR, "Herméneutique du témoignage," in E. Castelli, ed., *La testimonianza* (Rome, 1972), 35–61; H. MUSURILLO, *The Acts of the Christian Martyrs* (Oxford, 1972); E. PIACENTINI, *Il martirio nelle cause dei santi* (Rome, 1979); X. LÉON-DUFOUR, *Face à la mort: Jésus et Paul* (Paris, 1979); T. BAUMEISTER, *Die Anfänge der Theologie des Martyriums* (Münster, 1980); A. SOLIGNAC, "Martyre," *DSp*, 718–37; var., *Martiri: Giudizio e dono per la chiesa* (Turin, 1981); var., "Martyrdom Today," *Conc* 163 (1983); var., *Il sangue dei giusti* (Assisi, 1983); H. SCHÜRMANN, *Jesus ureigener Tod: Exegetische Besinnung und Aufblick* (Freiburg, 1976); J. JANSSENS, "Il cristiano di fronte al martirio imminente," *Greg* 66 (1985): 405–27; R. FISICHELLA, "Il martirio come testimonianza: contributi per una riflessione sulla definizione di martire," in var., *Portare Cristo all'uomo* (Rome, 1985), 2:747–67; C. NOCE, *Il martirio: Testimonianza e spiritualità dei primi secoli* (Rome, 1987); var., *La Iglesia martirial interpela nuestra animación misionera* (Burgos, 1988).

Rino FISICHELLA

MARXISM

I. IDEOLOGY

1. Concept

Marxism comprises the body of teachings of K. Marx (1818–1883) and F. Engels (1820–1895) and the various movements of thought and action inspired by them, and subsequently of and from N. Lenin (the pseudonym of Vladimir Ilyich Ulyanov, 1870–1924) and Mao Tse-tung (1893–1916).

To be accurate, we should speak of "Marxisms," since from the outset there has never been a single Marxism but several Marxisms with differing and sometimes even contrary interpretations (E. Bernstein, K. Kautsky, Rosa Luxemburg, G. V. Plekhanov). Indeed we might list the classic or orthodox Marxism of the founding fathers Marx and Engels, the "Marxism-Leninism" of Lenin, the "Marxism-Trotskyism" of Trotsky, the "Marxism-Stalinism" of Stalin (pseudonym of Joseph Vissarionovich Djugashvili (1879–1953), and "official Marxism," which is reflected in the Statute of the Communist Party, the Constitution and the legislation of the "real socialism" of the now-defunct USSR. We may also add Mao's Marxism, known as "Maoism," E. Bloch's "utopian Marxism," the "humanist" Marxism of R. Garaudy and the "anti-humanist" Marxism of L. Althusser. Add to these the "Marxism-revisionism" of V. P. Tugarinov and A. Schaff in Poland, of R. Richta and M. Machovec in Czechoslovakia, of G. Markus and A. Hegedüs in Hungary, that of a group of philosophers writing in the *Praxis* review (Zagreb), and another of a group of ethicists in Belgrade, and others still. Indeed, the body of movements of thought and action that we may call "Marxism" has many nuances, less philosophical than ideological, political, and economic.

Today, with the decline in the "Marxist driving force" (E. Berlinguer), with the agony and death of old-style Soviet Marxism and the command economy, despite the attempt at *perestroika* (reconstruction) by M. Gorbachev, we now speak of the post-Marxist era and of the heirs to those Marxisms, who will be trying to present "authentic Marxism" in its original form, with all the revisionisms and variations stripped away. Thus, for some, Marxism is not over but is only just beginning. The fundamental reason for this lies in its nature, which is comparable to a cultural civilization, such as that of Judaism, Christianity, Islam, or Buddhism — that is, to the great religious movements of the world.

The recent end of the USSR, as also the claims to autonomy made by the former constituent republics, should not make us forget the fact that Marxist ideology dominated a large part of the world for three-quarters of a century and that in certain countries it still persists. This major historical fact of the existence of Marxist ideology and the Communist Party amply justifies two articles devoted to Marxism in this book.

2. Doctrinal Elements

We shall mainly consider those doctrinal elements appropriated by official Marxism and professed in the countries of "real socialism" after the revolution of October 1917.

The philosophical form of the Marxist vision of the world is *dialectical materialism*; which denies the existence of God the creator of the world as a purely human invention and hence an unscientific — or, rather, antiscientific — hypothesis. It is "dialectical" inasmuch as it makes *matter* the first and supreme principle of everything.

Matter is eternal, internally dynamic, and in continual evolution. Everything emanates from matter in accordance with the laws of dialectic, which are very close to those of Hegel — that is, thesis, negation of the thesis, and negation of the negation. The third, Marxist phase differs from that of Hegel, which consists in synthesis. The final, qualitative, dialectical leap in evolution produced *humankind*, which represents the final fruit of the unstoppable energy dominating matter; its potentiality is almost infinite. Consequently, Marxism does not draw on the past for its models and norms of activity. Human thought does not have a merely reproductive character but is creative, in the sense of anticipating the future. The human person with its dignity is not the source of ethics and is of no importance for the epistemological criteria of the social norms. The purpose of human existence and the metaethical meaning of life are exclusively exterior to the person and

this-worldly. Here lies the reason why any genuine Marxist opposes transcendental reality — namely, it incapacitates human beings from resolving this-worldly problems, alienating them from the world and from themselves.

The object of *historical materialism* is the becoming of humanity, that is, of society. The subject is society under the aspect of its becoming-as-society. The basis of society is the economic structure, and any other structure is a reflection of the economic structure. The main factors determining human history are material ones. The transit from thesis to antithesis occurs by means of a dialectical leap.

The *world* is not a system whose structures should be preserved, but rather the raw material from which human workers should build their own world. People humanize the world by imposing their own ideas on it, gifted as they are with an agility that allows them to abandon existing forms for forms improved by them. The human being, worker and demiurge, produces a cultural world from a natural world. This human creation is qualitatively different from the natural world. We are talking of a natural world *humanized*. Human beings in the world and the world itself are the unique realities. By their knowledge of the natural world and by their own work, human beings transform the world into a place of happiness. The world is structured on two levels: the base and the superstructure. The base is the economy of the system of production; the superstructure comprises the sciences (philosophy, the natural sciences, law), religion, art, and social structure. Now, the economic order conditions the superstructure. If the base changes, the superstructure necessarily changes too. The changes that occur over the years within the economic structure are mainly quantitative, but once a certain base has been reached, they turn into qualitative changes and take form as revolutions. Such indeed is the dialectical leap. These revolutions are not mere acts of free will; they mainly spring from a natural necessity. At this point in the analysis, the unilateral dependence of the less material, or of the immaterial, on the material becomes apparent.

Thus is affirmed the *primacy of matter* in the human order and in the cultural world, its purpose being to realize and perfect all the conditions necessary for absolute earthly happiness. There is also a utopian, eschatological stage:

the collective will be the product of the final victory of communism. Humanity will be perfectly realized only in the final phase of human history, that is, in the perfect communist society. Human history thus includes a "transcendence," whether relative or immanent, the best-known theorist of which is E. Bloch. The previous phases are no more than preparatory; they prepare the transitions toward the final goal. In general, neo-Marxist thinkers no longer entertain the hypothesis of the perfect communist society, classless, with no state, and without any need for law, as human history's final stage of development.

Work is the main, and indeed only, means of humanizing nature. It is the central element of the Marxist dynamic and of historical materialism. By working, people transform the non-human world, enlarge themselves, create the world in their own image. This objectivization— or making a person into a thing—is necessary. Thus, when by their work people create a new world, they continually re-create themselves. In so transforming this world, they transform themselves. Consequently, the primary quality of work is its social character; this means that the subject of the work is not an individual but the collective working and creating the world through the individual.

Religion too depends on the economic order. It arises from forms of production that render people virtually incapable of mastering nature. Such human misery, the human inferiority with regard to antagonistic natural forces, has driven people to entrust themselves to a powerful higher being who can make them happy. But such a being is a fraud. He does not exist; he is a pure invention of unhappy, needy people. Hence religion is "the opiate of the people" (Feuerbach, Marx). It is the deepest, most radical, and hence most dangerous form of derangement, from which one must get free. The solution lies in the economy: the more perfect the economic order becomes, the more people subjugate nature, and the less right religion will retain to exist.

The *human being* is not seen as an individual, but as a part of the collective. Individual are a reflection of the structure of the society to which they belong. The more they reflect it, the more perfect they are. Their efforts must be directed toward belonging ever more totally to society. Thus the individual, in the collective, is a part of the whole and the faithful reflection of the whole of the whole, The essence of the individual is therefore identified with one's social being; each individual is a merely relative being. From birth onward, people as individuals have no personal natural, inherent, or intangible rights. There exists only a sort of citizen's right, which is derived from external sources such as the party, the state and its constitutional legislation, the natural laws, and the prescribed norms. So we are talking of an absolute, collectivist positivism, which has a heteronomous, temporary, relative system of law, always dependent on economic conditions and the will of other people—that is, the will of those in power.

As a result, people know themselves through the knowledge they have of others. This "other" is the collective. Subjectivity exists for communication, for person-to-person relationships. My self-awareness is born of the presence of the other within me. This other is not another individual or an indivisible "you" but a collective "we." Thus, ontologically speaking, the person does not exist. "Person" is understood exclusively in the ethical sense as personality, and this it becomes if, in practice, it acknowledges its relative being. Thus people become examples of "society-man" or, better still, "collective man" but, for all that, in no way enrich their own person by enriching the communities in which they live; they receive everything exclusively from society, and they give everything to society. So a man alienates himself from himself for the benefit of society, while becoming more and more impoverished in the core of his being as a man.

Within the context of the concrete collective in which people live, the individual is free and responsible. *Freedom* is the indispensable condition for an ethical life, but in a philosophical system where matter is the principal reality, primacy goes to the laws concerning matter— that is, to the laws of necessity. "Freedom of choice" here consists in knowing the necessity of the laws of matter and behaving ethically in accordance with this necessity. In other words, one must allow the laws of the process to act, without putting up obstacles, "External freedom" consists in interventions by society that keep reducing the freedom of the individual to the advantage of the society in which the individual lives. The third freedom is "eschatological freedom"—the freedom, according to official teaching, of communism's final phase.

Conscience, like all other elements of the ethical order in Marxism, has a quite different meaning from that in philosophical ethics in general, manifesting itself in an abstract relationship with the collective, of which the individual is but a tiny part. The individual conscience is the mirror of the concrete social environment. It is the collective voice manifesting itself in the individual's awareness of responsibility with regard to the community in which the individual lives. It is precisely in the conscience that the collective speaks as norm and "objective" categorical imperative. The conscience evolves, takes form, progresses to the same rhythm as the collective conscience. In official Marxism, freedom of conscience is understood exclusively as freedom of speech and freedom of the press, but within precise limits of conformity with the "interests of the people" and with the aim of consolidating and developing the well-being and progress of the collective.

So Marxism is at once historical and dialectical materialism. It came into existence as a reaction against Hegelian idealism, to the work of K. Marx. Society, or the collective, depends on the organizing of the means of production. The unfair distribution of the means of production leads to class war (capitalists vs. workers) which should have as its effect the final collapse of capitalism and the triumph of communism.

3. Marxist Atheism

The objective of Marxism and Marxists has been to form "atheist man" (*a-theos*, no-God, without God) in both the private sense and the collective sense of the system. *Theoretical* atheism is based on the ideologies of Marx, Feuerbach, Comte, Nietzsche, Freud, and others. *Practical* atheism, in contrast, draws its sustenance from agnosticism, hedonism, materialism, and nihilism. Both kinds have been taught and imposed by "real socialist" regimes on millions of Christian and non-Christian citizens with the aim of rooting out every form of religion or, if that proved impossible, of encouraging indifference to religion and of promoting practical materialism. Marxism, and more particularly Marxism-Leninism, thus

made one of its objectives the radical struggle against all organized religion, and especially against the antagonist regarded as the most dangerous, the enemy most hated: Christianity and, in its front line, the Catholic church.

Today, however, among the many theoretical "atheisms," the three major varieties absorbed and propagated by Marxism are gradually crumbling away; they no longer attract and no longer arouse interest. One is the brand of atheism known as *humanist*, which, with its anthropological and anthropocentric conclusions about the individual and the human race, proposes to make people more autonomous, more free, more independent, more mature, more important, and more powerful by putting them at the center of conflict with a "jealous" and "rival" God who enslaves them (Nietzsche), threatens their existence (Hegel, Feuerbach), deprives them of their rights and liberties and persecutes them (Sartre, Camus). Such an atheism no longer seems reasonable. Contemporary men and women are well aware that there is no scientific or philosophical basis for setting God and humanity in opposition. In the present state of the world, which is so tense and precarious (when one thinks of the problems of environmental pollution, genetic engineering, and nuclear energy), God once again becomes the sole guarantor of true peace and development, and the ultimate and effective protector of the common good against the structures of sin. The "death of God" has as its consequence the death of humanity and of the right functioning of our world and society, both political and economic. Hence the theories of humanist atheism evoke very little response in the consciousness of our contemporaries.

Much the same conclusion is reached with that atheism known as *scientific* in relation to science. The mentality of scientists has changed. If they follow up the theses of present-day epistemologists, they recognize how ill-based and illogical they are. The entirely mistaken tendency that consists in calling on science or the sciences in support of atheism becomes a *contradictio in adiecto*. What science could ever prove the nonexistence of God? What scientific method could produce a proof of this sort? "One may not be in agreement and reject the 'proofs' or human arguments which tend to prove the existence of God; one may criticise human concepts about God. But this criticism gets nowhere near touching the actual reality of God. So-called scientific atheism is an absurdity" (Poupard 1989). Quite simply, the question of God is a metaphysical and religious problem, not one that the physical sciences can resolve. It affects people qua human beings in their deepest, inner dimensions (metaphysical, religious, ethical) and cannot be resolved by any empirical science.

The third myth is *social* atheism, which speaks in the name of justice and preaches rebellion against exploitation, poverty, and every kind of social oppression. This atheism, however, transfers the problems of the past to our own period; that is, it applies rebellion against the ruling classes who used to make use of God to justify their own privileges to the ruling classes of today. But today's ruling classes no longer make use of God. The church, in fact, is the "voice in the wilderness" of the world, crying out against injustice and oppression, against poverty and atheistic Marxism, by invoking human rights, freedom, development, solidarity, and sharing; that is, the church strives to safeguard and protect human dignity at personal and communal levels. So rights, freedom, and justice can in no way constitute the object of a rebellion or of an accusatory harangue against God.

Now that these myths of theoretical atheism have collapsed—myths that different Marxisms have used, particularly official Soviet Marxism—and the system of "real socialism" has fallen apart, many Marxist specialists are changing course and beginning to admit unambiguously the "failure" of atheist Marxism. It is to be hoped that official Marxism, which is atheistic by definition, will go on losing ground, thanks to the new political and economic situation. Nonetheless, in the countries of yesterday's "real socialism," there remains the enormous problem of *practical* atheism, the fruit of the Marxisms propagated over many decades with all the means at the Communist regime's disposal. This practical atheism leads to today's *practical materialism*, with which goes a strong religious and moral *indifferentism*. Indeed, precisely here will be the new task of genuine Christianity, that is, what is called the "new" or "second" evangelization of cultures. For the negative fruits of Marxism, most particularly those of this oppressive and violent variant, namely Leninism and Stalinism, will

not be effaced from the hearts of future generations by a mere external change of political and economic systems.

4. Marxism-Leninism

Lenin distanced himself from the fathers of Marxism—Marx and Engels—on various points; as the system known as Marxism-Leninism took shape, it grew ever more Leninist than Marxist. Let us mention a few striking differences.

The first is the teaching on the *theory of the revolution*. For Marx and Engels, the socialist revolution requires a very high level of development of the productive powers, with an assured victory in almost all developed countries, but in conditions of objective socio-economic character. Lenin modifies these three theses: the revolution begins in a less-developed capitalist country, it does not break out simultaneously in all countries, and conditions of a purely subjective political character are enough. Furthermore, Lenin fights for a permanent revolution.

The second point of doctrinal and practical divergence concerns the *Communist Party* (→ MARXISM II). Marx and Engels wanted a "workers" party comprising the entire working class, and not a clique ruling and directing it from within. Lenin, however, at the Seventh Party Congress (1918), created the Russian Communist (Bolshevik) Party, which he put before class. This Leninist character of the party was subsequently to extend to all the parties of world communism and would still be found in the new name of the Communist Party of the Soviet Union (CPSU) adopted at the Nineteenth Party Congress (1952) under Stalin, and reinforced in the 1917 *Constitution* (K 77), with the notorious article 6, which states: "The Communist Party of the Soviet Union is the force that directs and guides Soviet society." This position of the CPSU lasted until 1990, when it was superseded by M. Gorbachev's "Presidential State."

The third point concerns *religion*. Theoretically, Lenin is in agreement with Marx when he states that religion is the opiate of the people. Lenin differed from Marx, however, in practice. Whereas Marx and Engels depended, ideologically speaking, on the "mythological school" (Bauer, Robertson, Drews), the "historical school" (Strauss, Renan, Harnack), and the "school of Tübingen" (Strauss, Feuerbach, C. Baur), Lenin followed an absolutely personal route — one more propagandist and more demagogic, not to say aggressive and violent, very close ideologically to the French encyclopedists of the eighteenth century. This route had already been traced by Engels. It does not much matter that the encyclopedists' struggle had nothing in common with Marxism at an ideological or practical level; the common point is their atheistic position, the struggle against the Christian religion. This commitment to "struggle" is even written into the statute of the CPSU (1961): "The party member is bound . . . to conduct a firm struggle against . . . religious prejudices" (art. 2). K 77, for its part, "guarantees to the citizens of the USSR the freedom . . . to make atheistic propaganda" (art. 52).

The fourth point of Leninism that differs from the original thought of Marx is the historical development of the concept of law. Let us first consider Marx's teaching, according to which law is not and cannot be natural, but rather is positive. Marxist law is consequently, by its nature, situated exclusively in the positive domain. As regards its *existence*, law appears in two periods: the first is transitory (which is going on now); the second is permanent (in the final classless society) and will survive the withering away of all law, even after the disappearance of the state. At an early stage, Marx would not even use the term "law," since he regarded it as tainted by the bourgeois conception. At a second stage, after grasping that this term had its roots in economics and history, beyond a mere juridical discipline, he affirmed it in proposing a new ontology admitting only material reality as the unique reality. Under the influence of Hegel, Feuerbach, Spinoza, the English and French materialists of the eighteenth century, and certain ancient philosophers such as Heraclitus and Democritus, Marx formulated two basic theses: (1) law forms an integral part of economic history, governed by economic evolution; and (2) law is neither immutable nor universal, above the categories of time, space, and history, since the being of humanity is not and cannot be an immutable reality. So there is no such thing as natural law, which in any case is a bourgeois system in the hands of the powerful, an enslaving and feudal system exploited by capitalists who have wrongly attributed a universal value to law. In a word, for Marx, all the doctrines that preceded his own thought are, in relation to historical materialism, those of conservative philosophies allied to the ruling class.

We should briefly mention Marx's utopian doctrine on the withering away of law and the state, although it is only of background interest for this study. This disappearance will occur once the conditions for the existence of law and the state completely disappear. This will require a certain period of "transition," during which the victorious proletariat assumes the responsibility of being the instrument of law and the state.

In following the stages of development in Marxist law and leaving aside many names (Kautsky, Plekhanov, Bukharin, and others) and their opinions (which did not always agree with each other or with official Marxism), it must be said that a double element again played an important role with Lenin: different practical and pragmatic needs were always engendered by new historical influences. So, the development envisaged by Marx and Engels has not, generally speaking, come to pass. Lenin, and even Stalin, followed the road imposed on them by objective *conditions*, which tended rather to strengthen than to enfeeble law and the state. This explains why E. P. Pashukahis's teaching in the 1930s was condemned; his fidelity to the thought of Marx on the "withering away" was regarded as dangerous. Since then, the lawbooks have done no more than reflect positions adopted by the CPSU. Stalin, Vyshinsky, and Yudin dictated to the legal theorists what the norms were according to which people had to think and behave. *Ex hypothesi*, by then, according to K 77, the legal process should have finally disintegrated.

5. Leninist Communism

The concept of communism relates to the socio-economic system based on the common ownership of goods. This sometimes fantastic theory is not new but over the centuries has known proponents and disciples such as Plato, More, Campanella, and Proudhon. The theorists of communism as a socio-economico-political system, however, are precisely those classic fathers of Marxism — Marx and Engels. Even here there exist various tendencies of communism as system. But the most violent, extreme, and rigorous is that of Lenin, who, after the revolution of 1917, created *bolshevism*—the specific and typical form of communism in the USSR.

It is interesting and significant that, already at the beginning of the century, after the failed revolution of 1905, a group of Russian thinkers should have prophesied the historic catastrophe of the Communist revolution, singling out the antireligious radicalism of the intelligentsia as the reason for the dominant totalitarianism. Berdyaev, Bulgakov, Struve, and Frank are the most representative names in the group writing for the *Vecchi* review in 1909, demonstrating that Marxism, having exhausted its "initial drive" from the theoretical point of view, manages to impose itself in its Leninist variation by passing itself off as the fundamentalist religion of a new humanity. Eighty years later, we see that their prophecy was accurate.

Despite these forecasts, this Marxist-Leninist brand of communism has exerted a powerful attraction in the world from the moment when, addressing the Russian people, disillusioned and exhausted by a land reform that had failed, Lenin, in the 1918 Constitution, launched the program of the Government of *Soviets* (art. 3). The Leninist call for justice, equality, and repression of exploiters could not have failed to capture the imagination of the disinherited masses of the czarist period in Russia. This type of Marxist communism, for the most part, abandoned subsequently in Soviet documents themselves, had a fascination at this period particularly attractive to peoples and individuals who felt themselves permanently oppressed by every type of power.

The internationalist revolutionary concept (→ MARXISM II), even under a constitutional form, is not however without precedents. Marx and Engels had already expressed and stressed it in the *Declaration of Rights of the Proletariat,* in the *Communist Manifesto* of 1848.

Lenin's attitude in 1917 and during the civil war was embodied in the Decree of 15 November 1917, on the sovereign rights of the peoples of Russia, issued by the Council of People's Commissars; his great preoccupation was to invite "the peoples of Russia to the greatest mutual confidence." In spite of this attempt on Lenin's part, Poland, Finland, Ukraine, Estonia, and Lithuania refused to accept the supremacy of the Russian Republic. The armistice of 15 December 1917 was followed by the peace of Brest-Litovsk of 3 March 1918. Belorussia, Ukraine, Georgia, Azerbaijan, and Armenia maintained their independence but were forced to join the USSR six years later, in 1924, after the victory of the civil war. This was a very unsettled and bloody phase in the history of the various peoples of the former czarist empire. The objective was the struggle for international, revolutionary world communism. This objective is clearly stated in the 1918 Constitution (chap. 3), which speaks of the "unshakable decision to tear humanity from the claws of finance capitalism and imperialism, which . . . have drenched the earth in blood" (art. 4), with the precise aim of preparing "a complete break with the barbarous politics of bourgeois civilization" (art. 5).

Revolutionary communist internationalism thus, according to Lenin, tends to create a socialism "in which there will neither be class divisions nor state power" (art. 9). He then clearly states "the certainty that Soviet power will resolutely advance along this road until the complete victory of the international workers' revolt against the yoke of capital" (art. 3). Moreover, the unionist Soviet state, united in a federation, would become the ideal model to imitate. Once world victory over the bourgeoisie had been achieved, the workers of all the countries in the world would form part of this worldwide unionist State.

We know how, after Hitler came to power, Stalin, aiming to avoid conflicts with other states by reducing grounds of contention to the minimum, brought the USSR into the League of Nations in 1934. His action was doubly significant, for he thereby recognized all the states with their "bourgeois" rights and also renounced working-class world revolution. At the same time, he gave up the idea of a Soviet Socialist world republic. Stalin's Constitution of 1936 clearly shows the effects of this, marking a change from the revolutionary phase of international communism to the phase guaranteeing national communism. It thus became the charter of a different kind of communism, which, instead of exalting the Communist Party of the USSR, exalted the state and, instead of upholding the communist internationalism of Marx and Engels, and that of Lenin too, put pan-Russian nationalism in first place.

Stalin was in search of certainty and stability, objectives that he attained by the well known usual radical means. Suffice it to think of the *Gosudarstvennoe Politicheskoe Upravlanie* (State Political Directorate), the infamous GPU, the abiding symbol of dictatorship, terror, anguish, blood, and death—all raised to constitutional level. Without entering into the debate as to whether Stalin was only a blind and superficial executive continuator of Lenin, as Medvedev, Solzhenitsin, and others think, one thing is certain: Stalin abandoned Lenin's internationalist line and, intending to maintain himself in power at all cost, had no scruples about liquidating his principal collaborators, who, as members of Lenin's circle, had been the first leaders of Bolshevism.

With Khrushchev's accession to power (1953–64), the cult of personality and police terror were eliminated. From Stalin's regime, however, there still remained the planned economy, institutional bureaucracy, pseudodemocratic procedures, and strict control over public debate and intellectual life. The Twentieth Party Congress of the CPSU in February 1956 was considered very promising. It formally condemned the excesses of the cult of personality that had developed under Stalin and proclaimed "collective leadership" with a worldwide program for a new strengthening of the building of communism on the international plane. It furthermore admitted the possibility of achieving the triumph of communism in many states without recourse to violence. The Warsaw Pact—signed on 14 May 1955 with Albania, Bulgaria, Poland, Romania, and Czechoslovakia, and in 1956 with East Germany, with the endorsement of the People's Republic of China—confirmed the weight the newly regrouped socialist countries maintained in the world. The program was clearly laid out: no more quarrels between Communist countries, which, within the context of the same ideology and following specific "national" roads, had as their common task the leading and building up of the proletariat of the *whole world*. Even under Khrushchev, however, the old Leninist stain did not fail to reappear. We recall what happened in Hungary in 1956, and the difficult relations with Communist China (1957–60), which were such that Mao himself accused the USSR of revisionism, that is, of substituting a different kind of communism for that of the "fathers," Marx, Engels, and Lenin.

When Brezhnev was in power, he sought to propose the USSR as model to the other countries in the world and the CPSU to other Communist parties as a statement of revolutionary Marxist-Leninist experiences. He thus decided to form a "new" state characterized by unparalleled improvements and renovations. To achieve these objectives, he promised to complete, in 1917, the new Constitution already begun under Khrushchev in 1962. The theory of Communist proletarian internationalism permeates the whole of K 77, which proved a first-rate instrument in the hands of the CPSU for installing a rigid centralism. Meanwhile, despite the fine words, we find ourselves once again in the presence of a type of Communist "predominant" internationalism, where the state remains subordinated to the CPSU as in the days of the Leninist Constitution. This is confirmed by a number of tragic events organized by Brezhnev, who, practically speaking, merely followed the same road as Lenin and Khrushchev in international revolutionary politics. Suffice it to remember the armed repression of the Prague Spring (1968), the bloody invasion of Afghanistan (1919), and what happened in Poland in 1981.

Communist internationalism sought to realize itself by using a larger nation (specifically the Russian nation in the USSR) as its instrument to subjugate smaller nationalities. The total failure of this policy of oppression has resulted in a sharp increase in nationalistic consciousness among those oppressed and humiliated minorities, who are now determined to pursue independence in the face of this unjust protectionism and are firmly opposed to Communist internationalism.

6. Ideological Failure

We are not saying that "real socialism" or Marxism in power has failed in every respect, but certainly at least in that of human rights. Let us consider just three of the best-known and most obvious phenomena.

Social Failure

Comparing the constitutional law of "real socialism" with international constitutional law (ratified by all the countries of the Eastern bloc), one discovers important differences on many points relating to the equality of human rights. The educational system was the exclusive monopoly of the state, with no possibility of schools other than those instituted by the authorities, with very few exceptions in the case of confessional schools. So all education could not but be Marxist-Leninist, antireligious, strictly secular. It was not a question of indifference about religion on the part of the state, but of a clear, atheistic, ideological choice throughout the field of scholastic instruction. Furthermore, the Marxist-Leninist worldview and the code of collectivist Communist morality had to be systematically taught to all citizens, particularly to the young in all classes until they completed their time at university, so that everyone should attain such conviction about and loyalty to communism as to be ready to defend it against its enemies. Teachers with religious beliefs found themselves cut off from access to the young, and religious students were discriminated against. From the point of view of international law, it was quite unacceptable that the whole educational system should be exclusively devoted to producing a type of "socialist man," without permitting any other views, K 77, like other "real socialist" constitutions, never uses the expression "human rights"; when speaking of rights, it uses the term "citizen rights."

In this context, the choosing of a vocation or profession was also not the free act of the individual; the choice, rather, was made by the state, which organized everything in terms of the economic and political system of a society in which the leading role was discharged by the party, with the inevitable acts of discrimination on social, ideological, political, cultural, and religious grounds. Favoritism or preferential treatment was common in the social order. In accordance with Marxist-Leninist doctrine, there was always a "legal" basis to justify discrimination of any sort. This discrimination took place the moment one embarked on a career in the public and political services; while there was much talk of equality, there was precious little of it. Once again, it is all too clear from this that "real socialism" allowed only one type of person or type of citizen, always willing to serve, without possibility of criticizing; otherwise one would be marked down as someone who "thought differently," or as a "dissident," and would be doomed to endure the psychiatric clinic, imprisonment, or forced labor.

Party and state hypocritically passed themselves off as the citizens' "benefactors," deserving of thanks and gratitude. Equal rights and liberties for all citizens were no more than a legal fiction, however, since only members of the CP were recognized as being "true" citizens.

Economic Failure

The basis of the economic system consisted in the socialist ownership of the means of production, under the form of "state property" (K 77, art. 10). Thus, land, subsoil, waters, forests, basic means of production in industry, construction and agriculture, means of transport and communication, the banks, the properties of commercial and communal enterprises and of other enterprises organized by the state, all urban housing, as well as other property needed for carrying out the commitments of the state were exclusively the property of the state (art. 11). The end envisaged was the material wellbeing of all and a standard of living far surpassing a capitalist economy and guaranteeing the growing material and spiritual needs of the citizens (art. 15). The result, however, was that throughout "real socialism," productivity stood below the minimum level, products were of poor quality, monthly pay was reduced to the minimum, and there was general impoverishment. Prophecies about the "liberation" of the workers from capitalist exploitation ended paradoxically in the fact of millions of "real socialism" workers being forced to seek work and a better reward for it in capitalist countries. With this money, they built houses or other things in socialist countries. There are still immense differences in the standard of living between capitalist and socialist countries. The paradox lies precisely in the fact that, for the Marxist, the basis of everything, in the collective, is production, which in fact has proved to be disastrous.

Political Failure

The ideal was to conquer the whole world, thanks to the internationalism proclaimed and propagated, and to set people free from any form of social, economic, or political alienation and oppression. The capitalist ruling classes were to have been totally eliminated from the world and replaced by the exploited and oppressed working classes: the "dictatorship of the proletariat" to begin with, then the "socialist brotherhood," and, finally, the "perfect, classless society." Yet, in all the countries of "real socialism," the Communist regime has managed to produce only a dictatorial and tyrannical system of government, led by the CP, maintained by the secret police, which has been entrusted with the task of eliminating millions of innocent people whose only crime has been to "think differently." Free thought did not exist even within the CP itself, where each member, in accordance with what was laid down by the statute, was enjoined to respect the decisions of the ruling organs. Those who, within the party, would not follow the line of the rulers (or better, that of the secretary-general), ended by finding themselves out of the party again and were regarded as "sick" members who needed treatment, having lost the faculty of sound, approved, Communist thinking. In this sense, freedom had always to be "in conformity with the interests of the people and the objective of consolidating and developing the socialist regime" (K 77, art. 50). The system was never to be criticized, and the possibility of serious self-criticism was considered even less, all the while the voices eulogizing the policy, the economy, and the CP continued to resound through all the means of communication, rigidly controlled and directed from above. This utopian system now has utterly collapsed, revealing its true face of misery and oppression.

Bibl.: K. MARX, *Oekonomisch-philosophische Manuskripte aus dem Jahre 1848*, vol. 1/3 (1932): 29–172; id., *Das Kapital*; vol. 1, *Marx-Engels Werke (MEW)*, 39 vols. (Berlin) 23 (1962); vol. 2, *MEW* 24 (1963); vol. 3, *MEW* 25 (1964); vol. 4, 26/1 (1965), 26/2 (1967), 26/3 (1968); id., *Grundriss der Kritik der politischen Oekonomie: Rohentwurf 1857–1858* (Berlin, 1953); id., *Aus der Kritik der Hegelschen Rechtsphilosophie: Kritik der Hegelschen Staatsrechts (paragraphs 261–313)*, *MEW*, vol. 1 (1957): 201–333; id., *Differenz der demokratischen und epikureischen Naturphilosophie*, in Karl Marx and Friedrich Engels, *Historisch-kritische Gesamtausgabe (MEGA)*, 7 vols. (Moscow, 1927–35), part 1, vol. 1; id., *Thesen über Feuerbach*, *MEW* 3:6.; id., *Zu Judenfrage*, *MEW* 1:347–77; id., *Das philosophische Manifest der historischen Rechtsschule*, *MEW*, 1:78–85; M. STIRNER, *Der Einzige und sein Eigentum* (Leipzig, 1845); V. I. LENIN, *Materi-*

alismus und Empiriokritizismus, vol. 14 (3rd ed.; 1873); F. ENGELS, *Anteil der Arbeit an der Menschwerdung des Affen* (1896), *MEW* 2:444–55; id., *Herrn Eugen Dührings Umwälzung der Wissenschaft* ("Anti Dühring"), *MEW*, 20:1–303; id., *Dialektik der Natur*, ibid., 305–570; id., *Ludwig Feuerbach und Ausgang der klassischen deutschen Philosophie*, *MEW*, 21:256–307; I. V. STALIN, "Über dialektischen und historischen Materialismus" (O dialekticeskom i istoriceskom materialisme), in *Geschichte der Kommunistischen Partei der Sowjetunion (Bolschewiki)* (Berlin, 1946), 126–60; G. A. WETTER, *Il materialismo dialettico sovietico* (Turin, 1948); id., *Der dialektische Materialismus: Seine Geschichte und sein System in der Sowjetunion* (Vienna, 1952); id., "Marxismo," *DTI*, 2:469–503; J. H. BOCHENSKI, *Der sovjet-russische dialektische Materialismus* (Berne, 1950); J. LACROIX, *Marxisme, existentialisme, personalisme* (Paris, 1951); E. BLOCH, *Prinzip Hoffnung*, vol. 2 (Frankfurt, 1959); G. GIRARDI, *Marxismo e Cristianesimo* (Assisi, 1966); H. GOLLWITZER, *Die marxistische Religionskritik und der christliche Glaube* (Munich/Hamburg, 1967); var., *L'ateismo contemporaneo: Il cristianesimo di fronte all'ateismo*, 4 vols. (Turin, 1967); E. CIMIC, *Savez komunista i religija* (Belgrade, 1969); L. BOGLIOLO, *Ateismo e Cristianesimo: Confronto dialettico* (Rome, 1971); G. H. PÖHLMANN, *Der Atheismus oder der Streit um Gott* (Gütersloh, 1977); F. RODÉ, *Uvod u moderni ateizem* (Celocev, 1977); P. POUPARD, ed., *L'Église devant le défi de l'athéisme contemporain* (Rome, 1982); id., *La fede e l'ateismo nel mondo: Indagine del Pontificio Consiglio per il dialogo con i non credenti* (Casale Monferrato, 1989); I. FUČEK, "Marxismus huius temporis in potestate constitutus de iuribus et libertatibus hominum," *Periodica* 72 (1983): 273–308; id., "Difficultés du Deuxième Monde," in *Commission théologiqui internationale*; P. DELHAYE and W. MURPHY, eds., *Les chrétiens d'aujourd'hui devant la dignité et les droits de la personne humaine* (Vatican City, 1985), 116–26; id., "Dostojanstvo Ijudske osobe u današnjem ateizmu (The dignity of the human person in contemporary communism)," in var., *U slу̌žbi čovjeka: Zbornik Nadbiskupa-Metropolite dr. Frane Franica* (Split, 1989), 89–121; M. J. BUCKLEY, *At the Origins of Modern Atheism* (New Haven/London, 1987).

Ivan FUČEK

II. COMMUNIST PARTY

What interests us is the guiding role of the Communist Party (CP) in "real socialism," its ideological dogmatism, and its monopoly of power in the Marxist-Leninist collective as it aspired to conquer the whole world. Whenever the party prevailed over the state, the desire for internationalism by means of world revolution created tension at the international level, which has on occasion reached a dangerously high pitch (e.g., in the confrontation over Cuba, the menacing diplomatic response in Brezhnev's last years in power, and then in Andropov's and in Chernenko's reigns). Alternatively, when the state has prevailed over the party, Leninist Communism has always found an opening for dialogue, a possibility of economic relations with other states (e.g., the pact between Stalin and Ritler, the Reagan-Gorbachev and Bush-Gorbachev conversations). Another feature of the party as it prevails over the state is that it serves as a model for all other Communist parties in the world, instead of seeking alliances between the USSR and other states. For our purpose, it will suffice to point out three obvious aspects of the history of the CPSU and of the CP in general: the evolutionary phase of the CP, the phase of its monopoly of power, and that of its decline.

1. The Evolutionary Phase

When K. Marx and F. Engels spoke of a "working-class party," they meant the whole working class. They did not want an elite party ruling from this class. This is very clear in the Communist Manifesto (1847–48), where it expressly says: "The Communists do not form a separate party opposed to other working-class parties. They have no interests separate and apart from those of the proletariat as a whole. They do not set up any sectarian principles of their own by which to shape and mold the proletarian movement." Thus, in France, the Communists join the Social Democratic party. In Switzerland, they support the radicals. In Germany, the CP is with the bourgeoisie. Communists, in a word, work everywhere in cooperation and understanding with the democratic parties in all countries. Thus, the Communists are that fraction of all the worker parties of each country that is the most determined to advance.

Lenin, however, had a different idea. The party ought *not* to embrace the entire working class. It not only should be a minority party but ought to become the *vanguard* of the class

because it is impossible under capitalism for the whole working class to raise itself to the party's level of awareness. The members of this vanguard must be revolutionaries by profession and must therefore submit to an iron discipline. The party should exercise control over the masses, assuming the direction of mass organizations (trade unions, social and cultural organizations, etc.). Against this theory, Trotsky objected that Lenin wanted to replace the proletariat by the party, and the party by its head. But from then on, in the constitutions of "real socialism" in the USSR and elsewhere, the CP had this strictly Leninist character, as was to become clear from 1917 onward.

Here we shall have to mention certain details in the life of Lenin (1870–1924), the better to understand the essence and structure of the CP, for his biography is essentially bound up with the history of the party as we know it. Lenin is its true founder. An atheist from childhood, he was convinced when still only a student of the ineffectiveness of the methods of radical populism, especially after his elder brother, Alexander, was sentenced to death for his active role in mounting an attempt on the life of Czar Alexander III (1887). Because of the part Lenin played in student disorders, he was expelled from Kazan University and temporarily sent to forced residence at Kukushkino, where he read the works of Chernyshevsky and so became acquainted with Hegel's philosophic materialism and dialectical method, which made his later studies of Marx and Engels easier. In 1890, having joined the Marxist circle in Kazan, he began reading the basic works of Marx, Engels, and Plekhanov. In 1893 he devoted himself to the preparation of Marxism in St. Petersburg; in 1895 he visited Western Europe, where he made contact with the Russian Marxists in Geneva (Plekhanov, Akselrod) and with Kautsky and Lafargue. Arrested once back in St. Petersburg, he was sent fourteen months later to Siberia; when released, he emigrated to Europe (1900), where he engaged in the polemic against populism. His influence within the Russian Social-Democratic Labor Party, which he joined in 1899, was important. He began publishing a paper called *Iskra*, with the aim of preparing the ground for the founding of the CP.

At the Second Congress of the Russian Social-Democratic Labor Party, Lenin obtained a large majority, and *Pravda* was declared to be the party's official organ. Thanks to the paper, Lenin was all the better able to impose his own line of thought. Shortly afterward, Plekhanov parted company with him. Consequently, after the publication of no. 52 (1903), Lenin had to give up editing *Pravda*. Plekhanov continued to edit nos. 53–112, until October 1905. In the struggle between the two party factions, that of the left, or "bolshevik," created by Lenin in 1903, had the upper hand. But in October 1905, neither Lenin nor the Bolsheviks played much part in the revolution. After the October revolution, Lenin had to flee to Finland; toward the end of 1907, he was forced to leave that country too and emigrate yet again.

During the First World War, he lived in Switzerland. In April 1917, Germany allowed him to return to Russia with a group of other revolutionaries. During his time abroad, he had written a number of books, notably *What Is to Be Done?* in which he develops his conception of the party as an organization of professional revolutionaries; then, *The State and Revolution* (1917), a very important work for the understanding of Leninism. On 3 April, Lenin arrived in Petrograd and the next day announced the famous *April Theses* on the tasks of the proletariat in the revolution, which showed an unheard-of audacity. Among other things, Lenin called for struggle against the provisional government, whatever its political persuasion, the placing of all power in the hands of the Soviets, and the formation of a "Soviet Republic" as a higher form of democracy, in which there would be no more police, army, or bureaucracy; the immediate nationalization of the banks and of all land, whereas the socialization of industry could be effected only by a gradual transition to socialism; the replacement of the name of the Russian Social-Democratic Labor Party (founded in 1898), already much compromised, by that of the Russian Communist (Bolshevik) Party, approved at the Seventh Party Congress in 1918. The party was to wait until Stalin in 1952, before receiving its new title of Communist Party of the Soviet Union at the Nineteenth Party Congress. Finally, Lenin envisaged the formation of a new Communist International, which was actually founded in March 1919. In his demands, however, Lenin found himself very isolated within his own party before the outbreak of the October 1917 Revolution. Only through his absolute conviction and

tenacious propaganda did Lenin manage to keep gaining ground within the party itself.

The *Communist International (Komintern)* (KI) was founded by Lenin as a world organization of parties, with an iron revolutionary discipline, such that all Communist parties in Europe, America, and Asia were subject to the common programs (one of the first of which was militant atheism) and to the decisions, binding upon all, of its organs—the congress and the executive committee. By a legal provision of Stalin's, this Komintern was abolished in 1943. It was also called the Third International, following Marx's First International of 1864, within which the earliest working-class' organizations took shape, and the Second International of 1889, which gave birth to the German Social-Democratic Party and the Russian Social-Democratic Party, with the Bolshevik left predominating (1903) under Lenin's leadership.

We should also mention the fact that, after the revolution of October 1917, Lenin's two constitutions, that of 1918 and the posthumous one of 1924, have an introductory section in the form of the CP program, with the statement that by means of *world* revolution the proletariat aims "to assure the victory of socialism in all countries" (1918 Constitution, art. 3) and to "tear humanity from the claws of finance capital and capitalism" (art. 4). The introduction to the Constitution of 1924 predicts that the USSR "will serve as a sure rampart against world capitalism and will accomplish a new and decisive step on the road to uniting the workers of all countries into a worldwide Soviet Socialist Republic." While Stalin's Constitution of 1936 has no such ambitions, Brezhnev's of 1977 (K 77) is, in contrast, a veritable political program of the CP.

2. The Phase of Power

Without even pausing to discuss to what extent the Soviet model of the state, described in Brezhnev's 1977 Constitution, is inspired by the teachings of Hobbes, Hegel, Marx, Engels, and Lenin, we see the following point clearly. Although the Preamble (para. 13.6) refers to "the Soviet people" and states that "the whole people" is above the socialist state and is the supreme authority, the infamous article 6 indicates otherwise. According to this article,

The Communist Party of the Soviet Union is the force that directs and guides Soviet society, the central nucleus of its political system and of state and social organizations. The CPSU exists for the people and at the service of the people. Armed with Marxist-Leninist doctrine, the CP determines the general perspective of the development of society and the line of the internal and external policy of the USSR, directs the great creative activity of the Soviet people, confers a planned and scientifically based character on its struggle for the victory of Communism. All party organizations operate within the framework of the constitution of the USSR.

"The CP . . . is the force." If we juxtapose the term "force," borrowed from the CPSU Statute of 1961, with the words "armed" and "struggle," two other terms from the same text, the military style becomes clear, even if, at first sight, we might suppose the reference to be to ideological, political, and ethical force.

"The CP . . . directs . . . Soviet society." The two expressions "force" and "direct" do not occur in Stalin's Constitution of 1936 (art. 126). Unlike Stalin, Brezhnev rehabilitated the CPSU, giving it the supreme position in Soviet society. It is the main, if not the unique, force directing the entire people, even the Supreme Soviet and the legislature, not in the sense that the functions of state are transferred directly to the CPSU but in the sense clearly stated as follows:

> In directing the activity of the Soviets, the [CPSU] does not substitute itself for them but delimits the functions of the organs of the Party and of the State. . . . The Party considers one of its most important tasks to be the consolidating, the improving in all possible ways, of the power of the Soviets, and safeguarding the subsequent development of socialist democracy.

This was how Brezhnev explained what is meant by the verb "direct" in his speech on the K 77 project, meaning thus to follow the thought of Lenin.

"The CP . . . guides Soviet society" toward the ends planned by the party. This is Lenin's, Khrushchev's, and Brezhnev's idea; Stalin, however, omitted it from his 1936 Constitution. "To orientate" means to set in the right direction, to engage, to direct, to lead correctly, in accordance with the idiosyncratic hallmark of the CPSU. The hallmark of an "infallible magisterium" as to doctrine, of "absolute precision" as to application, and of "mystification" as to intelligence and wisdom (R. G. Wesson).

"The CP . . . directs and guides . . . the central nucleus of its political system and of state and social organizations." This passage says a great deal more than is said in Stalin's 1936 Constitution, where the party itself is still "the central guiding nucleus" (art. 26). If therefore the party directs and orientates the "central nucleus" of the entire political system and all the state and social organizations, this means that there is absolutely nothing left that is not directed and orientated by the party. Thus, little by little, it becomes clear that the party is the "Soviet people" that establishes the rights, liberties, and obligations of the citizens, and even "the aims of the socialist State" (K 77, Preamble, para. 13.6). In a word, an authority without parallel.

"The CPSU exists for the people." This is the same as saying that, if the people were not directed by the party, there would be no point in the party's existence. Similarly, the CPSU is also "the heart of the [Soviet] organism," "inseparable from the people as a whole." To try to oppose the party and the people, says Brezhnev, or even to talk about "dictatorship of the Party" would be like trying to oppose, for example, the heart to all the rest of the human organism. By "organism," are we to understand the system or the people? In either case the results would be the same: if a heart attack were to occur, system and people both would die. This is exactly what did happen in East Germany, Hungary, Czechoslovakia, and elsewhere in 1989–90: the system disappeared when the CP disappeared.

"The CPSU . . . [is] at the service of the people." Inasmuch as everything is done on the basis of the will of the party, however, it is not by the will or aspiration of the people. To serve or be at the service of the people means that the party's task is to inform all the citizens of the Soviet collective as fully as possible of the party's objectives, so that all may adhere to them and follow them as the CPSU wishes.

"The CP, . . . armed with Marxist-Leninist doctrine" is a phrase that suggests a total control. It refers to the ideology by which reality, experience, and practice are measured and adjusted. Marxist-Leninist ideology—that is, mere worldly materialistic pragmatism—is more or less divinized or absolutized by the CPSU, so as to justify and defend its views and decisions for the development of society. The lines of "internal and external policy of the USSR" are determined in the same way. That is why no other, alternative, political thought is conceivable according to K 77, although opposing voices and the desire for change in a pluralist direction on the world stage may be very strong.

"The CP . . . directs the great creative activity of the Soviet people," not only as a charismatic enlivener of the country but as a driving force perfectly organized for "social and cultural" activity (arts. 19–27), for "guaranteed employment" (art. 40), for "scientific, technical, and artistic" activity (art. 47), always, however, "in conformity with the aims of building Communism." This same creative activity in all fields and at all levels in the USSR unfolds within the narrow limits conceded by the party, under its Argus-eyed vigilance and censorship.

"The CP . . . confers a planned and scientifically based character on its struggle for the victory of Communism." All decisions are taken in the course of debates within the CPSU. Both the planning and the execution have a "scientific" character, in accordance with the postulates of a materialistic worldview. But "scientific" in what sense? Is Marxist-Leninist ideology scientific? Once again, the term "scientific" is being improperly applied.

The final victory of Communism is envisaged only at the third phase of its evolution, after the "dictatorship of the proletariat" and after the state "of all the people," which henceforth characterizes "mature socialism." In it, the supreme goal of the state, of the people, and of the individual belonging to Soviet society is the "perfect society," where the state will no longer be necessary or even expedient, where law will disappear and where all will live an equal life in full "fraternal cooperation" (K 77, Preamble, para. 7) and in "friendship" (para. 4). While society is still on the way toward the third phase of Communist evolution, the supreme end of everybody's life (as moral norm) is that same future atheistic society, which is yet to be realized.

Stalin's Constitution of 1936 spoke only of the CPSU's struggle for "the consolidation and development of the socialist regime," whereas Brezhnev's K 77 reaffirms the struggle for the victory of Communism. This difference between the two constitutions marks a great step forward in achieving the goal of an international Communism.

A little before the publication of the new constitution, a new paragraph 3 was added to article 6, on the organizations of the CPSU "which act within the framework of the constitution of the USSR." Two explanatory articles (7 and 8) then follow: "The trade unions, the Young Communist League (Konsomol), the cooperative organizations" (art. 7), with all the others of the CPSU, in the new constitution become collaborators with, and various branches of, the party, whereas in Stalin's constitution they did not have anywhere near the same importance or such extensive responsibilities. This is a further sign that socialist society under the direction of the CPSU was gradually being transformed into a Communist society, the functions of which were to devolve on the party organizations. Without any doubt this was strange behavior, consisting in turning a blind eye to actual reality, which was moving in the opposite direction and preparing the collapse of "real socialism."

Analysis of K 77 clearly shows that at the apex of the pyramid of power in Soviet society sat the CPSU, the political, doctrinal, and ideological supremacy of which in the state appeared insurmountable. The CPSU was the primary determining factor of the state and, consequently, *above* the state, which was to act as its "basic instrument" (K 77, Preamble, para. 1), while legislation served it as an instrument subordinate to the state. The CPSU was thus the primary and supreme source of the rights and liberties of the Soviet individual. It is not to be wondered at if Brezhnev's K 77 calls the CPSU the "Soviet people," since everything outside the CPSU was nonpeople, nonreality, nontruth, nonliberty, nonintelligence, nonlife, nonhealth, and nonhumanity.

3. Total Collapse

This last phase, characterized by the end of the party-state, by the granting of plenary powers to the president, by the democratization and modification of structures, has itself been abortive and followed by total collapse.

Bibl.: C. D. KERNIG, "Die kommunistischen Parteien der Welt," in C. D. Kernig, ed., *Sowjetsystem und demokratische Gesellschaft* (Freiburg/Basel/Vienna, 1969); P. BISCARETTI DI RUFFIA and G. CRESPI REGHIZZI, *La Costituzione sovietica del 1977: Un sessantennio di evoluzione costituzionale nell'URSS* (Milan,

1979), 551–72; "Costituzione (Legge fondamentale) dell'Unione delle Repubbliche Socialiste Sovietiche approvata dalle VII sessione (straordinaria) della IX legislatura del Soviet Supremo dell'Urss il 7 ottobre 1977," in ibid., 509–47; A. PAGLIETTI, *La costituzione sovietica del 1977 nei suoi precedenti storici e nel quadro del costituzionalismo moderno* (Rome, 1980); R. .G. WESSON, *Lenin's Legacy: The Story of the CPSU* (Stanford, 1978); I. FUČEK, "Il sessantennio della morte di Vladimir I. Lenin (1870–1924)," in *Radio Vaticana-Studio* 28 (1984): 15–19; id., "Il fondamento dei diritti dell'uomo nella Costituzione sovietica," *CivCatt* (1983): 222–34; id., "Libertà religiosa nel diritto costituzionale di ispirazione marxista-leninista: confronto col diritto internazionale ratificato dal marxismo-leninismo ufficiale," in F. Biffi, ed., *I diritti fondamentali della persona umana e la libertà reliogiosa* (Rome, 1985), 637–41; id., "Human Rights and Freedom within Official Atheism," in R. Latourelle, ed., *Vatican II: Assessment and Perspectives Twenty-five Years After (1962–1987)* (New York, 1989), 3:199–236; The Russian text of the new "Statutes of the communist party of the Soviet Union," *Pravda* (March 7, 1986), 8; Also, the programmes . . . , 6.

Ivan FUČEK

MEANING, ULTIMATE, IN JESUS CHRIST

I. THE MEANING OF REVELATION. *1. The Recovery of the Objective Meaning. 2. In the Context of Gnosiology. 3. In the Context of Revelation. 4. Revealer and Revelation. 5. The Death of Jesus as Fullness of Meaning. 6. Consequences for a Theological Gnosiology.* (R. FISICHELLA)

II. QUEST FOR MEANING AND GIFT OF MEANING. *1. Search for Meaning. 2. The Gift of Meaning* (R. LATOURELLE)

I. THE MEANING OF REVELATION

1. The Recovery of the Objective Meaning

The presentation of revelation as renewed by Vatican II has restored a balance between the two elements constituting the revelatory event: God's revelation and the believer.

As theological history can easily show, there used to be a period when neglect of the recipient of revelation caused the very fact of the event to be lost from sight by reducing all revelation to its sole objective content, the truth of which was confirmed by external signs proving its divine origin.

Theologically speaking, fundamental theology should be able to advance a critical interpretation of the twofold acceptation of the meaning of revelation: on the one hand, the meaning of the event itself; on the other, the answer to the question posed by human nature on the meaning of existence.

Today, if revelation still claims it can provide the final answer to the question of meaning that rises in the human breast, this is because, already *in se* as event, it appears charged with meaning. Further, it is itself meaning, beyond which no more meaning can be had.

We therefore speak of the meaning of revelation as of its original sense—a sense that is distinguished from a general inherited sense which everyone possesses in virtue of being human. This, however, is the source and ground of meaning permitting the question about meaning to be asked, and this can be found intact in any age and any culture.

By meaning, we understand that which allows that true transparency to be achieved between essence and existence, whereby the former expends itself in the latter and the latter is the capacity and expression of the former. Meaning is perfect, exact consistency between that which is expressed and that which constitutes its definitive significance. Meaning is the ultimate end that exists of itself, finding the reasons for its finality in the internal dynamic of its own signification. In a word, meaning is that which appears and imposes itself as evident; it is the evidence itself which enables it to be known.

2. In the Context of Gnosiology

The existence of such meaning is that which is intuitively grasped as obvious by our epistemic activity. It exists, it is, it is perceived as that *quid* which is bestowed from everlasting and without which there can be no perception. By the "wonder" which enables us to have an ever more complete knowledge of the real, we discover that something has been given as existent. We are presented *sic et simpliciter* with an object and this it is that constitutes the evidence.

In deliberately opening up to what is outside us, we become apprised of the object's characteristics, which impose themselves on our consciousness as evidence. The evidence hence, the nature of the object as we see it, permits the first gnosiological object–subject relationship to come about. For we are characterized by our "ability to dispose of ourselves"; we are free to come out of ourself and to go back into ourself (*reditio in se ipsum*), to communicate the data of our cognitive divagations or to stay alone with the known object; in any case this dimension makes one fact obvious: the presence of something "other" than ourself.

In our gnosiological activity, we are always ready to accept the object of our knowledge into ourself; although we do not ourselves know, nor can we know, what will happen once we have accepted it into ourself. We are always faced with the unpredictability of what can happen. We can be transformed, or can refuse to change, according to our perception of having received a gift. . . . We shall always, however, be faced with the fact that we can discover a dimension of ourself which is precisely that of than new thing which we have just encountered: and hence our own potentiality for receiving some new manifestation.

By the same token, this allows us to grasp that our full realization—i.e., our potentiality for self-perception as a being able to know and dispose of itself—is possible only within the space of what we encounter. Our self-realization needs a knowledge that is outside ourself; our essence brings us to encounter that which we did not know before but which nonetheless is necessary for our self-explanation and realization.

In a word, the presence of the object brings a balance to the boundless pretensions of human knowledge. Since, on the one hand, it is true that personal awareness is unlimited and hence infinite in relation to itself, it is equally true that this limitlessness arises from the fact that objects are constantly presenting thmselves to be known. There is therefore an unlimited power for knowing things, but a power conferred by the *receiving* of knowledge through the presentation of the object. Our gaze therefore is unlimited, but this is because there is always something being offered to it.

3. In the Context of Revelation

In the act of revelation, theologically speaking, those features of complete freedom and transcendence must be manifested which are characteristics of God. From this it follows that the form of revelation bestowed on human beings is to be accepted as an expression of God's freedom in deciding to establish a relationship with us. Believers hence may never "pass judgment' on the forms in which revelation reaches them. It has to be accepted on its own terms and in the forms expressing God's freedom to communicate.

Identifying revelation with the person of Jesus of Nasareth as final and definitive expression of God's self-manifestation is what constitutes the distinctive feature of the Christian religion. This identification asserts that the figure of revelation is to be found in the mystery of the incarnation in which, in the historicity of a human being, the divine nature fully shares.

The form of revelation, hence, is given for us to know by means of the mystery which, to make itself understood, imposes the dialectic of a constant and reciprocal veiling and unveiling of the figure itself.

The figure of Jesus of Nazareth is therefore God's final and definitive communication to the human race, after which no further revelation of God is to be expected (*DV* 4). His person is revealed as an uninterrupted relationship with the mystery of the Trinity; for he reveals an awareness of being dependent on the Father and of being full of the Spirit; this makes him the *logos*, i.e., the first effective "public" expression of the mystery of God.

4. Revealer and Revelation

To say that Jesus Christ expresses the "evidence," the meaning of revelation, is to see that perfect accord and full conformity realized in him between revealer and revelation. Not only, therefore, does no greater revealer exist, but neither can anything new be revealed that he has not already expressed.

This identity between revealer and revelation rests on Jesus' own awareness; for this he evokes no less a testimony than that of the Father (Jn 5:31, 36–37). The words he utters are the Father's words (Jn 3:34); the signs he performs are those he has seen the Father perform (Jn 5:19, 36); this is because he is the Son and possesses all things, to such degree as to be the final *locus* of the judgment now completed once and for all (Jn 3:35).

That very "dependence" on the Father allows us to affirm that, humanly speaking, everything about God has been said in Jesus Christ and that he himself is the content of the revealed mystery.

Johannine theology too makes this clear, where it reports Jesus as having said: "My teaching is not *mine* but his who sent me" (Jn 7:17). By *didachē*, the evangelist means the public revelation that Jesus brings to completion in obedience to the Father's will; here, however, there is a special acceptation of the term, since the claim to know God's will is not said to be furnished by Scripture or the Torah. Instead, we encounter Jesus' repeated claim to be proclaiming, directly and without any mediation, the words and signs of God as he himself has learned them from the Father (Jn 8:28).

At the same time, however, we see a further fact revealed: what he reveals is *his*, and yet it is *not his* because it belongs to the Father. This referral to the Other does not, however, prescind from his own person, since the Father is present and actually working within him: "Whoever has seen me, has seen the Father" (Jn 14:9).

5. The Death of Jesus as Fullness of Meaning

The paradoxical dimension of the fullness of meaning can be seen in the death of Jesus of Nazareth on the cross. For in a unique event, the supreme sacrifice that anyone can voluntarily make of his own life, meets the very nature of God who reveals himself as a love that culminates in total self-giving.

In his death on the cross, the revelation Jesus makes of the Father is total, since in this death obedience to his will reaches its peak (Phil 2:8), and its revelatory content becomes transparent as a result.

The Son's existence is total obedience to and total reception by the Father. In this lies his freedom, by virtue of which he can say that he lays down "his life that he may take it again" (see Jn 10:17–18); for between him and the Father is identity of nature. This is that trinitarian love constituting the personal relationship which makes them Father and Son in the infinite and ceaseless giving and receiving to which the spiration of Love as the Third Person bears witness.

This *total* giving and receiving becomes humanly expressible in the death on the cross, since in the Son's death, and only in that, God reveals the climax of his activity: that of going to the very end. Certainly not a Plotinian climax by which, having reached the end, one is at the extreme and opposite point from where one set out, but that point at which the ending expresses the driving force of the beginning, since it discloses, and gives greater consistency to, the source itself which never loses intensity.

What, however, does become humanly meaningful is that this love is not an end in itself; rather, it is given "for the ungodly" (Rom 5:6). God does not give himself to die for the innocent, but takes the Innocent One as ransom for the guilty.

Each one of us, in our own individual lives, sees this death event come to pass and be addressed to us at that moment when we see and concretely experience our own sinfulness.

In the death of Jesus of Nazareth, therefore, meaning becomes a transparency of the divine nature and of the assumption into it of human nature; for God, crucified for human beings, bears our martyred flesh in the resurrection life of triune love.

6. Consequences for a Theological Gnosiology

An original and free meaning given to the believer is not without consequences for theological knowledge. For instance, theological "principles" could be extracted to become basic to a fundamental theology understood as epistemology (→ THEOLOGY II) of theological knowledge as such: we schematize them as follows:

a. Belief is a special form of human knowledge with regard to the revelation of God.

For believing does not mean renouncing the gnosiological dimension; rather, it entails recognizing that, already within the act of faith, some of the components exist that make us able to think of ourselves as free and potentially able to perceive the truth.

In this context, furthermore, believing is not primarily adherence to an abstract system of thought, such as might get us accused of being ideologists; no, it is an essentially person-to-person relationship that comes about with the person of Jesus of Nazareth as mediated by a living community. By believing, we put ourselves in that anthropological situation which makes our act one of great importance, because in it the kind of risk and self-giving to the "other" is of the highest order. As against the fragmentariness of human knowledge, believing is that kind of all-embracing awareness which welcomes the "other" into itself, so as to be able to initiate and make progress in self-knowledge.

b. The radical "newness" for human existence resides in the revealed event.

In our view, revelation ought above all to carry with it the component of something "radically new," a pure gift. This newness does not pertain to us nor derive from us, but is perceived by virtue of a movement from outside us, encountering us and able to lead us to knowledge of an existence perceived as indebted to the "other."

This potentiality for knowledge is provided by the kenotic act of a God who reveals himself and clearly encounters a creature, who as such is summoned to awareness of being open to receive the revelation (→ OBEDIENTIAL POTENCY).

This radical newness is to be found at two levels: that of the contents, and that of their understanding and explanation. The paschal event provides the interpretational key to this newness, since now the final victory over "the last enemy to be destroyed," death (1 Cor 15:24–26), has taken place within human history.

Starting from this newness, each of us is compelled to view the future in the words of the prophet: "Do not remember the former things, or consider the things of old. I am about to do a new thing; . . . do you not perceive it?" (Is 43:18–19). Here the "perceiving" is charged with that "wonder" which lets us see the truly new, that which did not exist in the past but which is now given and made visible.

The historicity of Jesus of Nazareth is the essential and constituent principle of knowledge of the faith.

The historicity of Jesus is not confined to the fact of his having lived on earth; it implies something more—his awareness of who and what he was and the way he conveyed this to others (→ CHRISTOLOGY I). By his presence and behavior, the teacher of Galilee changed the lives of his contemporaries; of these, to be more precise, a number of men and women gave up everything to follow him, since they believed in him and what he said as they saw the promises being fulfilled on which their hopes had been set.

This initial faith of theirs has made it possible for Jesus' own genuine awareness of his mission, his own relationship with God and the meaning of his saving death, to be handed down, even if indirectly, to our own times. As regards the way Jesus saw himself, NT theology has not handed down the Master's word (Heidegger: "*überwinden besagt nicht abstossen*"), but rather points out how faith knows and can express this.

The church is the formal dimension of knowledge of the faith (→ THEOLOGY III).

Were theology not to proceed from an ecclesial awareness and as contributing to the growth of the community, it would be only an esoteric sort of knowledge producing no results.

The church is not extraneous to revelation; the church is the depositary of revelation and mediates it down the ages. In their respective awareness of having a ministry to discharge, the bishop and his theologian should refer to this common matrix to ensure a proper updating of the revealed datum.

Rediscovering the dimension of the objective meaning of revelation does not imply depriving believers of feeling themselves to have been summoned by God and thinking of themselves as people to whom his communications are addressed. Quite the reverse: it means discovering and stressing a component of biblical anthropology which regards the individual as someone always "called," "employed" by God, and loved by him in the first place.

Such a view, however, shows us that human knowledge is always fragmentary; revelation is not determined by us but is made to us, so that each may "understand" and "believe" (Jn 20:31). Hence it is a free gift of the unconditioned activity of God. If it is necessary to talk about the meaning of revelation, this is in order that the believer may clearly understand that God and his mystery drive us ever onward toward the *semper maior.*

Bibl.: H. Urs VON BALTHASAR, *The Glory of the Lord: A Theological Aesthetics,* vol. 1: *Seeing the Form* (San Francisco, 1982); id., *Theologik,* vol. 1: *Wahrheit der Welt* (Einsiedeln, 1985); V. MELCHIORRE, *Essere e parola* (Milan, 1982).

Rino FISICHELLA

II. QUEST FOR MEANING AND GIFT OF MEANING

All human beings are confronted by a fundamental question: What is the meaning of life? But from the very outset this question itself is really two questions. The first has to do with the meaning, or a meaning, of the human condition; the second is concerned rather with meaning that is revealed and offered as a gift, namely, the revelation of God and the human person in Jesus Christ. This article will focus on the first question and simply sketch out an answer to the second, which is more fully developed in connection with revelation and its credibility.

1. Search for Meaning

Human beings are, first and foremost, a question about themselves and the ultimate meaning of their lives. They can no more escape this question than they can escape being themselves. Whether we like it or not, says Pascal in *The Wager*, we are all "committed": Who are we? Why do we exist? Where are we going? We cannot get rid of these questions without rejecting our very existence. We are riddles to ourselves and can do nothing worthwhile as long as we have not penetrated this mystery. Contemporary novelists, theologians, and philosophers are constantly insisting that the greatest of all problems is human beings themselves. Human beings know they must die, but they cannot abandon the question of what precedes and follows their disappearance from this world. As "rational" animals they have a thirst for meaning. And if the crisis of meaning becomes too intense with no resolution in sight, it ends in the tragedy of suicide—a denouement that annually carries off millions of human beings, especially from among the young between twelve and twenty years old.

In most instances, the meaning of life comes to us as an *inheritance* from the familial, social, and religious milieu into which we were born. From this point of view it can be said that there have been billions of meanings, beginning with the first faltering words of the human race and reaching down to our own time. To have some grasp of these we would have to review the range of models which philosophies, religions, and civilizations have developed in the course of the centuries. Here we would find ancient *Egypt*, which, after trying to overcome death by its own efforts (success, power), sank into passivity and fatalism in the face of the unpredictable course of history and the incomprehensible mystery of death; then, *Mesopotamia*, whose only answer was skepticism, which is as powerless in the face of life as in the face of death; then, the *Greek world*, which was imprisoned in the cyclical repetition of a history that lacks direction and is victim of the blind forces of fate; the *East*, which is tied to the wheel of life, on which birth, growth, and death are but participations in the one act of life itself, to which the individual always returns after being momentarily released from it by death; the *modern West*, which with Nietzsche substitutes the human person for God but soon sees Superman blown to pieces and replaced by Mind (Hegel) or society (Marx). In order to escape these servitudes, people have rushed madly into new enslavements: technology, class struggle, production and consumption, drugs, genetic manipulation, atomic war, and so on.

Faced with this torrent of contradictory meanings, people take a second step and ask: Is there no "true meaning" that triumphs at last and compels recognition? For brevity's sake, an attempt may be made to group all the attitudes taken toward life; with some simplification, all these attitudes may be reduced to four:

a. Enjoy life. A first attitude is to plunge into life "gluttonously," expecting it to offer an answer to all human aspirations. But such an attitude is in fact naïve and superficial. The decision to accept life without asking questions already implies a choice: the decision to free oneself from everything in life that imposes any constraints. This attitude implies taking oneself and no one else as model. Those who adopt it are trying to achieve fulfillment as though they were completely free subjects; but such an attempt can only fail, since on every side human beings come up against their finiteness and against constraints over which they have no control. The expectation of definitive fulfillment from one's own resources is the supreme delusion. In the end, human beings encounter the barrier of death. But we may not conclude from all this that the desire for fulfillment which lies deep in the human heart is therefore false and awakens no echo. The truth is that there is more in the human will-*willing* (Blondel) than in the will-*willed*, which finds expression in the immediate choices made. The admission that here on earth human beings cannot reach fulfillment by their own powers may be simply the other side of a desire to obtain fulfillment elsewhere and in an Other.

b. Pessimism and suicide. A second attitude is pessimism and nihilism. Defenders of this view prefer a radical solution to the games played by the "lovers" of life.

> Of what value are all these efforts to eliminate an illusory problem? A frank and brutal negation is better than all the hypocritical subterfuges and all the subtleties of thought. To taste death in everything perishable before one is oneself put in the grave; to know that one will be annihilated and to will this annihilation—*this* is for clear-sighted, free and strong minds the ultimate message of emancipation, courage and experimental certitude: at death everything is dead. (Blondel 1893:23)

What needs to be killed is not being, which does not exist, but the illusory will to be. We must expect nothing of life, because it has nothing to give. "To show up the deceitfulness of every instinct for self-preservation and survival is to bring humanity and the world the salvation that consists in nothingness: the nothing that consists in the absence of willing" (ibid., 29). Blondel's response to pessimism and nihilism as a solution is to say that it is impossible to conceive of or will nothingness except by willing something else. Human beings affirm nothingness only because they need a reality more solid than that which they find unsatisfactory. "In vain does one goad on thought and desire. In the *will to be*, the *will not to be*, and the *will not to will* there is always this common term, *to will*, whose inevitable presence dominates all forms of existence and annihilation" (ibid., 37). As a matter of fact, the will to nothingness has its origin in an absolute love of being that has been disillusioned by the inadequacy of phenomena, of appearances (ibid., 38-39). The person wills that there be something *consistent*. The question, then, is whether the surface will of those who proclaim the nothingness of existence is in accord with their deeper will that thirsts for a *true* existence.

c. Defiance and rebellion. A third attitude is rebellion. Ever since the nineteenth century, human beings have been discovering that they are no longer free, no longer masters either of themselves or of what is around them; servitude is imposed on them from every side. The result is the rebel (A. Camus): "I rebel, therefore we are." Even before Nietzsche, we find in Max Stirner (1806–1856) a deadly form of rebellion. Stirner simply sweeps away everything that could deny or adversely affect the individual. Truth for individuals (he said) consists in being conscious of being their own masters, their own owners. Ever since that time, the wave of rebellion has been constantly cresting and has moved from the realm of thought to the realm of history. *Nietzsche,* who takes the death of God for granted, combats everything that might attempt to be a spurious substitute for the vanished divinity. Salvation is achieved on earth and without any help from God; the only divinity is the individual spirit. *Marx,* for his part, seeks to liberate human beings from economic exploitation by subjugating nature and replacing the domination of the masters with that of their former slaves. Now, in obedience to history, the race is journeying toward a slavery such as has never been seen before. *Freud* seeks to set individuals free from determinisms and the chains imposed by unconquered determinisms. For *Jean-Paul Sartre,* as for *Albert Camus,* both life and death are absurd. In Sartre's view, there is no reason for our having been born, and we die by accident. Death robs human beings of their freedom and annihilates all possibilities of fulfillment. Camus starts with the same facts but draws a different conclusion. Life is absurd and lacks meaning: consequently, the only human greatness consists in accepting life with its absurdity and then using one's freedom to create a meaning in the very midst of absurdity. The attitude of rebellion rejects the idea of any true completion in humanity's present state or in any absolute located outside the person. This is a new version of stoicism. Human beings seek their greatness in defiance and cling to this. The error of rebels is not their claim to a supreme fulfillment, for it is to these heights that God invites us, but their attempt to attain by their own natural powers the divinization or perfect freedom to which they aspire.

d. Acceptance and openness. A final attitude consists in recognizing that human beings have within them a need of the absolute which in fact cannot be met in this life but which nonetheless is not impossible of fulfillment. In the face of death, which radicalizes the question of the human person, human beings become aware that they have within them an unconquerable aspiration for definitive self-fulfillment; on the other hand, death reveals to them their complete inability to ensure their own survival and fulfillment. Death confronts them with an inescapable choice: either they acknowledge that their life, insofar as it is projected toward, and aspires to, a greater degree of being, has a meaning (which means that they hope for a transcendent future, a survival after death); or they accept their life as utterly without meaning (then there is complete despair). Those who acknowledge that life has a meaning, which is connected with the meaning of death, admit that life is precarious and indelibly marked by finitude, but also that it is an initial given on which they can gradually build and come to experience themselves as a desire for a hoped-for absolute. They recognize that their freedom can achieve its fulfillment only with the help of a higher freedom that transcends theirs. They recognize that they are "persons," that is, conscious, free subjects who enter into an *accepted* relationship with the world, other persons, and the absolute, and that they "definitively" constitute themselves as persons by opening themselves to the Super-personal who grounds their awareness of being finite but also of being permeated by a will to infinity. But human beings have no say at all about the salvific decision of this higher Freedom which transcends their own. For here we enter into the world of the historical offerings of salvation to humanity. On the other hand, if a religion presents itself with the claim of being able to fulfill the deepest desires of human beings, to satisfy the thirst for the infinite that is devouring them, and indeed to surpass anything they can conceive, it would be unreasonable to reject this hypothesis of a revealed meaning that is offered and given to them. The human person must at least be open to the hypothesis of a possible word of God addressed to the human race in history. In its historical reality, Christian revelation seems to respond to this undefined but also irrepressible expectation of the human will.

2. The Gift of Meaning

Christianity answers the quest for meaning with the gift of meaning, a meaning revealed and offered to us in Jesus Christ. "The truth is that only in the mystery of the incarnate Word does the mystery of man take on light" (GS 22). Christ is seen as the great Presence that explains everything and interprets everything. Being the very Word of God made flesh among us, he is the *fullness of meaning* in a world that is searching for its *lost meaning.*

Christ is not only the irruption of God into human history but a "massive" irruption of meaning. The message of Christ reaches into the inmost depths of the human person, depths inaccessible to psychology and psychoanalysis, where knowledge and discourse fall silent and vanish as before a galaxy that flees from us and constantly eludes us. Christ is the key to the human riddle; he sums up and surpasses all anthropology. In fact, the mystery of Christ and the mystery of the human person are but a single mystery. But if human beings are to be revealed to themselves through Christ, this will be effected by the revelation of what is most intimate and profound in the mystery of Christ, that is, the mystery of his sonship. The secret of human beings, whether they know it or not, is that the love of God overshadows them; that they are loved and saved by the Father, in Christ and the Spirit. It is only when human beings discover this mystery that they can be fully revealed to themselves in all their greatness, which consists in this, that they are the object of God's loving kindness and are destined to accept the love of the Father that is revealed in Jesus Christ. It is in this participation and communion in the mystery of the trinitarian life that human beings are "fulfilled." The key to the mystery of the human person is that God, in Jesus Christ, wills to *re-generate* in every human being a son or daughter and to *in-spire* in them or *breathe into* them his Spirit of love, which is a spirit of sonship and daughterhood. The incarnation of the Son brings to light the dignity of the person, while the redemption reveals to us the value God sets on every human being. Consequently, far from being alien to human beings, revelation is so closely connected with their own mystery that without it they cannot know their own identity.

The questions that rise in the hearts of human beings are likewise the questions at the heart of revelation. We can try all the approaches we like to Christianity; one thing we can never eliminate is the *meaning* which Christ is for human beings and for the problems that go with their condition. Christ remains a mystery, but a mystery that sheds light and is the ever-gushing wellspring of meaning. When human beings become aware that the mystery of Christ echoes their own mystery and enters into their depths where it becomes closer to them than they are to themselves and does so in order to bring light and warmth to these depths, to the point of creating a fusion and a fission, then revelation is no longer simply "plausible," inasmuch as it introduces harmony into the person; it is now "credible." In other words, if it is true that Christ by his life and message is mediator of meaning and sole exegete of human beings and their problems; if it is true that in him human beings are able to "locate" themselves, understand themselves, fulfill themselves, and even surpass themselves; if, finally, the light which he projects on the human condition is as penetrating as I have described it, then the question of his identity arises. Must he not be, as he claims, the Son of the Father, God-among-us, the meaning of God and the human person, and the *gift of meaning*, since he is the Word of God?

Bibl.: M. BLONDEL, *Action* (1893; New York, 1984); P. TILLICH, *The Courage To Be* (New Haven, 1952); E. LEVINAS, *Totalité et infini* (The Hague, 1961); M. LÉGAUT, *L'homme à la recherche de son humanité* (Paris, 1971); M. ZUNDEL, *Quel homme et quel Dieu* (Paris, 1976); Vatican II, Constitution *Gaudium et Spes* (1965); R. LATOURELLE, *Man and His Problems in the Light of Jesus Christ* (New York, 1983); R. FISICHELLA, *Dieu existe, il s'est révélé: La Révélation et sa crédibilité* (Montreal/Paris, 1989); L. LEAHY, "La vie a-t-elle un sens?" *Nouveau Dialogue* (Nov. 1988).

René LATOURELLE

MESSIANISM

I. MESSIANIC EXPECTATION. *1. A Royal Messiah (50 B.C.E.–50 C.E.). 2. Messianic Expectation in Various Social and Religious Groups: Sadducees, Pharisees, Essenes, Popular Movements.* (G. ROCHAIS)

II. FULFILLMENT OF MESSIANISM. *1. The Messianic Hope (royal, priestly, prophetic, eschatological messianism). 2. Jesus the Messiah. 3. Faith in the Messiah* (R. FISICHELLA)

I. MESSIANIC EXPECTATION

Despite claims to the contrary, messianism in the strict sense played a relatively limited role in eschatology during the first century B.C.E. and the first century of our era. It was linked to the more fundamental theme of the reign of God, which in turn was linked to obedience to the Torah. In addition, expectation of the Messiah took quite different forms in different social or religious groups. Pharisees, Essenes, and Sadducees did not share the same hope with regard to the coming of the Messiah; the few texts from the Greek diaspora that speak of the Messiah offer nothing new; on the other hand, the messianic idea at work in the popular movements that arose at the death of Herod the Great and during the great revolt against Rome in 66–70 differed quite a bit from other messianic ideas.

The exposition here will be in two parts. In the first I shall show the constant elements found, across the spectrum of parties (Pharisees, Essenes, Greek diaspora), in the Jewish messianic hope of a royal Messiah; these constants are verifiable because of the continuity observable between pre-Christian texts and those following upon the destruction of Jerusalem in 70. This study will be based chiefly on *Psalms of Solomon* 17 and 18 and on the Qumran documents, and, as opportunity allows, on book 3 of the *Sybilline Oracles* and Philo of Alexandria's *Blessings and Curses*. The apocalypses dating from the end of the first century (4 Ezra and the Syriac *Apocalypse of Baruch*) as well as traditions contained in the ancient Palestinian Targum on the Pentateuch or in the *Testaments of the Twelve Patriarchs* (which in their final form are certainly Christian), will be used only to confirm evidence that can be dated with certainty. The Parables of Enoch (*1 Enoch* 37–71) will not be used because their date is uncertain. In the second part I shall explain how the messianic hope differed from group to group (Sadducees, Pharisees, Essenes), in order to bring out and contrast their differing conceptions of the royal Messiah.

A fairly important place will be given to popular messianic movements that preceded the ministry of Jesus of Nazareth.

1. A Royal Messiah (50 B.C.E.–50 C.E.)

Main Characteristics

The Messiah has an earthly origin. No text before the end of the first century C.E. speaks of his preexistence. The Messiah is a human being, an earthling. This point is clear from the claimants who presented themselves as royal messiahs in the first century and who are mentioned by Josephus: Judas ben Hezekiah, Simon, and Athronges after the death of Herod the Great (*Ant.* 17 §§ 271–84; *War* 2.4 §§ 55–65), or, again, Menahem or Simon ben Giora at the time of the Jewish revolt of 66–70; and finally Simon ben Kosibah during the second Jewish revolt. The only passage in which Philo of Alexandria speaks of the Messiah makes clear the latter's earthly origin: "For, according to the oracles (Nm 24:7 LXX) a man will appear who will lead armies and engage in battle and will subject many great nations" (*Blessings and Curses* 95). In the *Psalms of Solomon*, the Messiah king, though idealized, is a real human being of the line of David (*Pss. Sol.* 17:23–45). At Qumran, whatever the name he may be given (Messiah of Israel, Prince of the Congregation, Branch of David, etc.), the Messiah is always regarded as an earthly being. The same is true of the Palestinian Targum on the Pentateuch (PT Gn 49:10–12; Nm 24:7–9; 24:17–19). Still in the second century, Trypho says to Justin: "All of us await a Messiah who will be a man taken from among men, and Elijah who is to anoint him when he comes. If that individual proves to be the Messiah, let everyone know that he is a man taken from among men" (*Dial.* 49). The preexistence of the Messiah or the Son of Man does not seem to be attested before the end of the first century, in 4 Ezra and the Parables of Enoch (4 Ezra 12:31f.; 13:26, 51–52; 14:7–9; *1 En* 48:1–6; 62:7; see 39:6ff.; 40:5; 46:1–8).

As a human being, the Messiah belongs to the House of Judah or the House of Israel (PT Gn 49:10; Nm 24:17; *Testament of Judah* 24:1–5). The most widespread and most popular belief was that the Messiah would be the "son of David." In the *Psalms of Solomon* the Messiah is called "son of David." A number of texts from Qumran follow Jeremiah in calling the Messiah "Branch of David" (4QpIsa 2:21; 4QPBless 3–4; 4QFlor 1:11). But in the oldest messianic texts from Qumran this Davidic descent is not mentioned (4Q175 9–12; 1QSa 2:11–22; 1QS 9:11; 1QSb 5:20–29). The explanation seems to be that the Davidic line had been broken after Zerubbabel; because of this discontinuity the oldest messianic texts from Qumran would have been reserved with regard to the Messiah king belonging to the House of David and the tribe of Judah. Since no descendant of David could offer indisputable evidence of his claim, it was necessary to depend on a miracle not only for the coming of the desired king but for his very birth. The *Rule of the Congregation* (1QSa 2:11f.) issues a regulation regarding precedence for the time "when God will cause the Messiah to be born." The Hebrew verb (the reading is conjectural) signifies a divine intervention in the birth of the Messiah; the intention is probably to compensate for the break in the Davidic line. Finally, the claimants to messianic royalty whom Josephus lists did not belong to the Davidic line but, like David himself who was a guerrilla leader before being accepted as king by the people, sought popular recognition as Messiah.

The Manifestation of the Messiah: His Powers

The characteristics of the Messiah—his earthly nature; his descent, in a broad sense, from David—explain the language used in speaking of his manifestation.

Since he is a human being, the Messiah *will come* (CD 7:20; 19:10; 4QPBless 3; *Sib. Or.* 3:49) or *will arise* (CD 12:23; 14:19; 20:1; 4QpIsa 2:21; 4QFlor 1:11, 13). But the Messiah will not come or arise of his own accord; it is God who will *cause him to arise* or *will raise him up* (1QSb 5:27; *Pss. Sol.* 17:21; 18:5), or *will cause him to be born* (1QSa 2:11), *will send him* (*Sib. Or.* 3:652; 5:108). According to the apocalypses from the end of the first century, the Messiah is said to be kept in reserve for the end of days (4 Ezra 12:32; 13:26); as for his coming, it is said that *he will be revealed* (4 Ezra 7:28; 13:32; *2 Bar.* 29:3; 39:7; etc.).

But how will the Messiah show himself? How will people recognize that he is sent by God? According to the popular belief attested in the Gospels and in the stories of messianic prophets in Josephus the Messiah or messianic prophet will reveal himself and make his messiahship credible by miracles. There is nothing of this, however, in texts that can be dated with certainty. In apocalyptic texts from the end of the first century (4 Ezra; _2 Baruch_), the very coming of the Messiah is the decisive act that reveals him. The way in which he reveals himself—as a roaring lion emerging from a forest (4 Ezra 11:37; 12:31f.), as a lightning flash above a cloud (_2 Bar._ 53:1, 8–11)—is not to be taken literally; these are simply images whose value is purely symbolic. The Messiah will be certified as Messiah by his manifestation itself and by the work he will then undertake as judge, warrior, and peacemaker.

The Messiah will come at the end of time. God has settled upon a predestined day for his Messiah (_Pss. Sol._ 18:5), a day he alone knows (_Pss. Sol._ 17:21); this is described as the day of the Messiah (4 Ezra 13:52), as the day of his power (Ps 109:3 LXX), or also as a chosen day (_Pss. Sol._ 18:5).

The place of the Messiah's glorious manifestation is Palestine and, in particular, Jerusalem. Israel and Jerusalem are clearly mentioned in _Psalms of Solomon_ 17 and 18. It is to Mount Zion that the last enemy leader will be brought in chains, and there that he will be judged and put to death by the Messiah (_2 Bar._ 40:1–3). It is also on Mount Zion that the Messiah will stand to judge the nations that have come to do battle against him (4 Ezra 13:35–38).

In order that the Messiah may carry out his mission, God has endowed him with special qualities and powers. The _Apocalypse of Abraham_, a text that is difficult to date but which is after the fall of Jerusalem, sums up the Messiah's powers in a short sentence: "I will send my chosen one, having in him one measure of all my power" (31:1); in other words, all the properties of God himself are given to the Messiah in some degree. The passage that serves as support for all the references to the Messiah's powers in the Pseudepigrapha and in the Qumran texts is Is 11:1–5. Basing himself on this passage the psalmist writes: "For God made him powerful in the holy spirit and wise in the counsel of understanding, with strength and righteousness" (_Pss. Sol._ 17:37).

The eschatological hero combines in himself the virtues of both a judge and an ideal prince;

his supreme quality is justice or _righteousness._ This represented the ideal of all royalty in the East from earliest antiquity. The Messiah is a just or righteous king (_Pss. Sol._ 17:32). This justice is exercised toward both his own people and the nations (_Pss. Sol._ 17; 29; 32; 40): all will receive their due; peace and order will be maintained (1QSb 5:21–23); sinners will be punished, the just will live in peace. The word "justice" in these texts corresponds in part to what we still mean by justice today, especially in its legal and administrative application, but the phrase "righteousness of the Messiah" or "Messiah of righteousness" (4QPBless 3) says more. For in the Bible the term "righteousness" or "justice" is associated with salvation, liberation, and the establishment and maintenance of a certain quality of life for the people. The Messiah will assert the rights of his people against their oppressors, traitors, or outlaws, but also against the sinners who may exist in their midst. He will free them from slavery and oppression; he will bring about salvation and freedom in the face of all the dangers that threaten them; for Israel has a right to be free, rich, and prosperous and to be the first among all nations. The justice of the Messiah is the salvation of his people; justice and salvation are identical.

The Messiah will be righteous and _wise;_ righteousness and wisdom go together. As a righteous and wise king, the Messiah does not abide the wicked (_Pss. Sol._ 17:22–29, 41). His words are purer than precious gold; they are like the words of the holy ones in the midst of sanctified peoples (_Pss. Sol._ 17:43).

Righteousness and wisdom are accompanied by _strength._ These three powers, which are due to the gift of the Spirit that is given to the Messiah (Is 11:2), are found mentioned together in _Psalms of Solomon_ 17 and 18. In the time of salvation the Messiah will preside "in wisdom of spirit, and of righteousness and of strength" (_Pss. Sol._ 18:7). "For God made him powerful in the holy spirit and wise in the counsel of understanding, with strength and righteousness. And the blessing of the Lord will be with him in strength, and he will not weaken; his hope will be in the Lord. Then who will succeed against him, mighty in his actions and strong in the fear of the Lord?" (_Pss. Sol._ 17:37–40). In the Qumran collection of blessings God is asked to "raise you [the Prince of the congregation] up to everlasting heights, and as a fortified tower upon a high wall! [May you smite the peoples] with the might of your hand and ravage the earth with your scepter; may you bring death to the ungodly with the breath of your lips!" (1QSb 5:23–25). In the Palestinian Targum on Nm 24:7, the Messiah is "mightier than Saul," and in 4 Ezra he is compared to a lion that emerges from the forest rumbling and roaring as it faces an eagle (11:37; 12:31f.).

The Messiah's wisdom and strength come from his *reverence for God*. When this reverence acquires its full form, it becomes a freedom from sin, a characteristic that *Psalms of Solomon* 17 emphasizes: "He himself (will be) free from sin, (in order) to rule a great people. He will expose officials and drive out sinners by the strength of his word" (*Pss. Sol.* 17:36). The psalmist is not speaking here of a natural or inherent impeccability but rather, in accordance with the Jewish mentality, of the Messiah's freedom from any sinful action, something that is possible for those who live in a reverential fear of God and, being enlightened by God's Spirit, are able to obey the law of God; in other words, possible for those who are just in the biblical sense of this word. "He will be a righteous king over them, taught by God" (*Pss. Sol.* 17:32). "As the priests shall teach him, so shall he judge" (4QpIsa 2:27).

The Messiah embodies the religious and moral ideal of Israel (1QSb 5:20–29). His piety constitutes the heart of Israelite religion from its very beginnings and especially from the time of Isaiah: the reverential fear of God and trust in him prevent the Messiah from falling into the sin of pride that characterizes pagan nations which trust in human power and intelligence; but "he will not rely on horse and rider and bow, nor will he collect gold and silver for war. Nor will he build up hope in a multitude for a day of war. The Lord himself is his king, the hope of one who has a strong hope in God" (*Pss. Sol.* 17:33f.). Because he has wisdom and fear of God, he can be leader of his people and an example for them "under the rod of discipline of the Lord Messiah, in the fear of his God, in wisdom of spirit, and of righteousness and strength, to direct people in righteous acts, in the fear of God, to set them all in the fear of the Lord, a good generation (living) in the fear of God, in the days of mercy" (*Pss. Sol.* 18:7–9). Because he himself is holy, he can purify his

people from sin, from uncleanness and from paganism, make them holy, and create in them the moral and religious attitude that accompanies holiness, so that this people will be able to live a life consecrated to God (*Pss. Sol.* 17:26–29, 32:35f.). Finally, the gift given to the Messiah can be described in a single word of ancient Jewish terminology: he has received a special *blessing:* "The blessing of the Lord will be with him in strength, and he will not weaken" (*Pss. Sol.* 17:38); for this reason he in turn will be able to "bless the Lord's people with wisdom and happiness" (*Pss. Sol.* 17:35).

The Messiah's Role

The Messiah will have essentially a double role: first, to destroy or subject the enemies of Israel; then, to govern Israel in peace and holiness. The Messiah's activities as warrior and as peaceful ruler are often linked in the texts (1QSb 5:20–29; *Pss. Sol.* 17; *Sib. Or.* 3:652–60; 5:414–33; 4 Ezra 11–12; 13; *2 Bar.* 53–76); sometimes only his activity as warrior is mentioned (CD 7:20–8:2; *Sib. Or.* 5:108f.) and sometimes only his peaceful rule (*2 Bar.* 30). His activity as warrior is always mentioned before his peaceful reign, except in the blessing of the Prince of the Congregation (1QSb 5:20–29).

The first activity of the Messiah, when he comes or appears, will be to destroy or subject the enemies of Israel. In his prayer the psalmist asks God to send the Messiah

> to destroy the unrighteous rulers, to purge Jerusalem from gentiles who trample her to destruction; in wisdom and in righteousness to drive out the sinners from the inheritance; to smash the arrogance of sinners like a potter's jar; to shatter all their substance with an iron rod; to destroy the unlawful nations with the word of his mouth; at his warning the nations will flee from his presence; and he will condemn sinners by the thoughts of their hearts. He will gather a holy people whom he will lead in righteousness. . . . He will judge peoples and nations in the wisdom of his righteousness. And he will have gentile nations serving him under his yoke. (*Pss. Sol.* 17:22–26, 29–30)

According to *Sib. Or.* 3:652–54, the king whom God will send "will kill some, impose oaths of loyalty on others." According to *Sib. Or.* 5:418–19, "a blessed man came from the expanses of heaven ... [and] destroyed every city from its foundations with much fire and burned nations of mortals who were formerly evildoers." For Philo of Alexandria the Messiah is a strategist and military hero who "will lead armies and engage in battle and will subject many great nations" (*Blessings and Curses* 95).

At Qumran, in the blessing of the Prince of the Congregation, God is petitioned as follows:

> May the Lord raise you up to everlasting heights, and as a fortified tower upon a high wall! [May you smite the peoples] with the might of your hand and ravage the earth with your sceptre; may you bring death to the ungodly with the breath of your lips! ... May He make your horns of iron and your hooves of bronze; may you toss like a young bull [and trample the peoples] like the mire of the streets! For God has established you as the sceptre. The rulers ... [and all the kings of the] nations shall serve you. He shall strengthen you with His holy Name and you shall be as a [lion]. (1QSb 5:23–29)

In the *Damascus Document* it is said that "when he comes he [the Prince of the Congregation] *shall smite all the children of Seth*" (CD 7:20–21), that is, all those who were unfaithful to the reform instituted by the Teacher of Justice. In the very fragmentary pesher on Isaiah it is said that "the Branch of David ... shall rule over all the [nations]" and that "his sword shall judge [all] the peoples" (1QpIsa 2:24–25). The pitifully inadequate fragment that has come down to us of a commentary on Jacob's blessing of Judah in Gn 49:10 seems to emphasize the military aspect of the messianic monarchy—at least if one follows A. Caquot in translating lines 2 and 3 thus: "For what is established is the royal covenant, and the thousands of Israel are the foot soldiers" (4QPBless 2–3). Finally, in the annotated biblical *Florilegium*, Ps 2:1–2 is applied to the final battle of the nations against Israel: "Interpreted, this saying [Ps 2:1–2] concerns [the kings of the nations] who shall [rage against] the elect of Israel in the last days. This shall be the time of the trial to come over the house of Judah" (4QFlor 1:19–2:1).

The apocalypses of Ezra and Baruch, at the end of the first century, likewise expect a savior who will wipe out the enemies of Israel. In the vision of the eagle (4 Ezra 11:1–12:40) and the vision of the forest and the vine (2 Bar. 35–40), it is the fourth kingdom, that is, the Roman Empire, that the Messiah will destroy. In the vision of the eagle, the lion, who is identified with the Messiah (4 Ezra 12:31ff.) "will denounce them for their ungodliness and for their wickedness, and will cast up before them their contemptuous dealings. For first he will set them living before his judgment seat, and when he has reproved them, he will destroy them." In the vision of the forest and the vine, the last leader of the fourth kingdom is led in fetters to Mount Zion; there "my Anointed One will convict him of all his wicked deeds and will assemble and set before him all the works of his hosts. And after these things he will kill him (2 Bar. 40:1f.). In the vision of the man who came up from the sea, Ezra looks, "and behold, an innumerable multitude of men were gathered together from the four winds of heaven to make war against the man who came up out of the sea." The latter carved out a great mountain for himself and flew up upon it; his enemies became afraid and yet dared to fight.

> [When] he saw the onrush of the approaching multitude, he neither lifted his hand nor held a spear or any weapon of war; but I saw only how he sent forth from his mouth as it were a stream of fire, and from his lips a flaming breath, and from his tongue he shot forth a storm of sparks. All these were mingled together, the stream of fire and the flaming breath and the great storm, and fell on the onrushing multitude which was prepared to fight, and burned them all up, so that suddenly nothing was to be seen of the innumerable multitude but only the dust of ashes and the smell of smoke. (4 Ezra 13:5–11)

According to the interpretation given of this vision, at the manifestation of the Messiah all the pagan nations that hear his voice will leave their own lands and their wars with one another in order to fight against the Messiah. He, however, will convict them of their wickedness and, after showing them the torments they are to suffer, will destroy them by his decree, which is symbolized by the fire (4 Ezra 13:32–38). In the vision of the clouds and waters (2 Bar. 53–76), the perspective is more nationalistic and closer to the law of talion. The angel Ramael explains to Baruch the meaning of his vision of bright waters coming after black ones:

> This is the word. After the signs have come of which I have spoken to you before, when the nations are moved and the time of my Anointed

One comes, he will call all nations, and some of them he will spare, and others he will kill. These things will befall the nations which will be spared by him. Every nation which has not known Israel and which has not trodden down the seed of Jacob will live. And this is because some from all the nations have been subjected to your people. All those, now, who have ruled over you or have known you, will be delivered up to the sword. (2 Bar. 72)

Many passages of the ancient Palestinian Targum are also very meaningful. For in fact they transmit the same tradition which we find at Qumran, in the *Psalms of Solomon,* and in the apocalypses of Ezra and Baruch. It will be enough to cite this passage of Palestinian Targum on Gen 49:11:

How beautiful he is, the King Messiah
  who is to arise from those of the House
  of Judah.
He girds his loins and sets out for battle against
  his foes
  and slaughters both kings and princes.
He reddens the mountains with the blood
  of their slain
  and whitens the hills with the fat of their
  warriors.
His garments drip blood;
  he is like one who treads the grapes.

This stanza on the warrior Messiah combines Gn 49:11 with Is 63:2–3, to which it gives a messianic interpretation. But this interpretation is also attested in Rv 19:11–15; it is therefore ancient. On the other hand, the promise has to do first with the coming of the Messiah (PT Gn 49:10), then his victory in war against the enemies of his people (v. 11) and the final prosperity of Israel (v. 12). This sequence is also seen in the Qumran texts (1QSb 5:20–29), in the *Psalms of Solomon* (17:23–43), in the *Sibylline Oracles* (3:652–60), and in the apocalypses of Ezra and Baruch. It occurs again in PT Nm 24:7, where the essential hope is for national liberation, the gathering of the exiles into their own country, and the sovereignty of Israel. The activity of the warrior Messiah is described again in PT Nm 24:17–19, a passage cited several times in Qumran writings, and finally in the much later targums on the prophets (Tg. Is. 10:27; 11:4; 14:29–30; etc.).

Finally, Nm 24:7, according to the LXX, says that the kingdom of the man descended from Jacob is much larger than the kingdom of Gog, thus suggesting that the Messiah will conquer Gog, i.e., annihilate the peoples attacking Jerusalem. The fight against Gog is also mentioned in the Apocalypse (Rv 20:8) and in the targums (Jerusalem Targum 1 Ex 20:11; JT 1 Nm 24:17; JT 2 Nm 11:26).

The Messiah is thus the avenger of the people of Israel; he is their liberator (PT Nm 24:7; 4 Ezra 12:34; 13:26). He is also the protector of the people that shall have survived (4 Ezra 13:49; 2 Bar. 40:2).

The Messiah will bring many blessings to his people. He will restore Jerusalem and its temple (*Sib. Or.* 5:420–27); he will gather the scattered tribes (*Pss. Sol.* 17:26, 31; 4 Ezra 13:12f., 39–40). And according to *Pss. Sol.* 17:28 the Messiah will again distribute the gathered people on the land of Israel according to their tribes.

But at this period people expected that above and beyond these blessings given to the nation, the eschatological savior would introduce the survivors into a new order (4 Ezra 13:26); that he would fill them with joy (4 Ezra 7:28; 12:34) and, at their return to Israel, show them many miracles (4 Ezra 13:50); that he would bless the Lord's people with wisdom and joy (*Pss. Sol.* 17:35); and that he would restore to everyone the wealth which others had taken from them (*Sib. Or.* 5:416f.).

More particularly, people expected, in light of Is 11:19, that the eschatological hero would exercise just judgment in the midst of the saved community and would pour out his righteousness on the saved. According to the collection of blessings, God will renew the covenant of the community for the sake of the Prince of the Congregation, in order that he may restore the kingdom of God and the holy covenant, judge the poor with justice, and rule the lowly of the land with equity (1QSb 5:21–23). It was expected that he would lead a holy people in righteousness and govern the tribes of a people that is sanctified by God (*Pss. Sol.* 17:26). Would the eschatological savior grant forgiveness of sins? In Jewish literature forgiveness is reserved to God. The idea that the Messiah would be able to bring forgiveness through his expiatory sufferings was excluded. The acquittal from sin which the eschatological hero gives is the result of a judicial or administrative action; it is not an interior absolution. It is said that he will purify Jerusalem by making it holy as it was in the beginning (*Pss. Sol.* 17:30); that he will not allow wickedness to remain in the midst of the community or any who know wickedness to dwell any longer among them (v. 27); that he will rebuke princes and destroy sinners by his mighty word (v. 36); that no longer will Israel see terrible things happening to wretched mortals, or adulteries, or illicit love of boys, or slaughter, or din of battle (*Sib. Or.* 5:429–31); that he will shepherd the Lord's flock faithfully and righteously and will not allow any of them to stumble in their pasture (*Pss. Sol.* 17:40); that his mission is to discipline Israel (*Pss. Sol.* 17:42; 18:7); thus he will direct each person in righteous acts and in fear of the Lord, so as to set them all in the presence of the Lord (*Pss. Sol.* 18:8).

The community of the eschatological liberator is thus in practice a community of holy people; there will be no unrighteousness among them in his days; all shall be holy (*Pss. Sol.* 17:32); he will lead them all as equals, and arrogance will not exercise its tyranny among them (v. 41); they will form a good generation that fears the Lord (*Pss. Sol.* 18:9) as it lives through the last time of the holy ones (*Sib. Or.* 5:431).

The savior thus has two roles: he is the national and political liberator of the people, but also their spiritual and religious leader; the Messiah is at once king and savior, a political hero and a spiritual hero. The statement of Jesus that "my kingdom is not from this world" (Jn 18:36) was unthinkable on the lips of the Jewish Messiah as he is described in *Pss. Sol.* 17 and 18.

The age of the Messiah will be basically a time of peace, joy, and happiness for Israel. There will be profound peace in the days of the Messiah of Israel (Tg. Is. 11:6), and there will be an immense happiness. This happiness is described at length in the apocalypse of Baruch (*2 Bar.* 29; 73–74) and in the *Sibylline Oracles* (3:657–60; 5:420–33); it is also mentioned in the targums (PT Gn 49:12; Nm 24:18). The fathers of the second-century church (Papias, Justin) will use these biblical and paradisal images to describe the happiness of the elect on earth during the thousand-year reign.

The reign of the Messiah will be a time of peace, happiness, and joy for Israel. But what will it be for the nations? Speaking generally, we can say that the salvific activity and peaceful reign of the Messiah will be limited to Israelites living in Palestine. The nations will see the Messiah as, first of all, their enemy. According to a later rabbinic statement, the Messiah will be hard on the nations and easy on Israel. According to *Pss. Sol.* 17:28, the Messiah will not permit any alien or foreigner to dwell among the Israelites. The only nations to survive will be those that have not ruled over Israel (*2 Bar.* 72:26). In passages that do not presuppose the destruction of the nations, the eschatological hero is regularly seen as a sovereign who rules the peoples. His power extends over the entire world (*Sib. Or.* 2:653f.; 5:416); he keeps the pagan peoples under his yoke so that they may serve him (*Pss. Sol.* 17:30), and he judges the peoples and nations in the wisdom of his righteousness (*Pss. Sol.* 17:29). The eschatological hero is everywhere acknowledged as sovereign over the world, and the nations come from the ends of the earth to see his glory and to bring the scattered children of Jerusalem as a gift to him (*Pss. Sol.* 17:31; see 4 Ezra 13:13).

The duration of this reign is often not specified. In any case, the apocalypses of Ezra and Baruch regard it as temporary (4 Ezra 7:26–44; 12:31–34; *2 Bar.* 29–30; 39–40; 72–74). The duration of this intermediate reign is specified only in 4 Ezra 7:28, but the duration varies from translation to translation: it is "400 years" according to the Latin, Georgian, and first Arabic translations; "30 years" according to the Syriac translation; and "1000 years" according to the second Arabic translation. At the end of this reign the Messiah will die, as will all other human beings. The world will then return to its ancient silence for seven days, as at the beginning, so that no one is left alive. Then, at the end of the seven days, the world which is not yet awake will be awakened, and the world that is corruptible will perish (4 Ezra 7:29–31).

By way of a conclusion to this first section I shall attempt a synthesis of the material on expectation of the Messiah between 50 B.C.E. and 50 C.E.

During this period some circles (Pharisees, Essenes, apocalyptic writers) awaited the coming of a royal Messiah or even, at Qumran, of a priestly Messiah and a royal Messiah. This expectation was shared to a greater or lesser degree by the people, who probably heard it mentioned in the synagogal readings, if we accept that the traditions contained in the Palestinian Targum were known already in the first century; this messianic expectation was also known in the Greek diaspora. This royal Messiah was an earthly being, but one endowed with supernatural powers. The apocalypses from the end of the first century say that this Messiah has been kept in reserve by God for the end of days. It was expected that he would accomplish two things. The first was the political liberation of Israel: he would destroy or subject the pagan nations or the wicked. Second, he would establish, in a reassembled and united Israel, a social order that was just and conformed to the requirements of the law; he would once again give the Jewish state a prestige it had long since lost; he would bring about a universal acknowledgment of the one God. This dream was in the background whenever the name of Messiah was spoken. However, several points must be noted:

a. The expectation of the Messiah was subordinated to the much more basic theme of the reign of God, which in turn was connected with the observance of the Torah; it was not independent of this much more comprehensive eschatological expectation but was only one facet which some thought indispensable but which others did not even consider. The fact is that during the period with which we are dealing here, there were important works that did not mention the Messiah: the book of Wisdom, the Letter of Enoch (1 En 91–107); nor is there any mention of him in various documents that are contemporary with Jesus: Pseudo-Philo's *Book of Biblical Antiquities*, the *Testament of Moses*, and book 4 of the *Sibylline Oracles*. As we have seen, Philo speaks of him only once. In view of all this, is it really possible to speak of a "messianic fever," as many writers do? No, there are qualifications that must be made: the expectation of a Messiah was only one element of Jewish eschatology and was found only in some religious circles (Pharisees, Essenes) and some apocalyptic groups; it was known in the Greek diaspora (Philo, *Sibylline Oracles*) and shared to a greater or lesser degree by the common tradition (Palestinian Targum on the Pentateuch).

b. The renewal of messianism in the second century B.C.E. was undoubtedly due to devout persons, the Hasidim, who stood out against the persecution by Antiochus IV Epiphanes (see Dan and 1 En 90); subsequently, messianism developed as part of the opposition to the Hasmoneans. For, strangely enough, no messianic text from Qumran, except perhaps for 1QSb 5:20–29, and 1QM 5:1–2, seems to be directed against the Romans. Quite the contrary: all the messianic texts from Qumran seem to be directed against the Hasmoneans, who serve as a constant foil; it is this fact that explains the expectation at Qumran of either one or two Messiahs, depending on whether or not any given Hasmonean prince exercised the double function of king and high priest. On the other hand, it is the Romans who are envisaged in messianic texts from the Pharisaic world, apocalyptic circles, and the Greek diaspora.

c. The biblical texts on which this messianic expectation is based are very few in number; also significant is the fact that the same texts are used by the Pharisees, the Essenes, the apocalyptic writers, and the common tradition that is reflected in the Targum on the Pentateuch. The texts in question are essentially these: Gn 49:10–12; Nm 24; and Is 11; and, for the apocalypses, Dan 7. It is most significant that texts referring to the Davidic covenant are not cited, especially 2 Sm 7 and Ps 110. The Messiah is called Son of David, in a broad sense, in keeping with Is 11:1, or, again, Branch of David, after Jer 23:5. How is this lack of interest in the Davidic bloodline of the Messiah to be explained? Is it not due simply to the fact that people could no longer trace back this lineage? Consequently, we may suppose that God was expected to reestablish the lineage in a miraculous way by himself revealing or appointing the Messiah or "causing him to be born" (1QSa 2:11).

d. The messianism of the texts we have is purely national, political, and religious. How can this messianism be reconciled with the expectation of a truly transcendent salvation, resulting from a manifestation of God himself, that we find in other texts (*Testament of Moses*; *Book of Biblical Antiquities*)?

e. The messianism we have here, which despite some constants is rather diversified, is purely eschatological and ideological. The function of the Messiah is clearly more important than his person. Because it is ideological, it was able to exercise over first-century minds all the influence which any ideology exercises: the imagined society and the mental representations are not neutral but seek concrete embodiment. This is why, alongside this ideological messianism, the first century saw the rise of the popular messianic movements of which Josephus tells us. There is a real link between the nationalistic, political, and religious ideology contained in the texts we have been examining, and these popular messianic movements, as we shall see in the next section.

2. Messianic Expectation in Various Social and Religious Groups: Sadducees, Pharisees, Essenes, Popular Movements

The picture I have drawn of the royal Messiah may seem rather uniform across all the religious groups that shaped it: Pharisees, Essenes, apocalyptic circles, and even liturgical circles. But the comparative study of religions has demonstrated that it is by looking at what groups have in common that we perceive differences among them. In •his second section, then, it may prove worthwhile to look at the expectation of Messiah in light of the various religious and social tendencies at work in first-century Israel; greater space will then be given to the messianic ideas at work in some popular movements.

The Sadducees

The Sadducees must be considered separately. They did not assign the same value to all of the holy books, but it would be an exaggeration to say that they accepted only the Pentateuch as Scripture. In any case, the Torah, which was the basis of the Jewish law recognized by the Romans as by the Persians and Greeks before them, was the primary focus of Sadducean concern; as far as halakah was concerned, everything had to be based on the Torah, and the priests alone were its authentic interpreters, for the Sadducees rejected the idea of an oral law possessing an authority equal to that of the written law. The books that did not have the character of law—the prophets, Psalms, and other writings—could not claim to be the same privileged position as the Pentateuch. But as far as messianism was concerned a literal reading of the Pentateuch yielded very little material. The only texts accepted as messianic at this

time were Gn 49:10–12 (Jacob's blessing) and Nm 24:17 (oracle of Balaam). A messianic interpretation of these two passages required that they be linked to the promises given to David and his posterity; in other words, the prophetic books and the Psalms had to be invoked. At the same time, however, messianic promises in the prophetic books and the Psalms had less authority, in the eyes of the Sadducees, than the promises given to the patriarchs: promises regarding the holy land, the material prosperity of Israel, and the effectiveness of worship in obtaining this prosperity. But there is no evidence that the Sadducees did not expect a future manifestation of the Messiah. A popular messianism, however, with its uncontrollable bursts of enthusiasm, seemed to them dangerous, even for the nation. Menahem, a Sicarius, who played at being king, was captured and put to death by Eleazar, guardian of the Temple, at the beginning of the Jewish revolt (War 2.17.8–10 §§433–45). Simon bar Giora, too, at the beginning of the revolt, got into trouble with this provisional government in Jerusalem, which was led by the priestly aristocracy (War 4.9.3 §§503–4). And when messianic fervor began to rise with Jesus of Nazareth at its center, Caiaphas said that it was better that a single man die rather than that the nation should be destroyed (Jn 11:50). Moreover, it was due to delation by the Sadducees that Jesus was crucified by the Romans as a popular Messiah.

The Pharisees

The Pharisees based their messianic hope on Scripture in its entirety, and thus were already at odds with the Sadducees. Their messianism, which is well known, thanks to the observable continuity between the *Psalms of Solomon*, the Targums, and later rabbinic traditions, remained faithful to a royal messianism based on the testimonies of Scripture. Their messianic hope was basically nationalistic. The election of Israel and the promises made to the Davidic dynasty provided ideological support for the idea of the reign of God; that is, the reign of God in history depended on the fulfillment of these promises (→ KINGDOM/REIGN OF GOD). This fulfillment in turn was impossible apart from Israel's fidelity to the Torah. Even the restoration of political power through the coming of the Messiah had no purpose other than the complete return of the people to this fidelity. Religious nationalism was not seen as a kind of annexation of God; on the contrary, its purpose was that God should be served by Israel, and ultimately by the other nations as they in turn came to acknowledge him and submit to him.

This conception of a messianism that was purely royal separated the Pharisees from the Essenes and from the Sadducees. In addition, the Pharisees differed from the Sadducees in their behavior toward the occupying Romans. There could be no question for them of any acceptance of the Roman authorities as legitimate. They had broken with the Hasmonean dynasty out of fidelity to the Davidic royal line; they then distanced themselves from Herod the Great for the same reason. They could not now be false to themselves by officially accepting the occupying Romans. At the same time, however, the Pharisees were also against violent resistance, which could only do harm to the nation by imperiling the cultic and juridical autonomy that had been granted to it. The Pharisees relied on faithful observance of the law as the means of obtaining from God a messianic liberator. This liberator evidently played a political role in their view, but they were unwilling to hasten the hour of his coming by a rash activism. This is the reason why, during the revolt of 66–70, the Pharisees gradually dissociated themselves from military action; a tradition claims that at that time Johanan ben Zakkai left besieged Jerusalem for occupied territory in order to prepare the reorganization of the nation's institutions. The messianic expectation of the Pharisees differed in two respects from the messianism of the popular movements, to which I will turn shortly: the Pharisees awaited a Davidic Messiah, as is clear from the seventeenth *Psalm of Solomon* (v. 21) and from the Targums, whereas the popular movements did not share this conception of a Davidic Messiah, even if they regarded their leader as a worthy imitator of David. The second difference was that the armed resistance that the Pharisees rejected had a social and economic as well as a religious basis in the popular movements.

The Essenes

There is no doubt that the Essenes waited with some impatience for the fulfillment of the messianic promises that would bring about the liberation of Israel and the establishment of an ideal people. The theory of the two Messiahs— the Messiah of Aaron and the Messiah of Israel—is clear evidence of the priestly character of the religious party which the Qumran texts make known to us: the Branch of David was to be subordinate to the eschatological priest, within a holy people whose life would be centered in Jerusalem, its Temple, and its worship (1QSa 2:11–17). The role of the Messiah, who asks directives from the priests, the sons of Aaron, so that his conduct will be according to the law, is reduced to a political function (4QpIsa 2:27). His essential role, according to 1 QSb 5:23–29), seems to be the waging of the holy war that will free Israel from the yoke of pagans and of wicked persons within Israel. Religious nationalism controlled the thinking of the Essenes, as it did that of the Pharisees, and the Anointed One of Israel had a primarily political role in their eyes. This amounted to a very clear invitation to a political activism, for which the *War Rule* provided a program and a set of ideal, if not utopian, rules. It is all the stranger, then, that the Prince of the Congregation is mentioned only once in the *War Rule* (1QM 5:1). Royal messianism, originally aimed at the Hasmoneans, seems later on to have taken the Romans as its target. Archaeologists have discovered that the Qumran monastery was destroyed during the revolt of 66–70, which makes it probable that the Essenes took part in the struggle against the Romans.

Essene messianism is thus comparable to that of the Pharisees in respect of its nationalism and of the role assigned to the Messiah of Israel. However, the Essenes seem to have been more inclined than the Pharisees to violent resistance. The expectation of a Messiah of Aaron, who takes precedence over the Messiah of Israel, not only shows the priestly aspect of the sect but also distinguishes it from the Pharisees. The Essenes differ entirely from the Sadducees in their conception of the Messiah. On the other hand, they resemble the popular movements in two respects: like the latter, the Essenes seem committed to violent action, though in different contexts. Second, despite the stereotyped title "Branch of David," the Essenes did not necessarily expect the Messiah of Israel to belong to the Davidic blood line.

Popular Messianic Movements

The picture given of the Messiah by traditions stemming from Pharisee, Essene, Sadducee, and apocalyptic circles is basically eschatological and ideological. In parallel, but not without connection, to this idealized expectation of the Messiah, first-century Palestine experienced some popular movements that provide a concrete, palpable testimony to messianic activity in the time of Jesus. There were, among the people, several real, concrete movements under leaders who proclaimed themselves or were acknowledged to be kings; these movements and leaders exercised a real power in some parts of the country. We know of the movements from short, hostile accounts by Josephus. The latter attached no importance to the religious elements in this rather intense popular excitement; in his view, these movements were simply manifestations of anarchy on the fringes of official Judaism. It is admittedly difficult to discern the precise character of the aspirations that drove these groups of dissidents, but certain facts are obvious. It is clearly necessary to distinguish these popular messianic movements under leaders who claimed to be or were acknowledged as kings from the banditry that was rampant at the time; from the Sicarii, who came on the scene only toward the fifties; from the Zealots, who attracted attention only during the second year of the great Jewish revolt (therefore, in 67); and, finally, from prophetic movements. The reason for the distinction is that apart from the luckless attempt of Menahem the Sicarius, neither the leaders of the several groups named nor the prophets took the title of king. The prophets claimed rather to be the forerunners of the messianic age, and their claim usually lasted for only a short time; as soon as these prophetic movements appeared, they were crushed: thus Theudas (*Ant.* 20.97–98), the false prophet from Egypt (*Ant.* 20.168–71), and the Samaritan prophet (*Ant.* 18:85). In their intention and in their form, the manifestation and activity of these prophets differed from the truly popular messianic movements; there is, then, no point in examining them or, for that matter, the bandits, the Sicarii, and the Zealots. I shall restrict myself therefore to the messianic movements headed by leaders who sought acceptance as kings and who were regarded as

such by their followers and surely by a part of the population.

Josephus says that these movements arose at two clearly defined moments: during the revolt that followed upon the death of Herod the Great and during the great revolt against Rome in 66–70. Three movements that arose when Archelaus acceded to the throne call for remark: those of Judas ben Hezekiah, Simon, and Athronges. Josephus locates these movements, as well as other revolts, just before the war conducted by Varus. But it is hardly likely that all these movements arose simultaneously in 4 B.C.E. It seems rather that Josephus combines them by artificially lumping together events that must in fact have occurred at various points during the governorship of Archelaus. Even in Josephus's text the stories give the impression of a patchwork, for they are inserted between the call for help which Sabinus, besieged in Jerusalem, sent to Varus, the legate of Syria, and the actual coming of the latter (*Ant.* 17 §§269–85). Two other messianic movements under leaders who sought recognition as messiahs took place during the first Jewish revolt: those of Menahem and Simon bar Giora. The final messianic movement arose during the second Jewish revolt: the resistance led by Simon ben Kosibah, whom Rabbi Aqiba accepted as Messiah. I shall examine only those messianic movements that followed upon the death of Herod. Three points need to be considered: How explain that some leaders of popular movements took the title of king? Why did these revolts take place after the death of Herod the Great? What were the characteristics of these movements?

Although Josephus treats some leaders very unflatteringly, calling them bandits, he does say that some of them took or received the title "king." Thus Judas ben Hezekiah sought royal honors (*Ant.* 17 §274); Athronges boldly aspired to kingship and, after placing a diadem on his head, summoned a council to decide what course to take (*Ant.* 17 §§ 278–81). How explain this title of king which these leaders of rebellions claimed or which their followers and a segment of the people gave them?

Several factors may have played a part. We may say, first of all, that the ancient tradition of a king being anointed or acknowledged by the people (a tradition going back to Saul and David) may have been remembered and revived in moments of crisis. Just as David himself had been, so these leaders were initially leaders of groups of looters. Second, since the Davidic line disappeared after Zerubbabel, people expected that God would miraculously raise up a new Davidic king. Several texts make it clear that God himself would raise up the Messiah of the community of Israel, although his Davidic lineage is not mentioned (1 En 90:37; 1QSa 2:11). Finally, these movements of revolt took place at moments of crisis: at the death of Herod and during the two Jewish revolts. It was at moments of crisis, however, that the messianic hope was strongest; recall what had happened earlier during the persecution by Antiochus IV Epiphanes (book of Daniel; book of the Dreams of Enoch) and at the time when Jerusalem was captured by Pompey (*Psalms of Solomon*). If all three factors are taken in conjunction, it becomes possible to explain why the leaders of these revolts could take the title of king and could be acknowledged as kings by their followers and even by a segment of the population. On the other hand, we must not forget that the claim to kingship can also be explained by human factors: the ambition of leaders of movements and the longing for liberation on the part of their followers and of the segment of the population they controlled.

The second question can be quickly answered: Why did these revolts occur at the death of Herod the Great? Because this was a time of crisis and because such times revived the hope of liberation. From the economic and political points of view, Herod's reign was oppressive for the Jewish population and especially for peasants; but his security system was so strong and the measures it took were so severe that any revolt was impossible during his lifetime. On the other hand, it is easy to understand that revolts should break out at his death. Herod could not claim any legitimacy in the eyes of the people. He was half Jew and the very opposite of a popular leader. He was a puppet of the Roman authorities; he first had to conquer his kingdom and then rule it with the help of the Romans or of mercenaries whom he used as security forces. The Hellenistic style of his court and his bureaucracy were alien to the people.

The characteristics of these kings or popular messiahs were very different from those of the Messiah whom the Pharisees, the Essenes, and later the apocalypticists awaited. First of all, these popular kings were flesh-and-blood historical individuals, unlike the Messiah whom Pharisee, Essene, and apocalytpic circles awaited. Furthermore, these leaders were popular kings who trained their followers to free themselves from a tyrannical foreign government; they wanted to restore a more egalitarian society by putting an end to the socioeconomic privileges which certain classes of society enjoyed.

These kings had the characteristics which the people looked for. They were big men of great physical strength and courage; this was true of Simon and Athronges (*Ant.* 17 §§ 273, 278) and later on of Simon bar Giora. There is no doubt, however, that in the popular tradition the king chosen by God had to be a strong man or a warrior. This image of the hero or strong king sprang from the memory of the people. It was the image they had of David; in 1 Sm 16:18 Saul's servant reports to his master: "I have seen a son of Jesse the Bethlehemite who is skillful in playing, a man of valor, a warrior, prudent in speech, and a man of good presence; and the Lord is with him."

These popular leaders were of humble origin; the people did not look to the upper classes for their leaders. Simon had been a slave of King Herod, and Athronges a simple shepherd, like David himself (*Ant.* 17 §§273, 278); Judas was the son of a bandit and took up arms forty years after his father had been killed by Herod the Great. He was probably a peasant whom people looked upon as something of a hero because he was the son of a bandit.

The followers of Judas, Athronges, and Simon were probably peasants and craftsmen; many of them were desperate folk (*Ant.* 17 §271) who had probably lost their land as a result of the very difficult economic situation of the time. When Josephus says that the Pereans had chosen Simon as their leader because they were foolish and that they fought courageously rather than with ordered skill, he brings out something of the motives driving these people (*Ant.* 17 §§274–76). They were organized into companies for military purposes, and Athronges used his own brothers as commanders of various armed groups. He himself sought advice as to the course he should follow (*Ant.* 17 §§280–81).

These messianic movements had a twofold purpose: to gain liberation from Roman and Herodian domination and to restore the ancient ideal of social equality. Josephus says that they burned down the royal palaces in Sepphoris and Jericho, not only to avenge themselves for Herod's tyranny and to obtain weapons but also to recover the possessions taken from them by Herod's officials and stored in these palaces (*Ant.* 17 §274; *War* 2.4 §257). They doubtless also raided middle-class estates; their long-standing feeling of frustration and their resentment of the exploitation that had victimized them found expression in peasant uprisings and in an anarchic quest of equality.

These movements, which were founded on a desire for a religiously based equality and in which the leaders were regarded as kings, were more serious than mutinies or marauding bands. They were movements that took control of parts of the country in their respective areas: Galilee, Judea, and Perea. In Judea especially the movement led by Athronges lasted for a time until Roman or Herodian forces managed to conquer various groups of Athronges' followers. Archelaus finally persuaded the last of the brothers to surrender, but this did not happen until a number of years after the revolt (*Ant.* 17 §§281–84).

The messianic conception at work in these popular movements differed a good deal from the conceptions cultivated in various religious groups of the time. It was completely opposed to that of the Sadducees. The Sadducees were enemies against whom the rebels fought as much as they did against the Romans. On the other hand, unlike the Pharisees and Essenes, these popular movements did not wait for a Messiah; instead they chose, or followed, one with whom those involved could pursue the struggle for liberation; utopia gave way to practicality. At the same time, however, the messianic ideal at work in these movements was perhaps not so far removed from the picture the Pharisees had of the Son of David. What the Pharisees expected of the Messiah (according to *Pss. Sol.* 17) the movements were determined to make a reality now and by their own efforts. The eschatological war of liberation here became a present war; it was to be followed by liberation and an era of justice. This, at least, is what the followers of the movements hoped, and this was the motive for their taking up arms. The need they felt provided their faith with hands and strength for the struggle. If the religious motivation at work is not clear, it can

at least not be denied, and when Josephus treats these people as bandits, his attitude cannot be accepted unquestioningly.

In the time of Jesus, then, the messianic ideas abroad were more varied than a schematic analysis of the main currents of thought would suggest. Hopes for the future could take quite different forms; all were not messianic, as we have seen. Some circles took refuge in a dream that was very much detached from the political world: the *Testament of Moses* is a good example. In addition, ideas of the coming world that would follow upon the liberating activity of the Messiah were likewise wide-ranging, with spiritualizing tendencies being found side by side with very temporal views. The conception of the reign of God was no less varied, being often connected with whatever concept of the Messiah a group had. It is in relation to the beliefs and hopes of his contemporaries that Jesus must be situated. The impression of fuzziness that some Gospel passages give us when it comes to the messianic consciousness of Jesus can be explained by this background. How could Jesus have clearly defined himself as Messiah when the very word Messiah suggested such very different ideas? If this is the case, then an unavoidable question arises: Why did the first Christians feel obliged to sum up their hopes in a title that was initially only set alongside the name of Jesus of Nazareth but ended up being systematically linked to it in the form of "Jesus Christ"? Why did the first Christian generation believe it could not be faithful to Jesus except by naming him in a way that may not have been rejected by Jesus himself but had at least been accepted only with serious reservations and that in a Palestinian setting could only give rise to confusions? Why, if not because it was the title given to Jesus in death: "King of the Jews," i.e., Messiah, and because his death and resurrection transformed the meaning of "Messiah"? This is why in the face of every concept, secular or religious, of a glorious warrior Messiah, Christians proclaimed that which was unthinkable in the time of Jesus: a crucified Messiah, "a stumbling block to Jews and foolishness to Gentiles, but to those who are the called . . . a Messiah who is the power of God and the wisdom of God" (1 Cor 1:23f.).

Bibl.: La Bible: Écrits intertestamentaires, ed., André Dupont-Sommer and Marc Philonenko (Paris, 1987); M.-J. LAGRANGE, *Le messianisme chez les Juifs* (Paris, 1909); H. GRESSMANN, *Der Messias* (Tübingen, 1927); P. VOLZ, *Die Eschatologie der jüdischen Gemeinde* (Tübingen, 1934); L. CERFAUX, ed., *L'attente du Messie*, Recherches bibliques 1 (Paris/Tournai, 1954); S. MOWINCKEL, *He That Cometh* (Oxford, 1956); J. KLAUSNER, *The Messianic Idea in Israel* (London, 1956); A. S. VAN DER WOUDE, *Die messianischen Vorstellungen der Gemeinde von Qumran* (Assen, 1957); M.-A. CHEVALIER, *L'Esprit et le Messie dans le bas-judaïsme et le Nouveau Testament* (Paris, 1958); E. MASSAUX, ed., *La venue du Messie: Messianisme et eschatologie*, Recherches bibliques 6 (Paris/Bruges, 1962); var., *Il Messianismo: Atti della XVIII Settimana Biblica, Associazione Biblica Italiana* (Brescia, 1966); P. GRELOT, *L'espérance juive à l'heure de Jésus*, Jésus et Jésus-Christ 6 (Paris, 1978); A. CAQUOT, "Le messianisme qumrânien," in M. Delcor, ed., *Qumran: Sa piété, sa théologie et son milieu* (Paris/Louvain, 1978), 231–47; H. CAZELLES, *Le Messie de la Bible*, Jésus et Jésus-Christ 7 (Paris, 1978); J. COPPENS, *La relève apocalyptique du messianisme royal*, BETL 50 (Louvain, 1979); M. PEREZ FERNANDEZ, *Tradiciones mesiánicas en el Targum Palestinense* (Valencia/Jerusalem, 1981); E. M. LAPERROUSAZ, *L'attente du Messie en Palestine à la veille et au début de l'ère chrétienne* (Paris, 1982); H. J. GRESHOT, ed., *Jesus-Messias? Heilserwartung bei Juden und Christen* (Regensburg, 1982); J. NEUSNER, "Messianic Themes in Formulative Judaism," *JAAR* 52 (1984): 357–74; L. RUPPERT, "Die alttestamentlich-jüdischen Messias-erwartungen in ihrer Bedeutung für Zeit," *MTZ* 35 (1984): 1–16; R. A. HORSLEY and J. S. HANSON, *Bandits, Prophets and Messiahs: Popular Movements in the Time of Jesus* (Minneapolis/New York, 1985); R. A. HORSLEY, "Menahem in Jerusalem: A Brief Messianic Episode among the Sicarii—Not 'Zealot Messianism,'" *NT* 27 (1985): 334–48; E. NODET, "La dédicace, les maccabées et le Messie," *RB* 93 (1986): 321–75; P. SACCHI, "Esquisse du développement du messianisme juif à la lumière du texte qumrânien II Q Melch," *ZAWSup* 100 (1988): 202–14; W. HARRELSON, "Messianic Expectations at the Time of Jesus," *Saint Luke's Journal of Theology* 32 (1988): 471–95; S. ISSER, "Studies of Ancient Jewish Messianism: Scholarship and Apologetics," *Journal of Ecumenical Studies* 25 (1988): 56–73; J. H. CHARLESWORTH, *Jesus Within Judaism: New Light from Exciting Archeological Discoveries* (London, 1989).

Gérard ROCHAIS

II. FULFILLMENT OF MESSIANISM

For fundamental theology, messianism constitutes one of the most important yet difficult topics. For on it converge the most disparate findings of biblical/theological research, elements derived from Judaism, and also special NT theological data. Somehow all this must be synthesized around this nucleus.

If for some people messianism represents something fairly marginal to their own religious beliefs, for others it constitutes the basic element around which the newness of the faith revolves. In fact, we have here a phenomenon that holds OT and NT together; for messianism is essentially the sign of a hope that has never failed.

We might say that some four thousand years of religious history have gone by in the shadow of messianism. For the first two thousand years, a people hoped in different ways that the promise would come true; for the next two thousand years another people, a new one even if its roots were thrust down into the old, proclaimed that the promise has been kept and that it has definitively come true in Jesus of Nazareth. The phenomenon of messianism, as an aspect of religion, is not peculiar to Israel. Forms of messianism are to be found in ancient Egypt, in Mesopotamia, and in Greece. All peoples and cultures have their own ways of understanding, living, and expressing common phenomena. And in this sense we can call messianism an original creation of Israel, since in the religious/political forms that it took in that nation there are features that make it unique when compared with any other type of messianism.

1. The Messianic Hope

Hebrew *māšîaḥ*, with the corresponding Aramaic word *mešîḥâ*, is the participle of the verb *māšaḥ*, and means "anointed." In Greek this was rendered as *christos*, which came to be latinized as *christus*. It normally indicates the king or the high priest, but occasionally is used to denote someone with special functions, such as a prophet (1 Kgs 19:16), or a foreign king, as in the case of Cyrus (Is 45:1).

The Messiah thus is the anointed one, he who acts in accordance with God's will. As the oil that is brought for the anointing is special and conforms to the law (Ex 30:22–32), so he who is anointed with this oil is regarded as someone to whom special tasks are entrusted or, more precisely, someone consecrated to carry out a specific mission among the people.

In the OT, "messiah" possesses a particular connotation. Around the basic definition, different ideas and diverse aspirations take shape. Above all, messianism indicates a particular conception of history, moving toward fulfillment; it expresses the hope of salvation to be bestowed; and, lastly, it reflects the wait for a deliverer and the ushering in of a new political system.

Around the one term flow different emphases and meanings which move between religious and political coordinates typical of a theocratic system. This fluctuation of meanings does not allow an absolute and monolithic concept of messianism in the OT; as a kind of common denominator, however, one can trace a people's hopes which have taken form through the years of being led by a just and enlightened ruler.

Different messianic ideas came into being in the course of the OT period. We shall consider four of them: royal, priestly, prophetic, apocalyptic.

Royal Messianism

This is undoubtedly the idea that had the greatest effect on the history of Israel. From Nathan's prophecy to David onward (2 Sm 7:1–16), the royal dynasty begins to share in the sacral tradition of Israel. The titles earlier attributed to the people to indicate that it was "elect," "chosen," and "consecrated" to offer worship to God, are now applied to the king. He henceforth becomes the partner in a special relationship with Yahweh; with him a new covenant is struck, the sign of renewed commitment on God's part to save his people.

Beyond an immediate embodiment of the messianic figure, possibly suggested by the birth of the heir to the throne of the Davidic dynasty (in this context, the birth of Solomon to Bathsheba; see 2 Sm 12:13), Nathan's prophecy allows the glimpse of a promise which transcends that particular moment of time and is gradually accepted in Israel as a hoped-for and renewed commitment on God's part to intervene on behalf of his people.

The so-called *Royal Psalms* (Pss 2, 18, 20, 21, 45, 72, 89, 101, 110, 132) are a classic example of a reinterpretation, no longer only in a political but also in a spiritual light, of this messianic hope, which becomes entrenched in Israel. The figure of the royal Messiah gradually becomes transformed until it is no longer identified with the latest in the series of kings in the Davidic dynasty, but with the model of the perfect king, the one who will rule in accordance with Yahweh's will.

Priestly Messianism

The postexilic period, with the death of Zerubbabel, the last ruling prince of the Davidic dynasty, marks a new way of thinking with regard to the messianic hope. The person of the high priest, who begins to concentrate in himself the civil, military, and spiritual powers (see Zec 6:9–15), now represents the special mediation both of the covenant and of the promise of salvation. Just as King David had been promised an eternal covenant, so now the sacred writers insert into the tradition (Ex 40:15; Nm 25:13) the promise of an eternal priesthood made to Aaron and the entire priestly house.

Nearer to NT times, the overthrow of the Maccabees was to reproduce this messianic interpretation, which would be confirmed by the interpretation given in Qumran of the double Messiah: the Davidic Messiah and the "Messiah of Aaron," who would become the new priest (*archiereus christos*), the unique and definitive mediator of the covenant.

Prophetic Messianism

Prophetism is an institution peculiar to Israel. In different historical periods, it represents the critical consciousness watching over the purity of the faith. During the monarchy, the prophets were to be the sign of a higher authority than that of the king. In the period of the Babylonian captivity, they became a comforting presence for the people, and in postexilic times they concentrated the message of hope in their preaching.

The "day of the Lord" synthesizes their message, since it evokes both the people's obligation to observe the Torah and Yahweh's unchanging fidelity to his promise.

The figure of Moses, which was always to remain the prototypical image of the prophet in Israelite history, also signifies the hope that in the future one will arise like him, capable of renewing the signs and wonders of the exodus (Dt 18:15–18).

The year 585 B.C.E. is the climactic moment in the nation's calamities. In a single moment, the history of Israel seems to touch rock bottom, so much so that it might be thought of as over. The destruction of the Temple, deportation, exile, and collapse of the monarchy, all occurring at once, seemed to destroy hope forever.

And then the voices of three prophets ring out: Jeremiah, Ezekiel, and Deutero-Isaiah, representing a violent summons to hope in salvation, despite the deep sense of discouragement and skepticism lurking in the popular mind. As regards fulfillment of messianic expectation, eyes are now turned toward a point much farther away than the earlier royal tradition would have had it. Now the fulfillment of the promise is being spoken of no longer in the order of the Davidic line but rather as concerning the whole nation (Is 55:1–5).

Deutero-Isaiah is the prophet who, more than any other, provides this moment with the image most consonant with the messianic hope. Out of his own experience of life, he directs his eyes beyond his own self to reveal the portrait of a future prophet who would completely fulfill the prophetic mission.

In the Book of Consolation (Is 40–55), there are four passages of high poetry, commonly known as the "songs of the servant of Yahweh." Exegetes are still not in agreement over how these texts should be divided; a basic interpretation, however, on which most scholars agree, can be described in this way:

First song: Is 42:1–4: in this passage, the *mission* of the prophet is described. He is a chosen one, *anointed*, who has received a mission to proclaim Yahweh's law.

Second song: Is 49:1–6: this describes the servant's response; there is a correspondence between the biographical information and the difficulties which the nation itself is experiencing.

Third song: Is 50:4–9a: recalling the style of the Lamentations of Jeremiah, the servant expresses his trust in God, who will deliver him from his sufferings.

Fourth song: Is 52:13–53:1–2: this describes the servant's victory. The prophet's sufferings are revealed step by step: at first silent and docile, then weary and humiliated, next ill-treated and derided, finally so disfigured by suffering and insult that his face is no longer recognizably human. His suffering and death are described as *vicarious*, i.e., endured on behalf of the people, so that victory and salvation may come once and for all.

The importance these passages assume for theology is conditioned by the NT interpretation put on them. Jesus, in attempting to explain the mystery of his own death as a salvific event, used the figure of the suffering servant as one of his own particular ways of mediating revelation (→ CHRISTOLOGY III).

Eschatological Messianism

With the introduction of apocalyptic literature into Israel, messianic hope too acquired a new guise. The figures used to express it are no longer derived from the historical terrain of king, prophet, priest, or people, but from the intervention of God himself. Eschatological messianism is thus concerned with the mercy of God, who has chosen henceforward to intervene to save his people by means of his own representatives.

The angel of Yahweh, the *mal'ak Yhwh* (see Ex 23:22; Nm 22:22–35; Mal 3:1–2), is the concrete form the apocalyptic concept takes in preexilic times. The angel of Yahweh is encountered in two forms in the sacred texts: in some cases he is identified with God's actual presence (e.g., Gn 16:11; 31:11 [E], Ex 3:2 [J]; Nm 22:22–35); in others, however, he is distinct from God but is his most authoritative messenger, in such way that to disobey the angel is tantamount to disobeying Yahweh himself (Ex 23:22).

A second example is provided by the personification of Wisdom (Prv 1:20–23; Sir 24:10), who is described as combining within herself the functions of king, priest, and prophet. Wisdom "preaches" and "calls to conversion" (Prv 20:20–23), a typically prophetic activity; she serves in God's presence (see Sir 24:10, where the verb *leitourgein* is used), service peculiar to the priest. Finally, Wisdom is described as "begotten," "anointed" by God (Prv 8:12–36) like a Davidic king.

A last figure is provided by the Son of Man in

the vision of Dn 7:13–14, which will reappear in NT use, since it is the only form always and only to be found on the lips of Jesus, who uses it for choice as explaining his own type of messianic self-awareness.

2. Jesus the Messiah

These differing concrete forms of a single hope, in a remarkable way, take on new life in the days of Jesus. The Qumran community certainly plays a significant role in identifying the Teacher of Righteousness with the eschatological prophet of Dt 18:15. The Pharisees and other parties of the period, for their part, also kept alive the expectation of a more or less immediate deliverance; nor was there any lack of fanaticism embodied in various individuals, such as the Zealots with Theudas, or the "Egyptian" who is mentioned in Acts 21:37–38.

Popular religious euphoria, discontent with Roman rule, forced obedience to laws dictated by a pagan culture, and resentment at paying taxes to the exclusive enrichment of foreigners make it easy to see that messianic hope in the days of Jesus took on the form of an expectation of deliverance from all these kinds of injustice.

The wait for a political leader able to gather round himself enough people agreed on reversing the present situation of servitude and oppression is the datum and key for an understanding of this historic moment (→ MESSIANISM I).

Jesus, of course, never accorded himself the title Messiah. His behavior is consistent in shunning any formula that might identify him too plainly. The expression "Son of Man" (→ CHRISTOLOGY III) is the only one that recurs on his own lips and can be accepted as historical, precisely because of its fluidity of meaning.

The NT texts, however, often use the title Messiah, which gradually comes to be used as the Master's actual name. Here we see one of the most impressive phenomena of semantic evolution: the general feeling of hope becomes the precise proclamation of an event; this then gives support to a faith which henceforth transforms the adjective _christos_ into a proper noun, in order to attribute it to a historical personage, Jesus of Nazareth.

These transitions cannot be the fruit of the faith of only a handful of men and women. As children of their times, they too were bound up with the cultural/religious state of the nation, and their own messianic conception would not have gone beyond the bounds of a political deliverance.

The messianism, however, to which the NT introduces us is of another type: it is deeply original and totally unconnected with the popular expectations of the period in question.

In NT messianism, the general hope of a period is revealed instead as being rooted in the concretization of the word of a historical personage who, in a particular way, expresses his awareness of being God's definitive intervention among his people and the fulfillment of the promises of the past. With his coming and in his person, he affirms that the awaited messianic kingdom is being ushered in.

Generally speaking, a first impression to be gathered from the Gospels is the deep discretion with which this title is treated. Particularly in Mark's Gospel, one can see that on many occasions Jesus himself imposed silence on those keen to profess their faith in his messianic role (see Mk 1:34, 43–44; 3:12; 5:43). This fact is known as the _messianic secret._

The first person to have explored this phenomenon was W. Wrede (_Das Messiasgeheimnis in den Evangelien_ [Göttingen, 1901]) at the beginning of this century. Basing himself on Mk 9:9, he argued that the imposition of silence about Jesus' messianic calling was probably an action of the primitive community, which in this way was able to justify Jesus' actual preaching or alternatively his absolute absence of any messianic awareness.

Subsequent studies have shown the thesis to be biased and its interpretation too radical; among more representative writers, O. Cullmann and V. Taylor may be cited from the Protestant side, and E. Sjöberg and G. Minette de Tillesse from the Catholic. Thanks to these studies, the theme of the messianic secret has been largely anchored to the data derived from the history of Jesus of Nazareth. With the request for silence, he wished to protect and preserve the special nature of the messianic interpretation of his message and not subject it to the misunderstandings of his contemporaries.

Indeed, Mark, unlike the other evangelists, has adopted the messianic secret as his own peculiar characteristic and literary structure, but this is keeping faith with what Jesus himself used to say.

At a more specific level, it is quite possible to find passages that allow us to have a more direct knowledge of Jesus' messianic awareness as he himself expressed it. One of the basic texts with regard to this is the *logion* reported in Mt 11:2–6 (Lk 7:18–28). From prison, the Baptist sends his disciples to ask Jesus in plain terms if he is the Messiah. The way the question is framed, using the present participle *ho erchomenos*, reflects a popular conception of messianic expectation. That it is concerned with this expectation is confirmed by all John's preaching and by the very tone of his message. Speaking of his own mission, John sees it as preparing the way for someone who is "coming after me" (Mt 3:11), who has the winnowing fan in his hand to purge the threshing floor, so as to gather in the grain and the chaff in the fire (Mt 3:12, referring to Is 41:16 and Jer 15:7).

The Baptist, because of this, *explicitly* asks Jesus to pronounce on his messiahship: Was he the eschatological judge who would finally bring salvation by rewarding the righteous and punishing sinners, or would they have to go on waiting? Jesus' reply (Mt 11:4–5) seems only superficially to be evasive. For in fact what we have here is a plain and clear reply given to the Baptist, but not in the logic of the latter. Rather, in a train of thought that stands the Baptist's messianic concept completely on its head.

For the recalling of and referring back to the "*works* of the Christ" leave no doubts about Jesus' awareness in indicating that he is indeed the Messiah. Yet by referring to the works he is performing, he points out that his messiahship is sited at another level: not punishment and violence, but mercy and forgiveness become the distinctive signs of his messiahship.

The unexpected blessing that concludes the scene confirms what we have said. To proclaim someone to be blessed means first and foremost to make him or her a sharer in the messianic kingdom; yet here Jesus goes further. He asks the Baptist not to stop short at his own messianic conception, and hence not to "take offense"–i.e., not to stumble over accepting a new way in which this will be brought about, which Jesus embodies and which is willed by the Father.

This pericope, with its clear messianic connotation, plainly shows Jesus' attitude toward messiahship. He is certainly "he who is to come," but he will execute God's definitive judgment in a different way. The antiquity of the account (for what we have here is an *apophthegm*), combined with its total inconsistency with the mentality of the age, cannot but confirm the historicity of the incident.

Another example occurs in Mk 8:27–30: Peter, speaking for the Twelve, openly professes faith in Jesus as Messiah. Textual analysis shows that, editorially speaking, Mark seems to construct his Gospel in such a way as by stages to reach this point. The whole of the first part (Mk 1:1–8:26) is directed toward v. 29; all the second part (8:34–16:20) is made clear in the light of this verse. Everything seems to flow toward the description of the scene at Caesarea Philippi: literary evidence shows that the term *christos* has only been used once before, at 1:1; we encounter some "typological" incidents, such as Herod's questions (Mk 6:14–16) and the healing of the blind man of Bethsaida (8:22–26), which seem to have been created deliberately to produce a parallel with this scene; in a word, with this passage, we are at the heart of Mark's Gospel.

Jesus asks the disciples what the people think about the Son of Man; after various answers which express the various expectations, Peter professes: "You are the Christ." Jesus in this case too does not refuse the title; but as customary, especially in Mark (the messianic secret), he imposes silence on the disciples. From now on, however, his teaching, which before had a general character, now becomes precise, explicit, and clear (Mk 8:31). Jesus begins to talk of the Messiah's sufferings and death, images that seem all the more shocking, given that the expression "Son of Man" is being used, which directly recalls the glory and power of the eschatological Messiah. That this teaching was misunderstood and was not accepted is clear from Peter's own reaction (Mk 8:32–33: a logion certainly historical, given Jesus' harsh rebuke to Peter—unthinkable for the primitive community who accepted and venerated him as the leader of the apostles) and from the desertion and fear of some disciples (Mk 10:32; Jn 6:66).

The profession of messianic faith at Caesarea is to be found in all three Synoptics (and Jn 6:67–70 is generally regarded now as being the interpretation of that profession, which would give us a *multiple attestation*). It may, however, also be taken as a *necessary explanation* to clarify much of what would otherwise remain obscure, as for instance the sudden change in Jesus' teaching, the conflicting reactions of the disciples, and the rebuke administered to Peter. The historicity of all this is hard to question.

In these Gospel pages we are not merely witnessing the faith of the primitive community but, what is more, we are present at the revelation of the mystery of the person of Jesus, who comes to meet us as glorious Messiah, even though with the features of the suffering servant.

One last example demonstrating Jesus' messianic awareness and reasons for faith in him is to be found in the accounts of his trial, which, though in different versions, all share a common purpose—to show why Jesus was sentenced to death (see Mt 26:62–65; Mk 14:60–64; 22:67–71; Jn 18:12–40; 19:1–6).

What directly concerns us here comes from Jesus' interrogation by the high priest: "Are you the Christ?" Caiaphas, already out of patience with Jesus' long silence and the inconsistency of the evidence offered in court, tendentiously puts the question to him about his messianic identity.

Had Jesus answered in the affirmative, he would have directed the national leaders and the priests toward a political interpretation of his messiahship. The latter would easily then have been able to accuse him of inciting the people to rebel against the authority of the Romans. Had he answered in the negative, he would have disavowed all his teaching out of his own mouth.

The evasiveness of the first part of Jesus' answer: "You have said so" (Mt 26:64); "if I tell you, you will not believe" (Lk 22:67), is immediately corrected by the precision of the subsequent words in which he proclaims the glorious return of the Son of Man: "From now on you will see the Son of Man seated at the right hand of Power and coming on the clouds of heaven" (Mt 26:64).

In a word, the context of suffering and passion in which the question is put does not allow the proclamation of the glorious coming of the Messiah to be confused or identified with a political messiahship. The union of two figures, the Son of Man of Dn 7 and the glorious king of Ps 110, on the one hand permits the proclamation of the ushering in of the messianic kingdom in the person of Jesus but on the other clearly identifies the logic necessary for attaining this kingdom: vicarious passion and death as the sign of filial obedience to the Father's plan.

3. Faith in the Messiah

The faith of the post-paschal community is concerned with historical facts and, above all, with the Master's word. The disciples had "left everything" and followed the Lord (Mk 10:28), since, in their encounter with him, in his words and in his conduct, they had verified that the hope and promise in which they had been brought up to believe from birth had been realized in him.

Now, of course, in the logic of revelation, God's plan took a course that did not immediately tally with what they had been brought up to expect. Because of this, Jesus, in his originality and in accordance with his particular gift of teaching, introduced them little by little to an understanding of the modes in which a new kind of messianism would be fulfilled—one that henceforth had the characteristics of universality and was open to their individual involvement as believers and followers.

Jesus of Nazareth, the Messiah, gives notice to the Christian faith that henceforth salvation is only to be had in him. A generalized hope of deliverance, the product of diverse historical events, is now replaced by the certainty that, in Jesus the Messiah, God himself is intervening to save his people.

Furthermore, on the word of that Messiah, the believing community down to today continues to hope in the full and final achievement of deliverance. The presence of evil and injustice stimulates the new *messianic people* to be in harmony with their Lord. The certainty of salvation given in the event of the Easter mystery does not exonerate us, but rather obliges us to become the instrument of justice and mercy wherever evil still has the upper hand.

In studying messianism, fundamental theology can discover an element which, on the religious as on the merely cultural plane, is shared by other expressions of faith and by peoples inspired by a common hope for justice and deliverance.

There is one element, however, which is

specific and unique to our religion, which Christianity can never renounce: that of proclaiming the historical realization of messianism which occurred in Jesus of Nazareth, according to whom there can be no other messiahs except for him: "If anyone says to you, 'Look! Here is the Messiah!' or 'There he is!' do not believe it" (Mt 24:23). The Messiah has already come; the acknowledgment of his presence in history henceforth is in the people who unceasingly proclaim him as Messiah and Lord.

Bibl.: W. WREDE, *The Messianic Secret* (1901; Greenwood, S.C., 1971)); R. BULTMANN, *Theology of the New Testament* (New York, 1951); E. SJÖBERG, *Der Verborgene Menschensohn in den Evangelien* (Lund, 1955); V. TAYLOR, *The Gospel According to St. Mark* (London, 1957); W. ZIMMERLI and J. JEREMIAS, "παις," *TDNT* 5:636–717; A. GELIN, "Messianisme," *DBS* 5:1165–1212; var., *Attente du Messie* (Louvain, 1958); O. CULLMANN, *The Christology of the New Testament* (Philadelphia, 1959); id., *Christ and Time* (Philadelphia, 1964); W. EICHRODT, *Theology of the Old Testament* (Philadelphia, 1961); G. VON RAD, *Old Testament Theology*, 2 vols. (New York, 1962, 1965); F. HAHN, *The Titles of Jesus in Christology* (1963; New York, 1969); ASSOCIAZIONE BIBLICA ITALIANA, *Messianismo* (Brescia, 1966); J. BLINZER, *Processo a Gèsu* (Brescia, 1966); L. SABOURIN, *The Names and Titles of Jesus: Themes of Biblical Theology* (New York, 1967); J. COPPENS, *Le messianisme royal* (Paris, 1968); id., *Le messianisme et sa relève prophétique* (Gembloux, 1974); id., *La relève apocalyptique du messianisme royal*, BETL 50 (Louvain, 1979); G. MINETTE DE TILLESSE, *Le secret messianique dans l'évangile de Marc* (Paris, 1968); H. CONZELMANN, *An Outline of the Theology of the New Testament* (New York, 1969); N. FÜGLISTER, "Les bases vétérotestamentaires de la christologie du Nouveau Testament," in *MystSal 9* (Paris, 1972); var., *La venue du Messie* (Paris, 1972); var., *Il problema christologico oggi* (Assisi, 1973); G. VERMES, *Jesus the Jew* (London, 1973); E. SCHILLEBEECKX, *Jesus: An Experiment in Christology* (New York, 1974); A. GRILLMEIER, *Christ in Christian Tradition* (Atlanta, 1975); K. SCHUBERT, *Partiti religiosi ebrei del tempo neotestamentario* (Brescia, 1976); J. CABA, *El Jesús de los Evangelios* (Madrid, 1977); H. CAZELLES, *Le Messie de la Bible* (Paris, 1978); P. GRELOT, *L'espérance juive à l'heure de Jésus* (Paris, 1978); id., *Les poèmes du Serviteur: De la lecture critique à l'herméneutique* (Paris, 1981); M. BORDONI, *Gesù di Nazareth*, vol. 2 (Perugia, 1982); R. FABRIS, *Gesù di Nazareth: Storia e interpretazione* (Assisi, 1983); B. FORTE, *Jésus de Nazareth: Histoire de Dieu et Dieu de l'histoire* (Paris, 1984); E. SCHÜRER, *Geschichte des Jüdischen Volkes im Zeitalter Jesu Christi* (Hildesheim, 1964); C. I. GONZALES, *El es nuestra salvación: Cristología y Soteriología* (Bogotá, 1987); A. AMATO, *Gesù il Signore* (Bologna, 1988); G. CLAUDEL, *La confession de Pierre* (Paris, 1988); R. FISICHELLA, *La Révélation: La révélation et sa crédibilité* (Paris/Montreal, 1989).

Rino FISICHELLA

METHOD

I. SYSTEMATIC THEOLOGY. *1. Principal Models in the History of Theology. 2. Systematic Thinking.* (G. POZZO)

II. FUNDAMENTAL THEOLOGY. *1. The Need for a Discourse on Method. 2. Toward a Historical Memory. 3. Method of Integration* (R. FISICHELLA)

I. SYSTEMATIC THEOLOGY

Dealing with the problem of "method" of a cultural or scientific discipline means considering it not directly in its contents but in its formal and structural aspect. The doctrine of *theological method* is thus intended to expose the bases and presuppositions of theological knowledge, with a view to showing the value of affirmations about theological reflection in general and that concerned with individual and specific contents of faith. Whereas theology is defined as critical, methodical, and systematic reflection on the faith of the church, reflection on method has for its object the study of the norms, criteria, and operations that theology fulfills, for its theological activity to be carried out as it should.

We must be aware that theology has always accompanied the church's life through the centuries of history, presenting itself in different forms, borrowing an image to correspond to the demands and cultural baggage emerging from time to time in the concrete life of the church and the historical-cultural setting of the age. This changeability of theology's image, as against the unchangeability of the message and of the datum of revelation/faith, is determined not only by the various cultural categories used by theology for reflecting on the content of the faith to be proclaimed but also by the multiplicity of methods of which theology makes use to establish the mode of approach to understanding and studying the mystery of revelation/faith.

In this connection it seems useful and important—even in a very much synthesized way—to consider the figures and historical models of theological methodology and episteme, not just to serve as introduction for the present treatment of the doctrine of theological method in its overall historical-theological context, but also so that, through awareness of the historical origins of the principal models of theological episteme, we may better grasp the meaning and importance of the methodology now being proposed.

1. Principal Models in the History of Theology

The Patristic Period and the Sapiential Ideal

Patristics, having as its object the early centuries of Christian thought, studies the impact of the Christian revelation on Judaism, then on the philosophic culture of Greece and Rome. Patristics may be regarded as the "springtime" phase of theology, which, in its encounter/clash with Greco-Roman culture, asserts the novelty of Jesus Christ and the speculative consistency too, connected with the practical effect of the Christian message, as regards the various philosophical and religious currents of the day. Properly speaking, the works of the fathers lack a "systematic" character, but in them there appears, as a constant, a structurally biblical, salvation-historical approach and an attentiveness in seeking the various different levels of meaning in the biblical texts, which the latter offer the believer over and above what the merely philological datum has to show. A characteristic element: patristic theological reflection is furthermore the sapiential dimension and the theological and spiritual vibration of the fathers' thought, directed toward encouraging the growth of one's own interior life and of the Christian existence of one's neighbor. In the West, the ideal and example of AUGUSTINE of Hippo remained uppermost. For him, *intellectus fidei* (the understanding of faith) in its two variants (*credo ut intelligas* ["I believe in order to understand"] [theology] and *intelligo ut credas* ["I understand in order to believe"] [philosophy]) is at the service of the very practice of beatitude and Christian contemplation.

The same wide use of Neoplatonic dialectic and philosophy to illustrate the mysteries of the faith is constantly put at the service of salvation-historical consideration of the Christian religion in the concrete order of salvation.

Scholastic Theology in the Middle Ages

The high water mark of scholasticism in the thirteenth century, and especially THOMAS AQUINAS, demonstrated the limitations of patristic reflection and of the monastic theology of the early Middle Ages, mainly in the ontological and metaphysical development of the data of revelation. To go beyond the eclectic attitude of the fathers, scholastic theology sought a philosophic instrument that would be organically compatible with the logic of Christian thought. The medieval *Summae* thus are the expressions of a systematic rethinking of the data of the faith, directed toward the construction of a *theological synthesis*. Not wishing to underrate the variety of theological layout and choices of the different medieval schools (sufficient to mention the Dominican-Thomist and the Franciscan-Bonaventurist schools as examples), we can single out two main features as characterizing the episteme and theological methodology of the scholastics: (1) the fact that the deepening of the data of the faith, extracted from Scripture, from tradition, from the teaching of the councils and from the life of the church, by means of comparison with the conceptual equipment of philosophic thought—and Aristotelean thought in particular—more and more becomes the prime site for theology; (2) the increasingly determining role that the paradigm of technological work has taken over from the Aristotelean concept of "science" and from the acceptation that the first of the sciences is metaphysics.

This unitary and metaphysical character of scholastic theology was thrown into confusion by the fragmentation of knowledge caused by the philosophic nominalism of later scholasticism (fourteenth century) and by the rise of modern science with its relative inductive method.

Post-Tridentine and Manualistic Theology

In order to rediscover common ground among all the schools of Catholic theology after the Council of Trent so as to resist the spread of Protestantism, we have the rise of the so-called "dogmatic method" in connection with the discipline known as "dogmatic theology." The nucleus of theological reflection is in fact given by the dogmatic definitions of the magisterium. The process follows an order of explanation that involves different phases: enunciation of the dogmatic thesis, exposition of opinions, positive proofs derived from the authority of Scripture, the fathers, and the councils; proofs deduced from theological reasoning, solutions of the difficulties, and corollaries for the growth of spiritual life. In addition to this factor, we can mention two other characteristics of this methodological approach: orientation toward system and organized discourse, and the organization of theology into encyclopedias.

Manualistic theology (→ THEOLOGY VII), which in the nineteenth century and the first half of the twentieth developed into theological schools, is based on the preceding factors and consequently offers characteristics that may be summed up as follows: (1) The dominant concern is the desire to develop rational apologetic proofs, in reaction to the rationalistic currents of modern thought. The apologetic use of the sources of revelation (Scripture and tradition) is stressed to support the doctrinal interventions of the magisterium. (2) There is a tendency to juxtapose in a somewhat extrinsic way *auctoritas* and *ratio,* i.e., the data of the faith and the requirements of rational reflection. (3) Lastly, manualistic theology elevates the authority of the magisterium to first place in the scale of the various authorities, precisely in the sense that it leans *directly* on the magisterium's pronouncements and not on revelation as contained in Scripture and tradition.

The evolution of the ecclesial situation and the development of modern fields of research as regards the nature and method of theology will give an opportunity for rethinking the lines of theological methodology and for proposing a restructuring of theological studies.

Pointers and Perspectives of Vatican II

The thought of Vatican II on the nature and method of theology is expressed in *Optatam Totius* no. 16. The direction and scope of the renewal of theological method are to be understood on the basis of the renewed concept of "revelation" as it is set out in *Dei Verbum.* The decree *OT* teaches that Scripture is the basic point of the procedure, both because the development of biblical themes is at the root of the truth to be investigated more deeply, and also because Scripture is the "soul of theology" (*DV* 24). The conciliar directive goes on to take up the voice of the fathers of the church and the historical development of dogma, understood as the necessary route for understanding how to clarify the revealed datum. Dogmatic definitions are hence the end point of a long journey of faith within the life and thought of the church, and normative points for understanding the revealed message. Then follows the "speculative" phase of the theology, which consists in illuminating the saving mysteries of the faith as far as possible, keeping the example set by Thomas Aquinas especially in mind. Lastly, theology's final task is to show the continuity between biblical proclamation, history of faith, speculative reflection and liturgy, Christian piety and the edification of the church. In this context, the council invites us "to search for solutions to human problems with the light of revelation, to apply eternal truths to the changing conditions of human affairs, and to communicate such truths in a manner suited to contemporary man" (*OT* 16).

In conclusion, the conciliar exposition, while not seeking to impose a rigid scheme on theological method, points out some essential methodological orientations that cannot be disregarded and invites theological thought to reflect, in an organic, unitary way, on the basic principles of the centrality of Christ in the mystery of salvation, attention to human values, the pastoral and spiritual aim.

The Postconciliar Period

In the postconciliar period, numerous *figures* of theology have emerged, and this implies numerous methodological layouts, of which here, without attempting any evaluation of merit but solely for the purposes of information and by no means exhaustively, mention will be made to complete our brief historical survey.

a. Anthropological-transcendental figure. The anthropological development in theology leads to considering the discourse on humanity as the context, guideline, and angle of vision for all theological knowledge. Some authors in particular (Rahner, for instance) introduce the transcendental method as the basis for theological knowledge and for establishing the potential conditions for the subject to be able to think about and discuss a possible revelation of God.

b. Hermeneutic figure. This theological layout is particularly concerned with problems of language, of interpretation, and of reformulation of the doctrines of faith, so that they may be meaningful and speak the word of salvation to people today.

c. Orthopractical figure. In this epistemological model, the "praxis" constitutes the interpretational criterion of revelation and verification of what the revealed word means. The orthopractical figure of theology expresses itself in various forms (political theology, liberation theology, theology of development, etc.). Basic for an evaluation of liberation theology are the two instruments of the Congregation for the Doctrine of the Faith, *Libertatis Nuntius* (1984) and *Libertatis Conscientia* (1986).

d. Some authors also talk of models in prospect of "narrative theology," "eschatological theology," "aesthetic theology" (see Rocchetta, Fisichella, and Pozzo 1985).

The present treatment of theological method intends to remain within the perspectives of Vatican II and to articulate a systematic reflection on theological methodology by, first, considering the *bases* of theological method and by, then, describing the *process*, without claiming to go into specific problems but choosing rather to lay out the main lines of the organic structure of theological knowledge.

2. Systematic Thinking

Bases of the Doctrine of Theological Method

At the constituent origin of theology stands *revelation*, the source of the theological contents and basis of its certainties. The concept of revelation, present both in philosophic language and in religious experience, becomes meaningful in an absolutely unique manner when referring to Jesus Christ. For the Jesus Christ event is understood as being the definitive self-manifestation of God and the full and unsurpassable unveiling of the ultimate truth about humanity and history. The Jesus Christ event, understood in its unique and unrepeatable singularity, is the principle of a

knowledge and, in prospect, of a new science, distinct from all others. The revelation of God in Jesus Christ is not only a principle of transformation and of conversion of existence; it is also (because of this) the interpretative key for understanding the ultimate meaning of humanity and reality. On this presupposition theology is founded. The relationship revelation/faith/theology is hence one of mutual involvement, in the sense that the event of revelation in correlation to the response/acceptance of faith is the constituent principle of theology. Doctrine on theological method, while it must, from an intellectual point of view, respect the rules of a rigorous and disciplined procedure, cannot, however, leave aside *the specifically theological principle* that has a basic and normative function for methodology itself, and that is to say the reality of man as believer and theologian, who accepts the gift of God's love and truth and is converted to the gospel of salvation. From this basis it hence follows that only faith in the self-revelation of God in Christ fixes coordinates of comprehension adequate to the reality of which theology must treat. Here thus we also see the point of intersection between life and theological activity, between experience and reflection, and can also identify the presupposition making it possible for believers to translate their own intellectual requirements into a correct and organically structured procedure.

The considerations outlined above consequently show that it is not possible to make a correct and authentic, methodologically disciplined Catholic theology except on the postulate—which is also a formal principle—that the root of theological knowledge, precisely because it is knowledge, is knowledge of the faith, understood as awareness and understanding of the revelation of God in Jesus Christ (Jn 1:14; 1 Cor 1:2; see also *DV* 5). Theology of course, inasmuch as it is human "logos," in itself is structurally open to the acquisitions of philosophy, the sciences, and, generally speaking, all the logical, hermeneutic, and theoretical instruments that human thought discovers and makes use of. From the methodological point of view, this openness means that theology must always be alert to the promptings of culture and to knowledge of the historical consciousness, as also to the development and improvement of linguistic, logical, and critical instruments for bringing about the meeting between faith, church, and theological thinking on the one hand, and the demands of contemporary culture on the other. It is, however, equally necessary that the formulation of the theological method should take account of the fact that theology is "science of the faith" and that consequently it is impossible to understand the original and special modes of the *rationality* of theology, unless the *veritative structure of the faith* is itself taken into account and respected, with its own criteria of truth and authenticity. In particular, the actual, basic unity of knowledge/knowing the faith is the revelation of God completed in Jesus Christ and the church as the place where actual remembering of the Jesus Christ event takes place.

The conclusion is that the formulation of method in theology cannot be constituted exclusively or on the basis of criteria and norms which operate in other scientific disciplines, but must above all observe normative principles derived from knowledge of the faith and then make use of the contributions and critical means proper to metaphysical, historical, hermeneutic, and other forms of knowledge. So doing, theology can satisfy the requirements of being organic, systematic, logical, and unitary on the one hand, and the requirements of the knowledge of the faith on the other.

The Starting Point for
the Theological Procedure

The preliminary methodological requirement of any science is to isolate the topic and exactly formulate the question to which an answer is to be sought by appropriate means. Generally speaking, a given question arises from a fact or phenomenon already known in some sense but requiring to be known more profoundly and more exactly. Thus the *subject* constitutes the known element, and the *predicate* constitutes the element as yet not fully known, which is the object of research.

The *subject* of theology is the life and doctrine of faith of the church in the church's relation to the revelation of God, One and Three, and the *question* is: What does the doctrine of the revelation of God in Christ to which the faith and preaching of the church alike bear witness) mean and how can it be interpreted and made intelligible?

In this question, the subject is the ecclesial community itself, the doctrinal content of which is conscious, even if not necessarily justified and grasped in a reflected and critical manner. The *predicate* is the actual request to seize on the life and thought of the church in its relation to the revelation and mystery of God. This is achieved by projecting the experience and heritage of the church's doctrines of faith onto the plane of scientific, methodical, systematic reflection. In other terms: the starting point for systematic theology is contact made with the concrete experience of the ecclesial life of faith, i.e., with the modes by which the church, in history, reproduces the Christian event in its cognitive, doctrinal elements (*fides quae creditur*) and with the modes by which the community of believers leads its inner life and makes the Christian event (*fides qua creditur*) existentially its own. In connection with this, it is important to stress the personal dimension of theologizing, for this expresses the inner and personalized grasp of the faith and is reflected also in the way theological work is conducted, while of course this personal dimension must not lead to subjectivization and the theologian's identifying theology with his or her own autobiography. A further point: the faith-reality lived by the church is always a conditional reality. For, be it because of the psychological need of the individual who evinces an impulse, from the intellectual standpoint, to satisfy a desire to know, or be it because of the cultural shifts and turmoil which objectively throw doubt on the assertions and convictions of the faith, the theologian's task does not consist only in stating what the church's faith is, but in the duty of justifying the content of the faith on the basis of the sources of that faith; of presenting it in its historical continuity and in its development through the centuries, of explaining it in the context of revelation; of making it clear by illustrating its importance and its existential and historical relevance, so that people of any period can understand what their lives are for and what their ultimate destiny will be.

The starting point for a systematic process of reflection now having been made clear, let us deal with theology's basic twin tasks in the methodological sector:

a. Theology has to prove the link between the present-day faith of the church and the definitive saving event of Jesus Christ as unsurpassable revelation of the truth and charity of God. We may call this first basic task *auditus fidei:* it expresses the positive function of theology.

b. In a second phase, theology has to respond to the demands and challenges of present-day thought and culture by the contents of the faith comprehensible to the human intellect, by showing the practical and existential efficacy of the Christian message, by reaching an ever-deeper organic *synthesis* of the revealed truths. This second basic task for theology can be called *intellectus fidei;* it expresses the reflective and actualizing function of theology.

Positive Phase of Theology: Auditus Fidei

The *object* of positive theology is what results from having come to know the life and doctrine of the church. *The formulation of the question* is: How can we know and prove that the church's doctrine comes from Christ's revelation?

It is as well to make the point that this is not a matter of putting in doubt what knowledge of faith gives as certain, but of working through the critical approach to the datum of faith. The basis and clarification of the bond between the church's knowledge of faith and the principle of revelation are obtained by study of the normative testimony of faith, authorized to transmit Christ's teaching since formed by eye-witnesses and ear-witnesses of the historical happening of Jesus, which reached its climax in the Easter event. This testimony has been fixed in writing, in the NT, and hence has a foundational character for the faith of subsequent generations. This normative testimony, however, gets lived, handed on, and interpreted by the post-apostolic church. Ecclesial tradition is precisely this faithful and living transmission/interpretation/clarification/actualization of the testimony of apostolic faith. The whole people of God is involved in this "tradition," discharging a variety of duties among which, in a particular way, emerges the function of the MAGISTERIUM of the church with its duty of authenticating the interpretation and understanding of the revealed message. This magisterial office acquires irrevocable importance and significance in its dogmatic pronouncements and definitions.

Let us now consider the sources of theological knowledge and their undifferentiated use in positive theology.

Scripture. Use of the witness of Scripture in theological method presupposes the knowledge of what Scripture is, who its author is, and in what sense Scripture is the word of God. Furthermore, it presupposes a knowledge of the problems and use of the historical-critical method of biblical hermeneutics.

It is, however, opportune to recall the principle that Scripture, being the word of God, is not simply a historical-literary phenomenon, to be understood for the most part by the criteria used for any kind of writing from the past, but itself constitutes an event having its place in the project of the revelation of God in history. While it can indeed then be described in terms of historical-critical inquiry, Scripture is essentially something to be fully attributed to God's initiative, transcending the dimensions of human nature and human culture in its religious and doctrinal contents. So it must be understood that when the texts of the magisterium speak of Scripture, they unite this theme to that of tradition and to that of the magisterium, which enjoys the gift of authentically interpreting and faithfully expounding the word of God entrusted by Christ and the Holy Spirit to the apostles (DV 9).

In the light of the foregoing preamble, we may indicate some basic types of use of Scripture in positive theological reasoning:

a. The use of the biblical datum as *scriptural reasoning.* Here, with the confirmation of critical exegesis, systematic theology finds proof in Scripture justifying the derivation of a given doctrine of faith from revelation (e.g., the truth that the Holy Spirit is conferred in baptism).

b. The use of the biblical datum as *scriptural basis.* In this case the biblical datum, exegetically understood and clarified, offers only a part or only a starting point for justifying the provenance of a given doctrine from revelation. We can distinguish two cases. In the first, the modern reader, thanks to the results of exegesis, can see that a part of the truth of faith predicated is formally and explicitly contained in Scripture. For example, according to Paul, no one can be saved from sin and death except by the death and resurrection of Christ. Interpreting Rom 5, the Council of Trent indicates the exact way to follow for a full understanding of the Pauline message and for avoiding reductive interpretations about the doctrine of original sin. In the second case, the problem is one of singling out *in what measure* a truth taught by the church is present in the biblical testimony. (For example, the notion of *sphragis* (seal), while occurring in Scripture, does not mean exactly what the church was later to interpret it to mean with the doctrine of sacramental "character.") In other words, there can be doctrines of faith which the church teaches dogmatically but which only have a basis or starting point in Scripture, which have since been made explicit and been fully and correctly understood by tradition.

c. Lastly, there is the case where a doctrine of faith has nothing said about it in Scripture, whether formally explicit or technically formulated. In this situation, exegesis is not in a position either to give evidence of the meaning of the doctrine or of the starting point from which the path of explication sets out. In consequence, the believing reader and the theologian will have to have recourse to tradition (e.g., the dogma of the assumption of Mary). This, however, does not mean that some truths of faith are not contained in Scripture understood as the word of God; what it does mean is that the relationship between revelation, Scripture, and tradition has to take this dimension into account, i.e., that knowledge of Scripture is not enough for understanding the word of God. For the final and decisive determining of the revealed contents, there must always be recourse to tradition (liturgy, *sensus fidei* of the people of God, authoritative and authentic preaching of the magisterium).

To conclude, let us recapitulate by saying that the various uses of Scripture in theological method always postulate the result of historical-critical exegesis, directed toward extracting the technical and direct meaning of the biblical text, but going beyond this result since the use of the biblical datum in the reasoning of positive theology always has need of tradition, in the ways already explained, in order to understand the meaning and content of revealed doctrine. Furthermore, systematic theology must take account of two other basic criteria in

using the biblical datum: (1) the criterion of the *unity of the Bible* (any individual affirmation must be consistent with the overall message of Scripture); (2) the *christological* criterion (what is read in the Bible is not something complete *per se* but must be read in relation to him in whom all is made complete, Christ the Lord. Christ it is who leads to the deep and complete truth of what it says in the Bible).

The Ecclesial Tradition. Postulating the acquisitions of the church's self-comprehension with regard to the concept of tradition (DS 1501-3007-3386) we confine ourselves here to mentioning that, according to Vatican II, tradition transmits the word of God through the apostles and their successors *integre* ("in its full purity") down to today (*DV* 9). It gathers up not only the oral preaching but also the example of the life of Christ and the witness of the liturgy. What is more, the spiritual experience, doctrinal preaching, and scholarship of the faithful are elements that stimulate the progress of tradition in understanding revelation (*DV* 8). As regards the use of the data of tradition in theological method, there will be the preliminary need to distinguish various levels in interpreting the documents of tradition.

The level of *philological interpretation* consists in establishing the meaning of the text in its literal and grammatical structure. The level of *historical interpretation* aims at fixing what the author intended to say in the overall context of his writings and thought. The level of *dogmatic interpretation* aims at seizing on the transcendent sense enclosed in the documents of tradition. It must not be overlooked that in the human and historical witness of the documents of tradition, there may be a content of truth, derived from revelation, guaranteed by the presence of the Spirit, the universal guide.

This is why the use theology makes of the datum of tradition cannot leave the magisterium out of account, for this is the organ capable of singling out and fixing the dogmatic meaning of the testimony or doctrinal statement enshrined in tradition.

At this level precisely we encounter a knotty problem for theological method. For tradition is observed to put forward certain contents of truth with the same notions and words as date from the beginning of Christian preaching. Yet it puts other contents of truth into notions and words dating only from some given period. In connection with this, we may say that the greater part of present-day preaching of the faith—*linguistically speaking*—does not come directly from Christ and the apostles. The problem then arises: How can we explain this fact and what consequences does it have for correct theological method?

One answer to this question is that a shift of attention with regard to the many, many aspects of the mystery of the faith is a necessary condition for grasping the introduction of new terms in the church's doctrinal preaching (e.g., the concept of *homoousios* or the concept of "transubstantiation" or the concept of "sacramental character," and so one).

We can clarify all this as follows. For a period of time the church transmits a revealed content without formulating it technically. The introduction of new words and formulations always to express the same revealed content leads to a better thought-out, more consciously detailed knowledge of that same truth of faith which had been present in the lived awareness of Christian people in a preconceptual, pre-thought-out and perhaps only generalized way. In the transition from lived awareness to the knowledge and thought-out formulation, the magisterium always and necessarily has its place, for it alone can guarantee in the last resort that this transition and approach to the conceptual formulation takes place without manipulating and altering the revealed content itself.

For the probative reasoning of positive theology, it is therefore necessary to take account of the shifts of accent and degrees of concentration as regards the many aspects of the mysteries of the faith. Only thus can one be sure that the explication and historical soundings/developments of the ecclesial tradition are being conducted along the right lines.

Lastly, for theological method, it is important to emphasize the distinction between *doctrine-of-faith tradition* and *Christian theological/ cultural tradition*. The distinction prevents one from confusing the datum pertaining to the common faith of the church, the testimony of her liturgical life, of her spiritual experience, and of the dogmatic preaching of the magisterium, with the element pertaining to the theological and cultural convictions and opinions that happen to be present in the history of Christian thought. True, there is an interweaving often to be seen between the two elements; yet theology must draw proper distinction between what belongs to the tradition of faith, guaranteed by the magisterium, and what pertains to historically conditioned, intellectual models and perspectives that are not essentially bound up with the DEPOSIT OF FAITH. This, on the other hand, does not mean overlooking the educative and methodological importance of the thinkers and theologians (above all the fathers and doctors of the church) who have been accorded special recognition by the church itself.

In this context we may note certain basic characteristics of Christian authors that are to be kept in particular consideration: orthodoxy of teaching, holiness of life, recognition by the church and the ability to make the event of revelation comprehensible to human reason.

The mediation of the magisterium in theological knowledge. The affirmation that an intrinsic relationship exists between the ministry of preaching the true Word (see Ti 1:9; 1 Tm 1:10; 4:6; 2 Tm 4:3) and the apostolic succession leads to a consideration of the specific subject of the magisterium and the use of its documents in theological method.

a. Function of the documents of the magisterium: meaning and importance. The significance of the magisterium of the church is to be understood in the context of the *truth* of Christian doctrine. The documents of the magisterium are not therefore something extrinsic to or superimposed on Christian truth but are the explication of that truth. The service the magisterium performs for the saving truth is for the benefit of all Christian people, who are called to be inducted into the freedom of the truth.

The object of the magisterium's teaching is the word of God in all its amplitude: the magisterium's sphere of competence therefore is revealed doctrine (DS 3018). The ways in which the magisterium exercises its function are substantially two: (1) There exists a solemn and extraordinary way, the results of which are dogmatic pronouncements, irreformable in themselves and not by the consensus of the faithful (DS 3074). (2) And there exists an ordinary way, the results of which are not so much the final definition of a doctrine, nor the guarantee that a given content pertains to revelation; but rather, the *authentic* handing on of the substance of the Christian message, for it to be put into effect in the pastoral life of the church.

As regards dogmatic definitions, the magisterium's *charisma veritatis* concerns the possibility of declaring infallibly that the content of faith is revealed, on the presupposition that this same content has always been present in the deposit of faith, even though it may not have been thought out or formulated technically. In the formula dogmatically defining papal infallibility (DS 3015; 3017), the First Vatican Council also deliberately included the possibility that the church might define doctrines without necessarily claiming them to be divinely revealed. Doctrines of this sort, if proposed by the church in a definitive manner, must be accepted and acknowledged, even though the assent of divine faith is not due to them.

Hence, within the compass of irreformable, even though not divinely revealed, doctrines falls everything concerning the mysteries of salvation insofar as that without doctrinal clarification of the topic in question the effective proclamation of the revealed truths would be impossible. For instance, what concerns the moral natural law (the *preambula fidei*), the so-called *facta dogmatica*, such as the legitimacy of a council or of a pope, the canonization of saints, and so on fall within this sphere of competence.

As regards the preaching of the ordinary magisterium in the matter of faith and morals, the church's teaching (see *LG* 25) states that the aim is that of guiding the faithful to initiation in the central mysteries of salvation, by means of the various instruments of pastoral, liturgical, and catechetical activity. Preaching of this sort, while being authentic, does not intend to put forward doctrinal teaching in a definitive way, and so it is not in itself irreformable. To the teachings of the ordinary magisterium, therefore, the assent of faith is not due, nor is an irrevocable assent, but the religious deference of intellect and will is. "Religious" since it is not based on merely rational reasons but on the acknowledged singularity of the function of the pope and bishops to expound and preach—with the authority conferred by Christ through the apostolic succession—the contents of Christian doctrine

and Christian life. It should furthermore be remembered that, these being texts not of themselves irreformable, theological competence has a duty critically to deepen and develop the thinking of the magisterium.

As regards the *importance* of doctrinal definitions and particularly of dogmas, it is a matter of bearing in mind that dogmatic statements show what the church warns as not being compatible with the right understanding of revelation. The pronouncements of the magisterium do not claim positively to express the totality of the mystery of the faith; but for the believing conscience, they have inalienable value since on the one hand they refute heresy, which is invariably either a breach in or a reduction of the totality of the datum of the faith, and on the other they urge and guide theology to reexamine the message of salvation more and more deeply and to safeguard it from deviant and reductive interpretations.

b. Use of the documents of the magisterium and criteria of interpretation. The criteria and general principles for interpreting doctrinal texts of the magisterium with the aim of establishing their right use in theological method are as follows:

1. With any magisterial document, the first thing to do is to determine what it is aiming to teach, distinguishing between the intelligible doctrinal content and the forms or argumentational and illustrative schemes dependent on historically conditioned theological points of view.

This criterion entails consistently applying the declaration of Vatican I which, while aware of the church's progress in knowledge of revealed truth (DS 3020), taught that "to the sacred dogmas must be preserved the meaning once and for all time declared by the Church" (DS 3020). This teaching was confirmed by Pope John XXIII at the opening of the Second Vatican Council: "This certain and immutable doctrine . . . needs to be studied and expounded in the way our own age requires. For the substance of the ancient doctrine of the deposit of faith is one thing, and the way it is presented is another, though always with the same sense and meaning" (*AAS* 54 [1962]: 792; *GS* 62). The declaration *Mysterium Ecclesiae*, taking up this teaching, explains that here the pope speaks of the deposit of faith as being identical with the truths contained in this doctrine, and of truths that must be conserved in the same sense. The declaration goes on: "It is clear that the Pope admits that we can know the true and unchanging meaning of dogmas. . . . What is new and what he recommends in view of the needs of the times pertains only to the modes of studying, expounding and presenting that doctrine while keeping its permanent meaning" (*Mysterium Ecclesiae* no. 5). The document goes on to declare that "the dogmatic formulas of the church's magisterium were from the very beginning suitable for communicating revealed truth, and that as they are they remain forever suitable for communicating this truth to those who interpret them correctly" (no. 5). This does not mean that integrative and explanatory formulas other than those already fixed cannot be found, but "they would have to be approved by the magisterium and indicate the same meaning more completely" (no. 5). As a comment on this teaching, one may say by way of definition that the dogmatic formulas put forward and defined by the church express in objective and definitive (and hence not in approximative) manner the aspect or content of the revealed truths to which they refer. Even if the dogmatic formulas as such are not the ultimate object of faith, since faith is entirely directed toward the mysterious and transcendent mystery of God, they are nonetheless not the result of a subjective and merely historical and mutable representation of the mysteries of revelation.

2. One must distinguish between the various degrees of certainty and obligatoriness to which the magisterium intends to commit its own doctrinal authority. A dogmatic definition is one thing; pastoral instruction, or exhortation, or disciplinary directive, quite another.

3. One must distinguish in a document between the essential presuppositions for a dogmatic definition, such that once these are denied, the content of the definition is also denied, and the inessential presuppositions that pertain to contingent elements derived from the cultural notions of a given period.

4. Lastly, attention must be paid to the problem of distinguishing between the content or meaning of a dogma and its conceptual formulation. In this connection, it is a plain fact that,

in the doctrinal development of the themes of faith, there has been a linguistic transition or change from biblical notions to those contained in dogma (cf. *homoousios* in the Nicene Creed). This comes about because a biblical doctrine can express a revealed content in narrative terms or by a figurative expression. A biblical doctrine of this sort may need explaining in an altered historical context and require the separation of the doctrinal content from the figurative expression in order for its true, deep significance to be brought out. This separating is certainly to be observed in the history of tradition, and the magisterium has put forward some revealed contents in a figurative manner, just as the Bible does, and other revealed contents in a technically worked out, conceptual form. The transition from figurative to conceptual language can be defined as the process of interpreting the faith. In such a case, however, the content, which is always an intellectual element too remains unaltered and is recognizable to the intellect and communicable by the human word.

First conclusion. Reflection on the use of the sources of revelation and the documents of the magisterium shows us that Scripture, tradition, and magisterium always require reciprocal relationship and reference. The use of the biblical datum needs tradition and magisterium, since these latter alone can lead to a full and authentic understanding of the message of the biblical text. On the other hand, an understanding of tradition requires knowledge of Scripture, since tradition presupposes and depends on the original NT testimony. The use of magisterial texts ought always to take account of the wider context of tradition, in which the magisterial pronouncement takes place.

In its turn, the doctrine of today's church illuminates the interpretative horizon in which the meaning of the biblical and ecclesial message has to be correctly understood.

To conclude, theology proves the provenance from revelation of the doctrines of faith by a total and integral use of the sources of theological knowledge (Scripture, tradition, and magisterium). Without this totality, no valid chain of reasoning can be constructed, since without the overall frame offered by the testimony of Scripture, tradition, and the documents of the magisterium it is impossible to see *how and at what level* a truth of faith fits into the entirety of revelation. The history of faith, understood as the total union of Scripture, tradition, and magisterium down to the preaching of the faith today, allows us to recognize where and why certain aspects of Christian truth have been accentuated, thus accounting for the dogmatic explications and definitions concerned with explaining the revealed contents belonging to the *depositum fidei*.

Reflective Phase of Theology: Intellectus Fidei

The result of critical attention to the sources of the faith is the proof of the doctrine of faith's claim to truth, since it is derived from revelation. Hence the *object* of reflective theology is the church's doctrine and life inasmuch as they are derived from revelation or refer to revelation. Theology hence in the reflective phase always presupposes the truth of the faith and presupposes its critical basis to be in the principle of revelation. To formulate the *question* to which reflective theology has to reply, the relationship has to be considered between the theological data and human thought. Three main requirements have to be kept in mind: (1) the need to *illustrate* the content of faith *speculatively*, bearing in mind the doubts and difficulties raised by human reason or by human reason or experience; (2) the need to show the intrinsic consistency of a theological *synthesis* postulating the organic structure of Christian thought and doctrine; (3) the need for the truth of the faith to be up-to-date, so as to show the existential and practical importance of the mysteries of the faith and their ability to provide an answer to the profound longings of humanity and culture at the particular moment of time in which we live. To these three needs, we add the possibility that, in the course of an intellectual deepening of the faith, theology may discover some element as yet not made explicit, or as yet unformulated, and reflectively unclarified. The *explicative work* of reflective theology in this sense is an important and creative contribution for the whole church, committed as it is to penetrating ever deeper into an understanding of the mysteries of the faith.

On the basis of these introductory considerations, we can break down the methodological equipment of reflective theology into the following functional specializations: speculative function, and updating function of the *intellectus fidei*.

Before examining these functions individually, it is timely to consider some general premises of the epistemological order, which are relevant to the specific structure of the *intellectus fidei*.

As *intellectus fidei*, systematic theology has a duty of taking on the categories and cultural baggage of successive historical periods, in order to provide an exposition of the contents of faith, such as can meet the scientific and theological requirements of human thought and satisfy the requirement of a *theological synthesis* of the mysteries of the faith.

This taking on of the conceptual categories belonging to the cultural and theoretical sphere of thought objectively raises the problem of the confrontation between theology and philosophy (→ THEOLOGY V). Here we confine ourselves to pointing out the guiding principles for the use of philosophy in the speculative procedure of the *intellectus fidei* and subsequently presenting the basic methodological criterion for the construction of the theological synthesis.

1. *Intellectus fidei and philosophy.* For a right use of philosophical knowledge in the sphere of speculative theological reflection, the following principles and basic guidelines will need to be borne in mind:

a. The base principle is given by the fact that revelation manifests the truth of God in Christ Jesus and consequently requires and postulates that faith, as acceptance of/response to revelation, be both knowledge and true recognition of Jesus Christ's identity as revealer of the mystery of the father, and as logos of God.

Faith as *fides qua* entails trusting/existential/personal adhesion to the word of God revealed in Christ. Faith as *fides quae*, that is to say, as recognition of the revelation, entails the existence of a *doctrine* (*doctrina revelata*) and of an *activity* in conformity with and suitable to the truth of Christ.

b. Revealed doctrine structurally requires that human reason be rightly ordered to the truth, capable of knowing God starting from the creation (DS 3004, 3005; *DV* 6), and of learning the principles of moral life. The reception/transmission of revelation on the church's part therefore requires statements of universal, metaphysical import, i.e., that human beings are capable of truth, of enunciating true statements, of freely choosing the good. Such metaphysical implications of universal and objective import are essentially derived from revealed doctrine itself.

c. Faith (*fides quae*) as recognition of and adhesion to revelation intrinsically possesses the quality of being a legitimate mode of "knowing." Consequently, faith does not acquire its reasonableness from without, nor is there separation or extraneousness between "faith" and "knowing," between "faith" and "reason," even though faith and reason are distinct and not to be confused.

d. From the correct approach to the relationship between faith and reason (→ REASON/ FAITH) are derived certain implications for the relationship between theology and philosophy in theological method.

When faith seeks to understand itself critically and reflectively (*fides quaerens intellectum*), it requires theology. The origin of theology is therefore knowledge of the faith. To develop its critical and speculative task, however, theology also has need of philosophy. When faith/ theology encounters the human cultural sphere—i.e., a "cultivated reason"—it needs philosophic categories consistent with the requirements of the faith. Whereas by its nature philosophy claims to provide an interpretation of the totality of the real, the church's faith requires to be able to dispose of a philosophic reason which can grasp the truth about God, human nature, and the world, so that revealed doctrine can confirm these affirmations and raise them to the plane of revelation. This, after all, has been what the great masters of theological thought have striven to do: Augustine, Anselm, Thomas Aquinas, Bonaventura, Duns Scotus, and so on.

It is not a question of imposing a particular philosophic system on theology nor of making absolute a given model of thought, but of affirming as a matter of principle the possibility of and the need for right and true philosophic thinking which corresponds to the requirements of the faith.

In this context we see the opportuneness of Vatican II's reference to Thomas Aquinas as a value and an example to be pondered and imitated, without this reference's being interpreted in an exclusive and excluding sense.

In this perspective, the *intellectus fidei* is not the application of a technical philosophy to the understanding of revealed doctrine. *Intellectus fidei* does not depend on philosophic self-comprehension. On the other hand, philosophies are not "all the same" where *intellectus fidei* is concerned. The philosophic categories can be used as it may suit the faith, on condition that they be consistent with the requirements of revealed doctrine itself. In conclusion, it will be a good thing to keep the following points in mind:

First: the scientific nature of the *intellectus fidei* is intrinsic to its own nature, and the function of philosophy does not consist in putting order into a datum (the faith) which would in itself be disordered and without its own intrinsic unity. The function of the *intellectus fidei* is properly that of bringing out an order, a logical harmony, which is intrinsic to the revealed datum itself.

Second: the use of philosophic categories and models constitutes a means by which the *intellectus fidei* can show the intelligibility of revelation and go speculatively deeper into the mystery of the faith for the purpose of dialogue and for coming to grips with the philosophic terms in which human beings understand themselves and their culture today.

Thirdly: given that *revealed doctrine* contains and essentially entails metaphysical assumptions and universal gnosiological principles expressing the permanent structures of existence and thought (creaturely nature of human beings, capacity of the human mind to know the true and to do the right, ability of human language to express revealed contents, etc.), it requires philosophic thought that will be consistent and compatible with the true requirements of revelation/faith.

2. Intellectus fidei and theological synthesis. Reflection on the Christian mystery with the aim of a progressively deepening understanding of the *depositum fidei* can proceed only if it is constantly being integrated into and taking place within the totality of the doctrine of salvation, for that is the measure and rule of any inquiry and of any particular piece of rethinking. And thus reflective theology comes up against the requirements of the *theological synthesis*.

In connection with this, it is appropriate to consider the epistemological principle of the *analogy of the faith*, which pertains to the epistemological structure of theology itself. This principle says that speculative investigation of individual contents must in fact be conducted by way of singling out the relationships and connections between the truths of the faith, since only in this manner can determination be reached on the significance of the individual mysteries, and hence an organic synthesis of the doctrinal themes which are the object of reflection and systematization. The basis of this principle is indicated in the teaching of Vatican II, and particularly in the doctrine of the hierarchy of truths: "When comparing doctrines, they [theologians] should remember that in Catholic teaching there exists an order or 'hierarchy' of truths, since they vary in their relationship to the foundation of the Christian faith" (*UR* 11). Similarly *Mysterium Ecclesiae* affirms that "there exists an order and as it were a hierarchy of the church's dogmas, as a result of their varying relationship to the foundation of the faith. This hierarchy means that some dogmas are founded on other dogmas which are the principal ones, and are illuminated by these latter. But all dogmas, since they are revealed, must be believed with the same divine faith" (no. 4).

The aforesaid teaching constitutes a fundamental epistemological basis for the working out of the theological synthesis, since theology can penetrate the significance of the individual truths of faith only if it properly establishes the relationship between this one and that one by paying attention to the "hierarchical" reference to the basis of the faith, which is the revelation of God definitively completed in Jesus Christ. The principle of the analogy of the faith is therefore a basic rule for a correct theological methodology in the sector of *intellectus fidei*.

These general epistemic premises having been established, we shall now briefly illustrate the specific functions into which reflective theology is divided, with their respective methods.

a. The speculative function. *The response to the objections raised by reason.* Basically one can distinguish two types of objection. *The first is the insinuation that a contradiction exists between truth of faith and truth of reason.* To deal with this, theology will proceed by expounding the exact sense of the assertion of faith, to avoid misapprehensions about the meaning of the statement and so to refute the apparent contradictions, which in reality do not exist if the statement is properly understood. As regards the problems themselves, theology will next, with the instruments of logic, have to prove that human reasoning that persists in seeing a contradiction between faith and reason is wrong. The epistemological postulate that such a contradiction is impossible comes from the fact that a substantial homogeneity exists between the order of creation and the order of salvation (→ ANALOGY), by which the God who reveals a truth of faith is that God who has created human reason. *The second obstacle advanced by human reason is the attempt to rationalize and demonstrate the truth of faith* by reducing it to a mere truth of reason, and hence denying the revealed and absolutely gratuitous character of the truth of faith in question. In this case, human reason can be used to show the intrinsic evidence for the truth of faith, by the sole means of reflection. Theology will proceed by arguing the impossibility of an intrinsic demonstration of the truth of faith (e.g., the mystery of the triune nature of God) by reason alone, since the object in question necessarily transcends human philosophical capacity.

The response suggesting the reasonableness of the faith. A distinction must be drawn between two attitudes open to the believer. The first is that of someone who aims to make the revealed truth of faith intelligible by comparing it with the realities of human experience. The second is that of someone who intends to advance a reasoned argument by which to bring out the positive meaning of the message of faith for the fulfillment of human existence.

(1) The method of comparison. On the basis of the postulate that a substantial homogeneity exists between the order of creation and the order of salvation, although a qualitatively untranscendible difference always subsists (analogy), one may conclude that similarities exist between truths of faith and natural truths, *as regards the possibility of understanding the former.*

The methodological procedure puts one or more truths of faith into relationship with one or more truths of the natural and rational order (e.g., the analogy or similarity that Augustine sees between the inner, intimate life of the Trinity and the structure of the human soul, which he distinguishes into the faculties of memory, intellect and will). Clearly, theological reasoning depends for its soundness and plausibility on the ability of the human intelligence to maintain its theses, for theological reason here is not immune to possible error and approximation, which always endanger its accuracy. In the speculative field, theology possesses no strength other than that expressed by the reasons it manages to identify and the arguments it is able to produce.

(2) The method of correspondence. This aims at suggesting the value of doctrine by postulating its intellectual truth. The presupposition in this method is the conviction that Christian truth is *propter nos homines et propter nostram salutem*, i.e., that it is always a *saving truth*. Speculative theology seeks, hence, to work out a theoretical proposal offering valid reasons for why the Christian experience should be regarded as reasonable. In concrete terms, this means showing that the basic problems of human life (suffering, death, the yearning for personal self-fulfillment) are not created by revelation, nor do such problems create a response to revelation. Theological reason is, however, able to show that the radical problems of human existence in time find a *reasonable* response and definitive fulfillment (→ Meaning I) in the Christian revelation.

b. The explicative function. In this case it is not a question of the theological significance of a doctrinal content intelligible nor of replying to objections raised by human culture. The specific object is the perception of a line of reasoning or an aspect of the mystery that has not as yet been formulated in technically precise words and ideas. At the beginning of the process, neither nature nor importance on the doctrinal plane is known as yet. Elements exist, however, which suggest to the theologian that a theme of faith (e.g., Augustine's effort of thought to give technical formulation to the notion of original sin) needs to be defined with greater precision.

By synthesizing, it is possible to indicate the following methodological path for the explicative function of theology. First of all, there is the church's conviction that in the Catholic faith there can be no contradiction between the truths of faith. So, by putting one or more truths into relationship with the foundation and center of revelation, i.e., the Christ-event, the believer will see the reason that has prompted the discovery of a problem as yet unresolved by exact technical formulas. The method thus proceeds at two levels. First and foremost it is a question of discovering the thematic reality to be formulated, and this usually comes about by intuition. Second, an explicatory process takes place, so as to arrive at the formulation of the Christian content to be made explicit. The guarantee that the theological explication corresponds to the truth of revelation can only be given by the magisterium of the church. Nonetheless theology constitutes a necessary phase for reaching a statement of the revealed truth implicitly present in the *depositum fidei*.

The explicative reflection of theology achieves the clarification of the notion and revealed aspect not by means of a logical/deductive process but by an intuition of the mystery in question, which is developed by the relationship established between the problem to be clarified and the sum of the truths of salvation already known and particularly in relation to the mystery of Christ.

c. The function of updating. Theology is aware that there is an intrinsic link between the requirement to make the truth of the faith intelligible to the human mind by explicating the heritage of revelation and the missionary requirement to proclaim the gospel to all people "of every age and clime." This latter requirement represents theology's urgent need to be up-to-date, since it has to recover and renew its own awareness of mission based on the conviction of setting forth a universal and saving truth and set of values. Consistent with this objective, theology should be concerned with sensitivities, with the most effective instruments and with the language in which and by which it is called upon to express its own reflections. From the methodological point of view, it is essential to remember *two principles*. The first is that theology must be able to distinguish between the doctrinal contents of definitive nature and the illustrations and schemes of reasoning used to present these contents. The latter are always relative and contingent, while the former are unchanging.

The second principle is that a distinction must be made between the task of "scientific" updating and the task of "practical updating." Systematic theology satisfies the *pastoral* and updating aim insofar as it is *scientific and ecclesial*. This means that theology is up-to-date insofar as it is just itself and not insofar as it becomes something other than itself. Theology will accomplish its updating function in the sense that it has the task of making the reality of revelation/faith understood objectively, by taking up all the theoretical and practical acquisitions that are in some degree sound, which the conspectus of present-day human thought has to offer. Hence it is not a question of theology's giving up the rigorous requirements of its theological method by chasing after the modulations of contemporary culture in an uncritical and hasty way, but of assimilating—with critical discernment and starting from the judgment of the faith—those different ways of interpreting reality which human history on the march in search of the truth suggests and demands.

The task of present-day theological methodology is to achieve a deeper unity between the various aspects of theological inquiry, although these necessarily have to be differentiated during the process of theological work. A first aspect of this organic unity is the deep convergence of the positive and reflective functions of theology. For these functions do converge, inasmuch as they are expressions of a single higher knowledge, i.e., knowledge of faith. One may furthermore add that, in the doctrine of theological method, the "positive" and the "reflective" phases are not subordinate to one another but coordinate as different routes to a more adequate knowledge of the object in question. Both phases, however, are subordinate to the faith, which uses them as instruments to develop and deepen understanding of the revealed divine message. Furthermore, positive and reflective theology are not extraneous to the living tradition of the church. Therefore the unity between faith, church, and theology guarantees to the latter its legitimate autonomy in its scientific procedure, coordinating the results to a single end, which is the induction of human beings into knowledge of and intimate life in the mystery of God, who has revealed himself definitively in Christ as Father, Son, and Holy Spirit.

Bibl.: C. COLOMBO, "La metodologia e la sistemazione teologica," in var., *Problemi e orientamenti di Teologia Dogmatica* (Milan, 1957), 1–56; id., *Il compito della teologia* (Milan, 1982); W. KASPER, *Renouveau de la méthode théologique* (Paris, 1968); id., *The Methods of Dogmatic Theology* (Shannon, 1969); R. LATOURELLE, *Theology: Science of Salvation* (Staten Island, N.Y., 1969); B. LONERGAN, *Method in Theology* (New York, 1972); Z. ALSZEGHY and M. FLICK, *Come si fa teologia* (Rome, 1974); J. BEUMER, *Die theologische Methode* (Freiburg, 1977); J. ALFARO, "Theology and the Magisterium," in R. Latourelle and G. O'Collins, *Problems and Perspectives of Fundamental Theology* (New York, 1982), 340–56; W. KERN and J. NIEMANN, *Gnoseologia teologica* (Brescia, 1984); G. POZZO, "Il metodo nella teologia sistematica," in C. ROCCHETTA, R. FISICHELLA and G. POZZO, *La teologia tra rivelazione e storia* (Bologna, 1985), 255–351; J. RATZINGER, *Principles of Catholic Theology* (San Francisco, 1987).

Guido POZZO

II. FUNDAMENTAL THEOLOGY

Descartes in his *Discours sur la méthode* says: "My aim is not to teach the method that each should follow in order to conduct his reasoning to good effect, but only to show how I have tried to conduct mine." This quotation may well stand at the head of an article that in many respects opens onto problems still in the preparatory phase.

Discoursing on method has never been easy. Objective difficulties accompany reflection on its epistemological validity and on the resultant conclusions affecting theology, when compared with other sciences (→ THEOLOGY IV). Even so, discourse on method cannot be passed over. It should indeed be imposed with greater force, above all in the theological present which exhibits a number of ambiguities, whether over the precomprehension of the epistemological status of theology and at the same time over the role and function of the theologian, or over the mutual relationships between the various theological disciplines.

1. The Need for a Discourse on Method

Twenty-five years after the promulgation of
DEI VERBUM (18 November 1965), which marks
the *magna carta* for the renewal of fundamental theology, whereas we may certainly verify
the presence of a new style and new contents
allowing us to outline the identity of the discipline, we must still admit there are not a few
shadowy zones to be researched. One of the
first gaps that immediately come to mind is the
problem of method and of its peculiar nature in
relation to other theological disciplines.

General considerations apart, discourse on
method is all the more essential for fundamental theology since, as theological discipline, it
constitutes an epistemology for the whole
structure of knowledge of the faith. Different
elements converge on this subject, and these
emphasize both the many-sided nature of the
discipline, preventing us from giving it a
preestablished identity, and the plurality of its
contents and referents, obliging us to adopt
various different methodologies.

For a discourse on method in fundamental
theology, which is obviously determined by the
object of our inquiry, the time has come to
assess the twofold importance and function of
this discipline on the theological program
chart.

Starting from the Gazzada International Congress (6–11 September 1964; see the *Transactions*
in var., *Le deuxième symposium international
de théologie dogmatique fondamentale* [Turin,
1965]), one may see that there is consensus
henceforth between fundamental theologians
in regarding fundamental theology as a full
theological discipline in which two complementary requirements converge and are
expressed: the *dogmatic* and the *apologetic*.
The latter does not conflict with the former (and
vice versa): both are expressed rather as necessary *functions* so that the single discipline can
identify itself with the role that pertains to it:
i.e., the presentation of the event of REVELATION
and of its CREDIBILITY.

The object of study for fundamental theology
is therefore unique with regard to both dogmatic and apologetic reflection; but while for
the former we use a method that *investigates*
the content, for the latter *per contra* the
method employed is that of inquiry. With
investigation, we necessarily proceed by the

light of that revelation which we have already
accepted and believe to be the word of God.
With inquiry, however, we give play to the mind
which has not yet caught up with the truth in
which it believes. There is no dichotomy here:
only the acknowledgment of the presence of
the twofold requirement mentioned already,
which is accentuated in fundamental theology
on account of the person for whom it is designed
(→ FUNDAMENTAL THEOLOGY II), not only the
believer but also the "other."

Recognition of the apologetic urgency that a
nonbelieving recipient implies leads to the consideration that at least two elements must be
the direct object of study: (1) The need for a
critical presentation of the act of believing that
can assess the wholeness of the person, expressed
as epistemic subject and believing agent. This
is the phase in which, as regards content, the
act of faith is presented as a fully *free* act and
hence as a deeply human choice. (2) The presentation of the objectivity of the content which
is given by revelation and which hence can be
simply accepted by the subject as a gratuitous
act coming primarily from God.

Put in other terms, fundamental theology as
apologetics is committed to expressing the
evidence of the normative character of revelation, conferred by its own content, through a
gnosiological process favoring comprehension
and the free choice of the act of faith (*DV* 5).

More directly: given the methodological objective, it follows that fundamental theology,
being a *theological* discipline, is fully included
in methodology proper, which regulates knowledge of the faith; hence, in accordance with the
general characteristics leading to *auditus fidei*
and *intellectus fidei*. Insofar as it is a theological discipline but with a special apologetic
dimension, it does, however, need a method of
its own which will describe both the impact
with the analyzed content, and the addressee to
whom this must be conveyed.

a. As concerns the content: Fundamental
theology has as object the event of revelation
and its credibility. Both components, event and
credibility, find the principles within revelation
that set fundamental theology in motion and
make it exist.

Revelation, as historical event culminating in
the singularity and definitiveness of Jesus of
Nazareth, is conceived of as the decision of the

free and gratuitous intervention of God in history. The principle governing its credibility, furthermore, is not external to the event but intrinsic and given with the event itself; it is the very person of Jesus Christ who requires no other testimony than that of the Father (Jn 5:31–32; 8:13–18). This means that the object of inquiry is first and foremost the mystery of God in the dynamism and logic of his self-revelation.

First and foremost, however, this event is given to be known by means of a kenotic act on God's part, which in the mystery of his incarnation assumes the category of *historicity*; but also through the *mediation* of the community of the disciples, which transmits everything the Master has done and said, thus allowing future generations to encounter the Lord (see *DV* 7). To analyze these elements needs a methodology that can go scientifically through the data henceforth in our possession, so as to arrive critically at the truth which we have already accepted in faith.

As regards the dimension of the *historicity* of revelation, the point must be made that this is not like reducing something to a merely historical perspective, as though we were conducting straightforward archaeological research into raw facts. For to speak of historicity entails affirming the attainment of the historical awareness of a subject such as "Jesus of Nazareth" had and expressed about his own person (→ CHRISTOLOGY I). This means seeking to understand how much he revealed about his mission, about the role he fulfilled, about the impressions he left on his contemporaries, and, above all, about his attitude toward his own death. For in this event may be seen to converge the ultimate meaning he attached to his mission and his awareness of being the bearer of a revelation coming from God himself.

To deal with themes like these means approaching the historicity of a person, while knowing we are faced with an event that has all the characteristics qualifying it as *unique*, something that happens in history once and for all, and history itself can verify this. By virtue of the uniqueness and singularity which this person manifested and which cannot be put down to any kind of hyper-enthusiasm on the part of an individual subject, we then approach consideration about the purpose of all history; for he transcends the mere historical horizon, since he is able both to embrace it in its entirety

and to direct it beyond its immediate contingencies.

Historicity inevitably involves the understanding of how this event has come down to us: transmitted and mediated by people who, transformed by the faith, have been determined that the central nucleus of his message and the main features of his person should pass beyond the barriers of space and time, and so become universal.

To put it more plainly, with regard to our discourse on method, there is a clear need for various exegetical methodologies to furnish their own elements, so that the theological construct can be in conformity with and faithful to the original meaning intended by the author. E.g., it will happen that differing systems of linguistic analysis will go into the data of Scripture, of the fathers, of the heritage of tradition and magisterium, to show the relationship between formulation, historical/cultural context, and deeper meaning of the truth that was intended to be conveyed. Historiography with archaeology and the various hermeneutical sciences will have to develop a research technique so that, by means of external testimony, we may with greater objectivity reconstruct the datum furnished by the various narrations, which are conditioned by later, theological preoccupations. In a word, we realize that analysis of this one content encounters some twenty different methodologies which concur in solidifying the principle of *intellectus fidei*.

b. As concerns the addressee: A correct methodology cannot stop short with the content. It must perforce go on to sort out and apply rules to serve for conveying the results. Method is hence also determined by the referent to whom the content is addressed.

We have said already that fundamental theology has two types of addressees: believers and the "others." We have to give the former the *reasons* for what they believe and the latter reasons for at least being able to take the challenge of the faith seriously.

Also within the contours of method and because of these referents, we have to foresee aims and instruments of differing application. For believers, since they have the faith, will have to be trained to investigate its content with a critical intelligence coming primarily from within the act of believing, which as such already involves intellectual activity on the subject's part. For the "others," however, we must show, eventually, that already within the subject's ontological structure, "belief" is a determining component for self-realization, or (and furthermore) that, in believing, a series of "reasons" or "accumulation of possibilities" (Newman) appears, which can make life fully human.

2. Toward a Historical Memory

It must be honestly admitted that until Vatican II fundamental theology had progressively stressed the apologetic dimension, virtually identifying it with controversialist polemics. With disarming candor the manuals of the period show the special importance attributed to the two treatises _De Revelatione_ and _De Ecclesia Christi_. With the former, the authors proposed to legitimize the existence of Christianity as a revealed and hence supernatural religion, having as its founder Jesus Christ, the Messiah. Fulfillment of the ancient promises and Son of God-Christology were reduced to the _De legato divino_ and the analysis of christological titles (→ CHRISTOLOGY III). In the later treatise, the infallible authority of the Catholic church was demonstrated, since, by virtue of its marks, the church was the only legitimate successor to the church founded by Christ.

The apologetic method employed was directed to demonstrating the truth expressed in the thesis. Essentially, manualist theology (→ THEOLOGIES VII) had espoused the deductive method. The language employed betrays this at first glance; the terms "demonstrate" and "prove" play a determining role but are peculiar to this method.

Since reference to Scripture was without a correct hermeneutics and the methodology corresponded essentially to that of the _dicta probantia_, the resultant extrinsic nature of the arguments can be seen today in all its tragic clearness. Miracles and prophecies (taken as _external signs_) or the "marvelous expansion of the church" and the "sublimity of doctrine" (taken as _internal signs_) (in this sense, see the last texts still in the conciliar period by N. Dunas and G. De Broglie) were the objective signs advanced as clear and certain proofs of the supernaturality of revelation, inasmuch as they

were reached on the basis of a rational activity that left faith out of account.

This apologetic method was certainly faithful to the dictates of _Dei Filius_ ("God willed that to the interior helps of the Holy Spirit, there should be joined exterior proofs of His revelation; to wit, divine facts, and especially miracles and prophecies, which, as they manifestly display the omnipotence and infinite knowledge of God, are most certain proofs of His divine revelation, adapted to the intelligence of all men" (trans. C. Butler) (DS 3009), but simultaneously betrayed the full theological importance of the contents analyzed. In a word, a kind of certainty was achieved since, clearly, rational activity was put to work, but the characteristic of "evidence" which was internal to the signs was lacking, since these had essentially lost the referent that gave them meaning, i.e., Jesus of Nazareth.

Without wanting to go into the sort of judgments that an analysis and a major study would deserve, we can, however, detect an unconscious but continuous regression actuated by some schools of theology (we might for instance mention the treatises by Liebermann, Perrone, C. Pesch, Garrigou-Lagrange and Tromp, covering a span of about two centuries), which had lost sight of the original qualities in the intuitions of the fathers and the scholastics. The result was an "objective apologetics" based only on metaphysical arguments and unrelated to the believing subject. The absence of a methodology to show the historicity of the data, or at least of an exegesis to make a better job of contextualizing the contents, ended by laying apologetics open to the various schools of criticism later to be radicalized in modernism.

A careful reading of the apologetic fathers (→ APOLOGISTS) reveals that they were characterized by constant attention to the subject to whom their apologetics vere directed. Even though, of course, their primary concern was to present the _kerygma_ of the paschal mystery in its integrity, they never lost sight of the subject they were addressing. Jews and pagans were urged and prodded toward a direct encounter with the Holy Scriptures and the life of the Christian community; one need only think of Justin's apologies or the _Letter to Diognetus_. Of the same tenor are the writings of Clement of Alexandria, who composed a magnificent exhortation to conversion, the _Protrepticus_, and of

Origen in *Contra Celsum*, where he showed himself absolutely *au fait* with the writings of Celsus and employed a proper apologetic method: knowledge of the works of the person being addressed and an *ars maieutica* to bring out the truth from the very texts that seek to deny it.

Thomas Aquinas himself, seeking to safeguard the wholeness of the human act of believing as far as he could, was the first to distinguish between act of faith and judgment of credibility, based on the authority of the presence of God and of his grace. He does not, however, forget that the believer also needs elements to safeguard the humanity of his act for him: "non enim crederet nisi videret ea esse credenda vel propter evidentiam signorum sed propter aliquid huiusmodi" ("He would believe only what he sees he has to believe because of the conspicuousness of the signs [miracles] or something of the kind") (*ST* 2.2, q. 1 a.4). As the persons being addressed are different in different centuries, we witness the selection of new contents for discussion with a resultant modification of structure and method in apologetics. Deists, proponents of the Enlightenment, and rationalists in general were to be the addressees of the fundamental theologies of the sixteenth to eighteenth centuries; atheists and Marxists would be the targets for the nineteenth to twentieth. The common matrix for most of the treatises is essentially the defense of the supernaturality of revelation; the method adopted for the most part is the polemical/controversial one.

The various methodologies adopted, from that of "providence" by Deschamps to that of "authority" by Brunetière, from the more "psychological" one (following in the steps of Pascal) by Ollé-Laprune to the "historical" one by De Broglie, must all be given their due. Even so, it has to be recognized that they got farther and farther away from a *theological* motivation without realizing the serious dangers they were courting: on the one hand, they made a complete separation between faith and reason, falling pitifully into the pitfall devised by the Enlightenment, inasmuch as the credibility of the content of the faith was entrusted to proofs and signs reached by reason alone; on the other, getting farther and farther away from the one true content of revelation, the person of Jesus of Nazareth, they accentuated by turns either ecclesiocentrism (to the detriment of Christocentrism) or the subjectivism of individual experience (to the detriment of the objectivity and universality of the content).

In conclusion, it must be pointed out, there have been certain methodologies, their differing aims *notwithstanding*, which only today can be appreciated for their remarkable originality. PASCAL's apologetics or Simon's exegesis, DREY's historical research with the school of Tübingen, NEWMAN's *Grammar of Assent* and BLONDEL's *L'Action* caused sensations and polemics but had little or no impact on the theological methodology of their day.

3. Method of Integration

The effort directed during recent years toward presenting a renewed image of fundamental theology must not fail to devote itself with equal vigor also to the problems of method. The method of *immanence* in Blondel's interpretation, the *transcendental* in Rahner's project, the *psychological* one in Newman's attempt, or that of *correlation* advanced by Tillich, all play a significant role in this context as different and complementary methodologies to offer an apologetic interpretation of revelation. To dissipate our energies in these various methodologies, however, could cause a further fragmentation of the discipline, canceling out the results already gained. It therefore seems a matter of urgency to identify the route by which fundamental theology, as an individual theological discipline concerned with apologetics, can arrive at a method proper and peculiar to itself which, without absolutizing any one methodology, may instead contrive to amalgamate them all in a vision more homogeneous and consistent with its special nature.

The method of *integration* can be advanced as a possible solution.

By method of integration we mean to refer above all to the semantic meaning of the term. For "integration" indicates the possibility of making whole that which is not yet so by supplying needful and useful elements. With the method of integration, fundamental theology is equipped to deal within the mystery (which has already been theologically investigated) with the historical event which reveals it and which a community transmits by mediating it, and which therefore needs to be studied by a method of its own.

Integration within the mystery does not

debase the historical event inasmuch as the mystery—even though by virtue of a kenotic act—has made itself knowable by expressing itself in history and cannot be separated from the said historical structure if it is to speak to humanity and by humanity be grasped and accepted. So we have integration: hence an activity constituting a "going beyond" (*Aufhebung*, though not in the Hegelian sense) by which nothing that is given gets neglected nor dialectically absorbed, but is put as a whole into a more meaningful context.

The special object, therefore, continues to be expressing the faith, but in an intellectual form which, starting out from the faith, can take on board all critical instruments.

Given the primary choice of fundamental theology's precomprehension as "theology," it is obvious that the *dogmatic* (hence internal to the faith) dimension comes before the *apologetic* one of spreading and acquiring a knowledge external to the faith. This is, of course, not so as to preclude development or apologetic presentation, which by its nature has to seek for gnosiological forms and means by which the better to guarantee the universality of the datum; but rather, so as to give the totality of the datum, since this always remains a specific object of faith.

To take an example: Were miracles, prophecies, or signs of the times taken as eventual reasons for credibility, to be emptied of their original revelatory dimension (their intrinsic dependence on the person of Jesus of Nazareth, the revealer of the Father) which makes them primarily signs of God's presence and testimony of his love, what would they have to offer the believer and the "other" except sterile "signifiers" with no possible reference to their deeper "signified"?

By means of the method of integration, however, we may conclude that these retain their theological importance, since they are referred to the centrality of the mystery. Yet they are analyzed and studied with various methodologies (exegetic, historical, and so on) which guarantee their importance as signs. Only by integration in the theological interpretation, however, shall we be able to have an overall sight of the phenomenon, simultaneously guaranteeing the requirement of safeguarding the transcendency of God and the rationality and freedom of the subject.

By means of the method of integration, the addressee too will be fully respected. With the classic text "Always be ready to make your defense to anyone who questions (NRSV, "demands from") you an accounting for the hope that is in you" (1 Pt 3:15) as our starting point, we find two criteria that emerge relating to method: universality and questionability.

According to this text, believers ought to be prepared to give an account of their faith to "anyone," i.e., to one and all without exception. This means that fundamental theology must constantly be weighing up individual historical subjects, burdened with all the notions of the age. For these, analyses must be found that can mediate the original significance of the revealed content, but in such a way as to have an impact on each individual, so that revealed mystery finds answering resonance in individual history.

The text of the letter goes on to say "anyone who *questions* you" about your Christian hope. This means to say that fundamental theology must stay, with every means at its command, in that state of attention, of expectation, and of "questioning," so as not to evade any stirring that may eventually occur in the "other." This situation, on the one hand, obliges fundamental theology to be vigilant and, on the other, stimulates it itself to provoke questioning, so that, maieutically, each individual may discover a yearning for God and an understanding of his mystery. This involves being able to relate to those various disciplines better equipped scientifically to deal with social and cultural changes.

We may recognize that in this way fundamental theology shares in an altogether special manner in forming a theological *systematics*. For by this method, the datum produced, e.g., by historical-critical analysis, does not appear as an absolute and hence as a potential yielding to the thesis of an objective knowledge exclusive of rationality or, as later in the linguistic analyses, merely as a "control"; since this is actually *integrated* into that theological system which draws from the object itself the method with which to investigate it. In this context, however, systematic theological knowledge is guaranteed by a plurality of forms and methodologies which later show the all-embracing nature of the object of theology and the impossibility of reducing it to a "system" albeit a "theological" one.

Discourse on method cannot be reduced to a sterile array of instruments or techniques, such as a science or discipline may give itself to justify its own researches.

Method indicates much more, since it has the potentiality of accompanying truth itself in its progressive self-revelation to the epistemic subject. Method guides toward the true interpretation that fundamental theology puts on events by the light of the Event. This is why we must not be afraid to adopt a kenotic form, which sets out from the certainty of faith, takes on the forms of critical knowledge, and with these investigates the intelligence of that which it already knows to be true, so as to acquire a more complete and more humanly meaningful vision of the mystery.

Bibl.: G. DE BROGLIE, *Les Propheties Messianiques* (Paris, 1910); M. GRABMANN, *Die Geschichte der scholastischen Methode*, vol. 1 (Berlin, 1957); A. GABOARDI, "Theologia Fondamentale: Il metodo apologetico," in var., *Problemi e orientamenti di Teologia fondamentale* (Milan, 1957), 56–103; M. D. CHENU, *La théologie comme science au XIIIe siècle* (Paris, 1957); N. DUNAS, *Connaissance de la Foi* (Paris, 1963); G. DE BROGLIE, *Les signes de crédibilité de la Révélation chrétienne* (Paris, 1964); Y. CONGAR, *La Foi et la Théologie* (Paris, 1962); A. LANG, *Die theologische Prinzipienlehre der mittelalterlichen Scholastik* (Freiburg, 1964); R. LATOURELLE, "Apologétique et Fondamentale," in var., *Le deuxième symposium international de théologie dogmatique fondamentale* (Turin, 1965), 9–27; id., "Apologétique et Fondamentale. Problème de nature et de méthode," *Sal* 28 (1965): 256–73; id., *Theology: Science of Salvation* (Staten Island, N.Y., 1969); id., "A New Image of Fundamental Theology," in R. Latourelle and G. O'Collins, eds., *Problems and Perspectives of Fundamental Theology* (New York, 1982), 77–93; id., "Absence and Presence of Fundamental Theology at Vatican II," in R. Latourelle, ed., *Vatican II: Assessment and Perspectives Twenty-five Years After*, 3 vols. (New York, 1989), 3:378–416; W. KASPER, *Die Methoden der Dogmatik* (Munich, 1967); id., "Die Wissenschaftspraxis der Theologie," *HFT* 4:242–76; B. LONERGAN, *Method in Theology* (New York, 1972); E. SCHILLEBEECKX, *The Understanding of Faith* (London, 1974); J. BEUMER, *Die theologische Methode* (Freiburg, 1977); K. LEHMANN, "Apologetik und Fundamentaltheologie," *Comm* 7 (1978): 289–94; G. POZZO, "Il metodo nella teologia sistematica," in C. ROCCHETTA, R. FISICHELLA, and G. POZZO, eds., *La teologia tra rivelazione e storia* (Bologna, 1985), 255–347; R. FISICHELLA, *La rivelazione: evento et credibilità* (Bologna, 1985); id., "Metodo in Teologia Fondamentale," *Ricerche Teologiche* 1 (1990); D. TRACY, *Plurality and Ambiguity* (London, 1987), 28–46; R. LATOURELLE, "Spécificité de la théologie fondamentale," in J.-P. Jossua and N.-J. Sed, eds., *Interpréter: Hommage amical á Claude Geffré* (Paris, 1992), 103–22.

Rino FISICHELLA

MIRACLE

1. Problems of Approach. 2. Problems of Pre-understanding. 3. Historical Authenticity of the Miracles of Jesus. 4. Classification and Typology of the Miracle Stories. 5. Perspective of Each Evangelist. 6. Originality and Purpose of the Miracles of Jesus. 7. Catholic Idea of Miracle. 8. Definition of a Miracle. 9. Sign Values and Functions of Miracles. 10. Recognition of Miracles. 11. The Human Response to Miracles.

The only possible point of reference for thinking about miracles is the miracles of Jesus, i.e., the *foundational* signs of Christianity. Apart from Christ and salvation, miracles have no meaning. We must begin therefore with "the one who explains" and not with "that which is explained." The miracles of Jesus are the archetypes of all real miracles and the key to the intelligibility of these others, especially those connected with shrines and with causes of canonization. His are miracles at their source and within the setting that produces them; they are the signs that manifest the great presence among us of the living and thrice holy God. That is why in this article the theology of miracle is supported by the miracles of Jesus (historicity and purpose). This theology is preceded, however, by thoughts on problems of approach and pre-understanding, which are especially important in dealing with miracles.

1. Problems of Approach

In theology, as in the other sciences, questions of approach often play a determining role. The approach chosen may lead to impasses or irrepressible resistances, or on the contrary it may render the listener well disposed and promote understanding of the arguments offered. In recent decades theology has seen two changes of approach important enough to justify speaking of them as revolutionary: I am referring to the anthropological approach and the christological approach. This change of perspective has affected the theology of the signs of revelation and, in particular, the theology of miracles.

The present-day theology of miracles is characterized by a concern to connect it with the person of Christ. Between the nineteenth century and the second half of the twentieth, there was a shift in perspective from the object to the subject or person. Before Vatican II the signs on which emphasis was laid were the miracles and prophecies of Christ, the prophets, and the apostles. Miracles and prophecies were directly linked with the Christian message and indirectly with Christ, the author of that message. In a synthesis that was not entirely free of rhetoric but that was also not without a certain grandeur, the encyclical *QUI PLURIBUS* of Pius IX (1846) listed the "wonderful . . . lucid . . . arguments" showing that "the Christian faith is God's work" (DS 2779; ND 110). At Vatican I (DS 3034; ND 128) and in the anti-modernist oath (DS 3539), miracles and prophecies served as solid proof of "the divine origin of the Christian religion." The encyclical *Humani Generis* of 1950 repeated that "we are provided by God with such a wealth of wonderful exterior signs by which the divine origin of the Christian religion can be proved with certainty" (DS 2876; ND 146). In all of these texts the function of the signs is to *attest:* they enable us to establish with certainty the divine origin of the teaching on salvation. There is a clearly defined link between the Christian message and its divine origin.

Vatican II brought a change of perspective. Just as it personalized revelation, so it *personalized* its presentation of the signs of revelation. The latter are not detached entities accompanying the message of Christ like a passport or an ambassador's seal guaranteeing the authenticity of a letter. On the contrary, Christ is the fullness of revelation and is in his person the sign that authenticates his own revelation: he is the sign that *manifests* God by his entrance into history, flesh, and language, and at the same time the sign that bears *witness* to itself as God-among-us. "Jesus perfected revelation by fulfilling it through His whole work of making Himself present and manifesting Himself: through His words and deeds, His signs and wonders. . . . He confirmed with divine testimony what revelation proclaimed: that God is with us" (*DV* 4; ND 151).

The signs flow from the personal Center that is Christ himself. They are the multiform expression of the Son's epiphany in the midst of humankind. It is through his humanity that Christ reveals the Father; it is also by means of the incarnation that other human beings identify Christ as the Son of the Father. In the whole of his being, Christ is an enigmatic sign that calls for decipherment.

In the context of this return to a personalist and christocentric approach, it seems clear that an authentic theology of signs must center on the fundamental signs that contain all the others, namely, Christ and the church. A presentation of the signs that would disconnect them from their source, from their center, which is Christ, or would reduce their value to that of a juridical argument would be alien to the perspectives of the council and still more to those of the Scriptures.

2. Problems of Pre-understanding

The chief difficulty people face in studying the question of miracle, including the miracles of Jesus, has to do with the very idea of miracle, which they tend to reject before any examination of the facts offered for study. In the area of miracles more than anywhere else, "the die is cast" from the outset. Miracle stories, it is said, belong to another age, another mentality. To accept them as historical would be to display a naïveté as dismaying as it is anachronistic. We no longer believe in miracles, any more than we believe in fairies or ghosts. What is at issue, then, is the very possibility of a miracle in a self-sufficient universe.

The fact is that readers, believing or unbelieving, of the Gospel stories always read them with a certain *pre-understanding* or prior knowledge of God, humanity, and the universe; i.e., they read with *pre*-suppositions. This pre-understanding can be enriched and even altered and revised through contact with the facts. It can also harden and close in on itself, thus becoming a *pre*judgment, a blunt refusal. One thing is certain: all, be they believers or unbelievers, must make explicit the principles that guide their thinking. This is a minimum requirement for avoiding misunderstandings.

Most of the difficulties alleged by rationalists against miracles ever since the eighteenth century are based on the findings of sciences. On this basis rationalism asserts miracles to be either impossible or out of place. Any phenomenon said to be "miraculous" has a natural explanation that only needs to be discovered: drugs, credulity, suggestion, hypnosis, illusion, unknown forces. The history of religions is then brought to bear to confirm this hypothesis.

In the Name of Science as Interpreted by Philosophical Reason

At the beginning of the nineteenth century, Pierre Bayle devoted himself to showing the ridiculousness of belief in miracles. Miracles, he said, are contrary to reason, for there is nothing worthier of God's own greatness than for him to enforce the laws which he himself has established; nothing is less worthy of him than the belief that he intervenes to prevent the action of these laws. Baruch Spinoza in his *Theologico-Political Treatise* was the first theoretician of this position, which was to be repeated over and over after him. To say that something is contrary to nature is to deny the existence of an immutable God. "It is plain," says Spinoza, "that all the events narrated in Scripture came to pass naturally . . . like everything else, according to natural laws." "Miracles appear as something new only because of man's ignorance." David Hume (1711–1776) speaks of miracles in the tenth essay of his *Enquiry concerning Human Understanding*, which was published in 1748. The only foundation of our certainties, he says, can be the experience of our senses. This experience, however, shows that the laws of nature operate in a constant manner. Consequently, if someone claims that a miracle has occurred, we must reject their testimony, since "a miracle is a violation of the laws of nature; and as a firm and unalterable experience has established these laws, the proof against a miracle, from the very nature of the fact, is as entire as any argument from experience can possibly be imagined." In his *Philosophical Dictionary*, Voltaire takes Spinoza a step further. He regards a miracle as a contradiction in terms. God (people say)

might unsettle his machine, but only to make it go better; however, it is clear that, being God, he made this immense machine as best he could; if he had seen some imperfection resulting from the nature of the material, he would have attended to that in the beginning; so he will never change anything in it.

It is unworthy of God to imagine that he performs miracles for the sake of human beings, "To dare palm off miracles on God is really to insult him (if men can insult God); it's to tell him: 'You are a weak and inconsistent being.' It is therefore absurd to believe in miracles — in one way or another it dishonors Divinity." R. BULTMANN, who was heir to eighteenth- and nineteenth-century rationalism, gives a philosophical interpretation of the scientific mentality of our age and asserts that miracles are unintelligible in a world controlled by science. A distinction must be made, he says, between *Mirakel* and *Wunder*. A *Mirakel* is thought of as an exception to the laws of nature. "The idea of wonder as miracle [*Mirakel*] has become almost impossible for us today, because we understand the processes of nature as governed by law." For us, nature's "conformity to law" is the implicit or explicit basis of all our activity in the world. But while faith has no interest in *Mirakel*, which is a break in the determinism of natural law, it has a lively interest in *Wunder*, i.e., an event (*Weltgeschehen*) which obeys universal laws but in which I see an action of God (*Gottes Tat*). There is in fact "only one wonder [*Wunder*]: the wonder of the *revelation*, the revelation of the grace of God for the godless." A *Wunder* is an event in which faith, and faith alone, recognizes God revealing himself. Nothing has changed in the phenomenal order or in the web of laws. It is faith alone that sees in a natural healing a revelation of God's love to a human being who acknowledges himself or herself to be sinful and forgiven.

In the face of rationalism the apologetics of the period found itself in a bad position, for, by defining a miracle as a "breach of the laws of nature" and stripping it of its essential function as *sign of salvation in Jesus Christ*, the apologetes imprisoned themselves in the very universe from which they were claiming to escape. This caricature of miracles as "exceptions to the laws of nature" ended up being accepted by Christians, with the result that they came to regard as unseemly and even improper such a "break-in" by God into a universe that has its own intrinsic intelligibility. To allow miracles is to allow the intelligible and the unintelligible to coexist.

It is certainly hopeless to try to modify the rationalist position, especially if it claims to be exclusive and incapable of revision. Theologians can, however, place miracles in their proper context, which is salvation, and try to define them better. Above all, they must make known their own pre-understanding of the world, without trying to force it on others who refuse to share it. It is possible to line up the elements of this vision as follows.

a. It is true that the material universe becomes intelligible through its habitual submission to the laws of the universe, although a good number of these laws are statistical. On the other hand, reality in its entirety is not one-dimensional; i.e., it is not reducible to the material world and its network of inflexible laws. Reality as a whole is comparable rather to a pyramidal order in which no part is completely autonomous but all parts together form an organic whole that is ordered toward a summit which transcends the activity connaturally possible for each part. There is a hierarchy of intersubordinated orders: the order of the inorganic in which determinism reigns; the order of the organic with its finalities; the order of thought and art with its creativity; the order of religious and moral life with its freedom. In this hierarchy each lower order is ordered to the next higher order and thus integrated into the total order. The subhuman universe is ordered to human beings, and these in turn are open to the transcendent action of God. Miracles liberate the physical universe from its "limitations," elevate it, and enable it to play a part in the higher order of salvation. On the one hand, then, it is completely legitimate for the physical universe to derive its *habitual meaning* from the determinism of its laws; on the other, it is no less intelligible that God should, as first Cause and by a completely unmerited intervention in history and the universe, manifest his still more unmerited intervention in giving salvation through Jesus Christ. Miracles thus become traces and signs, in the visible universe, of the grace of salvation. They have their place in the religious order where God calls human beings to share his life.

b. Furthermore, if it is true that Christ, the incarnate Word, is the summit and goal of salvation, then miracles are to be seen as interventions of God in the time between the first creation and the final transformation of everything and everyone in Jesus Christ. Miracles are therefore an anticipation of the eschatological order with its new heavens and new earth: they are the future invading the present and giving it its meaning, for they manifest the transforming *dynamis* of God already at work in our world. The glorified body of Christ is a permanent miracle. In him the human race is re-created, and therefore the universe itself experiences the beneficent effects of this re-creation. In this perspective, which is that of Paul (Rom 8:19–21), miracles are not a problem; rather they force human beings to ask themselves what the ultimate meaning of history and the universe is. Paradoxically, it is miracles that become intelligible and explanatory.

c. Miracles can be perceived only by those who see the world as controlled and directed by a free and transcendent Being who acts at his own level as a creative and re-creative power and can establish interpersonal relations with human beings. A miracle, like revelation, is a call addressed to men and women in the depths of their being, at that level of interiority at which, as spiritual persons, they are open to God and his possible self-manifestation in history and in the world. A miracle supposes that human beings honestly acknowledge the finiteness of their existence and of their condition as beings "in need of salvation," as well as God's freedom to act in history and initiate an unparalleled dialogue with them. God's freedom is not exhausted by his creative act, as if it were a spring that dries up after its first outstreaming. God is infinite freedom, and his gratuitous initiatives are unpredictable and inexhaustible.

d. It is because of God's unpredictable love and infinite freedom that he decided to reveal himself to the human race and to save it through the incarnation and the cross, i.e., through what is most unlike himself, who is pure Spirit, namely, through the flesh, and that he also decided to continue this incarnational economy in an economy of signs that bear witness to the efficacious presence of salvation in our midst. Far from talking nonsense, those who locate miracles within this economy of salvation and freedom see in the divine action a *constellation of harmonies:* harmony of the signs with the intervention of God made flesh;

harmony of the signs themselves with one another; harmony of the signs with the human person who is made up of flesh and spirit. The miracles of Jesus have their place in the higher logic of love and salvation.

In the Name of the History of Religions

The historians of religion take over from the philosophers in explaining the presence of miracle stories in the Gospels. Undoubtedly (they say), preaching in a Hellenistic environment was responsible for clothing Jesus the prophet with the attributes of a Greek god, so that he came to be called Son of God, Savior, Lord. For propaganda purposes Jesus the miracle worker was described as the "divine man" (theios anēr) familiar to the Hellenistic world. The principal proponents of this theory are R. Reitzenstein, H. Windisch, L. Bieler, D. Georgi, and R. Bultmann. The truth is that after the recent books of D. L. Tiede and C. H. Holladay this theory is destined for oblivion. The sense of God's absolute transcendence was too highly developed on Jewish soil to allow for the attribution of divinity to human beings. The category "divine man" is absent from the OT and the NT alike. In addition, the technical sense given to "divine man" appears late in Hellenism, well after the time of Jesus.

In the Name of a Demythologizing Hermeneutic

Having observed the similarities between the literary structure of the Gospel miracle stories and the stories of wonders attributed to Apollonius of Tyana or the healer god Asclepius at Epidauros, the form critics, Bultmann chief among them, concluded that both are fables or legends. They make an invalid jump from a literary similarity to a value judgment on historical content. After all, from the literary point of view nothing more closely resembles a true account of an exceptional healing than a fictitious account. The most important factor in the case of Jesus is that the person who is at the center of the story is unprecedented in history and that the miracle itself has specific traits that are completely without parallel. The analysis of literary forms is not an infallible guide in making judgments about historicity.

Are the miracle stories of the Gospels to be eliminated because they are fictitious? Bult-

mann, for his part, thinks we must keep them but "demythologize" them and interpret them existentially. The important thing, in his view, is not the historical reality behind the story (this is often impossible to uncover or is simply nonexistent) but the meaning it contains, namely, that faith purifies, gives life, raises from the dead, and saves sinful but forgiven human beings. The tools of hermeneutic thus enable us to save the story while sacrificing the event. The miracle stories make it clear that revelation is food, light, and life.

All these attempts to withdraw miracles from their religious context and hail them before the judgment seat of philosophy and science have as their effect to distort the profound nature of miracles. Their reduction to "exceptions to the laws of nature" is a caricature. Miracles have meaning only in the one context in which, *as a matter of fact*, they appear, namely, the revelation of salvation in Jesus Christ.

3. Historical Authenticity of the Miracles of Jesus

If it is to be faithful to the nature of the gospel tradition and to the history of this tradition's formation, a study of the historical value of the miracle stories has no choice but to traverse the following stages:

(1) First of all, the historical value of the Synoptic tradition as a whole must be established.

(2) Second, it is important to analyze two logia of the *Quelle* in which Jesus himself explains the reality and meaning of his miracles.

a. In the first of these two logia Jesus takes formal note of his rejection by the three lake towns, which have not been able to recognize in his healings the signs of the coming of God's kingdom (Mt 11:20–24; Lk 10:13–15). Chorazin, Bethsaida, and Capernaum are privileged towns, being the first to witness and benefit from the activity of Jesus. Yet they have not understood the meaning of the works Jesus does. Their fate will therefore be worse than that of towns traditionally regarded as wicked (Tyre and Sidon) and sinful (Sodom). The *meaning* of the miracles of Jesus is obvious. Along with his preaching on the necessity of conversion in order to enter the kingdom, his miracles are overtures by God, calls to repentance and conversion in the face of the imminent coming of the reign of God. The inhabitants of the three towns have seen the wonders but have been unable to recognize in them the *signs* of the kingdom that the prophets had foretold. And yet the miracles are God's reign made visible, with its power to transform human beings totally.

b. The second logion, which is likewise taken from the *Quelle*, is the reply Jesus gives to the delegates from John the Baptist when they ask him to state his real identity: "Are you the one who is to come, or are we to wait for another?" Jesus answers them: "Go and tell John what you hear and see: the blind receive their sight and the lame walk, the lepers are cleansed, the deaf hear, the dead are raised, and the poor have good news brought to them. And blessed is anyone who takes no offense at me" (Mt 11:2–6; Lk 7:18–23). From the historical point of view, the passage is in an excellent position. The criteria of discontinuity and continuity or consistency can be applied in an exemplary way. The logion of Jesus contrasts with the Jewish mentality of the time and with the Baptist's conception of the Messiah; it also contrasts with the mentality of the early church, which emphasized the resurrection of Jesus rather than his miracles. The criterion of continuity also applies, since the logion is consistent with the teaching of Jesus on the central subject of his preaching, namely, the kingdom and the signs of the kingdom. It is consistent also with the theme that the preaching of the good news to the poor (in the parables and Beatitudes) is the radical sign of the coming of the kingdom; it is consistent, finally, with the style of Jesus, his habitual way of answering the sensitive question of his messiahship. He not only answers, but his answer goes well beyond the Baptist's question about the fact of his messiahship, since he describes God's reign as a reign of compassion, forgiveness, and grace. For the moment, Jesus embodies the coming of God's *agapē* into our world; judgment will come later on.

In these two logia, which belong to a very old tradition, Jesus connects his miracles with the coming of the kingdom he inaugurates in his person. His miracles are never prodigies for their own sake but are calls to conversion and repentance as indispensable conditions for entering the kingdom. The miracles are signs and at the same time works of Christ.

(3) Third, we can collect a number of pieces of evidence *pointing to the overall historical character* of the miracle tradition as a whole. These pointers derive their weight from their number and their presence at every point in both the Synoptic and the Johannine traditions.

A first fact is the important place occupied by miracle stories in our Gospels. In the Gospel of Mark, they occupy 31 percent of the text, or 209 verses out of 666. In the first ten chapters, which are devoted to the public ministry of Jesus (exclusive of the passion), the proportion becomes 47 percent (209 verses out of 405). In the Gospel of John, the first twelve chapters, which C. H. Dodd calls the "Book of Signs," are developed on the basis of the miracles of Jesus. In the Synoptics as in John miracles and preaching form an indissoluble whole, for both point to one and the same reality, namely, the coming of the reign of God. A good many stories emphasize the public character of the miracles and, consequently, the possibility of challenging their factuality at the time when the evangelical tradition was taking shape. The enemies of Jesus do not deny his thaumaturgic activity (enlightening in this regard is the very old passage on Beelzebul: Mt 12:26–27), but rather the source of this activity and the authority he claimed for himself on the basis of it. Finally, a passage in the Babylonian Talmud claims that Jesus was put to death for having practiced sorcery and led Israel into apostasy (*Sanhedrin* 43a). If the miracles occupy a place in the Gospels that is comparable in its extent only to the teaching of Jesus and to his passion, and if the early preaching and the evangelists themselves have as it were a "fixation" on the subject of miracles and connect them with the preaching of Jesus, to the point that neither makes sense without the other, then something extremely important must have happened which is worth examining in order to test its consistency.

(4) Fourth, turning to a stricter criteriology, we can apply to the miracle stories *criteria of authenticity* that are used in general history, while also taking into account that the Gospels are a "special case."

a. Criterion of multiple attestation. This criterion enables us to establish that the reality of the miracles of Jesus is attested in almost all the sources we have: Mark, the *Quelle*, Luke, Matthew, John, Acts, Letter to the Hebrews, the talmudic tradition, and the Apocrypha. Not only does the theme of miracles appear in the sources just listed; it is found also in the most varied literary genres: summaries, discourses, controversies.

b. Criterion of discontinuity. The fact that Jesus works miracles in his own name contrasts with the attitude of the prophets, who work miracles in the name of God, and with that of the apostles, who act in the name of Jesus. Furthermore, in some instances Jesus gives his miracles a meaning that goes against the Jewish mentality of the time, e.g., in the cure of the leper (Mk 1:40–41). In the time of Jesus the rabbis considered leprosy to be a specific punishment for certain sins. Lepers were judged to be people whom God was punishing, unclean people who were therefore excluded from the Temple and the community of Israel. Unlike the rabbis, Jesus does not avoid lepers; on the contrary, "moved with pity," he stretches out his hand to a leper to show that he is taking him under his protection; he touches him and says: "I will it; be clean." The attitude of Jesus to lepers, like his attitude to sinners, represents a break with the Judaism of his age. In the kingdom of God there are neither lepers nor healthy people but simply children of the Father.

c. Criterion of conformity or continuity with the basic teaching of Jesus on the definitive coming of the reign of God. The miracles are in fact inseparable from the theme of the inauguration of the kingdom: they manifest its coming and true nature. They are a sign of the kingdom and a component part of it. For the kingdom is not something static, but a dynamic reality that effectively changes the human condition and establishes the lordship of Christ over all things, including bodies and the cosmos. A miracle unaccompanied by an exhortation to acknowledge the coming kingdom and the person who has come to establish it is meaningless, an inexplicable event and nothing more. This is why when Christ works a miracle he also exhorts to conversion and to faith in his mission. This linking of inexplicable event with interior conversion is a unique phenomenon associated with the presence of Christ (Mt 11:20–24; Lk 10:13–15).

d. The style of the miracle stories. We find one and the same style in the miracles and in the teaching of Jesus, a style marked by simplicity, restraint, and authority, and this in a religious context characterized by exceptional purity and elevation. This style contrasts with that of the apocrypha and their thirst for the marvelous. If Gnosticism betrayed the gospel by reducing it to a doctrine, the apocrypha for their part betrayed it by looking to it solely for inexplicable events.

e. Internal intelligibility of the stories. Thus the fact of the resurrection of Lazarus, which is consistent with other stories of raisings from the dead in Mark and Luke and with the major fact of Jesus' own resurrection, is also perfectly consistent with its overall context, i.e., the Fourth Gospel as a whole, and especially with chaps. 5, 11, and 12. Furthermore, it sheds light on two important facts of the life of Jesus, namely, the decision of the Jewish authorities to do away with him, and the solemn entrance of Jesus into Jerusalem, which is attested by the three Synoptic Gospels. Only John's Gospel, however, sheds complete light on the event and gives a truly satisfactory explanation of it. John alone tells us: "The crowd that had been with him when he called Lazarus out of the tomb and raised him from the dead continued to testify. It was also because they heard that he had performed this sign that the crowd went to meet him" (Jn 12:17–18).

f. Divergent interpretations, substantial agreement. Substantial agreement of facts in the midst of redactional differences and even differences of interpretation is a solid indication of historicity. History and law constantly rely on this type of argument. Thus, in narrating the multiplication of the loaves John emphasizes more than Mark does the sacramental significance of the miracle. Mark, in his turn, emphasizes more than Luke does the christological significance of the miracle and shows Christ as the Good Shepherd who has compassion on these "sheep without a shepherd" (Mk 6:34). The Gospel of John provides many details peculiar to it. This substantial agreement amid differences of detail is backed by the criterion of multiple attestation, since the fact is attested by the six recensions of the Synoptic and Johannine traditions. Moreover, the event is depicted as a sign of the messianic and eschatological kingdom, in connection with the sign of the manna in the wilderness. Finally, if the event was not real, many facts remain unexplained.

g. The criterion of necessary explanation. This is an application of the principle of sufficient reason to the case of the Gospels. In the case of the miracles we find ourselves confronted with ten or so important facts which the critics can hardly dispute and which call for an adequate explanation: the popular excitement roused by the appearance of Jesus; the faith of the apostles in his messiahship; the place of the miracles in the Synoptic and Johannine traditions; the hatred of the high priests and the Pharisees because of the wonders worked by Jesus; the constant connection between the miracles and the message of Jesus on the definitive coming of the kingdom; the place of the miracles in the primitive kerygma; the presence of other signs given by Jesus that are on the same level and of the same quality (the profundity of a message that can decipher the human condition; the matchless love revealed by his life, suffering, and death; his glorious resurrection; the centuries-long activity of the church); the close connection between the claim of Jesus to be the Son of God and the miracles that show his dominion over sickness, sin, and death.

The fact that each of the criteria of historical authenticity used by historians generally and more recently by exegetes applies in a remarkable way to the miracles stories is a proof of historical reliability that is difficult to refute. Refutation is all the more difficult because the criteria *converge.* Few of the logia of Jesus are as well situated from the viewpoint of historical authenticity.

(5) Fifth, and lastly, we can examine the miracle stories one by one and test their historical coherence. This final task cannot be carried out in the limited space offered by this dictionary; I have undertaken it in my book *The Miracles of Jesus and the Theology of Miracles* (New York/Mahwah, 1988).

4. Classification and Typology of the Miracle Stories

Various aproaches have been taken to the classification of miracles. A classical distinction is between miracles performed on persons (healings, exorcisms, raisings from the dead) and miracles performed on the natural elements (sea, wind, bread, wine, fishes). This division is debatable, however, since in the final analysis miracles always have to do with persons. G. Theissen has proposed a classification that takes into account the nature of the relationship established between the wonder-worker and the beneficiary of the miracle, as well as the motives for the miracle. I adopt this classification with one exception.

a. Exorcisms. In the eyes of Jesus the deliverance of possessed persons is as important as the healing of the sick. These two liberating activities point to the same thing: the coming of the reign of God. On the other hand, since the mind of the time liked to attribute both sickness and sin to Satan, the distinction between an exorcism and a simple healing is not always made. In the typology of miracles I reserve the term exorcism for cases in which the demon is the wonder-worker's antagonist. These stories (there are six of them) share three characteristics: (1) The possessed persons are alienated from themselves; they lose the power of personal decision. (2) The wonder-worker's adversary is not the possessed persons but the demon, the former being only victim, only the terrain as it were on which the battle is fought. (3) Christ is dealing not with human beings but with the dark personal power that is Satan, whose kingdom he has come to destroy.

b. Healings. Healings are likewise related to the kingdom, but not as directly as exorcisms. Faith here plays a mediating role in relation to the power Jesus exercises of establishing the kingdom. The reason for the difference is readily explained. In the case of possessed persons, who are alienated from themselves and passive, there can be no call for faith. The situation is different for the sick, who enter into a direct relationship with the person of Jesus through faith. Three ways of expressing this faith can be distinguished: faith in the healing power of Jesus; an acclamation of faith following upon the miracle, especially in Luke; and faith that is identical with the conversion Jesus looks for as a response to his miracles (logion reproaching the lake towns).

c. Accreditation miracles. These miracles serve as justification for the behavior of Jesus and, at the same time, as criticism of a Pharisaic mentality that cannot see beyond the letter of juridical regulations. Consequently, these stories of healings all have controversy for their setting (Mt 12:14; Lk 14:13–17; Lk 14:1–6; Mk 1:40–45). All these healings have for their purpose to justify the merciful behavior of Jesus in the face of human narrow-mindedness and Pharisaic legalism. Their effect is to enkindle against him the hatred of the those in power and, in the end, to bring him to death.

d. Miraculous rescues and miraculous gifts. In these two types of miracles Jesus takes the initiative. In miraculous gifts he intervenes to the benefit of a crowd that has nothing to eat (Mk 6:36), invited guests who have no more wine (Jn 2:3), and fishermen who have caught nothing (Lk 5:5). The event is reported with very great restraint. Only the result is mentioned: hunger of the crowd satisfied, nets filled, abundant wine. Miraculous rescues have an even more dramatic setting (e.g., the stilling of the storm). In addition to their christological significance, these miracles also have an ecclesial bearing. Thus by stilling the storm Jesus protects his little flock against all storms. These miracles point to the new community of the saved that is gathered around Jesus.

e. Stories of raisings from the dead. Some authors (e.g., X. Léon-Dufour, G. Theissen) prefer to speak of "re-animation" or "bringing back to life" rather than "resurrection" or raising from the dead. It is of course legitimate to look for a vocabulary that is accurate and faithful to the reality conveyed. Those who speak of "re-animation" rather than of "raising from the dead" are evidently concerned to avoid some ambiguities. In the Gospel stories there is obviously no resurrection to glory like that of Jesus; nor is there a permanent return to life, but only a return to an earthly life that continues its normal course and ends in complete and definitive death. Lazarus has nothing to say about the next world, about a life after life. On the other hand, the Gospels are not treatises on eschatology. Having admitted all of this, we may ask whether the suggested word "re-animation" is not in its turn more ambiguous than the biblical and classical word "resurrection." Nowadays "re-animation" or "bringing back" has clinical overtones that are difficult to eliminate. In hospitals they talk of "bringing

someone back" from a short anesthesia; they try to "bring back" someone from drowning by means of artificial respiration; they "bring back" someone suffering a momentary cardiac arrest or a diabetic coma. Furthermore, is the word "re-animation" or "bringing back" faithful to the intention of the evangelists and of Jesus himself? In all the Gospel stories there is a common conviction: a return to life is impossible. For Jesus himself these raisings from the dead are signs of the coming of the kingdom: "The dead are raised up," he says in his answer to the emissaries of the Baptist (Lk 7:22; Mt 11:5). In the intention of the evangelists these miracles show that Jesus has power over death, just as he does over sickness and sin. All things considered, it seems preferable to speak of stories of "raisings from the dead," even though it is difficult to determine what stage of dying the individuals in these Gospel stories have reached. At the very least, a "raising from the dead" implies a return to life by someone who is on the irreversible path to death. The miracles of raising from the dead have a role to play in the eyes of Jesus and the evangelists. They are an important exercise of the unique power which Jesus possesses and by which the Son raises the dead just as the Father does. The *Jerusalem Bible* and the *Ecumenical Translation of the Bible* retain the term "raising from the dead," with which I agree, while waiting for specialists to propose a terminology that is clearly superior to that consecrated by centuries of usage.

5. Perspective of Each Evangelist

For Mark, the miracles are acts of power that show Jesus to be the one who will effectively establish the reign of God. In Matthew they show him to be the servant of Yahweh who carries out God's merciful intentions toward those oppressed by sickness and sin. Jesus, too, is the Lord who exercises his power. In Luke Jesus is the messianic prophet who brings deliverance and salvation. For John the miracles are signs of the glory of God that dwells in Jesus, as well as testimonies by the Father through the works he enables the Son to accomplish.

Mark does not associate any christological title with the miracles; in Matthew Jesus is servant of Yahweh and Lord; in Luke he is eschatological prophet; in John he is Son, Word, and Word made flesh, and the miracles manifest his properly divine glory. In substance, the evangelists see the miracles as having the meaning Jesus assigns them in his logia.

6. Originality and Purpose of the Miracles of Jesus

a. On the negative side, it can be said that Jesus refuses to confuse miracle and wonder. He will not let himself be put on the same level as a magician or a charlatan or even someone who possesses scientific secrets. The salvation he brings comes through the cross and will be known only at the point at which his mission will be fully accomplished.

b. On the positive side, a miracle *has for its purpose the salvation of the human person.* Jesus comes in order to restore human beings and give them the salvation for which they strive in vain. Miracles render visible this comprehensive restoration. Christ really expels demons, truly heals, truly restores to life, because he truly saves humanity. In the Synoptic tradition, however, Jesus is not called savior but simply the one who comes to save what was lost. This is why his miracles are connected with the conversion that brings human beings into the kingdom.

c. Miracles are performed *in view of a call to the kingdom.* This aspect is remarkably illustrated by the healing of the possessed man among the Gerasenes (Mk 5:1–20). This man has been stripped of everything: his somatic and psychic balance, his human dignity. He is estranged from himself and society. Jesus restores his human integrity as a thinking, responsible being, and reincorporates him into society; he turns the man into one who is personally and socially healthy. But the purpose of the miracle is not wholly achieved by this restoration to health; it includes a higher calling as well. The man who has received the miracle asks Jesus that he "might be with him" (Mk 5:18). Jesus tells him: "Go home to your friends, and tell them how much the Lord has done for you, and what mercy he has shown you" (Mk 5:19). Jesus turns a slave into a free human being and then into an evangelizer of the kingdom: "And he went away and began to proclaim in the Decapolis how much Jesus had done for him" (Mk 5:20). The miracle has mean-

ing only against this backdrop of God's plan for the race, namely, their entrance into the kingdom. Its purpose is both to liberate and to fulfill the human person. By means of his miracles Christ re-creates and re-forms human beings and raises them to an unexpected fullness of life. This accomplishment marks the dawn of the new creation.

d. A miracle establishes a new *personal and transforming relationship* between Jesus and its beneficiary. The latter is not asked scrupulously to practice magical rites but simply to enter by faith into a relationship with Jesus. During the lifetime of Jesus this faith is admittedly imperfect, but it takes the form at least of suppliant and confident petition to this man who proclaims the kingdom and in whom the power of God manifests itself. That a wonder should be thus connected with conversion and should establish an entirely new and personal relationship between Jesus and the beneficiary is a specific characteristic of Christian miracles.

e. The human being (whether the sick person or those who ask for the healing) has thus a *part* to play in the miracle, a *participation* that takes the form of an attitude of radical faith in Jesus or at least an attitude of readiness and openness. The first step to be taken by the recipient is to recognize that he or she is poor, helpless, "in need of salvation," to the point of crying out: "Son of David, have mercy on me!" (Lk 8:39). Without this minimum of participation by the recipient, even Christ is unable to act. If human beings close themselves and harden their hearts against the salvation offered to them, a miracle will only intensify their blindness and render the darkness within them more impenetrable. This call for human participation makes clear not only the power of God but also how weak he is in the face of human freedom—the supreme risk taken by a God who decides that the establishment of a people of sons and daughters, called to share his life, should depend on the response of love and not rejection.

f. The miracles are thus *inseparable from the cross.* Jesus personifies the reign of God, which destroys the reign of Satan. It is not surprising, therefore, that the light of the one should offend the darkness of the other. The exorcisms of Jesus are interpreted as the work of Beelzebul.

The healings he works for the lake towns lead not to conversion but to the hardening of hearts. The miracles of accreditation, performed on the Sabbath, arouse hatred and beget the decision to destroy Jesus. Even the miracle of the multiplication of the loaves is misunderstood and leads to desertion or doubt. The dialectic at work is that of the power and helplessness, the glorification and abasement of Jesus. Miracles are intended by their nature to lead human beings to the kingdom, but these human beings are able to see the *wonders* and yet close their eyes to the *signs*. Jesus brings a salvation that comes only through conversion; therefore his works, his miracles, are the occasion for a dramatic choice. To accept the signs is to accept Jesus and enter upon the path of conversion. And Jesus is finally condemned precisely because he rejects any other interpretation of his miracles except as signs of the kingdom and invitations to enter the kingdom through conversion (Jn 11:53).

g. The miracles of Jesus have an *"ecclesial" character.* Jesus is not a simple charismatic working on his own account and for his own day; he brings a universal salvation, the source of which never dries up. That is why he gives his disciples authority to proclaim the kingdom, along with power to heal the sick and expel demons (Mt 10:8), i.e., the same twofold power that he himself exercises. His miracles are signs of the community of salvation, which continues to offer the salvation that was begun in the community of the Twelve but is rendered permanent through the centuries and extended to all nations (Mt 16:15–18; Acts 5:12).

h. By means of the miracles of Jesus *the future invades the present.* In the person of Jesus the kingdom of God breaks into our world (Mt 12:28). Salvation becomes something of "today," something effectively operative. After the resurrection, when the church turns to Jesus, it does so in order to recall this past that established the kingdom and inaugurated a new world which awaits its completion. For the time being, signs come to us intermittently from the promised land, like interstellar light that gives us a glimpse of unsuspected dimensions.

i. Finally, the miracles of Jesus *are directed toward the unveiling of his person.* If Jesus alone brings the reign of God and eschatological salvation, the ultimate reason for this is to be found in the mystery of his person. This transcendence of Jesus at the very time when he was living his earthly life in Palestine showed itself only implicitly in the exercise of the salvation which he makes known through his works. Before Easter everything is already there, but at the same time everything needs to be understood. The ultimate meaning of the miracles of Jesus will be fully grasped only in the light of the ecclesial experience of Easter, which will make known the full identity of Jesus as Christ, Lord, and Son of God. Before Easter the actions are performed: they point others to the presence of a personal transcendence, but how could people at that time grasp the identity of the living God in the flesh and actions of the man Jesus?

7. Catholic Idea of Miracle

a. Biblical terminology. In the OT miracles are called *terata,* i.e., wonders. Deuteronomy and the NT often combine *sēmeia kai terata* ("signs and wonders") in order to describe a wonder in the order of the sacred. In other words, such *thaumasia,* or actions arousing wonder, and *paradoxa,* or unexpected events or actions, bring out the *psychological* effect of miracles: miracles are extraordinary events that arouse astonishment, wonder, and amazement in those who see them.

In the OT miracles are often described as *adynata,* i.e., works properly divine, because impossible for human beings. In the Gospel of Mark they are "works" (*erga*), i.e., works of Christ as Son of the Father. Mark and Matthew call them *dynameis,* i.e., manifestations and effects of the divine power. As works, miracles are part of the great work that God began with the creation of the world and completed with redemption, which is a new creation. As manifestations of power, they are connected with the divine *dynamis,* i.e., the all-powerful action by which God gives life and saves in both the natural and the supernatural order. These various terms, especially *erga* and *dynameis,* bring out the *ontological* aspect of miracles and show them to be transcendent works, that is, works impossible to creatures and requiring therefore a special intervention of divine causality.

Finally, in both the OT and NT, and especially in John, a miracle is called a *sēmeion*, a word that is often combined with *wonder*. A miracle is more than a wonder; it is also a sign from God. It is the vehicle of a divine meaning which one must be able to read in its context.

b. The data of tradition. The three aspects I have just listed (psychological, ontological, semiological) are to be found throughout the patristic and theological tradition, although the emphasis and focus have varied through the centuries. In particular, there has been a shift back and forth between the factual, ontological aspect, which stresses the element of transcendence of nature, and the semiological aspect, in which a miracle is seen primarily as a sign given by God.

Augustine stresses in particular the psychological and semiological aspects. A miracle is an unusual phenomenon that breaks the monotony of the everyday and therefore captures attention. In his apologetic dealings with pagans the impact of the sheer extraordinariness of a miracle is to serve as a springboard for its semiological function. By reason of their wonderfulness miracles stir carnal human beings, who are legion, to raise their gaze to heaven and contemplate the invisible realities of the world of grace.

In Anselm the emphasis is on the transcendence rather than the finality of miracles. Miracles are actions attributable to God alone, because they are beyond the powers of the entire created universe. The works of Thomas Aquinas show that he is aware of and acknowledges the three aspects of miracles that are mentioned in the Scriptures. But when he comes to define a miracle, his primary interest is in the effect produced and the cause capable of producing it, and he therefore firmly adopts the viewpoint of God, the transcendent agent: "An event is miraculous when it transcends the entire order of created nature" (*ST* 1, q. 110, a. 4c). God is the only cause proportioned to the ontological reality of the effect produced. He does not negate the order of nature, but in the case of a miracle he goes beyond it, because his action is at a different level. A miracle has its place in an order that is the total, universal order willed by God.

After Thomas, the scholastics followed the lead given in his definition of miracle rather than in his teaching on the subject, and they regularly defined miracle according to its ontological aspect as a strictly divine action, while showing little concern in practice for the other two aspects. Thus Pesch defines a miracle as "a sensible effect produced by God outside the order of nature" (*Praelectiones dogmaticae*). And Garrigou-Lagrange: "An event in the world, produced by God and falling outside the ordinary course of created nature in its entirety" (*De Revelatione* [ed. of 1950] 2:40). It was one of the merits of M. Blondel that he once again highlighted the semiological aspect of miracles. A miracle is a sign of the "abnormal" goodness which God manifests in the gospel of salvation. Postwar theology has been marked by an effort at a harmonious integration of the three essential aspects of miracles.

c. Data from the magisterium. While not attempting to derive from the documents of the magisterium a definition of miracle that they never intended to give, we can nonetheless find in them the three aspects that are constantly present in Scripture and tradition. Thus Vatican I regards miracles as *divine facts*, i.e., facts that have God for their author. Miracles are also *signs* of revelation: signs given to us by God to help us recognize that he has spoken to the human race. Vatican II speaks of the *works*, *signs*, and *miracles* by which Christ both makes known and attests to the divine origin of revelation. These three terms represent the three aspects of a miracle.

8. Definition of a Miracle

Using and grouping together the data of Scripture and tradition, I offer the following definition of a miracle: "A religious wonder that expresses, in the cosmic order (human beings and the universe), a special and utterly free intervention of the God of power and love, who thereby gives human beings a sign of the presence of his message of salvation in the world."

a. A wonder in the cosmic order. Quite obviously, wonder is not a synonym for miracle; rather, by reason of one of its aspects miracle has a place in the order of wonders. It is an extraordinary phenomenon that cuts across the regular course of events as observed down the ages. E.g., the cure of a leper: "'I do choose. Be made clean!' Immediately the leprosy left him" (Mk 1:41–42) or of man blind from birth. This was something never seen before, something unheard of. Its effect is shock, surprise, then astonishment.

b. A religious and sacred wonder. This having been said, excluded from the outset are all wonders occurring in a secular context, no matter how disturbing to the imagination, as well as everything belonging to the category of fantasy, magic, fairy tale, legend, and myth. For in a secular context a miracle would have no meaning or reason for existence. The explanation of phenomena in such a context, no matter how extraordinary they may be, is to be looked for in its proper setting, i.e., at the level of natural causes and in the secular order.

By "religious context" I mean a set of circumstances that gives the wonder, at least on the surface, the structure of a *divine sign.* A phenomenological study informs us of what these circumstances are. E.g., (1) a miracle comes after humble, trusting, persevering prayer by a sick person or that person's entourage. (2) It accompanies a life of heroic sanctity and is a sign of a complete union with God and a participation in his life-giving power (the Curé of Ars, Francis of Assisi, Francis Xavier). (3) It supervenes to authenticate a mission that claims to be from God; this was the case with the prophets, Christ, and the apostles. In all these instances there is a complete consonance between the wonder and the invocation of God's name, just as in the case of an interpersonal human relationship when one individual obtains from the other the answer sought, in accordance with the request made. In the case of the miracles of Jesus, the latter have their place in a still broader and more comprehensive context (message, holiness, suffering, resurrection, foundation of the church) and in the total economy in which God saves human beings through Christ. What we have here is a *constellation of signs* in which a miracle is simply one point of light among so many others.

c. A special, utterly free intervention of the God of power and love. The point I am emphasizing here is that miracles, as signs and anticipations of supernatural salvation, require an intervention of God that is no less special and utterly free (at least in the way it is produced) than salvation itself and that differs, therefore, from the ordinary divine conservation and government of the universe. A miracle is a work of the omnipotence of God. In its most striking aspect, i.e., as a wonder or extraordinary event, it seems to be "contrary to nature." In fact, however, it is rather "above nature" and transcends it, being a sign of the freely bestowed transformation of human beings and the universe by the divine love that saves and renews all things, not only in appearance but in truth, not only for the people of the past but for those of today and all times to come.

Obviously, when it comes to expressing what takes place at the phenomenal level as a result of God's action (which cannot be compared to the action of human beings), we can only stammer; we lack the needed words. Some people speak of a transcendence of habitual determinisms, a radical, sudden crossing of a boundary thought to be uncrossable; others speak of a stunning acceleration of the processes of restoration, in contrast to the temporality and continuity that characterize the phenomenal world, as though one had leaped the barrier of time and space, after the manner of the risen Christ who is no longer subject to distance and duration and allows us a fleeting glimpse of the world as glorified. God does not operate after the manner of an actor whose name is suddenly included in the credits of humanity, for he is omnipresent and acts at his own proper level, which is that of God, the first cause, who possesses all the sovereignty of the creator and remaker of humankind. Nature is not so much violated as restored, elevated, and dynamized. There is no decisive argument (if we exclude arbitrary positions or prejudgments) for putting miracles on the same level as ordinary events or happy coincidences. On the contrary, it is supremely consistent and intelligible that the gratuitousness inherent in the overwhelmning *event* of *God becoming flesh,* language, and crucified victim, should itself be "signaled" by events displaying the same gratuitousness, such as the restoration or transformation of bodily life by miracle and resurrection, and of the entire person by holiness. If Christ is among us as Son of the living God, it is to be expected that he would give signs expressive of his glory. The presence among us of God, the supreme Spirit, is literally "enormous": if such a presence is not accompanied by the presence in our world of events *signed* by God, who could ever guarantee that we are not the victims of the most colossal of deceptions? It is infinitely more difficult to accept the incarnation than to accept miracles. Maurice BLONDEL is on solid intellectual and religious ground when he says quite plainly that the seeming contradiction introduced by miracles "manifests in an analogous way the real derogation which the order of grace and charity introduces into the relationship of God and human beings." God "manifests his more-than-normal goodness by more-than-normal signs" (M. BLONDEL, "La notion et le rôle du miracle," *Annales de philosophie chrétienne* (July 1907): 337–61. If I add in my definition that the God who intervenes is the God of power and love, my intention is to make clear that a miracle is not purely a show of power but an action of love: a joint work of the Father and the Son, having its source in their mutual love. A miracle therefore does not reveal its true nature unless it is seen from the viewpoint of God as well as from the viewpoint of human beings.

d. A divine sign. A miracle is a sign that the message of salvation has come into the world. The important word here is *sign,* for a miracle, taken as a whole, is a *meaningful wonder,* a *sign-action.* This intentional or semiological aspect is the element that formally distinguishes miracles. The sign in this case is interpersonal and conveys a challenge; it is the vehicle of a divine intention and addresses human beings like a divine utterance, a concrete, urgent message in which God seeks to make them understand that salvation is at hand. Miracles are thus not historical events that are *closed in* upon themselves, but mediations that point to something beyond themselves. They make it known that the salvation proclaimed is true and real, because it is already present. The miracles of Lourdes have the same meaning: they point to salvation and to him who bestows them.

Miracles are always connected with the event of the message of salvation or revelation. This message may be that of the OT, announcing and promising salvation still to come, or of the Word of God that was made flesh and became an event in Jesus Christ, or it may be the message of the Church, which renders present and efficacious until the end of time the saving message uttered once and for all. Miracles are always in the service of the message, either as an element in revelation or as an attestation of that revelation's authenticity and efficacy.

9. Sign Values and Functions of Miracles

To say that a miracle is a sign is to raise the question of the functions miracles have as signs. Vatican I emphasized chiefly the corroborative or juridical function of miracles. As *divine facts, proofs,* and *signs,* the function of miracles is to establish "the divine origin of the Christian religion" (DS 3009, 3034; ND 119, 128). Vatican II recognizes that miracles have two functions: to *reveal* and to *accredit.* On the one hand, they are vehicles of revelation, just as the words of Christ are, and, on the other, they attest to the truthfulness of the witness given by Christ and to the authenticity of the revelation which he is in his person (*DV* 4). In thus highlighting these two functions of miracles, the magisterium does not claim to exhaust the wealth of meaning and expressivity that miracles contain. Miracles are in fact polyvalent signs; they act on several levels at once and point in several directions. The NT is the best witness to these varied functions of miracles; I shall list these in detail before systematizing them.

a. Signs of the power of God. Miracles are sign-events brought about by the power of God. In the Synoptics the miracles of Christ are epiphanies of the savior, manifestations of his universal and unlimited power. Christ acts in his own name. He heals with a word; he expels demons with a word; he calms the storm with a word; he raises the dead with a word. His power is limited only by human hatred, rejection, and rebellion. In the Gospel of John miracles are joint works of the Father and the Son; they show the power that resides in Christ as it does in the Father. Christ is God present among us, exercising the power of the living God over life and death. His glory is the glory of Yahweh himself.

b. Manifestations of Christ's love. Christ's miracles are manifestations of his active, compassionate love, which stoops to alleviate every kind of affliction. Sometimes the initiative is taken by Christ himself, who anticipates the pleas of human beings (multiplication of the loaves, raising of the son of the widow of Nain, healing of the man with the withered hand, healing of the crippled woman). Other miracles, however, are described as responses of Christ to petitions that are sometimes expressed in so many words, sometimes tacitly implied in a gesture or action (the blind men at Jericho, the Canaanite woman, the centurion, Jairus, Martha and Mary). God "visits" humanity in the depths of its infirmities. He has compassion; he is moved. Miracles are a response of the *agapē* of God to the pleas of distressed humankind. God is love, and this love takes a human form and a human heart in Christ, so that the intensity of God's love may be brought home to human beings.

c. Signs of the coming of the messianic kingdom. Seen from this angle, the miracles are connected with the broader theme of the fulfillment of the Scriptures. They signify that the reign of God which the prophets had foretold over the centuries has at last come. In Jesus of Nazareth the Messiah is present. Men and women are now healed of their infirmities and delivered from sin, and the good news is proclaimed. Healings and exorcisms show and prove that the reign of Satan is being dismantled and that the reign of God is now present (Lk 7:22; Mt 12:28). Wherever Christ is, the saving and life-giving power that the prophets had foretold is at work; it triumphs over sickness and death, as well as over sin and Satan. The kingdom is present and active. And in order that human beings may understand that the new world is present at the heart of the old, Christ *makes visible* the complete salvation which he is proclaiming.

d. Signs of a divine mission. Throughout the biblical tradition miracles have as their principal function to authenticate a mission as being from God. They have a kind of juridical function; they are the credentials of God's messengers. Thus Moses is "accredited" by the wonders which God works through him in the sight of all the people (Ex 4:1–9; 14:31). When Christ appears he must meet this traditional requirement (Mk 2:12; Mt 11:21; Jn 11:41–42). This juridical or probative or certificatory function of miracles is especially emphasized in the Gospel of John. "Many believed in his name because they saw the signs that he was doing" (Jn 2:23). Nicodemus (Jn 3:2), the man born blind (Jn 9:33), and the crowd (Jn 7:31) spontaneously invoke this argument. The juridical

function of miracles is more emphasized in the Acts of the Apostles than in the Synoptics. The miracles worked by the apostles are a testimony given by God: "The Lord . . . testified to the word of his grace by granting signs and wonders to be done through them" (Acts 14:3; 4:33). Miracles *accredit* the apostles and their preaching as authentic ambassadors of Christ.

e. Signs of the glory of Christ. From the viewpoint of other human beings miracles are signs, but from the viewpoint of Christ they are more accurately described as works of the Son. When considered as works, miracles are connected with Christ's consciousness of the mystery of his divine sonship; they are his activity as the Son in the midst of humanity. They also have as their function to accredit his mission as an envoy of God who is not a simple prophet or a purely human messiah but the Son of the Father and sharer in his knowledge (Mt 11:27) and omnipotence (Mt 28:18). Miracles are joint works of the Father and the Son; they point to Christ in his glory as the only Son. That is why Christ constantly refers his hearers to his miracles as being the Father's testimony in his behalf (Jn 5:36–37; 10:25). Because Christ's miracles manifest his power and signify him in his glory as the only Son, his person is the origin of these works and the center to which they draw others. The revelation mediated by the Son's works, like the revelation of his person, ends indeed in failure, but it is nonetheless meant to reveal his glory.

f. Revelation of the trinitarian mystery. The recognition that the miracles are joint works of the Father and the Son leads us into the mystery of the trinitarian life itself. If the works of Christ are also the works of the Father, who takes the initiative in everything, and if, on the other hand, they also belong to the Son, because the Father has given his own power to the Son in order that the Son may do the miracles as his own works, then they show that a unique covenant, a mystery of love, unites Father and Son. The miracles show that the Father is in the Son and the Son in the Father and that the two are united by a single Spirit (Jn 14:10–11; 10:37–38). Evidently, this revelatory depth of miracles emerges clearly only in the light of Christ's discourses and of John's reflections, which bring out their meaning.

g. Symbols of the sacramental economy. The coming of Christ inaugurates a new world, the world of grace. It effects a revolution, that of salvation through the cross. Miracles give a glimpse, as through a veil, of the transformation that has occurred. They are expressive images of the spiritual gifts offered to human beings in the person of Christ. In the Synoptics the symbolism of miracles can already be detected, especially in the stories of the healing of the paralytic, the leper, and the crippled woman and in healings effected by the laying on of hands. It is in the Gospel of John, however, that the symbolism of Jesus' actions emerges most clearly. The miracles of Christ reveal to us the deeper mystery of his person and of the economy of grace which he inaugurates by means of the sacraments, especially baptism (healing of the paralytic by Christ's words of forgiveness of sins and by the water of the regenerative pool; healing of the man born blind, in the pool of Siloam, by Christ the light of the world) and the Eucharist (multiplication of the loaves). The reason why the symbolism in John is so powerful is that it operates at several levels of depth. It is rooted, to begin with, in the incarnation. Miracles are the power of the Word made flesh being exercised through human gestures. The sight restored to the man born blind makes present and visible the power Christ has as source of light for the human race. But there is another reason why Johannine symbolism awakens such echoes in human beings: it is based on primordial human experiences that are tied to our deepest subconscious: water, light, fire, bread, life, safety. By making use of the great symbols of the human race, symbols already employed over the centuries in the OT, John gives the miracles of Jesus an evocative power and resonances that touch the very fibers of our being. But I must add that if John sees Christ as light, life, water, and bread, the reason is that Christ exists for us in his mission as Son sent by the Father, i.e., as the one who delivers human beings from the darkness of sin and death.

h. Signs of the transformation of the passing world. Miracles are, finally, prefigurative signs of the transformations that will take place at the end of time. For redemption must bring renewal to everything that has been touched by sin. In this context, miracles are signs, first of all, of the liberation and glorification of the body. The risen and glorified body of Christ is the visible anticipation of the ultimate destiny of humanity, called as the latter is to a communion of life with God; it is also proof that this glorification is already secretly at work in the world to transform it. Bodies set free, healed, made supple again, given new life, and raised from the dead already disclose the final triumph of the Spirit, who will give life to our mortal bodies and clothe them in incorruptibility. The material universe, too, awaits this transformation. Drawn in the wake of humanity, it must share in the glorification of human beings as it does in their sin. Paul (Rom 8:19–21) sees humanity and the universe as carried along by the movement of redemption toward their final glorification. In his view, the universe is destined not to be annihilated but to be transformed and glorified. Miracles foretell and inaugurate this definitive transformation that will take place when the power of God, having destroyed death and sin, will establish all things in an unfailing newness.

These various meanings of miracles are not independent of one another. On the contrary, each implies the others and sheds light on them, and we pass from each to the next without a conscious transition. It is possible, however, to group the essential *functions* of miracles in a systematic way, under four main headings.

(1) Miracles have the function, first of all, of *communicating:* they show God's intention of entering into a dialogue of friendship with human beings. They are, as it were, friendly, thoughtful greetings, a "visit" from God. The gospel of the kingdom blazes a way for itself along the paths of love.

(2) Second, miracles have a *revelatory* function. They are a constitutive element in a revelation that is realized by "words and deeds" (*DV* 2), by "signs and miracles" (*DV* 4). The message is that Christ has come to liberate, cleanse, and save human beings. Miracles show this message of salvation in action. Right before the eyes of men and women the miracles of Christ liberate and restore bodies. They are active words, eloquent actions. They too, in their own way, are good news, proclamation, message, light, words. Furthermore, in one sense, there is more in miracles than in dis-

courses. For revelation has an element of the ineffable which a discourse cannot capture. Miracles then come to the rescue and reveal a further meaning behind the words. By their power of suggestion and their dynamics as symbols, they speak to both senses and mind. If there had been no miracles that saved bodies and gave them new life, we would doubtless not have realized that Christ brings salvation to the whole human person. Miracles are an element in the kingdom, which is not something static but a dynamic force that is now changing the human condition and establishing the lordship of Christ over all things, including bodies and the cosmos.

(3) Third, miracles have the function of *attesting* or authenticating, as confirmatory, apologetic, juridical signs. Miracles are, as it were, letters of credit carried by the authentic messengers of God; they are the seal which God's omnipotence sets on a mission or message claiming to be from him. In the case of Christ, they attest to, or authenticate, the central claim of Christ to be not only God's messenger but the Son of the Father. At the same time, they prove that the gospel he proclaims is truly from God.

(4) From the viewpoint of the human beings who are the beneficiaries, miracles are *liberating, transforming interventions.* To individuals whose life is diminished by sickness; to men and women who are no longer counted among the living because they are not productive; to those excluded from the religious community because of a legal uncleanness; and even to those out of their senses, who are no longer in control of decisions regarding themselves: to all these Jesus restores physical and psychic integrity, human dignity, and, most importantly, deliverance from sin. He liberates them from sickness, from sin, and from all the prejudices that make outcasts of them. They are restored to themselves and once again enjoy normal relations with others. They are enabled henceforth to be their own masters, to choose their own direction, to make their own decisions: they are "new human beings." Not only that: Jesus turns slaves into disciples and heralds of the kingdom. This liberative and promotive function of miracles is calculated to appeal to our contemporaries, who aspire with indomitable spirits to freedom and full self-development. Miracles

speak to human beings at the very heart of their deepest longings. As a result, the credibility of miracles is greatly increased. By highlighting the liberation and transformation that the gospel proclaims, miracles accredit this gospel as authentic good news. A new humanity is about to be born in which yesterday's outcast or slave or prisoner is invited to enter into the realm of freedom that has been created by crucified and risen Love. Miracles serve Christ because they serve all human beings. On the day when men and women become aware of the newness that has been injected into history, they are quite close to the kingdom.

10. Recognition of Miracles

After what I have said about miracles as signs of the coming of the kingdom and of salvation in Jesus Christ, it is clear that they are addressed not solely to intellectual elites but to all men and women of good will. Miracles are addressed to the mass of those who, educated or not, have eyes to see, common sense, and good hearts. For, when all is said and done, the judgment of miracles as signs of God is a religious matter; the judgment is passed at the level of interiority at which human beings have either already decided that they are self-sufficient or, on the contrary, have become aware of their wretchedness and have admitted that they are poor, weak, helpless, and "in need of salvation."

The time of Jesus was undoubtedly a privileged one for miracles. The person and mission of Jesus provided the archetypal setting for miracles and the primordial reason for their very existence. His miracles, as I have said, were the "foundational signs" proving that *He who is* was present among us. The miracles of our day do not enjoy that privileged setting nor do they satisfy the urgent need of identifying Jesus as Christ and Lord. Furthermore, critical reason, which indeed existed in the time of Jesus, today more than ever requires the findings of medical expertise. It remains true, however, that science has something to say about only one aspect of the complex reality of miracles as wonders and religious signs.

a. Two levels of recognition. It is for the reason just given that I think the problem of the recognition of miracles should be studied first at the level of spontaneous recognition, i.e., the recognition elicited when individuals are suddenly confronted with a miracle; it makes no difference whether they are as simple and uneducated as the crowds in Galilee or as educated and demanding as people of the twentieth century: doctors, engineers, theologians, canonists. Theologians can then dissect and analyze each phase of the dialectic that leads the mind from the observed phenomenon to a judgment that this wonder is a sign from God, while always taking the original, spontaneous recognition as a guide. Spontaneous recognition and theological recognition are not to be opposed as religious and nonreligious, but as two levels and two ways of approaching the same event: the former intuitive, the latter discursive and systematic.

b. Spontaneous recognition. Since the point of departure in both cases is the understanding of miracle as a _complete, meaningful wonder,_ it is important to see what happens at the level of spontaneous recognition. I shall take as an example the cure of the man born blind (Jn 9) in order to grasp the dynamics of a miracle and the dialectic at work in the minds of those who recognize it as such. The striking thing about the story is the process of recognition and the variety of reactions from the witnesses, depending on their interior dispositions. Initially, all are shocked and agitated by this wonder that has suddenly appeared in their lives. Then come the attempts at explanation by minds in confused retreat, the recourse to hypotheses that try to make the event fit into the normal course of things: the man who is questioned is not the one who has been blind from birth, but only someone who looks like him; Jesus is not from God but from the devil because he does not observe the Sabbath; the parents who are questioned as witnesses refuse to commit themselves out of fear of the Pharisees; the man cured of blindness proves stubborn and constantly returns to the facts, restating that he was indeed blind from birth and that Jesus cured him; the adversaries treat Jesus as a sinner, while heaping insults on the healed man and finally expelling him from the synagogue. But the presence and increasingly compelling force of the only hypothesis that makes the event and its context coherently meaningful lead the blind man to acknowledge Jesus as his savior, while they "blind" those who claim to have the light.

c. Theological recognition. The striking thing about spontaneous recognition is the course followed by the mind: from the outset, unusual event and religious context are inseparably connected, and, in continuous process of comparison, a ceaseless back-and-forth from event to sign and sign to event, one gradually moves from the sensible sign to the same sign as authentically divine. The same is true at the level of theological recognition: the effort at recognition aims at an understanding of the event as a signifying totality. The problem of recognition is posed in a synthetic perspective, that is, one that never isolates the historically attested event from the meaning conveyed by the religious context in which it occurs. The identification of the sign is accomplished in a series of such approaches to the reality. In a true miracle there is an unbroken correspondence of signifier and signified; the factual and the intentional illumine one another, leading to a sure judgment on the authenticity of the sign.

d. Components of the sign and medical expertise. Since a miracle is a sign, each of its components must be subjected to study. These components are: the event itself as historically attested (this examination falls within the competence of the historian), as something unusual and out of the ordinary (this examination falls within the competence of the physician), and as located in a seamless religious context (this examination falls more directly under the competence of ecclesiastical authority). The study of the components of a miracle is thus an _interdisciplinary_ work. In this appeal to specialized competencies, there is no reason for theologians to be afraid of pushing the claims of sceince, even to the point of causing irritation, since they know that the final word on the claim of the event to be miraculous belongs to ecclesiastical authority, which in any case utters a judgment that is simply prudential and not infallible. Since most miracles take the form of healings, I shall pay greater attention here to the role of medical experts.

The role of physicians is not to say that an event is or is not a "miracle." In the past, indeed, they felt almost compelled to carry the entire burden of a verdict (because miracles were thought of as "exceptions to the laws of nature"). That time is over, because since then a better definition of a miracle and its components has been worked out. Physicians are asked to speak as physicians; it is in terms of their own competence that they are asked to evaluate what they observe. They do not have to take a position on whether or not miracles will occur in the next millennium; they no longer have to worry about whether miracles are many or few. In the time of Jesus the need was to prove the equation: Jesus of Nazareth is, *in reality*, the Christ, the Lord, the Son of the living God. But in the Jewish mind the supreme divine attribute was power. Jesus needed an identity card, a passport, and for this reason he showed himself to possess the attributes of divinity: power, holiness, wisdom. Today there is no longer the same urgent need of miracles. They continue, however, to be intermittent signs of the always active presence in history of the message of salvation. It is therefore utterly fitting that there still be miracles, while at the same time it is also fitting that they not abound.

This having been said, what should we expect of medical experts? First and foremost that physicians speak, observe, describe, and judge as physicians, with all the new technologies available, even the most sophisticated, and taking into account x-rays taken up to the moment of the cure and immediately after it. Even if medical authorities can show that techniques used in the past were incomplete and insufficient, the conclusion need not be that there was no divine intervention. The norms set down by Benedict XIV in 1740 serve to mark out the proper course for an examination of miracles, without claiming to limit or do away with this examination, especially when there is question of advancing further and to a greater depth. The more complete the work of the medical experts and the richer the resulting file, the better served will be the church's prudential judgment. In some medical circles experts feel, wrongly, a kind of allergic reaction to "instantaneous" or "almost instantaneous" as descriptions of the lightning rapidity of some cures. In fact, the words simply echo some of the Gospel stories: "Jesus said to him, 'Be made clean!' Immediately the leprosy left him"; "Take up your bed and walk"; "I will it. Be made clean." The purpose of the words is to point out that when God acts he acts as God, whether in miracles or in the incarnation. We have an irresistible tendency to assimilate the divine action to human action. The fact is that God is present to the world without being subject to the exteriority of space or the succession of moments in time. Among creatures space separates, while time gives the opportunity to bring them together and to organize and unify them. God, however, embraces the universe without having to traverse its various places; he is present to all times without having to change time zones in order to move toward what is ahead. He acts in space without having to bring together the separated points of space; he works in time, without having to spread himself out over time's continuum. A miracle is a supremely simple action on God's part; he produces it without having to traverse space and time, even though the result of this action has for us a before and an after. Miracles are not so much contrary to nature as they are above nature; they transcend it. They are intelligible actions, but on a divine scale. They are, for God, completely normal works, since it is proper to God to create and re-create. In short, God is God and has no need to "mimic" human beings. The unlikeness between God and human beings will always be infinite as compared to the likeness between them. That is why science will always be caught unawares, always taken aback, by the action of God. God eludes our measures, for he acts according to his own measure, which is that of God.

Miracles are now understood to be complex phenomena, such that their methodical recognition requires calling on the collaborative efforts of historians, medical experts, physicists, theologians, canon lawyers, and the experience of the church. The final judgment, which synthesizes all the elements that have been gathered, is prudential and not infallible; it belongs to the church.

11. The Human Response to Miracles

A healing may be an inescapable fact, but it is not necessarily recognized to be a divine sign. The recognition of a miracle is not simply a matter of mental acuity or technique but of a religious and moral attitude. To recognize a miracle is to open oneself to the mystery of God, who calls us in Jesus Christ; it is to acknowledge that human beings are needy and not self-sufficient. The development of such an attitude requires that men and women enter into those depths of themselves at which the question of life's meaning and human salvation is raised. One who is willing to accept salvation has renounced self-sufficiency, and nothing is harder for human beings that this "mortification," this death to the self. Depending on whether this attitude is present or absent, miracles will be interpreted in different ways: as signs from God or as disconcerting facts or as stumbling blocks. The Gospel stories illustrate the entire range of possible responses to miracles. Miracles are signs given by Christ to guide human beings to the kingdom and urge them to conversion, without ever forcing them. This is why the *concrete* recognition of a miracle normally takes place in a setting of grace which purifies and supports freedom. Miracles, after all, especially those of Jesus, confront human beings with the very meaning of their existence. But how is it possible that God should urge human beings to so decisive a choice without giving them the helps suited for bringing them through it? This efficacious historical presence of grace does not mean that human reason is incapable by itself of grasping the signs and their value (DS 3876; ND 146). Theological reflection can show that nothing in the dialectic leading from sign to signified is strictly beyond the power of reason to grasp. The efficacious historical presence of grace means simply that as a matter of fact the grace of God is at work as soon as there is question of human movement toward salvation; it is therefore at work in the signs no less than in revelation and faith. It is grace that in fact helps human beings correctly to interpret the signs and see the connection of these with salvation, just as it is grace that gives the courage to face the question which the perception of the signs inevitably raises in the case of Jesus.

Bibl.: A. MICHEL, "Miracle," *DTC* 10,2:1798–1858; A. VÖGTLE, J.-B. METZ, "Wunder," *LTK* 10:1255–65; J.-B. METZ, "Miracle," *SM* 4:45–46; T. G. PATER, "Miracle," *NCE* 9:886–95; A. VAN HOVE, *La doctrine du miracle chez saint Thomas et son accord avec les principes de la recherche scientifique* (Louvain, 1927); J. A. HARDON, "The Concept of Miracle from St. Augustine to Modern Apologetics," *TS* 15 (1954): 229–57; A. RICHARDSON, *The Miracle Stories of the Gospels* (London, 1956); R. BULTMANN, *Jesus Christ and Mythology* (New York, 1958); P. HAZARD, *La crise de la conscience européenne, 1680–1715* (Paris, 1959); L. MONDEN, *Le miracle, signe du salut* (Bruges/Paris, 1960); P. BIARD, *La puissance de Dieu* (Paris, 1960); J. KALLAS, *The Significance of the Synoptic Miracles* (London, 1961); A. LOCATELLI, *Dio e il miracolo* (Venegono inferiore, 1963); G. DE BROGLIE, *Revelation and Reason* (New York, 1965); H. VAN DER LOOS, *The Miracles of Jesus* (Leiden, 1965); C. MOULE, *Miracles* (London, 1965); M. TAGAWA, *Miracles et Évangile* (Paris, 1966); V. BOUBLIK, *Incontro con Dio* (Rome, 1968); F. MUSSNER, *The Miracles of Jesus* (Notre Dame, 1968); R. BULTMANN, "The Question of Wonder," in *Faith and Understanding* (New York, 1969), 247–61; K. KERTELGE, *Die Wunder Jesu im Markusevangelium* (Munich, 1970); R. PESCH, *Jesu ureigene Taten? Ein Beitrag zur Wunderfrage* (Freiburg, 1970); D. L. TIEDE, *The Charismatic Figure as Miracle Worker* (Missoula, Mont., 1972); G. THEISSEN, *Urchristliche Wundergeschichten* (Gütersloh, 1974); P.-E. LANGEVIN, "La signification du miracle dans le Message du Nouveau Testament," *Science et Esprit* 27 (1975): 177–82; F. LAMBIASI, *L'autenticità storica dei Vangeli: Studio di criteriologia* (Bologna, 1976); L. SABOURIN, *The Divine Miracles Discussed and Defended* (Rome, 1977); X. LÉON-DUFOUR, ed., *Les miracles de Jésus* (Paris, 1977); C. H. HOLLADAY, *Theios-anēr in Hellenistic Judaism: A Critique of the Use of This Category in New Testament Christology* (Missoula, Mont., 1977); R. LATOURELLE, *Finding Jesus through the Gospels* (New York, 1978); id., "Miracolo," *NDT* 931–45; id., "Miracle," *DSp* 10, fasc. 68–69, cols. 1274–86; id., *The Miracles of Jesus and the Theology of Miracles* (New York, 1968); A. WEISER, *Jesus Wunder: Damals und Heute* (Stuttgart, 1976); G. SEGALLA, "La soteriologia cristologica dei miracoli nei Sinottici," *Teologia* 5 (no. 2, 1980): 157–61; J. MARTORELL, *Los milagros de Jesús* (Valencia, 1980); G. ROCHAIS, *Les récits de résurrection des morts dans le Nouveau Testament* (Cambridge, 1981); N. L. GEISLER, *Miracles and Modern Thought* (Grand Rapids, 1982); H. VERWEYEN, "Il miracolo in Teologia fondamentale," in R. Fisichella, ed., *Gesù Rivelatore* (Casale Monferrato, 1988), 196–207; F. URICCHIO, "Miracolo," *NDT,* 954–78; R. LATOURELLE, "Le Christ et le miracle: Perspective théologique et expertise médicale," in A. Oliviéri and B. Billet, *Y a-t-il encore des miracles à Lourdes?* (Paris, 1990), 327–40; D. L. TIEDE, *Jesus and the Future* (Cambridge, 1990).

René LATOURELLE

MISSION

1. Introduction

Preamble

Rather than offer a complete treatise on missiology, we propose to show the justification and future outlook for mission as viewed by fundamental theology. We make bold to believe that fundamental theology is not only the best standpoint from which to understand the church's missionary calling but also the ideal way for linking up with the rest of the vast universe of theological science.

In line with the widespread view of contemporary scholars, we regard fundamental theology as the science called to deepen our understanding of revelation, starting out from revelation itself, and to justify the credibility of the Jesus Christ event. He throughout the centuries continues to be sacramentalized in the church, which claims to be that unique one willed by him.

We hold revelation to be the saving self-communication of God in Christ. It is definitive and eschatological, hence destined for all, since the Father "desires everyone to be saved and to come to the knowledge of the truth" (1 Tm 2:4).

The science of missiology seeks to study the theology of mission and the problems connected with it. Properly speaking, it does not form part of the core of fundamental theology but is one of the many major themes characterizing a specialization at the level of a master's degree or a doctorate. This topic is certainly a burning one, since the theme of mission today touches the sensibilities of many people holding very divergent views about the uniqueness of the saving role of Christ and particularly about the saving sacramentality of his church.

New Situations and Problems

Until recently, there was basic exegetical agreement over Christ's missionary "mandate." Divergences boiled down to conceptual differences with regard to the primary and various secondary ends of missionary activity, or with regard to the methodology of approaching other cultures and religions that were destined to pass through a CONVERSION that would transform them in depth.

When perchance some ethnic group or indeed some continent is discovered whose people have never heard about Jesus Christ, not a moment is lost before launching out on the adventure of evangelization, often sealed by martyrs' shedding their blood. The theoretical picture is straightforward and goes back, *sine glossa*, to Mt 28:10–20.

In recent years we have witnessed, as much among Catholics as among Protestants, a renewal of theological scholarship in general, and of missionary studies in particular. We are faced with a rapid succession of differing interpretations on the most serious theological topics, some half-baked and most conceived in haste. A new, positive, optimistic preconception has been created about the salvific role of other religions, which looks as though it might bury the validity of Christ's missionary mandate forever. So, especially among the Protestants, who have always set an example of missionary commitment in the past, the proposal has been advanced of a "moratorium," a pause and suspension of missionary activity.

Others have emptied mission of its dogmatic content and reduced its role to simply being a presence among "the others." Some propose to offer evidence of their own solidarity with those who are different not only or not so much because of the theological beliefs they profess but because of their state of economic underdevelopment or limited access to the services afforded by modern technology.

But, from another aspect, we also witness a resumption, not without lively discussion, of missionary activity, and an opening up of new frontiers for our specifically missionary congregations, as also for those for whom mission, understood as mission *ad gentes* and in geographically distant lands, constitutes only one component of their foundational charism. There has been a significant renewal of studies, an increase in types of approach, which have certainly thrown light on the theological origin of the church's mission, as well as on the particular spirituality of the missionary and the methodology for approaching those to be converted.

More and more monographs have appeared, the product of theoretical research or of years of experience in field work, dealing with every kind of topic from *kērygma* and evangelization to *didaskalia* and *koinōnia*; from *diakonia* and witness to incarnation, inculturation, acculturation of the gospel, and evangelization of cultures. This liveliness in research has given rise to dismay in lots of people, but joy, optimism, enthusiasm, and new availability for the missions in others.

Some people would be very happy to replace the word "mission" with EVANGELIZATION. From the histories of their respective uses, we can say that the term "mission," sometimes too with a secular significance indicating a representational function, refers rather to the initial kerygmatic proclamation. It is used particularly to indicate the "sending" on God's part *ad gentes*, with the task of carrying his message with its purpose of conversion and planting the church (cf. *AG* 6). The term "evangelization," with an exclusively religious and Christian significance, in use particularly from the second half of the last century, is used to indicate the actual content of the mission: the proclamation of the good news to all people, especially to non-Christians or the dechristianized (*EN* 52, 56). It is particularly used to indicate the work of catechesis and permanent Christian training, which embraces both the proclamation of eschatological salvation and the proclamation of human rights (cf. *EN* 22, 26, 27, 29, 33, 53, 54).

A first response, and for us a very valid one, to the question that we regard as central in the context of today's debate, and that is to say "for or against the mission," comes to us from Scripture itself, clearly revisited in accordance with the requirements, skills, and achievements of modern exegesis. But the uninterrupted practice of the church also has something to teach us. Its presence in the twentieth century is none other than the voice of the centuries in favor of one single hermeneutics of the missionary mandate of the Lord.

Since Vatican II, any reflection on mission ought to have as starting point and constant reference point what is said about the church and its indissoluble and vital relationship with the mission of the Son and of the Spirit, willed by the "fountain of love" that is the Father's charity (*LG* 1; *AG* 2). These are documents offering new light too for a reconsideration of OT and NT texts that bear on our subject. This link with the most holy Trinity is even more compelling than the actual mandate of Jesus (Mk 16:15; Mt 28:18–20) on which the missionary activity of the church is traditionally based. Our own ecclesiology too, following the example of the Orthodox, ought to get used to seeing the church as an icon of the Trinity. Ontologically the Church depends on the Blessed Trinity, and hence we should be shrewd enough to tap into every aspect of its dynamism.

2. In Holy Scriptures

In 1958, the Protestant G. F. Vicedome published a book very tellingly and appropriately entitled *Missio Dei*. For him, missionary work is nothing if not an external sign, extending down the centuries, of the dynamism of intra-trinitarian self-giving and communication that is reflected in the creation within time.

In the Old Testament

Rather than by being sent on a mission *in partes infidelium* (which is an absolute NT novelty, where a theology of mission was to develop based on the mission of the Son, the envoy of the Father), in the OT the spread of the Jewish religion came about by sympathy and other human motives, and we find references to a universal openness in God's gracious desire (cf. *AG* 2, 3) to save (cf. Is 40–45 and the book of Jonah, which are perhaps the only texts indicative of a missionary commitment among the Jews).

Only two texts make any explicit reference to being sent on a mission (Is 49:6; 61:1–3), but according to the exegetes, both are to be applied prophetically to the coming Messiah. Indeed, according to Lk 4:18–19, Jesus applied the second of these passages to himself at the outset of his mission.

Texts such as Dt 7:1; 9:1–3; Nm 33:51–52, which, if not interpreted in a religious sense, might lead to a mistaken interpretation of election (which is, however, always of a religious character) and thus seem a negation of this universal summons to salvation. In fact, God chose Israel precisely because it was weak and defenseless, the "fewest of all peoples" (Dt 7:7), with very negative qualities (Dt 9:6), more or less as the ideal arena for demonstrating the gratuitousness of his love. Even though in fact there was a tendency for the Jews to keep apart from other people, anyone who wished to live in accordance with the divine laws might be incorporated into the nation. Only if the laws are observed, however, will the people live as the elect and actually be so (Dt 7:12–13; Is 1:16–17; Jer 22:3).

Generally speaking, the prophets are those OT personages most resembling, by their vocation of hearing and spreading the word of God by word of mouth and in writing, the Christian missionaries of days to come. In their struggle against the exclusiveness of Judaism (which was always tempted to shut itself haughtily into the ghetto) and in foretelling the return of the Gentiles to the bosom of the Chosen People, the prophets—by bringing to mind the universalist themes of the earthly paradise, the covenant with Noah, and the call of Abraham—do indeed collaborate in preparing the true NT mission.

The *šeluhim,* or "apostles of the land of Israel," in contrast, constituted as it were committees of learned men for teaching religion but always and only to their own coreligionists, among whom they resolved and clarified religious difficulties; but they were not sent to the Gentiles to convert them.

The Babylonian captivity turned the Jews, without their realizing it, into missionaries of monotheism, a priestly people, magnet and beacon, "the servant of Yahweh," making proselytes everywhere. Nonetheless one may say that in the OT and generally in Judaism, there was no "mission" in the technical sense of the word.

In the New Testament

The NT books offer an abundant and varied panorama of missionary work. Besides talking of its going on, of its workers, of the people to be converted, and of the methodology to be followed, the Synoptics tell us of the testimony of the apostles as friends of the Lord and envoys *ad Hebraeos* and *ad gentes,* as teachers and witnesses of revelation. In Acts, the problem of universality in the primitive church is tackled in a straightforward way, where we are told of the serious misunderstandings that Peter and Paul had to face in defending it and their tireless missionary activity in founding communities among "the Gentiles." We find other information of the sort in the Epistles. John, for instance, offers the best of bases for a theology of mission by presenting Jesus as a missionary sent by the Father and by telling too of the mission of the Holy Spirit as the strength promised to the apostles and as the person giving life to the universal church by his continuous outpouring of charisms.

Jesus was sent by the Father (Jn 17:18, 21b; 20:21) to found the CHURCH with "the remnant of Israel" and the Gentiles (Gal 6:16); the two peoples are destined to become a *tertium genus.* To realize the plan, he chooses fellow workers

who are like laborers in his harvest (Mt 9:38), like shepherds of a scattered flock (Mt 9:36), like fishers of men (Mt 4:20; Mk 1:17; Lk 5:10), and like prophets (Eph 3:4–6; Lk 11:49; Rv 18:20). To these, freely chosen by God (Mt 10:8b), Jesus promises the fullness of the Holy Spirit (Jn 16:13a) and the full powers as described in Mk 3:14–15.

Criticism going back to R. Bultmann would have it that the passages containing Jesus' discourses about the apostles' mission *ad Hebraeos* (before Easter) and *ad gentes* (after Easter) were invented by the primitive community in its need to justify its own universalist openness, by attributing them to Jesus so as to silence the judaizing current, which was firmly opposed.

Without going into particulars set out in weighty studies on the subject by the *Formgeschichtemethode,* we may accept the conclusions relative to the missionary discourses of Jesus and to the two communities (Jewish-Christian and Gentile Christian), which have their origins in the missionary activity of the prepaschal community, the clearest statement of which is to be found in Mk 6:7–13, 30–31; Lk 9:1–6, 10; Mt 9:35–10:42; Lk 10:1–24. So too the command of the risen Lord, preserved in Mt 28:16–20; Mk 16:24–20(?); Lk 24:44–51, brings us back to the universal claims of Christ.

Exegetes are in agreement in identifying the missionary passages in the Synoptics; the "missionary discourses" are Mk 6:7–13, 30–31; Lk 9:1–6, 10; Mt 9:35–10:42; Lk 10:1–24; Mt 28:16–20; Mk 16:14–20(?); Lk 24:44–51, and a number of logia, some included in the discourses just mentioned, others reported here and there in different contexts. Thanks to studies already carried out, we can rediscover the original nucleus and typical condition of the postpaschal community by freeing the pericope from the adaptations certainly made by such a community and by ascribing the nucleus of it, with a high level of certainty, to the historical Jesus and particularly to his example, for, even though he had personally confined his apostolate primarily to the Jews and to his disciples, he had prepared the universal mission of his church.

We must not forget that missionary work began only after the apostles had been invested with "power from on high" (cf. Is 32:15; Wis 9:17; Lk 1:78; 24:48–49). The Master says: "You will receive power when the Holy Spirit has come upon you; and you will be my witnesses in Jerusalem, in all Judea and Samaria, and to the ends of the earth" (Acts 1:8). And right from the start, this "power from on high" is always checked as to its authenticity either by the *sensus fidei* or by the *munus apostolicum*.

In NT literature there is also abundant reference to a missionary apostolate that does not go back to the historical Jesus but is the product of a vision, of a hearing, of an apocalyptic understanding (1 Cor 9:1), of having seen him resurrected in vision (1 Cor 15:5–8), of having received the missionary charge from him (Gal 1:1), and so forth. This is the "apocalyptic" type of apostolate, based on revelations made by the Father and the glorified Christ. Between the two kinds of apostolate there is no conflict, whereas they are indeed differentiated from the apostolate of the synagogue.

A great variety of missionaries appear, male and female, called by different titles—prophets, apostles, teachers, messengers, servants, brothers, sisters-wives—but they seem all to have had the same assignments. Scholars debate their nature, as well as their relationship with the local hierarchy. It is certain, however, that along with the great apostles, these other disciples went as pilgrims all over the world to proclaim Christ and the gospel, knowing how to adapt it to the various catechetical needs of the church, in connection with James, Peter, John, or Paul. There was to be no lack of conflicts, quarrels, and polemics.

Jesus Christ was to synthesize all his saving activity in evangelization, in training his apostles, to whom he promises the Spirit, who will guide them in their missionary work. Forthwith and starting with them, a great current of missionaries, witnesses to the gospel, comes into being.

3. Carrying Out the Mandate in History

During the twenty centuries of Christianity, despite inactive phases due to various negative reasons such as ignorance of geography, simplification of the facts, and conflicting methodological interpretations, the church has given ample proof of the description given to it by Vatican II, when it says that "the Church is missionary by her very nature" (*AG* 2). The church has its raison d'être in the proclaiming of the gospel to all people and is rightly described as having been "divinely sent to all nations that she might be the 'universal sacrament of salvation'" (*AG* 1; cf. *LG* 48).

Missionaries, over the centuries, prompt of testimony, pushed ahead whenever the Christian Western world came into contact with new peoples, to evangelize them and, following the apostles' example, "preached the word of truth and begot churches" (Augustine, *PL* 36:508; cf. *AG* 1), seeking to establish the kingdom of God throughout the earth (cf. *AG* 6 with note 14).

The great stages can be divided thus: the church in the apostolic age and within the Greco-Roman world, with special mention of Paul's three great missionary journeys; the evangelistic activity in central Europe among the barbarian nations and the Slavs, and in the East among the Mongols and Muslims; the missions *ad gentes* of the sixteenth century, both in Latin America and in the Far East; the fourth stage, which begins with the founding of the Sacred Congregation *de propaganda fide* (1622); then that of the missionary revival of the last century, the crisis of the eighteenth century having been overcome, thanks to the new religious spirit and the appearance of many missionary congregations; finally, the period of the great papal encyclicals of our own century, the documents of Vatican II and Paul VI's magnificent *Evangelii nuntiandi* in which, starting from Christ the Evangelizer, he explains what evangelizing means and what the content, ways, recipients, workers, and spirit of evangelization are.

History tells us of the zeal of many a disciple of the Lord to make him known, and also of the difficulties and the quarrels among missionaries themselves over understanding how they should go about it. We know also about the development in ecclesial thinking on theological and scientific levels about a right understanding as a missionary community, of which the great documents of the modern magisterium are ample witnesses.

It is important to study the history of the missions so as to avoid past mistakes, especially those in missionary methodology made at different periods in the past. It should be remembered, however, and noted in passing that the deeper dimensions of the Christian missionary adventure may often elude historical and sociological analysis—namely, its divine origin and its inner drive due to the force of the Spirit.

4. Modern Missiology

According to Ad Gentes

The new ecclesiology worked out by Vatican II appears in *AG* and opens new horizons for missiology. It says that "the pilgrim Church is missionary by her very nature" (*AG* 2); that its only reason for existing is to be a missionary. The decree emphasizes that this is so, not only because of the Master's missionary mandate, but even more so because "it is from the mission of the Son and the mission of the Holy Spirit that she takes her origin, in accordance with the decree of God the Father" (*AG* 2). Because this is so, "this mission is a continuing one. In the course of history it unfolds the mission of Christ Himself" (*AG* 5). Earlier it is described as the realization of the Father's saving plan. So one may say that mission is central to the church, since Christ is central to it. Jesus, having clearly stated the need for faith and for baptism for salvation, has also declared the necessary sacramentality of the church, which is his Body (cf. *AG* 7).

Furthermore, "missionary activity is nothing else and nothing less than a manifestation or epiphany of God's will, and the fulfillment of that will in the world and in world history. In the course of this history God plainly works out the history of salvation by means of mission. By the preaching of the word and by the celebration of the sacraments, whose center and summit is the most holy Eucharist, missionary activity brings about the presence of Christ, the Author of salvation" (*AG* 9).

Basing itself on *LG* 1, 48, and elsewhere, *AG* 4 affirms that the Holy Spirit "instills into the hearts of the faithful the same mission spirit which motivated Christ himself." It emphasizes that this union of the Holy Spirit and the church and its missionaries is "to carry out [Christ's] saving work."

AG 6 offers the following description of missionary activity: "'Missions' is the term usually given to those particular undertakings by which the heralds of the gospel are sent out by the Church and go forth into the whole world to carry out the task of preaching the gospel and planting the Church among peoples or groups who do not yet believe in Christ." But the same section, besides referring to the territorial boundaries of those peoples and groups who do not

yet believe, goes on to tell us that such groups as have already been evangelized but for various reasons have lost their direction as Christians and have not as yet reached full development and maturity of Christian life are also the objects of missionary activity (cf. also *AG* 19).

Even though "missionary activity among the nations differs from pastoral activity exercised among the faithful, as well as from undertakings aimed at restoring unity among Christians," it states that "these two other activities are most closely connected with the missionary zeal of the Church" (*AG* 6). When this "activity wells up from the Church's innermost nature," it cannot ever fail. The young churches too must preach "the gospel to those still outside" (*AG* 6). Once a particular church has been "implanted," it ought immediately to become a missionary church. Since such churches are "bound to mirror the universal Church as perfectly as possible, let them rightly realize that they have been sent to those also who are living in the same territory with it, and who do not yet believe in Christ" (*AG* 20). This "mirroring" does not have a juridical but an ontological dimension. From it derives the fact that the missionary activity of the new church is essential to the whole church and lasts forever within it.

AG devotes much space to the soteriological dimension of mission, stating plainly that the church has a "saving mission" (*AG* 41). This salvation is understood not only in the eschatological sense but as something all-inclusive, even historical, touching all aspects of the human person. This work at times involves purification. By making Christ present, who is the Author of salvation, the church, "as a sort of secret presence of God . . . frees [the nations] from all taint of evil and restores to Christ [their] maker, who overthrows the devil's domain and wards off the manifold malice of vice" (*AG* 9). While the language is optimistic enough (cf. also *AG* 3, 11b), the need for an external salvation is clear.

We might point out *AG*'s insistence (cf. 3, 4, 9; cf. also *LG* 48) on the sacramental role of the church in the matter of salvation, precisely because this is one of the points contested by a certain kind of modern missiology, going back to the *missio Dei*, which tends to leave the church out of consideration. For even though God could achieve his aims by other means, he has of his own free will determined to do it sacramentally by means of his church, by analogy with what occurred in the mystery of the incarnation. This then is a further argument in favor of the urgency of evangelization (*AG* 7).

According to Evangelii Nuntiandi:
Attitude toward More Recent Tendencies

The first phase of enthusiasm after *AG* was soon followed by forceful criticisms. The source of this theological unease can be found in a series of ideological tendencies, which included a tendency toward exclusiveness, focusing only on one aspect of the missionary task, and a rejection of the definition of mission as "implanting the church," out of fear that this would be a matter of making copies of Western churches, while forgetting what *AG* 3 has to say about individual churches. The most serious danger seems to have come from too sociological an interpretation of missionary activity, beginning with the conception of the aims to be achieved, invariably using inductive-type criteria rather than deductive, theological criteria. Missiology, however, cannot lose its theological dimension; for it to become divorced from revelation is suicidal. Whereas the *AG* schema establishes a model of relationship conceived as *God—Church—World*, more recent thought prefers to rearrange them *God—World—Church*, following the thought that, respecting the SIGNS OF THE TIMES, it is up to the world now and then to set the agenda for the church (cf. J. C. Hoekendijk).

Paul VI's *EN* may be regarded as one of the most significant documents of the postconciliar period, having successfully integrated the theology of *AG* with most of the themes emerging with such unbelievable speed after the council. We note the definitive adoption of the term "evangelization," in preference to "mission" or "missionary activity" and "apostolate." As *AG* stressed the fact that the church is by its very nature missionary, so *EN* repeatedly says that "evangelizing is in fact the grace and vocation proper to the Church, her deepest identity" (*EN* 14; cf. also 13, 59, 60, 66).

The church fulfills this essential function insofar as it depends on Christ: "Having been born out of his having been sent, the Church in her turn is sent by Jesus. The Church remains in

the world when the Lord of glory returns to the Father. She remains as a sign—simultaneously obscure and luminous—of a new presence of Jesus, of his departure and of his permanent presence. She prolongs and continues him. And it is above all his mission and his condition of being an evangeliser that she is called upon to continue" (*EN* 15).

Section 75 reminds us that the church is an evangelizer thanks to the power of the Holy Spirit. The normal and desired, most visible and immediate fruit of evangelization is a new church (*EN* 15). Section 28 says that "in its totality, evangelization consists in the implantation of the Church." Evangelization is conceived of, not simply as an initial proclamation, but rather as an integral process embracing different aspects of the same reality.

At the time of the 1974 Synod, people began thinking of the whole mission of the church—everything it does—as the content of evangelization. Paul VI, in section 17, offers a list of elements, any one of which would be enough to absorb the actual definition of the concept. In fact, each is closely related to the others: "Thus it has been possible to define evangelization in terms of proclaiming Christ to those who do not know him, of preaching, of catechesis, of conferring baptism and the other sacraments. Any partial and fragmentary definition which attempts to render the reality of evangelization in all its richness, complexity and dynamism does so only at the risk of impoverishing it and even of distorting it. It is impossible to grasp the concept of evangelization unless one tries to keep in view all its essential elements" (cf. also *EN* 6, 21, 22, 24, 41).

Undeniably, *EN* describes the term "evangelization" in much richer form than *AG:* the final aim will be, as already said, the "implanting of the Church," which obviously entails the celebration of the sacraments, the changing of hearts, making people into new persons, who are able to make structures more just, more human, and less oppressive (cf. *EN* 15, 18, 23, 28, 36). An always indispensable element is witness, which must be present from the first contact, which some call, perhaps improperly, preevangelization (cf. *EN* 51). If there is no explicit proclamation of Christ, whatever type of commitment to other people in evangelization there may be, it will turn out hopeless or, if you prefer, useless: "There is no true evangelization if the name, the teaching, the life, the promises, the Kingdom and the mystery of Jesus of Nazareth, the Son of God, are not proclaimed" (*EN* 22).

There is insistence on the evangelization of cultures, on respect for their values, but when it mentions the salvation of those who have not yet been evangelized, it says that they can be saved "by ways which He alone knows" (*EN* 80), a position that, theologically speaking, would seem more restricted than that to be found in *AG*. A great deal of attention has been devoted to the theme of transmission, which has to be done with particular fidelity (*EN* 4, 15, 78–79). Paul VI rightly devotes section 48 to studying the evangelization of popular religiosity (→ RELIGION V). The pope dealt with issues deeply felt in the 1970s, such as the local church and its relationship with the universal church, proposing a very forward-looking solution (*EN* 62–65); the church's mission and progress, or the promotion of human rights; and the relationship between salvation history and world history; all these were tackled in a lucid, balanced, and (in our view) very successful way in chapter 3 of the apostolic exhortation.

5. Will the Mission of the Future Still Be to Proclaim Jesus Christ?

Recent Difficulties and Theological Muddles

In spite of the theological clarity of *EN*, some people still feel bewildered when having to cope with challenges possibly encountered before but now presented with new stridency. Even though *EN* declares that "evangelizing is the grace and vocation proper to the Church, her deepest identity" (*EN* 14), and again, that "she exists order to evangelize, that is to say in order to preach and teach, to be the channel of the gift of grace," increasingly discordant voices are to be heard.

In some circles, formerly active in missionary vocations, we see the notion of missionary and of mission *ad gentes* fade away. Others emphasize God's desire for everyone to be saved and deny any need to conform one's life to the demands of the gospel, to which in any case one adheres in faith, without any need to adhere to his church. The missionary's task, it is said, ought rather to be on the horizontal level; eschatological salvation may be left to God,

who "normally" reaches those to be saved in the religions to which they already belong: there is no point in putting oneself out only to upset them. Sometimes also the sense of the importance of the explicit proclamation of Christ's message is lost, giving place to the need for social-type denunciation or to dialogue, often too general and eirenic to produce much effect.

Against these positions and others like them, it must be emphasized that missionary work is the full mediation of salvation. From OT (e.g., Jer 7:25–26; 29:19; Ez 13:6; Hg 1:13) and NT history, its divine provenance is clear (Mt 3:13; Jn 20:21). Just as in the OT the mission is carried out with the strength of the Spirit (Ez 2:2–3; Zec 4:6b), so in the NT Jesus assures his disciples of his Spirit as strength for the mission and as guide, defender, and comforter of the missionaries (Jn 14:26; 16:12–13; Acts 6:10; 7:55–56; 10:19–20; 1 Cor 2:4, etc.). The mission is a work of salvation, the agents of which are God, who sends the Son (*missio Dei*), and the missionaries (*missio hominis*), who are the envoys of the church, who is the depository of Christ's salvation history (*missio ecclesiae*). The mission always has the same aim—the integral salvation of the human person—but it is realized in differing historical, geographic, religious, and cultural circumstances. When this salvific activity has the aspect of being a first proclamation and when the implantation of a new church is proposed, it takes the name of "missions *ad gentes*" and always entails the requirement of leaving home, of serving, and of fitting into something new.

The *plantatio ecclesiae* appears as end of the mission (*AG* 6) inasmuch as God wishes to save us, not individually but as forming a community of salvation (*AG* 1; *LG* 9, 13). One may say that there is a real Christian community once the gospel is accepted in faith, the Eucharist is celebrated, and there is one Shepherd (cf. *CD* 11; *AG* 19).

We must clear the ground of any suspicion or anxiety that the church engages in missions out of self-centeredness. It is indeed aware of being the instrument of salvation, but it obtains this role only from Christ—he is the "light of all nations" (*LG* 1), who habitually makes use of this his body.

Although not identifying itself with the kingdom of God, the church is at the service of the kingdom and on earth is its "initial budding forth" (*LG* 5). The church's only purpose is to usher in this kingdom of God throughout the world (*AA* 2), even though there is tension between church and kingdom, in that the ecclesial community and its structures must tend toward embodying the requirements of the gospel and the kingdom. That there should be tension is important and healthy. But tension does not mean opposition. There is common purpose, but no opposition, between the church's birth and the kingdom of God. By reflecting ideologically on this theme of the kingdom of God, we can easily pass on to asserting that the *missio Dei* is only and exclusively God's work; the church is a sign of God's commitment to the world, and Christ is only a model of devotion to his fellow beings.

Conversion—that is, conforming one's own life to the requirements of the gospel and to being a disciple of the Lord in his church and engaged in building his kingdom—must be looked on as a process involving one's whole life. Even though *AG* repeatedly speaks of it (13), some missiologists prefer not to hear this mentioned any more. If there is a real encounter with Christ, a break with one's previous mode of life is to some degree inevitable. Paul VI reminds us that God can salvifically reach "by ways which only he knows" (*EN* 80)—those whom the gospel message does not explicitly reach. But the question that ought always to form the basis for the church's missionary commitment is, "As for us, can we gain salvation if through negligence or fear or shame or as a result of false ideas we fail to preach it?" (*EN* 80).

History shows that the church has not been exclusively concerned with the eschatological saving of souls but has in modern times been promoting liberation and human and social improvement (*EN* 25). In recent years, in certain parts of the world the saving work of the Lord's church has been very largely reduced to a merely social and political liberation. We are reminded, however, that this work ought instead to be first of all religious and spiritual in nature, involving reconciliation with God (Rom 6:6; 8:23–24; 2 Cor 5:17–19; 1 Pt 1:18; Ti 2:5; Gal 6:15). Indirectly, all this will lead to structural changes too, able to improve the lot of anyone of any nation (*EN* 25; *GS* 42).

Great progress has been made in recent years in refining the concept, tasks, and mission of any given church, but especially of the young churches. The abiding task of each particular church should be to "assimilate the essential part of the gospel message, transpose it without the slightest alteration of its basic truth into the language understood by the people in question and then to proclaim it to them in that language" (*EN* 63).

Mission between Dialogue and Proclamation of the Uniqueness of Christ

The Indian M. Amaladoss maintains that the main causes of the missionary crisis are as follows: a more positive view of the salvific value of other religions, leading to a preference for dialogue rather than proclamation; a widening of the idea of mission to include all the church's activities, which seems to diminish the specific nature of the mission *ad gentes*; the perception that the church is now present everywhere, which seems to reduce the sense of urgency about going beyond present frontiers; an insistence on the responsibility of local churches, which seems to have brought on an identity crisis in the missionary institutes; last, a growing secularization and a shrinkage in missionary vocations among the older churches. In contrast, Amaladoss observes, a growing enthusiasm for evangelization may be noted in the young churches, conjuring up visions (dare we hope?) of a new missionary era.

Today the theme of salvation seems to bring people together, even non-Christians. It is and ought to be total and integral, historical and transcendent. Precisely because of this,

> it cannot be reduced into the framework of the merely earthly needs of the individual and society, nor can it be arrived at solely by the play of the dialectics of history. We are not in any real sense the saviours of ourselves: salvation transcends what is human and earthly; it is a gift from on high. There is no such thing as self-redemption; God alone saves us in Christ (cf. Acts 4:12–13; 1 Tm 2:5–6). (John Paul II, *L'Osservatore Romano*, 8.10.1988)

To remain faithful to what seems to us the Lord's plan as a result of serious and generally accepted exegesis, the testimony of the practice of church life over twenty centuries of history, and the repeated and solemn magisterial pronouncements of our own century, missiology must strive to overcome its guilt complex vis-à-vis those who accuse its agents of being church centered, preferring to see them more or less irenically and only socially committed to building a world more just and tolerable to live in.

Not merely from outside the church but actually from among the very members of the Christian/Catholic community, there seems to be a kind of unconscious plot to "de-missionize" the church, to use Mondin's expression. Cardinal Tomko talks of "self-emptying" of mission. D. Colombo offers a passionate and deeply felt study of all these problems, entitled *Missionari senza Cristo*. R. Panikkar sees a profound dichotomy between the historical Jesus and the Christ-Logos. Jesus of Nazareth is unique, but the Christ-Logos, who is superior to him, can appear in different but real ways in other religions and other historical figures. Is the Buddha, then, perhaps the Oriental incarnation of the Christ-Logos?

From these premises, P. Knitter was to affirm that "perhaps . . . other saviours and other revealers may be as important as Jesus of Nazareth." Perhaps with theological "intuition" but also certainly with exegetical superficiality, as I. de la Potterie rebukes him, Knitter will write another book, wondering whether Peter had not been exaggerating when he said that "there is salvation in no one else, for there is no other name under heaven given among mortals by which we must be saved" (Acts 4:12). The same author, more recently in another telling work (in collaboration with J. Hick), could bring himself to write that

> the stumbling block seems to be the content of the belief, which is central to Christianity, in the uniqueness of Christ. The basic premise of unitive pluralism is that all religions are, or can be, equally valid. This means that their founders, or the religious personalities that these religions reflect, are or can be equally valid. This however would open up the possibility that Jesus is "one among many" in the world of saviors and revealers. To acknowledge such a thing, for Christians, is simply out of the question. Or is it?

De la Potterie, relying also on the studies of noted expert J. Dupont, seeks to demonstrate the soundness of the traditional interpretation that holds Christ to be the only savior.

P. Knitter is not alone in thinking along these lines. Reference to the above-mentioned M.

Amaladoss will suffice: "In the present context of religious pluralism, has proclaiming Christ as the only Name in which human beings can find salvation and are called to become his disciples by baptism still got any meaning?" According to López-Gay, some "authors finally come to assert that a Christianity without Christ has more relevance for today's world than the presentation of the revelation and communication of God in Christ."

Scholars think the root of the present widespread confusion of ideas on subjects such as the theology of religions (→ RELIGION X), interreligious dialogue, and universal and ordinary sacramental value of the Christian/Catholic church for salvation, whether the theory of "anonymous Christianity" (→ ANONYMOUS CHRISTIANS) or implicitly such, is largely due to K. Rahner. Some of his radical disciples have reached the conclusion (perhaps not the same as that of their master and inspirer) that religions as such are just as effective and adequate a means of salvation as Christianity is.

Here is not the place to repeat the long debate and opposing positions adopted over this issue. That of H. U. von Balthasar, particularly in *Cordula*, is among the most significant. Even though twenty years have gone by since then, the vast quantity of literature now devoted to INTERRELIGIOUS DIALOGUE rather than to the evangelizing mission of Christ's church seems to tell us that von Balthasar was all too true a prophet.

The documents of the church tell us that non-Christian religions are a living reality that it cannot ignore, but it regards them as a "preparation for the gospel" (*LG* 16; *AG* 3; *NA* 26), with good and true elements, "seeds of the Word" (*AG* 11), fruit of the action of the Holy Spirit (*GS* 92–93; *RH* 12). These religions, however, also have negative elements, and the church knows that "often men [non-Christians], deceived by the Evil One, . . . have exchanged the truth of God for a lie, serving the creature rather than the Creator" (*LG* 16). Notice, though, that Vatican II, in statements that still seem more than valid, declares that "the Catholic Church rejects nothing which is true and holy in these religions" (*NA* 2), and that however dimly willed and sought in those religions, it can be purified and assumed by the Church (cf. *LG* 17; *AG* 11).

"The Church therefore has this exhortation

for her sons: prudently and lovingly, through dialogue and collaboration with the followers of other religions, and in witness of Christian faith and life, acknowledge, preserve, and promote the spiritual and moral goods found among these men, as well as the values in their society and culture" (*NA* 2). We need to regard dialogue and mission as intertwined realities. Interreligious dialogue is an integral element in the process of evangelization, but it can never replace or be a substitute for mission (cf. *EN* 27).

Missiology as viewed by fundamental theology brings us back to the need to present Jesus Christ as the definitive envoy—"missionary"—of the Father, end point of a divine pedagogy and starting point for a further spiritual journey to salvation. The proclamation of Jesus Christ as Savior is to be made, with attention to methodological achievements that are the fruit of twenty centuries of evangelization and that have recently been improved by conciliar and postconciliar reflection, and by the theology of religions and salvation. But it will be a proclamation never to be renounced. Only an overall, balanced, theological vision will keep us safe from damaging forms of extremism and allow our mission to be truly for the good of the many, hence good for the cause of the gospel.

Bibl.: J. BLAUW, *The Missionary Nature of the Church: A Survey of the Biblical Theology of Mission* (New York, 1962); K. RAHNER, "Christianity and the Non-Christian Religions," in *Theological Investigations*, vol. 5 (1962; London/New York, 1966), 115–35; id., "On the Importance of the Non-Christian Religions for Salvation," in *Theological Investigations*, vol. 18 (1978; New York, 1983), 288–96; id., "Anonymous Christians," in *Theological Investigations*, vol. 6 (1965; London, 1969), 390–98; id., "Anonymous Christianity and the Missionary Task of the Church," in *Theological Investigations*, vol. 12 (1970; London, 1974), 161–78; id., "Observations on the Problem of Anonymous Christian," in *Theological Investigations*, vol. 14 (1972; London, 1976), 280–95; H. R. SCHLETTE, *Die Konfrontation mit den Religionen* (Cologne, 1964); E. HILLMAN, *The Church as Mission* (New York, 1965); G. F. VICEDOM, *The Mission of God* (Saint Louis, 1965); id., "Christliche Mission und Entwicklungsdienst," *IKZ* 3 (1974): 215–29; J. MASSON, *Decreto sull'attività missionaria della chiesa* (Turin, 1966); J. JEREMIAS, *Jesus' Promise to the Nations* (London, 1967); H. Urs VON BALTHASAR, *Cordula ou l'épreuve décisive* (Paris, 1969); var., *Perché le missioni? Teologia delle missioni: studi e dibattiti* (Bologna, 1970); J. LÓPEZ-GAY, *Lo Spirito Santo e la missione* (Rome, 1971); id., "La misionologia postconciliar," in Fac. de teol. del norte de España, eds., *Estudios de misionología I: A los diez años del Decreto Ad Gentes* (Burgos, 1976), 15–54; G. W. PETERS, *A Biblical Theology of Missions* (Chicago, 1972); J. AMSTUTZ, *Kirche der Völker: Skizze einer Theorie der Mission* (Freiburg, 1972); A. SUMOIS, *Théologie missionnaire*, 5 vols. (Rome, 1973); A. R. TIPPETT, *Verdict Theology in Missionary Theory* (South Pasadena, CA, 1973); K. BOCKMÜHL, *Was heisst heute Mission?* (Giessen/Basel, 1974); G. COFFELE, *Johannes Christiaan Hoekendijk: Da una teologia della missione ad una teologia missionaria* (Rome, 1976); var., "Evangelization," *Conc* 114 (1979); A. ERBA, *Panorami di storia delle Missioni* (Rome, 1976); G. EVERS, *Storia e salvezza, Missione Religioni non cristiane e mondo secolarizzato* (Bologna, 1976); W. HOLLENWEGER, *Evangelism Today: Good News or Bone of Contention?* (Belfast, 1976); PAUL VI, "Apostolic Exhortation 'Evangelii Nuntiandi' on Evangelization," *Origins* (Jan. 8, 1976): 459–68; C. SALDANHA, *Divine Pedagogy: A Patristic View of Non-Christian Religions* (Rome, 1984); P. F. KNITTER, *No other name? A Critical Survey of Christian Attitudes Toward the World Religions* (Maryknoll, 1985); id., "Roman Catholic Approaches to Other Religions: Developments and Tensions," in *International Bulletin of Missionary Research* 8 (1984): 50–54; E. TESTA, "I principi biblici della missione," in var., *Missiologia oggi* (Pontificia Università Urbaniana, 1985), 11–47; var., *Missiologia oggi* (Rome, 1985); P. F. KNITTER and J. HICK, eds., *The Myth of Christian Uniqueness: Toward a Pluralistic Theology of Religions* (Maryknoll, 1987); K. MÜLLER, *Mission Theology: An Introduction* (Netteral, 1987); M. AMALADOSS, "Foreign Missions Today," in *East Asian Pastoral Review* 25 (1988): 104–17; var., "Vous serez mes témoins," *Spiritus* 113 (1988): 339–413; var., "Begegnung der Religionen," *TQ* 169 (no. 1, 1989); A. WOLANIN, *Teologia della missione* (Casale Monferrato, 1989); M. DHAVAMONY, "Mission in der nachkolonialen ära: neue Sicht auf neue Aufgaben," *IKZ* 3 (1974): 203–14; id., ed., *Evangelization, Dialogue and Development* (Rome, 1972); id., ed., *Prospettive di missiologia oggi* (Rome, 1982); J. M. VAN ENGELEN, "Tendenzen in der Missiologie der Gegenwart," *IKZ* 3 (1974): 230–47.

Gianfranco COFFELE

MODERNISM

Modernism in the strict, historical sense of the term is the name given to an intellectual crisis within Catholicism that came into the open at the end of the nineteenth century and the beginning of the twentieth. As historians look back from a later time, too many of them tend to attribute to modernism a unity and cohesiveness it never had. It formed a whole only in its global condemnation in the decree *Lamentabili* (17 July 1907) and the encyclical *Pascendi* (8 September 1907). It is possible, however, to detect some tendencies shared by a number of writers of the period: an attempt to free themselves from an ossified theology; an effort to reformulate the faith in a way adapted to modern men and women; and a testing of the foundations of Christianity with the help of new critical and historical methods. Inspired by a desire to help the church exert its spiritual influence on their contemporaries, the modernist writers represented an attempt to renew exegesis, history, and theology in response to thinking that had become suspicious of any and every dogmatism and was at home with new methods for the interpretation of texts.

It is not easy to give an outline of modernism because modernism is not easily isolated from the broader contemporary intellectual movement that was trying to make up for lost time in the "ecclesiastical sciences." In Germany, a current of liberalism in the universities and of Catholic reformism had developed throughout the nineteenth century, but it had nothing to do with modernism. In England G. Tyrrell (1861–1909) must be mentioned. In Italy, modernism had its place chiefly in the area of social action and religious culture, where it was associated with R. Murri (1870–1904), S. Minocchi (1869–1903), and E. Buonaiuti (1881–1946). It burst into public consciousness with the publication of A. Loisy's little "red book," *L'Évangile et l'Église* (Paris, 1902), which took the form of a historical defense not of the Roman system but of an enlightened Catholicism, in response to A. Harnack, who had just published his *Das Wesen des Christentums*, a historical defense of liberal Protestantism. Loisy's work was judged dangerous to faith; the same was even more true of the explanations that followed in his *Autour d'un petit livre* (Paris, 1903). In view of the number of his writings and also of the interest roused by the positions he took in exegesis and theology, it is not an exaggeration to call Loisy "the modernist par excellence." It is not right, however, to include among the modernists writers of this period who were innovators but who kept their distance from the doctrinal tendencies of modernism: M. Blondel, L. Laberthonnière, M.-J. Lagrange. Nor must we be too quick to make Kant, Schleiermacher, Renan, or even Newman the father of modernism.

Many of the positions Loisy adopted come within the purview of fundamental theology, since his modernist undertaking was based on a theology of revelation and of its development in the church.

1. Revelation as an Acquired Consciousness

Loisy sets out to strip revelation of all anthropomorphic ideas, i.e., those that regard revelation as a communication by God to humanity of ready-made and immutable ideas. He describes the original revelatory event in terms of "religious experience," "perception," "contact with the divine." This primordial religious experience finds expression in statements of faith and in doctrinal interpretations which believers formulate in the course of history as they become conscious of this gift of God. This consciousness, in which God is at work, is acquired by believers, and it is subject to the conditions and limitations affecting all human knowledge. Thus Loisy bases the development of revelation on the fact that the divine gift is continually given new expressions which are closely related to the culture of evolving humanity.

If we are to interpret correctly the much-discussed formula "revelation can only be the acquired consciousness which human beings have of their relationship with God" (*Autour d'un petit livre*, 195), a formula quoted and condemned in *Lamentabili*, we must understand it in light of a distinction Loisy makes between "living revelation" and "revelation formulated in human language." Living revelation is reducible to the embodiment in human beings of the divine mystery of which religion is the chief expression. The progressive human consciousness of the person's relationship with God is revelation in its human embodiment, which then takes the form of symbolic language and teaching. Revelation cannot exist unless human beings grasp and express it. Loisy is anxious to emphasize the active and indispensable role of human beings for whom "truth does not enter ready-made into their heads and . . . is never complete." Thus the truth of revelation does not escape being subject to the conditions governing all human truth, which is marked by historicity and relativity.

Loisy calls Christ "the Great Revealer," not so much because of the mystery of his person as because he is the one who has had the clearest and most intelligible "perception" of the relation between God and human beings. Christ's role was to bring to light what exists in the depths of all human beings, by enabling them better to understand what Loisy calls the "primitive revelation" or "unexplained revelation," i.e., the revelation that human beings carry, written in indistinct letters, in the depths of their religious consciousness. In his person, life, and teaching Jesus made clear what human beings have always vaguely understood: "God reveals himself to humanity in humanity, and humanity enters into a divine association with God" (*L'Évangile et l'Église*, 268).

In his *Through Scylla and Charybdis* (London, 1907), G. Tyrrell stresses even more than Loisy does the place of experience in revelation: In his view, revelation does not involve any communication of truths because it is an act of God with whom the believer enters into a mystical contact. The unformulated and non-conceptual contact with God finds expression in a kind of "prophetic knowledge," the elements of which are borrowed from the culture of the prophet who receives the revelation. Religious experience, which is the heart of revelation, is a gift which God can bestow on all human beings. But the prototypical experience that serves as a norm for believers is that of Jesus and of the apostles who were in direct contact with him. The expressions of their experience have an evocative power that can stir up in us an experience analogous to theirs. For Tyrrell, the expressions of faith have no value as reflecting objective reality. They are pure symbols that are conditioned by the cultural situation of an age, but they are useful to us as means of eliciting in us the experience of revelation and faith.

Because they reduced revelation too exclusively to an experience of the divine, the modernists failed to bring out the fact of God's self-communication in the history of salvation and in a special and definitive way in Jesus Christ. They nonetheless did highlight a real problem, namely, the distinction between truth in itself and truth as possessed by the human mind.

2. Access to Jesus

Loisy set about studying the foundations of Christianity with the aid of a historical method that had been emancipated from faith and dogma. He thought it possible to get back to the history of Jesus in its material content, without the mediation of the faith and religious purposes that underlay the production of the texts. Loisy stressed the literary genre of the Gospels: they are not essays in history but testimonies and expressions of the faith of the first disciples, who were attempting to give expression to real facts and their own religious experience. Even if some idealization and systematization of words and events were inevitable, he was convinced that it is possible to reach some consistent insight into the original, concrete form taken by the work and message of Jesus. In order to get back to Christ and his gospel, historians must look not only to the biblical texts but to the entire history of Christianity: "That which has emerged from the gospel shows the limitless power that was present in the work of Jesus." Loisy distinguished between the "historical Jesus" and the "Christ of faith," but, unlike BULTMANN later on, the distinction did not mean for him that knowledge of the historical Jesus has no role to play in faith.

Loisy did much to defend the historical reality of Jesus, but we must recognize that he did not penetrate deeply enough into the real nature of the intervention of Jesus in history and that he did not adequately bring out the originality of the message of Jesus and the transcendent and unique mystery of his person. He regarded the dogma of the divinity of Jesus as simply a learned Hellenistic expression, or perhaps a philosophical decipherment, of the transcendent and unique relationship between God and the historical person of Jesus.

3. Jesus and the Church

Loisy connects the establishment of the church "with a decision of the immortal Christ and not with an intention expressed by Jesus before his passion" (*Autour d'un petit livre*, 163). Jesus did not explicitly foresee a society that would have for its mission the spread of the gospel in future centuries. He preached the coming of the kingdom, which inevitably took on a particular social form. It is in this context that we must locate the words of Loisy which are so often cited to illustrate his eschatologism: "Jesus proclaimed the kingdom, and it was the church that came into being" (*L'Évangile et l'Église*, 155). The church came into being in order to continue the mission of Jesus during the period of waiting for the definitive coming of the kingdom; adaptation to the passage of time made the church's birth and evolution possible. Even though it claims not to change, the church has constantly changed, often despite its own will, in order that it may meet the needs of human beings. Loisy justifies the existence of the church as being in the service of the gospel, a service that has been shaped by the passing centuries. Its authority is no different from that of any teacher and any society. The church makes the revelation something always contemporary, and the whole of its history constitutes the ongoing revelation that has taken place down the centuries. As a historian, Loisy cannot prove that Jesus founded the church; but the church is not wholly alien to the thinking of Jesus. It follows him in the service of the gospel, which it must adapt to the changing conditions of human life. It effects this adaptation of the gospel through its teaching and the formulation of dogmas that serve to maintain a harmony between religious belief and the scientific development of humankind. Loisy used the historical method to show the development of sacramental practice and of the ecclesiastical institution. Many of his readers were surprised to learn that the origins and history of ecclesial practices and of dogmas were much more shaky and obscure than traditional theology made them appear. This introduction of history into Catholic theology is undoubtedly a major element in modernism.

4. Assessment of Modernism

Modernism is not reducible to the deviations that *Pascendi* isolated as alien to perennial Catholic thought. On the contrary, modernism derives its meaning and reality from the never-ending effort of Christian thought to explain the foundational events of Christianity. Modernism attempted to situate the Christian faith against a much broader backdrop than simply the traditional teaching of the church, and to find for this faith a language adapted to those transformations of the human mind of which the development of the modern sciences was both a symptom and an agent. Inasmuch as we have been hearing for thirty years about the renewal of exegesis and theology, it seems that the modernist project was not a priori unacceptable. Modernism was also the starting point for studies and for solutions that were condemned but that remain as questions in the program of fundamental theology. Modernism, and especially Loisy's thought, is of interest not so much for the solutions it offered as for the valid questions it elicited and formulated: the relative validity of expressions of truth; the truth of Scripture; the relation between history and dogma; the use of critical methods in exegesis; the development of dogmas; the entrance of history into theology. We must acknowledge the fact that many statements that were scandalous and even condemned at the time are now admitted or at least tolerated. Modernism was an undertaking by pioneers who were awkward, went too far, and made mistakes. They took the risk of using new critical and historical methods that they inherited from the still young history of religions, and they did so without enough of an effort in epistemology to keep them from becoming prisoners of a positivist and subjectivist mentality. Since their time the reconciliation of faith and reason has become possible because historical method and the sciences of religion have, on the whole, become self-critical and have developed a sense of their limitations; they have also gained a better understanding of the irreducible, specific, and transcendent elements in faith. Faith for its part has come to understand more clearly that the sciences, and especially history, can help it to unfold its riches and to become meaningful to the modern world.

Bibl.: P. Scoppola, *Crisi modernista e rinnovamento cattolico in Italia* (Bologna, 1961); E. Poulat, *Histoire, dogme et critique dans la crise moderniste* (Tournai, 1962); id., *Modernistica* (Paris, 1982); N. Provencher, *La révélation et son développement dans l'Église selon Alfred Loisy* (Ottawa, 1972); id., "La modernité dans le projet théologique d'Alfred Loisy," *Église et Théologie* 14 (1983): 35–45; G. Daly, *Transcendence and Immanence: A Study in Catholic Modernism and Integralism* (Oxford, 1980); var., *Le* *modernisme* (Paris, 1980); R. VIRGOULAY, *Blondel et le modernisme* (Paris, 1980).

Normand PROVENCHER

MODERNITY

The concept of modernity is a complex one, for it refers both to a historical process occurring within a limited time and space (from the sixteenth century to today, in the West) and to an ideology or rhetoric concerned with change, progress, and being in the vanguard. It has made its way into every area of life: art, technology, politics, moral values. Modernity implies an irresistible and irreversible break with the past because it claims to have at last brought true originality and progress. It presents itself as the flowering of a rationality that is giving birth to a quite unique civilization, while opposing all tradition, which it regards with suspicion, and bringing to bear a critical clarity of mind and an unprecedented creativity. Modernity judges what is old to be also outdated because its science and values are no longer effective and meaningful, and it regards progress and the transcendence of present reality as henceforth possible. Modernity is accompanied by crises and tensions in any given society, because it calls for choices and ways of living and thinking which it justifies by the standards of efficacy and originality.

1. Genesis and History of Modernity

In any and every social and cultural context the old and the new alternate and are at odds. Even the Middle Ages had its *via modernorum*. But modernity as a historical and polemical structure of change is to be found only in the West from the sixteenth century on, and it reached its full development only beginning in the nineteenth century.

According to school textbooks, the discovery of America by Christopher Columbus in 1492 marked the end of the Middle Ages and the beginning of modern times. At the start of this period the invention of printing, the discoveries of Galileo, and Renaissance humanism inaugurated a new way of looking at the world. Another factor was the Protestant Reformation, which divided Christendom but also introduced a new way of living the Christian faith, one that highlighted the freedom and autonomy of the person. During the seventeenth and eighteenth centuries the philosophical foundations of modernity were laid by the individualistic and rationalistic thinking promoted by Descartes and, later on, by the Enlightenment philosophers. The revolution of 1789 marked the beginning of the modern centralized, democratic state. The nineteenth century brought ever-new advances in science and technology, the rational division of labor, and urban development, all of which led to changes in moral outlook and the destruction of traditional cultures. The word "modernity" seems to have been used for the first time by Théophile Gautier in an article in the *Moniteur universel* for 8 July 1867: "On the one hand, the most extreme modernity, on the other an austere love of what is old."

From the nineteenth century to our own time, the ongoing break with the past has been constantly fostered by the increasing use of new sources of energy, more effective modes of production and transportation, and an ever more rational and anonymous organization of society. In our day, information and automation are helping to change the various areas of life in even more drastic ways. The massive, commercialized spread of cultural resources and the omnipresent intervention of the media (radio, television, video) are forming an attitude of change for change's sake, the content of the change being ephemeral and regarded as unimportant.

2. The Modern Mentality

The changes that have occurred since the nineteenth century have helped improve living conditions for humanity and have promoted the birth of modernity. While modernity is inexplicable without these changes, it cannot be identified with them but transcends them, because it is a way of thinking, a way of life, and a mentality, all of which have their specific traits and values: the dominant influence of measurable efficiency, the priority of structure over content and of image over thought, the promotion of rationality and activity at the expense of wisdom and contemplation, the value placed on consensus and public opinion which take precedence over truth. Modernity has also met with various kinds of resistance and has not avoided ambiguities that are reflected at present in the concern to safeguard the person as subject amid the ongoing homogenization of social life, in the fears and disappointments felt at blind development which threatens our fragile earth, and in the search for or pursuit of the irrational, the mysterious, or even the religious. There is thus a certain disenchantment in the face of modernity. Some people talk nowadays of "postmodernity," meaning by this that they have become less naïve and more realistic about the results of technology and the sciences and about the ability of these to give human life a meaning. People are clearer in their judgment on the successes of progress that is sought for its own sake to the detriment at times of the well-being of the individual. They are becoming skeptical about the search for the completest possible knowledge and about a way of life that no longer takes account of differences and of historical and cultural roots.

3. Christian Faith and Modernity

Secularization is the most visible way in which modernity has impacted on the Christian faith. A way of thinking and living without reference to God and his word has spread on a massive scale. Fundamental theology cannot evade the challenges of modernity if it wishes to be meaningful and to show itself credible to our age. The Christian faith has a long and rich history, but it is not the prisoner of its past. On the contrary, it is always new. Ever since the apostles did their preaching, it has shown itself to be possessed of an unqualified and all-embracing newness, for its origin is not in the dynamisms and needs of human beings, but in the very mystery of God's love. The images that best reflect its nature in contrast to an old world that is dying are the images of rebirth, everlasting youth, unending day, and new human being. The Christian faith has a new and unique message for modernity. In the face of the almost unlimited possibilities of modern science and technology, the Christian faith can urge the renunciation of all technologies except such as produce conditions making it possible to further those qualities of life that are necessary for human existence. It certainly encourages control of the elements, because it

knows that humanity is called upon to complete creation. But it also reminds human beings of the value of each person and of the truth that no single one of them may be sacrificed with the excuse that science is thereby advanced. Modern technology has too often become an end in itself, acknowledging no law but that of its own development and its own potentialities. But the Christian faith refuses to accept that science alone should decide on the meaning of human life. Moreover, the Christian faith gives rise to attitudes and concrete behaviors toward the sufferers whom modernity tends not to see. Fundamental theology can no longer limit itself to thinking about the Christian mystery within its own tradition or even within the framework of one or other philosophical tradition. It must emerge from its traditional cocoon and start listening to suffering human beings and meeting the challenges of culture shock. The practice and inculturation of the Christian faith are now part of the program of fundamental theology in the age of modernity.

According to modernity, human beings become autonomous by freeing themselves from their traditional guardians and even from God. The non-necessity of God for the achievement of human progress is a dimension of modernity. It must be acknowledged that the God whom modernity ignores is the God who was thought to be necessary for the running of the world and as the guarantor of the social order, but this was not the God of the Christian faith. One task of fundamental theology is to bring about a rediscovery of the God of the covenant, the God who gives himself to human beings in a completely unmerited way and with full respect for their autonomy and freedom, the God whose power is the power of love and of the law of grace. It must show that the mystery of God is not merely a response to a vague religious need and sense of helplessness. It must speak of the God who goes beyond all the expectations of the human heart and who, in one sense, is not necessary for successful human progress. It must make known the God who wills to communicate himself freely to human beings, and must show that it is possible for human beings to recognize him and be in communion with him. At a time when religion and the meaning of God are being eclipsed, fundamental theology must show that God is always present to human beings, even to those living in modernity and in God's apparent absence, an absence manifested in the cross of Jesus. In the eyes of Christian faith it is on the cross, where Jesus experiences the silence of God, that God saves the world and manifests his solidarity with those who suffer and die. Thus insofar as the theology of the cross reveals the true face of God, it is part of a fundamental theology that seeks to listen to modernity and show it the credibility of the Christian message.

Bibl.: J. LADRIÈRE, *Les enjeux de la rationalité: Le défi de la science et de la technologie aux cultures* (Paris, 1977); J. BAUDRILLARD, "Modernité," in *Encyclopedia Universalis*, vol. 11 (1980), 424–26; P. BERGER, *Facing Up to Modernity: Excursions in Society, Politics, and Religion* (New York, 1977); var., *Modernità: Storia e valore di un'idea* (Brescia, 1982); S. BRETON, "Le choc de la modernité sur la pensée philosophique et théologique," in *Théologie et choc des cultures* (Paris, 1984), 93–107; J. CHESNEAUX, *De la modernité* (Paris, 1984); R. VIRGOULAY, *Les courants de pensée du catholicisme français: L'épreuve de la modernité* (Paris, 1985); G. COTTIER, *Questions de modernité* (Paris, 1985); A. JEANNIÈRE, *Les fins du monde* (Paris, 1987); P. GISEL, *Albrecht Ritschl: La théologie en modernité* (Geneva, 1991); D. HARVEY, *The conditions of Postmodernity* (Oxford/Cambridge, 1991); S. CROOKS, J. PAKULSKI and M. WATERS, *Postmodernization* (London, 1992).

Normand PROVENCHER

MORAL EVIL

Evil takes endless forms, but the most radical evil has its source in the human heart. In the romantic period evil was equated with suffering, illness, and listlessness. Today, people disinfect human existence by denying sin. But we know very well that sin continues to exist and that, in addition, it is the supreme evil. Our everyday language is not mistaken when it distinguishes between one what *does* evil and what *is* evil, between evil *suffered* and evil *willed*. Suffering and death are called "human" because of the subject whom they affect; but in the strict sense sin alone is "human," because human beings alone are its free and responsible agents. It is what comes from the heart that renders a person evil (Mt 15:19–20). The discussion here will be of moral evil, sin, the black

tide of perverted love that smothers life. Since, however, SICKNESS and DEATH are elements in the stumbling block of evil, two other articles will deal with them as specific problems.

1. Appeasement or Rebellion

Before listening to Christ's answer, let us first look at two positions that are opposed to each other, while both are opposed to Christianity: the way of appeasement, which is a form of self-administered anesthesia, and the way of rebellion.

a. The first way tries to integrate evil into something that transcends it, namely, the order that reigns in the universe as a whole. For the moment (they tell us), we see only one side of reality: the scandalous side. But if our vision could encompass the whole of history, we would see injustice as but a temporary means of achieving an integral justice.

From this point of view, a "Christian" vision of the world that preaches resignation and says "things are not so bad," "everything will turn out right," or "good will conquer in the end," is strangely like the Marxist vision of history. According to MARXISM, the torment and despair we feel at the suffering of alienated and exploited humanity is due to our incomplete knowledge of history. The present hell is a necessary condition for entrance into a definitive order. The dialectic of contraries will yield a human race that is at last united and reconciled. In fact, it is the very degradation of the proletariat that will be the motive and energizing force of its liberation. The proletarian project, which is the result of despair, is leading to the establishment of a society in which there will be no masters and slaves and in which antagonisms hitherto inevitable will make way for a twofold harmony: of human beings among themselves and of human beings with the world. In order to focus the energies of men and women, it is enough for the moment to give them a glimpse of a higher state of ultratechnologized and ultradeveloped humanity in which each individual will profit through participation and each will find intellectual and affective fulfillment to the extent that he or she becomes an integral part of the system as a whole. The class struggle, while being a paroxysm of evil, also foretells the salvation of humanity.

The interplay of necessity and freedom remains ambiguous in the Marxist system. Are Marxists talking of freedom or of impeccability? The shift of the earthly paradise from the past to the future does not change the nature of the problem. Marxism's answer to the question of evil is a forced optimism. The way of appeasement or self-administered anesthesia is not an answer to the distress and horror caused by evil. If God exists and if he is Love, how can we justify him by saying that he sacrifices millions of innocent human beings for the sake of a harmony that will someday win out?

At times, we come across a still more radical solution. In past centuries human beings sinned, and sinned gravely, but they acknowledged themselves to be sinners and did not seek to evade the fact nor did they boast about it. The twentieth century is unique in that sin is denied or bracketed, even in Christian circles. Though obsessed by sin, by evil, people refuse to accept the burden of it; they shift the burden to institutions, structures, determinisms (hereditary, biological, psychic), or other people but never take it on themselves. They are concerned much more with collective liberation than with personal salvation. They disinfect human existence, as though it were comparable to the instruments that a surgeon uses. But when they thus maintain that everything is permitted and that human beings are pure, they remove the very possibility of the *fuller existence* that is connected with our condition as sinners who know we are sinners and are converted to Love.

It is certain, in contrast, that genuine Christianity has accepted the more difficult task when it insists, with the Scriptures, that the world has truly been willed by God and is the fruit of a deliberate intention. It is equivalently saying, in no uncertain terms, that evil exists because good exists. When it asserts that God wills the world, our present world, it opens itself to the question that Joan of Arc asks in Péguy's play: "But then why, my God, why so much evil? What kind of terrible game are you playing with us, Lord? How long, how long must we go on not understanding?" In the end, there are only two choices possible: to lay down one's weapons and surrender to God, or to rebel against him.

b. If people reject the Christian attitude, the only other attitude possible is rebellion.

In a sense, it is impossible not to rebel in the face of evil. Is there anyone who has not experienced the fits of rebellion that find expression in Job's curses? The torment we feel in the face of evil is like an obscure, dormant force that is always ready to spring up and is never perfectly under control. Thus when Christianity accepts in faith the scriptural judgment on the world—"And God saw that it was good"—it risks inciting a total, unqualified, and implacable rebellion against itself and God.

Dostoyevsky has given extremely dramatic expression to this rebellion in *The Brothers Karamazov*. When Christ returns to earth in order to renew the faith and courage of human beings, he is once again arrested and imprisoned. The Grand Inquisitor says to him:

> Is it you? You? . . . Do not answer, be silent. And, indeed, what can you say? I know too well what you would say. Besides, you have no right to add anything to what you have said already in the days of old. Why, then, did you come to meddle with us? For you have come to meddle with us, and you know it. But do you know what is going to happen tomorrow? . . . Tomorrow I shall condemn you and burn you at the stake. . . . Now you have seen those 'free' men. . . . You want to go into the world and you are going empty-handed, with some promise of freedom, which men in their simplicity and their innate lawlessness cannot even comprehend, which they fear and dread. . . . But in the end they will lay their freedom at our feet. . . . Instead of gaining possession of men's freedom, you gave them greater freedom than ever! . . . We have corrected your great work. . . . And men rejoiced that they were once more led like sheep. . . . Oh, we will convince them that only then will they become free when they have resigned their freedom to us and have submitted to us. (*The Brothers Karamazov*, trans. D. Magarshack [Baltimore: Penguin, 1958], 1:293–303)

The day when we discover that what should not be is and that evil seems to hoist its flag over all reality and prevail, we reach the point at which we ask ourselves: "Where is the greater guilt to be found: In human beings or in God? In the human self-centeredness and desire that unleash all evils, or in God who punishes the evil to which he himself has given rise along with freedom?" This somber question lies muffled in the tormented heart of every human being. People today are in rebellion against God—people like the poet Lautréamont, who committed suicide at the age of twenty-one while calling upon God to contemplate for all eternity the poet's undeserved punishment; or like Nietzsche: "God is dead. God remains dead. And we have killed him." Nietzsche died a madman, but with him the "rebel" was born.

Rebellion, in this context, is "the condemnation of God in the name of justice and of abhorrence of evil." In order to correct God's work freedom must be suppressed, but in order to suppress freedom, God must be suppressed, for no one rebels against a nonexistent God. Rebellion is directed against a God who exists and, more concretely, against the Christian God. Human beings want God to be silent so that they need not hear anything more about him or be any longer disturbed by him. They prefer to murder God so that they need not be subjected in the depths of their hearts to the questioning that condemns us.

Behind this rebellion against God lies not only an eternal rejection of all hope but also a rejection of the human condition itself. In rebelling against God, human beings render themselves capable of the worst horrors. For rebellion is a sweeping thing. In order to put an end to evil and change the human condition at whatever cost, people will sacrifice millions of beings to a progress that is conceived and carried out "on a human scale." In order to correct God's work, they expropriate freedom, and the result is an order of things worse than any of the evils to be corrected. When Marxists decide to impose what they regard as justice, they sacrifice whole sectors of the human race. The worst murderers in Shakespeare stopped at ten or so corpses because they were not driven by an ideology. Our century with its IDEOLOGIES ceaselessly piles up crimes in order to deliver us from all evil. To exterminate evil human beings exterminate God; but once God is crucified, they are at the mercy of humankind, the wolf capable of every ferocity.

What is it, in the final analysis, that makes rebellion possible? God did not will rebellion, but he did will freedom, and freedom makes rebellion possible. If we were simply minerals or robots, rebellion would be impossible. If we have the terrible, fearful power of saying no, it because we are free. Human beings are not simply piano keys; they are free, and their freedom means they can choose between rejection and love. Christ lets us have the last word.

"The scandal of the universe," Bernanos said, "is not suffering but freedom." But when we see human beings possessing such power that they can trigger the worst calamities, how can we not be tempted to say: "Is it really worth the cost? Why, Lord?"

If God were to excuse himself, it would not be for the evil he has done to us but for having made us *free*. He chose to create not only stones, animals, and computers but also persons, that is, beings capable of saying either yes or no, even to God. In creating "persons," he took the supreme risk. That is why he comes to us defenseless, as a child, with empty hands, or with arms stretched out on a cross, in order to prove to us that he really meant us to be free. God is willing that human beings should manifest their greatness by rebellion as well as by love. For Christians the problem is even more tragic, because freedom makes possible a rebellion that remains unchanged through eternity. In fact, the only truly decisive rendezvous with evil takes place in Gethsemane and on Calvary.

The only response to the folly of rebellion and evil is the folly of the cross. Out of respect for our freedom God has made known to us that the foolishness to which he would lead us is that of making ourselves helpless and defenseless, of surrendering to God and putting ourselves completely into his hands in faith and love. This seeming defeat is the only true wisdom. If rebellious human beings reject it, they destroy what is around them and destroy themselves with their violence. If we hold that the Innocent One died for all and as one struck by all, then in solidarity with this Christ we will surrender with him and join him in the final plea: "Father!" By forgiving and by surrendering to the Father, Christ shows the faith he places in human beings as capable of being converted to him; he also shows his trust in the Father, who is able to triumph over death through life. We remain in darkness, but under the stars. All those who have risen above their rebelliousness have refused to defend themselves and instead have surrendered to God: Paul, Augustine, and Francis of Assisi, as well as all the oppressed peoples who hope that by forgiving their oppressors and giving faithful, persevering witness to the Lord, they will win the conversion of human beings from oppressive rebellion to a love that confesses its sins (see C. Mesters, *La mission du peuple qui souffre* [Paris, 1986]).

2. Christ, Sinners, and Sin

In response to the unsatisfactory solutions offered by appeasement and rebellion, philosophers have multiplied qualifications that afford a better grasp of the problem. These qualifications serve as signposts on the way, but they do not answer the concrete questions human beings have when confronted by crime, hatred, injustice, and the martyrdom of the innocent. Christ does not offer us a metaphysical solution to the riddle of sin; he does offer a presence and an attitude.

We have no way of knowing God's views on sin except through Christ. If there is an understanding to be had, it must come from him. Now, from Genesis to the Gospels, from Hosea to John, the Scriptures constantly show God to us as a *lover*. Creation is a story with two characters in which God's yes looks for the creature's yes in return. If creation is to reach its completion, it needs the consent of human beings, because God creates not slaves but free persons. He is not a tyrant, but a lover; he invites, calls, asks: "If you want to!" God loves human beings enough to lay aside his power and run the risk of being rejected. If there is a hell, it is a hell that individuals will for themselves. For human beings can withdraw from this collaboration, drown out this call, and bring about a failure, an "un-creation" of the universe, but they cannot keep Love from continuing to love. As one comes to understand God and his love, one enters into abysses of both his tenderness and his weakness. By creating free persons, God is willing to be crucified by those who refuse to love him, but he cannot on that account stop being always "in love."

In the perspective given us by revelation we must reverse the perspective adopted by Camus and Ivan Karamazov. Instead of saying: "If evil exists, God does not exist," we must say: "If the martyrdom of the innocent is so terrible, it is because God exists and is a victim along with the innocent." The reason why sin is such a monstrous thing is that it attacks the infinite dignity of the human person. Only because God *is*, can evil have the horrible, scandalous face of a betrayal. In the innocent person it is God who is being aimed at; he is crucified along with the innocent. Sin is our very selves "in a state of rejection." When confronted by a human race that is stiff-necked, closed in on itself, immured in its rebellion, what can love do but continue to love, because God is Love? It can only continue to love like the husband who is wounded by his wife's betrayal but offers his wounded and agonizing fidelity in the hope that his love will finally be answered by love.

That is how Christ shows himself in his parables, in his attitudes, in his actions which are signs. Would we have acted as Christ did in dealing with the Samaritan woman? He offers this sinner the way to the highest level of reconciliation. Would we have chosen traitors like Peter and Judas and made them our righthand men? In Christ's eyes the most wretched of persons is capable of the greatest love: a thief, a wrongdoer, is the first candidate for the kingdom of heaven. The originality of Christianity consists in its having defined the relationship between human beings and God, between infinite wretchedness and infinite greatness, as one of "reciprocity." God expects to be loved in return, and out of love for our love, he leaves us the power either to turn away or to accept. That is the whole point of the parable of the prodigal son. God plays the game of freedom; he is silent when we turn away. When the son returns after wasting all that he had received, the father's attitude is not one of anger or concern for justice, or even forgiveness; instead the father waits for the son, sees him coming afar off, interrupts his excuses, sends for the robe, the ring, and the shoes, runs out to meet him, and embraces him, for he who suffers most loves most. God loves, but "in divine measure," with a love *completely different* from the love human beings have. Christ is the first victim of sin.

The washing of the feet gives advance expression to the attitude of Christ that will receive its final "shape" on the cross. As he celebrates his final meal with his disciples, Christ stoops and abases himself to wash their feet, including those of Judas. Here love and rejection meet, light and darkness, Christ and Satan, the power of evil and the omnipotence of love. For the omnipotence manifested here is that of weakness, abasement, poverty. Christ deliberately takes on the condition of a slave who is wholly at the mercy of others, who is wholly at the service of human beings, even for the service that consists in saving others at the cost of his own life. The supper, the washing of the feet, the cross: it is always love that gives itself, out of love, in order to disarm hatred and rejection. The human tragedy is that men and women do not believe in God's love for them.

3. The Only Response: The Crucified God

God's answer to the questions of human beings about the problem of evil is the disfigured face of his Son, "crucified for us." The sight of that face is the most decisive and staggering of all answers to the problem of evil. Without the cross God would have stayed on his side of the dividing line, and we on ours. But by means of the cross he puts himself on the side of the victims, the tortured, the oppressed, the humiliated. Human beings stand or fall in the presence of this face: "Lord, show us your face, and we shall be saved" (Ps 80:4).

The reader perhaps recalls the dramatic conversation described by Georges Bernanos in his *Diary of a Country Priest*, between the priest and the lady of the manor in the small village. The lady lost her child when it was quite young and is filled with hatred and rebellion against God. She has it in for God! The priest timidly ventures to speak to her of resignation. The countess replies: "Don't you think me resigned enough? If I hadn't been resigned!" Hardly aware of what he is saying, the priest continues: "God is not to be bargained with. We must give ourselves to Him unconditionally. Give Him everything. He will give you back even more." At this the countess cries out in wild rage: "Suppose that in this world or the next, somewhere was a place where God doesn't exist . . . I'd take my boy to that place . . . and I'd say to God: 'Now, stamp us out!'" The priest thinks of the sobs, the gasps of agony, torn from the throats of wretched human beings in the press of suffering. He says: "Madam, if our God were a pagan god or the god of the intellectuals. . . . He might fly to His remotest heaven and our grief would force Him down to earth again. But you know that our God came to be among us. Shake your fist at Him, spit in His face, scourge Him, and finally crucify Him: what does it matter? My daughter, it's already been done to Him. . . . Hell is not to love any more."

Then, at the end of her strength, exhausted by an interior struggle that has gone on for eleven years, the countess surrenders. With a quick gesture, she flings into the fire her child's lock of blond hair that she had kept with her in a locket as a witness against God. She has just escaped from a terrible loneliness because she has encountered disfigured Innocence and suddenly her heart broke open. Hope entered in, hastening there from the wide spaces, and invaded her like a great breath of spring. In Christ's gaze she has once again found peace, serenity, and boundless joy. The next night, doubtless broken by the agony she had lived with for so many years, the countess died, but as a woman reconciled to Love. Two hearts crushed in the same press, but Love had emerged victorious over hatred.

In like manner, if we want to understand and not run away, we must contemplate the cross, which is wiser than any explanation, stronger than any challenge, mightier than any violence. The supreme law governing this world is not a cosmic law but the law of the mysterious dialogue between human freedom, which has been endowed with the capability of saying the final word, and the freedom of God, whose final word is not a word but an act, a *passion* that shows us how far sin can go but, at the same time, how far love can go. Here rebellion is not beaten down from outside but is plunged into the abyss of Love. Here human beings meet not resistance but outstretched arms. In order to disarm us when we rebel, God offers us a superabundance of love. On the cross that stands at the crossroads of the centuries, torn and bloodied love is the counterweight that tips the scales, as it were, despite all the weight of our sins and offsets all our acts of hatred. The crucified Christ introduces into the world a love that is greater than all the hatred there may ever be.

We need, therefore, to reappraise all our ideas about God. When he sees his children choosing death by refusing to answer his call, he takes their place, he makes himself their "security." The cross thus takes us into a universe that is located completely outside the realm of justice, a universe of love—but a *love that is wholly other* and mysterious because it is divine in character. Nowhere is God more powerful than when he is powerless. If the mystery of evil is incomprehensible, the mystery of God's love is even more so.

The cross is love's ultimate attempt to break down our hatred, do away with our self-centeredness, and uncrucify God. But what is there about the human person, about this perverted race, that should elicit such excessive love, except the possibility that a love may come to birth in us, a new life be engendered that is forever free and liberated, a *child* be initiated into the life of the Trinity? The Christ who hangs on the tree of the cross urges human beings to put themselves into the Father's hands as the children conceived of his love.

The cross of Christ represents the extreme form of unreason and the most bewildering and illusory victory possible of the forces of evil over him who is life and power. But at the same time the cross is the revelation of a love that wins the day over evil, not by force or by love that overwhelms, but by an excess of love that consists in accepting death from the very hand of the beloved and enduring the punishment meant for the beloved, in the hope that rebellious love will become love again. The all-weakness of God then becomes the all-powerfulness of God. "Many waters cannot quench love, neither can floods drown it" (Song 8:7). Paul says: "We proclaim Christ crucified, a stumbling block to Jews and foolishness to Gentiles, but to those who are the called . . . the power of God and the wisdom of God. For God's foolishness is wiser than human wisdom, and God's weakness is stronger than human strength" (1 Cor 1:23–25). "Whoever does not love does not know God, for God is love" (1 Jn 4:8). What could Love do that it has not already done?

Henceforth we are the children of God, and his Spirit dwells in us. But in order to alter our condition in this manner, God had to become one of us; without himself knowing sin, he had to cross the gulf of absence that had been opened up by human rejection and rebellion. *Only* the action of the Son of God with his two natures, divine and human, could assume such a mission. Christ is the only point of convergence in which all things are fulfilled, surpassed, abolished, and replaced by the *one* work that God accomplishes as a human being and that God alone, as a human being, can accomplish. The seriousness of the crucified Christ who has been delivered up for us must be matched by the seriousness of our love, which allows all rebellion, all rejection, to be melted down in the white heat of the Trinity's love.

4. From Sin to Love

Christianity does not get rid of sin. It is not a religion of consolation or of escape but a religion of conversion. Christianity's answer to sin is the love that disarms by inviting human beings to lay down their arms out of love. The message of Christianity is a *message about the meaning of freedom and love* and about the omnipotent power of love. If there is any victory over evil, it is won by a love that rises above hate. Christ is Love in its pure state; that is why he can win the victory over our limited rebellions.

We give the name "conversions" to all these reversals of situation that can, in a moment, turn a sinner, a criminal, into a saint. Paradoxically, according to the gospel (Lk 15:17–20), it is the sinner, descending into hell, who is closest to the kingdom. Only too often, satisfaction with mediocrity keeps us from seeing the abysses within us; sinners, who are already at the bottom of the pit, often see them better than do the "just." Their wretchedness can even become a "shortcut" to love and speed them to God. God understands us, of course, but this does not mean that he connives with our cheating. What is asked of us is that we not refuse to recognize ourselves for what we really are, by classifying ourselves as honorable, "average" people. Sinners and criminals, who do not mistake themselves for someone else, already have in their hearts a breach through which mercy can enter in. They recognize themselves to be "sinners who are loved." Our resistance, our pharisaism, is stupid and spurious. We are all guilty; we all need to lay down our arms in the presence of love and acknowledge that we are prisoners of sin yet loved by God, and that we will never be loved with a love greater than his.

Christianity's answer to the problem of sin relativizes or dismisses a good many pseudo-solutions and declares them invalid:

1. The *moralistic* solutions, according to which the question of evil is answered by the satisfaction of a good conscience and by keeping one's distance from sinners. But those who take this approach forget that evil is installed in the human heart as something that is always and constantly possible.

2. The *Manichean* solutions, which conceive

of the world as a battlefield on which the good and the wicked meet or, more concretely, on which *we* do battle against *them*. It is a simplistic vision because wheat and tares are always intermingled in the affairs of this world. The supreme illusion is to claim to eliminate evil with a single blow in a final war to end all wars. It is an illusion because freedom and grace can shift at any moment, thus destroying the most solidly established boundaries.

3. The *Promethean* solutions, which regard evil as consisting wholly in an alienation that, because human beings lack knowledge and power, makes them dependent on natural and social forces; these, however, they will some day control with the aid of rational techniques. But nothing is more equivocal than this notion of controlling the world. Techniques can render human beings subservient to their fellows because they provide increasingly refined and despotic means of exploitation and manipulation; contemporary history offers abundant evidence that these threats are not imaginary.

Christianity is Promethean, but in its own special way, inasmuch as it associates human beings with the still-unfinished work of creation and redemption. But in proclaiming a salvation that is already accomplished, even if still to be completed, Christianity is both more optimistic than any optimistic philosophy and more pessimistic than any pessimistic view of the world. Both attitudes are fitting in a world that is not yet the definitive kingdom. We are all looking forward to a new world in which there will be no more tears or evil or death (Rv 21:4). But while we wait, the disproportion between what is coming and what we now see is so great that faith itself at times suffers attacks of vertigo. The sheer concentration of evil, its constantly renewed power, its extent, its proliferation, its exacerbated violence are all too overwhelming. As long as evil has the good sense to remain within certain limits, we can hold out. But at times it erupts with such savage spite that we are afraid of being engulfed by it. Could we have endured the treatment inflicted on the victims of Dachau, Buchenwald, Auschwitz, Treblinka, Cambodia, or Chile? We must be either pharisaic or naïve to claim that we would never have been sifted by the blows of evil and the horror of the injustice. Our faith remains exposed to the scandal of iniquity,

exposed to testing without the certainty of overcoming.

But if our faith is vulnerable, this is at least a sign that it exists! All of us are or will some day be sifted by evil that is unleashed upon us. But faith itself tells us that if all the consolations of earth cannot make up for evil, still less is there a proportion between the weight of glory that awaits us and is already here, and the weight of the evil we undergo. True enough, at certain moments evil seems to us more violent, more cruel, more ugly than anything we could have imagined; that is the hour of scandal, testing, and darkness. The testing shows us that we are not big enough to face the evil *alone*. But then, in a second stage, we discover that we are even less "fitted" for the immense good that is coming. The terrifying mystery of evil is answered by the still more impenetrable mystery of the happiness prepared for us. Two places, two hills, symbolize this mystery: Golgotha and Tabor. There is the weight of evil, but there is is the still greater weight of the glory that is coming, flooding in like the northern lights that transfigure a night already thronged with stars. Let us be willing not to triumph over evil with a heroic flourish but rather to be disarmed by love, because Christ before us laid down his arms in the face of our rejection and accepted the weakness of love.

Even in the presence of the cross, moral evil, connected as it is with freedom, remains a mystery; but the superabundance of love shown us in Christ projects such a superabundance of MEANING that it lights up even this abyss of darkness.

Bibl.: A.-D. SERTILLANGES, *Le problème du mal* (Paris, 1948, 1951); R. VERNEAUX, *Problèmes et mystères du mal* (Paris, 1956); X. TILLIETTE, *La légende du Grand Inquisiteur* (Paris, 1956); E. BORNE, *Le problème du mal* (Paris, 1958); id., "Mal," *DSp*, 74–75, cols. 122–36; C. JOURNET, *Le mal: Essai théologique* (Paris, 1962); P. ROQUEPLO, *Expérience du monde, expérience de Dieu* (Paris, 1968); F. HAINAUT, *Le mal: énigme scandaleuse, contestation radicale* (Paris, 1971); B. BRO, *Le pouvoir du mal* (Paris, 1976); M. ZUNDEL, *Quel homme et quel Dieu* (Paris, 1976); E. Y. YARNOLD, "Male," *NDT*, 815–34; P. EVDOKIMOV, *Dostoïevski et le problème du mal* (Bruges/Brussels/ Paris, 1978); P. GUILLY, "Mal," *Cath* 8:219–32; R. LATOURELLE, "The Power of Evil and Salvation through the Cross," in R. Latourelle, *Man and His Problems in the Light of Jesus Christ* (New York,

1983), 277–95; A. BONORA, "Male," *NDTB*, 870–87; M. FÉDOU, "Le christianisme et le problème du mal," *NRT* 113 (1991): 824–38.

René LATOURELLE

MYSTERY AND MYSTERIES

In the Bible, this concept has a thoroughly distinctive quality of an eschatological kind, with an implicit relatedness to historical events. The latter, however, point back to a common and unitary ground, so that the various uses of the word refer, via the inner connectedness of the realities they designate (*nexus mysteriorum*), to the originator and fulfillment of reality as such, i.e., to God, who is himself ultimately designated as a mystery. This, however, has a retroactive effect on the meaning of the word, insofar as it does not here signify merely the simply unknown, e.g., a riddle, a problem, or other such thing. Those expressions always connote something that should not exist and must be overcome, a demand by humans for a knowledge and resolution without which they cannot attain fullness in their lives. The riddle has to be solved. As long as it is not, there is discontent and a sense of burden, of lack. Mystery, in the Christian sense, is something totally different. It intimates its presence to humans in such a manner that they feel and understand not only that here no solution is possible, but that mystery must, for them, remain mystery, because only then is it meaningful to them and enduringly important, because only then does it constitute their happiness. Mystery is, as mystery, something good. Any attempt to resolve it must end in unhappiness for humans and place their salvation at risk. Moreover, such attempts are, in their basic intent, always ineffective because they are directed at an unsuitable object. God and his mystery are no object for humans.

Accordingly, the concept designates something that absolutely transcends human beings and is, for that reason, in no way directly graspable by them. They have to acknowledge it in its nature as transcendent to them. More precisely, this implies accepting something as a mystery; renouncing any hope of controlling or influencing it from the human side, because

that is an inappropriate expectation; and experiencing this, just as it is, as good and right, and thus as a cause for happiness. Even if this experience is, as such, unique, like God himself whom it concerns, similar experiences nonetheless occur in human life in the context of interaction with other persons. For another person, too, may never be reduced to an object of our behavior and control if we are to respect him or her as a person with the dignity that personhood implies. Thus one can speak of a mystery of personhood in relation to humans. In it is summarized everything that constitutes being a human. Its outer expressions are therefore all a means to understanding something of the mystery. To that extent, the one mystery unfolds itself in a profusion of concretizations which, as inherently related to that mystery, share in its mysteriousness. These observations make it necessary to attribute a personal character to mystery; whereas a problem, a riddle, or an uncompleted task are objective in character. These experiences also enter into the meaning of the concept of mystery in its application to God, to his self-expressions, or to his redemptive history of humanity and the world. That history, as pointing beyond the sphere of immanence and containing the claim of the biblical message, confronts humans with a reality that gives them cause to reassess their position. They feel themselves subject to higher jurisdiction, yet without being violated in their sense of self-worth or otherwise restricted. The personal mystery addresses itself to them in a variety of ways, thereby affording them an opportunity to attain genuine self-understanding, through which they recognize, and have to acknowledge, that their position corresponds in the best possible way to given actualities. In this connection, they also come to realize that they owe their being to the absolute mystery; that they remain bound to that mystery, which is itself unconditioned, whereas they are conditioned in precisely such a way as to have to answer for themselves before it. Basically, then, what is involved is God himself, who is just designated by the word "mystery" in a way that recalls to mind certain conditions of human familiarity with this word, conditions which, precisely in view of modern criticism and modern philosophical possibilities, must be absolutely heeded if one wishes to avoid captivation by unfounded conceptions and false ideas. Consequently, talk of mystery has acquired a changed standing and should, above all, be engaged in with more circumspection and discrimination than was previously possible. Use of the word must be guarded, especially in relation to the variety of individual manifestations that were traditionally represented, quite naively, as mysteries. Also, in order to preclude misunderstandings, the common distinctions between *mysteria stricte dicta* (mysteries in the full, strict sense) and derivative sorts of reality need to be used most sparingly and to be precisely defined. The difficulty lies in the fact, on the one hand, that the connection between God and creation must not be violated or restricted, that the interrelatedness in governance and dependence must be clearly and unalteredly expressed; but, on the other hand, that care must be taken to avoid any commingling or confusing of the noncreaturely and the creaturely. This task calls for an appropriate formulation and application of analogy. In it, the term "mystery" should thenceforth be strictly reserved for application to God and to whatever emanates directly from, and gives expression to, him. Evil, by contrast, should no longer be designated as *mysterium iniquitatis*, for reasons including the fact that in everyday language the concept of mystery tends to connote an attitude of joyous and hopeful expectation.

Against this background, it can then make sound and fruitful sense to rearticulate the traditional religious mysteries of the Trinity of God, the incarnation, and of divine grace as formulations of the mystery per se, namely, as the manifestation of the loving and self-bestowing God who redeems humanity and the world and becomes plainly evident in it as Creator. Viewed in this way, the reality of God that is understood as mystery acquires great significance for a fundamental theology that regards as its basic task the clarification of the question of God for modern humanity. Pointing in this same direction is the Second Vatican Council's commission to provide students in theological disciplines with an *introductio in mysterium Christi*. Considering the nature of the subject matter, that would seem to be part of the role of fundamental theology. In any case, such an introduction deals with the understanding of religion, Christianity, and the church precisely in the light of the mystery and takes this beyond any narrowly rational conception. The rationality proper to Christianity itself is naturally not thereby devalued but simply challenged, inasmuch as mystery, rather than supplanting rational endeavor, requires more consistent and more rigorous application of this, up to the point where it arrives, by its own means, at a boundary it can no longer go beyond. This incorporates modern criticism and enables it to be applied in religious thought, since, through the mystery that discloses transcendence, the critical attitude is transformed at every juncture into a listening and accepting one—without thereby becoming irrational—in which humans are no longer able, or permitted, to stand before the greater reality of God as anything but autonomous creatures with a thinking answerability that unfolds itself in acceptance and devotion. The latter are thus explained and justified in a precisely rational way, even if, by nature, they extend beyond the plane of mere reason. They draw their positive character from the ever-greater God as that beatific mystery which bestows itself upon humans in redemption and creation.

Bibl.: K. RAHNER, "Mystery," *SM* 1:133–36; id., "The Concept of Mystery in Catholic Theology," in *Theological Investigations*, vol. 4 (1960; London, 1966), 36–76; id., "Unity—Love—Mystery," in *Theological Investigations*, vol. 8 (1967; London, 1971), 229–50; id., "The Foundations of Belief Today" in *Theological Investigations*, vol. 16 (1979; New York, 1983), 3–23; id., "The Hiddenness of God" in ibid., 227–43.

Karl H. NEUFELD

N

NEWMAN, JOHN HENRY

In religious inquiry each of us can speak only for himself, and for himself he has a right to speak. His own experiences are enough for himself, but he cannot speak for others; he cannot lay down the law; he can only bring his own experiences to the common stock of psychological facts. He knows what has satisfied and satisfies himself; if it satisfies him, it is likely to satisfy others; if, as he believes and is sure, it is true, it will approve itself to others also, for there is but one truth. (*Grammar of Assent*, 385)

This expression alone should enable us to see why J. H. Newman (1801–1890) was considered one of the most controversial personalities of the last century. During his life he was violently attacked by Catholics and Anglicans alike. The latter thought of him as a traitor; by the former he was regarded with suspicion. On these impressions Newman himself comments in the *Apologia pro vita sua*, the autobiography written for the purpose of defending the motives behind his conversion. Through this narrative there shines the personality of an honest, serious, devout, and humble man.

Notwithstanding his elevation to the rank of cardinal by Leo XII in 1879, his writings remained the object of very different judgments for long after his death. Some hailed them as the harbingers of a practical philosophy and of *L'Action*; others perceived them as affording a foundation for modernist thought; while E. Przywara saw in Newman a bridge uniting Thomas Aquinas with modern thought; Prezzolini looked on him as the "chief of traditionalist Catholics."

Nevertheless, those who regarded Newman as an anti-intellectual, because he gave first place, with the Pascalian *raison du coeur*, to the psychology of experience, forgot that these reasons, though of the heart, were as far as he was concerned only *reasons*.

Finally there were others still who approached Newman not by a direct route, as the hard work of an honest seeker requires, but by means of others, and their interpretations of his works were not, especially in the beginning, particularly correct and faithful.

In the history of nineteenth-century APOLOGETICS, Newman stands alone. Like PASCAL, BLONDEL, TEILHARD, and a few others, he worked in a stagnant context that preferred the oversecure certainty of dogmatic metaphysical principles to the "situational" approach of a more pragmatical believer.

Newman's apologetic program, however, has its roots in an older and more fertile soil, that of Scripture and patristics. Brought up as an Anglican, he had more trust than Catholics had in the sacred text. His pastoral experience at St. Mary's and at Littlemore, which was to give life to his *Sermons*, enabled him to deepen his knowledge of and to comment on Scripture in a way that few exegetes and theologians of the period could emulate. The founding of the *Library of the Fathers* in 1835 had enabled him to find in the writings of the first-century fathers of the church the strength and courage to undertake the "second reformation" (*Apologia*, 51).

1. Essay in Aid of a Grammar of Assent

Though in many of the works of his fertile genius we find elements appropriate to an apologetic system—we need only think of the *University Sermons*, in which the theme of the relationship between faith and reason frequently recurs—it is nonetheless to the *Grammar of Assent* that we must turn to see the plan of a fundamental theology designed to provide a rational exposition of the faith for the ordinary person.

This was a theme that passionately engaged Newman for at least thirty years. In some notes written in 1860, he says: "How can one make use of reason where faith is concerned? How can one claim one has made use of one's intellect honestly and respectfully with regard to one's Creator? If a religion is open to *reason* and at the same time to *all*, there ought to be sufficient available reasons for rationally convincing each individual." In the *Grammar of Assent*, there come together, in a unique synthesis, those different problems that had been the object of Newman's studies, from the development of dogma to tradition, to the need to give a rational answer to the assent of faith.

His text does not make easy reading. Philosophy and theology share a common platform, without becoming confused, resting together in robust equilibrium; sometimes we even seem to be witnessing a reciprocal integration of the one with the other, It would, however, be ingenuous to think that in the *Grammar of Assent* theology has only a secondary role. After the more narrative, or catechetical, dimension—since recourse is had to daily experience and since the purpose of the book is to speak to the ordinary person—theology enjoys an authentically protagonistic role. For the true center of study is the faith of the believer and, more precisely, of the believer in the act of trying to discover those principles that will allow him or her to verify the certainty of his or her own decision of faith.

Of course, as a child of his times, Newman belongs to that current of thought deriving from Locke and Hume as the originators of an experiential empiricism; nevertheless, his "empiricism" is different, since it is simply a premise, not the final point of arrival. His studies therefore remain fully theological since deliberately framed by the light of faith; at the same time, they are fully apologetic since designed to give reason its peculiar role as the element common to all in their quest for and decisions of faith.

The *Grammar of Assent*, written in 1870, is made up of two main parts: in the first we study the relationship between *assent* and *apprehension*; in the second, between *assent* and *inference*. As the basis of this relationship, however, we study the role of the subject in its cognitive activity and, more specifically, in its religious dimension.

The context in which the work is placed is determined by two objections deriving from liberalism: (a) If religion aims to achieve the exercise of love and worship, why the need for a profession of faith? (b) Why should the certainty of adhesion to the faith be subordinate to the certainty of the proofs that it furnishes? In a word, we are faced with the difficulty of how to show the need for a professed act of faith and for it to be intelligible.

Newman's reply begins forthwith by analyzing the *modalities* of human knowledge. These are of a threefold order: (1) the *proposition*, which can be "notional" and "true" (e.g., "man is a rational animal," "Philip was the father of Alexander"), to which corresponds (2) *apprehension*, that act, i.e., by means of which a mean-

ing is assigned to the terms that compose the proposition, at the moment of their being interpreted. Contained in apprehension are the objects of sense perception; whereas "notional" apprehension allows progress and speculative knowledge, "real" apprehension, which is the more important, permits maintenance and conservation of what is known. This creates the *images* making possible our in-dwelling cognitive experience and, by means of the synthesizing faculty, gives rise to new thought forms. (3) Lastly, the act of assent "is in itself the absolute acceptance of a proposition without any condition" (*Grammar*, 13). This stands in relationship with apprehension and inference.

As we have said, the first part of the *Grammar* is devoted to the question of apprehension. Schematically, this is the dynamic by which Newman proceeds.

True assent allows the arousal in the subject of emotions and feelings that dynamically impel him toward action; notional assent, on the other hand, brings him to the contemplation of his mental images. This *schema*, carried into the realm of dogma, will offer the possibility of distinguishing between a true and a notional assent. The former is related to religion and brings life to its subject; the latter relates to theology and expresses the reflection of the intellect.

Assent in either case involves an absolute and permanent engagement; however, it gave Newman the opportunity to demonstrate that "sense sensations, instinct, intuition, supply us with facts, and the intellect uses them" (*Grammar*, 98). Thereby, an earlier dimension is recovered, that which recognizes a more universal horizon, natural religion—which is successively illuminated and interpreted by revelation.

Starting from this premise, Newman pursues his study by showing the movement of the human mind when it approaches "belief," i.e., the material object of faith. The proposition "I believe in one God" is analyzed within the horizon of apprehension and serves to establish a further principle which continues the previously made distinction: religion touches the propositions only as they affect the subject, only on one's own can one give a true assent; the general and the systematic, however, are the concern of theology, through which all that is notional material is object of reflection.

To encourage true assent and therefore to allow belief to become the motive force of life,

Newman has recourse to the feeling of *conscience,* since this, as moral sense and sense of duty, increasingly allows the subject to relate to his actions and to consistency of life. Consciousness of good and evil, however, does not arise out of inanimate things but is always a person-to-person relationship; it is at this point, hence, that the ethical principle is presented as the discovery of "the picture of a Supreme Governor, a Judge, holy, just, powerful" (*Grammar,* 110). At the same time, we discover the principle that guarantees true assent. For in the human (Newman was to say "in the infant"), images are created that go beyond the simple notion of godhead and give rise to a concrete living commitment, since they relate to the Creator, to him who rewards or punishes, but who in any case is a personal God to whom true and notional assent is given.

One conclusion to which this first part of the *Grammar* leads is that assent, true and religious, is given by the subject to revelation as presented in its unique and original unity:

> He who believes in the *depositum,* believes in all the doctrines of the **depositum.** And since he cannot know them all at once, he knows some doctrines, and does not know others; he may know only the Creed, nay, perhaps only the chief portions of the Creed; but, whether he knows little or much, he has the intention of believing all that there is to believe whenever and as soon as it is brought home to him. . . . All that he knows now as revealed, and all that he shall know and all that there is to know, he embraces it all in his intention by one act of faith. (*Grammar,* 152)

The knowledge of God that comes from revelation hence is not a speculative knowledge, but rather a reality that prompts to moral responsibility and calls for a total life commitment.

The second part of the *Grammar* is taken up with analyzing the relationship between assent and inference: an essential phase since it concerns the transition from probability to certainty.

Examination of the key terms used by Newman in this section will make it easier to grasp his argument.

Inference, first of all. A distinction is drawn between (a) "formal," which takes the form of reasoning, follows the rules of logic, and finds its most satisfactory form of expression in the syllogism; and (b) "non-formal," the reasoning that occurs spontaneously and naturally. Between inference and assent the difference is clean-cut. For with the first a proposition is accepted conditionally; with the second, absolutely.

As background to Newman's line of argument, we may detect Locke's thesis according to which one may only assent to propositions that are held to be true by virtue of the proofs adduced; for love of truth forbids one to go beyond the proofs and demonstration. For Newman, however, experience shows the weakness of this thesis; for one may give assent independently of inference.

The assent that is given unconditionally, Newman goes on, is always true acceptance and as such, hence, can never be granted only *sub conditione.* Truth is either accepted as such or rejected. This immediate assent to the truth is called "simple," i.e., the act itself by which assent is given. It is immutable per se; were modifying factors to intervene, these would only be in the order of the intensity of the experience, but not in the act as such.

From simple assent we have, however, to pass on to "reflected" assent or, more properly, *certainty.* At this point, *investigation* has to come into play; this is different from *inquiry.* Inquiry implies doubt; investigation does not (*Grammar,* 191). Someone who investigates does so because he wants to understand why something is credible and not have to fall into contradictions or revoke the truth to which he assents; he who inquires has not yet found and hence, per se, does not yet believe. In a word, reflected assent means being certain over the reasons and presuppositions of the assent that is given.

The problem, however, is not yet solved. How are we to pass on to absolute assent? Newman introduces the concept of *illative sense.* Though connection with Aristotelian *phronēsis* may first spring to mind, in the *Grammar* the concept is used in a special sense.

Whereas Aristotle's *phronēsis* is confined to the sphere of morals and expresses ethical judgment, in Newman the *illative sense* is open to the entire gnosiological compass. It is the judgment which investigates the true and which, beyond any individual technique, decides how and when to pass from inference to assent. It is a natural, intimate human activity; it keeps one in touch with the concrete world, develops by force of experience, and is ever present there where the subject is acting. In short, the *illative sense* is the principle that creates awareness and synthesis of the various probabilities which only when put together yield certainty. By means of the *illative sense* we are hence in a position to seize on the point of convergence of a series of data which, if taken singly, would only offer probability, but in the light of the illative sense which seizes on them as a whole begets certainty.

This reasoning concluded, the second part of the book too ends with a chapter devoted to the religious problem. Revelation, Newman argues, is not a philosophic text, nor is it a collection of abstract truths; rather, it is an authoritative teaching itself giving rise to faith and needing no external "proofs"; much less does it represent something subject to opinion. Revelation is a totality, a plain truth, a universality self-conferring; yet even here we can also show the need for assent.

Newman offers two pieces of data: (1) *natural religion*, which can be found present in everyone if one reflects on conscience, suffering, and sacrifice; (2) the "accumulation of probabilities," which constitutes the "essential principle" (*Grammar*, 411) of Newman's reasoning.

By analyzing various elements, the one independent from the other (e.g., natural religion, the historical religions and the sense of fulfillment present in them, the sense of sin, the Jewish religion, Jesus of Nazareth, the church), but taken as a whole, hence as of probabilities, Newman reaches the conclusion that

> there is only one religion which tends to fulfil the aspirations, needs, and foreshadowing of natural faith and devotion. It may be said, perhaps, that, educated in Christianity, I merely judge it by its own principles; but this is not the fact. For, in the first place, I have taken my idea of what a revelation must be, in good measure, from the actual religions of the world. . . . Besides, I do not here single out Christianity with reference simply to its particular doctrines or precepts, but for a reason which is on the surface of its history. It alone has a definite message addressed to all mankind. (*Grammar*, 430)

2. Applicability of Newman's Program

Newman's apologetic program has very modern features, able (one may think) to get a reaction from twentieth-century people. Here we find an "existential dialectic" which, by its inductive method, obliges reflection on the faith, starting out from one's human situation.

The first remarkable thing about the program is that the subject is reinstated as partner in the theological discourse. No longer abstract doctrine *in se* but, first and foremost, the *real human*, your actual human at grips with the decisive topic of MEANING. Everyone knows what personal experience is, and starting from this experience Newman succeeded in presenting the universal component of the Christian faith. He took experience for preference for his psychological interpretation, but did not confine himself to that. Taking in ethics and history too, he also produced that aspect of philosophy which may be regarded as preamble to the metaphysical thought of Blondel's *L'Action*. Newman could go no further, but the point in question certainly remains something that theological analysis cannot ignore.

The topic of history and historical consciousness (→ HISTORY I), ever-present in his works, suggests an originality anticipating our own theological period and not only ours.

The problems of faith, as tackled by Newman (so as to induce your actual human to live religiously) is another feature that emerges from this apologetic program. Faith is regarded as an all-embracing act, an *ensemble* of feeling, reason, and practice. Faith as response and need for *all* humans, since universality is keynote of revelation itself.

In the *Grammar*, an answer is provided for this problem: faith for all persons and for the whole person. The ordinary person, just like the specialist, can grasp the meaning of this act expressing the force of reason and the greatness of love.

Love is the protagonist in all Newman's writings: it constitutes the rediscovery of an inner, intimate need shared by everyone, originating in an act of love, the one visible in the death of Jesus:

> There is just one Name in the whole world that lives; it is the Name of One who passed His years in obscurity and who died a malefactor's death. Eighteen hundred years have gone since that time, but still it has its hold upon the human mind. It has possessed the world and it maintains possession. (*Grammar*, 490)

The unchanging need to believe will be presented to individuals in different terms and with different emphases. But, for Newman, this always rests on the truth "which is one alone," on the sense of sin, and on the concreteness of personal experience; but, as with the greatest apologists, at the basis of everything there is always the central theme of "the surrender of reason" before the mystery. This is not a passive, unfruitful surrender; the subject, having gone through all the stages of a proper rational process, and because of this, surrenders to obedient adoration.

Bibl.: J. H. Newman, *The Letters and Diaries of J. H. Newman*, 31 vols. (Oxford, 1978); id., *Parochial and Plain Sermons*, 8 vols. (London, 1869); id., *Grammar of Assent* (London, 1870); id., *The Works of Card. Newman* (London, 1908–1914); id., *Apologia pro vita sua* (New York, 1956); E. Przywara, *Religionsbegründung: M. Scheler und J. H. Newman* (Freiburg, 1923); R. Aubert, *Newman: Une psychologie concrète de la foi et une apologétique existentielle* (n.d.); id., *Le problème de l'acte de foi* (Louvain, 1945); J. H. Walgrave, *J. H. Newman: His Personality, His Principles, His Fundamental Doctrines* (Louvain, 1977); var., *J. H. Newman: Theologian and Cardinal* (Rome/ Brescia, 1981); P. Gauthier, *Newman et Blondel: Tradition et développement du dogme* (Paris, 1988).

Rino Fisichella

NEW AGE

Unlike the religious sects, New Age is the present-day expression of a not really organized, "vagabond" spirituality, which has emerged from modern faith in progress but is now directed toward the religious field and the spiritual transformation of humanity, with syncretic, evolutionist, ecological/holistic and millenarian characteristics.

1. Coming into the open in the turbulent manifestations of the generation gap around 1968, the concept goes back to the publications of the Theosophical Society and Alice Bailey (1880–1949). Her book, *The Reappearance of Christ* (1948), envisages the appearance of a new messiah, head of the spiritual hierarchy, which coincides with the imminent dawning of the Aquarian Age. According to the so-called Akasic chronicle, a period of universal harmony will be ushered in, exerting a strong mystical influence on social and political life and the spiritual self-realization of the individual. The programmatic expression of this "turning point" (Capra) was publicized in the musical *Hair* (1968). In accordance with ancient gnostic, hermetic, and astrological ideas (*magnus annus*, Plato, *Pol.* 269c) on universal history, the spring equinox (March 21) regresses by one sign of the zodiac once in about every 2,100 years, passing in our own century from the sign of Pisces into that of Aquarius. Given the symbolic representation of Christianity by the fish (*ichthys*) the age of the hierarchical church will then end and give place to a free spiritual awakening, guided by the Inner Master who represents all previous masters of religion. The new paradigm is expressed as a synthesis of four components: the Judeo-Christian tradition and the secular sciences, which—always affected by a gnostic/esoteric current, particularly obvious in times of crisis—today for the first time encounter the immediate challenge of the oriental religions and are hence stimulated to transcend their own limitations, in the face of the grave problems of world survival and of a nascent planetary culture. Among the programmatic texts deserving mention are the books of Baba Ram Dass (R. Alpert, 1973), Marilyn Ferguson (1976), David Spangler (1976), and Fritjof Capra (1980).

2. The characteristics of this global vision rest on the assumption of a polarity between human beings and cosmos (spaceship Earth) in a gigantic play of divine energies and constituting the ecosystem of divine manifestations (holism). In their mystical intuition of these laws, all religious and esoteric traditions, although by different routes, agree, deriving an equal value from them. A cosmic knowledge of such mysteries offers humanity the potential, by a process of awakening, for a gradual transformation of its consciousness, to culminate in the final realization of its divine nature. Whether based on various scientific theories (R. Sheldrake: morphogenetic fields; E. Jantsch: cosmic self-regulation; P. Russell: the Gaia hypothesis; S. Grof: transpersonal psychology), or on the perennial gnosis (Atlantis myth, pyramid wisdom), a single, global brain is postulated, which in the syntony of its multiple reactive cells (sensitive conspiracy) functions equally in the evolutive transformation of the individual self as in the ecological and social changes in the world.

With the dynamic of life itself put on a level with the evolution of its awareness in the illuminative process toward a conscious cosmos, the ways of salvation and their aims coincide and give rise to new metaphysical and ethical principles that transcend the anthropocentrism of a technological/rational culture in favor of a biocentric paradigm of depth ecology. The theory of human reincarnation through past and present lives, in conjunction with the law of moral retribution (*karma*), is the key to understanding be it the yearning for self-perfection, or the syncretism among the various spiritual traditions. In the presentation of these traditions and scientific theories, however, an eclectic foreshortening may be noted as well as a reluctance to produce convincing proofs.

3. Obviously answering to a spiritual vacuum and to the crisis of values in Western society, these pluralist ideas of the alternative religiousness also manifest themselves in new religious movements (e.g., Bhagwan Shree Rajnees, TM [transcendental meditation], and so on)—somewhat unstable forms of fluid membership in "audience cults" or "clientele cults" without any obligations about what you believe. Whereas the entire community revolves around a few magazines (*Astra*, for instance), authors (M. Ferguson, Shirley MacLaine), or the shared fascination with parareligious phenomena (e.g., UFOs), the clientele of mages, spiritual healers, astrologers, therapists, macrobiotic foods, ecological movements, and so one illustrates the americanization of religion as a consumer article. Yet contrariwise there is also a tendency to resacralize the biosphere by parareligious practices amalgamated from every cultural tradition. Emphasizing the primacy of personal experience and cultivation of harmonious relationships, activities unfold in a tight network of local groups of somewhat heterogeneous composition and with no institutional hierarchy. Exchange of ideas is made easier by the mass media and information technology.

4. The main components of the New Age could be thus systematized: (a) Salvation comes not from faith but from knowledge. (b) New Age is a syncretism, a mixture of elements (reincarnation, astrology, magnetism) borrowed from various traditions (Buddhism, Taoism, occultism). (c) New Age is a kind of pantheism:

God is not a person but a universal Energy. Human destiny exceeds the individual ego. One must broaden and deepen conscience, so as to merge into the cosmic energy. Through reincarnation, the limits of the ego are overstepped and the divine reached. (d) New Age is a millenarianism: it focuses on the coming of the "Great Initiate," who will inaugurate the marvelous era of the golden age. (e) New Age is a kind of esotericism, a more or less secret religion, into which one has to be initiated. (f) In spite of its vocational aspect, New Age is a sort of cerebralism: it tries to appropriate the still unknown and undeveloped powers of the brain, which are linked to the cosmic energies.

Under this rather disconcerting mixture, one can still detect signs of a search for harmony, and even for truth, which, for want of moving toward Christ, who is the real source of truth and salvation, turns to new magi.

5. The interpretation of religion in a pantheistic sense as the reestablishing of the sacred polarity between humanity and cosmos without the need for a transcendent God constitutes the first challenge to the Judeo-Christian tradition. The propagation of an Aquarian gospel (H. Dowling, 1908), with the baseless description of Jesus' initiation into the secret doctrines of the East, requires the integration of religious pluralism into the experience of the historicity of Christ. The postulate of a new "paganism" (*pagani* means "cultivators of the soil") as against the "religion of the city" (institutional church) today demands a second evangelization, a new contextualizing of Christianity in contemporary culture, and the creation of communities unitedly willing to bear clear ecumenical witness. In theological reflection, a deepening of trinitarian ontology, of cosmic Christology, and of pneumatology, besides the theology of religions, must demonstrate the truth of the Christian faith, in a basic dialogue, from its first beginnings to the progressive realization of a new age under the lordship of Christ (see *Dominum et vivificantem*, 53f.).

Bibl.: Baba R. Dass, *Be Here Now* (San Cristobal, 1971); F. Capra, *The Tao of Physics* (Berkeley, 1975); D. Spangler, *Revelation: The Birth of a New Age* (San Francisco, 1976); M. Ferguson, *The Aquarian Conspiracy* (Los Angeles, 1980); K. Wilber, *Up from Eden* (Garden City, N.Y., 1981); R. Stark and W. S. Bainbridge, *The Future of Religion* (Berkeley, 1985);

J. Vernette, *Jésus dans la nouvelle religiosité* (Paris, 1987); H. M. Enomiya-Lassalle, *Vivere in una nuova coscienza* (Rome, 1988); J. Sudbrack, *Nuova Religiosità* (Brescia, 1988); J. G. Melton, *Encyclopedia of American Religions* (3rd ed.; Detroit, 1989); G. Daneels, *Le Christ ou le Verseau?* (Mechelen, 1990); B. Bastian, *Le Nouvel Âge: d'où vient-il, que dit-il* (Paris, 1991); M. Gardner, *The New Age: Notes of a Fringe Watcher* (Buffalo, N.Y., 1988); A. Fortin, *Les galeries du Nouvel Âge* (Montreal, 1993).

Michael Fuss

O

OBEDIENTIAL POTENCY

By the expression *potentia oboedientialis* theology attempts, by the light of revelation, to describe that nexus concerning the possibility of relationship between God and human nature. In point of fact, the problem is that of the relationship between nature and grace. On the one hand, thought must be able to safeguard human freedom in relation to divine revelation; on the other, it must defend the priority, gratuitousness, and transcendence of God's activity.

It would be naïve to suppose that a question of this sort would not be the concern of fundamental theology. With *potentia oboedientialis* we face one of the omnipresent, if not explicitly stated, topics regulating all theological tradition. It is first of all to be found as the theme of a fundamental anthropology; then as an internal factor of revelation and of the incarnation; after this in problems concerning "natural" knowledge of God and faith; in the relationship between faith and reason; and, lastly, in questions concerning soteriology. Thus, from being marginal to theology, this theme constitutes one of its essential elements.

Formally speaking, *potentia oboedientialis* in current usage generally means the potency (*potentia*) that human beings have for receiving a specific character, which they do not of themselves possess but can only accept *obedientially* as a gift.

The legitimacy of this fundamental datum derives solely from theological reflection. As subjects, we conceive of ourselves as creatures, hence ontologically different from God, dependent on him, and aware of being unable to find fulfillment in ourselves but only in our relationship with the Creator. What is more, this line of thought—a genuinely Catholic understanding—proceeds in the light of the event of the incarnation, through which, historically, we see the archetypal relationship between God and human nature realized in the life of Jesus of Nazareth, which thus becomes the basis for our human claim to share in the divine life.

Hence in Christ there exists the totality of grace to be mediated to human nature; and therefore every grace is to be regarded as coming from Christ, even if we can only observe how in him human nature is *capax Dei* ("capable of God").

All patristic thought is strongly marked by this basic apprehension. Human nature is said to be "divinized," which is the same as saying that it is henceforth called to participate in that divine life which, in Christ, has already been realized in history. AUGUSTINE provides us with a first line of inquiry when he treats of the relationship between free will and grace. Human beings are free; but in order for them to do good they must first be *set* free; their *disponibilité* to grace must be wholly obediential.

But it is in THOMAS AQUINAS that we first encounter the technical terms *potentia oboedientiae* and *potentia oboedientialis* (*De Ver.* 3, 3, 3), to denote a passive potentiality of the human soul. In a classic passage (*ST* 3, q. 11, a. 1) we read:

> In the human soul, as in every creature, there is a twofold passive potentiality: one answers to a natural agent; the other to the first agent, who can bring any creature to some higher actuality, to which a natural agent cannot bring it. And this latter is usually called the "obediential potency" (*potentia oboedientiae*) of the creature.

Subsequently, this theme has undergone differing interpretations, notably in the work of Molina and his school. More directly, in harmony with modern theology, we may try, with Thomas's help, to reach a more authentic interpretation of the idea of *potentia oboedientialis*. For, according to him, the essential fulfillment of the human creature and the unconditional gift of our fulfillment cannot be regarded as contradictory concepts.

For this reason, the highest value has to be set on the unity of the human subject, which is expressed in its being as a *person*. Beyond every dualism (spirit/body, with the consequent division transcendence/immanence, or finite/infinite) the reality of the person is that which more than all else, from the outset, favors the unity and noncontradictoriness of the concepts and characteristics connected with it.

For the human subject, to be a *person* means self-comprehension and the capacity for self-realization by free acts. Now, in us, there is an opening to infinity, a constant dynamic of such openings, marked by our *desire* to be able to attain the object of our own knowledge. Furthermore, this very tension and desire make us more keenly aware of the finiteness of our own act of being.

This characteristic is also imprinted on our freedom, for we perceive in ourselves the desire for an ever greater freedom, and an opening toward an infinite freedom. This dimension allows us to discover ourselves as having the *disposition* toward being able to desire and perform either free acts, or the supremely free act by which we achieve self-realization.

The person is essentially freedom; this is expressed as supreme act when it is faced with the radical choice of accepting a greater freedom which does not pertain to it and to which it cannot lay claim, but which it can only receive. This is what characterizes the personal being as one which can carry out to the proper end and in accordance with its own nature acts that are proper to it.

In other words, we may say, the ultimate self-comprehension the subject can have, theologically, is that of a created being; this implies comprehension of a *distinctio realis* with the creator. Hence the creaturely being is always placed in a condition of relationship which is visible in its *disponibilité* toward being accepted. As creatures we cannot claim, but only receive as gift. At a creaturely level, therefore, there exists an availability (*potentia*) for accepting grace and hence for entering into possession (*oboedientia*) of a quality and characteristic that we do not possess of ourselves, nor can we, because of our creaturely nature, expect to possess.

The becoming aware of what has already been given in creation is also grace: a call to the obediential acceptance that is due to God. For only in this way is it possible to see that radical availability of the subject in regard to revelation. In a word, God, in creating, places within the creature the natural desire to know him; but the contingent nature of the created being—and this constitutes its essence—requires that this desire be directed at a personal level for it to be in all respects the complete act of a historical subject. This is necessary for the paradox of the relationship between God's transcendence and our human knowledge to be fully realized. For in this matter the initiative lies always and only with God, nor can human freedom, by

virtue of its own ontological structure, ever be in a position to form a direct relationship with God, unless God grants it the capacity either to become aware of it or to realize it.

The creaturely condition, assumed initially as the a priori of theological thought, necessarily entails, in this case too, that the rule of ANALOGY be maintained in force.

This dimension in no way diminishes the strength of the subject's freedom, since we realize this precisely when we become aware, and hence, as person, completely fulfill ourselves.

In conclusion, the person achieves self-comprehension in a historical reality. We do not mean to diminish the meaningfulness of the concept of *potentia oboedientialis* when we insert it into a dynamic "becoming" of the human being. In God's act of creation, we have already seen the act of a *potentia oboedientialis* being given to the subject as creature; nevertheless, the latter, as its existence unfolds, becomes more and more aware of its own being until it attains the plenitude of the beatific vision. In this dynamic, hence, *potentia oboedientialis* is not extraneous since the believer knows all too well that, as against the transcendency of grace, there remains the state of sin, and that, in spite of this, the desire for God keeps on growing within us.

Fullness of self-realization will thus be in the beatific vision; there we shall have a complete sharing in the divine life, where we creatures shall discover how good our choice has been and shall experience our freedom to the highest degree. At the same time we shall, however, see how unconditional the call was by which we were given what we had only dared desire.

Bibl.: P. ROUSSELOT, "Les yeux de la foi," *RSR* 1 (1910); A. GARDEIL, "Le désir naturel de voir Dieu," *RThom* 31 (1926): 381–410; id., "La vitalité de la vision divine et les actes surnaturels," *RThom* 31 (1926): 477–89; H. Urs VON BALTHASAR, "Der Begriff der Natur in der Theologie," *ZKT* 75 (1953): 452–64; id., *Spiritus Creator* (Einsiedeln, 1967); id., *Theo-drama: Theological Dramatic Theory*, vol. 2: *Dramatis Personae* (San Francisco, 1990); K. RAHNER, *Hearers of the Word* (New York, 1969); id., "Concerning the Relation between Nature and Grace," in *Theological Investigations*, vol. 1 (1954; London, 1961), 297–318; id., "Nature and Grace," in *Theological Investigations*, vol. 4 (1960; London, 1966), 165–88; H. DE LUBAC, *The Mystery of the Supernatural* (New York, 1967).

Rino FISICHELLA

ORIGEN

It may seem an anachronism to connect Origen and fundamental theology, since his theology knows no distinction between branches and is always simultaneously exegetical, spiritual, and speculative. However, he wrote the most important apologetic work of the ante-Nicene period, his *Against Celsus*, which was a refutation of the *True Discourse* of Celsus, a Middle Platonic philosopher who is extensively cited by his refuter. In addition, subjects belonging to fundamental theology are discussed in Origen's *Treatise on Principles (Peri Archōn)*, as well as in his commentaries and homilies.

1. God

It may surprise us to find that nowhere in his works does Origen attempt to prove the existence of God. Atheists were few at that period, and Celsus was far from being one. Origen, however, often returns to the subject of the incorporeity of God and of the soul, for these were points not understood by many Christians: the anthropomorphists, who took literally the anthropomorphisms of Scripture and therefore attributed to God bodily members and human passions; the millenarians or chiliasts, who took Rv 20:1–6 too literally and believed that in the "first resurrection," preceding the definitive resurrection, Christ and the martyrs would reign in the earthly Jerusalem for a thousand years. These people were not heretics, and Origen himself does not mention the incorporeity of God in the explanation that he gives of the rule of faith in the preface to his *Treatise on Principles*, even though the immediately following chapter (1.1) is devoted to this subject. It is indeed impossible for human beings here below to know God and talk of him without picturing him as human, and according to Origen this is one of the reasons for the incarnation of the Son, who became a human being in order to show us the divinity through his humanity.

That God created the world out of nothing is stated several times in the *Treatise on Principles* (see 1.3.3) and in the *Commentary on John* (1.17[18].103), in reliance on 2 Mc 7:28 and on the *Shepherd* of Hermas (Mandates 1[26].1), which Origen often treats as part of Scripture. The idea of providence is found in the Platonists and Stoics, but Origen and his disciple Gregory Thaumaturgus, in his *Panegyric on Origen*, give it a more personalist interpretation. The One of Plotinus, who was a fellow student of Origen, is concentrated wholly on itself, and providence—a providence that is hardly concerned with the person—is the responsibility of the second and third hypostases. But the Father, according to Origen, is constantly associated, both in creation and in providence, with the work of his Son.

2. Jesus

The discussion of Jesus occupies a good part of the first books of *Against Celsus*. Celsus examines the life of Jesus and finds at every step a reason for accusations or disbelief, with special attention to the death on the cross. Origen does not fail to reply. In his defense he uses several kinds of argument that have become classic. Jesus was foretold in the OT, and he completely fulfilled these prophecies; the same kind of reasoning is used in the *Treatise on Principles* (4.1) to prove the inspiration of the Scriptures, the argument being that Christ fulfilled the prophecies. Then, too, the miracles of Jesus did not work like magic, as Celsus claims when he compares them to prodigies occurring in paganism (see Francesco Moseto, *I miracoli evangelici nel dibattito tra Celso e Origene* [Rome, 1987]).

The fundamental argument for the miracles and entire mission of Jesus in this world comes from the extent, number, and depth of the moral conversions that he has brought about. His miracles had for their purpose the moral well-being of humanity, whereas the marvels invoked by Celsus the pagan were prodigies pure and simple, without any spiritual and moral relevance. Origen speaks from experience: he has taken note of the number and quality of the conversions produced by Christian preaching that delivers men and women from a life of selfish debauchery and leads them to virtue. Whereas the lawgivers of antiquity never succeeded in having foreigners adopt their laws, all areas of Origen's world are full of Christians, many of whom willingly suffer torture and death in order to be faithful to the faith that Jesus preached. The insufficiency of the human means at work in this preaching—the small number of the apostles, who in addition were uneducated—makes it all the clearer that its success was due to divine grace; the same holds for the lack of literary value in the Scriptures, which are vessels of clay that contain the word of God. The sufferings and maryrdoms endured by Christians are similarly invoked as proof of the truthfulness of their witness (*CCels* 3.27).

3. Revelation and Scripture

Both the Word and Scripture are revelation, according to Origen. Indeed, the two are not two different realities; they are both the word of God, and God does not have two words, but only one. Scripture is therefore an incarnation of the Word in written words, which are analogous to flesh; Scripture is therefore not an incarnation that would be a second incarnation alongside the incarnation in flesh. Rather, it exists in relation to the latter, which it prepares for (OT) or describes (NT), while awaiting the definitive fulfillment of the incarnation when humanity, now having been divinized in Christ and having become, as it were, interior to him, will see the Father with the very eyes of the Son. Scripture is thus identified in a way with the incarnate Word and, like the incarnation, is the work of the Spirit; it is not possible to understand the Scripture if one does not have within oneself the Spirit who inspired it. The charism of the sacred writer is closely allied to the charism of those who read and understand the Scripture; understanding of the Scripture is therefore also a revelation. Beyond the literal or historical or bodily meaning, which Origen considers to be, as it were, the raw material of what is said, prior to any interpretation, if this be possible (Origen differs here from our contemporaries, for whom the literal meaning is what the human author intends to express), a true understanding seeks to grasp the meaning intended by the Spirit, the spiritual meaning. The spiritual or allegorical meaning of the OT has to do with Christ and all the realities of the new covenant, for he is the key to the earlier Scriptures.

In taking this position, Origen bases himself on a number of NT passages, especially from Paul and John, the most important being 1 Cor 10:1–11, Gal 4:21–31, and 2 Cor 3:7–18. These passages show that certain OT episodes prefigure NT realities and that the OT remains veiled to those who have not converted to Christ. Furthermore, since revelation is first and foremost Christ himself, how could the OT be revelation if it did not in its entirety speak of Christ? But the NT, too, has a spiritual meaning, and this meaning is twofold. First, it applies to Christians what is said of Christ. Then it foretells the blessings of beatitude, but through a prophecy that is already a fufillment of what is prophesied. The gospel as we live it here below, the temporal or sensible gospel, differs from the eternal or intelligible or spiritual gospel only in the *epinoia*, or human concept of them. This means that they are not distinguished from each other in their *hypostasis* or *pragma*, i.e., their reality. In their reality they are but one (*ComJn* 1.8[10].44; see Henri Crouzel, *Origène et la "connaissance mystique"* [Bruges/Paris, 1961], 352–61). The only difference between them is in the way we know them: knowledge "in a mirror, dimly," here below, and "face to face" vision in eternity (1 Cor 13:12). This distinction implicitly contains the whole of Christian sacramentalism, beginning with Christ, the supreme "sacrament," the human being in whom "the whole fullness of deity dwells bodily" (Col 2:9).

Contrary to what has too often been said on the basis of hasty impressions, Origen does not scorn the literal sense, and many of his homilies are based chiefly on it. As one who was trained as a grammarian and philologist (see Bernhardt Neuschäfer, *Origenes als Philologe* [Basel, 1987]), he explains the literal meaning, often on the basis of all kinds of grammatical, scientific, historical, and geographic research, forays into Hebrew customs, and consultation of various manuscripts. We must not forget the colossal work of critical exegesis he undertook in order to reach a reliable text in his *Hexapla*. Beyond a doubt, he is the main critical and literal exegete of the ante-Nicene period and one of the most important in the whole of antiquity.

How, then, did he acquire a reputation for despising the literal meaning? It is because he occasionally says that in this or that text there is no literal meaning. But if we go by his definition of the literal meaning, which I gave earlier, it is quite true that there is no literal meaning when Scripture uses figurative language. Furthermore, the precepts of the OT that are juridical or ceremonial have been abolished by

Christ and therefore no longer have a valid literal meaning *for us*. The books that contain such precepts (e.g., Leviticus) have been given to us "to instruct us, on whom the ends of the ages have come" (1 Cor 10:11). They do, therefore, have a meaning for us, but this meaning can only be spiritual. In addition, there are some contradictions or at least oddities in the biblical text, many of which are due to the Septuagint translation, which Origen, despite some knowledge of Hebrew, regarded, as did all the fathers before Jerome, as the inspired and canonical text, the text that the apostles had given to the church (see *PArch* 4.3.1–3). On the other hand, what point is there to the stories contained in Scripture if we do not derive at least a moral lesson from them? Origen's purpose is not that of the historian or archaeologist but that of the pastor, whose concern is to help his readers or hearers make moral and spiritual progress.

In general, the spiritual meaning flows from the literal and is not simply a more or less arbitarily accommodated meaning; we should not be overly fussy about the few exceptions we may encounter. In many instances Origen takes as his starting point an allegorical explanation already given in the NT, which he explains, extends, and develops. When he does not find a spiritual meaning given in the NT, he suggests what comes to his mind, but he offers it modestly, not as an obligatory exegesis but as a possible interpretation, saying at times that he is ready to abandon his explanation if someone can provide him with a better one. The setting for the discovery of a spiritual interpretation is spiritual in the most exact sense of the word: the setting is prayer in which (as I said earlier) the Holy Spirit, present in the soul, plays the part of inspirer that he also plays in prophetic inspiration; thus a kind of spiritual illumination is given. If we are to understand Scripture according to its true meaning, we must have the *nous*, or mind, of Christ, and Origen says as much in a number of passages.

In a well-known passage at the beginning of his *Commentary on John* (1.4[6].23–24), Origen sees in John's Gospel the firstfruits of the gospel and says that the only person who can understand it is one who becomes another John, i.e., another Jesus, since John was given to Mary as her son, Jesus' appointed substitute for himself (Jn 19:26). Christ lives in such a person, and

therefore the person has the mind of Christ (1 Cor 2:16). Christ is the real author of the two Testaments (we saw earlier that the Word and the Scripture are but a single word of God), and according to a principle that goes back to the grammarian Aristarchus of Samothrace (217–145 B.C.E.), one will not properly interpret a text if one does not have within oneself the mind of the author (see Rolf Gögler, *Zur Theologie des biblischen Wortes* [Düsseldorf, 1963], 45–46). This philological principle helps us understand Origen's application of it in the theological order.

The spiritual meaning gets transferred from prayer to the preached homily and the written commentary. It thus retains its connection with a subject, in the philosophical sense of this word; i.e., this divine word is addressed to an individual mind. This does not mean, however, that it is not communicable. It is not necessarily a meaning valid for everyone, however, and therefore the preacher should use prudence in proposing it. For if the audience or readers have not reached the desired spiritual level, the interpretation can be harmful to them, and it is even possible that as a result of their misunderstanding they may harm their brothers and sisters. A certain spiritual disposition, which is a gift of grace, is necessary for expressing or accepting an interpretation of this kind.

There is, then, a correspondence and close connection between the two Testaments, and for this reason Origen triumphantly defends the value of the Old against the Marcionites and other gnostics who devalue it or even condemn it, along with its creator God, whom they distinguish from the Father of Jesus Christ. The OT contains the promise that will be fulfilled "in a mirror, dimly" in the NT and "face to face" in the state of blessedness (1 Cor 13:12). In some passages, though these are put right by others, Origen even exaggerates the importance of the OT when he maintains that some patriarchs and prophets have no less a knowledge of divine realities than the apostles did, although they did not see the fulfillment of the hidden mystery (*ComJn* 6.3–5[2].15–20). But further on in the same commentary on John (13.48.314–19), he speaks of the prophets as sowers and the apostles as reapers, in accord with Jn 4:36. According to other passages, it was at the transfiguration that Moses and Elijah received the full revelation of Christ; the other OT saints had to wait until the descent of Christ into the lower world after his death. Also to be noted is that the Pauline expression "in a mirror, dimly" is applied only to the time of the NT as distinguished from the eternal gospel. The phrase in question is never applied to the OT, which provides only a premonition, a desire, a hope, and not, like the NT, a real though imperfect possession of the "true" realities, the divine mysteries.

Scripture is not, however, the only revelation of God. Human beings find God first in their own nature because, like the angels (and the demons, but these denied their participation in God), they are created in the image of God, the Image of God that is always the Word. This doctrine plays a major role in human knowledge of God, for only like is able to know like, for it has this like within itself. Meditation on Scripture—*theia anagnōsis, lectio divina*—supposes as its backdrop this knowledge that is obtained through the image of God in oneself and that progresses with the help of grace and the exercise of the Christian life. Nor is this all. While rational beings are the only ones that are, strictly speaking, created in the image of God himself, all the beings of the sensible world are images of the divine mysteries. The Bible speaks constantly of these sensible beings. And these mysteries, which correspond to and include the Platonic ideas, are all contained in the Son of God, who, being Wisdom, is the intelligible world. In the final analysis, it is always the Word who reveals, whether through human nature or the sensible world or Scripture.

4. Human Free Will

A key idea controls Origen's conception of the human person, namely, free will. To this subject he devotes one of the best-known chapters of his *Treatise on Principles*, one of those that had the greatest influence on posterity. In it he answers the Scripture-based objections that were raised against this fundamental human prerogative. The emphasis that Origen places on free will is explained by the threats to the very existence of free will at that period: in paganism, from some philosophical sects as well as from astrology and the belief in *heimarmenē* (fate); in Christianity, from gnostics like the Valentinians, who allowed no role for free will either in the salvation of the "pneumatics" or in the damnation of the "hylics," since these outcomes were consequences of the natures with which the two types had been created.

Before speaking of free will, let me say a few words about the anthropological context in which it has its place. Human beings have three constituents, although it is perhaps preferable to speak of three tendencies, since this anthropology is more dynamic than ontological. The three are listed in 1 Thes 5:23 and, despite a rather widespread prejudgment, have little to do with the Platonic trichotomy. The three are, first of all, spirit (*pneuma, spiritus*), which is a participation in the Holy Spirit, the soul's trainer and mentor, and is a divine gift and not, properly speaking, part of the essence of a human being; it corresponds, with some qualifications, to the sanctifying grace of later theology.

The essential part of human beings is the soul (*psychē, anima*). Origen several times defines a human being as a soul that uses a body (e.g., *PArch* 4.2.7); the soul is the seat of the personality, of free will, and therefore of the participation of the human being in the image of God. But the soul is divided at its deepest level, not because it is created that way, but because of original sin as Origen conceives of this in light of his favorite hypothesis, the preexistence of souls. The higher part or, rather, tendency of the soul draws it toward the *pneuma*, whose pupil it is, and is designated either by the Platonic term *nous, mens*, "intelligence" (I shall not call it "spirit," lest it be confused with the *pneuma*) or by the Stoic term *hēgemonikon* or "dominant part" (Latin *principale cordis, principale mentis, principale animae*) or by the biblical term *kardia, cor*, "heart." But after the fall an inferior part or tendency was combined with the superior, drawing the latter to the carnal body. This inferior tendency is given several names, especially one taken from Rom 5:6–7: *phronēma tēs sarkos*, "thought of the flesh" (Latin, *sensus carnis* or *sensus carnalis*); sometimes it is also called simply *sarx* or *caro*, "flesh," which is always a pejorative term and refers not to the body but to this inferior part of the soul.

The "body" (*sōma, corpus*), which is the third constituent, can have a number of meanings. Most often, it designates the fleshly human body, but it can also designate the various kinds of body that Origen distinguishes in his story of human origins: the ethereal (the ether represents the most rarefied degree of matter) or "flashing" bodies of the angels, the preexisting intelligences, and the resurrected saints; the dark, dim bodies of the demons and resurrected wicked. For the body is the sign of the creature's condition, the Trinity alone being completely incorporeal, as the *Treatise of Principles* says on several occasions (1.6.4; 2.2.2; 4.3.15[27]). A fragment preserved by Methodius of Olympus (*De resurrectione* 3.17–18) even supposes that between death and resurrection the soul is clad in a bodily covering that is analogous to the "vehicle" of Middle Platonism. In keeping with a constant principle of Greek physics, which distinguishes between matter and the qualities with which it is invested, the passage from preexistent state to earthy state and then to risen state involves a change not of body but only of quality.

It is in this setting with its three stages—preexistence, present earthly life, and resurrected life—that the story of free will is located; it is given to the rational soul by God so that this soul may voluntarily unite itself to him, but it also makes possible the soul's refusal to surrender. According to Origen's favorite hypothesis, all rational creatures, which after the fall will become angels, human beings, or demons, were created together in complete equality. The only one set apart was the "intelligence" that was united to the Word and thereby made to be "in the form of God" (Phil 2:6) and completely impeccable—while still enjoying free will (a little further on we shall see the reason for this paradox). In his preexistent humanity Christ was thus the spouse of the preexistent church, which was made up of all the other "intelligences." These others lived in contemplation of God. But most of them refused, in varying degrees, to surrender themselves to God, either by a cooling of their fervor, which turned them into "souls" (*psychē*, "soul," is linked to *psychos*, "cold," the soul thus being a cooling of the original intelligence), or by a repugnance for contemplation, a *koros* or *satietas* that is analogous to the "acedia" that would later, in Eastern monasticism, be regarded as one of a monk's great temptations. This fall is the negative effect of the free will with which rational creatures had been endowed from the beginning.

According to their importance, these rational creatures were separated into angels, human beings, and demons, and the conditions under which human beings are born depends on the depth of their fall. The merciful punishment of the angels consists in their having to help human beings work out their salvation and also in having to govern the different realms of nature. The demons, for their part, in keeping with the evil choice they freely made, will employ themselves in hindering the salvation of human beings. Human beings have sinned but can be healed. God creates the sensible world for them as a testing ground; in order that they may live in this world, their previously etheral bodies take on an earthly character. In what does the test consist, this test of free will that will motivate the redemption wrought by Christ? Its nature can be inferred from Origen's constantly proposed concept of sin in its anthropological aspect. As I noted earlier, the realities of this earthly world are images of the divine mysteries. Their purpose is to arouse a desire for these mysteries by their beauty, but the soul must not settle down in them; that would be like journeying to a city but stopping at a signpost in the belief that one had already reached the goal. In other words, sin consists in wrongly, but deliberately, taking as an absolute that which is in fact only a deficient image of the absolute. When human beings on their journey to God detach themselves from what are only images—images admittedly innocent in themselves and tempting only because of human self-centeredness—they offer God a love that saves them.

God respects this free will, as does the Word, whose incarnation is not meant to compel human beings but to motivate them on their journey to God and to give them the strength to finish the journey. This outlook becomes clear from a disagreement with the Montanists, the sect to which Tertullian was a convert. Following some opinions held by Greeks in the matter of poetic and mantic inspiration, the Montanists maintained that when the Holy Spirit inspires prophets, he eliminates their mind, consciousness, and freedom and himself takes the place of these, so that the prophet becomes a mere instrument of the Spirit, the pick used to play the lyre (Epiphanius of Salamis, *Panarion* 48.4.1). Origen firmly opposes this view. The Holy Spirit, as it were, places the prophet in a state of superconsciousness and super-freedom; the prophet consciously and freely collaborates with the Spirit. Only the devil "takes possession" by clouding the intellect and immobilizing freedom. It is from this consideration of the way the Spirit works that Origen derives his most basic rule for the "discernment of spirits" (François Marty, "Le discernement des esprits dans le *Peri Archôn* d'Origène," *Revue d'Ascétique et de Mystique* 34 [1958]: 147–64, 253–74). The only other possibility he envisages is that in the case of the demons "their long-continued and deep-rooted wickedness may change from a habit into a kind of nature," thus jamming or blocking free will (*PArch* 1.6.3).

But in Origen's thinking free will is only a part of freedom, of which his spiritual teaching offers a fully Pauline conception, though he does not dwell at great length on it. Those who are faithful to God are free; those who are estranged from God become slaves, falling back under the weight of animal determinisms. This freedom finds its supreme manifestation in the human soul of Christ; his soul is like all other souls in that it is similarly endowed with free will, but the infinite charity that fills it because of its union with the Word makes it completely impeccable, taking from it the "accidentality" of creatures and giving it a share in the "substantiality" of the Trinity. On several occasions Origen extends this idea, in a measure, to the just, to the point of speaking (in a kind of boundary concept) of their immutability in good, while asserting elsewhere that every human being is a sinner. Just as in the soul of Christ "as a result of long custom" charity transformed "what formerly depended on the will . . . into nature" (*PArch* 2.6.5), so too does charity in the just, all due allowances being made. We see here the paradox of freedom: the wickedness of the demons, which long-standing custom has made part of their nature, blocks their free will; in Christ, and to a certain degree in the just, charity that long-standing custom has turned into a nature, exalts freedom, a freedom that flowers through union with God.

On several occasions, Origen poses the problem of reconciling free will and divine foreknowledge, e.g., in *Against Celsus* (2.18–20) in connection with Judas's betrayal. This is his answer: "The one who predicts the future event does not cause it to occur by predicting it; rather, the future event, which would occur even if not predicted, gives the seer the basis for predicting it." As for the famous theological problem of the reconciliation of free will and divine grace: there are indeed inadequate statements that are explainable by the fact that Origen lived before the problem was clearly stated in connection with Pelagius, but in his *Commentary on John* (4.36[20].181) Origen also gives an answer that the Council of Orange would not have repudiated. Despite Jerome's assertion, Origen was not the father of Pelagianism or even of Semipelagianism. The chapter on free will in his *Treatise on Principles* (3.1) reaches the same conclusions, provided it is read in its entirety.

5. Reason and Faith

The problem of relations between REASON and faith does not arise in the same way for Origen as it does for many moderns. For if the Word (*Verbe*) as word (*parole*) and revelation is the source of faith, it is also reason, because the Greek word *logos* means both word and reason. Reason is not alien to God and his Son, who is the eternal Reason (*Logos*) of the Father. This is why Origen reacts in a spirited way to Celsus's accusations that Christians surrender themselves to an irrational faith; he shows that, on the contrary, Christians make use of reason in a careful study of the sources and content of their faith. Christianity produces a real wisdom, even if this is quite often the opposite of pagan or atheistic wisdom, especially when it preaches the cross (*CCels* 1.91–103). A chapter in the *Treatise on Principles* (3.3.1–3) is entitled "The Threefold Wisdom" and gives an explanation of 1 Cor 2:6–7. The "wisdom of the world" is found in the various arts and sciences; of itself it provides no idea of God. But in his *Panegyric on Origen* (8.109–14) Gregory Thaumaturgus describes his master's teaching these sciences in a wholly religious spirit and, according to a fragment of the *Commentary on Romans* (Scherer, 230, 1.9ff.), explaining that the artisans who built and adorned the tabernacle were acting under the inspiration of the Spirit of God. For "the wisdom of God aids those who possess human wisdom and prepares themselves to receive divine wisdom."

The conclusion must be that "the wisdom of this world" by which "human beings conceive and understand what belongs to this world"

(PArch 3.3.2) does not of itself speak of God, although it is not incompatible with a religious vision. By the "wisdom of the rulers of this world," i.e., the angels or demons who govern the nations, is meant the sciences peculiar to each nation: "what people call the secret and hidden philosophy of the Egyptians, the astrology of the Chaldeans, the wisdom of the Indians who promise knowledge of higher realities, and also the many and diverse views of the Greeks about the divinity" (ibid.). With regard to Greek philosophy, the last entry in this list, in a number of passages Origen offers carefully qualified judgments that vary according to the school in question, although in general he is less optimistic than his own teacher, Clement, had been. His letter to Gregory Thaumaturgus agrees that Christians may make use of Greek philosophy in working out the "divine philosophy" of Christianity, and he himself uses it extensively in his own theological study (see H. Crouzel, _Origène et la philosophie_ [Paris, 1963]). But he does not conceal the fact that the application is tricky and that an incautious use of Greek philosophy may lead to heresy (_Letter to Gregory_, SChr 148).

As a general rule, it can be said that for Origen there is hardly any gap between revelation and reason, since both are the Logos, the Son of God. This usually means that—to use a distinction not familiar to Origen—reason has for him a meaning more supernatural than natural; the same can be said of the word _logikos_, "rational." The Son of God was the agent of creation on two counts: as Wisdom and as Logos. As Wisdom, he contained within himself the ideas in the Platonic sense, i.e., the plans of things, and the reasons in the Stoic sense, i.e., the seeds of the future creation. As Logos, he gave expression to these in real beings. But, as I said, human free will plays a role, and this is why both truth and error are to be found in philosophy. The use of philosophy requires that Christians exercise discernment, as Origen shows in the preface of the _Treatise on Principles_, for while the apostles delivered to Christians "all that they thought necessary," they left it to believers, who are inspired by the Holy Spirit, to investigate the "manner of being" and the "origin" of the realities that they, the apostles, had revealed to them. The apostles also left it to Christians to bring everything

together "into a body of doctrine . . . with the help of clear and compelling arguments," thereby establishing "the truth about each point," and "with the help of comparisons and statements, whether found in the sacred Scriptures or discovered by looking for logical consequences and following a correct reasoning process" (_PArch_ pref. 3 and 10).

Celsus accuses Christians of shunning a critical outlook and preferring blind faith. As we saw above, Origen answers that all Christians capable of doing so are urged to use their reason in studying and interpreting the Scriptures, but that few in fact are capable. The attitude of simple faith is the best thing for the majority; meanwhile, the moral effectiveness of Christian teaching is proof that the act of faith is reasonable (_CCels_ 1.9). Origen counterattacks: the philosophers themselves demand faith from their disciples. It is really by an act of faith that young persons attend one school rather than another, for they do not make the rounds of all the schools and try them out before settling on the one they will follow (1.10). Furthermore, faith is essential to any and every human life. Without it, no action is possible: people cannot sail the seas or marry or beget children or sow. They believe that everything will turn out well, although the outcome is in fact doubtful and failures are frequent. Yet without this trust they will not have the courage for any undertaking (1.11).

The faith of any given Christian may be the result of happy chance (which Christians call providence) or the product of a careful study of the truth. The mass of Christians are in the first category, a very small number in the second (_CCels_ 3.38). But all Christians, and not just the least educated among them need the attitude of faith; the knowledge and wisdom that spiritual men and women attain always have faith as their foundation.

6. The Natural Law

The idea of a natural law that comes from God and is contained in the very order of nature follows from the _koinai ennoiai_, "common notions"—i.e., moral concepts found in every human being. This idea of a natural law was inherited from Stoicism. Paul makes use of it in Rom 2:14–16. Origen, who makes quite frequent mention of these "common notions," appeals to natural law in *Against Celsus* and in his *Commentary on Romans*. In the former he does not deny Celsus's claim that the precepts of Christian morality are not original but are the same as those of all the other philosophies; he explains this by the existence of a natural morality that is written in every human heart (*CCels* 1.4). On the other hand, he rejects the relativism of Celsus, who says that people must observe scrupulously and exactly the laws and customs of their own country, even if these are contradictory to those observed in other countries (5.25). According to Origen's answer, a distinction must be made between the natural law, of which God is the author, and the written law of society, and the latter must be judged in the light of the former (5.37). A recent study of the various meanings of the word "law" in the *Commentary on Romans* (Reimer Roukema, *The Diversity of Laws in Origen's Commentary on Romans* [Amsterdam, 1988]) carefully examines each passage in which there is question of law and summarizes the various uses in its conclusion.

7. Human Beings and Animals

I end this article with a final question: What relation exists between the human soul and the souls of animals? The problem arose because there were those who accepted metempsychosis, a subject that was still being discussed by the philosophers. Contrary to what Rufinus and Jerome claim to have read in the *Treatise on Principles*, and despite several passages of Origen that have been preserved in Greek and whose meaning is beyond doubt, we find, even in the *Treatise on Principles* (2.9.3 at the end), that the rational soul of the human being, which is analogous to the angels by reason of its origin, is a primary being, while the mute animals (*alogoi*, having neither language nor reason) are secondary beings that God has placed at the disposal of humankind. This idea is developed at length in *Against Celsus* (4.74–99). Celsus attacks Christians who claim that God created the sensible world for the sake of human beings; he maintains that providence is not more concerned with human beings than with the rest of the universe, and he shows that animals are superior to human beings in many respects. Origen answers that reason enables human beings to exercise dominion over the animal world and places them on a quite different level (see Gilles Dorival, "Origène a-t-il enseigné la transmigrations des âmes dans les corps d'animaux? (à propos de *PArch* 1.8.4)," *Origeniana Secunda* [Rome, 1980]).

Bibl.: See the articles and books cited in the article. See also H. CROUZEL, *Théologie de l'image de Dieu chez Origène* (Paris, 1956); id., *Origen* (San Francisco, 1989).

Henri CROUZEL

ORTHODOXY

This word comes from the Greek words *orthē*, "right" or "correct," and *doxa*, "opinion" or "glory." While sometimes classical Greek authors placed these two words side by side (e.g., Plato, *Philebus* 11b), the adjective "orthodox" and the substantive "orthodoxy" came into common usage only in the Greek patristic period. Orthodoxy means correct or sound doctrine; it extends beyond a strictly theological context and can mean the accepted or established doctrine in any particular field of study. The precise word "orthodoxy" is not found in the NT, although its meaning is conveyed in a number of passages. Some texts speak about carefully handing on the message about Christ which had been received from earlier believers (1 Cor 11:2, 23; 15:1–3; 2 Tm 2:2). Both Paul (Gal 1:23) and Jude 3 speak of "the faith" in a way that connotes an identifiable doctrinal content. The Pastoral Letters place much emphasis on soundness of doctrine, using the word "teaching" (*didaskalia*) fifteen times and differentiating healthy teaching (1 Tm 1:10; 2 Tm 4:3; Ti 1:9; 2:1) from heterodox teaching (1 Tm 1:3; 6:3). The notion of sound doctrine underlies Paul's condemnation of those who preach "another Jesus" (2 Cor 11:4) or "another gospel" (Gal 1:6–9) and the condemnations of false teachers in 1 Tm 1:3–7; 2 Tm 3:1–9; 4:1–5. Thus, insofar as it is concerned about the handing on of correct doctrine as distinct from false doctrine, the NT provides a basis for later patristic usage of the word "orthodoxy," which became a common term among ecclesiastical writers especially after Eusebius (d. 339). By the time the councils of Ephesus (431) and Chalcedon (451) spoke of orthodoxy, the term connoted not simply right doctrine but the traditional and universal doctrine of the church, as handed down in an unbroken line from Jesus and the apostles.

The 1934 publication of W. Bauer's *Rechtgläubigkeit und Ketzerei im ältesten Christentum* challenged the traditional view that orthodoxy represented the original doctrinal content of Christian faith and that heresies were subsequent deviations. Bauer claimed that originally Christianity was a collection of doctrinally diverse groups most of whom were what would later be classified as heterodox. What later became known as orthodoxy was simply the doctrinal position of the Church of Rome, a position that gradually gained predominance during the third century, becoming the official Christian doctrine of the late Roman Empire. Bauer's thesis did not win wideranging acceptance, although it did demonstrate the difficulty of proving unanimity of doctrine in the earliest Christian decades.

In later history, the word "orthodoxy" was more frequently used among Eastern churches, which even had a yearly feastday of orthodoxy, than in the West, where the popes seemed to have avoided use of the term. The Second Vatican Council uses the adjective "orthodox" only once, stating that Marian devotion should keep within the bounds of orthodox teaching (*LG* 66).

For fundamental theology, the notion of orthodoxy raises several important areas for reflection. What is the relation between revelation and orthodoxy? Some have seen a kind of yardstick for orthodoxy in Vatican I's statement: "Moreover, by divine and Catholic faith everything must be believed that is contained in the written word of God or in tradition, and that is proposed by the Church as a divinely revealed object of belief either in a solemn decree or in her ordinary, universal teaching" (DS 3011). Here orthodoxy may be seen under its formal aspect—to be contained in Scripture or tradition and proposed by the church as revealed indicates that doctrine which is correct and therefore to be believed. This is a quantitative criterion for orthodoxy; orthodoxy comprises the doctrines that meet this criterion. Many theologians today suggest that greater attention needs to be paid to the material and qualitative aspects of doctrine. To believe in the central message of the gospel, the kerygma about the

saving death and resurrection of Jesus Christ, is already to believe in kernel the whole of Christian revelation. In this regard, Vatican II's statement about a "hierarchy of truths" (*UR* 11) would nuance Vatican I's more quantitative approach to orthodoxy.

Fundamental theology would also be interested in the relation between orthodoxy and faith. Because of the modern "turn to the subject," it has become clearer that the *fides qua*, or subjective aspect of faith, plays a significant formative role in a believer's grasp of the *fides quae*, or objective truth of revelation. Applied to orthodoxy, some have suggested that the pluralistic climate of contemporary society renders the act of faith on the part of any individual susceptible to a host of cultural and philosophic influences such that the complex subjective fabric of the faith of any individual resists facile categorization as orthodox or heterodox. Along this line, one needs to ask about the relation between orthodoxy and the *sensus fidelium*. The proclamation of two of the orthodox doctrines which are generally considered to be among the clearest examples of papal *ex cathedra* teachings, the doctrines of the immaculate conception and the assumption, was closely bound to the expressed faith of the vast majority of Roman Catholics. Fundamental theology needs to explore the ways in which one can "read" the *sensus fidelium*, as well as the theological significance of the *sensus fidelium* among divided Christians for that orthodox faith which provides part of the basis of full communion. Fundamental theology needs to show how orthodoxy can include, as it always has included, legitimate diversity. When a culture is sensitive to the historicity of all human endeavor and to the freedom and responsibility of individuals to seek truth, orthodoxy may connote a traditionalism that is not open to growth in truth and is even unthinkingly prejudiced against alternative, legitimate accounts of reality. However, by claiming to have a true message, Christianity of necessity claims to have an "orthodoxy." In this regard, the topic of orthodoxy brings one to the frontier between theology and philosophy. To some degreee, orthodoxy implies that Christianity can never remain neutral about any radically relative epistemology.

Bibl.: H. Rengstorf, "διδάσκω, διδασκαλία, ἑτεροδιδασκαλέω," *TDNT* 2:135–65; W. KASPER, "Zum Problem der Rechtgläubigkeit in der Kirche von morgen," in *Kirchliche Lehre: Skepsis der Gläubigen* (Freiburg/Basel/Vienna, 1970), 37–96; J. B. METZ, E. SCHILLEBEECKX, eds., "Orthodoxy and Heterodoxy," *Conc* 192, no. 4 (1987).

William HENN

ORTHOPRAXIS

Orthopraxis as a theological term has come into vogue rather recently under the impact of the "political theology" and "liberation theology" that developed from the late 1960s to the present. Theologians such as J. Moltmann, J. B. Metz, G. Gutiérrez, J. L. Segundo, and D. Soelle criticized the overly individualized preoccupations of Protestant neo-orthodox or Roman Catholic transcendental theology, calling for a greater attention to the social and political imperatives of the Judeo-Christian tradition. Moreover, these thinkers tended to accept a principle which, philosophically, has been associated with the work of Karl Marx, i.e., that it is more important to change the world than simply to interpret it. This social, future-oriented dimension of orthopraxis finds support in the tradition of papal social encyclicals, which began in the late nineteenth century and which provide part of the backdrop for collegial expressions of social doctrine such as Vatican II's *Gaudium et Spes*, the 1971 Synod of Bishops' *Justice in the World*, and the social doctrines of local episcopal conferences, the most notable example of which may well be the documents of the Episcopal Conference of Latin America (CELAM) from Medellín (1968) and Puebla (1975).

The word "orthopraxis" comes from the Greek words *orthē*, "right" or "correct," and *praxis*, "deed," "action," or "practice." Orthopraxis is evidently meant to be understood in comparison with orthodoxy. If orthodoxy concerns correct belief, orthopraxis is directed to correct action. Some would caution against identifying orthopraxis simply with action; rather it represents a critical relationship between doctrine or theory, on the one hand, and action or practice, on the other. Doctrine and action condition or mediate one another. Doctrine must prove its truth in practice; practice must be informed by doctrine and give rise to further doctrinal reflection.

The Bible has offered rich support for the fundamental importance of orthopraxis. The Hebrew Scriptures are divided into the categories of Law, Prophets, and Writings, each of which can be shown to have praxis as a principal aim. In recounting the history of salvation, the Law outlines the way of life of God's chosen people; in light of contemporary circumstances the Prophets challenge the people to a more faithful carrying out of that way of life; and the Writings discuss various ways in which the Law impinges on daily life. This practical sense is conveyed in such texts as Dt 30:14 ("No, it [the Law] is very near to you; it is in your mouth and in your heart for you to observe it") or Mi 6:8 ("He has told you, O mortal, what is good; and what does the LORD require of you but to do justice, and to love kindness, and to walk humbly with your God?"). Moreover, this practical dimension of the message of the Hebrew Scriptures has an ineradicable social side to it (see, e.g., Ex 20–23; Is 1:1–31; Am 1:6–7; 4:1–5). The NT continues to underline the importance of practice; Gal 5:6 speaks of "faith working through love." Jesus is recorded as saying, "Not everyone who says to me, 'Lord, Lord,' will enter the kingdom of heaven, but only the one who does the will of my Father in heaven" (Mt 7:21), and the criterion for eschatological judgment falls to one's praxis with regard to caring for one's fellow human beings (Mt 25:31–46). The dignity of the poor and the social obligations that are part of Christian discipleship appear repeatedly in the NT. Moreover, some have suggested that it is impossible to understand the message of the gospel without considering the praxis of Jesus, a praxis that had societal implications and that was directly related to his condemnation and death. For these, praxis becomes a hermeneutical principle, a way of reading the NT so as to bridge the gap that separates today's world from the horizons of the first century.

A significant task for fundamental theology will be to clarify the relation between orthodoxy and orthopraxis. Is orthopraxis in some way a criterion for orthodoxy such that un-Christian praxis mitigates one's ability to have correct belief? Furthermore, to what extent is orthopraxis a source for theology? The development of Basic Christian Communities, not only in Latin America but in other cultural milieus as well, has illustrated forcefully the role of experience in mediating the interpretation of revelation as contained in Scripture and tradition. What precisely is meant when one says that the experience gained in orthopraxis informs doctrine? Fundamental theology needs to attempt some answer to this question.

Another area of interest for fundamental theology is the relation between orthopraxis and the communion that is the church. In the past this communion has been often associated with right doctrine or orthodoxy. The term orthopraxis conjures up a contrast not only with orthodoxy but also, in a different way, with what might be called heteropraxis or heretical praxis. Some theologians have discussed the difficulties inherent in the celebration of the Eucharist by a community that encompasses both oppressed and oppressor, difficulties reminiscent of those faced by Paul in 1 Cor 11:17–34. Or, as another example, the social system of racial apartheid has been sometimes referred to as a "heresy." In both of these examples, the relation between orthopraxis and communion needs further elaboration.

While the word "orthopraxis" is somewhat new, the social and practical implications of faith to which it refers are as old as the oldest texts of Scripture. Today, reflection about orthopraxis will be a privileged point of dialogue between theology and the political and social disciplines.

Bibl.: J. MOLTMANN, _Theology of Hope_ (New York, 1967); J. B. METZ, _Theology of the World_ (London, New York, 1969); G. GUTIÉRREZ, _Theology of Liberation_ (New York, 1973); C. BOFF, _Theology and Praxis: Epistemological Foundations_ (Maryknoll, 1987); B. J. VERKAMP, "On Doing the Truth: Orthopraxis and the Theologian," _TS_ 49 (1988): 3–24.

William HENN

P

PASCAL, Blaise, and the Apologetics of the *Pensées*

1. A New Kind of Apologetic

Pascal's apologetic is original. His undertaking is not subordinated to a particular philosophy or science. It is nonetheless a philosophical apologetic; more exactly, it is an *anthropology*. In a universe in which human beings are adrift, a mystery to themselves and a mystery to others, Pascal tries to show how the Christian religion gives meaning to a seemingly absurd existence; his apologetic is thus a *theological anthropology*. The key to the mystery of the human person is to be found in Christ, the totality of meaning that makes it possible not only to decode the human condition but also to heal it.

Nowadays we might prefer to call Pascal's apologetic a HERMENEUTIC, i.e., a search for meaning, but one concerned less with proofs than with signs. It seeks to describe human existence by interpreting it as if it were a text. Pascal looks beyond the differences and oppositions, the breaks, discontinuities, and burstings of the mold and seeks to "decipher" the human condition. Moreover, his apologetic does not follow a linear order but is rather multidirectional and multidimensional. It is a search for and a discovery of a meaning on the basis of observations and figures that can be distributed and classified in different ways.

The search for meaning proceeds by analysis of the paradoxes attaching to the human condition and by way of the discovery of a high point that assumes and sheds light on these paradoxes.

Paradox, which plays a privileged role in Pascal's dialectic, is not for him a mere stylistic technique, a game of literary antitheses; rather, it sets forth the very terms of human reality as such. The paradox consists in the coexistence and the union of contraries; it amplifies these without resolving them. The characteristic Pascalian clash of themes—wretchedness and greatness, finite and infinite, time and eternity, flesh and spirit—is not his alone but belongs also to the gospel and to Paul, and describes the very movement of human existence: "Know, then, proud man, what a paradox you are to yourself" (B434 C438 K131).

Understanding of the paradox is not to be sought in an equilibrium in which the contraries are balanced off against one another and finally made to cancel one another out. What we should be looking for is not a balance or a symmetry but a *meaning* which has its source in a *higher point* that is able to explain and order divergent views. This higher point, which makes it possible to decipher the riddle of human existence, is supplied by Christianity, especially in its dogmas of original sin and redemption. Christian dogma, however, does not eliminate the terms of the paradox; rather, it shows them in a more glaring light. Christ is a point of rupture rather than of balance. Being himself a mystery, he explains the mystery of the human person by effecting a passage to a higher order: the order of the charity revealed by the cross. Christ alone deciphers the human condition.

2. Pascal's Dialectic

It is possible here only to sketch in broad outline the procedure followed in this new apologetic. Its originality consists in making the human person the central figure in the religious demonstration. In portraying this figure Pascal relies at times on images taken from mathematical physics (the human person having no set place in an infinite universe, abandoned, drifting, without point of reference), at times on images inspired by medicine (illness, search for an appropriate therapy). From the standpoint of phyics the need is to find a "high point"; from the standpoint of medicine it is to find a medicinal grace, a "remedy."

In a fragment that has become classical (B72 C84 K199) Pascal shows that human beings live in the midst of a spatial and temporal disproportion that is the sign of a still deeper disproportion which affects their very being. They have no place of their own in the universe where they might find their balance in relation to what surrounds them, for they are lost between the two abysses of the infinitely great and the infinitely small. Height, depth, center, periphery all lose their meaning in an infinite universe. What is this sphere whose center is everywhere and whose circumference is nowhere? Upon this vision of spatial infinities there is superimposed the vision of beings who know, but in their knowing are subject to two limitations: what they know they do not know either with certainty or completely.

Human beings find the paradox of finite and infinite at work again in the abyss of wretchedness and greatness in which their being is sunk. They look for truth, justice, and happiness, but in fact experience only uncertainty or error, injustice or violence, and disappointment or the mirage of happiness we call diversion. Everything ends in death. And yet the human person is great: "Through space the universe grasps me and swallows me up like a speck; through thought I grasp it" (B348 C256 K113). "Man is only a reed . . . but he is a thinking reed" (B347 C264 K200). His spirit is made for the infinite. Human wretchedness is due to an abyssal capacity that is open to the infinite but is never satisfied, to a thrust that never attains its goal. "Man infinitely transcends man" (B434, C438, K131), because in man there is something more than man. But, then, what is the human being? "How novel, how monstrous, how chaotic, how paradoxical, how prodigious! Judge of all things, feeble earthworm, repository of truth, sink of doubt and error, glory and refuse of the universe! Who will unravel such a tangle?" (B434 C438 K131).

Up to this point Pascal has been observing human beings, and watching them live and think, with the eye of a biologist or other expert who is responsible for drawing up a balance sheet. Readers are free to protest, should they wish, against the excessively somber colors of the description. And yet the analyses given by Nietzsche, Proust, Dostoyevski, Kafka, Mauriac, Malraux, Camus, and Sartre only continue and expand Pascal's insights and show that he is correct. Human beings, apart from the gospel, are hideous.

Apart from the Christian faith, human beings in the world can see no fate for themselves but absurdity ending in nothingness. What are they to do in the face of the mystery that they themselves are? Are they to go on living in indifference, unconscious of their past and unconcerned about their future? Pascal has such an indifferent person speak as follows:

I do not know who put me into the world, nor what the world is, nor what I am myself. I am terribly ignorant about everything. I do not know what my body is, or my senses, or my soul, or even that part of me which thinks what I am saying. . . .

I see the terrifying spaces of the universe hemming me in, and I find myself attached to one corner of this vast expanse without knowing why I have been put in this place rather than that. . . I see only infinity on every side, hemming me in like an atom or like the shadow of a fleeting instant. All I know is that I must soon die, but what I know least about is this very death which I cannot evade.

Just as I do not know whence I come, so I do not know whither I am going. All I know is that when I leave this world I shall fall for ever into nothingness or into the hands of a wrathful God, but I do not know which of these two states is to be my eternal lot. Such is my state, full of weakness and uncertainty. And my conclusion from all this is that I must pass my days without a thought of seeking what is to happen to me. (B194 C335 K427)

It is thus possible for unbelievers to accept a life of complete practical indifference. They need feel no discomfort about leaving aside any problems having to do with the deeper meaning of their lives. "To settle down in such ignorance is a monstrous thing, and those who spend their lives thus must be made to feel how extravagant and stupid it is by having it pointed out to them so that they are confounded by the sight of their own folly" (B195 C334 K428).

Pascal then applies himself to disconcerting libertines and stripping them of their certainties. He hopes to shake them from their torpor and send them in search of the truth. He wants to turn these experts in intellectual ease into "strangers" who are prey to the anxiety of being adrift, and thus to bring them to ask themselves the ultimate questions to which Christianity alone will provide answers. Unless libertines are thus shocked out of their complacency, no argument will have any effect on them; the result will be an academic debate and no more.

Pascal does not despair of effecting this kind of existential rift in the souls of unbelievers and launching them on this _search for meaning._ After all, their awareness of their own wretchedness should awaken them to their true vocation, since this vocation is an experiential call that they cannot drown out. But Pascal's strategy does not stop here. To the paradox of the human condition that needs to be decoded he adds another that is even more confounding and has to do this time with the demands of an authentic deciphering of the human condition.

Far from leaving the impression that the truth about the human person is to be found in a kind of naturalization of God, Pascal says bluntly: "What makes them believe is the Cross" (B588 C828 K842). Nothing else can teach us to know God and to know ourselves. "All Jesus did was to teach men that they loved themselves, that they were slaves, blind, sick, unhappy and sinful, that he had to deliver, enlighten, sanctify and heal them, that this would be achieved by men hating themselves and following him through his misery and death on the Cross" (B545 C689 K271).

There is no apologetic road save that of the cross. Pascal's entire description of the infinite universe and human beings adrift in it, of the mystery of wretchedness and greatness that dwells in them and tears them apart, has for its sole purpose to bring them to choose this road. The search for truth leads by way of the cross. This approach is another element in Pascal's originality. In addition to, and even more than, a doctrinal preparation, he sets down as a "preliminary" a "conversion of heart." In so doing he cuts short the objections of libertines and prepares them to read the historical signs and proofs. For, in point of fact, however reasonable the decision of faith may be and however impressive the accumulation of historical proofs, human beings get nowhere unless their passions have been brought under control and their hearts have been disposed to listen. "'I should have given up a life of pleasure,' they say, 'if I had faith.' But I tell you: 'You would soon have faith if you gave up a life of pleasure'" (B240 C457 K816). In order to see clearly one must rid oneself of fever and purify one's vision.

Pascal's apologetic thus advances by way of conversion of heart and by way of the cross. It makes use of historical proofs but intends them for those who are *disposed* by their consciousness of being incomprehensible to themselves and strangers to all things; for those who have correctly asked the question of life's meaning (origin and destiny) and now desire to find the truth with the help of the only light that can reveal it. This light comes from the cross of Jesus Christ, and human beings prepare themselves to receive it by mortifying their passions. This leap that is so perilous, so foolish in the world's eyes and so humiliating to the pride of the philosopher, cannot be better expressed than by the urgent warning: "Lest the cross of Christ be made of no effect."

Up to this point Pascal has been trying to disturb people and spur them to a search for the truth. He has also shown them the condition required for a successful search: they must dispose themselves to accept the truth, however disconcerting, by a conversion of heart.

Pascal first looks for an answer in the philosophers. These prove helpless to explain the human mystery in an authentic way. The Stoics opted for greatness and fell into pride; the skeptics opted for wretchedness and fell into a grievous indifference (B325 C392 K398). What the philosophers cannot do, the religions of humankind are likewise incapable of doing. Pascal interrogates in turn, but only briefly, Buddhism, Islam, and pagan religion. He does so in vain. Pascal's conclusion: Examine all the religions of the world; none of them gives a really decisive answer to the mystery of human beings and their destiny. All of these religions leave them unsatisfied and provide no real cure for their wretchedness.

3. Christ the Totality of Meaning

A definitive explanation of the human condition is possible only in Jesus Christ. "In Christ all contradictions are reconciled" (B684 C556 K257). He is the point at which all our paradoxes are resolved, not by establishing a balance or symmetry of contraries (sin–grace, greatness–wretchedness) but by a shift to a new order. Christ is the image of the new human being, and only God could have established this image; the world can neither call for it nor suspect it nor invent it. Adam becomes Jesus Christ, and each individual becomes a child of God in Jesus Christ. In Pascal's eyes, then, Christ is the center of everything; he is the reason for and meaning of everything: the whole of the human person and of God (B556 C602 K449). Christ does not depend on any figure, for in his case "the figure was drawn from the truth" (B673 C572 K826). Therefore the truth about human beings is found only in him. He alone explains the human paradox of greatness and wretchedness. For, on the one hand, "the Incarnation shows man the greatness of his wretchedness through the greatness of the remedy required" (B526 C677 K352); on the other hand, the cross manifests the "greatness of the human soul" (*Memorial*) which God mercifully calls to participate in his own life.

Christ not only explains the human condition in general; he also reveals human beings to themselves in their *personal mystery*. "Not only do we only know God through Jesus Christ; we only know life and death through Jesus Christ. Apart from Jesus Christ we cannot know the meaning of our life or our death, of God or of ourselves" (B548 C729 K417). Christ brings home to human beings the fact that they are self-centered, hardened, enslaved to their passions, and blind to God and their own destiny (B545 C689 K271). But as soon as they turn to him, their eyes are opened and they learn who they are and to whom they should commit themselves. Christ is therefore mediator in two ways: in the objective sphere, for he reveals to human beings the image of the living God and the image of the human person as God wants it to be; in the subjective sphere, too, for he supplies those who open themselves to God with the solid ground on which to build their existence; he gives them the living, filial outlook which is the source of their salvation.

Christ is truly the totality of meaning for human beings: he deciphers and he saves. He is light and healing, truth and life. Human beings do not discover their own meaning or achieve their own fulfillment in any wise man or any hero, but only in Jesus Christ crucified. In Christ sin has been taken over, but it has also been expiated and overcome; our sins have been acknowledged, forgiven and overcome by grace.

As Pascal sees it, there is only one explanation of the human person: the explanation given, by the Christian faith. Once the Christian truth has been projected upon the abyss that human beings are, once it supplies its account of their fall and greatness, unbelievers are more likely to be tempted by the Christian solution. There is continuity between the description of the human condition and the historical proofs. Pascal is aware that it is not enough to awaken respect for religion; its plausibility and credibility must also be established because God does not intend to ask for an irrational faith. His authority in asking

for faith will be based on solid arguments that are provided by the message itself and by prophecies, miracles, and holiness. This is enough, in Pascal's view, for those who are sincerely looking for the truth and are disposed to receive it with a humble heart and docility to grace. Those who are not won over will have to blame themselves for their stubbornness, that is, their lack of interest in the things that are above.

The guiding thread through the *Pensées* is Pascal's Christocentrism. In this respect there is a profound harmony between the *Memorial*, *The Mystery of Jesus*, the three orders, and the *Pensées*.

In the *Pensées* Pascal does not, or at least so it seems, start with Jesus and then turn back to other human beings. On the contrary, he turns his attention at great length to the latter, in order eventually to lead them to Christ. But in fact Pascal's procedure in the *Apology* is much closer than it seems to that adopted in the other two texts. Pascal, after all, is not a moralist or an analyst who finds delight in describing human beings and their internal contradictions; his primary purpose is to lead human beings to Christ. Like Augustine, Pascal is a "convert," and his *Apology* is a convert's project. As with Augustine and Paul, it was in the light of Christ that he studied the wretchedness and greatness of human beings, and it is this that makes his analysis such an astonishingly penetrating one. He looks at human beings, but only as seen in the new human being. It was in fact the mystery of Christ that enabled Pascal to make his way down into the abysses of the human person. Without the cross of Christ we would never have suspected how deep these abysses are. Jesus Christ is the summation of Pascal's *Pensées*. And in Jesus Christ the essential thing is the cross and the love it reveals.

Bibl.: Quotations from Pascal refer to the three following editions: B=Brunschvicg, C=Chevalier, and K=Krailsheimer (=Pascal, *Pensées*, trans. A. J. Krailsheimer [Baltimore: Penguin Books, 1966]); J. MESNARD, *Pascal: L'homme et l'oeuvre* (2nd ed.; Paris, 1956); id., "Blaise Pascal," *NCE* 10:1046–48; R.-E. LACOMBE, *L'apologétique de Pascal* (Paris, 1958); H. GOUHIER, *Blaise Pascal: Commentaires* (Paris, 1966); M. PONTET, *Pascal et Teilhard, témoins de Jésus-Christ* (Paris, 1968); P. SELLIER, *Pascal et S. Augustin* (Paris, 1970); P. MAGNARD, *Nature et histoire dans l'apologétique de Pascal* (Paris, 1975); H. BÜRKLIN, *Ein Gott für Menschen: Entwurf einer christo-*

zentrischen Anthropologie nach Bl. Pascal (Freiburg/ Basel/Vienna, 1976); R. LATOURELLE, "Christ, the Totality of the Signified," in Man and His Problems in the Light of Jesus Christ (New York, 1983), 29–88.

René LATOURELLE

PASCHAL MYSTERY

I. SUFFERING AND DEATH. 1. The Problem of Human Suffering. 2. The Death that Redeems All Suffering. 3. The Self-Attestation of Faith in the Cross (W. KERN)

II. THE RESURRECTION OF JESUS. 1. The Claim. 2. The Origins of Easter Faith. 3. The Easter Revelation. 4. Justifying Easter Faith. (G. O'COLLINS)

I. SUFFERING AND DEATH

Regardless of ways in which the twofold topic of "suffering and death" might be understood and treated as involving merely two degrees of the same basic thing, the two concepts—or rather realities—will be contrapuntally opposed to each other here as the suffering of *humans* and the death of *Jesus*. Human suffering is the question; the answer will be the death of the crucified Son of Man and Son of God.

1. The Problem of Human Suffering

Suffering as a Fact

That the amount of suffering in this world is immeasurably large, and the instances of evil innumerably many, is a conclusion so inescapable that anything said about it is already almost too much. Love between two human beings can turn into aversion and hatred leading to homicide or murder. As a consequence of long-escalating disputes, entire nations become caught up in enmities that unleash devastating wars. No end of innocent persons pose—with the woman who loses her children in one night of bombing—the question asked by Job: Why? Particularly the guiltless, and therefore unjustified, suffering of ill-treated or even tortured children (which has been called "the absolute evil") provokes outrage. It brought from Dostoyevsky's lips a cry of protest

against the world and its Creator. Camus echoed it: "I refuse, to the point of death, to love a creation in which children are martyred" (*La peste* [The Plague]; [Paris, 1947]). He conjectures that "the suffering of children can prevent" one "from arriving at faith. . . ."

From the Theodicy Problem to "Troubled Atheism"

The problem of the evil in the world was posed by Pierre Bayle (*Dictionnaire*, 1695–97) at the time of the modern intersection of the two preconditions for its rise: (1) the old conviction that there is an all-powerful, all-wise, and all-good governance of the world by God, and (2) the new claim by human reason to be able to pass critical judgment on the results of that. In 1710, Leibniz formulated the thus foreshadowed aporia both in name and as a demand: "theodicy," a justification of God (see Rom 3:4f.; Ps 51:6). His essay became the model for philosophical *optimism*: the perfect God could create only a perfect world. Despite the fact that the finitude of the world necessitates "metaphysical evil" — in which physical and moral evil are rooted— this world, when seen as a whole, is the best possible one; even though we may not comprehend *how* this is so, *that* it is so has a priori certainty. The subsequent period gave rise to a flood of apologies claiming to discern in the book of nature—and even in Alpine milk and cheese production (A. Kyburtz, 1753)—every conceivable sort of sign of God's creative wisdom. ("Theodicy" later became the title for the scholastic tractate on philosophical theology.) A shift from the mentality of optimism to *pessimism* was signaled in 1755 by the great earthquake of Lisbon. According to Hume, the course of the world gives no grounds for inferring the existence of a God who is at all concerned about the happiness and unhappiness of his creatures. Schopenhauer is the direct opposite of Leibniz: bankrupt from top to bottom, the world is the worst possible one, capable of arising only through blind unreason. E. v. Hartmann softens this radical pessimism somewhat by reducing it to the "claim that there is a negative balance of pleasure in the world"; ultimately, the nonexistence of the world remains preferable to its existence. J.-P. Sartre and A. Camus try to wrest from the *nihilism* (inaugurated in an optimistic spirit by Nietzsche) of their pessimistic theory a life that would, in practice, nevertheless be worth living. The failure of attempts to achieve a viable theodicy—which is, for the most part, what the record shows since Lisbon—is usually associated with agnosticism or explicit atheism. Precisely when such an attitude does not occur in militant form or with (pseudo-)scientific pretensions (like the until quite recently virulent "dialectical materialism"), but rather "only" addresses itself, as "troubled atheism," in disappointment and resignation to the many-sided experience of human suffering, it is (as will emerge later here) not theoretically refutable. (As early as the last century, the young writer, Georg Buchner, referred to human suffering as "the rock of atheism.")

Monism or Dualism?

Neither of these two metaphysical opposites can solve, through a quasi-ontological act of force, the theodicy problem. They turn out, under closer scrutiny, to be mere variants of optimism or pessimism. Kant (who, according to Goethe, had therefore most unbecomingly slobbered on his philosophical gown) remained adherent to the doctrine of inexpungeable "radical evil" in human nature. German IDEALISM, by contrast, monistically mediated everything negative, and especially humanity's original sin, by making it integral to a necessary developmental process involving God, world, and humanity as one: all of which implies and effects a breakthrough to self-consciousness, restructuring of the world, and cultural progress. Probably it was Hegel who most impressively charted the steps by which the Spirit, with an essential necessity that is also essentially freedom, manifests itself by externalizing itself as the extreme opposite of itself—namely, as the material world, as the finite consciousness of a single individual (Jesus of Nazareth), and as an ignominious death (on the cross at Golgotha)—in order, by just this means, to arrive at self-conscious reality in the world community of the Spirit that is represented by philosophers. Here evil remains just a sublimated, and to that extent transient, aspect of the greater whole; it heals the wound it inflicts, like the spear in the legend of the Holy Grail.

Dualism (examples of which are found above all in the history of religion) possesses, at least

seemingly, a greater closeness to reality and more persuasive force. It is most pronounced in Mazdaism and Parseeism, which derive from the teachings of Zoroaster (ca. 600 B.C.E.): of two twin spirits generated from the primal divinity, Ahura-Mazda, one opted for the good, true, and bright, and the other for the opposing power of the evil, and so on, and this choice is also faced by every human being. But when the world ends, Ahura-Mazda will establish his everlasting kingdom for those who are good (and to that extent pessimism is ultimately overcome). In a later version of this religion, a lord of darkness is opposed, as an equally primal and uncreated entity, to the lord of the realm of light. For Manichaeism (third century C.E.)—which is the radically dualistic form of Gnosticism—the world and humanity, as abnormal mixtures of good divinity (spirit) and evil body (matter), exist in a very bad state until such time as these principles have become separated again. Similar ideas were advocated earlier by Orphism, Pythagoreanism, and forms of Platonism resulting from one-sided interpretation of their master. Later resonances occur, e.g., in the German theosophist, Jakob Böhme (ca. 1600), and the late Schelling, who postulate a primal division of the one God into a bright/good principle of love and a dark/evil principle of wrath. By internally dividing the divine power, dualism aims to absolve the good God (the divine aspect) of responsibility for evil or for seemingly cruel permission of evil. That such a restriction—and thus annulment—of God's omnipotence still provides the least discrediting religious option is a widespread view today, even among some theologians.

An Attempt at Critical Questioning of Nihilism

Precisely that position which most comprehensively and fundamentally promotes the denial of everything positive in the world, of the existence of any sense or reason at all, can, it seems, serve to point the way here.

Toward the end of the eighteenth century in Germany, "nihilism" was a fairly common term for intellectual currents that were regarded as destructive; at the same time, the word _nihiliste_ appeared in France. In an early writing (1798), F. W. Jacobi characterizes nihilism as a form of idealism that succumbs to the danger of severing

Christian revelation from its origin, the earthly Jesus. In substance, this use of the word was—as Jacobi possibly did not realize—closely related to *nihilista*, which referred, in medieval Latin theology, to those who regard Christ's human nature (because it has no independent status) as of little, or even no, consequence. There were also those who took the view that Christianity, with its doctrine of a creation of the world "out of nothing," first prepared the way for nihilism; and that the *creatio* of the world is, after all, paralleled by the counter-concept of its *annihilatio* (something always possible given God's *potentia absoluta*). The notion of "nihilism" appears in its present-day, radically "nihilating" sense primarily in Nietzsche and Heidegger, both of whom regard it, however, as a (necessary) transitional stage to a new, positive perception and evaluation of humanity and the world.

Critical examination of nihilism may be opened with the at first rather unpromising observation that "nothingness" can be defined only as that which in no way *is*. The same sort of linguistic and conceptual necessity seems to obtain regarding all words (including the more specific ones) that express negative concepts. Even the mere *linguistic* designations of many negative kinds of experience point back to the positive ones that underlie them: dis-ordered-ness, in-appropriateness, un-harmoniousness, non-attainment, and so on. Also, the often-heard, resigned lament that everything is really "meaningless" can be understood only on the basis of a prior understanding of "meaning." Negative or—as formal logic puts it—privative concepts (like blindness, stupidity) are conceivable only through reference back to what they wholly or partially negate (e.g., sightedness, intelligence); they are secondary counterconcepts. It is not just a matter here of psychologically explainable habits of speech or thought but rather one of the *objective* state of affairs itself, of the logic of *reality*. Thomas Aquinas states not only that "*the understanding* of a negation is always based on an affirmation," but also that "the affirmation is *by nature* prior to the negation." And Aristotle had already summarized this relation as follows: "It is through the affirmation that the negation is understood, and the affirmation is prior; just as being, too, is prior to nonbeing"; or, in more lapidary phrasing: "But where there is the no, there is also the yes."

An example illustrative of this point suggests itelf here: What is the precondition in reality itself, in the concrete structure and function of the human body, of the fact that we can suffer *illness*? Being ill is an "a-normal" occurrence, a phenomenon involving either breakdown (or deficiency) or rampant growth. It, along with its causes and effects, lies either below or above the normal state that we call health (e.g., a bodily temperature above or below 98.6 degrees Fahrenheit). Only as a deviation from the normal state can illness manifest itself as bothersome, painful, hindering, or damaging; for *what* is hindered or damaged by it? *Only because of that does it exist at all.* Of course, some persons can always have been ill, from the time of their birth on; but even then, they are ill only because, in principle, given that basic organization of nature against which their particular condition appears as defective, they could, and should, be *healthy*. Without this fundamental predisposition to being healthy and the resultantly justified expectation that one should be healthy, illness would not be possible—not only at the level of our speech and thought but also in reality, *in natura rerum*.

Certain "thought-experiments" based on hypothetically imagined extremes, which cannot be detailed here, point in the same direction: to assume that the world is absolutely absurd is itself absurd; if everything were meaningless, nothing would be meaningless. What is the reason for (if there is "reason for" anything at all) the fact that people can come to prefer death to life? Because life failed to fulfill the expectations that they had associated with it? Because they had longed and striven for so much—even too much—of life? For what reason are we envious, jealous, or begrudging toward this or that person because of this or that thing? Possibly because our nature has a predisposition for extending its grasp unrestrictedly toward everything.

Such considerations come down to the following: inherent in the experience of meaninglessness is an always more fundamental demand for meaning. This does not, of itself, guarantee the *actuality* of meaning fulfillment, but it does attest to its inner, concrete *possibility*. Hence, fulfillment of the demand for meaning must not necessarily be real or ever become real; but the demand for meaning itself is fully real. It is an *actual* demand for a *possible* being.

This implies that even the most radical nihilism does not have the last word; one can, and must, raise questions that reach both beyond it and behind it.

This conclusion is confirmed by Albert Camus (1913–1950), who is generally regarded as the existentialist philosopher of absurdity: "There is no total nihilism. As soon as one says that everything is meaningless, one expresses something that has meaning. To reject any meaningfulness of the world is to suspend any sort of value judgment. But life in itself is a value judgment. . . ." "It is not possible to negate value judgments *absolutely*. To do so would be to deny the absurd [!]"; and in fact: "It is impossible for humans to despair completely." Many other literary, philosophical, and theological testimonies of this kind could be cited.

No Theoretical Resolution of the Theodicy Problem

The attempt to question the presuppositions behind radical nihilism, as a doctrine of last resort in the human interpretation of existence, may well be logically unobjectionable. That this, however, is of much existential significance for human beings, given the destiny of suffering affecting the world and their own lives, probably has to be doubted. But a similar sort of skepticism also seems appropriate regarding the (no doubt to a certain extent quite helpful) answer given by Christian tradition.

The following positions, which were staked out in the fifth century by Augustine, are as valid now as they were then:

Evil is, in its structure, only a (secondary) lack, a defect, or *privatio boni*.

Physical evil, or what is "bad" (e.g., illness, error), must be distinguished from moral evil, or what is properly "evil" (e.g., rape, lying). Natural catastrophes, by presenting a challenge to the spirit of invention, can serve to stimulate cultural development (but does that justify the ordeals and deaths of their victims?).

God cannot, in principle, will evil; that would contradict his holiness. He can only permit it in the sense of not willing to prevent it. (The notion of permission is, despite much opposition, an indispensable auxiliary concept.)

But why? Even the mere permitting must be justified, and the reason for it, which lies in God's providence, is the greater good that is indirectly achieved through the evil.

With this, the crucial stage of the problem has been reached. The most inhuman—in both form and degree—instances of abuse of human freedom lend a final pointedness to the question of why. The answer is often given that God merely respects the freedom of humans to decide for good or for evil, and that the state of the world just reflects that. But could not the God who, in omnipotence and infinite wisdom, created the world out of bountiful love have set it upon a different, and better, course, and can he not incline the hearts of humans in such a way that—without detriment to their freedom, indeed, with an even greater freedom—they turn toward the good and only the good? Why is there evil anyway? Why does God permit it? In a certain respect, one can understand why even theologians prefer to think of God as limitedly powerful rather than as the "Father" who—as it seems—malevolently or indifferently watches the misery of his "children." It is better that he be unable to prevent evil than that he be unwilling to do so. But even this "resolution" of the theodicy problem ultimately fails, as does everything that we humans say about it.

2. The Death That Redeems All Suffering

Philosophical Prologue: Death—A Promise of Life?

In a certain, very brutal sense, death puts an end to a person's life. But it is most feared as that which irrevocably breaks off the course of one's earthly life itself, as the worst form of physical evil. Does death only slam shut the door of life, or does it also throw open the hopeful prospect of new life?

All humans must die. And from the very first, the *whole* of human life is both overshadowed by and attuned to death; life is one long "sickness unto death," according to S. Kierkegaard. (One could speak of an extensive and intensive *universality* of death.) In death, everything is gathered together; it allows no more room to move, it seems to leave nothing else open. That probably explains the concluding, retrospective summary, customarily spoken after the burial, of the life of someone who has died; or, for instance, the cinematic replay of images from their lives that is supposed to flash, in split-second succession, before the mind's eye of victims of fatal accidents. In death, life seems to be plunged into the abyss of existing no longer. Death, who takes us all, takes us *from ourselves*; what is left for a while decays or crumbles. Where then—asked in imagistic terms—does death take us? Into "nothingness"? This is a cause of intense anguish for us humans. Fear of death is the most elementary form of fear. And what makes this so mercilessly acute for humans (in contrast to the animals) is their awareness of their own finitude and transience. Death "consumes the immanence of existence," as it were, before the dimming eyes of the dying person. This is what constitutes the (one is tempted to say "absolute") *negativity* of death—as well as the starting point for overcoming it.

Because death *"nihilates" everything* for everyone, it is the most radical instance of limitation. Thus a glance at the *dialectics of limitation* is appropriate here, with J. G. Fichte. And especially with G. W. F. Hegel: "Something is only known, or indeed, felt, as a limit or lack inasmuch as one is, at the same time, already beyond it." "The very fact that we recognize some limit is proof of our being beyond it, of our unlimitedness." The basic law that the experience of limitation equals the transcendence of limitation applies to all modes of the finite and the limited: "Nothing is so contingent and accidental that it does not have an inherent element of necessity" (Thomas Aquinas, *ST* 1, q. 86, a. 3). "For objective dialectics, the absolute is, in principle, contained in the relative" (Lenin, in context of Hegel studies). Nothing is so transitory that it does not include a dash of finality. Nothing wholly dumb: a spark of spirit inhabits it. Nothing only questionable: it begins, simultaneously, to answer itself (Aristotle: "The discovery of an aporia *is* its resolution" [*Eth. Nich.* 7.4]). Nothing is so open to manipulation and abuse that no glimmer of intractableness remains. In sum: nothing, wholly and fully, is purely worldly, merely human, *only* limited and finite. And nothing so mortal as to contain no life.

The negativity of death, precisely because of its all-embracing character, is impelled to move beyond itself, beyond its negation. It breaks out in the opposite of itself, in affirmation, the passing of what passes, the life beyond death. For that death should render "this negativity understandable to human existence" presupposes "that the latter understands itself with a view to the positivity of its being, . . . that this human existence is concerned with being and not with non-being, . . . with being whole, with being saved. . . . Its *not* is inscribed on the larger redemptive plan that human existence always projects for itself" (B. Welte, *Heilsverständnis* [Freiburg, 1966], 131–32). As a consequence of death's universality and negativity, the *"transcendentality"* of its (directional, internally impelled) self-surpassing would seem to intimate itself.

So far, so good (?). The reflections on death that were just conducted also—like the critical questioning of nihilism—remained abstract. Nor can allusion to heaven and hell satisfactorily "justify God" before the court of suffering humanity. But if what *humans say* about the "justice of God," about theodicy, is not sufficient, then what does *God do?*

Jesus' Crucifixion as a Paroxysm of Humanity's Passion

The hope that the cross of Jesus might shed light on the history of human suffering is, from the very start, faced with a great *videtur quod non* ("It seems not so"). Precisely the opposite seems to be the case. The crucifixion is the most ignominious method of execution known to the world. And is the crucifixion of *one* human being supposed to both ground and effect redeeming faith and eternal salvation for *all* human beings? This paradox will give us cause for thought.

The Scandal of the Cross. From the Celtic regions of the world to the Indian, it was customary to nail criminals to the cross as sacrifices to the gods. Among the Persians and Carthaginians (in North Africa), crucifixion was the punishment for the most grievous crimes against the state, for high treason. The Romans made crucifixion the typical form of punishment for slaves. Along with violent criminals, rebellious elements in the Roman provinces, e.g., in Judea, were also crucified. They usually stemmed from the lowest social classes, which, it was thought, had to be suppressed for the sake of public order. *Non sine* _metu_ ("Not without our resorting to fear") (Tacitus, _Annals_ 14.44.3) could the slavish rabble in Rome be kept under reasonable control. Short work was made of things: the emperor Domitian (ca. 90 C.E.) had a writer beheaded for caricaturing him in one of his books; the unfortunate scribe-slaves were crucified. At crucifixions, the tyranny and sadism of the executioners was given free play; that suited the vindictiveness and cruelty of the rulers as well as the masses. The most frightful aspect was the length of time that the victim was left hanging on the "woeful tree." The young Caesar is said to have been merciful enough to order captured pirates strangled before crucifixion. The public display of the naked, tormented victims was regarded as the ultimate humiliation, which visibly sealed their social expulsion and their religious condemnation. No ancient writer chose to linger at the scene of these cruel proceedings. The most detailed accounts are the passion narratives in the Gospels. In Greek and Latin fiction, the cross represents the worst threat facing the hero, thereby functioning to raise dramatic tension to a peak—but in no case is the hero actually allowed to suffer this degrading death: he is rescued just in time by a _deus ex machina_. For Cicero, the cross is "the harshest and ultimate form of punishment for slaves," "the cruelest and most abhorrent kind of execution"; he decries it as "this pestilence." Flavius Josephus judges it "the most pitiable form of death."

The Cross of Jesus: The Focal Point of Christian Faith. From the very beginning, Christianity has acknowledged the cross of Jesus as the basis and focal point of its faith. Paul had resolved, while with the community of Corinth, "to know nothing . . . except Jesus Christ, and him crucified" (1 Cor 2:2). He realized that he had been sent to preach the gospel—but to do so in such a way "that the cross of Christ might not be emptied," i.e., might not lose its power or meaning (1 Cor 1:17). The first two chapters of 1 Corinthians (1:17–2:9) are a "single magnificent" testimony to the fundamental—indeed, central—significance that the "message of the cross" (_ho logos tou staurou_, 1 Cor 1:18) has for Paul. But even "long before Paul, theological reflections and liturgical affirmations had emphasized Jesus' death as the advent of salvation"; and precisely Paul confirms this, for he

"accepts the different variations of this preaching," namely, the interpretations of Jesus' crucifixion as representation, reconciliation, redemption, and also as atonement and sacrifice. In this connection, Paul occasionally states quite expressly that he "passes on what he has received," i.e., that he is handing down earlier tradition (esp. 1 Cor 15:3–5; cf. 11:23–26); or the form of his communications makes clear his acceptance of the traditional interpretation (Rom 4:25; 8:34; 2 Cor 5:13; 13:4). In the early Christian hymn quoted in Philippians (2:6–11), it was probably Paul who underscored the extreme humiliation of Jesus' "becoming obedient to death" by himself interpolating the words "even death on a cross" (v. 8)! That Jesus himself had attributed, before the event, redemptive significance to his death has, admittedly, been called into doubt by some exegetes in recent decades; but later critical inquiries (esp. by H. Schürmann) adhere, for good reasons, to the view that, at the Last Supper, Jesus offered his disciples bread and wine as his body, which would be given, and his blood, which would be shed, for them or for "the many" (which means, for all).

The Paradox Inherent in Faith in the Cross. That the wretched death of a human being by hanging on a cross, which entailed that the one so treated was stigmatized as guilty of capital crime—that such a death should be, for all human beings, the source of life and of blessed communion with God, and thus the basis of their salvation and the focus of their faith, runs directly counter to all probability, to anything that human beings could possibly expect. Can anyone unwilling to dispense with reason even in matters of religion be asked to accept this paradox? The opponents of Jesus who stood beneath the cross at Golgotha called out to him to come down from the cross, and then they would believe he was the Messiah. This was vicious mockery, yet there is a grain of truth in their demand; someone executed by crucifixion is the Messiah—how utterly atrocious and scandalous!

The early Christians must initially have felt the same. Until the end of the second century, no representations (with likely reference to Jesus) of the tormented Crucified are known. (One exception is the mock-crucifix from Palatine Hill in Rome, a drawing on a wall of the imperial palace. From two lines that form a T hangs a little man—with the head of an ass. Another looks up at him. The accompanying inscription reads: "Alexamenos worshiping his god.") Around 200 C.E., Tertullian offers this explanation: "In ancient preaching, the mystery of the Cross had to be concealed in symbolic imagery. For had it been proclaimed openly, without imagery, it would have become an even greater scandal" (*Adv. Marc.* 3.18). As early as 150 C.E., Justin had already felt hard-pressed by critics: "Our madness consists, they declare, in the fact that we accord second place, after that of the immutable and eternal God, to a cruci- fied human" (*Apologia* 1.13.4); also, he tells of a Jew demanding proof that the Messiah "had needed to be crucified and to die, under legal condemnation, so ignominious and dishonor- able a death; for we cannot even imagine such a thing" (*Dial. Tryph.* 90.1).

Islam did not want to allow that Jesus— whom, along with Moses and Muhammad, it esteemed as a great prophet—was crucified: rather, someone else was executed in his place (*Qur'an* 4.157–59). (As early as the second cen- tury, Christian heresies began resorting to similar rescuing interpretations. According to Docetism [from *dokein*, "to appear"], Jesus possessed only the appearance of a body; accord- ing to Marcion, the crucifixion affected only Jesus' body, but not Jesus himself.) From more recent times—bypassing Goethe—there are these little-known words of Hegel: "The one who hangs from the cross is worshipped. This monstrous conjunct is what, for so many cen- turies, millions of God-seeking souls have fought over and been martyred for." Again: "In our socio-cultural context, this new religion would have had to take as its banner the equivalent of what the cross was then, namely, the gallows." Nietzsche referred to faith in the cross, supposedly pushed to undue prominence by Paul, as the *absurdissimum*.

> Modern people, with their jaded indifference to all Christian terminology, are no longer capable of emotional response to the element of the superlatively horrific that, for ancient taste, lay in the paradoxical notion of "God on the cross." Previously, there had never been, regardless of time or place, anything comparable in boldness of reversal, anything comparably frightful . . . to that notion: it heralded a revaluation of all ancient values. (Nietzsche)

Faith in the crucified God looks, "in the most terrifying way, like an incessant suicide of reason." Nietzsche, one of the most unrelenting critics of Christianity, probably grasped more acutely than anyone the kind of absurdity that faith in the cross represents for a nonbeliever.

Precisely Paul of Tarsus, the first and thus far (and perhaps forevermore) greatest Christian theologian, to whom we owe the earliest texts in the NT, has also mercilessly subjected himself, and us, to the impress and experience of this "most absurd" of possible things, to the gospel—that good and joyous message!—of the cross: consider here 1 Cor 1:17b–25. According to this, the cross of Jesus means a stumbling block (*skandalon*) for the Jews, who demand— as during the exodus from Egypt—signs of their God's power; and it means foolishness (*mōria*) for the Greeks, who seek intelligible worldly wisdom. However, precisely for one who does "not empty the cross of Christ [of its meaning]" (v. 17b), but rather embraces it in all its paradox- ical severity, the scandalously repulsive can become the promisingly attractive "message of the cross" (v. 18). The wounding shock then becomes a healing one. For those, namely, who are saved because they believe, the cross is not impotence and foolishness but the power of God and the wisdom of God. For—again a won- drous paradox—"God's foolishness is wiser than human wisdom, and God's weakness is stronger than human strength" (v. 25).

The Incomprehensibility of God, or the Credibility of the Incredible. The paradoxi- cality of Pauline theology takes one's breath away. On the whole, thought itself tends to fail for anyone who believes in the cross as the ad- vent of salvation. The passion of Jesus reaches its high point, which is an absolute low point, in the Crucified's cry of abandonment by God: "My God, why have you forsaken me?" (Mk 15:34; Mt 27:46). These words are vibrant with the question and plaint of the human being, Job; the passion of the whole of humanity re- sounds in them. They express most succinctly the contradictoriness of the event of the cross: the one abandoned by God abandons himself to God. He calls out to the very one who is not present. All the paradoxicality of faith in the cross has been compressed into the few words of this cry. On the one hand, Jesus seems to die not only in body but also in soul as he voices this cry. On the other hand, the cry is one majestic affirmation of the God of ultimate incomprehensibility. It acknowledges the divinity of God, and it both witnesses and seals that acknowledgment through death. In his divinity, God is, and must be (otherwise he would not be God, but similar to us), *the one who is incomprehensible to us.* And since (according to Heb 11:1) faith is "the assurance of things hoped for, the conviction of things not seen," that which at first—in its unique and unsurpassable contradictoriness (the crucified equals the savior of the world)—appears unbelievable could perhaps begin to glow with a hidden, deeper believability. To will to believe in the paradox of the cross—and Christianity stands or falls with that belief—is a challenge to confront the incomprehensibility of God. It is not enough just to accept Tertullian's *credo quia absurdum.* . . .

3. *The Self-attestation of Faith in the Cross*

What God Did. By our own devices, we humans can find no satisfactory answer to the question Why? in relation to human suffering. *God's* answer is the giving over of his Son to death—and, in fact, to a death on the cross. Through this, the theodicy problem is not theoretically resolved, but the suffering of the world is, in practice, redeemed. The suffering is redeemed, as well as the—in its own way equally tormenting—suffering over that suffering.

"For God so loved the world that he gave his only Son, . . . not . . . to condemn the world, but in order that the world might be saved through him" (Jn 3:16–17; cf. 1 Jn 4:9). Paul speaks similarly in the Letter to the Romans (8:32): "He who did not withhold his own Son, but gave him up for all of us, will he not with him also give us everything else?" And as an echo from Ambrose: "In order to save the servant, you gave up the Son." And as late as Kierkegaard: "The one who spared Abraham's first-born and only tested the patriarch's faith nevertheless did not spare his own, only-begotten Son" (*Journal,* entry dated 13 September 1839).

Jesus was not ordered to the beams of the cross against his will by God; he took the suffering freely upon himself (cf. Jn 10:17–18). As well, those who executed him were not destined or motivated by God to do so; they acted in accordance with their own—probably in their opinion good (cf. Lk 23:34) but de facto "objectively" bad—wills. God permits the evil (i.e., the killing of an innocent person) for the sake of a greater good, which does not *arise from* the evil as its supposed cause, but is only *occasioned by* the evil event, as *condicio sine qua non,* and has another source. But what, in the case of Jesus' death on the cross, is the "greater good," and what is its source?

The Revelation of Pardoning Love. Jesus' parable of the lost son (Lk 15:11–32) brings us close to the meaning of the mystery of the cross. The father allows his younger son, who will subsequently squander his inheritance on prostitutes, to embark on a path leading to misery, guilt, and remorse. He could have prevented this. But had the son been forced to remain at home, would he not have reacted with misunderstanding and protest, perhaps for the rest of his life? So the father permits him to set off on his unhappy, misguided journey. When, however, the ill-fated "lost son" returns home, the father rushes toward him in unrestrained love. The surprising, and almost dismaying, magnanimity of this behavior is highlighted by the counterexample of the older son, who insists unfeelingly on strict justice. The felt absence of the younger son is the precondition for the revelation of fatherly love in its new character as pardoning love, which absolves from pain and guilt.

Experience of crises and catastrophes in relations between people who love each other can cast a modern-day light on this biblical parable. A spouse goes astray; a friendship is betrayed. Then it may be that "everything is finished." However, it may also be that the situation is patiently endured and overcome, and that, through reconciliation and forgiveness, a new depth and intimacy of mutual understanding and attachment to one another are realized. Something similar also applies at the broader level of recent world events: through revolutionary change, peoples who were yoked for decades to the unfreedom of totalitarian regimes have come to experience, with a new intensity, what freedom means; and their experience can perhaps lead in other parts of the world to similar transformations of the political structure.

That Jesus' crucifixion is the revelation—something previously not to be expected or, indeed, even sensed as a possibility—of God's love is expressed most aptly, once again, by Paul: "God proves his love for us in that while we still were sinners Christ died for us" (Rom 5:8). God acts out of love. Indeed, "God *is* love" (1 Jn 4:16). "God, as love, hangs fully and utterly on the cross" (Simone Weil). Thus it can be said that "God's godliness is to be understood with a view to the occurrence of this death" (E. Jüngel), and that the cross is ultimately "the only possible definition of God and of humanity" (W. Kasper). Accordingly, God's self-definition becomes: crucified love. The incomprehensibility of love is now no longer the emptiest, but the fullest definition of the nondefinable. J. A. Möhler says of God that "his manifestation has occurred in the form of sacrificing himself for the sins of the world." Gregory of Nyssa (fourth century) elucidates the possibility of divine suffering as follows:

> That the almighty nature was capable of descending to the lowliness of the human evidences its power more than great miracles that transcend nature. . . . God's descent to the lowly is a certain superabundance of power for which contrariness to nature constitutes no obstacle. . . . The elevated appears in the lowly, yet the elevated is not thereby brought low.

God relinquishes his omnipotence by projecting it into the impotence of the one who—abandoned by humans and by God—is dying on the cross. In this, he reveals that "power" of love which does not descend triumphantly upon us humans but attracts and overwhelms us through its solidarity in suffering. God bends down to humans as "God in the form of a servant" (S. Kierkegaard); his all-mightiness becomes an "all-weakness" (G. Marcel). Jesus himself interprets the kenosis of his cross (cf. Phil 2:7) in terms of the eucharistic offering: "My body for you, my blood for all." It is the comprehensibly incomprehensible proof of his love. Crucified love divinely and infinitely outdoes ("undercuts") God's almighty creative love.

The Death of Death. It is important in the present context—and in Christian faith—that the cross be viewed not in isolation, as nothing but the gruesome, external process of execution at Golgotha, but rather as linked to its theological "inner side," Jesus' resurrection from the

dead. For it is the latter that is the one total *mysterium paschale.*

Already in the earliest of the NT texts, 1 Thessalonians (4:14; composed ca. 50 C.E.), Paul formulates the basic Christian affirmation in these few words: "we believe that Jesus died and rose." Even when Paul seems to speak only of Jesus' death, he nevertheless refers to this as a death "for us," thereby including its all-embracing and eternal redemptive effect. Early Christian missionary preaching has come down to us (in Acts) in differing versions, all of which share the same basic, bipolar structure: "This Jesus, whom you condemned to death on the cross, has been raised from the dead by God!" Similarly, 1 Peter interprets the basic assertion that "God raised him from the dead" (1:21) as follows: "Christ also suffered for sins once for all, the righteous for the unrighteous, in order to bring you to God. He was put to death in the flesh, but made alive in the spirit" (3:18; cf. 3:21f.).

It is significant "that pre-Pauline Christology, as recorded in early Christian hymns, regarded Jesus' ascension as having taken place directly from the cross" (E. Käsemann). From this it becomes evident once again how closely and indissolubly the event of Good Friday is linked to the succession of events (interpreted in Luke's Acts as having occurred over a period of fifty days) comprising the resurrection of Jesus, his ascension, and the sending of the Spirit, all of which coalesce to form the *Easter event* of death-and-resurrection. And only on the basis of the disciples' experience of the risen Lord was Jesus' death on the cross able to be grasped and believed in the profound dimension of its eternal redemptive significance for all humanity.

The death from which God's all-powerful love raised the Crucified to new life is *the death of death.* The death that exercises inescapable and ultimate power over the earthly destiny of humanity, and therefore arouses the greatest fear, stands for all those "powers and principalities" that bring suffering to humans. The NT recognizes them under various names. According to Paul, Jesus Christ has freed us from the law, sin, flesh, and (cf. 1 Cor 15) death. About this he says some dismaying things: "Christ ransomed us from the curse of the law by becoming a curse for us, for it is written, 'Cursed is everyone who hangs on a tree' [Dt 21:23]" (Gal 3:13); "For our sake he made him to be sin who knew no sin. . ." (2 Cor 5:21); or "The law of the Spirit of life in Christ Jesus has set you free from the law of sin and death" (Rom 8:2). Using a mythical mode of expression, Paul says that the "rulers of this age" did not know the wisdom of God hidden in Jesus, "for if they had [known it], they would not have crucified the Lord of glory" (1 Cor 2:8). Something similar is expressed in Justin's by no means only mythical conception that the powers of evil instigated the crucifixion without suspecting that, precisely through his sacrificial death, Jesus would "rob" them of their "booty," i.e., of human souls. In fact, it was—as they might well be called—the ideological, religious-political powers of his time that brought Jesus to the cross: Sadducean greed for possessions and power, legalistic Pharisaic justice, Zelotic liberation fanaticism. The victory by these powers was in reality their defeat. The death of the guiltless one that they achieved, together with Pontius Pilate, served to unmask their fatal tendencies. Because the divine power of life and love inherent in the crucified Son of God and of Man had endured death and overcome it from within, Augustine was able to express the world-shaking reversal that was the event of the cross—from its outer to its inner side; from cross to resurrection; from death to life—in the following words: *morte occisus mortum occidit* ("killed by death, he killed death"). The "powers," or ideologies, were the death of Jesus; Christ is the death of the powers.

Profounder Human Existence and Human Solidarity. "Ecce homo!" The heathen Pilate directed this exclamation at the one crowned with thorns, thereby attesting to the humanity of the "message of the cross." It is the "most Christian of titles" (T. Mann) because it is the most deeply human acknowledgment. In the Crucified, human life is pressed to its outermost limit, where nothing remains but naked existence, and indeed, beyond that to the point of loss of life itself. The God who identifies himself with the Crucified (because he became human in him) comes, however, to all those places where humans undergo suffering or annihilation (in Nazi concentration camps or Soviet gulags), and stands as guarantor for the identity that has been taken from them. At the profound level of human existence that is disclosed through Jesus' death on the cross,

human beings understand themselves as *those who can suffer.* They do not have to pretend that they are great and strong; they are permitted to be small and weak. They experience with Paul the fact that "when I am weak, then I am strong"; for "[God's] power is made perfect in [humans'] weakness." Hence, "about myself I will not boast, except about my weaknesses" (2 Cor 12:10, 9, 5). Even Jesus "was crucified out of weakness, but . . . lives by the power of God" (13:4). Paul knows what it means to be "always carrying about in the body the dying of Jesus" (4:10). The Gospels demand that one daily take the cross upon oneself, for this constitutes imitation of Jesus. The death of Jesus is the school for Christian life. *Coram crucifixo,* I am prepared to let God be God; and humans may then remain humans.

Faith in the cross does not lead to passivity in the face of suffering, and even less to masochistic rejoicing in it. On the contrary, everything negative is to be endured with patience, but also, insofar as possible, actively overcome in a spirit of comprehensive human solidarity. The life motto "with Christ," which Paul applies in various ways (as living and dying with; being crucified, buried, raised, and glorified with), alludes to the promise of his "for us," for us human beings, for all without any exception. Jesus is *the human being for* his countlessly many brothers and sisters. His blood "speaks more eloquently than that of Abel" (Heb 12:24)—calling not for revenge but for reconciliation. Thus the death on the cross calls, in its innermost essence, for resurrection. For the resurrection of *one* and *all.* That we humans might have life, and indeed, life in abundance (Jn 10:10, 17)—for this, Jesus gave his own life. If human existence (as earlier asceticism maintained) is a *continua mortificatio,* a perpetual process of mortification in all things—or, in more modern terms, an "experience of death in small doses" (A. Görres), then what decisively impels this is adherence, in solidarity, to the full implications of love of one's neighbor. This brings with it diverse conflicts, compromises, and renunciations, as well as (in certain circumstances of a kind not rare today in Latin America and elsewhere) the sacrifice of life. The cross of Jesus plants in world history the banner of universal solidarity. "He spread out his arms on the cross in order to embrace the limits of the world" (Cyril of Jerusalem, *Katecheseis*, no. 13, 28).

Concluding Fundamental-Theological Reflections. Faith in the cross, with all its paradoxicality, poses an enormous, unsurpassably demanding challenge to the human capacity for belief, and this can—indeed, initially must—appear to be a glaring argument against the credibility of the gospel. In the course of inquiring into the matter here, an attempt has been made to show that it is *an*—indeed, perhaps *the*—argument in favor of Christian revelation.

Humanity's search for deeper self-understanding, and also its approach to the world through a commitment to justice, freedom, and peace, can find no greater degree of justification and encouragement than is provided by the God of the Crucified. To be sure, even religion, Christianity, the church, and theology are not immune to ideologization and self-idolatry; perversion of them is, in fact, the worst kind possible (*corruptio optimi pessima*; the example of religious wars). But no divine being in the various world religions is as inherently resistant as the God of crucified love to being misused for pseudo-legitimation of the church as an end in itself or of some position of power. He is not a God for ceremonial occasions who floats triumphally above the world in radiance and glory. He is the God of everyday life and its small, or sometimes large, sufferings and joys. Therefore one can concur with the following words of the theologian D. Sölle: "The most accurate interpretation of human existence . . . is the Cross of Christ. Although Christianity's claim to absoluteness is also implicit in this proposition, it is no longer something asserted and demanded in an authoritarian way" (*Atheistisch an Gott glauben* [2nd ed.; Olten, 1969], 88).

Some results relevant to methodology in the theological discipline of fundamental theology are as follows. The "external" standards of credibility remain indispensable regarding the miracles performed by Jesus and—as their crowning, unsurpassable extreme—the resurrection experience that Jesus lives. However, the inner truth of the gospel should be accorded greater significance than was the case, in principle and in fact, previously: the truth of what Jesus not only communicated in words but

demonstrated in his life and death. Here his destiny in suffering death for us humans is an example. Is it *the* example?

Bibl.: G. W. Leibniz, *Essais de théodicée sur la bonté de Dieu, la liberté de l'homme et l'origine du mal* (Amsterdam, 1710); H. Schlier, *Mächte und Gewalten im Neuen Testament* (Freiburg, 1958); K. Jaspers, *Kleine Schule des philosophischen Denkens* (Munich, 1965); W. Kern, "Teodicea e cosmodicea mediante Cristo," *MystSal* 6:687–726; id., "Schöpfung bei Hegel," *TQ* 162 (1982): 131–46; id., "Gesù Cristo nella filosofia della religione di Hegel," in *I filosofi e Cristo* (Trente, 1990); id., *Atheismus, Marxismus, Christentum* (Innsbruck, 1979); id., "Das Kreuz Jesu als Offenbarung Gottes," *HFT* 2:197–222; G. Delling, *Der Kreuzestod Jesu in der urchristlichen Verkündigung* (Berlin, 1971); J. Moltmann, *The Crucified God* (New York, 1974); D. Arendt, ed., *Der Nihilismus als Phänomen der Geistesgeschichte* (Düsseldorf, 1974); P. Pöggeler, "Nihilist"; "Nihilismus," *ABG* 19 (1975): 197–210; H. Schürmann, *Jesus ureigener Tod: Exegetische Besinnung und Ausblick* (Freiburg, 1976); J. Choron, *Der Tod in abendländischen Denken* (Stuttgart, 1976); A. Paus, ed., *Grenzerfahrung Tod* (Graz, 1976); M. Hengel, "Mors turpissima crucis," in J. Friedrich et al., eds., *Rechtfertigung: Festschrift für Ernst Käsemann zum 70. Geburtstag* (Tübingen/Göttingen, 1976), 125–84; J. Friedrich, "Der stellvertretende Sühnetod Jesu," *Comm* 9 (1980): 1–25, 135–47; M. L. Gubler, *Die frühesten Deutungen des Todes Jesu* (Freiburg/Göttingen, 1977); P. Ariès, *L'homme devant la mort* (Paris, 1977); M. Riedel, "Nihilismus," in *Geschichtliche Grundbegriffe* 4 (1978), 371–411; B. Gherardini, *Theologia crucis* (Rome, 1978); E. Jüngel, *Tod* (Stuttgart, 1979); S. Scherer, *Das Problem des Todes in der Philosophie* (Düsseldorf, 1979); C. Andresen and G. Klein, eds., *Theologia crucis - Signum crucis* (Göttingen, 1979); J. Baur, "Weisheit und Kreuz," in *Zugang zur Theologie: En hommage à W. Joest* (Göttingen, 1979), 33–52; W. Weier, *Nihilismus: Geschichte, System, Kritik* (Paderborn, 1980); H. Weder, *Das Kreuz Jesu bei Paulus* (Göttingen, 1981); H. Ebeling, ed., *Der Tod in der Moderne* (Frankfurt, 1984); W. Beinert, ed., *Einübung ins Leben der Tod* (Regensburg, 1986); I. Levan-Stefanovich, *The Event of Death: A Phenomenological Enquiry* (Leiden, 1987).

Walter Kern

II. THE RESURRECTION OF JESUS

Christianity stands or falls with the belief that through the person and history of Jesus Christ, God has been definitively revealed. The climax of that self-manifestation was reached according to Vatican II's Dogmatic Constitution on Divine Revelation (*Dei Verbum* 4), with Christ's death and glorious resurrection, which were followed by the sending of the Holy Spirit.

The resurrection of the crucified Jesus is the decisive act that not only finally and unsurpassably revealed the tripersonal God but also inaugurated the end of history and the fullness of our salvation. Immediately after recognizing that the definitive high point of divine self-revelation took place at the first Easter and Pentecost, *Dei Verbum* at once points to the salvific import of that divine self-communication: Christ revealed "that God is with us to free us from the darkness of sin and death, and to raise us up to life eternal" (*DV* 4).

Fundamental theology should tackle at least four major questions here. What did the first Christians mean by their claim about Jesus' resurrection? How did they come to know about and believe in Jesus as risen from the dead? How did the resurrection of the crucified Jesus bring the definitive self-revelation of the tripersonal God? In what way can we legitimate Easter faith today?

1. The Claim

Evidence coming from the kerygmatic tradition quoted by Paul (e.g., 1 Cor 15:3b–5), from the pre-Pauline formulas about God (the Father) raising Jesus from the dead (e.g., Gal 1:1; 1 Thes 1:9–10), from the early formulas embedded in Peter's speeches at the beginning of Acts (e.g., Acts 2:22–24, 32–33, 36) and from other traditional material cited by various NT authors (e.g., Lk 24:34) shows that the claim about Jesus' resurrection from the dead goes back to the origins of the Christian movement. How then can one sum up the primary content of that claim coming from 30–50 C.E.—i.e., from the crucial two decades before Paul and then other NT authors began writing their works?

In essence, the first Christians asserted that through the divine power Jesus himself had been raised to life. The pre-Pauline tradition spoke of God raising Jesus (or his Son) from the dead (e.g., Rom 10:9; 1 Thes 1:10), or else it spoke of Jesus "being raised" (e.g., 1 Cor 15:4; Mk 16:6), implying that this had occurred "through the divine power." The *primary* claim was not that Jesus' cause continued or that the disciples had been "raised" to a new consciousness and the life of faith (when they came to see that Jesus was right about God), but that the crucified Jesus had been personally brought from the state of death to that of a new and lasting life. Of course, the pre-Pauline formulas recognized that the resurrection of Jesus had taken place in order to change and "justify us" before God (Rom 4:25). Nevertheless, in the first place the resurrection claim referred to what happened to Jesus himself.

It is clear that the first Christians did not present Jesus' resurrection as the mere resuscitation of a corpse—that simple return to life expected by 2 Mc 7, involved in the raising of Jairus's daughter (Mk 5:35–43), or envisaged by Herod's fear about John the Baptist coming back to life (Mk 6:16). Using a "vertical," spatial model of up and down (rather than the kerygma's more horizontal or temporal model of Christ as crucified, buried, raised on the third day and appearing to certain individuals and groups), early Christians also spoke or rather sang of Jesus as being "exalted" or "taken up" into divine glory (e.g., Phil 2:6–11; 1 Tm 3:16). This liturgical, hymnic language of exaltation cited from the pre-Pauline tradition indicates that the first Christians thought of Christ's resurrection as his glorious, final transformation. So far from being a mere reanimation, his resurrection was understood to have anticipated the general glorious resurrection expected by apocalyptic literature (e.g., Is 26:7–21; Dn 12:1–4) to take place at the end of history.

Paul and other NT writers followed this early tradition in both ways. They presented Jesus' resurrection as his glorious, definitive transformation (e.g., 1 Cor 15:20–58; Lk 24:26; Acts 13:34; 1 Pt 1:11). Second, they knew his resurrection to be the beginning of the final, general resurrection (e.g., 1 Cor 15:20; Col 1:18).

Thus far I have indicated the original and essential claims about the fact and nature of Jesus' resurrection from the dead. We turn now to the question: How did the first Christians know that this event had taken place?

2. The Origins of Easter Faith

During his ministry Jesus linked the present and coming rule of God to his own person and activity (e.g., Mk 1:15; Mt 6:10; 8:11; 12:28; Lk 12:8–9; 17:20–21). In proclaiming God's kingdom, he revealed a remarkable sense of personal authority, transforming in his own name the divine law (e.g., Mk 10:9; Mt 5:21–48). He acted with startling self-assurance when he set aside various interpretations of the Sabbath rest (Mk 3:1–5) and claimed the right to decide what should be done or not done on that sacred day (Mk 2:28). Further, Jesus exercised his extraordinary authority in a deeply compassionate fashion, identifying himself with the divine concern to forgive and definitively save sinful human beings (e.g., Mk 2:5, 17; Lk 7:48; 15:11–32; 19:1–10). Just as he understood his word and God's word to be identical, so he understood his presence and God's salvation to be identical.

Add too (a) the unique filial consciousness (e.g., Mt 11:27) he showed toward the God whom he addressed with astonishing intimacy as "Abba" (Mk 14:36) and (b) the sense of his messianic mission, which led (at least partly) to his being crucified on the charge of being a messianic pretender (Mk 15:26).

His death by crucifixion after condemnation by both religious and political authorities seemed to give the lie to Jesus' claim that in his person and activity the final divine revelation and salvation had come. He died apparently abandoned (Mk 15:34) and even cursed by God (Gal 3:13; 1 Cor 1:23). Some scholars have argued that Jews at the time of Jesus did not understand death by crucifixion to mean being cursed by God. But the evidence from Paul and Qumran (*Temple Scroll* 64:12) makes it clear that this "most wretched of deaths" (Josephus), unlike John the Baptist's decapitation and the forms of execution suffered by other martyred prophets (see Lk 13:34; Mt 23:35), symbolized rejection by God.

What can one reasonably hold about the situation of Jesus' disciples after his crucifixion and burial? It seems that during this ministry they had acknowledged him in some sense as Messiah (Mk 8:27–30), but could not accept his suffering destiny as Son of Man (Mk 8:31–33; 9:32; 10:35–45). The male disciples who had remained with Jesus fled at the time of his arrest, and Peter denied him. Condemned and crucified as a blasphemer and a false Messiah, Jesus died seemingly abandoned and cursed by the God whom he had called "Father dear." The evidence we have from the Gospels (e.g., Lk 24:13–24) agrees with what we should expect—that Calvary caused a profound theological crisis for the disciples and shattered their faith in Jesus and the God for whom he had acted.

Some writers have claimed a substantial degree of continuity between the pre-Easter and post-Easter faith of the disciples. This hypothesis argues that the disciples thought and prayed their way through the crisis of Calvary and reached the conclusion that Jesus had been right about God and must now be alive with his Father. In moving to their resurrection faith, the disciples were substantially helped by general Jewish beliefs about the divine vindication of martyred eschatological prophets and perhaps by specific things Jesus had said about his own post-death vindication, e.g., in terms of the kingdom (Mk 14:25) and the Son of Man (Mk 9:31; see also 8:31; 10:33–34). In this way some have argued that the appearances of the risen Lord and the discovery of his empty tomb were simply not necessary to call forth the disciples' Easter faith. Perhaps the "appearances" were no more than a way of expressing the psychological breakthrough, when the disciples finally saw the real truth about Jesus and drew the conclusion that he had to be alive and with God.

On several grounds such hypotheses about substantial continuity between the pre-Easter and post-Easter faith of the disciples do not stand up. First, the pre-Pauline tradition establishes that they believed the risen Jesus to be not merely a vindicated prophet but the Messiah (e.g., 1 Cor 15:3b). The OT messianic expectations included many kingly, priestly, prophetic, and eschatological elements. But there is no hard evidence that any Jews ever expected a Messiah who would be killed, let alone one who would be killed and then raised from the dead. Even more unthinkable and absurd was the idea of the resurrection of a crucified Messiah. Yet that was what the first Christians proclaimed. Their previous Jewish beliefs cannot account for such a uniquely new claim.

Second, as Wolfhart Pannenberg and others have rightly insisted, the Christian proclamation of the glorious, final resurrection of only one person (Jesus) was also something strikingly new. At that time the expectation of a general resurrection at the end of history was held by many Jews. Jesus' preaching presupposed such a general resurrection (e.g., Mt 8:11; Lk 11:32), and at least once he entered into debate about its nature (Mk 12:18–27). To his core group of followers he may have announced his vindication through resurrection (Mk 9:31), but neither that passion prediction nor the other two (Mk 8:31; 10:33–34) specify either the nature of his violent death (crucifixion) or the glorious eschatological nature of his resurrection. Hence neither from their Jewish beliefs nor from Jesus himself could the disciples have drawn what they began to proclaim—the final, glorious resurrection of one person (Jesus) in anticipation of a general resurrection that was still to come.

Third, the interpretation of the Easter *appearances* as no more than the disciples finally breaking through to the truth about Jesus does not correspond to what the NT witnesses indicate about the appearances. For these and other reasons, the thesis of a relatively smooth passage for the disciples from their pre-crucifixion faith to their post-Easter proclamation does not match the evidence.

We can set aside also the assertion, still occasionally made, that the disciples had been prepared to talk about the resurrection of Jesus by stories they had heard about dying and rising gods. As long ago as Celsus, the second-century critic of Christianity, it has been claimed that after the death of Jesus his disciples simply applied to their dead master the model of such deities as Dionysus, Isis, and Osiris, who were believed to rise each spring embodying the new life and fruitfulness that succeed the death and decay of winter. It is not hard to spot the differences between these stories and the case of Jesus. Unlike Jesus (whom the disciples had known personally), there is no reason to think any of these vegetation deities ever existed. Second, the disciples were claiming that Jesus had risen once-and-for-all from the dead, not that he returned each year from the underworld as nature turned from winter to spring. Third, it would have been extremely difficult for the disciples to draw on the model of vegetation deities. In first-century Palestine there is hardly a trace of any cults of dying and rising gods. For

these and other reasons, it is clear that prior beliefs about dying and rising gods did not move the disciples to start proclaiming Jesus' resurrection.

We are left then with two catalysts of Easter faith presented by the NT: primarily the disciples' encounter with the risen Lord, and secondarily the negative, confirmatory sign of his empty tomb.

Unlike the second-century apocryphal *Gospel of Peter* (9:35–11:45), our NT sources never claim that anyone witnessed the actual event of Jesus' resurrection. Instead, the pre-Pauline tradition (e.g., 1 Cor 15:3b–5), Paul (e.g., 1 Cor 15:6–8), the four Gospels and traditions on which the Gospel writers drew (e.g., Lk 24:34) testify that the risen and living Jesus appeared to certain individuals and groups, above all, "the twelve" or "the eleven" as Lk 24:33 more accurately calls that group after the defection of Judas. These sources vary as to where the appearances took place (Galilee? In and around Jerusalem?) or sometimes do not name any places at all (e.g., 1 Cor 15:5–8). The sources differ as to (a) whether Peter (1 Cor 15:5; Lk 24:34) or Mary Magdalene (Mt 28:9–10; Jn 20:11–18) was the first to see the risen Jesus, and (b) what may have been said during those encounters (e.g., Mt 28:16–20; Lk 24:36–49; Jn 20:19–23). But from these various sources we have multiple attestation for appearances to individuals (such as Mary Magdalene, Peter, and Paul) and groups, in particular, "the eleven." These appearances were the primary way the disciples came to know that Jesus had risen from the dead.

What were these appearances like? The evidence from Paul, the Gospels, and elsewhere supports the following conclusions. The appearances, while (a) not open to neutral observers, were (b) events of revelation that disclosed the (c) eschatological and (d) christological significance of Jesus, and (e) called the recipients to a special mission (f) through an experience that was unique and (g) not merely interior but involved some external, visual perception.

As regards (a), unlike the situation during his earthly ministry, the risen Jesus did not appear to enemies or outsiders. All those to whom he appeared were or at least became believers through that experience. The only (partial) exception to this generalization is found in Luke's version of Paul's Damascus road encounter. In two of the three accounts the apostle's companions hear the voice (Acts 9:7) or see the light from heaven (Acts 22:9), but on neither occasion do they see or communicate with Jesus himself. They function not as direct Easter witnesses but as external witnesses to Paul's dramatic experience.

Paul testifies to the revelatory nature (b) of his encounter with the risen Jesus (Gal 1:12, 16), who disclosed himself (c) as already living the definitive life of the end-times (1 Cor 15:20, 23, 45), and (d) as Christ and Son of God (1 Cor 15:3b–5; Gal 1:12, 16). In and through the appearances the risen Christ (e) called and sent Paul (1 Cor 9:1; Gal 1:11–17) and the other apostles (e.g., Mt 28:16–20) on their mission. Some try to interpret the postresurrection appearances as merely the first examples of experiences available to all later Christians. But the NT witnesses to (f) the unrepeatable nature of the appearances (e.g., Jn 20:29; 1 Pt 1:8), which came to an end with the call of Paul (1 Cor 15:8). The special nature of the appearances to the apostolic group corresponded to their once-and-for-all functions of testifying that the risen Christ was/is personally identical with the earthly Jesus and of founding the church through their Easter message. To do that they did not rely on the witness of others; they had seen the risen Christ for themselves and believed in him. Finally (g), unlike the experiences of the major OT prophets, the post-resurrection encounters were not primarily a matter of hearing (the divine word) but of seeing the risen Christ. The appearances were primarily visual (e.g., 1 Cor 9:1; 15:5–8; Mk 16:7; Mt 28:17; Jn 20:18) rather than aural.

The resurrection of Jesus was confirmed by the discovery of his empty tomb (Mk 16:1–8; Jn 20:1–2). The NT is aware that the empty tomb did not clearly establish resurrection. The absence of Jesus' body could be explained by supposing that it had been stolen or at least shifted elsewhere (Mt 28:11–15; Jn 20:2, 13, 15). But once given the primary positive sign (the appearances of the risen Jesus), the secondary negative sign of his open and empty grave confirmed the reality of his resurrection.

Some have argued that Mk 16:1–8 and later empty tomb stories neither convey nor intend to convey any factual information about the state of Jesus' tomb. They were simply imaginative ways of announcing the church's faith in

the resurrection and entirely derivative from the mainline proclamation of the crucified Jesus' resurrection and subsequent appearances (1 Cor 15:3–8). This legendary elaboration is usually supposed to have taken place over the ten or fifteen years between Paul's spare account of the appearances (1 Cor 15:5–8) and the writing of Mark's Gospel. However, careful exegesis of the two traditions (about the appearances and the empty tomb) shows up such differences that it is hard to see the first tradition producing the second. Important elements found in 1 Cor 15:3b–8 simply do not turn up in Mk 16:1–8, while Mark's story contains some major items of which 1 Cor 15:3b–8 knows nothing at all. The appearance traditions and the empty tomb story are independent and have independent origins. But is the empty tomb story historically reliable?

A reasonable case can be made for the basic reliability of the empty tomb story. Both the tradition behind Mark and that which entered John's Gospel testify to one (Mary Magdalene) or more women finding Jesus' grave to be open and the body missing. Early polemic against the message of his resurrection supposed that the tomb was known to be empty. Naturally the opponents of the Christian movement explained away the missing body as a plain case of theft (Mt 28:11–15). What was in dispute was not whether the tomb was empty but why it was empty. We have no early evidence that anyone, either Christian or non-Christian, ever alleged that Jesus' tomb still contained his remains.

Furthermore, the central place of women in the empty tomb stories speaks for their reliability. If these stories had simply been legends created by early Christians, they would have attributed the discovery of the empty tomb to male disciples rather than women. In first-century Palestine women were, to all intents and purposes, disqualified as valid witnesses. The natural thing for someone making up a legend about the empty tomb would have been to have credited the discovery to men, not women. Legend-makers do not normally invent positively unhelpful material.

All in all, accepting the empty tomb puts us in better agreement with the known data. The emptiness of Jesus' grave confirmed what the first Christians knew from witnesses to the appearances (e.g., Lk 24:34; Jn 20:18).

In this section I have sketched the kind of

answer that should be given to the question: How did the first Christians come to know about Jesus' resurrection? Much more could be added: e.g., to rebut the claim first made by Celsus in the second century that the witnesses to the appearances were hallucinating. Positively the nature and function of the postresurrection appearances should be studied in greater detail. Add too the need to examine how subsequent experiences (e.g., of the Holy Spirit and of the success of their mission) confirmed the disciples' Easter faith, which had been originally brought about through the appearances of the risen Jesus and the discovery of his empty tomb. That faith was also validated by their new insight into the point and purpose of Jewish history and Scriptures. The resurrection of the crucified Jesus gave their religion a sense of convergence and ending.

But it is time to fill out the teaching of *Dei Verbum*, that the resurrection of Jesus to which the first Christians witnessed was the definitive high point of God's self-revelation. In other words we turn from the *event* of resurrection (and the credibility of the signs, such as the appearances, manifesting it) to the Easter *mystery* itself, the fullness of the self-communication of the tripersonal God. This is a move from history (and matters accessible to critical historians) to eschatology and the revelation of God, who draws near to us out of that ultimate future already inaugurated by the resurrection of Jesus from the dead.

3. The Easter Revelation

When properly interpreted, the resurrection of the crucified Jesus is *the* truth about God from which everything else follows. Paul understands Jesus' resurrection (together with ours) to be the specifically Christian way of presenting God. To be wrong about the resurrection is to "misrepresent" God essentially, since Paul defines God as the God of resurrection (1 Cor 15:15). What the apostle says here negatively can be aligned with what he often writes positively of the God who has raised Jesus and will raise us with him (e.g., Rom 8:11; 1 Cor 6:14; 2 Cor 4:14; Gal 1:1; 1 Thes 1:9–10; 4:14). Whether positively or negatively, Paul defines the God revealed to and worshiped by Christians as the God of the resurrection.

From the revelation of this Easter mystery everything else follows. Further truths do no more than unfold what is implied by the resurrection of the crucified Jesus.

The cross, of course, is the great sign and characteristic of Christianity. Paul sums up his gospel as Christ crucified (1 Cor 1:18–24). Nevertheless, he does not claim, "If Christ be not crucified, your faith is futile." Still less does he say, "If Christ be not crucified, we are even found to be misrepresenting God." The crucifixion without its sequel in resurrection would not reveal God, effect our salvation, and bring into existence the church. The Preface to the Second Eucharistic Prayer does not stop with the words "for our sake he opened his arms on the cross." It continues: "He put an end to death and revealed the resurrection." In revealing the resurrection—i.e., in revealing himself as risen from the dead—Christ, so to speak, revealed everything. The self-manifestation of God reached its climax with Easter Sunday and the coming of the Holy Spirit. This teaching from *Dei Verbum* needs to he filled out in at least a little detail.

The resurrection revealed and illuminated Christ's relationship with the God whom he had called "Abba, Father dear." It disclosed that the life of Jesus had been the human life of the Son of God. By his resurrection from the dead, Christ was now known to be "Son of God" (Rom 1:3–4). Hence for Paul to meet the risen Jesus was to receive a special, personal revelation of the Son, which made Paul the great missionary to the Gentiles (Gal 1:16).

Another key title from early Christianity, "Lord," expressed the Easter revelation that Christ truly shared in the divine majesty and being. The Letter to the Romans quoted a pre-Pauline formulation that linked salvation with the confession of Jesus' resurrection and lordship: "If you confess with your lips that Jesus is Lord and believe in your heart that God raised him from the dead, you will be saved" (Rom 10:9). In Philippians, Paul cited and adapted an early Christian hymn that invited everyone in the universe to worship as divine Lord the exalted Jesus:

> he humbled himself and became obedient to the point of death, even death on a cross. Therefore God also highly exalted him and gave him the name that is above every name, so that at the name of Jesus every knee should bend, in heaven and on earth and under the earth, and

every tongue should confess that Jesus Christ is Lord, to the glory of God the Father. (Phil 2:8–11)

Easter stories from the Gospels state in a narrative form the call to adore the risen Jesus who is now revealed in his divine power and identity. In Matthew's final chapter, Mary Magdalene and the other Mary leave the tomb, meet Jesus, and "worship" him (28:9). Likewise the eleven disciples keep the rendezvous on the mountain in Galilee, and they "worship" Jesus when they see him (Mt 28:17). According to the last Gospel, it is only in the Easter situation that anyone acknowledges Jesus in the terms adopted by Thomas, "My Lord and my God" (Jn 20:28). It takes the resurrection to reveal fully that Jesus should be identified and worshiped as divine Lord.

The essence of Christian faith entails accepting the good news that in the power of the Spirit the incarnate and crucified Son of God has risen from the dead. Thus the doctrine of the Trinity points to and gathers up the self-revelation of God communicated through Christ's resurrection (understood in the light of the "prior" mysteries of creation, call of the Jewish people, incarnation and crucifixion, and the "posterior" mysteries of Pentecost and the eschaton).

Mark recalls a kind of appearance of the Trinity at Jesus' baptism. The Spirit descended "like a dove on him, and a voice came from heaven, 'You are my Son, the Beloved; with you I am well pleased'" (Mk 1:10–11 par.). At the resurrection the tripersonal God did not "appear" in any such way, and yet was revealed. Let us see some details.

Pre-Pauline formulations understood "God" (e.g., Rom 10:9) or "God the Father" (e.g., Gal 1:1) to have raised Jesus from the dead. The postexaltation worship of Jesus as divine Lord takes place "to the glory of God the Father" (Phil 2:11), while the Holy Spirit makes it possible for men and women to acclaim Jesus as divine Lord (1 Cor 12:3).

Since Paul does not fully and clearly distinguish between the risen Christ and the Holy Spirit (see 2 Cor 3:17; Rom 8:9–11), he nowhere as such says that Christ sent or sends the Spirit. Luke, and even more John, draws a clearer distinction between the risen Christ and the Spirit. Hence they can speak of the risen Christ sending the Spirit as the Father's promised gift (Lk 24:49) or "breathing" on the disciples and giving them the Holy Spirit (Jn 20:22).

First-century Christians understood in such trinitarian terms the events of Good Friday and Easter Sunday. In those events they experienced the climactic revelation of God. That revelation had something threefold about it, as Peter's address at Pentecost emphatically appreciates: "This Jesus God raised up, and of that all of us are witnesses. Being therefore exalted at the right hand of God, and having received from the Father the promise of the Holy Spirit, he has poured out this that you both see and hear" (Acts 2:32–33).

Undoubtedly we should be careful not to be anachronistic here. Christians had to pursue matters for several centuries before they came to a precise teaching on the divinity of Christ and the personal identity of the Holy Spirit. All the same, we find at the origin of Christianity a clear sense that the Father, Son, and Holy Spirit were revealed as acting in our human history, above all in the events of Good Friday, Easter Sunday, and their aftermath.

Thus far we have seen how the resurrection of the crucified Jesus finally disclosed the mystery of God. One could reflect on the ways Easter communicated or at least fully illuminated other such revealed truths as the creation of the world, the foundation of the church and its sacramental life. What comes earlier and later in the Nicene Creed can be rightly seen as introducing and unfolding the full sense of the central truth "he rose again."

In short, fundamental theology has the task of illustrating how the paschal mystery is the high point and fullness of God's self-revelation. In doing this, fundamental theologians take their cue from the origins of Christianity, which began with the Easter witnesses proclaiming the resurrection of the crucified Jesus. The first Christians knew themselves to be baptized into the paschal mystery (Rom 6:3–11). The Eucharist celebrated the death of the risen Lord in expectation of his final coming (1 Cor 11:23–26). It is consistent with all this to understand the resurrection as the focus and organizing center of the divine self-manifestation that is expounded and unpacked by our various articles of faith.

This treatment of Christ's resurrection has followed the characteristic trajectory of fundamental theology by moving from historical, apologetical considerations (sections 1 and 2 above) to dogmatic reflections (section 3). There still remains one major issue to be addressed: Why believe now in the risen Jesus?

4. Justifying Easter Faith

Is it a reasonable and responsible act to believe in Jesus Christ as truly risen from the dead? Can such faith be rationally justified?

Two factors have often been operating in this discussion about Easter faith. Some (wrongly) hold that historical reason, and indeed any use of our human reason, can never contribute to or legitimate faith. Otherwise we would turn faith into the work of our intellect and deny that it is a free gift of God to be freely accepted. This noble "fideist" option, however, ignores the fact that God works through our intellect to lend credibility to the decision of faith. Divine grace and human reason are, or at least can be, collaborative rather than opposing forces.

A second difficulty comes from the opposite camp of those who do not want to emancipate faith from history. They scrutinize and evaluate the evidence for the appearances of the risen Jesus, the discovery of his empty tomb, the dynamic rise of Christianity, and other pieces of relevant historical evidence for the truth of Jesus' resurrection. Their difficulty, however, will not easily go away: how can the probable or even highly probable conclusions of such historical investigation legitimate the unconditional and certain decision of faith? The short answer is that *by themselves* historical conclusions cannot validate such a decision. But, as we shall see, the converging signs that legitimate Easter faith include but are not limited to the relevant historical data from the first century.

A merely historical approach to the case for Jesus' resurrection risks forgetting that this is more than a matter from the past to be investigated and established (or refuted) to one's intellectual satisfaction. Accepting the truth of the resurrection and believing in the risen Christ are much more than a purely mental exercise about past claims and past facts. Easter faith goes beyond accepting the testimony of the Easter witnesses and confessing ("On the third day he rose again") to call for commitment ("We believe in one Lord, Jesus Christ") and confidence ("We look for the resurrection of the dead and the life of the world to come").

How then might we justify our free and grace-inspired option as those who "have not seen and yet believe" (Jn 20:29) in the risen Jesus? Trusting those who saw and believed (the apostolic witnesses to the resurrection) means accepting the testimony of persons who encountered the risen Jesus in a special kind of experience that, at least partly, was peculiar to them and hence lies beyond the range of possible experiences which we could simply as such repeat and hence verify for ourselves. Accepting the apostolic testimony also involves answering the fundamental questions about the nature, meaning, and destiny of our human existence. In a sense, this double approach to the legitimation of Easter faith is already prefigured in 1 Cor 15. The chapter opens by recalling the reliable testimony of those to whom the risen Jesus appeared (1 Cor 15:5–11). Then most of the rest of the chapter takes up the question of what that resurrection means for all of us who must face death. It is a meaning that gives credibility to the truth of Easter faith.

In short, the validation of Easter faith works "from the outside" and "from the inside." We need to hear the historical, public testimony coming to us, ultimately from Peter, Paul, Mary Magdalene, and the other original witnesses. At the same time, we look for signs "from the inside," acknowledging the ways in which belief in the risen Jesus correlates existentially with our deepest experiences and ultimate hopes. It offers us life, meaning, and love over against the death, absurdity, and hatred that threaten us. On the one hand, respect for the historical testimony keeps Easter faith from lapsing into mere wishful thinking. On the other hand, respect for our present experience saves us from the illusion that we could live and find faith by historical data alone.

As the creed indicates, we hold in common our faith in the risen Lord. We are the Easter people, who celebrate and experience together the presence of the risen Lord until he comes again.

Bibl.: R. E. BROWN, *The Virginal Conception and Bodily Resurrection of Jesus* (New York, 1973); P. PERKINS, *Resurrection* (New York, 1984); P. F. CARNLEY, *The Structure of Resurrection Belief* (New York, 1987); J. SCHMITT, "Résurrection de Jésus," *DBS* 10:487–582; G. O'COLLINS, *Jesus Risen* (New York,

1987); J. P. GALVIN, "The Origin of Faith in the Resurrection of Jesus: Two Recent Perspectives," *TS* 49 (1988): 25–44; G. O'COLLINS, *Interpreting the Resurrection* (New York, 1988).

Gerald O'COLLINS

THE PATRIARCHS AS MEDIATORS OF REVELATION

"God of Abraham, God of Isaac, God of Jacob, not of philosophers and scholars." Thus Pascal in his *Memorial*. Does the Bible ratify this insight? In trying to answer this question I will focus on three points: (1) the historicity of the patriarchal narratives; (2) the literary genre of these narratives; (3) the theological development within the narratives.

1. Historicity

Some authors deny that the narratives in Genesis have any historical value. Others defend this value against any and all attacks. The more prudent say that it is not impossible to recover the historical background of the narratives, especially for the patriarch Jacob. But one conclusion is becoming increasingly unavoidable: the patriarchal narratives are not historical writings in the modern sense of the term. The sacred writers had concerns different from those of modern writers, and in their works they have as it were deleted all traces that might lead us *directly* to historical personages and events. Even if the biblical texts contain elements of this kind, they are in the service of a purpose that transcends history pure and simple.

A serious inquiry can, therefore, start nowhere but in the texts. A hypothetical reconstruction of events is too rash and the results of historical labors too scanty to be able to supply a solid basis for a study of the religion of the patriarchs. But what is the literary genre of these texts?

2. Literary Genre of the Patriarchal Narratives

The patriarchal traditions are cast in the form of narratives. They must therefore be analyzed in terms of the categories proper to the narrative genre. Is it possible to be more specific? I have already excluded the possibility of regarding them as quasi "biographies" based on documents and witnesses the truthfulness of which can be tested and which report events of public interest. Another possibility that must be immediately eliminated is that the narratives are myths, even if disguised ones. Readers are not taken back to the origins, before time, in a world completely ruled by the standards of the sacred. Furthermore, there is no question here of "popular tales." In such tales, the personages are anonymous, time and place are left undefined, the laws of probability are suspended, and imagination is king. The primary purpose of tales is to amuse and not to produce convictions. Generally speaking, they reveal the desires and fears present in the unconscious in a given culture. This description does not apply to the patriarchal narratives. The patriarchs have names. The stories have definite settings in time and place. The narrative rarely passes beyond the boundaries of probability, and then only in very special circumstances. Finally, the biblical narrators are not satisfied to bewitch an audience; they want to be believed.

Scholars have more often suggested that the patriarchal narratives be put in the category of "legends," these being understood as sacral narratives about famous personages of the past and having as their purpose to edify (e.g., the *Golden Legend* of James of Voragine) or to explain the origin of a place, a cult, a custom, or a name (etiological legends). This explanation is not without its difficulties. First of all, the narratives do not always portray the patriarchs as models of virtue, far from it (but see Gn 18:18–19; 22:15–18; 26:5). Then, too, the narratives are not focused on the personages as such, but rather on the rich meaning of the events they experience. A comparison of these narratives with the *Little Flowers* of St. Francis would make the differences clear. Finally, while the patriarchs establish sanctuaries (Gn 12:7–8; 13:4, 18; 21:33; 22:14; 26:25; 28:12–22; 32:31; 33:20; 35:14–15) and are the source of certain customs (Gn 32:33), this aspect is rather secondary, and the majority of the narratives do not fall into this category.

The category that best defines the narratives in Genesis seems to "popular religious narratives." Some of the characteristics of these narratives make them similar to legends, but their primary purpose is not to edify or to justify a cult or practice. First and foremost, they recount experiences of the sacred. The narratives in Genesis seem to correspond quite well to this category. Four principal reasons may be given for this claim: (1) They describe the effects of the irruption of the divine into the consciousness and lives of the patriarchs. Their chief aim is describe the encounters of these men with the world of the numinous, the moments when they stumble across the frontier separating the present world from the world of God (see Gn 28:12–22; 32:23–33). These encounters give their lives an unexpected turn (see especially Gn 12:1–3; 22:1–2). (2) Experience takes precedence over personages (contrary to what happens in legends). (3) The personages are men of the people, and the addressees of the narratives can easily identify with them. There is no question of heroes or of uncommon adventures (as in epic or sacred legend), but of events connected with everyday life and, most often, with the private life of the family. (4) The element of the extraordinary is limited to the world of the sacred, the world of ultimate realities and values. This fact differentiates the extraordinary in these narratives from the element of the wonderful in tales, where it flowers in the realm of the imaginary and sinks its roots in the drives of the unconscious.

To summarize: the narratives have as their primary purpose to let the hearers or readers share a special kind of experience of God, since it is an experience that grounds the existence of the Israelite people as a believing people. It is therefore necessary to take these narratives seriously as narratives. Only a careful reading of them will make it possible to discern the shape of their specific message.

3. Religious Experience of the Patriarchs

To put it briefly, the faith of the patriarchs is a faith associated with a journey and a discovery. "Go . . . to the land that I will show you," God says to Abraham (Gn 12:1; see 22:1–2). The adventure on which Abraham sets out is a departure for an unknown destination with a divine promise as sole security. In the *Odyssey* Ulysses returns home. The Argonauts bring the golden fleece back with them. The Greek ideal is a return: either a return to the truth hidden within the self ("Know yourself," the Delphic

oracle tells Socrates) or a quest of a lost unity (e.g., the reunion of Ulysses and Penelope; for Plato, the return of the soul to the world of ideas). This cyclic ideal is found in most natural religions. Abraham, on the other hand, sets out to discover something completely new. He knows his starting point but not his point of arrival, which remains God's secret. The biblical narrative thus has two levels: on the one side, an omniscient God, and, on the other, a human being who seeks direction on the basis of signs given to him from on high. This aspect of the narrative makes Abraham very modern, in the sense that he must find his way by trial and error, alternately attempting and failing, while God often remains silent. On the other hand, God may suddenly intervene to give Abraham's life a completely unanticipated direction.

This aspect of the matter is heavily emphasized in the story of Abraham. He gets off the track in Egypt (Gn 12:10–20) and in Philistia (Gn 20). The promise of countless descendants is a dead letter for a long time. Abraham complains from the heart, and the setting of the nocturnal vision in Gn 15 reflects more than a state of mind: Abraham lives in the darkness of faith (Gn 15:5, 6, 12, 17). Then, in the depths of the night, God establishes a freely bestowed, unilateral, and unconditional relationship with the patriarch ("oath," rather than "covenant," Gn 15:18; see v. 17; 35:9–15), which brings out the transcendence of the divine favor. When God suddenly appears, consciousness comes up against its limits. The divine promise always surpasses understanding (see especially Gn 18:1–15). Finally, hardly is Isaac born when God asks for him in sacrifice (Gn 22:1–19). In the darkness of this trial Abraham learns to trust himself to "the Lord [who] will provide" (22:9, 14).

This same aspect appears again in the story of Jacob. His struggle with God during the night is one of the most striking images of it (Gn 32:23–33; see already Gn 28:10–20). Only at sunrise will Jacob, now injured in the hip, be able to identify his adversary and demand a blessing from him. The story of Joseph, for its part, will have this experience in its ultimate form, since God will never speak to him. He will find on his own the providential plan that gives meaning to the incidents of his life (see Gn 45:5–8; 50:19–21). In the final analysis, the patriarchal narratives may not tell us very much about the story of the patriarchs, but they do tell us how the patriarchs discovered the meaning of history, of which God is sole master.

Bibl.: T. L. THOMPSON, *The Historicity of the Patriarchal Narratives* (Berlin/New York, 1974); J. VAN SETERS, *Abraham in History and Tradition* (New Haven/London, 1975); P. GIBERT, *Une théorie de la légende: Hermann Gunkel et les légendes de la Genèse* (Paris, 1976); D. J. A. CLINES, *The Theme of the Pentateuch* (Sheffield, 1978); R. L. COHN, "Narrative Structure and Canonical Perspective in Genesis," *JSOT* 24 (1982): 3–25; J. SCULLION, "Märchen, Sage, Legende: Towards a Clarification of Some Literary Terms Used by Old Testament Scholars," *VT* 34 (1984): 321–36; P. GIBERT, *Bible, mythes et récits de commencement* (Paris, 1986); id., "Pour un 'bon usage' de l'histoire des patriarches," *Lumière et Vie* 188 (1988): 35–42; A. DE PURY, "Les traditions patriarcales en Genèse 12–35," *Lumière et Vie* 188 (1988): 21–34.

Jean-Louis SKA

PHILOSOPHY, CHRISTIAN

1. Historical Note

The expression "Christian philosophy" is not biblical. The NT uses the word "philosophy" only once, and then to signify a kind of gnosis or pre-gnosis whose seductions it denounces (Col 2:8). The early Christian writers were often critical of the philosophers (see Tatian, Hermas, and Tertullian, although the last-named derives some of the framework of his thinking from Stoicism). In some writers, such as Justin, the expression "our philosophy" or even "Christian philosophy" appears, but it means simply Christian teaching or, more broadly, Christian life, which is considered to be the only true philosophy. This approach further justifies the rejection of the philosophy of the philosophers. Some writers, however, do acknowledge the presence of seeds of truth in the great philosophers; they explain this by the supposed influence of the prophets or even by a kind of inspiration.

As reflection on the faith becomes more penetrating and theology begins to emerge, Christian thought tackles areas already explored by the philosophers, profits by their discoveries, and learns to use their conceptual and dialectical tools. Philosophy in turn is enriched and extended by this encounter and acceptance. This is true of Augustine and of Thomas Aquinas and the body of Scholastics, although rather differently in the two cases. Thomas Aquinas more clearly distinguishes the realm of theology from that of philosophy and makes a more methodical use of the latter. Nonetheless, as in Augustine, theological reflection incorporates a metaphysics and a moral philosophy. We can speak here of a Christian philosophy, but the expression itself hardly appears in these writers, or at least not in this sense.

Beginning in the thirteenth century, but above all in the modern period, there is an interest in philosophy for its own sake and not simply as a tool in theology. In a movement the reverse of the one just described, philosophy claims for itself areas that seemed to have been reserved to theology. The result is the emergence of a concept of Christian philosophy as distinct from theology and authentically philosophical. In fact, in the modern period "Christian philosophy" is generally used for the philosophy common to Christians, the set of doctrines which are *de jure* rational and which Christians hold to be in harmony with their faith and/or to be preambles of faith. The term sometimes has polemical overtones: thus the disciples of Descartes and especially of Malebranche like to give the name "Christian" to their philosophy, in which they find something of Augustine, in contrast to Scholasticism, which is linked to "pagan" Aristotle. But even then the expression was challenged, and for contrary reasons. Christianity has nothing to do with philosophy, or reason with faith. They are even incompatible. A "Christian philosophy" would imply a corruption and an abdication either of reason (→ FIDEISM) or of faith (→ RATIONALISM).

In the nineteenth century the term "Christian philosophy" occurs rather frequently, although the users were not concerned to give an exact definition of it. In France, 1830 brought the establishment of the *Annales de philosophie chrétienne*, which appeared until 1913, but in the early years of publication the philosophy offered was a traditionalism that was, at bottom, antiphilosophical. Once the

Scholastic and Thomist revivals began, the meaning of the phrase tended to become narrower. In 1879, the encyclical *Aeterni Patris*, which contains the expression "Christian philosophy," but only in its title, applied it chiefly to the teaching of Thomas Aquinas.

Beginning in 1928 and above all during the thirties, the idea of a Christian philosophy became the subject of lively discussions, especially in France. In lectures delivered in Belgium and especially in a famous paper to the Société Française de Philosophie, Émile Bréhier criticized the concept, chiefly on the grounds that it did not correspond to any historical reality. Other critics, such as Father Mandonnet, said that the concept embodied a contradiction, since philosophy cannot, by definition, accept any rule but reason. Still others, however, using various arguments (and understanding the expression somewhat differently among themselves), defended the validity of the idea: É. Gilson, J. Maritain, M. BLONDEL, G. Marcel, M. Nédoncelle, and others (see below). Since that period—for practical purposes, since 1935—the discussion has not advanced any further. The term "Christian philosophy" is sometimes used in the plural, not only to make room for other currents of thought besides Thomism but also to apply the idea in a weaker sense to doctrines not usually called Christian.

2. Semantic Field

Leaving aside such undifferentiated and polemically oriented terms as "Christian faith" and "Christian life," we find several different meanings for "Christian philosophy."

a. From the sociological and historical point of view Christian philosophy is the philosophy of Christians. But this usage is worth considering only (1) if there is question of Christians thinking as Christians (and not simply being put down as Christians on some list or other); (2) if one can show the influence of Christianity on the philosophical thinking in question and detect some original contribution by Christianity. This is the meaning of the term which Bréhier challenged and Gilson accepted.

b. The influence can vary quite a bit in character. The thinking of such men as Nietzsche and Feuerbach is unintelligible apart from Christianity, not only because Christianity is the enemy that gives meaning to their project, but even more because they owe to Christianity the breadth of horizon within which their project develops. But we do not speak of a Christian philosophy in the case of these thinkers, unless we are willing to stretch the meaning of words beyond any acceptable limit. The name is to be reserved for doctrines on which Christianity has a positive influence and in which reason moves along the lines of faith, finding and welcoming in the "revealed" that which is *de jure* accessible to it (the "revealable," in Gilson's terminology).

c. We are thus led to an idea of Christian philosophy that has to do with the content of the philosophy and more particularly with the accord between this content and Christian revelation. But an accord that is simply negative and allows the thinker without further ado to be both a Christian and a follower of a certain philosophy would not be a basis for speaking of a "Christian philosophy," especially if the "accord" does not suppose any influence from Christianity.

d. The situation is quite different for a philosophy whose positions agree with those of the faith or, more accurately, with the presuppositions of the faith (existence and oneness of God, creation, providences, etc.). Since in the teaching of the church these presuppositions are the goal which reason that is fully faithful to its light and its essential nature should attain, it can be said that such a philosophy is "naturally Christian." In fact, however, this kind of agreement is found in a complete form only where thought has already come in contact with Christian revelation. The viewpoints of history and of content thus match up. From this twofold point of view, the name "Christian" can be given to the philosophy of the "modern" age in its major representatives (Descartes, Malebranche, Leibniz, Locke in a pinch, but not Spinoza or Hume). The same cannot be said, or at least cannot be said in the same sense, of Kant, and still less of a philosopher like Aristotle, whose teaching, despite elements of truth that have allowed Christian thought to make use of it, developed independently of Judeo-Christian revelation.

e. In particular, the name "Christian" can be given to a philosophy that not only allows the thinker to accept even the nonphilosophical ("supernatural," "mysterious") parts of the Christian message, but also sees in human nature and activity a directed movement toward something beyond all "natural" ends and values, a radical dissatisfaction that causes the person to recognize the revealed message (though not required or anticipated) when it presents itself. Such a philosophy, *provided* it is authentically philosophical and does not make the affirmations of faith in any way a part of its reasoning and reflection, evidently deserves the name "Christian" in the highest degree (or, as Blondel prefers to say, the name "Catholic"). But it is this proviso that causes the difficulty here, as it does for "Christian philosophy" generally.

3. The Problem of Christian Philosophy

The problem is actually twofold, and we have already met it: (a) Is not the expression "Christian philosophy" a contradiction? Does it have a meaning? (b) Is there or has there ever been in fact a philosophy deserving of this name? If yes, how is the name understood?

Let me begin with the second question. It will not detain us for long. The works of É. Gilson (to cite but one thinker; he is not alone) have shown, in a way that may be regarded as definitive, the Christian originality of medieval philosophy, beginning with Augustine. It does not seem possible to think of Thomism, for example, as a simple offspring of the kind of Aristoteleanism that might just as well have developed outside the Judeo-Christian setting. Is it not noteworthy that the passages in which Thomas Aquinas shows his greatest metaphysical depth are most often found in his theological writings, even in a typically theological context and in connection with questions most typically theological (e.g., his teaching on the will, a teaching that is clarified and perfected through the theology of the Holy Spirit)? Furthermore, as I observed earlier, the whole of later philosophy betrays a Christian influence or at least broad expanses of it seem inexplicable apart from this influence.

But is all this enough to justify speaking of "Christian philosophy" in a strict sense of the words? The expression seems to ring as false as "Christian physics" or "Christian mathematics." Philosophy develops on the level of reason and allows no other norm. To call it "Christian" is to

apply to it a specification that comes from a different order of things and is therefore purely extrinsic to it, as when we speak of "French philosophy" or "German philosophy." But these comparisons are deceptive. Unlike physics or mathematics, philosophy deals with existential human problems and engages the person and its destiny; consequently it is in contact with religion and faith. This is why unity in faith unifies thinkers much more profoundly than unity in language. (Besides, the expressions "French philosophy" and "German philosophy" say something more than a shared language; they indicate a particular spirit, a particular way of thinking, attention to specific problems, specific examples and allusions, etc., all of which make clear, even in translation, the nation to which the writer belongs.)

Yet the fundamental difficulty remains. If "Christian philosophy" means something more than simply a philosophy acceptable to Christians and implies a positive influence of revelation (Christian philosophy thus meaning, historically, a "philosophy developed in a Christian setting and climate"), how is the strictly rational character of the philosophy to be safeguarded? Reason and faith, philosophy and word of God, are two essentially different things that cannot be combined without destroying each other.

It is possible, with Maritain, to distinguish between the *nature* of philosophy as a strictly rational search for truth, and its concrete *state* in the philosopher, where, if the philosopher is Christian, it profits from "objective contributions" (revealed truths that raise new questions for the thinker and lead him, in his effort to give answers, to improve his conceptual tools, just as experience and theories of physics press the scientist to perfect his mathematical tools and build new machines) and from "subjective sources of strength" (the action of grace as it heals spiritual blindness due to sin, but also, on the purely psychological level, a certain spiritual sensitivity and a perseverance in study due to interest in questions that non-Christians and nonbelievers regard as pointless and boring).

In any case, all thinkers are necessarily influenced by their environment as well as by their temperament and must subject what is thus given to them to an honest critique. The data of faith are no exception to this rule. Only that which, when thus critiqued, reason recognizes as belonging to its own domain can play a part in the construction of a philosophy.

Others, however, lay greater emphasis on the unity of the subject that is seeking an integral knowledge of reality than on the formal distinction of disciplines. Why should philosophy be deprived of the information given it by Judeo-Christian revelation? Among thinkers who take this attitude, although their approaches are quite different, are G. Marcel, M. Nédoncelle, the later Gilson, and perhaps even Sertillanges and E. Stein. To the objection that (Christian) philosophy thus understood merges into theology, one may answer that (1) theology requires an assent of faith at its outset, whereas philosophical reflection (e.g., on dogmas taken as hypotheses) is possible without this assent; (2) in any case, the focus of thought is different, since theology focuses on the mystery of God and looks at everything else in relation to it, while philosophy seeks to know reality as a whole and reaches God at the end of the process, as the one who gives reality its full intelligibility.

When all is said and done, one may be of the opinion that the notion of "Christian philosophy" departs too much from linguistic usage by excessively broadening the meaning of the word "philosophy." It might be more accurate to speak of "Christian wisdom."

Bibl.: É. Bréhier, "Y a-t-il une philosophie chrétienne?," *Revue de métaphysique et de morale* (1931): 131–62; J. Maritain, *De la philosophie chrétienne* (Paris, 1933); M. Blondel, *Le problème de la philosophie catholique* (Paris, 1933); M. Nédoncelle, *Existe-t-il une philosophie chrétienne?* (Paris, 1937); especially É. Gilson, *History of Christian Philosophy in the Middle Ages* (New York, 1955), chaps. 1 and 2 with precise bibliographical notes; and A. Henry, "La querelle de la philosophie chrétienne: histoire et bilan d'un débat," *Recherches et débats* 10 (Paris, 1955), 35–68, based on A. Renard, *Querelle sur la possibilité de la philosophie chrétienne* (doctoral thesis, Lille, 1941)

Joseph de Finance

PLATONISM AND CHRISTIANITY

Is it possible to speak of a "Christian Platonism"? In 1964 E. Ivánka published a collection of about fifty articles under the title *Plato christianus*; some of the articles dated from as much as thirty years earlier. One would not look to him for a final critical position, nor would one find this in R. Arnou's monumental article "Platonisme des Pères," which dates from 1935. Fortunately, not too long ago the encyclopedia *Catholicisme* gave the same title to a work that completes Arnou's and brings it up to date; it has the merit of clearing up an ambiguity. Whatever Plato's influence on Christian thought may have been, especially from the second century to the fifth, there has never been, and cannot be, a "Christian Plato" in the full sense of these two words. The only valid statement to be made is Pascal's: "Plato, to dispose people towards Christianity" (B219 K612; → Pascal, Bibl.). Another difficulty: it is not possible to distinguish the various Platonisms that R. Arnou discovered: "that of Plato, that of the beginning of the Christian era, that of Plotinus, and that of Plotinus's successors." There are certain constants: in every age "Platonists" have held fast to two watchwords: one must seek the truth with one's whole soul (*Republic* VII 518c8); only with pure hands may one touch what is pure (*Phaedo* 67b2).

When did Plato begin to influence Christian thought? One would look in vain for such influence in the NT. If one or other formulation in the Fourth Gospel, beginning with the prologue, suggests a comparison with a Platonic "homologue," there can be question only of an indirect echo, the most likely link being Philo of Alexandria; but even in this case, Lebreton tells us, connections between Philo and John are dubious.

Here, in chronological order, are some Christian writers who represent stages in the assimilation of Platonism.

Justin Martyr. The question of a direct influence of Plato arises for the first time in connection with Justin. Ever since J. Lebreton wrote his ground-breaking chapter on the subject, many authors have studied it; I need only name C. Andresen and Wolfgang Schmid (1952), N. Hyldahl and L. W. Barnard (1966), J. C. M. van Winden (1971), E. F. Osborn and R. Joly (1973). But Justin knew only a few passages of Plato himself, perhaps from an anthology, and too many uncertainties about Justin's sources prevent us from deciding to which Platonic school he belonged. It is enough, then, that we connect him with Middle Platonism; and in fact most of his contacts with Platonism are with Numenius, his contemporary and undoubtedly a Middle Platonist. Justin shares with Plato (see *Phaedo* 111b) his teaching on the vision of God, which is connected with the immortality of the soul; in Justin's view, however, both the vision and immortality are freely given gifts.

The Alexandrian School. Clement of Alexandria was the first of a series of Christian writers that would have ORIGEN as its most important representative but would also include such outstanding minds as Dionysius of Alexandria and, later on, Athanasius and Cyril of Alexandria. Clement, born around 150, succeeded Pantaenus as head of a school for catechumens in Alexandria. At a later date, persecution forced him to take refuge in Cappadocia, where he died around 215. His Platonism is based on a personal knowledge of the Platonic corpus (he is one of the few to have read it in its entirety), but he is closer to Middle Platonism. The reason why he thinks Plato so useful for Christian propaganda is that, like most Christian writers, Clement finds in Plato the best elements of Hebrew philosophy; such was already the tradition of Philo and the APOLOGISTS. A recent study of the way in which the *Stromata* of Clement assimilate Platonism reaches this conclusion: "If we are to reach the center of Clement's philosophy, our point of departure must be the main themes of Platonic thought."

Must we agree with H. Crouzel when he says of *Origen* that his "errors are reducible to the hypothesis of the preexistence of souls and to a tendency to subordinationism"? This is perhaps to minimize Origen's mistakes, many of which he shares with Clement. In any case, the "main Platonic themes found in Clement and Origen," which R. Arnou lists, became to a great extent elements of a Christian philosophy, and many pages of the *Phaedo,* the *Symposium,* and the *Phaedrus* would later be echoed in medieval mysticism.

While *Eusebius of Caesarea* can hardly be regarded as a thinker in his own right, his exceptional knowledge of Plato and Middle Platonism makes his works, especially his *Preparation for the Gospel,* a storehouse of texts which in many instances he alone has preserved for us. In my book *Eusèbe de Césarée commentateur,* the first chapter, "Eusèbe et l'héritage grec," devotes its opening section to "Eusèbe commentateur de Platon" and includes a list of Eusebius's citations and allusions; the parallels he draws between Plato and Moses serve the purposes already evident in Justin and Clement of Alexandria: to show the mingling of shadow and light that paganism presented to revelation. Sometimes Eusebius sees Plato as the supreme representative of pagan morality and as deserving the same blame; sometimes, perhaps most often, he dissociates Plato from the errors of his age and makes him the precursor of the apologists and their unwitting ally across the centuries.

Eusebius owes a great deal to Numenius, who represents Middle Platonism for him. Like the whole of Middle Platonism, Eusebius maintains that the transcendence of God requires a being who is intermediate between him and the world; he tries, not always successfully, to reconcile this philosophical idea with the Christian faith in a divine Word who is the second person of the Trinity, and he carries the subordinationism of Origen as far as is compatible with the Bible. The "second god" of his Greek models and of Numenius in particular seems to have impaired his orthodoxy; it brought him close to Arius, and at Nicaea he would be thought of as an Arian.

The Cappadocians and Neoplatonism. Though Numenius was the forerunner of Plotinus, the latter exerted hardly any influence before the end of the fourth century; his immediate disciples, Porphyry and Iamblichus, are closer to Numenius and the vague Platonism popularized by the *Chaldean Oracles,* a collection of hexameters that are rather mediocre productions but are not without depth of meaning. Proclus and Simplicius, the great pagan Neoplatonists of the fifth century, are the first to cite the *Oracles.* Beginning in the second half of the fourth century, Athens replaced Alexandria as an intellectual capital. Henceforth it was Plotinus, and no longer Numenius, who was the source of Christian Neoplatonism, as seen in Basil, Gregory of Nazianzus, and, above all, GREGORY OF NYSSA and Synesius. The last two, who unwillingly became bishops, did everything they could to reconcile their philosophy with their faith. Gregory of Nyssa has been the subject of many studies, the most important and penetrating of these being that of J. Daniélou.

A recent study has drawn a parallel between the *Phaedo* and the only dialogue written by Gregory of Nyssa, *On the Soul and Resurrection*. In this work Gregory's silences and reservations emerge clearly, for he is extremely careful not to contradict dogma; he hides his philosophical tendencies as best he can, but he remains first and foremost a Neoplatonist.

Synesius, for his part, never succeeded in completely unifying the three elements of his personality: his formation as a humanist and an orator, his Neoplatonic philosophy, and his Christian religion. The difficulty he had in accepting the resurrection of bodies threw him back constantly to Platonism.

At the end of the fifth century, Pseudo-Dionysius the Areopagite, a disciple of Proclus and yet a sincere Christian, provides us with a final example of these interior conflicts.

Bibl.: J. LEBRETON, *Histoire du dogme de la Trinité II* (Paris, 1928), 640–42, 405–84; R. ARNOU, "Platonisme des Pères," *DTC* 12, 2:2258–2392; E. IVÁNKA, *Plato christianus* (Einsiedeln, 1964); F. RICKEN, "Die logoslehre des Eusebios von Caesarea und der Mittelplatonismus," *Theologie und Philosophie* 42 (1967): 311–58; id., "Zum Rezeption der platonischen Ontologie bei Eusebios von Kaisarea und Athanasios," *Theologie und Philosophie* 53 (1978): 321–52; J. DANIÉLOU, *Platonisme et théologie mystique* (Paris, 1944); É. DES PLACES, "Les fragments de Numénius d'Apamée dans la Préparation évangélique d'Eusèbe de Césarée," in *Comptes rendus de l'Académie des Inscriptions et Belles Lettres* (1971), 455–62; id., "Numénius et Eusèbe de Césarée," in *Studia Patristica XIII* (Berlin, 1975), 19–28; id., *Platonismo e tradizione cristiana* (Milan, 1976); id., *Studia Patristica XV, Part I* (Berlin, 1984), 432–41; id., *Eusèbe de Césarée commentateur: Platonisme et Écriture sainte* (Paris, 1982); D. WYRWA, *Die Christliche Platonaneignung in den Stromateis des Clemens von Alexandria* (Berlin, 1983); G. MADEC, "Platonisme des Pères," *Cath* 50 (1986), 491–507; H. CROUZEL, *Origen* (San Francisco, 1989).

Édouard DES PLACES

PLURALISM, THEOLOGICAL

Theological pluralism should be understood within the overall context of pluralism as such.

The word "pluralism" generally refers to a situation in which a variety of systems of thought, worldviews, or explanations of reality coexist without any one of these having gained hegemony over the others. For a number of reasons pluralism may be said to characterize contemporary society as a whole. First of all, Western philosophy of the last several centuries has emphasized the role of the subject in the act of knowing, with the result that greater attention is paid to the personal and situational aspects of knowing. Emphasis is given not so much to the assertion of timeless truths as to evolving viewpoints and perspectives. The physical sciences too have illustrated the importance of frameworks, as can be seen, e.g., in such a revolutionary shift in worldview as that represented by the theory of relativity. The fields of history and hermeneutics, for their part, have focused attention on the fact that subjects are always to some degree conditioned by time and place. Moreover, the development of more effective means of mass communication has broken down cultural isolation to the effect that individuals are aware of and influenced by a wider range of points of view. The scientific ethic of free inquiry in its own way contributes to pluralism, as do political concepts such as freedom of speech and freedom of religion. All of these tend to promote the free exchange of ideas and the submission of various points of view on an equal footing before the open court of human reason and experience. The result is that contemporary society is strongly pluralistic; some say ineradicably so.

Pluralism can be distinguished from epistemological relativism. This latter affirms that all points of view are equally valid, a view that leads quickly to self-contradiction in that it admits the validity of its own denial. If, however, pluralism is understood as the position that a variety of conceptualizations can, without contradiction, complement one another in explaining a given reality, it need not be inconsistent with a critically realist epistemology which firmly rejects skepticism and which both claims certain knowledge of reality and explains how such knowledge is possible.

Theological pluralism refers to the situation in which theologians, in carrying out the task of theology that has been classically expressed as *fides quaerens intellectum* (faith seeking understanding), make use of various discourses of human thought and experience to explain the Christian message in terms that are both faithful to the inherited tradition and intelligible to contemporary human beings. To some degree, such theological pluralism is as ancient as Christianity itself. The NT makes use of a variety of expressions, themselves conditioned by the composition of the various communities of the primitive church, to express such important doctrines as the identity of Jesus Christ. Thus the various christological titles, some predominating among Jewish Christians and others among Gentile Christians, provide a concrete example of this early theological pluralism. The subsequent history of Christianity also witnesses to a legitimate diversity of approach in theology, such as the differences of perspective between oriental and occidental theology (see *UR* 17). For example, in explaining the effects of salvation, Eastern theologians emphasize the divinization of the creature, while Western theologians tend to focus on the overcoming of original sin. Moreover, within each tradition there was no little diversity. Augustine quotes Cyprian as saying "it is allowed to think differently, while keeping the right of communion" (*De baptismo* 3.3.5). Later, scholastic theology, under the influence of religious congregations and the new universities, exhibited a kind of pluralism in its various schools of thought, particularly those based either on the more traditional Platonic or the newly rediscovered Aristotelian ways of thinking. Moreover, such distinctions as that between *fides implicita* and *fides explicita* were employed by scholastic theologians to account for the unity in faith that obtains among the learned and the unlearned, a unity that admits substantial differences between such Christians in terms of what beliefs they explicitly profess. The sixteenth-century Reformation showed that some types of diversity in theology and, even more so, in doctrine are not compatible with unity among Christians. At the same time, some unsuccessfully tried to make room for unity among those who disagreed about some specific doctrines by distinguishing fundamental from nonfundamental articles of faith, an attempt that did not adequately treat the authority of revelation or of the magisterium of the church and on that account was eventually rejected by Pope Pius XI in *Mortalium Animos* of 1927. In general, Christian communities in the post-Reformation period stressed a unity in faith that was not appreciative of theological pluralism, a fact witnessed to not only by the increasing Roman Catholic emphasis on the doctrinal authority of the magisterium but also by the many unresolved doctrinal divisions among Protestant communities.

Theological pluralism is of interest to fundamental theology for a number of reasons. One reason for theological pluralism concerns the nature of Christian revelation itself, which, as God's self-manifestation, is incapable of fully adequate expression in human language. Paul writes: "How deep are the riches and the wisdom and the knowledge of God! How inscrutable his judgments, how unsearchable his ways!" (Rom 11:33). The Letter to the Ephesians speaks of the "unfathomable riches of Christ" (Eph 3:8). Thomas Aquinas captured some of this sense of the transcendent nature of revealed truth in an often quoted dictum: *articulus fidei est perceptio divinae veritatis tendens in ipsam* ("the article of faith is a perception of the divine truth leading to it") (*ST* II-II, 2, 6 ad 2), a phrase indicating that the expression of divine truth in human language is always pointing beyond itself to the greater divine reality which it can never capture. Since no expression is completely adequate to revealed truth, a plurality of expressions not only is possible but also can be beneficial if these complement one another and thus lead to a more complete grasp of that truth.

Another reason for theological pluralism can be found in the fact that revelation is received in faith according to the mode of the believer. The twentieth-century philosopher-theologian Bernard Lonergan has clarified some of the manifold and complex factors that differentiate subjects from one another. Such diversity in subjects leads quite inevitably to a variety in the ways in which revealed truth is received and expressed. While some diversity between subjects results from ignorance, error, or lack of conversion and leads to irreconcilably contradictory oppositions, not all variety need be of that kind. The Second Vatican Council blesses that diversity which represents the inculturation of the gospel, when, in its Decree on Missionary Activity, it encourages the local church to plant the seed of faith in the rich soil of the customs, wisdom, teaching, philosophy, arts, and sciences of its particular people (*AG* 22; for a liturgical application of this see *SC* 40).

The resulting multiplicity in discipline, liturgy, theology, and spirituality is seen as expressive of the catholicity of the church (see *LG* 23; *AG* 22; *UR* 4). The council comments several times about a legitimate variety even in the realm of theological expressions of doctrine (*UR* 17; *AG* 22; *GS* 62). Variety need not hinder the unity of the church but rather, on the contrary, could even promote it (*LG* 13; *UR* 16; *OE* 2). Not only the realm of culture (space) but also the realm of history (time) contains roots of theological pluralism. Here one should note that the development of doctrine implies a certain variation from one age to the next, so that the "faith delivered once for all to the saints" (Jude 3) has found expression in varying degrees of adequacy throughout the ages. Thus one can note a certain theological pluralism in the way historically separated figures such as Ignatius of Antioch, Irenaeus of Lyons, or Bonaventure speak about the one faith. Furthermore, this realm of the history of Christian thought must be considered against the backdrop of eschatology. Paul writes: "Now we see in a mirror, dimly, but then we will see face to face. Now I know only in part; then I will know fully, even as I have been fully known" (1 Cor 13:12). The indistinct nature of the vision of faith during this earthly pilgrimage guarantees a certain insufficiency that, in turn, allows for a margin of legitimate diversity among theologians.

By being directly related to revelation and its reception in faith, theological pluralism thus touches on several of the most vital concerns of fundamental theology. In addition, pluralism would need to be discussed in any theological epistemology, i.e., in any account of theology as a science, another issue within the regular provenance of fundamental theology. Perhaps most of all, theological pluralism raises the question of an adequate account of unity in faith. How does one distinguish that legitimate variety accepted and even praised by the Second Vatican Council from that diversity in faith which destroys the unity of the church? How does one distinguish theological pluralism from doctrinal indifferentism? The criteria for discerning what pertains to the legitimate diversity of faith expression would certainly include fidelity to revelation as expressed in Scripture and tradition, coherence with the *sensus fidelium*, and approval by the pastoral magisterium of the church. Here theological pluralism relates to the question of orthodoxy, seen as a norm for determining what positions remain within the unity of the faith.

Obviously, the questions raised by theological pluralism are directly relevant for the ecumenical movement, which to a large degree presupposes that unity in faith is a prerequisite for a greater sharing of life. If full communion must wait for the achievement of unity in faith, it is essential to clarify just what is meant by unity in faith, especially in light of the fact that some degree of theological diversity is legitimate. But as reflection about theological pluralism makes clear, the communion in truth that exists among Christians is complex, incorporating a very large number of different subjects into one unity of one faith. The challenge of explaining this communion in truth has not yet been adequately met.

Bibl.: Y. Congar, *Diversity and Communion* (1955; Mystic, Conn., 1985); Commissione Teologica Internazionale, "L'unità della fede e il pluralismo teologico," *CivCatt* (1973): 2, 367–69; D. Tracy, *Blessed Rage for Order: The New Pluralism in Theology* (New York, 1975); J. D. G. Dunn, *Unity and Diversity in the New Testament* (Philadelphia, 1977).

William Henn

POSITIVISM, HISTORICAL

Historical positivism, represented by Leopold von Ranke (1795–1886) and Theodor Mommsen (1817–1903), is of interest to fundamental theology because it expresses the conception of history that was dominant in the nineteenth century and for a long time inspired the judgments passed on the historical value of the Gospels. If this judgment is faithful to the norms of positivism, which aims to produce an accurate and complete picture of the past on the basis of "historically pure" sources, it can only be an unfavorable one, since the Gospels are obviously sources that have been "contaminated" by faith-inspired aims and by theological interpretation. It is proper, therefore, to examine the postulates of positivism.

The foundation of positivism is a naïve and uncritical epistemology. This considers the object of historical knowledge to be an already elaborated datum, and historical knowledge a recording or photograph, as it were, of this object. The objectivity of historical knowledge consists in perceiving the datum as it is (*wie es eigentlich gewesen*) and recording the facts in their raw state, in their original truth, apart from any interpretation. The ideal of historical positivism is to achieve the cold, neutral, impersonal precision of the natural sciences, such as botany, biology, and chemistry. Positivism stays strictly at the level of facts in their pure materiality.

It must be recognized that such an ideal is not only unattainable; it is contrary to reality. Von Ranke himself is obviously prompted by his Lutheran principles in his history of the Reformation. Facts are always accompanied by an individual or collective interpretation, without which indeed they would be unintelligible. To say that Kennedy was "assassinated" in Dallas is to assert more than a fact. If we were to limit ourselves strictly to facts, we would have to say: "During a visit to Dallas, Kennedy was found soaked in his own blood with two bullets in his body." The description "assassination" is already an interpretation of the fact and implies a deliberate intention on the part of one or more persons. In practice, every human fact proves to be both a fact and an interpretation, the latter taking the form of a judgment. Apart from the human mind, which apprehends and judges, there is only a chaos of data. Therefore, in the case of a historical fact, objectivity requires entering into the sphere of consciousness of the person who perceives and judges it.

In addition, every human fact is enriched by an indefinite number of interpretations waiting to be recognized or rediscovered. This activity of discrimination will always be incomplete, partial, and unilateral. Furthermore, the fact in its materiality is only one element among others in the process whereby a person carries out a project. One person brings a project into existence; others, the historians, apply themselves to retrieving this fact by interpreting the intention behind the project, with the help of an explanatory hypothesis. This is why the objectivity of any human fact whatsoever can be defined only by combining the contribution of the subject who brings the fact into being as an expression of his aim, and the contribution

of the other subjects who retrieve it by trying to interpret it.

Individual or collective subjective elements, which cannot be eliminated, always play a part in historical study, as they do in all the human sciences. Examples of such elements are (1) *The choice of perspective*. Thus the Counter-Reformation may be seen as a phase of a vigorous religious revival; for the history of art, however, it is a period a flagging energies. (2) *Affective choice*. Emotional factors play a determining role in judgments passed on persons or events. Thus, the war of 1939–1945 will be viewed in a different light by the French, the Germans, the English, the Americans, and the Russians respectively. The existential options of the historians—they are believers or unbelievers and have corresponding philosophical presuppositions—condition all of their work. Whether or not they are conscious of it, it inspires their selection of documents, their organization and interpretation of the materials, the synthesis they reach.

All this does not mean settling for a radical skepticism regarding the possibility of worthwhile historical research; it means only that clarity is needed about the nature of this research. A first step in the direction of objectivity is for historians openly to admit the perspective they are adopting and to state their presuppositions. They can then make room for another perspective, different from their own, and even renounce their own if there is good reason and if they are faced with solidly documented facts. Objectivity is in the first place a "search" for objectivity.

Historical research is thus not confronted by purely material facts that lack all meaning, but by an intention that has been embodied, a project that has been carried out. Historical research entails a *re-creative* interpretation of the intention that gave rise to a concrete history. It travels backward the path followed by living beings and endeavors to discover the intention of the subject through the action by which that subject shapes itself. Factual history and historical research are dependent each on the other. But historical knowledge is possible only because factual history is already "meaningful," intelligible. It follows from this that historical research is possible only on condition that it adopt, in the presence of factual history, an attitude both of affinity, so that it may "commune" with it, and of "distance," so that it may judge it correctly. "Understanding" always implies these two steps. It is _tradition_ that maintains both distance and continuity across distance.

The element of affinity is sometimes present from the outset, either because of chronological contemporaneity with the event and the setting in which it arose or because tradition preserves and communicates the horizon within which a document arose, and thereby makes possible a connatural reading of this text which is now chronologically distant. The exegete's work is simply to throw light on the text if it is obscure or ambiguous. But it can also happen that the tradition contains a series of readings or interpretations made through the centuries, within a cultural horizon that is different for each reading. In this case, it becomes necessary to reconstruct the original cultural setting and to discover the original meaning. This is the situation we find in the Gospels, which represent a series of successive rereadings of the life of Jesus.

What has thus far been said about history and historical knowledge already makes it clear that the Gospels are much more closely connected with the ideas of history and historical fidelity than the adherents of positivism realized. The Gospels tell us of the earthly life of Jesus, but inseparably from the deeper meaning it had for Jesus himself. To make the will of the Father his own and with it the abyss of love that led him to the cross: such is the fundamental project of Jesus. That the intention of the evangelists was in fact to convey the meaning of Jesus' life as a salvific self-offering can be seen in the importance they assign to the story of the passion. The fact is that two aspects are constantly being emphasized in the Gospels:

1. On the one hand, the event itself as an event that has "really occurred." But the Gospels also bring out the _meaning_ of the event—i.e., the meaning that belongs to the event itself, which is "intrinsic" to it. Meaning is therefore not something "superadded" by tradition: it is inseparable from the event. Meaning makes fruitful, but it is not made up out of whole cloth. Thus the death of Jesus is not simply a demise; the oblative character of this death is part of the reality itself. The function of the historian is to look beyond the several versions of this death and to reach the reality of the event, along with

its meaning. Here we have the element of truth in positivism: historical investigation must get back to the pre-Easter Jesus, in his totality as meaningful event.

2. On the other hand, though the event has a meaning, this meaning is not available to the merely curious, as a mere matter of "information"; rather it emerges in the form of a challenge, a call to conversion and an authentic life. The reality of Jesus is not neutral; it challenges the entire existence of those who encounter it. This is the valid element in the "new hermeneutic." Historians as such do not have to make decisions for others. They can, however, show that the call to a decision of faith is an intrinsic element in the message of Jesus. They can also show that the Christian interpretation of Jesus is coherent with the direction historically present in his life.

At the end of their investigation, historians always find themselves in the presence of events and meaning. They never end up with "meaningless" events. Their ambition, moreover, is not to lay hold of a dead, neutral past, in order then to contemplate it as aloof, uninvolved spectators (the myth of positivism), but to reach back to a pre-Easter Jesus who already has a meaning and is a source of meaning. The text as we have it is as it were the "precipitate" of a development of meaning through time, and historians endeavor to reconstruct the stages of the development and to ascertain its fidelity. The relationship between the text and the tradition regarding the Jesus event is gradually becoming clearer thanks to the combined efforts of history and hermeneutics.

Recent thought on the nature of history and on its ambitions and limitations, has to a large extent rehabilitated the gospels as a way of reaching Jesus. Historical investigation, viewed as a recreative interpretation of the project at work in lived history, shows that by introducing their readers to the ultimate meaning of the life of Jesus, namely, his self-giving to the Father for the salvation of humankind, the evangelists have located themselves at the heart of the story and its concerns. In the freedom they practice with regard to the coordinates of time and place they are more faithful to Jesus than the driest and most rigorous of chronicles could be.

Bibl.: R. ARON, _Introduction à la philosophie de l'histoire_ (Paris, 1948); J. HOURS, _Valeur de l'histoire_

(Paris, 1954); V. MELCHIORRE, *Il sapere storico* (Brescia, 1963); H.-G. GADAMER, *Le problème de la conscience historique* (Louvain, 1963); id., *Truth and Method* (New York, 1975); P. RICOEUR, *History and Truth* (Evanston, Ill., 1965); H.-I. MARROU, *The Meaning of History* (Baltimore, 1966); id., *Time and Timelessness* (New York, 1969); A. RIZZI, *Cristo verità dell'uomo* (Rome, 1972); P. FRUCHON, *Existence humaine et Révélation: Essais d'herméneutique* (Paris, 1976); R. LATOURELLE, *Finding Jesus through the Gospels* (New York, 1979).

René LATOURELLE

PROPHECY

1. Status Quaestionis. 2. Prophecy in OT Theology. 3. Jesus of Nazareth and Prophetic Christology (Jesus interpreted the Sacred Scriptures; Jesus uttered prophecies and performed prophetic actions; predictions of his passion and glorification; Jesus as visionary) 4. NT Prophecy. 5. Theological Value of Prophecy. (Rino FISICHELLA)

Confronting the subject of prophecy today is rather like looking at wreckage after a shipwreck. The little boat of the *argumentum ex prophetia*, tossed between the storm of calculated probabilities, usually operated by apologetic treatises, and the cloudburst of historical-critical methodology, is stranded today at Port Fundamental Theology, where no one seems very sure whether the wreck should be radically reconditioned or else completely dismantled.

Put before proceeding to a final sinking, it may be worthwhile to make one last effort to apply the various methodologies for a more biblical and theological use of the subject.

1. Status Quaestionis

First of all it must be said that the history of Christianity would be hard to understand without prophecy. It has played so important a part in theological thought that having to leave it would be to cast doubt on the vary object of the Christian religion.

The history of Israel too can only be understood by reference to the event of prophecy, inspiring and conditioning the more salient moments in the development of the people's life. The progressive revelation of monotheistic religion, as also the religious-political institutions of Israel, only make sense when set in their prophetic context.

Furthermore, the story of Jesus of Nazareth cannot prescind from a prophetic interpretation. By speaking and acting in the same way as the prophets, Jesus was understood to be a prophet by his contemporaries. In announcing, however, that the Baptist was to be regarded as the last of the prophets (Mt 17:10–13), he also paradoxically expressed his claim not to want to be confused with them; since he and his time were the final and unequivocal end to all fulfilling of the Law and Prophets (Mk 9:2–8; Mt 17:1–8; Lk 9:28–36).

Finally, the history of the church is marked through and through by the fact of prophecy. From the centrality of Jesus the Christ, "a prophet mighty in deed and word" (Lk 24:19), who is believed as the fulfillment and realization of ancient prophecy, the community lives in unceasing relationship with prophecy. Above all, the structure of the primitive community recognizes in the prophets one of the (actually institutional) fundamental principles of its existence (cf. Eph 4:11; 1 Cor 12:28). The church, then, in the course of its twenty centuries of history, has regarded prophecy as one of the normal charisms with which it is provided so as to perform its role as *mediatrix* of revelation in the world.

The essential role prophecy seems to discharge in the church's life notwithstanding, prophecy as one of the signs mediating the Christian revelation has been subjected to distinctly inconsistent treatment: rationalism has deprived it of any supernatural character whatever; the theological manuals, conversely (→ THEOLOGIES VII), have overrated its importance; lastly, historical-cultural criticism has limited its entire content to its mere *Sitz im Leben*, hence impeding its openness to theological interpretation and preventing any verification of its effects as they gradually occurred in the context of history.

To recover a sense of prophecy as sign of the credibility of revelation is not without its difficulties. The first one we encounter is in the order of a theological preconception about the category itself. The manualist tradition has bequeathed us a definition of prophecy which for many years has had a negative influence on theology and so on those various expressions of religious life connected with it. The classic treatises _De Revelatione_ agree in regarding prophecy as "certa predictio futuri eventus qui ex principiis naturalibus praesciri non potest" ("a prediction with certainty of a future event not predictable by means of human and natural knowledge") (for all, see C. Pesch, _Compendium Theologiae dogmaticae_, I: _De Legato divino_ [Freiburg, 1913], 54).

Here, as you can see, prophecy is limited to and identified with foretelling the future, and foreknowledge, linked immediately to the omniscience of God who, being "infinite intellect," can know everything, including future and potentially future events, and, being free, can miraculously reveal them.

A present-day preconception about prophecy should not deter us from recovering the biblical concept, and this, primarily, does not entrust the prophet with the responsibility for seeing what is to come; rather, it indicates the form by which Yahweh's word is communicated and preserved intact down the ages.

A second difficulty about the subject is due to the influence which, from the liberal school on, has been exerted on our understanding of NT prophecy. For a theory has come into existence that posits the presence of two, as it were, parallel churches in opposition to each other: the institutional one and the charismatic one. Fear of the prophetic charism, these authors conclude, was such that institution gained the upper hand over charisma, hence relegating prophecy to a subordinate role until it completely vanished from the scene.

From this order of ideas a view of the church came about that opposed the apostles to the prophets, exacerbating the tension between law and charism.

A reinterpretation of prophecy should certainly take account of the many different ways the churches have viewed themselves at different times in their history, but the interpretation must be an overall one, showing the unity in complementarity and not absolutizing one ministry in particular. Yet the various difficulties can be overcome if _interdisciplinary_ theological research converges on a center, which can be regained by painstaking exegesis and an overall theological view of the phenomenon.

The positive facts that can be obtained by a new kind of presentation of prophecy (let us say, e.g., by a more contextual foundation of Christo-

centrism, by a more authentic theology of history, by a balancing of the relationship between ministries and charisms, by a more meaningful grasp of the signs of the times . . .) prompt us to see beyond the problems and reach objectives that allow an easier presentation of the revealed event.

The very few studies which, the manuals aside, have been devoted to prophecy, have sought to bring the whole OT into relationship with the NT, thus overcoming the reductionist and mechanistic interpretation which relegated inquiry to verifying whether or not such and such a prophecy had been fulfilled. The consequence of this was that the OT came to be reinterpreted in the light of three categories: law, history, promise, which all three found their "fulfillment" in the NT and the Christian religion. Thus came into being a theology of the OT as "prophecy" of the NT, the latter reinterpreting the OT by giving it a "Christian sense."

But this praiseworthy attempt did not go beyond a Christian theology of the OT; the application of a _sensus plenior_ to the OT writings, while furnishing a Christian interpretation, did not admit the peculiar _autonomia_ which in any case the OT should possess as the sacred text of Judaism.

The Christian pretension to appropriate the OT and indeed to regard it as being orientated toward Christ throws light on the specific character of Christianity, but this does not remove the component of pretension arrogated toward the OT world. We maintain that it is possible to follow another route, which, while retrieving the salient traits of OT prophecy, would centralize the person of Jesus of Nazareth as _prophecy_ of the Father and, pointing out the specific quality of NT prophetism, would yield a theological interpretation more in keeping with the original nature of Christianity.

2. Prophecy in OT Theology

Unlike the surrounding peoples, who often confused prophecy with magic and ecstatic possession, Israel had a clear religious idea of the prophet. Semantically, the distinction is clear-cut between the biblical idea and that of the other religions: the _prophētēs_ of the LXX is confined to the _nābî_, identified as "he who speaks clearly on behalf of someone else," while Hebrew _qōsēm_, which means mage, is always

always rendered by *mantis*. The particular character of the Hebrew prophet stands out thus as a phenomenon that can be clearly related to the economy of revelation.

The OT prophet is a *traditus*, assigned and confined to the *dābār* Yahweh, whom he must obey by repeating his words (Is 48:17: "I am the Lord your God, who teaches you"). By virtue of this, the prophet becomes an "expert" in God; he experiences his "glory" (Ez 1:26–28), his binding force (Jer 15:16), the fascination of his holiness (Is 6:1–8).

As a man deeply involved in the history of his people, the biblical prophet sees covenant and Torah as the instruments most consonant with living at peace and keeping faith with the established pact. Religious awareness and political sense, however, point to an even deeper awareness that Yahweh is guiding history and directing it toward a future, the "day," when his covenant and self-manifestation will reach their climax, since linked to a profound inward change (Jer 31:31–37; Ez 34:11–30; 36:23–36).

Hence, to understand the OT prophets, we must first consider the unconditional nature of their *call*; for only within a vocational scheme can they be understood. For each of them, Yahweh's call is the basic event creating personal history and having, moreover, to be fixed in writing, because it must remain unchanged (Jer 1:2; Is 6:1; Ez 1:2; Hos 1:1).

In this call, presented as an act of deep love and implying a knowledge subsisting from the beginning: "from the mother's womb" or "even before birth," the prophet discovers his *mission*. He is the man sent to carry the word, a command that must be faithfully executed and requiring total availability, hence a willingness to accept every kind of suffering or even to lay down his life (Dt 18:15–22; 4:21–22; Is 52:13–53, 12; Jer 37–40).

Though proclaiming Yahweh's word is the main function, there is no concealing the fact that SILENCE and sign (→ SEMEIOLOGY I) are still the more expressive forms of prophetic communication. After that initial silence in which the prophet listens to his call and the content of the message to be proclaimed, his voice falls silent once more: God has spoken, what can be added to his word? (Is 8:16–20). This silence, deeper than any language, leads on to a deeper sense yet, that of the mystery which the prophet has just encountered. Thus, when speech does not seem adequate, the prophet performs signs that, at first sight only, appear illogical or crazy (see Jer 1:11; 18:1–12; 19:1–15; 24:1–10; 27:2–22; 32:6–15; Ez 4:1–3; 5:1–17; 24:1–27); in fact he himself will become a "sign" displayed to the whole nation (Ez 24:24; Jer 16), so that, by seeing him, they may be directed to the mystery he signifies.

In a word, the OT prophets are remarkable for their concreteness and consistency of life. They were men who put themselves at the service of Israel's sacred "tradition," marking out the history of their people. But the experience of God that they underwent and the responsibility for the message that they proclaimed were of their nature such as to transcend the narrow barrier of time and the confines of a single people and become the common heritage of the human race in a future that made plain what they had only promised and represented symbolically.

3. Jesus of Nazareth and Prophetic Christology

"The spirit of prophecy was quenched and exhausted in Israel with Haggai, Zechariah, and Malachi" (*Yoma* 9b); "until then, the prophets prophesied by the action of the Spirit; from them henceforth, give ear and hear the words of the sages" (*Seder 'Olam Rabbah* 30). These two sayings in the Talmud are an excellent guide to the Jewish attitude toward prophecy in the time of Jesus. The prophets have disappeared and the prophetic function is only acquired by virtue of high-priestly rank; otherwise, apocalyptic expectation alone keeps alive the sense of waiting for "someone like" Moses (Dt 18:15–18).

The figure of John the Baptist provides further information about conditions in the time of Jesus. It is impossible to leave the Baptist out of account, since the NT texts present him as part of the teacher from Galilee's story, and the Baptist's preaching was interpreted explicitly as a preparing of his way (Mt 3:1–3).

The person of the Baptist reminds us too strongly of the OT prophets for us to write him off merely as a wandering preacher. His ascetic manner of life, his call to the wilderness, his appeal to the fundamental themes of law and covenant, his preaching of conversion and practice of baptism are all elements that, even if given a theological interpretation by the evangelists, identify him as one of the great figures of classical prophecy. To some degree, moreover, his presence nourished a prophetic sense of hope among the people of his day.

Coming closer to home, it may be noted that the evangelists present Jesus of Nazareth as a prophet in two ways. In some cases they speak of him as *a* prophet (Mt 21:45), thus identifying him as one among many prophets in normal Jewish tradition; in others they describe him as *the* prophet (Jn 7:40), openly referring to the fulfillment of Dt 18:15–18. Interpretation of this data can provide material for a pre-paschal Christology of the utmost importance for an understanding of the relationship between Jesus and his contemporaries.

From straightforward textual analysis we can see that Jesus was called a prophet and was understood by people in the same terms as the prophets of old had been. The impact he made, whether on the crowds (Mt 21:11; Mk 6:15; 8:28; Lk 7:16) or on individuals (Lk 7:39; Mt 26:68; Jn 4:19; 9:17), was such as to make them feel they were in the presence of one of the classic figures of prophecy.

There are two explanations for the currency of this idea: either Jesus had himself explicitly said that he was a prophet, or else his behavior encouraged people to think so. The first hypothesis is hard to sustain. Even granting the historicity of the only passages where Jesus speaks explicitly about his own person and links it to those of the prophets (Mt 13:57; Lk 13:33), the context and scope of these pericopes are mainly concerned with violent death and the common fate in store for God's messengers. Besides, a mere two instances in the entire gospel tradition cannot be taken as a basis for this line of interpretation. Especially when these are compared with the explicit and continuous use of "Son of Man" and the establishing of the context of violent death, which further limits the field of interpretative activity. So we cannot pursue this hypothesis; Jesus therefore did not describe himself as a prophet, and this seems more than probable since it is consistent with his behavior and style, which were to evade any clear and explicit definition of himself.

So the second hypothesis is left: that Jesus behaved and spoke in the same style as the prophets. The "prophetic" texts that bear on this interpretation may be classified as follows:

a. Jesus interpreted the Sacred Scriptures. In this connection, the programmatic scene in Lk 4:16–30 takes on a special importance. Quoting the texts of the Fathers, Jesus applies the word of God to himself and illuminates his own times. Many other references may be adduced (cf. Lk 10:25; 18:18; 20:42); even so, the "actualizations" of the figures of the *Servant of Yahweh* in Deutero-Isaiah and the *Son of Man* in Daniel are what lend most substance to this model. More particularly we may consider the actual way in which Jesus interpreted the Scriptures, which was far removed from that of the rabbis and placed him, *qualitatively* speaking, on a different and higher level altogether (Mt 8:29).

b. Jesus uttered prophecies. First of all, this means that Jesus spoke in the style typical of the prophets and that in this sense he may also have made statements that bear on the future. We may consider the various *woes* uttered against Jerusalem (Mt 23:37), or against the Temple (Mk 13:1–2), or against "this generation" (Lk 11:49), or against the "daughters of Jerusalem" (Lk 23:28), and the *blessings* for people prepared to follow him (Mk 10:29), or for the weak and defenseless (Lk 12:32); and sundry other macarisms (Mt 5:3–12; Lk 7:23; Mt 11:6).

The text of Mk 13:1–2 mentioned above, which is clearly prophetic in form, contains to all intents and purposes a prophetic message attributable to the historical Jesus.

c. Jesus performed prophetic actions. Under this heading we must, above all, include the MIRACLES, seen as signs expressing the love and power of Jesus as envoy of the Father; there are, however, other actions of the type that calls classic prophetic activity to mind: e.g., the cursing of the barren fig tree (Mt 21:18); Jesus' writing on the ground while accusations are leveled against the woman taken in adultery and the accusers wait for him to pronounce judgment on her (Jn 8:1–11); his welcoming a little child to express the greatness of anyone who welcomes the kingdom of God (Mt 18:1–3); the expulsion of the traders from the Temple and the call to treat it as a holy place (Mk 11:15–18). In all these examples we have signs not immediately understood by the onlookers and therefore requiring explanation. The effect of this dialectic is once again to refer us back to the prophetic action by the revelation of its meaning.

d. Predictions of his passion and glorification. Jesus faced the prospect of a violent death with clear resolution. He made explicit reference to this historical awareness to the disciples: a prospect which, while linking his own fate to that of the prophets, at the same time separated him qualitatively from them by the meaning and interpretation he gave to his own death as vicarious atonement. While bearing in mind the role that the various redactions have played in formulating these predictions (see Mk 8:31–32; 9:30–32; 10:32–34), we may regard the texts as expressing a content deeply rooted in the person of the historical Jesus and in his awareness of his own identity. Texts referring to the resurrection as the final interpretation of the mystery of salvation should be regarded in the same way.

e. Jesus as visionary. This is not to say that the texts concerned with this topic are to be interpreted in a charismatic or ecstatic sense; it is sufficient to consider that Jesus had an immediate impact on the people he spoke to. Before they ever spoke, he instantly grasped what their thoughts and worries were (Mk 2:1; Mt 12:25; Lk 9:47). People cannot hide anything from him; they are transparent to him; he can read their hearts. Of the several texts referring to visions (see Mt 3:16; Mk 9:4; Lk 22:43), one in particular deserves attention because of its prophetic significance: "I watched Satan fall from heaven like a flash of lightning" (Lk 10:18). Rather than take this to be a visual manifestation of Satan, we should see it as lending credence to the fact that Jesus, thanks to his proclamation of the kingdom, could see that the power of evil was progressively being destroyed until the final victory over Satan himself.

The material organized under these five headings would justify the opinion of the multitude, as well as the first description of Jesus of Nazareth provided by the evangelists. The title "prophet" may therefore be listed among the first and most ancient bestowed on the teacher from Galilee; in it we see preserved the first impressions that Jesus' preaching and actions aroused in his contemporaries.

Yet a more careful reading of the texts shows that, even where Jesus is referred to as a prophet, a dialectic is immediately set up that tends to show the title's limitations and the need for transcending it (see Mt 21–23). Even in the presence of this prophetic figure, it is felt necessary to mention his awareness of being someone who was "more than" a prophet, "more than Jonah" (Mt 12:41), "greater than Solomon" (Mt 12:42), "greater than the Temple" (Mt 12:16).

With the use of the title "prophet," therefore, we are certainly looking at one of the oldest expressions of pre-paschal Christology; at the same time, however, we realize how impossible it would be to stop at this. There is such a wealth of usage in the sources that it obliges us to look at the figure in the round, rather than from any particular angle. Mark prefers using the title in connection with the fate of a violent death; Matthew sees it as the proper expression for revealing the fulfillment of the prophecies; Luke likes describing Jesus as the fulfillment of Dt 18:15 and hence as the new Moses; the Q source adds the connotation of Christ's superiority—he is to be regarded as "greater than" a prophet; lastly, John shows that the title, though a prerogative of Jesus as revealer, even so affords an incomplete interpretation of his mystery.

All of this leads us to conclude that the evangelists knew a "prophetic Christology," that this was one of the modes used for expressing the mystery of Jesus, but that, when referring to the prophets, only *analogically* could the title be applied to him. Even granting the similarities, the dissimilarities with the prophets were too obvious, whether concerning the authority with which he acted or his relationship with God. Jesus always and only acted in the first person, and this, for a prophet, was unthinkable. From the title "prophet," hence, it was necessary to pass on to that of "Christ" or "Son," since these more aptly expressed the novelty and uniqueness of his identity (→ CHRISTOLOGY III).

4. New Testament Prophecy

For a comprehensive evaluation of NT prophecy, we first must mention two characteristics that make it new with referrence to the OT. (a) The centrality of Jesus, who is henceforth proclaimed the Christ and thus the fulfillment of the ancient promises. This faith in Jesus and in his word, which had already been decisive for his disciples before the first Easter, led to a memorizing of his words and conduct. (b) The gift of the Spirit of the Risen One at Pentecost makes the community in Jerusalem, especially after the martyrdom of Stephen (Acts 6–7), aware of its universal missionary task.

The book of Acts mentions the presence of prophets: Barnabas in the list provided by Luke in Acts 13:1 figures first, along with "Simeon who was called Niger, Lucius of Cyrene, Manaen a member of the court of Herod the ruler, and Saul." But other information and precise names are also given: Agabus, who in Acts 11:28 makes a predictive prophecy about a famine, thus prompting the community to mutual aid; while the same man, in Acts 21:11, performs a prophetic gesture by binding Paul's hands and feet with his belt. In the same pericope we are told that the daughters of Philip the evangelist "had the gift of prophecy" (21:3); "Judas and Silas were prophets too" (15:32); according to some exegetes, even the martyr Stephen may have belonged to the prophetic group.

The fact that Lukan theology is apparently more concerned with presenting the prophetic *function* explains why it has nothing to say about the role the prophets played in the structure of the church.

Material to be found in the *corpus paulinum* could of itself furnish a theology of NT prophetism; for the sake of economy in this present study, we cite two texts as especially informative on the role of prophets in the primitive community.

1 Cor 12:28–30 and Eph 4:11 provide a first scheme of church order as regards those exercising a ministry in the community: in first place the apostles, then the prophets, then the teachers/evangelists.

The context of both passages is that of building the community into a basic unit, to be maintained by virtue of the gifts and, by means of these, of grace (*charis*) received from Christ himself.

The hierarchy of ministries and functions is thus an aspect of the "unique body of Christ" as presence and eschatological promise of the full revelation of God. Believers are admonished to accept the diversity of ministries and gifts, since these are necessary to constitute and diversify of the "body" (1 Cor 12:12–25). Writing to the Corinthians, who yearned for the greatest and most remarkable of gifts, that of speaking with tongues (glossolalia), Paul reminds them before all else of one basic principle: the need

for and equality of charisms. Those of them, therefore, who possess the more unusual gifts ought to honor the more ordinary ones, since charity is the foundation and rule of all (1 Cor 13:2; 14:1).

More careful reading of these texts shows that this is no mere "charismatic" interpretation of the church, but rather an actual institutional description of the community as it is. The apostle, in providing his list, describes the first three orders in precise and personal terminology: apostles, prophets, teachers; after these, however, the description becomes general and impersonal, no longer concerned with people but with activities: miracles, healings, government, glossolalia.

Agreed, Paul is not concerned with giving an accurate lesson church order. His particular concern is that God in Christ has established a precise order for the principal functions; for the rest, gifts abound, as the grace of the Lord disposes.

Thus, in the Christian community, prophets and prophecy are presented either as a *charismatic function* that all should exercise, since by virtue of their contact with other people they can be understood by them and so can build up the community (1 Cor 14:3, 29–32); or as an *institutional function*, forming part of the very foundation of the church (1 Cor 12:28), since it contributes to regulating the life of the community (1 Cor 14:12).

Read without prejudice or preconception, the NT texts lead us therefore to recognize the prophets as an "institution" (1 Cor 14:29, 32; 12:28; Rom 12:6; Eph 4:11; Acts 11:27; 21:9) and prophecy as a normal—even if brief and occasional—liturgical activity granted to certain believers (1 Thes 5:20; 1 Cor 14:1, 5, 24, 31, 39).

In the light of Pauline theology, there is no conflict here: prophets and prophetic activity specify the corresponding and diversified contribution made by individuals to the building up of the community. Whether it be thus the individual prophet, or the various believers who prophesy and who ought to aim at prophesying, they reveal and signify that the church, in its entirety, is built on the *Word of Jesus* and grows when this is actualized in the various situations of life.

On the basis of these texts it is more or less possible to reconstruct the identity of the NT prophet. Essentially the prophet is recognized as being moved by the Spirit of the risen Christ. The decisive role of the Holy Spirit in church life can be discerned at various levels, even in the taking of practical decisions (Acts 15:28; 5:3, 9). This is the context in which we have to interpret the fact that the Spirit raises up and inspires the prophets (Acts 2:18; 11:28; 19:6; 21:11; 1 Cor 12:28; 1 Pt 1:11; 2 Pt 1:21): no one can prophesy unless under the Spirit's prompting, which is always directed toward the building up of the community. This explains why the apostle feels it his duty to urge believers to want to prophesy; at the same time, however, he sees pneumatic activity and prophetic function as cause and effect: "Do not quench the Spirit, do not despise prophesying" (1 Thes 5:20); without these two realities there can be no growth for the church.

The prophet, moreover, is recognized as such by the church. Whether there is mention of a group of prophets or of an individual one, it is not the church that bestows the prophetic gift or raises up the prophet. No, the church welcomes both prophecy and the prophet as gift and ministry. By the same token, the prophet can only conceive of himself in relation to and in communion with the community.

For the community, then, the prophet discharges a function that may be summed up in these three points:

a. The prophet transmits the words and acts of Jesus. For this reason alone, the NT prophet is already substantially different from the OT prophet. The NT prophet does not primarily reinterpret the ancient Scriptures; rather, the NT prophet communicates and transmits the Master's word. The prophet does not speak in Yahweh's name nor proclaim any oracle of Yahweh. Instead, the prophet announces Jesus' words and speaks on his behalf. The prophecy is "the testimony of Jesus" (Rv 19:10); its purpose is to make the Lord's word present, alive, and immediate for the community. This explains why Paul unhesitatingly puts prophecy at the foundations of the church (Eph 2:20). Apostles and prophets, after all, are only making explicit what is uniquely necessary for the church: the word and activity of Jesus Christ, the "apostle" of the Father and his definitive "prophecy" in history.

b. The prophet is "guarantee" of the community's orthodoxy. Recognized as someone faithful to the Word that is made present under the action of the Spirit, the prophet is enabled to recognize as true the word transmitted by the apostle. Paul expressly uses this argument as a decisive factor in distinguishing the true prophet from the false (1 Cor 14:37).

c. The prophet, as Paul makes a point of reminding us, is called to "build up, encourage, and console" (1 Cor 14:3). By actualizing the word of Jesus, the prophet *exhorts* the people to live concretely in it, and *encourages* them by proclaiming the Lord's return in glory. Thus, by exhorting and encouraging, the prophet *builds up* the community which, thanks to the prophet, encounters the Master's very word.

Prophets can therefore be understood by the light of their own charism, without any need to confuse them with other people, even though obviously a clear line of distinction can never be drawn. Prophets are not apostles; the latter found and direct the community, whereas prophets are believers who accept apostles and their message. Neither are prophets teachers; the latter receive the Lord's word from apostles and prophets. Whereas teachers read and interpret the Scripture, prophets, as people of the Spirit, read all Scriptures in the light of Christ's word. Lastly, prophets are not evangelists, for the latter draw on personal experience of inspired activity to formulate a particular theology, whereas prophets are concerned with the immediate good of the community and with particular conditions arising in individual communities.

The prophet of the primitive church thus appears as that person who, under the action of the Spirit of the risen Christ, has the task of restating and actualizing the word and work of Jesus. The prophet is therefore one who looks backwards, orienting the community toward a present realization and a future expectation by bringing out the meaning of the person of Jesus Christ.

The prophet can with every justification be called the one who belongs to and creates tradition—where by "tradition" we mean the content that the apostles, personally or by the operation of the Spirit, received as a result of their relationship with the Lord (*DV* 7). By virtue of belonging to tradition, the prophets are to be regarded as persons of great innovative force, able to read the present perceptively and to propound the future.

When compared with the OT, NT prophecy exhibits undeniably new features. The most obvious of all is the great difference in the extent of the phenomenon. Whereas for Joel the universal event of prophecy remains a wish (Jl 3:1–2), here in contrast all believers, at least potentially, are in the condition of being able to prophesy.

What is even more striking is the fact that, in NT prophecy, any kind of *fear, judgment,* and *condemnation* has completely disappeared. Instead, the prophet is the one who infuses courage and brings a message of salvation. The event of the resurrection as the most obvious expression of Christ's victory and glorification has now imprinted an indelible mark on the relationship between the Christian and the Father. The prophet gives confidence and assurance that the resurrection affects all believers who are willing to make their lives an "offering pleasing to God"; henceforth our eyes are firmly fixed on the eschatological event.

From the *Didache,* the *Shepherd of Hermas,* Irenaeus, and the whole patristic period on, the prophet acquires a different physiognomy, and criteria are required for assessing prophetic sincerity. Prophecy, however, does not cease — at all events not because institutional stabilization has taken place to the detriment of the charismatic dimension. Rather, we may simply think that the Lord's words found their definitive form in the Gospels and apostles' letters and that these henceforth constituted the norm and principle point of reference in the lives of the various local communities.

Prophets do not disappear; they are only overshadowed in their particular charism and express themselves differently. The second and third centuries offer examples of men and women possessing characteristics similar to those of the prophets, but who in this period become *martyrs* and *confessors.* Nor was prophecy to fail in subsequent centuries: the Middle Ages were to see it linked to the symbolic imagination, most particularly as regards the expounding of Scripture. Hugh of St. Victor and Joachim of Fiore were to excel in this. The same point can be made if we take examples from that type of mysticism appropriately known as "prophetic"; here we could compose a list comprising famous and less well known

alike: Julian of Norwich, Catherine of Siena, Teresa of Avila, John of the Cross, Ignatius of Loyola, John Bosco, Adrienne von Speyer, and so on. This is only the start of a long and varied series of "prophets" going back to those whose names have been preserved for us here and there in the Acts of the Apostles.

All this leads to one further conclusion: the prophets and the prophetic charism cannot be relegated hastily only to the period of the primitive church; they are always a constituent part of the church and always possess a permanent and irreplaceable significance for the church.

5. Theological Value of Prophecy

Retrieval of the biblical data on the nature of prophecy enables fundamental theology to have a different perspective for its own line of reasoning.

Once the oppressive straitjacket of a knowledge of future events has been removed, prophecy can be thought of as that *particular form of revelation which, keeping word and sign united, permits us to grasp the dialectic between disclosure/concealment of the revealed content.*

Three elements contained in this need clarification:

a. Revelation is seen as a dialectical movement composed not of antitheses but of a constant going beyond. What is revealed seems clear, yet refers us to some further knowledge yet to be revealed. The person of Christ does not admit of being defined by human reason or language; instead, it remains ever open to that mysterious horizon — the intra-trinitarian life of God.

b. Prophecy is understood as an indivisible unity of word and sign. The word refers us to the sign and the sign in itself refers us to a further meaning. The word clarifies the sign where the latter seems ambiguous, and the sign serves to complete the form of words. This referring back and forth can, better than anything else, explain the dialectic of revelation.

c. Prophecy as such is not external to revelation but is one particular aspect of it. Hence, rather than being one of the signs of revelation, it is itself a form of revelation — hence entirely assumed by the dialectic of revelation as one of its forms of expression.

These clarifications show that prophecy, taken by fundamental theology to be one form expressive of revelation, can still today foster understanding of it and be an important way of mediating it.

Some further elements may give a clearer idea of the theological value of prophecy in a renewed understanding of the signs of credibility of revelation:

a. By recovering the centrality of Jesus of Nazareth, we can think of his revelation as a prophecy left in history as the permanent sign of salvation. This datum has a far from secondary value, for to say that *Jesus is the prophecy of the Father* is to sum up the sense of the NT in its totality. We have seen that only by analogy and reductively can the title "prophet" be applied to Jesus Christ; but to say that he constitutes the prophecy of the Father is to point out that his words and deeds, in an indivisible whole (*gestis verbisque intrinsece inter se connexis, DV* 2), constitute a permanent testimony left in history. An indivisible unity is to be found in the way word and sign complement each other, and this is typical of the language by which prophecy and revelation are expressed.

By the same token, we can say that a historical, permanent sign has been set within history and that this concentrates within itself the traits of fulfillment and finality, though at present it awaits its full realization.

A theology of history (→ HISTORY III) will have the task of showing how, with this datum, a principle is established by which direction may be given to the unpredictable vagaries of history. For prophecy directs all history to the final attainment of salvation in the eschatological encounter with the Lord who sums up all creation (Col 1:15–20; Eph 1:10; 2:14, 16).

Prophecy, as we have earlier established, is the word that guides the present of a community, but on a dual front: in the light of the event of Jesus of Nazareth, and in the expectation of his return in glory. So, interpreting the revelation of Jesus of Nazareth along these lines, as the prophecy of the Father, means involving the believer in a careful reading of the historical present, undertaken, however, in continuity with preceding tradition and with the awareness of a fulfillment to come.

b. It follows from this that prophecy exists in the church and in human history as a permanent form of memory, obliging us not to assume anything to be absolute but to see everything as relative in the light of the uniquely necessary.

In this way, God's word is presented to the modern world as that ultimate stimulus for us to discover the meaning of existence, but at the same time training each of us to take responsibility for ourselves.

The evidence of revelation, given prophetically, forces us believers to keep on questioning ourselves about the meaning of what has been revealed to us and at the same time thrusts us toward the supreme form of freedom, which is deciding to accept being directed to a hidden meaning within the mystery itself.

Assuming the tone of prophecy, theology affirms that revelation is given to us so that we can understand and believe. In other words, it takes a form that we can understand. Exegesis of 1 Cor 14:22–25 gives us to think of prophecy in this interpretative role. Preferring it to glossolalia, which scandalizes nonbelievers, Paul affirms that prophecy, in contrast, makes plain "the secrets of the heart," as a result of which believers and nonbelievers alike are convinced of God's presence in the midst of his people.

A willingness to pass on the datum of revelation ought to be observable in the testimony of believers who, in accordance with the Lord's command, are prepared to read the SIGNS OF THE TIMES. Here prophecy becomes the creating of new signs that actualize the message of salvation for contemporary needs. Hence the special need for recalling the world's attention to those universal values that can be proclaimed and lived in a specifically Christian way.

Prophecy then, as language addressed to people (1 Cor 14:1–5), stimulates theological research into discovering all sorts of new ways of communicating religious knowledge, so that revelation can be a contemporary answer to the meaning of belief and life.

c. Lastly, setting revelation in the light of prophecy means bringing out its specific content, which is God's compassionate love. Prophecy is never given in the form of condemnation, judgment, or fear; on the contrary, it is always and exclusively a word of encouragement, trust, and hope. The cross of Jesus of Nazareth is the prophetic sign of signs since, at it, each of us is forced to see the nexus between death and suffering, and the glory of God. The face of the Crucified is radiant with the Father's glory (2 Cor 4:6); this is the final message, for here the saving will of God has been entirely fulfilled.

A postbiblical prophecy not conforming to this typology would automatically rule itself out as a potential message of revelation. Since the death and resurrection of Jesus Christ, the church can only recognize as prophecy that which makes more evident the trinitarian love of God—a love that did not balk at the condemnation of an innocent to death for the salvation of sinners (Rom 5:6–10). Prophecy presenting itself in the garb of condemnation and striking fear and anguish is more likely to be the product of the severity of a reviled Montanism, never entirely eradicated from the Christian soul, than of a responsible trust in the Father's love.

e. Prophecy therefore trains believers to speak of revelation as of a *hope* entrusted to the church, for the church in turn to communicate to the world. It is that biblical hope which, while pointing to the future, does not view it as vague expectation but as certainty of the final accomplishment. It is generated by a promise that is experienced as true, made by someone who reveals himself or herself to be trustworthy.

Conclusion

Sometimes we ought to feel a bit anxious for the prophets. The world does not want them; the church lays claim to them, but only once they are dead. Often recourse to prophecy is determined by OT models, which in many respects are unacceptable today.

Christians are the children of a prophecy come true in the light of Golgotha; they therefore lay claim to the presence of prophets as signs of a love that goes to the lengths of total self-giving. The prophet, in the ultimate analysis, forces every one of us to give serious thought to our own existence in relation to the life of Jesus Christ for us, sinking ever deeper into cultures that at different levels proclaim themselves to be dead (for even indifference and the ephemeral are death to the reason), prophecy calls us back to the meaning of a life consistently led by the light of meaningful values.

To a world having more and more recourse to emotions in the hope of finding the truth about its future and, deceiving itself, presuming to know that which it cannot, the prophet speaks of a loyalty to the present, without which there can be no genuine future.

The activity of prophets today will be the more effective and salvific, the further removed they are from forms of excessive spiritualism or Montanism. To "aspire" to prophecy (1 Cor 14:1), for every believer, thus becomes the most coherent form of believing in revelation, since this can bear witness to the living and working presence of the Spirit at the heart of the world through the activities of those who witness to the Spirit (1 Thes 5:19).

Bibl.: P. DE BROGLIE, *Les prophéties messianiques* (Paris, 1904); K. RAHNER, *Visionen und Prophezeiungen* (Innsbruck, 1952); F. GILS, *Jésus prophète d'après les Évangiles synoptiques* (Louvain, 1957); P. BENOIT, *Traité de la prophétie* (Tournai, 1958); M. LODS, *Confesseurs et martyrs* (Neuchâtel/Paris, 1958); G. VON RAD, *Old Testament Theology*, 2 vols. (New York, 1962, 1965); P. GRELOT, *Sens chrétien de l'Ancien Testament* (Paris, 1962); id., *The Bible, Word of God: A Theological Introduction to the Study of Scripture* (New York, 1968); id., "Le rapport de l'Ancien et du Nouveau Testament en Jésus Christ," in R. Latourelle and G. O'Collins, eds., *Problems and Perspectives of Fundamental Theology* (New York, 1982), 186–205; E. KÄSEMANN, "Amt und Gemeinde im Neuen Testament," in *Exegetische Versuche und Besinnungen*, vol. 1 (Göttingen, 1965), 109–34; R. LATOURELLE, *Theology of Revelation* (Staten Island, N.Y., 1966); N. LOHFINK, *Propheti ieri e oggi* (Brescia, 1967); R. B. Y. SCOTT, *The Relevance of the Prophets* (London, 1968); A. DULLES, "The Succession of Prophets in the Church," *Conc* 34 (1968): 52–62; H. KRÄHMER et al., "προφήτης," *TDNT* 6:781–861; L. RAMLOT and E. COTHENET, "Prophétisme," *DBS* 8:811–1337; F. SCHNIDER, *Jesus der Prophet* (Göttingen, 1973); E. BOISMARD, "Jésus prophète par excellence d'après Jean 10, 24–39," in J. Gnilka, ed., *Neues Testament und Kirche* (Freiburg, 1974), 160–71; U. B. MÜLLER, *Prophetie und Predigt im Neuen Testament* (Gütersloh, 1975); B. REICKE, "Synoptic Prophecies on the Destruction of Jerusalem," in D. E. Aune, ed., *Studies in New Testament and Early Literature* (Leiden, 1977), 121–34; K. KERTELGE, ed., *Prophetic Vocation in the New Testament and Today* (Leiden, 1977); D. HILL, *New Testament Prophecy* (Atlanta, 1979); R. P. CARROLL, *When Prophecy Failed* (London, 1979); P. M. BEAUDE, *L'accomplissement des Écritures* (Paris, 1980); M. E. BORING, *Saying of the Risen Jesus* (Cambridge, 1982); W. A. GRUDEM, *The Gift of*

Prophecy in 1 Corinthians (Lanham, 1982); D. E. AUNE, *Prophecy in Early Christianity* (Grand Rapids, 1983); D. L. BAKER, *Two Testaments and Bible* (London, 1986); H. SIMIAN-YOFRE, "Old and New Testament: Participation and Analogy," in R. Latourelle, ed., *Vatican II: Assessment and Perspectives Twenty-five Years After (1967–1987)*, 3 vols. (New York, 1989), 1:267–98; R. FISICHELLA, "La profezia come segno della credibilità della rivelazione," in *Gesù Rivelatore* (Casale Monferrato, 1988), 208–26; H. Urs VON BALTHASAR, *The Glory of the Lord: A Theological Aesthetics*, vol. 5: *Theology: The Old Covenant* (San Francisco, 1991).

Rino FISICHELLA

PROPHETS

Two themes have been assigned for discussion in the present article: the prophet as mediator of revelation, and the prophetic call as a privileged moment of that mediation. It seems appropriate in a dictionary of fundamental theology to focus on the hermeneutical and methodological dimensions of these themes and to refer readers to the relevant articles in any good biblical dictionary for an extensive listing of pertinent texts and discussion of their detailed exegetical problems. Methodological reflection is all the more necessary in the present case, since a glance at some of the handbooks of fundamental theology published in the 1980s shows that in several instances the prophets are presented in ways that reflect exegetical positions current in the 1960s with no sign of awareness that the state of the question has changed rather considerably in the intervening decades.

Hence, the two particular themes mentioned above will be situated within the wider horizon of a general reading strategy of the prophetic texts. To be more precise, three such ideal types will be distinguished: a future-oriented reading, a past-oriented reading, and a transtemporal text-oriented reading. There may be some danger of oversimplification in this, but at least it can serve to bring to light important methodological questions that cannot be ignored with impunity.

1. Prophets as Foretellers

In the first type of approach the prophets are read primarily as foretelling in specific detail the life and mission of Jesus of Nazareth, the Messiah and Lord. Their significance is seen in the fact that they point to what, from their situation, lies in the future. With roots in the NT writings, this type of reading was greatly developed by second-century writers (especially Justin and Irenaeus). It continued in the following centuries and eventually formalized as the "proof from prophecy" of classical apologetics.

A salient characteristic of this type of reading is its considerable selectivity. The focus is naturally on those texts (in practice, not very many) that appear to lend themselves to this type of reading. There was even a tendency not only to stress but also to multiply the messianic texts; certain translation options of the Vulgate were influential here. But even so, large blocks of material in the prophetic books remained unamenable to this reading strategy (e.g., announcements of invasions, destruction, exile; critique of social abuses, of political maneuverings, and so on). Such material tended to be ignored or else put down to the "imperfect" aspect of the OT which is surpassed in the NT; others opted for the solution of allegorical readings.

The heavy concentration on a future-oriented reading of the texts in this perspective had its effect on the two themes in question here. The prophets were seen as mediators of revelation predominantly (or exclusively) insofar as they foretold the climax of revelation in Jesus Christ; the reading was Christo-referential. Then there was relatively little interest in the initial call of the prophets as a privileged moment of revelation, because the reading was not primarily prophet-referential, not particularly interested in the prophet's own experience and immediate audience.

How might this first reading strategy be evaluated? Three points could be noted. (a) The existence of a small number of texts, which can legitimately be termed "messianic," is admitted by practically all contemporary scholars. However, prescinding from those of fundamentalistic tendencies in the various Christian confessions, there is likewise agreement that a critical historical reading of those texts is unable to show that any of them contained from the start a direct and univocal foretelling of aspects of the life and mission of Jesus of Nazareth. Scholarly methodology is not able to conclude to a specific personal identification of the Messiah figure of the texts. Consequently, an apologetic "proof from prophecy," understood as rational historical argumentation, is not feasible. Matters are different for readers who already believe in Jesus as the Messiah; such readers can be reminded of various aspects of the life and mission of Jesus by some prophetic texts. But for these readers the prophetic texts have an anamnetic function, not an argumentative one; belief in Jesus as the promised savior is the presupposition, not the conclusion, of such a reading. The effect of this reading is not to ground faith but to deepen and enlighten it.

(b) When the apologetic "proof from prophecy" was taken in a strong sense, it was in danger of fostering (independently of personal intentions) an anti-Jewish attitude or even polemic. This would be the case if the argument took the form of a rational demonstration that the messianic texts are clear pointers to Jesus of Nazareth, which would imply that anyone of normal intelligence who accepts the scriptural authority of the prophetic texts and yet refuses to acknowledge Jesus as the Christ must be in subjective bad faith. Such a conclusion may well have played its part, together with various other factors of a socioeconomic and psychological nature, in giving rise to a widespread attitude of hostility to Jewish communities, especially in Europe in past centuries. The horrendous practical consequences of this are well known. After Auschwitz, these matters cannot be passed over in silence in a theological discussion of the use of prophetic texts.

(c) Finally, the drastic selectivity inherent in this strategy of reading the prophets is a decisive argument against its adequacy. Far too much of the prophetic literature has been in practice ignored or downgraded in the interests of the "foretelling" approach. This has the paradoxical effect of impoverishing a Christian reading of the prophetic texts.

2. Prophets as Extraordinary Religious Personalities

A second type of reading strategy focuses on what lies in the past behind the prophetic texts, namely, the historical figures of the prophets seen as exceptional religious personalities, whose inspired insights brought Israel's religion to a higher plane and in this way prepared for the stage of fulfillment in Jesus Christ. This type of reading emerged with the historical-critical approach to the Bible and developed in its early stages especially in Germany under the double influence of romanticism and idealism. The romantic influence encouraged an interest in the biography of the prophets, their personal vicissitudes and religious experiences. The idealist influence stressed the superiority of prophetic thought over the lower forms of cultic religion current among their contemporaries and often tended to set this contrast within the framework of an evolutionary view of the development of Israel's religion. Different authors were variously affected by these two influences, but there was a common tendency to value above all what was personal and original in the prophets and to depreciate the subsequent work of disciples, redactors, editors, and glossators who continued the process of formation of the prophetic books after the prophets themselves. These later contributions, usually termed "inauthentic," tended to be regarded for the most part as inept and at times even as a corruption of the original prophetic message.

It is within this second type of reading strategy that the two themes proposed for this article probably have their original *Sitz im Leben*. To speak of a prophet as a mediator of revelation seems to presuppose that one can elaborate a clear historical portrait of the prophet in question on the basis of the "authentic" material in the prophetic book and in other available sources, and that one can reconstruct the situation of the original audience to whom the prophet mediated the revelation in the first place. It is clear, furthermore, that the particular interest attached to the initial call experience of the prophet and its revelatory value is related to the person-centered biographical approach typical of that line of historical-critical study influenced by romanticism. One must add, of course, that themes, like text types, can move from their original *Sitz im Leben* and be used in other contexts; so one cannot conclude that the two themes in question here are inseparably linked to the second type of reading strategy. It is useful, however, to note their original setting.

How might this second reading strategy be evaluated? Again three points can be made. (a) An undoubtedly positive feature is that this type of reading recuperates much prophetic material, which had in practice been ignored by the "foretelling-of-Jesus" approach, and treats it as of at least potential significance for later readers. (b) Another positive value lies in "the acute awareness of the historical dimension and contextualized nature of the ministry of the prophets. (c) However, a definite weakness, which has become ever clearer to scholars in the second half of the twentieth century, is found in the unilateral focus on the prophetic personages at the expense of their writings. In its worst form, this attitude tended to see the prophetic books as regrettable obstacles which had to be dismantled critically as soon as possible in order to arrive at the *ipsissima vox* of the prophet himself, the only worthwhile object of study, the only repository of religious values of permanent validity. Fundamental theologians might need to consider to what extent an unconscious influence of this stance may not be present in their image of the prophets.

3. Prophets as Texts

The third ideal type can be described as text-oriented and trans-temporal. It is text-oriented in that it takes seriously the undeniable fact that the primary datum at the reader's disposal is the prophetic book, and it sees its primary task as being that of reaching a better understanding of that book in all its literary and historical complexity. It is trans-temporal in that the focus is not set unilaterally on one particular period (either the life of Jesus or the life of the prophet whose name is attached to the book) but comprises the whole temporal span in which the genesis of the book took place. Set out in chronological order (which, however, is not the operational order of exegetical work here), the temporal phases are these: all those factors prior to the prophet that influenced the way in which the message was formulated (tradition history); the prophet's own ministry and message insofar as this can be historically reconstructed; the various phases of transmission and development of the original prophetic material up to the formation of the book as we have it now (redaction history); a study of the completed book as a compositional (not an authorial) unity (final-form study). The tradition-history problematic was much developed in the 1950s and 1960s (G. von Rad's *Theology of the OT* is an outstanding example). Redaction-

history questions came to prominence and grew more sharply radical in the 1970s and 1980s (though, of course, one can find them before that period too). Final-form study has developed in the past two decades also under a variety of influences (structuralism, the canonical approach, attempts to apply various general theories of text and literature to the prophetic books).

How might all this have an influence on the formulation of the two themes suggested for this article? Three comments can be made. (a) A more nuanced presentation seems called for, in speaking of a prophet as a mediator of revelation. Insofar as one can propose a probable reconstruction of the historical ministry of a given prophet (and on this see the following comment), one will have to admit in the light of tradition-historical studies that the prophet's message was not a totally new revelation, that there was a considerable measure of dialogue with, and contestation of, earlier views—in brief, that the prophets were people of their time to a greater extent than one would have gathered from scholarly works of an earlier period. If so, then the question arises: Is it perhaps somewhat unilateral to focus so specifically on the prophets as mediators of revelation in the OT? Should we not expect also to read articles about the Deuteronomistic narrative theologians or the psalmists or the wisdom teachers as mediators of revelation?

(b) The historical reconstruction of the ministry of any of the prophets has become a much more difficult task in the light of the more radical redaction-critical studies of recent years. For example, the later editions of Otto Kaiser's commentary on Is 1–39 conclude that the historical contours of the life of Isaiah are shrouded in almost total obscurity; a similar conclusion has been reached for Jeremiah by Robert Carroll in his 1986 commentary on that book. Undoubtedly, there are other scholars who are more optimistic about the possibilities of recovering historical data about the ministry of the prophets (e.g., Hans Wildberger's commentary on Is 1–39 and the exceedingly optimistic commentary on Jeremiah by William L. Holladay), but the point is that the biographical approach is now a matter of considerable exegetical debate. It would be unwise for fundamental theologians to ignore the existence of these discussions and to continue to speak of "the prophets" as if there were few problems in reaching a consensus about their historical ministry. This affects one's use of the call narratives in the prophetic books, to take just one example. There is an increasing tendency among exegetes to read the "vocation texts" primarily (or even exclusively) as programmatic theological statements whose main purpose is not to supply biographical and psychological information about the prophet's experience but rather to offer a theological legitimation of the prophet's role and a summary of key points of the message. In this perspective, the call narratives do not give us direct access to privileged moments in the prophet's experience of revelation; instead, they are texts whose prominent position and programmatic content give them a privileged role in the structure of the prophetic book as a redactional composition.

(c) The difficulties of reconstructing a historical picture of the prophets involve also (according to some recent scholars) problems of role description. Two examples can be given. First, the Hebrew term *nābî*, translated as "prophet" ever since the Septuagint version, is the most common designation for the prophetic role in exilic and postexilic biblical writings, but it is doubtful whether the eighth-century prophets (Amos, Hosea, Isaiah, and Micah) ever used this title of themselves. Does an indiscriminate use of the term "prophet" tend perhaps to give an excessively uniform image of what may well have been a much more complex set of roles in Israel's religious history? Second, the syntagma *dĕbār YHWH* ("the word of the Lord"), generally presented as a specific feature of prophetic revelation, is in fact very rare in prophetic texts that can be dated with solid probability to the eighth century; it becomes frequent only in the exilic period and later (in Jer, Ezek, and the Deuteronomistic History). Again, does an indiscriminate generalization about the prophets as bearers of the *dĕbār YHWH* not run the risk perhaps of oversimplifying a more complex set of revelatory terms and roles?

To sum up, the current state of exegetical discussion about the prophets (meaning the books and the personages) is such as to suggest that fundamental theology should rethink the rationale of its traditional interest in, and discourse on, the prophets. The person-centered, naïvely experiential approach, which has been taken for granted in many works of fundamental theology up to now, needs to reflect on the new state of the question raised by recent exegetical research and its hermeneutical implications. Only thus can fundamental theology hope to remain in effective dialogue with biblical scholarship in this matter.

Bibl.: General Questions. A. G. AULD, "Prophets through the Looking Glass: Between Writings and Moses," *JSOT* 27 (1983): 3–23; J. BLENKINSOPP, *A History of Prophecy in Israel* (Philadelphia, 1983); O. KAISER, *Einleitung in das Alte Testament* (Gütersloh, 1984), 5; S. AMSLER et al., *Les prophètes et les livres prophétiques* (Paris, 1985); B. VAWTER, "Were the Prophets *nabis?*," *Bib* 66 (1985): 206–20; J. BARTON, *Oracles of God: Perceptions of Ancient Prophecy in Israel after the Exile* (London, 1986); D. L. PETERSEN, ed., *Prophecy in Israel: Search for an Identity* (Philadelphia, 1987); R. P. CARROLL, "Inventing the Prophets," *Irish Biblical Studies* 10 (1988): 24–36.

The Prophetic Vocation. B. O. LONG, "Berufung, I. Altes Testament," *TRE* 5:676–84; R. P. CARROLL, *From Chaos to Covenant: Uses of Prophecy in the Book of Jeremiah* (London, 1981), 31–58; D. VEIWEGER, *Die Spezifik der Berufungsberichte Jeremias und Ezechiels im Umfeld ähnlicher Einheiten des Alten Testaments* (Frankfurt, 1986).

Charles CONROY

Q

QUI PLURIBUS
(Encyclical)

This encyclical is of interest to two areas of fundamental theology: the relations between faith and reason, and the motives of credibility.

1. The primary purpose of the encyclical (9 November 1846) was to set forth the teaching of the church on relations between faith and reason. In this document Pius IX set down principles that would be repeated twenty-five years later by Vatican I. He says that there is no conflict between faith and reason, because both come from the very source of eternal truth; in fact, the two should support each other (DS 2776). Rationalism, an "enemy of divine revelation," seeks to subject the Christian religion to the conditions governing any "human work" or "philosophical invention," both of which are subject to the law of ceaseless progress. Pius IX responds to this attempt by declaring (a) that "our religion has been mercifully *revealed* by God to the human race" and "derives its power from the authority of this same *God who speaks*" (DS 2777); (b) that it is therefore the duty of human reason "to inquire diligently into the fact of revelation in order to be certain that God has spoken, and then to offer him an intelligent obedience"; (c) "that an unreserved faith must be given to God who speaks and that nothing is more in accord with reason itself than to accept and firmly adhere to all that has been established as revealed by the God who can neither be deceived nor deceive" (DS 2778). The encyclical thrice asserts a close connection between revelation, word, and faith, and explains each in terms of the others. It looks at revelation in its objective, active, and passive aspects successively. Objective: Christianity is a revealed religion ("religion" in the sense of "teaching," according to the interpretation given by Vatican I, which repeats this passage: DS 3020) in contrast to one that would be merely human teaching, the fruit of philosophical thought. "Active": the text treats the action of revealing and the action of speaking as equivalent. Passive: this has to do with the response of human beings to the God who reveals: faith is a response to God who speaks, an acceptance of what he reveals. Faith is, properly speaking, given to a person and accepts what that person says. The motive for this acceptance and obedience is the very word of God: the authoritative word of him who cannot be deceived (therefore no error) and cannot deceive us (therefore no lie). Faith is thus a reasonable obedience based on the truthful and infallible word of God himself. God's word is a testimony.

2. The encyclical is also of interest because it gives a coherent overview of the signs of revelation, thus introducing order into the traditional presentation, although it does not achieve the personalist perspective of Vatican II's document *Dei Verbum*, which presents Christ as both the source of all the signs and their center of convergence.

Listing, and organizing into a vast synthesis, all the signs that make it possible to establish with certainty the divine origin of Christianity, the encyclical links all the signs of revelation to Christ and his message. Christian faith, says the text, "has been confirmed by the birth of Jesus Christ, its author who also brings it to completion, by his life, his death, his resurrection, his wisdom, his miracles, his prophecies" (DS 2779). Vatican II likewise says that the life and works of Jesus Christ confirm revelation (*DV* 4). There are, however, important differences in the perspectives of the two documents. The encyclical focuses its attention chiefly on the *object of faith*, i.e., the salvific teaching that has Christ as its author; in Vatican II, Christ himself, Son of the Father and Word of the Father, is the main focus of attention. In the encyclical, the signs are connected with Christ but not by the close relationship that makes the person of the incarnate Word the center from which all the signs radiate. The text looks primarily to the fact that the *Christian faith* (in the sense of a doctrine to be believed) is *confirmed* by the life, words, and works of Christ, who is its author and perfecter. The encyclical does not express in as pregnant a way as *Dei Verbum* the fact that Christ *by his entire presence, by his entire self*, as well as by his words and works, both *completes* and *confirms* revelation. On the other hand, by its synthesizing presentation of the signs and its linking them with Christ, the text of the encyclical does anticipate the teaching and literary structure of Vatican II. It also stresses the point that the signs of revelation are not independent entities. They are connected with one another and shed light on one another: they come to us in a bundle as it were and they are effective by their convergence. They resemble a constellation rather than isolated meteorites.

The signs rendering revelation credible proceed from Christ and the church like rays of light from a single source. The needs of teaching cause us to separate what is united, at the risk of falsifying the reality.

René LATOURELLE

R

RAHNER, KARL

In the course of his professorial career, K. Rahner was active as a dogmatician at Innsbruck, Pullach, and Münster, and as a philosopher of religion at Munich. Fundamental theology was of decisive importance to his thinking, just as, conversely, his contribution profoundly influenced the development of fundamental theology. His work has been both theological and philosophical in character, an attribute sufficient in itself to ensure its fundamental-theological quality.

When Rahner arrived at Innsbruck in 1936, it was still uncertain which professorial chair he would assume. A position in fundamental theology had been vacant for some time. His doctoral research in theology could also be seen as qualifying him for this, even though it had centered on a speculative topic in patristics. Together with his earlier philosophical studies in Freiburg (im Breisgau), he possessed the kind of background that seemed to point toward future work in fundamental theology. Indeed, after his initial qualification as a university teacher (1937), Rahner was probably directly preparing himself along those lines, given that he devoted himself at that time to comprehensive study of the question of the role of philosophy within theology. His lectures at the Salzburg *Hochschulwochen* in the summer of 1937, later published under the title *Hearers of the Word*, deal with "an aspect of the ideal grounding of faith" (p. 30) that is made explicit only marginally, or not at all, in the normal pursuit of fundamental theology; consequently, Rahner himself calls his topic "*the* aspect of ideal fundamental theology that is usually much neglected in actual formulation of such theology," namely, "the ontology of the potentia oboedientialis for the free revelation of God" (p. 34). For that reason, this well-known work can at least also be regarded as a fundamental-theological essay, whose author sees something lacking in the usual fundamental theology of the time and attempts to supply it.

In fact, Rahner was not able to develop this approach further through his concrete teaching activities, since the vacant chair in fundamental theology at Innsbruck was assumed, in the autumn of 1937, by Rahner's former teacher in fundamental theology (transferring from the university at Valkenburg), P. K. Prümm, while Rahner embarked on his career as a dogmatician by lecturing on the doctrine of grace. That Rahner had not really anticipated teaching in that kind of area is suggested by the preface he provided in June 1938 to his written conspectus "De gratia Christi." He says there that he had been unable, for external reasons, to use the work of his teacher, H. Lange, as a textbook basis for his lectures, but had, for the convenience of his students, prepared a recapitulation of it. In so doing, he had rearranged the order of the material, had incorporated the treatise on the virtues of hope and love, and had adopted positions divergent from Lange's on a number of issues as well as provided supplementary bibliographic details. That he must have been conscious, when dealing with this topic, of its closeness to, yet also difference from, the fundamental-theological approach of *Hearers of the Word* is evident from a remark that he expressly added there, namely, that he was concerned "not with the potentia oboedientialis for supernatural *grace* as the ontological elevation of humans to participation in the life of God" . . . "but only with the potentia oboedientialis for hearing the possibly occurring *speech* of God" (p. 34). Rahner had conceived and structured the doctrine of grace fundamental-theologically, in the light of the *potentia oboedientialis*; this is made unambiguously clear by the basic concept of the "self-communication of God."

After these observations on the beginnings of his theological activity, it must be asked what form Rahner's relation to fundamental theology took in later stages of his teaching career. Two classical areas of traditionally fundamental-theological demonstration attracted his special interest during the war and postwar years: the question of God, which he approaches in a decidedly biblical-theological way, and the question of the church, which he deals with in mainly practical, pastoral-theological terms. In both cases, the concerns associated with the *demonstratio religiosa* and the *demonstratio catholica* were not overlooked, even if not particularly prominent. Regarding the *demonstratio christiana*, by contrast, Rahner had made, in his earlier years, only one (characteristically apologetic and so far ignored) contribution, namely, his commentary *Die protestantische Christologie der Gegenwart* [Present-day Protestant Christology] (1936). Not until after the Second Vatican Council, in the context of drawing together various occasional contributions to Christology, was this problem area further developed and elaborated.

In later theological debate, special attention had also become more intensely focused on the distinction made by Rahner in 1939 (together with H. Urs von Balthasar and in contrast to conventional fundamental theology) in the first main section ("Formal and Fundamental Theology") of his "Scheme for a Treatise of Dogmatic Theology" (*Theological Investigations* 1:19–23). That concise draft was not, however, worked out in detail and remained tied to the original but unrealized project of formulating a dogmatics. By the time this plan had become known to the public, in the fifties, other kinds of questioning had already become largely dominant. The proposal itself represents a historical document that provided the basis for speculations of various sorts.

For Rahner, in the decade before the Second Vatican Council, it was primarily the question of how to restructure theological studies and the training for the priesthood that caused him to reflect on fundamental-theological problems and led to his proposing a "basic curriculum." The Council accepted this idea in conjunction with its obligatory demand for an *Introductio in mysterium Christi*, which, to be sure, did not amount (materially or formally) to a simple realization of Rahner's conceptions. Nevertheless, in this lies what is probably Rahner's most directly influential contribution to fundamental theology. Rahner himself, however, was thinking here not of a replacement for fundamental theology but rather of an approach that was existentially attuned to the totality of faith and on whose basis fundamental-theological reflection—already highly elaborated and specialized in the meantime—would be able to develop. It would, of course, not then simply continue in the form in which it was pursued before but would have to adapt itself appropriately, in general and in particular, to its changed position. Impulses significant to this process also originated with Rahner, such as those that became thematic, by way of the

transcendental-theological kind of questioning and its corresponding approach, for the whole of theological thinking in the fifties and sixties. The attention given to the problem of the "conditions of possibility" on the side of the cognizing subject meant that simple continuous development of traditional philosophical deliberations or positive observation and appraisal of historical data in the framework of conventional fundamental theology were no longer permitted, quite apart from the fact that growing awareness of the efforts of non-Catholic theologians also made it necessary to assess various positions that were not without significance for Catholic fundamental theology. One need only think here of K. Barth's ideas on revelation, Bultmann's demythologization program, the new problem of the historical Jesus, and numerous results of recent exegesis, including associated conclusions about hermeneutics and the conditions for responsible research into Holy Scripture.

Beyond this, Rahner dealt directly with themes traditionally treated in fundamental theology, as, for instance, in *Inspiration in the Bible* (New York, 1961), *Episcopacy and the Primacy* (with J. Ratzinger; New York, 1962), *Revelation and Tradition* (with J. Ratzinger; New York, 1966), and elsewhere. In that way, he stimulated discussion and contributed to changes in the delineation of certain issues. This influence usually resulted in a more decided integration of individual themes into larger interrelational structures, so that the way was opened for overcoming the tendency to treat particular truths in positivistic isolation and relationless succession.

Even before, of course, there had been knowledge of the *nexus mysteriorum*; but concern for it had scarcely featured in fundamental theology because, for historical reasons, that theology had arisen primarily as an apologetic response to various, more or less randomly occurring, external challenges. For many, therefore, fundamental theology was regarded merely as an occasional collection of questions and answers that had been evoked in modern times by the Reformation, Enlightenment, criticism of religion, and so on, and had then been carried over into theological debate. It remained uncertain whether fundamental theology was at all capable of constituting an independent, self-coherent discipline, even if, in line with a conscious shift away from the concept of apologetics toward that of fundamental theology, this view became increasingly prevalent and justified. Rahner, it is true, was not solely a reinforcer of that development. His basic religious curriculum and demand for a formal and fundamental theology within the framework of dogmatics had the actual effect of possibly casting doubt on fundamental theology, as did the general elaboration of a transcendental theology, even though that may have been contrary to Rahner's express intention.

It was no mere coincidence that his understanding of revelation was articulated in terms of an analysis of humanity and its spatiotemporal situation, that is, through particular reflection on the physicosensory sphere (termed "world") and on history as the locus of conditioned freedom. All this was, however, not primarily fundamental-theological in intent, but anthropological, and was developed on the basis of data from theology of creation and redemption. The resultant view of humanity was perceived by many as a new discovery or new kind of emphasis; it had an immediate influence in fundamental-theological circles, inasmuch as it both called for and brought to consciousness a reconception of the possible relationship between God and humanity. The model for this relationship that had definitively underpinned traditional fundamental theology proved, in the light of deeper questioning, inadequate and unsustainable. This was confirmed by the Second Vatican Council with its Dogmatic Constitution on divine revelation, *Dei Verbum*, in the drafting of which Rahner played a committed role. But in this case, too, existing differences must not be glossed over; from Rahner's side, these are primarily explained by the fact that, in his thought, the status of revelation is conditioned in manifold ways by other themes that bear on it.

Precisely his christological reflections and essays demonstrate that Rahner is not concerned with theology of revelation in the usual understanding of that term. More and more unmistakably, what emerges as the core of his theological activity is the difficulty of gaining access, in our times, to the truth of Jesus Christ and to religious faith, an issue that is not even rightly perceived in theology of revelation. It is Rahner's practical-pastoral concerns that find expression in this viewpoint, giving him an open readiness, even at the close of his life, to consider new suggestions and methods, despite not normally aligning himself unconditionally with them. His receptiveness to orienting oneself primarily toward practice, to the political dimensions of theology, or to South American aspirations for liberation theology are well known. However, because of the controversiality of many of these propositions in the context of ecclesiastical and theological politics, it was no longer possible for him to achieve the degree of scholarly appropriation and critical deliberation that would have been desirable for full evaluation of the positive possibilities in such approaches. He often found it more urgent, in the face of some kind of narrowness or other, just to keep the field open for new contributions and to see that new approaches were not blocked in advance. It may well emerge, in the long run, that Rahner's most important service to fundamental theology consisted in his more than occasional laborious efforts to carry on discussions, or to get them restarted, or also to ensure that they were not broken off. For in and through those efforts he maintained a certain stance, defending positions with firmness while nevertheless striving to build bridges, and setting an example from which something decisive and indispensable can be learned by everyone entrusted with furthering the fundamental-theological project.

Bibl.: R. BLEISTEIN and E. KLINGER, eds., *Bibliographie K. Rahner 1924–1969* (Freiburg, 1969); id., *Bibliographie K. Rahner 1969–1974* (Freiburg, 1974); K. RAHNER, *Hearers of the Word* (New York, 1969); id., "Reflections on a New Task for Fundamental Theology," in *Theological Investigations*, vol. 16 (1975; New York, 1983), 156–68; id., "A Theology That We Can Live With," in *Theological Investigations*, vol. 21 (1983; New York, 1988), 99–114; P. IMHOF and H. TREZIAK, eds., "Bibliographie K. Rahner 1974-1979," in H. VORGRIMLER, ed., *Wagnis Theologie* (Freiburg, 1979), 579–97; P. IMHOF and E. MEUSER, eds., "Bibliographie K. Rahner 1979–1984," in E. KLINGER and K. WITTSTADT, eds., *Glaube im Prozess* (Freiburg, 1984), 854–71.

Karl H. NEUFELD

RATIONALISM

1. Explanation of the Concept

In philosophy, the term "rationalism" (from Latin: *ratio*, "reason," "understanding") refers to persuasions and theories holding that one can, by means of reason, adequately grasp reality and, conformably with that, act "reasonably." Rationalism stands in opposition to empiricism (on the epistemological plane), to irrationalism (on the plane of applied reason), and to utilitarianism and hedonism (on the ethical plane). It also runs counter to any sort of revelation-based religion, which naturally views the source of knowledge not as *reason*, but as *revelation*.

Karl Popper has introduced the distinction between "classical" and "critical" types of rationalism in *The Open Society and its Enemies* (1945).

2. Rationalism in the History of Philosophy

Initial approaches to Western rationalism can be found in Greek philosophy as early as the pre-Socratics. *Classical* rationalism, however, does not begin to take form until Socrates, who draws a strict distinction between genuine knowledge and mere opinion or belief. Genuine knowledge differs from mere opinion by virtue of being grounded. Its truth is secured through argued proofs. According to Aristotle, authentic knowledge comes about through recognition of the reasons that explain why something is as it is. He distinguishes between *indirect* knowledge (logical conclusions drawn on the basis of initial premises) and *direct* knowledge (insight into the truth of first principles). The classical example of this kind of cognitive ideal is represented by Euclidean geometry, in which certain ultimate propositions (axioms or postulates) are used as a basis for logically deducing all other propositions. All the propositions in such a system appear to have their truth secured: the initial ones through direct insight, and the others through logical deduction. Aristotle's conception of these things left its mark on medieval high scholasticism (e.g., THOMAS AQUINAS), and his influence can be traced right up to modern times.

But the basic problem is, and remains, that of *direct insight* into the highest truths. Modern rationalism attempts to find a solution to this.

Accordingly, it makes its appearance in two variant forms: as *intellectualism* (Descartes, Pascal, Spinoza) and as *empiricism* (Bacon, Locke, Berkeley). Intellectualism is generally also designated as rationalism. For intellectualism, intellectual intuition is the source of the direct knowledge; for empiricism, by contrast, the source is concrete experience. Kant attempts to achieve a synthesis of intellectualism and empiricism by replacing the previous realism with transcendental idealism, which is based on a transcendental formulation of the problem, namely, the question of the conditions of the possibility of knowledge. According to Kant, the certainty of knowledge is related not to an external reality but to the forms of experience, which are determined by the structures of the cognitive faculty. The Kantian solution, however, came under criticism from modern science, which was motivated by two "discoveries": (a) the discovery of non-Euclidean geometry, and (b) the formulation of non-Newtonian physics (Einstein).

Diverging from the ideal of classical rationalism (certainty of knowledge) is *critical rationalism*, as founded in the 1930s by Karl Popper (see *Logik der Forschung* [The Logic of Scientific Discovery]). The demand for secure knowledge is — as Popper shows — unrealizable. Critical rationalism therefore abandons that ideal and advocates a logically consistent *fallibilism:* no knowledge is absolutely certain because humans can always err when attempting to solve their cognitive problems. *Certain* knowledge is incompatible with the striving for *truth*. Popper's epistemological ideal is marked by a striving for substantial knowledge, and yet that always has the status of merely suppositional knowledge. In this sense, all knowledge is "hypothetical" — a fact that need not lead to relativism, since competition among the various theories produces at least approximate knowledge. Theories must therefore be subject to testing and able to be criticized. Instead of the demand for rational grounding, then, critical rationalism makes the demand for critical testing.

In critical rationalism, the search for truth, in the sense of a search for substantial knowledge, is thus not abandoned, just as (in contrast to Kantianism) there is a continuing adherence to critical "realism." Further, critical rationalism diverges from the striving of empiricism for "pure" experience, which, in its view, does not exist. Experience is always already "saturated with theory."

3. Rationalism and Modern Theology

In theology, "rationalism" is understood as implying the view that assent to faith rests on rational insight and that the truth of faith can be demonstrated by reasoned argument—but also that the credibility of faith is not positively provable. The First Vatican Council more than once condemned such rationalism (see DS 3028, 3032, 3041). Also included in the council's condemnation of rationalism was the view that the factuality of God's historically effected self-communication in human language is provable. Rather, all that is provable is the existence of a message claiming for itself the status of God's word. Even if this claim cannot ultimately be refuted by rational argument, the *truth* of the claim is recognized only in *faith*.

The answerability of faith in front of reason presupposes the possibility of demonstrating, prior to assent to faith, that, in the choice between faith and unbelief, unbelief remains arbitrary and thus cannot be responsibly justified. With that, however, the nonarbitrary nature of assent to faith has not been demonstrated. All that can be proved is that the accusation of arbitrariness is justified not in relation to faith but in relation to unbelief.

Ultimately, reason-based knowledge and faith-based knowledge cannot be mutually contradictory, even if they often stand in a conflict-like relationship to one another. Reason-based knowledge refers to the general knowledge of reality that can be attained independently of faith. Faith-based knowledge refers to knowledge for which one must have recourse to the self-communication of God. Reason-based knowledge stands primarily in a negative relationship to faith-based knowledge. Faith can neither be proved nor refuted nor made understandable by it. Hence, reason has, in relation to faith, not a supporting role, but rather a filtering one. This means (negatively expressed) that nothing contradictory to reason—which preserves its justified autonomy—can be believed. Such critically functioning reason protects faith from superstition, and faith has an interest, for its own sake, in such reason. One can confidently say that faith supports the independence of

reason and contradicts reason (through reasoned argument) if it offends against its own laws (though this is no proof of the truth of faith).

The expression "reason illumined by faith" characterizes the employment of reason within faith.

Bibl.: K. POPPER, *Die Logik der Forschung* (Vienna, 1934); id., *The Open Society and its Enemies*, 2 vols. (London, 1945); P. KNAUER, *Der Glaube kommt vom Hören: Ökumenische fundamentaltheologie* (5th ed.; Bamberg, 1968); H. J. POTTMEYER, *Der Glaube vor dem Anspruch der Wissenschaft, die Konstitution über den katholischen Glauben "Dei Filius" des 1. Vatikanischen Konzils und die unveröffentlichten voten der vorbereitenden Kommission* (Freiburg/Basel/Vienna, 1968); H. ALBERT, *Traktat über kritische Vernunft* (Tübingen, 1978); id., *Die Wissenschaft und die Fehlbarkeit der Vernunft* (Tübingen, 1982); id., *Freiheit und Ordnung* (Tübingen, 1986); id., *Kritik der reinen Erkenntnislehre* (Tübingen, 1987); K. HECKER, "Rationalism," in *SM* 5:184–87.

Bernd GROTH

REALISM, CHRISTIAN

1. Concept

The word "realism" (from the Latin *res*, "thing") has many meanings. In ordinary, non-philosophical language it signifies a cast of mind that attends chiefly to what things "really" are and not simply, or certainly not primarily, to what they could or should be, and that does not indulge in daydreaming or the play of images or ideas. To be a realist in this sense means to have one's feet on the ground and to grapple with things in all their unyielding reality. "Realism" is also used of literature, art, and language with almost the same meaning, though one that is hardly of interest in the present context: "realism" describes things as they are, calls them by their right name. Much more important is the philosophical use of the word. Here again there is a need to distinguish a fundamental meaning and more restrictive meanings. Realism, in the fundamental sense of the word, is the name given to every doctrine which acknowledges that things (persons or objects) have an *en-soi* and does not reduce them to representations or constructs of the mind or ideas. Realism thus understood is radically opposed to idealism (in the philosophical sense of this word). Since there are many forms of idealism, the same doctrine can be called "realism" from one point of view and "idealism" from another. For the thought in which things are said to subsist as "representations" can be (a) the thought of the philosopher: "solipsism" (things and persons exist only in me and for me), a view that has never been seriously professed; (b) the thought of society, humanity, all thinking beings; (c) an impersonal thought; (d) the thought or mind of God.

In contrast, the affirmation of the _en-soi_ reality of distinct persons can be called realism, but it can also be accompanied by an idealist denial of the reality of sensible entities. "Realism" has therefore come to signify specifically a doctrine that does affirm the reality of sensible things. Marxists, especially Lenin, wrongly identify realism thus understood with materialism, because they see materialism as the only possible alternative to idealism. It is to be noted, moreover, that in these debates between realism and idealism a distinction must be made between the ontological viewpoint and the critical viewpoint. It is one thing to say that others exist only in my thought; this position calls urgently for psychiatric treatment. It is another thing to say that I cannot prove apodictically the _en-soi_ existence of others, although I am convinced of it.

In an earlier age, "realism" had another limited meaning in connection with a problem debated in the Middle Ages: the problem of "universals," i.e., nouns that have a comprehensive or universal meaning, e.g., "man," which does not signify any individual human being. What is it that grounds this universality and guarantees that the word will have the same meaning when applied to different individuals? The Middle Ages supplied a whole range of answers, extending from realism in the fullest sense, and with its own specific outlook, to nominalism, which denied any reality to general ideas and recognized only individuals. The doctrine held by Thomas Aquinas and the great Scholastics, which based the value of general ideas on the abstraction of a common essence, a process made possible by the matter-form composition of things, is sometimes called "moderate realism."

2. Importance

Realism in the sense that I have called fundamental (i.e., realism as opposed to idealism) is undoubtedly something required by the Christian faith. The latter loses all its meaning if God is merely an idea or ideal that exists only in the consciousness and aspirations of human beings or in the requirements of Thought in general; in other words, if God is not first of all an _en-soi_, existing independently of what we think or believe and of everything that is not himself. In like manner, in the view of the Christian faith, Jesus, Mary, and the apostles are real beings who really lived in a real world, who really acted and really suffered — beings, then, who, at least in that sense, are historical. But the existence of persons is inseparable from the existence of things in the midst of which these persons live and act; things, like persons, cannot be reduced to simple "representations." Christ was really crucified on a cross that did not exist solely as an "object of thought." The doctrine of the sacraments, in particular, supposes that if signs are to signify, they must have a certain reality in themselves. The "real" presence of Christ in the Eucharist implies that the species by means of which he is present do not exist simply in our thought and our faith. (It is clear here that "realism" can have nuances of meaning: we also say that Christ is "really" with those who are gathered in his name, but in this context the adverb says simply that the presence is not illusory or purely subjective: Christ is present "through his Spirit." "Eucharistic presence" conveys a different meaning.)

There can be no doubt that the Gospels, and the whole of the Scriptures, are bathed in an atmosphere of realism — the realism of common sense, of the "experienced world" (_Lebenswelt_). This fact does, of course, leave room for an objection. The Bible (one may say) speaks the language of everyday life, but leaves the interpretation of it to us. It attributes to things — the cross of Christ, water, bread and wine, and so on — the same degree of reality that we ordinarily attribute to the things that surround us and that we use. The wood of the cross was as real as the wood of our furniture; the body of Christ was as real as our own bodies. But this outlook leaves completely untouched the question, What is the ontological status of the reality?

The Bible tells us nothing about the physical and metaphysical structures of material being, and faith does not demand of us any position on the subject. True enough, but this does not mean that faith can accept any and all positions. It cannot accept idealism, since idealism denies the real *en-soi* of things. (In addition, idealism contradicts the spontaneous and fundamental movement of thought, i.e., the affirmation of being and of the self as part of being, which is given to us in the form of really existing beings). This is not to say that there is no element of truth in idealism. Nothing compels us to hold a form of realism that denies any and all activity of the knowing subject in the elaboration and presentation of objects. We can legitimately say that perception, and even every form of knowledge, is already an interpretation; but this presupposes that there are things to interpret.

In another sense that is closer to the current understanding of the word, Christianity can be called "realist" insofar as it is not simply or primarily an intellectual construct or system of ideas but a living relationship between real persons, and develops not in the form of a discourse held together by logical connections but in the form of a history or, if one prefers, a discourse whose words are contingent events, free acts (L. Laberthonnière, *Le réalisme chrétien et l'idéalisme grec* [Paris, 1905]).

In regard to realism as a response to the problem of "universals," it is clear that a doctrine that would assert the reality of universal human nature to the point of regarding individuals and therefore persons simply as accidents of this universal nature and as at best lesser realities without any *en-soi* existence, would be incompatible with the Christian faith, which supposes the existence of persons endowed each with responsibility and open each to an individual destiny. Conversely, to deny any real community among individuals of a single species, and thus to make their unity purely nominal or at best ideal, would be to leave only a purely extrinsic solidarity between Christ and us. It comes as no surprise, therefore, that some fathers of the church professed, with regard to universals, a realism that is indeed less strict than that of Plato, but goes further, it seems, than the kind that the Scholastics mainly accepted. It is also in the light of this kind of realism that we can fairly interpret various trinitarian formulas of the early church which do not seem, at first sight, to assert more than a specific unity.

Joseph DE FINANCE

REASON/FAITH

1. The Various Levels of the Relationship

The problem of the relation between faith and reason comes into play at various levels and can therefore be made the object of methodological reflection in varying ways.

a. Quite directly, reason and faith are intertwined in every act of belief insofar as even the most freely arising instance of grace-given revelation is always apprehensible only within the horizon of some particular human understanding. Recognition of this fact, elaborated on the basis of the hermeneutics developed in the nineteenth century, profoundly affects every theological discipline today. It bears especially on the methodology of historical theology, which can succeed in transmitting earlier testaments of faith (including binding pronouncements of doctrinal office), in a form suited to present-day understanding, only through inquiry into the particular, and always differing, horizons within which that faith has articulated itself. As a result of the continued development of hermeneutics (particularly by M. Heidegger, R. Bultmann, H.-G. Gadamer, P. Ricoeur, and J. Habermas), it became increasingly evident that a certain philosophical difficulty is inherent in historical understanding: the grasping of any earlier horizon of understanding always occurs on the basis of a current preunderstanding that is itself historically conditioned. As part of the relevant historical task, this must itself be elucidated as fully as possible so that it does not enter into the general interpretative process in a covert way. Hence, the interpretation of testimonies of faith—like the encounter with God's word in direct, interpersonal communication—always involves interactive contention between different approaches that are all aimed at grasping the one, common matter of revelation.

b. Apprehension of revelation through reason

can also occur at the level of reflection about which horizon of understanding is likely to be most appropriate to God's word. Thus, the church fathers opted largely for Platonic thought, scholasticism (following Thomas Aquinas) for Aristotelian philosophy, and R. Bultmann for early Heideggerian existential analysis as providing the categorical framework in which the proclaimed word could be most adequately conceptualized theologically. This question about a *valid* (and not just practically *accepted*) categorical framework for theology— which is answered differently at different historical periods—is also an object of the hermeneutic understanding that brings to light the previously unrecognized historical conditionedness of particular statements. However, given the way that hermeneutics understands itself today and its assumption that all truth is in principle relative, one might question whether the search for greater adequacy of the specific forms of thought underlying theological statements can still be properly addressed— in other words, whether the present-day form of hermeneutic understanding satisfactorily reflects the conditions of the possibility of valid (and not just practically accepted) truth claims (see the remarks below on the concept of "first philosophy").

c. Beyond the ways in which reason plays a role directly (a) or reflectively (b) *within* faith, faith as a whole can be considered yet again as *opposed* to reason, especially in the sense of asking whether faith can possibly justify itself before reason. Inquiring into this dimension of their relationship has been understood, up to most recent times, as the essential task of fundamental theology (or of its predecessor, apologetics), and will also be the sole object of consideration in sections 2 and 3 below.

2. Three Basic Issues in Rational Justification of Faith

Central to Christian faith is the affirmation that God's enduringly valid self-communication to humanity was effected as a concrete historical fact. Given this, rational justification of faith is confronted with two fundamental tasks: (a) before the forum of *philosophical* reason, an account must be given about whether postulating such a thing as an enduringly valid revelation is at all meaningful; and (b) before

historical reason, both the possibility and the reality of a fact that is absolute in character, despite the contingent nature of everything historical, must be demonstrated.

More fundamentally, however, it must be asked whether the very attempt at a justification of faith "before reason" is not inadmissible or at least pointless. If, namely, what is understood by this is no purely theological scrutiny of the internal consistency of the statements of faith but a stepping before the "forum" of secular and not (yet) committedly Christian reason, then such a step would seem contrary to important statements in Holy Scripture about the darkness in which reason finds itself when it has not (yet) been seized by faith. Is it at all possible for faith to subordinate itself to the verdict of such secular reason without thereby surrendering itself?

These three basic issues have occupied fundamental theology, or apologetics, from the very start, although with an intensity that varies according to particular historical situations. First, a brief survey of their historical development is required.

3. The Historical Development of the Issues

New Testament

As a reason for prohibiting any extratheological justification of faith, reference is constantly made to the opposition, stressed by Paul, between the "wisdom of the world" and the "foolishness of the cross" (see 1 Cor 1–2). Here, however, it must be considered, first, that according to Paul the cross also has its understandability (see 1 Cor 1:18: *logos tou staurou*), and, second, that the "inexcusability" associated with the ungodly in Rom 1:20 presupposes, on the godly side and in principle, the possibility of understanding. Finally, it should be noted how strongly Paul emphasizes the need for reasoned explanation of religious discourse precisely with a view to those who are still uninstructed (cf. 1 Cor 14:14–19, 23–25). The first comprehensive attempt to justify Christian faith before secular reason may be seen in the two-volume Lukan work, whose author interprets the coming of salvation with Jesus Christ as the decisive fact of universal history. Rightly viewed as a guidepost for all apologetics and fundamental theology is the appeal, already voiced at the time of the first persecutions of Christians by the citizens of Rome, to be constantly ready to provide an account of the rational ground (*logos*) of Christian hope (cf. 1 Pt 3:15).

Patristicism

During the early period of the APOLOGISTS, Justin Martyr answered this appeal in an exemplary way. If his (first) "apology" (ca. 150) is directed to the Roman emperors, this does not mean that he simply subordinates his work to their judgment. Rather, he adverts to the universal tribunal of the divine Logos, which those he addresses also stand under. His detailed proof that the words and deeds of Jesus Christ had been proclaimed in advance by the prophets, and are thus certified by the Logos, is carried out in such a way as to enable him to show both the agreement of Christian revelation with the best in philosophy and the distortion of the true Logos in the theistic myths underlying the official Roman religion.

Faced with the penetrating criticisms made by the philosopher Celsus, ORIGEN, in his wide-ranging apology *Contra Celsum* (completed in 248), had to defend not only the meaning of Christian revelation but also the facts that are crucial to its uniqueness. The credibility of the miracles and the resurrection of Jesus is ultimately demonstrated, according to Origen, by the force of the testimonies of Jesus' followers, who were prepared to stand by what they proclaimed to the point of death.

Scholasticism

A characteristic aspect of the patristic justification of faith before reason is the fact that philosophy was not, at the time, viewed as an independent discipline vis-à-vis theology. This was reinforced by the widespread saying that the ancient philosophers had drawn on the texts of the OT. Again, ancient philosophy, especially in the Platonic tradition, had also understood itself to be theology. Given all this, it was easy for Christian theology to consider itself the replacer or fulfiller of philosophy.

In the early stages of scholasticism, however, as a consequence of relatively independent study of the *artes liberales* (especially at the cathedral schools, which had assumed leadership of the educational sphere from the eleventh century on), philosophy came to be recognized as a discipline methodologically distinct from theology. Still, this recognition occurred in quite varying forms, among which the approaches adopted by ANSELM OF CANTERBURY and THOMAS AQUINAS are particularly prominent.

The comprehensive inquiry into faith that was undertaken by AUGUSTINE already had as its motto *credo ut intelligam*, "I believe—in order that I may understand." In striving to uncover the rationality inherent in faith, this church father attempted—with a view, for instance, to late Platonic skepticism—to show that human reason, even in the act of doubting everything, is an image of the threefold God (see especially *Civ. Dei*, 11.26). This approach to justifying faith was continued by Anselm of Canterbury, though now, in view of the changed conception of scientific knowledge, with greater methodological and systematic consistency. According to his program of a *fides quaerens intellectum* ("faith seeking understanding"), sinful reason obscures to itself what is in fact its most essential possibility and actuality. When opened up to itself by faith, however, it can discover, through *rationes necessariae* and without recourse to the prescriptions of faith, its referredness to the God of Christian revelation. Stamped in the image of the threefold God, it is able to attain its end only through approximation to its archetype (*Monolog.*). In human reason's characteristic attempt to transcend all things, the existence becomes manifest of that *quo nihil maius cogitari potest* ("that reality greater than which none can be thought") (*Proslog.* 2–4; → GOD II). The essence of freedom consists in the affirmation of the good for its own sake (*rectitudo voluntatis servata propter seipsam* ("rectitude observed for its own sake"); *De ver.*; *De lib. arb.*). If freedom fails its essence, then God—as is also demonstrable on necessary rational grounds—can fulfill his plan for creation only through the representative self-sacrifice of his Son (*Cur Deus homo*).

THOMAS AQUINAS arrives at a fundamentally different approach, in which the question about humanity's inner referredness to revelation, or about a structural framework of understanding in which revelation discloses itself as conferring meaning upon human existence, is largely absent. In the context of critical confrontation with Islamic and Jewish scholars who introduced the work of Aristotle to the Christian West in the twelfth century, Thomas believes that he can extract conclusions about reason's natural capacity to know God from the philosophy of this pagan (→ GOD II). Such "natural theology," however, must then be strictly distinguished from "supernatural" revelation, whose central mysteries, like the Trinity and incarnation, essentially transcend human reason's possibilities of understanding. Justifying to reason the meaning of that revelation can imply only the rebutting of any arguments directed against it. The reality of the divine origin of supernatural revelation can be justified before reason solely through external signs, particularly miracles and prophecies, rather in the way that the content of a closed letter is certified as binding by the royal seal impressed upon it (see *Summa contra Gentiles* I, q.1; III, 1.43, a.1).

Modernity and the Enlightenment

An extrinsic relationship between faith and reason was already implicit in Aquinas's approach, with no inner link to the horizon of rational inquiry being ascribed to revelation; while miracles, in particular, appeared interesting solely because of their external value as "evidence," but no longer because of their meaning as signs. The view of revelation as something externally imposed on reason was considerably reinforced in the following period, first through the nominalistic conception of a voluntaristic God who, in his "potentia absoluta," is bound by no rational laws, and again through the image presented by Christian churches during the religious wars and absolutistic regimes that followed them, where whatever offered itself as binding Christian doctrine on the basis of the currently reigning constellation of state and church was regarded as positively revealed.

Owing to this, questions about such things as the possibility, in principle, of revelation's being binding on autonomous reason, or the meaningfulness or knowability of miracles, were posed with degrees of precision that varied according to the political environment — cautiously, at first, by the founders of English deism (Herbert of Cherbury, John Toland); then

in a spirit of radical hostility to the church by the forerunners of the French Revolution (Voltaire, the encyclopedists); and finally with increasing conceptual precision in the German-speaking countries, where, toward the end of the eighteenth century, relatively favorable conditions for an open dialogue between theology and philosophy began to emerge (Lessing, Kant, Fichte). The breakdown of trust in church tradition, along with the rise of historical criticism, had the result that not only the *meaning* of revelation but also the *fact* of original Christian revelation came increasingly under question, above all in the area of research on the life of Jesus that was introduced by H. S. Reimarus.

New Approaches and Reversals in the Nineteenth and Twentieth Centuries

Discussion of the relationship between reason and revelation took on a new perspective — as contrasted with that in the age of the Enlightenment — when, at the start of the nineteenth century, a move occurred toward more penetrating reflection on history as the lived dimension of human existence and the medium of any encounter with God (romanticism, German idealism). At first, important new departures in rational justification of faith, such as those by the Tübingen school (J. S. v. DREY, J. A. Möhler, J. E. v. Kuhn), by the circle around A. Günther and J. N. Ehrlich, by J. H. NEWMAN, and finally, at the end of the nineteenth century, in the philosophy of BLONDEL (→ IMMANENCE), made little headway against the dominant neoscholasticism favored by the church's doctrinal office (→ MODERNISM). Not until the second half of the twentieth century, and then primarily as a result of the revitalization of theological thought by the Second Vatican Council, did important aspects of these new departures gain effective recognition, coming under study for the first time in the Catholic sphere, along with the lively debate about the relation between reason and faith that had taken place, and was continuing, in the Protestant churches (Schleiermacher, liberal theology, dialectical theology, G. Ebeling, W. Pannenberg).

The Current State of the Question

In the present-day debate about the relationship between reason and faith, the need for an anthropological mediation of revelation is generally acknowledged. Having been influenced (via P. Rousselot and J. Maréchal) by M. Blondel, K. RAHNER initially pursued this question about the "hearer of the word" in the framework of a metaphysics of knowledge intended to achieve a reconciliation between Thomas Aquinas and Kant. In recent decades, however, under the influence of hermeneutics, linguistic philosophy (particularly after the late Wittgenstein), and sociocritical theory of discourse (J. Habermas), the search for structures of understanding constitutive of a universal, transtemporal reason conceived in relation to the individual subject was increasingly replaced by a concentration on the transcendental constitutedness of reason in its intersubjective, historical nexus of language and communication. From this perspective, the question—as posed by apologetics and fundamental theology—about justification of faith *before* reason appears relatively abstract and secondary in contrast to reflection—based on the inescapable pre-givenness of language for all modes of realizing human existence (including faith and theology)—about reason as it has already come to expression in any such instance.

On the one hand, analysis of this a priori factor can be directed (in the manner of hermeneutics and linguistic philosophy) primarily at the general linguistic structures of theological discourse (narrative theology, theology as autobiography, metaphor as the irreducible form of theological statements). On the other hand, however, the tradition of prophetic criticism suggests going beyond that (in the manner of critical theory of discourse) to inquire into the linguistic a priori of theology and its institutions, in the sense of how currently established power structures are expressed or concealed in such pre-givens (political theology, theology of liberation, feminist theology).

This turning of the anthropological mediatedness of revelation to the purposes of criticism of existing power structures, regarded as urgently necessary in the present-day debate, is nevertheless itself subject to the question of how valid standards can be obtained for its critical enterprise. The difficulty of this question is increased by the fact that, within the horizon of hermeneutics and linguistic philosophy, the search for comprehensively *valid* (not just historically *accepted*) standards seems idle. If linguistic criticism does not want to move in a

vicious (and not just hermeneutic) circle, then the problem of a "first philosophy," aimed at determining ultimately valid standards, presents itself as a means of orientation for hermeneutic understanding. Although there have been some important approaches (primarily along the lines of K.-O. Apel's transcendental pragmatics) to solving this problem (see Peukert; Hofmann), no systematically convincing treatment has (to this author's knowledge) yet been achieved.

In this outline of contemporary discussion of the relationship between reason and faith, what is essentially in focus is the MEANING of religion and revelation. Usually, the concrete conformation of faith is taken as the starting point for inquiry into either the "secular" structures of understanding implicit in it or the contribution made by Christian revelation to "post-Christian" thought, instead of something like an undialectical opposition between faith and "natural reason" being presupposed.

The question of how to justify affirmation of an ultimately valid historical fact before historical reason seems to have reached a certain stagnation today. An extrinsic approach to this task, by way of "external arguments of revelation" (see DS 3008), is rightly rejected as inappropriate on the basis of the newly formed concept of revelation in *DV* 1. Currently, fundamental theology believes that the demand for a justification before historical reason can be largely met as an offshoot of the "new search for the historical Jesus" that has been taken up since Bultmann. Scarcely given due consideration here, however, is the old dilemma— emphasized by Lessing, Kierkegaard, and dialectical theology—that the merely probable results of historically objectivizing research yield no appropriate foundation for providing an account of an unconditional commitment. Pathways toward a more adequate treatment of the question of the "factum Christianum" are emerging at present only in rough outline (Stuhlmacher; Verweyen).

Bibl.: W. GEERLINGS, "Apologetik und Fundamentaltheologie in der Väterzeit," in *HFT* 4:317–33; G. LARCHER, "Modelle fundamentaltheologischer Problematik in Mittelalter," in *HFT* 4:347–72; M. SECKLER, "Theologie als Glaubenswissenschaft," in *HFT* 4:180–241; W. KASPER, "Die Wissenschaftspraxis der Theologie," in *HFT* 4:242–77; M. SECKLER and M. KESSLER, "Die Kritik der Offenbarung," in *HFT* 2:29–59; E. CORETH, ed., *Christliche Philosophie im katholischen Denken des 19. und 20. Jahrhunderts*, 3 vols. (Graz, 1987, 1989); W. PANNENBERG, *Theology and the Philosophy of Science* (1973; Philadelphia, 1976); H. PEUKERT, *Wissenschaftstheorie Handlungstheorie Fundamentale Theologie* (2nd ed.; Frankfurt, 1978); J. B. METZ, *Faith in History and Society: Toward a Foundational Political Theology* (New York, 1979); F. SCHÜSSLER FIORENZA, *Foundational Theology: Jesus and the Church* (New York, 1984); H. VERWEYEN, *Christologische Brennpunkte* (2nd ed.; Essen, 1985); id., "Fundamentaltheologie: zum 'status quaestionis,'" *TP* 61 (1986): 321–35; P. STUHLMACHER, *Vom Verstehen des Neuen Testaments: eine Hermeneutik* (2nd ed.; Göttingen, 1986); P. HOFMANN, *Glaubensbegründung: Die Transzendental-philosophie der Kommunikationsgemeinschaft in fundamentaltheologischer Sicht* (Frankfurt, 1988).

Hansjürgen VERWEYEN

REDEMPTOR HOMINIS (Encyclical)

Just as *ECCLESIAM SUAM* was Paul VI's programmatic encyclical, so *Redemptor Hominis* is the programmatic statement of John Paul II. But while *Ecclesiam Suam*, which appeared while the council was in progress, is focused on the church, *Redemptor Hominis*, which appeared in 1979, is focused on Christ—and with good reason, since the historical context had radically changed in fifteen years. The most serious problems that the church and theology now had to face were problems of Christology. Under the influence of *Redemptor Hominis*, and not long after its publication, the International Theological Commission devoted its sessions in 1981, 1982, and 1983 to problems of Christology. People are today asking the most important of all questions: Was Christ truly God among us, in the flesh and language of Jesus? Is he really the one who alone can give meaning to our lives and an answer to our cries for help (in loneliness, otherness, suffering, evil, death)? Can he bring light into the depths within us and solve the riddle we are to ourselves? Is he truly, in the strict sense of the word, the "savior" of human beings, "salvation" in person? The encyclical *Redemptor Hominis*

seeks to answer these questions about the human person.

From its beginning the encyclical sets Christ before us as "the center of the universe and of history" (no. 1) and as redeemer of humankind and the world (no. 7). The encyclical is thus a kind of charter of the dignity of the *new human being* created by the blood of Christ.

Through the incarnation God has entered into the history of the human race:

> As a human being, [he] became one of its "subjects," one among countless others and, yet, always one who was unique. By means of the incarnation, God has given human life the meaning he intended it should have for the human person from the very beginning, He has given this meaning, moreover, in a definitive way. (no. 1)

Through *redemption*, the bond of friendship with God, which had been broken by man-Adam, was restored by Man-Christ (no. 8). More than any other, it is the human being in the age of progress who has need of *salvation*. "The world of this new age—the world of space flight and of hitherto unachieved scientific and technological conquests—" is at the same time a world that groans and looks for its own liberation (no. 8). The redeemer has in a unique and incomparable way entered "into the mystery of the human being . . . and reached the 'heart' of the human person" (no. 8). At this point John Paul II cites GAUDIUM ET SPES: "In reality it is only in the mystery of the Word made flesh that the mystery of man truly becomes clear" (no. 22). Christ alone, especially in his death on the cross, reveals to human beings the infinite love the Father has for them (no. 9).

> Human beings, therefore, who desire a profound understanding of themselves . . . must betake themselves to Christ with their anxieties and doubts, their weaknesses and sins, their life and their death. They must, as it were, enter into Christ with all that they are; they must "appropriate" and make their own the entire truth of the incarnation and redemption if they are to find themselves once again. (no. 10)

And the church, which unceasingly meditates on the mystery of Christ, "knows with the certainty of her faith that the redemption wrought by the cross has once and for all given human beings back their dignity and restored meaning . . . to their lives in this world" (no. 10).

When we familiarize ourselves with the mystery of redemption, we penetrate to the deepest part of the human person: the realm of the heart, of conscience, of life.

The third part of the encyclical deals not only with the human person and the human condition in general but more specifically with contemporary humanity. John Paul II has no doubt that Christ is the way for the human race at the end of the second millennium, because "salvation is in him alone" (no. 7).

The one goal that the church of today has is "that every person should find Christ" and "that Christ should make the journey of life with each individual in the power of the truth regarding man and the world that is contained in the mystery of the incarnation and redemption, and in the power of the love that radiates from this mystery" (no. 13). The church's concern is to lead human beings to Christ. This is why the encyclical can say, on the one hand, that "human beings are . . . the primary road the Church must travel in carrying out her mission: a road which Christ himself has opened up and which always leads through the mystery of the incarnation and redemption" (no. 14). For through his incarnation and redemption the Son of the Father is the sole *way* to the Father for human beings and the church, while human beings are the *way* the church must necessarily travel in carrying out its mission of gathering and saving the whole of the human race (no. 14).

Human beings today need Christ and his gospel because, despite all the technical progress that has been made, it is not clear that they have become more fully human. They live in fear, afraid that the fruits of their technical skills may turn into the instruments of their destruction. The encyclical asks: Has progress made them more "human," more mature spiritually, more responsible? Have the victories they have won been matched by a spiritual and moral progress? Is the human race moving in the direction of selfishness or of love? The idea of progress is a very ambiguous one. The church asks and must ask these questions if it is to be faithful to the gospel, for the church's mission is one of responsibility for human beings (nos. 15–16).

To all appearances, the world of technical progress still seems far from responsive to the demands of the moral order, of justice and love, far from thinking that "ethics is more important than technology, the person more important than things, and the spirit more important than matter." The essential thing, after all, is not to "have more" but to "be more." Is not the modern world like a vast illustration of the parable of poor Lazarus and the rich banqueter, with its scandalous contrast between affluent and starving societies? "Economic progress" should not become the sole criterion of "human progress." The present situation must change, but it will change only if human beings have a sense of moral responsibility and of respect for the "dignity and freedom" of each person (no. 16). The universal Declaration of Human Rights must not remain a dead "letter" but be made a reality in the "spirit" (no. 17).

René LATOURELLE

REINCARNATION

1. Various Forms of the Same Belief

Belief in reincarnation is belief that the soul, or psychic element in the human person, acquires a different body in successive lives and thus is "reincarnated." This belief is related to, but distinct from, belief in metensomatosis or transmigration and belief in metempsychosis. Belief in reincarnation is shared by several Eastern traditions (e.g., Hinduism and Buddhism) and, in the Greek tradition, by Orphism, Plato, and Pythagoras. The Theosophical Society and spiritualist and occultist groups developed a Western model of the belief at the beginning of the twentieth century; this model is widespread today. It is necessary, however, to distinguish between the various forms of the belief and to point out their meaning. It will be seen that while the Eastern and Greek forms are similar to each other, the direction taken by the Western form is quite different.

In Hinduism, in which the belief in reincarnation goes back to the Upanishads, successive reincarnations are governed by the law of *karma*, that is, the accumulation of merits and demerits in the course of previous incarnations. Incarnations will cease only when the chain of effects and causes is broken. The soul must free itself from *saṃsāra* by at last discovering the truth, i.e., by freeing itself from *māyā*, the illusion that the world is real. The soul will then experience enlightenment, blessedness, *samādhi*.

The experience of Gautama Sakyamuni, who became the Buddha (the Enlightened), is summed up in the "Four Noble Truths." Human beings must free themselves from suffering. To do this, they must suppress craving, or desire related to pleasure, which inevitably leads to further reincarnations. For craving, which is due chiefly to ignorance, engenders covetousness, hatred, and error, the "three roots of evil," from which spring actions and their fruits. Liberation through extinction of craving is a lengthy process that often requires more than the span of a human life. It leads to *nirvāṇa*, to protection against all suffering and all transmigration.

According to the Orphics, hardly has the soul left one body when it is reincarnated in another; the body (*sōma*) is looked upon as a prison (*sēma*). The cycle of reincarnations is unending for the noninitiated; the salvation of human beings consists in the cessation of these successive lives. For Pythagoras, too, human beings must be reincarnated in order to reach at last the complete purification of their being. Plato, for his part, thinks that some souls must even be reincarnated in animals if they are to achieve the purity needed for entrance into the abode of the gods. Reincarnation is a slow process of purification from the body and matter in order that the soul may gradually ascend to the divine.

The Western model of reinarnation is a reformulation of the Hindu model; it is syncretist and includes esoteric and occultist traditions. Reincarnation is a means of self-fulfillment and slow ascent to the divine Spirit. Rebirths correspond to a scale of merits; in this way they restore justice and follow a process of continuous ascent.

By comparison with the Hindu, Buddhist, and Greek forms of reincarnation, the Western, theosophical model shows a more optimistic conception of the human person. Reincarnation is not regarded here as a new and painful imprisonment of the soul, a hellish circle from which the soul must free itself, but as a new opportunity. In contrast with the idea of the body as a prison is the idea of an evolution, a development without any regression, since reincarnation is always in a human body.

The different models do, however, have a common substratum. The Hindu or Buddhist philosophy of *karma*, *saṃsāra*, and *mokṣa* (liberation) serves as their basis. Beings must be indefinitely reborn as long as they have not achieved their own liberation. According to the underlying anthropology, human beings consist essentially of a *spirit* (an immortal divine principle) that possesses a soul (to connect spirit with body) and a body (made of perishable matter). They are links in the cosmic chain, from which they must escape if they are to recover their original state and true nature. In addition, there is the conception of history as cyclical, in contrast to the linear conception of history represented by Christianity. Belief in reincarnation is thus part of a comprehensive conception of the human person, the world, and history.

2. Reincarnation or Resurrection

I have spoken of a "belief," and rightly so, for reincarnation cannot be scientifically proved, any more than can the Christian faith in the resurrection of the body. This point needs to be stressed, in view of the claim frequently made in the West that there are scientific, experimental proofs of reincarnation. These supposed proofs are based, on the one hand, on psychic memories or physical traces of earlier lives, and, on the other, on experimental communication with "disembodied" spirits that await reincarnation. There is no denying, of course, the existence of "memories" which a given subject's experience in his or her present life seems unable to explain. But the hypothesis of a previous life that is meant to explain such memories is only one hypothesis among others. The attribution of congenital physiological peculiarities to a previous life calls for even greater caution; there are other, more plausible explanations of these phenomena. Thus, if there are facts still unexplainable in the present state of science, this does not mean that the explanatory hypothesis of reincarnation, however legitimate it may be, can be said to be scientifically proved. It is an object of belief, of an assent springing from personal choice, just as is the Christian faith in the resurrection of the body.

But it is necessary to see clearly the differences between the two positions, as well as the global perspectives in which they have their place. Christian faith replaces the cosmic law of reincarnation with God's promise of resurrection for human beings.

According to the Christian faith, the body is not a negative part of human beings from which they must free themselves; the body is rather an integral part of their humanity. There can thus be no question of sloughing it off in order to acquire another in another life. There is only one life, and it is decisive for every human person, composed as this person is of spirit, soul, and body. Christianity thus highlights the divinely willed dignity of the person and of human life, as well as the power of human freedom.

But this God who personally wills and knows each human person is a loving God who will raise them to life, as he raised his own Son. For death was definitively conquered in the passion and resurrection of Jesus Christ; human beings have been delivered from death, so that there is now no point to reincarnation. In his suffering Jesus took upon himself the *karma* of the whole human race and has freed them from it. It is a fact, of course, that human beings, whose responsibility it is to draw near to God by a life of fidelity, remain subject to death. But this one death is meant to lead to a new form of life, including a new existence for the body as well. The resurrection at the end of time will bring to its ultimate goal the plan of salvation for the entire race, which God has been carrying out in the course of history. In the resurrection of the dead God will do for all human beings what he did on Easter morning for his Son, Jesus. The elect will be conformed, even in their bodies, to the unending life of the risen Christ.

Belief in reincarnation and Christian faith in resurrection are thus irreconcilable. They bring into play different conceptions of God and the human person, of history and the world. A choice must be made between them; this choice is a matter of faith.

Bibl.: A. Des Georges, *La réincarnation des âmes selon les traditions orientales et occidentales* (Paris, 1966); C. A. Keller, *La réincarnation: Théories, raisonnements et appréciations* (Bern, 1986); L.-V. Thomas et al., *Réincarnation, immortalité, résurrection* (Brussels, 1988); J. Vernette, *Réincarnation, résurrection, communiquer avec l'au-delà* (Mulhouse, 1988); id., "La réincarnation: Une croyance ancienne, répandue et séduisante," *Esprit et vie* 98 (1988): 655–62, 677–83, 694–700.

Jacques Dupuis

RELATIVISM, THEOLOGICAL

It is important not to confuse relativism with PLURALISM. Theological relativism reflects the change in mind-set and consciousness that has taken place in the nineteenth and twentieth centuries. Modern society is distrustful of all claims and positions that attempt to grasp the Absolute. Human beings, hitherto prisoners of their own corner of the world and their local traditions, have suddenly found themselves faced with a proliferation of religions and forms of wisdom. The result has been a spate of conflicts, exclusivist claims, and oppositions. People end with divergent positions which they look upon as all equal. This is relativism in its full form.

Relativism in its most general meaning is "the opinion that the truths man knows are valid only in the context of a particular finite system, that is the world of the individual's own sensibility, whereas there are other systems, equally valid, outside it" (K. Rahner and H. Vorgrimler, *Concise Theological Dictionary* [2nd ed.; London, 1981] 436). Relativism carried to this extent is absurd, for any system can then be immediately accused of being false by its opposite.

A relativism that asserts at one and the same time the validity of a claim and the validity of its contrary begets theologies that stand not side by side but face to face. Relativism is seductive in that it seems to "reconcile" the various religions and opposing theological systems. But the thing that is decisive for faith and salvation is objective realities in their relation to human beings, and neither these realities nor human beings are mere theses or abstract statements. Thus the claim that Christ truly rose from the dead is irreconcilable with the position that he did not rise. On the other hand, we can indeed say that we know God "by analogy" and that this fact justifies different approaches and formulations, which bring out better the richness of the reality and prevent us from clinging to a single formulation as though it were the reality itself. Pluralism maintains the identity of the reality being affirmed amid the diversity of expressions, all of which seek to convey the same meaning.

In recent decades there have been two periods during which pluralism seemed to be "flirting" with relativism. The encyclical *Humani*

Generis (1950) saw in the "new theology" signs of a (radical or limited) dogmatic relativism. According to the encyclical, some say that

> the mysteries of faith can never be formulated in notions that adequately express the truth, but only in approximate notions, which, as they say, are always subject to change, by which the truth is indicated up to a point, but at the same time necessarily deformed. Therefore, in their opinion, it is not absurd, rather it is absolutely necessary, that theology should constantly exchange old concepts for new ones, in accordance with various philosophies which it uses as its instruments in the course of time. So theology would express in a human way the same divine truths in different, and even to some extent opposite ways, which, however, they maintain, would mean the same thing. (ND no. 147; Latin text: *AAS* 42 [1950]: 566)

Another, vaguer kind of relativism has cropped up in the postconciliar period, especially in ecclesiology and Christology. With regard to the church, this kind of relativism says: "It matters little which church one chooses, since all have their value; all are responses to the search for salvation that goes on in every human being." In Christology, those who maintain that Christ was only a human being and those who maintain that he was God incarnate will alike claim to be Christians.

In fundamental theology, relativism is encountered chiefly in the kerygmatic theology of R. BULTMANN. Although he retained the major categories of Christianity, such as revelation, faith, miracle, resurrection, and salvation, by demythologizing them, Bultmann emptied them of their historical basis and gave them an entirely different meaning. He believed that this existentialist interpretation was necessary if Christianity is to be acceptable to contemporaries, who are allergic to the NT vision of Christ and his work.

Bibl.: G. LANGEVIN, "Les chances et les handicaps de la foi à notre époque," *ScE* 28/2 (1976): 48–68; J. SPLETT, "Relativisme," in *SM* 5:242–43; R. LATOURELLE, *Christ and the Church: Signs of Salvation* (New York, 1972); id. *Finding Jesus through the Gospels* (New York, 1979); M. B. SCHEPERS, "Relativism (Theological Aspect)," *NCE* 12:223–24; K. RAHNER, H. VORGRIMLER, in *Dictionary of Theology* (New York, 1981), 308–9.

René LATOURELLE

RELIGION

I. RELIGION: DEFINITION

1. Introduction

The term "religion" brings to mind different ideas for different people. Some consider it belief in God or the act of praying or of participating in the ritual. Others understand it to be the act of meditating on something divine; still others think that it has to do with emotional and individual attitude to something beyond this world. There are some who simply identify religion with morality. The way of studying the religious life of humanity depends to a large extent on one's experience with what one calls religious. Any scientific study of religion begins with a certain idea of religion, which leads to distinctions between what is religious and what is not religious. This advances research to make it more precise and critically more acceptable.

2. A Descriptive Definition

According to Cicero's well-known etymology of the term, the Latin word *religio* is derived from *re-ligere*, meaning "to be attentive," "to ponder and observe," "to keep together," as opposed to *negligere* ('to neglect, undermine"). Thus, religion means the conscientious fulfillment of duty, awe of higher power. The later apologist Lactantius (ca. 260–340 C.E.) believed that the word derived from *re-ligare*, meaning "to bind, hold together"– a close and lasting relationship to the divine. The human is connected to God by the bond of religiosity. In this perspective religion is a fact that enters in the domain of interiority and of human sentiment. Although there is no certainty about the correctness of these derivations, the latter was adopted by Augustine and dominated the theological views of the Middle Ages. Both meanings can be integrated to indicate the double aspect of religion—namely, the objective and subjective dimensions of the religious experience. The most important event that occurred in the later history of the word "religion" in Western culture is the transformation of its meaning from a primary reference to the ritual practice of a specific cult to a basic reference to a total system of beliefs and practices operating in a given society. The complexity and diversity of human religions, as well as the profound and ambivalent feelings they arouse, have produced a heterogeneous set of definitions of religion, many of which include evaluative assumptions and emphasize unduly one aspect of religious systems.

The word "religion" had its origin in pre-Christian language but entered Christian linguistic usage both in the Latin version of the Bible (the Vulgate) and in the writings of the Latin fathers of the church. In medieval Christianity, religion in its supreme and greatest degree signified monastic life with the three vows of poverty, chastity, and obedience. Hence, the religious person par excellence is the monk or the nun, and the religious state was considered the state of perfection.

Religion includes not only the beliefs, customs, traditions, and rites that belong to particular social groupings; it also involves individual experiences. Any conception of religion that stresses the communal aspect of religion to the exclusion of the individual's psychic life is defective since it is the individual's personal apprehension of the sacred or the divine that constitutes one of the most important features of religion. According to James Frazer, religion is "a propitiation or conciliation of powers superior to man which are believed to direct and control the course of nature and of human life. Thus defined, religion consists of two elements, a theoretical and a practical, namely a belief in powers higher than man and an attempt to propitiate or please them." He further explains that "belief clearly comes first, since we must believe in the existence of a divine being before we can attempt to please him. But unless the belief leads to a corresponding practice, it is not a religion but merely a theology" (*The Golden Bough* [abridged ed., London, 1925], 50).

Emile Durkheim puts emphasis on belief and practice within a social community:

A religion is a unified system of beliefs and practices relative to sacred things, that is to say, things set apart and forbidden—beliefs and practices which unite into one single moral community called a Church, all those who adhere to them. The second element of the definition is not less essential than the first; for by showing that the idea of religion is inseparable from that of the Church, it makes it clear that religion should be an eminently collective thing. "(*The Elementary Forms of the Religious Life* [Glencoe, Ill., 1954], 47).

The sociological theory developed by Durkheim claims that when individuals have the religious feeling of standing before a higher power that transcends their personal lives and impresses its will upon them as a moral imperative, they are indeed in the presence of a greater environing reality. This reality is not, however, a supernatural being; it is the natural fact of society. The encompassing human group exercises the attributes of deity in relation to its members and gives rise in their minds to the idea of God, which, in effect, is thus a symbol for society itself. There are many difficulties with this sociological theory of religion. It does not account for the universal reach of the religiously informed conscience, which on occasion goes beyond the boundaries of any empirical society and acknowledges a moral relationship to human beings as such. In the teaching of the great prophets, monotheism is brought home very powerfully: God loves *all* persons and summons all humans to care for one another as kin. This goes beyond the scope of an empirical society as used in the sociological theory, for humanity as a whole is not a society according to this theory. It also fails to account for the moral creativity of the prophetic mind. The moral prophet goes beyond the established ethical code and summons followers to acknowledge new and far-reaching claims of morality on their lives. Besides, this theory fails to explain the socially detaching power of conscience. An individual can be at variance with society with regard to many aspects of human life.

According to R. H. Thouless, any adequate definition of religion should include at least three factors: a mode of behavior, a system of intellectual beliefs, and a system of feelings. In order to find a complete and satisfactory definition of religion we must further inquire what is the particular mark of the conduct, beliefs, and feelings in question that characterizes them as religious. Thus, a definition might be the following: Religion is a felt practical relationship with what is believed in as a superhuman being or beings. Thouless explains the two terms that are important in the psychological study of religion: religious consciousness and religious experience. Religious consciousness is that part of religion which is present to the mind and is open to examination by introspection. It is the mental state of religious activity. Religious experience is a vaguer term used to describe the feeling element in religious consciousness—the feelings that lead to religious belief or are the effects of religious behavior. It is impossible to study religious consciousness alone; we have to investigate religious behavior as well (*An Introduction to the Psychology of Religion* [Cambridge, 1936], 3–4). According to William James, religious life consists in the belief that there is an unseen order and that our supreme good lies in harmoniously adjusting ourselves thereto. This belief and this adjustment are the religious attitude of the soul (*Varieties of Religious Experience* [New York, 1928], 26ff.).

N. Söderblom argued that the essential element in religion is neither formal belief nor organized worship but a response to the "tabu-holy" (*Das Werden des Gottesglaubens* [Leipzig, 1916], 211). Religion must mean, therefore, the human response to that power which one regards as sacred. The sacred in general is defined as the opposite of the profane. As soon as one attempts to give a clear statement of the nature, the modality, of that opposition, one finds difficulty. No formula, however elementary, will cover the labyrinthine complexity of the facts (Roger Caillois, *L'Homme et le sacré*, cited in Eliade, *Patterns of Comparative Religion* [London, 1958] xxi). Among the facts of this complexity Eliade includes taboo, ritual, symbol, myth, demon, God, etc. Religion differs from all other aspects of social life such as psychological, sociological, anthropological, because it is concerned with systems of belief as well as systems of relationship and action and because its systems of action are themselves directed to the sacred. In all societies people believe that the processes of nature and the success of human endeavor are under the control of supernatural beings beyond the range of everyday experience, whose intervention can change the course of events.

The general definition of religion designates relations of humanity to the sacred, the divine. Religion is the conscious and effective recognition of an absolute reality (the sacred or the divine) on which humanity is existentially dependent either in submission to it or in total or partial identification with it. This definition distinguishes religion from magic, which makes the divine submissive to the human; it includes theism (submission to God) and pantheism or panentheism or monism (a certain identification with the Absolute).

As religion consists in a relation of humanity to something that is felt by humans to be "absolutely the other," this "other" is presented in many ways as power, as person, as Absolute Reality, etc. Religion is not simply a human fact. In the religious experience a force felt to be superior to humanity intervenes in human life. Humanity itself feels unable to achieve what one wants by one's own power; hence the human person desires that the superhuman, supernatural Being responds to human aspirations in some way—however this intervention is conceived of in different religions. There is no pure natural religion: i.e., religion is not merely made by humans; religion is not merely human aspiration to the divine but also involves some kind of response to human aspirations on the part of the divine; a certain revelation is implied in this response. The religious person either himself or herself establishes symbols and rituals to ensure the divine intervention or historically receives from various kinds of mediations and intermediaries the divine response and help in realizing the goal of religion. The manifestation and intervention of the divine in human life and history have been called by historians of religions "hierophanies" (Mircea Eliade). The most sublime hierophany known to history is the incarnation as realized in Jesus Christ.

3. Religion and Magic

We have to distinguish clearly religion from magic. Scholars have indicated many points on this distinction that are included here; the most important ones being the following:

a. The attitude of humanity. Religion represents a submissive mind, whereas magic represents an overbearing, self-assertive attitude; it is submission versus control. A religious person treats the supernatural as subject, whereas a magician treats it as object. Magic consists in forcing the Numen; religion is submission—two wholly different psychological reactions, two different compartments of one large whole, which is supernaturalism. The essence of magic is admittedly coercion in the interests of one's imperative organic needs; genuine magic is supposed to enable one to influence the course of events by purely psychic means.

b. Relation to society. Religion is a matter for society, the church, whereas magic is the affair of an individual—organized cult versus individual practice. It is the unofficial practitioner who is the witch; in magic the individual is in the forefront.

c. The instrument. Magic is a technique that is supposed to achieve its purpose by the use of medicines; if they are used as mere tools, as a specific type of device, for attaining certain ends, then we are dealing with magic.

d. Purpose. Nearness or unity with the divine is religion; goals in life are envisaged by magic—means to an end. That is, magic, while an end in itself, represents religion. As a practice, magic is the utilization of this power for public or private ends; magic consists of actions expressive of a will for reality.

e. The additional factor. Personal beings of a mood versus powers calculable. Recognition of a transcendental order versus no transcendental reference to external supramundane powers. Whatever is addressed to nameless power is magic. The essential difference between magic and religion seems to be whether an action takes place as an *opus operatum* of itself or whether it addresses itself to a higher will, through which it strives to see its intention fulfilled. Religion is belief in some power in the universe greater than that of humanity itself. Magic is occult science; it is a reference to occult power.

In conclusion, magic differs from religion in that magic is manipulative in essence—although the manipulation is conducted in an atmosphere of fear and respect, marvel and wonder, similar to that which characterizes religious attitude. Religion means a direct action from the point of view of the agent, whereas magic can never be a direct method. For without an instrument there is no magic; one can never speak of "magic by nature." Magic is all devices, i.e., instruments.

In this context we have to make clear that although we do find phenomena that are religio-magical, we also come across cases where religious phenomena are not mixed with magic in any way. There are also cases in which magic alone is present without any mixture of religion.

4. Religion and Revelation

Among all religions, including the primitive religions, there is a consciousness of divine action. Among all known tribes and peoples are to be found in varying degrees both ascetical exercises and divine action in the religious practice. But among the primitive people the calling of the deity, its action in their life is acknowledged as the essential part of religion. Humanity's need of God asserts itself in many ways. This is especially seen in the higher religions more directly in what we call a type of religion that experiences and accentuates divine activity or prophetic revelation. In these manifestations there is a powerful intrusion of the divine into the human sphere.

Does God seek humanity or does humanity seek God? The alternative appears a foolish one. The right answer was given by the poet-mystic Rumi when he wrote that it is God himself who speaks in human invocation and prayer. In the Zoroastrian religion the former alternative is preferred. God sought out the chosen prophet, manifested himself to him, and called him to his work. It was rather the divine power that came to him to acknowledge the Ahura-mazda as the One unique supreme Being. Thus Zoroaster by a divine calling became the prophet of his people and his message became a revealed religion.

Prophetic religion in Israel is a founded religion, not a culture religion, ennobled by the intellect and religious feeling. It starts from a hisoric personality to whom it never ceases to refer. The importance of Moses as the founder of a relatively high form of ethical religion is recognized by all scholars of religion.

The Old Testament presents elevating and inspiring thought of God and a passionate zeal for love and justice; besides, its faith finds foundation or corroboration through historic events.

These characteristics have been intensified and brought to completion in the Gospel and in the Christian church. The truth of Christianity is indissolubly connected not only with an event, but with a person in history, Jesus of Nazareth. The exclusive claims of the Gospel and the church to have the truth and that of the man Jesus in the Fourth Gospel to be himself the truth, enhance the uniqueness of revealed religion. The fellowship established by Christ, the Redeemer, between the lost human soul and God, its creator, the new fellowship binding men together around the Savior in an eternal brotherhood, came into being with the Lord's preaching and mighty acts. When it was accomplished on the cross, the prisoners of sin, the world, and death were delivered and united into a new humanity. Its real center is a living personality, the incarnate Son, the risen Lord, who is the center of Christianity.

Very different is the case of Muhammad, who claimed to be simply a messenger of God Allah. He was convinced that a sacred book distinguishes the true religion from heathenism, and hence he gave his people the Qur'an, the eternal Word of God. God has announced his will through many prophets, and Muhammad is the prophet of Allah. He did not claim for his person moral perfection or superhuman mediation. He was only a man like others, only a preacher, the first Muslim (believer). He had sinned and needed forgiveness.

The Asian religions of Hinduism and Buddhism propose a different type of revelation, which is the direct and immediate experience of God or the Absolute in mysticism. Hence they are called mystical, as distinct from prophetic religions. Their sacred writings do not contain an account of God's dealings with humanity in history, but are rather a gradual human realization of the being of God and of humanity. It is humanity's search for the Real, the Light, and the Immortal, both in himself and in the world that surrounds him: "From the unreal lead me to the Real; from darkness lead me to light; from death lead me to immortality" (Brh. Up. 1.3.28).

Revelation signifies a free opening of God onto humanity; this is indispensable to every religion, given the fact that one cannot reach by oneself the knowledge of the absolute transcendence of God. Every religion as it exists in reality expects some intervention of God or of a supernatural being as response to the human search for the divine. Revealed religion is that in which God has revealed himself in a definite historical moment to a man who is a founder or a specialist of the sacred, e.g., Christianity, Islam, Judaism, Zoroastrianism. But Oriental religions can be called "revealed" in a mystical sense, i.e., in direct and immediate experience of God or of the Absolute. All religions are founded on faith, different only in the way in which this faith is justified. The foundation of faith can be an immediate, historical insertion of God who reveals his power, his will, and his nature by means of facts and words — or the tradition of the wise, mystics, seers, or ancestors. The faith of these two types is lived most seriously in absolute disponibility before God.

5. Religion and Faith

Religion and faith are linked with each other and are sometimes synonymous. Every believer is convinced of the absolute truth of his or her belief and is disposed to follow the consequences of this conviction, founding it formally and primarily not on verifiable logical or historical arguments but on faith transmitted from one generation to another. This does not mean that religion is fideistic or is based on an opinion insufficiently founded, but has a sense of tradition accepted as valid and authentic in religious matters. It is essential to faith that it has the character of totality of the religious act — not the fruit of a conclusion drawn from phenomena founded on the principle of causality, or a product of the intellect alone or that of the will alone. But it is an attitude of adoration of the soul, the most profound and absolute in the human person in his or her personal center.

W. Cantwell Smith argues that human religious life can be properly understood only if the notion of "religion" as an abstraction is eliminated. The concept "religion" is to be replaced by the two separate concepts of "a cumulative tradition" and "a personal faith." Smith criticizes scholarly attempts to describe a person's religious experience in terms of an impersonal entity called religion. He maintains that because religious phenomena are human expressions one must be sensitive to the particular character of the individual's involvement as one expresses oneself in prayer, ritual, or social responsibility. The investigator must distinguish between a religious person's personal faith and the cumulative tradition that is the object of the study of the historian and morphologist. Human faith can be studied by being sensitive to the living quality of religious persons who have exposed this faith in cultural forms. What Cantwell Smith says about the concept of religion is partly true. We have to take a personalist approach as a corrective to the purely objective studies that have emphasized an empirical methodology. But we understand by religion all that goes with the personal faith of a religious person.

When the awareness of the divine or the sacred becomes the center of personal life, all human functions, abilities, and decisions are informed by the special impact of this experience. As a religious term, faith does not mean what common speech takes it to mean; — i.e., an intellectual and emotional acceptance of something a person does not know with precision and cannot prove. This represents only a secondary character of the life of faith; besides, it shifts the focus from the transcendent source of faith to a concern with rules of logic and methods of empirical verification. These are only secondary considerations when we wrestle with the most profound elements of human experience. Faith is rather a way of living, not merely a way of thinking, that places human existence in the context of the sacred or the divine or the eternal reality. Faith is the self-conscious response to the sacred in all its mystery, revelation, power terrible and fascinating (*mysterium tremendum et fascinans*).

6. "Original" Religion, "Original" Monotheism, and "Original" Revelation

Wilhelm Schmidt, criticizing strongly the evolutionist interpretation of the origin of religion and of the idea of God, claimed that the origin of the human idea of God cannot be found without using a scientifically based historical method to distinguish and clarify various levels of within the primitive societies themselves. In the first volume of his book *The Origin of the Idea of God*, Schmidt argues that the most primitive tribes indicate through their beliefs and cultic practices a distorted but positive reflection of the earliest religious experience — the worship of a "High Being."

According to Schmidt, the foremost mark of the religion of primitive peoples is its fundamental monotheism; the essence of primitive religion consists in the peoples' belief in one Supreme Being, the recognition of their dependence on him, and of their obedience to his laws. The results of this new discovery, that monotheism is to be found in the most ancient religion and is the very heart of it, are diametrically opposed to the old evolutionist view that monotheism only appeared in later religions as a result of a long and complicated development. It must, of course, be held that monotheism is also present in religions, even if lesser deities exist alongside a Supreme Being, provided that it is held that the Supreme Being has created these deities, given them powers, assigned them functions, and will exercise a general superintendence over them. Even where one of these notes of supremacy is absent, monotheism still prevails, but in a weaker form.

"Primitive revelation" is that which the first parents of humanity received from God at the beginning of creation. After the fall they also received revelations about the savior. This revelation has been transmitted to posterity, which explains how humans can have common truths about God and about humanity's relation to God in diverse ways in different grades in the history of humanity. The truths found in other religions would be a residue of this "primitive revelation" (Schmidt). This has not been accepted by scholars, because it is difficult to retrace these truths in various religions and it is impossible to establish the continuity of the primitive tradition across the long human history that separates Adam from Abraham. "Primordial religion" is that which is supposed to have existed at the origin of humanity, either in the sense that this religion was considered to be the most perfect (thus one speaks of original monotheism) and degraded slowly into lower forms of religion (W. Schmidt) or in the sense of minimal state of religion such as animism or preanimisn or totemism, which evolves itself gradually into higher forms of religion such as monotheism (Tyler, Marrett, and Durkheim). Both these senses are not accepted by us for lack of historical evidence.

Although we do not admit Schmidt's primitive monotheism as a theory of the origin of religion, he and his followers have performed a service to the history of religions by stemming the influence of the theory of animism and showing the possibility of the nonanimistic hypothesis of religious origins. He has also shown the existence of the belief in the Supreme Being among the primitives, a fact that has often been neglected or denied by some scholars. In almost all primitive religions the idea of a Supreme Being is certainly found. Often enough this High God is regarded as the Creator and a moral Being who has laid down rules for the right relationships between human beings. We can distinguish two types of monotheism—explicit and implicit. Explicit monotheism is the belief in only one God to the exclusion of all other gods. Implicit monotheism is the belief in one God, only indirectly excluding other supreme Gods. Schmidt's primitive monotheism is implicit and can be admitted as it implies the belief in one supreme Being.

7. Current Critique of Religion

Let us review some of the present-day criticisms of religion, for they help us understand the true nature of religion.

It is alleged that religion involves us in a superstitious reliance on what is called *deus ex machina*, in a false supernaturalism or an outmoded metaphysics. This results in the diminution of human effort and the sense of human responsibility. This criticism has some validity if religion is meant to look on God as a useful problem solver or a convenient explanation for anything that goes wrong, for anything that might not be easily understood, for anything that happens because of human irresponsibility and stupidity. One's religious faith and reason should play much in the way of correcting false or superstitious notions about God or about God's relationship with the world and with human beings. But so long as we pray and worship and talk about the transcendent we are not delivered from the basic religious conviction, which, however we express it, most certainly implies some kind of belief about the way things are. We cannot pray or talk of the transcendent or even of an ultimate commitment without being prepared to state some kind of rationale for these things.

A further objection to religion states that it has to do with the individual's quest for salvation and is hence inherently egocentric. This may be true in some extreme cases but completely misses the point that one's personal salvation in religion is to be obtained through the fulfillment of one's duty to others in whatever state one finds in the name of the religious beliefs themselves. Humans, as social beings, are related to other humans and this relationship finds its profound reason in their personal relationship to God or the Absolute. The objection simply declares that the quest for salvation must have in view nothing less than all humanity. Although this condemns some distortions of religion, it reaffirms the purpose that lies at the heart of all true religion.

Again, it is said that religion easily becomes idolatry, a fetishism in which things meant to serve the cult become the objects of the cult. People fanatically become attached to particular dogmatic formulations or particular institutions. At times rules are absolute and immutable, etc. We have to respond by saying that religion itself carries out the examination of such idols and effects reforms from within. Every religious community has a power to renew itself and from time to time does in fact carry out the program of renewal.

8. Religion and Morality

Kant has shown convincingly that one need not know of God's existence in order to perceive the moral obligation to do good and avoid evil. No human can be excused for his or her evil deeds on the ground of being an atheist or an agnostic. But it does not follow from this that there is no relation between morality and God. "Only the existence of a personal God who is the Infinite Goodness can fulfill the message of moral values, and can ultimately justify the validity of this obligation" (von Hildebrand). Moral laws are not "respectable abstraction" but find their personal embodiment in the living God.

One need not be religious to perceive the absoluteness of moral values; but the religious person because of explicitly relating these values to God not only has a much deeper grasp of their nature but also can apprehend that no purely physical evil such as disease, suffering, starvation, and death can be compared in importance to a single offense against God. Not only are moral values perceived as rooted in God, but the religious person also perceives with clarity that the highest and the most sublime of all moral obligation is the response to God. Many thinkers have perceived that the ultimate seriousness of morality and its categorical character call for the existence of a personal God. The same is true of the fact that religion necessarily embraces morality. "No religion is from God which contradicts one's sense of right and wrong" (Newman). "Religion cannot thrive without ethics any more than ethics can thrive without religion" (von Hügel). Though religion and morality are distinct and religion cannot be simply identified with morality, still they are not separate but mutually inclusive even at the highest level of mysticism.

9. Religion and Mysticism

Mystical experience is primarily a fact charged with significance for the religious life of the mystic, for we must recognize the psychological existence of characteristic states that involve a certain type of consciousness in which the sensory symbols and notions of abstract and discursive thought seem, as it were, annihilated and in which the soul feels itself united in direct contact with the reality it possesses. Mystic feel that they have a deeper perception and greater light in their experience of the sublime reality, whatever it may be. This is the phenomenon that is commonly called mysticism.

The nature of mysticism can be glimpsed from a definition or description of it. First, mysticism is not the occult nor any of the paranormal phenomena such as mind reading, telepathy, or levitation. Although many authentic mystics may have had these powers, they are not essential to the mystical phenomenon as such. In order to include all types of mysticism we can say that mystical experience is a direct apperception of eternal being, whether this eternal being is conceived of in personal terms or simply as a state of consciousness. It is a suprarational, meta-empirical, intuitive, unitive experience of a timeless, spaceless, immortal, eternal "something," whether this something be a personal God, or a suprapersonal Absolute, or a mere state of consciousness. It is the realization of oneness with or in something that transcends the empirical self, whether this oneness be experienced in total identity or in intimate union. The common denominator in different types of mystical experience is the loss of the sense of personality or ego consciousness in a greater whole. Mystics feel themselves to be transplanted beyond time and space into an eternal "now" in which death can have no relevance, and the natural human natural condition is seen to be one of certain immortality.

This being the general definition of mysticism, we can now proceed to distinguish the three types of mystical experience: ecstatic, enstatic, and theist. In the ecstatic type of experience the soul feels itself to be merged in the undying life of all things. In this experience the barrier between the "self" and the "non-self," the experiencing subject and the objective world, seems to vanish, and all is seen as one and one as all. The core of the experience is that individuality itself seems to dissolve and fade away, and this brings joy and peace. This experience can be had by people of all religions and also by people who have no religion at all. Hence it is sometimes called nature mysticism. As a religious expression we see it related to the Zen enlightenment.

The second type of experience, enstatic, is that in which the soul plunges into its own deepest essence, from which all that is phenomenal, transient, and conditioned falls away, and it sees itself as unfractionably one and beyond all the dualities of worldly life. It is the experience of the absolute oneness or of the innermost spiritual essence of the self in its deepest being. When the absolute oneness of the spiritual self is experienced it can become a monist (nondualist) type of experience. The *Upanishads* interpret this as meaning that when one reaches this state, one then realizes that one is actually the Absolute; one is the Godhead itself, of which God is only the semi-illusory first emanation. No religion has any relevance except insofar as it is a pointer to the ineffable One who we all really are. This is the position of non-dualist systems.

The enstatic experience is like the ecstatic one in that in it both time and space are transcended. But whereas in the ecstatic experience the self seems to merge into the world and the world into the self, in the enstatic experience all multiplicity disappears and there is nothing but the unfractionable oneness. In the enstatic state, the unity of being is experienced within the self, an experience of the presence of the immensity of the divine in the soul. This is an experience of the spiritual self in its universality, totality, and expansiveness by the self itself.

The third type is the mysticism of the love of God. In the Hindu experience of supreme *bhakti* (love of God) we meet with this type of experience of the felt participation of the soul in the being of God. By *bhakti* the liberated person realizes God's nature through intuitive knowledge, for he or she knows God as he is in himself. The inmost self is beyond the kind of experience that says, "I want," "I desire," "I know." It has its own way of knowing, loving, and experiencing, which is a divine way, not a human way, a way of union, oneness, "espousal," in which there is no longer a separate psychological individuality drawing all good and all truth toward itself, and thus loving and knowing for itself.

The yogic and the nondualist experience has an immediate and direct contact with the inner center of the spiritual soul in its perfect interiority and totality, with the ultimate ground of the activities of the soul. In reality it is a descent into the very source of the ontological goodness in the being of the created soul. The danger in this type of mysticism is to defy or absolutize the experience of the self. In fact this has been the case of nondualists in India. This mistake is easy to make, unless one knows God either by faith or by experience, one can scarcely fail to mistake the image, once purified by asceticism and a total detachment from all temporal things, for the living God whom the image reflects. In the case of the mysticism of love of God the mystics, by means of intense love for God, experience a mystical union with him. Here a supernatural grace of God is at work, for this type of mysticism cannot be induced by human power of itself. However much humans may try, with all sorts of techniques and means, they will never achieve this mysticism of love which is felt to be a purely gratuitous gift of God. But with regard to the other types, the transcendental experience can be induced by techniques—of yoga, for instance, and by other means.

We have discussed the nature of mysticism and its various types rather at length because of its significance and importance to the contemporary religious scene both in the West and in the East, given the fact of the appearance of new religious sects and new religious movements under the influence of Eastern religions. The important thing to note here is that not all types of mysticism are religious; natural mysticism and profane mysticism have no relation whatsoever to the sacred, to the divine, or to God. They aim at self-perfection in various ways in order to have a greater spiritual mastery over oneself, to improve one's spiritual potency, and to dominate the empirical experience and life in which one finds oneself. These may be legitimate practices and may be useful in the technique of meditation, for instance, and also in the religious disciplines, although by themselves they are not necessarily religious.

Bibl.: W. Schmidt, *The Origin and Growth of Religion* (London, 1930); id., *Primitive Revelation* (St. Louis, 1939); M. Eliade, *Patterns in Comparative Religion* (London, 1958); H. Smith, *The Religions of Man* (New York, 1958); R. Otto, *The Idea of the Holy* (London, 1959); R. C. Zaehner, *At Sundry Times* (London, 1960); id., *Concordant Discord* (Oxford, 1970); G. Van Der Leeuw, *Religion in Essence and Manifestation* (New York, 1963); J. Wach, *The Comparative Study of Religions* (New York, 1963); W. C. Smith, *The Meaning and End of Religion* (New York, 1964); E. E. Evans-Pritchard, *Theories of Primitive Religion* (Oxford, 1965); A. Richardson, *Religion in Contemporary Debate* (London, 1966); L. Newbigin, *Honest Religion for Secular Man* (London, 1966); H. D. Lewis, *Philosophy of Religion* (London, 1967); S. Radhakrishnan, *Religion and Culture* (Delhi, 1968); F. J. Streng, *Understanding Religious Man* (Belmont, 1969); A. Von Hildebrand, *Introduction to a Philosophy of Religion* (Chicago, 1970); W. R. Comstock, ed., *Religion and Man* (New York, 1971); M. Dhavamony, *Phenomenology of Religion* (Rome, 1973); id., "Self-Understanding of World Religions as Religion," *Greg* 54 (1973): 91–130.

Mariasusai Dhavamony

II. Phenomenology of Religion

1. Introduction

First we must clarify the meaning of phenomenology of religion. As we understand it here, it does not refer to the philosophical school represented by Edmund Husserl and his followers such as Heidegger, Sartre, Merleau-

Ponty, which uses the phenomenological method by discussing five central concepts: description, reduction, essence, intentionality, and world. Understood in this way, phenomenology of religion is that part of phenomenological philosophy devoted to the study of religion. Again, phenomenology of religion is not philosophy of religion understood in the Hegelian sense. Hegel tried to organize all human activity such as art, law, religion, and so on, into a system and to apply philosophical methods of study to each sector; the philosophy of religion in this sense deals with the philosophical viability of religious doctrines and seeks to probe beneath the culturally conditioned forms of religious expression to their common presuppositions. In the sense in which we use it here, phenomenology of religion is the systematic treatment of the history of religions whose task is to classify and group the numerous and widely divergent data in such a way that an overall view can be obtained of their *religious* contents and the *religious* meaning they contain. It is better termed historical phenomenology of religion to avoid confusion with the philosophical discipline.

2. Historical Phenomenology of Religion

Chantepie de la Saussaye, one of the founders of the modern comparative study of religion, was the first to introduce phenomenology as a term and a concept within the science of religion (*Lehrbuch der Religionsgeschichte* [1st ed., 1887: "Die Phänomenologie der Religion," 48ff.]). This term is older than his textbook. Kant, Fries, and Hegel used the term in the sense of a philosophical theory about the process of knowledge. We cannot say for certain whether de la Saussaye borrowed the term from these philosophers or not; but he used the term not in the philosophical sense but in the context of the comparative study of religion inasmuch as the historian of religions not only studies separate facts but also compares them to get at their meaning. This usage of phenomenology preceded the development of Husserl's philosophy of phenomenology. De la Saussaye's phenomenology attempted to investigate the essence and meaning of religious phenomena and to group phenomena in a typological manner, independent of space and time. This early

phenomenology of religion was empirical and became a discipline of classification of religious phenomena. He presented a number of religious forms that occur universally and in all periods, such as gods, magic, divination, sacrifice, and prayer; and he has an entire section explicitly on mythology. He sounded a warning against structuralist or depth-psychological methods of discovering the supposedly hidden, unconscious meanings in myths: "It is not our task to find a rational nucleus in irrational stories, but to describe the origin and the development of a myth." However, the phenomenology of religion as treated by E. Lehmann and his contemporaries suffered both from general evolutionistic presuppositions of the time and from theological or antitheological bias.

The first important treatise on the phenomenology of religion was written by Gerardus van der Leeuw, who, respecting the religious data and their peculiar intentionality in his description of them, considered it the main task of the phenomenologist to illumine the inner structure of religious phenomena as specifically religious. But because he was not so much interested in the *history* of religious structures, he did not try to describe the particular structures in specific forms of religious life. Although he had been much influenced by *Gestaltpsychologie* and *Strukturpsychologie*, and Husserl's *Phänomenologie*, he remained a religious phenomenologist insofar as he paid attention in all his interpretations to the religious data as such and to their special intentionality, and he clearly argued for irreducibility of the religious phenomena to social, psychological, or rational functions. He went astray, however, in reducing the totality of all religious phenomena to the three *Grundstrukturen*: dynamism, animism, and deism. The most serious defect of his approach was his neglect of the history of religious structures, for even the most elevated of religious experiences (e.g., mystical experience) presents itself through specific structures and cultural expressions which are historically conditioned. His was not a historical phenomenology, but such shortcomings do not lessen the significance of his work.

The significance of Rudolf Otto's *Das Heilige* (Eng.: *The Idea of the Holy*) in the history of the scientific study of religion consists in the fact that, instead of studying the ideas of God and religion, it analyzes the modalities of the religious experience. Gifted with great psychological subtlety and well trained both as a theologian and as a historian of religions, Otto succeeded at the phenomenological understanding of the specific characteristics of religious experience. He concentrated chiefly on the non-rational aspect of religious experience, passing over its rational and speculative aspect, though not denying it.

The great master in the present-day phenomenology of religion is Mircea Eliade, whose aims and intentions are clearly formulated in his *Traité d'Histoire des Religions.* A religious phenomenon will be recognized as such only if it is grasped at its own level, i.e., if it is studied as something religious. To try to grasp the essence of such a phenomenon by means of psychology, sociology, anthropology, linguistics, or any other study is false; it misses the one unique and irreducible element in it, the element of the sacred. Obviously, there are no *purely* religious phenomena; no phenomenon can be solely and exclusively religious. Because religion is human it must for that very reason be something social, something linguistic, something cultural; one cannot think of humans apart from society, culture, and language. But it would be hopeless to try to explain religion as religion in terms of any one of those basic functions, which are really no more than another way of saying what humanity is. Eliade's books examine phenomenologically the various hierophanies, taking the term in its widest sense as anything that manifests the sacred. They study the various modalities of the sacred and show how they fit together in a coherent system. Religious wholes are not seen in bits and pieces, for each class of hierophanies forms in its own way a whole both morphologically (for it deals with gods and myths and symbols, etc.) and historically (for often the study must spread over many cultures divergent in time and space).

Mircea Eliade's writings have contributed much to what is called religious morphology or genetic phenomenology. He became aware of the serious inadequacy of van der Leeuw's approach and devoted his attention to the specific structures and cultural expressions in which religious life is expressed as they manifest themselves in history. According to Eliade, the task of the phenomenologist consists in understanding and expounding the religious value contained in the different patterns in which the sacred appears, as opposed to that of the profane, through symbols and myths. The pattern of religious behavior reveals itself as the imitation of the creative acts and models of the divine. These structures of awareness are historically and culturally conditioned. Hence his phenomenology can be considered genetic or historical.

It is true that Eliade gives the thematic presentation of certain religious phenomena, largely drawn from archaic and exotic thought forms and compared at the level of symbolism with little reference to their wider historical and social context. This is considered by him to be "history of religions," but his methodological stance clearly indicates his phenomenological leaning.

R. C. Zaehner, in his *At Sundry Times,* comes to grips with the problem of how Christians should regard non-Christian religions and how Christians could correlate them into their own. Zaehner tries to show how the main trend in Hinduism and Buddhism, on the one hand, and of Zoroastrianism, on the other, meet and find their fulfillment in the Christian revelation. He says,

> Christianity does fulfill both the mystical tradition of India as finally expressed in the *Bhagavad-gītā* and the Bodhisattva doctrine, and the hopes of Zoroaster, the Prophet of ancient Iran. In Christ the two streams meet and are harmonized and reconciled as they are nowhere else: for Christ fulfils both the law and the Prophets in Israel and the "Gospel according to the Gentiles" as it was preached in India and Iran.

R. C. Zaehner is showing not how Christianity is a reconstruction of the best elements found in world religions by piecing them together to form a whole but how the religious aspirations of world religions find their completion and fulfillment in the total and Christian revelation.

Geo Widengren considers the phenomenology of religion to be an established usage and approves an overall treatment of it. But its connection with history is essential in order to avoid the difficulty of presenting only a static impression of the religious phenomena. For Widengren, it is self-evident that sometimes there will be an overlapping between history and phenomenology. If the historical setting of the religious phenomena is of special importance for the phenomenological interpretation, then it will be necessary to present the corresponding phenomena in their own structures within a given particular religion. One cannot just pick one detail out of the structure of totality and treat it as typical and compare it with other typical phenomena, especially when a particular aspect of the phenomenon is sharply marked. Besides, the historical development can also be explained within the framework of an overall phenomenological treatment of a comparative nature.

C. J. Bleeker distinguishes three conceptions of the nature of the phenomenology of religion: (1) the older, descriptive school, which is content with classifying and describing the religious phenomena; (2) the typological procedure, by which the different types of religion are sketched and their religious significance brought out, without bothering much about the methodological presuppositions; (3) the phenomenological approach, which consistently applies the phenomenological principles in order to penetrate into the essence and structure of the religious phenomena. Bleeker himself adheres to the last approach. He has proposed three theoretical constructs to describe the task of the phenomenological study of religion. He distinguishes three dimensions in religious phenomena into which the phenomenologist must inquire: (1) the *theoria* discloses the religious meaning of the phenomena; (2) the *logos* of the phenomena penetrates into the structure of different forms of religious life where four different categories may be pointed out (constant forms, irreducible elements, points of crystallization, and typical factors); and (3) *entelecheia* is the phenomena in the way in which an essence reveals itself in the dynamics or development visible in the religious life of humanity.

R. Pettazzoni conceived of religious phenomenology as the religious understanding of history. Religious phenomenology and history are not two sciences but complementary aspects of the integral science of religion. He rightly reacted against a kind of phenomenology that claimed to be free of the inquiry into the historical origin and development of religious facts. He rightly observed that we

should hesitate to divide the science of religion into two different sciences, one historical and the other phenomenological. If the historical method were to insist exclusively on philological inquiry and were unduly interested in the cultural manifestations of religion and not in the essential values of religious life and experience, then it would miss the proper meaning of the religious fact itself. Here, as so often in religious studies, it is a case not of either religious phenomenology or history of religions but of both working in correspondence, analogy, and interconnection. In recent years many scholars have tried to combine both these intellectual operations, since both are equally valuable for an adequate knowledge of the *homo religiosus*.

However, we cannot admit Pettazzoni's theoretical position on religion. Brought up under the influence of Croce's historicism, he held that religion was a purely historical phenomenon and would in the course of time become obsolete and even disappear altogether, just like ancient Greek history or literature, epigraphy, or artifacts.

Some scholars use the term phenomenology of religion in a different sense—i.e., for the study of a particular religion as an organic structure within a certain period, disregarding the historical origin of the various ideas and practices while concentrating on their meaning to the believer. This notion of phenomenology of religion is not commonly admitted. The commonly accepted notion of phenomenology of religion is that it entails the comparative study of religious phenomena, its material being drawn from the history of individual religions. The material is arranged from a systematic rather than a historical point of view. For instance, one asks, What do the various religions believe about God? What ideas of God do we actually find in religions? Or what do they believe about evil, salvation, life after death, and so on?

3. Typology, Structure, Morphology

Phenomenology of religion does not try to compare religions with one another as large units but takes out similar facts and phenomena which it encounters in different religions, brings them together, and studies them in groups. The purpose is to gain a deeper and more accurate insight, for considered together as a group the data shed light on one another. In phenomenology we consider the religious phenomena not only in their historical context but also in their structural connection.

Typology is the study of types. A type is a pattern of traits of an individual, group, or culture that distinguishes it from other individuals, groups, and so on. Types are used on the assumption that they provide a means of classification of persons or groups that is useful for the purpose of analysis. An ideal type is a mental construct composed of a configuration of characteristic elements of a class of phenomena used in the analysis. The elements abstracted are based on observations of concrete instances of the phenomena under study, but the resultant construct is not designed to correspond exactly to any single empirical observation. The ideal type is an important methodological technique, a heuristic device, used to describe, compare, and test hypotheses relating to empirical reality. Such constructed types are made up of criteria (elements, traits, aspects, and so on) that have discoverable referents in the empirical world or can be legitimately inferred from empirical evidence, or both. The constructed type not merely provides a means of ordering data but also serves to facilitate generalization.

Structure is the underlying and relatively stable relationship among elements, parts, or patterns in a unified, organized whole. Structure is a connection that is neither merely experienced directly nor abstracted either logically or causally but is understood; it is an organic whole that cannot be analyzed into its own components but can from these be comprehended. Structure is reality significantly organized, but the significance belongs both to the reality and to the subject who attempts to understand it. It is therefore both intelligibility and understanding.

Morphology is the study of form, pattern, structure, or configuration; an integrated whole, not a mere summation of units or parts. Mental processes and behaviors cannot be analyzed, without remainder, into elementary units, since wholeness and organization are features of such processes from the start. Structure is the composition, arrangement of component parts, and organization of a complex whole, an organized whole, forming units of experience, with reference to the positional and functional interdependence of their parts. Structure function is a property or activity belonging to or dependent on the influence or action of a whole as such, and not on the action of any of the parts in the whole.

In the scientific study of religions the typology of religion is intended in various ways. Here the concept of type indicates something common to various religions and that which is typically unique and peculiar to every religion. When scholars investigate the specific core of individual religions, they seek to do a typology of religion, ascertaining the typical particularities of every single religion. This typology considers religions as wholes and as organisms that become the object of study and considers them from both sides—from the side of how much they typically have in common in their totality and from the side of their typical uniqueness in this totality.

The typology of religions can also be defined as division of religions according to a determinate principle. N. Söderblom, e.g., divided the world religions into animistic, dynamistic, and founded religions. F. Heiler divided them into mystical and prophetic religions. H. Frick divided them into religions of works and religions of mercy. The principle of division need not be necessarily just one; there can be many principles of division, which can differentiate religions in many categories. The purpose of the typology of religions is to explicitate the typically common characteristics that are found in the totality of each religion; i.e., it indicates more than just the typology of religions. There can be more than two or three of these constitutive, common characteristics of the "type" itself. At times the same religion can belong to more than one type. For instance, while Christianity pertains to the type of religion that is founded, prophetic, and of mercy, Islam also belongs to the type of religion that is founded, prophetic, but not to the type of religion of mercy. Hinduism is not of the type of a founded religion or of prophetic religion but one of mystical religions. Thus, there are many types of religions, and one religion can belong to more than one type of religion.

4. Aims of the Historical Phenomenology of Religion

There are several disciplines that deal with the religious phenomena. The philologist strives to interpret correctly the meaning a text that deals with a religious subject. The archaeologist aims at a reconstruction of the plan of an ancient sanctuary or at explaining the subject of a mythical scene. The ethnologist outlines the details of certain religious practices and rituals of "primitive" peoples. The sociologist tries to understand the organization and structure of a religious community and its relations to the secular life. The psychologist analyzes the religious experience of different persons. All these scholars study the religious data within the scope and limits of their own sciences, applying the methods than are proper to their own disciplines. These studies and their results help to widen and deepen our knowledge of religious phenomena but do not deal with the specific and essential nature of these religious phenomena. Since the religious phenomenon is human, it is also cultural, social, and psychological. Hence, it can be studied under the aspect of its cultural, social, psychological, and religious manifestation. Historical phenomenology of religions studies the phenomenon insofar as it is specifically religious, not so much as it is cultural, social, or psychological.

Phenomenology of religion does not confine itself to the verification and the analytical explanation of single data such as are studied separately by the various specialized disciplines. It seeks to coordinate the religious data with one another, to establish relations, and to group the facts according to those relations. If it is a matter of formal relations, phenomenology of religion classifies the religious data under types; if the relations are chronological, it makes them into series. In the former case, the science of religions is merely descriptive; in the latter case when the relationships in question are not merely chronological—when, in other words, the succession of events in time corresponds to an internal development, the science of religion becomes a historical science, the history of religions. It is not enough to know precisely what happened and how the facts came to be; what we want above all to know is the meaning of what happened. This under-

standing of the meaning of the religious phenomena can be obtained at two levels: historical and phenomenological. The historical meaning is common to that of nonreligious phenomena as well; but the phenomenological meaning probes into the religious phenomenon, not merely historical and sociocultural but specifically as religious. Certainly against a history of religions that is exclusively concerned with specialized philological research and interested more in the cultural manifestations of religion than in the essential values of religious life and experience, phenomenology represents a reaction as legitimate as it is laudable. In our view it is both history and phenomenology. Religious phenomena do not cease to be realities historically conditioned merely because they are grouped under this or that structure. Phenomenological understanding (Verstehen) runs the risk of ascribing a like meaning to phenomena whose likeness is nothing but the illusory reflection from a convergence of developments different in their essence; or, on the contrary, of not grasping the similar meaning of certain phenomena whose real likeness in kind is hidden under an apparent and purely external dissimilarity. Phenomenology knows that it depends on history and that its own conclusions always remain susceptible of revision in view of the progress of historical research.

Phenomenology, writes Pettazzoni, "gives the historical disciplines that sense of the religious which they are not able to capture. So conceived, religious phenomenology is the religious understanding (Verständnis) of history; it is history in its religious dimension." For safety's sake it should be made clear that the phenomenologist of religion operates with an understanding on two levels: first, the level of understanding of the place of a religious trait in a sociocultural milieu; second, the level of understanding of the general import of a religious element in a wider context, its theoretical meaning.

The historical phenomenology of religion is an empirical human science, making use of historic and phenomenological research. Its criteria of judgment are not derived from principles of any particular faith, Christian or non-Christian. It does not make value judgments of the phenomena it studies from the point of view of truth or supernatural efficacy; hence, it is not a normative science. It compares the religious phenomena of different religions not at all with the aim of proposing any exclusivism or syncretism. In the historical phenomenology of religion similarities are as important as differences between religions, and the proper and specific character of each religion is to be sustained. It compares only to deepen the meaning of the religious phenomena it studies.

5. The Phenomenological Method

We have explained before that the phenomenologist of religion studies the religious phenomena as specifically religious and concentrates on the religious signification of these data as presented by the history of religions. The religious trait is the most vital aspect of human life to the extent that phenomenologists remain fully away that religion is the deepest and noblest in the realm of human spiritual and intellectual existence, although phenomenologists know their limits in the task of penetrating into the depth of inwardness of a religious soul. Agnostics might claim that only they can be expected to achieve complete objectivity in this field of study, on the plea that they alone might be expected to be free from religious prejudice. Yet quite the reverse appears to be true. A careful reader of A. Dupont-Sommer's work on the Dead Sea Scrolls will realize how untrue such a claim is, for in his anxiety to make the Teacher of Righteousness of the scrolls into an almost exact counterpart of Jesus Christ, Dupont-Sommer permits himself to change, emend, and "complete" the text of the scrolls in a shocking way in what is supposed to be an academic discipline. Religion should certainly be studied rationally, for "reason is God's scale on earth," but it can never be fully grasped by reason alone. God is a tremendous Mystery, as Rudolf Otto points out. Hence, if the phenomenologist of religion does not know from personal experience what it means to pray, his or her view on prayer will be valueless.

Religious facts are subjective in the sense that they are the religious person's state of mind, his or her way of looking at things or interpreting them. At the same time these facts and their interconnections are objective in the sense that they are not the creation of the thinking mind of the religious person but that independent observers could verify them. By a convergence of different acts of understanding we may find out that a tribe holds ceremonies of expiation because it fears the anger of the gods; this conclusion is related to a body of independent evidence. There is the need to exclude the kind of subjectivity that would vitiate a piece of scientific research. Objectivity consists in letting the facts speak for themselves. This is what the principle of *epoché* means in the historical phenomenology of religion.

Epoché means the suspension of preconceived judgment before the phenomenon in order to let it speak for itself. A preconceived judgment or prejudice can be cultural, philosophical, or even theological with respect to other people's religion. Scholars must rid themselves of these prejudices to ascertain objectivity and fair-mindedness in research. They must put their own faith in parentheses; i.e., their faith must not interfere in the understanding of other faiths. Phenomenologists also should have empathy in the encounter with other religions. Empathy (*Einfühlung*) is the power of projecting one's own personality into the object of other people's faith so as to comprehend it fully. It is the power of understanding the behavior of another on the basis of one's own experience.

As scholars, phenomenologists must distinguish the task of explaining the meaning of the religious phenomena laid upon them by their discipline from the responsibility of judging these phenomena as belonging to one particular faith. It is not the work of phenomenologists to consider the grounds on which religious beliefs are held and to ask whether the religious judgments have objective validity. This is the domain of philosophy or theology of religion. But the fact that religious people make religious judgments which influence their actions and behavior and that they accept norms and rules in the expression of their religious convictions are matters of factual inquiry. That is to say, phenomenologists must inquire into the precise nature of religious convictions without being called upon to decide the religious or moral merit of the case.

The second principle of *eidetic vision* in the methodology of the phenomenology of religion has as its aim the search of the essential meaning of the religious phenomena. Understanding of the meaning of the religious phenomena is achieved always and solely through the understanding of expressions. The expressions include words and signs of any kind as well as the expressible behavior such as dancing. It is through expressions that we understand the other religious minds and enter them by rethinking, reexperiencing, empathy, and imaginative insight. Otherwise we would give the impression that we enter into other people's mind by a mysterious process of gazing directly into them. Understanding is the grasping of some mental content to which an expression points. Acts of understanding are the primary cognitive processes with which human studies must begin. This does not mean that they are infallible or that they cannot be further analyzed. Within the historical phenomenology of religion there are different types of understanding on different levels of complexity; but these types are unified in their purpose, which is to grasp the inner meaning of a religious phenomenon. This unity of purpose in the acts of understanding is what gives each discipline its specific character and avoids reductionism. To understand a poem is not the same as, and does not depend on, understanding the mental processes of its author, though certain features of the poem may be better understood if one knows them. Thus, to understand a religious act is not the same as, and does not depend on, the understanding of the mental processes of this act, which is to say that we cannot reduce the meaning of a religious fact to the psychological process of the same fact, though knowledge of the latter can help the knowledge of the former.

As we said before, understanding a religious phenomenon consists in empathy with another person's experiences, thoughts, emotions, and ideas. This act of understanding does not consist in a reproductive experiencing of another person's experience, emotion, and thought. Imitative or reproductive experiencing is not even a condition of understanding another's experience. For instance, one can be quite composed when one states that another is excited. A person in a state of joy can know that another person is sad; however, one should have previously experienced sadness oneself to really understand another person's sadness. Reproductive experiencing certainly yields a much clearer and detailed understanding of the experiences of other persons. If one has never experienced a religious act or ritual in some way, one would never be able to comprehend the meaning of this religious act from within.

But would not an approach of this kind to religious faiths of others involve subjectivism, given the fact that one starts to analyze the religious phenomena from one's own faith and experience? Some think that the only way to escape the accusation of partiality is to assert a priori the fundamental equality of all religions. Such a position is inadmissible, because the a priori assertion itself implies a judgment of value or rather begging the question. To assert a priori the fundamental equality of all religions it would be necessary to posit a metaphysical locus, so to say, above all particular religions, and such a perspective higher than the individual religions that actually exist is abstract and unreal. Moreover, the prime requirement of a comparative study of religions is the religious *epoché*, which does not imply surrender of one's own spontaneous religious convictions not yet purified by the phenomenological reduction but merely "placing in parentheses" their incidental modalities.

Scholars who belong to the historical school strongly reacted against phenomenology's claim that the essence of religious facts can be grasped. For them a religious phenomenon is exclusively a historical fact without transhistorical meaning or value. The quest for essences would involve the repetition of Platonic error. This is an unjust accusation, however; phenomenology of religion never pretended to be a science of the ultimate essences of religion. There are various kinds of essences of religion—empirical, philosophical, and theological. All that phenomenology intends to do is to understand the essence of the religious phenomenon, taken in the empirical sense of *the invariable structure* of a phenomenon that underlies every religious fact. On the other hand, some phenomenologists of religion have flatly stated that their phenomenology of religion has nothing to do with the historical origin and development of religious facts. This position also cannot be admitted. The essence of a religious fact is historically conditioned, and we cannot overlook history in the manifestation of the religious fact. The historical development of a fact does contribute to getting at new meanings or even to correct the older ones in the light of changing circumstances and contexts, and the essence itself of the fact, though invariable in some aspects, becomes variable in others. This kind of essence, as we have already said, is empirical, and every empirical thing can be made more precise and more adequate, as one gets new material in the investigation.

The historical school's insistence on philology, ethnology, and other historical disciplines is legitimate, for these give us the real, concrete character of the religious phenomena as they are manifest in human life and experience. We cannot impose arbitrary and a priori structures and meanings on the religious facts. Attentiveness to the historical origin and development of religious phenomena helps to avoid the imposition of structures which do not exist in the phenomena themselves. On the other hand, if the religious structures are completely historically conditioned and their meanings depend entirely on individual historical data, then we run the risk of historicism without paying attention to the meanings that are universal and common to many analogous phenomena. By saying that these phenomena are analogous, we cannot evade the consideration and importance of the common elements that are found in them; for every analogy argues for similar structures, which of course are at the same time different in various religions in which they manifest themselves. One should not be afraid of understanding the essence of the religious phenomena, i.e., of getting at the signification of the phenomena by comparing them in different historical contexts. To rely wholly on the historical development of these phenomena may mislead the investigator into taking them in one sense or in multiple senses without being aware of the sufficiently adequate meaning which can be arrived at only through phenomenological method.

Analogies are based on common elements, and a historian must consider both common elements and differentiations in order to arrive at a certain meaning. Mere typologies may give a certain meaning but not sufficiently clear and adequate presentation of the meaning, since typologies tend to give us only mere classification according to historical developments.

6. Conclusion

Students of phenomenology of religion use comparison as a basic interpretative tool to understand the meaning of such religious expressions as sacrifice, ritual, gods, and spirits. They seek to investigate the predominant characteristics of religion within historical-cultural contexts. Structurally similar religious acts, when compared, yield valuable meanings that explain the internal signification of these acts. The basic assumption in this approach is that the outward forms of human expression have an inner organizing pattern or configuration that can be outlined by the use of the phenomenological method. This method tries to find the structures that underlie historical facts and to comprehend them in their inner meaning as manifested through these structures with their laws and specific significations. It intends to gain an overall view of the ideas and motives that are of decisive importance in the history of religious phenomena. In short, it tries to decipher and interpret every kind of encounter of the human with the sacred.

A particular religious phenomenon is not to be deemed to have only one meaning; it may and does have many meanings for different participants in the religious act. By correlating what different participants perceive, the phenomenologist acquires an understanding beyond that of many individual participants. For example, the fire of the Vedic sacrifice can mean various things to the participants. Agni can be the god who consumes the sacrifice, is the priest and mediator between gods and humans who presents the sacrifice to the gods, and is the element that binds together the three worlds (heaven, atmosphere, and earth). While a particular religious adherent may not know the manifold meanings of a religious symbol, the phenomenologist studies the richness and vitality of the religious symbols by considering the different structural meanings of religious symbolism. Thus the religious meaning of a particular phenomenon for the individual participant or group of participants is never exhausted by the study of just one particular religion.

The phenomenological method does not yield a mere description of the phenomena studied, as it is sometimes alleged, nor does it pretend to explain the philosophical essence of the phenomena; for phenomenology is neither merely descriptive nor normative, as we have explained above. But it does give us the inner meaning of a religious phenomenon as it is lived and experienced by religious people. This inner meaning can be said to constitute the essence of the phenomenon. But the word "essence" should be understood correctly: what we mean is the empirical essence, which is liable to change if more material and better research impel us to. Phenomenology of religion is an empirical science, a human science that makes use of the results of other human sciences such as religious psychology, religious sociology, and anthropology. Still more, we can even say that phenomenology of religion is closer to the philosophy of religion than any other human science that studies religious phenomena, for it studies religious phenomena in their specific aspect of religiousness.

A phenomenological hermeneutic practices a sort of cutting across different religions to disengage from the multiplicity and diversity of religious phenomena common fundamental structures, essential forms, of all religious life together with the understanding of their profound signification. Thus it studies the notion of the sacred, the idea of God, myth, ritual, sacrifice, and finally the mystical experience. Across the variety of religious facts incorporated in particular spatio-temporal cultures, it attempts to find a universality that necessarily escapes a historian of a particular religion.

Bibl.: E. HIRSCHMANN, *Phänomenologie der Religion* (Würzburg/Anmuhle, 1940); R. PETTAZZONI, "History and Phenomenology in the Science of Religion," in *Essays on the History of Religions* (Leiden, 1954); J.-A. CUTTAT, *La rencontre des religions* (Paris, 1957); R. OTTO, *The Idea of the Holy* (London, 1959); G. MENSCHING, *Die Religion: Erscheinungsformen, Strukturtypen und Lebensgesetze* (Stockholm, 1959); B. KRISTENSEN, *The Meaning of Religion* (The Hague, 1960); F. HEILER, *Erscheinungsformen und Wesen der Religion* (Stuttgart, 1961); C. J. BLEEKER, *The Sacred Bridge* (Leiden, 1963); W. C. SMITH, *The Meaning and End of Religion* (New York, 1964); G. VAN DER LEEUW, *Religion in Essence and Manifestation* (New York, 1963); G. WIDENGREN, *Religions-phänomenologie* (Berlin, 1969); M. ELIADE, *The Quest, History and Meaning in Religion* (Chicago, 1969); id., *Patterns in Comparative Religion* (London, 1958); M. DHAVAMONY, *Phenomenology of Religion* (Rome, 1973); U. KING, "Historical and Phenomenological Approaches to the Study of Religion," in F. Whaling, ed., *Contemporary Approaches to the Study of Religion* (Berlin, 1984), 1:29–164; F. WHALING, *Contemporary Approaches to the Study of Religion* (Berlin, 1984).

Mariasusai DHAVAMONY

III. HISTORY OF RELIGIONS

1. Introduction

Every scientific study of religion has as its subject matter religious facts and their manifestations. Its material is taken from the observation of human religious life and behavior, as people manifest their religious attitude in acts such as prayer, sacrifice, and sacraments; their religious conceptions as contained in symbols and myths; their beliefs about the sacred, supernatural beings, gods, God, and so on. There are many specific disciplines that, although they treat of the same subject matter (i.e., religious phenomena), study it under specific aspects that are proper to the intent and scope of the particular discipline. Sociology of religion studies the interrelation of religion and society and the forms of interaction that take place between them. Anthropology of religion views religion as a cultural phenomenon in its many manifestations. In other words, it studies religious phenomena not as religious but as sociocultural. Psychology of religion treats of the religious function of the mind, partly dealing with the problem of the function of the individual mind in religious contexts (the individual-psychological aspect) and partly with the problem of the impact of the social religious life on its participants (social-psychological aspect). Its main area of reference is taken to be the religious experience of the individual or social unit. In brief, it studies the reactions of the human psyche—its responses, collective and individual, to the sacred or divine. Philosophy of religion examines critically and systematically the truth value of religious experience and expression in myths, symbols, and rites; discovers their meaning; and lays their ontological foundation and rational justification in the light of the principles of being. Thus it is a normative science that passes value judgments on religious phenomena. Theology of religions deals with the theological understanding of world religions in their relationship to Christianity, their salvific significance in the light of Christian revelation and faith. Theology of religions, being normative, judges in the light of Christian faith the salvific value of other religions. The history of religions is not a normative science; hence it does not pass value judgments on the epistemological or theological status or merit of the phenomena that are studied; it merely tries to understand their meaning.

2. History of Religions

There are many names that are currently used with reference to the history of religions. The *science of religion* is a very broad term which includes all kinds of studies of religion; hence it is too generic and does not indicate the specific field of the history of religions. *Comparative religion* or the *comparative study of religion* concerns itself with the history and comparison of religious phenomena as they manifest themselves in various religions. This brings out the comparative aspect of the study of religions. We prefer the term *history of religions*, which studies the religious phenomena historically and comparatively. Sometimes history of religions is identified with *phenomenology of religion* in order to signify the close connection between the history of religious phenomena and their structural meaning. We distinguish between these two disciplines, for

> phenomenology and history complement each other. Phenomenology cannot do without ethnology, philology and other historical disciplines. Phenomenology on the other hand gives the historical disciplines that sense of the religious which they are not able to capture. So conceived, religious phenomenology is the religious understanding of history; it is history in its religious dimension. Religious phenomenology and history are not two sciences but are two complementary aspects of the integral science of religion. (Pettazzoni, 1954)

Further, we have to make a distinction between the history of religions and the history of a particular religion. Many historians of religions, insofar as they specialize in one particular religion and at times in only one aspect or period of that religion, are called historians because they accept historical methods and work on historical presuppositions. Their works are valuable and sometimes even indispensable to build up an *allgemeine Religionswissenschaft*. But the history of religions that does not limit itself to one single religion or to one single aspect of religion but studies at least a few religions in order to be able to compare them tries to understand their modalities of

religious behavior, institutions and beliefs contained in myths, rituals, conceptions of high gods, and so one. Evidently it is in the second sense of the history of religions that we take it here. The material of history of religions is drawn from the history of particular religions but arranged from a systematic point of view rather than from the point of view of genetic development of the religious phenomenon.

Though distinct in scope from other disciplines such as sociology, anthropology, and psychology, which study the same religious phenomena, the history of religions has benefited from these sciences, which have brought and continue to bring important contributions to the study of religion. Certainly their data and conclusions help the historian of religions to understand the living context of the sources, for there is no such thing as a "pure" religious fact. Every religious fact is also social, psychological, and cultural; however, confusion of the scope and method of these sciences will lead only to reductionism—the theory that reduces religion to a kind of epiphenomenon of social, psychological, or cultural structure. Such reductionist theories have been proposed by sociologists such as Durkheim, by psychologists such as Freud, and by some anthropologists of both evolutionist and diffusionist types. The historians of religions consider religious phenomena as *religious* specifically, and not merely as social, psychological, or cultural; they concentrate on the religious signification of the phenomena insofar as they are related to the sacred.

History of religions does not confine itself to the verification and the analytical explanation of religious data; these are studied separately by the various specialized disciplines such as philology, archaeology, and ethnology and are related to historical investigation. History of religions seeks to coordinate religious data with one another, to establish relations, and to group the facts according to those relations. If it is a matter of formal relations, it classifies religious data under types; if the relations are chronological, it makes them into series. In the former case the science of religion is merely descriptive; in the latter it merely registers the origin and development of a religious phenomenon. But when the succession of events in time is seen in its internal development and the scholar understands its internal structure, then the science of religion becomes history of religions. This leads us to the subject of the method used in the history of religions.

3. The Method of the History of Religions

Methodology is the study of the special form of procedure in any branch of science in order to gain knowledge concerning the subject matter of that science under the particular aspect of the treatment of the subject. Methodology deals with the cognitive processes imposed by the problems that arise from the nature of its subject matter. We can say that a method is the systematic combination of cognitive processes, making use of specific techniques. Classification, conceptualization, abstraction, judgment, observation, experiment, generalization, induction, deduction, argument from analogy, and finally the understanding itself are cognitive processes. Different methods are distinguished in accordance with the variety of ways in which human thought can be organized and the different tasks to which it can be applied. In every scientific method there should be close and systematic relation between theorizing and experience. Observation and experiment furnish us with evidence for generalizations and hypotheses that are tested (verified or falsified) by making deductions from them and comparing these with the results of further observations and experiments.

The history of religions uses the scientific method as described above when it studies the religious phenomena. Its field of study consists of religious facts that are subjective and objective: subjective insofar as they deal with the thoughts, feelings, and intentions of religious people expressed in their outward acts; objective insofar as these expressions are objectified in myths, symbols, rituals, and external attitudes in different religions. The understanding of the expressions of these subjective states is what makes the given facts an act of religion such as worship, not mere movements. We call these states subjective in the sense that they take place in the human subject. Religion is primarily a phenomenon that takes place in a human subject and is expressed in signs and symbols. We can repeat the act of understanding of religious phenomenon and compare it with the acts of understanding of other observers and conclude that X is an act of worship, that Y is an act of sacrifice, and that Z is an act of prayer. Thus these facts assume the status of objectivity. In other words, religious phenomena are objectively ascertainable but subjectively rooted facts. Obviously it is by understanding the words and intentions of the participants in religious acts that one concludes to their religious character. That people behave in a religious way is a fact. The historian of religions has a preliminary understanding of what religious behavior is either from his or her own personal experience or from the experience of others.

At the same time the religious facts are objective in the sense that they are not the creation of the thinking mind but independent observers can verify them.

Some scholars think that the only way to escape partiality or prejudice in the study of religions, especially those different from one's own, is to assert a priori the fundamental equality of all religions. Such a position, as we see, is inadmissible because the assertion itself implies a judgment of value, or rather begging the question. To assert a priori the fundamental equality of all religions it would be necessary to posit a metaphysical locus, so to say, above all particular religions, and such a perspective higher than the individual religions that actually exist is abstract and unreal. Moreover, the prime requirement of a comparative study of religions is the suspension of all prejudice and a priori suppositions, which does not by any means imply surrender of one's own religious convictions.

Again, the act of understanding of religious phenomena is not an act of some mysterious—shall I say mystical—insight, based on some supernatural ability to penetrate the religious experiences of others. Knowledge of other peoples' religious faith is indirect, and inference about the religious states of others is based on their statements, gestures, products of work, and other observable data. Understanding of others' religious faith is based on the observation of human religious behavior and the products of human religious activity. Such a process of understanding can take place owing to two factors: first, that we have access to our own inner religious experiences, emotions, thoughts and ideas in various situations; second, that religious people are structured psychologically in a similar way. Here is then a question of inference by analogy. We can grasp only such mental states of another person that in some form, in some degree, and in some way have been included in our inner experience. What is totally alien to our inner experience remains outside the scope of our understanding. This is much more so with regard to understanding other people's religious behavior. We have to bear in mind also that various mental states are always experienced in a context, a social-cultural milieu in which a person lives. Through empathy historians of religions try to place themselves in the position of the adherent of another faith in order to understand the other's inner faith. As we see, the history of religions treats of the most vital aspect of human life to the extent that it remains fully aware that religion is the deepest and noblest in the realm of human spiritual and intellectual existence, although it knows its limits in the task of penetrating into the inner depths of a religious soul. If a student of religion does not know from personal experience of one's own life what it means to pray, one's views on prayer will be valueless.

4. The Historical Method

History as a human science is the study of particular, irreversible sequences of events in which the later ones are cumulatively affected by the earlier ones. The historical approach consists in the attempt to understand events by relating them to their historical context and to understand the whole context by moving from one event to another. The process of understanding events in their context and the process of understanding the context itself through these events are interdependent. The connections between the contents of events are themselves experienced, and this experience has to be recaptured by understanding. In order to understand this experience we place events in contexts different from the ones in which they occur. We see that they are of a certain type and can place them into a classificatory context. History obtains a meaningful complex of the sequences of events or expressions or clusters of events or expressions. Each sequence is unique because it is the result of a cumulative process and yet is similar to others; hence, it can be placed in a classificatory context.

There are various types of historians, depending on the way they want to do history. Here we are not speaking of the historians who write narrative history (_histoire-historisante_), battle history, or histories of great events. Nor are we concerned with the philosophers of history, e.g., Vico, Bossuet, Hegel, Dilthey, and Toynbee. We refer here to historians who primarily seek regularities, tendencies, types, typical sequences, and structures — and always within historical and cultural contexts. Such historians are interested in organisms, patterns, complexes, network of relations, intelligible wholes (_Zusammenhang, ensemble_), principles of coherence, and so on. These historians have their models and ideal types to help them represent the nature of the real. The intelligibility of an event derives from a generalization. E.g., the battle of Hastings, though fought once only, belongs to the class "battle" and is intelligible only when it is so considered. Any religious event has both uniqueness and generality; in an interpretation of it both of these characteristics must be taken into account. If the specificity of the religious fact were lost, the generalization about it would become so general as to be valueless. On the other hand, religious events would lose much, even all, of their meaning if they were not seen as having some degree of regularity and constancy, as belonging to a certain type of event, all instances of which have many common features. In order to have an intelligent understanding of a complex phenomenon, "we must know not only what it is, but also how it came into being" (F. Boas). As C. Lévi-Strauss remarks:

> When one completely limits one's study to the present period in the life of a society, one becomes first of all the victim of an illusion. For everything is history; what was said yesterday is history; what was said a minute ago is history. But above all one is led to misjudge the present because only the study of the historical development permits the weighing and evaluation of the interrelationship among the components of the present-day society. . . . How shall we correctly estimate the role, so surprising to foreigners, of the apéritif in French social life if we are ignorant of the traditional prestige value ascribed to cooked and spiced wines ever since the Middle Ages? (_Anthropologie Structurale_)

A people's traditional history cannot be overlooked, for it forms part of the religious thought of living people. We must distinguish between the effects of an event and the part played in the life of a people by the memory of that event, its representation in oral and/or written tradition.

In this context we have to make clear the two aspects of the analysis of structure. The structural analyst, confronted with a given religious phenomenon, attempts to isolate those factors within it that have remained constant. These are viewed as outside of time, given, perpetually present—hence synchronic—those elements which constitute the essence of the phenomenon. Then the analyst studies the temporal considerations, searching for factors that change with time, are subject to historical pressure, and are therefore diachronic. These diachronic aspects can be of two kinds: (1) those that move only in one direction over the course of time and are considered irreversible, and (2) those that seem to shift from one pole to another and back again and so are considered reversible. Such an analysis represents a radical and yet revealing simplification of a vast amount of material with regard to the same religious phenomenon. The themes are organized in such a way that their changes or continuities can readily be seen: some remain unchanged; others oscillate in importance; still others steadily increase or decrease in significance during the given period.

In historicism the emphasis is on the uniqueness of each historic period rather than on recurrent patterns or generalizations for all human behavior. According to the historicist approach, in studying any aspect of the social organization or culture of a people at a given time, the historian must trace its history to show how the particular form developed and to relate it to other aspects of the social-cultural system within which it takes place. A history of religions that takes the view that a religious phenomenon is best understood by analyzing only its historical development without paying attention to the development of generalized principles of religious behavior and without relating the specific and particular events to patterns of events yielding such principles must be included in the historicist approach to the study of religions. We cannot hold that history is concerned solely with the study of specific and unique events largely for their own sake. We fully grant that the historian cannot impose a priori structures or theories to explain the meaning of history; patterns and structures

originate from the study of historical phenomena themselves by means of which the historian can give generalized meaning for specific events.

5. The Comparative Method

Generally speaking, comparative method is the study of different types of groups of phenomena in order to determine analytically the factors that lead to similarities and differences in specific patterns of behavior. Usually it includes both the historical method and the cross-cultural method. This method involves the procedures that, while clarifying the resemblances and differences displayed by the phenomena, elicit and classify not only causal factors in the emergences and developments of such phenomena but also the patterns of interrelation within and between such phenomena.

It is necessary to take note of the difficulties involved in the use of the comparative method to yield *historical* accounts of growth as distinct from morphologies based on *contemporaneous* data. As M. Ginsberg points out, the use of the method neither proves nor implies the existence of genetic affinities or chronological sequences. Such limitations were not always taken into account in the nineteenth-century application of such methods to religious phenomena; this resulted in pseudo-historical and evolutionary conceptions of the phenomena. Comparative method is but an application of the general principle of varying the circumstances in order better to discover the causes of the phenomena.

Comparative method places analogous religious phenomena, e.g., certain forms of the idea of God, side by side and tries to define their structure by comparison. Similar facts and phenomena found in different religions are brought together and studied in groups in order to get at the signification of the phenomena. The purpose of such a method is to become acquainted with the religious thought, idea, or need that underlies the group of corresponding data. The comparative study of corresponding data often gives a deeper and more accurate insight into them than the consideration of each datum separately, for considered as a group, the data shed light on one another. It is important to note that comparison is not made to show that one religion is superior or inferior to another.

Comparison then is legitimately used both to relate and to distinguish, to find both parallels and distinctions. It would be impossible to understand the significance of a religious fact, say of the cosmic tree, without considering several of its variants, for each type or variety reveals with a particular intensity only certain aspects of the symbolism of the cosmic tree— e.g., *imago mundi, axis mundi*, center of the world, periodic regeneration of the universe, and so on. The nature of religious symbolism can be fully deciphered only when a number of examples from various religions have been examined. At the same time, only when a number of variants have been considered does their difference in meaning appear in full relief. Here arises a further question as to what internal reasons cause the same religious fact to possess different meaning, as to why such and such religion preserves a particular significance while other religions have rejected or modified it (M. Eliade).

The basic methodological problem is whether or not an objective study of a religious phenomenon could be achieved if the study interpreted the phenomenon in relation to historical and cultural context and at the same time retained some element of unique "religiousness" that could not be reduced to some other factor of existence. Students of the comparative study of religion, as we have explained previously, rightly insist that religious studies require a sensitivity to the particular aspect of human life that is religion as such or of the religious phenomenon as religious, which cannot be reduced to one or another aspect of human culture different from the religious. The comparative study of religion makes unbiased comparison of the religious data that have some common elements, such as sacrificial forms, theistic ideas, or prayer. The assumption is that there are some definable elements within human life that can be classified in terms of fundamental structures and that each classification has characteristic features which precisely determine the meaning of the phenomena. The comparative method seeks basic patterns or fundamental structures seen in a comparison of religious phenomena and regards it as the central feature by which the religious expression is understood.

The comparative investigation of the myth-and-ritual complex has led to the problem of interpreting the actual similarities that appear in different cultures. In this connection we must recall the highly spirited methodological debate that arose over the "Myth and Ritual School" or "Patternism," which insisted rather emphatically on the common elements in cultures and religions of the ancient Near East. The Gestalt psychologists have demonstrated the tendency of the mind to grasp selected composite forms and patterns as easily as simple ones and the more significant mental habit of impressing familiar patterns on groups of sensations and ideations. This makes it easier for comparative religionists to grasp the mechanism of transmission of myths. The following psychological principle of Gestalt is implied in the explanation of myths and cult practices: "The behavior of an element in a pattern is not determined so much by the class to which the element may belong as to the structure or pattern of which it forms part." S. H. Hooke, e.g., points out that the center of the cultus in the ancient Near East was the king, representing the god, and that the king as such was responsible for harvest, the prosperity of the cities, and finally for the well-being of the cosmos itself. G. Widengren estimated that this conception later gave rise to Iranian savior ideology and Jewish messianism. "Patternism" has been effectively dealt with by many scholars. H. Frankfort has shown that differences are more important than similarities. He has drawn attention to the fact that the pharaoh is considered a god or becomes a god, whereas in Mesopotamia the king is only the representative of a god. From this methodological debate we can conclude that the differences and similarities are equally important whenever we have to deal with historically related cultures. The fact that Spanish is different from the French and Italian does not prevent philologists from comparing these languages and tracing their common source, i.e. Latin, Hence the evaluation of the Myth-and-Ritual School reveals a confused methodology.

The following methodological recommendations are important for evaluating the significance of alleged parallels between Christianity and other religions. (*a*) A scholar must ascertain whether the supposed parallels were made plausible by selective description as the result of amalgamating heterogeneous elements drawn from various sources. If so, then such parallels would be imaginary. (b) If the parallels are really actual, then the scholar must find out whether they are mere analogies arising from similarity in more or less equal religious experience and in equality of outward conditions or whether there is borrowing one from the other. (c) Even when there is a question of borrowing one must critically make sure which religion is the real borrower. (d) Finally, one must attend to the profound differences a borrowed phenomenon undergoes in the new context of religious life and teaching.

6. *Religionsgeschichtliche Schule* (History of Religions School)

The first stage begins with Max Müller, the originator of the comparative study of religions, who formulated the principle *nihil in fide quod non ante fuerit in sensu* ("nothing in faith that was not first in sense perception"), and held that every knowledge—religious knowledge also—is based on sense perception. Humans did not begin by deifying grand natural objects or phenomena, but these gave rise to the feeling of the infinite in humans and also served as symbols for it. The gods of the ancient Indo-European religions—and by implication gods anywhere and at all times—are merely personifications of natural phenomena. The only way to reconstruct an ancient religion should be thorough philology.

Soon after Max Müller came the period in which folklorist, archaeological, and philosophical interests were added to the philological concern. The nineteenth century especially is characterized by a tremendous expansion of the frontiers of our knowledge of foreign religions. More specifically, many studies on Judaism, Gnosticism, the mystery religions, and other currents of thought and expression contemporary with the rise of Christianity came pouring in. Philological, historical, and anthropological methods which yielded such astonishing results in other fields were applied by professional theologians and amateurs to the study of the Christian religion. Many parallels and doublets between Christian and non-Christian religions were discovered and studied. For the first time, a comprehensive comparative study of religion became possible. Thus also appeared the possibility of seeing and interpreting Christianity not as an isolated fact but within the context of the much wider religious

and cultural history of humanity. Some theologians clamored for the substitution of the history of religions for Christian theology. The theory of isosthenia (equal validity) of Christian and non-Christian religions became predominant among some students of religion.

It was around this time that the *Religionsgeschichtliche Schule* formally came into existence, and its best representatives were Wilhelm Bousset, Wilhelm Heitmüller, and Richard Reitzenstein, This school sought to understand Christianity in relation to other religious movements and within the history of religions as a whole. These scholars had elucidated the alleged special contributions to the formation of Christianity of the Jewish, Hellenistic, Egyptian, Mesopotamian, Syrian, and Iranian religions and advocated the thesis that the Christian message could be explained purely as a reconstruction of foreign elements and influences.

Otto Pfleiderer (1836–1900), "the father of religious-historical theology in Germany," initiated the whole trend by declaring: "We can confidently say that Paul's theology would not have been what it is, if he had not drawn deeply on Greek wisdom as this was made available to him through the Hellenized Judaism of Alexandria." Let us take as an example the Pauline theology of baptism. This is what Pfleiderer affirms:

> We may permit ourselves to ask whether Paul, when from Corinth he wrote Romans chapter 6, was not aware of the rite of the Eleusinian mystery, the "bath of new birth," and described the sacramental significance of the Christian rite of baptism after this model. Just as in relation to the Lord's Supper he used the analogy of the pagan sacrificial meal, his mystical understanding of baptism may have stood in direct relation to the Greek mysteries.

Albert Eichhorn was convinced that the gap, as he conceived it, between what we may suppose to have happened at the Last Supper and the sacramental ideas that seem unmistakably to be present in Paul must be bridged through religious-historical investigation.

Wilhelm Heitmüller takes it as a proven fact that the origins of Paul's view of the sacrament are not to be found in the original Christian Gospel but even stand in contrast to it.

> The interpretation of baptism and the Lord's Supper stands therefore in unreconciled and

irreconcilable incongruity with the central significance of faith in Pauline Christianity, that is to say, with the purely spiritual and personal understanding of the religious relationship, which plays a leading role in Paul's own religion and in the world of his ideas.

The most noted scholar of this school is Richard Reitzenstein (1861–1931), who claimed for certain that Paul must have been profoundly influenced by the religious literature of the Hellenistic world when he set himself to proclaim the Jewish faith among the Gentiles. More specifically, faced with the problem of finding a pre-Christian belief in a Gnostic divine redeemer, Reitzenstein believed that he had found it in the supposed Iranian myth of redemption and that he could trace the origins of much that was Christian in this belief. R. C. Zaehner, an eminent Iranologist, disposes of this interpretation by saying that "the Iranian *Erlösungsmysterium* is largely Reitzenstein's invention." Further, M. Lidzbarski produced reliable translations of the Mandaean literature, especially the Ginza (Treasure). Here we find the heavenly redeemer, Manda da Hayye (the "knowledge of life"), who descends to earth to redeem lost souls from the powers of darkness back to the realm of light to which they belong. But it is admitted by all scholars that the Mandaean writings as we possess them belong to the seventh or eighth century C.E., though they may contain earlier material.

W. Bousset, one of the contributors to the development of the religious-historical school of interpretation, considered early Christianity as purely and simply a *Menschensohn-Dogmatik*—i.e., faith that identified Jesus with the expected Son of Man, but held that, having ascended into the heavens, Jesus was from henceforth absent from his church until the parousia. The belief in the present possibility of direct communion and fellowship with the exalted Lord on the part of the Christian springs from a false mysticism that is the illegitimate product of Hellenistic, rather than Jewish or properly Christian, religious devotion. Hence, Bousset roundly denied the existence of any *cultus* of Jesus among the original disciples, or of any idea of present communion with Christ in the original Jewish-Christian community.

C. H. Dodd has evaluated the conclusions of this school:

Too often the documents cited are of quite uncertain date, and we wander in a world almost as timeless as the world of the myth itself. When some more precise chronology is possible, it always, or almost always, turns out either that the document in question belongs to the fourth century or later, or that it belongs to an environment in which the influence of Christian or at least of Jewish thought is probable, so that it is hazardous to use the document to establish a pre-christian, non-Jewish mystery.

Suffice it to say that philological and historical exegesis alone is incomplete. Historians of religion should strive to understand their material in the context of ideas developed in and through the various methods of interpretation. For the Christian exegete and theologian the method is definitely different. The Qur'an, the Vedas and Upanishads, the Tripiṭaka, or the Lun Yü are not normative writings for the Christian exegete, whereas the Bible is so undoubtedly. Moreover the understanding of the Bible is directed by the authority that membership in the Catholic religious tradition and community provides. Finally, the present-day history of religions no longer admits the historicist fallacy found in the *Religionsgeschichtliche Schule*, namely, that norms may be attained from history itself.

Bibl.: R. PETTAZZONI, *Essays on the History of Religions* (Leiden, 1954); M. ELIADE and J. KITAGAWA, eds., *The History of Religions: Essays in Methodology* (Chicago, 1959); R. BASTIDE, ed., *Sens et usages du terme "structure" dans les sciences humaines et sociales* (The Hague, 1962); J. WACH, *The Comparative Study of Religions* (New York, 1963); H. RINGGREN and A. V. STRÖM, *Religions of Mankind* (Philadelphia, 1967); J. KITAWAGA, M. ELIADE, and H. LONG, eds., *The History of Religions* (Chicago, 1967); H. P. RICKMAN, *Understanding and the Human Studies* (London, 1967); C. J. BLEEKER and G. WIDENGREN, eds., *Historia Religionum*, 2 vols. (Leiden, 1969); M. DHAVAMONY, "The History of Religions and Theology," *Greg* 50 (1969): 805–37; var., *Problèmes et méthodes d'histoire des religions* (Paris, 1969); M. ELIADE, *The Quest, History and Meaning in Religion* (Chicago, 1969); id., *The Myth of the Eternal Return* (Princeton, N.J., 1954); U. BIANCHI, *La Storia delle Religioni* (Turin, 1970); U. BIANCHI, C. J. BLEEKER, and A. BAUSANI, eds., *Problems and Methods of the History of Religions* (Leiden, 1972); J. WAARDENBURG, *Classical Approaches to the Study of Religion*, 2 vols. (The Hague, 1973); E. SHAPPE, *Comparative Religion: A History* (London, 1975); var., *Le Scienze della*

Religione Oggi (Bologna, 1983); F. WHALING, ed., *Contemporary Approaches to the Study of Religion*, vol. 1: *The Humanities* (Berlin, 1984).

Mariasusai DHAVAMONY

IV. TRADITIONAL RELIGIONS

By the term "traditional religion" today we normally mean those religions that used to be associated with and/or still are associated with the illiterate peoples of the Third World, and which, on an erroneous, evolutionist assumption about their primordiality or about their inferiority to the great, classic, historical or universalist religions, used at one time to be described as "primitive religions."

Typical of peoples, ethnic groups, or communities of predominantly tribal structure and preindustrial economy, living in conditions of objective technological backwardness, subjected over many centuries to massive pressure from the historical and missionary religions (especially Islam and Christianity) which offer a manifest doctrinal superiority and act as vehicles of social progress, traditional religions have nonetheless demonstrated and continue to demonstrate, in varying regional contexts, a surprising vitality and creativity, to the point of symbolizing national identity and resistance in situations of forced cultural change and of assuming in some cases a role of conscious criticism of Western values. We may think for instance of all the syncretic Afro-Indo-American cults, which in actual fact represent as many religions in Latin America, or of the attitudes that in modern times characterize the cults of Africa and Oceania. Looking at things the other way, we may cite the influences exerted on the West and the challenges launched at that same modern culture by the traditional religions: to stay within the ambit of the examples already mentioned, the repercussions in the ecological field due to the religious respect the Amerindians have for nature; the capacity for interracial bonding and for building up the nation evinced by the syncretic cults of Latin America; the questioning of Western medicine by African traditional healers, whose therapeutic practice is never divorced from the spiritual and religious well-being of the whole personality; the territorial claims, based on religion but advanced in the name of civil, legal, and political rights of Western mold, of the Australian and Melanesian peoples.

In any attempt to give a general description of traditional religions and passing over individual, regional details, a number of special characteristics immediately stand out as distinguishing them, in normal situations, from Christianity. Let it be said at the outset that in no case will the complex of beliefs, actions, and customs that our Christian-Western culture regards as religious be clearly distinguishable in traditional cultures, which for their part are the bearers of the concomitant complex of beliefs, actions, and customs that we should describe as nonreligious: civic or profane, depending on whether we choose the (historical) dialectic civic/religious, or the (religious) dialectic sacred/profane. And this means, on the one hand, the absence in the non-Western culture of an explicit and objective notion of "religion" (a concept moreover very complex and elaborate even in the West, as our history shows), and on the other that everything in traditional cultures can be interpreted *sub specie religionis* (this, e.g., is the position of religious phenomenology), or that we can only speak of religion as an autonomous conceptual category in Western culture, which has historically drawn a distinction between the fields of religious and nonreligious activity (a position that has as scientific center the Roman school of history of religions founded by R. Pettazzoni).

Partly contingent on this premise is a first consideration: traditional religions, unlike Christianity (and other great universal religions in their historical maturity: → JUDAISM; ISLAM; BUDDHISM, etc.), figure as tightly interconnected with (and inseparable from) all the other aspects of the cultures individually expressing them and in particular with their respective economic systems. So, where we have farming populations (with more or less developed systems of agriculture, and this is the situation most widespread over all), we shall find a type of religion centered on the earth, variously deified or worshiped, and on the cult of the dead; whereas among hunter-gatherers and fishing peoples there prevails a complex of beliefs that hypostatize the hazardousness of their system of subsistence into the figure of some lord of the beasts (of land or sea), and among nomadic stock-raising peoples a religious system centering on a supreme sky-god.

A great influence is exerted on religious beliefs by social and political structure: the clan structure, which is a feature of most traditional societies, has its sanction on the religious plane through the mythicization of the ancestor-founder and the ritualization of solidarity and social control, while all individual life is governed by practices broadly speaking religious. In turn, the political structure is reflected in the system of beliefs by the mythical-ritual ratification of the social and political hierarchy in hierarchical societies (Africa, Polynesia), to the point of "deifying" the king in societies of monarchical structure (West Africa, pre-Columbian America) and in the appearance of religious forms of polytheistic type (whether original, or by diffusion from more advanced civilizations) in traditional societies of more complex, more articulated, and more diversified sociopolitical organization.

Another important element distinguishing traditional religions from the historical religions and especially Christianity, is the total absence of proselytizing. Traditional religions are tightly ethnic, often national, regional, or even community religions that neither form nor aspire to form a universal corpus of doctrine but, as will become clear later, are so many symbolic systems responding to specific and geographically limited cultural and social needs, rather than to intellectual and emotional ones.

To conclude the contrast between traditional religions and Christianity, it is right to stress the element chiefly characterizing non-Western cultures and hence non-Western religions as against Western culture and hence Western religion, and this is observable in the different approach that each has in its way of understanding the world: mythical and cosmologizing, the former; historical and anthropologizing, the latter. Traditional cultures demand of myth and of matters that, being mythical, have no date the function of establishing that part of reality which they recognize as and wish to be changeless and hence not subject to human intervention, so neutralizing human activity and hiding the future in a reassuring and protective way; whereas Western culture, developing along the lines laid down by Roman actualism and Chris-

tian free will, has progressively considered ever more ample portions of reality to be subject to change through the action of history. This is the same as saying that, whereas traditional cultures give cosmic dimensions to the real, Western culture tends to give it human ones. As an overstatement, we might say as an example of the foregoing that whereas at a traditional level the real is "divinized," in Western culture God has been "realized": the Word became human and so the beyond-history came down into history; the religious truth of revelation acquired a historical basis through the historical activities—life, passion, and death—of Christ.

With these preliminaries serving to illustrate the specific differences between Christianity and the traditional religions of non-Western cultures now behind us, we can take a closer and more detailed look at the morphology of the beliefs and ritual activities of the latter.

The belief in superhuman entities with powers different from and stronger than those of human beings. seems to lie at the root of many, if not of all, traditional religions; caution is dictated by the growing need for a critical reassessment of the older documentary sources, that is to say, of nonspecialist ethnographic reports by explorers, travelers, or missionaries who, owing to their own conditioning, may have misunderstood the cultures with which they came into contact. Nor will it be forgotten that in some cultures the supernatural actually assumes absolutely impersonal forms, as in the case of the Melanesian *mana*. Be that as it may, some of these entities are represented by the heroes of myths, or sacred stories, universally at traditional level (and not only at traditional level) forming the basis of reality, investing it with meaning and value. These mythical beings are typically inactual—i.e., inactive in the present and therefore not accorded worship. Whether by analogy with phenomena encountered in the higher religions or by the practical need for categorization, scholars have divided these mythical heroes into various recognizable types: creator, trickster, first human being, culture hero, mythical or totem ancestor, *dema*. Though the distinction may respond to functional needs, it is not to be found in the mythical deposit itself. For the fact is, all these mythical heroes perform foundational acts that are largely interchangeable—which done, their function is exhausted—and are only very rarely characterized in a personal sense. Accurate interpretation of ethnographic documentation shows assimilation to preconceived "mythological" or "divine" personalities at work, on the part of scholars conditioned by their own intellectual baggage. Take, for instance, the influence exerted by the Osiris myth on the conceptualization of the *dema* (the Melanesian mythical being who, having been put to death, dismembered, and buried, gives origin to foods) or, conversely, that of the Promethean myth on the conceptualization of the trickster (see below), even though, later, these conceptualizations have actually been used to explain the Egyptian and the Greek myths.

A more complex function as regards mythical heroes involves other superhuman entities that are regarded as existing and active in the present and therefore as recipients of worship, even if they can act at a mythical level to establish reality. In this case too, scholars have worked out a typology distinguishing between supreme being, lord of the beasts, Mother Earth, spirits (of nature, of the dead, tutelary spirits), ancestors, gods.

As regards ritual activities, traditional religions present two fundamental types of rites: *autonomous* ones not addressed to anyone in particular, and *cultic* ones, i.e., rites forming part of the cult of supernatural beings thought of as able to intervene actively in human affairs. Among the first we include magic rites and that vast category of rites of passage (i.e., rituals that at individual and/or collective level mark the most significant transitions from one state or condition to another, among which tribal initiation rites and New Year rites deserve special mention); cultic rites include prayer, sacrifice, and offering.

Since, as has already been said, in traditional cultures the religious sphere is not conceptually distinct from other effective fields of existence, frequently at the more "primitive" levels no "professional" specialization of a religious sort is to be found: the family head or tribal chief deals with "sacred" matters as he does with the "profane." Religious specialization coincides with greater specialization in all other human activities: it is therefore in those cultures with the more complex structure that we can find ritual practitioners properly so-called who, depending on circumstances, fill

their role by appointment or by personal vocation. Diviners, wizards, healers, and sorcerers are the most common "specialists" in religious matters to be encountered at traditional level, and the shaman deserves particular mention here. He is a type of ritual practitioner who by psychic or artificial means achieves a state of trance, in which he communicates with the spirits and from them obtains extraordinary divinatory and therapeutic faculties. Priestly classes properly so-called are, however, only found in the more complex and developed traditional cultures, in most cases characterized by religious forms of more or less polytheistic type (West Africa, Polynesia, pre-Columbian America).

In many traditional societies (North and South America, Africa, Oceania) in the colonial and postcolonial age, the figure of the prophet has assumed particular importance, often rising to be the leader of socioreligious movements of emancipationist type, whether in the political or in the cultural sense. The phenomenon of prophetism is still extremely important; throughout the Third World, owing to charismatic personalities, new sects or religions are springing up, mostly of syncretic type (i.e., which amalgamate elements of traditional religion with others derived from Christianity—on occasion, transcending a simple juxtaposition of these and taking on completely original connotations), which exert a strong grip on the native populations and are often characterized by proselytizing intentions actually derived from assimilating the ecumenical and missionary spirit of Christianity. These new religions, commonly called "spiritual," "charismatic," or "religions of healing" are symptomatic and indicative of the cultural malaise of traditional masses subjected to the increasingly traumatic impact of the modern age and its inconsistencies and, in the cases of open opposition to the missionary churches, of conscious criticism of the way the West had betrayed the commands of the gospel.

Let us now give a broad outline of the basic characteristics of traditional religions using a geographical criterion, while of course bearing in mind that the variety of cultures existing in the different areas makes this sort of systematizing not only reductionist but extremely artificial and homologistic. Indeed, if in some relatively isolated or restricted areas (for historical and/or geographical reasons: Australia, Melanesia, Polynesia, the subarctic zones of Asia and America) the respective cultures appear pretty homogeneous from the point of view of socioeconomic structure (the relevance of which to determining the type of religion has already been mentioned), other continents (North and South America, Africa) offer such a variety of situations as to make any generalization virtually impossible except by flattening out, leveling, abstracting, and thus substantially falsifying facts and problems.

The varied beliefs of the numerous Australian groups of hunter-gatherers find a certain unity in the enormous importance assumed by the mythical, half-human, half-animal heroes who, in the "Dream Time," laid down the lineaments of nature and of native culture, dictated the norms of social life and left sacred places and sacred objects on earth as the receptacle of their power and of the ritual systems that commemorate and reactualize their activities. The presence, as originally asserted, of the cult of a supreme sky-god does not, however, seem to tally with the facts. At the ritual level, tribal initiations are among the most complex, dramatic, and culturally significant, together with the rites to ensure the increase of animal and plant life (related—like many other aspects of Australians' social and religious life—to the debated phenomenon of totemism). The sorcerer and the healer—the former regarded as causing misfortune, illness, and death; the latter dispensing remedies (but often in the same person) —are recognized ritual practitioners, although all religious organization is lacking and the management of the "sacred" is diffused among all the elders according to a progressive *iter* marked by different stages of initiation.

The religions of Melanesia offer features similar, on the one hand, to Australian beliefs and, on the other, to the Polynesian, but generally speaking their own originality lies in the pragmatism that characterizes them. They are less "mystical" than Australian religions and less "binding" than Polynesian ones, leaving a wide margin for human initiative. Horticulturalists and fisherfolk, the Melanesians have evolved a rich mythology, believe in a multiplicity of spirits, and practice ancestor worship by means of complicated rites involving individual clans and/or entire villages, as in the case of the great renewal or New Year feast, at which

firstfruits are offered to the spirits of the dead. Initiation rites too, whether tribal or of secret societies, enjoy particular importance, and the former often merge chronologically and ideologically into the cult of the ancestors, thus guaranteeing continuity between the generations. Among groups that practice the raising of wild pigs, a great competitive feast is held at intervals of some years. At this, a *big-man*, to gain sociopolitical prestige, will make a show of sacrificing to spirits or mythical entities enormous numbers of animals, which are afterwards consumed orgiastically by those attending the feast. Witchcraft, in its ambivalent acceptance, is very prevalent, and all Melanesians often have recourse to magic spells in order to achieve their aims: the success or efficacity of a wizard or of a spell is believed to be determined by its respective *mana*, a sort of obscure power attributed without distinction to all kinds of spirits, people, and objects that may appear to have or to bring good luck.

Owing to the early and almost general conversion of the native population from traditional Polynesian religion to Christianity, we are forced to speak largely about the past, and the elements originally constituting traditional religion are now no more than memories of an age that the Polynesians themselves regard as being as remote as the age of myth. Originally, Polynesia presented a remarkably homogeneous culture: horticulturalists, pig rearers, and fisherfolk. Polynesian society was hierarchical to a degree, and some chiefs were so powerful as to be really kings. Religious organization depended on a priestly body enjoying immense prestige. Religious beliefs reflected the social order: the many deities, many of whom were genealogically related to one another, were organized into a sort of pantheon of hierarchical structure, at the apex of which were three ill-defined, mythical creator figures. All these supernatural beings had their own individual spheres of activity, representing a specific portion of reality. They could harm human beings or favor them and so, as the various heads of this and that, had to be appeased with continuous offerings at the many ceremonies conducted by the priests in the appropriate holy places. Furthermore, they could take trance-possession of individuals, and they protected wizards. A not insignificant role was also played by the spirits of the dead, with their ambivalent attributes. In addition to religious implications, *mana* had political-social ones, being understood as a quality in some way emanating from the godhead to confer success and prestige on individuals; so too taboo, a concept applied to everything sacred or forbidden, the violation of which entailed consequences of the mystical and/or social order. Particular mention must be made of the *"arioi"* society, of which Polynesians of either sex could become members by spirit-possession or by initiation. This too was rigidly hierarchical in structure and had as its role the performance of sacred games, rites, and shows. Its members enjoyed exceptional privileges and powers vis-à-vis the political authorities, living their lives in a ritual dimension totally different from that of ordinary people.

To a considerable degree the religions of the North and South American Indians reflect the variety of ecological, economic, and cultural situations to be encountered, given the vastness of the area in question. Some groups still live (and have lived for thousands of years) entirely by hunting and gathering; others live by farming; still others mainly by fishing, so that even the most abstract of generalizations would seem impossible to sustain. This notwithstanding, we can single out a close relationship with nature, religiously understood and treated as holy, as the unifying feature of all these systems of belief, be they never so diverse. Equally universal is the presence of a complex mythology and hence of an assortment of mythical heroes, among whom (especially, but not exclusively, in North America) the *trickster* stands out: a theriomorphic culture hero, often the opponent of the creator, characterized by particularly ambiguous behavior: founder and giver of important cultural elements, he is nonetheless a cheat, at once astute and foolish, the hero of adventures for the most part comic or coarse. Alongside the mythical heroes, we find, depending on the types of culture, supreme beings (Tierra del Fuego), lords of the beasts (in all hunter groups and among the Eskimos), earth and vegetation goddesses (in both Americas, among farming peoples and also, exceptionally, among hunter groups), spirits connected with the elements or cosmic and atmospheric events (practically everywhere), tutelary spirits of various sorts. These

last, to be found in both Americas, assume extreme importance in North America (except in the Southwest), being at the center of initiation rites and individual visionary practices designed to achieve a special relationship with a spirit. Acquisition of a tutelary spirit is also at the basis of shamanism, which recurs in various forms from the arctic zone (where it appears in its purest, prototypical aspect) to the other end of the land mass. A priesthood, more or less properly so-called, is only to be found in the Andes region, perhaps owing to the ancient influence of Inca civilization, and among the Navajo and Pueblo peoples in the Southwest of the United States. In either case, the ritual and ceremonial life is very dense with events, both at individual and collective level. The most important feasts are those of renewal, connected with the agricultural New Year and the beginning of the hunting or fishing season. Tribal initiations and those to secret societies and medical guilds (these last exclusively among the North American Indians) are some of the most powerful religious experiences in the individual and communal life of the natives.

The peoples of the Eurasian arctic and subarctic zones offer a certain homogeneity of beliefs — now largely supplanted by Christianity — with the accent on one or another particular component, depending on whether we are talking of groups ecologically determined to a lifestyle based on a hunting or a stock-raising economy respectively. As regards hunting and fishing peoples (who, apart from the Eskimos, include numerous Asiatic groups, among whom are the Siberians and the Ainu of the Japanese island of Hokkaido), religious beliefs, sustained by a complex mythology, are centered, as we might expect, on some lord of the beasts, often accompanied by a supreme being and a host of nature and tutelary spirits. Ritual activities are concentrated in the slack period for hunting and reach a climax with the opening of the season; the ritual practitioner is typically the shaman. The groups of stock-raisers, notably of reindeer (often the same ethnic group follows a different economic regime, whether as hunters or as pastoralists, depending on habitat: this is the case with many Siberian peoples — e.g., the Yukaghirs, Chukchi, Tunguses — whereas stock raising may always be presumed to have had a previous hunting phase — Lapps, Yakuts, Samoyedes, etc.)

mainly venerate a supreme sky-god, to whom they offer sacrifices at great annual feasts marking the seasonal cycle of stock raising, but their religious world is also peopled with many supernatural entities, among whom various tutelary spirits of wild animals take first place. Here too the shamanistic system predominates.

The African continent confronts us with an immense variety of religious beliefs, since it offers examples of virtually all ecological environments and socioeconomic regimes conditioned by them — hence of differing types of culture too. In Black Africa the gamut is run from the hunter-gatherer culture of the Pygmies in the equatorial forest and the Bushmen of the Kalahari to the farming culture of the great kingdoms of West Africa, passing through myriad societies of more or less primitive farmers and small or large-scale stock-raisers (Hottentots, Nilotics, Ethiopians). Because this is so, we do better to abstain from generalities and to stress the widespread and intense spirituality and integralism that characterize and unite all the many and diverse expressions of the African religious sense, in marked contrast to the materialism and individualism of the West. The task awaiting today's scholars is to undertake a historical reexamination of traditional African religions, whether because they have mistakenly been regarded as inert, static, and incapable of development — whereas in many cases their ability to adapt and respond creatively either to internal crises or to the new conditions imposed in the first place by colonialism and subsequently by modernization bears witness to a flexibility for which there must certainly have been historical precedent — or because the negative and positive preconceptions of informants, ethnographers, and theorists have too often affected their descriptions and judgments, they having in one way or another interpreted this diversity by their own concepts, reducing it precisely to these.

And this, in the last resort, if we are to grasp the spiritual treasure hidden in human beings, to whichever geographical, chronological, and cultural latitude they may belong, goes for any complex of beliefs.

Bibl.: V. LANTERNARI, *Movimenti religiosi di libertá e di salvezza dei popoli oppressi* (Milan, 1960); A. BRELICH, *Introduzione alla storia delle religioni*

(Rome, 1966); H. C. PUECH, ed., *Histoire des Religions*, vol. 18 (Paris, 1970); D. SABBATUCCI, *Sommario di storia delle religioni* (Rome, 1987); S. SUTHERLAND, L. HOULDEN, P. CLARKE and F. HARDY, eds., *The World's Religions*, 5th part: P. CLARKE, ed., *Traditional Religions* (London, 1988).

Danila VISCA

V. POPULAR RELIGION

1. The Study of Popular Religion

a. The investigation, analysis, and interpretation of the *religious phenomenon* is of broad interest in the field of the human sciences, given the concern of these sciences with the cultural or social problematic, which is intimately connected to the religious fact. Thus, religion and the phenomenon of popular piety arouse intense concern on the part of cultural anthropology and religious ethnology, the psychology and sociology of religion, the history of religious institutions and practices, the phenomenology and philosophy of religion, the theology of religions, and the theory of mission and pastoral theology. The field of observation and analysis is vast and diverse: religious folklore and popular traditions, magical or superstitious practices, popular festival and worship, and the elements of religious syncretism and cultural mix in the various manifestations of the social experience of religions, among the popular classes in particular, especially the peasantry, in their rites and celebrations, their legends and myths, their proverbs and refrains, their vital and social *ethos*.

The specific *methodologies* employed, like the *criteria* of interpretation of religious practices, are notably divergent. Thus, really or supposedly religious phenomena may be observed out of a merely anthropological and cultural interest or may be the object of a comparative investigation, whether of a historical character, in which case research will be interested in their evolution, or of a morphological and structural one. Finally, such phenomena, characteristic of human religiousness, may be interpreted in the perspective of certain antecedent naturalistic or positivistic, spiritualistic or materialistic, ideological or theological postulates. Accordingly, the phenomenology of popular religion may be regarded merely as the expression of a quest for existential security on the part of the popular classes, in the face of a cultural or social situation of misery and backwardness, oppression or unusual frailty. At other times, the religious fact is interpreted merely as a search for greater power, consent, or social and historical legitimation. Finally, the religious fact is rightly interpreted as the expression of popular faith.

b. In addition to the divergence of methodological presuppositions and hermeneutic criteria, we find a *conceptual diversity* in the manner in which the "popular" element is understood. At times, the popular is understood as a typical trait of the national idiosyncrasy of a people considered as the collective subject of a history and a culture, a society and a state, in terms of the experience of its piety. Or the popular is understood as a property of the popular strata, classes, races, or cultures *qua* subordinate and oppressed by other cultures, classes, or races. Or finally, the popular may be regarded as opposed to the official. In this case, popular piety signifies the religious experience and beliefs of particular human groups, by and large among the subordinate strata of society, which persist in a certain resistance to or divergence from official orthodox forms. Thus, one may speak, in very diversified fashion, of the piety of the Argentinian people or the Marian devotion of the Mexican or Andalusian people, of the legends or worship of the dead in Galician or Central American popular piety, or of various phenomena of Amerindian or African-American popular religiousness.

c. The popular manner of religious life is particularly conditioned by culture, both by that of the dominant class, and by that of the subordinate classes. The relationship between popular faith and popular culture can be regarded as a specific case of the relation between *religion and culture* in their mutual dialectical interaction. In all cultures marked by a theonomous situation—that is, cultures in which the irruption of the sacred acquires a peculiar intensity, religion offers culture its dimension of vital depth. This is the case in large cultural areas inspired by the great religions of the East—by Hinduism or by Buddhism—by the religion of Israel, or by that of Islam. The same occurs in nations marked by an in-depth contact with

Christianity. In turn, culture offers the forms of expression that bring great religious ideals and values to family and social life: absolute truth, sublime beauty, unconditional justice, and compassionate goodness.

The popular culture or subcultures of the subordinate classes or races may also, in a given space, offer forms of expression of faith or religious hope, the *ethos* of solidarity and siblingship, and the quest for reconciliation and peace, to religiousness or piety itself. Thus, the life of the ecclesial community as institution has always coexisted with manifold expressions of faith and popular religious experience, often charged with great religious sincerity and human authenticity in their expression of believing trust (*fides qua*) as well as of the objective content of faith (*fides quae*). Frequently, religious experience has been intimately intertwined with cultural or social realities, coloring popular language and art, and family and community life.

2. The Question of Popular Piety

a. It is customary to speak of *popular piety* when the form and manner of the religious experience takes on a more direct and simple character, in a search for an enhanced functionality, and a modality more accessible to the concrete individual or group. Thus, popular piety may readily overcome the barrier represented by a learned and conceptual, dogmatic and abstract manner of living one's religion or reflecting on one's faith. By adopting more spontaneous forms of experience of the religious sentiment—or at any rate forms that are more accessible to the cultural level of the persons concerned—popular piety tends to bypass the mediation of the priestly figure, which is felt to be absent or distant, if not indeed presenting an obstacle to religious communication. In popular piety, a kind of prayer is cultivated, frequently formulated in terms of an invocation of the intercession of a patron saint, that will be felt more effective for obtaining the desired object, in religious supplication for urgent or anguished human needs, especially those wants that beset the poorest and least protected strata of society.

It is not easy to elucidate the question of the relationship between a popular way and an official way of living one's religion. In many cases, a certain priority of the popular and spontaneous over the erudite and elaborate is observable. In numerous situations and circumstances, both forms of the life of piety have historically tended to coexist concretely, in a dialectical relationship: the normative, erudite form of the religious life tends to be nourished by the popular experience of religious feeling, which one seeks to frame in a theological, normative system. At times, popular faith is limited to the popularization of theological concepts in terms more akin to those of the culture of the subordinate classes. In language or gesture, piety or devotion, popular religiousness is frequently characterized by various *notes* like a certain spontaneity and wealth of communication in terms of the intuitive and symbolical, such as in the emotional and fantastic, the experiential and festive, or the celebrational and theatrical.

b. Popular piety includes a *broad range of phenomena*, vital and social, cultural and religious. At the popular level, religion is often enough experienced in a vital contact with the life cycle or with social reality. Thus, we find a religious celebration of birth, of the threshold of adolescence, of betrothal or marriage, of sickness or death. We also find a festive or celebrational consecration of work performed in a factory, especially at the moment of patronal or religious festivals. Christianity, as a universal religion, adopts the basic dialectic of biblical religion as a religion of creation and covenant, which consecrates, criticizes, or blesses nature and history. When evangelization has positively embraced the concrete human life of a people in their path to Christ, Lord of creation and mediator of the covenant, new forms of popular Christianity arise.

The phenomenology of piety or religiousness spans such a wide spectrum, however, that it is not immune to a high degree of *equivocity*, inasmuch as by popular religiousness, even in the case of popular Christianity or Catholicism, such a large variety of manifestations are understood, ranging from magical or superstitious expressions of an archaic, pre-Christian piety blended with devotions typical of the faith of the rural milieu, to other manifestations of the reappearance of traditions of popular Catholicism that serve to maintain the consciousness of a religious and social identity. Thus, we may speak of Amerindian or African-American influences on particular traits of Latin American Catholicism in its popular expression. Or we may analyze

popular forms of worship like pilgrimages or other festivals and devotions typical of a popular veneration of the Christian saints or representative of Marian devotion.

c. Of new importance for popular piety are the current movements of renewal in popular and lay pastoral practice, such as Bible study groups, base church communities, and neo-catechumenal or neo-Pentecostal groups, which often assume the function of educating and nourishing a sound popular piety in full communion with the church. In its relationship with popular groups and their characteristic experience of faith and piety, *church authority* has oscillated among various types of reaction, partly because of the nature of the religious phenomena themselves, and partly conditioned by historical circumstances. These reactions range from a condemnation of the phenomena in question as superstitious or magical to the rehabilitation of forms of legitimate devotion; from a toleration of imperfect forms of the believing experience to the proposal of admissible practices reconcilable with orthodoxy and canonical liturgy. In turn, the popular groups, in the various religious communities, have oscillated in their own relationship with authoritative, official instances, now sincerely accepting authoritative propositions, and now rejecting them or even camouflaging their reaction under various forms of religious *syncretism*. Still, the popular forms of religiousness must not necessarily be subjected to a negative judgment: they sometimes constitute splendid manifestations of an *inculturation of faith*, and of the adaptation of a universal religion to national, social, or cultural spaces characterized by an enormous diversity.

Bibl.: B. LACROIX and P. BOGIONI, *Les religions populaires* (Quebec, 1972); J. M. R. TILLARD et al., *Foi populaire, Foi savante* (Paris, 1976); L. MALDONADO, *Religiosidad popular* (Madrid, 1976); F. A. PASTOR et al., *Inculturazzione* (Rome, 1979); C. DUBOSQ, B. PLONGERON, and D. ROBERT, *La religion populaire* (Paris, 1979); V. BO, *La religiosità popolare* (Assisi, 1979); D. PIZZUTI and P. GIANNONI, *Fede popolare* (Turin, 1979); S. GALILEA, *Religiosidad popular y Pastoral* (Madrid, 1980); B. ADOUKONOU, *Jalons pour une théologie africaine* (Paris/Namur, 1980); F. A. ISAMBERT, *Le sens du sacré: Fête et religion populaire* (Paris, 1981); K. RAHNER, "The Relationship of Theology and Popular Religion," in *Theological Investigations*, vol. 16 (1975; London, 1979), 185–95;

F. A. PASTOR, "Ministerios laicales y comunidades de base," *Greg* 68/1–2 (1987): 267–305.

Félix-Alejandro PASTOR

VI. PHILOSOPHY OF RELIGION

1. A Complicated Matter

Among the many disciplines that, on various grounds, with different approaches and specific instruments of investigation, are concerned with the subject of religion—experiences, emotions, worship and traditions, individual and community life, inspiration, preaching and propagation, not excluding polemics and controversies—critical reflection is certainly due to the philosophy of religion. But this neither sets it apart from other sciences also concerned with religion (psychology, sociology of religion, history of religions, comparative religion, and so on) nor lays down, in any absolute and final way, an unambiguous epistemological criterion. Take, e.g., the *science* of religion, empirical, not prescriptive, "objective" and, as far as possible, a complete analysis of historical forms, reciprocal relationships with culture, politics, society, economy, environment. Or take the *phenomenology* of religion, which offers an overall survey of and imposes order on the complex phenomena of religious convictions and experiences. These examples are not accidental, for the same term is used in different senses and different methodologies within a philosophic context and otherwise; this rapid approach can have comparative justification. In rejecting hermeneutic-type assumptions which form the basis of the main systems of philosophy of religion (from Schleiermacher to I. Mancini) and by taking a different attitude to historical evolutionism, present-day philosophy of religion is faced with an enormous mass of archaeological, ethnological, historical, and psychological data on all religions, a vast and hardly definable sacral area concerning magic and taboo. Myth, rite, sacrifice, cult of the saints and of the dead, eschatology, apocalyptic, holy books, and revelation are topics to be investigated in a monotheistic/polytheistic/pantheistic framework which is hard to organize on a diachronic plane. There is a type of phenomenology which, by definition, seeks

to be as distant from abstract scientific objectivism as from a subjectivism all too easily a slave to prejudices and ideology and, maintaining reference, even if indirect, to the underlying question of the "essence of religion" (and of the "absoluteness of Christianity") as inescapable, seeks to strike a mean (and go beyond it) in *intentionality*. Without going any deeper into this philosophic treatment of phenomenology (not only Husserl but, more particularly, M. Scheler), the Christian is faced with a wealth of *semina verbi* and the long, slow, and contradictory *praeparatio evangelica* (e.g., human sacrifice, cannibalism, corpse eating, sacred prostitution, and the like) by means sometimes surprising.

The rationale of phenomenology (see van der Leeuw, *Phänomenologie der Religion* is the singling out of the *specific* so as to plot the variants on a *constant*. See W. Schmidt's monumental *Der Ursprung der Gottesidee* (12 vols.; 1912–55) for the demonstration of the constant presence, though with varying form and intensity, of the monotheistic concept of supreme being (historical-cultural method). It is a matter of individuating the architecture of the whole (the forest of trees) through language, symbols, rites, and myths. One must avoid creating ideologies (which occurs in a certain type of modernism); one must isolate and interpret religious phenomena without distorting them or using them to prove a point. With *Das Heilige* (1917), R. Otto brought phenomenology to a turning point by attacking the (deeply) entrenched cultural stereotype of the genetic explanation of religion, the product of rationalism, positivism, and evolutionism. The Marburg School that Otto founded was to go on studying the complex a priori, the numinous and irrational, moral and rational elements (note the subtitle "On the irrationality of the idea of the divine and its relationship to the rational") which make the sacred (*mysterium tremendum et fascinans*) something other than any naturalistic human structure. The contribution of R. Pettazzoni, who founded the Italian school of history of religions, has been decisive, being independent of the English tradition of comparative religion as also of the German *religionsgeschichtliche Schule*.

The permanent "philosophic" *questions* are, basically and in their own way, problems of the philosophy of religion, especially the question of God: his existence, attributes, and the possibility of and conditions for his communicating with human beings. We are not of course merely referring explicitly to "philosophy of revelation." Indeed, the scope of the disciplines is so vast and varied (taking into account the history of the church, of exegesis, of dogmas, spirituality, ecumenism) that the very concept of *religion*, fundamental in the modern age, has no precise signification. Starting from Greco-Roman tradition, the term varies in meaning; it is used in a general sense; it is synonymous with faith, order, law, sect. By way of the contribution of the fathers, of the great scholastic tradition and of humanism, we reach the Reformation and reformulation of the classic (medieval) dual concept faith-reason into the triad faith-religion-reason, the stress falling on the first of these terms, even though from Augustine to Calvin the second is of more frequent use. By way of religion-as-sentiment (from pietism to Schleiermacher) and its antithesis, the religion of reason (Kant, specifically), will emerge the concept of *religion*, and the transition from the theology of religion to the philosophy of religion as we know it today. But history (the prior events) and transition are what interest us. Also because we are convinced that the Kierkegaardian interpretation of faith as atypical model of philosophy of religion is inescapable.

Religion has its origins in religious experience, and reflection about religious experience is, from the experiential point of view, itself religious. But revelation does not of itself give rise to thought: a faith is necessary, while thought requires the freedom (a basic option) to interpret it, affirm it, or deny it. On the one hand, for instance, the philosophic faith of Jacobi: all human knowledge proceeds from revelation and from faith, since all attempts at proof lead to fatalism and we can only prove similarities; by faith, we know the finite and the infinite, the existence of our own bodies (*Briefe über die Lehre Spinozas* [1785]). On the other, mystical experience, e.g., that of Teresa of Avila or John of the Cross, for whom language is inadequate for expressing the inner experience and union with God, cannot be conveyed either by things created or by things thought. Socrates reaches the threshold of religious truth, i.e., of transcendence; on the other hand,

William of Auvergne (ca. 1180–1249) writes that there ought to be a single faith since the human race has a common origin and a single end: the Christian faith is the best guarantee, the only true religion. Lessing impenitently declares himself incapable of the leap to the transcendental; Hegel has the speculative presumption to accept, to explain, "to go beyond" faith with the concept. The ontology of Gioberti (and perhaps of Rosmini) postulates that the first reality known is not the finite being but the infinite and divine; as opposed to this, the traditionalists (or fideists) hold that the idea of God and his existence can only be revealed and hence only be known by faith. Though RATIONALISM was condemned in the Constitution *Dei Filius* at VATICAN I, the problem recurred with the immanentist conclusions of the modernists (see the decree *Lamentabili* and the encyclical *Pascendi* of 1907). What Jaspers has to say about subtle modern psychology is telling: declaring himself to be outside any religious faith, he speaks of a philosophic faith, the breath of freedom that fills and moves human nature to its depths, enabling it to rise above itself and attain the origin of its being (see *Vom Ursprung und Ziel der Geschichte*, 269). We might define this as "praeambulum fidei."

2. Philosophy of Religion: A Perennial Dimension of Thought

We may even try to spot in Spinoza (*Tractatus theologico-politicus* [1670]) the beginning, and in the various stages of the Enlightenment, the laborious and at times confused, instrumentalist statement, and in the romantic-idealistic flowering, the *definition* of philosophy of religion in the modern sense. But without lingering over the problems of such a definition (in space and time with all the attendant risks), we can collect into the whole philosophic ambit the elements of a specific line of thought covered by this heading. From within a fertile and uncontrolled *mythos* emerges the need for *logos* that points to a deity, "to One . . . very great" but beyond all anthropomorphism "of aspect" or "of thought," an immutable substance. In the sixth century B.C.E., Xenophanes (simplistic to label as a skeptic someone who, by means of sophist spirituality, anticipates the critique of *The City of God*) speaks of a "good wisdom" at once ethical, theological, and political, and which, paraphrasing a text in the Bible, we might say "comes from above." But the gods did not reveal all things to mortals at the beginning; this takes time—an argument taken up by Lessing in *Die Erziehung des Menschengeschlechts* (1780). He who feels within himself the "daemon" is not the "artificer of new gods," in contrast to the elders who assure the stability of the *polis* (Socrates in Plato's *Apologia*), but bears good witness to a provident creator-god and, by virtue of a concept of the deity free of spatial physicality, keeps far the friends of impiety and injustice (as also in Xenophon's *Memorabilia*).

Beyond *allegory* (which actually prompts us to attribute to the gods a human baseness of behavior that cannot be theirs, since evil cannot be attributed to them) is the *reality* of the gods, which has to be rediscovered. Ever, as in this case, there is evident in Plato the reciprocity of the *ideal* and the *real*. The *Summa Theologiae Platonis* (*Laws* 10), which was to become the foundation for the theology of the fathers and was to exert an uninterrupted influence on one entire interpretative line of spiritual-interiorist Christianity, begins from "universal" faith in God, to which all human beings can attain from existence, from beauty, from the order of things (see Rom 1). Though the soul is the principle of motion, the gods know, hear, and see all and take care of everything and everyone. They cannot be corrupted by human beings; the impiety of human beings is attributable to themselves and themselves alone.

There is also a "theology of Aristotle" (*Metaphysics* 12) based on his own cosmology, which starts from the continuity of movement and the principle "such that its substance be activity," "that which, without being moved, moves." Immobile principle that impresses an eternal and uniform movement, unmoved mover and, by an exquisitely metaphysical progression, "thought of thought . . . thought that thinks itself." Thomas Aquinas's comment is apt: the prime mover must be *substantia per se existens* and its substance, action; in it there is an essential reference of the *intellectus* to the *intelligere*, as of the *essentia* to the *esse*. But many centuries did not pass in vain, and though the acute and painful thought of Greek tragedy gave an existential and dramatic dimension to religious thinking (centered on the incurable con-

flict between fate and providence, necessity and freedom, fault and punishment, and in short between God and human nature), Christianity, on the one hand, brought the light of revelation and, on the other, stimulated thinkers to restate the problems with greater precision. The Aristotelian identification of first philosophy—metaphysics—and theology no longer works.

But the transition effected from *substance* to *divine substance* is not without its consequences, linguistic and conceptual. Substance, the Aristotelian "first category," the fundamental concept of metaphysics means, from Aristotle on through the fathers and the Scholastics up to Descartes, Spinoza, and Leibniz, a particular, unique, absolute, and supreme substance, this being the divine substance. This basic assumption for philosophy and for theological discussion about the nature of God (and of the Trinity), in its linguistic variety was to entail misunderstandings and confusions: *hypostasis, hyparxis, physis, essentia, substantia, natura* . . . and the final blow was dealt by empiricism, which objected to the idea of a substance *void* of characteristics, except for the answering criticism that a bundle of properties may define something.

The different conception of substance is what qualifies Plato "theologically" in relation to Socrates (and Aristotle in relation to Plato): the *ousia* is truly such on the eternal, abstract plane of reality, where "phenomenic" substance assumes an ambiguous significance. The deepening, in relation to the fact that only substances have corresponding ideas, that these are hierarchized and ordered by the Demiurge and that the One represents the apex of reality, prepares the way, not without the mediation of Aristotelian categories and Neoplatonism, for the earliest Christian philosophic and theological speculation.

For Aristotle, using analogy, the concept of substance can refer to the individual concretized by his materiality, and to God. Even if *ho theos* does not necessarily have a precisely monotheistic sense, it became the foundation of a monotheistic conception in the sense later developed by Neoplatonist commentators, and it undoubtedly exerted great influence on Christian writers. These confronted the problem of the unity (pure, unique being) and generality of God (first of all other beings) of Aristotelian "theology" with the Platonist notion to support them that the supreme god is absolutely one, simple, and unqualified. The second god is the one who is represented as polymorphous. This interpretation of the heavenly hierarchy, based on a reading of the *Parmenides*, became familiar to Christians through Eudorus of Alexandria and is witnessed to, e.g., in the *Gospel of Philip* and in Basilides. Not only will the *prōtē ousia* be the Father and the *deutera ousia* be the Logos, but there will also be mention of blood as the substance of the soul (Clement of Alexandria) and of the miracle of the water turned into wine as a change of substance (Origen). But, principally, the Logos is *ousia ousiōn*, whereas the Father is behind everything (see *Rep.* 509b: *epekeina tēs ousias*).

Inspired by Plato, Origen commenting on Jn 14:6 ("I am . . . the Truth") calls Jesus the "substance of truth" (*Contra Celsum* 8.12). In Philo, Clement, and Origen, the "idea of God" corresponds to the Logos, "place of ideas," "idea of ideas." All this is of course mediated by the experience that Christians themselves have of God, with various tonings-down and underlinings (mystical and pedagogic) all the way to *theologia negativa*.

3. Reason and Wisdom

The problem arises as to whether the other categories can be applied to God, and the conclusion is reached that God is not in time and space but time and space are within God. Athanasius claims that God is totally simple, has no accidents, has no need of anything to complete his substance, which, however, is *akatalēptos:* if "we call him God and Father and Lord," this is because we are trying to define him. Comparison with the biblical conception of God is fruitful: being, one, source, fire, spirit, light, life, love, good, father, lord, immanent and transcendent, all-providing and all-knowing. The concepts of *noēton phōs* and *pneuma*, e.g., are purified and spiritualized on this basis. Though Tertullian, in his peculiar Latin, calls God *corpus*, the acceptation of *spiritus* and the definition *unus* become widespread. All this was not to be without effects on the christological and trinitarian controversies and definitions: misunderstandings over *homo ousios* arose from the many senses of *ousia* and from the fear (in Eusebius, e.g.) of what we should (theologically) call *modernism*, whereas Athanasius succeeds

convincing us that the term merely contains more concentratedly (*pressius*) what is diffusely contained in revelation.

On the relationship between faith and reason (occasionally dialectical, ancillary, reciprocally autonomous or inevitably mixed up with one another), a conceptual clarification and observable disciplining develops, e.g., among the apologists and Alexandrians, and in the expressions *semina verbi* or *anima naturaliter christiana*.

After the polemical, apologetic, or anti-heretical phase comes the need for a "scientific" study of revelation, and this means an organized, complete, and precise doctrinal exposition, such as will not offend "intellectuals." It was no accident that the first, most famous school of theology should have been in Alexandria, the city founded by Alexander the Great in 331 B.C.E., the cradle of Hellenism, luminous center of intense cultural life, crossroads of civilization. With study of the sacred text went a preoccupation with the religious doctrines of the East, but more particularly classical Greek philosophy. Hence, the philosophic analysis of the contents of the faith and, under the influence above all of Plato, the allegorical interpretation of the sacred texts, practiced by Philo of Alexandria and even more by Clement, was erected into a system by Origen. For Philo, the allegorical interpretation is the truest one; the literal sense is as the shadow to the body. Allegory becomes the hermeneutical instrument of an ethical religious discourse establishing metaphysical principles—an epochal operation of inculturation by the rich and learned rabbi of Alexandria, whose loving study of the Scriptures was accompanied by a passion for theorizing: "I always have time for philosophising" (*De providentia* 2.215). To bring the word of God to a human audience, Philo spends his efforts in harmonizing the biblical message with philosophical ideas. The beginning is apodictic: "God is, thus, the first source and rightly so, since he it was who made this entire world spring forth" (*De fuga* 198). But there is a metaphysical dualism: as against God the absolute, the Creator, light, and measure of all things (as in Plato, *Laws* IV, 716c and against Protagoras), there is the world, multiplex, corruptible, material, and, in between, the world of ordered ideas (Philo is the first to speak of "intelligible world") with, as highest, the divine logos, wisdom of God, design and architect of the world. And human beings are modeled on the logos. "At the boundary between human nature and immortal nature, in such that we necessarily share in the one and the other and were created both mortal and immortal: mortal in body, immortal in mind" (*De opificio mundi* 135). In the Hellenistic climate of uncertainty and dissatisfaction with rationality, this is the basis for speculation on new relationships between reason and faith, on new prospects of salvation derived from revelation. It is a climate in which the very ancient *gnosis* revives and grows strong with its overall conception of being: cosmological, anthropological, soteriological, and the same, indeed accentuated, Manichaean conception of a dualism exacerbated by painful experience of evil and unfulfilled longing for total escape into a satisfying life of bliss. Here too the allegorical interpretation of revelation is a syncretic attempt to salvage oriental religious myths and Greek philosophic categories.

To become perfect, Philo says, human beings must run a course that carries them from encyclopedic ("encyclical") philosophic knowledge to (theological) wisdom:

> Truly, as the encyclical disciplines contribute to the acquiring of philosophy, so philosophy contributes to the acquiring of wisdom. Philosophy is the search for wisdom, and wisdom is the science of things divine and human and their causes. So, just as culture acquired by means of encyclical studies is the slave of philosophy, so too philosophy should be the slave of wisdom. (*De congressu* 79)

In comparison with biblical personalities, the mythical figure of Socrates grows pale: "Moses, . . . the man who explored immaterial nature, . . . directed his research in every possible direction; he tried to see the One clearly, on whom our most ardent desire is centered and who is the unique Good" (*De mutatione* 25–26).

These are the postulates of patristic exegesis which, on the basic distinction between the moral, the spiritual, and the mystical, was to develop a plurality of senses: anagogical, tropological, parabolical. Not only Platonizing ideas about the soul but Pauline anthropology of body-soul-spirit are at the basis of Origen's threefold system of the literal-moral-spiritual interpretation of Scripture which, with further stimulus from Augustine and Gregory, was to

be fixed scholastically by Augustine of Dacia: "*Littera gesta docet, quid credas allegoria. Moralis quid agas, quo tendas anagogia*" ("the letter teaches facts; allegory conveys what you are to believe; the moral interpretation teaches how you should conduct yourself; anagogy teaches where you are to tend, i.e., to the ultimate spiritual experience"). And Augustine of Hippo (*De doctrina christiana* 2.15) admonishes us not to lose our way among the literalists and allegorists: the Scriptures are misconstrued when unknown or ambiguous signs are imposed on them. But the picture is more complicated: there are heresies (e.g., gnosticism), one aspect of the virulent reaction of pagan classical philosophy. After turning the slow, broad headland of the first millennium (between John Scotus Erigena and Anselm of Canterbury), we have to wait for humanism and the Renaissance before we have a new methodological approach, admittedly in problematical terms, but lively and fruitful ones.

4. From Natural Theology to Philosophy of Religion

The book of Wisdom (chap. 13) calls those "stupid" who from the works have not been able to recognize the Artificer, and Rom 1 goes one better in accusing them of blindness and depravity. Then Paul (1 Cor 13) admits that sight is "like a mirror," like the metal ones of those days which, however brightly they were polished, still only reflected an indistinct image. The more enlightened among the apostles were not only to resume the dialogue with the authors of classical culture but were to identify the fruitful *semina Verbi* to be found in their philosophic and religious thought. The human *logos* is a sharing in the divine Logos; but in subsequent formulation, APOLOGETICS (demonstration — by stages, religious, Christian, Catholic) was to mark the transition from natural theology to the philosophy of religion. Even though the *sola fide* of the Reformation was to exclude recourse to apologetics, *The Apology and Confession of Faith* presented by the Waldensians to Duke Emmanuel Philibert in 1560 sounds the affirmation of faith in God and in his Son. The *Theology of the Early Greek Thinkers*, a right understanding of the Godhead by means of reason or "prime philosophy" which attains the (Supreme) Being, is systematized into three *genera: mythical* (fabulous, of the poets), *physical* (natural, of the philosophers), *civil* (of nations) by Varro (*Antiquities*), which is taken up later in *The City of God* (6.5.1). Cicero too had affirmed, long before Descartes' *Discourse of Method*, that true law and right reason conform to nature, which is diffused through all, constant and eternal.

Though IRENAEUS (*Adversus haereses* 40.20.7) had stated that "God's glory is the living man" (vistas open up toward liberation philosophy with an updated exegesis: "God's glory is the living poor man"), entailing the immediate theoretic and practical consequence that "human life is the vision of God," AUGUSTINE turns the accusations being leveled by pagans against Christians on their head by a violent critique of polytheism (*De Civitate Dei*) and by asserting that the realization of true religion in history is to be found in Christianity (*Epistolae* 102.12.5). But this introduction to truth is only the first step toward a higher reality which culminates in the doctrine of the Trinity (*De Trinitate*), set out by means of the category of relationship which, while preventing him from being very familiar with the concept of person, gives him ample means for developing the anthropological argument of the *vestigia* (*esse-nosse-velle; mens, notitia, amor; memoria, intelligentia, voluntas*) ("traces [to be-not to know-to will; mind, knowledge, love; memory, intelligence, will]"). This is not an explanation of the Trinity starting from human nature, of course, but an attempt to come to grips with human nature by starting from the trinitarian revelation. And human nature is remote from God *in regione dissimilitudinis* ("in the country of dissimilarity") (*Confessions* 7.10), a memory of Plato (between the nonexistence of nothingness and the immutable being of God) and an anticipation of Bernard's description of the *status naturae lapsae*: "*Nobilis illa creatura in regione similitudinis fabricata . . . de similitudine ad dissimilitudinem descendit*" ("state of fallen nature: 'This noble creature which was made in the domain of similarity . . . falls from similarity to dissimilarity'") (*De diversis, Sermo* 42.2). Bernard's very vigorous polemic against the dialectician Abelard is not intended to condemn dialectic but to warn against the emptying of the Christian mystery and to reaffirm the primacy of charity over logic. The region of sin and spoiled likeness is that into which we are born in con-

cupiscence and in which we live in the flesh; the will is *oblique* and philosophic knowledge leads into darkness (Bonaventure, *De donis Spiritus Sancti* 4.12).

But it is the only way of escape from theological solipsism (Peter Damian, *De divina omnipotentia*) and the charm of dialectic, which by different routes lead to a dangerous contempt for oneself and for the world (Innocent III, *De contemptu mundi sive de miseria conditionis humanae*) ("On despising the world, namely, on the wretchedness of the human condition").

Hatred of matter, contempt for the body under the weight of evil experiences, the yearning to escape from a repugnant world, and the ardent desire for a true, full, quiet life, had opposed a *gnosis* to a *pistis* in a revival, within Christianity, of a very ancient religious phenomenon. It was the task of Franciscanism, with its humane drive and feeling for nature, love for God and neighbor, and joy in suffering, to overcome the new forms of Gnosticism.

Augustine had already warned: *Aliud est esse rationalem, aliud esse sapientem* ("It's another thing to be rational and to be wise") and Bonaventure was to call revelation a certain inner light (*Com. in Sent*, II, 4, 2, 2). But warning is given that reason is needed to make the faith more intelligible, to confirm it, to interpret the Scriptures, reason being the autonomous source of philosophic knowledge (John Scotus Erigena). Dialectic is summoned to renew the study of theology: Fulbert, director of the episcopal school at Chartres does this, with the cautiousness due to the dogmas of the faith. But his pupil Berengarius of Tours (*De sacra cena adversus Lanfrancum* [The Last Supper against Lanfranc]) was to be condemned for his denial of the real presence, and Lessing's essay (*Berengarius Turonensis . . .* [1770]) would later be intended as a defense of a freedom of thought anticipating the Enlightenment.

With the *Monologion* (*Exemplum meditandi de ratione fidei* [A model of meditation about faith]) and the *Proslogion* (*Fides quaerens intellectum* [Faith seeking understanding]), Anselm of Canterbury (1033–1109) articulates the ontological proof whereby the believed-in existence of God is presented in a rationally inescapable way ("we believe that you are such that nothing greater than you can be imagined") because he is the unique being whose existence *in intellectu* is identified with existence *in re*. A very classic proof over which the greatest thinkers were to take sides: immediately against, Thomas Aquinas and later Kant, both of whom held the distinction between *in intellectu* and *in re* to be untenable; in favor, Descartes and Leibniz (with the rider: "if it is possible").

To avoid pantheistic-type misunderstandings, the Fourth Lateran Council (1215) was to warn: *Inter creatorem et creaturam non potest tanta similitudo notari, quin inter eos maior sit dissimilitudo notanda* (Between the Creator and the creature, dissimilarity is greater than similarity).

5. Toward the Age of Reason

Scholasticism, inaugurated by Anselm, reaches its apogee with Thomas Aquinas (1225–1274): The presumption is that the wise (those who make use of reason) are in a position to prove the existence of God. On this *praeambulum fidei*, knowledge of the God of faith, one in three, can be constructed. So Thomas, for whom human nature refers to God as cause and end, can with his deepest simplicity say: *Religio proprie importat ordinem ad Deum* (Religion is properly concerned with God) (*ST* part 2.2, q. 81, a. 1) which categorizes the Pauline affirmation: "What therefore you worship as unknown, this I proclaim to you" (Acts 17:23). God is the material object of all search: known by the natural light of human reason (*Summa contra Gentiles*) or by the supernatural light of divine revelation (*Summa Theologica*). But a perfect harmony between faith and reason requires that the aim of the latter be to set forth "the truth professed by the Catholic faith . . . by eliminating errors contrary to it" (1.2). It is theological work, even though in a dialogue with non-Christians, it uses rational arguments: the job of the wise is to consider supreme causes, the Truth source of every truth. The exposition proceeds, nicely articulated and apodictic in manner: God, existence and nature (1, 1); creation and creature (1, 2); God, ultimate end and supreme governor (1, 3); divine mysteries and eschatology (1, 4). In a word, God in himself, God the Creator, God the end, God the supernatural. Only the pedagogic method changes, but reason is always *manuducta fide*. For it is in the *Summa Theologica* that, nature and the ambit of *Sacra doctrina* having been defined, the problem of the existence of God is broached and the biblical assertion is proved in the famous five ways, which reformulate the

thought of Aristotle: motion, efficient cause, the contingent and the necessary, the gradation of things, and the government of nature.

(The argument *ex gubernatione*, which takes us back to the Stoics and the *nous* of Anaxagoras, in the *Contra Gentiles* refers back to John Damascene: impossible to separate the epistemological criteria of the two *Summae*). At the climax of a long process of assimilation, classical philosophy consolidates Christian dogma and, at the same time, human reason asserts its own rights.

Lest the tree of knowledge seduce (*Eritis sicut dei*) (you will be like God) and *libido sciendi* (lust for knowledge) be accompanied by *concupiscentia carnis* (concupiscence of the flesh) and lead to *desperatio salutis* (despising of salvation), wisdom must be *sapida scientia* (sapid science), or it becomes *ars diabolica* (diabolical skill). *Spiritualis intelligentia* (spiritual understanding) is the presupposition of Christian philosophizing, and the *caritas* of the redeemed, while reconciling us to God and our neighbor, makes it possible for us to have a general intuition of the beauty of the cosmic order. Reference to revelation is all the while taken for granted, not as incontrovertible proof (the risk of ideology) but as grace, a free gift soliciting human faith. The lure of the gnosis, medieval polemics (dialectic of sin/sin of dialectic) notwithstanding, had been largely soothed away by the Franciscan school; and a balance, never again to be achieved, in the Thomist system, was to lead to the reduction of being to thought (Descartes), then to perception (*esse est percipi* [to be is to be perceived] [Berkeley]) and, finally, to idea.

While recommending that one pay attention to the advice of others—books and authors—since knowledge grows by their successive contributions and is a progressive emergence into light, Roger Bacon (ca. 1214–1292) warns that theologians' concentration on the *quaestiones* should not distract them from studying the text (*Comp. studii Theol.*). In Raymond Lull, Christian enthusiasm and missionary zeal went with an irenic and ecumenical attitude aimed at clarifying the teaching of the various religions and demonstrating their fragmentary nature. This *Doctor illuminatus*, with his *Ars Magna*, dreams of an *Ars inventiva*, an organic, universal wisdom attainable by an intellect clothed in faith, illuminated by the faith. A convinced exposition, not an apologetic proof, of monotheism and immortality is offered in *The Book of the Gentile and the Three Sages*. From the anguish of the forest, from the darkness of error, the Gentile is drawn to the joy-conferring spiritual reality of the Jew, the Christian, and the Muslim, who in their turn are enlightened on the significance of five trees (divine virtues) surrounding a fountain (true doctrine) by "Intelligence," a mysterious and fascinating damsel, the depositary of the unique truth contained in the three religions. As the sages, having each serenely and with conviction presented his own religion, do not wait for the Gentile to choose any one of them, Lull breaks off with the promise that all three will go on meeting and conferring in their continued search for the true faith. This formulation of the old "Parable of the Three Rings," variously reworked until Lessing's *Nathan der Weise*, though it may present problems, is undoubtedly a high expression of civilization and true religion in an age that saw the passionate preaching of the Crusades and the waging of bloodthirsty religious wars.

A new age is dawning: a new spirit. But the newness is contained within the old wisdom in which Bible and Gospel are steeped and which keeps recurring in differing contexts.

> If someone living within Christendom goes to the house of God, to the true house of God, and has an accurate conceptual notion of God and prays to him but does not pray in the truth, and someone else who lives in a heathen land but prays with a passionate intensity even though his eyes rest on the image of an idol: who is nearer to the truth? One prays to God in the truth, even though he turns his eyes to an idol; the other does not pray to the true God in the truth and hence, in truth, adores an idol. (S. Kierkegaard, *Concluding Unscientific Postscript* [1848] SV VII, 168)

Analogously, Spinoza was to express himself extremely concisely in the *Tractatus theologico-politicus* of 1670: *Si quis vera credendo fiat contumax is revera impiam, et si contra falso credendo oboediens, piam habet fidem* ("If one in believing what is true becomes contumacious, his faith is actually ungodly. Contrariwise, if in believing what is false one remains obedient, he has a godly faith") (in *Opera*, ed. Gebhardt [Heidelberg, 1925] 3:158). And Augustine: *Gaudeat etiam sic et amet non inveniendo invenire, potius quam inveniendo non invenire te* ("Let him [who does not comprehend

this] rejoice even thus and be content rather by not discovering to discover Thee, than by discovering not to discover Thee") (*Confessions* 1.6.10). But adventures of the spirit involve their own risks.

6. Humanism and Antihumanism

The significant aspect of humanism lies in placing the human being at the center of attention, study, and care; in overcoming the rigid schemes of incontrovertible logic. Rather than an open revolt against medieval thought (which had neglected neither the *Studia humanitatis* nor human nature), it was its continuation, with a shift of interests, a greater religious inwardness, more moral, less codified, less defined, more open and tolerant.

In the same years as the divine poet was at work, Albertino Mussato (1251–1329) spoke of poetry as *divina ars, altera philosophia, theologia mundi*: the poet's function was to reveal beings. From antiquity, the divine poets have spoken to us of God in heaven, even if he whom we call God others have called Jove and others still have identified with some corporeal reality.

Philosophy and religion, alike the love and study of truth and wisdom—which is God—are autonomous, without coming into conflict, in reciprocal relationship but on a plane of parity. Such is the thought of Marsilio Ficino, who sees, in free and pluralistic philosophic research and a return to the past, the casting off of the chains of religious philosophy (be it Christian, Arabic, or Jewish) for an open and varied conception of the world. On a more religious plane, the Reformation, in conflict with these same humanistic values, was to take the search for truth and human dignity to extremes by denying "possession" of the truth and freewill and making the reality of faith prevail over that of religion. Quotations, translations, and imitations of the moralists or of classical moral thought (from Plato and Aristotle to Cicero, Plutarch, Seneca, Epicurus . . .) are not opposed but find a common harmony in an ultimate salvation, a (Christian) paradise, with the virtuous activity of a moral life in the *City*. From Cicero to Erasmus, the line of a tolerant eclecticism (*Ipsa natura ratio, quae est lex divina et humana* [Reason is nature itself, being at the same time divine and human law] [*De officiis* III, V]), which is not substantially different from the "follow nature . . . live according to nature," from Aristotle and the Stoics reaches right down to Thomas Aquinas. True, there is the risk of a return to paganism, denounced by Savonarola, or unstable balance, as in Nicholas of Cusa, between an irenic "peace of the faith" and the reaffirmation of the true Christian religion. But more than the *Conclusioni filosofiche, cabalistiche e teologiche* (of 1486), Pico della Mirandola's Promethean utopia that was doomed to failure, there remains the "Oration" *Della dignità dell'uomo* and the gleam, amid opinions and debates, of the "radiance of the truth." See also the Christian Platonism of Ficino (but a certain Aristotelian interpretation must not be overlooked which, by way of Alexander of Aphrodisias, emerges in *De immortalitate animae* (1516) by Pomponazzi, where it is not wrong to speak of "double truth"); and the efforts of Coluccio Salutati and Leon Battista Alberti to identify pagan fate and fortune with the biblical and Christian concept of Providence.

Philological meticulousness, brilliance of exposition, polemical vigor, as well as an acute freedom of conscience (not without certain ambiguities) justify Erasmus's claim to have converted humanism to the worship of Christ. The corrosive criticism of *In Praise of Folly* (1509) concerns the reform of the Christian religion (without sparing the Reformers) and the vanity of sciences and doctrines taken over from the ancients, present in Pico and treated by Agrippa of Nettesheim (*De incertitudine et vanitate scientiarum et artium atque excellentia verbi Dei declamatio* [1530]). To the complex phenomenon of humanism may also be ascribed the ferment of religious aspiration by way of magic, occultism, and hermeticism, which to some degree involves many of the authors already mentioned and also, above all, Giordano Bruno. Atypical but significant is the phenomenon of Machiavelli (*The Prince* [1513]), contrasted with the component of melancholy (brilliantly "described" by Dürer in the engraving of the same name) and utopianism (Thomas More, *Utopia* [1516]). The picture gradually grows more and more complicated, until we see the vanity of every doctrinal system, be it theological, scientific, literary, or moral (Agrippa, Montaigne, Erasmus); the corrosion and destruction of a universal natural law (Montaigne, Machiavelli); the abandonment of the classical-Christian-humanistic ideals of restraint, hier-

archy, balance, proportion (Telesio, Bruno, and especially the *Reformation*) until the transition from cabalistic or Aristotelian scientism to the pure empiricism which, with Bacon and Galileo, marks the beginning of a new age.

We must, to sum up, avoid facile talk identifying one kind of humanism with one kind of Christianity in a serene atmosphere of *anima naturaliter christiana*. There is also a Christian point of view that does *not* minimize the precarious, ambiguous, dramatic, irrational aspects of existence, where uneasy existence, a *status naturae lapsae*, a *status deviationis*, sees in salvation no easy or obvious way out. Folly widespread finds a response in the folly of the cross and in the paradoxical claim of salvation from folly through the folly of the cross. So the Christian is immersed in the mystery of history: between a response *already* given and a meaning *not yet* grasped. *Theologia negativa*, the *theologia crucis*, and "dialectical theology" are radical expressions not only of the incommensurability of the divine with the human, but also of the inescapability of the mystery of evil and temptation, which from the telling (even if debatable) reading in Job: *Temptatio vita hominis super terram* (7:1), leads on to the mystical experience: *Maxima temptatio est non temptari* (G. Groote) and to the disturbing and disillusioned *Quis non est temptatus, quid scit?*

The world, according to Groote, is a place of crime and transgression, toil and pain, futility and malice, delusion and despair. The harsh *militia Christi* portrayed in Athanasius's *Life of Antony*, by means of temptations, terrifying demonic apparitions, and hallucinating transformations of nature itself, is revived and updated for a Flanders sacked and put to fire and sword in the wars of religion, by H. Bosch, P. Brueghel, and other Flemish painters. A northern humanism of *insecuritas* and *indignitas hominis* of painters whom E. Castelli (*Il demoniaco nell' arte* [Milan, 1952]) calls theologians. The folly of rationality (the tree of knowledge) but also of religion and the religious Reformation and the prospect of the loss of identity, of anonymity (No one, *Niemand*), the radical demythologization of the *dignitas hominis* already explicit in the *De contemptu mundi* mentioned above and later taken up by Kierkegaard on different premises and with different results. While, on the one hand, Stoic themes were taken up again (Justus Lipsius, *De* constantia, 1584) and epicureanism remained in fashion (from the *De voluptate* of L. Valla [1431] to the *De vita, moribus et placitis Epicurei* in 8 books [1647] of the *doux prêtre* Gassendi), on the other, Agostino Steuco holds that all currents of philosophy can lead to Christian philosophy (*De perenni philosophia* [1540]), and Melchior Cano argues that natural reason is a *locus theologicus* (*De locis theologicis* [1563]).

7. Modern Acceptance

Francis Bacon distinguishes between divine philosophy (theology) and natural philosophy (theoretical and practical), and wishes empirics (experimental faculties) and dogmatics (rational faculties) to work together (*Novum Organon*); Galileo warns that physics tells us how the heavens move but not what goes on in heaven. But once again the problem of substance arises.

Whereas Aristotelian substance is defined in relation to its accidents, Cartesian substance is defined in relation to another substance and to the distinction between "thought" and "nature," which leads to the development of the substantial concept of the autonomy of thought. "By substance we mean nothing other than the thing that exists in such a way as to have no need of any other to exist" (*Princ.* 1.51). Whence the heteronomy of the substantiality of creatures and the autonomy of the divine substance as authentic autonomy of thought. Even if thought corresponds to certain requisites of the definition, it does, however, always refer to a body and, because of this, to a third (the first, ontologically speaking; we have mentioned Descartes' re-adoption of the "ontological proof"), which is God. "By the noun God I mean a certain infinite substance, independently and absolutely intelligent, absolutely powerful. . . . [By him] I and everything else, if it exists, have been created" (*Med.* III, 11–14). Descartes confidently concludes that substance cannot be *univocally* predicated of God and of others and that their relationship is a *creatio continua* (continued creation): "God is the cause of created things, not only *secundum fieri* (as becoming) but also *secundum esse* (as being)" (as he wrote to Gassendi).

Spinoza defined substance as *quod in se est et per se concipitur* (*Ethica*, def. III), i.e., that the concept of which, to be formed, has no need of the concept of anything else; the definition

of the *attributes* and the *modes* of being completes the interweaving of the concept of *substance* with the concept of *world*, with all those pantheistic implications that emerge in the *Spinozastreit*, documented in the Jacobi–Mendelssohn correspondence *On the Doctrine of Spinoza* (1785). The *Tractatus theologico-politicus* (1670) is looked on by some as the beginning of the philosophy of religion in its modern sense: the hermeneutics of the phenomenon of religion, of historical religion, of the traditions of a religion claiming to be revealed (Judeo-Christian) on the basis of *lumen naturale*. The biblical universal principle: the one God, omnipotent, provident, rewarder, is the foundational definition of true religion: obedience to God in the practice of justice and charity, without, moreover, having to look for relationships or affinities between faith and theology (obedience) on the one hand, and philosophy (the real) on the other. Scripture is examined by the light of nature, as is nature itself, taking care not to attribute anything to it that does not emerge clearly from its history. Except for everyone's right to think as he or she pleases, the result will not be "dogmas of truth" but "dogmas of piety" (obediential faith) in the acceptance of those principles that emerge clearly and constitute the basis for peaceful religious coexistence: God exists, i.e., a supreme being, unique, omnipotent, governing all; in the worship of God in obedience, justice, and charity, lies salvation; God forgives the sins of those who repent. Leibniz has to set out from a critique of Spinoza to affirm the plurality of substances, the infinite multiplicity of simple substances; but also a critique of Aristotelian substance with the definition of singular substance to define the subject: with all its predicates, past, present, and future; and a critique of Cartesian substance: "For if there is no 'vere unum,' every 'vera res' will cease to be" (A. Volder, 20-6-1703). He thus constructs a concept of substance, a unit systematically self-defined: the monad, the infinite multiplicity of monads.

It is their order, not the fact that creatures exist, that proves that God exists. So substance is defined as the expression of the original concept of the divine. Substance is the foundation of the harmony of the universe, the originating, constant, and absolute nature, without limitations, containing all possible reality. The ontological argument finishes with the proof of the possibility of the perfect being (all simple, purely positive qualities can coexist without contradiction). If it is possible, it exists (definitely) and is "existifying." Behold then the new relationship of substance with the world: we cannot derive concepts except in virtue of the original concept, so that nothing is in things except by God's influence, and we can think nothing in the mind except by God's idea: "All individual substances are different expressions of the same universe and of the same universal cause, that is to say, God" (*Pr. Ver.*). Onto the distinction between truth of reason (absolute) and truth of fact (contingents) in the *Nouveaux Essais sur l'entendement humain* (1704), was to be grafted the Lessing-Kierkegaard polemic. With *Essais de Théodicée sur la bonté de Dieu, la liberté de l'homme et l'origine du mal* (1710), Leibniz, while replying to Bayle's *Dictionnaire historique et critique* (1695–1697), founded modern theodicy.

In contrast to Cartesian rationalism, PASCAL, who stands outside the scholastic tradition, takes up the interiorist spiritual line in the *Pensées*, which, between the Scylla of dogmatism and the Charybdis of Pyrrhonism and unsatisfied by scientific answers (metaphysics too is a science; the metaphysical proofs of God's existence leave the human mind unsatisfied and unmoved), must gather up the *vestigia* of God, which are within him and outside him in the natural world. But this cannot be done without staking one's own existence in a *wager* that gives meaning to human existence because it makes God attainable. The God of Jesus Christ, not of the philosophers, to whom Pascal turns in personal, colloquial manner in the *Memorial*.

8. A Christianity without Mysteries

A religion without mysteries for a life without enigmas is the program of the vast, undefinable movement known as Deism, with its roots set deep in Renaissance culture. It rejects classical and scholastic speculation, assumes a particularly polemical attitude toward Christianity and points the way to the Enlightenment and rationalism. Deism is opposed to atheism but reluctant to embark on metaphysical questions about God; divine revelation—and the divine institution of the church—for Deism are meaningless questions. Only those religious and moral principles are

admitted that can be achieved by human reason; the myth, in its Christian-European, and notably English, ambit is precisely a "reasonable" Christianity without mysteries. One may think of Campanella and his *religio innata*, rather than of hermetic, magical, and pantheistic Bruno, but one must start with Herbert of Cherbury and his programmatic *De veritate prout distinguitur a revelatione, a verisimili, a possibili et a falso* (1624). Shaftesbury was to deepen the *Sensus Communis* (1709), the basis of all aesthetics and morals, but also of a religious sentiment imposed in the spirit of the Enlightenment and critical of Christianity. *Christianity not Mysterious* (1696) by J. Toland rules out the possibility of there being things contained in revelation that are superior to reason. The gospel may be interpreted freely and independently of ecclesiastical authority; all religions are manifestations of natural religion (another anticipation of the Enlightenment).

Immediately before, John Locke had published *Essay on the Reasonableness of Christianity as Delivered in the Scriptures*, a deist manifesto that envisages an immanent faith in an amplified natural revelation; a reason that is the orienting faculty that orders ideas; a worldly-political state separate from a religious-transcendental church. What matters for Locke is the freedom of the religious conscience from a state that should busy itself with civil well-being and a church that should not have the power to impose sanctions; and to reserve to reason the task of judging whether there is a revelation and what the words in which it is couched may mean (see *Essay concerning Human Understanding* IV, XVIII, 8). The need for revelation to conform to natural religion, for A. Collins, is the basis of free inquiry in matters of religion and free thought; it would be unworthy of a rational being to accept the impositions of authority. On the coincidence of Christianity (as of any religion) with natural religion, see also M. Tindal (*Christianism as old as Creation* [1730]).

David Hume belongs to the deist tradition in his critique of superstition and intolerant fanaticism, but combats it by a radical critique of its basis, reason, in its absolute adhesion to the empirical, with skeptical results. The *Dialogues concerning Natural Religion* (1779), and the *Natural History of Religion* (1757), reflect the refusal to transcend the empirical, the impossibility of defining a religious reality which, in its historical contingency, is mainly represented by excesses and degeneration. Just as religion is born of fear and ignorance, so it remains enveloped in hypocrisy and fanaticism, superstition and intolerance. Hume's assimilation of *natural belief* to natural credulity, superstition, and fanaticism is telling. Pure *philosophic* religion, indirectly and remotely postulated, anticipates the mythical *noumenon* of Kant, whereas his absolutization of the empirical as also of the immorality of religion is totally dogmatic. Hume rebuts the "design argument" with the refutation of analogy and the principle of causality (*post hoc non propter hoc*), he calls metaphysics and scholastic theology "sophistry and illusion," holds as utterly meaningless the question of the substance of the soul (as also any other question about substance), ascribes a "weak probability" to miracles, while certainty lies only in hope. In a word, if "popular religion" has its origin in human nature, "natural belief" is irreconcilable with faith in God; it has no religious significance.

From deistic influences in Germany developed an Enlightenment based on the rationalism of Wolff, who found perfect agreement between natural religion and reason. In the *Theologia naturalis* (2 vols., 1736, 1737), Wolff argued that the truths of Scripture can also be known merely by the right use of reason. The ambiguity of natural religion, which in point of fact is artificial and literary, a pale reflection of philosophic monotheism, was reinforced, with a few exceptions (Herder, Hamann), until Schleiermacher held it up to ridicule in his *Reden über die Religion* (1799).

A decisive contribution toward a *vernünftig* Christian religion (from Deism we are now moving decisively toward Kantian rationalism) is made by the liberal exegesis of J. S. Semler (*Apparatus ad liberalem N. Testamenti interpretationem* [1769]), who in a historico-evolutionary perspective distinguishes between the word of God (absolute) and the word of the Bible (with its psychological, sociological, and cultural garb); personal religion (inspired by the good, invisible activities of Christ) and public religion (established); religious experience and theological conceptualization. The biblical canon in its historical vicissitudes is regarded as any other literary text. No form is held to be complete or normative. The various books are not all of the same value. The original Christian message is one thing; its historical garb and psychological arrangement quite another. The same dogmatic formulas are to be seen in the historical evolution of church life.

Much of all this, with stress on the eschatological aspect of Christ's message, which excludes the idea of founding the church, is to be found in the *Apologie oder Schutzschrift der vernünftigen Verehrer Gottes* of H. S. Reimarus (1694–1768), which Lessing was to publish in 1778. Not by chance is Lessing the typical exponent of rationalistic enlightenment and apologist of natural religion, from which revealed or positive religion should depart as little as possible. History itself is the natural *place* of revelation, which is for the human race what education is for individuals. Christianity is the last of the positive religions, the forerunner of a future, rational religion of humanity, the prelude to a new, eternal gospel (*Die Erziehung des Menschengeschlechts* [1780]). The reduction of Jesus' message to a generalized philanthropy is one aspect of the "historicization" performed in the essay *Sulla dimonstrazione dello spirito e della forza* (1777), where, with reference to the Leibnizian distinction mentioned above, he says: "Contingent historical truths can never be the proof of unconditioned truths of reason." And in *Una Republica* (1778), we have one of the most famous concrete definitions of the spirit of the Enlightenment:

> If God held all truth tight in his right hand, and in his left only the unquiet aspiration to the truth, if he were to say to me: "Choose!" even at the risk of straying eternally in error I would humbly throw myself down at his left and say: "This one, Father; pure truth pertains to you alone."

9. The Fundamental Option

On the title-page of *Philosophical Fragments* (1844) Kierkegaard once again puts the problem: "Can there be a point of departure in history for an eternal consciousness? How can the beyond-history affect us? Can eternal bliss be constructed on historical knowledge?" As is well known, through the paradox of God-within-time—the hypothesis of Christian salvation—the philosophy of truth becomes the theology of salvation by the dialectic of the contemporaneity of Christ, as the concluding "Moral" proclaims: "Here we have assumed a new organ: Faith, a new postulate: consciousness of sin, a new decision: the Moment, a new Teacher: God in time." This entails the inversion of the Hegelian dictum "philosophy should beware of having anything to do with being edifying" (Preface to *Phänomenologie des Geistes*) in a program just as absolute and constant: "For edification and awakening." The problem of personal salvation in terms of eternal bliss is taken up again by Kierkegaard in the *Concluding Unscientific Postscript* (1848), where, in the section devoted to Lessing, together with homage to the Socratic awareness of the limitations due to the refusal to perform the *leap* of faith and intellectual honesty with regard to claims of Hegelian "going-beyond," there is the denunciation of the subtle pride of one who rejects the possibility of salvation. Socrates and the "edifying" are mediated to Kierkegaard by Hamann (*Sokratische Denkwürdigkeiten* [1759]), who represents another aspect of the nonrationalistic Enlightenment and who is hence unaffected by the rationalism of Kant or the "transcendental chatterings" of the "Prussian Hume." In the spirit of Pascal, Hamann denounces the dangerous breach between reason and nature, idealism and realism, just as the soul should not be severed from the body. Reason can also generate errors and needs sentiment, faith, revelation (human beings are the image of God), present in nature and in Scripture: the one and the other have to interpret the visible traces of the beautiful, creator-emulator spirit—revelation which is fulfilled in the Son. Religion is thus the prophet of the unknown God in nature, of the God hidden in grace, who by means of miracles and mysteries educates the reason to a loftier wisdom and raises our soul to highest hopes.

Awareness of the limitations of reason and consciousness of sin open human nature to the encounter with Christ; subjectivity is not the foundation of truth in itself but the personal relationship with the eternal truth that manifests itself *in persona Christi* in history. It is not a stubborn identity of thought and being but an ethical and ethical-religious knowledge. This search, for Kierkegaard, dates from the beginning: "To find a truth which is truth *for me*, to find *the idea for which I should live and die*" (*Papirer* [1835]), in the delusion of a fictitious harmony, of a false idyllic relationship of Christianity with the speculative reason in Hegel

and the *theologia speculativa* of the Hegelians. Equally mistrustful of Kantian "pure reason" and of Schleiermacherian *sentiment*, of Hegelian speculation and the "positive philosophy" of Schelling, which would claim to set out from existence to found existence, Kierkegaard, through the "school of the Greeks" and of Socrates, Augustine, Pascal, and Hamann, seeks God in Christ, without wasting time over proofs, over *praeambula*: "For, if God does not exist, it would of course be impossible to prove it, and if he does exist, then it would be folly to attempt it," and so on to the provocative "this *nota bene* of universal history" (*Philosophical Elements*, 31). But, not to charge Kierkegaard with an irrationalism that is not his, we must keep a clear distinction in mind, one he established: "The *absolute paradox* would be for the Son of God to become human, come into the world and move about in it without anyone's being able to recognise him. . . . The *divine paradox* is that he makes himself known, if not otherwise, by the fact of performing miracles; it is in this that his divine omnipotence is to be recognised, even if faith is needed to resolve his paradox" (*Papirer* [1842–43]). This has nothing in common with Hegelian dialectic and the disavowal of the principle of noncontradiction; but a resumption of a Christian theology which exalts the fundamental personal option, the leap of faith, *pari passu* with the inability of "proof" to bring God into human existence. In *contemporaneity* with Christ, with the response to Lessing's problem, this is a philosophy of history giving a new perspective to the relationship between *imitatio Christi* and Christology, even though with all its ecclesiological problems (of the historical and personal order). To freedom—the topic underlying the whole debate we are investigating—Kierkegaard gives one of the loveliest of definitions: "The most, at all events, that can be done for a being is to make him free. It needs omnipotence to be able to do this" (*Papirer* [1846]). From the ideal hypothesis, we have reached the threshold of faith: the (open) circle of a philosophy of truth that becomes theology of salvation—neither prolegomena to a Christian philosophy nor a chapter of apologetics (for Kierkegaard, apologetics means attack); neither derived from Schleiermacherian sentiment (even less so from the "positive philosophy" of Schelling) nor available for an ambiguous recycling in dialectical theology.

Enlightenment and *Populärphilosophie* go together for M. Mendelssohn and are the interpretative key and expositive criterion of philosophic thought and (Jewish) religious tradition. The *Phaedon*, on the immortality of the soul (1767), again takes up the Platonic argument of the spiritual nature of the soul, answers Pythagorean objections of psychological type and describes the fulfillment achieved by human nature in the afterlife. With *Jerusalem: Religious Power and Judaism* (1782), following on from the *Tractatus* of Spinoza, he presents Judaism not as a dogmatic religion but as a code of cultic laws and norms of life for the pursuit of a reasonable happiness, and gives a new dimension to the (Enlightenment's) myth of progress. In polemics with *Die Erziehung* of Lessing, he maintains that the individual progresses but the human race vacillates the while between certain limits. Enthusiastically received by Kant as an expression of freedom of conscience, this was violently attacked by Hamann (*Golgotha and Scheblimini*), who in this rationalistic interpretation of religion saw the possibility of faith under threat. In his wise *On the Question: What Does Enlightenment Mean?* (1784) he deals with an aspect of culture—the mission of human beings as individuals and as citizens, to combat prejudice, barbarism, and superstition. Kant's reply, with the famous introductory definition: "The Enlightenment is man's outgrowing a state of minority for which he has only himself to blame" and the exhortation *Sapere aude!* ("Dare to know!") emphasizes that even in things of the reason there is a greater need for clarity. The *Spinozastreit*, in which he opposed Jacobi over how Spinoza was to be interpreted, sees him insisting on the duty of removing doubts by rational reasons only and not acknowledging faith in eternal truths, as against Jacobi's contention, "All of us are born into the faith and we ought to remain in the faith, just as all are born into society and ought to remain in society. . . . By faith we know we have a body and outside us there exist other bodies and other thinking beings" (*Über die Lehre Spinozas*).

Mendelssohn put the finishing touches on his thought in *Morgenstunden*, a complete expression of philosophic theism, against materialism, against Spinozan pantheism but also against Kantian criticism. In it he reaffirms reason's capacity to know the real and attain to "scientific" concepts of the existence of God, *evident* existence, whether a posteriori (external and internal senses), or a priori (God is thinkable, therefore he really exists). Kant's reaction can be imagined. He saw in Mendelssohn's work a classic example of the illusion of reason ("dogmatising metaphysics"), where it confuses the subjective conditions of thinkability with the conditions of the ontological possibility of objects. In *What It Means to Orient Oneself in Thought* (1786), Kant had made the point about the Jacobi-Mendelssohn polemic by drawing attention once again to the danger of a thought that, by not taking reason's limitations into account, ended in fantasy and chimera. In *Der einzig möglich Beweisgrund zu einer Demonstration des Dasein Gottes* [1763]), the "necessary being" resulted from the analysis of the concepts of "possibility" and "existence": the basis of possibility is not to be found in the existence of things, since this postulates possibility. Having awakened from "dogmatic sleep" with the *Kritik der reinen Vernunft* (1781), Kant excludes the ontological, cosmological, and physico-theological proofs of the existence of God. But, reflecting on the interests of reason (What can I know? What should I do? What can I hope?), he reaches the "Ideal of the *Summum Bonum* as principle determining the ultimate goal of pure reason." God is a postulate. In the preface to the second edition (1787), he writes: "I therefore can never admit *God, freedom, immortality* for the necessary practical use of my reason, without at a stroke removing the speculative reason's claims to transcendental ideas." Hence the conclusion: "I have had to suppress *knowing* and substitute *faith* for it," after speaking at length "of the impossibility of an ontological proof of the existence of God" (ibid. 477–84), and "Of the impossibility of the physico-theological proof" (496–503).

In *Die Religion innerhalb der Grenzen der blossen Vernunft* (1793), from the *Summum Bonum* postulated as the basis of the moral law, Kant reaches a pure, rational faith and, by means of this the existence of God as adequate cause of the *Summum Bonum*. The concept of religion has nothing to do with the facts of a religious experience, giving rise to an ecclesial dogmatic system linked to a positive revelation and discharging its duties to God in a community of faithful in particular forms of worship. The concept concerns only the function of religion within human reason, its role in the coming of the real, universal kingdom of God, which conquers radical evil. Rational religion is put on the same plane as exegesis: "Thus rational religion and scriptural science are the competent interpreters and depositaries of a sacred document." In 1811, writing *Von den göttlichen Dingen und ihrer Offenbarung*, Jacobi took up a thought of Pascal ("We need to love divine things before we can know them") and ascribed to Kant the merit "of having made room for a faith that cannot be violated by the dogmatism of metaphysics."

Jacobi had been the first to speak of the nihilism to which idealism leads. In *Reden über die Religion* (1799), Schleiermacher asks himself: "What will the end of triumphant speculation, of perfect and full-blown idealism, be if religion does not balance it and does not allow it to present a higher realism?" and, still unaware of the danger of the quotation, exclaims: "Together let us reverently sacrifice a lock of hair to the *manes* of that excommunicate holy-man Spinoza!"

It is the response to the solicitations of a cultural environment dissatisfied with supernaturalistic solutions, as also with the coldly rationalistic approach, which, to be better understood, needs to be seen in the context not only of the subsequent *Der christliche Glaube*, but of the *Nachlass* of the *Hermeneutica* and of the *Dialectica*. In these works, the non-psychological or subjectivist sense of sentiment is made clearer, as well as the relationship between God and the world. The definition of religion as "feeling and taste for the infinite," as against the theorist-metaphysicians and the pragmatist-moralists, frivolous indifferentism, every kind of human folly, "from the inane fables of the savages to the most refined deism, from the uncouth superstition of our own people to the cobbled-up scraps — if the worst be told — of metaphysics and morals which we call rational Christianity."

The image that gives the best idea of it is chaos, plurality and diversity of the reflections of the infinite in the finite, where, from among the historical expressions of religion, Christianity emerges because Christ its founder had the most limpid and deepest intuition.

God who "is not all in religion, but only part, the Universe is there too" and who in the *Reden* is variously defined as universe, eternal, infinite, was subsequently to be defined in *Der christliche Glaube*. In maturity, Schleiermacher always rejected *Identitätsphilosophie*: God, the living God, is the original ground of being, metaphysically distinct, not identifiable with the totality of the finite and of the multiplex. By way of the *Dialectica*, intuition and feeling, feeling and taste for the infinite, in *Der christliche Glaube* has become "feeling of absolute dependence." After the first edition of the *Reden*, Schleiermacher avoided the term intuition in defining religion, so as to exclude any confusion with intuition of the Absolute which, for Schelling, defined the essence of philosophy. Like Fichte, he stood back from a conception of intellectual intuition, the contemplation of the Eternal within ourselves where the soul, in a direct relationship, becomes one with the Absolute though without losing its own individuality.

To Fichte, apparently, is addressed the apostrophe in the early pages of the second *Rede*: "What is the point of your metaphysics . . . your transcendental philosophy? It classifies the Universe and subdivides it into so many kinds of essence . . ." (68). As will be remembered, Fichte was heavily involved in the *Atheismusstreit* (even though Jacobi in *Idealismus und Realismus* claimed Fichte's transcendental philosophy was neither theistic nor atheistic), yet in the works *On the Grounds of Our Belief in a Divine Government of the Universe* (1798) and *The Vocation of Man* (1800), he held the existence of God as ground of the moral order of the world to be indubitable.

Herder had been no stranger to the formulation of Schleiermacherian feeling. For him, religion is existentially determined, directly touches the human soul, our most intimate awareness (*Von Religionen, Lehrmeinungen und Gebräuche* [1789]). So, most especially in *Ideen zur Philosophie der Geschichte der Menschheit* (1784–91), "religion above all, together with metaphysics, morals, physics and natural history, contributes to the history of humanity. Everywhere the great analogy of nature has led me to the truth of religion. . . . Nature is not an independent being, but *God is in all its works*." In chapter 6 of I, IV, "Man is formed by humanity and religion," and again, "Religion is the supreme humanity of man. . . . The first and last philosophy has always been religion."

Hegel was always critical of the *Reden* for violating the Jacobian principle of subjectivity (*Faith and Knowledge*).

In the *Phänomenologie des Geistes*, by delineating the scientific system of real knowledge on the premise that "only in the *concept* does truth find its element of existence," Hegel makes the most radical critique of romantic philosophy and of the "paltry feeling of the divine." Without appeal, this was intended to be the final judgment: "If in a man religion is based only on a feeling . . . then a dog would be the better Christian" (Preface to the *Philosophy of Religion*, ed. Hinrichs).

But the very completeness of the Hegelian system creates problems as is repeatedly pointed out in the Kierkegaardian critique, and "as is also to be seen from the results of the Hegelian "Right" and "Left." The so-called *Juvenile Theological Writings* mark his tormented and on occasion contradictory effort to detach himself from the weighty Kantian inheritance. *The Positivity of the Christian Religion* describes the transition from the loving message of Christ to the new positivity of an ethical Christianity, and *The Spirit of Christianity and Its Destiny* sees in the two natures of Jesus, human and divine, the meeting of the finite with the infinite. Finally, the *Fragment of a System* of 1800 clearly affirms that philosophy should end in religion, which alone can raise finite life to the infinite.

The *Lectures on the Philosophy of Religion* pass from the conception of religion, through the historical religions, to Christianity as the absolute religion. Neither feeling nor philosophic speculation are constituent elements of religion. The Enlightenment-rationalistic risk of religion's being reduced to the limitations of reason alone once being overcome, religion is knowledge of the relationship with God, of the relationship of the limited human spirit with the absolute spirit of God. Feeling raised to knowledge is the same religious doctrine expressed in images and this it is that we properly call *faith*. "That which is absolutely true, truth itself, reason by which all the world's enigmas, all the contradictions of deepest thought, all pangs of emotion, are resolved, the reason of eternal truth and eternal peace, that same absolute truth, the absolute satisfaction . . . the central and ultimate point in that thought which is uniquely knowledge, feeling of God" is the object of religion.

Philosophy and religion coincide: the former is representation; the latter is concept of the absolute spirit (art is intuition of it). They have content, needs, interests in common. "Philosophy is therefore theology and preoccupation with God or, rather, in God; it is *per se* serving God." After "the death of God" and the speculative Good Friday," this represents a new possibility for philosophic theology.

Schelling's case is emblematic. Sincere concern with religious problems especially in *Philosophie und Religion* (1804) and *Philosophische Untersuchungen über das Wesen der Menschlichen Freiheit* (1809), by way of the *Philosophy of Mythology*, leads to the *Philosophy of Revelation*; a doubtfully happy achievement of a speculative theology, a philosophic understanding of the Christian revelation or, rather, as to the speculation, the idealistic *Vollendung* which inevitably entails the emptying of revelation of its supernatural content, of its specific qualities. "This has nothing to do with speculative dogmatics, but with an explanation of Christianity, starting with its most exalted, historical character. This most exalted character, going back to the beginning of things, is fully explained. Underlying the theory of "powers," Christ is an individual but symbolic person, a finitization of the infinite, peak of the antique world of the gods, such that "the incarnation of God is thus the incarnation of eternity." Having affirmed the continuity of Christianity with paganism, the exegesis of *en morphē theou* (Phil 2:6) is the inevitable "speculative" result: "He is not true God, but *in the form* of God . . . the Son could not be spoken of in that intermediate state. . . . In his humanity, he does not divest himself of his divinity but of that false one. . . . For the Logos was de-divinised when he became an extra-divine power. . . . [H]e became human with everything in him that was not of the Father."

The "Right" interpreted the Hegelian *Aufhebung* as conservation of religion in philosophy. Significant and programmatic was the title *Zeitschrift für Philosophie und spekulative Theologie*, founded in 1837 and edited by I. H. Fichte with the collaboration of Weisse, Krabbe, and Vorländer. For the Hegelian "Left," the *Aufhebung* of religion had to be its final elimination in philosophy. Feuerbach, who had derided "positive philosophy" and Schelling's philosophy of revelation (ferocious too the attack by Engels, *Schelling und die Offenbarung* [Leipzig, 1842]), Schleiermacher's feeling and speculative theology, with *Das Wesen des Christentums* (1841) and *Das Wesen der Religion* (1843), reduces theology first to anthropology and then to philosophy. The dialectical materialism of Marx aims at demythologizing all superstructures, hence that of religion too: it is sufficient to get rid of the conditions giving rise to these: capitalism (*Economic and Philosophical Manuscripts* [1844]; *German Ideology* [1846]). It is worth remembering that the famous definition of religion as "the opiate of the people" (Introduction to the *Critique of Hegel's Philosophy of Law* [1843]) is in a context in which "religious misery is on the one hand the expression of actual misery and, on the other, a protest against actual misery. Religion is the sigh of the oppressed creature, the feeling of a heartless world, the spirit of a situation in which the spirit is absent."

But beyond these noble expressions, as we know, here the discourse became ideological: an ideology that today we have seen collapse.

Bibl.: M. Miegge, "Religione," in *Storia antologica dei problemi filosofici* (Florence, 1965), 1309f.; M. M. Olivetti, *Filosofia della religione come problema storico* (Padua, 1974); A. Babolin, ed., *Il metodo de la filosofia della religione*, 2 vols. (Padua, 1975); G. Ferretti, "Filosofia della religione," *DTI* 1:151–58; var., *L'ermeneutica de la filosofia della religione: Acts of the VIIe international colloquium on demythologisation* (Rome, 1977); I. Mancini, *Filosofia della religione* (3rd ed.; Casale Monferrato, 1986); E. Feil, *Religion: Die Geschichte eines neuzeitlichen Grundbegriffs vom Frühchristentum bis zur Reformation* (Göttingen, 1986); P. G. Grassi, ed., *Filosofia della religione: Storia e problemi* (Brescia, 1988); J. Schmitz, *Filosofia della religione* (Brescia, 1988); var., *In lotta con l'angelo: La filosofia degli ultimi due secoli di fronte al cristianesimo* (Turin, 1989).

Salvatore Spera

VII. Critique of Religion

Criticism of religion already existed, it is true, in (Greek) antiquity, in the early Christian period, and naturally, too, at the time of the Reformation. Nevertheless, modern criticism of religion (which acquired public significance in the middle of the nineteenth century through Feuerbach's projection theory) is a special type of criticism of religion. It is characterized by explicit, formally argued contestation of the existence of God and, in connection with that, rebuttal of the proofs of God's existence. Humans have the right, but also the duty, to justify the truth of religious faith, even before reason, to themselves and to others. Such explicit confrontation is demanded by their conscience. It is also demanded, however, by (Catholic) Christianity itself, since that, from the very first, does not understand itself as a leap into the uncertain, the coincidental, or the arbitrary. Admittedly, Christianity has always been engaged in debate with radical critics of its faith; in recent times, however, more systematic, philosophical-anthropological arguments have been put forward within criticism of religion; and these, in turn, have also become widely established in the general consciousness of modern "European" humanity.

The notion of "criticism of religion" is nevertheless not unambiguous. Hence, it is necessary to distinguish *intrareligious* from *interconfessional* criticism, or criticism directed at *another religion* from *atheistic* or *agnostic* criticism of religion. If reflection on religion leads, for whatever reason, to rejection of either religion or God's existence, then one speaks of criticism of religion in the narrower sense. It is in this atheistic sense that "criticism of religion" will be discussed here.

1. Conditions and Causes of Modern Criticism of Religion

a. The beginning of modern criticism of religion coincides with the age of Enlightenment and, in particular, its consequences. In the *Berlinische Monatsschrift* of 1784, under the title "An Answer to the Question 'What is Enlightenment?'" I. Kant wrote the famous sentences:

> Enlightenment is the emergence of humanity from its self-imposed stage of immaturity. Immaturity is the inability to use one's understanding without direction by another. Such immaturity is self-imposed when its cause lies not in lack of understanding but in lack of the resolve and courage to employ it without direction by another. "Sapere aude!", "Have the courage to make use of your own understanding!", is thus the motto of the Enlightenment.

Accordingly, it comes as no coincidence if the so-called "proofs of God's existence" are now subjected to critical examination by human reason alone, with any sort of "proof from authority" being rejected in advance. Kant himself, after all—by reducing all the proofs of God's existence known to him to the so-called ontological proof and rejecting that primarily through denial of the metaphysical possibility of knowing God—largely elaborated the foundation and fundamentals of modern criticism of religion.

If, however, human understanding concerns itself with the question of God's existence, then the following problems arise. The concept of "God" undoubtedly belongs among those that are hardest to convey through words and concepts. To be sure, theology has always endeavored to preclude or correct misunderstandings and over-simplistic conceptions of God. Nevertheless, in the practical context of catechesis and preaching, it remains difficult to impart an image of God that is reasonably free of mythological or anthropomorphic ideas. If, then, modern atheisms are represented largely (although not always) by thinkers who are familiar with Christian tradition and theological thought only, as it were, from the "outside," then criticism of religion, as contestation of God's existence, *can* be understood as rejection of a concept of God that is incompatible with the Christian understanding of God—even though by no means every atheistic argument rests solely on "misunderstandings." That is, there are certainly arguments advanced by criticism of religion that, other considerations notwithstanding, do challenge Christians to engage in reflection and reexamination.

b. A further condition of modern criticism of religion is the fact that the concept of "proof" acquires a meaning influenced by the exact sciences. If one recalls the affirmation by Vatican I that God can be known with certainty by the light of natural reason (DS 3026), it obviously implies no clear division between faith and knowledge (in the sense of "proof"). One can even say that traditional fundamental theology made things too easy for itself regarding so-called "proofs of God's existence"—something that was still justified as long as discussion of the question of God was directed at people who already believed (and thus experienced no real

problems about the question of God's existence); and yet, at the same time, that discussion could do justice to neither the seriousness, the concern, nor the arguments of criticism of religion. In short, it was forgotten that rationally compelling proofs of God's existence neither exist nor are possible, but that humans, even in relation to the question of God, are in the position of having to make a free decision based on conscience. In the view of Karl Rahner (and others), there would be a need today for a "mystagogics."

c. Articulated now more clearly than before, moreover, are all those arguments "against" God that relate to the theodicy question. The multitudinous forms—not caused by sin alone—of suffering, misery, and fear, of all human affliction and subjection to contingency, are cited to dispute the existence of a loving and caring God. Thus, for instance, S. Freud poses to his Protestant friend and minister Oskar Pfister the obvious question of how he conceives the suffering in this world to be reconcilable with God's love. Along with those kinds of argument (which cannot be further detailed here) human anxiety and the longing for certainty and security are criticized in a variety of forms. Thus, e.g., Nietzsche surmised:

> How does belief in God come about? The feeling of power, when it suddenly and overwhelmingly surges up in human beings—and such is the case with all strong feelings—arouses in them a sense of doubt about their own person; they dare not conceive of themselves as being the cause of this astonishing phenomenon—and thus they set up a stronger person, a divinity, to serve as that. . . . In summa: the origin of religion lies in extreme feelings of power that take human beings by surprise and seem alien to them. . . . Religion is a feeling of fear and terror before oneself. (Nietzsche 1930)

And B. Russell (a self-proclaimed agnostic) responds as follows to the question of what, down through the centuries, has caused people to believe in religions:

> I think mainly fear. Man feels himself rather powerless. There are three things that cause him fear. One is what nature can do to him. . . . And one is what other men can do. . . . And the third, which has a great deal to do with religion, is what his own violent passions may lead him to do—things which in a calm moment he

would regret having done. For that reason most people have a great deal of fear in their lives, and religion helps them to be not so frightened by these fears. (Russell 1974)

These (and any number of other) statements lead, of course, into the questions—to be considered next here—of the reasons and causes that, from the atheist viewpoint, explain the presence of belief in God.

d. Finally, brief reference may be made to the influence of modern history of religion and to the fact of ideological pluralism. Awareness of the multiplicity of religions in past and present, the geographical proximity in which differing religious communities often exist, a climate of pluralistic ideological freedom expressly favored in democratic societies—all this naturally affects the mentality of modern humanity in such a way that not only do questions arise about which is the true religion, but also the existence of God (or of "transcendental entities") in general is called into doubt, and questions likewise ensue about the reality of life after death.

2. The Argumentation of Criticism of Religion

A distinction must be made, within criticism of religion, between the form of basic argumentation and the different individual arguments. For that reason, one should preferably speak of *atheisms* (in the plural), since certain atheisms are mutually exclusive.

a. Given that no atheist or critic of religion contests the contingency of human situatedness within the manifold of experiences, the basic question of God's existence is decided through interpretation of those experiences. The believer considers such experiences impossible apart from the existence of God— without God, there could be no such experiences. The atheist, however, counters this by explaining that the undisputed fact that humans can think beyond their own inadequacies and thus arrive at the idea of God by no means proves the actual existence of God. In all the arguments of criticism of religion, there are undertones of repudiation of the so-called "ontological proof of God's existence," i.e., of unjustified reasoning *from the idea of God, or the wish for God, to the real existence of God.* This is well presented by R. Garaudy (during his

Marxist period): "Marxism asks itself the same questions, lives with the same sense of expectation toward the future, and is agitated by the same demands as the Christian; but it does not feel itself entitled to transform its question into an answer, its demand into a presence" (Metz and Rahner 1966)—the last words referring, of course, to the presence of God's existence. Also, in the same passage, he notes tersely: "My thirst does not prove the fount!" S. Freud bases his argument clearly on human wishful thinking. Belief in God is neurotic (because infantile) wishful thinking; however, as Freud sees it, whatever humans can—or even must—wish for themselves is by no means therefore a reality. What then remains decisive, of course (even if not every critic of religion expressly asks himself the question), is why, assuming that there is no God, there should be both religion and belief in God? No matter how diverse the answers to this question turn out to be, it is basic to every variety of criticism of religion that belief in God must be judged to be a *secondary consciousness* or a *secondary need* of human beings, with religion being rooted in some primary need that the believer does not recognize but that needs to be discovered and exposed by criticism of religion, and naturally has nothing to do with "God."

b. In what follows here, the important critics of religion can only be briefly mentioned (for fuller details, see Garaudy and Weger, eds. 1988).

The cursory references are certainly not enough to provide an adequate understanding of the arguments and issues. But Christians must ask themselves—and allow themselves to be asked—whether and to what extent their image of God may possibly need revision as a result of arguments advanced by criticism of religion.

Ludwig Feuerbach is no longer concerned, like Kant, about the knowability of God by human reason, but about the causes of belief in God. His basic conviction is that what we call "God" is in reality nothing other than the objectivized and conceptually reified consciousness of humans themselves, or of the human species.

> Religion, or at least the Christian one, is the *attitude adopted by human beings toward themselves,* or more correctly, *toward their nature,* but the attitude adopted toward their nature *as toward another nature. The divine*

nature is nothing other than human nature, or better, *the nature of human beings*, detached from the limitations of the individual, i.e., actual and physical, human being, and reified, i.e., *viewed and worshipped as another distinct and independent nature*—all the *attributes* of the divine nature are therefore attributes of human nature. (Feuerbach 1960)

It is through Feuerbach that the projection theory enters expressly into religious-critical thought.

Karl Marx, together with Friedrich Engels, was initially an "enthusiastic Feuerbachian" but later became convinced that Feuerbach had placed too much emphasis on developing a psychologico-genetic explanation of religion linked to the individual human being. To be sure, Marx was convinced that religion had been discredited by Feuerbach; this is why Marx himself wrote no systematic treatises against religion or against the existence of God. Nonetheless, Marx modifies Feuerbach's criticism of religion inasmuch as he characterizes religion as the "epitome of an inverted world." More concretely, since humans are first and foremost social beings, socioeconomic relationships are determinative of human consciousness at any given time. Human beings cannot but think in a way that reflects their particular social conditions; they are an "ensemble of social relationships." Because the history of humanity is nothing but a history of class conflict, a history of the exploitation of humans by humans, it follows that the ruling ideas of any time were always just the ideas of the ruling class. For Marx, it is self-evident that exploited humans have need of the "illusory sun" of religion. On the one hand, by means of their capacity for transcendence, they can imagine better living conditions beyond their own concrete, miserable circumstances; and on the other hand, they therefore require consolation through the promise of a better world, the hereafter, while overlooking the fact that the purpose behind unhealthy religion—which after all is only an expression of their earthly sufferings—can be achieved by fundamental alteration of economic relationships (nationalization of the means of production) and of the social order (abolition of all class distinctions). Accordingly, religion is "at once an *expression* of actual misery and . . . a *protest* against actual misery" (Marx and Engels in *MEW* 1959, vol. 4).

Sigmund Freud's criticism of religion stems, as could not otherwise be expected, from his depth psychology. For Freud, the function of religion consists in facilitating flight from "harsh reality." It involves a regression to infantile behavior. The adult person would like to be a child again; but since that is impossible, he or she escapes into what manifests itself as the symptoms of neurotic behavior. In this connection, religion is just *one* form of attempting to deal with life in a psychologically disturbed way. In a letter dated 1 January 1910, to his friend Ferenczy, Freud reports having experienced a flash of insight one night about the origin and function of religion: "The ultimate reason for religion is the helplessness of human beings" (Jones 1962)—a proposition that, seventeen years later, in his *Zukunft einer Illusion* [The Future of an Illusion], Freud elaborated as follows:

> The same person to whom children owe their existence, their father (perhaps more correctly, the parental authority represented by both their father and mother) has also protected and watched over them as weak, helpless children in their vulnerability to all the dangers lurking in the outside world; in his care, they have felt themselves safe. Having reached adulthood themselves, people are, it is true, aware that they now possess greater powers; however, their insight into life's dangers has also increased, and they rightly conclude that, at bottom, they still remain just as helpless and unprotected as they were in childhood, that, in relation to the world, they are still children. Hence, even now, they do not want to relinquish the protectedness that they had enjoyed in childhood. Yet they also have long since recognized that their father is a being narrowly circumscribed in power and hardly endowed with all good qualities. Therefore they fall back upon the remembered image of the father that they had so overestimated as children, elevate it to the status of divinity, and transfer it into the present and into reality. (Freud 1955)

In addition to these well-known critics of religion, many more critics and deniers of God's existence could be named. Of late, it can be observed that the number of atheistic critics of religion who make themselves known through scholarly publications is steadily diminishing. Apparently it has been recognized even from the side of criticism of religion that, just as there are no compelling proofs of God's existence, so there can be no strict proofs of God's nonexistence. Today critics of religion are more inclined to present themselves as agnostics, even if their arguments may lead, in the end, to atheism. As an example of an "atheistic agnostic" one could cite J. Améry, who speaks, in an essay made public originally as a radio talk, of "atheism without provocation." Améry proceeds on the assumption that, while he is able to understand traditional religious propositions, he nevertheless cannot believe them (e.g., "Above the starry firmament a kindly Father must dwell"). The statements of progressive theologians, by contrast, Améry is unable to understand, as when, for instance, it is explained that Christ arose from the dead via the "consciousness of certain people." Améry brings his ruminations to a close as follows:

> Those who lack belief—atheists or agnostics or whatever we might call them—do not know what to make of these new forms that are emerging before their eyes; they have the feeling that traditional religion is abandoning itself. They by no means react triumphantly; they only observe with polite astonishment the unfolding of a process that enables it to appear to them—the atheists—superfluous to intervene with free-thinking fervor. *The greatest provocation of atheism consists in the fact that it no longer provokes, nor wishes to provoke, at all.* (Améry 1971)

Were Améry right, then this would, in fact, be the desired success of atheism, its implicit or even explicit goal. Then atheism would be that which, basically, it had always aimed to be: an attitude that, whether for believers, doubters, or atheists, no longer arouses contradiction—an unquestioned, self-evident thing.

Bibl.: F. Nietzsche, *Der Wille zur Macht*, ed. H. Kröner, vol. 1 (Stuttgart, 1930); S. Freud, *Gesammelte Werke*, vol. 14 (London, 1955; see *Collected Papers*, 5 vols. [New York, 1959]); L. Feuerbach, *Das Wesen des Christentums*, ed. W. Bolin and F. Jodl, vol. 6 (2nd ed.; Stuttgart, 1960); K. Marx and F. Engels, *Manifest der kommunistischen Partei* (=*MEW*, vol. 4 [Berlin, 1959]); J. Jones, *Das Leben und Werk von S. Freud* (Berne, 1962); J. B. Metz and K. Rahner, *Der Dialog oder ändert sich das Verhältnis von Katholizismus und Kommunismus* (Reinbeck, 1966); J. Améry, *Widerspruche* (Stuttgart, 1971); B. Russell, *Bertrand Russell Speaks His Mind* (Westport, CT, 1974); R. Garaudy and K. H. Weger, eds., *Religionskritik von der Aufklärung bis zur Gegenwart:*

Autorenlexikon von Adorno bis Wittgenstein (Freiburg, 1988).

Karl-Heinz Weger

VIII. Psychology of Religion

1. Preliminaries

Definitions

Is there such a thing as a psychological science of religious phenomena? What is its subject matter, and how does the psychology of religion approach it?

Psychology, defined as a science of forms of behavior, comprises the study of behaviors and of their meanings. These implications of behavior are only partly conscious (motives), and those who study them often seek to elicit their meaning in terms of partly unconscious affective dynamisms, or underlying forces. Whether it is a matter of individuals or of groups, to elucidate meanings without resorting to arbitrary interpretation is the most difficult task assigned to psychology. On the one hand, a subject's explanatory or expressive language depends to a considerable degree on the form of discourse that is dominant in the groups to which that subject belongs—those of his or her social environment or culture. On the other hand, all psychological efforts are relational. They must be accompanied by continual self-criticism of the researcher's hypotheses, which are never wholly neutral, and of his or her interpretations, both when constructing the apparatus of research and in his or her personal reception of the language of the subjects, groups, or documents under examination. In spite of the variety of its methodological strategies, which I shall discuss later in this article, psychology defined as a "science of forms of behavior," whether descriptive, experimental, or clinical, also derives its "unity" from that very diversity (Lagache 1949).

Does *religion*, when scrutinized thus as a totality of observable, even measurable, behaviors, which are socially and culturally located, and the meanings of which are only partly associated with language, constitute a psychologically definable object or field?

Apparently not. Religiously motivated behaviors are immensely various and heterogeneous: chastity in the celibate but also sacred prostitution; forms of silent meditation but also prayer-wheels; orthodoxy but also prophetism; flight from the world but also presence in the world with the intention of reforming it; peaceful projects but also holy wars. From P. Johnson (1959) to R. Paloutzian (1983), from G. Milanesi and M. Aletti (1973) to B. Spilka, R. Hood, and R. Gorsuch (1985), from P. Pruyser (1968) to A. Vergote (1983), all authors of relevant manuals eventually come up against the disparate nature of religious phenomena and even of the definitions proffered in an attempt to place them in a single category, such as that of the "sacred" (R. Otto), which Mircea Eliade uses as a framework for his (debated) historical work. A philosophy of transcendence on Western lines, with or without any reference to the word "god," eventually obscures not only the variety of psychosociological *operations* that these two human sciences wish to examine more intimately, but the undeniable variety of their objectively instituted, positive "substance": traditions, linguistic constructions, writings, discourses, rites, and theologies. A strictly psychological solution, in restricted sociocultural environments, would be to retain as "religious" any observable behavior stated to be such by individuals or groups, in order either to delineate it precisely or to contest it. Then the psychology of religion would take as its object both phenomena of belief (for example) and those of nonbelief (see, in this regard, Vergote 1983). All research would comprise an examination of behaviors occurring where a symbolic system, a social institution, and a subjective life intersect. It would have to furnish the apparatus needed for the purpose (clinical observations, questionnaires, various correlations, experimentation in the strict sense), along the lines of psychological methods applied in any other field. It is probable that a polarity of this kind (belief–unbelief) is to be found in any culture on a continuum together with doubt, which would possibly be generalized as religious agnosticism.

The psychology of religion suffers from a lack of definition regarding its proper subject matter, but this neither blocks nor impedes its development. Biology has made considerable progress as a life science while ignoring speculative debates about the essence of life, by developing its own parameters on the basis of the paradoxical hypothesis according to which everything in life can be explained, measured, and even reproduced on the basis of its physicochemical makeup. Perhaps the same is true of the *psyche*, of that part of the human psychology which responds to scientifically established conditioning. This viewpoint was adopted and developed cogently by J.-F. Catalan (1986), to which I refer the reader to avoid any repetition in this article of references to the psychology of forms of spirituality, the vocation to dedicated celibacy, or its applications in pastoral psychology, which Catalan covers very efficiently. On the psychology of various spiritual topics, I also recommend Secondin 1987, or Godin 1986: chaps. 4 and 5; on the psychology of vocation, Godin 1975, and Rulla, Imoda, and Ridick 1978; on applications to pastoral relations, Godin 1983, Scharfenberg 1980, or Vaughan 1987; and on social practice in pastoral affairs, Nadeau 1987.

To locate and accord with the epistemological boundary by which the speculative sciences (philosophy, theology, etc.) and the empirical sciences are demarcated from religion, we may follow Paul Ricoeur in adopting the (Thomist) category of "systematic material causality" (1949), or have recourse to the propositions of Jean Ladrière (1984: vol. 2) in an original presentation of the articulations of (Christian) religious language.

Acquaintance with recent works of scientific psychology (both experimental and clinical) leads me to suggest that their utility is not mainly to provide theology with precise *answers* to some of its questions (e.g., about crises of belief in "ultimate purpose") but, *on the basis of its own methods*, to ask theology to pose questions *in a new way*. See an attempt along these lines by A. Godin (1988) and the general presentation of this problem by J.-H. Pohier (from 1967) also discussed by J.-P. Deconchy (1967). The latter concludes: "A believer should be able to admit that his or her thinking, belief and faith are to some extent controlled by a theology. In epistemology, however, he or she cannot admit that a theology controls his or her epistemology by deciding what is epistemologically more appropriate" (p. 148).

2. Historical Milestones: The Beginnings

At the beginning of this century, on either side of the Atlantic, a researcher took a psychological approach to religious phenomena. At Harvard, William James systematically studied the variety of the language by means of which subjects expressed their "religious experiences" (1902). This auspicious start was progressively marked by odd limitations, confirmed in other theoretical writings by James. The essential aspect of religion is to be found in an intense, joyous, and virtually mystical inward experience. All expressive language, indeed, forms part of a history, but is above all the history of an emotion (*Erlebnis*). The English language, like the French, has only one word for this, whereas there is a second word in German (*Erfahrung*). This leads us into an unconscious impasse revealed later by W. L. Brandt (1982). Christian thought is associated with a "revelation" (received in the community and testified to in the Scriptures) and finds theologically problematical the option that secures and privileges the inward experience (*Erlebnis*); this option implies a considerable risk of holding back the effectivity of psychology as a science for which religious facts are necessarily comprised in an active synthesis (*Erfahrung*) made in terms of, and confronted by realities of, a social and institutional order. In spite of some attempts to produce a kind of typology of various internal experiments, notably by R. V. Hood (1975: presentation of thirty-two short narratives to various groups whose answers were subjected to factor analysis), the composition of these stories (influenced by W. James and by W. T. Stace), poses various problems. The discovery of an *M* factor (general mysticism) distinct from an *m* factor (joy experienced in regard to knowledge obtained from an institutional religion), confirms the respect for James expressed by more recent researchers: "*Respect* for a man who, with unusual dedication, tried to give our science a due object and status; and *regret* that he led the psychology of religion into an impasse. For this reason, James remains, to adopt E. R. Goodenough's expression, "our giant and our despair" (Deconchy 1969).

At Geneva, Théodore Flournoy (1902) described the methodological limits of scientific research into the psychology of religion. It was necessary to abandon not only all questions about the existence or (implicit) truth of a transphenomenal reality, but any evaluation of the actively established formal religious relationship between subjects and a reality that they consider to be transcendent or divine. By thus requiring a process of ontologization, obviously present in the philosophy of religion and theology, to be sidestepped (*epoché*), psychology takes up what is in fact a classic position in many of the human sciences (e.g., economics) which defend their autonomy above all from interference by a political or religious power. This does not mean that it refuses to examine the *significance* in subjects or groups, religious or not, of the beliefs, rites, and myths that they accept or reject. It does not refuse to do so, just as it does not refuse to examine the significance of the word "god" and its use in order to discover its (linguistic, cognitive, affective) connotations in a sociocultural — indeed, Judeo-Christian — environment in which psychology aims to develop in accordance with Flournoy's principles. Psychology frees itself by affirming the scientific irrelevance of an "absolute knowledge" that believers would legimately attach to faith in a God-who-has-spoken-of-himself, or even an otherwise inexplicable "change" that their prayer may have directly produced in their bodies or psyches. This is the very condition of its progress as a psychological science.

Delays and Obstacles

The course described in the foregoing was not taken until half a century had passed. Initially, this was because first-class psychologists were still interested in research into exceptional features of religion, such as sudden conversions and ecstatic or mystical states (Leuba, Maréchal, Pacheu, Janet). In Germany the introspective method of examining states of consciousness, which were sometimes systematically induced (Girgensohn, Gruehn and his school; W. Keilbach and the journal *Archiv*, 1962–76), prevailed for a long time. Comparative studies of the course, religious or not, of meditation, with experimental and control groups (therapeutic Zen groups), were undertaken subsequently, but using a different scientific approach (van der Lans 1978, 1980), to demonstrate the importance of the referential framework in the production of experiences (*ervaringen*), whether religious or not.

Before 1950 a very few pioneers were convinced that the observation techniques (validated questionnaires, repeated measurements, attitude scales, significant correlations, projective images, free association, experimental methods, etc.) that had proved their utility in human psychology should be used to study religious behaviors according to the parameters or dimensions under investigation. Thus we may cite G. W. Allport (1935), who (perhaps unconsciously) wished to examine the differences between the extrinsic and intrinsic orientation of an individual's religiousness (1950); G. Castiglioni in 1928, evaluating the development of children's and then adolescents' vocabularies about God (1941); L. Thurstone (from 1929), constructing social attitude scales appropriate to the moral and religious fields (1954); A. Welford, the first to design an "experimental" approach to elicit more straightforward forms of prayer preferred by non-churchgoers but scarcely appreciated by churchgoers (1946).

Theoretically, the discovery was inevitable that the rich variety of religious languages and of the behaviors they supported undermined the pseudo-explanatory hypothesis of a "religious need," in the strict sense of a state of internal tension that demanded satisfaction in a specific object or action. In any case, psychology, which is an observational science, is quite incapable of establishing the existence of such a need, whether it has to do with God or immortality (not to be confused with a desire to avoid death).

The final cause of the delay was the churches' profound misunderstanding of the considerable development in clinical psychology and of its conceptualization (especially in regard to partly unconscious "desire") of psychic dynamisms and the accompanying theoretical systems of the various schools of psychoanalysis (mainly Freud and Jung). Not only was psychoanalysis (therapeutic analysts, clients, and theoreticians), in particular the Freudian version, condemned in 1950 because of such stereotypes as "pansexualism," but the entire symbolic order of religious cultures and the human beings active within them and drawing life from them or contesting them had to wait until the psychology of religion, without too much fuss, could benefit from its admirable progress both on the individual level (clinical psychology) and in

cultural anthropology. Research work and publications multiplied only after 1965, *inter alia* in the form of *re-readings of the scriptural texts* (see further Vergote 1972; Stein 1985; and Beirnaert 1988). Vergote (1975) offers a detailed discussion of the psychoanalytic contribution to anthropology, to historical-critical exegesis, and to the study of unusual phenomena "deserving of a psychological explanation (visions, instances of glossolalia)."

We are indebted to J.-P. Deconchy (1970 and 1987) for some invaluable documentation (in English and French) regarding the difficult birth of the psychology of religion and recent methodological developments. See also in English Wulff 1985; and Brown 1987; in Italian and for Italian publications, see Godin 1983: 245–59; Milanesi 1973; Filippi and Lanza 1981.

3. Old Questions Rephrased

In 1965, in order to bring some order into the area covered by the psychosociological study of religious phenomena, two sociologists. Y. Glock and R. Stark, proposed to divide these areas into a number of dimensions. Factor analyses revealed the value both of treating religion as "multidimensional" and of presenting these dimensions somewhat differently; the *cognitive* dimension (distinguishing knowledge from beliefs); the *ritual* dimension (distinguishing private practices from institutional liturgies); the *experiential* dimension (*Erlebnis*, experienced inwardly; or *Erfahrung*, a synthetic reaction experienced in relation to social or institutional realities); and the *consequential* dimension (the effect of commitment or recidivism in other fields: physiological, moral, ideological). Various studies, using questionnaires, revealed quite strong correlations between the cognitive (*beliefs*) and ritual (*services* attended), which is not surprising, but a very weak correlation between the experiential (*Erlebnis*) and the consequential (*commitment* in the secular field). This enables us to understand the polarization between two types of practicing believers: those who seek the mystical and those in quest of the ethical tendency in a religion.

I shall now select a few religious facts from the last twenty years which were efficiently gathered in the methodological sense and which enable the theologian "to see familiar topics in a new light.

Belief: God-Providence

Why does an event, whether happy or un-happy, occur? In 1966, J.-B. Rotter developed various instruments of assessment and dis-covered an unusual but well-defined division into two ways of thinking. Some subjects associate success or progress with their own behaviors, capabilities, or characteristics — in short, with factors that may depend on their personal "internal" control. "External" control, on the other hand, refers to individuals who situate positive or negative events beyond the reach of their personal control, whether they relate to the unavoidable (conditioning, deter-minisms) or to "powerful others" (Rotter 1966) and unforeseeable interventions, or evoke chance (good fortune or misfortune). The psy-chological interest of the location of control is the ability directly to situate a variety of religious beliefs in a larger whole. The *theory of attribution* made rapid strides in the United States in the form of exact research (R. Benson and B. Spilka) related to the external or inter-nalized image of God and to degrees of self-esteem (1973), and of a general theory (Spilka, Shaver, Kirkpatrick 1985) based on studies that included the differential variable in question: the event (gravity, proximity) and its context; the subject, his or her attitudes and motives (conscious, unconscious). Here, only one fact out of all this work will be taken as established.

When presented with these actual situations in the form of questionnaires or evocative stories, various religious groups (adult Chris-tians) attributed to "Providence" events that other, less-religious groups (criterion: feeling that God was close at hand) ascribed to "chance" (luck). These were serious events, e.g., rising floodwaters that carried off a neighbor's house and left the house of the narrator, a powerless witness, intact (see also Gorsuch 1983).

The astonishing devotional succcess of the notion of Providence (one of the divine attri-butes according to Thomist thinking), adduced to the detriment of the idea of *chance* or luck (a fortuitous event resulting from the conjunc-tion of blind or of humanly intended deter-minism), and a fairly late acquisition of the child mentality, is attributable to a desire to assuage human anxiety when unavoidably faced with such events. The idea of Providence tends to reduce anxiety and is psychologically

"functional." It is associated mainly with other divine attributes (omnipotence, loving-kind-ness, omniscience). Is it possible to rehandle these concepts, which sort ill with the NT revelation and its attitude to evil, in the light of the latter (a former proposition of Malevez 1960)? Are we faced here with a profound change in the notion of Providence or merely with an acknowledgment of its functional value, which the Christian sources ask us to set aside? It is not the function of psychology to judge this issue.

Belief: God-the-Father

Why not God-the-Mother? Surely, in a psy-chological sense, this designation, which has become a dogmatically permanent adjunct of Christian faith, does imply certain aspects of the mother figure. More than twenty years of rigorous and extensive research (more than fifteen applications in culturally varied en-vironments) have produced some far from negligible evidence on this question (Vergote et al. 1981).

Antoine Vergote's team has constructed a dif-ferential semantic scale (free association on the basis of stimulus words [Osgood]), a psycho-logical test that had already proved effective in other fields. In this scale, a nonreligious ques-tion demands an explanatory response before the subject can proceed further. The ideal father figure and the ideal mother figure (not the figures that your parents represented for you, but as you picture them for yourself in the image of the ideal father and the good mother) each comprise the suggested qualities and, according to circumstances, the appropriate degree of intensity (seven degrees). Results: some ideal qualities are predominantly attrib-uted to the mother alone and cluster around *availability* (*welcome, comfort, patience, refuge, security*); other traits more strongly accord with the father and form a constellation around the theme of *law* (*authority, decision, judgment, power, principle*). In addition, certain other qualities occur with less intensity in the mother image (*feminity, protection*) or in that of the father (*knowledge, strength, order*). These peripheral qualities vary significantly according to country (Belgium, Colombia) or culture (Indonesia, Philippines). Finally, the attribution of numerous (mainly central) qualities to the two parents, but less intensely now to the mother, now to the father, indicate that there is indeed a structure in (ideal) parenthood in which the two figures, however well differentiated, intermingle with one another in their ideal image. Psychologically, as Vergote rightly stresses, it is the culturally reinforced ideal image that is liable to be metaphorized or symbolized when "trans-ferred" to ("metaphorized in regard to") a divinity. (Vergote 1983: esp. 206–11). The parental qualities, effectively structured around *availability* and *law*, appear in semantics that express the image of God in all groups belonging to Christian culture. The maternal traits are quantitatively the most numerous for believers who still avow their faith in a Trinity or God-as-Father, but the less numerous paternal traits are attributed to the god figure more emphatically than in the case of the (real) father, which rarely happens in respect of maternal traits. Finally, in many cases, the above-mentioned "peripheral" maternal or paternal traits are attributed to the god figure *in accordance with cultural conditioning*.

These findings prompt certain questions for theology when using the Father's name. Does that name derive its entire meaning in the analogy from a *begetting–begotten* relationship (as in the definition of intratrinitarian life)? Must it differ depending on the empirical variety of *paternality–maternality*? Or is it a matter of retaining the Hebrew significance of Father as chief of the clan, tribe, or people—of the new people consisting of those whose response to the offer of an adoptive relationship takes the form of a "free relationship" (the Lord's brothers and sisters being those who hear the word and follow it)? Surely, in the same context, it is important for pastoral theology to choose an unambiguous form of discourse reflecting the fact that the traits of the mother figure (*comfort, protection, refuge, security, tenderness*) and the father figure (*authority, judgment, law, power, strength*) must necessarily change to a degree (which is irksome to the persisting inclination to dream of an enhanced mother and an enhanced father), if they are to express the novelty of a kingdom proclaimed and awaited according to the Spirit? Psychological research has been able valuably to enrich the circumstances of this option in all its psychopastoral openness. Of course, it does not have to make the actual choice.

Practice: Rites and Prayers

Forms of religious behavior possess a dimension most accessible to any kind of psychosociometric investigation. As we know, these behaviors show that so-called Western culture exhibits both a considerable diminution of traditional liturgical or ritual practices (mass attendance, frequency of confession) and a burgeoning of more or less primitive revivals (including those occurring at new centers of pilgrimage after apparitions). Psychologically speaking, a certain *omnipotence of desire* appropriate to early childhood ("Do what I want or I'll yell!") finds support in sacralized objects, sometimes difficult or painful practices, and more or less idealized individuals of the kind which the various religions of the world have always provided ("Do what I want with the help . . ."). This is functional religion, to be sure, for here desire expects to be satisfied as a result of its reliance on an omnipotent force (a religious aspect of desire) that is able to *change* the way in which things happen in harsh reality, and even as a result of its reliance on favorable causal mechanisms which result from the material nature of the objects used and from a meticulous observation of rites (the magic-play aspect). There are numerous investigations, inquiries, and observations in this regard. Among them I would single out, for the comparative variety of the groups studied, Brown 1967, 1968, on "prayers asking for favors."

I would also cite the rapid decline, in subjects between twelve and twenty years of age, of the opinion that there is an external causal relation (with no psychological explanation) between various prayers and the anticipated or expected results of those prayers. On the other hand, in certain situations described, many respondents of all ages hold that it is "all right" to pray, but differently. The language of love features several expressions of desire in which the granting of the desire is not the main aim of the request made. Surely a "revelational" religion of desires and divine projects provides action and prayer with a spiritual space where desires that are never wholly convergent can come together?

A probable objection would be that "requests for favors" (quasi miracles changing the course of events) are part and parcel of *popular religion*. The difficulty of defining what is "popular" is well known. It is probably more appropriate to recall the two ways of thinking about forms of belief—in an *external* or an *internal* control mechanism. These two approaches are found in all environments. But the special feature of a certain type of mysticism would seem to be its tendency to take the external nature of the control into the sphere of internal control, which is to be reshaped, reinforced, and even changed in an overwhelming, quasi-miraculous manner.

After fifteen years of research in the United States, it is impossible to treat in this way the case of *glossolalia* "presented as a miraculous gift resulting from a direc't intervention of the Holy Spirit." No recording has ever been made that confirms speaking in a foreign language that the glossolalic has not learned. Phonetic and linguistic analyses show that instances of glossolalia do not manifest certain typical features of all established languages or even of those invented in play. On the other hand, they have particular characteristics that show a certain relation between expressive phonemes not oriented to communication that are used by glossolalics even when the latter have different languages. This may suggest an unequally distributed capacity possibly akin to the thaumaturgic capability of healers. "It would be mistaken . . . to refer to a 'gift' which each individual receives and the other does not possess, in the sense of one gratuitously bestowed on a chosen few" (Suenens 1984). There is no objection to choosing to pray in tongues; it was a practice of several non-Christian religions. Prayer of this kind may profit from the accretion of meanings and symbolisms (e.g., the converse of the confusion of languages at Babel).

There is a fine work of psychological synthesis by H. N. Malony and A. A. Lovekin (1985). Do theology and pastoral theology have to choose between the "functional" or "revelational" meanings of rites and prayers? As a Christian psychologist, I think that it will always be a matter of compromise between human (religious) desires and desires that accord with the trinitarian spirit—a compromise, moreover, that is necessary if the Word has entered the reality of human history with a new project for the world (Godin 1986: chap. 7). Of course, "new" here means distinct from the expectations that religious persons may impose on God or gods (Sigmund Freud).

Mythic Language, Orthodox Discourse, and Prophetic Language

The history of religions shows that religions are transmitted, whether orally or in writing, not in instances of discourse but in *narratives* with symbolic meanings re-presented in gestural rites in which improvisations occur within a traditional and preordained framework or liturgical context. Every religion that, returning to its sources, produces narratives in mythic form—e.g., regarding the "origins" or to express the personality of its founder or founders—inevitably confronts the question of the movement of *myths*, which are culturally integrated and passively received (e.g., in the imagination of children) to the point where they are actively transformed into *symbols* with a religious significance. In Christian catechesis, the general opinion is that various beliefs should gradually shed their imaginary form to emerge eventually in a free and active faith. The contribution of R. Goldman (1964), in spite of his too narrowly cognitive operational framework, has been most helpful in making us aware of the average age before which the meaning of certain stories is inaccessible in most cases. On the other hand, at an early stage in the United States (from 1910), and with psychologically disastrous results, a certain degree of fundamentalism (literalism) in the interpretation of the Scriptures developed as a form of "antimodernism" in groups of an authoritarian tendency. This fundamentalism still influences certain ways of thinking, especially in France (Hervieu-Léger 1986, 1988) without giving rise to lasting perspectives capable of affecting a society deeply marked by desecularization (Hunter 1933). The various types of belief in Scripture (literalism, antireligiosity, mythosymbolism) inspired a questionnaire. R. A. Hunt's LAM (1972), which has been administered to very small population samples. If minimally adapted to particular sociocultural environments, it could be of great help in pastoral theology and thus to fundamental theology. More than forty-five years after *Divino Afflante Spiritu* (Pius XII, 1943), it would allow believers, on the basis, e.g., of the miraculous draught of fishes, to affirm their faith in the meaning of the narrative (the promise to the disciples that they will become "fishers of men") by stating whether they accept the draught of fishes as a miraculous *fact*, and would even allow nonbelievers to reject one or the other. It would be more beneficial to know where one stands in the churches and their various spiritual families.

J.-P. Deconchy has performed a quite different service with his two volumes of research into *orthodoxy* (1971, 1980). It is no longer a matter of describing and evaluating a state of belief, but of carrying out experiments that can reveal the structure and role of an essential dynamism within any institution that tries to maintain a certain way of thinking (ideology) or cognitive assent (beliefs). Strange to say, before 1971 the word "orthodoxy" did not occur in six of the major classic dictionaries of theology published after 1932. More modest or recent dictionaries hesitated between "right opinion" and "opinion that accords with a revealed teaching." The experiments focused first on the available religious lexis concerning "God" compared with other inductive words (house, father, etc.): the number of different words elicited for "God" is more limited, but above all it becomes more so as the situation of orthodoxy is (unconsciously) reinforced (inquiry conducted by a self-styled diocesan research center), and even more so if it is threatened (inquiry by a so-called center of rationalist thought). The other experimental procedures use "doxemes," or short propositions of belief, which have to be classified as true or false, absolutely obligatory or forbidden in my "church or group." Without citing the detailed procedures (see Godin 1972, 1983), we may now claim that the dynamic structure of orthodoxy comprises three dimensions: the psychosocial control mechanism of Belonging (*B*), avoidance of certain statements on the basis of Reason (*sR*), or the biblical corpus (*sC*). After a preliminary assessment of orthodoxy in a group, if the experiment introduces an assault on one of the three components, the second assessment elicits a compensatory, reinforcement of the other two. Across all of them, the information content is less important than the control of Belonging. Group cohesion is more significant than the meaning of the statements (*sR*), for instance. As for the relation to biblical references (*sC*), it is mainly used to support propositions accepted by the respondents, but is scarcely effective for propositions rejected "dogmatically." When *functional orthodoxy* is studied in this way, we find that subjects use

the biblical source less to investigate possible new propositions than to *ensure* that certain information *is "absolutely" safe* because it has already been checked by the group or church. This is psychological confirmation of the axiom that Tradition has the edge over Scripture. But does that really amount to theological wisdom when we recall that Scripture itself is a product of a tradition? New experiments (Deconchy 1982) have revealed other components that serve to support statements-doxemes called in doubt by scientific information: *utopianization* ("later on, those with the faith will have a better understanding of the proposition affirmed"), *eschatologization* ("the end of time will reveal fully what this or that proposition means") and *mysticization* ("in time . . . various religious authorities [the magisterium, theologians, mystics] will help us to see their truth"). Even in the case of propositions that are more deviant when measured against the structure of the orthodox system, this reinforcement "to come" is ascribed more often to mystics than to theologians or the magisterium. This tendency of the years 1975 to 1980 may change with circumstances.

Only now is J.-P. Deconchy's extensive work beginning to be known, commmented on, and utilized. Whether praised or unappreciated, it opens and closes on allusions to *the other dynamism*, that of *the* (messianic, prophetic) *Word*, which, together with orthodoxy, is included in "a diachronic model with an oscillating movement" and gives it its particular specificity among the ideologies. "It is probably located elsewhere . . . in the eminent originator, the 'messiah' in whom all the information is already present. . . . The group or church would thus be torn between bearing witness to its present structures and the wish to return to its sources and to its origins, all the way back to that privileged moment when there was no church . . ." (1971: 345)—when, one must add, there was as yet no refraction in four Gospels of that privileged time when emotion and imagination once again revolved about the Prophet. The very thrust of a reinforced orthodoxy would tend functionally to reduce revelation to an ideology, a set of propositions-*cum*-doxemes that would be as enforceable as dogmas. Here again proclamation demands interpretation. That spiritual space is once more available that allows Scripture once again to become the living Word, proclaimed in changing cultures, a product of the second Breath—who no longer speaks, like the Son, but inspires the pronouncements of those who come together in God's Name.

"If dogma means knowledge of the faith," one theologian has written, "perhaps we should stop taking only one formalized language seriously. Ideally, *a symbolic theology should unite biblical references, speculative thought and the evidence of contemporary debate in a single discourse*" (Geffré 1969: 96). Is this idea of uniting all these things *in the one discourse* a reasonable project or a mere dream? This particular theologian has cited three types of extremely varied language. A social psychologist has provided us with the results of complex but refined work that is difficult to refute on his own ground. The twofold meanings of symbols can never spare us the hard work of confirmation in the arena of "contemporary debate." If appropriately enlightened, the structure and thrust of orthodoxy cannot ignore fundamental theology.

Bibl.: W. JAMES, *The Varieties of Religious Experience* (New York, 1902); T. FLOURNOY, "Les principes de la psychologie religieuse," *Archives de Psychologie* 2 (1902): 33–57; G. CASTIGLIONI, "Ricerche ed osservazioni sull'idea di Dio nel fanciullo," *Vita e Pensiero* (Contributi 3) 1928; L. L. THURSTONE and E. J. CHAVE, *The Measurement of Attitudes* (Chicago, 1929); G. W. ALLPORT, "Attitudes" in C. Murchison, ed., *Handbook of Social Psychology* (Worcester, Mass., 1935), 798–884; G. CASTIGLIONI, "Il sentimento religioso di adolescenti," *Vita e Pensiero* (Contributi 9) 1941; A. T. WELFORD, "An attempt at an experimental approach to the psychology of religion," *British Journal of Psychology* 46 (1946): 55–73; D. LAGACHE, *L'unité de la psychologie* (Paris, 1949); P. RICOEUR, *Philosophy of the Will* (1949; New York, 1986); G. W. ALLPORT, *The Individual and His Religion* (New York, 1950); L. L. THURSTONE, "The Measurement of Values," *Psychological Review* 61 (1954): 47–58; L. MALEVEZ, "Nouveau Testament et théologie fonctionnelle," *RSR* 48 (1958): 258–90; P. JOHNSON, *Psychology of Religion* (New York, 1959); C. Y. GLOCK and R. STARK, *Religion and Society in Tension* (Chicago, 1965); J.-P. DECONCHY, "Peut-on parler de 'magie' chez l'enfant?" *MSR* 23 (1966): 217–36; J. B. ROTTER, "Expectancies for Internal versus External Control of Reinforcement," *Psychological Monographs* 80 (1966): 1–28; J.-P. DECONCHY, "Une tentative d'épistémologie de la pensée religieuse," *Arch. de sociol. des religions* 24 (1967): 141–48; J.-M. POHIER, *Psychologie et théologie* (Paris, 1967); L. B. BROWN, "Attitudes sous-jacentes dans les prières pour demander des faveurs" in A. Godin, ed., *From Cry to Word* (Brussels, 1968), 65–84; P. PRUYSER, *A Dynamic Psychology of Religion* (New York, 1968); C. GEFFRÉ, "Le langage théologique comme langage symbolique," in var., *Science et théologie* (Paris, 1969), 93-100; J.-P. DECONCHY, "La psychologie des faits religieux" in H. Desroche and J. Seguy, eds., *Introduction aux sciences humaines des religions* (Paris, 1970), 145–74; J.-P. DECONCHY, *L'orthodoxie religieuse* (Paris, 1971); R. A. HUNT, "Mythological Symbolism, Religious Commitment," *Journal for the Scientific Study of Religion* 10 (1972): 42–52; J. SCHARFENBERG, *Seelsorge als Gespräch* (Göttingen, 1972); A. VERGOTE, "Religion et psychanalyse," in *Encyclopaedia Universalis*, vol. 14 (1972), 38–39; P. BENSON and B. SPILKA, "God Images as a Function of Self-esteem and Locus of Control," *Journal for the Scientific Study of Religion* 12 (1973): 297–310; G. MILANESI and M. ALETTI, *Psicologia della religione* (Turin, 1973); R. W. HOOD, Jr., "The Construction and Preliminary Validation of a Measure of Reported Mystical Experience," *Journal for the Scientific Study of Religion* 14 (1975): 29–41; A. VERGOTE, "Psychanalyse et interprétation biblique," *DBS* 48–49 (1975): 252–60; A. GODIN, *Psychologie de la vocation* (Paris, 1975); L. M. RULLA, F. IMODA, and J. RIDICK, *Structure psychologique et vocation* (Brussels/Rome, 1978; English ed., Rome/Chicago, 1976); J. M. VAN DER LANS, *Religieuse ervaring en meditatie* (Nijmegen, 1978; 2nd ed., Deventer, 1980); J.-P. DECONCHY, *Orthodoxie religieuse et sciences humaines* (The Hague/Paris/New York, 1980); L. S. FILIPPI and A. M. LANZA, *Psicoterapia e valori umani* (Bologna, 1981); A. VERGOTE and A. TAMAYO, *The Parental Figures and the Representation of God* (Paris/New York, 1981); W. L. BRANDT, *Psychologists Caught* (Toronto, 1982); A. VERGOTE, *Religion, foi, incroyance* (Brussels, 1983); R. PALOUTZIAN, *Invitation to the Psychology of Religion* (Glenview, Ill., 1983); A. GODIN, *Psychology of Religious Vocations* (Washington, 1983); A. GODIN, *Psicologia delle esperienze religiose* (Brescia, 1983); J. D. HUNTER, *American Evangelicalism: Conservative Religion and the Quandary of Modernity* (New Brunswick, N.J., 1983); J.-P. DECONCHY, "Un vieux stéréotype idéologique: Les 'deux' religions," *Archives de sciences sociales des religions* 55 (1983): 175–81; A. GODIN, "Écoute et conseil," in *Initiation à la pratique de la théologie*, vol. 5 (1983): 47–76; R. L. GORSUCH and C. S. SMITH, "Attribution to God: An Interaction of Religious Beliefs and Outcomes," *Journal for the Scientific Study of Religion* 22 (1983): 340–52; L. LADRIÈRE, *L'articulation du sens*, Vol. 2: *Les langages de la foi* (Paris, 1984); J. L. SUENENS, "Entretien avec Fabien Deleclos," *Libre Belgique* (Apr. 30, 1984) p. 1 (see also J. L. SUENENS, *A New Pentecost* [New York, 1975]); H. N. MALONY and A. A. LOVEKIN, *Glossolalia* (New York, 1985); B. SPILKA, R. HOOD, and R. GORSUCH, *The Psychology of Religion: An Empirical Approach* (Englewood Cliffs, N.J.,

1985); B. Spilka, P. Shaver, and L. A. Kirkpatrick, "A General Attribution Theory for the Psychology of Religion," *Journal for the Scientific Study of Religion* 24 (1985): 1–20; D. W. Wulff, "Psychological Approaches," in F. Whaling, ed., *Contemporary Approaches to the Study of Religion* (Berlin/New York/Amsterdam, 1985); J.-F. Catalan, "Psychisme et vie spirituelle," *DSp* 12 (1986), 2570–2605; A. Godin, *Psychologie des expériences religieuses* (2nd ed.; Paris, 1986); D. Hervieu-Léger, *Vers un nouveau christianisme* (Paris, 1986); J.-P. Deconchy, "Les méthodes en psychologie de la religion: évolution récente," *Archives des sciences sociales des religions* 63 (1987): 33–83; J.-G. Nadeau, *La prostitution: une affaire de sens* (Montreal, 1987); B. Secondin, *Segni di profezia nelle Chiesa* (Milan, 1987); R. P. Vaughan, *Basic Skills for Christian Counselors* (New York, 1987); A. Godin, "Espérer en faisant mémoire: la crise des fins 'dernières' dans les croyances chrétiennes," in var., *Réincarnation, immortalité et résurrection* (Brussels, 1988), 91–132; D. Hervieu-Léger, "Les fondamentalistes," *Lumière et Vie* 186 (1988): 19–30.

André Godin

IX. Sociology of Religion

The sociology of religion, like other branches of sociology, has its own specific object and its own particular method. On the one hand, it studies the phenomenon of religion in its attitudinal, behavioral aspects and in its structure and dynamism deriving from the social nature of human beings. On the other, the approach uses methods appropriate to the observational sciences: hence, basically an inductive approach.

This rather general statement needs to be set out in more detail, both as to the object itself and as to the methodological implications. To this end, it is useful to present a brief but sufficient panoramic survey of the sociological approach to religion. For the sake of completeness, we shall add some considerations on contemporary problems.

With this in mind, and confining ourselves to the more important aspects, the basic points of our presentation can be set out as follows: (1) definition; (2) development of the sociology of religion; (3) religion as a multidimensional phenomenon; (4) modern themes and open questions.

1. Precise Definition of the Object

An initial delineation of the content of the sociology of religion shows two basic orientations: an essential concept of religion that seizes on its central and specific nucleus (substantial and exclusive delimitation); and a view based on the functions that religion develops in response to the fundamental hopes and expectations of human beings (functional and inclusive delimitation).

Each of these aspects, taken on its own, must be regarded as limited and hence unable to provide a base for a correct conception of the object of the sociology of religion. We need to adopt an approach that reconciles the two orientations and guarantees a new approach, which, while avoiding the shortcomings of each, will develop their positive aspects. This can be done by means of a series of transitions that elude any prejudicial choice and manifest an adequate heuristic capacity. A first phase consists of an empirical and amply comprehensive gathering of relevant information from various sources. The next phase is critical evaluation on the basis of historical, doctrinal, and sociocultural criteria. From these measures, a third phase yields an ample yet selective delimitation of the concept of religion: one rich in content and effective in method.

This procedure specifies the sociological approach to religion and demonstrates the justification for and basic plausibility of the object, both as to its direct content and as to its relational scope. It is therefore based on the share that religious phenomena have in the concept and dynamism of a given culture and social structure. It follows that the sociology of religion has as object those social and cultural phenomena of a religious character (e.g., cultural and social activities, roles, groups, and organizations originating from and molded by religious promptings) and religious phenomena (e.g., religious knowledge and experience, revelatory phenomena, relationship with super-empirical reality, etc.) with cultural and social characteristics.

Sociology studies and interprets the presence, structure, dynamism, and personal and social functions of these internal aspects and articulations, whether individually or in their interaction and interdependence. Furthermore, it explores the conditions and factors of continuity in time (traditional transmission), of generational transference (process of socialization), of assimilation, and of identification (personal and/or collective). Lastly, it analyzes the process of institutionalization, whether in general or in relation to individual cases.

Besides these constituent components, sociology observes the cultural and intercultural setting of a given religion and the complex of problems arising from this with regard to religion and sociocultural context. For now the traditional approach of the "dependent" and "independent" variables has been superseded or, better still, finished off; and a more complex and realistic relationship has been adopted, which is expressed in variable *autonoma*. This last theory holds that between religion and society there exists a multiplicity of active and passive relationships, to which the "cybernetic model" may be applied; this we have already been doing for some time. By this we can explain the persistence of a religious phenomenon, or its transformation, and also the various manifestations it may assume in a single context with the passing of time.

The sociology of religion tackles this complex of aspects with its own particular methodology—an inductive approach, such as is used by other branches of sociology. Such empirical study, moreover, is made with reference to the way individuals and groups perceive and live individual aspects of the religious phenomenon. The approach can be horizontal (comparing levels made up of components of various strata and different social categories) or longitudinal (in relation to the evolution of individual dimensions in the course of a people's or of a local community's history, as also of an individual person at different ages). Obviously these lists are possible in theory; but they cannot always, nor should they always, be used in every research project. They do, however, indicate the various matters that specific research work may take as its legitimate field.

2. Development of the Sociology of Religion

The sociology of religion has developed in parallel with general sociology. The beginnings are lost far back in time and constitute what is usually called the proto-historic phase. This is characterized by approaches on the part of other sciences, which we may call matrices, whose contributions, however, are nonspecific and not organic, but fragmentary and fortuitous. The systematic study of religious phenomena started once sociology began to get organized as a separate and autonomous science. From then on, there were any number of tentative sociological approaches to religion, though these obviously were conditioned by the philosophic and scientific climate of the last century.

In general terms, the development of the sociology of religion can be divided into three great periods, even though with contours none too clear. Basically we can distinguish a first period with a predominantly theoretical and general orientation; a second period with a predominantly empirical orientation, mainly confined to the study of religious practice; and a third period in which an orientation prevails where empirical and theoretical aspects are in equilibrium.

The Theoretical Orientation

This is a very important period, running from the earliest systematic attempts to the decisive and basic contributions of Durkheim and Weber. It is concerned with problems of a general nature with regard to religion and especially religion's relationship with society. Among the more prominent themes may be noted the problem of the origin of religion and the dynamics of the religious phenomenon *in se* and in relation to other social phenomena. Two currents in particular can be distinguished in the way the relationship with society is approached. The first one is known technically as the *theory of the dependent variable*; the second, adopting the opposite approach, is called the *theory of the independent variable*.

a. Religion as *dependent variable*. This view holds that religion is essentially a product of social conditions. Religion exists and persists as a phenomenon produced by society and experiences the influences of society's evolution. Here we find the early authors who dealt with the phenomenon of religion in the positivist climate of the last century: from A. Comte to R. Marx, from H. Spencer to E. Durkheim.

Durkheim's contribution is particularly important. While remaining substantially within the stream of the anthropologico-cultural thought of his day, he strengthens its more specifically sociological character by trying to arrive at a general theory of the origin and persistence of religion. The main points of Durkheim's theory, set out in his work *Les forces élémentaires de la vie religieuse,* can be synthesized as follows:

According to Durkheim, religion is a social fact, since it is born, becomes established, and develops in function of the group (or clan), which, in order to preserve itself from the danger of disintegration, projects outside itself the "group consciousness" (a sort of ideal personification of itself) as something superior, intangible, different, *sacred,* symbolized by the *totem.* Alongside static symbolism (the *totem*), stand narrative symbolism (myths) and operative symbolism (the cult), which make the group consciousness present to the individual psyche. All this needs to be lived and further developed, to be handed down to other generations. For this there has to be a fixed system of rules and structures, i.e., "a complex of beliefs and practices relative to sacred things, uniting in a single community, called church, all who adhere to them."

b. Religion as *independent variable.* Equally significant and convincing is the contribution of those who approach the relation between religion and society by standing the *schema* completely on its head and attributing to religion the function of independent variable. According to this view, it is important to study the dynamic of religions, their presence, and the role they have in social life. This role can best be depicted as being able to impress cultural orientations on society in order effectively to condition its development. Here sundry authors are to be found, including Hobhouse, Tawney, Troeltsch, and others more recent.

The most important author of all, however, is certainly Max Weber. He holds that religion plays an important role in the process of rationalizing the world, understood as a process of clarification and systematization of ideas seen in their normative force, by which they become effective motivations for social action. In this sense, religion performs an innovatory role and is a factor for social and even economic change.

This ability to influence is differentiated and depends on the metaphysics (immanentist or transcendentalist) on which a given religion is based, and on the ethical system (this-worldly or other-worldly) derived from this. The *immanentist* conception resolves the problem of the discrepancy between the real and the ideal world by passive and acquiescent attitudes that lead to contemplation or the godhead and an automatic and mechanistic view of the way the world works. The *transcendentalist* conception is based on the concepts of creation and of purpose in the creation and commits one to an active role in transforming the world. These two attitudes can be distinguished as mystical and ascetic respectively, connoting thus a greater emphasis in one direction or the other and ultimately giving rise to four basic types. According to Weber, the effect of religion on the nature of society consists mainly in a greater commitment and awareness of relationship with the world. This comes from what he calls worldly asceticism, which consists substantially in the strong identification between profession and concept of vocation (in German, he uses the term *Beruf*) in the religious sense. Weber expounds this approach in several of his writings, especially *Die Protestantische Ethik und der Geist des Kapitalismus.*

The Sociographic Orientation

After various other attempts to produce a synthesis, the sociographic orientation carries the day. Its initiator was G. Le Bras, who tried to reconstruct and analyze religious behavior particularly in relation to religious practice. In 1931, he published a questionnaire for a detailed examination and historical explanation of the state of Catholicism in the various regions of France. This approach was gradually followed by other scholars, such that in the 1960s it had become the dominant line of approach. It lends itself to establishing contact with the behavioral and aggregative state of religion, especially for pastoral use.

This approach is mainly descriptive, centered on the quantitative study of attendance at Sunday mass and at other forms of devotion, and the reception of the sacraments. The various surveys are then arranged according to demographic and territorial parameters, from which forms for classifying the material are derived, which show how and in what group or category of persons a given type of practice is more or less common. Other parameters of comparison have since been suggested, e.g., the relation between religion and industrialism, the effect of urbanization, the influence exerted by social and ecclesial organizational structures, the development of church membership, the incidence of the phenomenon of secularization.

Development of research along these lines did not have due commitment to content and method. A gap was apparent between research and general sociological theory, and applicational and methodological inadequacy was clear, because religious practice had been specially chosen as the main, often exclusive, analytical indicator. Such shortcomings give rise to unjustified and unbalanced inferences for the understanding of religious behavior.

Orientation Today

In recent years an observable change has come over research into the phenomenon of religion. Efforts have been made to avoid the defects in earlier sociologists' approaches, on the one hand, and those inherent in the sociographic orientation, on the other, by adopting a wider, more comprehensive, and at the same time more scientifically valid approach.

In this context, the widening of the coordinates of study and analysis acquires particular importance, tending as it does toward a multidimensional approach simultaneously embracing the various basic aspects of the phenomenon of religion. An approach of this sort takes account not only of religious practice but also of the cognitive component and the way it is symbolically expressed. Such an approach also insists on the communal component and hence on the processes of membership in and identification with a given religion. Lastly, it emphasizes the presence of an ethical component as deriving from religion and consisting in a particular complex of norms that regulate the behavior of the faithful.

In this orientation there has been a marked methodological development. Sociological method is applied more seriously and more vigorously, and this in turn has required more careful organization of the concepts and a consequent refining of the techniques or instruments in use. A significant contribution to practical research is the growing use of computers, which have made a greater complexity and sophistication possible in the processing of data, resulting in improvement in its interpretation.

3. Religion as a Multidimensional Phenomenon

It may well be imagined that so complex and articulated a phenomenon would be made up of many dimensions. This is generally affirmed, but if anything is to be made of it, the use of objective and acceptable criteria is essential. In particular, the following must be stressed: internal homogeneity, conceptual autonomy, anthropological foundation, workability of the concepts. There remains the fact, however, that in the transition to the practical individuation of the dimensions, differences will arise. These concern either the number of dimensions or the way each one of them is described. General opinion, however, singles out four main dimensions: beliefs, religious practice, community aspect, ethical implications.

Beliefs

These are commonly understood as being the complex of intuitive and cognitive elements perceived and felt not only as intellectual but also as experiential and willed fact, relative to a reality that is meta-empirical and hence by its nature unverifiable. In practice, this concerns the contents of the creed of each religion and each religion's teachings about God, the world, and humanity as aspects of "ultimate reality" and in their mutual relations. The beliefs constitute the basis of religious life. They give value and meaning to the rites, justify the organization not only as group but as *fellowship*; they give religious content and sanction to the moral norms.

Religious Practice

By this expression, we mean the gamut of rites organized and performed by the community (actions, words, symbols), by participating in which human beings manifest their relationship with God and strengthen their own religious feelings. In religious rites, three principal functions may be distinguished: expressive, instrumental, communal. The rites, taken all together, also have within them a series of distinctions that have become more or less well known and recurrent in literature on the subject. There are repetitive rites, depending on their inner nature and the effects that they produce, rites that can be performed by the community, others to be carried out by the individual, and so on.

The Communal Aspect

The phenomenon of religion has as constant characteristic that of being realized by the community. Membership and involvement of the individual in the community (which is basically held together by religious bonds) are derived either from the social nature of human beings or from the communal need for and performance of religious actions. Such a communal aspect can be observed at various levels. On the inter-religious plane, it concerns the general internal structuring (church or sect). On the internal organizational plane, however, it involves the qualitative and functional distinction between members (clergy and laity) and the division of territory (diocese, parish, etc.). On the personal plane are located membership, identification with one's own religious organization, and sharing in communal responsibilities.

The Ethical Dimension

Every religion offers values and goals that constitute an overall design for the individual and for society, presented as a response to the ultimate needs of existence. From it, therefore, norms and obligations are derived that regulate relationships between individuals and between these and the Godhead. With regard to ethics, religions present differing conceptions. One religion may insist on the definition of roles, the hierarchization and formal and exterior execution of the acts prescribed, and may present a socially conservative orientation (formal religion). Another religion, in contrast, may stress the improvement of the individual or of society, consistency of values, the superseding of ritualism, and may propose forms for renewing and transforming society (prophetic religion).

Before completing the brief exposition of the four dimensions of the religious phenomenon, two important observations must be made. The first concerns the presence of a relative interdependence between the different dimensions and hence the influence, under the forms of stimulus, motivation, consequence, or implication, of one of them on the others. A second observation, however, confirms the existence of

a certain conceptual and operative autonomy among the individual dimensions. Thus, it may be verified that a person (or group) excels in one dimension but not in another, with the prospect of finding oneself having to deal with incomplete and/or inconsistent forms of religiousness.

4. Modern Themes and Open Questions

The development of the sociology of religion is still in its early phases of growth, and there are many issues of content and methodology that still must be broached and thoroughly investigated. The number and quality of these issues depend on various natural factors, be they historical and cultural or epistemological. It is right at least to mention the most important present-day themes and open questions to which the sociology of religion *qua* science has to find correct answers today, taking account both of the object and what pertains to it, and of the method that should characterize our approach.

A first topic is the birth of new cults, which may be new religious movements generated from already existing religions, entirely autonomous and independent forms, or forms of a syncretic type. New cults have shown a great capacity for catching on, especially among the young. The speed with which they spread and the radical nature of their approach are impressive. Overall evaluation of them, however, tends suggest that they are fads, which, on the whole, show neither mass development nor particular durability.

Another interesting topic is the relationship between religion and society. Among the many practical ways in which religion and society are related, the link between liberation and religion stands out. There has been remarkable development along these lines not only in Latin America but in other places too. On the interpretative plane, it can be traced back to an updated version of the perennial problem of the relationship between religion and development seen from the sociopolitical viewpoint. It has given rise to an interesting and vital phenomenon, even though it has often been interpreted in a predominantly ideological, rather than properly scientific, way.

Also very important is the topic of grassroots religion. The revival of this phenomenon in recent years is well known, followed (as one might expect) by a vigorous debate on its conceptions and definitions and on its analytical and interpretative perspectives. The principal question is still whether to interpret the grassroots components merely as archaic, undeveloped, folkloric, or classist, or rather as a manifestation of something anthropologically perennial but typical of the way religious activities are performed when conducted on a massive scale.

Another important topic is religion in modern society. If we assume that the theory of secularization is outdated, there are three approaches: the theory of privatization (invisible religion), the theory of folkloric exteriorization (civic religion), and the theory of the persistence of the religious imperative in the quest for meaning, in new conditions but following original perspectives (transformed religion).

The chief methodological problem seems to be delimiting religious phenomena. This difficulty calls into question the status of sociology of religion as a branch of general sociology by reducing sociology of religion to one aspect of the sociology of knowledge. Further, there are those who believe that sociology of religion cannot maintain a satisfactory academic and scientific status. As far as these theorists are concerned, there are big problems in conducting empirical research within a given sociocultural context and in evaluating the acceptability and objectivity of the results (crisis over epistemological status). In this approach, however, there seems to be a hint of notions ideologically unfavorable to religion itself or to one historical religion in particular.

In conclusion, the acceptability of the basic theoretical assumptions of sociology of religion seem evident, as also the rightness of its methodological contribution. Obviously this way of approaching religion is not the only one, nor is it exhaustive, which is why, especially today, it presupposes and postulates various other types of approach to religion, such as theology, philosophy, history, and so on. This confirms the usefulness of an interdisciplinary approach and the prospect of in-put and contribution from various sciences for a better understanding of the religious phenomenon itself.

Bibl.: E. DURKHEIM, *The Elementary Forms of the Religious Life* (1912; New York, 1965); M. WEBER, *The Protestant Ethic and the Spirit of Capitalism* (1922; New York, 1958); J. WACH, *Sociology of Religion* (Chicago, 1944); J. FICHTER, *Social Relations in Urban Parish* (Chicago, 1954); G. LE BRAS, *Études de sociologie religieuse* (Paris, 1956); J. M. YINGER, *Religion, Society and the Individual* (New York, 1957); H. CARRIER, *Psycho-sociologie de l'appartenance religieuse* (Rome, 1960); T. O'DEA, *The Sociology of Religion* (New Jersey, 1966); T. LUCKMANN, *The Invisible Religion* (New York, 1968); P. L. BERGER, *The Social Reality of Religion* (London, 1969); R. ROBERTSON, *Sociological Interpretation of Religion* (Oxford, 1970); C. CAMPBELL, *The Sociology of Religion* (London, 1971); G. SCARVAGLIERI, *L'istituto religioso come fatto sociale* (Padua, 1973); id., *Sociologia della religione* (Rome, 1980); id., *Religione e società a confronto* (Reggio Emilia, 1982); G. MILANESI, *Sociologia religiosa* (Turin, 1974); var., *Religion and Social Change*, Acts of 13th CIRS (Lille, 1975); C. Y. GLOCK and R. N. BELLAH, *The New Religious Consciousness* (Berkeley, 1976).

Guiseppe SCARVAGLIERI

X. THEOLOGY OF RELIGIONS

1. Introduction

Theology of religions is a new field of study, just beginning to interest Christian thinkers who wish to carry on a fruitful dialogue with the adherents of non-Christian religions and to contribute to a better understanding of world religions. How is Christianity related to other world religions? Can Christianity any longer claim to be unique, given the fact that other religions propose themselves as means of ultimate human salvation? What is the theological basis for Christianity's rapport with other great religious traditions? Is it possible to be both evangelical and completely open to what Karl Jaspers calls "boundless communication" with Hinduism, Buddhism, Islam?

We Christians become more and more aware of rapidly growing religious pluralism in which we live from day to day in the midst of Muslims, Hindus, Buddhists and members of other religious traditions. Each of these faiths proclaims its own message of eternal truth and salvation. Christians too are faced with the problem of understanding other faiths in the light of Christian faith and commitment. They are faced with the theological problem of how to account for the diversity of religious life and each one's truth claim. Is Christianity the one, true, absolute religion meant for all humankind? Can Christianity at the same time recognize authentic religious values in other faiths? If Christ is the only true way to God and is the universal mediator between God and humanity, what can we say of other religions as ways of salvation, of other religious founders or prophets as showing the way of salvation? Are those of other faiths saved? What is the salvific value of other religions in the Christian perspective? Is there any kind of supernatural revelation in other religions?

2. The Christian Theology of Religions

The Christian theology of religions is the discipline that aims to answer the questions that arise from the theological implications of living in a religiously plural world. It makes its reflections on these implications in the light of Christian faith. Theology, being a normative science, judges in the light of Christian faith the validity of the religious claims of other religions. The theologian of religions makes value judgments on other religions from the point of view of truth and supernatural efficacy; the criteria of judgment are derived from the principles of Christian faith and revelation. The theology of religion differs from the philosophy of religion because the latter, though it is also a normative science, makes value judgments in the light of natural reason and not in the light of revelation.

There can be a theology of religions from the Hindu, Buddhist, or Islamic point of view insofar as these various religious adherents reflect on the meeting of world religions or on the relationship of their own particular religion to other religions in the light of their own faith. This is the reason why we call our discipline the Christian theology of religions. At this point, an interesting question arises. Can there be a universal theology of religions? A universal theology of religions is sometimes understood as the systematic reflection on religion, which includes all religions and is addressed not to a particular religious community but to all religious communities. This would mean that "theologians" would have to reflect and speak in a way that would be understandable by all, in a language shared by all, without thereby replacing particular religious language (Leonard Swidler). Such a universal theology of religions, in my view, is rather a philosophy of religion than a theology of religion, for theology is always a systematic reflection on one's own

faith in all its specificity and uniqueness, not merely in its common elements with other faiths.

Though the history and phenomenology of religion and the theology of religions are different in scope and method, still there is a close connection between the two disciplines. The theologian can and must make use of the results of the history and phenomenology of religions. The importance of this is proved by the fact that not only does this approach render the theologian capable of avoiding religious relativism and syncretism; it also permits the theologian positively to deepen and enlarge on his or her understanding of views, experiences, and norm on which theology is based. Theology is made living when the concrete religious experience and practice of religious persons is taken into account in the explanation and elucidation of the revealed truth, worship, and practice.

3. Contemporary Approaches to Other Religions

We can provide a concise presentation of the main paths that modern Christian theology has followed in its efforts to understand the relation between Christianity and other religions. Three main approaches have been proposed to resolve the tension between two fundamental axioms— first, that salvation is through Jesus Christ alone; and second, that God desires the salvation of all humans. The three approaches—exclusivist, inclusivist, and pluralist—reflect an emphasis on one or the other of these axioms.

The exclusivist attitude sees genuine knowledge and experience of God confined to Christian faith; there is only a blurred vision of God and little salvific value in other religions. It insists that all salvation comes from God alone through Jesus Christ. The inclusivist approach grants that genuine knowledge and experience of God may be found in other religious traditions but holds that the fullness of that knowledge and experience can be found only in Christianity. This position reconciles and holds together the axiom of the universal salvific will of God and the axiom that salvation comes only through God in Christ and his church. Thus it affirms both the value of other religions and the decisiveness of Christ. The pluralist approach, which claims to be a "Copernican revolution" in the theological approaches to other religions, maintains that other religions are equally salvific paths to the one God. It presents the different religious traditions as different expressions of a knowledge and an experience of God that are common to many traditions.

4. The Exclusivist Approach

In this view only the Christian faith is true and all other religions are false. Emile Brunner asserts that although primitive, polytheistic, and mystical religions make no claim to be revelations of universal validity, three world religions do make this claim. Of these, Zoroastrianism and Islam really reduce to a rationalistic, moralistic theism with no mystery of redemption. Judaism either awaits the Messiah—and thus does not claim a final revelation—or else it too reduces to the same type of theism. Brunner concludes that the claim of a universally valid revelation is in fact quite rare and that it appears in its fullness only in Christian faith. His thesis is that other religions are the product of the original divine religion in the creation and of human sin. He concludes:

> Whereas the relative theory of religion regards the basic element in all religions as the essence of religion, and all that distinguishes them from one another as nonessential, so far as biblical faith is concerned the exact opposite is true. It is the distinctive element that is essential, and all that the Christian faith may have in common with other religions is nonessential. (*Revelation and Reason*)

Hendrik Kraemer has proposed almost the same view. Making appeal to what he calls "biblical realism," he says that God's self-disclosing revelation in Christ is absolutely *sui generis*. If the idea of the fulfillment is to be applied to the gospel it can be only with reference to the promise of God given in previous acts of revelation and not to points of similarity in non-Christian faiths (Kraemer 1938). The dissimilarities and the antithesis are more significant than the similarities and points of contact. In the light of the revelation in Christ, we see in non-Christian religions only a fundamental misdirection of humanity and a groping for God, which find an unsuspected divine solution in Christ (ibid.).

Karl Barth, in his *Kirchliche Dogmatik*, has a long section headed: "The Revelation of God as the Abolition of Religion." He distinguishes between the Christian Faith, which is based solely on God's revelation of himself in Jesus Christ, and all religion, which is humanity's futile search for ultimate truth and meaning. This search is doomed to failure, because God is the wholly Other, and but for his condescension humans could not have known anything whatever about him. Religion is the vain attempt of self-righteous humans to erect their own truth and to justify themselves by their own works, their own piety, and their own pretension to discover God without the aid of divine grace. As such it is sinful unbelief. This attitude to other religions is often called dialectical, as the whole theology behind it is dialectical. It rejects the view that regards God as an "object" of theological reasoning (*via positiva*) and also the mystical notion that only what God is not is capable of being thought (*via negativa*), transcending the yes and no of these methods by means of a third approach (*via dialectica*), which affirms that God is known neither as object nor yet as merely negatively, but as subject, as the "Thou" who mysteriously and miraculously reveals himself to humans in his own unconditioned freedom. The Christian can say yes to other religions because they are in some way a response to the approach of the God whom the Christian worships. But the Christian must say no because they are a confused, distorted response. Thus the relation of the Christian Gospel to other religions is one of judgment and fulfillment—a judgment upon their sin and a fulfillment of their hidden origin in divine revelation.

5. The Pluralist Approach

This is also called an approach of relativity, a cultural relativism that asserts that each religion is the appropriate expression of its own culture. Thus, Christianity is the religion of the West; Hinduism is the religion of India; and Buddhism is the religion of Southeast Asia. The attitude of cultural relativism generally assumes that religion is a by-product of culture. There is an epistemological relativism which claims that we cannot know the absolute truth but only what is true for us. We believe that Christianity is true for us, but we cannot go on to affirm that it is the truth for all peoples, since they must be the judges of that. This kind of relativism results in syncretism, which is the effort to combine the various religions in order to bring them to a common denominator. Finally, we meet what is called teleological relativism, which holds that all religions are simply different paths to the same goal. So the path one chooses is only a matter of personal preference. But careful investigation has shown that the world religions have quite different conceptions of human fulfillment.

The pluralist approach at times has also an evolutionist aspect. Some Christian thinkers hold that at the heart of all religions is the same essence; it is identical to all as the intrinsic nature that lies hidden under all the religious forms. This essence of religion can be understood by doctrinal belief, by morals, or by experience. This could be described as mysticism (Hocking), the feeling of absolute dependence (Schleiermacher), the numinous sense of the holy (Otto), the recognition of all our duties as the commandments of God (Kant), or the personal encounter with God (Farmer). In this case the Christian interpretation of other religions will be that they contain the essence of religion in varying degrees of imperfection and partial realization, while Christianity constitutes the fullest manifestation of this essence.

6. The Inclusivist Approach

Christians do claim for Christ a unique position and maintain that Christianity is not merely one among many religions but in an absolute sense the religion for all. The claim of uniqueness can be understood in two senses: exclusive and inclusive. The exclusivist position, which we have outlined above, intends the claim to be exclusive—which means that Christ is to be taken to be the truth exclusively; the other religions and their central figures are considered to be false. The inclusive approach, on the contrary, holds that whatever is found to be true and good in other religions is claimed to be included and transcended in Christ and Christianity. This inclusivist position is certainly catholic. John's Gospel presents Jesus as saying: "No one comes to the Father except by me." But the same Gospel identifies in the man of Nazareth the eternal Logos, the utterance of God, which enlightens every person alive. This immense inclusiveness means that wherever God speaks, has spoken, or will speak through the great religious leaders such as Moses, the Buddha, Muhammad, Jesus is the embodiment of it. This NT claim of immense inclusiveness for Jesus Christ involves in principle all, anywhere and everywhere, that may be called the utterance (the Logos) of God. This claim does not mean that Christians have nothing to learn from other religions. Though they believe that all is summed up intensively in Christ, there is much extensively to learn from other religious followers. The claim of uniqueness for Christ concerns a uniqueness of total inclusion, not of exclusion. But the real stumbling block lies in attaching this all-inclusiveness to a particular historical figure who suffered under Pontius Pilate. Augustine wrote: "That the Word was in the beginning, and that the Word was with God and the Word was God, this I read [not, as he explains, in so many words, but in effect] in the books of the Neoplatonists; . . . but that the Word was made flesh and dwelt among us, I found not there" (*Confessions* 7.9.13–14). It is in Jesus that the salvific will of God is perfectly represented and put into effect. The risen and glorified Christ is hailed in the New Testament as the Lord of the universe, the cosmic Christ. The claim that in Jesus the Logos (God's utterance) was made flesh means that Jesus expresses, in a human personality, absolutely all that it is possible for God so to express. Jesus is God's last word in humanity. This does not deny that the same Logos might be expressed in its maximum possible completeness in whatever else humanity might one day evolve into, or at any other level of creation.

The church remains the means of access to Christ. It is the organization through which and in which the risen Christ himself maintains contact with those who believe in him. Christianity is not just a body of teaching; nor is it a matter of individuals following a great example; nor is the church a voluntary society of those who are concerned with Christ. The church is the body of Christ—i.e., the organism rather than the organization in which and through which God in Christ is acknowledged and worshiped.

7. Vatican Council II on Religions

We can distinguish between the fundamental religious experience and the socioculturally qualified religious experience as they are found in religions. We understand by the term "fundamental" the conscience and the religious experience that are known to be inscribed in the human being: that primary religious feeling which expresses itself in fundamental interrogatives, in human aspirations and endeavors. It refers to the religious capacity and the religious endowments and to their primary expression as they appear in every human being, apart from the sociocultural contents a cultural structure can imprint on them. This fundamental religious experience has been outlined in effective language by Vatican II as a phenomenon shared by the whole of humanity, and which lies at the basis of all religions. It can be called the *numus* from which the religions of the earth germinate. "What is a man? What is the meaning and the purpose of our life? What is goodness and what is sin? What gives rise to our sorrows and to what intent? Where lies the path to true happiness? What is the truth about death, judgment, and retribution beyond the grave? What, finally, is the ultimate and unutterable mystery which engulfs our being, and whence we take our rise, and whither our journey leads us?" (*NA* 1).

How does the theologian interpret this fundamental religious experience in the light of the Word of God? This universal fact of human experience refers to the primary fact of humans being creatures and to their destination in Christ, in whom all has been created, in whom everything subsists, and toward whom everything tends.

The council says that those also can attain to everlasting salvation who through no fault of their own do not know the Gospel of Christ or his church yet sincerely seek God and, moved by grace, strive by their deeds to do his will as it is known to them through the dictates of conscience (*LG* 16). The paschal mystery of Christ holds true not only for Christians but for all people of good will in whose heart grace works in an unseen way. For, since Christ died for all, and since the ultimate human vocation is in fact one, we ought to believe that the Holy Spirit in a manner known only to God offers to every person the possibility of being associated with this paschal mystery (*GS* 22). The council speaks of the ways and modes in which the salvific action of God reaches non-Christians, namely, through created realities (*GS* 36) and through an inner law (*GS* 16) and conscience (*DH* 3).

It speaks of the elements of truth and grace, found already among the nations as a secret presence of God (*AG* 9). The conduct of life and teachings proposed by non-Christian religions frequently reflect the ray of truth that enlightens all humans (*NA* 2). The council rejects nothing that is true and holy in these religions (*NA* 2) and recognizes the ascetic and contemplative traditions whose seeds were sometimes already planted by God in ancient cultures prior to the preaching of the gospel (*AG* 18). It remarks that human religious endeavors by which people seek God may sometimes serve as a guide to the true God, as a preparation to the gospel (*AG* 3). Whatever goodness or truth is found among them is looked on by the church as a preparation for the gospel (*LG* 16). Again, it teaches that those who have not received the gospel are related in various ways to the people of God (*AG* 16). It mentions first the Jews, then the Muslims and those who in shadows and images seek the unknown God, and those who without blame on their part have not yet arrived at an explicit knowledge of God but who strive to live a good life, thanks to God's grace.

The council has furnished these elements on which a theologian of religions has to reflect and build up a true theology of religions. What value do the non-Christian religions possess in the economy of salvation? What are they worth in God's eyes? Are they depositories of divine revelation, and can they be considered efficacious ways and means of salvation for their adherents? (1) Religions are the social and structural objectification of the fundamental religious feeling innate in humans. One's interior religious feeling is expressed spontaneously in objective and social forms and structures. In this external and social expression of the religious experience, the interior action of God in humanity is also reflected. From this point of view we can expect to find in the religions the presence or the reflection of the light "which enlightens everyone" (Jn 1:9). We can also say that in religions there is the objectification of that *instinctus Dei invitantis*, thanks to which, as Thomas Aquinas says, God calls people to salvation. Besides, we know from revelation that humans bear in themselves an image of God obscured by guilt and by the psychological conditioning induced by this. Humans are wounded by sin and carry in themselves an inclination to evil, to go against the will of God. Because of this we cannot consider religions simply as wholly luminous realities, depositories of the Spirit of God and objectification of the ways of the supernatural salvation. Insofar as religions are the expression of human creatureliness subject to the saving action of God, they must be considered depositories of real salvific values, objectifications of deeply human impulses sustained by the grace of God. But since humans are wounded by sin, we must regard religions as inevitably marked by human negativeness, with all the ambiguities that implies. Hence, there is the need of clear discernment of the heritage of the religions and the need for distinguishing between the various levels of each individual religion.

The problem of the relationship between religions and the Christian economy of salvation is a complex one. What kind of relationship does the self-communication of God that comes about in the church have with that which takes place in the sphere of non-Christian religions? Is there a divine revelation among non-Christians, and if this exists, what is its nature? What value should we attribute to the sacred books of non-Christian religious traditions? What is the theological statute of their founders and spiritual leaders of the past and of the present?

With regard to the question of the relationship of vital participation in divine communication between the religions and the Christian economy, we have to note first that this divine self-communication is called in the Bible "kingdom of God," justification, salvation, rebirth, new life, communion with Christ. It attracts light and life; hence, it is also called revelation, enlightenment, life, spirit, energy. This is a typically Christian terminology used to qualify the novelty of Christian revelation and experience. We cannot say that the reality denoted by these terms exists in the identical way outside of Christianity, since this would disregard the insistence with which the Christian sources outline the new experience in Christ. On the other hand, we cannot simply

say that this experience has nothing in common with that which precedes it, anticipates it and prepares it, since that would not respond to the divine plan as it is outlined in the same sources and which is at the basis of the missionary efforts of the apostles. The real solution, which would be faithful to the biblical tradition and to the conclusions of the phenomenology of religions, is to admit "various degrees of participation," thanks to which humans are informed of the divine economy. This gradualness of participation, in the span of a great unitary plan, is at the basis of John's prologue and of the first two chapters of the letter to the Romans, where the relationship between the salvific economy brought about in Christ and that of the OT and of those who have not received the Torah is clearly shown (P. Rossano).

Psychologically the divine self-communication can be explained by the fact that the fundamental religious experience, prior to any cultural expression, is the place and the normal and privileged point of contact of divine self-communication with humans. If the religious experience is totally wanting or distorted, Christian faith cannot take root, much less produce shoots. The seed of the divine Word falls on different kinds of soil and bears fruit according to the depth and fertility of the religious ground itself.

From the historical and phenomenological point of view also it is seen that the forms and structures of religious experience of humanity are the normal and constant means of expression of the Christian economy in history. In the biblical texts it is amply clear how revelation has been made accessible to humans through human religious categories to whom it was addressed. The history of theology, of the liturgy, of Christian spirituality has to take into account seriously the inculturation of faith in the spiritual and religious milieu of the people.

8. The Biblical and Patristic Views on Religions

The Bible recognizes and proclaims as positive and given by God for salvation the religious endowment of the human race, both in individuals and in peoples. Of course, the Bible strongly rejects its aberrations and errors. It announces a historic intervention of God with his people in view of all humanity, which is reached, elevated, and transformed in its religious spirit. Hence the religions appear, in their authentic and genuine elements, as the providential preparation for Christ, "in whom men find the fullness of religious life, and in whom God has reconciled all things to Himself" (*NA* 2).

In the whole Bible salvation history and revelation are interwoven with religion and its forms, and reach humans and react in them through the forms and categories inherent in the religious person. From the NT it is evident that the divine gift of faith is grafted onto the preliminary orders of "fear of God" and of submission to him; that the brotherhood and the Christian community fulfill the social aspirations common to religions; and that the same sacramentality of the holy acts (Baptism and the Eucharist) responds to the universal search for efficacious means of establishing contact with the divine.

The epoch of the fathers was very different from ours, and we must understand their approach to other religions in that light; dialogue was not their primary interest. Their fundamental attitude was one of struggle and opposition. God is present in every creature; all truth comes from him. Hence, Justin speaks of the "seeds of the Word," and Clement of Alexandria of a Hellenic Testament. Justin started with the maxim that reason (the germinal Logos) was what united humans to God and gave them knowledge of God. Before Christ's coming, humans had possessed, as it were, seeds of the Logos and had thus been enabled to arrive at fragmentary facets of truth. Hence, such pagans as "live with reason" were in a sense Christians before Christianity. The Logos had now assumed shape and became a man in Jesus Christ. Justin was very optimistic about the harmony of Christianity and Greek philosophy. The gospel and the best elements in Plato and the Stoics are almost identical ways of apprehending the same truth, admitting that the Greek philosophers had made serious errors. But he was sharply negative toward pagan cults and religious myths. Polytheism is crude, superstitious, and often immoral, a demonic counterfeit and caricature of the true religion, sown by evil powers to deceive people to give the impression that the gospel is just one more religious myth, in order to prevent people from rising above idolatry.

Similarities between Christianity and paganism in worship and myth are explained as imitations of the truth inspired by the devil, who with foresight and sagacity has tried to prejudice people against the gospel by caricatures of the incarnation, etc. There can not be reconciliation with counterfeit ideas of worship, and Justin rejects all syncretism which merges Christian story with Greek legends. But the higher philosophical truths about God were acquired by pagan philosophers either by derivation from the writings of Moses or through the exercise of the divinely given reason.

Every early Christian author is at pains to emphasize the absurdity and immorality of polytheism. Paganism has had its day, just like the civilization it founded; the new Christian dispensation has taken its place. Humanity is being renewed since the time of Christ and is destined to reach him. But the fathers had an attitude of esteem and respect for every pagan in good faith (Augustine, Justin, Clement, Basil). The truth is that for the fathers humanity belongs to God and at the same time it is completely one. They also affirm that God has never abandoned the Gentile nations even in the darkest hours of their history. What about the recognition of religious values to be found in pagan philosophies and religions? The answer is complex and delicate. A certain favor was accorded the philosophers; but none, or next to none, to the various religions. The pagan religions were identified with polytheism of the populace and were simply the work of the devil. They are an acknowledgment of the failure of human endeavor when left to itself, and they call for the advent of Jesus Christ.

The Catholic theology of world religions has taken two clearly marked lines.

9. Jean Daniélou and the Theology of Religions

Non-Christian religions express a dimension of human nature. Humans are fundamentally religious; they are capable of recognizing with their intelligence and ratifying with love their relationship to the divinity. This is true at the individual level, since the love of God is a condition of the complete realization of humanity, of human happiness. This is true also at the social level, since the religious act is a part of the temporal common good. The distinctive characteristic of religions is that they perceive the divine through its manifestations. The cosmic phenomena are signs in which humans of all times have perceived a divine presence. The presence of the divine is perceived still more strongly in human actions. Birth, beginning of adulthood, marriage, and death are always accompanied by religious rites. The seasonal rhythm of cosmos and of human life is celebrated in the liturgical cycle. The rites reproduce the exemplary actions of the divine beings in the realm of the archetypes. Thus the rites and myths express a fundamental experience by means of which one enters into communion with the divine, which transcends the human.

What is essentially a sign cannot be identified with the substance itself of religion. It was not the sun as a material object that religious people adored, but through the sun they adored the beneficent power which is the source of light and of life. The fact that religion is expressed through cultural structures does not mean that it is reducible to these structures. By means of the fundamental human relations one enters into communion with the Reality that transcends one. Finally, humans perceive the divine in their interior selves as distinct from themselves and as one who acts within them. They perceive their own proper limits and that which is of the absolute in them; they perceive the divine in the illumination of mind, inhabiting in the core of being and impelling them to search for God. The great religions are the historical expression of the religious act in humanity. Religions are one and diverse: one because they pertain to the same level of the experience, that of the divine. Each religion makes us aware of the ways in which humans have recognized God through the mediation of the world and have sought him beyond the world. Diversity is part of the essence of religions, and there are radical divergences in the religions themselves. The differences within Christianity reflect, in the unity of the unique faith that is necessarily one, the different types of the religious mentality that receive this faith, each in its own way.

The Judeo-Christian fact presents us with something absolutely different, because it is not simply a whole of various means of adoring God but is the witnessing of an event that con-stitutes sacred history. The Bible is a history that gives witness to the actions of God, of the invasion of history by the Word. Religions are a movement of humanity to God; revelation gives testimony of a movement of God toward humanity. The scope of all religions is to manifest God in the repetition of natural and human cycles. The object of revelation is a unique event, i.e., the event of Christ. If this event is unique, then the revelation ought to be necessarily unique which consists in believing in the reality of that unique event. Instead, the religions, created by human genius, attest to the value of important personages like the Buddha, Zoroaster, and Confucius, but are marked by the defects of what is human. Revelation is the work of God alone. Humans cannot advance any pretext to it, since they have no right to it. Being a pure gift of God, it is the infallible truth, which applies in a sense only to God. Religion expresses the desire that humans have for God, which they continuously posit in their lives. Revelation attests to God's response to this desire, conducting humans to salvation, which only Jesus Christ ascertains. Revelation is prophetic and eschatological, beyond the reach of humans. Revelation does not destroy religion but fulfills it.

Whereas religion is the realm of spiritual experience, i.e., experience of the divine, revelation is the realm of faith, which demands one to confide oneself in the experience of another who comes from above. This opposition between Christianity and other religions does not represent an incompatibility between them; it signifies a connection between them. The encyclical ECCLESIAM SUAM bears witness to the vitality of other religions and their values, which they continue to preserve. Christianity assumes the values of religions, purifies them, and transforms them without destroying them, because Christ has come to take possession of every person. What is of greater value is the *homo religiosus*. Salvation brought by Christ does not consist in substituting another reality in the place of that of nature. It is humanity whom the Word comes to save, and the human he has created is a religious one. Hence, the Word has come also to transform religious values. If human religious acts have been the point of insertion of the divine, these themselves signify also the fulfillment of the desire they have raised. This implies a new birth of the spirit which gives origin to the life of God. The relation between Christianity and other religions is reciprocal. Christianity is necessary in order that revelation be realized; but the effective quality of this realization depends on the quality of the religious person transformed by revelation. The dialogue of revelation with non-Christian religions passes through the problem of religion, i.e., the problem of the religious person.

Christianity does not consist in knowing God; for this religion is sufficient. But in reality, without Christianity other religions do not know the true God or, better still, do not know God truly. Christianity is not simply a religion; it is more than this—it is a salvific action of God.

Non-Christian religions belong to the realm of creation; hence to a different sphere from that of salvation. Religious sentiment forms part of creation. Because creation has been wounded by sin, religions are ambiguous and constitute obstacles for salvation. Religions have no means of salvation. They are not the ways of salvation, because only God saves one through Christ, who continues to work in the church. This does not mean that there are not some human elements in them, the most important of which are the religious, which are good even if they are more or less perverted. These elements have a role of preparation and constitute "stones of expectation" and wait to be assumed in the catholicity of the church, transformed and saved. Even though membership in the church is necessary for salvation, there are supplements to this belonging that always remain mysterious.

This is an intermediary position between the syncretism of liberal theology and the dialectical theology of Barth. It admits a certain value in religions but corrected by the affirmation of the transcendence of the dominion of faith above the dominion of religion. This theology is constructed on two foundations: missionary experience and the ecclesiocentric vision of salvation. The missionary perspective recognizes the good and true elements of religions but also their ambiguity and their being obstacles to conversion. The ecclesiocentric vision considers the church the unique instrument of salvation in history. Hence, religions do not contain any means of salvation but only the values that could and ought to be saved,

transformed, and integrated in the catholicity of the church. This line of theology is generally attributed also to de Lubac, Maurier, Bruls, Cornelis, with nuances of each of them.

10. Karl Rahner and the Theology of Religions

Christianity considers itself as the absolute religion, valid for all people. It cannot accord the same rights to any other religion. This conviction is based on the central fact of Christianity: Jesus Christ, the Word of God, who makes himself present concretely among humans. By his death and resurrection he has reunited the world to God, not in an allegorical or symbolic manner, but really, in the objective sense. Christ, who has worked out the salvation of all in historical reality, has willed the continuation of his work in a permanent historical actualization by instituting the church. This permanent historical actualization is precisely the religion that unites people to God.

Christianity has therefore an intrahistorical starting point in Jesus Christ. This implies that it ought to encounter humans as their legitimate and obligatory religion. Before this encounter with Christianity a non-Christian religion contains the elements of "natural" knowledge of God interspersed with human weakness due to original sin. But there are also found supernatural moments of grace, and on account of this can be a religion recognized as a legitimate. This position rests on the theological affirmation of the universal and effective salvific will of God with regard to all people. On the one hand, salvation is something specifically Christian, and there is no salvation outside of Christ. On the other hand, God has destined in a real and true manner this salvation for all. From these two elements it follows that humans are open to the influence of divine supernatural grace, which offers them an intimate communion with God and a participation in his life. Besides, non-Christian religions can have a positive sense; they should not be considered illegitimate, even when they contain many errors. From the fact that the follower of a non-Christian religion is under the influence of grace, it follows that this supernatural reality of grace ought to be found in that person's religion, in which the relation with the absolute is the specific, determining element. All humans ought to have the possibility of participating in an authentic and salvific relation with God. Given the social nature of humanity, one cannot realize this relation with God in an intimacy completely individual and outside of the religion of one's milieu, since the insertion of the individual profession of religion in a social and religious order is one of the essential elements of the true and concrete religion. The salvific will of God arrives at humanity by divine will and permission in one's concrete religion, in one's existential and concrete situation, in one's historical-cultural conditioning. This does not exclude anyone's right to be critical and to follow the religious impulses of reform within one's own religion.

In this perspective, Christianity does not consider one belonging to another religion to be simply non-Christian; that one rather is an "anonymous Christian." Rahner explains the meaning of this term thus:

> If it is true that the man to whom Christianity proposes its message is already originally, or at least could be, a man who is moved towards salvation; if it is true that this man finds his salvation, in a given circumstance, before the arrival to him of the proclamation of the Christian salvation; but if it is true that this salvation is the salvation of Christ, since outside of him there is no other salvation, then a man can be not only an anonymous theist, but can be called an "anonymous christian." (Rahner, "Anonymous Christians," 391–92)

Let us recall once again that this is seen in the Christian theological perspective, in the effort to give every true religious experience its intrinsic positive signification, without in any way offending the Christian belief that this is proper to Christianity alone.

The proclamation of the gospel does not transform into a Christian someone who is totally devoid of God and of Christ. It transforms an "anonymous Christian" into one who knows how to recognize objectively and reflexively, through the mediation of a social recognition in the church, his own Christianity in the depth of its essence of grace. This explicit affirmation of a Christian, once anonymous, is a phase of development of Christianity itself, the most elevated and necessary development of its essence. But the explicit preaching of Christianity is necessary, because without such a preaching one is already negatively an "anony-

mous Christian." This is necessary not only from the social structure of incarnation of grace and of Christianity but also because this conception, more clear and reflexive, offers humans the greater possibility of salvation than if they remained only anonymous Christians. Therefore, the church ought not to consider itself the only depository of salvation, in an exclusive sense for any other people.

The history of salvation is actualized in the history of the world. The history of salvation is distinct from profane history. The history of salvation explains profane history; through Christianity the history of the world is interpreted in the christocentric sense. The world has been created by the eternal Logos, derives from him, and ought to return to him. The world and its history have been created in view of the Logos of the incarnate God. The history of salvation is not restricted to the history of Israel and of the church. Universal or general history of salvation pertains to all humans. The history of humanity is interiorly transformed into the history of salvation by the dynamism of the redemptive grace of Christ. This is distinct from the special history of salvation that concerns Israel and the church. We ought to understand the universal history of salvation from the point of view of the special history of salvation. The history of salvation does not bear upon personal human decisions; it leaves its mark on all that humans do in history. Thus, it is possible to see religion as the social expression of the universal history of salvation. As such, religions are the ways of salvation offered by God to their adherents. As ways of salvation they are legitimate and conserve their value until they are called to surpass them in their encounter with the church. Not all followers of Rahner understand the term "ways of salvation" in the same way. Rahner founds the value of religions on the theology of grace and on the existence of "anonymous Christianity."

The universal salvific will of God is true and real; by this the action of God ought to be present even if it is in a hidden manner. The whole arch of human existence is constitutively shot through by the active presence of God. Every extrinsicism is to be excluded in the conception of the relation between nature and grace. Grace enters into the essential constitutive elements of humans, positing in them the supernatural existential as the historical constituent, before the divine gift of actual or habitual grace is given. This existential is supernatural because it transcends the constitutive elements of humanity, the possibility and the exigency of human nature. No legalism, because the universal salvific will of God is true and real; hence it is effective of something real. No extrinicism, because grace is not given as an extrinisic ornament without any convenience for it on the part of the human. Rahner's line is followed by Schoonenberg, Schlette, Thils, Heislbetz, Schillebeeckx, Fransen, Küng, Masson, Neuner, Nys.

11. Conclusion

Some contemporary authors insist on the paradigm change in the theology of world religions. This means that the basis and principal interest of every theological evaluation of other religions change from time to time; from their relationship with the church (ecclesiocentrism) to their relationship with Christ (Christocentrism); from this to their relationship with God (theocentrism). We should even go beyond this theocentrism to soteriocentrism; i.e., the primary concern of the theology of religions should not be "rightful belief" in the uniqueness of Christ but "rightful practice" with other religions, of the promotion of the kingdom of God and of its *sōtēria*, liberation, the well-being of humanity. The important emphasis here is on *paradigm* change. The term "paradigm" is used in a sense analogous to that proposed originally by Thomas Kuhn, i.e., a whole set of methods and procedures dictated by a central problem-solving model. It should be noted here that Kuhn had many reservations about the use of this concept of paradigm outside the specific area of scientific revolutions in which it was developed. Moreover, he has explained more precisely the way in which an "analogous" use of such a central term differs from the original. There are certain conditions to be verified and realized for using the paradigm change as a methodological device within the theological science. A central problem-solving model should not sacrifice the essential elements of Christian faith by undue stress on one element to the detriment of another for the purpose of pleasing everyone — nonbelievers and non-Christians. When a sociological or anthropological model is introduced within theology,

it has to be controlled in the light of revelation and tradition. In this perspective the theology of religions is at its initial stage; more research is needed to evaluate these methods.

Bibl.: K. BARTH, *Church Dogmatics*, vol. 2 (Edinburgh, 1956); H. KRAEMER, *Religion and the Christian Faith* (London, 1956); id., *The Christian Message in a Non-Christian World* (London, 1938); J. DANIÉLOU, "Christianity and Non-Christian Religions," in *The Word in History*, ed. T. P. Burke (London, 1968); id., *Essai sur le Mystère de l'Histoire* (Paris, 1960); R. PANIKKAR, *Religione e Religioni* (Brescia, 1964); id., *The Unknown Christ of Hinduism* (London, 1984); H. R. SCHLETTE, *Towards a Theology of Religions* (London, 1965); G. THILS, *Propos et problèmes de la théologie des religions non chrétiennes* (Tournai, 1966); id., *Présence et salut de Dieu chez les non-chrétiens* (Louvain-la-Neuve, 1987); K. RAHNER, "History of the World and Salvation-History," in *Theological Investigations*, vol. 5 (1962; London, 1966), 97–114; id., "Christianity and the Non-Christian Religions," in *Theological Investigations*, vol. 5 (1962; London, 1966), 115–34; id., "Anonymous Christians," in *Theological Investigations*, vol. 6 (1965; London 1969), 390–98; id., *Valore salvifico delle Religioni non cristiane*, Congrès international de missiologie (Rome, 1975), 3–11; HEISLBETZ, *Theologische Gründe der nichtchristlichen Religionen* (Freiburg, 1967); V. BOUBLIK, *Teologia delle Religioni* (Rome, 1973); P. ROSSANO, *Il Problema teologico delle religioni* (Rome, 1975); C. SMITH, *Towards a World Theology* (London, 1980); A. RACE, *Christians and Religious Pluralism* (New York, 1982); P. KNITTER, *No Other Name? A Critical Survey of Christian Attitude Towards the World Religions* (New York, 1985); G. D'COSTA, *Theology and Religious Pluralism* (Oxford, 1986); H. KÜNG, *Christianity and World Religions* (New York, 1986); M. DHAVAMONY, *Teologia delle Religioni* (Rome, 1986); id., ed., *Evangelization, Dialogue and Development*, Doc. Miss. 5 (Rome, 1986); J. HICK and P. KNITTER, eds., *The Myth of Christian Uniqueness: Towards a Pluralistic Theology of Religions* (New York, 1987).

Mariasusai DHAVAMONY

RELIGIOUS INDIFFERENCE

Religious indifference is by its nature difficult to detect. Lacking any specific discourse or arguments, and most often passive, it usually connotes a state of vagueness. Yet religious indifference is an observable phenomenon in our time and is becoming increasingly extensive and widespread, especially in the West. Two main kinds of indifference need to be distinguished: one obviously superficial, the other deep-going and radical.

1. Indifference to One's Own Religion

The first kind of indifference is that of individuals toward the religious confession to which they belong. Since the majority of the population in Western countries are Christian, the indifference here is chiefly an indifference to Christianity. In many persons we find a notable decline of interest in important elements of the Christian religion. The first sign is a slackening of liturgical practice, that is, the celebration of the Eucharist and the other sacraments. According to numerous polls, the number of those attending Sunday mass in recent years is 38 percent among the Catholics of Quebec, 16 percent among those of France, and 15 percent among those of Italy. Christians can, of course, remain believers even if they drop the practice of public worship; this practice is but one element in the more comprehensive Christian practice of a life lived according to the spirit of Jesus Christ in all situations, relationships, and activities. Liturgical practice remains, nonetheless, a test of religious vitality. Whether deliberately or through negligence, some Christians are not ready to confess their faith publicly and to share and celebrate it. A scientific inquiry has even shown that there is a correlation between the decline of Sunday practice and the decreasing importance assigned to the other elements making up the faith, namely, the principal beliefs, God, Jesus Christ, morality, prayer, and membership in the Christian community.

For all that, the collapse of liturgical practice does not mean an abandonment of religion. Réginald Bibby's work *La religion à la carte* (Montreal: Fides, 1988) presents the results of three national polls conducted from 1975 to 1985 on the religious situation in Canada in all the religious confessions. This sociologist reports that despite the decline in church attendance religious affiliations remain stable; people do not break their connection with the churches. In Quebec, for example, 88 percent claim affiliation, even though active membership is only 25 percent. On the other hand, people are anxious to keep up the rites of pas-

sage: 90 percent of Québecois turn to religious groups for baptisms, marriages, and funerals.

The conclusion is still more dismaying when the sociologist measures commitment by objective constants. Religious commitment has for its elements belief, private prayer, experience of God's presence, and fundamental religious knowledge. Sixty percent of Canadians believe in the three fundamental truths of the existence of God, the divinity of Jesus, and the future life, but only 20 percent show that these three main beliefs, private prayer, experience of God, and religious knowledge as a whole are integrated into their attitude of faith. This means that "only about 20 percent give some evidence that they make their own what might be called the traditional expression of an integral Judeo-Christian commitment. The religion of the great majority is a religion of isolated fragments." When the inquirer allows people to talk for themselves, he finds that 40 percent of Canadians regard themselves as committed Christians (but only a third of them display a good integration of the main dimensions of the faith); 40 percent regard themselves as uncommitted; and 20 percent declare that they are not religious. Moreover, they admit to making a selection of isolated elements of belief, practice, and worship.

Bibby concludes that religion has little influence on life. There are many who approach religion like consumers, taking a belief here and a practice there. "Canadians seem to keep their distance from Christianity or other religions as systems giving an overall meaning to life in its entirety. They accept fragments of Judeo-Christianity. . . . Canadians practice an à la carte religion" (p. 114). They tend to construct their religion from an à la carte menu. Some of them fill out their Christian menu with other supernatural beliefs. Whereas a religious confession proper calls for an organized and coherent synthesis, what we have here is rather a broken-down religion of isolated beliefs and occasional practices, a religion in the form of consumer goods that are put on the shelf with other commodities so that one can take them or leave them. The majority of people have no idea of commitment and make do with fragments of religion.

The life of faith is not easily measured. But the results of a poll, imprecise though they are, do give us facts. If one may attempt a brief interpretation of the facts, it must be noted that a sizable proportion of Christians are committed; signs of a Christian renewal and a sense of religious responsibility are everywhere observable. On the other hand, polls confirm the judgment that many believers pick and choose among the articles of the creed, the teachings of the church, and the applications of moral norms. In this attitude there is, first of all, the element of personal journey which must be recognized as part of the life of faith; all do not achieve the desired integration of the various dimensions of such a life, and there are inherent difficulties in this process of searching, understanding, and deepening participation. Allowance must also be made for the distinction between the essential and the secondary in the retinue of beliefs and practices: that which looks to the meaning of things rather than submission to precepts; that which gives priority to evangelical practice over concern for orthodoxy. Christianity is an experience before being a system. In addition, many believers are protective of an autonomy dearly won through the victories of modernity and are distrustful of systems, including religious systems.

Furthermore, this selection of bits and pieces from a fragmented religion can be due to the fact that these persons want to keep this or that belief, passage of the Gospel, moral standard, or teaching because it pleases them and is just what they need; consequently, they set the others aside. They choose what they want to keep and arrange everything in their own way. They provide themselves with a religion that causes them no trouble, and which they can use as they please. At this point they begin the slippery descent to the disappearance of their religious profession. At the level of knowledge they end up lost in confusion; at the level of practice they are inconsistent and risk losing their Christian identity. Consistency alone gives meaning to life and calls for progress beyond one's present stage and for spiritual growth. Such persons increasingly refuse to learn from the gospel. When they go further and acknowledge their lack of commitment, an observer may ask what roles these fragments of religion play in their lives. No matter how tightly they hold on to their religious affiliation out of fidelity to their heritage, no matter how much they want to hold on to the rites of passage for the sake of the small remaining

element of festivity, there can be no doubt that their religious sense is impoverished and that their religion is a purely private matter. When people accept this situation, they are close to a practical indifference toward the religion to which they belong, because they neglect whole areas of what makes up the life of faith.

There is, then, an indifference that brings with it a decomposition. These persons distance themselves not only from the ecclesial institution and its commandments but also from the community of believers and from constituent elements more and more intimately connected with the core of the faith. Their withdrawal shows in an abstention without any discussion, in a calm estrangement in small stages, or in a loss of the perception of the symbolic coherence of ideas and practices. This estrangement is often accompanied by distorted beliefs. Even when people join the crowd and say that they still believe in God, many of them identify God with some vital energy or higher power, an impersonal spirit, destiny, or fate. Their idea of Jesus Christ has been reduced to the idea of an exceptional person, a prophet, or a source of wisdom. Even while retaining a superficial conformity, some among them end up living as if God did not exist. Christians enter upon the way of indifference from the moment when they are unable to see how the Christian faith can inspire their human aspirations and their life as members of society. They have entered upon a process of distantiation that can lead to radical religious indifference.

The survey that the Roman Secretariat for Non-Believers conducted in 1985 revealed that this kind of indifference is the most significant religious phenomenon in such European countries as Italy (59%), France (25%), Germany, Switzerland, Austria, Portugal, and Sweden and the other Scandinavian countries. It is widespread in most of the South American countries, followed by Canada and the United States. It is also to be found in India, Korea, and New Zealand (Secrétariat 1988).

Despite everything that has been said, this kind of indifference is not radical. It does not necessarily cause persons to stop searching for a spiritual life. Some people even try to recover a faith through sects, forms of gnosticism, and the parasciences of the paranormal. They find in these something that gives meaning, as they link up with groups or gurus whose orders will supposedly bring unity into their fragmented lives. But here again individuals only acquire shreds of religion that are adjusted to meet their cognitive or affective needs. They are given access to religious consumer goods, without being led to any demanding conversion that goes beyond salvation through knowledge or mastery of their hidden pyschic energies or harmony with their bodies and the forces of the cosmos. Rather than open themselves to an Other who has revealed himself in Jesus as love and liberation, they are likely not to move beyond an individualistic preoccupation with themselves, their future, and their well-being. This return of religion has indeed a positive significance, but it remains ambiguous.

2. Religious Indifference in the Strict Sense

The second kind is religious indifference in the strict sense, and it is profound and radical. It is an indifference not only toward the religion to which one belongs but toward all religion and everything having to do with religion.

Religious indifference is the absence of interest in God and religion. Whether or not God exists, he is not a value. He is dead in the sense that he has ceased to be a vital value, an important reality. What we see here is not a well thought out rejection of God but a lack of interest. More than this, there is an insensibility when it comes to religion, an absence of concern about "religious matters."

This insensibility toward religion extends to the fundamental questions about the meaning of the human person and its destiny and the meaning of the world. The simple fact that human beings ask questions about themselves and their world implies that they are looking for what connects them with things other than themselves, with a Meaning that gives them meaning and directs them and their plans for themselves toward an Absolute or an Other who grounds their being. The word "religion" suggests the search for what binds (_religio_, _religare_). "Religion" also corresponds to the need of "collecting" oneself, finding oneself again, through a rereading and an interpretation of one's life, in order to be able to make a choice (_relegere_). Human beings are by their very nature open to the transcendent, whatever the name they may give to it. The fundamental search that the person undertakes is the locus

in which "faith" takes root in the Christian option, but also the locus of deliberate unbelief that implies a decision of conscience.

Individuals who are indifferent are unaware of this radical questioning, because they are so absorbed in their pragmatic interaction with the world and, often enough, are even stuck fast in the materialism of consumption. Any opening is blocked, all aspirations smothered, the transcendent horizon missing. Any spiritual restlessness has been drained away. Once religious questioning disappears, God disappears along with it. This indifference is a kind of spiritual numbness in which the person does not have the courage even to question and then scrutinize. It is an unbelief without any content, except in rare instances in which the very possibility of transcendence is disputed. Rather than being a commitment, it is a lack of concern in which the mind is otherwise occupied, if not completely undisciplined. It is sometimes even a flight, a defense mechanism against the distress involved in believing. Unlike atheists, who wrestle at length with the question of God, the indifferent simply do not care. This is the most radical form of unbelief.

"Most radical," because unbelievers include atheists who deny or reject the existence of God and try to give a rational justification for this denial; their ATHEISM is the other side of a positive faith in the complete autonomy of the human person, and it is often thematized in philosophical or ideological systems. Nonbelievers also include agnostics, who refuse to acknowledge God because they cannot acquire what they regard as certain or satisfactory knowledge of him, inasmuch as they cannot demonstrate his existence by human knowledge or verify it by the method used in the empirical sciences (→ AGNOSTICISM). Then there are the _freethinkers_, who perhaps acknowledge a vital force at work in the world but do not on that account admit the existence of a transcendent personal God; among freethinkers may be found deists, pantheists, and people who put their faith in humanity or in reason or whose creed is limited to declarations of the rights of the person. _Nonbelievers_ must also be listed: those who because of cultural heritage or family tradition are said to have no religion and are objectively ignorant of the God of the religions. The _indifferent_, for their part, not only take no stand on the existence or nonexistence of God, but in practice they even deny that the religious problem is a real one. The absence of God is nowhere so complete as here. Religious indifference is an attitude with little deliberation behind it and does not aim at being critical. It does not make a real choice "in the religious arena." It is an unbelief reached through lack of reflection. The energies of the indifferent are completely absorbed in meeting the needs of everyday life, so that no interest in the great problems of humanity and the competing visions of the world even passes the threshold of their consciousness. This indifference is the attitude least open to dialogue, since there seem to be no matters of common interest that might provide a meeting ground.

This religious indifference is difficult to measure. We do know that 10 to 20 percent of Québecois declare themselves to be unbelievers in God or Jesus Christ. Less than 5 percent of them say that they are atheists. We do not know how many are indifferent. Bibby's polls indicate, in addition, that in 1985 20 percent of Québecois, and of Canadians generally, say they "have no religion," without making any further distinctions. Fourteen percent of Canadians born before 1930, 18 percent of those born between 1931 and 1950, and 25 percent of those born between 1951 and 1967 says they "have no religion." Among young adults, therefore, there are more individuals who "have no religion." In France the number of those who "have no religion" is 15.5 percent, but the figure rises to 30 percent among those eighteen to thirty years of age; the proportion of indifferent people is not specified (see Clevenot 1987). Radical indifference is said to be widespread in Sweden and increasingly widespread in Europe and North America.

Is religious indifference simply an individual attitude, or is it a cultural phenomenon? It is doubtless both. We in the West have recently passed from a stage of opposition and emancipation, and even of unbelief and rejection, to a way of living without God, in which people are serenely unreligious. To some the question of God seems gratuitous, that of salvation a luxury. It is what goes on in the world that matters: one's job or profession, one's scientific and technological achievements, the happiness to be derived from comfort and money (which one has or desires to have). The young, according to some parents, display a religious indif-

ference so great that they do not think there can be anything other than material things, success to be pursued, and the goal of feeling good and taking advantage of what is going on. Religion means nothing to them. Is so radical a religious indifference be only a temporary attitude during a limited period in the life of the individual? It seems that it is the rare person who settles down permanently in such an extreme attitude.

But religious indifference is also to be considered a cultural phenomenon. Connected as it is with a mental universe for which religious considerations are increasingly irrelevant and which looks for its unity to a technocratic, scientistic, materialistic, or hedonist vision of the world, religious indifference is a phenomenon that spreads silently and smoothly, eliminating even the conditions that would make it possible to ask religious questions. People breathe it with the cultural air. Immersed as they are in things, immersed in the noise in which they keep increasing the decibels of their music, immersed in a world of sound that is overloaded with words so often trite, they have gotten rid of silence as a way to an inwardness in which the fundamental questions have a chance to emerge—and, with these questions, reflection on their activities. As long as this reflection is lacking, says Didier Piveteau, "all our efforts to awaken the young and pass values on to them are pathetically ineffective. We provide them with answers to questions they have never asked. . . . O happy solitude in which we can discover the treasure which each of us must find during our lifetime: ourselves!" There is also evident a blindness in regard to the spiritual. "The sphere of religion belongs to another planet which perhaps sends out signals, but people do not even attempt to interpret these on the rare occasions when they become conscious of their existence." The problem is that these people lack the intellectual and affective equipment that is indispensable for grasping the meaning of the spiritual.

> What seems to me to be lacking in the young, as indeed in our contemporaries, but to a greater degree in the young, is the possibility of imagining hope and the capacity for seeking meaning. They are like blind people set down in the midst of potential splendors but incapable of enjoying them because they lack the necessary sense organ. They do not reject God after having

known him or because they have known him. They quite simply do not suspect the existence of the reality; more than that, they feel no curiosity about it, no desire to inquire into what it might be. (*Lumen Vitae* [1983]: 183–91)

3. The Factors at Work

In order to understand this whole situation, we must go back to the causes or, better, the factors that explain it. I shall list only some of them, since they are many. To begin with, there is the major cultural change through which our Western societies are passing. This means, first, the shift to a scientific and technological society that is the result of the modern relation of human beings to nature and their world. Contemporary men and women characteristically concern themselves with action that effects change in nature and society. The logic governing their universe is wholly based on scientific rationality and its operational expression in technological rationality. They work furiously for ever greater progress. We all benefit from this labor of human genius, the development of the exact sciences, and the effects achieved, in order to improve our collective services, push back poverty, and restore human dignity.

But this same scientific and technological rationality runs the risk of going adrift when people are disposed to take it as an exclusive standard. It then extends its imperialistic sway to the whole of reality, thereby turning it into a one-dimensional world. Whatever works is regarded as good and worthwhile. Persons are valued according to their occupation, their competence, and above all by their accomplishments. Public issues are decided according to production and consumption and the exchange of activities, while human relations find themselves revolving around objects. This rationality is concerned with the "how" of things, not their "why" or finality. Some important human problems receive no consideration: life itself, love, the knowledge of why we live and die. Religion is reduced to a private matter. Faith is looked upon as something superfluous and useless or ineffective in this instrumental and functional society. Religious concerns disappear from the ken of those who have not the strength or the means of entering into themselves.

Scientific and technological rationality is coupled with the ideology of the consumer society. People produce in order to consume; they busy themselves in a frenzied way, without pausing to reflect and be open to everything that the other is. They lack the concentration needed if they are to ponder and try to clarify their vision of the world. They escape into noise. Another reason for their bustle is to escape their personal suffering. This is a society of appearances rather than being, a self-sufficient society. The attraction of material things blocks openness to the spiritual and to gospel values.

This is also a society in which the immediate, the spontaneous, the transitory, and the short-term hold sway; a society marked by a narcissistic turning in on the self, a pitching of one's tent in a little world all one's own. An American writer, Allan Bloom, speaks of a decline of the culture generally and a failure of the educational process to pay heed to the great books, including the Bible, and to the humanities, history, and philosophy. What is the human person? Where do I come from and where am I going? The young lack

> any real reason for not being satisfied with the present and for becoming aware that there are alternative solutions. . . . The desire for a beyond has diminished. . . . Because of their inability to interpret things, their souls are like mirrors that reflect not nature itself, but what there is around them. . . . Consciousness of both the depths and the heights is lacking; therefore they lack seriousness as well. (*L'âme désarmée* [Paris, 1987])

The paucity of integrated adult personalities to serve as models removes, for practical purposes, the possibilities of identification, opposition, or aggressivity and makes it harder for the young to build a true autonomy.

Another factor is the SECULARIZATION of society. This means the end of the dominant influence exerted by comprehensive religious or sacral visions on thought and by the church on the development of institutions. The autonomy of the secular is proclaimed. Secularization is, of course, a phenomenon that calls for a positive evaluation. Judeo-Christianity had already demystified a nature viewed in sacral terms. God is no longer seen as the stopgap for human ignorance and helplessness. The autonomy of the sciences, law, and politics has been successfully asserted. These are all good things in themselves. Secularization also contributes to preventing too immediate a recourse to Christianity: the latter must be discovered by other ways and taken into account in a different manner. Secular modernity also entails a segmentation or fragmentation of activities. Religion, which is identified with a sectorial universe, has little place in this society in which interesting activities are many and diverse. Individuals cannot take an interest in everything that is set before them in such profusion; therefore they make a selection and become indifferent to the rest. But the movement of secularization can deviate into secularism, i.e., a positively atheistic ideology that advocates the unqualified autonomy of scientific and technological rationality, to the point of radically excluding God from questions regarding the meaning of the world and the source of inspiration for the purpose of life.

In Quebec and other traditional societies, there has been a sudden shift from a universally accepted Christianity to pluralism. The widening of the mental universe to accept other currents of thought and the opening of Christianity to religious freedom have brought acceptance of a plurality of positions in religious questions. We see a kind of merry-go-round of competing religious trends, including a proliferation of sects and new "human potential" religions. This pluralism is certainly beneficial, but many people have lost their former self-coherence and have not found any to replace it. While room has been made for more personal choices in religious matters, there are many people who live amid shattered beliefs, and there are indifferent people whose attitude is "I'm not interested" or "I don't care." Relativism? Confusion? Inconsistency? There seems to be a slide from plurality to a neutrality in which everything is on the same level, as the aggressiveness of a short while ago has given way not to healthy confrontation but to indifference.

Many people talk of their disillusionment with the church; this is something deeper than mere resentment of clericalism. These people have a grudge against the religious model imposed on them in their childhood: a religion of commandments, prohibitions, mortifications, and obscurantism. They are still traumatized and pass on their frustration, through family and school, to the younger generations, which trot out the same complaints without themselves having known that past age. Oddly enough, both remain in a simplistic ignorance of developments in the church's life and of its evangelical renewal. Their starting point is an often-justified criticism of religion, but they do not always see that what they complain about is a local religious model that is really defective or antiquated, and they reject religion along with this cultural model. They are ignorant of the content of the faith and the interpretation it requires. Furthermore, the church in its preaching has not succeeded in translating the contents of the faith into contemporary cultural categories; too often it offers a morality consisting of norms which pay little heed to real human situations and to the demands of the adult conscience. Homilies too often show priests to be uneducated, behind the times, and trivializers of the word. Celebrations are mechanical and leave no room for silence and meditation. But Christians themselves are partly responsible because of their carelessness and their comfortable, privatized, and timid religion.

Finally, a by no means negligible factor is the job already done by the leaders of atheism in promoting the exaltation of the absolute self, in the sense that men and women are their own supreme being. There is also the stumbling block of evil, which calls into question the idea of an absolute God of goodness, as if God were to be held responsible for everything, as if the world were not contingent and fallible, and as if Jesus Christ had not given a meaning to evil by enduring it in his struggles. Then, too, there is always the difficulty of believing. And, of course, the freedom to remain indifferent.

4. Beyond Indifference

None of the factors listed nor all of them together inevitably lead to religious indifference. Modernity has the ability to make more room than ever before for all dimensions of the human being. Technology has some humanitarian spinoffs. A pluralist and secularized society represents an opportunity for faith by making personal choices necessary. All of this calls for responsible behavior, and this is what is at stake.

Nor has indifference completely taken over. We meet believers who are increasingly committed. There is also an unexpected return to religion among the followers of the NEW AGE religions; these individuals, bewildered by the spiritual void, bear witness in their own way to the thirst for belief and the need of belonging to a group. Of course, the frenzied clinging to beliefs, however esoteric and eclectic, and whatever the cost, can in some cases involve naïveté and ambiguity and is easily open to exploitation of all kinds. But, when all is said and done, the two kinds of indifference that I have described are becoming increasingly widespread.

The great challenge in acting against religious indifference is for each person to determine where he or she is, to clarify in a conscientious way his or her own existential situation as a citizen and as a man and a woman. In this way it becomes possible for individuals to make a fundamental choice with regard to the values they regard as primary, and to live accordingly. To make a fundamental choice is to choose a faith, whether religious or nonreligious, that is, Christianity, some other religion, or unbelief. Committed atheists and committed believers deserve respect: they have made a choice; they have taken one or other major religion seriously, either by adopting it for themselves or by justifying their rejection of it and replacing it with another set of principles. Unless persons are willing to let themselves be carried along the way of thoughtlessness, despair, or nihilism, they must identify and choose a faith. They must act in such a way, whether as Christians or as unbelievers, that the position they choose for themselves has the status of a faith. Those who are radically indifferent do not make a real, conscientious choice, for they are victims of a mass world.

What is faith if not the taking of a position that provides a foundation for human life and justifies one's reasons for living? To have a faith is to trust oneself to a "meaning" that precedes us and gives significance and direction to the human project. To have faith is to rely on this "meaning" so that one may take responsibility for the way one lives. It is to choose a key to understanding, a structure of meaning that calls for a certain manner of life and certain practices. There are in fact a number of positions that claim to solve the human problem: the Christian position, that of the other religions, that of a humanism without God. At this demanding level, unbelief can in fact be another faith, and the unbeliever another type of believer.

What Christians learn is that the Meaning, the Other, which they seek is not something but Someone. They discover that while the structure of meaning proper to the world and life is certainly made up of human values and universal ideals, the structure itself is ultimately grounded in a solid Meaning that is a personal being. They recognize in Jesus Christ that the Meaning they seek is a God who is Love, a God with a face and a message, a God who wishes to enter into covenant with human beings. In Christ they find God acting for them, and an interlocutor, and calls that are to be answered and that will lead humankind to its full humanity. As for unbelievers: the structure of meaning is here centered on a human value that is turned into an absolute; it becomes the ultimate goal of their existence, but Christians regard it—whether it be Humanity, History, Science, or anything else—as a substitute for God. Many people would do better to set aside scattered or superficial beliefs in favor of a faith that first rediscovers the center and then achieves unity, beginning with Christians.

It is uphill work overcoming the diffuse and thoughtless indifference that has become an established phenomenon of modern civilization. It is necessary to work on the conditions of access to the spiritual, to prepare the soil. It is necessary to revive an interest in humanitarian issues and in the future of the world, then an interest in the fundamental questions by which persons are awakened to the mystery of their origin and end, in order to avoid being unable to answer the final challenge put to them. It is necessary to promote a return to the center of the self in order there to hear its interior voices, to face up to its own mystery and to absurdity, and to regain the ability to listen, the readiness to let another speak to it.

Everything begins at the radical level at which individuals try to detach themselves from their lives, their conflicts, their tensions, and search for that which gives true life and enables them to build and act and hope. Everything begins at the level at which they must choose a kind of life, a project that fulfills their humanity and brings happiness. There they experience values and relate to ideals, but they also discover how precarious and almost impossible all this is if they do not have a decisive meaning and consistent support that provide reasons for living on amid their fragile successes, their ephemeral happinesses, their inadequacies in communicating and loving, and their failures, amid the interplay of competing interests, loneliness, and suffering, and in the face of death. The question quite naturally arises of God as creator, source, affirmation, and guarantee of what individuals are and do. But if this God exists, where does he make himself known? Where is he to be met? Who is he? If individuals have access to the Jesus of the Gospels, they can see this God as he lived, spoke, acted, and loved in his human experience. They will be able to grasp in him an unparalleled manifestation of the depths of God. They will be able to recognize in Jesus Christ the embodiment of the God of whom they have had obscure intimations and whom they meet at last as Love and Word for them. It is then that things fall into place, as they grasp the close connection between the actions and teachings of Jesus, on the one hand, and their own experience of life, on the other. They find their expectations confirmed and surpassed: they receive good news regarding life. To be Christian is to choose, decide on, a way of life. They must be converted and become individuals who possess something of the Spirit of Jesus, individuals-for-others, faithful to the causes Jesus promoted. They will gradually come to understand better the content of their faith and to put their knowledge into words that they themselves find believable and descriptions that are credible in today's world. They will be led to express their relationship with God in prayer, then in liturgy. They will discover, as part of the inherent thrust of Christianity, the importance of the community of their brothers and sisters in the faith, the community foreseen by Jesus, the community that is the church. They will commit themselves to consistent behavior at all levels of their human activity. All these are constitutive dimensions of the attitude of faith. Faith calls upon them to integrate all these dimensions and overcome the fragmentation of Christian behavior.

Obviously, then, Christian life belongs to the realm of experience. It implies a development, a learning process, a journey of growth. Many people think that because they cannot spontaneously integrate all these dimensions, they will never succeed in doing so. If there is development, then there is room for a process of maturation, for difficulties on the way, for doubt. The things of faith are never matters of evidence, not even the assertion that God exists. The culture no longer provides the presuppositions for religion as it did in the past: contemporary Western civilization is the first in history not to be religious. The development in question here, then, requires a labor of interpretation, purification, and authentication. Doubt represents a will to examine things, a time for answering objections, a way of refusing to be lied to, a critical need to go beyond naïve credulity and reach plausible convictions. The important thing is not to close the file on faith.

In the first type of indifference that was analyzed earlier there is one form of it that consists in a rejection of allegiance to any ecclesial institution. More specifically, indifference here means putting oneself beyond the reach of ecclesiastical authority; doing so is often the beginning of a process of loss of interest. We know, for example, the disastrous role played by the encyclical on contraception. People will be interested to know that the church is, first of all, a community in which Christians experience the Christian life in communion with one another. This community is structured; it has an organization and a power of leadership that are essentially a service. Christians who are prisoners of a maximalist conception of infallibility do not realize that infallibility is exercised only very rarely and that they are free to engage in discernment, and that they ought to play an important role in discussions which concern them: discussions of faith, morality, and practices, of the interpretation of the contents of these, and of challenges to this or that accepted view. This kind of involvement will suppose the establishment of small groups in which persons look beyond their prejudgments and examine things objectively, relearn the language of faith, return to its sources, and rethink Christian discourse with its demands for coherence and relevance to contemporary culture. In this way Christians are invited to exercise the *sensus fidelium*, which requires a work of enlightened interpretation by means of ecclesial dialogue. The church is a vast project brought into the world by Jesus; it demands the full involvement of all the members. It would be tragic if marginalization led to parting company and then to indifference.

Finally, far from refusing to have anything to do with secular society, Christians must make it the place of their life and activity. This society is called to make itself, in a transparent and balanced way, what the plan of its creator intends it to be. It is here that Christians are to be witnesses to the value of the human person and reject the flattening out caused by a society whose outlook is instrumentalist. It is here that they are to contribute to the renewal of their world, in complicity with the very noble principle at work in technological civilization, namely, the logic of transformation in the service of humanization. In the face of violence, the profit race, the threats of nuclear and genetic manipulation, and "the unbearable lightness of being," God reminds human beings of the true goal of human genius; he is the third party who inspires love, the guarantor of justice, the one who calls us to go beyond, the one who is our hope of salvation—and he is all this without exerting any determinism and without in any way detracting from our freedom. Salvation is not something superfluous. It is not found simply in a final other world, but is an everyday reality. Salvation is transfiguration and liberation: it implies a choice between growth toward fulfillment and degeneration toward loss. It is built up and put into practice in real life, at the heart of the human drama, until the work of a lifetime reaches its final form on the day of the passage through death. The project of the "kingdom of God" is that humanity should attain to its full humanness.

Bibl.: P.-A. Liégé, "Indifférence, indifférentisme," in *Catholicisme hier, aujourd'hui, demain* (Paris, 1962), vol. 5, cols. 1504–9; J. Girardi, "Réflexions sur l'indifférence religieuse," *Conc* 23 (1967): 57–64; *Conc*, no. 165: "Indifference to Religion"; *Lumen Vitae* 38/2 (1983): "Indifférence, incroyances et foi: quelle parole?"; Secrétariat pour les non-croyants, *L'indifférence religieuse*, Le point théologique 41 (Paris, 1983); *Athéisme et Dialogue*, vol. 20, nos. 2–3: *Athéisme, non-croyance et indifférence religieuse dans le monde: Diagnostic et orientations pastorales* (1985): P. Colin, "L'indifférence religeuse: discours anciens, questions nouvelles," *Études* 363/3 (March 1985): 393–404; M. Neusch, "Indifférence religieuse," in *Dictionnaire des religions* (Paris, 1985), 774–77; M. Clevenot, ed., *L'état des religions dans le monde* (Paris/Montreal, 1987); Secrétariat pour les non-croyants, *La foi et l'athéisme dans le monde*, Cultures et dialogue 3 (Paris, 1988); G. Pietri, "L'indif-férence religieuse: un aboutissement, Ses causes et ses limites," *Études* 371/4 (October 1989): 371–83.

André Charron

REVELATION

1. Introduction. 2. Methodological Premises. 3. Revelation in the Old Testament. 4. Revelation in the New Testament. 5. The Theme of Revelation in the Fathers of the Church. 6. New Questions and the Answers of the Magisterium. 7. Systematic Reflection: The Uniqueness of Christian Revelation. 8. Specific Features of Christian Revelation. 9. Conclusions

1. Introduction

In the context set by contemporary thought the theme of revelation is the focal point of all questions and all challenges. Western culture challenges the claim of Christianity to be the absolute, unconditional revelation for human beings. Meanwhile, Judaism, Islam, and Hinduism all make the same claim. Post-Christian people, especially in the West—whether atheist or indifferent, disappointed, bitter, or rebellious—all belong to a civilization that has been shaped by Christianity but has now lost its vitality and is incapable of producing anything but emptiness and absurdity—such people can no longer see Christianity as offering them anything; this is all the more the case since these people are abysmally ignorant of Christianity.

A crisis of such proportions cannot be overcome by superficial adjustments, but only by a rediscovery of the shattering and unprecedented intervention of God in the flesh and language of Christ. In the days of the Roman Empire Christianity had to do battle with paganism; today it must renew contact with post-Christian men and women who have abandoned or betrayed Christ. Pagans came to Christ; people today must be converted and return to him. As was said at the Synod of 1985 and in the apostolic exhortation *Christifideles Laici*, the peoples of the West require a "second evangelization."

Christianity indeed has something to say to human beings today, and especially to the peoples of the West, and this something is of critical importance. If Christianity is not able to say it, no power on earth, no ideology, no religion can take its place and say it. Since Christ is the supreme theophany, the God who both reveals and is revealed, the "concrete universal," he has a unique part to play that distinguishes Christianity from all the other religions which claim to be revealed and which challenge Christianity's central claim. Christianity is the only religion whose revelation is embodied in a person who presents himself as the living and unconditional truth, the truth that gathers up and unites in itself all the aspects of truth to be found in the course of humanity's history: the transcendent dimension that distinguishes the various Platonic currents of thought, the historical dimension that is emphasized in modern and contemporary thought, the interior dimension that is stressed in the several forms of existentialism. Christ is not simply the founder of a religion; he is immanent in human history and at the same time utterly transcends it. He alone therefore is the sole mediator of meaning, the sole exegete of the human person and its problems.

The people of our day must be helped to rediscover Christianity's primordial core, which is revelation, in all its freshness and to understand its specific nature. Any theology that seeks to be at once context oriented and systematic has no choice but to offer this help; its very nature compels it to do so.

2. Methodological Premises

A service that is clearly necessary is not on that account easily performed. The first difficulty is due to the different approaches taken by the theologians themselves. A number of theologians, Catholic and Protestant alike, have turned revelation into a "problem" and thus have made their theological reflection so "obscure" that they have managed, paradoxically, to "veil" that which they call "revelation," i.e., "unveiling." The fact is that they have chosen the unexplained as their starting point for throwing light on that which explains. Instead of letting themselves be carried by the stream of revelation itself and listening to what it says of itself, they have started from theological presuppositions.

a. This is true of such Protestant theologians as K. Barth, R. Bultmann, W. Pannenberg, and J. Moltmann. From the outset their thinking is conditioned by a theology of faith, of history, and of human existence. Some Catholic theologians, (overly) influenced by this recent theology, have developed their own thought on revelation within the perspectives of dialectical theology, existential hermeneutics, or a theology of praxis, instead of drawing upon the biblical and patristic traditions, which are doubtless less systematic but, on the other hand, are closer to the source in their inspiration.

b. Other theologians have taken the universal phenomenon of religion as their starting point. They see that all religions claim to have a revelation and display comparable patterns (mediators, rites, institutions); they conclude from this that Christian revelation is the highest form of a common experience. This comparative approach risks leading to the reductive views of a Schleiermacher or a Sabatier, or to the most extreme positions of the modernists. In fact, however, Christianity has its own normative sources — such as the gift of Christ himself — which elude all expectations and all common experiences.

c. Still other theologians, instead of starting with the "concrete universal" that is Christ, think it better first to develop a backdrop, namely, "transcendental revelation," i.e., the universal grace of salvation that is offered to every human being who comes into this world. Christic or "special" revelation is then seen as a more important episode, a more intense moment, within this universal revelation. Instead of starting with the concrete and known universal, these theologians start with a hidden and indeterminate universal that escapes the grasp of human consciousness. Neither the Scriptures nor the documents of the magisterium take this approach.

d. Still others, finally, take their cue from words, especially the word *reveal* (*apokalyptein*). But words too are a terrain full of booby traps. While the word *revelation* has indeed become the technical term for the self-manifestation and self-communication of God in Jesus Christ, the same is not true of the biblical sources. Thus in the OT "reveal" and "revelation" have an undeniable apocalyptic resonance and cover only part of a much more extensive reality. In the NT, a constellation of about thirty words serves to describe revelation in its active and passive aspects. In the OT the term "word" is far more important than "revelation"; in the NT the meaning of "word" deepens to the point of including the Logos of St. John. In reality, the term that comes closest to expressing what we mean today by revelation is "gospel." In conclusion: while the occurrence of certain words should alert us, it is not all-sufficient.

e. Are we then faced with an unanswerable question? Is it impossible to define the multi-faceted reality we call revelation? In my opinion, two criteria of discernment are available: first, do we find in the Christian tradition what is _meant_ today by the carefully defined technical term "revelation," as set before us in, e.g., _Dei Verbum?_ The aim of such a study is not to force texts to say what we mean today, but rather to see whether there is not present from the very beginning a luminous, initially distant and hardly perceptible line, consisting as it were of a series of dimly visible and discrete points, the unity of which the eye still has trouble seeing, but which gradually merge into limited units, then into an increasingly solid and increasingly bright line, until it becomes the dazzling light which is Christ, the mediator and fullness of revelation (_DV_ 2, 4). _Dei Verbum_, which is a point of arrival, is like a beacon that keeps inquirers from setting out on dead-end roads: it provides signposts for their search.

The second criterion calls our attention to the reality that is the response to what we call revelation. We are then surprised to see the astonishing variety of words that have "faith" for their counterpart. Thus Jesus _proclaims the good news_ and says: "Believe in the good news" (Mk 1:5); he _preaches_, he _teaches_, and urges people to faith (Mk 6:2, 5); he _bears witness_, even if people do not believe his testimony (Jn 1:1; 3:32); he _speaks_ and _says the truth_, but the Jews do not believe (Jn 8:46–47). The apostles in their turn _bear witness, preach, teach_, and urge people to faith in the risen Christ (Acts 2:41). Paul says: "So we _proclaim_ and so you have come to believe" (1 Cor 15:11). The _mystery_ that was hidden and then revealed is manifested and made known to all peoples "to bring about the obedience of faith" (Rom 16:25–26). In the OT as in the New, God _speaks_ in order to be heard (Heb 12:25) and believed (Heb 4:2). A single word describes the human response: _faith_, which is a response to a divine revelatory action that is expressed by a variety of concepts, since when faced with the mystery of God human beings

have no choice but to approach it from many angles and to stammer what they grasp of it.

In defining revelation I shall use the two criteria I have set down. In the limited framework of an article there can be no question of repeating the biblical, patristic, and theological inquiries already made in the _Theological Dictionary of the New Testament_, the _Supplément_ to the _Dictionnaire de la Bible_, the two fascicles of the _Handbuch der Dogmengeschichte_, or in monographs devoted to the theology of revelation. On the other hand, a systematic presentation of revelation would be impoverished without a developmental perspective. I have chosen a middle course, which consists in emphasizing points of continuity and discontinuity, signaling the diverse approaches taken, the high points, and the leading thinkers who were responsible for new directions. This kind of approach is not always taken, and yet it is a primary need of the reader: an approach that is both synchronic and diachronic, with priority given to a systematic presentation, but on the basis of sources that have been examined in a serious way.

3. Revelation in the Old Testament

The OT has no technical term for what we now call revelation, but instead uses a variety of words. Taken in its totality as a complex phenomenon that involves a multiplicity of forms, means, and expressions, revelation is presented as the experience of the unexpected action of a sovereign power, an action that alters the course of history for peoples and individuals. But this action is not a manifestation of raw power; rather it is seen as an encounter between a communicator and a recipient. Understood in a wide sense, revelation is a _dialogue_ of intelligent beings, of persons.

Stages and Forms of Revelation

a. _Terminology._ Eastern cultures used certain techniques in the attempt to learn the secrets of the gods: divination, dreams, casting of lots, omens, and so on. For a long time the OT retained these techniques to some extent, allowing them some value but stripping them of their links with polytheism or magic (Lv 19:26; Dt 18:10f.; 1 Sm 15:23, 28). It is also significant that Israel always refused to allow some of the classic techniques for gaining knowledge of the divine mind, especially hepatoscopy, which was used in sacrificial divination throughout the ancient East. Like most of the peoples of antiquity, the Hebrews accepted that God could use dreams to make his will known (Gn 20:3; 28:12–15; 37:5–10; 1 Sm 28:6). Joseph excels in the interpretation of dreams (Gn 40–41). Gradually, however, a distinction is made between dreams which God sends to genuine prophets (Nm 12:6; Dt 13:2) and those of professional diviners who spout false dreams (Jer 23:25–32; Is 28:7–13). The OT shows great reserve in regard to visions of God, be these direct or indirect. The important thing in theophanies is not the seeing of God but the hearing of his word. God's call to Abraham takes the form exclusively of divine speech (Gn 15:1ff.). It is also significant that Moses, who was able to converse with God as friend with friend (Ex 33:11), could not see his face (Ex 33:21–23). As for the prophets, even when they have visions, the essential thing is the words they hear. The revelation given to Samuel takes the form of an audition (1 Sm 3). In the OT vocabulary of revelation the roots most often used have to do with the action of communicating, saying, speaking, telling, so much so that the phrase "word of God" is the privileged description of divine communication. It is through his word that God gradually leads human beings to a knowledge of his interior life, until finally he gives the supreme gift: his very Word made flesh.

b. Patriarchal Revelation. Revelation first takes shape with Abraham and the patriarchs. The stories about the patriarchs are not, however, "historical" in the modern sense of this word: they are neither biographies nor myths nor popular tales nor legends, but "popular religious stories"; their aim is to share the experience of a particular kind of God, since this experience is the ground in turn of Israel's experience as a believing people. One might think that this foundational experience would take the form of an enlightenment and a knowledge of God after the manner of the Buddha. But there is nothing of this in the life of Abraham; there is rather a series of events and of decisions elicited by God and by his call: "The word of the Lord came to Abraham" (Gn 15:1). This God is a "disconcerting" God, a God who "unsettles": "Go . . . to the land that I will show you" (Gn 12:1; 22:1–2). Abraham experiences a departure into the unknown, strengthened only by a single guarantee: the promise of God. He knows that God is leading him, but in a direction of which he knows nothing (Gn 15:5, 6, 12, 17). Out of the depths of this night of faith arises a promise that is unmerited, unilateral, and unconditioned: Abraham will be given a countless posterity (Gn 17); this is followed by a change of name, *Abram* becoming *Abraham,* "father of a multitude." This promise seems indeed to be contradicted by the fact that Abraham and Sarah have no children. But God is faithful, beyond what is probable, beyond even what is possible. Sarah has a son. But hardly is this son born when God demands that he be sacrificed (Gn 22:1–19). In the darkness Abraham trusts himself to the God "who provides" (Gn 22:1–14). To this God who has shown himself to be the master of history and of life as well as the God of promises, Abraham responds with a total receptivity: his reaction is one of *faith* and *obedience.* Consequently Abraham becomes the "father of believers" (Rom 4:16). In this first stage of revelation, which is the prototype of all future revelations, God manifests himself through his action in history; this action takes the form of promise and fulfillment, of efficacious words that effect the salvation they promise. The counterpart of this promise is therefore not a "knowledge of God" but an obedient faith.

c. Mosaic Revelation. Revelation has its second decisive stage in the experience of the exodus, the salvific event that delivers Israel from slavery to the Egyptians and is accompanied by the self-manifestation of its author. In revealing his name to Israel by Moses, his mediator, God reveals not only that he exists but also that he is the only God and the only savior: "I AM WHO I AM" (Ex 3:14). Yahweh, and he alone, is always present, always active, always ready to save. By revealing his name God takes the side of Israel, which becomes his chosen one, then his partner in covenant. Liberation, election, covenant, law: these form an indivisible whole. The covenant and the Law are understandable only in the light of the entire process of liberation of which they are the crown. Through the covenant, Yahweh, who has proved his power and fidelity to Israel, makes this people his possession and becomes the leader of the nation. The "words of the covenant" (Ex 20:1–17) or "ten words" (*dĕbārîm:* Ex 34:28) express the exclusive claims of the God of Israel, as well as the moral demands made by the "holy" God who has entered into a covenant with a "holy people." In accepting the covenant Israel accepts a manner of life that corresponds to its calling. But salvation precedes election, covenant, and law. Henceforth Israel's destiny is linked to the will of God that has been historically expressed in, and founded on, the liberating event. In the exodus Israel experiences an encounter, but Yahweh is not reducible to this event. Through Moses he reveals his name and the *meaning* of the event. Israel is committed to a dialogic existence that is set in the framework of call and response. From the outset, revelation has its distinctive structure as *event/sign.* The dialectic of promise and fulfillment continues to operate. In revealing himself to the patriarchs and then to Israel as the God of history, God already gives his revelation its universal dimensions.

d. Prophetic Revelation. The word is addressed to the people, not directly, but through "mediators" (Ex 20:18). As mediator of the covenant and the Decalogue, Moses is the prototype of the prophets (Dt 34:10–12; 18:15–18). Although Joshua is presented as Yahweh's confidant and spokesman, it is only with Samuel (1 Sm 3:1–21) that prophetism begins to play its vital role and becomes a quasi-permanent phenomenon, in a form more charismatic than institutional, down to the fifth century.

The preexilic prophets (Amos, Hosea, Micah, and Isaiah) are the guardians and defenders of the covenant and the Law. In their preaching they invoke the justice and fidelity of the thrice holy God; but because Israel is unfaithful to the conditions of the covenant, the divine *dābār* most often utters condemnations and announces punishments (Am 4:1; 5:1; Hos 8:7–14; Mi 6–7; Is 1:10–20; 16:13; 28:13–14; 30:12–14). These punishments will not be withdrawn. This theme of the irreversibility and efficacy of God's word is clearly stated in Isaiah: "The Lord sent a word against Jacob, and it fell on Israel" (9:8). The word is utterly dynamic: it swoops down like an arrow and produces its effects in successive stages.

Jeremiah plays an important part in theological reflection on revelation, because he tries to establish criteria for discerning the authentic word of God. These criteria are: the fulfillment of the prophet's words (Jer 28:9; 32:6–8), fidelity to Yahweh and traditional religion (Jer 23:13–32), and, finally, the often heroic witness given by the prophet himself in carrying out his calling (Jer 1:4–6; 26:12–15).

Deuteronomy, which originated in northern circles that were influenced by the prophetic preaching of the ninth and eighth centuries, is located at the confluence of two currents: the law-centered current, which expresses the outlook of the priesthood, and the prophetic current. As a result of this twofold influence, the theology of the Law is developed more fully. Deuteronomy connects the Law closer than ever with the covenant: If Israel wants to live, it must put into practice all the words of the Law (Dt 29:28), because this Law, which has issued from the mouth of Yahweh, is a source of life (Dt 32:47). But Deuteronomy also includes in the Mosaic Law all the clauses of the covenant (Dt 28:69), i.e., the whole body of moral, civil, religious, and criminal law. Finally, the word of the Law is "interiorized": "The word is very near to you; it is in your mouth and in your heart for you to observe" (Dt 30:11–14). The essential command of the Law is to love God with one's whole heart and one's whole soul (Dt 4:29).

Parallel to the prophetic and deuteronomic currents, there develops a historical literature (Judges, Samuel, Kings), which offers in fact both a history of salvation and a theology of history. The covenant entered into by Yahweh and the conditions which he sets suppose that the course of events is determined by the divine will, which takes into account the attitudes of the chosen people. Once the covenant has been struck, Israel constantly used the categories of history in its thinking about religion. In the final analysis, it is the word of God that directs history and renders it intelligible. An important text in this historical literature is the prophecy of Nathan (2 Sm 7), which connects the covenant with the monarchy and establishes a royal messianism. As a result of this prophecy the Davidic dynasty becomes directly and permanently the covenant partner of Yahweh (2 Sm 7:16; 23:5) and the focus of salvation. Israel's hope rests henceforth on the king: initially the king of the moment, but then a future, eschatological king, as the infidelities of the historical kings make increasingly remote the expectation of a king who will fulfill the Davidic ideal. Nathan's prophecy is the point of departure for a theology which the prophets develop and which is eminently one of promise and turned to the future, more so than the theology of the covenant which looks primarily to daily life.

During the exile, the prophetic word, while not ceasing to be a living word, becomes more and more a written word. In this regard it is significant that the word entrusted to Ezekiel is written on a scroll which the prophet must eat and digest in order that he may preach its contents (Ez 3:1f.). An important characteristic of Ezekiel's prophetic activity is its pastoral tone. After the fall of Jerusalem (Ez 33:1–21) Israel no longer exists as a nation. At this point the message of Yahweh becomes one of comfort and hope for the demoralized exiles. Ezekiel undertakes to serve as a kind of spiritual director and to form a new Israel (Ez 33:1–9). While showing the people that the word which decreed and brought about punishment remains always a word of faithful promise, Ezekiel is also careful to keep them from mistaking its true nature: it is not enough to hear the word; they must also live it (Ez 33:31).

Second Isaiah (Is 40–55), which must be read in the context of the exile, reflects on the efficacy, at once cosmic and historical, of the divine *dābār*. The word's absolute sovereignty over creation is the foundation and guarantee of its all-powerful action in history. Because Yahweh brought all things into being out of nothingness through his word, he is master of the nations no less than of the forces of nature. He is both the point of departure and the goal of events; his word predicts, energizes, and brings to fulfillment. He holds in his hand the two ends of history (Is 41:4; 44:6; 48:12). Moreover, history is intelligible because it unfolds according to a plan which God's word gradually reveals to human beings, and his word never returns to him without having accomplished what he meant it to do (Is 55:10–12).

Clearly, it is due above all to prophetism that the revelation of Sinai always remains the core of all revelation, that it keeps its central place throughout the OT, especially in the period of the monarchy and during the exile, and that it is understood ever more fully. Now the originality of the prophets is due to their having been the recipients of a privileged experience, which occurred in most instances at the time of

their *call:* the prophets know Yahweh because he has spoken to them and entrusted his word to them. The prophets have been called to a special intimacy with God; they have been called to know his secrets (Nm 24:16–17) and plans (Am 3:7), so that they may interpret these to their fellow human beings.

This is the fundamental experience of the prophets: the word of Yahweh is in them (Jer 5:13). They are conscious that they have not brought this word into being, that it comes not from them but from God. They have received it, but in order that they may pass it on, broadcast it and make it known. Prophets serve as the *mouth* of Yahweh (Jer 15:19; Ez 7:1–2); they are *men of the word* (Jer 18:18). They live among other human beings as the divinely authorized interpreters of everything that happens in the world (storms, cataclysms, famines, prosperity), among human beings (sins, deaths, hardening of hearts), and in history (defeats, successes, the succession of empires). It is important to emphasize the objective and dynamic character of the prophetic word. Its first effect is to be seen in the prophets themselves who receive it. It acts in them like a devouring fire and an irrepressible force (Jer 20:8–9), like a dazzling light. Yahweh has *spoken;* the prophet must *bear witness.* Such is the experience of Amos (Am 3:8), Jeremiah (Jer 20:7–8), Isaiah (Is 8:11), Ezekiel (Ez 3:14), Elijah (1 Kgs 18:46), and Elisha (2 Kgs 3:15). Since the words of the prophet are God's word in human words, they share in the efficacy of God's word. They are never barren. God, nonetheless, is always in control, and his word acts according to his plan, which he gradually reveals and which is a plan of salvation and life. This is why at every point in the OT God is patient, answers prayers, lets himself be moved, and forgives.

The field in which the prophetic word operates is history: it is a word that *creates* and *interprets* history. For it is in history, as a result of God's interventions, that the Hebrew people experience the action of God in their behalf. The faith of Israel rests on these foundational events, and its creed consists in telling them over (Dt 26:5–10). The action of God which the prophets announce is doubly the work of the word. First, because it is the word of Yahweh that brings events about and directs their course: "the Lord God does nothing without revealing his secret to his servants, the prophets" (Am 3:7). In Israel's view, history is a process directed by Yahweh toward a goal which he wills. Second, the prophets not only announce history but interpret it. They see the divine meaning of events and make this known to others; they interpret history as seen by God. Event and interpretation are the two dimensions, as it were, of the one word of God. The history of salvation is a series of divine interventions which are interpreted by the prophets. Thus, through the events of the exodus as interpreted by Moses the Hebrew people come to know Yahweh as the living, personal, all-powerful, and faithful God who saves his people and makes a covenant with them so that he and they together may carry out a work of salvation (Dt 6:20–24). It follows that God, his attributes, and his plan are revealed not in an abstract way but in and through history. There is a progressive knowledge of God, but the progress is connected with events which the word of God announces, brings to pass, and interprets through the prophets. The progress takes the form of a *history that is meaningful.*

e. Sapiential Revelation. Although the sapiential literature of the OT is part of an international current of thought (Greece, Egypt, Babylonia, Phoenicia) that is attested from the second millennium B.C.E. on, this current of thought was soon turned by Israel into an instrument of revelation. The same God who enlightens the prophets uses human experience to reveal human beings to themselves (Prv 2:6; 20:27). Israel accepts human experience but interprets it and penetrates its meaning more deeply in the light of its faith in Yahweh. In addition, the data that are the subject of sapiential reflection are often part of revelation: history, the Law, and the Prophets. Wisdom, like the word, issues from the mouth of the Most High. Ultimately, wisdom too is identified with the word of God. The psalter, which took shape gradually in the course of history, is chiefly a response to revelation; however, it is itself also revelation, because the prayer of human beings brings out the full dimensions of revelation through the sentiments it expresses. The majesty, power, fidelity, and holiness of Yahweh that have been revealed by the prophets are reflected in the attitudes of believers and in the intensity of their prayer. The psalms are not only a mirror of revelation, but also the daily actualization of revelation in the worship of the Temple.

An element in sapiential revelation is the theme of cosmic revelation—i.e., revelation through creation—which represents a rather late stage in the development of inspired revelation. It was primarily through history that Israel came to know Yahweh, at the time when it experienced his liberating power in Egypt. Ceaseless meditation on this limitless power of Yahweh and on the way in which he freely uses the forces of nature in saving his people led, by an organic and homogeneous development, to a belief that he created the world. Israel came to understand that the same God who brought his people out of the nothingness of slavery also brought the world into being out of nothing. His sovereignty is universal: "By the word of the Lord the heavens were made, and all their host by the breath of his mouth. . . . For he spoke, and it came to be; he commanded, and it stood firm" (Ps 33:6, 9). When the word compels things, it creates; when it compels human beings, it becomes law. Because creation is something said by God, it too is revelation (Job, Proverbs, Sirach, Wisdom, Psalms, Rom 1:16).

Object and Character of OT Revelation

OT revelation has some quite specific characteristics that set it apart from every other kind of knowledge:

a. Revelation is essentially *interpersonal.* It is a self-manifestation of Someone to someone. Yahweh is at once the God who reveals and the God who is revealed, who *gives himself* to be known and who *makes himself* known. He enters into a covenant with human beings, first as a master with his servant, then gradually as a father with his child, a friend with his friend, a husband with his wife. Revelation leads to a communion with God for the sake of human salvation.

b. OT revelation is due to the *initiative* of God. Human beings do not discover God; Yahweh manifests himself, when he wills, to whom he wills, and because he wills. He is absolute freedom. He takes the first step in choosing, promising, and entering into covenant. And since his word is at complete odds with Israel's human and carnal expectations, he thereby makes the freedom of his plan even clearer. This freedom is also evident in the variety of means by which God chooses to reveal himself (the ways provided by nature, history, and human experience); in the variety of human beings he chooses (priests, wise men, prophets, kings and aristocrats, peasants and shepherds); in the diverse methods of communication (theophanies, dreams, oracles, visions, ecstasies, raptures, etc.); and in the variety of literary genres (oracles, exhortations, autobiographies, descriptions, hymns, poetry, sapiential reflection, etc.).

c. It is the *word* that gives the process of revelation its unity. The various Greek philosophies and the religions of the Hellenistic period focus on the vision of the godhead. OT religion, on the other hand, is a religion of the heard word. This predominance of hearing over seeing is an essential trait of biblical revelation. God speaks to the prophets and sends them forth to speak; they communicate God's plans and urge their fellow human beings to the obedience of faith. Their word does, however, pave the way for vision. While human beings do not yet penetrate to the innermost heart of the mystery, they do already have, through the word, an access to the mystery and a first grasp of it. Note, too, that the word shows the great respect God has for human freedom. He addresses himself to human beings and calls upon them, but they remain free to accept or reject. Finally, the word, which is the most spiritual form of human communication, is also the means par excellence of spiritual dealings between God and humanity. Sin consists in human beings hardening their hearts so as not to hear the word. Depending on whether they accept or reject revelation, it becomes life or death for them.

d. But the aim of revelation is *life and salvation* for human beings, a covenant that leads to communion. OT revelation acquires its momentum from the promise God made to Abraham, and it moves toward the fulfillment of that promise. The prophets see the present as only a partial actualization of a future that is announced, awaited, and prepared for, but still hidden. The present derives its full value solely from the promise, made in the past, of what will be in the future. Each prophetic revelation signifies a fulfillment of the word, but at the same time it gives the hope of an even more decisive fulfillment. History thus moves toward a fullness of time that will see the carrying out

of the divine plan of salvation in and through Christ.

Old Testament Concept of Revelation

According to the OT, revelation is the gracious and free intervention in which the holy and hidden God makes himself progressively known in the realm of history and in connection with historical events that he interprets through the word which he addresses to the prophets, using quite varied means of communication. God reveals not only himself but his saving plan of entering into a covenant with Israel and, through Israel, with all peoples, in order that he may bring to fulfillment in the person of his anointed one (Messiah) the promise he once gave to Abraham that in the latter's posterity he would bless all the nations of the world. This divine action is conceived of as the word of God urging human beings to faith and obedience; this word is essentially dynamic, and makes salvation a reality at the same time as it announces and promises it.

4. Revelation in the New Testament

The central NT insight is that between the two covenants an absolutely fundamental event has occurred: "Long ago God spoke to our ancestors in many and various ways by the prophets, but in these last days he has spoken to us by a Son" (Heb 1:1). In Jesus Christ, the Word interior to God, the Word in whom God knows all things and expresses himself totally, takes to himself the flesh and language of human beings; he becomes gospel or word of salvation in order to call his fellow men and women to the life that does not end. In Jesus Christ, the Incarnate Word, the Son is present among us and, using human language which we can understand and assimilate, he speaks, preaches, teaches, and bears witness to what he has seen and heard in the bosom of the Father. Christ is the summit and fullness of revelation, revealing God and revealing human beings to themselves: such is the great novelty, the inexhaustible mystery whose splendor the sacred writers unfold for us, each emphasizing a different aspect of it. Thus it becomes necessary to unify these different viewpoints and approaches, as we combine complementary views of one and the same cathedral, in order to grasp the complexity and richness of the whole.

The Synoptic Tradition

The key terms in the vocabulary of revelation (e.g., *apokalyptō, apokalypsis*) are not used in Mark. Consequently, here more than elsewhere, an exclusive attention to the saying in Mt 11:25–27; (par. Lk 10:21–22) and to the paired words "hide-reveal," "know-reveal" can lead into error. When the evangelists tell the story of Jesus, they are in fact simply narrating the manifestation of God in Jesus Christ, for Christ is the point of greatest concentration in this epiphany of God. The Gospel of Mark, in particular, traces the progressive manifestation of Jesus as Messiah and Son of the Father, the one who reveals himself and reveals the Father through his words, especially his parables, and through his works, especially his miracles, his examples, his passion, and his death, but who meets with rejection by his own people.

The terms that describe Christ's revelatory action are: preach (*kēryssein*) and teach (*didaskein*). Christ preaches the good news of the kingdom, and conversion as the way of entering it: "Repent, for the kingdom of heaven has come near" (Mt 4:17; Mk 1:14–15). This decisive news involves Jesus so directly that it makes him the beginning of the kingdom in his own person: "Today" the time of grace announced by the prophets is at hand (Lk 4:21). The "today" of the proclamation of the kingdom is accompanied by the "Here I am," the Rabbi, the Teacher who teaches with authority. His teaching is new, his authority is unparalleled (Mt 7:29), an authority that puts him on the level of God: "Amen," "But I say to you" (Mt 5:22, 28, 32). With Dt 18:18 in mind, the crowds look upon Jesus as *the* prophet who was to come at the end of time (Mk 6:14f.; 8:28; Mt 21:11). But when Jesus speaks of himself he never claims the title of prophet, because as revealer he is greater than the prophets (Mt 12:40; Mk 9:2–10; Mt 17:1–13; Lk 7:18–23; 9:28–36). He preaches and teaches, but in virtue of being the Son of the Father (Mt 7:21; 10:32–33; 11:25–27): "No one knows the Son except the Father, and no one knows the Father except the Son and anyone to whom the Son chooses to reveal him" (Mt 11:25–27). No one "knows" (Lk: *gignōskein*; Mt: *epigignōskein*), with an experiential knowledge, the nature and the interior, innermost life of the Son, except the Father; and no one knows the interior, innermost life of the Father, except

the Son. They know each other because they are face to face with each other as two equal magnitudes of the same order. And no one can share in this mystery of reciprocal knowledge without a freely given revelation. Christ, who is the Son, is the perfect revealer of the Father. To the disciples whom he has chosen he *grants* the favor of knowing the mysteries of the kingdom of heaven. The Father also reveals the mystery of the person of Christ to the "little ones" who recognize their poverty before God; but this revelation, too, is a gift of God, an interior light granted to them by the Father but withheld from the "wise" in their pride. This proclamation of the kingdom, as well as the revelation of Christ as Son of the Father, takes place through "actions and words," parables, i.e., and miracles, according to a strictly incarnational economy. Thus in the Synoptic tradition Christ is revealer insofar as he proclaims the good news of the kingdom of heaven and teaches the word of God with authority. In the final analysis, he reveals because he is the Son who knows the innermost life of the Father. The essential content of revelation is the salvation offered to human beings in the form of the kingdom of God which Christ proclaims and inaugurates. Christ is at once the one who proclaims the kingdom and the one in whom the kingdom becomes a reality.

The Acts of the Apostles

In continuity with the Synoptic tradition, the Acts of the Apostles presents the apostles as *witnesses* to Jesus, men who *proclaim* the good news and *teach* what they have received from the master. Witnessing, proclaiming the gospel, teaching: these belong to the apostle's role.

"Witness" is a title given to the apostles, and to them alone, because they alone have been associated with Christ throughout his public life and after his resurrection. They have followed Christ everywhere; they have sat at table with him before and after his resurrection. They alone have had direct, living experience of Christ, his person, his message, his deeds. They are witnesses, first and foremost of his resurrection (Acts 1:22; 2:32; 3:13–16; 4:2, 33; 5:30–31; 10:39, 41, 42; 13:31), but also, more broadly, of his entire career (Acts 1:21) from his baptism to his resurrection, and of his entire work, both that which led up to his suffering and resurrection and that which the resurrection in turn inaugurated. The testimony of the apostles is given in the power of the Spirit (Acts 1:8), who fills them with courage and confidence and acts in the hearts of those who hear them, so as to make God's word penetrate the soul and be accepted by faith (Acts 16:14). Again like Christ, the apostles proclaim the good news of salvation (Acts 2:14; 8:5; 10:42); they constantly "taught and proclaimed the word of the Lord" (Acts 15:35; 18:25; 28:31). Their function, then, is to be *witnesses* and *heralds*. Their message is dynamic and explosive; they cannot remain silent about the salvation given by Christ, for this is the only worthwhile news, the only news capable of transforming hearts and setting the world on fire so that love may be enkindled. The testimony of these apostle-witnesses is the object of our faith; it is testimony given not by words alone, but by examples of how we are to live, by attitudes and rites. This concrete, comprehensive testimony brings about the growth of the church under the action of the Spirit.

The Pauline Corpus

One pair of words, *mystery-gospel*, takes us to the heart of Paul's thought on revelation. The mystery, hidden initially, is then disclosed, preached, and made known, in order to elicit faith. This language calls to mind the older sapiential and apocalyptic literature; in addition, it lays greater emphasis on the *content* of revelation than on the revelatory action itself.

The *mystery*, which represents Paul's basic insight, undergoes an evident expansion of meaning in the course of his letters. In 1 Cor 2:6–10, the mystery is already defined as the plan of salvation that has been brought to fulfillment in Christ, but it is presented as a "wisdom" that has for its object the blessings which God intends for the elect and which can be understood only by those enlivened by the Spirit, since this wisdom has its source in the Spirit of God (1 Cor 2:10–16).

In Col 1:26, the mystery previously hidden is now disclosed and brought to fulfillment. It becomes a historical event, its aim being the participation of the Gentiles, no less than the Jews, in the blessings of salvation (Rom 16:26). The letter to the Ephesians broadens this vision still further (Eph 1:9–10). The mystery is defined as the unification of all things in Jesus Christ,

the bringing together of all beings on earth and in the heavens under a single Lord, who is Christ. The mystery of which Paul speaks is the divine plan of salvation, hidden in God from all eternity and now disclosed, by which God establishes Christ as the center of a new economy and makes him, through his death and resurrection, the sole source of salvation for both Gentiles and Jews and the head of all who exist, both angels and human beings. The mystery is the complete divine plan (incarnation, redemption, sharing in glory), which in the final analysis is reducible to Christ and his boundless riches (Eph 3:8). Concretely, then, *the mystery is Christ* (Rom 16:25; Col 1:26–27; 1 Tm 3:16). In his description of the mystery Paul initially emphasizes the call of the Gentiles to whom he is a "minister by a special call" (see Eph 3:8–9; 1 Tm 2:7; Rom 15:16); then, in the captivity letters, the mystery becomes principally Christ and participation in him: everything is "recapitulated" in him. The world, which was created in unity, returns to unity through Christ, the savior and universal Lord.

Once it has been revealed to chosen witnesses (Eph 3:5; Col 1:25–26), the mystery is made known to all human beings. In his practice, Paul makes "gospel" and "mystery" equivalent terms (Rom 16:25; Col 1:25–26; Eph 1:9–13; 3:5–6). Both are concerned with one and the same reality, namely, the divine plan of salvation, but each looks at this plan from a different angle. In the one case, there is question of a mystery that is hidden, then disclosed and manifested; in the other, of a good news, a message announced and proclaimed. Divine plan hidden and revealed; divine plan proclaimed: gospel and mystery have the same object or content. This object has two aspects: *soteriological*, i.e., the entire economy of salvation as accomplished through Christ (Eph 1:1–10), and *eschatological*, i.e., the promise of glory, which includes all the blessings of salvation, these being intended for the Gentiles as well as the Jews (Col 1:28; 1 Cor 2:7; Eph 1:18). The mystery made known to human beings through the preaching of the gospel becomes the plan of salvation that has reached the point of becoming a personal event. Instead of "gospel," but with the same meaning, Paul also uses the term "word" (Col 1:25–25; 1 Thes 1:6) or "word of God" (1 Thes 2:13; Rom 9:6; 1 Cor 14:36) or "word of Christ" (Rom 10:17). Through this word, which is God's message on human lips, it is always God who speaks and summons humanity (Rom 10:14), urging it to "the obedience of faith" (Rom 16:26; 1 Cor 10:5). "So we proclaim and so you have believed" (1 Cor 15:11).

Since the mystery is the union of Jews and Gentiles in Christ, the church becomes the definitive goal of the mystery, the radiant concretization of the divine economy, its visible and abiding expression. The plan of salvation is not only revealed, then proclaimed through the gospel; it is also made a reality in the church, the "body of Christ" (Eph 4:13). The founding of the church means that the time has come for the subjection of all things to Christ (Col 1:16). Just as Christ is the mystery of God rendered visible, so the church is the mystery of Christ rendered visible. The times are fulfilled; the salvation announced is at hand.

In Paul's view, however, a tension always remains between historical revelation and eschatological revelation, between the first and last epiphanies of Christ, the former veiled, the latter glorious (Phil 2:5–11). Beyond a doubt, the mystery, formerly hidden, is revealed "now" (Rom 16:25), and the preaching of the gospel takes place "now." But Paul therefore looks forward all the more eagerly to the eschatological revelation of the mystery, when the "revelation of our Lord Jesus Christ" will come in its fullness (1 Cor 1:7; 2 Thes 1:7), and when the glory of all who have become like Christ will also be revealed (Rom 8:17–19). This tension between history and eschatology, faith and vision, lowliness and glory, is characteristic of Paul.

According to Paul, revelation is the free and gracious action by which God, in and through Christ, makes the economy of salvation known to the world: makes known, i.e., his eternal plan to unite all things in Christ, the savior and head of the new creation. The communication of this plan is accomplished through the preaching of the gospel, which is a ministry entrusted to the apostles and prophets of the NT. The human response to the preaching of the gospel is the obedience of faith, which is achieved under the enlightening action of the Spirit. Faith in turn gives rise to a process of deepening understanding of the mystery, a process that will reach its term only in the revelation that comes with the vision of God.

The Letter to the Hebrews

The dominant term used here for revelation is "word." In a comparison of the two stages in the economy of salvation, the letter emphasizes the continuity between the two covenants, but at the same time the preeminence of the new revelation inaugurated by the Son. The new element which the letter to the Hebrews contributes to the history of revelation is twofold: a comparison between the old and new covenants; the grandeur of the demands made by the word of God.

Right from the opening two verses the letter gives prominence to the authority of NT revelation, while retaining the historical connection between the two stages of the history of salvation: there is continuity between the two economies (God spoke, God has spoken), but also there are differences (times, modes, mediators, addressees), and the excellence (superiority) of the new economy.

The continuity is due to God and his word. The absence of a direct object of the verb _lalein_ emphasizes the point that by means of his word God wills, first of all, to communicate with and enter upon a personal dialogue with human beings, for the sake of a communion with them. The letter states not the content of this communication but its addressees: the fathers, the prophets, us. But the word of God has a historical character: it differs according to period (the past, the present), mode of expression (the successive, partial, fragmentary, varied messages of the OT), and mediator (multiplicity of inspired recipients in the OT, as compared with the unity evident in the NT where everything is reduced to the person of the Son, who is heir of all things, the reflection of God's glory, and sole mediator in the sphere of revelation and in the sphere of priesthood). In the final analysis, it is the word that unifies the two covenants, and it is the person of the Son that accounts for the superiority of the new revelation over the old.

The second theme which the letter to the Hebrews emphasizes is the greatness and demands of the word of God, which are viewed at every point in terms of a comparison between the two covenants. We must pay greater heed to the gospel than to the Law (Heb 2:1) because of the absolute superiority of Christ. In the letter to the Hebrews the word of God has traits which call to mind those which it has in the OT, but these are now marked by a greater urgency, due to the presence of the Son in our midst. The word, which is active, effective, sharper than any two-edged sword (Heb 4:12–13) and always topical (Heb 3:7, 15; 4:7), rings in the ears of Christians in a constant today, urging them to enter into the rest of the Lord (Heb 3:7, 15; 4:11). The word in the NT calls for a fidelity and obedience that are proportioned to the origin and authority of its mediator, the Son.

Saint John: Gospel and Letters

Like Mark, John does not have such terms for revelation as *apokalyptō* and *apokalypsis*, nor the contrasting "hidden" and "unveiled." He does not use Paul's language of "mystery," but instead the language of Hellenistic circles: *zōē*, *logos*, *phōs*, *alētheia*, and *doxa*, these being seen as incarnated in the person of Jesus Christ. We find the verb *phaneroō* and, above all, a set of terms which all call for the response of faith: commandment (11 times), testimony (14), testify (33), speak (59), glory (18), truth (25), and word (40), as well as words which emphasize the acceptance of revelation, as, e.g., hear (58) and believe (98). The reason why John has a new set of words for revelation is that something new has been brought by Christ who is *already* God-among-us. In his person he is the Truth, the Word, the Light, the Life. There has been a qualitative leap. Christ makes the invisible God visible. The incarnation is revelation made a reality.

For John Christ is the Son who tells of the Father: he "testifies to what he has seen and heard" (Jn 3:32; 8:38). The Father in turn bears witness to the Son through the mighty *works* which he has given the Son to do (Jn 5:36) and through the *attraction* which he produces in souls, as he enables them to give their assent to the testimony of Christ (Jn 6:44–45).

From the outset, in his prologue, John equates Christ, Son of the Father, and the Logos. Christ is the eternal, subsistent Word, and revelation takes place because this Word has become flesh in order to tell us of the Father. The prologue takes the form of "Deeds of the Logos," a summary of the entire history of revelation in a passage of extraordinary density and power. But while the deeds begin with the creative action of the Logos, that which receives priority and explains everything else is the *drama of the Logos who becomes flesh*, who dwells among human beings, manifests his glory, and meets with rejection from his own. The prologue looks back and sees creation as a first manifestation of God and the Logos, and a first rejection by humanity. The light shone in the darkness (Gn 1:3), but humanity did not understand this first manifestation of the Word and darkened it (Jn 1:10; Rom 1:19–23; Wis 13:1–9). God then chose a people and made himself known to them through the Law and the Prophets; but this manifestation, like the first, ended in failure. The Word had come to his own, to his own house, "and his own people did not accept him" (Jn 1:11). Finally, the Logos became flesh and set up his tent among us. "No one has ever seen God. It is God's only Son, who is close to the Father's heart, who has made him known" (Jn 1:18). No one can see the invisible; if we know God, it is because in Christ *the Word became flesh*, became a *historical event* and, at the same time, the *exegete* of the Father and his love-inspired plan.

Three factors make Christ the perfect revealer of the Father: his preexistence as Logos of God (Jn 1:1–2), his entrance into the flesh and history (Jn 1:14), and his unbroken sharing of life with the Father, before the incarnation as well as after it (Jn 1:18). John thus gives revelation its maximal meaning and extension.

In virtue of his revelatory mission, which has its source in his life within the Trinity, Christ speaks and bears witness: he is the Son who tells of the Father (Jn 1:18), the witness who declares what he has seen and heard and who is faithful (Rv 1:5; 3:14). In the Synoptic tradition, Jesus is the Messiah who teaches, preaches, and proclaims the good news of the kingdom. In John, the full identity of the Messiah is made known: he is the Son of the Father. What the Son tells us is the interior life, the reciprocal love, of Father and Son: a love which the Father wills to communicate to all human beings, in order that all may be one. The goal of revelation is that humankind "may become completely one," and that they may thus know that the Father has sent the Son and that he loves human beings as he does his Son (Jn 17:23–25).

John tells us the final word about revelation: it is a work of love and salvation that has its origin within the Trinity. But when this revelation is shown to be a historical event, namely, the enfleshment of the Word, it becomes a stumbling block. It undermines human attitudes and judgments, even those of the OT. The tragic aspect of revelation is that men and women close themselves to the light, make themselves prisoners of the idol they take for God, and prefer to run to their own destruction. This is the drama described in the prologue and then repeated and illustrated by the miracle of the man born blind (Jn 9).

In light of the preceding survey it is possible to describe NT revelation as the sovereignly loving and free action by which, through an economy involving the incarnation, God makes himself known in his innermost life and makes known, too, the love-inspired plan which he has conceived from all eternity of saving all human beings and bringing them back to him through Christ. This divine action is accomplished through the exterior testimony of Christ and the apostles and the interior testimony of the Spirit who works from within to effect the conversion of human beings to Christ. The Father thus makes known and carries out his plan of salvation through the joint action of the Son and the Spirit.

5. The Theme of Revelation in the Fathers of the Church

We would look in vain to the fathers of the early centuries for the equivalent of a modern treatise on revelation, because these fathers do not see revelation either as a fact whose existence must be established, or as a problem to be solved. The first generations of Christians were still powerfully influenced by the great manifestation of God in Jesus Christ. For them, revelation is a self-evident fact. In their thinking, therefore, they are concerned less with "proving" that revelation is possible than with proclaiming to the whole world the overwhelming, unheard-of event of God's irruption among us in the flesh and message of Christ. The first problem, therefore, that arises for them is the problem of the _inculturation_ of Christian revelation in the Greek world. The resultant reflection is not yet systematic but is directly concerned with the requirements of the communities that have been evangelized or are to be evangelized. The theology of the early fathers is essentially "contextual," connected with the currents of thought of their times: Jewish objections, Gnosticism, and so on. No one has any doubts about the fact of revelation; all, rather, take revelation as the sole norm of interpretation.

In the contextual and occasional thinking of the early fathers of the church there is both _more_ and _less_ than in present-day thinking about revelation. Many problems raised today undoubtedly never entered into the consciousness of these early Christians. On the other hand, patristic thought possesses some inexhaustibly fruitful principles from which our contemporary systematic approach to revelation can draw profit. First, patristic thought is still close to the original event and develops within a comprehensive vision of the Christian mystery. It is inspired by Scripture and retains contact with the first witnesses. It draws upon the source and develops in that setting. All discourse is discourse about God who creates, saves, and reveals. In all the thinking of these fathers there is always an implicit theology of revelation. Second, in their effort to answer objections, heresies, and reductive views, the fathers of the church were led to evolve broad perspectives that would better illustrate the points of contact with other cultures and religions, but also the uniqueness and specific character of the Christian phenomenon. It was thus that they gave special attention to certain themes: the relationship (difference and unity) between the OT and NT; the progressivity to be seen in the stages of revelation, in the economy, and in the pedagogical aspect of the divine plan; the centrality of Christ; the tension in the mystery of God, which is revealed, yet always remains hidden; the need of the Spirit's action both in gaining access to revelation and in understanding it.

These broad perspectives, periodically renewed, end in imposing an image of Christian revelation in its totality: it is a landscape, each detail of which is illuminated by a flash of light at a particular moment of history. The impact on minds is greater than would be made by a uniformly dotted line of revelation. To use another comparison: by thrusting up, over the centuries, blocks of thought that are like islands emerging out of the Christian consciousness, patristic reflection ended up establishing archipelagoes and finally continents with well-defined contours as well as heights and lowlands. The contextual character of this reflection, with all its surprises, often leads us to sharper awareness and deeper understanding than does the kind of theological thinking that is linear and too neatly laid out. For these reasons, rather than work through the fathers of the church one after the other, I think it more useful to focus on some of the aspects of revelation on which they shed light.

In its first period, the postapostolic church lived in expectation of the Lord's immediate return; revelation, consequently, took on an eschatological coloring. Very soon, however, it was the problem of the interrelationship of the two testaments that became the focus of attention.

The Two Testaments: Unity and Progress

Judaizers wanted to give priority to prophetic revelation, while the followers of Marcion saw the two testaments as opposed to each other. The latter depicted Christ as the revealer of an utterly new God who had been unknown to the Jewish world. They set up a radical opposition between the God of the OT and the God of the NT. Between these two positions—on the one hand, an inadequate grasp of the newness of the gospel (this was the temptation of traditional Jewish circles) and, on the other, an insufficient appreciation of the OT and a rejection of it (à la Marcion)—Justin, Irenaeus, Clement of Alexandria, and Origen followed a middle path, emphasizing the continuity and profound *unity* of the two testaments. For these fathers, one and the same God is author of all revelation through his Word or Logos: creation, the theophanies, the Law and the Prophets, and the incarnation are the stages of the one, continuing manifestation of God in the course of human history. On the other hand they emphasize with equal clarity the *progress* made in moving from the one economy to the other. The fathers see this progress from different angles. According to Justin, there is a partial and obscure manifestation of the Logos in the OT; the manifestation is clear and complete in the NT. According to Irenaeus, in the OT there is a preparation, an education of the human race, hints and promises of the incarnation; in the NT there is the fulfillment and the gift of Christ. According to Clement of Alexandria, the OT contains enigmas and mystery; the NT

brings the clarification of the prophecies. According to Origen, in the OT the mystery is made known; in the NT it is fulfilled and possessed, there is a passage from shadows and images to truth, from letter and history to the Spirit.

The Theology of the Logos: Meeting Point of Two Cultures

Preaching to the pagans meant an encounter of the Christian message with a current of thought dominated by nonbiblical, philosophical categories. In order to make the gospel accessible to pagans, Christian thinkers adopted a philosophy that had been developed by Platonism and Stoicism, a philosophy that brought with it the danger that revelation would be seen primarily as a type of knowledge, a higher gnosis, to the detriment of its historical character. According to Plato, God is ineffable and does not intervene in history. In order to build a bridge between God's radical transcendence and his self-revelation in history Justin draws attention to the mediatorial function of Christ. For the Jesus of history is identical with the Logos, the Word of God, who appeared first to Moses and the prophets, and then was made flesh for the salvation of all humankind. Justin conceives of revelation as a soteriological process, but he tends to assign the Christ-Logos a universal scope and significance. This doctrine shows in the theme of the *Logos spermatikos* ("generative Logos"). Before Christ there existed *spermata tou Logou* ("seeds of the Logos"): these seeds are participations in the form of an inferior and partial knowledge, which only Christ, the incarnate Logos, can bring to completion. In virtue of this participation, pagan thinkers were able to perceive some rays of truth and to merit the title of Christians (*Apol.* 1.46.2–3). In thus making the Logos the focal point, Justin placed revelation under the sign of knowledge.

The esteem for and recourse to Greek philosophy that are already to be found in Justin are even more evident in Clement of Alexandria (died before 215), whose system of thought is based on a theology of the saving and revealing Logos. Clement does not hesitate to give priority to knowledge of God over salvation (*Str.* 4.136.5). By opting for a Logos who is source of light and truth, Clement makes revelation a

Christian "gnosis," thus responding to the desire for knowledge that was the inspiration of his cultural milieu. "The Father's face is the Logos, by whom God is brought out of his hiddenness and revealed" (*Paed.* 1.57.2; *Str.* 7.58.3–4). As Light of the Father, the Logos reveals everything that exists in the world, everything that enables human beings to understand themselves and to share in the life of God. Knowledge which God offers in its fullness and which brings salvation to human beings: such is the context in which revelation takes place. Only the incarnate Logos, and not the gnostic mysteries, bestows "the revelatory initiation of Christ." There is no doubt that knowledge of God has first place in Clement's thinking, even more than the history of salvation. Consequently, the Logos is our sole teacher. We are "God's pupils: it is his very own Son who gives us instruction that is truly holy" (*Str.* 1.98.4; *Prot.* 112.2). The incomparable superiority of Christianity is due to the fact that it has the Logos for its teacher (*Str.* 2.9.4–6), from whom it receives a teaching superior to any other. Before Christ came, philosophy had given the Greeks a kind of third testament to lead them to Christ. Once Christ came, philosophy is at the service of faith. It is now the incarnate Logos who teaches us how human beings can become children of God; he is the universal teacher who joins together the Law and the Prophets, and the gospel. The historical dimension of salvation is maintained by acknowledging stages, but it is subordinated to the principle of complete knowledge. True gnosis exists only in Christianity, but its source is God, who through it leads human beings to a salvation that is inseparable from Christ.

Origen (d. 253/254) also develops his ideas on revelation by taking at his starting point the Logos, who is the faithful image of God. "In the Word, who is God and image of the invisible God, we see the Father who begot him" (*Com. Jo.* 32.29). Revelation takes place because the Word becomes flesh and, in ways proper to the incarnation, i.e., through the flesh of his body and the flesh of Scripture, makes it possible for us to understand the invisible, spiritual Father. The Logos is mediator of a revelation that begins with creation and moves on to the Law and the Prophets, and the gospel. Revelation reaches its first summit in the incarnation of the Logos. But for Origen revelation is less a sudden descent of the Logos into history than

an advance of all things toward the Spirit. The incarnation of the Logos marks the beginning of a progressive knowledge that moves from shadows and images to truth. ORIGEN stresses the passage from preparations to fulfillment, but he stresses even more the passage from signs to reality: from flesh to spirit, shadows and images to truth, letter to spirit, temporal gospel to eternal gospel. The important thing is not so much the incarnation as the recognition and understanding, under the action of grace, of the coming of God. Thus Origen emphasizes, more than Clement does, the subjectivity of revelation. The enlightenment that was inaugurated by faith gives rise to a progressive understanding of revelation: a movement from an ever better understood temporal gospel toward the eternal gospel, i.e., the reality behind the mysteries dimly embodied in the temporal gospel. The content does not change, but it is gradually unveiled; it undergoes a spiritualization until it is definitively grasped in the vision of God. Origen, like Clement, welcomes the effort at an inculturation of Greek philosophy, but he does not go so far as to speak of a testament for the pagans.

The thought of the Alexandrians, whose aim was to bring the church out of its isolation and into an encounter with Hellenistic culture, represents a positive effort at reconciliation with the ancient world, but it also brings with it the danger of an excessive "intellectualization" of biblical revelation, since it conceives of this as a gnosis, a teaching, a higher doctrine. This current of thought, which runs the risk of cutting revelation off from its historical connections, exerted an influence on the whole of later theology, down as far even as the recent council. In the posttridentine period and in such theologians as Suarez and De Lugo, revelation is increasingly understood as a doctrine, a set of truths about God. The complaints voiced on the eve of Vatican II all emphasized the impoverishment which the idea of revelation had suffered due to an intellectualism that had reduced revelation to the communication of a system of ideas rather than to the manifestation and self-giving of a Person who is Truth.

Economy and Pedagogy of Revelation

If the patristic thought of the first centuries was able to avoid the dangers just mentioned, it was because it had never lost contact with the categories of the Bible. Above all, it never ceased to reflect on the history of salvation. This focus on history served to counterbalance a conception of revelation as pure knowledge. In this regard, the theology of IRENAEUS, which was a response to the Gnostics, is a point of reference which no historical account can overlook.

In a sense, the Gnostics raised the idea of revelation to its supreme height, inasmuch as, in their view, knowledge or gnosis came from on high by way of enlightenment. Gnosticism thus became a rival of Christianity by leaving history behind. It turned away from the historical Jesus and focused on the spiritual Christ. Christ retained his role as mediator, but in a distorted form; the church was therefore obliged to redefine this role more carefully in the context of the history of salvation.

In his response to Gnosticism, which opposed the NT to the OT, Irenaeus emphasizes the unity of the history of salvation. As a result, the theme of revelation is linked to the broader theme of the action of the Word of God, who is both creator and savior. With the aid of his concept of "economy" or "arrangement," Irenaeus stresses the organic unity of the history of salvation. The one God brings to fulfillment, through his one Word, a single plan of salvation that reaches from creation to the vision of God. Under the guidance of the Word the human race is born, grows, and matures until the fullness of time (AH 4.38.3).

To the Gnostics, who distinguished Christ from the fleshly Jesus, Irenaeus opposes the theme of the economy and makes the incarnation the high point of this economy that had its beginnings in the OT. More than that: since the Word is present to the whole of time, he reveals the creator God from the very beginning, from the moment of creation (AH 4.6.6; 2.6.1; 2.27.2). "Through both the Law and the Prophets the Word proclaimed himself and proclaimed his Father" (AH 4.6.6; 9.3). Finally, by his coming in the flesh, the Son "gave us all newness by giving us himself" (AH 4.34.1). The novel element of Christianity is the human life of the Word; this does not mean a new God, but a new manifestation of God in Jesus Christ. The incarnation is a theophany of the Word of God, and the advance which this marks consists in the human, fleshly presence of the Word, who has now become visible and palpable among human beings in order to make known to them the Father who remains invisible (AH 4.24.2). The OT is the time of the promise; the NT brings the fulfillment of the promise and the gift of the Word made flesh. The two TESTAMENTS form a tear-proof fabric. Irenaeus highlights the events of the history of salvation and closely connects the OT with the "fourfold gospel." The apostles are the link between Christ and the church (AH 1.27.2; 4.37.7), but Christ is the keystone of the entire building.

Almost all the fathers—notably Justin, Clement, Origen, Basil, Gregory of Nyssa, and Augustine—join Irenaeus in emphasizing this "economic" aspect of revelation. Revelation is seen as an infinitely wise plan of salvation which God conceives from all eternity and patiently carries out, following ways he foresees, preparing the human race, educating it, bringing it to maturity, and progressively revealing to it what it is capable of grasping at any moment. The fathers, and Irenaeus in particular, are fond of reviewing the steps taken by God to "accustom" human beings to his presence.

Connected with this idea of gradual stages is that of the period of waiting before the coming of Christ. The *Letter to Diognetus* says that humanity had to experience its helplessness before experiencing the fullness of salvation (salvation viewed as a drama). Irenaeus, Clement, and Origen (in some passages) develop the thesis of the divine pedagogy: God educates humanity to receive the fullness of divine gifts in the incarnation (optimistic view). For Augustine and for Origen (in other passages), the problem hardly arises, since the church is coextensive with humankind and began with the patriarchs. The truth of Christ was already known to the prophets of the OT.

In thus constantly recalling the stages of this economy and this pedagogy, the fathers are constantly asserting the historical nature of revelation: its profound connections with history in the preparation for it and the proclamation of it, in its fullness in Jesus Christ, and in its communication to the whole world through the apostles and the church. There are variations in this overall view, especially regarding the place assigned to the prophets and the apostles, as well as the importance assigned to philosophy. But for all the fathers revelation culminates in Christ, the Son of God, the incarnate Word or Logos and, therefore, the perfect revealer.

Central Place of Christ

All the fathers of the church see Christ as the high point, the culmination, of the history of salvation. As Word of God and Son of the Father, he assumes all the ways of being incarnate—word as well as action—in order to make the Father and his plan of salvation known to us. Most often, however, it is to the human words of Christ that they assign the principal role. This priority shows in the terms they use: word of God, word of Christ, good news or gospel, teaching, doctrine of the faith and of salvation, precepts, commandments, and ordinances of God or Christ, rule of truth, rule of faith, and so on. According to Ignatius of Antioch, Irenaeus, and Athanasius, incarnation and revelation are inseparable.

For Ignatius of Antioch the whole of revelation and the whole of salvation are to be found in the person of Christ. "There is only one God, and he has manifested himself through Jesus Christ, his Son, who is his Word that has come forth from silence" (*Magn.* 8.2; 6.1–2). All the manifestations of God in the OT were ordered to his definitive manifestation in the incarnation: "The knowledge of God is Jesus Christ" (*Eph.* 15.1; *Magn.* 9.1). To the Judaizers, who see the gospel and the prophets as opposed and who subordinate the gospel to the official records of the OT, Ignatius opposes the person of Christ, in whom everything is reduced to unity, hope, and fulfillment: "As for me, my official record is Jesus Christ; my inviolable records are his cross and his death and his resurrection and the faith that comes from him" (*Phil.* 8.1–2). Christ is "the Door through which Abraham, Isaac, and Jacob and the prophets and the apostles of the church all enter. All of them lead to oneness with God" (*Phil.* 9.1). Christ is the only savior and revealer.

Irenaeus likewise sees the whole of revelation as leading to the incarnation of the Son. "Through the Word made visible and palpable the Father made himself known" (*AH* 4.6.6). The incarnate Son does not provide us with a merely abstract knowledge of the Father; he is the Father's living manifestation. This does not mean that the Son is by his nature visible; he is by nature invisible, like the Father, but the incarnation makes him visible, and the many ways which the incarnation opens up enable him to manifest the Father (*AH* 4.6.6). Irenaeus

thus sees revelation as the epiphany of the Father through the Incarnate Word. Christ or the Incarnate Word is the visible, apprehensible one who manifests the Father, while the Father is the invisible one whom the incarnate, visible Son manifests. Irenaeus thus sets up a practical equivalence between the incarnation, viewed concretely, and revelation; the two are interchangeable.

Athanasius distinguishes two aspects in the manifestation of the Word through his incarnation: the manifestation of Christ as a divine person, and the communication by Christ of the teaching of salvation. Despite the Law and the Prophets human beings have forgotten God; they have sinned. Out of "condescension," out of love for humankind ("philanthropy"), and in order to restore the image of the Father in human beings, the Word of God became flesh (*De Inc.* 8), "the manifestation of God to humanity" (*De Inc.* 1). He contacts human beings at their level; as a result, they will be able to recognize, "through his bodily works, the Word of God who is in the body, and, through him, the Father" (*De Inc.* 14). Just as the invisible Word manifested himself through his work of creation, so the Incarnate Word makes himself known through his works of power, his miracles (*De Inc.* 16). Like Origen, Athanasius says: "The Word . . . became visible in his body in order that we might have an idea of his invisible Father" (*De Inc.* 54). Further, the incarnation enabled Christ to make the doctrine of salvation known to human beings (*De Inc.* 52) and to urge them to faith.

While acknowledging the central role of Christ, Greek theology is less attentive to the role of the incarnation as such. Thus Justin and Clement see Christ primarily as teacher and source of all truth, and revelation primarily as the communication of absolute truth and true philosophy. Origen stands at the meeting point of these two theologies. For him, Christ reveals in the sense that by means of his enfleshment we can gain an idea of the Word and, through the Word, the image of the Father, an idea of God himself. The Alexandrians looks upon Christ as the one who brings light to minds that are plunged in darkness. We see in these thinkers the Platonic nostalgia for the world of light and for its contemplation by the intellect.

Inaccessibility of God and Knowledge of God

The heresy of Eunomius, in the fourth century, caused the Cappadocians to go back to the problem of Christ's centrality, but from a new point of view. Eunomius was in effect saying that once the divine essence was revealed, it was no longer mysterious. In response to this error, Gregory of Nazianzus, Basil, and GREGORY OF NYSSA state it as their faith that God remains ineffable and inaccessible even after having revealed himself: he is the mysterious darkness whose depths no one can plumb completely. Even the great confidants of God, men like Moses, David, Isaiah, and Paul, say that the essence of God remains a mystery. What we know of the hidden depths of God comes to us from Christ. He alone penetrates the thick darkness of our ignorance. Our faith, says Gregory of Nyssa, comes "from our Lord Jesus Christ, who is the Word of God, Life, Light and Truth, God and Wisdom, and all this by his nature." "Let us be convinced that God has appeared in the flesh, and let us believe this only true mystery of religion, which has been passed on to us by the Word himself, who spoke directly to the apostles" (*C. Eunom.* 2.45.466–67).

Like the Cappadocians, John Chrysostom stresses the fact that God, even after revealing himself, remains the invisible, ineffable, inscrutable, inaccessible God who cannot be circumscribed or represented; he remains always abyss and darkness. What we know of God has been revealed to us by Christ and his Spirit (*Jo. Hom.* 15.1).

The Cappadocians, like the Alexandrians, are especially attentive to the subjective appropriation of truth and to its fructification in the soul through faith and the gifts of the Spirit. Under the enlightening action of the Spirit, the soul penetrates more and more deeply into the mysteries of the Son and the Father, in a never finished and ever more passionate search for truth. The Spirit sheds its light in the soul, which, under the influence of this enlightenment, becomes increasingly transparent and spiritual. The Spirit alone, says Basil, "knows the depths of God, and creatures receive from him the revelation of his mysteries" (*De Sp. S.* 24).

The Two Dimensions of Revelation

This emphasis on the enlightenment of believers by the Spirit leads us to a final characteristic of revelation that is stressed by most of the fathers of the church and is especially developed by Augustine, who derives it from John and also from Platonic and neoplatonic philosophy. To the exterior action of Christ who speaks, preaches, and teaches, corresponds an interior action of grace, which the fathers, following the Scriptures, describe as a revelation, an attraction, an interior audition, an illumination, an anointing, a testimony. At the same time as the church proclaims the good news of salvation, the Spirit works within the hearers to help them assimilate the word they have heard and make it bear fruit in them.

The Alexandrians emphasize this second dimension of revelation, but it is Augustine who more fully explains its function and working. The words of Christ are not mere human words, but have two dimensions, an exterior and an interior, because of the grace that accompanies and animates his words. Augustine develops this thought especially in his commentary on John 6:44: "No one can come to me unless drawn by my Father," and in his *De gratia Christi*, which is directed at Pelagius. To "come to Christ" means to experience a drawing by the Father; it means to believe. It was this drawing, which is a gift, that enabled Peter to confess Christ as Messiah. Christ speaks his words, but it is the Father who enables human beings to accept them, due to the drawing toward the Son which the Father produces in the soul. To *receive* the words of Christ, Augustine goes on to say, is not simply to hear them exteriorly, i.e., "with the ears of the body," but to hear them "in the depths of the heart" (*Jo. tr.* 106.6). To hear with the interior ear, to obey the voice of Christ, to believe: these are all one and the same thing (*Jo. tr.* 115.4). Augustine stresses this point: the word heard exteriorly is nothing unless the Spirit of Christ acts within us to make us realize that the word we hear is addressed to us personally: "Jesus Christ is our teacher, and his anointing instructs us. If this inspiration and anointing are lacking, the words will sound in our ears to no effect" (*Ep. Jo. tr.* 3.13). This grace is both attraction and light: an attraction that appeals to the forces of desire, a light that makes us see Christ as the truth in person. The Council of Orange, adopting the views of Augustine, would later say that no one can assent to the teaching of the gospel and perform a salutary act "without the illumination and inspiration of the Holy Spirit, who gives to all ease and joy in assenting to the truth and believing it" (DS 377; ND 1919)). Human beings receive a twofold gift from God: the gift of the gospel and the gift of the grace to assent to the gospel in faith (*De grat. Christi* 1.10.11; 26.27; 31.34). Put more universally: Christ, as Word of God, is the sole light of human beings and the source of all knowledge, natural as well as supernatural. Augustine delights to describe Christ in the language of John, as the Way, the Truth, the Light, and the Life.

Let me say by way of conclusion that the themes developed by the fathers of the church in connection with the points I have listed are too important not to be given a place in a theology of revelation. On a number of points, these themes dispel the darkness introduced by an approach developed outside the biblical categories or dependent on a rationalist philosophy.

For medieval thought on revelation see the article on THOMAS AQUINAS, the chief witness from that period.

6. New Questions and the Answers of the Magisterium

Viewed diachronically, the statements of the magisterium pick up without any break the thinking of the patristic and medieval periods. As a rule, the magisterium intervenes only to correct or condemn a serious deviation from the truth. During the first centuries and throughout the Middle Ages, the existence of revelation was never challenged. In any case, there was never an anathema or condemnation suggesting a denial of the fact of revelation or an adulteration of the concept. The controversies that occupied the attention of the church had to do mainly with the Trinity, the incarnation, and the mysteries of Christ. No one thought of denying or calling into question that God had spoken to humanity through Moses and the prophets and then through Christ and the apostles.

The fullest medieval statement of the idea of revelation is undoubtedly the one issued by the Fourth Council of the Lateran in 1215: "This Holy Trinity . . . communicated the doctrine of salvation to the human race, first through Moses, the holy prophets and its other servants, according to a well ordered disposition of times. Finally, the only-begotten Son of God, Jesus

Christ . . . showed the way of life more clearly" (DS 800–1; ND 19–20). Like the fathers of the church, the council stresses the themes of the economy and the development of revelation, which culminates in Jesus Christ. Like Bonaventure and Thomas Aquinas, it speaks of the doctrine of salvation. Revelation is the fontal action that precedes this doctrine, but it is the doctrine on which attention is focused. The word *revelation* is not yet used.

Until the convocation of the Council of Trent, the Protestant controversy with its *sola scriptura* principle, as well as the excesses of Protestant illuminism, which saw each believer as having an immediate revelation of the Spirit, caused theologians to turn their attention away from the historical and incarnational aspect of revelation and to become preoccupied chiefly with objective revelation, the message of faith, and the guarantees of its divine origin.

The Council of Trent and Protestantism

Though early Protestantism did not directly call the idea of revelation into question, it nonetheless threatened it. Thus Calvin (→ CALVINISM), in his *Institution de la religion chrétienne* (bk. 1, chap. 5, no. 2), allows that God manifests himself to human beings through the works of creation, but he immediately adds that human reason has been so seriously affected by Adam's sin that this manifestation remains useless to us. This is why God has given humankind not only "mute teachers" but also his divine word (bk. 1, chap. 6, no. 1). Thus, of the two traditionally recognized kinds of knowledge of God (through creation and through historical revelation), the first is discredited in favor of the second. Protestantism very soon tended to devalue all knowledge of God except his revelation in Jesus Christ. Moreover, at the same time as it asserted the principle of salvation through grace and through faith alone, it set forth the principle of the sovereign authority of Scripture. The rule of faith consists in Scripture alone, accompanied by the help which individuals receive from the Spirit, who enables them to understand what is revealed and therefore what they are to believe. The testimony of the Spirit in souls is inseparable from the word of God in the Scriptures. The Spirit alone sheds light on the word.

At first glance, Protestantism seemed to exalt

the transcendence of revelation, since it did away with any intermediary between the word of God and the soul that receives it. In reality, however, it compromised this transcendence, for while asserting the principle of the sovereign authority of Scripture, it resisted the authority of the church (DS 1477), whether located in its tradition or in the current decisions of its teaching office. Protestantism thus risked opting for an uncontrollable inspiration and thereby moving toward individualism or rationalism. This development reached its clearest form in liberal Protestantism, but it had begun as early as the eighteenth century.

The Council of Trent, for its part, endeavored to ward off the most immediate danger, namely, too exclusive a focus on Scripture to the detriment of the church and its living tradition. The conciliar decree on this subject was issued on 14 April 1546, and has this to say:

> The holy . . . Council of Trent . . . has always this purpose in mind that in the Church errors be removed and the purity of the Gospel be preserved. This Gospel was promised of old through the prophets in the Sacred Scriptures; Our Lord Jesus Christ, Son of God, first promulgated it from his own lips; He in turn ordered that it be preached through the apostles to all creatures as the source of all saving truth and rule of conduct. The Council clearly perceives that this truth and rule are contained in the written books and unwritten traditions which have come down to us, having been received by the apostles from the mouth of Christ Himself or from the apostles by the dictation of the Holy Spirit, and have been transmitted as it were from hand to hand. Following, then, the example of the orthodox Fathers, it receives and venerates with the same sense of loyalty and reverence all the books of the Old and New Testaments—for God alone is the author of both—together with all the traditions concerning faith and morals, as coming from the mouth of Christ or being inspired by the Holy Spirit and preserved in continuous succession in the Catholic Church. (DS 1501; ND 210)

Observe, first of all, that the word *revelation* does not appear in this paragraph: priority is given to the word *gospel*, in accordance with a widespread NT usage, i.e., the good news or message of salvation which Christ brought and fulfilled and which is to be preached to every creature (Mk 16:15–16). The council thus conforms to medieval usage and the language of the Council of the Lateran.

The "gospel," or doctrine of salvation, is the object of our faith. Looked at more systematically, the passage contains three statements: (a) the gospel has been given to humanity in stages: first *announced* by the prophets, then *promulgated* by Christ, and finally, at his command, *preached* to every creature by the apostles. This gospel is "the *source* of all saving truth and rule of conduct." (b) This saving truth and this rule of moral conduct, of which the gospel is the only source, are contained in the inspired books of Scripture and in unwritten traditions. (c) The council accepts with equal loyalty and equal reverence both the Scriptures (OT and NT) and traditions "coming from the mouth of Christ or . . . inspired by the Holy Spirit and preserved in continuous succession in the Catholic Church." This is why everything contained in the word of God, whether written or otherwise transmitted (DS 3011; ND 121), must be believed. The one message of the gospel, the one good news, is expressed in two distinct forms: written and oral. In Trent's Decree on Justification, the object of faith is again described as a doctrine, taught by Christ, transmitted by the apostles, preserved by the church, and defended by the church against all errors (DS 1520; ND 1924). In these documents the *message* of salvation, the *doctrine* taught by Christ, is undoubtedly seen as primary in revelation; the centrality of Christ as person, source, mediator, and fullness of revelation, takes second place.

The First Vatican Council and Rationalism

Here, for the first time, a council uses the word *revelation*. But the subject of discussion is not yet the nature and specific characteristics of this revelation, as will be the case at Vatican II, but the *fact* of its existence, its possibility, and its object. As at the Council of Trent, attention is focused less on the original revelatory action than on the result, the object of this action, i.e., the doctrine of the faith and its content: God and his decrees, his mysteries.

If we are to understand VATICAN I, we must recall its historical context. As a result of the European Enlightenment of the seventeenth and eighteenth centuries, the requirements of the thinking subject had come to occupy the first place in the Western consciousness. An inevitable result of this development was to raise the problem of a transcendent divine intervention.

Apart from the Catholic position on this point, three different answers were theoretically possible, and all three in fact were given. One was to reject the hypothesis of a revelation and transcendant action of God in human history: this was the response of Deism and progressivism (DS 3027–28; ND 116–17), which claimed an unqualified autonomy for reason. In this view, faith in a revealed religion meant contempt for the human mind; human beings must therefore cease to behave as "minors," always subservient, always tagging along behind the church. Another answer was to reduce revelation to an especially intense form of the religious sentiment that is universal among human beings: this was the response of liberal Protestantism and the extremists among the modernists. A third and final answer was to eliminate one of the two terms, namely, God. Thus the advocates of an absolute evolutionism, such as the Hegelians, still kept the word *revelation* but emptied it of all its traditional content. In this view, Christianity is simply a stage, now behind us, in the evolution of reason toward its total development.

In response to pantheism and Deism, Vatican I asserts the *fact* of a supernatural revelation, its possibility, its suitability, its purpose, its recognizableness, and its object. In order to understand the significance of the position taken, we must have in mind the individuals who for two centuries had dominated Western thought: individuals mostly Protestant who gradually drifted into RATIONALISM and materialism. In *Germany:* Wolf (1679–1754), Kant (1724–1804), Fichte (1762–1810), Schelling (1775–1854), Hegel (1770–1831), Schopenhauer (1788–1860), Schleiermacher (1768–1834), Strauss (1808–1874), and Baur (1792–1860). *English* rationalism was linked to the philosophy of Bacon (1561–1626), the materialism of Hobbes (1588–1679), and the sensualism of Locke (1631–1704). A continuing drift led to the positivism of Mill (1773–1836) and the scientific evolutionism of Spencer (1820–1903) and Darwin (1809–1882). In *France,* Voltaire (1694–1778) and Rousseau (1712–1778), along with the Encyclopedists, became the teachers of modern laicism. Locke's theories entered France through Condillac (1715–1780), while English positivism as repreesented by Hume, Spencer, and Darwin was introduced by Comte (1798–1857), Taine (1828–1893), and Littré (1801–1880).

As for the immediate context of the council, it is worth keeping in mind the fact that except for a short period of religious romanticism the nineteenth century was influenced above all by the English Deists and the French Encyclopedists. The very idea of the supernatural and of revelation, mystery, and miracle was called into question in educated circles, and the claims of Christianity were debated in the name of historical criticism and philosophy. The then still new science of religions challenged the claim of Christianity to transcendence. The Hegelian Left, in the person of Feuerbach, paved the way for the ATHEISM of Marx, while materialist explanations of the world and human life, developed under the influence of Spencer and Darwin, quickly won public favor.

The four chapters of the Constitution *Dei Filius* of Vatican I set forth the church's teaching on God, revelation, faith, and the relations between faith and reason. I shall concentrate here chiefly on the contribution of the second chapter, which has to do with revelation: less, however, with its nature than with the *fact of its existence,* its possibility, and its object.

In the first paragraph of this chapter (DS 3004; ND 113) the council distinguishes two ways by which human beings can come to know God: the ascending way, which takes creation (*per ea quae facta sunt*) as its point of departure, has the light of reason as its means of knowing, and reaches God, not in his inner life, but in his causal relationship to the world. The second way originates in *God who speaks,* God as author of the supernatural order, who makes himself, and the decrees of his will, known to his creatures. In speaking of the first way of reaching knowledge of God, namely, through the whole of creation, the council does not say whether or not grace is operative in the attainment of this knowledge. The main reason why it asserts that human reason can attain to knowledge of God is that it sees this truth affirmed by the Scriptures (Rom 1:18–32; Wis 13:1–9) and the entire patristic tradition and also that the denial of this truth would lead to religious skepticism.

The second way of reaching God is the supernatural way of revelation: "It pleased His wisdom and bounty to reveal Himself and His eternal decrees in another and a supernatural way, as the apostle says: 'In many and various ways God spoke of old to our fathers by the prophets; but in these last days He has spoken to us by the Son'" (DS 3004; ND 113). Although brief, this passage makes several important points about revelation: (a) It establishes the fact of supernatural and positive revelation as proposed by the OT and NT; (b) This action of God is essentially a favor from God, a gift inspired by love, an effect of God's "good pleasure" (*placuisse*). (c) Though revelation represents a free initiative on God's part, there is a reason for it: it was in keeping with God's wisdom and goodness. It was in keeping with the *wisdom* of God as creator and provider (DS 3001, 3003; ND 327, 413) that the truths of the natural order should be "known by everyone with facility, with firm certitude, and with no admixture of error" (DS 3005; ND 114), and also with his wisdom as author of the supernatural order, since if God raised human beings to this order he had an obligation to make its goal and the means to it known to them. Revelation was also in keeping with the *goodness* of God. The initiative taken by God in emerging from his hiddenness, addressing human beings, challenging them, and entering into personal communication with them is already a sign of his infinite kindness. But the fact that this communication not only facilitates the natural movement of human beings toward God but also makes them sharers in the secrets of his inner life, sharers "in the good things of God" (DS 3005; ND 114)—this is truly the mark of an infinite love. (d) The material object of revelation is *God himself* and the *eternal decrees* of his free will. The next paragraph (DS 3005; ND 114) shows that this object includes both truths accessible to reason and mysteries that transcend reason. By "God" is meant his existence and his attributes, but also the interior life of the three Persons. By "decrees" is meant the decrees concerning creation and the natural governance of the world, as well as those having to do with our elevation to the supernatural order: the incarnation, redemption, the call of the elect. (e) The entire human race is the beneficiary of revelation: it is as universal as salvation itself. (f) The passage from the letter to the Hebrews confirms this teaching about the fact of revelation; it also notes the advance from one covenant to the other. The citation, which fits closely into the text, gives us to understand that revelation is conceived of as God's word to humankind: *Deus loquens . . . locutus est.* The unity and continuity of the two covenants are due to the word of God, the word of the Son being the continuation and completion of the word of the prophets.

The second paragraph completes this initial definition with new specifications regarding the necessity, purpose, and object of revelation. (a) The council says that the reason why revelation is *absolutely necessary* is that "God in His infinite goodness has ordained man to a supernatural end, viz., to share in the good things of God" (DS 3005; ND 114). In the final analysis, then, it is God's intention to save that explains the need for a revelation of truths of the supernatural order. As for religious truths of the natural order, the council uses the language of Thomas to describe this revelation as morally necessary; the necessity here is not due to the object or to the active powers of reason, but to the present condition of the human race. Without revelation, these truths cannot be "known by everyone with facility, with firm certitude and with no admixture of error" (*ST* 1, q.1, a.1; 2–2, q.2, a.4). The encyclical *Humani Generis* (1950) speaks expressly of a "moral necessity." The object of revelation is still the same as that described in the first paragraph, but it is viewed here in terms of its proportion or disproportion to the powers of reason. (b) The word *revelation* can signify not only the action of revealing but also the result of this action, that is, the gift received, the truth revealed. Thus the council is led, in a quite natural transition, to consider revelation in its objective aspect, i.e., the message spoken or otherwise expressed. Repeating the words of the Council of Trent, Vatican I says that this revelation is conveyed in the written books and unwritten traditions "which have come down to us, having been received by the apostles from the mouth of Christ Himself, or from the apostles themselves by the dictation of the Holy Spirit, and have been transmitted as it were from hand to hand" (DS 3006; ND 216). But Vatican I adds something new, not found in Trent: it uses the word *revelation* to designate the content of the divine message: *haec porro supernaturalis* _revelatio._ The words spoken by God and contained in Scripture and tradition are the object of our faith. This is why the council says in the third chapter that "all those things are to be believed . . . which are contained in the word of God, written or handed down" (DS 3011; ND 219).

The human response to God's revelation is faith. The motive for this faith is the authority of God who speaks. Faith, says the council, accepts what is revealed "not because the intrinsic truth of things is recognized by the natural light of reason, but because of the authority of God Himself who reveals them, who can neither err or deceive" (DS 3008; ND 118). This statement evidently has the rationalists in mind. In thus distinguishing between faith and rational knowledge, natural evidence and the assent of faith, the council says equivalently, but without using the term, that God's word belongs to the realm of TESTIMONY. For in fact a message that calls for a response of faith, i.e., which asks for acceptance solely on the authority of the speaker, is in the proper sense a "testimony." On the other hand, faith itself is a gift from God. Using the words of the Council of Orange (DS 377; ND 1919) and the often repeated statements of the Scriptures, Vatican I declares: "No man can 'assent to the Gospel message,' as is necessary to obtain salvation, 'without the illumination and inspiration of the Holy Spirit, who gives to all joy in assenting to the truth and believing it'" (DS 3010; ND 120). The yes of faith to the preaching of the gospel is at the same time a free surrender to the movement of the Spirit.

Vatican I thus regards revelation in the active sense as an action of God for the salvation of humanity, an action by which he makes known himself and the decrees of his will. Yet it is clear that the council's attention is given primarily to revelation in the objective sense. In its Constitution on the Church the council equates revelation and deposit of faith: "The Holy Spirit was . . . promised to the successors of Peter . . . that, with His assistance, they might jealously guard and faithfully explain the _revelation_ or _deposit of faith_ that was handed down through the apostles" (DS 3070; ND 836).

The contribution of Vatican I is reducible to the following points: (1) assertion of the existence, possibility, necessity, and purpose of supernatural revelation; (2) definition of its principal material object: God himself and the decrees of his salvific will; (3) adoption of the term "revelation," in both its active and its objective senses; it thus becomes an official and technical term; (4) use of the analogies of word and (implicitly) testimony to describe this new and original phenomenon; (5) faith, which is a free acceptance of the preached gospel, is made possible by an interior action of the Spirit, who makes the heard message bear fruit. When compared to that of Vatican II, this contribution seems still minimal, but it has to be judged in its context.

The Modernist Crisis

When seen in the light of its ultimate purpose, modernism is the manifestation, in a new context, of an undertaking that must constantly be renewed, namely, to harmonize the data of revelation with history, the sciences, and cultures. The problem is too difficult to be solved at the first try. The effort of the modernists can be understood only in light of the changes which the church of the day had to face in a world being transformed at every level. The modernists' project was religious and intellectual, but they had the misfortune of coming on the scene at a time when an ill-prepared church was alarmed by increasingly antiauthoritarian thinking and felt itself being overwhelmed on every side. Instead of opening itself "to the world of its day," as Vatican II would do, the church thought only of defending itself and condemning. What a contrast between these two periods of history!

The factors at work in the shift of consciousness proper to a culture in gestation were too complex to be understood even by the individuals who have been lumped together under the rubric of "modernists." After all, how is it possible to link together and apply the same label to thinkers as different as M. Blondel, Msgr. Mignot, L. Laberthonnière, G. Tyrrell, Baron von Hügel, and A. Loisy? One thing is sure: no modernist would have recognized himself in the highly organized body of teachings that is presented in _Pascendi._ There was no common modernism but rather tendencies which at the time seemed to be leading to serious and inevitable deviations.

In the long course of reflection on revelation the antimodernist documents represent a moment of crisis in a church still lost in "the labyrinth of modernity" (E. Poulat) and being forced to launch out on uncharted paths. The documents of the period "testify" to a *transition*: churchmen were more concerned to protect and defend than to create and renew. A further point: the same authority cannot be assigned to the decisions of the Biblical Commission, the decree *Lamentabili*, the encyclical *Pascendi*, or the motu proprio *Sacrorum Antistitum* as to a council on the scale of Vatican II.

Reduced to its essentials, the thing the church feared in tendencies carried to their extreme by modernism was that historical revelation would be dissolved into a blind religious feeling which arises from the depths of the subconscious under the impulse of the heart and the inclinations of the will. At this point, modernism reached the positions taken by A. Sabatier. Revelation is reduced to a vague religious experience, and the various religions represent the emergence of this experience into the consciousness of individuals. It is easy to see that, given such deviations, the magisterium should vigorously defend both the historical and the transcendent character of revelation, as well as its doctrinal content. Without denying elements of immanence in revelation, the magisterium refused to reduce it wholly to the realm of immanence. In response to the excesses of modernism, which objected to the idea of revelation as a "divine deposit" or "collection of defined truths" and wanted to substitute for this a revelation that is a human creation emerging from the unconscious and gradually making its way from obscurity to clarity, from unformulated to formulated, the antimodernist oath said that the object of faith is "what has been said, attested to, and revealed by the personal God, our Creator and Lord" (DS 3542; ND 143/5). Revelation is the content of a message, a testimony. Elsewhere in the oath, this content is called doctrine, revealed word, gospel (DS 3538–50; ND 143–143/13). For the first time in an official document the three terms "word" (*dicta*), "testimony" (*testata*), and "revelation" (*revelata*) are used together (DS 3542; ND 143/5). Each of these words takes the content of the previous word and further defines it. *Word:* revelation is addressed to human beings and communicates God's plans to them; *testimony:* the word spoken calls for a

particular response, that of faith; *revelation* is a word that attests; whence the definition of revelation as *locutio Dei attestans*, a definition that would be used for decades and that condenses into a short formula what is said in the Scriptures and in the patristic and theological tradition. What God said, attested, and revealed, the church calls "revealed word," "doctrine of the faith," and "divine deposit" entrusted to it to be guarded without addition or alteration or change of meaning or interpretation. This doctrine is not from human beings but from God.

The antimodernist documents thus contribute a more precise terminology for treating of revelation; at the same time, they display an obvious inflation of the doctrinal aspect of revelation to the detriment of its historical and personal character. In this light it is easier to understand why the documents elicited an allergic response, in preconciliar theology, from such thinkers as de Lubac, Daniélou, Bouillard, von Balthasar, and Chenu, who objected to an intellectualism that tended to turn revelation into the communication of a system of ideas rather than the manifestation of one who is truth in person and goal of a history that has its culmination in Jesus Christ. The excesses of the antimodernist theologians produced a reaction that can be seen in *DEI VERBUM*. The complaints of preconciliar theologians were reducible to two: on the one hand, they feared the reduction of Christianity to an exaggerated intellectualism; on the positive side, they wanted a greater fidelity to what is found in Scripture and tradition. On Vatican II and *Dei Verbum*, see *DEI VERBUM* (commentary on revelation, chap. 1).

7. Systematic Reflection: The Uniqueness of Christian Revelation

Context

The present-day conciliar and postconciliar theology of revelation has not been produced by a spontaneous generation but is the result of a laborious process extending over many years and marked by dramatic tensions. It was born in a context of accelerated change that is well described in *Gaudium et Spes* (nos. 4–10). The scientific spirit has extended its reach to all realms of knowledge: the physical, biological, psychological, economic, and social sciences.

These sciences have, moreover, established themselves apart from philosophy. The philosophies now in favor are the philosophies of existence, of the person, of history, of language, and of praxis (see R. Winling, *La théologie contemporaine, 1945–1980* [Paris, 1983]).

Catholic interest in the theology of revelation was stimulated by the biblical and patristic renewals. One result of the return to the Bible was to give priority to the revelatory word and the revelatory action. In fact, in recent encyclopedias and dictionaries, the articles under the headings of word, language, revelation, and faith are often so extensive and detailed as to be real monographs. Furthermore, there has been a spate of works on fundamental ideas that are needed for an understanding of revelation (e.g., gnosis, mystery, epiphany, witness, testimony, word, truth). Even though the modern study of patristic theology on the theme of revelation has not advanced at the same rate, the theology of revelation has already benefited from the renewal of patristic studies, whether in the form of major collections (*Sources chrétiennes, Handbuch der Dogmengeschichte*) or in the form of monographs (e.g., on Origen, Irenaeus, the School of Alexandria, Gregory of Nyssa, Hilary of Poitiers, Augustine, and others). Meanwhile, Protestant theology has by its abundance and quality contributed greatly to the renewal of Catholic theology. I need only list some of the more important names: K. Barth, R. Bultmann, E. Brunner, H. W. Robinson, P. Tillich, H. R. Niebuhr, G. Kittel, and J. Baillie. Action, event, history, encounter, and meaning are some aspects that Protestant theologians like to emphasize. In the Catholic world, reflection on the status of theology, on the significance of preaching (kerygmatic theology, theology of preaching), on the development of dogma, and on faith have all acted as catalysts. The postwar period then saw the first essays in systematization; these became the starting point for an immense proliferation of monographs on revelation itself, on *Dei Verbum*, and on fundamental theology.

This new awareness of the importance of the theme of revelation did not come about without suffering or without victims. The theology of revelation was developed in a climate of tension between official teaching and scholarship that reflected the new currents of thought. The theology of the manuals was insufficiently

sensitive to the movement of history and to the interpersonal character of both revelation and faith. Its attention was focused more on the objective aspect of revelation than on the revelatory action itself. It was more concerned with preserving doctrine than with making a treasure yield its riches. Freedom of research was severely curtailed by the Holy Office. Typical in this regard was the debate over the "new theology," a debate marked by suspicions, denunciations, and suspensions from teaching.

Typology of Revelation

A good number of the seemingly irreconcilable positions taken in this area are due to the very complexity of revelation, its paradoxes, and the multiplicity of aspects which it manifests. The fact is that revelation is inexhaustibly rich, for it is at one and the same time action, history, knowledge, encounter, communion, transcendence and immanence, progress, economy, and definitive culmination. The sheer number and variety of elements to be considered constantly subject theologians to the danger of emphasizing one aspect to the detriment of another and thus of giving an unbalanced picture. Who would claim to bring out the whole splendor of a cathedral by approaching it from only one angle? It is this needed diversity of approaches that justifies such treatments as A. Dulles's *Models of Revelation* (New York, 1983).

We have already seen in this diachronic study how, due to the context, the reflection of each period has highlighted one or other aspect, without, however, excluding or denying the others. Under Greek influence, e.g., thinkers developed an approach that stressed chiefly the element of knowledge, of higher gnosis, in revelation, to the detriment of the element of personal self-manifestation. Later on, the Gregorian period, which found its climactic expression in Melchior Cano, posited a difference, amounting almost to a discontinuity, between the constitutive period of revelation and the entire subsequent period, which has for its task to expound, explain, and interpret the data of revelation, these being conceived as static and juridical. The result was to obscure the contemporaneity of revelation with the faith of each new believer. During the Enlightenment reason was turned into an absolute, capable of knowing everything: human beings no longer needed to receive anything from God. The response of Vatican I was to reassert revelation as a supernatural gift, although this council did not escape a certain extrinsicism that separated the action of revelation from the content of revelation, thus showing that it conceived of revelation as primarily a doctrine. At Vatican II, revelation was once again seen as centered upon Jesus Christ, who is God revealing, God revealed, and sign of revelation. Christ is the concrete universal whom we are urged to accept in faith.

Adopting a perspective that is both diachronic and synchronic, A. Dulles proposes five basic models of revelation, under which all others can be subsumed. (a) The first model conceives of revelation as primarily a *doctrine*, or body of teaching, that is formulated in propositions which the church offers us for acceptance by faith. The divine origin of this teaching is attested by exterior signs. This model is the one accepted by conservative Evangelicals and by neoscholasticism. It is also defended by the present-day integralist wing of the Catholic church. (b) In sharp contrast with this first model, a second places in the foreground the great events of the history of salvation, which culminate in the death and resurrection of Jesus and which make it possible to interpret past and future history. Revelation thus conceived calls for a response of indestructible hope in the God who promises salvation. This model is represented by O. Cullmann, W. Pannenberg, and G. E. Wright, although these thinkers place the emphases quite differently from one another. (c) In a third model, represented by F. Schleiermacher, A. Sabatier, and G. Tyrrell, revelation is conceived of as being first and foremost an interior experience of grace and communion with God, an experience that is a direct, immediate encounter with the divine. God communicates himself to the soul that abandons itself to his action, and this experience is the channel of salvation and eternal life. According to some of these thinkers, Christ remains the mediator of this experience. In any case, the human response to this mystical experience takes the form of devotional affectivity, the prayer of the heart. (d) A fourth model, represented by K. Barth, R. Bultmann, E. Brunner, and G. Ebeling, conceives of revelation as a "dialectical manifestation." Since God is the transcendent One, the Wholly Other, it is he who comes forth to encounter human beings, who then recognize him by faith. The word of God at once reveals and hides this manifestation of God. God's primacy is unqualified. The Bultmannians, however, stress the point that this unveiling of God is at the same time an unveiling to human beings of their sinful condition. (e) According to a fifth model, revelation has its privileged locus in a shift in the human person's ultimate horizon. What is meant is a new awareness which human beings acquire when confronted with the transcendent action of God who reveals himself, and with the human commitment to human history. Past events are of interest only insofar as they interpret the present. Revelation has power to save insofar as it contributes to a ceaseless restructuring of our experience and of the world itself. This model is represented, though with differing emphases, by M. Blondel, P. Tillich, K. Rahner, G. Baum, G. Moran, D. Tracy, and A. Darlap, and by the theology of liberation as this has developed under the influence of G. Gutiérrez and L. Boff.

Dulles endeavors to save the values of each of these models, not by giving one model a privileged place or by a combination of selected models or by harmonizing the several models, but by "going beyond" them in a way which he sees made possible by symbolic mediation and, concretely, by Christ the symbol who incorporates and completes all the preceding models.

I, too, think that Christ himself provides the only valid approach to revelation, for it is he, the Incarnate Word, who assumes everything, gives everything a new place, interprets everything, and decodes everything. I choose a totalizing approach to Christian revelation, one that makes it possible to bring out its "uniqueness" and its "specific features" and thus to identify it as such, while at the same time distinguishing it from other religions that likewise claim to be "revealed." I shall now set down the features which in my view are specific to Christian revelation.

8. Specific Features of Christian Revelation

Principle of Historicity

The first feature or trait that is specific to Christian revelation is the organic connection between revelation and *history*. It can be said, of course, that all religions are historical in a very general sense of the word, inasmuch as they coexist with history. Christian revelation is special, however, in that it not only exists in history and has its own history: it also develops through historical events, the deeper meaning of which is made known by authoritative witnesses, and it reaches its full form in a supreme event, namely, the incarnation of the Son of God, an event that takes place at a chronologically defined point and in a particular situation and context within universal history. Thus, unlike Eastern philosophies, Greek thought, and the Hellenic mysteries, which allow no place for history or attach little importance to it, the Christian faith is by its nature faced with "events" that have "happened." The Scriptures recount facts, present persons, and describe institutions. In other words, the God of Christian revelation is not simply a God of the cosmos but a God of unexpected interventions and irruptions into human history: a God who comes, intervenes, acts, saves. It would not be possible to speak of OT or NT revelation or of promise and fulfillment, apart from a series of events located in time and in a particular cultural setting, and apart from a series of mediators who act in God's name to make known the "meaning" of this history at it moves toward its definitive completion in Jesus Christ.

This organic connection between revelation and history has never been denied or forgotten, even though, down the centuries, it has sometimes received too little attention. Thus, as we saw above, Vatican I describes revelation as a divine activity whereby revealed doctrine, or the deposit of faith, is communicated to us. It cites Heb 1:1, but the implications of this passage do not play any important part in the description of revelation. Revelation is seen as a descending action which results in teaching about God, but the action has hardly any connection with history. The Christian mind has never forgotten this fundamental aspect of revelation, as is evidenced by the fact that the church has consistently rejected all the constantly reappearing forms of Gnosticism, from Marcion to Bultmann. Vatican II, however, judged it opportune to reassert firmly the historical character of revelation.

Sacramental Structure

Dei Verbum emphasizes no less strongly that revelation is not to be identified with the opaque tissue of historical events. Rather (it says) it is necessary to hold tight to both a history and its authentic interpretation, i.e., both to the fact, on the horizontal plane, and, in the vertical plane, to the *salvific meaning*, which is willed by God and made known by his authorized witnesses: the prophets, Christ, and the apostles. Revelation is both event and commentary on the event. To say that God reveals himself by words and actions (*verbis gestisque*) is to say that he indeed intervenes in history but mediately, through events, works, actions, and persons chosen to interpret these events. God truly communicates with humanity and speaks to it, but through a history that is meaningful and authoritatively interpreted. The event yields its full meaning only through the word. As I said earlier, without Moses the exodus would simply have been one migration among many. This sacramental structure distinguishes Christian revelation from every other form of revelation and avoids every appearance of Gnosticism or ideology. The clear assertion of this structure by *Dei Verbum* represents a revolution, whose implications are felt at every level. E.g., if it be true that Christian revelation takes place through the *verba et gesta* of Christ, then it follows that the transmission of this revelation is not reducible to the communication of a body of doctrine. If it were thus reduced, revelation would become a discourse about God and salvation, but would have no impact on life.

Dialectical Development of Revelation in the Old Testament

The historical nature of revelation affects its *development* as well as its *structure*. Its development takes place in accordance with a twofold dialectical movement: promise and fulfillment on the part of God, and meditative, trustful attentiveness on the part of Israel.

a. In the eyes of Israel, the important thing is not so much the annual cycle, in which everything begins repeatedly anew, as what God *has done, is doing,* and *will do* according to his promises. Promise and fulfillment give this three-dimensional time its dynamics. The present begins the future that has been announced and promised in the past. But the force that sets this history in motion and maintains its forward movement is the intervention of the God of the promise. For it is the promise that makes Israel conscious of history because the promise gives rise to hope of the future event. Because God is faithful to his promises, each new fulfillment leads to hope of a still more decisive fulfillment, and thus constitutes a kind of staging place in the continuous movement of history toward its ultimate goal. This is why Israel does not simply commemorate the past but sees it as a promise of the future. Even eschatological salvation is described in the category of promise, but of an expanded promise and of a fulfillment that will be a transfiguration of the past. The decisive event will be a new exodus, a new covenant, a universal salvation. Thanks to the promise, then, all of history is hastening toward the future and a definitive fulfillment of this history, although the fulfillment cannot be anticipated or clearly defined. On the surface the history of Israel may seem to be one of decline, a journey toward failure, but in reality, at the deeper level of the promise and the history of salvation, it is moving toward the time of fulfillment, which is the time of Christ.

b. The dialectic of promise and fulfillment that marks God's word is matched on the part of Israel by an attitude of meditative attention and of trust in the promise. Since history is the place where Yahweh reveals himself, Israel never stops meditating on the events associated with its birth and growth as the people of God. In particular, the events of the exodus, election, covenant, and Law add up to a kind of prototype for relations between Yahweh and his people, and this prototype provides the key for all later interpretation. In its present form the OT is the product of this centuries-long meditation, always on these same events, a meditation in which the people of God were guided by the prophets and the inspired writers. The great compilations which we call the Yahwist, the Elohist, the Priestly tradition, the Deuteronomist, and the Chronicler arise from this meditation; they represent rereadings of the history of salvation. The unity of the OT is due, therefore, not to the imposition of any logical system but to the succession of events which are promised and then brought to pass by God. The unifying principle is first and foremost the action of God in history, in keeping with a conception of time as not simply linear but as spiraling through circles of ever greater breadth and ever greater intelligibility. Finally, since revelation has taken the form above all of promise and fulfillment, the present time is always seen as a time of watchful waiting, of hope and trust. In Israel's eyes, to believe means to obey and trust; it means to acknowledge Yahweh as the only saving God and to trust oneself to his promises. Even while Israel journeys through time and has the painful experience of its failure and sinfulness, it also lives in expectation of the one who is coming and of the decisive salvation which he is bringing. Israel's hope intensifies as its distress deepens.

Incarnational Principle

Christian revelation is, then, historical. But a second feature must immediately be added which is even more specific to Christian revelation than its historicity, namely, that this revelation comes through the incarnation of the Son of God in the midst of humanity. The incarnation introduces the time of fullness, the moment when the rhythm of history rushes headlong as it were and comes to a point in the person of the Word made flesh. We have here something radically and unqualifiedly new. God not only enters into history but, in order to manifest himself, he takes to himself what is most unlike him: the body and flesh of a human being, with all the perils and limitations of language, culture, and institutions. Christ not only brings revelation: he *is* the revelation, the epiphany of God. And yet the opacity of the flesh becomes the privileged means by which God wills to manifest and give himself to us in a definitve way, in a revelation that will not fade away. The grace of God, says Paul, "has now been revealed through the appearing of our Savior Jesus Christ" (2 Tm 1:10). In Jesus Christ, the Agape of God, i.e., "the goodness and loving kindness [the *philanthropia* or love for human beings] of God our Savior," have "appeared" to us (Ti 3:4). In Jesus Christ, the life that was in God "was revealed to us" (1 Jn 1:2-3). Thanks to the sign which is Christ's humanity, John was able to see, hear, and touch the Incarnate Word. According to the Scriptures, then, the incarnation, in its concrete form, is the revelation of God himself in person. Christ is the epiphanic Word of God. The humanity of Christ is the *ex*-pression of God. In Christ, sign reaches its maximum expressiveness, for it is present to, and addressed by, the fullness of the signified in its fullest form, namely, God himself. Christ is the sacrament of God, the sign of God. *Dei Verbum* has articulated this incarnational principle in an exceptionally concise and substantial passage: "Thus it is he [Jesus Christ, the Word made flesh] who crowns and completes revelation by his whole presence and self-manifestation, and confirms it by attesting that God himself is with us" (*DV* 4).

The incarnational principle has numerous implications for the understanding of revelation:

a. First of all, it is necessary to stress the point that Christ's role as revealer results directly from the incarnation. Revelation and incarnation alike are part of the one mystery of the elevation of human nature and human language. "Incarnation" emphasizes the Son's assumption of flesh in a hypostatic union; "revelation" emphasizes the manifestation of God in the ways provided by flesh and language. But incarnation, like revelation, is the self-manifestation and self-giving of God. In revealing himself God gives himself, and in giving himself through the incarnation God reveals himself.

b. Second, if God truly "humanizes" himself in the incarnation, it follows that all the dimensions of the human are assumed and used to express this absolute person. Not only the words of Christ and his preaching, but also his actions, the example he gives, his attitudes, his behavior toward the lowly, the poor, the marginalized, all those whom others ignore, scorn, or reject, as well also as his passion and death, in short, his entire existence—all this is the means by which he reveals to us his own mystery, the mystery of the life of the Trinity, and our mystery as God's children. Christ involves his whole being in the work of revealing the Father and his love. We must say, therefore, that the love of Christ is God's love made visible and that the words and actions of Christ are the human words and actions of God.

c. Extending the application of this incarnational principle, we can say that by becoming incarnate the Word of God assumes the various cultures of the human race in order to proclaim Christian salvation to each people and to bring these cultures to their completion. Furthermore, although it is true that Christ belonged to a particular culture, nonetheless, by reason of his transcendence as the Absolute, he saves all cultures, including his own, from their deviations and offscourings, purifies them, rectifies them, elevates and completes them.

d. We will understand better the meaning of this incarnational economy if we note that what Christ comes to reveal to all human beings, namely, their status as children of God, means a *new way of life*, a *praxis*. But if this new way of life were revealed solely through oral teaching, the revelation would have been ineffective and without any real influence. God had to "illustrate" this new way of life *by living it*. That is why Christ, who within the Trinity is the Son of the Father, came among human beings to reveal to them their status as God's children and to do so by himself living as a child of God. It is through listening to Christ and contemplating him, through watching him act, that our status as God's children is revealed to us and we learn how God loves his Son and all other human beings, his adopted children.

The Unqualified Centrality of Christ

Since Christ is both the revealing mystery and the revealed mystery, both the mediator and the fullness of revelation (*DV* 2 and 4), it follows that he plays an utterly unique role in the Christian faith, a role that distinguishes Christianity from all other religions, including Judaism. Christianity is the only religion whose revelation is embodied in a person who claims to be living and absolute Truth. Other religions had their founders, but none of these (the Buddha, Confucius, Zoroaster, Muhammad) set himself up as the object of his disciples' faith. To believe in Christ is to believe in God. Christ is not simply the founder of a religion; he is both immanent in history and the completely transcendent One: one among countless others, but present there as the utterly unique One, the Wholly Other.

If Christ is among us as the Incarnate Word, then the signs that make it possible to identify him as such are not external to him, like a passport or a seal authorizing a mission, but emanate from the radiating personal center that is Christ himself. It is because he is in his person, in his innermost being, both light and the source of light that Jesus performs actions, proclaims a message, brings into the world a quality of life and love never before seen or imagined or experienced, and thus causes others to ask what his real identity is. The works, message, and behavior of Jesus belong to a different order; they show that the Wholly Other is present in our world. This man so close to us is in reality the transcendent One; this individual amid countless others is the utterly unique One; the homeless preacher is the Almighty; the man condemned to death is the Thrice Holy One. This double presence captures our attention and challenges us. In this man we see marks of weakness but also marks of glory, great enough to help us make our way into the mystery of his real identity. Jesus is himself the sign to be decoded, and all the other limited signs point to him like a bundle of converging indicators. This mystery of the recognition of the epiphany of the Son among human beings through the signs of his glory is another distinctive and at the same time scandalous feature of Christian revelation.

Principle of "Economy"

One of the principal merits of *Dei Verbum* is that it presents Christian revelation not as an isolated mystery but (following the patristic tradition) as a far-reaching "economy," i.e., as an infinitely wise plan which God unveils and brings to fruition in ways for which he has provided. This economy, which arises from the Father's initiative, enters into history and has its culmination in Jesus Christ, who is the fullness of revelation; it then continues on, under the action of the Holy Spirit, in the ecclesial community, through tradition and Scripture and under the sign of expectation of the eschatological consummation. All the elements of this economy support and shed light on each other and form a whole whose principle of unification and influence is Christ and the Spirit. Let me briefly explain this feature of Christian revelation.

In this economy the OT has the threefold function of preparation, prophecy, and prefiguration, for by making flesh and time his own the Word of God sets his mark on the entire time of the economy of salvation. All that precedes him is a *preparation* for his coming: preparation of a family according to the flesh, preparation of a social setting, preparation of a language as his means of expression, preparation of institutions (covenant, Law, Temple, sacrifices, etc.) and of great events (exodus, conquest, monarchy, exile, restoration), all of which turned the appearance of Christ on the scene into a revelation in a particular situation, a "contextualized" revelation.

Second, the OT as a whole is a *prophecy* of the Christ-event, i.e., it is an adumbration of the eschatological event, an adumbration that takes form over the centuries and arouses expectation and desire of the event itself, unforeseeable and unparalleled though this is in its concrete details. Only when the event comes to pass does the prophecy acquire its full meaning and force. Finally, the OT *prefigures* the eschaton, i.e., represents it symbolically; in this representation the ancient reality (events, institutions, persons) retains its status as historical fact, but at the same time it is enlarged, left behind, and transcended by the presence of Christ among us, our Emmanuel.

For when the Son is present among us, all newness is given to us. The event fulfills and surpasses the expectation.

At the same time, however, when the OT, understood in the light of the gospel, takes on a new meaning, it in turn bestows on the NT a substance and temporal density which it could not have of itself. It is not possible to understand the NT apart from the OT discourse, which is always present just beneath the surface. Without the interpretative key supplied by the OT, how many NT passages, such as the passover meal and the cup of the new and everlasting covenant, would still be obscure to us! As Christ walked along with the disciples on the way to Emmaus, he inaugurated a new era in exegesis, for in his person he *is* the exegesis of the OT, being as he is its outcome and fulfillment.

In Christ the foundational revelation reaches its highest point and acquires its definitive character. But this revelation had to be passed on and perpetuated through the centuries, in order that it might be as present and as relevant as on the first day. In the time of the church revelation enters into its period of expansion, its spread through societies and across time. Looked at as part of the "economy," this new phase of assimilation and inculturation is no less remarkable for its wisdom than the constitutive phase was.

Just as the fullness of revelation in Jesus Christ was prepared for by the election of a people, by a lengthy, patient, gradual formation of this people, and by the development of language and categories that help to express the good news, so the transmission of the revelation is not left to the tender mercies of history and individual interpretation. We need to bear in mind that the fullness of revelation was given to us not by the relatively common intervention of a prophet but by the extraordinary intervention of the Incarnate Word. In like manner, the transmission of revelation is safeguarded by a set of charisms or gifts which are the work of the Spirit: the charism of tradition's apostolic origin, the charism of scriptural inspiration, the charism of infallibility entrusted to the church's teaching office. Not only are these charisms at the service of revelation in order to ensure its faithful transmission; they are also interconnected and in the service each of the others (*DV*, chap. 2).

Such an "economy" is undoubtedly unparalleled, historically unmatched, but then are not Christ and Christianity also unique? If then it be true that a revelation given in history and by means of history cannot (it would seem) escape the vicissitudes of the historical process, we must at the same time never lose sight of the uniqueness of Christian revelation and the special character of its "economy": special in its preparation (election), its development (the prophetic movement), its definitive communication (Christ, the Incarnate Word), its transmission (tradition and inspired Scriptures), its safekeeping and interpretation (the church and the charism of infallibility). In short, just as Christ directs the constitutive phase of revelation, so the Spirit of Christ directs the phase of its spread through the centuries. This kind of unique and utterly individual economy makes it impossible to assimilate Christian revelation to any human gnosis or to other religions that also claim to be "revealed."

Uniqueness and Gratuitousness

Inasmuch as Christian revelation claims to be an intervention of God who acts in human history and climaxes his action with the incarnation of the Son, it is easy to see how it is unique and gratuitous.

Revelation does not come to us as knowledge to be discovered, knowledge communicated by a higher being, but as an unqualified novelty. It originates in the initiative of the living God whose creation of the cosmos does not exhaust the possibilities of his infinite freedom. The gift of revelation is an event that brings into existence a new creation, a new human being, a new calling, and a new way of life. It means a new human condition, one in which human beings become the children of God and the human race becomes the body of Christ. Such a divine initiative cannot be required or compelled by human beings.

If we accept that history is a constitutive element of the human person as embodied spirit, it follows that history is the place of a possible divine self-manifestation and that human beings must look to history in order to determine the time and place where salvation has perhaps reached out to the human race. But, that God has *in fact* emerged from his hiddenness and invited the human race to share his life and that he has in fact intervened in the field of human history, at this time and in this place rather than at some other, now rather than later—this depends on the mystery of his freedom.

This is one of the aspects that is already very strongly emphasized in OT revelation. It is not humanity that discovers God, but Yahweh who manifests himself when and to whom and as he wills. He is absolute freedom. He starts the process by choosing, promising, entering into covenant. And his word, which runs counter to Israel's human and carnal views, brings out even more clearly the freedom and gratuitousness of his plan. This freedom is also shown in the variety and multiplicity of the means he chooses in order to reveal himself. But it shines out above all in his decisive intervention, the incarnation. That God should decide to reveal himself and save humankind by taking to him the flesh and language of humanity and that he should decide to extend this economy by an economy of signs that are homogeneous with it—this is due to the unfathomable mystery of his love. Revelation is no less gratuitous and supernatural than the incarnation and redemption: all three are part of the mystery of the freely bestowed elevation of human nature.

Finally, human beings can only regard it as folly and madness that God should reveal the dimensions of his divine love to humankind (and invite them to share in it) through an economy containing the *cross*. And yet it is by casting himself down into the deepest and most incredible abyss of such a death on the cross that God in Jesus Christ shows his love to be that of one who is Wholly Other. Nowhere more than here is the utter freedom and gratuitousness of revelation to be seen.

As the manifestation of God in Jesus Christ, Christian revelation is a movement in which the mystery of God sheds its light on the mystery of the human person. The human person does not set parameters for God's action or dictate to him the most acceptable forms for his action to take. Rather it is God who becomes the measure for human beings and invites them to the obedience of faith. This is the constant perspective adopted in the Scriptures. Consequently, any conception of revelation that would tend to reduce it to the meaning which human beings are willing to allow it as part of their self-understanding would pervert one of the aspects of revelation that is most clearly attested in both the OT and the NT. Revelation is an utterly free gift of God. When Paul speaks of it he can only stammer in praise of God (Eph 1). Only by renouncing their own views and letting themselves be carried by the Spirit who murmurs within them can human beings grasp something of this mystery of gift and freedom.

With this gratuitousness and freedom of revelation we may connect its *uniqueness*. For, if Christ is the Word of God made flesh, if he is the Son of God present among us and the one in whom God's love for humanity is given its exhaustive expression, then we must conclude, with Vatican I and Vatican II, that the economy brought to fulfillment in and by him cannot be regarded simply as one episode in the history of revelation (*DV* 4). The revelation brought by Christ makes any third testament meaningless. We are now in the end-time. In Jesus Christ God has spoken his unparalleled word and has given us his only Son. All that God wanted to tell humanity about the mystery of God and the mystery of the human person has been said completely in the total and definitive word that is the Word of God.

Dialogical Character

In order to describe the unique relationship which revelation establishes between God and the human race through events and their interpretation, Vatican II follows the lead of the Scriptures and the entire patristic and theological tradition and uses the analogy of the word: God has spoken to humankind. As understood here, the analogy of the word includes the forms of communication attested in the Scriptures: words, dialogue, friendly conversation with human beings. But what depth this analogy reveals when it is applied to God and purified of all its deficiencies! For now it serves to describe the unprecedented encounter of the living God with his creatures through the mediation, first, of Moses and the prophets and then through the flesh, face, and voice of Christ, the Word that is spoken within God and has now been made flesh in order to call human beings and invite them to "communion" with him; the Word that was spoken and became good news; the Word given, handed over, sacrificed in the silence of the cross, where the extended arms and pierced heart speak out the supreme message: God is love. This dialogical structure marks the whole of OT and NT revelation.

As soon, however, as we speak of *analogy*, we are saying that there is as much, and even more, dissimilarity than similarity. On the one hand, it is true that revelation, like faith, engages the mystery of a person and not of a thing, of an "I" who addresses a "You"; an I who unveils the mystery of his own life and thereby makes it known to human beings that the full meaning of human existence is found in encounter with this I and in the loving acceptance of the gift he makes of himself. It is also true that the gospel is not simply an "ineffable"—faceless, without content—encounter with the living God, but rather a proclamation of salvation through Jesus Christ. By reason of its twofold character as message and challenge, within an unveiling of the mystery of God's person, for the sake of a communion of life, the phrase "word of God" obviously calls to mind what human beings mean by the term "word," namely, a higher form of social intercourse by which persons express and address themselves to others in order to communicate.

On the other hand, what a profound chasm there is between these human words and the words of revelation! The one who addresses human beings in the person of Jesus Christ is not simply a prophet but the transcendent One who comes very close to us, the One beyond our reach who becomes palpable, the Eternal One who enters time, the Thrice Holy One who in friendship approaches his creatures, though these have by their sins become wretched rebels against him. God meets these sinners at their own level, as a human being among human beings, and speaks to them through actions and words they can understand. Christ makes known to these sinners his innermost self, i.e., the mystery of his intimacy with the Father and the Spirit. The whole gospel in fact shows God making his love known to us (see Jn 13:1). He continues this revelation to the utmost that love can do. When Christ has exhausted all the resources of word and action and behavior, he gives the supreme witness, which is martyrdom. Thus all that is inexpressible in the Father's love for human beings finds expression in his gift of his Son. Nothing is left for human beings to do but to look and understand. John, who saw the outstretched arms, the water and blood flowing from the side, and the heart pierced by a lance, bears witness that God is Love. In Jesus Christ this Love both expresses itself and gives itself.

Sinners cannot open their hearts to this abyss of love unless there is an interior action that _re-creates_ them from within and enables them to accept the Wholly Other (Jn 6:44; 2 Cor 4:4–6; Acts 16:14). Human beings cannot assent to revelation and make it their own through faith unless they have been gifted with a new source of knowledge and love. The gospel message and the interior action of the Spirit thus constitute the two faces or dimensions of the one Christian revelation: two complementary dimensions which historical circumstances sometimes separate but which are meant, in the plan of salvation, to join and invigorate each other. For without the message human beings cannot know that salvation is coming to them nor can they know what God is doing within them through Christ and his Spirit; on the other hand, without the interior word addressed to

each of them individually, they are unable to surrender themselves to the invisible God and base their entire lives on him. For a chasm always separates human beings from God. They need security, and they find this in what they can touch and see, in an understanding of the universe they inhabit and in the taming of its forces. In revelation, they are called upon to base their lives not on the security their senses can afford but on the word of the invisible God. Without the interior action of the Spirit, they cannot "turn themselves around" and give up relying on what they can see, in order to entrust themselves, in reliance on a promise, to what they cannot see. Thus revelation is a reality objectively given in Jesus Christ, but only thanks to the Spirit can human beings make it their own. Christian revelation is both the self-manifestation and the self-communication of God in Jesus Christ, but under the action whereby the Spirit carries these into the minds and hearts of human beings.

By reason of its dialogical structure, which relates it to, but also distinguishes it from, the words of human beings, Christian revelation, understood as the word of God, is utterly original and special.

Revelation of God, Revelation of the Human Person

Human beings are riddles, mysteries, to themselves. For the deepest reality in them, that which provides the basic horizon against which their being and becoming take shape, is the very mystery of God who stoops to human beings, covers them with his love, and invites them to intimacy with the divine Persons. "In fact," says _Gaudium et Spes_, "only in the mystery of the Word made flesh does the mystery of the human person truly become clear. . . . In revealing the mystery of the Father and his love, Christ, the new Adam, fully reveals human beings to themselves and makes known to them their sublime vocation" (no. 22). "Whoever follows after Christ, the perfect man, becomes himself more of a man" (no. 41).

According to Bultmann, revelation simply makes known the meaning of our existence as sinners saved by faith; when we speak of revelation, we are speaking of human beings in their relation to God. It is true, of course, that revelation unveils for us the meaning of human existence, but (we must immediately add) it is by first revealing to us the mystery of God and of the trinitarian life that it thus reveals to us our own mystery as human beings. Christ is the light that enlightens all human beings, not by an illumination unconnected with them but in and by the very act of making known to us the mystery of the union of the Son with the Father in the Spirit. For God cannot in this way reveal the secret of his inner life except for the sake of a communion and sharing of that life with us.

Although revelation is not first and foremost an anthropology, it does have an anthropological purpose, to the extent precisely that it is light springing from the divine mystery and shed on the mystery of the human person. The greatness of human beings consists in their being called to know God and share his life. If, then, we are to see what is *specific* about Christian revelation in its relation to human beings, we must start from the source of light, i.e., Christ, and not from the darkness it is illumining.

Amid this chaos and darkness Christ appears as the *mediator of meaning:* the one in whom other human beings can locate themselves, unriddle themselves, understand themselves, attain to their completion, and even transcend themselves. When they listen to Christ, they learn something of the reason why they feel isolated, disoriented, anxious, despairing. A light-filled road stretches before them and illumines life, suffering, and death for them. The message of Christ is mysterious, but it is also an everflowing wellspring of meaning.

The essence of this message is that, left to themselves, human beings are only hatred and sin, selfishness and death, but that by grace absolute love enters their hearts in order to bestow on them, if they consent, its own life and love. Christ is the one in whom and through whom this gift is given to us. Being, as he is, Son of the Father within the Trinity and God made flesh in the midst of humanity, he makes us children of the Father, children who possess within us the Spirit of the Father and the Son, the Spirit of love, and he gathers all human beings into oneness in this love. In Christ, too, the deepest truth of the "mystery of others" is made manifest. "Others" are Christ, in whom the Father calls us to love all human beings. "Others" are the son of man, the suffering servant who went hungry and thirsty, was naked, sick, and abandoned, but who was also destined for the glory of the beloved Son. In Christ there are no more "strangers" but only children of the one Father and brothers and sisters of the one Christ. There is now only the love of the Father and the Son, and the love of human beings who are all brought together by the one Spirit. Freedom in turn takes the form of consent to the love that invades the human heart, of openness to the divine friend who asks us to share his life. Death itself is now less a break than a completion and a maturing, a passage of the son or daughter to the Father's house, the definitive encounter with the love that has been accepted in faith. It is in this that *salvation* resides.

The presence of Christ in the world thus proves to be the fulfillment of love. That is its *meaning* and the meaning which it gives to the human condition. If God is love (1 Jn 4:8–10), never has love for God been more like to that love than it was in Christ; never has it been invoked in a more gripping way. In a world ruled by self-interest and self-centeredness, Christ comes as love that is pure and without shadow, love ardent and faithful, love *given, handed over* to the point of sacrificing his life for the salvation of all: *dilexit . . . tradidit seipsum.* In Christ, human beings discover the existence of an absolute love that loves them in and for themselves, without any shadow of rejection, and they discover the possibility of dialogue and communion with this love. It is suddenly revealed to them that the *true meaning of human persons* is to enter freely into the current of the trinitarian life: to enter it "freely," i.e., as persons, without suffering dissolution or loss of the self in the absolute. The *ultimate meaning* of the human person is to respond to the gift of God, to accept this incomprehensible, overwhelming friendship, to answer in our puny way this offer of covenant with the infinite. In the Christian perspective, human beings find their ultimate fulfillment only in expectation and acceptance of the gift of God, the expectation and acceptance of love.

Tension between Past and Present

The message of faith achieved its definitive form through the testimony of Christ's witnesses and confidants, the apostles. At the same time, however, under pain of becoming a message that awakens no echo, it must remain as alive as it was on the day when it was first proclaimed. The people of the twentieth century must be as moved by the message of Christ as were the Jews, Greeks, and Romans of the first century, for the aim of the gospel is to give rise, in the human race, to a dialogue that will end only when history ends. The message was addressed to a particular milieu at a particular moment in time, and yet it must reach out to the human beings of every age, in their always unique historical situation, and answer their questions and their anxieties so as to put them on the way to God. The church transmits the message, but at the same time it must reexpress it in light of the culture, language, and needs of each generation.

Inevitably, then, there is a tension between _present_ and _past_. For, on the one hand, the church must not become attached to the letter of the past, thus succumbing to a kind of primitivism or a romantic view of the sources. And, on the other hand, it must not sacrifice Christ and his message under pretext of responding to the aspirations of the contemporary world, as Bultmann or the liberal Protestantism of the last century did.

In this work of never-ending interpretation and actualization of the message, the church is constantly exposed to a twofold danger: of neglecting the needed adaptation in the name of fidelity to the past, and of compromising the message itself under pretext of the need for perpetual revision. The church can fall victim to stagnation or immobilism or to the passing fashions of the day. One thing is sure: there is an inevitable tension between the past, which is given and peacefully possessed, and the still unclear and uncertain adaptation to the present and immediate future. The church is condemned to live dangerously.

Several pairs of terms—tradition and interpretation (of the message itself), gospel and inculturation (in the presentation of the message), tradition and development (in understanding and formulation)—express, each in its own way, this unique condition of Christian revelation.

In its preaching, the church makes clear its intention of omitting nothing from the message it has received, of changing nothing and introducing no novelty, but rather of keeping the message intact and proposing it according to its true meaning. On the other hand, it also

recognizes that it is obliged to understand the gospel as ever fresh and new, so that it may derive from it new answers to new questions. It must preach the gospel as good news for _today_. It must, says _ECCLESIAM SUAM_, "introduce the Christian message into the current of the thought, expression, culture, customs, and strivings of the human race in its present-day life and activity throughout the world" (no. 68; _AAS_ 56 [1964] 640–41). _GAUDIUM ET SPES_, for its part, recognizes that the church is passing through a new historical age and that at all times it has the responsibility "of scrutinizing the signs of the times and interpreting them in the light of the gospel," in order that it may answer the questions raised by the people of each generation (_GS_ 4). This document adds that "theological study . . . should not lose contact with the people of the day." By observing this rule, theology will help pastors: "they will be able to present the church's teaching on God, the human person, and the world, in a way more suited to our contemporaries, who will then more willingly accept their message" (_GS_ 62). This work of actualizing and presenting the word of God is the continuation of an uninterrupted tradition that started at the very beginning of the church. And in fact Vatican II did in many areas bring the gospel to bear on problems which earlier generations could hardly have imagined, because they are problems created by a new context.

This fidelity to the past, without being enslaved by it, this fidelity amid the process of making the gospel relevant, is admittedly paradoxical, but it is also a specific trait of Christian revelation. To appreciate the seriousness of this tension we need only think of the difficulties faced by many Protestant communions: some are fiercely attached to the letter of the gospel but lack genuine creativity (Protestant communities of a fundamentalist type); others, on the contrary, are overly preoccupied with our contemporaries and their philosophy and are ready, because of this, to sacrifice essential elements of the message. The church understands itself to the guardian of a past that is not a museum but an everflowing, always life-giving wellspring. It relies on the past in order to understand the present; it remains faithful to revelation without watering it down; it remains faithful to Christ without emptying him of his reality; and, on the other hand, it constantly repeats: Christ is present and alive *today*.

Tension between History and Eschatology

Just as there is a tension between past and present, so there is a tension between the revelation given through history and the revelation that will come with the parousia. The attention of many theologians today is focused on this final act of revelation, so much so that at times they upset the balance, so difficult to maintain, between the two terms of this new tension.

There can be no doubt that in the eyes of Scripture the decisive revelatory event has taken place in Christ. In him salvation has been announced and made a reality, and the future has begun. To say that revelation culminates and reaches its completion in Jesus Christ is to say that since Christ is God-among-us as Word of God, the dialogue with God has reached its climax, for in this dialogue God's purpose is not so much to give human beings a certain number of truths, as it is to communicate *himself* through his word. The goal of revelation is therefore attained when through the word love "appears" and when in this word God and human beings meet one another and enter into communion. But in Jesus Christ God has given and communicated himself wholly. Thus the revelation historically given in Jesus Christ is the decisive revelation, the revelation that feeds our faith, our hope, and our love.

The category of *now* (*nunc*) and *today* (*hodie*) characterizes historical revelation. When Christ becomes present, "the time is fulfilled" (Mk 1:15), "the fullness of time" is at hand (Gal 4:4). Though Paul ardently longs for the final self-manifestation of Christ, he nonetheless keeps repeating: it is "now" that the mystery formerly hidden is made known; it is "now" that the righteousness of God has been disclosed; it is "now" that the gospel is preached "so that we may present everyone mature in Christ" (Col 1:25–28). NT revelation is also presented, especially in John, as the *Here I am!* (*ecce*) of a person, namely, Christ, together with the salvation which he makes known and brings.

But this decisive characteristic of historical revelation does not exclude hope and expectation of the glorious Christ. The fulfillment which Christ embodies includes both an *already*

and a *not yet*. Thus while Paul is so zealous in preaching the revelation which Christ has brought, he is no less filled with longing for the eschatological revelation (1 Cor 1:7; 2 Thes 1:7). At the moment of his conversion he was chosen for an "apocalyspe" of the Son of God, but he still awaits the full manifestation of the *glory* of his Lord and the *glory* of all who are configured to Christ (Rom 8:17–19). For "what we will be has not yet been revealed" (1 Jn 3:2). Finally, the church constantly proclaims that the Lord is coming, that he will come. It awaits the return of the spouse and the shining manifestation of what already exists in faith.

It is necessary, however, to emphasize one point: there is an essential difference between the first and the final expectation of Christ, between the revelation given in history and the revelation at the parousia. In the OT, the promise has its fulfillment in a future that has not yet arrived. With the coming of Christ, however, the decisive event in relation to both past and future has now *happened*. With Christ the future has already been given, it has already begun. History has a threshold, an unexpected landing as it were on the ascending stairs, in the person of Christ, who is eternal life among us. Revelation does not simply define God and the human person as "nonworld," but proclaims that God is *in* the world, in order that human beings may live in the world but in movement now toward God in a *here* which is *already* eternal life; they thus begin in time a life that is outside the limits of time and that requires them, like Christ, to pass through temporal death and resurrection to eternal life. Christians have their future behind them, because in baptism they have already passed from death to life. If hope and expectation of the Lord are so strong in Paul and in the church, it is precisely because the decisive event has taken place and guarantees what is to come. If we hope for the *return* of Christ, it is because he has *already come*. It is not the parousia that explains the NT; rather it is the Christ-event, with all that it includes, that explains the future. The future is *certain* because the Christ-event has shed its light on the before and after, which until then were wrapped in darkness. It is the epiphany within history that guarantees the apocalypse, and it is this same epiphany that launches the church ever anew on the paths of conversion, rejuvenation, and holiness, so that it may be worthy to meet its Lord. Every future, that of Christ and that of Christians, will be the *future* of this *now*. The entire future is the future of the revelation given in Jesus Christ.

I think it extreme, therefore, to present revelation as if it were solely promise, expectation, eschatology, apocalypse. In this respect J. Moltmann's theology seems to me to be overly influenced by the pattern of OT revelation. We shall, of course, never reach the point of eliminating the real tension that exists between what has already occurred and what is still to come. Historical revelation itself bears clear witness both to the final manifestation of Christ and to his appearance in history. To reduce the one to the other or to eliminate one or other would thus mean infidelity to the content of revelation.

According to Vatican II, the revelation that befits our real condition as *viatores* or "pilgrims" is the one to which we are given access, and are enabled to make our own, in Christ, who, "by . . . making Himself present and manifesting Himself," "perfected revelation by fulfilling it" (*DV* 4). The council reserves the term revelation to describe first and foremost the historical manifestation of God through the Word made flesh. To describe God's manifestation through his creation the council speaks of his "enduring witness to Himself in created realities" (*DV* 3), and to describe the final event, the parousia, it speaks of the "glorious manifestation" of Christ (*DV* 4). The term "revelation" is thus reserved for God's historical self-manifestation and self-communication in Jesus Christ. Creation and parousia are called "manifestations" of God, while only the manifestation of God in history through the incarnation of the Word is given the name "revelation," which remains the consecrated technical term. Faith and hope are in movement toward the glorious return of Christ, but in Christ the future already belongs to us. When he comes, we shall discover, to our amazement and joy, the one who in faith has already been our everyday companion.

Christ the Criterion of Every Interpretation of Salvation

Christ is the point of departure for any and every theological reflection on salvation and revelation. He is the unique point of reference for the history of salvation and the history of revelation and the sole source of their intelligibility. He is *Archē* and *Telos*, the Beginning and the End, the one who gives all things their ultimate and unequivocal meaning. He is the key to the interpretation of the period preceding and following his coming as well as of all the forms of salvation that precede, are contemporaneous with, or follow upon his historical coming. This view of revelation in Christ as the universal criterion in regard to salvation and revelation is not a sign of contempt for or distrust of other religions; on the contrary, it is the only means of situating them and appreciating their value. To proceed in the opposite direction would be to substitute darkness for the full light and to ask the unexplained to explain the explainer. Consequently, I shall start from Christ, regarded as the "concrete universal," in my effort to determine the relationship between revelation, in the "technical" sense given to the word since Vatican II and *Dei Verbum*, and realities which are closely connected with it and are too often improperly called "revelation." Here, as elsewhere, terminological confusions quickly lead to a confusion of the realities signified.

Revelation and the History of Salvation

The history of salvation is coextensive with the history of the human race. God "ceaselessly kept the human race in His care, in order to give eternal life to those who perseveringly do good in search of salvation" (*DV* 3). But the council does not on that account identify revelation and salvation. Each phase of history that preceded Christ is part of the HISTORY of salvation, but it is not, strictly speaking, part of the history of revelation, since it is not aware of itself even as being part of the history of salvation. Apart from Christian revelation we cannot know with certainty what is going on at the heart of human history. Let me repeat this point: apart from the interpretation given to it by Moses in the name of God, Israel's migration from Egypt would not be part of the history of revelation but would simply be one of the countless migrations scattered through universal history. Salvation is everywhere present, but it is "fully revealed" only in Jesus Christ. It is Christ, taken together with the OT which announces him and prepares the way for him, who makes the history of salvation aware of itself and of its special character in relation to secular (political, juridical, social, economic, military, cultural) history. If this be the case, is it not better to follow the tradition of the church and reserve "revelation" and "history of revelation" for describing first and foremost the revelation given in and through Jesus Christ?

Transcendental (or Universal) Revelation and Special (or Christian, Historical, Categorical) Revelation

How then are we to describe the grace of salvation that is given to all human beings (a grace which some writers also call transcendental or universal revelation), and how are we to define its relationship to Christian revelation?

Let me begin by describing and identifying the reality in question. By "transcendental or universal revelation" is meant the direct and utterly free self-communication of God to every human being who comes into this world (in the present economy). This "elevating" action of God insinuates itself in a mysterious manner into the cognitive and volitional dynamism of the human person. Although it is not an object of reflexive and discursive consciousness, it is nonetheless present as the primary horizon, given along with human existence itself, within which human activity takes place. When human beings surrender to this grace in the depths of their consciences, then, even though they are ignorant of the existence of this grace and of its name and author, they achieve their salvation. It is one thing, however, to acknowledge this interior action of grace, and another to describe it as "revelation."

Scripture, for its part, tells us that the historical revelation given in Jesus Christ can be accepted only by a subjectivity that has been touched by grace. Scripture calls this interior action an "attraction" (Jn 6:44), an "enlightenment" comparable to the light of creation on the first morning (2 Cor 4:4–6), an "anointing" by God (2 Cor 1:22), a "testimony" of the Spirit (1 Jn 5:6), and, only once, an interior "revelation" (Mt 16:17). In the movement toward Christ that takes place in the acceptance of revelation by faith there is someone who acts first. But this interior action remains concealed, so much so that in Matthew 16:17 we see that Christ himself must tell Peter about this action of grace within him.

This interior action of God, which is identically the grace of salvation and of faith, is as it were the *interior dimension* of Christian revelation, for there are not two revelations, two gospels, but only two faces or dimensions of one and the same revelation, one and the same word of God. The interior grace is salvation offered, but not identified as such. It is only through historical, categorical revelation that the saving action of God becomes conscious and is made known in human categories. Only through the gospel do we know of the universal salvific will of God, as well as of the means of salvation that are at the disposal of all human beings. It is, of course, part of the economy of salvation that God's plan in Jesus Christ should be known, made known to others, and brought to the knowledge of the nations. It is also consonant with the rational nature of human beings that the choice of faith, which lays claim on the whole of the person's life, should be made by a conscience fully enlightened as to the seriousness and rightness of this choice.

Revelation, then, reaches its maturity or full form only when the history of salvation is known as positively and certainly willed by God. But the Christ-event alone is the complete and definitive event that not only emerges fully from anonymity but also resists every false interpretation of the history of salvation and is free of all ambiguity. Transcendental revelation remains radically ambiguous apart from the light shed on it by historical and categorical revelation. The directedness of human beings toward the future is an openness to an undefined horizon that can be given a pantheistic or theistic or atheistic interpretation. Only God's revelation in history can eliminate the radical ambiguity that envelops transcendental revelation.

I think it improper, therefore, to use a *theological* terminology that simply identifies history of salvation, grace of salvation, and history of revelation, thus giving the impression that revelation, in an unqualified sense, is first of all the grace of salvation which is given to human beings down the centuries, whereas Christian, historical, categorical revelation is simply a more important episode, a more intense phase of universal revelation, a kind of limited-area revelation, or a subsidiary of transcendental revelation. The truth is that the distinction between universal revelation (grace of salvation) and special revelation (in Jesus

Christ) gives a false idea of the reality. Authentic universal revelation is not anonymous; it is the revelation that takes place in Jesus Christ and bestows the grace of salvation on human beings, whether they come before him or after him. The thing that is *special* is the *concrete universal* realized in Jesus Christ, the absolute universal. This Christian universalism embraces the OT, which is a progressive unfolding of the full revelation, the germinal form of complete revelation, leading to Jesus Christ. If we look at all these factors in reverse order, we obscure the light and keep promoting a confusion that has no basis in Scripture or the magisterium, since for both revelation is seen as the incredible irruption into history of God among us. If we confuse this irruption at a particular moment with the anonymous and universally given grace of salvation which enters human beings without their knowing it, then we add to the already too numerous ambiguities that clutter up theology. *Dei Verbum* carefully avoids these misunderstandings. If we want a suitable word to define the action of this saving grace, we can follow Scripture and speak of an attraction, an illumination, or a testimony, or we can, with Thomas Aquinas, speak of an interior instinct or an interior word. If, in addition, we want to emphasize the fact that Christian revelation involves both an exterior gospel and an interior grace, or the joint action of Christ and his Spirit, we can speak of the interior dimension of the one revelation, the one word of God.

Revelation and the History of Religions

Since Christ is God-among-us and the fullness of revelation, it follows that he provides the only authentic interpretation of all the forms of salvation that preceded or were contemporary with or followed upon his historical coming. It is true that because the grace of salvation makes its action felt in a mind and heart that have the stamp of historicity, it tends to find objective expression in rites, practices, and language. Under the action of this grace human beings sense some mystery of salvation and grope after it. The great religions (e.g., HINDUISM, BUDDHISM), whose main goal is the liberation of human beings, are attempts to interpret this grace which acts within them without their realizing it and without their having a reflexive consciousness of it; but

because they lack a criterion whereby to judge, the interpretation they give of this hidden salvation contains, along with valid elements, other, human ingredients, as well as ambiguities, deviations, and errors. The great religions of human history stand in a positive relation to Christian revelation, but the quality and correctness of their content need to be improved. Christ alone, however, is "the fullness of religious life" (*Nostra Aetate* 2). Even the OT, if taken in isolation, does not give a complete and infallible interpretation of its own revelation, for it has as yet no knowledge of the definitive word that does away with its ambiguities, casts light on its figures, and disperses its shadows. Christ alone makes possible a complete understanding of the OT, as he does of all the religious experiences of the human race. Only the gospel of Christ, as proclaimed by the church, is an event which provides its own infallible self-interpretation, for the source of the interpretation here is God himself in Jesus Christ. The Word does, however, enlighten the various religions in different ways, so that they contain as it were rays of the truth which enlightens every human being who comes into this world (*Nostra Aetate* 2). These religions can be said to represent an *enlightenment* or a *manifestation* of God through the cosmos, through the ways of knowledge, or through other experiences, thus showing the Word acting on humankind: nothing eludes this action, which is the source and standard of all truth. Christian revelation, on the contrary, is a very specific reality, not to be confused with others that are related or contain only partial elements.

Revelation and Experience

In recent times, the theology of revelation has often been linked to the concept of *experience*; this concept, however, is quite ambiguous when applied to revelation. The linkage of revelation and experience originates with the liberal Protestantism of F. Schleiermacher and A. Sabatier. In a reaction against Kant, Schleiermacher (1768–1834) set out to reassert the value of religious feeling and experience. In his view, revelation merges with the immanent religious experience of human beings. What takes place in believers is a personal, imperfect repetition of the consciousness of God which Jesus had in a perfect degree. For A. Sabatier, as for Schleiermacher whom he follows, the essence of Christianity is to be found "in a religious experience, an interior revelation of God that occurred first in the soul of Jesus of Nazareth but occurs again, less luminously no doubt, but unmistakably, in the souls of all his true disciples" (*Esquisse d'une philosophie de la religion* [Paris, 1897], 187–88). Revelation is "a religious experience" that "must be able to be repeated and continued as a present revelation and individual experience" (ibid., 58–59). More recently, in his book *The Present Revelation: The Search for Religious Foundations* (New York, 1972). G. Moran wittingly or unwittingly makes his own the positions of Schleiermacher and Sabatier when he identifies revelation with interior personal experience. This personal experience is not bound to any norm. Scripture deserves respect, but the supreme guide is experience. Revelation is an experience involving two persons, subject to subject. According to Moran, once the objective aspect of the word is given priority, the idea of "Christian" revelation becomes an insurmountable obstacle. Revelation takes place in everyday experience.

A basic ambiguity shows itself once more in these views on the relationship of revelation and experience. Those who maintain them forget that revelation always involves a twofold gift: God *manifests and gives himself,* but there is also something *by means of which* we can receive this gift, namely, the *original, foundational experience* that is the self-consciousness of Jesus, the enlightenment given to prophets, the lived experience which the apostles had of Jesus. On the other hand, there is the acceptance of the foundational revelation by *faith* in the witnesses who were present when revelation was given. In the views I have described, faith in witnesses is confused with the experience of the founding revelation. Before taking the form of an experience of the ever actual word of God in our consciousness and daily life, revelation was, in its original form, an experience of this word in the consciousness of Jesus, the prophets, and the apostles. Our own experience is entirely under the control of faith; it is dependent, i.e., on faith and on the mediated experience of those who witnessed the constitutive revelation. Christian revelation does not involve simply a passage from a common experience to a more intense experience; it involves a qualitative leap, something utterly

new that comes about through the presence of God among us in his Son. The category "experience" is not adequate to explain revelation; to it must be added the historical mediation of Christ, the prophets, and the apostles, and the mediation of faith in these authoritative witnesses. These two kinds of experience may not be confused and assimilated to one another. A correct concept of Christian revelation avoids two extremes: an immanentism that for practical purposes does away with revelation in Jesus Christ, and an extrinsicism that would turn this revelation into an object exclusively of an assent of the mind to truths inaccessible to it.

If, then, we may speak of a real, conscious experience in the proper sense of the term, it is to be found first of all at the level of foundational revelation. Thus the self-consciousness of Jesus as Son of the Father is revelation *at its source.* The depth and extent of this self-consciousness are beyond our grasp. In Jesus there is a holy of holies, a sanctuary, for his origin is in the trinitarian life of God, which expresses itself in and through the humanity of Jesus. This self-consciousness does, however, become accessible to us in the signs and glimmers of it which the Gospels give us: through such words as ABBA, which points to a unique and utterly personal intimacy with the Father; in the parables describing the Father-Son relationship, e.g., the parable of the murderous vinedressers; or in the saying reported in Mt 11:27 and Lk 10:21–22, which shows that there exists in Father and Son a reciprocal knowledge which is also a communion of life. Prophets too enjoy a privileged experience, thanks to the light which overwhelms them, elevating their minds and enabling them to perceive what they would be incapable of discovering by themselves. So dazzling is this light that prophets grasp, without explicit reasoning, that God is the source of the light they have received and of the truth which this light reveals to them. Prophets are not only recipients of revelation through faith, as we are, but also vehicles of revelation and sources of its expansion. We have no way of grasping, however, the way in which the two levels of revelation—constitutive revelation and revelation received by faith—intermesh in the consciousness of prophets. Finally, the apostles had a unique and privileged experience of Christ

(1 Jn 1:1-3). We share in their experience of the Word of life only through the mediation of their testimony and through faith in this testimony. The experience to which they bear witness is inexhaustibly rich. No one can compete with the apostles when it comes to knowledge of Christ. Their experience is unique in the history of revelation; it marks the dawn of the new creation. The apostles did not transmit the whole of this bountiful experience, and indeed they could not have transmitted it in its entirety. Their preaching and even their manner of life could not express completely the ineffable part of this unique personal experience. What is set before us for our response of faith is the apostolic testimony, i.e., the testimony of those who saw and heard and who attest that they saw and heard. Faith in the testimony of Christ and the apostles is not, however, merely an assent of the mind; it is the fruit produced conjointly by preaching and interior grace. But in the normal dealings of God with humanity, this grace is not the object of a *conscious and reflexive experience* and cannot strictly be called "revelation."

Revelation and the Light of Faith

Following the lead of Scripture, the patristic tradition and theological reflection have always emphasized that revelation reaches into the human subjectivity, elevates it, and transforms it so that it may apprehend the gospel message as a living word addressed to it personally. The fathers and theologians have never failed to call attention to the combined action of the exterior word and the interior word. Can this interior grace, which echoes the exterior word and enables the soul to apprehend it, be therefore called "revelation"? As we saw earlier, the Scriptures use the words attraction, testimony, teaching, illumination, anointing, opening of the heart, and, sometimes, revelation. Thomas Aquinas speaks of an interior instinct (*ST* 2–2, q.2, a.9, ad 3) and an interior word.

Interior attraction and good news of the gospel are closely connected, but the attraction is not strictly speaking revelation; furthermore, we know of its existence only from the sources of revelation rather than from psychological reflection on the lived experience of our faith. The attraction of the true and of what is true for the person are so bound together in the dynamics of the intellect that apart from exceptional cases of mysticism, reflexive consciousness cannot distinguish them. The influence of this attraction is real and indeed decisive in the assent of faith, for it is what enables believers to adhere to the gospel and to the God of the gospel. It is first in the order of efficient causality, but it is not the gospel nor a new word. In a discourse that makes rigorous use of theological terms, the attraction cannot be described as "revelation": it urges persons to believe, it makes it possible for them to believe, but it retains its anonymity; it is rather an inspiration or illumination of the Spirit (DS 3010; ND 120). It can at times be called a *testimony* (in a broad but not improper sense) of the God who acts within and whose action carries the guarantee of uncreated truth. But this testimony remains obscure.

Let me define now the relationship between these two factors. They are complementary, they are ordered each to the other and constitute the two *dimensions*, as it were, of the one word of God. God calls and asks for faith through the gospel of Christ and the preaching of the apostles and the church and, additionally, through the interior inclination and attraction which he produces in the soul. There is thus a joint action of the exterior proclamation and the interior attraction. The attraction adapts itself to the exterior testimony, undergirds it, subsumes it, vitalizes it, and makes it fruitful. What Christ and the apostles say is carried into the soul by the Spirit, who causes it to take root there. The interior attraction has for its purpose to make this new and inconceivable world of the kingdom connatural to the person; it is at the service of the gospel. In the sphere of revelation the mission of the Spirit supplements and completes the mission of Christ. The gospel makes Christ and his plan of salvation known; the attraction causes it to be effectively received (disposes the soul to listen and gives the gospel power over it). Because of this interior dimension, revelation is a word of a unique kind. To its effectiveness as exterior word is added a special effectiveness which reaches into the depths of the subjectivity, into the heart of cognitive and volitional action, in order to initiate the response of faith. This grace that moves, rouses, calls, anticipates, and sustains is a grace of enlightenment, but it cannot on this account claim the name of "revelation."

Scandal and Superabundance

All the features or traits which I have been describing, taken together and with their qualitative distinctions, in their contrasts and multiplicity and complexity, make up the "face" of Christian revelation and account for its *specific character.* Christian revelation is therefore not faceless or lacking in contours; it is not so little distinguishable from other forms of religion that we must be content with a vague pan-revelationism. On the contrary, Christian revelation can be located in time and recognized by its well-defined characteristic features. But there is more to be said. The set of traits I have listed shows us that Christian revelation possesses two further characteristics which emerge when we consider this set of traits *as a whole:* these are the element of scandal and the element of superabundance.

a. Christian revelation appears, especially to the eyes of our contemporaries, to be something *scandalous* and even unintelligible. This trait applies to revelation at all its levels. There is the scandal, to begin with, of a revelation that comes to us in the frail and impermanent form of events and is therefore exposed to all the ups and downs of history. The scandal, second, of a revelation that makes its way to us through the flesh and language of the Incarnate Word, a tenuous figure, a point lost in the history of a culture and a nation, which themselves are as naught amid the great powers of this world. The scandal, finally, of a revelation whose spread through the centuries is entrusted to the hands of a church made up of wretched sinners. The self-emptying of God in the history of Israel, the self-emptying of the Son in the flesh of Christ, the self-emptying of the Spirit in the weakness of those who make up the church: these successive suppressions, as it were, of God, which are crowned by the scandal of love being supremely revealed in the visible, tangible form of a crucified man, turn all human ideas upside down. To tell the truth, this is not the kind of *extraordinariness* we would have expected from the Absolute and the Transcendent. And yet this very reversal of our human views, this scandal, is a fundamental characteristic of the revelation of God as the *Wholly Other.* Human beings will never succeed in coping with this scandal unless they rid themselves of their self-sufficiency and open themselves to the love offered to them.

b. A second characteristic that marks the combined features of revelation is the *superabundance* to be seen in the salvation which revelation makes known: superabundance in the means of communication and expression; superabundance in the ways of announcing and preparing for the climactic event, the incarnation of the Son; superabundance in the charisms that accompany and safeguard the spread of revelation through the ages (tradition, inspiration, infallibility); superabundance, finally, in the gifts and means of salvation. This superabundance, which already marks God's work in the universe, is also a characteristic of the history of salvation. The surprising thing is not the salvation offered to all human beings; it is rather the superabundance of salvation that accompanies the Christian revelation. By comparison with universal salvation and with the historical religions, Christian revelation represents a superabundance in the gifts of salvation that displays the prodigality of God in the new creation. The astonishing thing is the *superabundance of God's love* for sinful humanity. It is not inconceivable to us that God should emerge from his silence and declare his love for humankind. But that he should express this love so exhaustively, namely, in the gift of his very self and in the abyssal depths of the cross—*that* is the manifestation of an abounding and superabounding love. In the face of this "superabundance," which is a "signal" calling Christian revelation to the attention of all human beings, no other response is possible than love: "So we have known and believe the love God has for us" (1 Jn 4:16).

Revelation and the Trinity

The interpretative key that unlocks the secret of revelation is to be found, in the final analysis, in the mystery of mysteries: the Trinity, and especially in the theology of the trinitarian missions and of appropriation.

Revelation is the work of the entire Trinity: Father, Son, and Spirit. The Trinity unfolds its spiritual fruitfulness along the two lines of thought and love; whence the speaking of the Word and the spiration of the Spirit. The speaking within the Trinity is continued in a speaking that terminates outside the Trinity, and this is revelation. Christ's words have their origin in the communion of life between Father and Son, and for this reason they are the words of God. The Spirit prolongs the mission of Christ, but he does not do so by speaking of himself; rather he illuminaes the words of Christ in a communion of life with the Son, who is also in communion with the Father. Revelation is not the truth of a single person but the truth of the three persons. It has its roots in the communion of life of the three persons, and it translates this communion.

Although the Father, the Son, and the Spirit are a single source of revelation, it does not follow that the Trinity as such has no influence on revelation. Rather each of the persons acts according to effects which correspond in a mysterious way to what Father, Son, and Spirit respectively are within the Trinity.

As in all matters, the Father takes the initiative, since the Son receives everything from the Father: his nature and his mission. It is the Father who sends the Son to reveal his love-inspired plan (1 Jn 4:9–10; Jn 3:16); it is the Father who bears witness to the Son and his revelatory mission through the works he enables the Son to perform (Jn 10:25; 5:36–37; 15:24; 9:41); it is the Father, again, who draws human beings to the Son through an interior attraction which he produces in hearts (Jn 6:44).

Since within the Trinity the Son is already the eternal Word of the Father, the Word in which the Father completely expresses himself, he is ontologically qualified to be the supreme revelation of the Father to human beings and to initiate them into their life as the Father's children. Christ is the perfect revealer of the Father and his plan. But the Father's plan is to extend the very life of the Trinity to the human race. The Father's will is to beget his Son anew in each human being, to breathe forth his Spirit in them, and to join them to himself in the closest possible communion, so that all may be one as the Father and the Son are one, in the one same Spirit of love. If we accept the testimony of the Father to the Son, he makes us his very own children (Jn 1:12). Consequently, we receive a filial spirit, a spirit of love: "God has sent the Spirit of his Son into our hearts, crying, 'Abba! Father!'" (Gal 4:6).

While the Son "makes known," the Spirit "inspires." He is the warm breath of the divine thought. Christ sets the word of God before us; the Spirit adapts it to each of us and interiorizes

it so that it may remain in us. He makes the word "soluble" in the soul through the "ointment" which he pours out there. He makes the gift of revelation effective. It is the Spirit, too, who actualizes revelation for each generation down the centuries. The Spirit responds to the questions of each age by means of suggestions which are his gift.

In this way the Father, through the joint action of the Word and the Spirit, who are, as it were, his two loving arms, reveals himself to the human race and draws it to him. The movement of love by which the Father reveals himself to human beings through Christ, and the return of this love by human beings through faith and charity, are thus seen as immersed, so to speak, in the constant exchange of love that unites Father and Son in the Spirit. Revelation is an action that involves both the Trinity and humankind; it brings about an uninterrupted dialogue between the Father and the children whom he has acquired through the blood of Christ. It unfolds both at the level of historical events and at the level of eternity. It begins through word and faith, and it reaches its completion in the face-to-face vision.

9. Conclusions

I shall focus on three conclusions. The first one, obviously, will have to do with the very idea of revelation.

Idea of Revelation

Christian revelation is the self-manifestation and self-gift of God in Jesus Christ; it takes place in history, as history, and through the mediation of history, i.e., of events or actions that are interpreted by God's authorized witnesses. This manifestation has characteristics that are entirely specific to it and make of it something unique and unprecedented: historicity; sacramental character; dialectical, spiraling advance through time; incarnational principle; absolute centrality of Christ, the Word made flesh; "economy" and pedagogy; dialogue of love; revelation both of God and of human beings to themselves; tensions (past-present, history-eschatology). The uniqueness of this revelation makes Christ the key for interpreting everything that is connected with this revelation or resembles it: the universal grace of salvation; the experience of the historical religions; the illumination of faith. All these features of Christian revelation form, as it were, a vast galaxy of which Christ is the center, the universal reference point of interpretation. The uniqueness of Christian revelation makes it possible to identify it and at the same time to distinguish it from all the religions which likewise claim to be "revealed."

Implications for "Communication"

After what I have said about revelation and its specific features, it is quite clear that it is "communicated" in a different way from a philosophical system, a scientific discovery, or a piece of industrial technology. Revelation is communicated through *testimony*. Just as the testimony of Christ was inseparably both a *docere* and a *facere*, so the communication of the gospel includes both the practice of a filial way of life and the proclamation of the faith. In fact, it was by the combined testimony of their teaching and their life that the apostles passed on what they had learned about Christ "from living with Him and what He did" (*DV* 7). The church, in turn, "in her teaching, life, and worship perpetuates and hands on to all generations all that she herself is and all that she believes" (*DV* 8 and 10). The *communication* of revelation means that those who communicate and proclaim salvation are at the same time the living witnesses of a faith that has first enlightened and transformed their own lives. Otherwise the gospel is in danger of becoming an ideology, a system, a gnosis, an ethic.

In the Christian scheme of things, COMMUNICATION shares in the elevation of the human person by the incarnation and by grace. The mass media are, as it were, "gifted" with a new dimension that is due to the specific character of Christian revelation. For, (1) what is communicated is the gospel, the revealed, inspired, and efficacious word; (2) those who communicate and urge others to faith are themselves living witnesses of the gospel they set forth; (3) the hearers of the word are human beings in whom the Spirit of Christ is at work. The technologies used are the same (radio, television, film, press), but the reality communicated, the communicators, and the "hearers" all reflect a unique state of affairs.

The "Today" of Revelation

The "today" of the message of salvation that was proclaimed by Christ remains ever present and is addressed to every human being. Salvation comes *today*; the time for conversion is *today*. Salvation is not at the journey's end, but at each moment of our lives: today, now. Current injustices, ever-present war, terrorism, genocide: these should help to reactivate in each person a sense of the "today" aspect of the salvation which revelation makes known. Human beings are no less "hideous" than yesterday. Injustice and hatred elicit a desperate appeal to the Suffering Servant for a kingdom of justice and love. God still directs history as he did in the time of the patriarchs and the prophets. When we are stifled and suffocated by so much violence, the silence of God turns us to revelation. Human beings today are like those of the OT: they are waiting for peace, justice, truth, life, love, salvation. In the secret of their hearts they are looking for a meaning for everything in a world apparently without meaning. To these lost human beings who walk in darkness Christ, the fullness of revelation, says: I am the Way, the Truth, the Light, the Life, and Love. To all he says: I AM. Nothing is impossible to God, provided he finds us to be of "good will."

Bibl.: Encyclopedias, dictionaries, collective works: E. ROLLAND, "Révélation," in M. Brillant and M. Nédoncelle, eds., *Apologétique* (Paris, 1937), 197–229; J. DIDIOT, "Révélation divine," *DAFC* 4:1004–9; J. GUILLET and H. HAAG, "Révélation," *DBS* 10:586–618; K. PRÜMM, "Mystères," *DBS* 6:1–225; J. R. GEISELMANN, "Rivelazione," in H. Fries, ed., *Dizionario teologico* 3:162–73; N. JUNG, "Révélation," *DTC* 13(2): 2580–2618; G. RUGGIERI, "Rivelazione," in *Nuovo Dizionario di teologia*, 1332–1352; id., "Rivelazione," in *Dizionario teologico interdisciplinare* 3:148–66; C. COLOMBO, "Rivelazione," in *Enc. Cattolica* 10 (1953): 1018–25; G. GLOEGE, "Offenbarung," in *Die Religion in Geschichte und Gegenwart* (*RGG*) (3rd ed.; Tübingen, 1960), 1597–1613; H. FRIES, "Die Offenbarung," in *MystSal* (Einsiedeln/Zurich/Cologne, 1965), 1:159–235; M. SEYBOLD, P.-R. CREN, U. HORST, A. SAND, P. STOCKMEIER, "La révélation dans l'Écriture, la patristique, la scolastique," (Paris, 1974) (transl. of *Handbuch der Dogmengeschichte*, vol. 1, *Das Dasein im Glauben*, Fasc. 1a, *Die Offenbarung*, Freiburg 1977); C. DUQUOC, "Alliance et Révélation" in *Initiation à la pratique de la théologie*, 2:5–76; R. SCHNACKENBURG, H. VORGRIMLER, "Offenbarung," in *Lexikon für*

Theologie und Kirche 7:1104–16; J. JENSEN, "Concept of Revelation in the Bible," *NCE* 12:436–38; A. DULLES, "Theology of Revelation," *NCE* 12:441–44; S. WIEDENHOFER, "Révélation," in P. Eicher, ed., *Dictionnaire de théologie* (Paris, 1988), 664–72; W. EICHRODT, "Offenbarung im AT," *RGG* 4:1599–1601; N. SCHIFFERS, K. RAHNER, "Revelation," *SM* 5:342–55, 358–59; A. OEPKE, "Apokalyptō," *TDNT* 3:563–92; O. PROCKSCH, "Word of God in the OT," *TDNT* 4:91–100; H. WALDENFELS, L. SCHEFFCZYK, "Die Offenbarung von der Reformation bis zur Gegenwart," in *Handbuch der Dogmengeschichte*, vol. 1, fasc. 1b; W. KERN, H.-J. POTTMEYER, M. SECKLER, *Handbuch der fundamentaltheologie* (Freiburg, 1985, 1986), vol. 2; B. MAGGIONI, "Rivelazione," in *Nuovo Dizionario di Teologia biblica* (Turin, 1988), 1361–76.

Monographs and articles: J. BAIERL, *The Theory of Revelation* (New York, 1927); R. BULTMANN, *Der Begriff der Offenbarung im Neuen Testament* (Tübingen, 1929); H. HUBER, *Der Begriff der Offenbarung im Johannes Evangelium* (Göttingen, 1934); E. F. SCOTT, *The New Testament Idea of Revelation* (New York/London, 1935); K. BARTH, *Church Dogmatics*, vol. 1, 1 (Edinburgh, 1936); D. DEDEN, "Le Mystère paulinien," *ETL* 13 (1936): 403–42; H. W. ROBINSON, *Record and Revelation* (Oxford, 1938); id., *Inspiration and Revelation in the Old Testament* (Oxford, 1946); id., *Redemption and Revelation* (London, 1947); J. FEHR, *Das Offenbarungsproblem in dialektischer und thomistischer Theologie* (Leipzig/Freiburg, 1939); B. DECKER, *Die Entwicklung der Lehre von der prophetischen Offenbarung von Wilhelm von Auxerre bis zu Thomas von Aquin* (Breslau, 1940); R. GUARDINI, *Die Offenbarung: ihr Wesen und ihre Formen* (Würzburg, 1940); E. BRUNNER, *Offenbarung und Vernunft* (Zurich, 1941); S. MOWINCKEL, "La connaissance de Dieu chez les prophètes de l'A. Testament," in *Revue d'hist. et de phil. rel.* 22 (1942): 69–106; J. BRINKTRINE, "Der Begriff der Offenbarung im Neuen Testament," *Theologie und Glaube* (1942): 76–83; A. M. FAIRWEATHER, *The Word as Truth: A Critical Examination of the Christian Doctrine of Revelation in the Writings of Thomas Aquinas and Karl Barth* (London, 1944); L.-M. DEWAILLY, *Jésus Christ: Parole de Dieu* (Paris, 1945); H.-H. SCHREY, *Existenz und Offenbarung* (Tübingen, 1946); C. A. SIMPSON, *Revelation and Response in the Old Testament* (New York, 1947); K. BARTH, *Das Christliche Verständnis der Offenbarung* (Munich, 1948); H. SCHULTE, *Der Begriff der Offenbarung im Neuen Testament* (Munich, 1949); J. WOLFF, *Der Begriff der Offenbarung* (Bonn, 1949); V. WHITE, "Le concept de révélation chez saint Thomas," *L'Année théologique* 11 (1950): 1–17, 109–32; P. TILLICH, *Systematic Theology*, 3 vols. (Chicago. 1951–1963); G. E. WRIGHT, *God Who Acts* (London, 1952); S. VAN MIERLO, *La Révélation divine* (Neuchâtel, 1952); A. MARC, "L'idée de Révélation," *Greg* 34 (1953): 390–420; J. K. JEWETT,

Emil Brunners's Concept of Revelation (London, 1954); A. NEHER, *L'essence du prophétisme* (Paris, 1955); H. R. NIEBUHR, *The Meaning of Revelation* (New York, 1955); H.-M. FÉRET, *Connaissance biblique de Dieu* (Paris, 1955); E. FÜLLING, *Geschichte als Offenbarung* (Berlin, 1956); J. BAILLIE, *The Idea of Revelation in Recent Thought* (London, 1956); F. GILS, *Jésus Prophète d'après les Synoptiques* (Louvain, 1957); J. DANIÉLOU, L. BOUYER et al., *Parole de Dieu et liturgie* (Paris, 1958); M. HARL, *Origène et la fonction révélatrice du Verbe incarné* (Paris, 1958); H. SCHLIER, *Wort Gottes* (Würzburg, 1958); J. ALFARO, "Cristo glorioso, Revelador del Padre," *Greg* 39 (1958): 222–71; S. CAIAZZO, *Il concetto di rivelazione: Idea centrale della teologia di E. Brunner* (Rome, 1959); H. HOLSTEIN, "La Révélation du Dieu vivant," *Études* 81 (1959): 157–68; C. F. H. HENRY, ed., *Revelation and the Bible* (London, 1959); W. BULST, *Offenbarung, Biblischer und Theologischer Begriff* (Düsseldorf, 1960); J. G. S. THOMSON, *The Old Testament View of Revelation* (Grand Rapids, 1960); A. TORRES CAPELLÁN, "Palabra y Revelación," *Burgense* 1 (1960): 143–90; H. NOACK, *Sprache und Offenbarung* (Gütersloh, 1960); A. LÉONARD, A. LARCHER, C. DUPONT et al., *La Parole de Dieu en Jésus Christ* (Paris, 1961); P. S. BULGAKOW, *Dialog zwischen Gott und Mensch: Ein Beitrag zum christlichen Offenbarungsbegriff* (Marburg, 1961); W. ZIMMERLI, *Gottes Offenbarung* (Munich, 1961); A. NYSSENS, *La Plénitude de vérité dans le Verbe incarné: Doctrine de S. Thomas d'Aquin* (Baudouinville, 1961); H. GONZÁLEZ MORFÍN, *JesuCristo: Palabra y palabra de JesuCristo* (Mexico, 1962); J. BLANK, "Der Johanneische Wahrheitsbegriff," *BZ* 7 (1962): 163–73; J. CAHILL, "Rudolf Bultmann's Concept of Revelation," *CBQ* 24 (1962): 297–306; A.-C. DE VEIR, "Revelare-revelatio," *Recherches Augustiniennes* 2 (1962): 331–57; R. SCHNACKENBURG, "Zum Offenbarungsgedanken in der Bibel," *BZ* 7 (1963): 2–23; H. Urs VON BALTHASAR, *Word and Revelation* (1960; New York, 1964); id., *The Glory of the Lord: A Theological Aesthetics*, vol. 1 (San Francisco, 1982); K. RAHNER, R. LATOURELLE et al., *The Word* (New York, 1964); J. OCHAGAVÍA, *Visibile Patris Filius* (Rome, 1964); A. DULLES, "The Theology of Revelation," *TS* 25 (1964): 45–58; id., *Models of Revelation* (New York, 1983); id., "Revelation in Recent Catholic Theology," *Theology Today* (1967): 350–65; K. RAHNER and J. RATZINGER, *Revelation and Tradition* (New York, 1964); R. LATOURELLE, *Theology of Revelation* (Staten Island, 1966); G. MORAN, *Theology of Revelation* (New York, 1966); G. G. O'COLLINS, "Revelation as History," *The Heythrop Journal* 7 (1966): 394–406; H. R. SCHLETTE, *Epiphanie als Geschichte* (Munich, 1966); G. SEGALLA, "Gesù Rivelatore del Padre nella tradizione sinottica," *Rivista Biblica* 14 (1966): 467–508; E. GUTTWENGER, "Offenbarung und Geschichte," *Zeitschrift für Katholische Theologie* 88 (1966): 223–46; E. SIMONS, *Philosophie der Offen-*

barung (Stuttgart, 1966); K. McNAMARA, "Divine Revelation," *ITQ* 34 (1967): 3–19; E. SCHILLEBEECKX, *Revelation and Theology* (London/New York, 1967); J. ALFARO, "Encarnación y Revelación," *Greg* 49 (1968): 431–59; A. DULLES, *Revelation and the Quest for Unity* (Washington, DC, 1968); G. O'COLLINS, *Theology and Revelation* (Dublin, 1968); W. PANNENBERG, *Revelation as History* (New York, 1968); K. RAHNER, *Hearers of the Word* (New York, 1969); E. KLINGER, *Offenbarung im Horizont der Heilsgeschichte* (Zurich, 1969); H. WALDENFELS, *Offenbarung* (Munich, 1969); H. VERWEYEN, *Frage nach der Möglichkeit von Offenbarung* (Düsseldorf, 1969); T. CITRINI, *Gesù Cristo: Rivelazione di Dio* (Venegono, 1969); C. TRESMONTANT, *Le problème de la Révélation* (Paris, 1969); E. LÉPINSKI, *Essais sur la Révélation et la Bible* (Paris, 1970); E. CASTELLI, ed., *Rivelazione e Storia* (Rome, 1971); H. BOUILLARD, "Le Concept de Révélation de Vatican I à Vatican II" in var., *Révélation de Dieu et langage des hommes* (Paris, 1972); J. WALGRAVE, *Unfolding Revelation* (London, 1972); G. EBELING, *Wort und Glaube* (Tübingen, 1975); P. FRUCHON, *Existence humaine et Révélation* (Paris, 1976); P. RICOEUR, E. LÉVINAS, C. GEFFRÉ et al., *La Révélation* (Brussels, 1977); P. EICHER, *Offenbarung: Prinzip neuzeitlicher Theologie* (Munich, 1977); I. DE LA POTTERIE, *La Vérité dans S. Jean*, 2 vols. (Rome, 1977); P. KNAUER, *Der Glaube kommt vom Hören* (Cologne, 1978); G. VOLTA, "La nozione di Rivelazione dal Vaticano I al Vaticano II," in var., *La teologia italiana oggi* (Brescia, 1979), 195–244; S. BRETON, *Écriture et Révélation* (Paris, 1979); E. C. RUST, *Religion, Revelation and Reason* (Macon, 1981); B. TESTA, *Rivelazione e Storia* (Rome, 1981); H. PFEIFFER, *Offenbarung und Offenbarungswahrheit* (Trier, 1982); P. HELM, *The Divine Revelation: The Basic Issues* (London, 1982); J. W. ABRAHAM, *Divine Revelation and the Limits of Historical Criticism* (Oxford, 1982); H. PFEIFFER, *Gott offenbart sich: Das Reifen und Entstehen des Offenbarungsverständnis in ersten und zweiten Vatikanischen Konzil* (Frankfurt, 1982); H. DE LUBAC, *La Révélation divine* (Paris, 1983); A. SHORTER, *Revelation and Its Interpretation* (London, 1983); A. DARTIGUES, *La Révélation: du sens au salut* (Paris, 1985); J. ALFARO, *Rivelazione cristiana, fede e Teologia* (Brescia, 1986); A. TORRES QUEIRUGA, *La Revelación de Dios en la relatización del hombre* (Madrid, 1987); C. GEFFRÉ, "La Rivelazione e l'esperienza storica degli uomini," in R. Fisichella, ed., *Gesù Rivelatore* (Casale Monferrato, 1988), 87–99; T. CITRINI, "La Rivelazione, centro della Teologia fondamentale," in R. Fisichella, ed., *Gesù Rivelatore*, 87–99; R. FISICHELLA, *La Révélation: La Révélation et sa crédibilité* (Montreal/Paris, 1989); L. ELDERS, ed., *La doctrine de la révélation divine de S. Thomas d'Aquin* (Vatican City, 1990); J. DUPUIS, *Jésus Christ à la rencontre des religions* (Paris, 1989); H. VERWEYEN, *Gottes Letztes Wort* (Düsseldorf, 1991); T. G. GUARINO, *Revelation and Truth* (London/Toronto, 1993).

Treatises and manuals of fundamental theology: Most of these works contain one or several chapters concerning the theme of revelation. We include the most recent. J. ALEU, *Teología Fundamental* (Madrid, 1973); W. JOEST, *Fundamentaltheologie: Theologische Grundlagen und Methodenproblem* (Stuttgart, 1974); G. CAVIGLIA, *Le ragioni della speranza: Teologia fondamentale* (Turin, 1979); C. SKALICKY, *Teologia fondamentale* (Rome, 1979); A. BENI, *Teologia fondamentale* (Florence, 1980); H. WAGNER, *Einführung in die Fundamentaltheologie* (Darmstadt, 1981); G. O'COLLINS, *Fundamental Theology* (New York, 1981); G. BOF, *Teologia fondamentale* (Rome, 1984); F. SCHÜSSLER FIORENZA, *Foundational Theology: Jesus and the Church* (New York, 1985); H. WALDENFELS, *Manuel de théologie fondamentale* (Paris, 1990); H. FRIES, *Fundamentaltheologie* (Graz, 1985); A. KOLPING, *Fundamentaltheologie*, 3 vols. (Münster, 1968, 1974, 1981); S. PIÉ-NINOT, *Tratado di Teologia fundamental* (Salamanca, 1989).

René LATOURELLE

REVELATIONS, PRIVATE

After the coming of Christ no new revelation is to be expected concerning the fundamental situation of humanity in relation to its salvation. In and through Christ God has made fully known his universal plan of love. This revelation is regarded as having ended with the death of the last apostle. But during the present stage in the economy of salvation there is still room for divine revelations intended to enlighten the faithful about the way they should behave in the circumstances of their lives and to guide them in their practical, social, spiritual, and religious activities. The adjective *private*, which is added to distinguish them from the earlier revelation (sometimes called "public" because it is addressed, through the ministry of the church, to the human beings of every time and place), does not mean that these revelations are necessarily meant only for a single individual. In fact, they often apply to an entire group, an entire milieu, or even the entire church at a given moment of its history. It would undoubtedly be better to call these revelations "special" or "particular," as the Council of Trent does (DS 1540; 1566). This is the terminology I shall use here.

1. Sacred Scripture and particular revelations are not mutually exclusive. Revelations of the second kind are not to be defined by the fact that they are outside the biblical setting but by their object, purpose, and addressee. If these elements are particular, then the revelations are particular and remain such even if guaranteed by biblical inspiration, since the latter does not alter their characteristics but only ensures their authenticity. The Acts of the Apostles is full of examples. After having proclaimed on Pentecost the age of the Spirit, who works through visions, dreams, and prophecies (2:16–21), Peter learns through a particular revelation how he should act in regard to Cornelius the centurion (10:3–8). Paul is converted as the result of a revelation he receives on the road to Damascus (9:3–9), and he will be constantly guided in his missionary activity by particular revelations (16:9; 18:9; 20:23; 27:23–24), to which are to be added those revelations of a strictly personal and mystical kind about which he tells the Corinthians (2 Cor 12:1–6). Before the book of Revelation sets forth its symbolic visions having to do with the theology of history, it communicates to the various churches particular revelations which have to do less with doctrine than with the life of a specific community or even an individual (1:4–3:22). Finally, the Christian prophets whom the Pauline letters list immediately after the apostles (1 Cor 12:28; Eph 2:20; 4:11) do not limit themselves to exhorting, edifying, and interpreting, but sometimes have a real revelation to communicate from God (1 Cor 14:29–30). This last-named activity seems to be beyond all others the specific prophetic function.

2. In the patristic period two documents especially are to be noted: the *Didache*, which assigns prophets an important place in the community but also sets down rules for distinguishing between true and false prophets (11.7–12: SC 248:184–88), and the *Shepherd of Hermas*, whose numerous revelations of an apocalyptic kind are chiefly a call to repentance and conversion of life. Even a churchman like Cyprian attaches a great deal of importance to particular revelations, whether his own or those of his entourage, and he relies on them in his pastoral ministry (*Ep.* 11.3–4: CSEL 3:497–98)—a reliance which, however, did not please everyone (*Ep.* 66.10: CSEL 3:174). Augustine is more reserved.

He accepts the existence of private revelations, but he thinks it very difficult to distinguish between true and false ones (*De Genesi ad litteram* 12.13.28: PL 34:465).

3. Worth noting in the medieval period are the spiritual writings that take the form of collections of communications from God to holy women. One of the best known of these women is Bridget of Sweden (d. 1373). The Council of Basel had put on its agenda an examination of her revelations, and this was the occasion of the first systematic treatises on the discernment of particular revelations; these came from the pens of Jean Gerson (d. 1429), whose *De probatione Spirituum* urges prudence above all else, and John of Torquemada or Turrecremata (d. 1468), whose *Defensorium super revelationes S. Birgittae* formulates principles that were later adopted by theologians and spiritual writers.

4. In the modern period, the type of mystical theology that achieved predominance thanks to the Spanish school of the sixteenth century recommends an attitude of complete impartiality and detachment in regard to particular revelations. John of the Cross is extremely harsh, at least in the way he expresses himself. The desire for divine gifts and the pleasure taken in them are a major obstacle to union with God, since this union takes place only through pure faith. The attitude to be adopted is obvious: particular revelations are "not to be received," if they come, but on the contrary are to be "resisted" as dangerous temptations (*Ascent of Mount Carmel* 2.27.6). If they are truly supernatural, they will in any case produce their effect of grace, and if they are illusory, the soul will suffer no harm from its resistance. Teresa of Avila is more restrained in her judgment. Visions and revelations play an important part in her life and work. She is not satisfied simply to point out the risks and dangers; she always appreciates the possible good results (*Life*, chap. 25). From this time on, theoreticians of the spiritual life would classify particular revelations among the epiphenomena (i.e., secondary and accidental elements) of mystical experience, which consists essentially in the various degrees of infused contemplation.

And yet, in an extraordinary contrast, this later period has been characterized by an impressive series of major apparitions. Their message is addressed, via humble seers (women or children), to large sectors of the church and even to the universal church. In the seventeeth century there were the appearances of the Sacred Heart at Paray-le-Monial; in the nineteenth and twentieth there have been the Marian appearances at the Rue de Bac in Paris, at La Salette, Lourdes, Pontmain, Fatima, Beauraing, Banneux, and many others. It is impossible to discuss private revelations today without referring to these appearances, since the persons who appear speak, command, instruct, and confide secrets.

5. The criteria of discernment in deciding the authenticity or divine origin of this type of phenomena have gradually been codified. The first criterion is doctrinal and has to do with the orthodoxy of what a particular revelation says. It is not possible for God to contradict his own word, of which the church is the qualified interpreter. Any revelation will therefore be regarded as false if it contradicts a truth of faith or morality. The second criterion is psychological and has to do with the subjects who receive the revelation. Are they well balanced or do they display pathological tendencies? The third criterion is derived from the effects or spiritual fruits produced, whether in these subjects themselves or in those around them. And when the revelations are such as to create a widespread stir among the faithful, the church, in its judgment, takes into consideration the genuineness and breadth of the collective movement of prayer, conversion, and real fervor that flows from the revelations, as well, finally, as any miracles that (it is claimed) are clearly connected with them.

6. In what I may call the mechanism that is at work in particular revelations, there is no necessary opposition between the natural workings of the psyche and divine causality. Until recently it was generally accepted that as long as a natural explanation remains possible, there should be no recourse to a supernatural cause. But particular revelations are not miracles in the strict sense of the term. They do not necessarily suppose a special intervention of God that would suspend the laws of the human psyche. God can use, as his means of communication, the possibilities latent in the imagination, intelligence, and subconscious of the subject. The phenomenon would thus be natural as far as its psychic components are concerned, but supernatural by reason of the actual grace which activates and sets in motion the various processes that can be analyzed, described, and reconstructed by the psychological sciences; this does not mean that the impetus given by grace is itself scientifically observable, for it is of a different, transcendent, and absolutely spiritual order, so that psychology, left to itself in the presence of an event that is supposedly a revelation, will never be able to say that this event is only an ordinary psychic phenomenon.

7. Theologians are not in agreement about the assent to be given to particular revelations. There are two views on the subject. Suarez is the principal representative of the first (De fide, disp. 3, sect. 10, in his Opera omnia, ed. Vivès, 12:90–94). If the origin of the revelation is certain, then the revelation calls for an assent of divine faith, at least from the recipient of the revelation. The motive of faith is the authority of God's word. When this authority is present, it suffices to ground an assent of divine faith, no matter what the object is on which it puts its seal. The difference between divine faith in response to public revelation and divine faith in response to private revelations is purely accidental. In the first case, the revelation is set before us by the church, in the second by God directly, but the motive for the assent is the same in both cases, namely, the authority of God revealing. As for others besides the recipient of a private revelation, they too can and ought to give an assent of divine faith if they have suitable proofs and guarantees of the divine origin of this particular revelation. The Suarezian view has been taken up in our day by K. Rahner ("Les révélations privées. Quelques remarques théologiques," RAMy 25 [1949]: 509).

The second view is that of the modern Thomist school, though not of Thomas himself, since he never explicitly raised the question. It does not deny that a private revelation can give rise to an act of divine faith, but says that this happens only in a case in which God reveals to someone something of the supernatural mystery of God's inner life. The reason is that divine faith not only has the word of God as its motive but also has the mystery of God himself as its object. It is an assent to God when God speaks of God. If God bears witness to something outside his own mystery, there is no room for divine faith to come into play. The Thomist school thus tends to remove private revelations from the domain of divine faith, since these revelations do not usually have as their object truths not contained in public revelation, but are concerned rather with the practice, personal or societal, of Christian life. The assent for which they call is therefore an assent of human faith. By "human faith" is meant not just any assent but an assent that is firm because based on proofs obtained by the exercise of our critical faculties; that depends, not indeed on scientific evidence, but on moral certitude. This is the view taken by Y. Congar ("La credibilité des révélations privées," VSS no. 53 [1937]: 29–43).

8. It is for the magisterium, and in particular the papal magisterium, to express an authoritative judgment on private revelations, to the extent that these awaken a noteworthy echo in the church. When the judgment is one of approval, the approval is usually of a broad kind—i.e., the magisterium does not intend to commit itself authoritatively to a positive statement that the revelation really occurred. It simply permits the spreading of stories which claim to be revelations or to report revelations, and it does so because nothing has been found in them that is doctrinally objectionable or concretely inopportune. Thus the approval has only the negative value of a kind of *nihil obstat*. No one is obliged to believe the stories. This is clear from statements of the magisterium itself, whose practice was explained by Benedict XIV in the seventeenth century: "The approval which the church gives to a private revelation is simply a permission, based on a careful examination, to allow the revelation to be promulgated for the instruction and profit of the faithful. People may refuse their assent . . . to such revelations, even after these have been thus approved by the church . . . provided they do so for good reasons and without intending to cast scorn on them" (*De servorum Dei beatificatione* 2.32.11).

In some exceptional cases, e.g., Paray-le-Monial and Lourdes, because papal approval has been repeated so often and in so unqualified a form, it seems irreducible to a simple permission or a mere *nihil obstat*, but seems rather to

have at last become much more positive. The question has then been asked whether these approvals involve the infallibility of the magisterium or at least the exercise of some incontestable form of its authority. The answers given to the question vary. Unfortunately, they also prove ambiguous. What is it that the magisterium is supposedly guaranteeing in such cases? Is it only the intrinsic value of these revelations, considered from the viewpoint of the message they carry (such a guarantee would not cause difficulty), or is it also something that is less clearly within the scope of the magisterium, namely, the objective reality of the phenomenon (vision, apparition, locution) through which the revelations take form and are communicated?

9. The purpose of private revelations in the church is not the manifestation of new doctrinal truths but a practical direction given to human activity in particular concrete situations in the life of human beings, individually or collectively. Their aim is to "direct our conduct" (John XXIII, on the centenary of Lourdes: *AAS* 51 [1959]: 144). If such revelations do draw attention to certain truths of Christian doctrine, they do so not in order to add to the deposit of faith, but to help us understand the content of these truths in a way better suited to the life of charity, or to highlight and offer for the devotion of the faithful some aspect of the deposit that is insufficiently known or overly neglected. In general, the revelations take the form not so much of doctrinal statements as of moral demands, warnings, and exhortations. They always give an impulse and incentive to a more serious, intense, and fervent spiritual life by fostering growth in faith and in love of God or by urging apostolic and charitable undertakings. Though they occur irregularly and sporadically, these interventions have a permanent part to play in the life of the church to the extent that they are an exercise of prophecy, which according to St. Thomas has for its purpose to direct human activities (*ST* 2–2, q. 174, a. 6, ad 3).

Some people latch on to such events with a feverish hunger, though this may be excused when the legitimate need of experiential encounter with the divine is at work. Others, bearing in mind the lessons of experience, which shows that in this area human beings are easily deluded, react with excessive distrust and hostility. A proper use of private revelations requires avoiding both of these extreme attitudes.

Bibl.: L. VOLKEN, *Les révélations dans l'Église* (Mulhouse, 1961); R. LAURENTIN, "Fonction et statut des apparitions," in var., *Vraies et fausses apparitions dans l'Église* (Paris, 1973), 149–201; E. ANCILLI, "Le visioni e le rivelazioni," in var., *La mistica: fenomenologia e riflessione teologica*, vol. 2 (Rome, 1984), 473–81; P. ADNÈS, "Révélations privées," *DS* 13:482–92.

Pierre ADNÈS

ROSMINI, ANTONIO

Antonio Rosmini (1797–1855) is generally known as a philosopher, much less known as theologian. He seems to have been omitted from theological historiography for two reasons. First, there was the prejudicial shadow of condemnation: the *Post Obitum* (DS 3201–3241) was a decree pronounced on 14 December 1887, by which the Holy Office of the Inquisition censured, condemned, and proscribed forty propositions drawn from the *opera omnia Rosminiana* without adding any theological comment, and in *proprio auctoris sensu*, to make sure that the decree would not later be voided of relevance by the objections of people not prepared to learn and see Rosmini's genuine meaning in the condemned propositions, but only a distorted one.

The second reason was the *idealistic retrieval* of Rosmini for the history of philosophy by means of a faulty, modern hermeneutics that makes a false distinction between "Rosmini the philosopher" and "Rosmini the theologian and believer." For G. Gentile, indeed, Rosmini had to be purged of "those motives alien to science," significant references to his religious conviction, his Catholic faith, the missionary and apologetic aspect of his thought, which were to induce him to correct and emend Kant, "putting him into fancy dress" (G. Gentile, *Rosmini e Gioberti* [Pisa, 1898], 73).

Thus dominant critical opinion sees Rosmini as a real philosopher (maybe a minor one), passing over the theological structure of his thought. By the same token, Rosminian literature itself, bent on proving the philosophic greatness of this son of Rovereto and aiming to immunize him against the accusation of mysticism (the notion of a "religious genesis" in Rosmini's philosophy) promotes a hermeneutical approach to Rosmini's thought which insists on declaring and demonstrating the *philosophic truth* without, however, posing the critical problem (thus side-stepping the issue prejudicially a priori) of the eventual affirmation of a *true* philosophy within the existential and epistemological coordinates of religious faith. Supposing critical recognition of Rosmini's philosophizing to be possible and right without reference to his theology and faith, the literature of this type ends up sharing the interpretative results of modern hermeneutics, surreptitiously guaranteeing that very separation of philosophy and theology which Rosmini expressly abhorred; for this he identified as the main cause of the contemporary crisis in theology and of its inevitable swings between fideism and rationalism.

As opposed to current historical evaluation, a critically better informed judgment now seems possible: Rosmini is primarily a theologian, and he is a philosopher within a theologically determined movement of thought. As introduction to the course of our argument, suffice it in summary to mention: (1) his youthful project of restoring contemporary theology; (2) the centrality of Christ in the theological theme; (3) the importance of Christology maintained in the sphere of philosophy; (4) his originality as a theologian who, owing to his particular way of making the relationship work between reason and faith, philosophy and theology, seems to herald fruitful stimuli with regard to epistemological problems now being debated and to what fundamental theology today conceives to be its true function.

1. Contextual Theology and the Rosminian Reform

Though acknowledging and appreciating the presence of good theologians, such as the Jesuit G. Perrone (1794–1876), whose *Praelectiones theologicae* he often calls to mind, Rosmini was to reproach theology with having developed a documentative-controversialistic stance, while neglecting that better part of theological activity, i.e., the intellective penetration of dogma, positively obtained through the *auctoritates*. He identifies the main cause for decadence as the lack of a solid system of functional philosophy for the scientific exposition of revealed doctrine: the crisis is a philosophic one, directly produced by the separating of philosophy and theology, which has gone as far as it can go in modern times and to which Protestantism has contributed not a little.

In his day, however, the problem over theology could not be isolated from the context of church life in its entirety. The work *Delle cinque piaghe della santa chiesa* (1848) is an impassioned interpretation of the crisis through which the church was passing and of which the crisis in theology was only *one* sign.

The Rosminian way for restoring theology was thus identified with the task of *healing and refounding* philosophy by reviving the scholastic method of the golden age, with the aim of giving theology back its own capacity for speculation and its own unitary vision, prostrate as it then was in its discrete specializations. Already the *Inediti giovanili* of 1819–22 seem to document the deepening, in this very sense, of his notion of theology, already different from that practiced and accepted at the University of Padua in the early days of his theological training (1817–19).

The *Summa theologiae*, which Rosmini began translating in the years 1819–21 while he was already commenting on it at evening theological lectures in 1820, is held up as paradigm of reference for that need for rigor and systematic treatment, for unitary organization that was the most remarkable characteristic of the culture of the day, the Enlightenment. Reference to the *Summa* allowed Rosmini to attempt a unitary restructuring of theology without giving in to the rationalistic pressures of Wolff and the Enlightenment but recovering instead that *Christian philosophy* which has its origin in Catholic tradition and is symbolized by the fathers and Thomas. His failure to complete the work *De divi Thomae Aquinatis Studio apud recentiores theologos instaurando* may legitimately be justified by his deepening need to analyze Thomist thought in contemporary language, in order to *bring philosophy up-to-date:* a sound philosophy, thought out so as to restore theology, would have to be new, in continuity with the *philosophia perennis* of

Christian tradition, but aware of the critical pressure of modern philosophy.

The *Nuovo saggio sull'origine delle idee* (1830) claims to be the first step in his program of renovated Christian philosophy, which was to have reduced truth to system, acted as methodological unifier of all the sciences and reestablished theology as queen of the sciences by reconciling the *Sentences* with the freedom to philosophize.

For Rosmini, the undertaking assumed the scope of a truly encyclopaedic project. Quite the reverse of the *Encyclopédie française*, its aim was to restore reason to its own veritative capacities as against the sensism and subjectivism of contemporary philosophic thought. This ensured it would have a skeptical reception. Rosmini's apologia is an apologia for reason in the practical service of the Christian religion. For a reason that does not attain the object, the object of truth *per se*, is a reason destructive of morality and law, with harmful effects for the social, cultural, and political order—a reason that denies the supernatural, that is hostile to religion, and that alienates from the church. In the reclaiming of philosophy, therefore, there is also an aspect of missionizing for the church.

The cultural state of Europe at the end of the eighteenth and beginning of the nineteenth centuries found its own solution to the conflict between Enlightenment and traditionalism: currents diametrically opposed to one another, yet united in the same *hostility* to speculative reason. With the aim of restoring mind to its true rationality, Rosmini hit on the idea of a Christian encyclopedia. Such a project more than justified his decision to stop writing on theological topics, so as to devote his energies to philosophical and political ones.

2. The Centrality of Christ in Rosmini's Theology

Rosmini's theological works were left uncompleted and unpublished. The critical edition now in preparation organizes them as follows: (1) *Il linguaggio teologico* ("The language of theology"); (2) *Antropologia soprannaturale* ("Supernatural theology"); (3) *L'introduzione al Vangelo secondo Giovanni* ("Introduction to the Gospel of John"); (4) Minor theological writings; (5) *Il razionalismo che tenta di insinuarsi nelle scuole teologiche* ("Rationalism's attempt to infiltrate the theological schools").

From various standpoints, these precisely define the theme of the supernatural, regarded by Rosmini as the "religious question of our day," on account of the rationalist spirit which, having worked its way into theology via Protestantism and even having ensnared some Catholic theologians, refuses to recognize the real activity of God in the essence of the human soul, and weakens the supernatural by promoting naturalism.

Antropologia soprannaturale (1884), taking the concept of the supernatural as the proper starting point for theology, immediately fastens on the christological and trinitarian mystery: for the supernatural is, by identity, the grace of Christ acting within human nature. With Christ and by his means, it is the action of the whole Trinity. So, innocent Adam, sinful human nature, sanctified human nature, all—according to Rosmini—have Christ as point of reference. The grace of Christ—but the grace of Christ is Christ himself—unifies all thought. From the beginning, Christ as the "hidden Word" has been at work in the historical events of the creation, and then in the stages marking salvation history from the first sin to the coming of Christ; in this event the Word is "manifest" and works his redemption by the Holy Spirit, in that radical occurrence of encounter with God, which is the church where human beings receive the grace of the sacraments. Grace, determined in Christ, is that unitary element that prevents separate and independent study of human and divine nature. Human nature is human nature in-dwelt by the Triune God (grace is triniform, verbiform, spiritiform—a choice of language intended to safeguard the historical economy of revelation) and it is God who dwells in human nature. Beyond the conflict between anthropocentrism and theocentrism, the christocentric structure of the theological argument is amply documented: establishing the centrality of the activity of Jesus Christ, Incarnate Word of God, to whom all, from protology to eschatology, refers.

Rosmini's anthropocentrism is strictly methodological; his anthropology is not anthropocentric. For the theme of God finds its constant point of reference in human nature, not so much because there could be no talk about God unless by starting off from us and our capacity for speech but, more deeply, because in short the God we are talking about is the God who has manifested himself to a *partner* by creating us and redeeming us, i.e., by constituting us as persons and sanctifying us by his salvific work historically performed in Jesus Christ. Christ dead and risen is the "ground" of Christian doctrine, the "source of supernatural wisdom": with these expressions the *Introduzione al Vangelo secondo Giovanni* (1882) makes Christ the last condition for any further acquisition of theological truth. In the trinitarian context, even affirmation of the Father depends on that of the Word, notwithstanding that in the order of the processions of the divine persons, the Father is the "origin" of the Word. Hence the advantage of a methodology which, in the theological field, abolishes the danger of treating *one* God uncoupled from the *threefold* God, by resolutely affirming the Trinity as proper to Christian monotheism. The thematic deepening of the Rosminian argument about the intratrinitarian processions and the creation of the world should, beyond question, demonstrate his up-to-dateness as to content.

From Christ, of course, is derived the word *Christian* qualifying theology in general, inasmuch as in Christ, the personal manifestation of the Word to human beings, theology finds "new light" by which to interpret all the Scriptures, since his resurrection reveals their full meaning. Thus only Christian theology is, *stricto sensu*, theology. With the incarnation we have the maximum of the supernatural in concrete form, the end point of a developing activity of grace in world history, corresponding to a gradual growth in human capacity to know the truth: Rosmini can establish a "gradation" of knowledge and consequently of operative capacity between OT and NT, a growing supernatural awareness before the coming of Christ, to conclude at a given moment with the real novelty inaugurated by the presence of the Word himself—whence the centrality of Christ *in the history of revelation.*

Christ in person is the revealer. To us he reveals the "mysteries" and the "necessary truths," distinguished by Rosmini from the "contingent truths," such as the creation, the incarnation, and other matters of sacred history. These last also constitute the material revelation, but in a different way from the "mysteries."

They are nonrational yet positive truths, i.e., historical: as facts they are not necessary since conditioned by the divine will. Certainly the necessary truths are not extracted from the contingent truths as being their inner sense, so that fact may be explained as event and revelation be thought of as history, insofar as and because history has become the place or "form" of revelation. And yet the abundant use of the Greek fathers and the Scriptures confers a density on what Rosmini has to say about Christ the revealer that cannot be reduced to the intellectualism of verbal communication. Christ reveals the Father not only by words, but by "miracles" and "works." To the external and verbal revelation, Rosmini structurally links an inner-interior "verbiform" revelation which may be summarized as "substantial union" by which Christ "formally dwells in the souls of his Saints." Furthermore, Christ's revelation concerns all those things that the Son hears in the bosom of the Father, and hence communication of these things could only come about by the communication of his own person to the apostles, with the consequent perception derived from this. These indications and others too— as, e.g., the soteriological emphasis in Christ's teaching: Christ saves us by instructing us and his teaching can therefore be defined as "doctrine of salvation," "knowledge of salvation"— show in part Rosmini's ability to maintain the soteriological consistency of the truth as linked to the revelatory event of Christ, although within a "structural" mental context potentially inclined to think in noetic terms of revelation as propositional truths.

3. Christological Event and Philosophic Reason

Given the uniquenesss of the Christ-event, God himself within human history, the supernatural intelligence brought into the world could not, according to Rosmini, but make its beneficial influences felt at every level of human knowledge. Philosophic knowledge, the concise expression in Rosmini's day for the totality of the knowable, must hence be determined by the Christian revelatory event.

The effective importance of the christological event for the destinies of human rationality is abundantly documented in Rosmini's thought at two levels: (1) that of its historical interpretation, by which the history of the human conquest of meaning becomes as though catalyzed by this event—it is a history that progresses in relation to its "positive and personal knowledge of the Word," which can only take place with the incarnation; (2) that of his theoretical systematization, which starts out from the basic conviction, expressed in the *Introduzione alla filosofia* (1850), that "the effect of the Christian faith's being introduced into the world was to give an unexpected, marvelous, infinite development to human reason." It was necessary to show the conditions for this to be so, by presenting a philosophic system that openly proclaimed its explicit and intrinsic relationship with the truth of Christ or, rather, with the Truth, being Christ: putting itself forward without hesitation, without inferiority complexes, and without doubts about its own authenticity—or philosophic soundness—as the "theory of the Gospel and hence the philosophy of Christianity," according to the well-known statements in the preface to the *Nuovo saggio*. Because "the beginning of Christianity is therefore unique: the Truth. And Truth too is the beginning of philosophy."

Yet despite any christomonistic temptation to philosophize within religion, Rosmini adequately draws the distinction: in philosophy, truth is shown merely as "rule of the mind"; in religion, it is a divine person. Yet there is one sole Truth. It is the same, unique Truth.

A generalized pan-Christism having been avoided by the opportune distinction between Idea, present in the mind, and Jesus Christ the Word, an absolute separation would be intolerable because deviant, since the natural truth in the human mind is already actually "natural Christianity," inasmuch as it is a "twilight, I might call it, of the divine Word." This is the "spirit of philosophy" professed by Rosmini; it is the spirit generated by the deeply perceived relationship between his philosophy and the Christ; a clear relationship not to be disguised. The real theoretical coordinates for setting out the intrinsic relationship between *Word of God* and *Idea in Man* in the most objective way are found in the Rosminian theory of the "theosophical abstraction" in the creative process (theosophy). Here we only need to stress that to the Word in absolute manner pertains the character of "objective beginning" of all knowledge and of all intelligence, even of natural science, because he is "being known per se" and, therefore, that idea of being in the human mind is "intelligibility itself."

According to Rosmini, the idea of being is the first truth which human beings naturally embrace, since it is pure light blazing in the mind. Human rationality, as it develops in individual and collective history, moulds the truth into different forms, depending on progress and intellectual maturity. But, in the *Introduzione alla filosofia*, Rosmini is resolute: "Before all these forms, there is the same truth, and this is that ideal being in which all entities can be known." Now, who has ministered that pure truth anterior to all forms? First of all, therefore, there exists a divine magisterium "in which human beings believe by nature and not by reasoning, in such that even in the natural order, not only in the supernatural one, faith precedes reason." Rosmini thus points out a structural analogy between human rationality and supernatural rationality: human intellectual activity, reaching out toward truth, is always directed, whether on the natural or on the supernatural level, to the light of the one, same, unique teacher. Hence Rosmini's deep conviction: the Catholic faith is the "intimate friend" of reason and philosophy and, because of this, reason can take nothing away from her without destroying its own inner nature. The purity of reason is not contaminated by the presence of faith, but assured and made the brighter; this in condensed form is the thesis which Rosmini claims is borne out on the historical plane. The encounter between philosophy and Christianity caused a remarkable rebirth for philosophy.

The christological importance of philosophy signals the *originality of the Rosminian position in nineteenth-century theology*. His intention of showing the "metaphysical harmoniousness" of the truth revealed by Jesus Christ by no means tends to reduce the mystery, nor is it an attempt at one of his transcendental deductions. It is, however, a striving to explain the rational maximum possible on the basis of an incontrovertible conviction of a perfecting and completion of supernatural by creaturely truth, and a harmonious relationship between them. Such a relationship appears to perfection in the hypostatic union of the Incarnate Word. The execution of the task, plainly set forth in *Antropologia soprannaturale* of explaining the philosophy "which lies hidden in the bowels of

Christian theology" and is "assumed" and "pointed to by divine revelation," becomes the concrete space for the renewal of a contemporary theology wrecked and made sterile by theological positivism. In this sense, the originality of the Rosminian position in nineteenth-century theology is all still to be rediscovered and affirmed, even with regard to those great figures, widely associated with the theological renewal of the day, i.e., Moehler and Newman.

4. The Relevance of "Rosminian Theology" Today

In the framework of the foregoing considerations, theology, for Rosmini, is vigorously critical thought about the faith by means of the faith, hence science, theory, whose ultimate potentiality is to help us acquire an authentic, real, and sound philosophy as our methodical instrument for explaining and researching the dogmatic intelligence. Whence the dynamic interaction of two movements proper to his theologizing: the religious tradition is interpreted by Rosmini by means of his philosophy, but his philosophy is supported by tradition, since it is controlled by it point by point. What is at stake is the philosophy of the Christian tradition, which alone, as such, can serve the religious tradition by including itself as "function" of its self-understanding, in accordance with the critical and methodological rigor demanded by the scientific character of theology. Theology is the logos of religion. Because it is the logos, it appeals to philosophy. Because the logos is permanently being molded by the intentionality of the faith, this requires that the appeal to philosophy be logically preceded by philosophy's appeal to the faith: only the logos within the faith can consistently determine the logos of the faith, i.e., theology. Now, since for Rosmini theology is this philosophy applied to dogma, the consistency of his *figura* is bound up with the solution to the problem that it poses: the real, critically argued potentiality of this philosophy, in its philosophic truth, authenticity, and autonomy.

The underlying suggestion, however, remains paradigmatic for present-day epistemological problems, which, given the variety of theological positions, show the urgency of recovering *ad intra* the rationality of the faith. This rationality within the faith, in Rosminian terms, offers theology the possibility of existing by guaranteeing it its riches. This is the proper function of philosophizing within theology: to develop the philosophical thought immanent in theology since it is inherent in the faith, which, by making itself humanly intelligible, postulates and implies reason as such.

So then we may point out the place in fundamental theology where the encounter, the union, the fruitful collaboration of philosophy and theology, will take place: in this environment, the theologian, by being a theologian, should be able to be a philosopher without his theological activities being detrimental to the critical and intensive activity of philosophic thought. The present-day transition from apologetics to fundamental theology has acquired the truly *theological* character of an inquiry into the credibility and rationality of the faith: this is the appeal of the faith and within the faith to the overall rationality of the human mind. In this context may be placed Rosmini's theoretical contribution to determining the identity of a theological discipline of this sort. His attempt at a Christian encyclopedia would, according to Menke, have been the first type of apologetics capable of transcending the alternatives of objective and subjective fundamental theology. Beyond the preoccupation with demonstrating the acceptability of historical revelation by an intervention of pure reason, with the help of certain signs, or with reducing revelation to the completion of the transcendental quality in human nature, he attempts with the principles of the faith to develop a conception of reality higher and more consistent than any other. It is a matter of bearing witness by philosophizing to the fertility of the faith in relation to typical human problems, so that Christ may become the key to the human cryptogram. *Rosminian Christocentrism,* therefore: or, rather, for Rosmini, philosophy makes demands on the whole, but this whole cannot be autonomously conceived of in separation from the real whole which, for a believer, is Jesus Christ.

Fundamental theology, therefore, while legitimizing theological knowledge as a specific mode of knowing reality as regards the universal conditions of knowledge, *must also assume the task* of showing how an understanding of the faith can be expanded into an all-embracing conception of reality, consistently developing the reasons proper to philosophy by generating within itself the fruitful relationship between theology and believing philosophy. In the fundamental theology sector, by working out a philosophy in the faith, we reach the highest level from which to demonstrate the credibility of the revelatory Christian event to "others," and this is what fundamental theology, with its investigative character, is trying to do.

Bibl.: For a complete bibliography of works by or concerning Rosmini, see G. BERGAMASCHI, *Bibliographie rosminienne,* 6 vols. (Milan, 1967–82). A critical edition of his complete works is forthcoming: see G. FERRARESE, *Recherches sur les réflexions théologiques de A. Rosmini dans les années 1819–1828* (Milan, 1967); M. F. SCIACCA, *Interpretazioni rosminiane* (Milan, 1971); G. DI NAPOLI and R. BESSERO BELTI, *Problemi teologici ed ecclesiologici in A. Rosmini* (Stresa, 1972); F. CONIGLIARO, *Immanenza e trascendenza del soprannaturale in Rosmini* (Palermo, 1973); G. CRISTALDI, *A. Rosmini e il pensare cristiano* (Milan, 1977); K. H. MENKE, *Vernunft und Offenbarung nach A. Rosmini* (Innsbruck/Vienna/ Munich, 1980); F. EVAIN, *Être et personne chez A. Rosmini* (Paris/Rome, 1981); G. GIANNINI, *Esame delle quaranta proposizioni rosminiane* (Genoa, 1985); G. TAVERNA PATRON, *Antropologia e religione in Rosmini* (Stresa, 1987); G. LORIZIO, *Eschaton e storia nel pensiero di A. Rosmini* (Rome/Brescia, 1988); A. STAGLIANÒ, *La "teologia" secondo Antonio Rosmini: Sistematica-critica-interpretazione del rapporto fede e ragione* (Brescia, 1988).

Antonio STAGLIANÒ

RULE OF FAITH

Christian writers of the late second century mention with some frequency that their churches have a known "canon of truth," i.e., a set framework and content of church teaching, or more simply, a "rule of faith" (*regula fidei*). In some of these contexts we find concise summaries of the principal teachings, expressed in variable terms but with the same basic outline. These summaries indicate that the rule structures what was transmitted to catechumens by church teachers under the local bishop's supervision. The rule served the churches in outside contacts as a means by which to identify other believers or communities as orthodox. The rule relates to Scripture as the proper summary of its meaning and functions as the church's guideline in interpreting all the myriad contents of the biblical books as referring to a single divine economy of salvation.

Irenaeus of Lyon claims that although the churches throughout the world are quite distant from each other, and in spite of the fact that their members speak different languages, they nonetheless profess and preserve the same faith. Each church holds to the rule received from the apostles of Christ and their successors, namely, to believe in God, the Father Almighty, who created all that is; in Jesus Christ, the Son who became incarnate for our salvation; and in the Holy Spirit, who spoke through the prophets of Christ's birth, passion, resurrection, and ascension, of the future resurrection, of the coming manifestation of Christ in glory as just judge of all (*Adversus haereses* 1.10.1–2; cf. 1.9.4; 3.4.2; 4.33.7; *Demonstratio* 3). In North Africa, Tertullian also gives similar summaries of the rule of faith and argues from it as a recognizable and treasured possession in the churches (*De praescriptione* 13, 36; *De virginibus velandis* 1; *Adversus Praxeas* 2.1–2).

In the East, Clement of Alexandria speaks of the "ecclesiastical rule" of teaching, given by the apostles, which is "the understanding and practice of the divine tradition" (*Stromata* 6.124.4–5). This rule brings the law and prophets into harmonious unity with the new covenant in Christ (ibid. 125.2–3). The Lord himself is the source and ground of this true teaching (7.95.3–8), which has God as its object (ibid. 91.3), but such teaching is known and recognized by its faithful adherence to the ecclesiastical canon (ibid. 90.2). Origen's commentaries contain scattered references to the church's normative rule of faith, and, most importantly, his Preface to *De principiis* gives the rule in the form of a summary of essential Christian teaching, stemming from the apostles, and transmitted in plain terms to all Christians. The Christian speculation Origen undertakes in *De principiis* was to be framed and controlled by fidelity to the common canon of truths passed on from the apostles and held in the church, concerning God and creation, Christ, the Spirit and the Scriptures, and the human soul.

The second-century rule of faith was not a creed or confession with a verbally fixed formulation, although such more concise confessions did evolve in conformity with the rule (→ CREED). The rule, however, was connected with baptism as with the moment at which the believer came under its sway and guidance. The rule was consistently trinitarian in structure, and thus brought out the inherent unity of creation by the almighty Father with the economy of redemption, sanctification, and revelation, as realized by the Son and Holy Spirit. The rule was open to adaptation by orthodox teachers, especially when they were constrained to emphasize aspects of the transmitted faith contested by heretics. The rule led to formulations which emphasized the unity of the two testaments against Marcion, and to forms stressing the true entry of God's Son into the flesh of our humanity against the Gnostics.

The rule is the form and content of truth which authentic teaching transmits and which faith embraces. Faith lays hold of the truth of God, and faith then, as a lived relationship, is the canon which guides genuine Christian discourse. With faith as a rule, proper formulations of teaching are recognizable by their homogeneity with the transmitted body of teaching about God and his work. The formulated rule lays out the contours of a fully formed personal faith.

In controversy, the rule of faith served in unmasking false teachings by showing their discordance from the elements and symphonic unity of the church's normative body of teaching. Writings like the gnostic gospels, which claimed to come from contact with the risen Christ, could be excluded from Christian use by the demonstration of their deviation from the transmitted *corpus* of belief (cf. s.v. "canon of Scripture"). But the rule was not applied to the genuine prophetic and apostolic books as an ecclesiastical principle external to them. Instead the rule was the very meaning of the Scriptures themselves, as the churches came to express that meaning in the key elements of their common teaching.

For fundamental theology, the early rule of faith gives testimony to the inclusive unity of God's revelation of himself and of his saving work. The rule, thus, is a reflex of the single beneficent intention which underlies all the historical epiphanies of the Lord of Israel and the God and Father of Jesus Christ. The rule shows that from the beginning the mind of the postapostolic church was not distended by holding to a multitude of scattered fragments of belief, but was instead given over to a single "pattern of teaching" (Rom 6:17). This organic vision was centered on the historical words and deeds of Jesus, especially his cross and resurrection, but it embraced as well the abundant store of narrative, instruction, prophecy and prayer-forms found in the inherited Scriptures of Israel. It was a rule of faith to see the latter as one with the evangelical witness to Jesus and the new life given in his Spirit. The rule was, above all, a normative source of coherence through a single vision of God, creation, and human life in the historical world.

Christian faith has a determinate content, and the rule shows this to have been the case even immediately following NT times. This content, however, was not a compelling list of tenets formulated as propositions. The rule of faith shows the content to have been, instead, an ordered understanding of God's dealing with humankind as creator of all, savior of his fallen creation, and present power of illumination, sanctification, and guidance.

A basic moment in the work of Christian theology is to give an account of God and his economy in a way conformed to the perennially valid content and shape of the early rule of faith. Theology aims at further penetration into sense of the elements of belief and their manifold correlations with each other and with human life in the world. Theology continually tests the new emphases required in proclamation, instruction, and spirituality by new cultural circumstances. Theology strives as well for fresh syntheses. But all this has a given framework and order arising from faith itself, which has already laid hold of a primordial synthesis. Faith, as communion with the God of creation, salvation, and new life, is itself a rule and guide of Christian reflection and discourse.

Bibl.: D. VAN DEN EYNDE, _Les normes de l'enseignement chrétien dans la littérature patristique des trois premiers siècles_ (Gembloux/Paris, 1933), 281–313; H. E. W. TURNER, _The Pattern of Christian Truth_ (London, 1954), 307–78; B. HÄGGLUND, "Die Bedeutung der regula fidei als Grundlage theologischer Aussagen," _StTh_ 12 (1958): 1–44; R. TREVIJANO ETCHEVERRA, "Origenes y la Regula fidei," in H. Crouzel et al., eds., _Origeniana_ (Bari, 1975), 327–38; J. N. D. KELLY, _Early Christian Creeds_ (3rd ed.; London, 1976), chap. 3; M. JOURJOUR, "La tradition apostolique chez saint Irénée," _L'année canonique_ 23 (1979): 193–202; L. W. COUNTRYMAN, "Tertullian and the Regula fidei," _Second Century_ 2 (1982): 208–22.

Jared WICKS

S

SCHEEBEN, MATTHIAS JOSEPH

Scheeben was born in 1835 in Meckenheim (near Bonn). As a candidate for the priesthood in the archdiocese of Cologne, he went to Rome, where he pursued studies at the Collegium Germanicum et Hungaricum of the Pontificia Università Gregoriana (1852–59). The years in Rome were decisive for his work as a theologian. He acquired a good knowledge of the Greek and Latin church fathers as well as of the most important scholastic theologians. His teachers (Perrone, Passaglia, Franzelin, Schrader) belonged to the "Roman school." In 1853 he was ordained to the priesthood; then, after a brief period of pastoral activity (1860), he was appointed professor at the theological seminary in Cologne. He became one of the most esteemed Catholic theologians of the nineteenth century, and his large body of work continued to be influential in the twentieth century.

Scheeben is, first and foremost, a dogmatist. Thus he is interested less in the factuality and credibility of Christian revelation—the themes, of course, of classical apologetics as it had been developed since the eighteenth century—than in its content. The content of revelation forms an organic system of supernatural truths that contains no internal contradictions. To bring out the inner consistency of revelation is the task of the dogmatist. Scheeben is also not greatly interested in engaging in debate with contemporary philosophy or with outsiders. The justification of faith, in his view, occurs in faith's theological reflection on itself, in faith's accounting for itself to itself. This is, in fact, already fundamental theology in the modern sense. Scheeben did not, however, see or treat the matter in that way. But his attempt to focus on the reasonableness inherent in Christian faith furthers that tendency in early twentieth-century theology to develop reasoned arguments based on the content of revelation and faith ("revelation theology"). On the whole, Scheeben and his immanent justification of faith were influential primarily within the Catholic sphere, which does not imply that he did not also, in the context of the discussion surrounding VATICAN I, engage in outward-directed debate about apologetics. During the so-called culture-struggle (*Kulturkampf*), he defended the Catholic church against the RATIONALISM, naturalism, and liberalism of his time.

Scheeben's reflections on a theological epistemology and a doctrine of first principles are of the greatest significance; in particular, they pertain to the relationship between faith and knowledge, to the so-called teaching apostolate and its infallibility, and to theological analysis of the act of faith. Theological epistemology has to do with the transmission of revelation by the church, the establishment and scholarly treatment of the truths of faith, and the presuppositions and methodology of theology. Scheeben distinguishes between the objective principles of theological knowledge (revelation and its transmission, the teaching apostolate, tradition) and theological knowledge in itself (faith, the act of faith, faith and knowledge). Remarkably, theological epistemology begins with the emergence of the visible church, which puts itself forward as laying claim to be the authentic transmitter of God's revelation.

In Scheeben's theology, the category of the *supernatural* is of central significance. Against the rationalistic currents of his time, he emphasizes the *supernatural character* of *revealed truths*. At the same time, the preeminent goal of his theological endeavors is to exposit the organic unity of the natural and the supernatural. This concern is reflected in his thoughts on the relationship between nature and grace, knowledge and faith, and reason and revelation. He clearly marks theology off from philosophy, which, for him, is a rational discipline adhering to the natural principles of reason. Theology, as a religious discipline, is a system of knowledge based on propositions accepted in faith. It has its own epistemological principle (God's word) and its own material object (God).

Scheeben begins his theological activity in the period prior to the First Vatican Council. After humanity's liberation from its "self-imposed stage of immaturity" (Kant), certain questions in epistemology and theory of the sciences take on a new urgency: theology/philosophy, nature/grace, faith/knowledge, reason/faith, and so on are conceptual pairings in which such questions become evident and demand answers (Paul 1975). However, neither the *rationalistic* nor the *fideistic* model of thought can provide real answers. The first model eliminates faith, revelation, and theology altogether; the second, supplanting reason with faith, allows the distinction between faith and superstition to be blurred and exposes the content of faith to arbitrariness. The *separation* of faith and reason leads to "two-tiered thinking" (cf. the theory of the double truth); the intermixing of the two, on the other hand, leads to pan(en)theism of the sort also found, in particular, in the romanticism of that time.

Scheeben devotes the final main section (par. 104–10) of the *Mysterien des Christentums* (1st ed., 1865) to theological questions relating to epistemology and theory of the sciences. In the later, multivolume *Handbuch der katholischen Dogmatik*, "Theological Epistemology" appears as the first volume (1873–75). In the *Mysterien* (par. 109, he deals specifically with the relation between faith and reason. For him, these are two (subjective) "principles of knowledge," two "lights" which, although deriving from a single source (God), must nevertheless be distinguished in view of their *spheres of application*. Reason applies to nature, and faith to the supernatural. In relation to the mysteries of Christianity, there exists between the two a "service arrangement," which should not, however, be one in which reason is subject or subordinate to faith. It is not a slave relationship. Reason plays a thoroughly independent and irreplaceable role. Here, Scheeben invokes the image of the wedding of bride and bridegroom, of the relation between man and wife. The two natures in Christ can be viewed as analogous to the relationship between reason and faith, between philosophy and theology. Reason cannot generate from itself theological knowledge of God's mysteries "without the fertilizing seed of faith"; while faith is unable, apart from reason, to disclose and develop its content.

Scheeben belongs to no theological school nor can he be classed with any. His expositions are not always exactly clear, especially when he resorts to use of imagery. All this has hindered, rather than facilitated, understanding and appropriation of his work. The most diverse schools of thought have been eager to claim Scheeben for their own cause. His expositions

on the distinctive nature of theology sometimes seem to come close to "two-tiered thinking." In a way, his efforts to achieve a "wedding" of philosophy and theology lead—at a time when the great philosophical systems have broken down—to a theological version of late idealism (thus he has been called the "Hegel of Catholic theology") that takes little account of the historicality of thought and (especially in the late works) attempts to subordinate concrete realities to its conceptual system. According to Eugen Paul, Scheeben, influenced by ideas transmitted to him initially by Möhler (1796–1838), evolved a "romantic theology" of a Roman cast, which nonetheless, with the aid of the great representatives of theological tradition, developed into an independent system.

Bibl.: M. J. SCHEEBEN, *Nature and Grace* (St. Louis, 1954); id., *The Mysteries of Christianity* (St. Louis, 1946); id., *Dogmatique*, 4 vols. (Paris, 1877–82); var., *M. J. Scheeben: teologo cattolico d'ispirazione tomista*, Studi tomisti 33 (Rome, 1988); E. PAUL, "Matthias Joseph Scheeben (1835–1888)," with bibliography, in *Katholische Theologen Deutschlands im 19. Jahrhundert*, ed. H. Fries and G. Schwaiger (Munich, 1975), 2:386–408.

Bernd GROTH

SACRED SCRIPTURES

1. Sacred Scriptures and Word of God

The Second Vatican Council made its own the phrase "seeds of the Word" (*AG* 11), which some of the early fathers of the church had used in speaking of the religious traditions of the peoples to whom they were endeavoring to bring the Christian message. The expression applies directly to the sacred books of the various religious traditions of the human race and more especially to the writings which they think of as their "sacred scriptures." In some of these traditions—Hinduism, among others—the concept of "sacred scripture" is more fluid than it is in Christianity. A given sacred book, the *Bhagavad Gita*, e.g., may be recognized as "sacred scripture" (*śruti*) by some branches of religious HINDUISM, without necessarily being given the same value in other currents of thought, for which it belongs rather to "tradition" (smṛti) than to scripture. It is worth bearing in mind, however, that there is not always complete agreement among the different branches of Christianity on the canonicity of the sacred books (→ CANON OF SCRIPTURE); the Catholic tradition itself distinguishes between canonical and "deuterocanonical" books. The problem of canonicity is the problem of identifying the sacred writings which a religious community is to acknowledge as sacred scripture. But there is a more basic question: What is it that turns a sacred book into sacred scripture? The two questions are perhaps often confused—a confusion that does not make for theological clarity. In any case, the point I am interested in here can be put as a question: In view of what constitutes Sacred Scripture in Christian theology, can the "sacred scriptures" of the other religious traditions be recognized as such by theologians? If yes, then to what extent and in what way?

It is necessary to recall the distinctions that must be made between divine revelation, prophetism, and sacred scripture, although the realities indicated by these different words are interrelated in numerous ways. If we recall the holy "pagans" of the OT and the covenants God made with the human race and the peoples of the world (Gn 1–3; 9), we will be compelled to acknowledge that he has made his person known in the history of nations in such a way that theologians can speak of this manifestation as "divine revelation," even if this revelation is only a preliminary stage in the history of salvation and is directed beyond itself to Judeo-Christian revelation. On the other hand, it is being increasingly accepted today that the prophetic charism had antecedents outside Israel, both before Christ and even after him. The prophetic charism must, of course, be properly understood. It does not consist primarily in prediction of the future but rather in the interpretation, for the sake of a people, of the sacred history through which they are living, or the divine interventions in their history. Nor can "prophetic" religion and "mystical" religion be artificially opposed, since a mystical experience is the source of the prophetic charism.

The prophetic charism is not an exclusive privilege of Israel. The OT itself acknowledges as true prophecy from God the four oracles of Balaam of which the book of Numbers speaks (Nm 22–24). And in Christian antiquity the

Sybilline Oracles were sometimes regarded as prophetic.

In fact, the real problem is not the problem of revelation nor the problem of prophetism but the problem of sacred scriptures as containing the word of God that has been spoken to human beings in the course of the history of salvation (→ HISTORY V). For Christians, Sacred Scripture contains the record and remembrance of a divine revelation, and this in such a way that God himself is its author. This does not mean that the human authors of the sacred books, or the compilers who brought together oral or written traditions, did not have the full exercise of their human faculties and were not the real authors of their works. The title of author must be given both God and to the human writers, though at different levels. Sacred Scripture is "the word of God in the words of human beings." Because God is its author, it is not reducible to human talk about God; rather, it is the word of God himself. Because human beings are the authors, the words which God addresses to human beings are truly human words; indeed, nothing else would be intelligible to them. In order to explain the mystery of "God and human beings as coauthors," as it is uniquely embodied in Sacred Scripture, Christian theology appeals to the idea of "inspiration." The term "inspiration" has traditionally been understood to describe the fact that while respecting the activity of the human author, God guides this activity and makes it his own in such a way that what is written is in its totality God's word to humanity.

It is undoubtedly a weakness in the traditional theology of Sacred Scripture that the specific role of the Holy Spirit seems to be passed over in silence. The constant use of the word *inspiration* does not alter the situation, since the origin and deeper meaning of the word seem most often to have been forgotten or at least to have attracted little attention. Despite the church's profession of faith in the Holy Spirit who "has spoken through the prophets" (First Council of Constantinople), and despite the title of the encyclical *Divino Afflante Spiritu* and even what is said in the Constitution *Dei Verbum* (no. 11) of Vatican II, the current theology of Sacred Scripture continues to assert that God is the author in a rather indeterminate way, which does not do justice to the role of the third person, the Holy Spirit. "Divine inspiration" is understood as an action of God *ad extra*, an action common to the three persons, by reason of which God himself is author of the Scriptures. "Divine inspiration" seems to make no reference to an active presence of God's Spirit, who, by inspiring the sacred writers, impresses his personal seal on what is written. The theology of Sacred Scripture should once again, and to a greater degree than in the past, bring out the personal influence of the Spirit in the Scriptures. Only then will we have a theology of Sacred Scripture that makes possible a more open attitude toward the sacred scriptures of other religious traditions.

K. Rahner has emphasized the communal character of the Sacred Scriptures: the Bible is the church's book; it contains the word of God that is addressed to the ecclesial communion. This means that in the books which make up the Bible, and especially in the books of the NT, the church sees the authentic expression of its faith, as well as the word of God that is the basis of this faith. Sacred Scripture is thus a constitutive element in the mystery of the church, which is gathered together by the word of God. This does not require, however, that the sacred writers have been conscious of being moved by the Holy Spirit to write. It is accepted, too, that the charism of scriptural inspiration extends well beyond the group of authors to whom the various books are attributed. Often, in fact, these "authors" are "redactors" or "editors," who work with oral or written traditions already in existence. It may well be that the apocryphal gospels have preserved authentic sayings of Jesus.

If this be the case, then the question is whether Christian theologians can see in other sacred scriptures words of God that are inspired by the Holy Spirit and addressed by God to other religious communities. And, if the answer is that they can, then how are these words, words of God? Are we to see in them words originating in God, inspired by the Holy Spirit, and addressed to human beings? Or only human words about God? Or, again, only human words that are addressed to God and look for a divine response? If they are indeed original words of God, we must ask, further, how these words, spoken by God to human beings and contained in the sacred scriptures of various religious traditions, are linked to the decisive words which he has spoken to human-

ity in Jesus Christ and which are officially collected in the NT?

It must be accepted that the religious EXPERIENCE of the wise men and women of the nations is guided and directed by the Spirit. Their experience of God is an experience of his Spirit. It must also doubtless be accepted that this experience is not intended for these individuals alone. The initiative in every encounter between God and human beings belongs to God, and in his providence he has willed to speak to the peoples as such, through the religious experience of their prophets. In speaking to these individuals in the depths of their hearts, it is to their peoples that he has willed to manifest and reveal himself through his Spirit. In this way he has entered in a hidden manner into the history of peoples and has guided this history toward the fulfillment of his plan. The social character of the "sacred scriptures" of the nations can therefore be said to be willed by God. These scriptures represent the sacred heritage of a religious tradition in process of formation, not without the intervention of divine providence. They contain words of God to human beings in the words of the sages, inasmuch as the latter convey secret words spoken by the Spirit in the hearts of individuals, but intended by divine providence to lead other human beings to the experience of the same Spirit. To claim anything less would, it seems, be to underestimate the reality of God's self-manifestation to the nations.

What I have been proposing here is not the same as saying that the *entire* content of the sacred scriptures of the nations is God's word in the words of human beings. In the compiling of these sacred books many elements may have been introduced which represent only human words about God. Still less am I saying that the words of God contained in the sacred scriptures of the peoples are his final message to them, as if he had nothing more to say to them than what he had already said to them through their prophets. What I proposed above amounts to saying that insofar as the sages' personal experience of the Spirit is, in God's providence, a first personal step which God takes toward the various nations, and insofar, too, as this experience is authentically set down in their sacred scriptures, it is a personal word which God addresses to them through intermediaries he has chosen. In a true sense, although a sense which it is doubtless difficult to make more concrete, this word can be called an "inspired word of God," provided we do not take too narrow a view of these terms and provided that we take sufficiently into account the all-pervasive influence of the Holy Spirit.

2. Progressive and Diversified Revelation

The letter to the Hebrews (1:1) makes it clear that the word which God has spoken in Jesus Christ, in his Son, is his final word and, in this sense, his definitive word. In what sense, and how, is Jesus Christ the fullness of revelation? Where precisely is this fullness to be found? If we are to avoid confusion, we must say that the fullness of revelation is not, properly speaking, to be identified with the written words of the NT. The NT is the official record, the authentic memorial of this revelation. It has traditionally been said, with chronology in mind, that the record was complete at the death of the last apostle; it is preferable, however, to look at the matter from the point of view of the text and to say that the record was complete when the last of the books to be included in the NT had been composed. But this authentic memorial, which is part of Christianity's constitutive tradition, must be distinguished from the event which is Jesus Christ himself and to which authentic and authoritative witnesses render their testimony. It is the person of Jesus Christ, his works and words, his life, death, resurrection, or, in short, the event which is Jesus Christ, that constitutes the fullness of revelation. In Jesus God has spoken his final word to the world, a word to which nothing claiming to be divine revelation can be added. This is what the Constitution DEI VERBUM of Vatican II means when it distinguishes between the complete and perfect revelation given in the event which is Jesus Christ (no. 4) and its "transmission" in the NT, which is part of apostolic tradition (no. 7). The authentic remembrance of the event which the NT transmits is undoubtedly normative (*norma normans*) for the faith of the church in every age, but it is not on that account the fullness of God's word to humanity. The NT itself tells us that its report of the event is incomplete (see Jn 21:25).

If, then, we must attribute to the NT a special and unique charism of scriptural inspiration, the reason is that it contains the official record of the definitive revelation which God addresses to all human beings in Jesus Christ. Incomplete though the record is, the inspiration of the Holy Spirit places on it a seal of authenticity which allows the ecclesial community to see in it the official expression of its faith, i.e., the true meaning of what God has done for human beings in Jesus Christ. If the special influence of the Holy Spirit in the composition of the NT is to be understood correctly, it must be seen as an integral part of his action that creates the church.

The church was born on Pentecost as a result of the outpouring of the Spirit of the risen Christ. The presence of the Spirit among the first believers and his continual *paraklēsis* make the church an eschatological community that is commissioned to bear witness to the event, revelatory of God, which has occurred in the last times. The composition of the NT is an essential element in this creation of the church, since without it the ecclesial community could not give its authentic witness. Under a special influence of the Holy Spirit the earliest church recorded, for itself and the generations to come, the meaning of the event that was Jesus Christ. The record which the church made of this meaning is not only a word which God addresses to human beings through the personal experience of the Spirit which certain individual seers had; it is also God's definitive word to human beings, written down under the special guidance of the Holy Spirit by members of the eschatological community whom he filled with his presence. It is in this sense that the NT is a constitutive element in the mystery of the church.

But, once the unique character of the event that is Jesus Christ has been recognized and once the unique place which the official record of this event by the eschatological community of the church occupies in the mystery of God's revelation to the world has been asserted, there is still room for an open-ended theology of revelation and of Sacred Scripture. Such a theology will allow that before speaking his final word in Jesus Christ and even before speaking through the prophets of the OT, God had already spoken a first word to human beings through the prophets of the peoples, a word of which traces can be found in the sacred scriptures of the world's religious traditions. The final word does not exclude the first word, but rather presupposes it. Nor can it be said that God's first word is the one recorded in the OT, since the OT itself attests to the fact that God had spoken to other peoples before speaking to Israel. The sacred scriptures of the peoples, the OT, and finally the NT thus represent different ways and forms in which God communicates with human beings in a continual process of self-revelation. In the first stage, he lets seers hear in their hearts a secret word, of which at least traces may be contained in the sacred scriptures of the world's religious traditions. In the second stage, he speaks to Israel in an official way through the mouths of his prophets, and the whole of the OT is a record of this word. In these first two stages, the word of God, though differently in each case, is directed toward the full revelation that will take place in Jesus Christ. In this third and final stage, God speaks his definitive word in and through his Son, and it is to this that the NT bears official witness.

The sacred scriptures of the nations can contain only initial and hidden words of God; these words do not have the official character that must be assigned to the OT, and still less the definitive value that must be assigned to the NT. They can however be called words of God inasmuch as God speaks them through his Spirit. From the theological standpoint the sacred books that contain these words deserve in some valid sense the description "sacred scriptures." In the final analysis, the problem is one of terminology and depends on what is to be understood by "word of God," "sacred scripture," and "inspiration."

These terms can be given a narrow theological definition, as they have traditionally. It then becomes necessary to limit the application of them exclusively to the Scriptures of the Judeo-Christian tradition. But they can also be given a wider meaning which does not lack a valid theological basis and which allows them to be applied as well to the scriptures of the other religious traditions. Accordingly, "word of God," "sacred scripture," and "inspiration" do not express exactly the same reality at the different stages in the history of revelation and of salvation; at each stage, however, the terms truly signify a reality and can therefore be used of each stage, provided the necessary distinctions are kept in mind. For while it is undoubtedly important to preserve intact the unique impor-

tance of the word of God that is conveyed in Judeo-Christian revelation, it is no less important to acknowledge fully the value and meaning of the words of God that are contained in cosmic revelation. "Word of God," "sacred scripture," and "inspiration" are thus analogous concepts that apply differently to the several stages of a progressive and "differentiated" (C. Geffré) revelation.

The history of salvation and revelation is a single history (→ HISTORY V); in its various stages, cosmic, Israelite, and Christian, it carries, in different ways, the seal of the influence of the Holy Spirit. By this is meant that through the stages of his selfrevelation God in his providence personally directs the human race toward the goal he has set for it. The divine positive will that is at work in cosmic revelation as a personal revelation of God to the peoples of the earth includes his will that the peoples have their sacred scriptures as a "preparation for the gospel." The "seeds of the Word" contained in these scriptures are seminal words of God from which the influence of the Spirit is not absent. For this influence is universal; it extends to the words spoken by God to the human race at all stages of his lavish self-revelation.

Bibl.: K. Rahner, *Inspiration in the Bible* (New York, 1966); K. Rahner and J. Ratzinger, *Revelation and Tradition* (New York, 1966); M. Dhavamony, ed., *Révélation dans le christianisme et les autres religions*, Studia Missionalia 20 (Rome, 1971); id., ed., *Founders of Religions*, Studia Missionalia 33 (Rome, 1984); I. Vempeny, *Inspiration in the Non-Biblical Scriptures* (Bangalore, 1973); D. S. Amalorpavadass, ed., *Research Seminar on Non-Biblical Scriptures* (Bangalore, 1975); C. Geffré, "Le Coran, une parole de Dieu différente?" *Lumière et Vie* 32 (1983): 21–32; Groupe de recherche islamo-chrétien, *Ces Écritures qui nous questionnent: La Bible et le Coran* (Paris, 1987).

Jacques Dupuis

SECTS, CHRISTIAN

In general use, the meaning of "sect" is both vague and pejorative. Depending on the etymology chosen, it suggests the idea either of separation (from *secare*, "cut") or of following (from *sequi*, "follow").

In its current use, therefore, it signifies either a small group of followers who have seceded from a larger group, or the body of disciples of a heretical teacher. In either case the word is used only of groups that themselves reject the name because it conveys scorn and a departure from a norm. Within Christianity it is correlative to the word *church*, which is always given a positive connotation, with the result that every sect claims to be the/a church.

1. Theoretical Picture

Ever since Max Weber religious sociology has endeavored to isolate the content of the two opposed terms, "sect" and "church." According to Weber, a sect is a voluntary grouping, while a church is an institution for salvation. Ernst Troeltsch takes over and fills out Weber's categories.

Considered as a sociological type, a church is an established social body and an all-embracing institution endowed with priestly and sacramental power; a sect is a contractual group that opposes the ecclesiastical system and rejects all compromise with the world.

The dichotomy of sect and church has been taken over, developed, and refined by such writers as Joachim Wach, Leopold Van Weise, Howard Becker, and especially J. Milton Yinger, who develops the church-sect typology according to the principle of self-distancing in relation to universal Christianity. The extreme example of the sectarian type is the cult, which develops into a sect, and then into an established sect. Next comes the denomination, then the *ecclesia*, and finally the universal church which achieves the most complete form of universalism by bringing about the unification of society (the medieval church).

In theology the word *sect* is used of an ecclesiological type. Sect and church are inseparable types, since each is understood by reference to the other. Our theological understanding of sects depends very much on our understanding of the church. Sect and church differ essentially. A sect is not an underdeveloped expression of the church, but represents a specific theological type in the history of Christianity.

The specific character of a sect is not to be looked for in the movement of dissidence and secession nor in the heated protest against the established church. The specific characteristic is to be found rather in the combination of eschatological radicalism and illuminism. By separating the eschatological principle from the incarnational principle, a sect moves toward an exaggerated form of eschatology: toward eschatologism. And by separating the spiritual principle from the magisterial and sacramental principles, it ends in an abnormal development of the spiritual principle: in illuminism. A sect springs from the combination, at a given point in history, of eschatologism and illuminism. Its specific character consists in being the historical embodiment of this combination.

The many faces presented by sects are due both to the ways in which eschatologism and illuminism are combined and to the concrete expressions of these two fundamental principles, for these expressions determine the spiritual location of the sects and define their hermeneutical field. Eschatologism can take the form of millennialism, apocalyptic futurology, or sociopolitical utopianism. Illuminism can take the form of an excessive pursuit of charisms or revelations, or an unbridled religious enthusiasm, or a disembodied spiritualism, or, on the other hand, a calm pietism, a moderate pentecostalism, or a tranquil fideism. Behind their various faces, sects are always the same: all aim to get outside history by rising above it (illuminism) and moving ahead of it (eschatologism).

Sects have secondary characteristics that derive directly from their essential character. The first to be mentioned is a *dualism* that causes ruptures at all levels: between present and future, matter and spirit, body and soul, culture and gospel, reason and faith, world and church, human beings and God. The first member of these pairs is always evil, while the second is always good. This accounts for the emphasis on the corruptness of the present age, which is in the power of Satan and his henchmen, who control all institutions, even those that are religious. In the sociopolitical sphere, it accounts for a *contemptus mundi* (rejection of society) and a refusal to become involved in the structures of the present world, and, in the ecclesial sphere, for a rejection of ecumenical dialogue, as well as for missionary zeal and condemnation of the main churches (especially of the clerical system and the use of reason in theology).

Sects are also characterized by an ethical

radicalism. Having broken with society and dissented from the churches, sects live according to a radicalism that refuses any dialogue with history, science, and culture. This radicalism ensures doctrinal purity and moral rigorism while rejecting every kind of corruption, laxity, compromise, adaptation, and allowance for situations and the individual journeys of human beings. It interprets the demands of the gospel without appeal to the theological principle of economy. Sects are for the pure and the perfect.

In the realm of spiritual experience sects bear the stamp of FIDEISM. They offer a direct experience of God, Christ, or the Spirit. They reject the sacramental principle and tend to bypass all forms of mediation and all images. Faith, which for sects is essentially an act of trust and surrender, does not have to plumb its own foundations or provide itself with a reasoned theology. Sects are not interested in a hermeneutics of either their own origins or their meaning. They appeal to the heart and the will and call for a radical conversion.

Looking as they do to the future and what is above, rebelling against the established churches, and breaking with the world, sects keep in direct contact with the word of God that is set down in the Bible (and sometimes also in other "revelations"); the Bible is interpreted in a fundamentalist way, especially in contemporary sects. Rising above history, sects reject tradition and claim to hark back to the earliest Christian community, which they attempt to copy.

In summary, a sect is a group of lay believers in Jesus and/or in the Spirit, who have voluntarily come together around the Bible (and sometimes a secondary revelation) as their center, in order to form in this corrupt world the community of authentic Christians who reject compromise, practice a _contemptus mundi_, and await the imminent coming of the end and Christ's return.

2. History

Throughout the history of the church we see sects emerging that produced their own ecclesial systems and developed as rivals of the established churches. In the early church, protest groups of a sectarian kind seem to us today to have rather been schisms resulting from the denial of one or other essential truth. These movements of protest and rebellion, the best known of which are Marcionism, Montanism, Novatianism, and Donatism, belonged much more to the church type than to the sect type. Donatism, however, did approximate more closely to the sect type, since it rejected the imperial church of Constantine and made the holiness of the church depend on the holiness of its ministers and members.

In the Middle Ages the pauperist and penitential movements, such as the Waldensians, the Poor Men of Lyons, the Humiliati, the followers of Arnold of Brescia, the "Poor Catholics," the Poor of Lombardy, and the disciples of Henry of Lausanne, seem to have been dissident confraternities rather than sects. Their ascetic program, which was modeled on evangelical and apostolic poverty, was intended as a strong protest against the wealth and worldly luxury of the pope, cardinals, and upper clergy in general and against the weakening of eschatological expectation in an age in which the church thought of itself, in practice, as the kingdom. The Bogomils and Cathars, for their part, were religions of a gnostic kind, but did have sectarian traits. The Brothers and Sisters of the Free Spirit, the Franciscan Fraticelli and Spirituals, Joachimites, the Beguines and Beghards, and, later on, the Spanish Alumbrados and the Quietists: all these groups were typical manifestations of illuminist spirituality and only imperfectly correspond to the theological type we call a sect.

It was with the coming of the Protestant churches at the time of the Reformation that the sect type attained its full form. From that point on, sects developed only on the periphery of Protestantism. Most modern and contemporary sects are dissident expressions of the revivalist and protest movements that erupted within the Protestant and Anglican churches during recent centuries: the Pietist (seventeenth century), evangelical (eighteenth century; → CHURCH VII), eschatological (nineteenth century), and Pentecostal (twentieth century) revivals. The United States would not only quickly become the promised land for European sects, but would also provide fertile soil for the birth and multiplication of new sects.

Pietism would give birth in turn to a number of dissident sects, the best known of which are the Quakers or Society of Friends, the various conventicles of the Plymouth Brethren, usually known as "Darbyites," and the Society of United Brethren, known as the Moravian Brethren. Anglican evangelicalism, which was heir to Lutheran pietism, was to become a powerful leaven of dissidence. From it came Methodism, which in turn exercised a decisive influence on the whole range of sectarian movements and notably on the rise of sects of the evangelical type, which are still numerous today. Contemporary evangelicalism abounds in a multitude of small autonomous churches headed by various independent associations and in a whole constellation of sects that are strongly fundamentalist.

Modern Pentecostalism, which emerged from evangelicalism and the "holiness movements," was initially a collection of revival movements within Protestantism. Characterized as it was by the pursuit of unmediated experience of the Spirit and by the manifestation of charisms, Pentecostalism carried within it a strong leaven of dissidence that soon bore fruit. Alongside the pentecostalist assemblies there appeared a multitude of pentecostalist and neopentecostalist sects with quite varied names: Christian Tabernacle of the Gospel of the Last Times; Miraculous Temple of the Holy Spirit; Mission of the Holy Spirit. Each of these sects is under the unchallenged authority of a charismatic leader.

The eschatological revival or "second coming revival" (beginning of the twelfth century) is at the origin of Adventism which has developed into a number of sects: the Jehovah's Witnesses and the Worldwide Church of God (Herbert Armstrong), the latter being characterized by an Anglo-Israelism of which the Mormons, too, are a special instance.

Since the sixties the sectarian movement has expanded to an extraordinary degree. Evangelicalism and Pentecostalism have exploded in all directions; old sects have been revived and new ones have made their appearance. The "Jesus Movement" has found expression not only in song and music but in the establishment of a host of marginal communes, some of which (e.g., the Children of God) went on to become well-known sects.

While preserving the traditional characteristics of the sectarian type, contemporary sects are strongly marked, on the one, by a missionary zeal that is as inventive as it is tenacious and that is skilled in using both the print media and the electronic media to spread their message and win followers, and, on the other hand, by a fundamentalism that finds expression not only in a rejection of modernism, evolutionism, theological liberalism, communism, and secular humanism but also in support of the capitalistic structure and economic ideology now in operation in North America and Western Europe. The Unification Church (Moon) is a good example of this theological and sociopolitical position. Would it be overly bold to say that contemporary sects are, in general, socially reactionary and culturally conservative, and discourage political involvement? Is this not the necessary result of their categorically eschatological position, their privatist conception of faith, and their expectation of the imminent coming of the end?

3. Sects and Christianity

Throughout its history the church's overall attitude toward the sectarian movement has been one of rejection. Sects were regarded as schisms or heresies that endangered not only the unity of the church and Christian orthodoxy but the entire sociopolitical system. It was as heretics that sectarian groups were persecuted by the institutional church, which from the time of Theodosius the Great (395) did not hesitate to use violence and to have recourse to the secular arm.

Nowadays this attitude of total rejection is no longer necessary. Before being viewed as forms of secession and heresy, sects can be seen as essentially a specific model of Christianity, a parallel way of following Jesus and living the gospel. Modern sects are not so much heresies, i.e., denials of this or that Christian doctrine, as they are comprehensive interpretations of Christianity. Once sects are looked upon as expressions of a specific type of Christianity, they can no longer be totally rejected by the great churches.

To the extent that sects accept essential truths of Christian revelation, they are caught up in a movement that leads toward the fullness of Christianity. It is admittedly difficult to identify the essential truths of the Christian faith and the specific core of Christianity and to say precisely what elements of the system and doctrinal corpus of Christianity must be preserved if an individual is to qualify as a Christian or a group as a church. One example: if a group is to belong to the World Council of Churches it must explicitly profess that Jesus is Son of God and savior.

Without entering into all the theological distinctions, we may generalize and say that many contemporary sects can rightly bear the name "Christian," to the extent that they profess a body of Christian doctrine which can ensure an attitude of authentic faith and thus make it possible, with the help of grace, to lay hold of salvation in Jesus.

If sects are Christian groups, should we not understand them in the light of the principles of Christian ecumenism, according to which all the churches are only more or less successful rough drafts, more or less defective anticipations of the eschatological essence of the church? The *vestigia ecclesiae*, the "traces" or elements "of the church," that are found in the sects rightly belong to the one church of Christ. As we shift from an ecclesiology of traces or elements to an ecclesiology based on the whole, we are led to recognize in many contemporary sects not only elements of the church but also the soul of the church: the Holy Spirit who is laboriously building up the body of Christ.

Bibl.: E. Troeltsch, *Die Soziallehren der christlichen Kirchen und Gruppen* (Tübingen, 1912); H. Becker and L. Von Weise, *Systematic Sociology* (New York, 1932); E. T. Klark, *The Small Sects in America* (Nashville, Tenn., 1937); J. Wash, *Types of Religious Experience, Christian and Non-Christian* (Chicago, 1951); E.-U. Hoff, *L'Église et les sectes* (Paris, 1951); M.-B. Lavaud, *Sectes modernes et foi catholique* (Paris, 1954); J. Seguy, *Le phénomène des sectes dans la France contemporaine* (Paris, 1956); J. M. Yinger, *Religion, Society and the Individual* (New York, 1957); M. Colinon, *Le phénomène des sectes au XXe siècle* (Paris, 1959); K. Hutten, *Le monde spirituel des sectaires* (Neuchâtel, 1965); E. R. Sandeen, *The Roots of Fundamentalism: British and American Millenarianism 1800–1930* (Chicago, 1970); V. Synan, *The Holiness: Pentecostal Movement in the United States* (Grand Rapids, 1971); J. Seguy, "Églises et sectes," in *Encyclopedia Universalis*, vol. 5; J. Vernette, *Sectes et réveil religieux. . . . Quand l'occident s'éveille* (Mulhouse, 1976); J. Barr, *Fundamentalism* (London, 1977); W. R. Martin, *The Kingdom of the Cults* (Minneapolis, 1977); R. Bergeron, *Le cortège des Fous de Dieu* (Montreal, 1982); J. Le Bar, *Cults, Sects, and the New Age* (Huntington, Ind., 1989).

Richard Bergeron

SECULARIZATION AND SECULARISM

1. The Question of Secularization

a. Secularity is a characteristic phenomenon of modernity. In our age, at least in the Western world, human beings have come see themselves as genuinely autonomous, and as responsible for their overall situation. This cultural phenomenon is the result of a long, complex historical process, whose furthest roots are numerous and very diverse in character. Not only Greek culture but also biblical religion itself constitutes historical forces of singular efficacy as agents of secularization, in demythologizing cosmic nature and rendering human beings conscious of their ethical responsibility for their existence and destiny. Secularity walks hand in hand with a process of the concrete emancipation of human life and historical reason, in terms of a certain rigorous way of understanding knowledge even vis-à-vis the experience of religion, an experience that is always had in particular personal and social circumstances. The secularizing process seeks to understand the various sectors of life in a way immanent to human reality itself—which becomes ever more differentiated—independently of the metaphysical axioms or even certain religious norms of the past. The important thing for a scientific hypothesis is not its conformity with such metascientific systems, but its availability to verification or falsification, its usefulness or effectiveness. We even hear of a "cultural maturity," a term used to describe the phenomenon of the emancipation of scientific knowledge and the autonomy of human culture. Another characteristic of secular human beings is their concern with the present life, in its concrete factuality, and their abandonment of a nostalgia for the eternal, and rejection of a merely contemplative manner of experiencing religion. The secular human being likewise loses interest in the universe of "eternal ideas," concentrating all attention on the phenomenology and dynamics of what can be verified and "checked." Accordingly, secular human beings readily adhere to a kind of pragmatic empiricism, in whose spirit they have more esteem for facts than for grand metaphysical, political, or religious theories. In modern culture, life loses certain basic traits of the archaic world, undergoing a process of eclipse of conventional forms of experience of the sacred. Individual and social life is becoming more rational and more profane, with its insistence on a separation from, indeed a breach with, so many beliefs of a religious or cultural past. Again, numerous vital functions are winning emancipation from the tutelage of religious institutions, which produces a certain desacralization of cultural or social reality; and this can mean either a kind of religious decadence, or a kind of prophetic purification of the believing experience itself.

b. In our age and historical context, the religious affirmation must be experienced within the process of a *secularization* typical of modernity and characterized by the quest for a new humanism that will center on the responsible autonomy of the individual as the highest value. Secularity entails not only the twilight of the magical, superstitious universe of an archaic culture, but also a threat to the contemplative attitude characteristic of a Greek ontology or medieval theonomy. The secularization process involves breaking with a cultural tradition that had claimed to fuse time with eternity, and the finite with the infinite. In ethics and politics, in aesthetics and philosophy, the culture of ancient or medieval Christendom was theocentric; today, the culture of modernity is clearly anthropocentric, and specially concerned with contingent and historical, singular and concrete, reality. In order to appreciate the cultural distance that divides antiquity or the Middle Ages from modern times and today, we need only compare Plato's *Gorgias* or Aristotle's *Organon* with Descartes's *Discourse on Method* or Kant's *Critique of Pure Reason*. The same occurs in the area of religion, as we readily observe when we compare the *Confessions* of Aurelius Augustinus, Anselm's *Monologion*, or Bonaventure's *Itinerarium* with Schleiermacher's discourses *On Religion*, with Kierkegaard's *Concept of Angst,* or with Unamuno's *Agony of Christianity.* Philosophers and theologians are incapable of think-

ing upon human reality or speaking of God in the same way, or using the same categories, as it was possible to do so in bygone times. The secular situation is also characterized by the loss of a certain philosophical and theological language. According to some philosophers of culture, a new historical age is under way, marked by the functional, technical, and positive thought of the *homo urbanus* of the postmodern megalopolis, who abandons not only the mythic phase of the archaic world, but the ontological phase of the Greek *polis,* as well. Just as the archaic world, brought up on the Homeric or Babylonian myths, gave way to a Greco-Roman civilization, so Western Christian culture is experiencing a transition to a planetary civilization, through the process of cultural modernity, from Renaissance to Enlightenment, from the romantic idealism of the first existentialism to positivism and pragmatism, as the modern human being goes in pursuit of the new rationality and a new humanism.

c. How ought the historical phenomenon of secularization be judged from a religious viewpoint—as a lamentably negative occurrence, or as a religiously neutral process, or indeed as a theologically positive reality? In the eyes of a rigidly integralist or fundamentalist view, secularization is an essentially antireligious phenomenon. For a certain theological eclecticism, secularization is a religiously neutral phenomenon, consisting in the cultural defeat of thought models proper to a prescientific era: the secular human being, we hear, is no closer and no further away from religion and faith than the ancient or medieval one. But Christianity must take cognizance of the fact that, today, the proclamation of the gospel is addressed to someone culturally different: human beings who have been marked by the secularizing process. Finally, for the religious optimism of a certain theological progressivism, beneath the secularizing process we may discern the activity of God: secularity enables human beings to attain to their autonomy and maturity, as it delivers the evangelical proclamation from a false interpretation. The entire secularizing process is the logical consequence of a consciousness of *creaturely autonomy.* Our awareness of creatureliness strips the world of any numinous halo it may have had. The proclamation of the religious message concerning the activity of God in salvation history, and an awareness of a covenantal religion bestow on human beings an ethical sense in their life project and a social responsibility in their historical project. We discover ourselves as autonomous and personal, spiritual and responsible. Biblical faith has had a revolutionary impact. A theology of creation, exodus, and covenant has "desacralized" the human universe, as world, as history, and as religion.

d. The hostility of secular culture toward certain defective forms of the religious experience can actually coincide with a passionate affirmation of truth—one that dictates a polemic against any religious distortion deriving from fanaticism or superstition. Thus the culture of secular modernity may perform a corrective function with regard to certain contradictory traits of a false piety. Paradoxically, the secular critique of the fanatical intolerance or cruel tyranny flowing from a false idea of the religious imperative as ethical or political exigency may signify a moment of prophetical purification of religion itself.

Even regarded from a religious perspective, secular autonomy itself, as the expression of a responsible human liberty, both in the commitment of moral activity and in the process of a relentless search for truth, is not without a positive meaning, even for the believer. A theology of creation and covenant can only legitimize the autonomy of the human being as that of a free and responsible creature, and as a concrete opportunity for the construction of a historical future of solidarity and siblingship. This thesis of the "religious" value of secularity must correspond to an affirmation of the "secular" value of the religious. Precisely as an affirmation of the dialectical polarity of the divine and the human, purified of any schema of rivalry between the two, religion is capable of guaranteeing the legitimacy of secularity as the autonomous and free quest for justice and truth, solidarity and peace. The religious element has the capacity to correct any pretension to be able to absolutize what is relative in the various sectors of the human being's cultural or social life.

As unconditional experience of the sacred, whether in mystical contemplation or in the ethical option, religion offers human culture a depth dimension. In the name of the great religious ideals, faith can and should exercise a critical function: it ought to denounce any sort of contradiction or alienation present in human life as an expression of ethical wickedness or social injustice. Accordingly, it is impossible to agree with the thesis of the irreconcilability of the secular and the religious. The conflict that arises may spring from the different faiths animating the believer and the atheist; but it can also occur that the "God" the atheist denies is only a false image of God, which not even the Christians can legitimately accept, since it does not coincide with the "God of the gospel" (*GS* 19).

2. The Problem of Secularism

a. The secularity of modern culture, and the very process of secularization, become problematic when secular *autonomy* collides not only with an illegitimate form of political, cultural, or religious *heteronomy*, but with *theonomy* itself, as such—i.e., with precisely the irruption of the unconditional in the sacred. This occurs when secularity is transformed into a programmatic ideology of the denial of the absolute and the divine. Undeniably, a certain element present in secular humanism makes *secularism* its program, fostering sentiments of skepticism or aversion with regard to the possibility of an affirmation of God. For secularism, the very idea of God appears as alienating, useless, or impossible. First cropping up in a schema of rivalry, we are told, the idea of God is an alienating one, inasmuch as it would hypothetically deprive human beings of their autonomy and freedom, their self-determination and responsibility, and drive them out of the world toward an eschatological refuge. Instead of thinking about changing the world, in order to make it better and more human, the religious person seems to be limited to spending life in mere contemplation of eternity. In turn, religion seems only to serve to legitimate a system of historical or social structures of a conservative and patriarchal nature. When joined to religious experience, politics is sacralized. But in a sacred, hierarchical universe, there is no room for creative imagination and fantasy. Regarded as legitimated by a kind of divine right, historically anachronistic social structures become resistant to change. Furthermore, often enough the idea of God seems useless, as well, for improving human life, since concrete political options are now viewed against a merely intraterrestrial background—although in a second moment, in the case of the believer, such political options may be subsequently legitimated by a religious motivation. Finally, on the supposition of the demise of metaphysics and the impossibility of a strictly empirical verification of religious propositions, the idea of God seems impossible to be thought: after all, that idea becomes incredible for a philosophic consideration understood as a pure phenomenology of the social or as a mere structural analysis of linguistic games played out in various human situations. Consequently, the idea of God comes to be looked upon as a sort of fantasm, or trick with mirrors, and its eclipse from the awareness no longer sparks any great feeling of nostalgia.

b. Today, a critique of historical reason denounces countless intolerances and fanaticisms committed in the name of religious difference. Even the *problem of evil*, that thorn in the side of any theodicy, has returned, and with a new trenchancy, even in our secular era. It returns as a cry of protest against endless crimes of genocide and wars of extermination, against acts of economic he demonic triumph of terror. Current theological meditation also criticizes a false, ideological image of God conceived as an arbitrary, despotic dispenser of boons and afflictions, poverty and wealth, health or sickness. Besides being mythological or idolatrous, such an image becomes mythical and alienating, converting the reality of God into a questionable extension of the world.

To be sure, if we wish to give the name of "theism" to the supposedly religious system that identifies the image of the *deus otiosus* of mystical religion with the *motor immobilis* of the machine of the physical universe, or transforms the image of the *deus activus* of prophetical religion into a totem of religious nationalism, a form of "a-theism" can be legitimately proposed, as a rejection of a false image of the God of biblical revelation. But atheism as a program, and secularism as an ideology, can only constitute a serious challenge for the believer. At all events, a religious criticism of secularism will be able to purify Christianity's theological language, correcting its distortions

and renewing it in depth. Here, current theology has proposed a number of different alternatives, which may well stand in need of correction under some aspects, but which offer some orientations that seem to constitute irreversible options of the current theological task.

c. First, we may regard as irreversible the theological attention accorded divine revelation, and the awareness that, through this revelation, we genuinely know the living, free God. This theological conviction becomes explicit in what has been called the christocentric concentration of revelation. The word of God assumes in Jesus Christ its concrete eschatological definitiveness. Divine revelation does not offer us a fragmented multiplicity of abstractions, but very God, as almighty creator and as merciful, faithful parent. But the biblical message is also the literary objectification of a founding religious experience, and thus comes to be, as well, a human testimonial to the divine word. Here, we may also regard as irreversible the hermeneutical intent, and the existential impact of revelation: the *kerygma* reveals to us our authenticity and sincerity, or on the contrary, our lack of hope and faith. Jesus' way was one of a radical authenticity, and constitutes for us the opportunity for a concrete verification of our unconditional acceptance of God.

Again, we may regard as irreversible the defeat of theological idealism as a system, through an attention to the traumatic aspects of human existence and of vital concrete reality. As subject and addressee of theology, human beings appear in all their finitude and frailty—threatened by death as their tragic destiny, threatened by guilt as the possibility of existential alienation, threatened by the absurd and the void in their anguished spiritual journey, threatened by social evil and historical wickeness in their desire for the realization of community. This threatened human condition constitutes the concrete scenario of divine revelation, whose message becomes relevant— precisely in dialectical confrontation with finitude and alienation, with contradiction and evil—as a proclamation of faith and hope in the divine salvific power that enfolds human destiny.

d. The importance of accepting the secular condition of our era may also be regarded as an irreversible option of the current theological endeavor. This option will entail an acceptance of the impossibility of "thinking God," or speaking of the divine reality, after the fashion of a *deus ex machina*, upon which to call in situations of human helplessness. It will also entail an acceptance of the condition of unbelief and skepticism proper to our age, an era in which believers must affirm their faith, living it in profanity and secularity, without the possibility of an immediate empirical verification. In a secularized world, which organizes its consistency and its logic *etsi deus non daretur* (as if God did not exist), the believer suffers the provocation of the eclipse of the sacred, and the demise of the conventional forms of religious experience. Irreversible as well, therefore, will be the practical attention of theological reflection, which must address the malaise affecting so many Christians in their difficulty with the conventional manner of living their faith. During the time of the "silence of God," theology finds itself obliged to seek out a deeper meaning for personal faith along our life journey, finding a new language for the decisive problematic, and reanimating the tension of hope in the exercise of our freedom and in our commitment of love for our neighbor as "vicar of Christ."

In the quest for a new relationship between historicity and transcendence, we may also regard as irreversible an attention on the part of theology to the problems of praxis: theology must contribute to the splicing of an ethics of solidarity with a culture of secularity. Only in the immanence of history does the encounter with transcendence occur, in revelation and grace, and in the experience of faith and the option for justice. But the primacy of practice must not connote, for the believer, an illogical "Christian atheism," or the historical immanentism of an improper "earthly gospel." The argumentation that appeals to "incarnation" as a crisis of transcendence will only be coercive in terms of a "patripassianism" long since condemned by ancient tradition. Therefore the postulate of praxis and political involvement, in the immanence of history, cannot legitimate, for the believer, an authentic and sincere *fuga dei*. Nor will the admission of a possible "anonymous Christianity," any more than that of an inculpable form of purely theoretical atheism, justify an acceptance of nihilism as the legitimate heir of the Christian experience.

Accordingly, a theological reflection on the practical implications of the acceptance of the Christian *kerygma* may not be invoked to justify a breach with dogmatic tradition, even with respect to the theological language of "Christian theism" as an affirmation of the divine reality as absolute and unique, transcendent and personal. Were such an affirmation to be eliminated as the structure of an intellection of biblical religion itself, Christian revelation would become unintelligible, and lose its force of conviction and its raison d'être. Only God *in se* can found God *quoad nos*. A theological language of a "Christian theism," then, as a linguistic explicitation of the Christian affirmation of God, expresses a legitimate implication of faith, as it constitutes a necessary logical structure for its theoretical understanding and an indispensable presupposition for its free practical acceptance. Accordingly, a radical theology of the "death of God," understood as an acceptance of atheism as a proposition and secularism as a program, must be judged incompatible with Christianity as such.

Bibl.: P. Tillich, *The Religious Situation* (New York, 1932, 1956); D. Bonhoeffer, *Letters and Papers from Prison* (London, 1956); M. Stallmann, *Was ist Säkularisierung?* (Tübingen, 1960); S. Acquaviva, *L'Eclissi del sacro nelle civiltà industriale* (Milan, 1961); G. Vahanian, *The Death of God* (New York, 1961); J. A. T. Robinson, *Honest to God* (London, 1963); P. M. Van Buren, *The Secular Meaning of the Gospel* (London, 1963); A. T. Van Leeuwen, *Christianity in World History* (London, 1964); H. E. Cox, *The Secular City* (New York, 1965); D. Sölle, *Stellvertretung* (Stuttgart, 1965); T. J. J. Altizer and W. Hamilton, *Radical Theology and the Death of God* (Indianapolis/New York, 1966); K. Rahner, "Theological Reflections on the Problem of Secularization," in *Theological Investigations*, vol. 10 (1967; London, 1973), 318–48; T. Luckmann, *The Invisible Religion* (New York, 1967); J. B. Metz, *Zur Theologie der Welt* (Mainz/Munich, 1968); F. Gogarten, *Despair and Hope for Our Times* (Philadelphia, 1970); S. Acquaviva and G. Guizzardi, *La secolarizzazione* (Bologna, 1973); P. Glasner, *The Sociology of Secularization* (London, 1977); D. Martin, *A General Theory of Secularization* (Oxford, 1978).

Félix-Alejandro Pastor

SECULARITY

Difficulties arise when one tries to use the concept of "secularity." A careful study of it inevitably involves its correlatives: secularization and secularism. These two terms refer to highly complex sociocultural phenomena, and reflection on secularity, whether in the juridico-canonical sphere or in the philosophical, sociological, or theological spheres, must keep in close touch with these phenomena, as well as be open to a plurality of experiences. It is impossible in practice to speak of Christianity or secularization or religion in the singular, since they are phenomena that must be considered in their diverse historical and socio-cultural contexts. They are concepts that refer to basic vectors of human experience.

It may be asked whether it is still appropriate for theologians to reflect on secularity. Especially in the sixties this question was a central concern of all the human sciences. Beginning in the seventies, a counterattack was launched against secularization in the name of both politics and religion (e.g., the various liberation theologies, and political fundamentalism). However, neither the impressive revival of religion nor the movement for the liberation of the poor can serve as a substitute pure and simple for the process of secularization.

If we are to understand the present relationship of the church to secularity, it is important first of all to analyze the use of this concept in the documents of the magisterium. A way of life, namely, that of the secular institutes approved by Pius XII in 1947 in the Apostolic Constitution *Provida Mater Ecclesia*, also calls for attention, since secularity constitutes their primary mission, to be accomplished through profession of the evangelical counsels. In a second step I shall sketch the debate on secularization in its relation to Christian faith, and thus prepare the way for the question: Is "secularized" culture a test of Christian witness?

1. Emergence of the Concept of Secularity

"Secularity" is derived from the Latin *saeculum*, but the latter is not the only Latin word for "world"; there is also *mundus*. *Mundus* expresses the idea of space and is equivalent to the Greek *kosmos*, which signifies a universe in which all the elements are ordered to one another according to an internal logic that forms a closed system. *Saeculum* conveys the idea of time, which is expressed in Greek by *aiōn*, "age," "era" (the Sanskrit *àyus* and its compounds have the same meaning). *Mundus* reflects the Greek conception of the world as a place; *saeculum* reflects the Hebrew conception of the world as history. The Hebrew word *'olam* means both time and world, i.e., the temporal world. The Greek meaning of "world" dominated the theological tradition from the second-century apologists on. The result was that the word *secularity* lost the Hebrew sense of "world," in which "world" was thought of in terms of temporality and historicity. Exegesis of the OT has brought out this difference in meaning. It is impossible to overemphasize the importance of the recovery by theologians of the historical and temporal nature of secularity (see Cox 1965: 18–21).

The traditional use of the word *secular* pays no heed to the historical dimension. The adjective *secular* first appeared in the twelfth century; it referred to the "world" (*saeculum*), the lay state, and the temporal order, and was opposed to the sphere of ecclesiastics and religious. From the juridico-canonical viewpoint, a secular is one who lives in the world, as contrasted with one living a life according to rule. In the Middle Ages the noun *secularity* was rarely used to describe the state of the secular priest. Despite the seeming neutrality of juridico-canonical terminology, it in fact subordinates time to what is regarded as the realm of the sacred and of eternity. This leads to a depreciation of the secular in favor of the sacred and of religious and ecclesiastics. The temporality of the secular is relative and limited; temporal activities are less important than "sacred" activities. Furthermore, secular places are opposed to sacred places and the world of the beyond.

While it is a risky matter to define a particular age's conception of space and time, it is possible to single out its dominant aspect. Especially once Gregory the Great (540–604; *Moralia* I.14.20; V.13.30; XXXII.20.35 [*PL* 75:535, 695; 76:657]) had introduced the idea of a hierarchy of vocations, with monastic life serving as the ideal, Christian "perfection" was seen as belonging in its fullness to those men and women who "renounce worldly affairs." As applied to states of life, this view found expression toward the twelfth century in the concept of a two-part church: monks or clerics, and laypersons; men and women concerned with worship or the divine, and seculars. The relationship of human beings to the world and to the last things was given a specific cast. Greater attention to the last things obscured the eschatological meaning of history; the result was the primacy assigned to monasticism.

The Middle Ages held on to both terms: *mundus*/space and *saeculum*/time, but a problem remained nonetheless, namely, the association of the religious realm, the realm of ultimate things, with the concept *mundus,* and the association of the profane and less important realm with the concept *saeculum.* Nowadays the relationship of faith to the secular realm seems to be explained by the concept of secularity in the juridico-canonical and theological sense of the word, although the antimodernist outlook left its mark on this thinking down to Vatican II.

At the beginning of the century Catholicism posed the question of the relationship to the world in terms of the apostolate and of participation in the apostolate of the hierarchy. Some theologians and movements sought to free themselves from the Catholic ghetto and raised the question of a Christian secularity. The apostolate of the laity was thought of as taking three forms: the rechristianization of the structures of social life, direct evangelization, and the witness of a silent, hidden life.

Until Vatican II the increasing enthusiasm for lay action movements was not accompanied by any theological breakthroughs. On analysis, the so-called theology of "earthly realities" (G. Thils) proved to be based on a practical separation between nature and the supernatural rather than to be inspired by the idea that the secular has an essential connection with faith. Reflection on this theology ran into a stumbling block: a dualistic approach to eschatology and incarnation, humanization and evangelization. Secularity, in the sociological and theological sense of the term, was used almost exclusively in connection with states of life.

Vatican II grounds secularity in the mystery of Christ's incarnation: "For God's Word, through whom all things were made, was Himself made flesh and dwelt upon the earth of men. Thus he entered the world's history as a perfect man, taking that history up into Himself and summarizing it" (*GS* 38). The disciples of Christ share this secular condition, and "nothing genuinely human fails to raise an echo in their hearts" (*GS* 1), as Philippians 4:8 reminds us: "Whatever is true, whatever is honorable, whatever is just, whatever is pure, whatever is pleasing, whatever is commendable, if there is any excellence and if there is anything worthy of praise, think about these things." The council does not spell out the significance of the secularity of Christ for the church. It simply takes this as a basis for sketching the secularity of the members of the church: even if all the members participate in different ways in the secular nature of the church, the quality of secularity belongs in particular to the laity (*LG* 31) and the members of secular institutes (*PC* 11) and gives them a threefold duty: "to seek the kingdom of God," "engaging in temporal affairs," and "ordering them according to the plan of God" (*LG* 31). These three elements in combination are required for Christian secularity. While ordained ministers do share in the secularity of the church, "by reason of their particular vocation they are chiefly and professedly ordained to the sacred ministry" (*LG* 31). Finally, withdrawal from the world (*a mundo secessu: PC* 7) is a matter only for institutes of the contemplative life.

The documents of the 1987 synod on the laity and the postsynodal apostolic exhortation *The Lay Members of Christ's Faithful People* (*Christifideles Laici*) (1988) help us to define the present state of the thinking of the magisterium on secularity. The debate in which these documents play a part can be summed up in this question: Is the secularity of the laity a purely sociological phenomenon or is it also theological and ecclesial? From the sociological viewpoint secularity is the context of social life with its cultural changes, in which the laity play an active part. But secularity is not reducible to an activity that transforms the environment. The final Propositions of the synod state that the entire church has a secular dimension, although secularity calls to mind in particular the mission of the laity. The laity are "secular" in a sense that is not simply sociological but also, and primarily, theological, because they have a threefold mission: to "participate in the work of creation," to "free [it] from the influence of sin," and to "sanctify themselves" in the world (Proposition 4). Quoting a passage from the address of Paul VI to superiors and members of the secular institutes (1972), the apostolic exhortation says that the church "has an authentic secular dimension, inherent to her inner nature and mission, which is deeply rooted in the mystery of the Word Incarnate, and which is realized in different forms through her members" (no. 15). But, as Vatican II said, this trait belongs especially to the laity. Baptism gives a fundamental dignity shared by all Christians, and secularity is a "modality" of this dignity. Finally, the apostolic exhortation states clearly: "The Council considers their [the laity's] condition not simply an external and environmental framework, but as a reality destined to find in Jesus Christ the fullness of its meaning" (no. 15).

These statements suggest that secularity is being looked at from a spatial point of view and that its changing historical dimension does not define the nature of the church. Just as the laity are seen as being sent into the world from within the world, so secularity represents a direction or line of thinking that is seen as rather external to the life of the church. Discussion of the secular institutes would doubtless shed further light in this area. These institutes are officially engaged in, and are called to be engaged in, the experience of the secularity that affects the entire church. In their own discussions these institutes face, in a radical form, the questions being debated in Christian circles regarding the relationship of faith and the secular.

Born as they are of a determination to maintain an evangelical radicalism in the midst of the world, the secular institutes combine the problem of secularity and the problem of states of life in the church. They raise, first of all, the delicate question of a consecrated life lived *in saeculo et ex saeculo* (in the world and from within the world) (Lefebvre 1989). Consecration has traditionally been understood as a setting apart and as being realized in religious life. How, then, is it possible to combine consecration and a secular state? In the course of the history of the secular institutes (Angela Merici in the sixteenth century was the first to glimpse such a way of life) a tension has appeared between an increasingly pragmatic view of their own identity and the official vision of the onto-

logical character of the commitment to evangelical radicalism. This tension gives rise to discussion of such questions as these: Are the members of these institutes really laypersons? Have the institutes a specific connection with secularity? In the case of priestly secular institutes the question becomes even more critical: Since priests are men committed to the sacred, can they be inspired by the will to a truly secular involvement? The discussions in secular institutes are beset with problems arising from the fact that in defining its own nature the church still uses the categories of clergy and laity, ecclesiality and secularity, and eschatology and history. The institutes attempt to clarify their own status in the church by appealing to secularity, instead of explaining secularity in itself and in its relation to faith. Seen in this perspective, the precedence which being-in-the-world has over being-in-the-church from the standpoint of an ontology of culture remains an abstract principle. In the apostolic sphere, the kind of thinking that regards secularity as external to the gospel will see the problem as one of "suffusion" or "penetration" (*perfundere*), no less than of rapprochement, intervention, and integration into the world. The key formula of secular institutes—to live and act "in the world and from within the world" (PC 11)—only inverts the problem instead of solving it. For, whether Christians be regarded as coming from outside or from inside, they remain persons set apart in order then to inject something into the world, to "penetrate" the world. Given this perspective of "penetration," secularity is conceived of as a situation either *outside* the church or *inside* the church but not *of* the church. In order to give the various problems a new direction it will be necessary to bring into the discussion the theological literature of the last twenty-five years on the problem of secularization and the placing of religion at the very heart of secularity.

2. Secularization and Secularism

One's understanding of secularization depends on the view one takes of the secular and the sacred. The concept of secularization has, to begin with, a juridico-canonical meaning: the passage from the ecclesiastical state to the secular state, the alienation of ecclesiastical possessions to the advantage of civil authorities. In political history, it signifies the handing over of religious powers to the civil authority. In the sphere of culture, it means the doing away with cultural elements or symbols that are explicitly religious. Following this traditional conception of it, secularization is understood within the church as a diminishment (in state of life), a (political) loss, and a (cultural) failure. Hermann Lübbe brings all this out in his historico-political study of the history of the concept of secularization (Lübbe 1965).

The word *secularization* was used for the first time at Münster in 1803 by the French envoy delegated to negotiate the peace treaty of Westphalia. The issue there was to decide the conditions for the liquidation of the church's sociopolitical domination. The atmosphere at the beginning was one of neutrality, since the church admitted the validity of the secularization of some properties. But a possible judgment on the legitimacy or illegitimacy of the proceedings suggested a process in which political forces were at work.

The code of canon law bases its use of the term on this original sociopolitical usage. From a quite neutral viewpoint, secularization signifies here the authorized departure of a person from a religious order back to the lay state. But the secularized person loses certain privileges, in particular, that of teaching theology; this loss means a discrediting of the person.

In the sphere of political history, the occurrence of secularization created opposing parties: people in the church, who judged the actions to be illegitimate, and the civil authorities, who were convinced the actions represented sociocultural progress. According to historian Heinrich von Treitschke, there was wrongdoing on both sides. The church may have abused its ownership of property, but the takeover of property by the civil authorities was marked by greed (H. v. Treitschke, *Deutsche Geschichte im 19. Jahrhundert, I: Bis zum zweiten Pariser Frieden* [1927], 186ff.). But, independently of some wrongdoing on both sides, secularization was a necessary process, namely, the abolition of a theocracy that had become untenable. In time, the church finally saw the spiritual advantages of a secularization that turned it toward a greater authenticity. Although the conflicts have subsided, the en-

cyclopedias current in the fifties did not always view secularization as an irreversible choice made by society but, in some instances, still viewed it as a threat to a Christian culture.

The German language distinguishes two levels or areas of secularization: the historico-political area, for which the word *Säkularisation* is used, and the philosophical and cultural area, for which the word *Säkularisierung* is used. The philosophical and cultural meaning appeared for the first time in philosophies of history inspired by Hegel. Hegel himself, however, speaks of the "world-ing" (*Verweltlichung*) of the Christian faith: society turned worldly (*mondanéisée*) represents the historical fulfillment par excellence of Christianity, especially in the name of the principle of autonomy and freedom on which the French Revolution was based. The term *Säkularisierung* seems to signify the thesis that links Christianity and secularization. If Hegel does not use it, the reason is that he does not admit the ideological struggles which the term connotes. His vision of history is situated beyond conflicts of this kind.

The idea of a cultural secularization, as expressed in the term *Säkularisierung* (represented henceforth by "secularization"), was developed by analogy with the juridical and historico-political meanings, but with its point of reference in a secular philosophy and ethic, i.e., a philosophy and ethic removed from theological and ecclesiastical influences. The principal originators of this movement were Victor Cousin (1844) in France and Ernst Lass (1882) and Friedrich Jodl (1889) in Germany. Cultural secularization was concerned first and foremost with the area of education. In nineteenth-century Europe, the activities of the German Society for Ethical Culture (Die Deutsche Gesellschaft für Ethische Kultur), of which E. Laas and F. Jodl were directors, were evidence of this thinking: the society urged not only the separation of church and state but also neutral schools in which an autonomous public morality was to be taught in accordance with positivist technocratic principles; it promoted the principle of tolerance, although some of its members declared themselves outrightly hostile to religion and the churches. In England, the Secular Society, founded by George Holyoake in 1846, pursued the same objectives. It was here that the term "secularism" was coined to bring out the innovative nature of this association of free-thinkers. The antireligious ambiance of the mid-nineteenth century favored the emergence of this attitude. Holyoake, however, encouraged the coexistence of the secular with Christianity, to the extent that the latter promoted the well-being of all. Secularism found its philosophical basis in the "associationist" schools of James Mill and Jeremy Bentham and in the antitheism of Thomas Paine and Richard Carlile, as well as in positivist theory. It projected an ethics that looked solely to material conditions and contained no reference to transcendence. In Holyoake's view of coexistence, the deconfessionalization of civic institutions meant that these took no account of the transcendent character of Christianity's role in society. Theology has to do with the other world. Under the presidency of Charles Bradlaugh (1866) the Secular Society welcomed the materialistic and atheistic free-thinking of Ludwig Büchner's movement (1881). "Secularism" as a social project was compatible with either of two tendencies in regard to religion: tolerance or hostility.

At the beginning of the century secularization also meant the process whereby science became autonomous in relation to religion and religious authorities. In 1908 Richard Fester proposed a secularization of historical science and of the biblical and theological vision of the world. He did not engage in historico-political or cultural debates but directly challenged Catholic antimodernism, which was opposed specifically to the autonomy of science. But Fester's links to the freethinking of the Secular Society were an obstacle to a strictly scientific and neutral use of the concept of secularization. German sociology, in the persons of Ferdinand Tönnies and Max Weber, led to a turning point in the understanding of this concept. Although Tönnies never speaks of secularization, he sets out to determine the conditions for the passage from "community" (*Gemeinschaft*) to "society" (*Gesellschaft*) (F. Tönnies, *Community and Society*, trans. C. P. Loomis [East Lansing, Mich., 1957; Harper Torchbooks, 1963]). These are ancient categories, used, e.g., by Confucius, Plato, Aristotle, and Augustine. A world based on concord, morality, and religion has been replaced by one based on convention, politics, and public opinion. This change

represents, in Tönnies's view, a shift to a new kind of society that has no reference to religion. What he calls "society" is in fact a secularized community. He links the distinction between "community" and "society" with another, commonly used in other contexts, between "culture" and "civilization." The latter distinction is not neutral but is most often used in critiques of civilization. While Tönnies acknowledges the benefits which civilization has brought, he fears for culture. His hope is that the "scattered seeds [of the culture] . . . may remain alive and again bring forth the essence and idea of Gemeinschaft [community], thus secretly fostering a new culture amid the decaying one" (p. 231).

Max Weber, for his part, develops a neutral vision of secularization along the lines of a "disenchantment (*Entzäuberung*) of the world" (*Wirtschaft und Gesellschaft*, 1. Halbband [Tübingen, 1956]). He studies the connections between Calvinism and capitalism in Western Europe, capitalism being explained as the secular end result of a Christian faith that is Puritan in outlook. He regards capitalism as a product of secularization. The rationality that predominates in this type of society implies a "disenchantment" of the world. Weber passes no value judgment on this process, but does presuppose that it is inescapable. Against the ideological parties that emerged from the First World War Weber objects that they cannot agree on a genuine rationality, but represent rather the ancient gods who seek once again to control the way in which human beings live. He proposes a morality of existential freedom. Freedom of thought may not win salvation but at least it makes it possible to thwart ideological doctrines of salvation.

Ernst Troeltsch inherited the sociological contribution to the question of secularization. His own work deals with the theological aspect of the question (*Die Bedeutung des Protestantismus für die Entstehung der modernen Welt* [Munich/Berlin, 1911]; Eng. trans. *Protestantism and Progress: The Significance of Protestantism for the Rise of the Modern World* [Philadelphia, 1986]). Taking into account the connection between liberal theology and the modern world, he shows that Protestantism has made a major contribution to the process of "disenchantment" of the world. Thus he sees a continuity between secularized culture and Christian faith. In his view, modern culture is secularized Protestantism. He studies the problem of the future of the Christian faith. The process of secularization is a process of dissolution of the traditional faith. Confronted with the crisis of faith in this new setting, Troeltsch opts for a theological historicism in which the concept of secularization serves as a historical category. He takes no position on whether the process represents decline or progress, but simply accepts as priceless contributions the principles of freedom and individuality that are characteristic of the modern world and also inherent in the Christian faith. He fears, however, a failure to recognize the metaphysical and religious foundation of these principles and a resulting human self-sufficiency.

Among later positions on this subject, the most recent and the most important is that of Friedrich Gogarten, the first thinker to produce a theology of secularization. He gives his blessing to secularization and introduces a new distinction between secularization and secularism. As a result of the meaning given to "secularism" by the Secular Society, this term has come to be defined as the negation of continuity between faith and the modern, to the point of doing away with faith entirely. In his book, _Destin et espoir du monde moderne_ (Paris, 1970; German original 1953); Eng. trans. _Despair and Hope for Our Times_ (Philadelphia, 1970). Gogarten proposes a deeper theological understanding of secularization, and one that is still influential today.

In Gogarten's view, secularization is a result of the Christian faith, for it consists in a liberation of the human person from the forces at work in the world, and it is faith that has inspired this deliverance by changing the relationship of human beings to history. Conversely, secularization signifies a "world-ing" of the world and the end of the era of myth. In order to explain the new relationship which secularization expresses, Gogarten harks back to two biblical concepts: filiation and inheritance.

Salvation establishes a hitherto unknown relationship with God in which human beings are made his sons and daughters in their very being. Previously, in the infantile stage of human history, human beings were subject to the forces of the world (in the biblical sense) that had been established by the law. Faith consists in the acceptance of a new, radical, fundamental dependence on God as Father, creator, and justifier. Gogarten then goes on to explain the consequences of this sonship and daughterhood for the earthly life of human beings: the latter are given a complete freedom in relation to the world, in the sense that as heirs of creation they exercise a full control over it (Gal 4:1, 7). This control supposes that the basic dependence on God is extended through the acquisition of autonomy in action: the being that we have received from God achieves its fulfillment in our being-for-ourselves. These two poles, taken together, keep the creature in a balanced state. For Gogarten, then, secularization has its origin precisely in the constitution of the human person as a being-for-itself.

How does Gogarten see the erosion of secularization into secularism? In his view, there has been a perversion of historicity, as a result of which the direction which the development of the world ought to take remains still wrapped in mystery. Secularity is the acceptance of human historicity. The attitude which human beings, whether believers or not, take to the future as beings who are perpetually becoming and questioning, keeps them in secularity. If they claim to determine by themselves the direction of history and cease thereby to relativize their present projects, they fall into secularism.

Gogarten also rejects the Christian secularism that confuses faith and Christianity, with Christianity claiming to make salvation operative within history instead of leaving the final decision and operation to God and relying solely on faith. It is on this basis that Gogarten revises the usual conception of NT eschatology as being the final accomplishment of God's salvation, an accomplishment to which the entire stage that is the time of the church is ordered. In Gogarten's view, the phrase "everything passes" takes on a historical meaning and points to the relative nature of everything that makes up human life, including the historical forms of the expression of faith. The future always lies ahead of human beings and cannot be incorporated into their present plans. It is precisely faith that protects us from Christian secularism, because faith clearly differentiates human history from God's history. In Lübbe's judgment, the theology of secularization works with a more scientific use of the term _Säkularisierung_.

The Second Vatican Council does not use the concept of secularization. It does, however, refer to it indirectly when it envisages a legitimate "autonomy of earthly realities" (*GS* 38); it specifies what it means by this autonomy when it rejects a separatist outlook and insists on a "vital synthesis" of faith and life (*GS* 43). By the decisive direction which the council gives to relations between the church and the world in its Declaration on Religious Freedom (*Dignitatis Humanae*) it signals the end of the rejection in principle of secularization. This Declaration implies three major revisions: the church will no longer define its relationship to the state according to a logic of power; it abandons its antirevolutionary positions by ratifying human rights; it abandons any plans for a Christendom. Henceforward, state and religion coexist as autonomous entities. As for secularism, this is understood as a process whereby every reference to religion is deliberately eliminated. It is to be observed that the Propositions of the 1987 Synod on the laity speak of secularization but immediately shift to the concept of secularism, which is defined in these terms: "A vision of the human person and the world as autonomous, in complete abstraction from the dimension of mystery, this being neither taken into account nor denied" (*La Documentation Catholique*, no. 1909, col. 37). This definition is problematic: How can the scientific approach to reality be subordinated to mystery? Is it possible simply to identify human goals and the absolute future of God?

The "updating" which the council undertook liberated the critical and prophetic powers of the church. Thinking on church-world relations was now open to a "new" political theology that formally takes account of modernity and brings to light its consequence for Christian faith (see Johannes B. Metz, *Zur Theologie der Welt* [Munich, 1968]; Eng. trans. *Theology of the World* [London, 1969]), while also giving increased attention to the positions taken by such Protestant thinkers as Rudolf Bultmann, Paul Tillich, Dietrich Bonhoeffer, and John A. T. Robinson, as well as to the theologies of the secular city of Harvey Cox and Gibson Winter. Radical critiques of religion are formulated in connections with considerations on demythization, desacralization, and secularization.

Two important theological positions on secularization call for attention: those of Johannes B. Metz and Harvey Cox. They take up where Friedrich Gogarten's theology leaves off; each develops a thesis according to which the "world-ing" (Metz) or secularization (Cox) of the world has its origin in Christianity and in the power of Christianity acting in history. The end result of this process is a faith-world relationship that is far removed from the traditional dichotomy between the sacred and the profane (a dichotomy unknown to the biblical world). Metz challenges transcendental and personalist theologies, even that of his teacher, Karl Rahner. Cox distances himself from the "death of God" theologies (William Hamilton, Thomas J. J. Altizer, Paul van Buren). Both authors seek continuity with the Enlightenment, chiefly via Karl Marx, whom they understand as he is interpreted in the philosophy of Ernst Bloch, who takes a new approach to Marxism in his major work *Das Prinzip Hoffnung*. By his reflections on "anticipatory consciousness" and the "anticipatory dreams" that arise from the preconscious levels of the human person Bloch is able to supply Marxism with a "futurology." At the same time, however, he brings out the utopian project of the peoples of the Bible, as well as the reformist and political energies at work in their history but for a long time obscured by the church. More generally, both Cox and Metz loudly proclaim "the end of metaphysics." Metaphysics looks at reality from a static, realist, and substantialist point of view and does not allow us to think in terms of history, becoming, and time, for it conceives of change as something accidental in an immutable universe.

In his *Theology of the World* Johann Baptist Metz situates faith in relation to the new consciousness of the world that has resulted from the process of "world-ing." Faith must open itself to new situations and reflect on itself in the light of these. World-ing has its theological and biblical basis in God's incarnation and adopting of the world. In assuming humanity through his Son, God has adopted the world; this means that he has assumed it in its very worldness. In order to reconcile world-ing and adopting Metz uses the concept of otherness. God establishes a relationship of reciprocity with the world, assuming it as other. The saving restoration of the world is intended to make the world achieve this otherness. In a vital, ceaseless tension toward the God who is other, the world deepens its own worldness-otherness. God, who embraced the cosmos and predetermined it (cosmocentrism) seems to withdraw from the worldly sphere (anthropocentrism). This "disappearance" of God from the Greek vision of the world is experienced by many as a state of atheism. In fact, however, if atheism has become the current interpretation of this phenomenon, it is because faith has failed to keep its rendezvous with the world-ing of the world. The new religious relationship with the world involves numerous novelties. Autonomy in the management of the world, even in the midst of intersubjectivity, leads to a very marked pluralism of consciousnesses. A unified grasp of life becomes difficult. In the modern anthropocentric movement the categories in which experience of the divinity have hitherto been expressed are shattered. The Christian mission now has to unfold within a three-dimensional history: loss, salvation, and worlding-otherness as the context in which human freedom is exercised. By its contribution to the autonomization of the world Christianity makes it possible freely to take a position for or against salvation. The men and women of today, responsible as they are for the historical development of the world, are future-oriented: not in the contemplative attitude that used to mark their relation to the world-seen-as-nature, but in a constant will to transform the world-seen-as-history. This is why Metz opts for a theology that is political, eschatological, and critical.

This concern for action bearing on history paves the way for a radical turnaround on Metz's part. He attacks the abstract character of the various theses about secularization. His work _Faith in History and Society_ (New York, 1977; German original, 1968) gives the end result of this shift. He narrows his reading of modernity. After conceiving it initially as a comprehensive phenomenon of world-ing, he now understands it as a process of _emancipation_. He wants to correct the privatizing effects of the secularization thesis on faith. In his view, that kind of theology neutralizes the critical and transforming power of faith. He likewises rejects the identification of Christianity and secularization. He is gladdened, however, by the fact that the Enlightenment has proved itself a solid _locus theologicus_. Liberal theologies have the advantage of proclaiming a more demo-

cratic vision of the church, as well as freedom of conscience and of thought. But this liberalism and neoliberalism also bring with it the impasses of the Enlightenment, in particular the kind of citizen who is the Enlightenment's chief subject: the bourgeois. In his practical fundamental theology Metz wants to redirect theology toward the condition of the historical, concrete subject. Christianity is a praxis: _that_ is the meaning of evangelical radicalism.

In his _The Secular City_ Harvey Cox sets out to show the Judeo-Christian character of secularization. The fact that secularization thus originated is an opportunity for Christianity. Following Bonhoeffer, Cox proclaims "the end of religion." Secularization bids us take secularity as our starting point for talking about God and reinterpreting the Bible. The Scriptures tell of three events which are the source of secularization: the fact of creation leads to the _disenchantment_ of the world, the exodus to the _desacralization_ of the political order, and the Sinai covenant to the _deconsecration_ of values. Cox also picks out some characteristics of technological and urban civilization. I shall mention, first of all, the aspect of mobility. Sedentariness gives rise to _homo religiosus_, the human being with set traditions who does not welcome the novelties of God's ways. The entire history of salvation is a ceaseless effort to despatialize the divinity (the exodus) and to think of the world as history and becoming. A second point: the modern pragmatic attitude extends to the relation between subject and truth. Modern people are more interested in the functioning of things than in their substantial identity, as was the case in the age of metaphysics. The fundamental unity of humanity in Christ (Col 1:1–20) is not to be thought of as a predetermining source of historical direction; rather it leaves human beings the task of building their world in collaboration with God.

What are the limits of secularization? Although secularization is a healthy emancipation of humanity, it can nonetheless change for the worse and turn into secularism. Secularism is at hand when secularization turns into an ideology that overshadows the free expression of subjects and their experience. If we hark back to secularism as seen by Gogarten, Cox and Gogarten would be in agreement in seeing in secularism a radicalization of institutions and the development of a way of seeing and existing in isolation. Here the system withdraws into its own logic and changes into an ideology; it ceases to express itself through subjects. In this way even a Christian secularism can arise: one that is closed to the realms of historicity and of God's future, and therefore located outside of secularity. The process of secularization represents a reaction against this kind of Christian secularism. But if secularization in turn becomes an ideology, i.e., if it closes itself to subjects and their experiences, it too degenerates into secularism. Atheistic materialism and blind neoliberalism are to be seen as examples of secularism. The first wants to obscure the persistent religious outlook of subjects, and the second ignores those abandoned by economic liberalism. Challenging this last attitude, the Latin American liberation theologians attack secularization as a whole and see no value in the distinction between secularization and secularism.

The development of Cox's thought makes it possible to situate secularity in the perspective of the self-criticism of modernity. In 1973, in his *The Seduction of the Spirit*, he more clearly specifies the object of his criticism of religion. Bonhoeffer rejected a clericalizing religion that was closely allied with a reactionary politics and did not fully accept the human dimension of life. Following him and lightly dismissing the very idea of religion, the theologians of the early sixties opened their arms, without sufficient critical distance, to the visions of Marx, Freud, and even Nietzsche, and failed to grasp the complexity of the matter. In addition, there is the massive fact of religious experiences, especially in the countries of Eastern Europe, as well as the ever-present phenomenon of prayer. Theologians need to stop opposing gospel and religion and attempt instead to understand the new manifestations of the religious attitude. Eleven years later, in *Religion in the Secular City* (New York, 1984), Cox further locates his 1965 position within the horizon of the return to religion that is a growing movement. He analyzes the religious phenomenon in its unexpected resumption of links with politics, especially in American political fundamentalism and the Latin American theologies of liberation. But he does not therefore abandon his conviction that there must be a theology that works within secularity and continues the critique of religion that is an essential element of Judeo-Christianity. The fundamental role of Christian theology is to ensure that human history advances under the sign of liberation. Twenty years ago, his awareness of this role led him to undertake, in the footsteps of the prophets and Jesus, a sharp critique of religion in the light of secularization. Now after the abuse of power by reason and by political totalitarianism, what is needed is a critique of secularization in the light of religion, with concern for the poor playing a central role in this critique.

Two of the criticisms which Friedrich Gogarten, Johannes B. Metz, and Harvey Cox have brought against the secularization theologies deserve to be kept in mind. First, the claim that Christianity is the source of secularized society and the religion that marks "the end of religion" seems idealistic, since it masks the difficulty which the historical energies of the lay world have had in winning recognition of the autonomy of the various secular spheres. Following as it did upon Christianity according to Constantine, secularization undoubtedly meant a break with Christianity. As Hans Blumenberg sees it, therefore, the theses of secularization theology seem to be an opportunistic attempt at a retrieval of lost ground, following "the familar pattern of all self-preservation" (H. Blumenberg, *The Legitimacy of the Modern Age* [Cambridge, Mass., and London, 1983], 6). We are here thrown back on the distinction between secularization as a fact and secularization as an interpretation. Every interpretation of the process involves an ideological stance. The second criticism of Gogarten, Metz, and Cox is that the secularization theses forget about the rejected. In 1976, at a conference on the hermeneutics of secularization (convened by Enrico Castelli), Maurice Boutin remarked that F. Gogarten focuses his attention on the question of the meaning of secularization (the "what"), but forgets to raise the problem of those who are left by the wayside in this process of emancipation (the "for whose sake"). The theologians of liberation have been very much aware of this second aspect. Thinkers need to study not only the stakes in the relation between "faith and nonbelief," but also the implications of the relation between "faith and nonhumanity" (M. Boutin, "L'espace de la sécularité," in *Prospettive sulla secularizzazione* [Rome, 1976], 43–68). It is true that these points need to be taken into consideration, but do not the theologies and hermeneutics of secularization supply fundamental insights for reinterpreting Christianity in a secularized world? Do they not show the way for a theology of secularity that will indeed be able to shed light on the very nature of the church and of Christian witness?

3. Toward a Theology of Secularity

In 1976 Maurice Boutin described secularity as "the potential space" of both secularization and faith. A heteronomous vision of the world, proper to the geocentrist place of the human person in the universe (cosmocentrism), has been overturned in favor of an autonomous vision proper to heliocentrism (anthropocentrism). Now, human beings focus their gaze on the "periphery" of their experience and identify it as sacred or secularized. When they thus see their horizon in external terms, they form dualities: divine-worldly, sacred-profane, transcendence-immanence. Consequently, once the upheaval produced by heliocentrism has occurred, the entire religious vision is challenged. Boutin reminds us, however, that whatever the way in which human beings understand their place in the universe, they must take into account not only the "periphery" but also the "center," the place in relation to which they locate themselves. It is therefore possible for them to move beyond both a purely religious and a purely worldly vision of the world. Boutin calls this middle ground "the space of secularity" which makes possible both religion and secularization. The need is to understand how this potential middle ground is restructured in a heliocentrist system.

In light of these reflections on the possibility of both religion and secularization, the following observation seems called for: if we speak of the present phase of history, especially Western history, in terms of postmodernity or of a return to religion, we may keep alive the illusion of a possible return to the past. Given the growing complexification of social life, individuals and groups are bringing back traditional kinds of discourse and traditional settings. But does not this "return" hide a flight into the future as the crisis of modernity is recognized? We ought, then, come to the deeper recognition that religion is undergoing a metamorphosis.

A further observation has to do with the foundation on which Christian identity is built. Ecclesial secularity implies a recognition that the place where the Christian mission is to be carried out is the human heart which has been enlightened by the mystery of Christ (*GS* 22). The point on which the church focuses remains to some extent external to it, namely, the heart of Christ as source of salvation, and the heart of the human person as addressee of the proclamation of salvation. Secularity thus points to a continual detachment from self, in favor of the world and the future of God, and all this in Christ. To say this is to remind ourselves, in a vitally important way, that self-identity develops only in relation to the other. The secularized world is the no man's land in which God's freedom is safeguarded. Viewed thus, the process reminds us of the critical role played by pagans in the Bible. The secularized world is a place that makes possible the proclamation of faith as dialogue, i.e., as both assent and critique of the culture. It is this basic dimension of ecclesial secularity that gives it its theological content. Paul Valadier has maintained the necessity of a reciprocal challenge between the secularized world and the church:

> When faith meets its other, even a hostile other, when it listens to the other's objections, it discovers its hidden potentialities.... Because faith is thus lived out and asserts itself in confrontation with the other, it must struggle against the church's withdrawals into itself and must distrust the voices that call upon the church to find its identity within itself.... Let Christians learn rather to lose themselves, and they will find themselves in what they must become as they help the world to respond to the end for which it exists. (Valadier 1987: 237–38)

It follows that when secularity is seen exclusively in terms of social milieu or mission, the vision of Christian witness lacks an effective awareness of those aspects of secularity that are constitutive of the very experience of faith and its expression. John Paul II suggests this truth in his first encyclical *Redemptor Hominis* (March 1979), when he says that the human person in its concrete sociocultural conditioning is "the primary route ... the primary and fundamental way" for the church (no. 14). This is a truth that should determine the form Christian witness takes in secularity. Reflection on the structures of the church and on the church's entire way of being and acting must take into account the kind of religiosity at work in the contemporary world and the schemata used in the culture. Gabriel Vahanian speaks of a church that is in the avant-garde of society; but this, he says, requires that seculars with a wide variety of specializations participate and collaborate in the life of the church (*Dieu et l'utopie* [Paris, 1976]; Eng. trans. *God and Utopia* [New York, 1977]).

In light of the foregoing, we may question the relevance of the idea of "the consecration of the secular" that is used by the secular institutes (Lefebvre 1989). This concept implies separation. The incarnation, however, does not at all mean an alienation of human nature by God, but rather its recapitulation with the wholeness proper to it. When the world has been sanctified it remains the world; its world-ness is ratified. On the other hand, when the world is consecrated (in the proper sense of this word), it is set apart from what is profane (Lefebvre 1989:88–91; see also M.-D. Chenu, "La *consecratio mundi*," in J. Beyer, ed., *Études sur les instituts séculiers* 3 [Paris, 1966]). The sacramental role of the church is to turn the world into the kingdom of God, not by entering into it from the outside after setting it "spatially" apart, but by recognizing in it the calls and presence of God. The secularization theologians have learned to understand the insight of modern men and women in their criticism of religion. The God of the Bible is a creator, who relates to human beings and to history; this God refuses any spatialization and is the very opposite of the God of a religion that regards history as subordinated to it. At bottom, then, the modern movement resembles biblical desacralization. Is it not proving itself to be a movement for the legitimate secularization of the Christian God who has for too long been sacralized?

One thing is certain: the realization of a historical development toward a future that is open and mysterious is an irreversible acquisition of modernity. Science itself is revolutionizing our vision of reality by showing that it does not develop on a continuous and foreseeable trajectory (see, e.g., Brownian movement and catastrophe theory). When considering the autonomy of earthly realities, it is not enough to think of them simply as independent realities; they must be thought of rather as caught up in a process of perpetual movement and dif-

ferentiation, both in themselves and in their interrelationships. The same holds for the religious sphere. When Christianity limits secularity to an activity and a mission, it fails to see the profound changes that are taking place in contemporary societies and that call for a radically new interpretation of faith and its expressions. This reinterpretation goes hand in hand with recognition of the points where individual psychology and sociocultural organization converge and where culture and life are constantly interacting. After a period of uniformity during which orthodoxy and orthopraxis merged into one, faith and religious practice are now most often proving to be dissociated; this leads to the emergence of Catholic subcultures (see J. M. Donegani and G. Lescanne, *Catholicismes de France* [Paris, 1982]). Following upon industrialization, the technological age and urbanization are causing a frragmentation of religious affiliations. Field studies are making it possible to trace the twists and turns of a secularized culture that produces both a nonreligious vision of the world and a religious vision of a transformed world. Secularity is thus proving to be an emerging dimension *in* the life of the church, an extremely complex *locus theologicus* that calls for a fundamental theology which will draw upon the very source of experience.

Bibl.: Friedrich GOGARTEN, *Despair and Hope for Our Times* (1953; Philadelphia, 1970); Hermann LÜBBE, *Säkularisierung: Geschichte eines ideenpolitischen Begriffs* (Munich/Freiburg, 1965); Harvey COX, *The Secular City: Secularization and Urbanization in Theological Perspective* (New York, 1965); J.-B. METZ, *Faith in History and Society* (1968; New York, 1979); Enrico CASTELLI, ed., *Herméneutique de la sécularisation* (Paris, 1976); id., *Prospettive sulla secolarizzazione* (Rome, 1976); H. COX, *Religion in the Secular City: Toward A Postmodern Theology* (New York, 1984); Paul VALADIER, *L'Église en procès: Catholicisme et société moderne* (Paris, 1987); S. LEFEBVRE, *Sécularité et instituts séculiers: Bilan et perspectives*, Brèches théologiques 5 (Montreal, 1989).

Solange LEFEBVRE

SEMEIOLOGY

I. SIGN *1. From Signs to the Sign. 2. Epistemology of the Sign (historical dimension; mediating component; means of communication). 3. Apologetic Value.*

II. SYMBOL *1. Symbol in the Interdisciplinary Context. 2. Symbol in Theology. 3. Symbol in Fundamental Theology.*

I. SIGN

It is a human characteristic to seek for the sense and meaning of a reality beyond the spoken word. Human speech is a general phenomenon, which breaks down into differentiated forms bearing witness to the mystery and miracle of speech itself.

When the reality and its projection toward a further meaning unite in one, then human language becomes a sign.

Signs have always been a constituent part of apologetics: signs fleshed out Christianity's credibility and confirmed its divine origin.

Such is the context in which the various and frequent interventions of the magisterium over the last century and a half have to be understood. From the encyclical *QUI PLURIBUS*, by way of *Dei Filius* of Vatican I, to *Dei Verbum* and *Lumen Gentium* of Vatican II, we seem to be witnessing an evolution in the use and identification of signs. From a purely outward and extrinsic acknowledgment of their value, we have now reached the point of appreciating their intrinsic importance especially when Christ and the church are recognized as being the principal signs of the Christian revelation.

The theology underlying these interventions, at least until Vatican II, was always anchored in an exclusively objectivist interpretation of the revealed datum, and therefore was in no position to grasp the pregnancy and value of the sign in its relationship to its object.

1. From Signs to the Sign

To Vatican II can be ascribed the merit of presenting a threefold innovation as regards the understanding and use of signs.

a. One fact that clearly emerges is the *personalistic* interpretation of signs. These are not primarily singled out as facts, as things standing on their own, but are rather identified in the person of Christ and of the church (*DV* 2, 4; *LG* 1, 15). One may think of this change as a significant transition from signs to the sign. For the person of Jesus of Nazareth is the sign placed before human beings so that we can grasp the mystery of God. The church is the sign abiding in history to mediate and transmit the Lord's word.

The briefest of synoptic glances at the evolving drafts of *DV* 4 reveals that in the text *denuo emendatum* the person of Christ comes to predominate in the entirety of his historical existence (*tota suiipsius praesentia ac manifestatione*), as opposed to a fragmentary treatment of the various phases of his activity. The unity and uniqueness of his person come to be the source of other signs and the criteria of discernment for a complete understanding of them.

b. By emphasizing the person of Christ and of the church, *Dei Verbum* inevitably tends toward a *historical* view of signs. The total sign of revelation is sited at the climax of salvation history (*DV* 2), and abides as the principle of intelligibility for subsequent history (*LG* 48, 52).

Starting out from this *event*, God's various interventions in history take form as *signs* of his will to save (the creation, *LG* 16; the choice of a people, *DV* 14; the goal of history, *LG* 9).

c. Being historical, the signs are *aimed* at stimulating human beings in their quest for meaning (→ MEANING II). For everyone confronted with the concrete sign is summoned to seek out its deeper significance and reach a decision because of it. Signs therefore make us grasp, be it the unstoppable march toward knowledge of the truth which each of us ought to complete, be it the will to create new signs so that the saving word may remain visible in the world.

Personalization, historicization, and purpose can be said to characterize the council's renewal of the theology of signs. The first datum to be derived from postconciliar theology is identification of Christ as *the* sign of revelation and, in him, the church as *sacrament* or sign of the union of God and humankind (*LG* 1).

Though Vatican II led to the identification of the principal and basic sign of revelation, it is the task of postconciliar fundamental theology to provide a critical understanding of the sign.

2. Epistemology of the Sign

Theologically speaking, we must first explain what a sign is and then decide on its apologetic value.

What immediately strikes one in defining a sign is the great number of answers that get given. For the Stoics, the first people in the history of thought to leave a definition, it ran quite simply: that which seems to reveal something. Thomas Aquinas was to speak of sign as the sensible cause of a hidden effect: "per causam sensibilem quandoque ducimur in cognitionem effectus occulti" (*ST* 1, q. 70, a. 2). More recently, De Saussure defined sign as a union of the signified and the signifying; Peirce defines it as something by knowing which we know something else. In a word, we may think of the sign as it has always been handed down in the classic formula: "id quod inducit in cognitionem alterius."

More specifically, let us say that a sign *all that which, being historically based, allows knowledge of the mystery by creating the conditions for interpersonal communication.*

This, our own definition, allows us to assemble some of the sign's components:

a. The *historical dimension.* A sign, to be truly such, must have a reality which is knowable through normal sense channels. It should hence be a reality sited in the human sphere of cognition and be immediately perceptible as a signpost to a further meaning.

b. The component of *mediation.* The sign is an arbitrary union between something signified and something signifying it. By definition, the latter can never in itself exhaust what it signifies, without risk of the sign's being destroyed. The arbitrary character of the union may, in the course of time, undergo a modification of relationships; nevertheless, owing to "collective inertia" (De Saussure), the original meaning that gave life to the sign can never be completely set aside or altered.

c. As regards the relationship between signified and signifier, it is possible to create a number of different terminologies to accompany the general term, sign. Thus we have sign-pointer, sign-symbol, sign-ikon, sign-aesthetic, and others; these are semantic values referring to differing relationships between the two sign-components, but they do not in fact modify the basic reality, the sign itself.

d. A sign moreover creates *communication.* It is in fact created to communicate. It is suspended between the source that emits it and the person to whom it is directed. The sign is thus a means of communication that finds its sphere of meaning in a *context* that favors its being correctly understood.

We can thus already see a first series of elements taking shape as indispensable for identifying the sign. First of all, there must be a *consensus;* this means that the sign emerges from the sphere of the subjective; it cannot only be a sign for the individual since this would void the component of communication. The sign furthermore *stimulates* reflection, inasmuch as it stimulates the recipient to complete the transition between the reality signified and its signifier. Lastly, it prompts us to make a *decision* whether to accept the sign or refuse it; for no one can be neutral about the sign, since a choice is required to identify what is signified.

In a word, for a sign to be a sign, it must present itself to the *senses and hence be perceptible; it must be historical*, that is to say, contained in a sociocultural context; *signifying*, i.e., admitting to the comprehension of something signified and yet to be expressed, but not entirely contained in it; *universal*, i.e., that which creates consensus beyond the sphere of the individual.

In Scripture, it is possible to see a realized semeiology which contains the characteristics just described and favors the sign as the revelatory idiom best suited to expressing the very mystery of God.

For the people of the Bible, the sign had an essentially religious value.

It was the means by which the mystery became clear; it was no accident that Hebrew 'ōt was first rendered by *sēmeion* in the Greek of the Septuagint and then by *mystērion*, before the Vulgate translated it by *signum*.

Since God dwells in inaccessible light and we cannot picture him (Ex 20:4), the nearest means for expressing his relationship with his people will be the sign: a reality which expresses but cannot exhaust the content of the message. There is, as it were, a "theology of the sign," which can be described as a spiral moving toward a center. Progressively the thought of Israel is prompted to identify the signs of Yahweh's presence first of all revealed in *nature:* the rainbow is the sign of the universal covenant (Gn 9:12–17); the stars of heaven and the sands of the sea (Gn 15:5; Dt 10:22) are signs representing the many descendants who, by virtue of faith, will have Abraham as their ancestor; circumcision will show for all generations to come that the individual belongs to God and to that nation consecrated to him (Gn 17:10–11).

But in *history* too, signs may be found that point more directly to the mysterious relationship between Yahweh and his people. The deliverance from slavery in Egypt (Ex 13:11–16), the sojourn in the wilderness and the covenant struck at Sinai (Ex 13:18; Dt 4:6), the various liturgical feasts (Ex 12:21–28): all these happenings are seen as signs, to stand like milestones in Jewish history, so that people in future times can see concrete examples of how Yahweh has intervened on behalf of his people.

These signs have to be got by heart and acted out from time to time so that the sense of belonging to Yahweh and being consecrated to him may never fade.

In the prophetic books, the prophet himself is identified as the personal sign by which God reveals his will and plan of salvation to his people. Being himself a *sign* (Jer 16; Ez 24:24; Hos 2), the prophet multiplies signs, to convert the people and renew their faith (see Jer 1:18; 19; 24; 27; 32; Ez 4; 5; 24). There is, as it were, a divine pedagogy of signs, gradually preparing the way for the culminating appearance of the sign of signs: Jesus of Nazareth. For it is on the definitiveness of this sign that the NT writers construct their theology. Even if not entirely confirmed, Bultmann's theory of the presence of a *Semeionquelle* in John points to a strong tradition which regarded Christ's *sēmeia* and *erga* as a truly revelatory moment in history.

As against the disparate and disorganized presentation of the signs by the Synoptics, John offers a clear theology of the sign. From the "first of signs" (Jn 2:11) to the "many other signs" (20:30), the evangelist seems pretty much to plot the main line of his narrative by them. Above all, sign for him is a visible reality which impresses people; or, rather, it is what lets God's definitive presence in the midst of his people be discerned.

Jesus of Nazareth is a sign in his paschal mystery; to those who ask for *signs* to convince them of his divine origin, the only one he offers is the *sign* of Jonah (Mt 12:39–41; 16:1–4; Lk 11:29–32), to encourage them to make the act of faith and abandonment in his person.

As last and definitive sign of the Father, Christ too can multiply signs, to demonstrate the presence of the messianic kingdom beginning with his own person (Jn 11:47). Not only he; but those who believe in him will perform signs too, even greater ones, since everything now finds fulfillment in his person (Jn 14:12).

There is therefore a *dialectic* which is basic to an understanding of the value of signs in NT theology. First, it starts from Christ: in him, the sign is given to refer us to the greater mystery, which is the Father and the Spirit in the mutual love of the Trinity. The sign "Jesus of Nazareth" thus does not stop short with him but points beyond to the mystery of the Trinity. The second step of this dialectic lies in pointing toward the glory paradoxically present in the misery of suffering and death. Yet a further step is that which stimulates the believer to go beyond the typically striking and marvelous aspect of the signifier to recognize the contrasting presence of mercy and forgiveness (see Jn 6).

So the signs on the one hand encourage faith to be more genuine since they refer to its basic content, which is the mystery of God; on the other, they stimulate nonbelievers to try and perceive through them the presence of the mystery which can give meaning to life.

For a theological semeiology, therefore, the basic factor is the centrality of the historical event of Jesus as source and aesthetic sign of the revelation of God. The interpretative principle established by his PASCHAL MYSTERY teaches us to understand and discern all other signs (Jn 5:22; 6:30; 8:15; 12:48). Once again, the believer is put in the position of having to choose whether to halt at the miraculous, or to seize the deeper significance of the content of the faith.

3. Apologetic Value

From the point of view of *apologetics*, once the epistemological basis has been presented, the way this category can be used should be easily distinguishable from the way other theological disciplines are applied (e.g., sacramental theology, phenomenology of religion).

In our view, one particular use is that of the place of the sign within the problems over theological language. More than other linguistic expressions, the sign encourages the working out of a theological language (→ LANGUAGE II) aimed at presenting the mystery and its critical understanding. For the sign favors the dimension of referring onward to that which is signified and helps us to understand it, however inadequate human language may be in attempting to describe the divine mystery. And yet this process does not take place by absolutizing human language or by depriving it of one of its means of expression. For the sign necessarily points the way to the word, so as to remove it from the sphere of subjective interpretation or from ambiguity, to make possible its clarification.

By virtue, however, of its structure, the sign does not prevent us from reaching what is signified, which is beyond the sphere of the subjective. For the sign cannot be reduced either to an exclusively linguistic analysis, which would be unable to leave what is signified within its transcendent space; nor to be a mere empirical verification, as a result of which the constituent value of what is signified would be lost.

Paradoxically, the sign does entail metaphysical analysis, since it obliges us, in the signifying reality, to see present the signified reality as well; the way of expressing this is the typical language of "going further," beyond that which is represented, in order to attain, definitively, being itself.

The sign does not lie outside language; it is human language because it is a special activity of the person and, as such, encourages communication and mediation of the theological content even with the nonbeliever. Hence we are in the presence of a universal language which can create greater consensuses and make interdisciplinary exchanges easier. Analyzing it thus guarantees the possibility of motivating the act of believing as a free act because reinforced by the dimension of critical understanding.

Unlike imagery, which remains confined to the imagination and thought of the individual, the sign favors objectivity by the way it is expressed, and interpersonal communication.

The sign therefore becomes a challenge, since it represents that which we do not know how to say, or dare not say, and yet which we perceive to be true.

Bibl.: D. MOLLAT, "Le sémeion johannique," in *Sacra Pagina* (Paris, 1958), 2:209–18; G. DE BROGLIE, *Revelation and Reason* (New York, 1965); R. LATOURELLE, *Christ and the Church: Signs of Salvation* (New York, 1972); F. DE SAUSSURE, *Course in General Linguistics* (New York, 1959); U. ECO, *Il segno* (Milan, 1980); R. FISICHELLA, *La Révélation: La Révélation et sa crédibilité* (Paris/Montreal, 1989); H. J. POTTMEYER, "Zeichen und Kriterien der Glaubwürdigkeit des Christentums," *HFT*, 4:373–413; S. PIÉ-NINOT, *Tratado de Teología fundamental* (Salamanca, 1989).

Rino FISICHELLA

II. SYMBOL

The careless use of words is not without its consequences. It makes communication difficult and causes misunderstandings.

In theology we often see the words and symbol used indiscriminately.

Using them to mean the same thing may be admissible at a general level but will not always give us a clear notion of the theological concepts involved. Every author should make quite clear what semantic value he or she chooses to attach to sign and symbol, so that the reader may be in no doubt over what is intended.

1. Symbol in an Interdisciplinary Context

What symbol and symbolic function are is a matter of great debate, especially today. For the argument involves different disciplines and sciences which, putting more stress on some elements than on others, attach different meanings to one and the same thing. Thus Durkheim, studying the social value of religious symbolism, identifies it as signifying a "collective consciousness" which allows what is being represented religiously to be self-perpetuating in time. What is signified symbolically is thus not contained in the intrinsic reality but is added to it by the collective consciousness.

The psychoanalytical schools take another view, making symbol the main element on which, in the first instance, to base the interpretation of dreams. Various schools then interpret it according to their own ideas: Jung, for instance, seeing it as revealing a concrete, archetypal situation whether collective or individual. The better the symbol succeeds in expressing this atavistic belief, the more universal and meaningful it will be. Unlike him, Klein and Lacan today have recourse to symbol to express the figurative language of words.

On a more philosophic plane, the studies of E. Cassirer in the gnosiology of language are of fundamental importance. Symbol and symbolic function are held to signify any creative activity of the spirit. Myth, logic, and art are all of them symbolic forms, in which the signifying and the signified cannot be separated and distinguished; for all that is thought is thinkable only by means of mythical, logical, aesthetic symbols: "The symbol is no mere accidental clothing of thought, but its necessary and essential instrument" (1953–57: 1:20ff.).

For semantics, Morris's definition holds good; this places the symbol as "a sign produced by its interpreter, which acts as a substitute for other signs with which it is synonymous" (*Segni, linguaggio e comportamento* [Milan, 1948]). It therefore enjoys a wide autonomy but is more conventional too since produced by human, social agents.

Lastly, in the aesthetic perspective, the symbol is that which allows artistic expression of a transcendent reality.

2. Symbol in Theology

In the theological context, too, one may find varying views as to what symbol means.

Thus the Alexandrian school has gone down in the history of biblical exegesis as protagonist of a symbolic interpretation of revelation.

Within the Scriptures it is easy to recognize a symbolic system which seeks by symbols drawn from nature or human convention to convey a particularly revelatory content.

The OT is rich in symbolic actions attributed to prophets; one may think, e.g., of Jeremiah who takes an earthenware jug and, in the presence of the people's elders and senior priests, smashes it into a thousand pieces (Jer 19:1–15); what the symbol means is made clear by what the prophet says: "So will I break this people and this city, as one breaks a potter's vessel, so that it can never be mended" (19:11).

Other kinds of symbol may be found either as *personal names* (Jezreel: "God sows," in Hos 1:4; Shear-Jashub, Isaiah's son, which means "a remnant shall return," in Is 7:3; or Cephas, applied to Peter in Mt 16:18, to indicate his function in the church) or as *cryptic numbers*, which play an important part in the book of Revelation.

Contemporary dogmatic theology is indebted to K. Rahner's essay "The Theology of Symbol" (1966: 221–52) for an ontology of symbol. Starting from a general epistemological position which takes the symbolic entity per se as understood, inasmuch as it has to be "expressed to find its own essence," Rahner extends this principle to all theology, of which he was to say: "Theology could not be understood at all, were it not essentially a theology of symbols."

His various treatises too, such as those on the Trinity, Christology, ecclesiology, the sacraments, were to be invested with this ontological interpretation of symbol. Maintaining the mystery of the Trinity as central, Rahner singles out an *existential symbol* or *real internal symbol* which "is the appearance and perceptibility in space, time and history, in which an essence, by appearing, shows itself and, by showing itself, becomes present while it forms this appearance, which is truly distinct from itself" (*Kirche und Sakrament* [Freiburg, 1960], 34; Eng. *The Church and the Sacrament* [London, 1963]). The essential symbol is the internal phase of the reality itself, when giving itself and completing itself by means of the sign, while however remaining distinct from it. The entity is thus symbolic per se and expresses itself so as to possess itself; it gives itself to the "other" by coming out of itself and thus retrieves itself through knowledge and love. In a word, "symbol is the way of self-knowledge and general rediscovery of the self."

From this point of view, Rahner can think of symbol in three ways: first, as property of the entity that achieves its own perfection; second, as relationship between two entities; third, as expression by means of which knowledge and love of the self are brought about.

The symbol, seen theologically like this, is that which makes present, in its own special way, the saving reality of God.

3. Symbol in Fundamental Theology

In the context of fundamental theology, one of the first tasks to be taken in hand could be, to use Cassirer's words, to produce a "symbolic grammar," by which to single out the common elements and the differences between the various uses and applications of symbol, so as to make theological science epistemologically more consistent.

As apologetics, which comes into contact with the various philosophies, the basic task would be to build, as it were, a bridge between the new acceptation of symbol (with its value for hermeneutics) and theological usage. For symbol, rather than "saying" something, evokes the reality it symbolizes. This would then permit a suppleness in theologizing which, without falling prey to reductionism or passing fashion of any sort, would above all be able to retrieve the data which are peculiar to Scripture, which reposes what might be called a blind faith in symbol; for, by narrating and by evoking symbols, the sacred writer at once affirms the living and working presence of God and the incommunicability of his name. Furthermore, it would be possible to revive the content of patristic and medieval tradition, for this made symbolic interpretation a *via eminentiae*, as it were, for communicating the revealed message.

As for a hermeneutics of theological language, with reference to symbol, fundamental theology insists there be no indifference over usage or interchangeability with the sign. For the symbol, though belonging to the sign, is different from it because, at the moment of return from the symbolized to the symbolizing, it brings back with it a determining image of that which is symbolized (e.g., you can't very well substitute a donkey's head for a fox's mask, to express cunning; whether you say "fox," *volpe, Fuchs, zorro,* or *renard* is a matter of indifference, provided there is social agreement. This makes it legitimate for theology to use symbolic language in expressing itself, since this already has a certain immediacy and can be intuitively absorbed.

At all events, symbol reminds theology that the language of revelation cannot be reduced to mere "scientific" terms. Indeed, it obliges us to give serious consideration to the presence of the MYSTERY and to SILENCE as factors tolerating no reductionism of any sort. The symbol, once given and accepted, communicates its own independence of all linguistic restraints and invites us ever further toward that space that

opens on the infinite, to which only the imagination of the poet, the mystic, and the free spirit can attain.

Bibl.: E. CASSIRER, *The Philosopher of Symbolic Forms* (1923; New Haven, 1953–57); K. RAHNER, "The Theology of Symbol," in *Theological Investigations,* vol. 4 (1960; London, 1966), 221–52; A. M. DI NOLA, "Simbolo," in *Enciclopedia delle Religioni* 5:644–51; U. ECO, *Trattato di semiotica generale* (Milan, 1975); P. RICOEUR, *La métaphore vive* (Paris, 1975); id., *The Conflict of Interpretations: Essays in Hermeneutics* (1966; Evanston, Ill., 1974); V. MELCHIORRE, *Essere e parola* (Milan, 1984); S. BABOLIN, *Sulla funzione comunicativa del simbolo* (Rome, 1985); id., *Simbolo e conoscenza* (Milan, 1988).

R. FISICHELLA

SENSUS FIDEI

Sensus fidei, the believer's sense of faith, has become an object of reflection over the last decades, beginning with the Marian dogmas, and extending to the theology of revelation and to ecclesiology. Its explicit formulation has been consecrated by Vatican II, especially in the paradigmatic text of *Lumen Gentium* 12, as well as in various related notions presented throughout the conciliar documents (*sensus fidei,* PO 9; *sensus catholicus,* AA 30; *sensus Christianus fidelium,* GS 52; *sensus Christianus,* GS 62; *sensus religiosus,* NA 2; DH 4; GS 59; *sensus Dei,* DV 15; GS 7; *sensus Christi et Ecclesiae,* AG 19; *instinctus,* SC 24; PC 12; GS 18). Further, the *sensus fidei* is implicitly supposed in the text on the criteriology of the development of dogma in *Dei Verbum* 8.

The *sensus fidei* includes two related, but not coextensive, realities. On the one hand is the *sensus fidei* properly so called, which is a quality of the *subject,* upon whom the grace of faith, love, and the gifts of the Holy Spirit confers a capacity to perceive the truth of faith and to discern what is contrary to the same. The expression was coined by the high scholasticism of the thirteenth century (William of Auxerre, Albertus Magnus, Thomas Aquinas, etc.), and originates in an analysis of the faculties of faith in the believing subject. On the other hand, one speaks of a *sensus fidelium,* as well: that element in what the faithful believe and profess that can be grasped externally, *objectively*. This expression comes to us from the theologians of the latter half of the sixteenth century (Melchior Cano, Robert Bellarmine, Suarez, etc.), and springs from a study of doctrinal criteriology. By way of a development of the latter of these twin concepts, we have the *consensus fidelium*, or *universus ecclesiae sensus* of Trent (DS 1637), which adds the notion of universality to the assent involved, and refers to the situation in which the entire body of believers, "from the bishops down to the last member of the laity"— St. Augustine's expression, cited verbatim by the council (*LG* 12)—maintains the same faith. It is in this situation, Vatican II asserts, that the whole people of God cannot err. The council's formula is, *In credendo falli nequit*—"cannot err in matters of belief"—recalling the celebrated expression, *infallibilitas in credendo*, occurring in the conciliar debate (AS III/1: 198) and becoming classic with the post-Tridentine theologians, to be propagated by the manuals antedating Vatican II (H. Dieckmann, T. Zapelena, A. Lang, etc.). An assertion of this infallibility is legitimate, then, when the content of the proposition under consideration fulfills the following four conditions: when it is a matter of universal consent, when it refers to revelation, when it is the work of the Holy Spirit, and when it is recognized by the magisterium (cf. *DV* 8, 10; *LG* 12, 25). The correct interpretation of this concept of infallibility has been specified by the declaration of the Congregation for the Doctrine of the Faith *Mysterium Ecclesiae*, 2 (*AAS* 63 [1973]: 398 [EV 4, nos. 2567–69]).

The concept of *sensus fidei* in *Lumen Gentium* 12 comports the following theological elements. First, it is a "supernatural sense," which is "aroused and sustained by the Spirit," in terms of the basic concept of the free gift of faith. Second, it "characterizes the People of God as a whole": it belongs not to any sector of that people, but to all of its members. Finally, the text describes the effects of this gift: this people of God (1) "accepts not the word of men, but the very Word of God," (2) "clings without fail to the faith once delivered to the saints," (3) "penetrates it more deeply," and (4) "applies it thoroughly to life."

Besides proposing this explicit ecclesiological text, Vatican II implicitly cites the category of *sensus fidei* in a context of the handing on of revelation, and lists the elements of a criteriology of the development of Catholic dogma (*DV* 8). Among the four factors of that dogmatic progress ("the help of the Holy Spirit . . . the contemplation and study made by believers . . . the intimate understanding of spiritual things they experience, and . . . the preaching of those who have received through episcopal succession the sure gift of truth"), the third, especially, and to a certain extent the second, bear on the *sensus fidei*. Ultimately it is a matter of an extension of the activity with which the Holy Spirit generates faith: the development of dogma is nothing other than a deeper penetration of the faith, in terms of a description of that ongoing penetration in Vatican II: "To bring about an ever deeper understanding of revelation, the same Holy Spirit constantly brings faith to completion by His gifts," along the lines of Catholic tradition (*DV* 5, citing the Second Council of Orange, DS 377; Trent, DS 1525; Vatican I, DS 3010).

An effort to base the *sensus fidei* theologically finds in the NT clear testimonials to the reality of an organ of faith and its understanding, the work of the Spirit, in each of the baptized, as well as in the entire church. Thus, in various texts, we read of "the mind of Christ" (1 Cor 2:16), "spiritual insight" (Col 1:9), and "innermost vision" (lit., "enlightened eyes of the heart," Eph 1:18; cf. Jn 14:17; 16:13; Phil 1:9; etc.). On this basis, patristic and theological tradition frequently speak of the "eyes of the heart," "the eyes of the spirit," or the "eyes of faith." Suffice it to recall Augustine's expression: *Habet namque fides oculos suos* ("After all, faith has its eyes," Epist. 120.2.8 [*PL* 33:458]); as well as the words of Aquinas: *Per lumen fidei vident esse credenda* ("Through the light of faith, they see that these [things] are to be believed," *ST* 2-2, q. 1, a. 5, ad 1) and *oculata fide* with reference to Jesus' resurrection ("by a faith endowed with eyes," *ST* 3, q. 55, a. 2, ad 1). In turn, there appear axioms like that of an *ekklēsiastikon phronēma*, or a *sensus ecclesiasticus et catholicus* (Eusebius, Jerome, Cassian, etc.), a *sentire cum ecclesia* (Basil, Augustine, Leo the Great, etc.), and finally, a *sensus fidei*, which appears for the first time in Vincent of Lerins (d. 450: *Commonitorium*, chap. 23 [*PL* 50:669]), by way of a synthesis of his celebrated criterion for legitimate dogmatic growth: *quod ubique, quod semper, quod ab omnibus, creditum est* ("what has been believed everywhere, always, and by all," *Commonitorium,* chap. 2 [*PL* 50:640]).

The first more significant theological reflection on the epistemological and fundamental value of the *sensus fidei* is that of Melchior Cano, who situates it now in the context of tradition, now in that of the authority of the Catholic church: *Communi fidelium consensione* ("by the common consent of the faithful," *De locis theologicis* 3.3); *Ecclesia in credendo errare non potest* ("The Church cannot err in believing," ibid., 4.4). The question was subsequently addressed by two great apologists of the last century: J. Balmes (d. 1848), who refers to the providential "faith instinct" bestowed on believers by the Creator (*El Protestantismo comparado con el Catolicismo,* vol. 1, chap. 4), and John Henry Newman (d. 1890), who speaks of an "illative sense" that makes a "real assent" possible in matters of faith and conscience, and who sets down the conditions required for learning sacred doctrine from the *consensus fidelium* ("On Consulting the Faithful in Matters of Doctrine," par. 3). In the same century, two important theologians worked for a deeper understanding of the *sensus fidei* in a framework of tradition, in terms of a "comprehensive sense," in J. A. Möhler (d. 1838), and a "corpus of faith," in M. J. Scheeben (d. 1888).

In our own twentieth century, two main currents have dynamized this deeper understanding. The first has been the mariological movement, which culminated in the definition of the dogma of the assumption of the Blessed Virgin Mary (1950, DS 3900), and which gave a renewed impulse to a consideration of the *sensus fidei/fidelium* in the development of dogma. This movement emphasizes the notion that such development proceeds preeminently from the faith of a Christian people who recognize, in the Marian privileges, a revealed truth.

The second driving current has been the fruit of an ecclesiological renewal, especially that of the theology of the laity, which underscores the relationship between the *sensus fidei* and the prophetic function of the baptized. This aspect came in for emphasis even before Vatican II (Yves M.-J. Congar), is well recognized by that council, and has received further impetus with the bishops' synod on the laity (1987) and the apostolic exhortation *Christifideles Laici* (30 Dec. 1988), which, in treating of the faithful's sharing in the prophetic office of Christ,

explicitly speaks of a *sensus fidei* (cf. *LG* 12) joined to the grace of the word (*Christifideles Laici* 14). Postconciliar studies by private theologians, as well, have centered on the authentic epistemological importance of the *sensus fidei* for fundamental theology, and hence for a search for theoretical and practical criteria for an appeal to its use.

Accordingly, in synthesis: In order to grasp the authentic nature of the *sensus fidei,* one must consider it, first of all, in the context of Christian existence, which, on the basis of the "interior teacher" that is the gift of faith, makes possible a "judgment according to connaturality in matters of faith" (*ST* 2-2, q. 45, a. 2, c.). *Humani Generis* refers to this *connaturalitas* (DS 2324), which manifests the "connatural logic of Christian existence." In the second place, the *sensus fidei* must be situated in a context of the ecclesial communion that renders possible an intimate articulation between the "outward" magisterium of the apostolic college with its head and its successors, which has "the task of authentically interpreting the word of God, whether written or handed on" (*DV* 10; cf. *LG* 25), and the "inward" magisterium of the Spirit—present in all of the baptized and manifested in their participation in the prophetical function of Christ and the Church (cf. *LG* 12; 35; 37; *DV* 8)—as a *via empirica* of the living tradition of the church. Especially, in the post-Vatican years of our century, a more concrete exercise of the *sensus fidei* has inspired a search for practical routes. Some examples, among others: a new appreciation of the complementarity obtaining between the church taught and the church teaching, in the context of ecclesial communion; a recognition of the epistemological value precisely of "popular piety" and of "praxis" as "theological loci" and an expression of the *sensus fidei/fidelium*; or the exercise of ecclesial coresponsibility, especially on the part of the laity, in function of a new appreciation of the forms of "synodality" and consultation in the church.

Bibl.: L. M. Fernández De TroCóniz, "Sensus fidei": logica connatural de la existencia cristiana (Vitoria, 1976); J. Sancho, *Infalibilidad del Pueblo de Dios* (Pamplona, 1979); W. Beinert, "Glaubenssin der Glaübigen," in *Lexicon der katholischen Dogmatik* (Freiburg, 1987), 200f.; S. Pié-Ninot, "Aportaciones del Sínodo 1987 a la teología del laicado," *RET* 48

(1988): 321–70, 330, 362–64; Z. ALSZEGHY, "The Sensus Fidei and the Development of Dogma," in R. Latourelle, ed., *Vatican II: Assessment and Perspectives Twenty-five Years After*, 3 vols. (New York, 1988), 1:138–56.

Salvador PIÉ-NINOT

SIGNS OF THE TIMES

1. Recovery of an "Ancient" Term. 2. New Perspectives of Vatican II. 3. Outlines for a Theology of the "Signa Temporum" (Specific Criteria for Interpreting the Signs: To glorify Christ, To build up the church, To sum up all in Christ).

Constant attention to history and relating it to the gospel give rise, theologically, to the theme of the signs of the times.

"Signs of the times" is an ancient expression. Its gospel origin reminds us that we believers need constantly to scrutinize the world in which we live, so as to be able first to grasp these signs, whether positive or negative ones, as they appear, then to assess what they imply, and then to bring the stimulating and renovating force of the gospel to bear on them.

1. Recovery of an "Ancient" Term

The expression occurs for the first time in Matthew 16:2–3 (Lk 12:54–56). Regardless of the authenticity or otherwise of the text, which in all likelihood is a later interpolation, it is consistent with the dialectic with which Jesus invariably counters the requests of his listeners: their need to see a sign as proof of his divinity. As previously in 12:38–39, Jesus reminds them of the "sign of Jonah," which was to be the only one to convey the reality of his mystery. Here, however, having recourse to a simple metaphor drawn from the weather, the evangelist seems to be adding a further explanation to reveal both the absurdity of the request that the "Pharisees and Sadducees" address to Jesus and their inability to recognize him as the Messiah: "When it is evening, you say, 'It will be fair weather; for the sky is red.' And in the morning, 'It will be stormy today, for the sky is red and threatening.' You know how to interpret the appearance of the sky, but you cannot interpret the signs of the times."

As everyone knows, this is an invitation to use our heads, our brains, so as to be able to pierce to the root of things and so recognize what is essential in them.

The rediscovery of the value and significance of this category for the life of the church and theological thought we owe to the prophetic activity of John XXIII. The original meaning of the verse in Matthew was adapted by this pontiff to encourage Christians to take note of changes in the contemporary world and thus be able once again to proclaim Christ's gospel in terms that people can understand.

In the relevant document of the Second Vatican Council, *Humanae Salutis*, symbolically dated 25 December 1961, the text runs: "Indeed we make our own the recommendation of Jesus that one should know how to distinguish the signs of the times, and we seem to see now, in the midst of so much darkness, a few indications which augur well for the fate of the Church and of humanity" (*AAS* 54 [1962]: 5–13).

As against the "prophets of doom" ever ready to predict disasters as though the end of the world were constantly at hand (see the opening address to the council, 11 Oct. 1962), John XXIII proposed gospel optimism as the response to moments of crisis in the church and in society: a renewed spiritual strength with which to recognize the potentialities present in people of goodwill and the constant activity of the Spirit.

The same emphasis is also to be found in this pope's last encyclical *Pacem in Terris*, written a few months before his death. At the end of each chapter, John XXIII suggested the way certain signs of the times should be interpreted. Be it noted that the official Latin text—by who can say what editorial mystery—omits these words, although they always appear in all official translations of the encyclical.

Paul VI too used the expression in his first encyclical ECCLESIAM SUAM. The text points out the need of giving "a stimulus to the Church . . . to give careful consideration to the signs of the times, always and everywhere 'proving all things and holding fast that which is good' with the enthusiasm of youth" (*AAS* 56 [1964]: 609–10).

In the new climate which it was trying to create, especially in church/world relations, the council could not have agreed more with the foregoing. Repeatedly the term occurs in conciliar documents until officially formulated in

Gaudium et Spes. "Signs of the times," in this context, may be regarded as one of the more original formulations of the council as regards its pastoral aims.

It is useful at this point to mention some *explicit* texts in which the expression occurs, since these are fundamental to an understanding of this category, and are useful reference points for a theological interpretation of it.

It is easy to see how conciliar thinking developed when the texts are taken in chronological order:

a. "Today, in many parts of the world, under the inspiring grace of the Holy Spirit, multiple efforts are being expended through prayer, word and action to attain that fullness of unity which Jesus Christ desires. This sacred Synod, therefore, exhorts all the Catholic faithful to recognize the *signs of the times* and to participate skilfully in the work of ecumenism" (*UR* 4).

b. "This sacred Synod greets with joy the first of these two facts, as among the *signs of the times.* With sorrow, however, it denounces the other fact as only to be deplored. The Synod exhorts Catholics, and it directs a plea to all men, most carefully to consider how greatly necessary religious freedom is, especially in the present condition of the human family" (*DH* 15).

c. "[Priests] should listen to the laity willingly, consider their wishes in a fraternal spirit, and recognize their experience and competence in the different areas of human activity, so that together with them they will be able to read the *signs of the times*" (*PO* 9).

"To carry out such a task, the Church has always had the duty of scrutinizing the *signs of the times* and of interpreting them in the light of the gospel. Thus, in language intelligible to each generation, she can respond to the perennial questions which men ask about this present life and the life to come, and about the relationship of the one to the other. We must therefore recognize and understand the world in which we live, its expectations, its longings and its often dramatic characteristics" (*GS* 4).

From these texts alone it is already possible to see a continuous crescendo in conciliar teaching; starting from a view of life *within* the Christian community, by means of which the faithful are invited to work for unity among themselves, it passes by stages to recognize the presence of *external* signs affecting the church on two fronts: first, in the sphere of religious freedom; second, in acknowledging the advances of science, so as to be able to proclaim the gospel in a way that can be understood.

To these explicit texts, many other council texts may be added, in which reference to the *signs of the times*, though *implicit*, is perfectly clear. A quick survey of the relevant material will be helpful later for working out a "theology of the signs of the times" derived from Vatican II.

Two paragraphs in *Gaudium et Spes* are particularly important in this context:

> The People of God believe that it is led by the Spirit of the Lord who fills the earth. Motivated by this faith, it labors to decipher authentic signs of God's presence and purpose in the happenings, needs and desires in which this people has a part along with other men of our age. For faith throws a new light on everything, manifests God's design for man's total vocation, and thus directs the mind to solutions which are fully human. (*GS* 11)

It goes on to say:

> With the help of the Holy Spirit, it is the task of the entire People of God, especially pastors and theologians, to hear, distinguish and interpret the many voices of our age, and to judge them in the light of the divine Word. In this way, revealed truth can always be more deeply penetrated, better understood and set forth to greater advantage. (*GS* 44)

2. New Perspectives of Vatican II

Though conforming to time-honored teaching, it is easy to see, especially in theological thought, how these texts introduce the basic principles for verifying the council's intentions as regards the new relations the church should assume with human history and human activities in different sociocultural situations.

The following observations may contribute to a more general picture of the theology of the signs of the times as produced by Vatican II:

a. The first thing to be noted is the change in *language,* revealing the different view the church now takes of herself. For the Christian community now sees her as the servant of the word, which has been entrusted to her and which she has the duty of passing on to history.

The church and the contemporary world are together on a constant, endless journey to seek and find the entire truth (Jn 16:13). To every individual, she offers herself as companion in the search for the real will of God and hence for the welfare of the human race. To the men and women of our day, she offers her "community of faith," well aware that the activity of the Spirit who guides her also acts and ranges beyond her own spiritual boundaries (*LG* 8).

b. In order to accomplish the mission received from Jesus Christ, the church asks her contemporaries to help her attentively to construe the human phenomena and tensions which occur in history. The church that emerges from these texts is a "poor" church, a church that has shed any kind of presumptuousness and arrogance and is aware that truth is the common object of search and that she possesses it only in an eschatological perspective. This is why the duty of solidarity with all people comes out so strongly, as also the awareness of a universal commitment to achieve salvation, by which we are either all saved together, or else she does not fulfill the mission she has received.

She is a church who from the former standpoint of being the mistress in her relations with the world, returns to the status of discipleship, knowing that one alone is the master, Christ (Mt 23:10): "The Church herself knows how richly she has profited by the history and development of humanity. . . . The Church particularly needs the help of those who live in the world, are raised in different institutions and specialities and grasp their innermost significance in the eyes of both believers and unbelievers" (*GS* 44). Never in recent centuries have such clear and explicit words been heard from the magisterium about the world and about the help that the believing community asks of all people by virtue of their belonging to the human race and their competence in the scientific field. How many light-years these words are away from her formulae of perplexity and condemnation as regards the "world" and progress in the last century, there is no need to show. Thus the church has bravely rediscovered a new way of dealing with cultures and societies; to deny them would be to disregard the honest efforts that have been made in this direction; to disregard them would be to betray the spirit of Vatican II.

c. Commitment to the signs of the times obliges the church to pay permanent attention in her teaching to the diverse life situations and differing cultures underlying the various models of society. The world and its history are modified and alter in the course of only a few years; forms of progress and technology play a greater and greater role, and information in the modern world reaches peoples far away from one another; the gospel however has to be proclaimed and understood even in these situations, so that the message of salvation reaches every single person.

So the signs of the times can direct us to a more universal and general interpretation of the saving message, since they represent aspirations and the practical fulfillment of ideals which are the common heritage of the human race. In a certain way they belong to the pedagogy of revelation, since they can be identified as those seeds of life—the *logoi spermatikoi* so beloved of the fathers—which are placed in the world and in each individual's heart to make it easier for them to perceive God's activity as he constantly raises up new forces for the full realization of creation.

d. At the signs of the times, the church is stirred to develop her prophetic activity, since she is called to commit herself to reading the signs and pronouncing God's judgment on them. As concerns PROPHECY, which characterizes the Christian community, this judgment will always be within the perspective of salvation, inasmuch as coming from the very center of revelation which presents the crucified as definitive "place of salvation" as ultimate expression of the father's love.

In pronouncing this judgment, the community of believers dissociates herself from the various "prophets of doom" and, in the final analysis, recognizes the goodness of the creation in all its expressions, as well as the positive achievements of the human race where these are directed to the good of all. Hence she refers each of these expressions to the all-embracing scenario of the word of God, by which they can be fully illuminated and rightly directed (*GS* 40–90).

e. Lastly, the signs of the times spur us on to serious consideration of the eschatological factor, which is a characteristic of the Christian faith. For by these signs, all, believers and nonbelievers alike, are linked to a future as the definitive time and space for the fulfillment of ourselves and of all human history.

The signs of the times thus represent those necessary stages, for those of us who are still living as pilgrims, by which we may live with a vigilant and attentive spirit in expectation of the bridegroom who is to come. Though a state of vigilance is a gospel duty for the community, it is equally a duty for nonbelievers, for only thus will they be able to perceive how history and culture are evolving and hence be ready to answer the questions to which this must eventually give rise.

By commitment to this category, it would seem that the council had later come to favor that process of a personal application of an apologetic treatment of the sign which had already been initiated with *Dei Verbum* and *Lumen Gentium*.

In summing up the novelty of the council's teaching on this topic, we can say that two facts emerge as crucial: First, Jesus Christ is the source sign of revelation and, in keeping faith with him, the church is the sign synonymous with him; these are the abiding signs of God's presence and hence, basically, the true signs of the times. These revelatory signs orient history eschatologically and make it possible for historical development to reach its true end. They are signs of the times for our own times; for, impressed within themselves, they have the mark of universality, which makes them fully accessible in any times, and normative for each. Second, equally signs of the times are all those aspirations of the human race which make for progress and point the direction to acquiring more fully human conditions of life.

3. Outlines for a Theology of the "Signa Temporum"

If we wanted to sum up the various data already laid out with a view to a "definition" of signs of the times, so as to help us understand the phenomenon, we might say that they are *historical events which create a universal consensus, by which* the believer *is confirmed in observing God's changeless, dramatic activity in history and* the nonbeliever *is guided to make ever truer, more consistent and funda-* *mental choices tending to the general promotion of human values.*

This "definition" seeks to summarize some ideas which help toward identifying the signs of the times. First of all, we say *historical events;* this means that not all facts can be regarded as signs of the times, but only those that have the characteristic of being events. An event is that which constitutes a basic stage in the history of all; it may be described as a milestone on the human journey. It is so necessary as point of reference that one could not have a complete grasp of the history of a period, of a people, or of a culture, without it. So, to say that the signs of the times are events is to place them within a specific temporal dimension.

We say furthermore that there must be *universal consensus,* for which these signs somehow have to act as catalysts. They must evince the characteristic of universality; for everywhere their meaning must be accepted in its most genuine sense. The signs of the times are thus required to be the sign of the gradual coming together of the various human components which, leaving aside individual interests, tend toward the good of the human race.

In the "definition" we have given, a deliberate distinction has been drawn between the believer's and the nonbeliever's interpretation, first, to emphasize the note of universality of the signs which, being universal, must not be loaded either way; second, to encourage agreement on the importance of the signs before going on to interpret them; and last, to allow the believer to plan a proper religious campaign without any obligations toward the "other" (→ FUNDAMENTAL THEOLOGY II).

By *believers* therefore we mean those who are members of the Christian community and who because of this are called to interpret the signs of the times in the light of the word of God (*GS* 11; 44), and in them to see the creator's presence in a special way. By virtue of faith, believers will be led to identify each sign with the diverse manifestations of God's trinitarian love revealed in Christ. In surveying and identifying the signs, however, they will be called to follow the same road as the nonbelievers and will have to accompany them right to the end; but then they will be called on to go one step further, since they will have to arrive at the christological and ecclesial interpretation of the sign.

For *nonbelievers,* the signs of the times can

express the tensions, the aspirations of human beings to more human conditions of life. If however the signs have to create consensus, this means they also train nonbelievers to that consistent commitment, so that the unique truth about human beings and the creation can at last see the fullness of light. Yet, acting in company with believers, nonbelievers too may be prompted to a further demand and this can lead to questions about God and conversion to Christianity.

What has so far been said is mainly to do with describing the nature of signs of the times. For an overall view of the phenomenon, it is appropriate to add a few observations on how to discern the signs.

Inasmuch as the signs participate in the nature of sign (→ SEMEIOLOGY I), they hence form a relationship between that which signifies and that which is signified, but reading and interpreting this is often subject to ambiguity. How can the signs of the times be identified and who is competent to interpret them?

The council had already pointed out a number of different phenomena which, by their characteristics, seem to attest God's presence in the world and can be identified as signs of the times: the personal _holiness_ of the believer who bears witness to the newness of the gospel (_LG_ 39–42), the profound aspirations toward _religious freedom_ (_DH_ 15) and the respect for _human dignity_ (_GS_ 63–72), _martyrdom_ as the supreme sign of love and consistency for the ideal in life (_LG_ 42), the straining toward more human and universal _forms of culture_ (_GS_ 53–62), the pursuit of and drive toward _world peace_ (_GS_ 77–90). In the view of the fathers of the council, all these signs, as it were intuitively, refer back to God and create universal consensus.

How should we proceed, however, in singling out and interpreting other signs that history may from time to time produce?

Since, as we have said, the signs of the times are, above all, historical events, identifying them will have to be primarily entrusted to the human sciences. On a number of occasions and explicitly now, the church and the teaching of the magisterium have shown their confidence in science and in scientists (_GS_ 15; 44); to them it will fall to make a preliminary identification of the phenomena which create consensus and

which, in themselves, tend to influence societies to more human conditions of life. Once the signs are pointed out, interpretation can begin.

We hold, as a theological principle, that the qualified interpreter of the signs of the times has to be the _believing community_. The council says that the one who does the interpreting is the "church" (_GS_ 4) but immediately explains this statement by saying "all the People of God," especially "pastors and theologians" (_GS_ 44). As may be seen, an interpretation is given that for the one part refers to the whole community, and for the other singles out pastors and theologians, presumably by virtue of their ministry and competence.

More consistent with the description of the signs of the times, which we have already suggested, when it comes to interpreting them, we might apply what Paul VI taught in _Octogesima Adveniens_ as the right method of reading social phenomena, inasmuch as the community in question has to bear the great part. For he says: "It is up to the Christian communities to analyze with objectivity the situation which is proper to their own country, to shed on it the light of the Gospel's unalterable words and to draw principles of reflection, norms of judgment and directives for action" (_OA_ 3).

Here, in a few phrases, are the basic principles determining the way to deal with the signs of the times: identification, reading, interpretation, judgment, but within the community and with the specific competences of everyone.

The whole local church, therefore, becomes the interpreter of the signs of the times, involving the roles and charisms of everybody, but on a path "together with humanity" (_GS_ 40), because with them she forms the unique family of God.

In the same way as the community identifies the signs of the times which, as such, always have a positive component, since tending to the advance of the human race and the understanding of revealed truth, so too the community is called to identify _antisigns_ which, owing to the sinfulness of all, impede true progress and delay the action of global liberation.

The second phase having to be put into effect is that of interpreting the signs. Since believers and nonbelievers are at one in identifying them, it is important that a hermeneutical criteriology should not preclude this from taking place.

We therefore think that *general* criteria may be assumed in such as to express the common shared intention, and *specific* criteria to characterize the christological and ecclesial reading of believers.

Two criteria can be assumed as *general:* that of *human dignity,* favoring the recognition of all forms involving the freedom and improvement of the lot of the individual; and that of *justice,* which is to be regarded as the minimal and indispensable point of love, for with it everyone is enabled to live a decent human life.

Among the *specific* criteria, the theological claim will obviously play a major role, since it affects the community which, as such, is already living the reality that it proclaims. We think of three criteria and express them in biblical language:

a. To glorify Christ (Jn 16:14): for the signs of the times, insofar as they are rays of the glory of the Lord, should find full significance only in him. For this reason, every sign must return to Christ and tend to his glory, so as later to proclaim the victory of his death over every form of injustice and sin. The true signs of the times hence are recognizable because they bear within themselves this dynamic of transcending limitations and training us to recognize true freedom.

b. To build up the church (Eph 2:22): insofar as the believing community mediates revelation, it actually constitutes the abiding historical sign thereof, which can be perceived by everyone. The signs of the times ought to summon believers to the eschatological building up of the church, so that she may fulfill her mission by her diverse forms of participation in the life of the human race, If on the one hand the signs of the times train human beings to adopt more worthy ways of living, on the other they have to sustain the church on her way to meet the bridegroom. The various charisms and ministries which have been given for the building up of the church acquire their most vital importance here. The signs of the times are understood as expressions of God's love and activity because they are recognized as forms that teach the church how to react to history's demands with the strength of the gospel.

c. To sum up all in Christ (Eph 1:10): the signs of the times ought to encourage believers to keep their gaze permanently fixed on the "new heaven and the new earth" where every form of death will be done away forever. True signs of the times are therefore open to the fullness of that cosmic realization where all creation, history and humanity within it, will find their fulfillment. If the signs of the times were to stop short at the merely immediate or at a merely temporal realization, as far as the believers are concerned, they would lack all their driving force for the building of the future.

The reading once presented, the signs of the times can be traced back to their essential nucleus constituted by the very event of revelation, the love of the triune God. From the climactic point of this love, which consists in the death of the Son, other expressions and forms of love arise, since that unique sign persists as normative and always recognizable.

Attention to the signs of the times is something the church cannot renounce: the responsibility of everyone. With it, the rediscovery of everything lovely, good, and true to be found in our history and in the world we ourselves are building, becomes more immediate. But for believers, the signs have yet a further significance: the permanent presence of a God who, even after the event of the incarnation, continues to dwell in our midst and live among us.

Attention to the signs of the times, singling them out, reading them and interpreting them, cannot however exhaust the task of believers for they have to create newer and newer signs by which to show that revelation is still active today. A theology of signs that stopped short at the reading merely and had no will to continue raising up new signs, would always be lacking something essential. The criteria chosen above require believers to be ready to put forward new signs since they must always be watchful about life's different situations.

The signs of the times, therefore, present a challenge that the church puts to the world: for with these she invites everyone to live the historical present with all the intensity we can, yet never forgetting that our gaze must always be turned toward the future.

The capacity for perceiving and making new signs of the times will be proportionate to our capacity for reviving—yes, for today—the messianic times of God's presence in our midst. The word of the Lord invites us to do this: "Truly, truly, I say to you: he who believes in me will also do the works that I do; and greater works than these will he do, because I go to the Father" (Jn 14:12). For every believer this implies that we cannot remain in the world as passive spectators: the faith is testimony of a consistent and continuous work which lasts throughout our lives and knows no sabbath rest.

Bibl.: M. D. CHENU, "Signes des temps," *NRT* 87 (1965): 29–39; R. LATOURELLE, *Christ and the Church, Signs of Salvation* (New York, 1972); G. O'COLLINS, *Fundamental Theology* (London, 1981); C. BOFF, *Segni dei tempi* (Rome, 1983); K. FÜSSEL, "Die Zeichen der Zeit als locus theologicus," *FZPT* 31 (1984): 259–74; R. FISICHELLA, *La Révélation: La révélation et sa crédibilité* (Paris, 1989); L. GONZÁLEZ CARAVAIJAL, *Los signos de los tiempos: El reino de Dios está entre nosotros* (Santander, 1987); H. J. POTT-MEYER, "Zeichen und Kriterien der Glaubwürdigkeit des Christentums," *HFT* 4:373–413; S. PIÉ-NINOT, *Tratado de teología fundamental* (Salamanca, 1989).

Rino FISICHELLA

SILENCE

Theologians have neglected silence. In their keenness to become scientists, they have relegated this essential medium for theological thought to the realms of mysticism and spirituality, so running the constant risk of falling short of their purpose.

It is a paradoxical state of affairs when we have to speak or write about silence. On the one hand, it would be better never to mention it at all, since Heidegger's words, "There is no worse chatter than that which originates in speaking or writing about silence" (*Unterwegs zur Sprache* [Pfullingen, 1959]), seem to hang over our heads like the sword of Damocles; on the other, we feel we really must speak about it, to make people think about it and realize how much we need to recover it today.

Attempting to talk about silence is a kind of contradiction in terms, since we know that to express it we have to break it or at least suspend it. Yet this is the only way we can bring out the significance of silence and explain its function in creating intervals of meaning.

Fundamental theology can revive the study of silence on two planes at least. First, as theological epistemology, it must show that silence is method *in theologia*, inasmuch as it is the last expression to relate the object of inquiry with the epistemic subject. Second, it must make it a *locus theologicus*, so that believer and contemporary world alike be given the opportunity of encountering a sign that expresses, and directs toward, the presence of God.

1. Phenomenology of Silence

What is silence? We all know about it. We know a silence that separates, and a silence that denies; one that makes us anxious, another that expresses love; one that arouses suspicion and another that is the basis for friendship and understanding. We know moments of silence that are cold, even icy, and others that generate such serenity and peace we could wish they would last forever. Yet these experiences are only fragments of a greater silence that includes them all and gives them meaning: a silence guaranteeing that we can be, and understand ourselves as, free agents.

So from *silences* we must go back to that original *silence* which, being such, is as yet without emotive coloring but which nonetheless is the condition making possible that which we are writing about.

First, there is the silence that makes for thought and sustains it. This silence is no mere object of theoretical speculation, it is in fact what makes thought what it is. It is the precondition for the mind to be able to reflect; it is the original intuition, presenting itself visually to the intellect and thus already in existence, even though it cannot yet be put into words.

Silence is a reality, a fact that exists, allowing us to reflect and express ourselves and then revert to ourselves, so as to give full meaning to what we have thought and expressed. Hence we can say that silence is an original event, existing like life, death, faith, love, and so on. Perhaps, in a way, it contains all these, since it is identified with the very mystery of our existence. For, by taking us out of time and space, it inducts us into that original creative act by which we come into direct relationship with the creator.

Silence is not a pause due to our being tired of talking; it does not follow on when talking stops; not at all, it constitutes the essence of human language, since it is its original source and its ultimate end.

So speech and silence cannot be thought of as opposites, the presence of the one excluding and putting the other to flight; rather, they are the two aspects which make up human language as constituent element of the human being. So no conflict exists between silence and speech, but unity and integration, where silence, however, takes temporal and ontological precedence. There could be no speech without silence, yet there could be no real silence, were it not for suspension of speech.

Our first undertaking must be to devise an epistemology of silence. For it is not enough to show that it exists, nor to proclaim how important it is; first of all, we must show that silence belongs, as constituent element, to the human subject and that without it there is no human being.

Though we may accept Heidegger's dictum that "man is man inasmuch as he speaks" (ibid., 27), we should still not stop short at this stage in our thinking but should feel obliged to pursue our search for a yet more basic principle: language is sustained by silence.

Thus we need to pass from silence back to silence, to grasp what it is in itself and how we relate to it.

2. Silence and Speech

The first thing we note about silence is its relationship to speech. As we have already said, speech and silence constitute an inseparable duality in making up human language and the human being itself. Speech finds its true *Sitz im Leben* in silence.

The act by which speech occurs of itself puts an end to silence; yet the spoken word, as though by magic, reverts to and ends in silence, since silence is what endows it with *meaning*. Precisely at that moment when speech wells up from the thoughtful mind, when this ends to produce another silence, it acquires its full meaning. Speech incomplete, because interrupted or superimposed on something else, can never be properly understood; it will always be subject to differing interpretations and inevitably be ambiguous. It will just be "sound," anonymous, impersonal talk, without a referent, all at sea.

Completed speech, that is to say, complete in relation to the silence which gives rise to it and contains it, is fully meaningful since it evokes the silence which gave rise to it and which continually impresses new forms on it.

Speech, for its part, intervenes to end the silence of the indeterminate, of the void, of the undefined, even if once again silence lends precision to the spoken word. Hence speech, without its referent silence, would be an orphan, would lack depth and be dissipated in the superficial, in the indicative, but never could characterize a person-to-person relationship. There is, to sum up, an original meaning in everything that is said, and this is what sends us instantly back to the thought that generates it. It is there, we believe, that speech acquires its true significance, since there that relationship with silence is established which becomes the "space," the "place" where the thought that generates, the word expressed, and the meaning conveyed are all interconnected.

3. Silence and Person

The relationship between silence and speech inevitably sends us back to the being who seems to create the one and the other. "Seems" to create, since basically, in this matter of language, we all discover our own limitations or how to transcend them.

Certainly we create what we say; yet we never feel completely free in doing so. We do not create; rather, we belong to language. In any case we are debtors to another since we receive speech from the "other." Though we speak, it is only because *by nature* we are indebted to silence; though we want to understand, we can only do so if we create silence.

In silence we await the word and accept it; in a sense we create it because we make it "ours." Yet in the very silence allowing us intuition and reflection, we also discover how impossible it is to say all we want to say. A great part of ourselves remains silent, because the core of thought and the heart cannot be put into words.

For us, silence is also the condition for expressing our own freedom and experiencing ourselves as free agents. For silence arouses conflicting reactions in us; we do not know the wherefore of silence nor what there will be after the silence. Our being suspended in silence obliges us to make a choice. A dramatic situation, because we can fulfill or destroy ourselves. Only our freedom allows silence to be movement toward speech or to be motionlessly turned in on itself. Though silence fulfills us in speech, it can also destroy us if we are alone with it too long.

These elements allow us to show that language makes the human being, but only when silence is taken to be a constituent component, not an absolute one however.

In this context, the words of Ecclesiastes 3:7 (Sir 20:1–8) take on new meaning: "There is a time to keep silence and a time to speak," because in human wisdom, illuminated by grace, we create a balance between the two, to make a unity.

4. Silence in Scripture

The Bible makes a leitmotiv of silence when speaking about God. "Silence is the landscape of the Bible," the Jewish theologian A. Neher perceptively remarks in his stimulating study *L'exil de la Parole;* but perhaps we should take the paradox further by calling the Bible the book of the silence of God.

The logos is too Hellenistic a concept for us to understand what it truly means. Ignatius of Antioch puts it clearly in his letter *Ad Ephesios:* "The Father uttered a word and it was his Son, and the Word speaks ever in eternal silence and in silence must the soul listen to it."

Scripture expresses that original silence, the Father's first expression of love, which then becomes the obediential word of the Son and, hence, Spirit of love as a new silence going "beyond the word" and, within itself, containing the mystery of the Trinity.

From the silence is born revelation, which then becomes the historical and prophetic word, and hence the final word in the incarnation of the Son, but which in turn fades into a new silence as contemplation and responding faith.

The Bible is the first great witness to the grandeur of silence; not only does it treat it as a fact for human beings and the natural world, but makes it the background against which to situate the mystery of the revelation of God.

The OT, from a wealth of possible terms, for preference chooses those states related to silence rather than silence itself. The terms *dāmāh, sākat, hāsāh/hāšāh, hārāš, 'elem, hastēr pānîm,* cover a vast range of meanings running from silence understood as applying to night, sleep, death, to chaos and Sheol, and finally to indicate a dumb or lazy person. But at least twenty-five times, *hastēr pānîm* denotes the hiddenness-silence of God.

Historically speaking, the theme of God's silence emerges as linked to his hiddenness. The people beg God not to hide, not to forsake them, for otherwise history would come to an end and there would be no more people (see Dt 31:17–18; Jer 33:5–6; Is 54:7; Ez 24:33); the Psalms bear witness to the same ideas, converting the sense of fear into prayerful invocation (see Pss 30:8; 104:28; 143:7; 27:9; 102:3; 69:18).

A passage in Isaiah, however, would seem to be an attempt to treat the theme of human silence before the mystery of God. "Truly, thou art a hidden God" (Is 45:15; 8:17) at once conveys the mystery and the hope that it arouses in the believer.

God normally reveals himself in silence. The sojourn in the wilderness and the silence this picture naturally evokes stamp the entire relationship between Israel and Yahweh as one that is fulfilled in silence. The experiences of the prophets bear this out. More precisely, the narrative of the theophany to Elijah in 1 Kings 19:11–12; the prophet in the cave hears the rushing wind, but God is not in the wind; nor is he in the earthquake, nor in the fire; only when there comes the "murmur of a breeze" or, as more plastically some readings will have it, "in the voice of silence," only then does Elijah cover his face, knowing that he is in God's presence.

Likewise, Ezekiel adopts an impressive symbolism with silence: his silence becomes a sign of Yahweh's reproach for a people who are not prepared to listen. Those who will listen, like those who will not, are to take note of the prophet's silence, for this becomes the content of revelation and sign of discernment (see Ez 3:26–27).

Unlike human silence, which is often confused with quietness and absence of movement, God's silence is a dynamic source of all sorts of reactions. Before him, when he reveals himself, all fall prostrate in silent adoration: "The silence of praise is thine, O God" (Ps 65:2).

In Jesus of Nazareth, God's silence gives way to a definitive word about his life. He is the Word of God, the silence seems to stop; and yet many passages in the Gospels show that in this word there is still the silence of revelation.

Jesus' speech is his silence too; in this he reveals himself most deeply. Another passage from Ignatius of Antioch is very much to the point here:

> It is better to be silent and to be, than to speak and not to be. Teaching is a good thing, if the teacher acts. There is therefore one Master only, who spoke and what he said was done; but the things that he did without speaking are worthy of the Father. If we possess Jesus' word, we can also listen to his silence, so as to be perfect, so as to work through what we say and be known by what we do not. (PG 5:657–48)

To be the definitive Word of the Father, Jesus before all else has to be able to express the Father's silence: that which gives rise to triune love. Christ's own silence is grounded in that intratrinitarian obedience which initially consents to be uttered by the Father. With this in mind, we may consider the different moments in Jesus' life when the component of silence seems most suitable for expressing his relationship with the Father: "And he spent the night, alone, in prayer" (Mk 1:35; Mt 14:23).

Night and solitude automatically evoke the concept and fact of silence, and the prayer of Jesus to the Father on these intimate occasions could only be the silence of loving adoration.

Yet other passages allow us to see Jesus' attitude to silence. In Mark's account of Jesus, he lays great stress on this particular aspect of his character. On several occasions, he records that Jesus peremptorily ordered his disciples and other nothing, particularly on matters concerning his messiahship (see "messianic secret," → CHRISTOLOGY III). By the same token, we find a deep silence in the Lukan infancy narratives; consider too the silence of the trials; not to mention the silence of the judgment which simultaneously silences the accusations of the wicked and reveals the mystery of forgiveness (Jn 8:1–11).

But more indicative of revelation than any other is that silence beginning after the "cry" on the cross and lasting throughout Holy Saturday. That silence, when it seems God will speak no more through the Word of the Son, turns out to be the loudest of all revelatory language to proclaim the event.

The silence of death and the tomb bespeaks and reveals the depth of trinitarian love. The Son's sharing in the human condition reaches its extreme moment in the silence of Sheol.

The silent God is he who shouts his triumph-song over sin and death. The trinitarian love that emerged from the silent dynamism of Father, Son, and Spirit is now expressed as silence in sharing the condition of death. The God who dies in Jesus is the God who loves, but his silence indicates how much he loves: to the point of giving *all*, even to becoming dead among the dead, so that he can thus express the limit, the extreme point, which is then the beginning point, of his love.

After that silence—absolute since the only one placed in the world by God—all other suffering in silence, even the extreme example of Auschwitz and the extermination camps, will, to be fully grasped, have to be referred to the silence of Golgotha and Holy Saturday, for here, and here alone, God's silence about himself becomes the clarificatory word on sorrow, suffering, and the drama of human existence.

So even silence—and *above all* silence—speaks and expresses the revelation of God. Here we have no apophatic interpretation tending to the inexpressibility of God; rather, we have a positive conception of silence, by which it may become instrument and language for the powerful expression of revelation.

Not therefore silence as absence of speech, as though silence were imposed on us in obedience to the commandment not to create any image of God; rather, silence conceived as language with which to make the signs and words expressed fully comprehensible. In a word, we see Augustine's dialectic come true: *Verbo crescente, verba deficiunt* ("as the Word appears, the words fail").

5. Silence as a Sign of the Times

Silence can be regarded in fundamental theology also as being a sign of the times, able to express the tendency of human beings toward more humanly worthy conditions of life. While it is true that modern society and culture accord less and less space to silence, it is also true that we are becoming aware of how much we need to recover it.

The uneasy relationship between people and silence is not something we should get too agitated about, as though it were a negative effect of these past few decades; human beings have always been afraid of silence and tried to get away from it. Pascal frequently observes that his own contemporaries, rather than think about serious matters, preferred to go hunting (see *Pensées* 194; 168; 171); Kierkegaard in a valuable fragment says that, "in the state of the world today, all life is sick. Were I a doctor and someone asked my advice, I should reply: Create silence. Take the human race to silence." And R. Guardini, too, at the beginning of this century, observed: "We only have to look at the world about us to see to what a terrible degree silence has vanished; and it will vanish even faster, as idle chattering gains the upper hand." And on this topic, Jung seems to echo Pascal: "Noise is welcomed because it overcomes the instinctive warning of the danger within us. Those who are afraid of themselves seek rowdy company and deafening noise. Noise confers a feeling of security, as does the crowd, and that is why they like it. Noise protects us from painful thoughts, banishes worrying dreams. . . . It is so immediate, so overbearingly real, that everything else becomes a pallid phantom."

Lack of silence seems more dramatic today, now that we are more aware of the subhuman conditions in which so many other people live. Challenging noise, defending the environment and the natural world in general are only the tip of a greater critical awareness within us which is gradually being atrophied by the triumph of affluence. People today, especially in big cities, are bombarded non-stop, to destructive effect, by all kinds of meaningless words and noises: the noise of traffic, the shouts of people in the street, the disorderliness of an increasingly feverish mass tourism, the rush to meet deadlines and appointments, traffic signals, advertisements everywhere, graffiti on walls . . . in a word, an orgy of noises.

A regained sense of respect for the natural world and for life in various forms seems to be spreading fast, but this movement is doomed to fail if it is not basically concerned with silence.

The creation of areas of silence can allow a fresh encounter with ourselves and with our surroundings; this is a necessity, for we must escape from the noise tunnel in which we are losing our identity.

When the disciples returned from the first evangelistic mission but had not had a chance to talk to Jesus or even time to eat on account of the hurly-burly of the crowd, he invited them to come away "by yourselves to a lonely place," to be with him and rest and talk things over (Mk 6:30–32); this behavior should be taken very seriously, especially by believers today.

The monk is not the only concrete sign of the lover of silence. All mature human beings who have understood what life is about should feel it a duty to leave words awhile and recapture silence. The resumption of genuine person-to-person relationships, overcoming the barrier of individualism, a new way of tackling the world: all pass by way of silence.

Permanent silence is not called for, but silence ought always to be there, as "a moment," as "a space," from which we emerge to start communicating again. For in the wilderness we can only stay for forty years, or forty days, but not for a whole lifetime, since human beings are created with social natures.

Awareness of our loss and of our recovery of silence is a kind of maturity, giving rise to a much more effective awareness of belonging to and solidarity with a new humanism beyond the barriers of ideology and differences of language. Silence thus seems to be, as it were, that frontier zone for the recovery of MEANING and a sense of the grandeur of human language. This seems the more evident today owing to the multiplying and differentiating of languages, from the human one to the information technology now in common use. Once we have got—and it won't be long before we have—computers of the "fifth generation," able, that is to say, to program themselves: once faced with the marvel of mechanical language: we shall certainly be able to grasp the value of silence then. For we shall realize that, come what may, human language is the only language that can create silence and give it meaning. The machine will produce languages and formulae, the fruit of precision and the electronic brain, but we shall still produce meaning, since we have the power to choose and ordain silence.

Bibl.: M. PICARD, *Il mondo del silenzio* (Milan, 1951); K. RAHNER, *Encounters with Silence* (Westminster, Md., 1960); F. ULRICH, "L'uomo e la parola," in *MystSal*, vol. 4 (Brescia, 1970), 333–408; H. Urs VON BALTHASAR, "Word and Silence," in *Word and Revela-*

tion (New York, 1964), 165–91; id., *A Theological Anthropology* (New York, 1967); J. RASSAM, *Le silence comme introduction à la métaphysique* (Toulouse, 1980); A. NEHER, *L'exil de la Parole* (Paris, 1970); M. HEIDEGGER, *L'acheminement vers la parole* (Paris, 1976); M. BALDINI, *La parola del silenzio* (Turin, 1986); id., *Le dimensioni del silenzio: nella poesia, nella filosofia, nella musica, nella linguistica, nella psicanalisi, nella pedagogia e nella mistica* (Rome, 1988).

Rino FISICHELLA

SITZ IM LEBEN (Life Setting)

This expression entered our current vocabulary through the history-of-forms (*Formgeschichte*) school and is connected with the school's effort to reconstruct the prehistory of the Gospels, i.e., the period of oral tradition which lasted until the first written collections came into existence. In the first stage of reconstruction of the oral tradition scholars endeavor to isolate and identify the literary units which make up the Gospels; they then try to identify the *Sitz im Leben* or "life setting" or socioreligious context that explains their appearance and their formation in the life of the early church. These life settings, which are associated with the various activities of the church, are: missionary preaching, catechesis, worship, polemics.

René LATOURELLE

SKEPTICISM

1. Explanation of the Concept

Although the concept of "skepticism" stems most directly from the French word *sceptique* (skeptical; skeptic), it still also carries connotations of the original Greek word *skeptomai* (to examine searchingly). As a philosophical term, it is normally used to designate that philosophical orientation or attitude of mind that refrains from passing judgment because nothing about the truth or falsity of statements can be decided with adequate certainty.

Radical skepticism is self-contradictory, because the assertion "Everything is to be doubted" runs counter to its own implicit truth-claim. *Relative* or *limited* skepticism can occur in relation to certain specific areas (religion, ethics, aesthetics, etc.). Since Descartes, it is usual to speak of a *"methodological"* skepticism. Everything can, to be sure, be doubted; but one exception to this is the thinking ego of the person who doubts. Those who doubt everything obviously cannot doubt the fact that it is they themselves who are doubting. With that, Descartes hoped to overcome skepticism.

2. Skepticism in the History of Western Philosophy

Historically, skepticism appears as Janus-faced: both a *symptom of decadence* in declining civilizations and an *instrument* of enlightened thought.

In the philosophical thought of the West, skepticism emerges as a philosophical school in ancient Greece, primarily between 300 and 200 B.C.E. Three phases of development are generally distinguished: the early (Pyrrho, Timon), the middle or academic (Arcesilaus, Carneades), and the late or new (Aenesidemus, Sextus Empiricus). In common with other schools (e.g., Stoicism and Epicureanism), ancient Greek skepticism emphasizes the search for happiness. Like them, too, it views the prerequisite for this as being calmness of soul (ataraxia). In contrast, however, to other schools, which attempt to achieve that state by way of knowledge of the world, skepticism entirely dispenses with such knowledge. Having no knowledge, the skeptic is presumably untouched by the external world, and can thus attain the calmness of soul that is the condition of true happiness. The foregoing of knowledge is rationally justified through the impossibility of knowing truth or the world. Ancient philosophy evolves a peculiar conception of skepticism: critical scrutiny of thought does not ultimately lead to well-considered judgment, but ends in an aporia. The skeptic arrives at neither a positive nor a negative statement, but persists in the withholding of any judgment (*epochē*), like that donkey (indigenous to philosophy) which, equidistant from two equally large haystacks, starves to death because it presumably cannot decide in favor of either one.

Christianity engages, quite early on, in critical examination of skepticism. The starting point is the question of whether there is a transition from the doubts of thought to the certainty of faith, or also, perhaps, a justified coexistence of both. Absolute skepticism, however, is excluded from the very first. For Tertullian, "Athens" and "Jerusalem" stand in irreconcilable opposition. Christian faith completely excludes doubting and seeking. Dialogue between faith and skepticism is senseless. Augustine, too, endorses the opposition between certainty of faith and doubt (in *Contra Academicos*), but attempts to refute skepticism philosophically.

In medieval scholasticism, no skeptical currents are discernible. Initial approaches to such first reemerge in Duns Scotus and Ockham. Descartes's *cogito ergo sum* is aimed at overcoming, in principle, any sort of skepticism. Hume's skepticism about rational ethics and the principle of causation as a source of knowledge exerts a profound influence on the subsequent course of philosophical thought. For Hegel, skepticism is an essential stage in the unfolding truth of the whole. Nietzsche's skepticism issues in nihilism.

Today, skepticism is more a basic aspect of modern philosophizing than a specific direction in philosophy. As such, it safeguards intellectual freedom to engage in unreserved pursuit of truth against any attempts at dogmatization of thought.

3. Theological Assessment

Skepticism has never been explicitly condemned in any church document. Still, everything that has been said about agnosticism would also seem applicable to it.

Limited, or methodological, skepticism, in the sense of a "radical questioning," can nevertheless be quite legitimate, and can expose ambiguities in many areas by critically confronting seemingly self-evident things and questioning their presuppositions. The justification for such skepticism lies in the contingency of human cognition.

The relationship between faith and doubt (in the sense of a searching and questioning) is the central theological problem. For ultimately,

after all, faith does not represent a questionless cognitive possession. Christian faith is fully conscious of itself as a tension-filled complex of faith and doubt (see Mk 9:24). Paul invites the faithful to engage in critical examination of their own faith (see 2 Cor 13:5). The certainty of faith can be seen in the calmness with which it allows itself to be tested against all questions.

Skepticism also becomes theologically significant whenever human cognitive activity directs itself toward trying to derive a claim to absoluteness from Christian faith's connection with revelation. Faith itself remains fundamentally skeptical about promises of salvation through scientific knowledge. Even theology, as a cognitive discipline, is subject to the restrictions of human knowledge, and thus there is wide scope for application of a limited skepticism in it, too.

Wilhelm Weischedel (1905–1975) pursued extensive inquiries into the relation of skeptical thought to the question of God. He understands by skepticism a "radical questioning," which, as such, is a basic feature of modern philosophy. In contrast to Descartes, he sees the *process* of radical searching and questioning itself as being the indubitable fact, the "first certainty." In order for skeptical thought to arrive at the question of God, it must, for its part, be affected by a reality that cannot itself be called into question, one "that, instead, no matter how radical the questioning to which it is subjected, preserves and proves itself as a reality" (Weischedel, 20). In all its questionability, the questionable reality itself then appears as a *mystery*. Radical questionability and mystery are mutually conditioning. For this, Weischedel cites three examples: (1) that, regardless of the *contingency* of all being, something actually *exists*; (2) the *experience of death* and of *transience*; and (3) the world *as a whole*. The mysteriousness of reality is not invented or evoked, but discovered; indeed, it virtually forces its presence upon skeptical thought, it presses unavoidably toward it. Radical questioning would not be possible were there not first the mystery that provides the impetus for the questioning. Hence the mystery is what both conditions and enables the questioning. This mystery, as the reality that resists all questioning, Weischedel does not, however, wish to identify overhastily with the Christian God. Still, according to him, Christian faith ultimately refers to that which manifests itself, philosophically, as the mystery. Faith and philosophy, then, ultimately speak about the same thing in different languages: faith in symbolic language and philosophy directly.

Bibl.: W. Post, "Skeptizismus," in SM, vol. 4 (Freiburg/Basel/Vienna, 1969), 576–79; R. H. Popkin, "Scepticism," in *The Encyclopedia of Philosophy*, vol. 7 (New York, 1967), 449–61; R. Richter, *Der Skeptizismus in der Philosophie und seine Überwindung*, 2 vols. (Leipzig, 1904–05); H. R. Schlette, *Skeptische Religionsphilosophie: Zur Kritik der Pietät* (Freiburg, 1972); G. Schnurr, *Skeptizismus als theologisches Problem*, Forschungen zur systematischen und ökumenischen Theologie 14 (Göttingen, 1964); W. Weischedel, *Die Frage nach Gott im skeptischen Denken* (Berlin/New York, 1976).

Bernd Groth

SOLITUDE

A survey conducted in a large European country shows that for 65 percent of the people polled solitude or loneliness is the hardest trial they face. In a similar survey, this time among ecclesiastics, 90 percent of the students say that they fear loneliness more than death.

It is a paradox of the twentieth century that people constantly talk of communication, dialogue, and sharing, but have more than ever a sense of aloneness. They live together, work together, and think together. On the other hand, they feel they are not understood but are abandoned, repulsed, rejected. They experience loneliness as the bitterest form of poverty. It breaks down heart and spirit, as though the organism no longer had the antibodies needed to combat the void that is swallowing it up, as though it were afflicted by a "psychic AIDS." Persons feel exiled from themselves, with no one able or willing to join them.

Isolation and loneliness seem indeed to be one element in the *meaninglessness* felt in our society. If the subject is brought up in the context of this dictionary, it is chiefly because isolation (aloneness, solitude, loneliness) is inseparable from the human condition. In this respect, it is part of the mystery of the human person, of the person's condition as a "finite" creature before God. In its own way, it raises the question of *meaning:* a meaning that is partially accessible with human resources, but never fully discovered without an illumination from on high, from Christ.

As soon as we speak of solitude, we find we are using an ambiguous word. There are in fact many forms of solitude: a painful and enforced aloneness, imposed by events; a baneful and aggressive solitude, in the form of silence and isolation; finally, an aloneness that is fruitful, accepted, open and receptive (e.g., that of the saints or Christ himself). As a matter of fact, the only meaningful distinction is between harmful solitude, or isolation, and fruitful solitude, which alone is authentic. The problem is to move from isolation to the solitude of contemplation, from life in a state of *collapse* to life that is *successful.*

1. Forms of Solitude

A *first* form of solitude is imposed on us by the life-style of the modern world, especially in large cities. In small villages people know each other only too well. But in large cities, which bring so many people together and should therefore develop a sense of community, people in fact live in their separate cells or on parallel tracks, like branch lines of the subway, and in complete anonymity. There is no human warmth, only the indifference of icebergs. People may pass by their neighbor year after year without knowing the neighbor's name or giving their own. A neighbor is rarely what the word suggests: someone "close." Life within the great corporations, with their wilderness of offices and machines, hardly improves the situation. As a result of living with machines people risk dealing in a mechanical way with everything and everyone. The capacity for human encounter atrophies. Television rooms with their comfortable but isolated armchairs symbolize an indifference that ends in friendlessness, then in aggressive isolation.

A *second* form of forced solitude is that which results from a lack of understanding on the part of those who are close to us: relatives, friends, companions at work. This kind of loneliness is all the more painful in that it is caused by those on whom we should normally be able to rely most. It is found in families in which husband and wife live side by side but walled off from one another: this is the loneliness "together" of couples in conflict, engaged in open or secret war, until they finally "switch off" and get involved in affairs with occasional partners and in serial disorders. A further result of this situation is the loneliness of one-parent youngsters who no longer know to whom they belong and who become the classic prey to every temptation. This phenomenon of misunderstanding and resultant solitude is to be found in a no less virulent form in relations between the various classes of society (workers and bosses, unions and managements) and between the different generations: the tragic misunderstanding between children and parents (parents helpless or unnatural in their attitudes; children who leave home and slam the door behind them as they go off to join clandestine groups of idlers, misfits, or drug addicts).

A *third* form of forced, involuntary solitude, but the most painful and heart-rending of all, goes by the name of abandonment, neglect, rejection. Those who have experienced it want only to forget it, for it is an experience of total disintegration of their being. Such is the experience of ardent, zealous young priests who are left on their own in dechristianized, cold and numbing surroundings, in which there is no possibility of recouping their spiritual and intellectual energies. Such, too, is the lot of displaced persons or "refugees." Initially they are welcomed, but the honeymoon in their adopted country soon ends. On subways, trains, and buses their accent or their color quickly reveals the "foreigner." Few are the homes and still fewer the hearts that welcome them with the warmth of loyal friendship.

Turn now to those in the third or fourth stages of life. Such people are now common in our Western countries, where life expectancy has greatly increased. The elderly often feel like dead persons who have been granted a short reprieve; they spend the best part of their time in bed or watching television or sitting at the window and looking out at a world that no longer looks back at them, because they have nothing to contribute to society. They are hardly remembered except at election time! In some countries, entrance into a home is like entrance into the antechamber of death, where those beyond repair are put. It is not surprising that this kind of abandonment leads to bitterness and even to aggressive isolation.

Those most stricken with the loneliness of abandonment are the seriously ill and the chronically ill. They feel physically and socially diminished and spatially outcast. They no longer belong to the world of the living. As troublesome, unimportant persons in decline they often inspire disdain and the physical repugnance people feel when confronted with an object destined to rot in the grave or the charnel house. Others wait for them to die so that they may seize their inheritance. The seriously ill may emerge from this crisis purified and strengthened, but they may also sink into a "harmful solitude" that cuts them off from themselves and others.

There is, finally, the abandonment, neglect, and rejection that are the tragic lot of all those who are powerless before the brutal force of oppressive regimes, be these political, military, or economic. Every injustice committed in this world leaves its victim "alone" and tempted to suicide. Is this not the condition of peoples who have for centuries lived in "collective solitude": subjugated, oppressed, enslaved, trodden down, without even a hope of change, like a shipwrecked man who after each attempt to rescue himself feels as if he has been seized by the neck and pitilessly hauled back?

It must be said that the experience of forced solitude is a trial but not necessarily an existential failure. On the contrary, if it is lived through in union with Christ who is at once Solitude and Fullness, it can, like the solitude of contemplatives and the solitude of the suffering, become the most powerful spiritual energy in the world. Otherwise, it can turn into isolation, a harmful solitude.

2. Harmful Solitude or Isolation

Isolation is solitude that has turned *sour* instead of *mellow.* It can be seen in individuals who have known failure too early in their lives and have never accepted it or overcome it. Those who are isolated become bitter, aggressive, and belligerent toward everything and everyone. Those who are misunderstood and unloved become unloving in their turn; they are the scorned who answer with scorn. They drag out their lives and look upon everything and everyone with disillusionment. This temptation lies in wait for those who grow old and see their chances of success decrease and then disappear. "I gave what I had to give! The rest is their look-out!" A life that might have born fruit has become sterile.

Christian circles are not exempt from these tensions, which can be no less brutal than those seen in colonies of animals. If individuals do not subscribe to a particular group or ideology or trend, they are utterly excluded not only from power and favor but even from the air they need to breathe. Such circles, instead of expanding under the impulse of charity, become hells in which individuals isolate themselves, protect and defend themselves, or go on the attack. Encounters with others are for the purpose of knocking them down and crushing them. Fear is omnipresent, like a guillotine always ready to cut heads off. The *isolated* are indeed *frightful* and need to be *saved*.

3. The Ways Out of Solitude

There is only one real way out of solitude: upward, by rising above it. But this kind of fruitful aloneness is itself a *conquest*. It demands that persons practice recollection in order to find themselves, just as Christ went apart in order to pray and discover himself as Son through intimacy with the Father. Without recollection, withdrawal becomes arid, an intolerable desert. The purpose of getting out of the whirlpool and the eddies is to get into calm water. Persons return to themselves in order then to return to others enriched and with something to give.

Another factor in genuine aloneness is openness to others. Recollection and openness make up a single activity. In bringing persons back to their own center solitude reveals them to themselves as free and mysteriously and irreplaceably unique but also as finite and in need of knowing, loving, and acting if they are to achieve their fulfillment. If they do not know, love, and act they atrophy and die. Solitude also teaches them to see others with a purified eye, not as indifferent shadows nor as objects to be possessed, but as, like themselves, mysteries of freedom and uniqueness that reveal themselves only in revealing their secret and in freely given testimony. Exclusivism and totalitarianism are the enemies of genuine solitude. Only true solitude leads to authentic friendship and love. Human solitude then resembles the divine solitude, which is at once infinite plenitude and infinite self-surrender. Finally, true solitude leads to self-renewal. Those who enter into

their own hearts and open themselves to others create a new being for themselves. Genuine solitude is a source of progress, creativity, and integration. The dialectic proper to human life is a dialectic of solitude and communion; it has a two-phase rhythm. There is no real fruitfulness, intellectual or spiritual, without solitude.

4. Inevitable Radical Solitude

So much for authentic, fruitful solitude, but there is more to be said. For even under the most favorable conditions and in the best protected environments there always remains in the depths of our being a solitude that is radical and unavoidable; it is part of the mystery of our being as persons. To perceive that *we are* is to become aware that each and all of us are "secret cells," mysterious hiding places. At times, this awareness is felt as distressing, but it can be beneficial and turn into an appeal to the one who is present where no one else can enter in, closer to us than we are to ourselves; an appeal, too, to other solitudes like our own, those of the people around us who need us and with whom we feel a need to communicate in an unbroken exchange of sympathy and love.

This radical solitude is due to the mystery of our uniqueness (each of us is unique and inimitable), which relates us to the mystery of God's uniqueness. Whoever has not experienced this solitude has not penetrated very far into the depths of the human heart. This solitude is also due to our neediness. We are made for God and he alone can fulfill us. Whether we know it or not, we carry within us an unconquerable longing for God, a thirst for the infinite that God alone can slake. All human supports are frail: they will fail us or disappoint us. Some day or, in any case, on the final day we shall find ourselves alone before God, unprotected and with nothing to hide behind. This is our fundamental and unavoidable solitude. The sooner we become aware of it, the sooner our solitude will be filled, since he who is Plenitude will cover us with his love and will come to satsify our need.

This meeting of our solitude with Plenitude cannot take place amid din and racket but only in recollection and the silence that allows the soul to hear and open its door to the great presence. When we recollect ourselves in this way, the voice of God, which is like a gentle breeze, grows louder and can be heard. Solitude is then filled with the presence of the Other, a presence that brings light, warmth, new love, new strength, new joy, and harmony between God and ourselves. I once said to a woman suffering from terminal cancer, "You must feel very lonely at times"; she answered with a smile that was lit from within: "Oh no! When I am alone, there are always two of us here!" No one could put it better. Death, after all, is the meeting of our radical, innate solitude with the divine Thou who unveils his face at last. Death is solitude that has reached its full maturity, solitude that is crowned by Plenitude.

5. Christ and Our Solitudes

In our lives there are moments of loneliness that are due to fatigue or passing physical depression. We then turn to physicians or other experts. A friend, too, can help us through bad stretches. But even when we are able to "perform" normally at the physical level, we never succeed in eliminating the forms of human solitude or loneliness that inevitably mark every life. There are moments when human supports are useless. It is then that we must *turn our gaze* to Christ. For Christ offers no discourse about solitude, as he does, e.g., about our neighbor. He does indeed say: "I will not leave you orphans" (Jn 14:18), but that is not much. Here, more than ever, we must bear in mind that revelation takes place no less through the example and attitudes of Christ than through his formal statements. And in fact, Christ's answer to the problem of our solitude and loneliness takes the form *not* of a *discourse* but of an *attitude.*

If Christ had not experienced solitude, misunderstanding, abandonment, and rejection as we do, we could complain and remonstrate with him as Job does with God. But Christ has gone before us on the road of solitude, and has even entered the abyss; he experienced literally every form of solitude.

He experienced the *betrayal of friendship.* "He came to his own, and his own received him not" (Jn 1:11). He loved his people; he solaced them, with a mother's tenderness, in all their griefs; he enlightened and instructed them. Above all, he loved the Twelve and made them his companions on his journeys and at table. To the very end he calls them his "friends." Yet he

finds himself alone. They all desert him, even the most faithful. He becomes one "cut off," one who is "isolated." Peter denies him, Judas betrays him. Everyone abandons him; he alone abandons no one. Though rejected by all, he rejects no one.

At the moment of his passion, when arrested and bound as a criminal, Jesus falls into the power of his *enemies.* Thus the drama of his solitude is also a drama of a love that is hated, scorned, condemned, and crucified. Christ is alone and helpless, faced by the united opposition of his enemies. The weak, the jealous, the envious, the hate filled: all are there, united against him. Sin is there: raw, icy, cruel, brutal, on the offensive against the innocent. All speak with one voice: "Kill him! Crucify him! Get rid of him!" They *hand him over:* they pass him from hand to hand like something being bartered, until he reaches the executioner and the cross. Christ experiences all that hatred, cruelty, fear, envy, and weakness can make of us. He learns how eager human beings are to lie and to inflict suffering, degradation, and disgrace on all who do not think as they do. He feels what we feel in the darkest moments of our lives: that nothing can be expected of anyone! And yet he *remains faithful* to this human race that is capable of anything and everything. Not a word of reproach or revulsion or rejection. Jesus accepts us where we are: prisoners of our stubborn refusal, our self-made hell. All the sins of the world cannot separate him from the world and us or from the Father.

In Gethsemane Christ experienced an abyss of solitude that remains a mystery to us. The Gospel texts do, however, allow us to glimpse something of this frightful loneliness. Mark speaks of fear and distress. Jesus is crushed. He who came to reunite and gather together has achieved the opposite result: division. The "gatherer" has himself become a cause of division. He who had come to preach the kingdom has met with rejection of the kingdom by Israel. He has failed and experienced the greatest of all solitudes. Yet Jesus continues to proclaim the presence of him who seems to be absent; he remains faithful to the mystery of his own being as Son, and says: "*Abba!* Father!" Loaded down with the sins of the world and turned into a leper, Christ experiences the fearful loneliness, the heart-rending absence which sin creates between human beings and God. If anyone ever deserved to succeed, it was surely Christ, and yet he experienced failure, hatred, and rejection. In the horror of this solitude, in this darkness that is darker than night, he nonetheless says yes to the Father's will: "Not my will but yours." In this yes Christ remains turned to his Father, like a person holding tight to the hand that saves him, but unable to see the face of the savior. The solitude which Christ experiences, limitless and monstrous though it is as a human experience, is unable to cut him off from the Father. The abyss of his solitude is matched by his total abandonment to the Father. This, then, is the form his *discourse* on solitude takes: the form of an *attitude*, a *behavior*.

6. Creative Solitude in the Spirit

The radical, innate solitude which we carry within us as creatures will never depart from us until it is filled by him who is nothing but Plenitude. But there is another form of solitude that lies in wait for us daily to destroy us: the solitude of abandonment, of lack of understanding, of being forgotten, of undeserved failure. No life can escape this solitude, which is like the solitude of Christ. It can become a fearful thing, a martyrdom of the heart. It can be our lot, and we can see it being experienced by others around us, sometimes without their even suspecting it. Then it brings darkness and takes us to the cold, hard, steep wall of the cliff. We can see nothing any longer, nothing but the night! It is then that solitude can become evil and turn against us, against others, and against God. But it is also at this point that solitude can become an opportunity for rising above ourselves, for a leap upward! We must believe that Jesus, who remained faithful to the Father even in the abyss of abandonment and the silence of God, merited for us thé strength to say, with him and after him, in the terror of darkness: "Yes, Father! I do not see, I do not understand (for humanly there is nothing to understand), but I choose, I choose your will; I accept it, I embrace it, no matter where it leads me. I am your child, your child forever." Such fidelity is crucifying, but it has been made possible by the grace of the solitary one who was in agony and was crucified.

This solitude which is painfully and lovingly accepted is a fruitful solitude that rescues us from isolation. Those who acknowledge and accept such solitude will never again be alone. They are rescued from emptiness and from disgust with life, from all forms of skepticism, disillusionment, bitterness, rancor, and hatred. When solitude acquires such a sublime *meaning*, it renders credible the revelation that proposes such a vision of life. This fruitful and fulfilling solitude was that of the Curé of Ars, Francis of Assisi, Father de Foucauld, Isaac Jogues, and Father Kolbe. But we need not go so far afield. We should rather call to mind persons known to us who have experienced this fullness of joy and serenity in their solitude; persons who have lived their lives and endured trials sometimes heavier than they should have been, but who nonetheless have retained all their freshness of spirit and are capable of being deeply moved and feeling compassion, of listening and forgetting themselves, and of strengthening those whom they meet by their gentle unforgettable smile that radiates goodness and light because it is lit from within by the unique presence that fills every solitude for them. Solitude thus lived is akin to the solitude of those who suffer and those who pray: it is the most powerful spiritual force in the world. It is a perpetual prayer to the Son and the Father in the Spirit. At this level, we cannot any longer call any life a "failure," but only a "success."

Bibl.: L. LAVELLE, "Tous les êtres séparés et unis, in *Le mal et la souffrance* (Paris, 1940), 133–216; J.-B. LOTZ, *De la solitude humaine* (Paris, 1964); *Christus*, no. 19 (Jan. 1966); J. GUILLET, "Rejeté des hommes, abandonné de Dieu, in M. de Certeau and F. Roustang, eds., *La solitude* (Paris, 1967); D. VASSE, "De l'isolement à la solitude, in M. de Certeau and F. Roustang, eds., *La solitude* (Paris, 1967), 173–85; Simone de BEAUVOIR, *La vieillesse*, 2 vols. (Paris, 1970); R. LATOURELLE, "Christ and Human Solitude, in *Man and His Problems in the Light of Jesus Christ* (New York, 1983), 219–35; C. MESTERS, *La mission du peuple qui souffre* (Paris, 1986); P. TALEC, *L'annonce du bonheur: Vie et béatitudes* (Paris, 1988), 151–75.

René LATOURELLE

SUFFERING

Suffering consists in a feeling of loss, injury, or lack, be it physical or spiritual. At all levels of human existence it constitutes a religious problem insofar as it forces upon the sufferer various questions: How do I escape suffering? Why did suffering arise in the first place? This latter question seeks to prevent a repetition of the suffering and simultaneously opens wider perspectives about the significance of a painful existence. Some religions, like Hinduism and Buddhism, arose from the effort to overcome suffering: insofar as suffering is rooted in desire, desire has to be obliterated. Bliss, or nirvana, consists in either the suppression of individual consciousness or, alternately, in its expansion into universal consciousness, for individuality and the opposition that results from individuality give rise to desire. Usually individual consciousness is consigned to the realm of appearances, or *maya*, which has to be pierced by a transforming insight into being's ultimate reality and the consequential obliteration of individual consciousness. In the West, Stoicism likewise emphasized the unity of the cosmos—without postulating a radical monism—and sought to overcome pain by the "wider vision" of the balanced harmony of the universe, whose unity-in-plurality could be identified with the divinity. Such an insight supposedly suppressed individual desire and gave rise to a gentle feeling of joy. More radically, the American sect of Christian Science denies the reality of suffering and sickness, considering them but illusions to be conquered by meditation. Such solutions, however, fail to explain the existence of the apparent suffering; even if the suffering's ontological status is nonexistence, the finite consciousness really suffers its delusion, and it is not explained how such a dolorous appearance, a variation of metaphysical *nonbeing*, came to be and continues to subsist.

Both for polytheism and for metaphysical-ethical dualisms, e.g., Zoroastrianism and Manichaeism, tension and suffering structure reality. Although human beings are encouraged to struggle for virtue—often initiation rituals prescribe bearing pain manfully—polytheism threatens to subject human existence to the arbitrariness of conflicting deities while neither it nor any dualism adequately explains the metaphysical unity of existence; insofar as morality is grounded in being, this lack of unity threatens moral chaos.

As Israel advanced from henotheism to Deutero-Isaiah's magnificent monotheism, the problem of human suffering became ever more intense. Israel recognized its election in the covenant, which promised material blessings or curses as fitting recompenses for fidelity to the commandments or infidelity (Dt 28–30). But however much the straightforward measure of good rewarded, evil punished (e.g., Pss 1; 23; Prv 22:4) might be valid for small stable communities, experience showed that such a simple norm of justice cannot always suffice. So reward and punishment were often projected into the future (Pss 10; 13; 22; 37), and other reasons were offered for suffering. God employed sufferings medicinally to bring Israel and individuals to their senses and to obedience (Am 4; Hos 6:1–6; 11; Is 63:9–16). After conversion, suffering might purify the converted sinner (Ps 38; Zec 13:8f.). Moreover, God was known to test Abraham and the Jews in order to reward them for their fidelity (Gn 22; Dt 8:16; Ex 20:20; Ps 81). At times the promised reward seemed too long postponed or the amount of sufferings disproportionate to the sin committed (Pss 13:1f.; 35:17; Jer 12:4). Some just appealed to an almost mystical experience of God's presence (Pss 73; 16:5–11), and Job referred innocent sufferings to the mystery of God who not only created the universe's wonders (38f.) but also ruled over Behemoth and Leviathan, symbols of cosmic evil (40f.). Nonetheless, appeal to mystery does not answer rational questions, and Job's poetic wonder allows only so much repetition before transforming itself into Qoheleth's pious but skeptical wisdom. Apparently undeserved sufferings were explained also by the ancient sense of communitarian unity, or "corporate personality," a perception of social reality through which the individual was understood as a representative and constitutive member of the group. For weal and woe human beings share each other's fate, God's curses extending to three or four generations for one's offense, while his blessings continue for a thousand generations (Ex 20:5; Dt 5:9). Within such a perspective the sin of Adam and Eve affected all their descendants (Gn 3:16–19). But if all must suffer for one person's sin, inversely one can suffer for the sins of all, as the Servant songs testify (esp. Is 53:4–12). This solution of life after death was developed in late prophetic and sapiential literature (Dn 12:2f.; Wis 3:1–12; 5).

The danger lurking in the appeal to a reward on the other side was revealed in later rabbinic theology explaining the sufferings of the just in terms of divine purification of their peccadilloes so that their reward after death would be unalloyed; conversely, sinners prospered here lest the merits of their few good deeds claim a mitigation of their future punishment. Thus has the fundamental norm of the covenant, good rewarded, evil punished in this life, been inverted. Then, if all justice and lasting values are transposed from this world to the next, creation can no longer mediate knowledge of God, and atheism or Gnosticism threatens.

The atheistic protest against God has become more powerful in our times precisely because Christianity has proclaimed a God who cares for each individual (Mt 10:28–31) and in his beneficent love "makes his sun rise on the evil and on the good, and sends rain on the righteous and on the unrighteous" (Mt 5:44). How, many ask, can God be a loving Father if he permits so many innocent children to suffer horribly?

Before the plight of innocent sufferers Protestant theologians have stressed the impossibility of any natural theology and the absolute need of faith as a divine gift to make any sense out of life. Some developed a process theology whereby God is involved in the universe's becoming and suffers with it. J. Moltmann saw God suffering the death of Jesus on account of their loving union of wills; E. Jüngel interpreted Jesus' death as a constitutive part of the event of God, who, while remaining God, has entered historical becoming in order to conquer death and sin by suffering them. However moving these attempts to render God less immune to human suffering may be, they fail to explain the significance of human suffering, and they advance beyond Job's mystery only in increasing our wonder by projecting the sufferings back into God. The fact that God suffers does not lessen human sufferings; indeed, his suffering may increase the sufferings of those who love him.

Before examining the more adequate response to the dilemma of suffering offered by the NT as interpreted in the Catholic tradition, some preliminary reflections may circumscribe more exactly the issue. As already noted, suffering must be recognized as a reality, even if the "reality of an appearance," and any immediate recourse to God for a heavenly reward risks destroying knowledge of God through the world. Suffering seems almost inevitable for a corporeal being insofar as materiality implies divisibility, limitation, and possible collisions. To preclude entirely the possibility of corporeal suffering, the human being would have to be created without a body. But even for pure spirits pain remains possible insofar as they are limited, hence subject, to one degree or another, to the freedom of others. "Corporate personality" marks finite existence, all the more so in the Christian vision, where human beings, created in the image of the God who is love, are called to love their fellows; to refuse to acknowledge that link involves a sin as well as a denial of finite reality in its interrelatedness. Indeed, if men and women were considered just individuals, each responsible only for himself or herself, there would be no solidarity allowing atheists to protest against God in the name of "innocent sufferers." Moreover, the perception of limitation involves the recognition of a certain lack of plenitude, engendering desire and the pain of dissatisfaction. Actually to obviate every possibility of suffering, the individual would at least have to reduce all other free beings to the state of automata or become the infinite God. Thus, behind the desire to avoid all suffering may lurk the original sin of wishing to be like God (Gn 3:5, 22).

Given suffering and our finitude, this world cannot be the best or the wirst of all possible worlds. For whatever is limited can be surpassed. As finite, human sufferings cannot be absolute evils; instead, they can be relativized not only by the perceiver, whose attitude influences his perception, but also by reference to a greater reality or wider purpose. Thus sufferings often serve as a warning against greater evils or are entailed in a necessary discipline of body and soul that permits growth. Muscles are stretched and cells are broken down to build greater strength. Inversely, the easy life under the mango tree enervates and debilitates. The Greek adage, "Zeus adds learning to suffering" (Aeschylus *Agamemnon* 177f.), has been expanded by L. Bloy: "There are places in our hearts that do not yet exist and where suffering enters in order that they be." Furthermore, sufferings serve as a just punishment for sin, call men and women to conversion, help destroy selfishness, and open human beings to compassion and collaboration. Suffering for what is right can also reveal to human beings the meaning of their existence and contribute to a proper estimation of their own value. Indeed, were suffering impossible, life would be deprived of all challenge and adventure. Turning a pirouette on the top of the Empire State Building would be as risky as blowing one's nose. If persons attempted to escape the boredom of such an existence, their attempt at suicide would be frustrated since they could not harm themselves.

Not even death, anticipated in suffering, is an absolute evil. For from a world of tremendous suffering or absolute monotony death would be a liberation. In any world of pleasure and joy, life without death would ultimately result in the waning of wonder, the loss of spiritual powers, and monotony. As Shakespeare recognized, human mortality often makes values all the more precious: "This thou perceiv'st, which makes thy love more strong, / To love that well which thou must leave ere long" (Sonnet 73).

However ineluctably suffering is bound up with human existence, and however many benefits in may occasion, suffering can never be fully explained. To demand such an explanation would be to demand the irrational and the impossible for various reasons. First, insofar as suffering is always individual—the "mass of human sufferings" is an abstraction—the individual as such cannot be explained (individuum est ineffabile). Second, insofar as the sufferings are perceived as unjust—the core of the "problem of suffering"—every explanation is impossible. For an explanation implies a cause, which implies a necessity; hence if injustice were explained, it would be necessary, and an immoral universe would be an absurdity. Likewise, morality, since it appeals to freedom, cannot be reduced to a rational necessity. Morality also seems to involve suffering. Not only is there often a tension between pleasure and duty in our fallen world, but also the very cry for justice upon the recognition of its absence implies pain. Perhaps the pain of self-sacrifice must be included in morality lest an immediate recompense for good actions reduce morality to a higher form of selfishness. Only when a sacrifice is demanded are moral values properly appreciated.

These foregoing reflections should impede any facile rejection of God's existence because suffering exists. Indeed, to deny God's existence would neither solve nor alleviate the problem of suffering. The sufferings remain. If God does not exist, humanity loses every hope of a solution to its real and theoretical conundrums. Moreover, if this world of injustice alone exists, no recompense for all good and evil deeds occurs and justice becomes but a human construction and an illusion. Ultimately justice cannot be impersonal, for the intentions as well as the actions of human beings must be judged and rewarded; only an omniscient, omnipotent being can accomplish such justice.

A final observation concerns the alleged innocence of children. As many from Augustine to Freud observed, children are selfish, often vindictive, little brutes whose habits have to be corrected as they mature. In addition, Catholic theology maintains that after Adam's sin only Christ and his mother were absolutely sinless, and they both freely sacrificed themselves for sinners. Indeed, only Christ is God's Son by nature, all others become God's adoptive children by faith in Jesus (Gal 4:1–7; Jn 1:14f.). God sent the Spirit of his Son into the hearts of Christians in order that they cry "Abba, Father" (Gal 4:6; Rom 8:15). Since Jesus taught his disciples to call God Father, Christians must use that designation in the sense intended by Jesus. But Jesus explicitly entrusted himself to his Abba and his Father in Gethsemane and on the cross (Mk 14:36; Lk 23:46). Paul saw God's paternal love revealed in this, that he did not spare his own Son but gave him up for all; henceforth nothing, no matter how fierce or horrendous, need separate believers from the love of God in Christ (Rom 8:28–39).

Once sin had splintered the original unity of humankind, the world became an ambiguous place, in which the existence of a God of love might be doubted. So to give a sign of love and reconstitute humankind's unity, the eternal Son became a human person. This entrance of Love into a world of sin initiated a conflict leading to Jesus' death. That death revealed fully the meaning of his life of self-sacrificial love. For, though put to death by sinners, Jesus simultaneously offered himself freely to his Father and for humankind. As the total penetration of the assumed human nature by the divine personal freedom, Jesus' death simultaneously marked Love's conquest of death and sin, a victory that was eschatologically manifested in the resurrection. Henceforth the wounds of Christ's sufferings serve as the trophies of his victory and Christians have to be transformed into his death, crucified to the world, in order to share his life, which is salvation (Rom 6:1–11; Gal 2:19; 6:14; Jn 3:3–8; 5:24; 1 Jn 3:14). As in the OT, God's justice reigns supreme, but now the emphasis has been transposed to its justifying gratuity. God will reward the just and punish the evil in eternity, but the norm of judgment is Christ (Mt 25:32ff.). Furthermore, since the eschatological time has already broken in (Mk 1:15; Jn 5:24f.; Gal 4:4), salvation is already present in the world, in the union of love, that is Christ's body.

The individual's incorporation into the church's *koinōnia* then gives new meaning to his sufferings. They are a sharing in the sufferings of Christ, that overflow upon him (2 Cor 1:5; Phil 3:10); they also serve to fill up "what is lacking to Christ's afflictions for the sake of his body, that is, the church" (Col 1:24). As God's infinity does not exclude creatures nor does his omnipotence destroy human freedom, but both constitute their condition of possibility, so Christ's sufferings, sufficient in themselves to save all, open the way for humankind's contribution in love to the work of salvation. Corporate personality is revitalized in the church, and suffering finds its deepest meaning. Besides involving a call to conversion, a purification of sinful habits, or a test of fidelity, which is implied in the very exercise of freedom, suffering now becomes an invitation to join in Christ's redemptive work and a possibility of sharing more deeply in his self-sacrificial love. In this love the believer also participates in Christ's victory over sin and death, i.e., eternal life. God's continuing presence in history has thus revealed the mystery of love that in ways undreamt of by Job has dominated the forces of evil, conquering them by suffering them. God's self-sacrificial love also destroys human self-justification and protest against Adam's sin. Once Christ's overwhelming love is accepted, God's original plan of love, that bound all to each for weal and woe, can be accepted without recrimination, for where sin abounded, grace did more abound (Rom 5:12–21); the law of solidarity, which surpasses retributive justice, now works to our salvation. Thus through the mystery of Christ's redemptive love not only are all the explications of suffering offered in the OT synthesized but also suffering, the dross of human experience that other religions try to escape or mitigate, has been transmuted into a means of increasing love. Christ's victory on the cross has bestowed upon Christians the power of affirming and thanking God for the sorrows and trials, which affect their ever greater likeness to Christ, as well for the joys and the pleasant things of life. In Christ the shattered unity of existence is restored and found very good.

Although this redemptive understanding of suffering has long been embedded in Catholic tradition, it found an especially apt expression in the devotion to the Sacred Heart of Jesus. This devotion to Christ's pierced heart as the symbol of his love calling men and women to join in his work of redemption has been recommended to the faithful by many popes after the mystical revelations made to Margaret Mary Alocoque at Paray-le-Monial in France during the seventeenth century.

Bibl.: J. de Fraine, *Adam et son lignage* (Paris, 1959); C. Journet, *Le mal* (Paris, 1961); J. Moltmann, *The Crucified God* (New York, 1974); J. M. McDermott, "The Biblical Doctrine of Koinonia," *BZ* 19 (1975): 66–77, 219–33; id., "Il senso della sofferenza," *CivCatt* 137 (1986): 112–26; id., *Sofferenza umana nella Bibbia* (Rome, 1990); M. Flick and Z. Alszeghy, *Il Mistero della Croce* (Brescia, 1978); R. Latourelle, "Prophétisme et espérance des souffrants," in *Man and His Problems in the Light of Jesus Christ* (New York, 1982), 321–36; E. Jüngel, *God as the Mystery of the World* (Grand Rapids, 1983).

John M. McDermott

SUPERNATURAL

The word designates "that which goes beyond nature," but precisely the concept of "nature" is not clearly specified given the fact that it can also refer to the divine nature. A more precise meaning is "that which was not created and, as something uncreaturely, has effects on nature as the creaturely." For only when such effects are detectable can questions about the supernatural be sensibly posed at the level of the creaturely. The form of the word, and thus also the concept, exactly parallels that of *meta-physics* ("after," "behind," "beyond," and in this sense, "above" nature), even if, in both cases, the notions objectively referred to contain an implicit emphasis on directional priority of the above over the below. At any rate, these concepts presuppose the idea that reality is divided into different levels. The Christian expression "supernatural" denoted that aspect of reality which is not subject to the conditions of creation, but is nevertheless necessary both to reality and in view of it, while remaining beyond any sort of determination by creation.

In the light of Judeo-Christian revelation, a distinction of the preceding kind is inescapable, yet the problem of formulating adequate corresponding concepts leads to those aporias that accompany, and often mark out, the path of the concept of the "supernatural" through the history of theology. H. de Lubac, in his *Surnaturel* (1946), *Augustinisme et théologie moderne* (1965), and *The Mystery of the Supernatural* (London/New York/Montreal, 1967), has traced the most important contours of this historical path. The historical evidence of earlier use of the word in the late Middle Ages does not affect de Lubac's material discovery that the concept, in its theologically influential sense, stems from the controversy around M. Baius and C. Jansen, in which context it was linked to the notion that there were more or less independent and complete orders of the supernatural and the natural, and that this was the decisive component of a total system.

A supernatural order as such, even as a system, can hardly be conceived by humans, because they have no means of access to this reality that would enable them to pass over, or rise above, the creaturely. The transcendence of such an order must therefore be discoverable and demonstrable as immanent, without this having to imply that the supernatural has any essentially necessary tie to the creaturely. As de Lubac showed, it is even more dubious and risky to devise, as a counter concept, an order or system of pure nature. Such an attempt, rather than being able (as its defenders claim) to secure the total autonomy, gratuitousness, and freedom of the supernatural, is more likely to encourage the conclusion that the supernatural is superfluous and ultimately just a senseless doubling of what we experience as nature or creatureliness.

In fact, of course, this conception of the supernatural derives its content from that which is known, i.e., from the creaturely and natural, and then presents itself, having isolated its content from any creaturely limitations through abstraction, as a collocation of long-known elements on the allegedly higher plane. A representation arrived at in this way is unable, however, to express precisely that which is uniquely characteristic of the supernatural, and its usefulness is doubtful. In order to reach a different understanding of the matter, it is necessary to take into account, from the very first, the concept of God in the Judeo-Christian tradition (as was already intimated above when nature was identified with the created). God, as Creator, evidences himself in the full sense there where he attains the highest goal of his creative activity: his own self-communication to that which is not he. In view of this, the "supernatural" would be anything directly or indirectly constitutive of this self-communication, as well as anything affected by it insofar as it is so affected. Humans can gain knowledge of this on the basis of revelation; despite the fact that revelation bears upon the deepest aspects of their being, they cannot discover it by their own devices.

Grasping the specifically Christian sense of the supernatural requires that it be conceived with a view to God's full, definitive self-communication in Jesus Christ. Only in this light, too, does the concept of creation show those features that allow it to be recognized and assessed not merely as a designation for a neutral, objectlike state of affairs, but as the expression of a personal will and activity, and thus as itself something fundamentally personal. The summons to be children of God evokes the relation of the created to the supernatural, and also its directedness toward the supernatural, more fully and deeply than does the controversial *desiderium videndi Deum* ("desire of seeing God"). At the same time, the problem arises that a significance is thereby attributed to a historical event, under the limitations of space and time, that cannot, by nature, be attributable to any concrete historical fact. In order to overcome this difficulty, it seems indispensable to discover, in the general constitution of human nature, something that can suitably respond to the appearance of Jesus, i.e., those preconditions for grasping, understanding, and assenting that allow humans to recognize and acknowledge in Jesus Christ the communication of, and reference to, the supernatural. In this connection, K. RAHNER speaks of a "supernatural existential [i.e., mode of existing]" and of an open-ended, seeking Christology based on the anthropological refinement of the idea of an absolute savior who comes to meet the deep-rooted expectations which are part of man's created structure. H. DE LUBAC invokes a view common to thirteenth-century scholastics when he states—without in the least thereby calling into question the gratuitous character of grace or the free responsibility of humans for themselves—that "a spiritual creature has its goal not in itself, but in God" (*The Mystery of the Supernatural*). These basic positions have undergone subsequent development, with the element of grace being made more precise through association with either knowledge, freedom, or beauty. Accentuating either the true, the good, or the pleasing gives rise to still different orientations, which can also be set against one another. Whether this ultimately serves, however, to foster one-sided positions that gain attention at the expense of other emphases—each of which has its own particular validity—can only be determined by assessing the full details and implicit consequences of any given position. Also, the choice of a theological perspective on the general problem area itself is not something that can simply be made in all innocence.

The kind of meaning attributed to the supernatural in these variously accentuated theologies has implications especially for one's attitude and behavior toward the world. It is no accident that political theology and liberation theology have opposed privatized forms of religious life or a Christianity that is neutral or rejecting toward the world. Those who are basically concerned with the ultimate goal—whether understood in individual or social terms—should not overlook the fact that realization of that goal can be furthered or obstructed through their practical behavior toward earthly realities. The grace has been granted that can bring forth fruit, and the nature of the fruit will show whether it has been properly received and applied. Thus it must be accepted that God, as the goal for humans, is not placed before them precisely in

order to be exclusively awaited as the ultimate goal, but is communicated to them as the goal for here and today, for their behavior as Christians and for their present lives as Christians. The supernatural and the creaturely are not intermixed, yet they nevertheless form a unity; indeed, their interaction forces one to take positions and become committed, i.e., has the effect of setting tasks for Christians. In imposing its demands, the supernatural imparts to creaturely existence that inner tension which constitutes its life.

By means of these discernible effects, the supernatural can be indirectly experienced, although details of the possible forms of such experience cannot be given here. Obviously, the supernatural is present in such instances only as implicitly suggested, and requires, for its precise clarification, verbal specification through the revelatory word of God—or concretely, through Jesus Christ and his message—so that it becomes comprehensible to humans in its proper meaning. Broached here, then, is the christological character of the supernatural. Only since the appearance of Jesus has God's self-communication acquired a name and a face in the world. Talk of the supernatural must refer constantly back to this in order to secure that concept materially and formally, which is always necessary if misunderstandings and abuses are to be avoided. Above all, such reference shows that separating and isolating the orders of reality, as involved in the notion underlying the "two-tiered" theory, is inadmissible. Rather, it suggests a view analogous to the christological formula of the Council of Chalcedon, or to the truth of the incarnation. With that, it also offers a starting point for reflecting on the supernatural and its characteristic dynamics from the viewpoint of redemptive history. In traditional treatments of the topic, this aspect, along with certain others, was not given sufficient attention, which led to a one-sided, unbalanced view of the problem. But this one-sidedness was also worsened by treating the phenomenon in almost complete abstraction from supernaturally influenced persons or relegating the study of it to the areas of spirituality and piety. Hence it can be expected that conscious emphasis on the christological character of the supernatural will result in a new conception that will, in turn, stimulate theological reflection and allow this truth to become fruitful for other strands of theological thought as well; in any case, it will free the topic from the isolation into which it had slipped.

The history of the word is helpful only inasmuch as the term is absent from the language of the early church, begins to appear in the Middle Ages, then rapidly develops, from the time of posttridentine theology, into a specialized technical concept suffering from the sorts of one-sidedness noted above and from application in the context of a total theological system. Its adjectival form is earlier, and by far more widespread, than its substantival, which did not gain appreciable currency until the nineteenth century. As an independent noun, the concept proved particularly infelicitous, because it suggested a viewpoint and position presumed able to dispense completely with every necessary kind of referentiality.

Bibl.: H. DE LUBAC, _The Mystery of the Supernatural_ (New York, 1967); id., _Augustinisme et théologie moderne_ (Paris, 1965); id., _Petite catéchèse sur nature et grâce_ (Paris, 1980); H. BOUILLARD, _Comprendre ce que l'on croit_ (Paris, 1971).

Karl H. NEUFELD

SYMBOLISM

Certain areas of human life have a predilection for symbols; thus it is quite natural to find them in psychic, poetic, and religious activity. I shall begin by describing characteristics shared by different types of symbol, and then focus attention in particular on the meaning of the symbolic language found in the Sacred Scriptures.

The most basic characteristic of symbolic expression is that it combines representation and dynamic movement: a symbol is an image freighted with affects. The meaning for which a symbol is the vehicle is thus located at a preconceptual level, in the obscure realm of sensibility and affectivity. An image can represent something perceived or something invented by the subject: a unicorn as well as a wolf, a monster as well as a whale. It is the affects attached to images that give these their weight, quality, and diversity: a massive and undifferentiated affect like anxiety; one or other of ᵗhe sentiments that make up the gamut of

human affectivity; or, finally, a mixture of sometimes contradictory, sometimes complementary sentiments.

These affect-laden images give a human life its density and seriousness: they show the direction it is taking, its enthusiasms and reservations, its openness and its blockages. Understandably, they are the privileged object of psychotherapeutic investigation and activity. It is perhaps in psychoanalysis that the affective charge which gives life to certain images shows itself most clearly; the compulsive anxiety elicited every time that little Hans saw a certain kind of horse is a good illustration of the dynamic aspect of certain images. In like manner, the work of a poet harbors images heavy with the sentiments that are dominant in the author; these are the themes that "interest" him or her, to use Gaston Bachelard's word. Finally, it is well known that religious experience finds expression in images heavily invested with affects of the kind which Rudolf Otto brought to light in his classic work _The Idea of the Holy._

Images and affects are not established unchangeably, once and for all, in an individual; they are modified as the individual advnaces or regresses. Carl G. Jung assesses the psychic progress of a human being according to the images that regularly emerge in the process of individuation. For Carl Rogers the success of a therapy is judged by the emergence of new and differentiated sentiments, which succeed generalized sentiments that are hardly present to consciousness; conversely, regression is accompanied by images that give rise to anxiety. In like manner, progress in religious experience will be accompanied by, e.g., a transformation in the person's image of God and in the sentiments attached to it: the father replaces the tyrant, and love replaces fear; the feeling of distance yields to the certainty of a familiar presence.

Symbols do not express only the experience of individuals taken in isolation; they can also be shared by a group: nation, linguistic family, culture, religion. As a result, some symbols have a history and give rise to a tradition. In one type of Platonism the body can be looked upon as the prison of the soul, the place where the soul must pay its debts. In theistic religions the supreme divinity is paternal, is connected with the heavens, and maintains with humanity a relationship of speaking and listening. In a cosmo-biological religion, on the other hand, human beings are linked to the cosmos by a whole series of vital correspondences. Like individuals, groups can develop or regress. Paul Ricoeur, in his *The Symbolism of Evil*, has shown how in the OT Jewish tradition the symbols of evil are transformed, from stain, accompanied by blind terror, via sin, to which is added the fear of God's wrath, to guilt, accompanied by remorse of conscience. Each new image reinterprets and preserves within itself the images that have been superseded. Nietzsche takes an opposing view and interprets it as a sign of regression that the figure of Dionysus, who was central to the Greece that gave birth to the tragedies of Aeschylus and Sophocles, should have been replaced by Socratic figures in the works of Euripides and in the teaching of Socrates, and should have preserved only a subterranean existence in the Greek mysteries.

Furthermore, some experiences seem to be shared by all individuals, whatever their language, culture, or religion; consequently, the symbols that express these experiences are universal and can be called archetypes. Jung and his school in particular have emphasized the presence of primordial images that behave like foci of energy and transcend the limited spheres of individuals and groups.

Symbols do not convey meaning in the way that concepts do, but obey the laws of image and affect. They do not express a univocal meaning. Rather they signify to the extent that they form networks or "constellations" in which images having a certain kinship and eliciting similar affects point toward a meaning which they suggest without making explicit. Thus it is possible to study the symbols of a patient undergoing a psychoanalytic cure, a poet, or a religious leader. From the report on the "Rat Man," the works of Victor Hugo, or the writings of John of the Cross, it has been possible to extract symbolic "universes," which in each case display an original, coherent organization. This kind of study can be done at a broader level and take for its object the imaginative configuration of such cultural or religious movements as Romanticism, Christianity, or the Enlightenment. Finally, a still more comprehensive undertaking can be attempted: to bring together the symbolic materials, whatever their origin, that are found within certain well-defined structures. This is what Gilbert Durand has attempted in his *Les structures anthropologiques de l'imaginaire*. He takes as his starting point the three dominant reflexes of Betscheverian reflexology: the *vertical* dominant (posture), the *nutritive* dominant (swallowing), and the *sexual* dominant (rhythm). His thesis is that there are three great symbolic universes based on these three dominant reflexes. The first action is correlated with height, light, and sight, and with the techniques for separation and purification, these being symbolized by arms, arrows, and swords. The second action is correlated with the digestive descent, and suggests matter with depth, such as water and earth, as well as containers, such as cups and trunks. Finally, rhythmic actions are correlated with the rhythms of the seasons and the movements of the stars, and call to mind the many substitutes for these cycles: wheel, spinning wheel, and churn. Durand thus divides the entire realm of symbols into two regimes: one, diurnal, which is connected with postural activity, and another, nocturnal, which is connected with the digestive and sexual reflexes.

How do symbols merge into constellations so as to form a network, the extent and complexity of which can be so great as to give rise to a comprehensive vision of the world? I shall take as an illustration a symbol which human beings have always regarded as expressing their life with its cycles and crises, its sufferings and hopes, and which Mircea Eliade studies in chapter 4 of his *Patterns of Comparative Religion*.

Human beings see in lunar phenomena a model of their own behavior; they have used the moon and its activity to understand and express the character of their own life. The moon is the astral body that "measures" time by its own duration. It has a "life" marked by drama and pathos: it is born, grows, decreases, and dies. It is the embodiment of time inasmuch as it is in process and subject to transformation and death. The death of the moon is indeed not final, for after three days it rises again. This insight is the starting point for a vast synthesis in which human beings express their vision of the world and their own place in the cosmos. Like the moon, human beings are born, grow, decline, and die, but this death, too, cannot be final. Their hope of survival in and beyond death finds both its expression and its confirmation in the new moon that is born out of the death of the old moon.

This lunar "law" does not govern only human behavior; the entire universe is subject to it as to a principle that both unifies and organizes. Every form is subject to becoming and must return to a chaotic state; death is a regression, a return to formlessness. But regression and death are only one stage in the cyclical process: the stage in which forms fall back into rest and hibernate in expectation of a new birth. Death and darkness have a positive value; they are the cosmic night in which everything is at rest, and in which all forms are possible and all hopes permissible. Death is a state in which time is abolished and "slain," for the sake of an entrance into the transhistorical realm.

Lunar symbolism can even extend its reign to all spheres of the cosmos and form a completely coherent "system." Thus the whole of plant life is subject to the lunar process. Plants go through a constantly repeated cycle: they return to the seed state and they hibernate, while their potency is renewed to yield new vegetation in the spring. From the viewpoint of symbolism, earth and moon are completely interchangeable; both are places in which all forms have their start and in which all forms are resorbed with a view to their rebirth. The earth is the moon, and the moon is the earth. The waters also have their place in the lunar synthesis. In addition to being subject to a periodic rhythm, they are also germinative, like the moon and the earth; i.e., their function is to give birth to everything that takes form in the cosmos and also to resorb into themselves all the forms that have "seen their day." An aquatic disaster has a lunar character, and the hero who survives one in order to launch a new human race is the equal of the new moon that has passed through death. Other, no less important series of relations exist between the moon and women or the moon and the dead.

The "kinship" of these images shows us how a symbol like the moon can become the nucleus of a vast network in which each element takes on a meaning to the extent that it participates in an aspect revealed by the moon. In this way a multitude of objects become lunar symbols: snails, serpents, frogs, dogs, bears, and spiders; some plants, herbs, and shellfish; pearls and dew; spirals and lightning; distaffs and spindles.

This example helps us see how the law of images works. The objects I have listed do not derive their value from their literal, univocal meaning. They are interchangeable among themselves and identical with the moon, because all of them express the same fundamental pattern. This pattern thus unifies the entire universe and is the connecting element in a synthesis in which all objects in the world "hold together," being subject to one and the same law. Human beings are part of this cosmic synthesis because in it they recognize themselves and their condition. They accept and actualize their condition, which is compounded of suffering and greatness, of the threat of death and the desire to live forever, by subjecting it to a law that transcends them. In this way they share in the same manner of being as the remainder of the universe. Human beings and their activities thereby acquire a cosmic dimension. Reality par excellence manifests itself in them; they carry within them a reality that bursts the bounds of their individuality and bestows on them a "universal meaning."

Traces of this "surplus of meaning" or this "universal meaning" that is the mark of cosmic symbols can be founnd at the level of personal symbols. These symbols, these images charged with affects, express at the level of sensibility the overall mode of being of the human subject. This is to say that the meaning of which the symbol is the vehicle precedes any differentiation into particular faculties or powers, be these cognitive or affective, intellectual or sensible. The imagination is precisely this intermediate place through which meaning circulates freely between the various human functions: bodily demands are integrated with the highest levels of the psyche and the spirit; the spirit receives its needed sensible complement, and, finally, image and affect are adjusted to each other.

This preconceptual meaning that is present in symbols thus reveals the human subject as a whole, to the extent that it has its place in the world, along with its basic options in regard to itself, to others, and to God. Symbols reflect the existential condition of subjects who live out their fundamental choices in joy or sorrow, peace or conflict, wonder or disappointment, hope or despair, or in some mixture of sentiments that reinforce or contradict one another. Every symbol thus has a surplus of meaning to the extent that it hints at the openness of the subject to the whole of its world and suggests the element of the absolute that is present in its most essential options. Symbols are thus correlated with the absolute to which the human subject is open; they are, as it were, the resonance of the absolute in the sensibility and affectivity of the subject. Symbols are suited, more than concepts are, to giving a sense of the endless nuances attaching to the way in which one locates oneself in the totality of the universe.

When a symbol is a familiar one, understanding of it consists in following the movement of the image and being led spontaneously to that which the image suggests. But when we are introduced to a set of symbols that involve distance in time or in cultural space, we have to follow the long way round to the interpretation of them. With the help of various methods for reading a text, we can attain a grasp of what the text has in view, i.e., the kind of world set before us by the text itself.

People today come in contact with the Bible across a distance which it is the task of exegesis to bridge. In the Bible we find symbols that are rooted in the Judaic tradition while not being alien to other cultures or even to humanity as a whole. But even in the case of such symbols an understanding of them requires taking into account their place in a context of symbols wherein they acquire their meaning. Water, e.g., is an important symbol in the Scriptures. It takes on there a series of interconnected meanings which seem almost universal: water destroys forms, wipes out sins, purifies and regenerates; it contains the germs of all the possibilities of being. Yet, while other cultures have developed an aquatic cosmogony, the Bible reinterprets the symbol of water in a theistic context and, in the NT, in a christological context. As a result, while water is the source of all life and fruitfulness, it itself comes from God or Christ as from a deeper source. Water is connected with other symbols of life, such as wine or the earth; but the latter in turn are taken up into a set of properly theistic symbols, such as light, height, word, spirit, father, judge, and so on. When the symbol of water is reinterpreted in a theistic context, it in turn affects the meaning of the divine, which integrates the rhythms and cycles of life into the symbolism of water.

The meaning given to the divine is thus not univocal. The divine reveals itself to the extent that we explore the numerous symbols into which a people has, over the centuries, deposited the wealth of its varied experience as reflected in the complexity of its particular situations. The Jewish people wrote down its experience of the divine in its vocabulary, the many nuances of which, both representative and affective, express its encounter with its God. These symbols are rooted in a world of heights (God is light; he dwells in the heavens; he manifests himself to human beings on mountains); in a world of life (God is the source of the waters, of life and of fruitfulness); in a world of interpersonal relations (God is father, spouse, king); and so on. These representations elicit varied and contradictory sentiments: transcendence and familiar presence, fright and tenderness, jealousy and mercy, and so on.

In the NT, moreover, symbols not only point to the divine; they are identified with Jesus, as if they were all summed up in the unique symbol of the divine that is Jesus in his humanity. Jesus is at once the light of the world, the Word of the Father, the well of living water, the true Temple, the eschatological judge, the suffering servant, and so on.

To the extent that the revelation of God in Jesus Christ takes form in a language rich in symbols, it calls for a Christology that serves as a hermeneutics, a Christology that gathers up and explores the many meanings of the divine which have been enfleshed in time and space and have been made his own by the dead and resurrected Christ. It is through the endless process of interpretation that believers are able, on the basis of their religious experience in the church and with the help of various methods of reading, to understand the kind of world opened up to them by the Gospel text, a world often described as the reign of God or the new birth.

Bibl.: M. ELIADE, *Patterns in Comparative Religion* (New York, 1958); G. DURAND, *Les structures anthropologiques de l'imaginaire* (3rd ed.; Poitiers, 1969); B. J. LONERGAN, *Method in Theology* (New York, 1972); P. RICOEUR, *Interpretation Theory: Discourse and the Surplus of Meaning* (4th ed.; Texas, 1976).

Julien NAUD

SYNOPTIC PROBLEM

The first three Gospels resemble each other to such an extent that they can be printed in three parallel columns; whence the term *synopsis* and the name "Synoptic Gospels." It is possible, however, to speak of a synoptic *problem* because the similarities are accompanied by dissimilarities. The problem is not to "harmonize" the three Gospels but rather to explain this *concordia discors* through a historical and literary investigation of the mutual relations of the first three Gospels.

Mark, the shortest of the three, has only 661 verses. Almost all of the material in Mark is found in Matthew or in Luke or in both. Only 30 verses of the 661 are peculiar to Mark: two miracles, three short stories, one parable, a few sayings of Jesus, and a commentary on the Jewish practice of ritual washing. Matthew, which has 1,068 verses, contains the substance of Mark, except for 40 verses; 330 verses of Matthew are peculiar to him. Luke has 1,149 verses, of which 350 are taken from Mark, or, in other words, more than half of the first Gospel. Luke omits passages which he regards as repetitious or too harshly worded for his Gentile readers. He shows great freedom in his account of the passion. Most important, 548 verses out of 1,149 are peculiar to him: in particular, the infancy stories (132 verses), five miracle stories, and sixteen parables. Matthew and Luke have 235 verses in common which are not found in Mark. Those who hold the two-source theory think that this common material comes from another written source.

An extensive "narrative" section is common to the three Synoptics. Although this material does not constitute a "biography" of Jesus in any proper sense of the word, it does give a coherent view of his activity. Mark is the one who most faithfully reproduces this overview. Discourses form a sizable part of all three Gospels, but 235 verses, consisting of the sayings of Jesus, are common to Luke and Matthew. The substantial agreement between the three Gospels at the level of structure and even of formulation co-exists with noteworthy differences. Thus the 235 verses common to Luke and Matthew are grouped into six major discourses in Matthew, while in Luke they are scattered and made into shorter units. The differences are to be found even in important passages such as the Our Father, the Beatitudes, and the triple temptation of Jesus.

Before the nineteenth century the Synoptic problem did not arise. Readers were satisfied to "harmonize" the four Gospels; this outlook can be seen in the *De consensu Evangelistarum* of St. Augustine and was normative until the end of the Middle Ages. In fact, it was only with J. C. L. Geisler (1818) that scholars came to think of the *concordia discors* as a historical *problem*. The hypothesis now universally adopted among non-Catholics and accepted in practice by the majority of Catholic exegetes, with some nuances, is the two-source theory.

This theory can be summarized as follows. Matthew and Luke depend on Mark for the "narrative" parts of their Gospels, and on the *Quelle* (Source), or collection of the sayings of Jesus, for the words; the "source" itself has been reconstructed on the basis of the sayings common to Matthew and Luke. Mark is the earliest of our Gospels: it is responsible for the literary genre known as "gospel" and provides the general framework which its successors took over. But the source (Quelle) precedes the Gospel of Mark. This two-source theory obviously does not explain all the material in the Synoptics. Thus *Quellenkritik* has focused on the parts of Matthew (more than a fifth) and of Luke (more than a third) which are not explained by this theory. Luke, in particular, conducted his own investigations and had at hand sources peculiar to him.

As far as written sources are concerned, no hypothesis has succeeded in replacing the two-source theory or in carrying it further. It is to be noted that a number of Catholic exegetes accept the testimony of Papias and attribute to Matthew the apostle a Gospel that was written in Hebrew and that grouped together sayings of the Lord. In this view, this work of the apostle lent authority to the Greek Gospel known in his day, as well as to the revisions and interpretations of his work.

There is no literary dependence between Matthew and Luke. At the level of literary formulation, Matthew is more faithful to the *Quelle* than Luke is; this fact speaks in favor of connecting our canonical Gospel and the Aramaic work which Papias attributed to Matthew the apostle and which was subsequently translated into Greek and was known henceforth as *Quelle*. At the level of the organization of the material, Luke is more faithful than Matthew. Mark did not know of the *Quelle*.

The two-source theory remains the most satisfactory for practical purposes, but an adequate resolution of the Synoptic problem is not possible on the basis of literary dependences alone. Matthew and Luke have their own sources. In addition, we must always take into account the activity of oral tradition during the entire formation of the written Gospels. It is difficult to determine in an accurate way the influence of this oral activity, but it was constantly present.

Bibl.: L. Vaganay, *La question synoptique: Une hypothèse de travail* (Paris, 1954); F. J. McCool, "Synoptic Problem," *NCE* 13:886–91; X. Léon-Dufour, "Autour de la question synoptique," *RSR* 42 (1954): 549–84; A. Wikenhauser, *New Testament Introduction* (London, 1958), 221–53; A. Robert and A. Feuillet, *Introduction to the New Testament* (New York, 1965), 252–86.

René LATOURELLE

T

TEILHARD DE CHARDIN, PIERRE

Like Pascal, Teilhard (1881–1955) is interested in the human person, but as a phenomenon and in its totality; in the human person, but as part of the universe and the human collectivity, carried along through the infinite duration of the centuries and caught up in the vortex of evolution. He is interested in the world, but as a totality, including the natural, the religious, the Christian, and the supernatural. His vision of the world is single and unified, and the center of its unity is Christ. Teilhard is a man of all-embracing *synthesis*. For him, God is in the universe, and the universe is in God; Christ, the God-man, is in the universe, and this universe he makes his own and recapitulates. Teilhard felt himself pulled in two directions: toward the cosmos, and toward Christ. The two became ever more part of him, at first as seemingly independent parallels, but then coming together and becoming one in Christ, the single center of universal convergence.

1. Teilhard's Basic Intuition

According to Bergson, at the origin of every work and every body of thought there is a central intuition, which is something simple, infinitely simple, that language can spell out in detail and that is the leaven operative throughout an entire work. In Teilhard this intuition has to do with the meaning of the contemporary crisis. He is sure that Christianity and modern human beings, faith and science, though presently at odds, are indispensable to one another and complementary.

As a person deeply involved in the modern world through his commitment to science, Teilhard experienced both the aspirations of that world and its confusion. Important discoveries (e.g., by Galileo, Darwin, and Freud) had thrown the modern consciousness into confusion. In an earlier time, people were ignorant of the infinite extent of space and time; they lived in a static, nonevolving, reassuring world. In addition, the hope of

heaven provided a happy end to the wretchedness, sufferings, and inequities of the present world. Now this paradisal landscape had been darkened. A third personage now occupied the stage between God and human beings: the *world*, not simply as a physical reality, but as something to be built, something capable of setting in motion the energies of people. The static cosmos had turned out to be a cosmos in motion. There were henceforth a past and a future; the world had its genesis and course of growth; there was a past abyss into which everything sank behind us in the course of endless time, and a future abyss, equally unlimited, into which everything was hurling itself forward. The modern world is thus characterized by the discovery of the immensity of space and time, of an evolving world. Even more than Pascal could imagine, human beings today feel lost and meaningless in this spatial and temporal immensity. In the very moment of victory they feel powerless to use for human fulfillment the very values they claim to control and monopolize.

Teilhard's intuition and vocation are to be located at this precise point. He is convinced that despite everything, Christianity remains the only salvation of the modern world, of progress and evolution—provided it reflects anew on its own mystery, adapts its language, and recovers its power to attract; provided, too, that it adopts new attitudes in its contacts with the world and its action upon the world; provided, finally, that it "christifies" the legitimate values of the modern mind.

Teilhard found that he had a vocation as scholar, Christian, and priest. As a man passionately in love with the the world and with God, he felt called to reestablish a connection between the world of science as he knew it and Christianity, between the adorers of Christ and the adorers of the world, between the passionate concern to build the world and the passionate concern to win heaven. The twofold vocation as child of earth and child of heaven, which he saw both as his own and as implying a message for the people of his century, is the soul of his entire work. He possessed a simple intuition but also an energizing call.

2. Plan for an Apologetics

If we try to define Teilhard's work, we can agree with him that it is an *apologetics*, i.e., the reflection of a scientist on his faith with a view to determining whether and how science and faith can be harmonized. In "Outlines of a Dialectic of Spirit" (*Activation of Energy* [New York, 1970] 143), he offers his own work as an apologetics. He even describes the successive stages of this apologetics, or "dialectic." His first objective is to remove the barrier that for four centuries has repeatedly been set up between science and revelation, church and science. In a world controlled by science, Teilhard sets out to reconcile a religious and a scientific vision of the universe. From this point of view, says Msgr. de Solages, Teilhard "is the greatest apologist for Christianity since Pascal." C. Cuénot goes even further: Teilhard "developed a defense of Christianity, the demonstrative force of which is comparable and perhaps even superior to the thought of PASCAL or NEWMAN or Maurice BLONDEL."

Teilhard's aim is to lead scientists to realize that the convergent unity of evolution has meaning only if they admit not only the "ahead" of progress but also the "above" that effectively directs this advance from the outset. In this way he introduces the idea of transcendence as well as the idea of finality, and scientists would attack him for this. In addition, he thinks that without faith in a meaning and a successful outcome to life, human beings cannot continue to live and act. He thus prepares the way for acceptance of Christ, who alone can guarantee the future of the human person. In addition, Christianity alone can give a complete explanation of the evolving universe. Teilhard's goal is to christify evolution. When all is said and done, his project is to show scientists that in God and Christianity the evolution of the universe acquires a coherence that stands as a criterion of truth. But Teilhard does not want a conclusion that is reached, as it were, from the outside. He conceives of revelation and faith as an unexpected but fulfilling response to a mysterious call that rises from the depths of the cosmos and the human person. In this respect he is close to Pascal and Blondel.

No less an effort at rapprochement and understanding is required of Christians. If positions lost in dealing with the modern mind are to be regained, more than a revision is needed. What is needed is a total *conversion*. Christianity has, not without reason, been accused of treason to humankind, of antihumanism. Too

many Christians have given the impression that if one is to be a Christian, one must be opposed to progress. "While the Church verbally accepts certain results and certain prospects of progress, she seems 'not to believe in them.' Sometimes she gives her blessing but her heart does not go with it" ("Some Reflections on the Conversion of the World," in *Science and Christ* [New York, 1968], 126). If science and Christianity are to be reconciled, it will be necessary to rethink the Christian meaning of work, progress, research, and human effort. For the God who saves is also the God who has created. The church must be magnanimous in its acceptance of the world of progress and must truly believe in it. "To plunge into in order then to emerge and raise up. To share in order to sublimate. That is precisely the law of the Incarnation. . . . I believe that the world will never be converted to Christianity's hopes of heaven, unless first Christianity is converted (that it may so divinize them) to the hopes of the earth" (ibid., 127). As early as 1923 he was saying: "I believe in an Absolute which here and now manifests itself to us only through Christ. . . . There you have my entire apologetics. I can imagine no other" (*Lettres à Léontine Zanta* [Paris, 1965], 53). To the people of the twentieth century, so zealous for the progress of a universe that they have discovered to be limitless in space and time, Teilhard presents the figure of the cosmic Christ, who is an abyss of greatness in every direction and who embraces the universe as well as human beings and their progress. In 1943 he wrote: "By Super-Christ I most certainly do not mean another Christ, a second Christ different from and greater than the first. I mean the same Christ, the Christ of all times, revealing himself to us in a form and in dimensions . . . that are enlarged" ("Super-Humanity, Super-Christ, Super-Charity," in *Science and Christ*, 164).

3. Angle of Approach: The Entire Universe and the Whole of the Person on the Basis of a Phenomenology

The Teilhardian interpretation of the universe rests on two premises: a phenomenological approach to the human phenomenon seen as a whole, and an evolutionary vision of the universe.

The first premise is a *totalizing* vision of the

universe. In adopting this angle of approach, Teilhard is completely aware that he opens himself to opposition both from the pure scientists and from the philosophers and theologians. But he thinks that in the proximity of the Whole of things, physics, metaphysics, and religion become strangely convergent.

The "totality" of the phenomenon must become the object of science. But the center of the coherence of the real is not to be sought below, in its elements, but above, in the *human being* as perspectival and constructive center of the universe. The world is not headed downward but forward and upward. Teilhard reverses the data of the problem; for him, we are dealing with a world that has a direction and a finality.

A totalizing approach to the real supposes that the human person is assigned a preeminent place in the universe. Teilhard is convinced that it is impossible to penetrate deeply into the meaning of the universe if the latter is separated from the "human phenomenon," since the meaning of everything is to be found in the human person. But some qualifications are needed. When Teilhard looks at human beings, he does not consider them primarily in their psychological life, as Pascal does, nor in their nature as rational animals, as a philosopher might. Teilhard approaches them from without, in scientific fashion. Moreover, the object of his study is neither the individual nor abstract human nature but, rather, the mass of human beings, the human collectivity, the "human caravan," the human phenomenon, as it might be observed through a gigantic telescope that embraced all the centuries in its field of vision. In short, he studies human beings as a single block of reality. Hitherto thinkers have built a science of the universe without the human person and a science of the person with little relation to the universe. The need now is for a science that includes both the person and the universe.

Teilhard's phenomenology is thus not to be confused with that of Husserl, Merleau-Ponty, or Sartre, which takes the form of a careful analysis of the conscious act. It is a phenomenology not of consciousness but of nature. Teilhard uses the word "phenomenon" in its primary, prephilosophical sense as meaning everything that offers itself as an objective datum for knowledge and experimentation. His phenomenology has for its objects the realities of the external world and is related to the natural sciences. For philosophical phenomenologists it is human consciousness that gives meaning and value to things; for Teilhard, persons are the center of the universe because they are objectively the crown and goal of evolution. His phenomenology constitutes a first reflection that has the "observable" for its object, namely, nothing but the whole phenomenon.

Although this phenomenology has for its object the phenomena that offer themselves for scientific study, it is not simply to be identified with science; neither is it a pure metaphysics. Its ideal is to be a scientific reflection but one that embraces the totality of phenomena with a view to discovering their structure and unity. It is a sort of hyperphysics or ultraphysics that crowns the two abysses of Pascal with a third: an abyss of complexity. This new science combines the data of the special sciences, moves beyond the limits the latter set for themselves, and embraces the whole of earthly reality, from matter to the person. Its ambition is to bring all the data of human experience into a single vision that embraces everything from physics and chemistry to history and religion. In short, it embraces the human phenomenon in its totality and as an overarching whole. "Like the meridians when they approach the poles, science, philosophy and religion are bound to converge as they draw nearer to the whole. . . . It is impossible to attempt a general scientific interpretation of the universe without giving the impression of trying to explain it through and through" (*The Phenomenon of Man* [New York, 1959], 30). If the human phenomenon is completed by the Christian phenomenon, it is because Teilhard always looks at the human phenomenon in its totality and as completed in Jesus Christ. Teilhard's thought proves fascinating because it moves beyond the limits set by specializations and toward a vision that embraces the person in its totality. This ideal may leave the scientist skeptical, astonish the philosopher, and disconcert the theologian. But it has an undeniable attraction for those "in search of meaning," who look upon reality in all its complexity as a single whole.

4. The General Movement of the Universe: An Evolution

The second premise for understanding Teilhard's interpretation of the universe has to do with the basic intuition behind this vision; namely, that of evolution at work. The following points represent the essential lines of this vision. The universe forms a homogeneous whole, but it is subject to the movement of evolution. The universe is not static but is in process of genesis or formation; there is a cosmogenesis going on. In addition, this movement has a specific direction, for it obeys the law of growing complexity. The world is developing in time from something simple to something very complex, and their movement is accompanied by a correlative increase of interiorization, i.e., of consciousness.

Within evolution there are stages, qualitative leaps. Teilhard speaks of critical points, stages, crises, critical thresholds, critical stages, mutations, emergences, new orders, and discontinuities. But the same movement continues through these discontinuities. There are discontinuities but not breaks. Two such major discontinuities are the appearance of life and the appearance of thought. Science knows of only two critical points: biogenesis and noogenesis. Christianity tell us of still another unexpected passage, another decisive leap in which the vital drive reaches its completion: this point is Christ-Omega. Christ is the future of human beings, not only in the manner in which human beings are the future of the material universe (the natural term of the universe's evolution), but as one who represents a new kind of life and a new status for humanity that goes beyond previous expectations, fulfills them, and gives them an unanticipated completion. Pascal would say there has been a passage to a different order. Undoubtedly it is by his faith that Teilhard knows this, but he believes that the Christian phenomenon is capable of attracting and holding the attention of the scientist.

Before Teilhard, evolution had been materialistic. Everything was explained from below, in terms of the basic elements of matter; it was to the atom that scientists looked for the solidity of the universe. Teilhard, in contrast, starts from the top in looking for the axis of evolution, and he finds in the person the key to evolution. He endeavors to locate the human being at the heart of the world, without distorting either the human being or the world. Humanity's place in the universe as the thinking envelope enclosing the earth gives evolu-

tion its meaning and special nature. Not only does humanity represent a state of life that is absolutely new in the world, but in it the universe becomes capable of reflection. Human beings establish an organic link between the cosmos and personal existence.

5. The Ascent to Omega

From the phenomenological standpoint, humanity seems to be advancing toward a collective consciousness, a unity of the species, a superior pole of centering and reflection. This pole, Teilhard says, cannot be simply the human collectivity as such, even the collectivity as harmoniously united. The attractive force that centers humanity on itself must itself be a *person* to whom human beings can direct their love and in whom they can love their fellows.

This personal center, this ultimate pole of consciousness—which Teilhard calls Omega—is necessary in order to ensure the thrust and success of evolution. It is needed for reasons of love and survival or, equivalently, for reasons of irreversibility (or survival, immortality), polarity (or centering), and unanimity (or love). The vocabulary on this point fluctuates somewhat, but the two essential reasons that, as Teilhard sees it, require a personal and transcendent pole of evolution are *unanimization* (love) and the *irreversibility* of evolution.

First, there is the unification of humanity. The thrust present in humankind cannot reach its goal unless we acknowledge the existence, at the summit of the world and above our heads, of a Lover and a Lovable. "As such the collectivity is essentially unlovable. . . . It is impossible to give oneself to anonymous number" (*The Phenomenon of Man*, 267). Teilhard wrote in 1941:

> It is not a tête-à-tête or a corps-à-corps that we need. It is a heart-to-heart. This being so, the more I consider the fundamental question of the future of the earth, the more it appears to me that the generative principle of its unification is finally to be sought, not in the sole contemplation of a single Truth or in the sole desire for a single Thing, but in the common attraction exercised by a single Being. ("Some Reflections on Progress. I. The Future of Man as Seen by a Palaeontologist," in *The Future of Man* [New York, 1964], 75)

Love cannot be born and be established unless it encounters a heart, a face. The Omega Point must be the point at which all love one another because all love the same central point.

A second reason for postulating a personal and transcendent Omega is *irreversibility* (or immortality, or survival). Without a personal and transcendent mover ahead of us, evolution is not guaranteed because human action is not guaranteed. Put briefly, Teilhard's reasoning is as follows: Life has devoted billions of years to reaching the human being, i.e., self-consciousness. It would be absurd to think that this effort is vain and destined for self-destruction. Once a certain level has been reached, being cannot radically deny itself. Life would no longer be viable if it were not conscious, at least in its higher zone—in the human being—of being irreversible or immortal. To believe in the universe is to believe in its coherence. But a "directed" evolution ascending toward human beings would be incoherent and absurd if the human person (individual and collective), which is the higher fruit of evolution, must finally perish. The abolition of the ego after death would be the most serious possible regression and would contradict the very essence of evolution, which is an ascent toward mind and thus toward the human person. Human beings will not devote themselves to the work, seen as increasingly arduous, of advancing and unifying humankind, unless they are convinced that the effort demanded of them has some chance of being successful. The perspective of a total death, which would crush the individual or collective consciousness, would by that fact also frustrate any evolutionary ascent.

Evolution thus appears as a gigantic movement of unification and personalization that mounts up toward God. In a first phase, the human ascent to Omega appears as a search, an effort of humankind to achieve a fully conscious and deliberate formation of the community as such. But humanity cannot efficaciously and effectively tend to such a unity of mutual love unless it tends to a union of love with God-Omega. Evolution is an ascent to the human being, then an ascent of human beings to a union of love with their fellows, and finally an ascent to a union of all through union with a personal and transcendent God. After the biosphere and the noosphere, the consciousness of a personal Omega at the heart of the

noosphere gradually gives rise to the *theosphere*. In short, Omega must be *personal* in order to personalize and "amorize" evolution; it must be *transcendent* in order to consolidate evolution.

6. From God-Omega to God-Revealer

In his "Introduction to the Christian Life," written in 1944, Teilhard expressly says:

> Once the personality of God has been accepted, there is no longer any difficulty in the possibility, and even the theoretical probability, of a revelation, of a reflection, that is, of God on our consciousness; indeed they are seen to be eminently in line with the structure of things. In the universe, relations between elements are in all cases in proportion to the nature of these elements; they are material when between material objects, living between living beings, personal between reflective beings. Since man is personal, a personal God must influence him at a personal level and in a personal form: he must influence him intellectually and affectively. In other words he must "speak" to him. As one intellect to another, a presence cannot be dumb. (*Christianity and Evolution* [New York, 1971], 159–60)

It is another matter, of course, to establish the historical fact of such "speech."

"I begin to think in the most critical and positivistic parts of my being that the Christian phenomenon might well be what it claims to be . . . a revelation" ("Sketch of a Personalistic Universe," in *Human Energy* [New York, 1969], 92). No one who is open to an evolutionary and convergent vision of the universe as finding its completion in a point of superpersonalization of consciousness can fail to be open to the Christian fact, which presents itself as a reality of our present world. By reason of its creed, its existential value, and its extraordinary vitality, the Christian fact shows a remarkable similarity to all we know about the convergence of the universe on a transcendent and superpersonal Omega.

Christianity is distinguished by its affirmation of a personal God who directs the universe with wisdom, and of a revealer God who communicates himself to human beings by ways open to the intellect. In Jesus Christ this God partially immerses himself in matter and therein assumes control of evolution and becomes its head. As a human being among human beings, Christ directs, purifies and superanimates the general ascent of consciousness, of which he has become a part. By an action of communion and sublimation he unites to himself the total psychism found on earth. And when he has gathered, unified, and transformed everything, he will rejoin the divine center, which he has never left, and will close in on himself and his conquests. Then God will be all in all, and each element will reach its consummation at the same time as the universe does.

Christianity also demands attention for its existential and vital value. It addresses every human being and the whole person and compels recognition as one of the most vigorous and fruitful currents recorded in the history of the noosphere. Its value, quantitative and especially qualitative, is due to the appearance of an absolutely new state of consciousness: *Christian love.* For twenty centuries this Christian love has raised up and inspired to the point of heroism thousands of human beings who have made it their very life. In a world subject to the law of evolution and convergence, Christogenesis is to be seen as a continuation of the noogenesis in which cosmogenesis culminated. Christianity appears to be the only current of thought that is capable of embracing in a complete gesture the whole of the universe and the whole of the person.

In the eyes of modern people it is a religion's capacity for providing a meaningful interpretation of the world that determines its truth. For Teilhard, the religion that harmonizes best with the idea of a universe that is advancing by way of increasing complexity and consciousness toward a center of convergence and transcendence will also be the truest religion and the one that gives human life and action its maximal meaning. But among all the humanitarian and religious currents of our times, Christianity alone seems capable of effecting this synthesis in Jesus Christ. This coherence of the two phenomena ought to attract the attention even of unbelievers. Teilhard's phenomenological reflection and religious philosophy stop here.

7. Christ-Omega

The great discovery and great joy of Teilhard was his gradual identification of the Omega Point with the Christ of revelation. The great event of his life, he tells us, was to be the gradual identification of two suns: one of these stars being the cosmic summit postulated by a generalized evolution of a convergent kind, and the other being the risen Christ of the Christian faith. Teilhard does not confuse science and revelation. But when he compares his world vision, drawn from cosmic and organic evolution and its ascending drive, with what revelation has to say to him about the universe and humankind, he finds an astonishing coherence and harmony between the two. The same movement seems to embrace both: a movement upward, then a movement downward. In thus changing his perspective and looking at the world from above, Teilhard speaks now as a believer and takes his stand directly under the guidance of faith. In the light of revelation Omega is christified. "Christ possesses all the super-human attributes of Omega Point" ("Super-Humanity, Super-Christ, Super-Charity," 164). "Under the illuminating influence of Grace, our minds recognize in the unifying properties of the Christian phenomenon a manifestation (or a reflection) of Omega upon human consciousness, and so identify the Omega of reason with the Universal Christ of revelation" ("My Intellectual Position," in *The Heart of Matter* [New York, 1978], 144). Cosmogenesis and anthropogenesis exist for the sake of Christogenesis. To understand evolution is to understand the mysterious person of the risen Christ as the goal and point of convergence of evolution. But then we pass from philosophical hypothesis to historical fact, from phenomenological and philosophical analysis to the level of faith and Christology. As long as we stay at the level of the scientific analysis or philosophical interpretation of evolution, the features of Omega remain vague. It is revelation that shows the true identity of Omega: its name is Christ. Then, "instead of the vague centre of convergence envisaged as the ultimate end of this process of evolution the personal and defined reality of the Word Incarnate, in which everything acquires substance, appears and takes its place. Life for Men, Men for Christ, Christ for God" ("Social Heredity and Progress," in *The Future of Man*, 34). If we accept "that the Christ of Revelation is none other than the Omega of Evolution," then there is "the positive gleam of a way out at the highest point of the future. There is no longer any danger of our suffocating, for we are in a World whose peak certainly opens out *in Christo Jesu*" ("The Christic," in *The Heart of Matter*, 92).

As Teilhard sees it, this identification of Christ and Omega, this coherence and harmony between a religion of the christic type and an evolution of the convergent type are supported by and grounded in the Christology of Paul and John. "If the world is convergent and if Christ occupies its centre, then the Christogenesis of St. Paul and St. John is nothing else and nothing less than the extension, both awaited and unhoped for, of that noogenesis in which cosmogenesis—as regards our experience—culminates" (*The Phenomenon of Man*, 297). In "How I Believe" (1934), Teilhard sets forth his creed in the following articles: "I believe that the universe is an evolution. I believe that evolution proceeds towards spirit. I believe that spirit is fully realized in a form of personality. I believe that the supremely personal is the Universal Christ" (in *Christianity and Evolution*, 96).

8. The Universal Christ

The universal Christ is the total and totalizing Christ, "the organic centre of the entire universe . . . presented to us in the Gospels, and more particularly by St. Paul and St. John" ("Note on the Universal Christ," in *Science and Christ*, 14). In the incarnation, God christifies himself and thereby christifies the universe and human beings. The "christified universe" and the "universal Christ" are one and the same thing. The universal Christ is "he who, by his birth and his blood, restores every creature to his Father; the Christ of the eucharist and the parousia, the cosmic, consummating Christ of St. Paul . . . the physical pole of universal synthesis" ("Christianity and Evolution," in *Christianity and Evolution*, 179–80).

Teilhard's work certainly represents one of the most important contemporary efforts to expand and renew Christology. For him, the question is, What is the place of Christ in a world in which the immensity and complexity of the universe are being revealed on every side? We must develop and apply a Christology that is in keeping with the dimensions of the universe; i.e., we must recognize that in virtue of the incarnation and resurrection, Christ

possesses cosmic and universal attributes that make him the personal center of evolution. "To 'universalize' Christ is the only way we have of retaining in him his essential attributes . . . in a fantastically enlarged Creation" ("Some Reflections on the Conversion of the World," 124). It is also the only way of correcting and taking over all the modern attempts at pantheism.

Bruno was drawn by the solitary Christ, Francis by the poor Christ, Dominic by Christ the Truth, Ignatius by Christ the leader and king. Teilhard for his part is fascinated by the universal Christ, the center and head of the universe, present to every moment of the cosmic and human adventure to which he gives coherence from on high. For Teilhard, the universal Christ is his way of understanding the incarnation in all its fullness and with all its concrete implications. For him Christ is the incarnate Word with his prolongation and completion in the risen Christ and the eucharistic Christ.

The function of the universal Christ is thus based on the incarnation and resurrection. At this point I should emphasize that for Teilhard creation, incarnation, and resurrection are three very closed linked mysteries. In the plan for a universal ingathering of the universe, the Eucharist plays an important part. Through the Eucharist, which prolongs the incarnation, the omnipresence of Christ extends to the entire universe throughout the whole of its duration. As a matter of fact, ever since the creation of the world, a single decisive event has been taking place, namely, the divinization of the world through the incarnation and its prolongation, the Eucharist. The priestly action of Christ extends to the entire world. "From age to age, there is but one single Mass in the world: the true Host, the total Host, is the universe which is continually being more intimately penetrated and vivified by Christ. From the most distant origin of things to their unforeseeable consummation . . . the whole of nature is slowly and irresistibly undergoing the supreme consecration. Fundamentally—since all time and for ever—but one single thing is being made in creation: the body of Christ" ("Pantheism and Christianity," in *Christianity and Evolution*, 73–74).

The universal Christ is a synthesis of Christ and the universe. Teilhard discovers in this universal Christ what he had always dreamed of: the Christ who is head of the cosmic and human world, the recapitulator who is to hand everything back to the Father; the total Christ with the reality of his mystical body; the Christ who is all in all. This total and totalizing Christ—he is the true Omega Point. From the outset everything was ascending toward spirit through the attraction of the universal Christ. Toward the end of his life, in 1953, Teilhard wrote from New York that only one thing was clear to him about the future: "I wish to use the final years left to me as fully as possible in *christifying* . . . evolution. . . . To do that—and then to end well, that is, to die as a witness to this gospel" (*Nouvelles lettres de voyage* [Paris, 1957], 171–72).

9. Impact of Teilhard's Apologetics

The power of Teilhard's vision of the world is its ability to integrate; it omits no element but brings them all together in a dynamic vision. He succeeds in showing the universal coherence of the natural and supernatural universes in Jesus Christ. In this vision the physical, moral, social, and religious orders are taken up and unified in and through Christ.

Let me review quickly the elements of this coherence, which is the product of the meeting of two convergences, or better, of a "convergence" and an "emergence" (Christ). On the one hand, there is the cosmic convergence of a universe that is subject to a directed evolution that proceeds by a series of ever more complex and conscious arrangements to the level of spirit, and in the direction of an increasingly complex coreflection. The world is converging on itself in an irresistible and irreversible movement of unification. The human race is moving toward ever greater freedom and personality. On the other hand, under the action of the incarnate Word, for whose historical presence millennia of evolution prepared the way, an increasingly powerful dynamism of unification, personalization, and amorization is bringing about the gathering of all human beings in Christ, the head of the mystical body. The physical and the cosmic, the cosmic and the christic are moving toward an encounter. In a *converging* universe Christ is *emerging* to make his own and complete the cosmic convergence. Evolution preserves Christ (by making him possible), and at the same time Christ preserves evolution (by making it concrete and realiz-

able). Because Christianity puts *Some One* at the summit of space and time, it alone is in a position to dedicate itself to the success of a personalized and personalizing evolution.

Teilhard thinks and writes as scientist, philosopher, sociologist, theologian, mystic, prophet, and artist in giving expression to this synthesis (or rather this gigantic, stupendous fresco). It was almost inevitable that this synthesis on a colossal scale should not be understood by minds that are prisoners of a one-dimensional and monolithic universe. Teilhard, however, addresses himself primarily to the scientists of his day. His hope is that contemplation of this universal harmony, this supremely intelligible coherence that he finds in the universal Christ, will by its nature arouse in scientists an interest and attraction and perhaps even, under the motion of the Spirit, an acceptance and consent.

Bibl.: Pierre TEILHARD DE CHARDIN, *Oeuvres*, 13 vols. (Paris); G. CRESPY, *La pensée théologique de Teilhard de Chardin* (Paris, 1961); C. D'ARMAGNAC, "La pensée du Père Teilhard de Chardin comme apologétique moderne," *NRT* 84 (1962): 598–621; M. BARTHÉLEMY-MADAULE, *La personne et le drame humain chez Teilhard de Chardin* (Paris, 1967); P. SMULDERS, *La vision de Teilhard de Chardin* (Paris, 1964); E. RIDEAU, *La pensée de Pierre Teilhard de Chardin* (Paris, 1964); B. DE SOLAGES, *Teilhard de Chardin* (Lyons, 1967); R. FARICY, *Teilhard de Chardin's Theology of the Christian World* (New York, 1967); H. DE LUBAC, *La pensée religieuse du P. Teilhard de Chardin* (Paris, 1962); C. MOONEY, *Teilhard de Chardin and the Mystery of Christ* (New York, 1966); M. PONTET, *Pascal et Teilhard: Témoins du Christ* (Paris, 1968); R. D'OUINCE, *Un prophète en procès: Teilhard de Chardin dans l'Église de son temps* (Paris, 1970); L. BARJON, *Le combat de Pierre Teilhard de Chardin* (Québec, 1971); P. SCHELLENBAUM, *Le Christ dans l'énergétique teilhardienne* (Paris, 1971); R. LATOURELLE, "Pierre Teilhard de Chardin. At the Universal Center of Convergence," in R. Latourelle, *Man and His Problems in the Light of Jesus Christ* (New York, 1983), 89–158.

René LATOURELLE

TESTAMENTS, OLD AND NEW

I. PROMISE AND FULFILLMENT

Promise and fulfillment nowadays constitute a decisive element in the understanding of NT texts and indeed of the entire Christian economy; this is true not only for exegetes but for theologians and interpreters as well. Important progress has been made in this area thanks to both exegesis and hermeneutics. These advances show that the ideas of promise and fulfillment include much more than the argument from the fulfillment of prophecy, which has been a key chapter in treatises of fundamental theology or apologetics.

The renewal of biblical studies at the beginning of the present century promoted reflection on the ideas of promise and fulfillment. For France, mention may be made of the outstanding works that J. Touzard published in 1907–09. According to this author the changes in perspective can be summed up as follows: It is not possible to isolate the predictions of the prophets from their teaching; these predictions are at the service of their teaching on the coming sovereign rule of God over the world and on the establishment of an authentic religious life. Prophetic religion is rich in moral and religious truths, and the prophecies are in the service of this religion.

By focusing attention exclusively on the NT accomplishment of prophetic predictions, apologetics tended to see prophecies as enigmatic sayings that were unintelligible to the prophets' contemporaries. As a matter of fact, the predictions of the prophets did make sense to their hearers, whose faith and hope they kept alive and whose gaze they turned to the future. Prophecies thus had a literal OT meaning, the NT meaning being "deeper and ultimate," or "total." Finally, the predictions of the prophets did not necessarily have their definitive realization in the time of Jesus or the early church. Many of these prophecies continue to direct our eyes to the end of time, when God will definitively establish his reign and when the promises already realized in Jesus Christ will have their ultimate and definitive fulfillment. When the matter is seen in this perspective, it is possible to harmonize the *predictions* with the moral and religious teaching of the prophets as well as with the idea of *promise*, and the *accomplishment* of predictions with an idea that includes but also goes beyond that of accomplishment, namely, *fulfillment*. Such perspectives inevitably make believers more aware of the history of salvation as a whole and no longer only of the material accomplishment of predictions. They also involve the minds and hearts of believers in a real understanding of the prophets, and they emphasize the point that believers will be touched by the argument from prophecy if God in a mysterious way opens their hearts to it.

Toward the middle of the present century, the biblical renewal made some genuine syntheses possible. Although many names deserve to be cited, I shall mentions only those of J. Coppens (*Les harmonies des deux Testaments* [Tournai/Paris, 1949]) and P. Grelot (*Sens chrétien de l'Ancien Testament* [Tournai, 1962]; and *La Bible parole de Dieu* [Tournai/Paris, 1965]), both of whom authored substantial publications on this theme. The reader will be alerted by these two names to the fact that the problem of fulfillment has been taken up by two exegetes who aim at works of synthesis while being true to their profession of exegesis. As a result, the traditional argument from prophecies is considerably extended and becomes in the end a way of covering many thematic complexes of both the OT and the NT. J. Coppens has devoted several works to the various messianisms found in the Scriptures and to their fulfillment. P. Grelot has done the same, although his concerns are undoubtedly of a more theoretical order. His *Sens chrétien de l'Ancien Testament*, which was published in a series on dogmatic theology, sets forth all the possible links between the OT and the New, from the viewpoint both of the literal meaning and of the meaning of the realities thus expressed. Whereas Coppens's works assign an absolute priority to the literal meaning, to the exclusion of all attempts to approach the texts in other ways, P. Grelot studies the whole range of connections that the idea of a Christian meaning makes it possible to establish between the OT and the NT, whether by way of the *literal meaning* (the prophecies and their fulfillment) or by way of the *meaning of the realities* involved, which allows the emergence of typological, spiritual, or mystical senses and the placing of Christ fully at the center of history.

I stress the point that such syntheses were made possible by the biblical renewal of the first half of the twentieth century. That renewal brought with it an interest in the methods of historical and literary criticism, which focused the attention of exegetes on the value of the literal meaning. This meaning is thus the first to be taken into account in any effort to establish relations of promise and fulfillment. In regard to the prophetic argument used by the apologists of the nineteenth and early twentieth centuries, this serious concern for the literal meaning brought major changes of perspective. Many prophecies that had been interpreted as looking directly and exclusively to NT realities were found to be in fact connected with OT realities. One example is the Servant of Isaiah. This figure had been thought of as referring directly to Jesus Christ, but syntheses of biblical theology showed that this figure had first of all an OT meaning. It referred, e.g., to the remnant of Israel. In like fashion, the young woman of Is 7:14 referred to the wife of Ahaz, and her child would be Hezekiah. In this new approach, what became of the NT fulfillment? In order to do justice to the new acquisitions of critical exegesis, a theory of meanings had to be developed that would make it possible to establish real relations between OT prophecy and its NT fulfillment. Can this fulfillment be relegated to the category of theological, spiritual, or mystical meanings? Certainly not, for since the exegetical renewal was based on recognition of the solidity of the literal meaning, any lumping of the fulfillment meaning with theological or spiritual meanings would seem to deprive it of its value.

It was in order to resolve this theoretical problem that the idea of the "plenary (i.e., fuller) sense" or meaning was developed. This idea plays a key role in all the attempts at synthesis based on promise and fulfillment that made their appearance in and around the fifties. We saw earlier that Touzard spoke of a "total" or a "deeper" meaning. Back in the seventeenth century Richard Simon, a biblical critic, had already suggested a similar category when he spoke of a "theological or mystical or spiritual meaning," which he regarded as partly "literal in a way" and which he very carefully distinguished from the valueless "mystical fancies" that thrived here and there in his day. The term "plenary sense" seems to have been used first by A.

Fernandez in his *Institutiones biblicae*, published at Rome around 1920. It was taken up and developed in several syntheses, among which the following at least may be cited: R. E. Brown, *The "Sensus Plenior" of Sacred Scripture* (Baltimore, 1955), and also *CBQ* 25 (1963): 262–85; P. Grelot in most of his major works; J. Coppens, *Vom christlichen Verständnis des Alten Testaments* (Louvain, 1952); G. Courtade, "Les Écritures ont-elles un sens plenier?" *RSR* (1950): 481–99; P. Benoit, *RB* 67 (1960): 161–96; B. Vawter, *CBQ* 26 (1964): 85–96; and R. E. Brown, *ETL* 43 (1967): 460–69.

Although the supporters of the plenary meaning have sometimes differed in their explanations of it, it must be noted that for all of them the meaning in question is really present in the OT text at a deeper level of the strictly literal. The question, then, is whether or not the prophetic author was conscious of it. Opinions differ on this point. In any case, the idea of a plenary meaning makes it possible to give a solid basis in the literal meaning for the relationship between OT promises and their accomplishment in the NT.

The idea of a plenary meaning, which nowadays is rather ignored, did not win the support of everyone. Originating as it did, and being used exclusively in exegesis and in Catholic theology, it had its opponents, among whom must be mentioned H. DE LUBAC (*L'Écriture dans la Tradition* [Paris, 1966]). This specialist in patristic studies was too familiar with the tradition not to see that, in fact, a synthesis based on the plenary sense gave the literal meaning an importance it did not have in patristic syntheses based on the four senses. When the plenary sense is operative, the meanings derived from a living reading of Scripture by the tradition run the risk of being objectivized and regarded as already present in the letter of OT passages, whereas the need is to show how they hatch, as it were, in the practice of Scripture reading in the Christian communities.

The major theologies of the OT, especially, though not exclusively, those by Protestants, took other approaches to the relationship between promise and fulfillment. I shall focus here on those of W. Eichrodt, *Theologie des Alten Testaments*, 3 vols. (Leipzig, 1933–39; Eng. trans.: *Theology of the Old Testament*, trans. J. A. Baker; 3 vols. in 2 [London, 1951–

57]), and G. von Rad, *Theologie des Alten Testaments*, 2 vols. (Munich, 1960; Eng. trans.: *Old Testament Theology*, trans. D. M. G. Stalker; 2 vols. [Edinburgh, 1961–65]). But mention should also be made of E. Jacob, *Theologie de l'Ancien Testament* (Neuchâtel, 1965; Eng. trans.: *Theology of the Old Testament*, trans. A. W. Heathcote and P. J. Allcock [New York, 1958]), B. S. Childs, *Biblical Theology in Crisis* (Philadelphia, 1970), S. Amsler, *L'Ancien Testament dans l'Eglise* (Neuchâtel, 1960), among others. Using a cross-section method, Eichrodt sees relations between the OT and the NT in terms of constant elements in an overall structure that is one of the covenant. Prediction (*Weissagung*) must be brought into harmony with the broader notion of prophecy (*Prophetie*). In the NT, all the elements found within the covenant structure recur, but they are marked now with the seal of fulfillment. But this fulfillment needs to be properly understood, for it in turn refers us to the parousia for the definitive fulfillment.

In von Rad's work, the perspective is no longer that of a covenantal structure into which a series of specific elements is integrated, but rather a diachronic structure consisting of a history of traditions. The constant retrieval and actualization of older traditions is a characteristioc trait of the OT. The result would be an unfocused dispersal if von Rad did not see and emphasize a constant in this process, namely, the *kerygmatic intention*, which time after time allows Israel to take up the older tradition as a way of proclaiming the message of the one God at the present moment. Von Rad reflects on the "proof from Scripture" that is used by the NT writers. In his opinion, this phrase is too cumbersome to express all the nuances present in the idea that there are continuities between the OT and the Christ-event. He observes, quite rightly, that the proof from the Scriptures should not be separated from all the typological comparisons or parallels that are one of the original traits of the NT Scriptures. Typology seeks to establish between an OT event and a NT event a correspondence that expresses both continuity and gradation. It is therefore an essential tool in any effort to connect the OT and NT as promise and fulfillment.

Von Rad's theology of the OT has today become a kind of theological progenitor, so important has its influence been on the theo-

logies of history that have emerged since its publication. Among these I may mention the essays of W. Pannenberg, "Heilsgeschehen und Geschichte," *KuD* 5 (1959): 218–37 and 259–88 (Eng. trans.: "Redemptive Event and History," in his *Basic Questions in Theology*, trans. G. H. Kehm [London, 1971], 2:15–80), in which the author is concerned with promise and fulfillment, and of J. Moltmann, especially in his *Theologie der Geschichte* (Munich, 1965) (Eng. trans.: *The Theology of Hope*, trans. L. Leitch [New York, 1967]). The thought of these two men on promise and fulfillment should not be regarded as the same. Pannenberg's works lead him, in fact, to abandon completely the category of promise-fulfillment in favor of tradition history (see his remarks in his postscript to I. Berten, *Histoire, révélation, et foi* [Brussels, 1969], 145). Moltmann, on the contrary, keeps the idea of promise as a key element of his own thought and shows how promise and fulfillment ceaselessly support and refer back to each other.

We turn now to theologies specifically of the NT. Numerous detailed investigations into Scripture, promise, and prophecy have made it possible to develop more systematic studies. R. Bultmann in his day was interested in "The Significance of the Old Testament for the Christian Faith" (in *The Old Testament and Christian Faith: A Theological Discussion*, ed. B. W. Anderson [New York, 1963]) and "Promise and Fulfillment" (in *Faith and Understanding* [New York, 1969]). It is obvious that Bultmann thinks of relations between the OT and NT in terms not of the history of salvation but of existentiality. While the OT can be said to be a preparation for the NT, it is so, not in a historical sense (*historisch*), i.e., "as if the historical phenomenon that is the Christian religion had become possible only in virtue of a religious development to which the OT bears witness," but in a real sense (*sachlich*), i.e., the gospel can be preached only when human beings find themselves under law. It is in this sense that the OT can be regarded as placing human beings in a situation of "pre-understanding" (*Vorverständnis*) of the gospel. As for proofs drawn from the Scriptures, these cannot lead to the idea that Christ comes at the end of a series of predictions or promises that supposedly mark him down as the summit of history. Christ is the goal of history in the sense that he is the "eschatological terminus," by that very fact doing away with any preparation that would take the historical form of prediction, advance notice, or promise. The OT prepares for the NT by the fact that it is a failure. The ideas of covenant, kingdom of God, and people of God are eschatologized in the NT and are thereby radically different from the "intraworldly" use made of them in the OT. Christ, being an eschatological reality, signifies the failure of the OT, and only because it is a failure can the OT be called promise. "For human beings, nothing can function as promise except the failure of their ways and the knowledge they acquire that it is impossible to reach God directly in their intraworldly history and to identify this history wholly with the action of God" ("Promise and Fulfillment," 571).

As the typical representative of a theology that makes proclamation more important than history, Bultmann is poles apart from the theologies of history of a von Rad or a Moltmann. Among his most resolute opponents mention must be made especially of O. Cullmann and, in particular, his *Le salut dans l'histoire* (Neuchâtel, 1966; Eng. trans.: *Salvation in History*, trans. S. C. Sowers [New York, 1967]). Cullmann takes the exegetical material and shows that the category of salvation history, rejected by Bultmann, is indeed present in the NT writings and even in the thinking of Jesus, and that there is no reason for opposing a "precatholic" Luke, the supposed inventor of salvation history, to Paul, the supposed representative of a decision of faith that is untainted by any thought of salvation history. Having thus restored consistency to the NT writings, Cullmann shows how the unity of NT thought depends on the preaching of Jesus and how Jesus does in fact intend to bring the promises of the OT to their accomplishment, even while directing the gaze of his hearers to the fulfillment at the end of time.

There are other names that ought to be cited. Let me mention at least W. G. Kümmel, who in his day showed great mastery in handling the relation between history and eschatology in the NT texts (*Verheissung und Erfüllung* [Zurich, 1953]). E. Käsemann, a disciple of Bultmann, was able to go beyond his teacher and reinstitute a dialectical confrontation between history and eschatology that proves to be of great interest for the idea of fulfillment and that

takes us further, in my opinion, than the vision of history developed by Cullmann (see P.-M. Beaude, *L'accomplissement des prophéties* [Paris, 1980], 233).

At the present time, the ideas of promise and fulfillment still have a useful life ahead of them. They seem to prove an almost necessary path for Christian hermeneutics, since this has the unavoidable duty of explaining the insertion of the mystery of Jesus into the history of Israel and into general history. The work to be done, both exegetical and hermeneutical, is vast. By way of conclusion, let me mention two promising paths: (1) the development of intertestamental studies that will make it possible to analyze the ideas of promise and fulfillment as found in different circles in late Judaism; (2) the development of interest in the phenomenon of writing in all its aspects (linguistic, semiotic, sociological, etc.), since this provides new possibilities of theory formation (see, e.g., Beauchamp, 1976, 1990).

Bibl.: C. H. Dodd, *According to the Scriptures* (London, 1953); P. Grelot, *Sens chrétien de l'Ancien Testament* (Paris/Tournai, 1962); G. von Rad, *Old Testament Theology*, 2 vols. (New York, 1962, 1965); P. Beauchamp, *L'un et l'autre Testament*, 2 vols. (Paris, 1976, 1990); P.-M. Beaude, *L'accomplissement des Écritures* (Paris, 1980).

Pierre-Marie Beaude

II. The Relationship Between the OT and the NT in Romans

The study of the relations between the NT and the OT will always be illuminating. Several NT writers themselves bid us pursue it. According to John, for example, it is of *Christ* that Moses was writing (Jn 5:46). The first letter of Peter teaches that the prophets of the former covenant "prophesied of the grace that was to be yours" (1 Pt 1:10). Moreover, it was "the *Spirit of Christ* [who was] within them" and who through them "testified in advance to the sufferings destined for *Christ* and the subsequent glory" (1 Pt 1:11). Thus the OT prophets foretold, in their own way, the *paschal mystery* of Christ. Paul too, when he asserts that "in him [Christ] every one of God's promises is a 'Yes'" (2 Cor

1:20), shows that he often looks to the OT when he speaks of Christ Jesus.

It is possible to consider the relations between the OT and the NT in a general kind of way. In this study I have chosen to tackle the subject in a particular NT writing, the letter to the Romans. More specifically, I shall examine the OT citations with which Paul peppers the text of this letter.

Any careful reader of Romans will notice how often Paul refers to the OT. This practice gives rise to a number of questions: How many such references are there? From where do they come? What is their function? Do Paul's citations faithfully reflect the letter of the original texts and their original context?

1. Omnipresence of OT Citations.

The letter to the Romans cites no fewer than sixty-two passages of the OT (Koch 1986: 21–24). In Romans, more than in his other letters, Paul shows a special enthusiasm for the OT. He never cites the OT in 1 and 2 Thessalonians, Colossians, and Philippians. Ephesians refers to the OT but in passing, as it were, and without any great emphasis. Romans in fact contains a large number of the ninety-three OT citations that have been identified in the body of letters ordinarily attributed to Paul the apostle (Rom, 1 Cor, 2 Cor, Gal, Eph, Phil, Col, 1–2 Thes).

The OT citations found in Romans are taken chiefly from the Psalms (14 citations), Genesis (8), Deuteronomy (8), First Isaiah (7), Second Isaiah (7), and, finally, Third Isaiah (5). The thirteen remaining citations are from nine other OT books (Hb, Mal, Ex, Hos, Lv, 1 Kgs, Jb, Prv, and Jl). It seems, then, that the books to which Paul chiefly refers in writing Romans are the Psalms, Genesis, Deuteronomy, and, above all, Isaiah. In fact, in the whole body of his letters he shows a clear preference for these four books. He leaves aside the prophets Jeremiah, Ezekiel, and Daniel, as well as the historical books, such as the books of Samuel, Chronicles, and 2 Kings. In doing so, he reflects the preferences of his contemporaries (Koch, 47 n. 14). Like them, he cites only the books that Pharisaic and rabbinic Judaism later accepted as canonical after 70 C.E. He never cites, for example, Sirach or the book of Wisdom (E. Earle Ellis, "Paul's Use of Non-Canonical Literature," in Ellis 1957: 76–82).

This does not mean that he did not draw upon these writings (cf., e.g., Rom 1:18–23 and Wis 13:1–9), but only that he found it appropriate not to cite the texts.

A final note: in the letters to the Corinthians, Paul cites as belonging to the OT several passages for which we will search the Scriptures in vain (see 1 Cor 1:31; 2:9; 9:10b; 2 Cor 13:10).

2. The Original Text and the Pauline Citations

The Text of the Septuagint

Paul cites the OT from the Greek text of the Septuagint (LXX), or, more accurately, from a text of the LXX that had been hebraized before his day (Koch, 78–79). I thus refer constantly to the LXX, following throughout its numbering and versification of the Psalms.

Several citations in Romans show that Paul was reading the LXX text. For example, in Rom 15:10 he writes what the LXX has "*Rejoice*, O Gentiles, with his people" (Dt 32:43), whereas the Hebrew original has "*Praise*, O nations, his people!" Again, Rom 15:12 cites Is 11:10 from the LXX: "In him [the root of Jesse] *the Gentiles shall hope*," whereas the Hebrew text reads: "*The nations shall inquire of him* [the root of Jesse]."

Alteration of the Original Text

Paul sometimes uses a certain freedom in citing the Greek text of the OT. Rom 9:33 cites Is 8:14 freely, while ten other passages of the letter make stylistic changes in citing the OT (Rom 2:6; 9:9; 10:19; 11:4, 34, 35; 12:19; 14:11; 15:8, 11).

The apostle likes to change the word order for the sake of highlighting something that is of special interest to him. Thus Rom 11:3 emphasizes the murder of the prophets by beginning the citation of 1 Kgs 19:10 with the words "They have killed your prophets," although these words come at a later point in the original passage. So too, in Rom 10:21, in order to emphasize the guilt of the "disobedient and contrary" Jewish people, Paul calls attention to the words "all day long" by beginning with them: "*All day long* I have held out my hands to a disobedient and contrary people," even though in Is 65:2 the words come in the middle of the sentence.

Another stylistic modification of the LXX text can be seen in Rom 11:9b. Here Paul highlights "stumbling block" (*skandalon*), because this emphasis better suits a context of fall and rejection (see Rom 11:7–8, 10).

Paul often shortens the OT text in order better to bring out his own point of view (see Rom 3:10–12/Ps 13:1–3; Rom 3:15–17/Is 59:7–8). He then retains those parts of the original text that support his own thought.

The length of the passages that Paul cites varies considerably throughout the letter. At times he cites only a few words: "You shall not covet" (*ouk epithymēseis*) (Rom 7:7/Dt 5:21), or sometimes a brief but meaningful sentence: Yahweh is the one who "will repay according to each one's deeds" (*apodōsei hekastō kata ta erga autou*) (Rom 2:6/Ps 61:13). On other occasions, he often cites one or more complete verses (see Rom 11:9–10/Ps 68:23–24; Rom 11:26–27/Is 59:20–21).

Readers find themselves faced at times by collections of citations from various books of the OT. In some instances, such a series has for its purpose to express in several ways a single statement of Paul. There is no real progress in thought from one citation to the next. This is the case with Rom 15:9–12, where four OT texts (Ps 17:50; Dt 32:43; Ps 116:1; Is 11:10) provide—in Paul's mind, at least—four formulations of one and the same thought, which he has stated just before the group of citations: ". . . in order that the Gentiles might glorify God for his mercy." Each of the four texts that he goes on to cite (Rom 15:9b–12) contains either the same two words that he has just used ("Gentiles" and "glorify") or synonyms of them.

In this way Paul tries to lend his own thought the authority of the word of God. He gives a solid grounding in the religious tradition of Israel for seemingly new views of his own that may shock Jewish or Jewish-Christian readers.

Paul may have a different purpose in using a group of citations, namely, to give OT support to each part of his argument. This is the case in Rom 9:6–18, where he attempts to explain why Israel has not accepted Christ Jesus.

This refusal is a mystery or a historical scandal that Paul would like to understand. A first explanation suggests itself to Paul's mind: Can it be that the word of God, which according to the divine plan was to be received by "the descendants of Abraham," has failed because it was powerless, unable to carry out God's plan (Rom 9:6)? To this suggestion Paul reacts strongly: the true "descendants of Abraham" that the divine plan had in mind are the descendants whom *Isaac* gave his father, as Gn 21:12 (cited in Rom 9:7) had said. Second, the posterity in question is one born of a *promise*, as Gn 18:10, 14 (Rom 9:9) attests. Third, if Yahweh is accepted by one descendant of Isaac (namely, Jacob) rather than the other (Esau), this is because of a *free choice* on the part of God, who freely calls whomever he wishes, as we see him doing in Gn 25:23 and Mal 1:2–3 (Rom 9:12–13).

As we see, at each stage of Paul's reasoning a citation from Scripture—the word of God—is brought in to confirm, approve, or accredit Paul's thought. His recourse to the OT is here of a systematic kind.

3. Function of Old Testament Citations

My observations thus far give rise to an important question: What function do OT citations have in Paul? It seems indeed that the first function of such citations is to show that the teaching of the OT and that of Paul are in complete agreement. Whether the citations provide a purely verbal amplification of a Pauline theme, such as we see in Rom 15:9–12, or whether they confirm each step in a Pauline train of thought, as in Rom 9:6–18, the main purpose of these OT citations is the same: *to lend the authority of God's word to Paul's thought.*

Careless readers may fall into the trap of judging that Paul is simply setting forth the word of God that is contained in the Sacred Scriptures. They may think that there is complete agreement between Paul and the authors of the Sacred Scriptures. In fact, however, the citations are not the starting point of Paul's thought; ordinarily they do not even help his thought advance. They simply express his thought in various ways. Most importantly, it is by no means certain, as I shall go on to show, that Paul respects the meaning that the cited texts had in the OT.

Before coming to the important matter mentioned in the preceding sentence, I shall take up another question that I also raised implicitly a moment ago: What is the starting point in the interchange between the OT and Paul's own thought? Does Paul's thinking start with the

OT or with the Christian tradition? In my view, the apostle is reflecting first and foremost on the one gospel of Christ (Gal 1:7); then he goes back to the OT.

Rom 15:12–13

It undoubtedly does happen that one or another verse of Paul is, as it were, begotten of an OT text that he has just cited. For example, when Paul speaks in Rom 15:13 of the "God of hope," an expression he uses nowhere else in his letters, and if in the same passage he wishes that Christians "may abound in *hope* by the power of the Holy Spirit," it is undoubtedly because his citation from Is 11:10 in the preceding verse (Rom 15:12) ended with the words: "In him [the root of Jesse] the Gentiles shall *hope*." The word "hope" as used by Isaiah gives rise to Paul's wish in Rom 15:31, which speaks twice of hope (*elpis*).

Rom 15:9–12

The ordinary movement in Paul is the opposite of the one just illustrated. More commonly, an already-formulated thought of Paul determines the choice of citations subsequently made. We saw a moment ago how two words used by Paul himself in Rom 15:9 —"Gentiles" (*ethnē*) and "glorify" (*doxazein*) — call forth three citations from the OT that display the same two words, or synonyms in the case of "glorify" (*doxazein: exomologein, psallein, euphranein, ainein, epainein*).

Everything suggests that as Paul was dictating his letters, he turned back to the OT with his own thought already clear in his head, a thought inspired by the tradition springing from the gospel of Christ. He then looked to the OT either for clear and vivid expressions of his own thought or for scenes or events that would illustrate his thought.

Rom 3:21–4:25

The recall of the figure of Abraham is an excellent example of what I have just been saying. The letter to the Romans mentions Abraham for the first time at 4:1, i.e., after Paul has explained with noteworthy precision (Rom 3:21–31) that "a person is justified by faith apart from works prescribed by the law" (Rom 3:28). The apostle has first meditated on "the redemption

that is in Christ Jesus" (Rom 3:24) and on the atonement accomplished by Christ's blood (Rom 3:25). Only afterward is the spiritual history of Abraham (Rom 4) brought in to illustrate the thought previously developed (Rom 3:21–31).

The thoughts that Paul expresses in Rom 3:21–31 govern the reading he subsequently gives of the story of Abraham. For example, Why does Paul speak of the *righteousness* of Abraham only in the light of Gn 15:6: "[Abraham] believed the LORD, and the LORD reckoned it to him as righteousness"? Did Abraham not already act as a righteous man when Yahweh said to him in Gn 12:1: "Go from your country and your kindred and your father's house to the land that I will show you," and Abraham "went, as the LORD had told him" (Gn 12:4a)? Paul leaves out this episode in Gn 12:1–5 because he wants to link righteousness and faith in light of the gospel tradition that inspired Rom 3:21–31. But the words "righteousness" and "faith" do not appear in Gn 12:1–5, whereas they do occur, closely linked, in Gn 15:6. Only the latter passage is cited, therefore, because it alone clearly expresses Paul's personal thought.

Rom 4:19

Another proof that NT considerations guide Paul in his reading of the story of Abraham is the way in which he describes the God of Abraham as "the God . . . *who gives life to the dead*" (Rom 4:17), and then the bodies of Sarah and Abraham as being "already as good as dead" (Rom 4:19). The book of Genesis says indeed that "Abraham and Sarah were old, advanced in age" (Gn 18:11), but it never describes them as "already as good as dead."

But the paschal mystery, which is the heart of the Christian faith, inspires Paul to a new reading of the story of Abraham. The Christian faith, which speaks of "him who *raised* Jesus our Lord from the *dead*" (Rom 4:24), suggests to Paul the description of the God of Abraham as "the God . . . *who gives life to the dead*" (Rom 4:17) and of the bodies of Sarah and Abraham as "already as good as *dead*" (Rom 4:19). Thus a vocabulary taken from the paschal mystery, which speaks of *death* and a God who *raises from the dead*, is used in Rom 4 to tell the story of Abraham. The new Pauline reading of Abraham's experience does not falsify what is said in the OT but it does narrate the facts in a way that links them to the paschal experience of Christ. As a result, Abraham prefigures the disciples of Christ not only by his attitude of belief (Rom 4:12) but also by the very object of his faith: "The God . . . who gives life from the dead" (Rom 4:17). The birth of Isaac and the resurrection of Jesus will likewise be paralleled.

Paul is thus seen, at least in the letter to the Romans, as a disciple of Christ who feeds first of all on the religious tradition that springs from the gospel. Once he is well grounded in the Christian faith, he looks for signs, figures, symbols, or felicitous expressions in the OT writings.

4. Teaching Received from the Old Testament

At this point in my reflection two important questions regarding the OT citations in Romans come to mind. What are the aspects of Christian faith that Romans finds in the OT? And does Romans respect the original meaning of the OT passages that it cites? I shall handle these two questions simultaneously in order to avoid repetition.

God

a. A wise and omniscient God. Several of the OT citations in Romans speak of God. For example, Paul finds in Is 40:13 and Jb 41:3 exclamations of adoration of the wisdom and knowledge of God: "Who has known the mind of the Lord?" (Rom 11:45–35).

b. A faithful God. In Rom 11:2 God's *fidelity* to his people is recalled by a citation from 1 Sm 12:22: "God has not rejected his people," to which Paul adds: "whom he foreknew." These last words explain God's attitude of fidelity; it is because of the unmerited, prevenient love that God has for his people that Israel has not been rejected; this God is faithful "for his great name's sake" (1 Sm 12:22).

c. A God who judges and avenges. In another passage of Romans (2:6) Paul uses a psalm (61:13) as the basis for a teaching completely unknown to the psalmist. The latter is speaking of a just God who during this earthly life recompenses all persons according to their merits. Paul, however, finds in the passage a God who, *at the last judgment,* which begins

the next life, will see justice done. Paul thus reinterprets an OT text in light of the teaching of Christ (Mt 25:31–46).

Is 45:23 looks forward to the day on which the *pagan nations* will acclaim Yahweh as the only "righteous God and . . . Savior" (Is 45:21). But on this text Paul bases the claim that *every human being* will be judged by God and that therefore the judgment on any and every human being must be left to God (Rom 14:11). Here again Paul pretty well alters the meaning of the original. Thanks to a new context (the Christian faith), the text shifts from nations to individuals and then turns God the *Savior* (Is 45:21) into a universal *Judge.*

In Deuteronomy (32:35) Yahweh announces that he will intervene to punish the *pagan nations,* which are idolaters and enemies of Israel: "Vengeance is mine, and recompense, for the time when their foot shall slip." Paul changes the point of this text to a significant degree when he cites it in order to require individual Christians to "not repay *anyone* evil for evil," and to "leave room for the wrath of God" instead of avenging themselves (Rom 12:17, 19).

d. A merciful God. Though God is a stern judge, he remains merciful. Paul finds that two prophets, Hosea and Isaiah, have preached the doctrine that salvation is the fruit solely of God's mercy and not of our personal merits. God calls Israel his *people* and his *beloved* (Rom 9:25–26/Hos 2:1, 25) and *children of the living God* (Rom 9:26/Is 10:22–23; 1:10), although this people is steeped in sin (Hos 2:4–15).

Still on the subject of God's mercy, we may recall the passage in Romans (15:9a) in which Paul sees the *Gentiles* "glorify God for his mercy." He attributes to them the intention of David to sing his gratitude to Yahweh for rescuing him from his enemies: "I will confess you among the Gentiles, and sing praises to your name" (Rom 15:9b/Ps 17:50). Using the formula "as it is written," Paul simply applies to the *pagans* a text in which Scripture is speaking of David!

In Dt 32:43 the pagan nations are urged to praise Yahweh for the power and fidelity he has shown in *beating back the enemies of Israel, his people.* Paul uses this same passage in order to call upon the "Gentiles" to "rejoice" (as the LXX has it) at seeing the mercy of God exercised *in their behalf!* The OT text is expressing gratitude for Israel's happy lot: Yahweh has rescued it from its enemies, among whom the pagan "nations" undoubtedly figured. In Paul the happy lot becomes that of the pagan nations themselves. Yahweh's intervention *against* the "nations" now becomes an intervention *in their behalf!*

In the following verse of Romans (15:11) Paul gives a rather astonishing reinterpretation of Ps 116:1. A text that speaks of the fidelity of Yahweh to *Israel,* his people, becomes in Paul a text that speaks of the divine mercy shown to the *pagans,* whom the psalmist calls upon to praise God: "Praise the Lord, all you Gentiles" (Rom 15:11/Ps 116:1). It is not unimportant to observe how the Gentiles take the place of Israel; Paul had seen such a change take place during his own apostolate (Acts 28:28).

e. A God who acts in freedom. Our examination of (e.g.) Rom 3:21–31 and Rom 4 has shown us that Paul often proceeds as follows: he first states his convictions in his own words and then cites OT passages that will support his thought. That is how he proceeds in Rom 9:11–12. He first says that the plan of God unfolds by *his free choice* and does not depend on works but on him who calls. In other words, salvation is the result not of the works done by the person but of God's free choice, which the believer then accepts. This is indeed Paul's personal thesis, expressed in his own words (see Eph 2:7–10).

In support of these views Paul recalls the story of Esau and Jacob. Even before their birth God decides that the elder of the two sons shall serve the younger. In this decision Yahweh departs from the behavior familiar to Israel (Dt 21:15–17; Gn 43:33). He makes it clear that his choices are free; better, he makes clear the unmerited love that inspires his choices (Rom 9:13/Mal 1:2–3; see Gn 4:4–5; 1 Sm 16:12; 1 Kgs 2:15).

Thus God shows mercy to whom he will; he hardens those whom he will, as the story of Moses and the pharaoh makes quite clear. If God makes "all his goodness pass" before Moses and if he "proclaims the name 'The LORD'" before him, it is because he chooses to do so (Ex 33:19/Rom 9:15). In like manner, if Yahweh lets the pharaoh live through the plagues that ravage Egypt (Ex 9:16), it is because of a plan that Yahweh has freely conceived. All these are so many OT incidents and figures that serve to support Paul's views on a salvation that is a gift of God rather than a payment for works done by human beings (Rom 9:11–12).

Christ

Judging still by the witness of the OT citations which Paul scatters throughout Romans, he also uses the OT to gain a better knowledge of Christ and to make him known to others.

a. Thus Rom 10:18 cites v. 5 of Ps 18 (in which the psalmist contemplates the *glory of God* as shown in the firmament of the heavens) in order to proclaim that the *word of God* has resounded in "all the earth." The word of Christ fulfills what the psalmist said of the glory of God, for the latter shines out in the word of Christ. The sacred text that speaks of the one can also speak of the other at a different stage in the tradition.

b. Similarly, when Paul proclaims in Rom 10:13 that "everyone who calls on the name of the Lord shall be saved," he is using of the Lord *Jesus* a text of Joel that speaks of the Lord *Yahweh* (Jl 2:32 Heb.; 3:5 LXX). If Jesus has come to us as the "Yes" that God speaks in carrying out the promises made in the old covenant (2 Cor 1:20), he can work, for the benefit of all human beings, the wonders that Yahweh had done for Israel alone.

c. Christ fulfills the OT prophecies. Is 11:10 (LXX), for example, announces that the "root of Jesse" will some day arise "to rule the Gentiles," who will then put their hope in him. Paul cites this passage of Isaiah in order to proclaim that Christ, who through his resurrection (*anistamenos*) has become Lord of all the nations (Rom 15:12), brings to fruition the hope that the nations had placed in the "root of Jesse" (Rom 15:12). Thus Christ fulfills a great prophecy. He exercises the divine mercy toward the pagan nations, beyond anything they could have hoped for (Rom 15:8–9). The citation of Is 11:10 confirms this in Rom 15:12.

d. When Paul compares the insults that Christ received (Rom 15:3) with those heaped on the persecuted just man (Ps 68:10), he shows once again that Christ fulfilled in his own person a good many OT figures and events.

e. Throughout his ministry Paul undoubtedly came to see that Christ would lead the hearers of the gospel to life or to death, depending on whether they accepted him or rejected him; Christ emits a life-giving or death-dealing fragrance (2 Cor 2:16). Paul illustrates this truth by combining texts from Is 8:14 and 28:16 that speak of a stone that causes people to stumble or that keeps believers from wavering (Rom 9:33). In Paul's eyes Christ is the fulfillment of this image.

The Lot of Israel

Several of the OT texts cited in Romans had foretold the situation of Israel, which, in Paul's time, rejected Christ. A prophecy of Third Isaiah saw the pagan nations flocking to Yahweh, whereas a "rebellious" Israel turned away from him (Is 65:1–2). In Paul's view, the Israel of the Christian period was fulfilling this prophecy (Rom 10:20–21).

In contrast, the same prophet Isaiah foresaw the day when Yahweh would come as redeemer of Zion, whose children, "turning from transgression," would enter into a covenant with him thanks to the Spirit, who then rested on the prophet (Is 59:20–21). Paul sees in this passage the prophetic announcement of a conversion by which "all Israel will be saved," at the time when "the full number of the Gentiles [shall have] come in [into the Church]" (Rom 11:25–26). Paul thus sees in the OT the direction that history will one day take.

The Moral Life

The OT citations that we read in the Letter to the Romans also enable us to see how Paul found the main lines of his moral teaching in the OT.

When he seeks to confirm the basic law of Christian morality— "the one who loves another has fulfilled the law" (Rom 13:8)—he cites an OT text according to which the Decalogue and "any other commandment" are summed up in this precept: "Love your neighbor as yourself" (Rom 13:9/Dt 5:17–21; Lv 19:18b).

When urging Christians to forgive their enemies, Paul again calls upon a passage of the OT, this time from Proverbs (25:21): "If your enemies are hungry, feed them; if they are thirsty, give them something to drink" (Rom 12:20).

5. Salvation through Faith

a. Rom 1:17. As early as Rom 1:16–17 (a passage that states the two main themes of the letter), Paul maintains that "in it [the gospel] the righteousness of God is revealed *through faith [and] for faith*" (Rom 1:17a). In support of this central claim he immediately cites the prophet Habakkuk: "The one who is righteous will live by faith" (Hb 2:4/Rom 1:17b).

Like the text of Rom 1:17, Hb 2:4 is difficult to understand. Edouard Dhorme even regards it as "one of the most difficult verses" (*La Bible*, Bibliothèque de la Pléiade [Paris, 1959], 2:807). The prophet is speaking of those who are sincere or faithful, as opposed to those "whose soul is not upright." Moreover, in view of the way the text has habitually been cited in the tradition, it would be preferable to connect "sincerity" or "fidelity" with the verb "to live": "The just shall live by [their] fidelity." Habakkuk is not concerned, as Paul is, to define faith or to oppose the order of law to that of faith as the source of justification or salvation. He is speaking simply of the behavior of the upright person: such a person will live by serving God with sincerity or fidelity.

There is admittedly a common element in the divergent understandings that the prophet Habakkuk and the apostle Paul have of the same text (Hb 2:4); both are saying that the service of God or obedience to God is the right way to live or the true source of life. There is nonetheless a considerable distance between the thought of the two men. The prophet sees observance of the law as a service to be rendered to God, whereas Paul (Rom 1:17) sees this service as consisting of faith rather than works, including the work par excellence, which was, for Judaism, the observance of the law. Here again the letter to the Romans is using an OT text (Hb 2:4) because its words nicely express Paul's thinking. But once this text is placed in its original context in Habakkuk, its meaning is quite different from the meaning Paul sees in it. According to Habakkuk, observance of the law—motivated, admittedly, by fidelity to God—brings life to the upright; in Paul's thought, it is the life of faith, which for him is the opposite of observance of the law, that will be the source of life for the righteous. Once again Paul is adapting a citation from the OT to fit in with his own thinking.

b. Rom 10:5–10. The fundamental Pauline theme that we have just examined in Rom 1:17 appears again at the heart of Romans: righteousness and then salvation are given to everyone who believes (Rom 10:4b, 9).

In the *first stage* of his argument Paul wants to show that observance of the Mosaic Law could not lead to salvation. For this purpose he cites Leviticus: "The person who does these things [what is prescribed in the law] will live by them" (Rom 10:5/Lv 18:5). According to Paul's way of thinking, however, in saying this, Moses was in fact condemning the law as a way of life or salvation, because "through the law comes [only] the knowledge of sin" (Rom 3:20); the law does not give the strength to overcome sin. Human beings cannot fulfill the law completely.

If we go back to the context of Lv 18:5, we will readily see that Paul is reinterpreting the text by giving it a drift contrary to that which Moses gave it. For when Moses taught that "the person who does these things will live by them" (Rom 10:5/Lv 18:5), he was placing the emphasis on the gift of life. In his mind, the law was the source of life or salvation for those who observed it. Paul, however, places the emphasis rather on the observance (the *poiein,* or "doing") of the Mosaic law. But no one can observe the *entire* law (Gal 3:10), since "through the law comes [only] the knowledge of sin" (Rom 3:20). Consequently, no one will be saved by the law; rather, the law puts a curse on those who do not fulfill the *entire* law (Gal 3:10/Dt 27:26). In Rom 10:5, therefore, Paul has entirely changed the thought that Moses intended to express in Lv 18:5.

In the *second stage* of the demonstration undertaken in Rom 10:5, Paul tries to show that human beings are saved by faith (Rom 10:4) and that it is even *easy* to obtain salvation through faith. The apostle again offers a citation from the Pentateuch in support of his thinking: "The word is near you, on your lips and in your heart," so that one need only confess it to be saved (Rom 10:8/Dt 30:14).

But the citation from Deuteronomy (30:14) that Paul is here using has for its purpose in the OT to show how the *law* of Moses makes salvation easy. And in fact, in the religious setting in which Israel was living in the time of Moses, the Mosaic Law did at last make God's will known; it gave the people of Yahweh a wisdom and an exceptional understanding that made

salvation accessible (Dt 4:6). Thenceforth Israel would know clearly what the God whom it served wanted of it. But the proclamation of the gospel and, above all, the gift of the Spirit would change the situation: Christ would be "the end of the law" (Rom 10:4). The law would then become an obstacle to salvation (Rom 9:32–33), a "stumbling block."

It is clear, then, that in Rom 10:5, 8–9, Paul is turning against the law two texts (Lv 18:5; Dt 30:14) that in the thinking of Moses were meant to glorify the regime of the law as an easily traveled way of salvation.

6. Paul's Method

Is it possible, in the light of these passages in Romans that cite the OT, to determine Paul's method in using the OT?

I think it useful to call attention right off to Rom 2:24, which is especially enlightening in this regard. In this verse Paul is trying to make Jews aware of their sinful condition. He shows them one important consequence of this condition: "The name of God is blasphemed among the nations because of you" (Rom 2:24/Is 52:5 LXX). If we look at the context of this verse of Isaiah in the LXX, we see, on the one hand, an Israel reduced to a state of captivity and, on the other, pagans who scorn the God of these captives as powerless (Ez 36:20). According to Isaiah (52:5 LXX), then, Yahweh is blasphemed by the pagans because he has not been able to prevent the captivity of his people. It is the situation of the conquered people, and not their reprehensible moral conduct, that is responsible for the fact that "the name of God is blasphemed among the Gentiles because of [Israel]." But in Rom 2:24 it is the immoral behavior of the Jews (Rom 2:21–23) that scandalizes the pagan nations and causes them to "blaspheme the name of Yahweh."

Thus the text has different contexts in Isaiah and in Paul, and these give it quite different meanings. This fact does not seem to concern Paul. He seems to think it enough that the words of the citation, taken in themselves without regard for their original context, should give clear expression to his own thinking.

Conclusion

This examination of the OT citations found in the letter to the Romans is not sufficient to bring to light the whole of the influence that the OT may have had on Paul as he was writing this letter. The sixty-two citations from the OT do, however, reveal that on a good many particular points Paul had recourse to the Scriptures of the former covenant. For this reason they merit detailed study. They teach us, in fact, several things about Paul's relationship with the OT. We have learned, first of all, that the great majority of the citations in question are taken from four books (Is, Ps, Gn, Dt). It has become clear that the main function of the citations from the OT is not to provide a starting point for Paul's thinking; rather, they play a role in a personal synthesis that Paul has already achieved. This role is to provide new formulations of his thought on a particular point. The citations lend Paul's thinking the added prestige of the word of God; Paul is quite anxious to show that his teaching, revolutionary though it seems to be, is in agreement with the traditional Scriptures of Israel. I have noted the main themes in Romans that are supported by citations from the OT, namely, the person and activities of God and Christ, the lot of Israel, the moral life, and, finally, the central theme of the letter: salvation obtained through faith. Paul shows himself to be an author who is rather faithful in citing the letter of the OT as found in the Septuagint. He does, however, quite often make stylistic changes of minor importance. Again, he shortens the passage he is citing in order to call the attention of his readers to the points specific to his own thinking. I have drawn the reader's attention especially to the important point that Paul shows a surprising freedom in reinterpreting the OT passages that he cites. He interprets them without (it seems) taking into account the OT contexts from which he takes them and gives them a new setting in his letter. This procedure is rather surprising.

Readers may remember C. H. Dodd's contention is his remarkable book *According to the Scriptures: The Substructure of New Testament Theology* (London, 1952) that the evangelists and other spiritual masters of the early church ("Christian evangelists and teachers") had a whole context in mind when they cited an expression or verse from the OT: "Particular verses or sentences were quoted from [these large sections of the OT] rather as pointers to the whole context than as constituting testimonies in and

for themselves" (126). This thesis of Dodd does not seem applicable to Romans. Paul does not refer there to large sections or even to the immediate context of the texts he cites. He simply cites verses, or parts of verses, from the OT that seem to give clear expression to his personal views. The citations are reinterpreted to reflect views that the apostle has just expressed in his own words; they do not refer back to an OT context that Paul supposedly respects and that would supposedly explain his own thought. His citations have their value in and for themselves; i.e., the words as such of the citations have the merit first and foremost of giving clear expression to Paul's ideas. The OT context is, as it were, forgotten; a new context—that of the developing Christian tradition—often gives a new meaning to the OT passage. Paul's way of thus using the OT doubtlesss sheds some light on the way in which Jewish circles of his day, and especially the Pharisees, used the Scriptures.

Bibl.: E. E. ELLIS, *Paul's Use of the Old Testament* (Edinburgh, 1957); B. LINDARS, *New Testament Apologetic: The Doctrinal Significance of Old Testament Quotations* (London, 1961); D. A. KOCH, *Die Schrift als Zeuge des Evangeliums: Untersuchungen zur Verwendung und zum Verständnis der Schrift bei Paulus* (Tübingen, 1986).

Paul-Émile LANGEVIN

TESTIMONY

I. FORM OF REVELATION. *1. Testimony in a Secular Context. 2. Testimony as Way of Access to the Mystery of Persons. 3. Testimony in the Bible. 4. The Apostolic Testimony. 5. The Theme of Testimony in John. 6. From Testimony as Revelation to Testimony as Motive of Credibility.* (R. LATOURELLE)

II. MOTIVE OF CREDIBILITY (Testimony as Commitment). *1. Testimony in Vatican II. 2. Testimony in the Apostolic Exhortation* Christifideles Laici *(1988). 3. Fruitfulness of Personal Testimony. 4. Communal Testimony. 5. Necessity of Testimony. 6. Dynamics of Testimony. 7. Specific Character of Contemporary Testimony. 8. The Eucharist, Privileged Moment of Testimony.* (R. LATOURELLE)

I. FORM OF REVELATION

Over the course of about a century now, the category of testimony has gradually entered the vocabulary of the church. The term made a modest appearance in Vatican I, where it described the church insofar as the latter is, by its existence and whole presence in the world, "a great and perpetual motive of credibility and an irrefutable *testimony* of her divine mission" (DS 3013; ND, no. 123). Vatican II saw a massive irruption of the language of testimony; the theme is everywhere present. Such words as "testimony," "testify," and "witness" occur over one hundred times and are applied both to the church as a whole and to each group of Christians. The theme was taken up again with a new emphasis at the Synod of 1974, this time in the context of evangelization. Finally, the category of testimony is at the heart of present-day fundamental theology.

1. Testimony in a Secular Context

"Testimony" belongs to a set of analogies that the Scriptures use to introduce human beings to the riches of the divine mystery; these analogies include the categories of covenant, word, fatherhood, and sonship. If, then, revelation itself relies on the human experience of testimony to express one of the fundamental relationships between human beings and God, theological reflection is certainly justified in exploring the elements of this experience. In this analytical enterprise, revelation is undoubtedly normative and tells theologians the kind of purification and sublimation that the human reality must undergo if it is to be applied to the divine mystery. If the human experience were completely unrelated to the mystery of the divine being, the encounter of God and human beings would be impossible; there would be a place only for parallel monologues.

In its weakest use, *testify* or *attest* means to tell what one has seen and heard. Witnesses are persons who can inform others about events in which they have had a part or about persons or facts that they know; they can give a verbal account of what they know because they have seen and heard. Testimony is thus based on an experience of seeing or hearing. The most common setting for this kind of testimony is a trial. Even at this first level, belief in testimony requires a certain abdication of reason and a degree of trust, since the word of a witness becomes a substitute for experience for those who have not seen and heard.

In this judicial context testimony does not function simply as a source of information; rather, it is an account rendered in the interests of a judgment to be passed on events, on the motives of an action, on the character of a person. Testimony is meant to influence juries and judges, who rely on it as a proof while they think, evaluate, and decide. That is why the story told by a witness has more than a simple intellectual value (observation and description, information and report); it also has a moral value, being a deposition that derives a special weight from being given under oath. To testify in a trial is to take a position and declare onself for or against someone. Witnesses no longer simply tell a story or give a description, after the fashion of a journalist; they freely involve themselves and pass a value judgment.

This brings us to the second level of testimony, where witnesses fully involve themselves through their word, where they commit themselves in what they say. Thus, in giving testimony where someone's life is at stake, witnesses not only express their sincere conviction about the innocence or guilt of the accused; they also commit themselves wholly in their deposition. Their word implicates them personally. They are saying, equivalently: "I declare this person innocent; were I to deny their innocence, I would be denying myself." Existence and speech are coextensive here.

Occasionally—and this is the third level of testimony—witnesses will seal their commitment to the cause they are defending by making a public profession of their interior conviction, even to the point of sacrificing their lives. Most of the time, such a confession is uttered in a context of hostility and hatred from those who do not follow the same cause. When witnesses thus die in support of their testimony, they become *martyrs*, i.e., "witnesses." This kind of commitment that endangers life itself reflects back on the verbal testimony, which then ceases to be a mere narrative of things seen or heard and becomes an action and a tragic death. As a result, the word "testimony" has gradually come to be applied to the action of risking one's life, because this gift of life itself is the living evidence of the witnesses' interior conviction and dedication to the cause they are defending. At this point there is a semantic shift from testimony as word to testimony as action. It is the latter that gives meaning and value to the former. The fixed point of reference for this change of meaning is the *commitment* of the witnesses to their testimony. Here we find ourselves in the biblical context of testimony, for in the Bible the testimony of Christ, the supreme witness, is one in which speaking and acting are coextensive and in which his very being shines through.

2. Testimony as Way of Access to the Mystery of Persons

When witnesses fully commit themselves through word or action, they express themselves to the full extent of their existential freedom. At this point, testimony acquires an exceptional depth and dignity, since it has for its object the innermost mystery of personal being. At this level, more than in a trial, witnesses are identified with what they say. They intend to be present to their hearers and to make themselves transparent to them in the truth of their interior mystery. They may be mistaken and have illusions about themselves, yet their testimony is irrefutable because of the purpose that sustains it. Nothing can prevail against it.

When we leave behind the world of material things and move on to the level of persons, we are also leaving the world of evidence and entering the world of testimony. At this level, the scientific ideal—which in any case holds sway in only one of the central areas of human thought—is no longer valid.

At the level of intersubjectivity, which is the level of persons, we run up against mystery. Persons are not problems that can be packaged in formulas and reduced to equations. We have access to the inner life of persons only through their freely given testimony about themselves, through confidences that are in the strict sense revelations or unveilings of their inner mystery. The claim has been made that testimony yields an inferior kind of knowledge because it gives only probability and not certitude and because the standards of a particular scientific ideal do not apply to it. The claim shows a regrettable ignorance of the real issue. Knowledge through testimony is inferior only in cases in which, due to the nature of the object, we are able to obtain a direct, unmediated knowledge of the reality; it is not inferior, however, when we are dealing with the realities we call persons, for

here testimony is the only way of achieving union with them and sharing in their mystery.

Testimony is part of the mystery of freedom. Because this freedom is human, it is doubtless frail and always threatened. God alone can supply an absolute guarantee for his word, because he is eternally and absolutely identical with himself. In fact human experience tells us of the many kinds of involuntary errors that can be made, even by the most authentic persons. Nonetheless, despite this risk, testimony is a mark of the greatness and dignity of human beings, for it is a way of sharing in the autonomy and freedom of God himself.

In testimony, then, there is an element of solitude of which the witnesses cannot rid themselves and which makes them vulnerable, exposed to rejection. Even in the case of Jesus, whose experience of his identity as Son of the Father gives his word an unqualified certitude and value, his testimony was not guaranteed the reception it deserved, even though it was sealed with his blood.

The reason for this is that testimony, which has its ground in the core of human freedom, calls upon the freedom of those who receive it. Demonstration makes its appeal first and foremost to the understanding, but testimony also involves the will and love, in varying degrees. It calls for trust—a more or less profound trust that is measured by the importance of the object attested and of the values that testimony and its acceptance involves. When persons have recourse to testimony as their means of expression, they are already appealing for trust and committing themselves to telling the truth. They are committing themselves not to betray this trust and promising, at least implicitly, to be sincere and truthful. When we accept the testimony of others as true, we are already trusting them, for we are passing from autonomy to heteronomy; we are renouncing ourselves and putting ourselves in the hands of others. The very possibility of social intercourse among human beings depends in the final analysis on this trust that witnesses call for and on their tacit promise not to betray it. On the one side, then, we have the moral commitment of the witness and, on the other, the trust, which is already the germ of love, of those who accept the testimony. From the viewpoint, then, of both the hearer and the witness, testimony is something of the moral order and not simply of the intellectual.

In the extreme case in which persons risk their whole lives on the word of a witness, they show a trust, a total faith, that represents a profound love of the witness. In this respect, faith in Christ is a total self-giving of the person to Christ, a decision that commits the whole of one's personal and human existence. The whole person surrenders here to testimony that is absolute in character.

Consequently, we should not find it surprising that Christianity is a religion of testimony and faith. For revelation is essentially a manifestation of the personal mystery of God, who is supreme interiority. Christianity is a religion of testimony precisely because it is a manifestation of the mystery of the divine persons. That which Christ reveals is, when all is said and done, the personal mystery that he is as Son of the Father, incarnated in the flesh and language of the man Jesus. The apostles in turn bear witness to their close relationship with Christ, the Word of Life and Son of the Father, and with the Father and the Spirit; in their case, however, the relationship is marked by so privileged a communication that it cannot be shared. The entire gospel is a love-inspired sharing of a secret, a testimony of Christ to himself, to the life of the divine persons, and to the mystery of our condition as children of God.

3. Testimony in the Bible

It can be said, in very broad terms, that testimony as found in the Bible takes over the chasracteristics of human testimony, but at the same time heightens to the point of sublimating them. Under the pressure of the new reality that fills and energizes testimony in the Bible, there is an irruption of MEANING that affects the testimony in its height and depth and breadth.

In the OT, the chief kind of witness is the *prophet*. The originality of the prophets consists in the fact that they undergo a privileged experience and are chosen and sent by God. They know Yahweh because Yahweh speaks to them and entrusts his message to them. They are admitted to a special intimacy with God and called to share his knowledge, plans, and will so that they may be heralds of these among their fellow human beings. Prophets receive the word of God, not to keep it to themselves, but to pass it on, to make it known. They are the mouth of Yahweh, servants of the word, authorized interpreters of everything that happens in the world among human beings and in history, witnesses to Yahweh, often in a climate of hostility and persecution.

The *Israelite people* are also witnesses, chosen and called by Yahweh. Second Isaiah sums up in a single passage all the traits that characterize Israel as witnesses: "Bring forth the people who are blind, yet have eyes, who are deaf, yet have ears! Let all the nations gather together, and let the peoples assemble. Who among them has declared this, and foretold to us the former things? Let them bring their witnesses to justify them, and let them hear and say, 'It is true.' You are my witnesses, says the LORD, and my servant whom I have chosen, so that you may know and believe me and understand that I am he. Before me no god was formed, nor shall there be any after me. I, I am the LORD, and besides me there is no savior. I declared and saved and proclaimed, when there was no strange god among you; and you are my witnesses, says the LORD. I am God, and also henceforth I am He; there is no one who can deliver from my hand; I work and who can hinder it?" (Is 43:8–13).

Four characteristics set this witnessing people apart: First, the witnesses are not just any who come forth to offer testimony, but those who have been chosen and sent to testify. Second, the testimony has to do with the radical meaning of human experience; Yahweh bears witness to himself and presents himself as the one who gives meaning and coherence to all of human reality. Third, the testimony is meant to be proclaimed and broadcasted. Finally, this proclamation implies a commitment, not only in word, but in actions and way of life.

Thus the main aspects of testimony in its secular sense are retained, but the OT also introduces something new: the authority of the witnesses comes not from themselves but from their special calling and sending. It is possible to distinguish, in the mission of prophet-witnesses, two main forms, as it were, of activity, forms that sometimes come one after the other but most often are simultaneous: the activity of proclamation and the activity of vital commitment.

4. The Apostolic Testimony

The NT uses the category of testimony not just from time to time but repeatedly and deliberately. The statistic on the occurrence of *martys* (witness) and its derivatives (nouns and verbs) is highly significant, for the word occurs 198 times.

"Testify" and "witness" are found chiefly in the vocabulary of Acts and in the theology of Luke. "Testifying" is a characteristic activity of the apostles in the period after the resurrection. The title "witness" is given first and foremost to the apostles. There are four traits that cause them to be so described. First, like the prophets, they have been chosen by God (Acts 1:26; 10:41). Second, they have seen and heard Christ (Acts 4:20); they have lived in a close relationship with him (Acts 1:21-22) and therefore have a living, direct experience of Jesus the person and of his teaching and actions. They have eaten and drunk with him both before and after his resurrection (Acts 10:41). In short, they have been the close associates and table companions of Christ. Others may preach, but only the apostles can, in the strict sense, bear witness. Third, Christ has given them the mission of testifying to him (Acts 10:41), and in order that they may carry out their commission, they have been invested with the power of the Spirit (Acts 1:8). A final trait of the apostles as witnesses is commitment, an attitude that finds expression in an absolute fidelity to Christ and to his teaching, which is seen as the truth and as the salvation of humanity. Acts says over and over that the apostles proclaim the word of God with confidence (*parrēsia*), i.e., with a supernatural courage that is a fruit of the Spirit, who acts within them and overcomes their excessively human reactions to the difficulties of the apostolate, including timidity, human respect, fear of persecution, and death. Under the influence of this interior courage, the apostles declare: "We cannot keep from speaking about what we have seen and heard" (Acts 4:20). Their words are echoed by John: "What we have heard, what we have seen with our eyes, what we have looked at and touched with our hands, concerning the word of life . . . we . . . testify to it" (1 Jn 1:1-3).

Matthias had to fulfill these several conditions in order to take the place of Judas and become "a witness . . . to his resurrection." He had accompanied the apostles "during all the time that the Lord Jesus went in and out among us," i.e., from his baptism, which marked the beginning of his ministry, to his glorification as Christ and Lord (Acts 1:22; 2:36). There is thus no break in continuity between the earthly Jesus and the glorified Christ. The apostles are, as it were, the hinge joining the time of Jesus to the time of the church. It is also significant that at the beginning of Acts (1:13) Luke repeats the list of the apostles, thus showing that it is they who guarantee continuity between the pre-Easter and post-Easter communities. The name of Judas is not in this list, because he is henceforth replaced by Matthias, who has been appointed by God (Acts 1:26). The authority that witnesses have does not originate in them but in God, who sends or appoints them. Since Matthias has been called by God, has seen and heard Jesus, has a mind open to understand the Scriptures, and has been strengthened by the Spirit, he is qualified to transmit faithfully the knowledge of Jesus and to become a witness to his resurrection (Acts 1:21-26).

The testimony given refers both to what has been seen and heard and to the meaning of the events that have occurred. It is at once narrative and confession.

Inasmuch as the apostles have lived in a close relationship with Jesus, they are eyewitnesses and earwitnesses to his entire career from his baptism to his resurrection (Acts 4:20). Thus Peter says: "We are witnesses to all that he did both in Judea [or: in the country of the Jews=Galilee] and in Jerusalem" (Acts 10:39). But they are, first and foremost, witnesses to the resurrection, for this is the key event that gives authority to all that went before and all that will follow. This Jesus whom the Jews crucified has been raised up (Acts 5:31) and has appeared (Acts 10:40), "and we are witnesses to these things" (Acts 5:32)—an expression that recurs like a leitmotiv in the first part of Acts.

But the testimony is not concerned solely with the empirical, perceptible reality of the words and actions of Jesus. The apostles testify, above all, to the salvific significance of these facts. They are witnesses to the deeper meaning of his earthly life, namely, the salvation brought about by his death and resurrection (Acts 5:31; 10:42).

Acts 10:37-43 brings together in a single passage these two essential components of the apostolic testimony. Here Peter first recalls the events of the earthly life of Jesus: his ministry, miracles, crucifixion, death, resurrection, and appearances: His "message spread throughout Judea, beginning in Galilee after the baptism that John announced: how God anointed Jesus of Nazareth with the Holy Spirit and with power; how he went about doing good and healing all who were oppressed by the devil, for God was with him. We are witnesses to all that he did both in Judea and in Jerusalem. They put him to death by hanging him on a tree; but God raised him on the third day and allowed him to appear, not to all the people but to us who were chosen by God as witnesses, and who ate and drank with him after he rose from the dead" (Acts 10:37–41).

After this testimony to the earthly career of Jesus, the text continues with testimony that refers now to the interior, supernatural dimension of this historical reality. "He [Jesus] commanded us to preach to the people and to testify that he is the one ordained by God as judge of the living and the dead. All the prophets testify about him that everyone who believes in him receives forgiveness of sins through his name" (Acts 10:42–43). The vocabulary of this second part of the passage is still the vocabulary of testimony, but the reality attested eludes empirical observation, and yet it is part of the same object, for it expresses the deeper meaning, the inner nature, of that which eyes and ears have perceived. This Jesus of Nazareth, whom the apostles and the Jewish people saw and heard, is henceforth identified as Judge of the living and the dead. His death was not an ordinary death, like that of other human beings, for it saves us from sin and effects our salvation.

In the apostolic testimony described by Acts there is, then, an indissoluble union of historical event (horizontal dimension) and its religious and salvific meaning (vertical dimension). The same is true of Paul's kerygma. In Paul's eyes, the Jesus who was persecuted, crucified, put to death, raised up, and glorified is the Christ. Thus, far from denying or playing down the historical reality, the apostolic testimony reaffirms and confirms it, but in order to find its interior dimension that escapes the outward gaze. This testimony does not confer historicity on an event that never happened; it does bring to light the transcendent meaning of that which actually happened. Without Jesus (his deeds and his words), the testimony has no basis and collapses.

For the sake of completeness, a third element of the apostolic testimony must be mentioned. When the witnesses assert the *meaning* of the historical event, they are not offering an arbitrary interpretation but basing themselves on a real history: that of Jesus and that of the Jewish people. Thus when Peter declares the identity of Jesus on the day of Pentecost, he bases his interpretation on facts in the life of Jesus that justify such an interpretation, namely, his miracles, resurrection, and appearances. Peter makes this clear: "This Jesus, whom you crucified, God raised up, and of that all of us are witnesses" (Acts 2:36, 32). He says again: "Jesus of Nazareth, a man attested to you by God with deeds of power, wonders, and signs that God did through him among you, as you yourselves know. . . . God raised up" (Acts 2:22–24). The preaching of the resurrection itself is based on the appearances (Acts 10:40–41), and the latter in turn are asserted on the basis on intensely real experiences, such as eating, drinking (Acts 10:41; Lk 24:42), and touching (Jn 20:27). Peter's testimony to the *identity* of Jesus of Nazareth as Messiah and Lord is thus based on the historical reality of Jesus' life and deeds. The same concern is to be found in the Gospel of John (Jn 20:30–31). The apostolic testimony is thus related to history in two ways: because it proclaims the meaning of an event that it presupposes and reaffirms while interpreting it, and because the interpretation given is based on the real sayings and deeds of Jesus. Testimony involves not only a reference to Jesus but a deliberate reference to him. If Jesus did not in fact do what he did, then the apostolic testimony no longer has any value, and the gospel ceases to exist.

5. The Theme of Testimony in John

In John's writings, testimony reaches its greatest intensity as narrative, as confession, and as testimony interiorized. Christ is the great witness (Rv 1:5; 3:14); for Christ to "testify" amounts to manifesting or revealing the Father. "Testimony" describes Christ's revelatory activity, and it has for its object Christ himself in his personal mystery as the Son. Thus Christ bears witness by his entire being and throughout his entire existence. In his case, to testify is to reveal himself, to make himself known—to make known what he is and whence he comes, namely, from the Father. If this revelation reaches its climax on the cross, the reason is that the cross brings the supreme revelation of Christ, i.e., of the incomparable love of the Father for human beings, a love manifested in the incomparable love of Christ for those who belong to him.

In John's perspective, the testimony rendered by Christ has, to a greater extent even than the testimony of the prophets, a public and juridical character. His testimony is seen as a public deposition in the great trial in which the kingdom of God and the kingdom of Satan, Christ and the world, are the opposing parties. Testimony is given to Christ by John the Baptist, the Scriptures, John the apostle, and the Holy Spirit. But Christ's message meets with denial and hatred. When confronted with Christ, the Jews, who represent the whole world that is hostile to truth, reject his testimony and pass judgment on themselves. Christ's testimony thus brings about a division among human beings. But he continues his testimony to the end; he is the faithful and true witness (Rv 3:14).

Christ is thus witness in an unqualified sense: the witness who carries in himself the guarantee of his testimony. Yet human beings cannot accept, through faith, this testimony of the Absolute as manifested in the flesh and language of Jesus, unless they experience an interior attraction (Jn 6:44), which is a gift from the Father and a testimony of the Spirit (1 Jn 5:9–10). When this attraction operates, the testimony is interiorized almost completely, for it is said that those who believe in Christ *have in them* the testimony of God. The testimony that believers possess within them is the testimony that the Spirit renders to the Son. But while the testimony is interiorized, it never loses its connection with the word of Christ, who externalizes his own intimate dialogue with the Father. In like manner, John proclaims what he has seen and heard of the Word of life in order that others, through faith in his testimony, may enter into a sharing of life with the Father and the Son. Testimony as confession is never separated from testimony as narrative.

Biblical testimony is thus essentially religious. It is testimony about Someone: the God who saved (OT) or the God who gives salvation in Jesus Christ (NT). It is at the same time an outward proclamation of the good news of salvation and a commitment of the person (in word and deed) that may reach the point of the surrender of life itself in martyrdom. This element of *commitment* preserves a continuity between secular testimony and religious testimony. The outward testimony is matched by an interior testimony of the Spirit, who makes persons capable of opening themselves to the gospel and of assenting to it in faith. Without this interior testimony of the Spirit, the exterior testimony remains empty and barren. The NT idea of testimony does not yet explicitly include the testimony of blood, except in the Apocalypse, where the disciples of Christ are said to have won the victory "by the blood of the Lamb and by the testimony of their martyrdom, for they did not cling to life even in the face of death" (Rv 12:11). The transition to martyrdom is legitimate, however, since the truth attested in Christian testimony is the truth about death as redemptive. Martyr-witnesses testify to the victory of Christ's death and to his indestructible life. They testify to the absolute character of Christ, the supreme witness.

6. From Testimony as Revelation to Testimony as Motive of Credibility

What has been said about secular testimony and religious testimony makes it more understandable that revelation should be thought of as testimony. In the dealings of the three divine persons with human beings, there is an exchange of testimony that has for its purpose to offer revelation and nourish faith. There are three who reveal or give testimony, and the three are one. Christ testifies to the Father, while the Father and the Spirit testify to the Son. The apostles in turn testify to what they have seen and heard of the Word of life. Their testimony, however, is not the communication of an ideology or a scientific discovery or a new piece of technology but the proclamation of salvation that was promised and has at last become a reality.

In this perspective, testimony signifies above all the commitment of an authentically Christian life. This conformity of a human life to the gospel gives credibility and efficacy to the gospel. The salvation proclaimed has indeed become a reality, since the new self proclaimed by the gospel and given life by the Spirit is truly among us. Thanks to this testimony, others find themselves in the presence of the gospel as a reality enfleshed in the lives of flesh-and-blood persons. Truth and life echo each other and have become one. The gospel becomes transparently present. The message is embodied in the testimony, as the salvation foretold becomes salvation present. This agreement between the proclamation of salvation and the contemplation of salvation is itself a sign of the presence of God and the truth of the gospel. When testimony thus takes the form of a filial life style in which life comes from the Spirit, we shift from testimony as *revelation* to testimony as *motive of credibility*.

Bibl.: H. Strathmann, "μαρτυς," *TDNT* 4:474–508; B. Trépanier, "L'idée de témoin dans les écrits johanniques," *RUnOtt* 15 (1945): 27–63; C. Le Chevalier, *La confidence de la personne* (Paris, 1960); N. Brox, *Zeuge und Märtyrer* (Munich, 1961); E. Barbotin, *Le témoignage spirituel* (Paris, 1964); P.-H. Menoud, "Jésus et ses témoins," in *Église et théologie* (June 1969): 1–14; R. Latourelle, *Theology of Revelation* (New York, 1966), 52–59, 71–86; id., "Évangélisation et témoignage," in *Évangélisation*, Documenta missionalia 9 (Rome, 1975), 77–110; id., *Finding Jesus through the Gospels* (New York, 1979), 185–93; id., *Le témoignage chrétien* (Tournai/Montreal, 1971); P. Ricoeur, "L'herméneutique du témoignage," in E. Castelli, ed., *La testimonianza* (Rome, 1972), 38–84; S. Breton, "Philosophie du témoignage," ibid., 190–99; G. Geffré, "Le témoignage comme expérience de langage," ibid., 291–94; M. Nédoncelle, "Communication et interprétation du témoignage," ibid., 280–90; X. Tilliette, "Valeur et limite d'une philosophie du témoignage," ibid., 89–92.

René Latourelle

II. Motive of Credibility
(Testimony as Commitment)

The idea of commitment, which is inherent in that of testimony, establishes continuity between the two facets or aspects of testimony: testimony as *active*, when it refers to the revelation or intimate communication of God to human beings; and *passive*, when it refers to the attraction exerted by a life fully in accord with the gospel. When the lived gospel and the preached gospel correspond fully in a human life, this life becomes a motive of credibility, a sign of the truth of the gospel.

This kind of quiet, effective action, along with the word describing it, namely, "testimony," gradually won recognition in the preconciliar period, thanks to the various Catholic Action movements that taught that the laity should influence society not by trying to dominate it but by way of presence and inspiration from within. In a secularized world the church must be a community of energetic, active, responsible members who carry the gospel and the spirit of the gospel with them into their familial, professional, and social activities. Testimony works by infusing meaning and radiating life. The category of testimony has become so popular that it has even replaced "holiness" in contemporary parlance. Since the council, people prefer to say "a life of witness (testimony)" instead of "a life of holiness," when they are thinking of the attraction that someone's life has for those outside the church. This preference for the category of testimony can be clearly seen in the conciliar documents, as well as in the recent postsynodal document of John Paul II, *Christifideles Laici* (30 December 1988).

1. Testimony in Vatican II

This semantic shift is an expression of the profound change of perspective that occurred in the church between Vatican I and Vatican II. Vatican I offered the church (with its unity, holiness, worldwide development, stability, and fruitfulness) as a sign set up in the sight of the nations; Vatican II personalized and interiorized the sign that is the church, speaking rather of the testimony of Christians. Christians themselves by their holy lives, and Christian communities by the unity and love that characterize their life, constitute the sign that is the church. It is by living to the full their condition as children of the Father, redeemed by Christ and sanctified by the Spirit, that Christians bring home to others the fact that salvation is truly in our midst. That which Vatican I understood by the church as sign is now focused and concentrated in the category of testimony. Once this transposition has been seen, it becomes clear that the theme of testimony is one of the major and privileged themes of Vatican II. It recurs like a leitmotiv in all the constitutions and decrees of this council. In the view of the council, "to bear witness" or "to testify" means to confirm, by a life in accordance with the gospel, that the gospel is indeed true and the way to human salvation.

This testimony must take a form that is at once individual and communal. True, it is the entire *people of God* that must broadcast its living testimony by a fervent life of supernatural virtue. But "since the people of God lives in communities, especially in dioceses and parishes . . . [communities too] witness Christ before the nations" (*AG* 37). These general statements are then taken up and applied to each group of Christians.

Bishops and pastors must remember that "by their daily conduct and concern they are revealing the face of the Church to the world. Men will judge the power and truth of the Christian message thereby. By their lives and speech [may they] demonstrate that even now the Church, by her presence alone and by all the gifts which she possesses, is an unspent fountain of those virtues which the modern world most needs" (*GS* 43). *Priests* should "give living evidence of God to all men" (*LG* 41). They should remember that "by their daily life and interests they are showing the face of a truly priestly and pastoral ministry to the faithful and the unbeliever, to Catholics and non-Catholics, and that to all men they should bear witness about truth and life" (*LG* 28). With regard to *religious* the council says: "Let all religious therefore spread throughout the whole world the good news of Christ by the integrity of their faith, their love for God and neighbor, their devotion to the Cross, and their hope of future glory. Thus will their witness be seen by all, and our Father in heaven will be glorified" (*PC* 25). The *laity* are urged to give the same testimony of a holy life. Each of them "should stand before the world as a witness to the resurrection and life of the Lord Jesus and as a sign that God lives" (*LG* 38). *Teachers* in public schools are to "give witness to Christ, the unique Teacher, by their lives as well as by their teachings" (*GE* 8). In mission countries in particular, the unity and love characteristic of Christian life becomes an especially needed sign, for the entire church as presence and manifestation of Christ is concentrated in the persons of Christians. First and foremost, a *missionary* must "by a truly evangelical life, in much patience in long-suffering, in kindness, in unaffected love (cf. 2 Cor 6:4f.) . . . bear witness to his Lord, if need be, to the shedding if his blood" (*AG* 24). The laity share with missionaries the role of witness, since "wherever they live, all Christians are bound to show forth, by the example of their lives and by the witness of their speech, that new man which they put on at baptism and [the] power of the Holy Spirit" (*AG* 11). This general theme of witness or testimony is often further specified as to its object and orientation. The most frequent themes here are love, humility, service, unity, and poverty.

In the thinking of Vatican II the great sign that salvation has entered the world is undoubtedly a Christian life marked by unity and love, the testimony of a truly *committed* life, i.e., of human beings who live as God's children and as creatures made new, transformed, and enlivened by the Spirit. The new element in these statements is not the teaching itself, which is traditional, but the way in which the teaching is expressed, its vocabulary and emphases. In describing this holiness of life through which God gives us a sign that his kingdom has been established in Jesus Christ, the council allots a privileged place to certain expressions: the testimony or witness of a life, the living witnesses of Christ. This recourse to the category of *testimony as commitment* on the part of human beings, in response to *testimony as intimate communication* (i.e., revelation) on the part of God, shows that the council is concerned to speak a language that reflects the sensibilities and outlook of twentieth-century men and women. These men and women have been formed by personalist and existentialist thought and are repelled by a platonic, abstract holiness. If they are to be "touched" and to "surrender," it will only be due to the experience of a total dedication to God and to other human beings. But when we speak of holiness in terms of testimony, we suggest precisely this commitment of the whole person, body and soul, to the service of Christ and of those whom Christ has made his own, a commitment that accepts even the possibility of martyrdom. In the conciliar documents, martyrdom is regarded as "an exceptional gift and as the highest proof of love" (*LG* 42; see *PO* 13; *AG* 24; *UR* 4).

This sign—namely, testimony or witness—of the coming of salvation seems to be the one most attractive to our contemporaries. To persons jealous of their rights and autonomy, testimony comes marked by sobriety and unobtrusiveness; it draws without doing violence. To persons who measure all things by their effectiveness, testimony proposes actions, deeds; it says that the human condition can be changed because it has in fact been changed. To persons highly developed technologically but underdeveloped morally and showing a surprising psychological fragility, witnesses appear as healthy beings, people who are at peace with themselves and who radiate joy and peace despite suffering and death. A meeting with such people can rouse the desire to share in this kind of full life. I may add that in a pluralist and secularized society, the testimony of commitment is more needed than in the past. By their style of life more than by their words, Christians testify to the presence of salvation in the world. Their distinctive way of dealing with situations shared by all can inspire others to ask themselves: What is it that motivates these people?

2. Testimony in the Apostolic Exhortation _Christifideles Laici_ (1988)

The rise of the laity to prominence in the church is a movement that cannot be reversed. Laypersons are active in every area of life—not only in the areas of social work, charity, and pastoral work, but also at all levels of specifically religious education, from catechesis to research and university teaching. At the present time, hundreds of men and women are teaching theology in faculties throughout the world. In many countries they are clearly in the majority. This increased presence and influence of the laity in the church obviously brings with it an increased responsibility to give witness. It is this aspect that was stressed at the Synod of 1987 and in the exhortation _Christifideles Laici_ that followed in 1988.

"United to Christ, the 'great prophet' (Lk 7:16), and in the Spirit made 'witnesses' of the Risen Christ, the lay faithful are . . . called to let the newness and the power of the Gospel shine out everyday in their family and social life" (_CL_ 14). Immersed as they are in the world as their ordinary workplace, it is there that they

are to manifest Christ by "the testimony of a life of faith, hope, and charity" (_CL_ 15; _LG_ 31). They are urged to persevere in this witness even to the heights of holiness, since "the saint is the most striking witness to the dignity conferred on a disciple of Christ" (_CL_ 16). It can even be said that the renewal that the council looked for will depend in large part on the increased influence of the laity in the church and on the quality of their testimony. The part played by the laity is especially important in countries of the First World that are in urgent need of a second evangelization. "They must in a special way bear witness to the fact that the Christian faith constitutes the only fully valid response—consciously perceived and stated by all in varying degrees—to the problems and hopes which life presents to every person and every society" (_CL_ 34). The apostolic exhortation emphasizes that "the vital _synthesis_ which the lay faithful are able to effect between the gospel and the duties of everyday life will be the finest and most persuasive testimony that it is not fear but the following of Christ and attachment to his person that will determine how a person lives and grows" (_CL_ 34).

3. Fruitfulness of Personal Testimony

The facts confirm the claims of the council and the Synod on the Laity. To our contemporaries, the testimony of a committed life is the most decisive of all the signs that salvation has come in Jesus Christ. People deny, often bitterly, that God has the right to work miracles, i.e., the right to intervene in a universe that they regard as off-limits to him and reserved for the human species; they are more ready, however, to accept that God can act directly in the human heart to convert and transform it. If the words of John XXIII awakened such a profound echo in the hearts of human beings of every race and every confession, an echo that still persists, was it not because he spoke with the accents of authentic love, of the love of the Good Shepherd calling his flock? "Your duty is to cry the gospel from the housetops," said Charles de Foucauld, "not by your words but by your life." Yes, our contemporaries are looking less for preachers than for silent witnesses to the love of Christ, for men and women in whom the gospel exerts its power to attract. If such a meeting occurs, it can awaken the desire for salvation and make faith possible.

A few examples will suffice to illustrate the power of testimony to draw others. First, among converts. Conversion is almost always occasioned, or instigated, begun, or speeded up, by some initial shock. But according to converts themselves, this initial shock is most often produced by an encounter with a life of deep commitment in the spirit of radical adherence to the gospel. This was the case with Charles de Foucauld, Gabriel Marcel, G. K. Chesterton, Raïssa and Jacques Maritain, Ernest Psichari, Henri Ghéon, Thomas Merton, Edith Stein, and Karl Stern. Gabriel Marcel says: "Such meetings played a major role in my life. I met individuals in whom the reality of Christ was so vivid to me that I could no longer doubt it." And Daniel-Rops: "There is nothing more decisive than with your own eyes to see Christianity being lived and taking flesh." Sometimes the encounter with Christ occurs directly, in a mystical experience, such as A. Frossard had. In most instances, however, the decisive factor is an encounter, a coming face to face, with a life rooted in Christ. In this kind of encounter salvation becomes transparent. One does not infer salvation; one sees it being lived.

In the final analysis, it is not speeches that we must offer to others as they moan in distress but the precious gift of a life generously devoted to our fellow human beings. There is no other explanation for the powerful attraction exercised by such men and women as Father Maximilian Kolbe, who died at Auschwitz in 1941 when he sacrificed his life as a voluntary substitute for the father of a family who had been condemned to die of starvation; or Archbishop Oscar Romero, of El Salvador, who was assassinated in 1980 while celebrating Mass and thus became a martyr for his defense of the poor and the voiceless and for his protest against expulsions, persecutions, and tortures.

But we need not go back in time; we need only think of Mother Teresa. Muslims, Buddhists, believers, the indifferent, atheists—all bow down to the flame of love that she lights as she passes. All feel challenged by her, forced to ask questions, called to a revision of values and even to a complete conversion. Christ lives in her; in her he passes by, doing good. Speaking to the countries of the First World, she said: "The worst illness in today's world is neither leprosy nor tuberculosis, but the sense of being undesir-

able and abandoned by all; the greatest sin is the absence of love and charity, the terrible indifference to the neighbor who lies by the wayside, exposed to exploitation, corruption, destitution, and sickness. . . . Among you, the wealthy countries, there is a poverty of love, solitude, and immortality, and this is the worst illness in the world." Mother Teresa wants to lead the Western world out of the icy waters of selfishness and self-interest. She is neither sociologist nor economist nor politician. She does not go in for propaganda. In her eyes, love takes priority over "effectiveness"; immediate results are of little importance. It is love that radiates, illumines, warms, and gives without expecting a return. We sense in her a solid, intense love that is in communion with a light capable of dispelling the deepest darkness. As Christ was in his time, she is love present among us. She wants the last sight of even the most unfortunate of the dying to be of a gaze that envelops them with love. She is convinced that today's world needs love-filled hearts far more than it needs wheat-filled ships. Mother Teresa speaks to us of love through gestures inspired by love. Her life is not a proof but a showing forth of the love that dwells in her and energizes her. But by that very show of love she "proves" that the world is a livable place, provided that love succeeds in permeating it.

4. Communal Testimony

The testimony of an individual life conformed to the gospel is already a sign that salvation is present in the world. But how much more convincing is the sign if the testimony is given not only by individuals but by a group, or even a whole community, or even the whole church. Here the quality of the members of the community affects the quality of the community as such, as well as the _image_ of itself that the community conveys to the world. If this community lives by the gospel, it thereby asserts that it is controlled by the gospel, which it recognizes as the supreme value. When all or most of its members live by the gospel, the result is an image that is faithful to Christ and his Spirit. The testimony given by each of its members is nourished in turn by each testimony received. There is, as it were, a constant exchange from individual to community and from community to individual. A network of interpersonal relations, woven of justice, charity, peace, purity, gentleness, serenity, and mercy, is established among the members of the community. The communal testimony is an end result of this and is more than the mere sum or juxtaposition of individual testimonies. It constitutes a new and original reality.

The testimony given by the holy members of a community builds up a holy community that radiates the Spirit of Christ to all who draw near to it. Those coming in contact with this circle of people feel that they are breathing a livelier, more invigorating air. In contrast, when a community is divided, sin leads to sinful interpersonal relations. Everyday language is not mistaken when it speaks of sin having a body and face. The importance of this aspect of testimony, especially at the ecclesial level, may not be passed over in silence or played down. For, in the final analysis, it is the image that the church presents to the world that turns it into either an expressive, attractive sign or a negative sign of the salvation it preaches. Vatican II has impressed upon the Christian conscience the responsibility that the members of the church have for the formation of the image that the church presents to the world. The sign of the gospel can be obscured or even rendered void by the negative testimony of a scandalous Christianity. In its Decree on Missionary Activity the council says: "The division among Christians damages the most holy cause of preaching the gospel to every creature and blocks the way to the faith for many" (AG 6). And in the Decree on Ecumenism the council says that the division among Christians "provides a stumbling block to the world, and inflicts damage on the most holy cause of proclaiming the good news to every creature" (UR 1). Whenever the church no longer gives the witness of unity and love, but the witness of division and hatred, of factions, cliques, and exclusive groups, not only does it no longer draw men and women but it even turns them away from itself and thus from Christ, for it is through the church that we know Christ, and it is also through it that we measure the real effectiveness of the gospel.

In contrast, experience shows the drawing power exerted by the testimony of human beings gathered together in unity and love. Think, for example, of the community of young people at Sant'Egidio in Rome, which, because of its fervent prayer and manifold services of charity, has become a gathering place for many unbelievers as well as believers; or of the monastic community at Taizé, which was founded in 1940 and has become a mecca of prayer for visitors of every religious confession. Think, too, of the worldwide influence of L'Arche, a Christian association to help handicapped people, which was begun by Jean Vanier in 1964 at Trosly-Breuil in France. Here the doors are open to the most defenseless of all human beings: those with mental defects, who are condemned to live and die without hope of recovery. The remarkable thing about the Arche is the complete, even heroic, commitment to the service of these handicapped people, together with a spirit of prayer that would rouse the envy of the even the most fervent monks. Young people, thirty years of age on the average, devote the best years of their lives to helping persons whose wretched state can shake the composure of even the most balanced individuals. The goal, at the Arche, is to establish loving homes in which people can "feel" something of the love of the Word of life. Men and women who have had their fill of theories find here something they have never experienced before, something that can crack hearts open and allow love to enter in.

Think, finally, of the explosive witness given by rural families in the Macambria region of northeastern Brazil. These poor people display an unparalleled power—the power of God himself—which compels the rich to examine their consciences and be converted. The oppressed people of Brazil have no weapon but their suffering; these might have stirred in them a murderous hatred, but they have chosen the way of forgiveness. They see forgiveness as creative and able to conquer injustice at its root, thus turning the unjust into the just, the oppressor into a friend and brother or sister. Forgiveness breaks down the walls that separate and restores fraternal love. Forgiveness is the seed of justice. Oppressors, converted by the witness of the oppressed when the latter forgive, acknowledge their sins and are saved, liberated, and healed by the persevering and faithful testimony of oppressed persons who never stop forgiving. These local communities that bear witness to Christ even in the depths of their wretchedness are to be found throughout the world: in India, Nigeria, Central

America, and South America. The testimony of their forgiveness is the seed of a looked-for love: the love of the oppressor for the oppressed. Such was the testimony of Christ to his enemies.

These examples are chosen at random, but they convey a message. They attest that the *testimony of commitment*, of a life given over to Christ, is the most effective motive of the credibility of revelation. Salvation does not come as the conclusion of a syllogism; it is something we see living and active before us.

5. Necessity of Testimony

For Christianity, the testimony of a life in complete accord with the gospel is not simply something to be desired or highly commendable; it is an unqualified requirement, a necessity inherent in the nature of Christianity. There are several reasons for this:

a. First of all, Christianity requires the testimony of a life because it is not simply a system of philosophical or scientific thought to be communicated by teaching that does not commit either instructor or listener; it is a message of salvation and is connected with an event that has changed the meaning of the human condition and is an existential challenge to all who accept it. The gospel tells us that in Jesus Christ the human race is saved, that we are children of God and share even now in the life of the divine persons. If, then, Christianity were unable to make visible this change in the human condition that the gospel proclaims, it would admit failure. It is not enough to claim that the saving event has taken place but cannot be apprehended, that holiness is given but, paradoxically, gives no outward sign of its presence in the behavior of those who have received the Spirit. No, holiness must exist and in fact does exist; it can be encountered if one seeks it with a humble and docile heart. It bears witness to its presence in fruits of "love, joy, peace, patience, kindness, generosity, faithfulness, gentleness, and self-control" (Gal 5:22). In like manner, the church cannot be satisfied to claim that it is holy and has received from Christ the means of sanctifying human beings, while being unable, however, actually to sanctify them. The more the church talks of holiness, the more it must produce witnesses of salvation. The more it tells the story of salvation in Jesus Christ, the more

it must be able tell of victories won by the grace of salvation over human sinfulness. That is precisely the deeper significance of beatifications and canonizations. The church would not be what it is if it did not produce saints, i.e., fruits of salvation.

b. Second, the accord between gospel and life is necessary because the heart of the Christian message is the revelation of the infinite love that God shows to human beings through the love of Jesus Christ. But how are human beings, still ignorant of Jesus Christ, to believe in his love for them unless they have before their eyes the spectacle of other human beings who have already been won over by this love and have dared to dedicate their lives to it? How are human beings to be led into love of a person except by a love that is contagious? When Christians lead a fully evangelical life, those who see it see a God who is loved and a God who loves them. The love of Christians becomes for them a revelation of God's love. The love of human beings for one another becomes a sacrament or sign of God's love, the visible expression of his love for human beings.

c. Finally, the accord between gospel and life is necessary, because the gospel reveals a new way of living, a new life-style. But since this life-style in which God wills to educate human beings is at the same time sublime and unparalleled, how could God teach it except by concrete example? That is why Christ, the Son of God, the Witness par excellence, not only reveals to human beings their condition as sons and daughters but also initiates them into this kind of life by himself living as Son in their midst and before their eyes. It is also why witnesses to Christ are needed, saints who perpetuate in the church this filial life that Christ revealed and lived and who show to each generation the new style of life that is Christian life lived to the full.

In miracles, nature alone is affected; here human beings themselves are changed. The testimony of commitment makes visible to us the transformation of humanity that is worked by the influx of grace in Jesus Christ.

6. Dynamics of Testimony

The point here is to show how the testimony given by a life acts on the mind and heart of others to show them that the salvation proclaimed in the gospel and attested by Christ, the apostles, and authentic Christians is truly among us.

The testimony of a life is characterized by an unobtrusiveness. Saints make no demands, set down no requirements; they are satisfied to express by everything in their lives the supernatural reality in which they are immersed. The saint, says Bergson, "has felt truth flowing into his soul from its fountainhead like an active force. He can no more help spreading it abroad than the sun can help diffusing its light. Only, it is not by mere words that he will spread it" (*The Two Sources of Morality and Religion*, trans. R. A. Audra, C. Brereton, and W. H. Carter [1935; reprint, New York: Doubleday Anchor Books], 233). Holiness acts without doing violence, e.g., Mother Teresa. Its attraction consists in its very unobtrusiveness. While holiness is seemingly the weakest of signs, it is perhaps the most effective because it acts at the level of persons and appeals to the moral experience of each individual.

Holiness acts, first of all, as a *value*; i.e., by exerting the drawing power, the seductiveness, of something *good*. It reveals to those who encounter it a quality of life the existence of which they would not have even suspected apart from it and in which they secretly desire to share. It manifests to others, through a human life like their own, an ideal whose drawing power is never completely unfelt in the depths of their hearts. It does not explain the value of Christianity by proving it or eulogizing it; rather, it shows this value as present and active in a life that it has transformed. "Why is it . . . that saints have their imitators?" Bergson asks. "They ask for nothing, and yet they receive. They have no need to exhort; their mere existence suffices" (34).

While the highest values are the ones that leave the most room for freedom (the necessity of a value being in inverse proportion to its higher position), it is also true that their power to draw is in direct proportion to their nobility. Thus the sign of an authentic Christian life arouses, in those not closed to it, a lively desire to share in its splendor. Holiness is a call, not a form of pressure; it offers human beings the promise, as it were, of the fulfillment and self-transcendence to which they aspire. Few people will, in fact, effectively answer this unobtrusive

call, for it is a call to a new manner of life, one that is to be attained only at the cost of hard sacrifices. No matter. Noiselessly, and almost without seeming to intend it, the testimony of a life awakens attention, exerts an attraction, and in an unforced way initiates a movement by which souls may rouse themselves from their inertia and set out on the journey to God. They are now faced with a question. Will they, now that they have encountered holiness, "prefer a life in accordance with the love that has now been revealed to them personally through the mediation of another and by which they have been attracted and as it were tempted, or will they choose a self-centered life? The choice remains entirely free. . . . In any case, human beings are here roused from their indifference and confronted with a decision they cannot avoid" (Yves de Montcheuil).

To the really attentive gaze, holiness reveals a harmony between gospel and life. Holiness gives substance to the gospel and brings the gospel down into life. The gospel says that Christ is the Son of God who has come into the world to make us children of the Father, persons called to live as God's children and to share in the glory of Christ. In the saints we see this new human being whom the gospel proclaims, a being completely permeated by love, living and acting under the control of the Spirit. The saints let us see in their persons the salvation proclaimed and made a reality by Christ. In them gospel and life echo each other and become one. The saints show, and thereby prove, the ability of the gospel to transform human life. This accord between the gospel proclaimed and the gospel lived is a sign of the truth of the gospel. Saints bear witness by their presence in the world that salvation has been truly achieved, since the new human being that draws its life from the Spirit of love is truly in our midst.

This accord between gospel and life is all the more striking a sign in that it is not just any commonly occurring accord, but one involving *self-transcendence*. There is transcendence in the ideal (i.e., the gospel), and transcendence in reality. The saints make their appearance within a world in which sin, division, selfishness, and jealousy reign. Though they are human beings like us, they rise above our level of meanness and mediocrity. They breathe a purer air that is wafted from another world. Here in the present world they transcend the concrete, habitual ways of human action. Everyone knows that human beings can be magnanimous, but the magnanimity of Peter Claver to the blacks, of Vincent de Paul to the poor, of Jean de Brébeuf to the Hurons, of Charles de Foucauld to the Tuaregs, and of Mother Teresa to the "offscourings" of humanity goes far beyond any ordinary measure and has a dizzying effect on the beholder.

I may add that this transcendence is not vertical and single, as the heroism of martyrdom can be, but multiform and paradoxical. The lives of the saints repeat, in miniature, as it were, the paradoxes of the life of Christ. While present to the world and all its wretchedness, the saints give the impression of returning from unknown islands and bringing back exotic products with them. Though they are wholly focused on God, they are also filled with tender love of human beings. Though their humility and simplicity are fathomless, they are often fearless and ardent in speaking of God and claiming his rights. They are utterly pure and filled with repentance, yet they are convinced that they are the greatest sinners. They combine the obedience of a child with the liveliest creativity and initiative.

It is understandable that persons seeing this transcendent harmony between gospel and life, this love so intense and full, so constant and fruitful, should feel the desire to share in the universe of values that the testimony of an authentic Christian life reveals to them. The sight of holiness disposes men and women to listen to the gospel, for the gospel is already displaying itself before their eyes. In the final analysis, the power of the testimony of a life is due to the fact that *it shows salvation at work in our world.* The sign here is the splendor of the transformation that salvation brings about. Human beings themselves are changed and given a new life by the Spirit of love. The world is waiting for saints to pass through it. If holiness and the saints are invisible or absent, human beings live in a mist and die of cold.

7. Specific Character of Contemporary Testimony

What conditions must be met if personal and communal testimony is to be, for the people of our day, a sign that salvation has come in Jesus Christ? If this testimony is to be effective, it must take on new and quite specific characteristics.

a. People today are more alert than formerly to see whether Christians show respect for the human values acknowledged in the secular world, e.g., professional competence, efficiency in work, concern and respect for truth, honesty and humility in scientific work, frankness and sincerity in human relationships, consistency between words and actions, respect for one's given word, respect for freedom of conscience, respect for the property of others, and a sense of public service. Our contemporaries respect those who are committed to their tasks and carry them out with conscientious fidelity. They pay homage to those who are able to share not only in the joys but also in the sufferings and anxieties of the people among whom they live, and who endeavor to improve the social institutions of their country. If Christians show no respect, or too little respect, for these values acknowledged by the secular world, their profession of Christian faith, no matter how open and zealous, is likely to awaken no echo.

b. In former times, when a homogeneous Christendom existed and when nations were entirely Catholic, love had to be shown only to other Catholics; missionaries alone accepted the responsibility for carrying the gospel beyond the visible boundaries of the church. The situation is quite different today. In an increasingly unified world, walls of separation no longer exist, all the spiritual families (Protestants, Jews, Muslims, Buddhists, Hindus, etc.) and all the forms of belief and unbelief rub shoulders, come in contact, and merge. It is at the heart of this new humanity (in which enclosed areas of Christendom no longer exist) that the members of the church must bear witness to the love of Christ. As Charles de Foucauld put it very beautifully, each Christian must become "a universal brother or sister." Along the same line, R. Schutz has written: "Give us existential proof that you believe in God, that you indeed find your security in him. Prove to us that you live the gospel in its original freshness, in a spirit of poverty, in solidarity with all and not only with your own confessional family."

c. However, if the testimony of love is to become more universal, more ecumenical, and more missionary than in the past, it must also be intensified among Catholics themselves. Both in its local communities and as a worldwide community, the church that lives in the midst of other communities must show itself to be an especially fervent communion in the Spirit. It must become increasingly messianic and divine, and, by radiating an ardent love, give the world an effective sign of God's love present among us. To quote R. Schutz once again: "If Catholics are to be in solidarity with all the baptized, they must first of all be in solidarity, *within their own church*, with all the spiritual families that lend vigor to Catholicism. At this time in history we look for Catholics who do not reject one another. If the several currents of thought that show up there were to prevent dialogue, this would be an unparalleled ordeal for ecumenism." From this point of view the schism of Archbishop Lefebvre and, no less so, the intolerant attitudes of those who recognize no doctrinal paradigms except their own mental schemata, which they take to be absolute, undoubtedly constitute the most serious negative testimony for the church of the present day. The testimony of Catholics must indeed be a testimony of membership in the church, but also the church must promote, among the groups within it, the dialogue that it so forcefully called for at Vatican II. 8.

8. The Eucharist, Privileged Moment of Testimony

The place par excellence for the unity in love that constitutes personal and communal testimony is the Eucharist as assembly and as sacrifice. For the eucharistic celebration gathers up all the phases of Christ's life and all the phases of the church's life.

First, the Eucharist gathers up all the phases of the presence of Christ, for it presupposes the presence of Christ among human beings in the time of his mortal life, and it reminds us of this through the reading of the gospel. Furthermore, through the real presence of Christ in this sacrament, in which he gives himself as food, it presents a synthesis of the personal and spiritual presence of the glorified Christ with Christ as the Word made flesh in history.

The Eucharist also gathers up all the phases of the church's life. It is a memorial meal, a memorial of Christ's passion and saving death

that gave birth to his church. In the present, it is a communion of all the faithful in the living, glorified Christ, and a communion of the faithful among themselves in love. Finally, as banquet of hope, it prefigures and anticipates the eschatological banquet at which all the elect will be gathered around the table of the Lord. The Eucharist already effects a gathering in the unity produced by love, but at the same time it calls for an extension of this unity to all human beings, since not only does the eucharistic celebration represent the real and present unity of the members of one body, but it also launches a unifying movement that seeks to gather other human beings into the mystical body of Christ. Through those to whom he gives life and whom he feeds, Christ acts to bring about the growth of his body. While, then, the church is at all times the sign of the communion of love that the Trinity seeks to establish between human beings, it must be said that this sign is concentrated, as it were, and acquires its most expressive form, in the eucharistic assembly.

The people of our day want to find in the church, in Christian communities, and in every Christian a reflection of Christ's love—that pure and unshadowed, ardent and faithful love by which he gave himself completely, even to the sacrifice of his life, for the salvation of all. If, thanks to the testimony of committed Christians, the people of our day can encounter this love of human beings for their own sake, a love with no slightest hint of rejection, they will have discovered a new world and will desire to share in this fullness, for they will have discovered that God is love.

Bibl.: Y. DE MONTCHEUIL, *Problèmes de vie spirituelle* (Paris, 1947); M. NÉDONCELLE and R. GIRAULT, *J'ai rencontré le Dieu vivant* (Paris, 1952); P. BLANCHARD, *Sainteté aujourd'hui* (Paris, 1953); F. LELOTTE, *Convertis du XXe siècle*, 4 vols. (Paris/Brussels, 1953); K. Rahner, "The Church of Saints," in *Theological Investigations*, vol. 3 (1956; London, 1967), 111–26; E. SCHILLEBEECKX, *Christ, Sacrament of the Encounter with God* (New York, 1963); E. BARBOTIN, *Le témoignage spirituel* (Paris, 1964); R. LATOURELLE, "La sainteté, signe de la Révélation," *Greg* 46 (1965): 35–65; G. MARTELET, *Sainteté de l'Église et vie religieuse* (Toulouse, 1968); R. LATOURELLE, "La testimianza della vita del Popolo di Dio," in *Laici sulle vie del Concilio* (Assisi, 1966), 377–94; R. SCHULTZ, *The Power of the Provisional* (London, 1969); A.

Frossard, *Dieu existe, je l'ai rencontré* (Paris, 1969); R. Latourelle, *Le témoignage chrétien* (Tournai/ Montreal, 1971); id., "The Witness of Life," in *Christ and the Church, Signs of Salvation* (New York, 1972), 285–319; id., "Évangélisation et témoignage," in *Évangélisation* (Rome, 1975), 77–110; C. Mesters, *La mission du peuple qui souffre* (Paris, 1984); N. Cotugno, "La testimonianza della vita del Popolo di Dio, segno di Rivelazione alla luce del Concilio Vaticano II," in R. Fisichella, ed., *Gesù Rivelatore* (Casale Monferrato, 1988), 227–40; R. Latourelle, "Absence and Presence of Fundamental Theology at Vatican II," in R. Latourelle, ed., *Vatican II: Assessment and Perspectives Twenty-five Years After* (Mahwah, N.J., 1989), 378–415.

René Latourelle

THEOLOGY

I. Definition (R. Fisichella). II. Epistemology (R. Fisichella). III. Ecclesiality and Freedom (M. Seckler). IV. Theology and Science (M. Seckler). V. Theology and Philosophy (R. Fisichella).

I. Definition

Theology's basis and center is the revelation of God in Jesus Christ. Its particular objective is the critical understanding of the content of the faith so that the lives of believers may be fully significant.

Over the course of history, the coordinates for an understanding of the concept of theology have not always been the same. Insofar as it is *historical* thought about the faith and its contents, theology has undergone a constant evolution in its efforts to define itself, which can be identified with the very history of Christian thought.

The Greek term *theologia/theologein* is of non-Christian origin; in its earliest examples, *theologia* is connected with myth. Homer and Hesiod are called *theologoi* because of their particular activity in composing and singing the myths. Aristotle, dividing theoretical philosophy into mathematics, physics, and theology, identifies the last with metaphysics as being the *philosophia perennis* (*Meta.* 6.1.1025). The Stoics, as Augustine recalls, were among the first to use the term with a religious connota-

tion, identifying it as "ratio quae de diis explicatur" (*PL* 41. 180).

Only gradually, both in the East and in the West, did the Christian use of the term become widespread. For Clement of Alexandria, *theologia* meant "knowledge of things divine"; for Origen, it indicated the true doctrine about God and about Jesus Christ as savior. Eusebius was the first, however, to give John the Evangelist the title of *theologos* because in his Gospel he had written an eminent doctrine of God.

From Eusebius onward, therefore, *theologia* indicates the true doctrine, i.e., the Christian one, as opposed to the false doctrine taught by the pagans. Dionysius subsequently made a distinction (remaining valid up to our own day) between a mystical, symbolic, hidden theology that unites us to God, and another, more manifest, more philosophical theology tending to rational demonstration.

One last consideration worthy of note, which derives from the Greek fathers, is that of identifying *theologia* with doctrine concerning the Trinity, to distinguish it from doctrine concerning the incarnation, which was to be called *economia*. The monastic period (e.g., Evagrius Ponticus and Maximus the Confessor), finally spoke of *theologia* as the peak of knowledge and fullness of the gnosis, since it was brought about under the guidance of the Spirit.

As regards the West, it was primarily Augustine who pressed the religious use of the term into everyday culture and language. The intellect's attempt to understand the faith is the contemplation of a believing spirit who, in love, yearns to achieve the whole of what is loved.

In a word, for patristic thought, *theology* means the effort to penetrate ever further into understanding of Scripture and the word of God. The terms *theologia, sacra pagina,* or *sacra doctrina* are hence used indiscriminately, a terminology happily remaining intact right down to the twelfth century.

A first sign of change can be found in Boethius, who publicized Aristotle's categories of the "sciences." Alcuin started the Carolingian reform with the division of the arts into trivium and quadrivium; dialectic as the method of investigation began making more and more headway. And thus we reach the formulation of the earliest *Sententiae*, taken from the collected writings of the fathers, and the use of *grammatica.*

A growth in quality certainly occurs with the Anselmian concept of theology. Seeking to strike a balance between the monastic approach, largely nourished by the notion of the self-sufficiency of faith, and the dialectical approach, which tended to make the demands of reason absolute, Anselm created the principle of the *Quaero intelligere ut credam sed credo ut intelligam*, "I try to understand in order to believe, but I believe in order to understand." Loving faith wishes to know more; *ratio* is founded on *fides*, but is nonetheless autonomous in its research.

Above all, Abelard is remembered as the first to have effected the transition from a *sacra pagina* to a *theologia* understood as *scientia*, since from now on it became *quaestio*. The resistance put up by Bernard served for little to keep *theologia* relegated to the world of "non quasi scrutans, sed admirans." Thomas could not but ratify the approach of the Master of the Sentences, regarding *theologia* as a form of rational knowledge of Christian teaching; that which faith accepts as a gift, *theologia* unfolds and explains in the light of human understanding by its own laws.

Remaining faithful to the monastic current, Bonaventura maintained the accent on the role and presence of grace; after him, Duns Scotus was the greatest representative of this position.

During the same period, William of Ockham encouraged the input of criticism and nominalism. The humanist Erasmus of Rotterdam emphasized criticism to such a degree as to substitute it hencefore for the medieval *quaestio*. Melchior Cano marks the period of the return of the *auctoritates* with the LOCI THEOLOGICI, and the Tridentine period culminated in speculations on theological knowledge. The eighteenth century stressed the importance of having systems and the organizing of theological knowledge into encyclopedias. Finally, the encyclopedia *Aeterni Patris* registered a further change with an attempted return to Thomist thought, interpreted, however, in the light of new philosophical principles.

From the historical point of view, a complete study (and one likely to become a classic of theological literature) is provided by Y. Congar's article "Theologie" in *DTC*. What still needs to be said, however, is that theological understanding relates and adapts itself from time to time to different historical periods. An important characteristic of theological knowledge is the *historicity* of religious thought, which both allows the question about the intelligibility of the mystery to be kept alive and finds an answer such as to be consistent with the various achievements of human knowledge.

The change of perspective recently caused by Vatican II has removed theology far from the controversialist-apologetic context characterizing the four preceding centuries. Now theology can dialogue amicably with other cultures and with the sciences, showing that, with respect to the totality of knowledge, each is complementary with the others and has a part to play in improving human life (see *GS* 53–62).

Theology now lacks any single philosophical scheme of reference, this having been replaced by any number of reference points in differing philosophical systems. Having acquired a more rounded and deeper hermeneutical grasp of the biblical datum, theology defines itself more satisfactorily today in terms of a plurality of theologies reflecting the various methodologies acquired.

New problems, however, need to be addressed, as theology takes stock of itself once more. For example, theology must address the epistemological status of recent scientific advances. In addition, theology needs to take public responsibility for knowledge about the faith and the overcoming of any conflict there may be between theological knowledge as such and regional or contextual theology. Finally, the relationship between magisterium and theology needs to be clarified. Theology must identify the activities that are appropriate to itself as the ecclesial understanding of a communally held faith and the freedom of the epistemic subject in its scientific research.

RINO FISICHELLA

II. EPISTEMOLOGY

Fundamental theology, viewed as theological epistemology, should initially have answers to at least three basic questions with regard to theological knowledge: the source of theology, the determination of its content, and its self-justification as critical knowledge of the faith.

1. The Source of Theology

Theology's point of departure as reflective awareness of the faith lies in what we may call a believer's conscious wonder in the act of asking the question, "Why do I believe?" With the category of conscious wonder, we aim above all at reaching a datum common to the whole history of critical thought, where wonder is at the beginning of any consciousness of self-existence. It is the wonder that wells up in us when we think and find ourselves to be thinking beings with our place in history, in the world, able to plan for ourselves and for the world. This wonder allows us to see ourselves as active forces in the world, able to return to ourselves after leaving ourselves in order to learn and evaluate the real (*reditio in se ipsum*).

In a word, wonder stands at the origin of the human quest and understanding. It allows us to recapture what has gone before us; it decides what we and what the future will be. Without wonder, we should be unable to acquire fresh knowledge.

This can also be seen to happen in theological knowledge at the moment when the believer becomes aware of the gratuitousness of being called to living fellowship with God. It is the wonder of discovering ourselves to be capable of an act that, humanly speaking, characterizes existence and that is understood as something that cannot be claimed as a right but only accepted as a gift. In a word, it is the awareness of being a mystery and of having an infinite share in the mystery.

This wonder is not the fruit of the emotions but is a particular activity of the epistemic subject. For when the question "Why do I believe?" is asked, we may say that it wells up within faith; simultaneously, however, it gives rise to theology as critical inquiry into knowledge of this same faith.

Thus we can see that the context in which the questioning begins is determined from the start by the already-believing being. For there is a fundamental act that precedes the believer's reflective knowledge, and this is what provokes the onset of wonder, namely, the act of grace by which God summons each of us to faith. Before we can stand before God and explicitly utter his name as the expression of a personal intellectual activity giving content to faith, we thus are already known to God and called by him in Christ to salvation (cf. 1 Jn 4:10).

Conscious wonder and certainty about the call to salvation therefore constitute the necessary context in which our faith can take shape as product of thought. The condition, then, for theology to come into its own, particularly as regards other sciences (→ THEOLOGY IV), must necessarily involve its own peculiar characteristic of *paradox*.

The first paradoxical datum to emerge in this context affects both theology's object and its epistemic subject. For faith, as the basic point within which thought is born, so determines the content of the quest that this is already understood and accepted as an established truth and not as one that has to be proved. The revealed content, which gives rise to theology, is already considered and believed by theology as truth not needing to be proved but only to be grasped by the intellect and made communicable.

The paradox grows more acute when we consider that the truth given is not the fruit of abstract speculation but is a historical personage who lived a physical life on earth. As truth, a historical subject can lay claim to be acknowledged by the whole human race, himself providing the motive power of truth for the understanding of all history. But above all it is a truth manifesting all its paradoxicality in taking the death of Jesus of Nazareth as the criterion for expressing the ultimate truth about God. Humanly speaking, death constitutes the point most impenetrable to human knowledge and the most difficult to accept, since in it the hardship of existence reaches its climax (*GS* 18). Instead, in death we encounter that which expresses God's total self-giving to the human race.

In Jesus of Nazareth, theology receives both the object of its inquiry and the truth about human beings and their destiny. Passion, death, and resurrection all constitute the pledge of salvation, which is given in anticipation of our eschatological fulfillment.

Lastly, in this context, theology understands that *means* will be supplied that go beyond the categories of human knowledge. They are given because they belong to the economy of revelation, which comprises (1) the constant presence of the Spirit to guide the church in its understanding of the meaning of the word until the time that the truth has been completely attained (Jn 16:13); (2) the charisms that enable different believers, in their responsibility for one another, to build up the entire community (1 Cor 12–14); (3) infallibility in interpreting the true faith (*LG* 25); and (4) the *sensus fidei* as heritage of the entire people of God for discerning the true tradition (*LG* 12, 35).

From this paradoxical situation three principles at least may be derived that, for a correct theological appreciation, cannot be overlooked.

a. Because faith actuates theology, faith itself shows theology why the faith needs to be understood. Hence the intelligibility of the revealed datum is not a principle extrinsic to revelation but within it, and thus the principle setting theology in action.

b. Every theological reflection, except what is in the NT (that being, by its nature, to be accepted as *norma normans* for any theology), is historical and relativized by its own object. Freedom of scientific research hence cannot be to the detriment of orthodoxy on the content of the faith. Rather, such research should look openly at orthodoxy and obediently accept it.

c. Faith will provide theology with the main ways for attaining its content. With Anselm, we may identify these as *delectatio,* or joy at discovering the object of our search and thankfulness for having received it; *adoratio,* by which we perceive and understand the end of our journey, which flows into the profession of "rationally understanding that God is incomprehensible."

2. The Content of Theology

The content of theology is the revelation of God in Jesus Christ—in other terms, the comprehensive mystery of the incarnation. Theology is the "concretization of the Logos" (E. Peterson), which involves the entirety of Christian dogma, beginning with the unfathomable mystery of God and ending with the mystery of human nature.

Revelation thus constitutes the *basis* and the *center* of theology; its content is peculiar to itself. Nonetheless, the first content that will have to be made intelligible by the theological process is precisely that of the categories just mentioned.

Basis is that which, at a theoretical and temporal level, is a state of potentiality to know. Theoretically speaking, to speak of revelation as the basis or foundation of theology entails taking into account the presence of a threefold element: that which is accounted as already founded, that which is being founded, and that which has not yet been founded but that will be (for this terminology, see R. L. Hart, *Unfinished Man and Imagination* [New York, 1968], 83–97).

For theology, revelation thus constitutes a dynamic reality; from an initial event a later movement develops, allowing a historical understanding of it, past and present, but without having to preclude the future. The understanding we have of the event must refer us to it as to its formal and causal principle, since we have no possibility of knowing the foundation except by the foundation itself.

In other words, to affirm that revelation constitutes the basis of theology is the equivalent of recovering the prereflective component that entails the acknowledgment of a completely and radically new content that revelation alone can give. There is therefore the presentation of a *novum* that is given and that, by virtue of its evident truth, imposes itself as something that we believers cannot give ourselves but can only receive by revelation.

The most adequate knowledge that can be had of this *novum* is given by faith, this being the form of knowledge appropriate and corresponding to what is to be known. The threefold structuralization of the foundation of theology invites theological research, since it accepts what is already founded, includes what is being founded by the ceaseless faith of the church, and prepares for what has not yet been founded by constantly reaching out toward the eschatological event.

In speaking of revelation as the *center* of theology, we refer more specifically to the system of inquiry that we adopt. This means that all theological knowledge must be structured around revelation. First of all it must show that the formal principle of the various disciplines is one and the same, but equally that the mystery of revelation, from a scientific point of view, is complementary to other lines of research. In order to arrive at an all-inclusive dimension, theology must develop along with all other such lines (see *OT* 16; *Sapientia christiana*)

3. Critical Knowledge of the Faith

A final element to be justified is the fact that theology constitutes critical knowledge of the faith; put in classical terms, we have the first relationship between reason and faith (→ REASON/FAITH). To ask ourselves about critical knowledge of the faith is itself a theological datum, since, within the faith, believers, as epistemic subjects, possess an awareness conferring certainty.

Such an awareness perceived in the common experience of human knowledge, for knowing is an experience originating within us, by which we discern our own reality as thinking beings. This first, basic knowing is certainty itself, for we all *know* we *know*; we have an immediate knowledge constituted by our own existence and by our encounter with the external world. In its movement toward the external, knowledge is impaired by doubt, bringing knowledge itself into question: "scio me nescire." Yet this "not knowing" is directed toward new acquisitions of a knowledge not formerly known. There is therefore a twofold movement: we express the wish to know because we know we do not know, but this corresponds to a first knowing on which the certainty of knowing is based.

The believer's existence is also included in this certainty about salvation, which allows each of us to think of ourselves as called by grace to living fellowship with God. The wonder of this fact, giving rise in us to the question, Why do I believe? corresponds to the first, positive question that simultaneously gives rise to the certainty of a primary experience of faith and the need to go forward, since we discover that the mystery is still open and not completely known. The question about the need for knowing thus confers a first and basic certainty on the believer, since, by asking, we make an affirmation, even though our questioning directs us toward ever wider meaning and ever wider knowledge.

Theology, however, constitutes *critical* knowledge, i.e., knowledge that analyzes the relationship between the content of personal knowledge and that of the new object known. Such knowledge is therefore critical, leading to the conclusion of a process by means of which we reach a judgment. But judging means having found conformity between the original certainty and the content of the object; hence there will be critical judgment only when the essence of the known object has been reached and not merely some personal representation of it.

FAITH constitutes the believer's full and free response to the revelation of God (*DV* 5); it corresponds to the gift of grace with a totally human act in which "mind and will," synonyms for the totality of the person, are fully engaged in an indissoluble union. The truth that is accepted by faith is the fruit of the believer's consciousness of knowing; with that same act of faith we indicate the mutual relationship that must occur, on the epistemological plane, between our knowing and the object to be known. Faith thus expresses the form of knowledge corresponding to the nature of the object known; to be known, in a word, this object requires the knowledge of faith.

As believers, therefore, we know by believing; by knowing, we believe. In a single act, that of faith, the form of knowledge that is expressed by believing is thus present in a fully human way. Knowing, in relation to the revelation of God, is not different from believing, since it is the sole expression that can correspond to the object to be known.

The truth thus presented, however, is not an abstraction but turns on the historicity of Jesus Christ (→ CHRISTOLOGY I) as ultimate and definitive truth assigned to the human race, so that we can discover the meaning of existence. Theology, as critical knowledge of the faith that already knows, and knows this content to be true, has to show (for the most part following the lines of scientific knowledge and development) that there is complete harmony between what faith presents as true and what we understand as such. In other words, the content of our knowledge as believers comes to us from revelation accepted by faith, which is itself—as John of the Cross says—a kind of knowledge. By theology, inasmuch as it is critical knowledge, this content is analyzed and known by way of its component elements; thus historicity, language, behavior, and proclamation of Jesus of Nazareth all must be related critically to what faith already knows as true, so that the harmony may be brought about between faith and reason that gives the act of faith its essential humanity.

Hence, that which faith accepts in its believing is not debarred to reason but is in itself open to and given to reason because this very act of believing is already a particular form of knowledge.

Only a distorted vision of rationality and faith would separate the two elements and see them as strangers one to the other. Faith is no surrogate of the will faced with reason's inability to go further; nor is critical reason the unique form of knowing for human knowledge. Only the recovery of the relationship (in the light of an autonomous, even though complementary, research) between philosophy and theology can effectively demonstrate the legitimacy of knowledge by faith and the need for a faith properly known.

Bibl.: M. D. CHENU, *La théologie comme science au XIIIe siècle* (Paris, 1945); K. RAHNER, "Theology in the New Testament," in *Theological Investigations*, vol. 1 (1954; London, 1961), 79–148; id., "The Concept of Mystery in Catholic Theology," in *Theological Investigations*, vol. 4 (1960; London, 1966), 36–76; id., "The Historicity of Theology," in *Theological Investigations*, vol. 9 (1967; London, 1972), 64–82; id., "The Second Vatican Council's Challenge to Theology," ibid., 3–27; id., *Foundations of Christian Faith* (New York, 1978); Y. CONGAR, "Théologie," *DTC* 15:341–502; id., *La foi et la théologie* (Tournai, 1962); A. KOLPING, *Einführung in die katholische Theologie* (Munich, 1960); E. SCHILLEBEECKX, *Revelation and Theology* (London/New York, 1967); G. SÖHNGEN, "La sapienza della teologia sulla via della scienza," in *MystSal*, vol. 2 (Brescia, 1968), 511–608; H. Urs VON BALTHASAR, *Einfaltungen* (Munich, 1969); id., "Der Ort der theologie" in *Verbum Caro* (Einsiedeln, 1960), 159–72; id., "Théologie et sainteté," in *Dieu vivant*, no. 12 (1948): 17–32; R. LATOURELLE, *Theology: Science of Salvation* (Staten Island, N.Y., 1969); G. SAUTER, ed., *Theologie als Wissenschaft* (Munich, 1971); W. KASPER, *Glaube und Geschichte* (Mainz, 1970); B. LONERGAN, *Method in Theology* (New York, 1972); Z. ALZEGHY and M. FLICK, *Come si fa la teologia* (Rome, 1974); M. GATZMEIER, *Theologie als Wissenschaft* (Stuttgart, 1974); A. GRABNER-HAIDER, ed., *Theorie der Theologie als Wissenschaft* (Munich, 1974); B. CASPER, *L'ermeneutica e la teologia* (Brescia, 1974); W. PANNENBERG, *Epistemologia e teologia* (Brescia, 1975); id., *Basic Questions in Theology* (Philadelphia, 1971); C. VAGAGGINI, "Teologia," *NDT*, 1597–1711; P. EICHER, *Theologie: Einführung in das Studium* (Munich, 1980); T. TSHIBANGU, *La théologie comme science au XXe siècle* (Kinshasa, 1980); W. KERN, ed., *Die Theologie und Lehramt* (Freiburg, 1982); var., *Initiation à la pratique de la théologie*, vol. 1 (Paris, 1982); C. COLOMBO, *Il compito della teologia* (Milan, 1983); A. LOUTH, *Discerning the Mystery* (Oxford, 1983); G. THILS, *Pour une théologie de structure planétaire* (Louvain, 1983); M. MICHEL, ed., *La théologie à l'épreuve de la vérité* (Paris, 1984); W. KERN AND F. J. NIEMANN, *Gnoseologia teologica* (Brescia, 1984); R. FISICHELLA, "Cos'è la teologia," in C. Rochetta, R. Fisichella, and G. Pozzo, *La teologia tra rivelazione e storia* (Bologna, 1985), 163–252; J. ALFARO, *Rivelazione, fede e teologia* (Brescia, 1986); B. FORTE, *La teologia come compagnia, memoria e profezia* (Rome, 1987); J. RATZINGER, *Principles of Catholic Theology* (San Francisco, 1987); M. SECKLER, *Teologia, Scienza, Chiesa* (Brescia, 1988).

Rino FISICHELLA

III. ECCLESIALITY AND FREEDOM

1. Theology as a Function of Religion

As distinct from the study of religion and the philosophy of religion, as autonomous rational disciplines, all theology (with the exception of "philosophical" theology, which, as a subbranch of philosophy, is subject to philosophical norms) can be regarded as a vital function of religion itself. Hence, Christian theology is a function of Christian religion, just as each of the other religions has, or can have, its functional theology. Implicit in the concept of theology, then, is internal relatedness to a specific religion in a way presupposing both affirmation and membership of that religion. If these are absent, then the activity is not, conceptually, theology, but "free" (i.e., positionally unattached) philosophy of religion or study of religion. The requirement for internal relatedness to some religion, with corresponding affirmation and membership of that religion, is an objective component of the concept of theology, and not just a moral claim on the attitude of the theologian. Therefore, what is definitive for the concept of theology is not the religiosity of the individual but the religion-specific internality of the discipline. This means that what takes place in theology is the self-reflection and self-articulation of the particular underlying religion, and that theological work stands under obligation to the contents, norms, regulations, and goals of its particular religion. Accordingly, Catholic theology is that vital function of the church through which its understanding of its faith and its mission in the world, in all their dimensions, are researched and brought to theoretical expression.

By nature, theology (*theo-logia*, as religious discourse about God, *sermo de Deo*) is not necessarily something "scientific"; however, Christian theology has traditionally understood and organized itself primarily as a scientific discipline (in relation to various conceptions of scientificality, yet retaining its own sphere of competence in the context of theory of the sciences). Still, it is not a science that proceeds on the basis of rational principles (*secundum rationem*), but one that proceeds on the basis of biblical-Christian revelation (*secundum revelationem*); it is thus a religious science. The Christian faith (and fundamentally, the word of God within Christian faith) serves as the foundation, object, and goal of its scientific work, the methods of which must conform to the rules of rational discourse if they are to have the character of a science. The concept of religious science (*scientia fidei*), as a term for Christian theology, does not pertain primarily to the relationship of Christian faith to the sciences and refers not to a kind of science influenced by religion but to the inherently original scientific, scientifically structured character of the self-reflection and self-articulation of Christian faith. In the concept of religious science itself, therefore, are concentrated the irreducible—but thoroughly productive—tensions between revelation and reason, faith and knowledge, religion and science (religious truth and scientific method), and thus also between ecclesiality and freedom of theological research, both of which are essential to theology, although in a quite precise sense.

2. The Ecclesiality of Theology

In everyday language, the word "ecclesiality," which is burdened with various negative connotations, can mean many things: in a negative sense, servility, bias, and conformity; in a positive one, responsible participation—in a spirit of solidarity, critical sympathy, and pure *sentire cum ecclesia*—in the life and mission of the church. The ecclesiality of Christians and theologians, which is certainly to be presupposed, must be clearly distinguished from the ecclesiality of theology. In the former, it is a matter of the dispositions of persons, but in the latter, of a characteristic feature of theological

science; or in the former, of mental attitudes, and in the latter, of structures. To be sure, the two belong together, but it would be a misunderstanding to reduce the ecclesiastic character of theology, as it bears on the theory of the sciences, to the attitudes of theologians, or, in cases of conflicting opinion, to make the latter the decisive criterion of the former.

In contrast to study of religion and philosophy of religion, as autonomous rational disciplines, religious-scientific theology is to be conceived fundamentally as a vital activity of the church itself. From the viewpoint of the theory of the sciences, then, "ecclesiality" is an internal determinant of the status and function of theology. Hence, it has rightly been characterized as the Christian faith's own conceptual and linguistic project. Again, from the viewpoint of theory of the sciences, the church is not an external authority for its theology but is its supporting subject. Here, what is meant is primarily an internal, reciprocally conditioning relationship, and only secondarily an external, supportive role in the institutional-legalistic sense.

If theology is to be understood as fundamentally a function of the church, then attention must next be given to the meaning of the term "church." In certain linguistic usages, "church" refers merely to the office of the church, or to the hierarchy, or to any confessionally oriented institution. This can lead to theology's being rightly characterized, verbally, as a function of the "church," while what is really meant is only a function or subfunction of the office of the church, so that the ecclesiality of theology would consist in nothing more than its being an instrumental discipline auxiliary to church office. This would not be an accurate definition of the ecclesiality of theology. Instead, the actually supporting subject of theology is the church in its comprehensive sense, as the NT people of God, which exists as a richly articulated, complex, living reality. As a result of schisms in the church, Christian theology is virtually harnessed, on the one side, to the universality of the one church as a religious potency with its ecumenical dimensions and, on the other, to the various individual confessions that compose its concrete support. Just as the inner predetermination of Christian theology is to be truly Christian, in the sense of according with the substantial content of

Christianity, so it is to be radically ecclesiastical (as a vital function of the NT people of God), and at the same time unavoidably confessional (in view of the actually existing religious denominations that alone can support an ecclesiastic theology). Given the concrete nature of the relation between the ecclesiastical and its constituent confessions, it follows that the ecclesiality of theology is something multidimensional.

From the viewpoint of theory of the sciences, having the attribute of ecclesiality does not fundamentally preclude being, or having the capacity to be, scientific. Every kind of science operates on the basis of prescientifically constituted assumptions conditioned by aspects of the life environment. The decisive criterion of being scientific is the presence of methodological rationality and clarity in the relevant structures of discourse. Through its attribute of ecclesiality, theology is certainly obligated, as regards its positions and criteria, to the doctrine of the church; but that does not, in principle, give grounds for suspicion that it is inherently susceptible to partisan or ideological manipulation. For its appropriate and ultimate criterion is neither faith nor the community of the faithful (as the "people of God" and an "institution") but the word of God. Regarding the concept of a Christian religious science, there is a quite essential theological distinction between the *word of God* and *faith*. The former is the criterion for the latter, and not vice versa, even if the former first comes to us through the latter. Hence, the appropriate and supreme criterion of truth for theology (*norma suprema*) is not faith and not the church but the word of God (see *DV* 10; 21–25; *LG* 25). For theology, the church's attestation of faith is not the supreme norm but only the one that is concretely given, and therefore immediately binding, i.e., the "proximate" norm (*norma proxima*). The principle of the absolute priority and superiority of the word of God is not thereby annulled, even if, in practice and as a rule, it must be assumed that, for theology, the word of God presents itself, objectively and also as a criterion, through the medium of the church's witness and establishes itself there with binding validity. For this reason, it cannot in principle be claimed that the ecclesiality of theology would justify theology's being accorded merely official status within a church autocratically revolving

around itself or exercising control over the word of God.

Theology is, then, definitely a function of the church, or of the religious life of the church, and has to adapt itself to this fact in every aspect of its work. From the viewpoint of theological doctrine of first principles, this means that it is the role of hierarchical doctrinal office to pass definitive judgment, in accordance with the criteria of Christian faith, on the work of theology, and that such measures cannot in principle be regarded as illegitimate interventions or encroachments by an extradisciplinary authority. Since theology has a constitutive predetermination to articulate the faith of the church through its discourse, it is also the concern of the church to pass judgment on the success of those efforts. Since the supreme criterion for theology, however, is not the doctrine of the church in any or all of its historical forms but the word of God, attention to prophetic tasks, the duty to engage in transcending criticism, and the possibilities of dissent are also not, a priori, illegitimate. The word of God is the supreme criterion for theology and the church; all are obligated to stand by that and to conform to that (see *LG* 25), whether it is convenient or inconvenient to do so.

The "ecclesiality of theology" is to be understood as meaning not only its inner constitutedness as an ecclesiastical religious science but also its organically functional and vitally practical anchoredness in the life and mission of the church. From this viewpoint, the predetermined purpose of theology is fundamentally to serve, through religio-scientific activity, the word of God in the framework of the mission of the church. Its tasks are theoretical as well as practical in kind: cognitive disclosure and communication of God's word as the redeeming, orientating, and beatifying truth; work on constructive design and execution of the activities of the church; critical reflection (formal and material) on religious forms of language and ways of speaking; justification and defense of the truth of faith; and scientifically disciplined self-examination of the church together with critical accompaniment of its ongoing life. In these ways, theology makes an independent and active contribution to the mission of the church.

Another aspect of the ecclesiality of theology is its institutional anchoring in, and legal integration into, the church. In the case of ecclesiastical colleges and institutions, that is clear from the start, since they are supported by the church and are directly subject to canon law. For theological faculties in state universities, there are joint, state-canonical regulations designed to guarantee the ecclesiality of the theology that is intended to discharge official functions of the church. Since these legal relationships are to be understood as a consequence or expression of the ecclesiality that was discussed above in relation to theory of the sciences and practical life, what is involved here is essentially not just an external association with the church.

3. The Freedom of Theology

The question of the freedom of theology can be answered only on the basis of the points made above. As was the case regarding the ecclesiality of theology, the problems underlying the question of its freedom have two different sides (if one ignores the aspects pertaining to persons): one relating to theory of the sciences, and one to practice of the sciences.

From the nature of theology as a discipline constituted on the basis of the concept of ecclesiality, it follows that those bindings and functions are essential to it in accordance with which it is constituted as an ecclesiastical religious science. To that extent, its freedom is subject to constitutive and understandable limits that are justifiable within the theory of the sciences, for if the assumptions and principles supporting it were to be dissolved, it would itself be dissolved, i.e., be transformed into the study of religion or something similar. In accordance with theology's scientific structure, it, or the individual theologian as such, can therefore not lay claim to theological freedom in the sense of free choice of a fundamental orientation, but only in the sense of freedom for scientifically autonomous self-development on the basis of the operative foundations of theology as determined in theory of the sciences. What is often seen as the core of the issue of theological freedom— namely, the "liberation" of theology from ecclesiastical "guardianship"—is therefore, in fundamental terms, no less self-contradictory than a Christian theology "liberated" from Christian faith would be. A conception of religious science

that regarded its ecclesiality, in principle, as a shackle or hindrance to the free development of theology would thus be a contradiction in terms. In taking that approach, one would pay for the independence gained by it with the loss of the identity that is proper to theology. At the same time, such a "theology" would forfeit the special weight that accrues, and must accrue, to it precisely through the fact that it influences the community supporting it not from the outside (like the rest of the sciences) but internally and from within.

In a world of free sciences, theology is the only science not considered, at least theoretically, to be absolutely free. This view is correct insofar as the axiomatic and ecclesiastical tie connoted by the notion of ecclesiality is explicitly contained among theology's constitutive principles. There are, however, socially anchored, axiomatic ties in other sciences as well, even if their presence is less explicit. From the viewpoint of theory of the sciences, this does not, in principle, pose a hindrance to scientificality, i.e., to an appropriately subordinate freedom of research and teaching.

Like Vatican II (*GS* 62; cf. *LG* 37), canon law (*Codex Iuris Canonici* can. 218) accords to theological science, or to those persons pursuing that science, a justified freedom (*iusta liberatas*) of research and expression of opinion on the basis of disciplinary competence. This right to freedom of scientific research and opinion presupposes the general freedom to express one's opinion that is outlined, as a human or Christian right, in *Codex Iuris Canonici* can. 212 § 3 (in connection with *LG* 38); it cannot, however—given the special tasks to be pursued by theology and the special conditions applying to it as a science—be limited to that. The discourse of religious science must be able to follow, independently (if not unconditionally) and unobstructedly, the methods and rationality essential to a science if it is not to degenerate into a mere caricature of science. Here, at the level of scientific practice, theology has been subjected, down through its history, to many (at times unnecessary) obstructions of its freedom to develop, including—and specifically —from the side of church authorities, rather than at the level of theory of the sciences (although there, too, distorting conceptions have gained currency). The problem of the freedom of theology appears in a one-sided way if it is seen only in terms of an (unjustified) freedom *from* any ties, and not with a view to the freedom *for* the justified material and methodological self-development that is vitally necessary to any science. In addition to freedom in the sense required for the development of science in general, freedom of "expression of opinion" is also necessary to the life of theology and the fulfillment of its ecclesiastical tasks.

The results of competent theological research are formulated as "scientific doctrine" (or accepted scholarly opinion). Such "doctrine" has a special status. This is not only because the religious doctrine of the church itself must come to expression in it (as accords with the purpose of theology and the vocation of the theologian, who, in accordance with a *mandatum* [*CIC* can. 812; 818], teaches in the name of the church), although not in a formally authentic way (which is why theological doctrine hovers midway between mere private expression of opinion and official church doctrine). It is also because "scientific" doctrine always consists of argumentationally founded insights of a specialist nature and, in a certain respect, gives expression to cognitive compulsions that the theologian is not free to alter. Religio-scientific "freedom of expression of opinion" therefore transcends the plane of the rights of personal freedom in many respects. Its particular contents are far removed from the sphere of discretionary personal freedom; yet its being allowed free play is as important for scientific progress in research and consensus-formation as for the general ecclesiastical function of theology. Only thus can theology carry out its admittedly not independent but still—as compared with the authoritative doctrinal office of the church—relatively autonomous and self-regulated task. Not infrequently, too, dissenting views based on religio-scientific grounds can be an important step toward deepened knowledge of truth in theology and the church and can provide a stimulus to developments at the level of doctrinal office.

It is problematic to what extent the duty of obedience that applies to all the faithful (though subject to different gradations in accordance with *CIC* cen. 750–54) also affects religious science in its internal self-development. The ties implied by the attribute of ecclesiality, which distinguishes the discipline within the theory of the sciences, naturally remain fixed

and can be insisted upon. Beyond that, the authority of the church can, even regarding subordinate questions of theological practice, effect arrangements aimed at strengthening "religious obedience." Internal limits to this are set by what has been said above, first, about the normative status of the word of God, and second, about the bearing of considerations relevant to being a science.

Bibl.: W. VON LOEWENICH, *Glaube, Kirche, Theologie: Freiheit und Bindung im Christsein* (Witten, 1958); P. BRUNNER, "Gebundenheit und Freiheit der theologischen Wissenschaft," in P. Brunner, *Pro Ecclesia: Gesammelte Aufsätze zur dogmatischen Theologie*, vol. 1 (Berlin, 1962), 13–22; H. J. POTTMEYER, *Der Glaube vor dem Anspruch der Wissenschaft* (Freiburg, 1968); H. KRINGS, *Freiheit als Chance: Kirche und Theologie unter dem Anspruch der Neuzeit* (Munich, 1972); M. GATZEMEIER, *Theologie als Wissenschaft*, 2 vols. (Bad Cannstatt, 1974); W. PANNENBERG, *Theology and the Philosophy of Science* (Philadelphia, 1976); R. SCHAEFFLER, *Glaubensreflexion und Wissenschaftslehre* (Freiburg, 1980); M. SECKLER, *Im Spannungsfeld von Wissenschaft und Kirche* (Freiburg, 1980); id., *Die schiefen Wände des Lehrhauses* (Freiburg, 1988); id., "Theologie als Glaubenswissenschaft," *HFT* 4:190–241; E. JUNGEL, "Die Freiheit der Theologie," in E. Jungel, *Entsprechungen* (Munich, 1980), 11–36; H. M. MULLER, "Bindung und Freiheit kirchlicher Lehre," *ZTK* 77 (1980): 479–501; K. RAHNER AND H. FRIES, *Theologie in Freiheit und Verantwortung* (Munich, 1981); J. SIMON, "Zum wissenschafts-philosophischen Ort der Theologie," *ZTK* 77 (1980): 435–52; W. KASPER, "Die Wissenschaftspraxis der Theologie," *HFT* 4:242–47; id., "Wissenschaftliche Freiheit und lehramtliche Bindung der katholischen Theologie," in *Essener Gespräche zum Thema Staat und Kirche*, vol. 16 (Münster, 1982), 12–44, 45–68; M. HECKEL, *Die theologischen Fakultäten im weltlichen Verfassungsstaat* (Tübingen, 1986); J. RATZINGER, "Theologie und Kirche," *IKZ/Communio* 15 (1986): 515–33; id., *Principles of Catholic Theology* (San Francisco, 1987); H. PREE, "Freie Meinungsäußerung: Recht und Pflicht des Christen," *Anzeiger für die Seelsorge* 98 (1989): 3–5, 35–36.

Max SECKLER

IV. THEOLOGY AND SCIENCE

The conflict between Christianity and the sciences has long strained and tainted the mutual relationship of the two contending parties. In retrospect, it is one of the constant and distressing features of the whole modern period. Today, it is often viewed as merely the result of misunderstandings and other human shortcomings and is regarded partly as senseless—because lacking any justifying basis in fact—and partly as already settled or at least completely resolvable in principle. To this end, analytical and classificatory models are developed with the aim of removing any basis for the conflict, either by way of positively harmonizing the two or through showing that they are actually unrelated because of the kind of function proper to each. The worsening crises over the legitimacy of science, on the one hand, and the resurgence of religion (especially of religious mentalities of an irrational cast), on the other, have produced a diffuse consciousness of crisis that serves to undermine thought about concordance at a time when it has hardly begun. In this changing situation, Christian faith is faced with the question of how it should define itself, and what attitude it should adopt, regarding its relationship to science and the sciences. If one seriously reflects on this question in the context of the present state of relevant study and discussion, it quickly becomes evident, in a truly pressing way, that significantly more is at stake here than the usual view of the matter would lead one to suspect. The following considerations are intended to outline the essential dimensions of the current state of the problem while, at the same time, introducing into the discussion some germane points from the perspective of Christian faith's understanding of itself.

1. A Relationship of Essential Positive Subordination

The question of the relationship of Christian faith to science is not merely the question of an external relation. Also, it does not bear merely upon the external relations of theology to the rest of the sciences. Prior to that, and more fundamentally, it is a matter of a determination of internal relationships. Definitive here is the fundamental option that Christianity had already taken _in statu nascendi_, and was required to take by the very nature of Christian faith. Clearly dominant within Christianity's understanding of itself is a stress on the uniqueness and independence of the religious

act of belief, or of Christian faith, and thus on its differentiating distinctness from knowledge and science; at the same time, however, Christianity implies, in its very essence, a fundamental affirmation of reason and a positive attitude, in principle, to the rational sciences. To be sure, this option has not gone unchallenged in the history of Christianity; yet it has, by and large, remained valid as the fundamental option. This position need not be regarded primarily as implying an attitude of unreserved openness toward the world; rather, it is an objective consequence of the Christian understanding of creation as well as of the essential nature of the reality of faith, which is itself logos-like and logos-affirming. This gives rise to a relationship of essential positive subordination, which goes beyond mere indifference or nonopposition. Precise comprehension and articulation of this correlation is difficult to achieve and leads to antinomies, but at least in Catholic theology (despite differing theoretical models) there is generally prevailing agreement at a fundamental level. Actual instances of conflict in the relationship between theology and science, such as occurred primarily in the modern era, were thus regarded as conditioned, in principle, by human shortcomings. To this, however, have been added some new aspects that seriously complicate matters in relation to the problem.

2. Fundamentally Relevant Historical Problem-Complexes

Historically, theology has twice been faced with the fundamental task of making decisions of general principle on the basis of the option called for by the Christian understanding of creation and faith. In both cases, it was a matter of developing an appropriate attitude toward a concept of science or a scientific movement that had made its appearance within the horizon of theology. At issue here were problem-complexes that arose historically, but whose content was simultaneously representative of those two problematic points that—in relation to the present question—theology sees itself confronted with on a fundamental and lasting basis. Regarding both of those problem-complexes, Catholic theology moved—and moves—in the direction of a fundamental (if not unconditional and trouble-free) affirmation of science.

Internal Relation to Science

The first of the two cases occurred when the concept of science that was developed in Greek philosophy appeared on the horizon of Christianity as something available for possible use in the practice of theology itself. This can be observed as early as the time of the church fathers—generally, in the widespread affirmation (starting with the APOLOGISTS of the early church) of the Greek logos even in the framework of Christian religious reflection, and particularly in the structuring of theology on the model of an *epistēmē* (e.g., ORIGEN). In the course of the medieval appropriation of Aristotle, there occurred a fundamental transformation—justified on the basis of religious theology as well as theory of science—of theology itself into a science, or its self-organization on the model of a science (in the sense of the Aristotelian concept of science). At the same time, this theology, as a science among sciences, gained acceptance into the universities (the homes of the sciences), thus placing itself under the regulations governing institutionally organized science and the rituals of academic research and teaching. From then on, through its internal "scientification," along with its social and institutional integration into the world of the sciences, theology participated directly—i.e., by virtue of its own proper scientific capacity and scientific structure—in the process of the development of science.

Here, the relationship of theology to science is of quite another kind than would be the case, for example, with a prescientific or consciously nonscientific theology. An authority external to the sciences could maintain only external (or "foreign") relations with science, whereas the structure of interrelations between the sciences tends to exhibit the features typical of internal relationships. Inasmuch as theology subordinates itself to the requirements for being scientific and is itself active as a science, it not only genuinely participates in the distinctive aspects of scientific consciousness and in the good or bad fortunes of science but also gains the qualifications for working in partnership with the other sciences.

This continues to apply even if theology, as a religious science, occupies a somewhat special position—deriving from its tie to the religion supporting it—within the world of science. As distinct from those religious sciences for which religions, as historical phenomena, represent the object of study, Christian theology is committed to the scientific self-reflection and self-articulation of Christian faith, and represents, in this respect, the performance of a vital function of the religion itself. This aspect is significant here insofar as it imparts a special character to the relation of the religion itself to science. Inasmuch, namely, as Christian theology is both a vital function of Christianity and a participant in the carrying out of science, a directness of mutual relationship is implied; or at least this is so from the viewpoint of Christianity, which no longer sees itself just as something (amicably, antagonistically, or indifferently) opposed to science but must now, through the medium of religio-scientific theology, number science among its own vital functions and modes of self-realization—along with all the tasks, opportunities, and risks that might follow from such broadening and appropriation (and such as are, in fact, characteristic of the more recent history of Christianity).

In summary, it can therefore be stated that the relationship of theology to science, which, as a result of the "scientification" of theology, has fundamentally taken on the character of an internal relation between sciences, now also appears as part of the larger problem of the relationship between religion and science, and in such a way that it, too, no longer has just the character of an external relation. This complex structure of relations explains not only modern Christianity's own vital interest in science and the sciences but also the high degree of painful entanglements of the church with modern science.

External Relation to Science

The second case in which Christianity and theology were confronted, both historically and in principle, with the task of developing an appropriate position regarding the sciences occurred as a result of the emancipation of the sciences that began at the start of the modern age, and especially with the development, on foundations established by Descartes and Bacon, of the exact and empirical (natural) sciences. This emancipatory and developmental history was characterized by severe and incessant conflicts that have long tainted the relationship of both the church and ecclesiastical theology to secular science.

The causes of this lay partly in simple opposition between conservative and innovative forces, partly in inadequately clarified ideas about the different types and areas of knowledge, partly in the philosophical premises and ideological interests that were consciously or unconsciously at play, but above all in conflicting views about the cogency of the kinds of cognitive content involved in the contest between religious and rational knowledge. On the theological side, a severe handicap was posed by mistaken conceptions (reinforced by the Protestant position on Scripture) about the nature and scope of the authority of Scripture or about cosmologically conditioned elements in the biblical texts that—seemingly parts of scriptural inspiration itself—provided occasion for becoming entangled in unsustainable claims. For theology, all this resulted in a true *historia calamitatum*, with an endless series of defeats and ultimate withdrawals, in succession, from the areas of cosmology, geology, evolutionary biology, history, anthropology, psychology, etc. Along with this, theology, cramped by its dual character as religious science, was not infrequently caught between battle lines or became a victim of opposing loyalties. Objectively, however, it would be a mistake to try to lay the blame for these conflicts on one side only. The situation was not in every instance as clear-cut as in the case of Galileo, which has become an all-too-simplistic paradigm.

The highly symbolic treatment of the case of Galileo in the recent history of the church (i.e., the rehabilitation of Galileo by John Paul II, on 10 November 1979, before the Papal Academy of Sciences and on the basis of Vatican II) can be rightly understood as a fundamentally important gesture of peace, but the burdens of history cannot so easily be dispatched from the world. Despite the existence of a largely conciliatory atmosphere, it is by no means possible, even today, to regard the feelings of estrangement and mistrust as having been overcome. In addition, it must be seen that the conflicts of the past were by no means based solely on misunderstandings and inappropriate attitudes but also resulted from a collision between completely divergent understandings of the world itself whether those are objectively compatible or incompatible has still, even today, not been clarified as satisfactorily as those attempting to achieve harmonizing mediation often wish one to believe.

3. Incompatible Radical Alternatives?

A peace between religion and theology, on the one hand, and religion and modern science, on the other, that is based solely on changes in psychological "atmosphere," or that leads, by way of a stratagem involving a distinction of areas of competence and a separation of respective functions, to a relationless—and to that extent conflict-free—coexistence of the two contending parties must be considered non-genuine as long as the main problem has received no conclusive theoretical resolution. That problem lies primarily in the question of how scientific and religious consciousness should be mutually reconcilable when both represent, objectively and in their very roots, conflicting total positions on the questions of knowing reality and coping with existence. Distinctions like that between explaining nature and interpreting existence, or between instrumental knowledge of practical control and theonomous wisdom of spiritual redemption, cannot do sufficient justice to the radicalness of the alternatives, even if they can definitely defuse certain problems of relatively minor importance. The distinction between a plane of means and a dimension of ends is also unproductive when what is at issue are mutually exclusive totalistic alternatives.

The interconnections involved here can be more clearly grasped by viewing them in terms of two distinguishable subissues. One is the problem of atheism, and the other the question of cognitive competence.

The Problem of Atheism

It is well known that many of the great (natural) scientists were, as individuals, religious believers. However, both the inner logic of modern science and the prescribed goals that it subserves dictate that the question of God is to be marginalized. The methodological principle stipulating that the process of scientific explanation must forgo any recourse to "God as an explanatory factor," and that God must therefore be ignored a priori in the construction of scientific theories, is regarded today as unassailable. Concerning neither the correction of the planetary orbits nor the process of evolution (to cite but two examples) is it admissible to invoke the factor of God to bridge over gaps in knowledge. From the viewpoint of theory of science, this methodological atheism seems as compelling as, from the viewpoint of philosophy, it is far-reaching. It leads, in practice, to the elimination of God from the linguistic formulations, areas of study, and functions of science, as well as from the life-world of modern humanity that is so strongly influenced by these.

Even more momentous is the effect of the prescribed goal (under whose guidance modern science operates) that leads science to eliminate the factor of God from the practical dimensions of human existence by aiming to realize all rationally desirable goals, insofar as possible, through the application of atheistic techniques. Temporary gaps, failures, and limitations allow theology (which sees these as still presenting it with opportunities) a field of activity for the time being (and surely, in some connection, for all time, given the fundamentally irremovable contingency of our existential situation); it needs to be seen, however, that precisely this situation confirms and reinforces the fact that theology and science have the character of radical alternatives, and that the old "stopgap" theme thus recurs. Science, on the one hand, and religion (or theology), on the other, consequently appear as opposing—indeed, as fundamentally contradictory—ways of dealing with contingency. A theology (or religion) that was, in the context of human "praxis for overcoming contingency" (H. Lübbe), relegated to nothing more than the leftover area of those existence-threatening contingencies that resist (temporarily?) being overcome through scientific techniques, and are therefore, willing or not, to be overcome "religiously" (i.e., accepted out of God's hand), would have its area of responsibility virtually restricted, as it were, to "incurable diseases" and thus, in principle, to the science-resistant, darker sides of existence.

The Question of Cognitive Competence

The same danger of an ever more radically widening breach and of a fatal loss of substance can be made clear in terms of the issue of cognitive competence. Implicit in an outlook prevalent in modern criticism of religion and

theory of religion is the idea that religion represents, at least in fact, a prescientific form (as fantasy, myth, and "revelation") of gaining knowledge, of explaining existence, etc., which persists until it is replaced by science and gradually dislodged from all the areas of verifiable knowledge. The sciences that thus take over, in this respect, from religion and its theology, that surpass it in efficiency, reliability, testability, and progressive capacity, thereby wrest from theology its original cognitive competence. Here, too, in way analogous to the previously discussed situation regarding "praxis for overcoming contingency," theology finds itself relegated to temporary, residual functions within the cognitive enterprise that are perhaps humanly helpful, but also scientifically dubious.

This restrictive association with modes of knowledge alternative to science and areas of knowledge resistant to science can quite readily manifest itself even in religion-affirming contexts. Understanding religious knowledge as a supplementary alternative to scientific knowledge seems to leave room for peaceful, and perhaps even complementary and constructive, coexistence of the two mediators and modes of knowledge. In more recent theories of religion, the exclusion of religion from the areas of scientific cognitive competence and its association with the primary language of myth, symbol, and poetry is therefore often greeted as something positive, since it seems, after all, both to create room for religious "truths" and to enable a durable peace between the representatives of the two kinds of function. It needs to be seen, however, that the relationship between theology and science is thereby literally thrown back to its pre-Christian state. Religious truths and theological interpretations of existence that disengage themselves, in fundamentally irrefragable cognitive autonomy, from the rational logos and its responsibility to truth are ultimately condemned to forgo any effective validity as truth. The direction that is inevitably taken when this is done can be indicated by appellations such as "fundamentalism," "New Age mysticism," or indifference to truth regarding so-called religious paths to salvation.

The Claim to Truth of Christian Faith

Seen in terms of fundamental theology, therefore, with a view to the situation regarding the truth of God's word or the claim to truth of Christian faith, but also with a view to the unity of truth, it is necessary to resist decisively any reduction of religion and theology to cognitive areas that, at best, can be nothing more than objects of a science that adjudicates upon them, while they, for their part, are supposed no longer capable of representing, through a scientific (and scientifically relevant) cognitive competence proper to them, the truth that is their nominal province. The options taken in this matter by original Christianity, and down through the history of theology, are clear. As surely as religion can obtain its message from sources other than science, and as surely as the truth of Gospel does not conform to the science and wisdom of "this world," so surely would it be fatal for religion to seek its identity outside of the rational "logos," thus surrendering its own competence regarding salvation (cf. Rom 12:1).

Concretely, this means that, along with faithfulness to theology's primary anchoring in prescientific and extrascientific manifestations of truth, it must also, while continuing to pursue its own internal development, participate quite decidedly, genuinely, and cooperatively in the scientific cognitive process and the truth-seeking discourse of the rational sciences. It must do so not merely in the sense of making a maximally knowledgeable and competent contribution, as an external authority, to discussion of what others are doing, but in the manner of a self-commitment by theology to upholding its own scientific and (intersubjectively) scientifically relevant cognitive competence, most particularly in the elaboration and presentation of what is to be said about Christian faith, within it, and following from it. Only in that way can it give the messages of the Christian faith both presence and relevance within scientific consciousness itself. By making its own contribution, as far as it can, to the truth-seeking discourse of the rational sciences, and thus creating credibility and acceptance there for the substance of that contribution, it simultaneously corresponds to the maxim of modern consciousness according to which only that "can lay claim to unfeigned respect" which "has been able to survive free and open examination" (Kant).

4. Cooperation and Conflict

For the practical relationship of theology to the sciences, openness, cooperative solidarity, dialogue, and an interdisciplinary outlook are of great significance. An insular, and in that sense "pure," theology falls into cognitive isolation and becomes devoid of reality, distant from the world, incommunicative, and sectarian. Hence, it is not only with a view to what theology can contribute to the sciences but also in the interest of theology's own welfare that it must seek to engage in intensive and extensive interchange. This also corresponds to the truth-relevance of the Christian message, the universal mission of the Christian faith, the interrelatedness of specialized areas of study, and the conditions and tasks requisite to interpretative mediation. The need for dialogue, interdisciplinary work, and interchange is especially applicable to the areas of (1) reciprocal communication of research methods and findings, (2) discussion of leading interests and disciplinary presuppositions, and (3) attention to the common responsibility for science and its consequences. Above all, the ethical aspects of the alarming scientific-technological "progress" that is transforming the environment and threatening human existence are waiting to be dealt with. The crises in the goals and direction of a techno-economic civilization cannot be overcome without reflective attention to the metaphysical, anthropological, and eschatological considerations that provide a means of orientation. Here, theology certainly has at its disposal some helpful principles, but no ready-made solutions. The contribution that it has to offer in the interest of human affairs—including what it can bring to criticism of science—must, to be sure, derive basically from its own particular resources, but it can be realized only through working in solidarity with other disciplines.

At all events, what emerges from this is the need for co-operation, interdisciplinary work, dialogue, and partnership in a spirit of solidarity. Along with these go conflicts as well, and, in fact, not just those between science and nonscience but also those arising in the framework of an ultimately indivisible cognitive competence. In that framework, the notion of a total alternative, as discussed above, is an unavoidable, but also meaningful, topic of contention.

Bibl.: A. D. WHITE, *A History of Warfare of Science with Theology in Christendom* (New York, 1960; original, 1896); F. DESSAUER, *Begegnung zwischen Naturwissenschaft und Theologie* (Frankfurt, 1952); A. DEMPF, *Die Einheit der Wissenschaft* (Stuttgart, 1962); J. MOLTMANN, "Theologie in der Welt der modern Wissenschaften," in J. Moltmann, *Perspektiven der Theologie: Gesammelte Aufsätze* (Munich, 1968), 269–87; J. B. METZ and T. RENDTORFF, eds., *Die Theologie in der interdisziplinären Forschung* (Düsseldorf, 1971); W. HEISENBERG, *Schritte über die Grenze* (Munich, 1973); id., *Physics and Beyond: Encounters and Conversations* (New York, 1972); H. AICHELIN AND G. LIEDKE, eds., *Naturwissenschaft und Theologie: Texte und Kommentare* (Neukirchen-Vluyn, 1974); G. EBELING, "Überlegungen zur Theologie in der interdisziplinären Forschung," in G. Ebeling, *Wort und Glaube*, vol. 3 (Tübingen, 1975), 150–63; W. H. AUSTIN, *The Relevance of Natural Science to Theology* (London, 1976); W. PANNENBERG, *Theology and the Philosophy of Science* (Philadelphia, 1976); K. RAHNER, "The Relation between Theology and the Contemporary Sciences," in *Theological Investigations*, vol. 13 (1972; London, 1975), 94–104; id., "On the Relationship between Natural Sciences and Theology" in *Theological Investigations*, vol. 19 (1979; London, 1983), 16–23; L. SCHEFF-CZYK, *Die Theologie und die Wissenschaften* (Aschaffenburg, 1979); M. SECKLER, "Theologie, Wissenschaft unter Wissenschaften?" in M. Seckler, *Im Spannungsfeld zwischen Wissenschaft und Kirche* (Freiburg, 1980), 15–25; id., "Theologie, Religionsphilosophie, Religionswissenschaft," in M. Seckler, *Im Spannungsfeld zwischen Wissenschaft und Kirche* (Freiburg, 1980), 26–41; S. N. BOSSHARD, "Über die Dialogsfähigkeit der Theologie," *StZ* 203 (1985): 704–12; W. OELMULLER, *Wahrheitsansprüche der Religion heute* (Paderborn, 1982); J. SPLETT, "Wissenschaft, Grenzen zur Religion," *StZ* 205 (1987): 330–38; J. HUBNER, ed., *Der Dialog zwischen Theologie und Naturwissenschaft: Ein bibliographischer Bericht* (Munich, 1987); P. JORDAN, *Der Naturwissenschaftler vor der religiöser Frage: Abbruch einer Mauer* (Stuttgart, 1987); R. BERGOLD, *Der Glaube vor dem Anspruch der Wissenschaft: Der Dialog zwischen Naturwissenschaft und Theologie am Beispiel von Schöpfungsglaube und Evolutionstheorie* (Münster, 1988).

Max SECKLER

V. THEOLOGY AND PHILOSOPHY

"The idea of philosophy is mediation; that of Christianity, paradox." These pithy words of Kierkegaard well suggest the difficulties that arise from the relationship between theology and philosophy. Paul was well aware of the paradox when, writing to the Christians of Corinth, the Greek cultural center of his day, he said, "God chose what is foolish in the world to shame the wise." While the Greeks desire wisdom . . . we proclaim Christ crucified . . . foolishness to the Gentiles" (1 Cor 1:27–23).

In the modern age, Nietzsche perhaps has best grasped what the Christian paradox implies for philosophy. In *Beyond Good and Evil* he writes:

> People of today, who are too obtuse to understand the language of Christianity any more, no longer have any idea how fearful the paradoxical words "crucified God" were to a spirit of the ancient world. In no conversation had there ever been anything so daring, so terrible, something calling everything into doubt, something raising so many problems. Those words heralded a transmutation of all the values of the ancient world.

An initial difficulty, arising from the theological perspective, of the need to establish the relationship is caused by the fact that theology cannot define philosophy. For theology is permanently in the state of having to receive from philosophy the definition of what philosophy is. But, at this level, even the answer to what philosophy is determines a particular sort of philosophical thought, as a consequence of which, in the answer it provides, theology encounters one out of many possible philosophies. If, then, we are to speak about relationship, theology must fix on a definition of philosophy that includes its more universal features, leaving individual characteristics, whether historical or cultural, of this or that school.

At this level of "universal" acceptation, we may then think of philosophy as the science that is brought about by philosophizing. Philosophy is doing philosophy, it may be said *sic et simpliciter*; hence knowing that the answer to one of its definitions of self is what constitutes it a science is of the essence of philosophy. Criticism of its own presuppositions and basis is what makes simple reflection become philosophy. Doing philosophy will therefore be thinking philosophically, i.e., investigating the facts in search of the primal truth within them.

Once thought seeks truth, it starts distinguishing the essential from the superfluous, the authentic from the inauthentic, and hence opens up to every possible answer. Philosophical thought is hence characterized by dynamic openness, which of itself precludes any conclusion claiming to be accepted as definitive.

As well as by openness to an ever-wider form of knowledge, philosophy is also characterized by universality with regard to the object of investigation. Human personality and human existence constitute the object peculiar to philosophical investigation, since thinking subject and thought-of object are one of a piece. For _homo religiosus_, even the experience of the sacred and the reaching toward the absolute belong to the sphere of philosophical enquiry. Two data can thus characterize philosophy as science in its relationship to theology: (1) being constituted as a kind of knowledge tending to the universal principles of thought, hence a knowledge transcending the particular moment; and (2) presenting itself at the same time as a historical knowledge, hence thought subject to the cultural conditioning of different periods.

1. Elements Emerging from a History of the Relationship

The history of the relationship between theology and philosophy, which has often been over hastily identified with the relationship between reason and faith (→ REASON/FAITH) can be the _magistra vitae_ for the historic present—at least so as to avoid the forms of extrinsicism and absolutization that have often sacrificed the one science on the altar of the other.

When Christianity first became aware of itself, it was not a philosophy; the dimension of critical knowledge was foreign to the first believers. The basic theme of the proclamation to be converted had triggered the discovery of a new understanding of life. The convert, particularly if a rhetorician, jurist, or philosopher, saw in Christianity that meaning of life that in philosophy had been sought in vain. A passage from Basil bears clear witness to this fact.

> I frittered away much of my time in the service of vanity and lost all my youth in useless activities; for I devoted it to the acquisition of doctrines and of a wisdom that God had charged with folly (1 Cor 1:20). Suddenly, one day, as though I had woken up from a deep sleep, I raised my eyes to the marvelous light of gospel truth, realized the uselessness of the wisdom of the princes of this world, who will not last long now (1 Cor 2:6), bitterly repented of my wretched life and prayed that I might be granted a guide to direct me towards the princes of piety. (_Epistula_ 223.2)

To this overriding interest in conversion of life, we should add that during this period Christians did not attend the schools, which makes it easier to explain the accusation leveled against them that they were people without _logos_ and _nomos_—uncouth, devoid of culture or any ability to think, and capable only of making converts among the most ignorant and at the lowest levels of society (see Celsus in the _Alēthēs Logos_).

The church of the early centuries had no direct interest in a relationship between the two wisdoms. What was considered important was the way one lived; the matter of moral living marked the distinction between the pagan world and the Christian one.

Between the two, however, it is nonetheless possible to see a dual scheme of relationships coming into being: on the one hand, a wholesale repudiation of philosophical wisdom as against the discovery of divine wisdom (Tatian, Tertullian); on the other, a great openness and a critical and constructive dialogue (Justin, Minucius Felix). It cannot be denied, however, that the relationship of theology to philosophy was of the instrumental type, either to make the content of the kerygma intelligible to the pagans, or to strengthen the faith of believers. As the forerunner of Anselm, Origen states that "faith needs to be strengthened by reasoning . . . starting from commonly held ideas worked out by Greek philosophy" (_De principiis_ 1.7.1; 4.1.1).

Augustine deserves special mention. In him the currents of East and West converge, as it were, to such a degree as to constitute the first intimation of the medieval synthesis. In the _Soliloquia_ may be glimpsed the center of the Augustinian problem in this regard. To Reason, who asks, "What do you want to know?" Augustine replies, "Cupio Deum et animam scire" ("I yearn to know God and myself").

Reason continues, "Nothing else?" and Augustine answers, "Nothing else."

Here in Augustine, it would seem, we can find the nucleus of the relationship between faith and reason. For it occurs almost as a parenthesis to faith, so that the content of faith can be assimilated humanly, responsibly. It is in connection with the problem of human existence, rather than that of self-knowledge, that Augustine sees the relationship between human knowledge and that of the believer. To put the problem of human existence is like putting the problem of God, since human existence cannot be grasped at its deepest ontological reality except in relation to God.

Augustine's philosophy becomes an endless dialogue between creature and Creator that unfolds under the shield of love (*intellectus valde amat*, "The intellect loves strongly"). Searching for the truth and straining after it, for Augustine, are not a mere intellectual quest, as might be supposed in our modern way of thinking. For him, truth is the very life of the human mind; it is the interiority of the human subject that is found by penetrating ever deeper into the recesses of the self: "Do not go out; withdraw within yourself; truth inhabits the inner man, and if you find your nature changeable, rise above yourself."

The practice of philosophy therefore consists in nothing other than in deepening, stimulating, and searching for the truth that will then lead to all-truth; this is therefore thought of as given and as a gift to be accepted also by the intellect. "Reason does not create truth, it only discovers it; truth exists in itself before being discovered; once discovered, it renews us" (*De vera religione* 39).

We may therefore talk of a balance between faith and reason, since both revealed truth and rational truth converge on one another and furthermore, and above all, because they are present in the believer's concrete act of thinking. The believer is a human being, a thinking being, a constituent part of the natural order that investigates to what degree rational truth may be the basis for the truth of faith. The fields are both autonomous, but there are problems (e.g., the problem of evil, or that of history), the solution to which is given only by the wisdom of faith. In a word, philosophy indicates the purpose of human existence by means of natural truth, its point of departure being the

soul's awareness of itself, but revelation gives the means for its achievement.

The key word of this Augustinian synthesis seems to be that of truth, which is in God but which is incarnate in the Logos-Christ. The human soul hungers and thirsts for this truth, but it is a truth more like wisdom than like intellectual speculation; it is hence the mystery of humanity within the mystery of God. In Augustine faith and reason are thus two distinct values, but present and realized in the historicity of the believing subject.

The equilibrium reached with such difficulty in the Middle Ages, particularly in the happy intuitions of ANSELM and THOMAS AQUINAS, who understood the one as being within the other, was destroyed by the rise of a partial and biased interpretation of philosophical reason that, gradually, with the Enlightenment, was to become the unique criterion of knowledge and the unique source of certainty, relegating faith either to a nonknowledge or to a knowledge alternative to the philosophical one.

The different forms of recovering the relationship, especially that of neoscholasticism, were directed to discovering a means that would allow philosophy and theology to be reciprocally related. The means singled out was Christian philosophy, which had the advantage of moving on two fronts: the philosophical one, since it operated by speculative principles; and the theological one, since it was conceived in the light of the principles of revelation (→ PHILOSOPHY, CHRISTIAN).

In this context, we understand why the encyclical *Aeterni Patris* of Leo XIII stated that "putting philosophy to good use is required in order that theology may acquire and be invested with the nature, the character, the natural disposition of a true science (DS 3137).

It cannot be denied, however, that a perspective of this sort, if it seriously sought to recover a lost dialogue, was equipped only with a methodology extrinsic to the theological datum, which did not accord it its true value. For theology, if it is to follow an epistemological system, ought to be in a position to justify itself and, from within belief itself, first recover and then propose the principles that make faith a form of human knowledge.

The modern problem is still to some extent due to the absolute polarization of the two types of knowledge. For philosophy claims to possess overall knowledge, since it is able to express and explain reality in a definitive way and hence uniquely able to give meaning. Theology, for its part, makes the same claim by virtue of a knowledge that comes from revelation.

When two types of knowledge are thus opposed, the result is merely an encounter in which one type tends to exclude or absorb the other. The thought of Spinoza and Hegel shows the way theology gets absorbed by philosophy; that of Lamennais and late nineteenth-century traditionalism shows the reverse.

The views of Heidegger have significantly influenced the relationship between the two sciences up to our own day. His critique is well known: philosophy and theology are irreconcilable because of their respective *Ansatz*. Philosophy is characterized by questioning, for it owes its being to existence, the original source of the question and where reflection on meaning develops. It will always be characterized by openness and thus by the wonder to which interest in the existent as opposed to the nonexistent gives rise. Theology, by way of contrast, sees itself as an *Aufhebung* of existence, which accepts the *positum* of the event of the death of the innocent by virtue of faith. Theology thus does not arise from questioning but from believing, and this can never become a self-questioning on peril of self-destruction. "Those then who take their stand on the terrain of such a [biblical] faith can indeed in some degree follow our line of questioning and even take part in it, but cannot honestly ask, without ceasing to be believers . . . they can only behave 'as if.' . . . It is in such folly that philosophy consists . . . but for a genuinely Christian faith, philosophy is folly" (*Introduction to Metaphysics*).

2. As a Proposition

In this article, I am dealing with the relationship between theology and philosophy in terms of the principle *oportet philosophari in theologia*. Let us consider the two elements in this dictum.

1. The *oportet philosophari* is a necessity for theology, since by the act of speculation its concept and its language acquire universal value as regards intelligibility and communication.

2. To say *oportet philosophari in theologia* means to admit that the critical-reflective process does not come before or after theological knowledge but at the very time when it is being activated, since it is, precisely, a knowledge of the faith.

The *oportet philosophari in theologia* is possible if the following five propositions are borne in mind:

a. Revelation presents itself to believers as something completely and utterly new, bearer of the ultimate and definitive meaning of existence, which we cannot find out for ourselves (→ MEANING I). The essential nucleus of this revelation is concentrated in the event Jesus of Nazareth, who in human terms expresses the truth of and about God.

b. An understanding of the event does not come about by means of elements extrinsic to revelation but comes from the revealer himself. His person, life, actions, and words manifest the divine reality that he himself is. This his self-expression is normative for our understanding of the event itself inasmuch as it allows us to understand it as "referring onward" to a further mystery, that of the Trinity, and as a putting our trust in that.

c. Knowing Jesus of Nazareth is therefore the equivalent of entering into contact with a person, personal knowledge of whom is a "referring onward" to the mystery of the Trinity. At the same time, the highest form of knowing a person is that of putting our trust, for the sake of understanding ourselves, in an explanation that we already accept as a mystery.

d. Theology is not exclusively a reflecting on the *positum* of revelation; rather, it is to have knowledge of the fullness of the mystery of the incarnation, which has its epistemological principles within the event itself. As believers, we are thus introduced into a phase of more complete existence, allowing us actually to have knowledge of the mystery of God, but starting from the mystery itself.

A passage in John's Gospel is very significant in the light it sheds on this. "Why do you not understand what I say? It is because you cannot accept my word. You are from your father the devil, and you choose to do your father's desires. . . . But because I tell the truth, you do not believe me. . . . Whoever is from God hears the words of God. The reason why you do not hear them is that you are not from God" (Jn 8:43–47).

This pericope marks a central point in Jesus' preaching about the identity of his revelatory being. Neither the children of Abraham nor those of the devil can recognize him, but only those who are born of God. To put it more plainly, in this passage Jesus resumes the polemic with his opponents by taking up what he had already been saying: "He who is not of God" can know neither him nor his revelation (see Jn 3:6, 31; 8:23). "To be of God" is the same as being a child of God and, at the same time, as "one who belongs to the truth" (Jn 18:37). If we therefore claim to possess self-awareness, or trust only in our own truth, we can neither know God nor hear his voice and have even less claim to know ourselves, since we are not in the truth. "Being of God," however, is also the same as being *in* him, no longer in ourselves. By believing, we are all placed on a level of understanding that is no longer our own biased and fragmentary one, but God's. The act by which we recognize our own existence in God therefore entails our assuming the perspectives of the Other and hence their validity and universality as taking precedence over and authenticating our own.

e. The act of faith is an act that fully follows the subject's cognitive activity. To believe, therefore, is already to know (→ THEOLOGY II) and not only to know a content of faith but basically our own personal reality as that of subject faced with free choice whether to put our faith in or not to put our faith in the Other as the source of meaning and significance in life.

One possible solution for a correct relationship between theology and philosophy might be one that sees in this very *oportet philosophari in theologia* a form guaranteeing both the reflective component in theology and the real autonomy that each of the two sciences ought to have in accordance with the content and method of inquiry proper to each. There is a sort of circularity of relationship that starts from theology, of necessity gathers up philosophy, and then returns to theology once more.

The basing of theology on the word of God as *norma normans et non normata* reveals the awareness of a people who discover and thereby

choose, in that Word, the presence of an ultimate and definitive meaning addressed to them. Theology thus refers its own knowledge back to a received word that is itself intelligible and contains principles by which it can be understood.

This meaning of revelation and the objective evidence for it are what constitute the basis of theology itself. But the event revealed is given in the mystery of the incarnation; that signifies, in a historical event, that the trinitarian mystery of God allows itself to be expressed in human nature. The God who allows himself to be expressed in human nature is the God who kenotically always makes himself understood within this structure, even though the totality of his mystery can be given only in the eschatological event and final contemplation. In Jesus of Nazareth, therefore, God becomes utterable by human beings, who in this way and only in this way can have adequate access to the mystery of God.

For the Christian, the resurrection constitutes that definitive newness placed in the world and history as a principle of salvation and new life. Theology *knows* of the resurrection because it is in accepting this event that theology can begin to reflect; even though of this event theology knows only the fact that Jesus of Nazareth, once dead and buried, returns to live again in the fullness of life. The faith of the eyewitnesses, however, allows theology to check the accuracy of their statements and above all to know that there is complete identity between the Crucified and the Risen One.

From this event on, theology has to enter the critical dimension, working out concepts and the language in which to express them, so that the basis and content of the faith can be expressed and universally accepted. When critical activity begins, it establishes the various categories of thought that can be of most help in understanding the mystery of faith. Even so, this moment notwithstanding, theological thought of the critical type must return to the wider knowledge had by faith, in order to have an ever more all-embracing interpretation of the event itself.

The same thing happens when theology attempts to express the name of God. The point of departure will still be Scripture, which forbids the making of any image of God (Ex 20:4); setting out from this commandment, however,

Scripture says of God that he is Shepherd, Father, Bridegroom, and Rock. No one of these names expresses God, and yet each of them and all together can say who he is because, *by analogy*, the human mind expresses in this way what it has already learned by faith. But the same critical dimension will inform theology that God is not Shepherd, Father, Bridegroom, Rock, or anything else, since his name will ever remain the one he has given himself: Yahweh (Ex 3:14).

Philosophical reflection thus explains the content of faith by universalizing, but this refers us back to a theological knowledge that ends in the rational understanding that God is incomprehensible. If the relationship between theology and philosophy evinces this circularity, we may the more easily avoid instrumentalizing either of them and recognize their respective autonomy.

Theology is self-based in the word of God and for this reason can determine its epistemological basis starting from revelation. Philosophy retains its identity of questioning the real as presented to it and of universalizing it by the methods and means appropriate to it. Each follows a different path, yet they concur in the need to give meaning to their respective contents. By drawing closer to theology, philosophy can derive this radical newness of being from it, since coming from very being; theology, vice versa, will find the way conceptually to universalize the content of revelation.

A separation between the two sciences can lead only to mutual loss of a sense of reality. A renewed meeting, with the diverse autonomies in balance, will be possible only if theology and philosophy remain open to one another and are mutually aware of the limitations imposed on each by human thought-processes. If philosophy is aware that its constant relationship to reality is that of wonder, allowing it to keep formulating new questions, theology for its part knows that its position vis-à-vis revelation is always determined by the certainty of a future that will bring within itself, in the shared faith, the full event of revelation and its complete revelation (Jn 16:13; Rom 8:19).

Bibl.: M. HEIDEGGER, *Introduction to Metaphysics* (New Haven, 1959); id., *What Is Called Thinking* (New York, 1968); K. JASPERS, *Der philosophische Glaube* (Munich, 1963); B. WELTE, *Auf der Spur des Ewigen* (Freiburg, 1965); K. RAHNER, "Philosophy and Theology," in *Theological Investigations*, vol. 6 (1965; London, 1969), 71–81; id., "Philosophy and Philosophising in Theology," in *Theological Investigations*, vol. 9 (1967; London, 1972), 46–63; J. RATZINGER, *Introduction to Christianity* (New York, 1969); id., *Principles of Christian Theology* (San Francisco, 1987); J. MOLTMANN, *Perspektiven der Theologie* (Munich, 1968); W. PANNENBERG, *Basic Questions in Theology* (Philadelphia, 1970); V. MELCHIORRE, *L'imaginazione simbolica* (Bologna, 1972); id., *Essere e parola* (Milan, 1984); B. LONERGAN, *Philosophy of God and Theology* (New York, 1973); id., *Method in Theology* (New York, 1972); I. MANCINI, *Teologia, Ideologia, Utopia* (Brescia, 1974); G. EBELING, *Introduzione allo studio del linguaggio teologico* (Brescia, 1981); G. O'COLLINS, *Fundamental Theology* (London, 1981); H. Urs VON BALTHASAR, "Regagner une philosophie à partir de la théologie," in var., *Pour une philosophie chrétienne* (Paris, 1983), 175–87; J. ALFARO, *Rivelazione cristiana, fede e teologia* (Brescia, 1986); E. CORETH, ed., *Christliche Philosophie im katholischen Denken der XIX und XX Jahrunderts*, 2 vols. (Graz, 1987); G. COLOMBO, ed., *L'evidenza e la fede* (Milan, 1988); M. SECKLER, *Teologia, Scienza, Chiesa* (Brescia, 1988).

Rino FISICHELLA

THEOLOGIES

I. NATURAL THEOLOGY (G. LANE). II. TRANSCENDENTAL THEOLOGY (K. H. NEUFELD). III. NARRATIVE THEOLOGY (C. ROCCHETTA. IV. POLITICAL THEOLOGY (J. O'DONNELL). V. LIBERATION THEOLOGY (J. DUPUIS). VI. CONTEXTUAL THEOLOGY (M. CHAPPIN). VII. MANUALISTIC THEOLOGY (JARED WICKS).

I. NATURAL THEOLOGY

"Natural" theology was for a long time one of the subjects studied by Western philosophers. It was to be distinguished from theology pure and simple, i.e., the theology that was done in faculties of theology and was called, by comparison, "supernatural" or "sacred" theology. Natural theology was intended to be a methodical, critical study of God, his existence and attributes, and his relations with his creatures, but a study using only the mind's human (or "natural") powers. The other kind of theology was always meant to be as serious as possible a study of God, human beings, and the universe, but one that took as its points of departure or principal supports "special" revelations from God himself. When these revelations are called "supernatural," the intention is to indicate that their content could not have been grasped, deduced, or inferred by the exercise of the unaided human powers but only with the help of God, who is able to make up for the unavoidable inadequacy or limitations of these created powers. (An example of a supernatural revelation is the special destiny that no created being could attain by itself but that God has freely chosen to offer to human beings, along with his indispensable help in reaching it.)

Although many theologians still think it useful to do natural theology, many contemporary thinkers and philosophers have abandoned this discipline, which in their opinion deals with "religious" matters and therefore properly belongs to theologians alone (or to believers alone). After all, is there anything more religious than God himself or his plans or his expectations regarding his creatures? But in this attitude there is perhaps very often at work a mistaken notion of what is properly religious. Perhaps, too, it should be recognized that, contrary to a very widespread opinion, doing something _religious_ requires more than studying God or conducting an investigation into him or a rational discourse about him.

There are people who methodically study, for example, certain insects, with a view to knowing ever more about their anatomy, the food they eat, their way of reproducing themselves, their habitat, and their habits. These persons are said to practice "entomology." Others pursue systematic studies of atmospheric phenomena or the human heart or social behaviors in order to know more about these matters; they are said to practice meteorology or cardiology or sociology. If, then, still others carry on critical studies of God, and this solely in order to increase or improve their knowledge of this particular "object" (which they regard as existing or simply as possible or even simply as an idea whose more or less varying content intrigues them), they are obviously doing _theo_-logy. If, in addition, their purpose is simply to know more about this reality or this mere idea, it must undoubtedly be acknowledged that in their

studies they are not doing anything religious (either "supernaturally" religious or even "naturally" religious). In any case, they are not doing anything more religious than the other people are who pursue entomology or any other "ology."

What, however, would a properly "religious" activity involve? Careful reflection might yield the following description: individuals would be doing something religious if they were attempting to grasp, directly or indirectly, the expectations or attitudes that they believed a God could be having in their regard at this moment; or if they were attempting to manifest to this God the attitude that they themselves wanted to have toward him. Or, in other words, if they were trying by all sorts of means (cognitive or other) to recover, maintain, or deepen a "positive" relationship with this God, in order to improve their communication with him or to "encounter" him in a better way.

If such is, in essence, properly religious behavior, then clearly we would have to think, on the basis solely of the _texts_ of an Aristotle (for example), that this thinker was not engaged in any _religious_ activity when, in the part of his philosophy which he regarded as the most important and which he himself called "theology," he was endeavoring to reach a better knowledge or understanding of the being that is "pure act," or of the special way in which this God moves other beings (through finality), or of the principal and characteristic action of this God. We lack more explicit documents in this area, but it seems clear from the texts themselves that Aristotle's only purpose was to _gain an ever better knowledge_ of this particular being—that and that alone.

The case is quite different with those whom we know to be seeking a better knowledge of a God in whom they already believe, but only because they think (rightly or wrongly) that an increase in knowledge or understanding will enable them to achieve a more personal or deeper communication with him. Theirs is a properly religious activity. And if this search for knowledge and understanding is carried on in a methodical and critical way, with the help, if need be, of unifying or explanatory theories, then we must undoubtedly speak of a religious _theology_, i.e., an activity that is both religious and theological. Finally, this search would be "supernatural" or "natural," depending on whether the effort at understanding does, or does not, have recourse to data that no human being would be capable of discovering without a "revelation" (which in this case is said to be "supernatural") from God himself. (Clearly, it can often be difficult or even impossible to determine with certainty the purely natural components present in the *concrete* practice of religious and "supernatural" theology.)

Bibl.: J. F. DONCEEL, *Natural Theology* (New York, 1963); B. WELTE, *Auf der Spur des Ewigen* (Freiburg, 1965); id., *Heilsverständnis* (Freiburg, 1967); id., *Dal Nulla al Mistero assoluto* (1978; Casale Monferrato, 1985); K. RAHNER, *Hearers of the Word* (New York, 1969); D. BRAINE, *The Reality of Time and the Existence of God* (Oxford, 1988).

Gilles LANE

II. TRANSCENDENTAL THEOLOGY

The concept of transcendental theology, linked in a special way with the name of K. Rahner, is not unambiguous in usage. In general, it is taken to refer to the application in theology of either Kant's transcendental philosophy or essential aspects of it. This presupposes that the philosophical method of the philosopher from Königsberg is assumed to be at least partly compatible with theological reflection and that his thought is not judged to be completely opposed to Christianity. Details of the ever-changing critical debate about Kantian philosophy (especially among Catholic thinkers and theologians but equally on the part of the church's doctrinal office) cannot be entered into here, partly because it has still not been conceived in an adequate and well-reasoned way. Nevertheless, details of that debate are not absolutely necessary, insofar as transcendental theology is not dependent upon transcendental philosophy but essentially possesses its own theological arguments and makes use of transcendental philosophy in the way that patristic theology made use of a certain kind of Platonism, or scholasticism of a certain kind of Aristotelianism. And even if it has been precisely since Kant that clear consciousness of the problems surrounding such "making use of" has arisen, it is equally true that philosophical realities and methods are usefully at play whenever and wherever thinking occurs.

In connection with the question about "the basic theological discipline" (see *Schriften zur Theologie* 6:149–67), K. Rahner observed (in 1964) that the "new fundamental theology" would, to a large extent, have to be "transcendental," i.e., have to reflect on the conditions of the possibility, within the believing subject, of actualizing the contents of belief, in order to bring out more clearly the nature of the correspondence between the formal essence of revelation in general and its Christian content. From this viewpoint, transcendental theology was concerned not merely about the general question of the conditions of the possibility of Christian truth and its acceptance in belief; rather, this perspective was to be, from the very start, oriented toward the human being. Thus it would be bound up with an anthropocentric slant or orientation, although one in no way opposed to the fact that God himself is, and remains, the starting point and center of revelation and theology. It is just that the *pro nobis* of divine activity is taken seriously, on whose basis and in whose framework God becomes accessible and known to humans. That side of the mediation of revelation must undoubtedly have received too little attention, and may therefore have been long unrecognized and undervalued. This explains the heavy emphasis that was placed on it in recent theology after it and its associated problems were once again discovered. The study of Kant's transcendental philosophy has, incontestably, helped bring about that rediscovery. It has also contributed, however, to the emergence of a quick succession of differently conceived and accentuated versions of transcendental theology, which occasionally have little in common and even contend against one another.

Regarding the nature of the subject itself, every authentic sort of theology is actually transcendental, for it has to speak about God, doing so as the discourse of humans. It must, in any case, refer directly or indirectly beyond the immediately given sphere of life, action, and thought. In so doing, it inherently expands the natural human horizon of questioning and, in that way, asserts the possibility of the supernatural. That assertion reflects the situation of human beings, who are neither closed up within themselves nor capable of being sufficient unto themselves. A close analysis of this state of affairs enables recognition of the way in which humans are necessarily dependent upon certain demands for correspondence, although the exact form of those demands is not in any way a priori determinable. This is connected in no small degree with the fact that what determines the nature of these demands for correspondence is not, and cannot be, found in humans. Hence, humans have to accept, in principle, that they must correspond to something greater, and not vice versa. At the same time, what is involved is an authentic act of corresponding, even if the givenness and specification of the relevant demand stem from elsewhere.

This insight, which is fundamental to an understanding of transcendental theology, calls for a redefinition—to be taken seriously at least as a possibility—of the relationship between subject and object that was familiar and unquestioned in earlier philosophy. In the sphere of human cognition, there can be an "object" that is treated as an object, and is thus subject to the control of the knower, but that in reality is wholly beyond such control because it is the origin of all determining and controlling. To human apprehension, it nonetheless presents itself as an inner-worldly object, even if, through the way that it appears, it already serves notice of the claim that is really appropriate to it by nature and invites the human to a conversation. In other words, transcendental theology requires, as one of its initial steps, a reorientation on the part of theologians, who must become conscious of the difference between their cognition and viewpoint, on the one hand, and their place or role in reality, on the other, and must then accept the latter.

Transcendental theology thus proves to be a method in which the person applying it is also included; it is a special kind of theological questioning and reflecting produced by the fact that the message of Christianity is directed at humans and presents a challenge to them or seeks to achieve something through them. What is offered is intended for humans, in such a way that, without this orientation, it would not be the Christian message. Still, this basic fact is grasped by humans only insofar as they involve themselves with the claim and stimulus of the gospel, allowing it to speak to them and thereby to activate potentialities that are inherent within them—for listening, understanding, assenting, etc. To what extent these

potentialities are independently preexistent and to what extent they are partly constituted by the calling itself is difficult to determine, since a person can bring them to consciousness only in the process of their actualization, in which process, however, God and the person always work together. Precisely this working together underscores the fact that humans, in their very constitution, are necessarily oriented toward transcendence, insofar as this structure is demonstrably effective even in cases where it is expressly and thematically disputed.

Transcendental theology cannot be, and does not wish to be, _the_ form of theology; rather, it is an elemental part of theology, because faith always conditions the whole of existence historically and concretely. Any analysis of faith is also carried out in terms of transcendental theology and thus affects Christian truth and all the individual truths of faith, so that questions can be raised about its significance for the traditional articles of faith, about how they are to be understood, more profoundly grasped, and represented. A content-oriented application of this kind is relevant to particular truths in differing degrees but nonetheless serves to clarify the connections between the mysteries and to call to mind that, for a full understanding of the gospel, it is indispensable to see its individual statements as parts of an interconnected whole. A check is thereby provided on the tendency to view them in isolation, which, as regards the truth of revelation, has distorting and falsifying consequences. In a similar sense, the transcendental theological way of reflecting counteracts an overstatic and overlegalistic conception of revelation by effectively indicating that what is involved here is a vital process that repeatedly eludes any fixating grasp while relinquishing none of its precision and force.

In this respect, the transcendental-theological approach opens new access to precisely the missionary character of Christianity and provides an insight into the nature of convincing and of conviction, i.e., of testimony that achieves its purpose by stimulating further testimony. In that process, the message transcends itself, thus evidencing the basic structure also expressed in its content. In a world that is becoming more and more one, and where there are no longer any countries in which the Christian message is not in some way known or readily able to become known, it is no longer sufficient to understand missionizing in a merely spatiogeographic sense (i.e., where transcending equals expanding). The example discussed here shows how fundamental conceptual categories undergo broadening and change, and this can occur consciously and responsibly only with the help of thought that *is* transcendental-theological and *must* be so if it does not want to become dependent upon reflections that have, by nature, nothing to do with faith and theology.

Consequently, transcendental theology is concerned with the presuppositions behind, and the approach to, religious reflection itself. It enables the rediscovery and reemphasis, within the total phenomenon of Christianity, of those aspects that were not previously given specific attention—and did not, in the relevant circumstances, require such attention—but that are, in the present-day context, all the more urgently in need of consideration if, as accords with the gospel, the revelation of Jesus Christ is to continue to reach people today. It shows itself to be a now-necessary instrument of responsible religious accountability, regarding whose use, of course, its own proper rules apply.

Above all, it is necessary to note the peculiar indirectness of transcendental-theological religious reflection. The work of K. Rahner provides a clear example here. In this indirectness, the situation of human beings is once again evidenced, who have control neither over God nor over their relationship to God but nevertheless take a position in faith and thereby acknowledge, in their own proper way, God as their Redeemer and Lord. This God manifests himself to them with a human countenance in the form of Jesus Christ, so that it is not just coincidence that the questions of Christology were, and are, at the center of the exposition and debate surrounding transcendental theology. From every viewpoint here, the problem of the condition of the possibility presents itself, which means that Christology virtually demands a transcendental-theological approach, even if it need not adhere unconditionally to the concrete form and manner of the one developed by K. Rahner.

Meanwhile, in the context of these reflections, the question also arises about the nature of the relation between the fundamental-theological approach to christological truth and the dogmatic summarizing of that truth, i.e., about the necessary and legitimate independence of these disciplines precisely in their inalienable interconnectedness. It becomes conscious here, however, because transcendental theology already contains the elements for its reasoned solution.

Bibl.: P. ROUSSELOT, "Les yeux de la foi," *RSR* 1 (1910); K. RAHNER, "Transcendental Theology," *SM* 6:287–89; id., "Selbstmitteilung Gottes," *SM* 4:521–26; id., *Foundations of Christian Faith* (New York, 1978); L. B. PUNTEL, "Zu den Begriffen 'transzendental' und 'kategorial' bei K. Rahner," in H. Vorgrimler, ed., *Wagnis Theologie* (Freiburg, 1979), 189–98; F. J. NIEMANN, *Jesus als Glaubensgrund in der Fundamentaltheologie der Neuzeit: Zur Genealogie eines Traktats*, Innsbrucker Theologische Studien 12 (Innsbruck, 1983), 375–421; E. G. FARRUGIA, *Aussage und Zusage* (Rome, 1985), 198–215.

Karl H. NEUFELD

III. NARRATIVE THEOLOGY

The expression "narrative theology" is a programmatic title that, while having precedents in the work of K. BARTH and others, became current in theological language in the 1970s through the work of scholars such as the linguist H. Weinrich and theologians such as J. B. Metz, L. Wachinger, B. Wacker, C. Molari, and J. Navone, not to mention those such as L. Boff or E. Schillebeeckx, who do not deal with narrative theology but have built up their studies, in the sacramental and christological fields, within a basically narrative perspective.

1. "Narration" in Theology

The expression "narrative theology" does not mean simply having recourse to a theology composed of stories but recovering a way of practicing theology in constant attention to the original narration of the event of Jesus of Nazareth and retransmitting it in narrative style (*paradosis*). It reflects a theology skilled in analyzing the salvific narratives and the way they used to be presented and were charged with keeping alive the ecclesial community's narrative memory.

In this connection, it must be admitted that the road theological reflection is committed to completing is still a long one; at present, theology seems rather ill equipped to cope with the problem of narration. Theologians venturing into this field have a strong sense of moving in an environment that is very largely new to them and alien to their *forma mentis*.

Nature of Narration

Narration belongs to the literary genre of TESTIMONY; in it the narrator tends to take second place so as to make the facts and/or the protagonists speak for themselves. In the telling, it is not so much logical arguments that take pride of place but rather the sequence of events, with the remembered experiences, descriptions, and conclusions that flow from it. The past tense (or aorist) becomes the present, and it is this continuous present that makes the narration as though it were something actually happening now. The great storytellers are the ones who can bring the events they relate back to life today, almost as though they were remaking the story, re-creating it for their listeners. This presupposes the storyteller's real involvement in the story he or she is telling; otherwise it will merely be reduced to a cold or mechanical repetition of something quite detached, incapable of receiving new life and strength.

Effectiveness of the Narration

When the narration is effective, it can make those who hear it share in the facts related, the experience evoked. The story's effect may be emotive, arousing curiosity or sympathy, or may be of an encouraging, stimulating, or interpretative kind. There will always be an effect, even if only that of rejection of what has been narrated. With the narration it is as though we find ourselves in the presence of a symbol that strives to actualize the life-force expressed in the story. The memory of the past sparks off other memories, a force activating the happiness (or sorrow) of a love enjoyed (or lost), an experience allowing us to reorganize events apparently forgotten and give them new meaning. When memory of the past concerns historical facts that have brought about decisive changes, the telling of them is like a rebirth, a renewal of the task once undertaken, so as sometimes to present it as a "dangerous memory," involving awareness of a history yet to be realized, of a personal responsibility to be shouldered.

Truth of the Narration

The problem of the truth of the narration has to be tackled and resolved according to the literary genre to which it belongs. A story basing its truth on facts that have actually occurred is one thing; a narration obviously fictitious, such as an allegory or a parable, the truth of which resides essentially in what one is trying to convey by means of it, is another. Perception of the truth of a narration, in every case, involves at least two preconditions: discernment of the kind of story (historical, symbolic, mythological) and the identification of its specific purpose (what is the narrator trying to tell us?). Without being sure what these two factors are, we cannot be sure whether the story is true or what its message is. Every narration has its own heuristic character, which needs to be properly understood.

2. Reasons for a Narrative Theology

Apart from recovery of the semantic value of myth and more recent developments in the philosophy of language, the need for a narrative theology comes from a renewed awareness of the narrative aspect of Judeo-Christian revelation. While biblical language involves three essential forms of expression (*narratio, appellatio,* and *argumentatio*), narrative is the basic form, as well as being more common, fundamentally determining the other two.

From Jesus to Kerygma and Catechesis

The Gospels present Jesus as a storyteller. The early Christian community, confessing its faith in the risen Lord, is characterized as a community that *narrates* facts that have occurred. The faith is the invitation to follow Jesus of Nazareth, the Storyteller, as told by the community that meets to commemorate his Passover and proclaim it to one and all. The kerygma is the proclamation of lived events and experiences, made by someone who has seen and heard and who can therefore tell, after due consideration, the event of Christ and the facts of his life on earth from his birth to his death on the cross and his paschal appearances. The proclamation "He is risen. We are witnesses to this!" — core of the faith of the apostolic church — is a narration. Catechesis, developing on this fulcrum, assumes a mainly narrative form, as appears from the Gospels, which echo this in their overall structure and in individual literary units. Successive types of theological thought (e.g., the Pauline and the Johannine) are similarly rooted in the facts of Jesus of Nazareth and in the account handed down by the community, while developing their own doctrinal and moral interpretations.

The Faith as Narrated Homologia

The faith, especially as it is expressed in the creeds, retains an essentially narrative structure. It proclaims, by narrating, the story of trinitarian salvation—a story having its origin in the Father, Creator of heaven and earth, taking form in the mission of the Son and the mysteries of his life, and unfolding in the Spirit poured out on the church and the world, in expectation of the final parousia. The creed of the faith is the church's narrative *homologia*, a proclamation set out in the threefold figure of word proclaimed, word celebrated, and word lived, a proclamation that has within itself a testimony to be given and an appeal to the faith by which the ecclesial community can recognize itself and "utter" itself to the world. For the rest, the whole course of the faith is characterized by the hearing of a proclamation that turns into memory and is handed down in the church from generation to generation, always intact yet ever new.

A "New Innocence" in Narrative

The task of those theologians who engage in narrative theology is directed to rediscovering how today's theology can regain its narrative innocence without annulling the results of historico-critical investigation and the demands of a sound hermeneutics. The new developments in exegesis have not destroyed, as at one time was believed, the original riches of biblical and gospel narrative; on the contrary, these have made it possible to use them in a truer and more correct way. Naturally, this means moving from a more or less ingenuous narrative innocence to a "second innocence" if we are to take account of the demands of a careful exegesis, without ever forgetting that the revealed word is a living word, a question put to people of every age and clime, a memory that is never a neutral event but always a subversive one, capable of shattering the bounds of every false awareness

and of engaging every "hearer of the word" in a decisive option for the faith.

3. Narrative Theology and Systematic Theology

What is the relationship between narrative theology and systematic theology?

The Neoscholastic Model of Theology

The first point to note is the criticism that narrative theology leads back to the neoscholastic model of theology, which is itself accused of having assumed an exclusively argumentational character, inasmuch that the task of theology has largely sunk to that of merely deducing implicit or potential doctrinal conclusions from already-established dogmatic theses. The memory of biblical revelation, in consequence, has concerned only truths to be affirmed. This explains, for example, why modern handbook theology has finished by dropping the chapter concerned with the mysteries of the life of Christ, which contrastingly in Thomas Aquinas held a position of great importance. Analogous considerations might be advanced with regard to the theology of the Trinity, the church and the sacraments, and a good many other sectors of "theological knowledge." The impoverishment of modern theology is in large measure due to its having lost its ability to narrate the faith in terms of salvation history (*oikonomia*) and of "deeds and words having an inner unity" (*DV* 2), by overlooking the heuristic charge hidden in this form of proclamation. Rather than arguing, we need to go back to inspiring faith by telling the story of Jesus of Nazareth and the uniqueness of the events of his earthly life. The theologian is primarily a narrator of the Lord Jesus and a witness to his passover.

Narrative Theology and Argumentational Theology

This does not mean to say that narrative theology is to be set up in opposition to "argumentational theology"; it only means that narrating ought to be accepted as a constituent element of theological work. If theology narrates, it does so to lead people to reflect theologically on the contents of its narration, developing the implications of these and organizing them into an integral and properly articulated vision. The defect of argumentational theology was not that it argued but that it set out from, or reduced itself exclusively to, arguing, to the ultimate disregard of the fact that the faith is primarily structured as revelation that has become history, where event and word are constituent parts of a witness narrative and where care must therefore be taken not to reduce this merely to a system of abstract truths or propositions to be proved.

Historical Science and Narrative Theology

Narrative theology does indeed reason, but in a different manner from strictly systematic theology. If the latter leads to certainties within the framework of the logical concatenation of dogmatic principles and conclusions, narrative theology tries to justify affirmations of faith by showing the truth shining through the facts recounted or through the account of these facts in the faith of the church. Obviously, this way of practicing theology presupposes a close link with historical science, fundamental theology, and the history of dogma. It is not enough to say, "Jesus has risen"; we need to be able to tell people that "Jesus has *really* risen!" Only thus can our Christian proclamation be safeguarded against subjectivism and the arbitrary and be able to give "an accounting for the hope that is in you" (1 Pt 3:15). Historico-textual criticism is not only not opposed to narrative theology but is indispensable for determining the relationship existing between "history in the telling" and "history told," as also for the concomitant theological check on the truth enshrined in the story of the faith transmitted by the church.

Narrative Theology and Practical Theology

One last aspect to be stressed is the link existing between narrative theology and practical theology, the latter being understood in its widest acceptation from moral theology to the theology of praxis, from pastoral theology to catechesis. Contrary to what might be supposed, narrative theology has a deeply practical side to it. For narration calls upon the listeners' experience, involving them in the first person, even if for different reasons and on different levels. Narration tends toward communication, and communication presupposes a response, an encounter or a dialogue in which the listeners become involved as actors of what they are saying to one another, or relive in actualizing memory what is being told them. This aspect of narration has a performative value that it is no exaggeration to describe as sacramental. In this perspective, we come to understand the inseparable relationship existing in the church's faith between "word" and "sacrament" as macrosigns of salvation narratives, the one implying the other. When, for instance, in the eucharistic anamnesis we say: "On the night when he was betrayed . . . ," we are taking part in a narrative and functioning in the key of a narration that simultaneously becomes proclaimed word and sacramental event, making present what it recalls, making it live again in the today of the celebrating assembly and opening us to the future, by actuating in historic time the mystery set at the heart of the church.

4. Applicable Figures for Narrative Theology

Given what we have just said, it is easy to see in what a variety and large number of forms narrative theology can be applied to the various sectors of theological knowledge. In fact it can be applied, though with differing accentuation, to the history of religions and to fundamental theology, to biblical theology, to Christology, to sacramental, moral, and spiritual theology, to theological anthropology, to political and pastoral theology, and to catechesis. One might argue about some of these applications and about the way they should be conducted; their significance, however, cannot be doubted for recovering a way of "uttering God" and the event of salvation in terms of a living proclamation for the people of our age and every age.

Bibl. B. WACKER, "Teologia narrativa," *Conc* 5 (1973): 66–79; id., *Narrative Theologie?* (Munich, 1977); J. B. METZ, "A Short Apology of Narrative," *Conc* 85 (1973): 84–96; C. MOLARI, "Natura e ragioni di una teologia narrativa," in B. Wacker, ed., *Teologia narrativa* (Brescia, 1981), 5–29; J. NAVONE, "Teologia narrativa: una rassegna delle sue applicazioni," in *RdT* (1985): 401–23; id., ed., *Gospel Love: A Narrative Theology* (Maryknoll, N.Y., 1973).

Carlo ROCCHETTA

IV. POLITICAL THEOLOGY

Political theology is one of the major theological movements that developed in the 1960s, basically a European phenomenon, though closely related to other similar movements such as black theology in the United States and liberation theology in Latin America. Among the principal names associated with this movement are the Catholic theologian Johann Baptist Metz and the Protestant theologian Jürgen Moltmann.

In his book *An Alternative Vision: An Interpretation of Liberation Theology* (Mahwah, N.J., 1985), Roger Haight notes that one commonly makes a distinction between political theology and liberation theology first on the basis of geography, with political theology being restricted to the Northern Hemisphere, whereas liberation theology has flourished in the Southern Hemisphere. But beyond this it is commonly asserted that political theology has its roots in the tradition of Kantian philosophical agnosticism. The religious problematic of the First World is linked to the question of secularization: what place does faith have in a world where the word "God" is increasingly devoid of meaning? In contrast, Latin America is ostensibly religious. There the principal dialogue partner has been Marx, and the predominant problem is that of social injustice.

But Haight goes on to argue that in fact a similar problematic unites political and liberation theologies, namely, the post-Enlightenment crisis as regards the meaning of history. The Enlightenment, with its rejection of supernatural revelation and the Christian view of history, reduced reason to problem solving. Increasingly, human beings were left to try to resolve all human questions on the basis of technological reason. But the goal toward which a person should be liberated was left unclarified. Moreover, the Enlightenment made a sharp distinction between reason, which was public, and religion, which was private, so that the lonely individual was left to try to create his or her own meaning. In our own century, a succession of world wars, concentration camps, experiences of genocide, the disproportion of wealth between First and Third World countries, and the threat of nuclear holocaust have made even more radical the crisis of the meaning of history. How can Christian faith respond to this crisis? What is at stake is whether Christianity is viable as a public discourse, whether it has something concrete to offer to people caught in the apparent meaninglessness of historico-social existence, or whether indeed Christian belief is just another version of otherworldliness and hence opium for the people. Thus the problem of the credibility of faith as it is linked to the crisis of the meaning of history provides the link between political and liberation theologies.

As already indicated, political theology can be understood only within the context of the Enlightenment. In one sense the Enlightenment put an end to political theology, or at least the prevailing model of political theology. The Enlightenment, seeing the horror of the wars of religion, called for a sharp division between religion and politics. Religion was reduced to the private sphere. In place of religion the Enlightenment offered salvation through the use of human reason. However, contemporary criticism of the Enlightenment has shown that there is no such thing as pure reason. The Enlightenment philosophers claiming to worship the goddess of pure reason were in fact offering liberation only to the bourgeois. The turn to the subject proclaimed by the Enlightenment was in fact a version of rugged individualism and led to the capitalist system of our modern Western industrialized states. Today's criticism of the Enlightenment seeks to show how all reason is already historical reason. It criticizes the Enlightenment for excluding the negative aspects of history, for not reading history from the point of view of the victims and the oppressed. The Enlightenment reading of history was by no means neutral. Such thinkers as Marcuse, Horkheimer, and Adorno call for a new historical critical use of reason that faces squarely the negative dimension of history and from the negative seeks stimulation for new possibilities of liberation. As Marcuse notes, "The memory of the past can allow dangerous insights to arise and the established society seems to be afraid of the subversive content of memories" (cited by Moltmann, *The Experiment Hope* [Philadelphia, 1975], 103).

Another important factor in the development of political theology is the appropriation of Marx's insight regarding the relationship between theory and praxis. Marx criticized the Enlightenment idea that there is such a thing as pure reason. Contemporary philosophy, developing this line of thought, understands the relation between theory and praxis as a dialectical one. Theory arises from praxis and is in turn modified by praxis. By praxis one understands not unreflective activity but rather action infused and made conscious of itself by theory. Praxis could be defined as any human activity that has the power to transform reality and make it more human. In this context, Christian faith is not seen first of all as a theory but rather as a praxis. Christianity is a style of life, a way of being in the world. It is not an idea but a process of humanization and liberation. Believing in Christ is a mode of being and action in the world that is a participation in the movement of history itself. By such participation the outcome of the movement is already transformed.

These general reflections, which form the background for understanding the meaning of political theology, will become more concrete as we examine the representative positions of Moltmann and Metz.

Moltmann's early theology was popularly described as the theology of hope. In his early period he was strongly influenced by the neo-orthodox theology of Karl Barth. The accent lay on eschatology, and the gospel was read in terms of an eschatological hope for a new creation beyond the vicissitudes of our present suffering. Although Moltmann's theology was from the beginning future-oriented and although there was a Marxist element in that his dialogue partner was the Marxist philosopher Ernst Bloch, the accent lay on the totally other future, with little emphasis on the links between present and future. All this changed, however, in the early seventies as Moltmann began to dialogue with Horkheimer and Adorno and moved toward a theology of the cross and indeed toward a political theology of the Crucified.

Moltmann noted that theology, even in antiquity, indubitably had a political dimension. One of the hallmarks of Roman civilization was the link between the welfare of the state and the worship of the gods. Sacrifices to the gods guaranteed the state's well-being. Later, Constantine in adopting the Christian religion basically baptized the political religion of the Romans when he created the Christian empire. This idea prevailed in medieval Catholicism and even in classical Protestantism, for without the support of the princes Protestantism could never have survived. Although the Enlighten-

ment radically broke with this model, Moltmann contends that its effects are still felt in the modern civil religions such as the nationalisms of the nineteenth century. Although it is undesirable to return to the pre-Enlightenment model of political religion, Moltmann believes that we cannot be content with the individualistic view of religion, whereby faith consists merely in the proclamation of the rule of a holy God in individual hearts (Harnack).

Moltmann thus calls for a new model of political theology that he refers to as the model of correspondence. In this model one seeks to create a link between the eschaton, the ultimate future of the world, and the penultimate realities here and now. Moltmann recognizes that it is not possible to create a bridge from the penultimate to the ultimate. Only God can bring about his kingdom. But it is up to us to create anticipations of the ultimate future, to seek to make our present world a sacramental sign of his presence. Although one can do this only in fragmentary ways, nonetheless it is possible to create parables of the kingdom.

The center of Moltmann's project is the crucified Christ. First, Moltmann notes that we cannot depoliticize the cross of Christ. Jesus was condemned as a political revolutionary and threat to the state. Although Jesus was not a zealot, his message of ultimate allegiance to God's kingdom alone was in fact a threat to the sovereignty of all political systems. Moreover, the fact that in the resurrection God clearly manifested himself in union with the crucified Christ indicates that God is on the side of the poor, abandoned, and marginalized, with whom Christ identified. The resurrection of the crucified Christ puts every man and woman before a choice; either Christ or Caesar. In other words, God's identification with the crucified Christ has revealed that God's way is not that of power, the way of the master–slave relationship. Rather, God has revealed himself as suffering love, a God who has taken the part of the poor and the wretched of the earth. As Moltmann expresses it, "The crucified God is in fact a stateless and classless God. But that does not mean that he is an unpolitical God. He is the God of the poor, the oppressed and the humiliated. The rule of the Christ who was crucified for political reasons can only be extended through liberation from forms of rule which make men servile and apathetic and the political religions which give them stability" (*The Crucified God* [London, 1974], 329). Or again, "For those who recognize the Christ of God in the crucified one, the glory of God no longer shines on tne crowns of the mighty but alone on the face of the tortured Son of Man" (*The Experiment Hope*, 111).

Thus combining the negative dialectics of Horkheimer and Adorno with the theology of the cross, Moltmann is able to create a new hermeneutic for a political theology. The contemporary believer is not afraid to look at the negative experiences of suffering, death, loss of meaning, and god forsakenness. He or she recognizes that the history of the world has been the history of violence and that the world is littered with the corpses of the victims of such violence. But at the same time this negative element arouses in people the religious longing for the Totally Other, the kingdom of righteousness, where the murderer no longer triumphs over the victim and where the dead are raised. On the basis of negative dialectics alone, such a desire would be a mere longing for an impossible utopia, but on the basis of God's identification with the suffering of the world in the crucified Christ such suffering spurs Christians to create those correspondences to their hopes for the ultimate future that begin to transform our world and render it sacramental while at the same time making credible the Christian gospel of hope.

Turning now to the theology of Johann Baptist Metz, we can note immediately that his theology underwent a remarkable development in the years after the Second Vatican Council. His early work was written under the determining influence of Karl Rahner. Metz sought to deepen Rahner's transcendental approach and followed his master in developing the Kantian turn to the subject in the direction of a Christian anthropocentricity (see *Christliche Anthropozentrik* [Munich, 1962]). In the mid-1960s, however, Metz began to criticize Rahner's approach for being too individualistic. He wanted to understand the human person as a thoroughly social and historical being. Moreover, one noticed a significant shift in the meaning of the term "horizon." For Rahner, God is the infinite horizon implicit in every act of knowledge and will. Metz retains the notion of horizon but speaks of the ultimate horizon as the absolute future.

Thus, in dialogue with Marxism, Metz's thought is conspicuously more eschatological than is Rahner's. The gospel of the resurrection proclaims the absolute future of the world. This future, however, is not merely outstanding but gives us a criterion by which to judge and criticize present social reality.

Metz's theology is also more cross oriented than is Rahner's. We have seen above that Christian faith is a form of praxis. This praxis has its origin in the story that the gospel proclaims. Here again we see that Metz rejects the Enlightenment idea of pure detached reason. Christian faith is not based on an idea but on the story of Jesus. An important category that Metz introduces here is that of memory. One remembers the story of Jesus and his cross. The story of Jesus is the story of God's identification with the poor. It is the story of the promise of liberty. Like so many other stories, this story ends in the assassination of the liberator. But the resurrection proclaims that this story is not a tragedy because God has raised Jesus from the dead. He is alive and bears his message of liberation for the suffering victims of today's injustice. Therefore the Christian remembers the past for the sake of the present and the future. The memory of the past becomes itself a principle of criticism of the present in the light of the promised future. In this sense Metz speaks of a "dangerous memory" or of an "eschatologically oriented memory."

In addition to memory and narrative Metz introduces a third hermeneutical principle, that of solidarity. Modern post-Enlightenment cultures dominated by instrumental rational thinking are based on the principle of exchange. In effect, this means: "I will look after your interests if you look after mine." It is clear that such a basis for society is really a form of mutual egoism. The Christian command of love is excluded. A Christian basis for society would rather be founded on solidarity—i.e., on the need of the other. This solidarity extends to all victims of injustice and rejects the evolutionary view of progress whereby individuals can be sacrificed to the onward march of progress through technology. Solidarity extends even to the dead. Metz would agree with Horkheimer that if the longing for the Totally Other is not to be a flight from the negative reality of the dead victims of past oppression, it must also include hope for their resurrection and hence hope for their reconciliation with their murderers.

Turning to the ecclesiological implications of political theology, Metz argues that the mission of the church is to keep alive the dangerous memory of Jesus and to criticize existing institutions in light of his future. Metz recognizes that the church's relation to politics will be indirect. The church as such does not have a political program, nor does it identify with a political party. To do so would be to risk falling into ideology. Rather the church has a prophetic function in society, namely, to criticize existing injustices in the light of the kingdom Jesus preached. Naturally, in this eschatological perspective, the church will more easily align itself with the revolutionary movements of liberation than with those of conservative restoration. The church is on the side of the power of the future, not on the side of the status quo. At the same time, as a prophetic community, the church's own credibility depends on its willingness to critique itself as an institution and to let the dangerous memory of Jesus be the light that determines its own praxis and life-style.

Bibl.: J. B. METZ, *Theology of the World* (New York, 1969); id., *Faith in History and Society* (New York, 1980); J. MOLTMANN, *The Crucified God* (London, 1974); id., *The Experiment Hope* (Philadelphia, 1975); id., *Religion, Revolution and the Future* (New York, 1969).

John O'DONNELL

V. LIBERATION THEOLOGY

1. A New Way of Doing Theology

The inspiration for liberation theology came from the Second General Conference of Latin American Bishops, which was held at Medellín, Colombia, in 1968, on the subject "The Church in the Present-Day Transformation of Latin America in the Light of the Council." The aim of the conference was to apply to the vast Latin American continent, which contains almost half of the Catholic world, the new self-awareness that the church had developed at the Second Vatican Council, as well as the church's determination to open itself to the world and to

the problems of the human race. The bishops at Medellín showed exemplary courage as they strove to reach this goal by opening up new perspectives for the church's pastoral practice. Their striving was also realistic, for they took into account the concrete situation of a continent that, despite acknowledged differences between countries, has common traits that set it off from others: former colonization and the centuries-long influence of a Christianity imported from the West; underdevelopment and deep social disparities; the dehumanizing poverty of the masses; oppressive political regimes and economic dependence on a powerful neighbor to the North. Medellín took a stand for social change and political reform, condemned neocolonialism, committed itself to the poor through a preferential option, and set down the norms for a pastoral practice oriented to the people. The conference thus had a profound influence on a process that would lead to the development of a new theological project that embraced the entire continent.

The first systematic discussion of this new theological project was Gustavo Gutiérrez's book *Teología de la liberación* (1971; ET: *A Theology of Liberation*), a sketch of which had been published as an article two years earlier. From this point on, the new theology spread rapidly and produced a body of writings that soon became very extensive. As it developed, the theology doubtless took different forms. In fact, according to J. L. Segundo, it is possible to distinguish two liberation theologies in Latin America: one, still elitist, has been found chiefly in the universities; the other has developed among the people and with the people as its basis and has been more committed to a renewed appreciation of the traditional culture and especially of popular religion. Also to be taken into account is the fact that liberation theology quickly spread beyond the Latin American continent to the other continents of the Third World, where it has gradually developed specifically African and Asiatic forms. In the West it has even spread among various oppressed minorities, such as the blacks of the United States and the supporters of the feminist movement.

Notwithstanding all these different forms and the characteristics peculiar to the theological thinking of each of its major spokespersons, liberation theology is to be seen as a new and original theology. Despite the undeniable influences of Western theology on it (most of the liberation theologians did a substantial part of their studies in Europe), it vigorously asserts its differences from Western theology—and with good reason. It claims not only to be different; it claims also to be in opposition to Western theology, even of a "progressivist" kind, since the latter has its base in the other half of society and has developed within an opposite historical situation. Latin American liberation theology is done "from the underside of history," i.e., from the viewpoint of the oppressed people and at the heart of the people's historical development. It is not an academic exercise having as its addressee the "unbeliever" who must be brought to faith; it takes as its starting point the oppressed masses, those who are "nonpersons" (Gutiérrez) but who constitute a believing people involved in a process of human liberation. Even European "political theology" is not exempted from criticism, since it has developed in a different perspective and context and does not deal with the social reality of the Third World.

Liberation theology is thus an original way of doing theology. It is not a new form of theology in the sense that it deals with a new *object* or *theme* (theologies "of the genitive case"). It is not just one more among a variety of theologies, such as the theology *of* earthly realities, of hope, of politics, of revolution, of secularization, and so on. "Liberation theology offers not so much a new subject for reflection as *a new way of doing theology* (Gutiérrez). It represents a new and different "horizon" (L. Boff), an "attitude of mind or a special way of thinking the faith" (C. Boff) in terms of a historical situation. The first goal of liberation theology is to "liberate theology" itself (Segundo) from its elitist place in society and its academic character in order that it may engage in a hermeneutic and critical process, at a particular historical conjuncture and on the basis of a praxis of liberation. It can therefore be defined as "a critical reflection on liberating praxis in the light of faith" (Gutiérrez).

2. The Coordinates of Liberation Theology

Place and Subject of Liberation Theology

The theological locus of liberation theology is the people who make up the oppressed masses—the "poor," i.e., the classes of popular people, which are economically weak and subjected to social discrimination and whose subhuman living conditions are due to society's unjust structures. It is not enough to give economic "aid" to these poor through "caritative" action that keeps them in a state of dependence and even further consolidates the structures that oppress them. Nor is it enough to help them achieve a hypothetical "development" through random reformist activities, which in fact maintain the structures of a worldwide unjust system. The "epistemological break" that occurred in the sixties showed the insufficiency of the theory of development: the underdevelopment of some is a function of the development of others; the development approach ends in fact by widening the gap between the rich and the disinherited. The need, then, is to enable the poor to achieve an authentic human liberation; more accurately, it is to make them capable of liberating themselves, as their human dignity requires. Only a liberation strategy that can change social conditions and lead to structural changes can help the poor emerge from their situation of oppression. That is the kind of strategy that liberation theology brings into play.

While the poor are meant to be the authors of their own liberation, they are also the subjects or doers of the theology that supports and advances this liberation. Liberation theology is a theology of the people, before being a theology with the people and for the people. This does not mean that professional theologians have no part to play; it does mean that their role is to accompany. Their role is to help the poor articulate for themselves their own thoughts on a liberating practice in the light of revelation. To say this is to say also that professional theologians who claim to be theologians of liberation must identify themselves with the poor. It is not enough for them to support the cause of the poor; they must also be closely united with them by sharing their project and their action. They must become poor with the poor, to the point of feeling one of them; only then will they be able to articulate a theology that is developed in the theological place of the poor.

Praxis and Theologizing

Liberation theology is not a deductive theology that starts with abstract doctrinal principles and then, in a second stage, applies them to concrete reality. On the contrary, its aim is to be inductive, i.e., to move from experienced reality to reflection, from a liberating praxis to the work of theologizing. In other words, a liberating praxis lived through in faith is the first act; the development of a theology follows in second place. We may apply to liberation theology the Anselmian definition of theology as *fides quaerens intellectum* ("faith in search of understanding"), provided we are clear that the faith that comes first is not an abstract faith but one that is essentially engaged in a liberating praxis and is therefore contextual and militant. This practical faith—or, rather, this praxis of faith—has for its goal to change reality, to transform human relationships of dependence and domination so as to bring about an integral human liberation. The theological activity that follows will bring the involvement in liberating praxis to reflexive consciousness; it will evaluate this praxis in the light of the revealed word and the gospel message, while seeking in these the inspiration for a new involvement. "'Liberation theology' thus means a critical reflection on a human praxis . . . in the light of the praxis of Jesus and the requirements of the faith" (L. Boff).

While liberation theology is inductive and contextual inasmuch as it starts from the experienced real and allows itself to be challenged by historical reality, which it then endeavors to illumine with the light of revelation, it is also a hermeneutical theology. Its starting point is the context in which the church of the poor lives out its faith, and it seeks to interpret it in the light of the gospel message. Hermeneutical theology has been defined as "a new act of interpretation of the event that is Jesus Christ, on the basis of a critical correlation between the basic Christian experience, to which the tradition bears witness, and human experience today" (C. Geffré). The new interpretation of the Christian message emerges "from the interaction between, on the one hand, the reading, in the light of faith, of the foundational texts which bear witness to the original Christian experience, and, on the other, Christian experience today" (Geffré). But Christian life today is everywhere conditioned by the historical context—with its cultural, social, political, and religious components—in which it is lived. Hermeneutical theology thus involves a progressive and continuous interaction between present-day contextual experience and the witness of the foundational experience, the memory of which tradition keeps alive—and vice versa. This continuous interaction between context and text, between present and past, is what is meant by the "hermeneutical circle." In reality, however, we do not have a circle with two poles but a triangle and the reciprocal interaction of its three angles: the text or datum of faith, the historical context, and the present-day interpreter; or, in other terms: Christian memory, history in the making, and the ecclesial community or local church.

This description of hermeneutical theology and its method fits liberation theology perfectly, provided we correctly identify the three angles: the historical context is the situation of massive oppression and dehumanizing poverty of the toiling masses; the interpreter is this same people as engaged in a liberating praxis aimed at its own integral liberation; the datum of faith is first and foremost the liberating action of the God of Israel and the liberating praxis of the historical Jesus.

Three Mediations

Liberation theology attempts to articulate a reading of reality in terms of the poor and with a view to their liberation. In order to do this, "it uses the human and social sciences, applies a theological mediation, and calls for pastoral action in behalf of the oppressed" (L. Boff). The development of this reading can therefore be divided into three stages, which correspond to the three successive steps that are usually distinguished in pastoral work: see, judge, act. That is what is meant by three "mediations," or three stages, serving as tools in the theological process: the socioanalytic or historico-analytic mediation, which consists in searching out the causes of the oppressive situation of the poor; the hermeneutical mediation, which discerns the plan of God for the poor and the oppressed; and the practical mediation, which seeks to determine the course of action to be taken in overcoming the oppression in a way that is in accord with the divine plan. A quick review of these three stages is in order.

Liberation theology must begin by becoming informed about the real conditions of the poor, the forms of oppression, and their causes. This social and historical analysis is part of the theological process itself, an indispensable stage of it. This kind of analysis leads to a "dialectical" explanation of poverty and oppression, namely, poverty is the historical product of an economic and social system that exploits one class for the profit of another. It is a collective and conflictual phenomenon that can be eliminated only by replacing an unjust social system with a just one or, in other words, by a radical transformation of the very foundations of the economic and social system.

Is the social analysis practiced by liberation theology related to Marxist analysis, or is it clearly distinguishable from it? Without opting exclusively for Marxist analysis, liberation theology is not afraid to use it as a tool, to the extent that it is able to explain situations of poverty and their structural causes. But while liberation theologians say that they make free but critical use of Marxist analysis, they reject the charge made against them that they have succumbed to the Marxist ideology, i.e., that they have given in to dialectical materialism. Their intention is indeed to borrow from Marxism certain "methodological clues" that are useful for analysis, such as the importance of the economic factor and the need of attention to the class struggle and to the power that ideologies, including religious ideologies, have to hoax people. At the same time, however, they intend to keep a definitely critical attitude to Marxism as a materialistic and atheistic ideology. Liberation theologians are left, however, with the problem of an unstable balance between the adoption of Marxist analysis and the rejection of the Marxist ideology.

The second stage, or mediation, in the theological enterprise is the hermeneutical mediation. Once the situation of oppression and the mechanisms at work in it have been recognized, the question arises: What has the word of God to say about this situation? At this point, the discourse becomes formally theological, since the goal is to see the process of oppression and liberation in the light of faith. In order to do this, liberation theology applies a "hermeneutic of liberation," a new way of reading the Bible in

light of a situation of experienced oppression. This reading draws upon the great themes of the Old and New Testaments that are related to the subject and are in harmony with it: God as liberator of his oppressed people; in the Prophets, the rights of the poor and the demands of justice; the message of a new world; the kingdom of God for the poor; the liberating activity of Jesus and its political aspect; the mission of the church, which continues the activity of Jesus.

This reading is faithful to the basic message of revelation; at the same time, its contextual interpretation uncovers new meaning in the message. To understand this new meaning one must take divine revelation to mean the totality of the personal relationships into which God has entered with the human race in the course of history, and thus as an action that continues today in the history of liberation and salvation in which each people is engaged. This allows the hermeneutics of liberation to interpret the foundational texts in the light of an experiential situation and a praxis of liberation by bringing to light the "reserve of meaning" (J. S. Croatto) that the present conjuncture causes to emerge from those texts. In this way the word of God retains its sovereign role in the dialectic of text and new context, even while it is actualized in this context. The foundational meaning of the text is a function of its practical meaning: "The important thing is not so much to interpret the text of scripture as to interpret life 'according to the scriptures'" (C. and L. Boff). The hermeneutics of liberation seeks, therefore, to unleash the transformative energy of the biblical text in the present context of oppression; to this end, it highlights the social context to which the foundational word historically refers, i.e., the context of oppression in which Jesus lived and the political context of his death on the cross.

The third mediation that liberation theology uses is the mediation of praxis. As liberation theology has its point of departure in action (a liberating praxis), so it returns and leads back to action. It looks for practical, tangible results in relation not only to personal conversion but also to structural changes. For in the context of the injustice and oppression to which the "destitute of the land" are subjected, faith "cannot be satisfied with being also political; it is first and foremost political" (C. and L. Boff).

Liberation theology thus leads to pastoral action for justice and to the conversion and transformation of society. Its evangelical strategy favors nonviolent methods such as dialogue, persuasion, moral pressure, passive resistance, and so on, and turns to physical force only as a last resort.

In summary, it can be said that liberation theology is built, on the one hand, on a fundamental option for the poor and a praxis of liberation and, on the other, on the interarticulation of three mediations: a socioanalytic, a biblico-hermeneutical, and a practico-pastoral.

3. Key Themes in Liberation Theology

Only a quick reference to a few themes can be made here—to those having to do with God, with Jesus Christ, and with the church.

The God of the Bible Is the Father of the Oppressed

The God of liberation theology is the God of the exodus and the prophets. As the book of Exodus assures us, God hears the cry of the oppressed and determines to set them free. He takes the side of the poor and is partial to them; this partiality is based on the justice to which all have a right and which ought to be secured first for those to whom it has been refused. This God is a liberating God. The liberation of the Israelites from enslavement in Egypt is a political event that leads to the religious experience of an integral liberation, including liberation from sin and death. God is thus the God who works in history and not the God of metaphysical speculation. He reveals himself through history and through the establishment in the present world of his eschatological kingdom. It is in history that human beings encounter him, to the extent that they share in his liberating activity. The real choice in relation to God is not between faith and atheism but between faith and idolatry; i.e., the choice is between the God who liberates the poor in history and the ideas of God that human beings form for themselves and that reflect a social universe controlled by forces that enslave. These forces are idols, created by the hand of human beings in order to oppress the poor, who (it is thought) must be destroyed.

As for the Trinity within the Christian God, liberation theology sees in it a symbol and

paradigm of a human society and ecclesial community that are characterized by communion, participation, and equality. It therefore stresses the point that in God, unity does not precede the plurality of persons as though the latter were derived from it. It is necessary to reject any monarchy exercised by the Father, if this is taken to mean that the other persons are subordinate to him; this theory of "dependence," like the theory of an older monotheism, can serve to justify unitarian political regimes, as well as a rigidly hierarchized church. It is necessary to defend a God who is wholly a communion of persons and thus is guarantor of a society in which all are equals and a church in which all are brothers and sisters.

Jesus the Liberator

Oddly enough, in its early days liberation theology was accused of lacking a base in Christology. This lacuna was abundantly filled as time went on, for Christology is, as it ought to be, at the center of the thinking and literary production of the liberation theologians. What are the main traits of the Christology of liberation?

First of all, there is a large-scale return to the Jesus of history, to whom reference is constantly made. This is not something peculiar to liberation theology; liberation theology is not even the source of this return to Jesus of Nazareth. Post-Bultmannian historico-critical exegesis is once more confident that it is possible, if not to write a biography of Jesus, at least to get back, via the NT witnesses, to the historical person of Jesus in his essential originality. This explains why recent Western Christologies have likewise been marked by this large-scale return to the Jesus of history. This does not, of course, prevent liberation theology from having its own reasons for appealing first and foremost to him (while respecting historico-critical exegesis). It is the Jesus of history and not first of all the Christ of the apostolic faith who serves as the point of reference for a liberating praxis, and this by reason of his actions and his message, his options and his choices, and, finally, the political dimension of his mission and his death.

It is not enough, then, to assert the authentic and complete humanity of Jesus as "consubstantial" with our own, nor even to insist on his identification with the concrete historical condition of the human race. It is necessary, rather, to make his human history one's own, since it is in and through this history that God brings liberation and salvation to the human race. "The history of salvation is salvation in history" (J. Sobrino). It is also necessary to follow Jesus in his liberating praxis. To follow Jesus and "be his disciple" (which is not simple imitation) is indispensable for a knowledge of Christ that is not merely notional but real.

The kingdom of God is at the center of the activity and preaching of Jesus. It is God who establishes this kingdom in history, and he does so through the life and liberating activity of Jesus, as he does it subsequently through the death of Jesus by raising him up again. Liberation theology therefore emphasizes the connection between the kingdom of God that is being established and the actions and attitudes of Jesus. The kingdom is meant first and foremost for the poor; it is at work in Jesus' ministry of healing and in his exorcisms, in his choices and options, in his attitudes toward the established authorities, religious or political, of his day. Liberation theology lays particular stress on the political aspect of Jesus' activity and especially of his death on the cross. The messianic claims of Jesus cause him to be condemned to death for subverting the established order and for being a political revolutionary.

Readers must not make the mistake of thinking that liberation theology passes over in silence or neglects the fact that Jesus in his person is the Son of God. Liberation Christology is indeed an unswerving Christology "from below." At the same time, however, it professes (at the term of an organic process) the church's faith in the divine status of the Son of God, even if it offers criticisms of the traditional dogmatic formulations of the christological mystery. Its effort, nonetheless, is to discover in the human history of the Son of God the plan for the integral liberation of humanity that God is accomplishing in him. There is no break between the Jesus of history and the Christ of faith, even if orthopraxy precedes orthodoxy.

It is the death on the cross and the resurrection, which are the high point of the human history of Jesus, that completely reveal who he is and what kind of being he is, and who God is and what kind of God he is. Faith focuses on the resurrection, but it is the crucified Jesus who is raised up. It is therefore necessary to allow the mystery of the cross its full historical reality by interpreting it in light of the life of Jesus. But Jesus in his life finds himself in a conflict about God. The image he conveys is the image of a God who liberates by opposing the forces of oppression. That is why Jesus was condemned as a blasphemer and political agitator. The political and the religious orders are here conjoined; Jesus contradicted the prevailing conception of both. As for the resurrection: it shows the power of the divine love that dwelt in Jesus, and it puts a seal on his liberating activity.

The Church, Sign and Instrument of Integral Human Liberation

The ecclesiological model on which liberation theology is based is the "people of God" model that was spelled out by Vatican II in chapter 2 of *Lumen Gentium*. There the council says that the various ministries and functions must be conceived and organized within the fundamental reality of the church as a communion of all the members. Moreover, the mission of the church must be seen in its completeness. Evangelization includes, as an essential element, the promotion of justice and integral human liberation; it is a "liberating evangelization." This means that the poor themselves are the church; moreover, the entire church must become poor and be a church of the poor.

It is with this end in view that a vast network of "basic ecclesial communities" has developed that are mostly made up of ordinary people and cover virtually all parts of Latin America. These communities encourage personal relationships of communion and services; a variety of lay ministries come into being within them. The church thus becomes the people of God on the move, a community of communities that are organized for action in the service of an integral evangelization. It is of the utmost importance that these basic communities maintain indispensable links to the institutional church and its pastors.

The existence of the basic communities gave rise to the idea of a "church of the people" or a "church born of the people." The concept calls for caution to the extent that it seems to suggest that the church originates totally from the people, whereas in fact it is gathered by God and his word through the apostolic ministry. What the phrases are intended to mean, however, is that the church is first of all the "church of the poor," who are both the base and the center of the people of God. The meaning is also that if the church is to be faithful to the God of Jesus Christ, it must become conscious of itself in terms of the poor and the oppressed and become poor with them in order to share in their liberation. The term "people" in these phrases is not dependent on such Marxist categories as "proletariat" and "class struggle." The issue here is a "new way of being church," so that in our day the church may truly be a "historical sacrament of liberation" (Sobrino) and shift its center from itself to its Master and to the kingdom of God that is being established among the poor.

4. Liberation Theology and the Recent Central Magisterium

In the 1980s, the Congregation for the Doctrine of the Faith devoted two "instructions" to liberation theology. The first is entitled *Instruction on Certain Aspects of the "Theology of Liberation"* (1984); the second, *Instruction on Christian Freedom and Liberation* (1986). The two must be taken together, since in fact they complement each other. There is no room here to analyze the methodological, dogmatic, and ethical questions raised; still less is there room to take bearings in the ongoing debate and to determine the subjects on which there now seems to be agreement and those on which agreement is still distant. In general, while the first instruction drew attention to possible dangers and unsustainable positions, but without naming any particular theologian, the second developed in a positive way, but without any apparent connection with liberation theology, the Christian concept of freedom and a theology of salvation and liberation. Among the concerns of the Roman magisterium in the present debate over the church of the poor these must be certainly included: the need of an adequate method of social analysis, one not indebted exclusively to Marxist analysis, since this is falsified by an ideology; the concept of orthopraxy in relation to the concept of orthodoxy. The dominant concern, however, is to defend the transcendent dimension of the

Christian mystery against any danger of reducing salvation to the historical dimension of a human liberation or reducing ecclesial communion to an immanent historical project.

Bibl.: G. Gutiérrez, *Theology of Liberation* (Maryknoll, N.Y., 1973); id., *The Power of the Poor in History* (Maryknoll, 1983); J. van Nieuwenhove, *Les théologies de la libération latino-américaines*, Le point théologique 10 (Paris, 1974); id., ed., *Jésus et la libération en Amérique latine*, Jésus et Jésus Christ 26 (Paris, 1986); H. Assmann, *Practical Theology of Liberation* (London, 1975); L. Boff, *Teologia del cautivo y de la liberación* (Petropólis); J. M. Bonino, *Doing Theology in a Revolutionary Situation* (Philadelphia, 1975); E. Dussel, G. Gutiérrez, and J. L. Segundo, *Les luttes de libération bousculent la théologie* (Paris, 1975); id., *Histoire et théologie de la libération en Amérique latine* (Paris, 1977); id., *Histoire et théologie de la libération: Perspectives* (Brussels, 1981); J. L. Segundo, *Liberation of Theology* (New York, 1976); S. Galilea, *Teología de la liberación* (Santiago, 1977); P. Richard, *Mort des chrétiens et naissance de l'Église* (Paris, 1978); C. Geffré, *Le christianisme au risque de l'interprétation* (Paris, 1983); Congregation for the Doctrine of the Faith, "Instruction on Certain Aspects of the Theology of Liberation," *Origins* (Sept. 13, 1984); id., "Instruction on Christian Freedom," *Origins* (April 17, 1986); C. and L. Boff, *Salvation and Liberation* (New York, 1984); id., *Qu'est-ce que la théologie de la libération?* (Paris, 1987); J. B. Libânio, *Fé e política* (São Paolo, 1985); *Théologie de la libération: Documents et débats* (Paris, 1985); T. Witvliet, *A Place in the Sun: An Introduction to Liberation Theology in the Third World* (London, 1985); D. W. Fern, *Third World Liberation Theologies: An Introductory Survey* (New York, 1986); id., *Third World Liberation Theologies: A Reader* (New York, 1986); J. L. Segundo, *Theology of Liberation: Response to Cardinal Ratzinger* (Madrid, 1987); R. Gibellini, *Il debattito sulla teologia della liberazione* (Brescia, 1986); R. Marlé, *Introduction à la théologie de la libération* (Paris, 1988).

Jacques DUPUIS

VI. CONTEXTUAL THEOLOGY

One of the tasks of fundamental theology is to reflect on the epistemological status of theology; within the framework of this kind of reflection also comes the problem of the contextuality of theology itself. No theological text—not even a very abstract and speculative discourse on an eternal truth—is isolated from the reality of the theologian's situation and from the physical context in which such a discourse is delivered. This being the case, the language of theology, even while it has its own epistemological status on account of its object, does not enjoy a special or exceptional position.

1. Historical Facts: The Need for "Contextualization" Leads to a New Awareness of the Problem of Contextuality

Among Catholics, the explicit need for a contextualization of *theology as science* was first expressed in 1955 by a group of priests coming from Africa and Haiti. Earlier than this, in Africa, one could have observed certain practical activities along these lines in the field of liturgy and pastoral praxis, and—useful for theology—in the ambit of philosophy (the famous P. Tempels and his "Bantu Philosophy" of 1944). Among Protestants, attempts at a contextualized theology may be noted even before the Second World War, especially in India. For the use of the term "contextualization" we must, however, wait until the early 1970s (an early title is D. J. Elwood and P. L. Magdamo, *Christ in Philippine Context* [Quezon City, 1971]); especially after the Dar es-Salaam theological congress of 1976, which led to the founding of the Ecumenical Association of Third World Theologians, its use became very common. At the time when the term "contextualization" was introduced, the phenomenon itself had already developed and diversified in all sorts of ways.

The term "contextualization" retains the same basic meaning for everyone. It concerns an intentional and thought-out effort to do theology in and for a given context, an effort that, furthermore, is undertaken by people who belong to that context and make use of its own intellectual, religious, and spiritual resources. The aspect of intentionality and reflection constitutes the characteristic note, as against previous efforts to insert a theology into the context, along with all its social, cultural, political, economic, and religious dimensions. Efforts of this type have been made since the church first came into existence.

Skipping the ongoing debate over the possible divisions, subdivisions, classifications, and models, we may point out as the first type,

since chronologically it came earliest, the one represented by the initial need for an African theology and often specified by the term "indigenization" (which still gives rise to a few objections). The idea in this case is to make Christianity the indigenous religion of a given society and, as such, able to create a dialogue between the system of thought of the context in which it is placed and the Christian message. Within this type we may distinguish two models: *translation* and *inculturation.*

Translation consists in integrating certain traditional elements into ecclesial praxis, notably into liturgy and catechesis. In this case, efforts have to be made to justify the presence, in the context in question, of an ecclesial praxis deriving its own characteristics and particular contents from another context, which generated them originally but which in the course of the centuries has handed them down in a codified form. For theology, more particularly, the superculturality of revelation might favor this procedure. INCULTURATION uses a hermeneutics very differently based, namely, on culture itself, and—under the inspiration of *Ad Gentes* of Vatican II—indigenous religion too is already regarded as containing important values that can enrich the interpretation of revelation, allowing new dimensions to be discovered in it. Greater consideration, furthermore, is given to the question about the revelatory quality of non-Christian religions. The dogma of the uniqueness of Christ as revealer and savior does not exclude a deepening of this theme. At least in some theologies, the concept of revelation includes the fact of being hidden in various cultural contexts.

Contextualized theologies of this sort have arisen not only in Africa but also in quite a few Asian nations, e.g., India and the Philippines, where an openness to the great religions of the East is more in evidence.

At the level of contextualization, which is based on a priori assumptions tending to dialogue between various cultures, it is possible to detect the presence of this contextualized theology even in Europe. The THEOLOGICAL PLURALISM that has come into existence since Vatican II is the consequence of a pluralism of philosophical standards of reference with which theology normally has to enter into dialogue. The best-known example, in this period, is the one that applies to K. RAHNER, who deliberately proposes to reinterpret Thomism in transcendental terms.

Another type of contextualized theology, detectable about the mid-1960s, is the socio-economic one. According to this model, the idea is not only to make the Christian message acceptable in one specific context but to try to change that context, since it results from a combination of political oppression, economic exploitation, and racial discrimination. Such political, economic, and social change is willed in obedience to the Christian message, under its inspiration and with its help. Here a contextualized theology leads to a hermeneutics in function of a program of liberation. The method becomes inductive. The point of departure is concrete hope, which, as historic fact, gives rise to endless questions. Revelation, interpreted as the ceaseless activity of God in history, is questioned from a particular angle, in the hope of finding light by which to interpret the concrete situation and be able to change it for the better.

The best-known form of this, with the greatest impact, is *liberation theology*. This came into existence in the ecclesial environment of Latin America toward the end of the 1960s. Its foundations laid by Vatican II, it received its decisive impulse in the Assembly of the Latin American Episcopal Conference at Medellín in 1968. That same year, G. Gutiérrez gave a lecture on the subject of liberation theology; the subject is also to be found in a publication of his in 1971 and subsequently in his famous *Teología de la liberación* of 1972. The program aims at liberating oppressed and exploited peoples in the awareness that the Christian message of salvation implies and requires a social liberation too, and that the same message, with its inspiration and light, can contribute toward a liberation of this type.

This is preceded in time and as inspiration by the *political theology*, the product of the German academic environment of the 1960s. The first representatives of this were J. B. Metz (his earliest essays were written in 1961), J. Moltmann (with his important *Theology of Hope* of 1964), and D. Sölle. In the context of a society determined by a middle-class culture, this theology takes up the eschatological dimension of revelation. Its central point is the understanding that the kingdom of God cannot be reduced either to the sphere of the individual or exclusively to its expectation in the parousia.

While holding fast to the memory of the paschal event, political theology has as its program the orienting of believers toward a praxis of hope and love – in other words, toward expressions of freedom and justice especially within their own social dimension. The eschatological force, to use an expression of J. B. Metz, "deprivatizes" the activities of the believer by introducing them into the wider context, which is precisely the task of constructing the *polis*. However, the "eschatological reservation" i.e., the fact that we are always waiting for the Lord's return in glory, excludes any indentifying of the kingdom with any concrete social structure whatever; our eyes must always be fixed beyond any absolute that human beings may create, hence beyond any imaginable ideology. Political theology does not offer any specific political program of its own; it is rather conceived of as a function whose aim it is to arouse a critical attitude in Christians toward the society by which they are surrounded. In the thought of these authors, political theology is not meant to be a theology in its own right, but rather a function including and conditioning all theological thinking.

A different context, that of the ecclesial environment of black Protestants in the United States in the 1960s, gave rise to *black theology*. Radical militancy against discrimination (e.g., the Black Power movement) in the middle of the decade encouraged theological reflection, which became known with the publication of J. Cone's *Black Theology and Black Power* in 1969. The program is to fight racial discrimination and the biblical justification for it; it further tries to make the black population aware that salvation and liberation brought by Christ ought also to include the ending of discrimination and lead to the integral betterment of the blacks. In a word, it attempts to uproot the typical mentality of resignation. Some forms of this theology proclaim that Christian salvation is intended specially for blacks.

Again it was the unique context of the United States, with its dynamic democratic tradition (though evidently not completely so) that saw the rise of *feminist theology* in the 1960s. With the way prepared by a number of publications, the true beginning was probably in Mary Daly's book *The Church and the Second Sex* (1968). The program of this theology is the emancipation of women from the ideologies and subtle forms of discrimination and oppression that exist despite the democratic system. It wages war especially on the justification of such discrimination as based on arguments taken from the Bible and tradition; its main aim is directed to the revision of an image of God that is too male. It further tries to draw out the consequences for the life of the church; in particular, the finger is pointed at discrimination against women in various ecclesial activities, among which is that of the impediment to priestly ordination.

A new phase for the contextualization of theology begins when the program of a given contextualized theology gets adopted into a different context. Thus one has a black theology applied (and very urgently) in South Africa; a feminist theology, having found a ready echo in Europe (for a culture similar to but not the same as that of the United States), is now to be found, with somewhat different aims, in the Third World; a liberation theology (the object of attention in two instructions issued by the Congregation for the Faith, in 1984 and 1986, which, while rejecting some of its aspects, approved of certain others) is the one most liable to spread, not only in Latin America, but anywhere the masses live in degrading poverty and squalor, urging in every way, as it does, a complete liberation of the entire individual and of all individuals from oppressive economic, political, and religious structures. There are also the various forms of discrimination, especially against minorities. Different regions and different groups produce as many different liberation theologies.

2. Systematic Observations: Contextuality as Premise and Problem, as Risk and Riches

The need to contextualize theology arises under the stimulus of a missionary situation. For practical purposes, "missionary theology" can be called European or, if one prefers, Atlantic, so as to include the United States, Canada, and, in a remote way Australia and New Zealand. Though laying claim to universality, it is strongly conditioned by a different context in which the content to be handed on arose and took its form. And indeed, though not normally considered a contextualized theology, European theology is certainly contextual. Though following a deductive method (whether dogmatic and taking its point of departure from council definitions and decisions of the magisterium, or whether genetic, taking as point of departure the biblical datum and, successively, patristic, scholastic, and modern thought) and not the inductive one, like the new contextualized theologies, the choice of this method is also conditioned by a specific context; even if unconsciously, induction always precedes deduction.

The need for contextualization reveals a further aspect, namely, European theology sometimes assumed ideological form in the context of the colonization and exploitation of the Third World. There has to be an examination of the relationship between theological thought and the political and social problems of the First World too.

The programmatic aspect of contextualized theologies claims our attention all the more easily owing to the fact that traditional European theology was not, and still is not, any less programmatic. It discharges the function of continuing, purifying, and propagating church life in its many dimensions; divisions among Christians often gave a confessional accent to traditional ecclesial theology.

For European theology, meanwhile, there is the problem that its traditional program may no longer be sufficient; the context has changed because of secularization and growing religious indifference, shading off into AGNOSTICISM. Contextualization hence would mean encounter not only with other religions but with no religion.

If the need for contextualization outside Europe reveals contextuality as the inevitable premise of European theology, this discovery in turn makes us aware of the contextuality of every contextualization and of the problems this involves.

Contextualized theologies, which have to take account of their own contextuality, and European theology—which, being contextual, ought in a process of contextualization to think these matters out and make such situations more effective—are in the ultimate analysis both faced with the same problems. Problems of this sort ought also to be tackled with the help of the sociology of knowledge at a macrosociological level (the context of theology) and that of the sociology of science at a microsociological level (the situation of the theologian). This second level concerns, for instance, the academic level attained by individual theologians.

At the macrosociological level, the basic problem is how to individualize and define a context. What criterion should we adopt? Revelation offers no criterion. Salvation is universal, and the entire human race is destined to be the chosen people in the eschaton.

As criterion, some contextualized theologies suggest the division into a few big units; besides the (many!) theologies of the Third World, there would be those of the First and Second worlds. This sort of division, however, is somewhat problematic. If for the Third World we already have to talk of theologies in the plural, its conception of itself would be hard to define. Being formulated for the most part on the basis of economic factors (here problems arise already for theological discourse), the concept suggests further delineations. Why not then talk of Third Worlds in the plural, or of a Fourth World or even a Fifth. Another question: who is entitled to make a classification that will not be discriminatory? Parenthetically, we might also mention the fact that not every theology thought up *in* the Third World is a theology *of* the Third World.

No lesser problems arise over the identity of the so-called Second World. Regardless of the impact on theology, it must be said that since the events of 1989 the reality of the Second World eludes effective definition. Finally, the First World itself is no less problematic as a unitary concept. Australia and New Zealand are now searching for their own definition of their identity; the United States and Canada (now in an uneasy dialogue with the United States) are not to be identified with European nations, despite all the historical links that in fact exist.

Other contextualized theologies seem to point to an ethnic criterion. The problems associated with a criterion of this sort would spring from a cultural romanticism that would pay no attention either to negative elements of the past or to disagreements in the present or to inevitable development in the future. (Contextualized theologies are especially to be found among populations where the younger generations form the majority.)

Traditional historiography and political praxis suggest another criterion for identifying individual contexts: the easily identifiable

units formed by states. As realities, however, these are theologically irrelevant, for neither in the socioeconomic dimension nor in the cultural one (expressed particularly in language and predominant philosophy, nourished too by a common history and common traditions) can the actual frontiers be regarded as separating or uniting. Several states often share in a single culture, and some states are pluricultural. Perhaps it might be desirable to assume as context interstatal regions, e.g., the Mediterranean or, in a different continent, the Caribbean.

A second problem, linked to the foregoing thoughts, arises from the fact that every criterion adopted to identify or define a particular context—on which then to individuate the contextuality of theology and to construct its contextualization—could not remove the ever-present danger of a fragmentation of theology and its consequent isolation. The greatest and most easily incurred danger in contextualization carried to extremes is without doubt that of passing from an acritical and unscientific parochialism to a blind creation of ideology.

The risks of parochialism can be overcome by efforts that can become sources of riches. One thinks of joint research and study, which presupposes constant contact between theologians, of the exchange of publications, and of the functions performed by congresses, organizations, and, in a special way, international academic institutions.

The contextualization of theology thus ought to encourage a renewed quest for a "planetary" theology that would integrate all the various expressions without negating them; universality does not mean uniformity. Beyond the many contexts, there is still the common context of the whole human race, the basic unity of which ought to be stressed. Thanks to developments in communication, the world has become a global village, now in a phase of rapid urbanization and with a common culture, which in its technological aspect and democratic idealism originates from the First World. World problems—including the North-South divide, with the special aspect of population explosion and the threat of nuclear or ecological catastrophe—are the responsibility of all. The renewal of a theological discourse that will be relevant for this common context is urgently needed.

Such a planetary theology could not claim to be able to start from a blank slate, just as all regional theologies must recognize that revelation itself is irreversibly linked to a specific context and that its initial tradition has unfolded within a specific culture, i.e., the Judaic-Hellenistic-Roman one, subsequently passing into the European one. On the theoretical plane, the problems of the contextuality of theology, which is always a reflection on universal truth, ought to be tackled pretty much as if they were problems concerning the contextuality and the universality of revelation itself.

Bibl.: Bibliographical Instruments. *Exchange: Bulletin de Littérature des Églises du Tiers Monde. Bulletin of Third World Christian Literature* (Leiden, 1972); *Theologie im Kontext: Informationen über theologische Beiträge aus Africa, Asien und Ozeanien* (Aix-la-chapelle, 1980); A. AMATO, "Inculturazione — Contestualizzazione — Teologia in Contesto: Elementi di Bibliografia Scelta," *Sal* 45 (1983): 79–111. General Studies since 1980: T. RENDTORFF, *Europäische Theologie: Versuche einer Ortsbestimmung* (Gütersloh, 1980); D. RITSCHL, *Theologie in den Neuen Welten: Analysen und Berichte aus Amerika und Australasien* (Munich, 1981); H. WALDENFELS, *Theologen der Dritten Welt: Elf biographische Skizzen aus Afrika, Asien und Lateinamerika* (Munich, 1982); V. FABELLA and S. TORRES, eds., *Irruption of the Third World: Challenge to Theology* (Maryknoll, 1983); K. H. NEUFELD, ed., *Problemi e prospettive di Teologia Dogmatica* (Brescia), part 3; R. WINLING, *La théologie contemporaine (1945–1980)* (Paris, 1983); K. DICKSON, *Theology in Africa* (Maryknoll, N.Y., 1984); R. FRIELING, *Befreiungstheologen: Studien zur Theologie in Lateinamerika* (Göttingen, 1984); J. EM and M. SPANGENBERGER, eds., *Theologien der Befreiung: Herausforderung an Kirche, Gesellschaft und Wirtschaft* (Cologne, 1985); R. SCHREITER, *Constructing Local Theologies* (Maryknoll, N.Y., 1985); C. MILITELLO, ed., *Teologia al femminile* (Palermo, 1985); N. STROTMANN, *La Situación de la Teología: Aspectos — Perspectivas — Criterios* (Lima, 1985); *Théologies de la libération: Documents et débats* (Introduction by B. Chenu and B. Lauret) (Paris, 1985); T. WITVLIET, *A Place in the Sun: An Introduction to Liberation Theology in the Third World* (Maryknoll, N.Y., 1985); D. FERM, *Third World Liberation Theologies: An Introductory Survey. A Reader*, 2 vols. (Maryknoll, N.Y., 1986); R. GIBELLINI, *Il dibattito sulla teologia della liberazione* (Brescia, 1986); S. and W. SCHOTTROFF, eds., *Wer ist unser Gott? Beiträge zu einer Befreiungstheologie im Kontext der "ersten" Welt* (Munich, 1986); P. PUTHANAGADY, ed., *Towards an Indian Theology of Liberation* (Bangalore, 1986); S. AROKIASAMY and G. GISPERT SAUCH, eds., *Liberation in Asia: Theological Perspectives* (Anand, 1987); G. W. TROMPF, *The Gospel is not Western: Black Theologies from the Southwest Pacific* (Maryknoll, 1987); F. DUMONT, *L'institution de la théologie: Essai sur la situation du théologien* (Montreal, 1987); V. FABELLA and M. A. ODUYOYE, eds., *With Passion and Compassion: Third World Women doing Theology* (Maryknoll, N.Y., 1988); D. GELPI, *Inculturing North American Theology* (Atlanta, 1988); B. CHENU, *Teologie cristiane dei terzi mondi: teologia latino-americana, teologia nera americana, teologia nera sudafricana, teologia asiatica* (Brescia, 1988); M. SIEVERNICH, *Impulse der Befreiungstheologie für Europa: Ein Lesebuch* (Munich-Mainz, 1988).

Marcel CHAPPIN

VII. MANUALISTIC THEOLOGY

Between the two Vatican councils, Catholic theology found expression above all in the Latin handbooks of fundamental and dogmatic theology used in most seminaries and ecclesiastical universities. The organization, method, and content of these works constituted the theological "normal science" (T. Kuhn) imparted in the Catholic church before the dramatic appearance of new paradigms of thought and exposition in the wake of the Second Vatican Council. A brief account of the main characteristics of manualist fundamental and dogmatic theology can serve to deepen one's understanding of the drama and depth of the recent change.

1. Fundamental Theology

Examples of pre–Vatican II specialized manuals on revelation and fundamental theology are the frequently reprinted works of R. Garrigou-Lagrange (1st ed., 1918), H. J. Dieckmann (1925), S. Tromp (1930), and M. Nicolau (1950). The same general conception of the discipline and its procedures is also found in the initial volume of numerous textbook series, intended as four-year courses of systematic theology, e.g., by Christian Pesch (vol. 1, 1st ed., 1894), A. A. Tanquerey (1894), and L. Lercher (1927). The notable stability of method and content evident in the fundamental theology of these works can be traced back to the late eighteenth century. Of major importance, however, in the worldwide diffusion of this approach to the foundations of faith and theology were the treatises "De vera religione" and "De locis theologicis" in the nine-volume *Praelectiones theologicae* of Giovanni Perrone of the Roman College (d. 1876). Perrone's *Praelectiones*, first published in 1835–42, went through thirty-four editions, with a shorter compendium of them seeing forty-two editions down to 1888.

The principal components of fundamental theology in this manualist tradition were treatises on (1) the nature of religion; (2) the nature of divine revelation, with an exposition of its possibility and necessity for human beings, as well as the criteria by which God's revelation can be recognized for what it is; (3) the *demonstratio christiana*, which shows that Jesus of Nazareth is the fully accredited bearer of God's supernatural revelation to humankind; (4) the *demonstratio catholica*, which shows that the Catholic church was founded by Jesus and entrusted with the mission of transmitting, expounding, and defending divine revelation; and (5) the principal sources of faith's content and of theological work (→ *Loci Theologici*), namely, Scripture and tradition, from which dogmatic theology will gather its data and arguments in expounding the faith and contributing to its deeper understanding.

The centerpiece of manualist fundamental theology is the argumentation, based on historically trustworthy accounts found in the Gospels, (1) that Jesus actually *claimed* to be sent by God as envoy, legate, and spokesman in service of God's revelatory purpose; and (2) that Jesus *legitimated* his claim by the abundant evidence of his fulfillment of prophecy, by his miracles, and climactically by his resurrection from the dead. This demonstration yields the rational and historical conclusion that Jesus of Nazareth, with his messianic self-consciousness and his deeds of power, is credible as teacher and mediator of revelation. Jesus fulfills the criteriological tests for ascertaining the presence of revelation. The evidence for this "judgment of credibility" is, according to the manuals, publicly accessible to those who consult the documents, and the conclusion follows logically and suasively from the facts reported in the documents.

Among the specific marks of the classic manuals, one can first note their common understanding of God's revelation as instruction about otherwise unattainable truths. As such, revelation is easily susceptible of propositional formulation, including the formulation of doctrines about mysteries beyond the reach of natural reason. By revelation God gives us, above all, supernatural knowledge.

The manuals were marked as well by a shared hostility to approaching revelation under the guidance of the principle of IMMANENCE. Articulation of the correspondence between inner needs and the claim and content of revealed doctrines would shift attention to the realm of subjective interiority and could place limits on the content of revelation. The supernatural and positive character of God's communication could be endangered by such a method. The manuals created the environment of conviction that led to the condemnation of "modernism" by Pope Pius X in *Lamentabili* and *Pascendi* (1907), and manualist theology, confirmed by the condemnations and focused on objective historical criteria, was a primary vehicle of diffusion of argumentation contrary to modernism, down to 1960.

The scope of the manuals' demonstrations was not that of eliciting *faith* but instead of showing the credibility of the witness to revelation given by Jesus and his church. Credibility, in this system, imposes itself by the force of assembled evidence and arguments, independently of any inner enlightenment of "the eyes of faith" (Rousselot). Such a fundamental theology brings the mind to the threshold of faith. The movement of mind and will onward to faith is a further step beyond the judgment of credibility, a step in which God's grace attracts the human spirit to embrace and appropriate his word precisely because it is divine revelation. Faith rests on the authority of God himself, which imposes itself as the warrant for the truths to be accepted and giving certitude of an order quite different from the conclusion regarding credibility. But fundamental theology's demonstrations are still useful, since they set forth the external signs by which God recommends his legates to human reason. The assent of faith, while remaining supernatural, is thus shown not to be irrational, but instead an "obsequium rationi consentaneum" (Vatican I, DS 3009).

2. Dogmatic Theology

Since theological method is treated at length elsewhere in this work (→ METHOD), we give only a brief characterization of the treatises on God, Christ, grace, the sacraments, etc., presented in the dogmatic manuals of Catholic theology between the two Vatican councils.

The manuals practice the "regressive" method in their argumentation and exposition. This entails beginning from present-day teaching of the ecclesiastical magisterium and then showing how this doctrine was originally expressed in Scripture and then developed in the patristic and medieval expressions of Catholic faith. The sources are read in the light of what is taught and believed in the church of the theologian's own day. The intended result is an account of the harmonious development by sages down to what is explicit in present-day teaching. This method, long dominant in manualist practice, received official sanction from Pope Pius XII in *Humani Generis* (1950), who stated that the magisterium is to be the theologian's "proximate and universal norm of truth" and that the task of theology is to show how magisterial teachings are found explicitly or implicitly in Scripture and apostolic tradition (DS 3884; 3886).

The manuals are often termed "neoscholastic" and are at times said to have developed under the influence of Pope Leo XIII's *Aeterni Patris* (1879), with its endorsement of Thomas Aquinas as the model and norm of Catholic thought. However, upon closer examination, the manuals appear to diverge considerably from the universal scope and quest of wisdom found in the high-medieval *summae*. Manualist method was more deeply marked by the principles of Melchior Cano (→ LOCI THEOLOGICI) than by those of Thomas Aquinas. The manuals are children of their own time, the age of positivism, and give pride of place to the amassing of data to support their conclusions. The ten *loci* of Cano are considerably simplified in the manuals, which most typically follow their precise enunciation of church teaching by a standard three-step procedure of proof from Scripture, tradition, and the rational arguments showing the plausibility of the doctrine and its coherence with other certainties of the natural and supernatural order.

The manuals might well seem to have been instruments of indoctrination in fidelity to authoritative teaching. It is true that, in tendency, they ascribed the role of principal subject of theological activity to the conciliar and papal magisterium. But at the same time, the best manualist theologians were adept at a close and critical reading of magisterial documents. As the manualist established present-day doctrine, before having recourse to the sources, he carefully calibrated the exact weight of authority attached to the doctrinal thesis and to each of its parts. Essential to the system was the differentiated scale of "theological notes," which were applied in giving the doctrines presented a precise place on the descending scale of degrees of authority, from solemnly defined dogma down to a mere probability of theological opinion. Correspondingly, students were made aware of the different degrees of certitude found within one's global adherence to Catholic teaching.

3. Problems and Values

Manualist theology was beset with difficulties well before its wholesale repudiation after Vatican II. The Thomist tradition, for example, as cultivated by the school of Le Saulchoir, called attention to the instrumental role of the enunciation of doctrine by the church. The formulas are not the ultimate object of faith but are intermediate in faith's movement into union with the personal and saving truth of God himself. Manualist dogmatic method subordinated even Scripture to the overriding purpose of proving the doctrines of the day; instead, the latter should serve as aids and instruments in the understanding of God's own word, the revealed datum, as this has been articulated by his inspired prophets and apostles and especially by his Son.

Biblical studies, gaining momentum after World War II, showed that manualist fundamental theology was misconstruing the Gospels by treating them as historical chronicles. Christian personalism found completely alien the extrinsicism of the manuals' treatment of supernatural revelation and called insistently for attention to the resonances between what arises from the human heart and God's gift in Christ.

A theology of faith centered on submission to authoritative instruction was seen to distort the basic NT perception of revelation as God's invitation to communion of life with him. Vatican II, in *DV*, appropriated the latter view in an emphatically christocentric manner, and this sealed the doom of manualist fundamental theology.

However, it should well be recalled, in our postmanualist age, that the manuals kept theology in close touch with the life of the church of its own day. Their field of vision was indeed reduced to the sole consideration of the magisterium, to the neglect of the church's worship, *sensus fidelium*, and other signs of the Spirit, but their theology was kept from falling into an antiquarian treatment of the sources by its concern for enunciating with all due precision the present-day faith of the church.

Manualist fundamental theology may not have done justice to the richness of God's saving revelation, especially as this reaches its fullness in the person and life of Jesus himself. But that same theology showed an exemplary concern for relating revelation to human history and faith to human rationality. The manuals strove mightily to preserve the transcendence of supernatural revelation, but they did not for this reason flee from the realm of human thought and methodical discourse. The argument for credibility was a sustained effort to relate faith to reason. In our day credibility is articulated in a radically different manner. But the manualist tradition reminds one of the basic issues at stake here, namely, that faith be inserted into the center of human thinking, seeking, and loving, and there work out a communicable and intelligible account of its hope.

Bibl.: A. GABOARDI, "Teologia fondamentale: Il método do apologetica," in *Problemi e orientamenti di Teologia dommatica* (Milan, 1957), 1:57–103; G. THILS, *Orientations de la théologie* (Louvain, 1958); T. S. KUHN, *The Structure of Scientific Revolutions* (Chicago, 1962); M.-D. CHENU, "La théologie au Saulchoir," in *La Parole de Dieu*, vol. 1: *La Foi dans l'intelligence* (Paris, 1964), 243–67; B. WELTE, "Zum Strukturwandel der katholischen Theologie im 19. Jahrhundert," in *Auf dem Spur des Ewigen* (Freiburg, 1965), 380–409; R. LATOURELLE, *Theology: Science of Salvation* (New York, 1969); J. SCHMITZ, "La théologie fondamentale," in R. Van der Gucht and H. Vorgrimler, eds., *Bilan de la théologie du XXe siècle* (Tournai/Paris, 1970), 2:9–51; G. COLOMBO, "La teologia manualistica," in *La teologia italiana oggi* (Milan, 1979), 25–56; G. DALY, *Transcendence and Immanence: A Study in Catholic Modernism and Integralism* (Oxford, 1980); F.-J. NIEMANN, *Jesus als Glaubensgrund in der Fundamentaltheologie der Neuzeit* (Innsbruck/Vienna, 1983); G. HEINZ, *Divinam christianae religionis originem probare: Untersuchungen zur Entstehung des fundamentaltheologischen Offenbarungstraktat der katholischen Schultheologie* (Mainz, 1984).

Jared WICKS

THOMAS AQUINAS

If Thomas Aquinas is here chosen as a landmark for speaking of revelation in the medieval period, it is because he represents mature scholasticism and also because we do not find in later theologians any broader perspectives than those that he adopted, even if he does not have a theology of revelation in the modern sense of the phrase. After him and down to the twentieth century, terminology would become more precise and more technical, but thinking on the subject would not show any corresponding great gain in depth. The striking thing in Thomas, who died in 1274, is the rich multiplicity of aspects that he finds in the reality that is revelation: saving activity inspired by God's unmerited love; historical event that unfolds in time and reaches the human beings of every ages; divine action intermeshing with the psychological life of the prophets; sacred teaching communicated by Christ to his apostles and transmitted through them to the church; degree of knowledge located between natural knowledge, the knowledge of faith, and the knowledge of vision.

1. Revelation as Saving Action

The whole of theology, the entire life of faith, and the entire revealed datum come from revelation, but the revealed datum itself is not directly called revelation. "Revelation" signifies an action proceeding from God's gratuitous love and aimed at the salvation of the human race. Since this salvation is God himself in his interior life and is therefore an object that completely transcends the powers and exigencies of human nature, it was necessary that God himself make himself known to human beings in order to tell them of this end and of the way leading to it (*ST* 1, q. 1, a. 1c). However, since knowledge of the truths of the natural order concerning God and our relations with him is difficult for people to acquire without risk of error, God has revealed these truths as well, "in order that all might easily be able to have a share in the knowledge of God, and this without uncertainty or error" (*CG* 1, 4; *ST* 1, q. 1, a. 1c; see Vatican I, DS 3005; ND 114).

Thomas thus thinks of revelation in the *active* sense, as an action of God who freely and in his goodness provides human beings with truths that are necessary and useful for the attainment of their supernatural salvation. That which is revealed (the *revelatum*) is essentially the truths about God that are inaccessible to reason and therefore can be known only by way of revelation. That which can be revealed (the *revelabile*) is such truths that are not of themselves beyond the ability of reason to acquire but that God has revealed because they are useful in the work of salvation and because the majority of human beings, if left to their own resources, would not acquire a knowledge of them; these further truths, then, are part of the revealed datum. In short, the *revelatum* must be revealed, while the *revelabile* can be revealed (*ST* 1, q. 1, a. 3, ad 2).

2. Revelation as Historical Event

Revelation thus viewed is regarded by Thomas as a hierarchical action, marked by succession, progress, and a multiplicity of the forms and means of communication.

a. First, revelation is a *hierarchical* action. The truth of salvation comes to us like the water from a great spring, which reaches the plain only after having formed a series of pools: first the angels, according to the order within the heavenly hierarchies; then human beings, and, among these, first the greatest among them, namely, the prophets and apostles. The water spreads out to the multitude of those who accept it by faith, but it follows a similar course: those with a more extensive knowledge of it must transmit it and explain it to the simple faithful, who are obliged to hold explicitly only to the articles of faith (*ST* 2-2, q. 2, a. 6c). The phase of constitutive revelation is followed by the phase of applied revelation.

b. Second, revelation is marked by *succession*. It is not given all at once but in stages that represent partial fulfillments of the complete divine plan. Such was the richness of revelation that humanity needed centuries of preparation in order gradually to take possession of it and assimilate it (*Ad Heb.*, c. 1, lect. 1). Three ages, as it were, can be distinguished in the history of revelation; at the beginning of each a higher revelation is given from which others then flow. There is the revelation, given to Abraham, of the existence of a single God; this is the basis of patriarchal revelation and is addressed to only a few families. Then there is the revelation, given to Moses, of the name of God; this is the foundation of the prophetic era and is addressed to an entire people. Finally, there is the revelation of Christ, along with the revelation of the mystery of the inner life of God; this is the foundation of the Christian era and is addressed to the entire human race. God condescends to the weakness of humankind, allowing only as much light to filter through as human beings are capable of receiving (*ST* 2-2, q. 1, a. 7, ad 3).

c. A twofold movement is at work in the economy of revelation and determines the *dynamics of its progress*. On the one hand, there is the movement by which the deposit of revelation is gradually established, namely, the movement from the patriarchs to the prophets and on to the apostles. On the other, there is the movement that brings the human race closer and closer to the incarnation. The nearer Christ's coming, the nearer the fullness of revelation. Christ brings the springtime of grace, the time of fulfillment. "The ultimate perfection of grace became a reality in Christ; therefore the time of Christ is called the time of fullness (*ST* 2-2, q. 1, a. 7, ad 4).

d. Finally, revelation is *multiform*. In making himself known, God has not contemned any form of communication. In his commentary on the letter to the Hebrews (*Ep. ad Heb.* c. 1, lect. 1), Thomas stresses the extraordinary wealth and variety of God's ways, namely, the multiplicity and variety of the persons to whom revelation is addressed; the variety of psychological processes used (bodily, imaginary, and intellectual visions); revelations having to do with the past, the present, and the future; revelations given to instruct human beings or to punish them for their infidelities; finally, variety in the degree of clarity or obscurity. In Christ and his apostles the event of revelation reaches its climax and fullest form. This does not mean that the spirit of prophecy has disappeared. Some human beings are given it, not to make up for some deficiency in revelation, but to show human beings how they should act in light of the revelation already given (*ST* 2-2, q. 174, a. 6, ad 3).

3. Prophetic Revelation as an Intellectual Charism

Thomas focuses his attention chiefly on prophetic revelation (*De ver.* 12; *ST* 2-2, qq. 171–74; *CG* 3, 154). Modernists developed the false idea that Catholic revelation contains only truths that have, as it were, fallen from the skies; they would have profited from reading Thomas, who, centuries before, concerned himself with the psychological aspect of revelation as a divine action that intermeshes with the activity of the human psyche. His treatise on prophecy is marked by a surprising respect for the complex data of prophetic experience.

In discussing prophecy, Thomas distinguishes between prophetic *knowledge* and its use, i.e., the *denuntiatio* or publication of the prophecy (*ST* 2-2, q. 171, a. 1c). In a first stage, prophets experience the action of the divine light on them (*De ver.* 12.1c). Then, in a second stage, they proclaim. In this stage they choose images that accord with their own temperament and personal experience. How, concretely, does the unveiling take place that puts the prophets in possession of divine truth (*ST* 2-2, q. 171, a. 6c)? Like every form of human knowledge, prophetic knowledge involves representations (*acceptio rerum*) and a judgment, but both of these are raised to a higher level by the charism of prophecy; i.e., the judgment is made under the influence of a special light given to the prophets. "The formal element in prophetic knowledge is the divine light; it is from the unity of this light that prophecy derives its specific unity, despite the variety of the objects which the light makes known to the prophets" (*ST* 2-2, q. 171, a. 3, ad 3). What this light illumines is, after all, a datum of immense richness: historical event, behavior of human beings, interior visions, dreams, etc.

The essence of prophecy, however, does not consist in this representational element but in the divine light given to the seers so that they are able to discern, judge, and express God's

intentions. Thanks to the illumination they receive, prophets judge with certainty and without error the elements present in their consciousness and thus take possession of the truth that God intends to communicate to them. This illumination and this judgment truly unveil the divine thought to the prophets. Once they are thus enriched, they respond in a vital way. They are passive under the inspiration that elevates their minds, but they actively perceive the revelation given to them (*ST* 2-2, q. 171, 1, ad 4). They move beyond the level of images and reach the deeper truth to which the images point (*ST* 2-2, q. 173, 2, ad 2). The light that God grants is thus the essential element that marks prophets. But prophets in the full sense of the term are those who receive from God both the representations and the light by which to judge them (*ST* 2-2, q. 173, a. 2c). In revelation in the fullest sense of the term, "prophets possess the greatest certitude concerning the realities which they know through the gift of prophecy, and they regard it as certain that these truths have been divinely revealed to them" (*ST* 2-2, q. 171, a. 5c). This is why Jeremiah can say: "In truth the LORD sent me to you to speak all these words in your ears" (Jer 26:15). In the brilliant light given to them, the prophets perceive, without explicit reasoning (as one sees a cause in its effect), that God is the source of this light and the author of the truth that the light makes known to them. Prophets need no other sign; the light they receive is so intense that they are completely certain of its origin. This was true of Abraham as he prepared to sacrifice his son Isaac as a result of the illumination he had received (*ST* 2-2, q. 171, a. 5c). Teresa of Avila expresses herself in this same way (*Interior Castle*, Sixth Dwelling).

The action by which God communicates with human beings through created signs is called by Thomas *word of God* because of the analogy between God's action and human speech, which is likewise a communication of thought through signs. The interior word, in the case of the prophets, is identical with the divine illumination of the mind (*De ver.* q. 12, a. 1, ad 3). "Word," understood as communication between intelligent beings, is a category that includes human, angelic, and divine communication (*ST* 1, q. 107, a. 1c; q. 107, a. 2; *De ver.* q. 18, a. 3). As sound or gesture, "word" can be attributed to God only by metaphor, but as spiritual event and communication of thought, it implies no imperfection and can therefore be attributed to him. Just as in external speech we use words to convey meaning, so when God enlightens the prophets, he gives them a meaningful representation, a sign of his spiritual essence. It is in this way that God spoke to Adam, the patriarchs, and the prophets. These signs are evidently only imperfect representations of the divine mystery; nevertheless, by way of them, thanks to the light that enlightens the prophets, God introduces us into his life: he speaks to us.

4. Revelation through Christ and the Apostles

Thomas's thought on the revelatory function of Christ is less developed than his analysis of the prophetic experience. The *Summa* does, however, contain some very stimulating hints on the role of Christ and the apostles. The prologue of part 3, which deals with Christ the savior, begins as follows: Christ "has shown us the way of truth" so that through him we might go to the Father. When human beings want to make their thought known, they enflesh it in sounds or written symbols; so too, "God, desiring to make himself known to the human race, clothed in flesh within time the Word he had conceived from all eternity" (*In Jo.* c. 14, lect. 2). Through the flesh that he took, the Word speaks to us and we hear him (*In Jo.* c. 11, lect. 6). No one is better able than he to make truth known, for he is Light and Truth in person (*In Jo.* c. 18, lect. 6). Christ preaches and teaches by his actions as well as by his words (*In Jo.* c. 11, lect. 6), but unlike human teachers, he teaches interiorly as well as exteriorly (*In Jo.* c. 13, lect. 3; c. 3, lect. 1). He instructs his apostles by his preaching and by his Spirit (*In Jo.* c. 17, lect. 6), who makes known to them the meaning of the teaching. There is no doubt that in his thinking on revelation, Thomas gives pride of place to the result of the revelatory action, i.e., to the truth of the faith. His terminology is clear: to the totality of the knowledge that God has revealed to the prophets and apostles, Thomas gives the name "sacred doctrine," or "the teaching according to the revelation" contained in the Scriptures (*ST* 1, q. 1, a. 1c).

5. From Revelation to Church and Faith

God presented his truth directly to the prophets and apostles; to us he makes it known through the church. The church is, then, the infallible rule when it comes to presenting revealed truth (*ST* 2-2, q. 5, a. 3c, ad 2 and ad 3). The creeds that punctuate the history of the church express one and the same faith; they make revealed truth more explicit in order to counteract errors or incipient deviations. Most human beings have only mediate access to revelation, through the preaching of the church. God helps us in three ways to believe: through external preaching, through miracles that accredit this preaching, and "through an interior attraction, which is nothing else than an inspiration of the Spirit who thereby enables human beings to give their assent to some object of faith.... This drawing is necessary, since our hearts would not turn toward God unless he himself drew us to him" (*In Rom.* c. 8, lect. 6; *ST* 2-2, q. 2, a. 9, ad 3). The interior call of grace is the "testimony" given by the First Truth, which enlightens and instructs human beings interiorly" (*Quodl.* 2, q. 4, a. 6, ad 3). Thus God gives human beings two gifts: the gift of saving doctrine and the gift of the grace by which to accept this teaching in faith. Thomas does not give the name "revelation" to this action of grace, or at least he does not do so habitually; he describes it rather as a call, an attraction, a help, a movement, a testimony, and, above all, an interior instinct that comes to us from God as a personal call to each individual.

6. Revelation as a Degree of Knowledge of God

Revelation and faith are not ends in themselves but exist for the sake of the vision of God, since the end of the human person is to enter someday into the contemplation of God. In this sense, historical revelation is an imperfect knowledge, a phase in our initiation into the vision of God. Human beings can have three degrees of knowledge of God: in the first, they *rise* toward God with the aid of created things; in the second, God *descends* to them, stoops to them, reveals himself to them; in the third, human beings "*will be raised up* to see perfectly what has been revealed to them" (*CG* 4, 1). This consummation of revelation will take place only in our fatherland (*ST* 2-2, q. 5, a. 1, ad 1). Only then "will the First Truth be known, not by faith, but by vision.... Then human beings will be present with truth that is no longer wrapped in veils, but completely unveiled" (*CG* 4, 1). Through his word God leads us little by little into the mystery of his interior life.

Bibl.: THOMAS AQUINAS, *De Veritate*, q. 12; id., *Summa theol.*, 2a 2ae, q. 171–74; id., *CG.*, 53, c. 154; S. M. ZARB, "Le fonti agostiniane del trattato sulla profezia di S. Tommaso," *Angelicum* 15 (1938): 169–200; B. DECKER, "Die Analyse des Offenbarungsvorganges beim hl. Thomas im Lichte vorthomistischer Prophetietraktate," *Angelicum* 16 (1939): 195–244; id., *Die Entwicklung der Lehre von der prophetischen Offenbarung von Wilhelm von Auxerre bis zu Thomas von Aquin* (Breslau, 1940); V. WHITE, "Le concept de révélation chez S. Thomas," *L'année théologique* 11 (1950): 1–17, 109–32; B. DUROUX, *La psychologie de la foi chez S. Thomas d'Aquin* (Freiburg, 1956); A. NYSSENS, *La plénitude de vérité dans le Verbe incarné: Doctrine de S. Thomas d'Aquin* (Baudouinville, 1961); R. LATOURELLE, *Theology of Revelation* (Staten Island, N.Y., 1966), 159–80; J.-C. TORRELL, "Le traité de la prophétie de S. Thomas d'Aquin et la théologie de la Révélation," in L. Elders, ed., *La doctrine de la révélation divine de saint Thomas d'Aquin* (Vatican City, 1990), 171–95.

René LATOURELLE

TILLICH, PAUL

1. A Theonomous Philosophy

The religious meditation, philosophical reflection, and theological system of Paul Tillich (1886–1965) is dominated by his preoccupation with the "ultimate human problem," namely, a quest for the "unconditional" (*The Ultimate Concern*).

The Question of the Unconditional

From his earliest published writings, which were devoted to a study of Schelling's thought, Tillich addressed the problem of a philosophical understanding of religion (*Mystik und Schuldbewusstsein in Schellings philosophischer Entwicklung* [1912]). This "ultimate concern" is attested in all of Tillich's writings, especially in those devoted to the philosophical study of the concept of religion (*Religionsphilosophie* [1925]), or to the place of theology in the system of the sciences (*Das System der Wissenschaften nach Gegenständen und Methoden* [1923]), or to an analysis of the semiotics of the sacred and of the believing existence (*Religiöse Verwirklichung* [1930]), or to the study of the relationship between biblical revelation and human existence (*Biblical Religion and the Search for Ultimate Reality* [1955]). Tirelessly, Tillich searched for a "theonomous philosophy" of cultural and historical reality. His philosophical writings seek to situate the ethical or political, aesthetic or cultural problematic in the perspective of theonomy—whether he is discussing the relationship between religious values and reality or analyzing the religious foundation of ethical action. His political philosophy of "religious socialism" and his moral philosophy of the postmodern ethos constitute expressions of a theonomous ethics (*Protestantisches Prinzip und proletarische Situation* [1931]; *Love, Power, and Justice* [1954]). The same is true of his theoretical philosophical writings on culture or history, whether they analyze the tensions obtaining between freedom and destiny, or *kairos* and *logos*, or idealism and existentialism, or whether they propose his view of a "believing realism," or his notion of a "theology of culture" or his theory of the presence of the "demonic" in history (*Über die Idee einer Theologie der Kultur* [1919]; *Kairos und Logos* [1926]; *Philosophie und Schicksal* [1929]; *Das Dämonische* [1926]).

In Tillich, all theoretical or practical questions are contemplated in the perspective of the unconditional, in a quest for the revelation of its hidden presence in social or cultural reality, with a view to grasping the religious sense of the spiritual situation (*Die religiöse Lage der Gegenwart* [1926]). Thus is born and develops a religious thought in which culture and religion, political reality and prophetic principle, stand in stubborn confrontation, whether in the oscillating outward reality of culture or history, or in the inner world of doubt and faith (*Rechtfertigung und Zweifel* [1924]). Gradually an anthropology develops in the form of an ontology of existence that goes in search of the foundation or ground of being and meaning (*The Courage to Be* [1952]; *Morality and Beyond* [1963]). Tillich's autobiographical writings also testify to the importance of the dimension of depth as he felt it to be present in his personal trek (*On the Boundary* [1936]; *Autobiographical Reflections* [1952]). His religious meditations tirelessly propose the irruption of the unconditional in the depths of being and the presence of the eternal in the fleeting, propitious moment of the revelation of definitive truth (*The Shaking of the Foundations* [1948]; *The New Being* [1955]; *The Eternal Now* [1963]).

From his first works to his last, the recurrent theme of the Tillichian reflection is a constant search for the absolute, the infinite, and the definitive, as present in relative and contradictory contingent reality, in a dialectical confrontation between philosophical doubt and religious wisdom. This correlation became dominant to the point of constituting the methodical proposition and systematic response of his magnum opus of theonomous theology, in which autonomy and theonomy, doubt and faith, reason and revelation, ontology and theology, anthropology and Christology, existence and salvation, ethics and pneumatology, church and society, and history and eschatology stand in uninterrupted confrontation (*Systematic Theology*, 3 vols. [1951–63]).

The Philosophical Project

As a philosopher of religion, Tillich remained faithful to three fundamental convictions. First came the rigor of the methodical doubt of an interrogating reason. Second was the originality of the experience of the sacred as revelation and irruption of the unconditional. Finally, there was the paradoxical character of Christianity as a religion of grace. The main emphasis of Tillich's logic of believing reason is the unconditional character of religious content, and therefore the impossibility of founding it on any conditional reality, such as the world or the I, culture or history. Given the fact that, for Tillich, even metaphysics is defined by its thrust to express the unconditional in rational categories, theology can be developed only as a kind of theonomous metaphysics, inasmuch as its intent is a rational elaboration of religious content.

Tillich also develops a theory of the relationship between culture and religion, i.e., a philosophy of culture in a theonomous perspective. Here religion furnishes culture with the unconditional ground of the meaning of all reality; in turn, culture outfits religion both with the symbols of the unconditional and with the conditional forms of secular autonomy in all of the great areas of human values: truth in science, beauty in art, justice in society, love in community. Hence will follow the possibility of a religious analysis of cultural phenomena, in a transcendence of the diastasis between sacred and profane, and accordingly, the possibility of an authentic theology of culture.

In his theoretical philosophy, Tillich takes up his position on the borderline between idealism and existentialism. On the one side, he asserts the "principle of identity" between subject and object, denying that the conditions of the possibility of subjective experience are reducible to raw objectivity. The identity between thinking and being, as the principle of truth, enables one to get beyond any naturalistic or empiricist attitude. On the other side, in his practical philosophy, Tillich corrects the idealistic ethic of freedom through the application of a "principle of freedom" that addresses both an internal and an external freedom. The correspondence between the human mind and objective reality becomes evident in the "sciences of the mind," in their nature as systematic constructions of the thinking subject in search of the meaning of reality, in nature or art, in society or history. But Tillich sets limits to the claim of idealism to constitute absolute knowledge, underscoring the principle of difference observable in the frequent contradiction between the ideal and the real, certitude and doubt, happiness and *Angst*—in a word, between essence and existence.

In Tillich, then, on the theoretical plane as on the practical, idealism is affirmed, denied, and transcended. This transcendence of idealistic essentialism is effected through the integration of an "existential correction" in the system. On the individual level as on the social, the knowledge of truth is bound up with the situation of the knowing subject. Thus, a knowledge of essence becomes impossible without an acknowledgment of the conditions and contradictions of existence, whether as existential anguish on an individual level, or as class struggle on the social, historical level. With a view to a more adequate knowledge of existential reality, individual and social, Tillich employs two approaches typical of postmodernity: an existential psychoanalysis of Freudian origin, and a social dialectic stemming from Marx. This twin methodology led Tillich, on the individual level, to a certain existential

Stoicism, and on the social level, to a certain religious socialism.

As a concept of mediation between Lutheranism and socialism, Tillich developed the notion of *kairos*. The reign of God is far, and ever distant, but it becomes present in history as a critical judgment rendered upon a certain type of society, and as the shaping norm of a future kind of historical reality more nearly approaching the ideal of justice. Thus, a political philosophy centering on the project of a religious socialism finds its foundation in a particular philosophy of history, in which history is conceptualized as a lengthy journey toward the *novum* whose center coincides with the religious event of Christian revelation, so that this event appears as the principle of meaning of historical intelligibility and the authentic measure of history itself. The contrasting forces at work in history may be classified in terms of three qualities: as the demonic force of an oppressing, total power (*heteronomy*); as the emancipation of the human under the form of outright secularism (*autonomy*); or as the unconditional irruption of the sacred under the symbols of the exigency of prophetic religion (*theonomy*). The commitment to religious socialism is conceptualized exclusively in a theonomous perspective as the defeat both of demonic, heteronomous totalitarianisms and of the profane, exasperated secular autonomy typical of secularism and bourgeois decadence.

2. A Philosophical Theology

Tillich's *Systematic Theology* also develops the problematic of a "believing realism," in terms of the basic dialectic and correlation of the finite and the Infinite, the conditional and the unconditional, in a contemplation of the irruption of the Absolute in revelation and nature, in salvation history and grace.

The Method of Correlation

Tillich's theological system is conceived in the schema of a "bifocal ellipse." The twin foci of this ellipse are critical and ecstatic *reason*, which questions and contemplates, and the *revelation* of theonomy and mystery, which answers the human being's ultimate questions in the great religious symbols of Christianity. The human being and God constitute the basic theological correlation. Tillich's entire theo-

logical system is presented in five parts, preceded by an introduction on the nature and method of his *Systematic Theology*. Step by step, Tillich develops his thematics through his three volumes. The first volume, after the introduction, comprises the first two parts of the system, which are devoted to a study of the correlation between reason and revelation and between being and God. The second volume proposes the third part and is devoted to human existence and Christ. The third volume sets forth the two final parts, devoted to life and the Spirit, and history and the kingdom of God. But the basic dialectic remains the same throughout: the human being asks, and God answers; critical reason questions, and ecstatic revelation answers; finite being wonders about finitude, and God responds in the sphere of the unconditional and the sacred, as the Infinite and Absolute, in a self-revelation as Lord and Father. Alienated existence questions; Christ answers, as divine salvation and as expression of the "new being" in grace. Life, in its ambivalence of essential finitude and existential alienation, asks; the Spirit answers, in the dimension of religious depth and the authenticity of a "theonomous autonomy," through a process of prophetic discernment realized in concrete individual or social, religious or ecclesial, experience. History interrogates us, and the reign of God, with its unexpected, propitious *kairos*, furnishes us with the definitive eschatological answer.

In this way, Tillich's crowning work addresses, successively, the great questions of the human being and of Christianity, always in terms of the insuperable tension between philosophical reason, with its methodical doubt, and faith, with its unconditional certitude, which offers us the answer. Tillich's philosophical theology develops an ontology of essential finitude and existential alienation, vital ambiguity and historical ambivalence, in which many of the motifs of the philosophical culture of modernity find their echo, from Kant to Schleiermacher, from Schelling to Heidegger. A rereading of the great Pauline-Lutheran theme of justification in *sola gratia* synthesizes biblical motifs and postmodern ones—from Marx to Freud, for example, with regard to the question of existential alienation, individual and social. But the entire evangelical-Lutheran tradition passes through Tillich's Platonic-Augustinian filter of an understanding in search of faith, in the process of an inner way and the immediate certitude of a religious unconditional, in the ecstatic moment of a clinging to the Infinite. The *deus interior* of Augustine or the *deus supra deum* of Denis is Tillich's God as well. Profoundly modifying the outlook of evangelical fideism, against Luther Tillich will say that it is impossible to reach the *deus revelatus* apart from the religious experience of the *deus absconditus*.

Finite and Infinite

Tillich stresses the profound identity between the God of transcendence, in the dimension of the unconditional, and the God of the irruption of the sacred in the religious experience of Christian revelation. There are not two absolutes; thus, against Pascal, Tillich will say that the God of the philosophers and the God of Abraham are the same God, the only God. Eschatological revelation occurs in Christ, but its religious relevance is verified in the existential echo of the great Christian symbols. This means that revelation and its symbols become relevant only in an encounter with personal experience, mediated by the cultural and social situation. But for Tillich, the human condition is characterized by a finitude essentially open to the Infinite, and by an alienation existentially scored by vital and social contradiction. Human reality feels profoundly threatened — first, by death, as an attack on its essential finitude; second, by moral evil, as the concretion of an existential contradiction, as a rejection of the ethical quality of human reality; finally, by the absurd, as threat to the human condition as a spiritual tension in quest of a meaning in our own life and in history. God will be meaningfully revealed only in the methodical confrontation between that human condition, essentially and existentially threatened, and the symbols of Christian revelation, which express the irruption of the unconditional, the ultimate meaning of all reality. God is not available as one more object in the world. God is available only as the ultimate, absolute ground of being and meaning. Thus, God can be found only in the dimension of the unconditional.

Between the human being and God, between the finite and the Infinite, a maximal tension and a profound correlation prevails. For the human being, God is both ground and abyss. Theology must not content itself with explaining the kerygma of the past or trying to translate it in the present. Theological method will be fertile only when it succeeds in explicating the dialectic of meaning between religious reason, which investigates, and revelation, which proclaims to the believer its divine message. For the human being, the basic question underlying the problem of the traumatic quality of life or the tragedy of death, the question lurking beneath the provocation of the absurd or of evil, is precisely the question of being itself, and of the ultimate meaning of reality. A human being discovers himself or herself as a strange finitude, separated from its own foundation and nostalgic for the Infinite. Threatened by contradiction or evil, by a sense of guilt or by anguish in the face of death, by the opacity of meaning or by the transparency of the absurd, in proposing the question of the reality of being, the human being launches an interrogation into a power capable of resisting nonbeing — i.e., of resisting the physical or moral, personal or historical, force of destruction. This indestructible might, more real and more profound than any reality, and identified with the very fullness of being, is legitimately denominated God.

Like the question of the human being, the question of God is approached from a twofold viewpoint: theoretical and practical, essential and vital. Thus, God is regarded not only as *ipsum esse subsistens* ("the very subsisting being"), and the infinite plenitude of the power of being — corresponding, on the essential level, to the question of human finitude — but also, on a vital level, as the "eternal living," which, like anything else alive, transcends itself and returns to itself. God is not dead sameness but absolute fullness of life. *Qua* living, the divine reality is spiritual or personal; *qua* spirit, God is *in se* will and intelligence, power and self-awareness. Thus, the mysterious God is revealed as the infinite, unconditionally holy Being; as the eternal, omnipresent Living One; and as almighty, all-knowing absolute Mind, emerging from self in creation, sharing the suffering of the world in the redemption of all evil, and returning to self, reconciling all with the divine self in a consummated eschatology. For Tillich, the dynamics of the divine life furnish the meaning of the trinitarian doctrine in the great religions and Christianity.

In Tillich's mystical panentheism, the profound transcendental relation between finite reality and infinite Being is developed less in the key of Christian Aristotelianism than in an Augustinian Platonic view, as the self-bestowal of a Creator who undertakes a self-communication to the creature and so becomes a sharer in being. Thus, an ontological-theological *analogia entis* is founded. But between the alienated existence of the sinner and the divine holiness, which is paradoxically revealed in the cross, only an *analogia fidei* is possible, grounded in the justification of the sinner by faith and unmerited grace. Finally, between human reality and the Absolute, the basic relationship is that of an *analogia imaginis*, when the unconditional content of the divine reality communicates to the inner human being its inexhaustible meaning, through conditional forms or symbols of the Infinite. As a result of all this, human language concerning God will always be ontological, paradoxical, and symbolic.

Tillich's philosophical theology resolves itself into a philosophy of revelation that attempts to reflect on the experience of *homo religiosus* and the adherence of this being to Christianity, as a religion of synthesis, in a dialectical reconciliation of secular autonomy and a theonomous perspective, mystical identity, and ethical difference. In finally bringing his project of a theonomous metaphysics to completion, Tillich has bequeathed to us, in a Lutheran and evangelical key, the postmodern version of Christian Platonism. The mighty architecture of his theological system resounds with the echos of an age-old Christian thought that responds to the human yearning for the infinite and absolute, the unconditional and the sacred, and finds in Christ the emblematic paradigm of the "new being" and the *universale concretum* of humanity. However, it is his Christology that doubtless constitutes the *punctum dolens* of Tillich's system, by reason of its adoptionistic, neo-Nestorian accents, with the consequent bestowal upon his trinitarian doctrine, inseparably allied with the vitalistic irrationalism of Schelling's doctrine of the three potencies or powers, a certain quality reminiscent of pre-Nicene dynamic Monarchianism.

Nevertheless, many of the theses of Tillich's anthropology and his ethics, his ecclesiology and his theology of history, have contributed to the renewal of current theological debate. In his polemic against any heteronomy, Tillich constantly proclaims the primacy of theonomy over pure autonomy. His theonomous reading of ontology and ethics, culture and history, always comports an experience of the *numinosum*, characterized by the primacy of unconditional content over the conditional forms of religion itself. The theological ground of that primacy appears in the axiom of a Christian slogan that Tillich so generously adopted, programmatically, in his youth: "Impossibile est sine Deo discere Deum" ("It is impossible to know God without God himself teaching").

Bibl.: P. TILLICH, *Systematic Theology*, 3 vols. (Chicago, 1951–63); id., *Gesammelte Werke*, 14 vols. (Stuttgart, 1959–75); id., *Ergänzungs und Nachlassbände*, 6 vols. (Stuttgart, 1971–83); id., *Dogmatik* (Düsseldorf, 1986); id., *Main Works/Hauptwerke*, 6 vols. (Berlin, 1987–); W. and M. PAUCK, *Paul Tillich: His Life and Thought*, vol. 1: *Life* (New York, 1976); J. L. ADAMS, W. PAUCK and R. L. SHINN, eds., *The Thought of Paul Tillich* (San Francisco, 1985); F.-A. PASTOR, "La interpretación de Paul Tillich," *Greg* 66/4 (1985): 709–39; C. SCHWÖBEL, "Tendenzen der Tillich-Forschung," *Theologische Rundschau* 51/2 (1986): 166–223; R. ALBRECHT and W. SCHÜSSLER, *Paul Tillich: Sein Werk* (Düsseldorf, 1986); F. A. PASTOR, "Itinerario espiritual de Paul Tillich," *Greg* 67/1 (1986): 47–86; N. ERNST, *Die Tiefe des Seins* (St. Ottilien, 1988).

Félix-Alejandro PASTOR

TIME AND TEMPORALITY

Does time have a theological value? In other words, can it make a specific contribution to the effort, shared by all the theological disciplines, to acquire knowledge of God and his work? It seems that until quite recently the answer to this question would have been frankly negative; the heritage of Parmenides had almost replaced the intuition of Heraclitus. Today, however, a reversal in favor of time seems to be taking place, although at times without much discernment and sober thought. I must therefore give a very brief sketch of thinking about time, before pointing out a possible line to be taken in the question of time and theology.

1. The Rejection of Time by Cultures

The thinking mind has not had much love for time, doubtless because time is the measure of movement, the clock the measure of change; the mind looks for the stability that concepts give and, while it must make room for becoming, prefers the solidity of the points of reference that punctuate time, though they fail to capture it. In Greco-Latin culture, Christian as well as pagan, the immobile needs no justification, while movement can be understood only when clearly related to what denies movement. Two essentially fixed points make it possible to put up with mobility while waiting for it to cease: the point beyond the firmament where God abides motionless and eternal, and the center (of the soul or the world or . . .), whose fathomless depths are safe from any fluctuation. Between these two poles, which are perhaps really only one, time and movements that are unavoidable form a hierarchy according to the greater or lesser importance assigned them by the imagination. Thus for Aristotle the continuous circular movements in the vault of heaven are the most excellent and closest to the motionless divine, since they are repeated without alteration and are susceptible of exact measurement. In the *Timaeus* of Plato, in contrast, the meaningless gestures of newborn children are an evident sign of the finitude and even the malice of matter in motion.

Is it the primacy assigned to stability and repose that explains the catastrophic element in the stories people tell? Yes, to some extent, but not completely. Mircea Eliade has called attention to the spontaneous point of reference that is to be seen in stories that are supposedly universal and claim to describe the present situation of human beings. That reference point is *in illo tempore, in illa pulchra insula deserta,* i.e., somewhere outside space and time, because space and time are seen as always intrinsically marked not only by the limitation and finitude they derive from becoming but also by the malice and death that dwell in them; thus the repugnance felt toward time is a way of rejecting the sufferings that time brings. Consequently, since it is not possible to reascend the stream of time or to get outside of space, people try at least to exorcise the evil by singing spell-like stories of origins, by setting the boundaries of sacred places, which are thereby rescued from the guilty profaneness of space, and by performing rites that mark bodies with signs of nonbelonging to time and space and the evil that is in them. If the problem then arises of an ethic for behavior in this world, this ethic is defined in terms of the past, of the ways of the ancestors, of that which has always been done thus and so and, by its repetition, invalidates all novelty in movement, all change in space-time. Mysticism, finally, will always mean a contravention of time and movement because of an ineffable perception of the "beyond" (i.e., beyond space and time!) or an ineffable return to the center. Is it unwarranted to think that certain forms of modern thought conceal beneath their seeming intellectual rigor the same nostalgia for *in illo tempore?* I am thinking here of, for example, the Marx-Engels periodization of social history according to catastrophes; in addition, in this view revolution is regarded, though not expressly described, as the bloody liturgy of a return to the origins. There is something of the same in Heidegger's sketch of the history of metaphysics, where thought has been ceaselessly corrupted ever since the presocratics, who are credited with possessing a "truth" forever lost and never to be recovered except in one or another clearing at crossroads that lead nowhere.

These reflections, admittedly very summary, at least make it possible to lay out some of the conditions required for any theological thinking about time. A means must be found of dissociating suffering and evil from time, which certainly serves as vehicle for them but is not reducible to them. Time does not simply destroy; but how, then, does it build? In other words, how overcome the drift toward the past in thought about time and ground a hope for the future that justifies the present? At a more philosophical level, keys must be found that make it possible to put a value on becoming for its own sake and not simply to the extent that we can relate and reduce it to stability by way of circularity or an eternal return.

2. Christianity and Time: Ambiguities

One might think that since Christianity proclaims the resurrection of Jesus Christ and the incarnation of the Son of God, it provides the elements for a positive appreciation of time.

And so it does. The Scriptures focus attention on a very concrete stretch of history, from Abraham to Jesus Christ, and the inspired writers take the trouble to connect this stretch, by means of chronological information that is obviously fictive but nonetheless signifies the value of time, with the very beginning of the world's existence. After the resurrection, this Judeo-Christian strip of history broadens to include all the nations and the succession of generations; henceforward the deepest dimension of time is perhaps the dimension of mission, with its struggles that are carried on under the influence of the Spirit of Christ and in the invisible presence of Christ himself. As for Christ's return, we expect it within our present time; this implies that this time will not completely disappear but will be transfigured.

While Christianity had the basis for carrying on a reflection on time, it did not immediately do so. In fact, to the extent that the coming of Christ and his resurrection were regarded as marking the *fullness* (and therefore, in a sense, the "end") of time, it was natural for Christians to think of Christ's return as imminent; to the extent, therefore, that time continued to run, it could be seen only in a negative light, as the contrary of imminence and as a *delay*. Another consequence of the theme of the fullness of time combined with the first to blur the meaning of time. If everything is given along with the Christ who sends his Spirit, then the past has meaning only as an announcement and prefiguration of the fulfillment acquired in Christ, while the future is looked at less from the viewpoint of time as duration and newness than from the viewpoint of perfect union with God beyond time. While the spiritual exegesis of Scripture has a certain grounding in time in both the past of Israel and in the humanity of Christ, it focuses not on time but rather on "mystical" meanings that transcend time and reveal the true significance—allegorical or anagogical—of the Scriptures.

There are undoubtedly elements of these themes of time as delay or as the foundation (to be left behind) of allegory in the mystical and even millenarian chronologies that pop up from time to time, especially in moments of crisis, and that see the present age as the "sixth age" or the "evening of the world" or the "autumn of civilization." This kind of judgment is bound to entail a certain distancing from the present and

its circumstances, since any interest these have is diminished if the end is quite near. But it is possible that such chronologies have been and are still linked to rather profound residues of the hostility to time, some traits of which I sketched in the preceding section. In fact, a very strong, indeed almost essential, connection between sin and time has been heavily emphasized both in the East, with its theories of a "double creation" from Origen to Gregory of Nyssa and doubtless beyond, and in the West, with its overly pessimistic yet constantly renewed derivatives of the Augustinian theory of original sin. No one will deny that time is marked by sin. But that time is a "flower of evil" destined to disappear with that which caused it is another matter and represents an outlook that theologians have often been tempted to find too congenial. Moreover, in this perspective there is danger of focusing exclusively on the redemptive aspect of the Christian mystery, at the expense of its aspect of mediation and transfiguration. The events of the incarnation and cross are then no longer seen as giving a positive value to time but rather as a remedy for time that has been corrupted; as for the present, the only hope in the face of the complete triumph of evil would be "apocalypse" in the near future.

Thus the ambiguity found in some Christian judgments on time consists in the fact that on the positive side, Christianity gives a real significance to the basic reference points of time (the origin and the end and the paschal mystery), while on the other hand this realism is likely to be somewhat reduced by other considerations. Thus a particular interpretation of the theme of the fullness of time (denying all value to any further time), combined with a pessimistic assessment of the weight of evil (leading to some slackening of hope and thus in practice to a real growth of evil), can contribute to a lowering of esteem for the intellectual tools that might be applied to establishing the precise theological value of time.

3. Elements in the Consciousness of Time

A new consciousness of time as a structure that is constitutive of the world and the human person gradually developed between the end of the Middle Ages and our own day. It is important to distinguish the elements of this consciousness in order that we may understand the new data of the problem of "time and theology." Simplifying a good deal, I shall here reduce these elements to three: cosmology, science and technology, and history.

a. The image of the world has gradually changed from a static geocentric world in which human beings are kings, while the celestial spheres perform their perfect circular movements around the earth, to an expanding universe in which neither space nor time has a center but rather show themselves to be relatively (not absolutely) measurable dimensions of a universe in which the meaning of the human person is not immediately clear. Furthermore, Heisenberg's uncertainty principle, while not saying that completely unordered chance reigns, does underscore the limitations of a strictly logical kind of knowledge and reintroduces, even in cosmology, the category of *probability*, which Plato had entirely eliminated from epistemology and which Aristotle had retained only in the realm of ethics.

The appearance of human beings on this earth also belongs in time, to the extent that it becomes part of the history of life generally and of the animal species in particular. This history sheds light to some extent on the meaning of the corporeal stature of human beings, but it perhaps exacerbates the problem of death and in any case raises questions about the meaning to be ascribed to evolution.

b. Technology, which made creative leaps at major points in the Middle Ages and advanced in a more or less rectilinear fashion down to the industrial revolution of the eighteenth and nineteenth centuries, has altered the relation of human beings to their environment and, correspondingly, the relations of human beings among themselves. On the one hand, advances have become landmarks in time: *before* and *after* the water mill, the steam engine, electricity, etc. On the other, the experience and memory of progress have given rise to an outlook marked by *anticipation* and *research* (and thus, to some extent, the opposite of the religious perception of time as delay, of which I spoke above): "At the present time we do not yet know and are not yet able, in this or that area, but we are investigating and will surely

end up finding." Here again, time is thought of as infinite in extent. This is the case at least at the level of the unreflecting mind, for a more discerning analysis of the history of technology and a less naively progressivist view of the future lead to a more nuanced judgment. Nuances will also be supplied by the interpretation of the history of the social forms generated by economic and industrial development; the problem of a new form of poverty was seen as early as the Middle Ages, thus giving rise to the question of ethics and of the perversion of ethics in the history of a world that is undergoing constant technological development. This provides a new angle from which to approach the perennial question of evil and time.

c. The idea of history, which is already present in the background of technological and social evolution, came into existence because of various other factors. I shall mention only two here: a shift in the use of *memory* and an irreversible experience of *political* change.

In a world distinguished by an urgent need of anagogy combined with the weight of evil, memory is, on the one hand, a profound memory of God and the self and, on the other, remembrance and confession of sinfulness and sins. A perhaps decisive turning point can be seen at the Renaissance, when an entire civilization seemed to break with its immediate past, understood as the *via moderna*, and to invent a new model that appealed to older standards: the *via antiqua*. This substitution sometimes took an imaginary and mythical form, but it also found expression (and this is the important thing as far as the consciousness of time is concerned) in a twofold redirection of memory: the search for an attractive embodiment of one or another past (not only, e.g., the human being of antiquity but also the original texts of sacred Scripture) and, second, the criticism of the falsifications or simplifications of every kind by which the *via moderna* sought a solid grounding. A historical science that was future oriented and critical and had its basis in a humanistic project began to take form, and it gave rise to a new interpretation of the shape of human time.

Two fundamental events undoubtedly marked development in the political field and significantly influenced the human consciousness of time: the bull *Unam Sanctam* (1302) of Pope

Boniface VIII, which, contrary to the wishes of its author, signaled the end both of a unified Christendom and of the empire and ended the vitality of a particular conception, rooted in Plato, of authority and politics; and the French Revolution (1789), which set down the principle of a new kind of political organization in which civil society, state, and authority seek an articulation that does not depend on a strictly hierarchical principle.

The foregoing list of some elements or factors in the consciousness of time is certainly not exhaustive, but it should suffice to suggest a shift in mentality regarding time and history. I would like to summarize this shift by way of a conclusion to this section.

Time shows itself, first of all, to be a properly human dimension; it reveals itself in the twofold experience of *activity* and of *relationship*. In itself, then, time is disconnected from evil, since both action and communication are, in themselves, pure values.

Activity, first of all, is a given mode of production (and a corresponding form of consumption). Insofar as it is linked by memory to preceding and future modes, it manifests a certain consciousness of time, which is therefore connected with the experience human beings have of their own power. More subtly (and this applies above all to the type of "production" that is pure research), human beings sense that their scientific activity puts its mark on its result. Action and its yield are not completely separable, so that human time is in a way a part of the truth that work brings to light.

In a more definitive way than the relation of the human being to nature, the relation of person to person plays a determining role in the consciousness of time. If we "act," we act with others; in addition, many fields of human activity have for their object the establishment of social existence itself. But at this level the category of otherness is superimposed on the category of time. *The fundamental events are word-events* by which human beings create new situations of collaboration, coexistence, or oppression; in the succession of such word-events history, memory, and interpretation occur. At this level, time is defined as a history of freedoms and of the more or less irreversible structures that these freedoms create. We see immediately that the perception and interpretation of time is here connected with ethical

criteria whose provenance must be determined. Time can only be moral or immoral or a mixture of the two, and it is here that we again come upon the relationship among good, evil, and time, of which I spoke earlier. Here, too, to the extent that evil permeates time, the question of salvation arises.

But even before we come to action and relationship, where time is seen in its human dimensions, the problem arises of the *extremes* of time: for the individual, birth and death; for the human race, seen in an evolutionary perspective, its origin and possible disappearance; for the earth and, more broadly, for the universe, its origin and ultimate fate. Some of the factors involved in these matters can be reconstructed, with more or less scientific probability, on the basis of human time; in addition, some extrapolations are possible. The limits of knowledge cannot, however, be pushed back indefinitely; as a result, we cannot fail to find, in varying cultural contexts, certain questions looked upon as essential in any theology. There are the questions of the ultimate origin of each individual human being (a question that the ancients looked at from the viewpoint of the origin of the soul), of the real beginning of the human race, and of the beginning of the world. Then, too, there is the question of the dependence of all that is and moves on a Principle that is the origin of all existence. Finally, there is the urgent question of the end. What does death mean at the three levels of the person, the species, and the universe? As we shall see briefly in the following section, we are here at one of the points where the questions of God and of the meaning of Christianity arise. But we can already see that the epistemological status of such questions is not that which describes time as the measure of activity and relationships, for in dealing with the latter we are in time and have a language available for expressing time, whereas in the former we are situated at a boundary where time, like being itself, is received and not produced.

4. Theological Perspectives

On the basis of what has thus far been proposed, it is possible now to describe briefly the main lines of a study of the problem of "time and theology." The following subjects must be studied in succession: the relation between time and the covenant; what this relationship reveals to us regarding both human beings and God; possible points of meeting with the scientific study of space-time; finally, the impact of sin and evil.

a. If the fundamental events that give time its articulation are word-events, then in theology the category of time must be given an intrinsic connection with the category of covenant, for the latter can be described as a word of God set before human freedom. All the dimensions of time must find their proper interconnection in this free relationship with the word of God.

The liturgy is a not a sacred space-time unconnected with real space-time, the latter being looked upon as intrinsically corrupted by evil. Rather, the liturgy is the locus of an ever-new offering of the covenant concluded in Jesus Christ; it is an exercise of memory ("memorial") that brings the covenant already concluded into the present so that it may be once again heard and accepted. In this way the liturgy gives passing time its ultimate meaning. As a word-event involving humanity and God, the liturgy opens up an ethical way to the unprejudiced encounter of human beings with each other and to a well-regulated working of and upon this earth.

There is here perhaps a key to an understanding of the fact, at first sight quite strange, that the paschal mystery takes place at the center of time and not at time's end. The moment when the paschal mystery takes place is the moment when the covenant entered into with the Jewish people is extended to the Gentiles. But there was need precisely of time for this covenant to come about and for it gradually to change the meaning of human relationships and of the working of the earth.

b. It is possible, next, to start from this context and this effectiveness of the covenant as creative of time and to go on to God himself, who offers the covenant, and to the human beings who receive it. Perhaps the word "communion" expresses the ultimate meaning of time, for it expresses the purpose of the three human relationships (with God, other humans, and nature), whose proper integration is presupposed by authentic time. The word "communion" can also bring a new nuance to the eschatological conception of the human person, for it adds to the objectivist, visually oriented, and static theme of the "vision of God" the personal, affective, and dynamic theme of "being with" God and his Christ, of which Paul speaks.

In regard to God, who offers his word, establishes the covenant, and brings communion into being, it is possible, starting with the memorial of Jesus Christ, to enter into his interior life (the "immanent Trinity") and to seek, in the circumincession of Father, Son, and Holy Spirit, the paradigm for the covenantal process and therefore the ultimate foundation of time. When time is thus considered from the viewpoint of the covenant, it becomes a quasi-necessary category for the very knowledge of God. It is along this line, it seems to me, that recent studies of the "immutability" of God are to be interpreted. They are not, as has quite frequently been claimed, attempts to locate God in continuity with our movement but rather are efforts to find in God the origin not only of our being but also of our time (through application of analogy) and, reciprocally, to use the category of time (again through application of analogy), especially as seen from the viewpoint of the word-event, in order to understand the divine Trinity.

c. The connection between the theme of time as covenant and space-time as a dimension of the universe might be looked for in meditation on the idea of the beginning of the world and on the idea of the world's eschatological transfiguration. These themes have a double epistemological status that must be carefully worked out. Beginning of the world and end of time are, first of all, theological data, known through revelation. They express the fact that, if there is a world, this is ultimately in order that there may be a covenant; this explains why the world is not destined for icy darkness but will end as it began: in the orbit of the divine generosity. But it must be possible to connect this theological conviction with a physical reality; at this point, the second epistemological reflection, on the nature of a discourse on origin and end, has its place. Let me say briefly that this will be a discourse that is at once homogeneous with our existence, since it speaks of the beginning of the *time* in which have our being, and heterogeneous, since it speaks of time's *beginning* as such, which is, by any accounting, a limit concept. Once the proper nature of this type of language has been determined, the scientists must be allowed to speak, while we leave them time for research and avoid any kind of concordism (e.g., with the Big Bang theory).

It is not only the question of the world's beginning but the question of the very existence of the temporal world that has theological value. Science is able to determine with increasing accuracy the physical equations that express how the reality and vicissitudes of space-time make their appearance; it can also, to some extent, reconstruct the history of the galaxies, the history of the earth, the history of life and of the human being. But it is not possible to do more than formally record the fact that this history exists and that these formulas and narratives correspond to a real existence. If the desire for knowledge urges the inquirer on to ask why, then the question of creation becomes fully meaningful. Creation here is viewed not as beginning but as ongoing communication of being; at this level, time and being are not opposed because they are not located at the same level of scientific and philosophical investigation.

d. The question of evil can be faced next, the starting point being the origin of evil, namely, the breaking of the covenant, which was mysteriously enacted from the outset and has been constantly repeated. The question of evil is not the primary question because the covenant comes first, both in its initial offering and in its constant repetition in liturgical celebration. It is not possible, however, to set a correct value on concrete time unless one properly locates within it the consequences of the breaking of the covenant in the body and world of human beings as well as in their capacity for knowing and loving both God and other human beings. Seen from this angle, time does indeed manifest perversions at the level both of action and wisdom. But all this negativity cannot be regarded as primordial, otherwise we run the risk of interpreting temporality once again from the sterile vantage point of paradise lost, with all the forms this takes and all the nostalgias it brings with it.

Bibl.: O. CULLMANN, *Christ and Time* (1947; Philadelphia, 1964); P. RICOEUR, *Temps et récit*, 3 vols. (Paris, 1983–85); G. LAFONT, *Dieu, le temps et l'être* (Paris, 1986); S. W. HAWKING, *A Brief History of Time* (New York, 1988).

Ghislain LAFONT

TRADITION

The tradition of Christianity, like every other tradition, can be considered from various viewpoints: generally, as a phenomenon of human culture, from the perspective of anthropology and history; or more particularly, as an aspect of a self-identity, from the perspective of the self-understanding of the group supporting it—in this case, Christians. The Christian theologian reflects on Christian tradition both as a cultural phenomenon and from the perspective of Christian faith. Christian faith understands Christian tradition as an ongoing event whose protagonists are human beings and God.

Within Christian tradition—as in the case of every tradition—distinctions are made between the transmitted content (*traditum*, or *traditio obiectiva*), the process of transmitting and receiving (*actus tradendi et recipiendi*, or *traditio activa*), and the subjects (*tradentes*, or *traditio subiectiva*) of the tradition. Whereas other theological disciplines are interested more in the documents and content of Christian tradition (exegesis, dogmatics) or in its subjects (ecclesiastical history), fundamental theology reflects on the fundamental interrelations between the content, process, and subjects of tradition as well as on the norms and criteria of true Christian tradition.

1. Tradition as a Phenomenon of Human Culture

Our relationship to tradition today is contradictory. On the one hand, the authority and value of tradition are, in principle, disputed; on the other, there is growing realization that tradition is indispensable to the individual and to society. The fundamental loss of authority of all tradition rests, for one thing, on the experience that many traditional views and behavioral patterns have been overtaken by scientific-technical and social progress and have become outdated. This experience lends support to the demand, which has been increasing in modern times, for an autonomous self-grounding of humanity through reason. From the standpoint of this all-embracing demand, tradition was seen as a kind of prejudice and ideology from which humanity had to emancipate itself on its way to unlimited freedom. In the meantime, the crisis of modernity has necessitated a rethinking of this. We recognize that a total loss of tradition endangers freedom and humane values.

Nevertheless, a return to an immediately experienced relationship to tradition, as striven for in many New Age movements, or the mere restoration and conservation of particular traditions, as sought by fundamentalist traditionalism, is neither possible nor desirable. The gain in mature self-responsibility that has been won ought not to be reversed. What is possible today, and required, is a critical relationship to tradition that distinguishes between valuable and nonvaluable traditions and that appropriates the valuable traditions in a freely self-determining way. Adopting a critical relationship to tradition has itself a long tradition. In our cultural sphere, it begins with the transition from mythos to logos in Greek philosophy, is found in the Old and the New Testaments, and is not least evident in the case of Jesus.

Human beings are beings of tradition. They receive traditions and pass them on, they create traditions and terminate them. Handing things down is a cultural, social, and personal process. Tradition is a constitutive element of human culture. It rests on two basic anthropological facts: first, on the finitude, mortality, and historicality of human beings; and second, on the need to build on the experiences, knowledge, and skills acquired by others so that a culture can arise and develop. Among things handed down are skills, customs, rites, norms, stories, and doctrines. Tradition is, above all, tied to language. Language is a medium for handing things down and is itself tradition. Language and writing show that the very capacity for tradition has to be developed and handed down. Along with this, too, goes the emergence and evolving of certain functional roles (e.g., priest, teacher, judge, and master of any craft) and institutions (e.g., worship, law, school, and theater).

From a social viewpoint, tradition can be described as a diachronous and synchronous communicative process. Tradition exerts two kinds of social function. First, it promotes group cohesion and continuity. The traditional community is, at the same time, both the medium and the product of tradition. Again, tradition tends to diminish psychosocial stress and provide a means of orientation inasmuch as — in the face of a profusion of perceptual, conceptual, and behavioral possibilities that could prove humanly paralyzing — it makes available specific perceptual, conceptual, and behavioral models, or "guiding patterns." In the interest of securing normative traditions, every traditional community develops its relevant agencies of control. The communicative process of tradition is influenced jointly by those handing it down, those receiving it, and its particular content.

Tradition can support, and endanger, the personality of human beings. The fact that a person is born into a particular traditional community and comes under its sway means two things: first, that tradition makes possible the development of the personality; and second, that it can be so strongly determinative of individuals that their free development, in understanding and action, is hampered or prevented. Tradition is, therefore, simultaneously a destiny and a challenge. Personal (i.e., free and comprehending) appropriation of tradition is part of a critical relationship to tradition. Personal appropriation of tradition implies a need for interpretation. Both transmitter and receiver must bring tradition into relation with their particular situations and experiences and must also interpret for each other their remembered and current experiences, if living recollection is not to transform itself into dead traditionalism. Living tradition is interpretation and requires interpretation; it includes continuity and innovation. Hence, the process of handing it down is never without conflict.

All this implies an interactivity between the subjects and the content of tradition within the living progression of tradition. Transmitters and receivers pass on and receive the traditional content by interpreting it. In turn, the content of tradition determines, stamps, and alters not only the transmitters and receivers but also the process of tradition, its forms and institutions.

Christian tradition, as an interactive, communicative process sustained by human beings, is subject to the just-discussed anthropological conditions and laws. It can therefore be analyzed and assessed by anthropology and history, insofar as scholars in those disciplines also take the Christian self-understanding into consideration. Moreover, their findings have importance for theologians by enabling them to recognize the human and historical character of the process of Christian tradition and by directing their attention to the sorts of condition that hinder or promote the transmission of that tradition. From a theological viewpoint, however, Christian tradition is not simply the religious-Christian variant of a general human cultural phenomenon. Rather, the principle of Christian tradition is founded on the fact that, in Israel and in Jesus Christ, God has revealed himself once and for all as the salvation of humanity. From this fact stems the necessity for communicating and transmitting the news about that event and its redeeming power to all later generations.

2. The Principle of Christian Tradition

The process of Christian tradition begins with Jesus. He proclaims the Law and Prophets of Israel to be authoritative and interprets them critically from the standpoint of the will of God (Mt 5:17–48; 15:1–20; Mk 7:5–13). In the NT period, alongside the tradition of Israel as interpreted with a view to Jesus Christ, the testimony of the apostles about Jesus Christ becomes the other foundation of Christian tradition. Transmitted at first orally, this testimony is then recorded in writing in the Bible of the NT.

Already in the case of Paul, the figure of the apostle clearly emerges as the first and authoritative witness to, and transmitter of, Christian tradition. An apostle is one who (1) is a witness to God's self-revelation in Jesus Christ and (2) has been sent by the Lord to proclaim God's word (Gal 1:15–17). Paul himself is not only a direct witness of the Resurrected but also the transmitter of the testimony of the first apostles about the Last Supper and the resurrection of Jesus (1 Cor 11:23–25; 15:1–7), of the confession of faith (Rom 1:1–4; 4:24–25; 10:9), and of the hymns of the community (Phil 2:5–11). Like Jesus, Paul also has a critical relationship to tradition. He protests against Judeo-Christian traditionalism and insists on the true knowledge of Jesus Christ as the principle for interpreting Jesus' message (Gal 2:5–6; Phil 3:8–11).

From Paul's writings, as from the other texts of the Old and New Testaments, it becomes clear that the handing down of tradition takes place as a continual interpretive process in the light of new events and situations (the interpretation of the exodus by the prophets in relation to the Babylonian captivity; the interpretation of Jesus' message about God's unconditional love with a view to Paul's calling to the Gentiles; or the interpretation, in the Gospels, of the Jesus tradition in the light of Easter). Interpretation, as engaged in by Paul and the other hagiographers, is not only an expression of the general necessity for interpretation if tradition is to remain living; constant reinterpretation, in the Bible, is an expression of the truth that the Lord lives, is immediately present at all times, and desires to be testified to anew at each new point in time. Thus the Bible hands down not only the content of tradition but also models pertaining to its interpretation.

With increasing temporal distance from the original events, emphasis on the authority of the first apostolic testimonies and reference to the unbroken chain of tradition as the guarantor of the true preservation of the kerygma become more prominent. This begins with Luke (Lk 1:1–4), and leads to the idea of a handing down of teaching office in the Pastoral Letters (1 Tm 1:18; 4:11; 2 Tm 1:13–14; 2:2; 2 Pt 3:2) and to explication of the principle of Christian tradition by Irenaeus and Tertullian. In order to secure the apostolic tradition, the chain of testimonies is institutionalized in the form of the apostolic succession of bishops. As witnesses to the apostolic tradition, and as commissioned by Christ through the laying on of hands, bishops become the successors of the apostles and thus authentic bearers of tradition. For a long period, their authority receives mainly a material, and not a formal, foundation; their teaching must accord materially with the teaching of the apostles and the mother churches founded by the apostles, and also with Holy Scripture. One means, among others, of proving such material accordance is consensus.

It is not long before the question about the criteria of true tradition arises. As evidence of material accordance with apostolic tradition, Irenaeus and Augustine cite the consensus of the church fathers and the _regula fidei_ or _regula veritatis_. The _regula fidei_ does not have priority over Holy Scripture, nor does it refer to the church's doctrinal office. Rather, it consists of the clearer passages in Holy Scripture, "de scripturarum planioribus locis et ecclesiae auctoritate" (Augustine, *Doctr. chr.* 3.2.2; CChrSL 32, 77f.), and forms the first canon of the church. Vincent of Lerna, in his *Commonitorium* (434), describes the accepted practice for establishing truth in the church during the patristic period. In this connection, he is able to refer back to the Councils of Nicea and Ephesus. As criteria of true, universal doctrine, he cites *universitas* (catholicity), *antiquitas* (antiquity), and *consensio* (consensus) (of the council and the fathers) (*Commonit.* 2.3; CChrSL 29.41: "quod ubique, quod semper, quod ab omnibus," "what has been believed everywhere, always, and by all"). Along with apostolicity, catholicity has become an essential quality of true tradition. For Vincent, the council represents the link between synchronous and diachronous consensus. Conciliar decisions, however, become recognized as universal consensus only after they have been accepted by the church as a whole.

In the subsequent period, the concept of revelation is understood so broadly that, beyond the original apostolic tradition, later resolutions and customs of the church are also regarded as inspired and equally binding. Added to this is the fact that material legitimation of tradition on the basis of accordance with the apostolic kerygma is more and more replaced by its formal legitimation through (relative) age or through ecclesiastical authority. This conception of tradition threatens to immunize the church against any attempt at reform based on reference to the apostolic origin. No longer remembered is the warning by Tertullian that Christ had called himself the Truth, not the Custom (*De Virg. vel.* 1.1; CChrSL 1, 1209). The humanists and Reformers challenge the church to form a more critical understanding of tradition. In so doing, they are able to appeal to the examples of Paul and various church fathers.

Luther wishes, initially, to reject only those traditions that are not authorized through Holy Scripture, so as to restore the pure gospel to effective prominence. Later on, however, he replaces the principle of tradition with the principle of Scripture (*sola Scriptura*). Here, he remains caught up in the controversy associated with the late Middle Ages. Because the church of his time is in danger of forgetting the priority of Holy Scripture and of subordinating the material normativity of the apostolic kerygma to the formal normativity of ecclesiastical tradition, Luther takes precisely the opposite position, making Scripture the sole material and formal norm (*Sacra Scriptura sui ipsius interpres*, "Holy Scripture, which is its self-interpreter").

The Reformation leads the Council of Trent to adopt a more critical concept of tradition. In the "Decretum de libris sacris et de traditionibus recipiendis" of 1546 (DS 1501–5), the council takes up Luther's concern to preserve in the church the *puritas ipsa Evangelii* ("purity of the Gospel"). The gospel is the source of all saving truth and of the Christian order of life, which are contained "in written form and in unwritten traditions." These traditions are characterized more explicitly as "ab ipsius Christi ore ab apostolis acceptae, aut ab ipsis apostolis Spiritu Sancto dictante quasi per manus traditae ad nos usque pervenerunt." All the books of the Old and New Testaments and the inspired traditions stemming from the apostles, "tum ad fidem, tum ad mores pertinentes," are accepted and honored by the church "pari pietatis affectu ac reverentia."

With that, the traditions that qualify as binding are critically delimited: they must pertain to faith and morals and must derive from the apostles. A positive aspect, too, is that the gospel is designated as the *one* source of saving truth, a dynamic outlook to which Vatican II will later link up. Left open is what the binding content of tradition is and also the question of the material sufficiency of Scripture. Since, however, the council speaks of "traditions" in the plural, it suggests that they are materially distinct from Scripture rather than just differentiating them modally from Scripture. The external conjunction of the two forms of communication of the gospel remains as it was. The council is mainly interested in the modal or hermeneutic insufficiency of Holy Scripture. No one is allowed to interpret Scripture, insofar as it pertains to faith and morals, in a way opposed to the unanimous consensus of the fathers or to the meaning endorsed by the church, which alone may adjudicate on the true meaning and interpretation of Scripture (DS 1507).

After the Council of Trent, and because of considerations of theological controversy, the material distinction between Scripture and tradition gains acceptance again. With reference to the authority of the council, it is taught that the gospel is contained *partim* in Scripture and *partim* in the oral traditions—a formulation that the council had replaced with the more open wording *et . . . et.* Thus it becomes usual to speak of the two sources of revelation ("dual-source theory" of revelation). This conception asserts the material insufficiency of Scripture. Alongside it, there is the conception of a merely modal or hermeneutical insufficiency, according to which Scripture requires supplementation by tradition only as an aid to its correct understanding. The council's doctrine affirming that only the church may adjudicate on the true meaning of Scripture gives rise to a monopoly on interpretation by the church's doctrinal office, which increasingly appears as the sole bearer of tradition.

Not until Vatican II, with its dogmatic constitution *Dei Verbum* (1965), is a way offered that leads out of the blind alley represented, for theological debate, by the material delimitation between Scripture and tradition (*DV* 7–10). Linking up with what was said at the Council of Trent about the gospel as the one source of all saving truth (*DV* 7), it declares that sacred tradition and Holy Scripture spring from the same divine source and form an organic unity (*DV* 9). The special standing of Scripture within the process of handing down is emphasized. Scripture "*is* the word of God inasmuch as it is consigned to writing under the inspiration of the divine Spirit," while tradition *hands on* God's word, preserving and explaining it (*DV* 9).

With this, the relationship between Scripture and tradition tends to be defined modally; in tradition, namely, as the passing on of God's word by way of the interpretation of Scripture, "the sacred writings themselves are more profoundly understood and unceasingly made active in [the church]" (*DV* 8). Deciding on the question of the material sufficiency of Scripture was something that the council did not want to do. The indication that, through tradition, "the full canon of the sacred books" becomes known to the church (*DV* 8) need not be understood in the sense of a special content of tradition—the selection of canonical books is to be explained more from the insight into the canonicity of their contents that the church gained through occupying itself with these books. Also under-

standable in the modal sense is the compromise formulation: "it is not from sacred Scripture alone that the Church draws her certainty about everything which has been revealed" (*DV* 9).

The new determination of the relationship between Scripture and tradition, and particularly of the understanding of tradition itself, becomes possible through the deepening of the concept of revelation (*DV* 2–6) and of the concept of the church (*LG*): Just as revelation is understood no longer as a mere communication of individual truths but as the life-bestowing self-communication of the trinitarian God, in which he addresses humans as friends (*DV* 2), so tradition, too, is understood no longer as a mere collection of individual truths but as the life-bestowing presence of God's word, so that God "uninterruptedly converses with the Bride of His beloved Son" (*DV* 8). And just as revelation is depicted no longer as mere instruction but as occurring "by deeds and words" (*DV* 2), so the handing down of tradition occurs in the church's "teaching, life, and worship" (*DV* 8). Finally, just as the entire church is the people of God on the way to realization of the kingdom of God, so too "the entire holy people united with their shepherds" (*DV* 10) are the bearer of tradition. Understanding of the transmitted word of God increases not only through the preaching of the pastors but also "through the contemplation and study made by the believers" and "through the intimate understanding of spiritual things they experience" (*DV* 8).

Vatican II thus recovers a comprehensive understanding of tradition and its role in the life of the church, as well as bringing to light its theological and historical dimension. Attention is scarcely given, however, to the critical function of Scripture in relation to postbiblical tradition. Although this ecumenical desideratum has been left unresolved, the antinomy affecting theological debate in matters pertaining to the relationship between Scripture and tradition has been essentially overcome. This is confirmed by several ecumenical documents (Montreal, 1963; Malta, 1972; and others).

3. The Theological Concept of Tradition

Christian tradition can be grasped theologically as the ongoing self-transmission of the word of God in the Holy Spirit through the service of the church for the salvation of all humanity. The *primordial subject* of the history of its attestation, understanding, and interpretation in the church is the word of God itself, incarnated in Jesus Christ and livingly present in the Holy Spirit. The church is the *ministerial subject* of the transmission of the gospel. Only in the Spirit does the church become capable of the authentic handing on of God's word. Thus the church calls on the Spirit, as the power of effecting the renewed presence of God's word, when it remembers, in word and sacrament, the presence-effecting remembrance of Jesus Christ.

The *constitutive content* of tradition is the revelatory self-communication of God. Its culmination is God's handing his own Son over to human beings for us all (Rom 4:25; 8:32) and Jesus Christ's simultaneous handing himself over (Eph 5:2). God's redemptive act is communicated in the words of the preaching and in the eucharistic breaking of bread (1 Cor 11:23), not only verbally but really (verbal tradition and real tradition).

The *constitutive form* of tradition is the religious witness given by the apostles and their communities in "teaching, life, and worship" (*DV* 8), for it was in their faith that the church made its first response to revelation, as effected by the Spirit himself. The Holy Scripture of the NT, inspired by the Holy Spirit, attests to the apostolic faith (*traditio constitutiva*), and is therefore the norm for the ongoing tradition of the church (*traditio interpretativa et explicativa*).

Content and form should correspond to one another. Just as the constitutive content of tradition includes the *communicatio* of God himself and his incarnated Son and the *communio* with God, so the constitutive form of tradition in the apostolic communities includes the *communio*, with God and with one another, through the *communicatio* in the words of the preaching, the celebration of the Eucharist, and the caritas and social welfare work. Correspondence between content and form is the norm for the later church.

4. Norms and Criteria of Tradition

The supreme norm (*norma suprema, norma non normata*) of Christian faith and its transmission is the word of God alone—which

has become flesh in Jesus Christ and remains present in the Holy Spirit—and not any of its forms of attestation. For although the word of God is attested to in Holy Scripture, in the teaching, liturgy, and life of the church, and in the hearts of the faithful (2 Cor 3:3; 1 Thes 4:9; 1 Jn 2:28), it does not (owing to its eschatological character) exhaust itself in any of its forms of attestation. Rather, it generates, in great variety and fruitfulness, constantly new kinds of testifying.

The primary norm among the attestations to God's word (*norma normata primaria*) is Holy Scripture, in which the testimony of the prophets and apostles has been written down and is believed in by the church as the special work of the Holy Spirit. As a testimony of the *traditio constitutiva*, it sets the norm for, and also inspires, subsequent ecclesiastical tradition and can therefore be described as "the supreme rule of faith" [*suprema fidei regula*] (*DV* 21), in contrast to subordinate types of attestational authority.

The subordinate norm among the attestations to God's word (*norma normata secundaria*) is the binding religious tradition of the church, the *traditio interpretativa et explicativa*. On the basis of the assurance of Christ's enduring presence in his church (Mt 28:20) and of the lasting support of the Holy Spirit (Jn 14:16; 16:13), which promises the church an indestructibility or indefectibility (Mt 16:18), the church trusts that the Spirit will preserve it as "the pillar and bulwark of truth" (1 Tm 3:15). Therefore the "sense of faith" (*sensus fidei*) of the entire people of God (*LG* 12), along with (under certain conditions) the teaching office of the episcopal collegiality and of the pope (*LG* 25), are regarded as infallible. The various types of attestational authority in the church are described as *loci theologici*. In accordance with the understanding of tradition as a whole (*traditio obiectiva et activa*), we understand the *loci theologici* today not only as grounding bases for the objective delineation of ecclesiastical religious tradition but also as active testimonies of religious tradition.

From the norms, as the material principles of the faith and its tradition, we distinguish the criteria. By these we understand external or material attributes of a particular tradition that allow it to be critically examined with a view to determining whether it belongs to the binding religious tradition of the church or what is, in fact, its true meaning.

The criteria of belongingness to the binding religious tradition of the church, which is established through historical or current assessment, are (1) diachronous consensus (*antiquitas*), (2) synchronous consensus (*universitas*), and (3) the formal expressness with which the validity of a truth (whether as revealed or as necessary to the securing and explanation of revelation) is impressed upon pastors and theologians by teaching office (*formalitas*).

The hermeneutical criteria, used to determine the true meaning, the substantial weight, and the present-day significance of a religious tradition, are (1) historical inquiry, which clarifies the historical conditions behind the emergence and formulation of a tradition; (2) redemptive significance, with a view to which the tradition is to be interpreted as corresponding to God's redemptive intention (*DV* 8: "What was handed on by the apostles includes everything which contributes to the holiness of life, and the increase in faith of the People of God"; *DV* 11: "put into the sacred writings for the sake of our salvation"); (3) the "'hierarchy' of truths" (*UR* 11), according to which the normative weight of a tradition, in the context of tradition as a whole, is to be determined; and (4) the "signs of the times" (*GS* 4; 11), which enable a tradition to be interpreted, in teaching and practice, with a view to present-day conditions.

5. Pragmatics of Tradition

Along with elaborating a topics of the *loci theologici* of tradition, its criteriology and hermeneutics, fundamental theology should also develop a pragmatics of tradition. Up to now, the pragmatic interest of the fundamental-theological doctrine of tradition has been almost exclusively limited to the forms of activity of hierarchical doctrinal office. If, however, tradition is understood as a living process involving many subjects (pastors, theologians, and the rest of the faithful and their local churches) that all play differing roles, the pragmatic perspective must be widened. Vatican II has recognized (*DV* 23; *OE* 6; *UR* 16–17) the legitimate existence of a plurality of forms of local ecclesiastical tradition as an expression of the richness of the one "undivided heritage of the universal Church" (*OE* 1). From

the pragmatic viewpoint, this implies the need to structure the ecclesiastical order in such a way as to enable the development of the active supporting role of all the faithful as well as their communication and interaction with each other. What holds true for the *communio fidelium* within the local churches must also be expressed in the structuring of the whole church, as *communio ecclesiarum*, in the form of consultative and conciliar processes.

The right to active participation in supporting and structuring the tradition of the church implies, on the part of the faithful, the duty to acquire the competence needed for being true and devoted testifiers to the gospel. Active tradition presupposes listening to the word of God and appropriating the previous religious tradition of the church, implying also a metanoia in thought and action.

Bibl.: J. R. GEISELMANN, *Die heilige Schrift und die Tradition* (Freiburg, 1962); Y. CONGAR, *Tradition and Traditions* (New York, 1966); id., *The Meaning of Traditions* (New York, 1964); P. C. RODGER and L. VISCHER, eds., *Scripture, Tradition and Traditions: Rapport de la 4e conférence mondiale Foi et Constitution* (Montreal, 1963; London, 1964); K. RAHNER and J. RATZINGER, *Revelation and Tradition* (New York, 1966); J. BEUMER, "La tradition orale," in *Histoire des dogmes,* vol. 6 (Paris, 1967); H. G. GADAMER, "Tradition," in *RGG* 6:966–84; P. LENGSFELD, "Tradition," in *MystSal*, vol. 2 (Paris, 1969); J. PIEPER, *Überlieferung* (Munich, 1970); L. REINISCH, ed., *Vom Sinn der Tradition* (Munich, 1970); W. KASPER, "Tradition als Erkenntnisprinzip," *TQ* 155 (1975): 198–215; G. O'COLLINS, "Criteria for Interpreting the Traditions," in R. Latourelle and G. O'Collins (eds.), *Problems and Perspectives of Fundamental Theology* (New York, 1982), 327–39; M. SECKLER, "Tradition und Fortschritt," in *Christlicher Glaube in moderner Gesellschaft* 23 (Freiburg, 1982), 5–53; L. RORDORD and A. SCHNEIDER, *Die Entwicklung des Traditionsbegriffs in der Alten Kirche*(Berne, 1983); A. DULLES, "Das 2. Vatikanum und die Wiedergewinnung der Tradition in Glaube im Prozess," in *Festschrift K. Rahner* (Freiburg, 1984), 546–62; R. KAMPLING, "Tradition," in *Neues Handbuch theologischer Grundbegriffe*, vol. 4 (Munich, 1985), 221–35; H. J. POTTMEYER, "Normen, Kriterien und Strukturen der Tradition," in W. Kern and M. Seckler, eds., *Handbuch der Fundamentaltheologie*, vol. 4 (Freiburg, 1988), 124–52; D. WIEDERKEHR, "Das Prinzip Überlieferung," *HFT* 4:100–123; R. FISICHELLA, La *révélation et sa crédibilité* (Paris/Montreal, 1989); J. BUNNENBERG, *Lebendige Treue zum Ursprung: Das Traditionsverständnis Y.*

Congars (Mainz, 1989); H. WALDENFELS, *Manuel de théologie fondamentale* (Paris, 1990), 701–83.

Hermann J. POTTMEYER

TRENT, COUNCIL OF

In three working periods, 1545–47, 1551–52, and 1562–63, the Council of Trent created a body of doctrine and of disciplinary prescriptions that proved profoundly influential in shaping modern Roman Catholicism.

1. Historical Overview

The convening of the council by Pope Paul III (1534–49) had been delayed by political rivalries between the Catholic powers and by reluctance in Rome to espouse reform. The two interruptions were due to war and an epidemic in Trent, with the second break being prolonged by antipathy to the council on the part of Pope Paul IV (1555–59). From the beginning, Trent was a council of bishops, with the theologians having only advisory roles. The council's direction was in the hands of three cardinal-legates, who received regular and detailed instructions from the pope and his counselors.

Trent issued fourteen doctrinal decrees and thirteen decrees on reform of pastoral care and church discipline. In drafting its decrees, Trent took over selected points of doctrine from the Catholic controversialist theologians who had been disputing the claims of the Lutheran reformation for a quarter-century before the council began. Trent also drew on numerous reform memorials, with their lists of pastoral deficiencies and abuses in church administration, which had preceded the council, e.g., the reform programs presented to Pope Adrian VI in 1522 and the *Consilium de emendanda ecclesia*, submitted to Paul III by a commission of new cardinals in 1537. Trent brought a salutary clarification of Catholic doctrine on original sin, grace and justification, and the mass and the sacraments. The nature of the church, however, was left largely untouched in Tridentine teaching, with the consequence that doctrine forged later in the apologetic defense of the institutional church, e.g., by Robert Bellarmine, became dominant in ecclesiology down to the

twentieth century. The reform program suffered from a lack of a single overall vision and consequent fragmentation in confronting the many abuses to be rectified. The norms, however, did increase considerably the ability of bishops to govern their dioceses without local hindrance. The directives on priestly formation, together with the prescription that diocesan seminaries be instituted, left a deep mark on modern Catholicism.

2. Scripture and Church Traditions

For fundamental theology, Trent's decisive teachings concerned the normative sources of Christian doctrine. Before the council, numerous controversialist writers had already advanced arguments against the Reformation use of Scripture as the supreme and sole norm of doctrine and life and had contested the Reformation claim that Scripture has in itself a self-interpreting capacity (*sacra Scriptura sui ipsius interpres*, according to Luther). Johann Eck and Johann Cochlaeus had retorted that the Protestant use of the Bible as a critical norm against the church was destructive of the Bible itself, since it is the church that, by fixing the biblical canon, identifies and authenticates the books that are normative.

John Fisher drew together the main points of the Catholic case in his 1526 *Confutatio* of Luther. First, much in the Bible is in fact hard to understand, as 2 Pt 3:16 indicates. The Bible alone, instead of resolving controversies, actually leads to divisions and errors, as the history of heresy confirms. Second, there has developed in the church, under the lead of the Holy Spirit, a normative tradition of interpretation of the Bible, namely, the doctrine of the orthodox fathers and the ecumenical councils. Third, in the see of Peter the church has a *iudex controversiarum* to which recourse must be had when disputes break out over doctrine, forms of worship, and norms of Christian life. Finally, the apostolic writings, e.g., 2 Thes 2:15; Jn 20:30; 21:25, point to an oral communication of doctrine and rules beyond what is set down in the writings collected in the Bible, and some practices of the universal church derive from this nonwritten source. Similar arguments were advanced by other Catholic apologists, such as Johann Dietenberger, Nicholas Herborn, and Johann Dreido.

Trent's teaching on the transmission of revealed doctrine was framed in two decrees approved 8 April 1546. The first document (DS 1501–5) is the council's formal reception both of the biblical books and of apostolic traditions relevant to faith and morals as normative for Christians and in particular as being the testimonies on which Trent will base its own reaffirmations of transmitted teaching and its reform measures. A second document begins with a nuanced defense of the Latin Vulgate version of Scripture as "authentic" for church use, and then goes on to indicate norms for the correct interpretation of the Bible.

Trent's reception of the biblical books coincided with its formal clarification of the contents and limits of Scripture (→ CANON). Some members of the council, like the Augustinian Jerome Seripando, were open to a differentiation within the OT between books normative for faith and others, the deuterocanonical books, serving only to instruct in godly living. But the majority found this idea overly subtle and liable to weaken the remedy the council intended to bring to a disturbed situation of uncertainty and confusion. Even Seripando agreed that all the books of the traditional canon are inspired and inerrant, and so the more ample canon was formally laid down (DS 1502–3), following the list used by the Council of Florence in 1442 in its negotiations with the Coptic churches. The decree represents a sober but pointed expression of Trent's sense of speaking for a church that actually has its Bible "in possession" and so is able to declare definitively which books should be taken as "sacred and canonical" (DS 1504).

Trent's second major step was its reception along with Scripture of certain normative apostolic traditions. The Reformation had identified many church practices as abuses and many church laws (e.g., fasting, observance of holy days, clerical celibacy) as ecclesiastical encroachments on Christian freedom. Trent's response is a compact and grammatically intricate formulation (DS 1501) that presupposes that the apostolic church did exist, with living faith implanted in believing hearts, before the composition of the NT books. The starting point is the gospel of Christ, which is to be preserved in its purity, for this gospel is the one source of all saving truth and Christian practice. The body of doctrine and disciplinary norms coming from the gospel has not been exhaustively formulated in writing, and so certain unwritten traditions must be taken into earnest consideration, namely, those which come either from Jesus himself or from the Holy Spirit's "dictation" to the apostles.

However, not all traditions are definitive and normative for the church. Trent circumscribes considerably their ambit by explicitating its reception of what is (1) apostolic in origin and (2) transmitted in unbroken succession to the living, teaching, and worshiping church of today. Examples of such traditions would be the keeping holy of the first day of the week and the linking of the Lord's Supper with a liturgy of the word. Purely ecclesiastical usages are not considered here, since the council intended to lay down reform directives that in given cases could conceivably not receive some of these.

A third step of long-term importance was Trent's affirmation of the existence of a normative ecclesial interpretation of the Bible (DS 1507; → CHURCH VI). Here Trent expresses the church's sense of having a hold on the meaning of the biblical message, with the specification that this understanding is a continuous and ongoing part of the very being of the church. The text mentions the fathers of the church, thus calling to mind the controversialists' case for a normative patristic and conciliar "hermeneutical tradition." Because the church has an interior connaturality with the meaning of the biblical text, Trent's decree specifies that "it belongs to the church to judge the true meaning and interpretation of Holy Scripture." At the time of Trent, the term "magisterium" was not in use, but the reality seems present here, where Trent is appropriating what the controversialists had proposed about the existence and accessibility of a *iudex controversiarum* in the church.

The main conclusion, however, from the two decrees is that in determining how Christian doctrine should be formulated and Christian life and witness is to be shaped, an appeal to the Bible does not suffice by itself. One must consult other theological loci. The sense of the Bible is in the church, and so its interpretation is to be heard, along with its received ways of expressing the apostolic faith, in life and worship.

3. Reception of Trent

On the specific issue of the transmission of the gospel, we know that post-Tridentine Catholic theology and catechetics often went beyond the careful minimalism of the council's decree regarding the reception of traditions. Apologetic emphasis on the insufficiency of Scripture led to the conception of a purely oral doctrinal tradition deriving from Christ and his apostles and belonging to the substance of the faith. Thus, part of the gospel and some elements of saving revelation were thought to be expressed in the text of Scripture, while another part and other elements were passed on in a nonwritten manner. Here theology gave to Trent's reception of books and (*et*) traditions a further precision that the council had not espoused, for it had replaced the phrase *partim/ partim* with the simpler *et* just before the approval of the text. But theology gravitated to the conviction that Scripture and tradition are "two sources," parallel and diverse in content, instead of being two loci in which church and theology find concrete expressions of the one gospel. The historical work of J. R. Geiselmann, G. Tavard, Y. Congar, J. Ratzinger, and others has clarified the fruitful openness of the official Tridentine text, which left ample room for Vatican II to restate this doctrine on the basis of a quite different conception of the comprensive process of transmitting life and faith in the church (→ TRADITION).

A further issue concerns the true place of the Council of Trent and its documents in the broader horizon of early modern church history. Was Trent truly creative of the energy and militancy, along with the Roman centralization of rule and discipline, which characterized the Counter-Reformation church? Was Trent formative of those aspects of the ecclesiastical institution that Catholicism, in a major shift in self-understanding, began to transform at the Second Vatican Council? Two considerations seem important for framing the ongoing discussion of this question.

a. With increasing frequency today, historians highlight less the differences between early modern Protestant and Catholic beliefs and worship. More emphasis is now falling on the similarities that are found in the processes by which Protestants and Catholics, say around 1600, approached the indoctrination of youth,

training for church work, and church collaboration with state authorities. A general process of confessionalization took place in all the churches, as the normative doctrines were carefully formulated, structures of authority were clarified and hardened, and clear directives were laid down for the pastoral ministry. This thesis of E. W. Zeeden has been developed by W. Reinhard in his claim that the implementation of Tridentine reform was essentially a modernizing process, by which exigent standards were set for Catholic church professionals, modes of supervision and accountability were developed, and an extensive educational program tried to bring about the internalization of Christian norms. This is largely the transformation of Catholicism that Trent's documents had envisaged, but the council itself did not create the zeal and religious dedication of those who brought about this momentous ecclesial change. This latter was largely due to the new spirituality, especially that of Ignatius Loyola, which motivated the personnel of the confessionalized and modernizing church of the century and a half following Trent.

b. One way of implementing Trent's reform was the differentiated application of the new norms in the major dioceses under energetic bishops such as Daniele Bollani (Brescia), Gabriele Paleotti (Bologna), and Charles Borromeo (Milan). But by the pontificate of Sixtus V (1585–90), local implementations were brought decisively under the control of the pope and the supervision of his newly institutionalized curia. The aim was to promote effective reform in many places where it had made little headway. But the long-term result was that local pastoral initiative, well grounded in Trent's reform decrees, was largely smothered by the slow processes of centralized administration. Even the portrayals of Borromeo, canonized in 1610, were regulated so as to downplay his vigor as the episcopal reformer of a diocese, while highlighting his personal asceticism and his dignity as cardinal of the Roman Church. Such developments differ notably from the doctrine and reform measures formulated at Trent between 1545 and 1563.

Bibl.: H. JEDIN, *A History of the Council of Trent*, vol. 2 (London/New York, 1961), 52–98; J. R. GEISELMANN, *Die Heilige Schrift und die Tradition* (Freiburg, 1962); G. TAVARD, "Tradition in Early Post-Tridentine

Theology," *TS* 23 (1962): 377–405; G. ALBERIGO, "L'ecclesiologia del Concilio di Trento," *Rivista di storia della Chiesa in Italia* 18 (1964): 227–42; E. W. ZEEDEN, *Die Entstehung der Konfessionen* (Munich, 1965); Y. CONGAR, *Tradition and the Traditions: An Historical and a Theological Essay* (New York, 1966); J. RATZINGER, "Revelation and Tradition," in K. Rahner and J. Ratzinger, *Revelation and Tradition* (London, 1966), 26–78; H. O. EVENNETT, *The Spirit of the Counter-Reformation* (Cambridge, 1968); H. HOLSTEIN, "Le problème de l'Écriture et de la Tradition," in O. DE LA BROSSE et al., *Latran V et Trente*, vol. 1, Histoire des conciles oecuméniques 10 (Paris, 1975), 231–58; W. REINHARD, "Gegenreformation als Modernisierung?" *Archiv für Reformationsgeschichte* 68 (1977): 226–52; J. M. ROVIRA BELLOSO, *Trento: Una interpretación teologica* (Barcelona, 1979), 73–100; G. BEDOUELLE, "Le canon de l'Ancien Testament dans la perspective du concile de Trente," in J. Kaestli, ed., *Le canon de l'Ancien Testament: Sa formation et son histoire* (Geneva, 1984), 253–83; H. JEDIN and G. ALBERIGO, *Il tipo ideale del vescovo secondo la Riforma cattolica* (Brescia, 1985); G. ALBERIGO, "La 'réception' du concile de Trente par l'église romaine," *Irenikon* 58 (1985): 311–37; id., "The Council of Trent," in J. O'Malley, ed., *Catholicism in Early Modern Europe: A Guide to Research* (St. Louis, 1988), 211–26.

Jared WICKS

TRINITY AND REVELATION

One of the points of convergence between contemporary Catholic and Protestant theology is a renewed and deepened understanding of the act of revelation as God's self-disclosure and self-communication. According to this conception of revelation, which dominates the fundamental theology of this century, revelation does not in the first instance consist of propositions about the divine life but rather in the communication of God's being itself.

In the Protestant tradition it was Karl Barth who made this conception the center of his theology and drew the trinitarian implications in the first volume of his *Church Dogmatics*. Barth used the idea of revelation as the scaffolding upon which to construct his dogmatics. Exploiting the trinitarian dimension of revelation, he was able to ground his dogmatics in the triune God. For Barth, in contrast to Schleiermacher, the Trinity stands at the beginning of theology and undergirds every doctrine of Christian faith.

Barth's method is unashamedly from above. God's nature as such is hidden. The hiddenness of God corresponds to his transcendence. God can be known only if he gives himself to be known. Moreover, in the present situation of the human condition, human beings after the fall are unable to know God, who is present in the creation. All knowledge of God must therefore be through Jesus Christ.

The heart of Barth's understanding of revelation is christological. In Jesus Christ we have an event in which God makes himself known. God is the subject of revelation, and Jesus Christ is the content of revelation. Since God reveals nothing less than himself, there is a perfect identity between God the revealer and God the revealed. Revelation in the strict sense implies the doctrine of the incarnation.

Barth expresses the identity between revealer and revealed in various ways in order to bring out the full import of the meaning of revelation. Among such statements one can note the following: God reveals himself in this event, God is unveiled in this event, God reiterates himself to the world in this event, God interprets himself in this event, God is Lord in this event. One important aspect that deserves to be stressed is the historicity of revelation. Revelation is the event in which eternity and time meet. God's self-expression to the world is the event in which God becomes temporal. As Barth says, revelation requires historical predicates.

As a historical event, Jesus Christ is an event of our past human history. But one must go on to ask whether this event is over and done with or whether revelation is also contemporaneous. Barth answers that it is through the Holy Spirit that the act of revelation becomes a present event. Through the Holy Spirit, Jesus Christ becomes actual today. We are drawn into the revelation event and so come to share in the divine life itself. Through the Holy Spirit, God does not confront the human person as an object but dwells within the person as subject. Barth defines the Holy Spirit as the "revealedness" of the revelation-event.

Granted that God really reveals himself and not just information about himself, it follows that since God is triune in the act of revelation, he is also triune in his own eternal life. From the unity of revealed, revelation, and revealedness, Barth concludes that God from all eternity must be in himself Father, Son, and Holy Spirit. In this way Barth avoids any trace of modalism. God's threefoldness in the act of revelation corresponds to his threefoldness in the divine life.

In the postconciliar period, Karl Rahner, from the Catholic side, appropriated and deepened Barth's understanding of revelation and, on the basis of his trinitarian understanding of revelation, enunciated the thesis that the Trinity of the economy of salvation is the immanent Trinity and vice versa.

Although Rahner and Barth have similar conceptions of revelation, they have a different starting point and methodology. Rahner begins with the conviction that all theological statements are anthropological statements. Hence human beings, with their transcendence, are the starting points for theological reflection.

For Rahner, a human is that being for whom being itself is a question. Human beings question every aspect of reality, including themselves. Such questioning reveals that God is implicitly present as the horizon for their interrogation. Rahner's transcendental method analyzes humanity under the two aspects of knowledge and freedom. In knowing any finite object, the subject is drawn beyond the finite toward the Infinite. Human knowledge, therefore, has two dimensions—the objective or categorical, by which subjects know something in the world, and the transcendental, by which, implicitly in the act of knowing objects, subjects know themselves and God. The key to Rahner's argument here is that one can know the finite as finite only if one implicitly knows the Infinite as its condition of possibility. Rahner makes a similar analysis of human freedom. In choosing any object in the world, subjects are at the same time choosing themselves. Because human freedom is a transcendental dynamism toward the Infinite, no finite object is ever able to fill up the dynamism that a human being is. In recognizing the limits of all finite goods, subjects in the restlessness of their heart reach out to God, the absolute value.

According to this analysis, human beings are in the depths of their being an orientation toward Mystery. The religious dimension is an intrinsic constituent of human Dasein. Without Mystery as the horizon in which human beings live, they would not be able to grasp their life as a totality. They would be limited to individual aspects of their world and would not be able to question the totality of their being. In fact, human subjects always have an awareness of Mystery, but of Mystery as a distant, nameless horizon. People know that they are referred to this Mystery, but they do not know whether the Mystery wishes to draw near to them.

The first step of Rahner's analysis has shown that human beings, by the very fact of being creatures, have a natural revelation of God. God is given together with human Dasein. The heart of Christian faith, however, consists in the assertion that God wants to draw near to people. The first way in which this happens is through the mystery of grace. Through grace, God enters into the depths of human subjectivity.

For Rahner, "grace" is another word for the Holy Spirit. In this we see that the prime analogate of grace is uncreated grace. Rahner argues that this grace is given to every person, at least as an offer. Although the offer of grace is universal, it is nonetheless gratuitous. God could create a human nature without orienting it to grace, but in fact he has not done so. The originality of Rahner's proposal consists in his transcendental interpretation of grace. Grace is so intimate a part of the human being that God becomes a coconstitutive element of the human "I." Here Rahner suggests that the model of formal causality can illuminate the mystery of grace. The presence of grace in the human subject is analogous to the relationship of form and matter. They are intrinsically related to one another. Nevertheless the relation is quasi-formal, since God remains transcendent even in the act of bestowing himself. By the presence of uncreated grace in the human subject, the person is enabled to participate in the divine life. Hence Rahner affirms that in the bestowal of grace, God is the giver, the gift, and the condition of possibility of accepting the gift. Since participating in God's triune life transcends human capacity, the human person is not even able to accept this gift if the gift itself does not make this acceptance possible.

On the basis of God's universal desire to save, Rahner argues that grace has been offered to every person. If this is the case, then it follows that the history of the human race is coextensive with the history of grace. But in affirming this thesis, does Rahner in fact affirm too much? If grace is everywhere given, what is the significance of the history of salvation in the sense of God's saving deeds in the Old and New Testaments? In particular, in what sense is the Christ-event decisive for salvation?

If grace is God's offer of himself on the level of transcendentality, it is also true that every transcendental experience must be mediated objectively, categorically, and historically. Only if human begins are saved in their history as well as in their transcendentality can there be salvation in the full sense of the word.

Rahner thus argues that the Christ-event is the self-offer of God to the world in history. First of all, he tries to situate the Christ-event within the history of the world and within evolution itself. If all of history is a graced history, this history has an orientation and a goal—namely, Jesus Christ. Rahner says that we can look at evolution as a movement from below. Evolution is a process of becoming in which the lower gives rise to the higher. In the human being, evolution becomes conscious of itself. But the human being, in turn, is a dynamism toward God. As we saw above, the human is an orientation toward union with the Absolute Mystery. Seen from below, this movement of evolution arrives at an aporia with the emergence of the human being. From below, human being's union with Mystery remains an open question, for the Mystery is distant, silent, anonymous. But from the point of view of faith, we can see that the movement from below is complemented by a movement from above. God from above expresses himself and communicates himself in Jesus Christ. But such a self-communication is not just an intervention of God from on high. The whole of the evolutionary process was precisely a preparation for this self-expression. In this context we can understand Rahner's assertion, "The Incarnation of God is the unique and highest instance of the essence of the actualization of human reality, which consists in this: that man is, insofar as he abandons himself to the Absolute Mystery whom we call God" (K. Rahner, *Foundations of Christian Faith* [London, 1978], 218).

One of the ways in which Rahner expresses the truth of the incarnation is through the concept of the symbol (K. Rahner, "On the Theology of the Symbol," in *Theological Investigations* [London, 1966], 221–52). Rahner distinguishes between a sign and a symbol. The relation

between sign and signified is accidental, whereas that between symbol and symbolized is intrinsic. Rahner defines a symbol as "the self-realization of a being in the other which is constitutive of its essence." Applied to the incarnation, this means that the Logos creates the humanity of Jesus as its self-expression in the world. Here Rahner appeals to the patristic formula *assumptione creatur* to explain the relationship between the divinity and the humanity of Jesus. The human nature of Jesus never preexisted on its own. It was created and assumed by the Logos in one and the same act. In this way the humanity of the Logos is really the humanity of God, so that by contemplating the humanity, one sees the Logos and hence the Father, since the Logos is the Father's self-expression. In contrast, as a created reality, the human nature has its own autonomy. Divinity and humanity are not in competition. Rather, the relation between them is that of a direct proportion. The more the Logos is divine, the more the humanity is human.

To summarize Rahner's approach to revelation and the Trinity, one can say that the center of his theology is the self-revelation and self-communication of God, the Absolute Mystery, to the world. This self-communication takes place on the transcendental level through the gift of uncreated grace, or the Holy Spirit, to the human subject. The same self-revelation takes place on the historical level through the history of salvation, which culminates in the incarnation. In this interpretation of revelation we see that there is an exact parallel between theology and anthropology. Moreover, Rahner's approach to revelation shows that one can do justice to God's communication of himself to the world only if one understands the revelation-event in a trinitarian way. God the Mystery (Father) is present to men and women in the depths of their subjectivity (Holy Spirit) as well as in their concrete history (Jesus Christ). In other words, the immanent Trinity is the Trinity of the economy of salvation.

Another important way of understanding the event of revelation was introduced into Protestant theology by Gerhard Ebeling and has been recently appropriated for Catholic theology by Peter Knauer. According to this interpretation, the event of revelation is a Word-event. In the act of revelation the Word of God becomes a human word. Knauer asks how this is possible if God is not to become involved in the affairs of the world in a mythological way, which would compromise his transcendence. According to Knauer, the event of revelation is possible only if the measure of God's love for the world is the love of the Father for the Son. In seeking to place himself in relation to the world, God does not make human beings the measure of his love. Nor does God need a person as a dialogue partner. Rather, human beings are caught up into the love between the Father and the Son. The real relationship between God and the world is established in the incarnation. But here again humanity as such is not the term of God's relationship to the world, for in the incarnation the humanity of Jesus is not an independent hypostasis, nor does it have an independent existence apart from the Son. Rather, the humanity of Jesus is created by the Logos and united with the Logos in one and the same act. As a created reality, the humanity of Jesus is fully autonomous. As the humanity of the Logos, the humanity is God's own humanity. Like Barth and Rahner, Knauer stresses that the Word-event reaches its culmination when the person addressed is drawn into the event, so that he or she participates in God's own life. As Is 55:11 expresses it, the Word is efficacious. It accomplishes that for which it was sent. This accomplishment is nothing less than a person's participation in God's life. Hence the completion of the Word-event takes place through the Spirit, which establishes a real relation between God and human beings.

What all these approaches have in common is a profound understanding of the meaning of revelation as God's self-communication. As God's self-communication, revelation implies a strict identity between revealer and revealed (incarnation). However, this act of revelation cannot be understood merely as a past event. The once-for-all event of the incarnation becomes contemporaneous through the Holy Spirit by which human beings are enabled to share God's life. Since God the Father reveals himself in history through his Son and in grace through the Holy Spirit, we see that the structure of the revelation-event is trinitarian. And since God corresponds to himself in the act of revelation, it follows that God's own being is from all eternity trinitarian. Hence it is clear that a theological analysis of the act of God's

self-revelation leads us to the heart of the mystery of the Trinity.

Bibl.: K. BARTH, *Church Dogmatics*, vol. 1/1 (Edinburgh, 1936); K. RAHNER, *The Trinity* (London, 1970); P. KNAUER, *Der Glaube kommt von Hören* (Frankfurt, 1982); J. O'DONNELL, "Revelation and Trinity," in *The Mystery of the Triune God* (London, 1988), 17–39.

John O'DONNELL

TRUTH

In contemporary culture after Marx and Nietzsche, we find ourselves facing, say the philosophers, "an immense crisis over the idea of truth" (A. del Noce); we are witnessing a real and actual "elimination of the truth" (F. M. Sciacca). Not a few theologians too are feeling the influence of this, especially as regards the challenge by other religions. So as to take part in INTERRELIGIOUS DIALOGUE, some of them are tempted to concentrate on the salvific value of the various religions and to put the question of whether they are true or not (and ultimately, if not, why not) on hold. But the question about their truth cannot in fact be eliminated, if we want to avoid the danger of falling into syncretism or of reducing dialogue to a mere phenomenology of religions (→ RELIGION II). Now, if people wonder whether other religions are true, they ought in honesty to do as much for Christianity. But what would their benchmark be? For a Christian, it can only be Christian truth. But what exactly does this mean? Here, too, critical reflection is needed, for there is a danger either of reducing truth to dogma (for the Catholic) or of identifying it with one's particular theological traditions (for all Christians), hence with certain systems of ideas that do not necessarily belong to the essence of Christianity.

To make an evaluation of this kind, one therefore needs a criterion: one must set out from some given idea of truth. Many different concepts of truth are to be found in the history of philosophy; we could, e.g., mention Aristotle, Thomas Aquinas, Hegel, Marx, Nietzsche, Kierkegaard, Heidegger. But in the theological field, unfortunately, there seem to be many theologians who have no idea that there is such a thing as a properly Christian concept of truth and that this should be the basic norm for all theological work. What then is *Christian truth?* It would be going too far, as we have already said, to try to identify it with dogma: truth is wider than dogma, though it includes it. The Christian concept of truth can only be that of REVELATION itself, that of Holy Scripture, which is then taken up and actualized in tradition, sometimes with certain new emphases, which need always to be assessed in the light of the biblical concept, since Holy Writ, being the word of God, ought always to be "like the soul to theology" (see *DV* 24).

In short, we may say that according to Scripture, truth is indeed revelation—i.e., the gradual revelation in history of God's saving plan, which culminates in Jesus Christ. Already prepared in the OT, this conception is worked out in the NT, where it says that Jesus Christ is himself "the truth" (Jn 14:6) and that his work is prolonged by the activity of the Spirit in the truth of the church.

1. Biblical Conception of Truth

Old Testament

In the books of the OT, the Hebrew word *'emet* (truth) shows a clear-cut semantic evolution. In the oldest books it basically means solidity, stability, hence also fidelity (fidelity to the covenant). But after the exile, especially in the apocalyptic and sapiential tradition, "truth" gradually takes on a new sense, anticipating the NT: it comes to mean the revelation of God's plan—then also wisdom, the saving doctrine by which human beings ought to live.

It is significant that the noun "truth" is very often juxtaposed with "mystery" and used with verbs meaning not to conceal, to show, to reveal. As here, e.g., in Tb 12:11: "I am going to *tell* you the whole *truth*, hiding nothing from you. . . . It is right to keep the secret of a king, yet right too to *reveal* God's works openly." In one of the Qumran hymns, the author speaks of "the secret of *truth*"; in his turning to God, this is how he designates "your marvelous mysteries" (1QH 11:9–10). So we see that this conception of truth as revelation of the mystery is especially to be found in the apocalyptic and sapiential traditions. In Daniel's visions of the heavenly world, "the Book of Truth" (Dn 10:21)

is the divine book in which God's plan for the time of salvation is written (but still remains hidden). The book of Wisdom proclaims that when the eschatological judgment comes, the righteous "will understand the truth" (Wis 3:9). Then the wisdom of God's providential plan, which during their lives seemed to be "the paradox of salvation," will be fully revealed to their eyes (5:2).

New Testament

a. From that sapiential, apocalyptic, and eschatological background, the Christian notion of truth has gradually taken shape. The transition from the Jewish to the Christian conception appears clearly in a passage of Paul: he denounces the delusion of the Jews who boast of "having in the law the embodiment of knowledge and truth" (Rom 2:20), i.e., of finding the whole revelation of God's will in the Mosaic Law. For Paul, "the truth of the law" is henceforth replaced by "the truth of the gospel" (Gal 2:5, 14); "the word of truth" (Eph 1:13; c.f Col 1:5; 2 Tm 2:15) is "the gospel of your salvation." Christians, who have learned to know Christ (Eph 4:20), now know that the truth is in Jesus (4:21). But after his departure, i.e., from the moment when Christ was "taken up into glory," Christians also know that he remains with them until the end of the world (see Mt 28:20). Throughout this eschatological period, the "mystery of religion," or, in other words, the (past) mystery of God's self-manifestation in the flesh (1 Tm 3:16), is to be proclaimed in "the church of the living God," who thus remains "the pillar and bulwark of the truth" (3:15) for believers. This Christian truth, however, is intended for all: God desires "everyone to be saved and to come to the knowledge of the truth. For there is one God; there is also one mediator between God and humankind, Christ Jesus, himself human, who gave himself a ransom for all" (1 Tm 2:4–6).

In some of these NT texts one can still detect their apocalyptic origin. For Paul, it was his experience on the road to Damascus, when the Son of God was revealed to him (Gal 1:16). He had seen "the light of the gospel of the glory of Christ, who is the image of God." He had seen it blazing "in the face of Christ" (2 Cor 4:4, 6), so he could say he preached only "Jesus Christ as Lord" (4:5). He had not "tampered with God's word"; his ministry had always been "the open statement of the truth" (4:1–2). That truth was the truth of Christ.

b. This leads directly to John. Unlike the classical authors or the gnostic myths, John never locates truth in the absolute of the being of the transcendence of God. For him, truth/revelation is always linked to the temporal mission of Jesus, to his word and to the gift of the Spirit, then also to the acceptance of that truth by believers. "The Word became flesh . . . full of grace and truth" (Jn 1:14); "grace and truth came through Jesus Christ" (1:17). At the Last Supper, he himself said: "I am the truth" (14:6).

The novelty and audacity of an affirmation such as this were pointed out by Jerome: "In none of the patriarchs, in none of the prophets, in none of the apostles was there the truth: only in Jesus. For the others knew in part . . . they saw as in a mirror, confusedly. The truth of God appeared only in Jesus, who said without hesitation: I am the truth" (*In Eph.* 4.21; *PL* 26:507A). The man Jesus is indeed "the truth" for us, since in him was manifested the mystery of his divine sonship, in which we are called to share. The truth of which Jesus spoke was "the manifestation of himself to men and by means of the knowledge of himself the gift made to them of salvation" (Apollinaris of Laodicea).

The truth brought by the historical Jesus remains present also for John, after Jesus has left this world to go to the Father (see Jn 16:28). It is actualized in the church by the work of the Spirit. So John can write: "The Spirit is the truth" (1 Jn 5:7), and in his writings he regularly uses (and he alone in the NT) the expression "the Spirit of truth" (Jn 14:17; 15:26; 16:13; 1 Jn 4:7). The Spirit, Jesus had said, "will guide you into all the truth" (Jn 16:3). Not that he brings a new truth, different from Jesus' truth (Joachim of Fiore); but we need the Spirit of truth, who is the Spirit of Jesus (see Jn 1:33; 7:38–39; 19:34; 20:23) to remind us of and make us understand everything he said (Jn 14:26) and thus allow us to penetrate into the whole truth (16:13). So the truth will necessarily play a decisive role in the new life of the believer. To live like a Christian, for John, means living "in truth and love" (2 Jn 3). That truth is always the truth of Christ but actualized by the Spirit. The path of Christian life is described with many different formulas by John. When people are faced with Christ's

truth for the first time, the first thing they have to do is "do the truth" or take it into themselves. Under the influence of the truth that "abides in them," they will then gradually be able "to know the truth" and be guided in their behavior by that inner truth. The lives of true Christians will then consist in living "in the truth." The truth will inspire all their journey: brotherly love, adoration of the Father, personal sanctification. The more they become disciples of Christ and co-workers of the truth, the more will they be "set free by the truth," set free, i.e., by Christ himself, by the Son of God.

c. The essence of this biblical teaching on truth has been happily condensed by certain ancient authors: "Who persists in the memory of *Jesus* is in the *truth*" (maxim); "our title of *children* [of God] expresses the springtime of our entire lives; the truth which is in us does not grow old; and our whole mode of being is watered by that truth" (Clement of Alexandria).

2. Truth in Christian Tradition

Here a vast field for study opens before us, which is as yet unexplored. So we can touch only briefly on the main currents of Christian tradition in which the term truth has been used.

The Encounter with Hellenism

When Christianity spread into the Hellenistic world, it encountered the Greek and particularly the Platonic notion of truth. In Greek philosophy, truth is a metaphysical notion: truth designates the substance of being, the ultimate nature of things; according to Platonism, it exists in the world of ideas, in the transcendent world of the divine, which used to be called "the plain of Truth" (*Phaedrus* 248b). The Platonic tradition thus identifies God and Truth. One can understand, therefore, why some of the fathers are to say that "Truth is God" (Gregory of Nyssa, *Vita Moysis* 2.19). Augustine too speaks on various occasions of the *aeterna veritas* or of *Deus veritas*. Thomas Aquinas takes up the same conception, even when commenting on Jn 14:6, where Jesus says, "I am . . . the truth"; "He [Christ]," says Thomas, "is simultaneously the way and the end: the way according to his humanity, the end according to his divinity. And thus, as man, he says,

'I am the way'; and as God he adds 'the truth and the life'" (*In Ioan.* 1868). But John never says that God is truth in an ontological sense; for him, truth/revelation comes to us in the man Jesus, in his self-manifestation as Son of God. Therefore, an Orthodox theologian has acutely observed: "The sole starting-point for a Christian conception of truth is Christology" (J. D. Zizioulas). Another influence of the Greek world makes itself apparent, especially during the Middle Ages, when the Aristotelian and Thomist definition of truth comes into theological use: *adaequatio rei et intellectus* ("equivalence between reality and mind"). And so we come in post-Tridentine theology to speak of the truth of religious propositions, or (in the plural) of "Christian truths." But one cannot rationally identify Christianity with a list of truths (even dogmatic ones). This way of speaking was unknown to the entire ancient tradition and was abandoned by Vatican II, which went back to the biblical conception: *omnem veritatem in mysterio Christi conditam* ("all truth stored up in the mystery of Christ") (*DV* 26).

The Biblical Idea of Truth Present in Tradition

In tradition, in addition to the use of the notion of truth derived from Greek philosophy, we find in some of the fathers and in the liturgy a resumption and development of the biblical conception of truth, but sometimes with a stronger emphasis on its doctrinal aspect. Generally speaking, truth then designates the Christian faith, i.e., the divine revelation as it has been handed down in the church. This is the sense in which the formula *regula veritatis* (synonymous with *regula fidei*; → RULE OF FAITH) is to be understood, which was especially in use in the third century. Irenaeus said that the truth is "the teaching of the Son of God" (*Adv. haer.* 3, preface), but he also identified it with Christ himself: "our Lord Jesus Christ is the truth" (3.5.1). Elsewhere he identified truth with "the preaching of the church" (1.27.4), or with "tradition" (3.2.1). The Gnostics, on the other hand, as far as he was concerned, were *transfiguratores veritatis* (3.4.2), because "they had forsaken the truth" (1.18.2). Cerinthus too was called "the enemy of the truth" (3.3.4). An analogous use is found in the Latin world with Tertullian, but with a more apologetic and

polemical note: equivalents of *veritas* for him are *doctrina Christi, doctrina catholica, traditio,* and *praedicatio.* In the debate with non-Christians, he uses the expression *veritas nostra* (*Apol.* 4.3; 46.2) with pride, for Christians are *veritatis cultores* (15.8). Some authors rediscover the apocalyptic dimension of truth; Lactantius designates it with the expressions "the secret of the supreme God" (*De div. Instit.,* 1.1.5), "the mystery of truth" (5.18.11), "revealed truth" (6.18.2). Arnobius stresses the importance of truth in the encounter between Christians and non-Christians: "The Christian religion has been introduced into the world and has manifested the secrets (*sacramenta*) of the hidden truth" (*Adv. nat.* 1.3). We may also cite Gregory the Great: in introducing a saying of Christ in the Gospel, he does not normally use the formula *Iesus* (or *Christus*) *dixit,* but rather *Veritas dixit* (a usage that was to continue through the Middle Ages). The general tenor of Gregory's thought is pastoral, often spiritual and sometimes mystical. He wishes to show the importance of truth for Christian life: he designates it with such expressions as *veritatis eloquium, doctrina veritatis, lumen veritatis, pabulum veritatis.* The link between truth and faith is strongly emphasized. "We all, when in the fullness of faith we wish to give voice to something about God, are instruments of the truth (*organa veritatis sumus*)" (*Mor.* 30.81). Christians who have reached perfection of contemplation, Gregory explains, experience an authentic *revelatio veritatis* (*In I Reg.* 3.20). Holy souls in the church, Gregory further says magnificently, are *veritatis luce splendentes animas* (*Mor.* 19:17).

Let us now refer briefly here to the ancient liturgy, that "holy ark of Tradition" (Y. Congar). When addressing God, the prayers of the church often use the expression *veritas tua* to designate the revelation that comes from God for our salvation: "God, you show the light of your truth to those who are astray, so that they may return to the way of righteousness..." (Monday, third week in Eastertide). The identification of the light of truth with Christ is to be found in a Good Friday prayer (*agnita veritatis tuae luce quae Christus est*). But it is especially in the context of Christian life that the word truth recurs in a variety of formulas: *verbum veritatis, evangelica veritatis, divinae veritatis praeconium, confessio veritatis, veritatis assertor.* Also present is the aspect of the interiorization of the truth that must illuminate the Christian life spiritually, from within: "O God, by the grace of adoption you have made us children of light, grant that we be not swept away in the darkness of error but may ever remain transparent to the splendour of the truth" (13th Sunday in ordinary time). This very ancient prayer seems to have been inspired by the last passage of Gregory, quoted above.

A word too on Vatican II. In the council documents, the term "truth" is once more used in its biblical sense and in accordance with ancient traditional usage. We often find the following formulas: *veritas Dei, veritas revelata, evangelica veritas, christiana veritas, veritas salutaris*. The term truth designates the divine revelation that "is made clear for us in Christ" (*DV* 2). The christological concentration of the truth appears a number of times: "Christ Himself is the Truth and the Way. The preaching of the gospel opens them up to all" (*AG* 8; cf. *DH* 14; *DV* 24). But the council particularly speaks about the truth in connection with Holy Scripture. The ancient problems of "the absolute immunity from error in all Holy Scripture" (*DV* 12, pre-conciliar *schema*), which was inspired by the scholastic conception of truth, are henceforth overcome. In the definitive text, the constitution on divine revelation declares: "the books of Scripture must be acknowledged as teaching firmly, faithfully, and without error that truth which God wanted put into the sacred writings for the sake of our salvation" (*DV* 11). The truth of the Bible stands on the fact that Holy Scripture, being the instrument of the word of God, sets forth the divine revelation. The *veritas salutaris* of the Bible consists not in the absolute inerrancy of individual propositions but in the fact that all Scripture is ordained to the revelation of God's unique salvific plan. The truth of Scripture stands in its revelatory importance, by its gradual unfolding of salvation history. That dynamic conception of truth appears even more sharply in a text clearly biblically inspired (see Jn 16:13): "as the centuries succeed one another, the Church constantly moves forward toward the fullness of divine truth until the words of God reach their complete fulfillment in her" (*DV* 8).

2. Problems of Today

What the church seeks therefore is "divine truth," revealed truth that is also "our truth"

(Tertullian) This is the church's urgent invitation to modern theology, now immersed in a secularized world. The philosophers observe that scientific truth and the sense of history are "the two great myths of the twentieth century" (J. Brun). Someone else wonders whether, from the scientific point of view, "truth is possible" (E. Agazzi). Should we not rather say that scientific knowledge today is "the only source of genuine truth" (J. Monod)? Theology, for its part, has always been regarded as "the science of the faith" (*fides quaerens intellectum*); the truth that the theologian seeks to understand is not so much historical truth or human truth as revealed truth, truth of faith, which can only be understood from within the faith. In an address at Cologne (15 November 1980), Pope John Paul II said: "In a culture dominated by technology . . . the concept of truth becomes more or less superfluous, and is even on occasion explicitly rejected." Today's theologian must keep informed about the great advances in the human sciences and historical knowledge, but must also know that his/her formal object is something else: he/she must seek ever better to understand divine *revelation*, the word of God (*Dei Verbum*); must constantly seek "to arrive at the knowledge of the truth" (2 Tm 3:7). So the true theologian must always regard Holy Scripture as "the soul of theology"; Christian morality must always be "a morality of the faith" (Paul VI); biblical exegesis too must go beyond mere philological and historical research, ever better to understand, in the faith, what Paul called "the mystery of the gospel" (Eph 6:18). The closed-in world of modern immanentism expects (perhaps obscurely) of believers that they, at least they, like John the Baptist, will know how to "bear witness to the truth" (Jn 5:33) and help the people of our times to rediscover that *gaudium de veritate* (*Conf.* 10.33), of which Augustine dreamed so ardently his whole life long.

Bibl.: Var., "αλήθεια," *TDNT* 1:232–47; P. Guilloux, "Les conditions de la conquête de la vérité d'après saint Augustin," *RSR* 5 (1914): 489–506; R. Bultmann, "Untersuchungen zum Johannesevangelium, A. Alêtheia," *ZNW* 27 (1928): 113–63; G. W. Bromiley, "History and Truth: A Study of the Axiom of Lessing," *EvQ* 18 (1946): 191–98; M. Heidegger, *Platons Lehre von der Wahrheit* (Berne, 1947); F. Piemontese, *La "veritas," agostiniana et l'agostinismo perenne* (Milan, 1963); I. de la Potterie, "La verità in San

Giovanni," in *Atti della XVII settimana ABI* (Brescia, 1964), 123–44; id., *La vérité dans saint Jean*, 2 vols. (Rome, 1977); id., "History and Truth," in R. Latourelle and G. O'Collins, eds., *Problems and Perspectives of Fundamental Theology* (New York, 1982), 87–104; W. KASPER, "Die Warheit des Evangeliums," in *Dogma unter dem Wort Gottes* (Mainz, 1965), 58–109; G. KRETSHMAR, "Warheit als Dogma: Die alte Kirche," in H. R. Müller-Schwefe, ed., *Was ist Wahrheit?* (Göttingen, 1965), 94–120; J. GRANIER, *Le problème de la vérité dans la philosophie de Nietzsche* (Paris, 1966); H. MÜHLEN, "Die Lehre des Vaticanum II über die 'Hierarchia veritatum' und ihre Bedeutung für den ökumenischen dialog," *TG* 56 (1966): 303–35; V. GROSSI, "La ricerca cristiana della verità," *Aug* 10 (1970): 388–97; id., "'Regula veritatis' e narratio battesimale in sant'Ireneo," *Aug* 12 (1972): 437–63; M. DETIENNE, *Les maîtres de vérité dans la Grèce archaïque* (Paris, 1972); C. P. WIDMER, "La conception théologique de la vérité et le retournement épistémologique," *Istina* 18 (1973): 24–43; F. M. GENUYT, *Vérité de l'âme et affirmation de Dieu:*

Essai sur la philosophie de saint Thomas (Paris, 1974); J. D. ZIZIOULAS, "Vérité et Communion dans la perspective de la pensée patristique grecque," *Ir* 50 (1977): 451–510; T. D. QUINN, "'Charisma veritatis certum': Irenaeus, Adversus haereses, 4, 26, 2," *TS* 39 *(1978): 520–25;* K. HAACKER, "Il concetto biblico di verità," *Studi di teologia* 2 (1979): 4–36; W. BEIER-WALTES, "Deus est veritas: Zur Rezeption des griechischen Wahrheitbegriffes in der frühgriechischen Theologie," in E. Dassmann and K. Suso, eds., *Pietas* (Münster, 1980), 15–29; E. LANE, "'La règle de la vérité': Aux sources d'une expression de saint Irénée," in *Lex orandi lex credendi: Miscellanea P. Vagaggini* (Rome, 1980), 57–70; A. TASSI, "Modernity as the Transformation of Truth into Meaning," *IPQ* 22 (1982): 185–93; G. PENZO, *Friedrich Nietzsche o la verità come problema* (Bologna, 1984); J. MURPHY-O'CONNOR, "La 'vérité' chez saint Paul et à Qumran," *RB* 72 (1985): 29–76; E. AGAZZI, F. MINAZZI, and L. GEYMONAT, *Filosofia, scienza e verità* (Milan, 1989); H.-P. MÜLLER, ed., *Was ist Wahrheit?* (Stuttgart/Berlin/Cologne, 1989).

Ignace DE LA POTTERIE

U

UNIQUENESS AND UNIVERSALITY OF JESUS CHRIST

1. The Current Theological Debate

The question of the uniqueness and universality of Jesus Christ in the order of salvation is the key question for any Christian theology of religions. Although the question is as old as Christology itself, it is being asked in our day in a more urgent and radical way because of the contemporary context of religious pluralism and the intermingling of the various religious traditions; contemporary literature attests to this renewed raising of the question.

It is important at the outset to be clear about terms. The uniqueness in question here is not a relative uniqueness such as the comparative science of religion can affirm of every religious tradition by reason of its specific character, its distinguishing marks, and its differences from the other traditions. This kind of "relative" uniqueness—and only this kind—is accessible to scientific observation. Faith, however, and the theology that depends on it, goes further. The uniqueness of Jesus Christ in the order of salvation, as traditionally understood by the Christian faith, is an "absolute" uniqueness; i.e., Jesus Christ is necessarily constitutive for the salvation of all human beings; he is the universal savior. It must be said, however, that this uniqueness is ontological, not epistemological, as if it had to enter the field of consciousness. Furthermore, "relational" uniqueness (which is similar to "relative" uniqueness) does not do justice to the traditional Christian faith. That is, it is not enough to admit that even today the mystery of Jesus Christ is able, more perhaps than any other symbol, to inspire and foster a genuine religious life. Rather, it must be said that in God's plan this mystery is universally constitutive for salvation. Some writers prefer to speak of finality or centrality rather than of uniqueness. These other terms (they say) have the advantage of signifying that while the divine revelation in Jesus Christ is decisive and

in this sense final and central; it is not simply the only divine manifestation to the human race.

Oneness and universality: the two must be combined and kept together. Without universality, oneness would lead to exclusivism; separated from unity, universality would lead toward pluralism. But when combined, oneness and universality go together with an inclusive Christology. This becomes clear when we look at the terms in which the present-day discussion of the theology of religions is carried on.

Four main categories may usefully be distinguished in current theological opinion on the relationship of Christ and the church to the other religious traditions: (1) ecclesiocentric universe, exclusive Christology; (2) christocentric universe, inclusive Christology; (3) theocentric universe, normative Christology; (4) theocentric universe, non-normative Christology (J. P. Schineller). Three conceptions of the universe are brought face to face in this classification: ecclesiocentric, christocentric, and theocentric. At the same time, four christological positions are distinguished: exclusive, inclusive, normative, and non-normative.

It is to be noted that the theocentric conception of the world subsumes two views of Christ. The reason for this new model is that many writers regard the ecclesiocentric and christocentric perspectives as untenable nowadays; a new perspective is therefore needed. This new perspective is important, for it implies nothing less than a paradigm shift. According to the authors who propose it, it is henceforth impossible to connect universal salvation either with Jesus Christ explicitly confessed in the church that he founded or even with the mystery of Jesus Christ himself when regarded as effecting salvation beyond the boundaries of the Christian communities. Not only do they reject the idea of a necessary mediation of the church in the order of salvation; they also reject the universal mediation of Jesus Christ that is affirmed in Pauline theology, whatever more or less important (normative or non-normative) theological meaning one may continue to attribute to the person of Jesus Christ in the relations between God and the human race.

In the second case (the nonnormative), authors claim that God has manifested himself in different ways in the different religious traditions and that one may no longer regard his manifestation in Jesus Christ as in any way normative. In the first case (the normative), while recognizing that it is henceforth untenable to make universal salvation depend on the person and work of Jesus Christ (as the christocentric perspective does), authors nonetheless continue to give Jesus Christ a privileged place, in one or other manner, as the most perfect symbol or even the ideal model and, in this sense, as normative in the order of the divine-human relations that are meant by "salvation."

Although the four-part division has some value, many recent authors prefer a three-part classification. They distinguish, therefore, three perspectives: ecclesiocentric, christocentric, and theocentric, and, consequently, three basic positions, which are described respectively as exclusivist, inclusivist, and pluralist (A. Race). These three positions are easily identified, even though various distinctions can be made within each. The exclusivism that marks the ecclesiocentric perspective in the minds of its proponents is due to the church's confession that salvation comes exclusively through Jesus Christ. This is the thesis of H. Kraemer, who applies to the problem raised by the existence of various religions the dialectical theology of K. Barth, according to which the only valid knowledge of God is the one found in Christianity and given to human beings in Jesus Christ; the god of other religions is an idol.

An ecclesiocentric perspective does not indeed necessarily imply exclusivism as understood by H. Kraemer and as connected with a narrow interpretation of the axiom "Outside the church, no salvation." All Catholic theologians admit in fact the possibility of salvation outside the church, though they may have different ways of understanding its occurrence. Nonetheless, the ecclesiocentric perspective, even taken in this broader framework, needs to be transcended. In a theology of religions it is necessary to avoid an ecclesiological inflation that would distort perspectives. The church is a derivative mystery and entirely ordered to the mystery of Christ, and consequently it cannot be the standard by which the salvation of others is measured. This standard can be only Jesus Christ himself, who is constitutive for the salvation of all human beings and whose mystery is present and operative even outside the church. Such is the christocentric, or in-

clusive, thesis, of which K. Rahner is one of the principal proponents.

But the threefold division given above raises a serious challenge to this traditional christocentric perspective. Inclusive Christocentrism is opposed by a theocentric vision that is translated into a model bearing the rather ambiguous name "pluralism." A good number of recent writers support the paradigm shift that consists in moving from Christocentrism to theocentrism, from inclusivism to pluralism. In broad terms this means that if Christianity is sincerely seeking dialogue with the other religious traditions, then since such a dialogue is possible only on a footing of equality, it must begin by surrendering every claim to uniqueness for the person and work of Jesus Christ, when these are regarded as universally constitutive for salvation. This radical position is undoubtedly susceptible of being understood in different ways. I recalled earlier, with J. P. Schineller, two different understandings of the person of Jesus Christ as nonconstitutive for salvation: for some he remains nonetheless normative, while for others he is neither constitutive nor normative. Among those defending a "normative" Jesus are E. Troeltsch and, more recently, P. Tillich; among those opting for a "nonnormative" Jesus is John Hick.

The last-named advocates a "Copernican revolution" in Christology; this consists precisely in adopting a new paradigm by turning from the traditional christocentric perspective to a new theocentric perspective. Just as, after people had believed for centuries that the sun circles the earth, Galileo and Copernicus at last discovered that in fact the earth circles the sun, so too, after people have believed for centuries that the other religious traditions orbit around Christianity as their center, we must recognize today that the center around which all the religious traditions, including Christianity, orbit is none other than God himself. Such a change of paradigm necessarily implies the abandonment of all claims to a privileged importance, whether for Christianity or even for Jesus Christ himself. The fundamental choice, according to John Hick, is between ecclesiocentric exclusivism and theocentric pluralism, i.e., between a fundamentalist interpretation of the axiom "Outside the church no salvation" and a radical liberalism that sees the various manifestations of the divine in various cultures, including the manifestation in Jesus Christ, as all having the same fundamental equality amid their differences. Since ecclesiocentric exclusivism is untenable, the only remaining valid theology of the religions is a theocentric pluralism that leaves behind all Christian claims to a privileged and universal role for Jesus Christ and establishes an interreligious dialogue on a footing of real equality.

2. Belief in Jesus Christ as Alone Universal

The uniqueness and universality of Jesus Christ as traditionally professed by the Christian faith are to be understood in an absolute or unqualified sense: Jesus Christ is constitutive for the salvation of every human being. But the claim raises difficult questions, especially in the present climate of religious pluralism. In what does this uniqueness consist, and how is it to be understood? What is its theological foundation? In establishing it theologically, is it enough to appeal to certain human values set forth by Jesus: e.g., the values of the reign of God that he proclaims? Or to the projected human society that his action implies? Or, again, to the especially profound sense of the human person and its destiny as seen in the teaching of Jesus? Or even to the close filial relationship with God that he urges upon his disciples? Or—without excluding any of the above, but going further and deeper—do the uniqueness and universality of Jesus Christ have to be based in the final analysis on the mystery of his person and on his personal identity as Son of God? If this last is the case, then we realize immediately that only a "high" Christology will establish this uniqueness and universality with certainty. On the contrary, any Christology that remains on a functional level and refuses to take an ontological approach will, perhaps despite its intentions, be condemned to let the uniqueness of Christ rest on a fragile foundation. In any case, we must expect that the various theological opinions on the uniqueness and universality of Jesus Christ as savior will reflect the basic christological positions of their authors.

It must, then, be stated clearly that only the personal identity of Jesus Christ as the only Son of God provides a sufficient theological foundation on which to base his constitutive uniqueness as universal savior. Given this fact, contrary theological positions obviously become logical. For the two assertions go together: either Jesus Christ is the only Son of God, and then his universal mediation follows; or he is not the only Son, and the Christian claim regarding his constitutive uniqueness has no theological basis. But the assertion of the divine sonship of Jesus Christ is a matter of faith; it does not emerge from a reasoning process or from a comparative study of the religions of the human race. This fact, however, does not prevent this assertion, which is at the center of the Christian faith, from having to face serious objections in the present atmosphere of religious pluralism and of interreligious dialogue. The objections are concerned with the NT, the Christian tradition, and theology. It is necessary to answer them briefly.

The *New Testament* clearly asserts the universal mediation of Jesus Christ in the order of salvation. This is clear not only from a few texts that formally say as much (e.g., 1 Tm 2:5–6 and Acts 4:12) and from others that say it in other words but no less clearly (e.g., Jn 3:17 and Acts 5:31; 10:44–48; 17:24–31), as well as from christological hymns in which Christ is placed at the center of the divine plan (e.g., Eph 1:3–13 and Col 1:15–20). It is possible to go further and say that this is the message of the entire NT; it is the underlying core belief that at every point gives the NT its raison d'être and without which it would not have been written.

The same can be said of the divine sonship of Jesus Christ in the NT. This sonship is undoubtedly seen with increasing depth and clarity as we move from the initial apostolic kerygma (Acts 13:32–33) to the reflections of Paul (Rom 1:1–4), Hebrews (Heb 1:1–5), and John (Jn 5:18; 8:18–19; 10:30; 21:30) by way of the Synoptic Gospels (Mk 1:1; 15:39; Lk 1:32). Once again, the claim that Jesus Christ is Son of God can be said to be everywhere present just beneath the surface in the NT and to be indeed its decisive motif.

There is, by and large, no disagreement on what has just been said. The massive NT assertion of the uniqueness of Jesus Christ as savior is not denied. But some ask whether this assertion can and should be maintained in our present setting of religious pluralism. They suggest that, for various reasons and in various ways, it should be relativized. Recent hermeneutical studies show, after all, that the claim of the absolute uniqueness of Jesus Christ, which seems indeed to be the key for interpreting the entire NT, is due in fact to a historically conditioned worldview and ways of speaking that depend on a particular cultural context. This uniqueness can therefore no longer be regarded as _the_ referent of the gospel message, the untouchable core of the Christian message.

Critics note, further, that in the atmosphere created by the Jewish apocalyptic mentality, so permeated by eschatological expectation, it was natural for the early church to interpret the experience of God in Jesus Christ as final and unsurpassable. But this apocalytpic mentality was limited to a culture. The ultimacy that it assigned to the event of Jesus Christ cannot therefore be regarded as belonging to the essence of Christianity; it belongs rather to the fortuitous cultural setting in which Christianity was first experienced and presented. If Jesus had been met and interpreted in a different cultural context that implied a different philosophy of history, he would not have been looked upon as final or unique.

Since Paul is often thought responsible for the clear assertion of the uniqueness of Jesus Christ, critics suggest that if he had come in contact with the rich mystical traditions of the Eastern religions, he would doubtless have softened this unqualified and unnuanced claim. Or, turning now to John, critics note that he expresses the uniqueness of Jesus Christ in terms of incarnation. Incarnation, however, represents a mythic type of thinking, as does the concept of preexistence, which is linked to that of incarnation. But the language of myth must be taken as precisely that and therefore understood metaphorically and not literally. The myth of the incarnation needs to be "demythologized." This will lead into turn to the demythologization of Jesus Christ as absolute savior.

Critics observe, finally, that in the historical context in which Christianity came into existence, and given the opposition it encountered, it was natural for the disciples to present the way of Jesus as unique. This absolutist language is historically conditioned; it is a "language geared to survival."

What answer is to be given to these critiques? It is true that the mystery of Jesus Christ, as conceived in the NT, is located within a con-

cept of history that was inherited from Jewish culture and the religious history of Israel. It is no less true, however, that in return it gives that history a new and unexpected density. As far as Jewish eschatology and the apocalyptic mentality are concerned, it must be noted that the event of Jesus Christ shatters the Israelite understanding of the history of which it becomes a part. While it brings fulfillment to the messianic expectation of the last times, it does so in a transcendent manner by transforming it and going beyond it.

As regards Paul, he indeed did not experience the kind of religious pluralism we have today, but he did nonetheless have to pit his faith in Jesus Christ against not only the Jewish religion from which he emerged but also the Hellenistic culture that he encountered on his journey. The christological hymns may adopt the Jewish cosmology current at the time, but they assert nonetheless the absolute primacy of Jesus Christ and the cosmic dimensions of his coming and activity: he is beyond "thrones or dominions or rulers or powers" (Col 1:16). Those who accuse Paul of lightly made claims in his thinking on the absolute primacy of Jesus Christ are themselves guilty of an unfounded accusation.

As for John, he indeed is the first to use the concept of incarnation in order to account for the mystery of Jesus Christ (Jn 1:14); the concept of preexistence, however, is presupposed before him (see, e.g., Phil 2:6–11). It is also a fact that these two concepts lend themselves to erroneous interpretations. Preexistence is not an existence in a fictive time before time; "incarnation" does not mean that the divine existence is transformed into a human existence. What the incarnation of the Son of God does imply is that the Word really becomes a human being within history, while also having an eternal existence, independent of this becoming, in the mystery of God. That is what is literally meant by a word that is not reducible to a term out of myth. The prologue of the Gospel of John, which formulates the mystery of the personal identity of Jesus Christ in terms of the incarnation of the Word of God, is admittedly the culmination of lengthy reflection on the apostolic faith; it is also a legitimate end result of the dynamics at work in that faith. The functional Christology of the initial apostolic kerygma called for the ontological Christology of the Son-of-God-made-man.

There is little need to dwell on the claim that opposition to the Christian message led the church to assert the uniqueness of the way established by Jesus. Would not circumstances rather have quite naturally led the depositaries of the message to soften their claims about their master? Far from being "language geared to survival," the proclamation of Jesus Christ as savior is presented in the NT as "good news" for all human beings, and indeed good news that deserves forceful and courageous witness and even, if circumstances call for it, the ultimate witness of martyrdom.

While the universality of salvation in Jesus Christ is clearly stated in the profession of faith (see the creeds of Nicaea and Constantinople I), the patristic tradition provides only rare explicit reflections on his uniqueness. The reason is that in the eyes of the fathers, this uniqueness was at the very heart of the faith and beyond all theological suspicion. It was a doctrine that went undisputed because no one discussed it. What was indeed discussed was not the fact of Christ's uniqueness but the basis for it, namely, his personal identity as Son of God.

The question, then, in today's setting of religious pluralism is not whether the Christian tradition has in fact claimed unqiueness for Jesus Christ as savior. The challenge is rather to the why of the claim. One explanation would have it that the profession of faith in Jesus as savior is doxological in character; the significance of the profession must therefore be limited, since all doxological language originates in an impulse of faith that is loving but blind. But we must look at the real situation. This means, first of all, making a distinction between doxological texts and professions of faith or dogmatic decrees. Second, it means understanding that the element of doxology is not opposed to doctrinal content; doxological texts do not lack dogmatic value, any more than professions of faith and even dogmatic decrees lack a doxological element. The acknowledgment that certain documents have a doxological character does not mean they must be denied any dogmatic value. Note, too, that while faith is inspired by love, it is not therefore blind. On the contrary: faith gives a person new "eyes" with which to see the truth. In this sense, faith is its own confirmation; Christians know that what they believe is true.

A more serious and persistent objection is that the Christian doctrine of the uniqueness and divinity of Jesus Christ is the result of an undue hellenization of the Christian message, that this process started in the NT and was carried further in the postbiblical tradition. In response it must be said that if "hellenization" means that the content of the faith was transmitted by the tradition in the language of Hellenic and Hellenistic culture, the statement is true; in taking this course, the tradition was responding to the necessity of inculturating the message, a necessity of which we have become more explicitly conscious in our time. If, however, "hellenization" is taken to mean that first the biblical and then the postbiblical traditions falsified the content of the message by confusing it with Hellenistic philosophical speculation, nothing is further from the truth. It was precisely in order to preserve the Christian message and specifically the mystery of Jesus Christ from any adulteration by contemporary philosophies that the tradition decided to define this message and mystery in careful terms. To do so it had to use familiar concepts, but in using these to express the mystery, it gave them a new sense, a further, hitherto unknown meaning. The *homoousios* of the Council of Nicaea (325) is an eminent example of this procedure, but it is not the only one. We ought to speak, then, not of the hellenization but rather of the dehellenization of Christian dogma (B. Lonergan).

A growing number of theologians are saying that in the present context of religious pluralism the Christian claim of the absolute uniqueness of Jesus Christ has become untenable. The claim must be either moderated or abandoned if dialogue is to be possible. Jesus Christ will then no longer be constitutive for universal salvation; we may, however, continue to see in him the ideal and most inspiring symbol, the one that best responds to human aspirations, the perfect type or paradigm of relations between human beings and God. This view reflects a normative Christology in a theocentric universe, of which I spoke earlier. It is in this sense that Jesus Christ is, for E. Troeltsch, the purest revelation of the religious world.

Some theologians go further and abandon, as henceforth outdated, any Christian claim to the uniqueness of Jesus Christ, whether as constitutive or even as normative. Such is the price that must be paid if dialogue is to be possible. This is the thesis of a theocentric universe accompanied by a non-normative Christology. All religious traditions are fundamentally equal because they represent manifestations (different and all of them relative) of the divine in the various cultures of the human race. The "Copernican revolution" proposed by J. Hick is called the symbol of this theory. The theocentric perspective that he advocates for a theology of religions is closely connected with and logically based on a Christology of the "myth of God incarnate." In this view, Christian belief in the incarnation of the Son springs from a transposition of the message of Jesus into "mythic" language; this transposition was made by the Johannine and postbiblical tradition under the influence of Hellenism.

By way of reply it will be enough to refer the reader to what was said above, in connection with the tradition, about the problem of the "hellenization" or "dehellenization" of christological dogma, and to recall that the Christian faith refuses to allow the reduction of the divine sonship of Jesus Christ to a metaphorical sonship. The Christian faith is in an ontological sonship; this sonship is to be taken literally, even if, as is obvious, the concept of generation is an analogical concept that applies to God in an eminent way.

Another theological difficulty is that critics appeal to historical consciousness and the unavoidable relativity of all truth, even, and above all, revealed truth, even while allowing that this kind of relative truth is enough to justify an unqualified commitment of persons to the partial truth contained in their tradition.

To this argument must be opposed the unique character of the revelation that took place in Jesus Christ. For the transposition of the personal consciousness of Jesus as Son of God into communicable human concepts gives his unstinting revelation of himself and of God an objective value that is transcendent, incomparable, and unsurpassable.

A further problem: should not Christians practice what contemporary psychologists call a "hermeneutic of suspicion" in dealing with religious tradition and with their own in particular? A tree is known by its fruit. So, too, a religion is true to the extent that it makes men and women truly human, in themselves and in their relations with others. But can Chris-

tianity be said to have produced these human fruits in proportion to its exorbitant claims? If Jesus Christ is truly unique, should not the proof of this be seen in the life of believing Christian communities? Can it in fact be seen there?

It is necessary to point out the fallacy in the principle here invoked. Christianity makes no claim for Christians but only for Jesus Christ. It is he who is unique, not they. The Christian community undoubtedly has the mission of bearing credible witness to the mystery at work in it. It often betrays this mission, even without sufficiently realizing it. The fact remains, however, that the mystery of Jesus Christ and his uniqueness do not depend on the quality of the testimony of his disciples. He is God's gift to the human race, never to be withdrawn; God's fidelity does not depend on our Christian infidelities. It is therefore not true that the truth about Jesus Christ depends on the practice of Christians.

The verification principle reappears in another form. In this case, the suggestion is made that the practice of interreligious dialogue ought to be a criterion for judging the truth of any and every religious tradition, including the Christian. Christianity should therefore leave aside, at least provisionally, all claims to the uniqueness of Christ in order to engage in a real dialogue with others, as equals with equals. If Jesus Christ is really unique, it will be for the dialogue to manifest this; nothing else can establish it. From the practice of dialogue (it is said), "perhaps Jesus Christ will emerge (without being imposed on anyone) as the unifying symbol, the universally satisfactory and normative expression, of what God has in mind for the whole of history" (P. F. Knitter).

The question must be asked, however, How will dialogue lead to a rediscovery of faith in the uniqueness of Jesus Christ, once this belief has been bracketed, even provisionally? Faith does not come at the end of dialogue, nor can it be conceived of as a result of dialogue. Dialogue that is sincere neither requires nor allows the bracketing, even provisionally, of a person's faith. Note, too, that the rediscovery of the uniqueness of Jesus Christ that is here envisaged as a possible result of dialogue is not a rediscovery of the uniqueness professed by the Christian faith. A merely normative Christology is inadequate to account for the constitutive character of the mystery of Jesus Christ in the order of salvation.

Another suggestion is that an eschatological perspective be substituted for the traditional christological perspective. This new paradigm shift would mean focusing the theology of religions no longer on the Christ-event but on the reign of God that is being built up in the course of history and will at last reach its eschatological completeness; the focus would therefore be on the future and no longer on the past. When all is said and done, this is a way of ignoring Christocentrism to the advantage of a theocentric perspective: God and his reign are the goal of history, and all religions, Christianity included, are moving toward that goal.

Here again the facts must be taken into account. The theocentric perspective of the NT accepts that the reign of God must be extended in the course of history and reach its eschatological completion—but there is more to be said. Such a concentration on the reign of God undoubtedly makes it possible to move beyond an excessive "ecclesiocentrism," for the reign of God in history extends beyond Christianity and the church; the other religious communities and traditions of the human race are part of it. It is also true that Christianity and the other religious traditions are called to find themselves at one in the consummated reign of God beyond history. Does this therefore mean that the perspective of the reign of God effects a paradigm shift in relation to the christocentric perspective? This would be to forget that the reign of God of which we are speaking broke into history in Jesus Christ and by means of the Christ event; that it is by the joint action of the risen Christ and his Spirit that the members of other religious traditions share in the reign of God that is already present in history; and, finally, that the eschatological reign of God to which the members of all religious traditions are together invited is the reign both of God and of the Lord Jesus Christ. In Christian theology theocentrism and Christocentrism are inseparable. This is true even when the perspective of the reign of God is adopted, whether we think of the reign already begun in history or of the reign that will have its completion beyond history.

It is possible, then, following TEILHARD DE CHARDIN, to speak of a "wonderful convergence" of all things and all religious traditions in the

reign of God and in Christ the Omega, of a "mysticism of unification" toward which the spiritualities of East and West are all moving. But this convergence by no means overshadows the Christ-event. Christ is the end (Omega) because he is the beginning (Alpha), the center and the only point of reference. Finality, centrality, and uniqueness of the Christ-event are all aspects of one and same reality.

A Christian theology of the religions must be able to bring out the universal significance and cosmic dimensions of the mystery of Jesus Christ and of the Christ-event. In the final analysis, the only valid theological foundation of the uniqueness of Jesus Christ is his personal identity as Son of God. But to assert this is to make an act of faith; it cannot be otherwise. For, as Paul says, "No one can say 'Jesus is Lord' except by the Holy Spirit" (1 Cor 12:3).

Bibl.: H. KRAEMER, *La foi chrétienne et les religions non chrétiennes* (Neuchâtel, 1956); P. TILLICH, *Christianity and the Encounter of the World Religions* (New York, 1959); R. H. SCHLETTE, *Die Religion als Thema der Theologie* (Freiburg, 1963); E. TROELTSCH, *The Absoluteness of Christianity and the History of Religions* (Richmond, 1971); R. PANIKKAR, *The Unknown Christ of Hinduism* (London, 1972); J. HICK, *God and the Universes of Faiths: Essays in the Philosophy of Religion* (London, 1973); J. P. SCHINELLER, "Christ and Church: A Spectrum of Views," *TS* 37 (1976): 545–66; H. KÜNG, *On Being a Christian* (Garden City, N.Y., 1976); id., *Christianity among World Religions* (Edinburgh, 1986); K. RAHNER, *Foundations of Christian Faith* (New York, 1978); A. RACE, *Christians and Religious Pluralism: Patterns in the Christian Theology of Religions* (London, 1983); S. NEILL, *The Supremacy of Jesus* (London, 1984); M. DHAVAMONY, ed., *Founders of Religions* (Rome, 1984); L. NEWBIGIN, *L'universalité de la foi chrétienne* (Geneva, 1984); id., *The Finality of Christ* (London, 1969); P. F. KNITTER, *No Other Name? A Critical Survey of Christian Attitudes Toward the World Religions* (New York, 1985); K. CRAGG, *The Christ and the Faiths* (London, 1986); G. D'COSTA, *Theology and Religious Pluralism: The Challenge of Other Religions* (Oxford, 1986); J. RIES, *Les chrétiens parmi les religions* (Paris, 1987); J. HICK and P. F. KNITTER, eds., *The Myth of Christian Uniqueness: Toward a Pluralistic Theology of Religions* (New York, 1987); J. DUPUIS, *Jésus Christ à la rencontre des religions* (Paris, 1989.

Jacques DUPUIS

UNIVERSALE CONCRETUM

The concept of the *universale concretum* has proven helpful for the answering of certain questions arising in the specific fundamental-theological treatises *De religione* and *De revelatione*.

The church finds itself existing in a world of multitudinous religions and has to justify, in relation to them, its claim to being the community of salvation as willed by God, or the *vera religio*. It can be the *vera religio* only if it concentrates in itself and fulfills all the truth of all religions. It is capable of doing this because it is the "body" of the one who, as human and in all his limitedness, contains and lives the richness of all truth: Jesus of Nazareth. He and (through him) the church can be described in terms of the attribute of the *universale concretum*.

Divine revelation is not the disclosure of a dimension of the world that has always existed and of its history; rather, it is the unveiling of God's disposition for salvation. Since this is a decision made by a free God, it can be presented only through a historical, and therefore limited, event. But precisely such, if it is God's revelation, has an absolute relevance for the entire world. The person and life of Jesus of Nazareth is this event, which fulfills the requirements for being a "universale concretum."

Conceiving the universal and the concrete as belonging together has been attempted time and again by philosophers. All these attempts, however, were broken off before they arrived at their goal; either the universal was not truly conceived as concrete, or the concrete not truly as universal.

Only in the sphere of Christian theology was this attempt able to succeed—in the context, namely, of thoughtful reflection, based on belief in Easter, about the figure and significance of Jesus Christ. This occurs, for instance, in the case of Nicholas of Cusa, who often (but primarily in *De docta ignorantia*, 3.3) brings out the coincidence of the universality and concreteness of the revelatory events that culminate in Jesus Christ. To be sure, he does not speak here of *concretio*, but of *contractio*; so that what is repeatedly encountered is the conceptual combination *universalis contractio* or *universalis contracta* (*entitas*). In one way or another, all the major theological conceptions take account of the fact that Jesus of Nazareth

is the occurrence of God's revelation to the world, i.e., that he is the *universale concretum*.

In connection with the concepts of Adam and representation, OT and Jewish theology had set out on the path toward grasping the "universale concretum"; only in the context of believing reflection about Jesus of Nazareth, however, were such efforts able to lead to that goal. Decisive here is the aspect of "for many," or "for all," which characterizes his death on the cross and enables it to have redemptive significance. The *universale* of the *concretum* that is Jesus Christ, in his living and dying, comes to realization in his "pro-existence" (H. Schürmann, W. Breuning)—i.e., in his existence for others and for all. The condition of the possibility of this pro-existence is Jesus' being the incarnated word of God. It becomes humanly accessible through belief in Easter.

Already in the NT, the coincidence of the "universale" and the "concretum" that has become a reality in Jesus is thought out in constantly new forms. Above all, the Pauline and Johannine texts speak in a variety of ways of the universal scope of the coming of Christ: Jesus is God's word become flesh (Jn 1:14). Jesus is the new Adam (Rom 5:12–21; 1 Cor 15:20–22, 44b–49). Jesus is the mediator of creation and redemption (Rom 3:21–26; Eph 1:3–14). Jesus is the head of his body, the church, of which it is occasionally said (e.g., in the letters to the Ephesians and to the Colossians) that it has cosmic dimensions.

The biblical approaches have later been repeatedly reappropriated and developed in new forms. Irenaeus conceives the *concretum universale* that is Jesus Christ through the category of recapitulation. Christ comprehends in himself the whole of the world and its history. Thus Adam is reestablished in Christ. According to *Adv. haer.* 5.17.4, the crucified body of Christ, hanging from the beams of the cross, indicates the dimensions of the cosmos and embraces humanity—Jews and Gentiles—with both arms. Linking up with the prologue to the Gospel according to John, and in dialogue with Hellenistic philosophy, Justin described Christ as the true Logos, thereby realizing an additional possibility for conceiving Jesus Christ as a *concretum universale* (see *Apol.* 2.10.1). Other significant theologians of the early church continued to develop and deepen the Logos theme in Christology. Especially important here was Origen (e.g., *Hom. in Gen.* 1.1), who was then followed by many others.

In Greek patristic theology, the doctrine of "physical redemption" was also developed. According to that doctrine, although Jesus Christ, in becoming human, took on an individual human nature, he nevertheless entered, through it, into physical contact with the human race as a whole. Through that contact, he communicated to humanity the gifts of grace, redemption, and divinization. If it is to be universally effective, the incarnation presupposes the ontological oneness of humanity. The individual human being is a spatiotemporally limited participant in the one, universal "nature" of the human, i.e., in humanity regarded as a concretely existing entity. The ingress of the Word become flesh into a humanity understood in this way is a social phenomenon. The presence of Jesus Christ, the Firstborn, in humanity—which had, as a result of sin, lost its quality of being a likeness of God—brings redemption to that humanity, i.e., the restoration of its being a likeness of God. Gregory of Nyssa, in his *Major Catechetical Oration*, elaborated the doctrine of the physical redemption in an especially impressive form. Augustine developed, with constantly new variations, the theme of "Christus totus et caput et corpus" ("the whole Christ, head and body") (see *Sermo* 341.9.11; *Enarr. in Ps.* 37.6; etc.), thereby attempting to understand the "universale concretum" that is Jesus of Nazareth. Anselm of Canterbury's famous doctrine (as presented primarily in *Cur deus homo?*) of "representative satisfaction" is a way of illumining the universal scope of what was effected by Jesus Christ that has been especially influential in the history of theology.

Whether the medieval discussion, conducted mainly by Franciscan theologians and aimed at comprehending the relationship between *singulare* and *universale*, has anything to contribute toward understanding of the "universale concretum" that is Jesus Christ may be left open here. In any case, the work of Nicholas of Cusa, in which there is express mention of the "coincidentia" of *universale* and *contractum*, would probably not have been possible without the prior efforts of the Franciscan theologians. Martin Luther, in his controversy with Zwingli about the latter's conception of the Lord's Supper, attached great importance to the under-standing of the communication of idioms (interchange of the divine and human predicates) as a *praedicatio realis*, and not merely as a *praedicatio verbalis*. Only in this way, according to Luther, can that ubiquity (omnipresence) of Jesus' humanity be expressed without which the real presence of Jesus Christ in the eucharistic bread and wine would not be possible. Hence, Luther's doctrine of understanding the communication of idioms as real (rather than merely verbal) is also a way of reflecting on the mystery of Jesus Christ's being *concretum* and *universale*.

"God is love" (1 Jn 4:16). God, who in his essence is love, evidences that love to and through the world in history, and above all in the history of Jesus of Nazareth. In Jesus Christ, biblical revelation finds the centerpoint of its meaning and its most intense concentration. The occurrence of Christ, in its concrete uniqueness, comprehends in itself the whole of history and, indeed, the universe; the latter reaches its perfection in the universal pro-existence of the crucified and resurrected Christ. The concentration of the universal in the concrete uniqueness of the person and way of Jesus comes to christological expression in the dogma of the hypostatic union. In terms of theology of revelation, this union signifies the ontological oneness of Jesus Christ with God's word and God's redeeming action, and thus with God's revelation (see Col 2:9: "For in him the whole fullness of deity dwells bodily").

Bibl.: N. DE CUSA, *De docta ignorantia* (Minneapolis, 1985); R. HAUBST, *Die Christologie des Nikolaus von Kues* (Freiburg, 1956), 166–221; H. DE LUBAC, *Glauben aus der Liebe* (Einsiedeln, 1970), supplement; W. LÖSER, "Universale concretum als Grundgesetz der oeconomia salutis," in W. Kern, H. J. Pottmeyer, and W. Seckler, eds., *Handbuch der Fundamentaltheologie*, vol. 2 (Freiburg, 1985), 108–21, esp. 116–21. For the analysis of fundamental ideas: R. HÜBNER, *Die Einheit des Leibes Christi bei Gregor von Nyssa* (Leiden, 1974); T. VAN BAVEL and B. BRUNING, "Die Einheit des 'totus Christus' bei Augustinus," in P. Mayer and W. Eckermann, eds., *Scientia Augustiniana* (Würzburg, 1975), 43–75; H. MACKEY, "Singular and Universal: A Franciscan Perspective," *FrSA* 17 (1979): 130–64; G. GRESHAKE, "Erlösung und Freiheit, eine Neuinterpretation der Erlösungslehre Anselms von Canterbury," in G. Greshake, *Gottes Heil, Glück des Menschen* (Freiburg, 1983), 80–104.

Werner LÖSER

V

VATICAN I

1. The Challenge of the Period: The Pretension to Autonomy

The church that held the First Vatican Council was a church in search of certainties, a church that, by 1870, had already for a century been subjected to assaults regarding not only its power but also the basis of its very existence — namely, the possibility of the revelation of a personal God, Creator and Redeemer. Assaults, moreover, were not launched by some isolated thinker in unreadable books but were propagated, sometimes blatantly, in easily assimilated writings for an ever wider, educated public. (Voltaire and Rousseau were to have more influence in the nineteenth century than in their own.) These assaults, lastly, joined themselves to new models of political and social thought.

From the theoretical point of view, one could say these assaults had been hard to counter adequately from the start. Much eighteenth-century theological energy had been consumed in discussions and disputes (e.g., concerning Jansenism) conducted with a passion worthy of more important causes, and in a lesser degree ecclesiological problems turning on "episcopalism" in its various forms often joined in a marriage of convenience with the differing forms of jurisdictionalism.

It was a church in which uncertainty could only be increased by the traumatic experience of the French Revolution, for this not only wrecked a patriarchal and hierarchical political order in favor of Liberty, Equality, and Fraternity but led to a schism and, backed by the Terror, the dechristianizing of a nation known as the *Fille Aînée* of the church. In this church, any desire, however moderate, for democracy, as too any striving for liberty (the Irish and the Poles had plenty to strive about), raised the specter of anarchy and atheism, which were thought to be their inevitable result.

It was a church that had to come to grips with the fact that the restoration of the monarchy did not bring peace and harmony and that the specter was becoming more and more menacing — just look at 1848! This specter from now on had a new name: Communism. The Holy See's difficulties with Italy meanwhile gave the church a further negative experience. The theory of the masonic-Jacobin-liberal-Communist world plot easily took root and gained currency.

The analysis that saw the root of all the convulsions, both political and social, way back in the period of the Enlightenment was not far wrong. MODERNITY, with its concept of human autonomy that could and, in a certain sense, should be translated into the sociopolitical field was the product of a period of anthropocentrism and philosophical subjectivism (from Descartes to Kant), of the collapse of the ancient authorities invoked to explain the physical phenomena from anatomy (Vesalius, Malpighi, van Leeuwenhoek) to astronomy (Copernicus, Galileo, Keppler). Modernism equally was the product of the discovery of the ability to formulate and calculate the laws governing the universe, which now seemingly could be mastered (Newton), and also to make concrete and useful discoveries (to take a single example, Benjamin Franklin's invention of the lightning conductor). A new conception of the laws regulating society, in which there again was to be no more relying on ancient authorities, and the new analyses of the origin of authority and the formulation of inalienable human rights (Locke, Montesquieu, Rousseau) must be added to what has already been said. In a word, the church saw in rationalistic agnosticism the very fountain of anarchy.

The problem, being simplified in these terms, gave rise to the thesis that reaffirmation of a sound doctrine combatting agnosticism would also suffice to bring an ordered society to birth — one that could no longer do without religion. Thus the reaffirmation of the importance of the church would be achieved at the same time.

An importance, for the church, that was not to be limited solely to the religious fact but would have to be reaffirmed too as against the pretensions of modern governments which, apart from the question of revelation and the divine source of authority (the modern states too would have liked to maintain a principle of authority), excluded a sociopolitical doctrine based on transcendental moral principles, knowable from the natural law (given by God) and the revealed message.

2. The Response of Vatican I: The Principle of Authority

The need to combat AGNOSTICISM (the product of rationalism) in order thereby to combat anarchy, or the "immortal principles" of the French Revolution (which was only to be one link in the genealogy of errors prophesied by Bossuet as the fruit of the Protestant Reformation and still to be found in the magisterial documents of Leo XIII), is expressed in the answers given to the inquiry made by the Holy See among the curial cardinals and a group of residential bishops about the opportuneness of an ecumenical council. A first point in the program of the council is thus formulated: a condemnation of the errors now destroying the world, a condemnation already to be found in the *Syllabus* (Pius IX's Syllabus of Errors, 8 December 1864) but needing to be more solemnly reaffirmed. Pius IX himself wished this reaffirmation to be made.

The commission charged with drafting the schema on the Christian religion was hence to take the *Syllabus* as its starting point. In the first instance, the fathers were presented with a *schema* drawn up by J. B. Franzelin (1816–1886) and then modified by the theological commission. Anxiety about the entire social order, the basis of which—religion (i.e., the Catholic religion)—had to be reaffirmed, conditioned the first criticisms of the *schema* laid before the fathers. While beginning with the problems of materialism, pantheism, and rationalism (following the initial points of the *Syllabus*), and continuing with a series of themes of fundamental theology (the sources of revelation, the need for supernatural revelation, the distinction between divine faith and human knowledge, the need for reasons of credibility, the supernatural virtue of faith and the need for it, as well as freedom of assent, the mysteries of revealed religion, the relationship between human science and divine faith, and the immutability of dogmas), the *schema* also contains a whole series of dogmatic themes (Trinity, creation, incarnation and redemption, the supernatural order, sin, grace) directed in particular against the Viennese theologian A. Günther. The fathers insisted, because of the

worrying state of society, that it be limited to the basic and primary errors: materialism and atheism (Cardinal Rauscher of Vienna intervened here, as did various Italian bishops, who pointed to the crisis of faith among the masses). And so the Constitution *Dei Filius* was indeed to confine its attention to these first problems.

Anxiety over the political and social effects of the repudiation of divine authority is also expressed in the fathers' decision not to confine themselves to condemning errors but to formulate, above all positively, the correct teaching. This anxiety seems less present in the discussions on individual chapters and paragraphs. These discussions (brilliantly analyzed by H. J. Pottmeyer) are very technical, inasmuch as they seek to respond to the various positions deriving from the needs for autonomy of the thinking subject, for whom divine intervention by means of a transcendental revelation has become very hard to accept. With the council, we assist at the denial—on the part of Deism—of a revelation and of a possible transcendent activity of God in human history, and at the denial of the transcendent character of revelation, which gets reduced to a merely immanent reality and to the emptying of its significance in the context of an absolute evolutionism (Hegelians) that regards God and the universe as a single reality and therefore human reason as not substantially different from divine reason. At the council they also try to react directly to the solutions proposed by certain Catholic authors (already condemned by the magisterium in the previous decades) in order to overcome the same problems. This preoccupation of the fathers offers a hermeneutical key for interpreting the texts. In this context, rationalism and semirationalism are regarded as the most sinister errors (A. Günther, 1783–1863; G. Hermes, 1775–1831; J. Frohschammer, 1821–1893); to a lesser degree the solution of the traditionalists (F. de Lamennais, 1782–1854; A. Bonnetty, 1798–1879; L. de Bonald, 1754–1840; G. Ventura di Raulico, 1792–1861) and of the fideists (L. Bautain, 1796–1867), which, however, have to be rejected because they ultimately admit the claims of rationalism to be autonomous.

The Constitution was voted unanimously and promulgated on 24 April 1870. In its positive formulations and even more clearly in the anathemas, while correcting a number of specific errors, it above all sets out theologically the principle of authority as against the pretensions to autonomy. There can be no autonomy if (chap. 1) the world has been created by the free choice (against Hermes and Günther) of a personal, free, and transcendent God (against materialism and pantheism). There can be no autonomy if (chap. 2) this God can be known for certain by the light of reason as beginning and end of all things (against atheists and extreme traditionalists) and if, furthermore, he has revealed himself supernaturally (against Deists); this form constitutes the sole way by which human beings can attain knowledge of the supernatural realities (against the semirationalists). Instead of autonomy, the Constitution invokes (chap. 3) the obligatory response of faith, which accepts the truths revealed, not because reason could grasp them (against Hermes), but because of the will of the revealer, who also works supernatural signs, such as miracles and prophecy, as external reasons for belief (against rationalism). The act of faith, however, is always free (against Hermes). The *obedience* of faith extends to all truths proposed as such by the church; the church itself is also a reason for believing.

In the context of the antithesis between autonomy and authority, the relationship between supernatural faith and human science next needed to be dealt with (chap. 4), for science constituted the sphere in which the pretensions to autonomy arose in its most acute form. The response denies an absolute autonomy to reason, without denying reason's importance. On the one hand, the divine mysteries surpass reason, but on the other, reason can penetrate them to some degree. For there are not two truths, and there can be no contradiction between faith and reason, even though the former transcends the latter. Science has its role, but within established bounds. Dogmas, in conclusion, are essentially immutable.

This chap. 4 could well be regarded as the hermeneutical key to the whole document. Basically there exists a harmony between divine revelation and human knowledge, just as there is no contradiction between natural and supernatural revelation without having to subordinate the latter to the former. This reasoning can be extended to the relationship between the church and society. There can and

ought to be a harmony, without the church's being subordinated to the state, thus maintaining the church's superiority vis-à-vis the latter.

The document should not be read only against the background of autonomy discussed above, for its value and importance goes beyond a similar sphere. For the sake of fundamental theology, we may note that the Constitution, which later conditioned the treatises on the subject, had the great merit of dealing in a single document with the concept of revelation and its themes. It should furthermore be noted that the concept of revelation set out here is substantially limited to a collection of propositions; likewise miracles are considered only under the "exterior" aspect of their uniqueness, but not for their salvific content. The fathers reached balanced formulations on the role of human reason, the value of which is not denied but included in a vision creating harmony between nature and supernature and opening the way to the later development of fundamental theology; basically they do their best to respond to the problems of the period while giving a deeper insight into the faith and its fundamental principles. *In nuce*, the theme is already present, as V. A. Dechamps (1810–1883) pointed out, about the desire of the human heart—or in other words, the subject of immanence; here it is established that it cannot be the only thing, but it is not excluded. The fathers were probably more interested in the external reasons for credibility, hence their subsequent rebuke of extrinsicism. "While susceptible of further improvement, *Dei Filius* is still an irreplaceable basic text, and comparable to the Tridentine decree on justification" (G. Martina).

A second part of the council's program was also in part suggested by the *Syllabus*, especially the questions on the role of the church and its importance to civil society, as well as the rights of the church within the state, which political events had brought into debate for the past several decades. The intervention was, however, to be seen as a decisional statement at conciliar level in the centuries old debate about the church and its visible and hierarchical structure, a debate kept alive particularly by Protestants.

The fathers were presented with the first *schema* of a constitution on the church, containing the following chapters: (1) the description of the church as the mystical body of Christ; (2) the religion of Christ can be practiced only in the *societas* founded by him; (3) it is a society that is real, perfect, spiritual, supernatural, (4) visible, (5) one, (6) necessary for salvation, (7) not to be found outside the church, (8) indefectible, (9) infallible, (10) hierarchical, and (11) having the primacy of Peter. (Chaps. 12–14 deal with temporal power, the rights of the state, and the rights of the church in relation to the state.) The *schema* failed to please. The presentation of the church as the mystical body, although very biblical, was held to be too vague; note the preoccupation with the question of authority. Also the following chapters did not arouse much enthusiasm; oddly, because the biblical dimension was said to be lacking!

A *schema*, the first part of which had been emended mainly by J. Kleutgen (1811–1883), was withdrawn, since it was decided to present the chapter on the primacy as a separate *schema*, which dealt with the pope's ordinary, immediate, episcopal, and universal jurisdiction and his infallibility in matters of faith and morals. On the one hand, it was intended by these means to put an end to the debate not only with the Protestants and the Orthodox but also with the episcopalists ("Gallicanism") within the Catholic church itself, as may be seen in the defining formula; on the other, it was a general reaffirmation of the principle of authority, the authority of bishops too, as some early opponents to the infallibility definition had spotted. The discussion itself (see the good analysis by A. Houtepen), the object too of a controversial historical work (B. Hasler), does not always make the general context clear of being a response to the challenge of autonomy. The result—the Constitution *Pastor Aeternus* —was, however, received in the various chancelleries of Europe (Berlin, Vienna, Paris).

Pastor Aeternus is not only important for ecclesiology (→ CHURCH), for which it represents the triumph of ultramontanism, understood in the current sense of anti-episcopalist. The proclamation of the infallibility and universal jurisdiction of the pope also corresponds to the demands of politico-cultural ultramontanism, of which the nontheologian J. de Maistre (1753–1831) may be considered the father. He argued, "There is no order without religion, there is no religion without Chris-

tianity, there is no Christianity without the Church, there is no Church without the Pope, and there is no Pope without infallibility." Infallibility is another word for sovereignty.

Certainly the concept of infallibility very closely concerns various problems of fundamental theology. For it has bearing on the criteria concerning the true faith, the certainty of the faith, the problem of revelation "which came to an end with the death of the last apostle," the development of DOGMA, and the continuity of religious doctrine. It also is relevant for the problems about the relationship between ecclesiastical dogma and private conscience, between dogma and scientific research, and between religious experience and dogmatic formulas. As regards revelation, by an intervention of authority, it has been established that it has been entrusted to the church for it to communicate and interpret authoritatively; within the church, the pope in his turn exercises an authority that is opposed to any autonomous interpretations of revelation. Certainty is assured in the best possible way.

One might add that such a great and efficient authority both can and should also contribute to the reestablishing of the social order. In its historical perspective, the intense activity of the magisterium in constructing a social and political doctrine with the aim of inaugurating a new Christendom, modeled on a Middle Ages more imaginary than real, is also one of the fruits of the assertions of Vatican I. The church, founded on divine revelation and being its custodian, has something important to say to the world.

The *schemas* are put forward in the context of the third aim of the council, i.e., resolutions on certain disciplinary matters (obligations and authority of bishops, prelates, vicars general; clerical life; catechesis; religious orders; Eastern rites; missions; exemptions!) and are treated only partially, in a way that may be thought of, in the first instance, as an attempt to improve pastoral activity; insofar, however, as they envisage a better functioning of the church, the interpretative frame becomes wider. In a perturbed world, the church should bring a message of divine origin, proclaiming the existence of a basis for social order and, furthermore, pointing out how this order ought to be.

3. Final Observations

The documents of Vatican I cannot be read only as a key to the search for certainty; their significance ought not to be reduced to this. The reasoning according to which agnosticism led to anarchy could not be stood on its head in the thesis that victory over agnosticism would have restored Christendom at a stroke; new social models—even of advanced democracy (e.g., as in the United States)—did not automatically exclude the presence of religion and offered a freedom of action for the church that was unknown under the absolute kings, even if these did have such titles as "Most Christian," "Catholic," "Most Faithful," and "Apostolic."

The political consequences of modernity—the desire to base society and state on human rights and, as a consequence of this, to construct a liberal, and hence social, democracy—could be corrupted (Leninism, Stalinism) or interrupted (fascism), but they certainly could not be eradicated from the collective consciousness of the human race and its noblest representatives (see the pontifical magisterium on the subject). Theologically speaking, the dialectical concept of a theonomous autonomy was necessary.

Bibl.: Y. CONGAR, "L'ecclésiologie de la Révolution française au concile du Vatican sous le signe de l'affirmation de l'autorité," in var., *L'ecclésiologie du XIXe siècle* (Paris, 1960), 76–114; U. BETTI, *La costituzione dogmatica "Pastor Aeternus," del Concilio Vaticano I* (Rome, 1961); H. RONDET, *Vatican I, le concile de Pie IX: La préparation, les méthodes de travail, les schémas restés en suspens* (Paris, 1962); F. VAN DER HORST, *Das Schema über die Kirche auf dem I. Vatikanischen Konzil* (Paderborn, 1963); H. OTT, *Die Lehre des I. Vatikanischen Konzils: Ein evangelischer Kommentar* (Basel, 1963); R. AUBERT, *Vatican I* (Paris, 1964); H. MEYER, *Das Wort Pius IX, "Die Tradition bin ich": Päpstliche Unfehlbarkeit und apostolische Tradition in den Debatten und Dekreten des Vatikanum I* (Munich, 1965); H. J. POTTMEYER, *Der Glaube vor dem Anspruch der Wissenschaft: Die Konstitution über den katholischen Glauben "Dei Filius," des Ersten Vatikanischen Konzils und die unveröffentlichten theologischen Voten der vorbereitenden Kommission* (Freiburg, 1968); id., *Unfehlbarkeit und Souveränität: Die päpstliche Unfehlbarkeit im System der ultramontanen Ekklesiologie des 19. Jahrhunderts* (Mainz, 1975); var., *De doctrina Concilii Vaticani primi* (Vatican, 1969); G. SCHWAIGER, ed., *Hundert Jahre nach dem Ersten Vatikanum* (Stuttgart, 1970); J. GOMEZ-HERAS, *Temas dogmáticos del Concilio Vaticano I: Aportación de la Comisión Teológica preparatoria a su obra doctrinal, votos y esquemas inéditos,* 2 vols. (Vittoria, 1971); A. W. J. HOUTEPEN, *Onfeilbaarheid en hermeneutiek: De infallibilitas-concept op Vaticanum I* (Bruges, 1973); K. SCHATZ, *Kirchenbild und päpstliche Unfehlbarkeit bei den deutschsprachigen Minoritätsbischöfen auf dem I. Vatikanum* (Rome, 1975); A. B. HASLER, *Pius IX (1846–1878): Päpstliche Unfehlbarkeit und I. Vatikanischen Konzil: Dogmatisierung und Durchsetzung einer Ideologie* (Stuttgart, 1977); P. WALTER, *Die Frage der Glaubensbegründung aus innerer Erfahrung auf dem I. Vatikanum: Die Stellungnahme des Konzils vor dem Hintergrund der zeitgenössischen römischen Theologie* (Mainz, 1980); P. PETRUZZI, *Chiesa e società civile al Concilio Vaticano I* (Rome, 1984); G. MARTINA, *Pio IX, 1866–1878* (Rome, 1990).

Marcel CHAPPIN

VATICAN II

Once the upheaval of the modernist crisis had subsided, by about 1930, the dried-up, stunted, seemingly sapless tree of the church began to grow green again, to produce shoots, then to bud and extend branches out into the open in search of a little light. All this was an omen of Vatican II. For this council was not the result of spontaneous generation. It emerged from a context; it had been germinating for four or five decades. Consequently, before anything can be said of the event itself, its dimensions, its fruits and successes, some awareness is needed of the context that preceded and prepared for it.

1. The Antecedent Historical Context

The truth is that the council was a response to deep longings of Christianity and of the entire human race. The church could not continue in its attitude of distrust, its ghettoization, in the face of a society that was rapidly becoming planetary in scope and being renewed in its outlook, its customs, and its ways of being and acting. The church had to break its 150-year silence and enter into dialogue with a partner, at a time when the church itself was now so different from what it had been.

A Changing Society

Here are three factors in this change.

a. Rise of the Third World and end of colonialism in Africa and Asia and previously in the Americas in the nineteenth century. The dates and numbers speak for themselves: independence of Indonesia (1945), the Philippines (1946), and then India. The state of Israel came into being in 1948, and in 1951 Libya freed itself from British control. The years 1954–62 saw the struggles for the independence of Africa, with Sudan independent in 1956; Ghana in 1958, and then, around 1960, Congo (presently Zaire), Kenya, Uganda, and Madagascar. In 1970 Portugal ended its control of Angola and Mozambique. Indochina, which became Vietnam, liberated itself from French and American influence after years of bloody struggles. A new age had dawned. In the year 2000 the Third World will have a population of five billion, as compared with the billion and a half of the "developed" countries. This liberation of the African and Asian world has already had an immeasurable effect on the image that the church (hierarchy and faithful) presents of itself, as well as on its mentality, attitudes, customs, liturgy, and so on.

b. Worldwide industrialization. Meanwhile, in the Western countries, industry with its application of technology had transformed a society until then mainly agricultural; it increased a hundredfold the means and effectiveness of production, while drastically reducing the manpower needed. The result was the beginning of an exodus from the countryside to megalopolises (Mexico City, São Paulo, Shanghai, Tokyo, Calcutta, Beijing, Rio de Janeiro, and New York, each of which has more than ten million inhabitants); it was also the beginning of the many problems this concentration brought with it (drugs, unemployment, violence, terrorism, strikes, decreasing birth rate, immorality in many forms, and so on).

Finally, *television* took its place in the center of the home and transformed the world into a global village. We are living in a time when the entire world lives in the same present moment. The armchairs side by side in television rooms became the symbol of parallel silent monologues by individuals dwarfed before the little screen.

In the presence of changes on such a gigantic scale, was it any longer possible to speak of Christendom, state religion, or a Christian nation? What influence could the church exert in this pluralist and secularized world in which religions, races, and cultures rubbed shoulders and intermingled? For the moment, the world resembled an immense cauldron in which the best and the worst were mixed in together.

A Church in Quest of Itself

Everywhere, among laity and clergy alike, there was a vague sense of uneasiness. Even within the same regions progressivist and reactionary currents existed side by side. But new trends were taking increasingly clear shape, especially in three areas.

a. The laity were taking an increasingly important place in the church, an importance given concrete embodiment in the Catholic Action movements that were spreading rapidly across Europe and America under the influence of Canon Cardijn; in the birth of the secular institutes, whose members practiced the evangelical counsels while carrying on their professional occupations; and in the development of the theology of the laity, a project promoted by journals. The Catholic Action movements did not always have the success they hoped for, either because of the passivity of the masses or also because of the fears inspired by young people whom some thought were overly rebellious against authority. The real hope of these fearful ones was to build a new Christendom in a dechristianized world.

At the same time, the problem arose of the autonomy of the laity over against the clergy. Catholics carried on their activity in increasing independence of the Catholic Action movements and chose to act directly in the social sphere. The pressure of Communism and socialism forced the church to take a stand in *Rerum Novarum* and *Quadragesimo Anno*, and then, in *Mater et Magistra*, to warn against the excesses of capitalism. But the greatest difficulty for preconciliar Catholicism was the unbridged gap between theory and practice in the social area. Down to the eve of Vatican II the great majority of the faithful remained hostile to any idea of profound change. Starting in 1950, the scandalous underdevelopment of the Third World began to trouble Catholic circles, first at the level of documents (*Populorum Progressio*, Medellín, Puebla, *Laborem Exercens*), then at the level of reality. One thing was certain: even before Vatican II the rise of the laity had become irreversible. The foundations had even been laid for a theology of the laity (Y. Congar, _Vraie et fausse réforme dans l'Église_ [1950]).

_b._ A second characteristic of the renewal that had begun was the _return to the sources,_ especially to Scripture. This last, which for practical purposes had been put on the Index since the Reformation, regained its vitality and power through the Catholic Action movements, the distribution of Bibles, the multiplication of Bible study groups, and the commentaries on Scripture that accompanied the Sunday liturgy. The magisterium itself, in _Divino Afflante Spiritu_ (1943), gave new life to exegetes who had been broken by the modernist crisis. The increasingly widespread use of form criticism (_Formgeschichte_) as a method of literary analysis made it possible to examine in detail the history and prehistory of the Gospels. In patristics, collections such as Sources Chrétiennes and Ancient Christian Writers opened the sealed fountain of the fathers. This return to the sources led to a better understanding of the church as a mystery (H. de Lubac, _Catholicisme_ [1938]; Eng.: _Catholicism,_ 19; Encyclical _Mystici Corporis_ [1943]; beginning of the Unam Sanctam series, 1937). The approaches that would lead to _Lumen Gentium_ were gradually taking form.

_c._ The preconciliar period also saw the rise of an ever more intense _desire to restore the broken unity_ among Christians. This irresistible wave turned into the ecumenical movement, harbingers of which could be seen in the founding of the journal _Irénikon_ (1926), the work of Y. Congar (_Chrétiens désunis_ [1937]), and the establishment of the _Pro civitate christiana_ center by Don G. Rossi in 1939 and of the _Unitas_ center in Rome in 1950. These events prepared the way for the establishment of the Secretariat for Christian Unity by John XXIII in 1960.

There were other trends to which I shall return below: openness to the world; dialogue with science; liturgical renewal pursued with single-minded intentness; renewal of anthropology; better presentation of the Christian message in homilies, catechesis, and theology; emphasis on the specific character of Christianity in comparison with the other world

religions; abolition of Roman centralization and monolithic uniformity; and relations between church, gospel, and culture. For the time being, the pot was aboil in society and in the church, while people waited for a catalyst powerful enough to help and facilitate a seriously threatened unity.

2. Doctrinal Tensions within the Church

On the eve of Vatican II, all was not running smoothly at the center of the Catholic church, the Vatican. A first point to be stressed is that from 1944 to 1958 the post of secretary of state was not filled; Pius XII concentrated all power in his own hands and became an isolated pope, lacking adequate personal contacts and surrounded by advisers with the same mentality. The curia was in a period of stagnation.

Catholic thought itself was far from constituting a united bloc. On the one hand, there were the theologians, living on the periphery and listening to the demands of a new world; and, on the other, the conservatives, located rather in the Vatican, timid, scrupulous, or gripped by fear and panic and therefore turning aggressive and dangerous. One result was that a number of famous theologians became suspect and were disciplined. But in a fitting reversal, these persecuted indivuals were rehabitated and then became architects of the council, including even some cardinals (de Lubac, Daniélou). The accusers sank into oblivion.

This was the period when certain pastoral undertakings, such as the worker-priests in France, were condemned or halted. Some individuals, for example, J. Maritain, became suspect for defending the autonomy of lay Catholics in their temporal and political activity. Roman circles were likewise distrustful of John Courtney Murray, who regarded religious freedom as an essential right of the human person and not as a gift from a state that was bent on protecting Catholicism. Murray was silenced, until the declaration _Dignitatis Humanae_ of Vatican II, which marked the victory of his ideas.

More wide-ranging were the repercussions of the dispute over the "new theology" (_nouvelle théologie_), a dispute in which the targets singled out for attention were the Dominican and Jesuit seminarians at Le Saulchoir and Lyons-Fourvière, respectively, and in which the fiery Garrigou-Lagrange led the attack. In the encyclical *Humani Generis* (1950) Pius XII showed himself visibly concerned; he feared serious deviations regarding the very foundations of Christianity, especially the immutability of dogma, the importance of the pontifical teaching office, original sin, the relationship of nature and grace, the value of the motives of credibility, and so on. After a visit to Lyon-Fourvière by Édouard Dhanis, delegate of Father Janssens, general of the Jesuits, the latter ordered that the books and articles of Father Bouillard, Daniélou, de Lubac, and de Montcheuil be withdrawn from the libraries of the Society of Jesus; five professors were forbidden to teach. The Dominican General Suárez removed the provincials of Paris, Lyons, and Toulouse from their office and ordered the transfer of Fathers Boisselot, Féret, Chenu, and Congar. Among the Jesuits again, Teilhard de Chardin likewise became the object of suspicion and constant bans; in 1948 General Janssens prohibited him from teaching at the Collège de France. Teilhard was unable to teach or to publish during his lifetime, and he died in exile in New York. In Rome itself, under John XXIII, attacks on the Biblical Institute led to three already well-known professors being banned from teaching.

These contrasting trends, which lead even to the condemnation of the church's best theologians, shed a clear light on the climate in Rome on the eve of the council. People in many countries of Europe and the Americas were saying openly that if nothing changed, the worst was to be feared.

3. Vatican II as an Ecclesial Event

In fact a decisive event did occur, an event that was unexpected, especially in the form it took: a council, and indeed the greatest in history, announced by John XXIII on 25 January 1959. Pius XI had long ago thought of resuming Vatican I, which had been interrupted by war in 1870. He had even consulted some of the curial cardinals and bishops and had received the outline of a program, but in the end nothing happened. The plan was taken up again by Pius XII in 1948 but was immediately hindered by many differences of opinion. In the face of the accelerated rate of social change and the need of reestablishing unity among Christians, John XXIII made an irreversible decision to hold a

great ecumenical council. It was necessary to avoid a fatal delay in response to the needs, as had happened at the time of the Protestant Reformation. According even to Harnack, who knows but that if the Council of Trent had been convened fifteen years earlier, the tragedy of the Reformation might have been avoided? It was time now for the church to emerge from the silence in which it was living like an old lady draped in her outdated past and to speak at last to the men and women of our age so that it might serve them and lead them to Christ. Furthermore, the historical *kairos* was a favorable one, for when the council was held, the church had at last been liberated from political fetters and was able to profit from an exceptional team of great theologians. Today, now that these theological greats have passed from the scene, a Vatican II would be impossible. The council came "in the nick of time."

A preliminary commission head by Tardini and Felici was immediately formed for the organization of the work. As early as 5 June 1960, ten commissions were in place, sharing the job of preparing schemas, or position papers (*schemata*), to be discussed by the fathers. All of these commissions but one had as presidents cardinals from the Roman congregations; these were aided by conservative theological advisers. The first stage of the work produced over seventy position papers, most of them mediocre or even bad. As a result, when the council fathers began to meet, these papers were either rejected or sent back to committee for substantial reworking.

Vatican II lasted for four sessions, each two to three months long. The first session was opened by John XXIII on 11 October 1962; the last ended on 8 December 1965 under Paul VI. In his opening discourse John XXIII warned against the temptation of integralism and against issuing condemnations; he urged, instead, unity and a pastoral approach.

Vatican II was undoubtedly the most extensive effort at reform ever undertaken in the church, not only because of the number of council fathers (1,540 at the outset, as compared with 750 at Vatican I and 258 at the Council of Trent) and the near-unanimity in voting, which often beat all records (thus the constitution on revelation received only 6 negative votes out of 2,350; the constitution on the church, only 5 negative votes), but also and above all because of the scope of the subjects taken up: revelation, the church (its nature, constitution, members, missionary and pastoral activity), the liturgy and sacraments, the other Christian communities and the other religions, the laity, the consecrated life, the reform of ecclesiastical studies, religious freedom, education, relations between faith and culture and between church and world, and the communications media.

Vatican II was a uniquely original event. Earlier councils had for the most part been a response to heresies or specific, even regional, deviations. Even the Council of Trent held to a course within well-defined doctrinal lines: relation between Scripture and tradition, original sin, justification, sacraments. Vatican I was a Western and even European council. Vatican II was the first truly worldwide council. The percentages of participation were as follows: 33 percent from Europe, 13 percent from the United States and Canada, 22 percent from Latin America, 10 percent from Asia, 10 percent from Africa, 6 percent from the Arab world and Oceania, and the rest from others. For the first time, experts, whose numbers climbed from 201 to 480 under the influence of Paul VI, collaborated in the composition of the conciliar texts, thus giving a voice to ancient and rich cultural traditions. For the first time, too, a council had the courage to face utterly new problems: e.g., the alarming poverty of a large part of the human race, the many ways in which human freedom and essential rights are oppressed, the arms race, the threats of the annihilation of humanity, the practical quest of Christian unity, the contribution of literature and the arts to the life of the church. Because the sixteen conciliar documents occupy only a single volume, we may forget the immense labors carried on during this tumultuous period of the church's history. Those who look forward to an even more ecumenical council will doubtless have to wait for the parousia. As for those who refuse to acknowledge the authority of a council that mobilized so many energies and achieved such unanimity under the direction of two popes, do they not show the signs of blindness?

At the same time, however, the council was not a pleasure cruise. From the outset, there were seismic upheavals, sometimes disturbing in their intensity. How many schemas were blown out of the water, as it were, at the very beginning! How many others had a rough voyage and at times almost suffered shipwreck! And yet the whole affair was a success.

Here, succinctly, is the course the council took. The council began its work on 22 October 1962, with a discussion of the schema on the liturgy. Despite its favorable reception, it was subjected to further study and was promulgated only during the second session, on 4 December 1963. The schema on "the sources of revelation," which was controlled by a narrow and overly notional idea of the data of Scripture and tradition, was so strongly criticized that John XXIII sent it back to a joint commission whose members were taken from the theological commission and the Secretariat for Christian Unity. The schema was revised five times before being promulgated at the end of the council, on 18 November 1965. After a rapid review of the two schemas on the mass media and on union with the Orthodox, the council took up the schema on the church in December. After interventions by two cardinals, Suenens and Montini, and after a meeting with the pope, who urged rethinking the entire plan of the council in the "perspectives of a council for the world," this schema was sent back to be redone. These turnarounds may be attributed to the activity of the "experts" (periti) and the personal advisers of the bishops, for these individuals were much more aware of what was going on in the life of the universal church than were the theologians of the Curia. It was these experts and advisers who developed and fine-tuned the texts; they were the mainspring of the council. At the end of the first session, the schemas were reduced in number from 70 to 20.

Paul VI was in charge of the last three sessions. As early as 22 June 1963, the new pope decided that the council should continue. The set of moderators who were in charge of the discussions was reduced from ten to four. Of these four only Cardinal Agagianian represented the Curia. The other three—Lercaro (Bologna), Doepfner (Munich), and Suenens (Malines-Brussels)—made clear the will of Paul VI that the council should broaden its perspectives. The second session approved not only the constitution on the liturgy but also the decree *Inter Mirifica* on the communications media. During the third session the votes were taken on the decree on ecumenism, the constitution on the church, and the decree on the Eastern churches. The council also tackled, but in too precipitous a manner, such burning issues as religious freedom and schema 13 on the church in the modern world. A little feverishly and with some clashes, the fourth session voted on the final schemas. On 28 October 1965, the following were promulgated: (1) the decree on the pastoral office of bishops; (2) the decree on the adaptation and renewal of religious life; (3) the decree on the training of priests; (4) the declaration on Christian education; and (5) the declaration on the relation of the church to the non-Christian religions. On 18 November 1965, there followed the promulgation of the constitution *Dei Verbum* on revelation and the decree on the apostolate of the laity. Finally, 7 December saw the promulgation of the last four documents: the decrees on the missionary activity of the church and on the life of priests, the declaration on religious freedom, and the longest and most controversial constitution, that on the church and the world. Also on 7 December there was also proclaimed the "lifting of the excommunication" between Rome and Constantinople. The final meeting of the council took place on 8 December in the presence of representatives from eighty-one governments and nine international organizations. The council signaled the end of the post-Tridentine era, but the changes it brought about coincided with a crisis in Western civilization and with the advent of the secular city, two factors that were to muddy the waters in the postconciliar period.

4. John XXIII and Paul VI

It is impossible to speak of Vatican II without immediately calling to mind the two persons who dominated the council: John XXIII and Paul VI. With some simplification it may be said that John XXIII had the inspired idea of a council, decided to convoke it, and promoted it during the period of preparation and during the first session, and that Paul VI, who was in charge of the other three sessions, was the principal maker of the council, just as he was the effective agent of its application for a renewal of the spirit and structures of the church.

John XXIII

John XXIII has been interpreted as a visionary,

a fanatic, a man of impulse. He did indeed place unlimited trust in God, but his decision to convoke a council was in no way impetuous and unconsidered. His aim was to bring the church into twentieth-century history and society because he was convinced that the church is not a fortress or a museum but a garden that is constantly blooming. His purpose in convoking the council was to enable the church to respond better to the needs of the contemporary world, but in the framework of a deep respect for tradition. His pastoral concern is too well known to need commentary.

John XXIII hoped that the council would be a short one, but he also contemplated its prolongation with serenity, because he was aware that the council needed to ripen if it was not to die. It is also a fact that the council had a difficult, even chaotic beginning, but how was a break-in period to be avoided in an undertaking so gigantic and so much more difficult to program than the most sophisticated computer? John XXIII wanted the council to be a new Pentecost, but a Pentecost involving not now the little flock of the primitive church but a multitude. In fact, it very quickly became clear that more extensive planning was needed (this was the work of Paul VI) and that weeks and months had to be allowed for the formation of a "collegial consciousness" among the fathers (this was the work of time and the Spirit). Cardinal Montini, the future Paul VI, was undoubtedly the person best qualified to express a judgment on John XXIII's undertaking. Like most observers, Cardinal Montini was initially surprised by the pope's decision, but as early as 26 January 1960 he described the council to his diocese of Milan as "a historical event of the first magnitude, the greatest council ever celebrated in the history of the church." He saw in the pope's decision a pledge that the Holy Spirit was with Peter on his course as he led the church.

In Cardinal Montini's view, the pontificate of John XXIII was a period of Catholic rejuvenation and gave evidence of a phenomenal capacity for dialogue with all human beings for the sake of their salvation. He saw that John XXIII had been able to see the positive and not merely the negative side of the contemporary world. And he added that there was no need to change either the driving forces at work in the council or the direction the council was taking. More specifically, John XXIII had seen the need for a closer collaboration with the body of bishops, for the pursuit of unity with the separated churches, and for a more stable peace between peoples and social classes. Cardinal Montini was therefore one of the first to support John XXIII's bold undertaking. In a letter of 18 October 1962 to the secretary of state, however, he remarked that the council was ineffective because it lacked an "organic structure." He therefore offered a plan. The council, he said, should focus on a single theme—the church. He then sketched out the subjects for the three further sessions that he envisaged: a first on the mystery of the church, a second on the mission of the church, and a third on the relation of the church to the world. Such was in fact the order that the council would follow. Paul VI, then, recognized the timeliness and greatness of John XXIII's undertaking.

Paul VI

When Paul VI was elected pope after the death of John XXIII, he immediately set the council going again. He was well aware of the tensions between conservatives, progressives, and the undecided. The future of the council depended on him. One thing was certain: there was no question of retreating or of checking the forward movement inspired by hope and love. Paul VI set to work with incredible speed and efficiency. On 13 September 1963 he announced that the second session, set for 19 September, would deal with the church.

From beginning to end, Paul VI showed himself at once humble, clear-sighted, and courageous. His activity was marked both by a striving for the ideal and by a concrete realism that took into account the factual situations and circumstances that would condition the decisions to be made. The essential thing, in his eyes, was the renewal of the church and the rapprochement with the separated churches. At the beginning, his work consisted of planning ahead. The seventy-two original schemas were reduced to seventeen; sixteen would be finally voted on and promulgated. The thirteen lay observers present at the beginning became forty-two by the end. The pope more than doubled the number of experts.

Paul VI's thinking about the council focused on a single main idea: his desire, even his obses-

sion, was that the church should _become again_ what it _really is_ (_LG_), in order that it might better present itself to the world (_GS_). It can be said that the constitution _Dei Verbum_ is the fontal document of the council, while _Lumen Gentium_ begins a line of thought that climaxes in _Gaudium et Spes_. The council's masterpiece is the constitution on the church, which the other documents explain and clarify. Furthermore, in _Lumen Gentium_ it is the theme of the church as a _mystery of communion_ that gives meaning to the rest of the document.

In the view of Bishop Carbone, who is in charge of the conciliar archives, the most six important interventions of Paul VI at the council were (1) the _Nota praevia_ (regarding chap. 3 of _LG_), which seeks to maintain the connection between the sacramentality and the collegiality of the episcopal office (the _Nota_ says that a person is a member of the college of bishops through episcopal consecration and communion with the hierarchy); (2) the corrections made in the decree on ecumenism; (3) the intervention in favor of the schema on missionary activity; (4) the pope's determination that not only Islam and Judaism but also all the religions that, each in its own way, are in search of salvation should be included in the declaration on the non-Christian religions; (5) his request for a vote on the direction being taken in regard to religious freedom, before he addressed the United Nations in September 1965; and (6) his reservation to himself of the questions of the family and ecclesiastical celibacy.

To sum up: extreme positions must be avoided in comparing John XXIII and Paul VI. There was continuity between the two because both wanted the council and wanted its purpose, spirit, and success. There was continuity on the essential goal: _a church brought back to its sources and engaged in an up-to-date dialogue with the contemporary world._ Paul VI carried to completion the prophetic action of John XXIII; he brought the church into contemporary society.

5. The Gains Made by the Council

At the Level of Attitudes

Certain changes in which the conversion desired and effected by the council found expression have to do directly with fundamentals. Here are the main ones.

a. First of all, an attitude of *dialogue.* In this context "dialogue" is more than an exchange of words. It means a general attitude of openness to others, of mutual acceptance and self-giving, after the example of God himself, who took the initiative in emerging from his hiddenness and entering into dialogue with the world. The council itself was a dialogue in action with the other Christian communities, both Protestant and Eastern (*OE* 24–29; *UR* 14–18), but also with the non-Christian religions, especially Hinduism, Islam, and Judaism (*NA* 2–4), with the various forms of contemporary unbelief (*GS* 21), and with the masses of the indifferent that the secularized world has produced. This attitude of dialogue has also found expression at the level of several new structures created by Paul VI and John Paul II: Secretariat for Christian Unity, Secretariat for Non-Christians, Commission for Catholic–Muslim Relations, the Justice and Peace Commission, the Council for Culture. This attitude of dialogue is undoubtedly what has brought about the greatest change in the life-style of the church; its impact on fundamental theology has been so powerful that the term "apologetics," with its overtones of aggressiveness, has now fallen completely into disrepute.

b. Second, an attitude of *service.* The attitude of dialogue is accompanied by an attitude of service. The council offered a new image of pope and bishops, one in which the dominant element is the role of pastor. The magisterium itself is defined as servant of the word of God; it is not above the word but in its service (*DV* 10). In the exercise of their office, bishops "should announce the gospel of Christ to men, a task which is eminent among the chief duties of bishops" (*CD* 12).

c. Finally, an attitude of *seeking for MEANING.* The conciliar documents are broad instructions aimed at enlightening the people of God, whose chief desire is for meaning and internal intelligibility. The Christian message throws enough light on the depths of the human person to give rise to a spontaneous question: Is it not in this direction that the truth about human beings and about God is to be sought (*GS* 22)?

At the Level of Documents

At the level of documents, the gains made were spectacular.

a. The constitution *Dei Verbum,* which is still too little known, emphasizes the centrality of the word of God, but the "word" in question is Christ, the Word of God, Mediator and Fullness of revelation. The constitution also emphasizes the sacramental character of a revelation given through *actions* and *words,* in contrast to the earlier conception in which revelation was for practical purposes reduced to the spoken word, while the deeds, example, and behavior of Jesus were regarded as belonging to the realm of piety and popular devotion.

b. Scripture recovered its vital role in the Mass, where the liturgy of the word is inseparable from the liturgy of sacrifice, and also in Christian life, where Christians look to contemporary exegetes to bring out the relevance and topicality of God's word.

c. While *DEI VERBUM remains the source document for principles and method, Vatican II is nonetheless the council of ecclesiology. Among the gains made in this area, the following may be stressed: the emphasis on the trinitarian origin of the church; the church as both institution and mystery of communion; the image of the church as the people of God, which turned the former pyramid upside down by asserting the equality of all Christians by reason of their baptism; the recognition of the principle of collegiality and the principle of the ecclesial nature of the non-Catholic Christian churches.*

d. In the area of the *liturgy,* mention may be made of the reform of the celebration of mass. The revised celebration makes it much clearer than in the past that the people of God are a community that offers and sacrifices. Then, too, there are the other, subsequent reforms: the ritual of the sacraments; the divine Office; the new Code of Canon Law, in which Canon 1095 on marriage acknowledges that the lack of psychological maturity can be so great as to render invalid the consent of the partners and therefore the marriage itself.

e. The decree on ECUMENISM transformed yesterday's adversaries into separated brothers and sisters who are drawing near and who are given the name of churches and ecclesial communities. After having insulted one other for centuries, Christians are talking to one other, trying to understand one another, and finding themselves joined in work and prayer.

f. The decree *Perfectae Caritatis*, on the consecrated life, has had remarkable success by reason of the revision throughout the world of the laws and constitutions of religious communities and institutes of consecrated life.

g. After ecclesiology, ANTHROPOLOGY, which provides the subject matter of *Gaudium et Spes*, is the second major theme of the council. This anthropology, which is based on the biblical idea of the human person as created in the image and likeness of God, finds its highest expression in the statement: "Only in the mystery of the incarnate Word does the mystery of man take on light" (*GS* 22); the incarnate Word alone is the key to the human riddle.

h. The *dialogue with the other religions* is taken up in the decree on the relations between the church and the non-Christian religions (→ INTERRELIGIOUS DIALOGUE). While not forgetting the centuries of hostility between Catholics, on one side, and Muslims and Jews, on the other, the council urges mutual understanding and fraternal dialogue. These other human beings, who believe in the same God as we, are neither rejected nor accursed; they are sons and daughters of the same Father. Thus racism and discrimination are condemned.

i. Finally, although the decree *Inter Mirifica* seems to us today to be rather timid, it had the virtue of making the problem of the COMMUNICATIONS media one of the church's concerns.

To sum up: while the underlying nature of the church has not changed, the picture it presents of itself has been radically altered by the council. In the light of revelation Vatican II has gone more deeply into the central themes of Christianity and effected a new balance among them, including revelation, Scripture, tradition, liturgy, church, collegiality, relationship with the contemporary world, opening to the major religions of human history, and dialogue with all of humankind. The four main constitutions (*DV, LG, SC, GS*), which are rightly considered to be the four pillars of the council, are also the ones that have inspired the post-conciliar renewal. Admittedly, much remains to be done, but think of how much has changed in the areas of attitudes and documents! One would have to be either blind or cynical not to recognize the gains achieved.

6. Partial Successes

Here, quickly, are some of the problems that remain.

a. As the extraordinary Synod of Bishops in 1985 said: the council is still poorly understood and even unknown to many; it has been the object of "a partial and selective reading," a "unilateral presentation," and a "superficial interpretation" (Final Report, no. 4). Individuals select certain passages and use them to find in the council what they want to find in it.

b. The council has been received in different ways, depending on the openness of various cultural groups and depending, too, on the availablility or lack of the communications media. There are many who think this council was still too Western or even too Roman.

c. The council recognized that in the church there is pluriformity within unity. It also openly acknowledged the principle of collegiality. It did not, however, define the theological and juridical status of episcopal conferences. The positions taken by theologians on this subject have differed widely. Some allow the conferences only a pastoral and disciplinary role; others, on the contrary, assign them the role of intermediary authority between the local church and the universal church, a role in which they have an authority that is proper to them and not simply delegated, and a function that is both pastoral and doctrinal. In this last view, the conferences are comparable to "the ancient patriarchal churches" (*LG* 23).

d. The ecumenical dialogue has to some extent brought the churches closer, but it has also caused each of them to reflect on its own riches that it is not ready to sacrifice in order to return to the bosom of the Catholic church. The period of merely social meetings is now past; the time has come for major choices, and these cannot be made without difficult sacrifices. The divisions within the Catholic church, however, as well as the increasing authoritarianism of the Vatican, hardly encourage the return of churches accustomed to a greater freedom of action.

e. Some important documents have not had the impact they deserve: *Dei Verbum*, for example, and the decree on priests.

f. The image of the church as *people of God* held sway during the council but has since been overshadowed and has finally disappeared. Preference has been given to the image of the church as a mystery of communion, which seems to provide a greater bulwark against a democratic conception of the church.

7. Responses Begun during the Council and Continued Afterward

a. Sensitivity to the alarming poverty of a third of the human race found expression at the council in *Gaudium et Spes* (4:63–67), but it took Medellín, Puebla, and *Populorum Progressio* to make the preferential option for the poor a reality in the postconciliar period.

b. The problems of peace, war, and the nuclear threat were also mentioned by the council, but under the pressure of events in a more recent and still unfinished period of history, these problems have taken on terrifying proportions. The world today needs to defend itself against the temptation to suicide, which is fed by the drug traffic, against the ferocity of dictators, unbridled immorality, and the unchecked sale of arms around the world.

c. The vision of the human person that is set forth in *Gaudium et Spes* offers valuable, though still undeveloped, elements for a theology of human rights. Violation of human rights is a problem that has come to the fore chiefly in the postconciliar period. Among the points useful for such theological reflection the following may be mentioned: the principle that the human person is created in the image and likeness of God; the justice and love that characterize the covenant of God with humanity; the kingdom of God as based on solidarity among human beings and on the absence of discrimination. The problems of terrorism, abortion, genetic manipulation, racism, oppression in its many forms, diabolical torture, and massive migration show the urgency of a theological reflection on the dignity of the person and on human rights.

d. Gaudium et Spes devotes an entire chapter (*GS* 53–62) to cultural problems and the mutual relations between the gospel and cultures. The document could not, however, foresee the consequences of the cultural shift of the East to the West and of the infiltrations of the West into the East, the latter bringing with them the basest elements of the West. The problem of the coexistence of cultures and of intercultural or interreligious dialogue is becoming increasingly complex, especially where religious dialogue and political dialogue are identified, as, for example, in the Muslim world.

e. The council was aware that advances in "biology, psychology, and the social sciences" are enabling human beings to know themselves better and to exercise a direct influence on individual and social life by means of new technologies (*GS* 5). It was also aware that the church possesses no competence that would enable it to provide an immediate concrete solution to these new problems (e.g., in biotechnology) and to the ensuing moral problems that are studied in bioethics.

f. The decree on the laity anticipated the rise of this body, but it was not in a position to gauge the extent of the phenomenon. The 1987 Synod of Bishops and the subsequent pontifical Exhortation of 1988 attempted to define the specific mission of the laity in the church, but it is a long distance from theory to practice. In many countries of Europe and the Americas the majority of theologians, men as well as women, are laypersons; this is a new factor that will have to be taken into account. Laywomen in particular are painfully aware that their dignity and competence are not acknowledged at the level of practice.

8. Ambiguities That Remain

a. Hundreds of individuals worked on the composition and redaction of the conciliar documents. As a result, the overall unity of these documents suffered. The literary genres the documents make use of are many and varied: dogma, history, pastoral practice, social analysis. It is therefore difficult at times to reach agreement on the correct interpretation of a document or passage.

b. The council, like the new Code of Canon Law, remained torn between the idea, dominant for centuries, of the church as a juridical society, and the idea of the church as a mystery of communion. The council did not succeed in completely synthesizing these two visions, as anyone can see who reads chapters 1 and 2 of _Lumen Gentium_, where the focus is on the mystery of the church, and then chapters 3 and 4, where the focus is on the hierarchical structure of the church. Two ecclesiologies are here juxtaposed.

_c._ In a good many instances agreement was reached on wording, but not enough attention was paid to content. Thus all acknowledged the principle of collegiality, but some understood collegiality as a simply a social and pastoral practice, while others understood it as the exercise of an authority, doctrinal as well as pastoral, that is intermediate between the diocesan churches and the universal church. In the conciliar debates there was often talk of "injustices," but the meaning of this word remained ambiguous. In Communist countries the injustices were those committed by the Party, the many ways in which freedom was under attack. In other countries, the injustices were the sinful activities produced by a voracious and repugnant capitalism. In a good many Latin American countries, the injustices were the kinds of oppression and violence practiced by military dictatorships. In every case, however, the sufferers were the masses of the voiceless, who have neither wealth nor power.

9. Unfulfilled Hopes

Two (interconnected) examples will suffice. At the council the church spoke a great deal about itself, but not enough about Christ. The Synod of 1985 showed an awareness of this imbalance when it said in its final report: "The church makes herself more credible if she speaks less of herself and ever more preaches Christ crucified (cf. 1 Cor. 2:2) and witnesses with her own life." In other words, the council had vindicated the church (_LG_) and the human person (_GS_), but it should also have "vindicated" Christ in an important constitution. For the most acute problems that theologians must face today are problems of Christology.

Is it not significant in this respect that _Redemptor Hominis_, John Paul II's programmatic encyclical, should describe Christ as "redeemer of humanity" and "center of the cosmos and history," and that the International Theological Commission should have devoted its first three meetings (1981, 1983, 1985) to problems of Christology? The questions that people are asking today have to do with the very foundations of Christianity, which are to be found in Jesus Christ: with the person of Jesus, with his identity as God-among-us, with our knowledge of Jesus, with the means of gaining real contact with his teaching, his works (especially the miracles), his resurrection, his attitudes, his consciousness of being the Son of God, his plans for the church. In short, people today are asking the supreme question: Is Christ really God among us, in the flesh and language of Jesus? Is he the only one who can give meaning to our life and who knows its ultimate goal? The only one who can bring light into the depths within us and decode the riddle that we are to ourselves? These questions belong to a theological discipline known as fundamental theology, but the council preserved an impenetrable silence about it.

10. Reception of the Council Today

The reception of the council is a far from finished business. The great majority of the faithful realize that the council was a response to an urgent need, and they support it, sincerely and unconditionally. But the recent "Lefebvre affair" shows that a number of people have resisted and even rejected the council. Then there are those who keep alive a nostalgia for a past that can never return; there are those who still dream of a Vatican III, though they have never read Vatican II and, more important, have never assimilated its riches. Finally, there is the game played by those who work to diminish the importance of the council, to the point of making it meaningless, by highly sophisticated but no less treacherous talk about it. This last group says things like: "Let's not exaggerate the importance of Vatican II. Of its sixteen documents, three, after all, are only 'declarations.' The nine decrees simply repeat and flesh out the chapters of _Lumen Gentium_. _Gaudium et Spes_ is only a _pastoral_ constitution. The constitution on the liturgy deals chiefly with disciplinary and practical reforms. _Dei Verbum_ is a bone we can leave to the exegetes to chew on so that they'll be satisfied. The hard core of the council is _Lumen Gentium_ (and especially the *Nota praevia*), and this only repeats the traditional teaching of the church."

It will undoubtedly be several more decades before we can judge the real impact of Vatican II. We can, however, assume that human resistance will not succeed in making ineffective a council so visibly sustained by the power of the Spirit.

Bibl.: *Acta Synodalia S. Concilii Oecumenici Vaticani II*, 26 vols. (Rome, 1970–80); A. WENGER, *Vatican II*, 4 vols. (Paris, 1963–66); *Das Zweite Vatikanische Konzil*, 3 vols., suppl. to *LTK*; G. CAPRILE, *Il Concilio Vaticano II*, 5 vols. (Rome, 1963–66); G. MARTELET, *Les idées maîtresses de Vatican II* (Paris, 1967); R. AUBERT, M. D. KNOWLES and L. J. ROGIER, eds., *Nouvelle histoire de l'Église*, vol. 5: *L'Église dans le monde moderne* (Paris, 1975), 583–689; E. KLINGER and K. WITTSTADT, *Glaube in Prozess* (Festschrift K. Rahner) (Freiburg, 1984); G. ALBERIGO and J.-P. JOSSUA, eds., *La réception de Vatican II* (Paris, 1985); C. FLORISTÁN and J. J. TAMAYO, *El Vaticano II veinte años depués* (Madrid, 1985); J. RATZINGER, *Entretien sur la foi* (Paris, 1985); L. RICHARD, D. HARRINGTON, and J. W. O'MALLEY, eds., *Vatican II: The Unfinished Agenda* (New York, 1987); var., *The Church in Anguish: Has the Vatican Betrayed Vatican II?* (San Francisco, 1987); R. LATOURELLE, ed., *Vatican II: Assessment and Perspectives Twenty-five Years After (1962–1987)*, 3 vols. (New York, 1989), 1–122: especially the introduction of R. Latourelle and part I: the articles by G. Martina and H. Neufeld; Collection "Unam sanctam," vols. 51, 60, 61, 62, 65, 66, 67, 68, 70, 74, 75, 76 (Paris, 1966–70).

René LATOURELLE

W

WORLD COUNCIL OF CHURCHES (WCC)

1. "The World Council of Churches is a fellowship of churches which confess the Lord Jesus Christ as God and Saviour according to the Scriptures and therefore seek to fulfill together their common calling to the glory of the one God, Father, Son and Holy Spirit" (*Constitutions of the WCC*, I). This basis, accepted at the General Assembly of New Delhi in 1961 in substitution of the shorter one of 1948, is not meant to be a creed, nor a full statement of the Christian faith. It wants to say what holds the members together in the WCC, what is the starting point of their conversation and the foundation of their collaboration. The main function and purpose of the council is "to call the churches to the goal of visible unity in one faith and in one eucharistic fellowship expressed in worship and in common life in Christ, and to advance towards that unity in order that the world may believe." Other purposes are added, such as the facilitation of common witness, the support of the churches in their worldwide missionary and evangelistic task, common concern for service of human needs and the promotion of unity, justice, and peace between the peoples, the fostering of the renewal of the churches, and the maintaining of relations between various ecumenical bodies (*Constitutions of the WCC*, III). At the General Assembly of Vancouver (1963) the WCC described itself as "a preliminary expression of that unity which is God's will and gift for which Christians pray and work. It provides a forum for intensive encounter and exchange of Christian experiences, theological convictions and spiritual insights, as well as an ecumenical framework for the ever more inclusive cooperation of its member churches in common witness and service to the world" (*Taking Steps towards Unity*, § 31, in *Gathered for Life* [Geneva, 1983], 52). The WCC is thus not merely a tool in order to achieve unity. It realizes already in a provisional way the increasing unity and solidarity among the churches. The ecclesiological sig-

nificance of the WCC has been defined in 1950 by the so-called Toronto Statement, "The Church, the Churches, and the World Council of Churches" (*A Documentary History of the Faith and Order Movement*, ed. L. Vischer [St. Louis, 1963], 167–76). Officially this statement remains still the last word on the subject.

2. The decision to establish the WCC was taken in 1936 by two major movements that had worked for nearly two decades to bring various churches and church traditions together: the Faith and Order Movement and Life and Work (→ ECUMENISM). The idea survived the Second World War. The foundation itself took place at the first General Assembly at Amsterdam in 1948. The major events of the WCC were the General Assemblies held in Evanston, USA (1954), New Delhi (1961), Uppsala (1968), Nairobi (1975), Vancouver (1983), and Canberra, Australia (1991). A significant event was the full integration of the International Missionary Council, which originated from the 1910 International Missionary Conference of Edinburgh, into the WCC in New Delhi 1961. By this integration it became clear again how unity and mission are closely related. With the entrance of the Russian church and the Orthodox churches of other socialist countries, practically all the Orthodox churches had joined the council. The Geneva-based WCC counts over three hundred member churches, representing all Christian denominations. Its three program units—Faith and Witness, Justice and Service, Education and Renewal—show the extent of the council's concerns.

Among the absentees is the Roman Catholic church. After a first period of standing squarely aside, the Catholic church has established regular contacts with the WCC since the Second Vatican Council. Since 1965 they have been formalized in the Joint Working Group. This consultative group is intended to enable the Roman Catholic church and the WCC to evaluate together the development of the ecumenical movement and thus to be a challenge to the parent bodies by proposing new steps and programs and to further the collaboration between them. With membership rejected in 1969 as not yet appropriate, the present relation is seen as one of "fraternal solidarity" (Paul VI in his letter to the Fifth Assembly of the WCC, 1975, in *Breaking Barriers* [Geneva,

1975], 154). One of the most telling areas of collaboration is the official participation of twelve Catholic theologians in the work of the Commission of Faith and Order. SODEPAX has been a rather frustrating experience. After a brilliant start in 1968, this joint agency of the WCC and the Roman Catholic church for the building up of a greater awareness regarding questions of society, development, and peace, was more and more limited in its possibilities by its constituencies during the following mandates, and was finally dissolved in 1980.

3. Referring to the entry ECUMENISM, we mention here some conferences, programs, and statements of the WCC that have special relevance for the study of fundamental theology in an ecumenical perspective.

The very existence of the WCC raises fundamental theological problems. The intimate connection between unity and mission that presided the whole set-up of the council and remains institutionally present in the Commission for World Mission and Evangelism encouraged a theological reflection on mission, witness, and the meaning of salvation; on the absoluteness of the Christian faith and the dialogue with people of other faiths; and, last but not least, on the role of the churches in society and their responsibility for justice, peace, and the integrity of creation. In the 1970s the program Unity of Mankind and the Unity of the Church was established to study the interaction of these two unities. It was later discontinued as such but was taken up again in the program The Unity of the Church and the Renewal of Human Community.

The major issues are, however, connected with the models of Christian unity. Even if the WCC, according to the Toronto Statement, does not want to present a proper ecclesiology, the experience of living together brought the council to clarify some theological and ecclesiological items. It was in New Delhi (1961) that the council presented for the first time a unity formula, in which the aim of unity was somewhat described, stressing particularly its local dimension. In Uppsala (1968) the catholicity of the church was underlined. The Nairobi

Assembly (1975) described unity as *conciliar fellowship* (→ ECUMENISM), a model that was defined in Vancouver (1982) in strong eucharistic terms as a *eucharistic vision* that "encompasses the whole reality of Christian worship, life and witness, and tends — when truly discovered — to shed new light on Christian unity in its full richness of diversity" (*Gathered for Life*, 45).

Besides this more general problem some more particular problems of fundamental theology have been tackled in the WCC. Scripture and tradition were explicitly discussed at the World Conference of Faith and Order in Montreal (1963) and led to various other documents dealing with hermeneutical problems, with the meaning of councils and authority in the church. Apostolicity has been understood in a wider context that combines apostolicity of doctrine and of pastoral work with the apostolic succession in ministry. Important in this regard has been the study "Catholicity and Apostolicity" (1968) (*One in Christ* 6 [1970]: 452–82). Unity supposes a unity in faith and some form of common confessing of the faith. How can Christians confess the same apostolic faith that was expressed in Holy Scriptures and summarized symbolically in the creeds of the early church? This issue is tackled by the WCC in a major study process under the title "Towards the Common Expression of the Apostolic Faith Today." Many of these fundamental questions have been raised with new urgency in the light of the official responses to the Lima document entitled *Baptism, Eucharist, and Ministry.*

Bibl.: A. J. VAN DER BENT, *Vital Ecumenical Concerns* (Geneva, 1986); *Handbook, Member, Churches, World Council of Churches*, ed., A. J. van der Bent (Geneva, 1985); *A History of the Ecumenical Movement*, vol. 1: *1517–1948*, eds., R. Rouse and S. C. Neill (London, 1945); vol. 2: *The Ecumenical Advance: 1948–1968*, ed. H. E. Fey (London, 1970, 1986); *What in the World Is the World Council of Churches?* (Geneva, 1978); M. VAN ELDEREN, *Introducing the World Council of Churches*, Risk 46 (Geneva, 1990); Reviews of the WCC: *Ecumenical Review, International Review of Mission,* and *One World.*

JOS E. VERCRUYSSE

Z

ZUBIRI, XAVIER

1. Life

Xavier Zubiri Apalategui was born at San Sebastián, Spain, in 1898, and died, at Madrid, in 1983. He received his licentiate in philosophy from the University of Louvain in 1921, with a thesis directed by L. Noël, "Le problème de l'objectivité d'après Ed. Husserl: La logique pure." He received his doctorate in theology in Rome in 1920, and his doctorate in philosophy in Madrid in 1921 with a dissertation entitled "Ensayo de una teoría fenomenológica del juicio." In December 1926 he was appointed to the chair of the history of philosophy of the University of Madrid. He spent the years 1928–30 in Freiburg im Breisgau, attending the lectures of Husserl and Heidegger. He spent 1930–31 in Berlin, attending seminars of Einstein, Schrödinger, Köhler, Goldstein, and Mangold. Returning to Spain, he continued to teach at the university until 1936, when he moved to Rome. Prevented from returning to Spain by the outbreak of the Spanish Civil War (1936–39), first he lived in Rome, where he studied at the Biblical Institute and the Oriental Institute with Deimel, and then in Paris, where he attended seminars in physics (de Broglie) and Oriental languages (Labat, Benveniste, Dhorme, Delaporte). With the end of the civil war, he was able to return to Spain, where he taught from 1940 to 1942 at the University of Barcelona. In 1942 he left that university and moved once more to Madrid. There, from 1945 onward, he conducted private courses in philosophy, which were attended by the most important personalities of the Spanish intellectual life of those years. With a view to the continuation of this work, in 1947 the Sociedad de Estudios y Publicaciones was created, under whose auspices Zubiri exercised all of his later teaching activity, to the end of his life. Following his death, the Fundación Xavier Zubiri, devoted to the study of his thought, was established in Madrid (1989).

2. Works

Ensayo de una teoría fenomenológica del juicio. Madrid, 1923. *Naturaleza, Historia, Dios.* Madrid, 1945; 9th ed., Alianza Editorial, 1987; English trans., *Nature, History, God* (Washington, D.C., 1981); Italian trans., *Natura, Storia, Dio* (Palermo, 1990). *Sobre la esencia.* Madrid, 1962; 5th ed., Alianza Editorial, 1985; German trans., *Vom Wesen* (Munich, 1968); English trans., *On Essence* (Washington, D.C., 1980). *Cinco lecciones de filosofía.* Madrid, 1963; 4th ed., Alianza Editorial, 1985). *Scritti Religiosi.* Padua, 1976. *Inteligencia sentiente.* Madrid, 1980; 3rd ed., 1984. *Inteligencia y logos.* Madrid, 1982. *Ensayos de Antropología Filosófica.* Bogota, 1982; Italian trans., *Il problema dell'uomo: Antropologia filosofica* (Palermo, 1985). *Inteligencia y razón.* Madrid, 1983. *El hombre y Dios.* Madrid, 1984; 3rd ed., 1985. *Sobre el hombre.* Madrid, 1986. *Estructura dinámica de la realidad.* Madrid, 1989.

3. Thought

Zubiri's early formation was in Louvainian neoscholasticism. Through L. Noël's "immediate realism," he arrived at Husserl's phenomenology, which enabled him to make connections with the new philosophy of phenomenological inspiration, represented in Spain by Ortega y Gasset. Following his sojourn in Freiburg from 1928 to 1930, Heidegger's influence is evident in Zubiri's thought.

All of Zubiri's mature philosophy takes as its aim the discovery of a philosophically viable route for the phenomenological method, so that a philosophy might be established that could get beyond both classical realism and modern idealism. To this end, Zubiri transfers phenomenological investigation from "awareness" (Husserl), "life" (Ortega), and "understanding" (Heidegger) to "apprehension," in such a way that the primary object of philosophy would be the analysis of "human apprehension." Not that the philosopher cannot or need not study what things are, beyond the apprehension and independently of it; but such a study would lack radicality unless it was grounded on the previous and unshakable datum of what is given in apprehension *qua* given in it. Like awareness for Husserl, human apprehension has absolute priority in Zubiri and constitutes the ambit of "first philosophy."

There are two moments in the act of apprehension: the intellection of the thing, and the thing as intellected. For Zubiri, these moments are cognate, and neither has priority over the other. The old realism posited a priority of reality over reason, just as modern idealism posits a priority of knowledge over reality. The former gave rise to "metaphysics" in the classic —and somewhat pejorative—sense of the term; the second, to "theory of knowledge." Herein lie two most pernicious errors. When the philosophical problem is posed on the level of an adequate radicality, one promptly observes that knowledge and reality are cognate and therefore inseparable. This means that there is no knowledge without reality. But it also means that there is no reality without knowledge—or, as Zubiri prefers to say, that reality is the formal character of the actualization of things to the human being in apprehension. "Reality is the formal character—the formality—according to which that which is apprehended is something en propio, 'in its own' right, something de suyo, something 'of its own.' And to know is to apprehend something according to that formality." The elementary, primary, and radical knowledge, then, is not cognition, as Erkenntnistheorie would have it, but the apprehension of something according to the formality of reality. Indeed, this is what Zubiri calls "intellection." Thus, "in" apprehension (and not beyond it), "intellection" (i.e., the actualization of the thing in its formality as en propio or de suyo), and "reality" (i.e., the thing formally actualized as something en propio or de suyo) are inseparable terms. Classic phenomenology tells us that intellection and reality are intentional correlates. Zubiri thinks, however, that this is not a matter of relation but of something more radical, which he calls "respectivity." Nor is it a matter of intentionality—rather, something more profound is involved, which he calls "actuality." In synthesis, then: "Human intellection is formally the mere actualization of the real in the sentient intelligence." The science that studies this is no longer, strictly speaking, phenomenology but something distinct, which Zubiri calls "noölogy."

Human intellection is the mere actualization of the real. There are three terms here: "intellection," "reality," and "actualization." These are three moments of a single act—the act of "human apprehension," which is at once sentient and intellective. If, in terms of a long tradition going back to Greece, we call this sentient and intellective apprehension Nous, then we shall have to distinguish in it three moments: the intellective, or "noetic"; that of reality, or the "noematic"; and the moment of actualization, or the "noergic."

4. Binding

From 1935 on, Zubiri came to insist that things as de suyo not only are "actualized to" the human being in apprehension but, besides, "impose" themselves on that human being with a certain force. This force, which is that of things, imposes itself or impinges upon the human being in apprehension as (1) "ultimate"; (2) "enabling," or possibilitante; and (3) "impelling," driving. Human beings realize, render real to themselves—"in" (ultimacy), "from" (enablement or potentiation), and "by" (drive)—the reality actualized in apprehension. This character of fundamentality attaching to reality is what Zubiri calls the "power of the real." This power binds us intimately, nos religa, to reality. This is what Zubiri understands by binding. It is a primary datum arising from the mere description of what is given in the impression of reality, qua given in the same. Over against Heideggerian Geworfenheit, Zubiri believes it possible to assert the binding of human beings to reality.

5. God

Human apprehension is the elementary act of intelligence, but not the only one. Without apprehension, there would be no further acts; but without further acts, we should not know what things are beyond our apprehension of them—i.e., in the reality of the world. It is important to keep in mind that the word "reality" has two meanings in Zubiri: "reality as formality" (or reality qua given in apprehension) and "reality as fundamentality" (or reality beyond apprehension). Let us consider an example. In my apprehension of green, the latter thrusts itself upon me as something de suyo, something "of its own," qua distinct from me; this is what Zubiri calls "reity" (or reality "in" apprehension). Light is de suyo green (really green) in the apprehension. Could we not be sure of this, a physics of color would be impossible. But, what physics seeks is not only green as formal reality but the *fundamento* of green beyond its apprehension, in the reality of the world. Scientific reason has discovered this foundation in the electromagnetic theory, and green is defined as a wave of a certain length and determinate frequency. The object of reason (in the case of light, of scientific reason) is to move from apprehension, to move beyond it, in quest of what things are in the reality of the world.

The mistake woud be to think that all is reason or science and that therefore colors have no reality, only waves do. This is not an infrequent error in science. It is also a mistake, committed by philosophy from time immemorial, to confuse the formally real with the fundamentally real, and to think that the reality of green is identical in its apprehension and beyond its apprehension. The former error typifies naive idealism; the latter, naive realism. And Zubiri thinks that practically the whole of the history of philosophy has been divided between the two.

All of this is applicable to the topic of God. *Religación* is a fact, and really given in apprehension. It does not exhaust the problem of God, however, but it only poses it, just as the apprehension of light poses the problem of the physics of colors. *Religación* thrusts us beyond the act of apprehension in an effort to identify the *fundamento* of the power of the real. This quest must be rational—the work of one kind of reason—which in this case we shall call not scientific reason but theological reason. At all events, the method of reason is ever the same and consists, according to Zubiri, of four steps, which he calls (1) the system of reference, (2) the sketch, (3) the experiment or experience, and (4) verification. In an approach to the topic of God, these four steps consist concretely in a "will to truth," a "sketch of an absolutely absolute reality," an "experience of God," and "faith in God." Let us analyze these in succession.

The system of reference of the human being's rational journey to God is, obviously, the entire datum of apprehension—i.e., the power of the real, or *religación*. But in addition, the journey in search of the *fundamento* demands as a prerequisite what Zubiri calls, in an expression stemming from Nietzsche, the "will to truth." Although the analysis of this expression is very rich in nuances, in any case it means that the human being's access to God cannot be by

virtue of a mere "will to ideas," as classic speculative theology has thought. God, as existing, is not an idea but a reality-*fundamento*. The will to ideas has led philosophy to "entify" divine reality (transforming it into an "object") and to "logify" philosophical cognition (making of its intellectual approach a logical "proof"). On the contrary, the will to truth seeks not an object but the *fundamento* of *religación*—i.e., of the power of the real. This *fundamento* Zubiri calls deity. God, as existing, is not an idea but the reality-*fundamento*, and therefore something not only "sketched" with the mind, but also "experienced." The moment of the sketch is a moment of intelligence, of truth; that of experience, a moment of will. Only the authentic will to truth is genuine will to fundamentality, without which the rational journey to God is impossible. This is why we have called the will to truth its system of reference.

It is with, and from a point of departure in, this system of reference that reason must sketch the divine reality. The sketch is necessarily a rational, logical construction. This is how the so-called proofs of the existence of God have been attempted. Zubiri subjects them to a withering critique. In his opinion, the rational sketch concerning God must begin with the need to found worldly reality, especially human reality. Ultimate reality, due to its intelligence, is of a "transcendental" or "absolute" character; the human being is *ab-suelto* (ab-solved) or *desligado* (dis-connected) from any other reality. *Atqui*, at the same time, the human being is *religado* to reality. This leads Zubiri to say that the human being is a "relative absolute." *Atqui*, the rational sketch concerning God must have its starting point in the need to found the relatively absolute reality of the human being on an absolutely absolute reality—i.e., on an *absoluto de realidad*, an absolutely-real. This reality will have to be absolute person, "fundament" of all real things. This is the rational sketch concerning God.

But the sketch alone is not enough. In addressing the topic of God, or any other topic in which reason intervenes, the sketch must be followed by experiment, or experience. Let us consider, for example, how scientific reason behaves. Scientific hypotheses are sketches that must be verified or falsified by experience. Zubiri defines experience as the "physical assay [*probación*] of reality"; it is reality that, in experience, *aprueba* (approves) or *reprueba* (reprobates) the sketch. The *probación* that is experience, then, is endowed with a distinct character with each kind of reality sketched. Zubiri distinguishes four types of experience, which he names "experiment" (the *probación* proper to physical realities), "comprobation" ("proving," "checking" a mathematical reality), "compenetration" (interpersonal experience), and "conformation" (experience of life itself). It is obvious that the experience of God must consist neither in experiment nor in comprobation but in either compenetration or conformation. Now, the experience of conformation is more proper to moral realities, and that of compenetration more proper to religious realities. Whence Zubiri concludes that the experience of God—of God as existing—must be an experience of compenetration.

In order to have compenetration, two persons must be present. Now, the problem is whether God becomes present in the world. Zubiri thinks so, holding that the presence in question is what he has previously denominated *religación*, the "power of the real," and "deity." Thus what the moment of experience accomplishes is a reactualization of the apprehensive presence of the power of the real. *Atqui*, behind the sketch, this power of the real appears as the experience of a personal God in the world. Indeed, now the world appears as a "personal bestowal" of God, which produces in us a genuine *arrastre* (a drawing, an attraction). The *fundamento* draws us, hauls us—else we should be unable to approach it. This drawing, however, this "pull," which, at bottom, is the presence of God in things, requires of us an *entrega* (a surrender, a commitment). Our *entrega* is our voluntary response to the *arrastre*. Whence Zubiri concludes that compenetration proper to the experience of God is the compenetration between the presence of God as *arrastre* and the self-bestowal of the human being as *entrega*. The compenetration materializes between *arrastre* and *entrega*.

This experience of compenetration with God now enables us to reformulate the characters of ultimacy, enablement or potentiation, and drive or impulse, attaching ourselves to the power of the real, on a new and more profound level. Zubiri says that ultimacy is now transformed into attachment, which is the basis of

all worship and all sacrifice and the foundation of theological faith. As for enablement, this character of the power of the real is now experienced as supplication, in the form of prayer, which is the foundation of all theological hope. Finally, thrust or impulse is manifested to us in the form of refuge, the root of theological love. God is not an idea, or an unmoved mover, but the being to whom human beings attach themselves, whom they supplicate, and in whom they take refuge—i.e., a being with whom one compenetrates, and to whom one can pray. While the sketch has always corresponded to what Pascal called the God of the philosophers, the moment of experience confronts the God of the religions. There are not two gods but two inseparable moments of the rational approach and access of the human being to God.

In sum, experience by compenetration discovers a *personal bestowal of God*, in things and persons, in the form of an *arrastre* that calls for a *personal bestowal of the human being* upon God in the form of an *entrega*.

There remains the final moment of the method of reason—what Zubiri calls verification. This moment is important by virtue of the actual limitation of human rationality. Experience never altogether approves or reprobates the sketch. Thus, the latter is never altogether verified. The truth of reason is too weak for the verification process ever to be completed. To verify is an ever-open process, both logically and historically; it is, as Zubiri says, "to be verifying," in the present progressive tense.

Now, the same occurs with the topic of God. The moment of verification of the sketch, in the human being's journey to God, is called *faith*. Faith, for Zubiri, is not an assent to a judgment on the strength of the testimony of another but "la entrega a una realidad personal en cuanto verdadera"—surrender to, self-bestowal on, a personal reality *qua* true. Faith can be strong, but this does not militate against the need to keep it nourished; just as to verify is to keep on verifying, so to believe is to keep on believing. Faith must not be regarded as something acquired once and for all but as a continuous process. The will to truth, sketch, and the experience of God must be continually set in interface, and faith along with them. This enables us to understand why faith is a dynamic process, in which distinct levels or stages may be distinguished. Zubiri distinguishes three such stages: (1) "theological faith," as already described (*fe teologal*, objectively theological faith); (2) the "theological faith" proper to the positive or historical religions (*fe teológica*, reflexively theological faith); and (3) "Christian faith," the faith proper to the religion of deification.

Bibl.: For the life of Zubiri: C. CASTRO DE ZUBIRI, *Xavier Zubiri: Breve recorrido de una vida* (Santander, 1986). For an introduction to his thought, see D. GRACÍA, *Voluntad de Verdad: para leer a Zubiri* (Barcelona, 1986); A. FERRAZ, *Zubiri, Realismo Radical* (Madrid, 1987). The Xavier Zubiri seminar has published four volumes of studies concerning his works: *Realitas* vol. 1 (Madrid, 1974); vol. 2. (Madrid-Barcelona, 1976); vols. 3–4 (Madrid-Barcelona, 1979). At the end of vol. 2, there is a bibliography on Zubiri by the Swiss philosopher H. Widemer. At the "Fundación Zubiri," of Madrid there is a library and center of documentation concerning the thought of Zubiri.

Diego GRACÍA

ANALYTIC INDEX

This present index is intended to be the most complete possible but is not exhaustive. The words in small capital letters correspond to the articles in the dictionary. The subdivisions of longer and more complex words are indicated by small capitals in italics. The words in italics indicate important parts (or aspects) of a theme that has not been given particular treatment. The numbers refer to the pages of the dictionary where the subject in question is treated. The arrow (→) refers the reader to the words of the same index where he or she will find page references in the dictionary. This applies especially for words in italics.

— A. codifies certain principles of Christian hermeneutics   418
  → Credibility, Hermeneutics, History, Revelation, Theology

BALTHASAR, HANS URS VON   69-74
— epistemological principles of B.'s theology   69-70
— the *pulchrum* as the beginning moment of the understanding of
  revelation   70
— biblical *doxa* and B.'s aesthetics   71
— objective evidence of revelation and Christocentrism as oneness and
  singularity   71-73
— trinitarian love as a principle and synthesis of theology   73
— subjective evidence   73
— theological perspectives offered by B.   73-74
  → Beauty, Christocentrism

BARTH, KARL   74-77
— first appearance of the pastoral activity of B.   74-75
— occasion of the *Epistle to the Romans*   75
— accent on pure faith and the analogy of faith   75-76
— denial of the *analogia entis*   75-76
— his conception of revelation has exercised a great influence on ecumenical
  renewal   76-77
— his interpretation of Anselm   11-12, 75-76
— B.'s position on the Trinity   76-77
  → Analogy, Anselm of Canterbury

BEAUTY   77-78
— as transcendental   77
— in Scripture and in the history of the church   77-78
  → Balthasar, Imagination

Biblical Anthropology   17-21
— b.a. is dynamic   17-18
— dialogue between the biblical and the human sciences   17-18
— method to adopt in the study of b.a.   18
— use of images in the Bible   18-19
— a. and anthropomorphism   18-19
— b.a. is an a. of transformation of the human being in its entirety   19-20
— b.a. and theology   20
— b.a. as a solution to human limitations   20-21
— limitations of the human condition   20-21
  → Christian Anthropology, Death, Evil, *Gaudium et Spes*, Paschal Mystery,
  Suffering

Biblical Exegesis   298-306

Bloch, E.   477

BLONDEL, MAURICE   78-84
— B.'s thesis: *L'Action*   78
— dialectic of *L'Action*   78-83
— stages in the genesis of the supernatural   83-84
— B.'s apologetic is philosophical   83-84
  → Apologetics, Immanence, Pascal, Rahner

Buddha 85

BUDDHISM 84-88
— it is the world's oldest religion 84
— it developed itself in two currents: *Theravāda* (or *Hīnayāna*) and *Mahāyāna* 84
— Buddha, model and spiritual friend of humankind 85
— canonical sources of B. 84-85
— biography of Buddha Sakyamuni 85
— the *dharma* or doctrine of the Buddhist is contained in the four truths 85-86
— perspectives of dialogue with the Catholic Church 87
— wishes to overcome the problem of suffering 1013
— believes in reincarnation 816-817
→ Religion

BULTMANN, RUDOLPH 88-91
— biography 88
— methodological premises 88-89
— B. and the theology of kerygma 89-90
— necessity of demythologization 90-91
— B.'s Christology 90-91
→ Gospels, Hermeneutics

CALVINISM 92-94
— it is a complexity of theological reflections on the word of God, interpreted by Calvin 92
— biography of Calvin 92
— diverse themes from Calvinist teachings: God, Christology, pneumatology, Sacred Scripture, ecclesiology and sacraments, anthropology, faith, predestination 92-94

CANON OF SCRIPTURE 94-101
— concept of the c. 94-95
— Christian c. of the OT 95-96
— c. of the NT 97-98
— theological significance of the c. 98-101
— theory of "canonical criticism" 100
— theory of the "canon within the canon" 100
→ OT and NT, Apocryphal Gospels, Deposit of Faith, Gospels, Integrated Exegesis, Hermeneutics, Inspiration, Rule of Faith, Tradition

CATECHESIS 585
— with the *kerygma* and the *parenesis*, it constitutes a single process of evangelization 585
— articulates and explicates the *kerygma* 585-586
— in the first centuries, the c. ordinarily consisted in preparation for baptism 585-586
— differs from the *parenesis* 585-586
→ Kerygma, Parenesis, Theology

CERTITUDE 101-103
— opposes itself to opinion 101-102
— distinction between c. and belief 102

— h.c. as a perception of the historical sense 434
— h.c. and historical knowledge 434
— h.c. permits better understanding of the addressees of FT 322-336

COVENANT 267-273
— c. with Abraham is preceded by an election 267-268
— unique character of the Mosaic c. 269-270
— c. with David is the fruit of freedom 270
— the prophets tell of a new c. 271
— c. is a bond with election and the law 267-273
— c. in the spirit of Judaism 533-535
— c. is connected to the problem of the times 905-907
— c. and revelation 905

CONVERSION 191-193
— indicates a spiritual movement toward God 191
— *metanoia* in Scripture 191
— c. in the history of the church 191
— teaching of the church on c. 191-192
— various types of c.: theistic, Christian, ecclesial, personal 192
— interreligious dialogue encourages c. 520-523
— c. is needed for the reign of God 590
    → Church, Faith, Sign, Testimony

CREDIBILITY 193-209
— christological concentration on the study of c. 193-194
— soteriological horizon of c. 193-194
— various historical moments in the history of the theme of c.: Augustine,
    Thomas, Vatican I, Vatican II 194-197
— *analysis fidei* 195-196
— Gardeil and the rational demonstration of c. 197-198
— Rousselot and the "eyes of faith" 198-199
— systematic proposition of the theme of c.: c. as meaning 199-207
— c. as a fundamental problem of ecumenism 262
— the death of Jesus makes credible what is incredible 764-765
— martyr as a sign of c. 625-626
— miracle is the sign of c. 703-706
— c. and the meaning of the revelation 644-647
— testimony is the motif of c. 1051-1060
    → Church, Christology, Faith, Language, Martyr, Miracle, Prophecy, Revela-
    tion, Semeiology, Testimony

CREED 209-211
— c. has been known since the 4th century 209
— has deep roots in the NT 209
— since Nicea, c. has the function to express the orthodoxy and the commu-
    nion of the churches 210
    → Deposit of Faith, Dogma, Faith, Rule of Faith

CRITIQUE OF RELIGION 868-872
— is not a univocal concept 870
— exists since antiquity (classical times) 868
— since the arguments of Feuerbach, c.r. has acquired a public
    importance 870-871
— c.r. contests the existence of God and the proofs that support it 869-870

— apologetics guarantees theology as a science   250
— methodological structure of apologetics   250-251
— present state of research on D.   247-248

EARLY CATHOLICISM   252-257
— the work of S. Schultz deliberately carrying on the study of Ernst
  Käsemann   252
— analysis of the work   252-256
— criticism of the work   256-257
— e.c. and the church   253
    → Hermeneutics, Integral Exegesis

EASTERN CHURCHES (Oriental Churches)   179-181
— born of the schism following the Councils of Ephesus and of
  Chalcedon   179-180
— common elements with the Catholic Church   180-181
— moments of the dialogue from Vatican I to today   180-181
    → Church, Ecumenism

Ecclesiality and Freedom   1065-1069

ECCLESIAM SUAM   257-259
— encyclical of Paul VI on dialogue   257
— revelation is the prototype of the church-world dialogue   258
— object of the dialogue is the very life of God   258
— attitudes toward dialogue that the church adopts in the encounter with the
  world   258-259
    → Church, Interreligious Dialogue, Ecumenism, Revelation

ECCLESIOLOGY, FUNDAMENTAL   143-145
— origin of the tractate *De Ecclesia*   143-144
— various approaches of f.e.   143-144
— perspectives opened by Vatican II   144-145
— ecclesiality of theology   1065-1069
    → Fundamental Christology, Church, Vatican I, Vatican II

Economy   63-64, 433-434, 920, 934

ECUMENISM   259-267
— actual e. has various meanings   259
— *Unitatis Redintegratio* furnishes us with a definition of e.   259
— outstanding historical moments of e.   259-261
— e. makes certain problems of a theological character arise   261-267
— method of ecumenical theology   261-262
— credibility of the Christian message is a basic problem of e.   262
— various models of unity of the church   262-265
— search for unity arises from the problems that are also
  hermeneutical   265-267
— pluralism also interests e.   784
— Barth exercised a great renewing influence across the concept of
  revelation   76-77
    → Anglicanism, Calvinism, Ecclesiam Suam, Evangelical Churches, Hier-
    archy of Truths, Lutheranism, Orthodox Churches, World Council of
    Churches

— the "natural man" gains his place in h.h.   463
— the renaissance of classical values accompanies the renaissance of the human being   463-464
— h.h. is reached by grace and by harmony   464
— h.h. and anti-h.h.   465
— from a new h. the lay apologists arise   44-45
  → Humanism: Atheistic, Humanism: Christian, Literature

IDEOLOGY   490-494
— assists at the crisis of the ideologies   490-491
— problem of a science of i.   491
— problem of defining i.   491
— De Tracy is the first to introduce the theme   492
— Freud, Marx, Nietzsche and i.   493
— Paul Ricoeur has clearly posited the role of i.   493
— to obey the gospel, this is rebellion against i.   494
— faith and i.   493-494
— the check of Marxist i.   637-639
  → Evangelization, Faith, Marxism, Philosophy of Religion, Truth

Illative Sense   735-736

IMAGINATION   494-496
— furnishes the primary material for reflection by FT   494-495
— revelation presents itself in imaginative structures   494-495
— imaginative constructs give a sense of the real world   495
— imaginative constructs enter into a reciprocal relationship   495
— irreplaceability of imaginative constructs   496
  → Beauty, Language, Literature, Sign, Symbol

IMMANENCE   496-500
— concept introduced by Maurice Blondel   496-497
— the first attempt that looks to imply the complete autonomy of the human person and of revelation   497
— polemics and controversies in the Catholic world (498-499), especially the criticism of de Tonquédec   498-499
— i. precedes the supernatural existential of Karl Rahner   499
— i. is at the service of an integral apologetics   499-500
— influence of i. on contemporary FT   499-500
— de Lubac and the method of i.   228-229
  → Blondel, Hermeneutics, Language, Method, Obediential Potency

INCULTURATION   500-510
— i. indicates a special rapport between faith and culture   501
— i. has a special theological connotation   501
— i. indicates the active process to go inside of culture   501
— i. is a process of evangelization   501
— i. is a dynamic process   501
— i. is also as old as the history of salvation   502-504
— the incarnation is the most radical form of i.   502-503
— there exists a new ecclesial consciousness about i.   504-507
— indispensable elements for inculturated evangelization   507-508
— model of i.   508-510
— i. and Christology   134-135

— the forms of popular devotion sometimes constitute i.   851
  → Inculturation of the Gospel, Evangelization, Gospels, Addressees of FT

— INCULTURATION OF THE GOSPEL   510-514
— shows the interaction between a given culture and the message of
  Christ   510
— different historical moments   511-512
— decolonization and freedom make it necessary to rethink i.g.   512
— the incarnation is the point of departure   512
— it is necessary to have an anthropological discernment of cultures   512-513
— there are fundamental requirements to respect   513
— it is necessary to distinguish between faith and culture   513
— it is necessary to safeguard both unity and pluralism   513-514
— i.g. is also concerned with modern secular societies   513-514
  → Credibility, Inculturation, Evangelization, Addressees of FT

INDIFFERENCE, RELIGIOUS   896-905
— by its nature, it is difficult to circumscribe   896-897
— there exists an i. relative to religion proper   897-899
— the first indication is the relaxing of liturgical practice   897
— there exists an i. of decomposition   898
— there exists equally an i. with regard to religion in general   899
— there are both individual and cultural attitudes of i.   900
— it is necessary to go farther than i.   902-903
— the big challenge to i. is the interpretation of the self   903
  → Agnosticism, Atheism, Church: Motive of Credibility, Conversion,
  Credibility, Intelligence, Modernity, Religion, Skepticism, Secularization,
  Semeiology

Inference   735

INSPIRATION   515-518
— value of the theme of i. in FT   515
— particular stages in its history: Old Testament (515); New Testament
  (515-516); patristic and scholastic periods (516)
— interventions by the magisterium on i.   516-517
— identity of the sacred author   517
— precomprehension of the concept of truth   517
— i. and revelation   517-518
  → Faith, Sacred Scripture, Magisterium, OT and NT, Prophecy, Revelation,
  Truth

INTEGRAL EXEGESIS   291-298
— i.e. means the interpretation, the commentary, and the explication of the
  biblical text   291
— ultimate objective of e. is theological   291
— first task of i.e. is to establish the text   292
— e. seeks to discover the intention of the authors   294-295
— it is necessary to respect the actual text   292-294
— various methodologies   292-293
— e. and close reading   294
— theological principles that follow from *DV*   294-298
  → Canon, Dei Verbum, Structural Analysis, Sensus Fidei, Tradition

Intellectus Fidei   680-684

LANGUAGE, THEOLOGICAL   600-603
— essentials of t.l.   600
— speciality and difference of t.l. from other l.   601-602
— performativity of t.l.   601-602
— historicity of t.l.   602
— t.l. has developed a triple dimension: foundation, development, going beyond   602-603
— the martyr as l.   624
— the analogy is the law for t.l.   603
— t.l. is paradoxical   603
— t.l. is universal   603
— t.l. on God   351
    → Analogy, Communication, Credibility, Dogma, Hermeneutics, Integral Exegesis, Magisterium, Method, Revelation, Silence

LAW   267-273
— l. in Judaism   267-273
— the l. is a program of life in Judaism   540
    → Election, Justice

LAW AND GOSPEL   612-613
— the two must be preserved, but not separated   612
— Luther thought that their distinction was a great help for exegesis   612
— the distinction raises the problem of the essence of Christianity   612-613
    → Integral Exegesis, Lutheranism, Method

LAY APOLOGISTS   44-48
— the noncleric is able to be proposed   44
— the one who acquires the awareness of a new identity to move away from humanism   44-45
— originality of their contribution   44-45
— representative writers: in Italy, M. Leopardi (45); in Prussia: J. von Görres; F. B. von Baader (45); in Spain: J. D. Cortés (45-46); in France: J. de Maistre, R. de Chateaubriand and L. G. A. de Bonald (46-47)

LIBERATION THEOLOGY   1091-1097
— the first systematic discussion is due to Gutierrez   1091
— l.t. represents an original theological way   1091-1092
— the place of l.t.: the poor   1092
— the oppressed are the subject of l.t.   1092-1093
— l.t. is an inductive and contextual t.   1093
— three special mediations of l.t.   1093-1094
— the God of l.t. is the God of the Exodus   1095
— l.t. makes evident the political aspect of the action of Jesus   1095-1096
— the church is the sign and the instrument of liberation   1096
— l.t. and recent central magisterium   1097
— l.t. and the Christology of liberation   135-137
    → Christology, Justice, Marxism, Orthodoxy, Orthopraxis, Political Theology, Popular Religion, Kingdom/Reign of God

Life, Jewish, *see* Jewish Life

LITERATURE   604-605
— l. has the job of deepening the mystery of the human person   604
— human knowledge will be weakened without l.   604-605

— mediation of the m. in theological understanding   677
— judgment on private revelations belonging to the m.   953-954
   → Depost of Faith, Dogma, Method in Systematic Theology, Rule of Faith,
Tradition, Vatican I, Vatican II

MARTYRDOM   620-630
— semantic value and its evolution   620-622
— valuation of m. in the OT and the NT   621-623
— characteristic of m. in FT   623-625
— Jesus of Nazareth is the martyr   622-623
— m. is a language   624
— m. gives a meaning to death   625-626
— m. is a witness   624
— m. is a sign of the times   624-625
— m. in relation to its significance   625-626
— various definitions of m.   626-629
— Vatican II and m.   627
   → Church, Credibility, Death, Language, Paschal Mystery, Semeiology,
Testimony

Marx, Karl   476-477

MARXISM   630-644
— m. is an ensemble of doctrines   630-633
— its philosophical form is dialectic materialism   631
— object of historical materialism   632-633
— the primacy of the material is affirmed   633
— special considerations of M.: work, religion, human person, freedom,
conscience   631-633
— Marxist atheism   633-634
— Leninist M.   634-635
— Leninist communism   635-637
— social, economic, and political checks on the ideology of M.   637-639
   → Atheism, Communist Party, Ideology

Meaning of Faith, see Faith, Meaning of

Meaning of Revelation, see Revelation, Meaning of

MESSIANIC EXPECTATION   651-664
— the royal Messiah of earthly origin   652
— the miracles are his manifestation   652-653
— his greatest quality is justice   653
— the M. will liberate the people from slavery   653
— the M. possesses wisdom and strength   653-654
— the role of the M. is to destroy the enemies   654-655
— the M. will establish a new order   656-658
— the awaited M. is subordinate to the reign of God   658
— the Hasidim bring about the awaited M.   658
— messianism is a diverse phenomenon   658-659
— the awaited M. according to diverse social and religious groups   659-663
— the awaited M. and the arrival of the M.   664-670

MESSIANISM   651-670
— messianic waiting   651-664

— as a historical structure, m. is found in the West beginning in the 16th
century 723
— m. is a mode of thought and a style of life 723-724
— no one speaks of post-m. 724
— secularization is the most visible impact of m. on faith 724
— m. delays the non-necessity of God for humankind 724-725
— faith has an original word to say to m. 724-725
— m. must be evangelized because it is culture 286-287
   → Inculturation, Faith, Secularization

MORAL EVIL 725-732
— e. possesses an infinite number of forms 725
— here m.e. is treated 725
— reaction when facing e.: acquiesce or rebel 725-728
— Christ facing the sinner and sin 728-729
— God crucified is the answer to the problem of e. 728-729
— love conquers e. 730-731
— the Christian answer shuns pseudo-solutions 730-731
— e. is not defined as a mystery of iniquity 732-733
   → Death, Ideology, Paschal Mystery, Quest for Meaning and Gift of Meaning, Suffering

Motivum credentitatis 195

Motivum credibilitatis 195

Motivum fidei 195

MYSTERIES/MYSTERY 732-733
— secular concept of m. 732
— Christian interpretation of m. 732-733
— the [true] m. is God 732
— positive value of m. 732
— evil is not defined as *mysterium iniquitatis* 733
— Vatican II exhorts theology of have an "Introduction to the Mystery of
   Christ" 733
— rational justification of the m. 733
   → Rahner

NARRATIVE THEOLOGY 1084-1087
— this is a way to do t. 1084-1085
— nature and efficacy of the narration 1085
— each narration has a heuristic character 1085
— the early church community told the events of Jesus' life 1085-1086
— faith has a narrative structure 1086
— n.t. criticizes the neoscholastic, argumentative model 1086
— n.t. and practical t. 1087
   → Christology, Faith, Integral Exegesis, Language, Literature, Theology,
   Testimony

Natural Law 574-578

NATURAL THEOLOGY 1080-1082
— has been studied for a long time by philosophers 1080-1081
— numbers of contemporary theologians have abandoned n.t. 1081

— the limits of the apologetic that knows only of the fulfillment of prophecy   1033
— biblical renewal has favored a new synthesis   1033-1034
— the theory of the *sensus plenior* has been useful   1034
— various endeavors of theology of p. and f.   1035-1036
    → Old and New Testament: Relation between OT and NT, Integral Exegesis, Prophecy

PROPHECY   788-798
— actual problems connected to the prophetic argument   788-789
— need for interdisciplinary study   789
— p. in the OT   789-790
— Jesus of Nazareth as prophet, or prophetic Christology   790-792
— inadequacy of the title prophet, applied to Jesus   792
— p. in the NT: Acts and Paul   792-794
— particular traits for recognizing p.   794-795
— theological value of p.   795-797
— prophetic value in meeting the signs of the times   997, 796-797
— the OT is the p. of Christ   934-935
— prophetic revelation in Thomas Aquinas   1107-1108
    → Church, Credibility, Faith, Semeiology, Sensus Fidei, Sign, Signs of the Times, Symbol, Christological Titles

PROPHETS   798-801
— FT has made a partial reading of the p.   798
— p. have been perceived especially as seers   798
— historico-critical studies have made the prophets extraordinary religious personalities   799-800
— to make of the prophet a mediator of Christian revelation is a unilateral concession   799-800
— biographical dimension of the p. cannot be neglected   800-801
— FT must revise its positions to the same wave lengths as exegesis   800-801
— p. is a man of the word   905-907
— Jesus as prophet   119-120
— the p. and the martyr   622-623
— p. and prophecy in Islam   530-532
— p. of doom   995
    → Old and New Testament, Patriarchs, Prophecy, Revelation

PSYCHOLOGY OF RELIGIONS   872-881
— a clarification of concepts is indispensable   872-873
— beginnings of p.r.   874
— belief in God as providence   876
— belief in God as father   876-877
— religious behaviors are most accessible to p.r.   877-878
— p.r. and religious language   878-880
    → Religion, Symbol, Symbolism

Qu'ran   529-532

QUEST FOR MEANING AND THE GIFT OF MEANING   648-651
— the problem of meaning concerns the whole world   648
— we are not able to escape the problem of meaning   648
— various positions in facing the problem of meaning   648-650
— Christ, answer to the question of meaning   650-651

— the contemporary person has need of Christ   816
   → Ecclesiam Suam, Gaudium et Spes, Vatican II

REINCARNATION   816-818
— r. is a belief   816
— r. is a concept near to metempsychosis and metensomatosis   816
— r. is present in Hinduism and Buddhism   816-817
— is not subject to scientific proofs   817
— r. and resurrection are incompatible   817-818
   → Anthropology, Buddhism, Hinduism, Resurrection

RELATIVISM, THEOLOGICAL   818-819
— is not confused with pluralism   818
— is opposed to theological pronouncements   818
— according to _Humani Generis_, there is r.t. in the new theology   818-819
— theology of Bultmann and t.r.   819
   → Analogy, Bultmann, Pluralism: Theological

RELIGION
— critique of r.   868-872
— phenomenology of r.   827-836
— history of religions   836-844
— traditional r.   844-849
— popular r.   849-852
— philosophy of r.   852-868
— theology of religions   886-896
— psychology of r.   872-881
— sociology of r.   881-886
— r., according to Cicero, derived from _religere_   819-820
— according to Lactantius, derived from _religare_   819-820
— has a pre-Christian source   820
— r. also understands individual experiences   820
— r. is not simply a human act   821
— it is necessary to distinguish r. and magic   821-822
— r. and revelation   822-823
— r. and faith are linked and sometimes synonymous   823-824
— original r.   824
— there exists a modern critique of religion   825
— r. and morality   825-826
— r. and mysticism   826-827
— non-Christian r. and Christology   139-140

RELIGION, POPULAR   849-852
— field of observation and of analysis of p.r. is extended and
   differentiated   849-850
— p.r. has a direct and simple character   850
— p.r. touches a large range of phenomena   851
— p.r. is not exempt from ambiguity   851
— forms of p.r. sometimes constitute examples of inculturation   851
— Christology and p.r.   138-139

RELIGIONS, TRADITIONAL   844-849
— point out the religions of the illiterate populations of the Third World   844
— have strong links between them   844-845
— total absence of proselytism   845

Word of God   218-220

trans. by M. John-Baptist Porter, OCSO